PSYCHOLOGY

FRONTIERS AND APPLICATIONS

SIXTH CANADIAN EDITION

MICHAEL W. PASSER

University of Washington

RONALD E. SMITH

University of Washington

MICHAEL L. ATKINSON

Western University

JOHN B. MITCHELL

Brescia University College, Western University

Mc
Graw
Hill
Education

PSYCHOLOGY: FRONTIERS AND APPLICATIONS, SIXTH CANADIAN EDITION

Statistics Canada information is used with the permission of Statistics Canada. Users are forbidden to copy the data and redisseminate them, in an original or modified form, for commercial purposes, without permission from Statistics Canada. Information on the availability of the wide range of data from Statistics Canada can be obtained from Statistics Canada's Regional Offices, its World Wide Web site at www.statcan.gc.ca, and its toll-free access number 1-800-263-1136.

The Internet addresses listed in the text were accurate at the time of publication. The inclusion of a website does not indicate an endorsement by the authors or McGraw-Hill Ryerson, and McGraw-Hill Ryerson does not guarantee the accuracy of the information presented at these sites.

ISBN-13: 978-1-25-936942-1
ISBN-10: 1-25-936942-0

1 2 3 4 5 6 7 8 9   TCP   1 2 3 4 5 6 0 9 8 7

Printed and bound in Canada.

Care has been taken to trace ownership of copyright material contained in this text; however, the publisher will welcome any information that enables them to rectify any reference or credit for sub-sequent editions.

Portfolio and Prorgam Manager: *Karen Fozard*
Product Manager: *Scott Hardie*
Executive Marketing Manager: *Kelli Legros*
Product Developer: Brianna McIlwain
Senior Product Team Associate: *Marina Seguin*
Supervising Editor: *Jeanette McCurdy*
Photo/Permissions Research: *Derek Capitaine*
Copy Editor: *Valerie Adams*
Plant Production Coordinators: *Sarah Strynatka*
Manufacturing Production Coordinator: *Sheryl McAdam*
Cover Design: *Liz Harasymczuk*
Cover Image: © *Jordan Siemens/Getty Images*
Interior Design: *Liz Harasymczuk*
Page Layout: *MPS Limited*
Printer: *Transcontinental Printing Group*

MICHAEL W. PASSER, PH.D.

Michael Passer coordinates the introductory psychology program at the University of Washington, which enrolls about 2500 students per year, and also is the faculty coordinator of training for new teaching assistants (TAs). He received his bachelor's degree from the University of Rochester and his Ph.D. in Psychology from the University of California, Los Angeles, with a specialization in social psychology. Dr. Passer has been a faculty member at the University of Washington since 1977. A former Danforth Foundation Fellow and University of Washington Distinguished Teaching Award finalist, Dr. Passer has had a career-long love of teaching. Each academic year he teaches introductory psychology twice and a required pre-major course in research methods. Dr. Passer developed and teaches a graduate course on the Teaching of Psychology, which prepares students for careers in the college classroom, and has also taught courses in social psychology and attribution theory. He has published more than 20 scientific articles and chapters, primarily in the areas of attribution, stress, and anxiety, and has taught the introductory psychology course for almost 20 years.

RONALD E. SMITH, PH.D.

Ronald E. Smith is Professor of Psychology and Director of Clinical Psychology Training at the University of Washington, where he also has served as Area Head of the Social Psychology and Personality area. He received his bachelor's degree from Marquette University and his Ph.D. from Southern Illinois University, where he had dual specializations in clinical and physiological psychology. His major research interests are in anxiety, stress, and coping, and in performance enhancement research and intervention. Dr. Smith is a Fellow of the American Psychological Association. He received a Distinguished Alumnus Award from the UCLA Neuropsychiatric Institute for his contributions to the field of mental health. He has published more than 200 scientific articles and book chapters in his areas of interest and has authored or co-authored 29 books on introductory psychology, human performance enhancement, and personality, including *Introduction to Personality: Toward an Integration*, with Walter Mischel and Yuichi Shoda

(Wiley, 2004). An award-winning teacher, he has more than 15 years of experience in teaching the introductory psychology course.

MICHAEL L. ATKINSON, PH.D.

Mike Atkinson is Associate Professor of Psychology at Western University in London, Ontario. Dr. Atkinson received his B.Sc. from Dalhousie University in 1975 and his M.Sc. (1978) and Ph.D. (1982) from the University of Wisconsin, Madison. Dr. Atkinson's training is in social psychology, but his research and teaching interests place him more in the field of educational psychology. "Dr. Mike," as he is known to his students, has been featured in *Maclean's* magazine, *Media Television*, and The *Globe and Mail*. He has also received numerous teaching awards, including Western University's Professor of the Year award six times, as well as the Student's Council/Alumni Western Teaching Award of Excellence, and the Pleva Award for Excellence in Teaching. He has also received the 3M Canada Teaching Fellowship for his pioneering work in large-scale multimedia instruction, the "Superclass," and is a certified ISW trainer.

JOHN B. MITCHELL, PH.D.

John B. Mitchell is the Associate Academic Dean at Brescia University College, Western University. Dr. Mitchell received his B.A. and M.A. from Queen's University and his Ph.D. from Concordia University. Following completion of his Ph.D., he did post-doctoral research at the Douglas Hospital Research Centre in Montreal and at the University of Colorado Health Sciences Center in Denver. Dr. Mitchell has taught Introduction to Psychology at Boston College, Brescia University College, and Western University in classes that have ranged in size from 50 to 500 students. He has also taught courses in behavioural neuroscience, psychopharmacology, memory, research methods, and, more recently, educational psychology. In 2006, Dr. Mitchell received the Brescia University College Award for Teaching Excellence and is a certified ISW trainer. In 2016, Dr. Mitchell founded the Advanced Learning and Teaching Centre (the ALT Centre) at Brescia University College.

BRIEF CONTENTS

PREFACE   xiv

CHAPTER 1

Psychology: The Science of Behaviour   1

CHAPTER 2

Studying Behaviour Scientifically   36

CHAPTER 3

Biological Foundations of Behaviour   69

CHAPTER 4

Genes, Evolution, and Behaviour   107

CHAPTER 5

Sensation and Perception   141

CHAPTER 6

States of Consciousness   191

CHAPTER 7

Learning and Adaptation: The Role
of Experience   236

CHAPTER 8

Memory   276

CHAPTER 9

Language and Thinking   314

CHAPTER 10

Intelligence   356

CHAPTER 11

Motivation and Emotion   395

CHAPTER 12

Development over the Lifespan   447

CHAPTER 13

Behaviour in a Social Context   498

CHAPTER 14

Personality   549

CHAPTER 15

Stress, Coping, and Health   591

CHAPTER 16

Psychological Disorders   631

CHAPTER 17

Treatment of Psychological Disorders   682

APPENDIX: STATISTICS IN
PSYCHOLOGY   AP-1

ANSWERS TO THINKING
CRITICALLY   AN-1

GLOSSARY   GL-1

REFERENCES   RE-1

NAME INDEX   NI-1

SUBJECT INDEX   SI-1

CONTENTS

PREFACE   xiv

CHAPTER 1

PSYCHOLOGY: THE SCIENCE OF BEHAVIOUR   1

The Nature of Psychology   2
  Psychology's Scientific Approach   4
  Thinking Critically about Behaviour   6
  Psychology's Goals   8
  Psychology as a Basic and Applied Science   8
  Psychology's Broad Scope: A Simple Framework   8

Perspectives on Behaviour   10
  Psychology's Intellectual Roots   10
  Early Schools: Structuralism and Functionalism   11
  *The Psychodynamic Perspective: The Forces
    Within   12*
  *The Behavioural Perspective: The Power of the
    Environment   13*
  *The Humanistic Perspective: Self-Actualization and
    Positive Psychology   15*
  The Cognitive Perspective: The Thinking Human   16
  *The Sociocultural Perspective: The Embedded
    Human   18*

Research Foundations
Would You Marry Someone You Didn't Love?   20
  *The Biological Perspective: The Brain, Genes,
    and Evolution   20*

Focus on Neuroscience
The Neuroscience of Imaging Studies   22

Using Levels of Analysis to Integrate
The Perspectives   24

Frontiers
Culture, Language, and Behaviour   26
  An Example: Understanding Depression   27
  Summary of Major Themes   29

Psychology Today   29

Applications
Academic Performance Enhancement Strategies   32

CHAPTER 2

STUDYING BEHAVIOUR SCIENTIFICALLY   36

Scientific Principles in Psychology   37
  Scientific Attitudes   37

Research Foundations
Bystander Intervention   38
  *Gathering Evidence: Steps in the Scientific
    Process   39*
  Two Approaches to Understanding Behaviour   40
  Defining and Measuring Variables   41

Focus on Neuroscience
The Neuroscience of the Human Brain at Work   45

Methods of Research   46
  Descriptive Research: Recording Events   46
  *Correlational Research: Measuring Associations
    between Events   50*
  Experiments: Examining Cause and Effect   53

Threats to the Validity of Research   58
  Confounding of Variables   58
  Placebo Effects   59
  Experimenter Expectancy Effects   60
  Replicating and Generalizing the Findings   61

Frontiers
Does Esp Exist?   62

Ethical Principles in Human and Animal Research   63
  Ethical Standards in Human Research   63
  Ethical Standards in Animal Research   65

Critical Thinking in Science and Everyday Life   66

Applications
Evaluating Claims in Research and Everyday Life   66

CHAPTER 3

BIOLOGICAL FOUNDATIONS OF BEHAVIOUR   69

The Neural Bases of Behaviour   70
  Neurons   70
  The Electrical Activity of Neurons   71
  How Neurons Communicate:
    Synaptic Transmission   73

Applications
Understanding How Drugs Affect Your Brain   76

The Nervous System   79
  The Peripheral Nervous System   79
  The Central Nervous System   81

Research Foundations
Wilder Penfield and a Cortical Map   83
  The Hierarchical Brain: Structures and
    Behavioural Functions   87

Frontiers
Mirror Neurons and Autism Spectrum Disorder   97

Focus on Neuroscience
The Neuroscience of Music   103

CHAPTER 4

GENES, EVOLUTION, AND BEHAVIOUR   107

Genetic Influences   108
  Chromosomes and Genes   108

Focus on Neuroscience
Early Experience, Epigenetics, and Adolescence   111
  Behaviour Genetics Techniques   112

Applications
Gene Therapy and Genetic Counselling   113

Genetic Influences on Behaviour   118
  Heredity, Environment, and Intelligence   118
  Biological Reaction Range, the Environment,
    Personality, and Intelligence   119

Evolution and Behaviour   124
  Evolution of Adaptive Mechanisms   124
  Evolution and Human Nature   126
  Evolutionary Psychology   128

Frontiers
Heritability, Evolution, and Politics   129

Research Foundations
Gender Differences in the Ideal Mate   133

How Not to Think about Behaviour Genetics and
Evolutionary Psychology   138

CHAPTER 5

SENSATION AND PERCEPTION   141

Sensory Processes   143
  Stimulus Detection: The Absolute Threshold   144
  Signal Detection Theory   144

Focus on Neuroscience
The Neuroscience of Subliminal Perception and
Prosopagnosia   145
  The Difference Threshold   147
  Sensory Adaptation   148

The Sensory Systems   149
  Vision   149
  Audition   158
  Taste and Smell: The Chemical Senses   162
  The Skin and Body Senses   164

Frontiers
Sensory Prosthetics: Restoring Lost Function   167

Perception: The Creation of Experience   170
  Perception Is Selective: The Role of Attention   171
  Perceptions Have Organization and Structure   173
  Perception Involves Hypothesis Testing   175

Applications
Mona Lisa's Smile   176
  Perception Is Influenced by Expectations: Perceptual
    Sets   176
  Stimuli Are Recognizable under Changing Conditions:
    Perceptual Constancies   177

Perception of Depth, Distance, and Movement   179

Depth and Distance Perception   179
Perception of Movement   180

Illusions: False Perceptual Hypotheses   181

Experience, Critical Periods, and Perceptual
Development   184

Research Foundations
Critical Periods: The Role of Early Experience   185
Cross-Cultural Research on Perception   187
Restored Sensory Capacity   188

CHAPTER 6

STATES OF CONSCIOUSNESS   191

The Puzzle of Consciousness   192
Measuring States of Consciousness   193
*Levels of Consciousness: Psychodynamic
and Cognitive Perspectives   193*

Frontiers
Detecting Awareness   194
The Neural Basis of Consciousness   196

Circadian Rhythms: Our Daily Biological Clocks   197
Keeping Time: Brain and Environment   198
*Environmental Disruptions of Circadian
Rhythms   200*

Sleep and Dreaming   201
Stages of Sleep   201
Getting a Night's Sleep: Brain and Environment   204
How Much Do We Sleep?   204
Sleep Deprivation   205

Applications
A Good Night's Sleep   206
Why Do We Sleep?   207
Sleep Disorders   208
The Nature of Dreams   210

Focus on Neuroscience
Dreams and Daydreams   213

Drugs and Altered Consciousness   217
Drugs and the Brain   217
Tolerance and Withdrawal   218
Depressants   220

Research Foundations
Drinking and Driving: Decision Making in Altered States   222
Stimulants   223
Opiates   225
Hallucinogens   226
Marijuana   226
*From Genes to Culture: Determinants of Drug
Effects   227*

Hypnosis   230
The Scientific Study of Hypnosis   230
Hypnotic Behaviours and Experiences   230
Theories of Hypnosis   232

Some Final Thoughts   234

CHAPTER 7

LEARNING AND ADAPTATION: THE ROLE OF EXPERIENCE   236

Adapting to the Environment   237
How Do We Learn? The Search for Mechanisms   237
Habituation and Sensitization   238

Classical Conditioning: Associating One Stimulus
with Another   239
Pavlov's Pioneering Research   240
Basic Principles   240
Applications of Classical Conditioning   243

Applications
Learning, Virtual Reality, and Therapy   246

Operant Conditioning: Learning through
Consequences   247
Thorndike's Law of Effect   248
Skinner's Analysis of Operant Conditioning   248
*Antecedent Conditions: Identifying When to
Respond   250*
Consequences: Determining How to Respond   250
*Shaping and Chaining: Taking One Step at a
Time   254*
Generalization and Discrimination   254
Schedules of Reinforcement   255

Escape and Avoidance Conditioning 258
Applications of Operant Conditioning 259

Biology and Learning 261

Constraints on Classical Conditioning: Learned Taste Aversions 261
Are We Biologically Prepared to Fear Certain Things? 262
Constraints on Operant Conditioning: Animals That "Won't Shape Up" 263
Learning and the Brain 263

Cognition and Learning 264

Insight and Cognitive Maps 264

Focus on Neuroscience
Place Cells and Cognitive Maps 266
Cognition in Classical Conditioning 266

Frontiers
Animal Cognition 268
Cognition in Operant Conditioning 269

Observational Learning: When Others Pave The Way 270

Bandura's Social-Cognitive Theory 271

Research Foundations
Using Social-Cognitive Learning Theory to Prevent AIDS: A National Experiment 274

CHAPTER 8

MEMORY 276

Memory as Information Processing 277

A Three-Component Model 278

Research Foundations
In Search of the Icon 279

Encoding: Entering Information 283

Effortful and Automatic Processing 283
Levels of Processing: When Deeper Is Better 284
Exposure and Rehearsal 284
Organization and Imagery 285
How Prior Knowledge Shapes Encoding 287

Storage: Retaining Information 289

Memory as a Network 289
Types of Long-Term Memory 290

Retrieval: Accessing Information 292

The Value of Multiple and Self-Generated Cues 292
The Value of Distinctiveness 293
Context, State, and Mood Effects on Memory 294

Applications
Improving Memory and Academic Learning 296

Forgetting 297

The Course of Forgetting 297
Why Do We Forget? 298
Amnesia 300
Forgetting to Do Things: Prospective Memory 302

Frontiers
Methods to Enhance Memory 303

Memory as a Constructive Process 304

Memory Distortion and Schemas 304
The Misinformation Effect and Eyewitness Testimony 306
The "Recovered Memory" Controversy: Repression or Reconstruction? 307

The Biology of Memory 309

Sensory and Working Memory 309
Long-Term Memory 310

Focus on Neuroscience
How Are Memories Formed? 311

CHAPTER 9

LANGUAGE AND THINKING 314

Language 315

Adaptive Functions of Language 315
Properties of Language 316
The Structure of Language 317
Understanding and Producing Language 318
Acquiring a First Language 323

Bilingualism: Learning a Second Language 325
Linguistic Influences on Thinking 328

Focus on Neuroscience
The Bilingual Brain 329

Frontiers
Can Animals Acquire Human Language? 331

Thinking 334

Thought, Brain, and Mind 334
Concepts and Propositions 335
Reasoning 335
Problem Solving 338
Knowledge, Expertise, and Wisdom 344

Applications
Guidelines for Creative Problem Solving 345
Mental Imagery 347
Metacognition: Knowing Your Own Cognitive Abilities 350

Research Foundations
"Why Did I Get That Wrong?" Improving Students' Awareness of Whether They Understand Text MateriaL 351

CHAPTER 10

INTELLIGENCE   356

Intelligence in Historical Perspective 358

Sir Francis Galton: Quantifying Mental Ability 358
Alfred Binet's Mental Tests 358
Binet's Legacy: An Intelligence-Testing Industry Emerges 360

The Nature of Intelligence 361

The Psychometric Approach: The Structure of Intellect 361
Cognitive Process Approaches: The Nature of Intelligent Thinking 365
Broader Conceptions of Intelligence: Beyond Mental Competencies 367

The Measurement of Intelligence 370

Increasing the Informational Yield from Intelligence Tests 371
Theory-Based Intelligence Tests 371
Should We Test for Aptitude or Achievement? 371
Psychometric Standards for Intelligence Tests 372
Assessing Intelligence in Non-Western Cultures 377

Focus on Neuroscience
Brain Size and Intelligence 379

Heredity, Environment, and Intelligence 379

Group Differences in Intelligence 382

Applications
Early-Childhood Interventions: A Means of Boosting Intelligence? 382
Ethnic Group Differences 384
Sex Differences in Cognitive Abilities 386

Research Foundations
Effects of Hormonal Fluctuations on Perceptual and Motor Skills 388

Extremes of Intelligence 389

The Intellectually Gifted 389

Frontiers
Musical Training and Auditory Processing 390
The Intellectually Disabled 390
A Concluding Thought 393

CHAPTER 11

MOTIVATION AND EMOTION   395

Perspectives on Motivation 396

Instinct Theory and Evolutionary Psychology 396
Homeostasis and Drive Theory 396
Incentive and Expectancy Theories 397
Psychodynamic and Humanistic Theories 398

Hunger and Weight Regulation 400

The Physiology of Hunger 400

Focus on Neuroscience
Brain Activation and Food Cues 404

Psychological Aspects of Hunger 405
Environmental and Cultural Factors 407
Obesity 408

Applications
The Battle to Control Eating and Weight 410

Sexual Motivation 411

Sexual Behaviour: Patterns and Changes 411
The Physiology of Sex 412
The Psychology of Sex 414

Cultural and Environmental Influences   414
Sexual Orientation   417

Achievement Motivation   420

The Thrill of Victory, the Agony of Defeat   420
Achievement Goal Theory   420
Achievement Needs and Situational Factors   422
Family and Cultural Influences   422

Motivational Conflict   423

The Nature and Functions of Emotion   424

The Adaptive Value of Emotion   425
The Nature of Emotion   426

Frontiers
A New Emotion?   436

Theories of Emotion   438

The James-Lange Somatic Theory   438
The Cannon-Bard Theory   438
Cognitive-Affective Theories   440

Research Foundations
Cognition-Arousal Relations   442

CHAPTER 12

DEVELOPMENT OVER THE LIFESPAN   447

Prenatal Development   449

Genetics and Sex Determination   449
Environmental Influences   450

Infancy and Childhood   451

The Amazing Newborn   452
Sensory-Perceptual Development   454
Physical, Brain, and Motor Development   455
Cognitive Development   457
Social-Emotional and Personality Development   465

Frontiers
Social Media and Social Development   466

Applications
Understanding How Divorce and Remarriage Affect Children   473
Moral Development   475

Adolescence and Adulthood   478

Physical Development   479

Focus on Neuroscience
The Neuroscience of the Teenage Brain   481
Cognitive Development   483
Social-Emotional and Personality Development   487

Research Foundations
What Does It Take to Become an Adult?   490

CHAPTER 13

BEHAVIOUR IN A SOCIAL CONTEXT   498

Social Thinking and Perception   499

Attribution: Perceiving the Causes of Behaviour   499
Forming and Maintaining Impressions   503
Attitudes and Attitude Change   504

Social Influence   509

The Mere Presence of Others   509
Social Norms: The Rules of the Game   510
Conformity and Obedience   511

Research Foundations
The Dilemma of Obedience: When Conscience Confronts Malevolent Authority   514
Crowd Behaviour and Deindividuation   518
Group Influences on Performance and Decision Making   519

Social Relations   523

Affiliation and Interpersonal Attraction   523
Love   528
Prejudice and Discrimination   529

Applications
Making Close Relationships Work: Lessons from Psychological Research   530

Focus on Neuroscience
The Neuroscience of Stereotyping   532
Prosocial Behaviour: Helping Others   536
Aggression: Harming Others   540

Frontiers
Do Violent Video Games Promote Aggression?   545

CHAPTER 14

PERSONALITY 549

What Is Personality? 550

The Psychodynamic Perspective 550
Freud's Psychoanalytic Theory 551

Frontiers
Attachment Style and Abusive Romantic Relationships 556
Evaluating Psychoanalytic Theory 557

The Humanistic Perspective 558
George Kelly's Personal Construct Theory 559
Carl Rogers's Self Theory 559

Focus on Neuroscience
The Neurobiology of the Self 562
Research on the Self 565
Evaluating Humanistic Theories 566

Trait and Biological Perspectives 567
Cattell's Sixteen Personality Factors 567
Eysenck's Extraversion-Stability Model 568
The Five Factor Model 569
Traits and Behaviour Prediction 570
Biological Foundations of Personality Traits 571
The Stability of Personality Traits 571
Evaluating the Trait Approach 573

Social Cognitive Theories 573
Julian Rotter: Expectancy, Reinforcement Value, and Locus of Control 574
Albert Bandura: The Social Cognitive Perspective and Self-Efficacy 575

Research Foundations
Albert Bandura, Human Agency, and the Social Cognitive Perspective 576

Applications
Increasing Self-Efficacy through Systematic Goal Setting 578
Walter Mischel: The Consistency Paradox and If . . . Then . . . Behaviour Consistencies 581
Evaluating Social Cognitive Theories 581

Personality Assessment 582
Interviews 583
Behavioural Assessment 584
Remote Behaviour Sampling 584
Personality Scales 585
Projective Tests 586
Personality Theory and Personality Assessment 589

CHAPTER 15

STRESS, COPING, AND HEALTH 591

The Nature of Stress 592
Stressors 593
The Stress Response 594
Chronic Stress and the GAS 595

Stress and Health 597
Stress and Psychological Well-Being 597
Post-Traumatic Stress Disorder (PTSD) 598
Stress and Illness 599

Vulnerability and Protective Factors 601
Social Support 602

Focus on Neuroscience
The Neuroscience of Social Support 603
Hardiness 604
Coping Self-Efficacy 605
Optimism 605
Personality Factors 606
Finding Meaning in Stressful Life Events 607

Coping with Stress 608
Effectiveness of Coping Strategies 609

Research Foundations
Stress, Physical Contact, and Health: I Wanna Hold Your Hand 610

Frontiers
Mindfulness and the Stresses of Teaching 612
Bottling Up Feelings: The Costs of Constraint 613
Gender, Culture, and Coping 614

Health Promotion and Illness Prevention 615
How People Change: The Transtheoretical Model 616
Increasing Behaviours That Enhance Health 618
Reducing Behaviours That Impair Health 621

Combatting Substance Abuse 622
Psychological Approaches to Treatment and Prevention 623

Positive Psychology 627

Applications
How to Be Happy 628

CHAPTER 16

PSYCHOLOGICAL DISORDERS 631

The Scope and Nature of Psychological Disorders 632
What Is "Abnormal"? 632

Historical Perspectives on Deviant Behaviour 634

Diagnosing Psychological Disorders 636
The DSM-5: Integrating Categorical and Dimensional Approaches 637
Critical Issues in Diagnostic Labelling 638

Research Foundations
On Being Sane in Insane Places 639

Anxiety Disorders 641
Phobic Disorder 642
Generalized Anxiety Disorder 643
Panic Disorder 643
Obsessive-Compulsive Disorder (OCD) 644
Causal Factors in Anxiety Disorders and OCD 644

Focus on Neuroscience
The Neuroscience of Obsessive-Compulsive Disorder 645
Eating Disorders 648

Mood (Affective) Disorders 650
Depression 651
Bipolar Disorder 652

Prevalence and Course of Mood Disorders 652
Causal Factors in Mood Disorders 653

Applications
Understanding and Preventing Suicide 658

Somatic Symptom Disorders 660

Dissociative Disorders 662
What Causes Dissociative Identity Disorder? 662

Frontiers
Dissociative Identity Disorder: A Clinical and Scientific Puzzle 663

Schizophrenia 665
Characteristics of Schizophrenia 665
Subtypes of Schizophrenia 666
Causal Factors in Schizophrenia 667

Personality Disorders 671
Antisocial Personality Disorder 672
Borderline Personality Disorder 675

Disorders of Childhood and Old Age 677
Childhood Disorders 677
Dementia in Old Age 679

A Closing Thought 680

CHAPTER 17

TREATMENT OF PSYCHOLOGICAL DISORDERS 682

The Helping Relationship 683

Psychodynamic Therapies 684
Psychoanalysis 684
Brief Psychodynamic Therapies 686

Humanistic Psychotherapies 688
Client-Centred Therapy 688
Gestalt Therapy 690

Cognitive Therapies 691
Ellis's Rational-Emotive Therapy (RET) 692
Beck's Cognitive Therapy 693

Behaviour Therapies 694
Classical Conditioning Treatments 694

Focus on Neuroscience
The Neuroscience of Treating Unipolar Depression 695

Frontiers 697
Virtual Reality as a Therapeutic Technique 697
Operant Conditioning Treatments 699
Modelling and Social Skills Training 701

"Third-Wave" Cognitive-Behavioural Therapies 702
Mindfulness-Based Treatments 702

Cultural and Gender Issues in Psychotherapy 705
Cultural Factors in Treatment Utilization 705
Gender Issues in Therapy 706

Evaluating Psychotherapies 707
Psychotherapy Research Methods 708
Factors Affecting the Outcome of Therapy 711

Research Foundations
Drug versus Psychological Treatments for Depression:
A Randomized Clinical Trial 713

Biological Approaches to Treatment   715

Drug Therapies   715
Electroconvulsive Therapy   718
Psychosurgery   719
Mind, Body, and Therapeutic Interventions   719

Psychological Disorders and Society   721

Deinstitutionalization   722
Preventive Mental Health   723

A Final Word   725

Applications
When and Where to Seek Therapy   725

APPENDIX: STATISTICS IN
PSYCHOLOGY   AP-1

ANSWERS TO THINKING
CRITICALLY   AN-1

GLOSSARY   GL-1

REFERENCES   RE-1

NAME INDEX   NI-1

SUBJECT INDEX   SI-1

PREFACE

There is nothing more fascinating than the study of the mind and behaviour. But we didn't recognize this when we entered university. In fact, the study of psychology wasn't even on our radar screens. Some of us had planned careers in the "hard" sciences (M.P., M.A.) and others were focused on the "softer" side (R.S.). One of us (J.M.) was pretty sure he would pursue psychology, although philosophy was an attractive alternative. Then something unexpected occurred. Each of us took an introductory psychology course, and suddenly our life paths changed. Because of instructors who brought psychology to life, we were hooked, and that initial enthusiasm has never left us.

Now, through this textbook, we have the pleasure and privilege of sharing our enthusiasm with today's instructors and a new generation of students. We've endeavoured to create a thoughtfully integrated book and multimedia package that strikes just the right balance between student friendliness and scientific integrity—a teaching tool that introduces students to psychology as a science, while highlighting its relevance to their lives and society. We want students to experience, as we did, the intellectual excitement of studying the mind and behaviour. We also seek to help students sharpen their critical thinking skills, dispelling some commonly held myths. We have used clear prose, careful explanations, engaging examples, and supporting artwork to make the book and multimedia accessible to a wide range of students. All of this is done within a conceptual framework that emphasizes relations between biological, psychological, and environmental levels of analysis.

We are excited about the unique way in which our text is integrated with its pedagogy. This integration results in a learning package that "uses science to teach science." Specifically, we are impressed with research (e.g., Moreland et al., 1997; Pauk & Fiore, 2000) showing that recall of textual material is significantly enhanced by specific focus questions and learning objectives that serve as retrieval cues and help students identify important information and assess their mastery of the material. In addition, the opening vignettes are presented as Problem-Based Learning (PBL) case studies. PBL generates a deeper understanding of material and provides the student with critical problem-solving skills (see Aspy et al., 1993; Vernon & Blake, 1993). It is for precisely this reason that PBL is used in the curriculum of so many medical schools. Over the years, our students have profited from these pedagogical tools; consequently, we have retained these popular features from previous editions.

One of the fastest-evolving areas in psychology is neuroscience, particularly in the use of neuroimaging. By some estimates, published studies involving some aspect of neuroimaging have increased by 3000 percent over the past decade! We are now able to examine the neural substrates for most topics in psychology, including attitude change, fabricated memory, and psychological disorders, in addition to the more traditional topics of brain function and sensory processing. In an effort to embrace this fast-moving area of research, we continue to include a *Focus on Neuroscience* boxed feature in each chapter, which examines how neuroimaging provides a much more detailed understanding of how the mind and brain work.

Let's take a look at the features of our sixth Canadian edition.

OVERVIEW OF FEATURES

- **Problem-Based Learning:** Each chapter is structured around a set of tools to help students interact with the material at a level that exceeds reading alone. These tools include the chapter-opening vignette, which presents a real-world case related to the chapter topic; a margin icon throughout the chapter, which indicates when the discussion relates back to the case introduced in the vignette; and the *Gaining Direction* feature at the end of the chapter, which revisits the vignette and suggests some answers to the questions it poses. Together, these tools encourage students to apply the concepts they are learning to real-world situations.

- **Focus on Scientific Psychology:** Throughout the book, psychology is portrayed as a contemporary science without becoming excessively formal or terminological. The text focuses both on principles derived from research and on the methods by which good research is conducted.

- **Focus on Relations between Basic Science and Applications:** Whether in the context of students' personal lives or larger societal issues, many questions studied from a basic science perspective are inspired by real-world questions and issues, and basic research findings often guide solutions to social and individual problems. In this way, students can be guided by their knowledge in other aspects of their lives.

- **Levels of Analysis** emphasize how psychologists examine the interplay of biological, psychological, and environmental factors in their quest to understand behaviour. Topics explored include "Behaviour Genetics" (Chapter 4), "Aggression" (Chapter 13), and "Stress and Resilience" (Chapter 15).

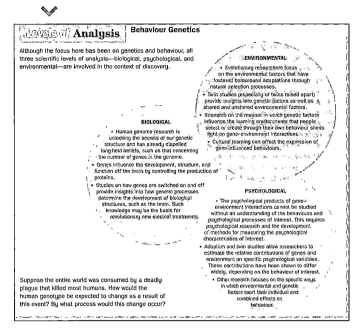

- To familiarize students with the text's pedagogical features, Chapter 1 includes a **Reader's Guide**—annotations written by the authors to draw attention to specific features and explain why they have been incorporated in the text.

- **Focus on Neuroscience** features highlight how rapidly developing cutting-edge technology is paving the way for groundbreaking imaging studies that give new insights into the workings of the human brain and its relationship to behaviour.

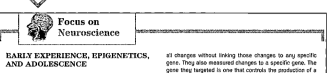

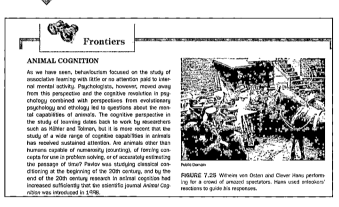

- **Frontiers** features highlight current and future directions in psychological theory and research, illustrating the dynamic nature of psychological science and the ways in which it can promote human development. New to the sixth Canadian edition are topics such as "Mirror Neurons and Autism Spectrum Disorder" (Chapter 3) and "Social Media and Social Development" (Chapter 12).

Frontiers

ANIMAL COGNITION

As we have seen, behaviourism focused on the study of associative learning with little or no attention paid to internal mental activity. Psychologists, however, moved away from this perspective and the cognitive revolution in psychology combined with perspectives from evolutionary psychology and ethology led to questions about the mental capabilities of animals. The cognitive perspective in the study of learning dates back to work by researchers such as Köhler and Tolman, but it is more recent that the study of a wide range of cognitive capabilities in animals has received sustained attention. Are animals other than humans capable of numerosity (counting), of forming concepts for use in problem solving, or of accurately estimating the passage of time? Pavlov was studying classical conditioning at the beginning of the 20th century, and by the end of the 20th century research in animal cognition had increased sufficiently that the scientific journal *Animal Cognition* was introduced in 1998.

Public Domain

FIGURE 7.25 Wilheim von Osten and Clever Hans performing for a crowd of amazed spectators. Hans used onlookers' reactions to guide his responses.

- **Research Foundations** features describe and critically evaluate a classic, high-interest study. Presented in a simplified journal format (introduction, method, results, discussion), the studies represent a diversity of research methods to help students learn the process of critical thinking. **Research Design** diagrams illustrate the research question, type of study, and variables for the study described in the *Research Foundations* feature.

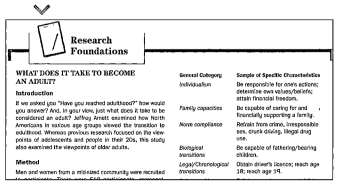

Research Foundations

WHAT DOES IT TAKE TO BECOME AN ADULT?

Introduction

If we asked you "Have you reached adulthood?" how would you answer? And, in your view, just what does it take to be considered an adult? Jeffrey Arnett examined how North Americans in various age groups viewed the transition to adulthood. Whereas previous research focused on the viewpoints of adolescents and people in their 20s, this study also examined the viewpoints of older adults.

Method

Men and women from a mid-sized community were recruited

General Category	Sample of Specific Characteristics
Individualism	Be responsible for one's actions; determine own values/beliefs; attain financial freedom.
Family capacities	Be capable of caring for and financially supporting a family.
Norm compliance	Refrain from crime, irresponsible sex, drunk driving, illegal drug use.
Biological transitions	Be capable of fathering/bearing children.
Legal/Chronological transitions	Obtain driver's licence; reach age 18; reach age 19.

- **Applications** features demonstrate how principles from basic psychological research can be applied to everyday life. Many of these features focus on important skills that can enhance students' learning and performance. Topics include "The Battle to Control Eating and Weight" (Chapter 11) and "How to Be Happy" (Chapter 15).

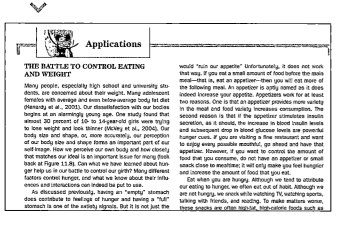

- **Thinking Critically** activities question a belief or information presented in the text, or pose a situation that requires analysis, and then ask students to construct an answer using their critical-examination skills. Students can then compare their answer to one provided on at the end of the book.

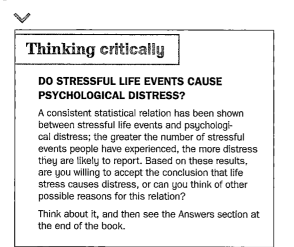

Thinking critically

DO STRESSFUL LIFE EVENTS CAUSE PSYCHOLOGICAL DISTRESS?

A consistent statistical relation has been shown between stressful life events and psychological distress; the greater the number of stressful events people have experienced, the more distress they are likely to report. Based on these results, are you willing to accept the conclusion that life stress causes distress, or can you think of other possible reasons for this relation?

Think about it, and then see the Answers section at the end of the book.

- **Directed Questions** appear in the margins of the text adjacent to important material. Students are to read the question before reading the material, and then answer the question after reading the material. The Directed Questions enhance concept mastery, serve as retrieval clues during study, and act as a performance feedback measure.

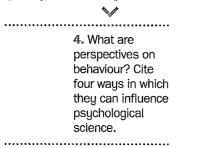

4. What are perspectives on behaviour? Cite four ways in which they can influence psychological science.

- **Each major section** ends with **In Review,** a bulleted interim summary that breaks the key content from each chapter into manageable segments.

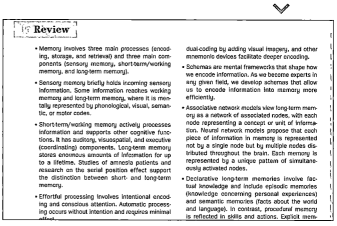

- At the end of each chapter, **Gaining Direction** features suggest some possible answers to the questions posed in the opening vignette. In the spirit of PBL, these answers are not definitive but merely suggest a set of issues to be explored and some sources of information. This feature helps students apply the newly learned material to real-world situations, thus enhancing their understanding of the text content and the use of psychology in real life.

- **Additional Pedagogical Features:** A textbook should inspire students and help them master the material at hand. To accomplish these goals, our book incorporates chapter outlines, boldfaced key terms, and a full end-of-text glossary.
- **Canadian Content:** Times have changed and work that once was considered classic is now performed in labs all across North America. Thus, we have included a large number of studies by both Canadian and U.S. authors. Bringing psychology to life for students, the text includes examples that are relatable for students, statistics that reflect the Canadian and North American context, and stories and vignettes that occur in Canadian locations.

LEARN WITHOUT LIMITS
■ connect

McGraw-Hill Connect® is an award-winning digital teaching and learning platform that gives students the means to better connect with their coursework, with their instructors, and with the important concepts that they will need to know for success now and in the future. With Connect, instructors can take advantage of McGraw-Hill's trusted content to seamlessly deliver assignments, quizzes and tests online. McGraw-Hill Connect is a learning platform that continually adapts to each student, delivering precisely what they need, when they need it, so class time is more engaging and effective. Connect makes teaching and learning personal, easy, and proven.

CONNECT KEY FEATURES:

SmartBook®

As the first and only adaptive reading experience, Smart-Book is changing the way students read and learn. SmartBook creates a personalized reading experience by highlighting the most important concepts a student needs to learn at that moment in time. As a student engages with SmartBook, the reading experience continuously adapts by highlighting content based on what each student knows and doesn't know. This ensures that he or she is focused on the content needed to close specific knowledge gaps, while it simultaneously promotes long-term learning.

Connect Insight®

Connect Insight is Connect's new one-of-a-kind visual analytics dashboard—now available for instructors—that provides at-a-glance information regarding student performance, which is immediately actionable. By presenting assignment, assessment, and topical performance results together with a time metric that is easily visible for aggregate or individual results, Connect Insight gives instructors the ability to take a just-in-time approach to teaching and learning, which was never before available. Connect Insight presents data that helps instructors improve class performance in a way that is efficient and effective.

Simple Assignment Management

With Connect, creating assignments is easier than ever, so instructors can spend more time teaching and less time managing.

* Assign SmartBook learning modules.
* Instructors can edit existing questions and create their own questions.
* Draw from a variety of text-specific questions, resources, and test bank material to assign online.

* Streamline lesson planning, student progress reporting, and assignment grading to make classroom management more efficient than ever.

Smart Grading

When it comes to studying, time is precious. Connect helps students learn more efficiently by providing feedback and practice material when they need it, where they need it.

* Automatically score assignments, giving students immediate feedback on their work and comparisons with correct answers.
* Access and review each response; manually change grades or leave comments for students to review.
* Track individual student performance—by question, assignment, or in relation to the class overall—with detailed grade reports.
* Reinforce classroom concepts with practice tests and instant quizzes.
* Integrate grade reports easily with Learning Management Systems including Blackboard, D2L, and Moodle.

Instructor Library

The Connect Instructor Library is a repository for additional resources to improve student engagement in and out of the class. It provides all the critical resources instructors need to build their course.

* Access Instructor resources.
* View assignments and resources created for past sections.
* Post your own resources for students to use.

INSTRUCTOR RESOURCES

* Instructor's Manual
* Validated Test Bank
* Alternate Test Bank
* Conceptual Test Bank
* Microsoft® PowerPoint® Lecture Slides

Superior Learning Solutions and Support

The McGraw-Hill Education team is ready to help instructors assess and integrate any of our products, technology, and services into your course for optimal teaching and learning performance. Whether it's helping your students improve their grades, or putting your entire course online, the McGraw-Hill Education team is here to help you do it. Contact your Learning Solutions Consultant today to learn how to maximize all of McGraw-Hill Education's resources.

For more information, please visit us online: http://www.mheducation.ca/he/solutions

ACKNOWLEDGMENTS

Every book, large or small, owes a great deal to the people behind the scenes. They keep the project going, offer support and assistance, and provide sage advice to the authors.

Thanks to Corey Isaacs for his dedicated work assisting with research and references, and making valuable content recommendations at the outset of the project. Thanks also to Lesley Atkinson and Debra Jared—your support keeps us sane.

Our heartfelt thanks to all the people at McGraw-Hill Ryerson who have nurtured this book over the past year: Scott Hardie (Product Manager); Jeanette McCurdy (Supervising Editor); Kelli Legros (Marketing Manager); Valerie Adams (Copy Editor); and Denise Foote (Group Product Development Manager).

And finally, a special thanks to Brianna McIlwain (Product Developer). You kept us on track, on time, and in focus. We simply could not have done this without you.

We also owe special thanks to our distinguished colleagues who recommended changes for the sixth Canadian edition of *Psychology: Frontiers and Applications*. We appreciate the time and effort graciously contributed by the following instructors:

Cheryl Wartman, *University of Prince Edward Island*
Kathy Foxall, *Wilfrid Laurier University*
Jason Leboe-McGowan, *University of Manitoba*
Jennifer Steeves, *York University*
Karsten Loepelmann, *University of Alberta*
Sally Walters, *Capilano University*
Joanne Lee, *Wilfrid Laurier University*

M.A. & J.M.

Psychology: The Science of Behaviour

CHAPTER ›

OUTLINE

The chapter outline is your roadmap to each chapter. Skim the outline before reading the chapter to get an overview of the chapter's topic.

The compass icon appears next to the opening story. Throughout the chapter, the icon will mark sections of text that may be relevant to this story.

THE NATURE OF PSYCHOLOGY

Psychology's Scientific Approach
Thinking Critically about Behaviour
Psychology's Goals
Psychology as a Basic and Applied Science
Psychology's Broad Scope: A Simple Framework

PERSPECTIVES ON BEHAVIOUR

Psychology's Intellectual Roots
Early Schools: Structuralism and Functionalism
The Psychodynamic Perspective: The Forces Within
The Behavioural Perspective: The Power of the Environment
The Humanistic Perspective: Self-Actualization and Positive Psychology
The Cognitive Perspective: The Thinking Human
The Sociocultural Perspective: The Embedded Human
  Research Foundations: Would You Marry Someone You Didn't Love?

The Biological Perspective: The Brain, Genes, and Evolution
  Focus on Neuroscience: The Neuroscience of Imaging Studies

USING LEVELS OF ANALYSIS TO INTEGRATE THE PERSPECTIVES

  Frontiers: Culture, Language, and Behaviour
An Example: Understanding Depression
Summary of Major Themes

PSYCHOLOGY TODAY

  Applications: Academic Performance Enhancement Strategies

Try to answer all these questions after you have read the opening story. When you see the compass icon throughout the chapter, consider which issue it might address, what information is provided, and what else you need to know.

Perhaps the most fascinating and mysterious universe of all is the one within us.
—Carl Sagan

 On March 24, 2015, Germanwings Flight 9525 crashed into the French Alps, killing all 150 people aboard. The Airbus A320 did not have any maintenance or mechanical problems. The investigation into the accident later revealed that the co-pilot, Andreas Lubitz, deliberately flew the plane into the mountains at 700 kilometres per hour. Lubitz was suffering from several psychological disorders and had recently been treated for suicidal tendencies.

In the summer of 2006, Derek Amato, a 39-year-old sales trainer,

© Derek Amato

What are the issues here?

What do we need to know?

Where can we find the information to answer the questions?

was fooling around at a friend's pool. His friend threw a football, Derek jumped for it, but missed and slammed his head into the side of the pool. He was diagnosed with a severe concussion and had intense headaches, memory loss, and a 35 percent hearing loss in one ear. Four days later, he was at his friend's place drifting in and out of consciousness. His friend had a small music studio and as Derek was sitting there he picked up a keyboard and started to play. Although he had no musical training at all, he played like a professional. His friend was stunned. Derek continued to play and compose music. He has written over 2500 pieces, composed scores for documentaries, and published a book. He's working on his third album and is preparing to go on tour.

Canadian biologist Anne Adams was suffering from a severe case of frontotemporal lobe dementia. She lost her ability to speak, but surprisingly, became an artistic genius. Her seminal work, *Unravelling Bolero*, is considered a forceful example of mathematics and art.

L et's begin our exploration of psychology with a quick exercise. Please read the paragraph below, unscrambling the words as you proceed.

Terms in boldface indicate new or important concepts. These terms are defined in the Glossary.

1. Define psychology and indicate what kinds of behaviours it studies.

Directed questions appear throughout each chapter. Read the question before you read the material in the text. After reading the material, try to answer the question.

Aoccdrnig to rscheearch at Cmabrigde uinervtisy, it deosn't mttaer waht oredr the ltteers in a wrod are, the olny iprmoetnt tihng is taht the frist and lsat ltteres are at the rghit pclae. The rset can be a tatol mses, and you can sitll raed it wouthit a porbelm. Tihs is bcuseae we do not raed ervey lteter by istlef but the wrod as a wlohe.

Type "jumbled words," "jumbled paragraph," or "scrambled letters" into a web browser. Dig around in the search results, and you'll find multiple sites and blogs about this paragraph. In 2003, it was all the rage. The paragraph spread across the Internet and reached countless email inboxes as people—amazed by how easily they could read it—passed it along. When we showed the paragraph to our students, most breezed through it, although some struggled (if you had trouble, that's okay; see the unscrambled version at the end of this chapter). Show the paragraph to some people you know and see how they do.

Do you accept the claim that if the first and last letters of a word remain intact "the rset can be a tatol mses and you can sitll raed it wouthit a porbelm"? From the paragraph's immense popularity, we speculate that many people do accept this statement. After all, the evidence is concrete; it's right before our eyes. Well, whether or not you accept it, take this challenge: Can you think of reasons why this particular jumbled paragraph is easy to read? Even better, can you create a short jumbled paragraph—keeping the first and last letters of words intact—that people find difficult to read? We'll return to this challenge later in the chapter.

So what does a jumbled paragraph have to do with psychology? If you personally view psychology as synonymous with *therapy, shrinks,* or *couches,* then your answer might be "not much."

But as we'll see, psychologists study a tremendous diversity of topics—including language and how we recognize words (Mousikou et al., 2010).

The jumbled paragraph raises other key psychological issues, such as how we acquire knowledge and form beliefs about our world, which we'll discuss in the conclusion of this chapter. Among the countless beliefs we hold and the claims we hear about human nature and behaviour, how do we separate fact from fiction and myth from reality? The science of psychology leads us to engage these questions.

THE NATURE OF PSYCHOLOGY

Psychology is the scientific study of behaviour and the mind. The term *behaviour* refers to actions and responses that we can directly observe, whereas the term *mind* refers to internal states and processes, such as thoughts and feelings, that cannot be seen directly and that must be inferred from observable, measurable responses. For example, we cannot directly see a person's feeling of love or admiration for someone else, but we can infer how the person feels based on observable verbal statements (e.g., "I love you"; "I really admire you").

When people hear the word *psychologist,* the first image that comes to their minds is often that of a therapist. This reaction is understandable, as a large number of psychologists work in a subfield called **clinical psychology:** the study and treatment of mental disorders. Many clinical psychologists diagnose and treat people with psychological problems in clinics, hospitals, and private practice. In addition, some are scientists who conduct research on the causes of mental disorders and the effectiveness of various treatments. Yet many psychologists have no connection with therapy and instead conduct research in other subfields (Figure 1.1). For example, **cognitive psychology** specializes in

(top) © StockTrek/Getty Images; (middle) © Gabe Palmer/Corbis; (bottom) © Royalty-Free/Corbis

FIGURE 1.1 Psychologists study diverse topics. Subfields that may not immediately occur to you include aviation and space psychology, educational psychology, and the law.

the study of mental processes, especially from a model that views the mind as an information processor. Cognitive psychologists examine such topics as consciousness, attention, memory, decision making, and problem solving. An area within cognitive psychology, called *psycholinguistics*, focuses on the psychology of language. The jumbled-word exercise relates directly to psycholinguistics.

To illustrate psychology's diversity, here a few other subfields:

- **Biopsychology/neuroscience** focuses on the biological underpinnings of behaviour. Biopsychologists examine how brain processes, genes, and hormones influence our actions, thoughts, and feelings. Some biopsychologists seek to explain how evolution has shaped our psychological capabilities (e.g., our capacity for advanced thinking and language) and behavioural tendencies (e.g., to act aggressively or altruistically).

- **Developmental psychology** examines human physical, psychological, and social development across the lifespan. For example, some developmental psychologists explore the emotional world of infants, while others study how different parenting styles psychologically affect children or how our mental abilities change during adolescence and adulthood.

- **Experimental psychology** focuses on such basic processes as learning, sensory systems (e.g., vision, hearing), perception, and motivational states (e.g., sexual motivation, hunger, thirst). Most research in this subfield involves laboratory experiments, often with nonhuman animals. Although this subfield is called *experimental* psychology, be aware that researchers in many psychological subfields conduct experiments.

- **Industrial-organizational (I/O) psychology** examines people's behaviour in the workplace. I/O psychologists study leadership, teamwork, and factors that influence employees' job satisfaction, work motivation, and performance. They develop tests to help employers identify the best job applicants and design systems that companies use to evaluate employee performance.

- **Personality psychology** focuses on the study of human personality. Personality psychologists seek to identify core personality traits and how different traits relate to one another and influence behaviour. They also develop tests to measure personality.

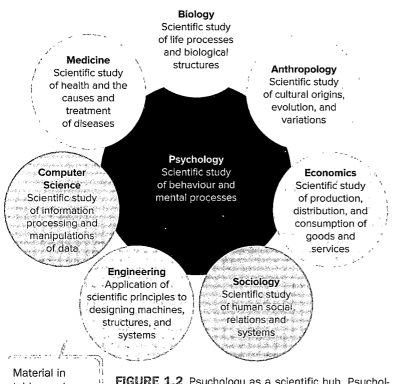

FIGURE 1.2 Psychology as a scientific hub. Psychology links with and overlaps many sciences.

Material in tables and figures can be just as important as the text. Be sure you read these sections.

- **Social psychology** examines people's thoughts, feelings, and behaviour pertaining to the social world: the world of other people. Social psychologists study how people influence one another, behave in groups, and form impressions and attitudes. They study social relationships involving attraction and love, prejudice and discrimination, helping, and aggression.

Note that topics studied in different subfields often overlap. Consider decision making, which is examined in all of the areas above. For example, a cognitive psychologist might study how wording the same information in different ways affects people's decisions; a social psychologist might study decision making in groups; and a developmental psychologist could examine how children's decision-making strategies change with age (Josyln et al., 2009; Toma & Butera, 2009). Moreover, many psychologists have interests that bridge different subfields. Thus, a clinical psychologist might be interested in the biological bases of how adolescents with anxiety disorders make decisions. She could have adolescents who do and who don't have an anxiety disorder perform decision-making tasks, and use brain-imaging techniques to compare the neural activity of the two groups (Krain et al., 2008).

We'll encounter other branches of psychology throughout the chapter, but we hope you already get the picture. Psychologists do study the causes of mental disorders, provide therapy, and evaluate therapy effectiveness, but their interests and research span the entire realm of behaviour. Indeed, the scope of modern psychology stretches from the borders of medicine and the biological sciences to those of the social sciences (Figure 1.2).

Psychology's Scientific Approach

Across psychology's diverse subfields, researchers share a common underlying scientific approach to studying behaviour. *Science* is a process that involves systematically gathering and evaluating empirical evidence to answer questions and test beliefs about the natural world. *Empirical evidence* is evidence gained through experience and observation, and this includes evidence from manipulating or "tinkering around" with things and then observing what happens (this is the essence of experimentation). For example, if we want to know how people's intellectual abilities change as they age, we don't rely on intuition, pure reasoning, or folk wisdom to obtain an answer. Rather, we collect empirical data by exposing people to intellectual tasks and observing how they perform. Moreover, in science these observations need to be *systematic* (i.e., performed according to a system of rules or conditions) so that they will be as objective and precise as possible (Shaugnessy et al., 2010).

Understanding Behaviour: Some Pitfalls of Everyday Approaches

Science is only one of many ways that we learn about human behaviour. Family and friends, great works of literature, secular and religious teachings, and the Internet and popular media all provide us with messages about human nature. Mix in our own intuitions (i.e., the knowledge that each of us acquires from years of personal experience interacting with people) and so-called "conventional" or "folk" wisdom, and we have potent ingredients for generating our personal beliefs about what makes people tick.

Unfortunately, in everyday life there are many ways in which these sources can end up promoting misconceptions. Other people—via conversations, books, the Internet, and other popular media—may provide us with information and insights that they believe to be accurate but really are not. Even personal experiences can lead us to form inaccurate beliefs. Although our experiences and everyday observations provide us with empirical information, unlike scientific observations, everyday observation usually is casual rather than systematic. Our own experiences also may be atypical and not representative of what most people experience.

As we'll explore in Chapter 9, misconceptions can also result from our own faulty thinking. For example, consider the following:

- We often take *mental shortcuts* when forming judgments—shortcuts that sometimes serve us poorly (White, 2009). Judging someone's personality based solely on stereotypes about his or her physical appearance would be an example of a mental shortcut (e.g., Kleider et al., 2012).

- Because many factors in real life may operate simultaneously to influence behaviour, we may *fail to consider alternative explanations* for why a behaviour has occurred and assume that one factor has caused it, when in fact some less obvious factor was the true cause (Elek et al., 2012; Lassiter et al., 2007).

- Once our beliefs are established, we often fail to test them further. In this vein, we tend to display a *confirmation bias* by selectively paying attention to information that is consistent with our beliefs and downplaying or ignoring information that is inconsistent with them (Mendel et al., 2011; Hart et al., 2009).

Using Science to Minimize Everyday Pitfalls

Yes, scientists are human too, and they may fall victim to all these pitfalls and to others that we'll discuss in the next chapter. But by adopting a scientific approach, psychologists can take concrete steps to avoid or at least minimize biases and problems that can lead to inaccurate conclusions. For example, rather than relying on imprecise casual observations, psychologists use various instruments (e.g., video recorders, questionnaires, brain-imaging devices) to objectively and precisely record people's responses. When directly watching people, several researchers can independently observe the same behaviours and compare their findings to ensure that their observations were reliable. To avoid perceiving illusory correlations, psychologists typically use statistics to analyze their data. To minimize drawing erroneous conclusions about what has caused what, psychologists often are able to examine behaviour under highly controlled experimental conditions in which they intentionally manipulate one factor, try to keep other factors constant, and see how the manipulated factor influences behaviour.

Science also is a public affair, as psychologists do publish their findings. Publication enables scientists to scrutinize and challenge each other's findings if they wish. This collective approach reduces the risk of confirmation bias. As new studies are conducted, the original findings are put to the test and may be contradicted, forcing scientists to modify their beliefs and conduct further research to sort out contradictory results.

To be sure, science has limitations and its own pitfalls. It is ideally suited to examining testable questions about the natural world. Psychologists can study such questions as "Do happy people differ from unhappy people in their degree of religiousness or spirituality?" and "What do people believe gives their life meaning?" But science cannot answer such questions as "Does God exist?" and "What is the meaning of life?" The former is a question of faith that is beyond scientific measurement; the latter is a question answered by personal values. As for pitfalls, poorly designed or poorly executed studies can produce misleading data that result in invalid conclusions.

Even when studies are designed well and conducted properly, "false starts" can occur in which other researchers later are unable to duplicate the original researchers' findings. Additionally, over time, new research often modifies or completely overturns existing scientific beliefs. But it's important to realize that these aren't weaknesses of the scientific approach. Rather, they reveal one of its great strengths: *In principle, science ultimately is a self-correcting process.* At any point in history, scientific knowledge represents a best estimate of how the world operates. As better or more complete information is gathered, that best estimate may continue to be supported or it may need to be changed. Understandably, to many people such change can be frustrating or confusing, as illustrated by the public uproar in 2009, when an expert medical panel issued new breast-cancer screening guidelines (Kolata, 2009). The panel stated that most women should start having regular mammogram tests at age 50, not at age 40 as recommended by prior, long-standing guidelines. Similarly, researchers in the Czech Republic reported that eating only two larger meals per day rather than multiple small meals actually leads to greater weight loss (Kahleova et al., 2012). To scientists, however, such changes represent an evolution of knowledge called *scientific progress.*

TABLE 1.1   Widely Held Beliefs about Behaviour: Fact or Fiction?

Directions: Decide whether each statement is true or false.

1. Most people with exceptionally high IQs are well adjusted in other areas of their lives.
2. In romantic relationships, opposites usually attract.
3. Overall, married adults are less happy than adults who aren't married.
4. Graphology (handwriting analysis) is a valid method for measuring people's personality.
5. A person who is innocent of a crime has nothing to fear from a lie detector test.
6. People who commit suicide usually have signalled to others their intention to do so.
7. When you negatively reinforce someone's behaviour, the person becomes more likely to behave that way.
8. On some types of mental tasks, people perform as well or better when they are 70 years old than when they are 20 years old.
9. Usually, it is safe to awaken someone who is sleepwalking.
10. A schizophrenic is a person who has two or more distinct personalities, hence the term *split personality*.

Answers: Items 1, 6, 8, and 9 are supported by psychological research. Item 7 is true by definition. The remaining items are false. (If you correctly answered 9 or 10 of these items, you've done significantly better than random guessing.)

The compass icon indicates that the material here may help us understand the opening story.

Thinking Critically about Behaviour

Because behaviour is so complex, its scientific study poses special challenges. As you become familiar with the kinds of evidence necessary to validate scientific conclusions, you will become a better-informed consumer of the many claims made in the name of psychology. For one thing, this course will teach you that many widely held beliefs about behaviour are inaccurate. Can you distinguish the valid claims from the invalid ones in Table 1.1?

Perhaps more important than the concepts you learn in this course will be the habits of thought that you acquire—habits that involve *critical thinking*. Critical thinking involves taking an active role in understanding the world around you rather than merely receiving information. It's important to reflect on what that information means, how it fits in with your experiences, and its implications for your life and society (Franco, Butler, & Halpern, 2015). Critical thinking also means evaluating the validity of something presented to you as fact (Levy, 2010; Vaughn, 2016). For example, when someone makes a claim or asserts a new "fact," ask yourself the following questions, just as a scientist would:

- What, exactly, is the claim or assertion?
- Who is making the claim? Is the source credible and trustworthy?
- What's the evidence, and how good is it?
- Are other explanations possible? Can I evaluate them?
- What is the most appropriate conclusion?

The Jumbled-Word Challenge

Let's think critically about the jumbled-word paragraph presented earlier. First, *what's the claim?* There are three, actually: (1) that people can read jumbled words without a problem as long as the first and last letters stay in place, (2) that people have no problems because we read words as a whole rather than as individual letters, and (3) that this finding is based on research at Cambridge University.

Second, *who is making the claim?* The jumbled paragraph's author is anonymous, which is *caution flag 1*. We can't evaluate the author's credibility and trustworthiness.

Third, *what's the evidence, and how good is it?* The evidence begins with an unsubstantiated claim that research was conducted at Cambridge. No reference information (researchers' names, publisher location, date) is given, which is *caution flag 2*. Indeed, scientists did no such research at Cambridge, although unpublished research at another university may have been the source (Davis, 2003; Rawlinson, 1999).

There's also the dramatic evidence of your own experience: reading the jumbled paragraph easily. But this is only one short paragraph. Also, overall, the transposition (i.e., switched ordering) of letters is minimal, which is *caution flag 3*, leading to the next question.

Fourth, *are other explanations possible* for why the paragraph is easy to read? We'll discuss reading more fully in Chapter 9. For now, consider the following:

- Of the words in the paragraph, 65 percent either aren't jumbled (because they have only one to three letters), or—with four-letter words—are "jumbled" only in that their second and third letters are switched (because there is only one possible transposition), which makes unscrambling them easy.

- Of words with five or six letters, in all but one case, the transposition is minor because only a single letter is out of sequence (e.g., for *mttaer*, only the *a* is out of order).

- Thus, in total, 83 percent of the words are either unjumbled or have only minor transpositions. This preserves much of the way the words sound when we read them. Further, these words provide contextual information in the sentence that makes it easier to anticipate the meaning of some of the few longer scrambled words.

In everyday life, you're unlikely to conduct a scientific study to test these alternative explanations, but you can gather additional evidence by constructing sentences with longer words and more complex transpositions and having some people try to read them. Try reading the following paragraph (the unjumbled version is revealed at the end of the chapter), and see if it changes your belief about the ease of reading jumbled words.

A plciaiiotn dieend the mtnaalueghsr of a clgaloeue, but was coincetvd and dlepoeelvd sreeve macedil cdointonis in posirn, wrhee he deid. Arnodiistitman of agctannlo-auit dgurs ptttnaioeed the eefctfs of atehonr durg, and rprsoiearty frliaue rleeutsd.

Lastly, *what is the most appropriate conclusion?* The claim that it's relatively easy to read words as long as the first and last letters are intact appears to be too broad and absolute. Stated as such, it's clearly wrong. Stated in qualified terms of "under some conditions" the claim has support, although one study found that even minor transpositions of interior letters slowed reading speed by 11 percent (Rayner, White, Johnson, & Liversedge, 2006). In some languages, however, such interior transpositions may make words very difficult, if not impossible, to read (Davis, 2003).

Of Astrology and Asstrology: Potential Costs of Uncritical Thinking

Suppose someone swallows the bait of the original jumbled-word paragraph and now erroneously believes that it's always easy to read words with transposed letters. Unless it's a smart-aleck student or worker who plans to turn in "jumbled" school papers or work reports (citing "scientific justification" for doing so), what's the harm in holding this little false belief? Perhaps the immediate personal consequences

are minimal, but misconceptions can add up and contribute to an increasingly misguided view of how the world operates.

Unfortunately, people uncritically accept many misconceptions that do have concrete harmful consequences. For example, in the hope of making their babies smarter, consumers have shelled out about $200 million annually for *Baby Einstein* videos that the Walt Disney Company advertised as educational, despite a lack of scientific support for its claim (Zimmerman et al., 2007). Under government and consumer group pressure, Disney eventually dropped the *educational* label and later agreed to partially refund consumers (Lewin, 2009).

Despite a lack of scientific evidence, people spend untold amounts of their hard-earned money to have their personalities analyzed and their futures forecasted by astrologers, graphologists (i.e., handwriting analyzers), tea-leaf readers, and other so-called "fortune tellers"—including rumpologists (sometimes referred to as *asstrologers*) who "read" people's buttocks to obtain their presumed psychic insights (Wyman & Vyse, 2008). Money aside, it's impossible to estimate how many people may have made major life decisions based on fortune tellers' bogus advice. It's also hard to know how many people have not only wasted money on bogus therapies for ailments, diseases, and mental disorders, but also experienced needless continued distress or further bodily harm by failing to employ scientifically validated treatments. Unfortunately, *pseudoscience*—a field that incorporates astrology, graphology, rumpology, and so on—is dressed up to look like science and it attracts many believers, despite its lack of credible scientific evidence (Figure 1.3). Critical scrutiny is important for all scientific claims, as

© Sidney Harris. ScienceCartoonsPlus.com. Reprinted with permission.

FIGURE 1.3 The popularity of pseudoscience.

illustrated by Bem's recent article claiming support for extrasensory perception (Bem, 2011). Daryl Bem is a highly respected researcher and the article was published in a prestigious journal. However, many other authors (e.g., Francis, 2012; LeBel et al., 2011) claimed that the data simply do not support the conclusions.

Psychology's Goals

2. What are the four goals of psychology? How are these goals linked to one another?

As a science, psychology has four central goals:

1. To *describe* how people and other animals behave
2. To *explain and understand* the causes of these behaviours
3. To *predict* how people and animals will behave under certain conditions
4. To *influence or control* behaviour through knowledge and control of its causes to enhance human welfare

As you will learn in Chapter 2, the scientific goals of understanding, prediction, and control are linked in the following manner: If we understand the causes of a behaviour and know when the causal factors are present or absent, then we should be able to successfully predict when the behaviour will occur. Moreover, if we can control the causes, then we should be able to control the behaviour. For scientists, successful prediction and control are the best ways for us to know whether we truly understand the causes of behaviour. We should also note, however, that prediction can have important practical uses that do not require a complete understanding of why some behaviour occurs. For example, a psychologist might find that scores on a personality test dependably predict school drop-out rates, without fully understanding the psychological processes involved.

Psychology as a Basic and Applied Science

3. How do the goals of basic research and applied research differ?

As scientists, psychologists employ a variety of research methods for developing and testing theories about behaviour and its causes. A distinction is sometimes made between **basic research,** the quest for knowledge purely for its own sake, and **applied research,** which is designed to solve specific practical problems. In psychology, the goals of basic research are to describe how people behave and to identify the factors that influence or cause a particular type of behaviour. Such research may be carried out in the laboratory or in real-world settings. Applied research often uses principles discovered through basic research to solve practical problems. Research methods will be discussed more fully in Chapter 2, but five research articles have been listed below to help you understand the difference between basic and applied research. These actual titles of articles appeared in psychological journals. Can you identify whether each study represents basic or applied research?

1. Two Forms of Spatial Imagery: Neuroimaging Evidence
2. The Prevention of Depressive Symptoms in Low-Income, Minority Children: Two-Year Follow-up
3. Increasing Seat Belt Use on a College Campus: An Evaluation of Two Prompting Procedures
4. Facial Structure Is a Reliable Cue of Aggressive Behaviour
5. Recognizing Speech under a Processing Load: Dissociating Energetic from Informational Factors

Check your answers at the end of the chapter.

Psychology's Broad Scope: A Simple Framework

Because we are biological creatures, living in a complex social world, psychologists study an amazing array of factors to understand why people behave, think, and feel as they do. At times, this diversity of factors may seem a bit overwhelming, but we would like to provide you with a framework that will greatly simplify matters. We call it **levels of analysis:** Behaviour and its causes can be examined at the *biological level* (e.g., brain processes, genetic influences), the *psychological level* (e.g., our thoughts, feelings, and motives), and the *environmental level* (e.g., past and current physical and social environments to which we are exposed).

Here is a brief example of how the framework can be applied. Consider a behaviour that you engage in every day: eating (Figure 1.4). At the biological level, various chemicals, neural circuits, and structures in your brain respond to bodily signals and help to regulate whether you feel hungry or full. At the psychological level, your moods, food preferences, and motives affect eating. Do you ever eat when you're not hungry—perhaps because you feel stressed or bored? The environmental level of analysis calls attention to specific stimuli (such as the appearance or aroma of different foods) that may trigger eating and to cultural customs that influence our food preferences.

The Psychological Level

The Environmental Level

The Biological Level

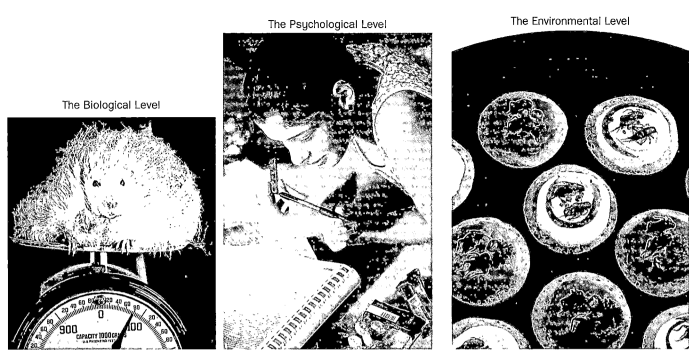

(left) Courtesy of Neal E. Miller; (centre) © Phanie/Photo Researchers, Inc.; (right) © Michael Freeman/Corbis

FIGURE 1.4 *Biological level* (left). This rat weighs about triple the weight of a normal rat. As we (or rats) eat, hunger decreases as certain brain regions regulate the sensation of becoming full. Those regions in this rat's brain have been damaged, causing it to overeat and become obese. *Psychological level* (centre). At times, we may eat out of habit, stress, or boredom. With a chocolate bar in hand and other candies lined up, this student is ready for some autopilot munching. *Environmental level* (right). Does a plateful of insect-topped crackers sound appetizing to you? Cultural norms influence food preferences.

Does the aroma of freshly baked treats ever make your stomach growl? How about the sight of duck feet or a mound of fish gills on a plate? To most Westerners, duck feet and fish gills may not be appetizing, but during a stay in China, we discovered that our hosts considered them delicious.

Mind–Body and Nature–Nurture Interactions

Form a mental picture of a favourite food, and you may trigger a hunger pang. Focus on positive thoughts when facing a challenging situation, and you may keep your bodily arousal in check. Dwell instead on negative thoughts, and you can rapidly stimulate the release of stress hormones (Borod, 2000). These examples illustrate what traditionally have been called *mind–body interactions*—the relations between mental processes in the brain and the functioning of other bodily systems. Mind–body interactions focus our attention on the fascinating interplay between the psychological and biological levels of analysis. This topic has a long history within psychology, and, as you will see throughout the textbook, it remains one of psychology's most exciting frontiers.

The levels-of-analysis framework also addresses an issue that has been debated since antiquity: Is our behaviour primarily shaped by nature (our biological endowment) or nurture (our environment and learning history)? The pendulum has swung toward one end or the other at different times in history, but today, growing interest in cultural influences and advances in genetics and brain research keep the nature–nurture pendulum in a more balanced position (e.g., Eagly & Wood, 2013; Rutter, 2014; Salvatore & Dick, 2015).

Perhaps most important, modern research increasingly reveals that nature and nurture interact (Masterpasqua, 2009; Moffitt et al., 2006). Just as our biological capacities affect how we behave and experience the world, our experiences influence our biological capacities. For humans and rats alike, continually depriving a newborn of physical contact, or providing a newborn with an enriched environment in which to grow, can influence its brain functioning and biological development (Rosenzweig, 1984). Thus, while it may be tempting to take sides, "Nature *or* nurture?" usually is the wrong question. As the levels-of-analysis framework implies, nature, nurture, and psychological factors must all be taken into account to gain the fullest understanding of behaviour. Later in the chapter, we'll provide a more detailed example of how looking at behaviour from multiple levels enhances our understanding.

- Psychology is the scientific study of behaviour and the mind. The term *behaviour* refers to actions and responses that we can directly observe, whereas the term *mind* refers to internal states and processes, such as thoughts and feelings, that cannot be seen directly and that must be inferred from observable, measurable responses.

- The primary goals of psychological science are to describe, explain, predict, and influence behaviour and to apply psychological knowledge to enhance human welfare.

- Basic research is the quest for knowledge for its own sake, whereas applied research involves the application of knowledge derived from basic research to solve practical problems.

PERSPECTIVES ON BEHAVIOUR

Psychologists' focus on biological, psychological, and environmental factors that influence behaviour is not new; this focus has been an integral part of psychology's history. But just how did psychology's scope become so broad? In part, it happened because psychology has roots in such varied disciplines as philosophy, medicine, and the biological and physical sciences. As a result, different ways of viewing people, called **perspectives**, became part of psychology's intellectual traditions (Figure 1.5).

4. What are perspectives on behaviour? Cite four ways in which they can influence psychological science.

FIGURE 1.5 Youth and beauty . . . or maturity and wisdom? What we perceive depends on our perspective. When you examine this drawing, you will see either a young woman or an old one. Now try changing your perspective. The ear and necklace of the young woman are the left eye and mouth of the old woman.

Source: Public Domain. "My wife and my mother-in-law. They are both in this picture - find them" by W.E. Hill.

In science, new perspectives are engines of progress. Advances occur as existing beliefs are challenged, a debate ensues, and scientists seek new evidence to resolve the debate. Sometimes, the best-supported elements of contrasting perspectives are merged into a new framework, which in turn will be challenged by still newer viewpoints.

If you have ever met someone who views the world differently from the way you do, then you know that perspectives matter. Similarly, perspectives serve as lenses through which psychologists examine and interpret behaviour. To illustrate this point, let's consider the case of Ray, who was a shy student when he first entered university. Ray knew he was shy, especially around women, yet he wasn't sure why. He had been nervous on the few dates he had gone on in high school. During his first term at university, Ray met some women he liked but was afraid to ask them out. He didn't make male friends either. By winter, he was depressed and his schoolwork suffered. After a good spring break visit with his family, Ray turned things around. He studied hard, did well in class, and made friends with some guys in the dorm. His mood improved and soon thereafter he met Kira. Kira was attracted to Ray but sensed his shyness, so she asked Ray out. They've been dating for a year and Ray is happy. He and Kira have even discussed marriage.

Soon we'll briefly look at Ray's case through the lens of six psychological perspectives. But first, to better understand how these perspectives evolved, let's examine psychology's roots and two of its earliest schools of thought.

Psychology's Intellectual Roots

Humans have long sought to understand themselves, and for ages the *mind–body problem* has occupied the centre of this quest. Is the mind—the inner agent of consciousness and thought—a spiritual entity separate from the body, or is it part of the body's activities?

Many early philosophers held a position of **mind–body dualism,** the belief that the mind is a spiritual entity not subject to physical laws that govern the body. But if the mind is not composed of physical matter, how could it become aware of bodily sensations, and how could its thoughts exert control over bodily functions? French philosopher and scientist René Descartes (1596–1650) proposed that the mind and body interact through the brain's tiny pineal gland. Although Descartes placed the mind within the brain, he maintained that the mind was a spiritual, nonmaterial entity. *Dualism* implies that no amount of research on the physical body (including the brain) could ever hope to unravel the mysteries of the nonphysical mind.

Another view, **monism** (from the Greek word *monos,* meaning "one"), holds that mind and body are one and that the mind is not a separate spiritual entity. To monists, mental events correspond to physical events in the brain, a position advocated by English philosopher Thomas Hobbes (1588–1679). Monism helped set the stage for psychology because it implied that the mind could be studied by measuring physical processes within the brain. The stage was further set by John Locke (1632–1704) and other philosophers from the school of **British empiricism,** which held that all ideas and knowledge are gained empirically— that is, through the senses. According to empiricists, observation is a more valid approach to knowledge than is pure reason, because reason is fraught with the potential for error. This idea bolstered the development of modern science, whose methods are rooted in empirical observation.

Discoveries in physiology (an area of biology that examines bodily functioning) and medicine also paved the way for psychology's emergence. By 1870, European researchers were electrically stimulating the brains of laboratory animals and mapping the surface areas that controlled various body movements. Additionally, medical reports were linking damage in different areas of patients' brains with various behavioural and mental impairments. This mounting evidence of the relation between brain and behaviour supported the view that empirical methods of the natural sciences could be used to study mental processes. Indeed, in the mid-1800s German scientists had already established a new field called *psychophysics,* the study of how psychologically experienced sensations depend on the characteristics of physical stimuli (e.g., how the perceived loudness of a sound changes as its physical intensity increases).

Around this time, Charles Darwin's (1809–1882) theory of evolution was generating societal shock waves. Opponents attacked his theory because it seemed to contradict philosophical and religious beliefs about the exalted nature of human beings. Evolution implied that the mind was not a spiritual entity, but rather the product of biological continuity between humans and other species. Darwin's theory also implied that scientists might gain insight about human behaviour by studying other species. By the late 1800s, a convergence of intellectual forces provided the impetus for psychology's birth.

Early Schools: Structuralism and Functionalism

The infant science of psychology emerged in 1879, when Wilhelm Wundt (1832–1920) established the first experimental psychology laboratory at the University of Leipzig in Germany (Figure 1.6). There he helped train the first generation of scientific psychologists. Among these were August Kirschmann and James Baldwin, both of whom were founding members of the Department of Psychology at the University of Toronto, and George Humphrey, who began the tradition of research in experimental psychology at Queen's University in Kingston, Ontario (Wright & Myers, 1982). One of Wundt's graduate students, Englishman Edward Titchener (1867–1927), later established a psychology laboratory in the United States at Cornell University. Wundt and Titchener believed that the mind could be studied by breaking it down into its basic components, as a chemist might break down a complex chemical compound. Their approach came to be known as **structuralism,** the analysis of the mind in terms of its basic elements.

In their experiments, structuralists used the method of *introspection* ("looking within") to study sensations, which they considered the basic elements of consciousness. They exposed participants to all sorts of sensory stimuli— lights, sounds, tastes—and trained them to describe their inner experiences. Although this method of studying the mind was criticized as being too subjective, and it died out after a few decades, the structuralists left an important mark by establishing a scientific tradition for studying cognitive processes.

In the United States, structuralism eventually gave way to **functionalism,** which held that psychology should study the functions of consciousness rather than its structure. Here's a rough analogy to explain the difference between

5. Contrast the positions of dualism and monism as they apply to the "mind–body" problem.

© Archives of the History of American Psychology— The University of Akron

FIGURE 1.6 At the University of Leipzig in 1879, Wilhelm Wundt established the first laboratory of experimental psychology to study the structure of the mind.

6. Compare the goals of structuralism and functionalism.

structuralism and functionalism: Consider your hands. A structuralist would try to explain their movement by studying how muscles, tendons, and bones operate. In contrast, a functionalist would ask, "Why do we have hands? How do they help us adapt to our environment?" The functionalists asked similar questions about mental processes and behaviour. They were influenced by Darwin's evolutionary theory, which stressed the importance of adaptation in helping organisms survive and reproduce in their environment.

William James (1842–1910), a leader in the functionalist movement, taught courses in physiology, psychology, and philosophy at Harvard University (Figure 1.7). James helped widen the scope of psychology to include the study of various biological and mental processes, and overt behaviour. Like Wundt, James trained psychologists who went on to distinguished careers. Among them was Mary Whiton Calkins (1863–1930), who became the first female president of the American Psychological Association in 1905 (Figure 1.8). Although functionalism no longer exists as a school of thought within psychology, its tradition endures in two modern-day fields: *cognitive psychology*, which studies mental processes, and *evolutionary psychology*, which emphasizes the adaptiveness of behaviour.

7. What causal factors are the focus of the psychodynamic perspective?

The Psychodynamic Perspective: The Forces Within

Have you ever been mystified by why you behaved or felt a certain way? Recall the case of Ray, the student described earlier in this chapter, who could not understand why he was shy.

© Archives of the History of American Psychology

FIGURE 1.8 Mary Whiton Calkins founded a psychology laboratory at Wellesley College, where she taught for over 30 years. She studied memory and dreams, and in 1905, she became the first female president of the American Psychological Association.

The **psychodynamic perspective** searches for the causes of behaviour within the inner workings of our personality (our unique pattern of traits, emotions, and motives), emphasizing the role of unconscious processes. Sigmund Freud (1856–1939) developed the first and most influential psychodynamic theory (Figure 1.9).

Psychoanalysis: Freud's Great Challenge

In late 19th century Vienna, Freud was a young physician intrigued by the brain's mysteries. Some of his patients experienced such symptoms as blindness, pain, paralysis, and phobias (i.e., intense unrealistic fears) that were not caused by any apparent bodily malfunction

© Science Photo Library/Photo Researchers, Inc.

FIGURE 1.7 William James, a leader of functionalism, helped establish psychology in North America. His multi-volume book *Principles of Psychology* (1890/1950) greatly expanded the scope of psychology.

Library of Congress Prints and Photographs Division, LC-3B19621

FIGURE 1.9 Sigmund Freud founded psychoanalysis. For more than 50 years, he probed the hidden recesses of the mind.

or disease. Thus, Freud reasoned that the causes must be psychological. Moreover, if patients were not producing their symptoms consciously, Freud reasoned that the causes must be hidden from awareness—they must be unconscious. Freud eventually treated his patients by using a technique called *free association,* in which the patient expressed any thoughts that came to mind. To Freud's surprise, patients eventually described painful and long-"forgotten" childhood experiences, often sexual in nature. After patients remembered and mentally "relived" these traumatic experiences, their symptoms often improved.

Freud became convinced that an unconscious part of the mind profoundly influences behaviour, and he developed a theory and a form of psychotherapy called **psychoanalysis**—the analysis of internal and primarily unconscious psychological forces. He also proposed that humans have powerful inborn sexual and aggressive drives and that because these desires are punished in childhood, we learn to fear them and become anxious when we are aware of their presence. This anxiety leads us to develop defence mechanisms, which are psychological techniques that help us cope with anxiety and the pain of traumatic experiences. Repression, a primary defence mechanism, protects us by keeping unacceptable impulses, feelings, and memories in the unconscious depths of the mind. All behaviour, whether normal or "abnormal," reflects a largely unconscious and inevitable conflict between the defences and internal impulses. This ongoing psychological struggle between conflicting forces is dynamic in nature, hence the term *psychodynamic.* To explain Ray's extreme shyness around women, Freud might have explored whether Ray is unconsciously afraid of his sexual impulses and therefore avoids putting himself into dating situations where he would have to confront those hidden impulses.

Freud's theory stirred great controversy. Even some of his followers disagreed with aspects of the theory, especially its heavy emphasis on childhood sexuality. Other psychologists viewed the theory as difficult to test. Nevertheless, Freud's ideas stimulated research on such topics as dreams, memory, aggression, and mental disorders. One review of over 3000 scientific studies examining Freud's ideas found support for some aspects of his theory, whereas other aspects were unsupported or contradicted (Fisher & Greenberg, 1996). But even where Freud's theory wasn't supported, it ultimately led to important discoveries. Additionally, Freud's work forever broadened the face of psychology to include the study and treatment of psychological disorders.

Modern Psychodynamic Theory

Modern psychodynamic theories continue to explore how unconscious and conscious aspects of personality influence behaviour (Barber & Sharpless, 2015). However, they downplay the role of hidden sexual and aggressive motives and focus more on how early relationships with family members and other caregivers shape the views that people form of themselves and others (Kernberg, 1984, 2000). In turn, these views can unconsciously influence a person's relationships with other people throughout life.

To explain Ray's shyness, a modern psychodynamic psychologist might examine Ray's conceptions of himself and his parents. Ray's shyness may stem from a fear of rejection of which he is unaware. This fear may be based on conceptions that he developed of his parents as being rejecting and disapproving, views that now unconsciously shape his expectations of how relationships with women and men will be.

The psychodynamic perspective dominated thinking about personality, mental disorders, and psychotherapy for the first half of the 20th century, and it continues to influence psychology and the practice of psychotherapy (Ryle, 2010). Although most contemporary psychological scientists reject Freud's particular version of the unconscious mind, modern psychological research has identified brain mechanisms that produce unconscious emotional reactions and has shown that many aspects of information processing occur outside of awareness (Bargh & Morsella, 2010; LaBar & LeDoux, 2006).

The Behavioural Perspective: The Power of the Environment

The **behavioural perspective** focuses on the role of the external environment in governing our actions. From this perspective, our behaviour is jointly determined by habits learned from previous life experiences and by stimuli in our immediate environment.

Origins of the Behavioural Perspective

The behavioural perspective has roots in the philosophical school of British empiricism. According to the early empiricist John Locke, at

8. What observations convinced Freud of the importance of unconscious and childhood determinants of adult behaviour?

9. In what sense, according to Freud, is the human in continuous internal conflict?

birth the human mind is a *tabula rasa*—a "blank tablet" or "slate"—upon which experiences are written. In this view, human nature is shaped purely by the environment.

In the early 1900s, experiments by Russian physiologist Ivan Pavlov (1849–1936) revealed how learning occurs when events are associated with each other. Pavlov found that dogs automatically learned to salivate to the sound of a new stimulus, such as a tone, if that stimulus was repeatedly paired with food. Meanwhile, American psychologist Edward Thorndike (1874–1949) examined how organisms learn through the consequences of their actions. According to Thorndike's (1911) *law of effect,* responses followed by satisfying consequences become more likely to recur, and those followed by unsatisfying consequences become less likely to recur. Thus, learning is the key to understanding how experience moulds behaviour.

Behaviourism

Behaviourism, a school of thought that emphasizes environmental control of behaviour through learning, began to emerge in 1913. John B. Watson (1878–1958), who led the new movement, strongly opposed the "mentalism" of the structuralists, functionalists, and psychoanalysts (Figure 1.10). He argued that the proper subject matter of psychology was observable behaviour, not unobservable inner consciousness. Humans, he said, are products of their learning experiences, and he issued the following challenge:

> Give me a dozen healthy infants, well-formed, and my own specialized world to bring them up in and I'll guarantee you to take any one of them at random and train him to become any type of specialist I might select—doctor, lawyer, artist, merchant-chief and, yes, even beggar-man and thief, regardless of his talents, penchants, tendencies, abilities, vocations, and race of his ancestors. (1925, p. 82)

Behaviourists sought to discover laws that govern learning, and they believed that the same basic principles of learning applied to all organisms. B.F. Skinner (1904–1990) was a leading 20th century behaviourist (Figure 1.11). Although Skinner didn't deny that people have thoughts and feelings, he maintained that "No account of what is happening inside the human body, no matter how complete, will explain the origins of human behaviour" (1989b, p. 18). Skinner believed that the real causes of behaviour reside in the outer world: "A person does not act upon the world, the world acts upon him" (1971, p. 211). His research, based largely on studying rats and pigeons under controlled laboratory conditions, examined how behaviour is influenced by the rewarding and punishing consequences that it produces.

In the case of our shy student, Ray, a behaviourist might focus on Ray's past dating experiences. In high school, the first time Ray invited a girl to a dance, he was turned down. Later, he had a crush on a girl and they went out once,

10. What are the important causal factors in behaviour within the behavioural perspective? How was this school of thought influenced by British empiricism?

© Culver Pictures, Inc.

FIGURE 1.10 John B. Watson founded the school of behaviourism. He published *Psychology as the Behaviorist Views It* in 1913.

© Sam Falk/Photo Researchers, Inc.

FIGURE 1.11 B.F. Skinner, a leading behaviourist, argued that mentalistic concepts were not necessary to explain behaviour and that learning principles could be used to enhance human welfare.

after which she turned him down. Though nervous, he asked out a few girls after that but was turned down each time. Such punishing consequences decreased the likelihood that Ray would ask someone out in the future. Fortunately, Kira asked Ray out, and the positive consequences they experienced on their first date reinforced their behaviour, increasing the odds that they would go out again.

Skinner believed that through "social engineering," society could harness the power of the environment to change behaviour in beneficial ways. His approach, known as *radical behaviourism*, was considered extreme by many psychologists, but he was esteemed for his scientific contributions and for focusing attention on how environmental forces could be used to enhance human welfare. In the 1960s, behaviourism inspired powerful techniques known collectively as **behaviour modification.** These techniques, aimed at decreasing problem behaviours and increasing positive behaviours by manipulating environmental factors, are still used widely today (Eldevik et al., 2010; Miltenberger, 2016).

Behaviourism's insistence that psychology should focus only on observable stimuli and responses resonated with many who wanted psychology to model itself on the natural sciences. Behaviourism dominated North American research on learning into the 1960s, challenged psychodynamic views about the causes of psychological disorders, and led to effective treatments for some disorders. But radical behaviourism's influence waned after the 1970s, as interest in studying mental processes expanded (Robins et al., 1999). Still, behaviourists continue to make important contributions, and their discovery of basic laws of learning was one of the greatest contributions made by 20th-century American psychology.

Thinking critically

ARE THE STUDENTS LAZY?

Imagine that you are a high school teacher. Whenever you try to engage your students in a class discussion, they gaze into space and hardly say anything. You start to think that they're just a bunch of lazy kids. From a radical behavioural perspective, is your conclusion reasonable? How might you improve the situation?

Think about it, and then see the Answers section at the end of the book.

Cognitive Behaviourism

In the 1960s and 1970s, a growing number of psychologists showed that such cognitive processes as attention and memory could be rigorously studied by using sophisticated experiments. This ability led some behaviourists to challenge radical behaviourism's view that mental life was off-limits as a topic for scientific study. A leading cognitive behaviourist is Albert Bandura (Figure 1.12), who was born in Alberta in 1925, received his B.A. from the University of British Columbia in 1949, and received his Ph.D. from the University of Iowa in 1952. Since 1953, he has taught at Stanford University, where he promotes the view that the environment exerts its effects on behaviour not by automatically "stamping in" or "stamping out" behaviours, as Watson or Skinner maintained, but rather by affecting our thoughts. In **cognitive behaviourism,** learning experiences and the environment affect our behaviour by giving us the information we need to behave effectively (Bandura, 1969, 2002). Cognitive behaviourism remains an influential viewpoint to this day.

A cognitive behaviourist might say that Ray's past dating rejections were punishing, leading him to expect that further attempts at romance would be doomed. In turn, these expectations of social rejection inhibited him from asking women out and even from making male friends.

The Humanistic Perspective: Self-Actualization and Positive Psychology

In the mid-20th century, as the psychodynamic and behavioural perspectives vied for dominance within psychology, a new viewpoint called *humanism* arose to challenge them both. The **humanistic perspective** emphasized free will, personal growth, and the attempt to find meaning in one's existence.

Humanists rejected psychodynamic concepts of humans as being controlled by unconscious forces, and rejected behaviourism's view of humans as mere reactors to the environment. Instead, such humanistic theorists as Abraham Maslow (1908–1970) proposed that each of us has an inborn force toward **self-actualization,** the reaching of one's individual potential (Figure 1.13). When humans develop in a supportive environment, the positive inner nature of a person emerges. In contrast, misery and pathology occur when environments frustrate our innate tendency toward self-actualization. Humanists emphasized the importance of personal choice, responsibility,

© Linda A. Cicero/ Stanford News Service

FIGURE 1.12 Albert Bandura has played a key role in merging the cognitive and behavioural perspectives into cognitive behaviourism.

....

11. What is cognitive behaviourism? How does it differ from radical behaviourism?

....

....

12. How does the humanistic conception of human nature and motivation differ from that advanced by psychoanalysis and behaviourism?

....

13. What is the conception of human nature advanced by the cognitive perspective?

© Diego Azubel/epa/Corbis

FIGURE 1.13 The humanistic perspective emphasizes the human ability to surmount obstacles in the drive toward self-actualization.

14. What does *Gestalt* mean? How does this meaning relate to the goals and findings of Gestalt psychology?

personality growth, and positive feelings of self-worth. To humanists, the meaning of our existence resides squarely in our own hands.

Thinking about Ray's shyness and loneliness, a humanist might say that no matter how many rejections Ray has had in the past, he must take personal responsibility for turning things around. A humanist also might wonder whether, in his first year at university, Ray's happiness and sense of self-worth were resting too heavily on his hope for a good romantic relationship. By focusing on building a few friendships, Ray wisely found another way to satisfy what Maslow (1954) called *belongingness*, our basic human need for social acceptance and companionship.

Few early humanists were scientists and, historically, humanism has had a more limited impact on mainstream psychological science than have other perspectives. Still, it has inspired important areas of research. Humanist Carl Rogers (1902–1987) identified key aspects of psychotherapy that led to constructive changes in clients. Humanistic concepts also stimulated research on self-esteem and self-concept (Verplanken & Holland, 2002).

Humanism's focus on self-actualization and growth is seen in today's growing **positive psychology movement,** which emphasizes the study of human strengths, fulfillment, and optimal living (Hogan, 2014; Lambert, Passmore, & Holder, 2015; Lopez, Pedrotti & Snyder, 2015). Rather than focusing on "what's wrong with our world" (e.g., mental disorders, conflict, prejudice), positive psychology examines how we can nurture what is best within ourselves and society to create a happy and fulfilling life.

The Cognitive Perspective: The Thinking Human

The **cognitive perspective** examines the nature of the mind and how mental processes influence behaviour. In this view, humans are information processors whose actions are governed by thought.

Origins of the Cognitive Perspective

Two of psychology's earliest schools of thought, structuralism and functionalism, reflected the cognitive perspective. Recall that structuralists attempted to identify the basic elements of consciousness, while functionalists explored the purposes of consciousness. Other pioneering cognitive psychologists, such as Hermann Ebbinghaus (1850–1909), studied memory.

By the 1920s, German scientists had formed a school of thought known as **Gestalt psychology,** which examined how the mind organizes elements of experience into a unified or "whole" perception ("Gestalt" roughly translates as "whole" or "organization"). They argued that perceptions are organized so that "the whole is greater than the sum of its parts." As an example, consider the illusion, discovered by Queen's psychologists Kang Lee and Alejo Freire (1999), shown in Figure 1.14. Although the oval windows through which you view the three faces are identical, for most people the one in which the internal features of the face are stretched appears longer, and the one in which the features are compressed appears shorter, than the window with the "normal" face. Another interesting point is that facial orientation is important. Slowly turn this page upside down and watch the difference in the size of the oval windows diminish. Gestalt psychologists believed that this tendency to perceive wholes is, like other forms of perceptual organization, built into our nervous system.

Gestalt psychology stimulated interest in such topics as perception and problem solving; but, like structuralism and functionalism, it eventually disappeared as a scientific school. As behaviourism's anti-mentalistic stance strengthened in North America during the 1920s and 1930s, the study of the mind was relegated to the back burner.

Renewed Interest in the Mind

In the 1950s, interest in studying cognitive processes regained ground. In part, this interest stemmed from psychologists' involvement during World War II in designing information

FIGURE 1.14 This illusion illustrates the Gestalt principle that the whole is often greater than the sum of its parts. The three ovals surrounding the faces appear to be of different size, but they are identical (see text). Prove this by measuring the length of each oval. This illusion can be reduced by inverting the page.

Source: Based on Lee K, Freire A, 1999, "Effects of face configuration change on shape perception: A new illusion" *Perception* 28(10) 1217–1226.

displays, such as gauges in airplane cockpits, that enabled military personnel (e.g., pilots) to recognize and interpret that information quickly and accurately. Computer technology, in its infancy at that time, provided new information-processing concepts and terminology that psychologists adapted to the study of memory and attention (Broadbent, 1958). A new metaphor developed—the mind as a system that processes, stores, and retrieves information—and it remains influential today.

On another front in the 1950s, behaviourists and linguists debated how children acquire language. The behaviourists, led by Skinner, claimed that language is acquired through basic principles of learning. The linguists, led by Noam Chomsky (b. 1928), argued that humans are biologically "preprogrammed" to acquire language and that children come to understand language as a set of "mental rules." This heated debate convinced many psychologists that language was too complex to be explained by behavioural principles and instead needed to be examined from a cognitive perspective.

Interest in cognition grew in other areas. For example, a theory by Swiss psychologist Jean Piaget (1896–1980), which explained how children's thinking becomes more sophisticated with age, gained widespread recognition in North America. Overall, psychologists' interest in mental processes swelled by the 1960s and 1970s—a period that sometimes is referred to as the *cognitive revolution*.

The Modern Cognitive Perspective

Cognitive psychology, which focuses on the study of mental processes, embodies the cognitive perspective. Cognitive psychologists study the processes by which people reason, make decisions, solve problems, form perceptions, and produce and understand language. Many, such as Elizabeth Loftus, study memory and factors that distort it (Figure 1.15). Cognitive psychologists explore the nature of attention and consciousness and have increasingly studied how unconscious processes influence behaviour.

Cognitive neuroscience, which uses sophisticated electrical recording and brain-imaging techniques to examine brain activity while people engage in cognitive tasks, is a rapidly growing area that represents the intersection

© Siner Jeff

FIGURE 1.15 Cognitive psychologist Elizabeth Loftus studies the nature of memory and how memories become distorted.

of cognitive psychology and the biological perspective within psychology. Cognitive neuroscientists seek to determine how the brain goes about its business of learning language, acquiring knowledge, forming memories, and performing other cognitive activities (Hans et al., 2013; Posner & Rothbart, 2007b).

From a cognitive perspective, we can examine Ray's shyness in terms of how he processes information. The few times he went on dates, Ray's nervousness may have caused him to focus on the slightest things that weren't going well, while failing to notice other cues that suggested his date was having a good time. Ray also may be remembering those events as much more unpleasant than they actually were, and his interpretation of past dating failures may be based on faulty reasoning. Ray believes he was rejected because of his personal qualities ("I'm not interesting enough") and therefore expects that future dates will also be unsuccessful. If Ray correctly attributed the rejections to some situational factor ("Clarissa was already interested in someone else"), then he would not necessarily expect other women to reject him in the future.

The Sociocultural Perspective: The Embedded Human

Humans are social creatures. Embedded within a culture, each of us encounters ever-changing social settings that shape our actions and values, our sense of identity, and our very conception of reality. The **sociocultural perspective** examines how the social environment and cultural learning influence our behaviour, thoughts, and feelings.

The Social Psychological Component

For over a century, *social psychologists* have studied how the presence of other people influences our behaviour, thoughts, and feelings (Triplett, 1898). The word *presence* includes actual physical presence (e.g., you're in a group), implied presence (e.g., you're dressing for a party, aware that at the party people will evaluate how you look), and imagined presence (e.g., driving a car, you slow down because you incorrectly think the car behind you is an unmarked police car). The social psychological approach overlaps with many other perspectives. For example, like behaviourism, social psychology pays special attention to how the environment influences our behaviour, but its emphasis is narrowed to the social environment. Consistent with a cognitive perspective,

much social psychological research examines social cognition: how people form impressions of one another, how attitudes form and can be changed, how our expectations affect our behaviour, and so forth. Intersecting the biological perspective (which we discuss next), social psychologists have increasingly examined the biological bases of social thinking and behaviour. For example, it appears that social pain, which can occur when people reject or ostracize us, shares many of the same brain circuits that underlie physical pain (Lieberman & Eisenberger, 2009).

The Cultural Component

Culture refers to the enduring values, beliefs, behaviours, and traditions that are shared by a large group of people and passed from one generation to the next. All cultural groups develop their own social **norms,** which are rules (often unwritten) that specify what behaviour is acceptable and expected for members of that group. Norms exist for all types of social behaviours, such as how to dress, how to respond to people of higher status, or how to act as a woman or a man (Figure 1.16). For culture to endure, each new generation must internalize, or adopt, the norms and values of the group as their own. Socialization is the process by which culture is transmitted to new members and internalized by them.

Throughout much of the 20th century, psychological research largely ignored non-Western groups. Even within Western societies, for decades participants in psychological research typically were White and came from middle- or upper-class backgrounds. There were important exceptions, however, such as research by Kenneth Clark (1914–2005) and Mamie Clark (1917–1983) and others, which examined how discrimination and prejudice influenced the personality development of African-American children (Clark & Clark, 1947; Figure 1.17).

Over time, psychologists increasingly began to study diverse ethnic and cultural groups. Today the growing field of **cultural psychology** (sometimes called *cross-cultural psychology*) explores how culture is transmitted to its members and examines psychological similarities and differences among people from diverse cultures (Schaller et al., 2010). Research findings in cultural psychology regarding differences in how Easterners and Westerners think and reason have challenged long-held assumptions about how the mind operates and highlight the influence of

15. Define culture and norms. What functions does a culture serve?

(left) Julie Jacobson/AP Photo/The Canadian Press; (right) © Eldad Rafaeli/Corbis

FIGURE 1.16 Social norms differ across cultures and over time within cultures. The idea of women engaging in aggressive sports or military combat is unthinkable in many cultures. A few generations ago, it was also unthinkable in Canada.

culture on our thought processes (Guan, Chen, Levin, Bond, Luo, Xu, & Han, 2015; Nisbett, Peng, Choi, & Norenzayan, 2001).

One important difference among cultures is the extent to which they emphasize individualism versus collectivism (Triandis & Suh, 2002). Most industrialized cultures of northern Europe and North America promote *individualism*, an emphasis on personal goals and self-identity based primarily on one's own attributes and achievements. In contrast, many Asian, African, and South American cultures nurture *collectivism*, in which individual goals are subordinated

Library of Congress Prints and Photographs Division, LC-USZ62-112521

FIGURE 1.17 Psychologists Kenneth Clark and Mamie Clark studied the development of racial identity among African-American children. Kenneth Clark also wrote books on the psychological impact of prejudice and discrimination.

to those of the group and personal identity is defined largely by the ties that bind one to the extended family and other social groups. The largest differences seem to exist between North Americans, who tend to both more individualistic and less collectivistic than individuals in most cultures, and Chinese, who show the opposite pattern (Jaing & Gore, 2015). However, even within a single culture there are variations in these characteristics—for example, between African Americans and European Americans (Oyserman, Coon, & Kemmelmeier, 2002). These differences are created by social learning experiences that begin in childhood and continue throughout our lives in the form of social customs.

Thinking about Ray's lonely first year in university, the sociocultural perspective again leads us to Ray's expectations of social rejection and beliefs about why past social rejections occurred. We also can ask how his cultural upbringing and other social factors contributed to his shy behaviour. Throughout his teen years, cultural norms for male assertiveness may have put pressure on Ray. His shyness may have evoked teasing and other negative reactions from his high school peers, increasing his feelings of inadequacy by the time he reached university. As for Ray and Kira's dating relationship, we might examine how norms regarding courtship and marriage differ across cultures. We consider cross-cultural attitudes toward love and marriage in our first *Research Foundations* feature.

16. Contrast individualistic and collectivistic societies.

Research Foundations

The *Research Foundations* feature in each chapter presents a classic study in some detail.

WOULD YOU MARRY SOMEONE YOU DIDN'T LOVE?

Introduction

Would you marry someone you did not love? According to one theory, people in individualistic cultures are more likely to view romantic love as a requirement for marriage because love is a matter of personal choice (Goode, 1959). In collectivistic cultures, concern for the extended family plays a larger role in marriage decisions.

Psychologist Robert Levine and his colleagues (1995) examined college students' views about love and marriage. Whereas previous research focused on American students, these authors studied students from 11 countries. They also examined whether students from collectivistic and economically poorer countries would be less likely to view love as a prerequisite to marriage.

Method

The researchers administered language-appropriate versions of the same questionnaire to 1163 female and male college students from 11 countries. The key question was "If someone had all the other qualities you desired, would you marry this person if you were not in love with him/her?" The students responded "No," "Yes," or "Not Sure." The researchers determined each country's economic status and collectivistic versus individualistic orientation from data gathered by previous cross-cultural investigators.

Results

Within each country, the views of female and male students did not differ significantly. In contrast, beliefs across countries varied strongly (Table 1.2). In India, Thailand, and Pakistan, most students said they would marry or at least consider marrying someone they did not love. In the Philippines and Japan, a sizable minority—just over a third—felt the same way. In contrast, students from the other countries overwhelmingly rejected the notion of marrying somebody they did not love. Overall, students from collectivistic

TABLE 1.2   Love and Marriage in 11 Cultures

If someone had all the other qualities you desired, would you marry this person if you were not in love with him/her?

Country	Percentage		
	No	Yes	Not Sure
India	24	49	27
Thailand	34	19	47
Pakistan	39	50	11
Philippines	64	11	25
Japan	64	2	34
Hong Kong	78	6	16
Australia	80	5	15
Mexico	83	10	7
England	84	7	9
Brazil	86	4	10
United States	86	4	10

and economically poorer countries were less likely to view love as a prerequisite to marriage.

Discussion

Among most of our own students, the notion that you marry someone you love is a truism. They are surprised—as perhaps you are—that many students in other countries would consider marrying someone they did not love. This study reminds us that as members of a particular culture, it is easy to mistakenly assume that "our way" is the "normal way."

As in all research, we must think critically and interpret the results carefully. For example, among those students who said they would marry someone without being in love, would it be accurate to conclude that they view love as irrelevant to marriage? Not necessarily, because other research has found that "mutual attraction/love" is viewed across most cultures as a desirable quality in a mate (Buss, 1989). Thus, the results of this study suggest only that in some cultures love is not viewed as an *essential prerequisite* to enter into marriage.

Source: Robert Levine, Suguru Sato, Tsukasa Hashimoto, and Jyoti Verma (1995). Love and marriage in eleven cultures. *Journal of Cross-Cultural Psychology, 26,* 554–571. Table 2. Copyright © 1995 SAGE Publications. Reprinted by permission of SAGE Publications, Inc.[1]

[1] The citation system used in psychology lists the authors, year of publication, title, journal or book, volume number of the journal, and page numbers.

17. What three classes of causal factors does the biological perspective focus on?

The Biological Perspective: The Brain, Genes, and Evolution

The **biological perspective** examines how brain processes and other bodily functions regulate behaviour. Biological psychology has always been

a prominent part of the field, but its influence has increased dramatically over recent decades.

Behavioural Neuroscience

Ray and Kira are in love. They study and eat together. They hold hands and kiss. Yet a year earlier, Ray was depressed. What brain regions, neural circuits, and bodily chemicals enable us to feel love, pleasure, and depression, and to read, study, and feel hunger? These questions pertain to **behavioural neuroscience** (also called *physiological psychology*), which examines brain processes and other physiological functions that underlie our behaviour, sensory experiences, emotions, and thoughts (Rolls, 2010).

An early pioneer of biological psychology, American Karl Lashley (1890–1958), trained rats to run mazes and then measured how surgically produced lesions (damage) to various brain areas affected the rats' learning and memory. His research inspired other psychologists to map brain regions involved in specific psychological functions (Figure 1.18). For example, at McGill University in Montreal, James Olds and Peter Milner (1954) discovered that some areas of the brain were specialized for providing animals with pleasurable sensations. As will be described in Chapter 8, W.B. Scoville and Brenda Milner (1957), in the course of treating a patient named H.M. who suffered from epilepsy, found that damage to some areas of the human brain was associated with severe memory loss. Another pioneer, Canadian Donald O. Hebb (1904–1985), proposed that changes in the connections between nerve cells in the brain provide the biological basis for learning, memory, and perception. His influential theory inspired research that eventually led to the discovery of **neurotransmitters**, which are chemicals released by nerve cells that allow them to communicate with one another.

Today, modern brain-imaging techniques allow psychologists to watch activity in specific

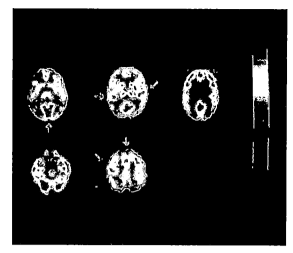

© Michael Phelps

FIGURE 1.19 Behavioural neuroscientists use positron-emission tomography (PET) scans to measure brain activity as people perform various tasks. Viewed from above, each image pictures a horizontal slice of the brain with the front of the brain at the top. Yellow and red indicate regions of greatest activity: visual task (top left), auditory task (top centre), cognitive task (top right), memory task (bottom left), and motor task (bottom right).

brain areas as people experience emotions, perceive stimuli, and perform tasks (Figure 1.19). Read more about imaging studies in the *Focus on Neuroscience* feature. These advances have led to new areas of study that link various psychological perspectives. For example, cognitive neuroscience—the study of brain processes that underlie thinking and information processing—represents an intersection of cognitive psychology and behavioural neuroscience.

Behaviour Genetics

Psychologists have had a long-standing interest in **behaviour genetics**, the study of how behavioural tendencies are influenced by genetic factors (Jaffee, Price, & Reyes, 2013; Plomin & Haworth, 2009). Animals can be selectively bred not only for physical traits, but also for such behavioural traits as aggression. This breeding is done over generations by mating highly aggressive males and females. In Thailand, where gambling on fish fights is a national pastime, selective breeding has produced the highly aggressive Siamese fighting fish. The male of this species will instantly attack his own image in a mirror.

Identical human twins, who result from the splitting of a fertilized egg and therefore have the same genetic makeup, are more similar to each other on many behavioural traits than are fraternal twins, who result from two different fertilized eggs and therefore are no more

18. What methods do behaviour geneticists use to investigate the role of genetic factors in animal and human behaviour?

© Archives of the History of American Psychology

FIGURE 1.18 Karl Lashley was a pioneer of physiological psychology (behavioural neuroscience). He examined how damage to various brain regions affected rats' ability to learn and remember.

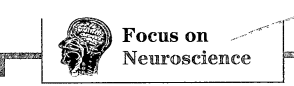

Focus on Neuroscience

THE NEUROSCIENCE OF IMAGING STUDIES

Early attempts to image or map the human brain relied on relatively inaccurate, and, in some cases, subjective, methods. Franz Joseph Gall and his colleague J.C. Spurzheim developed the "science" of phrenology in the early 19th century. According to historian E.G. Boring (1950), as a young boy, Gall had noticed a relationship between eye prominence and memory—he believed that those with pronounced eyes had superior memories. Gall went on to study the relationship between various mental characteristics and the shape of one's head, producing a number of mental maps based on the bumps and valleys found on the skull. Presumably, the bigger the bump, the more brain tissue underneath and, consequently, the more processing power. Gall's maps are completely inaccurate: Language and memory are not reflective of brain tissue behind your eyes. However, the general notion that different functions are mediated by different areas of the brain was an idea whose time had come.

Much of the early work on localization of function involved the examination of patients who had very specific brain injuries that resulted in a very specific mental or behavioural loss (e.g., the case of Phineas Gage discussed in Chapter 3). Upon autopsy, one could examine the nature and extent of the brain injury and relate this to functional loss. However, this method was not very exact and there were relatively few patients to examine. In the laboratory, it was possible to have much more precision. Shepherd Franz and his student Karl Lashley began a series of experiments in the early 1920s designed to investigate the effects of specific tissue loss. Using animal subjects, various brain areas were removed and results were noted. To their surprise, a great deal of cortex could be removed with relatively small losses in function. Many believe that the Franz and Lashley

studies are the source of the often-quoted myth that we use only 10 percent of our brain (we actually use it all).

With the development of new technologies, the focus has shifted to imaging the intact brain. Fox (1997) notes that the number of imaging studies is growing at an exponential rate. In the early 1980s, fewer than 15 imaging papers were presented, on average, at the annual meeting of the Society for Neuroscience. At the 2005 meeting, the number was up to 745. Tuomi shows a similar increase in PubMed studies (see Figure 1.20). In 2012, more than 20 articles using fMRI were published every day and the PubMed data base contains over 100 000 imaging studies (Tuomi, 2013). In every chapter of this text, we will highlight imaging studies in an effort to give a clearer understanding of the human mind.

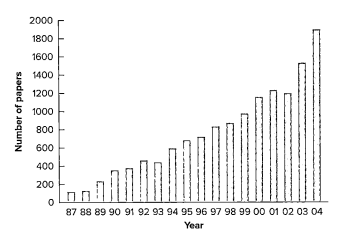

FIGURE 1.20 Growth in imaging abstracts at the annual Society for Neuroscience meeting (adapted from Fox, 1997).

Source: Tuomi, Ilkka. "Educational Neurosciences—More Problems than Promise?" Fig. 1. p. 10. (Bangkok 2013). © UNESCO 2013.

---

similar genetically than are non-twin siblings. This greater behavioural similarity is found even when identical twins have been reared in different homes and dissimilar environments (Lykken, 2006). Studies of twins and adoptees can tell us a great deal about the relative influences of genetics and parenting in children's behaviour, though measuring these influences can be tricky. For example, the parents who pass on their genes to a child also engage in parenting practices that are influenced by some of those same genes, making it difficult to tease apart the influences of nature and nurture on behaviour.

Thinking about Ray, perhaps he inherited a tendency to be shy. Some infants display an extremely shy, inhibited emotional style that seems to be biologically based and persists into adulthood (Kagan, 1989; Newman et al., 1997). Dating rejections may have reinforced Ray's natural reluctance to ask women out.

Evolutionary Psychology

In his theory of evolution, Darwin (1859) noted that within a species some members possess specific traits to a greater extent than do other members (Figure 1.21). Through a process he called **natural selection,** if an inherited trait gives certain members an advantage over others (such as increasing their ability to attract mates or escape from danger), these members

19. What is meant by natural selection? What is its role in physical and behavioural evolution?

FIGURE 1.21 Charles Darwin, a British naturalist, formulated a theory of evolution that revolutionized scientific thinking.

will be more likely to survive and pass on these characteristics to their offspring. In this way, species evolve as the presence of adaptive traits increases within the population over generations. Traits that put certain members at a disadvantage tend to become less common within a species over time because members having those traits will be less likely to survive and reproduce. As environments change, the adaptiveness of a trait may increase or decrease. Thus, through natural selection, a species' biology evolves in response to environmental conditions (Figure 1.22).

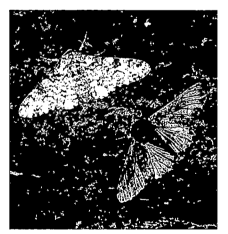

FIGURE 1.22 Natural selection pressures result in physical changes. The peppered moth's natural colour is that of the lighter insect. However, over many generations, peppered moths who live in polluted urban areas have become darker, not from the pollution but because moths who inherited slightly darker coloration blended better into their grimy environment. Thus, they were more likely to survive predators and pass on their "darker" genes to their offspring. However, a trip into the countryside to visit their light-coloured relatives could easily prove fatal for these darker urban insects.

Evolutionary psychology seeks to explain how evolution shaped modern human behaviour (Buss, 2005). Evolutionary psychologists stress that human mental abilities and behavioural tendencies evolved along with a changing body (Tooby & Cosmides, 2005). According to one theory, as our human-like ancestors developed new physical abilities (such as the ability to walk upright, thus freeing the use of the arms and the hands), they began to use tools and weapons and live in social groups (Pilbeam, 1984). Helping each other was important for the evolutionary fitness of the entire group (Kurzban, Burton-Chellew, & West, 2015). Certain psychological abilities—thought, language, and the capacity to learn and solve problems— became more important to survival as our ancestors had to adapt to new ways of living. Attraction to particular physical features such as facial symmetry may be an evolved adaptation, as a symmetrical face and smooth skin are indicators of a healthy potential mate (Rhodes, 2006). Our ancestors who were attracted to such features were more likely to have healthy babies and therefore to pass on those genes to future generations, compared to individuals who did not share this preference.

Within any generation, genetically based variations in brain structure and functioning occur among individuals. Ancestors whose brain characteristics better supported adaptive mental abilities were more likely to survive and reproduce. Thus, through natural selection, adaptations to new environmental demands contributed to the development of the brain, just as brain growth contributed to the further development of human behaviour.

Evolutionary psychologists also attempt to explain human social behaviour. The notion that evolutionary pressures have stimulated the development of brain mechanisms that allow us to learn, think, reason, and socialize more effectively is generally accepted today. However, one evolutionary theory (and there are many theories) is more controversial. **Sociobiology** (Wilson, 1980) holds that complex social behaviours are also built into the human species as products of evolution. Sociobiologists argue that natural selection favours behaviours that increase the ability to pass on one's genes to the next generation. These social behaviours include aggression, competition, and dominance in males, and cooperative and nurturing tendencies in females. Indeed, sex differences in reproduction are significant. For example, sociobiologists Martin Daly and Margo Wilson,

20. According to evolutionary psychology, how do biological and behavioural evolution influence each other?

21. According to sociobiology, what is the ultimate importance of evolved social behaviours? On what bases has this position been criticized by other theorists?

of McMaster University, note that females have a greater investment in the reproductive process. Women have less opportunity to reproduce (usually only one egg per month and, in Canada, produce only one or two children on average) than males. They also have a greater health risk during pregnancy and delivery, and in Canada, tend to be the primary caregiver after divorce. Thus, perhaps through natural selection men and women have become biologically predisposed to seek somewhat different qualities in a mate (Buss, 2007). A major point is that, in the eyes of sociobiologists, one's genetic survival (i.e., the transmission of one's genes) is more important than one's own physical survival. This principle can explain certain altruistic behaviours, including giving up one's life to save children or relatives. Although such behaviour is hardly in the survival interests of the individual, it serves a higher purpose: It keeps one's genes alive in the gene pool to live on in descendants (Sober & Wilson, 1998).

Many critics (e.g., Caporael, 1997) believe that sociobiology overemphasizes innate biological factors at the expense of cultural and social learning factors in explaining complex human social behaviour. Evolutionary theorists with a more cultural orientation suggest that the evolved brain structures that underlie psychological mechanisms (such as the ability to use language) developed to enhance adaptation to the demands of social and group living rather than simply to further the survival of one's genes.

22. What three levels of analysis allow us to incorporate causal factors suggested by each of the perspectives?

USING LEVELS OF ANALYSIS TO INTEGRATE THE PERSPECTIVES

As summarized in Table 1.3, psychology's six major perspectives (presented in the order we discussed them) provide differing conceptions of human nature. Fortunately, we can distill their essence into the simple three-part framework that we introduced earlier. Behaviour can be examined at biological, psychological, and environmental levels. At the *biological level of analysis*, we can study behaviour and its causes in terms of brain functioning, hormones, and genetic factors shaped over the course of evolution. At the *psychological level of analysis*, we might look to the

TABLE 1.3 Comparison of Six Major Perspectives on Human Behaviour

	Psychodynamic	Behavioural	Humanistic	Cognitive	Sociocultural	Biological
Conception of human nature	The human as controlled by inner forces and conflicts	The human as reactor to the environment	The human as free-agent, seeking self-actualization	The human as thinker	The human as social being embedded in a culture	The human as animal
Major causal factors in behaviour	Unconscious motives, conflicts, and defences; early childhood experiences and unresolved conflicts	Past learning experiences and the stimuli and behavioural consequences that exist in the current environment	Free will, choice, and innate drive toward self-actualization; search for personal meaning of existence	Thoughts, anticipations, planning, perceptions, attention, and memory processes	Social forces, including norms, social interactions, and group processes in one's culture and social environment	Genetic and evolutionary factors; brain and biochemical processes
Predominant focus and methods of discovery	Intensive observations of personality processes in clinical settings; some laboratory research	Study of learning processes in laboratory and real-world settings, with an emphasis on precise observation of stimuli and responses	Study of meaning, values, and purpose in life; study of self-concept and its role in thought, emotion, and behaviour	Study of cognitive processes, usually under highly controlled laboratory conditions	Study of behaviour and mental processes of people in different cultures; experiments examining people's responses to social stimuli	Study of brain-behaviour relations; role of hormones and biochemical factors in behaviour; behavioural genetics research

cognitive perspective and analyze how thought, memory, and planning influence behaviour. Borrowing from the psychodynamic and humanistic perspectives, we can examine how motives and personality traits influence behaviour. Finally, at the *environmental level of analysis,* the behavioural and sociocultural perspectives lead us to examine how stimuli in the physical and social environment shape our behaviour, thoughts, and feelings.

A full understanding of behaviour often moves us back and forth between these three levels. Consider Ray and Kira. When we describe the culture in which they were raised, such as its religious values and social customs,

we are operating at the environmental level of analysis. However, if Ray and Kira adopt those cultural values and make them part of their identities, this represents the psychological level of analysis. Similarly, we might describe a family environment as abusive, but also describe an abused child's tendency to worry and feel anxious, as well as discuss the chemical changes in the child's brain that underlie this anxiety, which moves us from the environmental, to the psychological, and then to the biological levels of analysis. The discussion in this chapter's *Frontiers* feature suggests some other ways in which the perspectives and levels might interact.

Review

- Several perspectives have shaped psychology's scientific growth. Each perspective views human nature differently and focuses on different causes of behaviour.

- Psychology's intellectual roots lie in philosophy, biology, and medicine. In the late 1800s, Wundt and James helped found psychology. Structuralism, which examined the basic components of consciousness, and functionalism, which focused on the purposes of consciousness, were psychology's two earliest schools of thought.

- The psychodynamic perspective calls attention to unconscious motives, conflicts, and defence mechanisms that influence personality and behaviour. Freud's psychoanalytic theory emphasized unconscious sexual and aggressive impulses and early childhood experiences that shape personality.

- With roots in 18th-century British empiricism, the behavioural perspective emphasizes how the external environment and learning shape behaviour. Behaviourists, such as Watson and Skinner, believed that psychology should study only observable stimuli and responses, not unobservable mental processes. They argued that the key to changing behaviour is modifying the environment. Behaviourists discovered basic laws of learning through controlled research with laboratory animals and successfully applied these principles to enhance human welfare.

- Humanists reject the notion that people are controlled by unconscious forces or merely react to environmental stimuli. Instead, the humanistic perspective emphasizes personal freedom and choice, psychological growth, and self-actualization.

- The cognitive perspective views humans as information processors who think, judge, and solve problems. Its roots lie in the early schools of structuralism, functionalism, and Gestalt psychology. Piaget's work on cognitive development, the study of linguistics, and the advent of computers sparked new interest in mental processes. Cognitive neuroscience studies brain processes that underlie mental activity.

- The sociocultural perspective examines how the social environment and cultural learning influence our behaviour and thoughts. Cultural psychologists study how culture is transmitted to its members and examine similarities and differences among people from various cultures. An orientation toward individualism versus collectivism represents one of many ways in which cultures vary.

- With roots in physiology, medicine, and Darwin's theory of evolution, the biological perspective examines how bodily functions regulate behaviour. Physiological psychologists study brain processes and other physiological functions that underlie our behaviour, sensory experiences, emotions, and thoughts. Behaviour geneticists study how behaviour is influenced by our genetic inheritance. Evolutionary psychologists examine behaviour in terms of its adaptive functions and seek to explain how evolution has biologically predisposed modern humans toward certain ways of behaving.

Frontiers

CULTURE, LANGUAGE, AND BEHAVIOUR

The behavioural and sociocultural perspectives emphasize the role of the environment in the development of behaviour. They tell us that we are moulded by our unique learning histories and shaped by the culture into which we are born. Our learning and cultural experiences influence not only our behaviour, but also how we view ourselves (i.e., our "cultural identity") and the world. The behavioural perspective seems straightforward: Our behaviour is shaped by learning. But just how does culture influence our behaviour?

Many researchers have argued that language and culture are intimately related (e.g., Vygotsky, 1962). In the most extreme version of this approach, Whorf (1956) suggested that language influences thought and cognition directly. According to Whorf, the language we use changes the way we think about the world. We can make cognitive distinctions among things we encounter only if we have a means to describe them. For example, Whorf suggested that a culture using a language without a past tense (such as the Hopi Indians of the United States) would have difficulty remembering past events.

The idea that culture, through language, *determines* how we think is a bit overstated, as various authors have suggested (e.g., Rosch, 1973). Nonetheless there are clear influences of both culture and language on cognition and behaviour. Consider some recent work by Li-Jun Ji at Queen's University. Ji and colleagues (Ji, Zhang, & Nisbett, 2004) recruited Chinese students at Hong Kong University and Beijing University. All students were bilingual—they spoke both English and Chinese. They were presented with two different sorting tasks. Each involved looking at sets of three words (e.g., *teacher, doctor, homework*) and deciding which two were most closely related. One task was presented in English, and the other in Chinese. Note that there are two ways to group the three words: either by category (teacher, doctor) or by relationship (teacher, homework).

A comparison group of European-American students at the University of Michigan (English only) had been tested in an earlier study. The results indicated very different sorting strategies by the European-American students compared to the Chinese students. At Michigan, the students sorted by category, more or less ignoring the possible relationships. The Chinese students used the opposite strategy. Their sorts reflected the relationships among the words, rather than category membership. Chinese students sorted this way regardless of their testing language, although the students from Beijing were more likely to use relationship sorts when the test language was Chinese. Most likely, the difference between the Hong Kong students and Beijing students reflects the age at which English is learned. For the Hong Kong students, English is learned much earlier, often in conjunction with formal language training. This early learning would result in a shared internal representational system for both languages.

Thus, according to Ji et al. (2004), culture influences these cognitive sorting patterns, independent of language. How is this possible? They suggest that the value of relationships is reinforced much more strongly in Chinese culture than in North American culture. Chinese people pay more attention to the social environment than do their American counterparts, who value autonomy (e.g., Ji, Schwartz, & Nisbett, 2000). These values are reflected in both the family and school environments and become an integral part of how the world is perceived. Language's influence fine-tunes these preferences, and yet it cannot overcome the influence of culture. Ji has also demonstrated the influence of culture on pain perception (Hseih, Tripp, & Ji, 2011), statistical thinking (Spina, Ji, Ross, & Zhang, 2010), and the importance of past versus future events (Guo, Ji, Spina & Zhang, 2012).

(left) © Ron Stroud/Masterfile; (right) Ariel Skelley/Getty Images

FIGURE 1.23 Culture and language influence cognition. The value that Chinese culture places on relationships and the contrasting value North American culture places on autonomy are reflected in the Chinese and English languages, and in turn in the way their respective speakers think and categorize concepts.

An Example: Understanding Depression

To appreciate how the biological, psychological, and environmental levels of analysis can help us understand an important behaviour, let us briefly summarize what is known about one of the most commonly experienced psychological problems in our culture, namely, depression.

Most of us have probably experienced feelings of sadness, grief, or "the blues" at some time in our lives. These feelings, often accompanied by such biological reactions as loss of appetite and sleep difficulties, are usually normal responses to negative events or meaningful losses that we have experienced. However, when these emotional responses remain intense over a long period, and when they are accompanied by thoughts of hopelessness and an inability to experience pleasure, we have crossed the boundary between a normal reaction and clinical depression (Rubin, 2000).

Depression has sometimes been referred to as the "common cold" of emotional disturbances because it is experienced by so many people. Even if we consider only severe depressive disorders, studies indicate that about 8–10 percent of Canadians can expect to experience depression in their lifetime. The rate for women is twice that for men (Gotlib & Hammen, 2010; Satcher, 2000).

Let's begin at the biological level of analysis. First, genetic factors appear to be involved in at least some cases (Edvardsen et al., 2009). In one study, relatives of people who had developed a major depression before age 20 were eight times more likely to eventually become depressed than were relatives of nondepressed people (Weissman et al., 1984).

Depression is also related to biochemical factors and sleep/wakefulness rhythms in the brain. Of special interest are certain chemicals, known as *neurotransmitters,* that are involved in the transmission of nerve impulses within the brain. One line of evidence proving that these substances are important is the fact that the most effective antidepressant drugs seem to operate by restoring a normal balance of these neurotransmitters (Deutschenbaur, Beck, Kiyhankhadiv, Muhlhauser, Borgwardt, Walter & Lang, 2016; Roland, 1997). Also, researchers have found disruptions in biological rhythms that underlie sleep and dreaming in the brain waves of depressed people (Buysse et al., 1997; Farina et al., 2003). If researchers interfere with the "depressive" brain rhythm by waking depressed people when it is occurring, those awoken feel less depressed afterward (Berger et al., 1997).

Moving from a biological to a psychological level of analysis provides additional understanding of depression and its causes. For example, many studies have shown that depression is associated with a particular thinking style in which the person interprets events in a pessimistic way (Beck, 2002; Strunk & Adler, 2009). Depressed people can find the black cloud that surrounds every silver lining. They tend to blame themselves for negative things that occur, while taking no personal credit for the good things that happen in their lives, and they generally feel that the world, the self, and the future are bleak and hopeless (Beck, 1991). The Canadian psychologist Norman Endler (1982) has provided an autobiographical account of what he himself felt like during a period of clinical depression.

Are some personality patterns more prone to depression than others? Many psychodynamic theorists believe that severe losses or rejections in childhood help to create a personality style that causes people to overreact to future losses, setting the stage for later depression. In support of this notion, studies of depressed patients show that they are more likely than nondepressed people to have experienced the loss of a parent through death or separation during childhood (Bowlby, 2000a; Brown & Harris, 1978). Depression is also related to childhood histories of abuse, parental rejection, and family discord (Esterbrooks, Kotake, Raskin, & Bumgarner, 2016; Li. D'Arcy, & Meng, 2015; Hammen, 1991). People who have been subjected to severe loss and neglect may develop pessimistic personalities that predispose them to slide into depression in the face of later life stresses. In addition, certain personality factors such as perfectionism, low self-esteem, and a lack of "mattering" make an individual more prone to depression (Cha, 2016).

Finally, the environmental level of analysis reveals several factors that play a major role in depression. According to the behavioural view, depression is a reaction to a non-rewarding environment. A vicious cycle begins when the environment provides fewer rewards for the person. As depression intensifies, such people feel so bad that they stop doing the things that ordinarily give them pleasure, a pattern that decreases environmental rewards still further. To make matters worse, depressed people complain a good deal, seek excessive reassurance and support from others, and generally become less likeable. These behaviours eventually begin to alienate others and cause them to shy away from the depressed person. The net result is a worsening environment with fewer rewards, a reduction in support from others, and the

23. What does the biological level of analysis tell us about the causes of depression?

24. What kinds of psychological causal factors have been identified in depression?

25. Which causal factors in depression are seen at the environmental level of analysis?

unhappiness and hopeless pessimism that characterize chronic depression (Hopko & Mullane, 2008; Lewinsohn et al., 1985; Nezlek et al., 2000).

The sociocultural environment also affects depression. Although depression is found in virtually all cultures, both its symptom pattern and its causes may reflect cultural differences. For example, feelings of guilt and personal inadequacy seem to predominate in North American and western European countries, whereas bodily symptoms of fatigue, loss of appetite, and sleep difficulties are more often reported in Latin, Chinese, and African cultures (Brislin, 1993; Lopez & Guarnaccia, 2000). Cross-cultural studies also have shown that in developed countries, such as the United States and other Western nations, women are about twice as likely as men to report feeling depressed, whereas no such sex difference is found in developing countries (Culbertson, 1997; Gibson, Baker, & Milner, 2016; Nolen-Hoeksema, 2006). In Canada, the rate is somewhat lower (about 8 percent; Health Canada, 2002). Why should this be? At present, we do not have the answer, but we must wonder what it is about more technologically advanced cultures that would produce a sex difference that does not show up in developing countries.

We'll discuss depression more fully in Chapter 16. For now, let's summarize the causal factors in depression that we've discussed by grouping them into the three levels of analysis (Figure 1.24).

> **This feature will appear in each chapter to help you compare and contrast levels of analysis.**

Levels of Analysis   Causal Factors in Depression

It's important to realize that some of the factors we've described above can act as a cause but also be an effect. For example, depression (cause) may lead to a decrease in social support (effect), and in turn, decreased social support (cause) can deepen the person's depression (effect). Also recognize that the causes of depression may vary from case to case, and that multiple causes can combine or interact with one another. **Interaction** means that the way in which one factor influences behaviour depends on the presence of another factor. For example, someone who experiences a minor setback may become depressed if she or he has a strong biological predisposition for depression or a highly pessimistic thinking style. The same setback might barely faze a person who has a weak biological predisposition for depression or an optimistic thinking style. Thus, just as boiling water softens celery and hardens an egg, the same environmental factor can affect two people differently, depending on their biological and psychological makeup.

You've now seen how a levels-of-analysis approach can be applied to examining depression. Focus on another aspect of human behaviour that interests you, and think about—even generally—how it might be examined at the biological, psychological, and environmental levels.

ENVIRONMENTAL
- Prior losses and rejections, especially early in life, may lead people to overreact to current losses or rejections.
- A significant decrease in pleasurable experiences may help trigger depression.
- Social support may decrease if people avoid the depressed person.
- Cultural norms may influence how people react to negative events and express unhappiness.

BIOLOGICAL
- People's genetic inheritance influences their susceptibility toward developing depression.
- Abnormal activity of neurotransmitters in the brain can cause depression.
- Antidepressant drugs restore more normal levels of neurotransmitter activity and relieve symptoms of depression for many people.

PSYCHOLOGICAL
- A pessimistic thinking style and negative interpretations of events may trigger or intensify depression.
- Perfectionistic expectations can make people overly sensitive to how other people evaluate them.
- Heightened sensitivity to loss or rejection may lead people to overreact to setbacks.

FIGURE 1.24

Summary of Major Themes

We have now surveyed the six major perspectives that shape psychological thought and the levels of analysis at which behaviour is studied. What has our excursion shown us about the science of psychology and its subject matter? The following principles are widely accepted by psychologists and are seen repeatedly as we explore the realm of behaviour:

- As a science, *psychology is empirical*, meaning that it favours direct observation over pure intuition or reasoning as a means of attaining knowledge about behaviour. In Chapter 2 and throughout the book, we study the empirical methods that are used to observe behaviour and identify its causes.

- Though committed to an objective study of behaviour, psychologists recognize that *our experience of the world is subjective* and that we respond to a psychological reality created by our own thought processes, motives, and expectations. Many of these influences operate beyond our conscious awareness.

- As our levels-of-analysis theme shows us, *behaviour is determined by multiple causal factors* that can interact with one another in complex ways. This interaction increases the challenge of understanding behaviour.

- *Nature and nurture* not only combine to shape our behaviour, but also influence each other. Our biological endowment helps to determine the kinds of experiences we can have, and biological processes are, in turn, influenced by our experiences.

- Behaviour is a means of adapting to environmental demands, and *psychological capacities have evolved* during each species' history because they facilitated adaptation and survival.

- Behaviour and mental processes are strongly affected by the *cultural environment* in which they develop. In an increasingly multicultural world, there is a growing need to understand and appreciate the role of cultural factors in behaviour.

PSYCHOLOGY TODAY

We will begin with a brief history of Canadian psychology. As shown in Table 1.4, Canadian universities were established by the British in the mid-1800s to educate their children, first in Nova Scotia and Upper Canada, and later, in the early 1900s, in Western Canada (Wright & Myers, 1982). The table also shows that psychology as an independent discipline is a very young science. Courses in psychology were taught in the early 1900s at all of the universities listed in the table, generally as part of Philosophy Departments (e.g., this was the case at Queen's University until 1948). The earliest independent Psychology Department was created at McGill University in 1924. Other universities taught psychology in combined "Philosophy and Psychology" Departments from the 1930s until the late 1950s (e.g., McMaster University, University of Alberta, University of British Columbia). In the 1960s, the number of graduate departments in psychology in Canada more than doubled; among the universities that developed graduate schools in that decade were Laval, Carleton, York, Waterloo, Calgary, Simon Fraser, and Victoria (see Wright & Myers, 1982).

Modern-day psychology in Canada and the United States is more diversified and robust

26. Summarize six important themes in contemporary psychology.

27. What is meant by the interaction of causal factors?

Review

- Factors that influence behaviour can be organized into three broad levels of analysis. The biological level of analysis focuses on brain processes, hormonal and genetic influences, and evolutionary adaptations that underlie behaviour. The psychological level of analysis examines mental processes and psychological motives, and how they influence behaviour. The environmental level of analysis calls attention to physical and social stimuli, including cultural factors, that shape our behaviour and thoughts.

- To understand behaviour, we often move back and forth between these levels of analysis. For example, when we are first exposed to cultural norms as children, those norms reflect a characteristic of our environment. However, once we adopt norms as our own, they become a part of our world view and now represent the psychological level of analysis.

- Biological, psychological, and environmental factors contribute to the development of depression. These factors can also interact to influence a given behaviour. It may take only a mild setback to trigger depression in a person who has a strong biological predisposition toward depression, whereas a person who does not have such a biological predisposition may become depressed only after suffering a severe setback.

TABLE 1.4   A Brief History of Canadian Psychology Departments by Founding Date*

University	Date Founded	Date Psychology Department Established
Dalhousie University	1838	1948
Queen's University	1841	1948
McGill University	1843	1924
University of Toronto	1850	1926
University of Ottawa	1866	1963
University of Manitoba	1877	1936
University of Western Ontario	1878	1931
McMaster University	1887	1958
University of Alberta	1908	1959
University of Saskatchewan	1908	1947
University of British Columbia	1915	1958
Université de Montréal	1919	1942

*Founding dates of the 12 Canadian universities with doctoral programs in psychology developed before 1960 (derived from data presented in Wright, M.J., & Myers, C.R. (1982). History of Academic Psychology in Canada. Toronto, ON: C.J. Ho.).

than ever before. Because of psychology's enormous breadth, no psychologist can be an expert on all aspects of behaviour. You have already encountered some of psychology's major subfields throughout the chapter, and Table 1.5 introduces several more.

For many people, the term *psychologist* evokes the image of a "therapist" or "counsellor." Although many psychologists are, in fact, clinical psychologists who diagnose and treat people with psychological problems, many other psychologists have no connection with therapy

TABLE 1.5   Major Specialty Areas within Psychology

Specialty	Major Focus
Animal behaviour (comparative)	Study of nonhuman species in natural or laboratory environments; includes genetics, brain processes, social behaviour, evolutionary processes
Cognitive and behavioural neuroscience	Examination of brain and hormonal processes that underlie behaviour; behaviour genetics and evolutionary psychology are sometimes grouped under cognitive and behavioural neuroscience
Clinical	Diagnosis and treatment of psychological disorders; research on causes of disorders and treatment effectiveness
Cognitive	Study of mental processes such as memory, problem solving, planning, consciousness, and language (psycholinguistics)
Counselling	Consultation with clients on issues of personal adjustment; vocational and career planning; interest and aptitude testing
Cultural/cross-cultural	Study of cultural transmission, psychological similarities and differences among people from different cultures
Developmental	Study of physical, mental, emotional, and social development across the entire lifespan
Educational	Study of psychological aspects of the educational process; curriculum and instructional research; teacher training
Experimental	Research (typically laboratory experiments, often with nonhumans) on basic processes such as learning, perception, and motivation
Industrial/organizational	Examination of behaviour in work settings; study of factors related to employee morale and performance; development of tests to select job applicants; development of machines and tasks to fit human capabilities
Personality	Study of individual differences in personality and their effects on behaviour; development of personality tests
Quantitative	Measurement issues and data analysis; development of mathematical models of behaviour
Social	Examination of how the social environment—the presence of other people—influences an individual's behaviour, thoughts, and feelings

in any form. These psychologists work as basic or applied researchers in their chosen subfield. Even within clinical psychology there are scientists who spend most of their time doing research on the causes of mental disorders and the effects of various kinds of treatment.

A career in most of the subfields described in Table 1.5 requires a doctoral degree based on four to six years of training beyond the bachelor's degree. Graduate training in psychology includes broad exposure to the theories and body of knowledge in the field, concentrated study in one or more of the subfields, and extensive training in research methods. In some areas, such as clinical, counselling, school, and industrial/organizational psychology, an additional year or more of supervised practical experience in a hospital, clinic, school, or workplace setting is generally required. Note, however, that psychologists who perform mental-health services are not the same as psychiatrists. Psychiatrists are medical doctors who receive additional specialized training in diagnosing and treating mental disorders.

The American Psychological Association (APA), founded in 1892, is the largest individual psychological association in the world. Its 150 000 members and 56 divisions represent not only the subfields shown in Table 1.5, but also areas that focus on psychology's relation to the arts, religion, the military, the environment, sports, social issues, the law, and the media (APA, 2002). The American Psychology Society (APS), a newer

organization consisting primarily of researchers, has grown to 20 000 members in just two decades (APS, 2009). Both the APA and the APS have international members in dozens of countries.

The actual number of psychologists in the different subfields of psychology in Canada is unknown. According to the Canadian Psychological Association's (CPA) Strategic Plan for 2008–2013, it has over 6000 members (this includes 1643 graduate and undergraduate students) in 32 different sections. The CPA, which was created by 38 psychologists in 1939, is the national Canadian organization for psychologists, but many psychologists do not belong to the CPA. We do know that there are over 11 000 clinical psychologists in Canada, according to a recent CPA survey, with the largest number, per capita, in Quebec. There are also many nonclinical psychologists with Master's and Ph.D. degrees working in school, university, hospital, industrial, and other settings who need to be counted.

Besides the fascinating subject matter of psychology, the rich variety of career options and work settings available to the well-trained professional attracts many people to a career in psychology. Figure 1.25 shows some of the major settings in which psychologists in the United States work (we should expect similar Canadian statistics). Many psychologists teach, engage in research, or apply psychological principles and techniques to help solve personal or social problems.

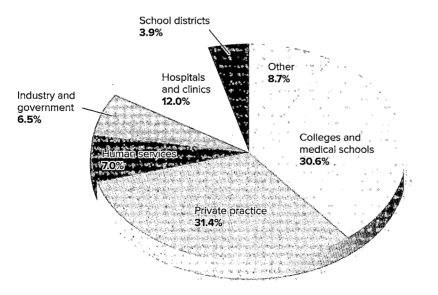

FIGURE 1.25 Work settings of psychologists.

28. Describe three important principles of effective time management.

Psychologists in all the areas shown in Table 1.5 engage in basic research and applied work. Some do one or the other; some do both. As we shall see throughout the book, we can apply psychological principles discovered through basic psychological research to many areas of our lives and to the solution of important social problems. For example, research on learning and memory conducted within the areas of educational and experimental psychology has provided practical guidelines that can enhance your academic performance. Our first *Applications* feature provides some research-based pointers that can help you be more successful in your coursework.

Applications

The *Applications* feature demonstrates how principles from basic research can be applied to everyday life.

ACADEMIC PERFORMANCE ENHANCEMENT STRATEGIES

Four classes of strategies—time management, study skills, test-preparation strategies, and test-taking skills—are particularly useful for increasing your learning and academic performance, both in this course and throughout your educational experience.

Effective Time Management

University life imposes conflicting demands that can challenge even the most organized student. However, if you manage your time efficiently, you can allocate the time needed for study and have a clear conscience when it's time for recreational activities and relaxation.

First, it is essential to develop a written schedule. You have exactly 168 hours in every week, no more, no less. A written schedule forces you to decide how you are going to allocate your time to meet particular course demands and increases your commitment to the plan. Begin your master schedule by writing in all your class meetings and other responsibilities, such as your job schedule. Then block in definite study times, taking into account how long you can study efficiently at one time and avoiding times when you are likely to be tired. Try to distribute your study times throughout the week. If possible, schedule some of your study times immediately before enjoyable activities so that you can use these as rewards for studying.

Once your study times are set, you are ready to apply the time management principle of *prioritizing* (Lakein, 1973). We all tend to work on routine or simple tasks while putting off the most demanding ones until we "have more time." Unfortunately, this method can result in never getting to the major tasks (such as a term paper or a major reading assignment) until it is too late to devote sufficient time to them. Prioritizing means asking yourself weekly or even daily, "What is the most important thing to get done?" Do that task first, then move to the second most important, and so on.

Often the large or important task is too big to complete all at once. Time management experts tell us to break down the large task into smaller tasks that can be completed at specific times (Haynes, 1997). Also, define each task in terms of a specific but realistic goal (e.g., the number of pages to be read or amount of material to be studied). Achieving these goals is rewarding, and such success strengthens your study skills and increases your feelings of mastery.

Like any other skill, time management requires practice. The important tasks are (1) creating written schedules, (2) prioritizing, and (3) constantly monitoring your progress so you can modify your weekly schedule as necessary. The effort put into time management is more than repaid. Working smart can be as important as working hard.

Studying More Effectively

Once you have planned your study time, you will want to use that time most effectively. *Where* you study can make a difference. Choose a place where you can concentrate and where there are no distracting influences. Most students can study better in a quiet library than in front of a TV or in the middle of a Student Union cafeteria. According to a principle of learning that we study in Chapter 7, an excellent practice is to choose a quiet place where you do *nothing* but study. In time, that place will become associated with study behaviours, and it will be easier to study there (Watson & Tharp, 1997).

How you study is vital to your academic success. Rather than simply reading material and passively letting it soak in, you must engage in an active learning process to study most effectively. Psychological research confirms the value of an active approach to learning (Glaser & Bassok, 1989). For example, when you read a chapter in a textbook, don't just start reading from the beginning. First, look over the chapter outline. Then go to the end of the chapter and read the chapter summary, which reviews the chapter's main points. You then will have a good idea of the information you are going to be processing.

The Directed Questions Method

One of the most effective study methods we've encountered in our many years of teaching psychology is what we've termed the *Directed Questions Method*. It is an active learning procedure that requires you to prepare questions about the material you are reading. Research has shown that responding to questions promotes better recall (Moreland et al., 1997; Pauk & Fiore, 2000). In a major review of the scientific literature on learning aids, Richard Hamilton (1985) reviewed

continued

35 different experimental studies in which the use of "adjunct questions" was compared with control conditions in which participants simply read textual material. He found that using questions like ours resulted in a superiority of about 20 percent in the retention of material. With our own students over the years, this approach has proven so successful that we chose to make it an integral learning tool in this text in the form of the directed questions found in the margins. These questions cover major facts and concepts you should know. Our directed questions can be supplemented by additional questions of your own. These questions will be an invaluable study aid when you prepare for tests. Here's how the directed questions method works.

As you read the material in a textbook, compose a question about each important point that is made. This forces you to actively identify what is being communicated. Put the number of the question in the margin next to the place where the answer is found. Do the same thing for your lecture notes. You can now study from your lists of questions and mentally recite the answers to yourself, referring back to your text and lecture notes to make sure that you are answering them correctly. The questions are written in such a way that they serve as a stimulus or prompt for the correct response, resulting in thorough learning.

The Directed Questions Method has two other benefits. Research shows that there is almost no relation between what students think they know and how well they actually perform on tests (Glenberg et al., 1987; Pressley et al., 1987). However, the specific questions that you prepare in the Directed Questions Method allow you to appraise your current level of mastery. Second, the method can reduce test anxiety. You are likely to go into a test more confident, and such confidence tends to enhance performance (Bandura, 1997). Active learning using any method, such as directed questions, requires more effort than passive reading does, but it results in more facts being absorbed and more principles being understood (Estes & Vaughn, 1985).

Preparing for Tests

Introductory psychology is not an easy course. In fact, it is often a very demanding one because of the sheer amount of material that is covered and the many new concepts that must be mastered. Many students who take the course are relatively new to university and don't realize that the price to be paid for success far exceeds the demands that existed in high school. Moreover, many students are not aware of how hard high achievers actually work. In one study, students in an introductory psychology class were asked to record the number of hours outside class that they devoted to the course over a period of several weeks. When the students who were failing the course were compared with those who were getting A grades, the researchers found that the failing students were spending only a third as many hours studying as were the A students (who were spending about two hours of active study for every hour spent in class). Yet the failing students *thought* they were studying as much as anyone else in the class, and

many were mystified that they were not doing as well as their high-achieving peers (Watson & Tharp, 1997).

The time management and study strategies we've discussed can be very helpful when preparing for tests. First, the written study schedule helps you allocate sufficient study time, distribute your learning of the material over time, and avoid the need to cram at the last minute. Cramming, or *massed learning,* is a less effective way to study because it is fatiguing and taxes your memory abilities. Moreover, it often increases test anxiety, which can interfere with both the learning process and actual test performance (Chapell et al., 2005; Sarason & Sarason, 1990). The ideal situation as you near an exam is to have a solid familiarity with the material through previous study and to use the time before the test to reinforce and refine what you already know at a more general level. The directed questions approach can pay big dividends in the final days before an exam if you've paid the price required to prepare them.

As you prepare for tests, it's also vital to repeatedly assess how well you understand the material. Unfortunately, research suggests that in general, students are not highly accurate in judging how well they comprehend textbook material that they've just read (Dunlosky & Lipko, 2007). This inaccuracy can lead to overconfidence as you prepare for tests. You should try to answer the directed questions in the margin after reading each section, but more importantly, you should assess your understanding later on, after a time delay (Thiede & Anderson, 2003). For example, after completing all the readings for your upcoming test, you can attempt to answer the directed questions again. Don't just look at a question and say, "Yeah, I know the answer"; actually verbalize or write out the answer and then refer back to the textbook to see whether your answer is accurate.

Test-Taking Strategies

Some students are more effective test-takers than others. They know how to take advantage of the kind of test they are taking (e.g., multiple-choice or essay format) to maximize their performance. This skill is called *test-wiseness* (Fagley, 1987).

1. Because you have a time limit in which to complete a test, use the time wisely. Check your progress occasionally to make sure that you are on track. Answer the questions you know first (and, in the case of essay exams, the ones that count for the most points). Do not get bogged down on a question you find difficult to answer. Mark it and come back to it later.

2. On essay exams, organize your answer before you begin writing. Make a rough outline of the points you want to make. On essay exams, try to cover all the critical points in enough detail to communicate what you know without needless verbiage.

3. On a test in an introductory psychology course, you are likely to have multiple-choice questions. As you read each multiple-choice question, try to answer it without looking at the alternatives. Then look at the answer options. If you

continued

find your answer among the alternatives, that alternative is probably the correct one. Nonetheless, read all the other alternatives to make sure that you choose the best one.

4. A widely held belief among both professors and students is that one should not change answers on multiple-choice tests because the first guess is most likely to be correct. Psychologists have studied this belief and have found it to be untrue. Ludy Benjamin and his colleagues (1984) reviewed 20 different studies that investigated the consequences of changing answers. They concluded that changing an answer is far more likely to result in a wrong answer becoming a correct one than vice versa. More recently, psychologists Justin Kruger, Derrick Wirtz, and Dale Miller (2005) obtained similar findings in a study of 1561 university students. The results are summarized in Figure 1.26. By a 2:1 ratio, more changed answers went from wrong to right than from right to wrong and, by nearly a 3:1 ratio, more students who changed answers ended up with higher rather than lower exam scores. Yet, most students still believed that as a general test-taking strategy, changing answers was harmful. Kruger et al. called this "the first instinct fallacy." Therefore, don't be reluctant to change an answer if you are fairly sure that another alternative is better. At the same time, don't out-think yourself by attaching some esoteric meaning to an alternative so that it could *possibly* be correct. Most multiple-choice alternatives are fairly straightforward and are not meant to trick you.

5. Many multiple-choice items have one or two alternatives that you can rule out immediately. Eliminate them first, and then choose your answer from the remaining alternatives, which are likely to have at least a grain of truth in them.

6. Some questions have "all of the above" as an alternative. If one of the other three or four alternatives is clearly incorrect, eliminate this option; if you are sure at least two of the other alternatives are correct but are not sure about the third, choose "all of the above."

The performance enhancement skills of time management, study skills, test-preparation strategies, and test-wiseness can help you improve your academic performance. Remember, however, that such skills are not acquired overnight; they require effort and practice. Psychology is an ideal course in which to acquire or refine them because the subject matter (e.g., learning, memory, problem solving, motivation) often pertains to the very principles you are perfecting. Some of the *Applications* features in other chapters also may help you enhance your academic performance. These include

- self-control of behaviour (see Chapter 7)
- improving memory (see Chapter 8)
- coping with stress—including test anxiety (see Chapter 15)

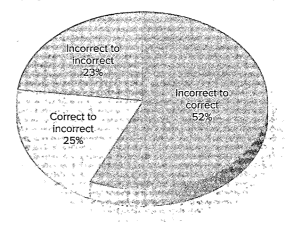

FIGURE 1.26 Researchers analyzed the eraser marks on 6412 exams taken by introductory psychology students. Contrary to popular wisdom, changing one's answer was twice as likely to result in gaining points than in losing points.

Source: Based on Kruger, J. Wirtz, D., & Miller, D.T. (2005) Counterfactual thinking and the first instinct fallacy. *Journal of Personality and Social Psychology*, 88, 725–735.

---

29. What does educational psychology research tell us about the effects of directed questions on retention of information? Why do they have these effects?

30. What kinds of strategies are used by test-wise students when they take tests?

- Psychologists specialize in numerous subfields and work in many settings. Their professional activities include teaching, research, clinical work, and application of psychological principles to solve personal and social problems.

- Psychologists today conduct research and provide services around the globe.

- You can use principles derived from psychological science to enhance your learning and increase your likelihood of performing well on tests. These include time-management principles, strategies for studying more effectively, test-preparation strategies, and techniques for test-taking.

Gaining Direction

The *Gaining Direction* feature takes you back to the opening story and presents some possible answers to the questions posed.

What are the issues?

The opening scenario for Chapter 1 deals with issues of depression, mental illness, suicide, brain structures, intelligence, and genius. Why would someone want to deliberately crash a plane? If the co-pilot wanted to kill himself, why did he have to take 150 people with him? Could this illness have been treated? What brain structures are involved? Could the disaster have been avoided? The brain plays a prominent role in the second story. How can someone with no musical or artistic talent suddenly become a virtuoso? What is the role of the damaged brain areas? How do they interact with other areas that promote genius? Is there a genius in all of us?

What do we need to know?

How is the brain organized?
How does one area of the brain interact with another?
Can a brain region suppress talent?
What is it that produces genius?
Can we all become a genius if we know how to alter the brain?
What causes depression?

Why are depressed individuals at a higher risk for suicide?
How can you treat depression?
Should individuals with a history of depression be allowed to care for others in high-risk situations?
How can psychological theory help us understand events in the "real world"?

Where can we find the information to answer these questions?

Look back at the icons in this chapter. What psychological principles (or research) are presented that may help us understand some of the issues? Look back on the section that discusses approaches to depression. Does this offer any clues to the causes of suicide? Are there any theories we should investigate? Which of the perspectives helps us understand depression best?

Consider the *Research Foundations* feature. There are cross-cultural differences in love . . . might there be cultural differences in mental illness? How might neuroimaging studies mentioned in the *Focus on Neuroscience* feature help us understand the biological underpinnings of intelligence and genius? What chapters of the text should we look at to find these answers?

Answers:

Jumbled paragraph 1

According to research at Cambridge University, it doesn't matter what order the letters in a word are, the only important thing is that the first and last letters are at the right place. The rest can be a total mess, and you can still read it without a problem. This is because we do not read every letter by itself but the word as a whole. (Note: In the jumbled version of this paragraph, the author of the paragraph misspelled *research* by adding an extra *h*.)

Jumbled paragraph 2

A politician denied the manslaughter of a colleague, but was convicted and developed severe medical conditions in prison, where he died. Administration of anticoagulant drugs potentiated the effects of another drug, and respiratory failure resulted.

Basic vs. applied research articles

1. Basic
2. Applied
3. Applied
4. Basic
5. Basic

Studying Behaviour Scientifically

CHAPTER ⟩
OUTLINE

SCIENTIFIC PRINCIPLES IN PSYCHOLOGY
Scientific Attitudes
  Research Foundations: Bystander Intervention
Gathering Evidence: Steps in the Scientific Process
Two Approaches to Understanding Behaviour
Defining and Measuring Variables
  Focus on Neuroscience: The Neuroscience
  of the Human Brain at Work

METHODS OF RESEARCH
Descriptive Research: Recording Events
Correlational Research: Measuring Associations
  between Events
Experiments: Examining Cause and Effect

THREATS TO THE VALIDITY OF RESEARCH
Confounding of Variables
Placebo Effects

Experimenter Expectancy Effects
Replicating and Generalizing the Findings
  Frontiers: Does ESP Exist?

ETHICAL PRINCIPLES IN HUMAN AND ANIMAL RESEARCH
Ethical Standards in Human Research
Ethical Standards in Animal Research

CRITICAL THINKING IN SCIENCE AND EVERYDAY LIFE
  Applications: Evaluating Claims in Research
  and Everyday Life

I have no special talents. I am only passionately curious.
—Albert Einstein

 Etienne LeBel has been getting a lot of attention lately. A graduate of Western University in London, Ontario, Dr. LeBel does research on prejudice, stereotyping, and on the replication of studies published in journals. It is this last area of interest that has caught the media spotlight. LeBel has commented that many of the classic studies in psychology are not really as strong as we would like to think. For example,

Castleski/Shutterstock

What are the issues here?

What do we need to know?

Where can we find the information to answer the questions?

the Festinger and Carlsmith (1959) study on cognitive dissonance has been cited by virtually every psychology textbook in the field and most research papers on the topic of attitude change. However, of the three dependent variables measured in the study, only one was significant.

He and 270 other researchers associated with the Reproducibility Project attempted to replicate 100 studies published in several journals in 2008. In only 39 cases was the same result found. The Festinger and Carlsmith study has also been heavily criticized by others, and LeBel notes that he has even received hate mail from senior colleagues. Nonetheless, the article by the Reproducibility Project was published in the prestigious journal *Science,* and other journals have started to revise their own reporting standards.

Psychology is not alone in this publication controversy—other authors have reported that only 6 of 53 papers in cancer biology journals could be reproduced.

Science frequently has all the mystery of a detective story. Something happens that we need to explain and we have to search for the answers in both obvious and the hidden places. When we find an answer, we have to test it against the facts to see if it will stand on its own. And if it doesn't make sense, we have to look harder before coming to a final conclusion.

In this chapter, we explore principles and methods that form the foundation of psychological science. These principles also promote a way of thinking—critical thinking—that can serve you well in many aspects of your life.

SCIENTIFIC PRINCIPLES IN PSYCHOLOGY

At its core, science is an approach to asking and answering questions about the universe around us. Certainly, there are other ways we learn about the world and ourselves—through reason, intuition, and common sense; religion and spirituality; the arts; and the teachings of family, friends, and others. What distinguishes science from these approaches is a process guided by certain principles: the scientific method (Fossion & Zapata-Fonseca, 2015). The scientific method was used by physicists and chemists for several centuries to make great progress in determining the laws of the physical sciences. Psychologists took much longer to adopt the scientific method for behavioural science because the subject matter is not as tangible as that in the physical sciences. Calculating the speed of a thrown ball by measuring time and distance is much more straightforward than measuring a person's intelligence. In this chapter, we explore in detail the principles and methods that form the foundation of psychological science.

Scientific Attitudes

Curiosity, skepticism, and *open-mindedness* are driving forces behind scientific inquiry. Like a child who constantly asks "Why?" the good scientist has an insatiable curiosity. And like a master detective, the good scientist is an incurable skeptic. Each claim is met with the reply "Show me your evidence," and even when a mystery appears to be solved, the good scientist asks, "Might there be a better explanation?" Scientists also must remain open-minded to conclusions that are supported by facts, even if those conclusions refute their own beliefs.

To illustrate the scientific approach to problem solving, let us examine a specific study (see the *Research Foundations* feature). Ideas for this study were prompted by the murder of Kitty Genovese in New York. Here is a synopsis of the story. Following the Kitty Genovese murder, two psychology professors in New York City, John Darley of New York University and Bibb Latané of Columbia University, met for dinner. They were so curious about how 38 people could witness such a violent crime and not even call the police that they decided to investigate further. Darley and Latané also were skeptical of the media's "bystander apathy" explanation; they believed it was unlikely that every one of the bystanders could have been apathetic. They noted that the bystanders could see that other neighbours had turned on their lights and were looking out their windows. Each bystander might have been concerned about Kitty Genovese's plight but assumed that someone else surely would help or call the police.

1. What key scientific attitudes did Darley and Latané display?

2. How does Darley and Latané's research illustrate the basic steps of the scientific process?

Research Foundations

BYSTANDER INTERVENTION

Introduction

Darely and Latané (1968) were moved by the story of Kitty Genovese in 1964. Genovese was a young woman who was attacked by a knife-wielding assailant as she returned to her New York City apartment. She was stabbed repeatedly and raped in an attack that lasted about 30 minutes, during which time her screams and pleas for help were witnessed by 38 of her neighbours. Yet none of them assisted her, and by the time someone had called the police, she had already died. Darely and Latané particularly wondered how 38 people could witness an attack and not do anything. What was it about an emergency situation that resulted in lack of action? They suggested that three decisions would have to be made before an individual would intervene in any emergency. First, the person would have to notice the event, then the event must be seen as an emergency, and finally, the individual would have to take responsibility for action. Furthermore, these decisions would be influenced by the number of bystanders present at the scene—the more bystanders, the less likely anyone would do anything. The following study was designed to test the effects of number of bystanders on reporting an emergency.

Method

Participants were seated in a small room and observed through a one-way window. They were either alone in the room, in a group of three, or with two other people (confederates) who actually worked for the experimenter. All participants were asked to fill out a questionnaire. After they finished the second page, "smoke" began to pour into the room through a wall vent. The smoke was actually a stage fog used for theatre productions. The confederates were instructed to ignore the smoke when it entered and to do nothing about it. Observers behind the one-way window recorded when participants first noticed the smoke, what they did while in the room, and at what time they left the room to report the smoke to the experimenter. If no one reported the potential emergency within six minutes, the experiment was terminated.

Results

Alone condition. Participants noticed the smoke within five seconds and would typically get up, go over to the vent, and examine it. On average, participants left the room and reported the smoke within two minutes after noticing it. Seventy-five percent reported the emergency before the experiment was stopped.

Confederate condition. In sharp contrast to the alone condition, only one person ever reported the smoke when two unresponsive bystanders were present. Average time to notice the smoke was 20 seconds. People in the room would attempt to clear the smoke by waving their hands, opening a window, and so forth, but they did not report the emergency.

Group condition. With three people in the room, we might expect at least one of them to react quickly. However, only four people reported the emergency and only one of them left room within four minutes after the smoke appeared. As in the confederate condition, the average notice time was 20 seconds.

All participants were interviewed after the experiment was over. Those people who had reported the smoke typically said that they were not sure what it was, but thought that it should be checked out. Participants who did not report the emergency constructed a number of possible scenarios for what the smoke might be, ranging from steam or smog to "truth gas" pumped in to insure accurate responses on the questionnaire.

Discussion

The results clearly support the unresponsive bystander effect. People were more likely to report the smoke in the alone condition than in either of the group conditions. Darley and Latané's decision-making model appears to be correct. Participants in the group conditions took four times longer to notice the smoke than those in the alone condition. Furthermore, people who did *not* help came up with a variety of explanations for the smoke that downplayed the emergency nature of the situation. It was smog or truth gas, not something that could be related to a fire. In essence, they had failed to interpret the situation as an emergency. Why might this occur? After all, participants could possibly be in danger. Darley and Latané suggest that in ambiguous situations, we tend to look to other people for information. So in the group conditions, you look at the other people in the room to see if they are concerned. If they do not seem to be concerned and no one is doing anything, you will consequently decide that this cannot be a real emergency. When you are alone, you do not have this source of information available, so you must decide for yourself what to do.

Design

Question: Does the number of bystanders witnessing an emergency influence helping behaviour?

Type of Study: *Experimental*

Independent Variables	**Dependent Variables**
Number of people in the room	• Time to notice the smoke • Time to report the emergency

Darley and Latané reasoned that the presence of multiple bystanders produced a *diffusion of responsibility,* a psychological state in which each person feels decreased personal responsibility for intervening. They performed several experiments to test their explanation.

Gathering Evidence: Steps in the Scientific Process

Science involves a continuous interplay between observing and explaining events. Figure 2.1 shows the following five steps, which reflect how scientific inquiry often proceeds.

Step 1: Identify a Question of Interest. Curiosity sparks the first step: identifying a question of interest. From personal experiences, news events, scientific articles, books, and other sources, scientists observe something that piques their interest, and they ask a question about it. Darley and Latané observed that nobody helped Kitty Genovese and then asked, "Why?"

Step 2: Gather Information and Form Hypothesis. Next, scientists determine whether any studies, theories, and other information that might help answer their question already exist. Then they form a hypothesis. Noting that each bystander probably knew that other bystanders were witnessing Kitty Genovese's plight, Darley and Latané proposed that a diffusion of responsibility reduced the likelihood that any one bystander would intervene. This tentative explanation is then translated into a **hypothesis,** a specific prediction about some phenomenon that often takes the form of an "If-Then" statement: "In an emergency, IF multiple bystanders are present, THEN the likelihood that any one bystander will intervene is reduced."

Step 3: Test Hypothesis by Conducting Research. The third step is to test the hypothesis by conducting research. Latané and Darley (1968) staged an "emergency" in their laboratory and recorded people's responses. Undergraduate participants were asked to fill out a questionnaire, either alone or in groups. Shortly after beginning the questionnaire, smoke began to pour into the room. Would anyone notice the smoke and would anyone seek help?

3. What is a hypothesis?

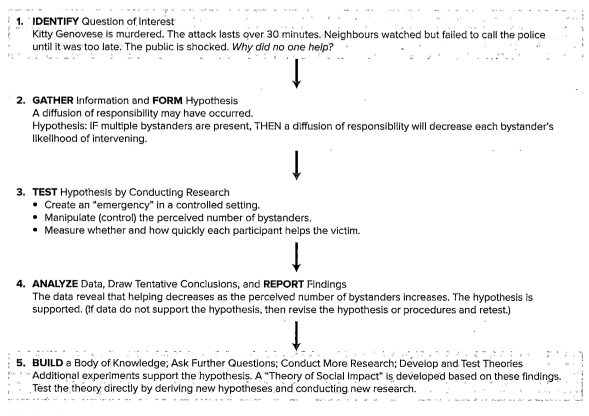

Examining bystander intervention: Why do people sometimes fail to help a victim in need during an emergency, even when there is little or no personal risk? What factors increase or decrease the likelihood that a bystander will intervene?

1. **IDENTIFY** Question of Interest
   Kitty Genovese is murdered. The attack lasts over 30 minutes. Neighbours watched but failed to call the police until it was too late. The public is shocked. *Why did no one help?*

2. **GATHER** Information and **FORM** Hypothesis
   A diffusion of responsibility may have occurred.
   Hypothesis: IF multiple bystanders are present, THEN a diffusion of responsibility will decrease each bystander's likelihood of intervening.

3. **TEST** Hypothesis by Conducting Research
   • Create an "emergency" in a controlled setting.
   • Manipulate (control) the perceived number of bystanders.
   • Measure whether and how quickly each participant helps the victim.

4. **ANALYZE** Data, Draw Tentative Conclusions, and **REPORT** Findings
   The data reveal that helping decreases as the perceived number of bystanders increases. The hypothesis is supported. (If data do not support the hypothesis, then revise the hypothesis or procedures and retest.)

5. **BUILD** a Body of Knowledge; Ask Further Questions; Conduct More Research; Develop and Test Theories
   Additional experiments support the hypothesis. A "Theory of Social Impact" is developed based on these findings. Test the theory directly by deriving new hypotheses and conducting new research.

FIGURE 2.1 Using the scientific method.

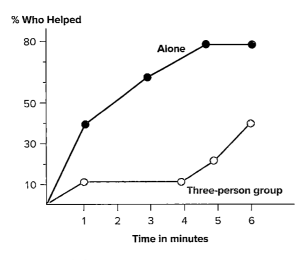

% Who Helped

FIGURE 2.2 Participants were in room either alone or with two other people. When smoke started entering the room, those who were alone were more likely to report the incident to the experimenter, and they did so faster than people in groups of three.

Source: Adapted from Latané and Darley (1968). Group inhibition of bystander intervention in emergencies. *Journal of Personality and Social Psychology, 10*(3), pp. 215–221.

Step 4: Analyze Data, Draw Tentative Conclusions, and Report Findings. At the fourth step, researchers analyze the information (called *data*) they collect, draw tentative conclusions, and report their findings to the scientific community. As Figure 2.2 shows. Latané and Darley found that most participants who were alone actually sought out the experimenter for help. In the groups of three, people were much less likely to define the situation as an emergency and to seek help. These findings support the diffusion of responsibility hypothesis and illustrate how research can contradict such common-sense adages as "There's safety in numbers."

Latané and Darley then submitted a report describing their research to a scientific journal. Expert reviewers favourably judged the quality and importance of the research, so the journal published the article. Publishing research is essential to scientific progress. It allows fellow scientists to learn about new ideas and findings, to evaluate the research, and to challenge or expand on it.

Step 5: Build a Body of Knowledge. At the fifth step, scientists build a body of knowledge about the topic in question. They ask further questions (e.g., What other factors affect bystander intervention?), formulate new hypotheses, and test those hypotheses by conducting more research. As evidence mounts, scientists may attempt to build theories. A **theory** is a set of formal statements that explains how and why certain events

4. What is a theory? How does it differ from a hypothesis?

5. Explain the major drawback of hindsight understanding.

6. What approach to understanding do scientists prefer? Why?

are related to one another. Theories are broader than hypotheses, and in psychology theories typically specify lawful relations between certain behaviours and their causes. For example, dozens of experiments reveal that diffusion of responsibility has occurred across many situations (Latané & Nida, 1981). Latané then combined the principle of diffusion of responsibility with other principles of group behaviour to develop a broad *theory of social impact,* which has been used to explain a variety of social behaviours (DiFonzo et al., 2013; Latané & Bourgeois, 2001). Scientists use theories to develop new hypotheses, which are then tested by conducting more research. In this manner, the scientific process becomes self-correcting. When research consistently supports the hypotheses derived from a theory, confidence in the theory increases. If predictions made by the theory are not supported, then it will need to be modified or, ultimately, discarded.

Two Approaches to Understanding Behaviour

Humans have a strong desire to understand why things happen. Why do scientists favour the preceding step-by-step approach to understanding behaviour over the approach typically involved in everyday common sense—hindsight?

Hindsight (After-the-Fact Understanding)

Philosopher Sören Kierkegaard stated, "Life is lived forwards, but understood backwards." Perhaps the most common method we use to try to understand behaviour in our everyday life is hindsight (i.e., after-the-fact) reasoning. Indeed, when you report the results of some of the research described in this book, you might hear the following comment: "Big deal—I knew that all along." However, there is a problem with using hindsight explanations based on common sense and folk knowledge to understand behaviour. For example, suppose two high school sweethearts promised each other undying love before going off to different universities and when they came home for the holidays they broke up. The well-known proverb "Out of sight, out of mind" can explain this result. But, suppose, instead, the opposite happened. When the sweethearts came home, they were more in love than ever and got married. The proverb "Absence makes the heart grow fonder" explains this result. So which proverb is true; or, are there other reasons for their behaviour— for example, the breakup occurred when sweethearts met new partners at university?

The main problem with relying solely on hindsight reasoning is that related past events can be explained in many creative, reasonable, and sometimes contradictory, ways. There is no sure way to determine which—if any—of the alternatives is correct. Despite this problem, hindsight reasoning can provide valuable insights and is often the foundation on which further scientific inquiry is built. For example, Darley and Latané's diffusion of responsibility explanation was initially based on after-the-fact reasoning about the Genovese murder.

Understanding through Prediction, Control, and Theory Building

Whenever possible, scientists prefer to test their understanding of "what causes what" more directly. If we understand the causes of a given behaviour, then we should be able to predict the conditions under which that behaviour will occur in the future. Furthermore, if we can control those conditions (e.g., in the laboratory), then we should be able to produce that behaviour.

Latané and Darley's research illustrates this approach. They predicted that because of a diffusion of responsibility, the presence of multiple bystanders during an emergency would reduce individual assistance. Next, they carefully staged an emergency and varied the number of bystanders. Their prediction was supported. Understanding through prediction and control is a scientific alternative to hindsight understanding.

Theory development is the strongest test of scientific understanding because good theories generate an *integrated network of predictions*. A good theory has several important characteristics:

- It incorporates existing facts and observations within a single broad framework. In other words, it organizes information in a meaningful way.

- It is testable. It generates new hypotheses and predictions whose accuracy can be evaluated by gathering new evidence (Figure 2.3).

- The predictions made by the theory are supported by the findings of new research.

- It conforms to the *law of parsimony:* If two theories can explain and predict the same phenomena equally well, the simpler theory is the preferred one.

Even when many successful predictions support a theory, it is never regarded as an absolute truth. It is always possible that future observation will contradict it, or that a newer, more accurate

"IT MAY VERY WELL BRING ABOUT IMMORTALITY, BUT IT WILL TAKE FOREVER TO TEST IT."

FIGURE 2.3 Is the scientist's claim of discovering an "eternal life potion" a testable hypothesis? Yes, because it is possible to show the hypothesis to be false. If people drink it but still die, then we have refuted the hypothesis. Therefore, it is testable. It is, however, impossible to absolutely prove true. Even after living for a million years, a person who drank the potion could die the next day.

theory will displace it. The displacement of old beliefs and theoretical frameworks by new ones is the essence of science (Klahr & Simon, 1999).

Finally, although scientists use prediction as a test of "understanding," this does not mean that prediction requires understanding. Even a child can predict that thunder will follow lightning without knowing why it does so. Our primeval ancestors undoubtedly could predict that eating certain plants would make them sick, without understanding principles of human physiology. But prediction based on understanding (i.e., "theory building") has important advantages: It satisfies our curiosity, increases knowledge, and generates principles that we can apply to new situations.

7. Describe the characteristics of a good theory.

Defining and Measuring Variables

Psychologists study variables and the relations among them. A **variable,** quite simply, is any characteristic or factor that can vary. People's sex, height, hair colour, age, income, and grade point average (GPA) are variables: They vary from one person to another, and many also vary within a given person over time.

Many variables that psychologists study represent abstract concepts that cannot be observed directly. For example, "self-esteem," "stress," and "intelligence" are concepts that refer to people's internal qualities. We might say that Tyra has high self-esteem, Shaun is intelligent, and Claire feels stressed, but how do we know this? We can't directly look inside their heads and see "self-esteem," "stress," and "intelligence"; yet such concepts must be capable of being measured if we are to study them scientifically.

Because any variable may mean different things to different people, scientists must define their terms clearly. And when conducting research, scientists must also define variables operationally. An **operational definition** defines a variable in terms of the specific procedures used to produce or measure it. Operational definitions translate abstract concepts into something observable and measurable.

To illustrate, suppose we want to study the relation between stress and academic performance among university students. How shall we operationally define our variables? "Academic performance" could mean a single test score, a course grade, or one's overall performance. For our study, let's operationally define it as students' final exam scores in an introductory chemistry course. We also have many options for operationally defining exam stress. How might you operationally define "exam stress" at a biological, psychological, and environmental level of analysis? Think about this, and then see Figure 2.4.

....
8. Why are operational definitions important?
....

Levels of Analysis | **Measuring Exam Stress**

Of course, we do not have to limit ourselves to one operational definition of stress or of academic performance. By incorporating multiple levels of analysis, we might measure students' pre-exam stress hormones and self-reported worry, their nervous habits during the exam, and the exam's difficulty. We can then examine how these different stress measures relate to immediate exam performance and students' overall GPAs. This strategy of measuring a conceptual variable (i.e., a "construct") in multiple ways can yield a much more complete picture than does using a single type of measure.

ENVIRONMENTAL
• We can measure aspects of the academic environment that create greater or lesser demands on students, such as the difficulty of the exam, the overall course grading scale, time pressures and room noise during the exam, and the level of achievement expectations set by the students' parents.

BIOLOGICAL
• Before, during, and after the final exam, we can physiologically measure students' stress hormone levels, heart rate, respiration rate, muscle tension, and sweating.

PSYCHOLOGICAL
• Two weeks before the final exam, we can administer a personality test to students that measures their self-reported, general level of anxiety over taking exams.
• Just before the final exam, we can ask students to report their level of worry, tension, and anxiety.
• During the exam, we can directly observe nervous behaviours, such as fingernail biting, foot wiggling, and hair pulling.

If you were designing a research study, what measures would you choose to operationally define exam stress?

FIGURE 2.4

(a)   (b)   (c)

(left) © Richard T. Nowitz/Photo Researchers; (centre) Comstock Images/Getty Images; (right) © Spencer Grant/PhotoEdit

FIGURE 2.5 (a) Self-report, (b) physiological, and (c) behavioural measures are important scientific tools for psychologists.

Measurement is challenging because psychologists study incredibly varied and complex processes. Some processes are directly observable, but others are not. Fortunately, psychologists have numerous measurement techniques at their disposal (Figure 2.5).

Self-Reports and Reports by Others

Self-report measures ask people to report on their own knowledge, beliefs, feelings, experiences, or behaviour. This information is often gathered through interviews or questionnaires. The accuracy of self-report measures hinges on people's ability and willingness to respond honestly, especially when research questions focus on sensitive topics, such as sexual habits and drug use.

Participants' self-reports may be distorted by a **social desirability bias,** the tendency to respond in a socially acceptable manner rather than according to how one truly feels or behaves. University of British Columbia researcher Delroy Paulhus (1991) suggests that researchers can minimize the social desirability bias by wording questions so that social desirability is not relevant or, if that is impossible, by guaranteeing respondents anonymity and confidentiality so they can respond honestly without fear of future consequences (e.g., questions about taking drugs or having unsafe sex). These measures presume respondents give honest responses. Paulhus, Harms, Bruce, and Lysy (2003) developed the Over-Claiming Questionnaire (OCQ) to measure the degree of a respondent's social

desirability bias. They had respondents rate their familiarity with a large number of items on a questionnaire, of which 20 percent didn't exist (e.g., cholarine). The social desirability bias is high when respondents confidently claim familiarity with a large number of nonexistent items.

We also can gather information about someone's behaviour by conducting interviews with or administering questionnaires to *other people,* such as parents, spouses, and teachers, who know the person. For example, job supervisors might be asked to rate workers' competence or motivation. As with self-reports, researchers try to maximize participants' honesty in reporting about other people.

Measures of Overt Behaviour

Another measurement approach is to record overt (i.e., directly observable) behaviour. In an experiment on learning, we might measure how many errors a person makes while performing a task. In an experiment on drug effects, we might measure people's **reaction time**—how rapidly they respond to a stimulus (such as the turning on and off of a light)—after ingesting various amounts of alcohol. In the bystander emergency experiment, Latané and Darley (1968) recorded whether and how quickly students reported a potential fire. In experiments on "thinking" in preverbal infants, researchers have measured how long infants look at various familiar and novel visual targets or if they turn to look at off-centred familiar versus novel sound sources.

9. Describe the major ways psychologists measure behaviour, and suggest a limitation of each method.

Psychologists also develop *coding systems* to record different categories of behaviour. While a parent and child jointly perform a task, we might code the parent's behaviour into such categories as "praises child," "assists child," and "criticizes child." Observers must be trained to use the coding system properly so that their measurements will be **reliable**—*consistent observations*. If two observers watching the same behaviours repeatedly disagree in their coding (e.g., one says the parent "praised" and another says the parent "assisted"), then the data are unreliable and of little use.

Humans and other animals may behave differently when they know they are being observed. To counter this problem, researchers may disguise their presence or use **unobtrusive measures,** which record behaviour in a way that keeps participants unaware that certain responses are being measured. For example, if we ask people to report their mood on a questionnaire, then they are aware that we're measuring their mood. Instead, we could have people perform tasks that assess their moods in ways that are not obvious to them, such as rating pleasant and emotionally neutral pictures, and reading various types of words (Kiecolt-Glaser et al., 2008). Robinson et al. (2012) report that thermal imaging also is a good predictor for mood state.

Psychologists also gather information about behaviour by using **archival measures,** which are records or documents that already exist. For example, to evaluate the effectiveness of a program to reduce schoolchildren's disruptive classroom behaviours, researchers have examined school records, which contained such things as student suspensions and number of trips to the principal's office, that were gathered both before and after the program was implemented (Pelham et al., 2005).

Psychological tests. Psychologists develop and use specialized tests to measure many types of variables. For example, *personality tests,* which assess personality traits, often contain questions that ask how a person typically feels or behaves (e.g., "True or False: I prefer to be alone rather than attend social gatherings."). In essence, such tests are specialized self-reports. Other personality tests present ambiguous stimuli (e.g., pictures that could have different meanings), and personality traits are judged based upon how a person interprets these stimuli.

Other psychological tests consist of performance tasks. For example, *intelligence tests* may ask people to assemble objects or solve arithmetic problems. *Neuropsychological tests* help to diagnose normal and abnormal brain functioning by measuring how well people perform mental and physical tasks, such as recalling lists of words or manipulating objects (Abramowitz & Caron, 2010; Goodale & Milner, 1992).

Physiological measures. Psychologists also record physiological responses to assess what people are experiencing. Measures of heart rate, blood pressure, respiration rate, hormonal secretions, and brain functioning have long been the mainstay of biopsychologists, but these measures have become increasingly important in many other areas of psychology (see this chapter's *Focus on Neuroscience* feature).

10. What is unobtrusive measurement?

In Review

- The scientific process proceeds through several steps: (1) asking questions based on some type of observation; (2) gathering information and formulating a testable hypothesis; (3) conducting research to test the hypothesis; (4) analyzing the data, drawing tentative conclusions, and reporting one's findings to the scientific community; and (5) building a body of knowledge by asking further questions, conducting more research, and developing and testing theories.

- In everyday life, we typically use hindsight to explain behaviour. Hindsight is flawed because there may be many possible explanations for behaviour and no way to ascertain which one is correct. Psychologists prefer to test their understanding through prediction, control, and theory building.

- A good theory organizes known facts, gives rise to additional hypotheses that are testable, is supported by the findings of new research, and is parsimonious.

- An operational definition defines a concept or variable in terms of the specific procedures used to produce or measure it.

- To measure behaviour, psychologists obtain peoples' self-reports and reports from others who know the participants, directly observe behaviour using unobtrusive measures, analyze archival data, administer psychological tests, and record physiological responses.

Focus on
Neuroscience

THE NEUROSCIENCE OF THE HUMAN BRAIN AT WORK

Neuroscientists use various techniques to identify localization of behavioural function in specific areas of the brain. They have used the case study method to test patients with damage to a specific area of the brain to uncover which of their abilities are preserved and which are lost, in an attempt to identify the functions of different brain structures (e.g., see Chapter 3; classic study of Phineas Gage). A modern example is the work of Mel Goodale, at the University of Western Ontario. In the 1990s, Goodale and Milner (1992) studied a patient (D.F.) who experienced carbon monoxide poisoning. D.F. suffered damage to one cortical visual processing area (the ventral stream) but had no damage in another cortical visual area (the dorsal stream; see Figure 2.6). When D.F. was shown objects (e.g., a rod), she couldn't identify them, their shape, or their orientation (i.e., she had lost visual object recognition). But when D.F. was asked to grab the rod presented in different orientations and positions, she showed normal anticipatory hand opening, rotated her hand into the correct orientation, accurately reached out and grabbed the rod (i.e., she had retained normal visually guided reaching). The case study of D.F. provided compelling evidence from purely behavioural data that visual object recognition and action are processed independently by the ventral and dorsal streams, respectively.

As discussed in Chapter 1, recent advances in brain-imaging technology have allowed neuroscientists to monitor neural activity in the intact brain of a person during mental or physical tasks (e.g., Talbot, 2003). PET and fMRI scans actually measure changes in local blood flow or oxygen content, which have been shown to reflect local neural activity (Logothetis et al., 2001). Neuroscientists have used brain-imaging technology to map the neural activity of clinical patients with psychiatric disorders (e.g., schizophrenia, Alzheimer's disease) and patients suffering from brain damage (e.g., Thompson et al., 2000; Partain, 2006), as well as to explore the development of normal and abnormal brain functions. Using imaging techniques, scientists have identified neural pathways involved in various mental operations, emotional regulation, language perception and

production, and visual perception and action. For example, James, Culham, Humphrey, Milner, and Goodale (2003) used fMRI scans to measure the activation level in D.F.'s ventral and dorsal streams during both visual recognition tests and object-directed grasping tasks. As predicted from the behavioural results, D.F.'s loss of visual object recognition was associated with absent/abnormal ventral-stream activation, while her dorsal stream regions showed normal activation during object grasping tasks. Finally, Valyear, Culham, Sharif, Westwood, and Goodale (2006) used fMRI to study the activity in the normal human brain and found the predicted differential ventral and dorsal stream activation during the performance of visual object recognition tasks versus object grasping (orientation) tests. Clearly, brain-imaging technology gives neuroscientists a powerful tool to study the localization of function.

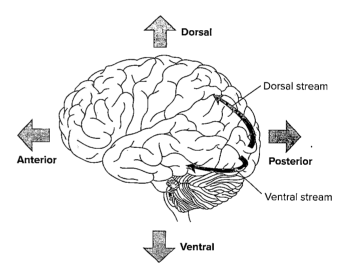

FIGURE 2.6 Navigating the brain. When discussing anatomy, we often use the standard terminology shown here. Thus, the dorsal stream runs along the upper surface of the cortex; the ventral stream runs along the bottom surface. In addition, we often use the terms *medial* to describe a structure toward the centre of the brain and *lateral* to indicate one toward the brain's outer surface.

Physiological responses can have their own interpretive problems, the main one being that we don't always understand what they mean. For example, if a person shows increased heart rate and brain activity in a particular situation, what emotion or thought is being expressed? Nevertheless, our knowledge about links between patterns of physiological activity and specific psychological processes is rapidly expanding (Rolls, 2010).

In sum, psychologists can measure behaviour in many ways, and each has advantages and disadvantages. To gain greater confidence in their findings, researchers may use several types of measures within a single study.

METHODS OF RESEARCH

Like detectives searching for clues to solve a case, psychologists conduct research to gather evidence about behaviour and its causes. The research method chosen depends on the problem being studied, the investigator's objectives, and ethical principles.

Descriptive Research: Recording Events

The most basic goal of science is to describe phenomena. In psychology, **descriptive research** seeks to identify how humans and other animals behave, particularly in natural settings. It provides information about the diversity of behaviour and may yield clues about potential cause–effect relations that are later tested experimentally. Case studies, naturalistic observation, and surveys are research methods commonly used to describe behaviour.

Case Studies: Treating Cases of Failure to Thrive (Starvation) in Human Infants

A **case study** is an in-depth analysis of an individual, a group, or an event. By studying a single case in detail, researchers typically hope to discover principles of behaviour that are true for people or situations in general. Data may be

11. What is a case study? Identify its advantages.

gathered through observation, interviews, psychological tests, physiological recordings, and task performance, or from archival records.

Case studies have several advantages. First, when a rare phenomenon occurs, this method enables scientists to study it closely. Second, a case study may challenge the validity of a theory or widely held scientific belief. Third, a case study can be a vibrant source of new ideas and hypotheses that subsequently may be examined by using more controlled research methods. Case studies have provided important insight into such diverse topics as brain functioning (see this chapter's *Focus on Neuroscience* feature), child development, mental disorders, and cultural influences. Consider the following example.

Normally, human infants gain weight rapidly after birth; not doing so can have a negative impact on their later physical and intellectual development. When medical causes are ruled out, this "failure to thrive" is related to poverty and/ or parenting neglect. Researchers at Surrey Place Centre in Toronto developed a training program for mothers with intellectual disabilities who are at high risk for infant neglect (Feldman, Garrick, & Case, 1997). First, the researchers recorded the child's weight weekly to diagnose failure to thrive *(baseline)*. Next, the mothers were instructed in feeding and nutrition for six weeks *(treatment)*. Finally, the child's weight was recorded over the next three years *(follow-up)*. The results are shown in Figure 2.7. Clearly, during the *baseline,*

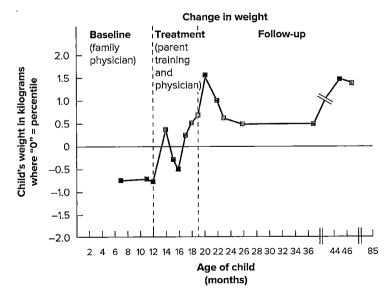

FIGURE 2.7 An example of a case study of a failure-to-thrive infant who stopped growing shortly after birth. Weight on the y-axis is given in kilograms relative to the 5th percentile (95 percent of the infants of that age are above the horizontal line at 0 on the y-axis). During the Baseline, the infant was 0.8 kg below the 5th percentile; but, during Treatment, when the parent received training in feeding and nutrition, the infant rapidly gained weight to a safe level. The infant remained at a normal weight for the next few years (Follow-up).

Source: Figure adapted from Feldman, M.A., Garrick, M., & Case, L. (1997). "The effects of parent training on weight gain of nonorganic-failure-to-thrive children of parents with intellectual disabilities." *Journal on Developmental Disabilities*, 5, 47–61.

this child remained small relative to the general population, rapidly gained weight to a safe level during *treatment*, and continued to thrive for the next few years during the *follow-up*, suggesting that the treatment program was very effective.

Case studies have several limitations. First, they are a poor method for determining *cause–effect* relations. In our failure-to-thrive case study, the treatment may have caused the infant's weight gain; alternatively, some other change in the mother's and infant's lives could have been responsible, or the symptoms may have ended simply because of the passage of time. Second, case study findings may not generalize to other people or situations. In the failure-to-thrive case study, perhaps the treatment was only beneficial for that particular mother. To establish the *generalization* of a principle (e.g., maternal education can reduce instances of failure to thrive), investigators must conduct more case studies, use other research methods, and test a variety of cultural groups. Third, observers may not be objective in gathering and interpreting the data. While this issue may not apply to our failure-to-thrive example (i.e., weight measures are relatively objective), *measurement bias* (also called *observer bias*) can occur in any type of research. Case studies are particularly worrisome because often they are based on an observer's subjective impressions. A skeptical attitude requires that claims based on case studies be followed up by more controlled methods before they are accepted. In everyday life, we should adopt a similar skeptical view. When encountering claims based on a case example or an anecdote, remember that the case may be atypical or the person making the claim may be biased. Try to seek out other evidence to evaluate the claim.

Naturalistic Observation: Bullying in Canadian Schoolyards

In **naturalistic observation,** the researcher observes behaviour as it occurs in a natural setting, and attempts to avoid influencing that behaviour (Figure 2.8). For example, by observing African chimpanzees in the wild, British researcher Jane Goodall (1986) and other scientists found that chimpanzees display behaviours, such as making and using tools, that were formerly believed to lie only within the domain of human capabilities (Lonsdorf, 2006).

Naturalistic observation is also used to study human behaviour. Consider bullying in schools, a topic that has received increasing attention from psychologists (Kanetsuna, Smith, & Morita, 2006). Were you ever bullied at school? If so, did any schoolmates step in to help? In a three-year

© Bill Aron/PhotoEdit

FIGURE 2.8 Psychologists conduct naturalistic observations in many settings, including the schoolyard.

study, psychologists recorded children's playground interactions during recess and lunch periods at two elementary schools in Toronto (Hawkins, Pepler, & Craig, 2001). Their main goal was to describe peer interventions during episodes of schoolyard bullying. How often do schoolmates intervene? What strategies do they use? Are peer interventions effective?

To answer these questions, the researchers developed coding systems so that the children's behaviour could be classified into meaningful categories. To illustrate, here are three of ten categories representing different intervention strategies:

- Verbal Assertion: Verbally requesting that the bullying stop (e.g., "Stop it," "Knock it off")
- Physical Assertion: Physically separating the bully and victim, but not physically attacking either one
- Physical Aggression: Hitting, pushing, shoving, or otherwise physically engaging the bully or victim

Overall, of the 306 bullying episodes observed, schoolmates were present 88 percent of the time but intervened in only 19 percent of the episodes. In order, the three most common types of intervention were verbal assertion alone, physical aggression alone, and verbal assertion combined with physical assertion. Recently, a number of schools have adopted anti-bullying policies, and those schools with such policies are indeed less likely to have problems with bullying (Azeredo, Rinaldi, deMoraes, Levy, & Menezes, 2015).

Like case studies, naturalistic observation does not permit clear causal conclusions. In the real world, many variables simultaneously influence behaviour, and they cannot be disentangled with this research technique. Bias in how researchers interpret what they observe is also possible. Finally, even the mere presence of an observer may disrupt a person's or animal's behaviour.

12. What are the major limitations of case studies?

13. What is naturalistic observation, and what is its major advantage?

14. What problems can occur when conducting naturalistic observations?

Thus, researchers may disguise their presence so that participants are not aware of being observed. Fortunately, when disguise is not feasible, people and other animals typically adapt to and ignore the presence of an observer as time passes. This process is called *habituation*, and researchers may delay their data collection until participants have habituated to the observers' presence.

Survey Research: Does Your Own Personality Match the Canadian National Character?

In **survey research**, information about a topic is obtained by administering questionnaires or interviews to many people. Political polls are a well-known example, but surveys also ask about participants' behaviours, experiences, and attitudes on wide-ranging issues. For example, Terracciano et al. (2005) addressed the following question: Does the stereotypical "national character" of a culture (with regard to neuroticism, extraversion, openness to experience, agreeableness, and conscientiousness) actually match the averaged scores for individual members of that culture on those personality characteristics? Eighty-six researchers administered two questionnaires (one measured "national character"; the other measured the respondent's own personality) to individuals from 49 cultures around the world, including students at York University (by L.E. Ayearst), the University of British Columbia (by D.L. Paulhus), and the University of Winnipeg (by P.D. Trapnell). Responses showed that there was a consensus on each culture's national character. However, the national character personality profile was significantly different from the averaged personality scores of individual members on the same characteristics. To illustrate, the national characters of the Canadian and U.S. samples were similar for neuroticism (e.g., anxiety, hostility, depression, impulsiveness) and agreeableness (e.g., altruism, compliance, modesty); but the averaged individuals' ratings on themselves were much higher for agreeableness and much lower on neuroticism for Canadians than for the U.S. respondents, and both profiles were significantly different from their respective national characters. Terracciano et al. concluded that while the cultural stereotype of a national character may define national identity, it does not reflect the actual, assessed personality traits of members of that culture.

Terracciano et al. surveyed only 3989 adults. So how is it possible to obtain accurate estimates of the stereotypic national character of various cultures? Two key concepts in survey research are population and sample. A **population** consists of all the individuals about whom we are interested in drawing a conclusion. Terracciano et al. wanted to know the stereotypic national character and actual personality characteristics of adult populations in 49 cultures. Clearly, it would be impossible to study everyone. Therefore, they surveyed a **sample**, that is, a subset of individuals drawn from the larger population of interest.

To draw valid conclusions about a population from a survey, the sample must be representative: A **representative sample** is one that reflects the important characteristics of the population (Figure 2.9). A sample composed of 80 percent males would not represent

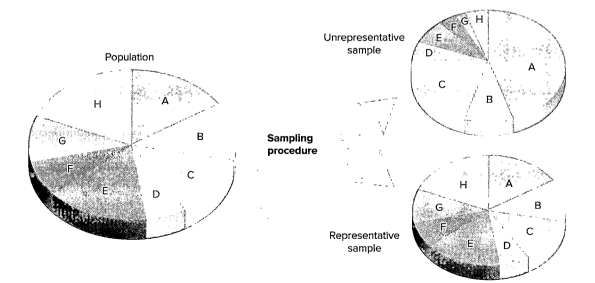

FIGURE 2.9 A representative sample possesses the important characteristics of the population in the same proportions. Data from a representative sample are more likely to generalize to the larger population than data from an unrepresentative sample.

a student body in which only 45 percent are men. To obtain a representative sample, survey researchers typically use a procedure called **random sampling,** in which every member of the population has an equal probability of being chosen to participate in the survey. A common variation of this procedure, called *stratified random sampling,* is to divide the population into subgroups based on such characteristics as gender or ethnic identity. If the population is 45 percent male, then 45 percent of the spaces in the sample would be allocated to men and 55 percent to women. Random sampling is then used to select the individual women and men who will be in the survey.

When a representative sample is surveyed, we can be confident (though never completely certain) that the findings closely portray the population as a whole. This is the strongest advantage of survey research. Modern political opinion polls use such excellent sampling procedures that, just prior to elections, they can reasonably predict who will win a national election from a sample of about 1000 people.

In contrast, unrepresentative samples can produce distorted results. Other things being equal, large samples are better than small ones, but it is better to have a smaller representative sample than a larger, unrepresentative one. A famous example is a mail survey of almost two million voters in 1936, which was carried out by *Literary Digest* magazine. This survey predicted that U.S. Republican presidential candidate Alf Landon would easily defeat Democratic candidate Franklin Roosevelt. When the election took place, Roosevelt won in a landslide!

How could a prediction based on two million people be so massively wrong? The answer is that the survey's sample was unrepresentative of the population that actually voted. The researchers obtained names and addresses from telephone directories, automobile registration lists, and magazine subscription lists. In 1936, most poor Americans did not have telephones, cars, or magazine subscriptions. Thus, the sample under-represented poorer socioeconomic groups and over-represented wealthier people: bad sample, bad prediction. In sum, always consider the nature of the sample when interpreting survey results.

The World Wide Web revolution in the 1990s produced a massive electronic interconnection of people around the world on the Internet, allowing psychologists to collect questionnaire data from thousands of subjects quickly and at virtually no cost compared with paper-based questionnaires and telephone surveys (see Kraut et al., 2004). For example, Nosek, Banaji, and Greenwald (2002) measured attitudes toward and stereotypes of social groups of over 1.5 million "drop-in" respondents at their website who were recruited through news media, links from other Internet sites and search engines, and word of mouth.

Internet questionnaires can be problematic because researchers do not have much control over data quality; respondents can lie about their ages, identities, and genders, and anonymity permits respondents to answer frivolously or maliciously. Also, sample bias can occur because, unlike randomly dialing telephone numbers, there is no method for randomly sampling the population of Internet users. Kraut et al. noted that Internet users in 2002 were more likely than the general U.S. population to be young, to be white, and to have children. Gosling, Vazire, Srivastava, and John (2004) evaluated these concerns by comparing personality questionnaire data from over 360 000 Internet respondents with that from 510 publications where traditional questionnaires were used. Gosling et al. acknowledged that Internet samples are not without flaws—their Internet sample was not representative of the general population—but their sample was more representative than the undergraduate psychology student samples used in many questionnaire studies. Moreover, Internet survey results have been shown to be less influenced by issues such as missing data and socially desirable responding than those of paper-based surveys (Truell, Bartlett, & Alexander, 2002; Wood, Nosko, Desmarais, Ross, & Irvine, 2006), suggesting that the Internet can be a useful research tool. Furthermore, recent research suggests that data from Internet surveys has similar properties to the same type of data collected by the standard paper-and-pencil format (Kalaitzaki, Birtchnell, Hammond, & DeJong, 2015; Vésteinsdóttir, Reips, Joinson, & Thorsdottir, 2015).

In scientific research, surveys are an efficient method for collecting a large amount of information about people's opinions, experiences, and lifestyles, and they can reveal changes in people's beliefs and habits over many years. But there also are several major drawbacks to surveys. First, survey data cannot be used to draw conclusions about cause and effect. Second, surveys rely on participants' self-reports, which can be distorted by social desirability bias, interviewer bias, peoples' inaccurate perceptions of

15. Explain what representative sampling is, and why survey researchers use it.

16. What are some advantages and disadvantages of survey research?

their own behaviour, and misinterpretation of survey questions. Third, unrepresentative samples can lead to faulty generalizations about how an entire population would respond. And finally, even when surveys use proper random sampling procedures, once in a while—simply by chance—a sample that is randomly chosen will turn out not to be representative of the larger population. Overall, in properly conducted professional and scientific surveys, this happens less than 5 percent of the time, but it does happen.

Note, in this chapter, while we give examples of descriptive statistics (e.g., line graphs in Figures 2.2 and 2.6, pie graphs in Figure 2.9, and percentage differences among groups), we focus on experimental design of studies rather than statistical procedures. A comprehensive introduction to statistical methods relevant to survey results and group observations are covered in the Appendix following Chapter 17.

Thinking critically

SHOULD YOU TRUST INTERNET AND POP MEDIA SURVEYS?

Tom fills out a political-attitude survey posted on the Internet. Claire mails in a dating-satisfaction survey that came in a fashion magazine to which she subscribes. Sam responds to a local TV news phone-in survey on a tax issue ("Call our number, press 1 to agree, 2 to disagree"). For each survey, can the results be trusted to reflect the general public's attitudes?

Think about it, and then see the Answers section at the end of the book.

Correlational Research: Measuring Associations between Events

What factors distinguish happily married couples from those headed for divorce? Do first-born children differ in personality from later-born children? Is monetary wealth related to happiness? These and countless other psychological questions ask about associations between naturally occurring events or variables. To examine such relationships, scientists typically conduct **correlational research,** which in its simplest form has three components:

1. The researcher measures one variable (X), such as people's birth order.

2. The researcher measures a second variable (Y), such as a personality trait.

3. The researcher statistically determines whether X and Y are related.

Remember that correlational research involves measuring variables, not manipulating them.

Naturalistic observation and surveys often are used not only to describe events, but also to study associations between variables. For example, in the naturalistic observation study of schoolyard bullying, the researchers examined associations between the children's sex and peer intervention (Hawkins et al., 2001). They found that girls were more likely to intervene when the bully and victim were female, and boys were more likely to intervene when the bully and victim were male.

Correlation Does Not Establish Causation

Diener and Seligman (2002) asked 222 university students to complete questionnaires measuring their general levels of positive and negative emotions, personality traits, social relationships, and

In Review

- The goal of descriptive research is to identify how organisms behave, particularly in natural settings. Case studies involve the detailed study of a person, group, or event. Case studies often suggest important ideas for further research, but they are a poor method for establishing cause–effect relations.

- Naturalistic observation can yield rich descriptions of behaviour in real-life settings and permits examination of relations between variables. Researchers must avoid influencing the participants they observe.

- Surveys involve administering questionnaires or interviews to many people. Most surveys study a sample of people that is randomly drawn from the larger population. Representative samples allow researchers to estimate the responses of the entire population. Unrepresentative samples can lead to inaccurate estimates. Survey results also can be distorted by interviewer bias or biases in the way participants report about themselves.

(a) Social relationships and happiness are correlated

(b) Bidirectionality problem

Does X cause Y?

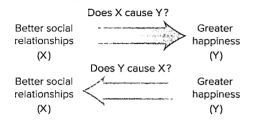

Does Y cause X?

(c) Third-variable problem

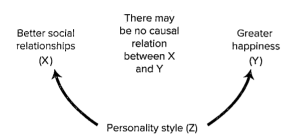

FIGURE 2.10 (a) Students who have better social relationships are happier. But why does this association occur? (b) Good social relationships could cause people to become happier or, conversely, being a happier person could make it easier to form good social relationships. This is the bidirectionality problem. (c) There may be no causal link between social relationships and happiness. Other variables, such as personality traits (e.g., having a more outgoing, agreeable disposition), may be part of the true common origin of better social relationships and of happiness. This is the third-variable problem.

satisfaction with life. They found that very happy people had stronger, more satisfying social relationships than unhappy people (Figure 2.10a). It is tempting to conclude from these findings that stronger social relationships cause people to be happier, but correlational research does not allow us to draw such a conclusion. First, the direction of causality could be opposite; perhaps being happy causes people to have stronger social relationships. For example, maybe happiness makes a person more receptive to going out and forming close relationships. In correlational research, you must consider the possibility that variable X (social relationships) has caused variable Y (happiness), that Y has caused X, or that both variables have influenced each other. This interpretive problem is called the *bidirectionality* (i.e., *two-way causality*) *problem* (Figure 2.10b).

Second, the association between social relationships and happiness may be artificial, or what scientists call *spurious* (not genuine). Although social relationships and happiness are statistically related, it may be that neither variable has any causal effect on the other. A third variable, Z, may really be the cause of why some people have better social relationships and also why those people are happier. For example, Z might be a certain personality style. Diener and Seligman also reported that very happy people were, in general, more outgoing and agreeable and tended to worry less. Perhaps this personality style makes it easier for people to establish good social relationships. At the same time, this style may help people soak up more joy from life and therefore feel happier. Thus, on the surface it looks as if social relationships and happiness are causally linked, but in reality this may be due to only Z (in this case, personality style).

This interpretive problem is called the *third-variable problem:* Z is responsible for what looks like a relation between X and Y (Figure 2.10c). As Z varies, it causes X to change. As Z varies, it also causes Y to change. The net result is that X and Y change in unison, but this is caused by Z, not by any direct effect of X or Y on each other. In sum, we cannot draw causal conclusions from correlational data, which is the major disadvantage of correlational research.

The Correlation Coefficient

A **correlation coefficient** is a statistic that indicates the direction and strength of the relation between two variables. Variables can be correlated either positively or negatively. A **positive correlation** means that higher scores on one variable are associated with higher scores on a second variable. Thus, social relationships and happiness are positively correlated so that more satisfying relationships are associated with higher levels of happiness. Similarly, people's height and weight are positively correlated (i.e., in general, taller people tend to weigh more).

A **negative correlation** occurs when higher scores on one variable are associated with lower scores on a second variable. Job satisfaction and job turnover are negatively correlated, which means that workers who are more satisfied with their jobs tend to have lower rates of turnover (e.g., quitting, being fired). Likewise, students' test anxiety and exam performance are negatively correlated (i.e., students with

17. Explain the main goal of correlational research and how it is achieved.

18. Why are we unable to draw causal conclusions from correlational findings?

19. How do positive and negative correlations differ?

20. How is a correlation coefficient interpreted?

| Thinking critically |

DOES EATING ICE CREAM CAUSE PEOPLE TO DROWN?

Nationally, ice cream consumption and drownings are positively correlated. Over the course of the year, on days when more ice cream is consumed, there tend to be more drownings. Are these two variables causally related? What causal possibilities should you consider?

Think about it, and then see the Answers section at the end of the book.

higher levels of test anxiety tend to perform more poorly on exams).

Correlation coefficients range from values of +1.00 to −1.00. The plus or minus sign tells you the direction of a correlation (i.e., whether the variables are positively or negatively correlated). The absolute value of the statistic tells you the strength of the correlation. The closer the correlation is to +1.00 (a perfect positive correlation) or −1.00 (a perfect negative correlation), the more strongly the two variables are related. Therefore, a correlation of −0.59 indicates a stronger association between X and Y than does a correlation of +0.37. A zero correlation (0.00) means that X and Y are not related statistically: As scores on X increase or decrease, scores on Y do not change in any orderly fashion. Figure 2.11 illustrates three **scatterplots**—graphs that show the correlation between two variables. (For more detailed information about the correlation coefficient, see the Appendix following Chapter 17.)

21. Explain how correlational research can be used to predict behaviour.

Correlation as a Basis for Prediction

Why conduct correlational research if it does not permit clear cause–effect conclusions? One benefit is that correlational research can help to establish whether relations found in the laboratory generalize to the outside world. For example, suppose that laboratory experiments show that talking on a telephone while operating a driving simulator causes people to get into more simulated crashes. Correlational studies, while not demonstrating a cause–effect relationship, can at least establish whether there is a real-world association between driver cellphone usage and automobile accident rates. (By the way, there is.) A second benefit is that correlational research can discover associations that are subsequently studied under controlled laboratory conditions. Third, for practical or ethical reasons, some questions cannot be studied with experiments but can be examined with correlational methods. We cannot experimentally manipulate how religious someone is, but we can measure people's religiousness and determine whether it is associated with other variables, such as personality traits.

Another benefit is that correlational data allow us to make predictions. If two variables are correlated, either positively or negatively, knowing the score of one variable helps us estimate the score on the other variable. For example, students' high school GPAs help admissions officers predict how well they are likely to do at university, as illustrated in the made-up data pictured in the scatterplot in Figure 2.12. You can see that higher high school GPAs are associated with higher first-year university GPAs. The scatterplot also shows that this positive

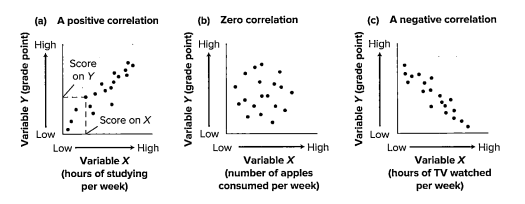

FIGURE 2.11 Scatterplots depict correlations between variables. The horizontal axis represents variable X, and the vertical axis, variable Y. Each data point represents a specific pair of X and Y scores, such as in (a) the number of hours a week a student studies (X) and that student's grade point average (Y). The three scatterplots show (a) a strong positive correlation, (b) a zero correlation (0.00), and (c) a strong negative correlation, for hypothetical sets of data.

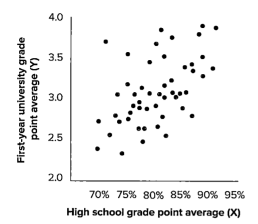

FIGURE 2.12 Data for a hypothetical sample of 50 students. The horizontal axis represents variable X, the students' high school grade point average (GPA). The vertical axis represents variable Y, the same students' first-year university GPA. Variables X and Y are moderately correlated because, while most students who had high grades in high school also had high grades in university, there were a number of cases in which high grades in high school were followed by low grades in university, and vice versa.

correlation is not perfect. Some students who have high school GPAs that are high achieve an average or a poor GPA in their first year at university; conversely, others with low high school GPAs excel at university. Still, even a moderate correlation between high school and university GPAs is useful to admissions officers, especially when high school GPAs are used with other variables—such as awards and extracurricular activities—that also help to estimate university performance.

Remember, we are not saying that higher high school GPAs *cause* better first-year university performance, only that they help to predict it. Similarly, business, government, and military organizations spend millions of dollars developing screening tests that correlate with work performance and therefore help to predict how well applicants will do on the job.

Experiments: Examining Cause and Effect

Do you ever drive while talking on a cellphone? Dalhousie University researchers Ishigami and Klein (2009) note that "there are more than 19.3 million cellphone subscribers in Canada" (p. 157), and talking on cellphones while driving is increasing. Fitch et al. (2013) report that drivers were talking on their phones almost 11 percent of the time that the vehicle was moving. Moreover, correlational studies reveal that cellphone (hand-held and hands-free) use while driving is associated with a substantially increased risk of having a vehicular collision (Dozza, Flannagan, & Sayer, 2015; McEvoy et al., 2005; Ishigami & Klein, 2009), fuelling the fire of a sometimes passionate public and political debate. But as you just learned, correlation does not establish causation. How then can we obtain a clearer causal picture?

In contrast to descriptive and correlational methods, experiments are a powerful tool for examining cause-and-effect relations. An **experiment** has three essential characteristics:

1. The researcher *manipulates (i.e., controls) one or more variables*. In the simplest possible experiment, the researcher manipulates one variable by creating two different conditions to which participants are exposed. For example, we could create a variable called "cellphone use" by randomly assigning half of our participants to drive without talking on a cellphone and assigning the other participants to drive while conversing on a hands-free cellphone. These would represent the two groups (conditions) in the experiment (i.e., Drive Only condition; Drive + Cellphone Use condition).

2. The researcher *measures whether this manipulation influences other variables* (i.e., variables that represent the participants' responses). For simplicity, let's focus on just

---

ⓘ Review

- Correlational research measures the association between naturally occurring variables. A positive correlation means that higher scores on one variable are associated with higher scores on a second variable. A negative correlation occurs when higher scores on one variable are associated with lower scores on a second variable.

- Causal conclusions cannot be drawn from correlational data. Variable X may cause Y; Y may cause X; or some third variable (Z) may be the true cause of both X and Y. Nevertheless, if two variables are correlated, then knowing the scores of one variable will help to predict the scores of the other.

Courtesy of Human Factors and Ergonomics Society

FIGURE 2.13 A simulator used in several experiments that examine how talking on a cellphone while driving affects drivers' performance. The simulator can be programmed to display various driving conditions, such as city (shown here) and highway traffic.

22. Describe the logic of experimentation.

23. What are independent and dependent variables? How are they related?

one measure of driving performance, called "braking reaction time": how quickly a driver depresses the car's brake pedal when another vehicle in front of the car slows down.

3. The researcher *attempts to control extraneous factors that might influence the outcome*

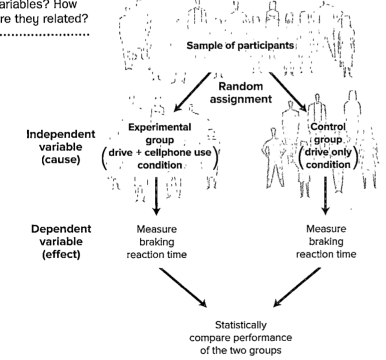

Independent variable (cause)

Dependent variable (effect)

Sample of participants

Random assignment

Experimental group (drive + cellphone use condition)

Control group (drive only condition)

Measure braking reaction time

Measure braking reaction time

Statistically compare performance of the two groups

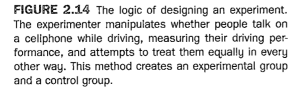

FIGURE 2.14 The logic of designing an experiment. The experimenter manipulates whether people talk on a cellphone while driving, measuring their driving performance, and attempts to treat them equally in every other way. This method creates an experimental group and a control group.

of the experiment. For example, while each participant is driving, there will be no passengers and no CD or radio playing. It also would be ideal to expose the Drive + Cellphone Use and the Drive Only participants to the same travel routes and also the same traffic and weather (e.g., temperature, visibility) conditions. By doing so, any differences we find in braking performance between the two groups could not possibly be due to these extraneous environmental factors. To achieve this type of rigorous environmental control, and also for ethical reasons of safety, let's do what most researchers have done: employ a highly advanced, realistic driving simulator in a laboratory environment rather than have people drive in actual traffic (Figure 2.13).

The logic behind this approach is straightforward:

- Start out with equivalent groups of participants.
- Treat them equally in all respects except for the variable that is of particular interest (in this case, cellphone use).
- Isolate this variable and manipulate it (create Drive Only and Drive + Cellphone conditions).
- Measure how the groups respond (braking reaction time).

If the groups respond differently, then the most plausible explanation is that these differences were caused by the manipulated variable (Figure 2.14).

Independent and Dependent Variables

The term **independent variable** refers to the factor that is manipulated or controlled by the experimenter. In our example, cellphone use is the independent variable. The **dependent variable** is the factor that is measured by the experimenter and that may be influenced by the independent variable. In this experiment, braking reaction time is the dependent variable. An easy way to keep this distinction clear is to remember that the dependent variable *depends on* the independent variable. Presumably, braking reaction time will depend on whether the driver is talking on a cellphone. The independent variable is the cause, and the dependent variable is the effect.

Our experiment thus far has only one dependent variable, but we could have many. In addition to braking reaction time, we could measure how frequently drivers fail to detect lights or road signs, and so on. This way, we could learn more about how cellphone conversations affect driving performance.

	Independent Variable (Cause)	Dependent Variable (Effect)
General level	Drive + Cellphone Use	Safe Driving
Operational level	Drive + Cellphone Use versus Drive Only	Braking reaction time

Experimental and Control Groups

The terms *experimental group* and *control group* are often used when discussing experiments. An **experimental group** is the group that receives a treatment or an active level of the independent variable. A **control group** is not exposed to the treatment or receives a zero-level of the independent variable. The purpose of the control group is to provide a standard of behaviour to which the experimental group can be compared. In our experiment, participants in the Drive + Cellphone group represent the experimental group (or experimental condition), and participants in the Drive Only condition represent the control group (or control condition).

Note that in an experiment, the *independent variable MUST HAVE at least two levels*. Many experiments have an experimental (treatment) and a control (no treatment) group. However, in some experiments, the concept of a control group may not apply. For example, in a taste-test experiment in which participants taste and rate how much they like Coca-Cola versus Pepsi-Cola, each drink represents an experimental condition and we simply make a direct comparison between them.

Experiments with one independent variable often include more than two experimental groups. In our driving-performance study, we could add a third condition in which other participants talk on a hand-held cellphone (rather than a hands-free phone) while driving, and even add other conditions in which participants don't converse on a cellphone but instead listen to the radio or talk with a passenger. The Drive Only participants would still represent the control group, and we could now compare how various types of potential distractions affect driver performance.

Two Basic Ways to Design an Experiment

One common experimental design is called a **between groups (or between subjects) design** because each group in the experiment is composed of a different set of participants. To draw meaningful conclusions, the various groups of participants must be equivalent at the start of the study. For example, suppose that in our experiment the Drive + Cellphone group displayed poorer driving performance than the Drive Only group. If the participants in the Drive + Cellphone group, on average, happened to have less driving experience or poorer vision than the Drive Only participants, then these factors—not talking on a cellphone—might have been why they performed more poorly.

To address this issue, researchers typically use **random assignment**, a procedure in which each participant has an equal likelihood of being assigned to any one group within an experiment. Thus, a participant would have a 50 percent chance of being in the Drive + Cellphone group and a 50 percent chance of being in the Drive Only group; that determination would be made randomly. This procedure does not eliminate the fact that participants differ from one another in driving experience, visual acuity, or other personal factors. Instead, random assignment is used to *balance these differences* across the various conditions of the experiment. It increases our confidence that, at the start of an experiment, participants in the various conditions are equivalent overall.

A second experimental design is called a **repeated measures (or within subjects) design;** in this design, each participant is exposed to all the conditions of an independent variable. For example, we could measure how skillfully the same people drive when talking on a cellphone versus when not talking on a cellphone. By doing so, such factors as the participants' driving experience and visual acuity are held constant across the different conditions of the experiment, and therefore we can rule them out as alternative explanations for any results we obtain.

This approach, however, can create problems if not used properly. Suppose that every participant drove the simulation the first time without conversing on the cellphone, and then drove it the second time while having phone conversations. If participants drove more poorly while talking on the cellphone, what would be the cause? Distraction created by the phone conversation? Perhaps. But perhaps the participants became bored, fatigued, or overconfident by the time they drove the route for the second time. To avoid this problem, researchers use **counterbalancing,** a procedure in which the order of conditions is varied so that no condition has an overall advantage relative to the others. Half the participants would drive the simulation first while having cellphone conversations, and then

24. Why are control groups important?

25. Why do researchers randomly assign participants to the conditions in an experiment?

26. Identify an alternative to using random assignment in experiments.

27. Why do researchers manipulate two independent variables in the same experiment?

drive it again without phone conversations. For the remaining participants, this order would be reversed.

Manipulating Two Independent Variables: Effects of Cellphone Use and Traffic Density on Driving Performance

To better capture the complexity of real life, researchers often study several causal factors within a single experiment by manipulating two or more independent variables simultaneously. Suppose we want to know how cellphone use *and* traffic density influence drivers' performance. We could design separate experiments, one to examine cellphone use and the other traffic density, but it typically is better to manipulate both independent variables within the same experiment. This approach allows us to examine not only (1) how cellphone use and traffic density each independently influence drivers' performance, but also (2) whether cellphone use has different effects, depending on whether traffic is heavier or lighter. In scientific terms, we are asking whether there is an interaction between cellphone use and traffic density. The concept of **interaction** means that the way in which one independent variable (X_1; e.g., cellphone use) influences the dependent variable (Y; e.g., driving performance) differs depending on the various conditions of another independent variable (X_2; e.g., traffic density).

As before, our first independent variable would be cellphone use (Drive Only versus Drive + Cellphone). But now we would add a second independent variable, "Traffic Density," by creating two or more conditions that differ in the amount of traffic that the driver encounters. For example, let's create "low density" and "high density" conditions by programming our driving simulator to display only one other car on the travel route, or many other cars on the travel route.

We now have two independent variables, each of which has two conditions: cellphone use (Drive Only, Drive + Cellphone) and Traffic Density (Low, High). As Figure 2.15a shows, combining these two independent variables within the same experiment creates four unique conditions: (1) driving only, in low traffic density; (2) driving only, in high traffic density; (3) driving while talking on the phone, in low traffic density, and (4) driving while talking on the phone, in high traffic density.

David Strayer and his colleagues (2003) conducted such an experiment. College undergraduates drove a simulated 40-mile (64-kilometre)

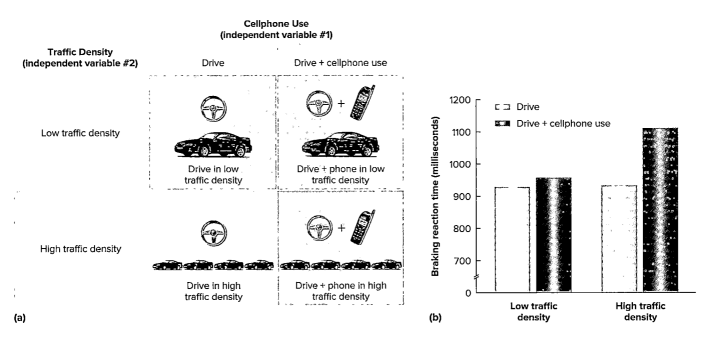

FIGURE 2.15 Cellphone use, traffic density, and driving performance. (a) Simultaneously manipulating two independent variables—cellphone use and traffic density—creates four conditions in this design. (b) Average braking reaction time to multiple decelerations by a simulated pace car.

Source: Data from Strayer, D.L., Drews, F.A., & Johnston, W.A. (2003). "Cell-phone induced failures of visual attention during simulated driving." *Journal of Experimental Psychology: Applied,* 9, 23–32.

route that had multiple lanes in each direction. Every student had cellphone conversations in some sections of the route and no phone conversations in the remaining sections. All phone conversations took place with a research assistant.

Each student's task was to follow a pace car travelling in the right lane. The low and high traffic-density conditions were created by randomly assigning each student to drive the entire route either with no other cars on the highway (other than the pace car), or with a steady flow of cars appearing in the left lane (high density condition).

For every student, the pace car braked and slowed down 32 times over the course of the route. If the student failed to brake in response, he or she would eventually collide with the pace car. The researchers measured several aspects of driving performance, including students' braking reaction time and whether they had any collisions.

Figure 2.15b shows the results for one of the dependent variables: braking reaction time. When traffic density was high, on average it took participants 179 milliseconds longer to depress their brake pedals when talking on the hands-free cellphone than when not talking on the phone. When traffic density was low, braking reaction times were only 29 milliseconds slower when talking on the phone. Strayer and his colleagues (2003) concluded that, overall, talking on a cellphone while driving caused drivers' responses to be more sluggish, especially when traffic density was high. In fact, three accidents occurred in the high-density, Drive + Cellphone condition, all involving participants' cars rear-ending the pace car. No accidents occurred in the other conditions. Table 2.1 summarizes key features of the research methods we have discussed, as well as some limitations of experiments, which we will discuss next.

TABLE 2.1 An Overview of Research Methods

Method	Primary Feature	Main Advantages	Main Disadvantages
Case studies	An individual, group, or event is examined in detail, often by using several techniques (observations, interviews, psychological tests).	Provides rich descriptive information, often suggesting hypotheses for further study. Can study rare phenomena in-depth.	Poor method for establishing cause–effect relations. The person or event may not be representative. Often relies heavily on the researcher's subjective interpretations.
Naturalistic observation	Behaviour is observed in the setting in which it naturally occurs.	Can provide detailed information about the nature, frequency, and context of naturally occurring behaviour.	Poor method for establishing cause–effect relations. Observer's presence, if known, may influence participants' behaviour.
Surveys	Questions or tests are administered to a sample drawn from a larger population.	A properly selected, representative sample typically yields accurate information about the broader population.	Unrepresentative samples may yield misleading results. Interviewer bias and social desirability bias can distort the findings.
Correlational studies	Variables are measured and the strength of the association is determined. Naturalistic observation and surveys also are often used to examine associations between variables.	Correlation allows prediction. May help establish how well findings from experiments generalize to more natural settings. Can examine issues that cannot be studied ethically or practically in experiments.	Correlation does not imply causation because of the bidirectionality problem and the third-variable problem, which can create a confounding of variables.
Experiments	Independent variables are manipulated and their effects on dependent variables are measured.	Optimal method for examining cause–effect relations. Ability to control extraneous factors helps rule out alternative explanations.	Confounding of variables, placebo effects, and experimenter expectancies can threaten the validity of causal conclusions.

THREATS TO THE VALIDITY OF RESEARCH

Although the experimental approach is a powerful tool for examining causality, researchers must avoid errors that can lead to faulty conclusions. **Validity** refers to how well an experimental procedure actually tests what it is designed to test. We will discuss two general classes of validity: internal and external validity. **Internal validity** represents the degree to which an experiment supports clear causal conclusions. If an experiment is well designed and properly conducted, we can be confident that the independent variable really was the cause of differences in the dependent variable. Such an experiment would have *high internal validity.* For example, because Latané and Darley's bystander experiment was conducted carefully and had proper controls, it had high internal validity. We can be confident that it was the presence of multiple bystanders (and not some other factor) that caused participants to help the seizure victim less often and more slowly. But if an experiment contains important flaws (see the next section for an example), it will have *low internal validity* because we no longer can be sure what caused the differences in the dependent variable.

Confounding of Variables

To introduce the concept of "confounding," consider an experiment on the "Mozart" effect. In 1993, Rauscher, Shaw, and Ky tested university students who were randomly assigned to one of three groups. The experimental group listened to 10 minutes of a Mozart sonata (an uptempo, "happy sounding" piece of music); one control group listened to 10 minutes of relaxation instructions; the other control group listened to silence. The Mozart group performed much better on a subsequent test of spatial abilities than the two control groups. This led the popular press to conclude that listening to music makes you smarter (see www.mozarteffect.com). What is wrong with this conclusion? Can you identify another major factor that could have produced these results? Perhaps students who listened to the music performed better on the spatial task because they were in a better mood or had a higher arousal level from having had an enjoyable experience compared with the no-music groups. Both factors—the independent variable (music versus no music) and another variable (mood: happy and excited versus neutral and bored)—differed between experimental and control groups. These two variables, like strands of a rope, were intertwined so that either one or both could have caused the group differences in performance.

William Thompson, at York University, and Glenn Schellenberg and Gabriela Husain, at the University of Toronto (2001), tested for this suspected confound by assigning university students to either a Mozart sonata (happy music) or an Albinoni adagio (sad music) group. Half of each music group heard 10 minutes of the music, while the other half sat in silence (control groups), at the end of which everyone was given the standard spatial abilities task (paperfolding and cutting). The results, shown in Figure 2.16, replicated the Mozart effect—those

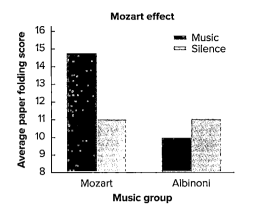

FIGURE 2.16 The Mozart effect—music enhancing performance on a cognitive task (paper-folding) relative to silent controls. In this two-factor study, two music groups, a Mozart (happy piece) group versus an Albinoni (sad piece) group, and silent controls are compared. The enhanced performance is likely due to the happy mood induction rather than Mozart's music in particular (see text for details).

hearing Mozart performed better than those who heard silence. However, the Mozart group also did better than the Albinoni group, which performed similarly to the silent control group. Clearly, improved spatial ability was not simply due to listening to music. Ratings of subjective enjoyment, positive mood, and arousal were also measured, and they were higher for those who heard Mozart rather than Albinoni. Thompson et al. used a mathematical adjustment to statistically "equate" the groups on mood/arousal/enjoyment and found that the difference between the Mozart and Albinoni groups' performances on the spatial task disappeared. Thus, they concluded that the Mozart effect is an artifact of arousal and positive mood.

Confounding of variables means that two variables are intertwined in such a way that we cannot determine which one has influenced a dependent variable. In the initial experiment on the Mozart effect, the mood level for the experimental and control group varied along with listening to Mozart or silence. The mood level is called a *confound* or a *confounding variable*.

	Group 1	Group 2	Group 3
Independent variable (presence of music)	Mozart	Silence	Relaxation
Confounding variable (mood/joy/activity level)	High	Low	Low

An essential point to remember is that this confounding of variables prevents one from drawing clear causal conclusions, and therefore it ruins the internal validity of the experiment. The simplest way to eliminate this problem is to keep the mood level constant across the different music conditions. If this were done—that is, if we used music by Handel and other composers, all of which induced a joyful, aroused mood, then we would expect that all the music groups would do better on spatial tests than the silent controls.

Confounding is a key reason why causal conclusions cannot be drawn from correlational research. Recall the third-variable problem shown in Figure 2.10. If variables X (e.g., level of happiness) and Y (e.g., quality of social relationships) are correlated, a third variable, Z (e.g., personality style), may be mixed up with X and Y, so we cannot tell what has caused what. Thus, Z is just another type of confounding variable.

Placebo Effects

In medical research, the term **placebo** refers to a substance that has no pharmacological effect. In experiments testing the effectiveness of new drugs for treating diseases, one group of patients—*the treatment group*—receives the actual drug being investigated (e.g., via pills or injections). A second group, the *placebo control group*, receives only a placebo (e.g., pills composed of inactive ingredients or injections of saline). Typically, participants are told that they will be given either a drug or a placebo, but they are not told which one they will receive.

The rationale for this procedure is that patients' symptoms may improve solely because they *expect* that the drug will help them. If 40 percent of patients receiving the actual drug improve, but 37 percent of the placebo-control patients show similar improvement, then we have evidence of a **placebo effect**: People receiving a treatment show a change in behaviour because of their expectations, not because the treatment itself had any specific benefit (Leech et al., 2012; Ray, 2000; Figure 2.17). In fact, verbal suggestion alone seems sufficient to generate a placebo effect for the treatment of itching (Darragh, Chang, Booth, & Considine, 2015).

Placebo effects decrease internal validity by providing an alternative explanation for why responses change after exposure to treatment. This problem applies to evaluating all

28. Explain why confounding decreases the internal validity of experiments.

29. Explain how the "placebo effect" can cloud the interpretation of research results.

FIGURE 2.17 Throughout history, placebo effects have fostered the commercial success of many products that had no proven physiological benefit. Herbal medicines are one of today's "health crazes." Do they really work? If so, is it because of placebo effects or the herbs' chemical properties? The best way to answer this question is through experiments that include placebo control groups.

types of treatments, not just those that test the effectiveness of drugs. For example, suppose that depressed patients improve (i.e., become less depressed) while receiving psychotherapy. Is this due to the specific procedures and content of the psychotherapy itself, or might it be merely a placebo effect resulting from their positive expectations that the therapy would help them? In the failure-to-thrive case we discussed earlier, the infant's weight gain may have been a placebo effect. The mother may have taken better care of her infant simply because of the attention she received from the researchers rather than the training she received in feeding and proper nutrition. Similarly, suppose that business managers feel more confident after taking a leadership training program or that anxious people become more relaxed after learning how to meditate. By carefully designing experiments to include placebo control conditions, researchers can determine whether behaviour change truly is caused by the various interventions or whether a placebo effect might have played a role.

30. Why do experimenter expectancy effects lower the internal validity of experiments?

31. How do researchers minimize experimenter expectancy effects?

Experimenter Expectancy Effects

Researchers typically have a strong commitment to the hypothesis they are testing. In psychology, the term **experimenter expectancy effects** refers to the subtle and unintentional ways researchers influence their participants to respond in a manner that is consistent

with the researcher's hypothesis. Scientists can take several steps to avoid experimenter expectancy effects. For example, researchers who interact with participants in a study or who record participants' responses are often kept blind to (i.e., not told about) the hypothesis or the specific condition to which a participant has been assigned. This makes it less likely that these researchers will develop expectations about how participants "should" behave.

The **double-blind procedure**, in which both the participant and the experimenter are kept blind as to which experimental condition the participant is in, simultaneously minimizes participant placebo effects and experimenter expectancy effects. In research testing drug effects, each participant receives either a real drug or a placebo but does not know which. People who interact with the participants (e.g., those who dispense the drugs or measure participants' symptoms) also are kept unaware of which participants receive the drug or placebo. This procedure minimizes the likelihood that the researchers will behave differently toward the two groups of participants, and it reduces the chance that participants' own expectations will influence the outcome of the experiment (Figure 2.18).

"IT WAS MORE OF A 'TRIPLE-BLIND' TEST. THE PATIENTS DIDN'T KNOW WHICH ONES WERE GETTING THE REAL DRUG, THE DOCTORS DIDN'T KNOW, AND I'M AFRAID, NOBODY KNEW"

FIGURE 2.18 Although the double-blind technique is a powerful tool for controlling participants' and researchers' expectations, scientists try to avoid the infamous "triple-blind procedure."

Replicating and Generalizing the Findings

Returning to our hypothetical experiment on cellphone use, let's suppose that participants' driving performance was impaired while they talked on their cellphones. If our experiment was conducted properly, then it will have high internal validity and thus we can be confident that talking on cellphones, and not some other factor, caused the driving impairment. There remain, however, other questions that we must ask: Would similar results be found with other types of participants or while driving under different road or traffic conditions?

This question focuses on **external validity,** the degree to which the results of a study can be generalized to other populations, settings, and conditions. Typically, judgments about external validity concern the *generalizability of underlying principles.* If talking on a cellphone impairs drivers' braking reaction time by 140 milliseconds in our experiment but only by 120 milliseconds in subsequent experiments with young drivers, then the 20 millisecond difference is not the issue. Rather, it is that the general principle—"talking on a cellphone *impairs* drivers' performance"—has successfully generalized to younger drivers.

To determine external validity, either we or other scientists need to replicate our experiment. **Replication** is the process of repeating a study to determine whether the original findings can be duplicated. If our findings are successfully replicated, especially when studying other types of participants and driving conditions, we become more confident in concluding that cellphone use impairs driving performance. Indeed, in simulation experiments, talking on a cellphone while driving has been found to interfere with driving performance in rural and urban environments of varying complexity, among younger and older drivers, and when using hand-held and hands-free phones (Ishigami & Klein, 2009; Strayer & Drews, 2004; Törnros & Bolling, 2006). In fact, younger drivers are more likely to use a cellphone while driving and they show smaller safety margins (Dozza et al., 2015).

In typical experiments, the responses of each participant are analyzed. When researchers review a number of experiments that are trying to replicate an effect, as Ishigami and Klein did, they use a **meta-analysis**—a statistical procedure for combining the results of different studies that examine the same topic to test the overall significance of the findings. In a meta-analysis, each study is treated as a "single participant," and its overall results are analyzed with those of the other studies. Meta-analyses inform researchers about the direction and statistical strength of the relationships between two variables. Many researchers consider meta-analysis to be the most objective way to integrate the findings of multiple studies and reach overall conclusions about behaviour.

Increasingly, psychologists are paying more attention to **cross-cultural replication:** examining whether findings generalize across different cultures. For example, researchers in Canada, Israel, Japan, and the United States attempted to replicate Latané and Darley's (1968) findings on bystander helping behaviour. Latané and Nida (1981) used a meta-analysis to review 66 bystander experiments, some performed in laboratories with students and others taking place in such real-life settings as subways, liquor stores, and workplaces. The number of bystanders who were present varied across different experiments, different types of helping behaviour were measured, and both women and men were tested. The vast majority of experiments confirmed the original finding.

Research findings that fail to replicate may lead to better research and new discoveries as scientists search for clues to explain why the results were different from one study to another. For example, not all experiments showed that driving impairment was due to cellphone use. Further research is needed to sort out the factors, such as different driving conditions, that might account for such results.

Studies that consistently fail to replicate the original results of earlier research may suggest that the original research was flawed or that the finding was a fluke. Even so, the scientific process has done its job and prevented us from getting caught in a blind alley. Ultimately, the accountability for the results of experiments rests with individual researchers and the scientific and academic community, a self-policing professional group. Psychologists are expected to use the highest standards for gathering their data and to hold their original data in trust for a reasonable period of time to give members of the research community an opportunity to examine the data. This chapter's *Frontiers* feature highlights why replication is such an important component of the scientific process.

32. How does external validity differ from internal validity?

Frontiers

DOES ESP EXIST?

Do you believe in ESP (extrasensory perception), such as mental telepathy (transmitting thoughts between minds), clairvoyance (remotely sensing a current object or event), or precognition (foretelling the future)? How about other paranormal phenomena? Surveys around the world reveal widespread public belief in the paranormal (Alcock, 2003). In a 2005 Gallup Poll, 73 percent of American adults stated that they believe in at least one of the following ten paranormal phenomena: "extra sensory perception (ESP—41 percent of the respondents acknowledged belief in this item), haunted houses (37 percent), ghosts (32 percent), [mental] telepathy (31 percent), clairvoyance (26 percent), astrology (25 percent), communication with the dead (21 percent), witches (21 percent), reincarnation (20 percent), and channelling spiritual entities (9 percent)" (Musella, 2005, p. 5). Many Canadian adults also hold paranormal beliefs (Lyons, 2005).

Should this surprise us? For decades, a steady diet of movies, TV shows, and novels has fed our imagination with characters who possess psychic abilities, such as telepathy (e.g., *The Mentalist; Medium; Ghost Whisperer;* Professor Xavier, *X-Men*), and psychokinesis: the direct mental influence of physical objects and systems (e.g., Yoda, *Star Wars;* Jean Gray, *X-Men;* Sylar, *Heroes*). Compared to nonbelievers, believers tend to be more open to new experiences and are more fantasy prone (Smith et al., 2009). Both correlational studies and experiments find an association between exposure to paranormal media content and belief in paranormal phenomena (Sparks & Miller, 2001).

Paranormal beliefs also have other sources. For one thing, many people claim to have had a paranormal experience (Kunzendorf et al., 2007). For another, popular books and websites written by parapsychologists (e.g., scientists from various fields who study paranormal phenomena) proclaim strong scientific support for several paranormal phenomena, including ESP (Parapsychology Association, 2008; Radin, 2009). However, many scientists and other skeptics say ESP does not exist. Believers and skeptics disagree about the rigour of some parapsychological research and about how high the standards of scientific evidence should be set. Adopting a scientific attitude means we should approach this issue with open-minded skepticism; that is, we should apply rigorous standards of evaluation, as we do to all phenomena (Cardeña, Lynn, & Krippner, 2000). Either way, the ability of independent investigators to replicate initial research findings is a central scientific standard.

When tested under controlled conditions in well-designed experiments and replications, claim after claim of psychic ability has evaporated. The Committee for Skeptical Inquiry, founded in 1976, consists of psychologists, other scientists, philosophers, and magicians who are experts in the art of fakery. To conclude that a phenomenon is psychic, the committee requires that presently known natural, physical, or psychological explanations be ruled out. To date, it has not judged any psychic claims to be valid.

What about paranormal demonstrations by self-proclaimed psychics, such as using mental powers to bend spoons? In 1964, James Randi, a magician and expert in the art of psychic fraud, began offering $10 000 to anyone who could demonstrate paranormal ability under his scrutiny. Today, the offer is $1 million and still no one has collected (although a Toronto psychic known as Nikki is seriously considering the challenge). Predictions made by leading psychics in national newspapers also yield dismal results (Emery Jr., 2001).

In 2011, however, Daryl Bem, a psychology professor at Cornell University, published a paper in a major scientific journal that outlined the results of nine studies that he claims demonstrate retroactive influences of future events on individuals' current responses (think premonition or precognition). By reversing the order of procedures from classic psychological studies, Bem purports to have measured effects on thinking of some cause that takes place in the future.

FIGURE 2.19 Modern society bombards us with scientific and pseudoscientific claims. Some publications do promote healthy skepticism and critical thinking, such as *Skeptical Inquirer* magazine.

Used by permission of the *Skeptical Inquirer* magazine (www.csicop.org)

continued

For example, in studies that look at effects of priming, or eliciting, emotions on activation of concepts in our minds, researchers typically report that presenting (even subliminally) a positive word to participants on a computer screen facilitates (i.e., speeds up) identification of subsequent positive images and slows identification of negative images. Likewise, priming negative emotions in a participant by flashing a negative word on a computer screen has been shown to facilitate identification of negative images compared to response times to positive images (Fazio, 2001; Klauer & Musch, 2003). Two of the studies that Bem reported involved a reversal of this procedure and of the priming effect: participants were faster to respond to positive words *before* they had been "primed" by a positive picture than in trials were the positive word was followed by a negative picture. Bem called this "retroactive priming," and argues that the presentation of the emotionally congruent images *after* the participants' responses to the words was facilitating those responses to the words, acting backwards in time.

This is a somewhat unusual example, given that the article was authored by a highly respected member of his field and published in a high ranking journal after critical review from a panel of professionals. Is it possible that premonition and precognition exist? Many researchers are skeptical, as evidenced by the controversy this article stirred up in the scientific community. Most responses to the article and to Bem's claims have focused on flawed methodology and unsound research practices (Wagenmakers, Wetzels, Borsboom, & Van Der Maas, 2011), while others have cited this publication as an example of some of the deficiencies and biases that exist in psychological science today (Lebel & Peters, 2011), as well as the crucial role of replication in drawing conclusions from research. So far it seems no one has replicated the findings reported by Bem (see Galek, LeBeouf, Nelson, & Simmons, 2012).

Critical thinking requires us to have a reasoned skepticism that demands solid scientific evidence but not a blind skepticism that rejects the unknown as impossible. In our opinion, at present there is no generally accepted, conclusive scientific evidence to support the existence of ESP. Research continues, and while the burden of proof lies with those who believe in the paranormal, evaluations of their claims should be based on scientific evidence rather than on preconceived positive or negative expectations.

🔲 Review

- An experiment has high internal validity when it is well designed and permits clear causal conclusions.

- Confounding occurs when the independent variable becomes mixed up with an uncontrolled variable. Confounding ruins internal validity because we can no longer tell which variable caused the changes in the dependent variable.

- Internal validity is weakened by (1) placebo effects, in which the mere expectation of receiving a treatment produces a change in behaviour, and (2) experimenter expectancy effects, which are the subtle ways a researcher's behaviour influences participants to behave in a manner consistent with the hypothesis being tested.

- The double-blind procedure prevents placebo effects and experimenter expectancy effects from biasing research results.

- External validity is the degree to which the findings of a study can be generalized to other populations, settings, and conditions. By replicating (repeating) a study under both similar and dissimilar circumstances, researchers can examine its external validity.

- Researchers can assess external validity by statistically combining the results of many studies that test the same variables by using meta-analysis.

ETHICAL PRINCIPLES IN HUMAN AND ANIMAL RESEARCH

Psychologists sometimes walk an ethical tightrope when they study important problems, weighing the knowledge and possible applications to be gained against potential risks to which research participants may be exposed. Investigators are obliged to adhere to a set of ethical standards based on both government regulations and guidelines developed by national psychological organizations.

Ethical Standards in Human Research

In Canada, university research in large part is funded by one of three national government agencies: the Canadian Institutes of Health Research (CIHR), the Natural Sciences and Engineering Research Council (NSERC), and the Social Sciences and Humanities Research

Council (SSHRC). These three agencies developed a "tri-council policy for ethical conduct for research involving humans," which universities must follow if they receive funding from any of the three councils. Universities are required to have ethics review boards (ERBs) that review the ethical issues involved in every research proposal (Figure 2.20). If a proposed study is considered ethically questionable, or if the rights of participants are not sufficiently protected, then the methods must be modified or the research cannot be conducted. The ERBs ensure that human participants have given informed consent and are ensured privacy and confidentiality.

The Canadian Psychological Association (CPA) published a "Canadian Code of Ethics for Psychologists" (2000, 3rd edition; **www.cpa .ca**; search "ethics") to cover the behaviour of psychologists engaged in research, direct service, teaching, administration, legal cases (e.g., as expert witnesses), or any other role related to the discipline of psychology. Psychologists must do the following:

- Protect and promote the welfare of participants.
- Avoid doing harm to participants.
- Not carry out any studies unless the probable benefit is proportionately greater than the risk.

33. Describe the major ethical issues in human research and how participants' rights are protected.

34. Why does some research involve deception? What ethical principle does deception violate?

- Provide **informed consent**—that is, explain all aspects of the procedure and ensure that the procedure is understood. Oral or written consent is usually required, and assurance is given that one can withdraw from the study without penalty. For those not able to give informed consent (e.g., children, seriously disturbed mental patients), consent must be obtained from parents or guardians.
- Take all reasonable steps to ensure that consent is not given under coercion.
- Ensure privacy and confidentiality.

The use of **incomplete disclosure,** or **deception,** that occurs when participants are misled about the nature of a study, is highly controversial. In and Latané and Darley's (1968) bystander experiment, for example, participants were not told that the researchers were studying how participants would respond to an emergency or that the procedures might cause them stress. They were misled about the true nature of the experiment. Proponents of deception research argue that, when studying certain types of behaviours, deception is the only way to obtain natural, spontaneous responses from participants. In other words, Latané and Darley's participants had to believe the emergency was significant and real. Clearly, incomplete disclosure violates the principle of informed consent. The guidelines permit incomplete disclosure only when no other feasible alternative is available and when the scientific, educational, or applied benefits clearly outweigh the ethical costs of deceiving participants. If incomplete disclosure is used, participants must be **debriefed**—told the true purpose of the study at the end of the experiment.

Most psychological studies do not involve incomplete disclosure, and deception research has decreased in recent decades (Nicks, Korn, & Mainieri, 1997). Still, many scientists oppose the use of deception under any circumstance, and the debate continues (Barrera & Simpson, 2012; Hertwig & Ortman, 2008).

What about ethics in the use of the Internet for surveys and observational research? Psychologists can do observational studies by joining virtual communities to record and analyze dialogues between participants (e.g., joining hate groups or therapeutic online groups). Pittenger (2003) notes that Internet researchers must take special care to ensure that they protect participants' privacy and confidentiality, obtain informed consent, and debrief participants. These actions can be difficult when

(top) © Annabella Bluesky/Photo Researchers, Inc.; (bottom) © Volker Steger/Photo Researchers, Inc.

FIGURE 2.20 Ethical standards are designed to protect the welfare of both human and animal subjects in psychological research.

deception is used (e.g., posting false comments designed to evoke reactions from members of hate groups or therapeutic online groups) because Internet respondents can drop out at any point in the study. Indeed, many authors suggest that standard review protocols be applied any Internet research (e.g., Graber & Graber, 2013; Saunders, Kitzinger, & Kitzinger, 2015). Despite ethical challenges, the research opportunities provided by using the Internet make efforts to overcome them worth it.

Finally, it should be noted that participants generally enjoy participating in psychological research. In a survey of several thousand introductory psychology students at Queen's University, 93 percent reported that their experiences as research participants were pleasant and informative.

Ethical Standards in Animal Research

According to the APA's Committee on Animal Research and Ethics (CARE, 2005), animals are subjects in 7 to 8 percent of psychological studies, including research done in both wild and controlled settings. Rodents and birds make up 90 percent of the animals studied; nonhuman primates account for another 5 percent. Some psychologists study these animals to discover principles that shed light on human behaviour, while others do so to learn about the behaviour of other species.

In Canada, both CPA and federal government codes of ethics state that experimental animals should not be subjected to pain, stress, or privation unless no alternative procedure is available and the research is justified by prospective scientific or educational benefits. This determination, however, is not always easy to make. For example, should researchers be allowed to inject a chemical into an animal's brain to study the relationship between brain-chemistry imbalance and memory impairment in humans? The Canadian

tri-council granting agency requires university ERBs (which usually include nonscientists) to review and approve all animal research proposals. Most ERBs follow the rules set down by the Canadian Council on Animal Care in its *Guide to the Care and Use of Experimental Animals, Vol. 1* (1993). This manual instructs researchers to provide humane care and treatment, minimize pain and discomfort, and avoid unnecessary use of experimental animals.

Most psychologists and university psychology majors believe that animal research is necessary for scientific progress in psychology (Plous, 1996a, 1996b). They do not agree with the American Anti-Vivisection Society, which maintains that animals should never be used in research "which is not for the benefit of the animals involved" (Goodman, 1982, p. 61). Proponents point to important medical and psychological advances made possible by animal research (Baldwin, 1993). For example, had Pasteur not subjected some dogs to suffering, he could not have developed the rabies vaccine that has saved the lives of countless animals as well as humans. Supporters ask such questions as "Does the prospect of finding a cure for cancer or identifying the causes of psychological disorders justify exposing some animals to harm?" Proponents also note that animal research has benefited animals. For example, using learning principles discovered in studies with dogs, researchers have changed the behaviour of coyotes, bears, and other wild animals that were endangering humans or livestock, thereby sparing those wild animals from extermination (Gustavson & Gustavson, 1985).

The use of animals in research continues to be debated both outside and within the psychological community (Hobson-West, 2012; Leven & Reppy, 2015). Although animal research has declined slightly in recent decades, the ethical questions remain as vexing as ever. What is encouraging is that the welfare of animals in research is receiving the careful attention it deserves.

35. What are the justifications for, and criticisms of, research in which animals are harmed?

Review

- Psychological research follows extensive ethical guidelines. In human research, key issues are the use of informed consent, the participants' right to privacy, the degree of risk, and the use of deception.

- Ethical guidelines require that animals be treated humanely and that the risks to which they are

exposed be justified by the potential importance of the research.

- Before human and animal research can be conducted, it must be reviewed and approved by ethics review boards that often include nonscientists.

CRITICAL THINKING IN SCIENCE AND EVERYDAY LIFE

We are exposed to a great deal of information about human behaviour—some of which is accurate and much of which is not. Especially in the popular media, we encounter oversimplifications, overgeneralizations, and *pseudoscientific misinformation:* bunk and psychobabble that is made to sound scientific. To be an informed consumer, you must be able to critically evaluate research and identify features that limit the validity of conclusions. Critical-thinking skills can also help you avoid being misled by claims made in everyday life, such as those in advertisements. Thus, enhancing your critical-thinking skills may be one of the most important benefits you will derive from your psychology course.

Throughout this chapter, you have seen how critical thinking, a healthy dose of skepticism, and the scientific method help scientists solve puzzles of mind and behaviour. As critical thinkers, we should recognize that our beliefs and emotions can act as psychological blinders that allow us to accept inadequate evidence uncritically, especially when this evidence supports our current views. This tendency does not mean that we should be so skeptical of everything that we end up believing nothing at all. Rather, we need to balance open-mindedness with a healthy skepticism and evaluate evidence for what it is worth. Critical thinking is the focus of the following *Applications* feature, which presents three examples of research claims for you to analyze.

36. As a critical thinker, what questions should you ask when someone makes a claim or assertion?

EVALUATING CLAIMS IN RESEARCH AND EVERYDAY LIFE

To give you an opportunity to practise critical-thinking skills, we present brief descriptions of a research study, an advertisement, and a newspaper article. Have some fun and see if you agree with the claims made. In each case, you can facilitate critical thinking by asking yourself the following questions:

1. What claim is being made?
2. Who is making the claim? Is the source trustworthy and credible?
3. What evidence is presented and how good is it?
4. Are there other plausible explanations for the conclusions being drawn?
5. What additional evidence would help to reach a clearer conclusion?
6. What is the most reasonable conclusion to draw?

Example 1: A Lot of Bull

Deep inside the brain of humans and other mammals is a structure called the *caudate nucleus*. Years ago, a prominent researcher hypothesized that this part of the brain is responsible for turning off aggressive behaviour. The scientist was so confident in his hypothesis that he bet his life on it. A microelectrode was implanted inside the caudate nucleus of a large, aggressive bull. The researcher stood before the bull and, like a Spanish matador, waved a cape to incite the bull to charge. As the bull thundered toward him, the researcher pressed a button on a radio transmitter that he held in his other hand. This sent a signal that caused the microelectrode to electrically stimulate the bull's caudate nucleus. Suddenly, the bull broke off its charge and stopped. Each time this sequence was repeated the bull stopped its charge. The researcher concluded that the caudate nucleus was indeed the "aggression-off" centre of the brain.

Stimulating the caudate nucleus caused the bull to stop charging, but does this demonstrate that the caudate nucleus is an aggressive-off centre? Why or why not? (Hint: What other bodily functions might the caudate nucleus help to regulate that would cause the bull to stop charging?)

Example 2: Vacations and Burglaries

A newspaper advertisement appeared many times in several American cities. The headline "While You're on Vacation, Burglars Go to Work" is followed by this statement: "According to crime statistics, more than 26 percent of home burglaries take place between Memorial Day and Labor Day" (U.S. holidays in late May and early September). The ad then offers a special summer sale price for installation of a home security system. In sum, the ad implies that burglaries are particularly likely to occur while people are away on summer vacation. How do you feel about this claim and its supporting evidence?

continued

Example 3: Will Staying Up Late Cause You to Forget What You Have Studied?

The headline of a newspaper article reads "Best Way to Retain Complex Information? Sleep on It, Researcher Says." The article begins, "Students who study hard Monday through Friday and then party all night on weekends may lose much of what they learned during the week, according to a sleep researcher." The researcher is then quoted as saying, "It appears skewing the sleep cycle by just two hours can have this effect. Watching a long, late-night movie the night following a class and then sleeping in the next morning causes students to not learn what they had thought they'd learn. They'll not lose it all—just about 30 percent."

Next, the experiment was described. University students learned a complex logic game and then were assigned to one of four sleep conditions. Students in the control condition were allowed to have a normal night's sleep. Those in Condition 2 were not allowed to have any sleep, whereas students in Conditions 3 and 4 were awakened only when they went into a particular stage of sleep (we'll learn about sleep stages in Chapter 6). A week later everyone was tested again. Participants in Conditions 3 and 4 performed 30 percent worse than the other two groups.

Re-examine the experimental conditions, and then identify what is wrong with the claims in the first paragraph.

Critical Analyses of the Claims

Analysis 1: A Lot of Bull

Perhaps the caudate nucleus plays a role in vision, memory, or movement, and stimulating it momentarily caused the bull to become blind, forget what it was doing, or alter its movement. Perhaps the bull simply became dizzy or experienced pain. These are all possible explanations for why the bull stopped charging. In fact, the caudate nucleus helps to regulate movement; it is *not* an aggression-off centre in the brain.

Analysis 2: Vacations and Burglaries

First, precisely how much is "more than 26 percent"? We don't know for sure but can assume that it is less than 27 percent, because it would be to the advertiser's advantage to state the highest number possible. The key problem is the Memorial Day to Labor Day time period, which typically represents between 26 and 29 percent of the days of the year. Therefore, about 26 percent of burglaries occur during about 26 percent of the year. Wow! Technically, the ad is correct: Burglars do go to work in the summer while you're on vacation. But the ad also may mislead people. Burglars seem to be just as busy as at other times of the year.

Analysis 3: Will Staying Up Late Cause You to Forget What You Have Studied?

It could be true that going to bed and waking up later than usual might cause you to forget more of what you studied. However, the article does not provide evidence for this claim. Look at the four conditions carefully. To test this claim, an experiment would need to include a condition in which a student went to bed later than usual, slept through the night, and then awakened later than usual. But in this experiment, the control group slept normally, and the three experimental conditions examined only the effects of getting no sleep or losing certain types of sleep.

When reading newspaper or magazine articles, look beyond the headlines and think about whether the evidence truly supports the claims. Were you able to pick out some flaws in these claims before you read the analyses? Critical thinking requires practice, and you will get better at it if you keep asking yourself the six critical-thinking questions listed earlier.

Review

- Critical thinking is an important life skill. However, we should also be open-minded to ideas that are supported by solid evidence, even when they conflict with our preconceptions.
- There is no generally accepted, replicable scientific evidence to support the existence of paranormal phenomena.
- In science and everyday life, critical thinking can prevent us from developing false impressions about how the world operates and from being duped in everyday life by unsubstantiated claims.

Gaining Direction

What are the issues?

For the opening scenario, we need to focus on the entire process of doing research. How do we design a study? How can we determine if it is a "good" study? Is there a difference between experimental research and correlational research? How do we determine when a study "worked"? Is it possible that results could be due to chance? Should we expect a study to be replicable? What do we do if we cannot get the same results? Are there possible biases in journal reporting that may lead to publication errors?

What do we need to know?

What is the scientific process for studying psychological phenomena?

What are independent and dependent variables? Are there any sources of bias that can enter into an experiment?

How can you control for possible bias?

How do you replicate a study?

How can you determine if an effect is due to chance?

Where can we find the information to answer these questions?

Look back over the chapter and identify the components of the scientific method. Then examine how we go about designing an experiment. What kinds of factors do we need to control? How do we determine statistical significance? Look at the factors that influence validity. Perhaps we need to conduct a meta-analysis. It would be a good idea to examine the studies mentioned by LeBel and his colleagues. Do you see any problems with them? Finally, we need to account for the failure to replicate—what should we do next?

Biological Foundations of Behaviour

CHAPTER ≫
OUTLINE

THE NEURAL BASES OF BEHAVIOUR

Neurons

The Electrical Activity of Neurons

How Neurons Communicate: Synaptic Transmission

Applications: Understanding How Drugs Affect Your Brain

THE NERVOUS SYSTEM

The Peripheral Nervous System

The Central Nervous System

Research Foundations: Wilder Penfield and a Cortical Map

The Hierarchical Brain: Structures and Behavioural Functions

Frontiers: Mirror Neurons and Autism Spectrum Disorder

Focus on Neuroscience: The Neuroscience of Music

> The brain is the last and grandest biological frontier, the most complex thing we have yet discovered in our universe. It contains hundreds of billions of cells interlinked through trillions of connections. The brain boggles the mind.
>
> —James Watson

 Most people will readily recognize Brad Pitt. The hair, mustache, and goatee are classic features. But if you ever meet Brad Pitt, he will probably not be able to recognize you again. Not because he sees so many people or because he does not pay attention. Brad Pitt cannot remember faces. It is as if the person's facial features were not committed to memory for him. He does realize that the face belongs to a person and could even tell you if the person is happy or sad. Once he knows who it is, he can remember everything about that individual. He just cannot tell you who the face belongs to. Many people have a similar problem, including primatologist Jane Goodall and neurologist Oliver Sacks.

DFree/Shutterstock.com

In severe cases of this disorder, individuals cannot even recognize themselves in a mirror.

What are the issues here?

What do we need to know?

Where can we find the information to answer the questions?

THE NEURAL BASES OF BEHAVIOUR

The brain is a grapefruit-size mass of tissue that feels like jelly and looks like a greyish cauliflower. One of the true marvels of nature, it has been termed "our three-pound universe" (Hooper & Teresi, 1986). To understand how the brain controls our experience and behaviour, we must first understand how its individual cells function and how they communicate with one another.

Neurons

Specialized cells called **neurons** are the basic building blocks of the nervous system. These nerve cells are linked together in circuits, not unlike the electrical circuits in a computer. At birth, your brain contained about 100 billion neurons (Bloom, 2000; Kolb & Whishaw, 1989). To put this number in perspective, if each neuron were a centimetre long and they were placed end to end, the resulting chain would circle the Earth more than 24 times.

Each neuron has three main parts: a cell body, dendrites, and an axon (Figure 3.1). The cell body, or *soma*, contains the structures needed to keep the neuron alive, and its nucleus contains the genetic information that determines how the neuron develops and functions. Emerging from the cell body are branchlike fibres called **dendrites** (from the Greek word for *tree*). These specialized receiving units are like antennas that collect messages from neighbouing neurons and send them on

to the cell body. There, in the soma, the incoming information is combined and processed. The surface of the cell body also has receptor areas that can be directly stimulated by other neurons. Extending from one side of the cell body is a single **axon,** which conducts electrical impulses away from the cell body to other neurons, muscles, or glands. The axon branches out at its end to form a number of *axon terminals*—as many as several hundred in some cases. Each axon may connect with dendritic branches from other neurons, making it possible for a single neuron to pass messages to as many as 50 000 other neurons (Kolb & Whishaw, 2003; Simon, 2007). Given the structure of the dendrites and axons, it is easy to imagine how there can be trillions of interconnections in the brain, making it capable of performing the complex psychological activities that are of interest to psychologists.

Neurons can vary greatly in size and shape. More than 200 different types of neurons have been identified using an electron microscopes (Nolte, 1998). A neuron with its cell body in your spinal cord may have an axon that extends almost a metre to one of your fingertips; on the other hand, a neuron in your brain may have an axon less than a millimetre long. Regardless of their shape or size, neurons share a common overall structure and function.

Neurons are supported in their functions by *glial cells* (from the Greek word for *glue*). Glial cells surround neurons and hold them in place. Glial cells also manufacture or transport nutrients, form the myelin sheath around some

1. Name the three main parts of the neuron and describe their functions.

2. Which structural characteristics permit the many possible interconnections among neurons?

3. How do glial cells differ from neurons? What three functions do they have in the nervous system?

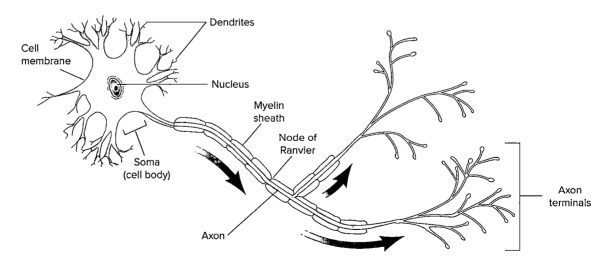

FIGURE 3.1 Structural elements of a typical neuron. Stimulation received by the dendrites or soma (cell body) may trigger a nerve impulse, which travels down the axon to stimulate other neurons, muscles, or glands. Some axons have a fatty myelin sheath interrupted at intervals by the nodes of Ranvier. The myelin sheath helps to increase the speed of nerve conduction.

axons, and absorb toxins and waste materials that might damage neurons. During prenatal brain development, as new neurons are being formed, glial cells send out long fibres that guide newly divided neurons to their eventual place in the brain (Fernichel, 2006). Within the nervous system, glial cells outnumber neurons about ten to one (Herculano-Houzel, 2014).

Another function of glial cells is to protect the brain from toxins. Many foreign substances can pass from the circulation into the different organs of the body but cannot pass from the blood into the brain. A specialized barrier, the **blood-brain barrier,** prevents many substances, including a wide range of toxins, from entering the brain. The walls of the blood vessels within the brain contain smaller gaps than elsewhere in the body, and they are also covered by a specialized type of glial cell (Cserr & Bundgaard, 1986). Together, the smaller gaps and glial cells keep many foreign substances from gaining access to the brain. Recent research has found evidence for much more complex glial function, such as a role in modulating the communication among neurons (Todd, Serrano, Lacaille, & Robitaille, 2006; Zhang & Haydon, 2005).

The Electrical Activity of Neurons

Neurons do two important things: generate electricity and release chemicals that allow them to communicate with other neurons and with muscles and glands.

Let's first consider how they generate electricity; how the nerve impulses occur. Nerve activation involves three basic steps:

1. At rest, the neuron has an electrical resting potential due to the distribution of positively and negatively charged chemicals (ions) inside and outside the neuron.

2. When stimulated, a flow of ions in and out through the cell membrane reverses the electrical charge of the resting potential, producing an action potential, or nerve impulse.

3. The original distribution of ions is restored, and the neuron is again at rest.

Let's now flesh out the details of this remarkable process. Like other cells, neurons are surrounded by body fluids and separated from this liquid environment by a protective membrane. This cell membrane is a bit like a selective sieve, allowing certain substances to pass through *ion channels* into the cell while refusing or limiting passage to other substances. An ion channel is quite literally

just that, a channel in the membrane that can open to allow certain ions to pass through.

The chemical environment inside the neuron differs from its external environment in significant ways, and the process that allows a nerve impulse to be is created involves the exchange of electrically charged atoms called *ions*. In the salty fluid outside the neuron, there are positively charged sodium ions (Na+) and negatively charged chloride ions (Cl−). Inside the neuron are large negatively charged protein molecules (anions or A−) and positively charged potassium ions (K+). The high concentration of sodium ions in the fluid outside the cell, together with the negatively charged protein ions inside, results in an uneven distribution of positive and negative ions that makes the interior of the cell negative compared to the outside (Figure 3.2), This internal difference of around 70 millivolts (thousandths of a volt) is called the neuron's **resting potential.** At rest, the neuron is said to be in a state of polarization. That is, the neuron is in some ways like a battery with an internal electrical potential that allows it to do work.

The Action Potential

In research that won them the Nobel Prize in Medicine and Physiology, neuroscientists Alan Hodgkin and Andrew Huxley found that if they stimulated the neuron's axon with a mild electrical stimulus, the interior voltage differential shifted suddenly from −70 millivolts to +40 millivolts. Hodgkin and Huxley had forced the axon to generate a nerve impulse, or *action potential*. An **action potential** is a sudden reversal in the neuron's membrane voltage, during which the membrane voltage momentarily moves from −70 millivolts (inside) to +40 millivolts (Figure 3.2). This shift from negative to positive voltage is called **depolarization.**

Exploring what happens in the neuron to cause the action potential, Hodgkin and Huxley found that the key mechanism is the movement of sodium and potassium ions across the cell membrane; Figure 3.2 shows what happens. In a resting state, the neuron's sodium and potassium channels are closed, and the concentration of Na+ ions is 10 times higher outside the neuron than inside it (Figure 3.2a). But when a neuron is stimulated sufficiently (Figure 3.2b), sodium channels open. Attracted by the negative protein ions inside, positively charged sodium ions flood into the axon, creating a state of *depolarization* (remember, when it comes to electrical charges, opposites attract!).

4. What causes the negative resting potential of neurons? When is a neuron said to be in a state of polarization?

5. What chemical changes cause the process of depolarization that creates graded and action potentials? How do these potentials differ?

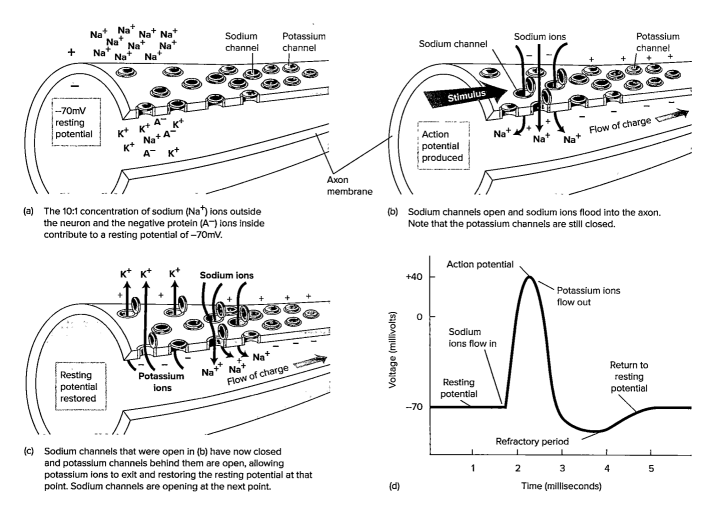

(a) The 10:1 concentration of sodium (Na⁺) ions outside the neuron and the negative protein (A⁻) ions inside contribute to a resting potential of −70mV.

(b) Sodium channels open and sodium ions flood into the axon. Note that the potassium channels are still closed.

(c) Sodium channels that were open in (b) have now closed and potassium channels behind them are open, allowing potassium ions to exit and restoring the resting potential at that point. Sodium channels are opening at the next point.

(d)

FIGURE 3.2 From resting potential to action potential. When a neuron is not being stimulated, a difference in electrical charge of about −70 millivolts (mV) exists between the interior and the surface of the neuron. (a) This resting potential is caused by the uneven distribution of positively and negatively charged ions, with a greater concentration of positively charged sodium ions kept outside the cell by closed sodium channels, and the presence of negatively charged protein (A−) ions inside the cell. In addition, the action of sodium-potassium pumps helps to maintain the negative interior by pumping out three sodium (Na+) ions for every two positively charged potassium (K+) ions pumped into the cell. (b) Sufficient stimulation of the neuron causes an action potential. Sodium channels open for an instant, and Na+ ions flood into the axon, reversing the electrical potential from −70 mV to +40 mV. (c) Within a millisecond, the sodium channels close and many K+ ions flow out of the cell through open potassium channels, helping to restore the interior negative potential. As adjacent sodium channels are opened and the sequence in (b) and (c) is repeated, the action potential moves down the length of the neuron. (d) Shown here are the changes in potential that would be recorded from a particular point on the axon. After a brief refractory period during which the neuron cannot be stimulated, another action potential can follow.

In an instant, the interior now becomes positive in relation to the outside, creating the action potential. In a reflex action to restore the resting state, the cell closes its sodium channels, and positively charged potassium ions flow out through their channels, restoring the negative resting potential (Figure 3.2c). Eventually, the excess sodium ions flow out of the neuron, and the escaped potassium ions are recovered. The resulting voltage changes are shown in Figure 3.2d.

Once an action potential occurs at any point on the membrane, its effects spread to adjacent sodium channels and the action potential flows down the length of the axon to the axon terminals, like a row of dominoes. Immediately after an impulse passes a point along the axon, however, there is a recovery period as K+ ions flow out of the interior. During this **absolute refractory period,** the membrane is not excitable and cannot generate another action potential. This places an upper limit on the rate at which nerve impulses can occur. In humans, the limit is about 300 impulses per second (Kolb & Whishaw, 2005). It also means that once an action potential starts it travels in only one direction, from soma along the axon to the dendrites.

It's all or nothing. One other feature of the action potential is noteworthy. For a specific type of neuron, action potentials occur at a uniform and maximum intensity, or they do not occur at all; this is the **all-or-none law.** Like pressing the shutter release of a camera, either there is enough change to trigger shutter release or nothing happens; pressing the shutter release button harder does not change this—it is hard enough to take a picture or nothing happens. Neurons function much the same. Either there is enough of a change to trigger an action potential or nothing happens. The negative potential inside the axon has to be changed from −70 millivolts to about −50 millivolts (the **action potential threshold**) by the influx of sodium ions into the axon before the action potential will be triggered. Changes in the negative resting potential that do not reach the −50 millivolts action potential threshold are called **graded potentials.** Under certain circumstances, graded potentials caused by several neurons can add up to trigger an action potential in the postsynaptic neuron, but changes below the threshold usually go no further.

For a neuron to function properly, sodium and potassium ions must enter and leave the membrane at just the right rate. Drugs that alter this system can decrease or even prevent neural functioning. For example, local anaesthetics such as Novocain and Xylocaine attach themselves to the sodium channels, stopping the flow of sodium ions into the neurons. This stops pain impulses from being sent by the neurons (Ray & Ksir, 2004).

The Myelin Sheath

Many axons that transmit information throughout the brain and spinal cord are covered by a **myelin sheath,** a fatty, whitish insulation layer derived from glial cells during development. The myelin sheath is much like the plastic insulation on an electrical wire. The myelin sheath is interrupted at regular intervals by the *nodes of Ranvier,* where the myelin is either extremely thin or absent. The nodes make the myelin sheath look a bit like sausages placed end to end (Figure 3.1). In unmyelinated axons, the action potential travels down the axon length like a burning fuse. In myelinated axons, electrical conduction can skip from node to node, and these "great leaps" from one gap to another account for high conduction speeds of more than 300 kilometres per hour.

The myelin sheath is most commonly found in the nervous systems of higher animals. In many nerve fibres, including important motor nerves in humans, the myelin sheath is not completely formed until after birth. The increased efficiency of neural transmission that results is partly responsible for the gains that infants exhibit in muscular coordination, such as the ability to walk, as they grow older (Cabeza et al., 2005).

The tragic effects of damage to the myelin coating can be seen in people who suffer from *multiple sclerosis.* This progressive disease occurs when the person's own immune system attacks the myelin sheath. The effect is much like stripping the insulation off of wires in an electrical circuit. Damage to the myelin sheath disrupts the delicate timing of nerve impulses, resulting in jerky, uncoordinated movements and, in the final stages, paralysis (Olsen & Akirav, 2015).

How Neurons Communicate: Synaptic Transmission

The nervous system operates as a giant communications network, and it requires that nerve impulses be communicated from one neuron to another. The famous Spanish anatomist Santiago Ramón y Cajal and the British scientist Charles Sherrington demonstrated that neurons were individual cells that did not make actual physical contact with each other, but communicated at a **synapse,** a functional (not physical) connection between a neuron and its target. Originally, this idea was controversial: How could a neuron influence the functioning of the heart, a skeletal muscle, or another neuron if these cells did not actually touch? The controversy persisted until the 1920s, when Otto Loewi in a series of simple but elegant experiments demonstrated that neurons released chemicals, and it was these chemicals that carried the message from one neuron to the next cell in the circuit (Loewi, 1935, 1960). Otto Loewi won the Nobel Prize for his discovery of chemical neurotransmission. With the advent of the electron microscope, researchers were able to actually see that there is indeed a tiny gap or space, called the **synaptic cleft,** between the axon terminal of one neuron and the dendrite of the next neuron.

Neurotransmitters

We now know that, in addition to generating electricity, neurons produce and release

6. What is the nature and importance of the myelin sheath? Which disorder results from inadequate myelinization?

substances called **neurotransmitters,** chemicals that carry messages across the synapse to either excite or inhibit the activity of the next cell. This process of chemical communication involves five steps: synthesis, storage, release, binding, and deactivation. In the *synthesis* stage, the chemical molecules are formed inside the neuron. The molecules are then *stored* in chambers called **synaptic vesicles** within the axon terminals. When an action potential comes down the axon, these vesicles move to the surface of the axon terminal and *release* the chemical neurotransmitter into the fluid-filled space between the axon of the sending (presynaptic) neuron and the membrane of the receiving (postsynaptic) neuron. The molecules of neurotransmitter cross the synaptic space and *bind* (attach) to **receptor sites**—large protein molecules embedded in the receiving neuron's cell membrane. These receptor sites have a specially shaped surface that fits a specific transmitter molecule, much like a lock accommodates a single key (Figure 3.3). Once the neurotransmitter has bound to a receptor site it can have an effect, much like the way your

room key (neurotransmitter) can have an effect (opening a door) when it is inserted in to the correct lock (receptor site).

Excitation, Inhibition, and Deactivation

The binding of a transmitter molecule to the receptor site produces a chemical reaction that can have one of two effects on the postsynaptic neuron, making it either more or less likely that the postsynaptic neuron will generate an action potential. In some cases, the reaction will depolarize (excite) the postsynaptic cell membrane by stimulating the inflow of sodium or other positively charged ions, making it more likely the neuron will reach the threshold to generate an action potential. Neurotransmitters that create depolarization are called *excitatory* transmitters. This stimulation, alone or in combination with activity at other excitatory synapses on the dendrites or the cell body, may exceed the action potential threshold and cause the postsynaptic neuron to fire an action potential.

In other cases, the chemical reaction created by the docking of a neurotransmitter at its

7. How do neurotransmitters achieve the processes of excitation and inhibition of postsynaptic neurons?

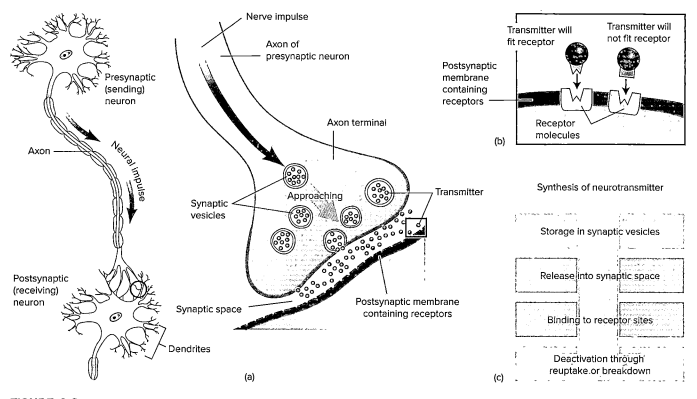

FIGURE 3.3 A synapse between two neurons. The action potential travels to the axon terminals, where it stimulates the release of transmitter molecules from the synaptic vesicles. These molecules travel across the synapse and bind to specially keyed receptor sites on the dendrite of the postsynaptic neuron (a). The lock-and-key nature of neurotransmitters and receptor sites is shown in (b). Only transmitters that fit the receptor will influence membrane potentials. (c) Neurotransmitter activity moves from synthesis to deactivation. If the neurotransmitter has an excitatory effect on the neuron, the chemical reaction creates a graded or an action potential. If the neurotransmitter has an inhibitory effect, the negative potential inside the neuron increases and makes it more difficult to trigger an action potential.

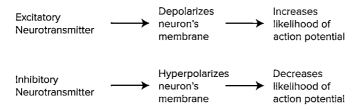

FIGURE 3.4 Neurotransmitters have either excitatory or inhibitory effects on postsynaptic neurons. Excitatory transmitters depolarize the postsynaptic neuron's cell membrane, making it less negative and thereby moving it toward the action potential threshold. Inhibitory neurons hyperpolarize the membrane, making it more negative and therefore more difficult to excite to an action potential.

receptor site will *hyperpolarize* the postsynaptic membrane by stimulating ion channels that allow positively charged potassium ions to flow out of the neuron or negatively charged ions, such as chloride, to flow into the neuron. This makes the membrane potential even more negative and makes it more difficult for excitatory transmitters at other receptor sites to depolarize the neuron to its action potential threshold. Transmitters that create hyperpolarization are thus *inhibitory* in their function (Figure 3.4).

Every neuron is constantly bombarded with excitatory and inhibitory neurotransmitters from other neurons, and the interplay of these influences determines whether the cell fires an action potential or not. The action of an inhibitory transmitter from one presynaptic neuron may prevent the postsynaptic neuron from reaching the action potential threshold, even if it is receiving excitatory stimulation from several other neurons at the same time. An exquisite balance between excitatory and inhibitory processes must be maintained if the nervous system is to function properly. The process of inhibition allows a fine-tuning of neural activity and prevents an uncoordinated discharge of the nervous system, as occurs in a seizure, when large numbers of neurons fire off action potentials in a runaway fashion.

Once a neurotransmitter molecule binds to its receptor, it continues to activate or inhibit the neuron until it is shut off, or *deactivated*. This deactivation occurs in two major ways (Fain, 1999). Some transmitter molecules are deactivated by other chemicals located in the synaptic space that break them down into their chemical components. In other instances, the deactivation mechanism is **reuptake,** in which the transmitter molecules are reabsorbed into the presynaptic axon terminal. When the receptor molecule is vacant, the postsynaptic neuron returns to its former resting state, awaiting the next chemical stimulation.

Most commonly used, and abused, psychoactive drugs influence one of these steps in chemical neurotransmission. Drugs may target the transmitter's receptor, binding to the receptor in place of the neurotransmitter, or one of the steps in the synthesis or release of the neurotransmitter. Drugs can also alter synaptic transmission by influencing how the transmitter is cleared from the synaptic cleft after it has been released. A drug's exact psychological effects, however, are determined not by its actions at the synapse, but by which specific chemical transmitter it targets. This chapter's *Applications* feature provides information on how some commonly used drugs influence neurotransmission.

Specialized Transmitter Systems

Through the use of chemical transmitters, nature has found an ingenious way of dividing up the brain into systems that are uniquely sensitive to certain messages. At present, 100 to 150 different substances are known or suspected transmitters in the brain, but there may be many more (Fain, 1999; Kolb & Whishaw, 2005). Each substance has a specific excitatory or inhibitory effect on certain neurons. The chemical specificity protects the brain from "crosstalk" and allows specific chemical systems to serve specific functions. Table 3.1 lists several of the more important neurotransmitters that have been linked to psychological phenomena.

Two widespread neurotransmitters are simple amino acids, glutamate, or glutamic acid, and gamma-aminobutyric acid, or GABA. Both glutamate and GABA are found throughout the central nervous system, and hence have some role in mediating virtually all behaviours. Glutamate is excitatory and has a particularly important role in the mechanisms involved in learning and memory. Improving one's memory, however, cannot be as simple as enhancing glutamate activity. Since it has a powerful excitatory

8. Describe two methods by which neurotransmitter molecules are deactivated at the synapse.

Applications

UNDERSTANDING HOW DRUGS AFFECT YOUR BRAIN

Drugs affect consciousness and behaviour by influencing the activity of neurons. According to Health Canada, 11 percent of Canadians between ages 15 and 19 smoke tobacco, and that number increases to 20 percent among Canadians aged 20 to 24 (Canadian Tobacco Use Monitoring Survey, Health Canada, 2012). These are the lowest rates since Health Canada began keeping tobacco use statistics in 1985. Among Canadians aged 15 to 24, 34 percent have used cannabis at some point in their life and 15.1 percent have used some type of illicit drug, such as ecstasy, cocaine/crack, or amphetamines, or hallucinogenic drugs like LSD (Health Canada, 2011). Alcohol is present at many university and college parties, in restaurants, at sporting events, and in the refrigerator or cupboard of many Canadian homes. In 2011, 71 percent of those aged 15–24 had used alcohol in the past year, and among drinkers in that age group, 21 percent exceeded Health Canada's low-risk drinking guidelines (Health Canada, 2011). Almost all students ingest caffeine in coffee, chocolate, cocoa, and soft drinks. Considering the amount of drugs that we ingest, it is important to have some knowledge of what these drugs are doing within the brain.

Most psychoactive drugs produce their effects by either increasing or decreasing the actions of neurotransmitters. An agonist is a drug that increases the activity of a neurotransmitter. Agonists may (1) enhance a neuron's ability to synthesize, store, or release neurotransmitters; (2) mimic the action of a neurotransmitter by binding with and stimulating postsynaptic receptor sites; or (3) make it more difficult for neurotransmitters to be deactivated, such as by inhibiting reuptake. An antagonist is a drug that inhibits or decreases the action of a neurotransmitter. An antagonist may (1) reduce a neuron's ability to synthesize, store, or release neurotransmitters; or (2) prevent a neurotransmitter from binding with the postsynaptic neuron by fitting into and blocking the receptor sites on the postsynaptic neuron. With the distinction between agonist and antagonist functions in mind, let's consider how some commonly used drugs work within the brain.

Alcohol is a depressant drug that has both agonist and antagonist effects. Although alcohol can have a wide range of effects, in the concentrations that people consume it, alcohol's effects are due to its agonist and antagonist actions (Levinthal, 2010). As an agonist, alcohol stimulates the activity of the inhibitory transmitter GABA, thereby depressing neural activity. As an antagonist, it decreases the activity of glutamate, an excitatory transmitter. The effect is a powerful slowing of neural activity that inhibits normal brain functions, including clear thinking, emotional control, and motor coordination. Sedative drugs, including barbiturates and tranquilizers, also increase GABA activity,

and taking them with alcohol can be deadly when their depressant effects on neural activity are combined with the alcohol's effects (Schatzberg et al., 2010).

Caffeine is a stimulant drug that increases the activity of neurons and other cells. It is an antagonist for the transmitter adenosine, which inhibits the release of excitatory transmitters. By reducing adenosine activity, caffeine helps produce higher rates of cellular activity. Although caffeine is a stimulant, it is important to note that contrary to popular belief, caffeine does not counteract the effects of alcohol and sober people up. What someone who has been drinking needs is a ride home with a driver who is sober—not a cup of coffee.

Nicotine is an agonist for the excitatory transmitter ACh. Its chemical structure is similar enough to ACh to allow it to fit into ACh binding sites and create action potentials. At other receptor sites, nicotine stimulates dopamine activity, which is an important chemical mediator for motivation and reward. This stimulation may help account for nicotine's powerful addictive properties.

Amphetamines are stimulant drugs that boost arousal and mood by increasing the activity of the excitatory neurotransmitters dopamine and norepinephrine. They do so in two major ways. First, they cause neurons to release greater amounts of these neurotransmitters. Second, they inhibit reuptake, allowing dopamine and norepinephrine to keep stimulating postsynaptic neurons (Ksir et al., 2008).

© Jim Arbogast/Photodisc/Getty Images

FIGURE 3.5 Brain activity is being altered in several ways in this scene. Nicotine from the cigarette smoke is activating acetylcholine and dopamine neurons, increasing neural excitation. The alcohol is stimulating the activity of the inhibitory transmitter GABA and decreasing the activity of an excitatory transmitter, glutamate, thus depressing brain functions. The possibility of a drink having been spiked with one of the powerful and potentially deadly "date rape" sedative drugs could place any of these women at great risk.

continued

Cocaine produces excitation, a sense of increased muscular strength, and euphoria. Like amphetamines, cocaine increases the activity of norepinephrine and dopamine, but it does so in only one major way: It blocks their reuptake. Thus, amphetamines and cocaine have different mechanisms of action, but both drugs produce highly stimulating effects on mood, thinking, and behaviour. The powerfully motivating and rewarding properties of these drugs is thought to be due to their actions on dopamine (Blum et al., 2012).

We should comment on two other drugs that, unfortunately, are also found on college campuses. Rohypnol (flunitrazepam, known as *roofies* or *rope*) and GHB (gamma hydroxybutyrate, known as *easy lay*) are so-called "date rape" drugs. Party-goers sometimes add these drugs to punch and other drinks in hopes of lowering drinkers' inhibitions and facilitating nonconsensual sexual conquest. These drugs are powerful sedatives that suppress general neural activity by enhancing the action of the inhibitory transmitter GABA (Levinthal, 2010). Rohypnol is about 10 times more potent than Valium. At high doses or when mixed with alcohol or other drugs, these substances may lead to respiratory depression, loss of consciousness, coma, and even death. Rohypnol also decreases neurotransmission in areas of the brain involved in memory, producing an amnesia effect that may prevent users from remembering the circumstances under which they ingested the drug or what happened to them afterwards. GHB, which makes its victim appear drunk and helpless, is now a restricted drug, and slipping it into someone's drink is a criminal act. Increasingly, women are being advised against accepting opened drinks from fellow revellers or leaving their own drinks unattended at parties (Figure 3.5).

effect, over-activation of glutamate will induce seizure activity within the brain, especially within the cerebral cortex. Whereas glutamate has a powerful excitatory effect, GABA is an inhibitory neurotransmitter. GABA is especially important for motor control and the control of anxiety. For example, the drugs most commonly used to treat anxiety disorders, the benzodiazepines, act by enhancing GABA activity. A commonly used drug, alcohol, acts, in part, to make the brain more sensitive to GABA, although in a less specific way than the anti-anxiety benzodiazepines. The symptoms of intoxication reflect the progressive inhibition of brain function with increasing GABA-induced inhibition.

Perhaps the best understood neurotransmitter is **acetylcholine (ACh)**, which is involved in memory and muscle activity. Underproduction of ACh is thought to be an important factor in *Alzheimer's disease*, a degenerative brain

9. Describe the roles of (a) acetylcholine, (b) dopamine, (c) serotonin, and (d) endorphins in psychological functions.

TABLE 3.1 Some Neurotransmitters and Their Effects

Neurotransmitter	Major Function	Disorders Associated with Malfunctioning
Glutamate (glutamic acid)	Excitatory; found throughout the brain; involved in the control of all behaviours, especially important in learning and memory	
GABA (gamma-aminobutyric acid)	Inhibitory transmitter; found throughout the brain; involved in controlling all behaviours, especially important in anxiety and motor control	Destruction of GABA-producing neurons in Huntington's disease produces tremors and loss of motor control, as well as personality changes
Acetylcholine (ACh)	Excitatory at synapses involved in muscular movement and memory	Memory loss in Alzheimer's disease (undersupply) Muscle contractions, convulsions (oversupply)
Norepinephrine	Excitatory and inhibitory functions at various sites; involved in neural circuits controlling learning, memory, wakefulness, and eating	Depression (undersupply) Stress and panic disorders (oversupply)
Serotonin	Inhibitory at most sites; involved in mood, sleep, eating, and arousal, and may be an important transmitter underlying pleasure and pain	Depression, sleeping, and eating disorders
Dopamine	Can be inhibitory or excitatory; involved in voluntary movement, emotional arousal, learning, motivation, experiencing pleasure	Parkinson's disease and depression (undersupply) Schizophrenia (oversupply)
Endorphin	Inhibits transmission of pain impulses	Insensitivity to pain (oversupply) Pain hypersensitivity, immune problems (undersupply)

disorder involving profound memory impairment that afflicts between 5 and 10 percent of all people over 65 years of age (Morris & Becker, 2005). Reductions in ACh weaken or deactivate neural circuitry that stores memories.

ACh is also an excitatory transmitter at the synapses where neurons activate muscle cells (Sherwood, 1991). Drugs that block the action of ACh, therefore, can prevent muscle activation, resulting in muscular paralysis. One example occurs in *botulism,* a serious type of food poisoning that can result from improperly canned food. The toxin formed by the botulinum bacteria blocks the release of ACh from the axon terminal, resulting in a potentially fatal paralysis of the muscles, including those of the respiratory system. The opposite effect on ACh occurs with the bite of the black widow spider. The spider's venom produces a torrent of ACh, resulting in violent muscle contractions, convulsions, and even death.

The neurotransmitter **dopamine** mediates a wide range of functions, including motivation, reward, and feelings of pleasure; voluntary motor control; and control of thought processes. Understanding the neurotransmitter dopamine has also had a profound impact on our understanding of several diseases. In Parkinson's disease, one specific group of dopamine-producing neurons degenerate and die. As dopamine is lost in the affected brain areas, there is a concomitant loss of voluntary motor control. The symptoms of Parkinson's disease are most commonly treated with a drug (L-DOPA) that increases the amount of dopamine within the brain. The treatment of emotionally disturbed people was revolutionized by the development the antipsychotic drugs; the drugs that started the so-called "psychiatric revolution" of the 1950s. These drugs are still widely used today. Antipsychotic drugs attach to dopamine receptors and block dopamine from having its effects. Such blockade of dopamine is effective in treating symptoms of schizophrenia, and led to the theory that schizophrenia is due to overactivity in specific dopamine systems (Howes, McCutcheon, & Stone, 2015). Dopamine has also been associated with the motivating and rewarding properties of the major drugs of abuse (Blum et al., 2012).

Quite a different mechanism occurs in the treatment of depression. Depression involves abnormal sensitivity to **serotonin,** a neurotransmitter that influences mood, eating, sleep, and sexual behaviour. Antidepressant drugs increase serotonin activity in several ways. Drugs like Prozac, known as selective serotonin-reuptake inhibitors (SSRIs), block the reuptake of serotonin from the synaptic space, allowing serotonin molecules to remain active and exert their mood-altering effects. Other antidepressant drugs work on a different deactivating mechanism; they inhibit the activity of enzymes in the synaptic space that deactivate serotonin by breaking it down into simpler chemicals. In so doing, they prolong serotonin activity at the synapse.

Endorphins are another important family of neurotransmitters. **Endorphins** reduce pain and increase feelings of well-being. They bind to the same receptors as the ones activated by opiate drugs, such as opium and morphine, which produce similar psychological effects. The ability of people to continue to function despite severe injury is due in large part to the release of endorphins and their ability to act as analgesics. We will discuss the endorphins in greater detail when we discuss pain.

Most neurotransmitters have their excitatory or inhibitory effects only on specific neurons

ⓘ **Review**

- Each neuron has dendrites, which receive nerve impulses from other neurons; a cell body (soma), which controls the vital processes of the cell; and an axon, which conducts nerve impulses to adjacent neurons, muscles, and glands.

- Neural transmission is an electrochemical process. The nerve impulse, or action potential, is a brief reversal in the electrical potential of the cell membrane as sodium ions from the surrounding fluid flow into the cell through sodium ion channels, depolarizing the axon's membrane. Graded potentials are proportional to the amount of stimulation being received, whereas action potentials obey the all-or-none law, occurring at full intensity if the action potential threshold of stimulation is reached. The myelin sheath increases the speed of neural transmission.

- Passage of the impulse across the synapse is mediated by chemical transmitter substances. Neurons are selective in the neurotransmitters that can stimulate them. Some neurotransmitters excite neurons, whereas others inhibit firing of the postsynaptic neuron.

that have receptors for them. Others, called **neuromodulators,** have a more widespread and generalized influence on synaptic transmission. These substances circulate through the brain and either increase or decrease (i.e., modulate) the sensitivity of neurons to their specific transmitters. Neuromodulators play important roles in functions such as eating, sleep, and stress. Thus, some chemical transmitters have very specific effects (neurotransmitters), whereas others (neuromodulators) have more general effects on neural activity.

THE NERVOUS SYSTEM

The nervous system is the body's master control centre. Three major types of neurons carry out the system's input, output, and integration functions. **Sensory neurons** carry input messages from the sense organs to the spinal cord and brain. **Motor neurons** transmit output impulses from the brain and spinal cord to the body's muscles and organs. Finally, there are neurons that link the input and output functions. **Interneurons,** which far outnumber sensory and motor neurons, perform connective or associative functions within the nervous system. For example, interneurons allow us to recognize a tune by linking the sensory input from

the song we're hearing with the memory of that song stored elsewhere in the brain. The activity of interneurons makes possible the complexity of our higher mental functions, emotions, and behavioural capabilities.

The nervous system can be broken down into several interrelated subsystems (Figure 3.6). The two major divisions are the **central nervous system,** consisting of all the neurons in the brain and spinal cord, and the **peripheral nervous system,** composed of all the neurons that connect the central nervous system with the muscles, glands, and sensory receptors.

The Peripheral Nervous System

The peripheral nervous system contains all the neural structures that lie outside of the brain and spinal cord. Its specialized neurons help to carry out the input and output functions that are necessary for us to sense what is going on inside and outside our bodies and to respond with our muscles and glands. The peripheral nervous system has two major divisions, the somatic nervous system and the autonomic nervous system.

The Somatic Nervous System

The **somatic nervous system** consists of the *sensory neurons* that are specialized to transmit

10. What are the three major types of neurons? What are their functions?

11. Differentiate between the central nervous system and the peripheral nervous system. What are the two divisions of the peripheral nervous system?

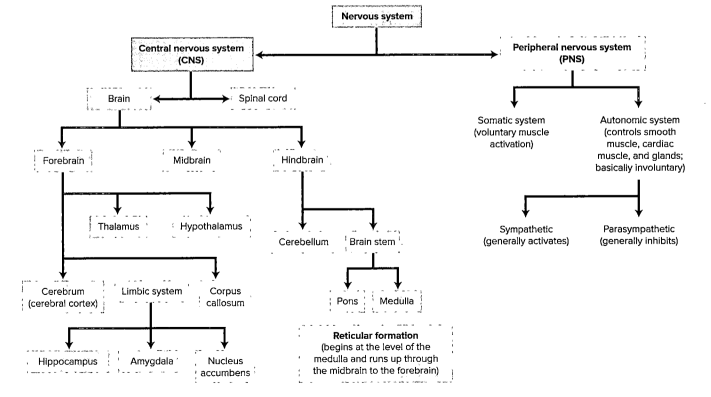

FIGURE 3.6 Structural organization of the nervous system.

messages from the eyes, ears, and other sensory receptors, and the *motor neurons* that send messages from the brain and spinal cord to the muscles that control our voluntary movements. The axons of sensory neurons group together like the many strands of a rope to form *sensory nerves*, and motor neuron axons combine to form *motor nerves*. (Inside the brain and spinal cord, nerves are called *tracts*.) As you read this page, sensory neurons located in your eyes are sending impulses into a complex network of specialized visual tracts that course through your brain. At the same time, motor neurons are stimulating the eye movements that allow you to scan the lines of type and turn the pages. The somatic system thus allows you to sense and respond to your environment.

The Autonomic Nervous System

The body's internal environment is regulated largely through the activities of the **autonomic**

nervous system, which controls the glands and the smooth (involuntary) muscles that form the heart, the blood vessels, and the lining of the stomach and intestines. The autonomic system is largely concerned with involuntary functions, such as respiration, circulation, and digestion, and it is also involved in many aspects of motivation, emotional behaviour, and stress responses. It consists of two subdivisions, the sympathetic nervous system and the parasympathetic nervous system (Figure 3.7). Typically, these two divisions affect the same organ or gland in opposing ways.

The **sympathetic nervous system** has an activation or arousal function, and it tends to act as a total unit. For example, when you encounter a stressful situation, your sympathetic nervous system simultaneously speeds your heart so it can pump more blood to your muscles, dilates your pupils so more light can enter the eye and improve your vision, slows down your digestive

12. Describe the two divisions of the autonomic nervous system, as well as their roles in maintaining homeostasis.

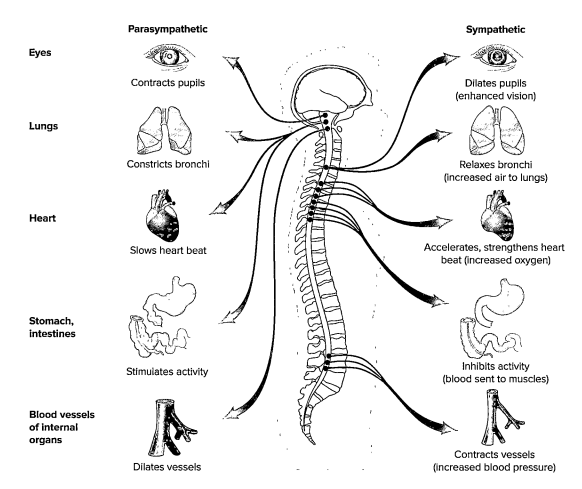

Parasympathetic		Sympathetic
Eyes		
Contracts pupils		Dilates pupils (enhanced vision)
Lungs		
Constricts bronchi		Relaxes bronchi (increased air to lungs)
Heart		
Slows heart beat		Accelerates, strengthens heart beat (increased oxygen)
Stomach, intestines		
Stimulates activity		Inhibits activity (blood sent to muscles)
Blood vessels of internal organs		
Dilates vessels		Contracts vessels (increased blood pressure)

FIGURE 3.7 The sympathetic branch of the autonomic nervous system arouses the body and speeds up its vital processes, whereas the parasympathetic division slows down body processes. The two divisions work together to maintain equilibrium within the body.

system so that blood can be transferred to the muscles, increases your rate of respiration so your body can get more oxygen, and, in general, mobilizes your body to confront the stressor.

Compared with the sympathetic branch, which tends to act as a unit, the parasympathetic system is far more specific in its opposing actions, affecting one or a few organs at a time. The **parasympathetic nervous system** slows down body processes and maintains or returns you to a state of rest. Thus, your sympathetic system speeds up your heart rate; your parasympathetic system slows it down. By working together to maintain equilibrium in our internal organs, the two divisions can maintain **homeostasis,** a delicately balanced or constant internal state. Some acts also require a coordinated sequence of sympathetic and parasympathetic activities. For example, sexual function in the male involves penile erection (through parasympathetic dilation of blood vessels) followed by ejaculation (a primarily sympathetic function; Masters et al., 1988).

The Central Nervous System

More than any other system in our body, the central nervous system distinguishes us from other creatures. This system contains the spinal cord, which connects most parts of the peripheral nervous system with the brain, and the brain itself.

The Spinal Cord

Most nerves enter and leave the central nervous system by way of the spinal cord, a structure that in a human adult is 40 to 45 centimetres long and about 2.5 centimetres in diameter. The spinal cord's neurons are protected by the vertebrae (bones of the spine). When the spinal cord is viewed in cross-section (Figure 3.8), its central portion resembles an *H* or a butterfly. The H-shaped portion consists largely of grey-coloured neuron cell bodies and their interconnections. Surrounding the grey matter are white-coloured myelinated axons that connect various levels of the spinal cord with each other and with the higher centres of the brain. Entering the back side of the spinal cord along its length are sensory nerves. Motor nerves exit the spinal cord's front side.

Some simple stimulus-response sequences, known as *spinal reflexes,* can be triggered at the level of the spinal cord without any involvement of the brain. For example, if you touch something hot, sensory receptors in your skin trigger nerve impulses in sensory nerves that flash into your spinal cord and synapse inside with interneurons. The interneurons then excite

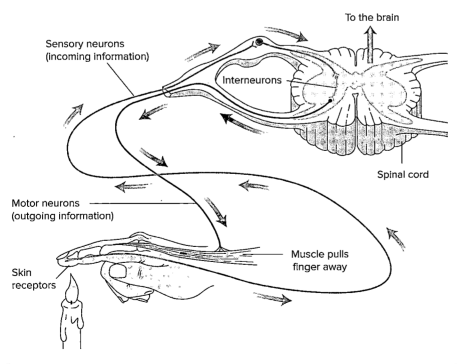

FIGURE 3.8 A cross-section of the spinal cord shows the organization of sensory and motor nerves. Sensory and motor nerves enter and exit the spinal cord on both sides of the spinal column. Interneurons within the H-shaped spinal grey matter can serve a connective function, as shown here, but in many cases, sensory neurons also can synapse directly with motor neurons. At this level of the nervous system, reflex activity is possible without involving the brain.

Labels in figure: To the brain; Sensory neurons (incoming information); Interneurons; Spinal cord; Motor neurons (outgoing information); Muscle pulls finger away; Skin receptors

motor neurons that send impulses to your hand so that it pulls away from the hot object. Other interneurons simultaneously carry the "Hot!" message up the spinal cord to your brain, but it is a good thing that you don't have to wait for the brain to tell you what to do in such emergencies. Getting messages to and from the brain takes slightly longer, so the spinal cord reflex system significantly reduces reaction time, and, in this case, potential tissue damage.

The Brain

13. How do spinal reflexes occur?

The 1.4 kilograms of protein, fat, and fluid that you carry around inside your skull is the real "you." It is also the most complex structure in the known universe and the only one that can wonder about itself. As befits this biological marvel, your brain is the most active energy consumer of all your body organs. Although the brain accounts for only about 2 percent of your total body weight, it consumes about 20 percent of the oxygen you use in a resting state (Simon, 2007). Moreover, the brain never rests; its rate of energy metabolism is relatively constant day and night. In fact, when you dream, the brain's metabolic rate actually increases slightly (Simon, 2007).

How can this delicate ball of greyish tissue discover the principle of relativity, build the Hubble Telescope, and produce great works of art, music, and literature? Answering such questions requires the ability to study the brain and how it functions. To do so, neuroscientists use a diverse set of tools and procedures.

Unlocking the Secrets of the Brain

More has been learned in the past three decades about the brain and its role in behaviour than was known in all the preceding ages. This knowledge explosion is due in large part to revolutionary technical advances that have provided scientists with new research tools, as well as to the contributions of psychological research on brain–behaviour relations. Investigators use a variety of methods to study the brain's structures and activities.

Neuropsychological tests.

14. Describe four methods used to study brain–behaviour relations.

Psychologists have developed a variety of *neuropsychological tests* to measure verbal and non-verbal behaviours that are known to be affected by particular types of brain damage (Vakil, 2012). These tests are used in clinical evaluations of people who may have suffered brain damage through accident or disease. They are also important research tools. For example, Figure 3.9 shows a portion of a Trail Making Test, used to test memory and planning. Scores on the test give an indication of the type and severity

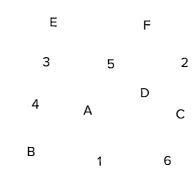

FIGURE 3.9 The Trail Making Test consists of a randomly scattered set of numbers and letters. On this timed test, the patient must connect the numbers and letters consecutively with a continuous line, or "trail" (i.e., A to 1 to B to 2 to C to 3, and so on). People with certain kinds of brain damage have trouble alternating between the numbers and letters because they cannot retain a plan in memory long enough, and poor test performance reflects this deficit.

of damage the person may have. Neuropsychological tests of this kind have provided much information about brain–behaviour relations.

Destruction and stimulation techniques. Experimental studies are another useful method of learning about the brain (Tatlisumak & Fisher, 2006). Researchers can produce brain damage (lesions) under carefully controlled conditions in which specific nervous tissue is destroyed with electricity, with cold or heat, or with chemicals. They also can surgically remove some portion of the brain and study the consequences. Most experiments of this kind are performed on animals, but humans also can be studied when accident or disease produces a specific lesion or when abnormal brain tissue must be surgically removed.

An alternative to destroying neurons is stimulating them, which typically produces opposite effects. A specific region of the brain can be stimulated by a mild electric current or by chemicals that excite neurons. Electrodes can be permanently implanted so that the region of interest can be stimulated repeatedly. Some of these electrodes are so tiny that they can stimulate individual neurons. In chemical stimulation studies, a tiny tube is inserted into the brain so that a small amount of the chemical can be delivered directly to the area to be studied. The neurosurgeon Wilder Penfield, of the Montreal Neurological Institute, pioneered brain surgery with an awake, interacting patient. Penfield stimulated specific points of cortex with a mild electrical current in an attempt to map out the functions of the cerebral cortex (see the *Research Foundations* feature).

Research Foundations

WILDER PENFIELD AND A CORTICAL MAP

Introduction

The idea that specific behaviours could be traced to specific brain areas emerged during the 19th century. The physiologists Gustav Fritsch and Eduard Hitzig found that electrical stimulation of discrete areas of a dog brain would reliably produce movements. The English neurologist John Hughlings Jackson published a series of papers detailing his observations of the behaviour of patients with brain damage. Paul Broca and Carl Wernicke found that damage to specific parts of the cerebral cortex were associated with specific language deficits. Such seminal work suggested that you could trace different functions, even sophisticated functions such as the ability to produce or comprehend language, to specific brain areas. The brain, it seemed, could be studied and understood much the way any other internal organ could be studied and understood.

Early in the 20th century, however, progress in understanding brain function within psychology slowed as behaviourism became the dominant orientation. Within psychology, the early and mid-20th century saw the work of Edward L. Thorndike, Ivan Pavlov, John B. Watson, and then B.F. Skinner gain prominence. Learning was king; it was learning, not brain structure, that determined what a person would become and do, learning was what turned one person into an artist and another into a thief. Furthermore, the behaviourists argued that psychology, as a science, should study only what was objectively observable: behaviour. According to the behaviourists, you could not tell, figuratively or literally, what was going on inside someone's head. But then a series of publications by a neurosurgeon rocked the field. The behaviourists had said that you could not study what was going on in the brain, but a neurosurgeon at the Montreal Neurological Institute was doing exactly that. The neurosurgeon was Wilder Penfield and studied the functions of specific areas of the brain with awake and alert surgical patients. Since the patients were fully conscious, they could describe and explain what they experienced during the procedure. Penfield performed brain surgery in this way primarily because the knowledge gained helped to guide his hand as a surgeon. As Penfield (1975) wrote, "The patient continued to be in the foreground of my concern, but in the background there was an urge to exploration" (ix).

Penfield worked mostly with patients who suffered from severe, uncontrollable epilepsy, and his task as a surgeon was to remove the damaged brain tissue that was responsible for the epileptic seizures. Since there are no pain receptors within the CNS, a patient could have local anaesthetics applied to the scalp and remain awake and alert during surgery without experiencing any undue discomfort. With the cooperation of such patients, Penfield explored the effects of small levels of electrical current applied to specific points on the surface of the cerebral cortex (Figure 3.10).

Method

The patient would have local anaesthetics applied to the scalp and remain awake and alert during surgery. When the brain was exposed, small levels of electrical current were applied to specific points on the surface of the cerebral cortex. Patients provided verbal reports of what they experienced during the stimulation and any visible body movement would be noted. Patient reports and the doctors' observations were transcribed for later analysis. Application of the electrical stimulation was done blind; the patient did not know where Penfield would stimulate and whether it would be applied to a new site or a previously tested site.

Results

Much of Penfield's early work concentrated on areas surrounding the central sulcus, the large fold separating the frontal cortex and the parietal cortex. Stimulation in front of this fold, within the frontal cortex, produced movement, and the movement produced was reliably related to the specific part of the cortex stimulated. For example, stimulation deep within the fold elicited movement of the toes and the feet, while stimulation to the side elicited movement of the face, mouth, or tongue. Stimulation behind the fold, in the parietal cortex, produced no movement; rather patients

The Canadian Press Archive Photo

FIGURE 3.10 Internationally renowned Montreal neurologist Wilder Penfield.

continued

reported somatic sensory experiences, such as a light touch, a brush, or an itch. The effects were repeatable and consistent across different patients. Penfield mapped the body onto the brain and his work produced the first functional maps of the motor cortex and sensory cortex (similar to the one in Figure 3.11).

Discussion

If Penfield had mapped only the motor cortex and the somatosensory cortex, his contribution to understanding the human brain would have been substantial, but Penfield also explored other areas of cortex, as guided by the surgical situation. Here, now, were reports not just of motor control and experiencing sensations of touch, but reports from patients of smelling roses, hearing voices, and recalling memories from their past—experiences likened to déjà vu elicited by mild electrical stimulation of the brain. In describing the reports of one patient, known as D.F., Penfield wrote, "D.F. could hear the instruments playing a melody. I re-stimulated the same point thirty times (!) trying to mislead her, and dictated each response to a stenographer. Each time I re-stimulated, she heard the melody again" (1975, p. 22). Another patient, M.M., reported somatic sensations, such as a tingling in the left thumb in response to stimulation at one point, but in response to stimulation of the temporal lobe, there were memories, or parts of memories: "activations of the stream of consciousness from the past" (Penfield, 1975, p. 24). The reports of memories were reliable within the same patient but less consistent across patients than the motor and somatosensory effects. In a minority of cases, the stimulation elicited unequivocal reports of memories or complex experiences such as hearing music, but in most cases, there was no subjective experience or only something vague and poorly defined.

Penfield mapped the body onto the brain for motor control and the sense of touch, and provided early tantalizing hints about the functions of the temporal lobes. In the decades since Penfield performed surgery, our interpretation of his results has grown increasingly sophisticated and our tools more elaborate and less invasive, although similar cortical mapping is still used. Our modern understanding of the cerebral cortex, like modern neurosurgery, owes a great deal to the pioneering work of Wilder Penfield.

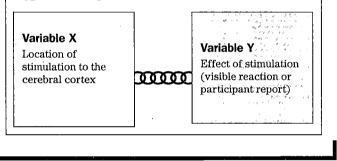

Design

Question: What are the functions of different areas of the cerebral cortex?

Type of Study: *Correlational*

Variable X
Location of stimulation to the cerebral cortex

Variable Y
Effect of stimulation (visible reaction or participant report)

A recent advance in these techniques is **transcranial magnetic stimulation** or **TMS** (Van De Ruit, Perenboom & Grey, 2015). TMS uses a magnetic coil placed close to the person's head to generate a magnetic field that disrupts activity in the brain region just under the coil. This allows the activity of specific brain areas to be disrupted temporarily without any form of surgery or other invasive action. Together with its use to explore the functions of brain areas close to the scalp, TMS has also been used to treat stroke, multiple sclerosis, migraine, and some chronic pain diseases (Groppa et al., 2012; Lefaucheur et al., 2012).

Electrical recording. Because electrodes can record brain activity as well as stimulate it, it is possible to "eavesdrop" on the electrical conversations occurring within the brain. Neurons' electrical activity can be measured by inserting small electrodes into particular areas of the brain or even into individual neurons.

In addition to measuring individual voices, scientists can tune in to "crowd noise" by placing larger electrodes on the scalp to measure the activity of large groups of neurons with the **electroencephalogram (EEG)** (Figure 3.12a, b). Although the EEG is a rather gross measure that taps the electrical activity of thousands of neurons in many parts of the brain, specific EEG patterns correspond to certain states of consciousness, such as wakefulness and sleep. Clinicians also use the EEG to detect abnormal electrical patterns that signal the presence of brain disorders. Researchers are especially interested in changes in the EEG record that accompany specific psychological events, such as presentation of a sensory stimulus. Changes in the EEG that accompany such events are called *event-related potentials* (ERPs).

Brain imaging. The newest tools of discovery are imaging techniques that permit neuroscientists to peer into the living brain (Figure 3.12c). The most important of these technological "windows" are CT scans, PET scans, and magnetic resonance imaging (MRI). CT scans and MRIs are used to visualize brain structure, whereas

15. How are CT scans, PET scans, and MRIs produced, and how is each used in brain research?

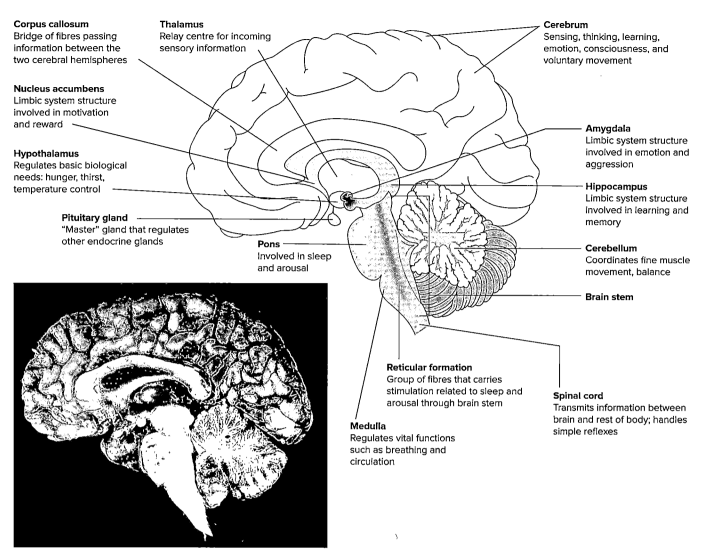

Corpus callosum
Bridge of fibres passing information between the two cerebral hemispheres

Thalamus
Relay centre for incoming sensory information

Cerebrum
Sensing, thinking, learning, emotion, consciousness, and voluntary movement

Nucleus accumbens
Limbic system structure involved in motivation and reward

Hypothalamus
Regulates basic biological needs: hunger, thirst, temperature control

Amygdala
Limbic system structure involved in emotion and aggression

Hippocampus
Limbic system structure involved in learning and memory

Pituitary gland
"Master" gland that regulates other endocrine glands

Pons
Involved in sleep and arousal

Cerebellum
Coordinates fine muscle movement, balance

Brain stem

Reticular formation
Group of fibres that carries stimulation related to sleep and arousal through brain stem

Spinal cord
Transmits information between brain and rest of body; handles simple reflexes

Medulla
Regulates vital functions such as breathing and circulation

(inset): © Martin M. Rotker/Science Source/Photo Researchers, Inc.

FIGURE 3.11 The major structures of the brain and their functions are shown as they would appear if the brain was sectioned at its midline, as in the photo.

PET scans and fMRIs allow scientists to view brain activity (Bremner, 2005).

Developed in the 1970s, **computerized axial tomography (CT) scans** use X-ray technology to study brain structures (Andreason, 1998). A highly focused beam of X-rays takes pictures of narrow slices of the brain. A computer analyzes the X-rayed slices and creates pictures of the brain's interior from many different angles (Figure 3.12d). Pinpointing where injuries or deterioration have occurred helps to clarify relations between brain damage and psychological functioning. CT scans are 100 times more sensitive than standard X-ray procedures, and the technological advance was so dramatic that its developers, Allan Cormack and Godfrey Hounsfield, were awarded the 1979 Nobel Prize for Medicine.

Whereas CT scans provide pictures of brain structures, **positron emission tomography (PET) scans** measure brain activity, including metabolism, blood flow, and neurotransmitter activity (Hornak, 2000; Ron & David, 1997). PET is based on the fact that glucose, a natural sugar, is the major nutrient of neurons. Thus, when neurons are active, they consume more glucose. To prepare a patient for a PET scan, a harmless form of radioactive glucose is injected into the bloodstream and travels to the brain. The energy emitted by the radioactive substance is measured by the PET scan, and the data are fed into a computer that uses the readings to produce a colour picture of the brain on a display screen (Figure 3.12c, g). Researchers can tell how active particular neurons are by measuring

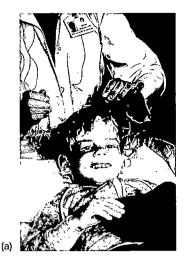

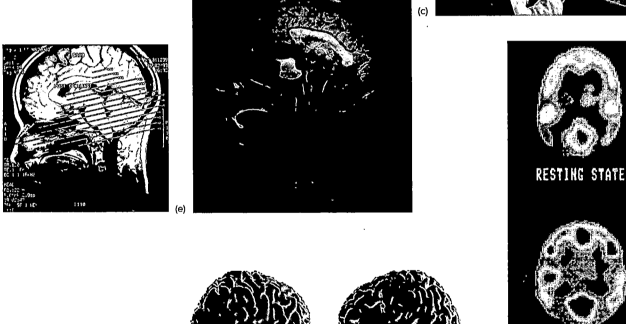

FIGURE 3.12 Measuring brain activity. (a) The electroencephalogram (EEG) records the activity of large groups of neurons in the brain through a series of electrodes attached to the scalp. (b) The results appear on an EEG readout. (c) Various brain scanning machines, such as the one shown here, produce a number of different images. (d) The CT scan uses narrow beams of X-rays to construct a composite picture of brain structures. (e) MRI scanners produce vivid pictures of brain structures. (f) Functional MRI (fMRI) procedures take images in rapid succession, showing neural activity as it occurs. (g) PET scans record the amount of radioactive substance that collects in various brain regions to assess brain activity.

the amount of radioactive glucose that accumulates in them. If a person is performing a mental reasoning task, for example, then a researcher can tell by the glucose concentration pattern which parts of the brain were activated by the task (Raichle, 1994).

Magnetic resonance imaging (MRI) combines features of CT and PET scans and can be used to study both brain structures and brain activity (Chakeres, Nornstein, & Kangarlu, 2000). MRI creates images based on how atoms in living tissue respond to a magnetic pulse delivered by the device. MRI can make out details one-tenth the size of what CT scans can detect, and it distinguishes much better between different types of brain tissue (Leondes, 1997). To obtain an MRI, the researcher places the part of the body to be studied in the hollow core of a long magnetic cylinder and exposes the atoms in the subject's body to a uniform magnetic field. The field is then altered, and when the magnetic field is shut off, the magnetic energy absorbed by the atoms in the tissue emits a small electrical voltage. The voltage is picked up by detectors and relayed to a computer for analysis. In addition to providing colour images of the tissue, MRI also can tell researchers which chemicals (such as neurotransmitters) are active in the tissue (Figure 3.12e).

The conventional MRI yields pictures taken several minutes apart. A *functional MRI (fMRI)* can produce pictures of blood flow in the brain taken less than a second apart (Baert et al., 1999). Researchers now, quite literally, can watch "live" presentations as different regions of the brain "light up" when subjects are given various types of tasks to perform. Researchers thereby can identify brain regions involved in specific psychological functions (Figure 3.12f).

Advances in brain research have made this area one of the most exciting frontiers of psychology. Driven by their intense desire to "know thyself," researchers studying the brain are beginning to expose its many secrets. Yet many important questions remain, which should not surprise us, for, as one observer noted, "If the brain were so simple that we could understand it, we would be so simple that we couldn't" (Pugh, 1977).

The Hierarchical Brain: Structures and Behavioural Functions

In an evolutionary sense, your brain is far older than you are, for it represents perhaps 500 million years of evolutionary development and fine-tuning (Striedter, 2005). The human brain can be likened to a living archaeological site, with the more recently developed structures built atop structures from the distant evolutionary past. The structures at the brain's core govern the basic physiological functions, such as breathing and heart rate, that keep us alive. These we share with all other vertebrates (animals having backbones). Built upon these basic structures are newer systems that involve progressively more complex functions: sensing, emoting, wanting, thinking, reasoning. Evolutionary theorists believe that as genetic variation and recombination sculpted these newer structures over time, natural selection favoured their retention because animals who had them were more likely to survive in changing environments. The crowning feature of brain development is the cerebrum, the biological seat of Einstein's scientific genius, Mozart's creativity, Mother Teresa's compassion, and that which makes you a unique human being.

The major structures of the human brain, together with their psychological functions, are shown in Figure 3.12. The brain traditionally has been divided into three major subdivisions: the hindbrain, which is the lowest and most primitive level of the brain; the midbrain, which lies above the hindbrain; and the forebrain.

16. In what sense might the structure of the human brain mirror evolutionary development?

In Review

- The nervous system is composed of sensory neurons, motor neurons, and interneurons (associative neurons). Its two major divisions are the central nervous system, consisting of the brain and spinal cord, and the peripheral nervous system. The latter is divided into the somatic system, which has sensory and motor functions, and the autonomic nervous system, which directs the activity of the body's internal organs and glands.

- The spinal cord contains sensory neurons and motor neurons. Interneurons inside the spinal cord serve a connective function between the two. Simple stimulus-response connections can occur as spinal reflexes.

- The autonomic nervous system consists of sympathetic and parasympathetic divisions. The sympathetic system has an arousal function and tends to act as a unit. The parasympathetic system slows down body processes and is more specific in its actions. Together, the two divisions maintain a state of internal balance, or homeostasis.

- Discoveries about brain–behaviour relations are made by using techniques such as neuropsychological tests, electrical and chemical stimulation of the brain, electrical recording, and brain-imaging techniques. Recently developed methods for producing computer-generated pictures of structures and processes within the living brain include CT and PET scans and MRI.

17. Which behavioural functions are controlled by the hindbrain structures, namely, the medulla, the pons, and the cerebellum? What occurs with damage to these structures?

The Hindbrain

As the spinal cord enters the brain, it enlarges to form the structures that compose the stalk-like **brain stem**. Attached to the brain stem is the other major portion of the hindbrain, the cerebellum.

The brain stem: Life support systems. The medulla is the first structure encountered after leaving the spinal cord. Well developed at birth, the 3.8 centimetre–long **medulla** plays an important role in vital body functions, such as heart rate and respiration. Because of your medulla, these functions occur automatically. Damage to the medulla usually results in death or, at best, the need to be maintained on life support systems. Suppression of medulla activity can occur at high levels of alcohol intoxication, resulting in death by heart or respiratory failure (Blessing, 1997).

The medulla is also a two-way thoroughfare for all the sensory and motor nerve tracts coming up from the spinal cord and descending from the brain. Most of these tracts cross over within the medulla, so the left side of the brain receives sensory input from and exerts motor control over the right side of the body, and the right side of the brain serves the left side of the body. Why this crossover occurs is one of the unsolved mysteries of brain function.

The **pons** (meaning *bridge* in Latin) lies just above the medulla, and it indeed serves as a bridge carrying nerve impulses between higher and lower levels of the nervous system. The pons also has clusters of neurons that help to regulate sleep and are involved in dreaming, and it contains motor neurons that control the muscles and glands of the face and the neck. Like the medulla, the pons helps to control vital functions, especially respiration, and damage to it can produce death.

The cerebellum: Motor coordination centre. The cerebellum (meaning *little brain* in Latin) does indeed look like a miniature brain attached to the rear of the brain stem directly above the pons. Its wrinkled cortex, or covering, consists mainly of grey cell bodies (grey matter). The **cerebellum** is concerned primarily with muscular movement coordination, but it also plays a role in certain types of learning and memory.

Specific motor movements are initiated in higher brain centres, but their timing and coordination depend on the cerebellum (De Zeeuw & Cicirata, 2005). The cerebellum regulates complex, rapidly changing movements that require exquisite timing, such as those of a ballet dancer or a competitive diver. Within the animal kingdom, cats have an especially well-developed cerebellum, helping to account for

their graceful movement abilities (Altman & Bayer, 1996).

The motor control functions of the cerebellum are easily disrupted by alcohol, producing the coordination difficulties that police look for in their roadside tests of sobriety (Ito, 1984). Intoxicated people may be unable to walk a straight line or touch their nose with their index finger (Figure 3.13). Physical damage to the cerebellum results in severe motor disturbances characterized by jerky, uncoordinated movements, as well as an inability to perform habitual movements, such as walking. The behavioural effects of a rapidly developing cerebellar tumour are apparent in the following clinical case:

> Ed could no longer walk a straight line. His gait involved wide separation of his legs. The timing of his steps was jerky and irregular, causing him to lurch from side to side. . . . By the fifth day he could no longer stand without assistance, and he began to display rapid and jerky eye movements. Ed was admitted to a hospital, where imaging techniques revealed a cerebellar tumor. Surgical removal of the tumor resulted in a marked improvement in his motor coordination. (Gazzaniga et al., 1979)

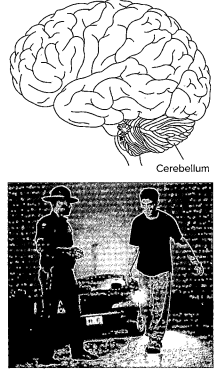

Cerebellum

© Brand X Pictures

FIGURE 3.13 The movement-control functions of the cerebellum are easily disrupted by alcohol, providing the neural basis for the sobriety tests administered by police.

The Midbrain

Lying just above the hindbrain, the **midbrain** contains clusters of sensory and motor neurons, as well as many sensory and motor fibre tracts that connect higher and lower portions of the nervous system. The sensory portion of the midbrain contains important relay centres for the visual and auditory systems. Here, nerve impulses from the eyes and ears are organized and sent to forebrain structures involved in visual and auditory perception (Kolb & Whishaw, 2003). The midbrain also contains motor neurons that control eye movements. For example, if you see movement out of the corner of your eye, midbrain activity causes your eyes to swing toward the source of the movement to identify it.

The reticular formation: The brain's gatekeeper. Buried within the midbrain is a finger-shaped structure that extends from the hindbrain up into the lower portions of the forebrain. This structure receives its name from its resemblance under a microscope to a *reticulum*, or net. The **reticular formation** acts as a kind of sentry, both alerting higher centres of the brain that messages are coming and then either blocking those messages or allowing them to go forward. The reticular formation has an *ascending* part, which sends input to higher regions of the brain to alert it, and a *descending* portion, through which higher brain centres can either admit or block out sensory input.

The reticular formation has attracted a great deal of interest from psychologists because of its central role in consciousness, sleep, and attention. The ascending reticular formation rouses higher centres in the brain, preparing them to receive input from our sense organs. Without reticular stimulation of higher brain regions, sensory messages do not register in conscious awareness, even though the nerve impulses may reach the appropriate higher areas of the brain. It is as if the brain is not "awake" enough to notice them. In fact, some general anaesthetics work by deactivating neurons of the ascending reticular formation, producing a state of unconsciousness in which the sensory impulses that ordinarily would be experienced as pain never "register" in the sensory areas of the brain involved in pain perception (Simon, 2007).

Sleep, wakefulness, and attention also are affected by the reticular formation. In a classic series of experiments in the late 1940s, researchers discovered that electrical stimulation of different portions of the reticular formation can produce instant sleep in a wakeful cat and sudden

wakefulness in a sleeping animal (Marshall & Magoun, 1997). As you might expect, severe damage to the reticular formation can produce a permanent coma (Pendlebury, 2007).

Attention is an active process in which only important or meaningful sensory inputs get through to our consciousness. Other inputs have to be toned down or completely blocked out or we'd be overwhelmed by stimulation. The descending reticular formation plays an important part in this process, serving as a kind of gate through which some inputs are admitted while others are blocked out by signals coming down from higher brain centres (Van Zomeren & Brouwer, 1994). If you can focus on these words and "block out" distractions such as other sights, sounds, and body sensations, then your reticular formation is doing its job.

The Forebrain

The most profound biological difference between your brain and that of other animals is the size and complexity of your forebrain, or *cerebrum*. The **forebrain** consists of two large cerebral hemispheres, a left side and a right side, that wrap around the brain stem. The outer portion of the forebrain has a thin covering, or cortex, and there are a number of important structures buried in the central regions of the hemispheres.

The thalamus: The brain's sensory input. The thalamus is located above the midbrain. It resembles two small footballs, one within each cerebral hemisphere. The **thalamus** is an important sensory processing and relay station, sometimes likened to a switchboard that organizes inputs from sense organs and routes them to the appropriate areas of the brain. The visual, auditory, and body senses (balance and equilibrium) all have major relay stations in the thalamus. In each case, nerve tracts from the sensory receptors (e.g., the eyes or the ears) are sent to specific areas of the thalamus. There they synapse with neurons that send the messages on their way to the higher brain regions that create our perceptions (Jones, 2006). Recent evidence indicates that the thalamus has functions that go beyond that of a simple relay station; it functions as an active, dynamic filter selecting what information is passed to higher brain regions (Alitto & Usrey, 2015). The only sense that does not send information through the thalamus is the evolutionarily ancient sense of smell.

The basal ganglia: Movement Surrounding and enveloping the thalamus is a group of at least five distinct structures that are collectively called the **basal ganglia.** The basal ganglia is

18. Describe the roles played by the ascending and descending reticular formation. Why is it called the "brain's gatekeeper"?

19. What is the role of the thalamus in sensory input, and possibly in thought and perceptual disorders?

critical for voluntary motor control. Whereas the cerebellum is critical for controlling reflexive, automatic, and rapid movements, the basal ganglia plays an important role in the deliberate and voluntary control of movement, especially in initiating voluntary movements. That you can reach out and pick up your coffee mug when you want to indicates that your basal ganglia is functioning. One example that illustrates the role of the basal ganglia is Parkinson's disease. In Parkinson's disease, the neurons that supply dopamine to the basal ganglia degenerate and die. Since dopamine is lost from the basal ganglia, the basal ganglia does not function properly, and the ability to initiate voluntary movement is lost. Initially, the signs of Parkinson's disease are small tremors of the hands and head, but as the basal ganglia loses more and more of its supply of dopamine, the tremors become shaking, then slow and jerky movements, then slow and jerky movements that can be performed only if there is assistance with initiating the movement. For example, many spouses, family, or friends of patients with Parkinson's disease have stories about how the patients will stop at a curb or a corner and stay frozen, apparently unable to move, but with a small push to get them started, they will begin walking again. When the basal ganglia has been largely depleted of dopamine and hence does not function, there is complete paralysis. Patients at the advanced stages of Parkinson's disease cannot move when they want to; they cannot get up from a chair, get out of bed, or hold a book. If, however, the movement depends on other, older brain structures, such as the cerebellum, they can perform it.

The hypothalamus: Biological drives. The hypothalamus (literally, "under the thalamus") consists of tiny groups of neuron cell bodies that lie at the base of the brain, above the roof of the mouth. The **hypothalamus** plays a major role in controlling many different basic biological drives, including sexual behaviour, temperature regulation, eating, drinking, aggression, and the expression of emotion. Damage to the hypothalamus can disrupt all these behaviours. For example, destruction of one area of a male's hypothalamus results in a complete loss of sexual behaviour; damage to another portion produces an overwhelming urge to eat that results in extreme obesity (Morrison, 2006).

The hypothalamus has important connections with the endocrine system, the body's collection of hormone-producing glands. Through its connection with the pituitary gland (the master gland that exerts control over the other glands of the endocrine system), the hypothalamus directly controls many hormonal secretions that regulate sexual development and behaviour, metabolism, and reactions to stress.

The limbic system: Memory and goal-directed behaviour. As we continue our journey up through the brain, we come to the limbic system: a set of structures lying deep within the cerebral hemispheres. These structures, which are shaped like a wishbone, have an important partnership with the hypothalamus. The **limbic system** helps to coordinate behaviours needed to satisfy motivational and emotional urges that arise in the hypothalamus, and it is also involved in memory. The limbic system appears to organize many instinctive activities in lower animals, such as mating, attacking, feeding, and fleeing from danger (Davis, 1992). Human behaviours are similarly organized into goal-directed sequences. If certain parts of your limbic system were injured, you would be unable to carry out organized sequences of actions to satisfy your needs. A small distraction would make you forget what you had set out to do.

Two key structures in the limbic system are the hippocampus and the amygdala. The **hippocampus** is involved in forming and retrieving memories. Damage to the hippocampus can result in severe memory impairment for recent events and an inability to transfer information from short-term memory to long-term memory (Scoville & Milner, 1957; Isaacson, 2002). The **amygdala** organizes emotional response patterns, particularly those linked to aggression and fear (LeDoux, 1998). Electrically stimulating certain areas of the amygdala causes animals to snarl and assume aggressive postures (Figure 3.14), whereas stimulation of other areas results in a fearful inability to respond aggressively, even in self-defence. For example, a normally aggressive and hungry cat will cower in fear from a tiny mouse placed in its cage. The amygdala is a key part of a larger control system for anger and fear that also involves other brain regions (Borod, 2000). An interesting recent study of two individuals with localized, bilateral damage to the amygdala found that the typical avoidance of risky financial decisions (so-called "loss aversion") was dramatically reduced in both patients (De Martino, Camerer, & Adolphs, 2010). This finding suggests that the amygdala has a role in inhibiting potentially risky actions.

An interesting feature of the amygdala is that it can produce emotional responses without the

20. What role does the hypothalamus have in motivated behaviour, hunger, pleasure-pain, and hormonal functions?

21. What is the possible relation between the hypothalamus and the limbic system regarding emotion and motivation? What roles do the hippocampus and amygdala play in psychological functions?

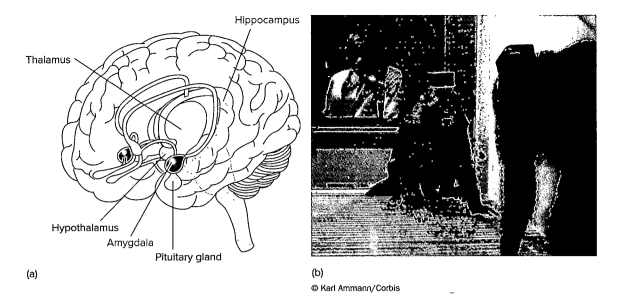

Thalamus

Hippocampus

Hypothalamus

Amygdala

Pituitary gland

(a)

(b)

© Karl Ammann/Corbis

FIGURE 3.14 The limbic system structures are shown in (a). Electrical stimulation of the amygdala, as in (b), can produce an immediate aggressive response.

higher centres of the brain "knowing" that we are emotionally aroused. This phenomenon may provide an explanation for clinicians' observations of "unconscious" emotional responses (LeDoux, 1998).

In 1953, James Olds and Peter Milner were conducting an experiment to study the effects of electrical stimulation of the reticular formation in rats. One of the electrodes missed the target and was mistakenly implanted in the hypothalamus. The investigators noticed that whenever this rat was stimulated, it repeated whatever it had just done, as if it had been rewarded for that behaviour. In a variety of learning situations, other animals with similarly implanted electrodes also learned and performed behaviours in order to receive what was clearly an electrical reward. Some rats would press a lever thousands of times an hour to receive the electrical stimulation, and would continue to do so until they dropped from exhaustion. The scientists concluded that they had found the "pleasure centre" in the brain (Olds, 1958; Olds and Milner, 1954; White & Milner, 1992; Wise, 1996).

Humans who have had electrodes implanted in their brains to search for abnormal brain tissue have reported experiencing pleasure when electrically stimulated in these same brain regions (Heath, 1972). One patient reportedly proposed marriage to the experimenter while being so stimulated. Thus, a misplaced electrode led to a discovery that neural events have important roles in motivation, and suggested that the hypothalamus was the brain area critical for motivation and reward.

Electrical stimulation of the hypothalamus activates neurons within that brain region and also activates axons that are going from neuron cell bodies in the midbrain to a limbic structure called the **nucleus accumbens**. It is the activation of axons going to the nucleus accumbens that is important for reward and motivation (Wise, 1996; Wise & Rompre, 1989). For example, Roy Wise, then of Concordia University in Montreal, has shown that the reward value of electrical stimulation of the hypothalamus can be either amplified or diminished by drugs that enhance or block, respectively, dopamine actions within the nucleus accumbens (Wise, 2004). This brain area has also been linked to the rewarding and motivating effects of drugs of abuse. Drugs such as cocaine, amphetamines, opiates, nicotine, and alcohol, all stimulate the release of dopamine in the nucleus accumbens of the limbic system (Blum et al., 2012). Other researchers, such as Alain Gratton of McGill University, have found that naturally occurring rewards such as food, sexually relevant cues, and sexual behaviour also lead to the release of dopamine from axon terminals in the nucleus accumbens (Hernandez & Hoebel, 1988; Mitchell & Gratton, 1991; Phillips et al., 1992). Interestingly, Gratton has shown that not only do drugs of abuse and preferred foods activate the nucleus accumbens, but also cues that reliably predict the arrival of drugs or food have a similar effect (Gratton & Wise, 1994; Kiyatkin & Gratton, 1994).

The Cerebral Cortex: Crown of the Brain

The **cerebral cortex,** a two-thirds centimetre-thick sheet of grey (unmyelinated) cells that form the outermost layer of the human brain, is the crowning achievement of brain evolution. Fish and amphibians have no cerebral cortex, and the progression from more primitive to more advanced mammals is marked by a dramatic increase in the proportion of cortical tissue. In humans, the cortex constitutes fully 80 percent of brain tissue (Kolb & Whishaw, 2003; Simon, 2007).

The cerebral cortex is not essential for physical survival in the way that the brain stem structures are, but it is essential for a human quality of living. How much so is evident in this description of patients who, as a result of an accident during prenatal development, were born without a cerebral cortex:

Some of these individuals may survive for years, in one case of mine for twenty years. From these cases, it appears that the human [lacking a cortex] sleeps and wakes; . . . reacts to hunger, loud sounds, and crude visual stimuli by movement of eyes, eyelids, and facial muscles; . . . may see and hear, . . . may be able to taste and smell, to reject the unpalatable and accept such food as it likes. . . . [They can] utter crude sounds, can cry and smile, showing displeasure when hungry and pleasure, in a babyish way, when being sung to; [they] may be able to perform spontaneously crude [limb] movements. (Cairns, 1952, p. 109)

Because the cortex is wrinkled and convoluted, like a wadded-up piece of paper, a great amount of cortical tissue is compressed into a relatively small space inside the skull. Perhaps 75 percent of the cortex's total surface area lies within its *fissures,* or folds. Three of these fissures are important landmarks. One large fissure runs up the front and along the top of the brain, dividing it into right and left hemispheres. Another major fissure within each hemisphere divides the cerebrum into front and rear halves, and the third fissure runs from front to rear along the side of the brain. On the basis of these landmarks, neurologists have divided each hemisphere into four lobes: **frontal, parietal, occipital,** and **temporal** (Figure 3.15).

Each of the four cerebral lobes is associated with particular sensory and motor functions (also shown in Figure 3.15). Speech and skeletal motor functions are localized in the frontal lobe. The area governing body sensations is located in the parietal lobe immediately behind the *central fissure,* which separates the frontal and parietal lobes. The brain's visual area is located in the occipital lobe at the back of the brain. Finally, messages from the auditory system are sent to a region in the top of the temporal lobe (Robinson, 1997). Although different areas of cortex are associated with specific functions, many complex behaviours involve the integrated activity

22. What are the four lobes of the brain, and where are they located?

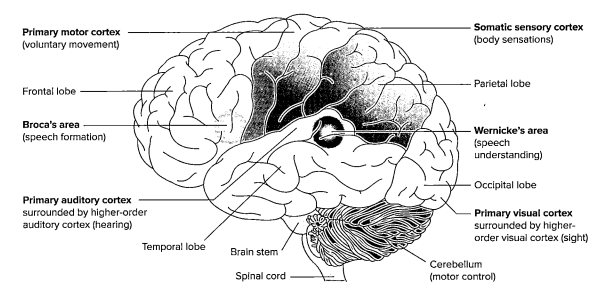

FIGURE 3.15 Division of the brain into frontal, parietal, occipital, and temporal lobes, and localization of sensory and motor functions in the cortex. The remainder is primarily association cortex, consisting of interneurons involved in complex psychological functions, such as perception and reasoning.

across many areas of cortex (see the *Focus on Neuroscience* feature). The large areas in Figure 3.15 that are not associated with sensory or motor functions (about three-fourths of the cortex) are *association cortex*, which are involved in mental processes such as thought, memory, and perception.

Most sensory systems send information to specific regions of the cerebral cortex. Motor systems that control the activity of skeletal muscles are situated in other cortical regions. The basic organization of the cortex's sensory and motor areas is quite similar in all mammals, from rats to humans. Let's explore these regions more closely.

The motor cortex. The **motor cortex**, which controls the 600 or more muscles involved in voluntary body movements, lies at the rear of the frontal lobe adjacent to the central fissure. Each hemisphere governs movement on the opposite side of the body. Thus, severe damage to the right motor cortex would produce paralysis in the left side of the body. The left side of Figure 3.16 shows the relative organization of function within the motor cortex. As you can see, specific body areas are represented in different parts of the motor cortex, and the amount of cortex devoted to each area depends on the complexity of the movements that are carried out by the body part. Note, for example, that the amount of cortical tissue devoted to your fingers is far greater than that devoted to your torso, even though your torso is much larger. If we electrically stimulate a particular point on the motor cortex, then movements occur in the muscles governed by that part of the cortex.

The sensory cortex. Specific areas of the cortex receive input from our sensory receptors. With the exception of taste and smell, at least one specific area in the cortex has been identified for each of the senses.

The **somatic sensory cortex** receives sensory input that gives rise to our sensations of heat, touch, cold, and our senses of balance and body movement (kinesthesis). It lies in the parietal lobe just behind the motor cortex, separated from it by the large fissure that divides the frontal lobe from the parietal lobe. As in the case of the motor system, each side of the body sends sensory input to the opposite hemisphere. Like the motor area next to it, the somatic sensory area

23. Differentiate between sensory, motor, and association cortex.

24. How are the somatic sensory and motor cortexes organized?

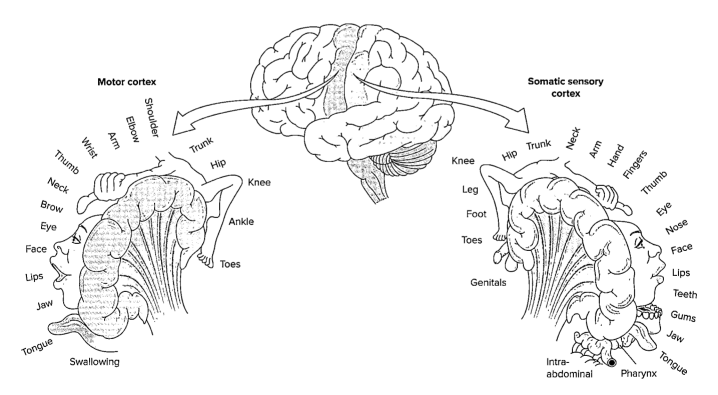

FIGURE 3.16 Both the somatic sensory cortex and the motor cortex are highly specialized so that every site is associated with a particular part of the body. The amount of cortex devoted to each body part is proportional to the sensitivity of that area's motor or sensory functions. Both the sensory and motor cortex are arranged in an upside-down fashion and serve the opposite side of the body.

Source: Adapted from Penfield/Rasmussen. *The Cerebral Cortex of Man.* © 1950 Gale, a part of Cengage Learning, Inc. Reproduced with permission. www.cengage.com/permissions.

is basically organized in an upside-down fashion, with the feet being represented near the top of the brain. Likewise, the amount of cortex devoted to each body area is directly proportional to that region's sensory sensitivity. The organization of the sensory cortex is shown on the right side of Figure 3.16, as is the proportion of cortex devoted to each body area. As far as your sensory cortex is concerned, you are mainly fingers, lips, and tongue. Notice also that the organization of the sensory cortex is such that the body structures it serves lie side by side with those in the motor cortex, an arrangement that enhances sensory-motor interactions in the same body area.

The senses of hearing and sight are well represented in the cortex. The auditory area lies on the surface of the temporal lobe at the side of each hemisphere. Each ear sends messages to the auditory areas of both hemispheres, so the loss of one temporal lobe has little effect on hearing. The major sensory area for vision lies at the rear of the occipital lobe. Here messages from the visual receptors are analyzed, integrated, and translated into sight. As in the auditory system, each eye sends input to both hemispheres.

Within each sensory area, neurons respond to particular aspects of the sensory stimulus; they are tuned in to specific aspects of the environment. Thus, certain cells in the visual cortex fire only when we look at a particular kind of stimulus, such as a vertical line or a corner (Hubel & Wiesel, 1979). In the auditory cortex, some neurons fire only in response to high tones, whereas others respond only to tones having some other specific frequency. Many of these single-cell responses are present at birth, suggesting that we are "pre-wired" to perceive many aspects of our sensory environment (Shair et al., 1991). Nonetheless, the sensory cortex, like other parts of the brain, is also sensitive to experience. For example, when people learn to read Braille, the area in the sensory cortex that receives input from the fingertips increases in size, making the person more sensitive to the tiny sets of raised dots (Pool, 1994).

The representation of the body along the somatosensory cortex shown in Figure 3.16 has the head oriented with the top of the face toward the top of the cortex and the chin lower down the side of the cortex. Philip Servos of Wilfrid Laurier University, together with colleagues at the University of California and the Robarts Research Institute of Western University, have provided evidence that this well-known representation may be wrong. Using fMRI measurements, Servos and colleagues found that stimulation of the chin increased activity within the somatosensory

cortex toward the top of the head, while stimulation of the forehead increased activity near the lower part of the somatosensory cortex (Servos, Engel, Gati, & Menon, 1999). That is, the representation of the face in the somatosensory cortex may be upside-down, with the chin toward the top. This position would better align the head with the rest of the body since an upside-down representation of the head within the somatosensory cortex would place the chin nearer the neck and shoulders.

Speech comprehension and production. Two specific areas that govern the understanding and production of speech are also located in the cortex (Figure 3.17). **Wernicke's area** in the temporal lobe is involved in language comprehension. The area is named for Carl Wernicke, who in 1874 discovered that damage to this cortical region left patients unable to understand written or spoken speech. **Broca's area** in the frontal lobe is necessary for normal speech production. The neural circuits in and around Broca's area are important for the ability to perform the sequences of fine-motor movements needed to speak, and are involved in the abilities to use grammar and find the correct

25. Where are Wernicke's and Broca's areas? How are they involved in speech?

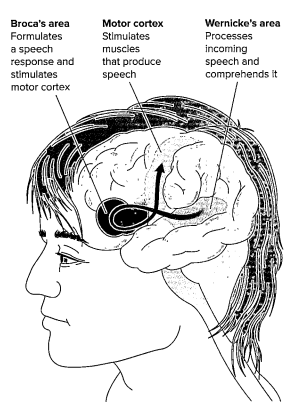

Broca's area	Motor cortex	Wernicke's area
Formulates a speech response and stimulates motor cortex	Stimulates muscles that produce speech	Processes incoming speech and comprehends it

FIGURE 3.17 Cortical areas involved in language. Wernicke's area is important in the comprehension of spoken or written speech. Broca's area is involved in the production of speech, and the motor cortex stimulates the speech production muscles.

word (Saffran, Schwartz, & Martin, 1980; Damasio, 1989). Its discoverer, Paul Broca, found that damage to this frontal area left patients with the ability to comprehend speech but not to express themselves in words or sentences. These two speech areas normally work in concert when you are conversing with another person. They allow you to comprehend what the other person is saying and to express your own thoughts (Werker & Tees, 1992). In this example, input is sent from the ears to the auditory cortex and is routed to Wernicke's area for comprehension. When you decide to reply, nerve impulses are sent from Wernicke's area to Broca's area, and impulses passed on from Broca's area to the motor cortex result in the mouthing of a verbal response. This sequence illustrates a key action principle of brain functioning: Even relatively simple acts usually involve the coordinated action of several brain regions.

Association cortex. Association cortex, found within all lobes of the cerebral cortex, is critically involved in the highest level of mental functions, including perception, language, and thought. These areas are sometimes referred to as "silent areas" because electrically stimulating them does not give rise to either sensory experiences or motor responses. This fact has probably helped to promote the widely cited myth that most humans use only 10 percent of their brain power. Nothing could be farther from the truth.

Damage to specific parts of the association cortex causes disruption or loss of functions such as speech, understanding, thinking, and problem solving. As we might expect, since the association cortex is involved in higher mental processes, the amount of association cortex increases dramatically as we move up the brain ladder from lower animals to human beings. It constitutes about 75 percent of the human cerebral cortex and accounts for humans' superior cognitive abilities. Our mass of association cortex has been described by one scientist as "evolution's missing link" (Skoyles, 1997). He suggests that its mental flexibility and learning capacity have allowed us to upgrade our cognitive skills and to acquire new mental skills specific to our human way of life, such as reading and mathematics, more quickly than could have occurred through natural selection alone. Pioneering work on how such activity is represented within the cortex was done by D.O. Hebb of McGill University (see Figure 3.18).

The importance of the association cortex is demonstrated in people who suffer from *agnosia*, the inability to identify familiar objects. One famous case was described by the neurologist

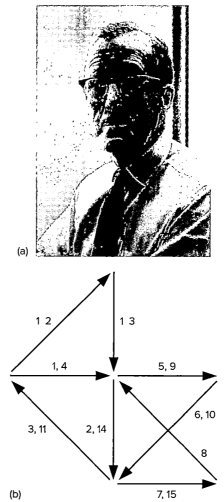

(a)

(b)

(photo): Chris F. Payne/The McGill News/McGill University Archives, Photographic Collection. PN000387

FIGURE 3.18 Donald Olding Hebb (1904–1985) was one of the towering figures in psychology and neuroscience during the 20th century. A native of Chester, Nova Scotia, Hebb received his undergraduate education at Dalhousie University and his Ph.D. at Harvard. After brief periods at the Montreal Neurological Institute, Queen's University, and the Yerkes Laboratories of Primate Biology, Hebb accepted a position at McGill University, where he published an enormously influential book, *The Organization of Behavior: A Neuropsychological Theory* (1949). Although he made many contributions, Hebb is best remembered and still frequently cited for his work on how learning, memory, and thought arise from activity within the cerebral cortex. Hebb proposed a mechanism for learning and memory (now called the *Hebb synapse*), an explanation of how groups of neurons formed circuits based on use (cell assemblies), and the idea that thought is the sequential activation of cell assemblies.

26. What is the role of the association cortex, the "silent areas"?

Oliver Sacks (1985). A patient, Dr. P., had suffered brain damage that disrupted communication between the visual cortex and cortical areas concerned with the nature of objects. Dr. P. could describe items in detail but could not identify them. On one occasion, "He reached out his hand and took hold of his wife's head, tried to lift it off, to put it on [his head]. He had apparently mistaken his wife for a hat!" (Sacks, 1985, p. 9).

The frontal lobes: The human difference. Some neuroscientists have suggested that the entire period of human evolutionary existence could well be termed the "age of the frontal lobe" (Krasnegor et al., 1997). This mass of cortex residing behind our eyes and forehead hardly exists in mammals such as mice and rats. The frontal lobes constitute about 3.5 percent of the cerebral cortex in the cat, 7 percent in the dog, and 17 percent in the chimpanzee. In a human, the frontal lobes constitute 29 percent of the cortex. The site of such human qualities as self-awareness, planning, initiative, and responsibility, the frontal lobes are in some respects the most mysterious and least understood part of the brain. As we explore in this chapter's *Frontiers* feature, the frontal cortex has recently been found to contain neurons that are active both when an activity is planned and performed, but also when watching another perform this action.

Early indications about the functions of the frontal cortex come from the tragic case of Phineas Gage. The year was 1848. As the Vermont winter approached, a railroad construction crew hurried to complete its work on a new track. As a blasting crew prepared its charges, the dynamite accidentally exploded. A spike more than a metre long and weighing almost 6 kilograms was propelled through the face and head of Phineas Gage, the 25-year-old foreman. The spike entered through the left cheek, passed through the brain, and emerged through the top of the skull (Figure 3.19). Dr. J.M. Harlow, who treated Gage, described the incident:

> The patient was thrown upon his back by the explosion, and gave a few convulsive motions of the extremities, but spoke in a few minutes. He . . . seemed perfectly conscious, but was becoming exhausted from the hemorrhage, . . . the blood pouring from the top of his head. . . . He bore his sufferings with firmness, and directed my attention to the hole in his cheek, saying, "the iron entered there and passed through my head." (Harlow, 1868, pp. 330–332)

Miraculously, Gage survived. Or did he?

> His physical health is good, and I am inclined to say that he has recovered. Has no pain in his head, but says it has a queer feeling that he is not able to describe. . . .

His contractors, who regarded him as the most efficient and capable foreman in their employ previous to his injury, considered the change in his mind so marked that they could not give him his place again. The equilibrium or balance, so to speak, between his intellectual faculties and animal propensities, seems to have been destroyed. He is fitful, irreverent, indulging at times in the grossest profanity (which was not previously his custom), manifesting but little deference for his fellows, impatient of restraint or advice when it conflicts with his desires . . . devising many plans of future operations, which are no sooner arranged than they are abandoned in turn for others. . . . His mind is radically changed, so decidedly that his friends and acquaintances say that he is "no longer Gage." (Harlow, 1868, pp. 339–340)

As the tragic accident to Phineas Gage shows us, biological and psychological processes are intimately related. Physical damage to Gage's brain changed his thinking and behaviour so radically that a psychologically different person emerged.

Much of what we know about the frontal lobes comes from detailed studies of patients who have experienced brain damage, starting with

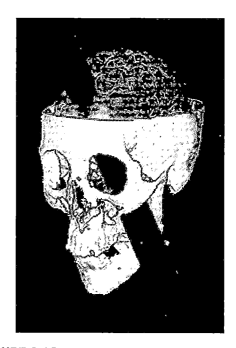

FIGURE 3.19 The brain damage suffered by Phineas Gage seemed to change him into a new person.
From: Damasio, H., Grabowski, T., Frank, R., Galaburda, A.M., Damasio, A.R.: The return of Phineas Gage: clues about the brain from the skull of a famous patient. *Science*, 264: 1102–1105, 1994.

Frontiers

MIRROR NEURONS AND AUTISM SPECTRUM DISORDER

A group of researchers at the University of Parma in Italy were studying the control of movement in monkeys when they made a surprising and completely unexpected discovery. The same neurons that became active when a monkey performed an action became active when it observed another monkey perform the same act (Rizzolatti et al., 1996; Rizzolatti & Sinigaglia, 2010). Not only did this happen when the monkey saw another monkey perform a behaviour, such as reaching for food, these neurons also became active when it saw one of the researchers reach for food. That is, these neurons seemed to react to the behaviour of another individual and what mattered was that the behaviour was a deliberate, intentional action that the monkey itself could perform in the future. These neurons are located most importantly in areas of the frontal cortex associated with the planning and execution of deliberate movements and in sensory areas of the parietal cortex (look back at Figure 3.15).

These neurons were named "mirror neurons" because they became active both when an individual performed an action and when that individual observed the same action performed by another. That is, these neurons "mirror" the behaviour of others. Whether I watch you reach for your coffee or I am planning and executing the same action to get my coffee, the activity in my mirror neurons is the same.

Mirror neurons have been suggested to serve a range of functions. One is that mirror neurons are important for observational learning. Observational learning is acquiring a new behaviour by watching someone else perform the behaviour (we will discuss observational learning in detail in Chapter 7). Mirror neurons that become active both when you watch someone perform a deliberate action and when you yourself perform that action would seem to be well-suited to a role in supporting observational learning (Molenberghs, Cunnington & Mattingley, 2009). We do not always imitate the behaviours we see others perform but mirror neurons still become active. This has led some to suggest that mirror neurons may instead contribute to our understanding of other peoples' behaviour (Gallese, 2013). They may also help us understand other peoples' emotional state and thus support reactions such as empathy (Braadbaart et al., 2014).

The exact functions of mirror neurons are still debated (Yang & Hofman, 2015), but it is clear that mirror neurons generate a pattern of activity within the observer's brain that closely matches what is happening within motor and sensory areas of the actor's brain. This may play a role in learning, understanding language, social interactions, the spread of emotional responses within a group, and in understanding others.

Autism spectrum disorder (ASD) is a group of developmental disorders characterized by deficits in social interactions, communication difficulties, stereotyped or repetitive behaviours, and, in some cases, cognitive delays (DSM-5, American Psychiatric Association, 2013). Autism and Asperger syndrome are the two best known disorders along this spectrum. The suggested role of mirror neurons in helping us understand the behaviour of others has led some researchers to suggest that problems in the development or functioning of mirror neurons may be important in ASD. Some findings have suggested that the mirror neuron system is affected in ASD (Hamilton, 2013), but findings are not consistent (Poulin-Lord et al., 2014).

Yang and Hofman (2015) reviewed and performed a meta-analysis on research publications on mirror neurons in ASD that used fMRI. Thirteen papers published between 2006 and 2015 (with almost half published in 2014 and 2015) met their criteria for inclusion. The results of their meta-analysis were that compared to typically developed control participants, those with ASD showed clear evidence of dysfunction in areas of the frontal and parietal cortices that are part of the mirror neuron system. The results of the meta-analysis indicated that during action observation and imitation, ASD participants showed deficits in mirror neuron activity. The brain areas affected are ones that are thought to help translate observed behaviour into our own motor commands (so-called sensory-to-motor remapping).

Master1305/Shutterstock

FIGURE 3.20 When we see someone perform a behaviour we generate the same pattern of activity in our mirror neurons as though we ourselves were performing that behaviour.

continued

Yang and Hofman concluded that these deficits may contribute to difficulties in being able to understand the actions of others.

The discovery of mirror neurons was surprise, at the time of their discovery no one had predicted anything like them.

There are still many questions about mirror neurons, but research on mirror neurons has implications for our understanding of learning, social interactions, our ability to understand others, emotional reactions, and even developmental disorders such as ASD.

Phineas Gage and progressing to the pioneering studies performed by Brenda Milner of McGill University. Frontal lobe damage results not so much in a loss of intellectual abilities as in a loss of the ability to plan and carry out a sequence of actions, and judge the order in which a series of events has occurred or will occur in the future (Milner, Petrides, & Smith, 1985).

The frontal cortex is also involved in emotional experience. In people with normal brains, PET scans show increased activity in the frontal cortex when these people are experiencing feelings of happiness, sadness, or disgust (Lane et al., 1997). In contrast, patients with frontal lobe damage often exhibit attitudes of apathy and lack of concern. They literally don't seem to care about anything.

A region of the frontal lobe known as the *prefrontal cortex* has received increasing attention in recent years. The **prefrontal cortex,** located just behind the forehead, is the seat of the so-called "executive functions." Executive functions, mental abilities involving goal setting, judgment, strategic planning, and impulse control, allow people to direct their behaviour in an adaptive fashion (Xue et al., 2009). Deficits in executive functions seem to underlie a number of problem behaviours. People with prefrontal cortex disorders seem oblivious to the future consequences of their actions and seem to be governed only by immediate consequences (Bechara et al., 1994). Phineas Gage, the railroad foreman described earlier, suffered massive damage to his prefrontal cortex when the spike tore through his brain (see Figure 3.19). Thereafter, he exhibited classic symptoms of disturbed executive functions, becoming behaviourally impulsive and losing his capacity for future planning.

A more ominous manifestation of prefrontal dysfunction was discovered by Adrian Raine and colleagues (1997; Steuber et al., 2006). Using brain-imaging techniques, the researchers studied 41 violent murderers who had pleaded not guilty by reason of insanity. The murderers' PET scans showed clear evidence of reduced activity in the prefrontal cortex. Their murderous acts, which were often random and impulsive in nature,

showed parallel evidence of failure in executive functions such as judgment, foresight, and impulse control. These early studies have led to research on the role of the frontal cortex in behavioural control, aggression, and criminal behaviour.

During the 1940s and 1950s, many thousands of psychiatric patients who suffered from disturbed and violently emotional behaviour were subjected to operations called *prefrontal lobotomies* (Shorter, 1998). The operation was performed by inserting an instrument with sharp edges into the brain, and then wiggling it back and forth to sever the nerve tracts that connected the frontal lobes with the subcortical regions associated with emotion. The calming effect was so dramatic that Egas Moniz, the developer of the technique, was awarded a Nobel Prize. However, the devastating side effects on mental functions that occurred as the executive functions were destroyed were equally dramatic, and the development of antipsychotic drugs resulted in the abandonment of this form of "treatment."

Hemispheric Lateralization: The Left and Right Brains

The left and right cerebral hemispheres are connected by a broad white band of myelinated nerve fibres. The **corpus callosum** is a neural bridge that acts as a major communication link between the two hemispheres and allows them to function as a single unit. Despite the fact that they normally act in concert, there are important differences between the psychological functions that are represented in the two cerebral hemispheres. **Lateralization** refers to the relatively greater localization of a function in one hemisphere or the other.

Medical studies of patients who suffered various types of brain damage provided the first clues that certain complex psychological functions were lateralized on one side of the brain or the other. For example, when Broca's or Wernicke's speech areas are damaged, the result is **aphasia,** the partial or total loss of the ability to communicate using language. Depending on the location of the damage, the problem may lie in recognizing the meaning of words, being unable to use

---

27. Describe the role of the frontal cortex in higher mental (including "executive") functions.

28. What is hemispheric lateralization, and what do we know about the functions that are concentrated in the left and right hemispheres?

grammar, or in both functions. C. Scott Moss, a clinical psychologist who became aphasic in both ways for a time as a result of a left hemisphere stroke, described what it was like for him:

> I recollect trying to read the headlines of the *Chicago Tribune* but they didn't make any sense to me at all. I didn't have any difficulty focusing; it was simply that the words, individually or in combination, didn't have meaning, and even more amazing, I was only a trifle bothered by that fact. . . . I think part of the explanation was that I had [also] lost the ability to engage in self-talk. In other words, I didn't have the ability to think about the future—to worry, or anticipate or perceive it—at least not with words. (1972, pp. 4–5)

When the right hemisphere is damaged, the clinical picture is quite different. Language functions are not ordinarily affected, but the person has great difficulty in performing tasks that demand the ability to perceive spatial relations. A patient may have a hard time recognizing faces and may even forget a well-travelled route or, as in the case of Dr. P., mistake his wife for a hat (Sacks, 1985). It appears that mental imagery, musical and artistic abilities, and the ability to perceive and understand spatial relationships are primarily right-hemisphere functions (Biller et al., 2006).

Even among individuals who have not experienced any brain damage and who do not have a history of abnormal brain function, the lateralization of function can be detected (Kimura, 1973). It is possible to present stimuli such as words or music, for example, in such a way that the information arrives first in one hemisphere. The information is quickly and efficiently transferred to the other hemisphere, but the hemisphere that received the information first has a head start on processing it. Subtle differences in the abilities of the two hemispheres can be detected by precisely measuring the speed and accuracy of subjects when the information is provided to one hemisphere before the other. Verbal stimuli such as letters and words are identified more quickly and accurately when they are presented in such a way that the information goes first to the left hemisphere while recognizing faces or melodies is faster and more accurate if that information goes first to the right hemisphere (Kimura, 1973).

The two hemispheres differ not only in the cognitive functions that reside there, but also in their links with particular types of emotions. EEG and imaging studies have shown that the right hemisphere is relatively more active when negative emotions such as sadness and anger are being experienced. Positive emotions such as joy and happiness are accompanied by relatively greater left-hemisphere activation (Marshall & Fox, 2000).

The split brain: Two minds in one body? Despite the lateralization of specific functions in the two cerebral hemispheres, the brain normally functions as a unified whole because the two hemispheres communicate with each other through the corpus callosum. The functions of the two cerebral hemispheres were most dramatically illustrated by a series of Nobel Prize–winning studies by Roger Sperry (1970) and his associates.

Like many scientific advances, this discovery resulted from natural human misfortune. Some patients suffer from a form of epilepsy in which a seizure that begins as an uncontrolled electrical discharge of neurons on one side of the brain spreads to the other hemisphere. Neurosurgeons found that by cutting the nerve fibres of the corpus callosum, they could prevent the seizure from spreading to the other hemisphere. Moreover, the operation did not seem to disrupt other major psychological functions.

Split-brain research was made possible by the way in which our visual input to the brain is "wired." Some of the fibres of the optic nerve from each eye cross over at the *optic chiasm* and travel to the opposite brain hemisphere (see Figure 3.21). Fibres that transmit messages from the right side of the visual field project to the left hemisphere and fibres from the left visual field project to the right hemisphere. We normally experience a unified visual world rather than two half-worlds because the hemispheres' visual areas are connected by the corpus callosum. When the corpus callosum is cut, however, visual input to one hemisphere cannot be sent to the other hemisphere.

In Sperry's experiments, split-brain patients focused on a fixation point, a dot on the centre of a screen, while slides containing visual stimuli (words, pictures, and so on) were flashed to the right or left side of the fixation point (Figure 3.22). When words were flashed to the right side of the visual field, resulting in their being sent to the language-rich left hemisphere, subjects could describe verbally what they had seen. They also could write what they had seen with their right hand (which is controlled by the left hemisphere). However, if words were flashed to the left side of the visual field and sent on to the right hemisphere, the subjects

29. What roles have (a) the corpus callosum and (b) the optic chiasm played in "split-brain" research? Is it reasonable to speak of separate "right" and "left" brains in normal people?

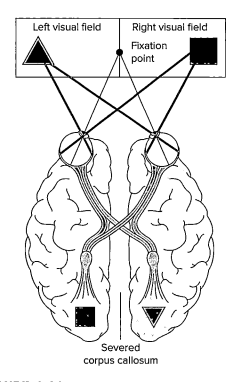

FIGURE 3.21 The visual system's anatomy made studies of split-brain subjects possible. Images entering the eye are reversed by the lens. Optic nerve fibres from the inner portion of the retina (toward the nose) cross over at the optic chiasm, whereas the fibres from the outer portion of the retina do not. As a result, the right side of each eye's visual field projects to the visual cortex of the left hemisphere, whereas the left visual field projects to the right hemisphere. When the corpus callosum is cut, the two hemispheres no longer communicate with each other. By presenting stimuli to either side of the visual fixation point, researchers can control which hemisphere receives the information.

could not describe what they had read on the screen.

The inability to describe stimuli verbally did not mean, however, that the right hemisphere was incapable of recognizing them. If a picture of an object (e.g., a hairbrush) were flashed to the right hemisphere, and the left hand (controlled by the right hemisphere) were allowed to feel many different objects behind the screen, the person's hand would immediately select the brush and hold it up (Figure 3.22c). As long as the person continued to hold the brush in the left hand, sending sensory input about the object to the "non-verbal" right hemisphere, the person was unable to name it. However, if the brush were transferred to the right hand, the person could immediately name it. In other words, until the object was transferred to the right hand, the left hemisphere had no knowledge of what the right hemisphere was experiencing.

Split-brain patients can function adequately in daily life because visual input is not usually restricted to only one visual field; we tend to normally scan the environment and move our gaze allowing visually information to fall in both the left and right visual fields and go to both hemispheres. The "split-mind" phenomena shown in the laboratory appeared because the patients were tested under experimental conditions that were specifically designed to isolate the functions of the two hemispheres. Nonetheless, the results of split-brain research were so dramatic that they led some people (and even some scientists) to promote a conception of brain functions

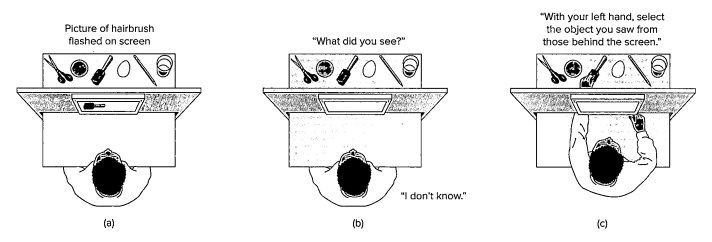

FIGURE 3.22 A split-brain patient focuses on the fixation point in the centre of the screen. In (a), a picture of a hairbrush is briefly projected onto the left side of the visual field, thus sending the information to the right hemisphere. In (b), the patient is asked to state verbally what she saw. She cannot name the object. In (c), she is asked to select the object she saw, and is able to find it with her left hand. If the object were transferred to her right hand, or if the word were flashed to the right side of the visual field, the information would be sent to the language-rich left hemisphere, and she would be able to name the object.

as being highly localized and restricted to one hemisphere or the other. Even today, we hear about "right brain" education programs and the untapped potential that they can release. Certainly, there is some degree of localization of brain functions, but a far more important principle is that in the normal brain, most functions involve many areas of the brain working together. The brain is an exquisitely integrated system, not a collection of localized functions.

Hemispheric lateralization of language. For many years, scientists have known that for most people language is primarily a left-hemisphere function. Why language tends to be localized in the left hemisphere is not clear, but it may have some undiscovered evolutionary significance (Gannon et al., 1998).

About 90 percent of people are right-handed, and among this majority, 95 percent have left hemisphere language dominance. Among left-handers, half have language in the left hemisphere, 25 percent have it localized in the right hemisphere, and the rest have language functions in both hemispheres. Those who use both hemispheres for language functions have a larger corpus callosum, perhaps because more interhemispheric communication is required (Springer, 1997).

Left-hemisphere lateralization is the case not only for spoken and written language, but also for non-verbal kinds of language, such as sign language. PET scans of neural activity show that, just as hearing people process speech with their left hemisphere, deaf people use the left hemisphere to decipher sign language. Likewise, a left-hemisphere stroke affects their ability to understand or produce sign language (Corina et al., 1992).

Realize, however, that even if your left hemisphere is dominant for language, this does not mean that your right hemisphere lacks language ability. PET scan studies measuring cerebral blood flow in the brains of normal people indicate that both hemispheres are involved in speaking, reading, and listening (Leondes, 1997; Raichle, 1994). One notable finding, however, is that males and females may differ in the extent to which certain language functions are lateralized. For example, when viewing randomly arranged vowels and consonants and asked if two nonsense words rhymed, women showed more activity in the right hemisphere than did men (Shaywitz et al., 1995). Brain-imaging studies indicate that during a language task men show greater left hemisphere activation, while women show activity in both hemispheres (Clements et al., 2006). Clinical observations of

stroke patients also suggest that there may be sex differences in the lateralization of certain aspects of language (Ciarello et al., 2009; Lindell & Lamb, 2008). On the whole, however, the brains of men and women are far more similar than they are different (Wallentin, 2009).

Plasticity in the Brain: The Role of Experience and the Recovery of Function

Learn to walk, acquire speech, read, fall in love, and your brain changes in a way that makes you a different person than you were before. Learning and practising a mental or physical skill may change the size or number of brain areas involved and alter the neural pathways used in the skill (Cicchetti, 2015; Posner & Rothbart, 2007a). This process of brain alteration begins in the womb and continues throughout life. It is governed in important ways by genetic factors but also is strongly influenced by the environment.

Neural plasticity refers to the ability of neurons to change in structure and function (Cicchetti, 2015; Kolb & Whishaw, 1998). Two aspects of neural plasticity—the effects of early experience on brain development and recovery from brain damage—are at the forefront of current research (Ethier, Gallego, & Miller, 2015).

Brain development is programmed by complex commands from our genes, but how these genetic commands express themselves can be powerfully affected by the environment in which we develop, including the environment we are exposed to in the womb (Fenichel, 2006). There is a long history of research indicating the importance of early experience for brain development and neural plasticity. Exposure of the developing fetus to drugs, such as alcohol, and other toxins can disrupt brain development and produce the lifelong mental and behavioural damage seen in fetal alcohol syndrome (Rangmar et al., 2015). There is evidence that being raised in a stimulating environment leads to lasting changes such

Thinking critically

DO THE SEXES DIFFER?

Does the evidence for activity in both hemispheres during a language task (Shaywitz at el., 1995) prove that women require the use of both sides of the brain for language? What kids of evidence would provide information about this question?

Think about it, and then see the Answers section at the end of the book.

30. How is language lateralized in the brain? Are there sex differences?

31. What is neural plasticity? How do age, environment, and behaviour affect plasticity?

In Review

- The human brain consists of the hindbrain, the midbrain, and the forebrain, an organization that reflects the evolution of increasingly more complex brain structures related to behavioural capabilities.

- Major structures within the hindbrain include the medulla, which monitors and controls vital body functions; the pons, which contains important groups of sensory and motor neurons; and the cerebellum, which is concerned with motor coordination.

- The midbrain contains important sensory and motor neurons, as well as many sensory and motor tracts connecting higher and lower parts of the nervous system. The reticular formation plays a vital role in consciousness, attention, and sleep. Activity of the ascending reticular formation excites higher areas of the brain and prepares them to respond to stimulation. The descending reticular formation acts as a gate, determining which stimuli get through to enter into consciousness.

- The forebrain consists of two cerebral hemispheres and a number of subcortical structures. The cerebral hemispheres are connected by the corpus callosum.

- The thalamus acts as a relay and filter through which impulses originating in sense organs are routed to the appropriate sensory projection areas. The hypothalamus plays a major role in supporting many different biological drives. The limbic system seems to be involved in organizing the behaviours involved in motivation and emotion.

- The cerebral cortex is divided into frontal, parietal, occipital, and temporal lobes. Some areas of the cerebral cortex receive sensory input, some control motor functions, and others (the association cortex) are involved in higher mental processes in humans. The frontal lobes are particularly important in such executive functions as planning, voluntary behaviour, and self-awareness.

- Although the two cerebral hemispheres ordinarily work in coordination with each other, they appear to have different functions and abilities. Studies of split-brain patients who have had the corpus callosum cut indicate that the left hemisphere commands language and mathematical abilities, whereas the right hemisphere has well-developed spatial abilities, but a generally limited ability to communicate through speech. However, recent findings indicate that language functions are less lateralized in women than in men. Positive emotions are believed to be linked to relatively greater left-hemisphere activation and negative ones to relatively greater right-hemisphere involvement. Despite hemispheric localization, however, most behaviours involve interactions between both hemispheres; the brain operates as a system.

---

as larger neurons with more dendritic branches, and greater concentrations of acetylcholine, the neurotransmitter involved in motor control and memory (Rosenzweig, 1984).

Research indicates that neural plasticity is not restricted to early development as was once thought. For example, experienced string musicians who do elaborate movements on the strings with their left hands had a larger right-hemisphere somatosensory area devoted to these fingers than did non-musicians. The corresponding left-hemisphere (right-hand) cortical areas of the musicians and non-musicians did not differ (Elbert et al., 1995). More recently, brain plasticity has been explored among healthy seniors and among those recovering from brain damage. Among healthy seniors, training in complex cognitive tasks was found, using MRI, to enhance neural activity, increase cerebral blood flow, and promote healthier white matter (Chapman et al., 2015).

Apart from practising cognitive tasks, motor practice can also lead to neural plasticity throughout life, including during one's senior years (Cai et al., 2014).

Recovery of function after injury. When an injury results in the destruction of brain tissue, other neurons must take over the lost functions of the dead neurons if recovery is to occur. At times the brain shows an amazing plasticity and recovery of function, as the following case illustrates:

> Jimmy was a healthy and normal 5-year-old child who awoke one day unable to speak and slightly paralyzed on the right side of his body. A blood vessel in his left temporal lobe had ruptured and an area of the brain "downstream" from the site of the stroke had died when its blood supply was cut off. For Jimmy's father, it was like

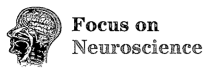

Focus on Neuroscience

THE NEUROSCIENCE OF MUSIC

Time to sit back and listen to some music—perhaps even sing along with one of your favourite songs. Music has been called the universal language; every known human culture has music and music plays an important role in many social activities (Levitin, 2008). Simple musical instruments, such as flutes made from the bones of birds, represent some of humankind's oldest artifacts and date from at least 42 000 years ago (Higham, 2012). Daniel Levitin of McGill University has turned the techniques of modern neuroscience to the study of one of our oldest social endeavours—making and listening to music.

Music activates a wide range of brain areas; there is no single "music centre" within the brain (Levitin, 2006). Different aspects of music are processed by different brain areas (Levitin, 2012). Different areas within the main auditory centres of the brain in the thalamus and the temporal cortex play a critical role in the early stages of processing music. Pitch, how high or low a note is, is represented by a strip of cortex arranged as a tonotopic map (or tone map), meaning that different pitches are represented by areas of the brain arranged in an orderly and predictable fashion, going from low to high pitch, like the keys of a piano keyboard. That is, notes that are adjacent in pitch are represented by adjacent areas of the primary auditory cortex in the temporal cortex. The different sounds made by different instruments, or timbre, are processed by a different area of the temporal cortex than where pitch is processed. This area is found along the sulcus, or fissure, that runs lengthwise along the middle of the temporal lobe. Tempo and rhythm involve areas of the cerebellum and the basal ganglia; as we discovered earlier, these are both areas associated with the control of movement. It is interesting that tempo and rhythm, aspects of music that tend to elicit movement coordinated with the music (such as toe-tapping, swaying, and dancing), are associated with activity in motor areas of the brain. Do you like music? Can music evoke an emotional reaction from you? Music has been shown to lead to the release of the neurotransmitter dopamine within the nucleus accumbens, an event associated with motivation and reward, and activity within the amygdala, a brain area associated with emotions. Finally, the most complex aspects of music, such as remembering melodies, expectations about rhythm, melody and harmony, and musical attention, involve areas within the frontal and prefrontal cortices (Levitin, 2012).

In an interesting recent study, Levitin and colleagues investigated how these aspects of music, processed separately, are put together so that we perceive a coherent and meaningful piece of music (Abrams et al., 2013). They measured brain activity with fMRI, and used a technique that allowed them to examine the integration of information over extended time periods. The ability to integrate information across an extended period of time is essential for the study of music; one or two notes in isolation do not make music—music requires the flow of notes over time. The goal of the research was to study the brain areas involved in the processing and integration of music that are common across people. The study included both male and female participants, all of whom were right-handed and who had little or no musical training. While brain imaging was done, the participants listened to a musical selection (music by the late-Baroque composer William Boyce) or to two different control conditions in which the temporal or spectral characteristics of the music were disrupted. That is, participants were tested listening to music or when listening to two other sets of sounds that contained the same simple auditory elements but that did not have the structure and qualities of music.

The researchers found a distinct set of brain areas that showed activity common across participants when they listened to the music but not to the control sounds. There was activity within the auditory areas of the thalamus and the temporal cortex of the right hemisphere. Several specific areas within the right frontal cortex showed activity during presentation of the music, as did both sides of the parietal cortex, but with greater activity in the right parietal cortex. There was also activity in areas of the cortex associated with planning movement. It is interesting that there was activity in the cortex involved in planning movement (premotor cortex); these were non-musicians, so they could not have been imagining how they would play the music they were listening to. This study showed that activity within auditory brain areas and in higher cortical areas, like the right frontal cortex and right parietal cortex, tracked aspects of musical structure over extended periods of time.

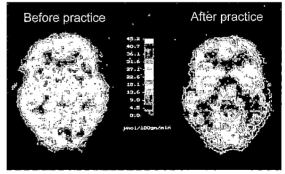

© Monte S. Buchsbaum, M.D., Mt. Sinai School of Medicine, New York, NY

FIGURE 3.23 Listening to music is not just hearing a series of sounds. Recent research has shown that distinct brain circuits are involved when you listen to music.

continued

The work by Daniel Levitin and his colleagues, as well as by other neuroscientists interested in music, has shown that when we listen to music our brains do not simply show the patterns of activity you would expect from listening to a series of sounds. Music generates a specific pattern of activity within the brain, a pattern that, as far as we know, is unique to music. Listening to music evokes consistent and distinctive patterns of brain activity in brain areas that extend beyond primary auditory areas to some of the highest and most distinctively human parts of the brain.

reliving a nightmare. His own grandfather had also suffered a left hemisphere stroke (late in life). The elderly man never recovered his speech and he remained partially paralyzed until his eventual death. But for Jimmy, the story had a happier ending. Within three months, Jimmy was again speaking normally, and his paralysis had disappeared completely. He was ready to resume the life of a normal 5-year-old. All that remained of his ordeal was a frightening memory. (Gazzaniga et al., 1979)

Neural reorganization had occurred in Jimmy's brain, allowing other neurons to take over the functions of those that had died. The outcomes for Jimmy and his grandfather also illustrate an important general principle: Brain damage suffered early in life is less devastating than damage suffered as an adult (Blosser, 2000).

The brain is clearly capable of greater plasticity early in life. In one study, researchers took neurons from the visual cortex of cats and then raised the neurons in a culture containing the nutrients needed for survival. They found that the neurons could survive and create new synapses with other neurons in the culture quite well if they were taken from kittens who were two to four weeks old but not if they were obtained from older animals (Schoop, Gardziella, & Muller, 1997).

Studies using the electron microscope may explain why such plasticity is possible early in life. The one- to two-year-old child has about 50 percent more brain synapses than mature adults do (Lomber & Eggermont, 2006). This greater availability of synapses may help to explain why children can recover from brain damage more quickly and completely than adults. But, sadly, the days of synaptic riches don't last forever. Unused or weaker synapses deteriorate with age so that the brain loses some of its plasticity (Huttenlocher, 2002). Moreover, cell death is programmed into every neuron by its genes, and what some neuroscientists refer to as the neuron's "suicide apparatus" is activated by a lack of stimulation from other neurons and by many other

32. Why do children typically show better recovery of function after brain injury?

33. Is it true that at birth you have all the neurons you will ever have?

unknown factors (Milligan & Schwartz, 1997). As a result, adults actually have fewer synapses in the brain than do children, despite their more advanced cognitive and motor capabilities.

Yet even adults can maintain or recover some functions after neuron death (Varney & Roberts, 1999). When nerve tissue is destroyed or neurons die as part of the aging process, surviving neurons can restore functioning by modifying themselves either structurally or biochemically (Lomber & Eggermont, 2006). They can alter their structure by sprouting enlarged networks of dendrites or by extending axons from surviving neurons to form new synapses (Shepherd, 1997). Surviving neurons may also make up for the loss by increasing the volume of neurotransmitters they release (Dwyer, 2007). Finally, recent research findings have begun to challenge the long-standing assumption of brain scientists that dead neurons cannot be replaced in the mature brain (Kempermann, 2005). The development of new cells (*neurogenesis*) has been demonstrated in the brains of rodents and primates within the hippocampus, which is involved in memory. In 1998, evidence for the birth of new cells in the human adult hippocampus appeared (Eriksson et al., 1998). Then, in what could be a landmark scientific discovery, psychologist Elizabeth Gould and her Princeton colleagues (1999) provided the first evidence of neurogenesis in the cerebral cortex of a primate. Using complex chemical and microscopic analysis techniques with adult macaque monkeys, Gould's team tracked newly developed neurons from their birthplace in subcortical tissue. The immature neurons migrated upward along myelinated nerve tracts into the association areas of the cerebral cortex, where they sprouted axons and extended them toward existing neurons. The researchers speculated that these new neurons may be involved in higher-order mental functions, such as complex learning and memory. If similar results are found in humans, whose brain structures and functions are similar to those of primates, new light could be shed on brain mechanisms of information storage and plasticity. It is even possible that degenerative mental disorders, such as Alzheimer's disease, represent a failure or decline in a previously unknown process of neuron regeneration in the mature brain.

Behavioural and lifestyle measures also can help to preserve brain functioning. In elderly people, for example, continued intellectual stimulation and activity seem to preserve synapses and their resulting cognitive functions, adding support to physiological psychologist David Krech's statement that "Those who live by their wits die with their wits" (Krech, 1978).

One controversial technique for neurogenesis involves the transplantation into the brain of neural stem cells—immature cells that can mature into any type of neuron or glial cell. These cells can be injected directly into the brain and, once in the brain, they can travel to any area, especially developing or degenerating areas. There they can detect defective cells and develop into healthy forms of the defective cells. How this is controlled and orchestrated is as yet unknown. Stem cells have been successfully transplanted into the spinal cords of injured animals where they have taken hold and organized themselves into neural networks (Jung et al., 2009). Although this work is at an early stage, it may herald what has never been done before—repair a severed spinal cord. Investigation of stem cell transplantation into the brain is also underway.

Levels of Analysis   Brain, Behaviour, and Environment

The focus of this chapter has been on the physiology of the nervous system. This system is the province of neuroscience. Yet, neuroscientists realize that their work at the biological level of analysis is only part of the fascinating and abiding mystery of how brain creates mind; indeed, of how brain *is* mind. Consider some of the findings we have reviewed in this chapter.

ENVIRONMENTAL

• Early environment, whether enriched or deprived, influences uences brain development and behaviour capabilities.

• Environmental rewards and punishments influence what we learn and the neural representations of that learning.

• The stimuli present at any particular moment trigger both biological (e.g., brain activation, hormonal, neurotransmitter) and behavioural processes.

• The culture in which we grow up plays an important role in psychological development and, as recent research shows, in how the brain operates.

BIOLOGICAL

• Every thought, feeling, or behaviour involves the action of the nervous system. In a real sense, our brain *is* the locus of who and what we are as a person.

• The biological level of analysis provides us with tools, such as brain scans, to study and directly measure the activity of the nervous system.

• Clinical studies of brain-damaged individuals by neurologists have provided much evidence concerning normal brain functions.

PSYCHOLOGICAL

• The psychological perspective provides discoveries on the nature and causes of both normal and abnormal cognition, emotion, and behaviour. These provide the basic phenomena that the biological perspective studies at a biological level.

• The psychological perspective provides the measures of psychological functions that allow us to relate them to biological factors, such as genetic or brain activation variables.

• Plasticity research shows us that psychological factors influence the brain just as the brain influences behaviour. New thought and behaviour patterns create the changes in the brain that underlie what we call learning, motivation, emotion, and personality development.

In summary, biological, psychological, and environmental factors are all involved in most behaviours, typically interacting with one another, and all of them can serve as either cause or effect.

FIGURE 3.24

Review

- Early experience has an especially profound effect on brain development, but neural plasticity can occur throughout life.

- Neural plasticity refers to the ability of neurons to change in structure and functions. Environmental factors, particularly early in life, have notable effects on brain development.

- A person's ability to recover from brain damage depends on several factors. Other things being equal, recovery is greatest early in life and declines with age.

- When neurons die, surviving neurons can sprout enlarged dendritic networks and extend axons to form new synapses. Neurons can also increase the amount of neurotransmitter substance they release so that they are more sensitive to stimulation.

- Recent findings suggest that the brains of mature primates and humans are capable of producing new neurons.

Gaining Direction

What are the issues?	In the June/July 2013 edition of *Esquire* magazine, Brad Pitt acknowledged that he has a lot of trouble recognizing faces. He simply cannot remember them. Apparently, he tried faking it for a while, but people were quite upset with him. They would perceive him as conceited and uncaring. But how is it possible to simply lose all memory of a person's face? To understand this, we need to examine normal brain	functioning, especially the processing of visual information. Brad Pitt, Jane Goodall, and Oliver Sacks all suffer from a form of sensory agnosia. Their processing of visual information is intact—the problem is one of interpretation. This neurological disorder is called *prosopagnosia* or "face blindness" and it affects up to 2.5 percent of the North American population.
What do we need to know?	How does the brain process sensory information? What is the role of the association cortex? How does one acquire the ability to identify objects?	How does one lose the ability to identify objects? What is visual agnosia? Is there more than one visual pathway in the brain?
Where can we find the information to answer these questions?	We need to examine the organization and function of the cortex. In particular, we need to look at the role of the primary projection areas. Is there an area responsible for visual processing? Is there only one of these areas? What would happen if you damage a visual area? In addition to the primary projection areas, the cortex	contains a number of association areas. Is there a visual association area? What happens when this area is damaged? Finally, consider the various areas that might be involved in object recognition. Might we be able to isolate an area that is responsible for facial recognition?

Genes, Evolution, and Behaviour

CHAPTER ❯
OUTLINE

GENETIC INFLUENCES

Chromosomes and Genes

  Focus on Neuroscience: Early Experience,
  Epigenetics, and Adolescence

Behaviour Genetics Techniques

  Applications: Gene Therapy and Genetic Counselling

GENETIC INFLUENCES ON BEHAVIOUR

Heredity, Environment, and Intelligence

**Biological Reaction Range, the Environment,
  Personality, and Intelligence**

EVOLUTION AND BEHAVIOUR

Evolution of Adaptive Mechanisms

Evolution and Human Nature

Evolutionary Psychology

  Frontiers: Heritability, Evolution, and Politics

  Research Foundations: Gender Differences
  in the Ideal Mate

**HOW NOT TO THINK ABOUT BEHAVIOUR
GENETICS AND EVOLUTIONARY PSYCHOLOGY**

> Psychology will be based on a new foundation.
>
> —Charles Darwin, 1859

(both): © Michael Nichols/Magnum

Identical twins Jim Springer and Jim Lewis met for the first time when they were 39 years old. They discovered each other through a landmark University of Minnesota study of twins who had been separated shortly after birth and raised by different adoptive parents. Although they had been raised in different families, the two Jims found that they had many things in common. Both had married twice and each had a son named James. Both men smoked—and even smoked the same brand of cigarette—and both preferred Miller Lite beer.

What are the
issues here?

Where can
we find the
information to
answer these
questions?

What do we need
to know?

Both worked as volunteers for their local police departments as part-time sheriffs, favoured poodles as pets, suffered from the same kind of headache symptoms when under stress, and bit their fingernails. Both Jims did woodworking as a hobby, and they were the only people in their respective neighbourhoods to have built a circular bench around a tree in their yard. When given a series of psychological tests, they were strikingly similar in their pattern of personality traits.

GENETIC INFLUENCES

1. Differentiate between genotype and phenotype.

Our physical development, including the development of the nervous system, is in large part directed by an elaborate genetic blueprint passed on to us by our parents. These biological characteristics set limits on our behavioural capabilities. However, our genetic endowment combines with environmental forces to determine our behaviour. Nature or nurture is not an appropriate dichotomy; it should be nature *and* nurture. Modern scientists realize that asking whether a particular behaviour is caused by genetic or environmental factors makes no more sense than asking if a triangle is formed by its sides or its corners. Instead, psychologists working in the field of behaviour genetics study the ways in which favourable or unfavourable environmental conditions can affect the genetically inherited potential of an organism.

Chromosomes and Genes

2. How does genetic transmission pass on from parents to offspring?

How are physical characteristics passed on from parents to their offspring? This question originated in antiquity, and the ancient Greek physician Hippocrates was one of the first to provide a semi-correct answer. Hippocrates suggested that semen contains not body parts, but rather some sort of design for the formation of the offspring. It was not until 22 centuries later that the wisdom of Hippocrates's answer was confirmed by Gregor Mendel, a monk whose research with garden peas in the 1860s marked the beginning of modern genetic theory.

Mendel showed that heredity involves the passing on of specific organic factors, not a simple blending of the parents' characteristics. These specific factors might produce visible characteristics in the offspring, or they might simply be carried for possible transmission to another generation. In any case, the offspring of one set of parents do not all inherit the same traits, as is evident in the differences we see among brothers and sisters.

Early in the 20th century, geneticists made the important distinction between **genotype,** the specific genetic makeup of an individual, and **phenotype,** the observable characteristics produced by that genetic endowment. A person's genotype is like the commands in a computer software program. Some of the directives are used on one occasion, some on another. Some directives are never used at all, either because they are contradicted by other genetic directives or because the environment never calls them forth. Thus, genotypes are present from conception and never change, but phenotypes can be affected by other genes and by the environment. For example, geneticists have discovered that chickens have retained the genetic code for teeth (Kollar & Fischer, 1980). Yet, because the code is prevented from being expressed, *hens' teeth* remains an expression for scarcity.

The union of two cells, the egg from the mother and the sperm from the father, is the beginning of a new individual. Like all other cells in the body, the egg and sperm carry within them the material of heredity in the form of rodlike units called *chromosomes.* A **chromosome** is a tightly coiled molecule of *deoxyribonucleic acid (DNA)* that is partly covered by protein. Indeed, the DNA is so tightly coiled that if the DNA in a single human cell were stretched out, it would be almost 2 metres long (Masterpasqua, 2009). The DNA portion of the chromosome carries the hereditary blueprint in units called **genes** (Figure 4.1). The many genes carried on each chromosome are like a giant computer file of information about your characteristics, potentials, and limitations. Every moment of every day, the strands of DNA silently transmit their detailed instructions for cellular functioning.

In humans, every cell in the body except one type has 46 chromosomes. The exception is the sex cell (the egg or sperm), which has only 23. At conception, the 23 chromosomes from the egg combine with the 23 from the sperm to form a new cell, the *zygote,* containing

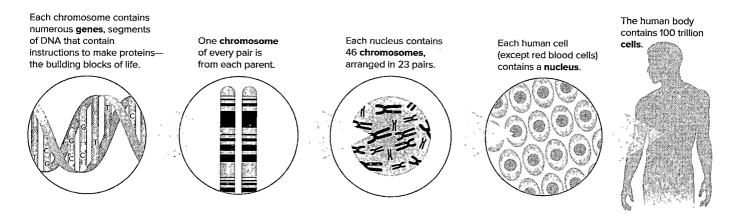

Each chromosome contains numerous **genes**, segments of DNA that contain instructions to make proteins—the building blocks of life.

One chromosome of every pair is from each parent.

Each nucleus contains **46 chromosomes,** arranged in 23 pairs.

Each human cell (except red blood cells) contains a **nucleus**.

The human body contains 100 trillion **cells.**

FIGURE 4.1 The ladder of life. Chromosomes consist of two long, twisted strands of DNA, the chemical that carries genetic information in the form of specific sequences of the substances adenine, thymine, guanine, and cytosine (A, T, G, and C). Every cell in the body (with the exception of red blood cells) carries within its nucleus 23 pairs of chromosomes, each containing numerous genes that regulate every aspect of cellular functioning. Human DNA has about 3 billion chemical base pairs, arranged as A-T or C-G units.

Source: Human Genome Project. (2007). Retrieved May 16, 2016, from http://www.genome.gov/.

46 chromosomes. The genes within each chromosome also occur in pairs, so that the offspring receives one of each gene pair from each parent. Every cell nucleus in your body contains the genetic code for your entire body. In all these cells (except for egg and sperm), there are two copies of each gene, one from your mother and one from your father. Alternative forms of a gene that produce different characteristics are called **alleles.**

Genes affect our body's development and functioning through one general mechanism: genes code for the production of proteins. The estimated 70 000 different types of proteins found in a human (Wahlsten, 1999) control the structure of individual cells and all the chemical reactions that go on within those cells, whether they are reactions necessary to sustain the life of the cell or are changes induced only periodically by experience or maturation. It is estimated that about half of all genes target brain structure and function (Kolb & Whishaw, 2003). Each individual gene carries the code for a specific protein, and when that gene is activated, the cell produces the specified protein. At different points in development, in response to different metabolic demands, or in response to different environmental factors, a gene may be activated and a protein produced or an already active gene may be "turned off," and the levels of a specific protein will then decrease. As the protein levels within a neuron change, there is a corresponding change in the function of that neuron and the neural circuits in which it participates.

Dominant, Recessive, and Polygenic Effects

Genotype and phenotype are not identical, because some genes are dominant and some are recessive. If a gene in the pair received from the mother and father is **dominant,** the particular characteristic that it controls will be displayed; if the gene is **recessive,** the characteristic will not show up *unless* the partner gene inherited from the other parent is also recessive. In humans, for example, brown eyes and dark hair are dominant over blue eyes and light hair. Thus, a child will have blue eyes only if both parents have contributed genes for blue eyes. Even if their traits remain hidden, however, recessive genes can be passed on to offspring.

In a great many instances, a number of gene pairs combine their influences to create a single phenotypic trait. This action is known as **polygenic transmission,** and it complicates the straightforward picture that would occur if all characteristics were determined by one pair of genes. It also magnifies the number of possible variations in a trait that can occur. Despite the fact that about 99.9 percent of human genes are identical among people, it is estimated that the union of sperm and egg can result in about 70 trillion potential genotypes, accounting for the great diversity in characteristics that occur, even among siblings.

Epigenetics: Environmental Effects on Genes

The term **epigenetics** was first used in 1940 to refer to lasting changes in gene expression

3. Compare dominant, recessive, and polygenic influences on phenotypic characteristics.

during development that were not due to genetic changes (changes to the genes themselves) but to changes around the genes—epigenetic changes (Isles, 2015). Epigenetics concerns lasting changes in gene function caused by external or environmental factors without any change in the DNA sequence itself. In the past 20 years research on epigenetics has exploded. A PsychINFO search of publications for the year 2015 using the keyword "epigenetics" returned 599 results, while a similar search for 1995 returned only 16. The study of epigenetics has changed our understanding of environment-gene interactions. Specific patterns of maternal behaviour (Zhang & Meaney, 2010), use of drugs of abuse (Cadet, 2016), nutritional intake (Wen et al., 2015), and even physical exercise (Kashimoto et al., 2015) can all lead to lasting changes in how our genes operate.

The processes of epigenetics work through a number of different chemical mechanisms that lead to lasting changes in how specific genes function without altering the DNA sequence. The mechanisms involved in epigenetics involve activating or silencing specific genes, or altering how a gene is expressed thus changing the gene product. For example, a process called DNA-methylation will turn a gene "off" preventing it from acting. Other processes can alter a gene so that the gene product is changed. For example, it has been shown that chronic cocaine exposure in rats alters the ratio of two specific gene products in the nucleus accumbens (Isles, 2015), a brain area important in motivation and reward as we saw last chapter. The changes in gene function are long-lasting and some can even be passed to subsequent generations (Isles, 2015; Zhang & Meaney, 2010). Together with helping us understand how the environment and our genes interact, epigenetics is gaining increasing attention in the study of psychosis and other disorders (Cadet, 2016; Pal et al., 2016). As we will see in Chapter 16, environmental factors such as stress are important risk factors for the development of a range of psychiatric disorders. Epigenetic studies are helping to explain how and why.

Throughout this chapter we emphasize that genes are expressed *in* an environment, and that behaviour is not the result of genes *or* the environment but of both. That is, genes and the environment interact. Epigenetics takes this even further and demonstrates that environmental factors can lead to lasting, even heritable, changes in how our genes function.

4. How can gene function change to affect behaviour long after the initial experience?

Prior to the modern study of epigenetics few would have predicted that the interaction of genes and the environment occurred at such a fundamental level or that the environment and external factors could lead to lasting changes in gene function. This chapter's *Focus on Neuroscience* feature explores how aversive early experience alters gene function in brain areas linked to emotion, learning, and memory during adolescence.

The Human Genome

In 1990, geneticists began the Human Genome Project, and in 2001, the genetic map was published, two years ahead of schedule (International Human Genome Sequencing Consortium, 2001; Venter et al., 2001). Canadian geneticists were involved in the Human Genome Project throughout, and a computer called Deep Maple (really!) at Toronto's Hospital for Sick Children provided the main computer database for the international effort.

The genetic structure in every one of the 23 chromosome pairs has been mapped by using methods that allowed the researchers literally to disassemble the genes on each chromosome and study the specific sequence of substances that occur in each gene (A, T, G, and C; Figure 4.1). The 3.1 billion letters in the entire human genome would fill 152 000 newspapers if printed consecutively. The Human Genome Project, along with Celera Genomics, reported a number of surprises when their projects were complete. They discovered humans have fewer genes than expected; a human has approximately 25 000 genes and not the 100 000 originally estimated (Human Genome Project, 2007). Indeed, we have about the same number as a fruit fly. The groups found that approximately 200 human genes may have arisen from genes that bacteria inserted into our early ancestors. As research continues to explore the functions of our genes, a new understanding of our genetic makeup may lead to the development of effective new medical treatments, to a revolution in how therapeutic drugs are developed, and to a whole new understanding of what makes a human and where we came from.

This chapter's *Applications* feature highlights how this understanding, together with the behaviour genetics techniques discussed in the next section, can raise questions and ethical issues associated with gene therapy, genetic screening, and access to genetic information.

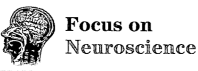

Focus on Neuroscience

EARLY EXPERIENCE, EPIGENETICS, AND ADOLESCENCE

Does early experience have a lasting impact? Does the impact of early experience differ from the impact of similar experiences later stages in life? Most people would say that yes, there is something special about early experience and the impact it has on later behaviour.

There are indeed good demonstrations of this belief. For example, in his classic studies on maternal behaviour and resistance to stress, Michael Meaney and his colleagues at McGill University found that variations in maternal care of rat pups during their first two weeks of life produced lasting changes in the behaviour of those animals. This early experience led to differences in the maternal behaviour of those animals when they were adults and to life-long changes in their ability to recover from stress (Champagne et al., 2006). As we will see in Chapter 12, the argument that early experience has a lasting impact is a well-established idea both within psychology and more broadly in our culture.

There has, however, been little understanding of the types of changes that can support changes in behaviour long after the actual experience. Recent advances suggest a role for epigenetic changes (Zhang & Meaney, 2010). As discussed in this chapter, epigenetics refers to a series of chemical modifications to the DNA that alters gene activity without changing the DNA itself. The importance of epigenetic mechanisms is that environmental factors, such as a stressful early experience, can lead to a long-lasting, even permanent, regulation of a gene. These epigenetic changes are candidates for the types of mechanisms that may support the lasting impact of early experience. That is, lasting, even heritable, changes may be due to epigenetic changes and not to genetic changes.

Adverse experiences early in life are known to increase the risk for later anxiety and mood disorders, and for persistent deficits in learning and memory (Maccari et al., 2014). The quality of early caregiving is important for later well-being, and caregiver maltreatment is an important risk factor. What mechanisms are involved in this situation has not been well understood.

Recently, Doherty and her colleagues (Doherty, Forster, & Roth, 2016) proposed that an epigenetic mechanism, such DNA methylation, may be involved. DNA methylation is a chemical process that attaches methyl groups to sites on the DNA. As a result, that gene is rendered less active or even left completely inactive. In this research, they examined two different classes of epigenetic changes in the adolescent brain after early adverse experiences. They measured what is referred to as global changes, which are epigenetic changes to the DNA as a whole and would include

all changes without linking those changes to any specific gene. They also measured changes to a specific gene. The gene they targeted is one that controls the production of a protein (brain-derived neurotrophic factor) that is important for brain development and for synaptic plasticity. These researchers specifically examined epigenetic changes in the amygdala and the hippocampus. As you will recall from Chapter 3, the amygdala is importantly involved in emotion, especially in fear- and anxiety-related behaviours, and the hippocampus is critically important for memory.

Doherty et al. (2016) used an animal model of caregiver mistreatment. For their first week of life, one group of rat pups were with a mother that was in a novel environment with little bedding material. A novel environment is stressful, so these pups were with a stressed mother and had inadequate nests. That was the caregiver maltreatment condition. It is worth noting that although a stressful and rather bare environment is aversive, this is a relatively low level of early maltreatment compared to the conditions that the young of many species—including human children—can find themselves. There was a group that also was with a mother that was placed in new environment but she had time to get used to it and recover from the stress. There was also ample bedding for this group. A third group was a control that had normal, ample bedding, and the pups and mother stayed in their usual home cage. Maternal behaviour was scored for appropriate caregiving behaviours (e.g., nursing, grooming the pups) and aversive caregiver behaviour (e.g., rough handling or avoiding the pups).

When these animals were adolescents, two different types of epigenetic changes were measured in the

© dpa picture alliance archiveAlamy Stock Photo

FIGURE 4.2 Epigenetic research using an animal model of caregiver maltreatment indicates that aversive experiences early in life can lead to a long-lasting change in gene function in brain areas linked to emotion, learning, and memory.

continued

amygdala and the hippocampus. Researchers measured both total methylation, which is a global change, and the methylation of a specific gene. Interestingly, male and female adolescents showed a different pattern of changes. Adolescent males showed an impact of early maltreatment on the global (nonspecific) measure in the hippocampus and amygdala, whereas adolescent females showed a change in the gene-specific measure in the amygdala and in a different part of the hippocampus. That is, a relatively mild form of early maltreatment had a lasting impact on epigenetic markers and the effect varied by sex and brain area.

Recent estimates are that 20 percent of adolescents are affected by some form of psychiatric disorder and that disorder will continue to adversely affect their life through adulthood (Giedd et al., 2014). Discovering how early stress, such as caregiver maltreatment, puts the mental health of adolescents at risk is important. There is much work to be done, especially in linking epigenetic changes to behavioural outcomes later in life. Nonetheless, this research suggests that one way early experience can have a lasting impact is by changing how genes function in specific brain areas. Knowing what is changed can potentially lead to preventative measures and successful treatment approaches.

Genetic Engineering: The Edge of Creation

Advances in molecular biology enable scientists to duplicate and modify the structures of genes themselves (Peacock, 2010). In **recombinant DNA procedures,** researchers use specific enzymes to cut the long threadlike molecules of genetic DNA into pieces, combine them with DNA from another organism, and insert the new strands into a host organism, such as a bacterium. Inside the host, the new DNA combination continues to divide and produce many copies of itself. Scientists have used this procedure to produce materials that are rare or difficult to obtain otherwise such as human growth hormone, used treat children who do not produce sufficient levels of this hormone for normal growth.

Molecular biologists have developed methods for inserting new genetic material into viruses that can infiltrate neurons and modify their genetic structure. These methods are now becoming part of the tool kit of physiological psychologists who wish to study genetic influences on behaviour. Gene-modification research by psychologists has focused on processes such as learning, memory, emotion, and motivation (Wahlsten, 1999). One procedure done with animals (typically mice) is to alter a specific gene in a way that prevents it from carrying out its normal function. This is called a **knockout procedure** because that particular function of the gene is eliminated, or knocked out. The effects on behaviour are then observed.

Although gene knockout studies are a powerful tool, researchers need to take great care when interpreting their outcomes. Very little

5. Describe the methods used in recombinant DNA research.

6. What is the knockout procedure, and how is it used by psychologists to study behaviour?

7. What is the percentage of genetic resemblance between parents and children, identical and fraternal twins, brothers and sisters, and grandparents and grandchildren?

behaviour is controlled by a single gene. Thus, the disruption of a behaviour after a gene knockout may help to identify one of the genes involved in the behaviour, but this identification does not mean that one gene is wholly responsible for the behaviour. It is also important to note that knocking out a single gene may disrupt a wide range of functions. Many of the substances found in the body do many different things in different areas of the brain and the body. Nonetheless, gene-modification techniques may one day enable us to alter genes that contribute to psychological disorders, such as schizophrenia.

Genetic engineering gives humans potential control over the processes of heredity and evolution. But these revolutionary techniques also give birth to a host of ethical and moral issues (Lucassen, 2012). How and when, if ever, should these techniques be used? To prevent genetic disorders? To propagate desirable human characteristics? To duplicate or clone exceptional people? What are the social and environmental consequences of using genetic engineering to greatly extend the healthy lifespan of people? Questions such as these are already topics of intense discussion, as scientific and technological advances carry us toward uncharted genetic frontiers.

Behaviour Genetics Techniques

Knowledge of the principles of genetic transmission tells us how genetically similar people are, depending on their degree of relatedness to one another. Recall that children get half of their genetic material from each parent. Thus, the probability of sharing any particular gene with one of your parents is 50 percent, or 0.50.

Applications

GENE THERAPY AND GENETIC COUNSELLING

Until recently, biological psychologists had to be content with studying genetic phenomena that occurred in nature. Aside from selective breeding of plants and animals for certain characteristics or studying the effects of genetic mutations, scientists had limited ways to study the effects of specific genes on behaviour. Technological advances now enable them not only to map the human genome and measure the genotypes of individuals but to modify genes themselves (Peacock, 2010).

In one gene-manipulation approach, the recombinant DNA procedure discussed earlier, scientists can join together segments of DNA from different sources, creating sections of DNA that are not found in nature. This new genetic material can then be inserted into a bacterium to produce many copies of the new DNA. The DNA can then be inserted into a virus that can enter the CNS and alter the genetic makeup of neurons within the brain. Modified genes have been used to study processes such as learning and memory, and to study disorders such depression and Alzheimer's disease. For example, gene knockout procedures have been used to prevent neurons from producing a chemical thought to be involved in the release of the neurotransmitter glutamate, and the effects on brain function and behaviour have been tested (Ohira et al., 2013). Researchers can also use a knock-in procedure to insert a new gene into an animal, rather than to remove the actions of an existing gene, as is done with a knockout procedure. For example, researchers have inserted a gene associated with Alzheimer's disease into the brain of mice and later tested the impact on neurotransmission, brain structure, and behaviour (Dumanis et al., 2013).

As we learn more about the human genome, the assessment and modification of genes heralds advances in the form of genetic screening and therapy. Currently, more than 1000 DNA-based genetic tests for specific diseases have been developed (National Institutes of Health, 2010). These include tests for susceptibility to Alzheimer's disease, cancers, and arthritis. Some tests are used to assist in diagnosis, other tests allow couples to assess the likelihood of conceiving children with gene-related health problems, and others help to identify a person's risk for cancers, heart disease, or some psychiatric disorders. There are now private companies that, for a fee, will process your DNA sample (usually obtained from a saliva sample) and report to you your risk for alcoholism, cancers, Alzhiemer's disease, Parkinson's disease, coronary heart disease, and other disorders.

This capability, however, brings with it serious practical and ethical issues (Lucassen, 2012). For example, the tests are not infallible and many tell you only about susceptibility or risk. Erroneous results or misinterpretation of results could cause great psychological suffering. Medical ethics experts also fear what would happen if insurance companies and employers had access to genetic testing results and the danger of having those kinds of decisions based on genetic screening. Canada is currently the only G8 nation that does not have laws against genetic discrimination. That is, there are no laws in Canada to prevent businesses, such as insurance companies, from using the results of genetic testing in a discriminatory way, such as denying insurance coverage for someone who carries the genetic risk for a specific disease. Embryonic screening gives parents increased knowledge of what their offspring might be like. Are parents entitled to make abortion decisions based on results that tell them whether a child is likely to be emotionally reactive, possibly obese, or lacking some characteristic valued by the parents (Valverde, 2010)?

Genetic testing combined with the ability to modify the genetic makeup of cells presents enormous potential for treating some of our most serious illnesses. Current gene therapy, however, is experimental and has not proven very successful in clinical trials (National Institutes of Health, 2010). Scientific work continues on the development of effective therapies. Gene-modification techniques may one day enable us to alter genes that contribute to psychological disorders, such as bipolar disorder and schizophrenia (McGuffin et al., 2005).

Genetic counsellors help people deal with issues, including ethical issues, that can arise from genetic testing (Groepper et al., 2015). A genetic counsellor provides

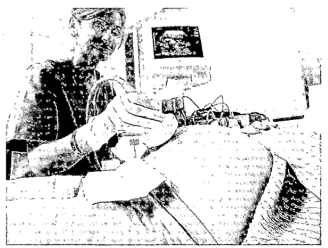

Juice Images/Getty Images

FIGURE 4.3 A genetic counsellor works with other healthcare professionals, such as obstetricians, to provide advice and support to a couple for whom pregnancy presents special risks because the unborn child may be affected by a genetic disorder.

continued

information on the inheritance of illnesses; addresses the concerns of patients, their families, and their healthcare providers; and supports patients and their families dealing with illness. Genetic counsellors usually work as part of a team, typically with a geneticist, physicians, and healthcare professionals from other specialties such as oncologists, obstetricians, dietitians, social workers, and nurses.

The goal of genetic counselling is to assist individuals in making decisions about healthcare. Clients may seek advice because they have a disorder or because of a family member's illness. Couples with a child affected by a genetic disorder may seek advice as they plan another pregnancy, and couples who are planning their first pregnancy may want to understand their future child's disease susceptibility, especially if they are planning a pregnancy late in life. Currently healthy clients may seek advice about lifestyle changes if they are at risk for developing a disease.

Genetic counselling in Canada is provided by individuals trained specifically as genetic counsellors or by nurses with additional training in genetic counselling. The Canadian Association of Genetic Counsellors was formed to support the development of genetic counselling in Canada and to increase public awareness of the issues involved. It also serves as the national accrediting body for genetic counsellors. Currently, four Canadian universities offer accredited Master's degree programs in genetic counselling: McGill University, the University of British Columbia, Université de Montréal, and the University of Toronto. Students entering these programs have a variety of undergraduate backgrounds, most commonly an undergraduate degree in biology, psychology, or social work. As genetic screening becomes more commonly available and more genetic tests are developed, the demand for genetic counselling is sure to grow.

Brothers and sisters also have a probability of 0.50 of sharing the same gene with one another, since they get their genetic material from the same parents. And what about grandparents? Here, the probability of a shared gene is 0.25 because, for example, your maternal grandmother passed on half of her genes to your mother, who passed on half of hers to you. Thus, the likelihood that you inherited one of your grandmother's genes is 0.50×0.50, or 0.25. The probability of sharing a gene is also 0.25 for half-siblings, who share half their genes with their biological parent but none with the other parent. An adopted child has no genes in common with his or her adoptive parents, nor do unrelated people share genes in common.

Behaviour geneticists are interested in studying how hereditary and environmental factors combine to influence psychological characteristics. One important question is the potential role of genetic factors in accounting for differences between people. The extent to which variation in a particular characteristic within a group can be attributed to genetic factors is estimated statistically by a **heritability coefficient.** It is easy to confuse two terms in this discussion. *Heredity* means the passage of characteristics from parents to offspring by way of genes; *heritability* means how much of the variation in a characteristic within a population can be attributed to genetic differences.

It is important to note that heritability refers to differences, or variance, in the trait across individuals and not to the trait itself. If a characteristic, such as weight, has a heritability coefficient of 0.60, this number does not mean that 60 percent of my body weight is due to my genes and 40 percent is due to my environment. If you look around at the other students in your psychology class, you will see a range of body weights. The heritability coefficient is a way of estimating how much of that variation is attributable to genetic factors. Furthermore, heritability applies only to differences *within* a

Review

- Heredity potential is carried within the DNA portion of the 23 pairs of chromosomes in units called *genes*. Genotype and phenotype are not identical because some genes are dominant while others are recessive. Many characteristics are polygenic in origin; that is, influenced by interactions of multiple genes.

- Genes influence the development, structure, and function of our body, including our brain, by controlling the production of proteins.

- Genetic engineering allows scientists to duplicate and alter genetic material or, potentially, to repair dysfunctional genes.

group, not to differences *between* groups. Consider the range of weights apparent within your psychology class, and now think of a different group, such as a group of individuals from a traditional hunter–gatherer society. Differences in body weight between your class and the hunter–gatherer group are most likely attributable to differences in the environment, such as differences in the availability of high-sugar and high-fat foods and the amount of physical exercise. You could calculate a heritability coefficient for each group and obtain estimates for the importance of genetic factors in explaining individual differences within each group, but your results could not be used to explain differences between groups. This point is widely misunderstood and misreported in the popular media.

In considering heritability estimates, such as those shown in Table 4.1, it is important to know what group was studied (the heritability estimates shown in Table 4.1 were obtained from studies of mostly middle-class North Americans). Why does knowing the group matter? If, for example, you were to obtain a heritability coefficient for intelligence from

TABLE 4.1   Heritability Estimates for Various Human Characteristics

Trait	Heritability Estimate
Height	0.80
Weight	0.60
Intelligence (IQ)	0.50–0.70
School achievement	0.40
Extraversion	0.36
Conscientiousness	0.28
Agreeableness	0.28
Emotional stability	0.31
Activity level	0.25
Impulsivity	0.45
Antisocial behaviour	0.41
Major depression	0.37
Anxiety disorder	0.35
Smoking	0.52
Problem drinking	0.26

Sources: Bouchard, C., Tremblay, A., Despres, J.P., Nadeau, A., Lupien, P.J., & Theriault, G. (1990). The response to long-term overfeeding in identical twins. *The New England Journal of Medicine*, 322, 1477–1482.; Dunn, J., & Plomin, R. (1990). *Separate lives: Why siblings are so different.* New York, NY: Basic Books.; Malouf, J.M., Rooke, S.E., & Schutte, N.S. (2008). The heritability of human behavior: Results of aggregating meta-analyses. *Current Psychology*, 27, 153–161.

a group of highly advantaged children, those with plentiful resources, enrichment, and educational support, then you would find a heritability coefficient with a high value. On the contrary, if you studied children with diverse backgrounds, those whose backgrounds range from impoverished to privileged, then you would find a heritability coefficient with a much lower value. How can the same characteristic, intelligence, have two very different heritability coefficients? Remember that the heritability coefficient is a statistical estimate of how much of the variability within a group is due to genetic factors. For the group of children from advantaged backgrounds, environmental factors that influence intelligence would be very similar from one individual to the next and so would be unable to explain individual differences. If the environment does not account for the variation in intelligence within this group, then the difference could be due to genetic factors, and the heritability coefficient would estimate a high value. Within the second group, which included children from a wide range of backgrounds, more of the differences can be attributed to differences in the environment, and hence the heritability estimate would be low.

Knowing the level of genetic similarity in family members and relatives provides a basis for estimating the relative contributions of heredity and environment to a physical or psychological characteristic (Plomin, 1997). If a characteristic has higher **concordance**, or co-occurrence, in people who are more highly related to one another, then this points to a possible genetic contribution, particularly if the people have lived in different environments.

One research method based on this principle is the **adoption study**, in which a person who was adopted early in life is compared on some characteristic both with the biological parents, with whom the person shares genetic endowment, and with the adoptive parents, with whom no genes are shared. If the adopted person is more similar to the biological parents than to the adoptive parents, then a genetic influence is suggested. If greater similarity is shown with the adoptive parents, then environmental factors are probably more important. In one study of genetic factors in schizophrenia, Seymour Kety and colleagues (1978) identified formerly adopted children who were diagnosed with the disorder later in life. They then examined the backgrounds of the biological and adoptive

8. How are adoption and twin studies used to achieve heritability estimates? What have such studies shown?

parents and relatives to determine the rate of schizophrenia in the two sets of families. The researchers found that 12 percent of biological family members also had been diagnosed with schizophrenia, compared with a concordance rate of only 3 percent of adoptive family members, suggesting a hereditary link.

Twin studies are one of the more powerful techniques used in behaviour genetics. *Monozygotic* (identical) twins develop from the same fertilized egg, so they share virtually all of their genes (there may be subtle differences such as variations in numbers of alleles and other copy variants) (Figure 4.4). Approximately 1 in 250 births produces identical twins. *Dizygotic* (fraternal) twins develop from two fertilized eggs, so they share 50 percent of their genetic endowment, like any other set of brothers and sisters. They occur once in 125 births.

Twins are usually raised in the same familial environment. Thus, we can compare concordance rates or behavioural similarity in samples of identical and fraternal twins, assuming that, if the identical twins are far more similar to each other than are the fraternal twins, then a genetic factor is likely to be involved. Of course, it is always possible that, because identical twins are more similar to each other in appearance than are fraternal twins, they might be treated more alike and therefore share a more similar environment. This environmental factor could partially account for greater behavioural similarity in identical twins. To rule out this environmental explanation for greater psychological similarity, behaviour geneticists have adopted an even more elegant research method. Sometimes they are able to find and compare sets of identical and fraternal twins who were separated very early in life and raised in *different*

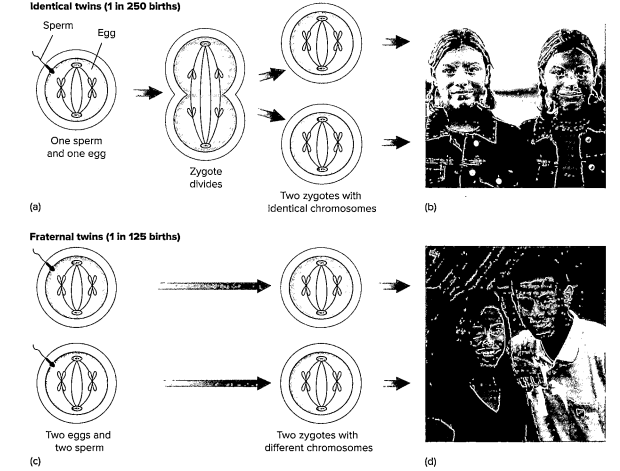

(b) © L. Clarke/Corbis; (d) © Jim Whitmer

FIGURE 4.4 Identical (monozygotic) twins come from a single egg and sperm as a result of a division of the zygote. They have all of their genes in common. Fraternal (dizygotic) twins result from two eggs fertilized by two sperm. As a result, they share only half of their genes.

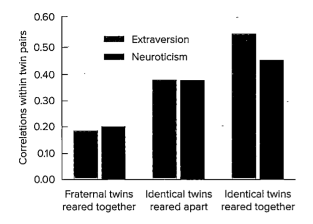

FIGURE 4.5 Degree of similarity on personality measures of extraversion and neuroticism of 24 000 pairs of twins who were reared together and apart.

Source: Data from Loehlin, J.C. (1992). *Genes and environment in personality development*. Newbury Park, CA: Sage.

environments (Lykken, Bouchard, McGue, & Tellegen, 1993). This design permits a better basis for evaluating the respective contributions of genes and environment.

Both adoption and twin studies have led behavioural geneticists to conclude that many psychological characteristics, including intelligence, personality traits, and certain psychological disorders, have a notable genetic contribution. Adoptive children frequently are found to be more similar to their biological parents than to their adoptive parents, and identical twins tend to be more similar to each other on many traits than are fraternal twins, even when they have been reared in different environments (Bazzett, 2008; Loehlin, 1992; Plomin & Spinach, 2004). Figure 4.5 shows the results of one such comparison. Three groups of twins—identical twins reared together and apart, and fraternal twins reared together—completed personality tests of extraversion (sociability, liveliness, impulsiveness) and neuroticism (moodiness, anxiousness, and irritability). The higher correlation coefficients reveal that the identical twins are more similar to each other than are the fraternal twins, and that the degree of similarity in identical twins on the trait of neuroticism is almost as great when they are reared in different environments as when they are reared together (Loehlin, 1992).

On the other hand, behaviour genetics studies also have demonstrated that environmental factors interact with genetic endowment in important ways. For example, one adoption study compared the criminal records of men who were adopted at an early age with the criminal records of their biological fathers and their adoptive fathers. A low incidence of criminal behaviour was found in the sons whose biological fathers had no criminal record, even when the adoptive fathers who reared them had criminal records. In contrast, the criminal behaviour of sons whose biological fathers had criminal records was very high, even when their adoptive fathers had no criminal records. This pattern clearly points to a genetic component in criminality. But one additional finding deserves our attention: The level of criminality was highest of all for those sons whose biological and adoptive fathers *both* had criminal records, suggesting a combined impact of genetic and environmental factors (Cloninger & Gottesman, 1987). In this case, heredity and environment combined to create a double whammy for society. This finding underscores the conclusion that genetic and environmental factors almost always interact with each other to influence behaviour.

9. Why are studies of twins raised together and apart especially informative? What findings have occurred in such studies?

GENETIC INFLUENCES ON BEHAVIOUR

Our unique characteristics as individuals arise from the combination of our learning experiences and the environment in which we behave acting on a substrate provided by our genetic makeup. All our behaviours reflect the interaction between genes and the environment. The best known and most fully explored (although still incomplete) studies of the genes–environment interaction involve intelligence and personality. Indeed, our growing understanding of intelligence has helped to elucidate how favourable and unfavourable environmental conditions act on genetically determined potential. Studies of personality have helped to illustrate how opportunities provided by the environment influence the expression of genetically based differences.

Heredity, Environment, and Intelligence

One of the most controversial questions in the history of psychology is the question: To what extent are differences in intelligence due to genetic factors, and to what extent does environment determine differences in intelligence? Since the 19th century, this question has been at the centre of controversy and, at times, bitter debate. Proponents on each side of this debate have marshalled strong arguments and sound supporting data. But can both sides be right?

Let's first examine the genetic argument. Suppose that intelligence is totally determined by genes. (No psychologist today would maintain that it is, but examining the extreme view can be instructive.) In that case, any two individuals with exactly the same genes would have identical test scores, so the correlation between the test scores of identical (monozygotic) twins would be close to +1.00. Nonidentical brothers and sisters (including fraternal twins, who result from two fertilized eggs) share only half their genes. Therefore, the correlation between the test scores of fraternal twins and other siblings should be substantially lower. Extending the argument, the correlation between a parent's test scores and his or her children's scores should be about the same as that between siblings, because a child inherits only half of his or her genes from each parent.

What do the actual data look like? Table 4.2 summarizes the results from many studies. As you can see, the correlations between the test scores of identical twins are substantially higher than any other correlations. Identical twins separated early in life and reared apart are of special interest because they have identical genes but experienced different environments. The correlation for identical twins raised apart is nearly as high as that for identical twins reared together, and higher than that for nonidentical twins raised together (Bouchard et al., 1990;

TABLE 4.2 Correlations in Intelligence among People Who Differ in Genetic Similarity and Who Live Together or Apart

Relationship	Percentage of Shared Genes	Correlation of IQ Scores
Identical twins reared together	100	0.86
Identical twins reared apart	100	0.75
Nonidentical twins reared together	50	0.57
Siblings reared together	50	0.45
Siblings reared apart	50	0.21
Biological parent—offspring reared by parent	50	0.36
Biological parent—offspring not reared by parent	50	0.20
Cousins	12.5	0.15
Adopted child–adoptive parent	0	0.19
Adopted children reared together	0	0.02

Sources: Based on Bouchard, T.J., & McGue, M. (1981). Familial studies of intelligence: A review. *Science*, 212, 1055–1059.; Bouchard, C., Tremblay, A., Despres, J.P., Nadeau, A., Lupien, P.J., & Theriault, G. (1990). The response to long-term overfeeding in identical twins. *The New England Journal of Medicine*, 322, 1477–1482.; Plomin, R., DeFries, J.C., & Fulker, D.W. (2007). *Nature and nurture during infancy and early childhood*. New York, NY: Cambridge University Press.; Scarr, S. (1992). Developmental theories for the 1990s: Development and individual differences. *Child Development*, 63, 1–19.

Plomin et al., 2007). Moreover, as Table 4.2 shows, IQs of adopted children correlate as highly with their biological parents' IQs as with the IQs of the adoptive parents who reared them. The pattern is quite clear: The more genes people have in common, the more similar they are in IQ. This strong evidence suggests that genes play a significant role in intelligence (Petrill, 2003).

Notice, however, that the figure for identical twins raised together is higher than the figure for identical twins raised apart. The same is true for other types of siblings raised together and raised apart. These findings rule out an entirely genetic explanation. Although one's genotype seems to be an important factor in determining intelligence test scores, it probably accounts for only 50 to 70 percent of the IQ variation among people in the United States (Bouchard et al., 1990; Plomin & Spinath, 2004). Thus, environment, too, contributes significantly to intelligence. Obviously, then, the question with which this section began is too simplistic. The real question should be as follows: How do heredity and environment *interact* to affect intelligence?

Biological Reaction Range, the Environment, Personality, and Intelligence

The concept of reaction range contributes to our understanding of genetic–environmental interactions. The **reaction range** for a genetically influenced trait is the range of possibilities—the upper and lower limits—that the genetic code allows. Thus, to say that intelligence is genetically influenced does not mean that intelligence is fixed at birth. Instead, it means that an individual inherits a range for potential intelligence that has upper and lower limits. Environmental effects will then determine where the person falls within these genetically determined boundaries. Each of us has a range of intellectual potential that is jointly influenced by two factors: our genetic inheritance and the opportunities our environment provides for acquiring intellectual skills. The diverse abilities measured by intelligence tests are undoubtedly influenced by large numbers of interacting genes, and different combinations seem to underlie specific abilities (Franić et al., 2015).

At present, genetic reaction ranges cannot be measured directly, and we do not know if their sizes differ from one person to another. But studies of IQ gains associated with environmental enrichment and adoption programs

suggest that the ranges could be as large as 15 to 20 points on the IQ scale (Dunn & Plomin, 1990). If this is indeed the case, then the influence of environmental factors on intelligence would be highly significant.

Some practical implications of the reaction range concept are illustrated in Figure 4.6. First, consider persons B and H. They have identical reaction ranges, but B develops in a very deprived environment and H in an enriched environment with many cultural and educational advantages. Person H is able to realize her innate potential and has an IQ that is 20 points higher than person B's. Now compare persons C and I. Person C actually has greater intellectual potential than person I, but ends up with a lower IQ as a result of living in an environment that does not allow that potential to develop. Finally, note person G, who was born with high genetic endowment and reared in an enriched environment. His IQ of 110 is lower than we would expect, suggesting that he did not take advantage of either his biological capacity or his environmental advantages.

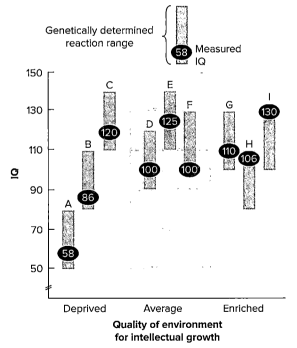

> **10.** How does the concept of reaction range illustrate the interaction between heredity and environment?

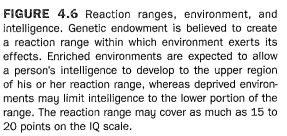

FIGURE 4.6 Reaction ranges, environment, and intelligence. Genetic endowment is believed to create a reaction range within which environment exerts its effects. Enriched environments are expected to allow a person's intelligence to develop to the upper region of his or her reaction range, whereas deprived environments may limit intelligence to the lower portion of the range. The reaction range may cover as much as 15 to 20 points on the IQ scale.

Evidence for these types of environmental effects comes from studies of children who are removed from deprived environments and placed in middle- or upper-class adoptive homes. Typically, such children show a gradual increase in IQ on the order of 10 to 12 points (Schiff & Lewontin, 1986). Conversely, when deprived children remain in their impoverished environments, either they show no improvement in IQ or they may even deteriorate intellectually over time (Serpell, 2000). These results remind us that intellectual growth depends not only on genetic endowment and environmental advantage, but also on personal characteristics that affect how much we take advantage of our gifts and opportunities.

11. Apart from genetic makeup, how else are monozygotic twins similar or the same?

Behaviour Genetics and Personality

Increasingly, personality theorists are working to trace differences in personality characteristics to specific differences in brain activity. Hans Eysenck was one of the first modern personality theorists to suggest that personality differences could be traced to differences in brain development or function. The personality dimension extraversion-introversion, for example, was argued to reflect differences in brain arousal (Eysenck, 1967). If such personality differences can be traced to specific aspects of brain development or function, then at least some genetic component would be expected.

Since Eysenck's pioneering work, research has indeed found evidence for specific genetic components of some personality characteristics (South et al., 2015).

One prominent personality trait theory is called the *Five Factor Model* (see Chapter 14). Five-factor theorists such as Robert McCrae and Paul Costa (2003) believe that individual differences in personality can be accounted for by variation along five personality dimensions or traits known as the *Big Five:* (1) Extraversion-Introversion (sociable, outgoing, adventuresome versus quiet, inhibited, solitary), (2) Agreeableness (cooperative, helpful, good-natured versus antagonistic, uncooperative, suspicious); (3) Conscientiousness (responsible, goal-directed, dependable versus undependable, careless, irresponsible); (4) Neuroticism (worrying, anxious, emotionally unstable versus well-adjusted, secure, calm); and (5) Openness to experience (imaginative, artistically sensitive versus unreflective, lacking in intellectual curiosity). Twin studies of the heritability of the Big Five personality traits have found heritability coefficients ranging from 0.42 (Agreeableness)

to 0.57 (Openness) (Bouchard, 2004). These results are consistent with studies of other personality variables, indicating that between 40 and 50 percent of the personality variations among people are attributable to genotype differences (Kandler, 2012). Although personality characteristics do not show as high a level of heritability as is found for intelligence, it is clear that genetic factors account for a significant amount of personality difference.

As discussed earlier, twin studies are particularly informative for studying the role of genetic factors because they compare the degree of resemblance between two individuals who share virtually all of their genes—monozygotic, or identical, twins—and two who do not—dizygotic, or fraternal, twins (Rowe, 1999). As noted briefly in the section "Behaviour Genetics Techniques," across many psychological characteristics monozygotic twins are more similar to each other than are dizygotic twins, suggesting a role for genetics. The issue, however, is complicated by the possibility that identical twins may also have more similar experiences than fraternal twins. Because identical twins are more similar than fraternal twins in appearance, size, and physical characteristics, others may treat them more similarly. Indeed, some parents even dress identical twins in the same clothes, making it almost impossible for the twins to be treated differently within many contexts (Figure 4.7). Even someone who knows the twins may confuse one for the other. One of us is married to an identical twin. Although she and her sister did not dress alike or even wear their hair in the same style, from her childhood to her adulthood, her grandparents called her by her own name about half of the time and by her twin's name about half of the time.

golf9c9333/Getty Images

FIGURE 4.7 Identical twins may be more similar because people treat them similarly, influenced by their identical appearance, size, and even clothing.

The ideal approach would be to compare personality traits in identical and fraternal twins who either were raised together or reared apart. If identical twins who were reared in different environments, by different adoptive families, are as similar as those reared together, a powerful argument could be made for the role of genetic factors. Moreover, this research design would allow us to divide the total variation among individuals on each personality trait into three components: (1) variation attributable to genetic factors; (2) variation due to a shared family environment among those reared together; and (3) variation attributable to other factors, such as unique individual experiences. The relative influence of these sources of variation can be estimated by comparing personality test correlations among four groups of twins: identical twins reared together, identical twins reared apart, fraternal twins reared together, and fraternal twins reared apart (Plomin & Caspi, 1999; Plomin et al., 2007).

Several studies have used this powerful research design to assess the genetic contribution to a range of personality traits (Lykken et al., 1993; Pederson et al., 1988; Rhee & Waldman, 2002; Tellegen et al., 1988; Yamagata et al., 2006). These studies have shown that identical twins are far more similar

in personality traits than are fraternal twins, and it makes little difference whether they were reared together or in different adoptive families. Contrary to what many personality psychologists had expected, family environment had little influence on personality differences in these studies.

One of the best known and largest of these studies was conducted by Lykken, Tellegen, and colleagues at the University of Minnesota. The so-called "Minnesota Twin Study" (in reference to the university and the participants, not the baseball team) assessed more than 400 pairs of twins, including Jim and Jim, whom we met at the start of this chapter. For those twins who were separated and reared apart, the median age at separation was 2.5 months, demonstrating relatively little shared experience within the same family environment. The results of this study are shown in Table 4.3. The four types of twin pairs completed measures of 14 different personality traits. Genetic factors accounted for 39 to 58 percent of the variation among people in personality trait scores. Surprisingly, the degree of resemblance did not differ much whether the twin pair were reared together or apart, showing that general features of the family environment, such as

12. According to the results of the Minnesota Twin Study, what factors were the most important in determining personality?

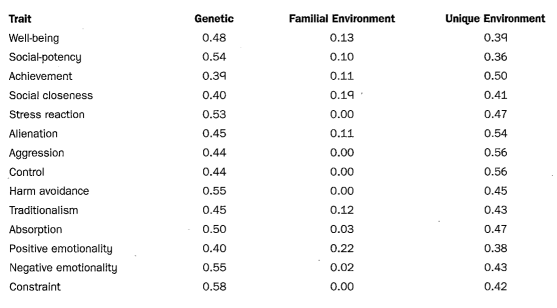

TABLE 4.3 Estimates of the Percentages of Group Variance in 14 Personality Traits Attributable to Genetic and Environmental Factors

Trait	Genetic	Familial Environment	Unique Environment
Well-being	0.48	0.13	0.39
Social-potency	0.54	0.10	0.36
Achievement	0.39	0.11	0.50
Social closeness	0.40	0.19	0.41
Stress reaction	0.53	0.00	0.47
Alienation	0.45	0.11	0.54
Aggression	0.44	0.00	0.56
Control	0.44	0.00	0.56
Harm avoidance	0.55	0.00	0.45
Traditionalism	0.45	0.12	0.43
Absorption	0.50	0.03	0.47
Positive emotionality	0.40	0.22	0.38
Negative emotionality	0.55	0.02	0.43
Constraint	0.58	0.00	0.42

Note: The variance estimates are based on a comparison of the degree of personality similarity in identical and fraternal twins who were reared together or apart.

Source: Data from Tellegen, A., Lykken, D.T., Bouchard, T.J., Wilcox, K.J., Segal, N.L., & Rich, S. (1988). Personality similarity in twins reared apart and together. *Journal of Personality and Social Psychology,* 54(6), June 1988, pp. 1031–1039.

emotional climate and degree of affluence, accounted for little or no variation in any of the traits. The absence of important effects of family environment, however, does not mean that experience does not matter. The individuals' unique experience, such as school experiences, social interactions, and individual learning experiences, was an important factor and accounted for 36 to 56 percent of the variation in individual personality traits. Even within the same family, individual children have different experiences while growing up, and it is this collection of unique experiences that help to shape personality.

Collaborative work by Tony Vernon at the University of Western Ontario and Kerry Jang at the University of British Columbia and their colleagues has demonstrated a genetic basis for a variety of personality and social dimensions. For example, Olson, Vernon, Harris, and Jang (2001) have shown that attitudes have an inherited component. They surveyed over 300 pairs of identical and fraternal twins on a wide variety of attitudinal and personality measures. Results indicated a significant genetic influence on 26 of 30 attitudinal measures and on 18 of 20 personality items. The highest heritability coefficients (all greater than 0.5) were found for attitudes toward reading books, abortion without restriction, playing organized sports, riding roller coasters, and the death penalty. A factor analysis revealed that, in general, attitudes toward preservation of life, equality, and athleticism had the highest genetic component. A "roller coaster gene" may sound like an absurd suggestion, and, as the authors cautioned, a direct and simple relationship between genes and attitudes is very unlikely. A more plausible explanation is that certain inherited factors (e.g., physical characteristics such as muscle coordination) may predispose individuals to prefer certain activities. That is, it is extremely unlikely that there is a "roller coaster gene" that accounts for the results. Genes do, however, control the development and function of physical characteristics, such as the development and functioning of the vestibular system, the inner ear, and other structures that give us our sense of balance. On the one hand, if your genetic makeup has resulted in a vestibular system that is easily disrupted, with the consequent feelings of dizziness and nausea, then you will not enjoy riding on roller coasters. On the other hand, if your vestibular system developed in a way that makes it more robust and less easily perturbed,

13. How might genes influence the tendency to enjoy reading or participating in organized sports?

© ermes ricci/MaXx Images

FIGURE 4.8 Genetic contribution to roller-coaster appreciation may be as simple as how genes develop one's sense of balance.

then that thrilling ride at the fair may give you exciting sensations of speed and movement without making you feel dizzy and nauseous (Figure 4.8).

Genetic influence has also been reported for a tendency to abuse alcohol (Jang, Vernon, & Livesley, 2000), a variety of personality disorder dimensions (Torgersen et al., 2012), seasonal mood changes (Jang, Lam, Livesley, & Vernon, 1997), anxiety, and novelty seeking (Vormfelde et al., 2006), and even for humour (Vernon et al., 2008) and political attitudes (Bell, Aitken Schemer, & Vernon, 2009). While there is a genetic component to these personality characteristics, the contribution of the environment is also important (Bell et al., 2009; Plomin, Asbury, & Dunn, 2001), as we saw earlier for intelligence. Figure 4.9 illustrates some of the biological, environmental, and psychological factors that we need to consider when analyzing behaviour from the perspective of behaviour genetics.

Levels of Analysis: Behaviour Genetics

Although the focus here has been on genetics and behaviour, all three scientific levels of analysis—biological, psychological, and environmental—are involved in the context of discovery.

ENVIRONMENTAL

- Evolutionary researchers focus on the environmental factors that have fostered behavioural adaptations through natural selection processes.
- Twin studies (especially of twins raised apart) provide insights into genetic factors as well as shared and unshared environmental factors.
- Research on the manner in which genetic factors influence the learning environments that people select or create through their own behaviour sheds light on gene–environment interactions.
- Cultural learning can affect the expression of gene-influenced behaviours.

BIOLOGICAL

- Human genome research is unlocking the secrets of our genetic structure and has already dispelled long-held beliefs, such as that concerning the number of genes in the genome.
- Genes influence the development, structure, and function off the brain by controlling the production of proteins.
- Studies on how genes are switched on and off provide insights into how genetic processes determine the development of biological structures, such as the brain. Such knowledge may be the basis for revolutionary new medical treatments.

PSYCHOLOGICAL

- The psychological products of gene–environment interactions cannot be studied without an understanding of the behaviours and psychological processes of interest. This requires psychological research and the development of methods for measuring the psychological characteristics of interest.
- Adoption and twin studies allow researchers to estimate the relative contributions of genes and environment on specific psychological variables. These contributions have been shown to differ widely, depending on the behaviour of interest.
- Other research focuses on the specific ways in which environmental and genetic factors exert their individual and combined effects on behaviour.

Suppose the entire world was consumed by a deadly plague that killed most humans. How would the human genotype be expected to change as a result of this event? By what process would this change occur?

FIGURE 4.9

In Review

- The more genetically similar two individuals, the higher the correlation between their IQ scores. The correlation between even genetically identical individuals, however, is not perfect, indicating an important role for the environment.

- Genetic factors contribute a reaction range for intelligence. Where within that range intelligence does develop depends on environmental factors.

- Identical twins are more alike than fraternal twins across a wide range of personality characteristics, indicating an important genetic component in personality traits. Together with genetic factors, an individual's unique experiences are important for personality; family environment has little impact.

- Genetic factors relevant for personality interact with the environment by predisposing an individual toward particular types of activities because of genetically influenced differences in brain activity, or other physical characteristics.

EVOLUTION AND BEHAVIOUR

In the misty forests and verdant grasslands of past eons, our early human ancestors faced many environmental challenges as they struggled to survive. If even one of your ancestors had not behaved adaptively enough to survive and reproduce, he or she would not have passed on his or her genes and you would not be here to contemplate your existence. In this sense, each of us is an evolutionary success story. As descendants of those successful forebears, we carry within us genes that contributed to their adaptive and reproductive success. The vast majority of genes we share in common with all other humans create the "human nature" that makes us like all other people.

The field of *evolutionary psychology* seeks to understand how behavioural abilities and tendencies have evolved over the course of millions of years in response to environmental demands. No behaviour by any organism can occur in the absence of **biologically based mechanisms** that receive input from the environment, process the information, and respond to it (Tooby & Cosmides, 1992). We begin life with innate biologically based mechanisms that enable us to take in, process, and respond to information, predisposing us to behave, feel, and even think in certain ways (Stearns & Hoekstra, 2005).

In humans, these inborn mechanisms allow us to learn, remember, speak a language, perceive certain aspects of our environment at

14. Define evolution and explain how genetic variation and natural selection produce adaptations.

birth, respond with universal emotions, and bond with other humans, among other things. Evolutionary psychologists also believe that important aspects of social behaviour, such as aggression, altruism, sex roles, protecting kin, and mate selection, are the products of evolved mechanisms. They are quick to point out that no behaviour as such ever evolves; what evolves are genetically produced physical structures that interact with the demands of the environment to produce a behaviour.

Evolution of Adaptive Mechanisms

Evolution

Evolution is a change over time in the frequency with which particular genes—and the characteristics they produce—occur within an interbreeding population. As particular genes become more or less frequent in a population, so do the characteristics they influence. Some genetic variations arise in a population through *mutations,* random events and accidents in gene reproduction during the division of cells. If mutations occur in the cells that become sperm and egg cells, then the altered genes will be passed on to offspring. Mutations help to create variation within a population's physical characteristics. This variation makes evolution possible.

Long before Charles Darwin published his theory of evolution in 1859, people knew that animals and plants could be changed over time by breeding members of a species that shared desired traits. Although Darwin knew nothing about genes, he knew that *something* must be passed on to the next generation through reproduction in order for evolution to occur. Darwin's landmark contribution was in specifying the process by which species change over time as they adapt to environmental demands.

Natural Selection

Just as plant and animal breeders "select" for certain characteristics, so, too, does nature. According to Darwin's principle of **natural selection,** characteristics that increase the likelihood of survival and ability to reproduce within a particular environment will be more likely to be preserved in the population and therefore will become more common in the species over time. As environmental changes produce new and different demands, some different characteristics may contribute to survival and the ability to pass on one's genes (Barrow, 2003).

Cartoon by Don Wright, © 2001. Reprinted with permission of Tribune Media Services.

FIGURE 4.10 Evolutionary principles are widely discussed, and widely enough known to be the subject of humour.

In this way, natural selection acts as a set of filters, allowing certain characteristics of survivors to become more common and those of nonsurvivors to become less common and, perhaps, even extinct over time. The filters also allow "neutral" variations that neither facilitate nor impede fitness to pass through and be preserved in a population. These neutral variations, sometimes called *evolutionary noise*, could conceivably become important in meeting some future environmental demand. For example, people differ in their ability to tolerate radiation (Vral et al., 2002). In today's world, these variations are of limited importance, but they could clearly affect survivability if a future nuclear war were to increase levels of radioactivity around the world. As those who could tolerate higher levels of radiation survived and those who could not perished, the genetic basis for radiation tolerance would become increasingly more common in the human species. Thus, for natural selection to work, individual variation must be present in a relevant species characteristic.

Evolutionary Adaptations

The products of natural selection are called *adaptations*. **Adaptations** allow organisms to meet recurring environmental challenges to their survival, thereby increasing their reproductive ability. In the final analysis, the name of the natural selection game is to pass on one's genes, either personally or through kin who share at least some of them (Dawkins, 2006). Some evolutionary psychologists believe this is why animals and humans may risk or even sacrifice their lives to protect their kin.

Let's apply these concepts to human evolution. We begin with the notion that an organism's biology determines its behavioural capabilities, and its behaviour (including its mental abilities) determines whether it will survive. In this manner, successful human behaviour evolved along with a changing body (Buss, 1995; Tooby & Cosmides, 1992).

One theory is that, when dwindling vegetation in some parts of the world forced apelike animals from the trees and required that they hunt for food on open, grassy plains, chances for survival were greater for those who were capable of *bipedal locomotion* (walking on two legs), thereby freeing the hands to use weapons that could kill at a distance (Lewin, 1998). By freeing the hands, bipedalism fostered the development and use of tools and weapons, and hunting in groups encouraged social organization. Social organization required the development of specialized social roles (such as "hunter and protector" in the male and "nurturer of children" in the female). It also favoured the development of language, which enhanced social communication and the transmission of knowledge. Our ancestors' emerging social organization provides an example of how changes contribute to evolutionary development. Social roles emerged as a result of biological predispositions, selection pressures (e.g., women who were sensitive to the needs of their young children likely had more of their children survive; men who provided for their children had more of their children survive), and emerging social organization. The social roles and social organization, shaped by evolutionary processes, themselves become selection pressures that help to shape the species as it continues to evolve (Geary, 2005; Tooby & Cosmides, 1992).

Tool use, bipedal locomotion, and social organization put new selection pressures on many parts of the body. For example, the teeth, the hands, and the pelvis all changed over time in response to the new dietary and behavioural demands. But the greatest pressure was placed on the brain structures involved in the abilities most critical to the emerging way of life: attention, memory, language, and thought. These mental abilities became important to survival in an environment that required the ability to learn quickly and solve problems. In the evolutionary progression from *Australopithecus* (an early human ancestor who lived about 4 million years ago) through *Homo erectus* (1.6 million to 100 000 years ago) to the human subspecies Neanderthal (75 000 years ago), the brain tripled in size, and the most dramatic growth occurred in the parts of the brain that are the seat of the higher mental processes (Figure 4.11). Thus, evolved changes in behaviour seem to have contributed to the development of the brain, just as the growth of the brain contributed to evolving human behaviour (Striedter, 2005).

Surprisingly, perhaps, today's human brain does not differ much from the Stone Age brain of our ancient ancestors. In fact, the Neanderthal had a slightly larger brain. Yet the fact that we perform mental activities that could not have been imagined in those ancient times tells us that human capabilities are not solely determined by the brain; cultural evolution is also important in the development of adaptations. From an evolutionary perspective, culture provides important environmental input to evolutionary mechanisms.

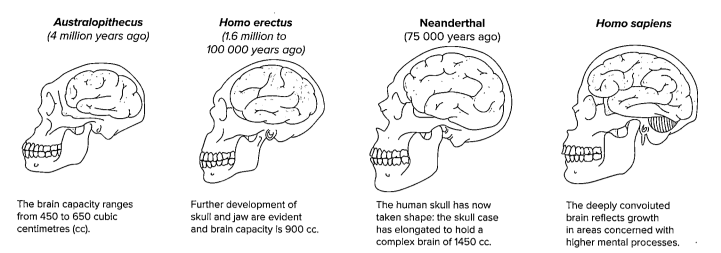

FIGURE 4.11 The human brain evolved over a period of several million years. The greatest growth occurred in those areas concerned with the higher mental processes, particularly attention, memory, thought, and language.

Some evolved biological mechanisms allow broad adaptations, such as the ability to learn a language, repeat behaviours that are rewarded and suppress those that are punished, reason logically, and imagine future events. Others are considered to be **domain-specific adaptations,** designed to solve a particular problem, such as selecting a suitable mate, choosing safe foods to eat, avoiding certain environmental hazards (snakes, cliff edges, spiders), detecting cheating and deception in others, and forming cooperative alliances with other people. Domain-specific mechanisms suggest that the human mind is not a general, all-purpose problem solver but rather a collection of specialized and somewhat independent *modules* that evolved to handle specific adaptive problems. As we shall see throughout the book, this modular approach to brain/mind functioning helps us understand many aspects of consciousness, problem solving, emotion, personality, and behaviour.

> **15.** Describe examples of human behaviour that suggest innate evolved mechanisms.

Thinking critically

NATURAL SELECTION AND GENETIC DISEASES

If Darwin was right about natural selection, then why do we have so many harmful genetic disorders? Consider, for example, cystic fibrosis, a hereditary disorder of European origin that clogs one's lungs with mucus and prevents breathing, typically causing death before age 30. Another example is sickle-cell anemia, which causes early deaths in many people of African descent. Can you reconcile the existence of such disorders with "survival of the fittest"?

Think about it, and then see the Answers section at the end of the book.

Evolution and Human Nature

Evolutionary psychologists suggest that the essence of human nature is the adaptations that have evolved through natural selection to solve problems specific to the human environment. We now consider a sampling of common aspects of human behaviour that will be discussed in greater detail throughout the book:

- Infants are born with an innate ability to acquire any language spoken in the world. The specific language(s) learned depends on which ones they are exposed to. Deaf children have a similar innate ability to acquire any sign language, and their language acquisition pattern parallels the learning of spoken language. Language is central to human thought and communication.

- Newborns are prewired to perceive specific stimuli. For example, they are more responsive to pictures of human faces than to pictures of the same facial features arranged in a random pattern (Fantz, 1961). They are also able to discriminate the odour of their mother's milk from that of other women (McFarlane, 1975). Both adaptations improve human bonding with caregivers.

- At one week of age, human infants show primitive mathematical skills, successfully discriminating between two and three objects. These abilities improve with age in the absence of any training. The brain seems designed to make "greater than" and "less than" judgments, which are clearly important in decision making (Geary, 2005).

(left): © Ryan McVay/Getty Images; (middle): © Royalty-Free/Corbis; (right): © 2009 Jupiterimages Corporation

FIGURE 4.12 The human smile seems to be a universal expression of positive emotion and is universally perceived that way. Evolutionary psychologists believe that expressions of basic emotions are hard-wired biological mechanisms that have adaptive value as methods of communication.

- Humans seem to have a need to belong and strongly fear being ostracized from the group. Social anxiety (fear of social disapproval) may be an adaptive mechanism to protect against doing things that will prompt group rejection (Baumeister & Tice, 1990).

- Humans, like other social animals, tend to be altruistic and helpful to other members of their own group. We tend to be especially altruistic toward relatives (Curry et al., 2015). Helping family members and relatives increases the likelihood that those people will be able to pass on the genes they share with you.

- As we will see in Chapter 11, there is much evidence for a set of basic emotions that are universally recognized (Ekman, 1973). Smiling, for example, is a universal expression of happiness and goodwill that typically evokes positive reactions from others (Figure 4.12). Emotions are important means of social communication that evoke psychological mechanisms in others (Ketellar, 1995).

- Our personal adaptations to life result from our interactions with immediate and past environments. Theorists propose that as the human brain evolved, it acquired adaptive capacities that enhanced our ability to learn and solve problems (Hofman, 2015). That is, we are predisposed to learn.

Review

- Evolutionary psychology focuses on biologically based mechanisms sculpted by evolutionary forces as solutions to the problems of adaptation faced by species. Some of these genetically based mechanisms are general (e.g., the ability to learn), but many are domain-specific (e.g., mate selection).

- Evolution involves a change over time in the frequency with which specific genes occur within an interbreeding population. Evolution represents an interaction between biological and environmental factors in both its original and later influences on behaviour.

- The cornerstone of Darwin's theory of evolution is the principle of natural selection, which posits that biologically based characteristics that contribute to survival and reproductive success increase in the population over time because those who lack the characteristic are less likely to pass on their genes.

Evolutionary Psychology

As is clear from the quotation that opens this chapter, Charles Darwin expected that an evolutionary analysis would be applied to behaviour, including human behaviour, and not just anatomy. Darwin himself wrote about human emotions and other behaviours, and some early psychologists, such as William James, continued that theme. As we discussed in Chapter 1, in their influential and controversial work in the mid-1970s sociobiologists such as E.O. Wilson argued that natural selection favours behaviours that increase the ability to pass on one's genes to the next generation. Despite this history, it is only within the past few decades that evolutionary psychology has become a major, and growing, perspective within psychology.

Although related, evolutionary psychology and sociobiology are different. The core principle of sociobiology is that the main purpose of the gene is to propagate itself. That is, the gene's purpose is to make more genes (i.e., reproduce). Evolutionary psychology focuses on the study of behaviour and the nervous systems from an evolutionary perspective and includes a wide range of behaviours, not just those directly linked to reproduction. An evolutionary analysis is being applied across a growing range of behaviours from traditional areas of evolutionary analysis, such as mating patterns, to personality traits and even consciousness (Bridgeman, 2003), and even to political attitudes (see the *Frontiers* feature). Whatever the specific topic, an evolutionary psychologist thinks about behaviour in terms of functions and how those functions contribute to the success and adaptability of the individual.

Personality

Behaviour genetics researchers attempt to understand how biological factors contribute to differences between individuals on personality traits. An approach called **evolutionary personality theory** (Buss, 1999, 2007) asks an even more basic question: Where did the traits come from in the first place?

A current theory of personality, the Five Factor Model we discussed earlier in this chapter, argues that the human personality has a limited number of basic dimensions. Researchers have argued that these basic personality traits are found universally across all humans. Why should we find these traits so consistently in cultures around the world? According to David Buss (1999), an evolutionary personality

16. According to evolutionary theorists, what is the origin of the basic personality traits?

theorist, they exist in humans because they have helped us achieve two overriding goals: physical survival and reproduction of the species. Traits such as extraversion and emotional stability were helpful in attaining positions of dominance and mate selection. Conscientiousness and agreeableness might be particularly important to group survival, as well as in reproduction and the care of children. Finally, because openness to experience may be the basis for problem solving and creative activities that could affect the ultimate survival of the species, there has always been a need for intelligent and creative people. Thus, evolutionary theorists regard basic personality traits as having been sculpted by natural selection pressures until they became part of human nature. They may also reflect the ways in which we are biologically prepared to think about and discriminate between people. Lewis Goldberg (1981) suggests that over the course of evolution, people have had to ask five basic questions when they interact with another person. In order of importance, these questions have survival and reproductive implications:

1. Is Person X active and dominant or passive and submissive? Can I dominate X or will I have to submit to X?

2. Is Person X agreeable and friendly, or hostile and uncooperative?

3. Can I count on X? Is X conscientious and dependable?

4. Is X sane (stable, rational, predictable) or crazy (unstable, unpredictable, possibly dangerous)?

5. How smart is X, and how quickly can X learn and adapt?

Not surprisingly, according to Goldberg, these questions map onto five basic personality traits. He argues that this is why factor analyses of trait ratings reveal the same five traits consistently across very diverse cultures. One issue that could arise from considering human personality from an evolutionary analysis is the range of human personality. If extraversion and openness to experience are adaptive and selected for, why, then, are we not all extraverted and open to new experiences? Extraversion is adaptive in some situations, but introversion can also be adaptive in some situations and in some social roles. Similarly, openness to experience is adaptive in many situations and social roles, but not all. One of the reasons that humankind has been so successful is that humans are a highly adaptable social species. In different times, in different

Frontiers

HERITABILITY, EVOLUTION, AND POLITICS

We tend to assume that people develop their political attitudes, such as their level of interest in politics and identification with a political party, based on social learning and socialization, which depends, importantly, on their family environment. We expect political leanings and interests to "run in families" because children are exposed to specific political discussions and attitudes from an early age, and relevant behaviours modelled by their parents and siblings. But does being politically engaged and politically left- or right-wing run in families because of heritability and not because of socialization processes? Both of the approaches we have encountered in this chapter, behaviour genetics and evolutionary psychology, are now being applied to political attitudes and behaviour (Lopez & McDermott, 2012).

Political interest—one's willingness to pay attention to politics—is one attitude that had been thought to be due to socialization processes. However, a twin study using two separate twin samples, one in Denmark and one in the United States, found a high degree of heritability for political interest (Klemmensen et al., 2012). With a total sample size of almost 4000 individuals, researchers were able to separate the relative contributions of genetic, familial environment, and unique environmental factors (see the discussions of behaviour genetics and personality earlier in this chapter). For both the Danish and the American samples, genetic factors and unique environmental factors played a significant role in political interest, whereas familial environment had a negligible impact.

If overall level of political interest has a heritable component, what about more specific political attitudes? Edward Bell and colleagues assessed a range of political attitudes among a sample of 570 adults that included 192 pairs of monozygotic twins and 78 pairs of dizygotic twins (Bell et al., 2009). Questions included general interest in national politics, feelings towards the major Canadian political parties, left/liberal versus right/conservative orientation, and six political attitude scales. As shown in Table 4.4, they found substantial genetic effects for four of the six political attitude scales, with heritability values ranging from 0.41 to 0.73. Level of political interest and left/liberal versus right/conservative identification also had an important genetic contribution. Unique environmental factors had a significant role in all attitudes measured, although it was less important than genetic contributions for most measures. As we have seen elsewhere in this chapter, there is a role for both heritability and unique personal experiences in explaining variations in behaviour. Genetic effects were also reported for feelings toward the major federal parties, party identification, and voting choice, with heritability values ranging from 0.33 to 0.62.

The principles of evolutionary psychology are also being applied to gain an understanding of political phenomena (Lopez & McDermott, 2012). For example, we know that

TABLE 4.4 Estimates of Group Variance in Political Attitudes Attributable to Genetic and Environmental Factors

	Genetic	Familial Environment	Unique Environmental
Political interest	0.62	–	0.38
Left/liberal vs. right/ conservative	0.57	–	0.43
Attitude scales			
Social conservatism	0.73	–	0.27
Environmentalism	–	0.56	0.44
Economic equality	0.58	–	0.42
State and social issues	–	0.46	0.54
Competition/business	0.41	–	0.59
Ethnic/racial minorities	0.52	–	0.48

Source: Adapted from Bell, E., Schermer, J. A., & Vernon, P. A. (2009). The origins of political attitudes and behaviours: An analysis using twins. *Canadian Journal of Political Science*, 42(4), 855–879. Reprinted by permission of SAGE Publications

after a competition testosterone levels tend to rise or stay stable in victors and to fall in losers. An evolutionary analysis may examine the impact of this phenomenon within the context of dominance hierarchies and the consequences on reproductive success (Archer, 2006). What about the impact in a very modern competition? Based on an evolutionary analysis, researchers predicted that the supporters of a losing political candidate would experience a post-election drop in testosterone, while supporters of the winning candidate would not. Stanton and colleagues (Stanton et al., 2009) tested 163 voters during the 2008 presidential election in the United States. They found that men who voted for the winning candidate, Barack Obama, had stable post-election levels of testosterone, while men who voted for either of the losing candidates showed a decline in testosterone levels. This pattern of testosterone change remained even when other factors that might influence results were controlled for (e.g., strength of support, timing of sample collection, levels of conservatism, social surroundings on election night). An evolutionary analysis is being applied to a range of topics within political science, such as leadership, aggression and conflict resolution, attitudes, and resource sharing. For example, the techniques, perspective, and analyses of evolutionary psychology have been applied to the new field of *evolutionary political science* (Lopez & McDermott, 2012).

We are a social species. Living in groups has been a successful and enduring feature of human nature. Natural selection has worked on the mechanisms that underlie political attitudes and behaviours as it has on other areas of human activity, and this relationship is being explored using the techniques and analyses we have encountered in this chapter.

environments, within different social roles, the range of personality characteristics that we can display has allowed us to adapt and thrive.

Mating Systems and Parental Investment

17. What is meant by parental investment?

The task facing any species is to insure not only the survival of the current generation, but also the survival of the next generation. A variety of strategies have evolved to solve this task. At one extreme are species that produce an extremely large number of offspring and offer little or no care, but enough of the young survive to continue the species. Many types of fish as well as other animals take this approach. Large numbers of eggs are laid, but many eggs are lost to predation and only a tiny proportion of hatchlings survive to adulthood. At the other extreme are species that produce few offspring but offer care and protection until the offspring are self-sufficient and capable of surviving on their own. The evolution of many animals, including humans, led to this later approach. Humans and most other mammals invest a great deal in a small number of offspring to protect and sustain the next generation in an environment with limited resources and danger of predation (Figure 4.13). From this basic dichotomy—little investment in many offspring versus large investment in few offspring—there are also differences between the sexes because of what females and males each contribute to reproduction. That is, one difference across species is in **parental investment**. Parental investment refers to the time, effort, energy, and risk associated with caring successfully for each offspring.

In one of the most influential papers in modern evolutionary theory, Robert Trivers (1972) described a theory in which he used sex differences in parental investment to explain different mating systems. An offspring of a sexually reproducing species has two parents, but the two parents do not necessarily make equal parental investment. Trivers argued that if parental investment is unequal, the parent who invests most in offspring will be more vigorously competed for and will be more discriminating when choosing a mate. One source of sex difference in parental investment is the simple fact of biology that male and female reproductive cells, or gametes, differ. Female mammals produce relatively few large, nutrient-rich gametes, that is, ova or eggs. Males produce many small, mobile gametes, the sperm. Investment continues to diverge during the nine months of human gestation, then delivery, and then breast-feeding

18. How does the idea of parental investment explain differences in physical size between the sexes?

19. What mating system described by Trivers fits with your experience of human society?

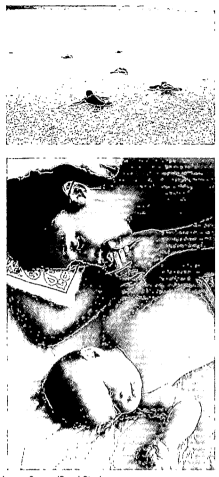

(top): © Image Source/PunchStock;
(bottom): © Cultura RM/Alamy Stock Photo

FIGURE 4.13 Some animals, such as the sea turtles shown here, produce enough offspring that even without protection or care enough will survive to adulthood to continue the species. Other species, such as humans, produce few young but offer extensive care until the offspring are self-sufficient.

(which can last up to four years in some human societies; Shostack, 1981). Although some components of parental investment can vary, there is, at the core, a sex difference due to the biological differences between male and female roles in reproduction.

If females of a species have high parental investment and necessary male parental investment is low, Trivers's theory predicts that polygyny would be most common. Female investment is high, so females will be competed for, and necessary male investment is low, so males can maximize their fitness by producing many offspring with many different females. Most mammals are polygynous, a mating system in which one male may mate with many females (**polygyny** means literally *poly-* "many"; *-gyn-* "females"). Such a system should lead to larger

© PhotoLink/Getty Images

FIGURE 4.14 Among polygynous species, such as the elephant seals shown here, natural selection has favoured large males, but there has been no such selection pressure on females. If the species is monogamous, then both sexes compete for mates, so there is no selection pressure for one sex to become significantly larger than the other.

and stronger males, since increased size and strength would confer an advantage in male-male competition. In general, it is true that the more polygynous the species, the greater the difference in size between males and females, with the males of the species larger than the females (Figure 4.14). The female, on the other hand, should be discriminating in choice of mate. She can produce a limited number of offspring, and each is a large investment. A poor choice by the female has important consequences: lower reproductive success, risk to her health, fewer of her children will survive to reproductive age, and opportunities for more successful matings missed.

If both female and male investment is high, then Trivers's analysis would predict a **monogamous mating system.** Equal, or approximately equal, parental investment would be expected if it is unlikely that a single parent can successfully raise the offspring (Dewsbury, 1988). Natural selection would favour genes that lead to parents staying together, at least until the young are self-sufficient. One reason that many species of birds (approximately 90 percent; Lack, 1968) are monogamous is that it is almost impossible for a single parent to successfully care for young. The eggs must be incubated, and the eggs and the flightless hatchlings need constant protection from predators. A lone parent faces the dilemma of staying at the nest to care for and protect eggs and hatchlings or leaving the nest to find food. A second parent that can share in incubation, protection, and foraging is an enormous advantage. If parental investment

is high among both females and males, then competition for a mate is not limited to one sex and monogamous species should show few sex differences in size and strength. Monogamous species show little sexual dimorphism in size or strength.

Of other possible mating systems, **polyandry,** in which one female mates with many males, is rare among mammals but occurs in some species of fish and insects, as well as in a small number of bird species. Within polyandrous species, it is the females who compete with one another for access to males. Consistent with a parental investment analysis, the females of polyandrous species are larger, stronger, more active, and more aggressive than males of the species.

The final mating system is one of **polygynandry,** or promiscuity, in which all members of the group mate with all other members of the group. Polygynandry is found among some primates, such as chimpanzees (Goodall, 1986), and is especially clear among bonobo chimps (Wrangham, 1993). For a highly social species such as bonobos, polygynandry is one possible way to reduce competition for a mate and may help bonobos be the most peaceful of all primates.

For humans, modern birth control techniques have altered much of the selective pressures for specific mating patterns based on parental investment in reproduction. But remember that human sexual psychology evolved over millions of years to cope with the pressures of adapting to the environment millennia before the advent of birth control. It is still the case that the human female has the greater necessary parental investment. But beyond the necessary minimal parental investment dictated by our reproductive physiology, it is clear that there is potential for both men and women to invest in children and that parental investment by the male does have an impact on the likelihood that the young will thrive.

Mate Preference

As just discussed, the theory of parental investment predicts that there will be competition for the sex with the highest parental investment. It also predicts that the sex with the greater parental investment will be more discriminating when selecting a mate. Evolutionary psychologists have argued that the most common and powerful mate preferences are all preferences that make the most sense from an evolutionary perspective. The results of a worldwide study of

20. How are male and female mate preferences similar? How are they different?

(left) Terry Allen/Alamy Stock Photo; (middle left) Grant Rooney Premium/Alamy Stock Photo; (middle right) © Photo Japan/Alamy Stock Photo; (right) Kwame Zikomo/Purestock/ SuperStock

FIGURE 4.15 Culture determines many details about how we live our lives, such as what is appropriate wedding attire. There is surprising consistency across cultures, however, in what men and women each look for in a mate.

mate preferences, for example, found considerable overlap between what men and women look for in a mate, but also reported differences (Figure 4.15; see the *Research Foundations* feature).

Women prefer older men as potential mates. Averaged over all cultures, women preferred men who were about three and a half years older. The actual worldwide average age difference between brides and grooms is three years, and in every culture studied, grooms were older, on average, than brides. That is, the actual marriage decisions of women match their expressed preferences. Evolutionarily this preference makes sense: Young adult males rarely have the respect, status, and access to resources that are achieved by older, more established males. Males in traditional hunter–gatherer societies have their peak access to resources in their late 20s, when status and physical strength are high, or later in life, when accumulated experience, skill, wisdom, and social status confer advantages, not when they are entering adulthood. Even within modern North American society, income, and hence access to resources, tends to increase with age.

Together with the woman's preference for a slightly older mate, women also show a preference for symmetrical faces and other signs of physical health (Thornhill & Gangestad, 2006). A symmetrical face is a sign that the person is free of parasites or has a genetic resistance to parasites, and has had a healthy and normal physical development (Gangestad, Haselton, &

Buss, 2007). Interestingly, these female preferences are most pronounced in parts of the world with high levels of pathogens (disease-causing organisms). In places where diseases such as malaria, plague, and yellow fever are most prevalent, male characteristics such as facial symmetry, robustness, intelligence, and social dominance—all signs of biological fitness—are especially important to women (Gangestad et al., 2006).

Given the large parental investment by women, and the added advantage to their children conferred by a mate who contributes to the care and rearing of those children, one would expect that women would prefer a mate who has demonstrated a willingness to contribute to a child's well-being (Buss, 2007). An interesting study by Peggy La Cerra (Buss, 1999) assessed whether women might have a preference for men who show signs of high parental investment. La Cerra showed female undergraduate students pictures of males in one of five conditions: (1) standing alone, (2) smiling and playing with an 18-month-old child, (3) ignoring a crying child, (4) with a child, but in an emotionally neutral pose with no male–child interaction, and (5) doing housework (vacuuming). The same set of males was shown in all conditions, so different ratings across the five conditions could not be due to the actual physical attractiveness of the men. Female undergraduates saw a series of 240 slides and then rated the males on a series of criteria, including how attractive the man was as a potential mate

21. Why do women in all cultures tend to marry older men?

22. Why do women and men find a symmetrical face attractive?

Research Foundations

GENDER DIFFERENCES IN THE IDEAL MATE

Introduction

How can we test the hypothesis that across millennia, evolution has shaped the psyche of men and women to be different? Evolutionary psychologist David Buss proposes that, as a start, we can examine whether gender differences in mate preferences are consistent across cultures. If they are, this would be consistent with the argument that men and women follow different, biologically based mating strategies that have developed during our evolutionary history. Buss hypothesized that across cultures

- men will prefer younger women because such women have greater reproductive capacity;
- men will value signs of physical health and fertility, such as attractiveness, more than women; and
- women will place greater value than men on a potential mate's earning potential, since such resources provide survival advantages for women and their children.

Method

A team of 50 scientists administered questionnaires to women and men from 37 cultures around the world. Although not randomly selected, the sample of 10 047 participants was ethnically, religiously, and socioeconomically diverse. Participants reported the ideal age for marriage for themselves and their spouse, rank-ordered 13 different qualities from least to most desirable in a mate, and performed a separate rating of the importance of 18 mate qualities.

Results

In every culture, men preferred younger women. Overall, men reported that the ideal age for marriage was 27.5 for men and 24.8 for women, a difference of 2.7 years. Women preferred older males, and actually preferred a slightly larger age difference; on average, women reported that the ideal age for men to marry was 28.8 and for women 25.4 years, a difference of 3.4 years. In every one of the 37 cultures, men valued physical attractiveness of a mate more than women did. In 36 of the 37 cultures, women valued a mate's earning potential more than men did. Buss concluded that the results strongly supported the predictions based on evolutionary theory. Table 4.5 shows the study's overall results.

Discussion

Buss's research provides evidence of remarkable cross-cultural consistency in gender differences in mate

TABLE 4.5 What Do You Look for in a Mate?

Women and men from 37 cultures rated each characteristic on a 4-point scale. From top to bottom, the numbers represent the order (rank) and the most to least highly rated characteristic, for Buss's worldwide sample. How would you rate the characteristics' importance?

	Preferred by			Preferred by	
	Women	**Men**	**Characteristic**	**Women**	**Men**
Mutual attraction/love	1	1	Refinement	10	9
Dependable character	2	2	Similar education	11	14
Emotional stability/maturity	3	3	Good financial prospect	12	13
Pleasing disposition	4	4	Good looks	13	10
Education/Intelligence	5	6	Social status	14	15
Sociability	6	7	Good cook/housekeeper	15	12
Good health	7	5	Similar religion	16	17
Desire for home/children	8	8	Similar politics	17	18
Ambitious	9	11	Chastity	18	16

Source: Data from Buss, D.M., Abbott, M., Angleitner, A., Asherian, A., Biaggio, A., Blanco-Villasenor, A., . . . Kuo-Shu, Y. (1990). International preferences in selecting mates: A study of 37 cultures. *Journal of Cross-Cultural Psychology*, 21, 5–47.

continued

preferences. Buss interprets the cross-cultural consistency as evidence that men and women follow different, biologically based mating strategies. Buss's conclusions have stimulated considerable debate, and some have argued that the cross-cultural consistency may reflect other factors, such as gender inequality (Wood & Eagly, 2000), and not our evolutionary past. It is important to note that there are many similarities in female and male mate preferences, and there are important differences in mate preferences cross-culturally. Indeed, as Buss wrote, "there may be more similarity between men and women from the same culture than between men and men or women and women from different cultures" (p. 17).

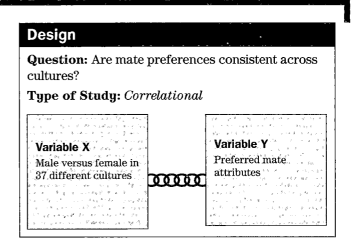

Design

Question: Are mate preferences consistent across cultures?

Type of Study: *Correlational*

Variable X
Male versus female in 37 different cultures

Variable Y
Preferred mate attributes

Source: David M. Buss (1989) Sex differences in human mate preferences: Evolutionary hypotheses tested in 37 cultures. *Behavioral and Brain Sciences, 12,* 1–49.

(see Figure 4.16). Women rated men who were interacting positively with the child the highest as a potential mate and rated the man ignoring the crying child the lowest. But it was not simply that the man interacting with the child portrayed an acceptable domestic scene; the man cleaning house was actually rated as less attractive than the man standing alone or the man and child shown in an emotionally neutral pose. That is, male attractiveness was enhanced by signs of parental investment and decreased by indifference toward a child in distress.

Interestingly, in parallel tests with male participants shown pictures of females in similar situations, it made no difference what the woman was doing. Whether the woman was interacting with a child, ignoring a crying child, standing alone, standing unemotionally next to a child, or vacuuming had no effect: Men's attractiveness ratings were the same across all conditions. Such findings among contemporary North American university students are what one would predict based on a parental investment analysis of mate preference.

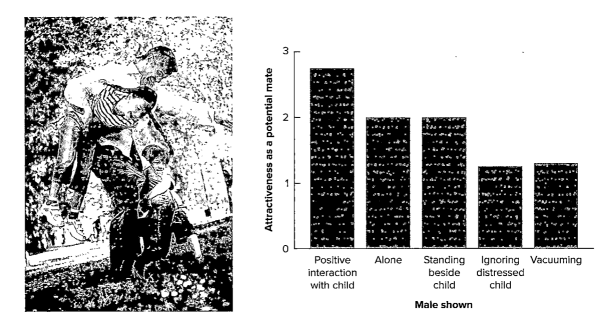

FIGURE 4.16 When rating males on attractiveness as potential mates, evidence of parental investment, such as positive emotional interactions with a young child, increases attractiveness ratings while evidence of low investment, such as ignoring a distressed child, decreases attractiveness.

© Max Power/Corbis; Source: Adapted from Buss, D.M. (1999). "Human nature and individual differences: The evolution of human personality." In L.A. Pervin & O.P. John (Eds.), *Handbook of personality: Theory and research* (2nd ed.). New York, NY: Guilford Press.

Male mate preferences have also been explored within an evolutionary perspective. Men tend to prefer women who display signs of youth and physical health, such as smooth skin, animated facial expressions, a high energy level, and a bouncy, youthful gait (Buss, 1999; Thornhill & Gangestad, 2006). The interpretation from an evolutionary perspective is clear: Males have evolved to value those characteristics that are associated with youth—and hence future reproductive potential—and with health. Remember that reproductive success includes the ability of the woman to remain in good health during pregnancy, to successfully carry the pregnancy to term, to have the energy and physical health to nurse the child, and to be able to care for and nurture the child until the child can eventually care for him- or herself.

Together with a strong male preference for signs of a woman's youth and health, research has also found a surprising degree of cross-cultural consistency in male rating of female physical attractiveness. For example, in one study (Cunningham et al., 1995), males of different races judged the attractiveness of women's faces shown in photographs. The photographs were of women of different ethnic groups, including Asian, Hispanic, Black, and White women. The average correlation in the attractiveness ratings between males of different racial groups was +0.95, a tremendously high correlation in psychological research. That is, males of all races agreed in their ratings of the photographs. Familiarity with or exposure to Western culture or to the culture of the model shown in the photograph did not influence attractiveness ratings.

For mate preferences to evolve, they must have had an impact on actual mating. Furthermore, although women's preferences powerfully control actual mating, the mate preferences between the sexes should at least be compatible. A clear example of the compatibility of mate preferences is the worldwide preference of women for older men and men for younger women. The impact of these preferences on actual mating is demonstrated by the worldwide prevalence of brides who are younger than grooms.

Altruism

Despite competition for mates, preferred foods, and safe places to sleep, social animals also help one another. There are two broad categories of helping: cooperation and altruism. **Cooperation** refers to situations in which one individual helps another and in so doing also gains some advantage. When you and your friends work together

on a project, you all benefit from one another's efforts and expertise. The adaptive value of cooperation is clear. As a species developed the behavioural repertoire that supported cooperation, groups of individuals became capable of accomplishing more than any individual could accomplish alone (Buss, 2007). Social animals benefit from cooperation in many activities, from finding food, to dealing with predators, to protecting their home territory, to caring for young. Many of the benefits of being a social species are based on cooperation.

Different from cooperation are acts of altruism. **Altruism** occurs when one individual helps another, but in so doing he or she accrues some cost. For example, when a bird emits a call to warn off a predator, the warning helps other members of the flock but puts the signaller in greater danger since it has advertised its location to the predator. In a series of classic studies, Sherman (1977) demonstrated that ground squirrels who sounded predator alarms to warn others of their colony were indeed at greater risk (Figure 4.17). Predators (weasels, badgers, coyotes) stalked and killed alarm callers at a far higher rate than noncallers. On the surface, altruism may not appear to make evolutionary sense: by engaging in altruism, individuals decrease the likelihood that they will survive.

© Richard R. Hansen/Photo Researchers, Inc.

FIGURE 4.17 This female ground squirrel has spotted a predator and is sounding an alarm call to warn other squirrels of the danger. In sounding an alarm, this female ground squirrel helps others of her colony but places herself at increased risk of being found and killed by the predator.

23. What is the difference between cooperation and altruism?

There are two important theories of altruism. The first, the **kin selection theory** of altruism argues that altruism developed to increase the survival of relatives (Hamilton, 1964; Curry et al., 2013). Many animals evolved living in small groups in which there was at least some degree of genetic relatedness across many group members. Even in large mixed groups, some members of the groups will be genetically related; there may be siblings, offspring, aunts or uncles, and other family members within the group. In showing altruism, one individual may perish, but if this increases the likelihood that genetically related individuals survive, the genes that support altruism will be selected for and spread through more and more members of the species across generations. The kin selection theory predicts that we should direct more acts of altruism toward relatives than toward nonrelatives. From squirrels (Sherman, 1977), to chimpanzees (Goodall, 1986), to humans (Curry et al., 2013), there is evidence that supports the contention that altruism is more likely to be shown toward kin than nonkin. As shown in Figure 4.18, as the degree of genetic relatedness decreases from 0.5 (e.g., siblings, parents) to 0.25 (e.g., half-siblings, aunts, uncles, nieces, nephews) to 0.125 (e.g., cousins, children of half-siblings), there is a concomitant decrease in altruism (Essock-Vitale & McGuire, 1985).

The second of the evolutionary theories of altruism is the **theory of reciprocal altruism.**

> 24. Combining the kin selection and reciprocity theories of altruism, who are you the most likely to help? Who are you the least likely to help?

This theory argues that altruism is, in essence, long-term cooperation (Trivers, 1971; Cosmides & Tooby, 1992). That is, one individual may help another, but that assistance will be reciprocated at some time in the future. If this theory of reciprocal altruism is correct, then social animals should remember who has helped them in the past and should help those individuals. Furthermore, they should not offer further assistance to individuals who have failed to reciprocate. It also requires a relatively stable social group; transient members are unlikely to be present to offer assistance at some later date (Figure 4.19). We have all experienced reciprocal altruism. If you help your roommates move, then you expect that, in the future, they will come to your assistance when you move. Likewise, if you have gone out of your way to pick up friends after work, then you expect that they would do the same when you need a ride. A large part of gossip is a public inventory of favours owed and repaid, and a public account of who is and who is not reliable for reciprocating (Barkow, 1992). Such reciprocal altruism between unrelated individuals has been observed in other social primates, such as bonobos (Surbeck & Hohmann, 2015).

These two theories of altruism, kin selection and reciprocity, are not incompatible. Kin selection theory offers an explanation of why we are more likely to act altruistically toward genetically related individuals, and why the likelihood of altruism decreases in an orderly way as genetic relatedness decreases. Reciprocity theory offers an explanation of why we also offer assistance to and request assistance from nonkin. However, altruism does not always occur; we do not always come to each other's aid. One of the challenges in the study of altruism is to identify what environmental factors increase and decrease the likelihood that we will engage in acts of altruism.

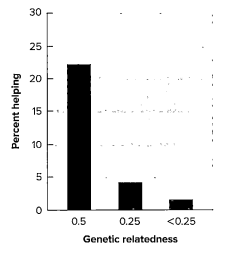

FIGURE 4.18 In a study of 300 adult women, 2520 instances of receiving help and 2651 instances of giving help were analyzed. The likelihood of giving and receiving help decreased as degree of genetic relatedness decreased.

Source: Adapted from Essock-Vitale, S.M., & McGuire, M.T. (1985). Women's lives viewed from an evolutionary perspective: II. *Patterns of helping. Ethology and Sociobiology,* 6, 155–173.

Tannis Toohey/Toronto Star via Getty Images

FIGURE 4.19 An act of altruism.

Aggression

One of the problems facing any animal is that the most valued resources are in limited supply. There are not enough of the best things to eat, safest places to shelter from predators, safest and most comfortable places to sleep, or most desirable mates. One possible solution to this problem is for animals to compete with each other or for a group to compete with another group to determine who has access to the resource. Evolutionarily, then, aggression may have developed as a means to protect one's mate, young, territory, or food, to co-opt others' resources, or to gain access to unclaimed resources. In many species of birds, for example, a male will attack other males of his species that approach his mate or his nest during the mating season. Fighting to protect one's territory or to usurp the territory and resources of others has been reported among a wide range of species, including lions, macaques, birds, and chimpanzees (Wilson, 1980; Goodall, 1986).

An important source of intraspecies aggression is competition for a mate. The rocks of the Galapagos Islands are densely populated by iguanas, and during mating there is a constant display of aggression with ritualized fighting and submissive postures by the losers (Eibl-Eibesfeldt, 1998). You are likely familiar with film footage of male rams, moose, or elk engaged in aggressive displays and physical confrontations during the mating season (Figure 4.20). Competition for a mate can be intense, and once a male and female have partnered, aggression may be used to protect one's mate from other suitors and the threat of sexual infidelity. Among humans, one of the most common causes of homicide is sexual jealousy,

most frequently two men fighting about a woman (Daly, Wilson, & Weghorst, 1982). Less extreme forms of aggression also occur within the context of winning or protecting a mate, and aggression may be used to inflict some cost on rivals. For example, both men and women belittle same-sex rivals, attempting to make their rivals appear less desirable (Buss & Dedden, 1990).

As animals evolved larger, more complex brains and more sophisticated mental functions, an important change occurred in competition: animals acquired the ability to recognize others and to remember past encounters. Unlike the constantly head-butting iguanas, birds and mammals could remember the outcome of a past conflict with another animal. Instead of having to compete anew each time there were resources to allocate or protect, social animals developed dominance hierarchies. Once a dominance hierarchy is established, and provided it is unchallenged, members of the group can determine access to resources without unnecessary, energy-expensive, and dangerous aggressive encounters. Hierarchies are established in the initial encounters between animals if the group is being formed or if a new member joins the group. Among social primates, such as chimpanzees, the dominant male is invariably physically large and experienced. Dominance position among primates is not, however, simply a matter of overt aggressiveness (Figure 4.21).

25. Evolutionarily, what function or functions does aggression serve?

© W. Perry Conway/Magma/Corbis

FIGURE 4.20 Male rams butting heads are an example of aggression that has developed evolutionarily.

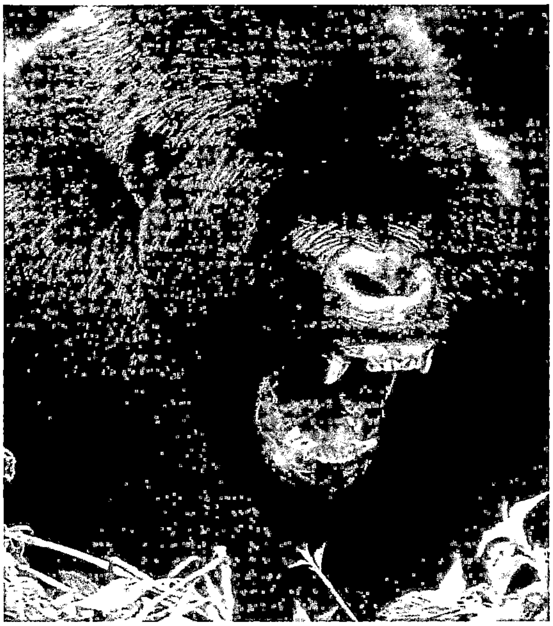

© Digital Vision/PunchStock

FIGURE 4.21 After establishing a dominance hierarchy, primates do not need to rely on aggressive behaviour to maintain dominant status.

The dominant male owes his position as much to his ability to form social alliances with other males, usually relatives, as he does to outright aggression (Goodall, 1971).

Within a group of social animals, aggression may occur in forming dominance hierarchies and if an animal challenges another in an attempt to better its position in the hierarchy. The dominance hierarchy, however, functions as much to decrease the amount of aggression within the group as it does to provide a context for aggression. Apart from settling order of access to resources in a way that avoids unnecessarily repeated conflict, there may be deliberate quelling of aggression. For example, dominant male chimpanzees, spider monkeys, and macaques have been observed to use their position to stop fighting among subordinates (Wilson, 1980).

In some contexts, then, aggression appears to make evolutionary sense: It functions to divide limited resources among a group, and those who are most skilled in physical confrontation or in forming social alliances, depending on the situation and the species, gain the most. Those physical and behavioural attributes that contribute to success should then be selected for and become more widespread within the species.

There is also, however, a pattern of aggression that has been observed only among chimpanzees and humans. Chimpanzees and humans form male coalitions to attack others as a group. For example, a member of Jane Goodall's Gombe team observed a group of eight young male chimpanzees form a fighting party that ventured into the territory of a neighbouring chimpanzee troop. Once there, they found and attacked a lone male chimpanzee, and then returned to their home territory (Wrangham & Peterson, 1996). The fighting party observed by the Gombe team did not gain any tangible benefit from having killed the other chimpanzee, although the actions of the group may have been related to establishing rank or status. Of the 4000 species of mammals, and more than 10 million animal species in total, only two, humans and chimpanzees, have been shown to form coalitions that have the express purpose of engaging in acts of potentially lethal aggression against members of their own species (Figure 4.22).

Such acts of aggression, by lone attackers or organized cooperative groups, are difficult to explain from any perspective, and traditional explanations, such as an aggression instinct or a drive to be aggressive, are clearly inadequate. However, the point is that many species, including chimpanzees and humans, evolved

26. Which members of a group are usually the most aggressive? Why?

Shaney Komulainen/The Canadian Press

FIGURE 4.22 The Oka Crisis confrontation between First Nations people and the Canadian Army featured this famous picture of an aggressive face-to-face showdown.

mechanisms that supported aggressive behaviours. The immediate situation, the environmental cues confronting the individual or group, can activate those mechanisms, whether such activation is related to the competition functions of aggression or is an aberrant display. The rich evolutionary history of species such as chimpanzees and humans has provided much behavioural flexibility, and that flexibility has great adaptive value. It does, however, also allow behaviours to occur in ways that become less rigidly tied to the original functions. The display of aggression is not invariant or inevitable as some early, simplistic instinct theories suggested, but rather is exquisitely sensitive to contextual cues. A male chimpanzee or human may live his entire lifetime without ever displaying overt aggression. Their evolutionary adaptations have provided the physical and psychological mechanisms that make them capable of displaying aggression, but it requires the appropriate eliciting stimuli for the expression of the behavioural potential.

HOW NOT TO THINK ABOUT BEHAVIOUR GENETICS AND EVOLUTIONARY PSYCHOLOGY

Evolutionary theory is an important and influential force in modern psychology. However, it is not without controversial issues, and some misconceptions about evolutionary theory exist.

First, let's consider some scientific issues. One has to do with the standards of evidence for or against evolutionary psychology. Adaptations are forged over a long period of time—thousands of generations—and we cannot go back to prehistoric times to determine with certainty what the environmental demands were. For this reason, evolutionary theorists are often forced to infer the forces to which our ancestors adapted, leading to after-the-fact speculation that is difficult to prove or disprove. Early instinct theory fell victim to the logical fallacy of circular reasoning, although the arguments of modern evolutionary psychology are much more sophisticated and guard against these errors.

Evolutionary theorists also remind us that it is fallacious to attribute every human characteristic to natural selection (Clark & Grunstein, 2005; Lloyd & Feldman, 2002). In the distant past, as in the present, people created environments that help to shape behaviour, and those behaviours can be passed down through cultural learning rather than through natural selection. Likewise, a capability that evolved in the past for one reason may now be adaptive for something else. For example, the ability to discern shapes was undoubtedly advantageous for prehistoric hunters trying to spot game in the underbrush. Today, however, few members of contemporary Western culture need to hunt to survive, but those shape-discriminating capabilities are critical in perceiving letters and learning to read.

While considering behaviour from an evolutionary perspective, it is important to avoid several other fallacies. One is **genetic determinism**, the idea that genes have invariant and unavoidable effects that cannot be altered—the idea that genes are destiny. It is simply not true that because our genes influence something, it is unavoidable or natural. For example, the discovery that early-onset diabetes has a genetic cause did not result in medical science abandoning diabetic patients because nothing could be done. Rather, the discovery allowed scientists to stop looking for a nonexistent viral or bacterial cause, freeing resources to increase understanding of the genetic basis and to develop ways to compensate for the missing enzyme. Researchers' increased understanding of the genetic basis of early-onset diabetes has changed the disease from a diagnosis of a slow death to a treatable condition. The expectation is that as our understanding of human genetics advances it will be possible to develop successful treatments for a range of diseases. One reason for the Human Genome Project has been that whether there is a genetic cause for a disease, such as for Alzheimer's disease, or a genetic predisposition, such as for breast cancer, if we know what gene products are involved, then effective treatments can potentially be developed.

Evolutionary theorists themselves argue against the idea that if something is genetically based it is somehow "natural" and therefore right. In one form, this led to the idea that nature's rule is "survival of the fittest" (a phrase coined by the philosopher Herbert Spencer, not by Charles Darwin). The idea is that those at the top of the social ladder are somehow the "best" people. This idea has been referred to as **social Darwinism.** The notion of the genetic superiority of those at the top of the social hierarchy has had destructive consequences, not the least of which was the eugenics movement of the early 20th century to prevent the "less biologically fit" (particularly immigrants) from breeding, and Nazi Germany's program of selective breeding designed to produce a "master race." As for the notion that genetically based behaviours are natural and must be accepted, we should remember that all behaviours are a function of both the person's biology and environment. We can regulate our own behaviour and exercise moral control, and this is often just as important to our survival (i.e., as adaptive) as are our biological tendencies. Likewise, we can choose to alter the environment to override undesired behavioural tendencies, and many of the laws and sanctions that societies enact serve exactly that purpose.

Another fallacy is the view that evolution is purposive, that there is a grand evolutionary scheme moving toward some end goal. There is, in fact, no plan in evolutionary theory; there is only adaptation to environmental demands and the natural selection process that results. The "nature's plan" concept (together with social Darwinism) has sometimes been used to support the morality of certain acts, even destructive ones. The usual strategy is for proponents of some idea to find an example of what they believe to be a comparable behaviour occurring in the natural world and to use that example to support their own behaviour or cause as "in accord with nature," and it will further humankind's natural progress toward some ideal state. To use this argument to define what is ethically or morally correct is not appropriate. Although there are regularities in natural events that define certain "laws of nature," judgments of morality are most appropriately based on cultural standards and philosophical considerations, and not on biological imperatives.

Review

- Parental investment refers to the time, effort, energy, and risk associated with caring successfully for each offspring. The sex that makes the greater parental investment will be more vigorously competed for and will be more discriminating when choosing a mate. Parental investment and the reproductive physiology of a species, together with environmental factors, have influenced the development of that species' mating system(s).

- Cross-culturally, women tend to prefer males who show signs of willingness to invest in children, physical health, earning potential, status, and ambitiousness. Consistent male preferences include physical attractiveness, good health, and younger women.

- Social species engage in acts of cooperation, in which all involved gain some benefit, and in acts of altruism, in which others benefit but the altruistic individual incurs some risk.

- Animals, including humans, are more likely to show altruism toward genetically related individuals than toward nonkin, according to the kin selection theory of altruism. Altruism among nonkin may contribute to the fitness of the individual by making it more likely that others will act altruistically toward them in the future, according to the theory of reciprocal altruism.

- Aggression may serve functions related to the protection of and allocation of resources, and the establishment of a position in a social dominance hierarchy. Among mammals, including all human cultures that have been studied, males, especially young males, are the most aggressive, since they are the group members that most actively compete.

Gaining Direction

What are the issues?

Is it possible that something as complex as personality has a genetic component? If so, then we would expect twins to show striking similarities in both physical characteristics and personality traits. This expectation is demonstrated dramatically in studies of twins who were separated at birth and later reunited. Such is the case with Jim Lewis and Jim Springer. Both were married twice and had a son named James. Both had the same habits and hobbies. They even liked the same brand of cigarettes and beer. Yet they did not meet each other until they were 39 years old. How do we account for this remarkable similarity? Is there a gene for choice of hobbies? Beer preference? Is genetics the factor that accounts for the similarity between the two brothers? If it is not genetics, then how can we explain the similarity?

What do we need to know?

How are traits passed from one generation to the next?
What effect do nature and nurture have on development?

Are complex traits inherited in humans?
Can personality have a genetic or biological component?
Why should we be interested in twins?

Where can we find the information to answer these questions?

To answer these questions, we must begin by looking at the basics. How do we inherit simple traits such as eye colour? Does the same mechanism underlie more complex behaviour patterns? How about traits such as intelligence or neatness? To answer these questions for humans, we turn to investigations of twins. If we can compare identical twins (who share 100 percent of their genetic material) who have been raised in separate environments (thus reducing any effects of nurture), then we can get a pretty good estimate of the effects of genetics on complex human behaviours. This is exactly what Bouchard and his colleagues have done at the University of Minnesota. In every case, the identical twins show a remarkable degree of similarity. You should consider whether there are other plausible explanations for this observed similarity, and how complex traits could be inherited.

CHAPTER 5

Sensation and Perception

CHAPTER **>**
OUTLINE

SENSORY PROCESSES
Stimulus Detection: The Absolute Threshold
Signal Detection Theory
  Focus on Neuroscience: The Neuroscience
  of Subliminal Perception and Prosopagnosia
The Difference Threshold
Sensory Adaptation

THE SENSORY SYSTEMS
Vision
Audition
Taste and Smell: The Chemical Senses
The Skin and Body Senses
  Frontiers: Sensory Prosthetics:
  Restoring Lost Function

PERCEPTION: THE CREATION OF EXPERIENCE
Perception Is Selective: The Role of Attention
Perceptions Have Organization and Structure

Perception Involves Hypothesis Testing
  Applications: Mona Lisa's Smile
Perception Is Influenced by Expectations:
  Perceptual Sets
Stimuli Are Recognizable under Changing Conditions:
  Perceptual Constancies

PERCEPTION OF DEPTH, DISTANCE,
AND MOVEMENT
Depth and Distance Perception
Perception of Movement

ILLUSIONS: FALSE PERCEPTUAL HYPOTHESES

EXPERIENCE, CRITICAL PERIODS,
AND PERCEPTUAL DEVELOPMENT
  Research Foundations: Critical Periods:
  The Role of Early Experience
Cross-Cultural Research on Perception
Restored Sensory Capacity

> All our knowledge has its origins in our perceptions.
> —Leonardo da Vinci

 In August 1933, three reporters for the *Saint John Telegraph* travelled to Moncton to investigate reports of a mysterious hill where cars ran uphill on their own. This was not the first time such stories had emerged. As early as 1880, area farmers noted that horses seemed to be straining with a loaded cart even though they appeared to be going downhill. If the carts were unhitched at the bottom of the hill, they would roll uphill on their own, as would barrels or bales! It was as if some mysterious magnetic force were pulling these items uphill.

Library and Archives Canada/J.R. Warren Collection/Accession 1977-036

What are the issues here?

What do we need to know?

Where can we find the information to answer these questions?

The three reporters were skeptical and spent the morning looking for the hill with strange magnetic powers. Indeed, they stopped at the bottom of every hill in and around Moncton waiting to see their 1931 Ford Roadster roll uphill. After hours of frustrating searching they stopped at the base of Lutes Mountain and got out of the car to stretch. To their surprise, the roadster calmly rolled uphill away from them.

There are at least ten magnetic or gravity hills in Canada and hundreds around the world. Not a single site has any unusual magnetic field.

Nature gives us a marvellous set of sensory contacts with our world. If our sense organs are not defective, we experience light waves as brightnesses and colours, air vibrations as sounds, chemical substances as odours or tastes, and so on. However, such is not the case for people with a rare and mysterious condition called **synaesthesia,** which means, quite literally, "mixing of the senses" (Cytowic, 2002; Simner & Hubbard, 2014). They may experience sounds as colours or tastes as touch sensations that have different shapes. Women are more likely to be synaesthetes than men (1 in 1150 versus 1 in 7150, respectively; Rice et al., 2005). Interestingly, Maurer and Mondloch (2006) have suggested that we are all born synaesthetic: The neural pathways of infants are fairly undifferentiated and lead to cross-modal perceptions.

The Russian psychologist A.R. Luria (1968) studied a highly successful writer and musician whose life was a perpetual stream of mixed-up sensations. On one occasion, Luria asked him to report on his experiences while listening to electronically generated musical tones. To a medium-pitch tone, the man experienced a brown strip with red edges, together with a sweet-and-sour flavour. A very high-pitched tone evoked the following sensation: "It looks something like a fireworks tinged with a pink-red hue. The strip of colour feels rough and unpleasant, and it has an ugly taste—rather like that of a briny pickle. . . . You could hurt your hand on this."

Sensory-impaired people such as those who experience synaesthesia provide glimpses into different aspects of how we "sense" and "understand" our world. These processes, previewed in Figure 5.1, begin when specific types of stimuli activate specialized sensory receptors. Whether the stimulus is light, sound waves, a chemical molecule, or pressure, your sensory receptors must translate this information into the only language your nervous system understands: the language of nerve impulses.

This process is called *transduction*. Once this translation occurs, specialized neurons called *feature detectors* break down and analyze the specific features of the stimuli. At the next stage, these numerous stimulus "pieces" are reconstructed into a neural representation that is then compared with previously stored information, such as our knowledge of what particular objects look, smell, or feel like. This matching of a new stimulus with our internal storehouse of knowledge allows us to recognize the stimulus and give it meaning. We then consciously experience a perception.

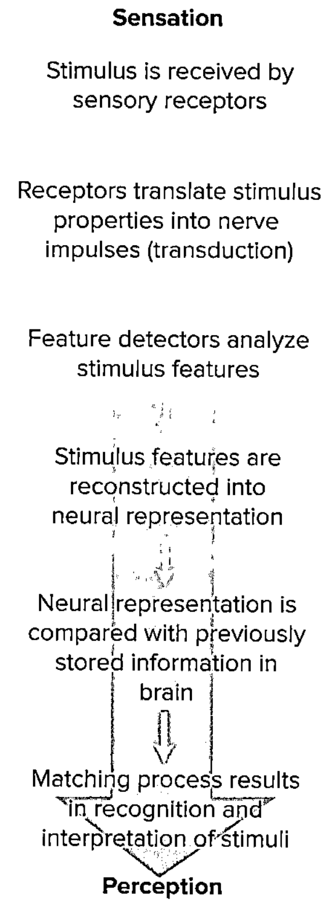

Sensation

Stimulus is received by
sensory receptors

Receptors translate stimulus
properties into nerve
impulses (transduction)

Feature detectors analyze
stimulus features

Stimulus features are
reconstructed into
neural representation

Neural representation is
compared with previously
stored information in
brain

Matching process results
in recognition and
interpretation of stimuli

Perception

FIGURE 5.1 Sensory and perceptual processes proceed from the reception and translation of physical energies into nerve impulses to the active process by which the brain receives the nerve impulses, organizes and confers meaning on them, and constructs a perceptual experience.

1. Describe the six stages that constitute the process of sensory processing and perception of information.

How does this process help us understand the mysterious mixing of the senses in synaesthesia? We know that specific parts of the brain are specialized for different sensory functions. In people with synaesthesia, there is some sort of cross-wiring, so that activity in one part of the brain evokes responses in another part of the brain dedicated to another sensory modality (Ward, 2008). Functional MRI studies have shown that for people with synaesthesia with word-colour linkages, hearing certain words is associated with neural activity in parts of the visual cortex. This activity does not occur in people without synaesthesia, even if they are asked to imagine colours in association with certain words (Nunn et al., 2002). Several explanations have been offered for the sensory mixing (Cytowic & Eagleman, 2009; Hubbard & Ramachandran, 2005). One theory is that the pruning of neural connections that occurs in infancy has not occurred in people with synaesthesia, so that brain regions retain connections that are absent in most people. In support of this theory, diffusion tensor imaging, which lights up white matter pathways in the brain, has revealed increased connectivity in patients with synaesthesia (Rouw & Scholte, 2007). Another theory is that with synaesthesia, there is a deficit in neural inhibitory processes in the brain that ordinarily keep input from one sensory modality from "overflowing" into other sensory areas and stimulating them. Whatever the processes involved, both normal perceptual processes and synaesthesia relate to one of the big mysteries in cognitive neuroscience called the *binding problem*. How do we bind all our perceptions into one complete whole while keeping its sensory elements separate? When you hold a rose in your hand, see its coloured petals, feel the petals' velvety quality, and smell its aroma, these disparate sensory experiences are somehow fused into your total experience of the rose. People with synaesthesia may create additional perceptions of that rose that are inconsistent with its physical properties.

In some ways, sensation and perception blend together so completely that they are difficult to separate, for the stimulation we receive through our sense organs is instantaneously organized and transformed into the experiences that we refer to as perceptions. Nevertheless, psychologists do distinguish between them. **Sensation** is the stimulus-detection process by which our sense organs respond to and translate

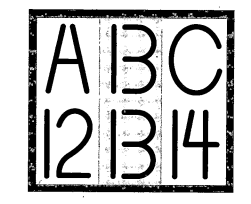

FIGURE 5.2 Quickly read these two lines of symbols out loud. Did your perception of the middle symbol in each line depend on the symbols that surrounded it?

environmental stimuli into nerve impulses that are sent to the brain. **Perception**—making "sense" of what our senses tell us—is the active process of organizing this stimulus input and giving it meaning (Mather, 2006; May, 2007).

Because perception is an active and creative process, the same sensory input may be perceived in different ways at different times. For example, read the two sets of symbols in Figure 5.2. The middle symbols in both sets of curved lines are exactly the same and they send identical input to your brain, but you probably perceive them differently. Your interpretation, or perception, of the characters is influenced by their *context*—that is, by the characters that preceded and followed them, and by your learned expectation of what normally follows the letter *A* and the number *12*. This simple illustration shows how perception takes us a step beyond sensation.

SENSORY PROCESSES

Locked within the silent, dark recesses of your skull, your brain cannot "understand" light waves, sound waves, or the other forms of energy that make up the language of the environment. Contact with the outer world is possible only because certain neurons have developed into specialized sensory receptors that can transform these energy forms into the code language of nerve impulses.

The particular stimuli to which different animals are sensitive vary considerably. The sensory equipment of any species is an adaptation to the environment in which it lives. Many species have senses that humans lack altogether. Carrier pigeons, for example, use

2. How do psychologists differentiate between sensation and perception?

Earth's magnetic field to find their destination on cloudy nights when they can't navigate by the stars. Sharks sense electric currents leaking through the skins of fish hiding in undersea crevices, and rattlesnakes find their prey by detecting infrared radiation given off by small rodents. Whatever the source of stimulation, its energy must be converted into nerve impulses, the only language the nervous system understands (Chaudhuri, 2013; Liedtke, 2006). **Transduction** is the process whereby the characteristics of a stimulus are converted into nerve impulses. We now consider the range of stimuli to which humans and other mammals are attuned and the manner in which the various sense organs carry out the transduction process.

As a starting point, we might ask the following: How many senses do humans have? Certainly there appear to be more than the five classical senses with which we are familiar: vision, audition (hearing), touch, gustation (taste), and olfaction (smell). For example, there are senses that provide information about balance and body position. Also, the sense of touch can be subdivided into separate senses of pressure, pain, and temperature. Receptors deep within the brain monitor the chemical composition of our blood. The immune system also has sensory functions that allow it to detect foreign invaders and to receive stimulation from the brain (Chiu, Heesters, Ghasemlou, Von Hehn, Zhao, Tran, Woolf, 2013; Nossal & Hall, 1995).

Like those of other organisms, human sensory systems are designed to extract from the environment the information that we need to function and survive. Although our survival does not depend on having eyes like eagles or owls, noses like bloodhounds, or ears as sensitive as those of the worm-hunting robin, we do have specialized sensors that can detect many different kinds of stimuli with considerable sensitivity. The scientific area of **psychophysics,** which studies relations between the physical characteristics of stimuli and sensory capabilities, is concerned with two kinds of sensitivity. The first concerns the absolute limits of sensitivity. For example, what is the softest sound or the weakest salt solution that humans can detect? The second kind of sensitivity has to do with differences between stimuli. What is the smallest difference in brightness that we can detect? How much difference must there be in two tones before we can tell that they are not identical?

3. What two kinds of sensory capabilities are studied by psychophysics researchers?

4. What is the absolute threshold, and how is it technically defined and measured?

Stimulus Detection: The Absolute Threshold

How intense must a stimulus be before we can detect its presence? Researchers answer this question by systematically presenting stimuli of varying intensities and asking people whether they can detect them. Because we are often unsure of whether we have actually sensed very faint stimuli, researchers designate the **absolute threshold** as the lowest intensity at which a stimulus can be detected correctly 50 percent of the time. Thus, the *lower* the absolute threshold, the *greater* the sensitivity. From studies of absolute thresholds, the general limits of human sensitivity for the five major senses can be estimated. Some examples are presented in Table 5.1. As you can see, many of our senses are surprisingly sensitive. Yet some other species have absolute thresholds that seem incredible by comparison. For example, a female silkworm moth that is ready to mate needs to release 2.8 billionths of a gram of an attractant chemical molecule per second to attract every male silkworm moth within a radius of 1.6 kilometres. Can humans perceive any stimulus that is actually below the absolute threshold? We discuss this matter in the *Focus on Neuroscience* feature.

Signal Detection Theory

I (M.W.P.) can remember lying in bed as a child after seeing a horror movie, straining my ears to detect any unusual sound that might signal

TABLE 5.1   Some Approximate Absolute Thresholds for Various Senses

Sense Modality	Absolute Threshold
Vision	Candle flame seen at approximately 50 kilometres on a clear, dark night
Hearing	Tick of a watch under quiet conditions at approximately 6 metres
Taste	Single teaspoon of sugar in approximately 7.5 litres of water
Smell	One drop of perfume diffused into the entire volume of a large apartment
Touch	Wing of a fly or bee falling on your cheek from a distance of 1 centimetre

Source: Based on Galanter, E. (1962). "Contemporary psychophysics." In R. Brown (Ed.), *New directions in psychology*. New York, NY: Holt, Rinehart & Winston.

Focus on Neuroscience

THE NEUROSCIENCE OF SUBLIMINAL PERCEPTION AND PROSOPAGNOSIA

A **subliminal stimulus** is one that is so weak or brief that, although it is received by the senses, it cannot be perceived consciously—the stimulus is well below the absolute threshold. There is little question that subliminal stimuli can register in the nervous system (Kihlstrom, 2008; Matthen, 2007; Merikle & Daneman, 1998). But can such stimuli affect attitudes and behaviour without our knowing it? The answer appears to be yes—to a limited extent.

In the late 1950s, James Vicary, a public-relations executive, arranged to have subliminal messages flashed on a theatre screen during a movie. The messages urged the audience to "drink Coca-Cola" and "eat popcorn." Vicary's claim that the subliminal messages increased popcorn sales by 50 percent and soft-drink sales by 18 percent aroused a public furor. Consumers and scientists feared possible abuse of subliminal messages to covertly influence the buying habits of consumers, and even to achieve mind control and brainwashing. The National Association of Broadcasters reacted by outlawing subliminal messages on American TV.

The outcries were, in large part, false alarms. Several attempts to reproduce Vicary's results under controlled conditions failed, and many other studies conducted in laboratory settings, on TV and radio, and in movie theatres indicated that there is little reason to be seriously concerned about significant or widespread control of consumer behaviour through subliminal stimulation (Dixon, 1981; Drukin, 1998). Ironically, Vicary admitted years later that his study was a hoax, designed to revive his floundering advertising agency. Nonetheless, his false report stimulated a great deal of useful research on the power of subliminal stimuli to influence behaviour. As far as consumer behaviour is concerned, the conclusion is that persuasive stimuli above the absolute threshold are far more influential than subliminal attempts to sneak into our subconscious mind, perhaps because we are more certain to "get the message."

Though consumer behaviour cannot be controlled subliminally, can such stimuli affect more subtle phenomena, such as attitudes? Here the effects are stronger (Arendt et al., 1997; Greenwald & Banaji, 1995). In one study, Jon Krosnick (1992) showed participants nine slides of a particular person and then measured their attitudes toward the target person. For half of the participants, each photograph was immediately preceded by an unpleasant picture (e.g., a face on fire) that was presented subliminally. The remaining participants were shown pleasant subliminal stimuli, such as smiling babies. Participants shown the associated unpleasant subliminal stimuli expressed somewhat

negative attitudes toward the person, indicating a process of subconscious attitude conditioning, whereas those who saw the positive subliminal stimuli did not.

Evidence consistent with subliminal perception can be seen when examining patients who have very specific types of brain damage. For example, individuals with prosopagnosia are unable to recognize familiar faces. In essence, they have a type of visual agnosia that is specific for faces. Such individuals typically have cortical damage in areas involved with object perception. In some cases, they may be aware that they are looking at a face, but they cannot tell you who the individual is. Nonetheless, they may be able to categorize the visual stimulus as a face, and some patients can correctly "guess" who the face belongs to. How can this happen if the stimuli cannot be perceived?

Consider the following study by J.K. Steeves and colleagues (2006). Steeves et al. studied patient D.F., a 47-year-old woman who suffered brain damage at age 34 from accidental carbon monoxide poisoning. D.F. has a great deal of difficulty recognizing the size, shape, and orientation of objects, but she is able to perceive colour. Thus, she is often able to recognize objects (e.g., an orange versus a tomato) based on colour and texture information alone. Similarly, people may be identified by nonfacial cues, such as clothing choice and voice pitch. Earlier studies using fMRI imaging (Culham, 2004; James et al., 2003) had identified specific lesions in D.F.'s cortex. In particular, damage was observed in the lateral occipital area (LOA) in both hemispheres (Figure 5.3). The LOA has been associated with object perception in the intact cortex. D.F. and three control participants with no brain damage were shown a series of face and object stimuli while imaging with fMRI. Activation was examined in the LOA and in a second area associated with facial processing: the fusiform gyrus. Here we find the fusiform facial area (FFA), a brain region specifically associated with facial perception (Barton, Press, Keenan, & O'Connor, 2002).

For all participants, including D.F., there was greater brain activation in the FFA when viewing faces than when viewing scenes. However, the control participants showed greater activation in the LOA as well when viewing faces. This area was damaged in D.F. Despite this damage, D.F. was able to accurately categorize the stimuli as faces versus objects 95 percent of the time. In a second test, D.F. was shown a series of 30 images (5 faces and 25 objects) and was asked to describe what they were. All five faces were accurately identified as a face, but not one of the objects was correctly described. In a third test, all participants were shown a series of 60 famous individuals (e.g., John F. Kennedy, Princess Diana) and were asked to name them or provide information about the individual if they could not come up with the name. The controls correctly

continued

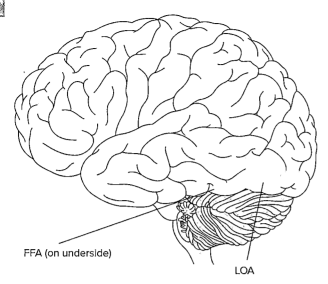

FFA (on underside)

LOA

FIGURE 5.3 Approximate locations of the lateral occipital area (LOA) and the fusiform facial area (FFA). The FFA is actually on the underside or ventral surface of the cortex.

is likely that D.F. uses certain heuristic rules to "identify" faces (e.g., elongated oval targets with skin tone are likely to be faces) even though she is not really aware that the stimulus is, in fact, a face. Second, this research emphasizes the importance of the case study to investigate psychological phenomena. D.F. is a unique individual who provides an extraordinary opportunity to examine the role of brain regions in visual processing. In addition, the combination of behavioural testing and fMRI imaging allows the researchers to precisely identify the regions and deficits involved with this disorder.

Finally, the study highlights the subtle manner in which subliminal stimuli may have an effect. Philip Merikle and his colleagues (e.g., Merikle & Skanes, 1992; Merikle et al., 2001) have argued that the effect is one of biasing perception—subliminal cues can bias what we perceive at a conscious level and may alter our conscious experience of those stimuli. Todorov & Bargh (2002) demonstrated that subliminal presentations of aggressively toned words cause people to judge the ambiguous behaviours of others as more aggressive and to increase their own tendency to behave more aggressively. More recently, Radel et al. (2013) have shown that exposure to subliminal motivational conversations results in greater perseverance on difficult tasks. How short can the subliminal exposure be? According to Sperdin, Spierer, Becker, Michel, and Landis (2015), 250 microseconds is enough. In a quarter of a millisecond, visually evoked potentials can be seen on an EEG recording. We may not be consciously aware of stimuli, but perhaps, like D.F., aspects of the stimuli are processed at a different level and are available for us to use in subsequent decisions.

identified 93 percent of the images; D.F. could not identify a single one.

There are three points we should take away from this study. First, it would appear that higher-order facial recognition is a complex process involving several brain regions, including the LOA and the FFA, in addition to the primary visual cortex. Nonetheless, an individual such as D.F. can glean a certain amount of information about visual stimuli even when one of these areas is severely damaged. It

the presence of a monster in the house. My vigilance caused me to detect faint and ominous sounds that probably would have gone unnoticed had I seen a comedy or a western earlier in the evening. Perhaps you have had a similar experience.

At one time it was assumed that each person had a more or less fixed level of sensitivity for each sense. But psychologists who study stimulus detection found that people's apparent sensitivity can fluctuate quite a bit. They concluded that the concept of a fixed absolute threshold is inaccurate because there is no single point on the intensity scale that separates nondetection from detection of a stimulus. There is instead a range of uncertainty, and people set their own **decision criterion,** a standard of how certain they must be that a stimulus is present before they will say they detect it. The decision criterion can also

5. Why do signal detection theorists view stimulus detection as a decision?

6. What kinds of personal and situational factors influence signal detection decision criteria?

change from time to time, depending on such factors as fatigue, expectation, and the potential significance of the stimulus. **Signal detection theory** is concerned with the factors that influence sensory judgments.

In a typical signal detection experiment, participants are told that after a warning light appears, a barely perceptible tone may or may not be presented. Their task is to tell the experimenter whether they heard the tone. Under these conditions, there are four possible outcomes, as shown in Figure 5.4. When the tone is in fact presented, the participant may say "Yes" (a hit) or "No" (a miss). When no tone is presented, the participant may also say "Yes" (a false alarm) or "No" (a correct rejection).

At low stimulus intensities, both the participant's and the situation's characteristics influence the decision criterion (Cataldo & Cohen,

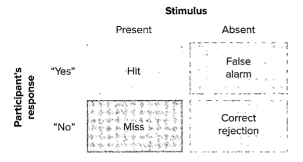

Stimulus

	Present	Absent
"Yes"	Hit	False alarm
"No"	Miss	Correct rejection

(Participant's response)

FIGURE 5.4 This matrix shows the four possible outcomes in a signal detection experiment in which participants decide whether a stimulus has been presented or not presented. The percentages of responses that fall within each category can be affected both by characteristics of the participants and by the nature of the situation.

2015; Colonius & Dzhafarov, 2006; Verghese, 2001). Bold participants who frequently say "Yes" have more hits, but they also have more false alarms than do conservative participants. Participants also can be influenced to become bolder or more conservative by manipulating the rewards and costs for giving correct or incorrect responses. Increasing the rewards for hits or the costs for misses results in lower detection thresholds (i.e., more "Yes" responses at low intensities). Thus, a Navy radar operator may be more likely to notice a faint blip on her screen during a wartime mission, when a miss might have disastrous consequences, than during a peacetime voyage. Conversely, like physicians who will not perform a risky medical procedure without strong evidence to support their diagnosis, participants become more conservative in their "Yes" responses as costs for false alarms are increased, resulting in higher detection thresholds (Irwin & McCarthy, 1998). Experience also plays a role in signal detection—experienced drivers respond more quickly to signs of danger partly because they have a lower threshold for detecting and identifying hazardous situations than do novice drivers (Wallis & Horswill, 2007). Signal detection research shows us that perception is, in part, a decision.

The Difference Threshold

Distinguishing between stimuli can sometimes be as important as detecting stimuli in the first place. When we try to match the colours of paints or clothing, very subtle differences can be quite important. Likewise, a

slight variation in taste might signal that food is tainted or spoiled. Professional wine tasters and piano tuners make their livings by being able to make very slight discriminations between stimuli.

The **difference threshold** is defined as the smallest difference between two stimuli that people can perceive 50 percent of the time. The difference threshold is sometimes called the *just noticeable difference (jnd)*. Fortunately, as the German physiologist Ernst Weber (pronounced *Veh-ber*) discovered in the 1830s, there is some degree of lawfulness in the range of sensitivities within our sensory systems. **Weber's law** states that the difference threshold, or jnd, is directly proportional to the magnitude of the stimulus with which the comparison is being made, and can be expressed as a *Weber fraction*. For example, the jnd value for weights is a Weber fraction of approximately 1/50 (Teghtsoonian, 1971). This number means that if you lift a weight of 50 grams, a comparison weight must weigh at least 51 grams in order for you to be able to judge it as heavier. If the weight were 500 grams, a second weight would have to weigh at least 510 grams (i.e., 1/50 = 10 grams/500 grams) for you to discriminate between them.

Although Weber's law breaks down at extremely high and low intensities of stimulation,[1] it holds up reasonably well within the most frequently encountered range, therefore providing a reasonable barometer of our abilities to discern differences in the various sensory modalities. Table 5.2 lists Weber

7. What is the technical definition of a difference threshold? How does Weber's law help us compare just noticeable difference (jnd) sensitivities in the various senses?

TABLE 5.2 Weber Fractions for Various Sensory Modalities

Sensory Modality	Weber Fraction
Audition (tonal pitch)	1/333
Vision (brightness, white light)	1/60
Kinesthesis (lifted weights)	1/50
Pain (heat produced)	1/30
Audition (loudness)	1/20
Touch (pressure applied to skin)	1/7
Smell (India rubber)	1/4
Taste (salt concentration)	1/3

Sources: Geldard, F.A. (1962). *Fundamentals of psychology.* New York, NY: Wiley.; Teghtsoonian, R. (1971). On the exponents in Stevens' law and the constant in Ekman's law. *Psychological Review, 78,* 71–80.

fractions for the various senses. The smaller the fraction, the greater the sensitivity to differences. As highly visual creatures, humans show greater sensitivity in their visual sense than they do in, for example, their sense of smell. Undoubtedly, many creatures who depend on their sense of smell to track their prey would show quite a different order of sensitivity. Weber fractions also show that humans are highly sensitive to differences in the pitch of sounds but far less sensitive to loudness differences.

Sensory Adaptation

8. What accounts for sensory adaptation? Of what survival value is adaptation?

Because changes in our environment are often most newsworthy, sensory systems are finely attuned to *changes* in stimulation (Rensink, 2002). Sensory neurons are engineered to respond to a constant stimulus by *decreasing* their activity, and the diminishing sensitivity to an unchanging stimulus is called **sensory adaptation.**

Adaptation (sometimes called *habituation*) is a part of everyday experience. After a while, monotonous background sounds are largely unheard. The feel of your wristwatch against your skin recedes from awareness. When you dive into a swimming pool, the water may feel cold at first because your body's temperature sensors respond to the change in temperature. With time, however, you become used to the water temperature.

Adaptation occurs in all sensory modalities, including vision. Indeed, were it not for tiny involuntary eye movements that keep images moving about the retina, stationary objects would simply fade from sight if we stared at them (Martinez-Conde, MacKnik, & Hubel, 2004). In an ingenious demonstration of this variety of adaptation, R.M. Pritchard (1961) attached a tiny projector to a contact lens worn by the participant (Figure 5.5a). This procedure guaranteed that visual images presented through the projector would maintain a constant position on the retina, even when the eye moved. When a stabilized image was projected through the lens onto the retina, participants reported that the image appeared in its entirety for a time, then began to vanish and reappear as parts of the original stimulus (Figure 5.5b).

Although sensory adaptation may reduce our overall sensitivity, it is adaptive because it frees our senses from the constant and the

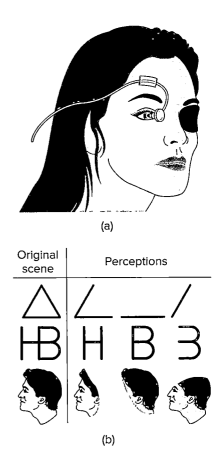

(a)

Original scene	Perceptions

(b)

FIGURE 5.5 (a) To create a stabilized retinal image, a person wears a contact lens to which a tiny projector has been attached. Despite eye movements, images will be cast on the same region of the retina. (b) Under these conditions, the stabilized image is clear at first, and then begins to fade and reappear in meaningful segments as the receptors fatigue and recover.
Source: (a) Drawing from R.M. Pritchard, 1961, "Stabilized Images on the Retina," Scientific American, 72–78. Reprinted by permission of Eric Mose, Jr.; (b) Adapted from Pritchard, 1961.

mundane to pick up informative changes in the environment. Sensitivity to such changes may turn out to be important to our well-being or survival—for example, by alerting us to potential threats. Sensory adaptation may be a "back-up measure" of sorts, for when we are not actively and consciously processing sensory stimuli in our environment. In one study, Castro-Alamancos (2004) reported that sensory adaptation was mostly absent in animals while they were alert and engaged in a behavioural learning task, whereas after the task was learned and had become routine, levels of alertness lowered and sensory adaptation returned.

- Sensation refers to the activities by which our sense organs receive and transmit information, whereas perception involves the brain's processing and interpretation of the information.

- Psychophysics is the scientific study of how the physical properties of stimuli are related to sensory experiences. Sensory sensitivity is concerned in part with the limits of stimulus detectability (absolute threshold) and the ability to discriminate between stimuli (difference threshold). The absolute threshold is the intensity at which a stimulus is detected 50 percent of the time. Signal detection theory is concerned with factors that influence decisions about whether or not a stimulus is present.

- Research indicates that subliminal stimuli, which are not consciously perceived, can influence perceptions and behaviour in subtle ways, but not strongly enough to justify concerns about the subconscious control of behaviour through subliminal messages.

- The difference threshold, or just noticeable difference (jnd), is the amount by which two stimuli must differ for them to be perceived as different 50 percent of the time. Studies of the jnd led to Weber's law, which states that the jnd is proportional to the intensity of the original stimulus and is constant within a given sense modality.

- Sensory systems are particularly responsive to changes in stimulation, and adaptation occurs in response to unchanging stimuli.

THE SENSORY SYSTEMS

Vision

The normal stimulus for vision is electromagnetic energy, or light waves, which are measured in *nanometres* (or one billionths of a metre). In addition to that tiny portion that humans can perceive, the electromagnetic spectrum includes X-rays, TV and radio signals, and infrared and ultraviolet rays (Figure 5.6). Bees are able to "see" ultraviolet light, and rattlesnakes can detect infrared energy. Our visual system is sensitive only to wavelengths extending from about 700 nanometres (red) down to about 400 nanometres (blue-violet). (You can remember the order of the spectrum, from higher wavelengths to lower ones, with the name ROY G. BIV—red, orange, yellow, green, blue, indigo, and violet.)

The Human Eye

Light waves enter the eye through the *cornea*, a transparent protective structure at the front of the eye (Figure 5.7a). Behind the cornea is the *pupil*, an adjustable opening that can dilate or constrict to control the amount of light that enters the eye. The pupil's size is controlled by muscles in the coloured *iris* that surrounds the pupil. Low levels of illumination cause the pupil to dilate, letting more light into the eye to improve optical clarity; bright light triggers constriction of the pupil.

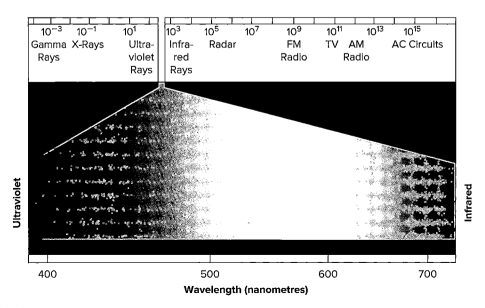

FIGURE 5.6 The full spectrum of electromagnetic radiation. Only the narrow band between 400 and 700 nanometres is visible to the human eye. One nanometre = 1 000 000 000th of a metre.

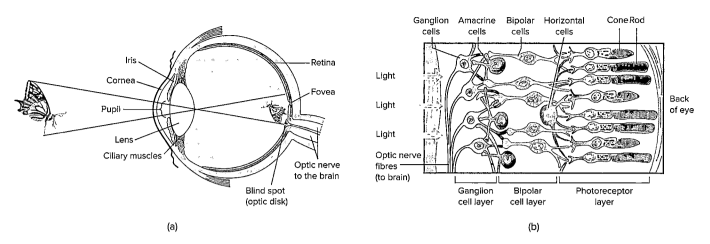

FIGURE 5.7 (a) This cross-section shows the major parts of the human eye. The iris regulates the size of the pupil. The ciliary muscles regulate the shape of the lens. The image entering the eye is reversed by the lens and cast on the retina, which contains the photoreceptor cells. The optic disk, where the optic nerve exits the eye, has no receptors and produces a "blind spot" as demonstrated in Figure 5.8. (b) Photoreceptor connections in the retina. The rods and cones synapse with bipolar cells, which in turn synapse with ganglion cells, whose axons form the optic nerve. The horizontal and amacrine cells allow sideways integration of retinal activity across areas of the retina.

Behind the pupil is the **lens,** an elastic structure that becomes thinner to focus on distant objects and thicker to focus on nearby objects. Just as the lens of a camera focuses an image on a photosensitive material (film), so the lens of the eye focuses the visual image on the light-sensitive **retina,** a multi-layered tissue at the rear of the fluid-filled eyeball. As seen in Figure 5.7a, the lens reverses the image from right to left and top to bottom when it is projected on the retina, but the brain reconstructs the visual input into the image that we perceive.

The ability to see clearly depends on the lens's ability to focus the image directly onto the retina (Pedrotti & Pedrotti, 1997). If you have good vision for nearby objects but have difficulty seeing faraway objects, then you probably suffer from **myopia** (nearsightedness). In nearsighted people, the lens focuses the visual image *in front of* the retina (too near the lens), resulting in a blurred image for faraway objects. This condition generally occurs because the eyeball is longer (front to back) than normal. In contrast, some people have excellent distance vision but have difficulty seeing closeup objects clearly. **Hyperopia** (farsightedness) occurs when the lens does not thicken enough and the image is therefore focused on a point *behind* the retina (too far from the lens). The aging process typically causes the eyeball to become shorter over time, contributing to the development of hyperopia and the need for many middle-aged people to acquire reading glasses (after complaining that their arms are not long enough to read newspapers and telephone books). Ironically, this age-related shortening of the eyeball often improves the vision of myopic people, for, as the retina moves closer to the lens, it

9. How does the lens affect visual acuity, and how does its dysfunction cause the visual problems of myopia and hyperopia?

10. How are the rods and cones distributed in the retina, and how do they contribute to brightness perception, colour vision, and visual acuity?

approaches the point where the "nearsighted" lens is projecting the image (Orr, 1998). Eyeglasses and contact lenses are designed to correct for the natural lens's inability to focus the visual image directly onto the retina. Recent research (Li, Polat, & Bavelier, 2009) suggests that playing action video games might also be effective in improving eyesight, even for older adults (Belchior, Marsiske, Sisco, Yam, Bavelier, Ball, & Mann, 2013). However, it's unlikely that playing video games will replace the need for corrective lenses!

Photoreceptors: The Rods and Cones

The retina, a multi-layered screen that lines the back surface of the eyeball and contains specialized sensory neurons, is actually an extension of the brain (Bullier, 2002). The retina contains two types of light-sensitive receptor cells, called *rods* and *cones* because of their shapes (Figure 5.7b). There are about 120 million rods and 6 million cones in the human eye.

The **rods,** which function best in dim light, are primarily black-and-white brightness receptors. They are about 500 times more sensitive to light than are the cones, but they do not give rise to colour sensations. The retinas of some night creatures, such as the owl, contain only rods, so they have exceptional vision in very dim light but no colour vision during the day (Dossenbach & Dossenbach, 1998). The **cones,** which are colour receptors, function best in bright illumination. Some creatures that are active only during the day, such as the pigeon and the chipmunk, have only cones in their retinas, so they see the world in living colour but have very poor night vision (Dossenbach & Dossenbach, 1998). Animals that are active during both day and night, as humans are, have a mixture of rods and cones. In humans, rods are found throughout the retina except in the **fovea,** a small area in the centre of the retina that contains only cones. Cones decrease in concentration as one moves away from the centre of the retina, and the periphery of the retina contains mainly rods.

Rods and cones send their messages to the brain via two additional layers of cells. **Bipolar cells** have synaptic connections with the rods and cones. The bipolar cells, in turn, synapse with a layer of about one million **ganglion cells,** whose axons are collected into a bundle to form the **optic nerve.** Thus, input from more than 126 million rods and cones is eventually funnelled into only one million traffic lanes leading out of the retina toward higher visual centres. Figure 5.7b shows how the rods and cones are connected to the bipolar and ganglion cells. One interesting aspect of these connections is the fact that the rods and cones not only form the *rear* layer of the retina, but their light-sensitive ends actually point *away from* the direction of the entering light so that they receive only a fraction of the light energy that enters the eye. Furthermore, the manner in which the rods and cones are connected to the bipolar cells accounts for both the greater importance of rods in dim light and our greater ability to see fine detail in bright illumination, when the cones are most active. Typically, many rods are connected to the same bipolar cell. They therefore can combine or "funnel" their individual electrical messages to the bipolar cell, where the additive effect of the many signals may be enough to fire it. That is why we can more easily detect a faint stimulus, such as a dim star, if we look slightly to one side so that its image falls not on the fovea but on the peripheral portion of the retina, where the rods are packed most densely.

Like the rods, the cones that lie in the periphery of the retina also share bipolar cells. In the fovea, however, the densely packed cones each have their own "private line" to a single bipolar cell. As a result, our **visual acuity,** or ability to see fine detail, is greatest when the visual image projects directly onto the fovea. Such focusing results in the firing of a large number of cones and their private-line bipolar cells. Some birds of prey, such as eagles and hawks, are blessed with not one, but two foveas in each eye, contributing to a visual acuity that allows them to see small prey on the ground as they soar high above the earth (Tucker, 2000).

The optic nerve formed by the axons of the ganglion cells exits through the back of the eye not

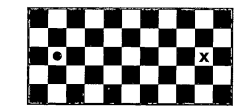

FIGURE 5.8 Close your left eye and, from a distance of about 30 centimetres, focus steadily on the dot with your right eye as you slowly move the book toward your face. At some point, the image of the X will cross your optic disk (blind spot) and disappear. It will reappear after it crosses the blind spot. Note how the checkerboard remains wholly visible even though part of it falls on the blind spot. Your perceptual system "fills in" the missing information.

far from the fovea, producing a *blind spot,* where there are no photoreceptors. You can demonstrate the existence of your blind spot by following the directions for the demonstration in Figure 5.8. Ordinarily, we are unaware of the blind spot because our perceptual system "fills in" the missing part of the visual field (Rolls & Deco, 2002).

Visual Transduction: From Light to Nerve Impulses

The process whereby the characteristics of a stimulus are converted into nerve impulses is called transduction. Rods and cones translate light waves into nerve impulses through the action of protein molecules called **photopigments** (Bonci, Neitz, Neitz, & Ventura, 2013; Wolken, 1995). The absorption of light by these molecules produces a chemical reaction that changes the rate of neurotransmitter release at the receptor's synapse with the bipolar cells (Burns & Arshavsky, 2005). The greater the change in transmitter release, the stronger the signal passed on to the bipolar cell and, in turn, to the ganglion cells whose axons form the optic nerve. If nerve responses are triggered at each of the three levels (rod or cone, bipolar cell, and ganglion cell), the message is instantaneously on its way to the visual relay station in the thalamus, and then on to the visual cortex of the brain.

Brightness Vision and Dark Adaptation

As noted earlier, rods are far more sensitive than cones under conditions of low illumination. Nonetheless, the brightness sensitivity of both the rods and the cones depends in part on the wavelength of the light. Research has shown that rods have much greater brightness sensitivity than cones throughout the colour spectrum *except* at the red end, where rods are

11. What is transduction, and how does this process occur in the photoreceptors of the eye?

relatively insensitive. Cones are most sensitive to low illumination in the greenish-yellow range of the spectrum (Valberg, 2006). These findings have prompted many cities to change the colour of their fire engines from the traditional red (which rods are insensitive to) to yellow-green in order to increase the vehicles' visibility to both rods and cones in dim lighting. Similarly, airport landing lights are often blue because this wavelength is picked up particularly well by the rods during night vision, when the cones are relatively inoperative.

Although the rods are by nature sensitive to low illumination, they are not always ready to fulfill their function. Perhaps you have had the embarrassing experience of entering a movie theatre from bright sunlight, groping around in the darkness, and finally sitting down on someone's lap. Although one can meet interesting people this way, most of us prefer to stand in the rear of the theatre until our eyes adapt to the dimly lit interior.

Dark adaptation is the progressive improvement in brightness sensitivity that occurs over time under conditions of low illumination. After absorbing light, a photoreceptor is depleted of its pigment molecules for a period of time. If the eye has been exposed to conditions of high illumination, such as bright sunlight, a substantial amount of photopigment will be depleted. During the process of dark adaptation, the photopigment molecules are regenerated, and the receptor's sensitivity increases greatly.

Vision researchers have plotted the course of dark adaptation as people move from conditions of bright light into darkness (Carpenter & Robson, 1999). By focusing light flashes of varying wavelengths and brightness on the fovea, which contains only cones, or on the periphery of the retina, where rods reside, they discovered the two-part curve shown in Figure 5.9. The first part of the curve is due to dark adaptation of the cones. As you can see, the cones gradually become sensitive to fainter lights as time passes, but after about 5 to 10 minutes in the dark, their sensitivity has reached its maximum. The rods, whose photopigments regenerate more slowly, do not reach their maximum sensitivity for about half an hour. It is estimated that after complete adaptation, rods are able to detect light intensities only 1/10 000 as great as those that could be detected before dark adaptation began (May, 2007; Stryer, 1987).

During World War II, psychologists familiar with the facts about dark adaptation provided a method for enhancing night vision in pilots

12. How is brightness sensitivity in rods and cones affected by the colour spectrum?

13. What is the physiological basis for dark adaptation? What are the two components of the dark adaptation curve?

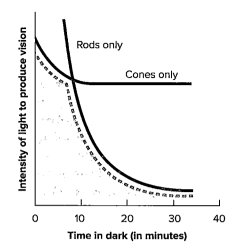

FIGURE 5.9 The course of dark adaptation is graphed over time. The curve has two parts, one for the cones and one for the rods. The cones adapt completely in about 10 minutes, whereas the rods continue to increase their sensitivity for another 20 minutes.

who needed to take off at a moment's notice and see their targets under conditions of low illumination. Knowing that the rods are important in night vision and relatively insensitive to red wavelengths, they suggested that fighter pilots either wear goggles with red lenses or work in rooms lit only by red lights while waiting to be called for a mission. Because red light stimulates only the cones, the rods remain in a state of dark adaptation, ready for immediate service in the dark. That highly practical principle continues to be useful to this day (Figure 5.10).

Colour Vision

We are blessed with a world rich in colour. The majesty of a glowing sunset, the rich blues and greens of a tropical bay, the brilliant colours of fall foliage all produce visual delights for us.

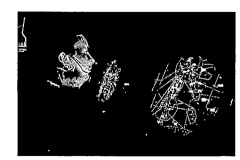

Matthew McVay/Stone/Getty Images

FIGURE 5.10 Working in red light keeps the rods in a state of dark adaptation because rods are quite insensitive to that wavelength. Therefore, they retain high levels of photopigment and remain sensitive to low illumination.

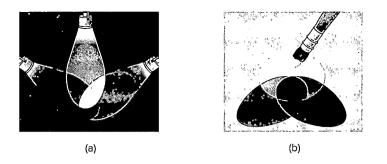

(a)   (b)

FIGURE 5.11 Additive and subtractive colour mixture are different processes. (a) Additive colour mixture. A beam of light of a specific wavelength directed onto a white surface is perceived as the colour that corresponds to that wavelength on the visible spectrum. If beams of light that fall at certain points within the red, green, or blue colour range are directed together onto the surface in the correct proportions, a combined or additive mixture of wavelengths will result and any colour in the visible spectrum can be produced (including white at the point where all three colours intersect). The Young–Helmholtz trichromatic theory of colour vision assumes that colour perception results from the additive mixture of impulses from cones that are sensitive to red, blue, and green (see text). (b) Subtractive colour mixture. Mixing pigments or paints produces new colours by subtraction—that is, by removing (i.e., absorbing) other wavelengths. Paints absorb (subtract) colours different from themselves while reflecting their own colour. For example, blue paint mainly absorbs wavelengths that correspond to nonblue hues. Mixing blue paint with yellow paint (which absorbs wavelengths other than yellow) will produce a subtractive mixture that emits wavelengths between yellow and blue (i.e., green). Theoretically, certain wavelengths of the three primary colours of red, yellow (not green, as in additive mixture), and blue can produce the whole spectrum of colours by subtractive mixture. Thus, in additive colour mixture, the primary colours are red, blue, and green; in subtractive colour mixture, they are red, yellow, and blue.

Human vision is finely attuned to colour; our difference thresholds for light wavelengths are so small that we are able to distinguish an estimated 7.5 million hue variations (Medieros, 2006). Historically, two different theories of colour vision have tried to explain how this occurs.

The trichromatic theory. Around 1800, it was discovered that any colour in the visible spectrum can be produced by some combination of the wavelengths that correspond to the colours blue, green, and red in what is known as *additive colour mixture* (Figure 5.11a). This fact was the basis of an important trichromatic (three-colour) theory of colour vision advanced by Thomas Young, an English physicist, and Hermann von Helmholtz, a German physiologist. According to the Young–Helmholtz **trichromatic theory**, there are three types of colour receptors in the retina. Although all cones can be stimulated by most wavelengths to varying degrees, individual cones are most sensitive to wavelengths that correspond to either blue, green, or red (Figure 5.12). Presumably, each of these receptor classes sends messages to the brain, based on the extent to which they are activated by the light energy's wavelength. The visual system then combines the signals to recreate the original hue. If all three cones are equally activated, a pure white colour is perceived.

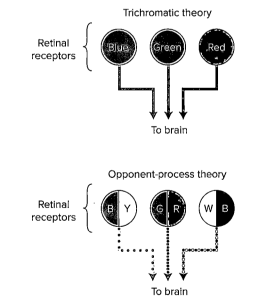

FIGURE 5.12 Two classic theories of colour vision. The Young–Helmholtz trichromatic theory proposed three different receptors, one for blue, one for red, and one for green. The ratio of activity in the three types of cones in response to a stimulus yields our experience of colour. Hering's opponent-process theory also assumed that there are three different receptors: one for yellow-blue, one for red-green, and one for black-white. Each of the receptors can function in two possible ways, depending on the wavelength of the stimulus. Again, the pattern of activity in the receptors yields our perception of the hue.

FIGURE 5.13 Negative colour afterimages demonstrate opponent processes occurring somewhere in the visual system. Stare steadily at the black dot in the centre of the flag for about a minute, then shift your gaze to a blank, white page. The opponent colours should appear.

14. Describe the Young–Helmholtz trichromatic theory of colour vision. What kinds of evidence support this theory, and what two phenomena challenge it?

Although the Young–Helmholtz theory was consistent with the laws of colour mixture, several facts did not fit the theory. For example, according to the theory, yellow is produced by activity of red and green receptors. Yet certain people with red-green colour blindness are able to experience yellow. This finding suggested to other scientists that there must be a different means of perceiving yellow. A second phenomenon that posed problems for the trichromatic theory was the colour *afterimage*, in which an image in a different colour appears after a colour stimulus has been viewed steadily and then withdrawn. To experience one yourself, stare steadily at the object in Figure 5.13 for a full minute, and then shift your gaze to a blank white space. Trichromatic theory cannot account for what you'll see.

15. Describe the opponent-process theory. What evidence supports it?

Opponent-process theory. A second influential colour theory, formulated by Ewald Hering in 1870, also assumed that there are three types of cones. Hering's **opponent-process theory** proposed that each of the three cone types responds to *two* different wavelengths. One type responds to red *or* green, another to blue *or* yellow, and a third to black *or* white. For example, a red-green cone responds with one chemical reaction to a green stimulus and with its other chemical reaction (opponent process) to a red stimulus (Figure 5.12). You have experienced one of the phenomena that supports the existence of opponent processes if you did the exercise in Figure 5.13. The colour afterimage you saw in the blank space contains the colours specified by opponent-process theory: The black portion of the flag appeared as white, and the green portion "turned" red. According to opponent-process theory, as you stared at the black and green colours, the

16. How does the dual-process theory of colour vision combine the trichromatic and opponent-process theories?

neural processes that register these colours became fatigued. Then, when you cast your gaze on the white surface, which reflects all wavelengths, a "rebound" opponent reaction occurred as each receptor responded with its opposing white or red reactions.

Dual processes in colour transduction. Which theory—the trichromatic theory or the opponent-process theory—is correct? Two centuries of research have yielded a win-win verdict for both sets of theorists. Today's **dual-process theory** combines the trichromatic and opponent-process theories to account for the colour transduction process (Valberg, 2006).

Trichromatic theorists, such as Young and Helmholtz, were right about the cones. The cones do indeed contain one of three different protein photopigments that are most sensitive to wavelengths roughly corresponding to the colours blue, red, and green (Valberg, 2006). Different ratios of activity in the red-, blue-, and green-sensitive cones can produce a pattern of neural activity that corresponds to any hue in the spectrum (Backhaus et al., 1998). This process is similar to that which occurs on your TV screen, where colour pictures (including white hues) are produced by activating combinations of tiny red, green, and blue dots.

Hering's opponent-process theory was also partly correct, but opponent processes do not occur at the level of the cones, as he maintained. When researchers began to use microelectrodes to record from single cells in the visual system, they discovered that certain ganglion cells in the retina, as well as some neurons in visual relay stations and the visual cotrex, respond in an opponent-process fashion by altering their rate of firing (DeValois & DeValois, 1993; Gegenfurtner & Kiper, 2003; Knoblauch, 2002; Pridmore, 2013). For example, if a red light is shone on the retina, an opponent-process ganglion cell may respond with a high rate of firing, but a green light will cause the same cell to fire at a very low rate. Other neurons respond in a similar opponent fashion to blue and yellow stimuli. The red-green opponent processes are triggered directly by input from the red- or green-sensitive cones in the retina (Figure 5.14). The blue-yellow opponent process is a bit more complex. Activity of blue-sensitive cones directly stimulates the "blue" process farther along in the visual system. And yellow? The yellow opponent process is triggered not by a "yellow-sensitive" cone, as Hering proposed, but rather by simultaneous input from the red- and green-sensitive cones (Valberg, 2006).

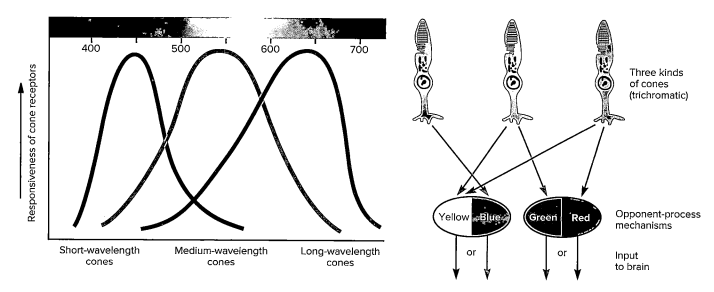

FIGURE 5.14 Colour vision involves both trichromatic and opponent processes that occur at different places in the visual system. Consistent with trichromatic theory, three types of cones are maximally sensitive to short (blue), medium (green), and long (red) wavelengths, respectively. However, opponent processes occur further along in the visual system, as opponent cells in the retina, visual relay stations, and the visual cortex respond differentially to red versus green, blue versus yellow, and black versus white stimuli. Shown here are the inputs from the cones that produce the red-green and blue-yellow opponent processes.

Colour-deficient vision. People with normal colour vision are referred to as *trichromats*. They are sensitive to all three systems: red-green, yellow-blue, and black-white. However, about 7 percent of the male population and 1 percent of the female population have a deficiency in the red-green system, the yellow-blue system, or both. This deficiency is caused by an absence of hue-sensitive photopigment in certain cone types. A *dichromat* is a person who is colour-blind in only one of the systems (red-green or yellow-blue). A *monochromat* is sensitive only to the black-white system and is totally colour-blind. Most colour-deficient people are dichromats and have their deficiency in the red-green system. Tests of colour-blindness typically contain sets of coloured dots such as those in Figure 5.15. Depending on the type of deficit, a colour-blind person cannot discern certain numbers embedded in the circles.

Analysis and Reconstruction of Visual Scenes

Once the transformation of light energy to nerve impulses occurs, the process of combining the messages received from the photoreceptors

17. What are the two major types of colour-blindness? How are they tested?

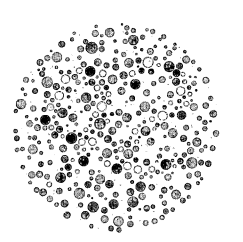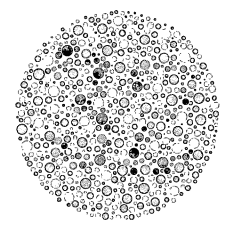

FIGURE 5.15 These dotted figures are used to test for colour-deficient vision. The first one tests for yellow-blue colour-blindness, the second one for red-green colour-blindness. Because the dots in the picture are of equal brightness, colour is the only available cue for perceiving the numbers in the chips.

into the perception of a visual scene begins. As you read this page, nerve impulses from countless neurons are being analyzed and the visual image that you perceive is being reconstructed. Moreover, you know what these black squiggles on the page "mean." How does this occur?

Feature detectors. From the retina, the optic nerve sends nerve impulses to a visual relay station in the thalamus, the brain's sensory switchboard. From there, the input is routed to various parts of the cortex, particularly the **primary visual cortex** in the occipital lobe at the rear of the brain. Microelectrode studies have shown that there is a point-to-point correspondence between tiny regions of the retina and groups of neurons in the visual cortex. As you might expect, the fovea, where the one-to-one synapses of cones with bipolar cells produces high visual acuity, is represented by a disproportionately large area of the visual cortex. Somewhat more surprising is the fact that there is more than one cortical "map" of the retina; there are at least 10 duplicate mappings. Perhaps this is nature's insurance policy against damage to any one of them, or perhaps the duplicate maps are somehow involved in the integration of visual input (Bullier, 2002).

Groups of neurons within the primary visual cortex are organized to receive and integrate sensory nerve impulses originating in specific regions of the retina. Some of these cells are known as **feature detectors.** They fire selectively in response to stimuli that have specific characteristics (May, 2007). Discovery of these feature detectors won David Hubel and Torsten Wiesel of Harvard University the 1981 Nobel Prize. Using tiny electrodes to record the activity of individual cells of the visual cortex of animals (Figure 5.16), Hubel and Wiesel found that certain neurons fired most frequently when lines of certain orientations were presented. One neuron might fire most frequently when a horizontal line was presented; another neuron would fire most frequently to a line of a slightly different orientation, and so on "around the clock." For example, a letter *A* could be constructed from the response of feature detectors that responded to three different line orientations: /, \, and –.

The discovery of feature detectors revolutionized vision research. Since then, scientists have found cells that respond most strongly to bars, slits, and edges in certain positions. Recent research also suggests that retinal ganglion cells may also function as feature detectors, passing the information along to higher

18. What kinds of feature detectors exist in the visual system? What is meant by parallel processing of sensory information?

Fritz Goro/The Life Picture Collection/Getty Images

FIGURE 5.16 A partially anaesthetized monkey views an image projected onto the screen while an electrode embedded in its visual cortex records the activity of a single neuron. This research by Hubel and Wiesel led to the discovery of feature detectors that analyze visual stimulus features, such as contours and shapes, movement, and colour.

structures (Sanes & Masland, 2015). Within the cortex, this information is integrated and analyzed by successively more complex feature detector systems to produce our perception of objects (Palmer, 2002). This process is illustrated by the illusion shown in Figure 5.17.

Other classes of feature detectors respond to colour, depth, or movement (Livingstone & Hubel, 1994; Smith, Snowden, & Milne, 1995; Zanker, 2010). These feature detector "modules" subdivide a visual scene into its component dimensions and process them simultaneously. Thus, as a red, white, and green beach ball sails toward you, separate but overlapping modules

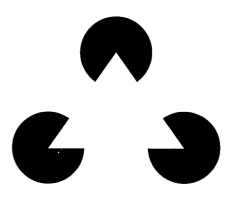

FIGURE 5.17 Is the white triangle "real"? It appears to be, because feature detectors that analyze the contours of the pie-shaped circles analyze the corners, and the brain fills in the "missing" lines. The contours are illusory, but they appear real. See what happens to the triangle if you cover up one or two of the circles.

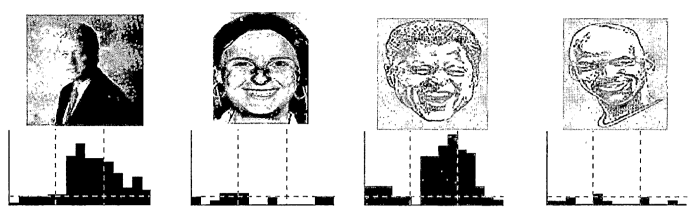

Neuron's Electrical Response

FIGURE 5.18 Single-neuron electrical recording in a patient's amygdala (which receives extensive visual input) revealed a neuron that responded to depictions of Bill Clinton but not to 47 other pictures showing other presidents, celebrities (e.g., Michael Jordan, far right), objects, landscapes, and geometric shapes. This neuron was apparently part of a neuronal network that had learned to recognize and represent the former U.S. president.

Source: From K. Koch, *The Quest for Consciousness: A Neurobiological Approach.* Fig 2.2, p. 30, 2004. Greenwood Village, CO: Roberts & Company Publishers. Reprinted by permission.

within the brain simultaneously analyze its colours, shape, distance, and movement by engaging in **parallel processing** of the information and constructing a unified image of its properties (Hubel & Weisel, 2005; Tarr & Vuong, 2002). In addition, brief, high-frequency "bursts" of firing in sensory neurons may function as feature detectors and can signal the occurrence of important stimuli in the sensory field (Marsat & Pollack, 2006). The final stages in the process of constructing a visual representation occur when the information analyzed and recombined by the primary visual cortex is routed to other cortical regions known as the **visual association cortex.** Here successively more complex features of

the visual scene are combined and interpreted in light of our memories and knowledge (Grossberg et al., 2005). If all goes correctly, then a process that began with nerve impulses from the rods and cones now ends with us "recognizing" the beach ball for what it "is" and catching it. Quite another conscious experience and response probably would occur if we interpreted the oncoming object as a water balloon.

Recently, scientists have discovered that neurons in the brain respond selectively not only to basic stimulus characteristics such as corners and colours, but also to complex stimuli that have acquired special meaning through experience. For example, brain scientists at the

In Review

- The senses may be classified in terms of the energy to which they respond. Through the process of transduction, these energy forms are transformed into the common language of nerve impulses.

- The normal stimulus for vision is electromagnetic energy, or light waves. Light-sensitive visual receptor cells are located in the retina. The rods are brightness receptors, and the less numerous cones are colour receptors. Light energy striking the retina is converted into nerve impulses by chemical reactions in the photopigments of the rods and cones. Dark adaptation involves the gradual regeneration of photo

pigments that have been depleted by brighter illumination.

- Colour vision is a two-stage process, having both trichromatic and opponent-process components. The first stage involves the reactions of cones that are maximally sensitive to red, green, and blue wavelengths. In the second stage, colour information from the cones is coded through an opponent-process mechanism further along in the visual system.

- Visual stimuli are analyzed by feature detectors in the primary visual cortex, and the stimulus elements are reconstructed and interpreted in light of input from the visual association cortex.

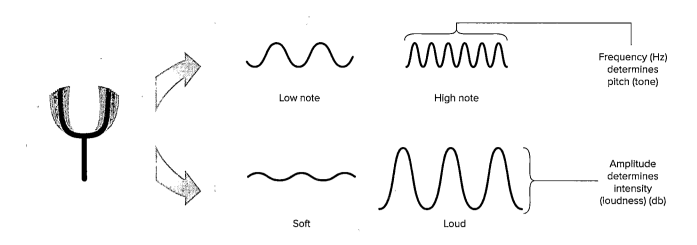

FIGURE 5.19 Sound waves are a form of mechanical energy. As the tuning fork vibrates, it produces successive waves of compression and expansion of air molecules. The number of maximum compressions per second (cycles per second) is its frequency, measured in hertz (Hz). The height of the wave above zero air pressure represents the sound's amplitude. Frequency determines pitch; amplitude determines loudness, measured in decibels (db).

University of California–Los Angeles who were recording from single neurons in the amygdala of a brain-damaged patient found a neuron that responded electrically to only 3 of 50 visual scenes. All of the three scenes involved former U.S. president Bill Clinton, but they differed considerably. One was a portrait, the second was a group picture that included Clinton, and the third was a cartoonist's representation of Clinton. Pictures of other celebrities, animals, landscapes, and geometric forms evoked no response (Figure 5.18). This neuron was likely part of a neural circuit that was created within the brain to register this particular celebrity (Koch, 2004).

Audition

The stimuli for our sense of hearing are sound waves, a form of mechanical energy. What we call *sound* is actually pressure waves in air, water, or some other conducting medium. When a stereo's volume is high enough, you can actually see cloth speaker covers moving in and out. The resulting vibrations cause successive waves of compression and expansion among the air molecules surrounding the source of the sound. These sound waves have two characteristics: frequency and amplitude (Figure 5.19).

Frequency is the number of sound waves, or cycles, per second. The **hertz (Hz)** is the technical measure of cycles per second; 1 hertz equals one cycle per second. The sound waves' frequency is related to the pitch that we perceive;

the higher the frequency (hertz), the higher the perceived pitch. Humans are capable of detecting sound frequencies from 20 hertz up to 20 000 hertz (about 12 000 hertz in older people). Most common sounds are in the lower frequencies. Among musical instruments, the piano can play the widest range of frequencies, from 27.5 hertz at the low end of the keyboard to 4186 hertz at the high end. An operatic soprano's voice, in comparison, has a range of only 250 to 1100 hertz (Aiello & Sloboda, 1994).

Amplitude refers to the vertical size of the sound waves—that is, to the amount of compression and expansion of the molecules in the conducting medium. The sound wave's amplitude is the primary determinant of the sound's perceived loudness. Differences in amplitude are expressed as **decibels (db)**, a measure of the physical pressures that occur at the eardrum. The absolute threshold for hearing is arbitrarily designated as 0 decibels, and each increase of 10 decibels represents a tenfold increase in loudness.

The decibel scale relates a physical quantity (sound intensity) to the human perception of that quantity (sound loudness). It is a logarithmic scale—that is, each increment of 10 decibels represents a tenfold increase in loudness. Table 5.3 indicates the decibel ranges of some common sounds as well as thresholds for hearing, hearing damage, and pain. Prolonged exposure at 150 decibels causes death in laboratory rats.

19. What are the two physical characteristics of sound waves, and which auditory qualities do these characteristics produce?

TABLE 5.3   Decibel Scaling of Common Sounds

Level in Decibels	Common Sounds	Threshold Levels
140	Jet fighter taking off at approximately 25 metres from plane	Potential damage to auditory system
130	Boiler shop	
120	Rock band	Human pain threshold
110	Trumpet automobile horn at approximately 1 metre	
100	Crosscut saw at position of operator	
90	Train whistle at 150 metres	Hearing damage with prolonged exposure
80		
70	Inside automobile in city	
60	Downtown city street (Toronto)	
50	Restaurant	
40	Classroom	
30	Hospital room	
20	Recording studio	Threshold of hearing (young men)
10		
0		Minimum threshold of hearing

Auditory Transduction: From Pressure Waves to Nerve Impulses

The transduction system of the ear is made up of tiny bones, membranes, and liquid-filled tubes designed to translate pressure waves into nerve impulses (Figure 5.20). At a speed of approximately 1200 kilometres per hour, sound waves travel into an auditory canal leading to the eardrum, a movable membrane that vibrates in response to the sound waves. Beyond the eardrum is the middle ear, a cavity housing three tiny bones (the smallest in the body, each the size of a grain of rice). The vibrating activity of these bones—the *hammer* (malleus), *anvil* (incus), and *stirrup* (stapes)—amplifies the sound waves more than 30 times. The first bone, the hammer, is attached firmly to the eardrum, and the stirrup is attached to another membrane, the *oval window,* which forms the boundary between the middle ear and the inner ear. The inner ear contains the **cochlea, a** coiled, snail-shaped tube about 3.5 centimetres in length that is filled with fluid and contains the **basilar membrane,** a sheet of tissue that runs its length. Resting on the basilar membrane is the **organ of Corti,** which contains about 16 000 tiny hair cells that are the actual sound receptors. The tips of the hair cells are attached to the tectorial membrane that overhangs the basilar membrane along the entire length of the cochlea. The hair cells synapse with the neurons of the auditory nerve which, in turn, sends impulses via an auditory relay station in the thalamus to the auditory cortex, which is located in the temporal lobe.

When sound waves strike the eardrum, pressure created at the oval window by the hammer, anvil, and stirrup of the middle ear sets the fluid inside the cochlea into motion. The fluid waves that result vibrate the basilar membrane and the membrane above it, causing a bending of the hair cells in the organ of Corti (Figure 5.20b). This bending of the hair cells triggers a release of neurotransmitter substance into the synaptic space between the hair cells and the neurons of the auditory nerve, resulting in nerve impulses that are sent to the brain. Within the auditory cortex, located in the temporal lobe, are feature detector neurons that respond to specific kinds of auditory input, much as occurs in the visual system (Musicek & Baran, 2006).

Coding of Pitch and Loudness

The auditory system transforms the sensory qualities of loudness and pitch into the language of nerve impulses (McDermott, 2014; Syka & Merzenich, 2005). In the case of loudness, high-amplitude sound waves cause the hair cells to bend more and release more neurotransmitter substance at the point where they synapse with auditory nerve cells, resulting in a higher rate of firing within the auditory nerve. In addition, certain receptor neurons have higher thresholds than others, so that they will fire only when

20. Describe how the middle and inner ear structures are involved in the auditory transduction process.

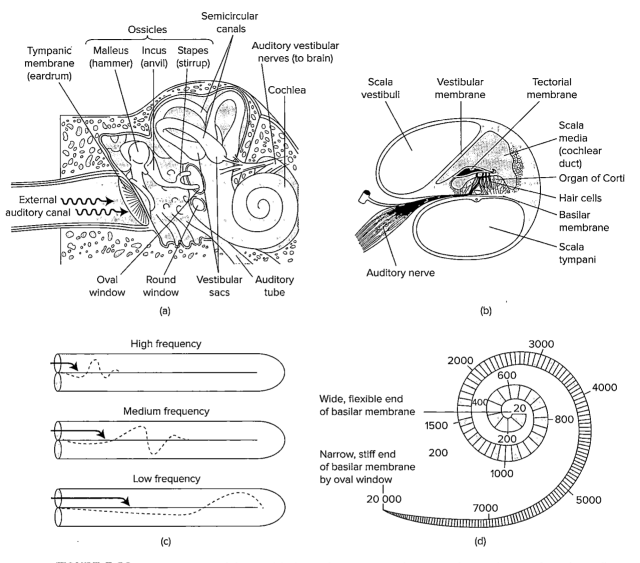

FIGURE 5.20 A cross-section of the ear (a) shows the structures that transmit sound waves from the auditory canal to the cochlea. There, sound waves are translated into fluid waves that stimulate hair cells in the organ of Corti (b). The resulting nerve impulses reach the brain via the auditory nerve. The semicircular and vestibular sacs of the inner ear contain sense organs for equilibrium. In (c), the fluid waves created by different sound frequencies are shown, and (d) shows the frequencies that maximally stimulate different areas of the basilar membrane. High-frequency waves peak quickly and stimulate the membrane close to the oval window.

21. Describe the frequency and place theories of pitch perception. In what sense are both theories correct?

considerable bending of the hair cells occurs in response to an intense sound. Thus, loudness is coded in terms of both the rate of firing in the axons of the auditory nerve and in terms of which specific hair cells are sending messages (Carney, 2002).

The coding of pitch also involves two different processes, one for frequencies below about 1000 hertz (approximately the midpoint of the piano keyboard) and another for higher frequencies. Historically, as in the case of colour vision, two competing theories were advanced to account for pitch perception. According to the **frequency theory** of pitch

perception, nerve impulses sent to the brain match the frequency of the sound wave. Thus, a 30 hertz (cycles per second) sound wave from a piano should send 30 volleys of nerve impulses per second to the brain. Unfortunately, frequency theory encounters a major problem. Because neurons are limited in their rate of firing, individual impulses or volleys of impulses fired by groups of neurons cannot produce high enough frequencies of firing to match sound wave frequencies above 1000 hertz. How then do we perceive higher frequencies, such as a 4000 hertz note from the same piano?

Experiments conducted by Georg von Bekesy (1957) uncovered a second mechanism for coding pitch and earned him the 1961 Nobel Prize. Bekesy cut tiny holes in the cochleas of guinea pigs and human cadavers and observed through a microscope what happened inside the fluid-filled cochlea when he stimulated the eardrum with tones of varying frequencies. He found that high-frequency sounds produced an abrupt wave that peaked close to the oval window, whereas lower frequency vibrations produced a slower fluid wave that peaked farther down the cochlear canal (Figure 5.20c). Bekesy's observations supported a **place theory** of pitch perception, suggesting that the specific point in the cochlea where the fluid wave peaks and most strongly bends the hair cells serves as a frequency coding cue (Figure 5.20d). Later it was found that, similar to the manner in which the retina is "mapped" onto the visual cortex, the auditory cortex has a tonal frequency "map" that corresponds to specific areas of the cochlea. By analyzing the specific location of the cochlea from which auditory nerve impulses are being received, the brain can code pitches such as our 4000 hertz piano note (Carney, 2002; Musiek & Baran, 2006).

Thus, like trichromatic and opponent-process theories of colour vision, which were once thought to contradict each another, frequency and place theories of pitch transduction have both proved to be applicable in their own ways. At low frequencies, frequency theory holds true; at higher frequencies, place theory provides the mechanism for coding the pitch of a sound.

Sound Localization

Have you ever wondered why you have two ears, one located on each side of your head? As is usually the case in nature's designs, there is a good reason. Our very survival may depend on our ability to locate objects that emit sounds. The two ears play a crucial role in *sound localization*. The nervous system uses information concerning the time and intensity differences of sounds arriving at the two ears to locate the source of sounds in space (Brown, 2013; Luck & Vecera, 2002).

Sounds arrive first and loudest at the ear closest to the sound. When the source of the sound is directly in front of us, the sound wave reaches both ears at the same time and at the same intensity, so the source is perceived as being straight ahead. Our binaural ("two-eared") ability to localize sounds is amazingly sensitive.

PROFESSOR MAYER'S TOPOPHONE.

© Culver Pictures, Inc.

FIGURE 5.21 This device, used in the late 1800s by sailors to increase their ability to locate sounds while navigating in thick fog, assisted in two ways. First, because the two ear receptors were much larger than human ears, they could capture more sound waves. More importantly, the wide spacing between the receptors increased the time difference between the sound's arrival at the two human ears, thus increasing directional sensitivity.

For example, a sound 3 degrees to the right arrives at the right ear only 300 millionths of a second before it arrives at the left ear, and yet we can tell which direction the sound is coming from (Yin & Kuwada, 1984). But, as Figure 5.21 shows, there is always room for improvement.

Nature's design often bests even human ingenuity. For example, the barn owl comes equipped with ears that are exquisitely tailored for pinpoint localization of its prey during night hunting. Its right ear is directed slightly upward, its left ear slightly downward. This allows it to localize sounds precisely in both the vertical and horizontal planes, and thereby to zero in on its prey with deadly accuracy.

Hearing Loss

In Canada alone, almost three million people (approximately 10 percent of the population) suffer from some form of hearing loss. On a North American basis, the figure is closer to 23 million. Of these, 90 percent were born with normal hearing (Sataloff & Thayer, 2006). They suffer from two major types of hearing loss. **Conduction deafness** is caused by problems involving the mechanical system that transmits sound waves to the cochlea. For example, a punctured eardrum or a loss of function in the tiny bones of the middle ear can reduce the ear's capacity to transmit vibrations. Use of a hearing aid, which amplifies the sounds

22. How does the structure of the auditory system permit humans to localize sounds? What sensory information is used by the brain in localization?

entering the ear, may correct many cases of conduction deafness.

Nerve deafness is an entirely different matter. It is caused by damaged receptors within the inner ear or damage to the auditory nerve itself, and it cannot be helped by a hearing aid. Although aging and disease can produce nerve deafness, exposure to loud sounds is a leading cause of nerve deafness. Repeated exposure to loud sounds of a particular frequency (as might be produced by a machine in a factory) eventually can cause workers to lose hair cells at a particular point on the basilar membrane, thereby causing hearing loss for that frequency.

Extremely loud music can take a serious toll on hearing. Figure 5.22 shows the devastating results of a guinea pig's exposure to a sound level approximating that of loud rock music heard through earphones. As Table 5.3 shows, even brief exposure to sounds exceeding 140 decibels can cause irreversible damage to the transducers in the middle and inner ears, and so can more continuous sounds at lower decibel levels. The rock band The Who used to hold the record for the loudest concert ever in 1976 (120 decibels at 50 metres from speakers), but they have been surpassed by a KISS concert in Ottawa, where the intensity was measured at 136 dB. The Foo Fighters also have a reputation for loud music. In 2012 a concert in Northern Ireland resulted in noise complaints from 24 kilometres away. The Canadian Hearing Society recommends that you protect your hearing by listening to music at safe levels (i.e., below 85 decibels). An iPod or similar personal music player can generate this decibel level when music is listened to through earbuds (Ballard, 2010).

Although hearing aids can do little to remedy nerve deafness, measures can be taken to prevent damage in people who are exposed to hazardous noise in the workplace (e.g., the use of noise-dampening ear protectors or noise-cancelling headphones).

Taste and Smell: The Chemical Senses

Gustation (taste) and **olfaction** (smell) are chemical senses because their receptors are sensitive to chemical molecules rather than to some form of energy (DiLorenzo & Youngentob, 2013). These senses are so intertwined that some scientists refer to a *common chemical sense* (Beauchamp & Bartoshuk, 1997; Halpern, 2002). Enjoying a good meal usually depends on the simultaneous activity of taste and odour receptors, as becomes apparent when we have a stuffy nose and our food tastes bland. People who lose their sense of smell typically believe they have lost their sense of taste as well (Beauchamp & Bartoshuk, 1997).

Gustation: The Sense of Taste

People who fancy themselves gourmets are frequently surprised to learn that their sense of taste responds to only four qualities: sweet, sour, salty, and bitter. Every other taste experience combines these qualities and those of other senses, such as smell, temperature, and touch. For example, part of the "taste" of popcorn includes its texture, its crunchiness, and its odour. In addition to its chemical receptors, the tongue is richly endowed with tactile (touch) and temperature receptors.

23. What are the two varieties of deafness, and how do they differ in their physical bases and in possible treatment?

24. Describe the stimuli and the receptors involved in gustation and olfaction. Why do researchers sometimes refer to a *common chemical sense?*

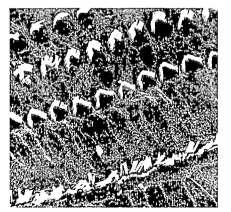 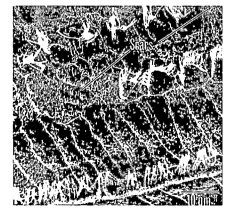

Micrographs by Robert E. Preston, courtesy of Professor J.E. Hawkins, Kresge Hearing Research Institute University of Michigan.

FIGURE 5.22 Exposure to loud sounds can destroy auditory receptors in the inner ear. These pictures, taken through an electron microscope, show the hair cells of a guinea pig before (a) and after (b) exposure to 24 hours of noise comparable to that of a loud rock concert.

Taste buds are chemical receptors concentrated along the edges and back surface of the tongue. Each taste bud is most responsive to one or two of the basic taste qualities, but responds weakly to the others as well. An additional taste sensation called *umami* increases the sensitivity of other taste qualities. This sensory response is activated by certain proteins, as well as by monosodium glutamate, a substance used by some restaurants for flavour enhancement. Humans have about 9000 taste buds, each consisting of several receptor cells arranged like the segments of an orange (Figure 5.23). A small number of receptors also are found in the roof and back of the mouth, so that even people without a tongue can taste substances. Hairlike structures project from the top of each cell into the taste pore, an opening to the outside surface of the tongue. When a substance is taken into the mouth, it interacts with saliva to form a chemical solution that flows into the taste pore and stimulates the receptor cells. A "taste" results from complex patterns of neural activity produced by the four types of taste receptors (Bartoshuk, 1998; Halpern, 2002).

The sense of taste not only provides us with pleasure, but also has adaptive significance in discriminating between nutrients and toxins (Born, Levit, Niv, Meyerhof, & Behrens, 2013; Scott, 1992). Our response to some taste qualities is innate. For example, newborn infants respond positively to sugar water placed on the tongue and negatively to bitter substances, such as quinine (Davidson & Fox, 1988). Many poisonous substances in nature have bitter tastes, so this emotional response seems to be "hard-wired" into our physiology (Hoebel, 1997; Small et al., 2003). In nature, sweet substances are more likely to occur in nutritious foods. Unfortunately, many humans now live in an environment different from the food-scarce environment in which preferences for sweet substances may have evolved (Scott & Giza, 1993). As a result, people in affluent countries over-consume sweet foods that are good for us only in small quantities.

Olfaction: The Sense of Smell

Humans are visually oriented creatures, but the sense of smell (olfaction) is of great importance for many species. Bloodhounds, for example, have poor eyesight, but an exquisitely developed olfactory sense that is about two million times more sensitive than ours (Thomas, 1974). A bloodhound can detect a person's scent in a footprint that is four days old, something no human could do.

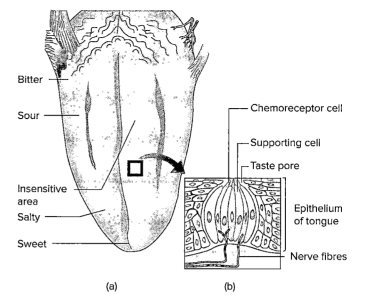

FIGURE 5.23 The receptors for taste are specialized cells located in the tongue's taste buds. The tongue's 9000 taste buds are grouped in different areas according to the taste sensation they produce. The centre of the tongue is relatively insensitive to the chemical molecules that constitute gustatory stimuli.

The receptors for smell are long cells that project through the lining of the upper part of the nasal cavity and into the mucous membrane. Humans have about 40 million olfactory receptors, dogs about one billion. Unfortunately, our ability to discriminate between different odours is not well understood. The most popular current theory is that olfactory receptors recognize diverse odours individually rather than by mixing the activity of a smaller number of basic receptors, as occurs in taste (Bartoshuk & Beauchamp, 1994; Wilson et al., 2004). Olfactory receptors have receptor structures that resemble neurotransmitter binding sites on neurons. Any of the thousands of potential odour molecules can lock into sites that are tailored to fit them (Buck & Axel, 1991; Pernollet, Sanz, & Briand, 2006). The receptors that fire send their input to the **olfactory bulb**, a forebrain structure immediately above the nasal cavity. Each odorous chemical excites only a limited portion of the olfactory bulb, and odours are apparently coded in terms of the specific area of the olfactory bulb that is excited (Dalton, 2002).

The social and sexual behaviour of animals is more strongly regulated by olfaction than is human behaviour (Alcock, 2005). For example, most of us find other ways to mark our territories, such as by erecting fences or spreading belongings over the table that we are using in the library. Whether humans have special

25. What is menstrual synchrony, and what evidence is there that pheromones are involved?

olfactory systems involved in the regulation of sexual and reproductive behaviour is a matter of some debate, but most researchers believe that there is no overwhelming evidence to support this. Nonetheless, some researchers believe that **pheromones,** chemical signals found in natural body scents, may affect human behaviour in subtle ways (Bartoshuk & Beauchamp, 1994; Monti-Bloch & Grosser, 1991; Rako & Friebely, 2004). One interesting but puzzling observation, known as **menstrual synchrony,** is the tendency of women who live together or are close friends to become more similar in their menstrual cycles. Psychologist Martha McClintock (1971) tested 135 university women and found that, during the course of an academic year, roommates moved from a mean of 8.5 days apart in their periods to 4.9 days apart. Another study of 51 women who worked together showed that close friends had menstrual onsets averaging 3.5 to 4.3 days apart, whereas those who were not close friends had onsets that averaged 8 to 9 days apart (Weller et al., 1999). Are pheromones responsible for synchrony? In experiments conducted at the Monell Chemical Senses Center in Philadelphia, 10 women with regular cycles were daubed under the nose every few days with underarm secretions collected from other women. After three months, the participants' cycles began to coincide with the sweat donors' cycles. A control group of women who were daubed with an alcohol solution rather than sweat showed no menstrual synchrony with a partner (Preti et al., 1986). In other studies, however, menstrual synchrony was not found for cohabitating lesbian couples or for Bedouin women who spent most of their time together, indicating that prolonged and very intensive contact may not be conducive to menstrual synchrony (Weller & Weller, 1997, 1998). The debate continues with arguments both for and against biochemical synchrony (Pettit & Vigor, 2015).

As anyone who has owned a dog or cat in heat could attest, odours strongly affect the sexual attractiveness of animals to other animals. On the other hand, there is no solid evidence to justify the recent rise in commercial sales of "pheromone substances" to humans who wish to become sexually irresistible. At this point, we would conclude that a good personality and good grooming are a better bet than a good pheromone.

The Skin and Body Senses

The skin and body senses include the senses of touch, kinesthesis (muscle movement), and equilibrium. The last two are called *body senses* because they inform us of the body's position and movement. They tell us, for example, if we are running or standing still, lying down, or sitting up.

The Tactile Senses

Touch is important to us in many ways. Sensitivity to extreme temperatures and pain enables us to avoid external danger and alerts us to disorders within our bodies. Tactile sensations are also a source of many of life's pleasures, including sexual orgasm. A lack of tactile contact with a caretaking adult retards physical, social, and emotional development (Harlow, 1958), and physically massaging newborn babies enhances their development (Cigales et al., 1997; Field et al., 1996; Canfield, 2006).

Humans are sensitive to at least four tactile sensations: pressure (touch), pain, warmth, and cold. These sensations are conveyed by receptors in the skin and in our internal organs. Mixtures of these four sensations form the basis for all other common skin sensations, such as itch.

Considering the importance of our skin senses, surprisingly little is known about how they work. The skin, a multi-layered elastic structure that covers 90 cm² and weighs between 2.7 and 4.5 kilograms, is the largest organ in our body. It contains a variety of receptor structures, but their role in specific sensations is less clear than for the other senses. Many sensations probably depend on specific patterns of activity in the various receptors (Schiff & Foulke, 2010). We do know that primary receptors for pain and temperature are *free nerve endings,* simple nerve cells beneath the skin's surface that resemble the bare branches of a tree in winter (Gracely et al., 2002). Nerve fibres situated at the base of hair follicles are receptors for touch and light pressure (Heller & Schiff, 1991).

The brain can locate sensations because skin receptors send their messages to the point in the somatosensory cortex that corresponds to the area of the body where the receptor is located. As we saw in Chapter 3, the amount of cortex devoted to each area of the body is related to that part's sensitivity. Our fingers, lips, and tongue are well represented, accounting for their extreme sensitivity to stimulation.

Sometimes the brain "locates" sensations that cannot possibly be present. This action occurs in the puzzling *phantom limb* phenomenon, in which amputees experience vivid sensations coming from the missing limb (Heavey, 2015; Warga, 1987). Apparently, an irritation of the nerves that used to originate in the limb fools the brain into interpreting the resulting nerve impulses as real sensations. Joel Katz and Ronald Melzack (1990) studied 68 amputees who insisted

26. What four tactile sensations are humans sensitive to? How are these sensations localized, and how are phantom limb sensations produced?

that they experienced pain from the amputated limb that was as vivid and "real" as any pain they had ever experienced. This pain was not merely a recollection of what pain used to feel like in the phantom limb; it was actually experienced in the present. The phantom limb phenomenon can be quite maddening: Imagine having an intense itch that you never can scratch, or an ache you cannot rub. When amputees are fitted with prosthetic limbs and begin using them, phantom pain tends to disappear (Gracely et al., 2002; Seilabipour, Fallah, Kazemi, & Shariat, 2013).

Pain

Pain receptors are found in all body tissues with the exception of the brain, bones, hair, nails, and nonliving parts of the teeth. Free nerve endings in the skin and internal organs respond to intense mechanical, thermal, or chemical stimulation and then send nerve impulses into the spinal cord, where sensory tracts carry pain information to the brain. Once in the brain, the sensory information about pain intensity and location is relayed by the thalamus to the somatosensory and frontal areas of the cerebral cortex (Fields, 2005). Reflecting the adaptive value of pain, brain recordings reveal that cerebral processing of pain occurs faster than for other kinds of tactile stimuli, permitting a more rapid response (Ploner et al., 2006). Other tracts from the thalamus direct nerve impulses to the limbic system, which is involved in motivation and emotion. These tracts seem to control the emotional component of pain (Zanker, 2010). Thus, pain has both a sensory and an emotional component. *Suffering* occurs when both painful sensations and a negative emotional response are present (Fordyce, 1988; Turk, 2001).

Spinal and Brain Mechanisms

Gate control theory, developed by Canadian psychologist Ronald Melzack and physiologist Patrick Wall (1982), was a major advance in the study of pain. **Gate control theory** proposes that the experience of pain results from the opening and closing of gating mechanisms in the nervous system (Turk & Melzack, 2001). Events in the spinal cord can open a system of spinal cord "gates" and allow the nerve impulses to travel toward the brain. However, other sensory input can partially or completely close the gates and blunt our experience of pain. For example, rubbing a bruise or scratching an itch can produce relief. Gate control theorists also suggest that acupuncture achieves its pain-relieving effects because the acupuncture needles stimulate mostly tactile receptors that close the pain gates.

From a psychological perspective, perhaps the most intriguing feature of gate control theory is that nerve impulses in fibres descending from the brain can also influence the spinal gates, thereby increasing or decreasing the flow of pain stimulation to the brain. This *central control mechanism* allows thoughts, emotions, and beliefs to influence the experience of pain and helps to explain why pain is a psychological phenomenon as well as a physical one.

Gate control and other theorists have traditionally viewed pain as solely reflecting the action of neurons. However, the immune system also plays a role in pain. Recent research has shown that *glial cells*, which structurally support and service neurons within the spinal cord, are involved in the creation and maintenance of pathological pain (Moayedi & Davis, 2013; Watkins & Maier, 2003). These glial cells become activated by immune challenges (viral or bacterial infection) and by substances released by neurons within the pain pathway. They then amplify pain by releasing *cytokines* (messenger molecules) that promote inflammation. This action may help account for that "ache all over" sensation that many of us experience when we are ill.

The Endorphins

In 1680, an English physician wrote, "Among the remedies which it has pleased Almighty God to give man to relieve his suffering, none is so universal and so efficacious as opium" (quoted in Snyder, 1977). Opiates (such as opium, morphine, and heroin) have been used for centuries to relieve pain, and they strongly affect the brain's pain and pleasure systems. In the 1970s, scientists discovered that opiates produce their effects by locking into specific receptor sites in brain regions associated with pain perception.

But why would the brain have built-in receptors for opiates unless there were some natural chemical in the brain for the receptor to receive? Later research disclosed what had to be true: the nervous system has its own built-in analgesics (painkillers) with opiatelike properties. These natural opiates were named **endorphins** (meaning "endogenous," or internally produced, "morphines"). Endorphins exert some of their painkilling effects by inhibiting the release of neurotransmitters involved in the synaptic transmission of pain impulses from the spinal cord to the brain (Fields, 2005). Endorphins are of great interest to psychologists because they may help to explain how psychological factors "in the head" can have such strong effects on pain and suffering.

In 2001, John-Kar Zubieta and colleagues published a landmark study that showed the endorphins in action within the brain. They injected a radioactive form of an endorphin into volunteer participants, then stimulated them with painful injections of salt water into the jaw muscles. Brain scans allowed the researchers to see which areas of the brain lit up from endorphin activity and to relate this activity to pain reports given by the participants every 15 seconds. The scans revealed a surge of endorphin activity within several brain regions, including the thalamus (the sensory switchboard), the amygdala (an emotion centre), and a sensory area of the cortex. As the endorphin surge continued over 20 minutes of pain stimulation, participants reported decreased sensory and emotional ratings of pain.

Acupuncture (Figure 5.24) is an effective pain-reduction technique that ultimately may be understood in terms of endorphin mechanisms. Injections of naloxone, a drug that counteracts the effects of endorphins, greatly decrease the pain-reducing effects of acupuncture (Oleson, 2002). This suggests that acupuncture normally releases endorphins to blunt pain sensations.

The Body Senses

We would be totally unable to coordinate our body movements were it not for the sense of **kinesthesis**, which provides us with feedback about our muscles' and joints' positions and movements. The receptors are nerve endings in the muscles, tendons, and joints. The information this sense gives us is the basis for making coordinated movements. Cooperating with kinesthesis is the **vestibular sense**, the sense of body orientation or equilibrium (Figure 5.25). The vestibular receptors are located in the *vestibular apparatus* of the inner ear (see Figure 5.20). One part of the equilibrium system consists of three *semicircular canals*, which contain the receptors for head movement. Each canal lies in a different plane: left/right, backward/forward, or up/down. These canals are filled with fluid and lined with hairlike cells that function as receptors. When the head moves, the fluid in the appropriate canal shifts, stimulating the hair cells and sending messages to the brain. The semicircular canals respond only to acceleration and deceleration; when a constant speed is reached (no matter how high), the fluid and the hair cells return to their normal resting state. That's why takeoffs and landings give a sense of movement, whereas flying at 800 kilometres per hour on a cruising airliner does not. Located at the base of the semicircular canals, the *vestibular sacs* also contain hair cells that respond to the position of the body and tell us whether we are upright or tilted at an angle. These structures constitute the second part of the body-sense system.

You have now learned a considerable amount about the principles underlying stimulus detection and transduction. As the *Frontiers* feature shows,

27. Describe the sensory principles that are applied to create sensory prosthetics for visually and hearing impaired people.

© Punchstock/Creatas

FIGURE 5.24 Acupuncture is a proven pain-reduction procedure. Gate control theory attributes its effects to the stimulation of sensory fibres that close sensory gates in the pain system. In addition, there is evidence that acupuncture stimulates endorphin release.

Corey Rich/Aurora Open/Getty Images

FIGURE 5.25 Kinesthesis and the vestibular sense are especially well developed in some people, and essential for performing feats like this one.

Frontiers

SENSORY PROSTHETICS: RESTORING LOST FUNCTION

Millions of people suffer from blindness and deafness, living in sightless or soundless worlds. War, accidents, or illness result in amputations that cost others important aspects of their sense of touch. Psychological research on the workings of the sensory systems is now being combined with technical advances in bio-engineering, resulting in **sensory prosthetic devices** that provide sensory input that can, to some extent, substitute for what cannot be supplied by a person's sensory receptors (Patil & Turner, 2008). In considering these devices, we should remind ourselves that we don't see with the eyes, hear with the ears, or feel with touch receptors. We see, hear, and feel with our brain. The nerve impulses sent from the retina, the organ of Corti, or the skin, are no different from those sent from anywhere else in the body.

Seeing with the Ears

One device, known as a *Sonicguide,* provides new "eyes" through the ears, capitalizing on principles of auditory localization. The Sonicguide, shown in Figure 5.26, works on the same principle as *echolocation,* the sensory tool used by bats to navigate in total darkness. A pair of eyeglasses contains a transmitter that emits high-frequency sound waves beyond the range of human hearing. These waves bounce back from objects in the environment and are transformed

Courtesy of the Department of Veterans Affairs

FIGURE 5.26 The Sonicguide allows a blind person to perceive the size, distance, movement, shape, and texture of objects through sound waves that represent the visual features of objects.

by the Sonicguide into sounds that can be heard through earphones. Different sound qualities match specific features of external objects, and the wearer must learn to interpret the sonic messages. For example, the sound's pitch tells the person how far away an object is; a low pitch signals a nearby object and becomes higher as the distance to the object increases. The loudness of the sound tells how large the object is, and the clarity of the sound (ranging from a static-like sound to a clear tone) signals the texture of the object, from very rough to very smooth. Finally, the sound-localization principle described earlier tells the person where the object is located in the environment by means of differences in the time at which sounds arrive at the two ears. The device has been tested on adults and children and works quite well. However, blind babies learn to use the sonic cues faster and more completely than anyone else.

The Seeing Tongue

At the University of Wisconsin, Paul Bach-y-Rita (2004) developed a tactile tongue-based, electrical input sensor as a substitute for visual input. The tongue seems an unlikely substitute for the eye, hidden as it is in the dark recess of the mouth. Yet in many ways it may be the second-best organ for providing detailed input, for it is densely packed with tactile receptors, thus allowing the transmission of high-resolution data. Moreover, its moist surface is a good conducting medium for electricity, meaning that minimum voltage is required to stimulate the receptors.

The stimulator, shown in Figure 5.27a, receives digital data from a camera and provides patterns of stimulation to the tongue through a 144-electrode array. The array can transmit shapes that correspond to the main features of the visual stimulus. Initial trials with blindfolded sighted people and blind people show that with about nine hours of training, users can "read" the letters of a Snellen eye chart with an acuity of 20/430, a modest but noteworthy beginning (Simpaio et al., 2001).

With continued development, a miniature camera attached to eyeglasses will transmit wireless data to a more densely packed electrode array attached to a dental retainer. In fact, the United States Food and Drug Administration has recently given the go-ahead for such a device—the BrainPort V100—to sold. The suggested retail price will be about $10 000 per unit. In addition to helping people who are blind, the device has both military and civilian applications. For example, it has been used to help soldiers locate objects in pitch-black environments, such as caves, where night-vision devices are useless. It could also aid firefighters as they search smoke-filled buildings for people to rescue.

Retinal Implants

Loss of vision may be the result of damage to the photoreceptors in the retina (as in macular degeneration). If this is the case, it may be possible to replace the receptors

continued

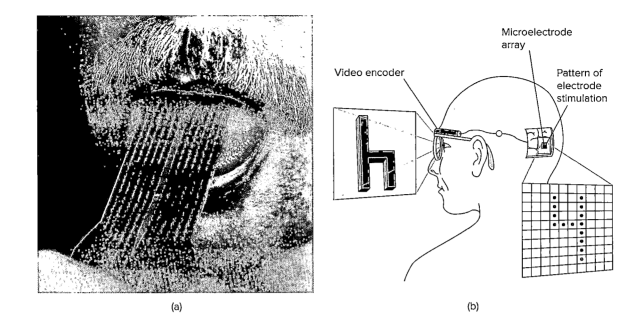

(a)

(b)

(left): © Jeff Miller/UW-Madison University Communications

FIGURE 5.27 Two approaches to providing artificial vision for the blind. (a) Bach-y-Rita's device converts digitized stimuli from a camera to a matrix of electrodes, which stimulate tactile receptors in the tongue to communicate spatial information to the brain. (b) Tiny electrodes implanted into individual neurons in the visual cortex produce patterns of phosphenes that correspond to the visual scene observed through the video camera and encoder. Note how the cortical image is reversed as in normal visual input.

with a prosthetic sensor. A digital camera, mounted to a pair of glasses, sends signals directly to an electrode array implanted in the retina. The array then stimulates the bipolar cells to produce a visual signal. The Argus II bionic eye system works on this principle and has been successfully implanted in over 100 people. Visual output is in light and dark contrast only, with an acuity of about 20/1260. However, this is enough to roughly perceive objects in space. Cost of the implant is about $100 000.

If the bipolar layer is also damaged, you may have to directly stimulate the ganglion cells. Sheila Nirenberg has designed just such a device. It too requires a digital camera input and a processor, but Nirenberg has deciphered the neural code used by the visual system providing a much more accurate input signal. The processor converts visual images into light pulses, which are then projected to the ganglion cells. The ganglion cells have been treated with light-sensitive proteins using gene therapy. Thus, the pulses are decoded at the ganglion cells and sent on to the brain. Nirenberg claims that the prosthesis virtually restores normal vision (Nirenberg & Pandarinath, 2012). To date, the procedure has only been used with rats, but Nirenberg's team has deciphered the visual code for monkeys as well.

Cortical Implants

When cells in the visual cortex are stimulated electrically, discrete flashes of light called *phosphenes* are experienced by both sighted and blind people. Because sensory neurons in the visual cortex are arranged in a manner that corresponds to the organization of the retina, a specific pattern of stimulation applied to individual neurons in the cortex can form a phosphene pattern that conforms to the shapes of letters or objects (Weiland & Humayun, 2008). The acuity of the pattern depends on the area of the visual cortex that is stimulated (the portion receiving input from the densely packed fovea produces greatest acuity) and on the number of stimulating electrodes in the array.

Building on this approach, researchers have developed the device shown in Figure 5.27b. It consists of a silicon strip containing thousands of tiny stimulating electrodes that penetrate directly into individual neurons in the visual cortex, where they can stimulate phosphene patterns. Eventually, a tiny TV camera mounted in specially designed eyeglasses will provide visual information to a microcomputer that will analyze the scene and then send the appropriate patterns of electrical stimulation through the implanted electrodes to produce corresponding phosphene patterns in the visual cortex. The researchers have shown that sighted participants who wear darkened goggles that produce phosphene-like patterns of light flashes, such as those provided by cortical stimulation, can quickly learn to navigate through complex environments and are able to read text at about two-thirds their normal rate (Liu et al., 2008; Normann et al., 1996, 1999). Blind people with the stimulating electrodes implanted in the visual cortex have also been able to learn a kind of cortical Braille for reading purposes. Although still experimental, a commercially available intracortical prosthetic device should appear in the near future.

continued

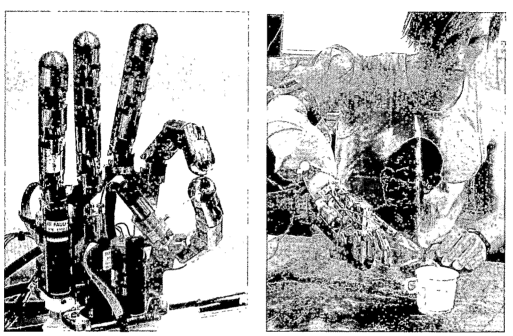

(both): © WENN.com/Newscom

FIGURE 5.28 Shown here without its skinlike covering, the SmartHand's leads connect to both sensory and motor nerves in the arm. The resulting motor control, combined with sensory feedback from the bionic hand's movements, allows an amputee to perform this precision act without dropping or crushing the soft plastic bottle.

Cochlear Implants

People with hearing impairments have also been assisted by the development of prosthetic devices. The cochlear implant is for people suffering from nerve deafness, who cannot be helped by mere sound amplification provided by normal hearing aids. A set of 22 electrodes is implanted in coil-like fashion around the cochlea to directly stimulate the auditory nerve. A microphone sends sound waves to a processor implanted in the bone behind the ear, and the processor breaks the sound down into its principal frequencies and sends electrical signals to cochlear areas associated with particular frequencies (Fayad et al., 2008). Electrical recording of cortical responses to sounds in people who had been deaf for more than two decades showed that in the months following installation of a cochlear implant, sounds increasingly "registered" in the auditory cortex (Pantev et al., 2006). With a cochlear implant, deaf people can hear everyday sounds such as sirens, and many can understand speech (Meyer et al., 1998; Parkinson et al., 1998). Although the substitution of 22 electrodes for the more than 16 000 hair cells that populate the intact cochlea cannot produce normal auditory experience, cochlear implants have helped many people partially restore their sense of hearing.

Recently, a revolutionary new device was implanted in three-year old Grayson Clamp. Grayson was born without cochlear nerves, so a cochlear implant simply would not work. Surgeons in Chapel Hill, North Carolina, implanted an auditory brain stem device directly onto the cochlear nucleus. The implant bypasses the inner ear and delivers auditory impulses directly to the brain, giving Grayson back his hearing (Hagen & Wilson, 2013).

The Bionic Hand That Restores Tactile Sensations

In 2009, researchers in Sweden and Italy announced the development of the SmartHand, a prosthetic device that restores the sense of touch in people who have lost their hands (ScienceDaily, 2009, November 11). The SmartHand contains 40 sensors that are connected to the sensory nerves in the arm of an amputee (Figure 5.28). Four motors, also linked to the brain through their attachment to motor nerves in the arm, allow patients to move the fingers in very precise ways. This prosthetic hand is the first to allow for the level of control of movement that comes only through tactile feedback. With it, an amputee can actually experience the feeling of stroking a loved one's cheek and can handle delicate objects with just the right amount of pressure. Recently, Antfolk et al. (2012) have suggested that the simple addition of an inflatable silicone pad can result in the experience of "real touch." Among the first to receive the device when it becomes commercially available will be returning soldiers from Iraq and Afghanistan who have lost their hands in battle.

Sensory prosthetics illustrate the ways in which knowledge about sensory phenomena, such as phosphenes, the organization of the visual cortex, sound localization, and the place theory of pitch perception, can provide the information needed to take advantage of new technological advances. Yet even with all our ingenuity, prosthetic devices are no substitutes for our normal sensory systems, a fact that should increase our appreciation for what nature has given us.

Review

- Sound waves, the stimuli for audition, have two characteristics: frequency, measured in terms of cycles per second or hertz (Hz), and amplitude, measured in terms of decibels (db). Frequency is related to pitch, amplitude to loudness. The receptors for hearing are hair cells in the organ of Corti of the inner ear.

- Loudness is coded in terms of the number and types of auditory nerve fibres that fire. Pitch is coded in two ways. Low-frequency tones are coded in terms of corresponding numbers of nerve impulses in individual receptors or by volleys of impulses from a number of receptors. Frequencies above 4000 hertz are coded according to the region of the basilar membrane that is displaced most by the fluid wave in the cochlear canal.

- Hearing loss may result from conduction deafness, produced by problems involving the structures of the inner ear that transmit vibrations to the cochlea, or from nerve deafness, in which the receptors of the inner ear or the auditory nerve are damaged.

- The receptors for taste and smell respond to chemical molecules. Taste buds are responsive to four basic qualities: sweet, sour, salty, and bitter. The receptors for smell (olfaction) are long cells in the upper nasal cavity. Natural

body odours produced by pheromones appear to account for a menstrual synchrony that sometimes occurs among women who are in frequent contact.

- Pain is a complex perception influenced by biological and psychological factors. At the biological level, the major pain receptors appear to be free nerve endings. Gate control theory attributes pain to the opening and closing of gates in the spinal cord and to influences from the brain. The nervous system contains endorphins, which play a major role in pain reduction.

- The skin and body senses include touch, kinesthesis, and equilibrium. Receptors in the skin and body tissues are sensitive to touch, pain, warmth, and cold. Kinesthesis functions by means of nerve endings in the muscles, tendons, and joints. The sense organs for equilibrium are in the vestibular apparatus of the inner ear.

- Principles derived from the study of sensory processes have been applied in developing sensory prosthetics for the blind and the hearing impaired. Examples include the Sonicguide, a device that provides visual information through tactile stimulation of the tongue, direct electrical stimulation of the visual cortex, and cochlear implants.

these principles have not only informational value for understanding how our sensory systems operate, but also applied value in helping people with sensory impairments.

PERCEPTION: THE CREATION OF EXPERIENCE

Sensory systems provide the raw materials from which experiences are formed. Our sense organs do not select what we will be aware of or how we will experience it; they merely transmit as much information as they can through our nervous system. Yet our experiences are not simply a one-to-one reflection of what is "out there." Different people may experience the same sensory information in radically different ways, because perception is an active, creative process in which raw sensory data are organized and given meaning.

To create our perceptions, the brain carries out two different kinds of processing functions

(Figure 5.29). In **bottom-up processing**, the system takes in individual elements of the stimulus and then combines them into a unified perception. Your visual system operates in

28. Differentiate between bottom-up and top-down processing of sensory information.

29. What two complementary processes occur in attention?

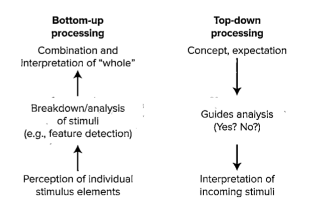

FIGURE 5.29 Bottom-up perceptual processing builds from an analysis of individual stimulus features to a unified perception. Top-down processing begins with a perceptual whole, such as an expectation or an image of an object, and then determines the degree of "fit" with the stimulus features.

a bottom-up fashion as you read; its feature detectors analyze the elements in each letter of every word, and then recombine them into your visual perception of the letters and words. In **top-down processing,** sensory information is interpreted in the light of existing knowledge, concepts, ideas, and expectations. Top-down processing is occurring as you interpret the words and sentences constructed by the bottom-up process. Here you make use of "higher-order" knowledge, including what you have learned about the meaning of words and sentence construction. Indeed, a given sentence may even convey a different personal meaning to you than to another person if you relate its content to some unique personal experience. Top-down processing accounts for many psychological influences on perception, such as the roles played by our motives, expectations, previous experiences, and cultural learning.

Perception Is Selective: The Role of Attention

As you read these words, 100 million sensory messages may be clamouring for your attention. Only a few of these messages register in awareness; the rest you perceive either dimly or not at all. But you can shift your attention to one of those "unregistered" stimuli at any time. (For example, how does the big toe of your right foot feel right now?) Attention, then, involves two processes of selection: (1) focusing on certain stimuli, and (2) filtering out other incoming information (Luck & Vecera, 2002; Similek & Frischen, 2013).

These processes have been studied experimentally through a technique called **shadowing.** Participants wear earphones and listen simultaneously to two messages, one sent through each earphone. They are asked to repeat (or "shadow") one of the messages word for word as they listen. Most participants can do this quite successfully, but only at the cost of not remembering what the other message was about. Shadowing experiments demonstrate that we *cannot* attend completely to more than one thing at a time. But we can shift our attention rapidly back and forth between the two messages, drawing on our general knowledge to fill in the gaps (Bonnel & Hafter, 1998; Sperling, 1984).

Inattentional Blindness

Electrical recording and brain-imaging studies have shown that unattended stimuli register in the nervous system but do not enter into immediate experience (Itti & Rees, 2005; Pitts et al., 2012). In the visual realm, scientists have coined the term **inattentional blindness** to refer to the failure of unattended stimuli to register in consciousness (Mack, 2003). We can look right at something without "seeing" it if we are attending to something else. In one study, research participants who were counting the number of passes made during a videotaped basketball game did not notice a woman wearing a gorilla suit who walked across the court, even though she remained in clear sight for more than five seconds (Simons & Chabris, 1999). Even if you are an expert with respect to the visual material, you can still miss unattended stimuli. Drew, Vo, and Wolfe (2013) asked experienced radiologists to examine lung X-rays for nodules. In the last case they looked at, a gorilla, 48 times the nodule size, was inserted. Eighty-three percent did not see the gorilla. Hanes (1991) reported that several experienced pilots training on flight simulators were so intent on watching the landing instruments, such as the air-speed indicator on the plane's windshield, that they directed their plane onto a runway containing another aircraft. Inattentional blindness is surely relevant to findings that cellphone conversations significantly reduce driving performance in experimental studies (e.g., Golden et al., 2003). It's a bad idea to drive while talking on the phone. It's also a bad idea to drink and drive, as alcohol ingestion increases inattentional blindness (Clifasefi et al., 2006).

Environmental and Personal Factors in Attention

Attention is strongly affected both by the nature of the stimulus and by personal factors. Stimulus characteristics that attract our attention include intensity, novelty, movement, contrast, and repetition. Advertisers use these properties in their commercials and packaging (Figure 5.30), especially sexually oriented stimuli that are very attention-grabbing (Krishna, 2009).

Internal factors, such as our motives and interests, act as powerful filters and influence which stimuli in our environment we will notice. For example, when we are hungry, we are especially sensitive to food-related cues. A botanist walking through a park is especially attentive to the plants; a landscape architect attends primarily to the layout of the park.

People are especially attentive to stimuli that have relevance to their well-being, a tendency that clearly has biological survival

30. Describe the results of shadowing experiments in relation to attentional capabilities.

31. What stimulus and personal characteristics influence attention?

FIGURE 5.30 Advertisers are adept at using attention-attracting stimulus characteristics in their advertisements. Personal characteristics are also important. What kinds of individuals do you suppose would be most attentive to this ad?

value (Oehman et al., 2001). This tendency is shown in experiments in which researchers measure how quickly people focus on and react to threatening versus nonthreatening stimuli. Thus, people are quicker to identify an angry-looking face in a crowd than a smiling face (Hansen & Hansen, 1988). If a fearful face or figure is projected on one side of the visual field and a neutral face or figure on the other, measurements of eye movements show faster movements toward the fearful stimulus, showing the capacity of threat-relevant stimuli to capture visual attention (Bannerman et al., 2009). Humans' ability to perceive and recognize objects in their peripheral visual field

is greater for naturalistic stimuli like animals than for artificial stimuli like letters or numbers (Thorpe, Gegenfurtner, Fabre-Thorpe, & Bülthoff, 2001). Increasingly, researchers are using more naturalistic sensory stimuli in studies of perception in an effort to better understand how we process real-life sensory information in our natural environment (Felsen & Dan, 2005).

In the sport of baseball, batters are sometimes forced to avoid pitched balls that might hit them. In an analogue of this process, Jeffrey Lin and colleagues (2009) seated participants in front of a video display, and then measured their reaction times in response to spherical images that sped from the background. The observers had significantly faster reaction times when the speeding object was coming toward their heads than when its trajectory would barely miss their heads. The investigators suggested that humans have developed a special visual system that unconsciously triggers protective responses to stimuli that are interpreted as threatening. As a real-life illustration of this principle, they point to the 2008 incident shown in Figure 5.31, when an Iraqi reporter hurled his shoes at former U.S. president George Bush during a joint news conference with Iraqi prime minister Nouri al-Maliki. Commenting on this scene, Lin stated, "If you look at the shoe-throwing video, you will see that the prime minister doesn't flinch at all. His brain has already categorized the shoe as non-threatening which does not require evasive action. But Bush has categorized the shoe as threatening and triggers an evasive dodge, all within a fraction of a second" (Schwarz, 2009).

FIGURE 5.31 Former U.S. president George Bush reflexively ducks as an Iraqi reporter hurls a shoe toward the podium, but Iraqi prime minister Nouri al-Maliki, does not.

Perceptions Have Organization and Structure

Have you ever stopped to wonder why we perceive the visual world as being composed of distinct objects? After all, the information sent by the retina reflects nothing but an array of varying intensities and frequencies of light energy. The light rays reflected from different parts of a single object have no more natural "belongingness" to one another than those coming from two different objects. Yet we perceive scenes as involving separate objects, such as trees, buildings, and people. These perceptions must be a product of an organization imposed by our nervous system (Davis & Johnsrude, 2007; Matthen, 2007). This top-down process of perceptual organization occurs so automatically that we take it for granted. But Dr. Richard, a prominent psychologist who suffered brain damage in an accident, no longer does:

> There was nothing wrong with his eyes, yet the input he received from them was not put together correctly. Dr. Richard reported that if he saw a person, he sometimes would perceive the separate parts of the person as not belonging together in a single body. But if all the parts moved in the same direction, Dr. Richard then saw them as one complete person. At other times, he would perceive people in crowds wearing the same colour clothes as "going together" rather than as separate people. He also had difficulty putting sights and sounds together. Sometimes, the movement of the lips did not correspond to the sounds he heard, as if he were watching a badly dubbed foreign movie. Dr. Richard's

experience of his environment was thus disjointed and fragmented. (Sacks, 1986, p. 76)

Another more extreme example of perceptual organization gone awry is synaesthesia, which we described at the beginning of this chapter. What, then, are the processes by which sensory nonsense becomes perceptual sense?

Gestalt Principles of Perceptual Organization

Early in the 20th century, psychologists from the German school of Gestalt psychology set out to discover how we organize the separate parts of our perceptual field into a unified and meaningful whole. *Gestalt* is the German term for "pattern," "shape," or "form." Gestalt theorists were early champions of top-down processing, arguing that the wholes we perceive are often more than (and frequently different from) the sum of their parts.

The Gestalt theorists emphasized the importance of **figure-ground relations**. We tend to organize stimuli into a central or foreground figure and a background. In vision, the central figure is usually in front of or on top of what we perceive as background. It has a distinct shape and is more striking in our perceptions and memory than the background. We perceive borders or contours wherever there is a distinct change in the colour or brightness of a visual scene, but we interpret these contours as part of the figure rather than background. Likewise, instrumental music is heard as a melody (figure) surrounded by other chords or harmonies (ground).

Separating figure from ground can be a challenging task (Figure 5.32), yet our perceptual

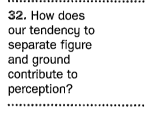

32. How does our tendency to separate figure and ground contribute to perception?

(both): WENN/YU Gallery Paris/Newscom

FIGURE 5.32 Figure-ground relations are important in perception. These amazing body paintings were created by Liu Bolin of Beijing. In a series known as "camouflage," the artist paints people from head to toe so they will blend in with the background.

FIGURE 5.33 This reversible figure illustrates alternating figure-ground relations. It can be seen as a vase or as two people facing each other. Whichever percept exists at the moment is seen as figure against background.

FIGURE 5.35 Fraser's spiral illustrates the Gestalt law of continuity. If you follow any part of the "spiral" with your finger, you will find that it is not really a spiral at all, but a series of concentric circles. The "spiral" is created by your nervous system because that perception is more consistent with continuity of the individual elements.

33. Define and give examples of the four Gestalt laws of perceptual organization.

systems usually are equal to the task. At times, however, what's figure and what's ground is not completely obvious, and the same stimulus may give rise to two different perceptions. Consider Figure 5.33, for example. If you examine it for a while, two alternating but equally plausible perceptions will emerge, one based on the inner portion and the other formed by the two outer portions. When the alternative perception (figure) occurs, what was previously the figure becomes the background.

In addition to figure-ground relations, the Gestalt psychologists were interested in how separate stimuli come to be perceived as parts of larger wholes. They suggested that people group and interpret stimuli in accordance with four **Gestalt laws** of perceptual organization: similarity, proximity, closure, and continuity. These organizing principles are illustrated in Figure 5.34.

What was your perception of Figure 5.34a? Did you perceive 16 unrelated dots, or did you view the stimulus as two triangles formed by

different-sized dots? If you saw triangles, your perception obeyed the Gestalt *law of similarity,* which says that when parts of a configuration are perceived as similar, they will be perceived as belonging together. The *law of proximity* says that elements that are near one another are likely to be perceived as part of the same configuration. Thus, most people perceive Figure 5.34b as three sets of lines rather than as six separate lines. Illustrated in Figure 5.34c is the *law of closure,* which states that people tend to close the open edges of a figure or fill in gaps in an incomplete figure, so that their identification of the form (in this case, a circle) is more complete than what is actually there. Finally, the *law of continuity* holds that people link individual elements together so that they form a continuous line or pattern that makes sense. Thus, Figure 5.34d is far more likely to be seen as combining components ab and cd than ad and cb, which have poor continuity. Or consider Fraser's spiral, shown in Figure 5.35, which is not really a spiral at all! (To demonstrate this,

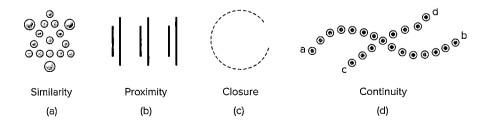

Similarity (a) Proximity (b) Closure (c) Continuity (d)

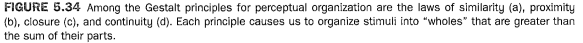

FIGURE 5.34 Among the Gestalt principles for perceptual organization are the laws of similarity (a), proximity (b), closure (c), and continuity (d). Each principle causes us to organize stimuli into "wholes" that are greater than the sum of their parts.

trace one of the circles with a pencil.) We perceive the concentric circles as a spiral because, to our nervous system, a spiral gives better continuity between individual elements than does a set of circles. The spiral is created by us, not by the stimulus.

Perception Involves Hypothesis Testing

"Recognizing" a stimulus implies that we have a **perceptual schema**—a mental representation or image—to compare it with. Our schemas contain the critical features of objects, events, and other perceptual phenomena (Wade & Swanston, 2001). They allow us to classify and identify sensory input in a top-down fashion.

Imagine, for example, that a person approaches you and calls out your name. Who is this person? If the stimuli match your inner representation of your best friend's appearance and voice closely enough, then you identify the person as your friend (McAdams & Drake, 2002). Many political cartoonists have an uncanny ability to capture the most noteworthy facial features of famous people, so that we can easily recognize the person represented by even the simplest line sketch.

Perception is, in this sense, an attempt to make sense of stimulus input, to search for the "best" interpretation of sensory information we can arrive at, based on our knowledge and experience (Carbon, 2014). Likening the process to the scientific enterprise described in Chapter 2, Richard L. Gregory (1966) suggested that each of our perceptions is essentially a hypothesis about the nature of the object or, more generally, the meaning of the sensory information. The perceptual system actively searches its gigantic library of internal schemas for the interpretation that best fits the sensory data.

An example of how effortlessly our perceptual systems build up descriptions or hypotheses that best fit the available evidence is found in the comic strips created by Gustave Verbeek in the early 1900s. The Sunday *New York Herald* told Verbeek that his comic strip had to be restricted to six panels. Verbeek wanted 12 panels, so he ingeniously created 12-panel cartoons in only six panels by drawing pictures like that shown in Figure 5.36a. The reader viewed the first six panels, then turned the newspaper upside down. Try this yourself, and you will find that a bird story becomes a fish story! The point is that you do not simply see an upside-down bird, even though the physical stimuli

(a)

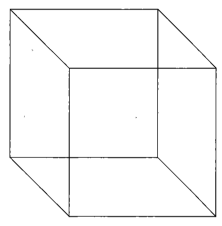

(b)

(top): Gustave Verbeek, "The Upside Downs of Little Lady Lovekins and Old Man Muffaroo: A Fish Story". First published in *The New York Herald*, circa 1904.

FIGURE 5.36 Two examples of how the same stimulus can give rise to different perceptions are found in a Gustave Verbeek comic strip (a) and the Necker cube (b). To produce the reversals, turn the comic strip panel upside down and stare at the cube. The front of the cube will suddenly become the back, and it will appear that the cube is being viewed from a different angle.

remain exactly the same. You see a radically different picture because the new stimulus closely matches another of your perceptual schemas.

In some instances, sensory information fits two different internal representations, and there is not enough information to permanently rule out one of them in favour of the other. For example, examine the Necker cube, shown in Figure 5.36b. If you stare at the cube for a while, you will find that it changes before your eyes as your nervous system "tries out" a new perceptual hypothesis. Another example is offered by our interpretation of the Mona Lisa as discussed in the *Applications* feature.

34. In what sense is perception a kind of hypothesis testing? What is the role of perceptual schemas in this process?

Applications

MONA LISA'S SMILE

Perhaps there is no better-known work of art in the world than the *Mona Lisa* by Leonardo da Vinci (Figure 5.37). The painting, completed in the early 1500s has been prized, stolen, and vandalized. It is a small painting (77 cm × 53 cm), presumably of Lisa Gherardini, and is undoubtedly the most visited and parodied piece of art in existence. It is worth an estimated $1 billion.

Leonardo was one of the first artists to use imaginary landscapes in painting. Prior to the Mona Lisa, backgrounds in portraits were exactly as they appeared in real life. He also was one of the first painters to use aerial perspective in his work—detail becomes "fuzzier" in the distance. But perhaps the most intriguing thing about the painting is the Mona Lisa's smile. Is she actually smiling in the portrait or is she serious? Viewers have reported both interpretations, often in the same viewing. What's going on?

Margaret Livingstone is a professor of neurobiology at the Harvard Medical School, specializing in the neurological underpinnings of vision. She has suggested (Livingstone, 2000) that the elusive quality of the Mona Lisa's smile is merely a by-product of the human visual system. Livingstone notes that the resolution of our visual system changes quite dramatically as we move away from the centre of the fovea. As you will recall, cones are found exclusively in the centre of the fovea and decrease as we move to the periphery. A small amount of movement from the centre of gaze results in acuity that is only about one-tenth of that in the centre of the fovea. In essence, targets falling at the centre of the fovea are in sharp focus, while those even a small distance away are blurrier. An image with a lot of detail (high spatial frequency) would be resolved much better at the fovea than in the peripheral retina (where we are more sensitive to lower spatial frequencies).

Livingstone (2000) applied selective filters to an image of the Mona Lisa so that it emphasized either high or low spatial frequencies. The high spatial frequency image (reflecting the centre of the fovea) resulted in fewer reports of smiling as compared to the low spatial frequency image (representative of the peripheral retina). Thus, as you gaze at the Mona Lisa, you will see her smiling if you are looking at her hands or at the background. In this fashion, her mouth falls on the peripheral retina and the perception of lower spatial frequencies emphasizes the smile. But when you look directly at her mouth, the smile fades away. Florian Hutzler at the Center for Neurocognitive Research in Paris notes that there is actually a smile hidden in low spatial frequencies around the mouth area. Looking directly at the mouth, you process the higher spatial frequencies and the smile disappears. In addition, Otero and Pablos (2009) have shown that the smile is more likely to be seen when gazing at the left side of the mouth. Perhaps features on the right side now fall in the peripheral retina where they are more likely to be seen as representative of a smile.

Was Leonardo aware of any of these visual processes? Perhaps. He intentionally blurred the expression around the eyes and mouth using a technique called *sfumato*. Thus, the Mona Lisa's smile and the perceived emotion remain ambiguous, adding to our appreciation of the artwork.

© Musée du Louvre, © Direction des Musées de France, 1999.

FIGURE 5.37 Leonardo da Vinci's famous painting, the *Mona Lisa*. Is she smiling at you?

Perception Is Influenced by Expectations: Perceptual Sets

On July 3, 1988, the warship *USS Vincennes* was engaged in a pitched battle with several speedy Iranian gunboats. Suddenly, the *Vincennes*'s advanced radar system detected an aircraft taking off from a military/civilian airfield in Iran and heading straight toward the American vessel. Radar operators identified the plane as an Iranian F-14 fighter, known to carry lethal air-to-surface missiles used earlier in a damaging attack on another U.S. warship. Repeated requests to the plane to identify itself yielded no response. The plane was now only 16 kilometres from the ship and, according to the crewmen watching on radar, descending toward the *Vincennes* on an attack course. When a final warning evoked no response, and the *Vincennes's* captain gave the command to fire on the plane. Two surface-to-air missiles streaked into the sky. Moments later, all that remained of the plane was a shower of flaming debris.

The jubilation and relief of the *Vincennes's* crew was short-lived. Soon the awful truth was known: The plane they had shot down was not an attacking F-14 warplane. Instead, it was a commercial airliner carrying 290 passengers, all of whom died when the aircraft was destroyed. Moreover, videotape recordings of the electronic information that the crew had used to identify the plane and its flight pattern showed conclusively that the aircraft was not an F-14 and that it had actually been climbing rather than descending toward the ship.

How could such a tragic error have been made by a well-trained and experienced crew with access to the world's most sophisticated radar equipment? At a Congressional hearing on the incident, several prominent perception researchers reconstructed the psychological environment that could have caused the radar operators' eyes to "lie."

Clearly, the situation was stressful and dangerous. The *Vincennes* was already under attack by Iranian gunboats, and other attacks could be expected. It was easy for the radar operators, observing a plane taking off from a military field and heading toward the ship, to interpret this as the possible prelude to an air attack. The *Vincennes's* crew was determined to avoid the fate of the other American warship, producing a high level of vigilance to any stimuli that suggested an impending attack. Fear and expectation thus created a psychological context within which the sensory input from the computer system was interpreted in a top-down fashion. The perception that the aircraft was a warplane and that it was descending toward the ship fit the crew's expectations and fears, and it became the "reality" that they experienced. They had a **perceptual set**—a readiness to perceive stimuli in a particular way. Sometimes believing is seeing.

Perceptual sets influence our social perceptions as well, as psychologist Harold Kelley (1950) demonstrated the day he invited a guest lecturer into his class. Half of the students in the class were given a set of introductory notes that described the guest as "industrious, critical, practical, determined and a rather *cold* person" (italics ours). The other half were given notes that described the visitor as "industrious, critical, practical, determined and a rather *warm* person." After the class, the students rated the guest lecturer and his presentation. Those who received the *cold* description interacted very little with him and later rated the guest lecturer as unhappy and irritable during the lecture. But those who got the *warm* description rated him as happy and good natured during the lecture, and they took part actively in the class discussion. They also rated his presentation more favourably. All of the students had seen and heard the *same lecturer*, or had they?

Stimuli Are Recognizable under Changing Conditions: Perceptual Constancies

When a closed door swings open, it casts a different image on our retina, but we still perceive it as a door. Our perceptual hypothesis remains the same. Were it not for **perceptual constancies** that allow us to recognize familiar stimuli under varying conditions, we would have literally to rediscover what something is each time it appeared under different conditions. Thus, you can recognize a tune even if it is played in a different octave, as long as the relations among its notes are maintained. You can detect the flavour of a particular spice even when it occurs in foods having very different tastes.

In vision, several constancies are important. *Shape constancy* allows us to recognize people and other objects from many different angles, as in the case of the swinging door. Perhaps you have had the experience of sitting up front and off to one side of the screen in a crowded movie theatre. At first, the picture probably looked distorted, but after a while your visual system corrected for the distortion, and objects on the screen looked normal again.

Because of *brightness constancy*, the relative brightness of objects remains the same under different conditions of illumination, such as full sunlight and shade. Brightness constancy

35. What is a perceptual set? What factors can create such sets? How did the *Vincennes* incident illustrate this concept? How is it involved in perceiving people?

36. What are the nature and adaptive value of perceptual constancies?

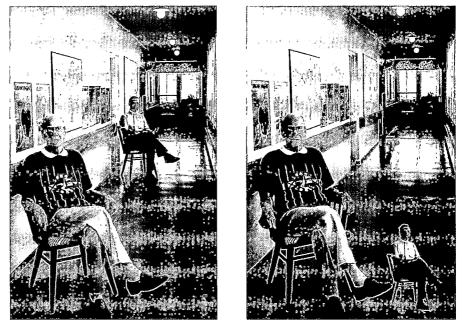

(both): © Jeffery Grosscup

FIGURE 5.38 Size constancy based on distance cues causes us to perceive the person in the background as being of normal size. When the same stimulus is seen in the absence of the distance cues, size constancy breaks down.

occurs because the ratio of light intensity between an object and its surroundings usually is constant. The actual brightness of the light that illuminates the objects does not matter, as long as the same light intensity illuminates both an object and its surroundings.

When we take off in an airplane, we know that the cars on the highway below are not shrinking and becoming the size of ants. *Size constancy* is the perception that the size of objects remains relatively constant even though images on our retina change in size with variations in distance. Thus, a man who is judged to be 180 centimetres tall when standing 2 metres away is not perceived to be 90 centimetres tall at a distance of 4 metres, even though the size of his image on the retina is reduced to half its original size (Figure 5.38).

Review

- Perception involves both bottom-up processing, in which individual stimulus fragments are combined into a perception, and top-down processing, in which existing knowledge and perceptual schemas are applied to interpret stimuli.

- Attention is an active process in which we focus on certain stimuli while blocking out other stimuli. We cannot attend completely to more than one thing at a time, but we are capable of rapid attentional shifts. Attentional processes are affected by the nature of the stimulus and by personal factors such as motives and interests. The perceptual system appears to be especially vigilant to stimuli that denote threat or danger.

- The Gestalt psychologists identified a number of principles of perceptual organization, including figure-ground relations and the laws of similarity, proximity, closure, and continuity. R.L. Gregory suggested that perception is essentially a hypothesis about what a stimulus is, based on previous experience and the nature of the stimulus.

- Perceptual sets involve a readiness to perceive stimuli in certain ways, based on our expectations, assumptions, motivations, and current emotional state.

- Perceptual constancies allow us to recognize familiar stimuli under changing conditions. In the visual realm, there are three constancies: shape, brightness, and size.

WHY DOES THAT RISING MOON LOOK SO BIG?

Just before bedding down for the night on a backpacking trip, a friend of ours poked his head outside of his tent and gasped to his wife, "Look at the moon! Just look at that moon!" Indeed, a gorgeous full moon had just come over the horizon, and it was so enormous that it dwarfed the mammoth peaks surrounding them. The couple gazed at it in wonder for a few minutes and then retired into their tent. Later that night, they looked out-side again only to see a rather small, ordinary full moon approaching the zenith.

You too may have exclaimed over the size of a rising moon, only to notice later that the moon, well above the horizon, seemed to have shrunk. What can explain this phenomenon?

Think about it, and then see the Answers section at the end of the book.

PERCEPTION OF DEPTH, DISTANCE, AND MOVEMENT

The ability to adapt to a spatial world requires that we make fine distinctions involving distances and the movement of objects within the environment. Humans are capable of great precision in making such judgments. Consider, for example, the perceptual task faced by a batter playing baseball (Figure 5.39). A fastball thrown

© Robert Michael/Corbis

FIGURE 5.39 The demands faced by a batter in judging the speed, distance, and movements of a pitched baseball within thousandths of a second underscore the capabilities of the visual perceptual system.

by a pitcher at 145 kilometres per hour from 18 metres will reach the batter who is trying to hit it in about 42/100 of a second. A curveball thrown at 130 kilometres per hour will reach the hitting zone in 47/100 of a second, a difference of only 5/100 of a second (but a world of difference for timing and hitting the pitch). Within the first 2 metres of a ball's flight from the pitcher's hand (an interval of about 25/1000 of a second), the batter must correctly judge the speed, type, and location of the pitch. If any of the judgments is in error, the hitter will be unable to hit a fair ball (Adair, 1990). The perceptual demands of such a task are imposing indeed (as are the salaries earned by those who can perform this task consistently). How does the visual perception system make such judgments?

Depth and Distance Perception

One of the more intriguing aspects of visual perception is our ability to perceive depth. The retina receives information in only two dimensions (length and width), but the brain translates these cues into three-dimensional perceptions. It does this by using both **monocular cues** (which require only one eye) and **binocular cues** (which require both eyes).

Monocular Depth Cues

Judging the relative distances of objects is one important key to perceiving depth. Because artists paint their portraits on a flat canvas, they depend on a variety of monocular cues to create perceptions of depth in their pictures. One such cue is patterns of *light and shadow*. The Dutch artist M.C. Escher skilfully used light and shadow to create the three-dimensional effect shown in Figure 5.40. The depth

37. Identify eight monocular cues for distance and depth.

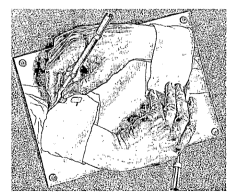

© 1948 M.C. Escher Foundation/Baarn-Holland, All Rights Reserved

FIGURE 5.40 Patterns of light and shadow can serve as monocular depth cues, as shown in *Drawing Hands* by M.C. Escher.

effect is as powerful if you close one eye as it is when you use both. Another cue, *linear perspective,* refers to the perception that parallel lines converge or angle toward each other as they recede into the distance. Thus, if you look down railroad tracks, they appear to angle toward each other with increased distance, and we use this as a depth cue. The same occurs with the edges of a highway or the sides of an elevator shaft. *Interposition,* in which objects closer to us may cut off part of our view of more distant objects, provides another cue for distance and depth.

An object's *height in the horizontal plane* provides another source of information. For example, a ship 8 kilometres offshore appears in a higher plane and closer to the horizon than does one that is only 1 kilometre from shore. *Texture* is a fifth cue, because the texture or grain of an object appears finer as distance increases. Likewise, *clarity* can be an important cue for judging distance; we can see nearby hills more clearly than hills that are far away, especially on hazy days. *Relative size* is yet another basis for distance judgments. If we see two objects that we know to be of similar size, then the one that looks smaller will be judged to be farther away. A final monocular cue is *motion parallax,* which tells us that if we are moving, nearby objects appear to move faster in the opposite direction than do faraway ones. All these cues provide us with information that we can use to make judgments about distance and, therefore, about depth.

The artist Raphael Sanzio was a master at using monocular depth and distance cues. *The School of Athens,* shown in Figure 5.41, illustrates seven of the monocular cues we have just described.

Binocular Disparity

The most dramatic perceptions of depth arise with binocular depth cues, which require the use of both eyes. For an interesting binocular effect, hold your two index fingers about 15 centimetres in front of your eyes with their tips about 2.5 centimetres apart. Focus on your fingers first, and then focus beyond them across the room. The two different views will produce a "third" finger between the other two. This "finger sausage" will disappear if you close either eye.

Many of us are familiar with the delightful depth experiences provided by "Magic Eye" photos and three-dimensional movies watched

School of Athens by Raphael. Scala/Art Resource, NY

FIGURE 5.41 *The School of Athens,* by Raphael Sanzio, illustrates seven monocular depth cues. (1) Linear perspective is produced by the converging lines of the corridor in the background. (2) The arches and the people in the background are smaller than those in front (relative size). (3) The back of the floor is in a higher horizontal plane than the foreground. (4, 5) The objects in the background are less detailed than the closer ones (texture and clarity). (6) Light and shadow are used to create depth. (7) The arches and people in the front of the painting cut off parts of the corridor behind them (interposition).

through special glasses. These devices make use of the principle of **binocular disparity,** in which each eye sees a slightly different image. Within the brain, the visual input from the two eyes is analyzed by feature detectors that are attuned to depth (Howard, 2002; Livingstone & Hubel, 1994). Some of the feature detectors respond only to stimuli that are either in front of or behind the point we are fixing our gaze upon. The responses of these depth-sensitive neurons are integrated to produce our perception of depth (Goldstein, 2002).

A second binocular distance cue, **convergence,** is produced by feedback from the muscles that turn your eyes inward to view a near object. You can experience this cue by holding a finger about 30 centimetres in front of your face, and then moving it slowly toward you. Messages sent to your brain by the eye muscles provide it with a depth cue.

Perception of Movement

The perception of movement is a complex process that requires the brain to integrate information from several different senses. Try this

38. Describe two binocular cues.

39. What is the primary cue for motion perception? How is stroboscopic movement used in motion pictures and TV?

demonstration: Hold your pen in front of your face. Now, while holding your head still, move the pen back and forth. You will perceive the pen moving. Now hold the pen still and move your head back and forth at the same rate of speed. In both cases, the image of the pen moved across your retina in about the same way. But when you moved your head, your brain took into account input from your kinesthetic and vestibular systems and "concluded" that you were moving but the pen was not.

The primary cue for perceiving motion is the movement of the stimulus across the retina (Sekuler et al., 2002). Under optimal conditions, a retinal image need move only about one-fifth the diameter of a single cone for us to detect movement (Nakayama & Tyler, 1981). The relative movement of an object against a structured background is also a movement cue (Gibson, 1979). For example, if you fixate on a bird in flight, the relative motion of the bird against its background is a strong cue for perceiving speed of movement.

The illusion of smooth motion can be produced if we arrange for the sequential appearance of two or more stimuli. Gestalt psychologist Max Wertheimer (1912) demonstrated this in his studies of **stroboscopic movement**, illusory movement produced when a light is briefly flashed in darkness and then, a few milliseconds later, another light is flashed nearby. If the timing is just right, the first light seems to move from one place to the other in a manner indistinguishable from real movement.

Stroboscopic movement (termed the *phi phenomenon* by Wertheimer) has been used commercially in numerous ways. For example, we have all seen the strings of successively illuminated lights on theatre marquees that seem to move endlessly around the border or that spell out messages in a "moving" script. Stroboscopic movement is also the principle behind motion pictures, which consist of a series of still photographs, or frames, that are projected onto a screen in rapid succession with dark intervals in between (Figure 5.42). The rate at which the frames are projected is critical to our perception of smooth movement. Early movies, such as the silent films of the 1920s, projected the "stills" at only 16 frames per second, and the movements appeared fast and jerky. Today the usual speed is 24 frames per second, which more accurately produces an illusion of smooth movement. TV presents images at the rate of 30 per second.

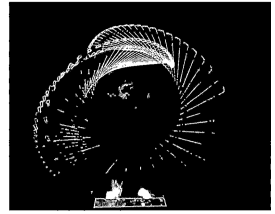

FIGURE 5.42 Stroboscopic movement is produced in moving pictures as a series of still photographs projected at a rate of 24 per second.

ILLUSIONS: FALSE PERCEPTUAL HYPOTHESES

Our knowledge of perceptual schemas, hypotheses, sets, and constancies allows us to understand some interesting perceptual experiences known as *illusions*. **Illusions** are compelling but incorrect perceptions. They can be understood as erroneous perceptual hypotheses about the nature of the stimulus. Illusions are not only intriguing and sometimes delightful visual experiences, but they also provide important information about how our perceptual processes work under normal conditions (Blakeslee & McCourt, 2015; Gregory, 2005).

Ironically, most visual illusions can be attributed to perceptual constancies that ordinarily help us to perceive more accurately (Frisby, 1980). For example, size constancy results in part from our ability to use distance cues to judge the size of objects. But distance cues sometimes fool us. In the Ponzo illusion, shown in Figure 5.43a, the depth cues of linear perspective (the tracks converging) and height in the horizontal plane provide distance cues that make the upper bar appear farther away than the lower bar. Because it seems farther away, the perceptual system concludes that the bar in the background must be larger than the bar in the foreground, despite the fact that the two bars cast retinal images of the same size. The same occurs in the vertical arrangement seen in Figure 5.43b.

40. In what sense is an illusion a false perceptual hypothesis? In what ways are constancies and context involved in producing visual illusions?

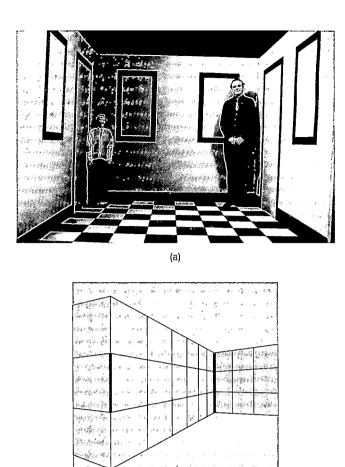

(a)

(b)

© Charles Walker/TopFoto/The Image Works

FIGURE 5.43 The Ponzo illusion. Which lines in (a) and (b) are longer? Measure them and see. The distance cues provided by the converging railroad tracks and walls affect size perception and disrupt size constancy.

Distance cues can be manipulated to create other size illusions. One occurs in a room constructed by Adelbert Ames. Viewed through a peephole with one eye, the scene presents a startling size reversal (Figure 5.44a). Our perceptual system assumes that the room has a normal rectangular shape because, in fact, most rooms do. Monocular depth cues do not allow us to see that, in reality, the left corner of the room is twice as far away as the right corner (Figure 5.44b). As a result, size constancy breaks down, and we base our judgment of size on the sizes of the retinal images cast by the two people.

The study of perceptual constancies shows that our perceptual hypotheses are strongly influenced by the *context*, or surroundings, in which a stimulus occurs. Figure 5.45 shows some examples of how context can produce illusory perceptions.

Some of the most intriguing perceptual distortions are produced when monocular depth cues are manipulated to produce a figure or scene whose individual parts make sense, but whose overall organization is "impossible" in terms of our existing perceptual schemas. Figure 5.46 shows three impossible figures. In each case, our brains extract information about depth from the individual features of the objects, but when this information is put together and matched with our existing schemas, the percept that results simply doesn't make sense. The "devil's tuning fork," for example (Figure 5.46c), could not exist in our

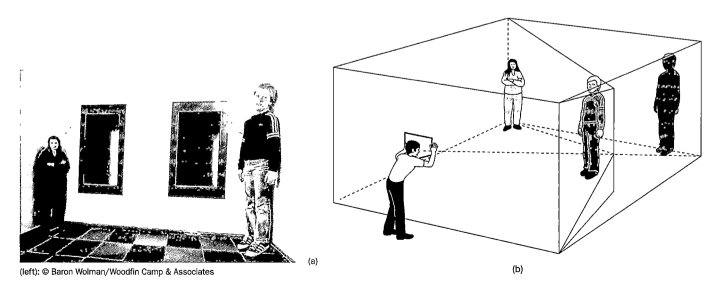

(a)

(b)

(left): © Baron Wolman/Woodfin Camp & Associates

FIGURE 5.44 The Ames Room (a) produces a striking size perception because it is designed to appear rectangular. However, as (b) shows, the room is actually trapezoidal in shape, and the figure on the left is actually much farther away from the viewer than the one on the right, making it appear smaller.

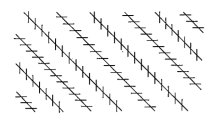

The long lines are actually parallel, but the small lines make them appear crooked.

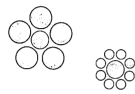

Which inner circle is larger? Check and see.

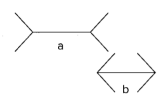

The Müller-Lyer illusion. Which line, a or b, is longer? Compare them with a ruler.

FIGURE 5.45 Context-produced geometric illusions.

Thinking critically

EXPLAIN THIS STRIKING ILLUSION

We'd like you to experience a truly interesting illusion. To do so, all you need is a piece of fairly heavy paper and a little patience. Fold the piece of paper lengthwise down the middle, and set it on a table with one of the ends facing you like an open tent, as shown in the figure below. Close one eye and, from slightly above the object, stare at a point midway along the top fold of the paper. After a while the paper will suddenly "stand up" and look like a corner viewed from the inside. When this happens, gently move your head back and forth while continuing to view with one eye. The movement will produce a striking perception. Can you explain what you now see?

Think about it, and then see the Answers section at the end of the book.

universe. It is a two-dimensional image containing paradoxical depth cues. Your brain, however, automatically interprets it as a three-dimensional object and matches it with its internal schema of a fork, a bad fit indeed. The never-ending staircase (Figure 5.46b) provides another compelling example of an impossible scene that seems perfectly reasonable when we focus only on its individual elements.

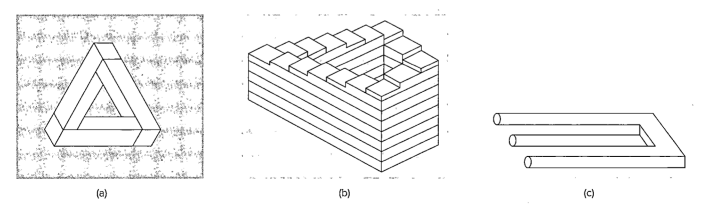

(a)   (b)   (c)

FIGURE 5.46 Monocular depth cues are cleverly manipulated to produce an impossible triangle, a never-ending staircase, and the "devil's tuning fork."

In Review

- Monocular cues to judge distance include linear perspective, relative size, height in the horizontal plane, texture, and clarity. These distance cues also help us judge depth. Depth perception also occurs through the monocular cues of light and shadow patterns, interposition, and motion parallax.

- Binocular disparity occurs as slightly different images are viewed by each eye and acted on by feature detectors for depth. Convergence of the eyes provides a second binocular cue.

- The basis for perception of movement is absolute movement of a stimulus across the retina or relative movement of an object in relation to its background. Stroboscopic movement is illusory.

- Illusions are erroneous perceptions. They may be regarded as incorrect perceptual hypotheses. Perceptual constancies help to produce a variety of context-produced illusions.

EXPERIENCE, CRITICAL PERIODS, AND PERCEPTUAL DEVELOPMENT

Development of sensory and perceptual systems results from the interplay of biological and experiential factors. Genes program biological development, but this development is also influenced by environmental experiences. For example, if you were to be blinded in an accident and later learned to read Braille, the area of the somatosensory cortex that

© The Image Works Archives/The Image Works

FIGURE 5.47 Eleanor Gibson and Richard Walk constructed this "visual cliff" with a glass-covered drop-off to determine whether crawling infants and newborn animals can perceive depth. Even when coaxed by their mothers, infants refuse to venture onto the glass over the cliff. Newborn animals also avoid the cliff.

is devoted to the fingertips would enlarge over time as it "borrowed" other neurons to increase its sensitivity (Pool, 1994). By the time they are old enough to crawl, children placed on a *visual cliff* formed by a glass-covered table that suddenly drops off beneath the glass ordinarily will not venture "over the edge" (Figure 5.47). This aversion may result from the interaction of innate depth perception abilities and previous experience (Gibson & Walk, 1960).

What might a lifetime of experience in a limited environment do to perceptual abilities that seem innate? The Bambuti pygmies, who live in the rainforests of Central Africa, spend their lives in a closed-in green world of densely packed trees without open spaces. The anthropologist C.M. Turnbull (1961) once brought a man named Kenge out of the forest to the edge of a vast plain. A herd of buffalo grazed in the distance. To Turnbull's surprise, Kenge remarked that he had never seen insects of that kind. When told that they were buffalo, not insects, he was deeply offended and felt that Turnbull was insulting his intelligence. To prove his point, Turnbull drove Kenge in his jeep toward the animals. Kenge's eyes widened in amazement as the "insects" grew into buffalo before his eyes. To explain his perceptual experience to himself, he concluded that witchcraft was being used to fool him. Kenge's misperception occurred as a failure in size constancy. Having lived in an environment without open spaces, he had no experience in judging the size of objects at great distances. Does such a limited environment affect your visual cortex as well? We discuss this possibility in the *Research Foundations* feature.

CRITICAL PERIODS: THE ROLE OF EARLY EXPERIENCE

Introduction

Our discussion of cultural factors in perception suggests that experience is critical to the development of perceptual abilities. For some aspects of perception, there are also **critical periods** during which certain kinds of experiences must occur if perceptual abilities and the brain mechanisms that underlie them are to develop normally. If the critical period passes without the experience occurring, it is too late to undo the deficit that results. How can we find out what the critical period is? Under normal circumstances, young organisms experience the environment into which they are born. Thus, we must arrange for the environmental experience to be absent. This basic methodology is behind a **deprivation experiment,** such as the one by Blakemore and Cooper (1970) described below.

Method

Recall that the visual cortex has feature detectors composed of neurons that respond only to lines at particular angles. What would happen if newborn animals grew up in a world in which they saw some angles but not others? British researchers Colin Blakemore and Grahame Cooper (1970) created such a world for newborn kittens. At birth, the kittens were housed in a dark room. At about two weeks of age, the kittens spent five hours each day in specially designed round chambers that had either high contrast vertical or horizontal stripes on the walls. Figure 5.48a shows one of the kittens in a vertically striped chamber. A special collar prevented the kittens from seeing their own bodies while they were in the chamber, guaranteeing that they saw nothing but the stripes. At five months of age, the kittens were no longer exposed to the vertical or the horizontal environment. Instead, they spent several hours each week in a well-lit furnished room. The remainder of the time was spent in the dark.

Results

The kittens quickly adapted to this "normal" environment and could easily navigate around the room. However, the kittens seemed to be "blind" to orientations that were perpendicular to the stripes in the special chambers. For example, a kitten raised in the horizontal environment would walk into vertical table legs. The cat would visually track a pencil held in a horizontal position, but showed no interest when the pencil was rotated to vertical. Blakemore and Cooper then proceeded to record from feature detector cells in the visual cortex by using bars of light at various orientations as the stimuli. The results for animals raised in the vertical environment are shown in Figure 5.48b. As you can see, these kittens had no cells that fired in response to horizontal stimuli, resulting in visual impairment. As you might expect, the animals raised in the horizontally striped environment showed the opposite effects. They had no feature detectors for vertical stimuli. Thus, the cortical neurons of both groups of kittens developed in accordance with the stimulus features of their environment. Blakemore and

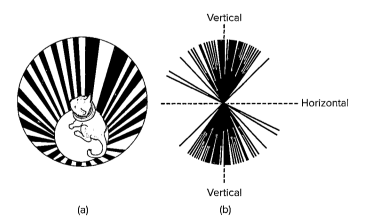

Vertical

Horizontal

Vertical

(a)   (b)

FIGURE 5.48 Kittens raised in a vertically striped chamber such as the one shown in (a) lacked cortical cells that fire in response to horizontal stimuli. The perceptual "holes" are easily seen in (b), which shows the orientation angles that resulted in evoked potentials from feature detectors.

Source: Adapted by permission from Macmillan Publishers Ltd.: *Nature,* 228, 477–478. C. Blakemore & G.F. Cooper, "Development of the Brain Depends on Visual Environment." Copyright © 1970, Nature Publishing Group.

continued

Cooper note that almost every cell examined showed this orientation specificity—there were no large areas of inactive cortex. The cells had adapted to their new environment rather than simply degenerating.

Discussion

The type of cortical change found by Blakemore and Cooper seems to be permanent. Using behavioural tests, Muir and Mitchell (1975) have demonstrated that kittens raised in a vertically striped chamber were able to discriminate vertical test patterns as well as kittens raised in a normal environment. However, their ability to "see" horizontal patterns was quite diminished, and showed no improvement whatsoever even after 30 months of exposure to a normal environment. Other cells in the cortex were not able to compensate for the loss.

Should we expect similar findings in humans? Daphne Maurer and her colleagues (e.g., Maurer & Lewis, 2001) have studied a number of children at the Hospital for Sick Children in Toronto who were born with cataracts and, consequently, were deprived of normal visual input. Upon surgical correction, these children were tested for visual acuity (i.e., the ability to distinguish patterns, gratings, or letters at various distances). Maurer found that upon correction, visual acuity of the children is about the same as that of newborns. Acuity does improve over time, but some effects of the early deprivation linger (e.g., sensitivity to fine detail). Apparently, the cortices of the children were influenced by the degraded visual input and the cells simply cannot function in the normal way. Maurer notes that the

critical period for visual acuity in humans seems to be from about birth until 10 years of age. A child born with cataracts that were not corrected before age 10 would show serious deficiencies in visual acuity.

Some perceptual abilities are influenced more than others by restricted stimulation. For example, monkeys, chimpanzees, and kittens have been raised in an environment devoid of shapes. Such animals distinguish differences in size, brightness, and colour almost as well as normally reared animals do. On the other hand, for the rest of their lives they perform poorly on more complex tasks, such as distinguishing different types of objects and geometric shapes (Riesen, 1965).

Design

Question: Does the environment influence the development of visual feature detectors?

Type of Study: *Experimental*

Independent Variable
Type of visual environment
• Vertical stripes
• Horizontal stripes

→

Dependent Variables
• Behavioural navigation around room
• Orientation specificity of visual cells

41. How do animal studies of restricted stimulation and human studies of restored vision illustrate the important role of critical periods for perceptual development?

As noted earlier, when light passes through the lens of the eye, the image projected on the retina is reversed, so that right is left and up is down. What would happen if you were to wear a special set of glasses that undid this natural reversal of the visual image and created a world like that in Figure 5.49? In 1896, perception researcher George Stratton did just that, possibly becoming the first human ever to have a right-side-up image on his retina while standing upright. Reversing how nature and a lifetime of experience had fashioned his perceptual system at first disoriented Stratton. The ground and his feet were now "up" and he had to put on his hat from the bottom up. He had to reach to his left to touch something he saw on his right. Stratton suffered from nausea and couldn't eat or get around for several days. Gradually, however, he adapted to his inverted world, and by the end of eight days, he was able successfully to reach for objects and walk around. Years later, people

who wore inverting lenses for longer periods of time did the same. Some were able to ski down mountain slopes or ride motorcycles while

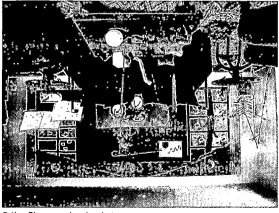

© Ken Rice. www.kenricephoto.com

FIGURE 5.49 Inverted vision would create a world that looks like this. Adaptation to such a world is possible, but challenging.

wearing the lenses, even though their visual world remained "upside down" and never felt normal for them. When they removed the inverting lenses, they initially had some problems, but soon re-adapted to the normal visual world (Dolezal, 1982).

Cross-Cultural Research on Perception

As far as we know, humans normally come into the world with the same perceptual abilities. However, from that point, the culture one grows up in helps to determine the kinds of perceptual learning experiences people have. Cross-cultural research can help to identify which aspects of perception occur in all people, regardless of their cultures, as well as perceptual differences that result from cultural experiences (Nisbett & Miyamoto, 2005; Posner & Rothbart, 2007b; Russell, Deregowski, & Kinnear, 1997). Although there are far more perceptual similarities than differences in the peoples of the world, the differences that do exist show us that perception can indeed be influenced by experience.

Consider the perception of a picture, which depends on both the nature of the picture and the characteristics of the perceiver. In Figure 5.50a, what is the object above the woman's head? Most North Americans and Europeans reply instantly, "A window." They also tend to see the family sitting inside a dwelling. But when the same picture was shown to East Africans, nearly all perceived the object as a basket or box that the woman is balancing on her head.

To them, the family is also outside, sitting under a tree (Gregory & Gombrich, 1973). These interpretations are more consistent with their cultural experiences.

In our earlier discussion of monocular depth cues, we used paintings such as that in Figure 5.41 to illustrate monocular depth perception. In Western culture, we have constant exposure to two-dimensional pictures that our perceptual system effortlessly turns into three-dimensional perceptions. Do people who grow up in cultures in which they are not exposed to pictures have the same perceptions? When presented with the picture in Figure 5.50b and asked which animal the hunter was about to shoot, tribal African people answered that he was about to kill the "baby elephant." They did not use the monocular cues that cause Westerners to perceive the man as hunting the antelope and to view the elephant as an adult animal in the distance (Hudson, 1960).

Illusions occur when one of our common perceptual hypotheses is in error. Earlier, we showed you the Müller-Lyer illusion (see Figure 5.45) in which a line appears longer when the V-shaped lines at its ends radiate outward than when they face inward. Westerners are very susceptible to this illusion. They have learned that in their "carpentered" environment, which has many corners and square shapes, inward-facing lines occur when corners are closer, outward-facing lines when they are farther away (Figure 5.51). But when people from other cultures who live in more rounded environments are shown the Müller-Lyer stimuli, they are more likely to correctly perceive the

42. What evidence is there that cultural factors can influence picture interpretations, constancies, and susceptibility to illusions?

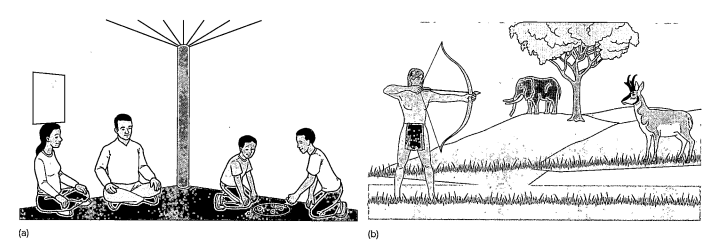

(a) (b)

FIGURE 5.50 (a) What is the object above the woman's head? East Africans had a far different answer than did North Americans. (b) Cultural differences also occurred when people were asked which animal the archer was about to shoot.

(a) Adapted from Gregory & Gombrich, 1973; (b) Adapted from W. Hudson, 1960, "Pictorial Depth Perception in Sub-Cultural Groups in Africa," *Journal of Social Psychology, 52,* 183–208. Copyright © 1960 Heldref Publications. Reprinted with permission of the publisher (Heldref Publications, www.heldref.org).

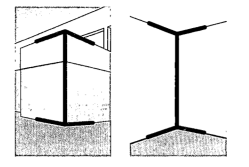

FIGURE 5.51 Perceptual experiences within our "carpentered" environment makes us susceptible to the Müller-Lyer illusion, which appears here in vertical form. Again, the vertical lines are the same physical length.

lines as equal in length (Segall et al., 1966). They do not fall prey to a perceptual hypothesis that normally is correct in an environment like ours that is filled with sharp corners, but is wrong when applied to the lines in the Müller-Lyer illusion (Russell, Deregowski, & Kinnear, 1997).

Cultural learning affects perceptions in other modalities as well. Our perceptions of tastes, odours, and textures are strongly influenced by our cultural experiences. A taste that might produce nausea in one culture may be considered delicious in another. The taste and gritty texture experienced as you chew a large raw insect or the rubbery texture of a fish eye may appeal far less to you than it would to a person from a culture in which that is a staple food.

Restored Sensory Capacity

Suppose it was possible to restore vision to a person who had been blind from birth after he or she reached adulthood. What would this person see? Could this individual perceive visually the things that he or she had learned to identify through other senses?

Scientists have studied the experiences of visually impaired people who acquired the ability to see later in life. For example, people born with cataracts grow up in a visual world without form. The clouded lenses of their eyes permit them to perceive light, but not patterns or shapes. One such person was Virgil, who had been almost totally blind since childhood. He read Braille, enjoyed listening to sports on the radio and conversing with other people, and had adjusted quite well to his disability. At the urging of his fiancée, Virgil agreed to undergo surgery to remove his thick cataracts. The day after the surgery, his bandages were removed. Neurologist Oliver Sacks recounts what happened next:

> There was light, there was colour, all mixed up, meaningless, a blur. Then out of the blur came a voice that said, "Well?" Then, and only then . . . did he finally realize that this chaos of light and shadow was a face— and, indeed, the face of his surgeon. . . . His retina and optic nerve were active, transmitting impulses, but his brain could make no sense of them. (Sacks, 1993, p. 62)

Virgil never was able to adjust to his new visual world. He had to touch objects to identify them. He had to be led through his own house and quickly would become disoriented if he deviated from his path. Eventually, Virgil lost his sight once again. This time, however, he regarded his blindness as a gift, a release from a sighted world that had become bewildering to him.

Virgil's experiences are characteristic of people who have their vision restored later in life. A German physician, von Senden (1960), compiled data on patients born with cataracts who were tested soon after their cataracts were surgically removed in adulthood. These people were immediately able to perceive figure-ground relations, scan objects visually, and follow moving targets with their eyes, indicating that such abilities are innate. However, they could not visually identify objects, such as eating utensils, that were familiar through touch, nor were they able to distinguish simple geometric figures without counting the corners or tracing the figures with their fingers.

After several weeks of training, the patients were able to identify simple objects by sight, but their perceptual constancies were very poor. Often they were unable to recognize the same shape in another colour, even though they could discriminate between colours. Years later, some patients could identify only a few of the faces of people they knew well. Many also had great difficulty judging distances. Apparently, no amount of subsequent experience could make up for their lack of visual experience during the critical period of childhood.

More recently, a woman in India was studied 20 years after she had cataracts removed at age 12 (Ostrovsky et al., 2007). Although the patient's visual acuity was below par, she did surprisingly well on complex visual tasks. Her results suggest that the human brain retains an impressive capacity for visual learning, even in children who are blind until early adulthood.

All these lines of evidence—cross-cultural perceptual differences, animal studies involving visual deprivation, and observations of congenitally impaired people whose vision has been restored—suggest that biological and experiential factors interact in complex ways.

Levels of Analysis Perception

The processes involved in sensation and perception illustrate the interaction of biological, psychological, and environmental factors.

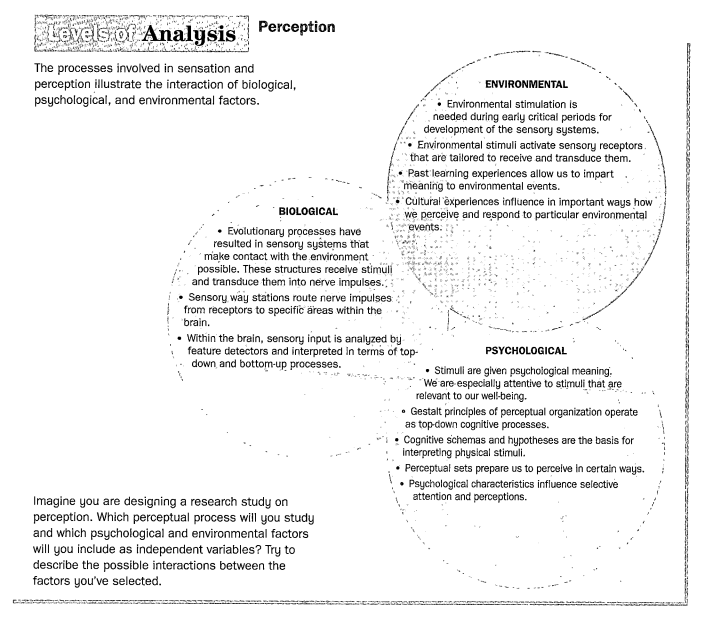

ENVIRONMENTAL
- Environmental stimulation is needed during early critical periods for development of the sensory systems.
- Environmental stimuli activate sensory receptors that are tailored to receive and transduce them.
- Past learning experiences allow us to impart meaning to environmental events.
- Cultural experiences influence in important ways how we perceive and respond to particular environmental events.

BIOLOGICAL
- Evolutionary processes have resulted in sensory systems that make contact with the environment possible. These structures receive stimuli and transduce them into nerve impulses.
- Sensory way stations route nerve impulses from receptors to specific areas within the brain.
- Within the brain, sensory input is analyzed by feature detectors and interpreted in terms of top-down and bottom-up processes.

PSYCHOLOGICAL
- Stimuli are given psychological meaning. We are especially attentive to stimuli that are relevant to our well-being.
- Gestalt principles of perceptual organization operate as top-down cognitive processes.
- Cognitive schemas and hypotheses are the basis for interpreting physical stimuli.
- Perceptual sets prepare us to perceive in certain ways.
- Psychological characteristics influence selective attention and perceptions.

Imagine you are designing a research study on perception. Which perceptual process will you study and which psychological and environmental factors will you include as independent variables? Try to describe the possible interactions between the factors you've selected.

FIGURE 5.52

Some of our perceptual abilities are at least partially present at birth, but experience plays an important role in their normal development. How innate and experiential factors interact promises to be a continued focus of perception research. Thus, perception is very much a biopsychological process whose mysteries are best explored by examining them from biological, psychological, and environmental levels of analysis (see Figure 5.52).

In Review

- Perceptual development involves both physical maturation and learning. Some perceptual abilities are innate or develop shortly after birth, whereas others require particular experiences early in life to develop.

- Cultural factors can influence certain aspects of perception, including picture perception and susceptibility to illusions. However, many aspects of perception seem constant across cultures.

- Visual deprivation studies, manipulation of visual input, and studies of restored vision have shown that the normal biological development of the perceptual system depends on certain sensory experiences at early periods of development.

Gaining Direction

What are the issues?

The opening scenario describes Moncton's Magnetic Hill. At first it seems that the phenomenon cannot possibly be true. How can cars roll uphill? However, if you've ever visited the site or watched a bus roll uphill on video (check out the link after this paragraph), you become intrigued. How can this be happening? We know that no magnetic or supernatural forces are involved, so what gives rise to this perception? There must be something about the geography of the hill or the way we see it that misleads our perceptual experience. What are the factors that help us perceive "up" from "down"? Are these cues available at Magnetic Hill? This scenario deals with image processing, Gestalt rules, and one of the most basic questions regarding perception: How do we construct reality from sensory experience?

http://www.travelvideo.tv/videos /newbrunswick/magnetichillvideo.html

What do we need to know?

How do we separate figure from ground?
What are the Gestalt rules of perception?
How do we perceive depth?

Can our expectations drive perceptual experience?
Can we be fooled by erroneous cues in the environment?

Where can we find the information to answer these questions?

A number of the chapter icons point to perceptual processes that influence how we see the world. We need to understand how we construct perception and then locate objects within this perceptual world. So-called "magnetic" or "gravity" hills are the result of an optical illusion. Typically, the hill is located in a wooded area where the horizon is obscured. Without access to the horizon, we have to use other cues to determine the lay of the land. Are the trees straight or angled? Does the shading suggest a hill or a valley? What does our sense of balance tell us? As we combine this information, it is likely that we come to believe that we are at the bottom of a hill when, in fact, we are standing at the top of the rise. Thus, a vehicle appears to roll uphill when it actually is rolling downhill. If you were to look at the water in the creek at the side of the road, you would see that it appears to run uphill as well, suggesting that the slope is not as you perceive it.

States of Consciousness

CHAPTER >
OUTLINE

THE PUZZLE OF CONSCIOUSNESS
Measuring States of Consciousness
Levels of Consciousness: Psychodynamic
  and Cognitive Perspectives
  Frontiers: Detecting Awareness
The Neural Basis of Consciousness

CIRCADIAN RHYTHMS: OUR DAILY
BIOLOGICAL CLOCKS
Keeping Time: Brain and Environment
Environmental Disruptions of Circadian
  Rhythms

SLEEP AND DREAMING
Stages of Sleep
Getting a Night's Sleep: Brain and Environment
How Much Do We Sleep?
Sleep Deprivation
  Applications: A Good Night's Sleep
Why Do We Sleep?
Sleep Disorders

The Nature of Dreams
  Focus on Neuroscience: Dreams and Daydreams

DRUGS AND ALTERED CONSCIOUSNESS
Drugs and the Brain
Tolerance and Withdrawal
Depressants
  Research Foundations: Drinking and Driving:
  Decision Making in Altered States
Stimulants
Opiates
Hallucinogens
Marijuana
From Genes to Culture: Determinants
  of Drug Effects

HYPNOSIS
The Scientific Study of Hypnosis
Hypnotic Behaviours and Experiences
Theories of Hypnosis

SOME FINAL THOUGHTS

Our normal waking consciousness is but one special type of consciousness,
whilst all about it, parted from it by the filmiest of screens, there lie potential forms of
consciousness entirely different.

—William James

 Lee Hadwin is a nurse from North Wales. But he is better known as "Klpasso," the artist who produces pencil drawings and works of fantasy. Lee does not know how he produces such work, because he can only draw at night when he is asleep. When awake, Lee has no artistic ability at all and is dumbfounded at the pieces he produces during the night.

Hadwin has been sleepwalking since he was four years old and began to draw works of art sometime in his teens. He now leaves art supplies out at night and routinely draws for 20 to 90 minutes. He awakes with a severe migraine, feeling totally exhausted.

He has been offered $7500 for one of his works, and he recently placed his entire collection of 100 pieces for sale on eBay. The asking price is $1.9 million.

Courtesy of Lee Hadwin

What are the
issues here?

What do we need
to know?

Where can
we find the
information to
answer these
questions?

Although the experience of Lee Hadwin is unusual, it demonstrates the surprising complexity of our conscious experience. We all drift into and out of various states of consciousness. By *state of consciousness*, psychologists mean a pattern of subjective experience, a way of experiencing internal and external events. You will also encounter the phrase *altered state of consciousness*, which refers to variations from our normal waking state. While daydreaming or passing from wakefulness to sleep, we may experience vivid images, and our nighttime dreams can seem just as real and emotionally charged as our waking perceptions.

1. Describe some basic characteristics of consciousness.

We also experience divisions of awareness. Consider this: Why don't you fall out of bed at night? You are not consciously aware of major postural shifts while soundly asleep, yet a part of you somehow knows where the edge of the bed is. Similarly, have you ever "spaced out" while driving, deeply engrossed in thought? Suddenly you snap out of it, with no memory of the kilometres just driven. While you were consciously focused inward, some part of you kept track of the road and controlled your responses at the wheel.

Philosopher David Chalmers (1995) notes, "Conscious experience is at once the most familiar thing in the world and the most mysterious." As we shall see, its mysteries span a range from normal waking states to sleep and dreams, drug-induced experiences, hypnosis, and beyond. When psychology was founded in the late 1800s, its "Great Project" was to scientifically unravel some of the puzzles of consciousness (Natsoulas, 1999). This interest waned during behaviourism's dominance in the mid-20th century, but resurgence of the cognitive and biological perspectives has sparked new research, forcing us to rethink long-standing conceptions about the mind (Figure 6.1).

THE PUZZLE OF CONSCIOUSNESS

What is consciousness, and how does it arise? In psychology, **consciousness** often is defined as our moment-to-moment awareness of ourselves and our environment. Among its characteristics, consciousness is

- *subjective and private.* Other people cannot directly know what reality is for you, nor can you enter directly into their experiences. As the author Charles Dickens observed, "Every human creature is constituted to be that profound secret and mystery to every other."

- *dynamic (ever-changing).* We drift in and out of various states throughout each day. Although the stimuli of which we are aware constantly change, we typically experience consciousness as a continuously flowing "stream" of mental activity, rather than as

(a)
(b)
(a) © Robert Frerck/Stone/Getty Images; (b) © A. Ramey/PhotoEdit

FIGURE 6.1 (a) During a Sufi religious ceremony in Istanbul, Turkey, whirling dervishes perform a spinning dance—a prayer in motion—that induces an altered state of consciousness. (b) Buddhists believe that meditation produces inner peace, facilitates insight and enlightenment, and opens a path to different dimensions of consciousness.

(left): © Anne Dowie; (right): Courtesy of the Cognitive Evolution Group, University of Louisiana Lafayette

FIGURE 6.2 Gordon Gallup (1970) exposed four chimps to a mirror. By day three, they used it to inspect hard-to-see parts of their own bodies and began making odd faces at themselves in the mirror. To further test whether the chimps knew the mirror images were their own reflections, Gordon anaesthetized them and put a red mark on their faces. Later, with no mirror, the chimps rarely touched the red mark. But on seeing the mark when a mirror was introduced, they touched the red spot on their face almost 30 times in 30 minutes, suggesting that the chimps had some self-awareness. Using a similar test in which a red rouge mark is placed on the tip of an infant's nose, researchers find that infants begin to recognize themselves in a mirror at around 18 months of age.

disjointed perceptions and thoughts (James, 1890/1950).

- *self-reflective and central to our sense of self.* The mind is aware of its own consciousness. Thus, no matter what your awareness is focused on—a lovely sunset or an itch on your back—you can reflect on the fact that *"you"* are the one who is conscious of it.

Finally, consciousness is *intimately connected with the process of selective attention,* as discussed in Chapter 5. William James noted that "the mind is at every stage a theatre of simultaneous possibilities. Consciousness consists in . . . the selection of some, and the suppression of the rest by the . . . agency of Attention" (1879, p. 13). Selective attention focuses conscious awareness on some stimuli to the exclusion of others. If the mind is a theatre of mental activity, then consciousness reflects whatever is illuminated at the moment—the "bright spot on the' stage"—and selective attention is the "spotlight" or mechanism behind it (Baars, 2007).

Measuring States of Consciousness

Scientists who study consciousness must find ways to operationally define private inner states in terms of measurable responses. The most common measure is *self-report,* in which people describe their inner experiences. Self-reports

offer the most direct insight into a person's subjective experiences, but they are not always verifiable. In contrast, *physiological measures* establish the correspondence between bodily states and mental processes. For example, EEG recordings of brain activity help to identify different stages of sleep throughout the night. Physiological measures are objective but cannot tell us what a person is experiencing subjectively. *Behavioural measures* also are used, including performance on special tasks, such as the *rouge test* (Figure 6.2). Behavioural measures are objective, but we still must infer the person's (or chimp's) state of mind. As you will discover in this chapter's *Frontiers* feature, the ability to measure consciousness can have a profound impact.

Levels of Consciousness: Psychodynamic and Cognitive Perspectives

A century ago, Sigmund Freud (1900/1953) proposed that the human mind consists of three levels of awareness. The *conscious* mind contains thoughts, perceptions, and other mental events of which we are currently aware. *Preconscious* mental events are outside current awareness, but can easily be recalled under certain conditions. For instance, you may not have thought about a childhood friend for years, but when

2. How do psychologists measure states of consciousness?

3. Explain Freud's three-level model of consciousness.

Frontiers

DETECTING AWARENESS

It reads like the plot for a horror movie or a short story by Edgar Allen Poe: As a result of brain injury, a person is rendered immobile and unresponsive, but is still conscious and aware of the surroundings, trapped inside his or her head, unable to move or communicate. Adrian Owen and his colleagues have been investigating whether such patients exist. He studies patients who have sustained brain injuries that result in what is called a vegetative state, or a minimally conscious state. The term "vegetative state" refers to a condition in which the individual appears to be awake, but shows no evidence of awareness (Figure 6.3). These patients have a sleep-wake cycle and when their eyes are open they may show simple behaviours such random eye movements, but they do not respond to sight, sound, or touch. That is, they appear to be awake but completely unaware. If these patients are conscious, how could you tell? How do you communicate with someone who cannot move or speak?

While he was at the University of Cambridge, Owen began his ground-breaking and controversial work with the study of a 26-year-old patient named Kate Bainbridge. Kate had been in a coma due to a viral infection. When the infection cleared and she came out of the coma, she entered a vegetative state. When you see a familiar face, an area of the temporal cortex called the fusiform face area (FFA) is activated. Owen tested Kate by showing her familiar faces while performing a PET scan. Amazingly, her FFA showed increased activity, just as you would expect if someone saw and recognized the faces (Menon et al., 1998). Kate was found to have significant brain function and responded well to rehabilitation; she is now in a wheelchair but otherwise active.

Gokhan Balci/Anadolu Agency/Getty Images

FIGURE 6.3 Patients in a vegetative state appear to be awake but show no awareness of their surroundings, and do not respond to sight, sound, or touch. Might some of these patients be conscious and aware, but unable to move or respond?

An important next step came when Owen and his team worked with a 24-year-old man, referred to as Patient 23 (Owen et al., 2006). Patient 23 had been in a vegetative state for five years after suffering brain damage in a car accident. When you imagine playing tennis and when you imagine finding your way around your house, different parts of your brain become active. Owen and his team used this finding with Patient 23. They told him to imagine playing tennis for "yes," and to imagine moving around his house for "no." Owen put Patient 23 into an fMRI and asked him questions. Incredibly, he answered: "Is your father's name Thomas?" *No.* "Is your father's name Alexander?" *Yes.* "Do you have any brothers?" *Yes.* "Do you have any sisters?" *No* (Owen et al., 2006). It was the first time anyone had communicated with a patient in a vegetative state.

Owen, now at Western University, is working to repeat the fMRI findings using an EEG (Cruse et al., 2012). Although an EEG does not have the precision of an fMRI and cannot measure activity deep within the brain, it is inexpensive, easy to use, and relatively portable. Developing techniques that allow answers to be detected with an EEG would allow faster, less expensive, bedside testing of vegetative patients. For patients far from the large medical centres that have expensive fMRI equipment and the highly trained personnel to perform the scans, an EEG may be a viable option.

Recently, Owen and his team reported a stunning breakthrough while working with normal healthy volunteers (Naci et al., 2013). Participants were asked to concentrate on "yes" or "no" to simple yes-or-no questions such as "Do you have brothers and sisters?" or "Are you younger than 21?" Using fMRI scans, researchers were able to identify answers with 90 percent accuracy. That is, participants could respond by concentrating on "yes" or "no," rather than using some other mental activity as a code, and the researchers could correctly identify what the participant had been thinking 90 percent of the time. Owen and his team are beginning to use this method to attempt communication with patients diagnosed as being in a vegetative state.

Owen's work has implications for diagnosis, clinical care and rehabilitation, medical ethics, and medical/legal decision making, but his findings and interpretation are controversial (Cyranoski, 2012). Some disagree with Owen's conclusion that these patients are conscious; they argue that responses are not a sign of consciousness but are involuntary and reflexive. Others object to what they consider too simple a view of consciousness. Disorders of consciousness, including vegetative state, are some of the least understood of all disorders. Owen's findings suggest that some of these patients may be aware of their surroundings and can communicate if the proper techniques are used. In 2010, Kate Bainbridge, the first vegetative state patient Adrian Owen tested more than a decade earlier, wrote to him, "It scares me to think of what might have happened to me if I had not had mine [PET scan]. It was like magic, it found me" (Cyranoski, 2012, p. 179).

someone mentions your friend's name, you become aware of pleasant memories. *Unconscious* events cannot be brought into conscious awareness under ordinary circumstances. Some unconscious content—such as unacceptable urges and desires stemming from instinctive sexual and aggressive drives, traumatic memories, and threatening emotional conflict—is kept out of conscious awareness because it would arouse anxiety, guilt, or other negative emotions.

Behaviourists roundly criticized Freud's model. After all, they sought to explain behaviour without invoking *conscious* mental processes, much less unconscious ones. Cognitive psychologists and many contemporary psychodynamic psychologists also take issue with specific aspects of Freud's model, which we describe more fully in Chapter 14. As psychodynamic psychologist Drew Westen (1998, p. 333) notes, "Many aspects of Freudian theory are indeed out of date, and they should be. Freud died in 1939, and he has been slow to undertake further revisions."

On a broad level, however, research strongly supports Freud's general premise: Nonconscious processes influence behaviour (Dimberg et al., 2000; Westen, 1998). Studies of *placebo effects* (see Chapter 2), *split-brain patients* (see Chapter 3), *subliminal perception* (see Chapter 5), and phenomena that you will encounter in upcoming chapters all indicate that mental processes can affect our behaviour without conscious awareness (Prinz, 2015).

The Cognitive Viewpoint

Cognitive psychologists reject the notion of an unconscious mind driven by instinctive urges and repressed conflicts. Rather, they view conscious and unconscious mental life as complementary forms of information processing (Hassin et al., 2005). As Daniel Reisberg (1997, p. 601) notes, unconscious mental activity is "not an adversary to the conscious mind. Instead, the cognitive unconscious functions as a sophisticated support service, working in harmony with our conscious thoughts." To illustrate, consider how we perform everyday tasks.

Controlled versus automatic processing. Many activities, such as planning a vacation or studying, involve **controlled (effortful) processing**, the voluntary use of attention and conscious effort. Other activities involve **automatic processing** and can be performed with little or no conscious effort. Automatic

processing occurs most often when we carry out routine actions or well-learned tasks. Learning to type, drive, and eat with utensils all involve controlled processing; you have to pay a lot of attention to what you are doing. With practice, performance becomes more automatic and brain areas involved in conscious thought become less active (Saling & Phillips, 2007). Through years of practice, typists, athletes, and musicians program themselves to execute highly complex skills with a minimum of conscious thought.

Automatic processing, however, has a key disadvantage: It can reduce our chances of finding new ways to approach problems (Langer, 1989). Controlled processing is more flexible and open to change. Still, automatic processing offers speed and economy of effort, and in everyday life most actions may be processed this way (Bargh & Chartrand, 1999). In fact, many well-learned behaviours seem performed best when our mind is on "autopilot," with controlled processing taking a backseat. The famous baseball player Yogi Berra captured this idea in his classic statement that "You can't think and hit at the same time." At tasks ranging from golf putting to video-game playing, experiments suggest that too much self-focused thinking can hurt task performance and cause people to "choke" under pressure (Beilcock & Carr, 2001).

Divided attention. Automatic processing also facilitates **divided attention**, the ability to perform more than one activity at the same time. We can talk while we walk, type as we read, eat while watching TV, and so on. Without the capacity to divide attention, every act would require our full attention and quickly overwhelm our mental capacity.

Although divided attention can be adaptive, it can have serious negative consequences in certain situations (Figure 6.4). For example, while engaged in a cellphone conversation, drivers leave less space between their cars and the cars in front of them and, especially during long conversations, they drive faster (Rosenbloom, 2006). Even the use of a hands-free cellphone has an impact: braking is delayed, the degree of braking is reduced, and anticipation of upcoming events is degraded (Treffner & Barrett, 2004), all of which are changes that would be expected to increase the chance of an accident. Divided attention can also degrade academic performance. Researchers from York University and McGill University have found that students performed more

4. How do cognitive psychologists view the unconscious?

5. What is automatic processing, and why is it important?

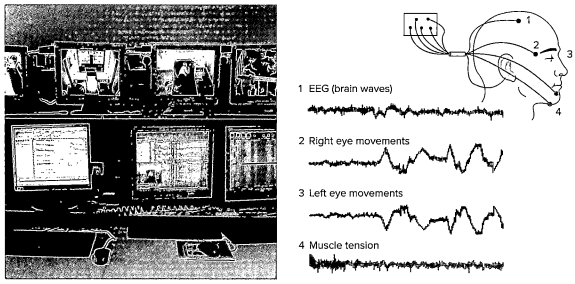

1 EEG (brain waves)

2 Right eye movements

3 Left eye movements

4 Muscle tension

(photo): © National Geographic Image Collection/Alamy Stock Photo

FIGURE 6.10 In a modern sleep laboratory, people sleep while their physiological responses are monitored. Electrodes attached to the scalp area record the person's EEG brain-wave patterns. Electrodes attached beside the eyes record eye movements during sleep. Muscle tension is recorded, and a neutral electrode is attached to the ear.

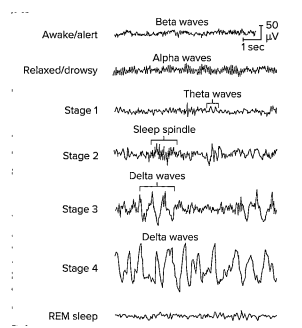

FIGURE 6.11 Changing patterns of brain-wave activity help to define the various stages of sleep. Note that brain waves become slower and larger as sleep deepens and that the general pattern of REM sleep is similar to that of stage 1.

Source: Adapted from Dement, W.C. (1978). *Some must watch while some must sleep.* New York, NY: Norton.; Hauri, P. (1982). *The sleep disorders* (2nd ed.). Kalamazoo, MI: Upjohn Corp.

11. What brain-wave patterns distinguish the first four stages of sleep?

12. Describe some major characteristics of REM sleep.

Stage 1 through Stage 4

As sleep begins, your brain-wave pattern becomes more irregular, and slower *theta waves* (3.5 to 7.5 cycles per second) increase.

You are now in *stage 1,* a form of light sleep from which you can easily be awakened. You will probably spend just a few minutes (or less) in stage 1, during which time some people experience images and sudden body jerks. As sleep becomes deeper, *sleep spindles*—periodic one- to two-second bursts of rapid brain-wave activity (12 to 15 cycles per second)—begin to appear. Sleep spindles indicate that you are now in *stage 2* (Figure 6.11). Your muscles are more relaxed, your breathing and heart rate are slower, and you are harder to awaken.

Sleep deepens as you move into *stage 3,* marked by the regular appearance of very slow (0.5 to 2 cycles per second) and large **delta waves.** As time passes, they occur more often, and when delta waves *dominate* the EEG pattern, you have reached *stage 4.* Together, stage 3 and stage 4 are often referred to as **slow-wave sleep.** Your body is relaxed, activity in various parts of your brain has decreased, and you are hard to awaken. After 20 to 30 minutes of stage 4 sleep, your EEG pattern changes as you go "back through" stages 3 and 2, spending a little time in each. Overall, within 60 to 90 minutes of going to sleep, you will have completed a cycle of stages 1-2-3-4-3-2. At this point, a remarkably different sleep stage ensues.

REM Sleep

In 1953, sleep researchers Eugene Aserinsky and Nathaniel Kleitman of the University of Chicago struck scientific gold when they identified a sleep stage unlike the rest. Every half minute or so, bursts of muscular activity caused the sleepers' eyeballs to vigorously move back and forth beneath their closed eyelids. Because of these *rapid eye movements* (REMs), this stage was called **REM sleep.** When Aserinsky and Kleitman awakened sleepers from REM periods, they discovered that a dream was almost always reported. Even people who swore they "never had dreams" recalled them when awakened during REM. At last, science had a window through which to examine dreaming more closely. Wait for a REM period, awaken the sleeper, and catch a dream.

During REM sleep, physiological arousal may increase to daytime levels. Heart rate quickens, breathing becomes more rapid and irregular, and brain-wave activity resembles that of active wakefulness. Men have penile erections and women experience vaginal lubrication. Because most dreams do not have sexual content, this REM-induced genital arousal is *not* a response to sexual imagery.

The brain also sends signals, making it more difficult for voluntary muscles to contract. As a result, muscles in the arms, legs, and torso lose tone and become relaxed. These muscles may twitch, but in effect you are "paralyzed" and unable to move. This state is called *REM sleep paralysis,* and because of it, REM sleep is sometimes called *paradoxical sleep:* Your body is highly aroused, and yet it looks like you are sleeping peacefully because you move so little.

REM sleep is often thought to be the only sleep stage in which we dream or even experience mental activity, but that is not correct. We also experience mental activity during non-REM sleep. REM dreams have their well-known story-like quality, with vivid sensory and motor elements and the perception of reality. When you are in a REM dream, you have the experience of sensing people, objects, and places, of moving and behaving, and of witnessing and participating in a series of real, if bizarre, events. When subjects are awakened from non-REM sleep, they often will report some type of mental activity (Foulkes, 1985). The non-REM dream is shorter than a REM dream (Stickgold et al., 1994). The non-REM dream is also less story-like, lacking the vivid sensory and motor experiences of a REM dream. The non-REM dream is often fixed and unmoving, resembling a tableau more than a story with a plot. Apart from non-REM dreams, mental activity that occurs during non-REM sleep also may resemble daytime thoughts, although in comparison to waking thoughts they are simple and jumbled. Indeed, some of the mental activity that occurs during non-REM sleep has even been referred to as *sleep thoughts* because of the closer resemblance to daytime thinking than to REM dreams (Foulkes, 1985).

Each cycle through the sleep stages takes about 90 minutes. Figure 6.12 shows that, as the hours pass, stage 4 and stage 3 drop out and REM periods become longer.

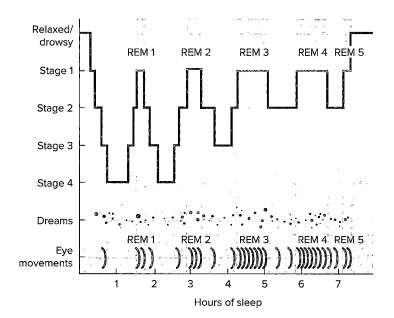

FIGURE 6.12 This graph shows a record of a typical night's sleep. People typically average four or five REM periods during the night. As the night wears on, we spend less time in the deepest stages of sleep and more time in REM sleep.

Getting a Night's Sleep: Brain and Environment

The brain steers our nightly passage into and through sleep, but it does not contain a single "sleep centre." Different aspects of the sleep cycle, such as falling asleep, REM sleep, and slow-wave sleep, are controlled by different brain mechanisms. Moreover, falling asleep is not just a matter of "turning off" the brain systems that regulate wakefulness. Separate systems "turn on" and actively promote sleep.

Areas at the base of the forebrain (called the *basal forebrain*) and within the brain stem are particularly important in regulating our falling asleep (McGinty & Sterman, 1968; Szymusiak, 1995). A different brain stem area—where the reticular formation passes through the pons—plays a key role in initiating REM sleep (Hobson et al., 1998). This region contains "REM-sleep On" neurons that periodically activate other brain systems, each of which controls a different aspect of REM sleep, such as eye movements, muscular paralysis, and genital arousal.

Sleep is biologically regulated, but the environment plays a role as well. The change of seasons affects sleep; in fall and winter, most

13. What brain areas help to regulate sleep onset and REM sleep?

14. How do sleep patterns change as we age?

people sleep about 15 to 60 minutes longer per night (Campbell, 1993). Shiftwork, jet lag, stress at work and school, and nighttime noise can decrease sleep quality (Saremi et al., 2008).

How Much Do We Sleep?

The question seems simple enough, as does the answer for many of us: not enough! In reality, the issue is complex. Figure 6.13 reveals that there are substantial differences in how much people sleep at various ages. Newborn infants average 16 hours of sleep a day, and almost half of their sleep time is in REM. But as we age, three important changes occur:

- We sleep less. On average, 15- to 24-year-olds average 8.5 hours of sleep per day, and elderly adults average just under six hours.
- REM sleep decreases dramatically during infancy and early childhood, but remains relatively stable thereafter.
- Time spent in stages 3 and 4 declines. By late adulthood, we get relatively little slow-wave sleep.

A parent or caregiver has likely told you that you need eight hours of sleep a night. We have all heard this, but is it true? Research has found that

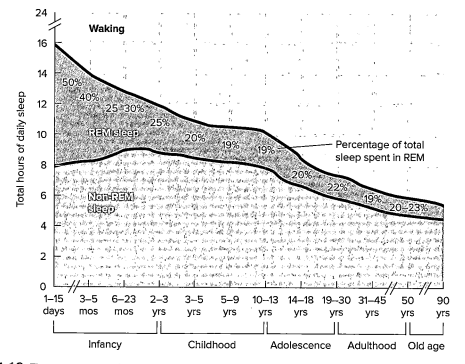

FIGURE 6.13 The percentage of sleep time in REM and non-REM sleep changes with age. Average daily sleep time decreases over the lifespan, and most of the decrease in non-REM sleep is due to decreasing delta sleep (stages 3 and 4). REM sleep time decreases throughout childhood and then is relatively stable through adulthood.

Adapted from H.P. Roffwarg, J.N. Muzio & W.C. Dement, "Ontongenic Development of Human Dream-Sleep Cycle," *Science, 152,* 604, Fig 1. Copyright © 1966, AAAS. Reprinted with permission from AAAS.

if we follow our own natural rhythms, with no clocks and scheduled routines, we sleep between 10 and 12 hours a night (Coren, 1996). How much sleep a person needs is influenced by genetic factors, work schedules, stress, age, lifestyle, and general health, among other factors (de Castro, 2002; Vincent et al., 2009; Williams, 2001). The most recent guidelines from the National Sleep Foundation (2016) suggest that adolescents should have eight to ten hours of sleep a night and young adults seven to nine hours. Although most of us may need eight to ten hours of sleep a night, some famous individuals have functioned well on surprisingly little sleep: British prime ministers Winston Churchill and Margaret Thatcher, U.S. president John F. Kennedy, and Napoleon Bonaparte all reportedly slept between 3 and 5.5 hours a night (Sharkey, 1993), and Leonardo da Vinci is reported to have slept as little as two hours a day. Whether we need eight or ten hours of sleep a night, how much time do we actually spend sleeping? Young adult Canadians sleep an average of eight hours and 18 minutes a night (Statistics Canada, 2005), but more than half of young adult Canadians sleep less than seven hours a night, and 30 percent less than six hours a night (World Association of Sleep Medicine, 2011).

Sleep Deprivation

Sleep deprivation is a way of life for many university students, and they are not alone. Almost half of us sacrifice some sleep to accomplish more work (National Sleep Foundation, 2000; Williams, 2001). Millions more lose sleep because of disorders.

Psychologists study sleep deprivation for its practical significance and to gain insight into why we need to sleep. June Pilcher and Allen Huffcutt (1996) meta-analyzed 19 sleep deprivation studies in which participants underwent either *short-term total sleep deprivation* (up to 45 hours without sleep), *long-term total sleep deprivation* (more than 45 hours without sleep), or *partial deprivation* (being allowed to sleep no more than five hours per night for one or more consecutive nights). Participants' self-reported mood (e.g., irritability, disorientation), responses on mental tasks (e.g., ability to concentrate, logical reasoning, word memory), and physical tasks (e.g., manual dexterity, treadmill-walking) were measured.

What would you predict? Would all types of deprivation affect behaviour, and which behaviours would be affected the most? Combining

across the different types of deprivation and behaviour, the results were remarkable: The "average" sleep-deprived person functioned only as well as someone in the bottom 9 percent of non-deprived participants. All three types of sleep deprivation had a negative impact on functioning. Mood suffered most, followed by cognitive and then physical performance, although *all three* behaviours showed significant impairment from sleep loss.

What about students who pull all-nighters or drastically cut back their sleep, and claim they still perform as well as ever? University students deprived of a single night's sleep perform more poorly on critical thinking tasks and show depressed mood, increased irritability, confusion, anxiety, and anger (Short & Louca, 2015). Sleep deprivation also has a physical cost. Sleep deprivation is associated with a range of health complaints including type II diabetes and insulin resistance, high blood pressure, headache, stomachache, increased allergic reactions, and lowered health-related quality of life (Paiva et al., 2015). See this chapter's *Applications* feature for tips on improving sleep quality.

Most total sleep deprivation studies with humans last less than five days, but 17-year-old Randy Gardner has the record for the longest scientifically documented period without sleep. He stayed awake for 11 days and 24 minutes as his project for a 1964 high school science fair in San Diego. Grateful sleep researchers received permission to study him (Gulevich, Dement, & Johnson, 1966). At times during the first few days, Randy became irritable, forgetful, nauseous, and intensely tired. By day five, he had periods of disorientation and distorted thinking. In the last four days, he developed finger tremors and slurred speech. Still, in his final day without sleep, he beat sleep researcher William Dement 100 consecutive times at a pinball-type game.

When Randy finally went to bed, he slept almost 15 hours the first night, and then returned to his normal amount of sleep within a week. In general, it takes several nights to recover from extended total sleep deprivation, and we do not make up all the sleep time that we have lost. Tony Wright was reported to have broken the record in 2007, but this was not confirmed, and Randy Gardner is widely accepted as the record holder. Guinness has since stopped carrying sleep deprivation as a category, on the grounds that it is a dangerous practice.

15. How do different types of sleep deprivation affect mood and performance?

Applications

A GOOD NIGHT'S SLEEP

You may have heard the witticism, "Do you know that awesome feeling when you get into bed, fall straight asleep, stay asleep all night and wake up feeling refreshed? No? Me neither." (Canadian Sleep Society, 2016).

Lack of sleep can have a serious impact on our well-being. Even short periods of sleep deprivation can have a large effect. Most students have had an "all-nighter" so they can complete a project, study for an exam, or have a movie marathon. Recent research found that among adolescents, the loss of a single night's sleep significantly depressed mood, and significantly increased confusion, anxiety, and anger (Short & Louca, 2015). The effect on anxiety was greater for female than for male students. Too little sleep can also affect physical health; too little sleep is linked to a range of health complaints including headache, neck and shoulder pain, stomachache, and insulin resistance (Paiva et al., 2015). That is, along with making you feel tired and irritable, too little sleep can also make you sick, angry, depressed, and anxious. Sleep is also known to be important for learning and memory consolidation (Horton & Malinowski, 2015).

Although we know how important sleep is for our well-being, most of us do not get enough sleep. Although there are large individual differences, the most recent guidelines from the National Sleep Foundation (2016) recommend that adolescents get eight to ten hours of sleep a night, while young adults should get seven to nine hours of sleep. However, according to one survey, 60 percent of Canadian adolescents and young adults average less than seven hours of sleep a night, and 30 percent get less than six hours of sleep a night (World Association of Sleep Medicine, 2011). That is, most of us are chronically sleep deprived.

wavebreakmedia/Shutterstock

FIGURE 6.14 Having sufficient sleep is important for our well-being, but a wide range of factors can interfere with our ability to fall asleep or stay asleep. There are, however, some simple steps that you can take that will improve your sleep quality.

Sleep experts at the National Sleep Foundation (2016), the BC Partners for Mental Health (HeretoHelp, 2016), and the Canadian Sleep Society (2016) have distributed guidelines known to promote healthy sleep habits. The most effective way to improve your sleep is to make small changes in behaviours that help to promote sleep and reduce those that interfere with sleep.

The most effective changes that help to promote healthy sleep are:

1. **Have a regular schedule.** Try to keep the same sleep and wake schedule every day, including on weekends. Deviating from this on occasion will happen and is not a reason for great concern, but the more you can stay with a regular schedule the better your sleep. People who go to bed at different times every day are much more likely to have sleep problems. Along with a regular bedtime, try to avoid bright light in the evening and expose yourself to sunlight in the morning. This will keep your circadian rhythms in check.

2. **Have a bedtime ritual.** Extend your routine from a regular bedtime to also having a relaxing routine that you practise just before going to bed. A relaxing bedtime routine helps to separate your sleep time from the rest of the day with its stress and excitement. As you develop and then consistently practise your relaxing bedtime ritual, it will help to train your body and brain that it is time for sleep (see information on conditioning in Chapter 7).

3. **Do not nap.** If you do not get enough sleep during the night, do not nap during the day. Some people can nap without it interfering with the quality or duration of their nighttime sleep, but for most people a daytime nap leads to problems falling asleep or staying asleep. If you do nap during the day, make it a power nap of no more than 30 minutes.

4. **Exercise regularly.** Even light to moderate exercise three times a week promotes improved sleep quality. Exercise can energize you so do not exercise too close to bedtime; avoid exercise within four hours of when you plan to go to bed.

5. **Your bedroom.** Your bedroom is your sleep environment. Does it promote sleep? When you want to sleep your bedroom should be cool (16–19°C), quiet, and dark. The bed and pillows need to be comfortable and free of allergens and other irritants.

6. **Avoid heavy meals in the evening.** Try to also avoid large or spicy meals before your bedtime. If you are hungry, have a light snack 45 minutes to an hour before bed.

7. **Avoid caffeine, alcohol, and nicotine in the evening.** Alcohol, nicotine, and caffeine all disrupt sleep and you should avoid them within at least two to three hours of bedtime. Caffeine is especially a concern with its

continued

powerful effect in delaying sleep onset. Caffeine and related compounds are found not just in coffee but also in dark tea, many soft drinks, chocolate, and in many over-the-counter medications such as pain relievers, cold remedies, and allergy medications. Among healthy young adults, the half-life of caffeine (the length of time it takes your body to eliminate half of the caffeine in your system) is five to six hours. Depending on your sensitivity to caffeine, you may need to avoid it for much longer than the three hours before bedtime. Alcohol may seem to make people sleepy, but alcohol disrupts the sleep cycle and powerfully suppresses REM sleep. Someone sleeping with alcohol in their system does not get a normal night's sleep.

8. **Relax.** If you have had a busy, active day and spent the evening studying, you cannot just turn that off and fall asleep. Along with having a specific bedtime ritual, spend at least an hour relaxing before trying to go to sleep. Spend that time listening to music or reading, but do not read something demanding or something that is going to make you angry or upset. Some people find electronic screens to be stimulating because of the nature of the light they emit, so be cautious about using a laptop or other electronic device or watching TV before bed.

9. **If you are not sleeping, get up.** If you cannot fall asleep or waken and cannot get back to sleep, get up and go to another room. We have all had the experience of lying awake watching the time get later and later. As we watch the minutes tick by we get more and more frustrated and

that makes it even harder to fall asleep. You cannot force yourself to fall asleep, and telling yourself that you *must* fall asleep is only going to make you feel stressed and anxious. If you cannot fall asleep within 30 minutes, get up, leave your bedroom, and do something relaxing— perhaps listen to music, meditate, have a warm uncaffeinated beverage, or take a warm bath. You do not have to wait for the full 30 minutes to elapse; if you are getting frustrated or anxious because you cannot fall back to sleep, get up and do something. It may take a few nights for this strategy to be effective, but it will become increasingly effective with practice.

Our sleep is controlled by a complex group of coordinated processes, and a wide range of medical, psychological, and lifestyle factors can disrupt it. If you are having persistent sleep problems, you may find it useful to keep a sleep diary. Recording your evening activities, sleeping habits, and sleep quality in a sleep diary can help identify common patterns or issues that interfere with your sleep. You can find many examples of sleep diaries online and, yes, there is an app for that. Be cautious about sleeping pills and other purported "sleep aids." There are circumstances when sleeping pills are necessary, but most compounds that promote sleep can lead to abnormal sleep cycles, and many have the potential for tolerance, dependence, and addiction.

If you try these strategies consistently and still experience sleep problems, you should speak to your doctor or a sleep professional.

Why Do We Sleep?

Given that we spend almost a third of our lives sleeping, it must serve an important purpose. According to the **restoration model,** sleep recharges our rundown bodies and allows us to recover from physical and mental fatigue (Hess, 1965; Walker, 2008). Sleep deprivation and night shiftwork studies strongly support this view: We need sleep to function at our emotional, mental, and physical best. In fact, we may need sleep to live. Laboratory rats deprived of all sleep usually die within a few weeks, and scientists are trying to pinpoint the physiological causes (Constantine et al., 1995; Cirelli et al., 1999).

If the restoration model is correct, activities that increase daily wear on the body should increase sleep. Evidence is mildly supportive. A study of 18- to 26-year-old ultra-marathon runners found that they slept much longer and spent a greater percentage of time in slow-wave sleep on the two nights following their 92-kilometre run (Shapiro et al., 1981). For the

rest of us mere mortals, a meta-analysis of 38 studies found that we tend to sleep longer by only about 10 minutes on days we have exercised (Youngstedt et al., 1997).

The biggest challenge is determining exactly what it is that "gets restored" in our bodies while we sleep. We do not know precisely, but some researchers believe that a cellular waste product called *adenosine* plays a role (Alam et al., 2009). Like a car's exhaust emissions, adenosine is produced as cells consume fuel. As adenosine accumulates, it influences brain systems that decrease alertness and promote sleep, signalling the body to slow down because too much cellular fuel has been burned.

Evolutionary/circadian sleep models emphasize that sleep's main purpose is to increase a species' chances of survival in relation to its environmental demands (Webb, 1974). Our prehistoric ancestors had little to gain and much to lose by being active at night. Hunting, food gathering, and travelling were

16. Explain the restoration and evolutionary theories of sleep.

accomplished more easily and safely during daylight. Leaving the protection of one's shelter at night would have served little purpose other than to become dinner for nighttime predators.

17. What evidence supports or contradicts the hypothesis that REM sleep serves a special function?

Over the course of evolution, each species developed a circadian sleep-wake pattern that was adaptive in terms of whether it was predator or prey, its food requirements, and its methods of defence from attack. For small prey animals, such as mice and squirrels, who reside in burrows or trees safely away from predators, spending a lot of time asleep is adaptive. For large prey animals, such as horses, deer, and zebras, who sleep in relatively exposed environments and whose safety from predators depends on running away, spending a lot of time asleep would be hazardous. Sleep may have evolved also as a mechanism for conserving energy (Berger & Phillips, 1995). Our body's overall metabolic rate during sleep is about 10 to 20 percent slower than during waking rest (Wouters-Adriaens & Westerterp, 2006). The restoration and evolutionary theories highlight complementary functions of sleep, and both contribute to a two-factor model of why we sleep (Webb, 1994).

Do specific sleep stages have special functions? To answer this question, imagine volunteering for a sleep deprivation study in which we awaken you only when you enter REM sleep; you can sleep through the other sleep stages. In this situation, two things will happen (beyond any unpleasant looks you may give us). First, on successive nights, we will have to awaken you more often, because your brain will be fighting back to get REM sleep (Figure 6.15a). Second, when the study ends, for the first few nights you probably will experience a *REM-rebound effect,* a tendency to increase the amount of REM sleep after being deprived of it (Figure 6.15b). REM-rebound occurs in many species, including humans (Rechtschaffen et al., 1999).

Results such as those shown in Figure 6.15 suggest that we need to have REM sleep. Several theories have proposed that REM sleep is vital for mental functioning, especially for processes related to learning and memory consolidation (Walker, 2005; Walker & Stickgold, 2006). As we saw earlier (see Figure 6.12), your brain is as active during REM sleep as it is during alert wakefulness. The high level of brain activity during REM sleep may help to strengthen the neural circuits involved in remembering important information from the preceding day (Maquet et al., 2000; Walker & Stickgold, 2006). Studies of REM sleep and learning among both

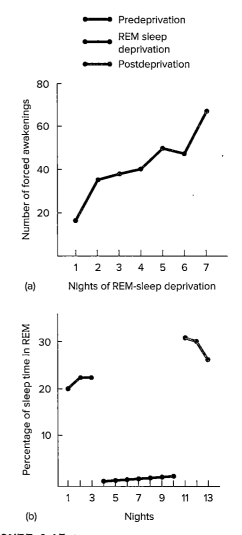

FIGURE 6.15 (a) In REM-sleep deprivation studies, participants start to go into REM periods more times with each passing night, as the brain tries to get REM sleep. (b) After REM deprivation ends, the sleeper spends more time than usual in REM sleep for a few nights. This is the REM-rebound effect.

Source: Data from Agnew, H.W., Jr., Webb, W.B., & Williams, R.L. (1967). Comparison of stage four and 1-REM sleep deprivation. *Perceptual and Motor Skills,* 24, 851–858.

humans (e.g., Maquet et al., 2000; Smith & Lapp, 1991) and animals (e.g., Smith & Rose, 1997) support the idea that REM sleep and learning are related, although exactly how REM sleep, memory, and learning are related is an ongoing area of research.

Sleep Disorders

The mechanisms involved in sleep are complex and can go wrong in a variety of ways. A staggering one-half to two-thirds of North American adults feel that they have some type of sleep problem (National Sleep Foundation, 2000).

Insomnia

True or False: Someone who falls asleep easily can still have insomnia. The statement is true, because **insomnia** refers to chronic difficulty in falling asleep, staying asleep, or experiencing restful sleep. Trouble falling asleep is most common among young adults, and difficulty staying asleep is most common among older adults. If you occasionally have trouble getting a good night's sleep, don't worry: almost everyone does. True insomniacs' sleep troubles are frequent and persistent.

Insomnia is the most common sleep disorder, experienced by approximately 10 to 40 percent of the population of various countries (Bartlett et al., 2008). Many insomniacs overestimate how much sleep they lose and how long it takes them to fall asleep: 20 minutes may seem like an hour. Certain people, called *pseudoinsomniacs*, complain of insomnia, but sleep normally when examined in the laboratory (Helmert Schneider, 1985). Despite a sound night of sleep, some pseudoinsomniacs awaken in the morning and claim that their insomnia was so bad that they didn't get any sleep at all (McCall & Edinger, 1992)!

Insomnia has biological, psychological, and environmental causes. Some people are genetically predisposed to insomnia. Medical conditions, mental disorders such as anxiety and depression, and many drugs can disrupt sleep (Lydic & Biebuyck, 1989). As we will see in Chapter 15, stress powerfully interferes with sleep and is a common cause of insomnia.

Narcolepsy

Some people suffer not from an inability to sleep, but from uncontrollably falling asleep. **Narcolepsy** involves sudden, uncontrollable sleep attacks that may last from less than a minute to an hour. No matter how much narcoleptics rest at night, sleep attacks can occur at any time. Narcolepsy is often associated with insomnia and REM sleep behaviour disorder (Dauvilliers et al., 2013). When a sleep attack occurs, narcoleptics may experience a sudden loss of motor control (cataplexy) and go directly into a REM sleep. These REM episodes can have intense, dreamlike images that are profoundly disorienting when the person awakes a few minutes later (Goodrick, 2014).

Our understanding of narcolepsy has changed dramatically in the past few years. In the early 2000s little was known about the causes of narcolepsy other than that there was a genetic predisposition (Mignot, 1998). For example, narcolepsy can be selectively bred in dogs (Figure 6.16). Modern sleep research has

18. Describe the major symptoms of narcolepsy and REM-sleep behaviour disorder.

(both): Barcroft Media/Getty Images

FIGURE 6.16 This dog lapses suddenly from alert wakefulness into a limp sleep while being held by sleep researcher William Dement. Narcolepsy occurs naturally in some dogs, and, by using selective breeding, researchers at Stanford's Sleep Disorders Center have established a colony of narcoleptic canines.

revolutionized our understanding of narcolepsy. Hypocretin is a peptide hormone produced in the hypothalamus that helps to regulate arousal, wakefulness, and appetite. Narcolepsy is now often associated with an insensitivity to hypocretin and in cases of narcolepsy with cataplexy even a complete lack of the hypocretin producing neurons in the hypothalamus (Dauvilliers, et al., 2013).

REM-Sleep Behaviour Disorder

Kaku Kimura and his colleagues in Japan (1997) report the case of a 72-year-old woman who, during a night's observation in a sleep laboratory, repeatedly talked, sang, and moved her hands and legs during REM sleep. One singing episode lasted three minutes. She was experiencing **REM-sleep behaviour disorder (RBD),** in which the loss of muscle tone that causes normal REM sleep paralysis is absent (Olson et al., 2000; Paparrigopoulos, 2005). If awakened, RBD patients often report dream content that matches their behaviour, as if they were acting out their dreams (Dyken et al., 1995). Unfortunately, the consequences of RBD can be severe:

> . . . a 67-year-old man . . . was awakened one night by his wife's yelling as he was choking her. He was dreaming of breaking the neck of a deer he had just knocked down. This patient had tied himself to his bed with a rope at night for 6 years as a protective measure, owing to repeated episodes of jumping from the bed and colliding with furniture and walls. (Schenck et al., 1989, p. 1169)

RBD sleepers may kick violently, throw punches, or get out of bed and move about wildly, leaving the bedroom in a shambles. Many RBD patients seen in sleep clinics have injured themselves while sleeping, and almost half have injured their sleeping partners (Schenck, Hurwitz, & Mahowald, 1993). Some researchers propose that brain abnormalities may prevent signals that normally inhibit movement during REM from being sent, but at present the causes of RBD are unknown (Iranzo & Aparicio, 2009).

Sleepwalking

Sleepwalking typically occurs during a stage 3 or stage 4 period of slow-wave sleep (Zadra et al., 2008). Sleepwalkers often have blank stares and are unresponsive to other people, but they seem vaguely conscious of the environment as they navigate around furniture, go to the bathroom, or find something to eat. Sleepwalkers

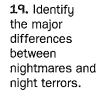

19. Identify the major differences between nightmares and night terrors.

often return to bed and awaken in the morning with no memory of the event. About 10 to 30 percent of children sleepwalk at least once, but less than 5 percent of adults do. If you did not sleepwalk as a child, then the odds are less than 1 percent that you will do so as an adult (Hublin et al., 1997). Sleepwalkers can injure themselves accidentally, such as by falling down stairs or wandering out of their homes.

A tendency to sleepwalk may be inherited, and daytime stress, alcohol, and certain illnesses and medications also increase sleepwalking (Hublin et al., 2001). Various treatments may be used, including psychotherapy, drugs, and routinely awakening children before the time they typically sleepwalk (Frank et al., 1997). But the most common "treatment" simply is to wait for children to outgrow it while creating a safe home environment so that the sleepwalker does not get injured. Contrary to common belief, awakening sleepwalkers is not harmful, although they may be confused for a few minutes.

Nightmares and Night Terrors

Nightmares are frightening dreams, and virtually everyone has them. Like all dreams, they occur more often during REM sleep and in the hours before we arise. Physiological arousal during nightmares is similar to levels experienced during pleasant dreams.

Night terrors (also called *sleep terrors*) are more intense than nightmares. The sleeper, usually a child, suddenly sits up and seems to awaken, letting out a blood-curdling scream. Terrified and aroused to a near-panic state, the person might thrash about in bed or flee to another room, as if trying to escape from something. Come morning, the person usually has no memory of the episode (Szelenberger et al., 2005).

Unlike nightmares, night terrors are most common during deep sleep (stages 3 and 4) and involve greatly elevated physiological arousal; heart rate may double or triple. Up to 6 percent of children, but only 1 or 2 percent of adults, experience night terrors (Ohayon et al., 1999). In most childhood cases, treatment is simply to wait for the night terrors to diminish with age.

The Nature of Dreams

Traditional aboriginal peoples of Australia speak of "The Dreaming." They view dreaming as a "parallel reality" connecting them to the spiritual world and a collective unconscious linked to their ancestral past (Dawson, 1993). The Dreaming involves stories of creation and beliefs that are passed on orally to educate each successive generation, and it defines their personal and cultural identities. Dreams also are a central guiding force in other cultures, such as the Senoi of Malaysia, who believe that events in dreaming and waking life influence one another (Greenleaf, 1973). Even in Western societies that generally attach less importance to dreams, many people believe that dreams can be meaningful (Morewedge & Norton, 2009).

When Do We Dream?

Mental activity occurs throughout the sleep cycle. When Jason Rowley and his colleagues (1998) awakened sleepers merely 45 seconds after sleep onset, participants reported visual images about 25 percent of the time. As this *hypnagogic state* (the transitional state from wakefulness through early stage 2 sleep) continued, mental activity became more dreamlike (Figure 6.17). In general, between 15 to 40 percent of sleepers report dreamlike activity when awakened within six minutes of falling asleep.

Research shows that we dream most when the brain is most active (Antrobus, 1991). Brain activity is higher during REM sleep than non-REM sleep, and we dream more during REM sleep. When awakened from REM sleep, people report a dream about 80 percent of the time, versus 15 to 50 percent of the time for non-REM sleep (Dement,

1978; Foulkes, 1962; Rowley et al., 1998). Brain activity also is higher in the final hours of sleep than it is during the earlier hours, thanks to our circadian sleep-wake cycle preparing us to rise for a new day. Thus, we dream more in the last few hours of both REM and non-REM sleep than during the same stages earlier in the night.

What Do We Dream About?

Much of our knowledge about dream content derives from 35 years of research using a coding system developed by Calvin Hall and Robert Van de Castle (1966). Analyzing 1000 dream reports (mostly from university students), they found that dreams are not nearly as strange as they are stereotyped to be. Most take place in familiar settings and often involve people we know. Certainly, some dreams are bizarre, but they often leave a lasting impression that biases our perception of what most dreams are like. As a case in point, have you ever dreamt that you were flying (under your own power, without a plane!)? Between one-third and one-half of university students say they have. Yet a study of 635 actual dream reports found only one dream that included flying (Snyder, 1970). This result suggests that dreams about flying are quite *un*common, but because they are so striking, many people can recall having such a dream at least once.

Given the stereotype of "blissful dreaming," it may surprise you that most dreams contain some

20. When do we dream the most? Why?

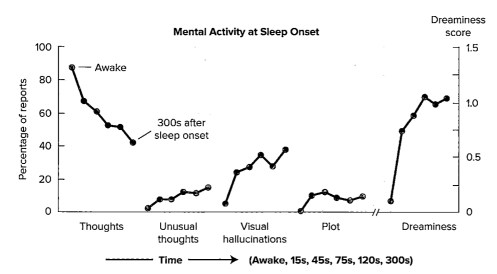

FIGURE 6.17 The mental activity of 11 male and female undergraduates was measured by self-report while awake and then 15, 45, 75, 120, and 300 seconds after sleep onset. Students slept at home, were awakened by computer, and the time of awakenings varied across different nights. In total, 477 reports of mental activity were collected. In general, after sleep onset, normal "waking-type" thoughts decreased, unusual thoughts and visual hallucinations (images that seemed "real") increased, and mental activity was more "dreamy." Unlike many REM dreams, however, mental activity after sleep onset rarely had a plot (e.g., a storyline).

Source: Adapted from Rowley, J.T., Stickgold, R., & Hobson, J.A. (1998). Eyelid movements and mental activity at sleep onset. *Consciousness and Cognition: An International Journal, 7*, 67–84.

negative content (Domhoff & Schneider, 2008). Hall and Van de Castle (1966) found that 80 percent of dream reports involved negative emotions, almost half contained aggressive acts, and a third involved some type of misfortune. They also found that women dreamt almost equally about male and female characters, whereas about two-thirds of men's dream characters were male. Although the reason for this gender difference is not clear, a similar pattern has been found across several cultures and age groups (Avila-White et al., 1999; Hall, 1984).

Our experiences, and current concerns can shape dream content (Bulkeley & Kahan, 2008). For example, in the weeks following the September 11, 2001, terrorist attacks, a study of 1000 Manhattan residents found that one in ten experienced distressing dreams about the attacks (Galea et al., 2002). Overall, it appears that up to 50 percent of our dreams contain some content reflecting the experiences of our most recent day (Botman & Crovitz, 1989; Harlow & Roll, 1992).

Other recent research has considered dreams as part of a continuum on which consciousness can from shift from alert wakefulness to daydreams to dreams. This chapter's *Focus on Neuroscience* feature explores this research.

Why Do We Dream?

Speculation about why we dream and whether dreams have special meaning has intrigued humankind for ages. Most scientific dream theories arise from the psychoanalytic, physiological, and cognitive perspectives.

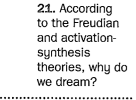

21. According to the Freudian and activation-synthesis theories, why do we dream?

Freud's psychoanalytic theory. Sigmund Freud (1900/1953) believed that the main purpose of dreaming is **wish fulfillment**, the gratification of our unconscious desires and needs. These desires include sexual and aggressive urges that are too unacceptable to be consciously acknowledged and fulfilled in real life. Freud distinguished between a dream's *manifest content*—the "surface" story that the dreamer reports—and its *latent content*, which is its disguised psychological meaning. Thus, a dream about being with a stranger on a train that goes through a tunnel (manifest content) might represent a hidden desire for sexual intercourse with a "forbidden" partner (latent content).

Although Freud sparked great interest in dreams and laid the groundwork for other dream theories, many contemporary researchers reject the postulates of his theory. They

conclude, for example, that there is little evidence that dreams have disguised meaning or that their general purpose is to satisfy forbidden, unconscious needs and conflicts (Domhoff, 1999; Fisher & Greenberg, 1996). Dream analysis has been criticized as highly subjective: The same dream can be interpreted differently to fit the particular analyst's point of view.

Activation-synthesis theory. Is it possible that dreams serve no special purpose? In 1977, J. Allan Hobson and Robert McCarley proposed a physiological theory of dreaming. When we are awake, neural circuits in our brain are activated by sensory input: sights, sounds, tastes, and so on. The cerebral cortex interprets these patterns of neural activation, producing meaningful perceptions. According to the **activation-synthesis theory**, during REM sleep the brain stem bombards our higher brain centres with random neural activity (the *activation* component). Because we are asleep, this neural activity does not match any external sensory events, but our cerebral cortex continues to perform its job of interpretation. It does this by creating a dream that provides the "best fit" to the particular pattern of activation that exists at any particular moment (the *synthesis* component). This accounts for the bizarreness of dreams: The brain is trying to "make sense" out of *random* neural activity. Our memories and experiences can influence the stories that our brain develops, and, therefore, dream content may reflect themes pertaining to our lives. In this limited sense, dreams can have meaning (Hobson, 1988; McCarley, 1998). However, dreaming does not serve any particular *function*—it is merely *a byproduct of REM neural activity*.

Critics claim that the activation-synthesis theory overestimates the bizarreness of dreams and ignores the fact that dreaming and mental imagery occurs during non-REM sleep (Solms, 2002). Nevertheless, this theory helped to revolutionize dream research by calling attention to a physiological basis for dreaming (Domhoff, 2005; Hobson et al., 2000).

Cognitive approaches. According to **problem-solving dream models**, dreams can help us find creative solutions to our problems and conflicts because they are not constrained by reality (Cartwright et al., 1977). Based on research with men and women undergoing divorce, Rosalind Cartwright (1991, p. 3) notes that those who dream ". . . with strong feelings, and

Focus on Neuroscience

DREAMS AND DAYDREAMS

We have all had the experience of our mind wandering while we are a passenger during a long, quiet trip, or listening to a speaker going on in a monotone voice about something that does not engage us. Thoughts in these situations may have included memories, future planning, reflection, or even emotional content and sensory information (have you ever had a song running in your head during a boring lecture?). You are awake, but your mind wanders and you even engage in daydreaming. As we discuss in detail in this chapter, dreams represent mental activity during sleep, typically REM sleep, also characterized by sensorimotor imagery and emotions, memories, and future planning. This agreement is more than coincidental. Researchers have noted similarities between reports of the subjective experiences that occur during daydreams and during dreams, and have asked whether the similarities are more than coincidental (Fox et al., 2013).

The first question is what do we know about brain activity during daydreams? Research that includes the measurement of neural activity during goal directed tasks will typically include rest periods. For example, if you are a participant in a study measuring activity in specific brain areas when you process and recognize images projected on a screen in front of you, viewing these images will be interspersed with periods of rest. The rest period is used to collect baseline data; in this example, what is brain activity when you are not processing and recognizing images. This baseline data is important to be able to detect where activity changes when you are engaged in the target task. During this quiet restful state, researchers identified what they called the "default mode network" (Raichle et al., 2001). There is a set of eight brain regions that are consistently *more* active during these "rest" breaks than when participants were actively engaged in a wide range of behaviours. The parts of the cortex associated with the default mode network include two areas within the prefrontal cortex, posterior cingulate cortex, the entorhinal cortex and parahippocampus within the temporal cortex, and the hippocampus. This network was given this name because it was suggested that its activity occurred as the "default," as the pattern of activity when we are doing nothing. But were these participants really doing nothing? When we are awake and alert but not engaged in any particular task, we rarely do nothing—mental activity does not stop. If I ask you to stop reading and just sit there for a few minutes, you are not really going to do nothing. You may wonder why I am asking you to stop reading, reflect on your day, picture a memorable image from the news, think about your favourite song, plan dinner, or remember a funny scene from *The Big Bang Theory* and smile. When asked to do nothing, an awake and otherwise alert individual will have his or her mind wander

and may daydream. It was suggested that that activity in default mode network, rather than reflecting an absence of mental activity, may actually represent the pattern of neural activity that occurs when we let our minds wander and daydream (Fox et al., 2013).

From the very beginning of modern research on sleep, researchers have been interested in what brain areas are active during different stages of sleep, and much attention has centred on REM sleep, with its association with dreaming sleep. It is important to note that REM sleep and dreams represent different phenomenon. Dreams are the sight-, sound-, movement-containing subjective experiences that occur while we sleep. The only way to know if someone is dreaming is to wake that person and ask what he or she was experiencing. REM sleep is a stage of the sleep cycle characterized by a specific pattern of brain activity, rapid eye movements, and a number of physiological changes. If someone is woken from REM sleep, more than 80 percent will report that they were dreaming (Domhoff, 2011). That is, REM sleep refers to a specific measureable stage of the sleep cycle; dreaming refers to the subjective mental experience. Researchers can say that they recorded brain activity during REM sleep and the assumption is that the individual was likely experiencing a dream during that time but we can never be certain

Fox and colleagues performed a meta-analysis of studies that used either PET or fMRI to measure brain activity during REM sleep (Fox et al., 2013). They found eight cortical areas that consistently increased activity during REM sleep. The areas activated includes those that involved in high-level visual processing and areas associated with memory, self-referential thought, and affective decisions. The known functions of these areas are consistent with the subjective experience of dreams. Interestingly, of these eight areas, seven are also components of the default mode network. The most complete overlap was within two regions of the medial prefrontal cortex and with medial temporal lobe structures associated with memory (entorhinal cortex, hippocampus). The overlap between brain areas active during REM sleep and the default mode network is specific to REM sleep. Changes in brain activity during other non-REM sleep stages occur in brain areas outside of default mode network. That is, the meta-analysis found that the cortical areas associated with REM sleep included many of the areas associated with the default mode network, a network also associated with daydreaming.

The idea that daydreams and nocturnal dreams are related has a long history. More than a century ago Sigmund Freud suggested that they shared the same underlying processes (Freud, 1908). It has been argued that dreams represent a more intense form of the mental activity

continued

that is also present in daydreams. Based on an analysis of the subjective experience of both dreams and of daydreams and based on an analysis brain areas that are active during both dreams and daydreams, Fox et al. (2013) and others (e.g., Domhoff, 2011) have argued that the evidence supports the contention that dreams represent a longer, immersive, more intense form of the same pattern of neural activity that also occurs during daydreams.

Fox proposed a model (Figure 6.18) that places waking, goal-directed thought, daydreams and dreams along a continuum. Their theory is that as activity in the default mode increases and activity in brain areas linked to executive function decrease, we move along this continuum and mental activity shifts from deliberate goal-directed thinking to mental activity characterized by the sensory laden, sometimes bizarre experience of our dreams. Similarities between the experience of daydreams and nocturnal dreams may be more than coincidental, and represent a single underlying continuum that reflects the balance of activity between two different brain networks.

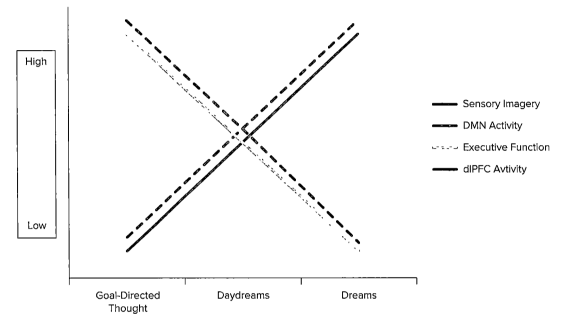

FIGURE 6.18 A model that places subjective mental experience from deliberate goal-directed thought to the types of mental activity that occurs during dreaming sleep along a continuum. Fox et al. (2013) proposed that as activity in the default mode network (DMN) increases, there is a corresponding increase in the types of mental activity that occurs during dreams such as sensory imagery. There is a corresponding decrease in executive function and activity in brain areas associated with executive function. The brain areas most strongly associated with executive function are the dorsolateral prefrontal cortex (dlPFC) and the anterior cingulate cortex.

Source: Fox, Kieran C. R., Savannah Nijeboer, Elizaveta Solomonova, G. W. Domhoff, and Kalina Christoff. 2013. "Dreaming as mind wandering: Evidence from functional neuroimaging and first-person content reports." *Frontiers in Human Neuroscience*, 7:412. Figure 3.

22. Describe the main assumption of cognitive-process dream theory. What evidence supports it?

who incorporate the stressor directly into their dreams, appear to 'work through' their depression more successfully than those who do not." But critics point out that, just because a problem shows up in a dream, this does not mean that the dream involved an attempt to solve it. We also may think about our dreams after awakening and obtain new insight, but this also is not the same as solving problems *while* dreaming (Squire & Domhoff, 1998).

Cognitive-process dream theories focus on the *process* of how we dream (Antrobus, 1991; Foulkes, 1982). Based on the modular model of consciousness, these theories propose that dreaming and waking thought are produced by the same mental systems in the brain. Consider that when three- and four-year-old children are awakened from REM sleep, they rarely report dreams, whereas eight- and nine-year-olds display some features of adult dreaming (Foulkes, 1982). Why should this be? According to David Foulkes (1999), it is because dreaming requires imagery skills and other cognitive abilities that young children have not yet developed sufficiently in waking life. As children's mental abilities develop with age, so does their ability to dream.

Research indicates far greater similarity between dreaming and waking mental activity than was traditionally believed

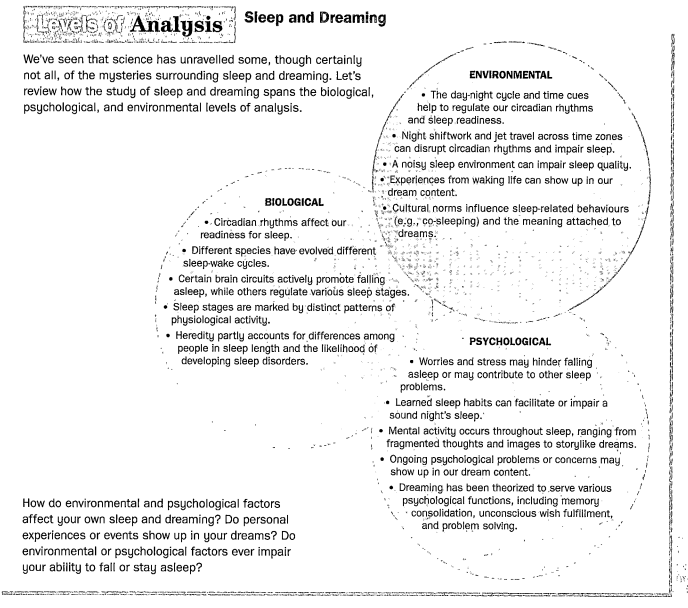

Levels of Analysis: Sleep and Dreaming

We've seen that science has unravelled some, though certainly not all, of the mysteries surrounding sleep and dreaming. Let's review how the study of sleep and dreaming spans the biological, psychological, and environmental levels of analysis.

ENVIRONMENTAL
- The day-night cycle and time cues help to regulate our circadian rhythms and sleep readiness.
- Night shiftwork and jet travel across time zones can disrupt circadian rhythms and impair sleep.
- A noisy sleep environment can impair sleep quality.
- Experiences from waking life can show up in our dream content.
- Cultural norms influence sleep-related behaviours (e.g., co-sleeping) and the meaning attached to dreams.

BIOLOGICAL
- Circadian rhythms affect our readiness for sleep.
- Different species have evolved different sleep-wake cycles.
- Certain brain circuits actively promote falling asleep, while others regulate various sleep stages.
- Sleep stages are marked by distinct patterns of physiological activity.
- Heredity partly accounts for differences among people in sleep length and the likelihood of developing sleep disorders.

PSYCHOLOGICAL
- Worries and stress may hinder falling asleep or may contribute to other sleep problems.
- Learned sleep habits can facilitate or impair a sound night's sleep.
- Mental activity occurs throughout sleep, ranging from fragmented thoughts and images to storylike dreams.
- Ongoing psychological problems or concerns may show up in our dream content.
- Dreaming has been theorized to serve various psychological functions, including memory consolidation, unconscious wish fulfillment, and problem solving.

How do environmental and psychological factors affect your own sleep and dreaming? Do personal experiences or events show up in your dreams? Do environmental or psychological factors ever impair your ability to fall or stay asleep?

FIGURE 6.19

(Domhoff, 1999). Consider that one reason many dreams appear bizarre is that their content shifts rapidly (Antrobus, 1991): "I was dreaming about an exam *and all of a sudden,* the next thing I knew, I was in Hawaii on the beach." (Don't we wish.) Yet if you reflect on the contents of your waking thoughts—your stream of consciousness— you will realize that they also shift suddenly. In fact, about half of REM dream reports involve rapid content shifts. But when people are awake and placed in the same environmental conditions as sleepers (a dark, quiet room), about 90 percent of their reports involve rapid content shifts (Antrobus, 1991).

Thus, rapid shifting of attention is a *process* common to dreaming and waking mental activity.

Toward Integration. Although there currently is no agreed-upon model of dreaming, some theorists have begun to integrate concepts from cognitive, biological, and modern psychodynamic perspectives. For example, John Antrobus (1991) has developed a model to explain how our sleeping brain creates dreams. As Figure 6.20 shows, the model incorporates findings on sleep physiology with the cognitive principle of modular consciousness.

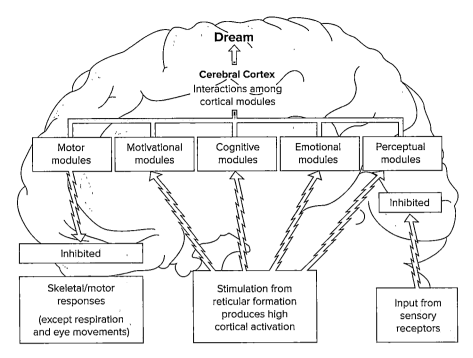

FIGURE 6.20 Antrobus's (1991) theory proposes that during REM sleep, the reticular formation stimulates various modules in the cortex. These modules interact, as they do during waking mental activity. The perceptual modules produce images that then are interpreted by the cognitive modules. Emotional modules may overlay an "emotional theme" to the dream, which stimulates the perceptual modules to produce additional images consistent with the theme. Because external sensory input is restricted, the brain attempts to provide the "best fit" interpretations of these internally generated images. Motor modules are active, but their output is blocked by REM muscular paralysis. This theory places greater emphasis than activation-synthesis theory on interactions between brain modules and proposes other mechanisms for non-REM dreams.

Though in need of more testing, these integrative models may signal the future of dream theorizing. As we described earlier, evidence is growing rapidly that unconscious cognitive, emotional, and motivational processes influence our waking life (Hobson, 2007). These models extend this view to our sleeping mental life.

Review

- EEG measurements of brain activity indicate five main stages of sleep. Stages 1 and 2 are lighter sleep, and stages 3 and 4 are deeper, slow-wave sleep. High physiological arousal and periods of rapid eye movements characterize the fifth stage, REM sleep. Several brain regions, including the brain stem, regulate sleep.

- The amount we sleep nightly changes as we age. Genetic, psychological, and environmental factors affect our sleep patterns and sleep length.

- Sleep deprivation negatively affects mood, mental performance, and physical performance. The restoration model proposes that we sleep to recover from accumulated physical and mental fatigue. Evolutionary/circadian models state that species evolved unique waking-sleeping cycles that maximized their chances of survival.

- Insomnia is the most common sleep disorder, but less common disorders such as narcolepsy and REM-sleep behaviour disorder can have extremely serious consequences. Sleepwalking typically occurs during slow-wave sleep, whereas nightmares occur most often during REM sleep. Night terrors create a near-panic state of arousal, typically occur in slow-wave sleep, and are most common among children.

- Dreams occur throughout sleep but are most common during REM periods. Unpleasant dreams are common, and there are gender differences in dream content. Our cultural background, current concerns, and recent events influence what we dream about.

- Freud proposed that dreams fulfill unconscious wishes that show up in disguised form within our dreams. Activation-synthesis theory regards dreaming as the brain's attempt to "fit" a story to random neural activity. Cognitive-process theories emphasize that dreaming and waking thought are produced by the same mental systems.

DRUGS AND ALTERED CONSCIOUSNESS

Like sleep and dreaming, drug-induced alterations in consciousness have mystified humans for ages. Three millennia ago the Aztecs considered hallucinogenic mushrooms to be a sacred substance for communicating with the spirit world (Diaz, 1997). Ancient peoples also attributed "magical" healing powers to drugs and used them recreationally for their mind-altering effects. Today, drugs are a cornerstone of medical practice and, as Figure 6.21 shows, psychoactive drugs are a pervasive part of social life. They alter consciousness by modifying brain chemistry, but drug effects also are influenced by psychological, environmental, and cultural factors (Kassel et al., 2010).

Drugs and the Brain

Drugs enter the bloodstream and are carried throughout the brain by small blood vessels, called *capillaries*. As we saw in Chapter 3, these capillaries contain a blood-brain barrier, a special lining of tightly packed cells that lets vital nutrients pass through so that neurons can function. The blood-brain barrier screens out many foreign substances, but some, including a variety of drugs, manage to pass through. Once inside, they alter consciousness by facilitating or inhibiting synaptic transmission (Heckers & Konradi, 2000; Julien, 2008).

Recall from Chapter 3 that synaptic transmission involves several basic steps. First, neurotransmitters are synthesized inside the presynaptic (sending) neuron and stored in vesicles. Next, neurotransmitters are released into the synapse, where they bind with and stimulate receptor sites on the postsynaptic (receiving) neuron. Finally, neurotransmitter molecules are deactivated by enzymes or reuptake. Psychoactive drugs act by influencing one or more of these steps in synaptic transmission.

How Drugs Facilitate Synaptic Transmission

An *agonist* is a drug that increases the activity of a neurotransmitter. Figure 6.22 shows that an agonist may enhance the production, storage, or release of a neurotransmitter; activate the postsynaptic receptor (or make it easier for the neurotransmitter to stimulate their receptors); or prevent the neurotransmitter from being deactivated. Consider two examples. Opiates (such as morphine, codeine, or fentanyl) are effective pain relievers. Opiates have this action by binding to and activating receptors that normally receive endorphins, a neurotransmitter that plays a major role in pain relief. An example of a psychoactive drug that acts in different ways is an amphetamine. Amphetamines are powerful stimulants, and they have this effect by amplifying the actions of the neurotransmitters dopamine and norepinephrine. Amphetamines

23. What is the difference between an agonist and an antagonist?

24. How do drugs increase and decrease synaptic transmission?

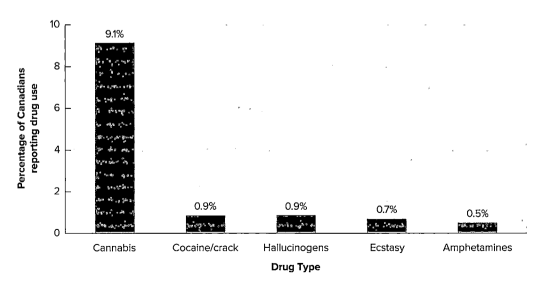

FIGURE 6.21 Percentage of Canadians 15 years of age and older who used illicit drugs during the past year, 2011. For comparison, 78 percent of Canadians 15 years of age and older reported using alcohol during the past 12 months.

Source: Data from the *Canadian Alcohol and Drug Use Monitoring Survey (CADUMS)—2011.* Health Canada, 2012. Reproduced with permission from the Minister of Health, 2016.

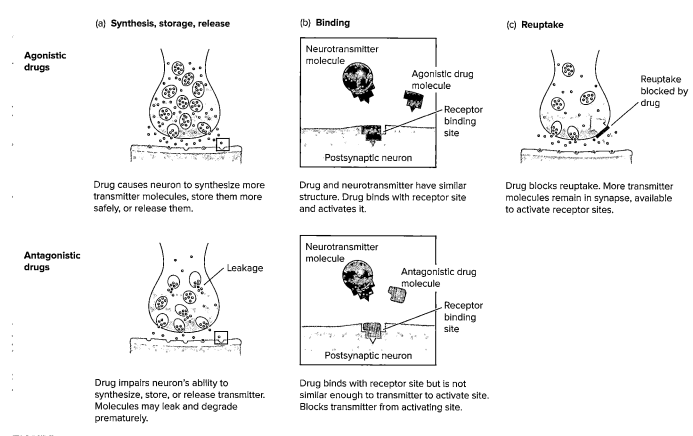

(a) **Synthesis, storage, release**

Agonistic drugs

Drug causes neuron to synthesize more transmitter molecules, store them more safely, or release them.

Antagonistic drugs

Leakage

Drug impairs neuron's ability to synthesize, store, or release transmitter. Molecules may leak and degrade prematurely.

(b) **Binding**

Neurotransmitter molecule

Agonistic drug molecule

Receptor binding site

Postsynaptic neuron

Drug and neurotransmitter have similar structure. Drug binds with receptor site and activates it.

Neurotransmitter molecule

Antagonistic drug molecule

Receptor binding site

Postsynaptic neuron

Drug binds with receptor site but is not similar enough to transmitter to activate site. Blocks transmitter from activating site.

(c) **Reuptake**

Reuptake blocked by drug

Drug blocks reuptake. More transmitter molecules remain in synapse, available to activate receptor sites.

FIGURE 6.22 (a) Agonists cause neurons to synthesize more neurotransmitter molecules, store them more safely, or release them. In contrast, antagonists impair neurons' ability to synthesize, store, or release neurotransmitters. (b) Agonists and neurotransmitters have similar molecular structure. The drug binds with the receptor site and activates it. In contrast, the antagonist binds with the receptor site but is not similar enough to the neurotransmitter to activate the site. The antagonist's placement prevents the real neurotransmitter from binding with and activating the site. (c) The agonist blocks reuptake of the neurotransmitter into the presynaptic neuron. More neurotransmitter molecules remain in the synapse and are available to activate the postsynaptic neuron.

cause neurons to release dopamine and norepinephrine, even if the neurons are not firing. Amphetamines also block the reuptake of these neurotransmitters, which allows dopamine and norepinephrine to remain in the synapse and to keep stimulating the postsynaptic neuron (Julien, 2008).

How Drugs Inhibit Synaptic Transmission

A drug that inhibits or decreases the actions of a neurotransmitter is called an *antagonist*. As shown in Figure 6.22, an antagonist may reduce the synthesis, storage, or release of a neurotransmitter, or prevent a neurotransmitter from binding to its receptors on the postsynaptic neuron. Many antagonists act on the postsynaptic receptors. For example, the drugs that began the so-called "psychiatric revolution" of the mid-1950s acted in this way. These drugs, the antipsychotics, are still used to treat schizophrenia, one of the most devastating forms of psychosis. (We will discuss schizophrenia in detail later in this book.) Antipsychotics bind to

dopamine receptors, but once bound they have no effect on the postsynaptic neuron. Instead, by occupying the receptor, they prevent the neurotransmitter dopamine from binding and acting on the postsynaptic neuron. That is, with schizophrenia there is too much dopamine activity, and if dopamine receptors are blocked by an antipsychotic, dopamine activity decreases toward normal levels, and many of the symptoms of schizophrenia improve.

Tolerance and Withdrawal

When a drug is used repeatedly, the intensity of effects produced by the same dosage level may decrease over time. This decreasing responsivity to a drug is called **tolerance.** As tolerance develops, the person must take increasingly larger doses to achieve the same physical and psychological effects. Tolerance stems from the body's attempt to maintain a state of optimal physiological balance, called *homeostasis.* If a drug changes bodily functioning in a certain

25. What is the relation among tolerance, compensatory responses, and withdrawal?

way, say by increasing heart rate, the brain will try to adjust for this imbalance by producing **compensatory responses,** which are reactions opposite to that of the drug (e.g., reactions that decrease heart rate). In effect, compensatory responses represent the body's way of fighting the invasion of drugs.

What happens when drug tolerance develops and the person suddenly stops using the drug? The body's compensatory responses may continue and, no longer balanced out by the drug's effects, the person may experience strong reactions opposite to those produced by the drug. This occurrence of compensatory responses after discontinued drug use is known as **withdrawal** (Diaz, 1997). For example, in the absence of alcohol's sedating and relaxing effects, the chronic drinker may experience increased heart rate, anxiety, and hypertension.

Learning, Drug Tolerance, and Overdose

Experiments by Shepard Siegel of McMaster University have shown that tolerance for various drugs partly depends on the familiarity of the drug setting (Larson & Siegel, 1998; Siegel, 1984). Figure 6.23 illustrates how environmental stimuli associated with drug use begin to elicit compensatory responses through a learning process called *classical conditioning.* As drug use continues, the physical setting triggers progressively stronger compensatory responses, increasing the user's tolerance. This

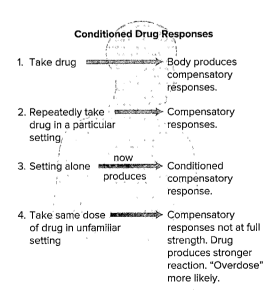

Conditioned Drug Responses

1. Take drug ⟶ Body produces compensatory responses.

2. Repeatedly take drug in a particular setting ⟶ Compensatory responses.

3. Setting alone now produces ⟶ Conditioned compensatory response.

4. Take same dose of drug in unfamiliar setting ⟶ Compensatory responses not at full strength. Drug produces stronger reaction. "Overdose" more likely.

FIGURE 6.23 Environmental stimuli that are repeatedly paired with the use of a drug can acquire the ability to trigger compensatory responses on their own.

helps to explain why addicts often experience increased cravings when they enter a setting associated with drug use. The environmental stimuli trigger compensatory responses, which, without drugs to mask their effect, cause the user to feel withdrawal symptoms (Bradizza & Stasiewkz, 2009).

There is a hidden danger in this process, particularly for experienced drug users. Compensatory responses serve a protective function by physiologically countering part of the drug's effects. If a user takes his or her usual high dose in a familiar environment, the body's compensatory responses will be at full strength—a combination of compensatory reactions directly to the drug and also to the conditioned environmental stimuli. But in an *unfamiliar* environment, the conditioned compensatory responses are weaker, and the drug has a stronger physiological net effect than usual.

Siegel (1984) interviewed heroin addicts who experienced near-fatal overdoses. He found that in most cases they *had not* taken a dose larger than their customary one. However, in 70 percent of the cases they *had* injected themselves in unfamiliar environments. Siegel concluded that the addicts were not protected by their usual compensatory responses, resulting in an "overdose" reaction.

Misconceptions about Drug Addiction and Dependence

Drug addiction, which is formally called **substance dependence,** represents a maladaptive pattern of substance use that causes a person significant distress or substantially impairs that person's life. Substance dependence is diagnosed as occurring with *physiological dependence* if drug tolerance or withdrawal symptoms have developed. You probably have heard the term *psychological dependence* used to describe situations in which people strongly crave a drug because of its pleasurable effects, even though they are not physiologically dependent. However, this is not a diagnostic term, and many drug experts feel it is misleading. They note that such cravings do have a physical basis because they are rooted in patterns of brain activity (Diaz, 1997).

Several misconceptions surround the issue of substance dependence:

- *Drug tolerance always leads to significant withdrawal.* It often does, but not always. Tolerance develops to marijuana and hallucinogens, such as LSD, yet at typical doses withdrawal symptoms are mild (O'Brien, 1997).

26. Describe some myths about drug dependence.

- *Physiological dependence is the major cause of drug addiction.* The image of a shaking alcoholic or "heroin junkie" desperately searching for a drink or a "fix" contributes to the perception that the motivation to avoid or end withdrawal symptoms is the primary cause of addiction. Certainly, the withdrawal symptoms contribute to drug dependence. But consider these points:

  - People become highly dependent on some drugs, such as cocaine, that produce only mild withdrawal (Kampmann et al., 2002). The pleasurable effects of these drugs—often produced by boosting dopamine activity—play a powerful role in drug dependence (Everitt et al., 1999).

  - Many drug users who quit and make it through withdrawal eventually start using again, even though they areno longer physiologically dependent.

  - Drug dependence is influenced by many factors beyond a drug's chemical effects, including genetic predisposition, personality traits, religious beliefs, peer influence, and cultural norms (Ehlers et al., 2010).

27. Explain how alcohol affects the brain.

Depressants

Depressants decrease nervous system activity. In moderate doses, they reduce feelings of tension and anxiety, and produce a state of relaxed euphoria. In extremely high doses, depressants can slow down vital life processes to the point of death.

Alcohol

Alcohol is the most widely used recreational drug in numerous countries. According to a recent national survey, 78 percent of Canadians ages 15 and over said they drank in the past year (Health Canada, 2012), and 17.4 percent of Canadians meet the criteria of being heavy drinkers (Statistics Canada, 2012). Canadians spent $20.9 billion on alcohol in 2012 (Statistics Canada, 2013). Tolerance to alcohol develops gradually but powerfully and leads to physiological dependence and a dangerous withdrawal syndrome. Alcohol withdrawal is one of the very few withdrawal syndromes that carry a risk of death.

As we discussed in Chapter 3, alcohol increases the activity of GABA, the main inhibitory neurotransmitter in the brain (Levinthal, 2010). By increasing the action of an *inhibitory* neurotransmitter, alcohol decreases brain activity. Alcohol also decreases the activity of glutamate, a major *excitatory* neurotransmitter, further decreasing brain activity (Kumar et al., 2009; Levinthal, 2010). Why then do many people report getting a "high" from alcohol and initially seem livelier when drinking? The answer is that the neural slow-down first depresses the action of inhibitory control centres in the cerebral cortex, so the person literally becomes "less inhibited" and feels euphoric. At higher doses, the brain's control centres become increasingly disrupted, thinking and physical coordination become disorganized, and fatigue and psychological depression may occur (Table 6.1).

Thus, alcohol's subjective effects seem to have an initial "upper" phase from the release of inhibitions, followed by a "downer" phase as brain centres become increasingly depressed (Marlatt, 1987). But both phases result from alcohol's action as a nervous system *depressant.* Unfortunately, some people respond to the "downer" phase by drinking even more alcohol in the hope that it will make them feel "high" again, a self-defeating strategy if ever there was one.

TABLE 6.1 Behavioural Effects of Alcohol

BAL	Hours to Leave Body	Behavioural Effects
0.03	1	Decreased alertness, impaired reaction time in some people
0.05	2	Decreased alertness, impaired judgment and reaction time, feeling of relaxation, release of inhibitions
0.10	4	Severely impaired reaction time, motor function, and judgment; less caution
0.15	10	Gross intoxication; impairments worsen
0.25	?	Extreme sensory and motor impairment, staggering
0.30	?	Stuporous but conscious, cannot comprehend immediate environment
0.40	?	Lethal in over 50 percent of cases

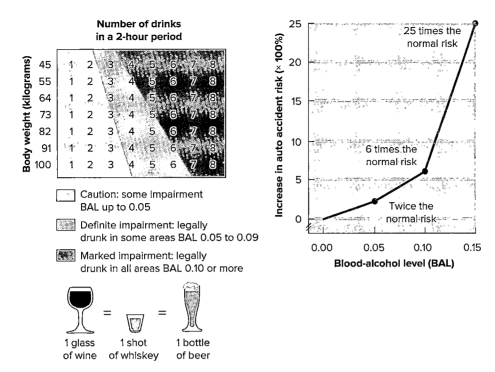

FIGURE 6.24 Relation between blood-alcohol level and risk of having an auto accident. At 0.08 to 0.10, the legal definition of intoxication in most American states and Canadian provinces, the risk is six times greater than at 0.00, and the risk climbs to 25 times higher at a BAL of 0.15.

Source: Based on National Safety Council, (1992). *Blood alcohol level and risk of having an automobile accident.* Washington, DC: Author.

The *blood-alcohol level (BAL)* is a measure of alcohol concentration in the body. Elevated BAL is linked to risky and harmful behaviours, such as having unprotected sex (Leigh & Stall, 1993). About 40 percent of American and Canadian traffic accident deaths involve alcohol (National Highway Traffic Safety Administration, 2006). As the BAL increases, reaction time, eye-hand coordination, and decision making are impaired (Figure 6.24).

Why do intoxicated people often act in risky ways that they wouldn't when sober? It is not simply a matter of lowered inhibitions; alcohol also reduces cognitive capacity. Intoxicated people display what Claude Steele and Robert Josephs (1990) termed **alcohol myopia,** a "shortsightedness" in thinking caused by the inability to pay attention to as much information as sober people (Cue et al., 2007). Drinkers start to concentrate only on those aspects of the situation (called *cues*) that stand out. As a result, in the absence of strong cautionary cues (such as warnings) to inhibit risky behaviour, drinkers do not think about the long-term consequences of their actions as carefully as when they are sober (MacDonald et al., 2000). The *Research Foundations* feature illustrates this effect.

Barbiturates and Tranquilizers

Physicians frequently prescribe barbiturates ("sleeping pills") and tranquilizers (anti-anxiety drugs, such as Valium) as sedatives and relaxants. Like alcohol, the vast majority of these drugs depress the nervous system by increasing the activity of the inhibitory neurotransmitter GABA (Grasshoff et al., 2008).

Barbiturates and tranquilizers are widely overused and powerful tolerance and physiological dependence can occur. As tolerance builds, addicts may take as many as 50 sleeping pills a day. At high doses, barbiturates trigger initial excitation, followed by slurred speech, loss of coordination, depression, and severe memory impairment. Overdoses, particularly when taken with alcohol, may cause unconsciousness, coma, and death. Sudden withdrawal after heavy use can cause death, so several months of gradual withdrawal may be needed before addicts lose their physiological dependence. Users often don't recognize that they have become dependent until they try to stop and experience serious withdrawal symptoms, such as anxiety, insomnia, and possibly seizures (Levinthal, 2010).

28. How does being intoxicated affect decisions about drinking and driving?

Research Foundations

DRINKING AND DRIVING: DECISION MAKING IN ALTERED STATES

Introduction

Most people have very negative attitudes about drunk driving and say they would not do it. They realize that the cons (e.g., risk of accident, injury, death, and police arrest) far outweigh the pros (e.g., avoiding cab fare, not leaving one's car behind). Why then do so many people decide to drive after they become intoxicated?

Tara MacDonald and her colleagues at the University of Waterloo examined how alcohol myopia affects decisions about drinking and driving. The authors reasoned that when intoxicated people decide whether or not to drive, they may focus on the pros or the cons, but do not have the capacity to focus on both. If some aspect of the situation that favours driving (a "facilitating cue") is made salient and captures the intoxicated person's attention (e.g., "It will only be for a short distance"), she or he will latch on to it and fail to consider the cons. But in general situations that do not contain facilitating cues, intoxicated people's feelings about driving should remain as negative as when they were sober.

Based on alcohol myopia principles, the authors made two predictions. First, intoxicated and sober people will have *equally* negative *general* attitudes and intentions toward drinking and driving. Second, intoxicated people will have less negative attitudes and greater intentions to drive than sober people in situations in which a facilitating cue or special circumstance is made salient.

Method

Laboratory Experiment

Fifty-seven male introductory psychology students, all regular drinkers who owned cars, participated. They were randomly assigned to either the sober condition, in which they received no alcohol, or the alcohol condition, in which they received three alcoholic drinks within an hour (the average BAL was 0.074 percent, just below the 0.08 percent legal driving limit in Ontario).

Participants then completed a drinking and driving questionnaire. Some items asked about *general* attitudes and intentions (e.g., "I will drink and drive the next time that I am out at a party or bar with friends"). Other items contained a *facilitating cue:* a special circumstance that suggested a possible reason for drinking and driving ("If I only had a short distance to drive home . . . [or] If my friends tried to persuade me to drink and drive . . . I would drive

while intoxicated"). Participants rated each item on a nine-point scale (1 = strongly disagree; 9 = strongly agree).

Party/Bar Diary Study

Fifty-one male and female university students recorded a telephone diary while at a party or a bar where they were going to drink alcohol. Some were randomly assigned to record the diary when they first arrived, and others recorded it just before they left. Based on participants' descriptions of how much alcohol they had consumed, the researchers estimated their BAL and identified two groups: sober participants (average BAL = 0.01), and intoxicated participants (average BAL = 0.11).

Results

The findings from both studies supported the predictions. Sober participants and intoxicated participants both expressed negative general attitudes about drinking and driving, and indicated they would not drive when intoxicated. But when the questions presented a facilitating cue, intoxicated participants expressed more favourable attitudes and a greater intention to drive than sober participants (Figure 6.25).

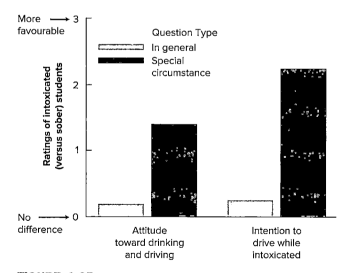

FIGURE 6.25 When general attitudes and intentions toward drinking and driving are measured, intoxicated and sober participants have similarly negative reactions. But when situations involving special circumstances (i.e., facilitating cues) are presented, intoxicated participants have less negative attitudes and intentions about drinking and driving than do sober participants.

Source: From Tara K. MacDonald, Mark P. Zanna, & Geoffrey T. Fong, (1995). Decision making in altered states: Effects of alcohol on attitudes toward drinking and driving. *Journal of Personality and Social Psychology, 68,* 973–985.

continued

Discussion

This study illustrates nicely how a person's physiological state (sober versus intoxicated) and an environmental factor (general situation versus special circumstance) interact to influence psychological functioning (attitudes and decision making). However, before accepting the researchers' claim that alcohol myopia caused the changes in intoxicated participants' responses, we need to think critically about other possible explanations for the results. The authors anticipated two other reasons why people might drive when drunk. First, perhaps drinkers do not realize how intoxicated they are. Second, perhaps intoxicated people overestimate their driving ability, a belief called *drunken invincibility*.

The authors tested and ruled out these explanations. Intoxicated participants believed they were *more* intoxicated than they actually were and estimated that they would drive *more poorly* than the average person. The authors also conducted a placebo control experiment in which some participants were convincingly misled to believe they were intoxicated. Results showed that the alcohol myopia effect occurred only for participants who truly had consumed alcohol and was not caused by participants' expectations.

The party/bar study examined decision making in a real-life but uncontrolled drinking situation, and therefore we cannot draw clear causal conclusions from it. The laboratory experiment examined behaviour in an artificial but controlled setting, permitting clearer causal conclusions. Because the authors conducted both types of research and obtained consistent findings, we can be more confident in their conclusions and the external validity (generalizability) of the findings.

Design

Question: If sober people hold negative attitudes toward drinking and driving, then why after becoming intoxicated do they decide to drive? Does focusing on "special circumstances" play a role?

Type of Study: *Experimental*

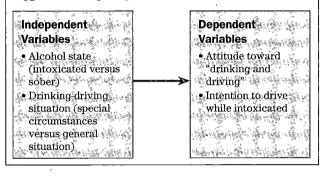

Independent Variables	Dependent Variables
• Alcohol state (intoxicated versus sober) • Drinking-driving situation (special circumstances versus general situation)	• Attitude toward "drinking and driving" • Intention to drive while intoxicated

Stimulants

Stimulants increase neural firing and arouse the nervous system. They increase blood pressure, respiration, heart rate, and overall alertness. They also can boost mood, produce euphoria, and heighten irritability.

Amphetamines

Amphetamines—popularly known as speed, uppers, and bennies—are powerful stimulants. They are prescribed to reduce appetite and fatigue, to decrease the need for sleep, and, sometimes, to reduce depression. Unfortunately, they are widely overused to boost energy and mood (Ghodse, 2007).

Amphetamines increase dopamine and norepinephrine activity. Tolerance develops and many heavy users start injecting large quantities, producing a sudden surge of energy and a rush of intense pleasure. With frequent injections, they may remain awake continuously for as long as a week, their bodily systems racing at breakneck speed. Injecting amphetamines greatly increases blood pressure and can lead to heart failure and cerebral hemorrhage (stroke); repeated high doses may cause brain damage (Ksir et al., 2008).

In schizophrenia, hallucinations and delusions are associated with excess dopamine activity. Imagine what happens when the brain's dopamine activity is boosted beyond normal levels by continuous or frequent amphetamine use: It causes schizophrenia-like hallucinations and paranoid delusions, a reaction called **amphetamine psychosis** (Medhus et al., 2015).

There is an inevitable "crash" when heavy users stop taking amphetamines. They may sleep for one or two days, waking up depressed, exhausted, and irritable. This crash occurs because neurons' norepinephrine and dopamine supplies have become depleted. Amphetamines tax the body heavily, and addicts have a short life expectancy.

One form of amphetamine is crystal methamphetamine, commonly referred to as *crystal meth*. Crystal methamphetamine comes in clear, slightly white or blue-white crystals, hence the street names of "ice," "crystal," and "glass." Crystal methamphetamine is inhaled or smoked and is a particularly potent form of amphetamine. Abuse of crystal methamphetamine has become widespread because of its long-lasting effects, its potency, and because it is relatively

29. How do stimulants affect brain functioning? Why does heavy use lead to a "crash"?

easy to make from commonly available ingredients. Crystal methamphetamine causes irritability, insomnia, loss of REM sleep, hyperactivity, confusion, hallucinations, anxiety, paranoia, and increased aggression. It has a powerful impact on the cardiovascular system, increases heart rate and blood pressure, and greatly increases the risk of stroke and heart attack. In high doses, methamphetamine also leads to hypothermia (a drop in core body temperature) and convulsions and can be fatal. Methamphetamine users often show pronounced tooth decay and lose their teeth abnormally quickly, a condition known as *meth mouth*.

Another drug that has been popular in recent years belongs to this class. MDMA (3, 4-methylenedioxymethamphetamine), commonly called **ecstasy,** is a derivative of amphetamine. Ecstasy acts on several neurotransmitters, including dopamine, but primarily alters serotonin functioning by causing the release of serotonin and blocking its reuptake (Parrott, 2002). Although MDMA was once considered to be a safe drug for enhancing awareness of emotions and sensations (Siegel, 1986), important adverse effects have become apparent. MDMA can cause cognitive deficits, sleep disturbances, sexual dysfunction, and impaired immune responses (Parrott, 2006). After the drug wears off, users often feel sluggish and depressed—a rebound effect partly due to depletion of serotonin within the brain (Travers & Lyvers, 2005). As shown in Figure 6.26, depletion of brain serotonin associated with long-term MDMA use, can persist long after drug use is stopped.

Cocaine

Cocaine is a powder derived from the coca plant, which grows mainly in western South America. Usually inhaled or injected, it produces excitation, a sense of increased muscular strength, and euphoria. Like amphetamines, cocaine increases the activity of norepinephrine and dopamine, but it does so in only one major way: It blocks their reuptake.

Cocaine was once widely used as a local anaesthetic in eye, nose, and throat surgery. Novocaine, a synthetic form of cocaine, is still used in dentistry as an anaesthetic. Because of its stimulating effects, cocaine found its way into health potions and tonics sold to the public to enhance health and emotional well-being. In 1885, John Pemberton mixed cocaine with the kola nut and syrup and developed a soda fountain drink that has become one of the icons of American beverages (Figure 6.27).

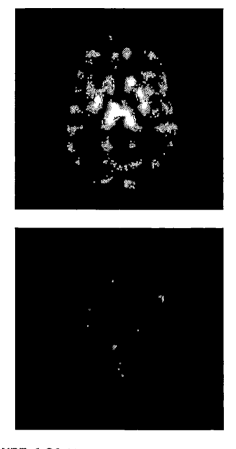

FIGURE 6.26 The top PET-scan image shows the brain of a person who has never used ecstasy. The bottom image shows the brain of a person who has used ecstasy 70 times or more over a period of at least 1.5 years but who stopped using the drug for several weeks before these images were taken. Areas of lighter colour indicate a higher density of special proteins (called *transporters*) necessary for normal serotonin reuptake. The darker image of the brain on the bottom suggests that there is damage to the serotonin reuptake system.

Source: McCann et al., 1998; © Dr. G.A. Ricaurte, Johns Hopkins University School of Medicine. Reprinted with permission from Elsevier Science The Lancet. "Positron emission tomographic evidence of toxic effect of MDMA ("Ecstasy") on brain serotonin neurons in human beings" *The Lancet* Vol. 352, Issue 9140, 31 November 1998, pages 1433–1437.

In large doses, cocaine can produce fever, vomiting, convulsions, hallucinations, and paranoid delusions (Smith et al., 2009). A severe depressive crash may occur after a cocaine high, particularly with repeated doses. *Crack* is a chemically converted form of cocaine that can be smoked, and its effects are faster, more intense, and more dangerous. Overdoses of crack cocaine can cause sudden death from cardiorespiratory arrest. Tolerance develops to many of cocaine's effects, but withdrawal symptoms are mild and the potential for physiological dependence is low. However, cocaine users

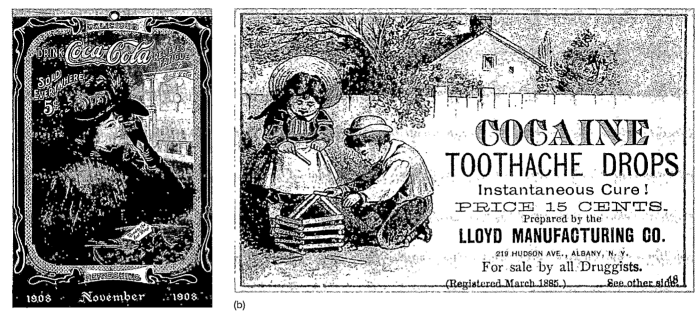

(b)

(top): The Advertising Archive, Ltd.; (bottom): © Corbis

FIGURE 6.27 When Coca-Cola was first produced, there was a clear reason why it relieved fatigue. It contained cocaine.

often develop strong cravings for the drug and the abuse potential is very high.

Opiates

Opium is a product of the opium poppy, a plant grown in hot, dry climates. Drugs derived from opium, such as morphine, codeine, and heroin, are called **opiates.** Opiates have two major effects. First, they provide pain relief. Second, they cause mood changes, which may include intense euphoria. The opiates oxycodone and fentanyl dramatically illustrate these two effects; they are powerful painkillers, but rapidly became widely abused drugs because of their potent mood-altering effects. Opiates bind to and stimulate receptors normally activated by endorphins, thereby producing pain relief. Opiates also increase dopamine activity, which may be one reason they induce euphoria (Flores et al., 2006). Endorphin receptors are found in many brain areas, which accounts for opiate effects on many brain functions, such as body temperature and hormone levels, and other functions, such as the control of the cough reflex (Levinthal, 2010). Heroin was originally marketed by the pharmaceutical company Bayer as a cough suppressant!

Fentanyl is an especially powerful synthetic opiate, even more potent than oxycodone. It has been reported that one person dies every three days in Canada as a result of using fentanyl (CBC, 2015). Some estimates are double that rate and suggest that at least two people die every three days from the drug (CCSA, 2015).

Fentanyl is used to treat patients with severe pain or to manage pain after surgery, especially among patients who have developed tolerance to other opiates. It is often administered as a skin patch, designed to slowly release the drug over 72 hours. Illicit use of fentanyl usually involves consuming the drug rapidly by smoking, injection, or chewing. Fentanyl is often mixed with other drugs such as heroin or cocaine and is used to make fake OxyContin pills (CCSA, 2015). Mixing fentanyl with heroin or cocaine amplifies the potency and potential dangers of those drugs, as well as introducing the toxicity associated with fentanyl itself. Drug users sometimes do not know that they are consuming fentanyl but think that they are injecting heroin or swallowing an oxycodone pill.

Experienced heroin users feel an intense, pleasurable "rush" within several minutes of an injection. For a time, users feel peaceful and non-aggressive, as if they are "on top of the world" with no concerns. Heroin users, however, often pay a substantial price for these transient pleasures. High doses can greatly reduce a person's breathing rate and may lead to coma. Overdoses can cause death (Morgan et al., 2008).

30. Describe the two effects of opiates.

© Claudia Andujar/Photo Researchers, Inc.

FIGURE 6.28 In some cultures, powerful hallucinogenic drugs are thought to have spiritual powers. Under the influence of peyote, this modern Native American shaman prepares to conduct a religious ceremony.

Hallucinogens

Hallucinogens are powerful mind-altering drugs that produce hallucinations. Some are derived from natural sources: Mescaline comes from the peyote cactus and psilocybin from mushrooms. Natural hallucinogens have been considered sacred in many tribal cultures because of their ability to produce "unearthly" states of consciousness and contact with spiritual forces (Figure 6.28). Other hallucinogens, such as LSD and phencyclidine ("angel dust"), are synthetic.

Hallucinogens usually distort or intensify sensory experience and can blur the boundaries between reality and fantasy. Users may speak of seeing sounds and hearing colours, of mystical experiences and insights, and of feeling exhilarated. They also may have violent outbursts, experience paranoia and panic, and have flashbacks after the "trip" has ended. The mental effects of hallucinogens are unpredictable. This unpredictability constitutes their greatest danger (Johnson et al., 2008).

31. What is the greatest danger of hallucinogens?

32. Explain three myths about marijuana.

Marijuana

Marijuana is a product of the hemp plant (*Cannabis sativa*). Some experts classify it as a hallucinogen, others as a sedative, and some feel it belongs in its own category (Levinthal, 2010). Marijuana is the most widely used illicit drug in Canada. Although estimates vary, most suggest that about a third of all Canadians have used marijuana at least once (Canadian Community Epidemiology Network on Drug Use, 2001; Centre for Addiction and Mental Health, 2001). Among some groups, use is even higher; almost 40 percent of high school students report having used marijuana within the past year (Patton, Brown, Broszeit, & Dhaliwal, 2001).

THC (tetrahydrocannabinol) is marijuana's major active ingredient, and it binds to receptors on neurons throughout the brain. You might wonder, as scientists have, why the brain would have specific receptor sites for a "foreign" substance such as marijuana. The answer is that the brain produces its own THC-like substances called *cannabinoids* (Devane et al., 1992; Stella et al., 1997). With chronic use, THC may increase GABA activity, which slows down neural activity and produces relaxing effects (Ksir et al., 2008). THC also increases dopamine activity, which may account for some of its pleasurable subjective effects (Maldonado & de Fonseca, 2002). Recent attempts to legalize marijuana use for medical purposes have stirred up waves of political controversy (Figure 6.29; Gottfried, 2000).

Certain misconceptions exist about marijuana. One is that chronic use causes people to become unmotivated and apathetic toward everything, a condition called *amotivational syndrome*. Another misconception is that marijuana causes people to start using more dangerous drugs. Neither statement is supported by

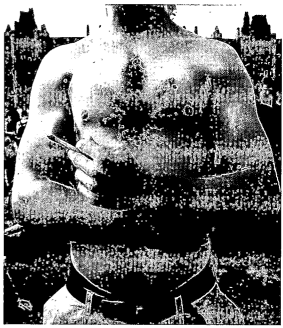

© Pawel Dwulit/The Canadian Press

FIGURE 6.29 The legal status of marijuana has long been a topic of debate in Canada. The use of marijuana has been legalized for certain medical purposes, such as helping cancer patients reduce some of the negative side effects (e.g., nausea) of chemotherapy. Further decriminalization, or even legalization of marijuana in Canada is hotly debated. In the United States, four states have legalized possession of marijuana, and it has been decriminalized in 18 states.

good scientific evidence (Ksir et al., 2008). A third misconception is that using marijuana has no significant dangers. This belief also is untrue. Marijuana smoke contains more cancer-causing substances than does tobacco smoke. At high doses, users may experience negative changes in mood, sensory distortions, and feelings of panic and anxiety. Marijuana can impair reaction time, thinking, memory, and learning, and can amplify the impact of other risk factors for psychiatric illness (Hall & Degenhardt, 2009).

Repeated marijuana use produces tolerance. At typical doses, some chronic users may experience mild withdrawal symptoms, such as restlessness. But users of chronically high doses who suddenly stop may experience nausea and vomiting, sleep disruptions, and irritability. About 10 percent of marijuana users develop dependence (Anthony, 2006).

From Genes to Culture: Determinants of Drug Effects

Table 6.2 summarizes some typical drug effects, but a user's reaction depends on more than the drug's chemical structure. Other biological, psychological, and environmental factors can influence the drug experience (Stewart, 2002).

At the biological level, animal research indicates that genetic factors influence sensitivity and tolerance to drug effects (Radcliffe et al., 2009). Genetic factors have been examined most extensively with alcohol. Rats and mice can be genetically bred to inherit a strong preference for drinking alcohol instead of water (He et al., 1997). Even in their first exposure to alcohol, these rats show greater tolerance than normal rats (Murphy et al., 1986).

Among humans, identical twins have a higher concordance rate for alcoholism than do fraternal twins (Lyons et al., 2006). Moreover, people who grow up with alcoholic versus non-alcoholic parents respond differently to drinking alcohol under laboratory conditions. Offspring of alcoholic parents typically display faster hormonal and psychological reactions as their blood-alcohol level rises, but these responses drop off more quickly as blood-alcohol levels decrease (Newlin & Thomson, 1997). Compared with other people, they must drink more alcohol over the course of a few hours to maintain their feeling of intoxication.

33. What evidence supports the hypothesis that genetic factors influence drug reactions?

TABLE 6.2 Effects of Some Major Drugs

Class	Typical Effects	Overdose Effects
DEPRESSANTS		
Alcohol	Relaxation, lowered inhibition, depressed/impaired physical and psychological functioning	Disorientation, unconsciousness, possible death at extreme doses
Barbiturates/Tranquilizers	Tension reduction, depressed reflexes and impaired motor functioning, induced sleep	Shallow breathing, clammy skin, weak and rapid pulse, coma, possible death
STIMULANTS		
Amphetamines	Increased alertness, pulse, and blood pressure; elevated mood; suppressed appetite; sleeplessness	Agitation, hallucinations, paranoid delusions, convulsions, heart failure, possible death
Cocaine		
Ecstasy		
OPIATES		
Opium	Euphoria, pain relief, drowsiness, impaired motor and psychological functioning	Shallow breathing, convulsions, coma, possible death
Morphine		
Heroin		
Oxycodone		
Fentanyl		
HALLUCINOGENS		
LSD	Hallucinations and "visions," distorted time perception, loss of reality contact, nausea, restlessness, risk of panic	Psychotic reactions (delusions, paranoia), panic that may lead to behaviour causing injury
Mescaline		
Psilocybin		
MARIJUANA	Mild euphoria, relaxation, enhanced sensory experience, increased appetite, impaired memory and reaction time	Fatigue, anxiety, disorientation, sensory distortions, and possible psychotic reactions

Growing up with alcoholic parents includes both genetic and social learning components. Animal studies have found that cross-fostered rat pups raised by an alcohol-consuming mother consume more alcohol than rat pups raised by mothers who do not drink alcohol (Honey & Galef, 2004). Animals, including humans, learn what to eat and drink, in part, by cues provided by the parents. Thus, the children of alcoholic parents could be at an increased risk of abusing alcohol for two reasons: genetic factors and exposure to a parent who abuses alcohol. Twin and adoption studies, however, have found that alcohol abuse among adoptees is correlated with alcohol abuse in their biological parents but not their adoptive parents (Cloninger et al., 1995; Heath et al., 2002). Overall, many scientists see evidence for a genetic role in determining human responsiveness to alcohol (Kuo et al., 2009).

34. Describe how environmental and psychological factors influence drug reactions.

At the environmental level, the setting in which a drug is taken can influence a user's reactions. As noted earlier, compensatory physiological responses to a drug can become associated with, and ultimately triggered by, environmental stimuli in the drug setting. The behaviour of other people who are sharing the drug experience provides important cues about how to respond, and a hostile environment may increase the chances of a "bad trip" with drugs such as LSD (Palfai & Jankiewicz, 1991).

Cultural learning also affects how people respond to a drug (Bloomfield et al., 2002). In many Western cultures, increased aggressiveness and sexual promiscuity are commonly associated with drunken excess. In contrast, members of the Camba culture of Bolivia customarily drink large quantities of a 178-proof beverage, remaining cordial and non-aggressive between episodes of passing out (MacAndrew & Edgerton, 1969). In the 1700s, Tahitians introduced to alcohol by European sailors reacted at first with pleasant relaxation when intoxicated, but after witnessing the violent aggressiveness exhibited by drunken sailors, they too began behaving aggressively (MacAndrew & Edgerton, 1969).

Cultural factors also affect drug consumption. Traditionally, American Navajo Indians do not consider drinking any amount of alcohol to be normal, whereas drinking wine or beer is central to social life and cultural identity in some parts of the world (Tanaka-Matsumi & Draguns, 1997). In some cultures, hallucinogenic drugs are feared and outlawed, whereas in others they are used in medicinal or religious contexts to provide new types of awareness and to seek advice from spirits (Dalgarno, 2007). In many countries, drug use varies across ethnic groups. Black and Hispanic Americans, for example, are less likely ever to have used alcohol, cocaine, marijuana, and hallucinogens than their White peers (Department of Health and Human Services, 1998).

Finally, at the psychological level, people's beliefs and expectancies can influence drug

▮ Review

- Drugs alter consciousness by modifying neurotransmitter activity. Agonists increase such activity, whereas antagonists decrease it.

- Tolerance develops when the body produces compensatory responses to counteract a drug's effects. When drug use is stopped, compensatory responses continue and produce withdrawal symptoms. Substance dependence represents a maladaptive pattern of substance use that causes a person significant distress or substantially impairs that person's life. It can occur with or without physiological dependence.

- Depressants decrease neural activity. The subjective "high" and liveliness associated with low alcohol doses occur because alcohol depresses the activity of inhibitory brain centres. Drinking contributes to poor decision making.

- Stimulants increase arousal and boost mood by enhancing dopamine and norepinephrine activity. Repeated use depletes these neurotransmitters and can cause a severe depressive "crash" after the drug wears off.

- Opiates increase endorphin activity, producing pain relief and mood changes that may include euphoria. Opiates are important in medicine but are highly addictive.

- Hallucinogens, such as LSD, powerfully distort sensory experience and can blur the line between reality and fantasy. The effects of hallucinogens are always unpredictable.

- THC, the main active ingredient in marijuana, produces relaxation and a sense of well-being at low doses but can cause anxiety and sensory distortion at higher doses. Marijuana can impair thinking and reflexes, and its smoke contains carcinogens.

- A drug's effect depends on its chemical actions, the physical and social setting, cultural norms, learning, and the user's genetic predispositions, expectations, and personality.

reactions (George et al., 2000). Experiments show that people may behave as if "drunk" if they think they have consumed alcohol even if they have not (Marlatt & Rohsenow, 1980). If a person's fellow drinkers are happy and gregarious, he or she may expect to respond in the same way. The cultural norm that a hallucinogen will enable contact with spirits provides the user with a powerful belief system and expectation that can shape the nature of the hallucinations and overall emotional reaction to the experience. As we learned in Chapter 5, we often perceive what we expect to perceive, and this applies to drugs; expectations powerfully influence the effects of a psychoactive drug.

Personality factors also influence drug reactions and usage. People who have difficulty adjusting to life's demands or whose contact with reality is marginal may be particularly vulnerable to severe and negative drug reactions and to drug addiction (Ray & Ksir, 1987). Chronic drug use among young people often is associated with a sense of meaninglessness and lack of direction in life (Newcomb & Harlow, 1986). Figure 6.30 illustrates some of the biological, environmental, and psychological factors that may determine drug experiences.

 **Drug-Induced States**

Drug-induced states involve an interplay of biological, psychological, and environmental factors. Let's summarize some of these factors.

ENVIRONMENTAL

- Cultural norms and experiences can shape users' drug attitudes and expectations.
- Repeated drug use in a particular setting can produce conditioned compensatory stimuli.
- The social context and behaviour of other drug users who are present can affect how a person responds to a drug.

BIOLOGICAL

- Drugs increase or decrease the activity of particular neurotransmitter systems.
- The body produces compensatory responses to counteract a drug's effect, possibly leading to tolerance.
- Withdrawal symptoms occur when drug use stops but the body's compensatory responses continue.
- Genetic factors influence biological reactivity to specific drugs.

PSYCHOLOGICAL

- Drugs can alter numerous aspects of psychological functioning, including mood, memory, attention, decision making, social inhibitions, and pain awareness.
- Users' attitudes and expectations about drugs can influence their psychological reactions to a drug.
- A user's level of personal adjustment can influence the likelihood of a negative drug reaction.

Suppose a person consumes enough alcoholic drinks within 30 minutes to reach a blood alcohol level of 0.08. In one case, suppose all the drinks are the same: all beers or all the same wine. In another case, suppose each drink is different: a beer, a glass of red wine, a shot of tequila. Would you expect the person to feel equally intoxicated in both cases?

FIGURE 6.30

HYPNOSIS

In the mid-19th century, the Scottish surgeon James Braid saw a performance of mesmerism—the use of animal magnetism—to influence behaviour. Braid thought that it was a fraud and so began an investigation into mesmerism that laid the foundation for the scientific study of hypnotism. He concluded that mesmerism was a state of "nervous sleep" produced by concentrated attention, and renamed it *hypnosis*, after Hypnos, the Greek god of sleep.

The Scientific Study of Hypnosis

Hypnosis is "a therapeutic technique in which clinicians make suggestions to individuals who have undergone a procedure designed to relax them and focus their minds" (American Psychological Association, 2016). Hypnosis draws great interest because some mental health practitioners use it as an aid in conducting therapy. Basic scientists explore whether hypnosis produces a unique state of consciousness.

Hypnotic induction is a process that creates a context for hypnosis. A hypnotist may ask the subject to sit down, relax, gaze at an object on the wall, and then in a quiet voice suggest that the subject's eyes are becoming heavy and tired. The goal is to relax the subject and increase her or his concentration. The procedures used in hypnotic induction are thought to be related to those used in meditation (Cahn & Polich, 2006).

Contrary to popular belief, people cannot be hypnotized against their will. Even when people want to be hypnotized, they differ in how "susceptible" (i.e., responsive) they are to hypnotic suggestion. **Hypnotic susceptibility scales** contain a standard series of pass/fail suggestions that are read to a subject after a hypnotic induction (Table 6.3). The subject's score is based on the number of "passes." About 10 percent of subjects are completely nonresponsive, 10 percent pass all or nearly all the items, and the rest fall in-between (Hilgard, 1977).

Hypnotic Behaviours and Experiences

It is widely claimed that hypnotized people experience substantial alteration in psychological functioning and behaviour. Let's examine some of these claims.

Involuntary Control and Behaving against One's Will

Hypnotized people *subjectively experience* their actions to be involuntary (Kirsch, 2001). If this is so, then can a hypnotist make people perform acts that are harmful to themselves or others?

In a classic experiment, Martin Orne and Frederick Evans (1965) found that hypnotized subjects could be induced to dip their hands briefly in a foaming solution they were told was acid and then to throw the "acid" in another person's face. This action might appear to be a striking example of the power of hypnosis to get people to act "against their will." However, Orne and Evans tested a control group of subjects who were asked simply to pretend that they were hypnotized. These subjects were just as likely as hypnotized subjects to put their hand in the acid or throw it at someone, and they performed this action of their own will.

Hypnosis does not involve any unique power to get people to behave "against their will" (Wagstaff, 2008). An authority figure can

35. Can everyone be hypnotized?

36. In what sense is hypnotic behaviour "involuntary"? Does hypnosis have a unique power to coerce people against their will?

TABLE 6.3   Sample Test Items from the Stanford Hypnotic Susceptibility Scale, Form C

Item	Suggested Behaviour	Criterion for Passing
Arm lowering	Right arm is held out; subject is told arm will become heavy and drop.	The arm is lowered at least 15 centimetres in 10 seconds.
Moving hands apart	With hands extended and close together, subject is asked to imagine a force pushing them apart.	Hands are 15 or more centimetres apart in 10 seconds.
Mosquito hallucination	It is suggested that a mosquito is buzzing nearby and lands on the subject.	Any grimace or acknowledgment of the mosquito is shown.
Posthypnotic amnesia	Subject is awakened and asked to recall suggestions after being told under hypnosis that she will not remember.	Three or fewer items are recalled before subject is told, "Now you can remember everything."

Source: Based on Wertzenhoffer, A. M., & Hilgard, E. R. (1962). *Stanford Hypnotic Susceptibility Scale: Form C.* Palo Alto, CA: Consulting Psychologists Press.

© AP Photo/Bookstaver

FIGURE 6.31 The "human plank" demonstration, a favourite of stage hypnotists, seems to demonstrate the power of the hypnotic trance. Most of the audience is unaware, however, that the average man suspended in this manner can support a person on his chest without hypnosis. In the photo, The Amazing Kreskin, a professional magician, demonstrates this fact with a group of unhypnotized men.

induce people to commit highly "out of character" and even dangerous acts, whether or not they are hypnotized. We will return to this idea later when we are discussing social psychology, authority, and the power of social roles.

Physiological Effects and Amazing Feats

Have you seen or heard about stage hypnotists who get an audience member to perform an amazing physical feat, such as the "human plank" (Figure 6.31)? A subject, usually male, is hypnotized and lies outstretched between two chairs. He is told that his body is rigid and then, amazingly, another person successfully stands on the subject's legs and chest. Similarly, hypnosis can have striking physiological effects. In one classic experiment, Ikemi and Nakagawa

Thinking critically

HYPNOSIS AND AMAZING FEATS

In the case of the human plank and in the allergy experiment, what additional evidence do you need to determine whether these amazing feats and responses really are caused by hypnosis? How could you gather this evidence?

Think about it, and then see the Answers section at the end of the book.

(1962) found that under hypnosis an allergic reaction to a toxic leaf could be prevented and an allergic reaction to a harmless leaf produced.

Should we attribute the human-plank feat and the unusual responses of the allergic people to unique powers of hypnosis? Here is where a healthy dose of critical thinking is important.

Pain Tolerance

Scottish surgeon James Esdaile performed more than 300 major operations in the mid-1800s using hypnosis as the sole anaesthetic (Figure 6.32). Experiments confirm that hypnosis can increase pain tolerance and that this is not due to a placebo effect (Milling, 2008). For patients who experience chronic pain, hypnosis can produce relief that persists for months or even years (Patterson, 2004).

We do not know exactly how hypnosis produces painkilling effects. Brain-imaging studies have found that hypnosis modifies activity in brain areas involved in processing painful stimuli. Nonhypnotic techniques, such as visual imagery and distractions, can, however, also alter activity in these brain areas and reduce the feeling of pain (Fardo et al., 2015).

Hypnosis and Memory

You may have seen TV shows or movies in which hypnotized people are given a suggestion that they will not remember something, either during the session itself (*hypnotic amnesia*), or after the hypnotic trance has ended (*posthypnotic*

37. Does hypnosis produce pain relief? Is this a placebo effect?

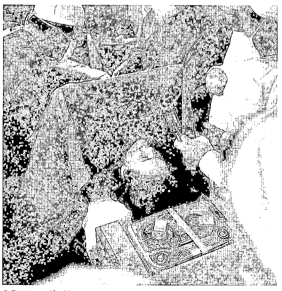

© Bettmann/Corbis

FIGURE 6.32 This patient is having her appendix removed with hypnosis as the sole anaesthetic. Her verbal reports that she feels no pain are being recorded.

amnesia). A "reversal cue" also is given, such as a phrase ("You will now remember everything") that ends the amnesia once the person hears it. Is this Hollywood fiction? Research indicates that about 25 percent of hypnotized university students can be led to experience amnesia (Kirsch, 2001).

In contrast to hypnotic amnesia, there is a popularly held view that hypnosis can enhance memory. The results of controlled experiments have revealed that, overall, hypnosis does not reliably improve memory (Lynn et al., 2009; Whitehouse et al., 2009). Hypnotized people do report more information, but much of that extra information is inaccurate. To make matters worse, the fact that they recalled these "memories" under hypnosis makes people feel more confident in the accuracy of the information (Burgess & Kirsch, 1999; Wagstaff et al., 2008). That is, memory is not more accurate under hypnosis, but people believe that it is.

Another concern is that some memories recalled under hypnosis may be *pseudomemories,* false memories created during hypnosis by statements or leading suggestions made by the examiner (Lynn et al., 2009). When hypnotized and nonhypnotized subjects are intentionally exposed to false information about an event. Highly suggestible people who have been hypnotized are most likely to report the false information as being a true memory and are confident that their false memories are accurate (Sheehan et al., 1992; Wagstaff, 2009). The increased suggestibility of hypnotized people makes them particularly susceptible to memory distortion (Scoboria et al., 2002). In 2007, the Supreme Court of Canada ruled that evidence obtained by using hypnosis should not be used as evidence in criminal cases because it is not sufficiently reliable.

38. According to the dissociation theory of hypnosis, why do hypnotic behaviours seem involuntary?

39. According to social cognitive theories of hypnosis, why do hypnotic behaviours seem involuntary?

Theories of Hypnosis

Hypnos may have been the Greek god of sleep, but hypnosis definitely is *not* sleep. James Braid, the Scottish doctor who pioneered the modern study of hypnosis, realized this and tried to change the name but it was too late; it became known as hypnosis. What then is hypnosis, and how does it produce its effects?

Dissociation Theories: Hypnosis as Divided Consciousness

Several influential researchers, such as Ken Bowers of the University of Waterloo and Ernest Hilgard of Stanford University, proposed **dissociation theories** that view hypnosis as an altered state involving a division ("dissociation") of consciousness (Kihlstrom, 2007). That is, hypnosis creates a *division of awareness* in which the person simultaneously experiences two streams of consciousness that are cut off from each other. One stream responds to the hypnotist's suggestions, while the second stream—the part of consciousness that monitors behaviour—remains in the background but is aware of everything that goes on. Hilgard refers to this second "part" of consciousness as the *hidden observer.*

Suppose a hypnotized subject is given a suggestion that she will not feel pain. Her arm is lowered into a tub of ice-cold water for 45 seconds and every few seconds she reports the amount of pain. In contrast to unhypnotized subjects, who find this experience increasingly painful, she will report feeling significantly less pain. But suppose the procedure were done differently. Before lowering the subject's arm, the hypnotist says, "Perhaps there is another part of you that is more aware than your hypnotized part. If so, would that part of you report the amount of pain." In this case, the subject's other stream of consciousness, the "hidden observer," will report a higher level of pain (Figure 6.33).

For Hilgard, this dissociation explains why behaviours that occur under hypnosis seem involuntary or automatic. Given the suggestion that "your arm will start to feel lighter and will begin to rise," the subject intentionally raises the arm, but only the hidden observer is aware of this. The main stream of consciousness that responds to the command is blocked from this awareness, and thus perceives that the arm is rising all by itself.

Social Cognitive Theories: Roles and Expectations

Nicholas Spanos of Carleton University was one of the leading proponents of a very different view of hypnosis. To Spanos and others, hypnosis does not represent a special state of dissociated consciousness (Dienes et al., 2009; Spanos, 1991). In general, **social cognitive theories** propose that hypnotic experiences result from expectations of people who take on the role of being "hypnotized." Most people believe that hypnosis involves a trancelike appearance, responsiveness to suggestion, and a loss of self-consciousness. People who accept the role of hypnotized participant conform to this role and develop a perceptual set—a readiness to respond to the hypnotist's suggestions and

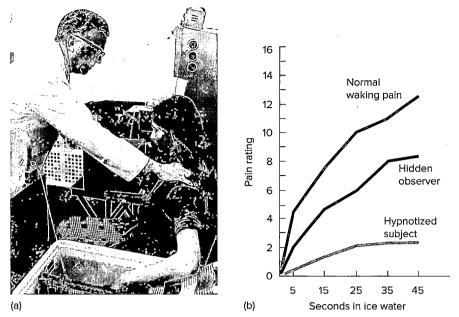

(a)   (b)   Seconds in ice water

(a) Courtesy News and Publications Service, Stanford University; (b) Data from Hilgard, E.R. (1977). *Divided consciousness: Multiple controls in human thought and action.* New York, NY: Wiley.

FIGURE 6.33 (a) This hypnotized subject's hand is immersed in painfully cold ice water. Placing his hand on her shoulder, Ernest Hilgard contacts her dissociated "hidden observer." (b) Pain intensity ratings given by a subject when she is not hypnotized, by the subject under hypnosis, and by the hidden observer in the same hypnotic state. The hidden observer reports more pain than the hypnotized subject, but less pain than the subject when she is not hypnotized.

to perceive hypnotic experiences as real and "involuntary."

In a classic study, Martin Orne (1959) illustrated the importance of expectations about hypnosis. During a classroom demonstration, university students were told that hypnotized people frequently exhibit spontaneous stiffening of the muscles in the dominant hand. Actually, this rarely occurs. An accomplice of the lecturer pretended to be hypnotized and, sure enough, he "spontaneously" exhibited hand stiffness. When students who had seen the demonstration were later hypnotized, 55 percent of them exhibited stiffening of the hand without any suggestion from the hypnotist. The control group participants did not see such a demonstration and none of these students exhibited hand stiffening when they were hypnotized.

Does social cognitive theory imply that people are faking or play-acting when they are hypnotized? Not at all. Role theorists emphasize that, when people immerse themselves in a social role, their responses are completely "real." Recall from Chapter 5 on perception that perceptual sets strongly influence how the brain organizes sensory information. According to social cognitive theory, many of the effects of hypnosis represent an extension

of this basic principle. The hypnotized subject perceives their behaviour as involuntary because this is what they expect, and because attention is focused externally on the hypnotist and the hypnotic suggestion (Kirsch, 2001).

Can the debate about hypnosis be resolved? Some psychologists believe the dissociation and social cognitive viewpoints can be integrated into a comprehensive theory (Kihlstrom, 1998; Woody & Sadler, 1998). Others disagree, saying it is time to discard some ideas of dissociation theory (Kirsch & Lynn, 1998a). The only sure bet is that hypnosis will remain a controversial topic for some time to come.

The Hypnotized Brain

Can peering inside the brain help us determine the nature of hypnosis? Presenting pain-reducing suggestions to hypnotized subjects decreases both subjective reports of pain and activity in brain areas that process pain information (Milling, 2008). Activity in brain areas linked to sensation and perception, memory and motor control have all been studied under hypnosis (Landry & Raz, 2015). These studies tend to support the conclusion that altered brain activity matches verbal reports while hypnotized (Dienes et al., 2009).

Social cognitive theorists argue that these findings do not resolve the issue (Kirsch, 2001). They note that hypnotic experiences are subjectively real, and if hypnosis alters brain activity this does not contradict the position that people's expectations are what lead them to become hypnotized in the first place. In sum, cognitive neuroscience provides insights into the hypnotized brain, but it will take more research to resolve the debate about hypnosis (Dienes et al., 2009).

SOME FINAL THOUGHTS

We have seen that consciousness can be studied scientifically at biological, psychological, and environmental levels. In so doing, we have learned that altered states are not as divorced from "normal" waking consciousness as had previously been thought. In a way, we all experience dissociated consciousness in the form of divided attention, and dreaming shares much in common with waking thought processes. As you learned in Chapter 1, expectations powerfully affect everyday waking perception. Now we see that our expectations and beliefs influence hypnotic and drug-induced experiences.

Consider the behaviour of the following participant in the *Research Foundations* experiment on drinking and driving earlier in the chapter. This university student consumed three non-alcoholic drinks but through taste and smell cues was convincingly led to believe that they were alcoholic. Prior to taking a Breathalyzer test, he estimated his blood-alcohol level to be 0.07, just below the 0.08 legal driving limit where he lived. He felt he was almost drunk! When told the drinks were non-alcoholic, he argued that there had to be a mistake. When shown his true Breathalyzer result of 0.000, he claimed it was rigged and refused to drive home until the effects of his "drinks" wore off (MacDonald et al., 1995)!

Clearly, we have a remarkable capacity to alter our own state of consciousness without being aware that we are responsible for causing the change. In fact, might this capacity to alter consciousness underlie dissociative identity disorder (DID)? Social cognitive theorists propose that, as with hypnosis, DID is a state in which people become deeply enmeshed in a role and sincerely come to perceive themselves as having multiple identities (Lilienfeld et al., 1999; Spanos, 1991). In contrast, dissociation theorists believe that DID represents a state of divided consciousness that usually develops as a protective reaction to extreme childhood trauma, such as prolonged sexual abuse (Gleaves, 1996; Putnam, 1998). Add to this mix the fact that some people intentionally fake DID, and you have an intriguing controversy that we explore in Chapter 16.

Along with the study of perception, probing the mysteries of conscious experience goes to the heart of understanding the subjective nature of "reality." On this matter, the century-old words of William James remain pertinent today:

> Our normal waking consciousness is but one special type of consciousness, whilst all about it, parted from it by the filmiest of screens, there lie potential forms of consciousness entirely different. . . . No account of the universe in its totality can be final which leaves these other forms of consciousness quite disregarded. (1902, p. 298)

Review

- Hypnosis involves an increased receptiveness to suggestion. Hypnotic susceptibility scales measure people's responsiveness to hypnosis.

- Hypnotized people subjectively experience their actions to be involuntary, but hypnosis has no unique power to make people behave "against their will." In experiments, hypnotized and unhypnotized people are equally likely to show striking physiological reactions and perform "amazing" physical feats. Hypnosis increases pain tolerance, but other psychological techniques also can reduce pain.

- Some people can be led to experience hypnotic and posthypnotic amnesia. Hypnosis, however, does not reliably improve memory or lead to the recall of forgotten information.

- Dissociation theories view hypnosis as an altered state of divided consciousness. Hilgard proposes that one stream of consciousness responds to the hypnotist's suggestions, while another stream (the hidden observer) stays in the background and is fully aware of everything going on. Social cognitive role theories state that hypnotic experiences occur because people have strong beliefs and expectations about hypnosis and are highly motivated to enter a hypnotized "role." People's actions are sincere but not the result of divided consciousness.

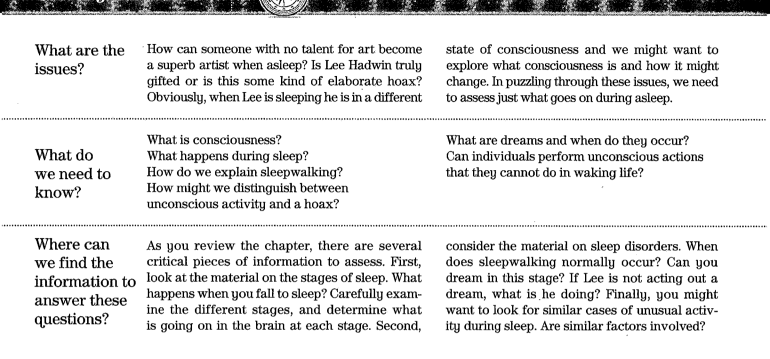

Gaining Direction

What are the issues?	How can someone with no talent for art become a superb artist when asleep? Is Lee Hadwin truly gifted or is this some kind of elaborate hoax? Obviously, when Lee is sleeping he is in a different	state of consciousness and we might want to explore what consciousness is and how it might change. In puzzling through these issues, we need to assess just what goes on during asleep.
What do we need to know?	What is consciousness? What happens during sleep? How do we explain sleepwalking? How might we distinguish between unconscious activity and a hoax?	What are dreams and when do they occur? Can individuals perform unconscious actions that they cannot do in waking life?
Where can we find the information to answer these questions?	As you review the chapter, there are several critical pieces of information to assess. First, look at the material on the stages of sleep. What happens when you fall to sleep? Carefully examine the different stages, and determine what is going on in the brain at each stage. Second,	consider the material on sleep disorders. When does sleepwalking normally occur? Can you dream in this stage? If Lee is not acting out a dream, what is he doing? Finally, you might want to look for similar cases of unusual activity during sleep. Are similar factors involved?

Learning and Adaptation: The Role of Experience

CHAPTER ❯
OUTLINE

ADAPTING TO THE ENVIRONMENT
How Do We Learn? The Search for Mechanisms
Habituation and Sensitization

CLASSICAL CONDITIONING: ASSOCIATING ONE STIMULUS WITH ANOTHER
Pavlov's Pioneering Research
Basic Principles
Applications of Classical Conditioning
  Applications: Learning, Virtual Reality, and Therapy

OPERANT CONDITIONING: LEARNING THROUGH CONSEQUENCES
Thorndike's Law of Effect
Skinner's Analysis of Operant Conditioning
Antecedent Conditions: Identifying When to Respond
Consequences: Determining How to Respond
Shaping and Chaining: Taking One Step at a Time
Generalization and Discrimination
Schedules of Reinforcement
Escape and Avoidance Conditioning
Applications of Operant Conditioning

BIOLOGY AND LEARNING
Constraints on Classical Conditioning:
  Learned Taste Aversions
Are We Biologically Prepared to Fear Certain Things?
Constraints on Operant Conditioning: Animals That
  "Won't Shape Up"
Learning and the Brain

COGNITION AND LEARNING
Insight and Cognitive Maps
  Focus on Neuroscience: Place Cells and
  Cognitive Maps
Cognition in Classical Conditioning
  Frontiers: Animal Cognition
Cognition in Operant Conditioning

OBSERVATIONAL LEARNING: WHEN OTHERS PAVE THE WAY
Bandura's Social-Cognitive Theory
  Research Foundations: Using Social-Cognitive
  Learning Theory to Prevent AIDS: A National
  Experiment

A man who carries a cat by the tail learns something he can learn in no other way.
— Mark Twain

 About one in five air passengers experience some degree of fear when they step aboard an airplane. Their heart and breathing rates increase. Their palms become sweaty, and their arousal levels are high. For 3 percent of air travellers, the arousal is so high that they are in a state of panic, even when sitting in the airport parking lot. These individuals have aviophobia. The fear and panic stems from a variety of sources: media reports, unusual sounds aboard the aircraft,

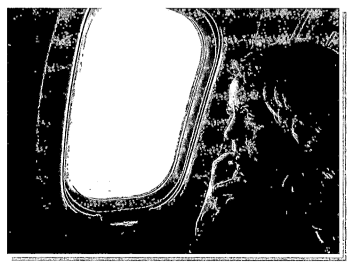
© Vicki Beaver/Alamy Stock Photo

What are the issues here?

What do we need to know?

Where can we find the information to answer these questions?

turbulence, and a general loss of control. Some take to driving all the way across Canada to avoid air travel completely.

In an effort to overcome this problem, people have turned to drugs, hypnosis, and audio self-help recordings. The self-help recordings have limited success, hypnosis works for some, and drugs, while reducing anxiety, do not really cure the problem. But recently, a new program run by Marc-Antoine Plourde of Montreal is showing a lot of promise. Plourde, a captain with Air Canada, runs the DePlour Training Centre, where individuals can sign up for a two-day course to reduce their fear. The course involves seminars on pilot training, aircraft design, and maintenance; a ride in a flight simulator; plus a graduation "liberty flight" from Montreal to Toronto. Together with a licensed therapist, Plourde explains the science of flight and the psychology of fear. During a demonstration of aircraft design, Plourde uses a model of an Airbus A330 to show how the wings are engineered to bend. However, he bends them a little too much (on purpose), breaking off the wing much to the astonishment (and shock) of the participants. Their worst fear realized, Plourde explains how this could not happen in the real world.

Does the program work? Plourde claims a 94 percent satisfaction rate and notes that only four of 500 people have failed to take the liberty flight. Apparently, dealing with the emotional anxiety is more important than stressing airplane safety. As Captain Tom Bunn, who runs a similar program in the United States, notes, "People tell us that they know that flying is safer than driving, but my car doesn't fall 30 000 feet [9100 metres] from the sky."

Reflect for a moment on how much of your behaviour is learned: telling time, getting dressed, driving, reading, using money, playing sports, and so on. Beyond such skills, learning affects our emotional reactions, perceptions, and physiological responses. Through experience, we learn to think, act, and feel in ways that contribute richly to our individual identity.

Learning is a process by which experience produces a relatively enduring change in an organism's behaviour or capabilities. The term *capabilities* highlights a distinction made by many theorists: "knowing how," or learning, versus "doing," or performance. For example, experience may provide us with immediate knowledge (e.g., you may receive instructions on how to perform a skill), but in science we must *measure* learning by actual changes in performance.

In this chapter, we explore basic learning processes. The first, *habituation* and *sensitization,* involve a change in behaviour that results from repeated exposure to a single stimulus. Next, we explore two forms of conditioning that involve learning associations between events, and hence have often been referred to as associative learning. *Classical conditioning* occurs when two stimuli become associated with each other. For example, seeing a dog and being bitten become associated such that one stimulus (seeing a dog) now triggers a new response (fear). In *operant conditioning,* we learn to associate

our responses with specific consequences. For example, we learn that smiling at others is followed by a friendly greeting. The study of associative learning has been central to the study of learning in psychology. Indeed throughout much of the history of psychology, "learning" was used to mean associative learning. Our examination of learning then considers *observational learning,* in which we learn by watching others behave. Finally, we consider the role of *cognition in conditioning.*

ADAPTING TO THE ENVIRONMENT

From the moment we are born, we encounter changing environments, each with its unique challenges. Some challenges affect survival, such as acquiring food and shelter. Others do not, such as deciding where to go on a date. But no matter the challenge, learning makes it possible for us to adapt to it. In fact, we can view learning as a process of *personal adaptation* to the ever-changing circumstances of our lives.

How Do We Learn? The Search for Mechanisms

Many of the key principles that we will discuss reflect important discoveries by the behaviourists (Bolles & Beecher, 1988). Within psychology,

1. Historically, how have behaviourists defined learning?"

2. What role does the environment play in personal and species adaptation?

behaviourists focused on *how* organisms learn, examining the processes by which experience influences behaviour. Behaviourists assumed that there are laws of learning that apply to virtually all organisms. For example, each species they studied—whether birds, reptiles, rats, monkeys, or humans—responded in predictable ways to patterns of reward or punishment.

Behaviourists treated the organism as a *tabula rasa*, or blank tablet, upon which learning experiences were inscribed. Most of their research was conducted with nonhuman species in controlled laboratory settings. Behaviourists explained learning solely in terms of directly observable events and avoided speculating about an organism's unobservable "mental state." The concept of learning calls attention to the importance of adapting to the environment. Whereas evolution focuses on species' adaption across many generations, learning represents a process of personal adaptation.

The resurgence of the *cognitive perspective,* an interest in *biological factors,* and the emergence of *cross-cultural psychology* also have expanded our understanding of learning. Cognitive and biological factors play important roles in learning (Dickinson, 1997; Shanks, 2010). As we have seen and will continue to explore in upcoming chapters, cross-cultural research highlights the important impact that culture has on what we learn—from social customs (*norms*) and beliefs, to our most basic perceptions of the world and ourselves (Figure 7.1; Super & Harkness, 1997). Culture's impact is not surprising, given that learning represents adaptation to the environment and culture is the human-made part of our environment (Herskovits, 1948). And yet, the learning mechanisms that foster this adaptation are universal among humans and, in some cases, occur across countless species.

Habituation and Sensitization

Imagine that you are sitting in a room studying. You notice that the clock makes an audible sound as the second hand moves to each new notch. Over time, as the tick occurs again and again, you notice it less and less, and eventually you do not register it at all. Now imagine that you hear a rustling sound outside your window at night. Although you think it must just be the wind in the trees, the sound startles you. You move to the window and experience an increase in arousal. The sound repeats and generates a stronger response in you, as you become increasingly fearful. These two examples illustrate the simplest forms of learning and

3. What is habituation, and what is its adaptive significance?

(top) © Oan Connell/The Image Works; (bottom) © George Houlton/ Photo Researchers, Inc.

FIGURE 7.1 People in different cultures learn different behaviours to adapt to their environment. Even the same general skill will take different forms depending on unique environmental features and demands.

demonstrate a change in behaviour because of the repeated presentation of a single stimulus.

Habituation is a decrease in the strength of response to a repeated stimulus. It may be the simplest form of learning and occurs across species, ranging from humans to dragonflies and sea snails (Glanzman, 2009). University of British Columbia psychologist Catherine Rankin has even demonstrated habituation in a microscopic worm (a nematode) that has only 302 neurons (Lau et al., 2013). Habituation serves a key adaptive function. You do not need to constantly respond to the pressure of clothing on your skin, to the sound of the ventilation system, or to the hum of distant traffic. If an organism responded to every stimulus in its environment, it would rapidly become overwhelmed and exhausted. By learning not to respond to uneventful familiar stimuli, organisms conserve energy and can attend to other stimuli that are important.

Habituation also plays an important role in enabling scientists to study behaviour. Whether observing animals in the wild or schoolchildren, a researcher's mere presence may initially disrupt participants' natural responses. Thus, before collecting data, observers often allow people and animals to habituate to their presence.

Habituation is different from sensory adaptation, which we discussed in Chapter 5. Sensory adaptation refers to a decreased sensory response to a continuously present stimulus. Habituation, on the other hand, is a simple form of learning that occurs within the central nervous system. You may habituate to a stimulus, but that sensory information is still available if it becomes relevant. For example, you habituate to the feeling of your clothing against your skin. That tactile information has been presented continuously with no important consequences, so you no longer notice it. If, however, there is reason to become aware of skin sensations, perhaps because of a wasp or a mosquito in your vicinity, you suddenly become keenly aware of all the light touches on your skin that a few seconds ago had shown habituation.

Sensitization is an increase in the strength of response to a repeated stimulus. For example, if a loud tone is sounded, an organism will show the startle reflex: They will orient to the sound; their muscle tension increases rapidly; and they jump and may vocalize. With repeated presentation of a loud tone, the startle response increases in intensity (Donahoe & Palmer, 1994). Have you ever touched a metal object, such as a door handle, and received a static electric shock? If you then touch another metal object and receive a second shock, you will

jump a little more, pull your hand back a little more quickly, and show a slightly stronger emotional reaction (the words you call out may also change). Each shock elicits a stronger response; that is, you have shown sensitization.

Like habituation, sensitization is found across a wide range of species, even among animals with very simple nervous systems (Cai et al., 2011). Sensitization tends to occur to strong or noxious stimuli (Donahoe & Palmer, 1994), and its purpose is to increase responses to a potentially dangerous stimulus.

CLASSICAL CONDITIONING: ASSOCIATING ONE STIMULUS WITH ANOTHER

Life is full of interesting associations. Do you ever hear songs on the radio or find yourself in places that instantly make you feel good because they're connected to special times you've had? When you smell the aroma of popcorn or freshly baked cookies, does it make your mouth water or stomach growl? These examples illustrate a learning process called **classical conditioning,** in which an organism learns to associate two stimuli (e.g., a song and a pleasant event), such that one stimulus (the song) comes to produce a response (feeling happy) that originally was produced only by the other stimulus (the pleasurable event).

Like habituation and sensitization, classical conditioning is a basic form of learning that occurs in mammals, birds, reptiles, fish, sea snails, and even insects (Kandel & Hawkins, 1992; Watanabe et al., 2008). Classical

4. What is sensitization, and why would you want to sensitize to the repeated presentation of a stimulus?

(a)   (b)

FIGURE 7.2 (a) Ivan Pavlov (the man with the white beard) is shown here with colleagues and one of his canine subjects. (b) In his early research, Pavlov measured salivation by using a simple device similar to the one shown here. In later research, a collection tube was inserted directly into the salivary gland.

conditioning involves *learning an association between stimuli*. Its discovery dates back to the late 1800s and an odd twist of fate.

Pavlov's Pioneering Research

In the 1860s, Ivan Pavlov was studying theology in a Russian seminary and preparing for the priesthood when his career plans unexpectedly changed. A new government policy allowed the translation of Western scientific publications into Russian. Before long, Pavlov read Darwin's theory of evolution and other works, which sparked in him a strong interest in the sciences (Windholz, 1997). Pavlov became a renowned physiologist, conducting research on digestion in dogs that won him the Nobel Prize in 1904.

To study digestion, Pavlov presented various types of food to dogs and measured their natural salivary response (Figure 7.2). But as often occurs in science, Pavlov was about to make an accidental but important discovery through astute observation. He noticed that with repeated testing, the dogs began to salivate *before* the food was presented, such as when they heard the footsteps of the approaching experimenter.

Further study confirmed Pavlov's observation. Dogs have a natural reflex to salivate to food but not to tones. Yet when a tone or other stimulus that ordinarily did not cause salivation was presented just before food powder was squirted directly into a dog's mouth, the sound of the tone alone soon made the dog salivate.

Pavlov's research team rigorously studied this process for decades, and this type of learning by association came to be called *classical* or *Pavlovian conditioning* (Pavlov, 1928). Many psychologists regard Pavlov's discovery as "among the most important in the history of psychology" (Dewsbury, 1997). But why all the fuss about dogs salivating to tones?

This question raises a major point about basic scientific research. As noted in Chapter 2, *what is paramount is the underlying principle being demonstrated, not the specific findings*. Classical conditioning performs a key adaptive function; classical conditioning alerts organisms to stimuli that signal the impending arrival of an important event. As Pavlov noted, if salivation could be conditioned, so might other bodily processes, including those affecting susceptibility to disease and mental disorders.

Basic Principles

What factors influence the acquisition and persistence of conditioned responses? Let us examine some basic principles of conditioning.

Acquisition

Acquisition refers to the period during which a response is being learned. Suppose we wish to condition a dog to salivate to a tone. Sounding the tone initially may cause the dog to perk up its ears and stare at us oddly, but not to salivate. At this time, the tone is a *neutral stimulus* because it does not elicit (i.e., trigger) the salivation response (Figure 7.3). Now, if we place

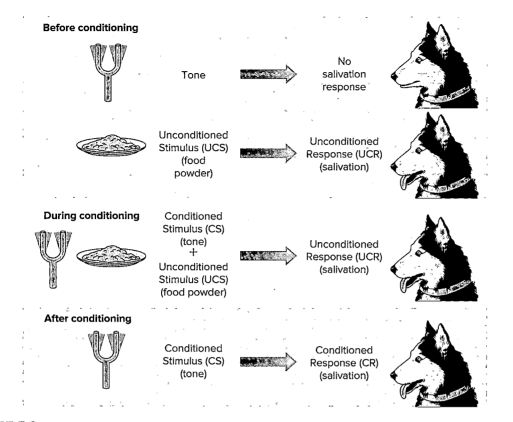

Before conditioning

Tone → No salivation response

Unconditioned Stimulus (UCS) (food powder) → Unconditioned Response (UCR) (salivation)

During conditioning

Conditioned Stimulus (CS) (tone) + Unconditioned Stimulus (UCS) (food powder) → Unconditioned Response (UCR) (salivation)

After conditioning

Conditioned Stimulus (CS) (tone) → Conditioned Response (CR) (salivation)

FIGURE 7.3 In classical conditioning, after a neutral stimulus such as a tone is repeatedly associated with food (unconditioned stimulus), the tone becomes capable of eliciting a salivation response.

food in the dog's mouth, the dog will salivate. This salivation response to food is reflexive—it's what dogs do by nature. Because no learning is required for the food to produce salivation, the food is called an **unconditioned stimulus (UCS)** and salivation is an **unconditioned response (UCR)**. Next the tone and the food are paired—each pairing is called a *learning trial*. After several learning trials, when the tone is presented by itself, the dog salivates even though there is no food. Through association, the tone has become a **conditioned stimulus (CS)** and salivation has become a **conditioned**

response (CR). Table 7.1 offers a quick reference to these classical conditioning terms.

Notice that we have two terms for salivation: *UCR* and *CR*. When the dog salivates to food, this UCR is a *natural, unlearned (unconditioned) reflex*. But when it salivates to a tone, this CR represents a *learned (conditioned) response*.

During acquisition, a CS typically must be paired multiple times with a UCS to establish a strong CR (Figure 7.4). Pavlov also found that a tone became a CS more rapidly when it was followed by greater amounts of food. Indeed,

······································
5. How do you create a conditioned salivation response in a dog?
······································

TABLE 7.1   A Quick Guide to Classical Conditioning

Term	Abbreviation	Description	Example
Unconditioned Stimulus	UCS	A stimulus that innately elicits a response	Food
Conditioned Stimulus	CS	A stimulus that gains value through learning	The sight of your favourite restaurant
Unconditioned Response	UCR	A reflexive, unlearned response to an innately important stimulus	Salivation in response to food
Conditioned Response	CR	A response elicited by a stimulus whose importance depends on past learning	Feeling hungry when you see your favourite restaurant

when the UCS is intense and aversive conditioning may require only one CS-UCS pairing (Richard et al., 2000). Someone who is in a car accident may develop a fear of cars or driving as a result of a single accident (Taylor et al., 2002). In the example of a fear of driving because of an accident, the stimulus (riding in a car) becomes a CS after only one pairing with an intense UCS (an emotionally and physically painful crash). Fear was the UCR, and it can become the CR triggered by the sight of cars or the thought of driving in a car (Taylor et al., 2002).

The sequence and time interval of the CS-UCS pairing also affect conditioning. Learning usually occurs most quickly with *forward short-delay pairing:* The CS (tone) appears first and is still present when the UCS (food) appears. In *forward trace pairing,* the tone would come on and off, and afterward the food would be presented. In forward pairing, it is often optimal for the CS to appear no more than two or three seconds before the UCS (Klein & Mowrer, 1989). Forward pairing has adaptive value because the CS signals the impending arrival of the UCS. Typically, presenting the CS and UCS at the same time (*simultaneous pairing*) produces less rapid conditioning, and learning is slowest, or does not occur at all, when the CS is presented after the UCS (*backward pairing*).

To summarize, classical conditioning usually is strongest when there are repeated CS-UCS pairings, the UCS is more intense, the sequence involves forward pairing, and the time interval between the CS and UCS is short.

Extinction and Spontaneous Recovery

If the function of classical conditioning is to help organisms adapt to their environment, then there must be a way of eliminating the CR when it is no longer appropriate. Fortunately, there is. If the CS is presented repeatedly in the absence of the UCS, the CR weakens and eventually disappears. This process is called **extinction,** and each presentation of the CS without the UCS is called an *extinction trial.* When Pavlov repeatedly presented the tone without the food, the dogs eventually stopped salivating to the tone (Figure 7.4). Occasional re-pairings of the CS (e.g., tone) and the UCS (e.g., food) usually are required to maintain a CR.

Even when a CR extinguishes, this does not mean that all traces of it are erased. If someone has been conditioned to respond to a specific location with fear, perhaps because that location was the scene of an accident, repeated exposure to that location (CS exposure) with no aversive consequences (no UCS), will lead to an extinction of the fear CR. However, if that person encounters that location again after a break, he or she will show a fear response. The extinguished CR, although weakened, has reappeared. This reappearance is called **spontaneous recovery,** which is defined as the reappearance of a previously extinguished

6. Under what circumstances are CRs typically acquired most quickly?

7. Explain the key factor in producing extinction of a CR.

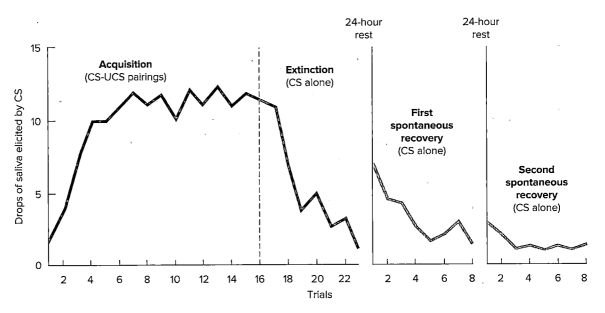

FIGURE 7.4 The strength of the CR (salivation) increases during the acquisition phase as the CS (tone) and the UCS (food) are paired on each trial. During the extinction phase, only the CS is presented, and the strength of the CR decreases and finally disappears. After a rest period following extinction, presentation of the CS elicits a weaker CR (spontaneous recovery) that extinguishes more quickly than before.

CR after a rest period and without new learning trials. As Figure 7.4 shows, the spontaneously recovered CR usually is weaker than the initial CR and extinguishes more rapidly in the absence of the UCS. The phenomenon of spontaneous recovery is why practical applications of extinction, such as treatment of phobias or other anxiety disorders, require multiple sessions. The abnormal CR, such as fear, may appear to have undergone extinction, but it will return in the future. With each set of extinction trials, the CR is progressively weakened, and with sufficient extinction training, spontaneous recovery is weak enough that it is not a problem.

Generalization and Discrimination

Pavlov found that once a CR is acquired, the organism often responds not only to the original CS, but also to stimuli that are similar to it. The greater the stimulus similarity, the greater the chance that a CR will occur. A dog that salivates to a medium-pitched tone is more likely to salivate to a new tone slightly different in pitch, than to a low- or high-pitched tone. Learning theorists call this **stimulus generalization:** Stimuli similar to the initial CS elicit a CR (Figure 7.5).

Stimulus generalization serves critical adaptive functions. An animal that ignores the sound of rustling bushes and then is attacked by a hidden predator will become alarmed by the sound of a rustling bush in the future (assuming it escapes). If stimulus generalization did not occur, then the next time the animal heard rustling it would become alarmed only if the sound were identical to that preceding the earlier attack. This absence of alarm does not

contribute to the animal's survival. Through stimulus generalization, the animal develops an alarm response to a range of rustling sounds. Some will be false alarms, but safe is better than sorry. The more like the original stimulus the new sound is, the stronger the response.

To prevent stimulus generalization from running amok, organisms must be able to *discriminate* (i.e., detect) differences between stimuli. An animal that becomes alarmed at every sound would exhaust itself from stress. It must learn to distinguish irrelevant sounds from those that may signal danger. In classical conditioning, **discrimination** is demonstrated when a CR (such as an alarm reaction) occurs to one stimulus (a sound) but not to others. Organisms can be taught, through conditioning, to behaviourally discriminate two stimuli that were initially treated the same way. Pairing the CS with the UCS combined with pairing similar stimuli with no consequence leads to a narrowing of response to the specific CS and a loss of generalized responses to other similar stimuli.

Higher-Order Conditioning

Imagine that we have exposed a dog to repeated tone-food pairings, and the tone is now a well-established CS that elicits a strong salivation response. Next, suppose that we present a neutral stimulus, such as a black square, and the dog does not salivate. Now, we present the black square just prior to sounding the tone but do not present any food. After repeated square-tone pairings, the square will become a CS and elicit salivation by itself (Figure 7.6). This process, discovered by Pavlov, is called **higher-order conditioning:** A neutral stimulus becomes a CS after being paired with an already established CS. Typically, a higher-order CS produces a CR that is weaker and extinguishes more rapidly than the original CR. The dog will salivate less to the black square than to the tone, and its response to the square will extinguish sooner.

Higher-order conditioning greatly expands the influence of conditioned stimuli and can affect what we come to value, like, fear, or dislike (Hussaini et al., 2007). For example, a child may value a gold star because that gold star was previously paired by social recognition and praise from the teacher.

8. Explain the adaptive significance of stimulus generalization and discrimination.

9. Explain the process of higher-order conditioning.

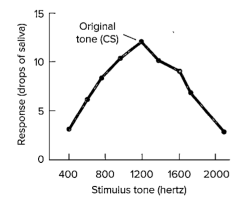

FIGURE 7.5 A stimulus generalization curve. An animal will salivate most strongly to the CS that was originally paired with the UCS. Progressively weaker conditioned responses occur as stimuli become less similar to the CS, as seen here with tones of lower or higher frequencies (pitch).

Applications of Classical Conditioning

Pavlov's belief that salivation was merely the tip of the classical conditioning iceberg has proven

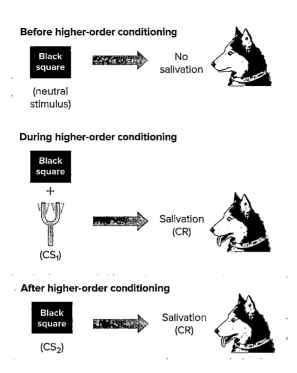

Before higher-order conditioning

Black square (neutral stimulus) ➡ No salivation

During higher-order conditioning

Black square + (CS₁) ➡ Salivation (CR)

After higher-order conditioning

Black square (CS₂) ➡ Salivation (CR)

FIGURE 7.6 Once a tone has become a conditioned stimulus that triggers salivation, we can now use it to condition a salivation response to a new neutral stimulus—a black square. The tone is the CS_1. The black square becomes the CS_2.

correct. Conditioning principles help us understand many diverse human behaviours and problems.

Acquiring and Overcoming Fear

Pavlov's discoveries enabled early American behaviourists to challenge Freud's psychoanalytic view of the causes of anxiety disorders, such as phobias. To explain a snake phobia, no Freudian assumptions about hidden unconscious conflicts or repressed traumas are needed. Instead, the behaviourist view is that snakes have become a fear-triggering CS because of pairing with an aversive UCS (such as injury) and stimulus generalization.

10. How does classical conditioning explain fear acquisition?

Does this explanation seem reasonable? It may, but it suffers from a serious limitation: Almost any explanation can seem plausible when it is provided *after* an event occurs. Behaviourist John B. Watson and his assistant Rosalie Rayner (1920) set out to obtain evidence that fear could be conditioned. They studied a number of infants, including, most famously, an 11-month-old infant named Albert, often referred to as *Little Albert*. One day, as Albert played in a hospital room, Watson and Rayner showed him a white rat. Albert displayed no sign of fear. Later, knowing that Albert *was* afraid of loud noises, they hit a steel bar with a hammer,

Courtesy of Professor Benjamin Harris

FIGURE 7.7 John Watson and Rosalie Rayner examine how Little Albert reacts to a Santa Claus mask.

making a loud noise as they showed Albert the rat. The noise scared Albert and made him cry. After several rat–noise pairings, the sight of the white rat alone made Albert cry.

To examine stimulus discrimination and generalization, Watson and Rayner exposed Albert to other test stimuli. Albert displayed no fear when shown coloured blocks, but furry white or grey objects, such as a rabbit and a bearded Santa Claus mask, made him cry (Figure 7.7). By the time Albert left the hospital, he had not been exposed to any treatment designed to extinguish his fear. Unfortunately, we do not know what became of Albert.

Thinking critically

WAS THE LITTLE ALBERT STUDY ETHICAL?

Review boards that oversee research ethics did not exist in the 1920s. Would you have approved Watson and Rayner's request to conduct the Little Albert study? Why or why not?

Think about it, and then see the Answers section at the end of the book.

Learning theory dominates our current understanding of specific phobias (Ollendick & Muris, 2015). The implication is clear: if a specific phobia was acquired through classical conditioning then exposure to the feared stimulus under neutral or positive circumstances should be an effective form of treatment. That is, if phobias are learned, they can be "unlearned."

In 1924, psychologist Mary Cover Jones successfully treated a boy named Peter, who had a strong fear of rabbits. Jones, who acknowledged Watson and Rayner's work, gradually extinguished Peter's fear by using the procedure shown in Table 7.2. Her approach provided

TABLE 7.2 **Using Exposure Training to Reduce Fear**

This table lists 10 of the 17 steps used by Mary Cover Jones to eliminate Peter's fear of rabbits.

Step No.	Peter's Progress
1	Rabbit anywhere in room triggers fear
2	Rabbit 4 metres away tolerated
4	Rabbit 1 metre away tolerated
5	Rabbit close in cage tolerated
6	Rabbit free in room tolerated
8	Rabbit touched when free in room
10	Rabbit allowed on tray of high chair
12	Holds rabbit on lap
16	Fondles rabbit affectionately
17	Lets rabbit nibble his fingers

Source: Adapted from Jones (1924) A laboratory study of fear: The case of Peter. *Pedagogical Seminary*, 31, 308–315.

the basis of what developed into current behaviour therapies, discussed in Chapter 17. They are called **exposure therapies** because their basic goal is to expose the phobic patient to the feared stimulus (CS) without any UCS, allowing extinction to occur. Although psychologists still debate the contribution of other factors, such as genetic influences (Ollendick & Muris, 2015), exposure therapy is effective in most cases.

Mental imagery, real-life situations, or both can be used to present the phobic stimulus. Exposure therapies are highly effective and represent one of behaviourism's important applied legacies (Hamm, 2009). Recently, clinical psychologists have used virtual reality (VR) as part of exposure therapy to successfully treat spider phobias, fear of flying, claustrophobia, fear of driving, and fear of heights (see the *Applications* feature).

Conditioned Attraction and Aversion

Much of what attracts and pleasurably arouses us is influenced by classical conditioning. Consider sexual arousal. An outfit or the scent of a partner's cologne can become a conditioned stimulus for arousal. Experiments show that pairing a neutral odour with pleasing physical massage increases people's attraction to that smell (Baeyens et al., 1996) and that people become sexually aroused to stimuli after those stimuli have been paired with sexually arousing UCSs (Rachman & Hodgson, 1968).

Classical conditioning also can decrease our arousal and attraction to stimuli. This principle is used in **aversion therapy,** which attempts to condition an aversion (a repulsion) to a stimulus that triggers unwanted behaviour by pairing it with a noxious UCS. To reduce an alcoholic's attraction to alcohol, the patient is given a drug that induces severe nausea when alcohol is consumed. Aversion therapies yield mixed results, often producing short-term changes that do not last or do not generalize outside of the environment where the learning occurred (Garbutt, 2009).

Conditioned attraction and aversion also play a role in attitude formation (Walther, 2002). Neutral stimuli can become attractive or unattractive by being paired with stimuli that already elicit positive or negative attitudes. Advertising executives are keenly aware of classical conditioning's power. They carefully link products and company logos to cute animals, attractive and famous people, humour, "fuzzy-warm" family images, and most of all, to pleasurable interactions with the opposite sex (Figure 7.9). And it works, marketing experiments show that this approach creates favourable attitudes toward novel products (Priluck & Till, 2004).

Behaviourists, such as John Watson, originally argued that an emotional reaction, whether it is fear or attraction, could be classically conditioned to any stimulus. We know now, however, that there are some constraints on learning. For example, it is easier to condition fear to some stimuli than others; we seem to be biologically prepared to easily learn to fear stimuli such as heights, snakes, spiders, and bats. Similarly, it is relatively easy to condition an aversion to a taste by pairing a taste and an illness, but it is very difficult to condition a similar aversion to a visual stimulus by pairing a visual cue and an illness. We will return to this issue later in this chapter when discussing constraints on classical and operant conditioning.

Beyond influencing fear, attraction, and aversion, classical conditioning also can affect our physical health. Allergic responses occur when the immune system overreacts and releases too many antibodies to combat pollen, dust, or other foreign substances (called *allergens*). When a neutral stimulus (such as a distinct odour) is repeatedly paired with a natural allergen (the UCS), it may become a CS that triggers an allergic CR (Irie et al., 2001). Classical conditioning can even increase immune system functioning (Saurer et al., 2008).

11. How is classical conditioning used in society to increase or decrease our arousal/attraction to stimuli?

Applications

LEARNING, VIRTUAL REALITY, AND THERAPY

The most widely accepted theory for the acquisition of anxiety disorders, such as phobias, is that these disorders are acquired through classical conditioning (Ollendick & Muris, 2015). Exposure to an environmental stimulus (CS) is paired with an aversive event (UCS), and as a result, the originally neutral stimulus comes to elicit an emotional reaction of anxiety or fear (CR). If we acquire anxiety disorders through conditioning, then conditioning procedures should be effective at treating these disorders. The most commonly used and most effective therapies for anxiety disorders, such as specific phobias, are based on a classical conditioning model.

These therapeutic approaches have been classified as exposure treatments because they all involve exposure to the phobic stimulus without aversive consequences. From studies of classical conditioning, we know that if a CS is presented repeatedly without any biologically important following event, the learned response will gradually diminish in strength. The traditional exposure therapy approaches have involved presenting the client with either the real, phobic stimulus, or exposure to a series of stimuli that gradually get closer to, and more like, the phobic stimulus. Such procedures, especially when combined with relaxation training, are very effective at treating anxiety disorders such as snake and spider phobias, fear of flying, and public-speaking anxiety. Exposure therapy with gradual introduction of the phobic stimulus is the treatment of choice for specific phobias (Antony & Swinson, 2000; Garcia-Palacios et al., 2002). In a variant of exposure therapy, the client imagines exposure to the feared stimulus rather than confronting the real thing. Clinical research has found that although imaginal exposure can be successful, real-world exposure (referred to as *in vivo* exposure) is superior (Krijn et al., 2004a).

Recent advances in computer and video technology have presented an innovative approach to treating anxiety disorders: the use of virtual reality (VR). VR uses real-time computer graphics and high-resolution three-dimensional visual displays, body tracking, sound, and, in some cases, other types of sensory input (e.g., tactile stimulation) to immerse clients in a computer-generated world. Via a computer, the therapist guides what happens within the client's virtual world (see Figure 7.8). This approach has been referred to as virtual reality exposure therapy (VRET). If you can overcome your fear of snakes, public speaking, or heights with exposure therapy, can that exposure take place in a virtual world? If VRET is effective, then the application of exposure therapy would be more practical in some cases (e.g., fear of flying, fear of heights). This therapy may also be more appealing for individuals who have avoided or abandoned therapy because exposure to the real stimulus generates such intense fear or is impractical.

Mauro Fermariello/Science Source

FIGURE 7.8 In VRET the client wears a VR display helmet (and, in some cases, other means of delivering sensory stimulation) and body position sensors, and is connected to a computer that generates the virtual environment. A therapist controls the virtual environment that the client explores. VR exposure therapy has been found effective for treating phobias, such as spider phobias, and related anxiety disorders.

One study of the effectiveness of VR to treat phobias involved clients with a spider phobia (Garcia-Palacios et al., 2002). Clients in this study had to meet a series of criteria, including the full diagnostic criteria for a specific phobia established by the American Psychiatric Association (DSM-5, American Psychiatric Association, 2013; and see Chapter 17). During treatment, clients donned a VR helmet and visited a virtual kitchen. Gradually, over a series of trials, clients received increasing exposure to a virtual spider. For example, they initially saw a virtual spider at a distance, later they came within arm's reach of a virtual spider, and eventually they were to touch the virtual spider. The goal of the VRET was to have the client hold a furry virtual tarantula within the cyber-kitchen and report low levels of anxiety. In a clever and creative twist, tactile feedback was provided by having the client's real hand explore a model spider while their virtual hand explored the cyber-spider. Across the course of this study, members of a wait-list control group showed no change in their spider phobias. Those who had experienced VRET showed significant and clinically meaningful improvement. Based on behaviour avoidance tests, measures of anxiety, a fear of spiders questionnaire, and a clinician's rating of the phobia, VRET exposure was found to be effective in treating the spider phobia.

continued

Similar approaches have been taken with other types of specific phobias, such as fear of flying, heights, and claustrophobia. A recent meta-analysis (Morina et al., 2015) found that VRET was as effective as *in vivo* exposure post-treatment and at later follow-up. VRET has been used mostly to address specific phobias, but has more recently been applied to post-traumatic stress disorder (PTSD). PTSD is a severe anxiety disorder that can develop in those exposed to severely stressful and traumatic events. PTSD is associated with severe anxiety and distress, painful and uncontrollable reliving of the traumatic event, emotional numbing, and in some cases with impulsive and self-destructive behaviour (we will discuss PTSD is greater detail in Chapter 15). VRET is currently being used to treat combat veterans and victims of terrorist attacks who have developed PTSD. Although more research on the use of VRET to treat PTSD is needed, currently available evidence indicates that VRET can be highly effective in treating PTSD among combat veterans and victims of terrorist attacks (Rizzo et al., 2015).

Interestingly, in a recent survey 70 clinicians were asked what interventions they predicted to increase over the next decade. VRET ranked fourth out of the 45 options provided, with other computer-assisted techniques occupying four out of the top five positons (Norcross et al., 2013).

Theories of phobias and related anxiety disorders that emerged from learning theory led to learning-based treatments that use graded exposure to the anxiety-provoking stimulus. These exposure therapies became the treatment of choice for a range of otherwise debilitating disorders, especially for specific phobias. Virtual exposure to cyber-spiders, enclosed space and airplanes are effective and provide practical benefits, such as improved client compliance. The use of VRET is expanding to successfully treat other anxiety disorders, such as PTSD, one of the most severe of all anxiety disorders.

The McGraw-Hill Companies, Inc./Lars A. Niki, photographer

FIGURE 7.9 Advertisers attempt to classically condition favourable consumer attitudes to products by associating products with other positive stimuli, such as physically attractive models.

OPERANT CONDITIONING: LEARNING THROUGH CONSEQUENCES

For all its power to affect our emotions, attitudes, physiology, and health, classical conditioning cannot explain how a dog learns to sit on command. Nor can it account for how we learn to drive cars, use computers, make friends, or be good citizens. Unlike salivating to a tone, these are not *elicited responses* automatically triggered by some stimulus. Rather, they are *emitted (voluntary) responses*, and they are learned in a different way.

In Review

- Classical conditioning involves pairing a neutral stimulus with an unconditioned stimulus (UCS) that elicits an unconditioned response (UCR). Through repeated pairing, the neutral stimulus becomes a conditioned stimulus (CS) that evokes a conditioned response (CR) similar to the original UCR.

- The acquisition phase involves pairing the CS with the UCS. Extinction, the disappearance of the CR, occurs when the CS is presented repeatedly in the absence of the UCS. Sometimes, spontaneous recovery occurs after a rest period and the CS temporarily will evoke a response even after extinction has taken place.

- Stimulus generalization occurs when a CR is evoked by a stimulus similar to the original CS. Discrimination occurs when a CR occurs to one stimulus but not another.

- Once a stimulus (e.g., a tone) becomes a CS, it can now be used in place of the original UCS (food) to condition other neutral stimuli. This is called higher-order conditioning.

- A wide range of bodily and psychological responses can be classically conditioned, including fears, sexual attraction, and positive and negative attitudes. Techniques based on classical conditioning are highly successful in treating fears and phobias.

12. What evidence led Thorndike to propose the "law of effect?"

Thorndike's Law of Effect

While Pavlov was studying classical conditioning, American psychology student Edward L. Thorndike (1898) was exploring how animals learn to solve problems. He built a special cage, called a *puzzle box*, which could be opened from the inside by pulling a string or stepping on a lever (Figure 7.10). Thorndike placed a hungry animal, such as a cat, inside the box. Food was put outside, and to get it the animal had to learn how to open the box. The cat scratched and pushed the bars, paced, and tried to dig through the floor. By chance, it eventually stepped on the lever, opening the door. Performance slowly improved with repeated trials, and over time the cat learned to press the lever soon after the door was shut.

Because performance improved slowly, Thorndike concluded that the animals did not attain "insight" into the solution. Rather, with trial-and-error, they gradually eliminated responses that failed to open the door, and became more likely to perform actions that worked.

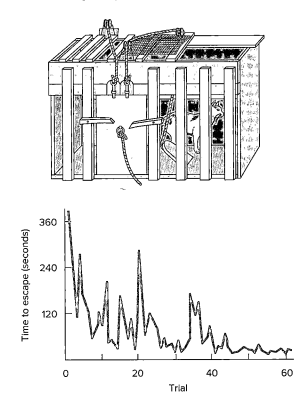

FIGURE 7.10 Through trial and error, cats eventually learned to open Thorndike's puzzle boxes to obtain food.

Source: Based on Thorndike, E.L. (1898). *Animal intelligence: An experimental study of the associative processes in animals.* New York, NY: Macmillan; Thorndike, E.L. (1911). *Animal intelligence: Experimental studies.* New York, NY: Macmillan.

Thorndike (1911) called this process *instrumental learning* because an organism's behaviour is instrumental in bringing about certain outcomes. He also proposed the **law of effect,** which stated that in a given situation, a response followed by a "satisfying" consequence will become more likely to occur, and a response followed by an unsatisfying outcome will become less likely to occur. The law of effect became the foundation for the school of behaviourism.

Skinner's Analysis of Operant Conditioning

Harvard psychologist B.F. Skinner was the leading American proponent of behaviourism throughout most of the 20th century. Skinner coined the term *operant behaviour,* meaning that an organism *operates* on its environment in some way; it emits responses that produce certain consequences. **Operant conditioning** (akin to Thorndike's instrumental learning) is a type of learning in which behaviour is influenced by its consequences (Skinner, 1938, 1953). Responses that produce favourable consequences tend to be repeated, whereas responses that produce unfavourable consequences become less likely to occur. Through operant conditioning, organisms learn to increase behaviours that benefit them and reduce behaviours that harm them.

Skinner designed a special chamber, called a **Skinner box,** to study operant conditioning experimentally. A lever on one wall is positioned above a small cup, and a food pellet automatically drops into the cup whenever a rat presses the lever (Figure 7.11). A hungry rat is put into the chamber and, as it moves about, it accidentally presses the lever. A food pellet clinks into the cup and the rat eats it quickly. We record the rat's behaviour on a *cumulative recorder,* and find that it presses the bar more and more frequently over time. Today, a computer can be programmed to control the delivery of stimuli and reinforcer and to record the responses.

Skinner identified several important types of consequences. For now, we focus on two: reinforcement and punishment. With **reinforcement,** a response is *strengthened* by an outcome that follows it. Typically, "strengthened" is operationally defined as an increase in the frequency of a response. The outcome (a stimulus or event) that increases the frequency of a response is a called a *reinforcer.* Food pellets are reinforcers because they increase the rat's frequency of lever pressing. Once a response becomes established, reinforcers maintain it: The rat keeps pressing the lever because it continues to receive food.

Punishment is the opposite of reinforcement; it occurs when a response is *weakened* by outcomes that follow it. Take our lever-pressing rat. Suppose we change things so that pressing the lever delivers a one-second electric shock, rather than food. If lever pressing decreases (which it will), then the electric shock represents a *punisher*—a consequence that weakens the behaviour. Notice that reinforcers and punishers are defined in terms of their observable effects on behaviour. If the food doesn't increase lever pressing, then for this particular rat it is not a reinforcer.

ABCs of Operant Conditioning

Skinner's analysis of operant behaviour involves three kinds of events: *antecedents* (A), which are stimuli that are present before a behaviour occurs; *behaviours* (B) that the organism emits; and *consequences* (C) that follow the behaviours. Thus,

IF *antecedent stimuli*   IF I say "Sit"

(A) are present
AND *behaviour*   AND my dog Jessie sits,

(B) is emitted,
THEN *consequence*   THEN she gets a tasty treat.

(C) will occur.

The relations between A and B, and between B and C, are called *contingencies.* Jessie's behaviour of sitting is contingent on my saying "Sit." The consequence of receiving food is then contingent on her response of sitting.

Before exploring operant conditioning more closely, we wish to emphasize two points. First, keep in mind the key differences between classical and operant conditioning:

• In classical conditioning, the organism learns an *association between two stimuli*—the CS and UCS (e.g., a tone and food)—that occurs *before* the behaviour (e.g., salivation). In operant conditioning, the organism learns an *association between behaviour and its consequences.* Behaviour changes because of events that occur *after* it.

• Classical conditioning focuses on *elicited* behaviours. The conditioned response is

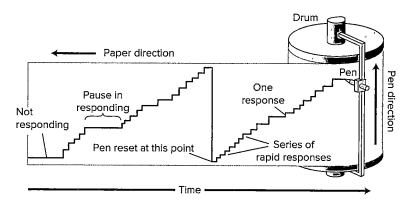

© Nina Leen, *Life Magazine* © *Time, Inc.*

FIGURE 7.11 With B.F. Skinner watching, a rat raises up and presses a lever in an operant experimental chamber (Skinner box). Pressing the lever turns on a light inside the chamber (notice the lever just below and to the right of the light). A food reinforcer is automatically delivered by the apparatus to the left of the box, and the rat's performance is displayed on a cumulative recorder.

triggered involuntarily, almost like a reflex, by a stimulus that precedes it. Operant conditioning focuses on *emitted* behaviours: In a given situation, the organism generates responses (e.g., pressing a lever) that are under its physical control.

Second, although classical and operant conditioning are different processes, many learning situations involve both. When your dog hears the can opener, he will run to you, wagging his tail and salivating. The sound of dinner being prepared is a CS that automatically triggers a

13. Identify two key differences between classical and operant conditioning.

CR of salivation. It also is a signal to your dog that if he comes to you (an operant response) he will be reinforced by the desirable consequence of being fed. Thus, one stimulus (the sound of the can opener) can have classical as well as operant functions, which appear to be processed through different neural pathways in the brain (Schmajuk & Holland, 1998).

Antecedent Conditions: Identifying When to Respond

14. Why are antecedent stimuli important in operant conditioning?

In operant conditioning, the antecedent may be a general situation or specific stimulus. Let's return to our lever-pressing rat. At present, simply being in the Skinner box is the antecedent condition. In this situation, the rat will press the lever. Suppose we place a light on the wall above the lever. When the light is on, pressing the lever dispenses food, but when the light is off, no food is given. The rat will soon learn to press the lever only when the light is on. The light becomes a **discriminative stimulus,** a signal that a particular response will now produce certain consequences. Discriminative stimuli "set the occasion" for operant responses.

Discriminative stimuli guide much of our everyday behaviour. If you are hungry, food on your plate is a discriminative stimulus to start eating. Classroom bells, the sight of your favourite restaurant, the words people speak to us, and the sight of a friend's face are all discriminative stimuli that set the occasion for us to make certain responses.

Consequences: Determining How to Respond

15. How does negative reinforcement differ from positive reinforcement and from punishment?

16. Explain how operant extinction, positive punishment, and negative punishment differ.

Behaviour is governed by its consequences. Two major types of reinforcement strengthen responses, and two major types of punishment weaken them. It is important to remember that reinforcement and punishment refer to whether the response is strengthened (reinforcement) or weakened (punishment), they do not refer to the emotional value of the event. It is also important to keep in mind that when discussing the consequences of behaviour the use of the terms "positive" and "negative" refer to something be added or something being taken away; they do not refer to whether something is good, or pleasurable, or aversive. You can think of "positive" as the plus sign (+) in arithmetic, something is added. Similarly, think of "negative" as the minus sign (–), something is taken away.

Operant behaviour also is weakened by extinction. Figure 7.12 shows these processes.

Positive Reinforcement

Behaviour is reinforced by desirable outcomes. Being *presented with* a stimulus we find pleasing represents a desirable outcome. A rat receives food for pressing a lever. We receive pay for performing a job. This process is called **positive reinforcement:** A response is strengthened by the subsequent *presentation* of a stimulus. The stimulus that follows and strengthens the response is called a *positive reinforcer.* Food, drink, comforting physical contact, attention, praise, and money are common positive reinforcers.

The term *reward* often is used as if it were synonymous with positive reinforcement. Behaviourists prefer the term *positive reinforcement* because it describes how consequences affect behaviour. In many instances, "rewards" do not function as positive reinforcers. Parents may "reward" a child with a new toy for cleaning her room, but if the child does not clean her room again, then the toy was not a positive reinforcer for that behaviour.

Negative Reinforcement

Receiving something pleasurable is a good outcome, but it's only half of the story. Getting rid of something we find aversive—or avoiding something we anticipate will be aversive—also is a good outcome. We take Aspirin to relieve headaches and we put on a sweater to warm up on a cold day. This process is called **negative reinforcement:** A response is strengthened by the subsequent *removal or avoidance* of a stimulus (see Figure 7.12). The stimulus that is removed or avoided is called a *negative reinforcer.*

It is easy to confuse negative reinforcement with punishment. Remember that the "negative" in negative reinforcement refers to something being taken away; it does not refer to the emotional impact. Reinforcement means that a response is strengthened. Hence, negative reinforcement is strengthening a response by removing some event or stimulus. For example, putting on a sweater is reinforced because it removes something aversive—being cold. Later in this chapter we will discuss in detail two important examples of negative reinforcement: escape conditioning and avoidance conditioning.

Operant Extinction

Operant extinction is the weakening and eventual disappearance of a response because

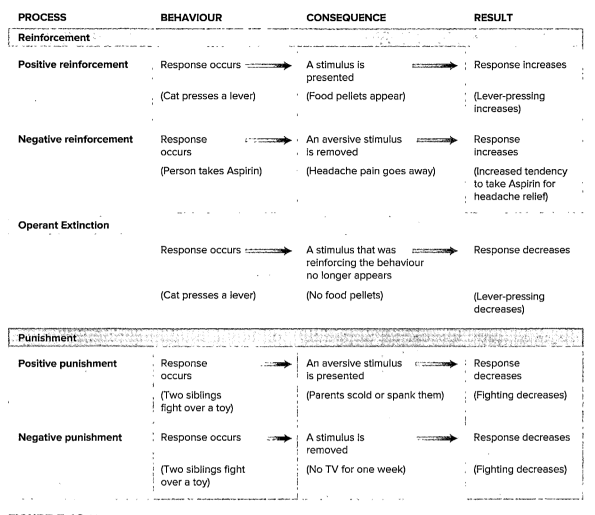

PROCESS	BEHAVIOUR	CONSEQUENCE	RESULT
Reinforcement			
Positive reinforcement	Response occurs ⟹	A stimulus is presented ⟹	Response increases
	(Cat presses a lever)	(Food pellets appear)	(Lever-pressing increases)
Negative reinforcement	Response occurs ⟹	An aversive stimulus is removed ⟹	Response increases
	(Person takes Aspirin)	(Headache pain goes away)	(Increased tendency to take Aspirin for headache relief)
Operant Extinction			
	Response occurs ⟹	A stimulus that was reinforcing the behaviour no longer appears ⟹	Response decreases
	(Cat presses a lever)	(No food pellets)	(Lever-pressing decreases)
Punishment			
Positive punishment	Response occurs ⟹	An aversive stimulus is presented ⟹	Response decreases
	(Two siblings fight over a toy)	(Parents scold or spank them)	(Fighting decreases)
Negative punishment	Response occurs ⟹	A stimulus is removed ⟹	Response decreases
	(Two siblings fight over a toy)	(No TV for one week)	(Fighting decreases)

FIGURE 7.12 Five major operant processes.

it is no longer reinforced. When previously reinforced behaviours no longer pay off, we are likely to abandon and replace them with more successful ones. If pressing a lever no longer results in food pellets, the rat eventually will stop making this response. If taking an Aspirin no longer relives your headaches, you will stop taking Aspirins.

The degree to which non-reinforced responses persist is called *resistance to extinction*. Non-reinforced responses may stop quickly (low resistance), or they may keep occurring hundreds or thousands of times (high resistance). People who solicit charitable donations do not stop just because 100 passersby in a row fail to give money. As we examine later, resistance to extinction is strongly influenced by the pattern of reinforcement that has previously maintained the behaviour. If you can identify the reinforcers that are maintaining an undesirable behaviour, operant extinction can provide a good alternative

to punishment as a method for reducing that behaviour (Putri, 2015).

Positive Punishment

Like reinforcement, punishment comes in two forms. One involves actively *applying* aversive stimuli, such as painful slaps, electric shock, and verbal reprimands. This is **positive punishment,** also called *aversive punishment*. A response is *weakened* by the subsequent *presentation* of a stimulus. Scolding a child for misbehaving is an obvious example, but so is a child's touching a hot stovetop. The pain delivered by the stovetop makes it less likely that the child will touch it in the future. Positive punishment often is subtle. A teenager wears a new blouse, and her close friends half-heartedly say "Uh-huh, nice," but their facial expressions betray dislike and the student stops wearing the shirt.

Positive punishment often produces rapid results, an important consideration when it is necessary to stop a particularly dangerous

17. Describe some disadvantages of using positive punishment to control behaviour.

of time. The first of these is a ratio schedule. On *ratio schedules,* a certain percentage of responses is reinforced. The key factor is that ratio schedules are based on the number of correct responses. In the workplace, this reinforcement method is called *pay for performance.* An example is being paid on a quota system—when you meet your quota you get paid. The second option is an *interval schedule* under which a certain amount of time must elapse between reinforcements, regardless of how many correct responses have occurred. The key factor is that interval schedules are based on the passage of time. An example would be receiving an hourly wage. It does not matter how many lattes your barista has made during the past hour, he still gets the same amount of money for having worked that hour.

Schedules of reinforcement can also vary as fixed versus variable schedules. With a *fixed schedule,* reinforcement always occurs after a specific—that is, fixed—number of responses or time interval. With a *variable schedule,* the required number of responses or the time interval varies at random around an average. Combining these dimensions creates four types of reinforcement schedules (Table 7.3).

Fixed-Ratio Schedule

On a **fixed-ratio (FR) schedule,** reinforcement is given after a fixed number of responses. For example, FR-3 means that reinforcement occurs after every third response, regardless of how long it takes for those responses to occur. Fixed-ratio schedules produce high rates of responding. That is one reason why some businesses prefer paying employees' wages based on a set number of items produced. FR schedules result in greater work output than hourly wages (Pritchard et al., 1980). If the ratio is gradually increased over time, many responses can be obtained with relatively few reinforcements.

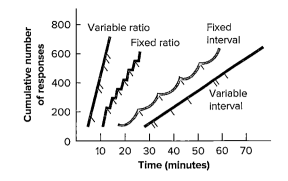

FIGURE 7.15 Each type of positive reinforcement schedule produces a typical cumulative response curve. The hash marks indicate the delivery of a reinforcer. Ratio schedules produce a high rate of responding, as shown in the steep slopes of the curves. Variable schedules produce a steadier rate of responding. Notice the prominent scallops in the fixed interval schedule; the subject learns to stop responding until the time interval for the next reinforcement approaches.

Some labour unions fight against the use of piecework wage systems, believing that they tempt employees to work to exhaustion.

FR schedules have a second characteristic effect. As shown in Figure 7.15, the organism often pauses briefly after each reinforcement, perhaps because the next response (or responses) is never reinforced.

Variable-Ratio Schedule

On a **variable-ratio (VR) schedule,** reinforcement is given after a variable number of correct responses, based on an average. A VR-3 schedule means that, *on average,* three responses are required for reinforcement, but the number of responses required will vary from trial to trial.

VR schedules, like FR schedules, produce a high rate of responding, but because the occurrence of reinforcement is less predictable on a VR schedule, there is less pausing after reinforcement. After all, the next response just

TABLE 7.3 **The Four Types of Partial Reinforcement Schedules**

	Fixed (F)	Variable (V)
Ratio (R)	FR: Reinforcement after completing a **constant number** of responses.	VR: Reinforcement after completing a **changing number** of responses.
	e.g., receiving a free coffee after having your loyalty card stamped 10 times	e.g., a variable and unpredictable number of responses need to occur before the slot machine pays off
Interval (I)	FI: Reinforcement is available after a **constant** length of **time**	VI: Reinforcement is available after a **changing** length of **time**
	e.g., receiving an hourly wage	e.g., email messages arrive at scattered and unpredictable times through the day

Brand X Pictures

FIGURE 7.16 Gambling is reinforced on a variable-ratio schedule. It is *ratio,* because the frequency of reinforcement is based on the amount of performance. On average, you will receive more payoffs when you pull the slot machine 100 times than when you play only 10 times. It is *variable,* because you never know when the next jackpot may occur.

might be reinforced. This leads to high, steady rate of responding, as shown in Figure 7.16. VR schedules also are highly resistant to extinction, because the organism learns that periods of no payoff eventually are followed by reinforcement.

Many gambling activities are maintained by VR schedules (Figure 7.16). A gambler, for example, may play a slot machine programmed to pay off an *average* of every 20 pulls (a VR-20 schedule). After eight pulls, our gambler receives a 10-coin payoff. After five more pulls, another payoff. But then, after 40 more attempts, nothing. He's frustrated but "hooked" by the VR schedule. The next attempt might be the one that pays off with a big jackpot, so our gambler plays again . . . and again.

Fixed-Interval Schedule

On a **fixed-interval (FI) schedule,** the first correct response that occurs after a fixed time interval is reinforced. Suppose a rat is pressing a lever on an FI-3 (minute) schedule. After a lever press is reinforced, for the next three minutes there will be no further reinforcement

regardless of the number of responses produced. Once these three minutes elapse, the next lever press is reinforced. The FI schedule's characteristic response pattern is shown in Figure 7.15. After each reinforcement, there is a pause, followed by increased responding as the time interval passes and the next reinforcement nears.

You likely have courses with scheduled midterm and end of term exams. Your study behaviour may resemble the pattern shown in Figure 7.15 for an FI schedule, reflecting relatively little studying during the period immediately following each exam, and an increasing amount of studying as the next scheduled exam approaches. This uneven performance rate is typical of FI schedules.

Variable-Interval Schedule

On a **variable-interval (VI) schedule,** reinforcement is given for the first response that occurs after a variable time interval. A VI-3 schedule means that, *on average,* there is a three-minute interval between opportunities to obtain reinforcement. Sometimes, responses only a few seconds apart may be reinforced; at other times the interval may be many minutes. As Figure 7.15 shows, because the availability of reinforcement is less predictable than with an FI schedule, the VI schedule produces a steadier response rate.

Pop quizzes represent a VI schedule. A course might average a quiz every two weeks, but they can occur anytime. Their unpredictable timing will produce a steadier approach to studying than regularly scheduled quizzes.

Partial Reinforcement, Learning, and Extinction

Reinforcement schedules significantly influence the rate of learning and extinction. Continuous reinforcement produces more rapid learning than partial reinforcement. However, continuously reinforced responses also extinguish more rapidly because the shift to no reinforcement is sudden and obvious.

Partial reinforcement produces behaviour that is learned more slowly but is more resistant to extinction, especially if the behaviour is reinforced on a *variable* schedule. If reinforcement has been unpredictable in the past, it takes longer to learn that it is gone forever. Most people do not continue to drop coins into a vending machine that doesn't deliver, because vending machines are supposed to operate on a continuous schedule. But it would take many pulls of a slot machine to recognize that it had stopped paying off completely. From our discussion you

23. Are variable or fixed schedules more resistant to extinction? Why?

could predict that the best way to promote fast learning and high resistance to extinction is to begin reinforcing the desired behaviour on a continuous schedule until the behaviour is well established. Then, shift to a partial (preferably variable) schedule that is gradually made more demanding. Knowing the impact of each type of schedule allows a psychologist to tailor the learning environment to produce the pattern of behaviour desired.

FIGURE 7.17 The shuttlebox is used to study escape and avoidance learning.

Escape and Avoidance Conditioning

Behaviour often involves escaping from or avoiding unpleasant situations. Simple escape situations include taking medications to relieve pain and putting on more clothes when we are cold. Examples of avoidance include putting on lotion to avoid sunburn and obeying traffic laws to avoid tickets. As you can recognize from these examples, escape and avoidance conditioning are both forms of negative reinforcement; an instance where the removal of an event or stimulus leads to an increase in behaviour.

In **escape conditioning,** organisms learn a response to terminate an aversive stimulus. If you are cold, you put on a sweater to escape the aversive state of being cold. Putting on a sweater is negatively *reinforced* by the desired consequence that you no longer shiver. Taking two Aspirin is negatively *reinforced* by the reduction of headache pain; you escape the pain.

In **avoidance conditioning,** the organism learns a response to completely avoid an aversive stimulus. That is, in avoidance conditioning we learn to respond before the aversive stimulus even begins. For example, if you put on a sweater *after* you feel chilled and it warms you, that is escape learning. If you put on your sweater *before* going outside and this prevents you from feeling cold at all, that is avoidance learning.

Escape and avoidance conditioning can be demonstrated experimentally (Zhuikov et al., 1994). For example, an animal is placed in a shuttlebox, a rectangular chamber divided into two compartments and connected by a doorway (Figure 7.17). The floor is a grid through which electric shock can be delivered to either compartment. When shock is turned on in the animal's compartment, it attempts to escape. Eventually, it runs through the door and into the other compartment. When shock is delivered

to that compartment, it can escape by running back to the original side. Running through the door removes the shock, which negatively *reinforces* this escape behaviour. Over a few trials, the animal learns to escape as soon as the shock is administered.

To study avoidance conditioning experimentally, researchers introduce a warning signal, such as a light, that precedes the shock by a few seconds. After a few trials, the animal learns that the light signals impending shock. It runs to the other compartment as soon as it sees the light, and thereby avoids being shocked. Once this avoidance response is learned, it often is hard to extinguish. This finding is puzzling, because the animal no longer experiences any shock after the light is turned on.

According to one model, the **two-factor theory of avoidance learning,** classical *and* operant conditioning are involved in avoidance learning (Mowrer, 1947; Rescorla & Solomon, 1967). For our rat, the warning light initially is a neutral stimulus paired with shock (UCS). Through classical conditioning, the light becomes a CS that elicits fear. Now operant conditioning takes over. Fleeing from the light is *negatively reinforced* by the termination of fear. This strengthens and maintains the avoidance response. Now, if we permanently turn off the shock, the avoidance response prevents extinction from taking place. Seeing the light come on, the animal will not "hang around" long enough to learn that the shock no longer occurs.

Two-factor theory helps us understand how many avoidance behaviours develop (Levis, 1989; Plaud & Plaud, 1998). However, it has trouble explaining some aspects of avoidance, such as why people and other animals develop phobic avoidance to some stimuli (e.g., snakes) much more easily than to others (e.g., squirrels). We will return to this issue a little later when we consider biology and learning.

24. Describe the role of negative reinforcement in escape and avoidance conditioning.

Applications of Operant Conditioning

Skinner was passionate about applying operant principles to enhance human welfare. In his bestselling books *Walden Two* (1948) and *Beyond Freedom and Dignity* (1971), Skinner set forth his utopian vision of how a "technology of behaviour" based on positive reinforcement could put an end to war, improve education, and solve a range of social problems. To his critics, Skinner's ideas conjured up images of people being manipulated like rats, of "Big Brother" controlling its citizens. But Skinner's point was that social influence is a natural part of human existence. Parents and children influence one another, as do employees and employers, teachers and students, friends, roommates, and romantic partners. We smile and say "please" to increase the chance someone will do us a favour. In Skinner's view, individual and societal problems are created by the *haphazard* use of reinforcement and overreliance on punishment.

Training Animals

Through shaping and chaining, animals can learn to perform some truly remarkable behaviours. Some are trained to be TV, movie, or circus performers, while others learn to assist people who are blind or have other disabilities (Figure 7.18). Law enforcement and military organizations also rely on operantly trained animals. Police dogs assist officers on routine patrol, and other dogs learn to use their sense of smell to locate hidden bombs, illegal drugs, and missing persons (Gazit & Terkel, 2003).

Some applications push the boundaries of ingenuity, such as using pigeons to assist

© Luc Marescot/Gamma

FIGURE 7.18 Because of injuries suffered in an accident, this woman cannot move her arms or legs. The monkey has been operantly trained to assist her with basic chores, such as eating.

in air-sea rescue. Pigeons have sharp long-distance visual acuity and a wide field of vision. Years ago, the U.S. Coast Guard put these abilities to good use by training pigeons to peck a key whenever they saw an orange object (Simmons, 1981). Orange, of course, is the international colour of life jackets. Three trained pigeons were then placed in a glass dome mounted underneath the search-and-rescue helicopter. Each pigeon had a different view outside, but together, they covered the entire 360° visual field. When a pigeon spotted an orange object in the ocean, it pecked a key connected to a particular directional signal in the cockpit. Depending on which pigeon was pecking at any moment, the pilot maintained or altered course and was guided to the victim's location.

Human Applications: Education, the Workplace, and Beyond

Walk into your local computer store and you likely will find shelves of educational software, teaching everything from geography and math to foreign languages. The effectiveness of such computerized instruction rests on two key principles championed by Skinner: *immediate performance feedback* and *self-paced learning.*

Skinner was deeply concerned about the inefficiency of traditional instructional methods (1961, 1989a). He developed mechanical teaching machines that presented material, quizzed the student, and provided immediate feedback. Students who did not learn the material the first time could repeat steps. Those who did learn the material could advance their machine to the next set of information. Personal computers turned Skinner's vision into an educational reality. *Computer-assisted instruction* also is found in business, industry, and the military (Tung et al., 2009).

A key behaviourist assumption is that poor performance occurs when the *environment* is not providing the proper consequences to reinforce the desired behaviour. **Token economies,** in which desirable behaviours are quickly reinforced with tokens (e.g., points, gold stars) that are later turned in for other reinforcers (e.g., prizes, recreational time), have been used to enhance academic performance, increase work performance, and aid treatment in group homes (Athens et al., 2007).

Finally, Skinner's work gave rise to a field called **applied behaviour analysis** (also known as *behaviour modification*), which

25. How has operant animal training helped humans?

26. In what broad ways has operant conditioning directly enhanced human welfare?

combines a behavioural approach with the scientific method to solve individual and societal problems (Kazdin, 1975; Matson, 2009). Essentially, a program (usually based on positive reinforcement) is designed and implemented to change behaviour, and its effectiveness is objectively measured by gathering data before and after the program is in place.

Applied behaviour analysis has been used to reduce an array of behaviour problems. It has been used in situations that have ranged from chronic hair pulling, to drivers' failure to use seat belts (Byrd et al., 2002), to safety improvements around stop signs (Van Houten & Retting, 2001). Applied behaviour analysis has been used to improve students' academic performance and social skills, enhanced elite athletic performance, and reduced unsportsmanlike behaviour (Hughes et al., 1998; Wilder et al., 2009). Workplace applications include increasing employee productivity, reducing injuries and accidents, enhancing the job interview skills of unemployed adults, and increasing energy conservation (Staats et al., 2000).

Review

- Thorndike's law of effect states that responses followed by satisfying consequences will be strengthened, whereas those followed by unsatisfying consequences will be weakened.

- B.F. Skinner analyzed operant conditioning in terms of relations between antecedents, behaviours, and consequences. Antecedents that signal the likely consequences of particular behaviours in a given situation are called *discriminative stimuli.*

- Operant behaviours are emitted (under voluntary control), whereas classically conditioned responses are elicited (reflexive). Classically conditioned responses are influenced by what happens before the behaviour (i.e., by the CS-UCS pairing), whereas operant behaviours are influenced by consequences that occur after the behaviour.

- Reinforcement occurs when a response is strengthened by an outcome (a reinforcer) that follows it. With positive reinforcement, a response is followed by the presentation of a positive stimulus, so the response becomes stronger. With negative reinforcement, a response is followed by the removal of an aversive stimulus, so again, the response becomes stronger.

- Operant extinction is the weakening and eventual disappearance of a response because it no longer is reinforced.

- Punishment occurs when a response is weakened by an outcome (a punisher) that follows it. With positive punishment, a behaviour is followed by the presentation of an aversive stimulus, and the behaviour becomes weaker. With negative punishment, a behaviour is followed by the removal of a positive stimulus, and the behaviour becomes weaker.

- Shaping, which uses the method of successive approximations, involves the reinforcement of behaviours that increasingly resemble the final desired behaviour.

- When behaviour changes in one situation because of reinforcement or punishment, and then this new response carries over to similar situations, this is called *operant generalization.* In contrast, when an operant response is made to one discriminative stimulus but not to another, this is called *operant discrimination.*

- On a continuous reinforcement schedule, every response is reinforced. Partial reinforcement may occur on a ratio schedule, in which a certain percentage of responses are reinforced, or on an interval schedule, in which a certain amount of time must pass before a response gets reinforced. In general, ratio schedules produce higher rates of performance than interval schedules.

- On fixed-ratio and fixed-interval schedules, reinforcement always occurs after a fixed number of correct responses or a fixed time interval. On variable schedules, the required number of responses or interval of time varies around some average.

- Learning occurs most rapidly under continuous reinforcement, but partial schedules produce behaviours that are more resistant to extinction.

- Escape and avoidance conditioning result from negative reinforcement. According to the two-factor theory, fear is created through classical conditioning. This fear motivates escape and avoidance, which is then negatively reinforced by fear reduction.

- Animals are operantly trained to perform in entertainment industries and to assist disabled people, the police, and the military. Human applications include teaching machines, computerized instruction, token economies, and applied behaviour analysis.

BIOLOGY AND LEARNING

For decades behaviourists assumed that they could condition virtually any behaviour an organism was physically capable of performing. Yet evidence mounted that "conditioned" animals did not always respond as they were supposed to. The behaviourist assumption was wrong because it ignored a key principle discussed at the outset of this chapter: Behaviour is influenced by an organism's evolutionary history (Crawford & Anderson, 1989).

Martin Seligman's (1970) concept of "preparedness" captures this idea. **Preparedness** means that, through evolution, animals are biologically "prewired" to easily learn behaviours related to their survival as a species. Behaviours contrary to an organism's natural tendencies are learned slowly, if at all. Let's consider some examples.

Constraints on Classical Conditioning: Learned Taste Aversions

Imagine eating or drinking something, and then becoming sick to your stomach. Perhaps it is food poisoning. Or perhaps, like cancer patients, it is chemotherapy that makes you ill. Pairing the smell and taste of food (CS) with a toxin or some illness-producing agent (UCS) can produce a CR called **conditioned taste aversion:** The taste and smell of the food now disgusts and repulses us (Garcia et al., 1985). It may even make us feel queasy, and we learn to avoid it. Cancer patients may develop aversions to foods they eat before treatment even though they know that the food did not cause their post-treatment stomach illness. Pairing food with nausea creates an aversion involuntarily.

Psychologist John Garcia pioneered numerous taste aversion experiments that challenged two basic assumptions of classical conditioning. First, behaviourists had assumed that the CS-UCS time interval had to be relatively short, usually within a few seconds. Garcia showed that animals learned taste aversions even though exposure to the taste (CS) was up to several hours—or even a day—before they became ill (UCR).

Second, in a classic experiment, Garcia illustrated how biological preparedness influences learned aversions (Garcia & Koelling, 1966). Whenever rats licked a drinking tube, they were simultaneously exposed to three neutral stimuli: sweet-tasting water, a bright light, and a buzzer (Figure 7.19). In one condition, half the rats were

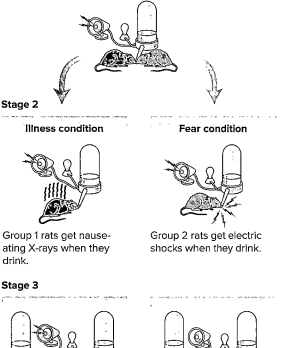

Stage 1: All Rats
When rats touch the drinking tube, sweet water is delivered and a light and buzzer turn on.

Stage 2

Illness condition

Fear condition

Group 1 rats get nauseating X-rays when they drink.

Group 2 rats get electric shocks when they drink.

Stage 3

Group 1 rats avoid the sweet water and prefer the plain water with the light and buzzer.

Group 2 rats still drink the sweet water, but avoid the plain water with the light and buzzer.

FIGURE 7.19 Biological preparedness in classical conditioning. This figure illustrates the design and main results of Garcia and Koelling's (1966) aversion experiment.

exposed to X-rays (UCS) upon drinking the water, which later made them ill (UCR). Would the rats develop an aversion to all three neutral stimuli? No, they avoided the sweet water but not the light or buzzer. Why did only the sweet taste become a CS? Because rats are biologically primed, or prepared, to form taste-illness associations, which means that in nature they most easily identify poisonous or "bad" food by its taste (or smell). Sounds and lights in nature don't make rats sick.

When rats in a second condition licked the tube, the light, buzzer, and sweet taste were all paired with an electric shock. Would the rats learn to fear all three neutral stimuli? No, they avoided the light and buzzer, but kept drinking the sweet water. This action also makes adaptive sense. In nature, sights and sounds—but not how food and drink taste—signal fear-provoking situations (e.g., a cat about to pounce). The same principle applies in humans. When a food makes us sick, we may develop an aversion to

27. How do learned taste aversions illustrate the concept of preparedness?

28. How has knowledge of learned taste aversions been applied to help animals?

it, but not to the friends we ate with. Furthermore, seeing the food again may repulse us, but it would not make us afraid.

Psychologists have applied their knowledge of conditioned aversions to save animals' lives. To prevent coyotes from killing ranchers' sheep, Carl Gustavson and his colleagues laced pieces of meat with lithium chloride, a nausea-inducing, non-lethal drug (Gustavson et al., 1974). The meat was wrapped in sheep hide and left out for coyotes to eat. The coyotes ate it, became ill, developed an aversion to the meat, and became less likely to kill sheep. This conditioning saved the lives of sheep and also of the coyotes, who otherwise would have been shot by ranchers. As part of wildlife management, researchers also have created conditioned aversions to various foods in other species, such as raccoons, wolves, and baboons (Gustavson & Gustavson, 1985). For an intriguing example of nature's own use of learned taste aversions, see Figure 7.20.

As mentioned earlier, a serious problem that can occur with patients receiving chemotherapy is that chemotherapy makes many patients extremely nauseous. Patients undergoing chemotherapy are thus exposed to the necessary conditions for the development of conditioned aversions: a CS (taste and smell of food at mealtime) is later followed by nausea (UCS), in this instance caused not by food but by the cancer treatment (Bovbjerg, 2006; Hickok, Morrow, & Roscoe, 2001; Stockhorst, Steingrueber, Enck, & Klosterhalfen, 2006). Patients receiving chemotherapy for cancer risk the gradual elimination of more and more items from their diets as they accumulate more and more conditioned aversions. This is especially important for children,

who do not have as long a learning history about foods as do adults. Although it may not be possible to completely prevent the development of conditioned taste aversions, it is possible to direct how they form. Darla Broberg and Ilene Bernstein (1987) gave child cancer patients unusual-tasting candy before their chemotherapy treatments. The candy, with its novel and unusual flavour, became the "scapegoat" for the children's taste aversions, protecting them from developing aversions to their normal foods.

Are We Biologically Prepared to Fear Certain Things?

Seligman (1971) and others (e.g., Öhman, 2008) proposed that humans, like other animals, are biologically prepared to acquire certain fears more readily than others. Case studies of phobic patients support this idea. The British psychologist Isaac Marks (1977) provided a famous example of this idea. A four-year-old girl saw a snake and then had her hand accidentally slammed in a car door. Although it was a car that injured her, she developed a lasting phobia not of cars or car doors, but of snakes.

Numerous experiments by Arne Öhman and his Swedish research team provide evidence of preparedness (Öhman et al., 1978; Öhman & Soares, 1998). For example, it has been shown that participants will easily develop conditioned fear responses to pictures of snakes, spiders, or angry faces, but not to pictures of flowers, houses, berries, or happy faces, even when the pictures are shown too briefly to be consciously perceived. Humans develop phobias to many stimuli, but most often we fear things that seem to

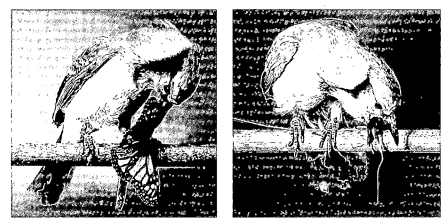

(both): Lincoln P. Brower

FIGURE 7.20 This blue jay has never eaten a monarch butterfly before and doesn't pass up an easy meal. Soon toxins in the butterfly cause food poisoning. The jay feels discomfort, vomits, and develops a conditioned aversion triggered by the sight of the monarch's brightly patterned wings. From now on, it will leave monarchs alone.

have evolutionary significance: snakes, spiders, other animals, and dangerous places. Although there are cases of it occurring, people rarely develop phobias to the things that really do injure, maim, and kill people in today's world; phobias to cars, cigarettes, knives, and guns are rare. Is this the result of evolution-based preparedness, or might it be due to learning experiences within our own lifetime? Through cultural transmission of knowledge, perhaps we come to expect that some stimuli can be dangerous, making us "cognitively" rather than "biologically" prepared to acquire certain fears. As children we all heard friends and relatives exclaim that snakes and spiders are frightening and repulsive. The role of cognitive factors in human fear conditioning continues to be examined (Davey, 1995), but one thing is clear: As with taste aversions, fear can be conditioned much more easily to some stimuli than to others.

Constraints on Operant Conditioning: Animals That "Won't Shape Up"

Two of B.F. Skinner's students, Keller and Marian Breland, became renowned animal trainers. They used shaping and chaining to train thousands of animals for circuses, advertising agencies, TV, and movies. Training usually was successful but not always. Sometimes the animals simply refused to behave according to the "laws" of operant conditioning (Breland & Breland, 1961, 1966).

On one occasion, the Brelands tried to train a chicken to play baseball. The game was arranged so that a small ball would roll toward home plate, and the chicken would pull a chain to swing a small metal bat. If the ball was hit, a bell would ring and the chicken would run to first base to get its food. The Brelands easily trained the chicken to pull the chain that swung the bat and to run to first base when it heard the bell. But when the ball was introduced into the game, utter chaos occurred. Whenever the chicken hit the ball, instead of running to first base to collect its food reinforcement, it chased the ball all over the playing field, pecking furiously at it, and flapping its wings. Try as they might, the Brelands could not extinguish these behaviours. End of training, and end of the chicken's baseball career. In this and many other examples, animals simply refused to "shape up."

The Brelands found that once a particular stimulus came to represent food, animals began to act as if it *were* food. The chicken pecked at the ball as if it were something to eat. In another

example, raccoons received tokens they were to deposit in a piggy bank. Rather than dropping the tokens into the bank, they kept rubbing their tokens together; an action raccoons naturally perform with food that has a hard shell. These behaviours are so deeply rooted in the animals' evolutionary history that it simply overrode the conditioning procedure. The Brelands called this **instinctive drift**: A conditioned response "drifts" back toward instinctive behaviour.

Experiments confirm that operant learning is constrained by biology. For example, it is relatively easy to train a pigeon to peck a novel object (such as a disc on a wall) for food reinforcers, because pigeons come into the world biologically primed to peck for food. Training a pigeon to peck an object to escape from electric shock is more difficult because in their natural environment pigeons do not escape from danger by pecking; they fly away.

Learning and the Brain

Biology and learning are deeply intertwined. Clearly, biology determines our ability to learn. The concepts of preparedness and instinctive drift illustrate how organisms are biologically predisposed to learn some associations more easily than others. Neuroscientists have found that certain brain regions, such as the nucleus accumbens, and certain neurotransmitters, such as dopamine, play a key role in regulating the ability to predict and experience reward (Platt & Pearson, 2016).

Yet, no single part of the brain "controls" learning. For example, the cerebellum plays an important role in acquiring classically conditioned movements—such as conditioned eyeblink responses—whereas the amygdala is centrally involved in acquiring classically conditioned fears (Carr, 2016; LeDoux, 1992). We examine the brain mechanisms underlying learning more closely when discussing memory in the next chapter (without memory, we could not learn from experience).

Biology affects learning, but experience and learning environments also influence our biological functioning (Wachs, 2000). Compared with their littermates who grow up in standard cages, young animals who are exposed to enriched environments—with toys and greater opportunities to learn—develop heavier brains with more dendrites and synapses, and with greater concentrations of various neurotransmitters (Rosenzweig, 1984). Experiments with humans find that infants who regularly receive stimulating "touch sessions" develop more mature movement patterns, are less stressed, and perform

29. What evidence led the Brelands to propose the concept of instinctive drift?

30. How do biology and learning influence each other?

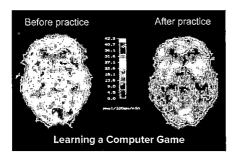

© Monte S. Buchsbaum, M.D., Mt. Sinai School of Medicine, New York, NY.

FIGURE 7.21. While learning a computer game, the brain of a novice player is highly active and uses a lot of energy, as indicated by the large yellow and red areas in the left PET scan. As the right scan shows, energy consumption decreases with experience.

31. How do the concepts of "insight" and "cognitive maps" challenge the behaviourist view of learning?

better on cognitive tests than infants who do not receive these sessions (Field, 2002).

In late adulthood, continued exposure to stimulating environments seems to slow down the decline in human brain functioning, as measured by better performance on intellectual and perceptual tasks (Goldstein et al., 1997; Schaie, 1998). In a sense then, every day you are alive, your brain continues its own "personal evolution"; its neural networks and patterns of activity are affected not only by your genetic endowment, but also, as Figure 7.21 shows, by your experiences as well.

COGNITION AND LEARNING

Early behaviourists believed that learning involves the relatively automatic formation of bonds between stimuli and responses. In classical conditioning, the CS elicits the CR: tone → salivation. In operant conditioning, a discriminative stimulus leads to an emitted response: Light comes on → a hungry rat presses the lever to obtain food. This behaviourist orientation came to be known as *SR (stimulus-response) psychology*. Behaviourists opposed explanations of learning that went beyond observable stimuli and responses. They did not deny that people had thoughts and feelings, but argued that behaviour could be explained without referring to such mentalistic concepts (Skinner, 1953, 1990).

Behaviourism guided much learning research from the early 1900s through the 1960s, and it remains influential (Reid & Staddon, 1998; Leighland, 2000). But even in psychology's early days, some learning theorists argued that between the stimulus (S) and the response (R) there was something else: the organism's (O) mental representation of the world. This model came to be known as the *S-O-R,* or *cognitive model* of learning. The cognitive perspective represents an important force in learning theory (Kirsch et al., 2004).

The study of animal cognition has expanded to include a wide range of topics, such as insight, cognitive maps, the role of cognition in classical and operant conditioning, and as we will discover later in this chapter's *Frontiers* feature—even numerosity.

Insight and Cognitive Maps

In the 1920s, German psychologist Wolfgang Köhler (1925) challenged Thorndike's behaviourist assumption that animals learn to perform tasks only by trial-and-error learning. Köhler exposed chimpanzees to novel learning tasks and concluded that they were able to learn by **insight,** the sudden perception of a useful relationship that helps to solve a problem. Figure 7.22 shows how one of his apes solved the problem of how to reach bananas that were dangling beyond reach. Köhler emphasized that the apes often spent time staring at the bananas and available tools, and then responded correctly, as if the solution suddenly appeared. Although the debate over animal insight continues, Köhler's work helped to place the cognitive learning viewpoint on the map.

Another cognitive pioneer, learning theorist Edward Tolman, studied spatial learning in rats. Look at the maze in Figure 7.23a. A rat runs to an open circular table, continues across, and follows the only path available to a goal box

(all): © Superstock

FIGURE 7.22 Sultan seemed to study the hanging bananas that were out of reach. After looking around, he suddenly grabbed some crates, stacked them, and obtained his tasty reward.

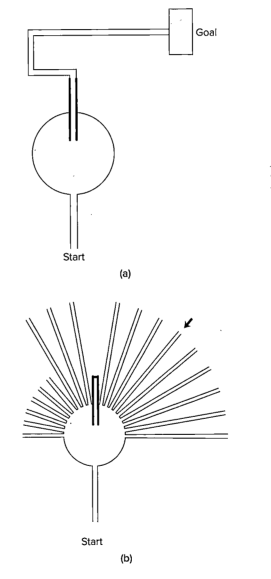

FIGURE 7.23 Rats first learned to run the simple maze shown in (a). When the maze was switched (b), many rats chose the fourth path to the right of the original route. Tolman proposed that the rats had developed a cognitive map of the maze.

Source: Adapted from Tolman, E.C. (1948). Cognitive maps in rats and men. *Psychological Review,* 55, 189–208.

Focus on Neuroscience

PLACE CELLS AND COGNITIVE MAPS

Edward Tolman's work on cognitive maps was widely influential and helped to foreshadow the rise of cognitive psychology in the 1950s and '60s. In 2014, John O'Keefe was awarded the Nobel Prize in Physiology or Medicine for work that renewed interest in cognitive maps. O'Keefe was awarded the Nobel Prize for his discovery of place cells in the hippocampus (O'Keefe & Dostrovsky, 1971).

A place cell is a type neuron in the hippocampus that becomes active when an animal is in a specific location in the environment (Wu & Foster, 2014). A specific place cell will have one or a few locations where it becomes active. Different cells represent different parts of the environment, and the firing pattern of these groups of place cells is thought to represent a cognitive map that supports recognition of different locations and enables the animal to successfully navigate in its environment (Figure 7.24). Place cells also become active in temporal sequences that are related to the order in which the animal has visited locations in the environment (Wu & Foster, 2014). Damage to the hippocampus causes a severe deficit in spatial memory (Morris et al., 1982), presumably because the place cells, and ability to process spatial location, are impaired as a result of the damage to the hippocampus.

Overall, it has been thought that individual place cells encode locations of the environment—and hence components of the cognitive map—each contributing a piece of map much the same way that each piece of a jigsaw puzzle contributes to the overall picture (Babichev, Cheng, &

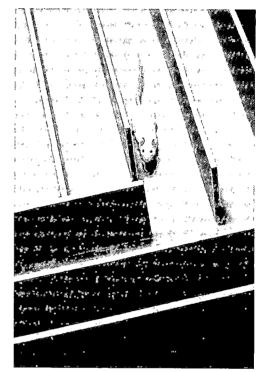

Will & Deni McIntyre/Science Source

FIGURE 7.24 Neurons in the hippocampus become active when an animal is in specific locations in the environment. These so-called *place cells* are thought to be important for the representation of cognitive maps.

containing food. After 12 trials, the rat easily negotiates the maze. Next, the maze is changed. The rat runs its usual route and reaches a dead end (Figure 7.23b). What will the rat do?

Tolman found that rats returned to the table, briefly explored most of the 18 new paths for just a few centimetres, and then chose one. By far, the largest number—36 percent—chose the fourth path to the right of their original route, which took them to about 10 centimetres in front of where the goal box had been. In short, the rats behaved as you would, given your advantage of seeing the maps in Figure 7.23.

Tolman (1948) argued that reinforcement theory could not explain this behaviour but that he could: The rats had developed a mental representation of the maze layout—a **cognitive map.** Neuroscience research has expanded on our understanding of cognitive maps and their neurobiological basis, as discussed in this chapter's *Focus on Neuroscience* feature. The

concept of cognitive maps supported Tolman's belief that learning does not merely "stamp in" stimulus-response connections. Rather, learning provides *knowledge,* and, based on their knowledge, organisms develop an *expectancy,* a cognitive representation of "what leads to what." Tolman's concept of expectancy remains a cornerstone of today's cognitive approaches to both classical and operant conditioning (Jeffery, 2008; Jensen, 2006).

Cognition in Classical Conditioning

Early American behaviourists believed that classical conditioning created a direct reflex-like connection between the CS (tone) and CR (salivation).

Cognitive learning theorists also argue that classical conditioning forms a CS-UCS link. In cognitive terminology, the link is an

32. Provide evidence that supports the "expectancy model" of classical conditioning.

Dabaghian, 2016). The situation, however, is more complex than this. For example, neighbouring place cells do not become active in neighbouring spatial locations, so it has been unclear how the activity of place cells fit together to form a cohesive cognitive map.

One question is about the type of map that is represented by the activity of place cells in the hippocampus. One possibility is that it is a geometric map, the type of map you might see of a city in which the geometry is represented; angles and relative distances are preserved and accurate. This is the type of map that you can look at and tell that one location is twice as far away as another—or that if you go north for two blocks and then turn west and go three blocks, you will arrive at your destination. Another type of map is a topological map. A topological map includes the relative order of locations and the connections between them, but there is little or no information about distance or geometry. A common example of this type of map is a subway map. The different subway stops are listed in the correct order but with little or no information about distances or absolute location. For example, if you are travelling on the green line of Montreal's Metro (subway) system, the subway map will show you that Place Des Arts is one stop east of the McGill stop, but there is no information about how far apart those two stops really are or if they are actually in a straight line as shown on the subway map.

In a recent study of place cells, Dabaghian and colleagues tested whether place cells in the hippocampus contributed to a geometric map or to a topological map. They recorded place cell activity in rats while the rats explored an environment, but the shape of that environment could change (Dabaghian et al., 2014). They recorded the electrical activity of place cells in the rat hippocampus as the animals navigated a maze to get a food reward (chocolate milk). The maze was constructed so that its arms could either be straight or curved. Changing the maze in this way, changing it from a straight line to a "U" shape to a zig-zag, does not alter the topology because the relative order of its various components—such as the positions of chocolate milk wells in the arms—are unchanged. It does, however, alter the maze's geometry. By changing the geometry of the environment but preserving the topology (what locations were connected to each other and in what order), the researchers could tell what type of map corresponded to place cell activity. As rats ran through different configurations of the maze, the activity of the place cells remained largely unchanged. That is, the place cells preserved the sequence of locations visited along the track even when the geometry of the track changed. This is what you would expect if the place cells represented a topological map but not a map that preserves the geometry of the environment. The research by Dabaghian et al. (2014) provides evidence that hippocampal maps have more in common with a subway map than with a street map. This work provides a framework for further experiments into place cell functions and important information for theories of cognitive maps.

Although it has been about 70 years since Tolman performed his original experiments on cognitive maps, and more than 30 years since O'Keefe first recorded place cells, we are still trying to understand how cognitive maps are developed and represented in the brain, and in developing a fuller theoretical understanding of cognitive maps (Babichev et al., 2016).

expectation that the CS will be followed by the UCS (Bolles, 1979; Hollis, 1997). This *expectancy model* states that the most important factor in classical conditioning is *not* how often the CS and the UCS are paired, but *how well the CS predicts (i.e., signals) the appearance of the UCS* (Rescorla & Wagner, 1972). It is important to note that the expectancy model does not refer to the conscious expectation of the UCS. The development of a CR is not the result of an individual's conscious inferences about the relationship between the CS and the UCS (Perruchet et al., 2015).

In a classic study Robert Rescorla (1968) demonstrated this principle in an experiment on fear conditioning. Rats in one condition received electric shocks (UCS), and each shock was preceded by a tone. As usual, the tone soon became a CS that elicited a fear response when presented alone. In a second condition, rats received the same number of tone-shock pairings as the first group, but they also received as many shocks that were not preceded by the tone. Would the tone become a CS for fear? According to traditional learning theory, the answer should be "Yes," because the number of tone-shock pairings was the same as in the first group. But the expectancy model predicts "No," because the tone does not reliably predict when the shock will occur. The results supported Rescorla's hypothesis: The tone did not elicit a fear response for the second group.

CS-UCS inconsistency also explains why we don't become conditioned to all the neutral stimuli that are present just before a UCS appears. For example, imagine a doctor testing your knee-jerk reflex. Many of us jerk slightly at the mere sight of that little rubber mallet moving toward our knee. Why doesn't this response occur to other stimuli that are present just before the hammer strikes, such as the sight of our doctor? Most of the time that we see

Research Foundations

USING SOCIAL-COGNITIVE LEARNING THEORY TO PREVENT AIDS: A NATIONAL EXPERIMENT

Introduction

In the 1990s, the African nation of Tanzania faced a growing AIDS crisis that was fuelled by risky sexual practices and widespread misinformation about HIV transmission (Bandura, 2006). HIV/AIDS was widely spread through heterosexual contact, such as between truck drivers and prostitutes who frequented the areas where truckers made stops.

To combat this crisis, the Tanzanian government and Radio Tanzania produced 208 episodes of a radio soap opera over several years. The content took advantage of principles from social-cognitive theory. In this five-year study, Peter Vaughan and his colleagues (2000) measured the effects of the radio program on listeners' attitudes and sexual practices.

Method

The soap opera featured three types of role models. Positive role models were knowledgeable about HIV/AIDS, minimized risky sex, and ultimately attained rewarding social outcomes. Transitional role models began by acting irresponsibly but eventually adopted safe sexual practices. Negative role models engaged in risky sex that led to adverse outcomes, including contracting HIV/AIDS and death.

The program's content had three goals. It was designed to (1) make listeners realize that they were at risk for contracting HIV/AIDS; (2) increase listeners' self-efficacy by showing them how to control risks; (3) have listeners reduce their number of sexual partners and to use condoms when having sex.

This prime-time soap opera was broadcast twice weekly to six geographic regions (e.g., the experimental regions) of Tanzania for five years. A seventh geographic region served as a control region for the first three years and received the radio program for only the final two years. Each year interviewers gathered information about participants' attitudes, sexual behaviours, and personal characteristics. One or more family members from roughly 2750 randomly chosen households participated.

Results

In the six experimental regions, the typical listener heard 108 of the 204 episodes, and about 80 percent said that the program helped them learn about preventing HIV/AIDS. Compared to people not exposed to the program, those who listened became more likely to believe that they were at risk

for contracting HIV/AIDS but that they could control this risk through safe sexual practices. Listeners spoke more often with their partners about HIV/AIDS, reduced their number of sexual partners, and increased their use of condoms. These findings were replicated in the seventh geographic region after it was switched from being a control condition to an experimental condition.

Discussion

This study illustrates how a scientific theory can guide the development of a treatment program that addresses a major societal problem. By cleverly turning the comparison region into an experimental region after three years, the researchers were able to test whether their initial findings would replicate.

Conducting large-scale research in the real world presents difficult challenges that can threaten a study's internal validity. Within each experimental region, the researchers could not control who tuned in to the radio programs. Indeed, listeners and non-listeners differed in several ways (e.g., listeners were somewhat better educated and wealthier) beyond just their exposure to the radio program. To minimize the chance that such factors would distort the results, the researchers statistically adjusted for these factors when they analyzed the data.

The study also relied heavily on participants' self-reports. But by gathering some objective data (such as increases in the number of condoms distributed in these regions), the researchers were able to corroborate some of the self-report measures.

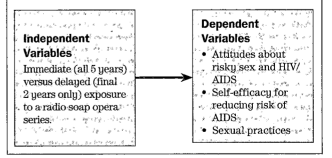

Design

Question: Can a radio soap opera series, designed using social cognitive learning principles, change people's attitudes and behaviour regarding risky sex?

Type of Study: *Field experiment*

Independent Variables
Immediate (all 5 years) versus delayed (final 2 years only) exposure to a radio soap opera series.

Dependent Variables
• Attitudes about risky sex and HIV/AIDS
• Self-efficacy for reducing risk of AIDS
• Sexual practices

Source: Peter W. Vaughan, Everett M. Rogers, Arvind Singhal, and Ramadhan M. Swalehe (2000). Entertainment-education and HIV/AIDS prevention: A field experiment in Tanzania. *Journal of Health Communication, 5,* 81–100.

Gaining Direction

What are the issues?	Fear of flying can be debilitating. It does no good to point out the statistics (e.g., you're 80 times more likely to be killed crossing the street than flying)—people with aviophobia simply will not process the information. So how can we treat this disorder? Plourde's approach is to get people back	in the air as soon as possible. Fear is aroused and confronted. Passengers fly in a flight simulator, and then board a real plane. How do they control their fear? How can they board a plane after a short, two-day program? Will the fear return? How was the phobia acquired in the first place?
What do we need to know?	How are phobias learned? What maintains the fear response? How can we extinguish the fear response?	Do extinguished responses recover? Why are other methods (e.g., self-help recordings) not as successful?
Where can we find the information to answer these questions?	There are two critical places in the chapter to examine. First, examine the section on classical conditioning. Most phobias are the result of a classically conditioned fear response. Look at the sections on the acquisition and generalization of classically learned responses. Next,	examine the material on acquiring and overcoming fear. In the classical model, the key to overcoming fear is exposure. In essence, exposure will extinguish the learned response. Escape and avoidance responses are relevant as well.

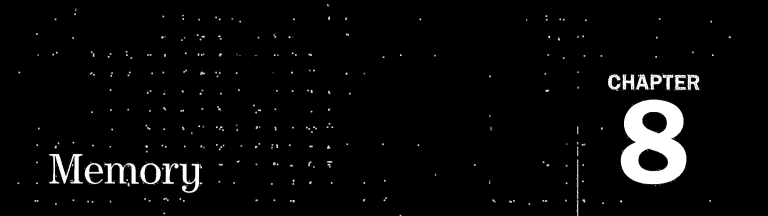
CHAPTER 〉
OUTLINE

MEMORY AS INFORMATION PROCESSING
A Three-Component Model
  Research Foundations: In Search of the Icon

ENCODING: ENTERING INFORMATION
Effortful and Automatic Processing
Levels of Processing: When Deeper Is Better
Exposure and Rehearsal
Organization and Imagery
How Prior Knowledge Shapes Encoding

STORAGE: RETAINING INFORMATION
Memory as a Network
Types of Long-Term Memory

RETRIEVAL: ACCESSING INFORMATION
The Value of Multiple and Self-Generated Cues
The Value of Distinctiveness
**Context, State, and Mood Effects
  on Memory**

Applications: Improving Memory
  and Academic Learning

FORGETTING
The Course of Forgetting
Why Do We Forget?
Amnesia
Forgetting to Do Things: Prospective Memory
  Frontiers: Methods to Enhance Memory

MEMORY AS A CONSTRUCTIVE PROCESS
Memory Distortion and Schemas
**The Misinformation Effect and Eyewitness
  Testimony**
**The "Recovered Memory" Controversy: Repression
  or Reconstruction?**

THE BIOLOGY OF MEMORY
Sensory and Working Memory
Long-Term Memory
  Focus on Neuroscience: How Are Memories Formed?

> The charm, one might say, the genius of memory is that it is choosy, chancy,
> and temperamental.
> —Elizabeth Bowen

What were you doing during the afternoon of October 25, 2006? You probably cannot remember, unless it was an important date for you such as a birthday. But Aurelien Hayman (pictured) can tell exactly what he was doing on that date. He remembers what he what he had for lunch, who he was with, what he was wearing, what the temperature was, and if anything happened in the news that day.

Aurelien, who was born in Cardiff, Wales, notes that his memory is somewhat limited. While he can tell you almost any fact about his life, his performance in university does not seem to be helped at all. He notes that his memory is like a visual file drawer that he can access, but only if he experienced the events himself.

Huw Evans/Rex Features/The Canadian Press

What are the
issues here?

What do we need
to know?

Where can
we find the
information to
answer these
questions?

There are only about 20 people in the world who are known to have this memory enhancement, including actress Marilu Henner. In almost every case, the superior memory started when they were about 14 years old.

Memory refers to the processes that allow us to record and later retrieve experiences and information. Memory is precious and complex, as illustrated by the case of H.M. (Henry Molaison). H.M. had most of his hippocampus and surrounding brain tissue surgically removed in 1953 to reduce severe epileptic seizures. The operation succeeded, but it unexpectedly has left H.M. with *amnesia*, or memory loss. He can discuss his childhood, teens, and early 20s, but has forgotten some events that occurred within the two years prior to surgery, and has lost the ability to form new memories. Typically, once an experience or fact leaves his immediate train of thought, he cannot remember it. Spend the day with H.M., depart and return minutes later, and he will not recall having met you. He forgets that he has recently eaten and reads magazines over and over as if he has never seen them before. What prevents H.M. from recalling new experiences, while leaving most of his pre-1953 memories intact? Why is it, as Figure 8.1 shows, that H.M. can learn and remember how to perform new tasks, yet swear each time he encounters these tasks that he has never seen them before? In this

chapter, we explore these and other fascinating questions about memory.

MEMORY AS INFORMATION PROCESSING

Psychological research on memory has a rich tradition, dating back to late 19th century Europe, when Hermann Ebbinghaus (1885) studied the rate at which new information is forgotten and Sir Francis Galton (1883) investigated people's memories for personal events. Decades later, the cognitive revolution within North American psychology and the advent of computers ushered in a metaphor that has influenced memory research since the 1960s: the mind as a processing system that encodes, stores, and retrieves information (Bower, 2000).

Encoding refers to getting information into the system by translating it into a neural code that your brain processes. Encoding is a little like what happens when you type on a computer keyboard, as your keystrokes are translated into an electrical code that the

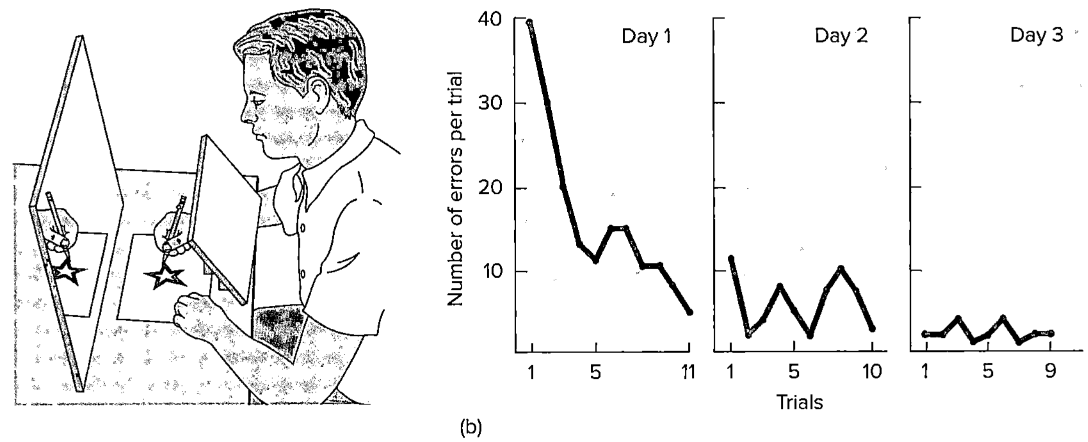

1. In what ways is memory like an information-processing system?

(a) (b)

FIGURE 8.1 (a) On this complex task, participants trace a pattern while looking at its mirror image, which shows their hand moving in the direction opposite to its actual movement. (b) H.M.'s performance rapidly improved over time, indicating that he had retained a memory of how to perform the task. Yet, each time he performed it, he stated that he had never seen the task before, and had to have the instructions re-explained.

Source: Adapted from B. Milner, 1965, "Memory Disturbances After Bilateral Hippocampal Lesions," in *Cognitive Processes and the Brain*, Peter Milner & S.G. Glickman, eds., Fig. 6, p. 108. Reprinted with permission.

computer can understand and process. **Storage** involves retaining information over time. Once in the system, information must be filed away and saved, as happens when a computer stores information on a hard drive. Finally, there must be a way to pull information out of storage when we want to use it, a process called **retrieval.** On a computer, retrieval occurs when you give a software command (e.g., "Open File") that transfers information from the hard drive back to the screen where you can view it. Keep in mind, however, that this analogy between human and computer is crude. For one thing, we routinely forget and distort information, and may "remember" events that never occurred (Laney & Loftus, 2010; Morris et al., 2006; Pickrell et al., 2003). Human memory is highly dynamic, and its complexity cannot be fully captured by any existing information-processing model.

Encoding, storage, and retrieval represent what our memory system does with information, and they could not take place without memory having some type of organization or structure. Thus, before exploring these processes in more detail, let us examine some basic components of memory.

A Three-Component Model

Our encounter with H.M. suggests an interesting possibility regarding how memory might be organized. If you told H.M. your name or read him a series of numbers, he could recall the information for a short time. Yet he could not form a lasting memory; once his train of thought changed, that information would be lost forever. Could it be, as William James (1890) suggested long ago, that

2. What is sensory memory? How did Sperling assess the duration of iconic memory?

memory has distinct yet interacting components, one temporary and the other more long-lasting?

The model shown in Figure 8.2 incorporates this assumption. Originally developed by Richard Atkinson and Richard Shiffrin (1968), and subsequently modified, it proposes that memory has three major components: sensory memory, short-term or "working" memory, and long-term memory. The model does not assume that each component corresponds to a specific structure within the brain. Rather, the components may involve interrelated neural sites, and memory researchers use these terms in a more abstract sense.

Sensory Memory

Sensory memory holds incoming sensory information just long enough for it to be recognized. It is composed of different subsystems, called *sensory registers*, which are the initial information processors. Our visual sensory register is called the *iconic store*, and in 1960, George Sperling conducted a classic experiment to assess how long it stores information (see this chapter's *Research Foundations* feature). As Figure 8.3 illustrates, the time course for visual sensory memory is very brief. Indeed, it is difficult, perhaps impossible, to retain complete information in purely visual form for more than a fraction of a second (Figure 8.4; Barsalou, 1992).

The auditory sensory register, called the *echoic store*, is studied by asking participants to recall different sets of numbers or letters that are simultaneously presented to their left and right ears via headphones. Echoic memory lasts longer than iconic memory. A nearly complete echoic trace may last about two seconds and a partial trace may linger for several more (Winkler et al., 2002).

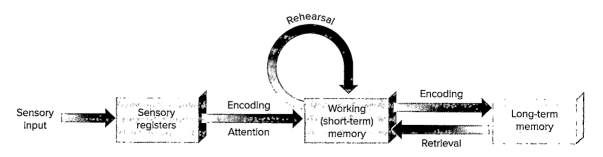

FIGURE 8.2 In this model, memory has three major components: (1) sensory registers, which detect and briefly hold incoming sensory information; (2) working memory, which processes certain information received from the sensory registers and information retrieved from long-term memory; and (3) long-term memory, which stores information for longer periods of time.

Source: Adapted from *The Psychology of Learning and Motivation: Advances in Theory and Research*, Vol. 2, K.W. Spence & J.T. Spence, eds. R.C. Atkinson & R.M. Shiffrin, "Human Memory: A Proposed System and Its Control Processes." Copyright © 1968 by Elsevier. Reprinted by permission.

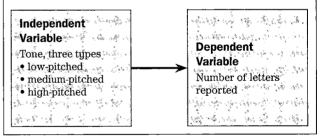

Research Foundations

IN SEARCH OF THE ICON

Introduction

How does information from some sensory input get translated into memory? Are we able to attend to all the information or is only some of it available? These questions were of central importance in George Sperling's pioneering work on iconic memory.

Method

Sperling (1960) had participants view matrices of letters such as the one shown in Figure 8.3. The matrix was presented for a very brief time (about 50 milliseconds). When asked to report what they had seen, participants could, on average, correctly identify only 4.5 letters (typically from the first row). Even if the presentation time was increased to 500 milliseconds or the number of letters was reduced, the results remained the same. Thus, it would appear that the memory span for a visual stimulus was quite limited—only about 33 percent of the display could be reported.

Sperling devised a method of **partial report** to demonstrate that much more information was actually available. In Study 2, the same matrices were presented, but when the visual stimulus was removed a tone was presented. For a high-pitched tone, participants were to report the letters in the first row. If the tone was low-pitched, the bottom row was to be reported. A medium-pitched tone called for a report of the middle row.

Results

Results indicated that approximately 75 to 90 percent of the letters could be correctly reported, regardless of the line they appeared in. Since the pitch of the tone was determined randomly, participants could not predict which line they needed to attend to until the stimulus display was gone.

Discussion

Sperling argued that some kind of memory trace must remain after the visual stimulus is removed. This trace is very short-lived (less than one second) but is available for scanning and, thus, any line in the matrix can be accurately recalled. However, when asked for a total report (recall as many letters as possible without the tone cue), the trace has faded by the time one line is reported.

This memory trace (referred to as an **icon;** Neisser, 1967) is a purely visual representation of the stimulus array. It is subject to interference by additional visual information, and its strength is affected by visual factors such as contrast and intensity. This notion of a sensory storage mechanism was quickly integrated into many models of memory and Sperling's 1960 paper remains one of the most cited studies in psychology.

Design

Question: Can participants report the letters from each row of a brief visual display if you cue the row for them to attend to?

Type of Study: *Experimental*

Independent Variable	Dependent Variable
Tone, three types • low-pitched • medium-pitched • high-pitched	Number of letters reported

Source: George Sperling (1960). The information available in brief visual presentations. *Psychological Monographs: General and Applied,* 74(11), 1–30.

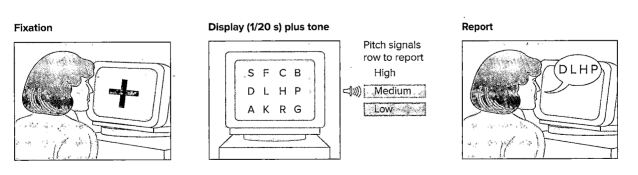

Fixation

Display (1/20 s) plus tone

S	F	C	B
D	L	H	P
A	K	R	G

Pitch signals row to report

High

◁))) Medium

Low

Report

D L H P

FIGURE 8.3 After a participant fixates on a screen, a matrix of letters is flashed for 1/20 of a second. In one condition, participants do not hear any tone and must immediately report as many letters as they can. In another condition, a high-, medium-, or low-pitched tone signals the participant to report the top, middle, or bottom row. If the tone occurs immediately, participants typically can report three or all four letters, no matter which row is signalled.

© Nick Daly/Photodisc/Getty Images

FIGURE 8.4 The arc of light that you see traced by a fiery baton, or the lingering flash that you see after observing a lightning bolt, results from the brief duration of information in iconic memory. Because of a slow camera shutter speed, this photo captures more arcs of light than you could actually see: Because your iconic memory stores complete information for only a fraction of a second, the image would quickly vanish.

Short-Term/Working Memory

Because our attentional capabilities are limited, most information in sensory memory simply fades away. But through selective attention, a small portion enters **short-term memory**, which holds the information that we are conscious of at any given time. Short-term memory also is referred to as **working memory**, because it consciously processes, codes, and "works on" information (Atkinson & Shiffrin, 1968; Baddeley, 2003).

Memory codes. Once information leaves sensory memory, it must be represented by some type of code if it is to be retained in short-term and eventually long-term memory. For example, the words that someone just spoke to you ("please buy some gum") or the phone number that you just looked up must somehow become represented in your mind. Such mental representations, or **memory codes**, can take various forms (Jackendoff, 1996). We may try to form a mental image (visual encoding), code something by sound (phonological encoding), or focus on the meaning of a stimulus (semantic encoding). For physical actions, such as learning sports or playing musical instruments, we code patterns of movement (motor encoding). Study of memory codes and their underlying neural mechanisms may provide a key to understanding how the brain represents and makes sense of information received through the senses (Tsien, 2007).

Note that the form of a memory code often does not correspond to the form of the original stimulus. For example, as you read these words (visual stimuli) you probably are not storing images of the way the letters look. Rather, you likely are forming phonological codes (saying the words silently to yourself) and, as you think about the material, semantic codes that represent their meaning (Lee, 2009). When people are presented with lists of words or letters and asked to recall them immediately, the errors that they make often are phonetic. They might recall a *V* instead of a *B* because of the similarity in how the letters sound (Conrad, 1964). Likewise, given word lists such as (1) *man, mad, cap, can, map;* (2) *old, late, thin, wet, hot;* and (3) *big, huge, broad, long, tall,* people become most confused recalling the first list, in which the words sound similar (Baddeley, 1966). Such findings suggest that phonological codes play an important role in short-term memory.

Capacity and duration. Short-term memory can hold only a limited amount of information at a time. Depending on the stimulus, such as numbers, letters, or words, it is believed that most people can hold no more than five to nine meaningful items in short-term memory, leading George Miller (1956) to set the capacity limit at "the magical number seven, plus or minus two," though others suggest that the number may in fact be as few as four (Cowan, 2001). However, the number of items in visual working memory may be up to 30 or more (Endress & Potter, 2014). To demonstrate Miller's limit, try administering the *digit-span task* in Table 8.1 to some people you know.

If our short-term memory capacity is so limited, how can we remember and understand sentences as we read? To answer this, read the line of letters below (about one per second), and

3. Describe the limitations of short-term memory, and how they can be overcome.

TABLE 8.1 Digit-Span Test

Directions: Starting with the top sequence, read these numbers at a steady rate of one per second. Immediately after saying the last number in each series, signal the person to recall the numbers in order. Most people can recall a maximum sequence of five to nine digits.

8 3 5 2
4 3 9 3 1
7 1 4 9 3 7
5 4 6 9 2 3 6
1 5 2 4 8 5 8 4
9 3 2 6 5 8 2 1 4
6 8 1 3 1 9 4 7 3 5
4 2 4 6 9 5 2 1 7 4 3
3 7 9 8 4 6 1 7 2 4 9 5

then cover it up and write down as many letters as you can remember *in the order presented.*

B I R C Y K A E U Q S A S A W T I

Did you have trouble remembering even half of these 17 letters in order? Now we rearrange (reverse) the letters and again ask you to write them down in order. Here are the 17 letters: "It was a squeaky crib." No doubt, you find this task much easier. The limit on short-term memory capacity concerns the number of meaningful *units* that can be recalled, and the original 17 letters have been combined into five meaningful units (words). Combining individual items into larger units of meaning is called **chunking**, and it can greatly aid recall.

Short-term memory is limited in duration as well as capacity. Have you ever experienced rapid forgetting, such as being introduced to someone, starting a conversation, and then suddenly realizing that you don't have the foggiest idea what her or his name was? Without rehearsal, the "shelf-life" of information in short-term memory is indeed short, perhaps lasting about 20 seconds. Lloyd and Margaret Peterson (1959) demonstrated this by presenting participants with three-letter syllables (all consonants), such as BSX, followed by a three-digit number, such as 140. Upon seeing the number, participants counted backwards by threes, which prevented them from rehearsing the letters. As Figure 8.5 indicates, after counting

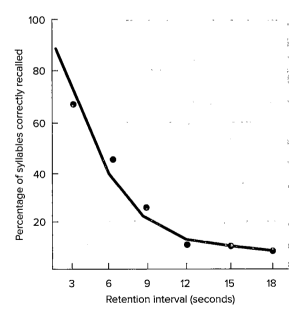

100 ─
Percentage of syllables correctly recalled

80 ─
60 ─
40 ─
20 ─

3   6   9   12   15   18
Retention interval (seconds)

FIGURE 8.5 Participants who were prevented from rehearsing three-letter syllables in working memory showed almost no recall of the letters within 18 seconds, illustrating the rapid forgetting of information in short-term memory.

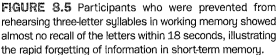

Source: Based on Peterson, L.R., & Peterson, M.J. (1959). Short term retention of individual verbal items. *Journal of Experimental Psychology*, 58, 193–198.

backwards for as little as 18 seconds, few syllables were recalled.

By rehearsing information, we can extend its duration in short-term memory indefinitely. This occurs when you look up a telephone number and keep saying it to yourself, either out loud or silently, while waiting to use a phone. This simple repetition of information is called **maintenance rehearsal.** In contrast, **elaborative rehearsal** involves focusing on the meaning of information or relating it to other things we already know. Thus, you could rehearse the term *iconic memory* by thinking about examples of iconic memory in your own life. Both types of rehearsal keep information active in short-term memory, but elaborative rehearsal is more effective in transferring information into long-term memory, which is our more permanent memory store (Gardiner et al., 1994; Mäntylä, 1986).

Putting short-term memory "to work." Picture the seemingly endless stacks of a library (representing long-term memory) and a tiny loading platform (representing short-term memory) outside the building. New books (pieces of information) rapidly arrive and, because there isn't enough space, knock other ones off the platform. According to the original three-stage model, items that remain on the short-term loading dock long enough—such as through maintenance rehearsal—eventually get transferred into the long-term library.

The original three-stage model of memory focused on short-term memory primarily as a loading platform or holding station for information along the route from sensory to long-term memory. Many cognitive scientists now reject this view of short-term memory as too passive and too sequential. Instead, they view short-term memory as a *working memory*—a "mental workspace" that actively and simultaneously processes different types of information and supports other cognitive functions, such as problem solving and planning, and interacts with long-term memory (Baddeley, 2010). Metaphorically, rather than a loading platform, working memory "is instead more like the office of a busy librarian, who is energetically categorizing, cataloging, and cross-referencing new material" (Reisberg, 1997, p. 139).

To illustrate how working memory stores information, processes it, and supports problem solving, add the numbers 27 and 46 "in your head." Your working memory stores the numbers, calls up information from long-term memory on "how to add," keeps track of the interim steps (7 + 6 = 13, carry the 1), and coordinates these mental processes.

4. Why do researchers refer to short-term memory as *working memory*?

5. Identify three components of working memory.

6. What is the serial position effect? Under what conditions do primacy and recency effects occur?

7. According to the three-component model, why do primacy and recency effects occur?

One model, proposed by Alan Baddeley (1998, 2007; Repous & Baddeley, 2006), divides working memory into four components. First, we maintain some information in an *auditory working memory* (the "phonological loop"), such as when you repeat a phone number, name, or new vocabulary terms to yourself mentally. A second component, *visual-spatial working memory* (the "visuospatial sketchpad"), allows us to temporarily store and manipulate images and spatial information, as when forming mental maps of the route to some destination. A third component, the *episodic buffer*, provides temporary storage space where information from long-term memory and from the phonological loop and/or visuospatial subsystems can be integrated, manipulated, and made available for conscious awareness. For example, after reading or hearing someone say, "How much is 87 plus 36?" your phonological loop initially maintains the acoustic codes for the sounds of 87 and 36 in working memory. Your visuospatial sketchpad also might maintain a mental image of the numbers. But to do this task, the rules for performing addition must be retrieved from long-term memory and temporarily stored in your episodic buffer, where they are integrated (i.e., applied to) information from the phonological and visuospatial subsystems. This creates the ingredients for the conscious perceptions that you experience as you perform the mental addition (e.g., "7 + 6 = 13, carry the 1 . . ."). The episodic buffer also comes into play when you chunk information. Finally, a control process, called the *central executive*, directs the action. It decides how much attention to allocate to mental imagery and auditory rehearsal, calls up information from long-term memory, and integrates the input. Many authors support this account of working memory (e.g., Norman, 2013) and research suggests that the prefrontal cortex, the seat of "executive functions" described in Chapter 3, is heavily involved in directing the processing of information in working memory (Nelson et al., 2000; Tsujimoto et al., 2004).

Long-Term Memory

As already noted, **long-term memory** is our vast library of more durable stored memories. Perhaps there have been times in your life, such as periods of intensive study during finals, when you have felt as if "the library is full," with no room for storing so much as one more new fact inside your brain. In reality, barring brain damage, we remain capable of forming new long-term memories until we die. And, as far as we know, long-term storage capacity essentially is unlimited. Once formed, a long-term memory can endure for up to a lifetime (Bahrick et al., 1994).

Are short-term and long-term memory really distinct? Case studies of amnesia victims, such as H.M., support this distinction, but another source of evidence comes from laboratory experiments in which participants with normal memory learn lists of words. Suppose that we present you with a series of unrelated words, one word at a time. The list might contain 10, 15, 20, or even 30 items. Immediately after the last word is presented, you will recall as many words as you can, in any order you wish. As Figure 8.6 illustrates, most experiments find that words at the end and beginning of the list are the easiest for participants to recall. This U-shaped pattern is called the **serial position effect,** meaning that recall is influenced by a word's position in a series of items. The serial position effect has two components, a *primacy effect,* reflecting the superior recall of early words, and a *recency effect,* representing the superior recall of the most recent words.

What causes the primacy effect? According to the three-stage model, as the first few words enter short-term memory, we can quickly rehearse them and transfer them into long-term memory. However, as the list gets longer, short-term memory rapidly fills up, and there are too many words to keep repeating before the next word arrives. Therefore, beyond the first few words, we cannot rehearse the items and they are less likely to get transferred into long-term memory. If this hypothesis is correct, then the primacy effect should disappear if we can prevent people from rehearsing the early words, say by presenting the list at a faster rate. Indeed, this is what happens (Glanzer, 1972).

As for the recency effect, the last few words have the benefit of not being "bumped out" of short-term memory by any new information. Thus, if we try to recall the list immediately, all we have to do is "read out" the last words while they linger in short-term memory. In sum, according to the three-stage model, the primacy effect is due to the transfer of early words into long-term memory, whereas the recency effect is due to short-term memory.

If this explanation is correct, then we should be able to wipe out the recency effect—but not the primacy effect—by eliminating the last words from short-term memory. This happens when the

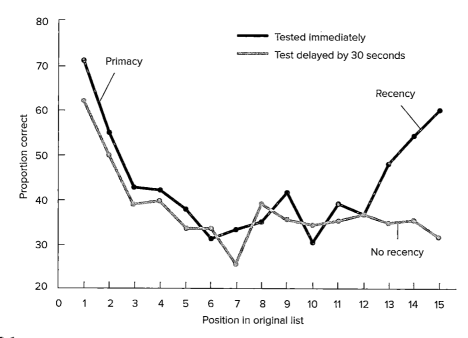

FIGURE 8.6 Immediate recall of word lists produces a serial position curve, in which primacy and recency effects are both evident. However, even a short delay of 30 seconds in recall (during which rehearsal is prevented) eliminates the recency effect, indicating that the later items in the word list have disappeared from short-term memory.

Source: Adapted from *Journal of Verbal Learning and Verbal Behavior* (now *Journal of Memory and Language*), 5, M. Glanzer & A. Cunitz, "Two Storage Mechanisms in Free Recall," pp. 351–360, Fig 2. Copyright © 1966, Elsevier. Reprinted by permission.

recall test is delayed, even by as little as 15 or 30 seconds, *and* you are prevented from rehearsing the last words. To prevent rehearsal, we might briefly ask you to count a series of numbers immediately after presenting the last word (Glanzer & Cunitz, 1966; Postman & Phillips, 1965). Now, by the time you try to recall the last words, they will have faded from short-term memory and been "bumped out" by the arithmetic task (six . . . seven . . . eight . . . nine . . .). Figure 8.6 shows that, indeed, under these delayed conditions, the last words are recalled no better than the middle ones, while a primacy effect remains.

Having examined some of the basic components of memory, let us now explore more fully how information is encoded into long-term memory, how it is stored, and factors that affect our ability to retrieve it.

ENCODING: ENTERING INFORMATION

The holdings of your long-term memory, like those of a library, must be organized in terms of specific codes if the information is to be available when you wish to retrieve it. In a library, new material is assigned a call number before it is placed in storage. As noted earlier, our "call numbers" come in various forms—semantic,

visual, phonological, and motor codes—that later enable us to activate information in long-term memory and access it. The more effectively we encode material into long-term memory, the greater the likelihood of retrieving it (Van Overschelde et al., 2005).

Effortful and Automatic Processing

Think of the parade of information that you have to remember: names, phone numbers, computer passwords, and mountains of schoolwork on which you expect to be tested. Learning such information involves *effortful processing*, encoding that is initiated intentionally and requires conscious attention. Rehearsing, making lists, and taking class notes illustrate effortful processing.

In contrast, have you ever been unable to answer an exam question, and said to yourself, "Why can't I answer this? I can even picture the diagram; it was on the upper portion of the left page"? Here incidental information about the diagram's location on the page (that you were not trying to learn) appears to have been transferred into long-term memory through *automatic processing*, encoding that occurs without intention and requires minimal attention.

8. Provide some examples of effortful and automatic processing in your own life.

Information about the frequency, spatial location, sequence, and timing of events often is encoded automatically (Gallivan et al., 2009). For example, if someone asks you what you did yesterday, you probably will have little trouble remembering your sequence of activities, despite the fact that you never had to sit down and intentionally memorize this information. Some processes (e.g., reading) are so automatic that we have difficulty switching to a more effortful style.

Levels of Processing: When Deeper Is Better

Imagine that you are participating in a laboratory experiment and are about to be shown a list of words, one at a time. Each word will be followed by a question, and all you have to do is answer "Yes" or "No." Here are three examples:

1. POTATO "Is the word in capital letters?"
2. horse "Does the word rhyme with course?"
3. TABLE "Does the word fit in the sentence, 'The man peeled the _____'?"

Each question requires effort but differs from the others in an important way. The first question requires superficial *structural encoding*, since you have to notice only how the word looks. Question 2 requires a little more effort. You must engage in *phonological* (also called *phonemic) encoding* by sounding out the word to yourself and then judging whether it matches the sound of another word. The last question requires *semantic encoding*, because you must pay attention to what the word means.

In this experiment, every word shown to you will be followed by a question similar to one of these. Unexpectedly, you will then be given a memory test. Which group of words will be recognized most easily: those processed structurally, phonologically, or semantically?

According to the **levels of processing** concept developed by Fergus Craik and Robert Lockhart (1972, 2008) of the University of Toronto, the more deeply we process information, the better it will be remembered. In the study just mentioned, semantic encoding involves the deepest processing because it requires us to focus on the *meaning* of information. Merely perceiving the structural properties of the words (e.g., capitalized versus lowercase) involves shallow processing, and phonemically encoding words is intermediate. You can see in Figure 8.7 that the results of a study conducted by Craik and Endel Tulving (1975) in Toronto support the value of deeper, semantic encoding.

9. Explain the concept of "depth of processing."

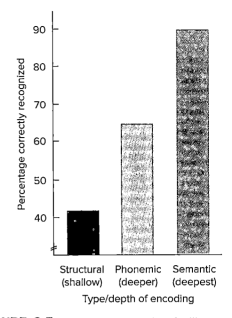

FIGURE 8.7 Depth of processing facilitates memory. Participants were shown words and asked questions that required superficial structural processing of a word, somewhat deeper phonemic processing, or deeper semantic processing. Depth of processing increased later recognition of the words in a larger list.

Source: Data from Craik, F.I.M., & Tulving, E. (1975). Depth of processing and the retention of words in episodic memory. *Journal of Experimental Psychology: General, 104,* 268–294.

Although many experiments have replicated this finding (Gabrieli et al., 1996), at times the concept of "depth of processing" can be difficult to measure. Suppose that some randomly assigned students study a chapter by creating hierarchical outlines and notes. A second group creates flash cards, jumbles them up, and rehearses them. Which study method represents deeper processing? If the first group performs better on a test, should we assume that they must have processed the information more deeply? To do so, warns Alan Baddeley (1990), is to fall into a trap of circular reasoning. Still, the levels of processing model has generated much research (Craik, 2002; Froger et al., 2008). Then again, there are situations in which few would argue with at least a broad distinction between shallow and deep processing. The following section discusses one of them.

Exposure and Rehearsal

Years ago a student came into my (M.W.P.) office after failing the first exam in introductory psychology. He told me he had been to all the lectures, completed the chapters ahead of time, and reread each chapter twice more just before the exam. Yet when I looked through his textbook, not a word or sentence had been underlined or highlighted. I asked whether he took notes as he read or paused to reflect on the information, and he said, "No." Instead, he read each chapter quickly, much like a novel, and assumed that merely by looking at everything three times the information would somehow "sink in."

Unfortunately, this student's approach stood little chance of success. To learn factual and conceptual information presented in most academic or job settings, we need to employ effortful, deep processing. Simple repeated exposure to a stimulus without stopping to think about it represents shallow processing. To demonstrate this, try drawing from memory a picture of a Canadian penny, accurately locating all the markings. Few of our students can do this. Thus, even thousands of shallow exposures to a stimulus do not guarantee long-term retention (Jones, 1990; Nickerson & Adams, 1979).

Rehearsal goes beyond mere exposure because we are thinking about the information. Of course, not all thinking is created equal, and neither is all rehearsal. As noted earlier, *maintenance rehearsal* involves simple repetition, as when silently repeating an unfamiliar phone number while waiting to use the phone. Maintenance rehearsal is most useful for keeping information active in short-term, working memory, and it may help to transfer some information into long-term memory (Naveh & Jonides, 1984; Wixted, 1991). However, it is an inefficient method for bringing about long-term transfer.

In contrast, *elaborative rehearsal* focuses on the meaning of information—we *elaborate* on the material in some way. Organizing information, thinking about how it applies to our own lives, and relating it to concepts or examples we already know illustrate such elaboration. According to Craik and Lockhart (1972, 2008), elaborative rehearsal involves deeper processing than maintenance rehearsal and should be more effective in transferring information into long-term memory. In contexts as varied as university students learning word lists to Grade 6 students learning CPR (cardiopulmonary resuscitation), experiments support the greater effectiveness of elaborative rehearsal (Gardiner et al., 1994; Mäntylä, 1986; Rivera-Tovar & Jones, 1990). Even thinking about examples of concepts that other people provide for us facilitates later recall (Palmere et al., 1983).

Organization and Imagery

Dining at the restaurant where J.C. is a waiter can be an awe-inspiring experience. Perhaps you would like a filet mignon, medium-rare, with a baked potato, and Thousand Island dressing on your salad? Whatever you choose, it represents only one of over 500 possible options that can be ordered (seven entrees × five serving temperatures × three side dishes × five choices of salad dressing). Yet, you and 20 or so of your best friends can place your selections with J.C., and he will remember them perfectly without writing them down. How does he do it?

Psychologists K. Anders Ericsson and Peter Polson (1988), who studied J.C., found that he invented an overall organizational scheme to aid his memory. He divided his customers' orders into four categories (entrees, temperatures, side dish, dressing) and then used a different system to encode the orders in each category. For example, he represented dressings by their initial letter, so orders of Thousand Island, oil and vinegar, blue cheese, and oil and vinegar would become TOBO.

Imposing organization on a set of stimuli is an excellent way to enhance memory. An organizational scheme can enhance the meaningfulness of information and also serve as a cue that helps to trigger our memory for the information it represents, just as the word *TOBO* jogs J.C.'s memory of the four orders of salad.

Hierarchies and Chunking

Organizing material in a *hierarchy* takes advantage of the principle that memory is enhanced by associations between concepts. Gordon Bower and his colleagues (1969) demonstrated this experimentally by presenting some participants with a logically organized list of words, based on a hierarchical tree like the one in Figure 8.8a. Other participants received the same words placed randomly within the tree. As Figure 8.8b shows, participants presented with a meaningful hierarchy remembered more than three times as many words.

Notice that the hierarchy in Figure 8.8a does not reduce the amount of information to be remembered. With or without it, there are the same number of words to learn. Rather, a logical hierarchy enhances our *understanding* of how these diverse elements are related, and as we proceed from top to bottom, each category can serve as a cue that triggers our memory for the associated items below it. Because the

10. How effectively do maintenance and elaborative rehearsal process information into long-term memory?

11. Why do hierarchies, chunking, mnemonic devices, and imagery enhance memory?

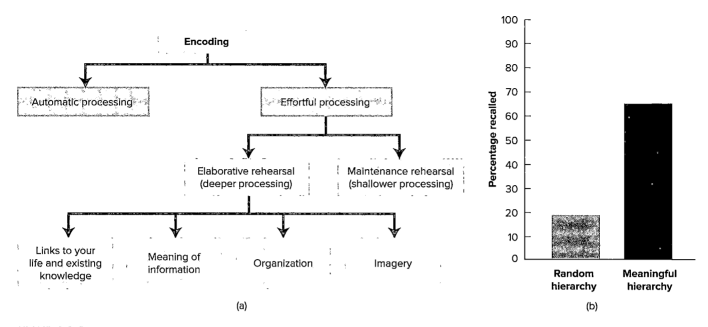

FIGURE 8.8 Words presented in a logically organized hierarchical structure (a) are remembered better than the same words placed randomly in a similar-looking structure (b).

Source: Bower, G.H., Clark, M.C., Lesgold, M.A., & Winzenz, D. (1969). Hierarchical retrieval schemes in recall of categorized word lists, *Journal of Verbal Learning and Verbal Behavior*, 8(3), 323–343. Copyright © 1969 Elsevier. Reprinted with permission from Elsevier.

hierarchy has a visual organization, there also is a greater possibility of using imagery as a supplemental memory code.

Chunking refers to combining individual items into a larger unit of meaning, and it widens the information-processing bottleneck caused by the limited capacity of short-term memory (Gobet et al., 2001; Miller, 1956). To refresh your memory, read the line of letters below to yourself (about one per second) and try to recall as many as you can, in the same sequence.

C T V Y M C A I B M K G B F B I

If you remembered four to eight of the letters in order, you did quite well. Now we can reorganize these 16 individual bits of information into five larger, more meaningful chunks: CTV, YMCA, IBM, KGB, and FBI. This rearrangement is easier to keep active in short-term memory and, should you be so motivated, to rehearse and transfer into long-term memory. A common example of chunking in everyday life is the way we encode and later retrieve phone numbers from long-term memory. Thus, if you periodically call someone who lives far away, you probably encode the number as a set of three chunks (e.g., 905-430-5147) rather than as 10 individual numbers.

Mnemonic Devices

The search for memory aids dates back thousands of years. In fact, the term *mnemonics*

(ne-MON-iks), which refers to "the art of improving memory," derives from the name *Mnemosyne*, the Greek goddess of memory. A mnemonic device is any type of memory aid. Hierarchies and chunking represent two types of mnemonic devices. So do acronyms, which combine one or more letters (usually the first letter) from each piece of information you wish to remember. For example, many students learn the acronyms HOMES and ROY G. BIV to help remember the names of the five Great Lakes of North America (Huron, Ontario, Michigan, Erie, Superior) and the hues in the visible spectrum— the "colours of the rainbow" (red, orange, yellow, green, blue, indigo, violet). Acronyms are one of the most popular mnemonic techniques among university students (Soler & Ruiz, 1996; Manolo, 2002).

Keep in mind that when you are learning new material, mnemonic devices do not reduce the amount of *raw* information you have to encode into memory. Rather, they reorganize information into more meaningful units and provide extra cues to help you retrieve information from long-term memory. When chunking seven digits into 430-5147, you still have to encode seven digits. And the acronym HOMES is useful only when you have also encoded the names of the Great Lakes into long-term memory. Thus, some researchers argue that acronyms—DAM—*don't aid* memory, or at least do so only when you are already familiar with the material (Carney et al., 1981, 1994).

Visual Imagery

How many windows are there in your home? Can you tell us, in as much detail as possible, what your bedroom looked like during your high school years? To answer these questions, you might try to construct and scan a series of mental images in your working memory, based on information that you draw out of long-term memory.

Allan Paivio (1969, 2006) proposes that information is stored in long-term memory in two forms: verbal codes and non-verbal (typically visual) codes. According to his **dual coding theory,** encoding information using both codes enhances memory, because the odds improve that at least one of the codes will be available later to support recall. In short, two codes are better than one, though dual coding is harder to use with some types of stimuli than others. Try to construct a mental image for each of the following: (1) fire truck, (2) light bulb. Now construct an image for these words: (1) jealousy, (2) knowledge. You probably found the second task more difficult, because the latter words represent abstract concepts rather than concrete objects (Sadoski et al., 1997). Abstract concepts are easier to encode semantically than visually.

Memory improvement books often recommend using imagery to dual-code information, and research supports this approach (Tye, 1991). The ancient Greeks developed an effective and well-known imagery technique called the *method of loci* (*loci* is Latin for "places"). To use this technique, imagine a physical environment with a sequence of distinct landmarks, such as the rooms in a house or places on your campus. In psychology classes, students can rapidly learn to use the 40 locations on the Monopoly game board as their visual reference (Schoen, 1996), or campus locations to remember shopping lists (McCabe, 2015).

To remember a list of items or concepts, take an imaginary stroll through this environment and form an image linking each place with an item or a concept. To remember the components of working memory, you might imagine walking into the administration building (central executive), then watching a band rehearsal in your gym (phonological loop), visiting an art class (visuospatial sketchpad), and finally, the offices of the campus newspaper (episodic buffer). Many studies support the method of loci's effectiveness (Massen et al., 2009).

How Prior Knowledge Shapes Encoding

Long-term memory is densely populated with semantic codes that represent the meaning of information. Typically, when we read, listen to someone speak, or experience some other event, we do not precisely record every word, sentence, or moment. Rather, we form a mental representation that captures the essential meaning or gist of that event. For example, in the two preceding paragraphs we described the method of loci. Can you recall those paragraphs word for word? More likely, what you have encoded is the gist—the general theme—that the method of loci involves forming images that link items to places.

Schemas: Our Mental Organizers

The themes that we extract from events and store in memory are often organized around schemas. A **schema** (plural: *schemas,* or *schemata*) is a "mental framework"—an organized pattern of thought about some aspect of the world, such as a class of people, events, situations, or objects (Bartlett, 1932; Koriat et al., 2000). We form schemas through experience, and they can strongly influence the way we encode material in memory (Tse et al., 2007). To demonstrate this, read the following paragraph:

12. What is a schema? Explain how schemas influence encoding.

> The procedure is actually quite simple. First you arrange things into different groups. Of course, one pile may be sufficient depending on how much there is to do. If you have to go somewhere else due to lack of facilities, that is the next step; otherwise you are pretty well set. It is important not to overdo things. That is, it is better to do too few things at once than too many. In the short run this might not seem important, but complications can easily arise. A mistake can be expensive as well. . . . After the procedure is completed, one arranges the materials into different groups again. Then they can be put into their appropriate places. Eventually they will be used once more, and the whole cycle will have to be repeated. However, that is part of life. (Bransford & Johnson, 1972, p. 722)

Asked to recall as much as you can of the preceding paragraph, you would probably have difficulty remembering much of it. Certainly, participants in the original experiment did. However, suppose we tell you that the paragraph is about a common activity: washing clothes. Now if you read the material again, you will find that the abstract and seemingly unrelated ideas suddenly make sense. Your schema—your mental framework for "washing clothes"—helps you organize these ideas and recall a great deal more.

This example illustrates that how we perceive a stimulus shapes the way we mentally represent it in memory. Essentially, schemas create a perceptual set, which is a readiness to perceive—*to organize and interpret*—information in a certain way.

Schemas, Encoding, and Expertise

When people who have never learned to "read notes" look at a musical score, they see an uninterpretable mass of information. In contrast, musicians see organized patterns that they can easily encode, eventually learning to play a piece "from memory." In music as in other fields, acquiring *expert knowledge* can be viewed as a process of developing schemas—mental frameworks—that help to encode information into meaningful patterns. From a neurological perspective, the active area involved in creating and using schema information is the medial prefrontal lobe (van Kesteren et al., 2014).

William Chase and Herbert Simon (1973) demonstrated the relation between expertise, schemas, and encoding in a classic study. Three chess players—an expert, an intermediate player, and a beginner—were allowed to look at a chessboard holding about 25 pieces for only five seconds. Then they looked away and, on an empty board, attempted to reconstruct the placement of the pieces from memory. This procedure was repeated over several trials, each with a different arrangement of pieces. On some trials, the chess pieces were arranged in *meaningful positions* that actually might occur in game situations. With only a five-second glance, the expert typically recalled 16 pieces, the intermediate player eight, and the novice only four. What may surprise you is that when the pieces were in *random positions* there was no difference in recall between the three players. They each did poorly, accurately recalling only two or three pieces.

What explains these results? We have to reject the idea that the expert had better overall memory than the other players, because he performed no better than they did with the random arrangements. But the concepts of schemas and chunking do explain the findings (Chase & Simon, 1973; Gobet & Simon, 1998). When the chess pieces were arranged in meaningful positions, the expert could apply well-developed

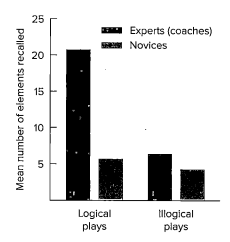

FIGURE 8.9 Diagrams of football plays were shown to football coaches (experts) and people who had played football but were not coaches (novices). Coaches, allowed to see each play for just five seconds, displayed excellent memory—but only when the plays were logical. Their well-developed football schemas were of little use when the patterns of Xs and Os were illogical. The findings are very similar to those obtained when expert and novice chess players tried to reproduce meaningful and random arrangements of chess pieces.

Source: Data based on Garland, D.J., & Barry, J.R. (1991). Cognitive advantage in sport: The nature of perceptual structures. *American Journal of Psychology, 104*, 211–228.

schemas to recognize patterns and group pieces together. For example, he would treat as a unit all pieces that were positioned to attack the king. The intermediate player and especially the novice, who did not have well-developed chess schemas, could not construct the chunks and had to try to memorize the position of each piece. However, if the pieces were not in positions that would occur in a real game, they were no more meaningful to the expert than to the other players. In this case, the expert lost the advantage of schemas and had to approach the task on a piece-by-piece basis just as the other players did. Similarly, football coaches show much better recall than novices do after looking at diagrams of football plays (patterns of Xs and Os) only when the plays are logical (Figure 8.9).

13. In what sense are schemas and expert knowledge related?

Thinking critically

WOULD PERFECT MEMORY BE A GIFT OR A CURSE?

If you could have a perfect memory, would you want it? What might be the drawbacks?

Think about it, and then see the Answers section at the end of the book.

You may not be an advanced chess player, but there are many areas in which you possess expert knowledge. You have used language for most of your life and have years of experience about how the world works. As the washing machine example illustrates, your own "expert schemas" strongly influence what you encode and remember.

One area that we are all "expert" in is survival. From a functional perspective, we should be extremely good at processing and remembering words and concepts related to survival. Nairne et al. (2007) demonstrated that this was indeed the case. If I ask you to imagine being stranded in a remote location and to give a list of everything you need to find food and water, protect yourself, etc., your memory for the words on the list is much better than if I ask you to generate items you need for a cross country move. This effect has been replicated by numerous authors (e.g., Bell et al., 2015; Nouchi, 2013). Apparently, it is very adaptive for us to encode and remember items related to survival.

STORAGE: RETAINING INFORMATION

After information is encoded, how is it organized and stored in long-term memory? Consider the following statements, indicating as quickly as possible whether each is true or false:

1. A raccoon has wings.
2 Moscow is in Russia.
3. A bat is a fish.
4. Coca-Cola is green.
5. An apple is a fruit.
6. Some fire engines are red.

Chances are, you were able to respond to each statement almost instantaneously. Considering their diversity, it is remarkable that you could access the information so quickly. The fact that we are able to perform such tasks routinely—that we can recall an incredible wealth of information at a moment's notice—has influenced many cognitive models of how knowledge is stored and organized in memory.

Memory as a Network

We noted earlier that memory is enhanced by elaborative rehearsal, which involves forming associations between new information and other items already in memory. The general principle that memory involves associations goes to the heart of the network approach.

Associative Networks

One group of theories proposes that memory can be represented as an **associative network,** a massive network of associated ideas and concepts (Bower, 2008; Collins & Loftus, 1975). Figure 8.10 shows what a small portion of such a network might be like. In this network, each concept or unit of information—fire engine, red, and so on—is represented by a *node* somewhat akin to each knot in a huge fishing net. The lines in this network represent associations between concepts, with shorter lines indicating stronger associations. For simplicity, Figure 8.10 shows only a few connections extending from each node, but there could be hundreds or more. Notice that items within the same category—types of flowers, types of fruits, colours, and so on—generally have the strongest associations and therefore tend to be clustered closer together.

Alan Collins and Elizabeth Loftus (1975) theorize that when people think about a concept, such as "fire engine," there is a *spreading activation* of related concepts throughout the network. For example, when you think about a "fire engine," related concepts, such as "truck," "fire," and "red," should be partially activated as well. The term **priming** refers to the activation of one concept (or one unit of information) by another. Thus, "fire engine" primes the node for "red," making it more likely that our memory for this colour will be accessed (Chwilla & Kolk, 2002).

The notion that memory stores information in an associative network provides one possible explanation for why hints and mnemonic devices help to stimulate our recall (Reisberg, 1997). For example, when someone says, "Name the colours of the rainbow," the nodes for "colour" and "rainbow" jointly activate the node for ROY G. BIV, which in turn primes our recall for "red," "orange," and so forth.

Neural Networks

The neural network approach provides a different and increasingly popular model of memory and cognition (Chappell & Humphreys, 1994; McClelland & Rumelhart, 1985). A neural network has nodes that are linked to one another, but these nodes are physical in nature and do not contain individual units of information. There is no single node for "red," for "fire engine," and so on. Instead, each node is more like a small information-processing unit. As an analogy, some proponents would say: Think of each neuron in your brain as a node. A neuron processes inputs and sends outputs to other neurons, but as far as we know, the concepts of "red," or "fire engine," or your mental image of an elephant are not stored within any single neuron.

14. Explain the concepts of associative networks and priming.

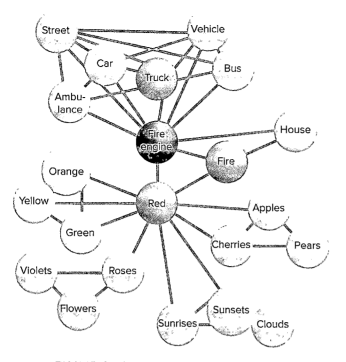

FIGURE 8.10 A network of concepts in semantic memory. The lines in the semantic network represent associations between concepts, with shorter lines indicating stronger associations.

Source: Adapted from A.M. Collins and E.F. Loftus, 1975, "A Spreading Activation Theory of Semantic Processing," *Psychological Review*, 82, 412, Figure 1. Copyright © 1975 by the American Psychological Association. Reprinted by permission of the author and the publisher.

For an interesting three-dimensional look at an associative network, check out the visual thesaurus at *www.visualthesaurus.com*.

15. How do neural network models differ from associative network models?

16. Use the concepts of declarative versus procedural memory, and explicit versus implicit memory, to explain the pattern of H.M.'s amnesia.

Where, then, is the concept "red" stored? In a **neural network,** each concept is represented by a particular *pattern* or *set of nodes* that becomes activated simultaneously. When node 4 is activated simultaneously (i.e., in parallel) with nodes 9 and 42, the concept "red" might come to mind. But when node 4 is simultaneously activated with nodes 75 and 690, another concept enters our thoughts. Looking across the entire network, as a multitude of nodes *distributed* throughout the brain fire in *parallel* at each instant and spread their activation to other nodes, concepts and information are retrieved and thoughts arise. For this reason, neural network models are often called *parallel distributed processing models (PDP)*. Researchers in many fields are using the neural network approach to model learning, memory, language disorders, and other cognitive processes (Botvinick & Plaut, 2006; Joanisse, 2009; Vogels, Rajan, & Abbott, 2005).

Types of Long-Term Memory

Think back to the nature of H.M.'s amnesia. Since his brain operation, H.M. has been unable to consciously recall new facts or personal experiences once they leave his short-term memory. Each time he meets you he will believe it is the first time. Yet with practice, H.M. learned new tasks, even though he would never remember having seen them before (Milner, 1965).

Based on research with amnesia patients, brain-imaging studies, and animal experiments, many cognitive scientists believe that we possess several long-term memory systems that interact with one another (Squire & Zola-Morgan, 1991; Tulving, 2002). This view is consistent with the concept, described in Chapter 6, that the mind involves distinct yet interrelated modules.

Declarative and Procedural Memory

Declarative memory involves factual knowledge, and includes two subcategories (Figure 8.11). **Episodic memory** is our store of factual knowledge concerning personal experiences: when, where, and what happened in the *episodes* of our lives. Your recollection that you ate pizza last night is an episodic memory. **Semantic memory** represents general factual knowledge about the world and language, including memory for words and concepts. You know that Mt. Everest is the world's tallest peak and that $e = mc^2$. Episodic and semantic memories are called *declarative* because, to demonstrate our knowledge, we typically have to "declare it"—we tell other people what we know.

H.M.'s brain damage severely impaired both components of his declarative memory, but this is not always the case. Some brain-injured children with amnesia cannot remember their daily personal experiences but can retain general factual knowledge, enabling them to learn language and attend mainstream schools (Vargha-Khadem et al., 1997).

In contrast to declarative memory, whose contents are verbalized, **procedural memory** (nondeclarative memory) is reflected in skills and actions (Cohen et al., 2005). One component of procedural memory consists of *skills* that are expressed by "doing things" in particular situations, such as typing, riding a bicycle, or playing a musical instrument. *Classically conditioned responses* also reflect procedural memory (Gabrieli, 1998). After a tone was repeatedly paired with a puff of air blown toward H.M.'s eye, he began to blink involuntarily to the tone alone (Woodruff-Pak, 1993). Although H.M. could not recall undergoing this procedure, his brain stored a memory for the association between the tone

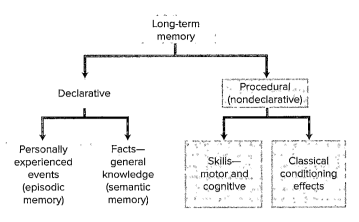

FIGURE 8.11 Some theorists propose that we have separate but interacting declarative and procedural memory systems. Episodic and semantic memories are declarative; their contents can be verbalized. Procedural memory is nondeclarative; its contents cannot readily be verbalized.

and the air puff, affecting his actions (he blinked) when subsequently exposed to the tone alone.

Explicit and Implicit Memory

Many researchers distinguish between explicit and implicit memory. **Explicit memory** involves conscious or intentional memory retrieval, as when you consciously recognize or recall something (Graf & Schacter, 1985). *Recognition* requires us to decide whether a stimulus is familiar, as when an eyewitness is asked to pick out a suspect from a police lineup or when students take multiple-choice tests. In recognition tasks, the "target" stimuli (possible suspects or answers) are provided for you. *Recall* involves spontaneous memory retrieval, in the sense that you must retrieve the target stimuli or information on your own. This occurs when you are briefly shown a

17. Describe some ways to measure explicit and implicit memory.

Review

- Memory involves three main processes (encoding, storage, and retrieval) and three main components (sensory memory, short-term/working memory, and long-term memory).

- Sensory memory briefly holds incoming sensory information. Some information reaches working memory and long-term memory, where it is mentally represented by phonological, visual, semantic, or motor codes.

- Short-term/working memory actively processes information and supports other cognitive functions. It has auditory, visuospatial, and executive (coordinating) components. Long-term memory stores enormous amounts of information for up to a lifetime. Studies of amnesia patients and research on the serial position effect support the distinction between short- and long-term memory.

- Effortful processing involves intentional encoding and conscious attention. Automatic processing occurs without intention and requires minimal effort.

- Deep processing enhances memory. Elaborative rehearsal provides deeper processing than maintenance rehearsal. Hierarchies, chunking,

- dual-coding by adding visual imagery, and other mnemonic devices facilitate deeper encoding.

- Schemas are mental frameworks that shape how we encode information. As we become experts in any given field, we develop schemas that allow us to encode information into memory more efficiently.

- Associative network models view long-term memory as a network of associated nodes, with each node representing a concept or unit of information. Neural network models propose that each piece of information in memory is represented not by a single node but by multiple nodes distributed throughout the brain. Each memory is represented by a unique pattern of simultaneously activated nodes.

- Declarative long-term memories involve factual knowledge and include episodic memories (knowledge concerning personal experiences) and semantic memories (facts about the world and language). In contrast, procedural memory is reflected in skills and actions. Explicit memory involves conscious or intentional memory retrieval, whereas implicit memory occurs when memory influences our behaviour without conscious awareness.

list of words and then are asked to recall them. With *cued recall,* hints are given to stimulate memory. If you cannot recall the word *hat* from the list, we might say, "It rhymes with *bat.*" In academics, essay, short-answer, and fill-in-the-blank questions involve recall or cued recall.

Implicit memory occurs when memory influences our behaviour without conscious awareness (Mulligan & Dew, 2009). H.M. was able to remember how to perform the mirror-tracing task, although he had no conscious awareness of having learned it. His memory for the task (in this case, procedural memory) was implicit.

In less dramatic ways, all of us demonstrate memory without conscious awareness. Riding a bicycle, driving, or performing any well-learned skill provides a common example. You may be consciously thinking about an upcoming school test or last night's party, while your implicit, procedural memory enables you to keep executing the skill.

Priming tasks provide another example. You might read a list of words (one word per second) that includes *kitchen, moon,* and *defend.* Later—even a year later—you are rapidly shown many word stems, some of which might be KIT____, MO____, and DE____, and are asked to complete each stem to form a word. You are not aware that this is a memory test. Compared with people not given the original list of words, you will be more likely to complete the stems with words on the original list (e.g., *MOon,* rather than *MOther*). The word stems have activated or "primed" your stored mental representations of these words—the information is still in your memory—even though you may be unable to consciously recall the original words (Bruss & Mitchell, 2009; Schacter, 1992).

RETRIEVAL: ACCESSING INFORMATION

Storing information is useless without the ability to retrieve it. Imagine looking for a specific title in a library, searching book by book because items are placed onto shelves without call numbers. In contrast, if we have a call number and the book is shelved correctly, we can easily gain access to it.

A **retrieval cue** is any stimulus, whether internal or external, that stimulates the activation of information stored in long-term memory. If someone asks you, "Have you seen Sally today?" the word *Sally* is intended to serve as a retrieval cue. Likewise, seeing a yearbook picture of a high school classmate can act as a retrieval cue

18. Why does having multiple, self-generated retrieval cues enhance recall?

that triggers memories of that person. *Priming* is a good example of how a retrieval cue ("fire engine," "MO____") can trigger associated elements ("red," "MOon") in memory, presumably via a process of spreading activation.

The Value of Multiple and Self-Generated Cues

Timo Mäntylä (1986) conducted a series of experiments that vividly show the value of having not just one, but multiple retrieval cues. In one experiment, Swedish university students were presented with a list of 504 words. Some students were asked to think of and write down an association for each word, while others were asked to think of and write down three associations. To illustrate, what three words come to your mind when you hear the word "banana"? Perhaps you might think of *monkey, peel,* and *fruit.*

The students had no idea that their memory for these words would be tested, and once the association task was completed, they were given an unexpected immediate recall test for 252 of the words. For some words, students were first shown the one or three associations that they had previously generated. As a control, for other words, they were first shown one or three associations that *another* participant had generated. Then they were asked to recall the original word.

The results were astounding. When the associations (i.e., retrieval cues) were self-generated, students shown one cue correctly recalled 61 percent of the words, and those shown three cues correctly recalled 91 percent. In contrast, when students were shown cues that someone else had generated, recall with one cue dropped to 11 percent and with three cues to 55 percent. Finally, when given another surprise recall test one week later on the remaining words, students still remembered 65 percent of the words when they were first provided with three self-generated retrieval cues, far better than any other condition.

In seven experiments, Mäntylä consistently found that having multiple, self-generated retrieval cues was the most effective approach to maximizing recall (Mäntylä, 1986; Mäntylä & Nilsson, 1988). Why might this be? On the encoding side of the equation, generating our own associations involves deeper, more elaborative rehearsal than does being presented with associations generated by someone else. Similarly, generating three associations involves deeper processing than thinking of only one.

On the retrieval side, these self-generated associations become cues that have personal meaning. And with multiple cues, if one fails, another may activate the memory. The implication for studying academic material is clear. Think about the material, and draw one or preferably more links to items you already have in memory.

The Value of Distinctiveness

You can perform the following quick exercise to demonstrate a simple point regarding memory. A list of words appears below. Say each word silently to yourself (about one per second), then when you see the word *WRITE*, look away and jot down as many words as you can recall, in any order. Here are the words: *robin, eagle, nest, crow, feather, goose, owl, tomato, rooster, fly, sparrow, nightingale, chirp, hawk, pigeon, WRITE.*

Recall that in the serial position effect, words in the middle of a list usually are recalled less well than those at the beginning or the end of the list. Yet, if you are like 95 percent of our students, you will have recalled the word *tomato*, which occurred in the middle. In this list, *tomato* is distinctive. It stands out from the crowd (or at least, from the flock) and catches our attention. Upon retrieval, it is less likely to "blend in" with all the other words. In general, distinctive stimuli are better remembered than non-distinctive ones (Bireta & Simels, 2009; Ghetti et al., 2002). This principle also applies to the events of our lives. In one study, university students were asked to list their three clearest memories (Rubin & Kozin, 1984). Distinctive events such as weddings, romantic encounters, births and deaths, vacations, and accidents were among the most frequently recalled.

Can we enhance the memorability of nondistinctive stimuli by associating them with other stimuli that help to make them distinctive? According to Mäntylä (1986), this is a key reason why students who generated their own three-word associations were able to remember almost all the 500 words on their list. Associating each word with three others helped form a distinctive, personally meaningful set of cues. Thus, when studying, one way to increase your recall when all the material "starts looking alike" is to make it distinctive by associating it with other information that is personally meaningful to you.

Flashbulb Memory: Fogging Up the Picture?

Do you recall what you were doing when a massive earthquake and tsunami hit Japan in 2011?

© RGB Ventures LLC dba SuperStock/Alamy Stock Photo

FIGURE 8.12 A flashbulb memory is a recollection that seems so vivid and clear that we can picture it as if it were a snapshot of a moment in time.

I (M.A.) distinctly remember waking up to reports of incredible damage and then watching as cameras captured the incoming waves (Figure 8.12).

Flashbulb memories are recollections that seem so vivid, so clear, that we can picture them as if they were a snapshot of a moment in time. They are most likely to occur for distinctive, positive or negative events that evoke strong emotional reactions (Curci & Luminet, 2009).

Because flashbulb memories are vivid and easily recalled, we are confident of their accuracy. But are they accurate? The day after the space shuttle *Challenger* blew up shortly after takeoff, Ulric Neisser and Nicole Harsch (1993) asked university students to describe how they learned of the accident, where they were, and so on. Reinterviewed three years later, about half of them remembered some details correctly, but they recalled other details inaccurately. A fourth of the students completely misremembered all the major details and were astonished by how inaccurate their memories were after reading their original descriptions.

In the seventh week after the 9/11 terrorist attacks, psychologist Kathy Pezdek (2002) asked 569 students attending college in New York City (Manhattan), Southern California, and Hawaii to complete a memory questionnaire. One item asked, "On September 11, did you see the videotape on television of the first plane striking the first tower?" Overall, 73 percent of the students said "Yes." Yet this was impossible, because the videotape of the first plane crashing was not broadcast until after September 11. Moreover, students who incorrectly responded "Yes" were more confident in their memory than the students who correctly said "No"! Similarly, after Princess

19. Do flashbulb memories always provide an accurate picture? Describe some evidence.

Diana died in a car crash in 1997, a study in England found that 44 percent of participants said that they had seen a videotape on the TV news showing the crash take place. No such tape was ever shown; in fact, it is highly doubtful that such a tape even exists, yet they were as confident in their memory as participants who said they never saw such a tape (Ost et al., 2002, 2008).

Memory researchers have studied the relation between confidence and accuracy with children and adults, inside and outside the laboratory, and for many types of events. Overall, confidence and accuracy are weakly related (Busey et al., 2000; Talarico & Rubin, 2003). People accurately recall many events—even after years pass—and typically are very confident when they do. But people often swear by inaccurate memories too. Even for a distinctive event, a memory can feel "like it just happened yesterday" when, in truth, it's foggy.

Context, State, and Mood Effects on Memory

Years ago, two Swedish researchers reported the case of a young woman who was raped while out for a jog (Christianson & Nilsson, 1989). When found by a passerby, she was in shock and could not remember the assault. Over the next three months, the police took her back to the crime scene several times. Although she could not recall the rape, she became emotionally aroused, suggesting implicit memory of the

event. While jogging one day shortly thereafter, she consciously recalled the rape.

Because this is a case study, we cannot be sure what caused the woman's memory to return. One possibility, the **encoding specificity principle,** states that memory is enhanced when conditions present during retrieval match those that were present during encoding (Tulving & Thomson, 1973). This enhancement occurs because stimuli associated with an event may become encoded as part of the memory and later serve as retrieval cues.

Context-Dependent Memory: Returning to the Scene

Applying the encoding specificity principle to *external* cues leads us to **context-dependent memory:** It typically is easier to remember something in the same environment in which it was acquired. Thus, upon returning to your elementary school or old neighbourhood, sights and sounds may trigger memories of teachers, classmates, and friends. As with the Swedish jogger, police detectives may take an eyewitness or crime victim back to the crime scene, hoping to stimulate the person's memory.

In a classic experiment, Duncan Godden and Alan Baddeley (1975) asked scuba divers to learn some lists of words underwater and some on dry land. As Figure 8.13 shows, when the divers were later retested in the two environments, lists learned underwater were recalled better

20. Explain how context-dependent and state-dependent memory illustrate the encoding specificity principle.

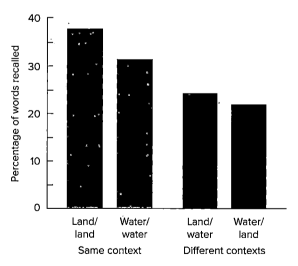

FIGURE 8.13 Context-dependent memory. Scuba divers who learned lists of words while underwater later recalled them better while underwater, whereas words learned on land were recalled better on land. Recall was poorer when the learning and testing environments were mismatched.

Source: Data from D.R. Godden & A.D. Baddeley, 1975, "Context-Dependent Memory in Two Natural Environments: On Land and Under Water," *British Journal of Psychology,* 66, 325–331. Reprinted by permission of the author. Photo: © Richard Hermann/Visuals Unlimited

underwater and those learned on land were better recalled while on land. Similarly, when randomly assigned university students studied material in either a quiet or noisy room, they later displayed better memory on short-answer and multiple-choice questions when tested in a corresponding (quiet or noisy) environment (Grant et al., 1998). Thus, if you take exams in quiet environments, try to study in a quiet environment.

The context or environment in which learning occurs may even influence the nature of the memory itself. Hupbach and colleagues (2008) claim that when new learning occurs in the same environment as prior learning, the context reactivates the earlier memory and as a result the new information modifies and updates the memory. When new learning occurs in a novel environment, on the other hand, the information is consolidated into a new episodic memory instead of modifying an existing memory.

State-Dependent Memory: Arousal, Drugs, and Mood

Moving from external to internal cues, the concept of **state-dependent memory** proposes that our ability to retrieve information is greater when our *internal* state at the time of retrieval matches our original state during learning. The Swedish jogger who was raped consciously remembered her assault for the first time while jogging. In her case, both context-dependent cues (similar environment) and state dependent cues (arousal while jogging) may have stimulated her memory.

Diverse experiments support this effect. Many students at the campus gym read course materials while exercising on a bicycle, treadmill, or stairclimber machine. Christopher Miles and Elinor Hardman (1998) found that material learned while we are aroused during aerobic exercise is later recalled more effectively if we are once again aerobically aroused, rather than at rest. Conversely, material learned at rest is better recalled at rest.

Many drugs produce physiological effects that directly impair memory, but state-dependency is another reason why events experienced in a drug state may be difficult to recall later while in a drug-free state (Figure 8.14). Experiments examining alcohol, marijuana, amphetamines, barbiturates, nicotine, caffeine, antihistamines, and other drugs have often found that information recall is poorer when there is a mismatch between the person's state during learning and testing (Carter & Cassaday,

Photofest

FIGURE 8.14 State-dependent memory. In the film *City Lights*, a drunken millionaire befriends and spends the evening partying with Charlie Chaplin after Chaplin saves his life. The next day, in a sober state, the millionaire doesn't remember Chaplin and considers him an unwanted pest. After getting drunk again, he remembers Chaplin and treats him like a good buddy.

1998; Rezayof et al., 2008). This finding *does not* mean, by the way, that drugs improve memory during initial learning.

Does state-dependent memory extend to mood states? Is material learned while in a happy mood or a sad mood better recalled when we are in that mood again? Inconsistent findings suggest that such *mood-dependent memory* is not a reliable phenomenon, although researchers continue to study whether it might occur under certain conditions (Ryan & Eich, 2000). Instead, there is more consistent evidence of **mood-congruent recall:** We tend to recall information or events that are congruent with our current mood (Teasdale & Fogarty, 1979; Fiedler, 2000). When happy, we are more likely to remember positive events, and when sad, we tend to remember negative events. This likelihood helps to perpetuate our mood and may be one factor that maintains depression once people have entered a depressed state (Pyszczynski et al., 1991). There is also evidence that some people experience *mood-incongruent recall,* which is thought to be related to negative mood regulation, or attempts to improve a negative mood state (Rusting & DeHart, 2000).

Clearly, many factors affect how we encode, store, and retrieve information. This chapter's *Applications* feature highlights some principles that are particularly relevant to helping you improve your memory.

21. Identify practical principles of encoding and retrieval that can be used to enhance memory.

Applications

IMPROVING MEMORY AND ACADEMIC LEARNING

Memory enhancement strategies fall into three broad categories (Park et al., 1990; Soler & Ruiz, 1996):

- *external aids,* such as shopping lists, notes, appointment calendars, and placing objects (such as keys) in the same location;
- *general memory strategies,* such as organizing and rehearsing information; and
- *formal mnemonic techniques,* such as acronyms and other systems that take training to be used effectively.

Overall, memory researchers most strongly recommend using external aids and general strategies to enhance memory (Park et al., 1990; Moe & De Benji, 2005). Of course, in situations such as "closed-book" exams, using external aids may land you in the dean's office! The following sound psychological principles can best enhance memory.

Use Elaborative Rehearsal to Process Information Deeply

Elaborative rehearsal—focusing on the meaning of information—enhances deep processing and memory (Gabrieli et al., 1996). Put simply, *if you are trying to commit information to memory, make sure that you understand what it means.* You may feel that we're daffy for stating such an obvious point, but let us ask you this: Do you always seek assistance when you encounter material that you have trouble understanding? Unfortunately, some students who find material confusing simply try to "learn" it by rote memorization, an approach that usually fails. The "directed questions" that appear in this book's margins can help you process the course material more deeply, and also serve as good retrieval cues.

Link New Information to Examples and Items Already in Memory

Once you understand the material, process it more deeply by associating it with information you already know. This association creates memory "hooks" onto which you can hang new information. Because you already have many memorable life experiences, *make new information personally meaningful* by relating it to your life.

Pay attention to examples, even if they are unrelated to your own experience. In one study, participants read a 32-paragraph essay about a fictitious African nation. Each paragraph presented a topic sentence stating a main theme along with zero, one, two, or three examples illustrating that theme. The greater the number of examples, the better the participants recalled the themes (Palmere et al., 1983).

Organize Information

Organizing information keeps you actively thinking about the material and makes it more meaningful. Before reading a chapter, look at the outline to determine how the material is logically developed. When studying, take notes from a chapter and use outlining to organize the information. This hierarchical structure forces you to arrange main ideas above subordinate ones and becomes an additional retrieval cue that facilitates recall (Bower et al., 1969).

Overlearn the Material

Overlearning refers to continued rehearsal past the point of initial learning, and it significantly improves performance on memory tasks (Driskell et al., 1992). In general, the greater the amount of overlearning, the greater the benefit. Moreover, much of this memory boost persists for weeks after overlearning ends. In short, just as elite athletes keep practising their skills, you should continue to rehearse material after you have first learned it.

Distribute Learning over Time

You have finished the readings and organized your notes for an upcoming test. Now it's time to study and review. Are you better off with *massed practice,* a marathon session of highly concentrated learning, or with *distributed practice,* several shorter sessions spread out over a few days? Research suggests that you will retain more information with distributed practice (Smith & Rothkopf, 1984; Underwood, 1970). It can reduce fatigue and anxiety, both of which impair learning.

Minimize Interference

Interference, as we soon will discuss more fully, occurs when one piece of information encoded in memory impairs our ability to remember some other piece of information. Distributed practice is effective because the rest periods between study sessions reduce interference from competing material. However, when studying for several exams on the same or consecutive days, there really are few rest periods. There is no simple solution to this problem. Suppose you have a psychology exam on Thursday and a sociology exam on Friday. Try to arrange several sessions of distributed practice for each exam over the preceding week. On Wednesday, limit your studying to psychology if possible. Once your psychology exam is over, turn your attention to your second test. This way, the final study period for each course will occur as close as possible to test time and minimize interference from other cognitive activities.

Studying before you go to sleep may enhance retention by temporarily minimizing interference, but, most of all, a

continued

typical university course load illustrates why overlearning is so important. Realistically, interference cannot be avoided, so study the material beyond the point where you feel you have learned it.

Use Imagery

Among formal mnemonic techniques, memory researchers view imagery as the most valuable (Park et al., 1990). As dual-coding theory predicts, images provide a splendid second "cognitive hook" on which to hang and retrieve information (Paivio, 1969, 1995). Instead of writing down

customers' orders, some restaurant waiters and waitresses form images, such as visualizing a man who has ordered a margarita turning light green. As one waitress remarked, "After a while, customers start looking like drinks" (Bennett, 1983, p. 165). Perhaps an image of a camera flashbulb with a big red X through it will help you remember that flashbulb memories often are less accurate than people think they are. In sum, although there may not be any "magic" or effortless way to enhance memory, psychological research has established numerous principles that you can use to your advantage.

FORGETTING

Some very bright people are legendary for their memory failures, or "absentmindedness." The eminent French writer Voltaire began a passionate letter "My Dear Hortense" and ended it "Farewell, my dear Adele." The splendid absentmindedness of Canon Sawyer, an English nobleman, once led him, while welcoming a visitor at the railroad station, to board the departing train and disappear (Bryan, 1986). Indeed, how we forget is nearly as interesting a scientific question as how we remember.

The Course of Forgetting

German psychologist Hermann Ebbinghaus (1885/1964) pioneered the study of forgetting by testing only one person—himself (Figure 8.15).

US National Library of Medicine

FIGURE 8.15 Hermann Ebbinghaus was a pioneering memory researcher.

He created over 2000 *nonsense syllables*, meaningless letter combinations (e.g., *biv, zaj, xew*), to study memory with minimal influence from prior learning, as would happen if he used actual words. A dedicated scientist, in one study Ebbinghaus spent over 14 000 practice repetitions trying to memorize 420 lists of nonsense syllables.

Ebbinghaus typically measured memory by using a method called *relearning* and computing a savings percentage. For example, if it initially took him 20 trials to learn a list, but only half as many trials to relearn it a week later, then the savings percentage was 50 percent. In one series of studies, he retested his memory at various time intervals after mastering several lists of nonsense syllables. As Figure 8.16a shows, forgetting occurred rapidly at first and slowed noticeably thereafter.

Perhaps you are dismayed by this finding, which suggests that we quickly forget most of what we learn. Ebbinghaus, however, studied so many lists that his ability to distinguish between them undoubtedly suffered. If you learned just one or a few lists of syllables, the general shape of your forgetting curve might resemble Ebbinghaus's over the first 24 hours, but the amount you forget would likely be much less. Moreover, when material is meaningful (unlike nonsense syllables), we are likely to retain more of it for a longer time.

Consider the forgetting curve shown in Figure 8.16b, based on a study examining the vocabulary retention of people who had studied Spanish in school anywhere from 3 to 50 years earlier and then rarely used it (Bahrick, 1984). Once again, forgetting occurred more rapidly at first, and then more slowly as time passed. Notice, however, that we are now employing a

22. Describe Ebbinghaus's "forgetting curve" and factors that contributed to his rapid, substantial forgetting.

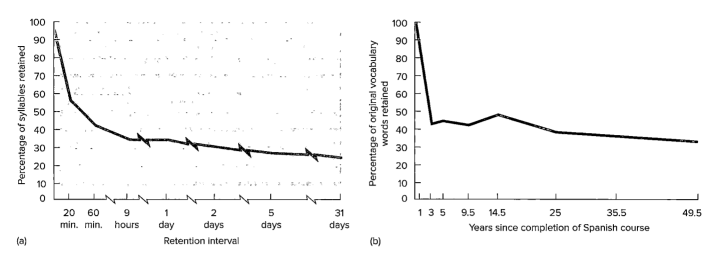

FIGURE 8.16 (a) Hermann Ebbinghaus's forgetting curve shows a rapid loss of memory for nonsense syllables at first, then a more gradual decline. The rapid decline is probably due to the meaningless nature of the nonsense syllables. (b) The forgetting of vocabulary from high school Spanish language classes follows a similar curve, except that the time frame is in years, not days.

Source: Data from (a) Ebbinghaus, H. (1885/1964). *öber das Gedächtnis: Untersuchungen Zur Experimentellen Psychologie* (*Memory: A contribution to experimental psychology*). (H.A. Ruger & C.E. Bussenius, Trans.). New York, NY: Dover. (Original work published 1885; and (b) Data from Bahrick, H.P. (1984). Semantic memory content in permastore: Fifty years of memory for Spanish learned in school. *Journal of Experimental Psychology: General, 113,* 1–29.

time frame of years rather than hours and days as Ebbinghaus did. Similarly, in another study, first- and second-year university students accurately recalled 73 percent of their grades from their last year in high school, and their recall for grades from earlier years was almost as good (Bahrick et al., 1996). Of course, although participants in these studies retained considerable information over time, their memory was far from perfect.

Why Do We Forget?

Given that some memories last a lifetime, why do we forget so much? Researchers have proposed several explanations for normal memory loss, emphasizing difficulties in encoding, storage, and retrieval.

Encoding Failure

23. Identify encoding, storage, retrieval, and motivational processes that have been hypothesized to contribute to forgetting.

If memory is in some respects like a giant library, then one reason we do not remember information is that the book was never put on the shelf. Many memory failures result not from "forgetting" information that we once knew well, but from failing to encode the information into long-term memory in the first place. Much of what we sense is not processed deeply enough to commit to memory, which is understandable given the flood of stimuli that enter the sensory registers every day.

We noted earlier that few people can draw a penny (or other coin) from memory, with accurate detail. Even when the task is made easier by requiring only recognition, as in Figure 8.17, most people cannot identify the correct coin (Jones, 1990; Nickerson & Adams, 1979). The details of a coin's appearance are not meaningful to most of us, so we do not encode them no matter how often we see coins in our daily lives.

At other times, we may notice information but fail to encode it deeply because we turn our attention to something else. Brad Bushman and Angelica Bonacci (2002) randomly assigned 328 adults to watch either a sexually explicit, violent, or neutral TV program. Nine commercial advertisements (e.g., for snacks, cereal, laundry detergent) appeared during each program. Immediately afterward and again a day later, the researchers tested viewers' memory for the ads. When analyzing their findings, Bushman and Bonaci adjusted for the fact that some of the TV programs were more interesting and arousing than others. Even so, at both time periods, viewers who watched the sexually explicit and violent programs remembered the fewest number of ads. Several factors might account for this, and, as the researchers proposed, one of them is encoding failure: All the viewers clearly saw the ads, but those watching the sexually

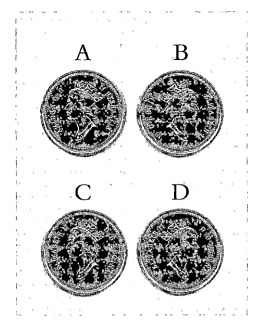

FIGURE 8.17 Which of the coins pictured here corresponds to a real penny? Most people have difficulty choosing the correct one because they have never bothered to encode all the features of a real penny. Which representation of the penny is correct? Check your answer at the end of the chapter.

Source: Adapted from Nickerson, R.S., & Adams, M.J. (1979). Long term memory for a common object. *Cognitive Psychology*, 11, 287–307.

explicit and violent programs likely were the most preoccupied with thoughts about the content of the shows.

Decay of the Memory Trace

Turning from encoding to storage, one early explanation for forgetting was **decay theory**, which proposed that with time and disuse the physical memory trace in the nervous system fades away. Decay theory soon fell into disfavour because scientists could not identify what physical memory traces were, where they were located, or how physical decay could be measured. In recent decades, however, scientists have begun to unravel some of the ways that neural circuits change when a long-term memory is formed. This research has sparked new interest in examining how these changes might decay over time (Villarreal et al., 2002).

Decay theory's prediction that the longer the interval of disuse between learning and recall, the less would be recalled, was also problematic. When participants learn a list of words or a set of visual patterns and are retested at two different times, they sometimes recall *more*

material during the second testing than during the first. This phenomenon, called *reminiscence*, seems inconsistent with the concept that a memory trace decays over time (Greene, 1992). In sum, scientists still debate the validity of decay theory (Brown et al., 2007).

Interference, Retrieval Failure, and the Tip-of-the-Tongue

According to *interference theory*, we forget information because other items in long-term memory impair our ability to retrieve it (Mayr, 2009; Postman & Underwood, 1973). Figure 8.18 illustrates two major types of interference. **Proactive interference** occurs when material learned in the past interferes with recall of newer material. Suppose that Charles changes residences, acquires a new phone number, and memorizes it. That night he sees a friend who asks for his new number. When Charles tries to recall it, he can remember only two or three digits, and instead keeps remembering the digits of his old phone number. Memory of his old phone number is interfering with his ability to retrieve the new one.

Retroactive interference occurs in the opposite direction. Here, newly acquired information interferes with the ability to recall information learned at an earlier time (Tulving & Psotka, 1971). Suppose Charles has now had his new phone number for several months and recalls it perfectly each time. If we ask him, "What was your old phone number?" Charles may have trouble remembering it, perhaps mixing up the digits with his new number. In general, the more similar two sets of information are, the more likely it is that interference will

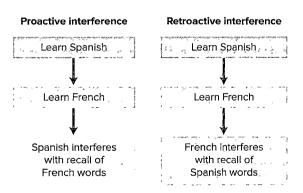

FIGURE 8.18 Interference is a major cause of forgetting. With proactive interference, older memories interfere with the retrieval of newer ones. With retroactive interference, newer memories interfere with the retrieval of older ones.

occur. You would probably experience little interference in recalling highly dissimilar material, such as French vocabulary and mathematical formulas.

Some researchers believe that interference is caused by competition among retrieval cues (Anderson & Neely, 1996; Runquist, 1975). When different memories become associated with similar or identical retrieval cues, confusion can result and accessing a cue may "call up" the wrong memory. Wixted (2004) has suggested that in fact *any* mental activity can interfere with not-yet-consolidated memories, even if the activity is not similar to the previously learned information. Retrieval failure also can occur because we have too few retrieval cues or the cues may be too weak (Tulving & Psotka, 1971).

Almost all of us have experienced the so-called *"tip-of-the-tongue" (TOT) phenomenon,* in which we cannot recall a fact or name (a target word) but feel that we are on the verge of recalling it. Often we keep recalling an incorrect word that sounds similar to or resembles the target word. TOT states are common, perhaps occurring on average about once a week (Brown, 1991). Eventually, we retrieve the correct answer about half the time, and when we cannot, we often recall related information that makes us feel "I really do know the answer" (Brown, 1991; Riefer et al., 1995).

Do TOT states always reflect a retrieval problem? In one experiment, Bennett Schwartz (1998) asked university students a series of general factual questions, some of which actually had no correct answer. Yet when asked these impossible questions, all students claimed at least once that the answer was on the tip of their tongue. In short, some TOT experiences seem to be illusory. Rather than retrieval failure, perhaps we never knew the answer to begin with (Lampinen & Schwartz, 2000).

Motivated Forgetting

Psychodynamic theorists and other psychologists suggest yet another reason for some forgetting. They maintain that motivational processes, such as **repression,** may protect us by blocking the recall of anxiety-arousing memories (Knafo, 2009; Singer, 1999).

During therapy sessions Sigmund Freud often observed that his patients remembered traumatic or anxiety-arousing events that had long seemed "forgotten." For example, one of

his patients suddenly remembered with great shame that while standing beside her sister's coffin, she had thought, "Now my brother-in-law is free to marry me." Freud concluded that the thought had been so shocking and anxiety arousing that the woman had *repressed* it— pushed it down into her unconscious mind— there to remain until it was uncovered years later during psychoanalysis.

The concept of motivated forgetting is controversial. Some evidence supports it, and other evidence does not (Follette & Davis, 2009; Karon, 2002). People certainly do forget unpleasant events (and pleasant ones as well), but it has been difficult to demonstrate experimentally that a process akin to "repression" is the cause of such memory loss or whether it is due to normal information-processing failure. Even more basically, if a person has not thought about an event for many years, does this necessarily indicate that the memory has been forgotten (McNally & Geraerts, 2009)? We will return to this topic shortly.

Amnesia

The most dramatic instances of forgetting occur in amnesia, which takes several forms. **Retrograde amnesia** represents memory loss for events that occurred *prior to* the onset of amnesia. For example, H.M. suffered mild memory loss for events in his life that had occurred during the year or two *before* his operation. A football player who is "knocked out" in a concussion, regains consciousness, and cannot remember the events just before being hit, is experiencing retrograde amnesia. In one study, Hassabis and colleagues (2007) reported that amnesiac patients with damage to their hippocampus were unable to imagine new experiences. Findings like these demonstrate the importance of memory systems and even memories themselves to everyday mental experience— without the ability to retrieve episodic memories we would be incapable of imagining new experiences.

Anterograde amnesia refers to memory loss for events that occur *after* the initial onset of amnesia. H.M.'s brain operation, and particularly the removal of much of his hippocampus, produced severe anterograde amnesia and robbed him of the ability to consciously remember new experiences and facts. Anterograde amnesia can also be produced by other conditions, such as *Korsakoff's syndrome,* which can

24. Describe the nature and some possible causes of retrograde, anterograde, and infantile amnesia.

result from chronic alcoholism and may also cause severe retrograde amnesia (Brand, 2007).

Dementia and Alzheimer's Disease

Dementia refers to impaired memory and other cognitive deficits that accompany brain degeneration and interfere with normal functioning. There are more than a dozen types and causes of dementia, and although it can occur at any point in life, dementia is most prevalent among elderly adults.

Alzheimer's disease (AD) is a progressive brain disorder that is the most common cause of dementia among adults over the age of 65. Half a million Canadians currently have Alzheimer's disease or a related dementia, and it is predicted that by 2035 the number of cases will reach 1.1 million Canadians (Alzheimer Society, 2010).

The early symptoms of AD, which worsen gradually over a period of years, include forgetfulness, poor judgment, confusion, and disorientation. Often, memory for recent events and new information is especially impaired. By itself, forgetfulness is not necessarily a sign that a person is developing AD. However, memory is the first psychological function affected, as AD initially attacks subcortical temporal lobe regions—areas near the hippocampus and then the hippocampus itself— that help convert short-term memories into long-term ones.

Alzheimer's disease spreads across the temporal lobes and to the frontal lobes and other cortical regions (Figure 8.19). As German physician Alois Alzheimer first noticed a century ago, patients with this disease have an abnormal amount of plaques and tangles in their brains. *Plaques* are clumps of protein fragments that build up on the outside of neurons,

whereas *tangles* are fibres that get twisted and wound together within neurons (Shepherd et al., 2009). Neurons become damaged and die, brain tissue shrinks, and communication among neurons is impaired as AD disrupts several neurotransmitter systems, especially the acetylcholine system. Acetylcholine plays a key role in synaptic transmission in several brain areas involved in memory, and drugs that help to maintain acetylcholine functioning have had some temporary success in improving AD patients' cognitive functioning (Ritchie et al., 2004).

Working memory and long-term memory worsen as AD progresses. If you read a list of just three words to healthy 80-year-old adults and then test their recall after a brief time delay, they will typically remember two or all three words. Patients with AD, however, typically recall either no words or one word (Chandler et al., 2004). Anterograde and retrograde amnesia become more severe, and procedural, semantic, episodic, and prospective memory can all be affected. Patients may lose the ability to learn new tasks or remember new information or experiences, forget how to perform familiar tasks, and have trouble recognizing even close family members.

What causes AD and its characteristic plaques and tangles? Scientists have identified several genes that contribute to early-onset AD, an inherited form of the disease that develops before age 65 (and as early as age 30) but accounts for only 5 to 10 percent of Alzheimer's cases (Belbin et al., 2009). For the more typical, late-onset AD, researchers have identified a gene called *ApoE* (on chromosome pair 19) as a major risk factor (Jonsson et al., 2013; Yuan et al., 2009). This gene helps to direct the production of proteins that carry

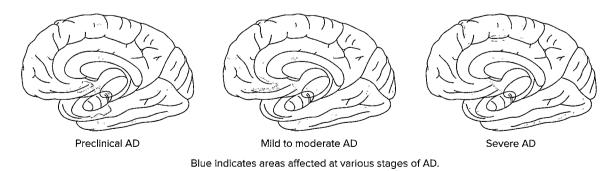

Preclinical AD   Mild to moderate AD   Severe AD

Blue indicates areas affected at various stages of AD.

FIGURE 8.19 The progression of Alzheimer's disease.

Source: National Institute of Health. (2002). Alzheimer's disease: Unraveling the mystery. NIH Publication 02-3782. Bethesda, MD. Retrieved from http://www.alzheimers.org/unraveling/unraveling.pdf.

cholesterol in the blood plasma, and high cholesterol and other risk factors for cardiovascular disease may likewise increase the risk of developing AD.

If you know someone who has AD, then you're aware that it involves much more than memory loss. Patients experience language problems, disorganized thinking, and mood and personality changes. Ultimately, they may lose the ability to speak, walk, and control bladder and bowel functions. We'll have more to say about the psychological, physical, and social aspects of dementia and aging in Chapter 16.

Infantile (Childhood) Amnesia

There is one type of amnesia that almost all of us encounter: an inability to remember personal experiences from the first few years of our lives. Even though infants and preschoolers can form long-term memories of events in their lives (Peterson & Whalen, 2001), as adults we typically are unable to recall these events consciously. This memory loss for early experiences is called **infantile amnesia** (also known as *childhood amnesia*). Our memories of childhood typically do not include events that occurred before the age of three or four, although some adults can partially recall major events (e.g., the birth of a sibling, hospitalization, or a death in the family) that happened before the age of two (Eacott & Crawley, 1998).

What causes infantile amnesia? One hypothesis is that brain regions that encode long-term episodic memories are still immature in the first years after birth. Another is that we do not encode our earliest experiences deeply and fail to form rich retrieval cues for them. Additionally, because infants lack a clear self-concept, they do not have a personal frame of reference around which to organize rich memories (Harley & Reese, 1999).

Forgetting to Do Things: Prospective Memory

Have you ever forgotten to mail a letter, turn off the oven, keep an appointment, or purchase something at the market? In contrast to *retrospective memory*, which refers to memory for past events, **prospective memory** concerns remembering to perform an activity in the future (Meacham & Singer, 1977). That people forget to do things as often as they do is interesting, because prospective memories typically involve little content (Baddeley, 1990). Often we need only recall that we must perform some event-based task ("Remember, on your way out, mail the letter") or time-based task ("Remember, take your medication at 4 p.m."). Successful prospective memory, however, draws on other cognitive abilities, such as planning and allocating attention while performing other tasks (Einstein et al., 2000; Marsh et al., 1998). The frontal lobes, which direct these executive processes, appear to be centrally involved in prospective memory (McDaniel et al., 1999).

Are people with better retrospective memory less likely to be forgetful on prospective memory tasks? Some findings suggest not, at least when retrospective memory is measured explicitly by recall and recognition tasks (McDaniel & Einstein, 1993). In one experiment, researchers assessed participants' retrospective memory ability by having them recall lists of words (Wilkins & Baddeley, 1978). Next, participants performed a prospective, simulated pill-taking task by carrying around a small box with a button. Four times a day at a specified time they had to remember to press the button, which time-stamped their response. Overall, participants who performed better on the word-recall task did not display better memory on the simulated pill-taking task.

During adulthood, do we become increasingly absentminded about remembering to do things, as a common stereotype suggests? Numerous studies support this view (Logie & Maylor, 2009; Vogels et al., 2002). Typically, in these studies, participants perform a task that requires their ongoing attention while trying to remember to signal the researcher at certain time intervals or whenever specific events take place. Older adults generally display poorer prospective memory, especially when signalling is time-based. However, when prospective memory is tested outside the laboratory by using tasks such as simulated pill-taking, healthy adults in their 60s to their 80s often perform as well as or better than adults in their 20s (Rendell & Thomson, 1993, 1999; Henry et al., 2004; Phillips et al., 2006). Perhaps older adults are more motivated to remember in such situations or rely more on a standard routine (Anderson & Craik, 2000). In sum, prospective memory—like other areas of memory—is far from simple. Want to remember things better? We offer some suggestions in the *Frontiers* feature.

METHODS TO ENHANCE MEMORY

While much of the latest research on memory has focused on neural mechanisms (e.g., Elhalal et al., 2014), there are a number of recent authors who have begun to explore methods for remembering things better. Surprisingly, many of these memory enhancement techniques are probably strategies that we have used before or thought about using. Let's examine a few of these.

Caffeine

Many people use caffeine, typically in the form of coffee, to enhance concentration and keep us awake. But does caffeine improve memory? Yassa (2015) reports that that caffeine can enhance memory for up to 24 hours. Participants who rarely used caffeinated beverages received a 200-milligram caffeine tablet or a placebo after exposure to a series of images. The next day they viewed another set of images, some of which were identical to those shown before while others were similar to the ones seen at training. Results indicated that those participants who had consumed caffeine were better at correctly identifying the similar images as new. It should be noted that caffeine was administered after the initial memory task rather than before in an effort to eliminate the potential effects of attention, focusing, and so on. So to enhance memory, you need to have that coffee *after* studying, not before.

Napping

Sleep is essential for the consolidation of memory, as we have seen earlier, but what about power naps? Studte et al. (2015) asked participants to learn a list of phone numbers, words, and unrelated word pairs such as "milk-taxi." Following the training session, half of the participants were allowed to nap for 45 minutes, while the others watched a DVD. When asked to recall the items on the list, the nappers were five times better at remembering the word pairs (an associative memory task). There was no enhancement for the single words or phone numbers. Interestingly, a large number of sleep spindles were observed on the EEGs of those who were napping, suggesting memory consolidation. Napping also improves memory in infants (Seehagen et al., 2015). Babies watched a researcher play with a hand puppet and then either napped or did not. When tested four and twenty-four hours later, the babies who a napped were better able to mimic the actions of the researcher with the puppet.

Curiosity

When we are really curious about an event, we attend to it very closely. This increased attention can have benefits for the memory of other material that occurs at roughly the same time. Gruber et al. (2014) asked participants a trivia question that they were curious about. While waiting for the answer to appear on the screen, they were shown a picture of a face. Those who were highly curious about the topic later remembered more of the answers and they were also better at remembering the faces that appeared while waiting. The researchers suggest that curiosity activates the hippocampus, enhancing memory for all things that occur during and around the topic in question.

Longhand Writing

Increasingly, more students are taking class notes on their computers rather than writing out the information using pen and paper. But is this the best way to learn and remember? Muller and Oppenheimer (2014) asked university students to watch video lectures and take notes either with a laptop computer or by writing out the information in longhand. Students were then given a test on the lecture material. Results indicated that those who wrote out the notes generally performed better than those who keyboarded. The researchers suggest that keyboarding is a relatively fast task and encourages taking down the information verbatim. Longhand requires you to listen and assimilate the information, resulting in better memory.

Chewing Gum

Many major league athletes are constantly shown on the field chewing gum. The claim is that it helps with focus and attention. But gum chewing can be beneficial for your memory as well. Morgan et al. (2014) asked participants to listen to a list of numbers and respond by pressing a button if they heard a sequence of odd-even-odd numbers (e.g., 5-8-3). Some participants were given gum to chew during the task and others were not. Results indicated that those who chewed gum had faster reaction times and were accurate at identifying the sequences. Apparently, chewing gum helps you to focus and remember better. But before you chew a wad of gum during your next test, research by Onyper et al. (2011) suggests that you have to stop chewing before you actually take the test. Students who chewed then stopped for five minutes before a test of memory performed better than those who did not chew at all *and* those who continued to chew gum during the tests.

- Retrieval cues activate information stored in long-term memory. Memory retrieval is more likely to occur when we have multiple cues, self-generated cues, and distinctive cues.

- We experience flashbulb memories as vivid and clear "snapshots" of an event and are confident of their accuracy. However, over time many flashbulb memories become inaccurate. Overall, memory accuracy and memory confidence are only weakly related.

- The encoding specificity principle states that memory is enhanced when cues present during retrieval match those that were present during encoding. Typically, it is easier to remember a stimulus when we are in the same environment (context-dependent memory) or same internal state (state-dependent memory) as when the stimulus was originally encoded. One exception is mood states, where we tend to recall information or events that are congruent with our current mood.

- Forgetting tends to be most rapid relatively soon after initial learning, but the time frame and degree of forgetting can vary widely depending on many factors.

- Because of encoding failure, we often cannot recall information because we never entered it into long-term memory in the first place.

- Decay theory proposes that physical memory traces in long-term memory deteriorate with disuse over time, but evidence of reminiscence contradicts this view.

- Proactive interference occurs when material learned in the past interferes with recall of newer material. Retroactive interference occurs when newly acquired information interferes with the ability to recall information learned at an earlier time.

- Psychodynamic theorists propose that we may forget anxiety-arousing material through repression, an unconscious process of motivated forgetting.

- Retrograde amnesia represents memory loss for events that occurred prior to the onset of amnesia. Anterograde amnesia refers to memory loss for events that occur after the initial onset of amnesia. Infantile amnesia is our inability to remember personal experiences from the first few years of our lives.

- Whereas retrospective memory refers to memory for past events, prospective memory refers to our ability to remember to perform some activity in the future.

MEMORY AS A CONSTRUCTIVE PROCESS

Retrieving information from long-term memory is not like viewing a taped replay on a video recorder. Usually, our memories of things past are incomplete and sketchy. In such situations, we may literally *construct* (or as some researchers prefer to say, *reconstruct*) a memory by piecing together bits of stored information in a way that intuitively "makes sense," and which therefore seems real and accurate (Schacter & Curran, 2000; Garoff-Eaton et al., 2006). Memory construction can be amusing at times. Many of us have a tendency to recall the world through slightly rosy glasses, which helps us feel good about ourselves. For example, when university students in one study recalled their high school grades, the worse the grade was, the less often students remembered it accurately. Students correctly recall almost all of their A's but only about a third of their D's (Figure 8.20).

Most important, errors were positively biased; students usually remembered their B's as having been A's, their C's as B's, and so on (Bahrick et al., 1996). Similar errors occur for recall of university grades (Bahrick et al., 2008). As we will see, however, memory construction also can have serious personal and societal consequences.

Memory Distortion and Schemas

Many years ago, Sir Frederick Bartlett (1932) provided an excellent illustration of memory construction. Bartlett asked residents of Cambridge, England, to read and then retell stories days, months, or years later. One story, "The War of the Ghosts," is a Pacific Northwest Indian tale about a man on a seal-hunting trip who meets a group of warriors and goes on a raid with them. During the raid, he discovers that his companions are ghosts; subsequently, he dies a supernatural death.

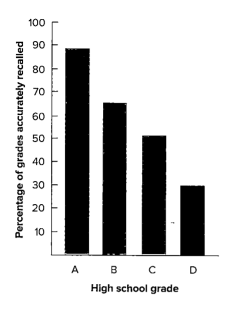

FIGURE 8.20 The lower the grade, the less likely university students were to accurately recall it. When students incorrectly recalled a grade, they almost always overestimated how well they did.

Source: Adapted from Bahrick, L.K. Hall & S.A. Berger, 1996, Accuracy and Distortion in Memory for High School Grades, *Psychological Science*, 7(5), 265–271, Table 2. Copyright © 1996 Association for Psychological Science. Reprinted by permission of Sage Publications.

Bartlett's participants, however, were 20th-century residents of England, not 18th-century Native Americans. When these English participants retold the story, they reconstructed it in a way that made sense to them. For example, one participant who retold the story 20 hours after reading it shortened the story and changed the plot significantly. Now the hero was fishing rather than hunting seals, the word *boat* was substituted for *canoe*, and most importantly the enemy—not the war party—were described as ghosts. Bartlett found that the longer the time interval between the reading and retelling of the story, the more the story changed to fit English culture.

Bartlett, who coined the term *schema*, believed that people have generalized ideas (schemas) about how events happen and that they use these ideas to organize and reconstruct their memories. In reading "The War of the Ghosts," our pre-existing schemas no doubt affect how we encode the story, but they also influence how we "fill in the gaps" and reconstruct the story when we later recall it.

In general, the use of appropriate schemas improves memory by helping us organize information as we encode and retrieve it. Remember that, whether we are a chess player, a coach, a musician, or simply an experienced user of language,

schemas are a key component of "expert knowledge." But schemas can exert a cognitive price. Fitting information into our schemas is sometimes like trying to squeeze a square peg into a round hole, requiring us to reshape and distort information so that it "makes sense" and fits in with pre-existing assumptions about the world.

Memory construction extends, quite literally, to how we visualize the world (Dickinson & Intraub, 2009). As Figure 8.21 illustrates, when university students look at photographs that have a main object within a scene, and then draw the pictures from memory, they consistently display *boundary extension*, remembering a scene as more expansive—as being "wider-angle"—than it really was (Intraub et al., 1996, 1998). In real life, objects occur against an expansive background, creating a schema for how we expect scenes to look. Thus, when remembering close-up images, our schemas

(a)

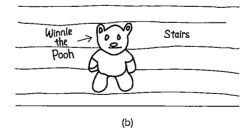

(b)

FIGURE 8.21 Boundary extension. (a) What you see. (b) What you remember. Helene Intraub and her colleagues (1996) have found that when people briefly look at close-up pictures, such as this one of a teddy bear, and then draw the pictures from memory, they unknowingly convert the image into a "wider-angle scene" in which the size of the main object (e.g., the teddy bear) shrinks. This effect is less likely to occur if the original picture already is a wide-angle scene.

Images courtesy of Helene Intraub. Intraub, H., Gottesman, C.V., Willey, E.V., & Zuk, I.J. (1996), Boundary extension for briefly glimpsed pictures: Do common perceptual processes result in unexpected memory distortions? *Journal of Memory and Language*, 35, 118–135.

25. How do Bartlett's research and studies of boundary extension illustrate memory construction?

lead us to "see beyond the edge" and retrieve a broader scene, not the one we saw.

The Misinformation Effect and Eyewitness Testimony

If memories are constructed, then information that occurs *after* an event may shape that construction process. This **misinformation effect,** the distortion of a memory by misleading post-event information, has been demonstrated in numerous studies (Porter et al., 2010; Sutherland & Hayne, 2001). Misinformation effects have been investigated most thoroughly in relation to mistaken eyewitness testimony. In fact, mistaken eyewitness identification is the source of more wrongful convictions in both Canada and the United States than all other sources together (Pezdek, 2012; Yarmey, 2001). In one celebrated case, Father Bernard Pagano, a Roman Catholic priest, was positively identified by seven eyewitnesses as the perpetrator of a series of armed robberies in the Wilmington, Delaware, area. He was saved from almost certain conviction when the true robber, dubbed the "gentleman bandit" because of his politeness and concern for his victims, confessed to the crimes. You can see in Figure 8.22 that there was little physical resemblance between the two men.

Two pieces of information may have affected the witnesses' memory. First, the gentlemanly and concerned manner of the robber is consistent with the schema many people have of priests. All else being equal, we will tend to make decisions in line with our schemas. Indeed, there is a high degree of consistency in the schemas that people have for "good guys" and "bad guys" in eyewitness situations (Yarmey, 1993). Second, before presenting pictures of suspects to the eyewitnesses, the police let it be known that the suspect might be a priest. Father Pagano was the only suspect wearing a clerical collar, and the witnesses' memories may have been strongly affected by this information (Rodgers, 1982; Tversky & Tuchin, 1989).

The misinformation effect can be subtle, produced by changing a single word while questioning an eyewitness. Imagine that after you witness a two-car crash, a police officer takes your statement and asks you, "About how fast were the cars going when they smashed into each other?" In a classic experiment, university students viewed a brief film of a car accident and then judged how fast the cars were going. Their judgments varied by almost 25 percent, depending on how the question was asked

(both): © Bettmann/Corbis

FIGURE 8.22 Seven eyewitnesses to armed robberies committed by Ronald Clouser (a) mistakenly identified Father Bernard Pagano (b) as the robber, probably as a result of information from police that influenced their memory reconstructions.

(Loftus & Palmer, 1974). The recalled speed became progressively slower when the words *smashed into* (65.3 km/h) were changed to *collided with* (62.9 km/h), *bumped* (61.0 km/h), *hit* (54.4 km/h), and *contacted* (50.9 km/h). Even your mood can enhance the misinformation effect. Van Damme and Seynaeva (2013) had students watch a movie while in a happy, sad or neutral mood. They were then exposed to misleading information. Participants were influenced by the misinformation and were more confident with their false beliefs in the sad condition.

Confusing the Source

Misinformation effects also occur because of **source confusion** (also called the *source*

26. Explain how source confusion contributes to misinformation effects.

monitoring error), our tendency to recall something or recognize it as familiar, but to forget where we encountered it. Suppose an eyewitness to a crime looks through a series of mugshots and reports that none of the individuals is the perpetrator. Several days later, the eyewitness is brought back to view a lineup and is asked to identify the person who committed the crime. In reality, none of the people in the lineup did, but one suspect was pictured in a mugshot that the eyewitness had seen days ago. "That's the person," says the eyewitness. Source confusion occurred because the eyewitness recognized that individual's face as familiar, but failed to remember that this familiarity stemmed from the mugshot. Instead, the witness mistakenly assumed that he or she saw the familiar-looking suspect committing the crime.

This scenario has been tested many times in experimental analogues. Participants who witness a staged event and later view mugshots are more likely to misidentify *innocent* suspects as having been involved in the event because of source confusion (Deffenbacher et al., 2006). Source confusion also occurs when participants are exposed to several misleading statements about an event that they have witnessed (Zaragoza & Mitchell, 1996; Dalton & Daneman, 2006). They eventually forget that the source of the misinformation (e.g., that a bare-handed thief wore gloves) was a statement made by someone else, and come to believe it was part of what they saw while witnessing the event.

Does post-event information permanently alter a witness's original memory, so that the original memory can never again be retrieved? Researchers debate the answer, but all agree that eyewitness reports can be influenced by post-event information. Results like these have raised concern about the reliability of eyewitness testimony not only from adults, but also from children in cases of alleged physical and sexual abuse.

Other Factors in Eyewitness Testimony

Misinformation effects are one source of inaccuracy in eyewitness testimony, but other factors may come into play as well. Imagine that a fight breaks out in a bar. An eyewitness insists that it was George who started the fight, not Paul. What are some possible sources of inaccuracy in this situation?

We might expect alcohol to be a factor. After people have been drinking, their memory for events may be less than accurate. Compared with people who have not consumed alcohol, a

blood-alcohol level of 0.10 resulted in less information being recalled from a staged theft, and more inaccurate identifications one week later (Yuille & Tollestrup, 1990). The effects of marijuana are much less pronounced (Yuille et al., 1998) and seem limited to a slight decrease in information recalled directly after an incident. One's ability to identify a possible perpetrator depends as well on the kind of information we have available. Identifications based on voice alone ("earwitness" identification) tend to be less accurate than those based on both visual and auditory cues, or on visual cues alone (Yarmey, 1993). Finally, we should note that, while men and women are equally inaccurate in their identifications, men tend to be more confident in their decisions (Yarmey & Yarmey, 1997).

The "Recovered Memory" Controversy: Repression or Reconstruction?

In 1997, a woman from Illinois settled a lawsuit against two psychiatrists and their hospital for $10.6 million. She alleged that her psychiatrists used hypnosis, drugs, and other treatments that led her to develop false memories of having been a high priestess in an abusive satanic cult. That same year, criminal charges were brought against a group of Houston mental-health professionals, alleging that they "used techniques commonly associated with mind control and brainwashing" with seven patients, creating false memories of having been abused in a satanic cult (*APA Monitor,* December 1997, p. 9). Yet, only years earlier, there had been a wave of cases in which adults—usually in the course of psychotherapy—began to remember long-forgotten childhood abuse and sued their parents, other family members, and former teachers for the alleged trauma (Figure 8.23).

In some cases it appears that accurate memories can indeed return after decades of post-trauma forgetting (Kluft, 1999; McNally & Geraerts, 2009). Yet memory loss after psychological trauma usually is far shorter, with memory returning over weeks, months, or perhaps a few years. In many cases of trauma the victim's primary problem is not memory loss but rather an *inability* to forget, which may involve recurrent nightmares and flashbacks (Ross et al., 1989). Experiments with adults and children also indicate that false memories of personal events can be created ("implanted") by suggestive questioning or comments, or merely by having someone imagine that the event took

27. Are younger and older children equally susceptible to misinformation effects and equally accurate in recalling traumatic events? Describe some evidence.

28. Do people ever forget traumatic personal events? Why are recovered memories and repression controversial topics?

© Shahn Kermani

FIGURE 8.23 In a famous 1990 repressed memory case, George Franklin was convicted of murdering Susan Nason, an eight-year-old girl killed in 1969. Franklin's 28-year-old daughter Eileen (shown above), who had been Susan's childhood friend, provided the key evidence. During therapy, Eileen recovered memories of her father sexually assaulting and killing Susan. A judge overturned the conviction after learning that Eileen's memories had been recovered under hypnosis. All the details about the case that Eileen recalled had been published in the newspapers, creating the possibility of source confusion in her memory. Eileen also had other recovered memories that were proven to be untrue, such as those of her father killing two other girls.

place (Laney & Loftus, 2005; Bruck et al., 1998; Herndon et al., 2014; Loftus & Pickrell, 1995). Many memory researchers are concerned that in "recovered memory therapy," therapists repeatedly suggest the possibility of abuse to people who already are emotionally vulnerable. Indeed, even when observers recognize that a therapist may be overly suggestive, ratings of competence remain high (Myers et al., 2015). Given everything psychology has taught us about forgetting, constructive memory, and the "fogging up" of even flashbulb memories, they argue that it is naive to take the accuracy of recovered memories of long-past events at face value.

The message from science is not that all claims of recovered traumatic memories should be dismissed (Brewin, 2012; Geraerts et al., 2007). Rather, it is to urge caution in unconditionally accepting those memories, particularly in cases where suggestive techniques are used to recover the memories (Follette & Davis, 2009; Gothard & Ivker, 2000). Some day it may be possible scientifically to separate true memories from false ones. Researchers have begun to establish that some types of true versus false memories are associated with different cognitive mechanisms (Geraerts et al., 2009) and even different patterns of brain activity (Abe et al., 2008), and true memories often are described in greater detail than false ones. But at present, these findings cannot be used to determine reliably whether any individual memory is true or false (Pickrell et al., 2003).

In Review

- Our schemas may cause us to remember events not as they actually occurred but in ways that fit with our pre-existing concepts about the world.

- At times, we may recall information that never occurred. Schemas, spreading activation, and priming are some of the reasons why this occurs.

- Misinformation effects occur when our memory is distorted by misleading post-event information, and they often occur because of source confusion—our tendency to recall something or recognize it as familiar but to forget where we encountered it.

- Like adults, children experience misinformation effects. Vulnerability is greatest among younger children and when suggestive questions are asked repeatedly. Experts cannot reliably tell when children are reporting accurate versus sincerely believed false memories.

- Psychologists debate whether recovered memories of child abuse are accurate and whether they are forgotten through repression or other psychological processes. Concern about the possibility of false memory has led many experts to urge caution in unconditionally accepting the validity of recovered memories.

THE BIOLOGY OF MEMORY

Since the early 1900s, the scientific quest to determine the biological basis of memory has taken some remarkable twists and turns. Karl Lashley, a pioneering physiological psychologist, spent decades searching for the *engram*—the physical "memory trace" that presumably was stored somewhere in the brain when a memory was formed. Lashley (1950) trained animals to perform various tasks, such as running mazes, and later removed or damaged (lesioned) specific regions of their cortex to see whether they would forget how to perform the task. No matter what small area was lesioned, the animals' memory remained intact. Large lesions affected memory, but even then, it didn't seem to matter where the lesion was made. Lashley never found the engram, and concluded that a memory is stored throughout the brain.

Other research initially suggested that, indeed, engrams exist. While performing neurosurgery, Wilder Penfield and his colleagues (1963) at the Montreal Neurological Institute electrically stimulated specific sites on the cerebral cortex of patients who were under local anaesthesia and fully conscious. Penfield reported that the stimulation sometimes triggered patients' memories. One patient reported seeing the office in which she had worked a long time ago, with a man leaning on her desk, pencil in hand. Unfortunately, when other researchers reviewed Penfield's data, they concluded that such instances were rare and probably involved inaccurate, "reconstructed" images (Loftus & Loftus, 1980). For example, people sometimes reported memories of being in places where, in fact, they had never been.

Perhaps most striking was James McConnell's (1962) discovery of "memory transfer." He classically conditioned flatworms to a light that was paired with an electric shock, eventually causing the worms to contract to the light alone. Next, he chopped them up and fed a chemical from their cells, RNA (ribonucleic acid), to a sample of untrained worms. Amazingly, the new worms showed some conditioning to the light. This result suggested that RNA might be a chemical engram, a "memory molecule" that stored experiences. Some scientists found memory transfer effects with rats, mice, and goldfish, but others were unable to replicate these findings. Controversy ensued, and McConnell gave up on the idea (Rilling, 1996). Yet, despite the inevitable "dead ends," neuroscientists have made considerable progress in understanding the biological bases of memory.

Sensory and Working Memory

Sensory memory depends on our visual, auditory, and other sensory systems to detect stimulus information (e.g., the sounds of "Hi, my name is Carlos"), transform it into neural codes, and send it to the brain, where sensory areas of the cerebral cortex initially process it. As working memory becomes involved in different types of tasks—remembering a person's name and face, recalling a list of numbers, learning a concept in your textbook—cortical networks located in different lobes of the brain become more active (Lehmann et al., 2010). For example, using visuospatial working memory to form a mental image of an object will activate some of the same areas of the visual cortex and other brain regions that become more active when looking at the actual object (Ganis et al., 2004).

The frontal lobes—especially the prefrontal cortex—play key roles in working memory (Christoff et al., 2009). The frontal lobes generally become more active during tasks that place greater demands on working memory. In one brain-imaging experiment, students paid attention to the meaning of words (i.e., deep, semantic encoding) or to whether the words were in capital or lowercase letters (i.e., shallow, perceptual encoding). Deeper encoding produced better memory for the words and greater activity in areas of the left prefrontal cortex, as Figure 8.24 shows (Gabrieli et al., 1996). The prefrontal cortex has also been shown to enhance memory by searching for commonalities and differences in material (Elhalal et al., 2014), presumably to facilitate further encoding.

The frontal lobes seem to be particularly important in supporting central-executive functions, such as allocating attention to the other components of working memory (Curtis & D'Esposito, 2003). This does not mean, however, that the central executive resides exclusively within the frontal lobes. Frontal-lobe damage often—but not always—impairs central-executive functions of working memory. Moreover, patients with intact frontal lobes but damage in other brain areas may exhibit central-executive impairments (Andrés, 2003). Thus, even the "master control" executive functions of working memory depend on a network of neural activity that connects regions across the brain.

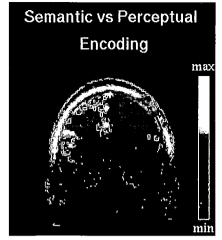

Semantic vs Perceptual Encoding

max

min

FIGURE 8.24 Four of the participants in this experiment performed shallow (i.e., perceptual/structural) encoding and deep (semantic) encoding tasks while undergoing functional magnetic resonance imaging (fMRI). Activity in a section of their prefrontal cortex was imaged every 1.5 seconds, yielding a total of 224 images per participant. The results, shown here for one participant, revealed that semantic encoding was accompanied by greater neural activity in specific regions of the left prefrontal cortex.

Long-Term Memory

Where are long-term memories formed and stored? Once again, multiple brain areas are involved, but the hippocampus and its adjacent areas appear to play important roles in encoding certain types of long-term memories (Lisman & Grace, 2005; Squire et al., 2004). We examine this matter in the *Focus on Neuroscience* feature.

Declarative Memory

The pioneering work of Brenda Milner at McGill University and her colleague W.B. Scoville led to the conclusion that the hippocampus and its adjacent tissue help to encode and retrieve long-term declarative memories (Milner, 1965; Rolls, 2000; Scoville & Milner, 1957). Like H.M., many patients with extensive hippocampal damage retain the use of their short-term memory but cannot form new, explicit long-term declarative memories—memories for new personal experiences and facts. For example, one patient could recall the names of presidents elected before his brain injury occurred but not the names of presidents elected after his injury (Squire, 1987). The hippocampus does not seem to be the site where long-term declarative memories are permanently stored, which explains why H.M. retained his long-term memories acquired earlier in life. Rather, it helps to gradually convert short-term memories into permanent ones.

According to one view, the diverse components of an experience—where something happened, what the scene or people looked like, sounds we heard, the meaning of events or information, and so on—are processed initially in different regions of the cortex and then gradually bound together in the hippocampus. This hypothetical and gradual binding process is called **memory consolidation** (Hardt et al., 2010). Once a memory for a personal experience is consolidated, its various components appear to be stored across wide areas of the cortex, although we retrieve and reintegrate these components as a unified memory. Semantic memories (factual information) also appear to be stored across wide-ranging areas of the brain. As John Gabrieli (1998) notes, "knowledge in any domain [e.g., for pictures or words] . . . is distributed over a specific, but extensive, neural network that often extends over several lobes" (p. 94). Several brain regions, including portions of the prefrontal cortex and hippocampus, appear to be involved in consciously retrieving declarative memories (Simons & Spiers, 2003; van Strien et al., 2009).

Although we have focused on the frontal lobes and hippocampus, memory formation also depends on other brain areas. For example, damage to the thalamus—the brain's major sensory relay station—can impair both the encoding of new memories and the retrieval of old ones (Hampstead & Koffler, 2009). In one famous case, a young U.S. Air Force technician named N.A. was injured in a freak accident (Squire, 1987). While his roommate was practising thrusts with a miniature fencing foil, N.A. suddenly turned around in his seat and was stabbed through the right nostril, piercing his brain and damaging a portion of his thalamus. The damage permanently limited his ability to form new declarative memories (Cohen & Squire, 1981). He also could not recall events from the two-year period prior to the accident, but over time this retrograde amnesia improved. In many cases, however, thalamic damage results in permanent, extensive anterograde and retrograde amnesia. Following a car accident in 1988, Terry Evanshen, a former CFL star receiver, awoke from a coma to find that his memory of everything prior to the accident had vanished. He could not remember how to speak, did not recognize his wife or daughters, and had no recollection of anything from the past 40 years. Terry had to relearn everything all over again.

Focus on Neuroscience

HOW ARE MEMORIES FORMED?

How does the nervous system form a memory? The answer appears to lie in chemical and physical changes that take place in the brain's neural circuitry. One possible mechanism is at the level of the synapse, while a different line of research, involving rats and other species with more complex nervous systems, supports the hypothesis that synaptic changes may be the basis for memory consolidation.

Synaptic Change and Memory

Eric Kandel (2001) and his colleagues have studied a marine snail, *Aplysia californica,* for more than 25 years—work for which Kandel received a Nobel Prize in 2000. *Aplysia* is no mental giant, but it can learn, form memories, and has only about 20 000 neurons (compared with 100 billion in humans) that are larger and easier to study than ours. For example, *Aplysia* retracts its gill slightly in self-defence when a breathing organ atop the gill is gently squirted with water. But if a squirt is paired with an electric shock to its tail, *Aplysia* covers up its gill with a protective flap of skin. After repeated pairings, *Aplysia* acquires a classically conditioned response and will cover its gill with the protective flap when the water is squirted alone. In other words, *Aplysia* forms a simple procedural memory. Kandel and his colleagues have traced the information of this procedural memory to a series of biochemical events that occur between and within various sensory neurons and motor neurons. How long these events last seems to be one key in determining whether short-term memories become long-term ones. If a single shock is paired with the squirt of water, certain chemical reactions shut off after a brief period and no permanent memory is formed. But with repeated pairings, these chemical reactions persist and a long-term memory forms. Days later, a squirt of water will still trigger a conditioned response. During the conditioning procedure, various sensory neurons become densely packed with neurotransmitter release points, and postsynaptic motor neurons (which cause the protective flap to cover the gill) develop more receptor sites. These structural changes result in a greater ease of synaptic transmission that may be the basis for memory consolidation (Abel & Kandel, 1998; Martin et al., 2000).

Long-Term Potentiation

A different line of research, involving rats and other species with more complex nervous systems, supports the hypothesis that synaptic changes may be the basis for memory consolidation. Here, researchers try to mimic (albeit crudely) a process of long-term memory formation by stimulating specific neural pathways with rapid bursts of electricity (say, 100 impulses per second for several seconds). They find that once this rapid stimulation ends, the neural pathway becomes stronger—synaptic connections are activated more easily—for days or even weeks (Wang & Morris, 2010). This enduring increase in synaptic strength is called **long-term potentiation (LTP).** LTP has been studied most extensively in regions of the hippocampus where neurons send and receive messages by using glutamate, the most abundant neurotransmitter in the brain (Lynch, 2004).

For LTP to occur, complex biochemical events must take place inside and between these neurons (e.g., Liu et al., 2013). Administering drugs that inhibit these events will block LTP. Moreover, mice can be genetically bred to be deficient in certain proteins required for LTP. These mice not only have impaired long-term potentiation, but also display memory deficits on a variety of learning tasks (Schimanski & Nguyen, 2005).

How does LTP occur? At least in some cases, when neural pathways are sufficiently stimulated, postsynaptic neurons alter their structure to become more responsive to glutamate. For example, postsynaptic neurons may change the shape of some receptor sites or may increase the number of receptor sites by developing additional tiny branches (spines) on their dendrites. Thus, in the future, presynaptic neurons will not need to release as much glutamate to stimulate postsynaptic neurons to fire. In sum, the formation of a long-term memory seems to involve long-lasting changes in synaptic efficiency that result from new or enhanced connections between presynaptic and postsynaptic neurons (Kandel, 2001; Wang & Morris, 2010).

A number of researchers now believe that memory consolidation in humans and other animals takes place during sleep (e.g., Buzsaki, 1989; Carr et al., 2011). When we are awake, memory traces are laid down in the hippocampus. But we need to move these traces to a larger information store and incorporate it with all of the other knowledge that we have. This seems to happen during slow-wave sleep (stages 3 and 4). Buzsaki first discovered how this works when he was a post-doctoral student at Western University. As he was trying to record from single cells in the rat hippocampus, he noted a burst of synchronized activity that disappeared very quickly. He referred to this burst of activity as a sharp wave ripple (SWR) and hypothesized that the purpose of this burst was to consolidate memory in the cortex. Buzasaki (1989) suggests that the neocortex sends out signals representing the various sensory inputs that have occurred. These signals are received and synthesized by the hippocampus and then broadcast back to the neocortex in an SWR. This ripple or index code (Leutgeb et al., 2005) is stored in the cortex for future retrieval. When we need this information, the ripple is replayed (Foster & Wilson, 2006). The information may be essential in learning and decision making (Jadhav et al. 2012), and memory strength has been correlated with reactivation in humans (Deuker et al., 2013).

29. What major roles do the hippocampus, cerebral cortex, thalamus, amygdala, and cerebellum play in memory?

The amygdala encodes emotionally arousing aspects of stimuli and plays an important role in helping us form long-term memories for events that stir our emotions (LaBar & LeDoux, 2006). As we discussed earlier, in laboratory experiments, most people remember emotionally arousing stimuli (e.g., film clips, slides) better than neutral ones. Damage to the amygdala eliminates much of this "memory advantage" from arousing stimuli (LaBar & Phelps, 1998).

Procedural Memory

Along with other parts of the brain, the cerebellum plays an important role in forming procedural memories (Hubert et al., 2009). This role helps to explain why H.M., whose cerebellum was not damaged by the operation, showed improved performance at various hand-eye coordination tasks (e.g., mirror tracing), even though he was unable to consciously remember having performed the tasks. Richard Thompson (1985) and his colleagues have examined another type of procedural memory. Studying rabbits, they repeatedly paired a tone (CS) with a puff of air to the eyes (UCS), and soon the tone alone caused the rabbits to blink. As the rabbits learned this conditioned response, electrical recordings revealed increased activity in the cerebellum. Later, Thompson found that removing a tiny portion of the cerebellum

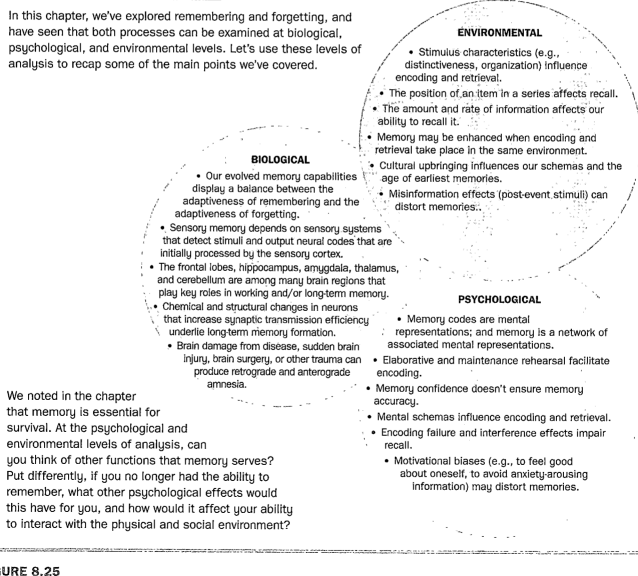

Levels of Analysis | Memory

In this chapter, we've explored remembering and forgetting, and have seen that both processes can be examined at biological, psychological, and environmental levels. Let's use these levels of analysis to recap some of the main points we've covered.

ENVIRONMENTAL
- Stimulus characteristics (e.g., distinctiveness, organization) influence encoding and retrieval.
- The position of an item in a series affects recall.
- The amount and rate of information affects our ability to recall it.
- Memory may be enhanced when encoding and retrieval take place in the same environment.
- Cultural upbringing influences our schemas and the age of earliest memories.
- Misinformation effects (post-event stimuli) can distort memories.

BIOLOGICAL
- Our evolved memory capabilities display a balance between the adaptiveness of remembering and the adaptiveness of forgetting.
- Sensory memory depends on sensory systems that detect stimuli and output neural codes that are initially processed by the sensory cortex.
- The frontal lobes, hippocampus, amygdala, thalamus, and cerebellum are among many brain regions that play key roles in working and/or long-term memory.
- Chemical and structural changes in neurons that increase synaptic transmission efficiency underlie long-term memory formation.
- Brain damage from disease, sudden brain injury, brain surgery, or other trauma can produce retrograde and anterograde amnesia.

PSYCHOLOGICAL
- Memory codes are mental representations; and memory is a network of associated mental representations.
- Elaborative and maintenance rehearsal facilitate encoding.
- Memory confidence doesn't ensure memory accuracy.
- Mental schemas influence encoding and retrieval.
- Encoding failure and interference effects impair recall.
- Motivational biases (e.g., to feel good about oneself, to avoid anxiety-arousing information) may distort memories.

We noted in the chapter that memory is essential for survival. At the psychological and environmental levels of analysis, can you think of other functions that memory serves? Put differently, if you no longer had the ability to remember, what other psychological effects would this have for you, and how would it affect your ability to interact with the physical and social environment?

FIGURE 8.25

Review

- Memory involves numerous interacting brain regions. Sensory memory depends on input from our sensory systems and sensory areas of the cortex that initially process this information.
- Working memory involves a network of brain regions. The frontal lobes play a key role in performing the executive functions of working memory.
- The hippocampus helps to consolidate long-term declarative memories. The cerebral cortex stores declarative memories across distributed sites. The amygdala encodes emotionally arousing aspects of events, and the cerebellum helps to form procedural memories. Damage to the thalamus can produce severe amnesia.
- Studies of long-term potentiation in several species indicate that as memories form, complex chemical and structural changes that enhance synaptic efficiency occur in neurons.

completely abolished the memory for the *conditioned* eyeblink but did not affect the rabbits' general (unconditioned) eyeblink response. Similarly, eyeblink conditioning fails to work with human patients who have a damaged cerebellum (Green & Woodruff-Pak, 2000).

In closing, we hope that this chapter has piqued your interest in understanding why we remember, forget, and sometimes misremember. We also hope that the chapter has provided some useful applied knowledge for you.

Gaining Direction

What are the issues?

Aurelien has a condition known as hyperthymesia—a heightened form of autobiographical memory. He can recall everything regarding personal memories of things he has done, but not more factual details that would be found in other memory stores. Why is this condition limited to autobiographical memory? How many kinds of memory stores are there? Is each type of memory encoded in the same fashion? Where in the brain might these memories be stored?

What do we need to know?

How does memory work?
How are memories stored?
Why do we forget material?
Is all memory processed in the same fashion?

Do people with hyperthymesia use different brain structures to process memory?
Is there such a thing as photographic memory?

Where can we find the information to answer these questions?

Look back at the compass icons in the chapter. You will find reference to the three-component model of memory, factors that result in maintaining memory (encoding), the influence of schemas, processes involved in retrieval and forgetting, and the construction of memory. Pay careful attention to the section on types of memory and the brain structures involved.

Answers:

In Figure 8.17, penny D is the actual penny—check it out while you still find some pennies in your pocket change.

CHAPTER

9

Language and Thinking

CHAPTER OUTLINE

LANGUAGE

Adaptive Functions of Language
Properties of Language
The Structure of Language
Understanding and Producing Language
Acquiring a First Language
Bilingualism: Learning a Second Language
Linguistic Influences on Thinking
  Focus on Neuroscience: The Bilingual Brain

  Frontiers: Can Animals Acquire Human Language?

THINKING

Thought, Brain, and Mind
Concepts and Propositions
Reasoning
Problem Solving
Knowledge, Expertise, and Wisdom
  Applications: Guidelines for Creative Problem Solving

Mental Imagery
Metacognition: Knowing Your Own Cognitive Abilities
  Research Foundations: "Why Did I Get That Wrong?"
  Improving Students' Awareness of Whether They
  Understand Text Material

> *Let language be the divining rod that finds the sources of thought.*
>
> —Karl Krauss

 In 1799, three hunters discovered a remarkable child in the forests of Aveyron, France. The child had grown up isolated from human contact for 12 years. He made few sounds but could walk upright. Some regarded him as only half-human and called him the *Wild Boy of Aveyron.* He was sent to Paris for training with a prominent physician, who named him Victor. Victor learned to read and write some words, but he never learned to speak.

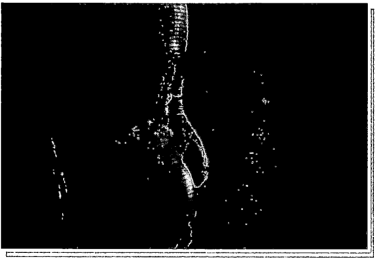

Midwestgal/Dreamstime.com/GetStock.com

What are the issues here?

What do we need to know?

Where can we find the information to answer these questions?

In 1970, 13-year-old Genie was discovered in Temple City, California. When Genie's mother and grandmother inquired with a social worker about resources for the blind, the social worker thought the girl appeared quite "strange." Over the next few weeks, the authorities learned that Genie had been kept isolated in a locked room for almost all her life. Her total spoken vocabulary consisted of two words: *stopit* and *nomore.* Over the next few months, her vocabulary increased, but she never mastered the ability to string words together. Most experts would agree that Genie's ability to speak seemed to be stalled at the level of an average two- or three-year-old.

In 1982, Dominique was discovered in Quebec at age five. She had been similarly abused: locked in the basement where her mother, grandmother, and the family cat would occasionally visit. Upon her rescue, she received language training from Aimee Leduc at Laval University. Dominique made quick progress in a number of mental abilities and seemed quite capable of fully acquiring language. Unfortunately, her foster placement did not work and she was institutionalized.

We humans are physically puny and relatively defenceless in comparison with some other species, but we dominate our world because we communicate more effectively and think better than other animals do. Humans have a remarkable ability to create *mental representations* of the world and to manipulate them in the forms of language, thinking, reasoning, and problem solving (Simon, 1990). **Mental representations** include images, ideas, concepts, and principles. At this very moment, through the printed words you are reading, mental representations are being transferred from our minds to yours. Indeed, the process of education is all about transferring ideas and skills from one mind to another.

LANGUAGE

Language has been called "the jewel in the crown of cognition" (Pinker, 2000) and "the human essence" (Chomsky, 1972). Much of our thinking, reasoning, and problem solving involve the use of language. In turn, these advanced cognitive processes build on the large store of knowledge that resides in memory, and they provide a foundation for intelligent behaviour.

Language consists of a system of symbols and rules for combining these symbols in ways that can generate an infinite number of possible messages and meanings. To most of us, using our native language comes as naturally as breathing, and we give it about as much thought. Yet using language actually involves a host of complex skills. **Psycholinguistics** is the scientific study of the psychological aspects of language, such as how people understand, produce, and acquire language. Before delving into some of these topics, let's consider some adaptive functions and characteristics of language.

Adaptive Functions of Language

According to anthropologists who have studied the skulls of prehistoric humans, the brain probably achieved its present form some 50 000 years ago (Pilbeam, 1984). Yet it took another 35 000 years before lifelike paintings began to appear on cave walls and another 12 000 years after that before humans developed a way to store knowledge outside the brain in the form of writing (Kottak, 2000). These time lags tell us that human thought and behaviour depend on more than the physical structure of the brain; although the structure of the brain may not have evolved much over the past 50 000 years, human cognitive and linguistic skills clearly have.

Over the course of evolution, humans adopted a more socially oriented lifestyle that helped them survive and reproduce (Flinn, 1997). Some evolutionary theorists believe that the use of language evolved as people gathered to form larger social units. As the social environment became more complex, new survival problems emerged: the need to create divisions of labour and cooperative social systems, to develop social customs and communicate thoughts, and to pass on knowledge and wisdom. The development of language made it easier for humans to adapt to these environmental demands (Dor, 2014; Pinker, 2003).

It is no coincidence, then, that every human culture, no matter how isolated or geographically remote, has developed one or more languages. Nor is it a coincidence that the human brain seems to have an inborn capacity to acquire any of the roughly 5000 to 6000 languages spoken across the globe. Humans have evolved into highly social creatures who need to communicate with one another and have the physical characteristics (e.g., a highly developed brain, a vocal tract) that allow them to do

1. What are some adaptive functions of language?

2. Describe key properties of language.

"GOT IDEA. TALK BETTER. COMBINE WORDS, MAKE SENTENCES."

© 2000 by Sidney Harris. ScienceCartoonsPlus.com. Reprinted with permission.

FIGURE 9.1 According to many theorists, the development of language was a major milestone in human evolution.

so in the most flexible way known: through language (Figure 9.1).

Language underlies so much of what we do that it is almost impossible to imagine functioning without it. Our conscious thinking usually takes the form of self-talk, or inner speech. Through language, we are also able to share our thoughts, feelings, goals, intentions, desires, needs, and memories with other people and thus interact socially in rich and diverse ways that would not otherwise be possible. Indeed, some authors have suggested that language and memory evolved at the same time (e.g., Gong & Shuai, 2015).

In ways small and big, language also is an extremely powerful learning mechanism. To get to a friend's house for the first time, you don't have to drive or walk all over the area (trial-and-error learning) or wait until someone shows up to lead the way (observational learning). Instead, you simply ask for directions or read a map. More broadly, in oral and written form—through storytelling, books, instruction, mass media, and the Internet—language puts the customs and knowledge accrued over generations at your fingertips.

Properties of Language

What is it that first captures your attention when someone uses a foreign language that you don't speak? Perhaps it is how different that language sounds or looks when written, or simply how incomprehensible it seems to you. Yet what is truly striking about the world's languages is not their differences but the underlying features that they share.

As we noted earlier, language is a system of symbols and rules for combining these symbols in ways that can generate an infinite number of messages and meanings. This definition encompasses four properties that are essential to any language: symbols, structure, meaning, and generativity. We will also describe a fifth property: displacement.

Language Is Symbolic and Structured

Language uses sounds, written characters, or some other system of symbols (e.g., hand signs) to represent objects, events, ideas, feelings, and actions. Moreover, the symbols used in any given language are arbitrary. For example, the Spanish, French, and German words for *dog* are *perro, chien,* and *hund,* respectively. None of these written words looks like a dog, and when spoken, there is nothing about how any one of these words sounds that makes it an intrinsically correct choice for representing the concept of "dog." In English, *gerk, kreg, woof, zog, professor,* or countless other words could be used to represent what we call a *dog,* but they aren't. (Even though "No Professors Allowed on the Lawn" has a certain ring.) Regardless of how the word *dog* came into being, it has an agreed-on meaning to people who speak English. The same holds true for all the other words we use.

Language also has a rule-governed structure. A language's **grammar** is the set of rules that dictate how symbols can be combined to create meaningful units of communication. Thus, if we ask you whether *zpflrovc* is an English word, you will almost certainly say that it is not. Why? Because it violates the rules of the English language; *z* is not to be followed by *pf,* and five consonants (*z, p, f, l, r*) cannot be put in an unbroken sequence. Likewise, if we ask you whether "Bananas have sale for I" is an appropriate English sentence, you will shake your head and say, "No. It should read: 'I have bananas for sale.'" In this case, "Bananas have sale for I" violates a portion of English grammar called **syntax,** the rules that govern the order of words.

You may not be able to verbalize the formal rules of English that are violated in these examples, but you know them implicitly because they are part of the language you speak. The grammars of all languages share common functions, such as providing rules for how to change present tense ("I am walking the dog") into the past tense ("I walked the dog") or a negative ("I didn't walk the dog"). Yet just as symbols (e.g., words) vary across languages, so do grammatical rules. In English, for example, we say "green salad" and "big river," which follow the rule that adjectives almost always come before the nouns they modify. In French and Spanish, however, adjectives often follow nouns ("salade verte," "rio grande"). Although language changes over time, with new words appearing regularly, new words and new phrases need to conform to the basic rules of that language.

Language Conveys Meaning

No matter the arbitrary symbols or grammatical rules used, once people learn those symbols and rules, they are able to form and then transfer mental representations to the mind of another person. Thus, you can talk with a friend about your courses, your favourite foods, how you feel, and so on. Based in part on the words you use and how they are organized, both you and your friend will extract meaning—and, it is hoped, the correct or intended meaning—from what is being said. But understanding **semantics**, the meaning of words and sentences, actually is a tricky business. For example, when you ask a friend "How did you do on the test?" and the reply is "I nailed it," you know that your friend is not saying "I hammered the test to the desk with a nail." Someone who is familiar with English knows from experience not to interpret this expression literally; someone just beginning to learn English might find this expression perplexing.

Language Is Generative and Permits Displacement

Generativity means that the symbols of language can be combined to generate an infinite number of messages that have novel meaning. The English language, for example, has only 26 letters, but they can be combined into more than half a million words, which in turn can be combined to create a virtually limitless number of sentences. Thus, you can create and understand a sentence like "Why is that sparrow standing underneath my pancake?" even though you are unlikely to have heard anything like it before.

Displacement refers to the fact that language allows us to communicate about events and objects that are not physically present. In other words, language frees us from being restricted to focusing on events and objects that are right before us in the present. You can discuss the past and the future, as well as people, objects, and events that currently exist or are taking place elsewhere. You can even discuss completely imaginary situations, such as a sparrow standing underneath a pancake.

The Structure of Language

Psycholinguists describe language as having a *surface structure* and a *deep structure*. They also examine the hierarchical structure of language, in which smaller elements are combined into larger ones. Let's look at both of these issues.

Surface Structure and Deep Structure

When you read, listen to, or produce a sentence, its **surface structure** consists of the symbols that are used and their order. As noted earlier, the syntax of a language provides the rules for ordering words properly. In contrast, a sentence's **deep structure** refers to the underlying meaning of the combined symbols, which brings us back to the issue of semantics.

Sentences can have different surface structures but the same deep structure. Consider these examples:

1. Sam ate the cake.
2. The cake was eaten by Sam.
3. Eaten by Sam the cake was.

Each sentence conveys the underlying meaning: that the cake ended up in Sam's stomach. Notice that the syntax of the third sentence is incorrect. English isn't spoken this way, except, perhaps, by the fictional *Star Wars* character Yoda. Still, in this case its meaning is clear enough.

Sometimes, a single surface structure can give rise to two deep structures, as happens when people speak or write ambiguous sentences. Consider this example:

> The police must stop drinking after midnight.

On the one hand, this sentence could mean that police officers need to enforce a curfew designed to prevent citizens from drinking alcohol after midnight. On the other hand, it could mean that if police officers go out for a few

3. Differentiate between surface and deep structure. Describe the hierarchy of language.

drinks after work, they need to wrap up their drinking by midnight.

In everyday life, when you read or hear speech, you are moving from the surface structure to deep structure: from the way a sentence looks or sounds to its deeper level of meaning. After time, you may forget the precise words used in the sentence, but you're likely to recall its essential meaning. In contrast, when you express your thoughts to other people, you must transform deep structure (the meaning that you want to communicate) into a surface structure that others can understand. Eloquent speakers and writers have the ability to convert their deep-structure meanings into clear and pleasing surface-structure expressions.

Thinking critically

DISCERNING THE DEEP STRUCTURE OF LANGUAGE

Figure 9.2 shows a grave marker in the Boothill Graveyard in Tombstone, Arizona, where many notorious outlaws and gunfighters are buried. Analyze the marker carefully, and then identify two possible meanings for the inscription.

Think about it, and then see the Answers section at the end of the book.

© Kay Smith

FIGURE 9.2 This grave marker in Boothill Graveyard illustrates an interesting relation between surface structure and deep structure.

The Hierarchical Structure of Language

Human language has a hierarchical structure, and its most elementary building block is the **phoneme,** the smallest unit of speech sound in a language that can signal a difference in meaning. Linguists have identified about 100 phonemes that humans can produce, including the clicking sounds used in some African languages, but no language uses all these sounds. The world's languages vary considerably in phonemes, some employing as few as 15 and others more than 80. English uses about 40 phonemes, consisting of the various vowel and consonant sounds, as well as certain letter combinations such as *th* and *sh*. Thus, sounds associated with *th, a,* and *t* can be combined to form the three-phoneme word *that*.

Phonemes have no inherent meaning, but they alter meaning when combined with other elements. For example, the phoneme *d* creates a different meaning from the phoneme *l* when it precedes *og* (i.e., *dog* versus *log*). At the next level of the hierarchy, phonemes are combined into **morphemes,** the smallest units of meaning in a language. Thus, *dog, log,* and *ball* are all morphemes, as are prefixes and suffixes such as *pre-, un-, -ed,* and *-ous*. Notice in Figure 9.3 that morphemes are not always syllables. For example, in English, *s* is not a syllable, but the final *s* on a noun is a morpheme that means "plural." Thus, the word *fans* has one syllable but two morphemes; *players* has two syllables but three morphemes. In every language, rules determine how phonemes can be combined into morphemes. English's 40 phonemes can be combined into more than 100 000 morphemes.

Morphemes, in turn, are the stuff of which words are formed. English morphemes can be combined into over 500 000 words, words into countless phrases, and phrases into an infinite number of sentences. Thus, from the humble phoneme to the elegant sentence, we have a five-step language hierarchy (see Figure 9.3). Beyond this basic hierarchy lies the sixth and most comprehensive level, that of **discourse,** in which sentences are combined into paragraphs, articles, books, conversations, and so forth.

Understanding and Producing Language

One day after a class discussion on language, a student told us about a humorous incident that had happened the evening before. Her husband answered a phone call, listened for five seconds, and hung up. "It was a prerecorded

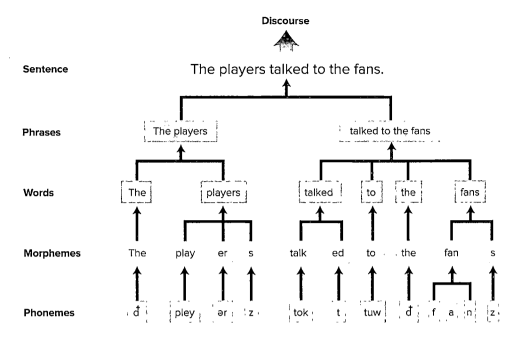

FIGURE 9.3 Human language is structured hierarchically, with phonemes being the most basic unit. The row of phonemes contains symbols used by linguists to denote particular sounds.

telemarketing call," he said. "Some company called Pressgrits." "Pressgrits. That's a really weird name," she replied. And then it dawned on her. She was expecting an automated call from a company called Express Scripts to confirm an order. Later, she found out that this had indeed been the confirmation call.

How can a voice on the phone produce the words *Express Scripts,* which the student's husband hears as "Pressgrits"? Did he need to clean out his ears? Hardly. He simply failed to perceive the morpheme *Ex,* which left *Press* for the first word. And by saying both words rapidly, as the prerecorded voice did (try it five times, fast), you'll realize that phonetically, *pressscripts* and *pressgrits* are not that far apart. Most importantly, the student's husband had no context for interpreting the message. Later on, when our student listened to a callback of the same message, she heard "Express Scripts" because she knew what to expect. Context, as you'll see, plays a key role in understanding language.

The Role of Bottom-Up Processing

To understand language, your brain must recognize and interpret patterns of stimuli—the sounds of speech, shapes of letters, movements that create hand signs, or tactile patterns of dots used in Braille—that are detected by your sensory systems. And just like other perceptual tasks, extracting information from linguistic stimuli involves the joint influence of bottom-up

and top-down processing (concepts that you may recall from Chapter 5). In **bottom-up processing,** individual elements of a stimulus are analyzed and then combined to form a unified perception. Analyzing the hierarchical structure of spoken language as a set of building blocks that involve the use of phonemes to create morphemes and the combination of morphemes to create words reflects a bottom-up approach.

Likewise, as you read this sentence, specialized cell groups in your brain are (1) analyzing the basic elements (e.g., contours, angles of lines) of the visual patterns that are right before your eyes and (2) feeding this information to other cell groups that lead you to perceive these patterns as letters. We then recognize words either directly by perceiving the visual patterns of letters or indirectly by first translating those visual patterns into auditory codes, as happens when you sound out in your head the phonemes and morphemes created by the letter sequences (Bernstein & Carr, 1996). Words and their grammatical sequence then become the building blocks for sentences, and sentences the building blocks for discourse. But at every step in this bottom-up sequence, including pattern recognition, our understanding of language also is influenced by top-down processing.

The Role of Top-Down Processing

In a famous farmers' market, there used to be a store called The Bead Store. The store sold

4. Explain the role of bottom-up and top-down processes in language. Use speech segmentation and pragmatics as examples.

beads for making jewellery. Tourists would often walk by and ask "Where's the bread?" The store's sign said *Bead,* but these patrons perceived the word as *Bread,* a function perhaps of their mental set (i.e., a perceptual expectation) that they were in a farmer's market that sold food. It got so bad for the merchants that they eventually put up a sign saying "We Don't Sell Bread."

In **top-down processing,** sensory information is interpreted in light of existing knowledge, concepts, ideas, and expectations. In Chapter 5, we discussed how people's unconscious expectations (i.e., mental sets) literally shape what they visually perceive. As the Bead Store example illustrates, people looked at a stimulus pattern on a store sign that said *Bead,* but *Bread* is what they saw.

Language by its very nature involves top-down processing, because the words you write, read, speak, or hear activate and draw on your knowledge of vocabulary, grammar, and other linguistic rules that are stored in your long-term memory. That's why if we write "Bill g_ve th_ pe_cil to h_s fr__nd," you can probably interpret the words with little difficulty ("Bill gave the pencil to his friend"), despite the absence of several bottom-up elements.

Let's consider another example of top-down processing. Have you ever listened to someone speak a foreign language in which you aren't fluent and found that it was difficult to tell where one word ended and the next began? Even if you have studied that language for a term or two in school, native speakers may seem to talk so quickly that you can't distinguish the individual words they are saying. Conversely, they would have the same problem listening to you speak English. Despite all the sophistication of modern computers and software, many still struggle with human voice recognition.

How is it, then, that in your native language this process of **speech segmentation**—perceiving where each word within a spoken sentence begins and ends—seems to occur automatically? When you read a sentence, the spaces between words make segmentation easy. But when people speak, they don't pause in between each pair of words. In fact, when psycholinguists measure the sound energy produced as people utter sentences, they find that the decreases in energy output between words often are smaller than the decreases between segments within the same words. To illustrate, say "We hope you have a nice day" out loud and at a normal speech rate. Did you distinctly segment each whole word, creating a sound energy break between each one? Or were your segments more like "We ho pew ha va nice day"? Moreover, in English about 40 percent of words consist of two or more syllables that are vocally stressed (i.e., emphasized) when spoken (Mattys, 2000). Thus, in these and other words, the auditory breaks that we hear in speech often do not correspond well to the physical breaks produced by the spaces in written sentences.

Psycholinguists have discovered that we use several cues to tell when one spoken word ends and another begins (Cunillera et al., 2006). For example, through experience we learn that certain sequences of phonemes are unlikely to occur within the same words, so when we hear these sounds in sequence we are more likely to perceive them as the ending or beginning of an adjacent word.

We also use the context provided by the other words in a sentence to interpret the meaning of any individual word. In two classic experiments, Irwin Pollack and J.M. Pickett (1964) recorded the conversations of four female university students and text passages spoken by four adult men. The researchers then played back one-, two-, three-, or four-word segments taken from these recordings to 38 university students. For example, from the words ". . . of the world was covered in ice," the researchers created the segments "of," "of the," "of the world," and "of the world was" and asked participants to identify the first word in the segment. Remarkably, when participants listened to one-word excerpts, and thus had to identify a word based on its sound alone, they could do so on average only 35 to 62 percent of the time, depending on the voice of the particular speaker. When participants listened to the four-word segments, they were able to identify the initial word between 70 and 100 percent of the time, depending on the speaker. In sum, the availability of context made the job of identifying individual words much easier.

Pragmatics: The Social Context of Language

Suppose that you call up a friend and someone else answers the phone. You ask, "Is Bill there?" The person says, "Hang on," and goes to get Bill. Or imagine that a passerby asks you "Do you have the time?" You say, "10:20" and part ways. In these cases, the questions really are shorthand for "Is Bill there, and if so, please go get him and tell him to pick up the phone" and "I'm not wearing a watch, so please tell me what time it is right now." You wouldn't expect the person who answered the phone to merely say "Yes" and then wait until you gave more instructions ("Uh, okay, would you please go get him?"). Nor would you respond to the request "Do you have the time?" merely by saying "Yes, I do" and then walking away.

Instead, you and the other people involved in these communications understand the social context and rules for how to respond. Likewise, if a friend says, "I need you to explain this material to me. Do you have the time?" you wouldn't say "10:20" and walk away. In this context, you understand that "Do you have the time?" means "Can you take a few minutes to help me?"

These examples illustrate that it takes more than having a vocabulary and arranging words grammatically to understand language and communicate effectively with others. It also involves **pragmatics,** a knowledge of the practical aspects of using language (Cummings, 2005; McNally, 2013). Language occurs in a social context, and pragmatic knowledge not only helps you understand what other people are really saying, but also helps you make sure that other people get the point of what you're communicating. In essence, pragmatics is another example of how top-down processing influences language use and it is essential for language acquisition (Clark, 2014; Ryder & Leinonen, 2014).

Psycholinguists have identified social rules that guide communication between people (Arundale, 2005; Grice, 1975). One rule states that messages should be as clear as possible (Figure 9.4). Thus, depending on whether you talk with an adult who is fluent in your language, a foreign visitor who barely speaks your language, or a young child, you usually adjust your speech rate, choice of words, and sentence complexity.

Thinking critically

THE SLEEPING POLICEMAN

You're on vacation in England, driving to a countryside bed-and-breakfast to spend the night. You stop in a small town to get directions. A storekeeper tells you to take a left turn a mile up the road, drive "until you come to the sleeping policeman," and then take a right. What do you imagine "the sleeping policeman" (or "The Sleeping Policeman") might be?

Think about it, and then see the Answers section at the end of the book.

Pragmatics also depend on other aspects of the social context. For example, when you write a term paper or go for a job interview, you normally would use a more formal tone than when writing an email or speaking to friends. Thus, when a university student sent an email to her instructor (it wasn't to one of us) that read "I can't find tomorrow's assignment could you pleeeeez send it to me pleeeeez, could ya, could ya?" the instructor sternly let the student know about her violation of pragmatics, namely, that the style of the message was completely inappropriate for the context.

Language Functions, the Brain, and Sex Differences

Language functions are distributed in many areas of the brain, but the regions shown in Figure 9.5 are especially significant. As discussed in **Chapter 3,** Broca's area, located in the left hemisphere's frontal lobe, is most centrally involved in word production and articulation (lower-right brain scan). This area is also

5. What sex differences exist in the brain's language processing?

© Jim Toomey. Reprinted with special permission of King Features Syndicate.

FIGURE 9.4 A breakdown of pragmatics. Although most of us might understand the underlying meaning of "Can I see you again?" it seems that in this case our suitor made an error in his choice of words.

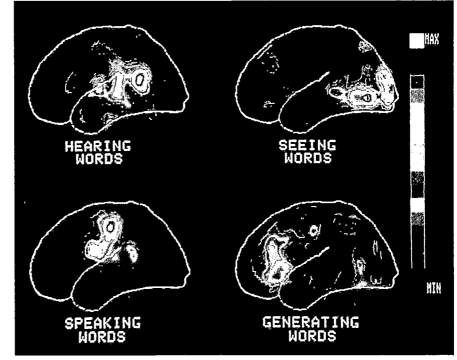

Marcus Raichle, Washington University, St. Louis, Mcdonnell Center for High Brain Function

FIGURE 9.5 Brain areas involved in various aspects of language. In these PET scans, regions of white, red, and yellow show the greatest activity. Notice in the upper-left image that Wernicke's area (in the temporal lobe) is especially active when we hear words, and in the lower-right image that Broca's area (located in the frontal lobe) is especially active when we generate words.

involved in the hand motor-control system, which explains why people often "talk with their hands" (Gentilucci & Volta, 2008). Wernicke's area, in the rear portion of the temporal lobe, is more centrally involved in speech comprehension (upper-left scan). People with damage in one or both areas typically suffer from **aphasia,** an impairment in speech comprehension and/or production that can be permanent or temporary (LaPointe, 2005). The visual area of the cortex is also involved in recognizing written words. In a fascinating study, Bedny et al. (2015) have show that the visual cortex will respond to spoken words in children who were blind from birth. Without visual input, language processing recruits part of the primary visual cortex through plasticity.

Years ago scientists noted that men who suffer left-hemisphere strokes are more likely than women to show severe aphasic symptoms. In female stroke victims with left-hemisphere damage, language functions are more likely to be spared, suggesting that more of their language function is shared with the right hemisphere.

Brain-imaging research by Susan Rossell and her colleagues (2002) supports this hypothesis. In their study, men and women engaged in a language task in which words and nonwords were presented on each side of a computer screen. Participants had to identify which was the real word as quickly as possible by pressing one of two computer keys. Functional MRIs (fMRIs) were recorded during the task and during a nonlanguage control task. As the image in Figure 9.6 shows, men exhibited greater left-hemisphere activation (red areas) during the language task, whereas women's brain activation occurred in both the left and right hemispheres. Maximum activation occurred in regions corresponding to Broca's area and Wernicke's area. Neural systems involved in several aspects of language may be organized differently in women than in men, but because this finding has been successfully replicated in some studies but not others, more research is needed to sort out why these inconsistencies occur (Gleason & Ely, 2002; Sommer et al., 2004; Démonet et al., 2005). Further, as a critical thinker, you should recognize that if men's and women's brains differ overall in some aspects of language processing, this finding does not establish by itself whether the sources of those differences lies in our genes or possible gender-differences in language socialization (Kaiser et al., 2009).

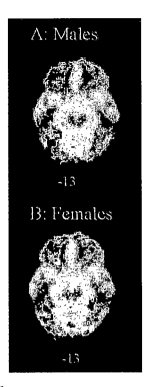

FIGURE 9.6 Brain activation, as recorded by fMRI, is shown in the red areas. For males, the left hemisphere is more active than the right hemisphere during this language task. Females' activation patterns are distributed in corresponding areas of both the left and right hemispheres, indicating less lateralization of language functions than in the males' brains. The yellow activation patterns occurred in response to a control (nonlanguage) task.

Source: Rossell, S.L. et al. (2002). Sex differences in functional brain activation during a lexical visual field task. *Brain and Language*, 80(1), 97–105, Figure 1, p. 102; *Brain and Language* Copyright © 2003 Elsevier. Reprinted with permission from Elsevier.

Acquiring a First Language

Language acquisition is one of the most striking events in human cognitive development. It represents the joint influences of biology (nature) and environment (nurture). Many language experts believe that humans are born linguists, inheriting a biological readiness to recognize and eventually produce the sounds and structure of whatever language they are exposed to (Chomsky, 1965; Clowey, 2014; Pinker, 2000).

Biological Foundations

Several facts suggest a biological basis for language acquisition. First, human children, despite their limited thinking skills, begin to master language early in life without any formal instruction. Moreover, despite their differences at the phoneme level, all adult languages throughout the world—including sign languages for the deaf that developed independently in different parts of the world—seem to have common underlying structural characteristics. Language acquisition thus represents the unfolding of a biologically primed process within a social learning environment (Chomsky, 1987; Kuhl, 2004).

Whether born in Toronto, Taiwan, or Tanzania, young infants can perceive the entire range of phonemes found in the world's languages. Between 6 and 12 months of age, however, they begin to discriminate only those sounds that are specific to their native tongue. For example, Japanese children lose the ability to distinguish between the *r* and *l* sounds because their language does not make this phonetic distinction, but children exposed to English continue to discriminate these sounds as they mature. Likewise, Japanese-speaking children learn the syntactic rule to put the object before the verb ("Ichiro the ball hit"), whereas English-speaking children learn the syntactic rule that the verb comes before the object ("Ichiro hit the ball").

The linguist Noam Chomsky (1987) proposed that humans are born with a **language acquisition device (LAD)**, an innate biological mechanism that contains the general grammatical rules (which he terms *universal grammar*) common to all languages. Among the principles inherent in LAD are that languages contain such things as noun phrases and verb phrases that are arranged in particular ways, such as subjects, predicates, and adjectives. Chomsky likened LAD to a huge electrical panel with banks of linguistic switches that are thrown as children hear the words and syntax of their native language. For example, for a child learning to speak English, the "switch" that indicates whether to insert a pronoun before a verb (as in "*I* want") is set to yes. But in Spanish, the same switch is set to no, because the applicable verb (in this case, *deseo*) already includes the first-person singular and inserting a pronoun is not necessary. In this manner, universal grammar becomes calibrated to the grammar and syntax of one's native tongue.

Social Learning Processes

Given the required biological foundation, social learning plays a central role in acquiring a language (Pruden et al., 2006). Early on, mothers and fathers attract their children's attention and maintain their interest by conversing with them in what has been termed *child-directed speech*, a high-pitched intonation that seems to be used

6. How do biological factors influence language acquisition?

7. How do social learning factors influence language acquisition?

FIGURE 9.7 Language development depends not only on the brain's biological programming device but also on exposure to one's language. Childhood is an important sensitive period for such exposure.

all over the world (Fernald et al., 1989). Parents also teach their children words by pointing out objects and naming them, by reading aloud, and by responding to the never-ending question "What dat?" (Figure 9.7).

The behaviourist B.F. Skinner (1957) developed an operant conditioning explanation for language acquisition. His basic premise was that children's language development is strongly governed by adults' positive reinforcement of appropriate language and non-reinforcement or correction of inappropriate verbalizations. However, most modern psycholinguists doubt that operant learning principles alone can account for language development. For one thing, children learn so much so quickly. By second grade in elementary school, children have acquired about 5000 to 6000 words (Biemiller & Slonim, 2001). Moreover, observational studies have shown that parents do *not* typically correct their children's grammar as language skills are developing. Rather, parents' corrections focus primarily on the

"truth value" (or deep structure) of what the child is trying to communicate. Thus, they are less likely to correct a young child who says "I have two foots" than they are to correct one who says "I have four feet," even though the latter statement is grammatically correct (Brown, 1973).

As this point also shows, much of children's language is very different from that of their parents, and thus it can't be explained simply as an imitative process. Nonetheless, social learning is a crucial contributor to language acquisition, and the interplay between biological and environmental factors is a given for most modern theorists. Psychologist Jerome Bruner (1983) proposed the term **language acquisition support system (LASS)** to represent factors in the social environment that facilitate the learning of a language. One could say that when LAD and LASS interact in a mutually supportive fashion, normal language development occurs.

Developmental Timetable and Sensitive Periods

As biological factors (including the maturation of speech-production mechanisms) and experiential factors combine their influences, language acquisition proceeds according to a developmental timetable that is common to all cultures. As shown in Table 9.1, children progress from reflexive crying at birth through stages of cooing, babbling, and one-word utterances. By two years of age, children are uttering sentences called *telegraphic speech* that at first consist of a noun and a verb (e.g., "Want cookie"), with nonessential words left out as in a telegraph message. Soon, additional words may be added (e.g., "Daddy go car"). From that point on, speech development accelerates as vocabulary increases and sentences become more grammatically correct. In the short span of five years, an initially non-verbal creature has come to understand and produce a complex language.

In Chapter 5, we saw how the normal development of perceptual abilities requires certain kinds of sensory input early in life. A study of children who were born deaf and received cochlear implants early in life showed significant advantages in language and speech perception among children who received an implant before the age of two compared to children who received one at three or four years of age (Svirsky, Teoh & Neuburger, 2004). Some linguists are convinced there is also a sensitive period from

TABLE 9.1   Course of Normal Language Development in Children

Age	Speech Characteristics
1–3 months	Infant can distinguish speech from nonspeech sounds and prefers speech sounds (phonemes). Undifferentiated crying gives way to cooing when happy.
4–6 months	Babbling sounds begin to occur. Child vocalizes in response to verbalizations of others.
7–11 months	Perception of phonemes narrows to include only the phonemes heard in the language spoken by others in the environment. Child moves tongue with vocalizations ("lalling"). Child discriminates between some words without understanding their meaning and begins to imitate word sounds heard from others.
12 months	First recognizable words typically spoken as one-word utterances to name familiar people and objects (e.g., *da-da* or *block*).
12–18 months	Child increases knowledge of word meanings and begins to use single words to express whole phrases or requests (e.g., *out* to express a desire to get out of the crib); primarily uses nouns.
18–24 months	Vocabulary expands to between 50 and 100 words. First rudimentary sentences appear, usually consisting of two words (e.g., *more milk*) with little or no use of articles (*the, a*), conjunctions (*and*), or auxiliary verbs (*can, will*). This condensed, or telegraphic, speech is characteristic of first sentences throughout the world.
2–4 years	Vocabulary expands rapidly at the rate of several hundred words every six months. Two-word sentences give way to longer sentences that, though often grammatically incorrect, exhibit basic language syntax. Child begins to express concepts with words and to use language to describe imaginary objects and ideas. Sentences become more correct syntactically.
4–5 years	Child has learned the basic grammatical rules for combining nouns, adjectives, articles, conjunctions, and verbs into meaningful sentences.

infancy to puberty during which the brain is most responsive to language input from the environment. Support for a sensitive period comes from studies of children who lived by themselves in the wild or who were isolated from human contact by deranged parents. One such child, found when she was six years old, immediately received language training and seemed to develop normal language abilities (Brown, 1958). In contrast, language-deprived children who were found when they were past puberty seemed unable to acquire normal language skills despite extensive training (Clarke & Clarke, 2000; Curtiss, 1977). We should note that some authors (e.g., White et al., 2013) have reminded us to consider that there is considerable neural plasticity and transfer of training in auditory learning. Thus, we are not exactly sure of how wide or narrow the critical period might be.

The importance of early language exposure applies to any language, not just spoken language. Because sign languages share the deep-structure characteristics of spoken languages, deaf children who learn sign language before puberty develop normal linguistic and cognitive abilities, even though they never hear a spoken word (Marschark & Mayer, 1998). In contrast, deaf people who are not exposed to sign language before age 12 show language-learning deficits later in life (Morford, 2003).

Bilingualism: Learning a Second Language

For those of us labouring to learn a second language, there are models to inspire us. M.D. Berlitz, inventor of the system for teaching languages that bears his name, spoke 58 of them. Sir John Bowring, once the British governor of Hong Kong, could speak 100 languages and read 100 more. And some sort of record must be held by Benjamin Schulze (1699–1760), who could recite the Lord's Prayer in 215 languages (Bryan, 1986). Somewhat more modestly, only about 18 percent of Canadians (including 43 percent of those living in Quebec) report that they speak both English and French (Statistics Canada, 2013).

A second language is learned best and spoken most fluently when it is learned during the sensitive period of childhood. Much of the evidence argues that the vocabulary of a language can be learned at any age, but mastery of the syntax, or grammar, depends on early acquisition (Bialystok, 2001). After about age seven, mastery of English grammar, for example, becomes progressively more difficult (Johnson & Newport, 1989, 1991). One concern with the early learning of multiple languages is that children will confuse the two languages. Young bilingual children do sometimes mix their two languages, but as McGill University's Fred Genesee has shown, children begin

8. What factors affect the learning of a second language and its effects on thinking?

to differentiate their two languages by two years of age, perhaps younger, and such code mixing is not a lasting or important source of confusion (Nicoladis & Genesee, 1997).

The study of bilingualism has special importance in Canada, with our two official languages and policy of multiculturalism. During the past 40 years, the study of second language learning has often focused on the Canadian development and practice of French-immersion programs in the educational system. The idea of French immersion programs originated with a group of English-speaking parents in St. Lambert, Quebec. The parents wanted their children to acquire proficiency in French so that they would be able to function in the majority language of the province and also to improve relationships with francophone Quebecers (Genesee & Gandara, 1999). This group of parents began to work with Wally Lambert, a psychologist at McGill University, and a French immersion program was developed. The first French immersion class in Canada opened in September 1965. From these modest beginnings, the French immersion program has grown tremendously; more than 300 000 Canadian students are now enrolled in immersion programs (Genesee & Gandara, 1999).

Some of the early research on bilingualism suggested that having to learn two vocabularies and sets of grammar put bilingual speakers at a disadvantage. Lambert (Lambert, 1992; Lambert et al., 1993), however, found quite the opposite. When matched on background variables, bilingual speakers scored at least as well as monolinguals on performance tests. More recent research has found that bilingual children actually show superior cognitive processing when compared with their monolingual peers (Bialystock et al., 2010; Barac & Bialystock, 2012). On average, French immersion students outperform monolingual students in reading (Allen, 2004). Ellen Bialystok, at York University, has found that bilingual children better understand the symbolic nature of print, even before they can read (Bialystok, 1997). Bilingual children also perform better than monolingual children on perceptual tasks that require them to inhibit attention to an irrelevant feature of an object and pay attention to another feature (Bialystok & Martin, 2004). For example, suppose you sit in front of a computer screen like the one shown in Figure 9.8. There's a box in the lower-left corner with a red square above it and a box in the lower-right corner with a blue circle above it. Next, a stimulus appears at the top of the screen—either a blue square or a red circle. At first, your task is to place the stimulus into the box that has the

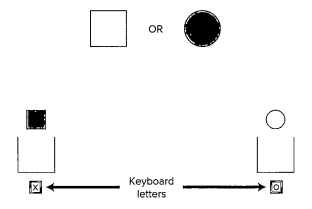

FIGURE 9.8 Measuring your ability to ignore irrelevant details. This figure shows one of the attention-inhibition tasks used by Bialystok and Martin (2004).

Source: From E. Bialystok & M. Martin, 2004, "Attention Inhibition in Bilingual Children: Evidence from the Dimensional Change Card Sort Tasks," *Developmental Science, 7*(3), 325–339, Fig 1b. Copyright © 2004 Wiley/Blackwell. Reprinted by permission of Blackwell Publisher.

same colour. If a blue square appears, you press the letter *O* on the keyboard to drop it into the lower-right box. If a red circle appears, you press the *X* key to drop it into the lower-left box. After several trials, however, we switch the rule. Now your task is to sort each stimulus by its shape, not by its colour: Drop blue squares into the left box and red circles into the right box. This new rule requires you to ignore the colour of each stimulus, which just a moment ago was foremost in your mind, and instead to selectively focus your attention on the shape of the stimulus.

Positive correlates of bilingualism, such as greater flexibility in thinking and better performance on standardized intelligence tests, have been discovered in a number of countries, including Switzerland, South Africa, and Canada. For children who are entering into a new language group, such as the children of recent immigrants, research has found that non-English-speaking immigrant children perform best in bilingual educational settings in which they are taught in both their native language and English. Compared with similar children who are placed in English-only classrooms, those in bilingual classes are less likely to drop out of school and they develop higher self-esteem, achieve better academic performance, and have better English fluency (Thomas & Collier, 1997).

Learning a Second Language: Is Earlier Better?

Given that children are language sponges, it seems obvious that a second language would be learned best and spoken most fluently when acquired early in life. Some psycholinguists believe that there is a critical period for learning a second language that ends in childhood or possibly in the early teens. If this is the case, it would not be possible for people who begin to learn a second language in high school or university, or after emigrating as late teens or adults to a foreign country, to achieve the fluency of native speakers. What do you think about this hypothesis?

In one sense, it does appear that the earlier one learns a second language, the better. If you start to learn a second language in childhood, then by the time you reach age 25 to 30, let's say, you will have had many more years of exposure to that language than if you had first started to learn it in your late teens. Thus, "age of acquisition" can easily be confounded with "years of exposure and practice." As a critical thinker, realize that to test the biologically based critical-period hypothesis, researchers must try to compare the proficiency of people who are "early" versus "late" second-language learners yet who also have had a similar amount of overall exposure to that second language.

In one well-known study, Jacqueline Johnson and Elissa Newport (1989) studied university students and faculty members who had emigrated from Korea or China to the United States when they were either 3 to 16 years old ("early arrivals") or 17 to 39 years old ("late arrivals"). Overall, the early- and late-arrival groups had nearly identical years of exposure to English since coming to the United States. Johnson and Newport presented these individuals with 276 English sentences that were either grammatically correct (e.g., "Every Friday our neighbour washes her car.") or incorrect (e.g., "Two mouses ran into the house this morning."). The participants were asked to judge the correctness of each sentence. A sample of native-born Americans also took this grammar test.

The findings strongly supported the critical-period hypothesis. Overall, the early arrivals performed far better than the late arrivals. Moreover, even among the early arrivals, those who had arrived by age seven mastered English grammar just as well as native-born Americans, whereas immigrants who had arrived between the ages of 8 and 10 and between 11 and 16 did progressively worse on the grammar test (Figure 9.9). The 17- to 39-year-olds showed the poorest understanding of grammar and, within this age group, breaking the data down by age subgroups made little difference: Immigrants who had arrived after age 30 performed as well, for example, as those who had arrived in their late teens (Johnson & Newport,

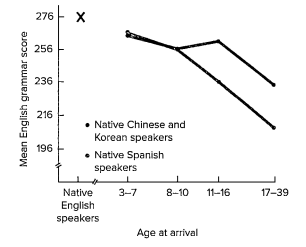

FIGURE 9.9 Age and proficiency of learning a second language. The X represents the grammar score of native-born Americans. The blue line shows the relation between age of arrival in the United States by Korean and Chinese individuals and their scores on a 276-item test of English grammar, compared with native-born Americans. The red line shows the relation between age of arrival in the United States by native Spanish speakers and their scores on a 274-item version of the same grammar test.

Based on data from Johnson, J.S., & Newport, E.L. (1989). Critical period effects on universal properties of language: The influence of maturational state on the acquisition of English as a second language. *Cognitive Psychology*, 21(1), 60.; Birdsong, D., & Molis, M. (2001). On the evidence for maturational constraints in second-language acquisition. *Journal of Memory and Language*, 44, 235-249.

1989). These findings suggest that because late arrivals had missed a critical period for learning a second language, it mattered little at what age they started to acquire English.

Other findings, however, complicate the picture. David Birdsong and Michelle Molis (2001) used the same grammar test in a study of native Spanish speakers who had immigrated to America at different ages and were now either faculty members, students, or employees at a university. Once again, despite having a similar amount of overall exposure to English, early-arriving immigrants (i.e., arrival by age 16) performed much better than late-arriving immigrants (i.e., arrival after age 16). But unlike the previous study, performance among early arrivals generally remained high all the way through age 16 (Figure 9.9). And among the late arrivals, age did make a difference. It was not as if some biological second-language acquisition switch got completely turned off by the end of childhood or even by the late teens. Overall, immigrants who arrived in their 20s, though not as proficient as early arrivals, still performed better than those who arrived in their 30s or 40s.

In addition, Adamuti-Trache (2013) has shown that older immigrants to Canada have fewer language learning opportunities, which contributes to poorer second language acquisition in this population.

Differences in the patterns of findings across studies have led researchers to debate whether there is a biologically based critical period for second-language acquisition and, if so, at what age range it ends. Moreover, some studies suggest that to speak a second language with the fluency and accent of a native speaker, people must begin to acquire that language in childhood. Other studies find that even after mid-adolescence, some second-language learners acquire the proficiency (if not quite the perfect accent) of native speakers (Bialystok, 2001; Birdsong & Molis, 2001).

9. Is there a critical (or sensitive) period for acquiring a second language? Discuss the evidence.

The issue of whether earlier is better—or, more precisely, whether earlier is biologically better—is far from resolved. One study, for example, found that the better grammar proficiency of early- versus late-arriving immigrants to the United States seemed to be due not to a biological critical period but to the greater amount of formal education in English that the early arrivals had received (Flege et al., 1999). Still, the two studies just discussed, along with most others, support the general principle that it is more difficult to learn a second language in adulthood than in childhood. Overall, at present, the data suggest that there may at least be a *sensitive* (rather than a *critical*) period for learning a second language that extends through mid-adolescence. The *Focus on Neuroscience* feature for this chapter examines brain areas involved in bilingualism.

Linguistic Influences on Thinking

10. How does language influence thinking?

Does the language we speak shape how we think? The linguist Benjamin Lee Whorf (1956a) took an extreme position on this matter, contending in his **linguistic relativity hypothesis** that language not only influences but also determines what we are capable of thinking.

If the linguistic relativity hypothesis is correct, then people whose cultures have only a few words for colours should have greater difficulty in perceiving the spectrum of colours than do people whose languages have many colour words. To test this proposition, Eleanor Rosch (1973) studied the Dani of New Guinea, who have only two colour words in their language, one for bright warm colours and the other for dark cool ones. She found that contrary to what

strict linguistic determinism would suggest, the Dani could discriminate among and remember a wide assortment of hues in much the same manner as can speakers of the English language, which contains many colour names. Similarly, in the Amazon, the language of the Mundurukú people contains few words for geometric or spatial concepts, yet Mundurukú children perform as well on many geometric and spatial tasks as American children (Dehaene et al., 2006).

Other research, however, comparing English children and Himba children from Africa, suggests that colour categories in a given language have a greater influence on colour perception than Rosch's study of the Dani suggested (Davidoff, 2004). The English language contains 11 basic colour terms, whereas the Himba language has only five. Himba children made fewer distinctions among coloured tiles than did English children. For example, Himba children categorized under the colour term *zoozu* a variety of dark colours, such as dark shades of blue, green, brown, purple, red, and the colour black. English children distinguished among these colours and remembered the different hues better when retested on which ones they had seen earlier.

Still, most psycholinguists do not agree with Whorf's strong assertion that language *determines* how we think. They would say instead that language can *influence* how we think, categorize information, and attend to our daily experiences (Newcombe & Uttal, 2006). Language can also colour our perceptions, the decisions we make, and the conclusions we draw (Figure 9.10). Consider, for example, the ability

© Digital Vision/Getty Images

FIGURE 9.10 Sexist language influences our perceptions, our decisions, and the conclusions we draw. Which of these people would you assume is the chairperson of this committee? Might you consider the question differently if we said "Which of these people would you assume is the chairman of the committee?"

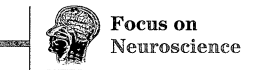

Focus on Neuroscience

THE BILINGUAL BRAIN

Is a second language represented in the same parts of the brain as the native language? One intriguing set of findings comes from studies of bilingual people who experience a brain trauma (e.g., from a tumour or a stroke) and subsequently develop an aphasia. In some bilingual patients, the same linguistic ability—such as understanding the meaning of words—may be impaired to different degrees in each language, or impaired in one language and not the other (Fabbro, 2001). Moreover, when brain damage produces similar impairments in both languages, patients may experience some simultaneous recovery in both languages, or recovery in one language but not the other. These findings suggest that there is variability among people in how bilingual abilities are represented in the brain, but also that in some cases, each language is represented by at least partially distinct neural networks.

Brain-imaging studies shed further light on this issue. At the University of Milan, Daniela Perani and her colleagues (1998) used PET scans to measure cortical activation patterns in the brains of English-speaking Italians as they listened to stories read aloud in Italian and in English. People who were highly proficient in English and who had learned this second language before the age of ten showed representation of the two languages in the same cortical areas. The two languages had, in a sense, become one, accounting for the fluent participants' ability to use the languages interchangeably. In contrast, less fluent Italians who had learned English later in life showed brain activity in different areas, depending on whether they listened to stories in Italian or English.

In general, it appears that when people acquire a second language early in life or learn it to a high degree of proficiency later in life, both languages use a common neural network (Démonet et al., 2005). However, the classic language areas may show some fundamental changes (Jasinska & Petitto, 2013). Yet even within this common

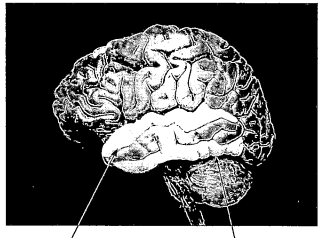

Superior temporal gyrus   Inferior temporal gyrus
© Royalty-Free/Corbis

network, some brain regions become more active when fluent bilinguals use the language to which they have been less extensively exposed (usually the second language). For example, fMRI imaging suggests that even though roughly the same brain regions are involved in first and second language processing, there are some subtle differences. In the left inferior frontal gyrus, different centres are activated for first versus second language processing, but there is no distinction in the superior temporal gyrus or the inferior parietal cortex (Marian et al., 2003; Stein et al., 2012). Thus, despite a person's fluency in both languages, this difference may suggest that the person has to exert more conscious effort to process the less dominant language (Hulstijn, 2005; Marian et al., 2003). In contrast, people who learn a second language only moderately well later in life show more variability in their patterns of neural activation; at least in certain cases, some of the specific brain areas that process each language are distinct.

---

of sexist language to evoke gender stereotypes. In one study, college students read one of the following statements about psychology:

> The psychologist believes in the dignity and worth of the individual human being. He is committed to increasing man's understanding of himself and others.

> Psychologists believe in the dignity and worth of the individual human being. They are committed to increasing people's understanding of themselves and others.

The students then were asked to rate the attractiveness of a career in psychology for men and women. Those who had read the first statement rated psychology as a less attractive profession for women than did the students who read the second statement, written in gender-neutral language (Briere & Lanktree, 1983). Apparently, the first statement implied that psychology is a male profession (when, actually, the majority of psychology doctorates awarded over the past decade went to women). In such ways, language can help to create and maintain stereotypes.

Language not only influences how we think but also may influence how well we think in certain domains. For example, English-speaking children consistently score lower than children from Asian countries in mathematical skills such as counting, addition, and subtraction (Miller et al., 2005). One reason may be the words and symbols the languages use to represent numbers. Asian languages make it far easier to learn the base-10 number system, particularly the numbers between 10 and 100. For example, in Chinese, the number 11 is "ten-one," 12 is "ten-two," and 13 is "ten-three." In contrast, English speakers struggle with such words as eleven, twelve, and thirteen, which bear little conceptual relation to a base-10 mode of thinking. Regardless of their counting proficiency, American and British children fail to grasp the base-10 system by age

five; in contrast, by age five, many Chinese children understand this concept, enabling them to do addition and subtraction with greater ease (Miller & Stigler, 1987). In this manner, the English language appears to hamper the development of skills in using numbers, whereas Asian languages seem to facilitate the development of mathematical skills.

In sum, language provides the foundation of many human behaviours and capabilities, and in this chapter we have touched on only a few of its complexities. As a central topic of psychological research, it continues to be studied vigorously at the biological, psychological, and environmental levels of analysis (Figure 9.11). You may wonder if humans are the only species to use language. We examine this question in the *Frontiers* feature.

11. Does evidence support the view that apes can acquire human language? Why or why not?

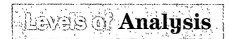 Language

We've seen that language is a complex cognitive activity jointly shaped by biology and the social environment. Let's consider how some of the factors we have discussed represent the biological, psychological, and environmental levels of analysis.

ENVIRONMENTAL

- Social learning experiences guide language acquisition, beginning with early caretaker speech that exposes infants to the phonemes of a particular language.
- Formal educational experiences facilitate language development and are integral to learning to read.
- Extensive exposure to a bilingual environment influences the number of languages that children acquire.
- There are cultural variations in word use, such as in the number of words used to identify colours or the degree of sexist language.

BIOLOGICAL

- Acquiring language depends on brain maturation; it also modifies the brain.
- There appears to be a maturational critical or sensitive period for acquiring normal language capabilities.
- Using language involves a network of brain structures; among bilingual speakers, whether the two languages share the same network depends on age of acquisition and other factors.
- Hemispheric lateralization for language may differ between men and women.

PSYCHOLOGICAL

- Cognitive processes (e.g., attention, memory) are involved in learning a language's symbols and grammatical rules.
- Bottom-up and top-down processes influence our ability to recognize speech and to read.
- Bilingualism appears to influence other cognitive abilities.
- Language influences how we think.

Consider this possible interaction between the biological and environmental levels of analysis. Suppose a highly proficient bilingual speaker, raised from birth in a bilingual home, studies a third language in university and eventually learns it well. Would you expect all three languages to share a common brain network?

FIGURE 9.11

Frontiers

CAN ANIMALS ACQUIRE HUMAN LANGUAGE?

Nonhuman species communicate in diverse ways. Chimpanzees grunt, bark, scream, and make gestures to other chimps. Dolphins make clicking sounds and high-pitched vocalizations (Figure 9.12). Many species use special calls to warn of predators and to attract mates (Alcock, 2005).

Communication also abounds in the insect world. Honeybees use a repertoire of body movements—so-called "dances"—to communicate. When a honeybee discovers nectar, it returns to the hive and performs a turning "waggle dance" (von Frisch, 1974). The dance's pattern and duration convey information about the nectar's location, which other bees receive by sensing vibrations as they stay in contact behind the dancer. Using this information and odour cues, they can zero in on the food source. Honeybees also vibrate their bodies from side to side in a "grooming invitation dance" that signals other bees to come by and help clean them (Land & Seeley, 2004).

In some species, communication shows interesting parallels to human language. Just as humans have different languages, each songbird species has its own songs. Remarkably, some songbirds also have local dialects, as humans do (Catchpole & Rowell, 1993). Thus, experts can tell whether a male white-crowned sparrow lives in certain areas north, south, or east of San Francisco by how it sings. And just as humans have a sensitive period in childhood for language acquisition, some songbirds will not sing normally in adulthood unless they hear the songs of their species while growing up (Wilbrecht & Nottebohm, 2003).

Although other species can communicate in intriguing and sophisticated ways, the capacity to use full-fledged language has long been regarded as the sole province of humans. Several decades ago, some scientists attempted to challenge this assumption by teaching apes to use human language.

Washoe: Early Signs of Success

At first, investigators tried to teach chimpanzees to speak verbally, but chimps lack a vocal system that would permit humanlike speech. A breakthrough came in 1966 when Allen Gardner and Beatrice Gardner (1969) took advantage of chimps' hand and finger dexterity and began teaching American Sign Language to a ten-month-old chimp named Washoe. They *cross-fostered* Washoe: They raised her at home and treated her like a human child. By age five, Washoe had learned 160 signs. More important, at times she combined signs (e.g., "more fruit," "you tickle Washoe") in novel ways. For example, when a researcher showed Washoe a baby doll inside a cup and signed "What that?" Washoe signed back "Baby in my drink." Other researchers also had success. A gorilla named Koko learned more than 600 signs (Bonvillian & Patterson, 1997), and a chimp named Lana learned to communicate via visual symbols on a specially designed keyboard (Rumbaugh, 1990).

Project Nim: Dissent from Within

At Columbia University, behaviourist Herbert Terrace (1979) taught sign language to a chimp he named Nim Chimpsky— a play on the name of linguist Noam Chomsky. But after years of work and videotape analysis of Nim's "conversations," Terrace concluded that when Nim combined symbols into longer sequences, he was either imitating his trainer's previous signs or "running on" with his hands until he got what he wanted. Moreover, Nim spontaneously signed only when he wanted something, which is not how humans use language. Terrace concluded that Nim had not learned language.

Not surprisingly, some ape-language researchers disputed Terrace's conclusions. They agreed that although apes signed mainly to request things, other types of communication also occurred. For example, Chantek, an orangutan who had been taught a symbol for "dirty" in regard to feces and urine, spontaneously began applying the symbol to spilled food, soiled objects, and toilets (Miles et al., 1996). At Central Washington University, Roger Fouts and Deborah Fouts continued working with Washoe and other cross-fostered chimps. They intentionally refrained from signing in front of Loulis, Washoe's adopted son, and found that Loulis acquired over 50 signs by observing other chimps communicate (Fouts et al., 1989). The chimps also signed with one another when humans were not present, and signing occurred across various contexts, such as when they were playing, feeding, and fighting (Cianelli & Fouts, 1998).

"Although humans make sounds with their mouths and occasionally look at each other, there is no solid evidence that they actually communicate with each other."

Copyright © 2004 by Sidney Harris. ScienceCartoonsPlus.com. Reprinted with permission.

FIGURE 9.12 Human scientists debate whether dolphins and other animals use language. Could the opposite also be occurring?

continued

Kanzi: Chimp versus Child

Sue Savage-Rumbaugh of Georgia State University has worked extensively with a chimpanzee species called the bonobo (Figure 9.13). At age one, a bonobo named Kanzi spontaneously showed an interest in using plastic geometric symbols that were associated with words. By age four, with only informal training during social interactions, Kanzi had learned more than 80 symbols and produced a number of two- and three-word communications. Kanzi typically combined gestures and symbols that he pointed to on a laminated board or typed on a specially designed keyboard. For example, Kanzi created the combinations "Person chase Kanzi," "Kanzi chase person," and "Person chase person"

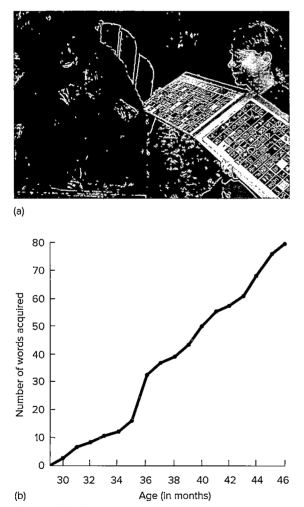

(a)

(b)

(a) Courtesy of Sue Savage-Rumbaugh; (b) E.S. Savage-Rumbaugh, K. McDonald, R.A. Sevick, W.D. Hopkins & E. Rupert, 1986, "Spontaneous Symbol Acquisition and Communicative Use by Pygmy Chimpanzees (Pan Paniscus), Jounal of Experimental Psychology: General, 115, 220, Fig 1. Copyright © 1986 by the American Psychological Association. Reprinted by permission.

FIGURE 9.13 Can a chimpanzee acquire language? (a) Using complex symbols, a bonobo communicates with psychologist Sue Savage-Rumbaugh. (b) This graph shows the rate of Kanzi's symbol acquisition over 17 months of informal training.

to designate who should chase whom during play. Kanzi also responded readily to spoken English commands.

Savage-Rumbaugh and her colleagues (1993; Segerdahl et al., 2006) also tested Kanzi's ability to understand unfamiliar spoken sentences under controlled conditions. For example, when told "Give the doggie a shot," Kanzi picked up a toy dog, grabbed a toy hypodermic needle, and gave the dog a shot. Kanzi also appeared to understand syntax. Given slightly different requests, such as "Make the [toy] snake bite the [toy] doggie" and "Make the doggie bite the snake," Kanzi responded appropriately. For comparison, one of the researcher's daughters, Alia, was tested under the same conditions between the ages of two and two-and-a-half. Kanzi correctly responded to 74 percent of the novel requests and Alia to 65 percent. In short, Kanzi was comprehending speech at the level of a human toddler. Savage-Rumbaugh has also demonstrated that Kanzi and his half-sister can use emotion-laden words such as "happy" and "hurt" appropriately, suggesting that apes can both feel emotion and communicate about emotion in a symbolic fashion (Lyn & Savage-Rumbaugh, 2013).

Is It Language?

What should we conclude about apes' language abilities? Recall that human language (1) is symbolic, (2) is structured, (3) conveys meaning, (4) is generative, and (5) permits displacement. Evidence is strongest for the first and third criteria. Apes, undisputedly, are capable of communicating with symbols and hand signs, and they can learn a small vocabulary of several hundred words. However, whether the apes perceive the symbols and signs as words in the sense that humans do is still unclear. As for conveying meaning, realize that just as toddlers can convey meaning by using one- or two-word utterances, apes can convey meaning by using one- or two-symbol communications (e.g., "banana" or "give banana"), and they have also produced longer symbol strings that, at least some of the time, convey meaning. As for structure, both sides can point to examples of how apes follow—and violate—rules of grammar. Lastly, the evidence for generativity and displacement is limited and controversial.

Critics—even those impressed by Kanzi's feats—are not persuaded. Some believe that ambiguous ape communications are interpreted as language because the researchers erroneously assume what must be going on inside the apes' minds. Conversely, proponents believe the data show that great apes can acquire rudimentary language skills (Segerdahl et al., 2006). If it were anatomically possible, argues Sue Savage-Rumbaugh, Kanzi would be speaking.

At present, neither side in the debate has convinced the other. If nothing else, this intriguing scientific work should remind us to appreciate something that we often take for granted, namely, the seemingly natural ease with which humans acquire a native language.

continued

We do know that many of the necessary components for acquiring language are not unique to humans. The "mirror system hypothesis" (Rizzolatti & Arbib, 1998) states that imitation of manual gestures—an ability observed in all primate species—was the initial seed for the development of language in our hominid ancestors. Arbib (2005) argues that a key component in the evolution of human language was a system of mirror neurons in Broca's area that permit imitation of manual gestures, which was the basis for a gestural precursor to spoken language. The same system of mirror neurons exists in monkeys' brains in an area analogous to Broca's area called premotor area F5. Other research shows that the ability of newborns to tune to certain properties in speech—and to distinguish various speech sounds—is also present in tamarin monkeys (Ramus et al., 2000), suggesting that humans' ability to acquire speech is based partly on perceptual and neurobiological mechanisms that may be common to all primates, and perhaps other species.

Recently, Perlman and Clark (2015) reported that a gorilla named Koko engages in verbal and breathing-related behaviours, such as movements of the larynx, tongue, and lips, when making sounds. This control over vocalization could represent a precursor to speaking. Finally, dolphins appear to communicate with each other in a manner similar to human speech. By manipulating structures in their nasal cavities, they are able to modulate the "whistle" sound when they greet each other (so-called "signature-identifying whistles"). Hodson (2014) reported that one researcher (Denise Herzing) was able to translate some of the whistle sounds using a sophisticated telemetry device. Perhaps one day we will have the ability to actually communicate with another species.

Review

- Human languages across the globe share the same underlying features. Language is symbolic and structured, conveys meaning, is generative, and permits displacement. Language has many adaptive functions, such as facilitating cooperative social systems and allowing people to transmit knowledge to one another. Scientists believe that humans have evolved an innate capacity for acquiring language.

- The surface structure of a language refers to how symbols are combined; the deep structure refers to the underlying meaning of the symbols. Language elements are hierarchically arranged: from phoneme to morpheme to words, phrases, and sentences. Discourse involves higher-level combinations of sentences.

- Understanding and producing language—including pattern recognition of words and the hierarchical structure of language—involve bottom-up and top-down processing.

- In infancy, babies can perceive all the phonemes that exist in all the languages of the world. Between 6 and 12 months of age, their speech discrimination narrows to include only the sounds specific to their native tongue. By ages four to five, most children have learned the basic grammatical rules for combining words into meaningful sentences.

- Language development seems to depend heavily on innate mechanisms that permit the learning and production of language, provided that the child is exposed to an appropriate linguistic environment during a sensitive period that extends from early childhood to puberty.

- Although research findings are not entirely consistent, it appears that a second language is most easily mastered and fluently spoken if it is learned during a sensitive period that ranges from early childhood possibly through mid-adolescence. Bilingual children tend to perform better than monolingual children on a variety of cognitive tasks.

- In general, it appears that when people acquire a second language early in life or learn it to a high degree of proficiency later in life, both languages share a common neural network.

- Language influences what people think and how effectively they think. Expansion of vocabulary allows people to encode and process information in more sophisticated ways.

- Researchers have attempted to teach apes to use hand signs or keyboard symbols to communicate in language-like fashion. At best, apes are capable of learning, combining, and communicating with symbols at a level similar to that of a human toddler. Skeptics question whether apes can learn syntax and generate novel ideas.

THINKING

Can pure thought move mountains? Perhaps not yet, but pure thought can play a video game. In a scene that could be taken right out of a science-fiction movie, 19-year-old Tristan Lundemo looks at a video screen located next to his hospital bed and, without speaking a word or lifting a finger, makes a red electronic cursor (similar to the paddle in the video game *Pong*) move up, down, left, or right, merely by thinking it (Paulson, 2004). In this literal mind game, Lundemo tries to move the cursor quickly enough to strike rectangular targets that pop up and then disappear from random locations on the video screen.

Thought, Brain, and Mind

Lundemo is a patient with epilepsy who agreed to participate in a brain-computer interface study while undergoing diagnostic tests at Seattle's Harborview Medical Center (Figure 9.14a). During a session, the researchers attach 72 electrodes to Lundemo's scalp to record his brain's electrical activity. A computer analyzes the patterns and intensity of these brain signals and uses that information to control the movement of the cursor on the video screen. It's not quite that simple, however, as computer and human essentially have to adapt to each other and learn the precise patterns of thought that will make the cursor move. Lundemo was a fast study (as was the computer), and in two days he mastered the task. Electric mind over electronic matter.

As Lundemo notes, "I just think up, up, up or over left, left, left and it moves" (Paulson, 2004, p. A15). Figure 9.14b shows that several brain regions become most active when Lundemo's thought moves the cursor in a particular direction. The pattern of brain activity changes when he has a thought that moves the cursor in a different direction. Researchers hope that this technology eventually will improve the lives of people who have lost limbs or are paralyzed.

As we discussed in Chapter 6, according to some neuroscientists, conscious thought arises from the unified activity of different brain areas. In essence, of the many brain regions and connecting circuits that are active at any instant, a particular subset becomes joined in unified activity that is strong enough to become a conscious thought or perception (Koch, 2004). The specific pattern of brain activity that composes this dominant subset varies from moment to moment as we experience different thoughts and respond to changing stimuli. Even altering one's thought from "move up" to "move down," "move left," or "move right" produces a different pattern of brain activity. Although we're still far from understanding exactly how the brain produces thought, it is clear that from a biological level of analysis, thought exists as patterns of neural activity.

Subjectively, at the psychological level, thinking may seem to be the internal language of the mind—somewhat like "inner speech"—but it actually includes several mental activities. One mode of thought does indeed take the form

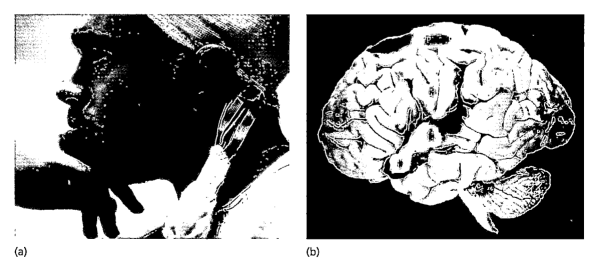

(a)   (b)

FIGURE 9.14 The power of pure thought. (a) With electrodes attached to his scalp underneath the bandage, Tristan Lundemo uses his thoughts to control the movement of a cursor on a video screen. (b) Various brain regions become active when Lundemo moves the cursor in a particular direction.

of verbal sentences that we say or hear in our minds. This is called **propositional thought** because it expresses a proposition, or statement, such as "I'm hungry" or "It's almost time for dinner." Another thought mode, **imaginal thought,** consists of images that we can see, hear, or feel in our mind. A third mode, **motoric thought,** relates to mental representations of motor movements, such as throwing an object. All three modes of thinking enter into our abilities to reason, solve problems, and engage in many forms of intelligent behaviour. In this chapter, however, we'll focus on propositional and imaginal thought.

Concepts and Propositions

Much of our thinking occurs in the form of **propositions,** statements that express ideas. All propositions consist of concepts combined in a particular way. For example, "college students are intelligent people" is a proposition in which the two concepts "college students" and "intelligent people" are linked by the verb *are* (Figure 9.15). **Concepts** are basic units of semantic memory—mental categories into which we place objects, activities, abstractions (such as "liberal" and "conservative"), and events that have essential features in common. Every psychological term you are learning in this course is a concept. Concepts can be acquired through explicit instruction or through our own observations of similarities and differences among various objects and events.

Many concepts are difficult to define explicitly. For example, you are quite familiar with the concept "vegetable," yet you might have difficulty coming up with an explicit definition of what a vegetable is. However, you can quickly think of a good example of a vegetable, such as broccoli or carrots. According to Eleanor Rosch (1977), many concepts are defined by **prototypes,** the most typical and familiar members of a category or a class. Rosch suggests that we

often decide which category something belongs to by its degree of resemblance to the prototype.

Consider the following questions:

Is an eagle a bird?

Is a penguin a bird?

Is a bat a bird?

According to the prototype view, you should have come to a quicker decision on the first question than on the last two. Why? Because an eagle fits most people's "bird" prototype better than does a penguin (which is a bird, though it lacks some essential prototypic features, such as the ability to fly) or a bat (which is not a bird, even though it flies). Experiments measuring how quickly participants responded "Yes" or "No" to the preceding questions have found that it does indeed take most people longer to decide whether or not penguins or bats are birds (Rips, 1997).

The use of prototypes is perhaps the most elementary method of forming concepts. It requires that we note *only* similarities among objects. Thus, children's early concepts are based on prototypes of the objects and people they encounter personally. They then decide whether or not new objects are similar enough to the prototype to be a "Mommy," a "cookie," a "doggie," and so on (Smith & Zarate, 1992). Because prototypes may differ as a result of personal experience, there is considerable room for arbitrariness and individual differences in prototypic concepts. Thus, one person's "terrorist" can be another person's "freedom fighter."

Reasoning

One aspect of intelligent thinking is the ability to reason and think logically. Such thinking helps us acquire knowledge, make sound decisions, and solve problems. Reasoning helps us avoid the hazards and time-consuming efforts of trial and error. Philip Johnson-Laird (2010; Johnson-Laird et al., 1992) proposed that we reason about an observation (e.g., viewing a triangle) by constructing mental models of each possibility based on that observation and our existing knowledge ("this is a square," "this is a triangle"), and then compare each possibility to determine which most closely matches our experience. This process of constructing and comparing mental models suggests that reasoning is based not on formal rules of inference as previously thought, but on internal representations of our world combined with our knowledge about the world.

12. What are concepts, and how do they enter into propositions? How are prototypes involved in concept formation?

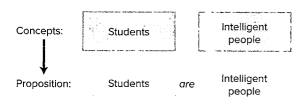

FIGURE 9.15 Concepts are building blocks of thinking and reasoning. Concepts can be combined into propositions to create simple and complex thoughts, and the propositions can serve as the basis for reasoning and discourse.

Deductive Reasoning

Two types of reasoning underlie many of our attempts to make decisions and solve problems (Figure 9.16). In **deductive reasoning,** we reason from the top down, that is, from general principles to a conclusion about a specific case. When people reason deductively, they begin with a set of *premises* (propositions assumed to be true) and determine what the premises imply about a specific situation. Deductive reasoning is the basis of formal mathematics and logic. Logicians regard it as the strongest and most valid form of reasoning because the conclusion *cannot be false* if the premises (factual statements) are true. More formally, the underlying deductive principle may be stated: Given the general proposition "if X, then Y," if X occurs, then you can infer Y. Thus, to use a classic deductive argument, or *syllogism,*

If all humans are mortal (first premise), and

if Socrates is a human (second premise),

then Socrates must be mortal (conclusion).

Inductive Reasoning

In **inductive reasoning,** we reason from the bottom up, starting with specific facts and trying to develop a general principle. Scientists use induction when they discover general principles, or laws, as a result of observing a number of specific instances of a phenomenon. After Ivan Pavlov observed repeatedly that the dogs in his laboratory began to salivate when approached by the experimenter who fed them, he began to think in terms of a general principle that eventually became the foundation of classical conditioning (i.e., repeated CS-UCS pairings produce a CR). A college student who experiences repeated

negative consequences when she gets drunk may eventually conclude that binge drinking is a high-risk behaviour to be avoided.

An important difference between deductive and inductive reasoning lies in the certainty of the results. Deductive conclusions are certain to be true *if* the premises are true, but inductive reasoning leads to likelihood rather than certainty. Even if we reason inductively in a flawless manner, the possibility of error always remains because some new observation may disprove our conclusion. Thus, you may observe that every person named Jordan you have ever met has blue eyes, but it would obviously be inaccurate to reason that, therefore, all people named Jordan have blue eyes.

In daily life and in science, inductive and deductive reasoning may be used at different points in problem solving and decision making. For example, psychologists often make informal observations (e.g., hearing about crime victims such as Kitty Genovese who do not receive help when many bystanders are present). These specific observations may prompt them to construct an initial explanation (e.g., diffusion of responsibility) for the observed phenomenon. This is inductive reasoning, so the explanation could be wrong even if it is consistent with all the known facts. Therefore, scientists move to a deductive process in which they design experiments to formally test specific *if-then* hypotheses, moving now from a general explanatory principle to a specific observation (the experiment's results). If the results of these experimental tests do *not* support their hypotheses, the scientists conclude that their explanation or theory cannot be correct and needs to be revised or discarded.

13. Distinguish between deductive reasoning and inductive reasoning. How do irrelevant information, belief bias, and framing influence reasoning?

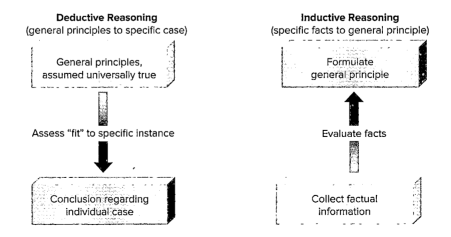

FIGURE 9.16 A comparison of deductive and inductive reasoning.

Stumbling Blocks in Reasoning

The ability to reason effectively is a key factor in critical thinking, sound decision making, and problem solving. Unfortunately, several factors may prevent us from selecting the information needed to draw sound conclusions.

Distraction by irrelevant information. Distinguishing relevant from irrelevant information can be challenging. Consider the following problem. As you solve it, analyze the mental steps you take, and do not read on until you have decided on an answer.

> Your drawer contains 19 black socks and 13 blue socks. Without turning on the light, how many socks do you have to pull out of the drawer to have a matching pair?

As you solved the problem, what information entered into your reasoning? Did you take into account the fact that there were 19 black socks and 13 blue ones? If so, you're like many of Robert Sternberg's (1988) Yale University students who did the same thing, thereby making the problem much more difficult than it should be. In this case, all that matters is how many *colours* of socks there are. It wouldn't matter if there were 1000 socks of each colour; once you have selected any three of them, you are bound to have at least two of the same colour. People often fail to solve problems because they simply don't focus on the *relevant* information. Instead, they take into account irrelevant information that leads them astray.

Belief bias. **Belief bias** is the tendency to abandon logical rules in favour of our own personal beliefs. To illustrate, let us consider an experiment in which college students were asked to judge whether conclusions followed logically from syllogisms like the following:

> All things that are smoked are good for one's health.
>
> Cigarettes are smoked.
>
> Therefore, cigarettes are good for one's health.

What do you think? Is the logic correct? Actually, it is. If we accept (for the moment) that the premises are true, then the conclusion *does* follow logically from the premises. Yet students in one study frequently claimed that the conclusion was not logically correct because they disagreed with the first premise that all things smoked are good for one's health. In this case, their beliefs about the harmful effects of smoking got in the way of their logic. When the same syllogism was presented with a nonsense word, such as *ramadians* substituted for *cigarettes*, the errors in logic were markedly reduced (Markovitz & Nantel, 1989). Incidentally, we agree that the conclusion that cigarettes are good for one's health is factually false. However, it is false because the first premise is false, not because the logic is faulty. Unfortunately, many people confuse factual correctness with logical correctness. The two are not at all the same.

Johnson-Laird (2001) suggests that whereas people construct mental models of the possibilities compatible with a set of premises to determine if a given conclusion is valid, errors in deductive reasoning often occur because people fail to consider all possible models. The stronger your belief in a particular topic, the more you reject other possibilities and the stronger the bias effect (Pennycook et al., 2013). Klauer and colleagues (2000) have suggested that belief bias occurs when people construct only one mental model representing the premises and the conclusion (or its logical negation), leading to biased reasoning. In addition, the more difficult the problem, the stronger the belief bias (Brisson et al., 2014). On the other hand, research using event-related fMRI suggests that emotion may play a role in belief bias—different brain areas were observed to be related to reasoning processes, including activation of the ventral medial prefrontal cortex, a region associated with emotion, when reasoning was influenced by belief bias (Goel & Dolan, 2003).

Emotions and framing. When we evaluate problems or make decisions, at times we may abandon logical reasoning in favour of relying on our emotions—"trusting one's gut"—to guide us (Slovic & Peters, 2006). And even when we try to reason logically, emotions may still creep into the picture.

Reasoning also can be affected by the particular way that information is presented to us, or *framed*. **Framing** refers to the idea that the same information, problem, or options can be structured and presented in different ways. For example, in one classic study, college students who were told that a cancer treatment had a 50 percent success rate judged the treatment to be significantly more effective and expressed a greater willingness to have it administered to a family member than did participants who were told that the treatment had a 50 percent failure rate (Kahneman & Tverksy, 1979). Representing outcomes in terms of positives or negatives has this effect because people tend to assign greater costs to negative outcomes (such as losing $100) than they assign value to an equivalent positive outcome (finding $100). The proposition that "there is a 50 percent chance of failure" evokes thoughts about the patient's dying and causes the 50–50 treatment to appear riskier (Slovic et al., 1988). Similarly, graphs or other visual displays can be designed to make identical information "look different" and, thus, influence people's judgments and decisions (Diacon & Hasseldine, 2007).

Framing influences how we perceive information and can interfere with logical reasoning. This may be especially so when choices are framed to highlight potential positive or negative outcomes, thereby triggering emotions—such as fear, anger, or sadness—that may alter our perceptions of the risks associated with various choice options (Slovic & Peters, 2006). Framing also can enhance reasoning, however, as you'll now see as we discuss problem solving and decision making.

Problem Solving

14. Summarize the four major stages of problem solving. Why are problem framing and mental sets important?

Humans have an unmatched ability to solve problems and adapt to the challenges of their world. People can systematically use inductive and deductive reasoning to solve problems. Such problem solving proceeds through four stages (Figure 9.17). How well we carry out each of these stages determines our success in solving the problem.

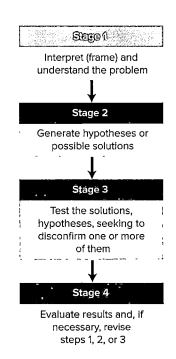

Stage 1
Interpret (frame) and understand the problem

Stage 2
Generate hypotheses or possible solutions

Stage 3
Test the solutions, hypotheses, seeking to disconfirm one or more of them

Stage 4
Evaluate results and, if necessary, revise steps 1, 2, or 3

FIGURE 9.17 Stages of problem solving.

Understanding, or framing, the problem. Most of us have had the experience of feeling totally frustrated in our attempts to solve a problem. We may even think that the problem is unsolvable. Then someone suggests a new way of looking at the problem, and the solution suddenly becomes obvious. How we mentally *frame* a problem can make a huge difference. Consider the following problem (illustrated in Figure 9.18):

> Train A leaves Winnipeg for its 50-kilometre trip to St. Boniface at a constant speed of 25 kilometres/hour. At the same time, Train B leaves St. Boniface, bound for Winnipeg at the same speed of 25 kilometres/hour. An energetic crow leaves Winnipeg at the same time as Train A, flying above the tracks toward St. Boniface at a speed of 60 kilometres/hour. When the crow encounters Train B, it turns and flies back to Train A, then instantly reverses its direction and flies back to Train B. The supercharged bird continues this sequence until Trains A and B meet midway between Winnipeg and St. Boniface. Try to solve this problem before reading on: *What is the total distance the bird will have travelled in its excursions between Trains A and B?*

Many people approach the problem as a distance problem, which is quite natural because the question is stated in terms of distance. They try to compute how far the bird will fly during each segment of its flight between trains A and B, sometimes filling up several pages with increasingly frenzied computations in the process. But suppose you approach the problem by asking not how far the bird will fly but *how long* it will take the trains to meet. The crow will have flown the same period of time at 60 kilometres/hour. Now that you have reframed it as a time problem, the problem becomes much easier to solve. (Check your solution against the answer given at the end of the chapter.)

As you can see, our initial understanding of a problem is a key step toward a successful solution. If we frame a problem poorly, then we can easily be led into a maze of blind alleys and ineffective solutions. If we frame it optimally, then we at least have a chance to generate an effective solution. A knack for framing problems in effective ways that differ from conventional expectations has been called *outside-the-box thinking;* it is a prized ability in many academic and work environments.

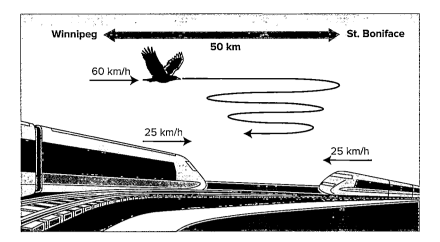

FIGURE 9.18 The crow-and-trains problem. (The answer appears at the end of the chapter.)

Generating potential solutions. Once we have interpreted the problem, we can begin to formulate potential solutions or explanations. Ideally, we might proceed in the following fashion:

1. Determine which procedures and explanations will be considered.

2. Determine which solutions are consistent with the evidence that has so far been observed. Rule out any solutions that do not fit the evidence.

Testing the solutions. Consider the possible solutions that remain. If a solution requires you to choose between specific explanations, ask if there is any test that should give one result if one explanation is true and another result if a different explanation is true. If so, evaluate the explanations again in light of the evidence from that test. In essence, this is what scientists do when they design experiments.

Let us consider a common difficulty in the process of discovering and applying solutions to problems. Consider problem 1 in Figure 9.19:

> You have a 21-cup jug, a 127-cup jug, and a 3-cup jug. Drawing and discarding as much water as you like, how will you measure out exactly 100 cups of water?

> Try to solve all seven problems in Figure 9.19 in order, and write down your calculations for each one before reading on. Does a common solution emerge? If so, can you specify what it is?

As you worked the problems, you probably discovered that they are all solvable by the same formula, namely $B - A - (2 \times C) =$ desired amount. In problem 1, for example, $127 - 21 - (2 \times 3) = 100$. If you discovered this, it gave

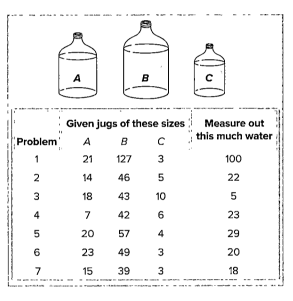

	Given jugs of these sizes			Measure out this much water
Problem	A	B	C	
1	21	127	3	100
2	14	46	5	22
3	18	43	10	5
4	7	42	6	23
5	20	57	4	29
6	23	49	3	20
7	15	39	3	18

FIGURE 9.19 Luchins's water jugs problems. Using containers A, B, and C with the capacities shown in the table, how would you measure out the volumes indicated in the right-hand column? You may discover a general problem-solving schema that fits all seven problems.

you a logical formula that you could apply to the rest of the problems. And it worked, didn't it? However, by applying this successful formula to problems 6 and 7, you may have missed even easier solutions for these last two problems, namely $A - C$ for problem 6 and $A + C$ for problem 7.

Abraham Luchins (1942) developed the water jugs problems to demonstrate the manner in which a **mental set**—the tendency to stick to solutions that have worked in the past—can result in less-effective problem solving. Luchins found that most people who worked on problems 6 and 7 were blinded by the mental set they had developed by working the first five problems. In contrast, people who had not worked on problems 1 through 5 almost always applied the simple solutions to problems 6 and 7. Studies of mental sets show how easy it is to become rigidly fixated on one particular approach that has been successful in the past.

Evaluating results. The final stage of problem solving is to evaluate the solutions. As we saw in the water jugs problems, even solutions that prove successful may not be the easiest or the best. Thus, after solving a problem, we should ask ourselves, "Would there have been an easier or more effective way to accomplish the same objective?" This question can lead to the development of additional problem-solving principles that may be applicable to future problems.

The Role of Problem-Solving Schemas

15. What are problem-solving schemas? Distinguish between algorithms and heuristics. Describe the means-ends and subgoal analysis heuristics.

In solving problems, people often learn to employ shortcut methods that apply to specific situations (Rips, 1997). **Problem-solving schemas** are like mental blueprints or step-by-step scripts for selecting information and solving specialized classes of problems. We have all learned a great many of them, from schemas for cooking dinner to schemas for studying and mastering academic course content (Figure 9.20). Once we master them, we seem to know what to do without having to engage in step-by-step formal problem-solving procedures.

Algorithms and heuristics. *Algorithms* and *heuristics* are two important strategies for problem solving. **Algorithms** are formulas or procedures that automatically generate correct solutions. Mathematical and chemical formulas are algorithms; if you use them correctly, you will always get the correct answer. Consider another example of an algorithm. If the letters of a word are scrambled in random order to produce an anagram like *teralbay*, we can identify the word by using a process in which we rearrange the eight letters in all possible combinations—all 40 320 combinations, that is. As you can see, using algorithms can be very time-consuming. You might therefore decide to use some rule-of-thumb strategy, such as trying out only consonants in the first and last positions, because you know that more words begin and end in consonants than in vowels. When we adopt rule-of-thumb approaches like this, we are using heuristics.

Heuristics are general problem-solving strategies that we apply to certain classes of situations. *Means-ends analysis* is one example of a heuristic (Newell & Simon, 1972). In **means-ends analysis,** we identify differences between the present situation and the desired state, or goal, and then make changes that will reduce these differences. Assume, for example, that you have a 30-page paper due at the end of the term and have not begun working on it yet. The present situation is no pages written; the desired end state is a 30-page paper. What, specifically, needs to be done to reduce that discrepancy, and how are you going to do it?

You would be foolish to decide, "There are 30 days until the paper is due, so all I have to do is write one page a day." This approach is likely to result in a 30-page paper, but it is unlikely to result in one that will earn a passing grade. Instead, you would be wise to use another heuristic known as **subgoal analysis,** formulating subgoals, or intermediate steps, toward a solution. In this case, your expertise as a student will likely lead you to break down the task of writing a paper into subgoals, such as (1) choosing a topic, (2) doing library and Internet research on the topic to get the facts you need, (3) organizing the facts within a general outline of the paper, (4) writing a first draft or specific sections of the paper, (5) reorganizing and refining the first draft, and so on. In so doing, a huge task becomes a series of smaller and more manageable tasks, each with a subgoal that leads you toward the ultimate goal of a quality 30-page paper.

The value of setting subgoals can be seen in the Tower-of-Hanoi problem, which is explained in Figure 9.21. Breaking this task into subgoals

© Digital Images/Getty Images

FIGURE 9.20 Experienced snowboarders and skiers learn schemas for various types of snow, and the discriminations made possible by these schemas can affect planning and decision making. This boarder might approach a slope covered with "powder" differently from one covered with "corn" or "hardpack" because of their different effects on the board and potentially on the boarder's safety.

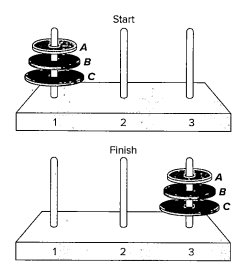

Start

A
B
C

1   2   3

Finish

A
B
C

1   2   3

FIGURE 9.21 The Tower-of-Hanoi problem. The object is to move the rings one at a time from peg 1 to peg 3 in no more than seven moves. Only the top ring on a peg can be moved, and a larger ring can never be placed on top of a smaller one. (The answer appears at the end of the chapter.)

helps us solve the problem. The first subgoal is to get ring C to the bottom of peg 3. The second subgoal is to get ring B over to peg 3. With these two subgoals accomplished, the final subgoal of getting ring A to peg 3 is quite easy. The solution requires planning (hypothesis formation), checking, and revising hypotheses. The correct seven-step sequence of moves appears at the end of the chapter.

Heuristics enter not only into problem-solving strategies but also into a wide range of decisions and judgments, from judgments about other people, to judgments about our own health, to decisions about buying products (Katapodi et al., 2005). As we shall see, heuristics can also contribute to errors in judgment.

Uncertainty, Heuristics, and Decision Making

Few decisions in everyday life can be made with the absolute certainty that comes from applying some mathematical formula or other algorithm. Typically, the best we can hope for is a decision that has a high probability of a positive outcome. Because we seldom know what the exact probabilities are (e.g., how likely it is that the stock market will be up or down when you need your money in the future, or how probable it is that a new dating relationship will become permanent), we tend to apply certain heuristics to form judgments of likelihood. These heuristics can serve us well, but they also can lead to errors in judgment (Kaheman, 2011; Kaheman & Klein, 2009).

In daily life, we routinely make decisions about what other people are like. Suppose, for example, you are given the following description of a young woman:

> Linda is 31 years old, single, outspoken, and very bright. She majored in philosophy. As a student, she was deeply concerned with issues of discrimination and social justice, and she also participated in anti-nuclear demonstrations.

Now rate the likelihood that each of the following hypotheses is true. Use 1 to indicate the most likely statement, 8 to indicate the least likely statement, and any number between 2 and 7 to indicate the likelihood of the second most likely statement.

_____ Hypothesis A: Linda is active in the feminist movement.

_____ Hypothesis B: Linda is a bank teller.

_____ Hypothesis C: Linda is active in the feminist movement and is a bank teller.

Cognitive psychologists Daniel Kahneman and Amos Tversky (1982) used this problem in a series of experiments that studied the role of heuristics in judgment and decision making. They showed that certain heuristics underlie much of our inductive decision making (drawing conclusions from facts) and that their misuse results in many of our thinking errors. Let us examine how that occurs.

The representativeness heuristic. "What does it look (or seem) like?" This decision is probably the first faced by our perceptual system when it processes incoming stimuli. Earlier, we discussed the importance of prototypes in concept formation. We use the **representativeness heuristic** to infer how closely something or someone fits our prototype for a particular concept, or class, and therefore how likely it is to be a member of that class. In essence, we are asking, "How likely is it that this [person, object, event] *represents* that class?" In this case, does Linda seem like a feminist? This question is a perfectly logical one to ask ourselves. Sometimes, however, our use of representativeness can cause us to make decisions that fly in the face of logic.

For example, what was your order of likelihood judgments concerning Linda? Figure 9.22 shows the mean likelihood estimates that university students attached to each statement (a low number indicating greater likelihood). First of all, there is a clear tendency to favour hypothesis A (Linda is a feminist). This tendency is not

16. What role do uncertainty and heuristics play in decision making? How do the representativeness and availability heuristics distort probability judgments?

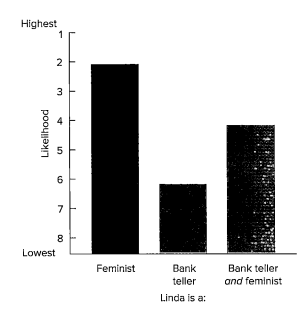

FIGURE 9.22 Illogical judgments. This graph shows the mean likelihood judgments made by participants on the basis of the description of Linda (top left column). Overall, people judge it to be more likely that Linda is a bank teller and a feminist rather than just a bank teller. Logically, this is impossible.

Based on Tversky, A., & Kahneman, D. (1982). "Judgements of and by representativeness". In D. Kahneman, P. Slovic, & A. Tversky (Eds.), *Judgement under uncertainty: Heuristics and biases* (pp. 23–31). Cambridge, MA: Cambridge University Press.

surprising; the description does make her sound like a feminist. However, the significant finding is that hypothesis C (Linda is a feminist bank teller) was favoured over hypothesis B (Linda is a bank teller). But this cannot possibly be correct. Why not? Because everyone who is both a feminist and a bank teller is also *simply* a bank teller. Furthermore, there are many bank tellers who are not feminists, and Linda could be one of them. Stated differently, any person is more likely to be simply a bank teller than to be a bank teller *and* a feminist—or, for that matter, a bank teller and anything else. People who say that hypothesis C is more likely than hypothesis B (and about 85 percent of people given this problem do so) violate the logical principle that the combination of two events cannot be more likely than either event alone.

Tversky and Kahneman believe that the reason people make this sort of error is that they confuse representativeness with probability. Linda represents our prototype for a feminist bank teller better than she fits our prototype for a bank teller. Therefore, we erroneously think the former is more likely than the latter. Notice how this argument fits with the ideas about memory discussed in Chapter 8. On the one hand, the

description of Linda as "outspoken" and "concerned with issues of discrimination and social justice" serves a *priming* function, activating the elements in memory that are associated with the concept of "feminist," so it is hard to think of Linda without thinking of a feminist. On the other hand, there is nothing in Linda's description that would activate the concept of "bank teller." Thus, if Linda is to be a bank teller at all, we think she must be a feminist bank teller. Kahneman (2011) notes that the use of representativeness reflects what he calls *System 1 thinking*—we respond reflexively to situations in order to quickly identify the situation at hand and respond to any perceived danger.

The availability heuristic. Another heuristic that can sometimes lead us astray is the **availability heuristic,** which causes us to base judgments and decisions on the availability of information in memory. We tend to remember events that are most important and significant to us. Usually that principle serves us well, keeping important information at the forefront in our memories, ready to be applied. But if something easily comes to mind, we may exaggerate the likelihood that it could occur. For example, consider each of the following pairs and choose the more likely cause of death:

- murder or suicide?
- botulism or lightning?
- asthma or tornadoes?

When Paul Slovic and his colleagues (1988) asked people to make these judgments, 80 percent chose murder over suicide as the more likely cause of death, 63 percent chose botulism over lightning, and 43 percent chose tornadoes over asthma. In actuality, public health statistics show that people are 25 percent less likely to be murdered than to kill themselves, that lightning kills 53 times more people than botulism does, and that death by asthma is 21 times more likely than death as a result of a tornado. Yet murder, botulism, and tornadoes are more highly and dramatically publicized when they do occur and, thus, are more likely to come to mind.

A recent memorable event can increase people's belief that they may suffer a similar fate. After the terrorist hijackings of September 11, 2001, airline bookings and tourism declined dramatically within the United States for a significant period. Demand for office space in landmark high-rise buildings also declined, and many businesses sought space in less conspicuous suburban settings. Similarly, in the summer of 1975, when Steven Spielberg's movie *Jaws* burned into people's memories graphic images of a great white shark devouring swimmers at a New England seaside town, beach attendance all over the country decreased. In fact, *Jaws* was blamed for a drop in tourism on the New England coast so dramatic that in the summer of 1976 many beachfront resorts nearly went bankrupt. The images available in memory—even though the movie was clearly fiction—increased people's perceived likelihood that they, too, could become shark bait.

Thus, at times the representativeness and availability heuristics can lead us astray by distorting our estimates of how likely an event really is. In other words, they can blind us to the *base rates*, or actual frequencies, at which things occur. In general, it's always best to find out what the actual probabilities are and make judgments on that basis; that's the strategy that allows insurance companies (and casinos) to flourish.

Confirmation Bias and Overconfidence

Sometimes one of the most challenging tasks is obtaining new evidence to test a hypothesis or solution. But what's the best type of evidence? Here is a principle that may seem puzzling to you: The best thing we can do to test our ideas is to seek evidence that will *disconfirm* them, rather than look for evidence that supports them. Why? Because the most informative piece of evidence we can obtain is one that rules out a hypothesis or an idea. Disconfirming evidence proves conclusively that our idea *cannot* be true in its current form. In contrast, confirming evidence only supports our idea. It doesn't prove it with certainty, for it is possible that some future observation will disconfirm it or that another explanation fits the facts even better. Especially in the area of causal beliefs, you can be absolutely sure when you're wrong about something, but you can't be absolutely sure when you're right because there might be a better explanation or an impending observation that calls your belief into question.

Following this disconfirmation principle is easier said than done, because people are often unwilling to challenge their cherished beliefs. Instead, they are prone to fall into a trap called **confirmation bias,** tending to look for evidence that will confirm what they currently believe rather than looking for evidence that could disconfirm their beliefs. Often, when people have strong beliefs about something—including beliefs about themselves—they are very selective in the kinds of information they expose themselves to (Chen et al., 2006). They seek out like-minded

people, compatible mass media sources and Internet sites, and recall feedback from others that confirms their beliefs about themselves. The fact that people find it difficult or even upsetting to test and challenge their ideas, particularly those to which they are strongly committed, can be a major obstacle to getting the evidence needed to make a correct decision.

Confirmation bias often contributes to a distorted sense of how correct our opinions and beliefs are. **Overconfidence,** the tendency to overestimate one's correctness in factual knowledge, beliefs, and decisions, is another reason people do not challenge their beliefs. This tendency, like confirmation bias, is widespread. In one study, college students were asked at the beginning of the academic year to make predictions about how likely it was (from 0 percent to 100 percent) that they would experience any of a long list of personal events, such as dropping a course, breaking up with a romantic partner, or joining a fraternity or sorority. They also indicated how confident they were in their probability estimates (i.e., how likely it was that they would be correct). At the end of the following semester and at the end of the academic year, they indicated which events had in fact occurred. As shown in Figure 9.23, confidence exceeded accuracy overall, and the difference

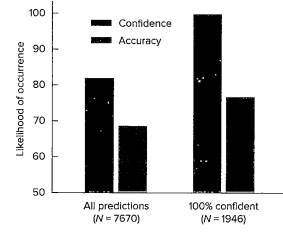

FIGURE 9.23 Displaying overconfidence. Overconfidence is illustrated in the discrepancy between the accuracy with which students predicted that specific events would occur to them during the coming academic year and the degree of confidence that they had in their predictions. Overall, accuracy was considerably lower than confidence level, even for those events for which the students expressed complete certainty.

Source: Based on Vallone, R.P., Griffin, D., Lin, S., & Ross, L. (1990). Overconfident prediction of future actions and outcomes by self and others. *Journal of Personality and Social Psychology,* 58, 582–592.

17. When making decisions, why is disconfirming evidence important? How does overconfidence contribute to confirmation bias?

18. Discuss some factors that inhibit and facilitate creative problem solving.

19. What roles do schemas play in knowledge acquisition and expertise?

between the two was equally great when the students were originally 100 percent confident in their predictions (Vallone et al., 1990). Similar overconfidence effects have been found in studies involving investment professionals, military strategists, weather forecasters, and other populations. It apparently stems from people's need to see themselves as knowledgeable and competent (Blanton et al., 2001).

Overconfidence and confirmation bias can be potent adversaries in our search for correct predictions and decisions. When we're confident in the correctness of our views and reluctant to seek evidence that could prove them wrong, we can easily be blinded to the truth. The *Applications* feature discusses some aspects of creative problem solving.

Knowledge, Expertise, and Wisdom

Knowledge forms a foundation for expertise and wisdom. Each culture passes down its knowledge and world view from one generation to the next through language, instruction, and socialization. This vast library of knowledge, shaped by cultural learning and by other environmental experiences (including trial-and-error learning), also supports the reasoning, decision-making, and problem-solving skills that we have been discussing in this chapter.

Acquiring Knowledge: Schemas and Scripts

One way to think about knowledge acquisition is as a process of building schemas. Most broadly, a **schema** is a mental framework, an organized pattern of thought about some aspect of the world. Concepts and categories represent types of schemas, and together they help you build a mental framework of your world, such as "interesting versus dull people" or "easy versus hard exams." Algorithms and heuristics also are types of schemas—problem-solving schemas—that provide you with mental frameworks for solving certain types of problems.

Another type of schema, called a **script,** is a mental framework concerning a sequence of events that usually unfolds in a regular,

Review

- In deductive reasoning, we reason from general principles to a conclusion about a specific case. Inductive reasoning, in contrast, involves reasoning from a set of specific facts or observations to a general principle. Deduction is the strongest and most valid form of reasoning, because the conclusion cannot be false if the premises are true. Inductive reasoning cannot yield certainty.

- Unsuccessful deductive reasoning can result from (1) failure to select the appropriate information; (2) failure to apply the appropriate deductive reasoning rules, particularly in novel situations; and (3) belief bias, the tendency to abandon logical rules in favour of personal beliefs.

- Problem solving proceeds through a number of steps: (1) understanding the nature of the problem, (2) establishing initial hypotheses or potential solutions, (3) testing the solutions against existing evidence to rule out hypotheses that do not apply, and (4) evaluating results.

- Problem-solving schemas are shortcut methods for solving specialized classes of problems. They are stored in long-term memory and can help to overcome the limitations of working memory. Expertise results from acquiring a range of successful problem-solving schemas through training and practical experience, as well as knowing when to apply them.

- Algorithms are formulas or procedures that guarantee correct solutions. Heuristics are general strategies that may or may not provide correct solutions. Means-ends analysis is one commonly used heuristic. The representativeness heuristic is the tendency to judge evidence according to whether it is consistent with an existing concept or schema. The availability heuristic is the tendency to base conclusions and probability judgments on what is readily available in memory. Humans exhibit confirmation bias, a tendency to look for facts to support hypotheses rather than to disprove them; and they suffer from overconfidence, a tendency to overestimate their knowledge, beliefs, and decisions.

- In some situations, divergent thinking is needed for generating novel ideas or variations on ideas. Functional fixedness can blind us to new ways of using an object or a procedure, thereby interfering with creative problem solving. In some cases, a period of incubation permits problem solving to proceed on a subconscious level while giving the problem solver psychological distance from the problem.

Applications

GUIDELINES FOR CREATIVE PROBLEM SOLVING

Creativity is the ability to produce something that is both new and valuable (Sternberg, 2006). The product may be virtually anything, from a creative painting to a novel approach to solving a problem. In this case, we will be concerned with creative problem solving.

Research on reasoning offers insights into how effective and creative problem solvers think and how they approach problems. In some ways, as experts so often demonstrate, there is no substitute for experience, for it teaches us useful heuristics and problem-solving schemas. Yet one of the marks of creativity is the ability to break out of conventional schemas when the occasion demands it and to engage in **divergent thinking,** the generation of novel ideas that depart from the norm (Guilford, 1959). In part, this means being able to apply concepts or propositions from one domain to another unrelated domain in a manner that produces a new insight. It also means refusing to be constrained by traditional approaches to a problem (Sternberg, 2006). Creative people are, in this respect, intellectual rebels. The constraints created by the tried-and-true can be difficult to overcome.

Consider, for example, the nine-dot problem in Figure 9.24. Many people have difficulty solving this problem. Did you? If so, it is probably because you imposed a traditional but unnecessary constraint on yourself and tried to stay within the boundary formed by the dots. But nothing in the statement of the problem forced you to do so. To solve the problem, you have to think outside the box.

Creative problem solvers are often able to ask themselves questions like the following to stimulate divergent thinking (Simonton, 1999):

• What would work instead?

• Are there new ways to use this? How else could it be used if I modified it in some way? By adding, subtracting, or

rearranging parts, or by modifying the sequence in which things are done, could I make it more useful?

• Do the elements remind me of anything else? What else is like this?

Use some of these questions when trying to solve the candlestick problem illustrated in Figure 9.25.

Solving the problem requires using some of the objects in unconventional ways. Many people, however, are prevented from doing so because of **functional fixedness,** the tendency to be so fixed in their perception of the proper function of an object or a procedure that they are blinded to new ways of using it.

Sometimes creative solutions to problems seemingly appear out of the blue, suddenly popping into our minds in a flash of insight after we have temporarily given up and put the problem aside. **Incubation** is the name given to this phenomenon; it is as if the problem is incubating and being worked on at a subconscious level (Cattell, 1971). Sometimes the best approach when we are stymied by a problem is to put it aside for a while and gain a bit of psychological distance from it. Perhaps this causes mental sets and other biases to dissipate somewhat, allowing a new idea to emerge (Anderson, 1985). In addition, as time passes, new internal or external stimuli may activate a different perspective on the problem, aiding its solution.

As you can see, creative problem solving involves many of the principles discussed earlier in the chapter. We see the operation of means-ends reasoning, the testing of hypotheses, and the need to overcome biases that may cause us to overestimate or underestimate the likelihood of certain outcomes. Here are some other general problem-solving guidelines:

1. When you encounter a new problem you haven't solved before, ask yourself if it is similar to other problems you've solved. Maybe the schema for solving a problem with similar features can be modified to solve this one. Take advantage of the storehouse of knowledge in long-term memory.

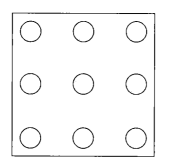

FIGURE 9.24 The nine-dot problem. Without lifting your pencil from the paper, draw no more than four straight lines that will pass through all nine dots. (The answer appears at the end of the chapter.)

FIGURE 9.25 The candlestick problem. Using these objects, find a way to mount the candle on a wall so it functions like a lamp. (The answer appears at the end of the chapter.)

continued

2. Make a true effort to test your ideas. Try to find evidence that would disconfirm your ideas, not evidence that would confirm what you already believe. For example, if you are asked to accept statement X as true, see if you can imagine situations in which X would be false. Beware of the human tendency toward confirmation bias.

3. Be careful not to confuse representativeness with probability. The bird you see that looks too big to be a sparrow but just the right size to be a rare Patagonian warbler is probably . . . a big sparrow; the odds are overwhelmingly in favour of its being a sparrow because there are so many more sparrows (even big ones) than Patagonian warblers.

4. Make use of the means-ends problem-solving heuristic. Ask yourself what you are trying to accomplish, what the present state of affairs is, and what means you have for reducing the discrepancy.

5. Don't be afraid to use a pencil and paper. Orderly notes and schematics can substitute for our rather limited working memory and allow us to have more information at hand to work with.

almost standardized order. For example, if we tell you that "John and Linda went to the movies," these mere seven words convey a lot of information because "going to the movies" is a fairly standardized (i.e., scripted) activity. You can reasonably assume that John and Linda got to the theatre, waited in the ticket line and bought tickets (or bought them online), entered the theatre where someone checked their tickets, bought a snack, found seats, and so on. The scripts that you learn—"attending class," "shopping," "driving," and so on—provide knowledge to guide and interpret actions. In sum, your knowledge grows as you acquire new scripts, concepts, and other types of schemas; as your existing schemas become more complex; and as you form connections between schemas.

The Nature of Expertise

Schemas help to explain what it means to be an expert. Masters and grand masters in chess can glance at a chessboard and quickly plan strategies and make adjustments in the heat of competition. The world's best players can store in memory as many as 50 000 board configurations, together with the locations of the individual pieces (Chase & Simon, 1973). For years, world chess champion Garry Kasparov's sophisticated schemas enabled him to regularly defeat chess-playing computers that used logical rules, even those capable of logically analyzing up to 100 000 moves per second. It took Deep Blue, a 1273 kilogram behemoth capable of calculating at a rate of 200 million positions and 200 000 moves per second, to finally defeat the schemas within Kasparov's 1.4 kilogram brain (Figure 9.26).

Whether in medicine, science, sports, politics, or other fields, experts have developed many schemas to guide problem solving in their field, and just as critically, they are much better

© Adam Nadel/AP Photo

FIGURE 9.26 Chess master Gary Kasparov has developed chess schemas that make him a worthy opponent for even the most sophisticated computers, including IBM's Deep Blue.

than novices at recognizing when each schema should be applied (Montgomery et al., 2005). Applying the correct mental blueprint provides a proven route to solving a problem quickly and effectively.

Expert Schemas and Memory

Consider what the ability to flexibly apply schemas means in terms of what we know about human memory and pattern recognition. As you learned in Chapter 8, schemas reside in long-term memory. Because they rely on learned schemas, experts take advantage of their spacious long-term memory. They can quickly analyze a problem deductively, select the retrieval cues needed to pull the appropriate schema from memory, and apply the schema to solve the problem at hand (Horn & Masunaga, 2000). In contrast, novices who haven't yet learned specialized schemas must use general problem-solving methods in working memory, the space-limited blackboard of the mind (Newell & Simon, 1972). In so doing, they tax their working memory—the weakest link in the human mind.

When people develop expertise, their brain functioning changes in ways that increase processing efficiency. This change occurs even in animals. Thus, as macaque monkeys in one study became experts in categorizing objects, brain recordings revealed quicker and stronger activity in the specific neurons that responded to the important features used to categorize the stimuli (Sigala & Logothetis, 2002).

What Is Wisdom?

Anthropologist Peter Collings (2001) notes that, as in many cultures, the Inuit living in the Arctic of western Canada accord their elders special status and great respect (Figure 9.27). Young and old Inuit alike regard wisdom as a key component of aging successfully. To them, wisdom reflects "the individual's function as a repository of cultural knowledge and his or her involvement in community life by interacting with younger people and talking to them, teaching them about 'traditional' cultural values" (p. 146).

Does the Inuit conception of wisdom coincide with yours? If not, how would you define wisdom? Until the past 20 years, relatively few psychologists explored this issue, but their interest in studying wisdom has grown considerably since then. To German psychologist Paul Baltes and his colleagues, **wisdom** represents a system of knowledge about the meaning and conduct of

© Lawrence Migdale

FIGURE 9.27 Among the Inuit of the Canadian Arctic, wisdom involves extensive cultural knowledge, involvement in community life, and teaching young people about cultural values.

life (Baltes & Kunzmann, 2004). What, then, are the components—the types of schemas—that make up this system of knowledge? One way to answer this question would be to study the characteristics of people who are widely esteemed for their wisdom. Yet, say Baltes and Kunzmann, this approach is not ideal, because "Wise persons are approximations to wisdom, but they are not wisdom" (2004, p. 290). Instead, Baltes and his colleagues took another approach, reviewing numerous cultural, historical, philosophical, religious, and psychological views of wisdom (Baltes & Staudinger, 2000). They concluded that wisdom has five major components:

1. *Rich factual knowledge about life.* This includes knowledge about human nature, social relationships, and major life events.

2. *Rich procedural knowledge about life.* Such knowledge includes strategies for making decisions, handling conflict, and giving advice.

3. *An understanding of lifespan contexts.* This includes an awareness that life involves many contexts, such as family, friends, work, and leisure.

4. *An awareness of the relativism of values and priorities.* This includes recognizing that values and priorities differ across people and societies.

5. *The ability to recognize and manage uncertainty.* This ability stems from an awareness that the future cannot be fully known.

You can readily see from this discussion that expertise and wisdom, though they may partly intersect, are not the same. For example, being an expert does not guarantee the breadth of qualities and knowledge that comprise wisdom. True wisdom, say Baltes and Staudinger, is hard to achieve, for it combines extraordinary scope with "a truly superior level of knowledge, judgment, and advice . . . used for the good or well-being of oneself and that of others" (2000, p. 123).

Mental Imagery

Having spent most of this chapter discussing language and the types of thought that primarily involve what we subjectively experience as inner speech, let's turn to another mode of thought: *mental imagery*. A **mental image** is a representation of a stimulus that originates inside your brain rather than from external sensory input. Nighttime dreams are among the most common forms of mental imagery. During

20. What are some components of wisdom? How do wisdom and expertise differ?

daydreaming, people may intentionally create and manipulate mental images to get a break from reality or relieve boredom. Many elite athletes receive psychological training in how to effectively use mental imagery to rehearse skills, and people from all walks of life may use mental imagery to help to solve problems. By using mental imagery to conduct experiments in their minds, Sir Isaac Newton and Albert Einstein gained insights that led to the discovery of several laws of physics. In a daydream at age 16,

> Einstein imagined himself running alongside a light beam and asked himself the fateful question: what would the light beam look like. Like Newton visualizing throwing a rock until it orbited the earth like the moon, Einstein's attempt to imagine such a light beam would yield deep and surprising results. (Kaku, 2004, p. 43)

Although people have mental images that subjectively involve sounds, tastes, smells, and so on, visual mental images are the most common and most thoroughly researched. Thus, we'll focus on them here.

21. Why was Shepard and Metizer's mental rotation study important? What did they find?

Mental Rotation

Take a look at the objects shown in Figure 9.28. In each pair, are the two objects different, or are they the same object that has simply been rotated to a different orientation? This activity is called a *mental rotation task.* Typically, people rotate one object in their mind's eye until it lines up sufficiently with the other object to permit a same–different judgment. (By the way, in pairs (a) and (b), the objects are the same. In pair (c), they are different.)

In 1971, the journal *Science* published an experiment by psychologists Roger Shepard and Jacqueline Metzler that helped place the study of mental imagery on the scientific map. At a time when cognitive psychology was still in its infancy and emerging from under the shadow of behaviourism's half-century-long dominance, this elegant experiment demonstrated that mental images could be studied by gathering objective data, rather than by relying exclusively on people's subjective self-reports.

Shepard and Metzler presented each participant in their study with 1600 pairs of rotated objects, including the objects shown in Figure 9.28. Upon seeing each pair, participants pulled one of two levers to signal whether the two objects were

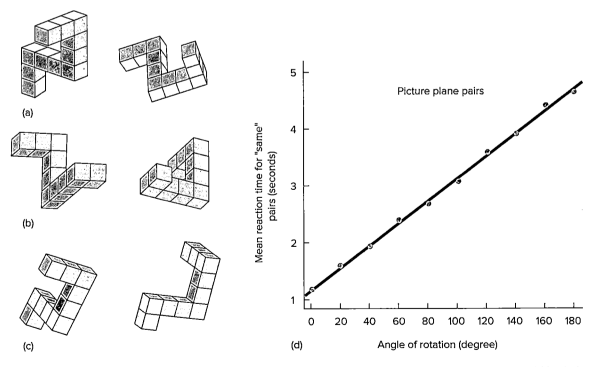

FIGURE 9.28 Mental rotation. (a, b, c) These are three of the many pairs of objects used in Shepard and Metzler's (1971) mental rotation study. (d) This graph shows the average number of seconds it took participants to decide that the two objects in each pair were similar, as a function of the initial angle of rotation. Factoring in the time that it took to make a physical response, participants' speed of mental rotation was approximately 60 degrees per second.

Source: Adapted from R.N. Shepard & J. Metzler, 1971, "Mental Rotation of Three-Dimensional Objects," *Science,* 171, Figures 1 & 2. Reprinted with permission from the American Association for the Advancement of Science.

the same or different, and their speed of response was measured. In 800 of the pairs, the objects within the pair were identical and were rotated from each other at an angle of either 0, 20, 40, 60, 80, 100, 120, 140, 160, or 180 degrees. The two objects in pair (a) and pair (b) in Figure 9.28, for example, are rotated 80 degrees from each other. Because the two objects in pair (c) differ from each other, the concept of angle of rotation does not apply.

Subjectively, the participants reported that they were able to mentally rotate the objects as if the objects existed physically in three-dimensional space (i.e., they could rotate the objects vertically, horizontally, and from front to back) but that the speed of this mental rotation process was limited. Shepard and Metzler's key finding concerned the pairs in which the two objects were the same. On these trials, the greater the difference in rotation between the two pictured objects, the longer it took participants to reach their decision. Moreover, as Figure 9.28d shows, this relation was linear. Shepard and Metzler (1971) concluded, "If we can describe this process as some sort of 'mental rotation in three-dimensional space,' then . . . the average rate at which these particular objects can be thus 'rotated' is roughly 60° per second" (p. 703).

Are Mental Images Pictures in the Mind?

Many researchers believe that mental images, while not literally pictures in the mind, function in ways analogous to actual visual images and are represented in the brain as a type of perceptual code (Kosslyn et al., 2006). If this is the case, then mental images should have qualities similar to those that occur when we perceive objects and scenes in the real world. For example, if the objects portrayed in Figure 9.28 were real objects, you would be able to physically rotate them in three-dimensional space. Shepard and Metzler's (1971) experiment suggested that mental images likewise can be rotated within mental space.

Mental imagery as perception. Based on studies by Stephen Kosslyn, a leading researcher in the field of mental imagery, let's consider an example that illustrates the perceptual nature of mental imagery. Take a look at the island shown in Figure 9.29, and notice that it contains seven landmarks (e.g., a hut, lake, hill, beach), each of which is marked by a red dot. Suppose that after giving you time to memorize this map, we ask you to close your eyes and focus on a mental image of the map. Next, we ask you to (1) focus on a particular landmark (say, the beach), (2) scan the map until you come to the hill, and

FIGURE 9.29 Imagine an island. This island is similar to one used in Kosslyn et al.'s (1978) mental imagery scanning study.

Source: From S.M. Kosslyn, T.M. Ball & B.J. Reiser, 1978, "Human Perception and Performance." *Journal of Experimental Psychology*, 4(51), Fig 2. Copyright © 1978 by the American Psychological Association. Reprinted by permission of the author and the publisher.

(3) press a button (which measures your response time) when you find the hill. On another trial, we might ask you to start at the tree and scan the map until you come to the lake. In total, you will end up taking 21 of these mental trips as you scan once between every possible pair of locations.

In the real world, visually scanning between two objects takes longer when they are farther apart. When Stephen Kosslyn and his colleagues (1978) conducted the actual experiment, they found that the greater the distance between the two locations on the mental image of the map, the longer it took participants to scan and find the second location. This result supports the view that mental images involve a spatial representation. Kosslyn (1978) also conducted experiments that indicated that the size and level of detail of mental images can be changed in ways that correspond to perceiving actual objects.

Mental imagery as language. Some researchers challenge the view that mental images originate from visual codes that are stored in the brain. Instead, they argue that mental imagery is more closely tied to language than to visual perception (Pylyshyn, 2003). According to this view, for example, when you create a mental image of a brick wall, you are not pulling a visual code that represents a brick wall directly out of your long-term memory. Rather, you may subjectively experience a mental image of a brick wall that seems visual, but in reality "brick wall" is being represented by linguistic concepts that are brought together to form propositions ("brick," "bonded with," "mortar," "stacked," "vertical," "spread," "horizontal"). But it must be more than that. Graham et al. (2014) had participants perform a demanding isometric exercise. During a break, half rested quietly, while the other half imagined performing the exercise. All participants then did a second isometric exercise. Those who imagined the exercise during the break were more fatigued during the second effortful task. As the title to their paper suggests, "It wears me out just imagining it!"

Mental Imagery and the Brain

If mental imagery is rooted in perception, then people who experience brain damage that causes perceptual difficulties might also be expected to show similar impairments in forming mental images. In most instances, this seems to be the case, but there are exceptions. For example, some patients who have damage on one side of the brain (usually, the right hemisphere) suffer from a condition called *visual neglect:* They fail to visually perceive objects on the other side (e.g., the left side) of their visual field. If you showed patients who have left-side visual neglect the picture of the island in Figure 9.29 and asked them to draw a copy, they would draw the right side of the island but fail to copy the left side. However, in some cases, if you were to ask the patients to draw the picture from memory (by calling up a mental image of the picture of the island) rather than to copy it (which relies on direct visual perception), they would be able to draw the entire island (Halligan et al., 2003). Most often, however, damage to brain regions involved in perception also disrupts people's ability to form mental images.

Brain-imaging studies of healthy people reveal that many brain regions that become more active when people perceive actual objects also become more active when people form mental images of those objects (Berger & Henrik Ehrsson, 2014; Ganis et al., 2004; Slotnick et al., 2012). Moreover, researchers have found evidence of neurons, called *imagery neurons,* that fire in response to a particular stimulus regardless of whether it is visual (a photo of a baseball) or imagined (a mental image of a baseball). Altogether, studies of brain functioning suggest that while mental imagery and visual perception

do not map onto all the same neural components, there is a lot of overlap between these two processes (Slotnick et al., 2005).

Metacognition: Knowing Your Own Cognitive Abilities

Have you ever had a friend or classmate say to you after an exam, "I don't understand why I got this question wrong" or "I don't understand how I got such a low grade—I thought I really knew this stuff"? Have you ever felt that way?

Recognizing What You Do and Don't Know

To cognitive psychologists, the term **metacognition** refers to your awareness and understanding of your own cognitive abilities. For example, comprehension has to do with understanding something, such as a concept that you just read about. You may *think* you understand the concept, but in actuality you may or may not understand it. Metacognition has to do with truly knowing whether you do or do not understand the concept. The particular component of metacognition that we're discussing in this case is *metacomprehension.* In other words, people who display good metacomprehension are accurate in judging what they do or don't know, whereas people with poor metacomprehension have difficulty judging what they actually do and don't understand. They may typically think they understand things that, in fact, they don't, or they may often think they don't understand things that they actually do.

Metacomprehension is only one aspect of metacognition. Another component, called *metamemory,* represents your awareness and knowledge of your memory capabilities. For example, suppose that you try to memorize a list of definitions or facts. Your ability to accurately judge how well you will be able to remember those items for an upcoming test reflects one aspect of metamemory. In this discussion, however, we'll focus on metacomprehension.

As a student, your ability to effectively monitor what you do and don't know is an important ingredient in studying efficiently (Koriat & Bjork, 2005; Schraw, Crippen, & Hartley, 2006; Son & Metcalfe, 2000). Some students excel at this. Unfortunately, many studies have found that when it comes to reading text material, students, overall, are only mildly to moderately accurate in judging how well they understand what they are reading. Our *Research Foundations* feature examines one technique for improving students' metacomprehension.

22. Does research, including brain research, support the view that mental images are perceptual in nature? Explain.

23. What is metacognition? Identify two types of metacognition, and provide examples.

Research Foundations

"WHY DID I GET THAT WRONG?" IMPROVING STUDENTS' AWARENESS OF WHETHER THEY UNDERSTAND TEXT MATERIAL

Introduction

According to psychologists Keith Theide and Mary Anderson, this study is the first to examine whether students' meta-comprehension for text material can be enhanced by requiring them to write summaries of that material. Theide and Anderson hypothesized that students who write delayed summaries of passages of text material will show better metacomprehension than students who write immediate summaries or no summaries. Presumably, the task of writing delayed rather than immediate summaries taps more powerfully into students' long-term memory and provides them with a better opportunity to assess whether they truly understand what they have read.

Method

Ethnically diverse samples of 75 and 90 university students taking introductory psychology participated, respectively, in Experiment 1 and Experiment 2. The students in each experiment read six passages of text material, with each passage focusing on a different topic (e.g., black holes, global warming, genetics, intelligence, Norse settlements). In Experiment 1, the passages were each about 220 words long, whereas in Experiment 2 they were much longer (1100 to 1600 words) and more similar in style to material presented in textbooks.

Students in each experiment were randomly assigned to one of three groups. In the no-summary group (control group), they read all six passages and then rated their comprehension of each passage ("How well do you think you understood the passage?") on a scale ranging from 1 ("very poorly") to 7 ("very well"). In the immediate-summary group, students summarized each passage immediately after they read it and then, after finishing all six summaries, rated their comprehension of each one. In the delayed-summary group, students read all six passages before summarizing each one and then rating their comprehension of each passage.

All students, after rating their comprehension, took a multiple-choice comprehension test for each passage that included both factual and conceptual questions. These tests enabled Theide and Anderson to measure how well students' *beliefs* about their comprehension (measured by the rating scales) correlated with their actual comprehension (measured by their test scores). The Design box summarizes the basic design of this research.

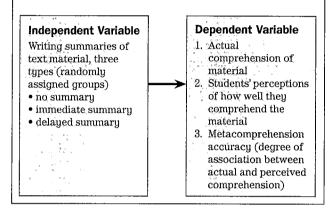

Design

Question: Will writing summaries of text material that they have read improve students' accuracy in judging how well they understand that material?

Type of Study: *Experimental*

Independent Variable	Dependent Variable
Writing summaries of text material, three types (randomly assigned groups) • no summary • immediate summary • delayed summary	1. Actual comprehension of material 2. Students' perceptions of how well they comprehend the material 3. Metacomprehension accuracy (degree of association between actual and perceived comprehension)

Results

In all three conditions, there was a positive correlation between students' comprehension ratings and comprehension scores, but in the no-summary and immediate-summary groups, this correlation was only weak to moderate. The critical finding was that in both experiments, students in the delayed-summary group were much more accurate than the other students in judging whether they knew or didn't know the material. In other words, the correlation between their comprehension ratings and their comprehension test scores was much stronger (Figure 9.30).

The data also revealed that, overall, the three groups did not differ in their comprehension ratings or in their test performance. In other words, students in the delayed-summary group did not feel that they knew the material better, and in fact they didn't. Rather, summarizing the passages after a time delay helped them become more accurate in distinguishing the material they did know from the material they didn't.

Discussion

Both experiments supported the researchers' hypothesis: Students' ability to accurately determine how well they understood passages of text improved greatly when they summarized that material after a time delay. Because the delayed-summary group did not rate their comprehension higher or perform better on the comprehension tests than

continued

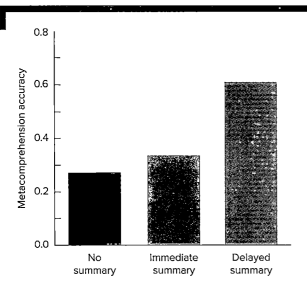

FIGURE 9.30 Writing summaries helps us recognize what we do and don't know. Students who wrote delayed summaries of text material showed far better metacomprehension than did students who wrote immediate summaries or no summaries.

Source: Reprinted from *Contemporary Educational Psychology*, 28(2), K.W. Thiede & M. Anderson, 2003, "Summarizing can improve metacomprehension accuracy," pp. 129–160, Fig 3. Copyright © 2003 Elsevier. Reprinted by permission.

Source: Keith W. Theide and Mary C.M. Anderson (2003). Summarizing can improve metacomprehension accuracy. *Contemporary Educational Psychology*, 28, 129–160.

the other groups, we want to take special care in making sure that you do *not* reach the wrong conclusion of "So what if metacomprehension improved? The students didn't do better on the test."

Realize that the students in this experiment were not allowed to go back and study the text passages again before taking the comprehension tests. Therefore, students in the delayed-summary group did not have the opportunity to act on their superior metacognitive knowledge (i.e., to bone up on the material that they accurately felt they didn't know). But in real-world test situations, students who are better at recognizing what they know and don't know can indeed put that information to efficient use in the days and the hours before a test. They can allocate more time to studying the material they have found difficult and less time to the material that they already understand. Students with poor metacomprehension may end up allocating their study time less efficiently, ignoring material that they think they know but truly don't. Indeed, Theide and Anderson found in Experiment 2 that when all the students were asked to identify the passages of text that, hypothetically, they would select to restudy for an exam, students in the delayed-summary group were the most likely to accurately select the passages that they had learned least well.

Further Advice on Improving Metacomprehension

24. Based on the Research Foundations feature and other research, describe some ways to enhance meta comprehension.

In Chapter 1's *Applications* feature, we discussed several study strategies that can enhance your academic performance. As a student, you also want to be able to accurately assess your understanding of how well you know the material *before* it's time to take a test. One way to do this is to take advantage of practice tests, such as those found in study guides. Trying to memorize specific questions and answers from practice tests—as some students do—will do little to help you assess your broader understanding of the material. Instead, seriously study the material first and then try to answer the questions. For each question, rate how confident you are that your answer is right; this may help you develop a better sense of whether your metacomprehension is good.

The study discussed in the *Research Foundations* feature found that writing delayed summaries improved students' metacomprehension, and other research finds that writing summaries boosts actual comprehension of

text material (Winne & Hadwin, 1998). Many university textbooks provide preview questions or review questions in each chapter. In this textbook, there are focus questions in the margins of each chapter. Use these focus, preview, or review questions as the basis for writing brief summaries of the text. It's not magic. It takes time and effort. But in writing these summaries, if you find yourself struggling to remember the material or if you have a hard time articulating the main concepts, then you have gained the knowledge that you need to restudy this material or seek assistance in trying to understand it.

Finally, you may consider assessing your confidence on your answers to multiple choice questions as you answer them. Couchman et al. (2015) found that confidence ratings of each question were better predictors of overall performance than students perceptions of how well they knew the material before or after the exam.

In closing this chapter, Figure 9.31 provides a levels-of-analysis summary of some of the aspects of thinking that we have discussed.

Levels of Analysis | Thinking Processes

We have now covered diverse aspects of human thought. The subjective experience of thinking fits squarely within the psychological level of analysis, but as we now recap, research on thinking spans the biological, psychological, and environmental levels of analysis.

ENVIRONMENTAL

- Irrelevant information can impair reasoning.
- How a question is framed influences our ability to reason logically.
- The resemblance of a stimulus to a prototype can prompt the proper or improper use of the representativeness heuristic.
- Dramatic, vivid events may lead us to overestimate the likelihood of such future events.
- Cultural and educational experiences foster expertise and wisdom.
- Following instructions to write a delayed summary of textbook material increases students' metacomprehension.

BIOLOGICAL

- Conscious thoughts exist as patterns of neural activity.
- Developing expertise changes brain functioning in ways that improve processing efficiency.
- In general, during mental imagery the brain's activity corresponds to that of visual perception.
- Often, brain damage that disrupts visual perception also impairs mental imagery.

PSYCHOLOGICAL

- Much of our thinking involves concepts and takes the form of propositional thought.
- Belief bias can impair logical reasoning.
- We often rely on heuristics to solve problems and make decisions.
- At times the representativeness and availability heuristics, confirmation bias, and overconfidence may impair our decision making.
- To solve problems in their fields, experts make more effective use of schemas than do novices.
- In some ways, mental images function analogously to visual images.

Consider this possible interaction between the environmental and psychological levels of analysis. Do you think that educational experiences or training about thinking errors and biases would reduce people's future tendency to display such errors and biases?

FIGURE 9.31

In Review

- At the level of the brain, thoughts are patterns of neural activity. At the level of the mind, thoughts are propositional, imaginal, or motoric mental representations.
- Concepts are mental categories, or classes, that share certain characteristics. Many concepts are based on prototypes, the most typical and familiar members of a class. How much something resembles the prototype determines whether the concept is applied to it. Propositional thought involves the use of concepts in the form of statements.

- In deductive reasoning, we reason from general principles to a conclusion about a specific case. Inductive reasoning involves reasoning from a set of specific facts or observations to a general principle. Deduction is the strongest and most valid form of reasoning because the conclusion cannot be false if the premises are true. Inductive reasoning cannot yield certainty.
- Unsuccessful deductive reasoning can result from (1) failure to select relevant information; (2) failure to apply the appropriate

deductive-reasoning rules, particularly in novel situations; (3) belief bias, the tendency to abandon logical rules in favour of personal beliefs; and (4) emotional reactions and framing effects.

- Problem solving proceeds through several steps: (1) understanding the nature of the problem, (2) establishing initial hypotheses or potential solutions, (3) testing the solutions against existing evidence, and (4) evaluating the results of these tests.

- People use several types of problem-solving schemas. Algorithms are formulas or procedures that guarantee correct solutions. Heuristics are general strategies that may or may not provide correct solutions. Means-ends analysis is a common heuristic. The representativeness heuristic is the tendency to judge evidence according to whether it is consistent with an existing concept or schema. The availability heuristic is the tendency to base conclusions and probability judgments on what is readily available in memory.

- Humans exhibit confirmation bias, a tendency to look for facts to support hypotheses rather than to disprove them. They also suffer from overconfidence, a tendency to overestimate their knowledge, beliefs, and decisions.

- In some situations, divergent thinking is needed for generating novel ideas or variations on ideas. Functional fixedness can blind us to new ways of using an object or a procedure, thereby interfering with creative problem solving. Sometimes, a period of incubation permits problem solving to proceed on a subconscious level while giving the problem solver psychological distance from the problem.

- Knowledge acquisition can be viewed as a process of building schemas, which are mental frameworks. Scripts, which are one type of schema, provide a framework for understanding sequences of events that usually unfold in a regular, almost standardized, order.

- Experts rely heavily on schemas that they have developed from experience. Compared with novices, experts have more schemas to guide problem solving in their field and are much better at recognizing when each schema should be applied. Schemas also enable experts to take greater advantage of long-term memory.

- Wisdom represents a system of knowledge about the meaning and conduct of life. According to one model, wisdom has five major components: rich factual knowledge, rich procedural knowledge, an understanding of lifespan contexts, an awareness of the relativism of values and priorities, and the ability to recognize and manage uncertainty.

- A mental image is a representation of a stimulus that originates inside the brain rather than from external sensory input. The objective, quantifiable study of mental imagery received a huge boost from research examining people's ability to mentally rotate objects.

- Mental images of objects seem to have properties that are analogous to the properties of actual objects (e.g., you can rotate them, visually scan them). Thus, one viewpoint holds that mental images are basically perceptual in nature. A second viewpoint proposes that mental images actually are based on language. Overall, brain research offers more support to the imagery-as-perception view.

Gaining Direction

What are the issues?

The opening vignette describes the tragic cases of Victor, Genie, and Dominique. These three children were more or less isolated from birth. Their interaction with adults was severely restricted, and it appears that they were rarely, if ever, spoken to. When rescued, they all began to use speech, but only Dominique continued to develop normal language abilities. Was there something different about Dominique's case? Why did she appear to develop normally, whereas Victor and Genie did not? Such tragic cases provide us with an opportunity to examine the "forbidden experiment." Should we investigate language development in this fashion? Are there ethical concerns?

What do we need to know?

How does human language develop?
Is experience necessary for language acquisition?
What are the properties of a language?
Is there a sensitive period for language learning?

How did Victor's, Genie's, and Dominique's isolation differ?
How do we learn language?
Is it ethical to study abused children?

<table>
<tr><td>**Where can we find the information to answer these questions?**</td><td>You might want to start by reviewing the information on general issues in language acquisition. Pay close attention to what we know about the biological underpinnings of language and how experience shapes our use of language.</td><td>Note as well the material on second language learning. The *Frontiers* feature on language acquisition in animals will also be helpful. A wealth of information on isolated children can be found at http://feralchildren.info.</td></tr>
</table>

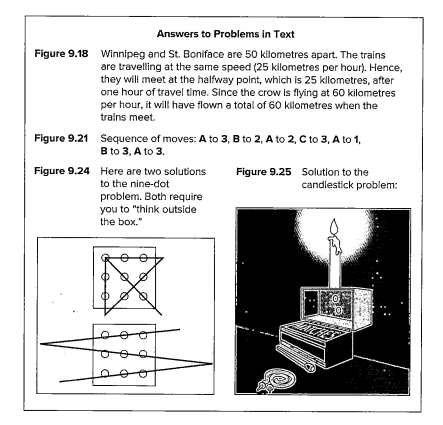

Answers to Problems in Text

Figure 9.18   Winnipeg and St. Boniface are 50 kilometres apart. The trains are travelling at the same speed (25 kilometres per hour). Hence, they will meet at the halfway point, which is 25 kilometres, after one hour of travel time. Since the crow is flying at 60 kilometres per hour, it will have flown a total of 60 kilometres when the trains meet.

Figure 9.21   Sequence of moves: **A** to **3**, **B** to **2**, **A** to **2**, **C** to **3**, **A** to **1**, **B** to **3**, **A** to **3**.

Figure 9.24   Here are two solutions to the nine-dot problem. Both require you to "think outside the box."

Figure 9.25   Solution to the candlestick problem:

Intelligence

CHAPTER **>**
OUTLINE

INTELLIGENCE IN HISTORICAL PERSPECTIVE

Sir Francis Galton: Quantifying Mental Ability

Alfred Binet's Mental Tests

Binet's Legacy: An Intelligence-Testing
  Industry Emerges

THE NATURE OF INTELLIGENCE

The Psychometric Approach: The Structure of Intellect

Cognitive Process Approaches: The Nature of
  Intelligent Thinking

Broader Conceptions of Intelligence:
  Beyond Mental Competencies

THE MEASUREMENT OF INTELLIGENCE

Increasing the Informational Yield from
  Intelligence Tests

Theory-Based Intelligence Tests

Should We Test for Aptitude or Achievement?

Psychometric Standards for Intelligence Tests

Assessing Intelligence in Non-Western Cultures

  Focus on Neuroscience: Brain Size and Intelligence

HEREDITY, ENVIRONMENT, AND INTELLIGENCE

GROUP DIFFERENCES IN INTELLIGENCE

  Applications: Early-Childhood Interventions: A Means
  of Boosting Intelligence?

Ethnic Group Differences

Sex Differences in Cognitive Abilities

  Research Foundations: Effects of Hormonal
  Fluctuations on Perceptual and Motor Skills

EXTREMES OF INTELLIGENCE

The Intellectually Gifted

  Frontiers: Musical Training and Auditory Processing

The Intellectually Disabled

A Concluding Thought

> Many highly intelligent people are poor thinkers. Many people of average intelligence
> are skillful thinkers. The power of a car is separate from the way the car is driven.
> —Edward De Bono

 In the 1988 Oscar-winning movie *Rain Man*, the inspiration for Dustin Hoffman's character was Kim Peek. When Peek came into this world on November 11, 1951, he was born without a corpus callosum, and a damaged cerebellum. Although he did not walk until the age of four, he began to demonstrate some special abilities early in his life. By 20 months of age, he was able to memorize every book read to him—in a single reading. By the time he was three years old, he could use the dictionary, look up words alphabetically, pronounce them correctly, and remember the

© Universal/courtesy Everett Collection/The Canadian Press

What are the
issues here?

What do we need
to know?

Where can
we find the
information
to answer the
questions?

definition. Peek could tell you practically anything about world history, geography, sports, movies, and literature. In all, his expertise spanned 14 different content areas. He read and memorized over 7600 books and, knowing your birthday, could tell you without hesitation on what day of the week you would turn 65 years old.

Peek had autism and his tested IQ was over two standard deviations below normal. He died in 2009.

 In Western cultures, being smart is typically thought of as having good mental skills that are instrumental to succeeding in school and in higher-level jobs and occupations. As we shall see, people with good mental skills do indeed do better in school and on the job in our culture. But if we view intelligence in a broader perspective as the ability to respond adaptively to the demands of a particular environment, we see that other cultures are less impressed with the products of Anglo-Saxon education than we are. It's important to remember, then, that intelligence is not something that has concrete existence; it is, instead, a socially constructed concept (Sternberg, 2004; Figure 10.1).

In previous chapters, we have explored general principles of human learning, memory, thinking, reasoning, and problem solving. In all these areas, we have seen that people differ widely in how effectively they learn, remember, think, and behave. Is it therefore the case that some people are generally more intelligent than others? If so, can we measure these differences and use the measures to predict success and failure in real-life settings? What is the nature of intelligence, and what factors account for the differences we observe in people's cognitive, emotional, and behavioural skills? Attempts to answer these questions have influenced our culture enormously. Today, there exists a multi-billion-dollar intelligence-testing industry. You yourself have undoubtedly taken mental ability tests for educational or occupational reasons.

As we shall see, however, even after more than a century of research and theory development, there are still sharp disagreements about what intelligence is. In our discussion, we use the following definition, which accommodates most viewpoints: **Intelligence** is the ability to acquire knowledge, to think and reason effectively, and to deal adaptively with the environment.

(top): © Creatas/AGE Fotostock; (bottom): ton koene/Alamy Stock Photo

FIGURE 10.1 The skills required to adapt successfully to environmental demands may differ from culture to culture, suggesting to some theorists that what constitutes intelligence may be somewhat culture-specific.

1. What is our working definition of intelligence?

INTELLIGENCE IN HISTORICAL PERSPECTIVE

Historically, two scientists with entirely different agendas played seminal roles in the study and measurement of mental skills. The contributions of Sir Francis Galton and Alfred Binet set the stage for later attempts to measure intelligence and discover its causes.

Sir Francis Galton: Quantifying Mental Ability

Sir Francis Galton was a cousin of Charles Darwin and was strongly influenced by Darwin's theory of evolution (Figure 10.2). In his book *Hereditary Genius* (1869), Galton showed through the study of family trees that eminence and genius seemed to occur within certain families. No intellectual slouch himself, young Francis wrote a childhood letter to his sister that contained the following: "My dear Adele, I am 4 years old, and I can read any English book. I can say all of the Latin substantives and adjectives and active verbs besides 52 lines of Latin poetry."

Galton's research convinced him that eminent people had "inherited mental constitutions" that made them more fit for thinking than their less successful counterparts. Exhibiting his own belief bias, Galton dismissed the fact that the more successful people he studied almost invariably came from privileged environments.

Galton then attempted to demonstrate a biological basis for eminence by showing that people who were more socially and occupationally successful would also perform better on a variety of laboratory tasks thought to measure the "efficiency of the nervous system." He developed measures of reaction speed, hand strength, and sensory acuity. He even measured the size of people's skulls, believing that skull size reflected brain volume and hence intelligence.

In time, Galton's approach to mental-skills measurement fell into disfavour because his measures of nervous-system efficiency proved unrelated to socially relevant measures of mental ability, such as academic and occupational success. Nonetheless, Galton's work created an interest in the measurement of mental abilities, setting the stage for the pioneering work of Alfred Binet.

Alfred Binet's Mental Tests

The modern intelligence-testing movement began at the turn of the 20th century, when the French psychologist Alfred Binet was commissioned by France's Ministry of Public Education to develop the test that was to become the forerunner of all modern intelligence tests (Figure 10.3). Unlike Galton, with whom he had trained, Binet was interested in solving a practical problem rather than supporting a theory. Certain children seemed unable to benefit from normal public schooling. Educators wanted an objective way to identify these children as early as possible so that some form of special education could be arranged for them.

2. How did Galton and Binet differ in their approaches to measuring mental abilities?

US National Library of Medicine

FIGURE 10.2 Sir Francis Galton pioneered the study of intelligence with his studies of hereditary genius.

US National Library of Medicine

FIGURE 10.3 Alfred Binet developed the first intelligence test to assess the mental skills of French school children. His test launched the modern intelligence-testing movement.

In developing his tests, Binet made two assumptions about intelligence: First, mental abilities develop with age. Second, the rate at which people gain mental competence is a characteristic of the person and is fairly constant over time. In other words, a child who is less competent than expected at age five should also be lagging at age ten.

To develop a measure of mental skills, Binet asked experienced teachers what sorts of problems children could solve at ages three, four, five, and so on, up through the school years. He then used their answers to develop a standardized interview in which an adult examiner posed a series of questions to a child to determine whether the child was performing at the correct mental level for his or her age (Table 10.1). The result of the testing was a score called the **mental age.** For instance, if an eight-year-old child could solve problems at the level of the average ten-year-old, the child would be said to have a mental age of ten. For the French school system, the practical implication was that educational attainment could be enhanced if placement in school were based at least in part on the child's mental age. An eight-year-old child with a mental age of six could hardly be expected to cope with the academic demands of a normal classroom for eight-year-olds.

The concept of mental age was subsequently expanded by the German psychologist William Stern to provide a relative score—a common yardstick of intellectual attainment—for people of different chronological ages. Stern's **intelligence quotient (IQ)** was the ratio of mental age to chronological age, multiplied by 100: $IQ = $ (mental age/chronological age) $\times$ 100. Thus, a child who was performing at exactly his or her age level would have an IQ of 100. In our previous example, the child with a mental age of ten and a chronological age of eight would have an IQ of $(10/8) \times 100 = 125$. A 16-year-old with a mental age of 20 would also have an IQ of 125, so the two would be comparable in intelligence even though their ages differed.

TABLE 10.1   Sample Problems from the Stanford-Binet Intelligence Test That Should Be Answered Correctly at Particular Ages

Age 3—Child should be able to
- Point to objects that serve various functions, such as "goes on your feet."
- Name pictures of objects such as *chair* and *flag*.
- Repeat a list of two words or digits—e.g., *car, dog*.

Age 4—Child should be able to
- Discriminate visual forms such as squares, circles, and triangles.
- Define words such as *ball* and *bat*.
- Repeat 10-word sentences.
- Count up to four objects.
- Solve problems such as "In daytime it is light; at night it is . . ."

Age 6—Child should be able to
- State the differences between similar items such as *bird* and *dog*.
- Count up to nine blocks.
- Solve analogies such as "An inch is short; a mile is . . ."

Age 9—Child should be able to
- Solve verbal problems such as "Tell me a number that rhymes with tree."
- Solve simple arithmetic problems such as "If I buy 4 cents' worth of candy and give the storekeeper 10 cents, how much money will I get back?"
- Repeat four digits in reverse order.

Age 12—Child should be able to
- Define words such as *muzzle*.
- Repeat five digits in reverse order.
- Solve verbal absurdities such as "Bill's feet are so big he has to pull his trousers over his head. What is foolish about that?"

---

3. Why do today's intelligence tests no longer use the concept of mental age? How is IQ now defined?

Today's tests no longer use the concept of mental age. Although the concept works pretty well for children, many of the basic skills measured by intelligence tests are acquired by about age 16 through normal life experiences and schooling, so that Stern's quotient is less useful for adults. Moreover, some intellectual skills show an actual decline at advanced ages. If we applied Stern's definition of IQ to a 20-year-old who performed at the typical level of an 80-year-old, we would have to say that the 20-year-old's IQ was 400! To deal with these problems, today's intelligence tests provide an "IQ" score that is not a quotient at all. Instead, it is based on a person's performance relative to the scores of other people the same age, with a score of 100 corresponding to the average performance of that age group.

Binet's Legacy: An Intelligence-Testing Industry Emerges

Lewis Terman (Figure 10.4), a professor at Stanford University, was intrigued by Binet's work. He revised Binet's test for use in the United States, translating it into English and rewriting some of its items to improve their relevance to American culture. Terman's revised test became known as the *Stanford-Binet*. By the mid-1920s, it had become widely accepted in North America as the gold standard for measuring mental aptitude. The Stanford-Binet contained mostly verbal items, and it yielded a single IQ score.

At about the time that the Stanford-Binet test was introduced in 1916, the United States entered World War I. One of Terman's students

4. What was Wechsler's concept of intelligence? How do the Wechsler scales reflect this concept?

FIGURE 10.4 Lewis Terman imported the intelligence test developed by Binet to the United States and revised it as the Stanford- Binet Scale. The Stanford-Binet became the standard for future individually administered intelligence tests and is still used today.

at Stanford, Arthur Otis, had been working on a group-administered test of intellectual ability. This test became the prototype for the *Army Alpha,* a verbally oriented test that was used to screen large numbers of U.S. Army recruits for intellectual fitness. Because some recruits were unable to read, a non-verbal instrument using mazes, picture-completion problems, and digit-symbol tasks was also developed and given the name *Army Beta.* Before the war's end, more than 1.7 million men had been screened for intelligence using these tests.

Inspired by the success of the Army Alpha and Beta for measuring the intelligence of large numbers of people in a group setting, educators clamoured for similar instruments to test groups of children. New group tests of intelligence, such as the Lorge-Thorndike Intelligence Test and the Otis-Lennon School Ability Test, soon appeared and became an important part of educational reform and policy. Many school districts use these or similar tests routinely, and you are likely to have taken one or more of them during your earlier school years.

Two decades after Terman introduced the American version of Binet's test, psychologist David Wechsler developed a major competitor to the Stanford-Binet. Wechsler believed that the Stanford-Binet relied too much on verbal skills. He thought that intelligence should be measured as a group of distinct but related verbal *and* non-verbal abilities. He therefore developed intelligence tests for adults and for children that measured both verbal and non-verbal intellectual skills. In 1939, the Wechsler Adult Intelligence Scale (WAIS) appeared, followed by the Wechsler Intelligence Scale for Children (WISC) in 1955, and the Wechsler Preschool and Primary Scale of Intelligence (WPPSI) in 1967. The Wechsler scales have undergone several revisions. Today, the Wechsler tests (WAIS-IV and WISC-V) are the most popular individually administered intelligence tests in North America (Newmark, 2005). Following Wechsler's lead, the Stanford-Binet has also been revised to measure a wider range of mental abilities. Later in the chapter, we'll take a closer look at the Wechsler tests, as well as other measures that assess various classes of mental skills.

Intelligence has long been a major focus of psychological research, much of which has been inspired by questions that, even after a century of research, continue to evoke disagreement and controversy (Bartholomew, 2004; Naglieri, 2015). Should we regard intelligence as a single aptitude or as many specific abilities? Is intelligence an innate mental capacity, or is it a product of our upbringing? What kinds of brain processes underlie mental skills? Are there actually multiple intelligences, including some that may have little to do with mental skills? These and other questions have inspired a fascinating odyssey of scientific discovery. We begin with the most basic question of all: Just what is this attribute we call *intelligence?*

THE NATURE OF INTELLIGENCE

Psychologists have used two major approaches in the study of intelligence (Sternberg et al., 2003). The *psychometric approach* attempts to map the structure of intellect and to discover the kinds of mental competencies that underlie test performance. The *cognitive processes approach* studies the specific thought processes that underlie those mental competencies.

The Psychometric Approach: The Structure of Intellect

Psychometrics is the statistical study of psychological tests. The psychometric approach to intelligence tries to identify and measure the abilities that underlie individual differences in performance. In essence, it tries to provide a measurement-based map of the mind.

Factor Analysis

Psychometric researchers have long sought to identify the mental abilities of the human mind. How many are there? Are there dozens, or are there perhaps only one or a few basic abilities that underlie performance across diverse tasks? What is the nature of these abilities?

To answer questions like these, researchers administer diverse measures of mental abilities and then correlate them with one another. They reason that if certain tests are correlated highly with one another—if they "cluster" mathematically—then performance on these tests probably reflects the same underlying mental skill. Further, if the tests within a cluster correlate highly with one another but much less with tests in other clusters, then these various test clusters probably reflect different mental abilities. Thus, researchers hope to determine the number of test clusters and to use this information to infer the nature of the underlying abilities.

When large numbers of tests are correlated with one another, many correlation coefficients result, and it is difficult to determine by visual examination the actual patterning of the test scores. Fortunately, a statistical technique called **factor analysis** reduces a large number of measures to a smaller number of clusters, or factors, with each cluster containing variables that correlate highly with one another but less highly with variables in other clusters. A factor allows us to infer the underlying characteristic that presumably accounts for the links among the variables in the cluster.

To illustrate with a highly simplified example the kind of clustering of tests that we are interested in, consider the small correlation matrix in Table 10.2, based on only six different mental ability tests. (There might be as many as 10 to 15 tests in an actual study.) Examination of Table 10.2 reveals two clusters of tests. Tests 1, 2, and 3 correlate highly with one another. Tests 4, 5, and 6 also show high positive correlations with one another. But tests 1, 2, and 3 do not correlate highly with tests 4, 5, and 6. This indicates that the two sets of tests are measuring different abilities. A factor analysis would tell us that there are two different factors.

5. How is factor analysis used in the study of intelligence?

TABLE 10.2 Correlations among Six Cognitive Ability Tests

Test	1	2	3	4	5	6
1	1.00	0.84	0.79	0.46	0.39	0.43
2		1.00	0.87	0.51	0.48	0.54
3			1.00	0.47	0.50	0.48
4				1.00	0.88	0.91
5					1.00	0.82
6						1.00

But what are these two sets of tests measuring? The factor analysis cannot answer this question; it can only identify the clusters for us. It's now up to us to examine the nature of the tests within each cluster and decide what the underlying factors might be. Suppose that test 1 is a measure of vocabulary, test 2 measures reading comprehension, and test 3 requires respondents to complete sentences with missing words. Because all three tasks involve the use of words, we might decide to call the underlying factor "verbal ability." Inspection of tests 4, 5, and 6 might reveal that all of them involve the use of numbers or mathematical word problems. We might therefore decide to name this factor "mathematical reasoning." What matters is that we have now reduced six variables to two variables, based on the correlations among them, and we have arrived at some idea of what the underlying abilities might be.

We should note, however, that the two clusters of tests we've identified are not totally unrelated to each other. The verbal and mathematical scores are also correlated with each other, though at a much lower level than within the clusters. This fact suggests that although the verbal and mathematical factors are clearly distinct from each other, they also share something in common, perhaps some more general mental ability that cuts across both verbal and mathematical abilities. This pattern of results anticipates one of the major controversies in the field of intelligence: Is intelligence a general mental capacity, or does it consist of separate and specific mental abilities?

The *g* Factor: Intelligence as General Mental Capacity

The psychometric argument for intelligence as a general ability was first advanced by the British psychologist Charles Spearman (1923). He observed that school grades in different

....

6. What kinds of evidence supported the existence of Spearman's *g* factor?

....

subjects, such as English and mathematics, were almost always positively correlated but not perfectly. Spearman found the same to be true for different types of Stanford-Binet intelligence test items, such as vocabulary questions, arithmetic reasoning problems, and the ability to solve puzzles. Were he to look at the correlation matrix in Table 10.2, he would be impressed by the fact that the verbal-ability cluster and mathematical-reasoning cluster are correlated with each other at about the 0.40 to 0.50 level. He would regard these correlations as evidence that verbal and mathematical abilities, while clearly different, also reflect a more basic or general mental capacity that contributes to them.

Spearman concluded that intellectual performance is determined partly by a ***g* factor**, or general intelligence, and partly by whatever special abilities might be required to perform that particular task. Spearman contended that because the general factor—the *g* factor—cuts across virtually all tasks, it constitutes the core of intelligence. Thus, Spearman would argue that your performance in a mathematics course would depend mainly on your general intelligence but also on your specific ability to learn mathematics.

Today, many theorists continue to believe that the *g* factor is the core of what we call *intelligence*. Moreover, *g* matters a great deal as a predictor of both academic and job performance. Nathan Kuncel and his colleagues (2004) performed a meta-analysis of 127 studies involving 20 352 participants in numerous educational and work settings. They concluded that the same general mental ability is significantly related to success in both areas of life. Taking this argument a step further, Frank Schmidt and John Hunter (2004) concluded that measures of the *g* factor predict job success even better than do measures of specific abilities tailored to individual jobs. Summarizing the research evidence, David Lubinski, a prominent intelligence researcher, concluded, "*g* is clearly the most important dimension uncovered in the study of cognitive abilities to date" (2004, p. 100). General intelligence also predicts memory gain through consolidation during sleep (Fenn & Hambrick, 2015). Finally, Sternberg and Kaufman (2012) note that the vast majority of research on intelligence has focused on establishing the importance of *g* and its correlates to such an extent that future work will be directed elsewhere.

Intelligence as Specific Mental Abilities

Spearman's conclusion about the centrality of the *g* factor was soon challenged by L.L. Thurstone of the University of Chicago. While Spearman had been impressed by the fact that scores on different mental tasks are correlated, Thurstone was impressed by the fact that the correlations are far from perfect. Thurstone therefore concluded that human mental performance depends not on a general factor but rather on seven distinct abilities, which he called **primary mental abilities** (Table 10.3). Thus, Thurstone would focus on the two clusters of test scores shown in Table 10.2 and attach special significance to the high correlations within each cluster. He would expect that performance on a given verbal or mathematical task would be influenced more by the specific skills represented in the relevant cluster than by any *g* factor.

Following Thurstone's lead, other investigators claimed to have found many more specific cognitive factors. One prominent theorist maintained that there are more than 100 distinct and measurable mental abilities (Guilford, 1967). Other theorists suggest fewer abilities but maintain that intelligence is more complex than a single *g* factor.

For practical reasons, educators tend to find the specific-abilities notion of intelligence more attractive and useful than the general mental ability model (Mayer, 2000). They are more interested in identifying the specific mental skills involved in learning subjects such as reading, mathematics, and science. They are also interested in helping children increase the specific mental abilities that are needed for success in various subjects. For such purposes, general mental ability measures such as an overall IQ are less useful than are measures of specific cognitive abilities that can point to a student's areas of strength and weakness. Additionally, it may appear more feasible to enhance specific mental skills than to raise general intelligence.

Crystallized and Fluid Intelligence

Raymond Cattell (1971) and John Horn (1985) proposed a new model of intelligence (Figure 10.5). They broke down Spearman's general intelligence into two distinct but related subtypes of *g* (with a correlation of about 0.50). **Crystallized intelligence (g_c)** is the ability to apply previously acquired knowledge to current

7. What led Thurstone to view intelligence as specific mental abilities?

8. Differentiate between crystallized and fluid intelligence, and indicate their relation to aging and types of memory.

TABLE 10.3 Thurstone's Primary Mental Abilities

Ability Name	Description
S—Space	Reasoning about visual scenes
V—Verbal comprehension	Understanding verbal statements
W—Word fluency	Producing verbal statements
N—Number facility	Dealing with numbers
P—Perceptual speed	Recognizing visual patterns
M—Rote memory	Memorizing
R—Reasoning	Dealing with novel problems

Source: L.L. Thurstone, 1938, *Primary Mental Abilities.* Copyright © 1938 by The University of Chicago Press. Reprinted with permission.

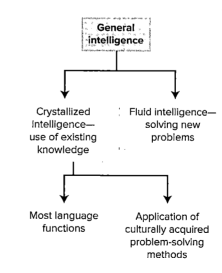

FIGURE 10.5 Crystallized and fluid intelligence. Raymond Cattell and John Horn made an important distinction between crystallized and fluid intelligence. Crystallized intelligence is based more strongly on previous learning and experience, whereas fluid intelligence is a more creative type of intelligence.

problems. Vocabulary and information tests are good measures of crystallized intelligence. Crystallized intelligence, which is the basis for expertise, depends on the ability to retrieve previously learned information and problem-solving schemas from long-term memory (Horn & Masunaga, 2000; Hunt, 1997). It is dependent on previous learning and practice.

Cattell and Horn's second general factor is **fluid intelligence** (g_f), defined as the ability to deal with novel problem-solving situations for which personal experience does not provide a solution. It involves inductive reasoning and creative problem-solving skills such as those discussed in the previous chapter. Fluid intelligence is dependent primarily on the efficient functioning of the central nervous system rather than on prior experience and cultural context. People high in fluid intelligence can perceive relations among stimulus patterns and draw inferences from relationships. The Tower-of-Hanoi and nine-dot problems you worked on in Chapter 9 are fluid-intelligence tasks.

Fluid intelligence requires the abilities to reason abstractly, think logically, and manage information in working (short-term) memory so that new problems can be solved on the blackboard of the mind (Hunt, 1997; Jaeggi et al., 2008). Thus, long-term memory contributes strongly to crystallized intelligence, whereas fluid intelligence is particularly dependent on efficient working memory.

The g_c-g_f model is based in part on what has been learned about intellectual development in adulthood (Berg, 2000). Cattell and Horn concluded that over our lifespan, we progress from using fluid intelligence to depending more on crystallized intelligence. Early in life, we encounter many problems for the first time, so we need fluid intelligence to figure out solutions. As experience makes us more knowledgeable, we have less need to approach each situation as a new problem. Instead, we simply call up appropriate information and schemas from long-term memory, thereby utilizing our crystallized intelligence. This is the essence of wisdom (Kunzman & Baltes, 2003).

Because long-term memory remains strong even as we age, performance on tests of crystallized intelligence improves during adulthood and remains stable well into late adulthood. In contrast, performance on tests of fluid intelligence

9. Describe Carroll's three-stratum psychometric model and how it originated. How does it relate to the previously discussed models?

begins to decline as people enter late adulthood (Daniels et al., 2006; Schaie, 1998). The fact that aging affects the two forms of intelligence differently is additional evidence that they represent different classes of mental abilities (Horn & Noll, 1997; Weinert & Hany, 2003). Furthermore, different brain areas are active during tasks associated with fluid and crystallized intelligence (Colom et al., 2009). Haasz at al. (2013) have shown that fluid intelligence is related to increased connectivity in the brain's white matter, while crystallized intelligence seems to be more associated with frontal and parietal lobe grey matter.

Carroll's Three-Stratum Model: A Modern Synthesis

In their attempts to specify the nature of intellect, psychometric researchers have been administering measures of mental abilities for more than a century. The many tasks they have used have probably left no cognitive stone unturned. In an attempt to synthesize the results of prior research, John B. Carroll (1993) used factor analysis to reanalyze more than 460 different sets of data obtained by researchers around the world between 1935 and 1980. Carroll's analysis resulted in an integrative model of intelligence that contains elements of Spearman's, Thurstone's, and Cattell-Horn's models. The **three-stratum theory of cognitive abilities** establishes three levels of mental skills—general, broad, and narrow—arranged in a hierarchical model. As shown in Figure 10.6, at the top, or third stratum, of the model is a g factor thought to underlie most mental activity. Below g at the second stratum are eight broad intellectual factors arranged from left to right in terms of the extent to which they are influenced by (or correlated with) g. Fluid intelligence is most strongly related to (or "saturated with") g, and crystallized intelligence is next, indicating the importance of the Cattell-Horn factors. The other broad abilities at the second stratum involve basic cognitive functions such as memory and learning, perceptual abilities, and speed of mental functioning, some of which resemble Thurstone's primary mental abilities. Finally, at the first stratum of the model are nearly 70 highly specific cognitive abilities that feed into the broader second-stratum factors. On average, these specific ability measures

General (Stratum III)

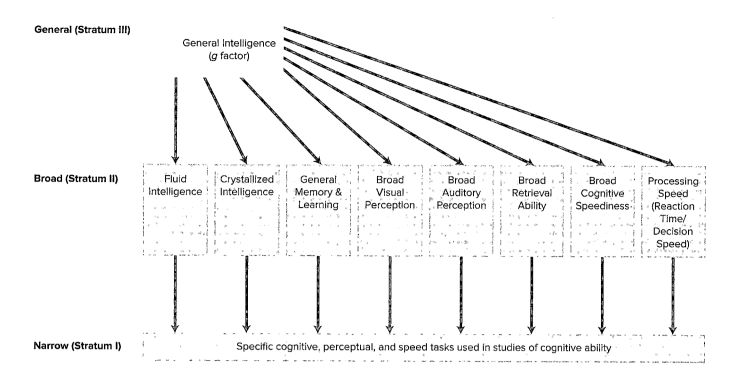

Broad (Stratum II)

Narrow (Stratum I)

FIGURE 10.6 A modern model of intellect. John B. Carroll's three-stratum model of cognitive skills is based on a reanalysis of more than 400 data sets. The model builds upward from specific skills to a *g* factor at its apex. The lengths of the arrows from Stratum III to Stratum II represent the contribution of the *g* factor to each Stratum II ability.

Source: Adapted from Carroll, J.B., "A Modern Model of Intellect," from *Human Cognitive Abilities: A Survey of Factor-Analytic Studies.* (Appendix B: Hierarchical Factor Matrix Files). Copyright © Cambridge University Press, 1993. Reprinted with permission.

tend to correlate around 0.30 with one another, reflecting the common *g* factor at the top of the model. Carroll believes that the three-stratum model encompasses virtually all known cognitive abilities and provides the most complete and detailed map of the human intellect derived from the psychometric approach to intelligence.

Cognitive Process Approaches: The Nature of Intelligent Thinking

Psychometric theories of intelligence are statistically sophisticated ways of providing a map of the mind and describing *how* people differ from one another (Birney & Sternberg, 2006). What psychometric theories don't explain is *why* people vary in these mental skills. **Cognitive process theories** explore the specific information-processing and cognitive processes that underlie intellectual ability. Recall that this was the logic behind Galton's early attempts to relate thinking ability to speed of reaction and sensory acuity. Robert Sternberg (1988, 2004, 2007) is a leading proponent of the cognitive processes approach to intelligence.

His **triarchic theory of intelligence** addresses both the psychological processes involved in intelligent behaviour and the diverse forms that intelligence can take. Sternberg's theory divides the cognitive processes that underlie intelligent behaviour into three specific components (Figure 10.7).

Metacomponents are the higher-order processes used to plan and regulate task performance. They include problem-solving skills such as identifying problems, formulating hypotheses and strategies, testing them logically, and evaluating performance feedback. Sternberg believes that metacomponents are the fundamental sources of individual differences in fluid intelligence. He finds that intelligent people spend more time framing problems and developing strategies than do less intelligent people, who have a tendency to plunge right in without sufficient forethought.

Performance components are the actual mental processes used to perform the task. They include perceptual processing, retrieving appropriate memories and schemas from long-term

10. Differentiate between psychometric and cognitive process approaches to intelligence.

Types of Intellectual Competence

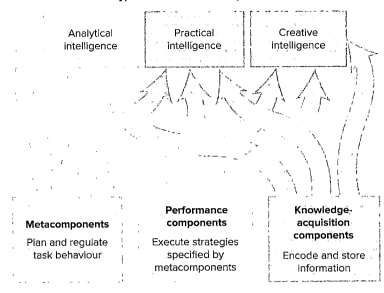

FIGURE 10.7 Sternberg's triarchic theory includes three different types of intelligence and three classes of cognitive processes that underlie each type of intelligence.

memory, and generating responses. Finally, **knowledge-acquisition components** allow us to learn from our experiences, store information in memory, and combine new insights with previously acquired information. These abilities underlie individual differences in crystallized intelligence. Thus, Sternberg's theory addresses the processes that underlie the distinction made by Cattell and Horn between fluid and crystallized intelligences.

Sternberg believes that there is more than one kind of intelligence. He suggests that environmental demands may call for three different classes of adaptive problem solving and that people differ in their intellectual strengths in these areas:

11. What three classes of psychological processes and forms of intelligence are found in Sternberg's triarchic theory?

1. *Analytical intelligence* involves the kinds of academically oriented problem-solving skills measured by traditional intelligence tests.

2. *Practical intelligence* refers to the skills needed to cope with everyday demands and to manage oneself and other people effectively.

3. *Creative intelligence* comprises the mental skills needed to deal adaptively with novel problems.

Sternberg has shown that these forms of intelligence, while having a modest underlying *g* factor, are also distinct from one another. Consider,

for example, the relation between academic and practical skills. In one study, adolescents in Kenya were given one set of analytical tests measuring traditional academic knowledge and another set measuring their knowledge of natural herbal medicines used to treat illnesses, a kind of practical knowledge viewed by villagers as important to their survival. The results indicated that the practical intelligence measure of herbal knowledge was unrelated to (and sometimes negatively correlated with) the academic measures (Sternberg et al., 2001). Sternberg also found that Brazilian street children were very proficient at the math required to carry on their street businesses, despite the fact that many of them had failed mathematics in school (Sternberg, 2004).

Sternberg believes that educational programs should teach all three classes of skills, not just analytical-academic skills. In studies with elementary school children, he and his colleagues have shown that a curriculum that also teaches practical and creative skills results in greater mastery of course material than does a traditional analytic, memory-based approach to learning course content (Grigorenko et al., 2002). As Sternberg's work illustrates, cognitive science is leading us to a focus on understanding and enhancing the mental processes that underlie intelligent behaviour.

Broader Conceptions of Intelligence: Beyond Mental Competencies

Traditionally, intelligence has been viewed as *mental competence*. Some psychologists think this is too limited a definition to capture the range of human adaptations. They believe that intelligence may be more broadly conceived as relatively *independent intelligences* that relate to different adaptive demands.

Gardner's Multiple Intelligences

Harvard psychologist Howard Gardner (2003) is one of the strongest proponents of this view. Inspired by his observations of how specific human abilities are affected by brain damage, Gardner advanced a theory of multiple intelligences. The number of intelligences has varied as Gardner's work has progressed; he currently defines eight distinct varieties of adaptive abilities, and a possible ninth variety (Davis et al., 2011; Gardner, 2000):

1. *Linguistic intelligence:* the ability to use language well, as writers do

2. *Logical-mathematical intelligence:* the ability to reason mathematically and logically

3. *Visuospatial intelligence:* the ability to solve spatial problems or to succeed in a field such as architecture

4. *Musical intelligence:* the ability to perceive pitch and rhythm and to understand and produce music

5. *Bodily-kinesthetic intelligence:* the ability to control body movements and skilfully manipulate objects, as demonstrated by a highly skilled dancer, athlete, or surgeon

6. *Interpersonal intelligence:* the ability to understand and relate well to others

7. *Intrapersonal intelligence:* the ability to understand oneself

8. *Naturalistic intelligence:* the ability to detect and understand phenomena in the natural world, as a zoologist or meteorologist might

In recent writings, Gardner (2000) has also speculated about a ninth possible intelligence, which he calls *existential intelligence*, a philosophically oriented ability to ponder questions about the meaning of one's existence, life, and death.

Gardner's first three intelligences are measured by existing intelligence tests, but the others are not. Indeed, some of Gardner's critics insist that these other abilities are not really part of the traditional concept of intelligence at all and that some of them are better regarded as talents. However, Gardner replies that the form of intelligence that is most highly valued within a given culture depends on the adaptive requirements of that culture. In Gardner's view, the abilities exhibited by Albert Einstein, Sidney Crosby, and a street-smart gang leader exemplify different forms of intelligence that are highly adaptive within their respective environments (Figure 10.8). Gardner further suggests that these different classes of abilities require the functioning of separate but interacting modules in the brain. Gardner's approach, though provocative, remains controversial because it goes far beyond traditional conceptions of intelligence as mental skills.

Emotional Intelligence

Another form of adaptive ability lies within the emotional realm, and some theorists believe that emotional competence is a form of intelligence. According to John Mayer and Peter Salovey, **emotional intelligence** involves the abilities to read others' emotions accurately, to respond to them appropriately, to motivate oneself, to be aware of one's own emotions, and to regulate and control one's own emotional responses (Mayer et al., 2004).

According to Mayer and Salovey, emotional intelligence includes four components, or branches, as shown in Figure 10.9. The Mayer-Salovey-Caruso Emotional Intelligence Test (MSCEIT) includes specific tasks to measure each branch. *Perceiving emotions* is measured by people's accuracy in judging emotional expressions in facial photographs, as well as the emotional tones conveyed by different landscapes and designs. *Using emotions to facilitate thought* is measured by asking people to identify the emotions that would best enhance a particular type of thinking, such as how to deal with a distressed co-worker or plan a birthday party. To measure *understanding emotions*, people are asked to specify the conditions under which their emotions change in intensity or type; another task measures people's understanding of which basic emotions

12. What kinds of abilities are included in Gardner's multiple intelligences?

13. Describe the four branches of emotional intelligence and how they are measured.

(left) © ZUMA Press, Inc./Alamy Stock Photo; (middle) Ottawa Citizen/The Canadian Press; (right) Carlos Osorio/Toronto Star via Getty Images

FIGURE 10.8 According to Howard Gardner, these people's abilities exemplify forms of intelligence that are not measured by traditional intelligence tests. Geddy Lee of the Canadian rock band Rush (a) possesses high musical intelligence, whereas Sidney Crosby (b) and Rick Mercer (c) exhibit high bodily-kinesthetic and interpersonal intelligence, respectively.

blend together to create subtle emotions, such as envy or jealousy. Finally, *managing emotions* is measured by asking respondents to indicate how they can change their own or others' emotions to facilitate success or increase interpersonal harmony.

The scoring method for the MSCEIT tasks yields high reliability among expert scorers; it produces scores for each branch, as well as a total emotional intelligence score. Mayer and Salovey view these tasks as ability measures in the same sense that a Wechsler scale measures

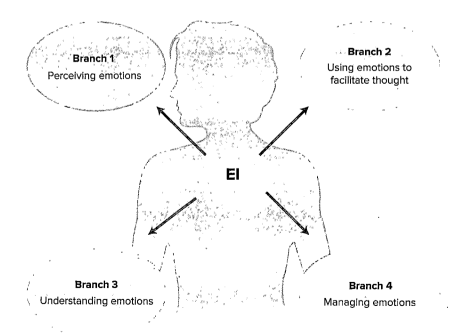

Branch 1
Perceiving emotions

Branch 2
Using emotions to facilitate thought

EI

Branch 3
Understanding emotions

Branch 4
Managing emotions

FIGURE 10.9 The structure of emotional intelligence (EI). Four specific branches of emotion-detection and control abilities are assumed to underlie emotional intelligence.

Source: Based on Mayer, J.D., Salovey, P., & Caruso, D.R. (2004). Emotional intelligence: Theory, findings, and implications. *Psychological Inquiry*, 15, 197–215.

mental abilities. As in the case of mental intelligence, it seems important to measure what people can actually do rather than simply asking them how competent they are. Other measures of emotional intelligence, which ask people how competent they are in emotional areas, tend not to correlate highly with the MSCEIT or predict competent behaviours as well (Mayer et al., 2004).

Proponents of emotional intelligence point to the important adaptive advantages of emotional skills in meeting the challenges of daily life, and they believe that the ability to read, respond to, and manage emotions has evolutionary roots. Emotionally intelligent people, they suggest, form stronger emotional bonds with others; enjoy greater success in careers, marriage, and child-rearing; modulate their own emotions so as to avoid strong depression, anger, or anxiety; and work more effectively toward long-term goals by being able to control impulses for immediate gratification. In the end, some people who are high in emotional

intelligence may enjoy more success in life than do others who surpass them in mental intelligence (Salovey & Pizzaro, 2003). They also tend to use more effective coping strategies (Saklofske et al., 2007) and report lower levels of depression and greater life satisfaction (Petrides et al., 2007).

As is the case with Gardner's multiple intelligences, emotional intelligence has its critics. Landy (2005) argues that many claims of a relation between emotional intelligence and success in the workplace have not been scientifically scrutinized. A recent study at the University of Ottawa (Humphrey-Murto et al., 2014) indicated that emotional intelligence as measured by the MSCEIT was not predictive of success in medial school, even though the MSCEIT is being considered as a screening test for medical school admission. Some psychologists believe that the concept of intelligence is being stretched too far from its original focus on mental ability (e.g., Matthews et al., 2004). They would prefer a

In Review

- The psychometric approach to intelligence attempts to map the structure of intellect and establish how many different classes of mental ability underlie test performance. A newer approach, the cognitive processes approach, focuses on the specific thought processes that underlie mental competencies.

- Factor analysis can be applied to correlations among test scores to identify clusters of measures that correlate highly with one another and therefore are assumed to have a common underlying factor, such as verbal ability or mathematical reasoning.

- Spearman believed that intelligence is determined both by specific cognitive abilities and by a general intelligence (g) factor that constitutes the core of intelligence. Thurstone disagreed, viewing intelligence as a set of specific abilities. Thurstone's position is best supported by observed distinctions between verbal and spatial abilities.

- Cattell and Horn differentiated between crystallized intelligence, the ability to apply previously learned knowledge to current problems, and fluid intelligence, the ability to deal with novel problem-solving situations for which personal experience does not provide a solution. They argued

that over our lifespan, we show a progressive shift from using fluid intelligence to using crystallized intelligence as we attain wisdom.

- Carroll's three-stratum model is based on reanalyses of hundreds of data sets. Mental abilities are represented at three levels, with general intelligence (g) at the apex and highly specific cognitive and perceptual skills at its base. Carroll's model may be the most accurate psychometric representation of human cognitive abilities.

- Cognitive process theories of intelligence focus on the elementary information-processing abilities that contribute to intelligence. Sternberg's triarchic theory of intelligence includes a components subtheory that addresses the specific cognitive processes that underlie intelligent behaviour.

- Sternberg and Gardner maintain that there are distinct forms of intelligence beyond the traditional concept. Sternberg differentiates between analytical, practical, and creative intelligence, and Gardner proposes nine different kinds of intelligence. The theory of emotional intelligence refers to people's ability to read and respond appropriately to others' emotions, to motivate themselves, and to be aware of and in control of their emotions.

14. How is Wechsler's view of intelligence reflected in the Wechsler tests? What kinds of scores do they provide?

different term, such as *emotional competence,* to distinguish this concept from the traditional mental-skills concept of intelligence. But emotional-intelligence proponents respond that if we regard intelligence as adaptive abilities, we ought not limit ourselves to the purely cognitive realms of human ability. The debate concerning multiple intelligence continues to rage and promises to do so into the future.

So far we have explored the nature of intelligence. Let's now examine more closely how individual differences in intelligence are measured.

THE MEASUREMENT OF INTELLIGENCE

Today, the Wechsler tests (WAIS-IV and WISC-IV) are the most popular individually administered intelligence tests in North America (Kaplan & Saccuzo, 2009). They provide a good illustration of how intelligence is assessed and show excellent psychometric properties (e.g., Benson et al., 2013).

Recall that Wechsler believed that intelligence tests should measure a wide array of different mental abilities. His tests reflect that conviction. The WAIS-IV consists of a series of subtests that fall into four "index scales"—Verbal Comprehension, Perceptual Reasoning, Working Memory, and Processing Speed. A psychologist can therefore plot a profile based on the scores on each of the subtests to assess a person's pattern of intellectual strengths and weaknesses. The test yields five summary scores: one for each of the index scales and a Full-Scale composite IQ based on all of the scales (Figure 10.10). For some purposes, it is useful to examine differences between the Verbal IQ and the Performance IQ. For example, individuals from an impoverished environment with little formal schooling might score higher on the performance subtests than on the verbal subtests, suggesting that their overall IQ might be an underestimate of their intellectual potential. Sometimes, too, various types of brain damage are reflected in large discrepancies between certain subtest scores (Goldstein, 2000; Strauss et al., 2006).

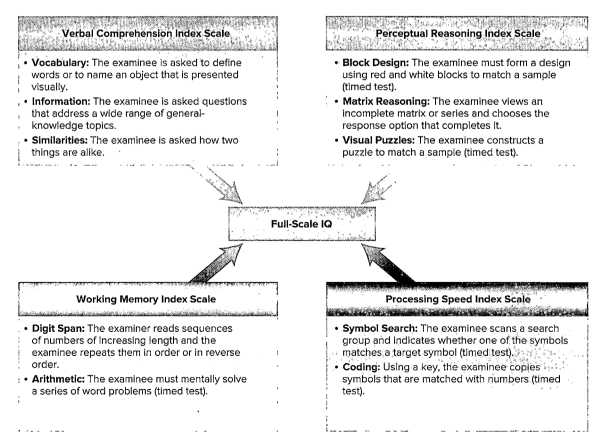

FIGURE 10.10 Scales and subscales of the Wechsler Intelligence Scale for Adults IV (WAIS-IV).

Source: Based on Coalson, D.L., & Raiford, S.E. (2008). WAIS-IV: Technical and interpretative manual. San Antonio, TX: Pearson.

Increasing the Informational Yield from Intelligence Tests

Revisions of both the Stanford-Binet and the Wechsler scales have been responsive to advances in the understanding of the mental processes that underlie intelligence. The original Stanford-Binet yielded a single IQ score based mainly on verbal items, but today's test samples a wider range of abilities and provides, in addition to a composite IQ score, separate scores for Verbal Reasoning, Abstract/Visual Reasoning, Quantitative Reasoning, and Short-Term Memory. The WISC-IV, used to assess children between ages 6 and 11, provides, in addition to its Full-Scale IQ, separate scores for Verbal Comprehension, Perceptual Organization, Freedom from Distractibility, and Processing Speed. These scores make the tests more useful for understanding test takers' intellectual strengths and weaknesses and possibly planning educational interventions for them. Measurement of specific abilities is also supported by the finding that as children mature, their general intelligence remains stable, but specific abilities become increasingly more differentiated (Kane & Brand, 2006). Many other tests of specific cognitive skills are currently in use, providing many tools for assessing both children and adults (Bartholomew, 2004; Groth-Marnat, 1999).

Theory-Based Intelligence Tests

Advances in the theory of intelligence have stimulated the development of new instruments to test the specific abilities dictated by the theories. For example, the Cattell-Horn distinction between crystallized and fluid intelligence has had a strong impact on the field of intelligence testing. Several recently developed tests, such as the Kaufman Adolescent and Adult Intelligence Test and the Woodcock-Johnson Psycho-Educational Battery, are specifically designed to measure fluid and crystallized abilities separately (Kaufman & Kaufman, 1997; Woodcock, 1997). The Kaufman test has three crystallized-ability subscales and three fluid-ability scales, and test results yield separate g_c and g_f IQs, as well as a composite, or full-scale, IQ. The crystallized-intelligence scales require respondents to define words, listen to and answer questions about a detailed news story, and study two sets of words, such as *"animal* and *vampire"* and *"baseball* and *stick"* and then produce a word that relates to both, such as *bat.* The fluid-intelligence subtests require respondents to break mystery codes, solve logic problems, and associate words with complex drawings and then "read" sentences composed only of the drawings. The Kaufman and Woodcock-Johnson tests have become quite popular in educational, job-screening, and clinical settings.

Sternberg's triarchic model of intelligence has inspired the development of a new test as well. The Sternberg Triarchic Ability Test (STAT) measures the three forms of intelligence identified in his model—analytic, practical, and creative. This test can be useful in identifying students' levels of each of the three types of intelligence so that school curricula can be individualized to capitalize on their strengths and thereby optimize learning and school performance.

Should We Test for Aptitude or Achievement?

Using written tests for selection purposes highlights an issue that Binet faced and that continues to plague test developers today: Should we test a person's abstract "aptitude for learning," or should we test what a person already knows? Consider an example. In selecting applicants for post-secondary education, we could give students either an **achievement test** designed to find out how much they have learned so far in their lives, or we could present them with an **aptitude test,** containing novel puzzle-like problems that presumably go beyond prior learning and are thought to measure the applicant's potential for future learning and performance.

The argument for achievement testing is that it is usually a good predictor of future performance in a similar situation. If a student learned a lot of academic material in high school (and therefore scored well on the test), he or she is likely to also learn a lot in college or university. The argument against achievement testing is that it assumes that everyone has had the same opportunity to learn the material being tested. In post-secondary selection, for example, a given applicant's test score could depend on whether that person went to a good school rather than on his or her ability to learn in college or university.

15. How have theories of intelligence influenced recently developed tests?

16. Describe the controversy involving aptitude versus achievement tests in relation to the measurement of intelligence.

The argument for aptitude testing is that it is fairer because it supposedly depends less on prior knowledge than on a person's ability to react to the problems presented on the test. The argument against aptitude testing is that it is difficult to construct a test that is independent of prior learning. Further, such a test may require an ability to deal with puzzles that is not relevant to success in situations other than the test itself.

In fact, most intelligence tests measure a combination of aptitude and achievement, reflecting both native ability and previous learning (Lubinski, 2004). This combination approach has raised major scientific and social issues concerning the meaning of test scores, the extent to which improvement can be fostered by educational experiences, and the usefulness of the measures for describing mental competence and predicting performance in non-test situations.

Tests of mental skills have become a staple of Western societies. They are used to make important educational, occupational, and clinical decisions, as well as to set social policy. These measures also have become important scientific tools for cognitive psychologists who study the development, stability, operation, and modification of cognitive functions. We will now consider the scientific standards required for psychological tests.

Psychometric Standards for Intelligence Tests

A **psychological test** is a method for measuring individual differences related to some psychological concept, or construct, based on a sample of relevant behaviour in a scientifically designed and controlled situation. In the case of intelligence testing, intelligence is the *construct* and scores obtained on the test are its *operational definition*. To design a test, we need to decide which specific behaviours serve as indicators of intellectual abilities. Then we need to devise test items that allow us to assess individual differences in those behaviours. We will, of course, need evidence that our sample of items (a sample, because we can't ask every conceivable question) actually measures the abilities we are assessing. As in designing an experiment (see Chapter 2), we want to collect *a sample of relevant behaviour* under standardized conditions, attempting to control for other factors that could influence responses to the items. To understand how psychologists meet these requirements, we must examine three key measurement concepts: *reliability, validity,* and *standardization*. We should note that these standards apply to all psychological tests, not just intelligence measures.

Reliability

Reliability refers to consistency of measurement. As shown in Table 10.4, reliability can take several forms when applied to psychological tests. It can refer to consistency of measurement over time, consistency of measurement by the items within the test itself, or consistency in scores assigned by different examiners.

One of the most important forms of reliability is consistency over time. If you step on your bathroom scale five times in a row, you should expect it to register the same weight each time unless you have a very unusual metabolism.

> **17.** Define the three types of test reliability.

TABLE 10.4   Types of Reliability and Validity in Psychological Testing

Types of Reliability	Meaning and Critical Questions
Test-retest reliability	Are scores on the measure stable over time?
Internal consistency	Do all the items on the measure seem to be measuring the same thing, as indicated by high correlations among them?
Interjudge reliability	Do different raters or scorers agree on their scoring or observations?
Types of Validity	
Construct validity	To what extent is the test actually measuring the construct of interest (e.g., intelligence)?
Content validity	Do the questions or test items relate to all aspects of the construct being measured?
Criterion-related validity	Do scores on the test predict some present or future behaviour or validity outcome assumed to be affected by the construct being measured?

Likewise, if we assume that intelligence is a relatively stable trait (and virtually all psychologists do), then scores on our measure should be stable, or consistent, over time. Where psychological tests are concerned, this type of measurement stability over time is defined as **test-retest reliability,** which is assessed by administering the measure to the same group of participants on two (or more) separate occasions and correlating the two (or more) sets of scores.

After about age seven, scores on intelligence tests show considerable stability, even over many years (Gregory, 1998). Over a short interval (two to 12 weeks), the test-retest correlation of adult IQs on the WAIS-IV is 0.95, or nearly perfect (Coalson & Raiford, 2008). Correlations between IQs at age nine and age 40 are in the 0.70 to 0.80 range (Plomin & Spinath, 2004), indicating a high degree of stability. In a Scottish national sample, scores on a test of general intelligence administered at age 11 correlated 0.66 with scores on the same test at age 80 (Deary et al., 2004). Thus, relative to his or her age group, a person who achieves an above-average IQ at age nine or age 11 is very likely to also be above the average for 40- or 80-year-olds when he or she reaches those ages. Even while children's cognitive skills are developing rapidly during middle childhood, IQs are quite stable, with test-retest coefficients around 0.90 (Canivez & Watkins, 1998).

Another form of reliability, **internal consistency,** has to do with consistency of measurement within the test itself. For example, if a Wechsler subtest is internally consistent, all its items are measuring the same skill, as evidenced by high correlations among the items. In accord with this requirement, the individual items within the Wechsler subtests correlate substantially with one another (Gregory, 1998). Using a Canadian sample, Hale et al. (2014) report reliable clusters of items on the WISC-IV.

Finally, **interjudge reliability** refers to consistency of measurement when different people observe the same event or score the same test. Ideally, two psychologists who independently score the same test will assign exactly the same scores. To attain high interjudge reliability, the scoring instructions must be so explicit that trained professionals will use the scoring system in the same way.

Validity

As a general concept, **validity** refers to how well a test actually measures what it is designed to measure. As in the case of reliability, there are several types of validity (Table 10.4).

As noted earlier, intelligence is a concept, or mental construct. **Construct validity** exists when a test successfully measures the psychological construct it is designed to measure, as indicated by relations between test scores and other behaviours that it should be related to. If an intelligence test had perfect construct validity, individual differences in IQs would be due to differences in intelligence and nothing else. In reality, this ideal is never attained, for other factors, such as motivation and educational background, also influence test scores.

Two other kinds of validity contribute to construct validity. **Content validity** refers to whether the items on a test measure all the knowledge or skills that are assumed to underlie the construct of interest. For example, if we want the Arithmetic subtest of the WAIS-IV to measure general mathematical reasoning skills, we would not want to use only addition problems; we would want the items to sample other relevant mathematical abilities as well, such as subtraction, division, and fractions.

If an intelligence test is measuring what it is assumed to measure, then the IQ it yields should allow us to predict other behaviours that are assumed to be influenced by intelligence, such as school grades or job performance. These outcome measures are called *criterion measures*, and **criterion-related validity** refers to the ability of test scores to correlate with meaningful criterion measures. A critical issue for intelligence tests is the extent to which they predict the kinds of outcomes we would expect intelligence to influence, such as school and job performance. Let us examine this aspect of validity.

Intelligence and academic performance. Intelligence tests were originally developed to predict academic and other forms of achievement. How valid are they for this purpose? Actually, they do fairly well and far better than personality factors do (Kaia et al., 2007). Correlations of IQ with school grades are in the 0.60 range for high school students and in the 0.30 to 0.50 range for university students (Kuncel et al., 2004). In general, then, people who score well on the tests tend to do well academically. Likewise,

18. What is validity? Describe three kinds of test validity.

19. How well do IQ scores predict academic, job, and other life outcomes?

university entrance examinations used in the United States (such as the SAT) do predict university grades, with correlations slightly below 0.50 (Willingham et al., 1990). This correlation, which is about the same magnitude as the correlation between people's height and weight, is high enough to justify using the tests for screening purposes but low enough to necessitate the use of other predictors (such as high school grades) in combination with SAT scores.

Another measure of general intelligence used in selecting graduate students, the Miller Analogies Test, successfully predicts a variety of performance criteria, including grades, faculty ratings, comprehensive examination scores, and number of years required to attain the advanced degree, with validity coefficients ranging from 0.35 to 0.58 (Kuncel et al., 2004). There is little doubt that measures of intelligence successfully predict academic performance.

Job performance, income, and longevity. Intelligence test scores also predict military and job performance. General mental ability predicts both occupational level and performance within one's chosen occupation (Schmidt & Hunter, 2004). Intelligent individuals are far more likely to attain prestigious occupations. One study followed siblings raised together, thereby controlling for home background. When the siblings were in their late 20s, mental ability measures collected during young adulthood were related to their annual adult incomes. Siblings with IQs of 120 or more were, on average, earning $18 000 more than siblings of average intelligence (Murray, 1998). Intelligence correlates 0.50 to 0.70 with the level of socioeconomic status that people attain in adulthood (Lubinski, 2004).

People with higher intelligence perform better on their jobs, and the more complex the job, the more strongly intelligence is related to performance (Hunter & Hunter, 1984). The relation is particularly striking during the job-training period, when the superior learning ability of highly intelligent people helps them shine (Schmidt & Hunter, 2004). Furthermore, intelligence predicts job performance better than does job experience, specific abilities, or personality traits (Schmidt & Hunter, 2004). On a broader level, national IQ predicts technological achievement and national economic success (Gelade, 2008).

Intelligence predicts other life outcomes as well. People high in intelligence show better recovery from brain injuries (Stern, 2006). Moreover, intelligence literally predicts life and death. In 1932, every child in Scotland who had been born in 1921 was administered an intelligence test. These children and another similar-age cohort of children tested in 1947 were followed as their lives unfolded (Deary et al., 2004). Higher childhood intelligence was associated with significantly greater survival to age 76 in both men and women, but the results were particularly striking for women (Figure 10.11). Another sample of Scots born in the 1950s shows a similar pattern (Leon et al., 2009).

How shall we account for these results? Is it possible that cognitive ability is a reflection of general fitness to survive (Der et al., 2009)? The researchers suggest the possibility that lower childhood intelligence may in some cases be influenced by prenatal or postnatal events that

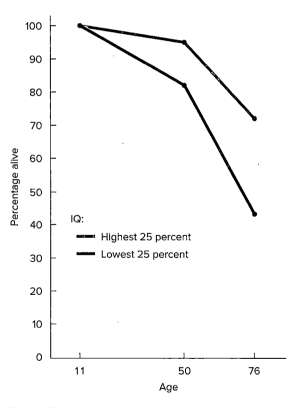

FIGURE 10.11 Does intelligence predict lifespan? This graph shows the relation between IQ assessed at age 11 and survival at ages 50 and 76 in women followed in the Scottish Mental Survey.

source: Data from Whalley, L.J., & Deary, I.J. (2001). Longitudinal cohort study of childhood IQ and survival up to age 76. *British Medical Journal*, 322, 819–822.

also impair later health. Or perhaps good brain development is related to optimal development of other bodily organs as well. But it is also possible that intelligent people are more likely to engage in healthy behaviours and to avoid unhealthy ones, or that higher intelligence allows people to live and work in safer physical environments or to enjoy better nutrition, thereby helping them live longer and healthier lives.

Standardization

The third measurement requirement, **standardization**, has two meanings: (1) the development of norms and (2) rigorously controlled testing procedures. The first meaning of standardization is especially important in providing a meaningful IQ score. It involves the collection of **norms**, test scores derived from a large sample that represents particular age segments of the population. These normative scores provide a basis for interpreting a given individual's score, just as the distribution of scores in a course exam allows you to determine how well you did relative to your classmates. Normative data also allow us to recalibrate the distribution of test scores so that an IQ of 100 will remain the "average" score even if the general population's test performance changes over time.

When norms are collected for mental skills (and for many other human characteristics), the scores usually form a **normal distribution,** a bell-shaped curve with most scores clustering around the centre of the curve. On intelligence tests, the centre of the distribution for each age group from childhood to late adulthood is assigned an IQ score of 100. Because the normal distribution has known statistical properties, we can specify what percentage of the population will score higher than a given score. Thus, as Figure 10.12 shows, an IQ score of 100 cuts the distribution in half, with an equal percentage of the population scoring above and below this midpoint. The farther we move from this average score of 100 in either direction, the fewer people attain the higher or lower scores. The figure also shows the percentage of people who score above certain IQ levels. On modern intelligence tests, this method of assigning an IQ score has replaced the original formula of mental age divided by chronological age. Interestingly, your calculated IQ can change depending on how you standardize the data. Both Harrison et al. (2015) and Miller et al. (2015) have shown that Canadians' calculated IQ changes depending whether one uses the American norms or the Canadian norms (it is lower with the Canadian norms). This may reflect smaller sample sizes and has important implications for educational classifications.

The Flynn effect: Are we getting smarter? The relative nature of the IQ allows its meaning to be preserved even if performance changes within the population. A notable discovery by New Zealand researcher James Flynn (1987, 1998) suggests that much of the world's

> **20.** What are the two meanings of standardization?

> **21.** What is the Flynn effect? What explanations have been suggested?

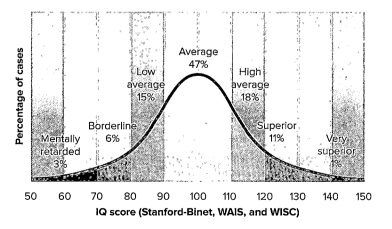

FIGURE 10.12 The bell curve of intelligence. When administered to large groups of people, intelligence tests yield a normal, or bell-shaped, distribution of IQ scores that has known statistical properties. The mean of the distribution is set at 100. It is possible to specify for any given score which percentage of the standardization group achieved higher or lower scores. Common descriptive labels are shown relative to the bell-shaped distribution. The range of scores from 90 to 110 is labelled *average* and includes nearly half of the population.

population is scoring progressively higher on intelligence tests. This "rising-curve" phenomenon (also called the *Flynn effect*) has resulted in IQ increases of 28 points in the United States since 1910 and a similar increase in Britain since 1942. On average, IQs in the West have increased about 3 points per decade, meaning that today's average IQ would be about 115 if the tests were scored according to the norms used in 1955. The increase seems to be occurring to the same degree for both men and women and for different ethnic groups (Truscott & Frank, 2001).

The reasons underlying the Flynn effect are not clear, but several possibilities have been suggested (Flynn, 1998; Neisser et al., 1998). One possibility is that better nutrition has helped fuel the IQ increase. Height has also increased dramatically over the past century, and it, like increased brain functioning, may be due to nutritional gains (Lynn, 2009). Other explanations focus on the environment. Richer and more complex learning environments that require more complex coping may have increased mental abilities. Likewise, technological advances may have helped shape the kinds of analytical and abstract reasoning skills that boost performance on intelligence tests. Whatever the reasons, however, the rising-curve phenomenon means that the intelligence score distribution has to be recalibrated upward periodically if the average IQ is to remain at 100, the traditional midpoint of the intelligence range.

22. Explain the nature and value of dynamic testing.

Testing conditions: Static and dynamic testing. Test instructions and procedures are designed to create a well-controlled, or standardized, environment for administering the intelligence test so that other uncontrolled factors will not influence scores. Tests like the Stanford-Binet and Wechsler scales have very detailed instructions that must be closely adhered to, even to the point of reading the instructions and items to the person being tested (Figure 10.13). The goal is to make sure that all testees are responding to as similar a stimulus situation as possible so that their scores will be solely a reflection of their ability. This traditional approach to testing is called **static testing.**

Some theorists suggest that the static approach to testing may reveal an incomplete picture of a person's abilities by measuring only the products of previous learning. In **dynamic testing,** the standard testing is followed up with

© Stefanie Felix/The Image Works

FIGURE 10.13 When administering intelligence tests, psychologists use consistently applied instructions and procedures to create a standardized testing environment.

an interaction in which the examiner gives the respondent guided feedback on how to improve performance and observes how the person utilizes the information. This part of the session provides a window to the individual's ability to profit from instruction and improve performance, and may disclose cognitive capacities not revealed by static testing.

Let's look in on a dynamic testing session with a five-year-old child who is being tested for educational purposes. Daniel is impulsive in the classroom, and the teacher wants to know how best to instruct him. The child has been asked to draw a picture of a person (a task common to several intelligence tests) and has hurriedly scribbled a poorly formed figure that merits a low score. The examiner wants to see how much Daniel can improve with feedback:

> Wow, Daniel. I can really tell that that's a boy. I see a head, two arms, and two legs. He even looks like he could be running, because his legs are kind of bent. Now we're going to work together to see if we can get this picture to look more like a boy. I think we need to think real hard about some more parts that people have and just where they need to go. I also noticed that you did this really fast, and that made this look kind of wobbly. So I'm going to help you slow down a bit so you can make this boy stand really straight. (Lidz, 1997, p. 283)

By testing the limits of Daniel's competencies and his ability to profit from various kinds of feedback, the dynamic tester may gain a fuller picture of his mental skills and may be able to make better educational recommendations. Dynamic testing can be particularly useful when people have not had equal learning opportunities, as occurs in disadvantaged groups. Equally important is the fact that dynamic feedback tends to improve test scores, and these new scores often relate more highly to educational outcomes than do the original test scores (Lidz, 1997). Dynamic testing can be particularly useful and revealing when testing people from cultures that are not accustomed to taking Western-style tests (Sternberg, 2004), as well as children with learning disabilities (Tzuriel, 2000).

Assessing Intelligence in Non-Western Cultures

Special challenges await the psychologist who wants to assess intelligence in non-Western cultures. Traditional intelligence tests such as the WAIS and the Stanford-Binet draw heavily on the cognitive skills and learning that are needed to succeed in Western educational and occupational settings. They tend to have strong verbal content and to rely on the products of Western schooling. Taken into a cultural context where *smart* is defined in different ways and requires other kinds of adaptive behaviour, such tests cannot hope to measure intelligence in a valid fashion (e.g., Suzuki et al., 2014). For example, the WAIS does not measure the ability to create herbal medicines, construct shelters, or navigate in the open sea. Robert Sternberg (2003, 2004) has advanced a *theory of successful intelligence* in which intelligence is whatever is required to meet the adaptive demands of a given culture. Sternberg believes that fundamental mental skills (the metacomponents described earlier) are required for successful behaviour in any culture. These include the ability to mentally represent problems in a way that facilitates their solution, to develop potential solutions and choose successfully from among them, to utilize mental resources wisely, and to evaluate the effects of one's action plans. What differs is the kinds of problems to which these basic intellectual skills are applied (Sternberg & Grigorenko, 2006). People from different cultures may think about the same problem in very different ways (Nisbett, 2003).

Two main approaches have been taken to meet the challenges of cross-cultural intelligence

assessment. One is to choose reasoning problems that are not tied to the knowledge base of any culture but that reflect the ability to process and evaluate stimulus patterns. The problem shown in Figure 10.14 resembles one on the Raven Progressive Matrices, a test that is frequently used to measure fluid intelligence (Raven, 1962). On this non-verbal task, you must detect relationships and then decipher the rules underlying the pattern of drawings in the rows and columns of the upper figure. Finally, you must use this information to select the figure that is the missing entry from the eight alternatives below. The Raven test has been used in many cultures and measures a general mental capacity that is also measured by traditional intelligence tests in our culture (Jensen, 1998). Scores on the Raven correlate positively with measures of IQ derived from traditional tests, yet they seem to be more "culture fair."

A second and more challenging approach is to create measures that are tailored to the kinds of knowledge and skills that are valued in the particular culture. Such tests may measure how smart an individual is in terms of the practical skills and adaptive behaviours within that culture. Scores may be unrelated or even negatively correlated with other measures of intelligence, yet they may predict successful functioning within that culture (Sternberg, 2004). If intelligence is defined as the ability to engage in culture-specific adaptive behaviour, then who is to say that the culture-specific measure is not a valid measure of intelligence in that context?

Galton resurrected: Intelligence and neural efficiency. The scientific study of intelligence began in part with Sir Francis Galton's attempts to develop measures of nervous system efficiency that might underlie mental skills. As noted earlier, these attempts fell into disfavour because scores on his measures were unrelated to one another and to external criteria of success. As tools for directly measuring brain functions become more sophisticated, however, Galton's legacy lives on in current attempts to relate neural measures to IQ (e.g., Posthuma et al., 2001, 2002).

Two types of evidence suggest that this line of research may bear fruit. The first comes from electrophysiological studies of

23. How is intelligence assessed in non-Western cultures?

24. What evidence exists that brain size and neural efficiency underlie high intelligence?

25. What evidence is there that intelligence might involve neural efficiency?

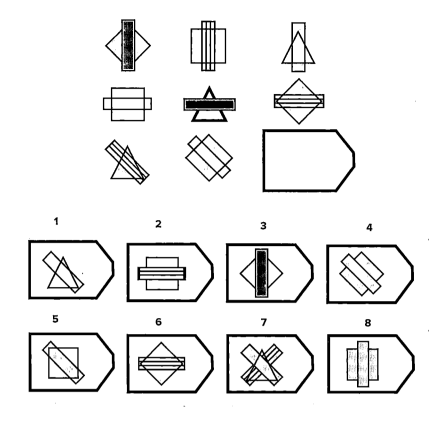

FIGURE 10.14 Culture-fair measurement? This problem is similar to those on the Raven Progressive Matrices test. This non-verbal measure tests fluid-intelligence ability, requiring subjects to perceive relationships and decipher the rules underlying the pattern of drawings in the rows and columns of the upper figure and then to select the figure that is the missing entry from the eight alternatives below. (The answer appears at the end of the chapter.)

Source: Adapted from P.A. Carpenter, M.A. Just & P. Shell, 1990, "What One Intelligence Test Measures," *Psychological Review*, 97, 404-431, Fig 2. Copyright © 1990 by the American Psychological Association. Reprinted by permission.

brain responses to visual and auditory stimuli. Modest relations have been shown between traditionally measured IQ and both the nature and speed of the brain's electrical response to stimuli. These electrical responses may reflect the speed and efficiency of information processing in the brain (Barrett & Eysenck, 1992; Caryl, 1994).

The second line of evidence comes from studies of brain metabolism. PET scans of people's brains taken while they engage in problem-solving tasks have shown lower levels of glucose consumption in people of high intelligence, suggesting that their brains are working more efficiently and expending less energy (Haier et al., 1993). Intelligence also involves speed of processing, which relates to the efficiency of neural connections (Hunt, 2007). Whether these findings herald a new way of measuring intelligence is an unanswered question. The proof of this pudding will be in the ability of such measures to predict external achievement criteria, as traditional intelligence tests do.

Some neuroscientists believe that individual differences in *brain plasticity*—the ability of the brain to change by forming new connections among neurons in response to environmental input—may be the key neural factor underlying differences in intelligence (Luders et al., 2009; Rushton & Davison, 2009). The ability to quickly establish new neural networks would increase processing speed and efficiency, and people with brains capable of greater plasticity would therefore develop better intellectual skills. This suggestion receives support from evidence that there may be a critical period for the growth of new neural circuits that ends at about age 16, the same age period by which crystallized intelligence seems to achieve stability (Garlick, 2002). Some authors have even suggested that size of one's brain may be critical. We examine this idea in the *Focus on Neuroscience* feature.

Focus on Neuroscience

BRAIN SIZE AND INTELLIGENCE

The brain is clearly the locus of intellectual activities. For a brain to operate more efficiently, it makes sense that having more neurons, or more connections among them, might be advantageous, especially if they were in the areas most involved in processing information. This notion has spurred attempts to relate brain size with intelligence. As noted in Chapter 3, evolutionary evidence indicates a progressive increase in brain size as humanoid species evolved over the ages. Particularly evident is growth in the parts of the brain involved in higher mental functions, especially the cerebral cortex and frontal lobes (Kolb & Whishaw, 2005). Not surprisingly, therefore, scientists have revisited Sir Francis Galton's original hypothesis that individual differences in brain size might be related to intellectual competency.

One intriguing way of testing this hypothesis is to study the brains of dead geniuses to see whether they differ from the brains of less-brilliant people and, if so, how. After Albert Einstein's death in 1955, a Missouri physician removed and preserved his brain. The brain has undergone several analyses by neuroscientists over the years. The examinations have shown that Einstein's brain was *not* larger than average overall; in fact, it was actually smaller than average in some regions. But it was indeed bigger in some ways. His parietal lobes were densely packed with both neurons and glial cells, which produce nutrients for neurons and support them. As a result, his parietal lobes were about 15 percent wider than normal. So densely was this brain area packed that some major fissures were no longer visible. Significantly, this area of the brain is involved in mathematical thinking and visuospatial functions—precisely the kinds of abilities that seemed to underlie Einstein's creative genius (Witelson et al., 1999).

Prior to 1990, the research involving brain size and intelligence with living individuals required a rather crude measure of brain size—the size of the skull. This is a rather crude measure to be sure (Luders et al., 2009). Nonetheless, the correlations using this measurement were about 0.20, suggesting a very modest relationship between brain size and intelligence (Rushton & Davison, 2009). In more recent research using MRI imaging techniques, the correlation has been shown to be in the 0.35 to 0.45 range, and even as high as 0.60 when the most precise measures of general intelligence (*g* factor) are used (Haier et al., 2009; McDaniel, 2005).

These findings are intriguing, but before you conclude that the larger your brain is, the more intelligent you're likely to be, consider these points:

- Neanderthals, ancient humans hardly known for their intellectual brilliance, had slightly larger brains than we do (Kolb & Whishaw, 2005).
- Women and men have virtually identical mean IQs, but women's brains are smaller on average (Ankney, 1992).
- Other research, beginning with Galton's, indicates that brain size is minimally related to intelligence, and the meaning of even this weak correlation is not clear. Does larger brain mass cause intelligence, do lots of "intelligent" interactions with the environment facilitate brain growth, or do other factor(s) cause both brain mass and intelligence?

The size of certain brain areas may indeed result in more efficiency on certain types of tasks. Colom et al. (2008) report that the thickness of the prefrontal, frontal, and parietal lobes was correlated with measures of both fluid and crystallized intelligence. Gregory et al. (2016) have demonstrated that the degree of folding or gyrification in the prefrontal cortex is related to general cognitive ability. Haier et al. (2005) have shown that different amounts of white and grey matter are devoted to intelligence in men and women. In general, men have about 6.5 times as much grey matter (related to general intelligence) as women do, but women have almost ten times the amount of white matter. Thus, it would appear that males have greater information-processing capacity, but women have superior connectivity. This variation could well explain reported sex differences in cognitive abilities (see this chapter's *Research Foundations* feature). In addition, the areas related to general intelligence tended to be more centralized (e.g., in the frontal lobe) in women than in men. These anatomical differences would appear to occur early in biological development (Schmithorst & Holland, 2007).

HEREDITY, ENVIRONMENT, AND INTELLIGENCE

Genes and environment both influence intelligence, but they rarely operate independently of one another. The environment can influence how genes express themselves, as when prenatal factors or malnutrition retard gene-directed brain development. Likewise, genetic factors can influence the effects produced by the environment. For example, genetic factors influence which environments people select for themselves, how they respond to the environment, and how the environment responds to the person (Plomin & Spinath, 2004; Scarr & McCartney, 1983).

26. What evidence supports a genetic contribution to intelligence, and how much IQ group variation is accounted for?

Review

- Most modern intelligence tests, such as the Wechsler scales, measure an array of different mental abilities. In addition to a global, or full-scale, IQ, they provide scores for each subtest and summary scores for broader abilities, such as verbal and performance IQs. Some recent tests are derived directly from theories of intelligence. The Kaufman scale provides separate scores for crystallized and fluid intelligence, and Sternberg's STAT measures analytical, practical, and creative intelligence.

- Achievement tests measure what has already been learned, whereas aptitude tests are assumed to measure potential for future learning and performance. Most intelligence tests measure combinations of achievement and aptitude, for it is difficult to separate past learning and future learning potential.

- Three important standards for psychological tests are reliability (consistency of measurement over time, within tests, and across scorers), validity (successful measurement of the construct and acceptable relations with relevant criterion measures), and standardization (development of norms and standard testing conditions).

- IQ scores successfully predict a range of academic, occupational, and life outcomes, including how long people live. Such findings indicate that intelligence tests are measuring important adaptational skills.

- The Flynn effect refers to the notable rise in intelligence test scores over the past century, possibly due to better living conditions, more schooling, or more complex environments.

- In dynamic testing, standard test administration is followed by feedback and suggestions from the examiner and a retaking of the test, thus allowing an assessment of how well the person profits from feedback and how intellectual skills might be coached in the future. Dynamic testing provides information that static testing does not, and retest scores sometimes relate more strongly to criterion measures.

- Intelligence testing in non-Western cultures is a challenge. One approach is to use tests that are not tied to any culture's knowledge base. Another approach is to devise tests of the abilities that are important to adaptation in that culture. These culture-specific abilities may bear little relation to the mental skills assessed by Western intelligence tests.

- Recent physiological evidence suggests that the brains of intelligent people may function more efficiently. Brain size is not significantly related to intelligence, but the neural networks laid down in the process of brain development may be extremely important. One current theory is that differences in brain plasticity may underlie intelligence.

As we saw in Chapter 4, intelligence clearly has a strong genetic component, with heritability coefficients ranging between 0.50 and 0.70 being reported consistently in both twin and adoption studies (Plomin et al., 2007). This indicates that more than half, and perhaps more than two-thirds, of the within-group variation in IQ is attributable to genetic factors. Overall, the pattern is quite clear: The more genes people have in common, the more similar they tend to be in IQ. In identical twins, the IQ correlation remains at about 0.80 from age four through adulthood. In adulthood, correlations for fraternal twins drop to around 0.40. Doubling this difference in correlations yields a heritability coefficient of 0.80 in adulthood, indicating that genetic factors become even more important as we age (Plomin & Spinath, 2004). One reason may be

that new genes come on line to affect intelligence as more-advanced cognitive processes emerge during development. Another is that genetic influences snowball during development as people create and select environments that are compatible with their genetic characteristics.

Although genes are important foundations of the *g* factor (Bouchard, 2014; Plomin et al., 2007), there clearly is not a single "intelligence gene." The diverse abilities measured by intelligence tests are undoubtedly influenced by large numbers of interacting genes, and different combinations seem to underlie specific abilities (Lykken, 2006; Plomin & Spinath, 2004). The newly acquired ability to measure the genome directly has led to a search for specific genes and gene combinations that underlie intelligence. This search brings us ever closer to an understanding of the neurological basis for human cognition, and a handful of candidate genes associated with intelligence have already been identified (Deary et al., 2006; Posthuma & de Geus, 2006).

Genes are not the whole story, however (Daw et al., 2015). As we noted in Chapter 4 (Table 4.2), IQ correlations for identical twins raised together are slightly higher than those for identical twins raised apart. The same is true for other types of siblings raised together and raised apart. This rules out an entirely genetic explanation. Although one's genotype is an important factor in determining intelligence test scores, environment seems to account for 30 to 50 percent of the IQ variation among people. Both shared and unshared environmental factors are involved (Schermer et al., 2015). Behaviour-genetic studies indicate that between a quarter and a third of the population variability in intelligence can be attributed to shared environmental factors, particularly the family environment (Figure 10.15). The importance of the home environment is also shown in studies of children who are removed from deprived environments and placed in middle- or upper-class adoptive homes. Typically, such children show a gradual increase in IQ on the order of 10 to 12 points (Scarr & Weinberg, 1977; Schiff & Lewontin, 1986). Conversely, when deprived children remain in their impoverished environments, they either show no improvement in IQ, or they actually deteriorate intellectually over time (Serpell, 2000). Scores on

general intelligence correlate around 0.40 with the socioeconomic status of the family in which a child is reared (Lubinski, 2004).

Recall also the Flynn effect, the notable IQ increases that have occurred in Western countries during the last century. It's highly unlikely that genetic changes can explain such gains. More likely, they are due to better and longer schooling during the past century, more-complex and stimulating environments provided by better-educated parents, and by technological advances (even TV and video games), as well as better nutrition (Greenfield, 1998). Although the environment we live in may be more complex, fast-paced, and stressful than it was a century ago, it is also more conducive to learning the mental skills that are assessed on measures of intelligence.

As we might expect, educational experiences can have a significant positive impact on intelligence. Many studies have shown that school attendance can raise IQ and lack of attendance can lower scores (Ceci & Williams, 1997). It appears that the opportunity to practise mental skills such as those assessed on cognitive tests is important in solidifying mental skills. Research on intelligence has had a strong impact on educational curricula, and much has been learned about what, when, and how to teach. School-related gains in intelligence are most likely to be observed under the following conditions (Mayer, 2000):

- Rather than "teaching to" general mental ability, help students learn the specific cognitive skills and problem-solving approaches that

27. How much do family and school environments contribute to intelligence?

(left): © Jim Cummins/Corbis; (right): © Tomasz Tomaszewski/National Geographic/Getty Images

FIGURE 10.15 Shared family environment has a significant influence on intelligence, accounting for between a quarter and a third of IQ variation in children.

28. What effects have been shown in early-intervention programs for disadvantaged children?

underlie success in particular subjects. This is an outgrowth of education's increasing de-emphasis on the *g* factor and renewed emphasis on the development of specific mental skills.

- Replace the traditional emphasis on repetition and rote learning of facts with instruction in *how* to learn, critically think about, and apply course content. In this approach, teachers function as "mental coaches."

- Rather than waiting until low-level skills have been mastered before teaching learning tools such as memory-enhancement strategies, apply this "learning to learn" approach from the very beginning so that the skills are applied to even the most-basic course content.

Many children begin their lives in conditions that are not conducive to developing intellectual skills. An important outgrowth of intelligence research is the attempt to intervene early in the lives of such children. The *Applications* feature examines several of these programs and what they've accomplished.

GROUP DIFFERENCES IN INTELLIGENCE

Some of the most controversial issues in the study of intelligence revolve around group differences. Ethnic and social-class differences exist, as do differences between men and women. The meaning of these differences—and their

Applications

EARLY-CHILDHOOD INTERVENTIONS: A MEANS OF BOOSTING INTELLIGENCE?

The belief that early-childhood education can influence the life success of poor children can be found in the 18th-century writings of the French social philosopher Jean-Jacques Rousseau. In the United States today, that belief translates into the annual expenditure of more than $10 billion on early-intervention programs designed to reverse the downward course of cognitive and social development, school dropout rate, and joblessness that is so often seen in children from low-income families (Ramey et al., 1998).

In the 1960s, researchers and educators in the United States began to design early-childhood intervention programs, such as Head Start, in an attempt to compensate for the limited learning environments of disadvantaged children. Head Start began as a summer program and gradually increased in scope. But even when it was extended to a full school year, Head Start was only a half-day program that did not begin until age four. The results were disappointing. Within two years, Head Start children were performing in school no better than children who had not attended Head Start (McKey et al., 1985).

What had gone wrong? Was the Head Start program too little, too late? How much might a more intensive program begun earlier in life help disadvantaged children? These questions inspired several notable intervention programs, namely, the Abecedarian Program and the High/Scope Perry Preschool Program.

Participants in the Abecedarian Program were healthy infants born to impoverished families in a southern U.S. community. Many were African-American. The children were

© Banana Stock/AGE Fotostock

FIGURE 10.16 The Abecedarian Program provided intensive preschool learning experiences for low-income, high-risk children. Here a trainer in an early-intervention program teaches number concepts to preschool children.

randomly assigned to an experimental preschool program or to a control group whose families received normal social services. The preschool group was given an intensive early-childhood educational program beginning when they were six months old and continuing until they began kindergarten at five years of age. Within an educational child-care setting, highly trained preschool personnel exposed the children to many stimulating learning experiences designed to foster the growth of cognitive skills (Figure 10.16). At age five, the preschool program ended, but half of the preschool

continued

children and half of the control children were enrolled in a special home-and-school educational program during the first three years of school. This experimental design allowed the researchers to test the effects of early versus later intervention.

The long-term effects of the program have now been evaluated. By the time the children had been in the program for one year, they tested 18 IQ points higher than the control group. By age 15, the IQ advantage of the children in the preschool condition had decreased to about five points, but they also had higher scores on standardized tests of reading and mathematics than did the control-group children. Only about half as many had been held back a grade or placed in special education.

A particularly notable IQ effect was found for children in the preschool condition whose mothers were mentally retarded, having IQs below 70. In this sample, every one of the children who had the early intervention attained an IQ at least 20 points higher than their mother's, with an average difference of 32 IQ points. No such effect was found in the control group (Landesman & Ramey, 1989). A difference of this magnitude is truly remarkable for children of mentally retarded parents, one reason being that such parents are unable to provide much in the way of intellectual stimulation for their children. Apparently, the preschool program provided the environmental stimulation needed for normal intellectual development to occur.

What of the control-group children who did not attend the preschool program but were exposed to the special program from five to eight years of age? This delayed training had little effect on any of the outcome measures. Also, the later training had almost no added effects on the children who had been in the preschool program. It thus appears that early intervention has a much stronger effect than does later training. By the time disadvantaged children are in school, it may be too late to influence their future cognitive development to any great degree (Ramey & Ramey, 1998).

The Abecedarian Program showed positive intervention effects that were still apparent in adolescence. What effect does early intervention have on later adult functioning? Here, we turn to another program, the High/Scope Perry Preschool Program, carried out with African-American children who lived in an impoverished area of Ypsilanti, Michigan. The participants were considered at high risk for educational and social problems. They were two or three years old when they were matched on IQ and family variables and randomly assigned to either an intensive preschool program or a control group that did not receive the program. The intervention continued for three years.

The two groups of children have been followed up into adulthood and the results are encouraging. Figure 10.17 compares what happened to the two groups in the 22 years after the program ended. The early-education group had lower crime rates, required less welfare

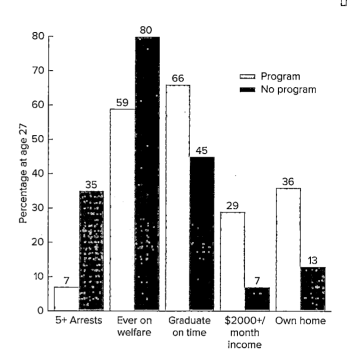

FIGURE 10.17 Effects of early intervention. This graph shows the differences by age 27 between disadvantaged children who received the High/Scope Perry Preschool Program and matched control children.

Source: Schweinhart, Lawrence J., and David P. Weikart. Figure 5.1, "Major Findings at Age Twenty-Seven." In *Social Programs That Work.* © 1998 Russell Sage Foundation, 112 East 64th Street, New York, NY 10021. Reprinted with permission.

assistance, exhibited better academic performance and progress, and had higher incomes and home ownership. A cost-benefit analysis showed that the early-intervention program provided taxpayers with a return of $7.16 for every dollar invested in the program (Schweinhart & Weikart, 1998).

Does early intervention work? The Abecedarian and High/Scope Perry programs suggest that it can provide social, intellectual, educational, and psychological dividends if the program is intensive enough and administered very early in life (Masten & Coatsworth, 1998; Reppucci et al., 1999). A more recent early-intevention program conducted with low-birth-weight children, also considered at risk for later cognitive impairment and academic failure, showed significant IQ gains of seven to ten points, but only for those children who had attended the program for at least 400 days between the ages of two and three (Hill et al., 2003). We should also note that the positive effects of early-intervention programs seem to occur only for disadvantaged children, for whom quality programs offer learning opportunities and support that the children would not experience at home. Such programs do little for middle- and upper-class children who already have those resources in their homes (Hetherington, 1998).

political, social, and educational implications—has often sparked bitter debate and, at times, discriminatory policies. It has also inspired stereotypes about certain groups and influenced the self-image of group members.

Ethnic Group Differences

Some of the most contentious debates in psychology have concerned the existence and meaning of ethnic and racial group differences in intelligence. Discussions of intellectual differences between ethnic groups and between men and women touch on deeply held notions of social equality. Consider the case of J. Philippe Rushton at Western University. Rushton (1995) suggested that on over 60 measures, ranging from intelligence, to brain size, to a host of physical and social variables, there was a consistent pattern: Individuals of East Asian descent scored the "highest," those of African descent scored the "lowest," and Caucasians fell in the middle. There was an immediate flurry of political activity following Rushton's announcement of these findings at a conference. Rushton was investigated by both the Ontario Provincial Police and the Ontario Human Rights Commission. The premier of Ontario called for his dismissal, and the university was forced to cancel all classes taught by Rushton for safety considerations. Over the past two decades, there have been many supporters of Rushton's right to publish articles on these matters, while many others have argued that the work encourages hatred and, consequently, violates the Ontario Human Rights Code. Similar observations have been reported in the United States. For example, in 1969, in the midst of the civil rights struggle, an article in the *Harvard Educational Review* by Arthur Jensen sparked debate and, in many quarters, outrage. Jensen concluded that because the heritability of intelligence is substantial, genetic differences are "strongly implicated" in ethnic group differences in intelligence. A quarter century later, in a *New York Times* bestseller titled *The Bell Curve*, Richard Herrnstein and Charles Murray (1994) painted a pessimistic picture of the future for ethnic groups that lag behind in genetically influenced mental competencies. Like Jensen's article, *The Bell Curve* evoked considerable controversy. There are numerous articles that support the Asian, Caucasian, and African

rankings (e.g., Lynn & Cheng, 2013; Rushton, 2012), but because the questions under scrutiny are complex and the evidence does not warrant any simple conclusions, the debate is unlikely to be resolved any time soon.

Where ethnic groups are concerned, everyone agrees on certain facts. Today, there are consistent differences in the average intelligence test scores of members of different racial and national groups. National comparisons indicate that Japanese children have the highest mean IQ in the world (Hunt, 1995). Their mean score of 111 places 77 percent of Japanese children above the mean scores of North American and European children. Within the United States, significant ethnic differences also exist. Asian Americans test slightly below White American norms on verbal skills but somewhat higher on tests related to spatial and mathematical reasoning. Hispanic people who have become U.S.-acculturated score at about the same level as White Americans. African Americans score, on average, about 12 to 15 IQ points below the White American average (Jencks & Phillips, 1998).

This, of course, does not mean that all White Americans and Hispanic Americans test lower than Asian Americans or that all African Americans test lower than the other ethnic groups. There is great overlap among group IQ distributions, and in all groups, some individuals score at the highest levels. Nonetheless, the average group differences are large enough to have practical consequences, such as ethnic differences in academic achievement. However, a recent report by Nisbett et al. (2012) suggests that the gap is narrowing, but it still exists—although other authors (e.g., Woodley & Meisenberg, 2012) suggest that these conclusions are not justified. The unanswered question is as follows: Where do these differences come from? Much work is currently underway to separate science from myth (Fish, 2002).

Are the Tests Biased?

Keep in mind that these group differences apply to test scores, which are the standard operational definition of the construct we call *intelligence*. Some have expressed concerns that these tests underestimate the mental competence of minority group members because the tests are based on Euro-American White culture and therefore are culturally biased.

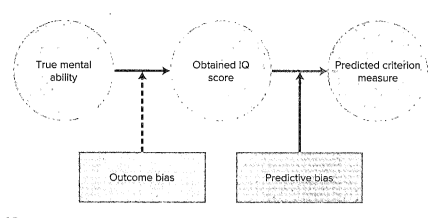

FIGURE 10.18 Test bias can take two forms. Outcome bias would occur if the nature of the test items significantly underestimated true mental ability because of factors such as cultural relevance. Predictive bias would occur if test scores predicted criterion measures accurately for one group, but not for another.

Test bias can actually take two forms (Figure 10.18). **Outcome bias** refers to the extent that a test underestimates a person's true intellectual ability. **Predictive bias** occurs if the test successfully predicts criterion measures, such as school or job performance, for some groups but not for others (Serpell, 2000).

Defenders of intelligence tests dismiss both types of bias. They point out that ethnic group differences appear throughout intelligence tests, not just on those items that would, at face value, appear to be culturally biased (Jensen, 1980, 1998). They also point out that intelligence test scores predict the performance of minority group members as accurately as they predict White people's performance (Barrett & Depinet, 1991; Kuncel et al., 2004). For example, even though African Americans as a group score lower than White Americans, the tests predict academic and occupational performance with equal accuracy for both racial groups, indicating that they are measuring relevant mental skills (Hunt, 1995). Test critics remain unconvinced, asserting that current measures can be outcome-biased in underestimating the mental skills of ethnic minorities.

What Factors Underlie the Differences?

The next dispute about racial differences is a rather different one. The nature–nurture discussion tentatively accepts the differences in measures of mental abilities as being real and then asks why they exist. Consider the differences between White Americans and African Americans. On the nurture side, there is no question that a higher proportion of White than African-American children are raised and schooled in enriched environments that optimize the development of cognitive skills. However, social changes over the past 25 years have provided African Americans with greater access to educational and vocational opportunities and have coincided with an increase in African-American IQs that has reduced the IQ difference between African Americans and White Americans by about a third (Barnett & Camilli, 2002). These shrinking ethnic differences also extend to reading and mathematics achievement tests in Grades 1 through 12, as well as to standardized university entrance exams in the United States (Block, 2002).

People who are impressed by this decreasing test gap tend to attribute ethnic differences to environmental differences that could be changed, ranging from nutritional factors to educational opportunities (Grigorenko, 2003; Nisbett, 1998). Meredith Phillips and colleagues (1998) analyzed a wide range of family-environment factors in relation to intellectual differences between five- and six-year-old African-American and White children. They concluded that family-environment factors alone could account for about two-thirds of the test score gap. Figure 10.19 provides an agricultural analogy of how environmental factors (in this case, rich or poor soil) can produce group differences even for a genetically influenced variable.

The key role played by the social environment also may be illustrated by a historical example involving a different minority group. Early in the 20th century, the average

29. What explanations have been offered for differences in IQ between ethnic groups?

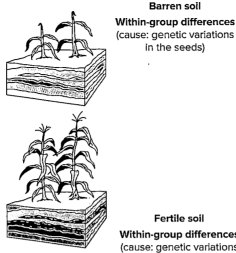

Barren soil
Within-group differences
(cause: genetic variations in the seeds)

Between-group differences
(cause: the soils in which the plants were grown)

Fertile soil
Within-group differences
(cause: genetic variations in the seeds)

FIGURE 10.19 Heredity and environment. The interaction of heredity and environment is shown in this agricultural analogy. Seeds planted in fertile soil will be, on average, larger than those planted in barren soil. This between-groups variability is attributable to environment. Within each field, however, plants will also differ in size as a result of genetic factors. Applied to intelligence, this analogy indicates how between-group differences could result from environmental factors despite the fact that intelligence has a strong genetic component.

30. What sex differences exist in cognitive skills? What biological and environmental factors might be involved?

Italian-American child had an IQ of 87, about the same as the average score of African Americans today. Henry Goddard (1917), a leading hereditarian researcher of the time, concluded that 79 percent of Italian-American immigrants were "feebleminded," posed a danger to the U.S. gene pool, and should not be allowed to immigrate to the United States. Today, the average Italian-American student obtains an above-average IQ (Ceci, 1996). Obviously, genetic changes in Italian Americans could not produce a gain of this size over such a short time. Cultural assimilation and educational and economic opportunity seem much more reasonable explanations for this pronounced increase in test scores.

Another factor worth noting is a tendency, even among some scientists, to overemphasize genetic differences between groups. Indeed, where measured directly, genetic differences, like test scores, tend to be greater *within* any given racial group than they are between racial groups (Block, 2002). For example, both African Americans and White Americans exhibit greater genetic variation among themselves than that which exists between the average African American and the average White American.

Sex Differences in Cognitive Abilities

Men and women differ in physical attributes and reproductive function. They also differ in their performance on certain types of intellectual tasks. The gender differences lie not in levels of general intelligence but rather in the patterns of cognitive skills that men and women exhibit (e.g., Pezzuti & Orsini, 2016). Men, on average, tend to outperform women slightly on certain spatial tasks, such as the ones shown in Figure 10.20. Men are more accurate in target-directed skills, such as throwing and catching objects, and they tend to perform slightly better on tests of mathematical reasoning (Gallagher et al., 2000). Women, on average, perform better on tests of perceptual speed, verbal fluency, and mathematical calculation and on precise manual tasks requiring fine-motor coordination (Collins & Kimura, 1997; Lippa, 2005). Although typically small, these ability differences have been reported quite consistently by researchers (Halpern, 2004; Hampson & Kimura, 1992; Hines, 2005). Keep in mind, however, that men and women also vary considerably among themselves in all these skills, and the performance distributions of males and females overlap considerably.

**Problem-solving tasks
favouring women**

**Problem-solving tasks
favouring men**

Women tend to perform better than men on tests of perceptual speed, in which people must rapidly identify matching items—for example, pairing the house on the far left with its twin.

Men tend to perform better than women on certain spatial tasks. They do well on tests that involve mentally rotating an object or manipulating it in some fashion, such as choosing which of the three objects at right is the same as the one on the left.

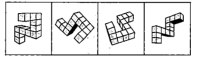

On some tests of ideational fluency, for example, those in which people must list objects that are the same colour, and on tests of verbal fluency, for example, those in which participants must list words that begin with the same letter, women also outperform men.

Men also are more accurate than women in target-directed motor skills, such as guiding or intercepting projectiles.

L _ _ _	Limp, Livery, Love, Laser, Liquid, Low, Like, Lag, Live, Lug, Light, Lift, Liver, Lime, Leg, Load, Lap, Lucid . . .

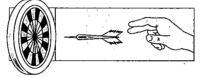

FIGURE 10.20 Male–female cognitive differences. Some of the most consistent gender differences in cognitive abilities reported in the scientific literature occur on tasks like these.
Adapted from Kimura, D. (1992). Sex differences in the brain. *Scientific American, 267*, 119–195.

Psychologists have proposed explanations for these gender differences, citing both biological and environmental factors. The environmental explanations typically focus on the socialization experiences that males and females have as they grow up, especially the kinds of sex-typed activities that boys and girls are steered into (Crawford & Chaffin, 1997). Prior to the early 1980s, for example, boys were far more likely than girls to play sports that involve throwing and catching balls, which might help to account for their general superiority in this ability. Evolutionary theorists have also weighed in on the differences, suggesting that sex-role specialization developed in ancestral environments. Men's roles, such as navigating and hunting, favoured the development of the visuospatial abilities that show up in sex-difference research. Women's roles, such as child-rearing and tool-making activities, favoured the development of verbal and manual-precision abilities (Joseph, 2000).

From a biological perspective, these differences may reflect structural differences in the brains of men and women. For example,

Burgaleta et al. (2012) report that sex differences in mental rotation tasks are related to the amount of grey matter (favouring males), while differences in verbal skills are related to the amount of white matter (favouring females). Increasingly, biological explanations have focused on the effects of hormones on the developing brain (Halpern & Tan, 2001; Hines, 2005). These influences begin during a critical period shortly after conception, when the sex hormones establish sexual differentiation. The hormonal effects go far beyond reproductive characteristics, however. They also alter brain organization and appear to extend to a variety of behavioural differences between men and women, including aggression and problem-solving approaches (Hines, 2005; Lippa, 2005).

Do hormonal factors also influence cognitive performance later in life? Several studies have shown that fluctuations in women's hormonal levels during the menstrual cycle are related to fluctuations in task performance. This research is discussed in the *Research Foundations* feature.

Research Foundations

EFFECTS OF HORMONAL FLUCTUATIONS ON PERCEPTUAL AND MOTOR SKILLS

Introduction

Gonadal steroids have been shown to influence sex-linked behaviour in a variety of nonhuman species (e.g., Hines & Gorski, 1985). Much of this work has focused on reproduction, but other behaviours (such as bird song) may be influenced as well. Could some of the sex differences in cognitive abilities among humans also be influenced by hormonal fluctuation? This intriguing question is addressed in the following study by Hampson and Kimura (1988).

Method

Thirty-four women with regular, spontaneous menstrual cycles were recruited for the study. The average age of the participants was 24.65 years and most (32) were right-handed. All participants were tested twice, approximately six weeks apart. For each woman, one testing session was scheduled during menstruation (day 3, 4, or 5). At this time, levels of estrogen and progesterone are low. The second testing session took place when levels of estrogen and progesterone were much higher—seven days before the onset of menstruation (the midluteal phase). Order of testing was counterbalanced across all participants.

At each of the sessions, the women completed a battery of cognitive and motor tests. These tests included the portable Rod-and-Frame test (Oltman, 1968; Witkin et al., 1962) and three tests of manual coordination. The Rod-and-Frame test requires the participant to align a rod to the true vertical position when it is presented against a tilted background. Typically, men are more accurate at this test than women are. The manual coordination tests included

finger tapping (tapping a telegraph key with the index finger), pegboard assembly (inserting pegs into a board to assemble various targets), and a test of manual sequencing in which participants first learn a series of movements and are then tested under speeded conditions. The women also completed a mood inventory prior to each session.

Results

The women were significantly less accurate on the Rod-and-Frame task during the midluteal phase than during menstruation (see Figure 10.21). The rod was set more degrees off true vertical when levels of estrogen and progesterone were high. In contrast, performance on the manual coordination tasks was better during the midluteal phase than during menstruation. Participants assembled more peg components, required less time on the speeded manual coordination task, and achieved higher accuracy during the midluteal phase. The mood inventory revealed no significant differences in affect for the two sessions. Thus, mood cannot account for any of the observed differences.

In a separate study, results were obtained for a group of women who were on oral contraceptives. Their performance

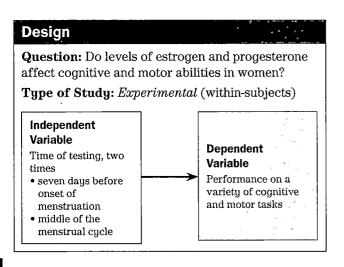

Design

Question: Do levels of estrogen and progesterone affect cognitive and motor abilities in women?

Type of Study: *Experimental* (within-subjects)

Independent Variable		Dependent Variable
Time of testing, two times • seven days before onset of menstruation • middle of the menstrual cycle	→	Performance on a variety of cognitive and motor tasks

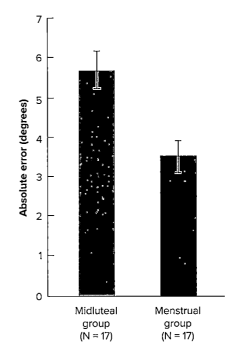

FIGURE 10.21 Rod-and-Frame performance.

Source: Hampson, E., & Kimura, D. (1988). Reciprocal effects of hormonal fluctuations on human motor and perceptual-spatial skills. *Behavioral Neuroscience*, 102(3), pp. 456-459. Reprinted with permission by American Psychological Association.

continued

on speeded tasks was even better than that of the midluteal group. This result could be expected given the elevated levels of estrogen and progestin from the oral contraceptives.

Discussion

The women in this study performed differently at different phases of their menstrual cycles. When levels of estrogen and progesterone were high (midluteal phase), the women performed the tasks faster and with greater accuracy. However, when these hormonal levels were lower (during menstruation), performance declined. It is interesting to note that the size of the performance difference due to these hormonal fluctuations is about 70 percent of the reported difference between men and women on these tasks.

Kimura has also demonstrated that there are reliable differences in these skills based on sexual orientation

(Hall & Kimura, 2005). On a throw-to-target task, heterosexual men outperformed heterosexual women, but gay men were less accurate than heterosexual men, and lesbian women were more accurate than heterosexual women. These results held when sports history and hand strength were controlled. Whether these observed differences in motor skills based on sexual orientation reflect biological underpinnings remains a subject for further research.

Finally, it should be noted that a more recent study measured a wide range of sex hormones in men and women before they performed a variety of cognitive tasks. Men and women showed the typically reported differences in cognitive skills, but no relations were found between any of the measured hormones and cognitive performance (Halari et al., 2005). Thus, the role of sex hormones in adulthood remains unclear.

Source: Hampson, E., & Kimura, D. (1988). Reciprocal effects of hormonal fluctuations on human motor and perceptual-spatial skills. *Behavioral Neuroscience, 102*(3), 456–459.

EXTREMES OF INTELLIGENCE

Because of the many genetic and environmental influences on intelligence, there are individuals at both ends of the intelligence distribution who have unusual mental abilities. At the upper end are the "intellectually gifted"; at the low end are those labelled *intellectually disabled* or *cognitively disabled*.

The Intellectually Gifted

At the top end of the intelligence bell curve are the intellectually gifted, whose IQs of 130 or higher place them in the top 10 percent of the population. Their high IQs do not mean that they are good at everything, however. As we might expect from the theories of multiple intelligences, many are enormously talented in one area of mental competence but quite average in other domains. Even with IQs over 150, large discrepancies are often found between verbal and spatial-mathematical skills (Achter et al., 1996). Thus, a mathematical prodigy who figures out rules of algebra on his own at age three may have relatively unexceptional verbal skills. But what accounts for prodigious talent? We examine one possibility in this chapter's *Frontiers* feature.

Only a small percentage of gifted children attain true eminence in later life. Eminence

seems to be a special variety of giftedness. Joseph Renzulli (2002) has studied this rare group, and he believes that their success is a product of three interacting factors. The first is highly developed mental abilities—not only general intelligence but also specific mental abilities related to one's chosen field. Thus, Einstein was blessed with unusual mathematical and spatial abilities (but not exceptional verbal skills). The second factor is the ability to engage in creative problem solving—that is, to come up with novel and unconventional ideas, to judge their potential value, and to apply them to challenging problems (Sternberg & Davidson, 2005). The third factor is motivation and dedication. Eminence involves a great deal of elbow grease and a determination to attain the highest levels of performance. Studies of eminent scientists, artists, musicians, writers, and athletes reveal that they tend to work much harder and dedicate themselves more strongly to excellence than do their less eminent counterparts (Simonton, 2001). Given that the person has the requisite level of intelligence, these nonintellectual factors become especially important. Many eminent figures, including Sigmund Freud and Charles Darwin, showed no signs of being exceptionally gifted as children, but their motivation and dedication helped them achieve greatness in their professions.

31. What factors allow gifted people to become eminent?

Frontiers

MUSICAL TRAINING AND AUDITORY PROCESSING

What distinguishes the thought processes of the gifted? Some theorists believe that gifted children think in the same way as average children but simply do it much more efficiently (Jackson & Butterfield, 1986). Others disagree. When they see a child capable of memorizing an entire musical score after hearing it once, they conclude that this ability is based on a different quality of thinking that involves great intuition and a passion for the specific domain in which the child excels (Winner, 2000). However, a growing body of evidence suggests that musical training may promote enhanced auditory skills and help in the development of cognitive processing.

Musical training can result in actual changes to the auditory system (Hannon & Trainor, 2007). For example, individuals who have learned to play the piano show more reactivity in the auditory cortex to piano notes, as compared with those without musical training (Pantev et al., 1998). In a recent review, Kraus and Chandrasekaran (2010) argue that these changes reflect neural plasticity and result in part from experience—the amount of neural activity was correlated with the age at which an individual learned to play the piano. Moreover, observed changes in function and structure can be shown to be *caused* by musical training. Longitudinal studies of children randomly assigned to either a music training program or an art training program reveal structural changes favouring musical training in the primary auditory cortex as well as the motor cortex (Hyde et al., 2009). Kraus and Chandrasekaran (2010) argue that these studies indicate strongly that musical training results in changes to brain structure that enhance the processing of musical information throughout one's life.

But does enhanced musical processing transfer to any other tasks? Kraus and Chandrasekaran (2010) report that musical training results in superior processing of pitch, timing cues, auditory information in general, and even speech. In a wide variety of studies, the physical encoding of sound (cortical and subcortical) was positively correlated with an individual's amount of musical training.

Kraus and Chandrasekaran (2010) are careful to point out that there has been much debate over whether musical experience can influence general cognitive abilities (recall our discussion of the Mozart effect in Chapter 2). But these results are intriguing. Musicians can more easily incorporate sound patterns when learning a new language (Wong & Perrachaone, 2007), and children with musical training have better language and reading skills than those without training (Overy, 2003; Tallal & Gaab, 2006). Musical training requires attentional skills, good memory strategies, and implicit learning—all skills that are related to language and intelligence. It is not such a big leap to suggest that musical training may indeed improve one's cognitive functioning, and in essence, enhance intelligence. In fact, a recent study suggests that musical training results in higher executive functioning in both children and adults, enabling them to process information faster (Zuk et al., 2014). In any event, musical training results in a host of benefits, and Kraus and Chandrasekaran (2010) suggest we rethink the role of music in the education system, particularly in the early years.

Like children at the low end of the competence continuum, intellectually gifted children often need special educational opportunities (e.g., Callahan et al., 2015). They may become bored in

Thinking critically

ARE GIFTED CHILDREN MALADJUSTED?

The image of the introverted, socially awkward, and unhappy "nerd" is familiar to all of us. Gifted children are often depicted in the media as unathletic, interested in intellectual activities that do not excite most students, and socially inept. Is there truth in this stereotype? What would you expect research on gifted children to show?

Think about it, and then see the Answers section at the end of the book.

regular classrooms and even drop out of school if they are not sufficiently challenged (Phillipson & McCann, 2007). Yet many school systems have de-emphasized programs for the gifted in the same spirit of egalitarianism that places cognitively challenged children in regular classrooms. Increasingly, parents of gifted children are enrolling their children in special camps and extracurricular programs to provide the needed intellectual stimulation and exposure to peer groups with common interests and abilities (Winner, 2000).

The Intellectually Disabled

Approximately 3 to 5 percent of the North American population, or about 10 million people, are classified as having intellectual disability disorder. In the DSM-IV-TR, the American

TABLE 10.5 **Adaptive Capabilities of Cognitively Challenged People over the Lifespan (DSM-IV-TR)**

Category	Percentage of Intellectually Disabled Population	Birth through Age 5	Age 6 through Age 20	Age 21 and Older
Mild: 50–70 IQ	85	Often not noticed as delayed by casual observer but is slower to walk, feed him- or herself, and talk than most children.	Can acquire practical skills and master reading and arithmetic to a third- to sixth-grade level with special education. Can be guided toward social conformity.	Can usually achieve adequate social, vocational, and self-maintenance skills. May need occasional guidance and support when under unusual social or economic stress.
Moderate: 35–50 IQ	10	Noticeable delays in motor development, especially in speech. Responds to training in various self-help activities.	Can learn simple communication, elementary health and safety habits, and simple manual skills. Does not progress in functional reading or arithmetic.	Can perform simple tasks under sheltered conditions, participate in simple recreation, and travel alone in familiar places. Usually incapable of self-maintenance.
Severe: 20–35 IQ	4	Marked delay in motor development. Little or no communication skill. May respond to training in elementary self-help, such as self-feeding.	Usually walks, barring specific disability. Has some understanding of speech and some response. Can profit from systematic habit training.	Can conform to daily routines and repetitive activities. Needs continuing direction and supervision in protective environment.
Profound: below 20 IQ	1	Gross disability. Minimal capacity for functioning in sensorimotor areas. Needs nursing care.	Obvious delays in all areas of development. Shows basic emotional responses. May respond to skills training in use of legs, hands, and jaws. Needs close supervision.	May walk, need nursing care, have primitive speech. Usually benefits from regular physical activity. Incapable of self-maintenance.

Source: Reprinted with permission from the *Diagnostic and Statistical Manual of Mental Disorders*, Text Revision. Copyright © 2000, American Psychiatric Association.

Psychiatric Association devised a four-level system that classifies intellectual disability as mild, moderate, severe, or profound on the basis of IQ scores. Table 10.5 describes these classifications. As you can see, the vast majority are mildly disabled, obtaining IQs between about 50 and 70. Most members of this largest group, given appropriate social and educational support, are capable of functioning adequately in mainstream society, holding jobs, and raising families. Progressively greater environmental support is needed as we move toward the profoundly disabled range, where institutional care is usually required. The DSM-5 has shifted away from basing these distinctions totally on IQ scores and requires a test of adaptive functioning in addition to IQ.

Mildly disabled children can attend school, but they have difficulties in reading, writing, memory, and mathematical computation. Many of these difficulties result from poorly developed problem-solving strategies. They often have deficiencies in the executive functions discussed in Chapter 3: reasoning, planning, and evaluating feedback from their efforts (Molfese & Molfese, 2002).

Intellectual disability has a variety of causes: some genetic, some due to other biological factors, and some due to environmental causes. Genetic abnormalities account for about 28 percent of all intellectual disability disorder cases (Winnepenninckx et al., 2003). More than 500 different genetic causes of intellectual disability have been identified (Brown & Percy, 2007; Bulayeva et al., 2015). For example, *Down syndrome* (formerly called *mongolism*), which is characterized by mild to severe mental disability, is caused by an abnormal division of the twenty-first chromosome pair.

Heritability plays a different role in mild disability than it does in profound disability (Plomin & Spinath, 2004). Cases of profound intellectual disability are more likely to be caused by genetic accidents instead of an inherited genotype (Zechner et al., 2001). Therefore, profound intellectual disability does not run in families. In one study of 17 000 children, about half of 1 percent were profoundly disabled. None of these children's siblings had an IQ below 85, and their mean IQ was 103. In contrast, the siblings of the 1.2 percent who were

32. How do causal factors differ for mild and profound intellectual disability?

mildly disabled had mean IQs of 85, and a third of the siblings had IQs below 75 (Nichols, 1984).

Intellectual disability can also be caused by accidents at birth, such as severe oxygen deprivation (anoxia); and by diseases experienced by the mother during pregnancy, such as rubella or syphilis. Likewise, drugs and alcohol taken by the mother—especially in the first weeks of pregnancy when a woman is often unaware she is pregnant—can cause neural damage and intellectual disability. Despite this range of potential causes, in a significant majority (75 to 80 percent) of intellectually disabled people, no clear biological cause can be found. Experts theorize that these cases may be due to undetectable brain damage, extreme environmental deprivation, or a combination of the two.

In the United States, federal law requires that cognitively disabled children, who were formerly segregated into special education classes, be given individualized instruction in the "least restrictive environment." This has resulted in the practice of *mainstreaming*, or *inclusion programs*,

© Richard Hutchings/PhotoEdit

FIGURE 10.22 To an increasing extent, children of low intelligence have been included in normal classrooms rather than being confined to special education programs.

which allows many cognitively challenged children to attend school in regular classrooms and experience a more normal peer environment (Figure 10.22). Although not embodied in Canadian federal law, similar practices are followed by all the provinces. Each provincial education act

Review

- Intelligence is determined by interacting hereditary and environmental factors. Genes account for between 50 and 70 percent of population variation in IQ. Shared family environment accounts for perhaps one-fourth to one-third of the variance during childhood, but its effects seem to dissipate as people age. Educational experiences also influence mental skills. Heredity establishes a reaction range with upper and lower limits for intellectual potential. Environment affects the point within that range that will be reached.

- Intervention programs for disadvantaged children have positive effects on later achievement and life outcomes if they begin early in life and are applied intensively. They have little effect when applied after school begins or with middle- or upper-class children.

- Heritability estimates of intelligence can vary, depending on sample characteristics. In impoverished families, shared environment was more important than genes, whereas the opposite was found in affluent families. Twin studies also show that heritability effects on intelligence increase in adulthood.

- Cultural and ethnic differences in intelligence exist (though they may be narrowing), but the relative contributions of genetic and environmental factors are still in question. Evidence exists for

both genetic and environmental determinants. Whether intelligence tests exhibit outcome bias in underestimating the mental abilities of minorities is a point of contention, but the tests do not appear to have predictive bias.

- Although the differences are not large, men tend as a group to score higher than women on certain spatial and mathematical reasoning tasks. Women perform slightly better than men on tests of perceptual speed, verbal fluency, mathematical calculation, and fine-motor coordination. Both environmental and biological bases of sex differences have been suggested.

- Even people with IQs in the 150s often show discrepancies in specific skills. Those who achieve eminence tend to have, in addition to high IQs, high levels of interest and motivation in their chosen activities.

- Cognitive disability can be caused by a number of factors. Biological causes are identified in only about 28 percent of cases. Cognitive disability can range from mild to profound. The vast majority of disabled individuals are able to function in the mainstream of society, given appropriate support. Genetic factors seem relatively unimportant in profound intellectual disability, but they seem to play an important role in mild disability, which is more likely to run in families.

outlines a policy of inclusion—exceptional students (whether disadvantaged or gifted) must be integrated into the regular classroom.

In today's world, intellectual skills have become increasingly important for successful adaptation. General intelligence, or the *g* factor, captures the kinds of general mental flexibility needed to cope with novelty, read the environment, draw conclusions, and choose how and when to act (Lubinski, 2004). In addition to the importance of general mental ability, more specific skills, such as those at the first and second levels of Carroll's three-stratum model, may be needed to cope successfully with more narrowly defined situations and task demands. To an increasing degree, the study of intelligence is focusing on these real-life adaptations and on ways to help people develop and apply their intellectual abilities.

A Concluding Thought

In the preceding chapters, we have seen how humans learn, how they remember what they've learned, and how they think and solve problems. Language, thinking, and intelligent behaviour are intimately related to one another and to the processes of learning and memory. As we have also seen, intelligent behaviour has many causal factors. Some of these factors are summarized in Figure 10.23.

Levels of **Analysis**   Intellectual Functioning

In the preceding chapters, we have seen how humans learn, how they remember what they've learned, and how they think and solve problems. Language, thinking, and intelligent behaviour are intimately related to one another and to the processes of learning and memory. As we have also seen, intelligent behaviour has many causal factors. We now summarize the biological, psychological, and environmental factors we have discussed in this chapter.

ENVIRONMENTAL

- Shared and unshared learning environments that interact with biological reaction range influence intellectual development.
- Cultural factors influence which behavioural capabilities are prized, adaptive, and defined as intelligent.
- Sex roles influence the development of stereotypes concerning sex differences in specific abilities.
- Administration of intelligence measures may place culturally different people at a disadvantage.

BIOLOGICAL

- Genetic factors account for significant group variation in intelligence. They help to establish a biological reaction range that sets limits on the impact of environmental factors.
- Brain size and neural efficiency are underlying factors for intellectual performance.
- Sex hormones play a role in certain types of mental abilities and appear to contribute to the modest sex differences erences that exist in certain cognitive abilities.

PSYCHOLOGICAL

- There exists a general intelligence factor (*g* factor) that underlies other, more specific abilities.
- Specific cognitive and perceptual skills influence more specific task performance.
- Other cognitive skills underlie personal and emotional intelligence, as well as specific competencies described in Gardner's multiple intelligences and Sternberg's triarchic theory.
- Motivational factors clearly influence intellectual outcomes.

Considering Sternberg's triarchic theory, can you formulate a hypothesis about how biological or environmental factors might be related to his definitions of analytical, practical, and creative intelligence?

FIGURE 10.23

Gaining Direction

What are the issues?	The opening story describes the case of Kim Peek, the individual on whom Dustin Hoffman's character in the film *Rain Man* was based. Peek had savant syndrome. He could perform a number of extraordinary mental feats (such as counting), but his measured IQ was below normal. How could this be? If intelligence is a single entity, then Peek should not have been able to perform lightning-fast calculations and	still test below normal in intelligence. Alternatively, the way we measure intelligence might be flawed—it failed to account for Peek's abilities. But perhaps intelligence is more than a single entity. Perhaps there are many ways to demonstrate intelligent behaviour. We also may want to address the issue of autism because there is a relationship between autism and savant syndrome.
What do we need to know?	What is intelligence? Are there competing theories of intelligent behaviour? How do we measure intelligence?	Is the measurement of intelligence biased in any fashion? What can savants do? What causes savant syndrome?
Where can we find the information to answer these questions?	You should have a look at the various theories of intelligence, paying particular attention to how intelligence is defined and how it is measured. How can you account for Peek's abilities? Do you need to consider the issue of multiple intelligences? Is it possible that some kind of measurement error could be involved? Information	on autism and savant syndrome would be very useful. Two excellent Internet resources are the Society for Treatment of Autism (www.autism .ca) and Dr. Darold Treffert's site on savant syndrome (www.wisconsinmedicalsociety.org /professional/savant-syndrome).

Answers

The correct choice in Figure 10.14 is geometric form number 5. Can you specify why?

Motivation and Emotion

CHAPTER >
OUTLINE

PERSPECTIVES ON MOTIVATION
Instinct Theory and Evolutionary Psychology
Homeostasis and Drive Theory
Incentive and Expectancy Theories
Psychodynamic and Humanistic Theories

HUNGER AND WEIGHT REGULATION
The Physiology of Hunger
  Focus on Neuroscience: Brain Activation
  and Food Cues
Psychological Aspects of Hunger
Environmental and Cultural Factors
Obesity
  Applications: The Battle to Control Eating
  and Weight

SEXUAL MOTIVATION
Sexual Behaviour: Patterns and Changes
The Physiology of Sex
The Psychology of Sex

Cultural and Environmental Influences
Sexual Orientation

ACHIEVEMENT MOTIVATION
The Thrill of Victory, the Agony of Defeat
Achievment Goal Theory
Achievement Needs and Situational Factors
Family and Cultural Influences

MOTIVATIONAL CONFLICT

THE NATURE AND FUNCTIONS OF EMOTION
The Adaptive Value of Emotion
The Nature of Emotion
  Frontiers: A New Emotion?

THEORIES OF EMOTION
The James-Lange Somatic Theory
The Cannon-Bard Theory
Cognitive-Affective Theories
  Research Foundations: Cognition-Arousal Relations

One can never consent to creep when one feels an impulse to soar.
—Helen Keller

Dr. Larry Farwell, a former member of the Harvard Medical School, has developed a new technique for determining guilt or innocence. "Brain fingerprinting" involves the monitoring of brainwaves to determine whether or not a suspect has details of a crime or other information stored in the brain. Suspects are shown words or images that would be accessible only to someone

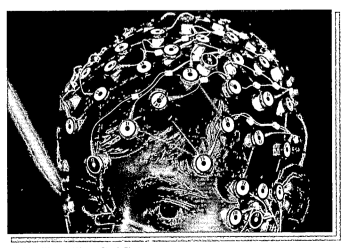
© Adrian Weston/Alamy Stock Photo

What are the issues here?

What do we need to know?

Where can we find the information to answer these questions?

who was actually at the scene of the crime. By monitoring brainwaves, the investigator can determine whether or not the suspect recognizes these images.

Dr. Farwell's testimony was instrumental in exonerating Terry Harrington, a convicted murderer who was serving a life sentence in Iowa. Brain fingerprinting revealed that the information in Harrington's brain did not match the details of the crime but, in fact, were consistent with his alibi. Unlike polygraph examinations, brain fingerprinting has been ruled admissible in U.S. courts.

The term *motivation* often triggers images of people who persevere to attain their dreams and stretch the boundaries of human achievement. But to psychologists, motivational issues are broader. What motivates eating, sexual behaviour, thrill seeking, and affiliation? **Motivation** is a process that influences the direction, persistence, and vigour of goal-directed behaviour. The word *motivation* derives from the Latin term meaning "to move," and psychologists who study motivation identify factors that move us toward our goals, whether they are obtaining food, a mate, success, or even peace and quiet.

1. According to evolutionary psychologists, how does the concept of adaptive significance help us understand human motivation?

PERSPECTIVES ON MOTIVATION

Psychology's diverse theoretical perspectives view motivation through different lenses. Let's examine some of their basic motivational concepts.

Instinct Theory and Evolutionary Psychology

Darwin's theory of evolution inspired early psychological views that instincts motivate much of our behaviour. An **instinct** is an inherited predisposition to behave in a specific and predictable way when exposed to a particular stimulus. Instincts have a genetic basis, are found universally among all members of the species, do not depend on learning, and have survival value for the organism. William James (1890) proposed about three dozen human instincts, and by the 1920s, researchers had proposed thousands (Atkinson, 1964).

Human instinct theories faded because there was little evidence to support them and they often relied on circular reasoning. Why are people greedy? Because greed is an instinct. How do we know that greed is an instinct? Because people are greedy. This explains nothing. As discussed in Chapter 4, behaviour geneticists now use twin and adoption studies to examine hereditary contributions to human motivation more productively.

Modern evolutionary psychologists propose that many "psychological" motives have evolutionary underpinnings that are expressed through the actions of genes (Buss, 2007; Palmer & Palmer, 2002). From this perspective, the *adaptive significance* of behaviour is a key to understanding motivation. For example, why are we such social creatures? Presumably, affiliation produced survival advantages—such as shared resources and protection against predators—that afforded our ancestors a greater opportunity to pass on their genes to successive generations. Over the ages the genes of "affiliative people" made up an increasing part of the human gene pool, and we became biologically predisposed to be social rather than reclusive.

Homeostasis and Drive Theory

Your body's biological systems are delicately balanced to ensure survival. For example, when you are hot, your body automatically tries to cool itself by perspiring. When you are cold, your body generates warmth by shivering. In 1932, Walter Cannon proposed the concept of **homeostasis,** a state of internal physiological equilibrium that the body strives to maintain.

Maintaining homeostasis requires a sensory mechanism for detecting changes in the internal environment, a response system that can restore equilibrium, and a control centre that receives information from the sensors and activates the response system (Figure 11.1). The control centre functions somewhat like the thermostat in a furnace or an air-conditioning unit. Once the thermostat is set at a fixed temperature, or *set point,* the sensors detect significant temperature changes in either direction. The control unit responds by turning on the furnace or the air conditioner until the sensor indicates that the set point temperature has been restored, and

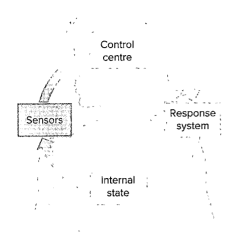

Control centre

Sensors

Response system

Internal state

FIGURE 11.1 Your body's internal environment is regulated by homeostatic mechanisms. Sensors detect bodily changes and send this information to a control centre, which in turn regulates a response system that restores bodily equilibrium.

then turns it off. Homeostatic regulation also can involve learned behaviours. When we're hot, we not only perspire, but also may seek a shady place or deliciously cool drink.

According to Clark Hull's (1943, 1951) influential **drive theory** of motivation, physiological disruptions to homeostasis produce *drives*, states of internal tension that motivate an organism to behave in ways that reduce this tension. Drives such as hunger and thirst arise from tissue deficits (e.g., lack of food and water) and provide a source of energy that pushes an organism into action. Hull, a prominent learning theorist, proposed that reducing drives is the ultimate goal of motivated behaviour.

Homeostatic models currently are applied to many aspects of motivation, such as the regulation of hunger, thirst, body temperature, weight, and sleep (Meunier, Malzahn, & Boersma, 2014). Drive theory is, however, less influential than in the past. For one thing, people often behave in ways that seem to increase rather than reduce states of arousal, as when people skip meals to diet or flock to tension-generating horror movies.

Incentive and Expectancy Theories

Whereas drives are viewed as internal factors that "push" organisms into action, **incentives** represent environmental stimuli that "pull" an organism toward a goal. To a student, a good grade can be an incentive for studying.

Incentive theories focus attention on external stimuli that motivate behaviour, though historically the concepts of incentives and drives were often linked. Clark Hull (1943, 1951) argued that all reinforcement involves some kind of biological drive reduction (e.g., food is an incentive because it reduces the drive of hunger), but this view is no longer held. Modern incentive theory emphasizes the "pull" of external stimuli and how stimuli with high incentive value can motivate behaviour, even in the absence of biological need. We have all had the experience of finishing a meal, and hence having no biological need for more food, but quite happily eating dessert when someone places our favourite cake or pie on the table. In this situation, behaviour is motivated not by biological need but by the incentive value of the external stimulus (the dessert). Incentive theories of motivation have been powerfully applied to the study of drug abuse (LeBlanc, Maidment, & Ostlund, 2014; Stewart, 2000). An incentive theory of drug use argues that seeking and administering a drug is motivated by the positive incentive value of the drug's effect. Heroin users, for example, will find and inject heroin because the drug makes them feel good, not because of a biological heroin drive or a desire to escape withdrawal.

Why is it, however, that people often respond differently to the same incentive? In part to address such questions, expectancy theories of motivation include the value of incentives, but take a cognitive perspective. Incentive theories had more in common with classical conditioning (e.g., Stewart, 2000) than with cognition, but expectancy theory has broken from this tradition and given a larger role to cognition (Erez & Isen, 2002). Consider James, Lenora, and Harrison, students in a calculus class all with similar math aptitude. Yet James studies hard in hopes of getting an A, whereas Lenora and Harrison put in just enough effort to pass with a C. How can we explain the differences in the behaviour of these three students?

According to the cognitive perspective, the answer lies in their thoughts about this situation. One important cognitive approach, called **expectancy × value theory** (or simply expectancy theory), proposes that goal-directed behaviour is jointly determined by two factors: the strength of the person's expectation that particular behaviours will lead to a goal, and the value the individual places on that goal—often called *incentive value* (Brehm & Self, 1989). These two factors are multiplied, producing the following equation: *Motivation = expectancy × incentive value*. James works hard because he

2. How are homeostatic and drive concepts of motivation related?

3. According to expectancy × value theory, why might people respond differently to the same incentive?

believes that the more you study, the greater the probability of getting an A, and he values an A highly. Lenora also believes that studying hard will lead to an A, but getting an A in calculus holds little value for her. In contrast, Harrison values an A, but does not believe that working hard will produce a high grade because the course is too hard.

Many cognitive theorists distinguish between **extrinsic motivation,** performing an activity to obtain an external reward or avoid punishment, and **intrinsic motivation,** performing an activity for its own sake—because you find it enjoyable or stimulating. Students who read their textbooks only because they want to get good grades are showing extrinsic motivation. Students who read their textbooks because they find them interesting and want to learn more are showing intrinsic motivation.

Can external incentives ever decrease motivation? According to the *overjustification hypothesis,* giving people extrinsic rewards to perform activities that they intrinsically enjoy may "overjustify" that behaviour and reduce intrinsic motivation (Bright & Penrod, 2009). In essence, if we begin to perceive that we are performing for the extrinsic rewards rather than for enjoyment, the rewards will turn "play" into "work." It is surprisingly common for people to report that an activity is no longer as enjoyable once they begin to be paid for it. A student who, for example, makes jewellery as a hobby (i.e., she simply enjoys the activity) and then begins to sell the jewellery will commonly report a marked decrease in the intrinsic pleasure of the activity.

Psychodynamic and Humanistic Theories

The psychodynamic and humanistic perspectives view motivation within a broader context of personality development and functioning, but take radically different approaches. Freud's (1923) psychoanalytic theory highlighted the motivational underworld. To Freud, much of our behaviour results from a never-ending battle between unconscious impulses struggling for release and psychological defences used to keep them under control. Energy from these unconscious motives—especially from instinctive sexual and aggressive drives—is often disguised and expressed through socially acceptable behaviours. Thus, hidden aggressive impulses may fuel one's career as a trial lawyer, businessperson, or athlete.

4. Explain Maslow's concept of a need hierarchy. Do you agree with this model?

Although research offers little support for Freud's "dual-instinct" model, his work stimulated other psychodynamic theories that highlighted different needs, such as needs for self-esteem and relatedness to other people (Adler, 1927; Kohut, 1977). Today's diverse psychodynamic theories continue to emphasize that, along with conscious mental processes, unconscious motives and tensions guide how we act and feel (Westen, 1998).

Humanist Abraham Maslow believed that psychology's other perspectives ignored a key motive: our striving for personal growth. Maslow (1954) distinguished between *deficiency needs,* which are concerned with physical and social survival, and *growth needs,* which are uniquely human and motivate us to develop our potential. He proposed the concept of a **need hierarchy,** a progression of needs containing deficiency needs at the bottom and growth needs at the top (Figure 11.2). Once our basic physiological needs are satisfied, we focus on our needs for safety and security. After these needs are met, we turn our attention to needs at the next highest level, and so on. **Self-actualization** represents the need to fulfill our potential, and it is the ultimate human motive. To echo an army recruiting slogan, self-actualization is striving to "be all that you can be."

Critics question the validity of Maslow's need hierarchy and argue that the concept of "self-actualization" is vague (Heylighen, 1992). How does the hierarchy explain why prisoners of war endure torture rather than betray their comrades or why millions of women live in constant hunger to be thin? Still, the model draws valuable attention to the human desire for growth, incorporates a wide range of psychological and biological motives, and has influenced thinking in such diverse fields as philosophy, education, and business (Muchinsky, 2000).

Thinking critically

IS MASLOW'S NEED HIERARCHY VALID?

Does the concept of a need hierarchy, shown in Figure 11.2, make sense to you? How do you feel about the ordering of needs in Maslow's hierarchy?

Think about it, and then see the Answers section at the end of the book.

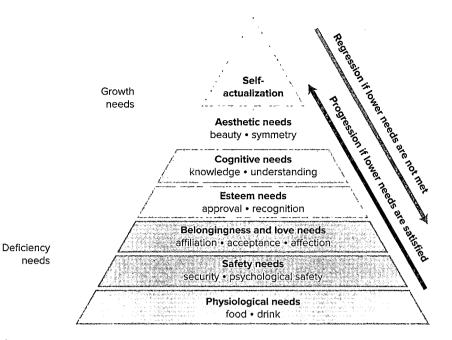

FIGURE 11.2 Maslow proposed that needs are arranged in a hierarchy. After meeting our more basic needs, we experience need progression and focus on needs at the next level. If a need at a lower level is no longer satisfied, we experience need regression and focus once again on meeting that lower-level need. Critics wonder whether people might focus on belonging, love, esteem, and higher-level needs even when their physiological and safety needs are not met. What do you think?

A more recent humanistic theory of motivation has been advanced by Edward Deci and Richard Ryan (1985, 2009). **Self-determination theory** focuses on three fundamental psychological needs: competence, autonomy, and relatedness. People are most fulfilled in their lives when they are able to satisfy these fundamental needs. On the other hand, when these needs are not met, there can be consequences for both psychological and physical well-being (Deci & Ryan, 2009).

Competence motivation reflects a human need to master new challenges and perfect skills. This need motivates much exploratory and growth-inducing human behaviour. The need for *autonomy* (or self-determination) is satisfied when people experience their actions as a result of free choice without outside interference. *Relatedness* refers to our desire to form meaningful bonds with others. At first glance, relatedness may seem opposed to autonomy, but the two actually complement each other. When true relatedness is achieved, people often feel freer to be themselves. Adolescents who feel that their autonomy is acknowledged and supported by their parents feel a strong sense of relatedness to their parents (Ryan & Lynch, 1989). Similarly, workers who are given freedom to develop their own plans (increased autonomy) experience an increased emotional bond with their employer and company (Tremblay et al., 2009). Self-determination theory has been applied to other areas, such as the work by Ronald Ferguson, of Concordia University in Montreal, and his analysis of social media's effectiveness in engaging others in charitable causes (Freguson et al., 2015).

The importance of self-determination theory's three basic needs has been strongly supported by research. They appear to have independent and additive effects on positive outcomes such as psychological well-being, happiness, worker performance and satisfaction, positive social relationships, and a sense of meaningfulness in life (Deci & Ryan, 2009; Sheldon et al., 2003). The most positive psychological outcome of all results from a balance among the three needs (Milyavskaya et al., 2009).

In sum, each of these theoretical approaches raises provocative questions about human motivation and has strong proponents and critics, just as some perspectives no doubt resonate more than others with your own views about motivation. Taken together, they underscore the complexity of behaviour and the value of studying it from multiple levels of analysis.

5. What are the three needs identified in self-determination theory?

- Motivation is a process that influences the direction, vigour, and persistence of behaviour. Evolutionary psychologists propose that in our ancestral past, motivational tendencies that had adaptive significance were more likely to be passed from one generation to the next, eventually evolving into genetically based predispositions to act in certain ways.

- Homeostatic models view motivation as an attempt to maintain equilibrium in bodily systems. Drive theories propose that tissue deficits create drives, such as hunger, that motivate or "push" an organism from within to reduce the deficit and restore homeostasis.

- Incentive theories emphasize the role of environmental factors that "pull" people toward a goal. The cognitive expectancy × value theory explains why the same incentive may motivate some people but not others.

- Psychodynamic theories emphasize that unconscious motives and mental processes guide much of our behaviour. Humanist Abraham Maslow proposed that needs exist in a hierarchy, from basic biological needs to the ultimate need for self-actualization.

- Self-determination theory focuses on three psychological needs: competence, autonomy, and relatedness.

We begin that analysis with one of our most basic motives: hunger.

HUNGER AND WEIGHT REGULATION

If you could give up all food forever and satisfy your hunger and nutritional needs with a daily pill, would you? Eating is a necessity, but for many people it also is one of life's delicious pleasures. Thus, while biology provides a "push" to eat, the anticipated and actual good taste of food offers a powerful "pull" (Bolles, 1980). Indeed, numerous biological, psychological, and environmental factors regulate our food intake.

The Physiology of Hunger

Eating and digestion supply the body with the fuel it needs to function and survive. **Metabolism** is the body's rate of energy (or caloric) utilization, and about two-thirds of the energy we normally use goes to support *basal metabolism*, the resting, continuous metabolic work of body cells. Several mechanisms attempt to keep the body in energy homeostasis by regulating food intake (Woods & Seeley, 2002). There are "short-term" signals that start meals by producing hunger and stop food intake by producing *satiety* (the state in which we no longer feel hungry as a result of eating). Your body also monitors "long-term" signals based on how much body fat you have. These signals adjust appetite and metabolism to compensate for times when you overeat or eat too little in the short term.

Before we describe some of these signals, consider three points. First, many of us believe that hunger occurs when we begin to "run low on energy," and that we feel "full" when immediate energy supplies are restored (Assanand et al., 1998). Your body does monitor its immediate energy supplies, but this information interacts with other signals to regulate food intake. Thus, hunger is not necessarily linked to immediate energy needs (Pinel, 1997; Woods et al., 1998). Second, homeostatic mechanisms are designed to *prevent* you from "running low" on energy in the first place. In evolutionary terms, an organism that does not eat until its energy supply is low (in any absolute sense) would be at a serious survival disadvantage.

Finally, researchers believed that there is a *set point*—an internal physiological standard—around which body weight (or more accurately, our fat mass) is regulated (Powley & Kessey, 1970). This view holds that if we overeat or eat too little, homeostatic mechanisms will return us close to our original weight, our set point. Although this idea is well ingrained in popular culture, some researchers, such as John Pinel at the University of British Columbia, believe it is flawed (Pinel, 1997; Pinel, Assanand, & Lehman, 2000). They propose that, as we gain or lose weight, homeostatic mechanisms kick in and make it harder to keep gaining or losing weight, but do not necessarily return us to our original weight. Over time, we may "settle in" at a new weight.

Signals That Start and Terminate a Meal

Is hunger produced by those familiar muscular contractions ("hunger pangs") of an empty

6. Describe some physiological signals that initiate hunger.

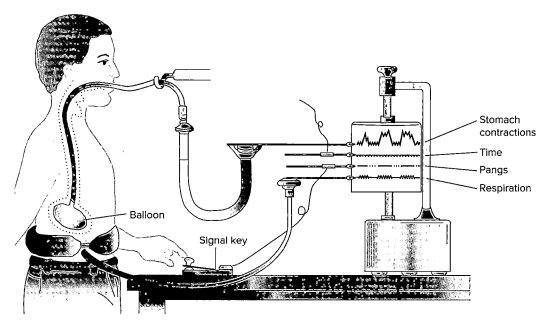

FIGURE 11.3 A.L. Washburn swallowed a balloon and inflated it in his stomach. A machine recorded stomach contractions by amplifying changes in the pressure on the balloon, and Washburn pressed a telegraph key every time he felt a hunger pang. Hunger pangs occurred when the stomach contracted.

Source: Based on Cannon, W.B., & Washburn, A.L. (1912). An explanation of hunger. *American Journal of Physiology, 29,* 441–454.

stomach? In an early experiment, A.L. Washburn showcased a unique scientific talent: He swallowed a balloon. When it reached his stomach, the balloon was inflated and hooked up to an amplifying device to record his stomach contractions. Washburn then pressed a key every time he felt hungry (Figure 11.3). The findings revealed that Washburn's stomach contractions did indeed *correspond* to subjective feelings of hunger (Cannon & Washburn, 1912). But did they *cause* the "experience" of hunger?

Surprisingly, other research indicates that "hunger pangs" do not depend on an empty stomach, or any stomach at all! Animals display hunger and satiety even if all nerves from their stomach to their brain are cut, and people who have had their stomach surgically removed for medical reasons continue to feel hungry and "full" (Brown & Wallace, 1980). Thus, other signals must help to trigger hunger.

When you eat, digestive enzymes break food down into various nutrients. One key nutrient is **glucose,** a simple sugar that is the body's (and especially the brain's) major source of immediately usable fuel. After a meal, some glucose is transported into cells to provide energy, but a large portion is transferred to your liver and fat cells, where it is converted into other nutrients and stored for later use. Sensors in the hypothalamus and liver monitor blood glucose concentrations. When blood glucose levels decrease, the liver responds by converting stored nutrients back into glucose. This action produces a drop-rise glucose pattern; a pattern that can powerfully generate feelings of hunger.

As we eat, several bodily signals combine and ultimately cause us to end our meal. *Stomach and intestinal distention* are "satiety signals" (Stricker & Verbalis, 1987). The walls of these organs stretch as food fills them up, sending nerve signals to the brain. This does not mean that the stomach literally has to be "full" for us to feel satiated. Nutritionally rich food seems to produce satiety more quickly than an equal volume of less nutritious food, suggesting that some satiety signals respond to food content.

Patients who have had their stomachs removed continue to experience satiety not only because of intestinal distention, but also because of chemical signals (Collier & Johnson, 2004). The intestines respond to food by releasing several hormones—called *peptides*—that help to terminate a meal. For example, **CCK (cholecystokinin)** is released into your bloodstream by the small intestine as food arrives from the stomach. It travels to the brain and stimulates receptors in several regions that decrease eating. Hungry animals injected with CCK will stop feeding or reduce the size of their meals, and humans who receive small doses of peptides report feeling full after eating less food (Gibbs et al., 1973; Konkle et al., 2000). See Table 11.1.

7. What physiological signals cause us to stop eating?

TABLE 11.1 **Some of the Signals That Control Eating by Increasing or Decreasing Hunger**

Signal	Source	Effect
Glucose	blood glucose levels monitored by hypothalamus, liver	drop-rise pattern increases hunger
CCK	released into bloodstream by intestines	decreases hunger
Leptin	secreted into bloodstream by fat cells	decreases hunger
Neuropeptide Y	secreted by neurons within the PVN of the hypothalamus	increases hunger
Ghrelin	secreted into bloodstream by stomach, small intestine	increases hunger

Whereas CCK decreases feelings of hunger, another peptide hormone increases feelings of hunger and eating. **Ghrelin** is released into the bloodstream by the stomach and small intestine and is now thought to be one of the most important signals for hunger among humans (Schüssler et al., 2012). People given an injection of ghrelin report feeling hungry and, given the opportunity to eat, will consume more food than participants given injections of saline (Schmid et al., 2005). Ghrelin has also been reported to increase thoughts about food and mental images of food, especially the mental image of a favourite meal (Schmid et al., 2005). Your ghrelin levels are highest just before meal-time, they decline rapidly after eating, and then they begin to rise again as the next meal approaches. Ghrelin release can also be triggered by food-related cues, such as pictures of food (Schüssler et al., 2012).

Signals That Regulate General Appetite and Weight

Fat cells are not passive storage sites for fat. Rather, they actively regulate food intake and weight by secreting **leptin**, a hormone that decreases appetite (Halaas et al., 1995). As we gain fat, more leptin is secreted into the blood and reaches the brain, where receptor sites on certain neurons detect it. These leptin signals influence neural pathways to decrease appetite and increase energy expenditure (Woods et al., 1998, 2000). See Table 11.1.

Leptin is a "background" signal. It does not make us feel "full" like CCK and other satiety signals that respond directly to food intake during a meal. Instead, leptin may regulate appetite by increasing the potency of these other signals (Woods & Seeley, 2002). Thus, as we gain fat and secrete more leptin, we tend to eat less because these mealtime satiety factors make us feel full

8. Explain how leptin regulates appetite. How did scientists learn about leptin's role?

sooner. As we lose fat and secrete less leptin, it takes more food and a greater accumulation of satiety signals to make us feel full. In essence, high leptin levels may tell the brain "There is plenty of fat tissue, so it's time to eat less."

Evidence for leptin's important role grew out of research with genetically obese mice (Coleman, 1978; Zhang et al., 1994; Figure 11.4). A gene called the *ob* gene (*ob* = obesity) normally directs fat cells to produce leptin, but mice with an *ob* gene mutation lack leptin. As they gain weight, their brains do not receive this "curb your appetite" signal, and the mice overeat and become obese. Daily leptin injections reduce their appetites and increase their energy expenditure, and the mice become thinner. Another strain of obese mice produces ample leptin, but because of a mutation in a different gene (the *db* gene), their brain receptors are insensitive to leptin (Chen et al., 1996; Halaas et al., 1995). The "curb your appetite" signal is there, but they can't detect it, and become obese. Injecting

AP Photo/The Rockefeller University

FIGURE 11.4 The mouse on the left has an *ob* gene mutation. Its fat cells fail to produce leptin, and it becomes obese. Leptin injections help such mice return to normal weight, as seen in the mouse on the right.

these mice with leptin does not reduce their food intake and weight.

Are these specific *ob* and *db* gene mutations a major source of human obesity? Probably not, for both genetic conditions seem to be rare in humans (Clement, 1999). However, when they do occur, these conditions are associated with extreme obesity, suggesting the importance of normal leptin functioning in human weight regulation. Might leptin injections be the "magic bullet" that would help most obese people lose weight? Unfortunately, there is reason for doubt, because obese people already have ample leptin in their blood because of their fat mass (Jequier & Tappy, 1999; Ravussin & Gautier, 1999). For currently unknown reasons, their brains appear to be insensitive to that information.

Brain Mechanisms

Many parts of the brain—ranging from the primitive brain stem to the lofty cerebral cortex—play a role in regulating hunger and eating (Logue, 1991; and see this chapter's *Focus on Neuroscience* feature). But is there a "master control centre"? Early experiments pointed to two regions in the hypothalamus (Stellar, 1954). Areas near the side, called the *lateral hypothalamus (LH)*, seemed to be a "hunger on" centre (Figure 11.5). Electrically stimulating a rat's LH causes it to start eating, and lesioning (damaging or destroying) the LH causes it to refuse to

eat, even to the point of starvation (Anand & Brobeck, 1951).

In contrast, structures in the lower-middle area, called the *ventromedial hypothalamus* (VMH), seemed to be a "hunger off" centre. Electrically stimulating the VMH caused even a hungry rat to stop eating, and lesioning the VMH produced gluttons who ate frequently and doubled or tripled their body weight (Hetherington & Ranson, 1942). Medical case studies of people with damage to these hypothalamic areas also found that normal weight regulation was disrupted (Gazzaniga et al., 1979).

As scientists explored further, they learned that, although the LH and VMH played a role in hunger regulation, they were not really "hunger on" and "hunger off" centres (Pinel, 1997; Schwartz, 1984). For example, rats with LH damage stop eating and lose weight in part because they develop trouble swallowing and digesting, and they become generally unresponsive to external stimuli, not just to food. Moreover, axons from many brain areas funnel into the hypothalamus and then fan out again upon leaving it. Cutting these nerve tracts anywhere along their path—not just within the hypothalamus—duplicates some of the effects of the LH and VMH lesions (Schwartz, 1984).

Researchers are examining how various neural circuits within the hypothalamus regulate food intake. Many pathways involve the **paraventricular nucleus (PVN),** a cluster of neurons packed with receptor sites for various transmitters that stimulate or reduce appetite (Figure 11.5). The PVN appears to integrate several different short-term and long-term signals that influence metabolic and digestive processes (Berthoud, 2002). One transmitter, *neuropeptide Y,* is a powerful appetite stimulant (Leibowitz, 1992). Rats in one experiment quickly became obese when they received three daily injections of neuropeptide Y into their PVN for ten days. Their food intake doubled, their fat mass tripled, and their total body weight increased sixfold (Stanley et al., 1986).

A fascinating finding about leptin and the PVN in rats may help to explain why we become so hungry when trying to lose weight. When leptin reaches the hypothalamus, it seems to *inhibit* the activity of neurons that release neuropeptide Y into the PVN, and therefore appetite is reduced. But when rats lose fat, less leptin is secreted and therefore neuropeptide Y neurons become more active, increasing appetite (Woods & Seeley, 2002). See Table 11.1.

9. What evidence suggested that the LH and VMH were hunger "on" and "off" centres? What evidence suggests otherwise?

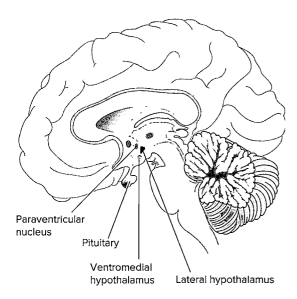

FIGURE 11.5 Various structures within the hypothalamus play a role in regulating hunger, thirst, sexual arousal, and body temperature. The lateral hypothalamus (LH), ventromedial hypothalamus (VMH), and paraventricular nucleus (PVN) are involved in hunger regulation.

Paraventricular nucleus

Pituitary

Ventromedial hypothalamus

Lateral hypothalamus

Focus on Neuroscience

BRAIN ACTIVATION AND FOOD CUES

Whether it is through media displays or a grocery store, we are constantly presented with a wide range of food choices. We are an affluent society and for many of us there is easy access to high-fat and high-sugar foods, as well as to healthy alternatives such as fruits and vegetables. However, much of our eating is motivated not by survival needs, but by the pleasure we obtain from highly palatable foods (Berthoud, 2006). As the proportion of the population that is overweight or obese continues to increase, understanding food choices is taking on even greater importance.

Brain imaging techniques, such as fMRI, have been used to investigate which brain areas are involved in our reactions to food and that are important for food choice (see Figure 11.6). Brain areas that have been found to be activated by pictures of high-calorie foods (e.g., chocolate cake, doughnuts, cheeseburgers, and French fries) include midbrain brain areas often associated with motivation and reward such as the nucleus accumbens and the ventral tegmental area (VTA), as well as the cingulate cortex and insula (Murdaugh, Cox, Cook, & Weller, 2012). Interestingly, it has been found that the extent of brain activation evoked by pictures of high-calorie foods significantly predicts the success of a 12-week weight-loss program. Murdaugh and colleagues (2012) found a positive correlation between weight change and the level of activation recorded within the nucleus accumbens, VTA, anterior cingulate cortex, and insula in response to pictures of highly palatable foods. There was also a greater response to the highly preferred foods in areas associated with visual processing within the occipital lobe, and in areas involved in attention within the frontal cortex and parietal cortex, suggesting greater attention to food. That is, the higher the weight at the end of the 12-week weight loss program and at a nine-month follow-up, the greater the activation in brain regions associated with motivation and with attention in response to pictures of high-calorie foods at the start of the program. In other words, those participants who showed the smallest brain response to pictures of food lost the most weight, whereas those who showed the greatest brain activation in motivation- and attention-linked brain areas lost the least weight.

Among weight-conscious people (i.e., those that are trying to lose weight or maintain a low weight), self-regulation is important. You would expect that if someone is deliberately trying to control his or her weight, brain activation elicited by food cues would reflect this. In a study using healthy, normal-weight (BMI 18–25) young adult women, brain activation was measured while the participants viewed pictures of fattening foods (e.g., chocolate cake) or neutral

© McGraw-Hill Education

FIGURE 11.6 When we are presented with a preferred food, or even just a picture of the food, brain areas within the midbrain associated with motivation are powerfully activated. If you are trying to control your weight, areas within the prefrontal cortex linked to self-control are activated at the same time.

pictures (office supplies) (Smeets, Kroese, Evers, & Ridder, 2013). As expected, food pictures increased activity in midbrain areas associated with motivation and reward, especially in the nucleus accumbens. Those participants who were the most concerned about weight control also showed increased activity in the visual cortex, suggesting greater visual attention to pictures of food. Interestingly, those participants who were the most concerned about weight control also showed enhanced activity in areas of the prefrontal cortex associated with self-regulation and the ability to inhibit responses.

continued

So far, we have discovered that brain areas generally linked to motivation (nucleus accumbens, VTA, insula) are activated by food cues, and the extent of that activation can predict the success of a weight-loss program. If you are trying to control your weight, pictures of highly palatable foods will also activate areas within the prefrontal cortex associated with self-control and the ability to inhibit behaviour.

What about food choice? We are frequently presented with a wide range of food choices in the cafeteria, in vending machines, on restaurant menus, and in our own refrigerators and cupboards. In a recent study (Charbonnier, van der Laan, Viergever, & Smeets, 2015), healthy normal-weight participants viewed pictures of either high-calorie foods (e.g., doughnuts, potato chips, chocolates), low-calorie foods (e.g., watermelon slices, carrot sticks, bananas), or office supplies (e.g., pencils, push tacks, a calculator). While brain activation was being measured using fMRI, participants were asked to choose between two equally liked foods, one high in calories and one low in calories. When two non-food items were shown, participants were asked simply to choose one of the products. Participants were more likely to choose the low-calorie food items; 57 percent of choices were for the low-calorie option. The brain areas activated by both low- and high-calorie foods were similar to those that have been reported previously, the midbrain areas associated with motivation and reward. When making food choices, brain areas that have previously been associated with decision making and with attention were active—areas such as the insula, cingulate cortex and areas within the temporal cortex. That is, the evidence would suggest that brain areas linked to decision making in other situations are also active when we make food choices.

An interesting recent study (van der Laan, Barendse, Viergever, & Smeetsm, 2015) investigated food choice and impulsivity. Impulsivity includes lower behavioural inhibition, increased sensitivity to reward, and favouring immediate rewards over long-term consequences. There is a positive correlation between impulsivity and BMI; those who score the highest in impulsivity tend to also have a higher BMI, and impulsivity is associated with a higher preference for high-sugar and high-fat foods and increased snacking (van der Laan et al., 2015). Individuals high on impulsivity show stronger activation in the nucleus accumbens, VTA, and amygdala in response to pictures of highly palatable foods and in response to pleasant tastes (Ker et al., 2014), and show a stronger activation in the nucleus accumbens when choosing a high-calorie food compared to low-calorie food (van er Laan et al., 2015). That is, those who score high in impulsivity are more sensitive to reward based on behavioural measures; they also show increased activation in the nucleus accumbens when presented with pleasant tastes, pictures of highly palatable foods, or when allowed to choose a high-calorie food.

It is interesting to note that none of the brain areas identified in these studies are specific to food. The evidence is that the brain areas activated by pictures of food are also important in the response to other motivationally relevant stimuli. Pictures of highly palatable foods can also activate brain areas linked to self-regulation, visual attention, and stimulus evaluation. The picture of brain activity emerging from recent fMRI studies of our responses to food cues is consistent with earlier discussions of the modular mind. That is, the brain areas identified in this research seem to be specialized by task (e.g., attention, motivation, response inhibition), not by the nature of the stimulus presented.

In summary, midbrain limbic structures, especially the nucleus accumbens, play a special role in the motivational value of food (Castro, Cole, & Berridge, 2015). The brain areas most commonly linked to motivation and reward, the nucleus accumbens, VTA and insula, are powerfully activated by food cues, especially if it is a preferred or highly palatable food. The extent of that activation is correlated with success in weight control, and is also influenced by personality factors such as impulsivity. At the same time that the motivation-associated brain areas are active, other brain areas may also become active. For example, those who are concerned about their weight show activation in brain areas linked to self-control and response inhibition.

As we learn more about our response to food, not only does it increase our understanding of the brain and how our brain processes food-related cues, but it may also help lead to more successful interventions for those whose weight falls outside of the healthy range.

Psychological Aspects of Hunger

From a behavioural perspective, eating is positively reinforced by the good taste of food and negatively reinforced by hunger reduction. Cognitively, we develop an expectation that eating will be pleasurable, which becomes an important motivator to seek and consume food. Even the mere thought of food can trigger hunger, as you may find by closing your eyes and concentrating on the aroma, sight, and taste of your favourite dish.

Attitudes, habits, and psychological needs also regulate food intake. Have you ever felt "stuffed" after gobbling up part of a meal, yet finished it and even had dessert? Beliefs such as "don't leave food on your plate" and conditioned habits ("autopilot" snacking while watching TV) may lead us to eat even when we do not feel hungry. Conversely, countless dieters intentionally restrict their food intake even though they *are* hungry.

(left): © The Granger Collection; (middle): © Museo del Prado, Madrid/Peter Willi/SuperStock; (right): © The McGraw-Hill Companies, Inc./Lars A. Niki photographer.

FIGURE 11.7 Throughout much of Western history, a full-bodied woman's figure was esteemed. This is illustrated by (a) Peter Paul Rubens's 17th-century painting *The Three Graces*, and by (b) actress Lillian Russell, who represented the American ideal of feminine beauty a century ago. In recent decades, the norm of "thin = attractive" has evolved, as illustrated (c) by this contemporary fashion model.

10. Describe some factors that contribute to the pressure women feel to be thin.

Especially for women, such food restriction often stems from social pressures to conform to cultural standards of beauty (Figure 11.7). Studies of *Playboy* magazine centrefolds, beauty pageant contestants, and fashion models indicate a clear trend toward a thinner, leaner, and increasingly unrealistic "ideal" female body shape between the 1950s and 2000s (Owen & Laurel-Seller, 2000). The culturally defined "ideal" female body has changed again in recent years, adding an ultra-fit physique in addition to extreme thinness (Homan et al., 2012). Correspondingly, relative to men, over the past 50 years, women have become increasingly dissatisfied with their body image (Feingold & Mazzella, 1998).

A classic study by April Fallon and Paul Rozin (1985) suggests an additional reason why this is so. University women overestimated how thin they needed to be to meet men's preferences, whereas men overestimated how bulky they should be to match women's preferences (Figure 11.8). Women also perceived their body shape as heavier than ideal, whereas men viewed their body shape as close to ideal. As Fallon and Rozin noted, "Overall, men's perceptions serve to keep them

satisfied with their figures, whereas women's perceptions place pressure on them to lose weight" (1985, p. 102). Researchers continue to find results similar to Fallon and Rozin's (Carlson & McAndrew, 2004; Demarest & Allen, 2000).

People who perceive themselves as heavy tend to have lower self-esteem, and this relation is stronger among women than men (Pila et al., 2015). According to Barbara Fredrickson and Tomi Ann Roberts's (1997) *objectification theory*, Western culture teaches women to view their bodies as objects, much as external observers would. This perspective increases body shame and anxiety, which in turn leads to eating restriction and even eating disorders (Fredrickson et al., 1998). Laboratory experiments suggest that women do indeed restrict eating to restore self-esteem (Mori et al., 1987). Work by Eva Pila and her colleagues at the University of Toronto has shown body weight-related shame, higher among females, is important in decreasing self-esteem (Pila et al., 2015).

The norms that "thin = attractive" and "you can never be too thin" are strongly ingrained by

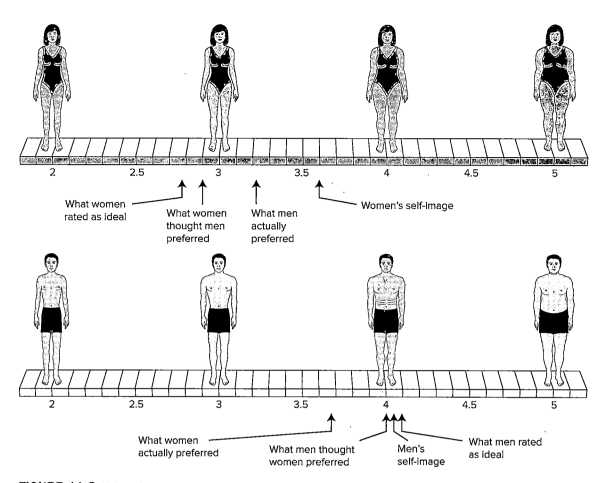

What women rated as ideal

What women thought men preferred

What men actually preferred

Women's self-image

What women actually preferred

What men thought women preferred

Men's self-image

What men rated as ideal

FIGURE 11.8 University women overestimated how thin they needed to be to conform to men's preferences and viewed their own body shape as heavier than ideal. In contrast, men overestimated how bulky they should be to conform to women's preferences but viewed their body shape as close to ideal.

Source: Data from Fallon, A.E., & Rozin, P. (1985). Sex differences in perceptions of desirable body shape. *Journal of Abnormal Psychology, 94*, 102–105.

adolescence and have a powerful impact even early in adolescence. As early as the Grade 8, many girls have adopted the belief that they have to be thin to be popular with boys (Halpern et al., 1999), and girls as young as ten years old diet to look thinner (McVey et al., 2004). Such social pressures and beliefs can lead to a high level of dissatisfaction with one's own body. As few as one in five adolescent and young adult females report being happy with their weight, even when body weight is within a normal, healthy range (Halpern et al., 1999; Huon et al., 2002; Kenardy et al., 2001).

Environmental and Cultural Factors

Although not very sensitive to manipulation of biological variables such as overfeeding, underfeeding, or changes in the caloric density of the diet, people are very sensitive to changes in environmental stimuli, such as portion size, the number of people present during a meal, the amount that others eat, and the variety of foods available (Levitsky, 2005). We will consider a few of the most important environmental variables that influence how much we eat.

Food availability is the most obvious environmental regulator of eating. For millions of people who live in poverty or famine-ravaged regions, food scarcity limits consumption. In contrast, abundant low-cost food (including high-fat foods) in many countries contributes to a high rate of obesity among children and adults (Wadden et al., 2002).

Food taste, variety, and serving size all powerfully regulate eating. Good-tasting food positively reinforces eating and increases food consumption, but during a meal and from meal to meal, we can become "tired of eating the same thing" and terminate a meal more quickly (Rolls et al., 1981). In contrast, food variety

11. Identify several environmental and cultural factors that influence eating.

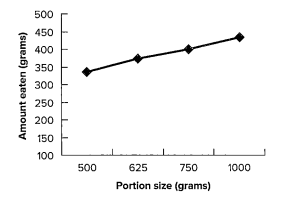

FIGURE 11.9 Participants were presented with a macaroni and cheese lunch in one of four portion sizes, and the amount of food eaten increased with portion size. This was true for both men and women, and for normal-weight and overweight participants (data shown is for the subject groups combined).

Source: Data from Rolls, B.J., Morris, E.L., & Roe, L.S. (2002). Portion size of food affects energy intake in normal-weight and over-weight men and women. *American Journal of Clinical Nutrition, 76*, 1207–1213.

increases consumption, which you know all too well if you attend buffet meals. The amount of food served also influences how much we eat. In one study participants were presented with a macaroni and cheese lunch in one of four different portion sizes (Rolls et al., 2002). Although participants did not differ in self-reported hunger or how much food they predicted they would eat before the lunch, the larger the portion they were given, the more they ate. Those presented with the largest portion size ate, on average, almost 100 grams more macaroni and cheese than those presented with the smallest serving (Figure 11.9). That represents an additional 676 kJ (162 calories) consumed just because of a larger serving size.

Through classical conditioning we learn to associate the smell and sight of food with its taste, and these food cues can trigger hunger. Eating may be the last thing on your mind until your nose detects the sensuous aroma wafting from a bakery, a pizzeria, or a popcorn machine. Dr. Harvey Weingarten (1983), then at McMaster University, demonstrated that rats that have eaten recently and are not hungry (i.e., they have food available but ignore it) will eat when presented with sounds and lights that they have learned to associate with food. Similarly, does the musical jingle of the neighbourhood ice cream truck tweak your hunger?

Many other environmental stimuli affect food intake. We typically eat more when dining with other people than when eating alone, in part because meals take longer (de Castro, 2002). Cultural norms influence when, how, and what we eat. In countries such as Spain and Greece, people often begin dinner in the late evening (say, around 9:00 P.M.), by which time most North Americans have long finished their supper. And although we like variety, we usually feel most comfortable selecting from among familiar foods and often have difficulty "getting past" our squeamish thoughts about unfamiliar dishes.

Obesity

The heaviest known man and woman in recorded history, both Americans, weighed 635 kilograms and 545 kilograms at their respective peaks in 1978 and 1987 (*Guinness Book*, 2000). (After hospitalization and dieting, the man lost 418 kilograms over 16 months, and the woman lost 417 kilograms over seven years.) Health Canada guidelines suggest that a body mass index (BMI, the ratio of weight to height— kg/m^2) between 25 and 29.9 is considered overweight, and a BMI over 30 is considered obese. According to recent statistics, more than half of adult Canadians (52.5 percent) are either overweight or obese, with 19.8 percent of men and 16.8 percent of women classified as obese (Statistics Canada, 2013). Among Canadian children, almost 20 percent are overweight and 8 percent are obese. Statistics Canada reported a 500 percent increase in childhood obesity between 1980 and 2004. Not only does obesity pose a health risk, but it can also expose the individual to stereotypes and prejudice (Teachman et al., 2003).

Obesity is often blamed on a lack of willpower, a weak character, or emotional disturbances, but research does not consistently find such psychological differences between obese and non-obese people (Faith et al., 2002). Some scientists hypothesize that eating is an attempt to cope with stress (Wallis & Hetherington, 2004) or that obese people react more strongly than non-obese people to food cues, such as the appearance or taste of food (Stice et al., 2008). But again, evidence that these factors cause obesity is mixed (Greeno & Wing, 1994).

Genes and Environment

Do you know people who seem to gain weight easily and other envied souls who eat even more food without adding weight? Data from over 25 000 pairs of twins and 50 000 other biological and adoptive family members point to heredity as one source of such differences. Heredity influences our basal metabolic rate and tendency to store energy as either fat or lean tissue (Bouchard et al., 1990). Overall, genetic factors appear to account for about 40 to 70 percent of the variation in body mass among women and men (Maes et al., 1997; Comuzzie & Allison, 1998). Identical twins reared apart are about as similar in body mass as identical twins reared together, and adopted children resemble their biological parents more closely than their adoptive parents (Stunkard et al., 1990).

More than 200 genes have been identified as possible contributors to human obesity, and in most cases, it is the combined effect of a subset of genes—rather than "single-gene" variations—that produces an increased risk (Comuzzie & Allison, 1998). However, although heredity affects our susceptibility to obesity, so does the environment. Genes have not changed much in recent decades, but obesity rates in Canada and the United States have increased significantly. According to experts such as James Hill and John Peters (1998), the culprits are

- an abundance of inexpensive, tasty, high-fat foods available almost everywhere;
- a cultural emphasis on "getting the best value," which contributes to the "supersizing" of menu items; and
- technological advances that decrease the need for daily physical activity and encourage a sedentary lifestyle.

The Pima Indians of Arizona provide a striking example of how genes and environment interact to produce obesity. Despite the fact that the Pimas are genetically predisposed to obesity and diabetes, both conditions were rare among tribe members before the 20th century (Savage & Bennett, 1992). Their native diet and way of life prevented their genetic predisposition from expressing itself. But, particularly among Pimas born after World War II, obesity rates increased dramatically as they adopted a Westernized diet and sedentary lifestyle (Price et al., 1993; Esparza et al., 2000). Today, they have one of the highest rates of obesity (and diabetes) in the world. In contrast, Pimas living in northwest Mexico, who still eat a more traditional diet and perform more physical labour, have an obesity rate much lower than that of their Arizonan counterparts (Ravussin et al., 1994).

Dieting and Weight Loss

Unfortunately, weight gain tends to promote additional weight gain, in part by altering body chemistry and energy expenditure (Logue, 1991). For example, obese people generally have higher levels of insulin (a hormone secreted by the pancreas) than people of normal weight, which increases the conversion of glucose into fat. Substantial weight gain also makes it harder to exercise vigorously, and dieting slows basal metabolism because the body responds to food deprivation with decreased energy expenditure. Along with a genetic predisposition to obesity, these factors cause many obese people to maintain excess weight with fewer calories than people who are gaining the same weight for the first time. In contrast to earlier reports, however, there is no consistent evidence that the body's energy-saving metabolic slowdown becomes more pronounced with each weight loss attempt (Brownell & Rodin, 1994, National Task Force, 1994). Thus, whether repeated "yo-yo dieting" makes it more difficult to lose weight is debatable.

Are diets doomed to fail? The common adage that "95 percent of people who lose weight regain it within a few years" evolved from just one study decades ago. According to Albert Strunkard, one of the researchers, 100 obese patients were "just given a diet and sent on their way. That was state of the art in 1959" (Fritsch, 1999). Certainly, achieving weight loss is not easy, and combining healthy eating (reduced energy input) with exercise (increased energy output) has a greater chance of success than dieting alone. But in truth, we do not have good estimates of weight-loss success rates, partly because people who succeed (or fail) on their own without going to clinics or treatment programs are rarely heard from (Schachter, 1982). For example, the National Weight Control Registry (2000) has a database of over 2000 successful, long-term dieters who, on average, have lost about 27 kilograms and kept it off for about five years. About half of these participants did so on their own, without any type of formal program (see the *Applications* feature for more information about how to control eating and weight).

Health concerns motivate some dieters, but psychological and social concerns are the primary motivators for many others. Many *non-obese* adolescent girls and women diet, including those of average and below-average weight (Miller et al., 2000; McVey et al., 2004).

12. What evidence suggests a genetic role in obesity? How does obesity among the Pima Indians illustrate a gene–environment interaction?

13. Why is it especially hard for obese people to lose weight? Are diets doomed to fail?

THE BATTLE TO CONTROL EATING AND WEIGHT

Many people, especially high school and university students, are concerned about their weight. Many adolescent females with average and even below-average body fat diet (Kenardy et al., 2001). Our dissatisfaction with our bodies begins at an alarmingly young age. One study found that almost 30 percent of 10- to 14-year-old girls were trying to lose weight and look thinner (McVey et al., 2004). Our body size and shape, or, more accurately, our perception of our body size and shape forms an important part of our self-image. How we perceive our own body and how closely that matches our ideal is an important issue for many (look back at Figure 11.8). Can what we have learned about hunger help us in our battle to control our girth? Many different factors control hunger, and what we know about their influences and interactions can indeed be put to use.

As discussed previously, having an "empty" stomach does contribute to feelings of hunger and having a "full" stomach is one of the satiety signals. But it is not just the sheer mass of food in the stomach that helps us feel full and slows our eating. Acting through mechanisms that are not yet well understood, what is in the stomach also matters. Nutritionally rich food makes us feel fuller than an equal volume of food with little or no nutritive value. Nutritionally rich food is lower in fats and calories than nutritionally empty food, and it will make you feel fuller faster.

The incentive value of the foods in front of us is also important. Cues that predict the arrival of food, such as the smell of popcorn, the sight of a favourite restaurant, or the sound of a steak sizzling on a barbecue, can all make us feel hungry, even when we do not need food. Controlling the response to such food cues is not a matter of willpower. The smell, sight, and even sound of a favourite food can stimulate the release of the hormone insulin (Rodin, 1978, 1981), and secretion of insulin is associated with increased hunger (Rodin et al., 1985). Ghrelin levels are associated with hunger and increased food consumption, and research has shown that even pictures of food can trigger the release of ghrelin (Schüssler et al., 2012). The mere sight of one's favourite food increases feelings of hunger and food cravings, and increases heart rate, blood pressure, salivation, and gastric activity (Nederkoorn et al., 2000). If you can, avoid such cues. We certainly do not want to isolate ourselves in a sterile and boring environment, but knowing that such cues have a powerful physiological impact can help us to control them. Do not ask to see the dessert tray, with its array of attractive, high-incentive delicacies, unless you plan to eat one.

If you eat a small amount of food before a meal, will you eat more or less of the main meal? Many of us have been warned by a parent that a snack too close to mealtime

would "ruin our appetite." Unfortunately, it does not work that way. If you eat a small amount of food before the main meal—that is, eat an appetizer—then you will eat more of the following meal. An appetizer is aptly named as it does indeed increase your appetite. Appetizers work for at least two reasons. One is that an appetizer provides more variety in the meal and food variety increases consumption. The second reason is that if the appetizer stimulates insulin secretion, as it should, the increase in blood insulin levels and subsequent drop in blood glucose levels are powerful hunger cues. If you are visiting a fine restaurant and want to enjoy every possible mouthful, go ahead and have that appetizer. However, if you want to control the amount of food that you consume, do not have an appetizer or small snack close to mealtime; it will only make you feel hungrier and increase the amount of food that you eat.

Eat when you are hungry. Although we tend to attribute our eating to hunger, we often eat out of habit. Although we are not hungry, we snack while watching TV, watching sports, talking with friends, and reading. To make matters worse, these snacks are often high-fat, high-calorie foods such as chips, peanuts, or doughnuts. Do not put that bowl of chips on the table beside your favourite reading or TV chair.

You can lose weight by consuming a constant number of calories and increasing energy expenditure (i.e., exercising) or you can lose weight by decreasing the number of calories that you consume without changing your energy expenditure. It is important to know, however, that weight loss through exercise is not the same as weight loss through dieting. If weight is lost because of an increase in exercise, that weight is subsequently regained much more slowly than if the weight is lost because of dietary restriction alone (Wainwright et al., 1990). Weight loss through diet is due to a loss of both lean body mass and fat, whereas weight loss through exercise is due to a loss of fat. If weight is lost through exercise, there is a consequent increase in the ratio of muscle to fat (since only fat is lost), and that generally leads to an increase in basal metabolic rate (Vanltallie & Kissileff, 1990). The heightened basal metabolism will help to burn calories, even when you are not exercising.

It is also important to consider stress and stress coping (we will discuss stress and coping with stress in detail in Chapter 15). In an interesting study investigating the "freshman 15"—the expectation that students gain 15 pounds (almost 7 kg) during their first year of university—Boyce and Kuijer (2015) found that stress played an important mediating role. First-year university students with a higher BMI at the start of the university year and who also had high levels of stress gained the most weight. Interestingly, students with the lowest BMI and who also experienced high stress tended to lose weight. Students with effective stress coping experienced little weight change. In order to control

continued

unhealthy weight changes and to help control weight, it is important to know effective stress-reduction techniques and coping strategies.

We go to great lengths, sometimes tragically unhealthy ones, to control our weight. The study of hunger has demonstrated that many different factors contribute to the control of appetite and weight. Some, such as our genetic endowment, are beyond our control, but others, such as exposure to food-related cues, types of food eaten, and how we arrange our meals, are within our control, and they can have a dramatic effect on how much food we eat, without resorting to the current fad diet.

Review

- The body monitors several chemicals involved in energy utilization. Changing patterns of glucose usage provide one signal that helps to initiate hunger. The hormone ghrelin powerfully increases feelings of hunger. Upon eating, hormones such as CCK are released into the bloodstream and signal the brain to stop eating. Fat cells release leptin, which acts as a long-term signal that helps to regulate appetite. The hypothalamus and other brain regions play a role in hunger regulation.

- The expected good taste of food motivates eating, and the thought of food can trigger hunger.

Our memory, attitudes, habits, and psychological needs affect our food intake.

- The availability, taste, variety, and amount of food powerfully regulate eating. Through classical conditioning, neutral stimuli can acquire the capacity to trigger hunger. Cultural norms affect our food preferences and eating habits.

- Heredity and the environment affect our susceptibility to becoming obese. Homeostatic mechanisms make it difficult to lose substantial weight.

SEXUAL MOTIVATION

Why do people have sex? If you are thinking, "Isn't it obvious?" let's take a look. Sex often is described as a biological "reproductive drive," yet people usually do not have sex to conceive children. Moreover, a drive to reproduce does not explain why people masturbate, have oral sex, use birth control, and have sex into their 70s and 80s. Pleasure, then, must be the key. Evolution has shaped our physiology so that sex feels good; periodically, this leads to childbirth, and our genes are passed on. But consider the following:

- In a study asking adolescents why they have sex, both genders cited peer pressure far more often than sexual gratification (Stark, 1989).

- In the 1920s, British sex researcher Helena Wright found that most women she surveyed viewed sex as an unenjoyable marital duty (Kelly, 2001).

- Many women find their first sexual intercourse disappointing (Sprecher et al., 1995). Some sex researchers call this reaction "Peggy Lee syndrome," named for a singer who had a hit song titled "Is That All There Is?" (Hyde & DeLamater, 2000).

- About 10 percent of American men and 20 percent of women report that sex is not pleasurable (Laumann et al., 1994).

In reality, people engage in sex for a host of noble and not-so-noble reasons: to reproduce, obtain and give pleasure, express love, foster intimacy, build one's ego, fulfill one's "duty," conform to peer pressure, get over a broken relationship, and for millions of people worldwide, to earn money (Byer et al., 1999).

Sexual Behaviour: Patterns and Changes

Because most people are reluctant to let researchers into their bedrooms, scientists typically learn about people's sexual activities by conducting surveys. Alfred Kinsey and his colleagues (1948, 1953) at Indiana University conducted the first large-scale American sex surveys in the late 1930s. One of the best and more recent U.S. surveys, based on a nationally representative sample of 18- to 59-year-olds, found that about 70 percent of people in this age group have sex with a partner at least a few times per month (Figure 11.10; Laumann et al., 1994; Michael et al., 1994). Overall, single adults who cohabit (are not married but live with a sexual partner) are the most sexually active, followed by married adults. Single adults who do not cohabit are the least active.

The survey also found that, although men and women have sex with a partner about

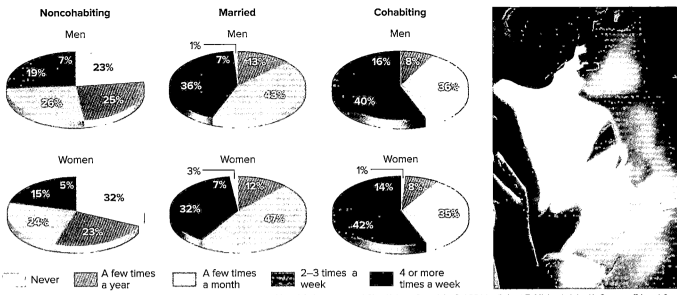

Noncohabiting	**Married**	**Cohabiting**

Never | A few times a year | A few times a month | 2–3 times a week | 4 or more times a week

(left): Adapted from *Sex in America* by Robert T. Michael, John Gagnon, Edward O. Laumann and Gina Kolata. Copyright © 1994 by Robert T. Michael, John H. Gagnon, Edward O. Laumann and Gina Kolata. Reprinted by permission of Little, Brown & Company (U.S. and U.K.), and Brockman, Inc.; (right): Ingram Publishing.

FIGURE 11.10 Frequency of sex over the past 12 months by gender and marital status among adult men and women.

equally often, men masturbate and fantasize about sex more often than women do. About 25 percent of men and 10 percent of women masturbate one or more times per week, and 60 percent of men and 40 percent of women report masturbating at least once a year. The common belief that adults masturbate simply because they do not have a sex partner is *false:* 85 percent of men and 45 percent of women with regular sex partners masturbate at least once a year.

Overall, males tend to have their first sexual intercourse experience one to two years earlier than females (CDC, 2002), but by the end of high school, similar proportions of males and females have had sexual intercourse at least once, and a high proportion of high school–aged youth are sexually active. For example, in 2002 Health Canada reported that 23 percent of Grade 9 males and 19 percent of Grade 9 females had engaged in sexual intercourse; by Grade 11, 40 percent of males and 46 percent of females had engaged in sexual intercourse (Canadian Youth, Sexual Health and HIV/ AIDS Study, Health Canada, 2004). Premarital intercourse has become more common in many countries over the past half-century. Changing social norms, a trend toward sexual activity at a younger age, and a tendency to delay marriage have all contributed to an increase in premarital sex.

Some findings suggest, however, that these premarital trends may be levelling off and

possibly reversing (CDC, 2002). This may be a response to an increased cultural emphasis on the depth of relationships (Wade & Cirese, 1992) and to the crisis concerning AIDS and other sexually transmitted diseases (STDs). According to the World Health Organization, worldwide more than 1 million sexually transmitted infections are acquired every day (World Health Organization, 2015). Sexually transmitted infections include infections that may be asymptomatic; that is, the infection is present but the individual does not show disease symptoms or shows only mild symptoms.

The Physiology of Sex

In 1953, William Masters and Virginia Johnson began a landmark study in which they examined the sexual responses of 694 men and women under laboratory conditions. In total, they physiologically monitored about 10 000 sexual episodes in which volunteers masturbated, had intercourse, and performed other sexual activities. By putting a camera into a transparent penis-shaped case, Masters and Johnson were able to film vaginal reactions during simulated intercourse.

The Sexual Response Cycle

Masters and Johnson (1966) concluded that most people go through a four-stage **sexual response cycle** when sexually aroused (Figure 11.11). During the *excitement phase,* arousal builds rapidly. Blood flow increases to

14. Explain the stages of the sexual response cycle.

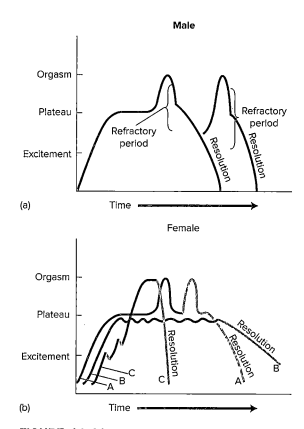

FIGURE 11.11 Masters and Johnson discovered a four-stage pattern of sexual response. (a) In males, there is a refractory period after orgasm during which no further response is possible. (b) In females, pattern A represents one or more orgasms followed by resolution, pattern B shows a plateau stage with no orgasm, and pattern C shows an orgasm with no preceding plateau stage.

Source: Based on Masters, W., & Johnson, V. (1966). *Human sexual response*. London, UK: Churchill.

arteries in and around the genital organs, nipples, and women's breasts, pooling and causing these body areas to swell (this process is called *vasocongestion*). The penis and clitoris begin to become erect, the vagina becomes lubricated, and muscle tension increases throughout the body. In the *plateau phase,* respiration, heart rate, vasocongestion, and muscle tension continue to build until there is enough muscle tension to trigger orgasm.

During the *orgasm phase* in males, rhythmic contractions of internal organs and muscle tissue surrounding the urethra project semen out of the penis. In females, orgasm involves rhythmic contractions of the outer third of the vagina, surrounding muscles, and the uterus. In males, orgasm is ordinarily followed by the *resolution phase,* during which physiological arousal decreases rapidly and the genital organs and tissues return to their normal condition. During

the resolution phase, males enter a *refractory period* during which they are temporarily incapable of another orgasm. Females may have two or more successive orgasms before the onset of the resolution phase, but Masters and Johnson reported that most women experienced only one. Moreover, sexual response varies across people and time, and this four-stage model represents only an "average." People may experience orgasm on some occasions but not others, and orgasm is neither the only goal nor necessarily the ultimate goal of all sexual activity.

Hormonal Influences

As with hunger, the hypothalamus plays a key role in sexual motivation. It controls the pituitary gland, which regulates the secretion of hormones called *gonadotropins* into the bloodstream. In turn, these hormones affect the rate at which the *gonads* (testes in the male and ovaries in the female) secrete *androgens,* the so-called "masculine" sex hormones such as testosterone, and *estrogens,* the so-called "feminine" sex hormones such as estradiol. Note that, despite these labels, both men and women produce androgens and estrogens.

Sex hormones have *organizational effects* that direct the development of male and female sex characteristics (Breedlove, 1992; Byer et al., 2002). In the womb, male and female embryos form a primitive gonad that has the potential to develop into either testes or ovaries. If genetically male, the embryo forms testes about eight weeks after conception. Then, as the testes release sex hormones during a key period of prenatal development, there typically is sufficient androgen activity to produce a male pattern of genital, reproductive, brain, and other organ development. Years later, as part of this pattern, the hypothalamus stimulates an increased release of sex hormones from the testes when the male reaches puberty. In contrast, a genetically female embryo does not form testes and, in the absence of sufficient androgen activity during this prenatal period, a female pattern of development ensues. As part of this pattern, at puberty the hypothalamus stimulates the release of sex hormones from the ovaries on a cyclical basis that regulates the female menstrual cycle.

Sex hormones also have *activational effects* that stimulate sexual desire and behaviour. The activational effects of the sex hormones begin at puberty, when the individual's gonads begin to secrete sex hormones. Mature males have a relatively constant secretion of sex hormones, and their readiness for sex is largely governed

....

15. Describe the organizational and activational effects of sex hormones. How do the activational effects differ in humans versus nonhumans?

....

by the presence of environmental stimuli (e.g., a receptive female). In contrast, hormone secretions in female animals follow an "estrus" cycle, and they are sexually receptive only during periods of high estrogen secretion (i.e., when they are "in heat"). Sex hormones also influence human sexual desire, as when the hormonal surge of puberty results in increased sexual motivation for most people. But in humans, normal short-term hormonal fluctuations have relatively little effect on sexual arousability (Morrell et al., 1984). Women may experience high sexual desire at any time during their menstrual cycle.

In men and women, androgens—rather than estrogens—appear to have the primary influence on sexual desire (Hyde & DeLamater, 2003; Napi, 2015). However, desire does not go up and down like a yo-yo as blood levels of sex hormones change. Rather, a baseline level of certain hormones, such as testosterone, appears necessary to maintain sexual desire. Women who have had their androgen-producing organs (ovaries, adrenal glands) removed for medical reasons experience a gradual loss of sexual desire that can be reversed by administering sex hormones (Buster et al., 2005). Similarly, most men who are castrated (have their testes removed) experience a gradual decrease of sexual desire. But, particularly if the man is sexually experienced, sexual responsiveness declines more slowly than sexual desire. In some cases, men continue to have sexual intercourse for years after they have been castrated (Hyde & DeLamater, 2000), which is one reason why castrating sex offenders is not a guaranteed method of preventing future rapes.

The Psychology of Sex

16. What psychological factors stimulate and inhibit sexual functioning?

17. How do cultural norms and environmental stimuli influence sexual behaviour?

Sexual arousal involves more than physiological responses. It typically begins with desire and a sexual stimulus that is perceived positively (Walen & Roth, 1987). Such stimuli can even be imaginary.

Sexual Fantasy

Sexual fantasy is an important component of many people's lives. Among 18- to 59-year-old American adults, about half of men and a fifth of women fantasize about sex at least once a day (Laumann et al., 1994). Fantasy illustrates how mental processes can affect physiological functioning. Indeed, sexual fantasies alone may trigger genital erection and orgasm in some people, and are often used to enhance arousal during masturbation (Byrne & Osland, 2000).

Most men and women also fantasize at least occasionally during sexual intercourse (Leitenberg & Henning, 1995), as comedian Rodney Dangerfield acknowledged with his quip, "Last time I tried to make love to my wife nothing was happening, so I said to her, 'What's the matter, you can't think of anybody either?'" However, in contrast to what Dangerfield's joke implies, sexual fantasy typically is not a response to dissatisfaction with one's partner. Rather, people who are more sexually active also tend to fantasize more (Kelly, 2001).

Desire, Arousal, and Sexual Dysfunction

Psychological factors not only can trigger sexual arousal, but also inhibit it. A person may be anticipating an evening of lovemaking, or be engaged in sexual activity, and then become "turned off" by something a partner does. Many people who are physiologically capable of becoming sexually aroused simply do not have the desire. About one in three women and one in six men report that they lack an interest in sex (Laumann et al., 1994).

Other people desire sex but have difficulty becoming or staying aroused. Stress, fatigue, and anger at one's partner can lead to temporary arousal problems. Sexual dysfunction refers to chronic, impaired sexual functioning that distresses a person. It may result from injuries, diseases, and drug effects, but some causes are psychological. About 10 percent of men report difficulty maintaining an erection, and about 20 percent of women have difficulty lubricating and becoming aroused (Laumann et al., 1994). Performance anxiety can cause both types of problems, and arousal difficulties also may be a psychological consequence of sexual assault or childhood sexual abuse (Rumstein & Hunsley, 2001).

Cultural and Environmental Influences

The psychological meaning of sex depends strongly on cultural contexts and learning. For example, some religions discourage or prohibit premarital sex, extramarital sex, and public dress and behaviour that arouses sexual desire (Figure 11.12). In turn, most people who view themselves as very religious believe it is important to bring their sexual practices into harmony with their religious beliefs (Janus & Janus, 1993).

Cultural Norms

Anyone who doubts culture's power to shape the expression of human sexuality need only

(left): © BananaStock/JupiterImages; (right): © A. Majeed/AFP/Getty Images

FIGURE 11.12 Habits of dress that many people take for granted in some societies, such as wearing tank tops, short-sleeve shirts, and tight jeans, are unacceptable in other cultures because they would be considered sexually provocative.

examine sexual customs around the globe. Consider that childhood sexuality is suppressed in our culture but is permitted and even encouraged in others. In the Marquesas Islands of French Polynesia, families sleep together in one room and children have ample opportunity to observe sexual activity. When a baby boy is distressed, Marquesan parents may masturbate the child. Boys and girls begin to masturbate at age two or three, and most engage in casual homosexual contacts during their youth. When they reach adolescence, an adult of the opposite sex instructs them in sexual techniques and has intercourse with them (Suggs, 1962).

Although North Americans are less sexually permissive than the Marquesans, they are not as repressive as the inhabitants of Inis Beag, an island off the coast of Ireland. Sex is a taboo topic among these people, and nudity is abhorred. Only infants are allowed to be completely naked. The genders are separated from early childhood until marriage, and during marital sex both partners keep their underwear on. Sexual revulsion is so intense that dogs and other animals are often beaten if they are caught licking their genitals. In contrast to Marquesan women, who customarily experience orgasm in sexual interactions,

orgasm among the women of Inis Beag is rare and viewed as abnormal (Messenger, 1971). Clearly, what is considered proper, moral, and desirable varies enormously across cultures.

Arousing Environmental Stimuli

The environment affects sexuality not only through cultural experiences, but also by providing sexually arousing stimuli. A lover's caress can trigger sexual desire in an instant. So too can watching a partner undress, which ranks second only to vaginal intercourse as the sexual activity that most men and women find appealing (Laumann et al., 1994).

Erotic portrayals of sex can trigger arousal and sexual behaviour as long as people perceive those stimuli positively (Davis & Bauserman, 1993). In one study, Julia Heiman (1975) measured the genital arousal and self-reported arousal of sexually experienced university students as they listened to tape recordings of erotic and non-erotic stories from popular novels. Women and men experienced sexual arousal to descriptions of explicit sex but not to descriptions devoid of sexual content (romantic or general conversations). Both genders showed the strongest arousal when erotic stories focused on the female character, and when she was the one who initiated sex.

Pornography, Sexual Violence, and Sexual Attitudes

18. According to social learning and catharsis principles, how should viewing pornography affect sexual aggression? What does research find?

By today's standards, depictions of sex in popular novels are a tame form of erotica. Sexually explicit magazines and movies, telephone sex lines, nude dance clubs, and Internet "cyberporn" constitute a multi-billion-dollar pornography industry. The rapid growth in access to the Internet has been accompanied by a dramatic increase in the availability of pornography, and consumption of pornography has been increasing since the 1970s (Price et al., 2015). One study of more than 800 undergraduate and graduate students found that about two-thirds (67 percent) of the male students and almost half (49 percent) of the female students agreed that viewing pornography was acceptable (Carroll et al., 2008). When it came to use of pornography, the same study found that 87 percent of the male students and 31 percent of the female students reported using pornography.

Statistics Canada has reported that 39 percent of adult Canadian women have had at least one experience of some form of sexual assault (Statistics Canada, Measuring Violence Against Women, 2006). Contrary to a common belief, as Figure 11.13 shows, most sexual assaults are *not* committed by strangers (Brennan & Taylor-Butts, 2008). Given the appalling incidence of sexual assault in some countries, the public and scientists alike have asked whether exposure to pornography fosters sexual violence against women.

Two psychological viewpoints are especially relevant to predicting pornography's effects. According to *social learning theory*, people learn through observation. Many pornographic materials model "rape myths"—that sex is impersonal, that men are entitled to sex when they want it, and that women enjoy being dominated and coerced into sex (Malamuth, 1998). Men who view such materials should become more likely to treat women as objects and sexually aggress toward them. In contrast, Freud and other psychoanalysts advocated a *catharsis principle*, which states that as inborn aggressive and sexual impulses build up, actions that release this tension provide a "catharsis" that temporarily returns us to a more balanced physiological state. Thus, viewing pornography—especially materials that contain aggressive or violent content—should provide people with a safe "outlet" for releasing sexual and aggressive tensions, and should decrease sexually aggressive behaviour toward women.

Correlational studies of real-world sexual violence do not clearly support either viewpoint. For example, although some sex offenders use pornography to arouse themselves in preparation for a crime, overall, they do not report having been exposed to pornography at a younger age or to a substantially larger degree than males in general (Bauserman, 1996). More broadly, some countries with high rape rates have little pornography, whereas others have a great deal. In some countries, pornography is widely available but rape rates are low (Bauserman, 1996).

To isolate pornography's possible effects on behaviour, controlled experiments are needed. In one such experiment, Edward Donnerstein and Leonard Berkowitz (1981) randomly divided male university students into four groups. Group 1 saw a nonsexual film of a talk show. Group 2 watched a sexually explicit film in which a young couple made consensual love. Groups 3 and 4 watched explicit depictions of a woman being sexually assaulted by two men. In one film (Group 3)—a "rape myth" version—the woman resisted at first but then became a willing sexual participant. In the other film (Group 4), she was shown resisting and then suffering during the entire experience.

Next, in a supposedly unrelated second experiment, these male participants interacted with a woman (who was actually an accomplice of the

Who Commits Sexual Assault?

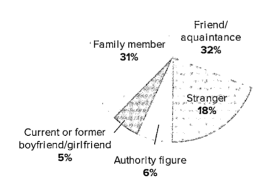

FIGURE 11.13 According to Canadian police-reported data for 2007, the victim knew the perpetrator in 82 percent of sexual assaults; only 18 percent of sexual assaults were committed by a stranger. Family members and friends/acquaintances were the most likely to commit a sexual assault (Brennan & Taylor-Butts, 2008).

Source: Data from Brennan, S., & Taylor-Butts, A. (2008). Sexual assaults in Canada 2004 and 2007. Canadian Centre for Justice Sta-tistics Profile Series. Statistics Canada. Cat. No. 85F0033M. p. 13.

changes and expressive behaviour, which, in turn, can affect what we think about the situation and about ourselves (Forgas, 2000; Frijda et al., 2005).

Emotion is a dynamic ongoing *process*. Thus, any of its four elements can change rapidly as the situation and our responses to it influence one another. For example, as anger begins to escalate during a disagreement, you might choose to make a conciliatory response that evokes a positive reaction or apology from the other person, helps to defuse the situation, and reduces your negative appraisal of the other person and your level of emotional arousal. This dynamic, ever-changing property of emotional reactions makes them a challenging "moving target" for scientific study.

Eliciting Stimuli

Emotions do not occur in a vacuum. They are responses to situations, people, objects, or events. We become angry *at* something or someone; fearful or proud *of* something; in love *with* someone. Moreover, the stimuli that trigger cognitive appraisals and emotional responses are not always external; they can be internal stimuli, such as mental images and memories. Most of us can work up a state of anger simply by recalling or imagining a painful injustice or insult from the past, or evoke warm feelings by recalling significant positive experiences.

Innate biological factors help to determine which stimuli have the greatest potential to arouse emotions (Panksepp, 2005). Newborn infants come equipped with the capacity to respond emotionally with either interest or distress to events in their environment (Galati & Lavelli, 1997). Adults, too, may be biologically primed to experience emotions in response to certain stimuli that have evolutionary significance. As discussed in Chapter 7, fear responses can be classically conditioned more easily to pictures of snakes and spiders than to more innocuous stimuli, such as flowers, when these stimuli are paired with mild electric shocks (Öhman & Wiens, 2005).

Learning also influences the ability of particular objects or people to arouse emotions. Previous experiences can make certain people or situations eliciting stimuli for emotions. In Chapter 7, we encountered Little Albert who had learned a fear of white rats and other white furry objects. The mere sight of one's lover can evoke feelings of passion, and the sight of a disliked person, an instantaneous feeling of revulsion that seems almost reflexive in nature.

On the broadest level, cultures have different standards for defining the good, the bad, and the ugly, and these standards affect how eliciting stimuli will be appraised and responded to emotionally. Physical features that provoke sexual arousal and feelings of infatuation in one culture, such as ornamental facial scars, may elicit feelings of disgust in another. In Western societies, recent increases in the popularity and acceptability of body piercing and tattoos illustrate how quickly cultural standards can change.

The Cognitive Component

You are walking across campus with a group of people from one of your classes when you encounter a person you met at a party the previous night and to whom you are attracted. The person looks at you as you warmly say "Hello," responds with a blank stare, and then turns away without responding. Which emotions would the following thoughts trigger in you?

- "Oh no! What a total put-down. What do my classmates think of me now?"
- "What a jerk, ignoring me like that."
- "Just like always. I'll never find anyone who likes me."
- "What a relief! Now I won't be distracted from my usual 50-hour study week and my thimble collection." Embarrassed? Angry? Depressed? Relieved? As you think, so shall you feel.

Cognitions are involved in virtually every aspect of emotion. They can evoke emotional responses, they are part of our subjective experience of the emotion, and they influence how we express our emotions and act on them. A situation may evoke pleasure or distress, depending on how we appraise it. For example, sexual stimulation may elicit anger, fear, or disgust instead of pleasure if it is deemed inappropriate or unwanted.

Appraisal processes. Emotions are always responses to our perceptions of the eliciting stimuli. While all perceptions involve attaching meaning to sensory stimuli, the appraisals involved in emotion are especially evaluative and personal; they relate to what we think is desirable or undesirable for us or for the people we care about (Lazarus, 2006).

Both conscious and unconscious processes are involved in appraisals (Feldman-Barrett et al., 2007). Often we are not consciously aware of the appraisals that underlie emotional

31. In what sense can eliciting stimuli be external or internal? What are the roles of biological and learning factors?

32. How can learning influence emotion?

33. How do cognitive appraisals enter into emotion? Do they need to involve conscious thought?

responses. Some appraisals seem to involve little more than an almost automatic interpretation of sensory input based on previous conditioning (Smith & Kirby, 2004). Indeed, most strong emotions are probably triggered initially in this automatic fashion, after which we may appraise the situation in a more reasoning manner. Even at this more "cognitive" level, however, our habitual ways of thinking may occur with little or no awareness on our part (Clore & Centerbar, 2004; Phelps, 2005). We often fail to appreciate how arbitrarily we interpret "the way things are."

The idea that emotional reactions are triggered by cognitive appraisals rather than external situations helps to account for the fact that different people (or even the same person at different times) can have very different emotional reactions to the same object, situation, or person (Figure 11.22). Statements such as "I have a new attitude toward her now" or "I've decided what's really important in life" reflect changes in appraisals of certain situations or people.

Culture and appraisal. Like theorists who study the situations that elicit emotion in various cultures, those who study cognitive appraisal have looked for cross-cultural similarities and differences in the thoughts and perceptions that precede emotions (Scherer, 1984; Smith & Ellsworth, 1985). Respondents in a variety of cultures have been asked to recall events that evoked certain emotions and then to answer questions about how they appraised or interpreted the situations. In one study conducted in 27 different countries, the researchers found

34. What evidence exists for (a) universal and (b) culturally determined appraisals? Provide examples of each.

strong cross-cultural similarities in the types of appraisals that evoked joy, fear, anger, sadness, disgust, shame, and guilt (Wallbott & Scherer, 1988). In another cross-cultural study comparing American and Asian people in Japan and Hong Kong, Robert Mauro and his colleagues (1992) found that Americans reported feeling happiness, pride, and hope more frequently than did the Japanese. The Japanese, in turn, reported more frequent feelings of shame and regret than did people from Hong Kong. Nonetheless, whenever any of these emotions did occur, similar appraisals were involved, regardless of the culture.

Despite these cross-cultural commonalities in appraisal, the same type of situation also can evoke different appraisals and resulting emotional reactions, depending on one's culture (Mesquita & Markus, 2005). Consider, for example, the circumstance of "being alone." For Tahitians, being alone is appraised as an opportunity for bad spirits to bother a person, and fear is the most common emotional response. Among the close-knit Utku, an Inuit culture, being alone signifies social rejection and isolation, triggering sadness and loneliness. In Western cultures, being alone may at times represent a welcome respite from the frantic pace of daily life, evoking contentment and happiness (Mesquita et al., 1997). Thus, where appraisals are concerned, there seem to be certain universals, but also some degree of cultural diversity in some of the more subtle aspects of interpreting situations (Mesquita et al., 1997; Scherer, 1998).

The Physiological Component

One of the first things we notice is the bodily changes that occur when our feelings are "stirred up." Many parts of the body are involved in emotional arousal, but certain brain regions, the autonomic nervous system, and the endocrine system play especially significant roles.

Affective Neuroscience. The brain's involvement in emotion is complex, and many aspects are not well understood. It is clear, however, that emotions involve important interactions between cortical and subcortical areas (Damasio, 2005).

Subcortical structures, such as the hypothalamus, the amygdala, the hippocampus, and other limbic system structures play major roles in emotion (Figure 11.23). If animals are electrically stimulated in specific areas of the limbic system, they will growl at and attack anything that approaches them. Destroying the same

35. Which subcortical and cortical structures are involved in emotion?

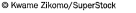

© Kwame Zikomo/SuperStock

FIGURE 11.22 Differences in appraisal can trigger entirely different emotional reactions, as in this instance. What kinds of appraisals are likely occurring in these people?

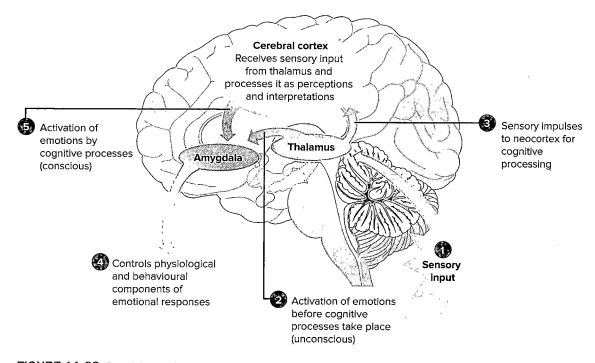

Cerebral cortex
Receives sensory input
from thalamus and
processes it as perceptions
and interpretations

5 Activation of
emotions by
cognitive processes
(conscious)

Amygdala

Thalamus

3 Sensory impulses
to neocortex for
cognitive
processing

4 Controls physiological
and behavioural
components of
emotional responses

1 **Sensory
input**

2 Activation of emotions
before cognitive
processes take place
(unconscious)

FIGURE 11.23 Parallel neural processes may produce conscious and unconscious emotional responses at about the same time. LeDoux's research suggests that sensory input to the thalamus can be routed directly to the amygdala in the limbic system, producing an "unconscious" emotional response before cognitive responses evoked by the other pathway to the cortex can occur.

sites produces an absence of aggression, even if the animal is provoked or attacked (Sotres-Bayon, Cain, & LeDoux, 2006). Other areas of the limbic system show the opposite pattern: lack of emotion when they are stimulated and unrestrained emotion when they are removed (Thompson, 1988).

The cerebral cortex has many connections with the hypothalamus and limbic system, allowing constant communication between cortical and subcortical regions. Cognitive appraisal processes surely involve activities in the cortex. Moreover, the ability to regulate emotion depends heavily on the executive functions of the *prefrontal cortex,* which lies immediately behind the forehead (Gross, 1998).

Groundbreaking research and theorizing by psychologist Joseph LeDoux (1986, 2000, 2006) has revealed important links between the cortex and the limbic system. As shown in Figure 11.23, the key brain structures in this model are the thalamus, which routes sensory input to various parts of the brain, the amygdala, which helps to coordinate and trigger physiological and behavioural responses to emotion-arousing situations, and the cortex, where sensory input is organized as perceptions and evaluated by the "thinking" or linguistic part of the brain. LeDoux's key discovery was that the thalamus sends messages along

two independent neural pathways, one travelling to the cortex and the other directly to the amygdala. This means that the amygdala can receive direct input from the senses and generate emotional reactions before the cerebral cortex has had time to fully interpret what is causing the reaction. LeDoux suggests that this primitive mechanism (which is the only emotional mechanism in species such as birds and reptiles) has survival value because it enables the organism to react with great speed. Shortly afterward, the cerebral cortex responds with a more carefully processed cognitive interpretation of the situation. This may be what occurs when a hiker sees an object that looks like a snake and jumps out of the way, only to realize an instant later that the object is a rope. That is, there is emotional processing by areas such as the amygdala without conscious awareness.

The existence of a dual system for emotional processing may help to explain some puzzling aspects of our emotional lives. For example, most of us have had the experience of suddenly feeling emotional without understanding why. LeDoux (2000) also suggests that people are capable of having two simultaneous emotional reactions to the same event, a conscious one occurring as a result of cortical activity and an unconscious one triggered by the amygdala. This might help to explain instances in which

36. How does LeDoux's theory explain unconscious emotional phenomena?

people are puzzled by behavioural reactions that seem to be at odds with the emotion they are consciously experiencing: "I don't know why I came across as being angry. I felt very warm and friendly."

Brain activity is also involved in the regulation of emotional behaviour. Of particular interest is the prefrontal cortex, the seat of executive function involving reasoning, planning, decision making, and the control of impulsivity. Deficits in prefrontal functions allow emotions to be expressed in an unregulated manner that can have negative consequences (Boes et al., 2009).

Neuroscientist Candace Pert (1997) argues that, because all the neural structures involved in emotion operate biochemically, it is the ebbs and flows of various neurotransmitter substances that activate the emotional programs residing in the brain. For example, dopamine activity appears to underlie some pleasurable emotions, and endorphins may also play a role, whereas serotonin and norepinephrine may play a role in anger (Damasio, 2005). When the final story of the brain and emotion can at last be told, it will undoubtedly describe complex interactions between brain chemicals and neural structures.

Hemispheric activation and emotion. Years ago in Italy, psychiatrists treated clinically depressed patients with electroshock treatments to either the right or the left hemisphere. The electric current temporarily disrupted activity in the hemisphere to which it was applied. With the left hemisphere knocked out (forcing the right hemisphere to take charge), patients had what physicians termed a *catastrophic* reaction, wailing and crying until the shock effects wore off. When shock was applied to the right hemisphere, allowing the left hemisphere to dominate, the patients reacted quite differently. They seemed unconcerned, happy, and sometimes even euphoric. A similar pattern of emotions was noted in patients in whom one hemisphere had been damaged by lesions or strokes. Left hemisphere damage, particularly in the frontal lobe, accentuated negative emotions such as depression; right frontal damage was linked to indifference or euphoria (Gainotti, 1972).

These findings suggest that left-hemisphere activation might underlie certain positive emotions and right-hemisphere functioning negative ones (Sutton, 2002). To test this proposition, Richard Davidson and Nathan Fox obtained EEG measures of frontal lobe activity as people experienced various emotions (Davidson & Fox, 1988; Fox & Davidson, 1991). They found that when

people felt positive emotions by recalling pleasurable experiences or watching a happy film, the left hemisphere was relatively more active than the right. But when sadness or other negative emotions were evoked, the right hemisphere became relatively more active. This pattern seems to be innate. Infants only three to four days old showed a similar pattern of hemispheric activation when given sucrose solutions, which evoke positive reactions, or a citric acid solution, which apparently disgusts them (Davidson & Fox, 1988).

People differ in their tendency to experience positive or negative emotions. Individual differences in typical or *resting* hemispheric activation, measured under emotionally neutral conditions, seem related to this tendency. Davidson and Fox (1989) found that human infants with resting right-hemisphere dominance were more likely to become upset and cry if their mothers left the room than were those with left-hemisphere dominance (Figure 11.24). In adults, a higher resting level of right-hemisphere EEG activity appears to be a risk factor for the later development of adult depressive disorders (Marshall & Fox, 2000; Tomarken & Keener, 1998).

The association of the right hemisphere with negative emotions and the left hemisphere with positive emotions has become widely accepted (Ng, Fishman, & Bellugi, 2015; Sutton, 2002).

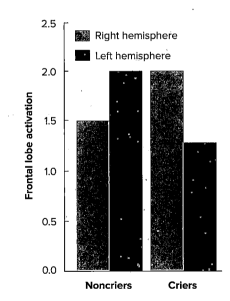

FIGURE 11.24 Resting activation in the left and right frontal hemispheres differs in infants who later reacted with distress or no distress when their mothers left. The criers showed relatively greater right-hemisphere activation, the noncriers greater left-hemisphere activation.

Source: Data from Davidson, R.J., & Fox, N.A. (1989). Frontal brain asymmetry predicts infants' response to maternal separation. *Journal of Abnormal Psychology, 98*, 127–131.

37. Which neurotransmitters are involved in specific emotional responses?

38. What clinical and research evidence is there to support a "left-right" theory of hemispheric activation differences for positive and negative emotions?

Autonomic and hormonal processes. You are afraid. Your heart starts to beat faster. Blood is drawn from your stomach to your muscles, and digestion slows to a crawl. You breathe harder and faster to get more energy-sustaining oxygen. Your blood sugar level increases, producing more nutrients for your muscles. The pupils of your eyes dilate to let in more light so you can see the danger better. Your skin perspires to keep you cool and flush out waste products created by extra exertion. Your muscles tense, ready for action.

Some theorists call this state of arousal the *fight-or-flight response*. It is produced by the sympathetic branch of the autonomic nervous system and by hormones from the endocrine system. The sympathetic nervous system produces arousal within a few seconds by directly stimulating the organs and muscles of the body. Meanwhile, the endocrine system pumps epinephrine, cortisol, and other stress hormones into the bloodstream. These hormones produce physiological effects like those triggered by the sympathetic nervous system, but their effects are longer lasting and can keep the body aroused for a considerable length of time.

Thinking critically

CAN YOU FOOL A LIE DETECTOR?

The polygraph, or lie detector, measures physiological changes normally outside of our intentional control. Does that make it infallible?

Think about it, and then see the Answers section at the end of the book.

Do different emotions produce different patterns of arousal? On the one hand, many investigators conclude that complex and subtle emotions such as jealousy and tenderness do not involve distinct patterns of arousal (Panksepp, 1998). On the other hand, autonomic patterns do show subtle differences in certain basic emotions, such as anger and fear (Levenson, 1992). For example, heart rate speeds up in both fear and anger, but there are differences in where the blood gets pumped (Ekman et al., 1983). Anger causes more blood to flow to the hands and feet, whereas fear reduces blood flow to these areas (providing a scientific basis for the colloquial expression "cold feet"). But whether people can detect such subtle physiological differences in a manner that would allow them to identify and label their emotions is an unanswered question.

We cannot easily control autonomic nervous system activation with exposure to emotion-evoking stimuli. This simple observation led to the idea that changes in physiological arousal might tell us whether someone is lying or telling the truth. The rationale is that when people lie, they should become anxious and that increase in anxiety will be reflected in physiological responses such as increases in heart rate, respiration, and skin conductance (which increases because of sweat gland activity). On the contrary, if they are answering honestly, then no change in physiological arousal would be expected. The instrument used to measure such changes is the **polygraph**, the famous, or infamous, "lie detector" (Figure 11.25). Although controversial, research has found an especially high rate of false positives, identifying an

39. How are the sympathetic and endocrine systems involved in emotion? Do different emotions have different patterns of autonomic arousal?

40. What considerations and research evidence challenge the validity of the "lie detector"? What kinds of errors are most likely?

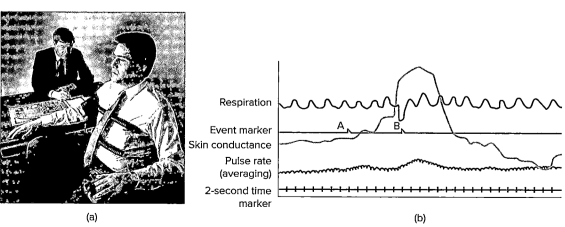

(a) Guy Bell/Alamy Stock Photo

FIGURE 11.25 The polygraph (a) records physiological changes (b) that are part of emotional responses. Between points A and B, an emotionally loaded question was asked. Within two seconds, the effects of the question were visible in the subject's respiration, skin conductance, and pulse rate. Does this mean he was lying?

innocent person as guilty, with polygraph tests (Lykken, 1981, 1984; Honts & Perry, 1992).

The Behavioural Component

So far, we have examined the situational, cognitive, and physiological components of emotion. We now turn to the directly observable behaviours that are part of emotional responses.

Expressive behaviours. Although we can never directly experience another person's feelings, we can often infer that someone is angry, sad, fearful, or happy on the basis of his or her emotional displays, or **expressive behaviours.** When exposed to slides showing angry or happy faces, university students responded with subtle facial muscle responses that denote displeasure or pleasure within a third of a second (Dimberg & Thunberg, 1998). Sometimes, too, others' emotional displays can evoke similar emotional responses in us, a process known as **empathy.** Perhaps you have found yourself experiencing the same emotion as the central character while reading a novel or viewing a movie. Professional actors sometimes find that they become so immersed in the expressive behaviours of a character they are playing that the boundaries between self and role begin to fade. Kirk Douglas reported one such experience after he played Vincent Van Gogh in the movie *Lust for Life:*

41. What evidence exists for fundamental emotional patterns of expression?

I was close to getting lost in the character of Van Gogh . . . I felt myself going over the line, into the skin of Van Gogh. . . . Sometimes I had to stop myself from reaching my hand up and touching my ear to find out if it was actually there. It was a frightening experience. That way lies madness . . . I could never play him again. (Lehmann-Haupt, 1988, p. 10)

Evolution and emotional expression. Where do emotional expressions come from? In his classic work, *The Expression of Emotions in Man and Animals* (1872/1965), Charles Darwin argued that emotional displays are products of evolution that developed because they contributed to species survival. Darwin emphasized the basic similarity of emotional expression in animals and humans. For example, both wolves and humans bare their teeth when they are angry (Figure 11.26). As Darwin explained it, this behaviour makes the animal look more ferocious, and thus decreases its chances of being attacked and perhaps killed in a fight. Darwin did not maintain that all forms of emotional expression are innate, but he believed that many of them are.

Like Darwin, modern evolutionary theorists stress the adaptive value of emotional expression (Izard, 1984; Plutchik, 1994; Tomkins, 1991).

(left): © Thomas Kitchen & Victoria Hurst; (right): © The beauty archive/eStock Photo

FIGURE 11.26 Similarities among species in the expression of certain basic emotions convinced Darwin and other theorists that some expressive behaviours have an evolutionary origin.

Two key findings suggest that humans have innate or **fundamental emotional patterns.** First, the expressions of certain emotions (e.g., rage and terror) are similar across a variety of cultures, suggesting that certain expressive behaviour patterns are wired into the nervous system. Second, children who are blind from birth seem to express these basic emotions in the same ways that sighted children do, ruling out the possibility that they are learned solely through observation (Eibl-Eibesfeldt, 1973). The fundamental emotional patterns proposed by three leading evolutionary theorists are shown in Table 11.3. As discussed in this chapter's *Frontiers* feature, a new emotion, referred to as elevation has recently been proposed. Other emotions are argued as resulting from some combination of these innate emotions. The evolutionary view does *not* assume that all emotional expressions are innate, nor does it deny that innate emotional expressions can be modified or inhibited as a result of social learning.

Facial expression of emotion. Most of us are fairly confident in our ability to "read" the emotions of others. Although many parts of the body can communicate feelings, we tend to concentrate on what the face tells us. Most lower animals have relatively few facial muscles, so

TABLE 11.3   Fundamental or Primary Innate Emotions Proposed by Three Leading Evolutionary Theorists

Carroll Izard	Silvan Tomkins	Robert Plutchik
Anger	Anger	Anger
Fear	Fear	Fear
Joy	Joy	Enjoyment
Disgust	Disgust	Disgust
Interest	Interest	Anticipation
Surprise	Surprise	Surprise
Contempt	Contempt	
Shame	Shame	
	Sadness	Sadness
	Distress	
Guilt		
		Acceptance

Source: Based on Izard, C.E. (1984). "Emotion-cognition relationships and human development." In C.E. Izard, J. Kaga, & R.B. Zajonc (Eds.), *Emotions, cognition and behavior.* Cambridge, UK: Cambridge University Press.; Tomkins, S.S. (1991). *Affect, imagery, consciousness, Vol. 3: Anger and fear.* New York, NY: Springer.; and Plutchik, R. (1991). *The emotions.* Lanham, MD: University Press of America.

their facial expressions are limited. Only monkeys, apes, and humans have enough well-developed facial muscles to produce a large number of expressions.

The development of sophisticated measuring procedures, such as the Facial Action Coding System (FACS) by Paul Ekman and Wallace Friesen (1987), have permitted the precise study of facial expressions. The FACS requires a trained observer to dissect an observed expression in terms of all the muscular actions that produced it. The system is so complex that it takes about 100 minutes to score each minute of observed facial expression (Ekman et al., 1988).

Although facial expressions can be valuable cues for judging emotion, even people within the same culture may learn to express the same emotions differently. Thus, some people have learned to appear very calm when they are angry. Fortunately, we usually know something about the situation to which the person is reacting, and this often is an important basis for judging emotions. For example, if a woman is crying, is she crying because of sadness or because of happiness? A background showing her being declared the winner of a lottery will result in a different emotional judgment than one showing her at a graveside. Many experiments have shown that people's accuracy and agreement in labelling emotions from pictures is considerably higher when the pictures show a background situation (Keltner & Ekman, 2000).

Across many cultures, women have generally proven to be more accurate judges of emotional expressions than men (Ekman, 1982; Zuckerman et al., 1976). Perhaps the ability to accurately read emotions has greater adaptive significance for women, whose traditional role within many cultures has been to care for others and attend to their needs (Buss, 2005). This ability may also result from cultural encouragement for women to be sensitive to others' emotions and to express their feelings openly (Taylor et al., 2006). However, it is important to note that men who work in professions that emphasize these skills, such as psychotherapy, drama, and art, are as accurate as women in judging emotions, suggesting that these skills can be learned (Rosenthal et al., 1974).

What of Darwin's claim that certain facial expressions are universal indicators of specific emotions? Modern researchers have approached this question by determining the extent to which people in different cultures

42. What results concerning emotional perception, sex differences, and universal expressions of emotion have been found by using the FACS?

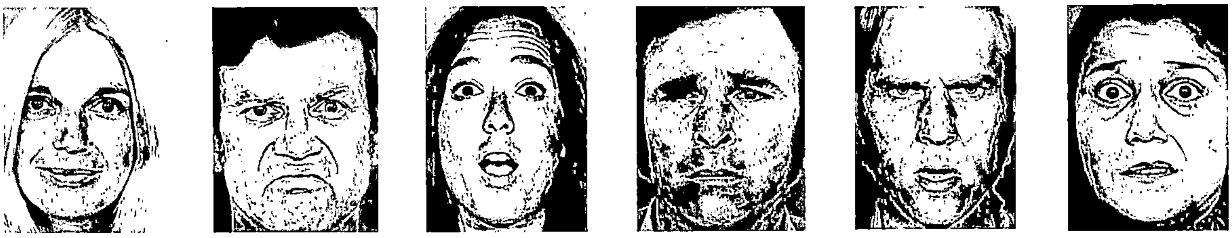

	Happiness	Disgust	Surprise	Sadness	Anger	Fear
United States (N = 99)	97%	92%	95%	84%	67%	85%
Brazil (N = 40)	95%	97%	87%	59%	90%	67%
Chile (N = 119)	95%	92%	93%	88%	94%	68%
Argentina (N = 168)	98%	92%	95%	78%	90%	54%
Japan (N = 29)	100%	90%	100%	62%	90%	66%

FIGURE 11.27 Percentage of agreement in judgments of facial expressions of emotion by people in five different cultures.

Source: (data): Ekman, P. (1973). *Darwin and facial expression: A century of research in review.* New York, NY: Academic Press.; (photos) © P. Ekman and W.V. Friesen, *Pictures of Facial Affect.* Consulting Psychologists Press, Palo Alto, CA, 1976

agree on the emotions being expressed in facial photographs (Ekman, 1973; Russell et al., 1997). The results of one such study are shown in Figure 11.27. You can see that there is generally high agreement on these photos of basic emotions, but also some cultural variation. Other researchers have found levels of agreement ranging from 40 to 70 percent across a variety of cultures, well above chance but still far from perfect (Russell, 1994).

In an interesting study of facial expressions, Matsumoto and Willingham (2006) analyzed the facial expressions of medal winners in the judo competition at the 2004 Olympic Summer Games, held in Athens, Greece. Using photographic and videotaped records, they analyzed the facial expressions of winners immediately after completing the medal-winning match and again later when they received their medals. Matsumoto and Willingham used the FACS coding system developed by Ekman and Friesen to score the facial expressions of 84 winning athletes from 35 countries. Their results support the argument that the facial expressions displayed spontaneously in an emotion-evoking situation can be considered to be universal.

Cultural display rules. The norms for emotional expression within a given culture are called **display rules.** Certain gestures, body postures, and physical movements can convey vastly different meanings in different cultures.

For example, using the familiar upright thumb gesture while hitchhiking in certain regions of Greece and Sardinia could result in decidedly negative consequences, such as tire tracks on one's body. In those regions, an upright thumb is the equivalent of a raised middle finger in North America (Morris et al., 1979). Likewise, spitting on someone is a sign of contempt in most cultures. Yet the Masai tribe of Africa traditionally considered being spat on a great compliment, particularly if the person doing the spitting is a member of the opposite sex (Thomson, 1887). One can only imagine what a Masai singles bar would be like.

Do emotional expressions differ across cultures in the same way that gestures do? To some extent they do, since the display rules of a particular culture dictate *when* and *how* particular emotions are to be expressed. In the Orissa culture of India, sticking out one's tongue is the display rule for expressing feelings of shame (Menon & Schweder, 1994). Some Asian cultures, such as the Japanese, are more subdued in their expression of emotion in public settings than are Europeans and Americans (Mesquita et al., 1997). Within the Utku Inuit culture, the expression of anger is nearly absent. The only exceptions occur toward individuals who have been ostracized by the community and toward dogs, who are the frequent targets of vented aggression (Briggs, 1970). A number of emotion theorists, including Silvan Tomkins (1991), Paul Ekman (1994), and Carroll Izard (1989), conclude

43. What are cultural display rules? How do they affect emotional behaviour?

that innate biological factors and cultural display rules combine to shape emotional expression.

Instrumental behaviours. Emotional responses are often "calls to action," requiring some sort of response to the situation that aroused the emotion. A highly anxious student must find some way to cope with an impending test. A mother angered by her child's behaviour must find a nondestructive way to get her point across. These are **instrumental behaviours,** directed at achieving some goal.

Batja Mesquita, Nico Frijda, and Klaus Scherer (1997) analyzed cross-cultural studies and concluded that instrumental actions fall into five broad categories: moving toward others (e.g., love), moving away from others (fear, revulsion), moving against others (anger), helplessness, and submission (and see the *Frontiers* feature). Within each of these broad categories, many different goal-directed behaviours can occur. Whether an instrumental behaviour will be successful depends on the appropriateness of the response to the situation, the skill with which it is carried out, and the level of emotional arousal that accompanies the behaviours.

People often assume that high emotional arousal enhances task performance, as when athletes try to "psych themselves up" for competition. Yet, as students who have experienced extreme anxiety during tests could testify, high emotional arousal can also interfere with performance. In many situations, the relation between emotional

arousal and performance seems to take the shape of an upside-down, or inverted, U. As physiological arousal increases up to some optimal level, performance improves. But beyond that optimal level, further increases in arousal impair performance. It is thus possible to be either too "flat" or too "high" to perform well.

The relation between arousal and performance depends not only on arousal level, but also on task complexity (Yerkes & Dodson, 1908). Task complexity involves how complicated the task is, how much precision is required to do the task, and how well the task has been learned. Generally speaking, as task complexity *increases*, the optimal level of arousal for maximum performance *decreases*. Thus, even a moderate level of arousal can disrupt performance on a highly complex task.

Figure 11.28 illustrates these two principles. Note that the inverted U relation applies for all three tasks and that the more complex the task, the lower is the optimal arousal level. One other feature of Figure 11.28 is worth noting: Performance drops off less at high levels of arousal for the simple task than for the others. In fact, even the highest levels of arousal can enhance performance of very simple tasks, such as running or lifting something. This fact may account for seemingly "superhuman" feats we hear about occasionally, such as one incident in which a highly distraught 46 kilogram mother lifted up the front end of a truck to free her child, who was trapped under one of its wheels (*Honolulu Star-Bulletin*, January 6, 1980).

44. How do level of arousal and task complexity combine to affect task performance?

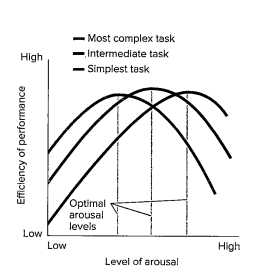

(middle): © Duomo/Corbis; (right): © Ingram Publishing/SuperStock

FIGURE 11.28 The relation between arousal and performance often takes the form of an inverted U, with performance declining above and below an optimal arousal level. However, the more difficult or complex a task is, the lower is the optimal level of arousal for performing it. For which of the performances shown, (b) or (c), should optimal arousal be lower?

Frontiers

A NEW EMOTION?

As discussed in this chapter, there is wide agreement that there are a limited number of basic human emotions—emotions found universally among all humans. There is debate about whether these are the six basic emotions originally identified by Ekman and Friesen (1987) in their groundbreaking work, or some modification, such as the contributions of evolutionary psychologists shown in Table 11.3. If you examine the emotions listed in Table 11.3 or illustrated in Figure 11.27, all of these emotions are familiar; no one will read these lists and be surprised by anything in the lists or confused about what they mean. There is discussion about how many fundamental emotions there are and how many of our emotion responses are combinations of these fundamental emotions, but no one has proposed a new emotion for a very long time. No one, that is, until the beginning of the 21st century.

Early in this century, psychologist John Haidt proposed a new emotion. This new emotion was labelled "elevation" (see Figure 11.29; Ellithorpe, Ewoldsen, & Oliver, 2015; Haidt, 2000, 2003). Elevation was defined as the emotion evoked by witnessing a morally beautiful or virtuous act (Haidt, 2000), and is an emotional sense of meaningfulness, a feeling of being connected to humanity, of wanting to help others and to be a better person (Ellithorpe et al., 2015). It is associated with the physical sensations of a lump in the throat, a general "tingly" sensation, and a feeling of dilation, or swelling, of the chest (Haidt, 2000).

Elevation is a positive emotional experience, but it is not simply positive affect. For an experience to elicit elevation it must include something deeper, something that can be described as inspiration or connectedness (Ellithorpe et al., 2015). Positive affect, such as feeling happy, can be elicited by stimuli such as jokes, slapstick comedy, amusing word-play, or situations where something good happens to someone you like. Similarly, feeling good about oneself or about a situation can be elicited by compliments, aesthetically pleasing surroundings, or goal achievement. All of these can generate positive affect, but not elevation. That is, elevation is more than a positive emotional reaction. The situations that elicit it are things such as watching someone perform altruistic acts or an inspirational message (Ellithorpe et al., 2015; Haidt, 2001, 2003; Oliver et al., 2012). For example, Silvers and Haidt (2008) used a video clip from the *Oprah Winfrey Show* in which a man described how he was spared from a life of poverty and deviance due to the positive influence of his music teacher to evoke elevation, and a video featuring the comedian Jerry Seinfeld to generate happiness without elevation.

It has been argued that the function of elevation is to promote altruism and prosocial behaviour. In an early study on elevation, participants who watched a video expected to generate elevation (a video about Mother Teresa) were more likely to report a desire to help others, to improve themselves, and to engage socially (Haidt , 2000). There is also evidence that elevation increases the amount of money one is willing to donate to a charity (Freeman, Aquino, & McFerran, 2009), although this effect is not always reported (Ellithorpe et al., 2015). Compared to participants who watched either an emotionally neutral documentary or a humorous video, participants who watched a video that generated elevation were more likely to volunteer to participate in a uncompensated part of a putative memory experiment, and they spent more time engaged in a tedious activity thought to be helpful to someone else (Schnall, Roper, & Fessner, 2010). That is, there is evidence to support the

David H. Lewis/Getty Images

FIGURE 11.29 Witnessing selfless acts of compassion and altruism has been suggested to elicit the emotion of elevation, a feeling of meaningfulness, connectedness, and desire to help others.

continued

idea that eliciting elevation has important and unique consequences for altruistic and prosocial behaviour.

One interesting recent study (Ellithorpre et al., 2015) on elevation included what is called the noise blast task, a measure of aggression. Initially, participants watched either a video intended to elicit elevation or a funny video, and participants were led to believe they had a choice over which video they watched. After watching the video, participants engaged in the noise blast task. In this task participants are told that they will compete with another person in a reaction time test, and whoever is faster will be rewarded with money. The slower player, however, will hear an uncomfortable blast of noise (hence the name "noise blast" task). Participants could set the noise level for their opponent, and were told that their opponent would set the level of noise that they would be exposed to if they lost. As you might guess, participants were actually playing against a computer, and the task was rigged so that each participant would win and lose an equal number of times at random intervals. The only exception was that all participants lost on the first trial. On that first trial, the (computer) opponent was faster and the real participants all lost and were blasted with the loudest allowable noise. That is, as a participant your first experience was to be blasted with the loudest possible noise and think that your opponent had picked that noise level. What do you do now, when you can set the noise level for the next trial? Do you retaliate and set the noise level to maximum? Participants who both believed they had chosen the video they watched and who had seen the elevating video were the least likely to retaliate of all of the groups in the study. Along with evidence for elevation increasing altruism, there is at least preliminary evidence that it can also decrease aggression, as measured by a decrease in retaliation.

Although there is great deal still to be done, there are some intriguing results from studies of the proposed new emotional state of elevation. We experience this emotion when we see others perform selfless and inspiring acts or receive inspirational messages, and it has been suggested that this emotion functions to promote prosocial behaviours such as acts of altruism and cooperation and that it may lower aggression.

Review

- The primary components of emotion are the eliciting stimuli, cognitive appraisals, physiological arousal, and expressive and instrumental behaviours. Individual differences in personality and motivation affect the experience and expression of emotion, as do cultural factors.

- Although innate factors can affect the eliciting properties of certain stimuli, learning can also play an important role in determining the arousal properties of stimuli.

- The cognitive component of emotional experience involves the evaluative and personal appraisal of the eliciting stimuli. The ability of thoughts to elicit emotional arousal has been demonstrated clinically and in experimental research. Cross-cultural research indicates considerable agreement across cultures in the appraisals that evoke basic emotions but also some degree of variation in more complex appraisals.

- Our physiological responses in emotion are produced by the hypothalamus, the limbic system, and the cortex, and by the autonomic and endocrine systems. There appear to be two systems for emotional behaviour, one involving conscious processing by the cortex, the other unconscious processing by the amygdala.

- Studies suggest that negative emotions reflect greater relative activation of the right hemisphere, whereas positive emotions are related to relatively greater activation in the left hemisphere.

- The validity of the polygraph as a "lie detector" has been questioned largely because of the difficulty of establishing which emotion is being expressed.

- The behavioural component of emotion includes expressive and instrumental behaviours. Different parts of the face are important in the expression of various emotions. The accuracy of people's interpretations of these expressions increases when situational cues are also available. Based in part on similarities in facial expression of emotions across widely separate cultures, evolutionary theorists propose that certain fundamental emotional patterns are innate. They agree, however, that cultural learning can influence emotional expression in important ways.

- Research on the relation between arousal and performance suggests that there is an optimal level of arousal for the performance of any task. This optimal level varies with the complexity or difficulty of the task; complex tasks have lower optimal arousal levels.

For complex tasks, the relation between arousal and performance is different. High emotionality can interfere with the ability to attend to and process information effectively. Thus, people may underachieve on intelligence test items that require complicated mental processing if they are too anxious, and the performance of air-traffic control officers can suffer in highly stressful circumstances (Joslyn & Hunt, 1998; Pierce et al., 1998). On physical tasks, muscle tension can interfere with the skilful execution of complex movements. For example, in the sport of golf, which requires precise and complex movements, the optimal level of arousal should be quite low. Robert Weinberg and Marvin Genuchi (1980) studied the effects of anxiety on performance during an intercollegiate golf tournament. Before the tournament began, they administered a questionnaire to identify players who were low, moderate, or high in performance anxiety. Although the three groups of golfers were similar in ability and performed equally well during practice rounds, their golf scores differed sharply during the anxiety-arousing tournament rounds. On the first day of competition, the average performance of golfers in the low-anxiety group was five strokes better than the performance of those in the high-anxiety group. On the pressure-packed last day of the tournament, this difference rose to nearly seven strokes. The moderate-anxiety group had intermediate scores.

45. Compare the James-Lange (somatic) and Cannon-Bard explanations for emotional perception and labelling.

THEORIES OF EMOTION

Emotions involve complex interactions among eliciting stimuli, thoughts, physiological responses, and behaviours (see the Levels of Analysis feature, Figure 11.37, at the end of this chapter). For more than 100 years, theorists and researchers have explored the nature of these interactions.

The James-Lange Somatic Theory

In 1890, the eminent psychologist William James ignited considerable controversy with this counterintuitive statement:

46. How does research on animals and people deprived of sensory feedback bear on the validity of the James-Lange and Cannon-Bard theories?

> Common sense says . . . we meet a bear, are frightened, and run; we are insulted by a rival, are angry, and strike. The hypothesis here to be defended says that this order of sequence is incorrect . . . and that the more rational statement is that we feel sorry *because* we cry, angry *because* we strike, afraid *because* we tremble. (emphasis added, 1890–1950, p. 451)

At about the same time that James advanced his theory, a Danish psychologist named Carl Lange reached a similar conclusion, so the theory was attributed to both men. Today, the *James-Lange theory* lives on as the **somatic theory of emotion** (Papanicolaou, 1989). To proponents of this theory, body informs mind; our physiological reactions determine our emotions. We know we are afraid or in love only because our bodily reactions tell us so.

The Cannon-Bard Theory

It was not long before the James-Lange theory was challenged. In 1927, the physiologist Walter Cannon fired back. He pointed out that people's bodies do *not* respond instantaneously to an emotional stimulus; several seconds may pass before signs of physiological arousal appear. Yet people typically experience the emotion immediately. This would be impossible according to the James-Lange theory. Cannon and his colleague L.L. Bard concluded that cognition must be involved as well.

The *Cannon-Bard theory* proposed that, when we encounter an emotion-arousing situation, the thalamus simultaneously sends sensory messages to the cerebral cortex *and* to the body's internal organs. The message to the cortex produces the experience of emotion, and the one to the internal organs produces the physiological arousal. Thus, neither cognition nor arousal causes the other; they are independent responses to stimulation from the thalamus. The James-Lange and Cannon-Bard theories are compared in Figure 11.30.

The Role of Autonomic Feedback

The James-Lange and Cannon-Bard theories differ on one critical point. According to the James-Lange theory, feedback from the body's reactions to eliciting stimuli tells the brain that we are experiencing an emotion. Without such feedback, there would be no emotional response. In contrast, the Cannon-Bard theory maintains that experiencing emotion results from signals sent from the thalamus to the cortex, not from bodily feedback. Is there any situation that would provide a test of whether bodily feedback is necessary?

In fact, there is. What if organisms were deprived of sensory feedback from their internal organs so that they never knew when these organs were aroused? Would they be devoid of emotional reactions? To answer this question, Cannon (1929) carried out experiments with animals in which he severed the nerves that provide feedback from the internal organs to

James-Lange

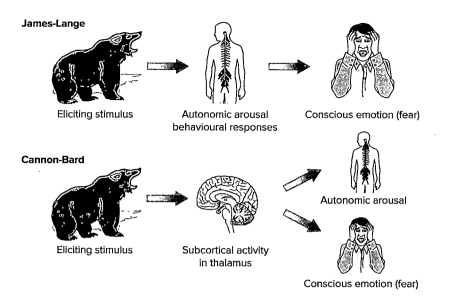

Eliciting stimulus   Autonomic arousal   Conscious emotion (fear)
behavioural responses

Cannon-Bard

Eliciting stimulus   Subcortical activity   Autonomic arousal
in thalamus

Conscious emotion (fear)

FIGURE 11.30 Two early theories of emotion continue to influence current-day theorizing. The James-Lange theory holds that the experience of emotion is caused by somatic feedback and physiological arousal. According to the Cannon-Bard theory, the thalamus receives sensory input and simultaneously stimulates physiological responses and cognitive awareness.

the brain. He found that even after surgery, the animals still exhibited emotional responses, supporting his theory over that of James and Lange.

But perhaps people are different from other species. Obviously, Cannon's animal experiments could never be replicated with people, but nature provides a tragic parallel. Like Cannon's animals, people whose spinal cords have been severed in accidents receive no sensory feedback from body areas below the injury. Given this fact, what are their emotional lives like? To find out, Kathleen Chwalisz, Ed Diener, and Dennis Gallagher (1988) administered self-report measures of emotional experience to people who had sustained spinal injuries. For comparative purposes, the same measures were administered to individuals having physical handicaps that did not affect sensory feedback, and to a group of non-handicapped people.

As shown in Figure 11.31, the people with spinal cord injuries did not differ from the other two groups in the reported intensity of either their positive or negative emotions. Indeed, some reported that they frequently experienced very intense emotions—sometimes more intense than those they had experienced before their injury. Moreover, people with upper and lower spinal cord injuries—who differed in the amount of bodily feedback they could receive—did not differ in the intensity of their emotions. These results, like those of Cannon's animal studies, appear to cast doubt on the claim that arousal feedback from the body is absolutely

necessary for people to experience intense emotion. But let us take this issue one step further.

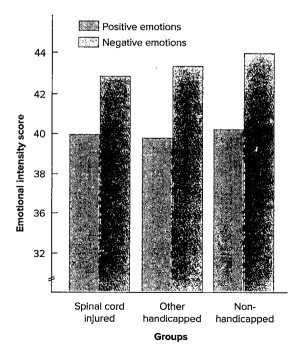

FIGURE 11.31 Intensity of positive and negative emotions reported by people with spinal cord injuries, by handicapped people with no spinal damage, and by non-handicapped people. The lack of differences casts doubt on the assertion that feedback from physiological arousal is essential for the experiencing of normal emotional responses.

Source: Data from Chwalisz, K., Diener, E., & Gallagher, D. (1988). Autonomic arousal feedback and emotional experience: Evidence from the spinal cord injured. *Journal of Personality and Social Psychology,* 54, 820–828.

47. What is the facial feedback hypothesis? What research evidence supports it? What might be the role of vascular feedback?

48. How did Lazarus and his colleagues show that appraisals influence level of arousal?

The Facial Feedback Hypothesis

Arousal feedback is not the only kind of bodily feedback the somatic theory considers important. Facial muscles involved in emotional displays also feed messages to the brain, and these muscles are active even in patients with spinal injuries who may receive no sensory input from below the neck. According to the **facial feedback hypothesis,** this feedback to the brain might play a key role in determining the nature and intensity of emotion that we experience, as the James-Lange theory would suggest (Adelmann & Zajonc, 1989; McIntosh et al., 1997; Soussignan, 2002).

Research shows that positive or negative emotional responses can indeed be triggered by contraction of specific facial muscles. Especially noteworthy are studies in which participants do not know that they are activating muscles used in specific emotional expressions. In one such study, Fritz Strack and his colleagues (1988) found that when participants held pencils in their teeth, activating muscles used in smiling (Figure 11.32a), they rated themselves as feeling more pleasant than when they held the pencils with their lips (Figure 11.32b), which activates muscles involved in frowning. Participants also rated cartoons as funnier while holding pencils in their teeth and activating the "happy muscles" than while holding pencils with their lips (Figure 11.32c). In another study, Robert Zajonc and his colleagues compared the subjective experiences of subjects who

pronounced different sounds, such as *eee* and *ooh.* Saying the *eee* sound, which activates muscles used in smiling, was associated with more pleasant feelings than saying the *ooh* sound, which activates muscles involved in negative facial expressions (Zajonc et al., 1989). Perhaps photographers should force us to say "cheese" not only when they take our picture, but also later when they show us proofs that not even our mothers could love.

Cognitive-Affective Theories

Nowhere are mind–body interactions more obvious than in the emotions, where thinking and feeling are intimately connected. Cognitive-affective theories focus on the ways in which cognitions and physiological responses interact (Clore & Centerbar, 2004). Historically, Richard Lazarus and Stanley Schachter have been major figures in this approach.

Lazarus (2001) emphasizes the link between cognitive appraisal and arousal, and argues that all emotional responses require some sort of appraisal, whether we are aware of that appraisal or not.

The fundamental premise is that in order to survive, animals (humans particularly) are constructed biologically to be constantly evaluating (appraising) their relationship with the environment with respect to significance for well-being. . . . If a person (or

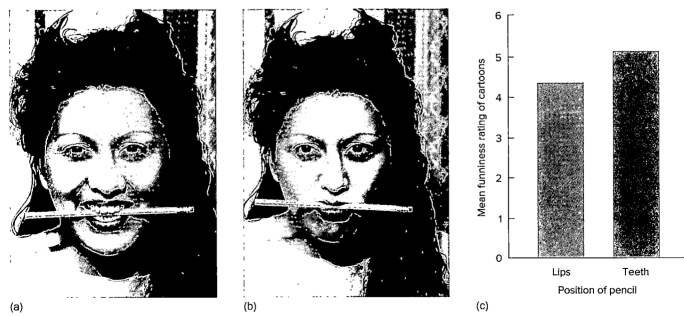

(a)   (b)   (c)

(photos): © Tony Freeman/PhotoEdit

FIGURE 11.32 Holding a pencil in the teeth (a) so as to activate the muscles used in smiling evokes more pleasant feelings than holding the pencil in one's lips (b), which activates muscles used in frowning. This finding (c) provides support for the facial feedback hypothesis.

Data from Strack, F., Martin, L.L., & Stepper, S. (1988). Inhibiting and facilitating conditions of facial expressions: A non-obtrusive test of the facial feedback hypothesis. *Journal of Personality and Social Psychology, 54,* 768–777.

animal) appraises his or her relationship with the environment in a particular way, then a specific emotion, which is tied to the appraisal, always results; and if two persons make the same appraisal, then they will experience the same emotion regardless of the actual circumstances. (Lazarus, 1991, p. 825)

It is worth emphasizing a key difference between the Cannon-Bard and the cognitive-affective theories of emotion. According to the Cannon-Bard theory of emotion, when you encounter a specific environmental cue, a matching emotion is triggered. That is, which emotion you experience is importantly determined by what is in the environment. For example, the sight of a bear triggers fear or hearing an insult triggers anger. The cognitive-affective theories, however, argue that what matters is how you appraise, or interpret, environmental stimuli. The sight of a bear can elicit fear, but if the bear is perceived as an impressive and noble animal, the emotion may be awe. Similarly, hearing an insult may trigger anger, but that same comment may be interpreted as a cutting and valid personal criticism and trigger sadness, or it may be interpreted as sarcasm and elicit happiness and laughter. That is, for Lazarus and Schachter, what matters is not what environmental cue confronts you but how you appraise it. For Cannon and Bard, a specific stimulus would be expected to consistently trigger the same emotion, whereas for Lazarus and Schachter it would trigger the same emotion only if the appraisal was the same; a stimulus could trigger as many different emotions as there are different appraisals.

As noted earlier, the appraisal itself need not be a conscious thought; it may be some automatic perception that does not enter conscious awareness. Once the appraisal has triggered the arousal response, arousal cues may feed back into the ongoing appraisal process. Thus, if you feel yourself becoming aroused in the presence of another person, you may begin to appraise the person as more desirable and attractive than before.

Like Lazarus, Stanley Schachter emphasized the link between cognition and arousal, and he developed the best known of the cognitive-affective theories of emotion. He was intrigued with the question of how we know both *what* we are feeling and *how strongly* we are feeling it. Schachter's **two-factor theory of emotion**, also called the *Schachter-Singer theory of emotion*, states that arousal and cognitive labelling based on situational cues are the critical ingredients in emotional experience. The intensity of physiological

Schachter's Theory

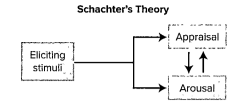

FIGURE 11.33 Stanley Schachter's two-factor theory focuses on the interactive role of cognition and arousal. Schachter emphasized the role of appraisals of the environment in our labelling of the emotions we experience.

arousal tells us *how strongly* we are feeling something, but situational cues give us the information we need to tell us *what* we are feeling—fear, anger, love, or some other emotion (Schachter, 1966). Lazarus would agree, viewing these cues as an important determinant of the appraisal process (Figure 11.33). Thus, both view situation, cognition, and arousal as highly interrelated.

A classic, and creative, test of Schachter's two-factor theory was performed by Dutton and Aron (1974) of the University of British Columbia. Dutton and Aron arranged for either a male or a female research assistant to approach males who were crossing two different bridges and ask them to participate in a study of creativity. Participants were asked to complete a short questionnaire and write a short story based on a picture shown to them by the research assistant. The participants were then told that they could contact the research assistant if they had any questions and were given the researcher's name and phone number. The participants were recruited on one of two different bridges. One was the Capilano Suspension Bridge, a 137-metre-long suspension bridge 76 metres above a section of rapids. The other was a wide, sturdy cedar bridge only 3 metres above a small stream. Dutton and Aron reasoned that, if Schachter was correct, when males crossed the swaying, anxiety-provoking suspension bridge and met the attractive female research assistant, they would attribute their arousal to the female research assistant. The results supported a cognitive-appraisal theory. Participants who had crossed the suspension bridge included more sexual imagery in their stories and were more likely to later call the female research assistant than participants who had crossed the low, sturdy cedar bridge (Figure 11.34). For participants met by the male research assistant, it did not matter which bridge they crossed, sexual imagery and later behaviour were similar between bridges. Two classic experiments performed by Lazarus and Schachter that also explored the links between cognition and arousal are described in the *Research Foundations* feature.

49. According to Schachter, what influences perceptions of emotional intensity? What tells us which emotion we are experiencing?

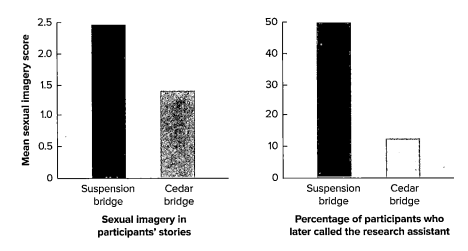

FIGURE 11.34 Results from Dutton and Aron's classic 1974 experiment in the Capilano Canyon. Male participants who experienced increased arousal from crossing a suspension bridge included more sexual imagery in their stories and were more likely to later call the research assistant, attributing this arousal to the female research assistant.

Source: Data from Dutton, D.G., & Aron, A.P. (1974). Some evidence for heightened sexual attraction under conditions of high anxie-ty. *Journal of Personality and Social Psychology*, 30, 510–517.

Research Foundations

COGNITION-AROUSAL RELATIONS

Manipulating Appraisal to Influence Arousal

Introduction

Richard Lazarus and his University of California colleagues examined how differences in cognitive appraisal can influence physiological arousal. To do so, they needed to measure physiological arousal in response to visual stimuli that were held constant for all participants, while influencing the manner in which these eliciting stimuli were appraised. If people in different appraisal conditions showed different arousal responses to the same eliciting stimuli, it would support the notion that arousal is influenced by appraisal.

Method

The researchers monitored university students' physiological responses while they watched an anthropology film, *Subincision in the Arunta*, which depicts in graphic detail an aboriginal puberty rite during which the penises of adolescent boys are cut with a jagged flint knife. The film typically elicits a high level of physiological arousal in viewers (and, according to the researchers, many leg-crossing responses in males). The dependent variable, measured by recording electrodes attached to the participants' palms, was changes in electrical skin conductance caused by sweat gland activity.

To study the effects of participants' appraisal of the filmed visual stimuli on arousal, the researchers experimentally varied the film's soundtrack. Four different soundtrack conditions were used to manipulate the independent variable:

1. A *trauma* soundtrack emphasized the pain suffered by the boys, the danger of infection, the jaggedness of the flint knife, and other unpleasant aspects of the operation.

2. A *denial* soundtrack was just the opposite; it denied that the operation was excessively painful or traumatic, and emphasized that the boys looked forward to entering

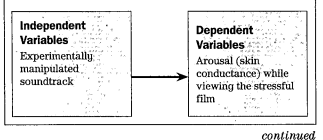

Design: Lazarus

Question: Can experimentally manipulated cognitive appraisals influence physiological arousal responses to external stimuli?

Type of Study: *Experimental*

Independent Variables	Dependent Variables
Experimentally manipulated soundtrack	Arousal (skin conductance) while viewing the stressful film

continued

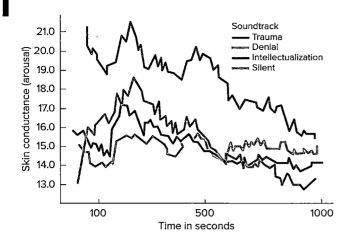

FIGURE 11.35 Appraisal influences arousal. Participants who viewed a film showing a tribal subincision rite in vivid detail exhibited different levels of physiological arousal, depending on the soundtrack that accompanied the film.

Source: From J. Speisman, R.S. Lazarus, A. Mordkoff & L. Davidson, 1964, "Experimental Reduction of Stress Based on Ego-Defense Theory," *Jounal of Abnormal and Social Psychology*, 68, 373, Fig 1. Copyright © 1964 by the American Psychological Association. Reprinted by permission of the author and the publisher.

adulthood by undergoing the rite and demonstrating their bravery.

3. The *intellectualization* soundtrack, also designed to produce a more benign appraisal, ignored the emotional elements of the scenes altogether and focused on the traditions and history of the tribe.

4. In a *silent* control condition, the film was shown without any soundtrack at all, leaving viewers to make their own appraisals.

Results

As shown in Figure 11.35, the soundtracks produced markedly different levels of arousal. As predicted, the trauma soundtrack resulted in the highest arousal, followed by the silent film condition, which likely evoked dire appraisals as well. The denial and intellectualization soundtracks, designed to create more benign appraisals, resulted in much lower levels of arousal. This classic study supported Lazarus's contention that appraisal can influence arousal.

Manipulating Arousal to Influence Appraisal

Introduction

Is the reverse also true? Can level of arousal influence people's appraisal of an eliciting stimulus? To test this hypothesis, one must cause people to experience different levels of arousal without knowing the true reason. The level of arousal should then be attributed to whatever eliciting stimuli are present in the situation.

Method

In Stanley Schachter's laboratory at Columbia University, participants were told they were in a study involving the effects of a new vitamin, called suproxin, on visual perception. The researchers directly manipulated the level of physiological arousal by injecting participants with one of three different substances. In one condition, participants received epinephrine, a stimulant that increases arousal. In a second experimental condition, participants received a tranquilizer drug that would decrease arousal. A placebo control group received a saline injection that would have no effects on arousal. The experimenters told all participants that the suproxin injection would have no side effects (when, in fact, the epinephrine and tranquilizer would begin to have immediate and opposite effects on arousal). Then, while presumably waiting for the vitamin to take effect, the participants were shown a short movie "to provide continuous black-and-white stimulation to the eyes." The movie was a comedy that included a slapstick chase scene. The experimenters hypothesized that the participants in the two drug conditions would attribute their heightened or lowered level of arousal to the funniness (or lack thereof) of the film, because they would know of no other reason why they should feel as they did.

Results

Participants were observed from behind a one-way mirror while they watched the movie. The observers, who were unaware of which participants had received which injections, recorded how frequently the participants smiled, grinned, laughed, threw up their hands, slapped their legs, or doubled over with laughter. These behaviours were combined into an "amusement score" that served as the dependent variable measure of how funny the participants found the film to be.

It appears that arousal cues can indeed influence one's appraisal of the situation. As Figure 11.36 shows, the results supported the experimenters' hypothesis that level of arousal would influence participants' appraisal of

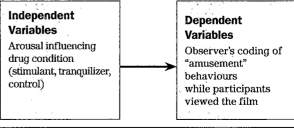

Design: Schachter

Question: Can experimentally manipulated arousal levels influence cognitive appraisals of external stimuli?

Type of Study: *Experimental*

Independent Variables	Dependent Variables
Arousal influencing drug condition (stimulant, tranquilizer, control)	Observer's coding of "amusement" behaviours while participants viewed the film

continued

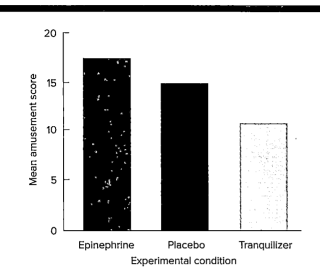

Experimental condition

FIGURE 11.36 Arousal influences appraisal. Participants were injected with epinephrine, a tranquilizer, or a placebo to affect arousal and then were shown a humorous film. The amount of amusement they displayed varied with their state of arousal.

Source: Data from Schachter, S., & Wheeler, L. (1962). Epinephrine, chlorpromazine, and amusement. *Journal of Abnormal and Social Psychology, 65,* 121–128.

Sources: Joseph Speisman, Richard Lazarus, Arnold Mordkoff, and Les Davison, 1964. Experimental reduction of stress based on ego-defense theory. *Journal of Abnormal and Social Psychology, 68,* 367–380; and Stanley Schachter and Ladd Wheeler, 1962. Epinephrine, chlorpromazine, and amusement. *Journal of Abnormal and Social Psychology, 65,* 121–128.

the film. The aroused participants in the epinephrine group found the film funnier than the tranquilized participants did, and the placebo control group fell in the middle. Thus, a person injected with epinephrine might think, "Here I am watching this film and getting all excited. This film's really funny!"

Discussion

These two studies were among the first to experimentally manipulate appraisal and arousal so as to study their effects on each other. In the first study, even though it was not possible to completely control for participants' own tendencies to appraise situations in certain ways, the four soundtrack conditions did have effects on the arousal responses of participants as they watched the subincision film. When Schachter and Wheeler turned Lazarus's procedure around and manipulated arousal levels with the stimulant and tranquilizing drugs, they found the expected differences in appraisal of the films. Moreover, they were able to measure these differences in terms of observable behaviour.

Taken together, these two studies show that appraisal influences arousal and that arousal can influence appraisal, demonstrating the two-way causal relation between cognition and arousal shown in the model of emotion originally presented in Figure 11.21.

In Review

- Several past and present theories posit causal relations among emotional components. The James-Lange/somatic theory maintains that we first become aroused and then judge what we are feeling. The Cannon-Bard theory proposes that arousal and cognition are simultaneously triggered by the thalamus. Cognitive appraisal theory states that appraisals trigger emotional arousal. According to Schachter's two-factor theory, arousal tells us how strongly we feel, while cognitions derived from situational cues help us label the specific emotion.

- The facial feedback hypothesis, derived from the James-Lange/somatic theory, states that feedback from the facial muscles associated with innate emotional displays affects cognitive and physiological processes. Recent evidence supplies support for the theory.

- Because of the two-way relations between the cognitive and physiological components of emotion, it is possible to manipulate appraisals and thereby influence the level of arousal. Arousal changes can also affect appraisal of the eliciting stimuli.

Levels of Analysis | Emotion

As we have seen, emotion involves complex interactions between mind, body, and the environment. As such, its study spans the biological, psychological, and environmental levels of analysis. Here is a summary of the factors that need to be taken into account for an understanding of emotion.

ENVIRONMENTAL

- Many eliciting stimuli arise in the external environment.
- Individual and cultural learning experiences can affect emotional expression and experience.
- Some environmental stimuli are primed by evolutionary factors to be eliciting stimuli.

BIOLOGICAL

- Genetic factors influence emotional reactivity from the moment of birth.
- Brain structures, especially the amygdala, other limbic structures, and the cortex, are part of a two-component emotional system that can operate at both conscious and unconscious levels. The hemispheres differ in the emotions associated most strongly with them.
- Neurotransmitter systems play an important role in the neural activations and inhibitions that underlie emotion.

PSYCHOLOGICAL

- Cognitive processes play an important role in the emotional response system, generating emotions, and guiding instrumental and coping responses.
- Cognitive appraisals and physiological arousal influence each other.
- Knowledge of cultural norms for emotional expression influence both emotional experience and expression.

How might cognitive appraisal processes influence right and left hemisphere responses to environmental stimuli, and which emotions would be expected to result?

FIGURE 11.37

Gaining Direction

What are the issues?	The opening scenario for Chapter 11 deals with a new approach to forensic neurology called *brain fingerprinting*. The basic idea is to present details of a crime to a suspect and then monitor the suspect's brainwaves. The developers argue that familiar information generates	a very specific response pattern (known as *P300*). Such a pattern is not emitted for new information. Issues surrounding this scenario range from the specifics of brainwave patterns, to the reliability of testing, to the use of such a technology in court.
What do we need to know?	How reliable and valid is brain fingerprinting? What is P300? How are brainwaves measured?	Is this procedure any different from polygraph testing? What happens when someone is lying?
Where can we find the information to answer these questions?	You should begin by reviewing the information on polygraph testing. What specifically is measured by the polygraph, and what does brain fingerprinting assess? Is brain fingerprinting a more reliable method? Why? You will probably want to look back at Chapter 2 and consider	what type of information constitutes a valid scientific claim. As a general background source, look for information on lying and deception. A leading authority in this area is Dr. Paul Ekman at the University of California Medical School, San Francisco.

Development over the Lifespan

CHAPTER >
OUTLINE

PRENATAL DEVELOPMENT
Genetics and Sex Determination
Environmental Influences

INFANCY AND CHILDHOOD
The Amazing Newborn
Sensory-Perceptual Development
Physical, Brain, and Motor Development
Cognitive Development
Social-Emotional and Personality Development
  Frontiers: Social Media and Social Development

Applications: Understanding How Divorce
and Remarriage Affect Children
Moral Development

ADOLESCENCE AND ADULTHOOD
Physical Development
  Focus on Neuroscience: The Neuroscience
  of the Teenage Brain
Cognitive Development
Social-Emotional and Personality Development
  Research Foundations: What Does It Take
  to Become an Adult?

There are only two lasting bequests we can hope to give our children. One of these is
roots; the other, wings.
—Hodding Carter

Almost 40 percent of infants in North America and Europe under the age of two have used an iPad. No, they do not really understand how to use the tablet nor can they choose and launch apps. But they can follow the images and trace actions with their fingers. Plus, iPads have the added advantage of keeping children occupied. Proponents argue that iPad usage helps to develop eye–hand coordination, promotes number recognition, and is a useful developmental tool. Others suggest that such technology may interfere with a child's social and perceptual development. Some go as far as suggesting that we have no idea what these devices might do to the developing brain.

Currently, there are over 800 apps available for kids from birth to age two. You can also buy a baby bouncy seat with an attachment to hold an iPad.

Cultura Creative (RF)/Alamy Stock Photo

What are the
issues here?

What do we need
to know?

Where can
we find the
information to
answer these
questions?

1. Explain how cross-sectional, longitudinal, and sequential designs differ.

Developmental psychology examines changes in our biological, physical, psychological, and behavioural processes as we age. To accomplish this, developmental psychologists often use special research designs (Figure 12.1) to investigate age-related changes. Suppose we wish to study how intellectual abilities change from age 10 to age 60. Using a **cross-sectional design,** we would compare people of different ages at the same point in time. Thus, we could administer intellectual tasks to 10-, 20-, 30-, 40-, 50-, and 60-year-olds. We would test each person and compare how well the different age groups perform. The cross-sectional design is widely used because data from many age groups can be collected relatively quickly, but a key drawback is that the different age groups, called *cohorts,* grew up in different historical periods. Thus, if 60-year-olds have poorer intellectual abilities than 30-year-olds, is this due to aging or environmental differences (e.g., poorer nutrition, poorer medical care, less education) growing up in the 1950s and 1960s versus the 1980s and 1990s?

To avoid this problem, a **longitudinal design** repeatedly tests the same cohort as it grows older. We could test a sample of 10-year-olds this month and then retest them every 10 years, up to age 60, thus ensuring that everyone is exposed to the same historical time frame. Unfortunately, a longitudinal design is time-consuming and, as years pass, our sample may shrink substantially as people move, drop out of the study, or die. Furthermore, suppose we find that intelligence declines at age 60. Is this really due to aging or developmental experiences unique to our particular cohort? Researchers can answer this question by using a **sequential design** that combines the cross-sectional and longitudinal approaches. That is, we can repeatedly test *several* age cohorts as they grow older and determine whether they follow a similar developmental pattern. This design is the most comprehensive, but also the most time-consuming and costly.

These research approaches provide much of our knowledge about human development, which we now explore from conception through death. We begin with the *prenatal period,* approximately 266 days during which we develop from a single-cell organism barely larger than a pinhead into a wondrously complex newborn human.

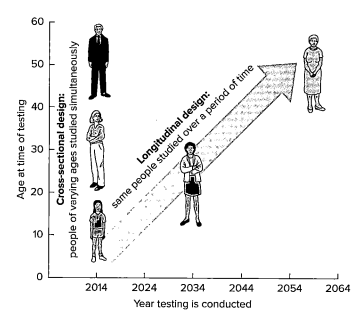

FIGURE 12.1 Using a cross-sectional design, we would test different age groups in the year 2014 and compare their performance. Using a longitudinal design, we would test one age group and then retest them every 10 years until age 60. Using a sequential design (there are many types), we might test 10- through 60-year-olds in the year 2014 and then retest them every 10 years until age 60. Suppose that in the year 2014 the 60-year-olds perform worse than younger adults. Also suppose that, as the 10- through 50-year-olds age, their performance worsens at age 60. We are now more confident that this decline, replicated over different age cohorts, represents a true effect of aging.

PRENATAL DEVELOPMENT

Prenatal development consists of three stages (Figure 12.2) of physical growth. The *germinal stage* constitutes approximately the first two weeks of development, beginning when one sperm fertilizes a female egg (ovum). This fertilized egg is called a **zygote.** Through repeated cell division the zygote becomes a mass of cells that attaches to the mother's uterus about 10 to 14 days after conception.

The *embryonic stage* extends from the end of the second week through the eighth week after conception, and the cell mass now is called an **embryo.** Two life-support structures, the placenta and umbilical cord, develop at the start of this stage. Located on the uterine wall, the *placenta* contains membranes that allow nutrients to pass from the mother's blood to the umbilical cord. In turn, the *umbilical cord* contains blood vessels that carry these nutrients and oxygen to the embryo, and waste products back from the embryo to the mother. Supplied with nutrients, embryonic cells divide rapidly and become specialized. Bodily organs and systems begin to form, and by week eight the heart of the two-centimetre-long embryo is beating, the brain is forming, and facial features, such as eyes, can be recognized.

At the ninth week after conception, the embryo is called a **fetus.** During this *fetal stage,* which lasts until birth, muscles become stronger and other bodily systems continue to develop. At about 24 weeks the eyes open, and by 28 weeks the fetus attains the *age of viability,* meaning that it is likely to survive outside the womb in case of premature birth (Hetherington, Parke, & Locke, 1999).

Genetics and Sex Determination

A female's egg cells and a male's sperm cells each have only 23 chromosomes. At conception, an egg and sperm unite to form the zygote, which now contains the full set of 23 *pairs* found in other human cells. The 23rd pair of chromosomes determines the baby's sex. A genetic female's 23rd pair contains two X chromosomes (XX), so-called because of their shape (Figure 12.3). Because women carry only X chromosomes, the 23rd chromosome in the egg is always an X. A genetic male's 23rd pair contains an X and a Y chromosome (XY). Thus, the 23rd chromosome in the sperm is an X in about half of the cases and a Y in the other half. The Y chromosome contains a specific gene, known as the **TDF (testis determining factor) gene,** that triggers male sexual development. The union of an egg with a sperm cell having a Y chromosome results in an XY combination and, therefore, a boy. A sperm containing an X chromosome produces an XX combination and so a baby girl.

How does the Y chromosome determine male sex characteristics? At roughly six to eight weeks after conception, the *TDF* gene initiates the development of testes. Once formed, the testes secrete sex hormones called *androgens* that continue to direct a male pattern of organ development. If the *TDF* gene is not present, as happens with an XX pair on the 23rd chromosome,

2. What determines the sex of a child?

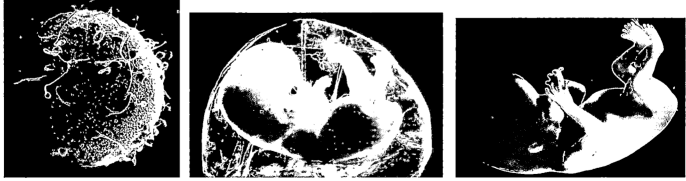

(left): © David M. Phillips/The Population Council/Photo Researchers, Inc.; (middle): © Biophoto Associates/Photo Researchers, Inc.; (right): © John Watney Photo Library/Photo Researchers, Inc.

FIGURE 12.2 These remarkable photos show (a) the moment of conception, as one of many sperm cells fertilizes the ovum, (b) the embryo at six to seven weeks, and (c) the fetus at three months of age.

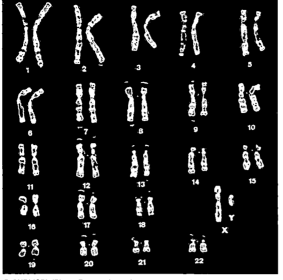

FIGURE 12.3 Most human cells contain 23 pairs of chromosomes. Each pair consists of one chromosome from each parent. The 23rd pair determines a person's sex. In males, the 23rd pair, which is shown in the lower right area of the photo, consists of an X chromosome and a Y chromosome. In females, the 23rd pair contains two X chromosomes.

testes do not form and—in the absence of sufficient androgen activity during this *prenatal critical period*—an inherent female pattern of organ development ensues (Hyde & DeLamater, 2000).

Environmental Influences

Teratogens are environmental agents that cause abnormal prenatal development. The placenta prevents many dangerous substances from reaching the embryo and fetus, but some harmful chemical molecules and diseases can pass through. For example, if the mother contracts rubella (German measles)—especially when the embryo's eyes, ears, heart, and central nervous system are beginning to form early in pregnancy—it can cause blindness, deafness, heart defects, and intellectual disability in the infant (Plotkin, 2006).

Sexually transmitted diseases can pass from mother to fetus and produce brain damage, blindness, and deafness, depending on the disease. Among pregnant women with untreated syphilis, about 25 percent of fetuses are born dead. Likewise, without treatment during pregnancy or delivery by Cesarean section, about 25 percent of fetuses born to mothers with human immunodeficiency virus (HIV) also are infected (Meleski & Damato, 2003).

3. How do STDs, alcohol, and other drugs affect prenatal development? Identify other broad classes of teratogens.

As we will discuss in detail in Chapter 15, stress is an important concern for many people and our lives seem to only get increasingly stressful. There has been concern over whether or not maternal stress affects the developing fetus and whether there are any lasting consequences. Robert Coplan of Carleton University has investigated maternal anxiety during pregnancy and infant temperament (Coplan, O'Neil, & Arbeau, 2005). This research has found that maternal anxiety is associated with greater infant distress reactions and difficulty in recovering from distress at three months of age. Although this could be due to a range of factors other than the impact of maternal stress on the developing fetus, such as differences in postnatal care associated with anxiety, genetic predisposition to anxiety disorders, and so forth, subsequent research has led to the conclusion that prenatal exposure to stress and the stress hormones is an important risk factor for later mental health problems, including anxiety and depression (Davis et al., 2013).

Mercury, lead, radiation, and many other environmental toxins can produce birth defects, as can many drugs. **Fetal alcohol spectrum disorders (FASD)** involve a range of mild to severe cognitive, behavioural, and physical deficits caused by prenatal exposure to alcohol (Coates, 2015). One disorder within this spectrum, **fetal alcohol syndrome (FAS),** involves a cluster of severe developmental abnormalities. FAS children have facial abnormalities and small, malformed brains (Figure 12.4). Psychological and social impairments include intellectual disability, attentional and perceptual deficits, impulsivity, and poor social skills (Murthy et al., 2009). Other children exposed to alcohol in the womb may display fewer or milder impairments.

The threshold levels of alcohol exposure needed to produce FASD, or FAS specifically, are not known. About one-third to one-half of infants born to alcoholic mothers have FAS, but even social drinking or a single episode of binge drinking can increase the risk of prenatal damage and long-term cognitive impairment. Because no amount of prenatal alcohol exposure is safe, women should not drink if there is any chance that they are pregnant.

Nicotine is another known teratogen. Maternal smoking increases the risk of miscarriage, premature birth, and low birth weight (Kirchengast & Hartmann, 2003). Because of

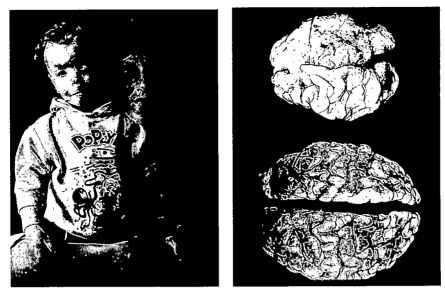

(left): © George Steinmetz; (right): © Streissguth, A.P., & Little, R.E. (1994). "Unit 5: Alcohol, Pregnancy, and the Fetal Alcohol Syndrome: Second Edition" of the Project Cork Institute Medical School Curriculum (slide lecture series) on Biomedical Education: Alcohol Use and Its Medical Consequences, produced by Dartmouth Medical School.

FIGURE 12.4 Children who suffer from fetal alcohol syndrome (FAS) not only look different (left), but have brains that are underdeveloped compared with those of normal children (right).

In Review

- Cross-sectional designs compare people of different age groups at a single point in time. A longitudinal design repeatedly tests the same age group as it grows older. A sequential design tests several groups at one point in time and then again when they are older.

- Prenatal development involves the zygote, embryonic, and fetal stages.

- The 23rd chromosome in a mother's egg cell always is an X chromosome. If the 23rd chromosome in the father's sperm cell is an X, the child will be genetically female (XX); if a Y, the child will be born genetically male (XY).

- Illness, drug use, and environmental toxins can cause abnormal prenatal development.

second-hand smoke, regular tobacco use by fathers also has been linked to low infant birth weight and increased risk of respiratory infections (Wakefield et al., 1998). There is evidence that caffeine, the most widely used drug in the world, can also influence fetal brain development (Mioranzza et al., 2014). Caffeine may affect the embryonic development of both the cerebral cortex and the hippocampus. Babies of pregnant mothers who use heroin or cocaine are often born addicted and experience withdrawal symptoms after birth. Their cognitive functioning, motor skill development, and ability to regulate their arousal and attention may also be impaired (Bennett et al., 2013; Wahlsten & Sarman, 2013).

INFANCY AND CHILDHOOD

Studying infants poses interesting challenges. During research studies, infants may start to fuss, cry, drool, spit up, soil their diapers, or simply fall asleep! Experiments must be designed to keep infants alert and "on task," a difficult job because they are easily overwhelmed by novel, highly stimulating environments and rapidly become bored by bland environments. Optimal test settings are difficult to achieve and change with age during the first year of life. Finally, because infants can't describe their experiences, researchers must find clever ways to use those responses that

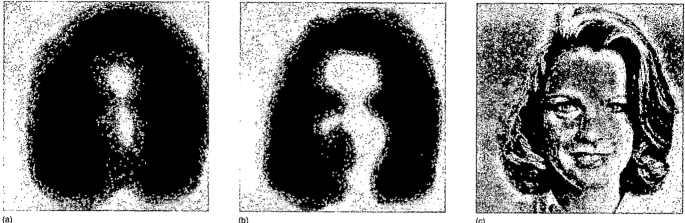

(a)

(b)

(c)

© Ryan McVay/Getty Images

FIGURE 12.5 Seeing through an infant's eyes. These three images approximate the visual acuity of an infant at (a) age one month, (b) three months, and (c) 12 months.

infants can make, such as sucking and looking, to draw inferences about their capabilities and preferences.

The Amazing Newborn

William James (1890) suggested that the newborn's world is a "buzzing, blooming confusion"—that is, that they are passive, disorganized, and have an empty mind. This view is no longer tenable, given our knowledge of prenatal sensory-motor development; the tactile, auditory, and chemical perceptual systems have been stimulated and are operating at birth. By contrast, the visual system receives little fetal stimulation, making it a candidate for identifying innate capacities.

Newborn Sensation and Perception

Infants are very nearsighted; their visual acuity is about 20/800, or 40 times worse than normal adult acuity of 20/20 (Maurer & Lewis, 2001; see Figure 12.5). Although nearsighted, infants can focus on an object 20 to 40 cm away, the distance to the mother's face for a breastfeeding infant. In a pioneering study, Robert Fantz (1961) used the **preferential looking procedure** to study infants' visual preferences. He placed infants on their backs, showed them two or more stimuli at the same time, and filmed their eyes to record how long they looked at each stimulus. Infants preferred complex patterns, such as realistic or scrambled drawings of a human face, to simple patterns and solid colours (Figure 12.6).

4. How can scientists measure a newborn's sensory capabilities and perceptual preferences? What are some of those preferences?

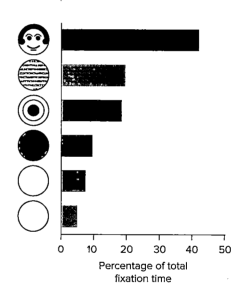

FIGURE 12.6 Whether two days old or two to three months old, infants preferred to look at complex patterns rather than simple patterns or solid colours.

Source: Based on Fantz, R.L. (1961, May). The origin of form perception. *Scientific American*, 66–72.

Finally, newborns readily turn toward off-centred auditory (e.g., rattles or voices sounded opposite one ear) and tactile (e.g., touching the cheek) targets (Muir, Humphrey, & Humphrey, 1994) and odours (e.g., Soussignan, Schaal, Marlier, & Jiang, 1997). Thus, newborns orient to significant stimuli in their environment, the most important being their mother's face, voice, and smell, optimizing their access to food, warmth, and social stimulation.

Newborn Learning

Although babies will track objects with their eyes from birth, infants are very near-sighted. Tests of visual acuity indicate that up to about one month of age, infants are very near-sighted and can see at 6 metres what normally sighted adults can see at 60 to 120 metres (Kellerman & Arterberry, 2006; see Figure 12.5). Infants, however, can focus on objects that are 20 to 40 centimetres away, the distance to the mother's face for a breastfeeding infant.

Colour vision also develops rapidly after birth. A newborn can perceive few colours, but by three months of age the three types of cones and their circuits are functional, and infants can perceive the full range of colours (Kellman & Arterberry, 2006).

The **preferential looking procedure** (Fantz, 1961) is used to study infants' visual preferences. In this procedure, preference is inferred by measuring how long the infant looks at one visual stimulus compared to another. Infants tend to prefer complex patterns to simple patterns and solid colours (Figure 12.6), and prefer yellow and blue over other colours (Taylor et al., 2013).

Philip Zelazo and colleagues at McGill University (e.g., Swain, Zelazo, & Clifton, 1993) used an auditory habituation procedure to study infant memory. They recorded two-day-olds' head-turning toward an off-centred, recorded speech sound (e.g., "Tinder"). After about 16 presentations, infants stopped turning to face the now familiar sound. They were not simply fatigued because (1) by the end of habituation, many infants were turning away from the sound, perhaps trying to avoid it; (2) they readily turned toward a novel sound (e.g., "Beagle"), indicating that they could discriminate between some adult speech sounds; and (3) partial habituation to the sound lasted for at least 24 hours. Finally, using the habituation procedure, Barbara Morrongiello at the University of Guelph (Morrongiello, Fenwick, & Chance, 1998) has shown that newborns rapidly learn to associate particular sounds with particular objects, including the mother's face and voice.

Newborns can learn through classical and operant conditioning, and imitation. Blass, Ganchrow, and Steiner (1984) followed a touch on newborns' foreheads (the CS) with the delivery of milk to their mouths (the UCS). After a few pairings, newborns turned toward the food source and puckered their lips (the UCR) during the CS. When the food was withheld during extinction, they cried, reflecting that they were upset when learned expectancies were violated. Through operant conditioning, newborns learn that they can "make things happen." For example, three-day-olds learned to suck a plastic nipple with a certain pattern of sucking bursts to activate a tape recorder playing their mother's voice, as shown in Figure 12.7b (DeCasper & Fifer, 1980).

Meltzoff and Moore (1977, 2000) reported that newborns will imitate some adult facial

5. Can newborns learn through classical and operant conditioning, as well as imitation?

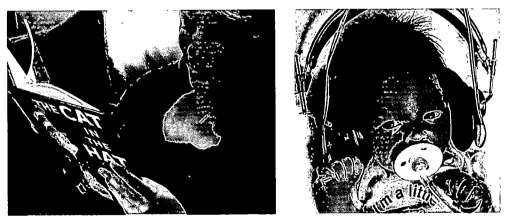

(left): © The McGraw-Hill Companies, Inc./Jill Braaten photographer; (right): © Dr. Melanie Spence, University of Texas, Dallas

FIGURE 12.7 (a) Twice a day during their last six weeks of pregnancy, mothers read out loud the same passage of a nursery rhyme from Dr. Seuss's story, *The Cat in the Hat*. (b) Two or three days after birth, newborns were able to turn on a recording of their mother reading either the *Cat in the Hat* or an unfamiliar rhyme by sucking on a sensor-equipped nipple at different rates. Compared with infants in a control condition, these newborns more often altered their sucking rate on a sensor-equipped nipple in whichever direction (faster or slower) selected the familiar rhyme (DeCasper & Spence, 1986).

Courtesy of Dr. Andrew Meltzoff

FIGURE 12.8 Young infants have been found to reproduce tongue protrusion after watching an adult model. Here researcher Andrew Meltzoff models the behaviour and records an infant's response.

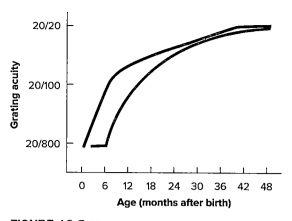

FIGURE 12.9 The normal developmental function for visual acuity (the blue line) consists of a rapid improvement in grating acuity during the first year of life followed by a more gradual improvement during the next few years until adult levels are reached by three to four years of age. The critical/sensitive period for damage to visual acuity as a consequence of early visual deprivation lasts for the first ten years of life in humans. Although acuity may be damaged following early visual deprivation, the effect is partially reversible when vision is restored. This point is illustrated by the results of a case study of an infant born with cataracts (red line). For this infant, grating acuity was still at the newborn level when the cataracts were removed at about six months of age, after which grating acuity rapidly improved to almost normal levels. Although grating acuity becomes almost normal for such visually deprived infants, other aspects of their visual perception remain abnormal.

Source: Adapted from Maurer, D., & Lewis, T.L. (2001). "Visual acuity: The role of visual input in inducing postnatal change." *Clinical Neuroscience Research*, 1, 239–247.

expressions (Figure 12.8). They suggest that this innate ability helps infants recognize people and engage them in social exchange. In sum, infants are born with mechanisms that help them respond to caretakers and important events in their environment.

Sensory-Perceptual Development

Newborns' crude sensory-perceptual abilities improve rapidly. Their visual field in each eye expands to almost adult size by six months of age, while acuity improves in a continuous developmental function from 20/800 at birth to 20/100 by six months of age, and then progresses more slowly until it reaches adult levels by about four years of age (Maurer & Lewis, 2001). This developmental function is shown in Figure 12.9. Researchers, using visual habituation and preference procedures, have shown that around three to four months of age, infant pattern perception is organized according to certain Gestalt principles (e.g., closure and proximity; Quinn, Brown, & Streppa, 1997), and depth perception appear at about 3.5 months (Fox et al., 1980). Other Gestalt principles appear later in a steplike fashion (Quinn & Bhatt, 2006).

Not all perceptual developmental functions show improvement with age during infancy. For example, a U-shaped function exists for sound localization—the remarkable ability of newborns to turn toward sounds at birth

6. Why might a perceptual function show a decline and then improvement during infancy?

disappears in the second month of life and returns again at four to five months of age (Muir & Hains, 2004). Possible reasons for this drop in responding include a lack of practice, interest that is captured by visual targets, and a change in how the behaviour is controlled as the cortical structures mature and take control of what had been subcortically driven reflexes. Other examples of U-shaped functions are discussed shortly.

Auditory pattern perception is also relatively advanced in young infants, who can detect tiny changes in adult speech sounds that differentiate one word from another (called *phonemes*) by one to two months of age. Janet Werker (1989) and colleagues at the University of British Columbia found that six-month-olds rapidly learned to turn their heads to receive a visual reward (a toy that lights up) whenever they heard one repeated phoneme (the "b" sound in *bah*) change to another (the "d" in *dah*). They were equally good at detecting changes in phonemes not found in their parents' language (e.g., two ways to pronounce a "t" sound in Hindi) that their mothers could not detect. The infants lost this latter ability by 12 months of age, as they began to speak words in their native language, demonstrating an early case of "use it or lose it" (Werker & Byers-Heinlein, 2008). However, the ability is not entirely lost since adults could learn to discriminate these non-native phonemes after extensive training.

Young infants also appear to perceive music as adults do, according to the research of Laurel Trainor, at McMaster University, and colleagues. For example, six-month-olds will look longer to hear a pitch change that adults find pleasant (or consonant) than to hear a pitch change that adults rate as unpleasant (or dissonant; Trainor, Tsang, & Cheung, 2002). As early as two months of age, infants remember a short melody after listening to it repeated 15 times; and they discriminate it from a novel melody (Plantinga & Trainor, 2009). Masataka (2007) hypothesized that this primitive early musical appreciation reflects an early stage in the evolution of our communication system composed of melodies (also found in nonhuman primates) rather than words.

To summarize, sensory-perceptual processes are exercised in the uterus, and they all, including vision, operate at some level at birth. Most improve rapidly during the first year of life but some perceptual abilities appear rather suddenly several months after birth while others decline temporarily or disappear during the first year of life. The reasons for the U-shaped developmental functions are not clear.

Physical, Brain, and Motor Development

Thanks to **maturation**, the genetically programmed biological process that governs our growth, our bodies and movement (motor) skills develop rapidly during infancy and childhood. The **cephalocaudal principle** reflects the tendency for development to proceed in a head-to-foot direction. Thus, as you can see in Figure 12.10, the head of a fetus (and infant) is disproportionately large because physical growth concentrates first on the head. The **proximodistal principle** states that development begins along the innermost parts of the body and continues toward the outermost

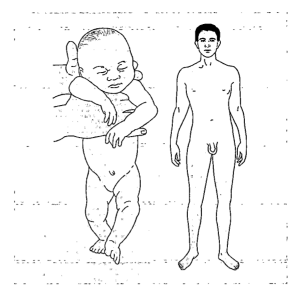

FIGURE 12.10 The cephalocaudal principle. Compared with adults, a newborn's head is disproportionately large relative to the rest of the body, reflecting the tendency for development to proceed in a head-to-foot direction. In a fetus, the head represents an even greater proportion of the body (look carefully at Figure 12.2c).

parts. Thus, a fetus's arms develop before the hands and fingers and at birth infants can control their shoulders, but not their arm or hand muscles.

The Young Brain

No organ develops more dramatically than the brain (Kolb, 1989). At birth, the newborn's brain is far from mature and has reached only about 25 percent of its eventual adult weight. By six months of age, however, the brain reaches 50 percent of its adult weight. As Figure 12.11 shows, neural networks that form the basis for cognitive and motor skills develop rapidly. The first brain areas to mature fully lie deep within the brain and regulate basic survival functions, such as heartbeat and breathing. Among the last areas to mature is the frontal cortex, which is vital to our highest-level cognitive functions.

Rapid brain growth during infancy and early childhood slows in later childhood (Sowell et al., 2001). Although five-year-olds' brains have reached almost 90 percent of their adult size, brain maturation continues. New synapses form, unnecessary synapses are pruned back and lost, association areas of the cortex mature, and the cerebral hemispheres become more highly specialized.

7. Explain how nature and nurture jointly influence physical growth and motor development during infancy.

At birth

1 month

3 months

15 months

24 months

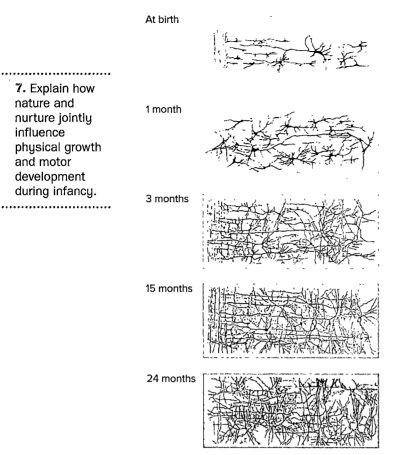

FIGURE 12.11 These drawings show sections of the human cortex at different ages early in life. Moving from birth through the first 24 months of life there is a dramatic increase in the number and complexity of connections between neurons as the neural network becomes increasingly intricate. The types of processing possible in the complex neural network present at 24 months could not be supported by the simple, partially formed network present at birth.

Source: Reprinted by permission of the publisher from *The Postnatal Development of the Human Cerebral Cortex, Vols. I–VIII*, by Jesse LeRoy Conel, Cambridge, Mass.: Harvard University Press. Copyright © 1939, 1941, 1947, 1951, 1955, 1959, 1963, 1967 by the President and Fellows of Harvard College. Copyright © renewed 1967, 1969, 1975, 1979, 1983, 1987, 1991.

Motor Development

Motor development tends to follow a regular, stage-like sequence, as illustrated by examples of North American motor-scale norms shown in Figure 12.12. While infants vary in the age at which they acquire a particular skill, the sequence in which each skill appears is similar across infants. Some motor skills also follow a U-shaped developmental function. For example, the newborn stepping reflex (and others) usually drops out after one to two months of age and reappears around 12 months of age, when most North American infants attempt to walk. This motor skill is hidden, not lost (Fisher & Ridley-Johnson, 1984).

Environmental and Cultural Influences

Although physical and motor development are guided by genetic programs (i.e., maturation), they are also influenced by experience. Diet is an obvious example. For example, a large randomized study done at 31 maternity hospitals in Belarus found that consistent breastfeeding was linked with improved cognitive development (Kramer et al., 2008). Chronic, severe malnutrition not only stunts general growth and brain development, but also is a major source of infant death worldwide (Pelletier & Frongillo, 2003). Along with proper nutrition, babies thrive in an enriched environment—one in which they have the opportunity to interact with others and to manipulate suitable toys and other objects (Needham et al., 2002). Physical touch, too, affects growth in infancy. Massaging premature and full-term human infants accelerates their weight gain and neurological development (Field et al., 2006).

Experience also can influence basic motor skill development (see Figure 12.13). For example, reaching and grasping training at three months of age has been shown to have lasting effects on reaching and object exploration (Libertus, Joh, & Needham, 2015). Cross-cultural studies tell a similar story. Compared to North American infants, infants raised in urban China begin crawling six to eight weeks later and begin walking one to two months later. It has been argued this is because the Chinese children have less space for crawling because of smaller houses and that concerns about hygiene mean that Chinese parents are reluctant to have infants on the ground (He, Walle, & Campos, 2015). Thus, developmental differences are not due to biological differences, but are more likely the result of economic and cultural factors and differences in parenting.

Clearly, experience plays a critical role in the development of sensory, perceptual, motor, and physical development. Our discussion of physical growth and perceptual-motor development reinforces three points that apply across the realm of human development:

- *Biology sets limits on environmental influences.* The best nutrition will not enable most people to grow 2.15 metres tall, and no infant can be toilet trained before the nerve fibres that help to regulate bladder control have matured biologically.

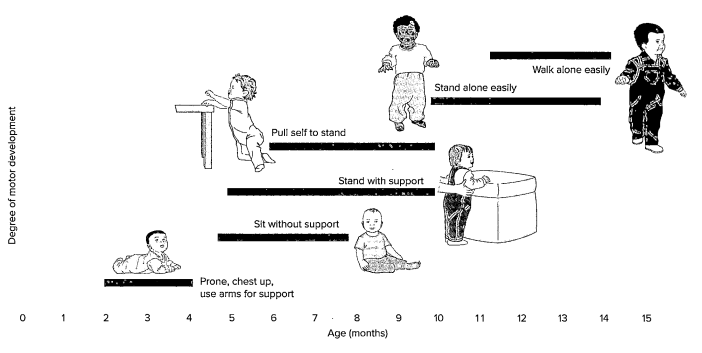

Walk alone easily

Stand alone easily

Pull self to stand

Stand with support

Sit without support

Prone, chest up,
use arms for support

Degree of motor development

Age (months)

FIGURE 12.12 Infant motor development occurs in an orderly sequence, but the age at which abilities emerge varies across children. The left end of each bar represents the age by which 25 percent of children exhibit the skill; the right end represents the age by which 90 percent have mastered it.

- *Environmental influences can be powerful.* Nurturing environments foster physical, sensory-motor, and psychological growth, while impoverished environments can stunt growth.

- *Biological and environmental factors interact.* Enriched environments enhance brain development. In turn, brain development facilitates our ability to learn and benefit from environmental experiences. Physical deprivation early in life can lead to permanent deficits.

KidStock/Getty Images

FIGURE 12.13 Experience helps us acquire complex motor skills, such as those involved in riding a bicycle.

Cognitive Development

What are the thought processes of a child like, and how do they change with age? Swiss psychologist Jean Piaget (1926, 1977) spent over 50 years exploring these questions, and his ideas have influenced generations of developmental researchers (DeVries et al., 2000).

Piaget's Stage Model

Early in his career Piaget worked for French psychologist Alfred Binet, the pioneer of intelligence testing. Piaget became intrigued by the patterns of errors children made on test questions, with children of the same age often making similar mistakes. He came to believe that the key issue in understanding how children think was not whether they got the right answers, but *how* they arrived at their answers.

Piaget relied on observational research, carefully watching children and listening to them reason as they tried to solve problems. He proposed that children's thinking changes *qualitatively* with age, and that it differs from the way adults think. Piaget believed that cognitive development results from an interplay of maturation and experience, and he viewed children as natural-born "scientists" who actively explore and seek to understand their world.

Review

- Newborns have poor sensory acuity, but they can distinguish between different visual patterns, speech sounds, odours, and tastes. They display perceptual preferences, learn through classical and operant conditioning, and may have a primitive capacity for imitation.

- Sensory, perceptual, and motor abilities have several different developmental functions. Most rapidly improve during the first year of life. Some newborn perceptual-motor responses temporarily decline during the first few months after birth and then recover during the first year of life.

- The cephalocaudal principle reflects the tendency for development to proceed in a head-to-foot direction. The proximodistal principle states that development begins along the innermost parts of the body and continues toward the outermost parts.

- Experience is critical for normal development; sensory and motor development can be delayed or accelerated by experience.

To achieve this understanding, the brain builds schemas (or schemata), which are organized patterns of thought and action. (Schemas were also discussed in Chapter 9.) Think of a schema as an "internal framework" that guides our interaction with the world. For example, infants are born with a sucking reflex that provides a primitive framework—a schema—for interacting with physical objects. To the infant, the world is meant to be sucked. In a sense, sucking is a basic way in which the infant "knows" the world. Similarly, when a child says "doggie" to describe the family pet, this word reflects an underlying schema—a concept or framework—that the child is using to understand this particular experience.

Cognitive development occurs as we acquire new schemas, and as our existing schemas become more complex. According to Piaget, two key processes are involved. **Assimilation** is the process by which new experiences are incorporated into existing schemas. When a young infant encounters a new object—a small plastic toy, a blanket, a doll—she will try to suck it. She tries to "fit" this new experience into a schema that she already has: objects are suckable. Similarly, a child who sees a horse for the first time may exclaim "big doggie." After all, the horse has four legs and a tail, so the child tries to make sense of this new experience by applying her familiar schema: "doggie."

Accommodation is the process by which new experiences cause existing schemas to change. As the infant tries to suck different objects, she will eventually encounter ones that are too big to go into her mouth or that taste bad. Similarly, the child who calls a horse a "big doggie" eventually will realize that this "big doggie" doesn't bark, sit, fetch, or otherwise behave like a dog. This imbalance or *disequilibrium* between existing schemas and new experiences ultimately forces those schemas to change. Thus, the infant's "suckability" schema will become more complex; some objects are suckable, some are not. The child's "doggie" schema also will change, and she will begin to develop new schemas for "horsey," "kitty," and so on. This may not seem earth-shaking to us, but to them, their understanding of the world has changed fundamentally. Every time a schema is modified it helps to create a better balance, an *equilibrium,* between the environment and the child's understanding of it.

Cognitive growth thus involves a give-and-take between trying to understand new experiences in terms of what we already know (assimilation) and having to modify our thinking when new experiences don't fit into our current schemas (accommodation). As Table 12.1 shows, Piaget charted four major stages of cognitive growth.

Sensorimotor stage. In the **sensorimotor stage,** from birth to about age two, infants understand their world primarily through sensory experiences and physical (motor) interactions with objects. Their reflexes are the earliest schemas that guide thought and action, but as sensory and motor capabilities increase, babies begin to bang spoons, take objects apart, and realize that they can "make things happen."

For young infants, said Piaget, "out of sight" literally means "out of mind." If you hide six-month-old Cindy's favourite toy from view, she will not search for it, just as if the toy no longer existed (Figure 12.14). At around eight months, Cindy will search for and retrieve the hidden toy. She now grasps the concept of

8. Describe assimilation and accommodation. How are they related to cognitive development?

TABLE 12.1 Piaget's Model of Cognitive Development

Stage	Age (years)	Major Characteristics
Sensorimotor	Birth to 2	• Infant understands world through sensory and motor experiences • Achieves object permanence
Preoperational	2–7	• Emergence of symbolic thought • Symbolic thinking; child uses words and images to represent objects and experiences; pretend play • Thinking displays egocentrism, irreversibility, and centration
Concrete operational	7–12	• Child can think logically about concrete events • Grasps concepts of conservation and serial ordering
Formal operational	12 on	• Adolescent can think more logically, abstractly, and flexibly • Can form hypotheses and test them systematically

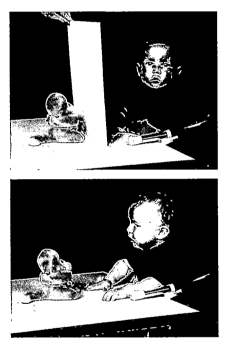

(both): © Goodman/Photo Researchers, Inc.

FIGURE 12.14 During the early sensorimotor period, a baby will reach for a visible toy (a), but not for one that has been hidden from view while the infant watches (b). According to Piaget, the child lacks the concept of object permanence; when something is out of sight, it ceases to exist.

object permanence: the understanding that an object continues to exist even when it no longer can be seen.

Infants begin to acquire language after age one, and toward the end of the sensorimotor period they increasingly use words to represent objects, needs, and actions. Thus, in the space of two years, infants have grown into thinkers who can plan, form simple concepts, solve some

problems mentally, and communicate their thoughts to others.

Preoperational stage. At around age two, children enter a **preoperational stage** in which they represent the world symbolically through words and mental images, but do not yet understand basic mental operations or rules. Rapid language development helps children label objects and represent simple concepts, such as that two objects can be "the same" or "different." Children can think about the past ("yesterday") and future ("tomorrow," "soon"), and can better anticipate the consequences of their actions. Symbolic thinking enables them to engage in "make believe," or pretend play.

Despite these advances, their cognitive abilities still have major limitations. The preoperational child does not understand **conservation,** the principle that basic properties of objects, such as their volume, mass, or quantity, stay the same (are "conserved") even though their outward appearance may change (Figure 12.15). For example, four-year-olds often say that the taller beaker in Figure 12.15 has more liquid in it than the shorter one. You understand that the liquid can be poured back into the short beaker to return to the original equal state of affairs, but children's thinking at this age displays *irreversibility:* It is difficult for them to reverse an action mentally. You also pay attention to height and width, recognizing that the liquid is "taller" because the beaker is narrower. Preoperational children exhibit *centration;* they focus (centre) on only one aspect of the situation, such as the height of the liquid.

Preoperational children's thinking also reflects **egocentrism,** difficulty in viewing the world from someone else's perspective.

9. How do infants develop cognitively during the sensorimotor stage?

10. Identify some achievements and limitations of children's thinking in the preoperational stage.

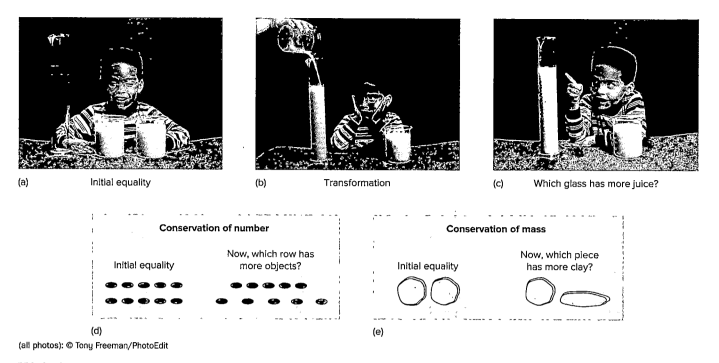

(a)   Initial equality   (b)   Transformation   (c)   Which glass has more juice?

Conservation of number		Conservation of mass	
Initial equality	Now, which row has more objects?	Initial equality	Now, which piece has more clay?

(d)   (e)

(all photos): © Tony Freeman/PhotoEdit

FIGURE 12.15 (a, b, c) Conservation of volume. At the end of this sequence (from left to right), when the preoperational child is asked which beaker contains more liquid, he points to the taller one. (d) Conservation of number. Two rows with an equal number of objects are aligned. After one row is spread out, preoperational children will say that it has more objects than the other row. (e) Conservation of mass. Preoperational children watch as one of two identically sized clay balls is rolled into a new shape. They typically will say that it now has more clay.

By "egocentrism," Piaget did not mean "selfishness," but rather that children at this stage believe that other people perceive things in the same way they do (Figure 12.16).

Concrete operational stage. Between about seven and 12 years of age, Piaget found that children in the **concrete operational stage**

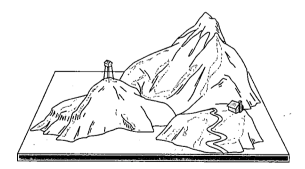

FIGURE 12.16 Piaget used the three-mountain problem to illustrate the egocentrism of young children. Suppose that a preoperational child named Ted is looking at the mountains just as you are. Another child, Susan, is standing at the opposite (far) side of the table. Ted is asked what Susan sees. Because Ted is able to see the road, he will mistakenly say that Susan also can see it, indicating that he has failed to recognize Susan's perspective as different from his own.

could perform basic mental operations concerning problems that involve tangible (i.e., "concrete") objects and situations. They grasped the concept of reversibility, displayed less centration, and easily solved conservation problems. They grasped the concept of serial ordering, easily arranging a set of objects along various dimensions (e.g., from "shortest" to "tallest"). These children also formed mental representations of a series of actions (e.g., drawing a map showing the route to get to school).

However, concrete operational children often have difficulty with hypothetical problems or problems requiring abstract reasoning; they often show rigid types of thinking. To demonstrate this, ask a few nine-year-olds the following question: "If you could have a third eye, where on your body would you put it? Draw a picture." Then ask them to explain their reason. David Shaffer (1989) reports that nine-year-olds typically draw a row of three eyes across their face. Their thinking is concrete, bound by the reality that eyes appear on the face, and their justifications often are unsophisticated (e.g., "so I could see you better"). Many find the task silly because "Nobody has three eyes" (Shaffer, 1989, p. 324).

Formal operational stage. Piaget's model ends with the **formal operational stage** in which individuals think logically about both concrete and abstract problems, form hypotheses, and systematically test them. Formal thinking begins around 11 to 12 years of age, and increases through adolescence (Ward & Overton, 1990).

Children entering this stage also begin to think more flexibly when tackling hypothetical problems, such as brainteasers, and typically enjoy the challenge. Shaffer (1989) reports that 11½- to 12-year-olds provide more creative answers and better justifications to the "third-eye problem" than do nine-year-old concrete thinkers. One child placed the eye on the palm of his hands so that he could use it to "see around corners." Another placed it on top of his head, so that he could "revolve the eye to look in all directions."

Assessment of Piaget's Theory: Stages, Ages, and Culture

Tests of Piaget's theory conducted around the world yield several general findings. First, according to Queen's University cross-cultural psychologist John Berry and his colleagues (Berry et al., 2002), the general cognitive abilities associated with Piaget's four stages occur in the same order across cultures. For example, children understand object permanence before symbolic thinking blooms, and concrete reasoning emerges before abstract reasoning.

Second, children acquire many cognitive skills and concepts at an earlier age than Piaget believed (Wang et al., 2005). Even three-and-a-half- to four-and-a-half-month-olds display a basic grasp of object permanence when they are tested on special tasks that require them only to look at events rather than physically search for a hidden object. For example, Baillargeon (1987) found that four-month-olds have a basic understanding that two solid objects cannot be in the same place at the same time (Figure 12.17), suggesting that four-month-olds have a sense of object permanence. Even more surprising, five-month-old infants are sensitive to the number of objects present and stare longer if a scene violates the number of items that should be present; details are given in Figure 12.18 (Wynn et al., 1998).

Third, *cognitive development within each stage seems to proceed inconsistently.* A child may perform at the preoperational level on some tasks, yet solve other tasks at a concrete

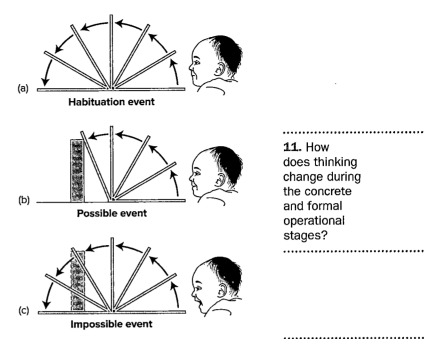

(a) **Habituation event**

(b) **Possible event**

(c) **Impossible event**

FIGURE 12.17 (a) Habituation. Renée Baillargeon (1987) repeatedly exposes young infants to a screen that slowly rotates 180 degrees. Eventually, they habituate and become bored. Then the infants watch as a box is placed in the screen's path. (b) Possible event. The screen rotates, conceals the infant's view of the box, and then stops as the box blocks it. (c) Impossible event. The screen rotates, conceals the view of the box, and continues a full 180 degrees because the box is secretly removed. Infants stare longer at the "impossible" than at the "possible" event, as if they are surprised that the box did not stop the screen. This response can happen, reasons Baillargeon, only if the infants understand that the box continues to exist even when concealed from view (i.e., object permanence).

Source: Adapted from Baillargeon, R. (1987). "Object permanence in 3 1/2- and 4 1/2-month-old infants." *Developmental Psychology*, 23, 655–664.

11. How does thinking change during the concrete and formal operational stages?

12. In what major ways does research support and contradict Piaget's basic ideas?

operational level (e.g., Marini & Case, 1994). This challenges the idea that development proceeds in distinct stages: A child at a given stage should not show large inconsistencies in solving conceptually similar tasks.

Fourth, *culture influences cognitive development.* Piaget's Western perspective equated cognitive development with scientific-logical thinking, but "Many cultures . . . consider cognitive development to be more relational, involving the thinking skills and processes to engage in successful interpersonal contexts" (Matsumoto & Hull, 1994, p. 105). In Africa's Ivory Coast, the Baoulé people most strongly value a social intelligence that reflects the skills to get along with others and be respectful and responsible (Dasen et al., 1985).

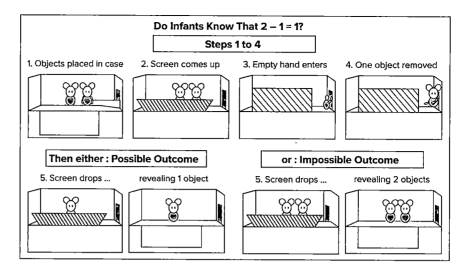

FIGURE 12.18 A violation-of-expectancy experiment. Five-month-old infants watch the sequence of events shown in steps 1 through 4. Then, in step 5, they witness a "possible" or "impossible" event. Infants stare longer at the impossible event, suggesting that they were expecting only one object and are surprised to see two objects still there. In other words, they understand that 2 – 1 should equal 1. In another experiment, in steps 1 to 4, infants watch 1 object being added to another object. Then the screen is raised and lowered, revealing either two objects ("possible event") or just one object ("impossible event"). Once again, infants stare longer at the impossible event, suggesting that they understand that 1 + 1 should equal 2.

Source: Adapted with permission from Macmillan Publishers Ltd: K. Wynn, 1992, "Addition and Subtraction by Human Infants," *Nature*, 358 (6389) p. 749. August 27, 1992. Copyright © 1992.

Fifth, and most broadly, *cognitive development is more complex and variable than Piaget proposed* (Larivée et al., 2000). All children progress from simpler to more sophisticated thinking, but they don't necessarily follow the same developmental path.

Although research challenges many of Piaget's ideas, he revolutionized thinking about cognitive development. His work still guides many researchers, called *neo-Piagetians,* who have modified his theory to account for the issues we have just discussed (Becker, 2004).

Vygotsky: The Social Context of Cognitive Development

Piaget acknowledged that social factors influence children's thinking, but he focused mainly on children's independent exploration of the physical world. By contrast, Russian psychologist Lev Vygotsky (1935/1978) highlighted how the sociocultural context interacts with the brain's biological maturation. To illustrate, suppose that five-year-olds Ray and Juanita have similar scores on cognitive tests, but neither child can solve Piaget's conservation problems. However, after guidance from a parent, teacher, or older sibling, Juanita can now solve these problems. Ray, even with assistance, just doesn't understand. Are these two children really at the

same cognitive level? Vygotsky says no, introducing a concept called the **zone of proximal development:** the difference between what a child can do independently and what a child can do with assistance from adults or more advanced peers.

Why is the zone of proximal development important? First, it helps us recognize what children may soon be able to do by themselves. Second, it emphasizes that people can help to "move" a child's cognitive development forward within limits (the "zone") dictated by the child's biological maturation. For example, parents who assist a child on scientific tasks may push the child's understanding further along by using age-appropriate but cognitively demanding speech (e.g., introducing scientific concepts) rather than simpler speech (Tenenbaum & Leaper, 2003). Similarly, having older siblings around the house may stimulate a younger child's cognitive development, as long as the child's brain is mature enough (Ruffman et al., 1998).

Information-Processing Approaches

In contrast to Piaget's stage approach, many researchers view cognitive development as a continuous, gradual process in which the same set of information-processing abilities becomes more

13. What is the zone of proximal development and why is it important?

efficient over time. For example, young children may be unable to solve conservation problems because they don't search for key information or are unable to hold enough pieces of information simultaneously in memory (Siegler, 1996).

Information-search strategies. Look at the two houses in Figure 12.19. Are they identical? This visual scanning task is easy for you or me but not for young children. Elaine Vurpillot (1968) recorded the eye movements of three- to ten-year-olds during tasks like this one. Preschoolers often failed to compare each window in the house on the left to the corresponding window in the house on the right, but older children methodically scanned the houses. In short, older children are better able to search systematically for relevant information (Merrill & Lookadoo, 2004).

Processing speed, attention, and response inhibition. Processing speed, attention and the ability to inhibit responses all show improvements with age (Kali, 1991; Rose et al., 2012). As shown in Figure 12.20, processing speed improves rapidly across childhood and then changes more gradually during adolescence. Older children are also better able to focus their attention and inhibit responses to distractions (Luna et al., 2004). For example, if children are

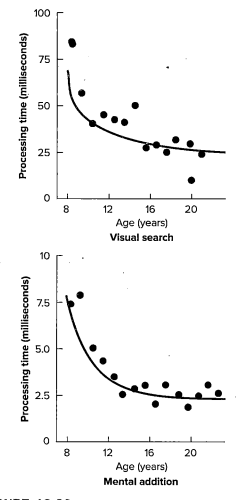

FIGURE 12.19 Stimuli used by Vurpillot to assess visual inspection through filmed eye movements. Preschoolers fail to scan the pictures systematically, which often leads them to claim that the two houses are identical.

Source: Based on Vurpillot, E. (1968). "The development of scanning strategies and their relation to visual differentiations." *Journal of Experimental Child Psychology*, 6, 632–650. Fig 1. Copyright © 1968 Elsevier. Reprinted with permission.

14. Describe how information-processing capabilities improve during childhood. How is this relevant to the continuity-discontinuity debate?

FIGURE 12.20 These two graphs show how information-processing speed for visual search and mental addition tasks becomes faster with age. The relatively rapid rate of change between age eight and about 12 slows during adolescence. A similar nonlinear pattern also occurs in name retrieval, mental rotation, and other cognitive tasks.

Source: Data from Kail, R. (1991). "Developmental change in speed of processing during childhood and adolescence." *Psychological Bulletin*, 109, 490–501. Fig 7. Copyright © 1991 Elsevier. Reprinted with permission.

asked to sort cards by one rule (e.g., colour) and then the rule is changed and they need to sort using a different feature (e.g., shape), young children will often revert to the old rule even when they can correctly describe what they are supposed to be doing (Davidson et al., 2006).

Working memory and long-term memory. Children's working memory improves with age (Gathercole et al., 2004; Rose et al., 2012). If you read older children a list of words, numbers, or sentences of increasing length, they will be able to store more of that information in working memory and repeat more of it to you than will younger children. Older children also can retain and manipulate visuospatial information in working memory more effectively than younger children. For example, they can perform mental-rotation tasks (see Chapter 9) more easily, and if you asked them to draw you a map to a friend's house several blocks and a few turns away, they would likely have little difficulty. A younger child might be able to lead you to the friend's house but would have difficulty drawing the route.

Older children are also more likely than younger children to use strategies to improve memory (Schneider et al., 2004). In one study, when given lists of words or numbers to remember, preschoolers rarely used rehearsal spontaneously, whereas eight- to ten-year-olds could often be heard rehearsing words or numbers, repeating them under their breath (Flavell, 1970). This strategy helps older children to hold information in working memory and to process it into long-term memory.

Theory of Mind: Children's Understanding of Mental States

15. At what age do children begin to understand other people's thinking? How have researchers established this?

The term **theory of mind** refers to a person's beliefs about the mind and the ability to understand other people's mental states; that is, we have theories about the contents of other peoples' minds. We use these assumptions to explain and predict our own and other people's behaviour, and to be able to take another's perspective. Piaget believed that children younger than six or seven have trouble recognizing what other people are thinking. Consider the following story:

> Susie puts a candy bar inside a green box on the table, and then she goes away. Then her mother takes the candy bar out of the box and puts it inside a red bag on the bed. Susie doesn't see her mother do this. Later, Susie comes back and wants to get her candy because she is hungry. Where will Susie look for her candy bar?

On problems like this, called "false belief tasks," very young children will say that Susie will look in the red bag, as if Susie had the same knowledge that they have. This example shows what Piaget's concept of egocentrism is all about: not being able to understand how someone else perceives a situation (Müller & Carpendale, 2011). By four years of age, many children will choose the green box, recognizing that Susie does not have the information they do. They comprehend that Susie's mental state—her "mind"—is different from theirs (Astington & Gopnik, 1991). By five to six years of age, most children pass such false belief tasks. Finally, using culturally equivalent tests, researchers studying young children from African tribal societies, Canada, China, Japan, the United Kingdom, and the United States found similar results (Ruffman et al., 1998).

Lying and deception also reflect a theory of mind. Evidence clearly indicates that those who understand false beliefs are more likely to lie, starting as early as three years of age (Talwar & Lee, 2008). They will also understand the difference between a mistake and a lie. For both a mistake and a lie, what I say is wrong. The difference is that in one case, the lie, I recognize that you do not know what is going on inside my mind and so I can deceive you.

In Review

- According to Piaget, cognitive development depends on processes of assimilation and accommodation, and occurs in four stages: sensorimotor, preoperational, concrete operational, and formal operational.
- Although the general cognitive abilities associated with Piaget's four stages occur in the same order across cultures, children acquire many cognitive skills at an earlier age than Piaget believed.
- Vygotsky emphasized that cognitive development occurs in a sociocultural context. Each child has a zone of proximal development, reflecting the difference between what a child can do independently and what the child can do with assistance from others.
- Information-processing capacities improve with age. Older children search for information more systematically, process it more quickly, and display better memory.
- Children begin to develop a theory of mind (beliefs about another person's knowledge, feelings, intentions, etc.) at around three to four years of age.

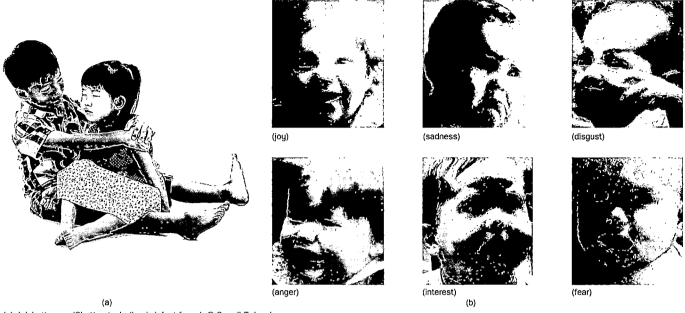

(joy) (sadness) (disgust)

(anger) (interest) (fear)

(a)

(b)

(a): kdshutterman/Shutterstock; (b: six infant faces): © Carroll E. Izard

FIGURE 12.21 (a) Emotional responses communicate our internal states, and they can influence how others respond to us, providing us with the aid and comfort we need. (b) Young infants display a variety of basic emotions.

Social-Emotional and Personality Development

Children grow not only physically and mentally but also emotionally and socially. They form attachments and each child displays a unique *personality*—a distinctive yet somewhat consistent pattern of thinking, feeling, and behaving.

Early Emotions and Emotion Regulation

Emotional responses communicate our inner states to other people and influence how others respond to us. Although infants can't describe their feelings, Figure 12.21 illustrates that their facial expressions, vocalizations, and other behaviours provide a window into their emotional lives (Izard, 1982). By crying, they express distress; by focusing their gaze and staring at objects and people, they express interest. Around the world, within about six months after birth, infants begin to express joy and surprise ("peekaboo, I see you!"), and distress branches out into the separate emotions of disgust, anger, fear, and sadness (Lewis, 2000).

Around 18 months of age, infants begin to develop a sense of self. They are able to recognize themselves in a mirror and this growing self-awareness sets the stage for envy, embarrassment, and empathy to emerge. After age two, as toddlers learn about performance standards and rules that they are supposed to

follow, they begin to display pride and shame. Around the same age, they also display guilt— as evidenced by avoiding eye contact, shrugging shoulders, and making facial expressions (Kochanska et al., 1995).

Just as emotional reactions become more diverse with age, so does **emotion regulation,** the processes by which we evaluate and modify our emotional reactions. Young infants may suck their thumbs or a pacifier, turn their heads away from something unpleasant, or cling to a caretaker to soothe themselves. To reduce distress, toddlers may seek out a caretaker, cling to a doll or teddy bear, fling unpleasant objects away, and learn to smile, pout, or throw a tantrum to get what they want. Once they acquire language, children can reduce distress by talking to themselves and other people.

As children age, their emotional expressiveness and ability to regulate their emotions become part of their overall emotional competence, which in turn influences their social behaviour and how well their peers and other people like them. Children who frequently display sadness or who can't control their anger are less likely to be popular, and emotional competence remains important for well-being as children develop (Eisenberg, 2002).

Socialization influences children's emotional development, as parents, teachers, and peers

Frontiers

SOCIAL MEDIA AND SOCIAL DEVELOPMENT

In 2009 the Daily Mail news service reported a story about two Australian girls that dramatically illustrates the impact of social media on youth (Daily Mail, 2009). The two girls, ages 10 and 12, became trapped in a storm drain but luckily had cellphones with them. They used the cellphones not to call for help, but to update their status on Facebook. The girls were rescued when a friend saw their status updates and contacted authorities.

The introduction and growth of social networking sites and mobile computing has raised concerns about the impact of social media on development. Parents are concerned that social media use may adversely affect their children's school achievement and social skills (O'Keefe & Clarke, 2011). With the rapid expansion of social media and the use of so-called "third screens" (screens other than TV and computer), there has been a shift from face-to-face communication to electronic communication, even among children (Rideout et al., 2010). The impact of social media may be especially important during late childhood when face-to-face communication with peers and adults is considered to be critically important for social and emotional development (Denzin, 2010).

In an interesting recent study, Roy Pea and colleagues (Pea et al., 2012) investigated the impact of media use on social development of during late childhood (ages 8 to 12), the same age group as our two trapped Australians. During late childhood friendships are increasingly important, exposure to risky behaviour must be dealt with, there is greater responsibility and autonomy, and social life shifts from family-centred to peer-centred. This is the age of Erikson's stage of industry vs inferiority, when social life expands into school and peer relationships and the child's main task is to develop social competence.

Pea his and colleagues investigated social media and feelings of social well-being in a sample of 3461 American and Canadian girls 8 to 12 years old. They divided media use and communication into seven categories: watching video content (e.g., TV, YouTube, movies); listening to music; reading or doing homework; emailing or sending messages, including posting on Facebook; texting or instant messaging, including Facebook chat; talking on the phone; and face-to-face communication. The researchers were

especially concerned with social well-being, which included feelings of social success, social normalcy and the number of friends that parents considered a bad influence. The measure of social success included items such as having close friends and feeling understood and valued by peers. Social normalcy included items such as feeling normal when compared to peers and feeling accepted by peers. The average amount of total media use was 6.9 hours per day, a little lower than has been reported by others studying this age group (e.g., Rideout et al., 2010), but still a substantial amount of media use.

Pea and his colleagues found that watching video had a strong negative association with feelings of both social success and normalcy, while face-to-face communication was positively associated with both social success and normalcy. Time spent reading or doing homework had a small but statistically significant negative relationship with feelings of social success and normalcy. Overall, the results indicated that watching video, multitasking (simultaneous use of multiple media sources), and online communication were associated with negative social and emotional outcomes. Conversely, face-to-face communication was associated with positive social and emotional outcomes. High levels of face-to-face communication were associated with greater social success, stronger feelings of normalcy, more sleep, and having fewer friends that the children's parents considered to be a bad influence.

Although these results are correlational, trading face-to-face communication for some forms of online activity is associated with a cost for youths' social well-being and social development. The authors concluded, "our society is experiencing an unprecedented shift in media ecology. The choices that our children are making—when and how they engage with these media and in what situations—are shaping their social relationships, social well-being, and time availabilities for school-related study and other activities" (Pea et al., 2012, p. 335). As illustrated by the two Australian girls trapped in the storm drain, the choices are not always the smartest.

Source: Pea, R. Nass, C., Meheula, L., Rance, M., Kumar, A., Bamford, H., Nass, M., Simha, A., Stillerman, B., Yang, S., & Zhou, M. (2012). "Media use, face-to-face communication, media multitasking, and social well-being among 8- to 12-year-old girls". *Developmental Psychology*, 48(2), 327–336.

---

serve as models and reinforce children for some types of emotional responses but not others (Ahn, 2005). Recently, the role of social media in development has drawn attention, as we explore in this chapter's *Frontiers* feature. But as we will now explore, heredity also contributes to children's basic emotional-behavioural style.

Temperament

From the moment of birth, infants differ from one another in **temperament,** a biologically based general style of reacting emotionally and behaviourally to the environment. Some infants are calm and happy; others are irritable and fussy. Some are outgoing and active; others are shy and inactive. Indeed, within any age group—children, adolescents, or adults—people differ in temperament (Fox et al., 2005).

In a pioneering, ten-year longitudinal study, Alexander Thomas and Stella Chess (1977) had parents describe their babies' behaviour. Most infants could be classified into three groups. "Easy infants" ate and slept on schedule, were playful, and accepted new situations with little fuss. "Difficult infants" were irritable, were fussy eaters and sleepers, and reacted negatively to new situations. "Slow-to-warm-up infants" were the least active, had mildly negative responses to new situations, but slowly adapted over time. Subsequently, the difficult infants were most likely to develop emotional and behaviour problems during childhood.

This study was admired but also criticized for relying on parents' reports of their infants' behaviour. Other researchers directly observed infants and identified temperamental styles that differed from those described by Thomas and Chess. Although some research has found that temperament is only weakly to moderately stable during the first two years of life (Carnicero et al., 2000), a recent study of more than 7000 children found that temperament was stable when children were tested at three, five, and six years of age (Bould et al., 2013).

Consider shyness, which forms part of a more general temperament style called *behavioural inhibition.* Inhibited infants are quiet and timid; they cry and withdraw when they are exposed to unfamiliar people, places, objects, and sounds. Uninhibited infants are more sociable, verbal, and spontaneous. Research by Jerome Kagan and his colleagues (1988) found that about 20 to 25 percent of infants displayed this inhibited pattern, which remained moderately stable during infancy. They also studied these infants until age seven-and-a-half. For the vast majority— those who were only mildly to moderately inhibited or uninhibited between the ages of one and two—their temperament did not predict how shy or outgoing they would be as children. But for infants who were *highly* uninhibited or inhibited, the findings were different. Highly uninhibited infants tended to become sociable and talkative seven-year-olds, whereas highly inhibited infants developed into quiet, cautious, and shy seven-year-olds (Kagan, 1989). A more recent study found results consistent with this pattern. Baker and colleagues working with a sample of 100 infants in Wales found that both high fearfulness and high fearlessness, similar to Kagan's high inhibition and disinhibition, were stable across the first three years of life (Baker et al., 2012).

Thinking critically

SHY CHILD, SHY ADULT?

We have just seen that very shy or very outgoing infants tend to retain these traits into early childhood. Do you think that the very shy or outgoing child grows into a shy or outgoing adult? In general, does childhood temperament predict adult behaviour?

Think about it, and then see the Answers section at the end of the book.

Erikson's Psychosocial Theory

Psychoanalytic psychologist Erik Erikson (1968) believed that personality develops through confronting a series of eight major **psychosocial stages,** each of which involves a different "crisis" (i.e., conflict) over how we view ourselves in relation to other people and the world. Each crisis is present throughout life, but takes on special importance during a particular age period. As Table 12.2 shows, four crises occur in infancy and childhood:

- *Basic trust versus basic mistrust.* Depending on how adequately our needs are met, and how much love and attention we receive during the first year of life, we develop a basic trust or basic mistrust of the world.

- *Autonomy versus shame and doubt.* During the next two years, children become ready to exercise their individuality. If parents unduly restrict children or make harsh demands during toilet training, children develop shame and doubt about their abilities and later lack the courage to be independent.

- *Initiative versus guilt.* From age three through five, children display great curiosity about the world. If they are allowed freedom to explore and receive answers to their questions, they develop a sense of initiative. If they are held back or punished, they develop guilt about their desires and suppress their curiosity.

- *Industry versus inferiority.* From age six until puberty, the child's life expands into school and peer activities. Children who experience pride and encouragement in mastering tasks develop *industry*—a striving to achieve. Repeated failure and lack of praise for trying leads to a sense of *inferiority.*

Although critics argue that Erikson's model lacks detail and question its stage approach,

16. What does Erikson's model imply about the stability of personality?

TABLE 12.2 · Erikson's Psychosocial Stages

Age (years)	Major Psychosocial Crisis
First year	Basic trust vs. basic mistrust
1–2	Autonomy vs. shame and doubt
3–5	Initiative vs. guilt
6–12	Industry vs. inferiority
12–20	Identity vs. role confusion
20–40	Intimacy vs. isolation
40–65	Generativity vs. stagnation
65+	Integrity vs. despair

17. How does attachment illustrate the concept of a sensitive period?

the model successfully captures several major issues that developing children confront. Because each stage of life creates new opportunities, personality is not fixed in childhood. Yet, as Erikson proposed, and as some research supports, successfully resolving each crisis helps to prepare us to meet the next (Hazen & Durrett, 1982; Kahn et al., 1985). Like the early chapters of a novel, themes that emerge in childhood help to set the stage for the unfolding story of our lives.

Attachment

18. How did Harlow demonstrate the importance of contact comfort?

The young of some bird species, including ducks and geese, and a few mammals, such as shrews, show a powerful form of attachment. Austrian ethologist Konrad Lorenz (1937) called it **imprinting,** a sudden, powerful, biologically primed form of attachment (Figure 12.22a). Imprinting involves a *critical period.* In mallard ducklings, for example, the strongest imprinting takes place within one day after hatching, and by two-and-a-half days the capacity to imprint is lost (Hess, 1959).

19. According to Bowlby, what are the phases of attachment in infancy?

In humans, **attachment** refers to the strong emotional bond that develops between children and their primary caregivers. There is no immediate post-birth critical period when contact is required for infant–caregiver bonding, as with imprinting. Instead, the first few years of life seem to be a *sensitive period* when we most easily form a secure bond with caregivers that enhances our adjustment later in life (Sroufe, 2002; Figure 12.22b). Although it is difficult to form strong first attachments to caregivers later in childhood, it is still possible.

The attachment process. For decades, people assumed that infant–caregiver bonding resulted primarily from the mother's role in satisfying the infant's need for nourishment. Harry Harlow (1958) tested this notion by separating infant rhesus monkeys from their biological mothers shortly after birth. Each infant was raised in a cage with two artificial, "surrogate" mothers. One was a bare wire cylinder with a feeding bottle attached to its "chest." The other was a wire cylinder covered with soft terry cloth, without a feeding bottle (Figure 12.23).

Faced with this choice, the infant monkeys became attached to the cloth mother. When exposed to frightening situations, the infants ran to the terry cloth figure and clung tightly to it. They even maintained contact with the cloth mother while feeding from the wire mother's bottle. Thus, Harlow showed that *contact comfort*—body contact with a comforting object—is more important in fostering attachment than is the provision of nourishment.

Around the same time, other researchers studied human attachment in Africa, Europe, and North America (Ainsworth, 1967; Bowlby, 1958). Based on this work, British psychoanalyst

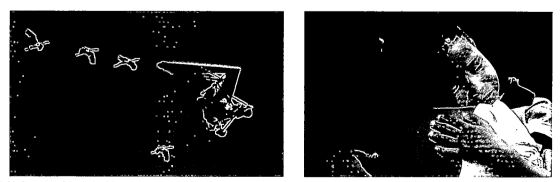

(left): Courtesy of Operation Migration, www.operationmigration.org; (right): Studio 1One/Shutterstock

FIGURE 12.22 (a) Canadian wildlife sculptor Bill Lishman imprinted Canada geese hatchlings to the sight of his ultralight airplane. Although the geese have now matured, the ultralight still represents "mother" to them, and they follow it in flight. (b) In humans, infant-caregiver attachment is more complex and forms over a much longer period.

© Harlow Primate Laboratory

FIGURE 12.23 Infant monkeys reared from birth with a cloth-covered surrogate clung to it as they would a real mother, and they preferred to remain in contact with the terry cloth mother even though the wire mother satisfied nutritional needs.

John Bowlby (1969) proposed that attachment during infancy develops in three phases:

* *Indiscriminate attachment.* Newborns cry, vocalize, and smile, and they emit these behaviours toward everyone. In turn, these behaviours evoke caregiving from adults.

* *Discriminate attachment.* Around three months of age, infants direct their attachment behaviours more toward familiar caregivers than toward strangers.

* *Specific attachment behaviour.* By seven or eight months of age, infants develop their first meaningful attachment to specific caregivers. The caregivers become a "secure base" from which the infant can crawl about and explore the environment.

As an infant's attachment becomes more focused, two types of anxiety occur. **Stranger anxiety,** distress over contact with unfamiliar people, emerges around age six or seven months, and ends by 18 months of age. When approached by, touched by, or handed over to a stranger, the infant becomes afraid, cries, and reaches for the caregiver. **Separation anxiety,** distress over being separated from a primary caregiver, typically begins a little later, peaks around age 12 to 16 months, and disappears between two and three years of age, showing an inverted U-shaped age function. Both forms

of anxiety show a similar pattern across many cultures (Figure 12.24).

These responses, which coincide with infants' increasing cognitive and physical abilities, may be adaptive reactions shaped over the course of evolution (Bowlby, 1973). At an age when infants master crawling and then learn to walk, fear of strangers and separation may help to prevent them from wandering beyond the sight of their caretakers, especially in unfamiliar situations.

Around age three or four, as children's cognitive and verbal skills grow, they develop a better understanding of their attachment relationships. According to Bowlby (1969), a stage of *goal-corrected partnership* emerges in which children and caregivers can describe their feelings to each other and maintain their relationships whether they are together or apart.

Types of attachment. Infants develop different types of attachment with their caretakers. Canadian psychologist Mary Ainsworth (1913–1999) and her colleagues (1978) developed the **Strange Situation Test (SST),** a standardized procedure for examining infant attachment. The infant, typically a 12- to 18-month-old, first plays with toys in the mother's presence. Then a stranger enters the room and interacts with the child. Soon the mother leaves the child with the stranger. Later the

20. Does separation anxiety follow a similar pattern across cultures? What is the adaptive value of separation anxiety?

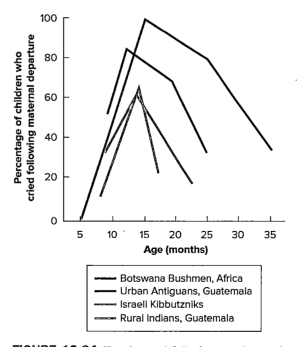

FIGURE 12.24 The rise and fall of separation anxiety in infancy shows a similar pattern across cultures.

Source: Based on Kagan, J., Kearsley, R.B., & Zelazo, P. (1978). *Infancy: Its place in human development.* Cambridge, MA: Harvard University Press.

stranger leaves and the child is left alone. Finally, the mother returns.

In the mother's presence, "securely attached" infants explore the playroom and react positively to strangers (Ainsworth et al., 1978; Ainsworth, 1993). They are distressed when she leaves and happily greet her when she returns. In contrast, there are two types of "insecurely attached" infants. "Anxious-resistant" infants are fearful when the mother is present, demand her attention, and are highly distressed when she leaves. They are not soothed when she returns and may angrily resist her attempts at contact. "Anxious-avoidant" infants show few signs of attachment and seldom cry when the mother leaves and don't seek contact when she returns. A fourth form of attachment is disorganized attachment, sometimes referred to as disorganized-disoriented attachment. Infants that shows disorganized attachment may appear disoriented and confused, or they may show contradictory behaviours, such as simultaneously trying to get close to the mother and freezing or striking out when the mother tries to comfort them.

Across most cultures studied, about one-half to three-quarters of infants are securely attached. Babies in Canada (Pederson, Gleason, Moran, & Bento, 1998) and the United States (Posada et al., 2002) who appear securely attached in the SST have mothers who are rated as more consistently responsive and sensitive to their babies' needs than infants classified as insecure. Moreover, securely attached infants appear to be better adjusted socially during childhood. Establishing a secure attachment early in life also may help to foster a capacity for compassion and altruism that carries forward into adulthood (Mikulincer & Shaver, 2009). This research lends credence to Erikson's view that establishing a stable, trusting relationship with a caregiver is an important component of early social development.

Attachment Deprivation

If infants and young children are deprived of a stable attachment with a caregiver, how do they fare in the long run? Harry Harlow studied this issue under controlled conditions. At six months of age, "isolate" monkeys were returned them to the monkey colony. Exposed to other monkeys, the isolates were indifferent, terrified, or aggressive. When they became adults, some female isolates were artificially inseminated, and as parents they were highly abusive toward their first-borns (Harlow & Suomi, 1970).

The conclusion is that being raised without attachment to a real, interactive caregiver produced long-term social impairment.

Isolation. What of isolate human children? Remember Victor, the Wild Boy of Aveyron discussed in Chapter 9, who was abandoned early in life and lived alone in a forest until about 12 years of age. He was severely impaired after his isolation and showed only limited recovery after intensive remedial training (Itard, 1962). Did the lack of human contact stunt Victor's development or did brain damage that was possibly present at birth?

In the 1960s, twin boys in Czechoslovakia were forced by their father and stepmother to live in extreme isolation beginning at 18 months of age. The twins were discovered at age seven, emotionally and socially retarded, with the cognitive development of a three-year-old and speech skills of a two-year-old. Jarmila Koluchova (1972, 1991) studied the boys for more than 20 years and found that they became firmly attached to their foster family. Their IQ increased to normal levels, and they became well-adjusted, happy, sociable adolescents and young adults.

Why the difference between Victor and the Czech twins? Perhaps a critical difference was that the twins' isolation ended and rehabilitation began when they were younger, at age seven, when the brain was still maturing and capable of catching up. Moreover, in their first year of recovery, the twins were well cared for in a home that allowed them to interact with younger, nonthreatening preschool children.

Children raised in orphanages. Developmental psychologists have studied orphans to address the question of whether it is necessary to have a primary attachment figure during the hypothesized sensitive period, in the first year of life. An impressive Canadian study was initiated after the overthrow of the Romanian dictator Nicolae Ceausescu in 1989. Thousands of orphans were discovered housed in state-run orphanages under deplorable conditions, including the absence of a primary attachment figure (Figure 12.25). Elinor Ames and her colleagues at Simon Fraser University, and Kim MacLean now at St. Francis Xavier University, conducted a longitudinal study of a large group of Romanian orphans adopted into Canadian homes (Chisholm, 1998). They compared three groups matched for age and sex: early (adopted before four months of age) and late (adopted after at least eight months in an orphanage) Romanian

21. How do studies of monkey and human child isolates, and of children in orphanages, help us discover whether attachment involves critical or sensitive periods?

22. Why might Victor's recovery have been so limited, compared with that of the Czech twins?

© Josef Pelleross/The Image Works

FIGURE 12.25 In the 1980s, about 100 000 Romanian infants and children were warehoused in filthy, disease-ridden orphanages where they were often left unattended for days and had no opportunity to bond with caretakers. Studies of Romanian infants who were adopted into American and Canadian homes before age two showed that about a third formed secure attachments, in contrast to the more typical 60 percent figure found in attachment studies. Still, that so many formed secure attachments is a testament to their resilience in bouncing back from extreme adversity.

adoptees, and Canadian-born non-adoptees. After two years, when attachment was assessed using a separation-reunion procedure, the late-adoptees displayed more insecure attachment behaviours that were related to more behaviour problems, lower IQ scores, and more parental stress. The late adoptees also showed more indiscriminate "friendly" behaviour, indicating a possible lack of specific attachment.

Factors other than a lack of a sensitive, early attachment figure may have contributed to the attachment and other problems shown by the Romanian late-adopted children. Barbara Tizard and Jill Hodges (1978) studied children raised in orphanages where the nurses were attentive, but high staff turnover prevented children from forming a stable bond with any caregiver. Those adopted between ages two and eight years formed healthy attachments with their adoptive parents, although in adolescence many had difficulty forming peer relationships because they appeared to need "too much attention" (Hodges & Tizard, 1989).

In sum, it appears that infancy is a sensitive (not critical) period in which an initial attachment to caregivers forms most easily and facilitates subsequent development. Prolonged attachment deprivation creates developmental

risks, but when deprived children are placed in a nurturing environment at a young enough age, many if not most become attached to their caretakers and grow into well-adjusted adults. Clearly, although unfavourable environments can significantly impair development, some children exposed to extreme adversity are highly resilient and thrive in later life (Mersky & Topitzes, 2009).

The Daycare Controversy

As a child, did someone other than a parent regularly care for you during the day (Figure 12.26)? In Canada, more than half (54 percent) of parents with children aged four and under use some form of child care (Statistics Canada, 2014). The most common forms of daycare in Canada are (1) daycare centres, (2) home daycares, and (3) private arrangements, such as by grandparents or other relatives.

High-quality daycare provides a stimulating environment with well-trained caretakers, few children per caretaker, and low staff turnover, whereas poor daycare provides the opposite (Marshall, 2004). In either case, many parents worry about how child care will affect their child's development. In the most comprehensive research project to date, psychologists working with the National Institute of Child Health and Human Development (NICHD) Early Child Care Research Network began studying approximately 1400 American children from birth. Here are some major findings:

- *Attachment.* Overall, as measured by the strange-situation procedure, high-quality child care did not disrupt infants' or very young children's attachment to their parents, even when they attended daycare for many hours a week. When several negative factors combined—the

23. Does daycare impair infants' attachment? Does it seem to have long-term effects on children?

Liquidlibrary/Jupiterimages

FIGURE 12.26 Today, many preschoolers are cared for during the day by someone other than a parent or other family member.

child care was poor, the child spent many hours there, and parents were not sensitive to the child at home—the risk of insecure attachment increased (NICHD, 2001).

- *Social behaviour.* Comparing the social development of children who experienced child care versus those raised exclusively by their mothers, virtually no significant differences emerged through age four-and-a-half (NICHD, 2006). Among child-care children, spending a lot of time in child care was associated with more behaviour problems by age four-and-a-half, but this relation disappeared by Grade 3 (NICHD, 2002; Vandell et al., 2005).

- *Cognitive performance.* Overall, as with social development, children's cognitive development by age four-and-a-half did not differ significantly depending on whether they experienced child care or were raised exclusively by their mothers (NICHD, 2006). Among children in child care, exposure to higher-quality care was associated with better cognitive performance (NICHD, 2006).

Concerns about disrupted parent–child relations also surface when parents divorce. Our *Applications* feature examines this societally important issue.

Styles of Parenting

Beyond the issues of divorce and remarriage, how do different child-rearing practices affect children's development in general? After studying how parents interacted with their preschool children, Diana Baumrind (1967) identified two key dimensions of parental behaviour. The first is *warmth versus hostility.* Warm parents communicate love and caring for the child, and respond with greater sensitivity and empathy to the child's feelings. Hostile parents express rejection and behave as if they did not care about the child. The second dimension is *restrictiveness versus permissiveness.* Parents differ in the extent to which they make and enforce rules, place demands on children, and discipline children. As Figure 12.27 shows, combining these dimensions yields four parenting styles that are associated with different patterns of child development (Linver et al., 2002).

Authoritative parents are controlling but warm. They establish clear rules, consistently enforce them, and reward children's compliance with warmth and affection. They communicate high expectations, caring, and support. This style is associated with the most positive childhood outcomes (Baumrind, 1991). Children with

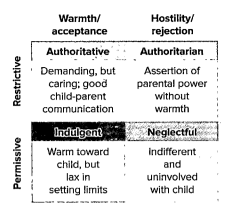

	Warmth/ acceptance	Hostility/ rejection
Restrictive	**Authoritative** Demanding, but caring; good child-parent communication	**Authoritarian** Assertion of parental power without warmth
Permissive	**Indulgent** Warm toward child, but lax in setting limits	**Neglectful** Indifferent and uninvolved with child

FIGURE 12.27 Four styles of child-rearing. Combining the two basic dimensions of parental behaviour (warmth-hostility and restrictiveness-permissiveness) yields four different styles of child-rearing.

Source: Adapted from Maccoby, E.E., & Martin, J.A. (1983). "Socialization in the context of the family: Parent-child interaction." In E.M. Hetherington (Ed.), *Handbook of child psychology: Socialization, personality, and social development.* New York, NY: Wiley.

authoritative parents tend to have higher self-esteem, are higher achievers in school, and have fewer conduct problems.

Authoritarian parents also exert control over their children, but do so within a cold, unresponsive, or rejecting relationship. Their children tend to have lower self-esteem, be less popular with peers, and perform more poorly in school than children with authoritative parents (Dornbusch et al., 1987).

Indulgent parents have warm and caring relationships with their children, but do not provide the guidance and discipline that helps children learn responsibility and concern for others. Their children tend to be more immature and self-centred (Patterson, 1982).

Neglectful parents provide neither warmth nor rules and guidance. Their children are most likely to be insecurely attached, have low achievement motivation and disturbed relationships with peers and adults at school, and be impulsive and aggressive. Neglectful parenting is associated with the most negative developmental outcomes (Ainsworth, 1989).

Do these findings extend to adolescence? Laurence Steinberg and his colleagues (1994) studied several thousand high school students in California and Wisconsin. They found that, overall, authoritative and neglectful parenting were, respectively, associated with the most positive and negative developmental outcomes. Many of the findings held true across African-, Asian-, Caucasian-, and Hispanic-American students (Lamborn et al., 1991).

24. In the short and long term, how do children generally respond to parental divorce? What factors enhance their adjustment to divorce and remarriage?

25. What parenting styles are associated with the most and least positive child outcomes?

Applications

UNDERSTANDING HOW DIVORCE AND REMARRIAGE AFFECT CHILDREN

Divorce is more common than it was 30 years ago. According to Statistics Canada data for 2008 (the last year for which data are available, Statistics Canada no longer reports divorce rate), 41 percent of marriages will end in divorce by the 30th wedding anniversary. Family breakups create a stressful life transition for both parents and children, and almost everything in the child's daily life changes. Many parents remarry, which leads to a second major transition for children as they become part of a stepfamily. Research tells us how these major life events affect children.

How Does Divorce Affect Children?

Many children report that parental divorce is one of the most painful experiences of their lives. In the short term, children may experience anxiety, fear, anger, confusion, depression, and behavioural, social and academic problems at school.

In the long term, children of divorce remain at greater risk for various difficulties, including academic problems, troubled social relationships with family members and peers, low self-esteem, and depression (Dawson-McClure et al., 2004; Kelley, 2012). When they become adolescents, children of divorced parents are more likely to drop out of school, be unemployed, use drugs, and become unmarried teen parents. In adulthood, they are more likely to experience conflict in relationships, unemployment, depression (particularly among women), and have a higher divorce rate (Huurre et al., 2006; Wauterickx et al., 2006). The extent of this risk, however, depends critically on care before, during, and after the divorce.

The risk of emotional, behavioural, social, and academic problems for children of divorced parents is more than double that of children whose parents have been continuously married (Kelley, 2012). However, one cannot assume that divorced-family children will have problems. Divorce is an important life stress for children and adolescents, but the impact will depend on a number of factors including the child's age, cognitive and emotional strengths and vulnerabilities and temperament, the presence of peer support and other sources of social support, the parents' behaviour, the amount of contact with the noncustodial parent, and the amount of conflict between the parents before, during, and after the divorce (Jordan, 2016). As a major stress, divorce can act to amplify the impact of other risk factors present in the child's life, but its impact can also be lessened by various protective factors, such as social support.

Research has not found a consistent sex difference; both sons and daughters can be affected by divorce, although males tend to be at higher risk for externalizing and females for internalizing disorders (Jordan, 2016; Kelley, 2012). The child's age at the time of divorce is also an important factor for later consequences. Each age has its own challenges and developmental tasks (see our discussion of social-emotional and personality development in this chapter) and the developmental stage of the child at the time of divorce is an important consideration (Jordan, 2016).

The first year after a divorce is the hardest, but beginning in the second year most children begin to adjust (Kelley, 2012). By three years after the divorce, close to 80 percent of children of divorce are within the average range on measures of adjustment (Kelley, 2012).

Should We Stay Together for the Sake of the Child?

Many parents considering divorce wonder whether they should stay together for the child's sake. Research consistently supports the finding that children are psychologically, emotionally, and socially healthier if divorce ends a marriage in which there is open conflict between the parents than if that situation continues (Kelley, 2012). High marital conflict can cause the children to feel "caught in the middle" in the battle between their parents, and this worsens the impact of the divorce (Amato & Afifi, 2006). Children living with married but contentious parents have poorer school achievement, lower self-esteem, and more behaviour problems than children from divorced families. That is, the risk to the future health and adjustment of children is greater in a family in which there is open conflict than it is if divorce ends such a family situation.

How Do Children Respond to Remarriage and Stepfamilies?

Forming a stepfamily temporarily disrupts children's relationships with the remarried custodial parent and typically increases children's short-term problem behaviours. In turn, such behaviour can increase the risk of marital conflict between the stepparents (Jenkins et al., 2005). It can take several years for parents and children to adjust to their new roles within the stepfamily. In general, young adolescents seem to have the most difficulty coping with the transition into a stepfamily.

In remarriages, children may be hostile and reject the stepparent, especially when the stepparent attempts to be a strong disciplinarian. Children usually adjust better to living in a stepfamily when the custodial parent is warm but firm and has primary responsibility for discipline, and when the stepparent is warm but supports the custodial parent's authority (Bray & Berger, 1993).

continued

Making It Better or Worse

Divorce and the ensuing changes to daily life are a major life stress for children and a significant risk factor for a range of problems. The extent of that risk can be powerfully influenced by the parents' behaviour before, during, and after the divorce (Amato & Afifi, 2006; Kali & Barnfield, 2015; Kelley, 2012).

To reduce the risk parents should:

- explain what is happening and what the child can expect in the weeks and months ahead;
- reassure the child that he or she is still loved;
- reassure the child that they will still be the child's parents;

- encourage the child to be open with his or her feelings and discuss those feelings with the parents, including the anger and fear that sometimes emerge; and
- remain involved in the child's life.

The risk is amplified and made worse by parents who:

- fight or insult each other in front of the child;
- criticize their ex in front of the child;
- compete with each other for the child's attention and affection;
- use the child as a way to get back at the ex; and
- involve the child in mediating disputes.

Gender Identity and Socialization

Parenting also influences children's development in other ways, such as helping children develop a **gender identity,** a sense of "femaleness" or "maleness" that becomes a central aspect of our personal identity (Gelman et al., 2004). Early in life, infants display some knowledge about gender. Poulin-Dubois and her colleagues (1988, 1994) at Concordia University presented infants with pairs of male and female pictures, along with a male *or* female vocal recording. Infants at 9 and 12 months of age looked longer at the female picture when it was paired with the female voice, and by 18 months, they matched both male and female voices with the appropriate pictures. However, it's not until between two and three years of age that most children develop a basic gender identity; they can label themselves (and others) as being either a boy or a girl, but their understanding of gender is still fragile. Just as young children often report that a cat wearing a dog mask has suddenly become a dog, they may believe that a boy wearing a dress is a "girl" and that a girl can grow up and become a man. **Gender constancy,** which is the understanding that being male or female is a permanent part of a person, develops around age six or seven (Szkrybalo & Ruble, 1999).

As gender identity develops, children also acquire **sex-role stereotypes,** which are beliefs about the types of characteristics and behaviours that are appropriate for boys and girls to possess. **Socialization,** which refers to the process by which we acquire the beliefs, values, and behaviours of a group, plays a key role

26. How does socialization shape children's beliefs about gender?

in shaping our gender identity and sex-role stereotypes. Every group, including our family and cultural groups, has norms that set standards for expected and accepted behaviour. Through socialization, we ultimately internalize these expectations and standards, and they become part of our identity (Martin & Ruble, 2004). Sex-role stereotypes are no exception.

Sex-typing involves treating others differently based on whether they are female or male. From infancy onward, girls and boys are viewed and treated differently. Fathers use more physical and verbal prohibition with their 12-month-old sons than with their daughters, and they steer their sons away from activities that are considered stereotypically feminine (Snow et al., 1983). In fact, University of Montreal researcher Daniel Paquette (2004) theorized that while mothers play a comforting role in times of stress, fathers encourage their children, especially males, to take risks to explore their environment. Paquette and Bigras (2010) found that fathers gave toddlers more leeway to take risks than mothers did and that this freedom allowed them to better explore their environment. Finally, even when their sons and daughters display equal interest and aptitude in science, fathers and mothers are more likely to believe that sons have the greater interest and will find science easier (Tenenbaum & Leaper, 2002). Indeed, when parents interact with their one- to eight-year-olds at science exhibits in a children's museum, they are much more likely to explain the exhibits to their sons than to their daughters—even though the children rarely ask for such explanations (Figure 12.28; Crowley et al., 2001).

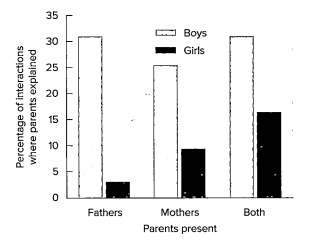

FIGURE 12.28 Fathers and mothers provided more explanations to their one- to eight-year-old sons than to their daughters while engaged with science exhibits at a children's museum. Similar results were obtained regardless of the children's age.

Source: Adapted from K. Crowley, M.A. Callahan, H.R. Tenenbaum, & E. Allen, 2001, "Parents Explain More Often to Buys than to Girls During Shared Scientific Thinking," *Psychological Science*, 12(3), 258-261, Fig 1. Copyright © 2001 Association for Psychological Science. Reprinted by permission of Sage Publications.

Sex-role stereotypes also are transmitted through observational learning and operant conditioning (Figure 12.29). Children observe parents, other adults, peers, and TV and movie characters, and often attempt to emulate what they see (Bandura, 1965). In ways both obvious and subtle, others approve of us and reinforce our behaviour when we meet their expectations, and disapprove of us when we don't. In turn, this influences the way children think about gender. Some children as young as two or three years of age display sex-role stereotypes in their ability to identify objects, such as hammers and brooms, as "belonging with" one gender or the other (Campbell et al., 2004). By age seven or eight, stereotyped thinking is firmly in place; children believe that boys and girls possess different personality traits and should hold different occupations as adults (Miller & Budd, 1999).

As children make the transition to adolescence and enter junior high school, they generally display more flexible thinking about gender. Some come to believe that traditionally masculine and feminine traits can be blended within a single person—what is called an *androgynous* gender identity—as when a person is both assertive and compassionate. During the remaining junior high and high school years, some adolescents maintain this view. Overall, however, stereotypes about men's and women's psychological traits seem to become a little more rigid, and most people continue to adhere to relatively traditional beliefs (Alfieri et al., 1996).

Moral Development

All societies attempt to teach their members right from wrong. How does children's moral thinking change as they grow older?

Kohlberg's Stage Model

Drawing on Piaget's model of cognitive development, Lawrence Kohlberg (1963, 1984)

(left): © Simon Marcus/Corbis; (right): © Rosanne Olson/Digital Vision/Getty Images

FIGURE 12.29 In subtle and not so subtle ways, cultures socialize most female and male children in gender-stereotypic ways.

developed a highly influential theory of moral reasoning. He presented children, adolescents, and adults with hypothetical moral dilemmas such as the following:

> Heinz's wife was dying from cancer. A rare drug might save her, but the druggist who made the drug for $200 would not sell it for less than $2000. Heinz tried hard, but he could only raise $1000. The druggist refused to give Heinz the drug for that price even though Heinz promised to pay the rest later. So Heinz broke into the store to steal the drug. What do you think? Should Heinz have stolen the drug? Why or why not?

Kohlberg was interested not in whether people agreed or disagreed with Heinz's behaviour, but in the reasons for their judgment. He analyzed responses to various moral dilemmas and concluded that there are three main levels of moral reasoning, with two substages within each level (Table 12.3).

Preconventional moral reasoning is based on anticipated punishments or rewards. Consider reasons given for stealing the drug. In stage 1, children focus on punishment: "Heinz should steal the drug because if he lets his wife die he'll get into trouble." In stage 2, morality is judged by anticipated rewards and doing what is in the person's own interest: "Heinz should steal the drug because that way he'll still have his wife with him."

27. How do preconventional, conventional, and postconventional moral reasoning differ?

Conventional moral reasoning is based on conformity to social expectations, laws, and duties. In stage 3, conformity stems from the desire to gain people's approval: "People will think that Heinz is bad if he doesn't steal the drug to save his wife." In stage 4, children believe that laws and duties must be obeyed simply because rules are meant to be followed. Thus, "Heinz should steal the drug because it's his duty to take care of his wife."

Postconventional moral reasoning is based on well thought out, general moral principles. Stage 5 involves recognizing the importance of societal laws, but also taking individual rights into account: "Stealing breaks the law, but what Heinz did was reasonable because he saved a life." In stage 6, morality is based on abstract, ethical principles of justice that are viewed as universal: "Saving life comes before financial gain, even if the person is a stranger. The law in this case is unjust, and stealing the drug is the morally right thing to do."

Kohlberg believed that progress in moral reasoning depends on general cognitive maturation and the opportunity to confront moral issues, particularly when such issues can be discussed with someone who is at a higher stage of development. Moral education programs based on Kohlberg's theory have been applied in schools, prisons, and with at-risk youth (Higgins, 1991).

TABLE 12.3 Kohlberg's Stages of Moral Reasoning

Level of Moral Reasoning	Basis for Judging What Is Moral
Level 1: Preconventional	Actual or anticipated punishment and rewards, rather than internalized values
Stage 1: Punishment/obedience orientation	Obeying rules and avoiding punishment
Stage 2: Instrumental/hedonistic orientation	Self-interest and gaining rewards
Level 2: Conventional	Conformity to the expectations of social groups; person adopts other people's values
Stage 3: Good child orientation	Gaining approval and maintaining good relations with others
Stage 4: Law and order orientation	Doing one's duty, showing respect for authority, and maintaining social order
Level 3: Postconventional	Moral principles that are well thought out and part of one's belief and value system
Stage 5: Social contract orientation	General principles agreed upon by society that foster community welfare and individual rights; recognition that society can decide to modify laws that lose their social utility
Stage 6: Universal ethical principles	Abstract ethical principles based on justice and equality; following one's conscience

Source: Adapted from Kohlberg, L. (1963). "The development of children's orientations toward a moral order: I. Sequence in the development of moral thought." *Human Development*, 6, 11–33., 1963; Kohlberg, L. (1984). *The psychology of moral development: Essays on moral development (Vol. 2)*. New York, NY: Harper & Row.

Culture, Gender, and Moral Reasoning

Studies of moral reasoning from North, Central, and South America, to Africa, Asia, Europe, and India indicate the following overall:

- From childhood through adolescence, moral reasoning changes from preconventional to conventional levels (see Figure 12.30).

- In adolescence and even adulthood, postconventional reasoning is relatively uncommon (see Figure 12.30).

- A person's moral judgments do not always reflect the same level or stage within levels (Eckensberger & Zimba, 1997).

Critics claim that Kohlberg's theory has a Western cultural bias. Fairness and justice are Kohlberg's postconventional ideals, but in many cultures the highest moral values focus on principles that do not fit easily into Kohlberg's model, such as respect for all animal life, collective harmony, and respect for the elderly (Iwasa, 2001).

Carol Gilligan (1982) argues that Kohlberg's emphasis on justice also reflects a male bias. She claims that highly moral women place greater value than men do on caring and responsibility for others' welfare. Overall, however, evidence of gender bias is mixed. Women use justice reasoning when the situation calls for it, and men use reasoning based on caring and relationships when appropriate. Nevertheless, Gilligan's analysis reinforces the key point that high-level moral reasoning can be based on values other than justice (Gump et al., 2000).

Moral Behaviour and Conscience

Moral reasoning does not necessarily translate into moral behaviour. Researchers have proposed that for children to conform to their culture's moral standards, they must understand that there are moral rules, be able to control their impulses to engage in forbidden behaviour, and experience some negative emotion when they violate these rules.

By the age of two, children understand that there are rules for behaviour, and their emotional expressions suggest that they experience guilt when they break a known rule. Children's ability to stop themselves from engaging in forbidden behaviour develops slowly, but even toddlers can do so at times. This internal regulatory mechanism, often referred to as *conscience*, tends to restrain individuals from acting in destructive or antisocial ways when they are not being monitored by parents or other adults (Kochanska et al., 2005). Internalizing the societal values transmitted by parents or other caretakers provides the basis of a moral conscience. Children are most likely to internalize their parents' values when they have a positive relationship with them, when parents establish clear rules and provide explanations that facilitate children's awareness of parental values, and when discipline is firm but not harsh (Laible & Thompson, 2000).

Children's temperament also enters into the picture. Fearful, inhibited children tend to internalize parental values more easily and at an earlier age than less fearful children, particularly when their parents provide gentle discipline. For relatively fearless, uninhibited children,

28. What aspects of Kohlberg's model have been supported? What are its limitations?

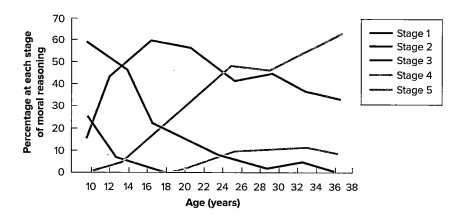

FIGURE 12.30 In this study based on Kohlberg's model, 58 American boys responded to moral dilemmas for more than 20 years. As they aged, preconventional morality (stages 1 and 2) decreased and conventional morality (stages 3 and 4) took precedence during adolescence. Postconventional moral reasoning was not common at any age.

Source: Based on Colby, A., Kohlberg, L., Gibbs, J., & Lieberman, M. (1983). "A longitudinal study of moral judgment." *Monographs of the Society for Research in Child Development*, 48(1–2, Serial No. 200).

In Review

- Erikson proposed that personality development proceeds through eight major psychosocial stages. Each stage involves a major crisis, and the way we resolve it influences our ability to meet the challenges of the next stage.

- Temperament reflects a pattern of reacting emotionally and behaviourally to the environment. Temperament remains stable across in infancy and childhood.

- Infant–caretaker attachment develops in three phases, and infants experience periods of stranger and separation anxiety. Secure attachment is associated with better developmental outcomes in childhood and adolescence than insecure attachment. For most children, daycare does not disrupt attachment.

- Parenting styles vary along dimensions of warmth–hostility and restrictiveness–permissiveness. The children of authoritative parents generally display the best developmental outcomes.

Gender identity begins to form early in childhood, and socialization influences children's acquisition of sex-role stereotypes.

- Divorce disrupts children's psychological adjustment in the short term and, for some children and adolescents, is associated with a long-term pattern of maladjustment.

- Kohlberg proposed that moral reasoning proceeds through three levels. Preconventional moral judgments are based on anticipated rewards and punishments. Conventional morality is based on conformity to social expectations, laws, and duties. Postconventional moral judgments are based on well-thought-out moral principles. Critics argue that the model contains cultural and gender biases.

- Moral behaviour is governed by many factors, including observational learning, temperament, attachment, and emotional development.

however, whether discipline is gentle or harsh is less important. A secure attachment with warm parents, rather than fear of punishment, appears to motivate fearless children to internalize their parents' standards. Thus, the development of moral behaviour is linked not only to children's moral thinking but also to their emotional development, attachment, and temperament (Kochanska et al., 2004).

ADOLESCENCE AND ADULTHOOD

In some cultures specific ceremonies or activities represent *rites of passage* that mark a transition from childhood into adulthood (Figure 12.31). But what of **adolescence,** the period of development and gradual transition between childhood and adulthood? Alice Schlegel and Herbert Barry (1991) found that among almost 200 nonindustrial societies worldwide, nearly all recognize some type of transition period between childhood and adulthood. Yet in many societies this period is brief and is not marked by a special term analogous to *adolescence.*

The lengthy period called *adolescence* is largely an invention of 18th- to 20th-century Western culture (Valsiner & Lawrence, 1997). In preindustrial times, biological maturity was

Anders Ryman/Alamy Stock Photo

FIGURE 12.31 A First Nations girl participates in a ceremony that initiates her into womanhood.

a major criterion for adult status. In many cultures, for example, girls were expected to marry once they became capable of bearing children. But as the Industrial Revolution brought new technology and a need for more schooling, recognition of adult status was delayed and the long transition period of adolescence evolved.

Adolescence differs from **puberty,** a period of rapid physical maturation in which the person becomes capable of sexual reproduction. Although the developmental periods overlap, puberty is a biologically defined period whereas adolescence is a broader social construction (Spear, 2000). Puberty is an important aspect of adolescence, but adolescence is also ushered in and out by changes in thinking, interests, social circumstances, and parental and societal expectations. In research studies, 12- to 18-year-olds—give or take a year at each end—are typically considered to be adolescents, but it's essential to keep in mind that the transitions into and through adolescence, and out of adolescence into adulthood, are gradual (Arnett, 2001).

Physical Development

We now explore some key developmental changes that occur in adolescence and adulthood, beginning with changes in the body's physical processes and capabilities. Note that when we talk about *young adulthood* (approximately 20 to 40 years of age), *middle adulthood* (roughly, one's 40s through early 60s), and *late adulthood* (approximately age 65 and older), these terms—like *adolescence*—represent social constructions rather than distinct biological stages.

Puberty

During adolescence, puberty ushers in important bodily changes as the brain's hypothalamus signals the pituitary gland to increase its hormonal secretions. Pituitary hormones stimulate other glands, speeding up maturation of the *primary sex characteristics* (the sex organs involved in reproduction). Hormonal changes also produce *secondary sex characteristics* (nonreproductive physical features, such as breasts in girls and facial hair in boys).

The pubertal landmark in girls is *menarche,* the first menstrual flow. For boys, it is the production of sperm and the first ejaculation. In North America and Europe, these events occur most often around age 11 to 13 for girls and

12 to 14 for boys (Kaltiala-Heino et al., 2003). Considerable variation, however, occurs among people and cultures.

The physical changes of puberty have psychological consequences. The hormones that steer puberty affect brain function and can influence mood and behaviour (Peper & Dahl, 2013). Whether puberty occurs early or late also matters. Overall, early maturation tends to be associated with fewer negative outcomes for boys than for girls. Early-maturing boys are at somewhat heightened risk for engaging in delinquent behaviour and using drugs (Kaltiala-Heino et al., 2003). However, the physical strength and size that they acquire often contribute to a positive body image, success in athletics, and popularity among peers. In contrast, although some early-maturing girls welcome their changed appearance, the weight gain that comes with puberty results in a negative body image for others. Moreover, early physical maturation may exposes girls to greater social and sexual pressures that they are not ready for emotionally. Thus, compared with girls who mature later, early-maturing girls typically feel more self-conscious about their bodies and are more likely to eventually develop eating disorders, problems in school, major depression, and anxiety (Graber et al., 2004).

The Adolescent Brain

Compared with infancy and early childhood, overall brain growth slows from childhood to adolescence (Sowell et al., 2001). Longitudinal studies using fMRI techniques have shown that brain activity in children differs from that in adolescents, which in turn differs from that in adults (Giedd, 2004; Goddings et al., 2014). Cortical white matter within the frontal cortex increases linearly with age especially in areas that are important for impulse control and abstract thought. In contrast, nonmyelinated grey matter in the frontal cortex peaks at around 11 years of age for girls and a year later for boys, presumably reflecting the pruning of unnecessary cells by maturation and experience. This maturation of neural networks permits more-efficient communication between brain regions.

Neural restructuring is especially prominent in the prefrontal cortex and the limbic system, regions that play a key role in planning and coordinating behaviours that satisfy motivational goals, emotional urges, and behavioural control (Wu et al., 2016). There are changes in

29. Describe some factors that influence adolescents' psychological reactions to experiencing puberty.

30. How does the brain change during adolescence?

the corpus callosum, a structure that allows the two hemispheres of the brain to communicate with each other (see Chapter 3). This structure changes significantly during adolescence, increasing in area by up to 10 percent within a two-year period (White & Nelson, 2004). Silveri and colleagues (2006) studied the relationship between maturational changes in frontal cortex and corpus callosum and behavioural impulse control and response inhibition. They used an fMRI procedure that measured the integrity and speed of neural transmission by the white matter in the corpus callosum. They found a significant relationship between increases in the degree of white matter and both impulse and inhibitory control scores. More details on the teenage brain are given in this chapter's *Focus on Neuroscience* feature.

Physical Development in Adulthood

Young adults are at the peak of their physical, sexual, and perceptual functioning. Maximum muscle strength in the legs, arms, and other parts of the body is reached at age 25 to 30. Vision, hearing, reaction time, and coordination are at peak levels in the mid-20s (Hayslip & Panek, 2002).

Physical status typically declines at mid-life (Troll, 1985). For example, the active visual field that expanded in the first six months of life begins to shrink in the 20s; and by late adulthood this "tunnel vision" interferes with tasks, such as driving, in which a quick reaction to peripheral input is important. During middle adulthood muscles become weaker and stiffer, especially among sedentary people. After age 40 the *basal metabolic rate*, the rate at which the resting body converts food into energy, slows and this produces a tendency to gain weight. The efficiency of oxygen consumption decreases, and it is harder for middle-aged adults to maintain the physical endurance needed for sustained exercise. Around age 50 women's ovaries stop producing estrogen; they lose their fertility and experience *menopause*, the end of menstruation. Men remain capable of fathering children, but their fertility gradually declines in middle age.

Despite this decline, many middle-aged adults are in excellent health and are vigorously active. Growing experience in job and recreational skills can offset much of the age-related physical decline. From climbing mountains to running marathons, middle-aged adults may achieve physical goals well beyond those attained by many younger adults.

The physical changes of middle adulthood become more pronounced in late adulthood. Lean body mass decreases while the amount of fatty tissue tends to increase, bones lose calcium becoming more brittle and slower to heal, and hardened ligaments make movements stiffer and slower (Weg, 1983). But with regular exercise, good nutrition, and the right attitude, many adults maintain physical vigour and an active lifestyle well into old age (Figure 12.32). A wonderful example of this is Olga Kotelko, a Canadian track and field athlete who, at age 91, was called "one of the world's greatest athletes" (Grierson, 2010). After retiring from teaching in 1984, she took up slow-pitch softball, and then at age 77 she *started* training for track and field. By 2010, at the age of 91, she held 23 age-graded track and field world records.

The Adult Brain

During the earliest years of adulthood, the brain's neural networks generally continue to become more efficiently integrated (Luna et al., 2004). But like other parts of the body, the brain declines later in adulthood. In a longitudinal study, psychologist Susan Resnick and her colleagues (2003) used magnetic resonance imaging to measure the loss of brain tissue among 92 men and women over a four-year period. The participants were 59 to 85 years old at the start of the study, and none of them exhibited abnormal cognitive impairments. On average, over the next four years, they lost tissue at a rate of 5.4 percent per year in the brain regions studied, with the

© Ken Fisher/Getty Images

FIGURE 12.32 Many older adults maintain a physically active lifestyle.

Focus on Neuroscience

THE NEUROSCIENCE OF THE TEENAGE BRAIN

At one time it was thought that all of the important aspects of brain development were completed by early childhood. It has, however, become clear that brain maturation continues until the early 20s, with important changes occurring during adolescence. These changes occur most prominently in brain areas linked to processing emotional information, response inhibition and behavioural control, planning and executive function, and sensitivity to reward (Goddings et al., 2014).

The neural systems involved in processing emotional information are functional very early in life but the ability to discriminate emotional expressions and then to control one's emotional response emerges later. As we discussed in Chapter 11, both the amygdala and areas within the prefrontal cortex are critical for detecting and processing emotionally relevant stimuli and for generating and controlling our subsequent response. Some interesting recent research has found that these brain areas mature at different rates (Goddings et al., 2014). The amygdala appears to be fully functional by puberty, but the prefrontal cortex does not reach full maturity until early adulthood. In an interesting recent study, Wu and colleagues (Wu et al., 2016) investigated age-related changes in activation and functional interactions between the amygdala and the prefrontal cortex.

Healthy participants between 7 and 25 years old performed an emotional facial expression assessment task while brain activity was recorded using fMRI (Wu et al., 2016). In the task, participants saw a target facial expression at the top of a display and two faces at the bottom of the display. One of the lower faces matched the facial expression shown in the target and the participant's task was to indicate which of the lower facial expressions matched the target. Facial expressions tested included both emotionally positive (e.g., happiness) and emotionally negative (e.g., fear, anger) expressions. Control trials asked participants to match geometric shapes. As you would expect, processing emotional facial expressions generated significant activation in the amygdala and in areas within the prefrontal cortex as compared to processing geometric shapes. Interestingly, evaluation of the functional connectivity between the amygdala and prefrontal cortex changed with age. For children the pattern of activity indicated excitatory signalling from the early-maturing amygdala to the developmentally immature frontal cortex. Among young adults, this pattern was reversed, indicating control of the amygdala by the prefrontal cortex. Adolescence was the time when this shift occurred. That is, Wu and colleagues found that during adolescence there was a change in processing emotional facial expressions from a bottom-up excitatory signal generated by the amygdala to a top-down regulatory pathway controlled by the prefrontal cortex.

Adolescence is often associated with increases in novelty and sensation seeking, and an increase in these behaviours during adolescence may have adaptive value. Enhanced novelty and sensation seeking can lead adolescents to explore new environments, new social relationships, and new activities, all of which can help them establish their independence and help in the acquisition of new skills (Steinberg, 2008). These same changes, however, can have unfortunate, even dangerous, consequences if sensation seeking strays into experimentation with drugs of abuse, taking physical risks, or unsafe sex.

Researchers such as Beatriz Luna (Luna et al., 2013) have explored whether there is a neurobiological underpinning to these changes. In a series of studies that used fMRI while participants engaged in a cognitive control task during which the availability of reward was varied, Luna and colleagues assessed both reward-relevant brain areas and brain areas involved in cognitive control. The cognitive control task was suppressing the urge to look toward a suddenly appearing visual cue and instead looking away from it. In this situation, reward (the possibility of winning $25 for successful performance) was varied. The ability to exert control over this behaviour continues to improve through adolescence and is associated with maturation of the parietal cortex, motor areas (e.g., basal ganglia), and especially areas within the prefrontal cortex, the latest to mature of these brain areas. That is, the brain circuit needed to exert cognitive control is present in childhood and during adolescence the connections to the prefrontal cortex are strengthened and then mature in early adulthood. There is a different developmental pattern within the brain circuit involved in processing reward value. As we discussed earlier, key areas of this circuit include the amygdala, prefrontal cortex, and especially the nucleus accumbens. This circuit does not just show a steady developmental growth or maturation; adolescence is a period of heightened reward sensitivity. Adolescents show increased sensitivity to reward compared to both younger and older comparison groups. This difference is most striking in the nucleus accumbens, the brain area most powerfully linked to motivation and reward (see Chapters 3 and 6).

These results indicate that during adolescence cognitive control over behaviour is present but still developing and there are limitations with that control. During this time the brain area most powerfully linked to motivation and reward, the nucleus accumbens, shows enhanced activity in response to reward availability. That is, control is still developing and is inconsistent but sensitivity to reward is amplified.

Adolescence is also often characterized as a time when youth stay up too late, sleep in until noon, and generally

continued

cannot—or do not want to—function on the same clock as the rest of society. This is commonly attributed to lifestyle choices, with adolescents and young adults simply choosing to stay up late, which then forces them to sleep in or be overly tired the next day. But is this just a lifestyle choice?

Recently, attention has been drawn to the difference between social time, the daily schedule set by social convention, and biological time, the daily rhythms set by our internal biological clock. It has been argued that adolescence is a time when the social clock and the biological clock are not in sync (Kelley et al., 2015). There is also evidence that from mid-adolescence until the early 20s, the amount of sleep one needs changes. That is, there are at least two aspects to the sleepy teen: the amount of sleep needed and the pattern, or timing, of that sleep.

The length of time a person needs to sleep each day declines steadily from infancy through late adulthood except for a transient increase during adolescence (Ruger et al., 2012). The smooth decline in the amount of sleep needed is interrupted and from early/mid-adolescence until the early 20s, a time when the amount of sleep needed each day actually increases compared to younger and older individuals. Yes, the sleepy teen does actually need more sleep.

There is also a shift in circadian rhythms, with a shift to later sleep and wake times (Kelley et al., 2015). As we discovered in our discussion of circadian rhythms, our master clock is the suprachiasmatic nucleus (SCN; see Chapter 6). The SCN coordinates all of our circadian rhythms and, with entrainment from external cues such as the light, keeps us functioning on a 24-hour clock. In adolescence and early adulthood, there are changes and the timing of the circadian clock shifts later, delaying the time at which one can fall asleep, and leading to a later sleep time and later wake time (Kelley et al., 2015).

This combination, a later time when one can fall asleep and the need for more sleep, leads to the well-known picture of a teen who stays up late and who cannot get out of bed in the morning. This mismatch between social clock and biological clock can have serious consequences. Many studies of adolescents and young adults find evidence of chronic sleep deprivation, with those in their late teens showing the greatest effects (de Souza & Hidalgo, 2014; Kelley et al., 2015). As we saw in Chapter 6, sleep deprivation is associated with a range of problems including difficulty concentrating and poor cognitive performance, irritability, anxiety, depression, digestive problems, weight gain, and increased risk of developing diabetes.

It is important to keep in mind that developmental changes during adolescence do not excuse sensation seeking that is directed to unhealthy or dangerous behaviours, emotional overreacting that is inconsiderate of others, self-indulgence, or even sleeping through morning classes. As we have seen when considering social-emotional development and cognitive development, changes continue throughout the lifespan and the emotional, cognitive, social, and biological changes that occur interact in complex ways. Yurgelun-Todd pointed out that while "there are neurobiological components to teen behaviour (this) doesn't discount the effects of environmental or social factors, nor does it absolve teenagers of accountability" (Packard, 2007, p. 22). Recent neuroscience research is finding changes that are often surprisingly consistent with the changes one might posit based on the work of psychologists such as Erikson, Piaget, and Vygotsky. The behavioural, emotional, and cognitive mechanisms that allow self-control, abstract thought, and reflection are present from a very young age; they just take longer to mature than was once thought.

Recent brain-imaging and behavioural studies indicate that during adolescence cognitive control is still developing; there is increased sensitivity to reward, which can lead to impulsive behaviours and sensation seeking; top-down control over emotional responses is still maturing and may not be exerted consistently; and changes in circadian rhythms increase the amount of sleep needed and shifts the sleep cycle to later sleep and waking times. Sound like anyone you know?

In Review

- In Western cultures, puberty marks the onset of adolescence. Hormones that steer puberty also can affect mood and behaviour. Generally, early maturation is a more positive experience for boys than it is for girls.

- During adolescence, neural restructuring is especially prominent in the prefrontal cortex and the limbic system, regions that play a key role in planning and coordinating behaviours that satisfy motivational goals, emotional urges, and moral decisions.

- Young adults are at the peak of their physical, sexual, and perceptual functioning in their 20s.

- Declines in physical processes (perception, bone density, basic metabolic rate, flexibility, etc.) begin in the 30s, and become more pronounced in late adulthood, but an active lifestyle, good nutrition, and a positive attitude can offset many age-related declines.

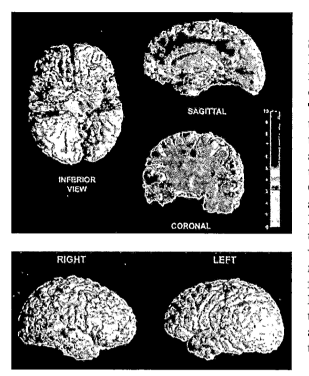

FIGURE 12.33 These photographs portray the average amount of brain-tissue loss that 92 men and women, ages 59 to 85 (who did not have brain disease), experienced over a four-year period. Areas in red had the greatest loss.

Resnick, S.M., Pham, D.L., Kraut, M.A., Zonderman, A.B., & Davatzikos, C. (2003). "Longitudinal magnetic resonance imaging studies of older adults: A shrinking brain." *Journal of Neuroscience*, 23(8), 3295–3301. Fig 6, p. 3300.

frontal and parietal lobes showing the greatest loss (Figure 12.33). Participants who were very healthy experienced less tissue loss than those who experienced medical problems, but still, even among physically and mentally healthy older adults, tissue loss is normal as the brain ages.

Cognitive Development

Supported by continuing brain maturation and learning experiences, cognitive changes during adolescence can be as dramatic as physical ones. Does Figure 12.34 strike a familiar chord? Teenagers can spend a lot of time thinking about themselves and their social circumstances. Such thinking reflects **adolescent egocentrism,** a self-absorbed and distorted view of one's uniqueness and importance (Elkind, 1967; Galanaki, 2012). Elkind (1967) proposed that adolescent egocentrism has two main parts. First, adolescents often overestimate the uniqueness of their feelings and experiences, which Elkind called the *personal fable.* This is reflected in statements such as "Nobody's ever felt love as deeply as ours." Second, many adolescents feel that they are always "on stage" and that "everybody's going to notice" how they look and what they do. Elkind called this sensitivity to social evaluation the *imaginary audience.*

Adolescents who think more egocentrically are somewhat more likely to engage in risky behaviours, perhaps in part because of a sense of invulnerability (Greene et al., 2000). At the same time, it's not clear that this self-consciousness truly reflects a thinking bias. Some theorists view teens' greater self-reflection as a natural outgrowth of the search for individuality and of realistic social consequences that teens face (Bell & Bromnick, 2003).

Reasoning and Information Processing in Adolescence

Abstract reasoning abilities increase substantially during adolescence. Adolescents can more easily contemplate hypothetical issues, ranging

31. Discuss how adolescents' reasoning abilities change, and the ways in which their thinking is egocentric.

Copyright © ZITS. King Features Syndicate. Reprinted with permission of TorStar Syndicate Services.

FIGURE 12.34 According to David Elkind (1967), this type of thinking reflects adolescent egocentrism.

from scientific problems (Figure 12.35a) to questions about social justice and the meaning of life. They reason more flexibly than children and use both deductive and inductive problem-solving, described in Chapter 9. Recall that in Piaget's (1970) view, this signifies that adolescents have moved beyond concrete operational thinking and entered a new stage of cognitive development: formal operational thinking.

Consider the pendulum problem in Figure 12.35b. Which variable(s)—length of the string, weight of the object, how hard it is pushed, and release point (height in the arc)—influence(s) how quickly the pendulum oscillates? This problem is best solved by forming and testing an organized set of deductive hypotheses (e.g., "*If* string length is a factor, *then* the swing time with a short versus long string should differ"). Concrete operational children struggle with this task (Inhelder & Piaget, 1958). For example, when they adjust the string length, they often adjust the weight as well, making it impossible to draw a conclusion about either variable. In contrast, adolescents think more systematically and manipulate one variable at a time while holding the others constant.

Continued improvements in information-processing capacities help abstract thinking to develop and foster better performance across a wide range of tasks. Although advancing more slowly than during childhood, the speed with which adolescents process information quickens, their working memory becomes more efficient, and they become better able to ignore distracting information, suppress irrelevant responses, and stay focused on the task at hand. Information-processing speed and visuospatial working-memory abilities approach adult-like levels by middle adolescence, and the ability to suppress task-irrelevant responses by late adolescence (Luna et al., 2004). Task performance does differ for different types of reasoning, and partly depends on formal schooling and exposure to scientific-abstract tasks. Even with schooling, however, many teens and adults struggle with formal operational tasks. Some people frequently use abstract reasoning, but others rarely do.

Changes in Adulthood

Post-formal operational thinking. Piaget believed that formal operational thinking was the fourth and final stage of cognitive development. He argued that adults do not develop new modes of thinking; rather, they simply use formal operations in new and more complex ways. Several theorists disagree, proposing a fifth stage of cognitive development called **post-formal thought,** in which people can reason

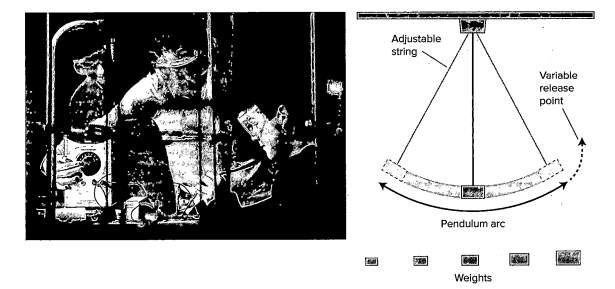

FIGURE 12.35 (a) When adolescents attain formal operational thought, they can use deductive reasoning to solve scientific problems systematically. (b) The materials for the pendulum problem used by Inhelder and Piaget include an adjustable string and a set of weights. The problem is to determine what factors influence how long it takes the pendulum to move through its arc. String length is the only relevant factor: the shorter the string, the less time it takes the pendulum to swing back and forth.

logically about opposing points of view and accept contradictions and irreconcilable differences (Rakfeldt et al., 1996; Lamport & Richards, 2003). Post-formal thinkers also realize that, from social behaviour to ethics and politics, life involves many interacting factors (Kramer, 1983). When reasoning about social problems, post-formal thinkers engage in complex thought and are more likely to acknowledge opposing points of view and see both sides of a disagreement as having legitimate arguments.

Information processing and memory. The University of Toronto's Fergus Craik concluded that, in general, information-processing abilities decline during adulthood, but the age at which they begin to decline and the amount of decline can vary substantially (e.g., Craik & Salthouse, 2000). Consider these examples:

- *Perceptual speed* (reaction time) begins to decline steadily in early adulthood, by some estimates as soon as one's early 20s (Salthouse, 2004). As adults grow older, it takes them longer to visually identify and evaluate stimuli, such as when looking at two patterns of lines and deciding whether they are the same. It takes longer to remember an item's context (source memory), especially under time pressure (Benjamine & Craik, 2001). But a loss of perceptual speed may be only part of the reason that older adults perform more slowly on such tasks. By late adulthood, people may process such information more conservatively, essentially trading off slower response times to gain greater accuracy in their judgments (Ratcliff et al., 2006).

- *Memory for new factual information* declines during adulthood. With increasing age, adults generally find it harder to remember new series of numbers, names, and faces of new people, and new map directions. On some tasks, such as recalling lists of unrelated words, performance worsens somewhat by the late 30s and then steadily declines after age 50 (Salthouse, 2004). Certain types of verbal memory, however, decline more slowly with age. Thus, the ability to immediately repeat meaningful sentences decreases more slowly than the ability to repeat single, unrelated words. Even in late adulthood, healthy adults do well in recognizing familiar stimuli from long ago, such as the faces of high school classmates (Bahrick et al., 1975).

- *Spatial memory* declines with age, according to Concordia's Cooney and Arbuckle (1997)

and Kessels and Postma (2006). For example, Uttl and Graf (1993) measured memory for the location of objects in an office setting or a museum and found that spatial memory remains constant in adulthood and begins to decline in the 60s.

- *Recall* declines more strongly than recognition, because recall requires more processing resources (Craik & McDowd, 1998; Arbuckle et al., 1992).

- The effects of aging on *prospective memory*—the ability to remember to perform some action in the future—are less clear (McDaniel et al., 2003). By late adulthood, people generally display poorer prospective memory than young adults in time-based laboratory tasks (e.g., remembering to push a button every 15 minutes). On event-based tasks (e.g., remembering to push a button whenever a light comes on), age differences are less consistent. Moreover, when tested outside the laboratory, older adults may perform as well as young adults, even when the tasks (e.g., simulated pill taking) are time-based. However, when older people remember that they are supposed to execute a task ("Ah, I'm supposed to call Sylvia") and something temporarily delays them from performing it, they will be less likely to remember to perform the task immediately after the delay ends (McDaniel et al., 2003).

Intellectual changes in adulthood. How do intellectual abilities change in adulthood? Although it was once thought that IQ scores began to decrease between ages 30 and 40 (Doppelt & Wallace, 1955), researchers made a breakthrough by examining separate intellectual abilities rather than overall IQ. They studied *fluid intelligence*, which reflects the ability to perform mental operations (e.g., abstract and logical reasoning, solving spatial problems), and *crystallized intelligence*, which reflects the accumulation of verbal skills and factual knowledge (Horn & Cattell, 1966). Cross-sectional research typically found that fluid intelligence began to decline steadily in early adulthood, whereas crystallized intelligence peaked during middle adulthood and then began to decline in late adulthood (Figure 12.36a).

Was this early decline in fluid abilities really a function of aging or instead the result of different experiences encountered by the various generations? The older adults may have had less

32. Discuss how information-processing abilities and memory change throughout adulthood.

33. How do intellectual abilities change with age? To what extent does the answer depend on the research design used?

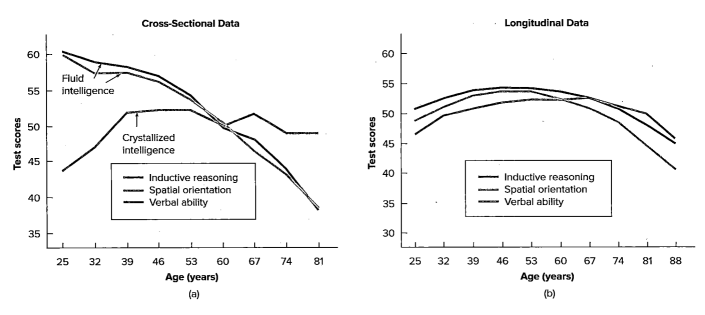

FIGURE 12.36 (a) Cross-sectional data indicate that fluid abilities (reasoning and spatial task performance) begin to decline in young adulthood, whereas crystallized intelligence (verbal ability) begins to decline in late adulthood. However, (b) longitudinal data from the same study indicate that *both* fluid and crystallized intelligence remain fairly stable through young and middle adulthood and do not decline significantly until late adulthood. The longitudinal and cross-sectional data are consistent in showing that crystallized abilities decline at a later age than fluid abilities.

Source: Adapted from Schaie, K.W. (1994). "The course of adult   intellectual development." *American Psychologist*, 49, 304–313.

exposure to scientific problem solving in school or jobs that required less use of abstract intellectual skills. Such factors could have depressed their scores artificially.

To answer this question, Warner Schaie and colleagues (1994, 2005) began a study in 1956 that has now involved several thousand adults. This study uses a sequential design, incorporating longitudinal and cross-sectional components. The longitudinal data do not support an early decline in either fluid or crystallized intelligence. Rather, most abilities are relatively stable throughout early and middle adulthood and do not reliably decline until late adulthood (Figure 12.36b). But both the cross-sectional and longitudinal data, along with findings from other studies, indicate that fluid intellectual abilities typically begin to decline at an earlier age than crystallized intelligence, such as verbal abilities, which are similar at ages 25 and 88 (Singer et al., 2003).

Age-related intellectual declines are partly due to poorer perceptual speed, memory, vision, and hearing (Fristoe et al., 1997). Thus, we find a bigger intellectual decline during old age when test questions call for quick responses (i.e., timed tests) than when they involve unlimited or ample time (untimed tests). This decrease in intellectual speed shows up in various real-world tasks, such as learning to use a computer. Although 75- to 89-year-olds may take longer to acquire computer skills and need more assistance than their 60- to 74-year-old counterparts, the key is that many retain the intellectual capacity to learn (Echt et al., 1998).

Use It or Lose It? Maintaining Cognitive Functioning

The average intellectual decline in old age shown in Figure 12.36 is a bit deceiving, since it is disproportionately influenced by a minority of Schaie's older participants who showed very pronounced declines. For each intellectual ability, Schaie found that about 70 percent of his participants *maintained* their level of functioning between ages 67 and 74, and 65 percent maintained it between ages 74 and 81.

Can we predict who will maintain their level of intellectual functioning the longest? As in the case of maintaining physical fitness, the moral for intellectual fitness appears to be "use it or lose it" (Clarkson-Smith & Hartley, 1990). In Schaie's (1994, 2005) longitudinal research, he found that adults who retained their level of cognitive functioning tended to engage in more cognitively stimulating jobs and personal activities (e.g., reading, travel, continuing education), to marry a spouse with

34. Identify some factors associated with greater retention of cognitive abilities during late adulthood.

greater intellectual abilities than their own, and to maintain a higher level of perceptual processing speed. Singh-Manous, Hillsdon, Brunner, and Marmot (2005) conducted a longitudinal study on 10 308 civil servants beginning in the mid-1980s, when they were 34 to 55 years of age. Their physical activity was assessed five years later and again, along with cognitive function, after ten years. Low physical activity levels were associated with cognitive decline, especially in fluid intelligence. That is, regular physical exercise and perceptual-motor activities help to preserve cognitive abilities in late adulthood (Allmer, 2005; Newson & Kemps, 2006).

Current research suggests that practice can boost many adults' performance on particular mental tasks—no trivial matter (Delahunt et al., 2009; Petrosini et al., 2009). For example, video games that require fast reaction times, computer-based memory and attention exercises, and regular participation in problem-solving groups to prepare for a community competition are among many training activities that have been found to improve older adults' performance on specific cognitive tasks (Smith et al., 2009; Stine-Morrow et al., 2008). It is important, however, to avoid unrealistic expectations about the effectiveness of mental exercise as a "sure-fire treatment" to prevent cognitive decline or reverse existing dementia; there is simply too much that we still do not know about aging and age-related changes (Low & Anstey, 2009).

Social-Emotional and Personality Development

G. Stanley Hall (1904), the first psychologist to study adolescence, viewed it as a time of "storm and stress." As they cross the bridge between childhood and adulthood, adolescents may grapple with issues concerning parental and peer relations, career goals, gender roles and ethnicity, sexuality, drug use, politics, and religion. Although some adults recall adolescence as a period of conflict and alienation, others find it to be a positive, relatively carefree period of life (Arnett, 1999).

Adolescents' Search for Identity

"Who am I?" "What do I believe in?" Erik Erikson (1968) proposed that such questions reflect the pivotal crisis of adolescent personality development, which he termed *identity versus role confusion* (see Table 12.2). Erikson believed that an adolescent's "identity crisis" (a term he coined) can be resolved positively, leading to a stable sense of identity, or can end negatively, leading to confusion over one's identity and values.

Building on Erikson's work, James Marcia (1966, 2002) studied adolescents' and young adults' search for identity. Marcia classified the "identity status" of each person as follows:

- *Identity diffusion.* These teens and adults had not yet gone through an identity crisis. They seemed unconcerned or even cynical about identity issues and were not committed to a coherent set of values.

- *Foreclosure.* These individuals had not yet gone through an identity crisis either, but for a different reason: they committed to an identity and set of values before experiencing a crisis. For example, some automatically adopted peer-group or parental values without giving these values much thought.

- *Moratorium.* These people wanted to establish a clear identity and were currently experiencing a crisis but had not yet resolved it.

- *Identity achievement.* These individuals had gone through an identity crisis, successfully resolved it, and emerged with a coherent set of values.

35. Identify some of the different ways that adolescents approach the challenge of establishing an identity.

Review

- Improvements in information-processing processes (speed, memory) foster increases in abstract reasoning during adolescence. However, many teens and adults continue to struggle on formal operational tasks (e.g., the pendulum problem); while some people frequently use abstract reasoning, others rarely do so.

- Information-processing capacities decline steadily after reaching one's 30s. However, longitudinal data show that many intellectual abilities do not begin to decline reliably until late adulthood.

- Remaining physically and cognitively active can maintain cognitive function with advanced age.

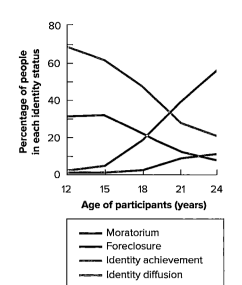

36. To what extent are parent-teen relationships characterized by "storm and stress"?

FIGURE 12.37 Based on interviews in one study, this graph shows the percentage of participants in each of Marcia's four identity statuses at various ages. These data suggest that most young people attain identity a few years later than Erikson suggested.

Source: Adapted from Meilman, P.W. (1979). "Cross-sectional age changes in ego identity status during adolescence." *Developmental Psychology,* 15, 230–231.

As shown in Figure 12.37, most young adolescents are in identity diffusion or foreclosure; they have not experienced an identity crisis. But, with age, many identity-diffused teens think more deeply about who they are, and most teens in foreclosure reconsider their prematurely adopted values. They experience an identity crisis, and more than half successfully resolve it by young adulthood.

Identity, of course, is not a simple concept, and our sense of identity has multiple components (Camilleri & Malewska-Peyre, 1997). These include (1) our gender, ethnicity, and other attributes by which we define ourselves as members of social groups ("daughter," "student," "athlete"); (2) how we view our personal characteristics ("shy," "friendly"); and (3) our goals and values. Typically, we achieve a stable identity regarding some components before others, and changing situations may trigger new crises and cause us to re-evaluate prior goals and values.

Culture plays a key role in identity formation, one that goes beyond the simple idea that we view ourselves as belonging to certain cultural groups. Our cultural upbringing influences the very way we view concepts such as "self" and "identity." If you grew up in an individualistic culture, your sense of identity assumes that you are an autonomous individual, with clear boundaries separating you from other people. But in collectivistic cultures, the concept of "self" is traditionally based more strongly on the connectedness between people (Kagitáibasi, 1997). Thus, the question "Who am I?" is more likely to be answered in ways that reflect a person's relationships with family members, friends, and others. Still, keep in mind that we are talking about relative differences. Across cultures, people's sense of identity incorporates elements that involve autonomy from—and interdependence with—other people (Mascolo & Li, 2004).

Relationships with Parents and Peers

When it comes to teenagers' relationships with their parents, is "storm and stress" the rule or the exception? In a national survey, about 80 percent of American teens reported thinking highly of, and enjoying spending time with, the parents with whom they lived at home (Moore et al., 2004). About two-thirds of the teens reported an overall positive relationship with their parents.

Likewise, research in China, the Netherlands, Canada, and with various American ethnic groups suggests that teen–parent conflict is not as severe as often assumed (e.g., Chen et al., 1998). For example, Andrew Fuligni (1998) studied 1341 female and male American students in Grades 6, 8, and 10. The students came from immigrant and native-born families of Mexican, Chinese, Filipino, and European ancestry. He found that among both sexes and all four ethnic groups, teenagers' level of conflict with mothers and fathers was low.

Most adolescents also state that if they face a serious problem, they can confide in one or both parents (National Center on Addiction and Substance Abuse, 2005). Yet many adolescents also feel that for various reasons, including the right to preserve their independence, it is acceptable to lie to their parents at times. As Figure 12.38 shows, in one study most high school students said that they had lied to their parents on several issues in the past year (Jensen et al., 2004).

Some parents and teenagers do struggle a lot, and parent–teen conflict is correlated with other signs of distress. For example, those who report more conflict with parents also display higher levels of school misconduct (e.g., skipping school), more antisocial behaviour (e.g., getting into fistfights), lower self-esteem, more drug use, and less life satisfaction (Caughlin & Malis, 2004; Chen et al., 1998). Recalling the principle that correlation does not equal causation, we must

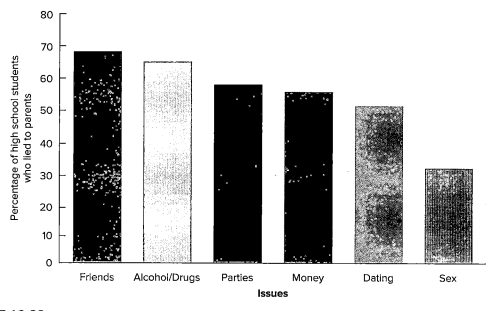

FIGURE 12.38 In one study, 229 students attending a public high school were asked how often they lied to their parents about six issues. For each issue, this graph shows the percentage of students who reported lying to their parents at least once during the past year.

Source: Jensen, L.A., Arnett, J.J., Feldman, S.S., & Cauffman, E. (2004). "The right to do wrong: Lying to parents among adolescents and emerging adults." *Journal of Youth and Adolescence*, 33, 101–112. Fig. 1, p. 106. With kind permission from Springer Science & Business Media.

consider that although parent-teen conflict may be a cause of teens' psychological problems, it also is likely to be caused *by* such problems.

In every city, town, and village in Canada, teens like to spend time hanging out with friends. Peer relationships increase in importance during adolescence, and some studies find that teenagers spend more time with peers than doing almost anything else. But this pattern may be stronger in Canada and the United States than in Europe or Asia, where teens generally place a relatively stronger emphasis on family relationships (Chen et al., 1998).

Adolescent friendships are typically more intimate than those at previous ages and involve a greater sharing of problems. Peers can strongly influence a teenager's values and behaviours, thereby facilitating the process of separating from parents and establishing one's own identity. For some adolescents, however, experiences with peers increase the risk of misconduct, such as skipping school, damaging property, or using drugs (Larson et al., 2006). Fortunately, peer pressure *against* misconduct typically has an even stronger effect, and closeness to parents is an added buffer that helps many teenagers resist peer pressure to engage in risky behaviour (Chen et al., 1998). Also, Hastings and Grusec (1997) found that conflict between Canadian teens and their parents was

reduced when the parents accurately perceived their teens' cognitions and affect. So, despite increased peer influence during adolescence, parental influence remains high on political, religious, moral, and career issues. Indeed, the so-called "generation gap" is narrower than is often assumed.

Although parent–teen conflict may contribute to teens' psychological problems, we should remember that it also is likely to be caused by such problems. And, of course, not all adolescent negative behaviour can be blamed on peers or parents; for example, aggressive behaviour may have a genetic component (Guo, 2006).

37. How do peer relationships change during adolescence?

The Transition to Adulthood

In traditional cultures, marriage typically is the key transitional event into adulthood (Arnett, 2001). Through socialization, males develop skills that will enable them to protect and provide for a family of their own, and females learn skills needed eventually to care for children and run a household. Marriage signifies that, in the eyes of the culture, each partner has acquired these skills and is deemed capable of raising a family.

In industrialized societies, how do we know when someone has become an adult? This chapter's *Research Foundations* feature examines this question.

Research Foundations

WHAT DOES IT TAKE TO BECOME AN ADULT?

Introduction

If we asked you "Have you reached adulthood?" how would you answer? And, in your view, just what does it take to be considered an adult? Jeffrey Arnett examined how North Americans in various age groups viewed the transition to adulthood. Whereas previous research focused on the viewpoints of adolescents and people in their 20s, this study also examined the viewpoints of older adults.

Method

Men and women from a mid-sized community were recruited to participate. There were 519 participants, representing three age groups: 13- to 19-year-olds, 20- to 29-year-olds, and 30- to 55-year-olds. Participants rated ("Yes" or "No") whether each of 38 specific characteristics "must be achieved before a person can be considered an adult." These characteristics were presented in random order and represented six general categories of criteria for judging adult status. These categories and some sample items appear in the accompanying table. Each participant also was asked, "Do you think that you have reached adulthood?" The answer options were "Yes," "No," and "In some respects yes, in some respects no." The Design box summarizes key aspects of the method.

General Category	Sample of Specific Characteristics
Individualism	Be responsible for one's actions; determine own values/beliefs; attain financial freedom.
Family capacities	Be capable of caring for and financially supporting a family.
Norm compliance	Refrain from crime, irresponsible sex, drunk driving, illegal drug use.
Biological transitions	Be capable of fathering/bearing children.
Legal/Chronological transitions	Obtain driver's licence; reach age 18; reach age 19.
Role transitions	Full-time employment; establish career; finish education, get married.

Design

Question: How do people of various ages view the transition to adulthood?

Type of Study: *Correlational*

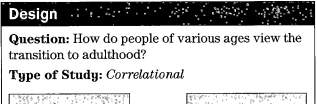

Variable X

Age, three groups
- ages 13 to 19
- ages 20 to 29
- ages 30 to 55

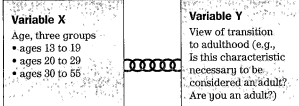

Variable Y

View of transition to adulthood (e.g., Is this characteristic necessary to be considered an adult? Are you an adult?)

Results

What qualities were judged as necessary to be considered an adult? Regardless of age group, about 90 percent of participants endorsed the importance of accepting responsibility for one's actions. Establishing one's own values and beliefs, seeing oneself as an equal with one's parents, and attaining financial independence were the next most frequently chosen qualities among all age groups. Items such as "reaching age 18," "employed full-time," and "marriage" were endorsed by only 47, 32, and 13 percent of participants, respectively. In fact, if you look at the six general categories shown in the Method section, they are listed in the overall order of importance, as determined by the average ratings of all the items in each category. Overall, there was strong consistency in how the various age groups viewed the importance of these characteristics.

In contrast, substantial age differences emerged in whether participants viewed themselves as having reached adulthood. As Figure 12.39 shows, among adolescents (average age 16 years), fewer than a fifth said that they had reached adulthood. Among people in their 20s (average age 24 years), almost half said that they had reached adulthood. Still, in both of these age groups, the transitional "yes and no" response was most common. Only among people in mid-life (average age 42 years) did most view themselves as having fully attained adulthood.

Discussion

Along with other research conducted across North America, this study reveals that on the psychological road to adulthood, biological, legal, chronological, and role transitions take a backseat. *Individualism*—becoming a responsible, independent person—was judged to be the single most

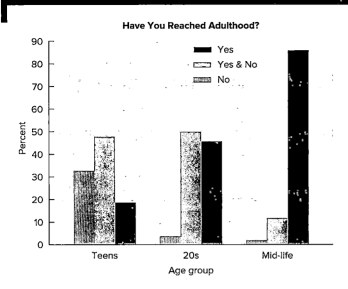

Have You Reached Adulthood?

■ Yes
▭ Yes & No
▦ No

(y-axis) Percent — 0, 10, 20, 30, 40, 50, 60, 70, 80, 90
(x-axis) Age group — Teens, 20s, Mid-life

FIGURE 12.39 Have you reached adulthood? This graph shows the percentage of people in their teens, 20s, and 30s to mid-50s (mid-life) who felt that they had not, had partially, or had fully reached adulthood.

Source: Jeffrey J. Arnett (2001). Conceptions of the transition to adulthood: Perspectives from adolescence through midlife. *Journal of Adult Development*, 8, 133–143. Fig. 2, p. 140. With kind permission from Springer Science & Business Media.

important general criterion. Still, in making the transition from adolescence to adulthood, multiple factors appear to come into play for most people.

This study had several strengths. It addressed an interesting question, one likely to assume great personal relevance for many people at some point in their lives. The 38 characteristics for judging adulthood status were carefully chosen on the basis of prior research, and the participants represented a broader age range than in previous studies.

All studies have limitations, however, and as a critical thinker, you should recognize that this study employed a cross-sectional design. The findings tell us, at a given point in time, how various age groups view the transition to adulthood. It would be interesting to study the same participants by using a longitudinal design and, thus, examine more precisely how people's views of "becoming an adult" change as they grow older. Additionally, most participants in this study (84 percent) were White. As Arnett notes, although the overall findings were consistent with those of studies conducted elsewhere in North America, the question of whether the transition to adulthood is viewed differently among various ethnic groups and among people from other cultures needs closer examination.

Source: Jeffrey J. Arnett (2001). "Conceptions of the transition to adulthood: Perspectives from adolescence through midlife." *Journal of Adult Development, 8,* 133–143.

Stages versus Critical Events in Adulthood

Many researchers view adult social development as a progression through age-related stages (Levinson, 1990). According to Erik Erikson (1959/1980; look back at Table 12.2), *intimacy versus isolation* is the major developmental challenge of early adulthood (ages 20 to 40). Intimacy is the ability to open oneself to another person and to form close relationships. This is the period of adulthood in which many people form close adult friendships, fall in love, and marry.

Middle adulthood (ages 40 to 65) brings with it the issue of *generativity versus stagnation*. Through their careers, raising children, or involvement in other activities, people achieve generativity by doing things for others and making the world a better place. Certainly, many young adults make such contributions, but generativity typically becomes a more central issue later in adulthood (Slater, 2003).

Late adulthood (age 65 and older) accentuates the final crisis, *integrity versus despair.* Older adults review their lives and evaluate

their meanings. If the major crises of earlier stages have been successfully resolved, the person experiences integrity: a sense of completeness and fulfillment. Older adults who have not achieved positive outcomes at earlier stages may experience despair, regretting that they had not lived their lives in a more fulfilling way.

Consistent with Erikson's model, many goals increase in importance as people age, and successfully resolving certain life tasks contributes to mastering others (McAdams & de St. Aubin, 1998). Critics caution that we should avoid viewing early, middle, and late adulthood as strict stages in which one life task takes over while others fade away. Although older adults are more concerned about generativity and integrity than are younger adults, they remain highly concerned about intimacy (Sheldon & Kasser, 2001).

Another way to view adult social development is through the major life events that people experience. Sigmund Freud (1935) once defined psychological adjustment as "the ability to love and work," and many key life events revolve around these two themes.

Marriage and Family

Around the world, most people marry or form another type of family union at some point in their lives, and family structures can vary widely both across and within various cultures. The "average" family in North America and some other parts of the world has changed in several ways over recent generations. For example, Baby Boomers were born a few years after the end of World War II, and their children (born in the 1960s through the early 1980s) became known as *Generation X*. As Figure 12.40 shows, compared with the families that Baby Boomers grew up in, members of Generation X are more likely to have experienced parental divorce, had two working parents, had a smaller number of siblings, and yet maintained a similar level of closeness to their parents (Bengtson, 2001).

Adults typically expect much from marriage, but a high divorce rate in many countries indicates that marital happiness is by no means automatic. Successful marriages are characterized by emotional closeness, positive communication and problem solving, agreement on basic values and expectations, and a willingness to accept and support changes in the partner (Cordova et al., 2005). On average, marital satisfaction declines over the first few years after the knot is tied (McNulty & Karney, 2004). This decline does not mean, however, that most couples are unhappy. They are still satisfied, just a little less so. In a sense, the honeymoon is over.

The birth of a first baby dramatically alters the way couples spend their time. For many couples, marital satisfaction decreases in the year or two after their first child is born (Cowan & Cowan, 2000). Compared with husbands, wives are more likely to leave their outside jobs, spend more time parenting, and feel that their spouses are not helping enough. Disagreements over the division of labour and parenting are a major contributor to the drop in marital satisfaction (Frisco & Williams, 2003).

Over a broader age period, cross-sectional studies suggest a U-shaped relation between marital satisfaction and progression through major life events. The percentage of couples reporting that they are "very satisfied" in their marriage typically is highest before or just as the first child is born, drops during child-rearing years, and increases after all the children have left home (Orbuch et al., 1996). Contrary to the popular "empty nest" stereotype, most middle-aged couples do not become significantly depressed or suffer a crisis when their children leave home (Chiriboga, 1989). Couples maintain meaningful relationships with their children but have more time to spend with each other and pursue leisure activities.

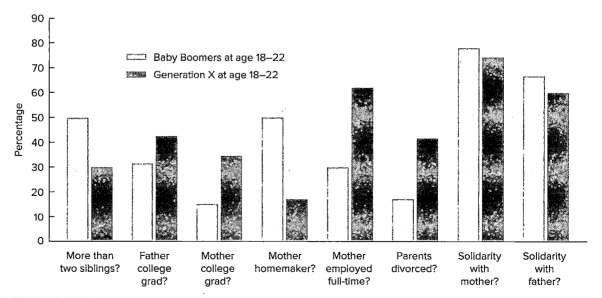

FIGURE 12.40 Growing up in different generations. Baby Boomers were surveyed when they were 18 to 22 years old and asked to identify various characteristics of the families in which they had grown up. A generation later, when the Baby Boomers' children (Generation X) had turned 18 to 22 years old, they answered the same survey questions as their parents had.

Source: V.L. Bengtson, 2001, "Beyond the Nuclear Family: The Increasing Importance of Multigenerational Bonds," *Journal of Marriage and the Family*, 63(1), 1–16, Fig 2. www.interscience.wiley.com. Reprinted by permission of the publisher.

Despite the stresses that accompany marriage and parenthood, studies around the globe find that married people experience greater subjective well-being than unmarried adults (Keyes & Waterman, 2003). They tend to be happier and live longer. Although raising children is demanding, parents often report that having children is one of the best things that happened in their lives.

Cohabitation. Some couples in committed relationships *cohabit*—that is, live together without being married. According to Statistics Canada, 8.6 percent of the adult population cohabited in a "common-law" relationship in 2012. Couples may cohabit as a permanent alternative to marriage, but many more people do so as a "trial marriage" to determine if they are compatible before tying the knot. In Sweden, premarital cohabitation appears to be the norm among newlyweds (Duvander, 1999). Not all premarital cohabitation leads to marriage; Manning and Smock (2002) found that the probability of cohabiters expecting to marry depended in part on the socioeconomic status of the man.

Thinking critically

COHABITATION AS A "TRIAL MARRIAGE"

What would you predict? Do couples who live together before getting married have a lower, higher, or similar rate of divorce compared to couples who do not live together before they get married? Why?

Think about it, and then see the Answers section at the end of the book.

Attachment revisited. Before we leave marriage and parenthood, note that, according to attachment theory, security of attachment influences the relationships adults form with their partner and their children. Adults' security of attachment with their mothers has been classified by using interviews (e.g., Benoit & Parker, 1994) and questionnaires (e.g., Webster, 1997). The proportions of secure, avoidant, and resistant attachment styles are similar for adults and infants, at least for Canadian and American samples, and adult attachment styles are related to social relationships (Goldberg, 1991). For example, a disproportionate number of adults with various behavioural problems (including criminal behaviour; e.g., Wand, Hudson, & Marshall, 1996) have a history of insecure attachment.

Diane Benoit and Kevin Parker (1994) conducted a longitudinal study on 96 Canadian infants, their mothers, and their grandmothers. They found 88 percent agreement in attachment classification of mothers and their infants, and 65 percent agreement across the three generations—much greater than expected by chance. Benoit and Parker's results suggest that the patterns of attachment are passed on from one generation to the next. However, along with attachment, difficult temperaments, poverty, and other factors may also be involved.

Establishing a Career

In the adult world, one of the first questions a new acquaintance typically asks is "So, what do you do?" A career helps us earn a living and defines an important part of our identity. Work provides an outlet for achievement, gives us structure, and is a significant source of social interactions. Having satisfying relationships at work is especially important in collectivistic countries (Siu, 2003).

According to Donald Super (1957), a pioneer in the field of vocational psychology, from childhood through our mid-20s, we first enter a *growth stage* of career interests in which we form initial impressions about the types of jobs we like or dislike. This stage is followed by a more earnest *exploration stage* in which we form tentative ideas about a preferred career and pursue the necessary education or training.

From the mid-20s to mid-40s, people often enter an *establishment phase*, during which they begin to make their mark. Initially, they may experience some job instability. After college, for example, many people are likely to change careers at least once. Eventually, careers tend to become more stable, and people enter a *maintenance stage* that continues into late adulthood. Finally, during the *decline stage*, people's investment in work tends to decrease, and they eventually retire.

Although this general model is useful, people's career paths vary, and this is especially true for women. Overall, compared with their fathers and mothers at the same age, today's young women hold higher career aspirations (Bengtson, 2001). Still, family responsibilities, which fall disproportionately on women even when their married partners have similar job status, are a major cause of women's work gaps outside the home, of reductions to part-time work status, or of delayed entry into the workforce (Smithson et al., 2004). After raising a family, many women enter the workforce for the first time, reinvigorate an earlier career, or return to college to prepare for a new one. Career gaps also occur when adults must temporarily leave the workforce to care for their elderly parents. As in raising children, women disproportionately fill this elder-care role.

Mid-Life Crisis: Fact or Fiction?

Popular wisdom holds that, along the developmental path of career and family, people hit a massive pothole called the mid-life crisis. Is it true? Daniel Levinson and his colleagues (1978, 1986) longitudinally studied 85 men and women and found that many experienced a turbulent mid-life transition between the ages of 40 and 45. They began to focus on their mortality and realized that some of their life's dreams pertaining to career, family, and relationships would not come true.

Critics note that Levinson's sample was small and nonrepresentative. In fact, there is considerable evidence that the notion of a full-blown, turmoil-filled mid-life crisis is largely a myth (Lachman, 2004). Research conducted around the world shows that happiness and life satisfaction generally are unrelated to age (Diener et al., 1999). In one study of adolescents and people in young, middle, and late adulthood from eight Western European countries, about 80 percent of each age group reported they were "satisfied" or "very satisfied" with their lives (Ingelhart & Rabier, 1986). Moreover, people in their 40s do not have higher rates of divorce, suicide, depression, feelings of meaninglessness, or emotional instability than younger or older adults (Figure 12.41; McCrae & Costa, 1990; Kessler et al., 2005).

In sum, adults surely experience conflict, disappointment, frustration, and worry as they enter

38. Is the mid-life crisis a myth? Discuss the evidence.

39. Does retirement cause psychological problems for most retirees? Under what conditions are such problems most likely?

mid-life, but so do people of all ages (Wethington, 2000). As Erikson emphasized, there are major goals to achieve, crises to resolve, and rewards to experience in every phase of life.

Retirement and the "Golden Years"

Older adults are the fastest-growing segment of the population in many countries, including Canada. In 2012, according to Statistics Canada, the median age in Canada was 40.0 years, the oldest it has ever been. There are almost as many Canadians 65 and older (5 186 822) as there are younger than 15 (5 663 163); a record 14.9 percent of the total population was over 65. Furthermore, the age group between 55 and 64—a group of people that will soon retire—is at a record high of 4 491 528 (almost 13 percent of the Canadian population)!

Retirement is an important milestone. Some adults view it as a reminder that they are growing older, but many look forward to leisure and other opportunities they were unable to pursue during their careers. Most retired people do not become anxious, depressed, or dissatisfied with life because of retirement itself, although those who have strong work values are most apt to miss their jobs (Hyde et al., 2004).

The decision to retire or keep working typically involves many factors, such as one's feelings about the job, leisure interests, physical health, financial security, and family relationships. Family income, leisure time, and family roles change with retirement, and married couples often experience increased marital stress after a spouse retires, especially if the other spouse is still working. Over time, however, they typically adjust to their new circumstances and marital quality is enhanced (Moen et al., 2001).

Some people, of course, do not have the luxury to choose their work status. They may be forced into retirement by job layoffs or mandatory retirement ages, or feel compelled to keep working for economic reasons. These circumstances can have a significant impact on well-being. Whether in their 50s, 60s, or 70s, adults who are working or retired because this is what *they* prefer report higher life satisfaction and better physical and mental health than adults who are involuntarily working or retired (Shultz et al., 1998). Of course, declining physical and mental health also may be factors that lead people to retire in the first place. Thus, biological, psychological, and environmental factors noted in Figure 12.42 continue to exert their influence on development and jointly shape how people navigate their golden years.

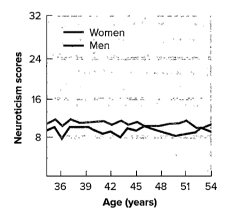

FIGURE 12.41 In a national health survey of over 10 000 men and women, the percentage of individuals measured to have "emotional instability" remained steady between the ages of 33 and 54.

Source: From McCrae, R.R. & Costa, P.T. (1990). *Personality in adulthood.* New York, NY: Guilford Press.

 **Lifespan Development**

We've seen in this chapter that aging is a biological process intertwined with psychological and environmental components. Using these three levels of analysis, let's highlight some of the main points we've covered.

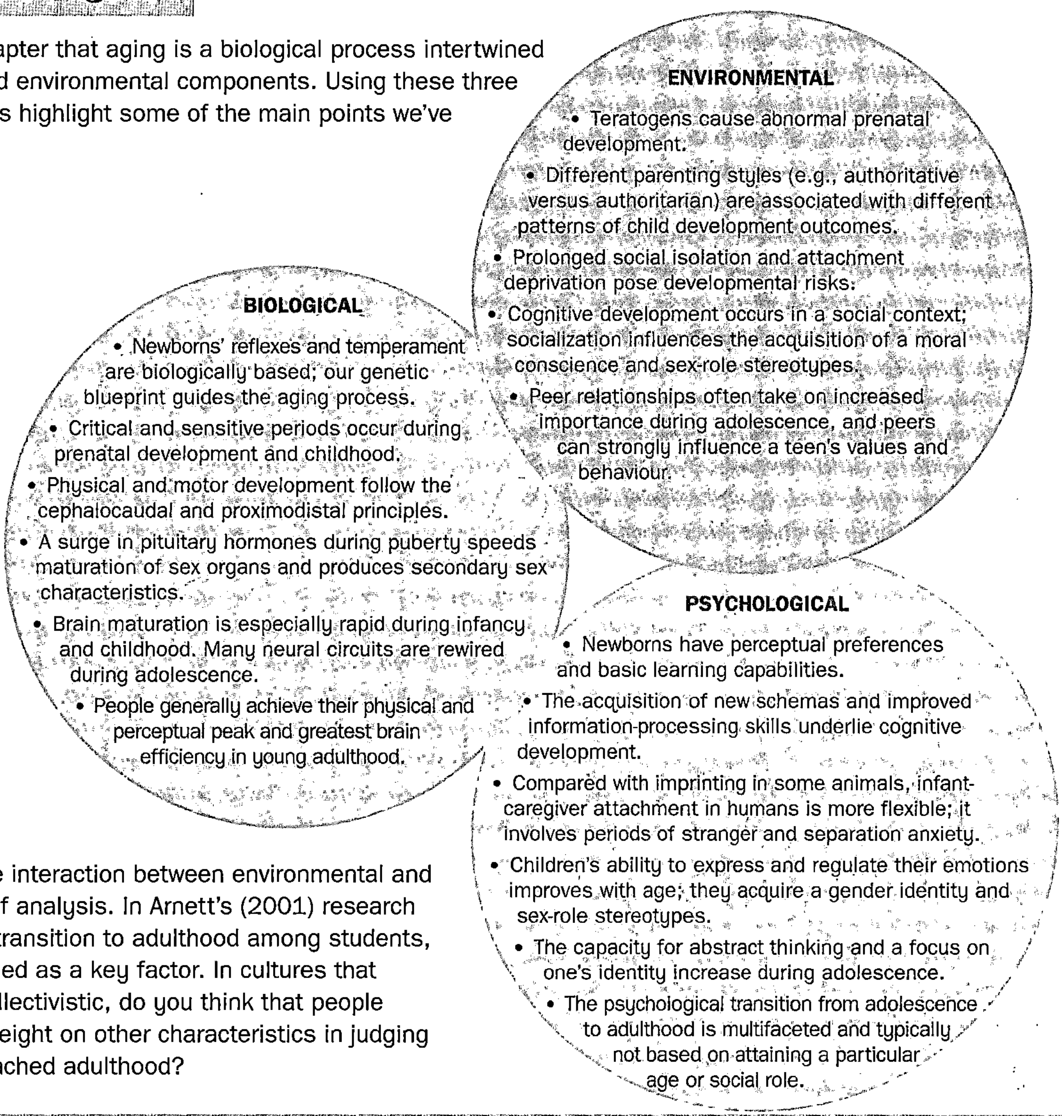

ENVIRONMENTAL

- Teratogens cause abnormal prenatal development.
- Different parenting styles (e.g., authoritative versus authoritarian) are associated with different patterns of child development outcomes.
- Prolonged social isolation and attachment deprivation pose developmental risks.
- Cognitive development occurs in a social context; socialization influences the acquisition of a moral conscience and sex-role stereotypes.
- Peer relationships often take on increased importance during adolescence, and peers can strongly influence a teen's values and behaviour.

BIOLOGICAL

- Newborns' reflexes and temperament are biologically based; our genetic blueprint guides the aging process.
- Critical and sensitive periods occur during prenatal development and childhood.
- Physical and motor development follow the cephalocaudal and proximodistal principles.
- A surge in pituitary hormones during puberty speeds maturation of sex organs and produces secondary sex characteristics.
- Brain maturation is especially rapid during infancy and childhood. Many neural circuits are rewired during adolescence.
- People generally achieve their physical and perceptual peak and greatest brain efficiency in young adulthood.

PSYCHOLOGICAL

- Newborns have perceptual preferences and basic learning capabilities.
- The acquisition of new schemas and improved information-processing skills underlie cognitive development.
- Compared with imprinting in some animals, infant-caregiver attachment in humans is more flexible; it involves periods of stranger and separation anxiety.
- Children's ability to express and regulate their emotions improves with age; they acquire a gender identity and sex-role stereotypes.
- The capacity for abstract thinking and a focus on one's identity increase during adolescence.
- The psychological transition from adolescence to adulthood is multifaceted and typically not based on attaining a particular age or social role.

Consider this possible interaction between environmental and psychological levels of analysis. In Arnett's (2001) research on the psychological transition to adulthood among students, "individualism" emerged as a key factor. In cultures that are relatively more collectivistic, do you think that people would place greater weight on other characteristics in judging whether they have reached adulthood?

FIGURE 12.42

Death and Dying

It was a grand birthday party. Jeanne Calment (Figure 12.43) was born in France ten years after the American Civil War. By age 60, she had lived through a world war and the invention of the radio, telephone, motion picture, automobile, and airplane. Still to come was another world war, TV, space flight, computers, and the Internet. Calment rode a bicycle until age 100 and her 120th birthday was a grand affair. When a reporter asked how her future looked, Jeanne replied with a wry sense of humour, "Very brief."

All of us eventually face death. Like other aspects of lifespan development summarized in Figure 12.42, death can be viewed at several

levels; it is an inevitable biological process, but one with important psychological and environmental components.

In her pioneering work on dying, Elisabeth Kübler-Ross (1969) found that terminally ill patients often experienced five stages as they coped with impending death. *Denial* typically came first, as the person refused to accept that the illness was terminal. Next, denial often gave way to *anger* and then to *bargaining*, such as "Lord, please let me live long enough to see my grandchild." *Depression* ushered in the fourth stage, as patients began to grieve. Finally, many experienced *acceptance* and a resigned sense of peacefulness.

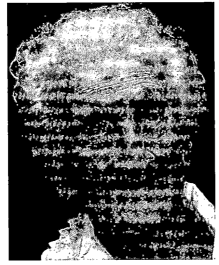

Francois Mori/AP Photos/The Canadian Press

FIGURE 12.43 Jeanne Louise Calment of Arles, France, was born in 1875 and died in 1997 at the age of 122. Calment's life is the longest that has been verified.

© Reuters/Corbis

FIGURE 12.44 Many cultures honour a person's death with a ceremony that involves family, friends, and the wider community. In some cultures, this occasion is traditionally sombre; in others, it is a joyous celebration.

40. Why is it incorrect to say that there is a "normal" or "proper" way to confront death?

It is essential to keep in mind that these stages do not represent a "normal" or "correct" way to face death, and that terminally ill patients' reactions may not typify those of people facing death under other circumstances (Doka, 1995). Even among terminally ill patients, some move back and forth between stages, do not experience all the stages, or look forward to death (Schulz & Aderman, 1980).

Kübler-Ross's ideas have become widely known, but her research and model have remained topics of discussion and debate (Maciejewski, 2007; Roos, 2013). It is important to keep in mind that Kübler-Ross studied terminally ill patients and described the process of dying among those individuals. Her model, however, has also been applied to describe how people deal with loss, trauma, and bereavement. Extensive research by George Bonanno indicates that when people deal with loss or trauma they do not pass through Kübler-Ross's stages of grief, but tend to be surprisingly resilient (Bonanno, 2009; Mancici & Bonanno, 2012).

Beliefs and customs concerning death vary across cultures (Figure 12.44) and individuals (Werth et al., 2002). To some, death means the complete end of one's existence. Others believe in reincarnation or that the soul enters an afterlife. Death also means different things to people of different ages (Cicirelli, 1998). Older adults typically have lost more friends and loved ones, and have thought more about their own deaths than have younger people. Understandably, the elderly are more accepting of their own deaths than any other age group (Kalish & Reynolds, 1977). In the midst of a fatal heart attack, one 81-year-old man reassuringly told his family, "It's my time. It's been a good life." We should all wish for this blessing of a fulfilled life's journey.

Review

- Erikson proposed that intimacy versus isolation, generativity versus stagnation, and integrity versus despair are the main crises of early, middle, and late adulthood.

- Young adolescents often show egocentrism in their social thinking. The search for identity is a key task of adolescence. With age, teens who have not experienced an identity crisis become more likely to do so, and most resolve it successfully.

- During adolescence, peer relationships become more important and intimate. Most teens maintain good relations with their parents.

- In North America, the most important criterion for a transition into adulthood is becoming a responsible, independent person. In traditional cultures, marriage is a common marker of this transition.

- In general, married people tend to be happier and live longer.

- For many couples, marital satisfaction tends to decline in the years following the birth of children, but it increases later in adulthood. Adult-mother attachment styles are related to social relationships and may be passed on from one generation to the next.

- Work serves important psychological and social functions. Overall, women experience more career gaps and their career paths are more variable than men's. Most adults do not experience a full-blown "mid-life crisis." Similarly, most retired people do not become more anxious, depressed, or lonely because of retirement.

- Many terminally ill patients experience similar psychological reactions as they cope with their impending death, but beliefs and feelings about death vary with culture and age, and there is no "normal" way to approach death.

Gaining Direction

What are the issues?	Brain development in infants is a very complex activity. Perceptual development requires exposure to and interaction with the environment. But what happens if we replace the "real world" with a technology-based virtual world? Will the brain develop in a normal fashion or	will development be influenced by the screen images? How are we ever going to test this properly? Is there any evidence of enhanced development using technology? Is this really any different from letting kids watch television?
What do we need to know?	What is the normal path of brain development? Does a virtual world result in a virtual brain? Can kids really see the screen properly? Will concentrating on the screen harm vision?	Does prolonged use of a tablet result in digital dependency? How much use is appropriate? Can apps help young children learn?
Where can we find the information to answer these questions?	We need to begin by looking at the abilities of the newborn and consider both sensory and brain development. There are not a lot of studies on infant tablet usage, so we might have to look for research on television or even see if there are any appropriate animal	studies in this area. One consideration would be infant's visual acuity—are they straining their eyes watching the screen? Finally, we should consider what it means to be digitally dependent and whether early usage promotes this disorder.

CHAPTER 13

Behaviour in a Social Context

CHAPTER ≫   **SOCIAL THINKING AND PERCEPTION**

OUTLINE   **Attribution: Perceiving the Causes of Behaviour**
Forming and Maintaining Impressions
Attitudes and Attitude Change

SOCIAL INFLUENCE
The Mere Presence of Others
Social Norms: The Rules of the Game
Conformity and Obedience
  Research Foundations: The Dilemma of Obedience:
  When Conscience Confronts Malevolent Authority
Crowd Behaviour and Deindividuation
Group Influences on Performance
  and Decision Making

SOCIAL RELATIONS
Affiliation and Interpersonal Attraction
Love
Prejudice and Discrimination
  Applications: Making Close Relationships Work:
  Lessons from Psychological Research
  Focus on Neuroscience: The Neuroscience of
  Stereotyping
Prosocial Behaviour: Helping Others
Aggression: Harming Others
  Frontiers: Do Violent Video Games Promote
  Aggression?

> Without the human community, one single human being cannot survive.
> —The Dalai Lama

At approximately 12:30 P.M. on September 13, 2006, Kimveer Gill parked his car on Boulevard de Maisonneuve in Montreal. He popped the trunk and removed a Beretta semi-automatic carbine, a Glock 9mm handgun and a shotgun. He then proceeded to the entrance of Dawson College and opened fire. As he entered the college, he made his way to the cafeteria, where he reloaded the weapons and began to shoot people at random. Two police officers who had been visiting the school responded immediately and exchanged fire with Gill. He was shot in the arm by one of the officers, and shortly afterwards, he turned his weapon on himself and died at

Peter McCabe/The Canadian Press

What are the issues here?

What do we need to know?

Where can we find the information to answer these questions?

12:48 P.M. In less than 20 minutes, Gill had killed one woman and injured 19 other people, 8 critically. Fortunately, all 19 people recovered. When police searched Gill's home, they found a number of firearm accessories, a letter of apology, and a letter praising the actions of Eric Harris and Dylan Klebold, the Columbine shooters.

Gill's blog at the Goth site vampirefreeks.com contained photos of all his weapons, articles on his various interests, and information suggesting that the shooting was premeditated. Gill's screen name was "fatality 666" and he commented that he would become known as the *Angel of Death*. He liked violent video games and was a fan of *Postal, Blood, 25 to Life,* and *Doom.* It is rumoured that he also liked *Super Columbine Massacre.* In his profile, Gill wrote, "Work sucks . . . School sucks . . . Life sucks . . . What else can I say? Life is like a video game, you gotta die sometime."

To date, there have been over 145 shooting incidents at schools, colleges, and universities in North America. Over 300 people have been killed.

As social beings, we belong. We spend our lives in a stream of social environments that profoundly shape how we behave, think, and feel. In this chapter, we explore the field of social psychology, which studies how we think about and perceive our social world (*social thinking* and *social perception*), how other people influence our behaviour (*social influence*), and how we behave toward other people (*social relations*).

SOCIAL THINKING AND PERCEPTION

Beyond decision making, we spend a great deal of time thinking about our social world. We hold countless attitudes and beliefs, wonder about why people act as they do, and develop impressions of people. Social psychologists have devoted considerable attention to these three aspects of social thinking and perception.

Attribution: Perceiving the Causes of Behaviour

In everyday life, we often make **attributions**, judgments about the causes of our own and other people's behaviour and outcomes (Figure 13.1). Was my A on the mid-term because of hard work and ability, or was it just an easy test? Did Bill criticize Carl because he is a rude person, or was he provoked? Attributions influence our subsequent behaviour and emotions. If I attribute my A to hard work and ability, I will feel greater pride and continue to exert more effort than if I attribute it to an easy test (Weiner, 1985). In the courtroom, jurors' attributions about a

© Bruce Ayres/Getty Images

FIGURE 13.1 "He's been under a lot of stress lately." "He only thinks about himself. What a jerk!" Depending on which attribution she makes for her husband's outburst, this woman may respond with understanding or anger.

defendant's behaviour influence their decisions about guilt versus innocence.

Personal versus Situational Attributions

Fritz Heider, a pioneer of attribution theory, maintained that our attempts to understand why people behave as they do typically involve either personal attributions or situational attributions (Heider, 1958; Stewart et al., 2010). *Personal (internal) attributions* infer that people's behaviour is caused by their characteristics: Bill insulted Carl because Bill is a rude person; my A on an exam reflects my high ability. *Situational (external) attributions* infer that aspects of the situation cause a behaviour: Bill was provoked into insulting Carl; I received an A because the test was easy.

How do we decide whether a behaviour is caused by personal or situational factors? Suppose you ask Kim for advice on whether to take a particular course (say, Art 391) and she tells you that the course is terrible. Is Art 391 really terrible

1. What types of information lead us to form a situational rather than a personal attribution?

2. Describe the fundamental attribution error and the self-serving bias. How do cultural norms affect these attributional tendencies?

(a situational attribution), or did something about Kim (a personal attribution) lead to this response? According to Harold Kelley (1973), three types of information determine the attribution we make: *consistency, distinctiveness,* and *consensus.* First, is Kim's response consistent over time? If you ask Kim again two weeks later and she still says that Art 391 is terrible, then consistency is high. Second, is her response distinctive? If Kim dislikes only Art 391, then distinctiveness is high. If she thinks that most of her courses are terrible, then distinctiveness is low. Finally, how do other people respond? If other students agree with Kim that Art 391 is terrible, then consensus is high. But if they disagree with her, then consensus is low.

As Figure 13.2 illustrates, when consistency, distinctiveness, and consensus are all high, we are likely to make a situational attribution: The course is terrible. But, when consistency is high and the other two factors are low, we make a personal attribution: Perhaps Kim is overly critical or just doesn't like university.

At times, people do respond thoughtfully and take consistency, distinctiveness, and consensus information into account when making attributions. But, at other times, people take mental shortcuts and make snap judgments that bias their attributions (Ross & Nisbett, 1991). Interestingly, Brosch et al. (2013) have shown that when people take situational information into consideration, the dorsolateral prefrontal cortex is involved, indicating more thoughtful top-down processing of the information. Dispositional

attributions are more closely linked to the medial prefrontal cortex (Moran et al., 2014).

Attributional Biases

Social psychology teaches us that the immediate social environment profoundly influences behaviour. Yet we often form negative opinions about the participants in these studies because we tend to make a **fundamental attribution error:** We underestimate the impact of the situation and overestimate the role of personal factors when explaining other people's behaviour (Neuschatz et al., 2008; Ross, 2001).

In a classic experiment, university students read either a favourable or unfavourable speech about Cuban president Fidel Castro, presumably written by a member of a university debating team (Jones & Harris, 1967). They then estimated the writer's attitude toward Castro. Half the students were told that the debate team member freely chose the favourable or unfavourable position. The others were told that the favourable or unfavourable viewpoint had been assigned by the debate coach—it was not the debater's choice. Figure 13.3 shows that when the speech was freely chosen, students logically assumed that the debater had a correspondingly positive or negative attitude about Castro. Yet, when told that the role was assigned, students paid insufficient attention to this situational factor and still perceived that the pro-Castro and anti-Castro debaters had different personal beliefs. Similarly, people make the fundamental

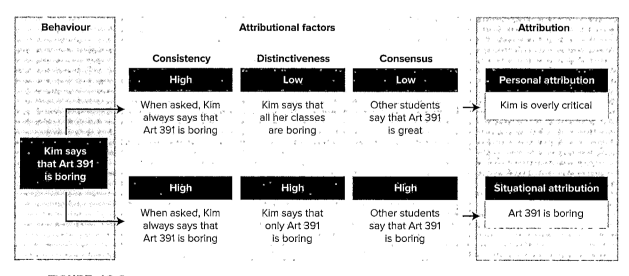

FIGURE 13.2 According to Harold Kelley, consistency, distinctiveness, and consensus information help us determine whether to make personal or situational attributions for someone else's behaviour. Note that in both examples, above, consistency is high. If a person's behaviour has low consistency (suppose that sometimes Kim says Art 391 is boring, and other times she says it's interesting), we typically attribute the behaviour to transient conditions (e.g., changes in Kim's mood) rather than to stable personal or situational factors.

Source: Based on Kelley, H.H. (1973). The process of causal attribution. *American Psychologist, 28,* 107–128.

**Attitude attributed
to speaker**

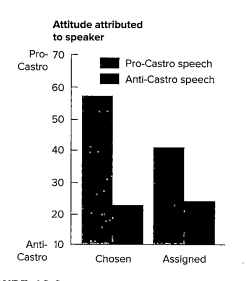

FIGURE 13.3 These data illustrate a fundamental attribution error. When told that a debate coach had assigned a team member to write a pro- or anti-Castro speech, university students still attributed a more anti-Castro attitude to the writer of the anti-Castro speech.

Source: Data from Jones, E.E., & Harris, V.A. (1967). The attribution of attitudes. *Journal of Experimental Social Psychology*, 3, 2–24.

NBC/Courtesy Everett Collection/The Canadian Press

FIGURE 13.4 Unlike Mr. Spock, the logical and emotionless Vulcan from the series *Star Trek*, actor Leonard Nimoy has feelings just like the rest of us. TV and movie fans make the fundamental attribution error when they expect media stars to have the same traits as the characters they play. The title of Nimoy's autobiography, *I Am Not Spock*, emphasizes this point.

attribution error on the basis of actors' professional roles: They expect TV and movie stars to have the same personal traits as the characters they play (Tal-Or & Papirman, 2007). Figure 13.4 illustrates this example.

The fundamental attribution error applies to how we perceive other people's behaviour rather than our own. As comedian George Carlin once noted, the slow driver ahead of us is a "moron," and the fast driver trying to pass us is a "maniac." Yet we do not think of ourselves as a "moron" or a "maniac" when *we* are driving slowly or trying to pass another driver. One reason for this is that we have more information about the present situation when making judgments about ourselves, as when we are driving slowly to follow unfamiliar directions. Second, the perceptual principle of figure-ground relations comes into play. When you watch others behave, they are the "figure" that stands out against the background. But when we behave, we are not "watching" ourselves. We are part of the background, and the situation that we are in stands out. If you watch yourself on a videotape, you now become the figure, and are more likely to make personal attributions about your own behaviour—as if you were observing someone else (Storms, 1973).

Is the fundamental attribution error inevitable? Certainly not. Recall that Eric Harris and Dylan Klebold went on a shooting rampage in 1999 killing 12 of their Columbine High School

schoolmates and a teacher. In the following days, Gallup Polls found that most Americans rated situational factors such as parenting, gun availability, TV and movie violence, and media coverage of past shootings as bearing considerable blame. On one set of questions, only 11 percent made a personal attribution for the shooters' behaviour, such as "mental problems," "bad kids," "anger," or "wanting attention" (Gillespie, 1999; Saad, 1999).

When people have time to reflect on their judgments or are highly motivated to be careful, the fundamental attribution error is reduced (Burger, 1991; Gilbert & Malone, 1995). The Columbine shooting was preceded by a tragic string of similar and highly publicized incidents across the United States. The American public was already highly engaged in this issue and had considerable time to think about the causes of school violence. Similarly, when a 14-year-old boy opened fire at the W.R. Myers High School in Taber, Alberta, one week after Columbine, we were ready to think about the possible situational determinants of such behaviour.

When it comes to explaining our own behaviour, we tend to protect our self-esteem by displaying a **self-serving bias:** making relatively more personal attributions for successes and more situational attributions for failures (Ross & Nisbett, 1991). In one study of athletes' post-game statements, successes tended to be attributed to personal factors, such as "We played great defence and hung in there," whereas losses were more frequently attributed to external causes, such as poor officiating or "Everything they shot was going in" (Lau & Russell, 1980). The strength of the self-serving bias depends on various factors, ranging from one's psychological state to cultural norms. Depressed people, for example, often display the opposite attributional pattern—taking too little credit for successes and too much credit for failures—a pattern that helps to keep them depressed.

Culture and Attribution

Just as culture influences how we perceive the physical world (see Chapter 5), it also affects how we perceive the social world. Consider the fundamental attribution error. Many studies suggest that the tendency to attribute other people's behaviour to personal factors reflects a Westernized emphasis on individualism (Triandis, 2001). In a study by J.G. Miller (1984), participants of varying ages from India and the United States attributed causality for several behaviours. As Figure 13.5 shows, with increasing age, participants from India made more situational attributions and those from the United States made more personal attributions. Similarly, American university students and British schoolchildren make more personal attributions for other people's criminal behaviour than do Korean university students and Nigerian schoolchildren, who come from less individualistic cultures (Na-Eun-Yeong & Loftus, 1998; Pfeffer et al., 1998; Tyson & Hubert, 2002).

Culture also influences attributions for our own behaviour (Singh et al., 1979). Modesty is highly valued in China's collectivistic culture, and Chinese university students take less credit for successful social interactions than do American students, while accepting more responsibility for their failures (Anderson, 1999).

Beyond influencing the types of attributions that we make, our cultural background also seems to affect the way we go about making attributions. Consider that East Asians, in general, tend to hold a more holistic view of the universe than Westerners (Nisbett et al., 2001, 2008). This view, reflected in the belief that all events are interconnected and therefore cannot be understood in isolation, leads East Asians to develop more complex views about the causes of behaviour. Accordingly, Incheol Choi and colleagues (2003) predicted and found that compared with European-American college students, Korean college students scored

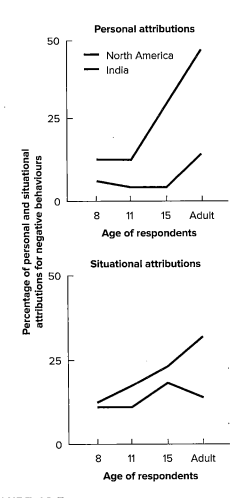

FIGURE 13.5 With increasing age from childhood to adulthood, North Americans show a greater tendency to make personal attributions for other people's behaviours. In contrast, participants from India show an increased tendency to make situational attributions.

Source: Data from J.G. Miller, 1984, Culture and the Development of Everyday Social Explanation, *Journal of Personality and Social Psychology, 46*, 961–978, Table 2. Copyright © 1984 by the American Psychological Association. Reprinted by permission of the author and the publisher.

higher overall on measures of holistic thinking and also took a greater amount of information into account when making causal attributions for other people's behaviour.

Importantly, this relation between holistic thinking and the use of information was also found within each culture. Among the American students and among the Korean students, those who thought more holistically than their peers took more information into account when making attributions (Choi et al., 2003). Thus, the *same underlying psychological principle*—a link between holistic thinking and beliefs about causality—seems to account for information-seeking differences between cultures as well as among individuals within each culture.

Forming and Maintaining Impressions

As social beings, we constantly form impressions of other people, just as they form impressions of us. Attributions play a key role in impression formation: Does a person's behaviour say something about her or him, or is it caused by the situation? Other factors, however, also affect how we form and maintain impressions.

Primacy versus Recency: Are First Impressions More Important?

Try this simple exercise: Tell some people that you know a person who is "intelligent, industrious, impulsive, critical, stubborn, and envious." Tell others that this person is "envious, stubborn, critical, impulsive, industrious, and intelligent." Then ask for their impression of this person. Both groups receive the same information but in reverse order. In a classic experiment, Solomon Asch (1946) found that the person in the first description was perceived more positively—as being more sociable and happier—than the person in the second description. In another experiment, participants read a two-paragraph story about a boy named Jim. One paragraph described Jim as outgoing, the other as introverted. Participants' impression of Jim was influenced more strongly by whichever paragraph they read first (Luchins, 1957a).

When forming impressions, the **primacy effect** refers to our tendency to attach more importance to the initial information that we learn about a person. New information can change our opinion, but it has to "work harder" to overcome that initial impression for two reasons. First, we tend to be most alert to information we receive first. Second, initial information may shape how we perceive subsequent information. Imagine a student and an athlete who, respectively, get off to a great start in class or training camp. The teacher and the coach attribute high ability to these people, but, suppose that as time goes on, performance declines. To maintain their positive initial impression, the teacher and coach need only attribute the performance decline to fatigue, a drop in motivation, or a string of bad breaks.

Primacy is the general rule of thumb in impression formation, especially for people who dislike ambiguity and uncertainty (Kruglanski, 2004). We seem to have a remarkable capacity for forming snap judgments based on small amounts of initial information

(Ambady & Skowronski, 2008), and some evolutionary psychologists propose that evaluating stimuli quickly (such as rapidly distinguishing friend from foe) was adaptive for our survival (Krebs & Denton, 1997). But we are not slaves to primacy. Primacy effects decrease—and *recency effects* (giving greater weight to the most recent information) may occur—when we are asked to avoid making snap judgments, are reminded to carefully consider the evidence, and are made to feel accountable for our judgments (Luchins, 1957b; Webster et al., 1996).

Mental Sets and Schemas: Seeing What We Expect to See

Imagine that we are going to a party and I tell you that the host, George, is a distant, aloof, and cold person. You meet him and try to make pleasant conversation. George doesn't say much in response to your questions, avoids eye contact, and doesn't ask you about your life. A bit later, you say to me, "You were right; he's really a cold fish." Now let's roll back this scene. Suppose that I had described George as nice, but extremely shy. Later, when you try to make conversation, he doesn't say much, avoids eye contact, and doesn't ask you about your life. You say to me, "You were right; he's really shy." Same behaviour, different impression. This example reminds us of a key perceptual principle highlighted in Chapter 5. Whether perceiving objects or people, the same stimulus can be "seen" in different ways. Our mental *set*, which is a readiness to perceive the world in a particular way, powerfully shapes how we interpret a stimulus (see Figure 5.2).

What creates our mental sets? One important factor that we have encountered throughout the book is *schemas*, mental frameworks that help us organize and interpret information. By telling you that our host is "cold," "shy," or "distracted," I activate a set of concepts and expectations (your schema) for how such a person is likely to behave. Although the host's behaviour can be interpreted in multiple ways, you "fit" his behaviour into the particular schema that is already activated.

A **stereotype**, which is a generalized belief about a group or category of people, represents a powerful type of schema. In one experiment, participants watched a videotape of a nine-year-old girl named Hannah and were asked to judge her academic potential. Half of the participants were told that Hannah came from an upper-middle-class environment and that her parents had white-collar careers. Other participants were told that Hannah came from a poor neighbourhood and that her parents were blue-collar

3. Why do primacy effects occur in impression formation? How can they be reduced?

4. How do mental sets shape the way we perceive people? How do stereotypes create mental sets?

workers. On the videotape, Hannah performed at an average level, answering some difficult questions and missing some others. Although all participants saw the same performance, those who thought Hannah came from an affluent setting rated her higher in ability than did those who thought she came from a disadvantaged background (Darley & Gross, 1983). In a real sense, participants' stereotypes about blue-collar and white-collar workers created a mental set that biased their perception of Hannah's subsequent behaviour.

Self-Fulfilling Prophecies: Creating What We Expect to See

5. Explain how our incorrect expectations can become self-fulfilling.

Seeing what we expect to see is only one way we confirm our initial expectations and impressions. A **self-fulfilling prophecy** occurs usually without conscious awareness, when people's erroneous expectations lead them to act toward others in a way that brings about the expected behaviours, thereby confirming the original impression. Returning to our "party" example, if you expect the host to be cold and aloof, your behaviour toward him may change in subtle ways. You make conversation, but perhaps you smile less, stand farther away, or give up a little earlier than you would have if I had told you that George was a great guy. His reserved response, in part, could be a reaction to *your* behaviour (Figure 13.6).

Self-fulfilling prophecies have since been demonstrated in hundreds of studies across different countries and settings, including schools, business organizations, the military, sports, and dating and marital relationships (Madon et al., 2006; Shapiro et al., 2007). In interacting with others, our initial, unfounded expectations can influence how we behave toward them, thereby shaping their behaviour in a way that ultimately confirms our expectations.

Attitudes and Attitude Change

In 1935, Gordon Allport called attitude "social psychology's most indispensable concept" (p. 798). Our attitudes help to define our identity, guide our actions, and influence how we judge people (Maio & Olson, 2000). Indeed, attitudes help to steer the course of world events, from political elections, to war, to the latest fashion craze.

An **attitude** is a positive or negative evaluative reaction toward a stimulus, such as a person, action, object, or concept (Crano & Prislin, 2006; Gawronski, 2007). Whether disagreeing with a governmental policy or agreeing with a movie review, you are expressing evaluative reactions. Sometimes, as shown in Figure 13.7, our attitudes are supported by an extensive personal belief and value system.

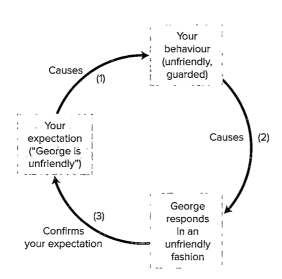

FIGURE 13.6 The self-fulfilling prophecy begins when a false expectation that we have about someone else influences how we treat that person. Next, influenced by our behaviour, the person responds in a particular way. Finally, we interpret the person's behaviour as evidence that our expectation was correct all along—unaware of the role that we played in shaping the person's behaviour.

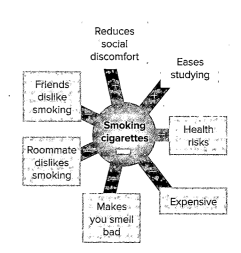

FIGURE 13.7 The components of a person's attitude toward smoking. Around the attitude object (smoking cigarettes) are beliefs related to smoking. The plus and minus signs show the positive or negative value the person associates with each belief. The minus sign in the centre indicates the resulting overall negative attitude toward smoking cigarettes.

Source: Adapted from Sears, D.O., & Kinder, D.R. (1985). Whites' opposition to busing: On conceptualizing and operationalizing group conflict. *Journal of Personality and Social Psychology*, 48, 1141–1147.

Do Our Attitudes Influence Our Behaviour?

If we tell you that, according to research, people's attitudes strongly guide their behaviour, you might reply, "So what? That's just common sense." But consider a classic study by Richard LaPiere (1934). In the 1930s, he toured the United States with a young Chinese couple, stopping at 251 restaurants, hotels, and other establishments. At the time, prejudice against Asians was widespread, yet the couple—who often entered the establishment before LaPiere did—was refused service only once. Later, LaPiere wrote to all the places they had visited, asking if they would provide service to Chinese patrons. More than 90 percent of those who responded stated they would not. In a similar study, Page (1999) reported that landlords in Windsor and London, Ontario, were less likely to want to rent to a potential tenant if that person identified himself or herself on the phone as an individual with AIDS.

In LaPiere's study, we cannot be sure that the people who expressed negative attitudes in the survey were the same individuals who, months earlier, had actually served the Chinese couple. Yet the discrepancy between stated prejudicial attitudes and nondiscriminatory behaviour seemed so overwhelming that it called into question the "common-sense" assumption of attitude-behaviour consistency. Decades of better-controlled research, however, indicate that attitudes do predict behaviour (Hunecke et al., 2010). Three factors help to explain why the attitude-behaviour relationship is strong in some cases but weak in others.

First, attitudes influence behaviour more strongly when counteracting situational factors are weak. Financial incentives, conformity and obedience pressures, deindividuation, groupthink, and other conditions may lead people to behave in ways that are at odds with their inner convictions. According to the **theory of planned behaviour** and similar models (Ajzen, 1991, 2015; Fishbein, 1980), our intention to engage in a behaviour is strongest when we have a positive attitude toward that behaviour, when *subjective norms* (our perceptions of what other people think we should do) support our attitudes, and when we believe that the behaviour is under our control. Based on this approach, researchers have successfully predicted numerous behaviours, including whether people will undergo breast cancer screenings,

seek HPV vaccination, become smokers, use condoms, attend church, donate blood, and seek out therapy (Armitage, 2005; Blanchard et al., 2002; Courneya et al., 1999; Elliot et al., 2007; Fisher et al., 2013; Rutter, 2000; Sieverding et al., 2010; Yardley & Donovan-Hall, 2007). Attitudes are even a strong predictor of your desire to avoid physical exercise and remain a couch potato (Prapavesis & DeJesus, 2015). But if situational factors are strong, we may defer. For example, Aschemann-Witzel et al. (2014) followed a group of young Danish shoppers who held positive attitudes towards organic foods. If the price was very high, they avoided buying organic.

Second, *attitudes have a greater influence on behaviour when we are aware of them and when they are strongly held.* Sometimes we seem to act "without thinking," out of impulse or habit. Attitude-behaviour consistency increases when people consciously think about their attitudes before acting (Powell & Fazio, 1984; White et al., 2002). In addition, attitudes are stronger and more predictive of behaviour when they are formed through direct personal experience, rather than through second-hand, indirect information (Millar & Millar, 1996).

Third, *general attitudes are better at predicting general classes of behaviour, and specific attitudes are better at predicting specific behaviours.* For example, Martin Fishbein and Icek Ajzen (1974) found almost no relation between people's general attitudes toward religion and 70 specific religious behaviours (such as the frequency of praying before meals or attending services). However, when they combined the 70 specific behaviours into a single "global index" of religious behaviour, the relation between general religious attitudes and overall religious behaviour was substantial. Similarly, Zanna, Olson, and Fazio (1980) found a general composite index of over 90 separate religious behaviours (referred to as a *multiple-act behavioural criterion*) was reasonably correlated with general attitudes ($r = 0.54$), whereas the correlation with specific behaviours was quite low ($r = 0.09$ to 0.38).

Does Our Behaviour Influence Our Attitudes?

As we have just seen, under the proper conditions, people's attitudes guide their behaviour. But attitude-behaviour consistency is not a one-way street: We also may come to develop attitudes that are consistent with the way we

6. Why did LaPiere's study raise doubts about attitude-behaviour consistency?

7. Discuss three broad conditions under which attitudes best predict behaviour.

behave (McKimmie et al., 2009). Why should this be?

Self-justification. Imagine that you volunteer for an experiment, arrive at the laboratory, and perform two extremely boring tasks, emptying and filling a tray with spools over and over, and repeatedly turning 48 pegs stuck into holes. After 60 minutes of the laboratory equivalent of being bitten to death by ducks, the experimenter enters, thanks you for participating, and asks for your help. You are told that it is important for the next student to begin the study with a "positive attitude" about the tasks and that all you have to do is tell the student that the boring tasks are interesting. Depending on the condition to which you have been randomly assigned, the experimenter offers to pay you either $1 or $20 for, essentially, lying to the next participant. To help out, you agree to do so. Afterwards, you go to the psychology department's main office to collect your money and fill out a "routine form" that asks how much you enjoyed the tasks in the experiment.

Make a prediction: Comparing participants who received $1 and those who received $20 with a control group that simply rated the boring tasks without telling any lie beforehand, which of the three groups rated the task most positively? Why?

Common sense might suggest that participants paid $20 would feel happiest about the experiment and rate the task most highly. However, as Figure 13.8 shows, and as Leon Festinger and J. Merrill Carlsmith (1959) predicted, participants who were paid $1 gave the most positive ratings. Indeed, they actually rated the boring tasks as slightly enjoyable!

According to Festinger's (1957) **theory of cognitive dissonance,** people strive for consistency in their cognitions. When two or more cognitions contradict one another (such as "I am a truthful person" and "I just told another student that those boring tasks were interesting"), the person experiences an uncomfortable state of tension that Festinger calls *cognitive dissonance,* and becomes motivated to reduce this dissonance.

The theory predicts that, to reduce dissonance and restore a state of cognitive consistency, people will change one of their cognitions or add new cognitions. Participants who received $20 could justify their behaviour by adding a new cognition "Who wouldn't tell

8. What causes cognitive dissonance, and how can it produce attitude change?

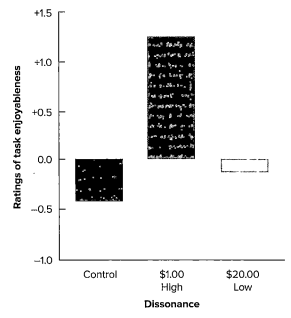

FIGURE 13.8 Participants lied to a fellow student by saying that a boring task was interesting. Those offered $1 to lie later rated the task most positively. Presumably, they reduced their cognitive dissonance about lying by convincing themselves that the task was interesting after all. Participants offered $20 had an external justification to lie, experienced little dissonance, and therefore did not need to convince themselves that the task was enjoyable. They and control participants who had not lied rated the task less favourably than did the $1 group.

Source: Based on Festinger, L., & Carlsmith, J.M. (1959). Cognitive consequences of forced compliance. *Journal of Abnormal and Social Psychology,* 58, 203–210.

a little lie for $20?"—and there was little reason for them to change their attitude toward the boring tasks. Those who had lied for only $1 could not use this trivial monetary gain to justify their behaviour. But, if they could convince themselves that the tasks were actually enjoyable, then they wouldn't have lied after all! In short, they changed their attitude about the task to bring it more into line with how they had behaved.

Behaviour that is inconsistent with our attitude is called *counterattitudinal* behaviour, and it produces dissonance only if we perceive that our actions were freely chosen rather than coerced. Dissonance is maximized when the behaviour threatens our sense of self-worth or produces negative consequences that were foreseeable (Stone & Cooper, 2001; Petty & Wegener, 1998). For example, Powers & Jack (2013) argue that returning merchandise to stores is the result of dissonance induced by the negative consequence of purchasing a less than desirable product.

Dissonance, however, does not always lead to attitude change. People can reduce dissonance by rationalizing that their attitude or their behaviour wasn't important, by finding external justification, or by making other excuses (Buunk & Dijkstra, 2001; Gosling et al., 2006; McKimmie et al., 2009). In surveys of over 3300 Scandinavian adolescents and adults, people who drank alcohol despite having negative attitudes toward drinking often emphasized that "Other people drink more than I do." As researcher Klaus Mäkelä (1997) noted, the general rationalization seemed to be "I may not be perfect, but other people are still worse."

Despite the many ways to reduce dissonance, the theory has successfully inspired researchers to change people's attitudes by inducing them to engage in counterattitudinal behaviours. For example, university students who agree to write essays advocating positions opposite to their own (such as supporting a tuition increase) often shift their attitudes in the direction of the essay they have produced (Croyle & Cooper, 1983; Stalder & Baron, 1998). Mediators in labour disputes occasionally use this principle by asking company executives and labour leaders to switch roles for a time and present each other's arguments.

Self-perception. If we observe someone campaigning for a political candidate, we likely will assume that this person has a positive attitude toward the candidate. If we see someone exerting great effort to achieve a goal, we will judge, logically, that the goal is important to that person. In short, we infer what other people's attitudes "must be" by watching how they behave. According to Daryl Bem's (1972) **self-perception theory,** we make inferences about our own attitudes in much the same way: by observing how *we* behave. Knowing that, for very little external justification ($1), you have told a fellow student that the boring experimental tasks are enjoyable, you logically conclude that "deep down" you *must* feel that the tasks were at least somewhat enjoyable. In Bem's view, your attitude is not produced by a mysterious concept called *cognitive dissonance.* Rather, you simply observe how you have acted, and infer how you *must* have felt to have behaved in this fashion.

Self-perception theory and cognitive dissonance theory both predict that counterattitudinal behaviour will produce attitude change. One key difference, however, is that dissonance theory assumes that we experience heightened physiological arousal (tension produced by dissonance) when we engage in counterattitudinal behaviour. Do we? At least in some instances, it appears that this does happen (Harmon-Jones et al., 1996).

Moreover, if unpleasant arousal motivates attitude change, then factors that reduce arousal should reduce attitude change. When research participants experience arousal from dissonance-producing behaviours but are led to believe that their arousal is a side effect caused by a pill (which in reality is a placebo), they do not change their attitudes to be more in line with their behaviour (Cooper, 1998; Zanna & Cooper, 1974). The pill gives participants an external justification (albeit a false one) for their arousal.

In general, dissonance theory better explains why people change their views after behaving in ways that openly contradict their clearly defined attitudes, particularly when such behaviours threaten their self-images. However, in situations in which counterattitudinal behaviour does not threaten one's self-worth and we have weak attitudes to begin with, such behaviour is less likely to create significant arousal—yet people still may alter their attitudes to be more consistent with the way they have behaved. In this case, self-perception theory may provide the better explanation. Thus, both dissonance theory and self-perception theory appear to be correct but under different circumstances (Fazio et al., 1977; Tesser & Shaffer, 1990). Both theories, however, agree that *our behaviours can influence our attitudes.*

Persuasion

Whether through political speeches, advertisements, or discussions with family and friends, persuasion is a fact of everyday life (Maio & Olson, 2000). Persuasion involves a *communicator* who delivers a *message* through a *channel* (e.g., in writing, verbally, or visually) to an *audience* within a surrounding *context* (e.g., a cultural setting; Petty & Cacioppo, 1986). Here, we briefly examine three components that have been studied extensively.

The communicator. Communicator credibility—how believable the communicator is—often

9. According to self-perception theory, why does counterattitudinal behaviour produce attitude change?

10. What evidence supports dissonance theory? What evidence favours self-perception theory?

11. Identify communicator and message characteristics that increase persuasiveness.

12. Describe the central and peripheral routes to persuasion. For whom is the central route more likely to be effective?

is the key to effective persuasion. In fact, audience members who do not enjoy thinking deeply about issues may pay little attention to the content of a message and simply go along with the opinions of a highly credible source (Chaiken & Maheswaran, 1994). Credibility has two major components: *expertise* and *trustworthiness* (Schul et al., 2004; Tobin & Raymundo, 2009). The most effective persuader is one who appears both to be an expert and to be presenting the truth in an unbiased manner (Hovland et al., 1953), as well as one who advocates a point of view contrary to his or her own self-interest (Petty et al., 2001). Perceived expertise may be particularly important when the issue is complex (Cooper et al., 1996; Cooper & Neuhaus, 2000).

Communicators who are physically attractive, likable, and similar to us (such as in interests or goals) also may persuade us more effectively, which is why advertisers spend millions of dollars hiring likable, attractive stars to promote their products (Messner et al., 2008).

The message. In trying to persuade someone, is it more effective to present only your side of the issue or to also present the opposition's arguments and then refute them? A meta-analysis indicates that, overall, the *two-sided refutational approach* is more effective (Allen, 1991). Especially when an audience initially disagrees with a message or is aware that there are two sides to the issue, the audience will perceive a two-sided message as less biased.

In stating your position to an audience that disagrees with you, should you "go for broke" and present extreme arguments, hoping that the audience will compromise by moving toward your position? Or should you present a position that is only moderately discrepant with their viewpoint? A highly credible communicator can afford to present a more discrepant viewpoint than a low-credibility communicator (Aronson et al., 1963), but in general, a *moderate degree of discrepancy* is more effective (Bochner & Insko, 1966).

Messages that attempt to persuade by arousing fear can be effective under certain conditions (Wood, 2000). Overall, fear arousal works best when the message evokes *moderate fear* and provides people with effective, feasible (i.e., low-cost) ways to reduce the threat (Johnson, 1991; Witte & Allen, 2000). If the message is too frightening, people may reduce their anxiety by simply denying the message or the communicator's credibility.

The audience. A message loaded with logical arguments and facts may prove highly persuasive to some people yet fall flat on its face with others. According to Richard Petty and John Cacioppo (1986), there are two basic routes to persuasion. The **central route to persuasion** occurs when people think carefully about the message and are influenced because they find the arguments compelling. The **peripheral route to persuasion** occurs when people do not scrutinize the message but are influenced mostly by other factors, such as a speaker's attractiveness or a message's emotional appeal. Attitude change that results from the central route tends to have a deeper foundation, lasts longer, and predicts future behaviour more successfully.

Under what conditions will we follow the central route? Petty and Cacioppo (1986) suggest that we tend to process a message more closely when it is personally relevant: when it actually will affect us in some way. Typically, high personal relevance or high involvement with an issue will result in central processing. But this is not always the case. One reason is that people differ in their *need for cognition.* Some enjoy analyzing issues; others prefer not to spend much mental effort (Cacioppo et al., 1983, 1996). People who have a high need for cognition tend to follow the central route to persuasion. In forming attitudes about consumer products, for example, they are influenced by information about product characteristics (Wood & Swait, 2002). In contrast, people with a low need for cognition are more strongly influenced by peripheral cues, such as the attractiveness of the person who endorses the product (Haugtvedt et al., 1992).

Sorrentino and his colleagues at the University of Western Ontario (e.g., Sorrentino et al., 2005) have reported also that people differ in their approach to new information. Those who are uncertainty-oriented look for information, particularly in situations that are new and unpredictable. In contrast, certainty-oriented individuals avoid such situations, particularly when the information is self-relevant. Thus, uncertainty-oriented people follow the central route when issues are personally relevant, but those who are certainty-oriented do not. In fact, they are more likely to rely on peripheral information when the information is self-relevant and are more influenced by factors such as speaker attractiveness or expertise.

⟨🔍⟩ **Review**

- Consistency, distinctiveness, and consensus information jointly influence whether we make a personal or situational attribution for a particular act.

- The fundamental attribution error is the tendency to attribute other people's behaviour to personal factors while underestimating the role of situational factors. The self-serving bias is the tendency to attribute one's successes to personal factors and one's failures to situational factors.

- Although our impressions of people may change over time, our first impression generally carries extra weight. Stereotypes and schemas create mental sets that powerfully shape our impressions.

- Through self-fulfilling prophecies, our initially false expectations shape the way we act toward someone. In turn, this person responds to our behaviour in a way that confirms our initially false belief.

- Attitudes are evaluative judgments. They predict behaviour best when situational influences are weak, when the attitude is strong, and when we consciously think about our attitude.

- Our behaviour also influences our attitudes. Counterattitudinal behaviour is most likely to create cognitive dissonance when the behaviour is freely chosen and has negative implications for our sense of self-worth or produces foreseeable negative consequences.

- To reduce dissonance, we may change our attitude to become more consistent with how we have behaved. In situations where our attitudes are weak and counterattitudinal behaviour doesn't threaten our self-worth, we may change our attitudes through self-perception.

- Communicator, message, and audience characteristics influence the effectiveness of persuasion. Communicator credibility is highest when the communicator is perceived as expert and trustworthy. Fear-arousing communications may be effective if they arouse moderate to strong fear and suggest how to avoid the feared result. The central route to persuasion works best with listeners who have a high need for cognition; for those with a low cognition need, the peripheral route works better.

SOCIAL INFLUENCE

Patricia, a novice piano player, makes more mistakes after her parents enter the room to listen to her practise. Shawn donates money to a charity after seeing his co-workers contribute. Jenna, a university student, picks up the slack on a class project because other members of her group are not pulling their weight. These diverse situations share one basic ingredient: They all involve social influence.

The Mere Presence of Others

Norman Triplett (1898) helped to launch the field of social psychology by testing a deceptively simple hypothesis: The presence of others energizes performance. Triplett, who loved bicycle racing, analyzed the records of numerous competitions. In some races, cyclists performed individually against the clock; in other races of similar distance, they performed together in a "pack." As Triplett predicted, cyclists' average speed per mile was much faster in group races than in individual races. Next, in a laboratory experiment, Triplett had children perform a simple physical task as rapidly as they could, either alone or in the presence of another child (called a *coactor*) who independently performed the same task. Again,

performance improved when people were in each other's presence (Triplett, 1898).

Many early studies replicated this finding; the *mere presence* of coactors or a passive, silent audience enhanced performance. Even ants carried more dirt when in the presence of other ants (Chen, 1937). Yet, other experiments found that performance on learning tasks worsened when coactors or an audience were present.

In 1965, Robert Zajonc proposed a theory to explain this seeming paradox. First, the mere physical presence of another person (or member of the same species) increases our arousal. Second, as arousal increases, we become more likely to perform whatever behaviour happens to be our *dominant response* (i.e., our most typical response) to that specific situation. When a task is difficult and complex, and we are first trying to learn it, our dominant response is to make errors. Therefore, performing in front of an audience or with coactors should impair performance. But when a task either is simple or is complex but well learned, our dominant response usually is to perform the task correctly. In these situations, performing in the presence of others enhances performance (Figure 13.9). This phenomenon is called **social facilitation,** an increased tendency to perform one's dominant response in the mere presence of others (Blascovich et al., 1999).

13. Under what conditions does the mere presence of other people enhance or impair performance? Why?

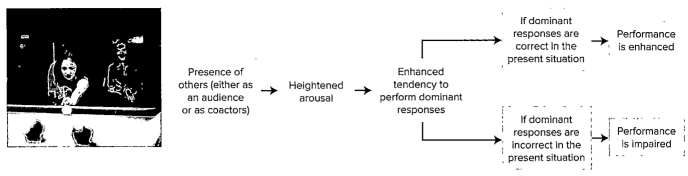

© PhotoAlto/SuperStock

FIGURE 13.9 Social facilitation of dominant responses. Whether this pool player's performance improves or worsens when other people are watching depends on whether she is highly skilled or a novice (Michaels et al., 1982). Zajonc's (1965) theory of social facilitation proposes that the presence of other people increases our arousal, which then makes us more likely to perform our dominant responses. If a dominant response (e.g., stroking the pool cue in a particular way) happens to be correct—as typically occurs on simple tasks or complex tasks that have been mastered—then performance will be enhanced. But if a dominant response is incorrect—as often occurs when a novice is trying to learn a complex task—then the presence of other people most likely will impair performance.

Social facilitation occurs in species ranging from cockroaches and fruit flies to rats and hens (Duncan et al., 1998; Thomas et al., 2002). Meta-analyzing the results of 241 studies involving almost 24 000 participants, Charles Bond and Linda Titus (1983) found that social facilitation produced small but reliable effects on human performance. In one study, James Michaels and his colleagues (1982) identified pairs of pool players who had either above average or below average skill. Then four observers (researchers) sauntered over to the pool tables at the student union building to watch the players. As predicted, the presence of an audience improved the performance of the accomplished players (whose dominant responses were assumed to be correct) but worsened the performance of the less skilled players (whose dominant responses were assumed to be incorrect). Social facilitation may be the most basic of all social influence processes, and it has an important practical implication: When learning complex tasks, minimize the presence of other people.

Social Norms: The Rules of the Game

Years ago, a professor we knew gave his class an unusual assignment: Without doing anything illegal, students were to violate some "unspoken rule" of social behaviour and observe people's reactions. One student licked her plate clean at a formal dinner, receiving cold stares from other guests. Another boarded a city bus, sat down next to the only other passenger, and said "Hi." The passenger sat up stiffly and stared out the window. The assignment ended when a third student entered class—attired only in a thin coat of oil.

Social norms are shared expectations about how people should think, feel, and behave,

and they are the cement that binds social systems together (Morris et al., 2001; Schaller & Crandall, 2004). Some norms are formal laws and regulations, but many are implicit and unspoken. As the "break-a-norm" examples illustrate, such norms often regulate daily behaviour without our conscious awareness; we take them for granted—until they are violated.

A **social role** consists of a set of norms that characterizes how people in a given social position ought to behave. The roles of "university student," "professor," "police officer," and "spouse" carry different sets of behaviour expectations. Because we may wear many hats in our daily life, *role conflict* can occur when the norms accompanying different roles clash. University students who hold jobs or have children often experience role conflict as they try to juggle the competing demands of school, work, and parenthood.

Norms and roles can influence behaviour so strongly that they compel a person to act uncharacteristically. In a classic study by Phil Zimbardo (Zimbardo et al., 1973), students at Stanford University were recruited to participate in a two-week-long simulation of prison life. Half were assigned the role of guards and half the role of prisoners. Guards wore uniforms and mirrored glasses, and the prisoners were housed in cells in the basement of the psychology building. Within six days the simulation had to be stopped because the guards became so brutal in their treatment of the prisoners that the experimenters became worried about the prisoners' well-being. Prisoners were awakened in the middle of the night for roll call, forced to do push-ups with a guard's foot holding them down, made to clean toilets with their hands, and so on. The guards in the Stanford Prison Study were well-adjusted students, yet norms related to the role of "guard" and to

14. How do norms and roles guide our behaviour?

concepts of "crime and punishment" seemed to override their values, leading to dehumanizing treatment of the prisoners.

Culture and Norm Formation

Social norms lose invisibility not only when they are violated, but also when we examine behaviour across cultures and historical periods. In doing so, we see that social customs we take for granted as "normal"—from gender roles to sexual practices and views of love and marriage—are merely arbitrary (Figure 13.10). Norms regulate even such subtle aspects of social behaviour as the amount of *personal space* that we prefer when interacting with people (Li, 2001; Li & Li, 2007). For example, Japanese sit farther apart when conversing than Venezuelans do, and Americans prefer an intermediate distance (Sussman & Rosenfeld, 1982). Italians and Greeks are more likely to touch while interacting than are Europeans from more northern regions (Remland et al., 1995).

Indeed, it is difficult to imagine any society, organization, or social group functioning well without norms. In a classic experiment, Muzafer Sherif (1935) found that even randomly created groups develop norms. The task involved an optical illusion called the *autokinetic effect:* When people stare at a dot of light projected onto a screen in a dark room, they begin to perceive the dot as moving, even though it really is stationary. When Sherif tested university students individually over several trials, each student perceived the light moving a different amount, from a few centimetres to almost 30 centimetres.

Later, the students were randomly placed into groups of three and made further judgments. As the members within each group heard one another's

judgments over several sessions, their judgments converged and a group norm evolved. The participants did not explicitly communicate or "decide" to develop a group norm; it just happened. Moreover, just as norms vary across cultures, the norm that evolved for how far the dot of light moved varied from group to group, and it was not the simple average of the original judgments (Figure 13.11). When participants were retested *individually* a year later, their judgments continued to reflect their group's norm (Rohrer et al., 1954).

Sherif's finding has been replicated in other countries and with different types of tasks (Khoury, 1985). Whether at a cultural level or in small random groups, humans placed together seem to develop common standards for behaviour and judgment. Indeed, Bennett and Sekaquaptewa (2014) were able to induce a norm of embracing diversity that lasted throughout the year simply by having a faculty member talk about egalitarian social norms at the beginning of the term. Ridout and Campbell (2014) were also able to reduce alcohol use in a sample of university students by promoting safer levels of consumption via Facebook.

Conformity and Obedience

Norms can influence behaviour only if people conform to them. Without *conformity*—the adjustment of individual behaviours, attitudes, and beliefs to a group standard—we would have social chaos. It is no accident, therefore, that all social systems exert overt and subtle pressures on their members to conform.

FIGURE 13.10 The evolution of norms across time and cultures. The Academy Award–winning movie *Million Dollar Baby* portrayed an aspiring professional female boxer—an activity that women would be barred from in many countries and women were barred from decades ago in the United States.

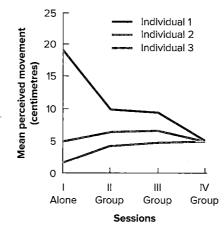

FIGURE 13.11 In Sherif's experiments, individuals' autokinetic judgments made alone (session I) began to converge when they were made in the presence of two other participants (sessions II, III, IV). Each mean is based on 100 judgments per session. These data are from one of the three-person groups.

Source: Based on Sherif, M. (1935). A study of some social factors in perception. *Archives of Psychology* (No. 187).

"Well, heck! If all you smart cookies agree,
who am I to dissent?"

FIGURE 13.12 Often we conform to a majority
because we believe that their opinion "must be right."

15. Explain
the difference
between
informational
and normative
social influence.

Why Do People Conform?

Psychologically, our desire to understand the
world and respond to it effectively provides one
basic motive for conforming (Biener & Boudreau,
1991). As Figure 13.12 illustrates, at times we follow the opinions or behaviour of other people
because we believe they have accurate knowledge
and what they are doing is "right." This is called
informational social influence. We also may
conform to obtain rewards that come from being
accepted by other people, while at the same time
avoiding their rejection. This is called **normative
social influence** (Deutsch & Gerard, 1955).

Solomon Asch's (1951, 1956) landmark conformity experiments illustrated both types of
influence. In the experimental condition, groups
of university students performed several trials
of a simple visual task, shown in Figure 13.13.
Only one member of the group, however, actually was a participant. The rest were accomplices
(called *confederates*) of the experimenter. Group
members sat around a table and were called on
in order. The real participant sat next to last.
According to plan, every confederate intentionally gave the same wrong answer on some trials.
Imagine, for example, that the first member says
"Line 1." (You think to yourself, "Huh?"). Then the
next four members also say "Line 1." (You wonder, "Can this really be?"). Now it is your turn.

Would anybody conform to the group's incorrect judgments? Asch found that a quarter of the
participants never conformed, a quarter conformed frequently, and the rest conformed once
or a few times. Overall, participants conformed
37 percent of the time, compared with a mere 1
percent error rate in a control condition in which
people judged the lines by themselves. This conformity rate stunned many scientists since the
task was very easy and the confederates did not
overtly pressure participants to conform.

16. Identify
some situational
factors that
influence
people's degree
of conformity.

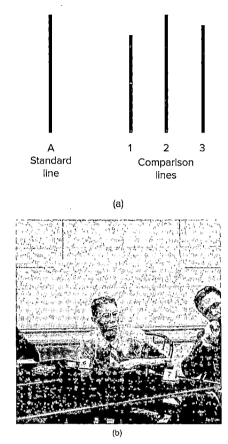

FIGURE 13.13 (a) In Asch's (1956) conformity experiments, students were asked to judge which of three
comparison lines was the same length as the standard
line. They performed this task for 18 trials, using a different set of standard and comparison lines each time.
(b) Upon hearing other group members unanimously
say that "Line 1" is the correct match, the participant
wonders whether his own judgment (Line 2) is correct.

During debriefing discussions with the experimenter after the task was over, many participants
said they were puzzled by the difference between
their own and the group's perceptions. Some
felt that the group was wrong but went along to
avoid "making waves" and possible rejection. This
behaviour reflects normative social influence.
After several trials, other participants succumbed
to informational social influence and began to
doubt their eyesight and judgment.

Factors That Affect Conformity

Asch demonstrated that complex social behaviour could be studied scientifically under controlled conditions. In subsequent experiments
he manipulated different independent variables
and measured their effects on conformity. Consider two examples:

- *Group size.* Conformity increased from about 5 to 35 percent as group size increased from one to four or five confederates, but, contrary to common sense, further increases in group size did not increase conformity. Participants were just as likely to conform when there were four or five confederates giving incorrect answers as when there were 10 or 15.

- *Presence of a dissenter.* When one confederate (according to plan) disagreed with the others, this greatly reduced real participants' conformity. Even when the dissenter gave an incorrect answer (e.g., the majority said "Line 3" and the dissenter said "Line 1"), participants made many fewer errors. The key is that, when someone else dissents, this person serves as a model for remaining independent from the group.

Would Asch's participants have conformed less if the task had been made more important to them, say, by offering a financial incentive for giving correct answers? As Figure 13.14 shows, when the correct answer is obvious (the task is easy, as was Asch's), conformity decreases when the consequences of going along with the group's erroneous judgment are made more costly (Baron et al., 1996). But, when we are less sure of the right way to behave (the task is hard), conformity increases as the stakes become higher.

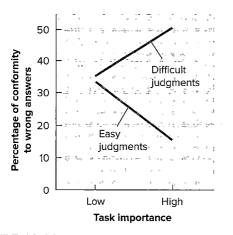

FIGURE 13.14 In this experiment, university students made a series of eyewitness memory judgments. For each judgment, one participant and two accomplices were shown a slide of a person. Next, they had to pick out that person from a second slide showing four people. The second slide was presented for five seconds (easy task) or half a second (hard task), and the accomplices intentionally gave wrong answers on some trials. Participants were told that the task was important (including a possible $20 prize for high accuracy) or unimportant. The high incentive decreased conformity on the easy task, but increased conformity when the task was difficult.

Source: Based on Baron, R.S., Vandello, J.A., & Brunsman, B. (1996). The forgotten variable in conformity research: Impact of task importance on social influence. *Journal of Personality and Social Psychology, 71,* 915–927.

Around the globe, conformity in face-to-face situations tends to be greater among research participants from collectivist cultures, in which group harmony is valued more highly than in individualistic cultures. Overall, gender differences in conformity have been weak or non-existent (Bond & Smith, 1996; Cinnirella & Green, 2007).

Minority Influence

Although majority influence is powerful, in some cases a minority of the group's members may influence the majority's behaviour (Clark, 2001). Serge Moscovici (1985) proposes that, to maximize its influence, the minority must be highly committed to its point of view, remain independent in the face of majority pressure, and be consistent over time, yet appear to keep an open mind. Dissenting information presented by the minority may cause majority members to change their view, at least on a private level (Butera & Levine, 2009; Maass & Clark, 1984). In reviewing almost a hundred studies, Wendy Wood and her colleagues (1994) found that minority influence is strongest when it maintains a highly consistent position over time. However, if the minority appears too unreasonable, deviant, or negative, it may cause the majority to become entrenched or lead some people to shift their attitudes even further away from the minority's position.

Obedience to Authority

Like conformity to a group, obedience to an authority figure is inherently neither good nor bad. As an airplane passenger, you would not be amused if the co-pilot disregarded the pilot's commands simply because he or she "didn't feel like obeying," putting the flight and your life at risk. Without obedience, society would face chaos.

But obedience can also produce tragic results. After World War II, the famous Nuremberg trials were held to judge Nazi war criminals who had slaughtered millions of innocent people in concentration camps. In many instances, the defence offered by the defendants was that they had "only followed orders." In the massacre of men, women, and children at My Lai during the Vietnam War, American soldiers accused of atrocities gave the same explanation. No doubt we will hear the cry "I was just following orders" again as accountability is judged for more recent mass atrocities in Kosovo, Rwanda, and elsewhere around the globe.

Just as the Nuremberg court did, many of us reject justifications based on obedience to authority as mere rationalizations, secure in our conviction that we would behave more humanely in such situations. But would we? Let's consider the answers provided by Stanley Milgram in this chapter's *Research Foundations* feature.

17. Under what conditions is the minority most likely to influence the majority?

18. Describe Milgram's obedience experiment. Do you believe the results would be similar today? Why or why not?

Research Foundations

THE DILEMMA OF OBEDIENCE: WHEN CONSCIENCE CONFRONTS MALEVOLENT AUTHORITY

Introduction

Stanley Milgram wanted to examine conformity in a more powerful situation than Asch had. Rather than have participants judge lines, Milgram thought about testing whether people would conform to group pressure and give electric shocks to a protesting victim. But he realized that a control condition was needed to measure how much shock people would give without group pressure. Here the experimenter would instruct each participant to give the shocks. As he thought about it, Milgram wondered: Would ordinary citizens obey such malevolent orders? How far would they go? At that moment, Milgram shifted his focus from conformity to obedience. Fuelled by his desire to better understand the horrors and lessons of the Holocaust, Milgram conducted 18 obedience experiments between 1960 and 1963 (Milgram, 1974).

Method

The following experiment was conducted twice, first with 40 men and then with 40 women. Participants ranged in age from 20 to 50 years and represented a cross-section of occupations and educational backgrounds.

In the laboratory, each participant met a middle-aged man who was introduced as another participant, but who actually was a confederate. They were told that the experiment examined the effects of punishment on memory. Then, through a supposedly random draw (it was rigged), the real participant became the *teacher* and the confederate became the *learner*. The teacher presented a series of memory problems to the learner through a two-way intercom system. Each time the learner made an error, the teacher was instructed to administer an electric shock, using a machine that had 30 switches, beginning with 15 volts and increasing step-by-step to 450 volts. As the teacher watched, the learner was strapped into a chair in an adjoining room and hooked up to wires from the shock generator (Figure 13.15). The learner expressed concern about the shock and mentioned he had a slight heart problem.

Returning to the main room, the experimenter gave the teacher a sample shock (45 volts) and then ordered the experiment to begin. Unbeknownst to the teacher, the learner actually did *not* receive any shock and intentionally committed many errors. The learner made verbal protests that were standardized on a tape recorder, so that they were the same for all participants.

As the learner's errors mounted, the teacher increased the shock. If the teacher balked at continuing, the experimenter issued one or more escalating commands, such

© 1965 by Stanley Milgram. From the film *Obedience,* distributed by Penn State, Media Sales

FIGURE 13.15 The participant (teacher) saw the learner being strapped into the chair.

as "Please continue," "You must continue," and "You have no other choice." At 75 volts the learner moaned when the teacher threw the switch. At 150 volts the learner's reaction was "Ugh!!! Experimenter! That's all. Get me out of here. I told you I had heart trouble. My heart's starting to bother me now. Get me out of here, please . . . I refuse to go on. Let me out." Beyond 200 volts he emitted agonized screams every time a shock was delivered, yelling "Let me out! Let me out!" At 300 volts the learner refused to answer and continued screaming to be let out. At 345 volts and beyond, there was only silence. Full obedience was operationally defined as continuing to the maximum shock level of 450 volts.

Participants wrestled with a dilemma: Should they continue to hurt this innocent person, as the experimenter commanded, or should they stop the learner's pain by openly disobeying? Most participants became stressed. Some trembled, sweated, laughed nervously, or in a few cases, experienced convulsions. But would they obey? Make a prediction: What percentage of people obeyed to 450 volts, and were there any gender differences?

Results

When Milgram asked psychiatrists, professors, university students, and middle-class adults to predict the outcome,

continued

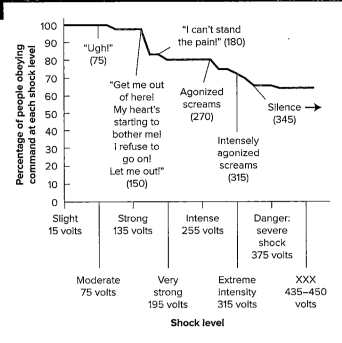

FIGURE 13.16 This graph shows the percentage of male participants who continued to shock the learner through various voltage levels. The pattern for women was similar.

Source: Based on Milgram, S. (1974). *Obedience to authority: An experimental view.* New York, NY: Harper & Row.

they estimated a 1 percent obedience rate. Indeed, most participants balked or protested at one time or another and said they would not continue. But ultimately, 26 of the 40 men and an identical 26 of 40 women (65 percent) obeyed to the end (Figure 13.16).

Discussion

Milgram's research has generated controversy for decades (Blass, 2000). On one level, its ethics were harshly criticized (Baumrind, 1964): Participants were deceived, exposed to substantial stress, and risked long-lasting negative effects to their self-image. Milgram countered that the research was so socially significant as to warrant the deception, that participants were carefully debriefed afterward, and that psychiatric follow-ups of a sample of obedient participants suggested no long-term ill effects. Weighing the costs and benefits, do you believe that this research was justified?

Researchers also debate why obedience was high, but many agree with Milgram's view that participants psychologically transferred much of the "responsibility" for the teacher's fate to the experimenter (Blass & Schmitt, 2001).

Source: Stanley Milgram (1974). *Obedience to Authority.* New York: Harper & Row.

While administering the shock, some participants stated that they "were not responsible" for what happened. Others asked, "Who is responsible if something happens to the learner?" When the experimenter replied, "I am responsible," participants felt greater freedom to continue. Yet they were the ones flipping the switch.

Would similar results occur today? We suspect so. For 25 years after Milgram's research, experiments in different countries, in "real-world" settings, and with children, adolescents, and adults yielded depressingly consistent results (Miller, 1986). In the 1980s, Dutch researchers Wim Meeus and Quinten Raaijmakers (1986, 1995) conducted 19 obedience studies. In one, 92 percent of male and female participants completely obeyed an experimenter's orders to repeatedly disrupt the performance of a job applicant (actually a confederate) taking a very important job screening test. The applicant pleaded to no avail with participants to stop.

How would you have responded? Almost all of our own students say they would have disobeyed. So suppose we conduct the experiment today, but with real electric shock and with you as the learner. The teacher will be a randomly selected student from your class. Are you confident that this student will disobey? Few of our students express such confidence. In short, virtually all of us are confident that we would not obey, but we are not so sure about other people—and in turn they are not so sure about us.

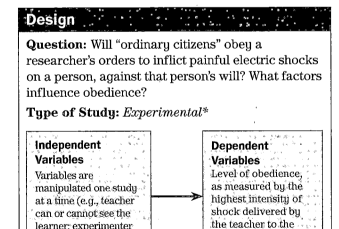

Design

Question: Will "ordinary citizens" obey a researcher's orders to inflict painful electric shocks on a person, against that person's will? What factors influence obedience?

Type of Study: *Experimental**

Independent Variables	**Dependent Variables**
Variables are manipulated one study at a time (e.g., teacher can or cannot see the learner; experimenter gives orders in person or by phone)	Level of obedience, as measured by the highest intensity of shock delivered by the teacher to the learner

*The situation is systematically changed from study to study and effects on behaviour are observed.

Factors That Influence Destructive Obedience

By changing various aspects of the experimental situation, Milgram and other researchers obtained obedience rates ranging from 0 to more than 90 percent.

- *Remoteness of the victim.* Obedience was greater when the learner was out of sight. When the teacher and learner were placed in the same room, obedience dropped to 40 percent. Furthermore, when the teacher had to make physical contact and force the learner's hand onto a "shock plate," obedience dropped to 30 percent (Figure 13.17).

- *Closeness and legitimacy of the authority figure.* Obedience was highest when the authority figure was close and perceived as legitimate. When the experimenter left the scene and gave orders by phone, or when an "ordinary person" (a confederate) took over and gave the orders, obedience dropped to about 20 percent.

- *Cog in a wheel.* When another "participant" (actually a confederate) flipped the shock switch and real participants had to perform only another aspect of the task, 93 percent obeyed. In short, *obedience increases when someone else does the "dirty work."* In contrast, when Harvey Tilker (1970) made participants feel fully responsible for the learner's welfare, not a single person obeyed to the end.

- *Personal characteristics.* Milgram compared the political orientation, religious affiliation, occupations, education, length of military service, and psychological characteristics

© 1965 by Stanley Milgram. From the film Obedience, distributed by Penn State, Media Sales.

FIGURE 13.17 In one of Milgram's studies (Touch Proximity), the teacher was ordered to physically force the learner's hand onto a shock plate after the learner refused to continue. Here, 30 percent of participants obeyed fully to 450 volts. Although touch proximity strongly reduced obedience, the fact that a significant minority still obeyed raises considerable concern.

of obedient versus disobedient participants. Differences were weak or non-existent. Likewise, gender was not consistently related to obedience rates (Milgram, 1974; Shanab & Yahya, 1977).

Lessons Learned: From the Holocaust to Airline Safety

What lessons shall we draw from this research? Certainly, it is *not* that people are apathetic or evil. Participants became stressed precisely because they did care about the learner's welfare. Neither is the lesson that we are sheep. If we were, obedience would be high across all situations, which is not the case. Rather, Milgram sums up a key lesson as follows:

> ... it would be a mistake ... to make the simple-minded statement that kindly and good persons disobey while those who are cruel do not ... often, it is not so much the kind of person a man is as the kind of situation in which he finds himself that determines how he will act. (1974, p. 205)

In other words, by arranging the situation appropriately, most people—ordinary, decent citizens—can be induced to follow orders from an authority figure they perceive as legitimate, even when doing so contributes to harming innocent people. The applicability of this principle to the Holocaust and other atrocities seems clear (Blass, 2008; Saltzman, 2000). During the Holocaust, obedience was made easier because most of the personnel working at the concentration camps were cogs in a horrendous wheel: They didn't pull the switch to flood the chambers with gas but instead performed other tasks. Their victims also were "remote" at the moment of their murder. Furthermore, to lessen concentration camp workers' feeling of responsibility, Hitler's subordinate Heinrich Himmler told them in manipulative speeches that only he and Hitler were personally responsible for what took place (Davidowicz, 1975). Keep in mind, however, that the participants in Milgram's studies did show stress and remorse, unlike many of the Holocaust perpetrators (Fenigstein, 2015).

Does obedience research suggest that we are not responsible for following orders? This is a moral and legal question, not a scientific one. But this research should heighten our sense of responsibility and awareness of the pitfalls of blind obedience and prevent us from being so smug or naive as to feel that such events "could never happen here." We should note that Milgram's results hold true today and not just decades ago.

Burger (2009) conducted a partial replication of the Milgram experiment, but the shock level went to only 150 volts (where participants began to stop in the original experiment). The procedures used by Burger were fully reviewed by the American Psychological Association and deemed to be ethical. Consistent with Milgram's original report, 65 percent of those tested obeyed fully.

Increased sensitivity to the power of obedience pressures also has concrete applications. As an airline passenger, there are times when you would want the co-pilot to challenge a pilot's commands, such as when the pilot's actions pose a clear threat to flight safety. But, traditionally, co-pilots have been reluctant to do this (National Transportation Safety Board, 1979). Actual cockpit recordings and flight simulator experiments suggest that several jetliner crashes might have been prevented had co-pilots been more assertive in taking over control or questioning pilots' decisions (Foushee, 1984; Helmreich, 1997). For example, there were reports of disagreement between the pilot and co-pilot on the ill-fated Swiss Air flight 111 (Figure 13.18).

Detecting and Resisting Compliance Techniques

From telemarketers and salespeople to TV and Internet advertisements, would-be persuaders often come armed with special *compliance techniques:* strategies that may manipulate you into saying "Yes" when you really want to say "No." By learning to identify these techniques, you will be better able to withstand them.

The powerful **norm of reciprocity** involves the expectation that when others treat us well, we should respond in kind. Thus, to get you to comply with a request, I can do something nice for you now—such as an unsolicited favour—in hopes that you will feel pressure to reciprocate later when I present you with my request (Cialdini, 2008). As Figure 13.19 illustrates, the Hare Krishna Society (a religious group) cleverly used "flower power" to manipulate the norm of reciprocity and raise millions of dollars in donations.

Now consider the **door-in-the-face technique:** A persuader makes a large request, expecting you to reject it (you "slam the door" in the persuader's face), and then presents a smaller request. Telemarketers feast on this technique. Rather than ask you directly for a modest monetary donation to some organization or cause, they first ask for a much larger contribution, knowing that you will say no. After you politely refuse, they ask for the smaller contribution. In one experiment, after people declined an initial request to donate $25 to a charity, they were more likely to donate $2

19. Identify four common compliance techniques and explain how they work.

© STRJOH/Jonathan Hayward/The Canadian Press

FIGURE 13.18 On September 2, 1998, Swiss Air flight 111, carrying 215 passengers and 14 crew members, crashed off the coast of Peggy's Cove, Nova Scotia. Indications arose later that there was a disagreement between the pilot and co-pilot, in which the co-pilot acquiesced.

© Owen Franken

FIGURE 13.19 In the 1970s, members of the Hare Krishna Society approached passersby and gave them a small flower. If a passerby refused, the member said, "Please. It is a gift for you." Reluctantly, people often accepted. Then the member asked for a donation. People felt pressure to reciprocate, donated money, and often threw the flower away.

than were participants who were directly asked for $2 (Wang et al., 1989). To be effective, the same persuader must make both requests (or at least, be present at both (Terrier et al., 2013). The persuader "compromises" by making the second, smaller request, so we feel pressure to reciprocate by complying (Lecat et al., 2009). Refusing the first request also may produce guilt, and complying with the smaller request may help us reduce guilt or feel socially responsible (Tusing & Dillard, 2000). Door-in-the-face works for a variety of requests, including cutting back on smoking (Pansu et al., 2014).

Using the **foot-in-the-door technique,** a persuader gets you to comply with a small request first (getting the "foot in the door") and later presents a larger request (Eastwick et al., 2009). Imagine receiving an email message from a stranger requesting help. It's a student who needs to collect data for a class project and asks if you would fill out a 20-minute online questionnaire about your dietary habits. Would you do it? In an experiment with French college students, 44 percent complied (Guéguen, 2002). Now let's turn to a different condition of this experiment. Imagine receiving an email from a stranger who asks for simple advice about a word-processing program. It takes less than a minute to reply, and you do (as did all the participants in this condition of the experiment). Once the person gets the foot in the door, a second email appears minutes later, asking if you would help with a class project by filling out a dietary questionnaire. In this condition, many more students—76 percent—complied.

With a final technique, **lowballing,** a persuader gets you to commit to some action and then—before you actually perform the behaviour—he or she increases the "cost" of that same behaviour (Cialdini, 2008). Imagine negotiating to buy a used car for $8000, a "great price." The salesperson says, "I need to confirm this with my manager," comes back shortly, and states, "I'm afraid my manager says the price is too low. But you can have the car for only $400 more. It's still a great price." At this point, you are more likely to go through with the deal than you would have been, had the "real" $8400 price been set at the outset.

Both lowballing and the foot-in-the-door technique involve moving from a smaller request to a larger, more costly one. But with the foot-in-the-door approach, the smaller and larger requests often involve different acts (e.g., giving advice, filling out a questionnaire) and the larger request is made after you finish complying with the smaller request. In lowballing, the stakes for the *same behaviour* are raised after you commit to it but *before* you consummate the behaviour. Having made a commitment, you may find it easier to rationalize the added costs or may feel obligated to the person to whom you made the commitment.

By recognizing when compliance techniques are being used to manipulate your behaviour, you are in a better position to resist them. Consider the norm of reciprocity. Robert Cialdini (2008), an expert on influence techniques, suggests that the key is not to resist the initial gift or favour; instead, accept the unsolicited "favour," but if the person then asks you for a favour in return, recognize this as a manipulative technique. As Cialdini notes, "The rule says that favors are to be met with favors; it does not require that tricks be met with favors" (1988, p. 53). Similarly, if a telemarketer asks you to agree to a large request and then after you decline immediately asks for a smaller commitment, respond by thinking or even saying, "I see: the door-in-the-face technique." Of course, you can still choose to comply if you believe it is the right thing to do. The goal is not to automatically reject every social influence attempt but to avoid feeling coerced into doing something you don't want to do.

Crowd Behaviour and Deindividuation

Years ago in New York City, a handyman sat perched on a ledge for an hour while a crowd of nearly 500 people on the street below shouted at him to jump. Fortunately, police managed to rescue the man. New York is hardly alone, as Australian psychologist Leon Mann (1981) found when he analyzed newspaper reports of 21 cases in which crowds were present when a person threatened to jump off a building. In 10 cases, the crowd had encouraged the person to jump.

What could prompt people to encourage distraught human beings to end their lives? In the 19th century, French physician Gustave LeBon (1895) suggested that the anonymity that exists in mobs leads to a loss of personal identity and a weakening of restraints that prompt people to engage in behaviours they would not perform as individuals. This condition is called **deindividuation,** a loss of individuality that leads to disinhibited behaviour (Festinger et al., 1952). The concept of deindividuation has been applied to diverse types of antisocial behaviour, from cheating and stealing, to riots by sports fans, to acts of genocide (Staub, 1996).

But what is the primary aspect of deindividuation that disinhibits behaviour? Tom Postmes and Russell Spears (1998) meta-analyzed 60 deindividuation studies and determined that *anonymity to outsiders* was the key. Conditions that make an individual less identifiable to people *outside* the group reduce feelings of accountability and, slightly but consistently, increase the risk of antisocial actions. Postmes and Spears suggest that being anonymous to outsiders enhances the individual's tendency to focus on his or her identity with the group and makes the person more responsive to emerging group norms.

Reinforcing the importance of anonymity to outsiders, Mann (1981) found that people were most likely to encourage a potential suicide victim to jump when the crowd was large and it was dark outside. During the Stanford Prison Study, no names were used and guards had to be called "Mr. Correctional Officer." All guards wore identical uniforms and reflecting sunglasses that prevented the prisoners from making direct eye contact. The guards were unaware that their behaviour was being monitored by the experimenters, and antisocial norms evolved from the role of "tough prison guard" adopted by those participants who spontaneously took over leadership roles (Zimbardo et al., 1973). These factors led Zimbardo to conclude that deindividuation was a key factor in the cruelty exhibited by the guards. Reducing anonymity—and thereby increasing public accountability—may be the most basic approach to counteracting deindividuation.

Group Influences on Performance and Decision Making

Much of our behaviour occurs in groups, from family and friendship groups to social clubs, work groups, and athletic teams. People often form groups to make decisions or perform tasks that are too complex or physically demanding to be accomplished by one person (Figure 13.20). We now consider some factors that enhance or interfere with group productivity.

Social Loafing: Failing to Pull Your Own Weight

In 1913, Max Ringelmann, a French agricultural engineer, measured the force that men exerted while pulling on a rope as hard as they could. Individually, the men averaged 63 kilograms of pull. In groups of three, you might expect a combined pull of about 3×63 kilograms = 189 kilograms, and 504 kilograms for groups of eight. But this isn't what happened. The total pull in three- and eight-man groups was 16 percent and 51 percent below expectations, respectively.

Why did this happen? Perhaps the men didn't coordinate the timing of their pull precisely, and there was a loss of mechanical efficiency. Or perhaps each person exerted less effort when in a group. To resolve this issue, Alan Ingham and his colleagues (1974) led blindfolded participants to believe that they were pulling a rope (connected to a force meter) either alone or in groups of various sizes. In reality, participants were always alone, and therefore any performance drop had to be due to diminished effort.

20. Describe deindividuation and how conditions in the Stanford Prison Study may have fostered it.

(left): Ammit Jack/Shutterstock; (right): © Digital Vision/Getty Images

FIGURE 13.20 Whether for recreational, volunteer, or work activities, much of human behaviour occurs in groups.

Overall, participants exerted 18 percent less force when they thought they were in a group.

The tendency for people to expend less individual effort when working in a group than when working alone is called **social loafing.** In contrast to social facilitation experiments, in which a person performs a task individually (in front of an audience or with a coactor) and *does not pool* her or his effort with anyone, social loafing involves collective performance. Thus, contrary to what common sense might tell you, when university students and high school cheerleaders are asked to be as loud as possible, they individually clap, shout, and cheer *less* loudly when performing as a group than when they are alone (Hardy & Latané, 1986).

Social loafing also occurs on cognitive tasks, such as when people have to evaluate written materials, make decisions in simulated juries, and monitor the concentration of gases in the air (Hoeksema et al., 1998). Why does social loafing occur? Steven Karau and Kipling Williams (1993, 2001) propose a *collective effort model:* On a collective task, people will put forth effort only to the extent that they expect their effort to contribute to obtaining a valued goal. In support of this model, their meta-analysis of 78 social loafing studies revealed that social loafing is *more* likely to occur when

- people believe that individual performance within the group is not being monitored;
- the task (goal) has less value or meaning to the person;
- the group is less important to the person; and
- the task is simple and the person's input is redundant with that of other group members.

Fatigue also seems to increase social loafing. By having participants work on various cognitive tasks for 20 hours without sleep, Dutch researchers demonstrated that we are more likely to "skate by" on other group members' shoulders when we are tired (Hoeksema et al., 1998). Social loafing also depends on gender and culture (Karau & Williams, 1993). It occurs more strongly in all-male groups than in all-female or mixed-sex groups, possibly because women may be more concerned about group outcomes than men. Participants from individualistic cultures (Canada and the United States) exhibit more social loafing than people from collectivistic cultures (China, Japan, Taiwan), in which group goals are especially valued.

Social loafing suggests that, in terms of group performance, "the whole is less than the sum of

its parts." But this is not always the case. Social loafing may disappear when individual performance is monitored (Lount & Wilk, 2014; Pearsall et al., 2010) or when members highly value their group or the task goal (Karau & Hart, 1998). In fact, to achieve a highly desired goal, some members may engage in *social compensation:* They will work harder in a group than alone if they expect that their colleagues either don't have enough ability or will slack off (Hart et al., 2001).

Group Polarization: Going to Extremes

Groups are often called on to make key decisions. Governments, educational institutions, and corporations frequently develop policies through committees. The fate of defendants often rests in the hands of juries. Such decisions are often entrusted to groups because they are assumed to be more conservative than individuals and less likely to "go off the deep end." Is this assumption correct? It is, as long as the group is generally conservative to begin with. In such cases, the group's final opinion or attitude likely will be even *more conservative.* But, if the group members lean toward a more liberal or risky viewpoint to begin with, the group's decision will tend to become *more liberal or riskier.* This principle is called **group polarization:** When a group of like-minded people discusses an issue, whether face to face or through email, the "average" opinion of group members tends to become more extreme (Krizan & Baron, 2007).

Why does group polarization occur? One reason, reflecting *normative social influence,* is that individuals who are attracted to a group may be motivated to adopt a more extreme position to gain the group's approval. A second reason, reflecting *informational social influence,* is that during group discussions people hear arguments supporting their positions that they had not previously considered. These new arguments tend to make the initial positions seem even more valid (Sia et al., 2002).

Groupthink: Suspending Critical Thinking

After the U.S. military ignored warning signs of imminent attack by Japan in 1941, the fleet at Pearl Harbor was destroyed in a "surprise" attack. In 1961, President John F. Kennedy and his advisors launched the doomed Bay of Pigs invasion of Cuba. In 1972, five men broke into Democratic Party offices at the Watergate hotel, and the following cover-up forced President Richard Nixon to resign. According to Yale University social psychologist Irving Janis (1983), the decision makers involved in each of these

21. What is social loafing and when is it most likely to occur?

22. Identify two causes of group polarization.

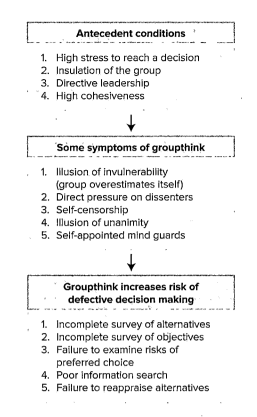

Antecedent conditions

1. High stress to reach a decision
2. Insulation of the group
3. Directive leadership
4. High cohesiveness

↓

Some symptoms of groupthink

1. Illusion of invulnerability (group overestimates itself)
2. Direct pressure on dissenters
3. Self-censorship
4. Illusion of unanimity
5. Self-appointed mind guards

↓

Groupthink increases risk of defective decision making

1. Incomplete survey of alternatives
2. Incomplete survey of objectives
3. Failure to examine risks of preferred choice
4. Poor information search
5. Failure to reappraise alternatives

FIGURE 13.21 Antecedents, symptoms, and negative effects of groupthink on decision making.

Source: Adapted from Janis, I.L. (1983). *Groupthink: Psychological studies of policy decisions and fiascos* (2nd ed.). Boston, MA: Houghton Mifflin.

historical blunders fell victim to a process called **groupthink,** the tendency for group members to suspend critical thinking because they are striving to seek agreement.

Janis developed the concept of groupthink, shown in Figure 13.21, after analyzing historical accounts of group deliberations that resulted in disastrous decisions. He proposed that groupthink is most likely to occur when a group

- is under *high stress* to reach a decision;
- is *insulated* from outside input;
- has a *directive leader* who promotes her or his personal agenda; and
- has *high cohesion,* reflecting a spirit of closeness and ability to work well together.

Under these conditions, the group is so committed to reaching a consensus, while remaining loyal and agreeable, that members suspend their critical judgment. Particularly when facing a collective threat, the group's desire to maintain a positive view of itself may lead members to reach agreement without carefully weighing opposing views (Turner et al., 2007).

Various symptoms signal that groupthink is at work. For example, group members who express doubt are faced with *direct pressure* to stop "rocking the boat." Some members serve as *mind guards* by preventing negative information from reaching the group. Ultimately, members display *self-censorship* and withhold their doubts, creating a potentially disastrous *illusion of unanimity* in which each member comes to believe that "everyone else seems to agree with the decision" (Figure 13.22).

Groupthink principles have been applied to diverse situations. In the business world, groupthink can contribute to poor management decisions that adversely affect the

23. What are some causes, symptoms, and consequences of groupthink?

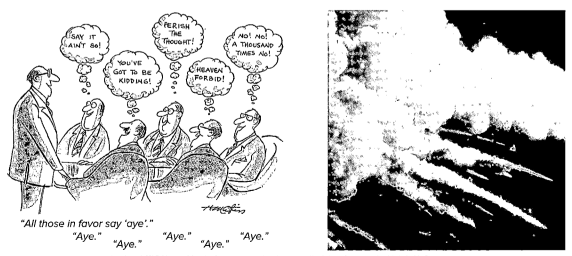

"All those in favor say 'aye'."
"Aye." *"Aye."* *"Aye."* *"Aye."* *"Aye."*

FIGURE 13.22 (a) The illusion of unanimity occurs when group members collectively fail to speak their true minds. (b) This illusion contributed to the ill-fated decision to launch the space shuttle *Challenger* on January 28, 1986. The *Challenger* exploded shortly after takeoff, killing all the astronauts on board.

financial value and public reputation of a company (Eaton, 2001). In crime investigations, groupthink may lead the investigative team to prematurely reach agreement on a particular interpretation of the case without adequately considering other alternatives (Kerstholt & Eikelboom, 2007).

Many aspects of groupthink were present during the decision process leading up to the fatal launch of the space shuttle *Challenger* in 1986 (Esser & Lindoerfer, 1995; Moorhead et al., 1991). The engineers who designed the rocket boosters had strongly opposed the launch, fearing that subfreezing weather would make rubber seals too brittle to contain hot gases from the rocket. NASA, however, was under great stress, and leadership was directive. This shuttle mission was to be historic, carrying America's first civilian into space. There had been several delays and NASA did not want another one. To foster an illusion of unanimity, a key NASA executive polled only management officials, excluding the engineers from the final decision-making process (Magnuson, 1986). Thanks to mind guarding, the NASA official who gave the final go-ahead was never informed of the concerns expressed by the engineers.

In the days leading up to the fiery disintegration of the space shuttle *Columbia* as it reentered Earth's atmosphere in 2003, engineers, supervisors, and some NASA officials intensely debated whether *Columbia's* left wing had sustained damage because of a mishap during launch. But as the Columbia Accident Investigation Board found, tragically, "dangerous aspects of NASA's 1986 culture . . . remained unchanged" (2003, p. 198). For example, stress was high, key managers were isolated from outside expert opinion, and a "need to produce consensus at each level" filtered out dissenting information on safety risks (p. 198).

Can groupthink be prevented? Janis suggests that the leader should remain impartial during discussions, regularly encourage critical thinking, bring in outsiders to offer their opinions, and divide the larger group into subgroups—to see if each subgroup independently reaches the same decision. Of course, even groups that display poor decision-making procedures may still end up making a correct decision, or at least may "get away" with a bad one (Raven, 1998). Conversely, critical debate does not guarantee a positive outcome, but it does enhance the odds.

Review

- A social norm is a shared rule or expectation about how group members should think, feel, and behave. A social role is a set of norms that defines a particular position in a social system.

- People conform to a group because of informational social influence and normative social influence. The size of the majority and the presence or absence of dissenters influence the degree of conformity. Minority influence is strongest when the minority maintains a consistent position over time but does not appear too deviant.

- Milgram's obedience research raised strong ethical concerns and found unexpectedly high percentages of people willing to obey destructive orders. Such obedience is stronger when the victim is remote and when the authority figure is close by, legitimate, and assumes responsibility for what happens.

- People often use special techniques to get us to comply with their requests. These compliance techniques include the norm of reciprocity, the door-in-the-face technique, the foot-in-the-door technique, and lowballing.

- Deindividuation is a temporary lowering of restraints that can occur when a person is immersed in a group. Anonymity to outsiders appears to be the key factor in producing deindividuation.

- Social loafing occurs when people exert less individual effort when working as a group than when working alone. Social loafing decreases when the goal or group membership is valued highly and when people's performance within the group can be individually monitored.

- When the members of a decision-making group initially share the same conservative or liberal viewpoint, the group's final decision often reflects a polarization effect and becomes more extreme than the average opinion of the individual members.

- Cohesive decision-making groups that have directive leaders, are under high stress, and are insulated from outside input may display groupthink, a suspension of critical thinking to maintain cohesion and loyalty to the leader's viewpoint.

SOCIAL RELATIONS

Our relations with other people take many forms. Here we explore four types of social interaction that help to define who we are, both individually and collectively: attraction, prejudice, altruism, and aggression.

Affiliation and Interpersonal Attraction

What makes your life meaningful? To many people, close relationships are one key. Abraham Maslow (1954) viewed belongingness and love as basic psychological needs, and considerable research indicates that "... the need to belong is a powerful, fundamental, and extremely pervasive motivation" (Baumeister & Leary, 1995, p. 497).

Why Do We Affiliate?

Humans are social beings and affiliate in many ways (Figure 13.23). Some theorists argue that, over the course of evolution, individuals whose biological makeup predisposed them to affiliate were more likely to survive and reproduce than those who were reclusive. By affording greater access to sexual mates, more protection from predators, an efficient division of labour, and the passing of knowledge across generations, a socially oriented lifestyle had considerable adaptive value (Flinn, 1997; Kottak, 2000).

Craig Hill (1987) suggests that, psychologically, we affiliate for four basic reasons: to obtain positive stimulation, receive emotional support, gain attention, and permit social comparison. **Social comparison** involves comparing our beliefs, feelings, and behaviours with those of other people. This comparison helps us determine whether our responses are "normal,"

Ingram Publishing/SuperStock

FIGURE 13.23 Affiliation brings us companionship, intimacy, love, and also basic social contact. To satisfy these desires, we form friendships, interact with family members, join groups, converse with strangers, and flock together in crowds.

and enables us to judge the level of our cognitive and physical abilities (Festinger, 1954).

People differ in how strongly they desire to affiliate. In one study, university students who scored high on a personality test of *need for affiliation* made more friends during the semester than did students who scored low (Byrne & Greendlinger, 1989). In another study, high school students wore beepers over a one-week period. They were signalled approximately every two hours, and then recorded their thoughts and activities. Participants with high need for affiliation were more likely than their peers to report they were thinking about friends and wishing they could be with people (Wong & Csikszentmihalyi, 1991).

People with high need for affiliation also show a stronger *psychological sense of community*—the feeling of being part of a larger collective and being engaged with others in pursuing common goals (Burroughs & Eby, 1998). People with a strong sense of community are more likely to engage in extracurricular school activities and to keep abreast of local and national news (Davidson & Cotter, 1997). Clearly, our desire to feel connected can express itself in many ways.

Many situational factors affect our tendency to affiliate. For example, fear-inducing situations increase our desire to be with others (Schachter, 1959). During emergencies, as in the aftermath of earthquakes, floods, and hurricanes, many people find themselves bonding to strangers (Humphriss, 1989). When afraid, we prefer to be with people who have been through the feared situation we are facing. This way, we can gauge the normalcy of our reactions and learn information about what to expect. In one study, hospital patients awaiting open-heart surgery expressed a stronger desire to have a roommate who already had been through the surgery than a preoperative roommate like themselves (Kulik & Mahler, 1989). And, when such patients were assigned to postoperative rather than preoperative roommates, they became less anxious and later recovered from surgery more quickly (Kulik et al., 1996).

Initial Attraction

Attraction is the first phase of most friendships and romantic relationships. What causes us to "connect" with some people, but not others?

Proximity and mere exposure: "Haven't I seen you somewhere?" People cannot develop a relationship unless they first meet, and proximity (nearness) is the best predictor of who will cross paths with whom. In today's increasingly

24. According to evolutionary and social comparison viewpoints, why are humans such social creatures?

25. How does fear influence affiliation?

wired world, friendships and romances sometimes develop after strangers make initial contact through Internet chat rooms, social-networking sites, or email. Still, physical proximity matters. We interact most with people who are physically closer (Latané et al., 1995). Residents in married-student apartments are more likely to form friendships with other residents who live close by; students placed in assigned classroom seats are more likely to become friends with students seated nearby (Back et al., 2008); and many adults meet their spouse or current dating partner at school, work, or place of worship (Festinger et al., 1950; Michael et al., 1994). In fact, if we are thinking about affiliating with other people, we actually see ourselves as physically closer to others (Stel & Koningsbruggen, 2015).

Proximity increases the chance of frequent encounters, and over 200 experiments provide evidence of a **mere exposure effect:** Repeated exposure to a stimulus typically increases our liking for it. No matter the stimuli—university classmates, photographs of faces, random geometric shapes, foreign words, and so on—so long as they are not unpleasant and we are not oversaturated, exposure generally enhances liking (Monahan et al., 2000; Winograd et al., 1999). This effect occurs even when we are not consciously aware of the repeated exposures (Hansen & Wänke, 2009).

Similarity: Birds of a feather. When it comes to attraction, folk wisdom covers all the bases. On the one hand, "opposites attract." On the other, "birds of a feather flock together." So which is it? The evidence is overwhelming: People most often are attracted to others who are similar to themselves (Byrne, 1997). For psychological attributes, similarity of attitudes, beliefs, and values seems to matter the most (Buss, 1985).

In the laboratory, university students' degree of liking for a stranger can be predicted very accurately simply by knowing the proportion of similar attitudes that they share (Byrne, 1997; Byrne & Nelson, 1965). This similarity-attraction relationship has been found across many groups, including people in Mexico, India, and Japan who ranged from Grade 4 students to retirees. Outside the laboratory, Donn Byrne and his colleagues (1970) matched university students on a brief 30-minute date, pairing people with partners who had either highly similar or dissimilar attitudes. Students were more attracted to similar partners, talked with them more during the rest of the semester, and had a stronger desire to date them. One reason we like people with similar attitudes is that they validate our view of the world.

So like mismatched roommates Felix Unger (an uptight neatnik) and Oscar Madison (a carefree slob) in the classic movie *The Odd Couple,* do opposites ever attract? At times, of course. But much more often, opposites repel (Krueger & Caspi, 1993; Rosenbaum, 1986). When choosing potential friends or mates, we typically screen out people who are dissimilar to us. And, when dissimilar people do form relationships, they tend not to last as long (Byrne, 1997). As Diane Felmlee (1998) found, dissimilarity increases the risk of "fatal attractions": We initially find some characteristic of another person appealing, but over time we come to dislike it. In short, what is intriguing and different today may repel us tomorrow!

Physical attractiveness: Spellbound by beauty. It may be shallow and in many ways unfair, but most people seem drawn to beauty like moths to a flame (Figure 13.24). In many studies, when men and women rate the desirability of hypothetical short-term dating partners, their judgments are influenced most strongly by how good-looking the person is.

Consider the heterosexual college students who participated in a recent speed-dating survey at a southeastern U.S. public university (Luo & Zhang, 2009). Prior to the actual speed-dating sessions, the researchers measured the students' interests, values, personality characteristics, and other personal factors. Eight research team members also rated each student's physical attractiveness based on a photograph of the student taken moments prior to their particular speed-dating session. At a session, each speed date lasted five minutes and immediately afterwards, participants rated their desire to see that person again. The results were as follows: For men and women, their desire to date the partners they met depended far more strongly on the partner's physical attractiveness than on any other characteristic the researchers measured.

In other research, psychologists have measured people's physical attractiveness and personal characteristics, and then randomly paired them on actual blind dates. In one classic study with university students, the partners' physical attractiveness was the only factor that predicted students' attraction (Walster et al., 1966).

Women and men who dated physically attractive partners liked them more and had a stronger desire to date them again. Similarly, among 100 homosexual men who researchers paired together for a date, men's liking for their partners and desire to date them again were most

26. How and why does proximity influence affiliation and attraction?

27. Do birds of a feather flock together, or do opposites attract? Describe the evidence.

(left): © PhotoAlto/Alamy Stock Photo; (right): © Sid Bahrt/Photo Researchers, Inc.

FIGURE 13.24 Hey, good lookin'! The way that both sexes initially judge someone is influenced by that person's attractiveness and other physical features. We are not alone. Many species, such as these Frigate birds (male on the left), have evolved distinct features and ritualized mating displays to attract a potential mate's attention.

strongly influenced by the partners' physical attractiveness (Sergios & Cody, 1986).

What motivates our desire to affiliate with attractive people? One factor may be the widespread stereotype that "what is beautiful is good"; we often assume that attractive people have more positive personality characteristics than unattractive people (Dion et al., 1972; Feingold, 1992). The popular media reinforce this stereotype. Analyzing five decades of top-grossing Hollywood movies, Stephen Smith and his colleagues (1999) found that good-looking male and female characters were portrayed as more intelligent, moral, and sociable than less attractive characters. However, attractiveness can work against you if you are in need and asking for help (Fisher & Ma, 2014). Because we are often judged by the company we keep, we also may prefer to associate with attractive people to buttress our self-esteem. Self-conscious people, who are highly concerned about how they come across to others, are especially likely to gravitate toward attractive people (Richardson, 1991; Snyder et al., 1985).

Lest you conclude that beauty is the key to happiness, we should note that physical attractiveness during the university years is unrelated to life satisfaction in middle age (Kaner, 1995). And physically attractive people do not necessarily have the highest levels of self-esteem (Major et al., 1984), although attractiveness has been shown to be related to psychological well-being (Datta Gupta et al., 2015). Beauty is sometimes linked with self-doubt, because highly attractive

individuals may attribute the positive responses of others solely to their "surface" beauty rather than to their inner personal qualities.

Although we are attracted to "beautiful people," we are most likely to have a dating partner or spouse whose level of physical attractiveness is similar to our own: a **matching effect** (Feingold, 1988). In this case, "birds of equally attractive feathers flock together." One reason for this is that the most attractive people may match up first and be "taken," then the next most attractive, and so on (Kalick & Hamilton, 1988). Another factor is that, to lessen the risk of rejection, some people may refrain from approaching potential dating partners who are more attractive than they are (Huston, 1973). Among dating couples, those who are best matched on attractiveness are most likely to fall deeply in love, and couples who eventually marry are more similar in attractiveness than dating couples in general (White, 1980).

Facial attractiveness: Is "average" beautiful?
Given beauty's power, what makes a face physically attractive? Beauty may be in the eye of the beholder, but within and across cultures, people are seeing through similar eyes; their ratings of facial attractiveness agree strongly (Langlois et al., 2000).

Look at face 3 and face 5 in Figure 13.25. The first thing you need to know is that these people don't exist. These photos are composites, "averaged" male and female faces created digitally by blending 16 photographs of young men and

28. Identify two factors that may underlie the desire to affiliate more with attractive people than unattractive people.

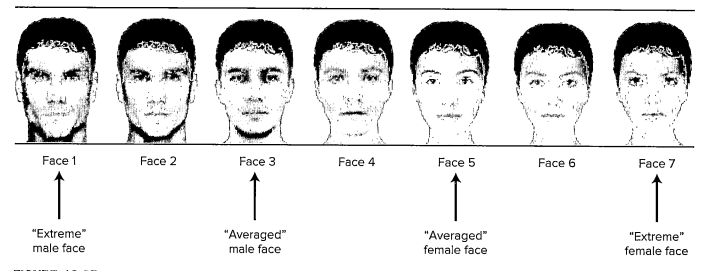

Face 1   Face 2   Face 3   Face 4   Face 5   Face 6   Face 7

"Extreme" male face   "Averaged" male face   "Averaged" female face   "Extreme" female face

FIGURE 13.25 Judging beauty. Which male face do you find most attractive? Which female face? Faces 3 and 5 are "averaged" composite photographs digitally created by blending photos of 16 men and 16 women, respectively. These averaged composites were then digitally altered to accentuate either masculine or feminine features. Faces 1 and 7 are extremely masculinized and feminized, respectively; faces 2 and 6, moderately so. Face 4 blends the masculine and feminine features. In actual experiments, masculinization-feminization changes typically are done very gradually, creating many more choices than you see here.

Source: Adapted with permission Johnston, V.S. et al. Male Facial Attractiveness: Evidence for Hormone-Mediated Adaptive Design. Fig. 1, p. 255, *Evaluation and Behavior* 22. pp. 251–ßß267. Elsevier Publishing.

16 photographs of young women (Johnston et al., 2001). Using different sets of photographs, studies in North America, Europe, and Asia consistently find that people typically rate "averaged" male and female faces as more attractive than almost all the individual faces used to create the composites (Langlois & Roggman, 1990). Moreover, people perceive individual faces as more attractive when those faces are digitally modified to look more like the "averaged" face (Rhodes et al., 2001). One reason that averaged faces seem more attractive is that they are more symmetrical, and people prefer facial symmetry (B. Jones et al., 2004). However, even when viewing faces from the side, where symmetry is not an issue, averaged faces are still rated as more attractive.

As Gestalt psychologists noted, in visual perception, the whole is more than the sum of its parts. As individual facial features—noses, eyes, lips, and so on—conform more to an "averaged" norm, we perceive the "whole face" as more attractive. But keep in mind that some individual faces, which deviate from their composite, are rated the most attractive overall. Moreover, as Figure 13.25 shows, some researchers have taken composite faces and digitally altered them to appear progressively more masculine (e.g., larger jaw and brow ridges) or more feminine (e.g., fuller lips, a narrower jaw). Consistently, people perceive moderately feminized faces as the most attractive (Johnston et al., 2001; Perrett et al., 1998). In contrast, depending on the study, male faces that have been somewhat masculinized or feminized are rated as the most attractive.

As Attraction Deepens: Close Relationships

Budding relationships grow closer as people share more diverse and meaningful experiences(Altman & Taylor, 1973). *Self-disclosure*—the sharing of innermost thoughts and feelings—plays a key role (Dindia, 2002). In friendships, dating relationships, and marriages, more extensive and intimate self-disclosure is associated with greater emotional involvement and relationship satisfaction. This relation is reciprocal. Self-disclosure fosters intimacy and trust, and intimacy and trust encourage self-disclosure.

Social exchange theory proposes that the course of a relationship is governed by rewards and costs that the partners experience (Thibaut & Kelley, 1959). Rewards include companionship, emotional support, and the satisfaction of other needs (van de Rijt & Macy, 2006). Costs may include the effort spent to maintain the relationship, arguments, conflicting goals, and so forth. The overall *outcome* (rewards minus costs) in a relationship can be positive or negative.

29. According to social exchange theory, what factors influence whether a relationship will deepen, be satisfying, and continue?

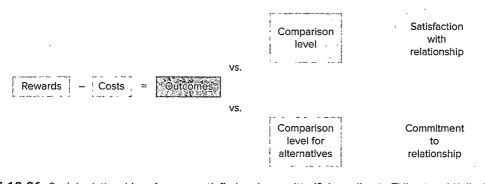

FIGURE 13.26 Social relationships: Are you satisfied and committed? According to Thibaut and Kelley's (1959) social exchange theory, rewards minus costs equal the outcome of a relationship. Comparing our outcomes with two standards, the comparison level and the comparison level for alternatives, determines our satisfaction and commitment to the relationship, respectively.

Outcomes are evaluated against two standards (Figure 13.26). The first, called the *comparison level*, is the outcome that a person has grown to expect in relationships, and it influences the person's *satisfaction* with the present relationship. Outcomes that meet or exceed the comparison level are satisfying; those that fall below this standard are dissatisfying. The second standard, called the *comparison level for alternatives*, focuses on potential alternatives to the relationship, and it influences the person's degree of *commitment*. Even when a relationship is satisfying, partners may feel low commitment if they perceive that something better is available. In turn, the partners' sense of commitment helps to predict whether they will remain together or end their relationship in the future (Sprecher, 2001).

Sociocultural and Evolutionary Views

According to social exchange theory, a partner's desirable characteristics can be viewed as rewards, whereas undesirable characteristics represent costs. But what specific characteristics do people desire in a partner? In a massive study involving 10 000 men and women from 37 cultures around the world, evolutionary psychologist David Buss and his colleagues asked people to identify the qualities they sought in an ideal long-term mate (Buss, 1989; Buss et al., 1990). Overall, for both sexes, mutual attraction/love, dependable character, emotional stability, and a pleasing disposition emerged (in that order) as the most highly rated of the 18 characteristics evaluated.

The importance attached to many qualities, however, varied considerably across cultures. For example, whereas North American men and women viewed refinement/neatness as having only modest importance, Iranian men and women viewed it as the most important quality they desired in a mate. In many cultures, a mate's chastity (no previous experience in sexual intercourse) was viewed as last or near-last in importance, but in China and India, men and women viewed chastity as an important quality in a mate.

There are also remarkably consistent sex differences in mate preferences across cultures. Men tend to place greater value on a potential mate's physical attractiveness and domestic skills, whereas women place greater value on a potential mate's earning potential, status, and ambitiousness. Men tend to desire a mate who is a few years younger, whereas young and middle-aged women tend to desire a mate who is a few years older (Alterovitz & Mendelsohn, 2009). Men also are more likely to desire and pursue a greater number of short-term romantic encounters than are women (Schmitt et al., 2001).

As we discussed in detail in Chapter 4, some evolutionary psychologists argue that these sex differences reflect inherited predispositions, shaped by natural selection in response to different adaptive problems that men and women have faced over the ages (Gangestad et al., 2006). According to the *sexual strategies theory*, ancestral men who were predisposed to have sex with more partners increased the likelihood of fathering more children and passing on their genes. Such men may have perceived a woman's youth and attractive appearance as signs that she was fertile and had many years left to bear children (Buss, 1989). Ancestral women, however, maximized their reproductive success by selecting mates who were willing and able to commit time, energy, and other resources (e.g., food, shelter, protection) to the family (Buss, 1989).

Do men and women have different biological wiring when it comes to romantic attraction

30. Describe some gender differences in mate preferences.

and relationships? *Social structure theory* proposes that most of these sex differences in mating strategies and preferences occur because society directs men into more advantaged social and economic roles (Eagly & Wood, 1999, 2006). As this theory predicts, in cultures with more gender equality, many of the sex differences in mate preferences shrink. Women place less emphasis, for example, on a mate's earning power and status, and men and women seek mates more similar in age. Men's tendency to place more emphasis on a mate's physical attractiveness, however, does not decrease in such cultures. But it is still a leap, say critics, to conclude that sex differences in mating preferences reflect a hereditary predisposition rather than some other aspect of gender socialization that may be consistent across cultures.

This issue is far from settled, but perhaps the most important point to realize is the notion that men and women come from "different planets" when it comes to attraction, romance, and close relationships is more pop psychology than reliable science (Hazan & Diamond, 2000). Sex differences exist, but cross-cultural differences tend to be stronger. That is, men and women within the same culture are typically more similar to one another than are men from different cultures or women from different cultures (Buss et al., 1990).

Love

Love must be a powerful motive if it indeed "makes the world go round," but which type of love does this? In his book *The Art of Loving*, psychoanalyst Erich Fromm (1956) identified five fundamental types of love: parental love, erotic (sexual) love, self-love, love for humanity, and love of God. Restricting ourselves to friendships and romantic relationships, poet Elizabeth Barrett Browning's insight, "How do I love thee? Let me count the ways" is most applicable.

Types of Love

Passionate love involves intense emotion, arousal, and yearning for the partner (Hatfield, 1988). We may ride an emotional roller coaster that ranges from ecstasy when the partner is present to heartsickness when the person is absent. **Companionate love** involves affection, deep caring about the partner's well-being, and a commitment to "being there" for the other (Caspi & Herbener, 1990; Hatfield, 1988). Both

types of love contribute to satisfaction in long-term romantic relationships (Sprecher & Regan, 1998). In general, passionate love is less stable and declines more quickly over time than companionate love, but this does not mean that the flames of passionate love inevitably are extinguished (Tucker & Aron, 1993).

The distinction between passionate and companionate love is one of psychology's most basic. However, Robert Sternberg (1988, 1997) proposes a three-component **triangular theory of love** that focuses on *intimacy* (closeness, sharing, and valuing one's partner), *commitment* (the decision to remain in the relationship), and *passion* (feelings of romance, physical attraction, and sexual desire). Research suggests that these three qualities do a good job of capturing the way people commonly think about love (Aron & Westbay, 1996).

Figure 13.27 shows that different combinations of these components characterize seven types of love (plus "non-love," which is the absence of all three components). Sternberg proposes that the ultimate form of love between people—*consummate love*—occurs when intimacy, passion, and commitment are all present.

The Cognitive-Arousal Model: Why Does My Heart Pound?

Our culture believes in the concept of love, and we are exposed to love themes from childhood.

31. How does Sternberg's model expand on the passionate-companionate love distinction?

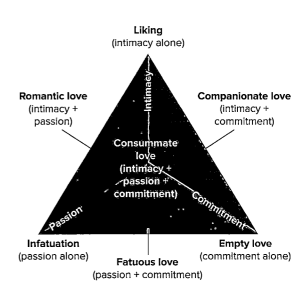

FIGURE 13.27 According to Sternberg, different types of love involve varying combinations of intimacy, commitment, and passion. Consummate love involves the presence of all three factors, whereas non-love represents the absence of all three.

Woman meets Prince Charming; they fall in love, get married, and live happily ever after. By adolescence, we are eagerly awaiting the glories of love.

According to the **cognitive-arousal model of love,** the passionate component of love has interacting cognitive and physiological components (Berscheid, 1984; Hatfield & Rapson, 1987). Primed with our beliefs and expectations about love, when we experience high arousal in the presence of someone whom we perceive as attractive and desirable, we may conclude that we must be "falling in love." This model suggests that emotional arousal actually caused by some other factor may sometimes be misinterpreted as love. This phenomenon is known as **transfer of excitation:** arousal due to one source is perceived ("misattributed") as being due to another source (Zillmann, 1984).

Remember the Capilano Suspension Bridge experiment by Donald Dutton and Arthur Aron (1974) that we discussed in Chapter 11? As you will recall, an experimenter approached male participants as they crossed over one of two bridges just north of Vancouver. Participants who crossed the narrow, wobbly, and arousing Capilano Suspension Bridge included more sexual themes in their stories than did participants who crossed a wide, sturdy non-arousing bridge. Dutton and Aron (1974) concluded that men's sexual attraction toward the woman was increased by the arousal produced by being on the suspension bridge, and a meta-analysis of over 30 experiments supports this model (Foster et al., 1998). When we are in the presence of someone we find attractive, other sources of arousal—whether a wobbly bridge, physical exercise, or a frightening movie—increase our sexual attraction even if we recognize those outside sources. If we are not aware of these sources, our attraction increases even more.

As you might expect, love does seem to have a neurological component. The ventral tegmental area of the brain is triggered when you think about the person you love. This results in the release of dopamine, which is related to pleasure. People who are in love, show greater activity in the entire reward structure of the brain (Song et al., 2015). Other neurotransmitters are affected as well. For example, norephinephrine increases and serotonin decreases. The result is an increase in heart rate and blood pressure, and we tend to become almost obsessive in our thoughts about our loved one. Finally, the prefrontal cortex shows lower activity levels (Zeki, 2007)—indicating that we are likely to engage in riskier behaviours.

Of course, for close relationships to develop and endure, they need more than passion alone. Intimacy, self-disclosure, and commitment provide a basis for the trust and friendship that sustain and increase love. As this chapter's *Applications* feature highlights, other behaviours also help to make close relationships successful.

Prejudice and Discrimination

Walk into a party, classroom, job interview—any social situation—and just by looking at your body build people will start to form an impression of you (Crandall et al., 2001). If they perceive you as "overweight," for example, then you may be judged as less likable, as having poorer will power and social skills, and as being more unhappy with yourself than your nonfat peers (Crandall & Martinez, 1996; Carr & Friedman, 2005).

Attractiveness matters too. Both children and adults tend to form less favourable impressions of people who are less attractive. They expect them to have less desirable personality traits and to achieve less success and happiness in life, even though correlational studies typically find that such variables are unrelated or only weakly related to attractiveness and other facial features (Dion et al., 1972; Zebrowitz et al., 1996).

Perhaps above all, ethnicity and gender matter. They are likely to be the first characteristics someone notices about you, and like so many other personal qualities, can be the basis for prejudice and discrimination (Fiske, 2002). **Prejudice** refers to a negative attitude toward people based on their membership in a group. Thus, we *prejudge* people—dislike them or hold negative beliefs about them—simply because of their gender, ethnic or religious identity, sexual orientation, and so on. This type of prejudging is more likely to found in people with lower levels of education and lower levels of income (Carvacho et al., 2013). **Discrimination** refers to overt behaviour: It involves treating people unfairly based on the group to which they belong.

Overt and Covert Prejudice: Have Times Changed?

Even in this day and age, overt prejudice and discrimination are in abundant supply. Armed conflicts based on ethnic or religious divisions continue across the globe; supremacist groups and

32. Explain how transfer of excitation can influence our feelings of love.

33. Based on marital research, give some advice to a newlywed couple about behaviours that will help to keep their relationship strong.

Applications

MAKING CLOSE RELATIONSHIPS WORK: LESSONS FROM PSYCHOLOGICAL RESEARCH

Close relationships go through good times and bad, persisting or dissolving over time. Consider marriage. Though highly intimate, this union often is fragile. In North America, about half of first marriages end in divorce, and the failure rate for second marriages is higher. How can people make their close relationships more satisfying and stable? Recent research on marriage suggests several answers that also may be applied to dating relationships and friendships.

For decades, most marital research simply asked people about their marriages. But as Figure 13.28 shows, researchers are now bringing couples into laboratories to videotape their interactions and to chart their facial and physiological responses as they discuss emotionally charged issues (Gottman et al., 1999; Kiecolt-Glaser et al., 1998). Rather than focusing only on unhappy couples to find out what is going wrong in their relationships, researchers also are studying happy couples to discover the secrets of their success.

Using these methods and new marital interview techniques, psychologists have predicted whether marriages will last or dissolve with impressive accuracy (Carrere et al., 2000). In one laboratory study, John Gottman and his colleagues (1998) collected behavioural and physiological data from 130 newlywed couples as they discussed areas of marital conflict (e.g., in-laws, finances, sex) during the first six months of their marriage. Six years later, participants

© Andrew Brusso

FIGURE 13.28 In John Gottman's "love lab," married couples (husband visible in rear) are filmed while interacting. Facial expressions, actions, heart rate, breathing rate, perspiration, fidgeting, and other responses are measured.

reported being happily married, unhappily married, or divorced. Using data collected while the couples were newlyweds, the researchers predicted which marriages would end in divorce with 83 percent accuracy, and the degree of marital satisfaction in still-married couples with 80 percent accuracy.

Surprisingly, the amount of anger expressed by husbands and wives in their laboratory interactions predicted neither stability nor happiness six years later. Instead, the crucial factor was the manner in which couples dealt with their anger. Particularly important were four behaviours that Gottman (1994) calls "The Four Horsemen of the Apocalypse": *criticism, contempt, defensiveness,* and *stonewalling* (listener withdrawal and nonresponsiveness).

Couples headed for unhappiness or divorce often exhibit these behaviours while discussing conflict, thereby escalating their conflict and negative emotions. When the wife criticizes the husband, he often stonewalls and withdraws from her attempts to reach some resolution. Her resulting frustration leads to stronger emotional displays and criticism, and the interaction degenerates into exchanges of contempt in which the partners tear down each other. Once this negative cycle develops, even positive overtures by one spouse are likely to evoke a negative response from the other (Margolin & Wampold, 1981).

Happily married couples experience conflict and anger, too, but do not allow the spiral of negativity to get out of control. Instead, they make frequent "repair attempts" to resolve their differences in a spirit of mutual respect and support. Gottman and his colleagues (1998) found that in happy marriages, the wife often introduced the conflict topic in a softened or low-intensity manner, rather than with sarcasm, criticism, and strong emotion. Next a key factor occurred: The husband responded to the issues she raised in a concerned and respectful manner that de-escalated negative emotion. A husband who turns off the TV and listens to his wife, or who says, "I can see you're upset, so let's work this out," demonstrates that her concerns are important to him. In happy marriages, after the husbands' responsiveness de-escalated the conflict, couples tended to "soothe" each other (and themselves) with positive comments and humour, resulting in more emotionally positive interchanges and lowered physiological arousal.

Happily married partners also make the effort to get to know each other's psychological world—their fears and dreams, philosophy of life, attitudes, and values—and they continually update their knowledge. This "love map," as Gottman calls it, allows each partner to be more responsive to the other's needs and to navigate around relationship roadblocks (Gottman et al., 1998; Gottman & De Claire, 2002). Such behaviour contributes to an essential aspect of happy marriages: a deep and intimate friendship between

continued

TABLE 13.1 How Strong Is Your Relationship?

Answer each question True (T) or False (F):

I can tell you about some of my partner's dreams.	T	F
We just love talking to each other.	T	F
My partner is one of my best friends.	T	F
My partner listens respectfully, even when we disagree.	T	F
We generally mesh well on basic values and goals in life.	T	F
I feel that my partner knows me pretty well.	T	F

The greater the number of "True" answers, the stronger your relationship. Courtesy of John Gottman.

Source: Gottman & De Claire, 2002. *The relationship cure: A five-step guide to strengthening your marriage, family, and friendships.* New York, NY: Three Rivers Press

the partners. Gottman (1994; Gottman & Silver, 2012) notes that the lessons of happy marriages can be applied to other types of close relationships. Affirmative answers to the questions in Table 13.1 suggest that such relationships are on solid psychological ground.

hate crimes persist (Figure 13.29); and people's race, gender, religion, and sexual orientation spark unfair treatment (Herek, 2000). In some ways, however, the most blatant forms of prejudice and discrimination have decreased in many countries. Racial segregation is no longer sanctioned by government policy in the United States and South Africa, and opinion polls indicate that fewer people express prejudiced attitudes toward other ethnic groups than was the case decades ago.

Although prejudiced attitudes truly seem to have faded a bit, in many ways modern racism, sexism, and other forms of prejudice have gone underground and are more difficult to detect (Brochu et al., 2008; Dovidio et al., 2005; Dovidio et al., 1997). Many people consciously hide their prejudices, expressing them only when they feel it is safe or socially appropriate. In other cases, people may honestly believe that they are not prejudiced but still show bias when tested in sophisticated ways (Fazio et al., 1995; Olson & Fazio, 2003).

To measure covert prejudice, Anthony Greenwald and his colleagues (1998) developed an

© Royalty-Free/Corbis

FIGURE 13.29 Prejudice reveals itself in many subtle and not-so-subtle forms.

implicit association test in which a series of word-pairs, such as "black—pleasant" and "white—pleasant" are flashed on a computer screen. As soon as you see each pair, your task is to press a computer key as quickly as you can, and this represents your reaction time. The principle underlying this test is that people react more quickly when they perceive that the two words in each pair are associated with each other (i.e., the words "fit" together) than when they don't fit together. Thus, without conscious control, a person prejudiced against Blacks will react more slowly to the "black—pleasant" pair than to the "white—pleasant" pair. The larger the discrepancy in reaction times, the stronger are the person's underlying negative attitudes. Greenwald and his associates found large reaction time differences of this kind even among White males who claimed—in response to standard questions—to have no prejudice toward Blacks. Likewise, Japanese and Koreans, whose nations have a history of conflict, react differently toward pairs such as "Japanese—pleasant" and "Korean—pleasant."

Prejudiced attitudes may surface when we are cued to think in negative ways. Esses and Zanna (1995) had students listen to music that put them in a good, bad, or neutral mood. They then generated a set of traits for a variety of ethnic groups (e.g., English Canadians, Pakistanis) and rated how positive or negative they felt each trait was. The data indicated that English-Canadian students rated other ethnic groups more negatively when they were in a bad mood but not when they were in a good mood. Thus, the way we are feeling can influence how we think about others. Recent research has attempted to identify the neural basis for these reactions. We examine this work more closely in this chapter's *Focus on Neuroscience* feature.

34. How do psychologists use reaction time tasks to detect people's covert prejudice?

Focus on Neuroscience

THE NEUROSCIENCE OF STEREOTYPING

Researchers wanting to study stereotyping acknowledge that modern versions of prejudice are more covert, more implicit than they were in the past (e.g., Esses & Hodson, 2006; Greenwald et al., 1998). Rather than directly indicating that a particular group is disliked, prejudice is more likely to show up as increased reaction time when the names of targeted groups are paired with positively toned adjectives (e.g., Black—pleasant). What neural circuits might we expect to be involved in this kind of reaction?

Recent work has focused on the amygdala. Activity in the amygdala can reflect a quick assessment of the potential threat posed by an emotionally laden stimulus (Adolphs et al., 1994; Nelson, 2013). Thus, if an individual perceives an out-group member as threatening, we should observe heightened amygdala activity. This result has been reported by several researchers (e.g., Chekroud, et al., 2014; Cunningham et al., 2004; Eberhardt, 2005) in studies where participants simply look at faces of in-group and out-group members. Indeed, amygdala activation can be observed even when the target face is presented subliminally (Cunningham et al., 2004) and the strength of activation is correlated with measures of implicit racism (Phelps et al., 2000).

Which facial features might trigger such a response? While there are many possible features to examine (e.g., size of nose, straightness of hair), one that seems an obvious candidate is skin tone. Variations in skin tone are related to perceptions of favourability (lighter skin tones are preferred), even by same-race judges (e.g., Maddox & Gray, 2002). Perhaps looking at skin tone itself will activate the amygdala. Ronquillo et al. (2007) presented photographs of both Black and White faces to participants (White males) while being scanned with fMRI. The faces had been colour adjusted by using Photoshop so that participants saw both light-toned and dark-toned versions of each face. Their task was simply to decide whether the individual presented was older or younger than 24 years. Consistent with previous findings, greater activity was observed in the amygdala for

Black faces than for White faces. However, the dark-toned White face resulted in as much activity as observed with the Black faces (see Figure 13.30). There was a nonsignificant decrease observed for the light-toned Black faces.

Ronquillo et al. (2007) suggest that these subtle differences are the bases of stereotype formation. Phenotypic features such as dark skin tone are detected at the level of the amygdala and in a largely automatic fashion result in stereotypic bias. We are likely to have a negative-affective response to individuals who possess this feature, regardless of their group membership. How fast does all of this happen? Ito and Bartholow (2009) and others (e.g., Kubota & Ito, 2007) have found EEG spikes (event-related potentials) within 180 milliseconds following the presentation of an out-group target.

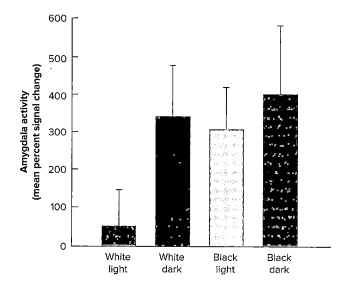

FIGURE 13.30 Amygdala activity in response to Black and White faces (after Ronquillo et al., 2007).

Source: Data from Ronquillo, J., Denson, T.F., Lickel, B., Lu, Z., Nandy, A., & Maddox, K.B. (2007). The effects of skin tone on race-related amygdala activity: An fMRI investigation. *Social Cognitive and Affective Neuroscience, 2*(1), 39–44.

Cognitive Roots of Prejudice

Whether overt or subtle, prejudice and discrimination are caused by a constellation of factors, including historical and cultural norms that legitimize differential treatment of various groups. Here, we examine several cognitive and motivational causes of prejudice.

Categorization and us-them thinking. To organize and simplify our world, we have a normal

35. Identify cognitive processes that foster prejudice.

perceptual tendency to categorize objects and people. At times, this helps us react to the environment quickly and to predict others' behaviour (Ito & Cacioppo, 2000). But our automatic tendency to categorize people also helps to lay a foundation for prejudice (Dovidio et al., 1997; Glick & Fiske, 1999).

Categorization leads to the perception of "in-groups" and "out-groups," groups to which we do and do not belong, respectively. In turn, in-group versus out-group distinctions spawn two common biases. First, we display *in-group favouritism*, a tendency to favour in-group members and attribute more positive qualities to "us" than to "them." In-group favouritism emerges in laboratory experiments across the globe, even when participants are assigned to temporary groups based on the flip of a coin or some trivial characteristic (Reichl, 1997; Tajfel, 1970). *Out-group derogation* reflects a tendency to attribute more negative qualities to "them" than to "us." Although people may display both biases, especially when they feel threatened, in-group favouritism is usually the stronger of the two (Hewstone et al., 2002).

Second, people display an *out-group homogeneity bias*. They generally view members of out-groups as being more similar to one another than are members of in-groups (Du et al., 2003; Brauer, 2001). In other words, we perceive that "they are all alike," but recognize that "we are diverse" (Linville & Jones, 1980). The mere fact that we identify people as "Asian," "Hispanic," "Black," and "White" reflects such a bias, because each of these ethnic categories contains many subgroups. In one study, Anglo-American university students were less likely to distinguish among "Hispanic" subgroups than were Cuban-American, Mexican-American, and Puerto Rican–American university students (Huddy & Birtanen, 1995). But just like Anglo students, the Cuban-, Mexican-, and Puerto Rican–American students also engaged in us-them thinking: They saw their own subgroup as distinct from the others but did not differentiate between the other two Hispanic subgroups.

Stereotypes and attributional distortions. Categorization and in-group biases lead us to respond quickly to out-group members based on perceived group characteristics—stereotypes—rather than based on their individual characteristics. Recall that merely labelling Hannah's parents as "blue-collar" or "white-collar" created a mental set that shaped how people perceived her behaviour (Darley & Gross, 1983). Similarly, 73 percent of White university students who observed a videotape of a Black man shoving a White man perceived the behaviour as "violent," but when the tape showed a White man shoving a Black man, only 13 percent of students saw it as violent (Duncan, 1976). Figure 13.31 illustrates how racial and gender stereotypes affect our perceptions.

36. How can people maintain their stereotypes in the face of contradictory information?

(a)   (b)

FIGURE 13.31 (a) Who is holding the razor knife? Allport and Postman (1947) showed this picture to one person, who then told another, who then told another, and so forth. Typically, by the sixth telling, the Black man was erroneously described as holding the razor. (b) Which person contributes most strongly to this research team? When the drawing shows an all-male group, all-female group, or mixed-sex group with a male at the head of the table (seat 3), participants say that the person in seat 3 is the strongest member. But in this mixed-gender drawing, most male and female participants do not pick the woman in seat 3. Instead, they pick one of the two men (Porter & Geis, 1981).

Source: (a) From *The Psychology of Rumor*, by G.W. Allport (L. Postman, 1947, Henry Holt & Co. Reprinted by permission of Robert Allport; (b) based on Porter, N.P., & Geis, F.L. (1981). "Women and nonverbal leadership cues: When seeing is not believing." In C. Mayo & N.M. Henley (Eds.), *Gender and nonverbal behavior*. New York, NY: Springer-Verlag.

What happens when we encounter individual members of out-groups whose behaviour clearly contradicts our stereotypes? One possibility is that we may change our stereotype; but someone who is motivated to hold on to a prejudiced belief can "explain away" discrepant behaviour in several ways. For example, the out-group member may be seen as an "exceptional case" or as having succeeded at a task not because of high ability but because of good luck, special advantage, or some other situational factor (Stewart et al., 2010).

Motivational Roots of Prejudice

People's ingrained ways of perceiving the world—categorizing, forming in-groups and out-groups, and so forth—appear to set the wheels of prejudice in motion, but motivational factors affect how fast those wheels spin.

37. According to realistic conflict theory and social identity theory, what are the motivational roots of prejudice?

Competition and conflict. According to **realistic conflict theory**, competition for limited resources fosters prejudice. In the United States and Europe, hostility toward minority groups increases when economic conditions worsen (Green et al., 1998; Catalano et al., 2002; Hovland & Sears, 1940; Pettigrew & Meertens, 1995). Originally, it was believed that a threat to one's personal welfare was the prime motivator of prejudice, but research suggests that prejudice is triggered more strongly by a *perceived threat to one's in-group* (Tajfel et al., 2004). In a classic study by Sherif et al. (1961), students at a summer camp were divided into two groups ("The Rattlers" and "The Eagles"). When the groups had to compete with each other for scarce resources, hostility and derogation of the out-group was maximized. Likewise, among Whites, prejudice toward Blacks is not related to personal resource gains and losses, but to the belief that White people as a group are in danger of being overtaken (Bobo, 1988).

Enhancing self-esteem. According to **social identity theory,** prejudice stems from a need to enhance our self-esteem. Some experiments find that people express more prejudice after their self-esteem is threatened (such as by receiving negative feedback about their abilities) and that the opportunity to derogate others helps to restore self-esteem (Fein & Spencer, 1997). Self-esteem, however, is based on two components: a personal identity and a "group" identity that reflects membership in various groups (Tajfel & Turner, 1986). We can raise self-esteem by associating ourselves with our in-group's accomplishments, and, conversely,

38. Discuss how self-fulfilling prophecies and stereotype threat perpetuate prejudice.

threats to the in-group threaten our self-esteem. Our group identity thus creates a tendency to take pride in one's in-group while also derogating out-groups (Perdue et al., 1990). Compared with relatively unprejudiced people, prejudiced individuals show greater concern with accurately determining who is an in-group versus out-group member (Blascovich et al., 1997).

How Prejudice Confirms Itself

Self-fulfilling prophecies are one of the most invisible yet damaging ways of maintaining prejudiced beliefs. A classic experiment by Carl Word and his colleagues (1974) illustrates this point. The researchers began with the premise—supported by research at the time—that Whites held several negative stereotypes of Blacks. In the experiment, White male university students interviewed White and Black high school students who were seeking admission into a special group. The participants used a fixed set of interview questions provided by the experimenter. Unknown to them, each applicant was an "accomplice" who had been trained to respond in a standard way to the questions. The findings indicated that these White participants sat farther away, conducted shorter interviews, and made more speech errors when the applicants were Black. In short, their behaviour was discriminatory.

But this is only half the picture. In a second experiment—a job interview simulation—White male undergraduates served as *job applicants*. Through random assignment they were treated either as the White applicants had been treated in the first experiment, or as the Black applicants had been treated. In other words, for half the participants, the interviewer sat farther away, held a shorter interview, and made more speech errors. The findings revealed that White participants who were treated more negatively performed worse during the job interview, were less composed, made more speech errors, and rated the interviewer as less friendly. In short, these experiments suggest that an interviewer's negative stereotypes can lead to discriminatory treatment during a job interview, and this discriminatory behaviour can cause the applicant to perform more poorly—ultimately confirming the interviewer's initial stereotype.

Stanford University psychologist Claude Steele (1997) has demonstrated another debilitating way that prejudice ends up "confirming itself." His concept of **stereotype threat** proposes that stereotypes create a fear and self-consciousness among stereotyped group members that they will "live up" to other people's stereotypes. For example, in a study comparing female and male college students who major in various fields, women majoring in the traditionally "male" fields of math, science, and engineering reported the highest level of stereotype threat (Steele et al., 2002). They were more likely to feel that they (as well as other women in their major) had been targets of sex discrimination and that because of their gender, other people (including their professors) expected them to have less ability and do more poorly. Stereotype threat can occur even if the group members do not accept the stereotype themselves. Given the stereotype that "Blacks are not as intelligent as Whites," Black university students who take a difficult test perform more poorly than White students when the test is described as "an intelligence test." But Blacks perform as well as Whites when the items are described merely as being a "laboratory task." Stereotypes that Whites are inferior to Asians in math, and that women are inferior to men in math, produce analogous results. When a difficult standardized math test is given in situations that activate these stereotypes, Whites and women perform more poorly than when the test is presented in a more neutral way (Aronson et al., 1999; Spencer et al., 1999).

Reducing Prejudice

Psychologists are interested not only in the causes of prejudice but also in identifying ways to reduce it. With some success, they have implemented many techniques aimed at changing the way people categorize one another and think about in-groups and out-groups (Hewstone et al., 2002; Kawakami et al., 2000).

The best-known approaches to prejudice reduction are based on a principle called **equal status contact:** Prejudice between people is most likely to be reduced when they (1) engage in sustained close contact, (2) have equal status, (3) work to achieve a common goal that requires cooperation, and (4) are supported by broader social norms (Allport, 1954).

In 1954, the United States Supreme Court handed down a momentous decision in the case of *Brown v. Board of Education,* ruling that school segregation based solely on race violates the constitutional rights of racial minorities. Providing key testimony, several psychologists stated that segregation contributed to racial prejudice and hostility.

Did school desegregation reduce prejudice? Walter Stephan (1990) reviewed more than 80 evaluation studies of desegregation programs and concluded that increasing direct contact through desegregation did not, in and of itself, consistently reduce racial prejudice. Indeed, some studies found that prejudice increased after desegregation.

Why weren't the results more positive? First, the condition of equal status contact was often not met, and contact when status is unequal serves only to perpetuate both groups' negative stereotypes of each other. Second, in many integrated school situations, close and personal contact between group members did not occur. Black and White students were sometimes placed in different "learning tracks" that minimized in-class contact, and they tended to associate only with members of their own ethnic group outside of class. Third, classroom experiences focused on individual rather than cooperative learning. And finally, intergroup contact was often not supported by broader social norms. In the early years of desegregation, many White politicians, parents, teachers, and school officials militantly opposed school integration.

When intergroup contact takes place under proper conditions, however, prejudice often decreases (Krahe & Altwasser, 2006; Pettigrew & Tropp, 2000). In school settings, *cooperative learning programs* place children into multiracial learning groups. Contact is close and sustained, each child is accorded equal status, and each has responsibility for learning and then teaching other group members one piece of the information that is needed for the group to succeed in its assignment (Aronson & Patnoe, 1997). Overall, such programs reduce prejudice and promote appreciation of ethnic group differences (Johnson & Johnson, 2000; McKown, 2005).

Beyond equal status contact, cooperative learning programs enable children to forge a common group identity, much as athletes on a team or members of a military unit form a group identity. Adopting a common identity is another factor that helps to reduce prejudice among group members (Dovidio et al., 2000).

Research investigating the cognitive mechanisms that underlie prejudice and stereotyping suggests that the automatic activation of stereotypes can be reduced. Kawakami and colleagues (2000) demonstrated that training in negating stereotypes reduced subsequent stereotype activation in participants. Gawronski and colleagues (2008) have since argued that in fact *affirmation* of counter-stereotypic associations is much more effective than negation of stereotypic associations in reducing stereotype activation. Mentally processing a statement such as "Not all African Americans are criminals" involves the breakdown of the statement into several components, including the pairing of Africans and criminality, and the presence of the negation (i.e., the word "not," which reverses the meaning of the rest of the sentence). For this reason, extensive training in negating stereotypes can have the ironic effect of actually *increasing* stereotype activation.

Using simulations to reduce "shooter bias." In several highly publicized cases during the past decade, police officers investigating a crime have shot and killed unarmed Black men. The officers, faced with a split-second decision about whether to shoot, mistakenly perceived that these men were either reaching for or holding a weapon. Was the victims' race a factor in these shootings? Social psychologists devised experiments in which college students and other adults quickly had to decide whether to shoot armed and unarmed White and Black suspects who appeared on a computer screen during a video simulation. The results revealed a "shooter bias" in which participants—both White and Black participants in some studies—were more likely to shoot unarmed suspects who were Black (Correll et al., 2002). Miller et al. (2012) have shown that this bias extends to people who are simply perceived as different from you. Participants were randomly assigned a personality type (red or green) and then shown images of other people who had a similar or different personality type. Sometimes the person in the image had a weapon, sometimes not. Participants had 600 milliseconds to decide whether or not to shoot. Results indicated that people were more likely to shoot unarmed suspects if they were different.

In computer simulation experiments with students and police officers, E. Ashby Plant and colleagues have been able to reduce this shooter bias (Plant & Peruche, 2005; Plant et al., 2005). The shooting simulation program, like those used in other experiments, was designed so that White and Black criminal suspects were equally likely to be armed or unarmed. Over time, with repeated exposure to the simulation program, the shooter bias that students and police officers displayed on the earlier trials disappeared. As the researchers note, these findings are only a promising first step that await further testing in a more rigorous police academy training program.

39. According to sociobiologists, what is the evolutionary basis of helping behaviour?

40. How do social norms, self-reinforcers, and empathy influence helping behaviour?

Prosocial Behaviour: Helping Others

Helping behaviour comes in many forms, from heroic acts of bravery and charitable donations to tutoring a classmate or returning a lost wallet. It characterizes the entire being of people such as Mother Teresa, who devoted her life to the world's poor. Acts of violence often grab the news headlines, but we should not lose sight of the mountains of good deeds performed around the world each day (Figure 13.32).

Why Do People Help?

What motivates prosocial behaviour? The debate over this question has practical consequences and profound implications for our conception of human nature. In Chapter 4, we considered the evolutionary principle of kin selection. Let's examine some more environmental explanations.

Social learning and cultural influences. Socialization, modelling, and reinforcement play a key role in fostering prosocial behaviour and attitudes (Eisenberg & Mussen, 1989; Janoski et al., 1998). Beginning in childhood, we are exposed to helpful models and taught prosocial norms. Recall from Chapter 7 that children were more likely to place several dogs' welfare above their own if they had first seen adults rescue a puppy on a TV program (Sprafkin et al., 1975). A survey of nearly 200 studies suggests that TV programs that model acts of kindness and helping have a strong positive effect on viewers' prosocial behaviour (Hearold, 1986).

Two social norms are especially relevant to helping behaviour (De Cremer & van Lange, 2001; Miller et al., 1990). First, the *norm of reciprocity* states that we should reciprocate when others

© Ken Gillespie Photography/Alamy Stock Photo

FIGURE 13.32 Like these rescue workers, many people seek out careers or join volunteer organizations that allow them to help other people.

treat us kindly. Second, the *norm of social responsibility* states that people should help others and contribute to the welfare of society. We are reinforced with approval when we adhere to these norms, receive disapproval when we do not, and observe that other people receive praise for conforming to these norms. Eventually, we internalize prosocial norms and values as our own, enabling powerful *self-reinforcers* such as pride, self-praise, and feelings of satisfaction to maintain prosocial behaviours even when external reinforcement is absent. If we remind people about these norms in the lab, they are more likely to help even when bystanders are present (Abbate et al., 2013).

Studies in Europe, Asia, and North America confirm that socialization matters (Eisenberg & Valiente, 2002). Children are more likely to act prosocially when they have been raised by parents who have high moral standards, who are warm and supportive, and who encourage their children to develop empathy and "put themselves in other people's shoes" (Janssens & Dekovic, 1997; Krevans & Gibbs, 1996). However, there also are cross-cultural differences in beliefs about when and why we should help (Eckensberger & Zimba, 1997). Joan Miller and her colleagues (1990) found that Hindu children and adults in India believe that one has a moral obligation to help friends and strangers, whether their need is serious or mild. In contrast, when a person's need for assistance is mild, American children and adults feel less obligated to help and view helping as more of a choice.

Empathy and altruism. Are all prosocial acts, regardless of how noble they appear, ultimately motivated by self-reinforcement, or do we have a capacity for *altruism*, the desire to aid another without concern for oneself? According to C. Daniel Batson's **empathy-altruism hypothesis**, altruism does exist, and it is produced by *empathy*, the ability to put oneself in the place of another and to share what that person is experiencing (Batson, 2006; Batson et al., 2002).

In one study, female students' empathy for another female participant (actually an accomplice) was increased or decreased by leading them to believe that her values were either similar or dissimilar to their own (Batson et al., 1981). Then, by a rigged coin flip, the accomplice was selected to receive supposedly painful electric shocks while performing a task, while the real participant acted as an observer. When the experiment began, the accomplice expressed great fear of the shocks. At this point, the participant was told that she could leave after watching only two shock trials or, if she wished, could change

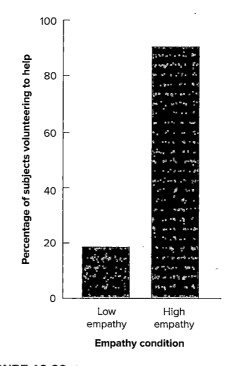

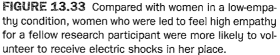

FIGURE 13.33 Compared with women in a low-empathy condition, women who were led to feel high empathy for a fellow research participant were more likely to volunteer to receive electric shocks in her place.

Source: Data from Batson, C.D., Duncan, B.D., Ackerman, P., Buckley, T., & Birch, K. (1981). Is empathic emotion a source of altruistic motivation? *Journal of Personality and Social Psychology*, 40, 290–302.

places with the woman, thereby saving her from the trauma of being shocked. Consistent with the empathy-altruism hypothesis, Figure 13.33 shows that high-empathy participants were much more likely to voluntarily change places.

As critical thinkers, we need to ask whether participants exchanged places not by virtue of empathy, but because they would have felt guilty for not doing so. Or perhaps, as the **negative state relief model** proposes, high empathy causes us to feel distress when we learn of others' suffering, so by helping them we reduce *our own* personal distress—a self-focused goal, not an altruistic one (Cialdini et al., 1987). Indeed, there are many reasons for acts of helping, but Batson's research suggests that at least some prosocial behaviour is motivated by unselfish goals and not by the reduction of guilt, sadness, or one's own distress (Batson et al., 1997). Given that altruistic behaviour has been observed in children as young as 18 months of age and even in young chimpanzees (Warneken & Tomasello, 2006), it seems likely that Batson is correct. Other researchers are not convinced, however, and the larger philosophical debate as to whether people are ever truly altruistic rages on (Cialdini et al., 1997).

Thinking critically

DOES PURE ALTRUISM REALLY EXIST?

Do you believe that people ever help one another for purely altruistic reasons? Or is even a small degree of egoism always involved?

Think about it, and then see the Answers section at the end of the book.

When Do People Help?

41. Identify two key ways (two stages of intervention) in which the presence of other bystanders often inhibits people from responding to an emergency.

Ordinary citizens often go to great lengths to help strangers, but, as the infamous Kitty Genovese murder (discussed in Chapter 2) illustrates, at times bystanders fail to assist victims who are clearly in distress (Figure 13.34). What influences whether a bystander will intervene?

Bibb Latané and John Darley (1970) view bystander intervention as a five-step process (Figure 13.35). First, a bystander will not help unless she or he notices the situation. Imagine that as you walk along a street, you hear two people yelling and then hear a single scream coming from inside a house. You've noticed the situation, but now what? In everyday life, many social situations are ambiguous, and step 2 involves deciding whether this is an emergency. Is someone really in danger? To answer this question, we often engage in *social comparison:* We look around to see how other people are responding. You might say to yourself, "No one else seems concerned, so it mustn't be anything too serious." In Kitty Genovese's murder, some bystanders mistakenly thought that because nobody else intervened they were merely witnessing a "lover's quarrel" that didn't warrant their "butting in" (Darley & Latané, 1968).

George Widman/AP Photo

FIGURE 13.34 Why do bystanders sometimes fail to assist a person in need?

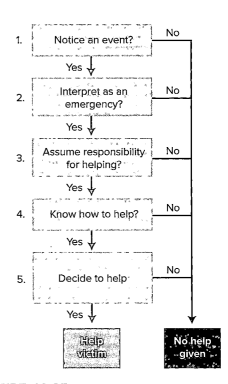

FIGURE 13.35 Bystander intervention in an emergency situation can be viewed as a five-step process. If the answer at each step is "Yes," help is given.

Source: Based on Latané, B., & Darley, J.M. (1970). *The unresponsive bystander: Why doesn't he help?* New York, NY: Appleton-Century-Crofts.

Laboratory experiments confirm the importance of social comparison. In one classic study, participants were filling out a questionnaire when smoke started to pour into the room from underneath a locked side door (Latané & Darley, 1968). Among those who were alone, three-quarters left the room to report the smoke. But when three participants were in the room together, only 38 percent of the groups reported the smoke. Astonishingly, most groups kept working while the room filled with smoke. Each person looked around, saw that nobody else was doing anything, and became convinced that the smoke didn't represent an emergency!

If you conclude that a situation is an emergency, then you move to the next step: assuming responsibility to intervene. If you are the only person to hear someone screaming, then responsibility for helping falls squarely on you. But if others are present, there may be a *diffusion of responsibility*—"If I don't help, someone else will"—and if each bystander has this thought, the victim won't receive help. In the Kitty Genovese murder, many bystanders who *did* interpret the incident as an emergency failed to intervene because they were certain that someone must already have called the police

(Darley & Latané, 1968). Similarly, in an experiment in which university students were isolated in individual cubicles and listened to another student who indicated he was having a seizure, participants were less likely to assist the seizure victim if they believed that other bystanders were present (Darley & Latané, 1968).

If you take responsibility, whether you actually intervene still depends on a fourth factor, your *self-efficacy* (confidence) in dealing with the situation. Sometimes we fail to help because we don't know how or believe that our help won't be effective. In one survey, 269 university students and faculty indicated they had witnessed a public episode of child abuse, yet only a quarter reported that they had intervened (Christy & Voigt, 1994). Of those who intervened, 71 percent said that they had been certain about what to do. Among those who did not intervene, 80 percent said they were *not* certain about what action to take.

Finally, a bystander might decide not to intervene because of the perceived costs (Dovidio et al., 1991). Potential costs include not only possible physical danger, but also negative social consequences, such as "appearing foolish" by trying to help inappropriately.

As this model indicates, the common-sense adage "there is safety in numbers" is not always true when it comes to receiving help. Many experiments find a **bystander effect:** The presence of multiple bystanders inhibits each person's tendency to help, largely because of social comparison or diffusion of responsibility. This inhibition is more likely to occur when the bystanders are strangers rather than friends (Latané & Rodin, 1969). Markey (2000) reports that the bystander effect occurs even when communicating over the Web. A general request for help ("Can anyone tell me how to look at someone's profile?") was sent to 200 chat groups over a 30-day period. Assistance came more slowly from larger chat groups than from smaller ones.

Beyond the bystander effect, other factors also help to explain why people may be helpful on some occasions but not on others. First, we are more likely to help when we are in a *good mood* (Salovey et al., 1991). Ironically, *pre-existing guilt*—feeling guilty about something we have recently done—also increases helping (Regan et al., 1972). Apparently, assisting others eases our guilt, even when the two actions are unrelated. Observing a *helpful role model,* such as someone assisting a stranded motorist or donating blood, increases prosocial behaviour (Sarason et al., 1991). Certain drugs such as MDMA (ecstasy) may influence emotional empathy and, thus, result in increased helping (Hysek et al., 2014). Finally, we help more when there is a lack of time pressure and we are *not in a hurry.*

Whom Do We Help?

Some people are more likely to receive help than others. Three prominent factors are the following:

- *Similarity.* Perceiving that a person is similar to us increases our willingness to provide help. The similarity may be in dress, attitudes, nationality, music preference or other characteristics (Clark & Giacomantonio, 2013; Dovidio, 1984), and it may make it easier for us to identify with the victim's plight.

- *Gender.* Women are more likely to receive help than men *if* the bystander is male (Eagly & Crowley, 1986). Women and men are equally likely to be helped by female bystanders.

- *Perceived responsibility.* People are more likely to receive help when their need for aid is viewed as being caused by factors beyond their control (Blader & Tyler, 2002; Weiner, 1996). Thus, people who are homeless because of a natural disaster are more likely to receive help than those who are perceived as being homeless because they are unwilling to work.

Because our attributions regarding why a person needs help can be inaccurate, this last factor—perceived responsibility—can take an odd twist. Ironically, one factor that can lead attributions astray is a belief that the world is a just place. The **just world hypothesis** (Lerner, 1980) holds that, because people want to view the world as fair, they perceive that people get what they deserve and deserve what they get. This belief may lead some people to conclude that victims of rape, AIDS, and other misfortunes somehow *deserve* their fate (Ford et al., 1998; Landstrom et al., 2016; Wyer et al., 1985). This irrational blaming of victims may reduce people's feelings of responsibility to help.

Increasing Prosocial Behaviour

Can prosocial behaviour be increased? "Mandatory volunteerism" is one approach used in some high schools, universities, and businesses. Obviously, the students and workers who are required to donate their time to charitable organizations provide a valuable service, but do these

42. Whom are we most likely to help? How might the belief in a just world inhibit us from helping?

programs increase participants' intrinsic volunteerism later in life? Unfortunately, research results are mixed (Janoski et al., 1998; Stukas, 1999). The outcome probably depends on the personal rewards that volunteers experience and their increased awareness of human needs.

Another approach, consistent with social learning theory, is to expose people to prosocial models. Psychologists used prosocial modelling as part of a nationwide program to increase blood donations (Sarason et al., 1991). Students in 66 high schools watched an audiovisual program showing high-school donors giving blood. Compared with a control condition presented with a standard appeal from the local blood bank, the prosocial video increased blood donations by 17 percent.

Research suggests that developing feelings of empathy and connectedness with others also may make people more likely to help (Eisenberg, 2000). Margaret Clark and her colleagues (1987) found that people who felt a greater sense of connectedness to their communities were more likely to experience a need to be socially responsible and help others. Even group musical training in children increases connectedness and prosocial behaviour (Schellenberg et al., 2015).

Finally, simply learning about factors that hinder bystander intervention may increase the tendency to help someone in distress. Arthur Beaman and his colleagues (1978) exposed some university students to information about the *bystander effect*. Control participants did not receive this information. Two weeks later, more than half of the students who had learned about the bystander effect provided aid to the victim of an accident (staged by the researchers), compared with only about a quarter of the control group participants.

Aggression: Harming Others

We love. We nurture. We help. But as current events and the history of humankind attest, we also harm. In humans, *aggression* represents any form of behaviour that is intended to harm another person, and it can be analyzed at biological, environmental, and psychological levels.

Biological Factors in Aggression

Is aggression rooted in heredity? From bulls, roosters, and dogs to laboratory mice and rats, animals can be selectively bred over generations to be more or less aggressive (Lagerspetz et al., 1968). In some species, such as the stickleback

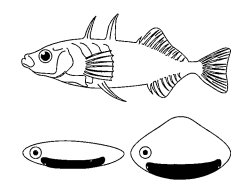

FIGURE 13.36 During the mating season, the male stickleback fish develops a red belly. The sight of another red-bellied male—a potential rival for a mate—reflexively triggers an attack by the first male. The key releaser stimulus for this fixed action pattern is the red marking. A male stickleback will not attack a realistic-looking male model that has no red belly but will attack unrealistic fish models that have this red marking.

Source: Based on Tinbergen, N. (1951). *The study of instinct.* Oxford, UK: Clarendon Press.

fish shown in Figure 13.36, certain aggressive behaviours represent a fixed-action pattern that is reflexively triggered by specific environmental stimuli. Humans do not display such rigid, reflexive aggressive responses, but behaviour geneticists argue that heredity partly determines why some people are more aggressive than others. Identical twins are more similar in their aggressive behaviour patterns than are fraternal twins, even when the identical twins are raised in different homes with presumably different social environments (Bouchard et al., 1990; Coccaro et al., 1997; Beatty et al., 2002). Sociobiologists propose that a genetic predisposition toward aggression can be traced to evolutionary adaptation (see Chapter 4). As in nonhumans, aggression at the proper time helped our ancestors compete successfully for mates, food, and shelter, defend territory, and survive against attack. This aggression increased the odds that such individuals would pass their genes on to the next generation (Rushton, 1989).

The search for biological causes of aggression also has led researchers deep within the brain, to the *hypothalamus, amygdala,* and other subcortical structures (Adams, 2006; Falkner et al., 2014; Siegel et al., 1999). Electrically stimulate certain neural pathways in a cat's hypothalamus, and it will arch its back and attack. Surgically destroy areas of the amygdala—an approach that sometimes has been used with violent human criminals—and in many species defensive aggression will decrease (Aggleton, 1993). There is, however, no

43. What evidence supports a genetic role in aggression?

44. Describe some brain regions and body chemicals that play a role in aggression.

single brain structure that "turns on" and "turns off" aggression. Different types of aggression—defending oneself, defending one's offspring, predatory aggression, establishing dominance, and so forth—may involve different neural circuits (Siegel et al., 1999).

Aggression also involves activity of the *frontal lobes,* and the important role that the frontal lobes play in impulse control (Hawkins & Trobst, 2000). Adrian Raine and his colleagues (1998) examined the brain functioning of 24 adults who had murdered someone, either out of emotional, momentary impulse, or as a planned predatory act. PET scans revealed that both groups of murderers showed more subcortical activity than a control group of non-murderers, but the impulsive murderers also had lower frontal lobe activity. Deficient frontal lobe activity may make it more difficult to regulate aggressive impulses generated by subcortical brain regions (Raine, 2002).

Just as there is no single brain centre for aggression, there is no one "aggression chemical." In humans and other animals, however, atypically low levels of *serotonin* activity may play a role in impulsive aggression, as when people lash out from emotional rage (Audero et al., 2013; Siegel et al., 1999; Siever et al., 1999; Moore et al., 2002). When a drug designed to boost serotonin activity is administered to men who physically abuse their partners and also to psychiatric patients who have difficulty controlling aggressive impulses, both groups show a relatively weak response to the drug (Rosenbaum et al., 1997).

And what about the sex hormone *testosterone,* which is found in males and also in females (though in smaller amounts)? In many species of mammals, higher testosterone levels contribute to greater *social aggression:* unprovoked aggressive acts that are designed to establish a dominance hierarchy among members of the same species. Injecting adult males with testosterone increases social aggression, whereas castration decreases it. But in humans and other primates, the association between testosterone and aggression is weaker and less consistent (Pinel, 1997; O'Connor et al., 2002).

Aversive Environmental Stimuli: Beyond Frustration

Aggression is influenced not only by biology, but also by our present environment and past learning experiences (Eron, 2000; Rotton & Cohn, 2000). Frustration, which occurs when some stimulus or event interferes with our progress toward a goal, often contributes to aggression. In 1939, several leading psychologists proposed the **frustration-aggression hypothesis,** stating that (1) frustration inevitably leads to aggression, and (2) all aggression is the result of frustration (Dollard et al., 1939).

Both of these sweeping assertions have since been disproved. From human infants to adults, frustration does increase the risk of verbal or physical aggression (Calkins & Johnson, 1998). At the workplace, it contributes to acts of employee hostility, theft, and sabotage (Spector, 1997). But people do not always respond to frustration by aggressing. Instead, they may exhibit despair, resignation, or non-aggressive ways of dealing with conflict (Björkqvist, 1997).

The second postulate is false as well. Aggression can be increased not only by frustration, but also by exposure to a wide range of aversive stimuli (Berkowitz, 1990). For example, *painful stimuli* can trigger irritability and aggression in humans and other animals. *Provocation* is another stimulus to aggress. Experiments with university students confirm that we often retaliate against someone who insults us or causes us physical harm (Ohbuchi & Kambara, 1985). In other species, even animals that are normally passive and prefer to flee when attacked will fight if they become cornered (Enquist & Leimar, 1990).

Crowding can trigger aggression in many species. In humans, when people feel crowded and believe they have little control over the situation, they report greater stress, have higher levels of stress hormones, and tolerate frustration more poorly (Fleming et al., 1987). For some motorists, increasingly congested roads and being trapped in inescapable traffic jams set the stage for high stress and aggressive acts of "road rage" (Figure 13.37). These aggressive acts are slightly lower for motorcycle riders, who are more vulnerable than drivers (Rowden et al., 2016).

45. Identify some major types of environmental stimuli that increase the risk of aggression.

Gabriela Medina/Blend Images/Getty Images

FIGURE 13.37 Increasingly crowded roads and stressed drivers have made road rage an international problem.

Heat also increases the risk of aggression (Anderson, 2001; Bushman et al., 2005). Assaults, rapes, family disturbances, and riots increase in summer months. These correlational findings are supported by several controlled experiments. In one, Dutch police officers were exposed to two temperature conditions (27° and 21°C/80.6° and 69.8°F) and shown firearm-training videotapes portraying interactions with crime suspects (Vrij et al., 1994). When the temperature was hotter, police perceived suspects as more threatening and responded with greater aggression. Recently, several authors (e.g., Anderson, 2012; Mares, 2013) have suggested that global warming has the effect of increasing violence, particularly in disadvantaged neighbourhoods.

Learning to Aggress: Reinforcement and Modelling

46. Discuss how reinforcement and modelling contribute to aggression.

47. How do cognitive factors determine whether we will respond to a stimulus aggressively?

Aggression, like other behaviours, is influenced by learning (Anderson & Bushman, 2002). Non-aggressive animals can be trained to become vicious aggressors if conditions are arranged so that they are consistently victorious in fights with weaker animals. Conversely, if conditions are arranged so that an animal is defeated in its early battles, it becomes submissive. The younger an animal is when it first suffers repeated defeats, the more submissively it will react to attacks by other animals (Zillmann, 1979).

Reward affects human aggression in much the same way. In one study of four-year-old nursery-school children, the investigators recorded a total of 2583 aggressive acts and their consequences. Children became increasingly aggressive when their aggressive behaviour produced positive outcomes for them (as when an aggressive act resulted in another child's giving up a desired toy). Children whose aggressive behaviour was unsuccessful or who experienced unpleasant consequences were less likely to be aggressive in the future (Patterson et al., 1967). Unfortunately, about 80 percent of the aggressive behaviours were rewarding for the aggressor.

Aggression also can be learned by observing others (Huesmann, 1997). As Albert Bandura's (1965) famous "Bobo doll" experiments clearly demonstrated, children learn "how to aggress" even when they witness an aggressive model being punished (Chapter 7). Later, if the punishing agent is not present, or if rewards are available for aggressing, children may reproduce the model's actions. Correlational studies, while not establishing cause and effect, find that aggressive and delinquent children tend to have parents who frequently model aggressive behaviour (Bandura, 1973; Stormshak et al., 2000).

Psychological Factors in Aggression

Numerous psychological factors influence whether we behave aggressively in a particular situation (Anderson & Bushman, 2002). From face-to-face and cyber (email, chat) aggression among schoolmates to gang violence, "road rage," and war, people may employ several types of *self-justification* to make it psychologically easier to aggress toward others (Lanier, 2001; Pornari & Wood, 2010). Aggressors may blame the victim for imagined wrongs, thereby convincing themselves that the victim "deserves it." They may minimize the seriousness of their own aggression by believing that other people's acts are even more repulsive, or by displacing responsibility. They may also "dehumanize" their victims by stripping them of human qualities and regarding them as objects or animals.

Perceived intent, empathy, and emotional regulation. Other cognitive factors, such as the *attribution of intentionality*, affect how we respond to provocation. When we perceive that someone's negative behaviour toward us was intended or controllable, we are more likely to become angry and retaliate (Betancourt & Blair, 1992; Graham et al., 1992). Unfortunately, people who are generally angry and aggressive tend to perceive others as having greater hostile intent, which may contribute to a vicious cycle of aggression (Epps & Kendall, 1995).

Our degree of *empathy* for someone also influences how we react to provocation. When people offend us and then apologize, the likelihood that we will forgive them depends, in part, on how well we can understand their viewpoints (McCullough et al., 1997). And even when we don't forgive, whether we respond to provocation calmly or lash out depends on our *ability to regulate our emotions*. Some children and adults seem to be more physiologically reactive to provocation than others, and reduced frontal lobe activity may impair the ability to control aggressive impulses (Raine et al., 1998). But cultural norms and cognitive factors also influence how we regulate our emotions and manage conflict (Bjoerkqvist, 1997). Thus, when nonviolent married men listen to audiotaped interactions designed to induce anger, they respond with more anger-controlling thoughts than do men with a history of domestic abuse (Eckhardt & Kassinove, 1998).

Psychodynamic processes. Sigmund Freud believed that human aggression is instinctive, a view shared by the famous ethologist Konrad Lorenz (1966) and some modern psychodynamic thinkers (Raphling, 1998). Freud proposed that, in a never-ending cycle, aggressive impulses build up over time, eventually have to be released, and then build up again. His principle of **catharsis** stated that performing an act of aggression discharges aggressive energy and *temporarily* reduces our impulse to aggress. But how does one do this in a world in which violence is discouraged and punished? One method of releasing aggressive impulses is to channel them into socially acceptable "aggressive" behaviours, such as participating in verbal debates, vigorous exercise, competitive sports, hunting, and so forth. Another approach is to discharge aggressive impulses *vicariously* by watching and identifying with other people who behave aggressively.

If people cannot express their aggressive impulses in direct or disguised forms, will the unreleased pressures build up to an explosion point? In some cases, seemingly meek or unassertive people commit shocking and brutal crimes. These individuals, whom psychologist Edwin Megargee (1966) describes as having *overcontrolled hostility,* show little immediate reaction to provocation. Instead, they bottle up their anger and, over time, the pressure to aggress builds up. At a critical point, they erupt into violence. Often, the provocation that triggers their destructive outburst is trivial. For example, one ten-year-old boy with no previous history of aggression stabbed his sister more than 80 times with an ice pick after she changed the channel during his favourite TV show. After the aggressive outburst, such people revert to their former passive, unassertive state (Quinsey et al., 1983).

Cases of overcontrolled hostility are consistent with the concept of catharsis, but other research results are not. For example, when people are aroused by just-completed vigorous physical exercise, it is easier—not harder—to provoke them to aggression (Bushman & Bonacci, 2002). Psychodynamic theory also predicts that viewing violent pornography should help people discharge aggressive impulses, but, as noted in Chapter 11, this is not what happens. After watching scenes of rape and sexual coercion, men act *more* aggressively toward women (Donnerstein & Berkowitz, 1981). And what about watching violent movies and TV programs? Do these activities help people "blow off steam," as some stars in the entertainment industry claim?

Media Violence: Catharsis versus Social Learning

Many movies, as well as fiction and non-fiction TV programs, are saturated with violence. According to psychodynamic theory, movie and TV violence should be a cathartic pot of gold. But social learning theorists argue that, by providing numerous aggressive models—including many who are reinforced—media violence is more likely to increase viewers' aggressive behaviour than to reduce it (Anderson et al., 2010; Huesmann, 2007). From a social learning perspective, it is particularly disturbing that

- 40 percent of violent incidents on TV were initiated by "good guys" whom viewers were likely to perceive as attractive role models and identify with;
- about 75 percent of violent scenes contained no remorse or penalty for violence, and the "bad guys" went unpunished in 40 percent of the programs; and
- only 15 percent of TV programs portrayed long-term negative consequences of violence (National Television Violence Study, 1998).

Headline-making "copycat" acts of violence clearly illustrate social learning effects. Still, hundreds of millions of people view media violence, and such horrendous acts thankfully are rare. What, then, are the more general effects of media violence on aggression? Over the past 30 years, hundreds of experiments and correlational studies have shed light on the "catharsis versus social learning" debate.

To most experts, the verdict is clear: The preponderance of evidence favours the social cognitive view (Eron, 2000; Gentile, 2007; Huesmann, 2010; Johnson et al., 2002). Exposure to TV and movie violence is related to the tendency of both children and adults to behave aggressively (Huesmann et al., 2003).

For example, using data collected over 22 years, Leonard Eron (1987) found that American children who had watched greater amounts of TV violence at age eight were more likely to have committed serious criminal activity by age 30 (Figure 13.38). In Finland, Vappu Viemeroe (1996) found that boys and

48. According to the catharsis and social learning viewpoints, what role does media violence play in regulating human aggression?

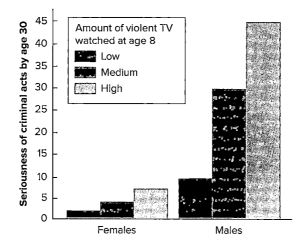

FIGURE 13.38 Children who watched more violent TV at age eight committed more serious criminal behaviour by age 30. Although criminal behaviour is higher overall for males than for females, the general pattern of results is the same. These findings are correlational (can you think of alternative explanations for this TV-crime relation?), but, in conjunction with controlled experiments, the weight of evidence convinces most experts that viewing media violence has psychological consequences.

Source: Data from Eron, L.D. (1987). The development of aggressive behavior from the perspective of a developing behaviorism. *American Psychologist, 42,* 435–442.

girls who had watched more violent TV when they were seven to nine years old were more likely to have been arrested by their mid-20s. In Belgium, Jacque Leyens and his colleagues (1975) went into a facility for high-school-age juvenile delinquents and held a special "movie week" in which they showed different groups of boys either violent or nonviolent movies each night. The result: Among boys who watched the violent films, physical and verbal aggression increased.

Media violence appears to exert its effects through multiple avenues (Huesmann, 1997; National Television Violence Study, 1998):

- Viewers learn new aggressive behaviours through modelling.
- Viewers come to believe that aggression usually is rewarded or, at least, is rarely punished.
- Viewers become desensitized to the sight and thought of violence, and to the suffering of victims.
- Viewers' fear of becoming a target of crime or violence increases.

Before you become completely disillusioned and toss out your TV, there are some

49. Based on research, how does media violence affect people's behaviour and attitudes?

50. According to learning principles, how might violent video games teach people to behave aggressively? Does evidence support this view?

qualifications that we should consider. First of all, some people are more influenced by TV violence than others. For example, Eron (1987) notes that boys tend to be more susceptible to media violence effects than girls (see Figure 13.38 again). In addition, aggressive behaviour does not occur in a vacuum— in most cases, some kind of negative stimulus (e.g., insult, provocation, extreme heat, high arousal level) must be present. Finally, the highest level of aggression is observed when the cues present in the TV program are similar to those encountered in the actual situation. Wendy Josephson (1987) at the University of Winnipeg asked boys in Grade 2 or 3 to watch either a violent or nonviolent program. Both shows were action-oriented, but the violent show involved a lot of gunplay between a police SWAT team and gang members. The SWAT team kept in constant communication with one another by using walkie-talkies. After watching the program, the boys were asked to play a game of floor hockey while observers coded their behaviour for aggression. However, before starting the match, the players were "interviewed" by the experimenter in a manner similar to pre-game interviews at actual hockey games. For some of the boys, the experimenter used a microphone and for others, a walkie-talkie.

The highest level of aggression was found in the boys who watched the violent program and who were interviewed with a walkie-talkie. The lowest level was reported for those who watched the nonviolent show. Apparently, the presence of the aggressive cue (the walkie-talkie) stimulated more aggression because of its association with the violence in the film clip. Similar results of increased aggression following exposure to aggressive cues have been reported in both laboratory (e.g., Berkowitz & LePage, 1967) and field settings (e.g., Boyanowski & Griffiths, 1982).

Beyond movies and TV, the question of whether violent video games promote aggression also has raised public and scientific concern. In July 2000, the St. Louis County (Missouri) Council passed an ordinance to penalize businesses that allow people under the age of 18 to play violent video games without parental consent (Jurkowitz, 2002). This decision has since been overturned by a U.S. federal appeals court, but it still highlights the issue of video game violence. What does science have to say? This chapter's *Frontiers* feature looks at this issue in more detail.

Frontiers

DO VIOLENT VIDEO GAMES PROMOTE AGGRESSION?

On a summer's eve in 2008, four bored teenagers from New Hyde, New York, decided to go on a crime spree. Seeking to emulate the behaviour of the lead character in the violent video game *Grand Theft Auto IV,* they beat and robbed a victim, broke into garages, attempted a carjacking, and tried to rob a man driving a van before being arrested by the police (Crowley, 2008, June 27). In August of 2013, an eight-year boy shot and killed his grandmother after playing the same game. Over a decade earlier, in April 1999, two students went on a shooting rampage in Columbine High School, Colorado, killing a teacher and 12 students, and wounding others. The killers were avid players of many violent video games, most notably the "first-person shooter" games *Doom* and *Doom 2* (Block, 2007).

In North America and Europe, crimes such as these reinforce public, political, and scientific concern about the effect of violent video games (Glock & Kneer, 2009). Yet such tragic cases cannot, by themselves, provide clear answers. Many factors play a role in aggression, and trying to isolate how any single factor contributed to a crime after the fact typically involves much speculation. Had the four teens, the eight-year-old, or the two Columbine shooters never played a violent video game (or watched a violent movie), would they still have committed those crimes?

Keep in mind that in other school shootings, the killers have had little, if any, expertise with violent video games (Ferguson, 2008). Moreover, many millions of people play violent video games (and watch violent media) and don't commit violent crimes. So, in an interview on the TV station CNN, was the president of the Interactive Digital Software Association correct when he stated, "I think the issue has been vastly overblown. . . . There is absolutely no evidence, none, that playing a violent video game leads to aggressive behaviour" (Lowenstein, 2000, May 12; quoted in Anderson & Bushman, 2001, p. 353)?

Even back then, experiments in which researchers directly manipulated people's exposure to violent video games provided such casual evidence. In what remains one of the better experiments to this date, Roland Irwin and Alan Gross (1995) randomly assigned 60 seven- and eight-year-old boys to play with a violent or nonviolent video game for 20 minutes. Afterwards, each child engaged in a ten-minute "free-play" period with another boy (an accomplice). Next, as each participant competed against this boy on a task for a prize, the boy (according to plan) cheated. Compared with participants who had played the nonviolent game, those who had played the violent game displayed more physical and verbal aggression toward inanimate objects (e.g., toys), more verbal aggression toward the other boy during the free-play period, and more physical aggression toward the boy during the competition.

What Research May Show

Let's think critically about these results. Did the violent content of the video game increase the children's aggression, or was it simply a more exciting game? Heart rate measures recorded before and during video game play indicated that the game's content was not more arousing, strengthening the conclusion that the game's content was the key factor. Other experiments with college students have found that briefly playing violent video games, at least in the short term, increases subsequent aggressive behaviour and physiologically desensitizes students to scenes of real-world violence (Carnagey & Anderson, 2005; Carnagey et al., 2007).

Some correlational studies also suggest a possible link between playing violent video games and getting into physical fights (Gentile et al., 2004; Rudatsikira et al., 2008). But as a critical thinker, remember that correlation doesn't establish causation. Recall the bidirectionality problem: perhaps getting into fights produces consequences (e.g., anger, frustration) that prompt people to play video games. Also consider the third-variable problem: perhaps people who have a more hostile personality to begin with play more violent video games and also get into more fights. Indeed, in one study, adolescents exposed to more violent video games did score higher on personality tests of hostility (Gentile et al., 2004). So the researchers adjusted their statistical analyses to take this possible confounding factor into account. They found that violent video game exposure was still correlated—albeit weakly—with a tendency to get into more physical fights.

© Sylent-Press/ullstein bild/The Image Works

FIGURE 13.39 Do children who play graphically violent video games become desensitized to violence and more likely to behave aggressively toward other people?

continued

Several longitudinal studies have examined video game violence. For example, two studies of adolescents in Germany and one of adolescents and children in Finland found that exposure to violent video games helped to predict physical aggression or delinquency 24 to 30 months later (Hopf et al., 2008; Möller & Krahé, 2009; Wallenius & Punamäki, 2008). In contrast, a one-month longitudinal American study involving older participants (with an average age of 28 years) found no link between playing an online violent video game and subsequent aggression (Williams & Skoric, 2005). Aldachi & Willoughby (2013) followed students throughout high school and report that the more competitive video gamers were indeed more aggressive. But they attribute this to the competition factor rather than the violence per se. The same students were also more violent if they were engaged in competitive gambling.

The Big Picture

Based on the most comprehensive meta-analysis of violent video game research to date, which covers 136 studies and 130 296 participants in Western countries and Japan, Craig Anderson and his colleagues (2010a) concluded that playing violent video games increases people's aggressive behaviour, cognition, and emotions, and also desensitizes them to violence. Most of these associations are weak, but they all support social-cognitive models of aggression. As for practical importance, Anderson and his colleagues note,

> When effects accumulate across time, or when large portions of the population are exposed to the risk, or when consequences are severe, statistically small effects become much more important (2010a, p. 170).

As an analogy, think of some factor (shoe or ski design, anxiety) that reduces a sprinter's or ski racer's time in a competition by only two-tenths of a second. In many circumstances, this might be trivial, but in the Olympics, it could mean the difference between a gold medal and no medal at all.

As in the case of mass media research, debate about violent video games still exists. Based on their own considerably smaller meta-analysis and concerns about the methods used in many studies, Christopher Ferguson and John Kilburn (2009) believe that it's premature to conclude that violent video games cause aggression. Researchers have also swapped critiques about whose meta-analysis approach is more appropriate (Anderson et al., 2010b; Ferguson & Kilburn, 2010).

We agree that more research, and especially more complete longitudinal research, is needed. But based on the evidence available now, the conclusion that exposure to video game violence is more likely to increase than decrease aggression is more reality than myth. In fact, the American Psychological Association has recently taken a stand on this issue noting that there is definitely a link between violent video games and aggression. The APA is less sure whether or not this can lead to actual crimes. This doesn't mean that everyone who plays violent video games becomes more aggressive, angrier, or desensitized. After Australian researchers exposed adolescents to a violent video game for 20 minutes, 72 percent showed no significant change in feelings of anger. But among those who changed, almost three times as many experienced increased (20.6 percent) rather than decreased (7.4 percent) anger (Unsworth et al., 2007). In a more recent study, Hasan et al. (2013) report that playing an aggressive video game for three consecutive days results in more aggression and an increase in hostile expectations about the behaviour of others. Certainly, the overwhelming majority of children, teens, and adults who play violent video games don't go out and assault or kill people. But aggression comes in many forms—physical and verbal, obvious and subtle—and even the potential for a small increased risk of aggression among some people some of the time can have important consequences.

 **Review**

- Proximity, mere exposure, similarity of attitudes, and physical attractiveness typically enhance our attraction toward someone. Relationships deepen as partners self-disclose and exchanges between them become more intimate and broader. Social exchange theory analyzes relationships in terms of the rewards and costs experienced by each partner.

- The qualities that people find most attractive in a mate vary somewhat across cultures. Evolutionary theorists propose that gender difference in mate preferences reflect inherited biological tendencies, whereas sociocultural theorists believe that these differences result from socialization and gender inequities in economic opportunities.

- Partners are more likely to remain happily married when they understand each other and deal with conflicts by de-escalating their emotions and providing mutual support.

- Overt prejudice has decreased in some ways, but people may hide their prejudice or be unaware of subtle prejudices they harbour.

- Prejudice stems partly from our tendency to perceive in-groups and out-groups. People typically display in-group favouritism and an out-group homogeneity bias. Perceived threats to one's in-group and a need to enhance one's self-esteem can motivate prejudice.

- Prejudice often is reduced when in-group and out-group members work closely together, with equal status, on tasks involving common goals and under conditions of broader institutional support.

- Some theorists propose that through kin selection and reciprocal altruism, evolution has helped to shape a genetic predisposition toward prosocial behaviour among humans. Social learning theorists emphasize how social norms, modelling, and reinforcement shape prosocial attitudes and behaviour.

- The presence of multiple bystanders may decrease bystander intervention through social comparison processes and a diffusion of responsibility for helping. We are most likely to help others when we perceive that they are similar to us and not responsible for their plight.

- Prosocial behaviour can be increased by enhancing people's feelings of empathy for victims and providing prosocial models.

- Heredity influences the strength of an organism's tendency to aggress. The hypothalamus,

amygdala, and frontal lobes play especially important roles in certain types of aggression.

- Provocation, heat, crowding, and stimuli that cause frustration or pain increase the risk of aggression. Learning experiences help to shape a tendency to behave more or less aggressively. People are more likely to aggress when they find ways to justify and rationalize their aggressive behaviour, perceive provocation as intentional, and have little empathy for others.

- Most research supports the social-cognitive theory prediction that watching movie and TV violence, and playing violent video games, increase the risk that children and adults will act aggressively.

Levels of **Analysis** | Aggression

We've just seen that biological, psychological, and environmental factors all contribute to aggressive behaviour. Let's recap some of these factors.

ENVIRONMENTAL

- Stimuli that produce frustration (i.e., that block goal accomplishment) increase the risk of aggression.
- Painful stimuli, heat, and crowding increase the risk of aggression.
- Past and present reinforcement for aggression affects the likelihood of current aggressive behaviour.
- Exposure to live models and media models who display aggression can promote the social learning of aggression.

BIOLOGICAL

- Within a species, heredity partly accounts for individual differences in aggressiveness.
- The frontal lobes, amygdala, hypothalamus, and other brain regions play key roles in regulating aggression.
- Serotonin is among the major neurotransmitters that regulate aggression.
- Higher testosterone levels contribute to greater social aggression in many mammalian species.

PSYCHOLOGICAL

- Aggression is more likely when a potential provocation is perceived as intentional.
- A lack of empathy for a potential target increases the risk of aggression toward that person.
- People denigrate and dehumanize potential targets to self-justify acts of aggression.
- Impaired reasoning may decrease the ability to regulate hostile feelings.

In the social influence section of this chapter, we discussed how norms, conformity, obedience, and group processes affect behaviour. Think about the relevance of these social influence factors in accounting for human aggression. For example, in what contexts do these factors promote or inhibit aggression, and how do they shape the form that aggression takes?

FIGURE 13.40

WHAT IS PERSONALITY?

The concept of personality arises from the fascinating spectrum of human individuality. We observe that people differ meaningfully in the ways they customarily think, feel, and act. As one group of theorists noted, each of us is in certain respects like *all other* people, like *some other* people, and like *no other* person who has lived in the past or will exist in the future (Kluckhohn & Murray, 1953).

The concept of personality also rests on the observation that people seem to behave somewhat consistently over time and across different situations. From this perceived consistency comes the notion of "personality traits" that characterize individuals' customary ways of responding to their world. Although only modest stability is found from childhood personality to adult personality, consistency becomes greater as we enter adulthood (Caspi & Roberts, 1999) and personality traits among adults tend to remain consistent across time (Specht, Luhmann, & Geiser, 2014). Nonetheless, even in adulthood, there remains a capacity for meaningful personality change (Lewis, 1999). Combining these notions of individuality and consistency, we can define **personality** as the distinctive and relatively enduring ways of thinking, feeling, and acting that characterize a person's responses to life situations.

The thoughts, feelings, and actions that are seen as reflecting an individual's personality typically have three characteristics. First, they are seen as components of identity that distinguish that person from other people. Second, the behaviours are viewed as being caused primarily by internal rather than environmental factors. Third, the person's behaviours seem to "fit together" in a meaningful fashion, suggesting an inner personality that guides and directs behaviour (Figure 14.1).

1. What two common observations give rise to the concept of personality?

2. What three standards are used to evaluate the usefulness of a personality theory?

Perhaps more than any other topic, the study of personality has been guided by the psychodynamic, humanistic, biological, cognitive, and sociocultural perspectives. These perspectives provide different conceptions of what personality is and how it functions. As one pair of observers noted, "It seems hard to believe that all the theorists are talking about the same creature, who is now angelic and now depraved, now a black-box robot shaped by reinforcers and now a shaper of its own destiny, now devious . . . and now hardheadedly oriented to solid reality" (Stone & Church, 1968, p. 4). Yet this very diversity arises from the fact that the theorists have their own personalities that influence how they perceive and understand themselves and their world. No doubt you will find some of the theories more in accord with your own life views than others. But for personality psychologists, their subjective "truth" is less important than their *usefulness* as scientific theories. As discussed in Chapter 2, a theory is scientifically useful to the extent that it (1) provides a comprehensive framework within which known facts can be incorporated, (2) allows us to predict future events with some precision, and (3) stimulates the discovery of new knowledge. We will evaluate each of the theories we describe in terms of these scientific standards.

THE PSYCHODYNAMIC PERSPECTIVE

Psychodynamic theorists look for the causes of behaviour in a dynamic interplay of inner forces that often conflict with one another. They also focus on unconscious determinants of behaviour. Sigmund Freud's psychoanalytic theory was the first and most influential of these theories, and his ideas continue to influence Western thought today.

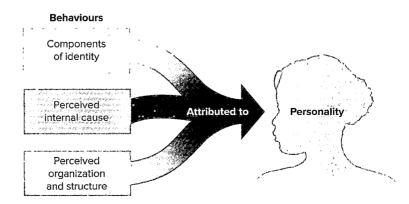

FIGURE 14.1 Perceived characteristics of behaviours that are seen as reflecting an individual's personality.

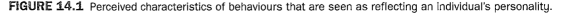

Freud's Psychoanalytic Theory

Freud (1856–1939) spent most of his life in Vienna, where he attended medical school with the intention of becoming a medical researcher concentrating on brain functioning (Figure 14.2). A pivotal event in his life occurred when he was awarded a fellowship to study in Paris with the famous French neurologist Jean Charcot. Charcot was treating patients who suffered from a disorder called *conversion hysteria* in which physical symptoms such as paralysis and blindness appeared suddenly and with no apparent physical cause. Freud's experiences in treating these patients convinced him that their symptoms were related to painful memories and feelings that seemed to have been repressed, or pushed out of awareness. When his patients were able to re-experience these traumatic memories and unacceptable feelings, which were often sexual or aggressive in nature, their physical symptoms often disappeared or improved markedly.

These observations convinced Freud that an unconscious part of the mind exerts great influence on behaviour. He began to experiment with various techniques to access the unconscious mind, including hypnosis, free association (saying whatever comes to mind, no matter how trivial or embarrassing), and dream analysis. In an attempt to relieve painful bouts of depression he was experiencing, Freud conducted an extensive self-analysis based on his own dreams. Freud's work on dream analysis culminated in the publication of his book *The Interpretation of Dreams* in 1900. The book sold only 600 copies in its first six years, but his revolutionary ideas began to attract followers. His theory also provoked scathing criticism

© Corbis

FIGURE 14.2 Sigmund Freud is shown here with his daughter Anna, who also became an influential psychoanalytic theorist.

from a Victorian society that was not ready to regard people as seething cauldrons of sexual and aggressive impulses.

Freud based his theory on careful clinical observation and constantly sought to expand it. Over time, psychoanalysis became a theory of personality, an approach to studying the mind, and a method for treating psychological disorders.

Psychic Energy and Mental Events

Inspired by the hydraulic models of 19th-century physics, which emphasized exchanges and releases of physical energy, Freud considered personality to be an energy system, somewhat like the steam engines of his day. According to Freud, instinctual drives generate **psychic energy**, which powers the mind and constantly presses for either direct or indirect release. For example, a buildup of energy from sexual drives might be discharged directly in the form of sexual activity or indirectly through such diverse behaviours as sexual fantasies, farming, or painting.

Mental events may be *conscious, preconscious,* or *unconscious.* The conscious mind consists of mental events that we are presently aware of. The preconscious contains memories, thoughts, feelings, and images that we are unaware of at the moment but that can be called into conscious awareness. Memories of your 16th birthday reside in your preconscious mind. If mention of your 16th birthday resulted in you thinking about it, that prompt triggered the movement of those memories from your preconscious to your conscious mind. Because we are aware of their contents, we are likely to see the conscious and preconscious areas of the mind as the most prominent. Freud, however, believed that these areas are dwarfed in both size and importance by the unconscious mind, a dynamic realm of wishes, feelings, and impulses that lies beyond our awareness. Only when impulses from the unconscious are discharged some way, such as in dreams, slips of the tongue, or some disguised behaviour, does the unconscious reveal itself.

The Structure of Personality

Freud divided personality into three separate but interacting structures: the *id*, the *ego*, and the *superego*. The **id** exists totally within the unconscious mind (Figure 14.3). It is the innermost core of the personality, the only structure present at birth, and the source of all psychic energy. The id has no direct contact with reality and functions in a totally irrational manner.

3. Which clinical phenomena convinced Freud of the power of the unconscious mind?

4. How did hydraulic systems of his time contribute to Freud's psychodynamic concepts?

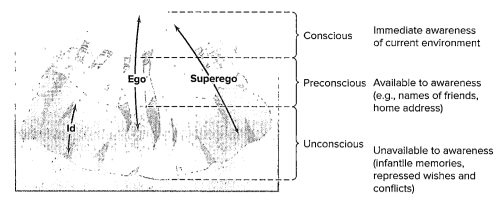

FIGURE 14.3 Freud's own representation of his three-part conception of personality shows the relation of the id, ego, and superego to the conscious, preconscious, and unconscious areas of the mind. Note how relatively small the conscious portion of the mind is compared with the unconscious.

Source: Adapted from Smith, B.D., *Psychology: Science and Understanding*, Fig 14.2, 1998. New York: McGraw-Hill. Reprinted by permission of The McGraw-Hill Companies, Inc.

5. Discuss the roles of the pleasure principle, the reality principle, and identification in relation to Freud's three personality structures.

6. Why is the ego sometimes referred to as the "executive of the personality"?

7. How and why do defence mechanisms develop? What specific forms do they take?

Operating according to the **pleasure principle,** it seeks immediate gratification or release, regardless of rational considerations and environmental realities. Its dictum: "Want . . . take!"

The id cannot directly satisfy itself by obtaining what it needs from the environment because it has no contact with the outer world. Therefore, in the course of development, a new structure develops that has direct contact with reality. The **ego** functions primarily at a conscious level, and it operates according to the **reality principle.** It tests reality to decide when and under what conditions the id can safely discharge its impulses and satisfy its needs.

The last personality structure to develop is the **superego,** the moral arm of the personality. According to Freud, the superego developed by the age of four or five, and was the repository for the values and ideals of society. These ideals are internalized by the child through identification with his or her parents, and by explicit training about what is "right," what is "wrong," and how the child "should" be. With the development of the superego, self-control takes over from external controls of rewards and punishments. Like the ego, the superego strives to control the instincts of the id, particularly the sexual and aggressive impulses that are condemned by society. Whereas the ego tries to delay gratification until conditions are safe and appropriate, the superego, in its quest for perfection, tries to block gratification permanently. For the superego, moralistic goals take precedence over realistic ones, regardless of the potential cost to the individual. Thus, the superego might cause a person to experience intense guilt over sexual activity even within marriage because it has internalized the idea that sex is "dirty."

With the development of the superego, the ego is squarely in the eye of a psychic storm. It must achieve compromise between the demands of the id, the constraints of the superego, and the demands of reality. This balancing act has earned the ego the title "executive of the personality."

Conflict, Anxiety, and Defence

The dynamics of personality involve a never-ending struggle between the id trying to discharge its instinctive energies and the opposing forces generated by the ego and the superego. When the ego confronts impulses that threaten to get out of control or is faced with dangers from the environment, anxiety results. Like physical pain, anxiety serves as a danger signal and motivates the ego to deal with the problem at hand. In many instances, the anxiety can be reduced through realistic coping behaviours, as when a person who is extremely angry at someone works out the problem through rational discussion. However, when realistic strategies are ineffective in reducing anxiety, the ego may resort to **defence mechanisms** that deny or distort reality. Some of the defence mechanisms permit the release of impulses from the id in disguised forms that will not conflict with the limits imposed by the external world or with the prohibitions of the superego. The major defence mechanisms are described in Table 14.1.

Psychoanalysts believe that repression is the primary means by which the ego "keeps the lid on the id." In **repression,** the ego uses some of its energy to prevent anxiety-arousing memories, feelings, and impulses from entering consciousness. Repressed thoughts and wishes remain in the unconscious, but they may be

TABLE 14.1 Psychoanalytic Ego Defence Mechanisms

Defence Mechanism	Description	Example
Repression	An active defensive process through which anxiety-arousing impulses or memories are pushed into the unconscious mind.	A person who was sexually abused in childhood develops amnesia for the event.
Denial	A person refuses to acknowledge anxiety-arousing aspects of the environment. The denial may involve either the emotions connected with the event or the event itself.	A man who is told he has terminal cancer refuses to consider the possibility that he will not recover.
Displacement	An unacceptable or dangerous impulse is repressed, and then directed at a safer substitute target.	A man who is harassed by his boss experiences no anger at work, but then goes home and abuses his wife and children.
Intellectualization	The emotion connected with an upsetting event is repressed, and the situation is dealt with as an intellectually interesting event.	A person who has been rejected in an important relationship talks in a highly rational manner about the "interesting unpredictability of love relationships."
Projection	An unacceptable impulse is repressed, and then attributed to (projected onto) other people.	A woman with strong repressed desires to have an affair continually accuses her husband of being unfaithful to her.
Rationalization	A person constructs a false but plausible explanation or excuse for an anxiety-arousing behaviour or event that has already occurred.	A student caught cheating on an exam justifies the act by pointing out that the professor's tests are unfair and, besides, everybody else was cheating, too.
Reaction formation	An anxiety-arousing impulse is repressed, and its psychic energy finds release in an exaggerated expression of the opposite behaviour.	A mother who harbours feelings of hatred for her child represses them and becomes overprotective of the child.
Sublimation	A repressed impulse is released in the form of a socially acceptable or even admired behaviour.	A man with strong hostile impulses becomes an investigative reporter who ruins political careers with his stories.

expressed, as slips of the tongue or in dreams. They may even be channelled into socially desirable behaviours through the defence mechanism of **sublimation,** completely masking the forbidden underlying impulses. For example, hostile impulses may find expression in tracking down criminals or being a successful trial lawyer. Although Freud described several defence mechanisms, his primary interest was in repression. His daughter Anna Freud, also a psychoanalyst, extended his ideas and described many of the defence mechanisms shown in Table 14.1.

Defence mechanisms operate unconsciously, so people are usually unaware that they are using self-deception to control anxiety. Freud argued that excessive reliance on defence mechanisms, with their denial or distortion of reality, was a primary cause of maladaptive or dysfunctional behaviour.

Psychosexual Development

Freud's clinical experiences convinced him that personality is powerfully moulded by experiences in the first years of life. He proposed that children pass through a series of psychosexual stages during which the id's pleasure-seeking tendencies are focused on specific pleasure-sensitive areas of the body called *erogenous zones* (Table 14.2). If there is either inadequate or excessive gratification at any of these stages,

8. What happens if there is deprivation during a stage of psychosexual development?

TABLE 14.2 Freud's Stages of Psychosexual Development

Stage	Approximate Age	Erogenous Zone	Key Task
Oral	0–2	Mouth	Weaning
Anal	2–3	Anus	Toilet training
Phallic	4–6	Genitals	Resolving Oedipus complex
Latency	7–puberty	None	Developing social relationships
Genital	puberty on	Genitals	Developing mature social and sexual relationships

then *fixation* at that stage occurs and instincts stay focused, or fixated, on that stage's erogenous zone. Freud's theory of psychosexual development is the most controversial part of his work. Many theorists reject Freud's assertions about childhood sexuality as well as the notion of specific psychosexual stages in the development of personality. Although there is evidence that childhood experiences, such as emotional attachments, do indeed influence the development of personality (Westen et al., 2008), there is little to support the idea that personality development unfolds in the manner theorized by Freud.

Research on Psychoanalytic Theory

Freud was committed to testing his ideas through case studies and clinical observations. He believed that careful observations of everyday behaviour and clinical phenomena were the best source of evidence. He opposed experimental research, believing that the complex phenomena he had identified could not be studied under controlled conditions (Rosenzweig, 1992). Most modern psychologists do not believe that clinical observations are sufficient proof of a theory, although they do acknowledge the difficulty of studying psychoanalytic concepts under controlled laboratory conditions (Carver & Scheier, 2003; Mischel et al., 2004).

Although limited, research continues to address aspects of psychodynamic theory. For example, research on defence mechanisms and repression continues (Cramer, 2007), as does research into who is likely to be a target of projection (Govorun, Fuegen, & Payne, 2006). Much of the research into psychodynamic theory is in a clinical context, as were Freud's original observations.

According to Freud's theory of psychosexual development, we develop our personality as we pass through a series of discrete developmental stages, each defined by an erogenous zone, a bodily source of pleasure. If there is either excessive or inadequate gratification at a particular stage, then fixation at that stage occurs and adult personality is affected.

Despite this research interest, a major shortcoming of psychoanalytic theory is that many of its concepts are ambiguous and difficult to operationally define and measure (Westen & Gabbard, 1999). How, for example, can we measure the strength of an individual's id impulses or study processes that are by definition unconscious and inaccessible to the person?

Cognitive psychologists have developed methods to identify and measure nonconscious

processing of information, and a growing body of research has shown that much of our moment-to-moment mental and emotional life does occur outside our awareness (e the discussion of subliminal perception in Chapter 5, and automatic processing in Chapter 6). On the biological front, cognitive neuroscience has provided methods for tapping into mental processes as they occur by measuring brain activity (D'Esposito, 2003). Although some researchers are using these tools to test hypotheses derived from Freudian theory with greater scientific precision, there is relatively little current research attempting to assess psychoanalytic theory.

Freud's Legacy: Neoanalytic and Object Relations Approaches

Freud's ideas were so revolutionary that they generated disagreement even within his circle of disciples. *Neoanalysts* were psychoanalysts who disagreed with certain aspects of Freud's thinking and developed their own theories. Among them were Alfred Adler, Karen Horney, Erik Erickson, and Carl Jung. The neoanalysts believed that Freud did not give social and cultural factors a sufficiently important role in the development and dynamics of personality. In particular, they believed that he stressed infantile sexuality too much (Kurzweil, 1989). The second major criticism was that Freud laid too much emphasis on the events of childhood as determinants of adult personality. Neoanalytic theorists agreed that childhood experiences are important, but some neoanalysts, such as Erik Erikson, believed that personality development continues throughout the lifespan as individuals confront challenges that are specific to particular phases in their lives.

In contrast to Freud's assertion that behaviour is motivated by inborn sexual and aggressive instincts and drives, Alfred Adler (1870–1937) insisted that humans are inherently social beings who are motivated by *social interest,* the desire to advance the welfare of others. They care about others, cooperate with them, and place general social welfare above selfish personal interests (Figure 14.4). In contrast, Freud seemed to view people as savage animals caged by the bars of civilization. Perhaps influenced by his own struggles to overcome childhood illnesses and accidents, Adler also postulated a general motive of *striving for superiority,* which drives people to compensate for real or imagined defects in themselves (the *inferiority complex*) and to strive to be ever more competent in life.

9. Explain how neoanalytic theorists Adler and Jung departed from Freudian theory. What is the focus of the object relations approach?

© PhotoEdit

FIGURE 14.4 In Alfred Adler's theory, people have an inborn social interest that can cause them to put society's welfare above their interests. Mother Teresa's selfless service to others is one striking example.

Like Adler, Carl Jung (1875–1961) was Freud's friend and associate before he broke away and developed his own theory of **analytic psychology.** Jung expanded Freud's notion of the unconscious in unique directions. For example, he believed that humans possess not only a *personal unconscious* based on their life experiences, but also a *collective unconscious* that consists of memories accumulated throughout the entire history of the human race. These memories are represented by **archetypes,** inherited tendencies to interpret experience in certain ways. Archetypes find expression in symbols, myths, and beliefs that appear across many cultures, such as the image of a god, an evil force, the hero, the good mother, and the quest for self-unity and completeness.

Following Freud's death in 1939, a new psychodynamic emphasis known as *object relations* became highly influential. **Object relations** theorists, including Melanie Klein (1991), Otto Kernberg (1976), Margaret Mahler (1968), and Heinz Kohut (1975), focus on the images or mental representations that people form of themselves and other people as a result of early experience with caregivers. Whether realistic or distorted, these internal representations of important adults—for example, of the mother as kind or malevolent, the father as protective or abusive—become lenses, or "working models" through which later social interactions are viewed, and these relational themes exert an unconscious influence on a person's relationships throughout life (Shaver &

Mikulincer, 2009). People who have difficulties forming and maintaining intimate relationships tend to mentally represent themselves and others in negative ways, expecting painful interaction and attributing malevolence or rejection to others (Kernberg, 1984; Nigg et al., 1992). These working models often create self-fulfilling prophesies, influencing the recurring relationships people form with others (Fraley & Shaver, 2009). See the *Frontiers* feature about adult attachment style and abusive romantic relationships for more about the impact of attachment style.

John Bowlby's (1969, 2000b) attachment theory, discussed in Chapter 12, is an outgrowth of the object relations approach. Research relating early attachment experiences to later adult relationships is yielding provocative results. For example, university students with a history of positive early attachments tend to have longer and more satisfying romances (Shaver & Clark, 1996). In contrast, child-abusing parents often have mental representations of their own parents as punitive, rejecting, and abusive (van Ijzendoorn, 1995). Table 14.3 shows descriptive statements that characterize people who manifest secure, avoidant, and anxious-ambivalent adult attachment styles. Studies by Benjamin Hankin and colleagues

TABLE 14.3   Attachment Styles in Adult Relationships

Question: Which of the following best describes your feelings?*

A. I find it relatively easy to get close to others and am comfortable depending on them and having them depend on me. I don't often worry about being abandoned or about someone getting too close to me.

B. I am somewhat uncomfortable being close to others; I find it difficult to trust them completely, difficult to allow myself to depend on them. I am nervous when anyone gets too close, and often, love partners want me to be more intimate than I feel comfortable being.

C. I find that others are reluctant to get as close as I would like. I often worry that my partner doesn't really love me or won't want to stay with me. I want to merge completely with another person, and this desire sometimes scares people away.

*The first type of attachment style is described as "secure," the second as "avoidant," and the third as "anxious/ambivalent."

Source: Based on Shaver, P., Hazan, C., & Bradshaw, D. (1988). "Love as attachment: The integration of three behavioral systems". In R.J. Sternberg & M.L. Barnes (Eds.), *The psychology of love.* New Haven, CT: Yale University Press.

Frontiers

ATTACHMENT STYLE AND ABUSIVE ROMANTIC RELATIONSHIPS

Researchers who study abusive romantic relationships have noted that involvement in such relationships tends to repeat over time (Dutton, 2006). Does this occur by chance, or do people with specific personality patterns somehow seek out one another to re-create destructive relationships marked by psychological abuse? One possibility is that adult attachment styles predispose people to prefer romantic partners who fit their working models of intimate relationships. To test this hypothesis, Vivian Zayas and Yuichi Shoda (2007) studied the romantic partner preferences of women with a history of victimization and of men with a history of abusing women in romantic relationships.

Two groups of women were identified for the study. One group consisted of 32 women who reported being victims of frequent psychological abuse in their most recent long-term romantic relationship. On the measure of abusive behaviours, these women reported: *isolation and emotional control* (e.g., "My partner tried to keep me from seeing or talking to my family"); *undermining self-esteem* (e.g., "My partner treated me like I was stupid"); *jealousy* (e.g., "My partner was jealous of my friends"); *verbal abuse* (e.g., "My partner swore at me"); and *emotional withdrawal* (e.g., "My partner sulked and refused to talk about a problem"). The second group of 33 women were in low-abuse relationships; they reported that such experiences occurred seldom or never in their most recent romantic relationship.

The women participated in a computer dating procedure in which they indicated how much they would like to date each of 16 different men. The descriptions of the men, presented as personal ads, varied in desirability as a dating partner and potential for being abusive.

The women viewed each of the 16 personal ads (without pictures) on an experimenter-constructed website. The personal ads were compiled from actual self-descriptions provided by a group of male university students and were rated by a separate sample of women on desirability as a dating partner and potential for being abusive. The descriptions created potential male dating partners who fell into three categories: potentially abusive; undesirable as a dating partner but not abusive; and desirable as a dating partner and not abusive. The high-abuse and low-abuse women viewed each of the descriptions and made a series of choices, finally selecting the one person they were most interested in getting to know better. The women in each group also completed a self-report measure of attachment style.

In a second part of the study, male students were administered the psychological abuse questionnaire. The researchers identified 46 men who were abusive and 47 who reported inflicting little or no psychological abuse. These two groups of men also engaged in a computer dating procedure in which they chose a potential dating partner based on personal ads (again, no pictures). They chose from personal ads that were designed to express either high or low attachment anxiety.

The researchers first examined the relationship between attachment anxiety and past abuse. In agreement with previous research, they found that the high-abuse women were significantly more anxious about their close relationships and fearful of losing them; that is, they showed high levels of attachment anxiety.

The dating preferences of the two groups of women are shown in Figure 14.5. The low-abuse women preferred a

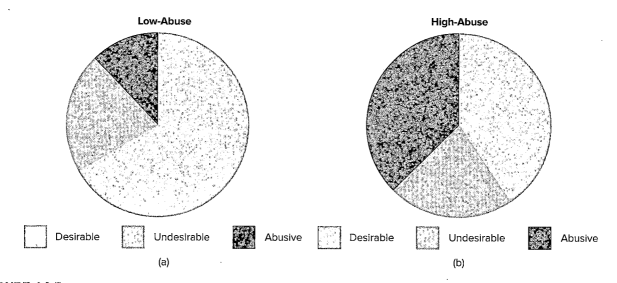

FIGURE 14.5 Percentages of women who chose each type of dating partner. Women had a history of little or no abuse in their romantic relationships and were low in attachment anxiety (Low-Abuse, panel a), or had experienced high levels of psychological abuse in their recent romantic relationships and were high in attachment anxiety (High-Abuse, panel b).

Source: Zayas, V. & Shoda, Y. (2007). Predicting preferences for dating partners from past experiences of psychological abuse: Identifying the psychological ingredients of situations. *Personality and Social Psychology Bulletin, 33,* 123–138.

continued

desirable partner and very few chose one of the potentially abusive men. In contrast, the high-abuse women were three times as likely to choose one of the potentially abusive men; they were about as likely to choose a potentially abusive partner as a desirable one.

The men's dating preferences also showed a notable contrast. The majority of non-abusive men (72.3 percent) preferred a woman who was low in attachment anxiety. In contrast, a majority of abusive men (60.9 percent) chose a potential dating partner who was high in attachment anxiety.

This study illustrates the potential usefulness of concepts derived from object relations theory in understanding human relationships. In this study, we see evidence that people may perpetuate self-injurious and destructive relationship patterns. Women with histories of abuse in romantic relationships might be expected to steer clear of future relationships of this kind. Instead, they are as likely to choose a dating partner who has been judged by others to be impulsive, possessive, jealous, aggressive, hostile, degrading, and potentially violent as they are to choose a desirable and non-abusive partner. Men's personality characteristics also influence their choice of potential romantic partners. Men without a history of abusing women show little desire to relate to insecure, relationship-anxious women. In contrast, abusive men are drawn to women who are more likely to become dependent on them and therefore tolerate their behaviour as they act out their hostility within the relationship.

Source: Zayas, V. & Shoda, Y. (2007). Predicting preferences for dating partners from past experiences of psychological abuse: Identifying the psychological ingredients of situations. *Personality and Social Psychology Bulletin*, 33, 123–138.

(2005) examined the relationship between adult attachment dimensions and symptoms of emotional distress (e.g., anxiety, depression). Avoidant and anxious-ambivalent attachment predicted depressive symptoms, and anxious attachment predicted anxiety symptoms. Anxious and avoidant attachment also predict poorer response to psychotherapy (Shorey & Snyder, 2006). Abuse by a caregiver can put a child at risk of developing disorganized attachment. Children with disorganized attachment may appear disoriented and feel detached from what is happening around them. As adults, they often have difficulty making sense of their own experiences, struggle with emotional and social relationships, and are at an increased risk for the development of anxiety and depression (Beeney et al., 2016; Lecompte, Moss, Cyr, & Pascuzzo, 2014).

The lasting impact of attachment patterns is also apparent in the finding that some forms of early attachment are associated with personality disorders among both adolescents and adults (Errázuriz, Constantino, & Calvo, 2015; Weinstein et al., 2014). Disorganized attachment (discussed in Chapter 12) is of particular concern and has been linked to personality disorders and other mental health challenges among adults (Beeney et al., 2016).

Attachment theory predicts that once attachment styles are set down by childhood experiences, they continue to play themselves out in adult relationships. Our *Frontiers* feature explores the possibility that this can result in abusive romantic relationships.

Today, a large proportion of psychodynamic theorists and clinicians claim to rely more heavily on object relations concepts than on classical psychoanalytic theory. The concepts in object relations theories are also easier to define and measure, making them more amenable to research.

Evaluating Psychoanalytic Theory

Although it has profoundly influenced popular culture, psychology, psychiatry, and other fields, psychoanalytic theory has often been criticized on scientific grounds. One reason is that many of its specific propositions have not held up under the scrutiny of research (Fisher & Greenberg, 1996). Another major problem with psychoanalytic theory is that it is hard to test, not because it doesn't explain enough, but because it often explains too much to allow clear-cut behavioural predictions (Meehl, 1995). For example, suppose we predict on the basis of psychoanalytic theory that participants in an experimental condition will behave aggressively, and they behave instead in a loving manner. Is the theory wrong, or is the aggression being masked by the defence mechanism called *reaction formation* (which produces exaggerated behaviours that are the opposite of the impulse)? The difficulty in making clear-cut behavioural predictions means that some psychoanalytic hypotheses are untestable. Science, including the science of human behaviour, progresses by the development of theories and

10. Why is it difficult to test psychoanalytic theory? What is the current status of unconscious processes and psychosexual development?

Review

- Freud's psychoanalytic theory views personality as an energy system. Personality dynamics involve modifications and exchanges of energy within this system. Mental events may be conscious, preconscious, or unconscious.

- Freud divided the personality into three structures: id, ego, and superego. The id is irrational and seeks immediate instinctual gratification on the basis of the pleasure principle. The ego operates on the reality principle, which requires it to test reality and mediate between the demands of the id, the superego, and reality. The superego is the moral arm of the personality.

- The dynamics of personality involve a continuous conflict between impulses of the id and counterforces of the ego and superego. When dangerous id impulses threaten to get out of control or when danger from the environment threatens, the result is anxiety. To deal with threat, the ego may develop defence mechanisms, which are used to ward off anxiety and permit instinctual gratification in disguised forms.

- Freud's psychosexual theory of personality development held that adult personality is basically moulded by how children deal with instinctual sexual urges.

- Neoanalytic theorists modified and extended Freud's ideas in important ways, stressing social and cultural factors in personality development. Modern object relations theorists focus on the mental representations that people form of themselves, others, and relationships.

---

the rigorous testing of hypotheses based on those theories. Many personality theorists have rejected psychoanalytic theory on the grounds that it cannot be tested.

Freud's emphasis on the unconscious was scorned by a Victorian society that emphasized rationality and was condemned as unscientific by generations of personality psychologists with a behaviourist orientation. Research over the past 20 years, however, has vindicated Freud's belief in unconscious events by showing that nonconscious mental and emotional phenomena do indeed occur and can powerfully affect our behaviour (Bargh & Chartrand, 1999; Erdelyi, 1995). Then again, the nonconscious processes that have been experimentally demonstrated are far different from those proposed by Freud (Kihlstrom, 1999). Accepted nonconscious mental processes, such as automatic processing (see Chapter 8), are very different from the types of phenomena that Freud placed in the unconscious mind. Rather than a seething cauldron of forbidden wishes and desires, current research is unearthing what one theorist described as "a kinder, gentler unconscious" (Greenwald, 1992).

11. What is self-actualization? How does this concept conflict with Freud's conception of human nature?

THE HUMANISTIC PERSPECTIVE

Humanistic theories were in part a reaction to Freud's conception of the human as being driven by "those half-tamed demons that inhabit the human beast" (Freud, 1900, p. 202). Instead, humanists embrace a positive view that affirms the inherent dignity and goodness of the human spirit. They emphasize the central role of conscious experience, as well as the individual's creative potential and inborn striving for **self-actualization,** the total realization of one's human potential (Figure 14.6). As described in Chapter 11, humanist Abraham Maslow considered self-actualization to be the ultimate human need and the highest expression of human nature.

Hero Images/Getty Images

FIGURE 14.6 The motivations underlying behaviour are much different for humanistic theorists than they are for Freudians. In the view of humanistic theorists such as Maslow and Rogers, creative and artistic accomplishments like this one are a product not of intrapsychic conflict and sublimation but of an innate tendency toward self-actualization.

George Kelly's Personal Construct Theory

A theory developed by George Kelly (1905–1967) in the 1950s had a strong influence on personality theory and on the development of clinical psychology (Kelly, 1955). According to Kelly, people's primary goal is to make sense out of the world, to find personal meaning in it. When they are unable to do so, they experience uncertainty and anxiety. To achieve understanding, they try to explain and understand the events of their lives, and they test this understanding in the same way scientists do: by attempting to anticipate, to predict.

Kelly's primary interest was how people construct reality. They do so by their individual system of **personal constructs,** which are cognitive categories into which they sort the people and events in their lives. In Kelly's theory, the personal construct system was the primary basis for individual differences in personality.

As noted in our discussion of concept formation in Chapter 9, perception and thought involve categorizing. From birth onward, Kelly maintained, stimuli are categorized, given meaning, and reacted to in terms of the categories, or personal constructs, into which they are placed. Every person has her or his own pattern of preferred personal constructs, which vary in personal importance. For example, your constructs of "good" or "successful" may differ from those of the person sitting next to you in class. By understanding these constructs, the rules an individual uses to assign events to categories, and her or his hypotheses about how the categories relate to one another, Kelly believed that we can understand the person's psychological world. If we can understand the individual's internal world, then we can understand and predict that person's behaviour.

The same event can be categorized, or perceived, in entirely different ways by different people. For example, suppose that two lovers break up. One observer may construe the event as "simple incompatibility"; another may think that one person was "jilted" by the other; another might describe the breakup as the "result of parental meddling"; another might call it "a terrible development"; and a fifth might see it as "a blessing in disguise."

Rather than evaluating alternative constructions according to whether or not they are true (which we cannot know), Kelly examined the consequences of construing in particular ways. For example, if one of the people in the broken relationship interpreted what happened as "being rejected," Kelly would try to discover the consequences for the person of construing the situation in that way. If the construction led to bad outcomes, such as feelings of worthlessness or the conclusion that "no one will ever love me, and I'll never get involved again," then the task would be to find a more useful and healthier alternative construction. Kelly, a clinical psychologist, saw psychotherapy as a way of demonstrating to clients that their constructions are *hypotheses* rather than facts. Once clients realize this, they can be encouraged to test the hypotheses that govern their lives, just as scientists do, and to replace maladaptive ones with more useful ones.

In order to help clients experiment with new viewpoints and behaviours, Kelly developed a therapeutic technique called *fixed-role therapy*. He wrote role descriptions and behavioural scripts for his clients that differed from their typical views of themselves. For example, a shy person might be asked to play the role of a more confident and assertive person for two or three days, to think and act like a confident person. Kelly and the client would practise the role within the therapy setting to be certain that the client had a command of the required behaviours and the view of the world that a confident individual would have. Kelly hoped that by trying out the new role, the client might gain a firsthand appreciation for the ways in which different constructions and behaviours could lead to more satisfying life outcomes. Kelly suggested that a willingness to experiment with new roles and ways of thinking can help all of us develop in ways that enhance our lives.

Carl Rogers's Self Theory

Carl Rogers (1902–1987) was one of the most influential humanistic theorists. In contrast to Freud, Rogers believed that our behaviour is not a reaction to unconscious conflicts but a response to our immediate conscious experience of self and environment (Rogers, 1951). He believed that the forces that direct behaviour are within us and that, when they are not distorted or blocked by our environment, they can be trusted to direct us toward self-actualization.

The Self

The central concept in Rogers's theory is the **self,** an organized, consistent set of perceptions of and beliefs about oneself (Rogers, 1959). Once formed, the self plays a powerful role in guiding our perceptions and directing our behaviour. **Self-concept** is now a more widely used term than "the self" and conveys much the same meaning as intended by "Self."

Rogers theorized that, at the beginning of their lives, children cannot distinguish between themselves and their environment. As they interact with their world, children begin to distinguish between the "me" and the "not-me." Self-concept continues to develop in response to our life experience, though many aspects of it remain quite stable over time. There are also cultural influences on our self-concept. For example, Asian collectivist cultures exhibit an extended sense of self that can include close relatives (Wang et al., 2012).

Once the self-concept is established, there is a tendency to maintain it, for it helps us understand ourselves in relation to the world. We therefore have needs for **self-consistency** (an absence of conflict among self-perceptions) and **congruence** (consistency between self-perceptions and experience). Any experience we have that is inconsistent with our self-concept, including our perceptions of our own behaviour, evokes threat and anxiety. Well-adjusted individuals can respond to threat adaptively by modifying the self-concept so that the experiences are congruent with the self. But other people choose to deny or distort their experiences to remove the incongruence, a strategy that can lead to what Rogers termed "problems in living."

Suppose that an important aspect of a young man's self-concept is the belief that he is so charming and handsome that every woman finds him irresistible. He meets a young woman whom he finds very attractive but who shows a total lack of interest in him. This incongruence between his self-concept and his experience produces threat and anxiety because his basic view of himself is challenged. On the one hand, he could react adaptively by modifying his self-concept to acknowledge that he is not, after all, irresistible to *all* women. On the other hand, he might resolve the incongruence by distorting reality. He might deny the woman's lack of interest ("She's just playing hard to get"), or he might distort his perception of the woman ("She would have to be crazy not to appreciate how special I am—thank heaven I found out in time").

The self-consistency knife can cut in both directions, however. At the other extreme, consider a young man who believes that he is totally undesirable to women. If an attractive woman expresses interest, he might appropriately revise his self-concept in a positive direction. But it is often as difficult for people with negative self-concepts to accept success as it is for those with unrealistically positive self-concepts to accept failure (Rogers, 1959). Thus, he might find it necessary to give a congruent explanation ("She's just trying to be nice. She doesn't really like me."). Such interpretations will allow the young man to maintain his negative image of himself.

To preserve their self-images, people not only interpret situations in self-congruent ways, but they also behave in ways that will lead others to respond to them in a self-confirming fashion (Swann & Bosson, 2008). As Rogers frequently noted, people are pushed by self-consistency needs to behave in accord with their self-concepts (Figure 14.7).

According to Rogers, the degree of congruence between self-concept and experience helps to define one's level of adjustment. The more inflexible people's self-concepts are, the less open they will be to their experience and the more maladjusted they will become (Figure 14.8a). If there is a significant degree of incongruence between self and experience, and the experiences are forceful enough, the defences used to deny and distort reality may collapse, resulting in extreme anxiety and a temporary disorganization of the self-concept.

This chapter's *Focus on Neuroscience* feature explores how modern neuroscientific techniques, such as brain imaging, are being used to explore the self.

Self-Esteem

Self-esteem refers to how positively or negatively we feel about ourselves, and it is a very important aspect of personal well-being, happiness, and adjustment (Diener, 2000; Lilienfeld et al., 2010). That is, if self-concept is how we perceive and describe ourselves, self-esteem is our affective evaluation of that description. The feelings included in self-esteem can be illustrated by the types of items found on measures of self-esteem (Table 14.4). In adulthood, there are only small differences in overall self-esteem between men and women (Larsen & Buss, 2010; Pan, 2015); however, during late adolescence, males report having higher self-esteem than females do (Pan, 2015). Levels of self-esteem, however,

12. Describe the roles of self-consistency and congruence in Rogers's self theory. How do these concepts relate to adjustment?

13. How do differences in self-esteem affect behaviour?

"I can't say I like the looks of that bunch."

FIGURE 14.7 Tendencies to behave in accordance with one's self-concept at times can have ominous implications.
The New Yorker Collection 1971 Dana Fradon from cartoonbank. com. All Rights Reserved.

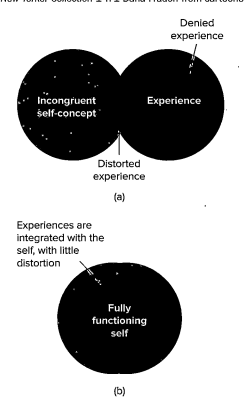

FIGURE 14.8 Rogers defined psychological adjustment in terms of the degree of congruence between self-concept and experience. Maladjustment (a) occurs when a person faced with incongruities between self and experience distorts or denies reality to make it consistent with the self-concept. In contrast, extremely well-adjusted, or fully functioning, people integrate experiences into the self with minimal distortion (b), so they are able to profit fully from their experiences.

Source: Rogers, C.R. (1951). *Client-centered therapy*. Boston, MA: Houghton Mifflin.

tend to be stable across development, with correlations between + 0.50 and + 0.70 from childhood to old age (Trzesniewski et al., 2003; Yang et al., 2016).

Self-esteem is related to many positive behaviours and life outcomes. People with high self-esteem are less susceptible to social pressure, have fewer interpersonal problems, are happier with their lives, achieve at a higher and more persistent level, and are more capable of forming satisfying love relationships (Baumeister, 1999). In contrast, people with a poor self-image are more prone to psychological problems such as anxiety and depression, to physical illness, and to poor social relationships and underachievement (Heimpel et al., 2002).

TABLE 14.4   Items Similar to These Found on Measures of Self-Esteem*

1. I believe I am a worthwhile person.
2. There are many things I would change about myself if I could (reverse scored).
3. I approve of myself as a person.
4. I have many positive traits.
5. I like who I am.
6. There are many things I do not like about myself (reverse scored).

*Items are answered on a 5-point scale ranging from strongly disagree to strongly agree.

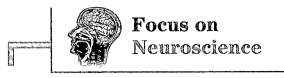

Focus on Neuroscience

THE NEUROBIOLOGY OF THE SELF

Our self-esteem, how positively or negatively we feel about ourselves, has an important influence on our well-being; positive self-esteem is associated with lower risk of anxiety and depression, more successful social and emotional relationships, and greater life satisfaction (Lecompte et al., 2014; Pan, 2015). As discussed in more detail elsewhere in this chapter, our self-esteem is our emotional evaluation of our self-concept, the emotional reaction to how we perceive ourselves. Another important influence on our self-esteem is how we believe others perceive and evaluate us (Yang et al., 2016). That is, self-esteem includes both an intrapersonal perspective, how we evaluate ourselves, and an interpersonal perspective, how others evaluate us.

Questions that have recently been asked are what brain areas support self-concept and self-esteem and whether the two different aspects of self-esteem, the intrapersonal and the interpersonal, are related to activity within different brain regions. The self-evaluation that is the central feature of self-esteem might be expected to be associated with activity in brain areas generally associated with affect, many of which were discussed in Chapter 11. But our self-esteem is also influenced by how others evaluate us and by what we believe others think of us. It has not been clear what brain areas might be associated with this aspect of self, with processing how others evaluate us.

In an interesting recent study, Yang and colleagues (Yang et al., 2016) asked participants to reflect on the self or on a celebrity, and to reflect on what others said about them or about the celebrity. While participants were engaged in these tasks, brain activity was assessed using fMRI. This design allowed the researchers to evaluate whether self-esteem is associated with brain activation related to both self-evaluation and processing evaluations about the self provided by others.

The study involved 25 healthy university students who completed the Rosenberg Self-esteem Scale, the most widely used measure of self-esteem and then had brain activity measured using fMRI. For information from others about the self, the researchers had other students rate potential participants on different personality adjectives, half of which were positive (e.g., friendly) and half of which were negative (e.g., childish). Students were also asked to rank a celebrity (a well-known athlete) on the same set of adjectives.

This allowed the researchers to ask participants four different questions while brain activity was monitored:

1. How well does this adjective describe you?
2. How well does this adjective describe the celebrity?
3. Do you agree with how others described you?
4. Do you agree with how others described the celebrity?

There was a strong positive correlation between self-esteem scores and how much participants agreed with positive descriptions of them provided by others, and a strong negative correlation between self-esteem scores and how much they agreed with negative deceptions of them provided by others. This would indicate that participants did attend to and process the different adjectives and assess their accuracy.

Participants' self-esteem scores were positively correlated with activity in the orbitofrontal cortex when processing adjectives about the self. The orbitofrontal cortex is an area within the medial prefrontal cortex (mPFC) immediately above and behind the eyes at the very front of the brain. The orbitofrontal cortex and more generally the mPFC are important parts of the network involved in emotional processing and have important connections with brains areas, such as the amygdala and anterior cingulate cortex, known to be important for emotion. These results are consistent with the findings of other studies that have found that the mPFC is active when people process information about themselves (e.g., Kim & Johnson, 2014).

When the evaluation was not of the self, but was about what others said about them, a somewhat different pattern of activity was found. Self-esteem scores were positively correlated with activity in the mPFC, the posterior cingulate cortex, and structures within the temporal cortex when participants evaluated what others said about them. That is, along with the mPFC, self-esteem was related to the brain areas often associated with cognitive processing during evaluation of feedback about the self provided by others.

Interestingly, there were also increases in activity within a group of structures referred to as the *default mode network,* which we encountered in Chapter 6, which are associated with reflection and mind-wandering. Although changes in activity were not correlated with self-esteem scores, processing information about the self was associated with increased activity within parts of the default mode network.

The neuropeptide oxytocin has been reported to influence activity within the default mode network (Scheele et al., 2014), especially within frontal regions such as the mPFC and anterior cingulate cortex. Furthermore, results of several research studies have indicated that oxytocin may be involved in processing information about the self, and is involved in some way in making distinctions between self and others (Zhao et al., 2016). Past results, however, have been inconsistent. The overlap between areas known to be influenced by oxytocin, such the mPFC and parts of the default mode network, and its effects on making distinctions between self and other has led

continued

researchers to investigate oxytocin's role in self-concept and self-esteem.

In one recent study (Zhao et al., 2016), university student participants were randomly assigned to a placebo group or to a group that was treated with oxytocin. Participants were administered either the placebo or oxytocin by nasal spray, a procedure that has been shown to increase oxytocin levels in cerebrospinal fluid. After the nasal spray, participants completed a number of questionnaires including measures of anxiety, personality traits, positive and negative affect, self-esteem, and feelings of connectedness with others. Participants then had brain activity measured using fMRI while they evaluated how accurately positive (e.g., kind) and negative (e.g., lazy) adjectives described them, a family member, a classmate, or a stranger.

Brain imaging found that making judgments about the self increased activity in areas of the frontal cortex, especially mPFC and cingulate cortex. Interestingly, oxytocin decreased activity in the mPFC, and also decreased functional connectivity between the mPFC and the anterior cingulate cortex and other structures within the default mode network. This decrease in the interactions between the mPFC and the anterior cingulate cortex was negatively associated with self-esteem. That is, the mPFC was active when making judgments about the self, as compared to making judgments about others, and this activity was suppressed by oxytocin.

Oxytocin also decreased reaction times; participants made their decisions about whether or not an adjective accurately described them or others more quickly if treated with oxytocin. Participants were tested unexpectedly with a memory task for the adjectives after scanning was completed. We usually remember descriptions about self more accurately than descriptions about others. Oxytocin eliminated the preferential memory for self information over other information. That is, oxytocin improved the speed of decision making on all judgments and, at the same time, weakened the usually superior memory for self over descriptions of others.

These results further support a critical role for the mPFC in self. Oxytocin reduced activity in the mPFC and interactions between the mPFC and anterior cingulate cortex and this decrease was associated with a weakened distinction between self and others.

The results of studies such as those by Yang et al. (2016) and Zhao et al. (2016) indicate a critical role of the mPFC, anterior cingulate cortex, and parts of the default mode network in supporting distinctions between self and others, and an association between activity in these brain areas, especially areas within the mPFC, and an individual's self-esteem. It is interesting to note that the brain areas that are most powerfully linked to self-concept and self-esteem are the phylogenetically newest—they are the most distinctly human of all brain areas—and are also the last brain areas to mature during an individual's development.

Research by Joanne Wood and Sara Heimpel at the University of Waterloo has examined the influence of successes on those with low self-esteem. They found, perhaps counter-intuitively, that while success bolsters the self-esteem of those already high in self-esteem, success generates self-doubt and anxiety among those low in self-esteem (Heimpel, Wood, Marshall, & Brown, 2002; Wood, Heimpel, & Michela, 2003; Wood et al., 2005).

Earlier work by these researchers found that self-esteem has an impact on how people act to regulate their mood. In response to failure, participants with low self-esteem were less likely to express a desire to improve their mood than were participants with high self-esteem. Although those with low self-esteem knew what to do to improve their mood (e.g., watch a comedy, visit friends), they did not engage in these behaviours when in a negative mood (Heimpel et al., 2002). Not only did those low in self-esteem not attempt to improve a bad mood, they even worked to depress a good mood. After experiencing a positive event in their own lives, people with low self-esteem reported that they deliberately thought about things that would calm their excitement, that would make them feel less good about themselves and their success, or that would distract them from the success (Wood, Heimpel, & Michela, 2003).

Danielle Gaucher, of the University of Winnipeg, and colleagues found that self-esteem is also linked to expressive behaviour, such as emotional expressivity and self-disclosure. Self-esteem is an important determinant of expressivity because expressive behaviours leave one vulnerable to rejection. Those with low self-esteem are particularly averse to social rejection, so they are usually less expressive than those with high self-esteem (Gaucher et al., 2012). Consistent with this finding, Jessica Cameron at the University of Manitoba reported that high self-esteem contributes to the willingness to accept social risk such as that involved in initiating a potential romantic relationship (Cameron et al., 2013).

What conditions foster the development of high self-esteem? Children develop higher self-esteem when their parents communicate unconditional acceptance and love, establish clear guidelines for behaviour, and reinforce compliance while giving the child freedom to make decisions and express opinions within those guidelines (Coopersmith, 1967; Harrington et al., 1987). One study showed that when low–self-esteem children were exposed to highly supportive youth sport coaches who gave them much positive reinforcement and encouragement, the children's self-esteem increased significantly over the course of the sport season (Smoll et al., 1993). Apparently, the positive feedback caused the children to revise their self-concepts in a positive direction.

The value of high self-esteem has been well publicized and has led to a wide range of self-help books, educational programs, child-rearing manuals, and other resources meant to help people elevate their feelings of self-worth. But is high self-esteem always beneficial? Unstable or unrealistically high self-esteem may be even more dangerous to the individual and society than low self-esteem. When unstable or inflated self-esteem is threatened, individuals may react aggressively, even violently, to protect their self-esteem (Baumeister, Smart, & Boden, 1996). Indeed, the higher one's self-esteem, the greater the vulnerability to ego threats (Baumeister et al., 1996). Recently, it has been recognized that the pursuit of self-esteem can also be a source of problems. When you attempt some new task, such as learning to snowboard, tackle a new and challenging university course, or join a band, do you do it to master the task? Or do you do it because success will enhance your self-esteem and validate your abilities? If the goal is enhanced self-esteem, achieving your goal imparts a feeling of worth and value, but the emotional benefits may be only temporary (Crocker & Park, 2004). Furthermore, a failure when the goal is enhanced self-esteem is more damaging to the individual than a failure when the goal is to master the task (Crocker, 2002; Crocker & Park, 2004). If the goal is enhanced self-esteem, people feel particularly challenged to succeed and may react to threats or perceived threats in ways that are destructive or self-destructive. When the pursuit of self-esteem is successful it does have emotional benefits, but the pursuit of self-esteem can also have costs, such as decreasing learning and leading to poor self-regulation and poor mental and physical health (Baumeister & Leary, 1995; Crocker, 2002; Deci & Ryan, 2000).

The Need for Positive Regard

Rogers believed that we are born with an innate **need for positive regard**—that is, for acceptance, sympathy, and love from others. Rogers viewed positive regard as essential for healthy development. Ideally, positive regard received from the parents is unconditional—that is, independent of how the child behaves. **Unconditional positive regard** communicates that the child is inherently worthy of love. *Conditional positive regard,* however, is dependent on how the child behaves. In the extreme case, love and acceptance are given to the child *only* when the child behaves as the parents want.

People need positive regard not only from others but also from themselves. We all want to feel good about ourselves. Thus, a **need for positive self-regard** also develops. Lack of unconditional positive regard from parents and other significant people in the past teaches people that they are worthy of approval and love only when they meet certain standards. This fosters the development of **conditions of worth** that dictate when we approve or disapprove of ourselves. A child who has experienced parental approval when behaving in a friendly fashion, but disapproval whenever she became angry or aggressive, may come to disapprove of her own "angry" feelings, even when they are justified. She may, therefore, come to deny in herself all feelings of anger and struggle to preserve a self-image of being totally loving. Rogers believed that conditions of worth can tyrannize people and cause major incongruence between self and experience, together with a need to deny or distort important aspects of experience. Conditions of worth are similar to the "shoulds" that populate Freud's superego.

Fully Functioning Persons

Toward the end of his career, Rogers became particularly interested in people who had achieved self-actualization. As Rogers viewed them, **fully functioning persons** do not hide behind masks or adopt artificial roles. They feel a sense of inner freedom, self-determination, and choice in the direction of their growth. They have no fear of behaving spontaneously, freely, and creatively. Because they are fairly free of conditions of worth, they can accept inner and outer experiences as they are, without modifying them defensively to suit a rigid self-concept

14. What conditions affect the development of self-esteem?

15. How do conditions of worth develop and how can they hinder adjustment?

or the expectations of others. Thus, a fully functioning unmarried woman would be able to state quite frankly that her career is more important to her than a role as a wife and a mother *if* she truly felt that way, and would act comfortably on those feelings. In a sense, she could be true to herself (Figure 14.8b).

Research on the Self

By giving the self a central place in his theory, Rogers helped to stimulate a great deal of research on the self-concept (Robins et al., 1999; Phillips & Silvia, 2005). Two topics at the forefront are (1) the development of self-esteem and its effects on behaviour, and (2) the roles played by self-enhancement and self-consistency motives.

Thinking critically

IS SELF-ACTUALIZATION A USEFUL SCIENTIFIC CONSTRUCT?

Self-actualization is a central concept for humanistic theorists such as Maslow and Rogers. Consider what you have learned about formulating a psychological construct and evaluating a theory according to scientific principles. Can you see any problems with establishing the existence of this core motivation from a scientific perspective?

Think about it, and then see the Answers section at the end of the book.

Self-Verification and Self-Enhancement Motives

Rogers proposed that people are motivated to preserve their self-concept by maintaining self-consistency and congruence. Modern researchers call this need **self-verification**, and it has received considerable research support. In one study, researchers measured university students' self-concepts. In a later experiment, the students interacted with other participants and received fake feedback from them in the form of adjectives that were either consistent or inconsistent with their self-concept. Later, when the students were asked to recall and identify the adjectives that had been attributed to them, they showed greater recall for the consistent adjectives, suggesting that people selectively attend to and recall self-consistent information (Suinn et al., 1962).

Self-verification needs are also expressed in people's tendency to seek out self-confirming

relationships. One study found that if people with firmly held negative self-views marry spouses who appraise them favourably, they tend eventually to withdraw from the marriage. Such people are more likely to remain with spouses who agree with the negative image they have of themselves. In contrast, people with positive self-concepts prefer spouses who share their positive view of themselves (Swann et al., 1992).

Rogers also suggested that people have a need to regard themselves positively, and research confirms a strong and pervasive tendency to gain and preserve a positive self-image. These processes are known as **self-enhancement** (Brown, 1998; Swann, 1966). Several self-enhancement strategies have been identified. For example, people show a marked tendency to attribute their successes to their own abilities and effort, but to attribute their failures to environmental factors. Furthermore, most people rate themselves as better than average on virtually any socially desirable characteristic that is subjective in nature (Steele & Baumeister, 1999). The vast majority of businesspeople and politicians rate themselves as more ethical than the average. In defiance of mathematical possibility, about 80 percent of high school students rate themselves in the top 10 percent in their ability to get along with others. Even people who have been hospitalized after causing auto accidents rate themselves as more skilful than the average driver (Pyszczyncki & Greenberg, 1987). Indeed, as evidence on self-serving biases in self-perception continues to accumulate, researchers are concluding that positive illusions of this sort are the rule rather than the exception in well-adjusted people and that these self-enhancement tendencies, or "positive illusions," contribute to their psychological well-being (Taylor & Brown, 1988; Taylor et al., 2000).

Culture, Gender, and the Self

Culture provides a learning context in which the self develops. Individualistic cultures such as those in North America and northern Europe place an emphasis on independence and personal attainment, whereas collectivistic cultures such as those found in many parts of Asia, Africa, and South America emphasize connectedness between people and the achievement of group goals (Cross & Markus, 1999; Triandis, 1989). What kinds of self-concept differences would you predict in people from these two types of cultures?

In one study, American and Japanese university students were given a self-concept

16. Define self-verification and self-enhancement. What research evidence is there to support these processes?

17. What cultural and gender differences have been found in self-concept research?

questionnaire on which they listed their five most important attributes. The researchers then classified each statement according to whether it referred to a personal attribute (e.g., "I am honest"; "I am smart"), a social identity (e.g., "I am an oldest son"; "I am a student"), or something else, such as a physical trait. As Figure 14.9 shows, the Americans were far more likely than the Japanese to list personal traits, abilities, or dispositions, whereas the Japanese more frequently described themselves in social identity terms. Thus, the social embeddedness of the collectivist Japanese culture was reflected in their self-perceptions, as was cultural individualism in the Americans' self-concepts (Cousins, 1989).

Gender-role socialization provides us with **gender schemas,** organized mental structures that contain our understanding of the attributes and behaviours that are appropriate and expected for males and females (Bem, 1981). Within a given culture, gender schemas tell us what the typical man or woman "should" be like. In Western cultures, men tend to prize attributes related to achievement, emotional strength, athleticism, and self-sufficiency, whereas women

especially prize interpersonal competencies, kindness, and helpfulness to others (Beyer, 1990; Brown, 1998; Marsh, 1990). In a sense, men in Western cultures tend to develop more of an individualistic self-concept, emphasizing achievement and separateness from others, whereas women's self-concepts tend to be more collectivistic, emphasizing their social connectedness with others (Watkins et al., 2003; Bresnahan et al., 2005). Nonetheless, we should keep in mind that significant individual differences exist within each gender group, with many women being highly individualistic and many men collectivistic (Brown, 1998).

Evaluating Humanistic Theories

Humanistic theorists focus on the individual's subjective experiences. What matters most is how people view themselves and the world (Nye, 1996). Some critics believe that the humanistic view relies too much on individuals' reports of their personal experiences. For example, psychoanalytic theorists maintain that accepting what a person says at face value may easily lead to erroneous conclusions because of the always-present influence of unconscious factors. Some critics also believe that it is impossible to define an individual's actualizing tendency except in terms of the behaviour that it supposedly produces. This would be an example of circular reasoning: "Why did the person achieve such success? Because of self-actualization." "How do we know self-actualization was at work? Because the person achieved great success."

Though humanism may indeed seem nonscientific to some, Carl Rogers (1959) dedicated himself to developing a theory whose concepts could be measured and whose laws could be tested. One of his most notable contributions was a series of groundbreaking studies on the process of self-growth that can occur in psychotherapy. To assess the effectiveness of psychotherapy, Rogers and his colleagues measured the discrepancy between clients' *ideal selves* (how they would like to be) and their *perceived selves* (their perceptions of what they are actually like). The studies revealed that when clients first enter therapy, the discrepancy typically is large, but it gets smaller as therapy proceeds, suggesting that therapy may help the client to become more self-accepting and perhaps also more realistic. Rogers and his colleagues also discovered important therapist characteristics that either aid or impede the process of self-actualization in therapy. This research will be described in Chapter 17.

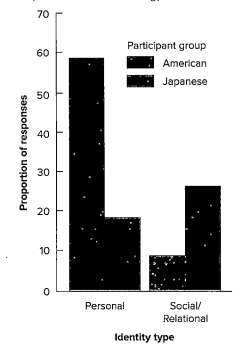

FIGURE 14.9 Cultural differences in the self-concept. Percentages of personal identity and social/relational self-attributes given by Japanese and American university students as key aspects of their self-concepts.

Source: Data from Cousins, S.D. (1989). "Culture and Self-Perception in the United States and Japan," *Journal of Personality and Social Psychology,* 56, 124–131, Table 2 (adapted). Doi: 10.1037/0022-3514.56.1.124. Copyright © 1989 by the American Psychological Association. Reprinted by permission of the author and the publisher.

- Humanistic theories emphasize the subjective experiences of the individual and thus deal with perceptual and cognitive processes. Self-actualization is viewed as an innate positive force that leads people to realize their positive potential, if not thwarted by the environment.

- George Kelley's theory emphasizes the subjective experiences of the individual and how we make sense out of the world and find personal meaning in it. He focused on the manner in which people differ in their construction of reality by the personal constructs they use to categorize their experiences.

- Carl Rogers's theory attaches central importance to the role of the self. Experiences that are incongruous with the established self-concept produce threat and may result in a denial or distortion of reality. Conditional positive regard may result in realistic conditions of worth that can conflict with self-actualization. Rogers described a number of characteristics of the fully functioning person.

- Rogers's theory helped to stimulate a great deal of research on the self-concept, including studies on the origins and effects of differences in self-esteem, self-enhancement and self-verification motives, and cultural and gender contributions to the self-concept.

Several recent developments have renewed scientific interest in humanistic concepts. For example, work by Mark Baldwin of McGill University has contributed to our understanding of the impact of implicit (nonconscious) self-esteem (Sakellaropoulo & Baldwin, 2006) and the interactions between social threat, stress, and self-esteem (Dandeneau et al., 2007). Recent advances in measuring brain activity are enabling psychologists to study self-processes as they occur at the biological level, as we saw in this chapter's *Focus on Neuroscience* feature.).

TRAIT AND BIOLOGICAL PERSPECTIVES

How do people differ in personality? The goals of trait theorists are to describe the basic classes of behaviour that define personality, to devise ways of measuring individual differences in personality traits, and to use these measures to understand and predict a person's behaviour.

The starting point for the trait researcher is identifying the behaviours that define a particular trait. But here we have an embarrassment of riches. Years ago, the trait theorist Gordon Allport went through the English dictionary and painstakingly recorded all the words that could be used to describe personal traits. The result was an imposing list of 17 953 words (Allport & Odbert, 1936). Obviously, it would be impractical if not impossible to describe people in terms of where they fall on each of nearly 18 000 dimensions. The trait theorist's goal is to condense all these behavioural descriptors into a manageable number of basic traits that can capture personal individuality.

Two major approaches have been taken to define what Allport (1937) called "the building blocks of personality." One approach is to propose traits (e.g., "dominance," "friendliness," or "self-esteem") on the basis of intuition or a theory of personality. A more systematic approach uses the statistical tool of **factor analysis** to identify clusters of specific behaviours that are correlated with one another so highly that they can be viewed as reflecting a basic dimension, or trait, on which people vary. For example, you might find that most people who are socially reserved also avoid parties, like quiet activities, and enjoy being alone. At the other end of the spectrum are people who are very talkative and sociable, like parties and excitement, dislike solitary activities such as reading, and constantly seek out new acquaintances. These behavioural patterns define a general factor or dimension that we might label *introversion-extraversion* (or simply *extraversion*). At one end of the dimension are highly introverted behaviours, and at the other end are highly extraverted behaviours (Figure 14.10). Presumably, each of us could be placed at some point along this dimension in terms of our customary behaviour patterns. In fact, as we shall see, factor analytic studies have found introversion-extraversion to be a major dimension of personality.

Cattell's Sixteen Personality Factors

If you were asked to describe and compare every person you know, how many different traits would it take to do the job? It is in their answers to this question that trait theorists

18. In what way is factor analysis based on correlation, and how is it used to identify personality traits?

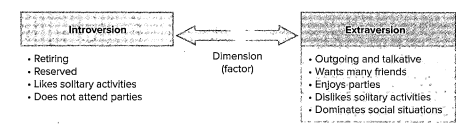

FIGURE 14.10 Factor analysis allows researchers to reduce many behaviours to a smaller number of basic dimensions, or factors. A factor consists of behaviours that are highly correlated with one another and, therefore, are assumed to have common psychological meaning. Here, we see the kinds of behaviours that might fall on the two ends of the introversion-extraversion dimension. The two groups of behaviours are negatively correlated with one another.

begin to part company. Because factor analysis can be used and interpreted in different ways, trait theorists have cut up the personality pie into smaller or larger pieces. For example, the pioneering trait theorist Raymond B. Cattell (1965, 1990) asked thousands of people to rate themselves on numerous behavioural characteristics and also obtained ratings from people who knew the participants well. When he subjected this mass of data to factor analysis, he identified 16 basic behaviour clusters, or factors. These personality dimensions are shown in Figure 14.11. Using this information, Cattell developed a widely used personality test called the 16 Personality Factor Questionnaire (16PF) to measure individual differences on each of the dimensions and provide a comprehensive personality description. He was

able to develop personality profiles not only for individuals, but also for groups of people. For example, Figure 14.11 compares average scores obtained by creative artists and Olympic athletes.

Eysenck's Extraversion-Stability Model

Among trait theorists, some, like Cattell, proposed a large number of basic traits. At the other extreme was the British psychologist Hans Eysenck (1916–1997), who proposed surprisingly few basic traits (Figure 14.12a). In his original theory, Eysenck proposed only two basic dimensions, although he later added a third (Eysenck, 1967, 1991). Eysenck called his original basic dimensions of personality

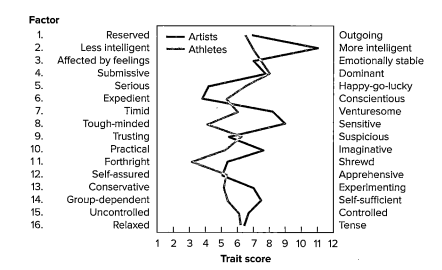

FIGURE 14.11 Cattell identified 16 basic personality traits through factor analysis. Here we see personality profiles (mean scores) for Olympic athletes and creative artists on the 16PF, the test developed by Cattell to measure the traits.

Source: Based on data from Cattell, R.B. (1965). *The scientific analysis of personality.* Chicago, IL: Aldine.

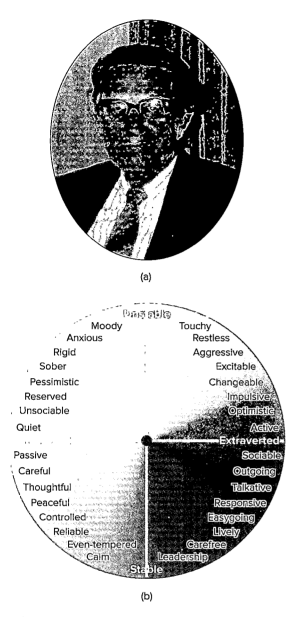

(a)

(b)

FIGURE 14.12 According to Hans Eysenck (a), various combinations of two major dimensions of personality, Introversion-Extraversion and Stability-Instability, combine to form the more specific traits shown in (b).

(a): © Randy J. Larsen, 1987.; (b): From H.J. Eysenck, *The Biological Basis of Personality*, Figure 12, 1967. Courtesy of Charles C Thomas, Publisher, Ltd., Springfield, Illinois.

Introversion-Extraversion and *Stability-Instability* (which he first referred to as *Stability-Neuroticism*). Eysenck argued that personality within the normal range could be understood with only these two basic dimensions.

Extraversion reflects the tendency to be sociable, active, and willing to take risks; the Introversion end of the scale represents a tendency toward social inhibition, passivity, and caution. The Stability-Instability dimension represents a continuum from high emotional stability and poise at the Stability end, to moodiness, a tendency to worry excessively, easily provoked guilt feelings, and anxiety at the Instability end.

Eysenck's Extraversion-Stability model is shown in Figure 14.12b. The two basic dimensions, Extraversion-Introversion and Stability-Instability, intersect at right angles, indicating that these two dimensions are independent, or uncorrelated. Thus, knowing how extraverted a person is tells us nothing about her level of emotional stability; she could fall anywhere along the Stability-Instability continuum. The secondary traits shown around the periphery of the circle reflect various combinations or mixtures of the two primary dimensions. Thus, someone who scores high on emotional stability and high on extraversion is a carefree, lively person who tends to be well-adjusted and seek leadership roles. In contrast, someone who scores high on instability (neuroticism) and high on extraversion tends to be touchy, aggressive, and restless. With even subtle variations along one or both dimensions, different combinations of these two basic dimensions can produce very diverse personality patterns.

Although Eysenck continued to emphasize these two "supertraits," he added a third dimension to his theory of personality (Eysenck, 1991, 1993). Eysenck called this third factor *Psychoticism-Self Control*. Unfortunately, the choice of the name *Psychoticism* evokes an image of pathology, but scoring high on this scale does not mean that someone is developing some type of psychosis (Eysenck, 1993). By *Psychoticism*, Eysenck meant someone who was creative and had a tendency toward nonconformity, impulsivity, and social deviance.

The Five Factor Model

Other trait theorists argued that Cattell's 16 dimensions may be more than are needed and that Eysenck's two or three may be too few. Their factor analytic studies suggest to them that five "higher-order" factors, each including several of Cattell's more specific factors, are all that are needed to capture the basic structure of personality (McCrae & Costa, 2003). These theorists also believe that these "Big Five" factors may be universal to the human species, since the same five factors have been found consistently in trait ratings within diverse North American, Asian, Hispanic, and European cultures (e.g., Ispas, Iliescu, Ilie, & Johnson, 2014; John & Srivastava, 1999).

19. What does *OCEAN* stand for in the Five Factor model?

The Big Five factors are shown in Table 14.5, together with behaviours that express those traits. (The acronym *OCEAN*—for Openness, Conscientiousness, Extraversion, Agreeableness,

TABLE 14.5 The Big Five Personality Factors and Their Behaviours (Facets)

Big Five Factors	Behaviours (Facets)
Openness	Ideas (curious)
	Fantasy (imaginative)
	Aesthetics (artistic)
	Feelings (excitable)
	Values (unconventional)
Conscientiousness	Competence (efficient)
	Order (organized)
	Dutifulness (not careless)
	Achievement striving (thorough)
	Self-discipline (not lazy)
	Deliberation (not impulsive)
Extraversion	Gregariousness (sociable)
	Assertiveness (forceful)
	Activity (energetic)
	Excitement-seeking (adventurous)
	Positive emotions/ cheerfulness (enthusiastic)
	Warmth (outgoing)
Agreeableness	Trust (forgiving)
	Straightforwardness (not demanding)
	Altruism (warm)
	Compliance (not stubborn)
	Modesty (not a show-off)
	Tender-mindedness (sympathetic)
Neuroticism	Anxiety (tense)
	Angry hostility (irritable)
	Depression (not contented)
	Self-consciousness (shy)
	Impulsiveness (moody)
	Vulnerability (not self-confident)

Source: Based on McCrae, R.R., and Costa, P.T., *Personality in Adulthood: A Five-Factor Theory Perspective*. 2003, 2008, New York: Guilford Press. Reprinted by permission of Guilford Publications, Inc.

20. What are the predictive advantages of (a) broad general traits and (b) narrow, specific ones? What's the research evidence?

and Neuroticism—may help you remember them.) Two of the five factors, Extraversion and Neuroticism, overlap with Eysenck's theory, and two other factors, Conscientiousness and Agreeableness, are similar to Eysenck's Psychoticism factor. Proponents of the Five Factor Model believe that when a person is placed at a specific point on each of these five dimensions by means of a psychological test, behaviour ratings, or direct observations of behaviour, the essence of his or her personality is captured (McCrae & Costa, 2008).

What do you think about that conclusion? Your reaction may be one of skepticism, since it seems that there *must* be more to individuality than can be captured by only five dimensions. However, we should remember that, as discussed in Chapter 5, the incredible number of colours that humans can discriminate is based on the activity patterns of only three types of cones. Thus, the many variations that can occur from the blending of five personality dimensions could account for enormous variation in the pattern of people's behavioural tendencies.

Traits and Behaviour Prediction

Trait theorists try not only to describe the basic structure of personality, but also to predict real-life behaviour on the basis of a person's traits. Even if a limited number of general traits such as the Big Five seem adequate to describe important features of personality, it is entirely possible that a larger number of specific traits such as Cattell's would be more likely to capture nuances of behaviour within particular situations and therefore would be better for predictive purposes.

Measurements of the Big Five factors and real-life behavioural outcomes seldom show correlations beyond 0.20 to 0.30 (e.g., Paunonen, 2003). In recognition of these findings, the Big Five Model now includes six subcategories or *facets* under each of the five major factors (Table 14.5). The most important personality test to measure the Big Five is the NEO Personality Inventory (NEO-PI). The NEO-PI now provides scores on each of the facets as well as the corresponding major factor. These more-specific dimensions allow for more-accurate behavioural predictions (McCrae & Costa, 2008). For example, the Positive Emotions/Cheerfulness facet of Extraversion is more highly related to life satisfaction than is the total Extraversion score that includes all six facets (Schimmack et al., 2004).

Research has found a powerful association between the Big Five personality traits and health, with different personality traits associated with an increased or decreased risk of a number of serious health problems (Hampson, 2012). For example, Weston, Hill, and Jackson (2015) found that high levels of Conscientiousness lowered the risk of stroke, high blood pressure, diabetes, and arthritis; Openness was protective against stroke, heart disease, high blood pressure, and arthritis; while Neuroticism increased the risk of developing heart disease, lung disease, high blood pressure, and arthritis. While personality traits clearly are risk or protective factors for a range of diseases, the mechanisms involved are not well understood. The expectation is that different personality traits influence health by influencing lifestyle choices and specific behaviours, such as communication with health care professionals, and these behaviours then have an impact on health (Hampson, 2012; Weston et al., 2015).

Biological Foundations of Personality Traits

Both nature and nurture influence the development of personality traits, but their contributions differ depending on the trait in question (Plomin & Caspi, 1999). Biological explanations for personality differences focus on three levels. Some researchers search for differences in the functioning of the nervous system (Pickering & Gray, 1999). As discussed in Chapter 4, there is evidence that genes make an important contribution to personality (e.g., Munafo, 2009). Some psychologists have also used evolutionary principles to explain why these traits exist among humans (Buss, 1999; and see Chapter 4). In considering the biological perspective for personality, keep in mind the role of behaviour genetics and the evolutionary explanations that we explored earlier.

Hans Eysenck (1967) was one of the first modern theorists to suggest a biological basis for major personality traits. He linked Introversion-Extraversion and Stability-Instability to differences in individuals' normal patterns of arousal within the brain. He started with the notion that there is an optimal, or preferred, level of biological arousal in the brain. Eysenck believed that extreme introverts are chronically *overaroused;* their brains are too electrically active, so they try to minimize stimulation and reduce arousal to get down to their optimal arousal level, or "comfort zone." In contrast, the

brains of extreme extraverts are chronically *underaroused,* so they need powerful or frequent stimulation to achieve an optimal level of cortical arousal and excitation. The extravert thus seeks social contact and physical arousal, likes parties, takes chances, is assertive, and readily suffers from boredom.

Whereas Introversion-Extraversion reflects a person's customary level of cortical arousal, Stability-Instability represents the suddenness with which shifts in autonomic nervous system arousal occur. Unstable people have hair-trigger nervous systems that show large and sudden shifts in arousal, whereas stable people show smaller and more gradual shifts (Pickering & Gray, 1999). Eysenck also called this stability dimension *Neuroticism* because he found that people with extremely unstable nervous systems are more likely to experience emotional problems that require clinical attention.

Eysenck believed that the arousal patterns that underlie Introversion-Extraversion and Stability-Instability have genetic bases. As we learned in Chapter 4, a growing body of evidence supports his view. Eysenck believed that, although personality is strongly influenced by life experiences, the ways people respond to those experiences may be at least partly programmed by biological factors.

Other personality researchers continue to link personality traits to biological foundations. For example, DeYoung (2013) has linked the neurotransmitter dopamine to both Extraversion and Openness. Other researchers are exploring associations between brain activation, assessed using fMRI, and the Big Five personality traits (e.g., Ikeda et al., 2014).

The Stability of Personality Traits

Personality traits are defined as enduring behavioural predispositions—they should thus show some degree of stability over time and across situations. As far as stability over time is concerned, the research literature shows evidence of both stability and change (Caspi & Roberts, 1999; Roberts et al., 2008). Some personality dimensions tend to be more stable than others. For example, introversion-extraversion, as well as temperamental traits such as emotionality and activity level, tend to be quite stable from childhood into adulthood and across the adult years (Eysenck, 1990; Zuckerman, 2005).

Certain habits of thought may also be fairly stable. One is our tendency to think optimistically or pessimistically. Melanie Burns and

21. In Eysenck's theory, what are the biological bases for individual differences in Extraversion and Stability?

TABLE 14.6 Sample Items from a Trait Measure of Optimism-Pessimism*

1. In uncertain times, I usually expect the best.
2. Overall, I expect more good things to happen to me than bad.
3. If something can go wrong for me, it will.
4. I rarely count on good things happening to me.

*Items on the Life Orientation Test are answered on a 5-point scale ranging from strongly disagree to strongly agree.

Source: M.F. Scheier, C.S. Carver & M.W. Bridges, 1994, Distinguishing Optimism from Neuroticism (and Trait Anxiety, Self-Mastery, and Self-Esteem): A Reevaluation of the Life Orientation Test, *Journal of Personality and Social Psychology, 67,* 1073, Table 6. Copyright © 1994 by the American Psychological Association. Reprinted by permission of the author and the publisher.

Martin Seligman (1989) coded diaries and letters that elderly people had written approximately 50 years earlier for the tendency to respond either optimistically or pessimistically to life events. The elderly people also completed a questionnaire that measured their current optimistic-pessimistic tendencies. Although little consistency over time was shown for dealing optimistically or pessimistically with positive events, Burns and Seligman found a stable tendency to respond with optimism or pessimism to negative life events. The authors suggested that this tendency to be pessimistic might constitute an enduring risk factor for depression, low achievement, and physical illness, and they are presently studying such linkages. Table 14.6 contains items from the Life Orientation Test (Scheier & Carver, 1985) used by personality researchers to measure the disposition to be optimistic or pessimistic.

When it comes to stability of behaviour across situations, personality again shows both a degree of stability and some capacity for change (Mischel & Shoda, 1999). Because behaviour always results from a person interacting with a situation, we would be foolish to expect people to behave in the same manner from situation to situation. Even on a trait as central as honesty, people can show considerable behavioural variability across situations. In a classic paper, Walter Mischel (1984) found that among university students the trait conscientiousness varied across situations. A student might be highly conscientious in one situation (e.g., coming to work on time) without being conscientious in another (turning in class assignments on time).

22. How does research evidence bear on the assumption of stability across time and across situations?

23. What three factors make it difficult to predict behaviour on the basis of individual personality traits?

Three factors make it difficult to predict on the basis of personality traits how people will behave in particular situations. First, personality traits interact with other traits as well as with characteristics of different situations. This melding accounts for the incredible richness we see in personality, but it also poses a challenge to psychologists who want to predict behaviour. When two or more traits, such as honesty, dominance, and agreeableness, influence a behaviour in a particular situation, our ability to predict on the basis of only one of the traits is bound to be limited (Ahadi & Diener, 1989).

Second, the degree of consistency across situations is influenced by how important a given trait is for the person. A person for whom honesty is a central component of the self-concept may show considerable stability across situations in honest behaviours because feelings of self-worth may be linked to living up to moral standards regardless of the circumstances (Kenrick & Funder, 1991).

Third, people differ in their tendency to tailor their behaviour to what is called for by the situation. This personality trait is called **self-monitoring** (Table 14.7). People who are high in self-monitoring are very attentive to situational cues and adapt their behaviour to what they think would be most appropriate. On the one hand, extreme self-monitors resemble behavioural chameleons who act very differently in different situations. Low self-monitors, on the other hand, tend to act primarily in terms of their internal beliefs and attitudes rather than the demands of the situation. The saying "What you see is what you get" applies well to low

TABLE 14.7 Sample Items from the Self-Monitoring Scale*

1. In different situations and with different people, I often act like very different persons.
2. I am not always the person I appear to be.
3. I have trouble changing my behaviour to suit different people and different situations.
4. I would not change my opinion (or the way I do things) in order to please someone or win their favour.

*Items 1 and 2 are keyed *true* and items 3 and 4 *false* for self-monitoring.

Source: Based on Snyder, M. (1987). *Public appearances/ private realities: The psychology of self-monitoring.* New York, NY: W.H. Freeman.

self-monitors, and such people show greater consistency across situations than do high self-monitors (Snyder, 1987).

According to some trait theorists, the stability and distinctiveness that we see in personality do not come from the fact that we behave the same way in every situation. Rather, they result from our exhibiting an *average* amount of extraversion, emotional stability, agreeableness, honesty, and other traits across many different situations (Epstein, 1983; Kenrick & Funder, 1988). Nonetheless, if they wish to understand more about these interactions among personality traits, situations, and behaviour, personality researchers need to define the relevant characteristics of both the person and the situation (Shoda & Mischel, 2000).

Evaluating the Trait Approach

Despite differences of opinion concerning the nature and number of basic personality dimensions, trait theorists have made an important contribution by focusing attention on the value of identifying, classifying, and measuring stable, enduring personality dispositions. Several challenges confront trait theorists, however. More attention must be paid to how traits interact with one another to affect various behaviours if we are to capture the true complexity of personality (Ahadi & Diener, 1989; Choca et al., 1992; Smith et al., 1990).

In evaluating the trait perspective, we must remember the distinction between description and explanation. To say that someone is outgoing and fun-loving *because* she is high in extraversion is merely to describe the behaviour with a trait name, not to explain the inner disposition and how it operates. Traditionally, the trait perspective has been more concerned with describing the structure of personality, measuring individual differences in personality traits, and predicting behaviour than with understanding the psychological processes that produce the traits (McAdams, 1992). Eysenck's theory of brain arousal is a notable exception, since it attempts to explain the biological bases for behavioural differences produced by extraversion and stability. Research linking variations in personality traits to differences in brain structure and function continues and is adding to our knowledge of personality traits (e.g., De Young, 2013; Karimizadeh et al., 2015).

SOCIAL COGNITIVE THEORIES

The psychology of learning has great relevance for understanding personality. Many behaviours ascribed to personality are acquired through classical conditioning, operant conditioning, and modelling (Bandura, 1999b). However, the learner is not simply a passive reactor to environmental forces. Instead, as the cognitive perspective tells us, the human is a perceiver, thinker, and planner who mentally interprets events, thinks about the past, anticipates the future, and decides how to behave. Whatever effects the environment has are filtered through these cognitive processes and are influenced—even changed—by them. **Social cognitive theorists** such as Julian

24. How does the distinction between explaining behaviour and describing behaviour apply to trait theory?

Review

- Trait theorists try to identify and measure the basic dimensions of personality. They disagree about the number of traits needed to adequately describe personality. Cattell suggested 16 basic traits; other theorists insist that as few as five may be adequate. Eysenck posits three major dimensions, including extraversion and stability. Prediction studies indicate that a larger number of more-specific traits may be superior for prediction of behaviour in specific situations.

- Traits have not proved to be highly consistent across situations, and they also vary in stability over time. Individuals differ in their self-monitoring tendencies, and this variable influences the amount of cross-situational consistency they exhibit in social situations. Traits interact not only with situations but also with one another, thereby producing inconsistency.

- Biological perspectives on traits focus on differences in the nervous system, the contribution of genetic factors, and the possible role of evolution in the development of universal human traits and ways of perceiving behaviour. Introversion-Extraversion, for example, has been linked to a person's level of brain arousal.

25. How does reciprocal determinism apply to an individual's personality pattern? Specify the two-way causal links.

26. Define Rotter's concepts of expectancy and reinforcement value and explain how they jointly influence behaviour.

27. Describe Rotter's concept of locus of control and how it affects behaviour.

Rotter (1954, 1966), Albert Bandura (1986, 1999a), and Walter Mischel (1973, 1999) have combined the behavioural and cognitive perspectives into an approach to personality that stresses the interaction of a thinking human with a social environment that provides learning experiences.

To understand behaviour, psychodynamic, humanistic, and trait theorists emphasize internal, personal causes of behaviour, such as unconscious conflicts, self-actualization tendencies, and personality traits. In a sense, they account for behaviour from "the inside out." In contrast, radical behaviourists emphasize environmental causes and view humans as reactors to external events (Parker et al., 1998). To them, behaviour is to be explained from "the outside in." Social-cognitive theorists take an intermediate position, focusing on both internal and external factors. They believe that the debate about whether behaviour is more strongly influenced by personal factors or by the person's environment is basically a meaningless one (Fleeson, 2004; Smith & Shoda, 2009). Instead, according to the social cognitive principle of **reciprocal determinism** (Bandura, 1978), the person, the person's behaviour, and the environment all influence one another in a pattern of two-way causal links (Figure 14.13).

Julian Rotter: Expectancy, Reinforcement Value, and Locus of Control

In 1954, Julian Rotter (whose name is pronounced so it would rhyme with "motor") laid the foundation for today's social cognitive approaches. According to Rotter, the likelihood that we will engage in a particular behaviour in a given situation is influenced by two factors: expectancy and reinforcement value. *Expectancy* is our perception of how likely it is that certain consequences will occur if we engage in a particular behaviour within a specific situation. *Reinforcement value* is basically how much we desire or dread the outcome that we expect the behaviour to produce. Thus, a student who strongly values academic success and expects that studying will result in high grades is quite likely to study. Note that this approach makes use of reinforcement, a central behaviourist concept, but views its effects within a cognitive framework that emphasizes how we think about our behaviour and its expected outcomes.

Locus of Control

One of Rotter's most influential concepts is **internal-external locus of control,** an expectancy concerning the degree of personal

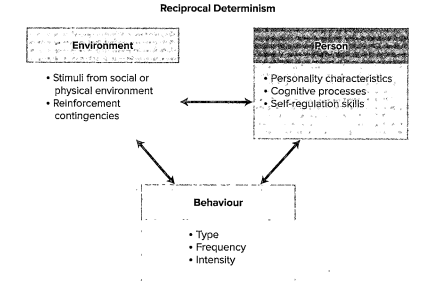

FIGURE 14.13 The social cognitive concept of reciprocal determinism states that the characteristics of the person, the person's behaviour, and the environment all affect one another in reciprocal, or two-way, causal relations.

control we have in our lives. People with an internal locus of control believe that life outcomes are largely under personal control and depend on their own behaviour (Figure 14.14). In contrast, people with an *external* locus of control believe that their fate has less to do with their own efforts than with the influence of external factors, such as luck, chance, and powerful others. Table 14.8 contains items from Rotter's (1966) Internal-External (I-E) Scale, used to measure individual differences in locus of control.

Locus of control is a highly researched personality variable (Steptoe & Wardle, 2001). Quite consistently, people with an internal locus of control behave in a more self-determined fashion (Burger, 2000). Internal university students achieve better grades than do external students of equal academic ability, probably because they link their studying to degree of success and work harder. Internals are more likely to actively seek out the information needed to succeed in a given situation (Ingold, 1989). Interpersonally, internals tend to be independent but cooperative in their dealings with others and are more resistant to social influence, whereas externals tend to give in to high-status people whom they see as powerful others. Internals are more likely than externals to engage in health-promoting behaviours, such as exercising regularly, maintaining a healthy diet, using seat belts, and abstaining from smoking (Steptoe & Wardle, 2001; Wallston, 1993).

Geoff Howe/The Canadian Press

FIGURE 14.14 Research shows that people with an internal locus of control are more likely to take an active role in social change movements.

TABLE 14.8   **Sample Items from Rotter's Internal-External Scale***

Choose statement a or b.

1a. Many times I feel that I have little influence over the things that happen to me.

1b. It is impossible for me to believe that chance or luck plays an important part in my life.

2a. The average citizen can have an influence in government decisions.

2b. The world is run by the few people in power and there isn't much the little guy can do about it.

3a. In the long run, people get the respect they deserve in this world.

3b. Unfortunately, an individual's worth often passes unrecognized, no matter how hard one tries.

---

*1b, 2a, and 3a are the internal alternatives.

Source: Adapted from Rotter, Julian B. (1966), Generalized expectancies for internal versus external control of reinforcement, *Psychological Monographs: General & Applied*, 80(1), No. 609, 1–28. Table 1, pp. 11–12. Copyright © 1966 by the American Psychological Association. Adapted with permission of the author and the publisher. No further reproduction or distribution is permitted without written permission from the American Psychological Association.

Internal locus of control is positively related to self-esteem and feelings of personal effectiveness, and internals tend to cope with stress in a more active and problem-focused manner than do externals (Jennings, 1990). They are also less likely to experience psychological maladjustment in the form of depression or anxiety (Hoffart & Martinson, 1991). Locus of control is called a *generalized expectancy* because it is thought to apply across many life domains.

Albert Bandura: The Social Cognitive Perspective and Self-Efficacy

Albert Bandura has made major contributions to the development of the social cognitive approach. His early studies of modelling, described in Chapter 7, helped to meld the psychology of learning with the cognitive perspective. Bandura's social learning analyses of aggression, moral behaviour, and behavioural self-control demonstrated the wide applicability of the social cognitive approach (Bandura, 1973, 1988, 1991). His concept of human agency is central to the social cognitive perspective (see this chapter's *Research Foundations* feature).

Research Foundations

ALBERT BANDURA, HUMAN AGENCY, AND THE SOCIAL COGNITIVE PERSPECTIVE

Introduction

Albert Bandura's research and theory has been critical in establishing, popularizing, and expanding the social cognitive perspective in psychology. His research is known as rigorous and creative, his theoretical writing as clear, carefully argued, and based on a solid empirical foundation. Albert Bandura (Figure 14.15) is widely considered one of the most influential of all psychologists and was selected as *the* most influential psychologist of the modern era by the American Psychological Association. These are lofty heights for someone born in the small northern Alberta town of Mundare (population 715). Bandura received his undergraduate degree from the University of British Columbia and his graduate training at the University of Iowa. In 1953, he joined the faculty of Stanford University in California and he has spent his academic career there.

© Linda A. Cicero/Stanford News Service

FIGURE 14.15 The research and theories of Albert Bandura have been instrumental in establishing the social cognitive perspective in psychology.

Bandura laid much of the foundation of the social cognitive perspective, and his research and theories about human agency, self-efficacy, observational learning (see Chapter 7), and reciprocal determinism continue to be widely influential. Bandura began his career when behaviourism was the dominant perspective in psychology. He argued, however, that our behaviour is not controlled simply by stimuli in our environment and the immediate consequences of our behaviour. Bandura wrote, "If actions were performed only on behalf of anticipated external rewards and punishments, people would behave like weather vanes, constantly shifting direction to conform to whatever influence happened to impinge upon them at the moment" (2001, p. 7).

In a classic study that laid some of the early foundation for Bandura's agentic perspective (and was important for his work on observational learning), Bandura and Carol Kupers tested seven- to nine-year-old children in a bowling game (Bandura & Kupers, 1964).

Method

Children, seven to nine years of age, played a bowling game. They were told that they could reward themselves with candy (M&Ms) for their performance, and it was left to the child to decide when and how much candy he or she should receive. Before their turn at the bowling game, some of the children watched an adult or another nine-year-old bowl and reward themselves verbally and with candy for their performance. The models differed in the standard that they used to determine if they should reward themselves or not. Some children watched a model who made positive statements about self and took candy only when they scored 20 points or more out of a possible 30 points. Other children saw a model take candy as a reward for scores as low as 10 points. The children were then allowed to bowl and reward themselves when they thought it appropriate. Scoring of the bowling game was fixed so that all the children achieved the same pattern of scores across the different bowling attempts. A final group of children were assigned to a control condition; they bowled and rewarded themselves without the experience of first watching a model.

Results

If the children saw an adult or peer model, the criteria used by the model had a powerful impact on the child's own criteria for self-reinforcement (Figure 14.16). Children who saw a model with a high performance standard themselves adopted a more stringent performance criterion for self-reinforcement than did the children who watched a model with a low standard. Children in the control condition took candy

continued

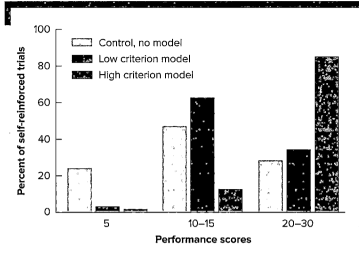

FIGURE 14.16 Percentage of trials in which children took candy as a reward for their performance in a bowling game. Children who previously watched a model with a high criterion for self-reinforcement rewarded themselves only for similarly high levels of performance (highest score obtained was 30 points). Children who had watched a model with a lower criterion for self-reward reinforced themselves for lower levels of performance.

Source: Adapted from Bandura, A., & Kupers, C.J. (1964). Transmission of patterns of self-reinforcement through modeling. *Journal of Abnormal and Social Psychology*, 69, 1–9.

independently of their performance in the bowling game. Based on these findings, Bandura and Kupers argued that although externally applied reinforcements are clearly important, self-administered reinforcement and punishment may be particularly important in governing behaviour. In the bowling experiment, children could set any criteria they wanted, but they adopted a criterion that they had observed and applied it to their own behaviour, even if doing so meant that they received less candy.

Discussion

Bandura and Kupers wrote,

> . . . people typically make self-reinforcement contingent on their performing certain classes of responses which they have come to value as an index of personal merit. They often set themselves relatively explicit criteria of achievement, failure to meet which is considered undeserving of self-reward and may elicit self-denial or even self-punitive responses; on the other hand, they tend to reward themselves generously on those occasions when they attain their self-imposed standards. (1964, p. 1)

If you think about this, we are sure that you can identify examples from your own life. All of us have had occasions when we met our goal on a test, an exam, or another

challenge and followed this success with a night off from working, buying ourselves a treat, or some other act of self-reinforcement.

We have also had the experience of not meeting our performance standard and so not self-reinforcing. Indeed when we fail to meet our own self-imposed standards we may engage in some self-punitive behaviour such as negative verbal comments about self or denying ourselves an activity ("I didn't do well enough on that test to allow myself a camping trip/shopping trip/movie night/party this weekend").

Children not only adopt performance criteria that they have seen modelled, but models can also influence a particularly difficult decision: forgoing a reward that is available now for a larger reward that will be available at some time in the future. Bandura and Walter Mischel, his colleague at Stanford, found that children would sacrifice a small but immediately available reward in favour of a delayed but more valuable reward if they saw a model behave in this way (Bandura & Mischel, 1965). That is, behaviour was controlled not by the immediacy of a reward in front of the child but by the behaviour they saw modelled by others, even when that meant delaying reward to a future time. These early studies of the social origins of a child's self-motivation and self-regulation provided new and experimentally testable alternatives to older conditioning explanations, to explanations based on the subconscious, and to personality trait theories. If a child is going to adopt specific performance criteria, even when doing so means less reward, and is willing to sacrifice an immediate reward for a better reward sometime in the future, that child is acting in accordance with the concept of human agency as outlined.

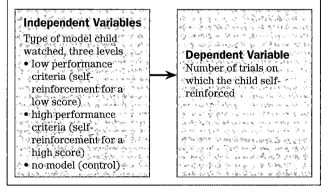

Design

Question: Will children adopt the performance criteria they see modelled, even if it means obtaining less reward?

Type of Study: *Experimental*

Independent Variables	Dependent Variable
Type of model child watched, three levels • low performance criteria (self-reinforcement for a low score) • high performance criteria (self-reinforcement for a high score) • no model (control)	Number of trials on which the child self-reinforced

28. What does Bandura mean by human agency? What are the four components of human agency?

29. Define self-efficacy. What four sources of information influence efficacy beliefs?

A concept central to Bandura's work, and to social cognitive theory, is the idea of human agency, the idea that humans are active agents in their own lives. Bandura argued that we are not just at the mercy of the environment—we make plans and set goals, and then we behave in ways that help us reach our goals. We are self-reflective and self-regulatory. Human agency is a process, not a trait or a characteristic, and includes four aspects: intentionality, forethought, self-reactiveness, and self-reflectiveness. By intentionality, Bandura meant that we plan, modify our plans, and act with intention. We also show forethought; we anticipate outcomes, set goals, and actively choose behaviours relevant to those goals. Self-reactiveness refers to the process of motivating and regulating our own actions, the processes that we use when we modify our goals, monitor our progress toward those goals, and, when necessary, change strategies. With self-reflectiveness, we think about and evaluate our own motivations, values, and goals (Bandura, 2001).

Bandura has argued that much of our behaviour, and especially our social behaviour, is guided by the process of human agency, not by the learning phenomenon explored by Pavlov, Watson, and Skinner, not by the repressed urges of a Freudian subconscious, and not by personality type or trait. We plan, act with intention, anticipate outcomes, set goals, actively choose behaviours, and regulate our own actions. How we engage in these processes is set in part by our learning history, including past models, and by our reciprocal interactions with others in our environment.

Self-Efficacy

According to Bandura (1997), a key factor in the way people regulate their lives is their sense of **self-efficacy,** their beliefs concerning their ability to perform the behaviours needed to achieve desired outcomes. People whose self-efficacy is high have confidence in their ability to do what it takes to overcome obstacles and achieve their goals (see this chapter's *Applications* feature).

Applications

INCREASING SELF-EFFICACY THROUGH SYSTEMATIC GOAL SETTING

Positive self-efficacy beliefs are consistently related to success in behaving effectively and achieving goals. This has led Bandura and other social cognitive theorists to have a strong interest in practical measures for enhancing self-efficacy.

When people are successful and when they attribute their success to their own competencies (internal locus of control), their self-efficacy increases and assists them in subsequent goal-directed efforts (Maddux, 1999). Moreover, successful people usually have mastered the skills involved in setting challenging and realistic goals, figuring out what they need to do on a day-by-day basis to achieve them and making the commitment to do what is required. As they achieve each goal they have set, they become more skilful and increase their sense of personal efficacy (Bandura, 1997).

Not all goal-setting procedures are created equal, and it is important to apply research-based principles that make goal-setting programs most effective (Locke & Latham, 2002). Here are some research-derived guidelines for effective goal setting:

1. **Set specific, behavioural, and measurable goals.** The first step in changing some aspect of your life is to set a goal. The kind of goal you set is very important, because certain kinds of goals encourage us to work harder, enjoy success, and increase self-efficacy.

Specific and fairly narrow goals have been shown to be far more effective than general "do your best" goals (Locke & Latham, 2002). A goal such as "improving my tennis game" is less likely to be helpful than "increasing the percentage of serves I put in play by 20 percent." The latter goal refers to a specific behaviour that you can focus on and measure.

One of the most important aspects of goal setting is systematically measuring progress toward the goal. The importance of this aspect was shown in a study by Bandura and Daniel Cervone (1983) in which participants worked on a strenuous bicycle-pedalling task over a number of trials. Two independent variables were manipulated: (a) whether the participants were given specific improvement goals, and (b) whether the participants were given feedback about their performance on the previous trial. A control condition got neither goals nor feedback and provided a basis for evaluating the effects of goals and feedback, alone or in combination. The dependent variable was the speed and power with which the participants pedalled.

As shown in Figure 14.17, simply having goals was not enough, nor was feedback effective by itself. The

continued

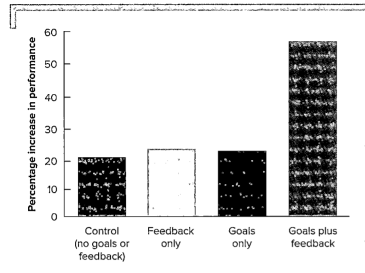

FIGURE 14.17 The effects of improvement goals and performance feedback on performance improvement on a grueling bicycling task. Clearly, the combination of explicit goals and performance feedback resulted in the greatest improvement in performance.

Source: Data from Bandura, A., & Cervone, D. (1983) Self-evaluative and self-efficacy mechanisms governing the motivational effects of goal systems. *Journal of Personality and Social Psychology,* 45(5), Nov 1983, 1017–1028. Copyright © 1983 by the American Psychological Association. Reproduced with permission. The use of APA information does not imply endorsement by APA.

participants who had both goals and feedback showed by far the greatest improvement. This result shows how important it is to find a way to measure your progress toward the goal so that you get performance feedback and can see your improvement. Visible movement toward realistic goals builds self-efficacy.

2. **Set performance, not outcome, goals.** Many of our goals relate to outcomes in the future, such as "getting an A in this course." You are more likely to achieve such goals if you use the means-ends heuristic discussed in Chapter 9 and think about the specific things you must do to achieve that outcome goal. Performance goals (what one has to do) work better than outcome goals because they keep the focus on the necessary behaviours. A performance goal might be "read the book and outline the lecture notes for one hour each day." Achieving this performance goal can also be measured quickly and repeatedly, giving you

constant feedback. Many people focus on outcome goals and forget what has to be done on a day-to-day basis to achieve them. It has been said that there are three kinds of people in this world: those who make things happen, those who wait for things to happen, and those who wonder what happened. Make sure you're someone who makes things happen.

3. **Set difficult but realistic goals.** Moderately difficult goals challenge and motivate us and give us a sense of hope. When reached, they increase self-efficacy. Easy goals do not provide a sense of accomplishment, and extremely difficult goals do not provide the success experiences you need to increase self-efficacy.

4. **Set positive, not negative, goals.** Chapter 7 discussed the advantages of positive reinforcement over punishment. Working toward positive goals, such as "getting a B," is better than avoiding a negative consequence, as in "not flunking." Again, positive goals keep you focused on the positive steps that you need to take to achieve them.

5. **Set short-range as well as long-term goals.** Short-range goals are important because they provide the opportunity for immediate mastery experiences, and they keep you working positively. A long-term goal such as "graduating with honours" can easily be broken into a series of subgoals that you can be working toward right now. Short-term goals are like the steps on a staircase leading to the long-term goal. As they are accomplished, they not only provide mastery experiences, but also lead you toward your ultimate goal. In reaching any goal, "divide and conquer" is a cliché that works.

6. **Set definite time spans for achievement.** It is said that the road to hell is paved with good intentions. To keep a goal-setting program on track, it is important to specify the dates by which specific performance goals or subgoals will be met, together with the behaviours needed to attain them in that time span.

Goal setting is a motivational technique that has resulted in remarkable improvement in productivity in many work, social, and academic settings (Locke & Latham, 2002). Moreover, for purposes of increasing self-efficacy, it has the added advantage of providing the repeated mastery experiences that are the most powerful sources of efficacy information.

A good deal of research has been done on the factors that create differences in self-efficacy (Figure 14.18). Four important determinants have been identified (Bandura, 1997; Maddux, 1999). The most important is our previous *performance attainments* in similar situations. Such experiences shape our beliefs about our capabilities. For example, as shown in Figure 14.19, university women who felt that they had

mastered the martial arts and emotional control skills taught in a physical self-defence training program showed dramatic increases in their belief that they could escape from or disable a potential assailant or rapist (Weitlauf et al., 2000). Bandura stresses that self-efficacy beliefs are always specific to particular situations. Thus, we may have high self-efficacy in some situations and low self-efficacy in others. For

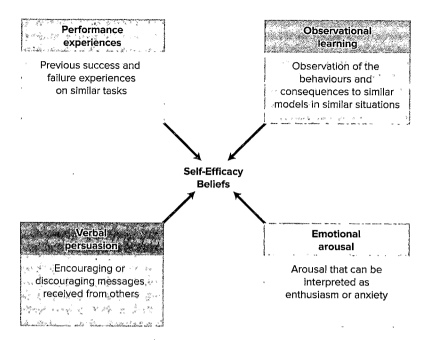

Performance experiences

Previous success and failure experiences on similar tasks

Observational learning

Observation of the behaviours and consequences to similar models in similar situations

Self-Efficacy Beliefs

Verbal persuasion

Encouraging or discouraging messages received from others

Emotional arousal

Arousal that can be interpreted as enthusiasm or anxiety

FIGURE 14.18 Four classes of information that affect self-efficacy beliefs.

Source: Based on Bandura, A. (1997). *Self-efficacy: The exercise of control.* New York, NY: W.H. Freeman.

example, the women who mastered the physical self-defence skills did not feel more generally capable in all areas of their lives, despite their enhanced self-defence efficacy.

A second source of information comes from *observational learning*—that is, observing others' behaviours and their outcomes. If you observe a person similar to yourself accomplish a particular goal, then you are likely to believe that if you perform those same behaviours, you will also succeed. A striking example of how

powerful such expectations can be comes from the world of sports. At one time, physiologists insisted that it was physically impossible for a human being to run a mile in less than four minutes, and no one in the history of track and field had ever done it. When the Englishman Roger Bannister broke the four-minute barrier in 1954, that limiting belief was shattered. The impact on other runners' performance was immediate and dramatic. In the year following Bannister's accomplishment, 37 other runners broke the

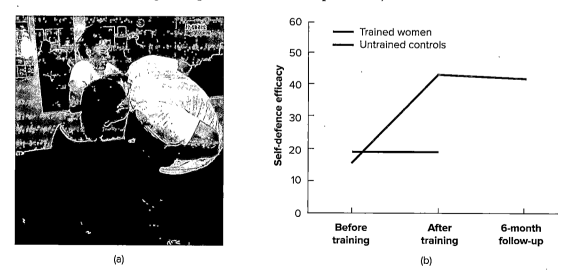

(a)

(b)

FIGURE 14.19 Physical self-defence training (a) has dramatic effects on women's self-efficacy to perform the behaviours needed to defend themselves. (b) The physical defence self-efficacy scores in this study could extend from 6 to 60.

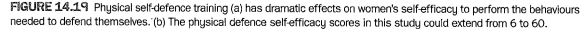

(a): © William Thomas Cain/Getty Images; (b): Based on data from Weitlauf, J., Smith, R.E., & Cervone, D. (2000). Generalization effects of coping skills training: Influences of self-defense training on women's efficacy beliefs, assertiveness, and aggression. *Journal of Applied Psychology, 85,* 625–633.

barrier, and the year after that, nearly 300 runners did the "impossible." Apparently, a great many people came to believe that "if he can do it, so can I."

Third, self-efficacy can be increased or decreased by *verbal persuasion*. The messages we get from other people who affirm our abilities or downgrade them affect our efficacy beliefs. Thus, inspirational teachers who convey high standards and a "you can do it" conviction can inspire their students to great accomplishments.

Finally, high *emotional arousal* that is interpreted as anxiety or fatigue tends to decrease self-efficacy. Then again, if we find ourselves able to control negative arousal, it may enhance efficacy beliefs and subsequent performance. For example, test-anxious students who mastered relaxation skills showed increases in their belief that they could remain relaxed and focused during tests, and their performance on tests increased as well (Smith, 1989).

Efficacy beliefs are strong predictors of future performance and accomplishment (Bandura, 1997). They become a kind of self-fulfilling prophesy. In the words of Henry Ford, "Whether you believe you can do something or you believe you can't, you're probably right."

Walter Mischel: The Consistency Paradox and If . . . Then . . . Behaviour Consistencies

Walter Mischel is a third key figure in the development of modern social cognitive theory. Mischel, along with Bandura, became part of the "cognitive revolution" that occurred during the 1960s. Mischel argued that a more cognitive approach to personality was required, one that takes into account not only the power of situational factors, but also how people characteristically deal mentally and emotionally with experience. He has argued for the importance of personal constructs, individual ways of perceiving and understanding events, in behaviour.

In 1984, Walter Mischel triggered an upheaval in the study of personality. We expect people to behave in a consistent way over time and across situations. Indeed, if someone we know behaves in a way that is inconsistent with his or her past behaviour, we tend to make excuses for the person's atypical behaviour (e.g., "She must be tired," "He's feeling really stressed"). As mentioned earlier in this chapter, Mischel (1984) studied the personality trait of conscientiousness among university students and found that

the consistency was much less than expected. A student may be highly conscientious in one situation without being conscientious in another situation. Other studies revealed similar inconsistencies in behaviour. So although we expect and perceive a high level of consistency in people's behaviour, the actual level of consistency is surprisingly low. This has been referred to as the *consistency paradox*. For some, this lack of consistency called the very idea of personality traits into question. One reaction was the argument that if personality traits were so unimportant, perhaps only the situation mattered and we might not even need a concept of personality to account for behaviour (Mischel & Shoda, 1998, 1999). Mischel argued, however, that both personality and the situation are important.

Mischel has formulated a personality theory, called the *cognitive-affective personality system* (CAPS), in which both the person and the situation matter (Mischel, 1999, 2004; Mischel & Shoda, 1998). According to this view, there is a dynamic interplay between the characteristics that a person brings to the situation (e.g., encoding strategies, expectancies, beliefs, goals, emotion, self-regulatory processes) and the characteristics of the situation. It is this interaction that accounts for behaviour. That is, behaviour results from relatively stable personal dispositions and with cognitive-affective processes that interact with a specific situation. This view proposes what have been referred to as **if . . . then . . . behaviour consistencies**, which suggests that there is consistency in behaviour, but it is found within similar situations. For example, *if* Mark gets angry at his partner, *then* he will shout and become aggressive; however, once the *if* changes, so does the *then: If* Mark becomes angry with his boss, *then* he will withdraw and sulk. Behaviour, Mischel argues, is consistent, but we should not expect some form of global consistency. We expect, and find, consistency within similar situations. Mischel's interpretation does make sense of our experiences; how you behave with your friends, for example, is consistent, but it is different from how you behave when you visit your grandmother (for the sake of your friends, we hope it is different).

Evaluating Social Cognitive Theories

A strength of the social cognitive approach is its strong scientific base. It brings together two perspectives, the behavioural and the cognitive, that have strong research traditions. The

Review

- Social cognitive theories are concerned with how social relationships, learning mechanisms, and cognitive processes jointly contribute to behaviour. A key concept is reciprocal determinism, relating to two-way causal relations among personal characteristics, behaviour, and environment.

- Rotter's theory viewed behaviour as influenced by expectancies and the reinforcement value of potential outcomes. His concept of locus of control is a generalized belief in the extent to which we can control the outcomes in our life.

- Bandura's concept of self-efficacy relates to our self-perceived ability to carry out the behaviours necessary to achieve goals in a particular situation.

- According to Walter Mischel, behaviour results from relatively stable personal characteristics interacting with specific situational cues. Hence, a person's behaviour is consistent in similar situations but may not be consistent across different situations.

constructs of social cognitive theory can be defined, measured, and researched with considerable precision. As a result, the social cognitive approach has advanced our understanding of how processes within the person and characteristics of the situation interact with each other to influence behaviour. Another strength is its ability to translate insights derived from other perspectives into cognitive-behavioural concepts (Carver & Scheier, 2000; Mischel et al., 2004).

Social cognitive theory also helps to resolve an apparent contradiction between the central assumption that personality produces stability in behaviour and research findings that people's behaviour is not very consistent across different situations. Social cognitive theory suggests that the inconsistency of a person's behaviour across situations is actually a manifestation of a stable underlying cognitive-affective personality structure that reacts to certain features of situations.

PERSONALITY ASSESSMENT

If we were to introduce you to a woman you have never met and give you one week to provide a complete personality description of her, what would you do? Chances are, you would seek information in a variety of ways. You might start by interviewing the woman and finding out as much as you could about her. Based on your knowledge of the theories we have discussed, what questions would you ask her? Would you ask about early childhood experiences and dreams? About how she sees herself and others? Would you be interested in the kinds of traits embodied in the Big Five or in Eysenck's dimension of Introversion-Extraversion? Would

you want to know how the woman customarily feels and responds in various situations? Your answers to these questions and your other assessment decisions would in some sense reflect your own theory of what is important in describing personality.

You probably would not be content simply to interview the woman. You may also decide to interview other people who know her well and get their views of what she is like. You might even ask them to rate her on a variety of traits, such as those found in Cattell's model of personality or in the Five Factor model, and you could ask the person you are studying to rate herself on the same measures to see if her self-concept agrees with how others see her.

Finally, you may decide that it would be useful to actually observe how the woman behaves in a variety of situations. You would want to observe her in such a way that you got as "natural" and characteristic a sample of her behaviour as possible. This information, together with that obtained from the person and those who know her best, may provide a reasonable basis for a personality description.

Figure 14.20 shows some of the major methods that psychologists use to assess personality characteristics. As you can see, they use some of the same methods you might have chosen: the interview; trait ratings and behaviour reports; and behavioural assessment, or direct observation, and measurement of the person's behaviour. In addition, they have developed several types of psychological tests, including objective self-report measures and "projective" tests that ask respondents to interpret ambiguous stimuli, such as inkblots or pictures. Finally, physiological measures can be used to measure various aspects of personality, such as emotional reactivity or levels of cortical arousal.

30. Cite six methods that can be used to measure personality variables.

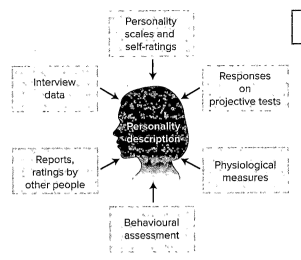

FIGURE 14.20 Measurement approaches used to assess personality.

CRIMINAL PROFILING: ANALYZING THE CRIMINAL MIND

Television shows such as *Criminal Minds* and *CSI: Crime Scene Investigation* depict special agents who help solve crimes by creating personality profiles of likely perpetrators. But what is the scientific verdict on the usefulness of criminal profiling? Does it help solve crimes?

Think about it, and then see the Answers section at the end of the book.

An interesting and novel approach to assessing personality is only beginning to be explored: the use of personal websites. According to Statistics Canada, 80 percent of Canadians aged 16 or older used the Internet in 2010, and Canadians are often online—76 percent of Canadians use the Internet at least once a day. The use of personal websites has grown rapidly in recent years and although the exact number of personal websites is not known, they have become an increasingly common and popular medium for self-expression (Vazire & Gosling, 2004). We make identity claims by how we dress, by how we decorate our homes and offices, and by which logo we have on our backpacks. We make judgments about others people's personality based on these identity claims, such as how they look (Naumann et al., 2009). Identity claims made in a personal website allow even greater control and even greater chance for self-expression since virtually every detail is the result of a decision by the website author. This control allows the website author to be much more deliberate and calculating in creating his or her online identity than is possible in other areas. Personality impressions based on personal websites show surprisingly good agreement with personality assessment based on more traditional measurements, such as the BFI (Big Five Inventory; Vazire & Gosling, 2004). Vazire and Gosling concluded, "When viewing a website, observers form clear, coherent impressions of the author, and they tend to agree about what the author is like. Furthermore, their impressions are largely correct" (2004, p. 130).

The task of devising valid and useful personality measures is anything but simple, and it has taxed the ingenuity of psychologists for nearly a century. To be useful from either a scientific or practical perspective, personality tests must conform to the standards of reliability and validity discussed in Chapter 10. *Reliability,* or consistency of measurement, takes several forms. A test that measures a stable personality trait should yield similar scores when administered to the same individuals at different times (test-retest reliability). Another aspect of reliability is that different professionals should score and interpret the test in the same way (interjudge or inter-rater reliability). *Validity* refers to the most important question of all: Is the test actually measuring the personality variable that it is intended to measure? A valid test allows us to predict behaviour that is influenced by the personality variable being measured. Research on test reliability and validity is an important activity of personality psychologists, and good measures of personality are an absolute must for scientific research on personality and for ethical clinical application (Domino & Domino, 2006).

Interviews

Interviews are one of the oldest methods of assessment. Long before the invention of writing, people undoubtedly made judgments about others by observing them and talking with them. Interviewers can obtain information about a person's thoughts, feelings, and other internal states, as well as information about current and past relationships, experiences, and behaviour.

Structured interviews, frequently used to collect research data or make a psychiatric diagnosis, contain a set of specific questions that are administered to every participant. An attempt is

31. What is a structured interview? What are its advantages over informal approaches?

made to create a standardized situation so that interviewees' responses to more-or-less identical stimuli can be interpreted and compared.

Good interviewers do not limit their attention to what an interviewee says; they also look at how she or he says it. They note interviewees' general appearance and grooming, their voice and speech patterns, the content of their statements, and their facial expressions and posture. Sometimes, attitudes that are not expressed verbally can be inferred from behaviour, as in this instance:

> During the interview she held her small son on her lap. The child began to play with his genitals. The mother, without looking directly at the child, moved his hand away and held it securely for a while. . . . Later in the interview the mother was asked what she ordinarily did when the child masturbated. She replied that he never did this—he was a very "good" boy. She was evidently entirely unconscious of what had transpired in the very presence of the interviewer. (Maccoby & Maccoby, 1954, p. 484)

The interview is valuable for the direct personal contact it provides, but it has some limitations. First, characteristics of the interviewer may affect how the person responds in ways that can affect the validity of the information. The validity of information obtained in an interview also depends on the interviewee's desire to cooperate, respond honestly, and report accurately what the interviewer is trying to assess. Some interview data may be valid, others invalid.

Despite its limitations, the face-to-face interview is essential for certain purposes. A clinical psychologist needs to observe and converse with someone who is being considered for admission to a mental hospital. Interviews are often used in research.

Behavioural Assessment

Personality psychologists sometimes can observe the behaviours they are interested in rather than asking people about them. In **behavioural assessment,** psychologists devise an explicit coding system that contains the behavioural categories of interest. Then they train observers until they show high levels of agreement (interjudge reliability) in using the categories to record behaviour. Behavioural assessment can provide valuable information about how frequently and under what

conditions certain classes of behaviour occur (Haynes, 2000). For example, this method was used by social cognitive researchers to measure the "behavioural signatures" of verbally aggressive children in summer camp environments (Shoda et al., 1994).

Behavioural assessment requires precision in defining the behaviours of interest and the conditions under which they occur. For example, observers studying a young child who is having problems in school do not simply say "Jerry is disruptive." Instead, they try to answer the question, "What, specifically, does Jerry do that causes disruption?" Once they have identified Jerry's specific behaviours, the next questions are "How often and under what conditions does the disruptive behaviour occur?" and "What kinds of outcomes do the behaviours produce?" Answers to these questions can be particularly important, not only in measuring differences in people's personality characteristics, but also in identifying potential situational causes of their behaviour (Greene & Ollendick, 2000).

Remote Behaviour Sampling

It is not practical or possible for behavioural assessors to follow people around from situation to situation on a daily basis. In addition, assessors are frequently interested in unobservable events, such as emotional reactions and thinking patterns, that may shed considerable light on personality functioning. Through **remote behaviour sampling,** researchers and clinicians can collect samples of behaviour from respondents as they live their daily lives (Figure 14.21). A tiny computerized device carried by respondents pages them at randomly determined times of the day. When the "beeper" sounds, respondents record their current thoughts, feelings, or behaviours, depending on what the researcher or therapist is assessing (Csikszentmihalyi, 1990; Singer, 1988; Stone et al., 2000). Respondents also may report on the kind of situation they are in so that situation-behaviour interactions can be examined. The data can either be stored in the computer or transmitted directly to the assessor.

Remote sampling procedures can be used over weeks or even months to collect a large behaviour sample across many situations. This approach to personality assessment holds great promise, since it enables researchers and clinicians to detect patterns of personal functioning that might not be revealed by other methods.

32. How are behavioural assessments designed, and what three questions are they designed to answer?

33. Describe remote behaviour sampling procedures and the types of reports that can be collected.

© Wei Yan/Masterfile

FIGURE 14.21 In remote behaviour sampling, a computerized device resembling a cellphone is used to collect responses from participants—such as ratings of their mood at a certain time—as they live their daily lives.

Personality Scales

Personality scales, or inventories, are widely used for assessing personality in both research and clinical work. Personality scales are termed *objective* measures because they include standard sets of questions, usually in a true-false or rating scale format, that are scored by using an agreed-upon scoring key (Nezami & Butcher, 2000). Their advantages include the ability to collect data from many people at the same time, the fact that all people respond to the same items, and ease of scoring. Their major disadvantage is the possibility that some people will choose not to answer the items truthfully, in which case their scores will not be valid reflections of the trait being measured. To combat this threat to validity, some widely used tests have special *validity scales* that detect tendencies to respond in a socially desirable manner or to present an overly negative image of oneself.

The items on personality scales are developed in two major ways. In the **rational approach,** items are based on the theorist's conception of the personality trait to be measured. For example, to develop a measure of introversion-extraversion, we might ask ourselves what introverts and extraverts would be likely to say about themselves, then write items that capture those kinds of self-descriptions (e.g., "I love to be at large social gatherings" or "I'm very content to spend time by myself"). One frequently used measure developed by using the rational approach is the NEO-PI, which measures the Big Five personality traits of Openness, Conscientiousness, Extraversion, Agreeableness, and Neuroticism (Costa & McCrae, 1992).

In a second approach to personality test development, known as the **empirical approach,** items are chosen not because their content seems relevant to the trait on rational grounds, but because previous research has shown that the items were answered differently by groups of people known to differ in the personality characteristic of interest. The empirical approach was used to develop the **Minnesota Multiphasic Personality Inventory (MMPI;** Hathaway & McKinley, 1983), the most widely used personality inventory. Developed in the 1940s, the MMPI was originally designed to provide an objective basis for psychiatric diagnosis. Its 567 true-false items consist of statements that were answered differently by groups of patients who were diagnosed as having specific psychiatric disorders (e.g., hysteria, paranoia, and schizophrenia) than they were by a non-psychiatric comparison sample of "normal" people. The items vary widely in content; some are concerned with attitudes and emotions, others relate to overt behaviour and symptoms, and still others refer to the person's life history.

The revised MMPI-2, like the original, has ten clinical scales and three validity scales (Table 14.9). The validity scales are used to detect tendencies to either present an overly positive picture or exaggerate the degree of psychological disturbance. The clinical scales were originally intended to measure severe personality deviations such as schizophrenia, depression, and psychopathic personality, and they do. In addition, however, the pattern or *configuration* of scores obtained on the various scales also reveals important aspects of personality functioning in people who do not display such disorders. The MMPI-2 is used not only for personality description and as an aid to psychiatric diagnosis, but also as a screening device in industrial and military settings.

34. Contrast the rational and empirical approaches to personality test development. Give an example of a test developed by each approach.

TABLE 14.9 **The Validity and Clinical Scales of the Minnesota Multiphasic Personality Inventory-2 (MMPI-2) and the Behavioural Characteristics Associated with High Scores on the Scales**

Scale	Abbreviation	Behavioural Correlates
Validity scales		
Lie	L	Lies or is highly conventional
Frequency	F	Exaggerates complaints, answers haphazardly
Correction	K	Denies problems
Clinical scales		
Hypochondriasis	Hs	Expresses bodily concerns and complaints
Depression	D	Is depressed, pessimistic, guilty
Hysteria	Hy	Reacts to stress with physical symptoms, lacks insight into negative feelings
Psychopathic Deviate	Pd	Is impulsive, in conflict with the law, involved in stormy relationships
Masculinity-Femininity	Mf	Has interests characteristic of the opposite sex
Paranoia	Pa	Is suspicious, resentful
Psychasthenia	Pt	Is anxious, worried, high-strung
Schizophrenia	Sc	Is confused, disorganized, disoriented, and withdrawing from others
Hypomania	Ma	Is energetic, active, restless
Social Introversion	Si	Is introverted, with little social contact

Responses on the MMPI-2 are scored and then plotted on a graph, or profile sheet, that reflects the degree to which the individual's responses resemble those of the psychiatric groups. Figure 14.22 shows the MMPI profile

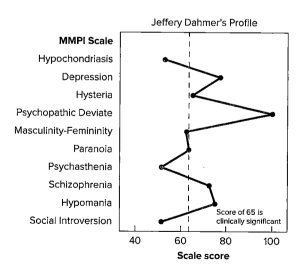

FIGURE 14.22 The MMPI profile of convicted mass murderer Jeffrey Dahmer reflects his severe psychological disturbance and is consistent with his pattern of unrestrained and vicious victimization of others. Scores greater than the dotted line are considered clinically significant.

Source: Caldwell, A.B. (1994). *The profile of Jeffrey Dahmer* (videotape). Los Angeles, CA: Caldwell Report, Inc.

of mass murderer Jeffrey Dahmer, who mutilated and dismembered his victims, sometimes eating their body parts. According to MMPI expert Alex B. Caldwell (1994), several aspects of this profile are consistent with his bizarre and destructive behaviour. The extraordinarily high score on the Psychopathic Deviate scale reflects an extreme antisocial impulsiveness coupled with a total lack of capacity for compassion and empathy. His victims in all likelihood were regarded as little more than objects to satisfy his perverse needs. Caldwell viewed the profile as reflecting Dahmer's sense of being fated or doomed to repeat his acts until he was caught (the high Depression score), together with an absence of fear that, in normal people, might inhibit murderous behaviour (the low Psychasthenia [anxiety] score). Although the profile clearly indicates his high level of psychological disturbance (a normal score on each scale is 50), it also reflects an ability to mask his pathology and put up the normal façade that for years fooled law enforcement officials.

Projective Tests

Freud and other psychodynamic theorists emphasized the importance of unconscious factors in understanding behaviour. By definition, however, people are unaware of unconscious dynamics, so they cannot report them to interviewers or on questionnaires such as the NEO-PI or the MMPI. Therefore, other methods were needed to assess them. The assumption underlying **projective tests** is that, when a person is presented with an ambiguous stimulus whose meaning is not clear, the interpretation attached to the stimulus will have to come partly from within. Thus, the person's interpretation may reflect the "projection" of inner needs, feelings, and ways of viewing the world onto the stimulus.

Rorschach Inkblots

The Rorschach test consists of ten inkblots, five in black and white and five in colour. The person being tested is shown each one in succession and asked, "What does this look like? What might it be?" (Figure 14.23). After responding, the person is asked what specific feature of the inkblot (e.g., its shape or its colour) caused it to be seen in that manner. Examiners write down the responses word for word. They also carefully note subjects' behaviour during testing, including gestures, mannerisms, and expressed attitudes. They categorize and score responses in terms of the kinds of objects reported, the features attended to (e.g., the whole blot, coloured portions, tiny details), and the emotional tone associated with particular types of responses (Erdberg, 2000).

Interpretations made by Rorschach examiners are often based on what the responses seem to symbolize. For example, people who see peering eyes and threatening figures in the inkblots are likely to be viewed as projecting their own paranoid fears and suspicions onto the stimuli.

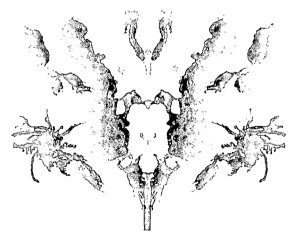

© Science Museum/SSPL/The Image Works

FIGURE 14.23 During a Rorschach test administration, the person being tested is shown a series of inkblots similar to this one and is asked to indicate what each resembles and what feature of the stimulus (e.g., its shape or its colour) makes it appear that way.

A problem is that different examiners may interpret the same response very differently, producing unreliability between examiners. In an attempt to minimize clinician subjectivity in interpreting Rorschach responses, John Exner (Exner & Erdberg, 2005) developed a Comprehensive System with specific coding categories and scoring criteria. Although this system created greater uniformity in scoring, the usefulness of the test for predicting behaviour is still hotly debated (e.g., Dawes, 1994; Wood, Nezworski, Lilienfield, & Garb, 2003). A recent meta-analysis, however, did find good test-retest stability when the Comprehensive System scoring was used (Gronnerod, 2003), and others, such as the University of Windsor's Stephen Hibbard, have presented evidence that the Rorschach is clinically useful (Hibbard, 2003). Many psychodynamic clinicians maintain their faith in the usefulness of the Rorschach, insisting that they find it useful for gaining insight into unconscious processes.

Thematic Apperception Test

The Thematic Apperception Test (TAT) consists of a series of pictures derived from paintings, drawings, and magazine illustrations. Although the pictures are more ambiguous than most photographs (Figure 14.24), they are less ambiguous

Photo Researchers, Inc./Alamy Stock Photo

FIGURE 14.24 A picture from the Thematic Apperception Test. Subjects are asked to make up a story about the picture, covering specific questions such as those listed in the text. These stories are analyzed for recurrent themes that are assumed to reflect significant aspects of personality.

35. What is the assumption underlying projective tests? Describe two widely used projective tests.

than the Rorschach inkblots. Respondents are asked to describe what is going on in each scene, what has led up to the current situation, what the characters are thinking and feeling, and what the outcome of the situation will be. The stories are analyzed for recurrent themes that are assumed to reflect important aspects of the respondent's personality. These might include the kinds of relationships depicted in the stories, the types of motives and feelings that are attributed to the characters, whether positive or negative outcomes occur, and factors that produce such outcomes, such as personal weakness or forces in the environment.

The TAT, like the Rorschach, has the problem of non-standardized or subjective interpretation of responses, which can result in different interpretations of the same stories. Since not everyone can be right, the possibility of erroneous interpretations is obvious. Hibbard (2003) and Bram (2014) have found that when specific systems have been developed to score stories, the TAT has proven to be a useful and valid test. As discussed in Chapter 11, this method is used by researchers to measure motivational variables such as achievement needs. The TAT appears to provide a more valid measure of these needs than do objective self-report measures of the

 **Levels of Analysis**   **Conceptions of Personality**

As we have now seen, diverse conceptions of personality have focused on different aspects and mechanisms of personality functioning. An understanding of how personality accounts for individual differences in behaviour requires analysis at biological, psychological, and environmental levels of analysis.

ENVIRONMENTAL

- Early relationships with parents and other significant figures dating back to infancy underlie personality differences and working models of the world (psychoanalytic, neoanalytic, and object relations theorists).
- Environmental factors can support or interfere with the natural tendency toward self-actualization (humanistic theorists).
- Shared and (especially) unshared environment interact with genetic predispositions, including temperament (biological theorists).
- Past social learning experiences, cultural learning, and current situational factors interact with personal factors to create behavioural signatures (social cognitive theorists).

BIOLOGICAL

- Global personality dispositions are shaped by evolutionary forces, and individual differences in these dispositions occur because they interact with environmental forces that require particular adaptations, including cultural factors (evolutionary psychology theory).
- Genetic factors account for significant amounts of group variance on most personality variables (behaviour genetics).
- Individual differences exist in customary levels of cortical arousal and the speed with which arousal shifts occur (Eysenck).
- Temperamental differences present from birth form a foundation for the development of personality traits.

PSYCHOLOGICAL

- Psychodynamic processes involving impulses, defences, unconscious conflicts, and psychosexual developmental factors shape adult personality (Freud).
- Differences in object relations and attachment styles develop during development.
- The self-concept and drive toward self-actualization influence how we behave. Self-verification and self-enhancement processes are self-related motives (Rogers).
- Individual differences in behaviour are attributed to presumably stable personality traits (trait theorists).
- Cognitive-affective personality factors interact with situational and social learning factors to create person-situation interactions that constitute behavioural signatures (social cognitive theorists).

How would we expect a physically abusive childhood environment to affect children who are high and low in Eysenck's dimension of Stability?

FIGURE 14.25

same motives, showing stronger relations with motivated behaviour (Ferguson, 2000; McClelland, 1989). Despite such exceptions, however, objective measures of personality have generally been found to have better reliability and validity than projective measures (Nezami & Butcher, 2000; Groth-Marnat, 2003).

Personality Theory and Personality Assessment

Personality assessment is intimately related to theory. Theories provide us with a framework that specifies how thoughts, feelings, and bodily processes relate to one another and behaviour (Figure 14.25). Assessment provides tools for measuring personality variables and testing the theory. A clinician's or researcher's theoretical perspective therefore influences which assessment approach he or she is likely to use.

Projective techniques are favoured by psychodynamic theorists who believe that people's responses to tests such as the Rorschach and TAT reveal unconscious processes. Humanistic theorists favour self-report measures of the self-concept and personal aspirations (Wylie, 1989). Social cognitive researchers use behavioural assessments and ask people to rate their expectations about what will happen in the future and how well they will do in particular situations. Remote behaviour sampling is also useful in studying interactions between the person and the situation. Paper-and-pencil inventories such as the MMPI and the NEO-PI are favoured by trait theorists who want to measure specific personality traits and by behaviour geneticists who want to estimate genetic contributions to traits through twin or adoption studies. Researchers interested in biological processes that underlie personality functioning, such as emotional reactivity or brain processes, use physiological measures. All these assessment methods have their place in studying personality and can help to illuminate important aspects of individuality.

Review

- Methods used by psychologists to assess personality include the interview, behavioural assessment, remote behaviour sampling, physiological measures, objective personality scales, and projective tests.

- The major approaches to constructing personality scales are the rational approach, in which items are written on an intuitive basis, and the empirical approach, in which items that discriminate between groups known to differ on the trait of interest are chosen.

- The MMPI-2 is the best-known test developed with the empirical approach. The NEO-PI, developed via the rational approach, measures individual differences in the Big Five factors.

- Projective tests present ambiguous stimuli to subjects. It is assumed that interpretations of such stimuli give clues to important internal processes. The Rorschach inkblot test and the Thematic Apperception Test are the most commonly used projective tests.

Gaining Direction

How can you assess personality? We are faced with such assessments in the media all the time—horoscopes are readily available in the daily paper. But how can a horoscope capture personality? For that matter, what is personality anyway? Some theories discuss crisis or decision points required for "proper" development. Others focus on the achievement of developmental goals for particular purposes. Thus, it would seem that personality is the result of interacting with a demanding environment, using the resources that nature has given us. But just how does this result in a stable set of characteristics that we call *personality?* Is it really determined by the stars . . . or might there be other forces (which we may or may not be aware of) at work?

What are the issues?

What do we need to know?	What is personality? How is personality acquired? How do we measure personality? Is there any evidence for consistent personality traits?	What happens when a person fails to develop personality in a "normal" fashion? Is personality stable across the lifespan?
Where can we find the information to answer these questions?	Look back at the compass icons in this chapter. There are many theories of personality (e.g., Freud's psychodynamic theory, Rogers's self theory, the trait approach), and you should be familiar with each of them. What do each of these theories say about "normal" development?	How would you explain a particular personality type? Note how we measure personality (e.g., by using a scale) and compare this to how a horoscope is constructed. Which method has more validity?

Stress, Coping, and Health

CHAPTER > THE NATURE OF STRESS

OUTLINE
Stressors
The Stress Response
Chronic Stress and the GAS

STRESS AND HEALTH
Stress and Psychological Well-Being
Post-Traumatic Stress Disorder (PTSD)
Stress and Illness

VULNERABILITY AND PROTECTIVE FACTORS
Social Support
Focus on Neuroscience: The Neuroscience
of Social Support
Hardiness
Coping Self-Efficacy
Optimism
Personality Factors
Finding Meaning in Stressful Life Events

COPING WITH STRESS
Effectiveness of Coping Strategies
Research Foundations: Stress, Physical Contact,
and Health: I Wanna Hold Your Hand
Frontiers: Mindfulness and the Stresses of Teaching
Bottling Up Feelings: The Costs of Constraint
Gender, Culture, and Coping

HEALTH PROMOTION AND ILLNESS
PREVENTION
How People Change: The Transtheoretical Model
Increasing Behaviours That Enhance Health
Reducing Behaviours That Impair Health

COMBATTING SUBSTANCE ABUSE
Psychological Approaches to Treatment
and Prevention

POSITIVE PSYCHOLOGY
Applications: How to Be Happy

> Life is largely a process of adaptation to the circumstances in which we exist.
> —Hans Selye

 It was looking like a relaxing weekend for Koby Soto in January of 2016. He was taking a break from his law-school studies and had planned to meet his partner later that day. Then around noon, he received a call out of the blue—his partner was breaking up with him. Koby was stunned. He had thought that everything was going well, but the call indicated that it was not.

Koby tried to focus on other things, but was pretty upset all day. Later that night as he tossed around in bed, he noticed that his heart rate was elevated. So he decided to launch his Fitbit app. It was then that he saw the results of the break-up call. His heart rate jumped to 88 beats per minute (BPM) at the exact time of the call and remained high for the rest of the day, peaking at 118 BPM. It looked like he spent the entire day at the gym.

The Fitbit has also been credited with predicting a pregnancy and saving the life of a teacher whose heart rate had soared to 190 BPM following a seizure.

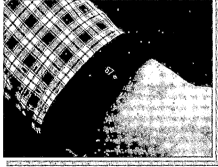
Jeffrey Blackler/Alamy Stock Photo

What are the
issues here?

What do we need
to know?

Where can
we find the
information
to answer the
questions?

Some people are exposed to extraordinarily stressful environments and thrive, while others develop a range of stress-related disorders while living in what many would consider relatively benign circumstances. What allows some people to function at a high level despite stress when others in the same situation would be devastated? The answer will show us that our psychological and physical well-being depends on complex interactions among environmental demands, the personal and environmental resources that we have to deal with them, the individual vulnerabilities that make us susceptible to certain kinds of problems, and protective factors that help to shield us from the ravages of stress.

We experience a high level of stress in our daily lives. Among Canadians aged 15 and older, 23 percent agreed that most days they felt "quite a bit" or "extremely" stressed (Statistics Canada, 2015a). A third of Canadian adults show symptoms of chronic stress (Canadian Mental Health Association, 2009). Of course, university students do not need to be reminded that there are many sources of stress in their lives. Considering how commonly we experience stressors of various types, it is important to understand the impact of stress, and those factors that can either lessen or worsen the impact of that stress.

THE NATURE OF STRESS

Psychologists have viewed stress in three different ways: as a stimulus, a response, and an organism-environment interaction. Some define stress in terms of eliciting stimuli, or events that place strong demands on us. These situations are termed **stressors**. We use the term *stress* in this "stimulus" fashion when we make statements such as "There's all kinds of stress in my life right now. I have three exams next week, I lost my backpack, and my car just broke down."

Stress also has been viewed as a *response* that has cognitive, physiological, and behavioural components. Thus, a person might say, "I'm feeling all stressed out. I'm tensed up, I can't concentrate because I'm really worried, and I've been flying off the handle all week." The presence of negative emotions is an important feature of the stress response and links the study of stress with the field of emotion (Zautra, 2003).

A third way of thinking about stress combines the stimulus and response definitions into a more inclusive model. Here stress is viewed as a *person-situation interaction*, or, more formally, as a *transaction* between the organism and the environment (Lazarus, 1991, 1998). The transactional conception of stress forms the basis for the model shown in Figure 15.1 and will guide our discussion of stress. From this perspective,

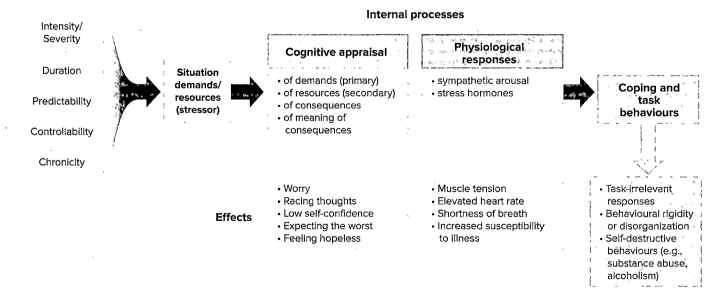

FIGURE 15.1 Stress involves complex interactions among situational factors, cognitive appraisal processes, physiological responses, and behavioural attempts to cope with the situational demands. Stressor characteristics that increase stress responses are shown. The lower panels show potential cognitive, physiological, and behavioural stress responses that can interfere with well-being.

stress is a pattern of cognitive appraisals, physiological responses, and behavioural tendencies that occurs in response to a perceived imbalance between situational demands and the resources needed to cope with them. You will recognize this as an adaptation of the general model of emotion presented in Chapter 11.

Stressors

Stressors are specific kinds of eliciting stimuli. Whether physical or psychological, they place demands on us that endanger well-being, requiring us to adapt in some manner. The greater the imbalance between demands and resources, the more stressful a situation is likely to be. Stressors can range in severity from *microstressors*—the daily hassles and everyday annoyances we encounter at school, on the job, and in our family relations—to very severe stressors. *Catastrophic events* often occur unexpectedly and typically affect large numbers of people. They include such events as natural disasters, acts of war, and concentration camp confinement (Figure 15.2). *Major negative events* such as being the victim of a major crime or sexual abuse, the death or loss of a loved one, an academic or career failure, or a major illness, also require major adaptation. As we shall see, all three classes of stressors can have a significant negative impact on psychological and physical well-being (Aldwin, 2007; Zautra, 2003).

 In addition to intensity or severity, several other characteristics of stressors have been identified as important and are listed in Figure 15.1. In general, events that occur suddenly and unpredictably, and that affect a person over a long period of time seem to take the greatest toll on physical and psychological well-being (Taylor, 2009).

Measuring Stressful Life Events

Sometimes it is possible to verify the life events a person has experienced. We may know that a person has lived through a natural disaster or lost a loved one to death. In other cases, researchers must rely on people's self-reports. To study linkages between life events and well-being, researchers have devised **life event scales** to quantify the amount of life stress that a person has experienced over a given period of time (e.g., the last six months or the past two years). The life event scale shown in Table 15.1 asks people to indicate not only whether a particular event occurred, but also their appraisal of whether the event was positive or negative, and whether it was a major event (defined as having a significant and long-term impact on the person's life) or a "day-to-day" event (Smith et al., 1990). Moreover, additional information can be obtained. For example, respondents might be asked to rate the predictability, controllability, and duration of each event they experienced, permitting an analysis of these factors as well. Life event scales have been widely used in life stress research. Like other self-report measures, however, they are subject to possible distortion and failures of recall.

Some early theorists believed that any life event that requires adaptation, whether negative or positive in nature, is a stressor (Holmes & Rahe, 1967; Selye, 1956). Because later research showed that only negative life changes consistently predicted adverse health and behavioural outcomes, most modern researchers now define stress in terms of negative life changes only (Cohen et al., 1995; Lazarus, 1998). Indeed, positive life events sometimes counter or even cancel out the negative impact of negative events (Thoits, 1983).

1. Describe three ways that theorists have defined the term *stress.*

(left): © Shaul Schwarz/Getty Images; (right): Mario Beauregard/The Canadian Press

FIGURE 15.2 Stressful life events can vary from catastrophic ones to microstressors, or "daily hassles." Both classes of stressor take their toll on physical and psychological well-being.

TABLE 15.1 Sample Items from a Self-Report Measure of Positive and Negative Life Events

Experience	Happened in Last Six Months?		Good or Bad?		"Day-to-Day" or "Major"	
Parents discover something you didn't want them to know	No	Yes	Good	Bad	Day-to-day	Major
Pressures or expectation by parents	No	Yes	Good	Bad	Day-to-day	Major
Receiving a gift	No	Yes	Good	Bad	Day-to-day	Major
Having plans fall through (not going on a trip, etc.)	No	Yes	Good	Bad	Day-to-day	Major
Losing job (quitting, getting fired, getting laid off, etc.)	No	Yes	Good	Bad	Day-to-day	Major
Making honour roll or other school achievement	No	Yes	Good	Bad ·	Day-to-day	Major
Making love or sexual intercourse	No	Yes	Good	Bad	Day-to-day	Major
Something good happens to a friend	No	Yes	Good	Bad	Day-to-day	Major
Work hassles (rude customers, unpleasant jobs, etc.)	No	Yes	Good	Bad	Day-to-day	Major
Death of a friend or family member	No	Yes	Good	Bad	Day-to-day	Major

Source: Scale used in Smith, R.E., Smoll, F.L., & Schutz, R.W. (1990). Measurement and correlates of sport-specific cognitive and somat-ic trait anxiety: The Sport Anxiety Scale. *Anxiety Research*, 2, 263–280.

The Stress Response

2. What four types of appraisal occur in response to a potential stressor? How do these correspond to primary and secondary appraisal?

We respond to situations as we perceive them. The starting point for the stress response is, therefore, our appraisal of the situation and its implications for us. As Figure 15.1 indicates, four aspects of the appraisal process are of particular significance:

1. appraisal of the *demands* of the situation (primary appraisal);

2. appraisal of the *resources* available to cope with it (secondary appraisal);

3. judgments of what the *consequences* of the situation could be; and

4. appraisal of the *personal meaning*, that is, what the outcome might imply about us.

Let us apply these appraisal steps to a real-life situation. You are about to have an important job interview. According to Richard Lazarus (1991), you will first engage in a **primary appraisal** of this situation as being either benign, neutral/irrelevant, or threatening in terms of its demands (how difficult an interview it will be) and its significance for your well-being (how badly you want or need the job). At the same time, you will be appraising your perceived ability to cope with the situation, that is, the resources available to deal with it. Lazarus calls this resource appraisal step **secondary appraisal.** Coping resources include your knowledge and abilities, your verbal skills, and your social resources, such as people who will give you emotional support and encouragement. If you believe that the demands of the interview greatly exceed your resources, you will likely experience stress.

You will also take into account the *potential consequences* of failing to cope successfully with the situation, including both the seriousness of the consequences and the likelihood that they will occur. Will you be able to pay your tuition if you perform poorly and don't get the job? How likely is it that you will fail? Appraising the consequences of failing as very costly and very likely to occur increases the perceived stressfulness of the situation.

Finally, the *psychological meaning of the consequences* may be related to your basic beliefs about yourself or the world. Certain beliefs or personal standards can make people vulnerable to particular types of situational demands. For example, if your feelings of self-worth depend on how successful you are in situations like this one, you may regard doing poorly during the interview as evidence that you are a worthless failure.

Distortions and mistaken appraisals can occur at any of the four points in the appraisal process, causing inappropriate stress responses. People may overestimate the seriousness of the situation, they may underestimate their own resources, they may exaggerate the seriousness of the consequences and the likelihood that they will occur, or they may have irrational self-beliefs that confer inappropriate meaning on the consequences (e.g., "If I don't succeed at this, it means I am and always will be a total loser"). The fact that appraisal patterns can differ from person to person in so many ways helps us understand why there can be so much individual variation in the way people respond to the same event or situation, and it also helps us understand why some people are particularly vulnerable to certain types of demands.

As soon as we make appraisals, the body responds to them (Kemeny, 2004; Taylor, 2009). Although appraisals begin the process, appraisals and physiological responses mutually affect one another (Sun, 2005). Autonomic and somatic feedback can affect our reappraisals of how stressful a situation is and whether our resources are sufficient to cope with it. Thus, if you find yourself trembling as you enter the interview room, you may appraise the situation as even more threatening as you did initially.

Chronic Stress and the GAS

Endocrinologist Hans Selye, of the University of Montreal, was a pioneer in studying the body's response to stress (Selye, 1976). He described a physiological response pattern to strong and prolonged stressors that he called the **general adaptation syndrome (GAS)**. The GAS consists of three phases: alarm reaction, resistance, and exhaustion (Figure 15.3).

In response to a physical or psychological stressor, animals exhibit a rapid increase in physiological arousal. This *alarm reaction* occurs because of the sudden activation of the sympathetic nervous system and the release of stress hormones by the endocrine system. The sympathetic nervous system has an activating effect on the smooth muscles, organs, and glands of the body. Sympathetic nervous system activation, for example, leads to an increase in heart rate and respiration, dilates the pupils, and slows digestion. This alarm reaction helps the body deal with the source of the stress. The slowing of digestion leads to blood being diverted from the digestive system to muscle. The increased heart rate and respiration means that the extra blood arriving at your skeletal muscles contains extra oxygen. Pupil dilation makes our eyes more sensitive to light and enhances vision.

There is also an endocrine, or hormonal, stress response (Miller et al., 2007). Perception of a threat leads a cascade of messages from the hypothalamus within the brain to the pituitary gland at the base of the brain, and then from the pituitary gland to the adrenal glands. The adrenal glands produce a number of different hormones, but during a period of stress the most important is **cortisol**. Cortisol triggers an increase in blood sugars, in part by acting

3. Describe the three stages of Selye's GAS.

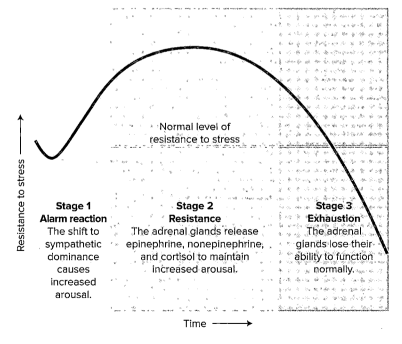

FIGURE 15.3 Hans Selye described the general adaptation syndrome. When a person is exposed to a stressor, the alarm reaction mobilizes the body's resources. During the stage of resistance, stress hormones maintain the body's defensive changes, and the body signs characteristic of the alarm reaction virtually disappear. But, if the stress persists over a long time, the body's resources become depleted and exhaustion occurs; the organism can no longer cope and is highly vulnerable to breakdown.

Source: Figure, "Hans Selye's General Adaptation Syndrome," from *The Stress of Life,* 2nd ed., by Hans Selye, p. 476, 1976. New York: McGraw-Hill. Reprinted by permission of The McGraw-Hill Companies, Inc.

on the liver. Thus, the extra blood arriving at your skeletal muscles contains additional sugar, along with the additional oxygen. Cortisol also suppresses the immune system (Chiappelli, 2000). If you are injured, this action of cortisol suppresses inflammation so that injured tissues do not swell. The powerful anti-inflammatory effects of cortisol are well demonstrated by the use of cortisone, which the body converts to cortisol, to treat the joint inflammation of tennis elbow, bursitis, and some cases of arthritis. The stress hormones are especially important for your ability to function despite the presence of a stressor; but, persistent secretion of cortisol is associated with a number of serious clinical conditions, such as depression and anxiety disorders (Holsboer & Ising, 2010).

Sympathetic nervous system activation and the hormonal response help you deal with the stressor. The stress response has been characterized as the "fight-or-flight" response, and in many ways that is an apt description. Your ability to confront the source of stress ("fight") or retreat from it ("flight") is enhanced by the stress response. You are more sensitive to visual stimuli, movement is faster and stronger, and injury is less likely to generate movement-limiting swelling; your body is primed and ready to act.

The alarm reaction stage cannot last indefinitely, however, and the body's natural tendency to maintain the stable internal state of homeostasis results in parasympathetic nervous system activity. The parasympathetic nervous system functions to reduce arousal. Despite attempts to return to homeostasis, if the stressor continues, the stress response also continues, although sympathetic nervous system activity is partially muted by the opposing parasympathetic nervous system. With continued exposure to stress, the body remains on red alert and enters the second stage, resistance.

During the stage of *resistance*, the body's resources continue to be mobilized so that the person can function despite the presence of the stressor. Resistance can last for a relatively long time, but the body's resources are being depleted. How long the stage of resistance can last depends on the severity of the stress, the individual's general health, available support (such as social support), and other factors. Elevation of heart rate and respiration, suppression of digestion, suppression of the immune system, and changes in blood sugar levels cannot continue indefinitely without exhausting the body. Eventually, remaining bodily resources are no longer sufficient and the stage of resistance comes to an end.

If the stressor is intense and persists for too long, the body may reach the stage of *exhaustion*, in which the body's resources are dangerously depleted. It is during the stage of exhaustion that there is increased vulnerability to disease and, in extreme cases, collapse and even death (Hancock & Desmond, 2000; Holsboer & Ising, 2010). When a person leaves

 **Review**

- Stress has been viewed by various theorists as a stimulus; as a response that has cognitive, physiological, and behavioural components; and as a person-situation interaction—that is, a transaction between the person and the environment.

- A transactional model of stress specifies interactions among situational factors, cognitive appraisal processes, physiological responses, and behavioural attempts to cope. This model by its nature predicts individual differences in response to stressors.

- Stressors are events that place physical or psychological demands on organisms. The stressfulness of a situation is defined by the balance between demands and resources. Life events can vary in terms of how positive or negative they are, as well as in predictability, controllability, chronicity, and other dimensions that affect their impact.

- Cognitive appraisal processes play an essential role in people's responses to stressors.

People appraise the nature of the demands, the resources available to deal with them, their possible consequences, and the personal meaning of these consequences. Distortions at any of these levels can result in inappropriate stress responses.

- The physiological response to stressors is mediated by the autonomic and endocrine systems, and involves a pattern of arousal that mobilizes the body to deal with the stressor.

- Selye described a general adaptation syndrome (GAS) that describes the changes that occur during chronic stress. The changes progress through the three stages: alarm reaction, during which the stress response is activated; resistance, during which bodily resources are mobilized to allow you to function despite the stress; and exhaustion, during which resources are depleted and stress-induced illness occurs.

the stage of resistance and enters the stage of exhaustion is again determined by a number of factors, especially the severity of the stress, the person's ability to cope with stress, and his or her general health. The more severe the stress, however, the sooner the body will reach the stage of exhaustion. Selye argued that whichever system of the body is the weakest will be the first to be affected during the exhaustion stage. If, on the one hand, because of maturational, genetic, or experiential factors, a person's cardiovascular system is at risk, then that will be the first system to break down during the stage of exhaustion. If, on the other hand, a person's immune system is weak, then that person may develop diseases related to immune system dysfunction or show evidence of weakened immune function.

A mild form of this process is familiar to students who deal with periods of stress, such as during the end of an academic term. You continue to function despite the stress of term-end deadlines and final exams (resistance), only to become ill when the stressors end and the vacation begins.

STRESS AND HEALTH

Selye's work inspired a generation of medical and psychological researchers to explore the effects of stress on both physical and psychological well-being. As we will now see, stress can result in physical and psychological deterioration. One conclusion is that a physical mobilization system sculpted by evolution to help organisms deal with life-threatening *physical* stressors may not be as adaptive for dealing with the *psychological* stressors we face in modern life. As noted by one medical authority, "Stone Age physiological and biochemical responses to emotion have become inappropriate in a Space Age setting, and can pave the way to psychosomatic diseases" (Carruthers, 1981, p. 239).

Stress and Psychological Well-Being

Effects of stress on psychological well-being are clearest and most dramatic among people who have experienced catastrophic life events. Anthony Rubonis and Leonard Bickman (1991) surveyed the results of 52 studies of catastrophic floods, hurricanes, and fires. In the wake of natural disasters, they found an average increase of 17 percent in rates of psychological disorders such as anxiety and depression.

Some stressors are so traumatic that they can have a strong and long-lasting psychological impact (Resick, 2005). Several decades after the horror of the Holocaust, psychological scars remain for Jewish survivors of the Nazi concentration camps (Nadler & Ben-Shushan, 1989; Valent, 2000a; Zahava & Ginzburg, 1998). Many survivors are still troubled by high levels of anxiety and recurrent nightmares about their traumatic experiences. Children who lost their parents and siblings continue to experience sudden fears that something terrible will happen to their spouses or children whenever they are out of sight. Depression and crying spells are also common, as are feelings of insecurity and difficulties in forming close relationships. As one researcher reported, "child survivors (now in their 50s and 60s) . . . despite their outward normalcy, remain entrapped in this survival mode" (Valent, 1998, p. 751).

Long-lasting psychological symptoms have also been found among soldiers who experienced the trauma of combat. Twenty years after the 1982 Lebanon war, Israeli soldiers who had experienced combat reported more psychological, social, and health problems than did a matched group of veterans who had not experienced combat (Zahava et al., 2006).

Women who experience the trauma of rape sometimes find that its aftermath can be almost as stressful as the incident itself. Many victims experience a reaction known as the **rape trauma syndrome** (Burgess & Holmstrom, 1974). For months or even years after the rape, victims may feel nervous and fear another attack by the rapist. Many victims change their place of residence but continue to have nightmares and be frightened when they are alone, outdoors, or in crowds. Victims frequently report decreased enjoyment of sexual activity long after the rape, even when their ability to have orgasms is not affected (Feeny & Foa, 2000; Holmes & St. Lawrence, 1983). In one long-term study of rape victims, a quarter of the women felt that they had not recovered psychologically six years after the rape (Meyer & Taylor, 1986).

Fortunately, the majority of stressors that people experience are not as severe as concentration camp confinement, combat, or rape. How do more typical but less serious stressors affect psychological well-being? To answer this question, researchers have examined the relation between self-reported life events and measures of psychological well-being. Findings consistently show that the more negative life events people report on measures such as the one shown in Table 15.1, the more likely they are also to report symptoms of psychological distress (Holahan & Moos, 1990; Holsboer &

4. What are the characteristics of the rape trauma syndrome?

5. Describe three possible causal paths between self-reported stress and distress.

Ising, 2010). We might therefore be tempted to conclude that "stress causes distress." This causal interpretation is shown in path 1 in Figure 15.4, but it may not be accurate because the data are correlational in nature and other causal interpretations are possible. For example, path 2 reverses the first causal interpretation, suggesting that people's levels of distress may influence their reporting of negative life events. That is, distressed people may be more likely to remember negative things that have happened to them. Or they may tend to view more events as negative, resulting in higher negative life change scores. Psychological distress also might cause more negative events to occur in people's lives because of their own behaviour. For example, distressed people tend to evoke negative reactions from others (Coyne et al., 1991; Joiner et al., 1992).

6. Describe four common features of PTSD.

A third causal possibility, shown in path 3, is that a third variable causes both negative life events and psychological distress. The personality trait of **neuroticism** might be one such factor. People who are high in neuroticism have a heightened tendency to experience negative emotions and get themselves into stressful situations through their maladaptive behaviours (Eysenck, 1989; Suls et al., 1998). In one longitudinal study of Dutch adults, Johan Ormel and Tamar Wohlfarth (1991) found that initial scores on a neuroticism scale were related positively to both the number of stressful events and the amount of psychological distress reported over the next six years. Thus, we are again reminded that stressful life events are part of a network of causal relations that involve ongoing transactions between people and situations. It appears that stressful life events can function as both cause and effect (Cohen & Edwards, 1989; Suls et al., 1998).

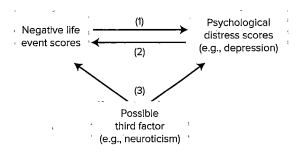

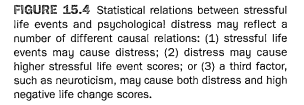

FIGURE 15.4 Statistical relations between stressful life events and psychological distress may reflect a number of different causal relations: (1) stressful life events may cause distress; (2) distress may cause higher stressful life event scores; or (3) a third factor, such as neuroticism, may cause both distress and high negative life change scores.

DO STRESSFUL LIFE EVENTS CAUSE PSYCHOLOGICAL DISTRESS?

A consistent statistical relation has been shown between stressful life events and psychological distress; the greater the number of stressful events people have experienced, the more distress they are likely to report. Based on these results, are you willing to accept the conclusion that life stress causes distress, or can you think of other possible reasons for this relation?

Think about it, and then see the Answers section at the end of the book.

Post-Traumatic Stress Disorder (PTSD)

Post-traumatic stress disorder (PTSD) represents what can happen to victims of extreme stress and trauma. PTSD is a severe anxiety disorder that is caused by exposure to traumatic life events—that is, to severe stress. Four major groups of symptoms occur with PTSD:

- severe anxiety, physiological arousal (the stress response), and distress;

- painful, uncontrollable reliving of the event(s) in flashbacks, dreams, and fantasies (Pitman et al., 2000);

- emotional numbing and avoidance of stimuli associated with the trauma; and

- intense "survivor guilt" in instances where others were killed but the individual survived (Valent, 2000b).

Some individuals with PTSD also show self-destructive and impulsive behaviour.

The study of PTSD arose in part from studies of soldiers who had witnessed the horrors of an active war zone. One study found that the incidence of PTSD was seven times greater for Vietnam veterans who had spent significant time in combat and were wounded than it was for other Vietnam-era veterans (Centers for Disease Control [CDC], 1988). Another study found that within 12 months of combat exposure, 27.8 percent of veterans developed PTSD (Prigerson et al., 2002). Civilian victims of war are even more likely to develop PTSD than are soldiers. Amy Ai and colleagues (2002) found that 60.5 percent of the refugees from the bloody civil war in Kosovo showed signs of PTSD. Traumas caused by human perpetrators, such as war, rape, assault, and torture, tend to cause more severe

Prakash Singh/AFP/Getty Images

FIGURE 15.5 The devastation and loss of life caused by the 2004 Indian Ocean tsunami traumatized millions of people in 11 countries. One effect of the trauma was the development of post-traumatic stress disorder in many people, particularly those who were personally affected by the destruction.

PTSD than do natural disasters (Figure 15.5; O'Donohue & Elliot, 1992). Following exposure to a severe trauma, women are more likely to develop PTSD than are men. Although anyone can develop PTSD if they are exposed to a sufficiently severe trauma, the likelihood of developing PTSD is influenced by the victim's social support, the presence of significant childhood stresses, personality factors, coping strategies, and pre-existing psychological conditions (American Psychiatric Association, 1994). However, if the trauma is sufficiently severe, such as the trauma suffered by the victims of violent rape, the likelihood of developing PTSD is high regardless of the presence of mitigating factors.

Terrorist acts can be a powerful trigger for the development of PTSD. Interviews with more than a thousand adult residents of Manhattan found that 7.5 percent manifested symptoms consistent with PTSD in the five to eight weeks following the September 11, 2001, destruction of the World Trade Center. Among those living closest to the World Trade Center, the rate of PTSD was 20 percent (Galea et al., 2002). PTSD does not necessarily develop immediately after the trauma. Although PTSD usually develops within three months, in some cases it can be many months or even years before PTSD fully emerges (American Psychiatric Association, 1994; Meyer & Taylor, 1986).

The severe problems caused by PTSD can also increase later vulnerability to other disorders. One study found that women who had developed PTSD had double the risk of developing alcohol-related problems in the future (Breslau et al., 1997). The unpredictability of who will develop

PTSD, the severity of PTSD, and the ensuing problems caused by PTSD all highlight the importance of prompt and careful post-trauma intervention (Sorenson, 2002; Kaysen et al., 2013). If post-trauma intervention is available for the victims of rape or torture, they can be spared one of the most severe stress-related disorders.

Between the 1870s and 1990s it is estimated that 150 000 Aboriginal children attended residential schools across Canada (Joseph, 2014). The intention of the residential school program was to educate Aboriginal children and assimilate them into the dominant Canadian culture. Children, some as young as four years old, were removed from their families, communities, and culture and sent to live at a residential school (Joseph, 2014). A significant number of residential school children alleged psychological, physical, and sexual abuse (Brasfield, 2001; Joseph, 2014). Most residential schools had closed by the mid-1980s, but it was not until 1996 that the last federally funded residential school was closed.

For most Aboriginal children who attended a residential school there was no lasting impact other than what is experienced by many children who attend a boarding school for an extended period of time (Brasfield, 2001). For a significant minority of residential school students, however, there were lasting problems. The symptoms experienced by these individuals include recurrent intrusive memories, nightmares, flashbacks, avoidance of anything that might remind them of the residential school experience, increased risk of alcohol and drug abuse starting at a very young age, emotional detachment, relationship difficulties, loss of and avoidance of cultural knowledge, and anger management problems (Brasfield, 2001). This set of symptoms is similar to PTSD and has been called the **residential school syndrome** (Brasfield, 2001). The most important differences between PTSD and residential school syndrome are the significant cultural impact and the outbursts of violent anger associated with alcohol and drug abuse that occur with residential school syndrome (Brasfield, 2001).

Stress and Illness

Stress can combine with other physical and psychological factors to influence the entire spectrum of physical illness, from the common cold to cancer, heart disease, diabetes, and sudden death (Lovallo, 2005; Marsland et al., 2002; Segerstrom & Miller, 2004). Sometimes the effects are immediate. On the day of the 1994 Los Angeles earthquake, the number of sudden deaths due to

7. What are some of the delayed effects of stress?

8. By what physiological and behavioural mechanisms can stress contribute to illness?

heart attacks in that city increased from an average of 35.7 per day during the 7 previous days to 101 fatalities (Leor et al., 1996).

Other effects of major stressors on physical well-being are less immediate but no less severe. Within a month following the death of a spouse, bereaved widowers and widows begin to show a higher mortality rate than married people of the same age who have not lost a spouse (Kaprio et al., 1987). People who experience the chronic stress of caring for a spouse suffering from Alzheimer's disease have a significantly increased risk of developing their own health problems (Vitaliano et al., 2004). Sklar and Anisman (1981) at Carleton University found that stressful life events also increased the risk of developing cancer.

Statistics Canada (Health Reports, February 2004) reported that adults who experienced high stress during 1994–95 were at increased risk of developing chronic health conditions by 2000–01. The chronic health conditions included arthritis and rheumatism, bronchitis or emphysema, and stomach or intestinal ulcers. For men, the risk of heart disease was also increased; for women, the risk of asthma and migraines was increased. Each additional stressor reported during 1994–95 increased the chance of reporting a chronic health problem six years later by 6 percent among men and by 8 percent among women. For someone experiencing several different stressors, the increased risk of developing a chronic health problem quickly becomes substantial. For example, experiencing just three lasting stressors—such as financial worries, difficulties in a relationship, and problems at work or school—increase the risk of developing a chronic health condition by 18 percent among males and by 24 percent among females.

A traumatic life event can worsen an already existing medical condition, as in the case of a seven-year-old African-American girl with sickle-cell anemia:

> This little girl was bused to a new elementary school in a white neighborhood. . . . She and other black children were met with cries by angry whites to "go back to where you belong!" The little girl was quite upset by the incident. After some time at the school she went to the principal's office crying and complaining of chest pains. She died later that day in the hospital, apparently from a sickle-cell crisis brought on by stress. As she died, she kept repeating "go back where you belong." (Friedman & DiMatteo, 1989, p. 169)

Linkages between long-term stress and illness are not surprising, for physiological responses to stressors can directly harm other body systems. For example, the secretion of stress hormones by the adrenal gland is an important part of the stress response. These hormones affect the activity of the heart, and excessive secretions can damage the lining of the arteries. By reducing fat metabolism, the stress hormones also can contribute to the fatty blockages in arteries that cause heart attacks and strokes (Kimble, 1992; Willenberg et al., 2000).

Stress also can trigger illness by causing a breakdown in immune system functioning (Segerstrom & Miller, 2004; Taylor, 2009). Janice Kiecolt-Glaser and her colleagues (1998; Kiecolt-Glaser et al., 2002) have shown that stress-induced weakening of the immune system is one possible reason for increased risk of illness. For example, in one study, Kiecolt-Glaser and colleagues (1998) brought 90 newly married couples into a laboratory and asked them to discuss areas of conflict in their relationship. They coded the couples' behaviour during the discussions and measured their physiological and immune responses. Among those couples whose interactions became hostile during the conflict discussions, measurable decreases in immune function occurred within 24 hours (Figure 15.6). Similar results were observed in an older sample of 31 couples who had been married an average of 42 years. In this older sample, one of the immune functions that decreased after hostile interchanges helps to protect against influenza and pneumonia, leading causes of death in elderly people.

Stress also can contribute to health breakdown by causing people to behave in ways that increase the risk of illness. For example, people with adult-onset diabetes frequently can control

Monkey Business Images/Shutterstock

FIGURE 15.6 Research has shown that the stress produced by marital conflict can produce a decrease in immune function.

their disease by means of medication and diet. When under stress, however, diabetics are less likely to regulate their diets and take their medication, resulting in an increased risk of serious medical consequences (Brantley & Garrett, 1993). People are more likely to quit exercising when under stress, even if the primary reason they began exercising in the first place was to reduce stress (Stetson et al., 1997). Stress may also lead to smoking, alcohol and drug use, sleep loss, undereating and overeating, and other health-compromising behaviours (Taylor, 2009).

The stress hormones, such as cortisol, have an important effect on the brain and cognitive function (Holsboer & Ising, 2010). The hippocampus, important for learning and memory (as discussed in Chapter 3), is especially sensitive to cortisol (Vouimba et al., 2007). Prolonged exposure of the hippocampus to elevated stress hormone levels leads to deterioration of the hippocampus similar to that seen in old animals (Landfield et al., 1978, 1981). Michael Meaney and his colleagues at McGill University have found that elevated levels of this stress hormone are associated not only with physical deterioration of the hippocampus, but also with memory impairment. A history of efficient stress recovery, and so less exposure of the brain to stress-related hormones, is associated with preservation of the hippocampus and memory in old age (Bagot et al., 2009; Meaney et al., 1991). That is, high levels of this stress hormone lead to deterioration of the hippocampus and memory function, but a history of low exposure can leave an old animal relatively unscathed by the passage of time.

If high levels of stress-related hormones are detrimental, can anything protect us from the inevitable stresses of life? Michael Meaney and colleagues found that if rat pups were given additional stimulation (daily handling) during the first week of life, they showed faster recovery from stress during adulthood (Meaney et al., 1988). Similarly, work with nonhuman primates has found that mild early life stress strengthens emotional, cognitive, and hormonal resistance to stressors later in life (Parker, Buckmaster,

Justus, Schatzberg, & Lyons, 2005). That is, mild stresses early in life may serve to inoculate the individual against subsequent stressors. Recent research has found that the additional stimulation can be applied by the mother, not just imposed by an experimenter. Subtle differences in maternal behaviour, such as differences in grooming, can lead to enhanced ability to recover from stress when that animal reaches adulthood (Bagot et al., 2009; Caldji, Diorio, & Meaney, 2000; Meaney, 2003). Interestingly, female rat pups who received the additional early stimulation themselves show differences in maternal behaviour when they eventually become mothers, and the differences are such that their pups also grow to recover from stress more efficiently and behave differently as mothers (Bredy, Weaver, Champagne, & Meaney, 2001; Zhang & Meaney, 2010). That is, once an animal has received the type of early stimulation that enhances their stress-recovery, concomitant changes in maternal behaviour allow this to be passed from generation to generation.

Are there comparable phenomena among humans? Although this research is in an early stage, results indicate that experiences humans have when they are young have a lasting impact on stress hormone levels and the efficiency with which a person recovers from stress (Lupien et al., 2001; Meaney, 2003). Prolonged elevation of stress hormone levels is associated with a number of clinical conditions, including depression and anxiety disorders (Holsboer & Ising, 2010). There is evidence that childhood abuse interferes with the ability of the hippocampus to control the stress response and this is then associated with an increased risk of suicide (McGown et al., 2009).

VULNERABILITY AND PROTECTIVE FACTORS

Some individuals seem able to tolerate extremely demanding stressors over a long period of time; others appear to quickly fall prey to even relatively minor stressors. **Vulnerability factors** increase people's susceptibility

9. Differentiate between vulnerability and protective factors, and give examples of each.

to stressful events. They include lack of a support network, poor coping skills, tendencies to become anxious or pessimistic, and other factors that reduce stress resistance. In contrast, **protective factors** are environmental or personal resources that help people cope more effectively with stressful events. They include social support, coping skills, and personality factors, such as optimism.

Social Support

10. What evidence exists that social support is a protective factor? In what ways can it protect against stressful events?

Social support is one of the most important environmental resources (Wills & Shinar, 2000; Suls & Wallston, 2003). The knowledge that we can rely on others for help and support in a time of crisis helps to blunt the impact that stress has (Figure 15.7). In contrast, social isolation is an important vulnerability factor. Studies carried out in the United States, Finland, and Sweden carefully tracked the well-being of some 37 000 people for up to 12 years. Even after taking into account medical risk factors such as age, smoking, high blood pressure, high cholesterol levels, obesity, and lack of physical exercise, the researchers found that people with weak social ties were twice as likely to die during the period of the study as those with strong ties (House et al., 1988). The relation between social isolation and poor health was stronger for men than for women.

One way that social support protects against stress is by enhancing immune system functioning. Robert Baron and his colleagues (1990) studied distressed people whose spouses were being treated for cancer. The participants agreed to be injected with an antigen so that their immune responses could be measured (an antigen will trigger an immune reaction). As Figure 15.8 shows, the immune systems of the spouses who rated themselves high in social

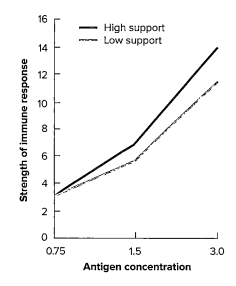

FIGURE 15.8 Relation of social support to immune function in spouses of cancer patients. Immune cell activity in response to antigens was greater in spouses high in social support, particularly at high antigen levels that place people at increased risk.

Source: Data from Baron, R.S., Cutrona, C.E., Hicklin, D., Russell, D.W., & Lubaroff, D.M. (1990). Social support and immune responses among spouses of cancer patients. *Journal of Personality and Social Psychology, 59*, 344–352.

support produced more immune cells, particularly at high levels of the antigens, than did the immune systems of those who indicated lower social support in their lives. These results may help to explain why people who have high levels of social support are more disease-resistant when they are under stress (Hampson & Friedman, 2008).

Social support has a number of stress-buffering benefits apart from enhancing immune function. First, people who feel that they are part of a social system experience a greater sense of identity and meaning in their lives, which in turn results in greater psychological well-being (Cohen, 1988; Tix & Frazier, 1998). Second, social networks reduce exposure to other risk factors, such as loneliness, and having the backing of others can increase feelings of control over stressors. Finally, friends can apply social pressure to prevent people from coping with stressors in maladaptive ways (e.g., through alcohol or drug use). Any of these buffering effects can help to counteract the impact of stressful life events. Social support is also explored in this chapter's *Focus on Neuroscience* feature.

Studies of children who have experienced traumatic events have repeatedly highlighted the role of social support in helping blunt the impact of the terrible stressors they

© Purestock/Getty Images

FIGURE 15.7 Social support is one of the strongest protective factors against stress.

11. What environmental factors make some children highly resistant to stressful environments?

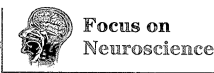

THE NEUROSCIENCE OF SOCIAL SUPPORT

One of the most consistent findings in the study of physical and psychological well-being is the profound impact of social support. Research has consistently found that individuals living under stressful conditions benefit from social support, including profound benefits to their physical health. For example, stress can activate the immune system and increase the release of substances that lead to inflammation. With prolonged exposure, these inflammatory substances are known to endanger health. Notably, they may increase many of the processes involved in the development and spread of cancer (Muscatell et al., 2016). Among breast cancer patients, inflammation is associated with a recurrence of the cancer and with increased mortality. Muscatell and colleagues found that among women who had been treated for breast cancer there was a significant negative correlation between social support and the presence of inflammatory substances in their blood (Muscatell et al., 2016). That is, the higher the level of social support that these cancer survivors had, the lower their levels of dangerous inflammatory agents and, one would predict, the better their long-term chance of staying cancer-free.

Those with good social support live longer, healthier, happier lives. But how does having a friend that you can talk to or someone to give you a hug when you need it affect your physical health? What is the link between social support and how your body and brain function?

Social support may alter our reaction to potential stressors in at least two different ways. Social support may limit what we consider a threat and hence lead to fewer situations in which we generate a stress response. That is, those with good social support may feel less threatened, so they are less likely to interpret a situation as stressful (Cohen & Wills, 1985). Alternatively, social support could lessen the stress response after it has been generated by allowing more effective coping and recovery (Eisenberger et al., 2007). That is, individuals with greater social support may respond normally to stress but be better able to then cope with and recover from that stress. These two explanations are not mutually exclusive. Social support could allow both a more benign appraisal of one's life and the ability to recover from stress more effectively.

These two explanations suggest the involvement of different brain areas. The first, that those with good social support are less likely to appraise a situation as stressful, suggests an involvement of the amygdala. As we saw in Chapters 3 and 11, the amygdala is well known to play an important role in appraising and mediating the response to threats (LeDoux, 2006). Muscatell et al. (2016) also assessed brain activity in response to a potential threat. Participants viewed either threatening facial expressions or

control shapes while brain activity was assessed using an fMRI. The researchers found a significant negative correlation between social support and activity in the left amygdala when participants viewed threatening facial expressions. That is, the higher the level of social support the cancer survivor had, the less activation occurred in their left amygdala when processing a potential threat. These results support the first suggestion: that those with good social support appraise situations as less threatening, and they implicate the amygdala in this. It is worth noting that these are the same participants referred to earlier who also showed lower blood levels of dangerous inflammatory substances. The impact of social support on threat-induced activity in the amygdala is thought to be responsible, at least in part, for the difference in immune system activation.

Thus, it would appear that one way that social support may alter the impact of stress is to decrease activity in the amygdala when we process a potentially threatening situation, leading to lessened reactivity to that situation. That is, those with good social support process situations as less threatening.

The other explanation, that those with good social support are better able to recover from stress, suggests that social support would be associated with changes in brain areas that regulate and control the stress response once it is activated. Among the brain areas that can regulate the stress response, the prefrontal cortex (PFC) is a prime candidate. Areas within the PFC help to regulate emotionality and provide powerful feedback control over the stress response helping to shut down the stress response once the stress is over (Romeo & McEwen, 2006; Urry et al., 2006). Thus, social support could be associated with better health by acting to modulate activity within brain areas such as the PFC that allow individuals to control the stress response and better recover after the stress.

In an interesting study, Naomi Eisenberger and colleagues (Eisneberger et al., 2007) investigated the role of brain areas, including the PFC, in the association between social support and stress. To obtain a measure of social support, they signalled participants at random times during the day for 10 days. When signalled, participants were to answer a set of questions about the nature of support received in their most recent social interaction. Participants then had brain activity measured using fMRI scans while they played "Cyberball." Cyberball is a game of catch played on a computer with three players. Unbeknownst to the participant, two of the players were actually controlled by a computer program and the participant being scanned was the only real (i.e., human) player. One scan was done while all three players (the real player and two computer-controlled players) played a cooperative game of Cyberball in which approximately half of the throws went to the human participant. In an immediately following game, the human

continued

player received seven throws early in the game and then the two computer players stopped throwing the ball to the human player. Participants reported that being excluded from the game by the other players generated feelings of social distress, anxiety, frustration, and irritation. The researchers found areas within the PFC in which increased activity was associated with lower levels of past social support and increased cortisol secretion to the stress of social exclusion. That is, low levels of past social support were associated with both a larger stress response and a change in activity in the PFC. These results are consistent with the second suggestion, that past social support limits the stress response and helps us recover from the stress, and suggests involvement of the PFC.

Taken together these studies indicate that receiving social support protects our health by both decreasing our reaction to potential threats and by improving our recovery once we are stressed. The brain areas implicated in these functions include the amygdala and the prefrontal cortex.

In a recent study, Inagaki and Eisenberger (2016) asked what is in some ways the opposite question: We know that *receiving* social support contributes to physical and emotional health, but what about *giving* social support? Does giving social support have an impact on how we respond to stress? In this study, the researchers had participants either hand-write a letter to a close friend who they thought needed support or, in the control condition, write about the route they take to get to school or work. Participants who wrote the letter of support were instructed to write what they thought would be the most helpful for their friend, whether that was advice, comfort, emotional support, or some combination of these. After the letters or route descriptions were complete, participants were stressed using the Trier Social Stress Test (TSST). Briefly, in the TSST participants are given five minutes to prepare a five-minute speech that they then deliver to a panel of judges. Immediately after giving their speech, participants are asked to count backwards from 2083 by 13s, again in front of the non-supportive judges. Participants' speeches and math performance are videotaped and they are told the recordings will be scored. As you can imagine, giving a speech with little time to prepare and doing difficult mental arithmetic aloud in front of a panel of evaluators is very stressful. Interestingly, those who wrote the supportive letter showed significantly less sympathetic nervous system activation to the TSST. That is, those who had just engaged in providing social support to a close friend were less stressed by the situation.

Both giving and receiving social support help us deal with stress and contribute to our health and well-being (Figure 15.9). We are beginning to understand how receiving support influences brain activity and how that may then change the hormonal stress response and activation of the sympathetic nervous system. Both helping others and being helped is good for your health.

SpeedKingz/Shutterstock

FIGURE 15.9 Research has found that receiving social support influences functioning of brain areas such as the amygdala and frontal cortex, and this helps to limit and control the stress response. Recent research has found evidence that giving social support also decreases the stress response. That is, in the interaction shown here there are benefits to both the person being hugged and the hugger.

experienced (Garbarino, 1995; Garmezy, 1983; Masten & Coatsworth, 1998; Werner & Smith, 1982; see Table 15.2). Summarizing the findings of her 30-year longitudinal study of such children, psychologist Emmy Werner noted, "Without exception, all of the children who thrived had at least one person that provided them with consistent emotional support—a grandmother, an older sister, a teacher or a neighbor" (*New York Times,* October 13, 1987, p. C11).

Hardiness

In the 1970s, Suzanne Kobasa of the University of Chicago began an intensive study of 200 executives who worked in highly stressful jobs. She found that some of them responded to their circumstances with psychological distress and physical illness, whereas others continued to function well both physically and psychologically. How did the two groups differ? The answer came in the form of three beliefs that constituted a stress-protective factor that she termed **hardiness.** The "three *Cs*" of hardiness are *commitment, control,* and *challenge.*

Hardy people are committed to their work, their families, and their other involvements, and they believe that what they are doing is important. Second, they view themselves as having control over outcomes, as opposed to feeling powerless to influence events. Finally,

12. What three *C* beliefs underlie the protective factor called hardiness?

TABLE 15.2 Personal and Environmental Factors That Contribute to Stress-Resilience in Children

Source	Characteristic
Individual	Good intellectual functioning
	Appealing, sociable, easygoing disposition
	Self-efficacy, self-confidence, high self-esteem
	Talents
	Faith
Family	Close relationship to caring parent figure
	Authoritative parenting: warmth, structure, high expectations
	Socioeconomic advantages
	Connections to extended supportive family networks
Extrafamilial context	Bonds to prosocial adults outside the family
	Connections to prosocial organizations
	Attending effective schools

Source: Masten, A.S., & Coatsworth, J.D. (1998). The development of competence in favorable and unfavorable environments: Lessons from research on successful children. *American Psychologist, 53*, 205–220, p. 212.

they appraise the demands of the situations as challenges, or opportunities, rather than as threats. As a result, demanding situations not only become less stressful, but they can actually stimulate higher levels of performance (Kobasa et al., 1985).

Of these three hardiness components, control apparently is the strongest active ingredient in buffering stress (Funk, 1992; Steptoe, 2000; Taylor, 2009). A five-year longitudinal study showed that women who felt in control of their lives did not show increases in future illness when stress increased, whereas those low in perceived control did (Lawler & Schmeid, 1992).

A concept related to hardiness and sometimes confused with it is resilience. Whereas hardiness refers to characteristics that help one cope with stress, resilience refers to unexpectedly good recovery, or even positive growth, following stress, including after extreme adversity (Bonanno et al., 2007). A child who grows up in poverty in an abusive family but who becomes a healthy, successful adult shows resilience. A parent who loses a child and from that experience starts a foundation to help others suffering from a similar tragedy shows resilience. It is not

simply recovering from distress and adversity; resilient individuals recover from trauma more quickly and effectively than expected and, in some cases, the experience triggers a period of positive personal growth (Bonanno et al., 2007). Resilient individuals use humour, positive emotions, social support, optimism, and positive thinking to recover (Southwick et al., 2005; and see Table 15.2 for the characteristics of resilient children). Once considered rare, recent research suggests that resilience is much more common than expected following trauma and loss (Mancici & Bonanno, 2012).

Coping Self-Efficacy

When confronted by a stressor, one of the most significant appraisals we make is whether or not we have sufficient resources to cope with the demands (Bandura, 1997; Bandura, 2000). Small wonder, then, that **coping self-efficacy**—the conviction that we can perform the behaviours necessary to cope successfully—is an important protective factor (Bandura, 1989). Even events that are appraised as extremely demanding may generate little stress if we believe that we have the skills needed to deal with them.

Self-efficacy is always specific to the particular situation: Can I handle *these* demands? Previous successes in similar situations increase efficacy; failures undermine it (Bandura, 1997). People also can increase efficacy expectancies by observing others cope successfully and through social persuasion and encouragement from others. Finally, experiencing a low level of physiological arousal in the face of a stressor can convey a sense of strength and ability to cope, demonstrating another way in which arousal can affect appraisal.

Feelings of self-efficacy may fortify our bodies as well as our minds against stressful events. An intriguing finding is that when people experience an increase in self-efficacy while confronting a stressful situation, their immune system actually begins to function more effectively (Wiedenfeld et al., 1992).

Optimism

Positive affect is linked to better health and longer life (Pressman & Cohen, 2005), and a critical aspect of positive affect is our view of the future. Our beliefs about how things are likely to turn out also play an important role in stress. Optimists have a rosy view of the future, expecting that in the long run, things will work

13. What four types of information increase coping self-efficacy?

14. What evidence is there that optimism or pessimism affects the response to stress?

out well. Pessimists tend to focus on the black cloud surrounding any silver lining. Pessimistic people are at greater risk for helplessness and depression when they confront stressful events (Peterson & Park, 1998). Edward Chang (1998) found that optimists appraised themselves as being less helpless in the face of stress and adjusted better to negative life events than did pessimists. Recent research indicates that optimism is good for your health as well as your happiness (Peterson & Park, 1998; Carver & Scheier, 2000). In one study, infectious illnesses and number of doctor visits were counted over a one-year period for optimistic and pessimistic university students. Pessimists had about twice as many illnesses and visits to doctors as did optimists (Peterson & Seligman, 1987).

Another study followed women receiving breast cancer treatment for five years. On average, pessimists died sooner than optimists, even when the physical severity of the disease experienced by both groups was the same at the beginning of the five-year period (Levy et al., 1989).

The increased vulnerability to disease and death may lie in a link between pessimism and reduced immune functioning in the face of stress. A study of law students during the stressful first year of law school revealed that optimists had higher levels of immune system functioning (Segerstrom et al., 1998).

Longitudinal studies suggest that pessimists may suffer more illnesses over their lifetimes and may die at younger ages from both natural and accidental causes. At age 25, members of the Harvard classes of 1939–1944 completed questionnaires from which a measure of optimism–pessimism was later derived. Since that time, they have been studied and have had periodic physical checkups. The researchers found that pessimism at age 25 predicted poorer health beginning at about age 45, perhaps because pessimists (who tend to expect the worst) were less likely to engage in self-protective patterns of healthy behaviour, such as regular exercise and good dietary habits (Peterson et al., 1988).

Personality Factors

Can your personality make you more or less vulnerable to illnesses such as coronary heart disease and cancer? There is increasing evidence that the answer is yes.

Consider, for example, a personality style known as the Type A personality. Those with **Type A personality** tend to live under

great pressure and are demanding of themselves and others (Shaw, 2000). Their behaviours include rapid talking, moving, walking, and eating. They have an exaggerated sense of time urgency and become very irritated at delays or failures to meet their deadlines (Figure 15.10). Type A people are also characterized by high levels of competitiveness and ambition, as well as aggressiveness and hostility when things get in their way. They stand in sharp contrast to those with **Type B personality,** who are more relaxed, more agreeable, and have far less sense of time urgency (Strube, 1989). Several large-scale studies suggest that even when other physical risk factors, such as obesity and smoking, are taken into account, Type A men and women have about double the risk for coronary heart disease (CHD; Haynes et al., 1980; Rosenman et al., 1975).

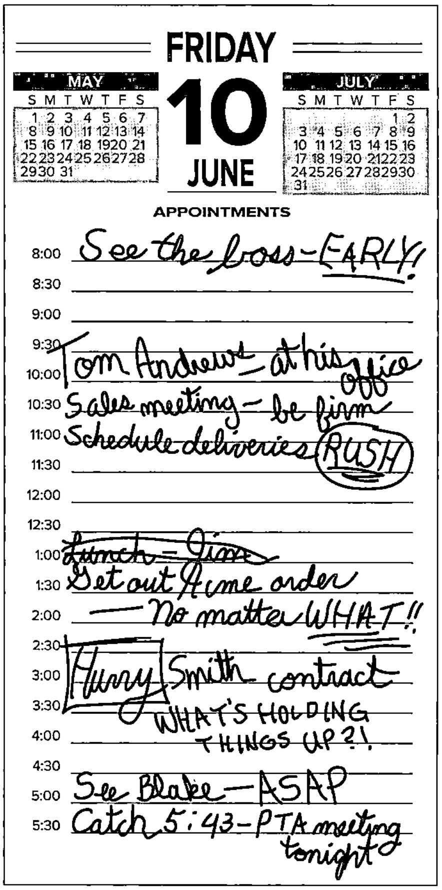

FIGURE 15.10 The Type A personality experiences a constant sense of time urgency as well as irritable impatience and hostility. The owner of this appointment book died of a heart attack shortly after the date on this schedule.

Source: Based on Carver, C.S. & Schler, M.F., *Perspectives on Personality EDTN* 1st Ed. © 1988. Reprinted by permission of Pearson Education, Inc., New York, New York. p. 119.

15. Describe Type A and Type B personalities.

Not all components of the Type A pattern increase vulnerability to CHD. The fast-paced, time-conscious lifestyle and high ambition apparently are not the culprits. Rather, the crucial component seems to be negative emotions, especially hostile or aggressive feelings. The Type A behaviour pattern virtually guarantees that these people will encounter many stressful situations, such as time pressures of their own making and barriers that anger them (Booth-Kewley & Friedman, 1987; Friedman, 1991). A cynical hostility marked by suspiciousness, resentment, frequent anger, distrust, and antagonism seems particularly important (Barefoot et al., 1989; Miller, 2000). This aspect of the Type A pattern is likely to alienate others, produce conflict, and reduce the amount of social support they receive. As we discussed earlier, social support is powerfully related to physical and emotional health, so anything that acts to decrease social support is a powerful risk factor for illness. Adding to the risk equation is the tendency of Type A people to overreact physiologically to events that arouse anger, a biological factor that may contribute to their tendency to develop heart disease (Fichera & Andreassi, 1998; Taylor, 1999).

Among the Big Five personality factors that we discussed in Chapter 14, conscientiousness seems to have the strongest links to physical health and longevity. In one study, a large group of children were followed for over 70 years. Those children who were judged by their parents and teachers to be highly conscientious at age 11 have lived significantly longer and are about 30 percent less likely to die in any given year (Friedman et al., 1995). Conscientious people were less likely to engage in risky behaviours, and therefore less likely to die from violent deaths in accidents or fights. They were also less likely to smoke and drink to excess and more likely to exercise regularly, eat a balanced diet, have regular physicals, and follow medical prescriptions when ill. Thus, the effects of being

carefree and careless add up during one's life and can be quite harmful in the end.

Considerable evidence exists that personality plays a role in health and longevity (Contrada et al., 1999). Researchers continue to explore links between personality and health, and their findings may shed important light on psychological processes that can affect physical well-being.

Finding Meaning in Stressful Life Events

Humanistic theorists emphasize the human need to find meaning in one's life, and the psychological benefits of doing so (May, 1961; Watson & Greenberg, 1998; Yalom, 1980). Some people find personal meaning through spiritual beliefs, which can be a great source of comfort in the face of crises (Mascaro & Rosen, 2006). Researchers have studied people who recently lost a family member to death. In following up with the survivors over a period of 18 months, the researchers discovered that people who were able to find meaning in the loss experienced less distress during the first year. Finding a sense of meaning from their own process of coping with the loss (e.g., by growing spiritually) had even longer-term positive effects (Davis et al., 1998).

Religious beliefs can be a double-edged sword, however. They can either decrease or increase stress, depending on their nature and the type of stressor to which they are applied. In one study of medically ill elderly adults, poorer physical and psychological adjustment occurred in patients who viewed God as punishing them, saw themselves as the victims of demonic forces, expressed anger toward God, clergy, or church members, or questioned their faith (Koenig et al., 1998). Religious beliefs may have positive effects in dealing with some types of stressors but not others. Such beliefs seem to help people cope more effectively with losses, illnesses, and personal setbacks. In contrast,

16. What is it about Type A patterns that increase an individual's risk for health problems?

17. Which personality factor is most strongly linked to good health?

18. In what ways do spiritual and religious beliefs affect the response to stressful events?

In Review

- Social support is an important protective factor for people who are confronting stressors. Such support has both direct and buffering effects that help people cope with stress.

- Hardiness is a protective factor against stress. Hardy individuals are characterized by commitment, feelings of personal control, and a

tendency to perceive stressful situations as a challenge.

- Other protective factors are self-efficacy and optimism. Spiritual beliefs often help people cope more effectively with stressful life events, but certain religious beliefs are negatively related to adjustment.

Levels of Analysis — Stress and Coping

Stress involves complex interactions among environmental, cognitive, physiological, and behavioural processes. As such, its study occurs at all the levels of analysis that characterize psychological research.

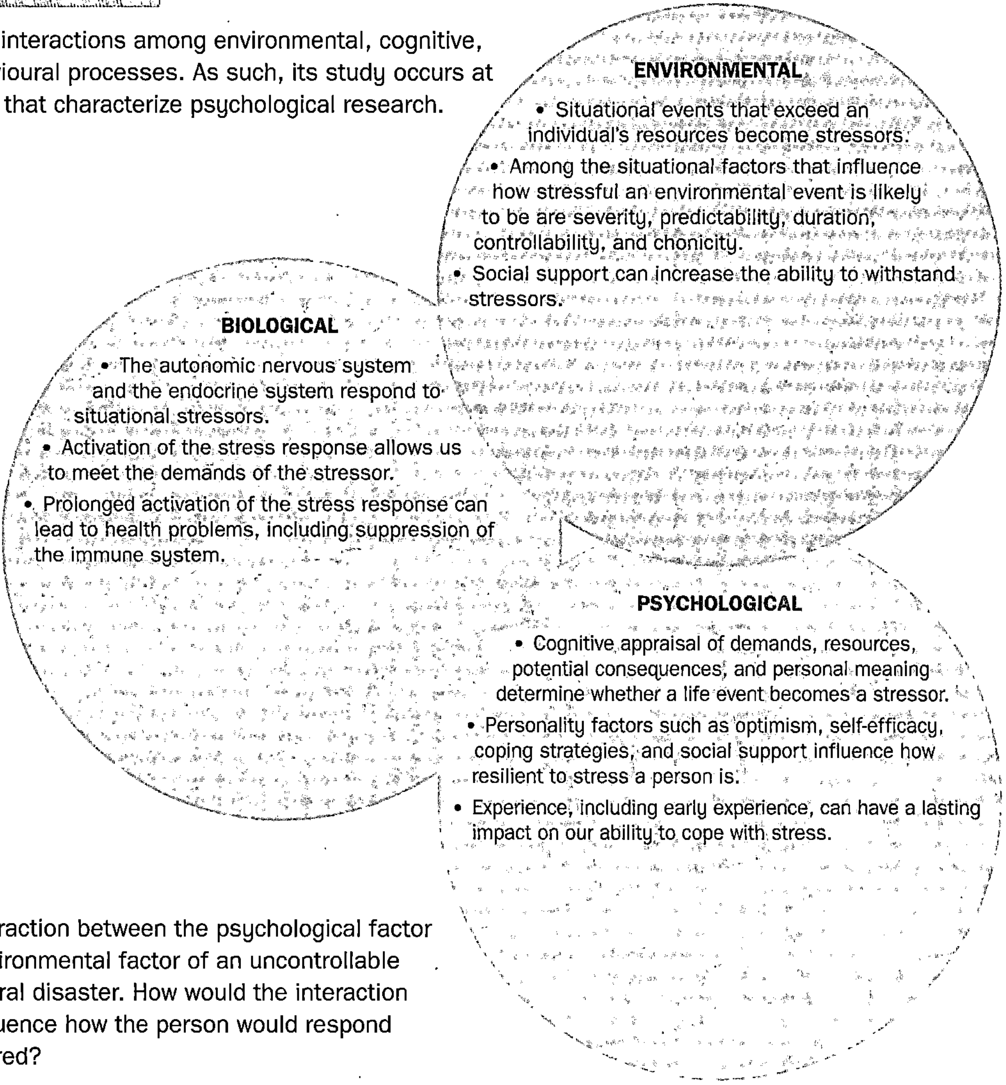

ENVIRONMENTAL
- Situational events that exceed an individual's resources become stressors.
- Among the situational factors that influence how stressful an environmental event is likely to be are severity, predictability, duration, controllability, and chronicity.
- Social support can increase the ability to withstand stressors.

BIOLOGICAL
- The autonomic nervous system and the endocrine system respond to situational stressors.
- Activation of the stress response allows us to meet the demands of the stressor.
- Prolonged activation of the stress response can lead to health problems, including suppression of the immune system.

PSYCHOLOGICAL
- Cognitive appraisal of demands, resources, potential consequences, and personal meaning determine whether a life event becomes a stressor.
- Personality factors such as optimism, self-efficacy, coping strategies, and social support influence how resilient to stress a person is.
- Experience, including early experience, can have a lasting impact on our ability to cope with stress.

Consider a possible interaction between the psychological factor of optimism and the environmental factor of an uncontrollable stressor, such as a natural disaster. How would the interaction of these two factors influence how the person would respond when the disaster occurred?

FIGURE 15.11

they can increase the negative impact of other stressors such as marital problems and abuse, perhaps by inducing guilt or placing internal pressures on individuals to remain in the stressful relationship (Strawbridge et al., 1998).

As we now have seen, a variety of biological, cognitive, and environmental factors influences stress and its effects on us. Figure 15.11 summarizes these important influences.

COPING WITH STRESS

My courage sank, and with each succeeding minute it became less possible to resist this horror. My cue came, and on I went to that stage where I knew with grim certainty I would not be capable of remaining more than a few minutes. ... I took one pace forward and stopped abruptly. My voice had started to fade, my throat closed up and the audience was beginning to go giddily round. (Aaron, 1986, p. 24)

This account of stage fright was given not by a novice actor in his first play, but by Sir Laurence Olivier, considered by many to be the greatest actor of his generation. Few people were aware that for most of his career, Olivier experienced a private hell before every performance. His audiences saw only what happened once he stepped onto the stage: another flawless performance. Olivier had a remarkable ability to purge the terror from his mind, relax his body, and concentrate fully on his role once showtime arrived (Aaron, 1986).

Although there are countless ways people might respond to a stressor, coping strategies can be divided into the three broad classes shown in Figure 15.12. (Carver et al., 1989; Folkman & Lazarus, 1988; Smith et al., 1999). **Problem-focused coping** strategies attempt to confront and deal directly with the demands of the situation, or to change the situation so that it is no longer stressful. Examples include studying for a test, going directly to another person to work out a misunderstanding, and signing up for a course in time management to deal with time pressures.

Rather than dealing directly with the stressful situation, **emotion-focused coping** strategies attempt to manage the emotional responses that result from it. As Figure 15.12 shows, some forms of emotion-focused coping involve appraising the situation in a manner that minimizes its emotional impact. A person might deal with the stress from an interpersonal conflict by denying that any problem exists. Other forms involve avoidance or acceptance of the stressful situation. Thus, a student might decide to deal with anxiety about an upcoming test by going to a party and forgetting about it. Or, informed that he has a terminal illness, a man might simply accept grim reality, realizing that there is nothing that can be done to change the situation.

A third class of coping strategies involves **seeking social support**—that is, turning to others for assistance and emotional support in times of stress (see the *Research Foundations*

feature in this chapter). Thus, the man with the terminal illness might choose to join a support group for the terminally ill, and the student might seek help in preparing for the test.

Effectiveness of Coping Strategies

Which of the three general classes of coping strategies would you expect to be most generally effective? Whenever we ask this question in our classes, the majority of students vote for problem-focused coping. This response is understandable, since many people approach problems with the attitude that if something needs fixing, we should fix it.

What does the research literature say? Charles Holahan and Rudolf Moos (1990) studied coping patterns and psychological outcomes in more than 400 adults over a one-year period. They found that problem-focused coping methods and seeking social support were associated with favourable adjustment to stressors. In contrast, emotion-focused strategies that involved avoiding feelings or taking things out on other people predicted depression and poor adjustment. Other studies have yielded similar results. Among both children and adults, and across many different types of stressors, emotion-focused strategies that involve avoidance, denial, and wishful thinking seem to be related to less effective adaptation (Aldwin, 2007; Ben-Zur, 2009). There are, however, adaptive emotion-focused strategies, such as identifying and changing irrational negative thinking and learning relaxation skills to control arousal. Physical

19. Define and give an example of the three major classes of coping strategies.

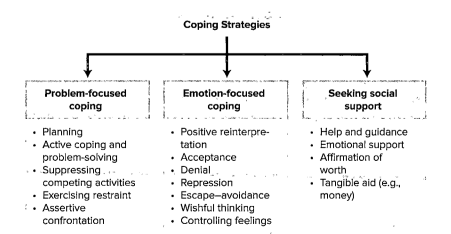

Coping Strategies

Problem-focused coping	**Emotion-focused coping**	**Seeking social support**
• Planning	• Positive reinterpretation	• Help and guidance
• Active coping and problem-solving	• Acceptance	• Emotional support
• Suppressing competing activities	• Denial	• Affirmation of worth
• Exercising restraint	• Repression	• Tangible aid (e.g., money)
• Assertive confrontation	• Escape–avoidance	
	• Wishful thinking	
	• Controlling feelings	

FIGURE 15.12 Coping strategies fall into three general categories: (1) problem-focused coping, consisting of active attempts to respond to situational demands; (2) emotion-focused coping, directed at minimizing emotional distress; and (3) seeking or accepting social support.

Research Foundations

STRESS, PHYSICAL CONTACT, AND HEALTH: I WANNA HOLD YOUR HAND

Introduction

Social isolation has emerged as a major health risk. Among married people, higher marital quality is associated with lower rates of infectious illness, faster recovery from injury, and a lower rate of mortality (Robles & Kiecolt-Glaser, 2003). A likely mechanism for the protective effects of supportive relationships is their effect on emotional responding. Good marital relationships provide security and support that reduce negative emotional responding in the face of threat. In this study, the effects of a spouse's physical expression of support (in this case, hand-holding) on both self-report and neural responses to a threatening situation were assessed.

Method

Sixteen highly satisfied married couples agreed to take part in the study and received payment for their participation. The couples were told that, as part of the study, the wife would receive a number of electric shocks while her brain responses were monitored. Functional MRI (fMRI) was used to provide an ongoing measure of the brain's response to the experimental procedures. After being acclimated to the scanning device in a first session and completing measures of marital satisfaction, the couples returned for a second session in which the experiment was conducted.

As the woman lay in the scanner, shock electrodes were attached to her ankle and the woman watched a black panel on which either of two visual displays occurred. If a red X appeared (the threat cue), the woman knew that there was a 20 percent chance that she would receive a painful electric shock at the end of a ten-second waiting period. If a blue O occurred (the safety cue), she knew that she would not be shocked on that trial. Each woman received a shock on random trials after 20 percent of the threat cues.

In random order, 12 threat cues and 12 safety cues occurred within each of three blocks of trials that made up the experimental conditions. Support occurred in the form of having one's hand held during the procedure, a behaviour that is used to express soothing and support in both humans and primates under conditions of threat. In one block of trials, the wife held the hand of her spouse. In a second block of trials, an anonymous and unseen male experimental assistant held the woman's hand. In the third block, no one held the woman's hand. The order of exposure to the three experimental conditions was systematically varied (i.e., counterbalanced) to control for potential order effects. In this within-participants experimental design, each woman was therefore exposed to all three experimental conditions in random order (as compared with a between-groups design in which participants are randomly assigned to only one experimental condition). At the end of each trial block, the woman rated how unpleasant the situation was and how much fear arousal she was experiencing.

Results

Two sets of dependent variables were measured. One was the women's ratings of unpleasantness and fear arousal. The innovative feature of this study was that the researchers also scanned the brain to measure how much activity occurred in 17 cortical and subcortical areas known to be involved in fear and emotional control. They compared brain activity on threat and safety trials during the three experimental periods.

As shown in Figure 15.13, the women's subjective experiences of threat and fear-arousal differed in the experimental conditions. When spouses were holding their hands, they found the situation less unpleasant than when their hands were being held by a stranger or not at all. They also reported less physiological arousal when their spouses held their hands, but having one's hand held by a stranger also reduced arousal somewhat.

As expected, the brain's emotional response was significantly lower during the safety trials than during the threat trials. More important, the fMRI recordings of brain activation yielded dramatic proof that social support, particularly from a spouse, reduces the brain's response to threat. In all, eight areas of the brain showed significant differences during the experimental conditions, and in all instances, the spouse's hand-holding was associated with the lowest activation. However, hand-holding by a stranger was also associated with less activation.

One other important finding occurred. Despite the fact that all the couples were in satisfying marriages, the researchers found that even in this restricted marital-satisfaction group, satisfaction scores were significantly correlated with reduced brain activation on the threat trials when the woman was holding the spouse's hand. This relation did not occur when the woman held a stranger's hand.

Discussion

The stress-buffering role of social support is well established, but how and where in the brain it produces its protective effects is largely unknown. This study not only supports the stress-buffering effects of a quality marital relationship, but also points to places in the brain where the effect is manifested, thereby increasing our understanding of brain mechanisms of emotion and emotional control. One structure that was sensitive to marital quality was the hypothalamus, which plays a major and widespread role in the

continued

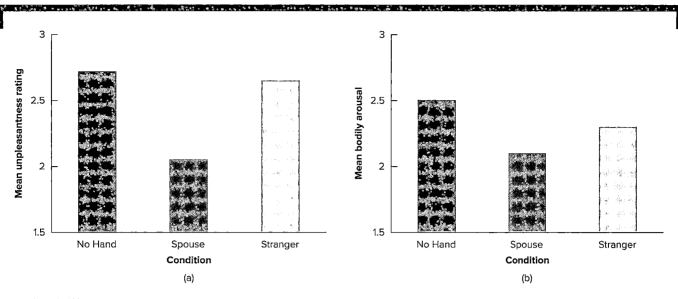

FIGURE 15.13 Mean ratings of unpleasantness (a) and bodily arousal (b) when the participant's hand was not being held (No Hand) or being held by a spouse or a stranger.

Source: Adapted from Coan, J.A., Schafer, H.S., & Davidson, R.J. (2006). Lending a hand: Social regulation of the neural response to threat. *Psychological Science*, 17, 1032-1039. Reprinted by permission of SAGE Publications.

release of stress hormones that adversely affect immune function and emotional arousal. The finding that spousal hand-holding depressed hypothalamic activation may help to explain links found in other research between marital quality and health.

Like many important studies, this research raises additional questions. Would the same findings occur if the husband were being shocked and the wife was doing the hand-holding? What would occur in couples who had less-happy marriages than the participants in this study? Would other, nonmarital intimate relationships and friendships produce similar effects? Another question arises from our discussion of adult attachment styles in Chapter 14. Given the high levels of marital satisfaction in the couples who were studied, we might assume that most of them had secure attachment styles. Therefore, the buffering effect of spousal soothing and support could well vary according to the attachment styles of the participants, which are known to produce individual differences in how people relate to others while under stress (Mikulincer & Shaver, 2009).

These and other questions await further investigation. In the meantime, this study provides important information about the neural systems and processes through

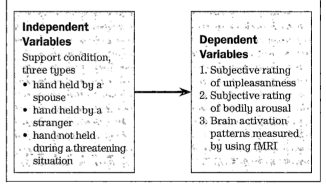

Question: When women face a threatening situation, does physical contact with a loved one reduce their stress response?

Type of Study: *Experimental*

Independent Variables	**Dependent Variables**
Support condition, three types • hand held by a spouse • hand held by a stranger • hand not held during a threatening situation	1. Subjective rating of unpleasantness 2. Subjective rating of bodily arousal 3. Brain activation patterns measured by using fMRI

which the stress-buffering and health-enhancing effects of social soothing and high-quality attachment relationships occur.

Source: Coan, J.A., Schaefer, H.S., & Davidson, R.J. (2006). Lending a hand: Social regulation of the neural response to threat. *Psychological Science, 17*, 1032–1039.

exercise is also well-established for effectively reducing stress (Aldwin, 2007). These emotion-focused methods can reduce stress responses without avoiding or distorting reality, and can be effective ways of dealing with stress (Chiauzzi et al., 2008).

Despite the evidence generally favouring problem-focused coping strategies, attempts to change the situation are not always the most adaptive way to cope with a stressor. When we cannot change the situation, problem-focused coping may do us little good and could even

Frontiers

MINDFULNESS AND THE STRESSES OF TEACHING

As we have seen, stress can exact a devastating toll on a person's physical and psychological well-being. A wide range of techniques for protecting oneself from the ravages of stress have been explored. One approach, mindfulness, has received increasing attention in recent years. Jon Kabat-Zinn, a pioneer in this approach, defined mindfulness as "Paying attention in a particular way: on purpose, in the present moment, and nonjudgmentally" (Kabat-Zinn, 1994, p. 4). That is, mindfulness has three interrelated components (Roeser et al., 2013). The first is to be fully and deliberately aware of your environment, emotions, thoughts, and actions—no running on auto-pilot. The second is to focus your attention on the current moment rather than ruminating on the past or anticipating the future. Finally, it includes experiencing each moment as it is without judgment or bias based on expectations, wishes, or fears. Mindfulness training has similarities to some forms of Buddhist meditation, but is independent of any religious context.

Mindfulness has been found to be useful in helping reduce stress, regulate emotions, and improve health and well-being (Carmody & Baer, 2008; Khoury et al., 2013). For example, Tavis Campbell, Linda Carlson, and colleagues at the University of Calgary tested the effects of mindfulness-based therapy with female cancer patients. They found that mindfulness-based therapy led to fewer recurrent, past-oriented negative thoughts about oneself (i.e., less rumination), and lower blood pressure for those whose blood pressure had been high (Campbell et al., 2012). Mindfulness training is starting to be used with many different groups, including those who experience high levels of work-related stress.

Although rewarding in many ways, teaching has been found to be a particularly stressful occupation (Johnson et al., 2005). The high social, cognitive, and emotional demands of working with up to 30 children or youth at one time, having to maintain high levels of attention for prolonged periods, the need for flexibility and creativity, the workload, and management of difficult students are among the factors that contribute to high levels of stress and the risk of burnout among teachers (Roeser et al., 2012).

In an interesting recent study, Robert Roeser and colleagues assessed the impact of mindfulness training on elementary and secondary school teachers in western Canada and the United States (Roeser et al., 2013). The mindfulness training program lasted 11 sessions spread over eight weeks, and included guided mindfulness and yoga practice, group discussions of mindfulness, small group practice sessions, two lectures about mindfulness, and a series of homework assignments in which the participants applied some aspect of mindfulness training to their teaching each week. Teachers were randomly assigned to either mindfulness training or a wait-list control; 54 teachers were assigned to the mindfulness group and 59 to a wait-list control. At the start of the study, the two groups did not differ significantly in age, teaching experience, or any of the stress-related measures. The impact of mindfulness training was assessed immediately after the training was completed and again at a three-month follow-up.

The researchers found that mindfulness training resulted in a decrease in self-reported job stress, and in fewer symptoms of anxiety and depression both post-training and at the three-month follow-up (Figure 15.14). Teachers who received

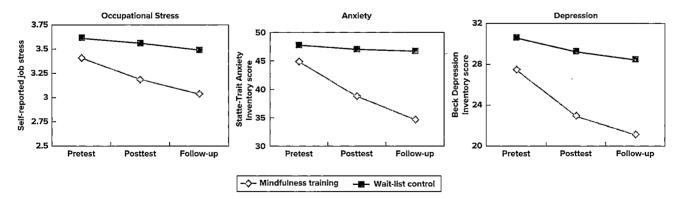

FIGURE 15.14 The impact of mindfulness training on elementary and secondary school teachers in Canada and the United States. Mindfulness training had a beneficial impact on occupational stress, and on symptoms of anxiety and depression; all three were lower among teachers who received mindfulness training than among teachers in a wait-list control group. The graphs show mean pretest, post-training, and three month follow-up scores for each group.

Source: Data from Data from Roeser, R.W., Schonert-Reichl, K.A., Jha, A., Cullen, M., Wallace, L., Wilensky, R., Oberle, E., Thomson, K., Taylor, C., & Harrison, J. (2013). Mindfulness training and reductions in teacher stress and burnout: Results from two randomized, waitlist-control field trials. *Journal of Educational Psychology*, 105, 787–804.

continued

mindfulness training also reported fewer symptoms of burn-out such as emotional exhaustion, depersonalization, and an absence of feeling of accomplishment. There was also a small but significant positive impact of mindfulness training on a measure of focused attention and working memory capacity. The researchers did not find an effect on resting heart rate or blood pressure.

Mindfulness training helped teachers deal more effectively with the stresses of their occupation. The improvement in the teachers' well-being is not only a benefit to them, but you would expect that it will also benefit their students. As a result of mindfulness training, the teachers experienced less occupational stress and fewer symptoms of burnout, anxiety, and depression, and can thus better meet the cognitive, emotional, and social demands of teaching (Roeser et al., 2013). This should lead to a better learning environment for the students, and a healthier one for the teachers.

Source: Roeser, R. W., Schonert-Reichl, K. A., Jha, A., Cullen, M., et al. (2013). Mindfulness training and reductions in teacher stress and burnout: Results from two randomized, waitlist-control field trials. *Journal of Educational Psychology, 105*, 787–804.

make things worse. In such cases, emotion-focused coping may be the most adaptive approach we can take; if we cannot master the situation, we can prevent or control maladaptive emotional responses to it (Auerbach, 1989; Taylor, 1991; and see the *Frontiers* feature in this chapter). Of course, reliance on emotion-focused coping is likely to be maladaptive if it prevents us from acting to change situations in which we actually *do* have control.

The important principle is that no coping strategy or technique is equally effective in all situations. Instead, effectiveness depends on the characteristics of the situation, the appropriateness of the technique, and the skill with which it is applied. People are likely to adapt most effectively to the stresses of life if they have mastered a variety of coping techniques and know how and when to use them most effectively.

There are some coping strategies that are not only ineffective, but dangerous. One too common means of dealing with stress is to use a drug, often alcohol, to regulate negative stress-induced emotions (Gottfredson & Hussong, 2013). Such use of an unprescribed drug to alleviate stress, anxiety, or other symptoms is referred to as *self-medication*. The image of a person returning from a stressful workday and immediately pouring a glass of whiskey, grabbing a beer, or preparing a martini to "unwind" is so common that it is a standard scene in movies, plays, and television shows—and in many peoples' lives. Alcohol, a depressant, lessens the emotional impact of stress, including symptoms of PTSD (Kaysen et al., 2013). This promotes future self-medication with alcohol because of negative reinforcement (Miranda et al., 2002) and can lead to increasing alcohol consumption, with all of the associated health risks.

Another concerning maladaptive coping strategy is *self-injury*. Self-injury, also called self-harm, is deliberately harming oneself without suicidal intention. Cutting is the most common form of self-injury, but burning, scratching or preventing wounds from healing, hitting, hair pulling, and ingesting toxic or inedible substances also occur (Muehlenkamp, 2005; Nixon, 2008). Self-injury is often associated with a history of emotional or sexual abuse (Moskowitz et al., 2013). It can occur at any age but is most common among adolescents (Nixon et al., 2008). Although the reasons for self-injury are complex and not fully understood, in some cases self-injury is used as a coping mechanism to provide temporary relief from intense feelings of anxiety and stress (Nixon et al., 2008).

Bottling Up Feelings: The Costs of Constraint

Is there any truth to the popular wisdom that when we are stressed out and upset, it's good to talk with someone about it? Denise Sloan and Brian Marx (2004) studied college students who had experienced traumatic life events. The students completed measures of stress symptoms and depression, and reported the number of days that they had been sick since the beginning of the school term. In an experimental condition, participants were then asked to write about the traumatic event, whereas participants in a control condition did an unrelated task. Physiological arousal was recorded while participants performed their respective tasks.

One month later, the students again completed the measures of psychological symptoms and sick days. Although students had not differed from one another initially, they did differ

20. Can disclosing upsetting experiences to others enhance well-being? Cite relevant data.

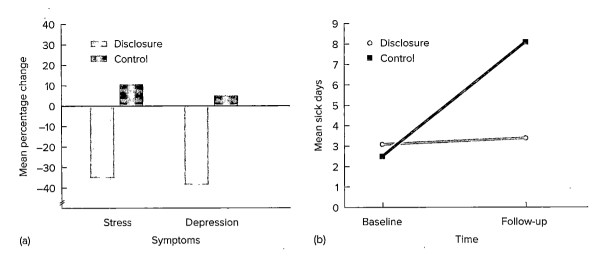

FIGURE 15.15 Does disclosure help? These data show the effects of written disclosure concerning a previous traumatic life event on (a) subsequent stress symptoms, depression, and (b) number of self-reported sick days.

Source: Based on Sloan, D.M., & Marx, D. (2004). A closer examination of the structured written disclosure procedure. *Journal of Consulting and Clinical Psychology, 72,* 165–175.

21. How do gender and cultural factors affect the tendency to use particular coping strategies?

at the one-month follow-up. Those who had written about their trauma showed significantly lowered stress and depression scores, and they also had missed fewer classes during that month (Figure 15.15). Sloan and Marx (2004) concluded that cues that accompanied the trauma became conditioned stimuli that trigger distress. Writing or talking about the traumatic event provides exposure to these cues and the exposure allows extinction to occur (see discussions of exposure therapy in Chapter 17). Recent research, however, suggests that the impact of disclosure lessens over time (Sloan, Fienstein, & Marx, 2009).

If expressing one's emotions can have benefits, what is the impact of keeping one's feelings bottled up? While constantly venting strong negative feelings is not a good way to make friends and influence people, an inability to express negative feelings can also have its costs. Some studies have reported relations between cancer development and the use of denial or repressive coping

strategies (Suls & Wallston, 2003; Taylor, 2009). In one recent study, suppressing one's emotions was associated with poorer self-reported health and greater stress among women with breast cancer (Tamagawa et al., 2013).

Gender, Culture, and Coping

Many factors, including gender roles and culture, influence our tendency to favour one coping strategy over another. Although men and women both use problem-focused coping, men are more likely to favour it as the first strategy they use when they confront a stressor (Matud, 2004; Tamres, Janicki, & Helgeson, 2002). Women, who tend to have larger support networks and higher needs for affiliation than men, are more likely than men to seek social support (Billings & Moos, 1984; Schwarzer, 1998). Women also are somewhat more likely than men to report using emotion-focused coping (Carver et al., 1989; Pearlin & Schooler, 1978). This general pattern of coping

Review

- Three major ways of coping with stressors are problem-focused coping, emotion-focused coping, and seeking social support.

- Problem-focused coping and seeking social support generally relate better to adjustment than emotion-focused coping. However, the outcome of a coping strategy depends on its appropriateness to the situation and the skill with which it is carried out. In situations involving low personal control, emotion-focused coping may be the most appropriate and effective strategy.

- The ability to appropriately express one's emotions is associated with healthier stress management, while bottling up ones' emotions may present a health risk.

- Both gender and culture influence coping strategies. Men tend to use problem-focused coping more while women tend to use social support and emotion-focused coping. Those in collectivist cultures tend to favour social support and emotion-focused coping.

preferences is consistent with the socialization that boys and girls traditionally experience. In most cultures, boys are pushed to be more independent, assertive, and self-sufficient, whereas girls are expected to be more emotionally expressive, supportive, and dependent (Chaplin, Cole, & Zahn-Waxler, 2005; Tsai et al., 2007).

Cultural differences in coping have also been found. North Americans and Europeans show a tendency to use problem-focused coping more than do Asian and Hispanic peoples (Essau & Trommsdorff, 1996; Tsai, Levenson, & McCoy, 2007). The latter two groups tend to favour greater use of emotion-focused coping and social support. Asians also show a greater tendency to avoid the stressful situation, particularly interpersonal stressors, reflecting their culture's emphasis on interpersonal harmony (Elliot, Chirkov, Kim, & Sheldon, 2001).

HEALTH PROMOTION AND ILLNESS PREVENTION

Over 99 per cent of us are born healthy and made sick as a result of personal misbehavior and environmental conditions. (Knowles, 1977, p. 58)

During the 1960s and 1970s, evidence began to accumulate that psychological factors were critically involved in physical health. By the late 1970s, research had been published on the behavioural treatment or management of pain, enuresis, migraine headaches, sexual dysfunction, essential hypertension, presurgery apprehension and postsurgery recovery, alcohol abuse, and obesity. Evidence supporting the importance of psychological factors in the development of coronary heart disease, hypertension, and a variety of stress-related medical disorders had also appeared (Matarazzo, 1980). In 1979, the Surgeon General of the United States issued a report that concluded that improvements in health are more likely to result from efforts to prevent disease and promote health than from new drugs and medical technologies (U.S. Public Health Service, 1979).

That conclusion is borne out by comparing the leading modern causes of death in North America to those in 1900. As Figure 15.16 indicates, the leading culprits in Canada have changed from influenza, pneumonia, tuberculosis, and gastroenteritis to cancer, heart disease, and stroke. The major killers of the early 1900s have been largely controlled by medical advances. In contrast, the death rate has

22. What changes have occurred in the major causes of death since the beginning of the 20th century? How do these changes suggest the potential contributions of health psychology?

Death rates per 100 000

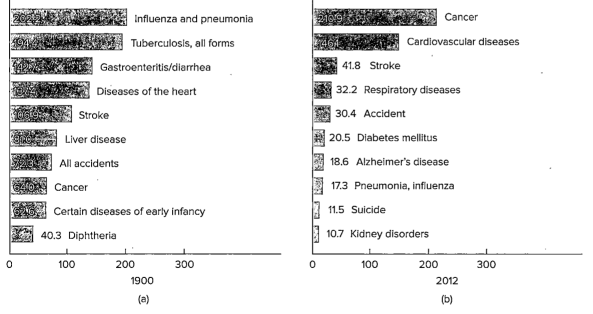

FIGURE 15.16 The top 10 leading causes of death in North America in 1900 (a) and in 21st-century Canada (b). Modern causes of death are more attributable to health-endangering behaviours, whereas in the past, infectious diseases were the leading causes of death.

Sources: Based on data from Sexton, M.M. (1979). Behavioral epidemiology. In O.F. Pomerleau & J.P. Brady (Eds.), Behavioral Medicine: Theory and Practice. Baltimore, MD: Williams & Wilkins.; Murphy, S.L. (2000). Deaths: Final data for 1998. National Vital Statistics Reports (NCHS), 26, 73.; Centers for Disease Control and Prevention. (2002). Statistics on addictive behaviors. Atlanta, GA; Statistics Canada (2015), Leading causes of death, total population, by age group and sex, Canada. CANSIM table 102-0561.

TABLE 15.3 Behavioural Risk Factors for the Leading Causes of Death in North America

Disease	Risk Factors
Heart disease	Tobacco, obesity, elevated blood pressure, cholesterol, sedentary lifestyle
Cancer	Tobacco, improper diet, alcohol, environmental exposure
Cerebrovascular disease (stroke)	Tobacco, elevated blood pressure, cholesterol, sedentary lifestyle
Accidental injuries	Safety belt non-use, alcohol, home hazards
Chronic lung disease	Tobacco, environmental exposure

Source: Based on McGinnis, M. (1994). The role of behavioral research in national health policy. In S.J. Blumenthal, K. Matthews, & S.M. Weiss (Eds.), *New research frontiers in behavioral medicine: Proceedings of the national conference.* Washington, DC: NIH Publications.

23. What are the two major categories of health-related behaviours? Give an example of each type.

24. Describe the transtheoretical model and the rationale for stage-matched interventions.

doubled for heart disease and tripled for cancer since 1900. As shown in Table 15.3, these diseases and today's other killers are strongly influenced by behavioural factors. Health authorities estimate that half the early mortality (deaths occurring prior to the life expectancy age within a culture) from the ten leading causes of death can be traced to cigarette smoking, excessive alcohol consumption, insufficient exercise, poor dietary habits, use of illicit drugs, failure to adhere to doctors' instructions, and other self-defeating behaviours, such as risky sex practices and failure to wear auto seat belts (Centers for Disease Control, 1994; Taylor, 2009).

Recognition of the crucial role that behaviour plays in health maintenance has added impetus to the field of **health psychology,** which studies psychological and behavioural factors in the prevention and treatment of illness and in the maintenance of health (Elovainio & Kivimaki, 2009). Research by psychologists has helped to identify many of the psychological and social causes of risky health behaviours, and the clear need for lifestyle interventions has spurred attempts around the world to promote positive changes in such behaviours (Suls & Wallston, 2003; Taylor, 2009). This effort is also driven by attempts to contain rising medical costs. Total health care costs in Canada have risen from $37 billion in 1984 to over $137 billion in 2009 (Canadian Institutes for Health Information, 2009). That equates to $4089 per person for health care costs in Canada in 2009. With Canada's aging population, health care costs are expected to continue to increase. Prevention of illness by modifying people's health behaviour before they ever become ill has the potential to result in both financial savings and the avoidance of illness-produced human distress.

Health-related behaviours fall into two main categories. **Health-enhancing behaviours**

serve to maintain or increase health. Such behaviours include exercise, healthy dietary habits, safe sexual practices, regular medical checkups, and breast and testicular self-examination. **Health-compromising behaviours** are those that promote the development of illness. They include smoking, fatty diets, a sedentary lifestyle, and unprotected sexual activity. Psychologists have developed programs that are focused on both categories.

How People Change: The Transtheoretical Model

To increase health-enhancing behaviours and reduce health-impairing ones, we need to understand the processes that underlie behaviour change in general. In the 1980s, psychologists James Prochaska and Carlo DiClemente began to study the process that occurs as people modify their thoughts, feelings, and behaviours in positive ways, either on their own or with professional help. Their research resulted in a **transtheoretical model** that identified six major stages in the change process (DiClemente, 2003; Prochaska & DiClemente, 1984). The model, shown in Figure 15.17, does not assume that people go through the stages in a smooth sequence. Longitudinal studies have shown that many people move forward and backwards through the stages as they try to change their behaviour over time, and many people make repeated efforts to change before they finally succeed (Davidson, 1998; Burkholder, Evers, Burbank, & Riebe, 2002). It is assumed, however, that failure at a given stage is likely to occur if the previous stages have not been mastered.

The first stage is *precontemplation.* In this stage, people have no desire to change their behaviour. Often, they don't perceive themselves as having a problem, or they deny that

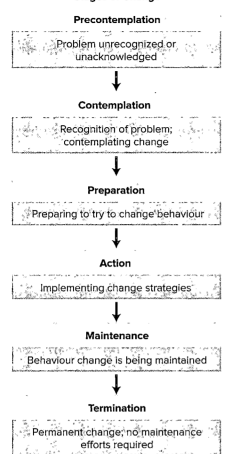

Stages of Change

Precontemplation

> Problem unrecognized or unacknowledged

↓

Contemplation

> Recognition of problem; contemplating change

↓

Preparation

> Preparing to try to change behaviour

↓

Action

> Implementing change strategies

↓

Maintenance

> Behaviour change is being maintained

↓

Termination

> Permanent change; no maintenance efforts required

FIGURE 15.17 The transtheoretical model identifies a series of phases through which people pass as they modify their behaviour. People may move up and down through the stages several times before they reach the final stage of termination.

Source: Prochaska, J.O., Johnson, S., & Lee, P. (1998). "The transtheoretical model of behavior change." In S.A. Shumaker & E.B. Schron (Eds.), *The handbook of health behavior change* (2nd ed.). New York, NY: Springer.

their behaviour has negative consequences. For example, public opinion polls suggest that there may be as many as 10 million people in the United States who still refuse to believe that smoking leads to premature death (Prochaska et al., 1994). Some precontemplators who do perceive a problem feel powerless to change their behaviour, so they have no inclination to try.

Some precontemplators move on to the stage of *contemplation*. Here the person perceives a problem or the desirability of a behaviour change but has not yet decided to take action. Thus, some smokers are well aware of the health risks of their habit, yet they are not ready to make a decision to quit. Until the perceived benefits of changing outweigh the costs

or effort involved, contemplators will not take action.

In the *preparation* stage, people have decided that they want to change their behaviour but have not actively begun to do so. Typically, they are developing a plan to take action within the next month to accomplish the change. People in this stage have often begun making small changes, such as reducing the number of cigarettes they are smoking or identifying conditions that affect the behaviour they want to change.

In the *action* stage, people actively begin to modify their behaviour and their environment. For example, they stop smoking altogether. Success at this stage hinges on the behaviour control skills necessary to carry out the plan of action. The action stage requires the greatest commitment of effort and energy.

If the person has been successful in avoiding relapse and has controlled the target behaviour for six months, he or she is in the stage of *maintenance*. This does not mean that the struggle is over. Many people lapse back into their former behaviour pattern at various times, as would be expected when one is trying to change deeply ingrained habits. The big challenge is not to give up when a lapse occurs and abandon the change program. It typically takes smokers three to five cycles through the action stage before they finally beat the habit, and New Year's resolutions are typically made for five or more consecutive years before they are finally carried out successfully (Prochaska et al., 1994; Schachter, 1982). The message is clear: If at first you don't succeed, don't give up. Instead, acquire the behavioural skills you need to succeed.

The final stage, *termination*, occurs when the change in behaviour is so ingrained and under personal control that the original problem behaviour will never return. It is the ultimate goal for all people who seek change.

The transtheoretical model is important because it helps us understand how people change and it has important applied implications. For example, we know that different intervention procedures are needed for people at various stages. Psychologists have therefore developed ways of determining what stage people are in so that they can apply *stage-matched interventions* designed to move the person toward the action, maintenance, and termination stages. Precontemplators need consciousness-raising information that finally convinces them that there is a problem, as well as social support to change (DeVries et al., 1998). Contemplators often need a "wake-up" emotional experience that increases their motivation to change or causes them to re-evaluate themselves in relation to the behaviour. For example, a serious auto accident while intoxicated may finally convince a problem drinker that this behaviour has to change. In the preparation stage, the person needs to develop a specific plan (ideally based on the goal-setting procedures described in Chapter 14) and have the skills to carry it out before action is likely to be successful. Only when the person is ready for the action stage are change techniques, however powerful, likely to have their intended effect.

Increasing Behaviours That Enhance Health

25. What is aerobic exercise? What evidence is there that it promotes health and longevity?

During the 1970s, the role of behaviour in maintaining health and living longer became evident as researchers began to study the effects of lifestyle. Figure 15.18 shows the results of one longitudinal study of nearly 7000 adults. The researchers studied the relation of seven good-health practices to life expectancy. These included sleeping seven to eight hours per day, eating breakfast, not smoking, rarely eating between meals, being at or near one's prescribed body weight, engaging in regular physical activity, and drinking only small to moderate amounts of alcohol. For men and women alike, these behaviours predicted a longer life. A higher mortality rate among those with poor health practices began to appear in men between the ages of 45 and 64 and in women

between 55 and 64 (Belloc, 1973). Let's examine some of these health-enhancing behaviours and what can be done to encourage them.

Exercise

The couch potato lives! (But apparently, not very long.) A sedentary lifestyle is a significant risk factor for a variety of health problems, including coronary heart disease, diabetes, and obesity (Taylor, 2009). Despite this widely publicized fact, only about a third of adult North Americans engage in regular physical activity (Ehrman, 2003; National Center for Health Statistics, 2008). Inactivity has helped to double the rate of obesity since 1900, despite a 10 percent decrease in daily caloric intake over the same period (Friedman & DiMatteo, 1989).

Aerobic exercise is sustained activity, such as jogging, swimming, and bicycling, that elevates the heart rate and increases the body's need for oxygen. This kind of exercise has many physiological benefits. In a well-conditioned person, the heart beats more slowly and efficiently, oxygen is better utilized, cholesterol levels may be reduced, faster adaptation to stressors occurs, and more calories are burned (Baum & Posluszny, 1999; de Geus, 2000).

Exercise is associated with both physical health and longevity (Figures 15.18 and 15.19). A study that followed 17 000 Harvard undergraduates into middle age revealed that death rates were one-quarter to one-third lower among moderate exercisers than among those in a less active group. Surprisingly, perhaps,

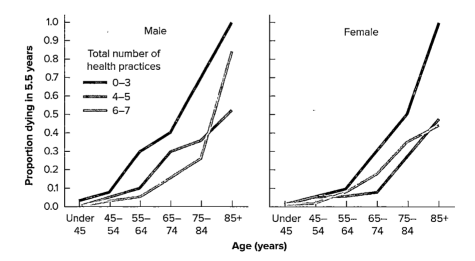

FIGURE 15.18 Relation between the number of positive health practices and longevity in men and women. Those who adhered to few of the health practices experienced earlier mortality, with the pattern appearing earlier for men than for women.

Source: Adapted from Belloc, N.B. (1973). Relationship of health practices and mortality. *Preventive Medicine, 2,* 67–81.

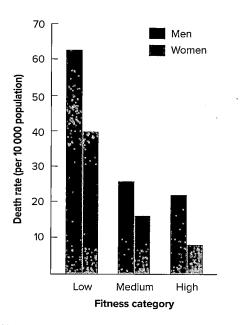

FIGURE 15.19 Aerobic exercise is an important health-enhancing behaviour that contributes to physical well-being. Significantly higher death rates occur for both men and women who are low in physical fitness.

Source: Based on Blair, S.N., Kohl, H.W., III, Paffenbarger, R.S., Jr., Clark, D.G., Cooper, K.H., & Gibbons, L.W. (1989). Physical fitness and all-cause mortality: A prospective study of healthy men and women. *Journal of the American Medical Association,* 262, 2395–2401.

very high levels of exercise were not associated with enhanced health; instead, moderate exercise (burning 2000 to 3500 calories per week) on a regular basis produced the best health benefits (Paffenbarger et al., 1986). Performing at 70 to 85 percent of maximal heart rate nonstop for 15 minutes three times a week is related to reduced risk for coronary heart disease (Dishman, 1982). Most experts suggest that a regular (three times per week) program of aerobic exercise performed at 60 to 85 percent maximal heart rate for 20 to 60 minutes per session has a host of health benefits.

Findings like these have inspired behavioural interventions designed to promote regular exercise. Typically, these programs have an educational component that provides information on the benefits of regular exercise and the best ways to exercise. They may also include other components of behaviour change, such as goal setting, writing explicit contracts that specify an exercise regimen, monitoring one's exercise behaviour on a daily basis, and increasing social support by choosing an exercise partner or group.

Despite the demonstrated benefits of regular exercise, people have a strong tendency either to avoid doing it or to discontinue it after

a short period. When employers offer exercise programs to their employees, it is uncommon for more than 30 percent of employees to participate. On the one hand, dropout rates of 50 percent within six months are quite typical in virtually all the exercise programs that have been studied (Dishman, 1988; Chenoweth, 2002). On the other hand, people who are able to persist for three to six months are likely to continue, since exercise becomes a healthy habit (McAuley, 1992).

What factors predict dropout? This research question is important because, once the risk factors are identified, measures can be taken to counteract them. Research has shown that general attitudes toward physical fitness do *not* predict adherence or dropout; the attitudes of dropouts and people who adhere to their exercise programs are equally favourable (Suls & Wallston, 2003). However, low self-efficacy for success in exercising regularly ("I can't do this"), Type A personality ("Sorry, too busy to exercise"), inflated estimates of current physical fitness ("I'm already in great shape from walking from my couch to the refrigerator"), and inactive leisure-time pursuits (such as watching TV and walking to the refrigerator) all predict dropout (Martin & Dubbert, 1985; Wilcox & Storandt, 1996). The strongest social-environmental factor related to dropout is lack of social support from friends, family, or other exercisers (Ehrman, 2003).

Psychologists have been able to increase compliance by helping exercisers identify these impediments and prepare specific strategies to deal with them before they occur (Rosen, 2000; Simkin & Gross, 1994). For example, people who anticipate feeling "too tired" to work out at the end of the day might prepare a set of self-statements about how much better they will feel after exercising. If people are not receiving social support and encouragement from others, they could also arrange for a pleasurable activity after exercise so as to positively reinforce their exercising (Courneya, 1995).

Weight Control

In 2014, 20 percent of Canadians aged 18 and older were obese and a total of 54 percent of adult Canadians were either overweight or obese (Statistics Canada, 2015b). The rate of being overweight or obese has more than doubled among adults and tripled among children in the past 25 years (Figure 15.20). Obesity is a risk factor for a variety of chronic diseases, such as cardiovascular disease, kidney disease,

26. How large are exercise dropout rates? What factors predict dropout and compliance?

27. Why is yo-yo dieting an undesirable practice?

28. What are the major behaviour-change techniques used in behavioural weight control programs?

© RGB Ventures LLC/SuperStock/Alamy Stock Photo

FIGURE 15.20 An alarmingly large percentage of North American adults and children are overweight, increasing health risks. Family-based interventions are directed at modifying bad dietary habits, such as high-fat diets.

and diabetes (Baum & Posluszny, 1999). Women who are 30 percent or more above their recommended weight are more than three times more likely to develop heart disease than normal-weight women (Manson et al., 1990). For reasons yet unknown, fat that is localized in the abdomen is a far greater risk factor for cardiovascular disease, diabetes, and cancer than is excessive fat in the hips, thighs, or buttocks (Taylor, 2009). The accumulation of abdominal fat is increased by **yo-yo dieting** that results in big up-and-down weight fluctuations. Such dieting markedly increases the risk of dying from cardiovascular disease, an excellent reason to avoid this practice (Hafen & Hoeger, 1998; Rodin et al., 1990).

Behavioural intervention for weight loss usually begins with a period of self-monitoring in which clients keep careful records of what they eat, how much they eat, and under what circumstances. This is designed to make them more aware of their eating habits and to

identify situational factors (antecedents) that affect their eating. They then are taught to take control of those antecedents. For example, they make low-calorie foods, such as raw vegetables, freely available, while limiting high-calorie foods in the house. Stimulus control techniques are then used, such as confining eating to one location in the house and eating only at certain times of the day. Because overeaters tend to wolf down their food and overload their stomachs, clients also learn to slow down their eating by putting down eating utensils until the food is chewed and swallowed, and by pausing between mouthfuls. These behaviours reduce food intake and allow clients to pay attention to how full they are. They are told to savour each mouthful of food. The goal is to eat less but enjoy the food more. Finally, they chart the amount of food they eat to provide constant feedback, and they arrange to reinforce themselves for successful performance. These behavioural practices are combined with nutritional and attitudinal guidelines. Table 15.4 shows specific guidelines from a highly successful weight-reduction program developed by Yale psychologist Kelly Brownell (1994).

Research shows that the addition of an exercise program increases the positive effects of the behavioural eating control program (Jeffery & Wing, 1995; Wadden et al., 1997). High levels of physical activity are associated with initial weight loss and maintenance of the weight loss, and physical activity adds to the effectiveness of other weight loss methods, such as dietary change. Many people are able to attain gradual weight loss of about one kilogram per week for up to 20 weeks, and to keep the weight off over two years, whereas others are less successful (Jackson et al., 1999; Taylor, 2009).

TABLE 15.4 A Sample of Effective Behavioural Weight Control Techniques

Keep an eating diary.	Keep problem foods out of sight.
Examine your eating patterns.	Serve and eat one portion at a time.
Prevent automatic eating.	Use gradual shaping for behaviour change.
Examine triggers for eating.	Distinguish hunger from cravings.
Do nothing else while eating.	Focus on behaviour, not weight loss.
Eat in one place.	Cope positively with slips, lapses.
Put fork down between bites.	Keep an exercise diary.
Pause during the meal.	Understand benefits of exercise.
Shop on a full stomach.	Know calorie values of various exercise activities.
Buy foods that require preparation.	Program exercise activity.

Source: Adapted from Brownell, K.D. (1994). *The LEARN program for weight control.* Dallas, TX: American Health.

Reducing Behaviours That Impair Health

We now turn our attention to several types of health-impairing behaviours. We begin with a class of behaviours that prior to the 1980s was not considered a major health threat. Although a number of serious diseases can be transmitted through sexual contact, the majority of them can be successfully treated. In the early 1980s, however, a mysterious and lethal sexually transmitted disease emerged.

On June 5, 1981, the Centers for Disease Control reported the first case of acquired immune deficiency syndrome (AIDS). In the decades that followed, AIDS grew from an unknown disease into a devastating worldwide epidemic for which there is currently no medical cure, although there has been progress in treatment. According to the World Health Organization (2016), almost 71 million people have been infected with the HIV virus and about 34 million have died. The number of AIDS-related deaths peaked in 2005 and has since declined, but in 2014 there were still more than a million people worldwide who died of AIDS-related illnesses. In Canada there were 2570 new HIV infections in 2014, again a lower rate than the peak infection rates of the 1990s and early 2000s (Public Health Agency of Canada, 2015). An estimated 75 500 Canadians were living with HIV/AIDS at the end of 2014. The AIDS epidemic threatens to overwhelm the world's health-care financing and delivery systems.

AIDS is caused by the *human immunodeficiency virus (HIV)*, which cripples the immune system by killing cells that coordinate the body's attack against invading viruses, bacteria, and tumours, which become the actual killers. Because the AIDS virus changes rapidly, vaccines at present are ineffective in preventing its spread. Moreover, the incubation period between initial infection and the appearance of the disease may be as long as ten years, meaning that an infected person unknowingly may pass on the virus to many other people. The major modes of transmission are direct exposure to infected semen, vaginal fluids, and blood through either homosexual or heterosexual contact, the sharing of infected needles in intravenous drug use, and exposure to infected blood through transfusion or in the womb.

Prevention Programs

In the absence of a vaccine, the only existing means of controlling the AIDS epidemic is changing the high-risk behaviours that transmit the virus. In this respect, AIDS is as much a psychological problem as a medical one. In recent years, principles derived from educational psychology, social psychology, and the psychology of learning have been applied in designing and carrying out prevention programs. Such programs typically are designed to (1) educate people concerning the risks that attend certain behaviours, such as having sex without using a condom; (2) motivate people to change their behaviour and convince them that they can do so; (3) provide specific guidelines for changing the risky behaviours and teach the skills needed for change; and (4) give support and encouragement for the desired changes (O'Leary et al., 2001).

Early AIDS interventions were directed at homosexual men, who were originally the major at-risk group. In this population, a major mechanism of HIV transmission is anal intercourse without use of a condom. In one early prevention study (Kelly et al., 1989), 42 homosexual men went through a program that provided them with information about the risks accompanying unprotected intercourse, helped them develop and rehearse strategies for avoiding high-risk situations (such as sexual relations with strangers), and taught them how to be more assertive in refusing to engage in high-risk behaviours such as sexual relations without a condom. Another group of 43 homosexual men also completed the program after serving as an initial control group.

Both groups were assessed before and after the first group went through the program, and then were followed for eight months after completion of the program to assess long-term behaviour changes. As shown in Figure 15.21, the intervention program resulted in substantial and lasting changes in the use of condoms during sexual activity. Similar programs are now being conducted with adolescent populations, in which unprotected heterosexual intercourse is resulting in a surge of new infections (Jemmott et al., 1998). A more recent study done with homeless HIV-positive adults resulted in 34 percent fewer risky sexual acts and 72 percent fewer sexual encounters with partners who were HIV-negative or of unknown status compared with an untreated control group (Rotheram-Borus et al., 2008). Another target for intervention is heterosexual women, who not only are the fastest-rising segment of the HIV population, but who also have the potential to infect their babies (Stevens & Bogart, 1999).

Even when something as urgent as AIDS prevention is involved, research has shown that the

29. What is the scope of the worldwide AIDS crisis?

30. Summarize the four features of most AIDS prevention projects, and the outcomes of a program directed at homosexual men. How do cultural factors influence outcomes?

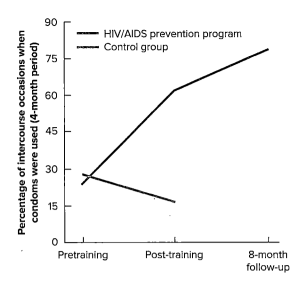

FIGURE 15.21 Effects of an HIV/AIDS prevention program for homosexual men on their use of condoms during sexual activity. The program educated the men on the risks involved in sexual behaviours (especially unprotected sex), promoted use of condoms, and taught them coping skills to deal with high-risk situations.

Source: Data from Kelly, J.A., St. Lawrence, J.S., Hood, H.V., & Brasfield, T.L. (1989). Behavioral intervention to reduce AIDS risk activities. *Journal of Consulting and Clinical Psychology*, 57, 60–67.

success of prevention programs depends on the extent to which the individual's social system supports the desired changes. When the use of condoms runs contrary to the values of an individual or a cultural group, people may continue to engage in high-risk behaviours even though they have been informed of the dangers involved (Herdt & Lindenbaum, 1992; Huff & Kline, 1999). Interventions, like the social-cognitive learning theory-based approach we discussed in Chapter 7, that take social and cultural factors into account have a greater likelihood of succeeding. Likewise, within both homosexual and heterosexual populations, and particularly among adolescents and young adults, many individuals continue to have an irrational sense of invulnerability to infection, and this belief contributes to a failure to engage in safe sexual practices (Kelly, 2001). Counteracting these barriers to safe sexual behaviour is a major challenge for health psychologists.

COMBATTING SUBSTANCE ABUSE

Substance abuse exacts a fearsome toll on society. There were 1082 Canadians killed in alcohol-related traffic accidents in 2010 (Pitel & Solomon, 2013). According to the World Health Organization, alcohol causes 2.5 million deaths a year worldwide (CBC, 2011). Most alcohol-related deaths are from accidents, alcoholic liver cirrhosis, cancer, cardiovascular disease, and alcohol-related suicide. According to recent statistics 23 percent of adult men and 18 percent of adult women in Canada meet the criteria to be classified as heavy drinkers (Statistics Canada, 2016). Alcohol abuse affects not just the drinker: For every person who has a problem with alcohol, an average of four other people's lives are adversely affected on a daily basis (Levinthal, 2005).

Other varieties of substance abuse also have adverse effects. Tobacco use damages both smokers and those who breathe their second-hand smoke. Smoking tobacco is the most important risk factor for the four leading causes of death in Canada (cancer, heart disease, stroke, and lung disease) and about 37 000 Canadians die each year as a result of smoking tobacco (Canadian Cancer Society, 2016). According to Health Canada, 18 percent of adult Canadians smoked either daily or occasionally in 2014 (Statistics Canada, 2016b). This represents a decrease from previous years and is the lowest smoking rate reported. People typically begin smoking during their teenage years, and among those 12 to 19 years of age, 7.7 percent of males and 8.3 percent of females smoked in 2014; these are the lowest rates of teen smoking that Health Canada has reported (Statistics Canada, 2016b). This low rate of teenage smoking may forecast a lower smoking rate among adults as that generation ages. Currently, however, the smoking rate jumps dramatically among young adults and is higher among 20- to 34-year-olds than any other age group. Among young adults, almost 30 percent of males and 19 percent of females smoked in 2014.

The total cost of substance abuse in Canada for 2002 was estimated to be $39.8 billion; tobacco accounted for $17 billion, alcohol for $14.6 billion, and illegal drugs for $8.2 billion (Rehm et al., 2006). Together with the economic costs, alcohol and drug use has a social cost (Figure 15.22). In approximately half of physical assaults and half of sexual assaults there is evidence that alcohol or illicit drugs had been used by the perpetrator (Statistis Canada, 2004). Moreover, substance abuse is highly associated with psychological disorders, often being part of a larger pattern of maladjustment in both adolescents and adults (Miller, 1997).

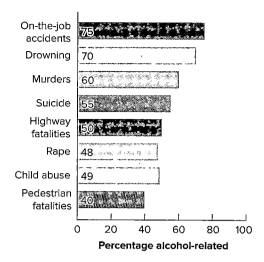

FIGURE 15.22 Societal costs of alcohol abuse, showing the percentage of common negative events that are alcohol-related.

Source: Data from Carroll, C.R. (1993). *Drugs in modern society.* Madison, WI: Brown & Benchmark.

Psychological Approaches to Treatment and Prevention

A variety of psychological principles discussed in earlier chapters has been applied to the treatment of substance abuse (Cadet, 2016; Marlatt & Witkiewitz, 2002; Taylor, 2009). Disappointing results from traditional psychotherapy, such as long-term psychodynamic approaches, and limited effectiveness of biological treatments, pointed the way to cognitive-behavioural approaches, which have proven to be more cost-effective and successful in reducing abuse (Institute of Medicine, 1990; Marlatt et al., 1998; Miller & Leukefeld, 1995).

Motivational Interviewing

If smokers, problem drinkers, drug abusers, and others who practise self-defeating behaviours are to change, they must increase their awareness of their problems, have a desire to take action, and believe that they can change (Miller & Rose, 2009). Rather than confronting people with their problems (which often drives away people who need help), the technique of **motivational interviewing** leads people to their own conclusions by asking questions that focus on discrepancies between the current state of affairs and individuals' ideal self-images, desired behaviours, and desired outcomes. Focusing on these discrepancies may help to motivate change. Consider the following exchange:

Client: I really don't believe I have a drinking problem.

Counsellor: You're the best judge of that. May I ask how many drinks you have a day?

Client: Oh, it varies. Probably five or six.

Counsellor: Is that about what you'd like to be drinking?

Client: Well, I'd probably be better off if I cut down a little—maybe to three or four.

Counsellor: How would that be helpful to you?

Client: Well, I could study better and reduce the arguments with my roommate. I can get pretty nasty when I'm buzzed. I hate being nasty. I'm not that kind of person. Our relationship is going downhill, and I'd hate to lose a friend.

Counsellor: Well, you know, you don't have to have a big problem in order to want to make a change. I'm sure you could do so if you really want to.

Client: I can see that I'd be more the person I want to be if I worked on this.

Counsellor: And I'd be happy to help you make your change.

Following a client's decision to pursue behaviour change, the counsellor helps the client set specific goals and select from a menu of behaviour-change strategies the ones he or she would like to employ. Thereafter, the counsellor provides feedback and support for the client's efforts.

Motivational interviewing has proven to be an effective and low-cost treatment approach for substance abusers (Miller & Rollnick, 2002). In one large-scale study of alcohol abuse patients, a four-session motivational interviewing intervention proved to be as effective as a 12-session program modelled on Alcoholics Anonymous (AA; Project MATCH Research Group, 1997). More than 20 other studies have demonstrated the effectiveness of motivational interviewing with problem drinkers (Vasilaki et al., 2006).

31. What are the major goals and techniques of motivational interviewing?

Multimodal Treatment Approaches

All substance-abuse behaviours are resistant to change, and for good reason. Some people may be more vulnerable than others because of genetic factors (Ducci & Goldman, 2008). Craving, caused by either psychological need or physical dependence, is a huge barrier to overcome. Negative emotions, such as anxiety, irritability, or depression, which are the temporary results of abstinence, cause many people who successfully quit to have relapses. Past conditioning may create stimuli that trigger the behaviour in certain common situations. For example, coffee drinking or social situations are linked with smoking for many individuals, thus encouraging lapses in behavioural control when those stimuli are present. The numerous factors that encourage smoking, drinking, or drug abuse make these behaviours very hard to change.

Psychologists are therefore willing to combine anything that has proven effective into what they hope will be a more powerful behaviour-change "package" to apply when people are ready to make a change. These **multimodal treatments** often include biological measures (e.g., the use of nicotine patches to help smokers who are trying to quit), together with psychological measures such as the following:

- aversion therapy, in which the undesired behaviour is associated with an aversive stimulus, such as electric shock or a nausea-producing drug, in an attempt to create a negative emotional response to the currently pleasurable substance;

- relaxation and stress-management training, which help the person adapt to and deal with stressful situations. A procedure called *mindfulness meditation* has become an important tool in the treatment of addictive behaviours (McCown & Reibel, 2010);

- self-monitoring procedures that help the person identify the antecedents and consequences of the abuse behaviours;

- coping and social skills training for dealing with high-risk situations that trigger abuse;

- marital and family counselling to reduce conflicts and increase social support for change; and

- positive reinforcement procedures to strengthen change.

This broad-based multimodal approach appears to produce favourable outcomes for many people who have substance addictions. For example, in one of the more successful multimodal treatment outcome studies, 427 alcoholic patients were followed for 12 to 20 months after completing an in-patient program that included aversion therapy (using a drug that produces nausea when alcohol is consumed), personal counselling, and coping skills training. Follow-up assessments revealed that 65 percent were totally abstinent for one year

after treatment. The best outcome occurred in cases where urges to drink had been eliminated (presumably by aversion therapy) and alternate coping skills were increased through the use of cognitive-behavioural techniques such as those just described (Smith & Frawley, 1993). Despite these encouraging results, typical treatment results are less favourable: Long-term maintenance of behaviour changes often occurs in fewer than 30 percent of treated individuals, whether the target behaviour is smoking, drinking, or some other substance abuse (Ockene et al., 2001). The goal of many researchers is therefore to develop increasingly more effective treatment packages.

Relapse Prevention

High dropout rates are a major problem in treating substance abuse. For example, the AA program seems to be moderately effective in reducing drinking if people remain in the program and adhere to its procedures (Morgenstern et al., 1997). Yet only 10 percent of those who begin the AA program remain in it, become abstinent, and remain abstinent for a year (Tonigan et al., 1996). Aversion therapy programs, such as Antabuse treatment, suffer from the same dropout problem. Overall, fewer than 30 percent of treated alcoholics remain improved one year after treatment, and 80 percent of people who quit smoking relapse within a year (Baker et al., 1987; Baum et al., 1997). Virtually every behaviour change program has the same problem, even New Year's resolutions. These self-initiated change attempts are maintained for more than four months by only 40 to 45 percent of people (Marlatt & Kaplan, 1972; Norcross et al., 1989).

Why do people relapse into their problem behaviours, and what can be done to prevent relapse? Research on these questions led G. Alan Marlatt and Judith Gordon (1985) to develop the model of relapse shown in Figure 15.23, together with an intervention known as *relapse prevention*. Research with substance abusers showed that most **relapses** (a return to the undesirable behaviour pattern) tended to occur after the person had suffered a **lapse** (a one-time "slip") when confronted with a high-risk situation. High-risk situations included stressful events, interpersonal conflicts, social pressure to perform the undesirable behaviour, being in the company of other individuals using the substance, and experiencing negative emotions (Lijffijt, Hu, & Swann, 2014; Marlatt, 1996).

32. What kinds of behaviour-change procedures are employed in multimodal treatments for substance abuse?

33. How severe is the problem of relapse in substance abuse treatment?

34. What is the difference between a lapse and a relapse? How does the abstinence violation effect contribute to relapse?

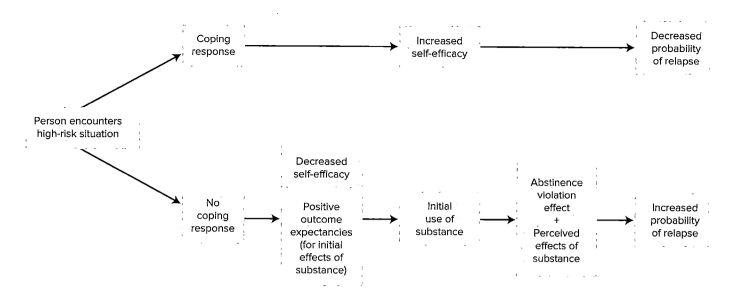

FIGURE 15.23 A model of relapse prevention. Relapse is most likely to occur as a result of inadequate coping skills for dealing with high-risk situations, a focus on anticipated positive effects of substance use, and a resulting abstinence violation effect that causes the person to feel incapable of successful change and to abandon attempts at behaviour control.

Source: Based on G.A. Marlatt & J.R. Gordon, 1985, *Relapse Prevention: Maintenance Strategies in the Treatment of Addiction*, p. 38, Figure 1-4. New York: Guilford Press. Reprinted by permission of Guilford Publications, Inc.

Increased likelihood of relapse occurred when people had not developed strong enough coping skills to deal successfully with the high-risk situation. Consequently, they felt a lack of self-efficacy for resisting the temptation, or they allowed expected positive benefits (such as enjoyment of the substance or anticipated stress reduction) to prompt their decision to perform the undesirable behaviour. A lapse would then occur, followed by a critically important reaction called the **abstinence violation effect:** The person became upset and self-blaming over the failure to remain abstinent and viewed the lapse as proof that he or she would never be strong enough to resist temptation. This self-blaming sense of hopelessness placed people at great risk of abandoning all attempts to change, and in many cases, a total relapse would occur. In contrast, people with sufficient coping skills who confront high-risk situations feel confident in their ability to handle them and are far less likely to relapse, even if they slip once in a while.

Relapse prevention strategies involve teaching people that a lapse means nothing more than the fact that they have encountered a situation that exceeded their current coping skills. Moreover, the episode has given them valuable information about the specific situational, cognitive, and emotional antecedents that they must learn to handle more effectively. When they master the needed skills, they will be better able to resist high-risk situations. Attention is then directed at learning and practising the required skills so that self-efficacy improves. The continuing focus is on "progress, not perfection."

Relapse prevention, which was developed from a research-based theory of why people relapse, is increasingly being incorporated into many behaviour change programs (Marlatt, 1996). It is an important addition to the transtheoretical model, since being prepared for occasional lapses helps people move more smoothly from the preparation stage to the action and maintenance stages (DiClemente, 2003). Building in relapse prevention training appears to increase the effectiveness of many behaviour change programs (Taylor, 2009). As a stand-alone approach to alcohol abuse, studies have shown relapse prevention to have an overall effectiveness equal to AA programs, even though it is usually a much briefer intervention (Ouimette et al., 1997).

Harm Reduction Approaches to Prevention

Substance abuse not only has negative effects on physical well-being, but often results in other severe consequences, such as self-defeating sexual and aggressive behaviours. **Harm reduction** is a prevention strategy that is designed not to eliminate a behaviour, but rather to reduce the harmful effects of a behaviour when

35. How does relapse prevention treatment attempt to keep lapses from becoming a relapse? How effective is this approach?

36. What is a harm reduction approach, and how does it differ from an abstinence-based one?

it occurs (MacCoun, 1998; Weingardt & Marlatt, 1998). In the area of drug abuse, harm reduction approaches include needle and syringe exchange programs to reduce the spread of HIV infections. Another example is methadone maintenance programs for heroin addicts that are targeted at reducing their need to engage in criminal activity to feed their heroin habit. The reasoning is that, even if an addictive behaviour cannot be eliminated, it is possible to modify how often and under what conditions it occurs, and thereby to minimize its harmful effects on the person and society.

Many university students fail to realize the extent to which they place themselves in harm's way through their use of alcohol. In one national study carried out by the Harvard School of Public Health, binge drinking was defined as having more than four (for women) or five (for men) drinks at a time on at least three occasions during the previous two weeks (Wechsler et al., 1994). Data from 18 000 students at 140 U.S. universities revealed that 50 percent of the males and 40 percent of the women met this bingeing criterion; yet, less than 1 percent saw themselves as having an alcohol problem. However, the dangerous consequences of their drinking became clear when binge drinkers were asked about alcohol-related problems (Table 15.5). Frequent binge drinkers were seven to ten times more likely than moderate drinkers to engage in unplanned and unprotected intercourse, to suffer injuries, to drive under the influence of alcohol, to damage property, and to get into trouble with

37. How serious are the consequences of heavy drinking among university students?

38. What methods and outcomes occurred in Marlatt et al.'s alcohol harm reduction study with high-risk university students?

TABLE 15.5 Percentage of Binge-Drinking University Students Who Reported Drinking-Related Problems

Missed a class	61%
Forgot where they were or what they did	54%
Engaged in unplanned sex	41%
Got hurt	23%
Had unprotected sex	22%
Damaged property	22%
Got into trouble with campus or local police	11%
Had five or more alcohol-related problems in school year	47%

Source: Data from Wechsler, H., Davenport, A., Dowdall, G., Hoeykins, B., & Castillo, S. (1994). Health and behavioral consequences of binge drinking in college: A national survey of students at 140 campuses. *Journal of the American Medical Association*, 272, 1672–1677.

the police. At schools with the highest alcohol consumption rates, non-drinkers and moderate drinkers were two to three times more likely to report physical assault, sexual harassment, destruction of their property, and interruption of their sleep and studying by heavy drinkers. Some university women (obviously, sound sleepers) complained that they woke up Sunday after Saturday night to find a strange man in bed with their roommate (and all too frequently, the heavy-drinking roommate didn't know him either).

Previous attempts to convince heavy-drinking university students to abstain from alcohol have met with limited success (Marlatt, 1998). Typically, it seems, problem drinkers laugh all the way to the liquor store after being told to simply stop drinking. As a result, a new generation of intervention programs is focused on helping drinkers control how much and under what conditions they drink so as to reduce harmful consequences to themselves and others. In one harm-reduction project carried out at a large U.S. university, incoming freshmen were screened for alcohol problems before they arrived on campus (Marlatt et al., 1998). Once on campus, those identified as problem drinkers were randomly assigned to either an intervention condition or to a no-treatment control condition. Over the next two years, the students in both conditions regularly reported on their alcohol consumption and alcohol-related problems. People who knew them well also furnished reports, and high agreement between the two sources of data indicated that the students were being truthful and accurate. Students' degree of alcohol dependence (craving for alcohol and withdrawal symptoms when not drinking) was assessed through psychological tests and interviews.

The brief intervention, occurring in the winter of the freshman year, was based on the motivational interviewing approach described earlier. The goal was to prevent or reduce harmful consequences of drinking by increasing motivation to make constructive changes rather than to stop students' drinking. Clinical psychologists met with each student individually for one session. The interviewer reviewed the drinking data submitted by the student over the previous academic term and gave individualized feedback in graphic form. The graph compared the student's drinking rates with university student averages, which were invariably much lower. This feedback actually surprised many students. Because most of their friends drank as much as they did, they thought the same was true for university students in general. Potential risks for heavy drinkers (such as those shown in Table 15.5) were pointed out. The psychologists also told the students about the physiological effects of alcohol, including the biphasic effect described in Chapter 6 (an initial stimulating effect followed by a depressive one) to show that the expectation that "drinking more will make me feel better" is incorrect. Environmental risk factors, such as being in a fraternity or sorority, or having heavy-drinking friends, were also discussed when relevant.

The interviewers were never confrontational but instead helped students evaluate their situation ("What do you make of this? Are you surprised?"), to think about present and possible future problems ("Would you be worried about something like this happening to you? What impact would it have on your life?"), and to consider the possibility of change. Specific goals of behaviour change were left to the student and not imposed by the interviewer. Later, during the winter of their second year in university, students in the intervention condition were mailed individualized feedback on their self-reported drinking data and alcohol-related problems over the previous year so that they could evaluate possible changes in their situations.

Did this very brief program have positive effects on the at-risk students? At the end of two years, the students in the intervention group were drinking less than were the students in the control condition, but still nearly 80 percent more than the average university student. However, only 11 percent of the intervention students were judged to be alcohol-dependent, compared with 27 percent in the control group. Although they continued to have more alcohol-related problems than did a comparison group of average university students, the intervention group had far fewer alcohol-related problems than did the untreated high-risk group (Figure 15.24). Thus, despite the lack of an explicit focus on reducing drinking, the brief one-session intervention had significant positive effects. In particular, students learned to moderate their drinking when in potentially hazardous situations, thereby reducing harmful consequences.

Changing health-related and substance abuse behaviours is challenging. That is why advances from theory development and research are such important foundations for interventions, and why program evaluations provide important information on how to make them

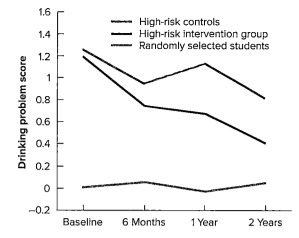

FIGURE 15.24 Effects of a brief harm-reduction intervention based on motivational interviewing. One year and two years after the intervention, high-risk drinkers who underwent the program still reported more alcohol-related problems than the average university student, but fewer than the high-risk drinkers in the control group.

Source: Data from Marlatt, G.A., Baer, J.S., Kivlahan, D.R., Dimeff, L.A., Larimer, M.E., Quigley, L.A.,...Williams, E. (1998). Screening and brief intervention for high-risk college student drinkers: Results from a 2-year follow-up assessment. *Journal of Consulting and Clinical Psychology*, 66(4), Aug 1998, 604–615. Copyright © 1998 by the American Psychological Association. Reproduced with permission. The use of APA information does not imply endorsement by APA.

better. Moreover, given the widespread nature of health-endangering behaviours, even modest increases in success are socially significant. For example, an estimated 18 million people try to quit smoking each year (Wetter et al., 1998). Even if an improved intervention results in an increase of only 10 percent in the success rate, this translates into 1.8 million additional people (plus those affected by their second-hand smoke) whose health and life expectancy are positively affected.

POSITIVE PSYCHOLOGY

Although the term "positive psychology" was first used by the humanistic psychologist Abraham Maslow (1954), current usage and meaning is based on Martin Seligman's inaugural address when he became president of the American Psychological Association in 1998 (Seligman, 1999). Seligman continues to be one of the leading proponents of positive psychology. He has argued that since the 1950s psychology has focused too strongly on pathology—on treating illness and repairing the harm caused by inadequate parenting, past traumas, unresolved conflicts, inappropriate

Applications

HOW TO BE HAPPY

As research has accumulated on factors that relate to happiness, psychologists have been able to offer advice based on data rather than intuition (Seligman, 2002; Snyder & Lopez, 2007). Most psychologists believe that happiness, like a successful romantic relationship, is something that one must work at (Diener & Biswas-Diener, 2008). Here are some psychological research-derived suggestions that may help you maintain and enhance personal happiness:

- *Spend time with other people, and work to develop close relationships.* Research consistently suggests that good relationships provide the strongest basis for life satisfaction. Even if you tend to be introverted, form at least a few close relationships, and nurture them. Make time for social interactions.

- *Look for ways to be helpful to others, and reach out to the less fortunate.* Try to make a positive difference in the lives of others. Doing so will increase your sense of self-worth, add meaning to your life, and deepen relationships with those whose lives you touch. It will also help put your own problems in perspective and direct your energies away from self-absorption. There is a lot to be said for the proposition that we receive by giving. In one five-year longitudinal study of elderly people, Stephanie Brown and her colleagues (2003) found that those who gave help and support to friends, relatives, and family members had lower mortality rates than those who did not, even when health and other quality-of-life variables were statistically controlled. Likewise, highly sociable people are more resistant to infectious diseases, despite their greater exposure to other people who might be contagious (Cohen et al., 2003). Martin Seligman (2002) believes that truly authentic and lasting happiness awaits those who utilize their virtues and strengths (i.e., your kindness, integrity, enthusiasm, perseverance) "in the service of something larger to obtain meaning" (p. 263).

- *Seek meaning and challenge in work.* Enjoying one's work is a prime ingredient of happiness. If you feel stuck doing something that provides little gratification, be it your job or your major, consider looking for something more satisfying. Everyone has to make a living, but many people spend their lives doing things they do not derive satisfaction or meaning from—hardly a recipe for a happy life. Even if you love your work, strive for balance between work and personal pursuits. People on their deathbeds rarely if ever express the wish that they had spent more time at the office.

- *Set meaningful personal goals for yourself, and make progress toward them.* Whether in work, school, or relationships, engaging in goal-directed activity and seeing yourself moving toward your goals will provide a basis for life satisfaction and foster feelings of being in greater control of your life. Many people find that spiritual development (religiously based or not) confers meaning in their lives.

- *Make time for enjoyable activities.* One of the benefits of time-management skills is the ability to schedule everyday activities that provide pleasure around school, work, and other obligations. Make time for a hobby, reading, and recreational activities. If time management is an issue for you, see Student Services at your university; most have time management workshops.

- *Nurture physical well-being.* Many studies show that even moderate physical exercise contributes to emotional well-being (Morgan, 1997). Exercise provides a temporary respite from life's stressors. When done in a social context, it adds the benefits of social interaction as well. People who exercise, get sufficient sleep, and practise good dietary habits tend to be more stress resistant and satisfied with themselves and their lives (Taylor, 2009).

- *Be open to new experiences.* Some of our most pleasurable experiences occur when we try new things. It is easy to fall into a rut, so whether it is travelling, developing a new hobby, or taking a course on a new subject, be open to doing something you haven't done before.

- *Cultivate optimism, and count your blessings.* As we have seen, cognitive appraisals influence emotions and the stress response. An upbeat, optimistic approach to life is linked with subjective well-being. Try to look on the positive side of things, to see demanding events as challenges and opportunities rather than threats. Learn to appreciate and be grateful for even the mundane, average day in which nothing bad happens to you. There is a Buddhist saying: "Happiness is a day without a toothache." All of us have much to be happy about and thankful for, but that we tend to take for granted. Focus more often on these typically ignored aspects of good fortune.

© Fancy/Alamy Stock Photo

FIGURE 15.25 Two of the keys to happiness are to spend time with others, and to make a positive difference in the lives of others.

learning, biological factors, and various personal characteristics. The goal of positive psychology is to shift some of the focus away from a disease model and towards a science that concentrates on positive human experience (Seligman & Csikszentmihalyi, 2000). Positive psychology attempts to improve well-being not by treating illness, but by exploring those things that make life worth living.

Positive psychology is not simply encouragement to be happy, or a collection of pop psychology self-help books (see this chapter's *Applications* feature). Like the other areas of psychology we have explored in this book, positive psychology is a science. Positive psychology uses the scientific method and the research tools that psychologists have developed to study human behaviour. It is also worth noting that the emphasis on positive experience and well-being does not mean that psychology

should ignore negative experience and illness. It *is* important to study and treat psychological disorders. The argument made by Seligman and others is that the treatment of illness should be one goal of psychology, but not the only goal. By studying positive experiences, positive individual traits, and positive social institutions, this perspective explores what makes one healthy rather than what makes one sick. This is in many ways a shift from the treatment of illness to the prevention of illness by promoting psychological health.

Positive psychology focuses on happiness, well-being and life satisfaction, personal strengths, wisdom, creativity, imagination, and the characteristics of positive groups and positive institutions (Hefferon & Boniwell, 2011). Positive psychology, for example, considers happiness to be a mix of *hedonic* and *eudaimonic* well-being (Hefferon & Boniwell,

Review

- The transtheoretical model identifies six stages through which people may move during the process of successful long-term behavioural change: precontemplation, contemplation, preparation, action, maintenance, and termination. The model has inspired stage-matched interventions focused on the individual's current stage, with the intent of moving the person to the action, maintenance, and termination stages.

- Exercise is an important health-enhancing behaviour that affects both physical and psychological well-being. Numerous behavioural interventions have been developed to promote exercise, but many people fail to adhere to exercise programs. One factor that influences adherence is social support. People who are able to stick with it for three to six months have a better chance of adhering thereafter.

- About a third of the North American population is obese. Behavioural weight-control programs feature self-monitoring, stimulus control procedures, and eating procedures designed to help people eat less but enjoy it more. The addition of an exercise program to weight-control procedures enhances weight loss.

- Because HIV infection is caused by high-risk sexual and drug-abuse behaviours (e.g., sharing needles), a prevention approach is essential. Behavioural changes have been accomplished in homosexual populations, and efforts are centring on high-risk heterosexual populations, such as teenagers. Cultural factors sometimes

conflict with safe sex practices, increasing the challenges of reducing health-endangering behaviours.

- Substance abuse is highly associated with other disorders and is often part of a larger pattern of maladjustment. Multimodal treatments combine a number of techniques, including aversion training, stress-management and coping-skills training, and positive reinforcement for change. A promising new approach is motivational interviewing, a nonconfrontational procedure designed to engage the person's own motivation to change self-defeating behaviours.

- Relapse prevention is designed to keep lapses from becoming relapses by building effective coping skills to deal with high-risk situations and countering the abstinence violation effect when lapses occur. This approach enhances the effects of many behaviour-change programs.

- Harm-reduction approaches attempt to reduce the negative consequences that a behaviour produces rather than to focus on stopping the behaviour itself. Examples include needle exchange programs for drug addicts and programs designed to reduce the destructive consequences of binge drinking in university students.

- Positive psychology involves the study of positive experiences, positive individual traits, and positive social institutions to understand what makes one healthy, happy, creative, and satisfied with one's life.

2011), although this view is not universally held (Biswas-Diener et al., 2009). Hedonic well-being includes high levels of positive affect and low levels of negative affect. Eudaimonic well-being is a feeling of meaning and purpose in life, often derived from helping others.

Seligman and Csikszentmihalyi wrote, "our message is to remind our field that psychology is not just the study of pathology, weakness, and damage; it is also the study of strength and virtue. Treatment is not just fixing what is broken; it is nurturing what is best" (2000, p. 7). Positive psychology can be viewed as the scientific study of health and well-being. Much of what we have discussed in this chapter—hardiness, resilience, optimism, coping, promotion of healthy behaviours, and so on—fit within the new context of positive psychology.

Gaining Direction

What are the issues?	We all get stressed out from time to time. But what does this really mean? What does stress do to the body? Is there some way to detect any changes we might experience? The nature	of stress is complicated and we need to understand why we get stressed and how we can cope with it.
What do we need to know?	What is stress? What changes happen to the body? Are these changes good or bad for you? Can we control our stress response?	What if experience prolonged stress? Can stress result in psychological disorders? How does a tracking device like Fitbit work? What is a safe level of arousal?
Where can we find the information to answer these questions?	We need to start by looking the stress response. What are stressors and what do they do? Examine the model by Hans Selye in Figure 15.3. Each stage produces a different stress response. Are these detectable by something like a Fitbit?	Also look at the section on stress and health. What does prolonged stress do to the body? Finally, there are protective factors for stress. Did Koby Soto have these available?

Psychological Disorders

CHAPTER ❯
OUTLINE

THE SCOPE AND NATURE OF PSYCHOLOGICAL
DISORDERS
What Is "Abnormal"?

HISTORICAL PERSPECTIVES ON DEVIANT
BEHAVIOUR

DIAGNOSING PSYCHOLOGICAL DISORDERS
The DSM-5: Integrating Categorical and Dimensional
    Approaches
Critical Issues in Diagnostic Labelling
    Research Foundations: On Being Sane in Insane Places

ANXIETY DISORDERS
Phobic Disorder
Generalized Anxiety Disorder
Panic Disorder
Obsessive-Compulsive Disorder (OCD)
Causal Factors in Anxiety Disorders and OCD
    Focus on Neuroscience: The Neuroscience of
    Obsessive-Compulsive Disorder
Eating Disorders

MOOD (AFFECTIVE) DISORDERS
Depression
Bipolar Disorder

Prevalence and Course of Mood Disorders
Causal Factors in Mood Disorders
    Applications: Understanding and Preventing Suicide

SOMATIC SYMPTOM DISORDERS

DISSOCIATIVE DISORDERS
What Causes Dissociative Identity Disorder?
    Frontiers: Dissociative Identity Disorder: A Clinical
    and Scientific Puzzle

SCHIZOPHRENIA
Characteristics of Schizophrenia
Subtypes of Schizophrenia
Causal Factors in Schizophrenia

PERSONALITY DISORDERS
Antisocial Personality Disorder
Borderline Personality Disorder

DISORDERS OF CHILDHOOD AND OLD AGE
Childhood Disorders
Dementia in Old Age

A CLOSING THOUGHT

How come when we talk to God we're praying, but when God talks to us we're schizophrenic?
—Lily Tomlin

Kingston, Ontario's Tony Rosato is an exceptional comedian. He has been a cast member on both *SCTV* and *Saturday Night Live*, and has appeared in several movies. But Tony's career and life started to fall apart in 2005. He began complaining to the police that his wife Leah and family were missing and that they had been replaced by imposters. Whenever he saw Leah he would demand to know what she had done with his wife and daughter. Leah fled their home and filed for sole custody of their daughter. The interactions became so intense that Tony

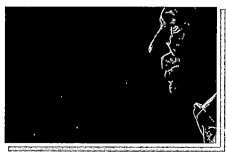

Steve Russell/ZUMApress/Newscom

What are the
issues here?

What do we need
to know?

Where can
we find the
information
to answer the
questions?

was eventually charged with criminal harassment. He refused to plead insanity (he did not believe that he had a mental problem) and spent the next two years in jail awaiting trial. The average sentence for such a criminal harassment conviction is one day in jail with two years' probation.

Tony's case was heard in 2007. The judge refused to give Tony a criminal record, but he remained on three years' probation. Since that time, Tony has returned to Toronto. Both he and Leah are trying to re-establish their marriage.

Tony was diagnosed with Capgras syndrome. Other people with Capgras believe that their pets or even appliances have been replaced by imposters.

THE SCOPE AND NATURE OF PSYCHOLOGICAL DISORDERS

Psychological disorders have a major impact on individual and societal well-being. Consider these recent statistics from government reports (Canadian Mental Health Association, 2016; Mental Health Commission of Canada, 2012; National Institute of Mental Health, 2008):

- At any given point in time, one in five Canadians suffers from a diagnosable mental disorder.
- Nearly half of all North Americans between the ages of 15 and 54 will experience a psychological disorder at some time in their lives.
- Psychological disorders are the second leading cause of disability, exceeding physical illnesses and accidents.
- Medications used to treat anxiety and depression are among the most frequently prescribed drugs in North America.
- One adolescent commits suicide every 90 seconds in North America.
- Four thousand Canadians commit suicide every year; 90 percent of these were diagnosed with a mental disorder.
- Twenty-four percent of all deaths among 15- to 24-year-olds are due to suicide.
- Each year, more than a million students withdraw from universities in North America because of emotional problems.
- One in four North Americans will have a substance abuse disorder during his or her lifetime. The loss to North American businesses is over $120 billion annually, much of which stems from the sharp decline in job productivity.

- In developed economies such as Canada and the United States, psychological disorders account for over 15 percent of the financial burden of illness, more than the burden caused by all cancers.

These cold statistics, startling though they may be, cannot possibly capture the intense suffering that they reflect. They cannot communicate the confusion and terror felt by the schizophrenic patient whose psychological world is disintegrating, the intense personal misery of a depressed person who is sinking into a quagmire of hopelessness, or the suffering endured by the families and friends of those who have psychological disorders.

This chapter is therefore not just about the problems of "someone else." Even if you do not at some point in your life experience a psychological disorder, statistics suggest that a family member, friend, or acquaintance almost surely will.

What Is "Abnormal"?

Defining what is normal and what is abnormal is no easy matter, as there are many measures we could apply. Here are several possibilities (Bassett & Baker, 2015; Leising et al., 2009; Wakefield, 2006; 2013):

1. The personal values of a given diagnostician
2. The expectations of the culture in which a person currently lives
3. The expectations of the person's culture of origin
4. General assumptions about human nature
5. Statistical deviation from the norm
6. Harmfulness, suffering, and impairment

Most people would not find criteria 1 and 5 satisfactory bases for judging a person to be disordered. Where criterion 1 is concerned, the diagnosis could depend on arbitrary and unusual beliefs of the person making the judgments, such as a conviction that women should never work. Where deviation from the norm (criterion 5) is concerned, an extremely well-adjusted or highly intelligent person would be judged abnormal.

Criteria 2 through 4 reflect cultural or even more widespread beliefs about what is appropriate, so that judgments about what is normal and what is abnormal can differ depending on the time and the culture. For example, cannibalism has been practised in many cultures around the world (Walker, 2001). In contemporary Western culture, however, such behaviour would be viewed as extraordinarily pathological. To cite a more realistic example, until December 15, 1973, homosexuality was officially considered a form of mental illness. On that day, however, the trustees of the American Psychiatric Association voted to remove homosexuality from the psychiatric classification system—surely, the quickest and most widespread cure in the history of psychiatry. Despite this formal change in the psychiatric status of this sexual orientation, some people in our society continue to view homosexuality as an indicator of psychological disturbance, illustrating to some the arbitrary nature of abnormality judgments (Herek, 2002).

Despite the arbitrariness of time, place, and value judgments, three criteria inherent in criterion 6—distress, dysfunction, and deviance—seem to govern decisions about abnormality, and one or more of them seem to apply to virtually any behaviour regarded as abnormal (Wakefield, 2006; 2013). First, as shown in Figure 16.1, we are likely to label behaviours as abnormal if they are intensely *distressing* to the individual. On the one hand, people who are

Distressing to
self or others

|

**Judgment
of
abnormality**

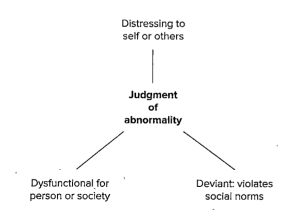

Dysfunctional for   Deviant: violates
person or society   social norms

FIGURE 16.1 Abnormality as a social construct. Whether a behaviour is considered abnormal involves a social judgment made on the basis of the three D's: distress, dysfunction, and deviance.

excessively anxious, depressed, dissatisfied, or otherwise seriously upset about themselves or about life circumstances may be viewed as disturbed, particularly if they seem to have little control over these reactions. On the other hand, personal distress is neither necessary nor sufficient to define abnormality. Some seriously disturbed mental patients are so out of touch with reality that they seem to experience little distress, and yet their bizarre thought processes and behaviours are considered very abnormal. And although all of us experience suffering as a part of our lives, our distress is not likely to be judged abnormal unless it is disproportionately intense or long-lasting relative to the situation.

Second, most behaviours judged abnormal are *dysfunctional* either for the individual or for society. Behaviours that interfere with a person's ability to work or to experience satisfying relationships with other people are likely to be seen as maladaptive and self-defeating, especially if the person seems unable to control such behaviours. Some behaviours are labelled as abnormal because they interfere with the well-being of society. But even here, the standards are not cut-and-dried. For example, is a suicide bomber who detonates a bomb in a public market a psychologically disturbed individual, a criminal, or a patriot?

The third criterion for abnormality is society's judgments concerning the *deviance* of a given behaviour. Conduct within every society is regulated by *norms*—behavioural rules that specify how people are expected to think, feel, and behave. Some norms are explicitly codified as laws, and violation of these norms defines criminal behaviour. Other norms, however, are far less explicit. For example, it is generally expected in our culture that one should not carry on animated conversations with people who are not present, nor should one face the rear of an elevator and stare intently into the eyes of a fellow passenger (don't try this unless you want to see an elevator empty out quickly). People are likely to be viewed as psychologically disturbed if they violate these unstated norms, especially if the violations make others uncomfortable and cannot be attributed to environmental causes.

To summarize, both personal and social judgments of behaviour enter into considerations of what is abnormal. Thus, we may define **abnormal behaviour** as behaviour that is personally distressing, personally dysfunctional, and/or so culturally deviant that other people judge it to be inappropriate or maladaptive. There is great variety in the behaviours that are

1. Cite the "three Ds" that typically underlie judgments that behaviour is abnormal.

TABLE 16.1 A Sample of Major Diagnostic Categories in the DSM-5

1. Anxiety disorders: Intense, frequent, or inappropriate anxiety, but no loss of reality contact; includes phobias, generalized anxiety reactions, and panic disorders.

2. Mood (affective) disorders: Marked disturbances of mood, including depression and mania (extreme elation and excitement).

3. Somatic symptom disorders: Physical symptoms, such as blindness, paralysis, or pain, that have no physical basis and are assumed to be caused by psychological factors.

4. Dissociative disorders: Psychologically caused problems of consciousness and self-identification, including amnesia and multiple personalities (dissociative identity disorder).

5. Schizophrenic and other psychotic disorders: Severe disorders of thinking, perception, and emotion that involve loss of contact with reality and disordered behaviour.

6. Substance-related and addictive disorders: Personal and social problems associated with the use of psychoactive substances, such as alcohol, heroin, or other drugs. Also includes behavioural dependencies such as gambling disorder.

7. Neurodevelopmental disorders: Disorders that begin in childhood such as autism spectrum disorder and attention-deficit/hyperactivity disorder.

8. Eating disorders: Include anorexia nervosa (self-starvation) and bulimia nervosa (patterns of bingeing and purging).

9. Personality disorders: Rigid, stable, and maladaptive personality patterns, such as antisocial, borderline, and narcissistic disorders.

Source: Based on American Psychiatric Association, 2013. *Diagnostic and statistical manual of mental disorders* (5th ed.). Arlington, VA: American Psychiatric Publishing.

judged to be abnormal in contemporary society. Indeed, well over 300 disorders are included in the current manual of the American Psychiatric Association—the *Diagnostic and Statistical Manual of Mental Disorders, Fifth Edition,* (DSM-5). Table 16.1 shows some of the major categories.

HISTORICAL PERSPECTIVES ON DEVIANT BEHAVIOUR

Psychological disorders are not just a modern problem. The pages of history are filled with accounts of prominent people who suffered from psychological disorders (Figure 16.2). The Bible describes King Saul's mad rages and terrors. Tamerlane, the 14th-century Mongol conqueror of much of Europe and Asia, delighted in constructing pyramids made up of as many as 40 000 human skulls. The composer Mozart developed marked paranoid symptoms and was convinced he was being poisoned during the time he was composing his *Requiem.* Abraham Lincoln suffered recurrent bouts of depression throughout his life and was, on one occasion, so depressed that he failed to show up for his own wedding. Winston Churchill also periodically suffered from severe depression, referring to it as his "black dog." Contemporary celebrities Howie Mandel and Cameron Diaz both

(left): © Stephen Lovekin/Getty Images; (middle): © Bettmann/Corbis; (right): Frank Arcuri/The Canadian Press

FIGURE 16.2 Winston Churchill suffered from severe depression during his lifetime. Celebrities Cameron Diaz and Howie Mandel have reported obsessive-compulsive issues involving germ contamination.

have publicly discussed their obsession with germs, which causes Mandel to avoid pushing elevator buttons or shaking hands and compels Diaz to wash her hands many times a day and open doors with her elbows.

Throughout history, human societies have explained and responded to abnormal behaviour in different ways at different times, based on their values and assumptions about human life and behaviour. The belief that abnormal behaviour is caused by supernatural forces goes back to the ancient Chinese, Egyptians, and Hebrews, all of whom attributed deviance to the work of the devil. One ancient treatment was based on the notion that bizarre behaviour reflected an evil spirit's attempt to escape from a person's body. To release the spirit, a procedure called *trephination* was carried out. A sharp tool was used to chisel a hole about 2 centimetres in diameter in the skull (Figure 16.3). It seems likely that in many cases trephination successfully eliminated abnormal behaviour by putting an end to the patient's life.

In medieval Europe, the demonological model of abnormality held that disturbed people either were possessed involuntarily by the devil or had voluntarily made a pact with the forces of darkness (Figure 16.4). The killing of witches was justified on theological grounds, and various "diagnostic" tests were devised. One was to bind a woman's hands and feet and throw her into a lake or a pond. Based on the notion that impurities float to the surface, a woman

Witches' Sabbath: The He-Goat. 1798 Museo Lazaro Galdiano, Madrid Spain. Giraudon/Art Resource, NY

FIGURE 16.4 This painting by Francisco de Goya reflects the widespread belief that disordered people were possessed by the devil. *Sabbath* portrays the weekly gathering of Satan and the witches he possessed.

who sank and drowned could be posthumously declared pure (a pronouncement that must have been enormously comforting to her loved ones). Of course, a woman who floated was in *real* trouble. During the 16th and 17th centuries, more than 100 000 people with psychological disorders were identified as witches, hunted down, and executed.

Centuries earlier, about the 5th century B.C., the Greek physician Hippocrates suggested that mental illnesses were diseases just like physical disorders. Anticipating the modern viewpoint, Hippocrates believed that the site of mental illness was the brain. By the 1800s, Western medicine had returned to viewing mental disorders as biologically based and was attempting to extend medical diagnoses to them. The biological emphasis was given impetus by the discovery that *general paresis*, a disorder characterized in its advanced stages by mental deterioration and bizarre behaviour, resulted from massive brain deterioration caused by the sexually transmitted disease syphilis. This was a breakthrough—the first demonstration that a psychological disorder was caused by an underlying physical malady.

2. Describe the demonological perspective on abnormal behaviour and its implications for dealing with deviant behaviour.

3. What was the historical importance of discovering the cause of general paresis?

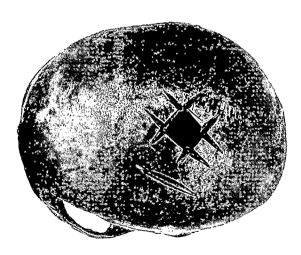

© Kjell Sandved/Visuals Unlimited, Inc.

FIGURE 16.3 An early treatment for disordered behaviour was trephination, in which a hole was chiselled through the skull to release the evil spirit thought to be causing the abnormal behaviour. Some people survived the operation, but many died from it.

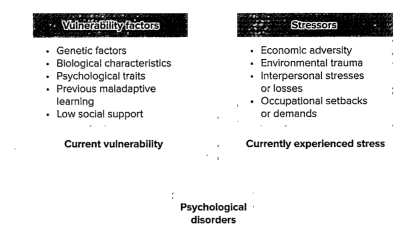

FIGURE 16.5 The vulnerability-stress model. This popular conception attributes behaviour disorders to interactions between personal vulnerability factors and life stressors. Personal vulnerability factors contribute to maladaptive efforts to cope with life's challenges.

In the early 1900s, Sigmund Freud's theory of psychoanalysis ushered in psychological interpretations of disordered behaviour. As we shall see, psychodynamic theories of abnormal behaviour were soon joined by other models based on behavioural, cognitive, and humanistic concepts. These various conceptions focus on different classes of causal factors and help to capture the complex determinants of abnormal behaviour. The importance of cultural factors has also received increasing attention. Although many questions remain, these perspectives have given us a deeper understanding of how biological, psychological, and environmental factors can combine to cause psychological disorders.

Today, many psychologists find it useful to incorporate these factors into a more general framework. According to the **vulnerability-stress model** (sometimes called the *diathesis-stress model;* Figure 16.5), each of us has some degree of vulnerability (ranging from very low to very high) for developing a psychological disorder, given sufficient stress. The *vulnerability,* or predisposition, can have a biological basis, such as our genotype, over- or under-activity of a neurotransmitter system in the brain, a hair-trigger autonomic nervous system, or a hormonal factor. It could also be due to a personality factor, such as low self-esteem or extreme pessimism, or to previous environmental factors, such as poverty or a severe trauma or loss earlier in life. Likewise, cultural factors can create vulnerability to certain kinds of disorders (Johnson & Johnson, 2014; Tinsley-Li & Jenkins, 2007).

But vulnerability is only part of the equation. In most instances, a predisposition creates a disorder only when a *stressor*—some recent or current event that requires a person to cope—combines with the vulnerability to trigger the disorder (Calvete et al., 2015; van Praag, 2004). Thus, a person who has a genetic predisposition to depression or who suffered a traumatic loss of a parent early in life may be primed to develop a depressive disorder *if* faced with the stress of a significant loss later in life. As we shall see, the biological, psychological, and environmental levels of analysis have all contributed to the vulnerability-stress model and our understanding of behaviour disorders and how they develop.

DIAGNOSING PSYCHOLOGICAL DISORDERS

Classification is a necessary first step toward introducing order into discussions of the nature, causes, and treatment of psychological disorders. To be scientifically and practically useful, however, a classification system has to meet standards of reliability and validity. **Reliability** means that clinicians using the system should show high levels of agreement in their diagnostic decisions. Because professionals with different types and amounts of training—including psychologists, psychiatrists, social workers, and general physicians—make diagnostic decisions, the system should be couched in terms of observable behaviours that can be reliably detected and should minimize subjective judgments (American Psychiatric Association, 2000). **Validity** means that the diagnostic categories should accurately capture the essential features of the various disorders. Thus, if research and

4. How does the vulnerability-stress model illustrate person-situation interactions?

5. What is meant by reliability and validity of diagnostic classification systems?

clinical observations show that a given disorder has four behavioural characteristics, the diagnostic category for that disorder should also have those four features. Moreover, the diagnostic categories should allow us to differentiate one psychological disorder from another.

The DSM-5 (and the DSM-IV-TR prior to May 2013) is the most widely used diagnostic classification system in North America (although in much of Europe, a different classification system—the *International Statistical Classification of Diseases*—is often used. The current version is ICD 11). For each of its more than 350 diagnostic categories, the DSM-5 contains detailed lists of observable behaviours that must be present in order for a diagnosis to be made.

The DSM-5: Integrating Categorical and Dimensional Approaches

The American Psychiatric Association has revised the diagnostic system for assessing mental disorders and it was released as the DSM-5 in 2013. Panels of experts on each disorder studied the research literature and suggested revisions to the system (American Psychiatric Association, 2010).

The DSM-IV-TR was a *categorical* system, in which people were placed within specific diagnostic categories. The highly specific behavioural criteria in the DSM-IV-TR diagnostic categories clearly have improved reliability over earlier versions (Brown et al., 2001; Nathan & Lagenbucher, 1999). One trade-off, however, is that the criteria are so detailed and specific that many people—as many as 50 percent—don't fit neatly into the categories (Westen et al., 2004). Moreover, people who receive the same diagnosis may share only certain symptoms and look very different from one another. Finally, the categorical system does not provide a way of capturing the severity of the person's disorder,

nor can it capture symptoms that are adaptively important but not severe enough to meet the behavioural criteria for the disorder.

An alternative (or supplement) to the categorical system is a *dimensional* system, in which relevant behaviours are rated along a severity measure. Such a system is based on the assumption that psychological disorders are extensions different in degree, rather than kind, from normal personality functioning. As an example, consider the dimension of behaviour that extends from normal, adaptive conscientiousness to the maladaptive extremes seen in a person with a compulsive disorder (Table 16.2). The maladaptive exaggeration of what is a normally adaptive personality style, or inability to engage in the adaptive behaviours, can be applied to virtually all disorders (Brown & Barlow, 2009). Likewise, it appears that much of the comorbidity that exists among current diagnostic categories, such as anxiety and depression, reflects variations in the same underlying factors, such as activity in the behavioural inhibition system or the personality trait of neuroticism (Brown, 2007; Widiger & Smith, 2008). Representing individuals along basic personality or symptom dimensions was attractive to the experts on the DSM-5 revision panels because they believed that such a system may better represent the uniqueness of each individual and avoid the one-size-fits-all disadvantages of being assigned to a particular diagnostic category (American Psychiatric Association, 2010).

In May 2013, the American Psychiatric Association released the DSM-5. Although diagnostic categories are retained, the proposed system incorporates, as mentioned, dimensional scales that are used to rate the presence and severity of specific symptoms and personality characteristics. A prime example is in the personality disorders, where six basic dimensions of disordered personality functioning—Negative

TABLE 16.2   From Conscientious Personality to Obsessive-Compulsive Personality Disorder: A Dimensional View

Adaptive Conscientiousness	Subclinical	Disordered	Severely Disordered
"I do what I'm supposed to do. I have a strong work ethic, and I take pride in my work. I like to take my time and do things right."	"I feel as if I need to work on things until I get them right so that others will not disapprove of me if they find even one small mistake."	"I can't put something aside until it's perfect, even if it's plenty good enough to meet my obligations and needs."	"I check and recheck my work until I'm sure that no one could find fault with what I've done. I can't stop worrying that it's not perfect."

Source: Adapted from Millon, T., & Davis, R. (2000). *Personality disorders in modern life.* New York, NY: Wiley.

Emotionality, Schizotypy (odd thinking and behaviour), Disinhibition, Introversion, Antagonism, and Compulsivity—are rated by clinicians to define a set of six personality disorders. Figure 16.6 shows how different combinations of the personality dimensions (and their more specific behavioural facets) give rise to antisocial and borderline personality disorders (described later in this chapter). Some of the basic personality dimensions clearly reflect the maladaptive extremes of the traits in the Five Factor Model of normal personality described in Chapter 14 (Widiger et al., 2009). These factors—Extraversion, Agreeableness, Conscientiousness, Neuroticism, and Openness to experience—are thought by proponents to be universal dimensions of personality. One beneficial consequence of the proposed DSM-5 approach to the diagnosis of personality disorders is that it helps to link normal and abnormal personality functioning. Moreover, the dimensional severity ratings that clinicians will give to the behaviours involved in each diagnostic category in the DSM-5 will result in a fine-grained description that better reflects each person's individuality while also

6. What effects does psychiatric labelling have on social- and self-perceptions?

helping clinicians develop an effective treatment strategy (Paris, 2013; Skodol & Bender, 2009).

Critical Issues in Diagnostic Labelling

Beyond their clinical and scientific utility, diagnostic labels can have important personal, social, and legal consequences for the people who receive them.

Social and Personal Implications

Once a diagnostic label is attached to a person, it becomes all too easy to accept the label as an accurate description of the *individual* rather than of the *behaviour*. It then becomes difficult to look at the person's behaviour objectively, without preconceptions about how he or she will act. It also is likely to affect how we will interact with that person. Consider for a moment what your reaction might be if you were informed that your new next-door neighbour had been diagnosed as a "sexual psychopath." It would be surprising indeed if this label did not influence your perceptions and interactions with that person, whether or not the label was accurate. We discuss these implications in this chapter's *Research Foundations* feature.

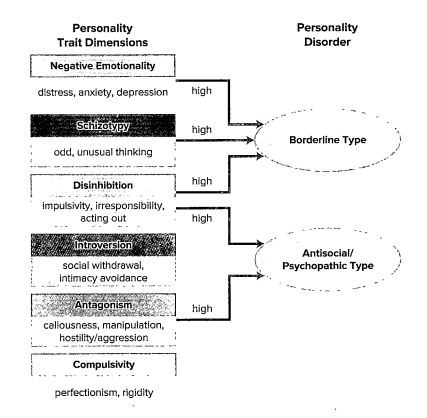

FIGURE 16.6 The DSM-5 Task Force proposed six basic personality dimensions, with high ratings indicating greater psychological impairment. Here we see which of these personality trait dimensions are most prominently involved in borderline and antisocial/psychopathic personality types.

Research Foundations

ON BEING SANE IN INSANE PLACES

Introduction

How do we come to know when someone is "insane"? For that matter, can we tell when someone is "normal"? Of course, we could administer a battery of tests and use the classification system from the DSM-5. But what if someone were to simply walk into a treatment facility complaining of hearing voices? Would he or she perhaps be viewed as suffering from a mental disorder? The implications of such behaviour were examined in this classic study by Davis Rosenhan (1973).

Method

Rosenhan arranged for eight "pseudopatients" (five men and three women) to present themselves at the admissions desk of 12 mental hospitals across the United States. Most were older, and they came from a variety of backgrounds (three psychologists, a psychiatrist, a pediatrician, a painter, and a housewife, plus Rosenhan himself). All were sane. The pseudopatient arrived at admissions complaining of hearing voices. If asked about the voices, the pseudopatient indicated that the message was unclear, but contained the words *hollow, empty,* and *thud.* The voice was not familiar but was of the same sex as the pseudopatient. Nothing further was ever said about the symptoms or about hearing voices. If questioned by any member of the staff, the pseudopatients gave accurate details from their own life history and indicated that they no longer heard voices. They participated in all aspects of the hospital environment as directed by the staff. Each person was to appear as "normal" as possible and to convince the staff that they should be released.

Results

All eight pseudopatients were admitted to the hospital with a diagnosis of schizophrenia, and upon discharge the diagnosis of "schizophrenia in remission" was indicated. Not a single member of the staff at any of the hospitals realized that these patients were, in fact, perfectly sane. Interestingly, many of the patients at the various hospitals did see through the ruse, often commenting that the pseudopatient was not a real patient—that he or she was probably a journalist or a professor. The average stay at the hospital was 19 days, with a range from 7 to 52 days.

After hearing about some of these results, many hospitals claimed that such an error would never happen at their institution. So Rosenhan arranged the following demonstration. The staff at a large teaching and research hospital was told that sometime during the next three months, one or more pseudopatients would present themselves at the admission desk. The staff members were asked to rate each new patient during this time frame and indicate the likelihood that the patient was a fake. During the three-month period, 193 patients were admitted. Of these, 41 were determined with a high degree of confidence by at least one staff member to be pseudopatients. Nineteen were rated as suspect by at least one staff member and a psychiatrist. Not a single person was, in fact, a pseudopatient—all were real.

Beyond the issues of simply failing to detect both sanity and insanity, it is interesting to note how the staff responded to the pseudopatients. Once the individuals were labelled as "schizophrenic," every behaviour performed by these individuals was viewed as consistent with this label. For example, the pseudopatients kept journals during their stay. This journal writing was interpreted as symptomatic of paranoid delusions. Details of family history were reinterpreted in a manner consistent with the diagnosis. Rosenhan concludes that we must be cautious in both using and interpreting the labels we place on others.

Discussion

Although the results of this experiment are compelling, we must remember that the staff members at the various hospitals were responding with the best interests of the pseudopatients in mind. As Spitzer (1975) has noted, it would have been unprofessional of them to respond in any other fashion. Nonetheless, Rosenhan's demonstration points out the difficulty of deciding just what is "normal." It should be noted that the Canadian Mental Health Act would prohibit the lengthy institutional stays reported by Rosenhan (1973). If a psychiatrist determines upon interview that you are a danger to yourself or society, you may be held involuntarily for up to 72 hours. You must be reassessed within that time. If the psychiatrist still believes that you are a threat, you can be held for an additional two weeks, after which there must be another assessment. The pseudopatients in the Rosenhan study would likely have been discharged within the first three days.

Diagnostic labels may also add to the burden of psychological disorders if the person with the disorder or others react negatively to the labels (Corrigan, 2005). When people become aware that a psychiatric label has been applied to them, they may accept the new identity implied by the

continued

label and develop the expected role and outlook. Because psychiatric labels often carry degrading and stigmatizing implications, the effects on morale and self-esteem can be devastating. Moreover, a person may despair of ever changing and therefore give up trying to deal with life circumstances that may be responsible for the problems. In this way, the expectations that accompany a label may result in a self-fulfilling prophecy, in which expectation becomes reality. Because of the stigma attached to "mental illness," many people with psychological disorders do not seek treatment. Of course, a psychiatric label can be a double-edged sword, and the other side of this stigmatizing concern is that the label will evoke sympathy, understanding, and support from others (Lilienfeld et al., 2010).

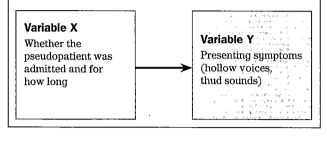

Design

Question: Will ordinary people be admitted to a mental institution if they simply demonstrate symptoms?

Type of Study: *Participant observation*

Variable X Whether the pseudopatient was admitted and for how long	→	**Variable Y** Presenting symptoms (hollow voices, thud sounds)

7. Differentiate between the legal concepts of competency and insanity. What is the current burden of proof in insanity hearings?

Legal Consequences

Psychiatric diagnoses also have important legal consequences (Schlesinger, 2007). Individuals judged to be dangerous to themselves or others may be involuntarily committed to mental institutions under certain circumstances. When so committed, they lose some of their civil rights and may be detained indefinitely if their behaviour does not improve.

The law tries to take into account the mental status of individuals accused of crimes. Two particularly important legal concepts are competency and insanity. **Competency** refers to a defendant's state of mind at the time of a judicial hearing (not at the time the crime was committed). A defendant judged to be too disturbed to understand the nature of the legal proceedings may be labelled as "not competent to stand trial" and institutionalized until judged competent.

Insanity, a far more controversial issue, relates to the presumed state of mind of the defendant at the time the crime was committed. Defendants may be declared "not guilty by reason of insanity" if they are judged to have been so severely impaired during the commission of a crime that they lacked the capacity either to appreciate the wrongfulness of their acts or to control their conduct. In 1992, Canada officially changed this verdict to "not criminally responsible on account of mental disorder (NCRMD)." It is important to understand that insanity is a legal term, not a psychological one.

The insanity defence has long been hotly debated. Despite the fact that the insanity plea is entered in only one of every 500 felony cases in North America (Canadian Department of Justice, 2010) and that in most cases the Crown/ prosecution agrees that the person was indeed insane, it has become more difficult to plead insanity successfully. Until two decades ago in the United States, the prosecution was required to prove that the defendant was *not* insane when the crime was committed. Today, the burden has shifted to the defence to prove that the client was too impaired at the time of the crime to be held accountable for it. A recent U.S. Supreme Court decision (*Clark v. Arizona*, 2006) gave the option of not considering mental illness as evidence in criminal trials, further increasing the difficulty of mounting an insanity defence.

To balance punishment for crimes with concerns about a defendant's mental status and possible need for treatment, Canada and an increasing number of U.S. jurisdictions have adopted a verdict of "guilty but mentally ill."

Thinking critically

"DO I HAVE THAT DISORDER?"

When people read descriptions of disorders, whether physical or psychological, they often see some of those symptoms or characteristics in themselves. In medical education, this is sometimes termed "medical students' disease." If you experience such concerns as you read about the various psychological disorders in this chapter, how should you decide whether you have a problem worthy of professional attention?

Think about it, and then see the Answers section at the end of the book.

This verdict imposes a normal sentence for a crime but sends the defendant to a mental hospital for treatment. Defendants who are considered to have recovered before serving all their time are then sent to prison for the remainder of the sentence. However, Canada's new Criminal Insanity Bill would make it more difficult for high-risk offenders to leave a psychiatric facility in the first place.

ANXIETY DISORDERS

All of us have experienced anxiety, the state of tension and apprehension that is a natural response to perceived threat. But in **anxiety disorders,** the frequency and intensity of anxiety responses are out of proportion to the situations that trigger them, and the anxiety interferes with daily life.

Anxiety responses have four components: (1) a *subjective-emotional* component, including feelings of tension and apprehension;

(2) a *cognitive* component, including subjective feelings of apprehension, a sense of impending danger, and a feeling of inability to cope; (3) *physiological* responses, including increased heart rate and blood pressure, muscle tension, rapid breathing, nausea, dry mouth, diarrhea, and frequent urination; and (4) *behavioural* responses, such as avoidance of certain situations and impaired task performance (Barlow, 2002; Simms et al., 2012; Figure 16.7).

Anxiety disorders take a number of different forms, including phobic disorders, generalized anxiety disorders, and panic disorders. Post-traumatic stress disorder (PTSD; discussed in Chapter 15) and obsessive-compulsive disorder were considered anxiety disorders in the DSM-IV-TR, but the DSM-5 considers them separate disorders. Two statistics are commonly used in epidemiological research. *Incidence* refers to the number of *new* cases that occur during a given period. *Prevalence* refers to the number of people who have a disorder during a specified

8. Describe the four components of anxiety.

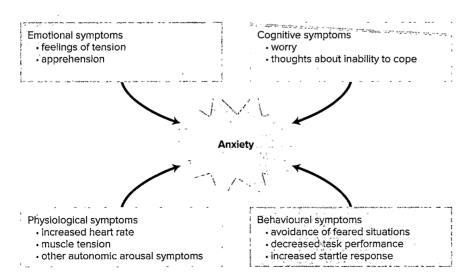

FIGURE 16.7 Anxiety consists of subjective-emotional, cognitive, physiological, and behavioural components.

period of time (i.e., both new and previously existing cases). Large-scale population studies indicate that anxiety disorders are the most prevalent of all psychological disorders in North America, affecting 18.6 percent of the population during their lifetimes (Kessler et al., 2005). Figure 16.8 shows lifetime prevalence rates for various anxiety disorders (based on DSM-IV-TR classification). All of the anxiety disorders tend to occur more frequently in females than in males (16 percent versus 9 percent in Canada respectively). In more than 70 percent of cases, anxiety disorders interfere significantly with life functions or cause the person to seek medical or psychological treatment (Narrow et al., 2002).

9. What is a phobia, and what are the three major types?

Phobic Disorder

Laura's fear of the water dates back to her childhood. She recalled her mother, who had a similar fear, vividly describing an incident in which

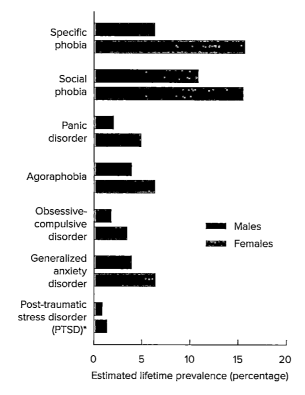

FIGURE 16.8 Lifetime prevalence rates for the anxiety disorders in men and women. All the disorders occur more frequently in women.

Source: Based on Kessler, R.C., Berglund, P., Demler, O., Jin, R., Merikangas, K.R, & Walters, E.E. (2005). Lifetime prevalence and age-of-onset distributions of DSM-IV disorders in the National Comorbidity Survey replication. *Archives of General Psychiatry, 62*, 593–602.

one of her own childhood friends had drowned at a school picnic. Laura's fear of water intensified after she breathed in some water and panicked when she was "dunked" by a playmate at a swimming pool. She floundered and was sure she was going to drown until a lifeguard pulled her to safety. For the past 15 years, Laura has avoided outings that would take her into deep water. Although she knows how to swim, she dreads the thought of going swimming. She makes excuses to avoid boating trips and once turned down a free trip to Hawaii because of the anxiety she knew she would experience flying over the ocean.

Phobias are strong and irrational fears of certain objects or situations. The word was originally derived from *Phobos*, the Greek god of fear, whose likeness was painted on masks and shields to frighten enemies in battle. Today's phobic fights a different kind of battle, with fears of a less realistic, but no less intense nature.

People with phobias realize that their fears are out of all proportion to the danger involved, but they feel helpless to deal with these fears. Instead, they make strenuous efforts to avoid the phobic situation or object. Among the most common phobias in Western society are **agoraphobia,** a fear of open and public places; **social anxiety disorder** (formerly known as **social phobia**), excessive fear of situations in which the person might be evaluated and possibly embarrassed; and **specific phobias,** such as fears of dogs, snakes, spiders, airplanes, elevators, enclosed spaces, water, injections, illness, or death. Animal fears are common among women, and fear of heights, among men (Curtis et al., 1998). Phobias can develop at any point in life, but many of them develop during childhood, adolescence, and early adulthood. Many social phobias evolve out of extreme shyness during childhood (Beidel & Turner, 2007). Once phobias develop, they seldom go away on their own, and they may broaden and intensify over time (Stein & Hollander, 2002).

The degree of impairment produced by a phobia depends in part on how often the phobic stimulus is encountered in the individual's normal round of activities. For example, fear of flying (aviophobia) is a common phobia that occurs in some 25 million North Americans (Kessler et al., 2005). An airplane phobia may be a relatively minor inconvenience for a person who never needs to travel by air, but it may be a debilitating condition for an executive who has to travel frequently. Some people simply refuse to fly even at great personal inconvenience (Figure 16.9).

FIGURE 16.9 Many people suffer from a fear of flying. One famous figure is John Madden, formerly a professional football coach and currently a TV analyst, who travels to his weekly assignments (sometimes separated by thousands of kilometres) in a specially equipped motor home.

Generalized Anxiety Disorder

On initial assessment, Dr. N, who is manifestly tense, complains of never being entirely free of a sense of impending disaster, although he cannot further specify the nature of this anticipated catastrophe. He notes a number of signs of autonomic hyperarousal that he experiences on virtually a daily basis, emphasizing in particular excessive sweating, which has become a source of embarrassment. He is medicating himself for persistent attacks of diarrhea. He complains of an inability to attain a refreshing level of sleep even on those rare occasions when he can count on a few uninterrupted off-duty hours, and his very few waking "leisure" hours are filled with restless irritability. (Carson et al., 1988, p. 195)

Dr. N is suffering from a **generalized anxiety and worry disorder (GAD)**, a chronic state of diffuse, or "free-floating," anxiety that is not attached to specific situations or objects. In such cases, the anxiety may last for months on end, with the signs almost continuously present. Emotionally, Dr. N feels jittery, tense, and constantly on edge. Cognitively, he expects something awful to happen but doesn't know what. Physically, he experiences a mild chronic emergency reaction. Dr. N sweats, his stomach is usually upset, he has diarrhea, and so forth.

As we might expect, this disorder can interfere markedly with daily functioning, even if the symptoms are not continually present for the six months required for a formal diagnosis (Kessler & Wittchen, 2002). The person may find it hard to concentrate, make decisions, and remember commitments. One large-scale study found that 5 percent of people between the ages of 15 and 45 reported having experienced the symptoms of generalized anxiety and worry disorder. In fact, our beliefs about worrying and control are highly correlated with the development GAD (Koerner et al., 2015). Onset tends to occur in childhood and adolescence (Wittchen et al., 1994).

Panic Disorder

In contrast to generalized anxiety disorder, which involves chronic tension and anxiety, **panic disorders** occur suddenly and unpredictably, and they are much more intense. The symptoms of panic attacks can be terrifying. It is not unusual for victims to feel that they are dying (Ballenger, 2000).

In most cases, panic attacks occur out of the blue and in the absence of any identifiable stimulus. It is this unpredictable quality that makes panic attacks so mysterious and terrifying to their victims. Many people with panic attacks develop *agoraphobia*, a fear of public places, because of their fear that they will have an attack in public. In extreme cases, they may fear leaving the familiar setting of the home, and agoraphobics have been known to be housebound for years at a time because of their "fear of fear" (Milrod et al., 1997). This case shows the development of an agoraphobic pattern:

As the attacks continued, Ms. Watson began to dread going out of the house alone. She feared that while out she would have an attack and would be stranded and helpless. She stopped riding the subway to work out of fear she might be trapped in a car between stops when an attack struck, preferring instead to walk the 20 blocks between her home and work. Social and recreational activities, previously frequent and enjoyed, were severely curtailed because an attack might occur. (Adapted from Spitzer et al., 1983)

Formal diagnosis of a panic disorder requires recurrent attacks that do not seem tied to environmental stimuli, followed by psychological or behavioural problems. These typically involve persistent fear of future attacks or agoraphobic responses. Panic disorders with or without agoraphobia tend to appear in late adolescence

10. How does a generalized anxiety disorder differ from a phobic disorder? How does it differ from a panic disorder?

11. What occurs in a panic disorder, and how do these experiences frequently result in development of agoraphobia?

or early adulthood and affect about 6 percent of the population over their lifetimes (Kessler et al., 2005). Even more common are occasional panic attacks. In one survey of Canadian students, 34 percent reported having had at least one unexpected panic attack within the previous year, usually during periods of extreme stress (Norton et al., 1985). Under DSM-5 criteria, these students would *not* be diagnosed as having a panic disorder unless they developed an inordinate fear of having future attacks.

Obsessive-Compulsive Disorder (OCD)

A thirty-eight-year-old mother of one child had been obsessed by fears of contamination during her entire adult life. Literally hundreds of times a day, thoughts of being infected by germs would occur to her. Once she began to think that either she or her child might become infected, she could not dismiss the thought. The constant concern about infection resulted in a series of washing and cleaning rituals that took up most of her day. Her child was confined to one room only, which the woman tried to keep entirely free of germs by scrubbing it— floor to ceiling—several times a day. Moreover, she opened and closed all doors with her feet, in order to avoid contaminating her own hands. (Rachman & Hodgson, 1980)

This woman was diagnosed as having an **obsessive-compulsive disorder (OCD)**. OCD and related disorders are considered separate in the DSM-5, but we will discuss them in this section because of their relation to anxiety. Such disorders usually consist of two components, one cognitive and the other behavioural, although either can occur alone. **Obsessions** are repetitive and unwelcome thoughts, images, or impulses that invade consciousness, are often abhorrent to the person, and are very difficult to dismiss or control. This mother was tyrannized by thoughts and images of contamination. **Compulsions** are repetitive behavioural responses—such as the woman's cleaning rituals—that can be resisted only with great difficulty. Compulsions are often responses to obsessive thoughts and function to reduce the anxiety associated with the thoughts (Clark & O'Conner, 2005; De Silva & Rachman, 1998). Once the mother had performed her compulsive cleanliness acts, she was relatively free from anxiety, at least until the thoughts of contamination intruded once more.

In this case, the woman's germ obsession clearly interfered with her life, as well as her daughter's. One man's obsession resulted in a far more favourable outcome: Louis Pasteur's discovery of a process for eliminating destructive micro-organisms and limiting fermentation in milk, beer, and other liquids. His tireless work on this invention was fuelled in part by his own obsession about contamination and infection. Pasteur refused to shake hands with others and had a ritual of vigorously wiping his plate and glass before dining (Asimov, 1997).

Behavioural compulsions are extremely difficult to control. They often involve checking things repeatedly, cleaning, and repeating tasks endlessly. If the person does not perform the compulsive act, he or she may experience tremendous anxiety, perhaps even a panic attack. Like phobic avoidance responses, compulsions appear to reduce anxiety and be strengthened through a process of negative reinforcement because they allow a person to avoid anxiety (Jenike, 1998).

In the DSM-5, specific types of OCD have been included such as hoarding disorder, hair-pulling disorder (trichotillomania), and skin-picking disorder (exoriation).

Recent studies have found the lifetime prevalence of OCD in the United States and Canada to be about 1.6 per 100 people. Onset typically occurs in the 20s (Kessler et al., 2005). We examine some of the brain mechanisms involved in OCD in this chapter's *Focus on Neuroscience* feature.

Causal Factors in Anxiety Disorders and OCD

Anxiety is a complex phenomenon with biological, psychological, and environmental causes, and all three levels of analysis have provided major insights into the development and maintenance of anxiety disorders. Within the vulnerability-stress model presented earlier, any of these factors can create predispositions to respond to stressors with an anxiety disorder (Beidel et al., 2007; Velotis, 2006).

Biological Factors

Genetic factors may create a vulnerability to anxiety disorders (Blackwood, 2000; Jang, 2005). Where clinical levels of anxiety are concerned, identical twins have a concordance rate (i.e., if one twin has it, so does the other) of about 40 percent for anxiety disorders, compared with a 4 percent concordance rate in fraternal twins

12. Differentiate between obsessions and compulsions. How are they typically related to each other?

13. What evidence is there for a genetic predisposition to anxiety disorders? What form might the vulnerability factor take?

Focus on Neuroscience

THE NEUROSCIENCE OF OBSESSIVE-COMPULSIVE DISORDER

Obsessive-compulsive disorder (OCD) can be debilitating. The behavioural compulsions are difficult to control and may result in physical damage to the individual. For example, excessive handwashing may result in severe skin abrasions. Why do people engage in such potentially damaging behaviours?

Neuroimaging (fMRI, PET, and CT) has helped to shed light on two underlying neural circuits involved in OCD. In a recent review, Friedlander and Desrocher (2006) examined the data on both models. The executive dysfunction model (e.g., Rapoport, 1991) suggests that the underlying problem lies in impulse control and behavioural inhibition. The modulatory control model (e.g., Saxena et al., 1998) posits a different mechanism, reflecting lack of control of socially appropriate behaviours. According to the executive dysfunction model, the problem is an inability to inhibit behaviours viewed as inappropriate for a particular situation. Friedlander and Desrocher (2006) suggest that this model would predict altered activity in the prefrontal cortex (in particular, regions to the back and the side of the prefrontal cortex). However, they also suggest that the caudate nucleus (a major structure in the basal ganglia) should be involved, since it is richly connected to the prefrontal cortex and helps to regulate limbic system activity, especially with respect to the completion of behaviours. However, the findings seem to be mixed, with several showing increased volume of the caudate, and others showing a decrease or no difference (e.g., Baxter et al., 1988; Robinson et al., 1995; Szeszeko et al., 2004). Furthermore, the involvement of the prefrontal cortex is more likely to be seen in adults than in children. The data are more consistent regarding activity in the thalamus, which serves as a major relay station for incoming information. For example, using PET scans, Perani et al. (1995) report that thalamic abnormality is directly related to OCD symptom severity.

More compelling support is found for the modulatory control model. In general, the evidence (e.g., Sawle et al., 1991) supports increased metabolism in the orbitofrontal (the prefrontal lobe directly behind the eyes) and medial (toward the middle) prefrontal cortex. Beucke et al. (2013) have shown a heightened degree of activity in these brain circuits. These areas have been implicated in the control of socially appropriate behaviours and motivation. If these areas do not function properly, the individual may display a variety of inappropriate, impulsive behaviours, and may fixate on one aspect of the environment. Friedlander and Desrocher (2006) suggest that dysfunction in the orbitofrontal cortex and associated areas may be responsible for the generation and persistence of obsessive thought. Abnormalities were also observed in the cingulate gyrus, which is connected to both the frontal lobes and the limbic system.

These imaging studies suggest the involvement of two separate pathways contributing to OCD. Friedlander and Desrocher (2006) argue that the executive dysfunction model is best equipped to explain compulsions and that the neural wiring should be found in the prefrontal-caudate-thalamus circuit (Figure 16.10). The modulatory control model is focused on obsessions, and the underlying pathway involves the orbitofrontal cortex and the cingulate. Early identification of abnormalities in either route may help with the timing of effective treatment for OCD.

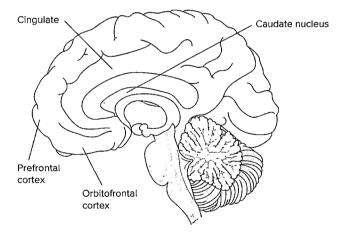

FIGURE 16.10 Areas involved in OCD. Research indicates that obsessions are likely generated through an orbitofrontal-cingulate pathway, while compulsions involve a prefrontal-caudate-thalamus circuit.

(Carey & Gottesman, 1981). Recent research indicates that as much as 61 percent of the population variance in panic disorder and 44 percent of the agoraphobia variance is genetically influenced (Gelernter & Stein, 2009). Although such findings indicate a genetic predisposition, the concordance rate even in identical twins is far from 100 percent, indicating the significance of psychological and environmental factors.

David Barlow (2002) suggests that such vulnerability may take the form of an autonomic nervous system that overreacts to perceived threat, creating high levels of physiological arousal. Larson and colleagues (2006) found, for example, that the amygdala play a threat-detection role in phobias, resulting in a brief but strong response to feared objects that is not present in response to nonphobic stimuli or among nonphobic individuals. Hereditary factors may cause overreactivity of neurotransmitter systems involved in emotional responses (Brown & Barlow, 2009; Mineka et al., 1998). Exposure to stress early in life is also associated with changes in various neurotransmitter systems, resulting in increased responsiveness to stress (Heim & Nemeroff, 2001).

The search for biological processes associated with anxiety disorders has focused on several neurotransmitters in the brain. One such transmitter is GABA (gamma-aminobutyric acid). As mentioned in Chapter 3, GABA is an inhibitory transmitter that reduces neural activity in the amygdala and other brain structures that stimulate physiological arousal. Some researchers believe that abnormally low levels of inhibitory GABA activity in these arousal areas may cause some people to have highly reactive nervous systems that quickly produce anxiety responses in response to stressors (Bremner, 2000). Such people might also be more susceptible to classically conditioned phobias because they already have a strong unconditioned arousal response in place, ready to be conditioned to new stimuli. In support of this hypothesis, brain scans showed that patients with a history of panic attacks had a 22 percent lower concentration of GABA in the occipital cortex than age-matched controls without panic disorder (Goddard et al., 2001). Other transmitter systems, particularly serotonin, may also be involved in the anxiety disorders (Akimova et al., 2009).

As noted earlier, women exhibit anxiety disorders more often than men do (Leibenluft, 1999). In a large epidemiological study of adolescents, Peter Lewinsohn and colleagues (1998) found that this sex difference emerges as early as seven years of age. The contributing role of biological factors is suggested by Lewinsohn's finding that, even when 11 psychosocial factors (including negative life events, self-esteem, and social support) that differentiated males from females were controlled for statistically, the large sex difference remained.

Such findings suggest a sex-linked biological predisposition for anxiety disorders, but social conditions that give women less power and personal control may also contribute (Kessler et al., 1994; Craske, 2003). As in other instances of sex differences, it seems likely that biological, psychological, and environmental factors combine in complex ways.

Finally, we should recall the possible role of evolutionary factors in predisposing people to fear certain types of stimuli that might have had survival significance in the past, such as snakes, spiders, storms, and heights. As discussed in Chapter 7, evolutionary theorists believe that biological preparedness makes it easier for us to learn to fear certain stimuli, and may explain why phobias seem to centre on certain classes of "primal" stimuli and not on more dangerous modern ones, such as guns and electrical power stations (Ohman & Soares, 1993).

Psychological Factors

Psychodynamic theories. Anxiety is a central feature of psychoanalytic conceptions of abnormal behaviour. According to Freud, **neurotic anxiety** occurs when unacceptable impulses threaten to overwhelm the ego's defences and explode into action. How the ego's defence mechanisms deal with neurotic anxiety determines the form of the anxiety disorder. Freud believed that in phobic disorders, neurotic anxiety is displaced onto some external stimulus that has symbolic significance in relation to the underlying conflict. For example, in one of Freud's most celebrated cases, a little boy named Hans suddenly developed a fear of horses and the possibility of being bitten. To Freud, the phobia resulted from the boy's unresolved Oedipus complex. The powerful horse represented Hans's father, and the fear of being bitten symbolized Hans's unconscious fear of being castrated by his father if he acted on his sexual desire for his mother.

Obsessions and compulsions are also ways of handling anxiety. According to Freud, the obsession is symbolically related to, but less terrifying than, the underlying impulse. A compulsion is a way of "taking back," or undoing, one's unacceptable urges, as when obsessive thoughts about dirt and compulsive handwashing are used to deal with one's "dirty" sexual impulses. Finally, generalized anxiety and panic attacks are thought to occur when one's defences are not strong enough to control or contain anxiety, but are strong enough to hide the underlying conflict.

Although psychoanalytic theory has stimulated considerable thinking about the causes and treatment of anxiety disorders, the notion of anxiety disorder symptoms as symbolic expressions of underlying conflicts has not received much research support (Fisher & Greenberg, 1996). Cognitive and behavioural approaches are far more influential today in guiding research on anxiety disorders and their treatment.

14. How might GABA be related to anxiety disorders? How might the biochemical factor in panic disorder be different?

15. What factors might produce the sex difference seen in the prevalence of anxiety disorders?

16. How does psychoanalytic theory explain the development of anxiety disorders?

Cognitive factors. Cognitive theorists stress the role of maladaptive thought patterns and beliefs in anxiety disorders (Brown & Barlow, 2009). Anxiety-disordered people "catastrophize" about demands and magnify them into threats. They anticipate that the worst will happen and feel powerless to cope effectively (Clark, 1988; Mineka et al., 1998). Attentional processes are especially sensitive to threatening stimuli (Bar-Haim et al., 2007). Edna Foa and colleagues (1995) asked social phobics (1) how likely it was that they would embarrass themselves in a social situation and (2) how serious and costly the consequences of performing poorly would be for them. Compared with non-phobics, the social phobics judged both the likelihood and the costs to be much higher. Interestingly, these judgments were restricted to social situations. The social phobics did not differ in their likelihood and cost judgments in nonsocial situations.

Cognitive processes also play an important role in panic disorders. According to David Barlow (2002), panic attacks are triggered by exaggerated misinterpretations of normal anxiety symptoms, such as heart palpitations, dizziness, and breathlessness. The panic-disordered person appraises these as signs that a heart attack or a psychological loss of control is about to occur, and these catastrophic appraisals create even more anxiety until the process spirals out of control, producing a full-blown state of panic (Figure 16.11). Helping panic patients to replace such "mortal danger" appraisals with more benign interpretations of their bodily symptoms (e.g., "It's only a bit of anxiety, not a heart attack") results in a marked reduction in panic attacks (Barlow, 1997; Craske, 1999).

Anxiety as a learned response. From the behavioural perspective, anxiety disorders result from emotional conditioning (Öhman, 2000; Mineka & Zinbarg, 2006). Some fears are acquired as a result of traumatic experiences

that produce a classically conditioned fear response (Waters et al., 2009). For example, a person who has a traumatic fall from a high place may develop a fear of heights (a CR) because the high place (CS) was associated with the pain and trauma of the fall (UCS).

Classical conditioning cannot be the whole story, however, because many phobics have never had a traumatic experience with the phobic object or situation that they now fear (Bruce & Sanderson, 1998; Menzies & Clarke, 1995). Most people who are afraid to fly have never been in an air crash themselves. So how did they learn their fear? Clearly, phobias also can be acquired through observational learning. For example, televised images of air crashes can evoke high levels of fear in some people. Yet most people do not develop phobias under these conditions, so there must be still more going on. It may be that biological dispositions and cognitive factors help to determine whether a person develops a phobia by observing a traumatic event. Thus, if a person has a biological disposition toward intense fear, and if the person comes to believe that "sooner or later, the same thing will happen to me," the likelihood of developing a phobia on the basis of observational learning may increase.

Once anxiety is learned, it may be triggered either by cues from the environment or by internal cues, such as thoughts and images (Pitman et al., 2000). In the case of phobic reactions, the cues tend to be external ones relating to the feared object or situation. In panic disorders, on the other hand, the anxiety-arousing cues tend to be internal ones, such as bodily sensations (e.g., one's heart rate) or mental images (such as the image of collapsing and having a seizure in a public place; Craske, 1999).

People are highly motivated to avoid or escape anxiety because it is such an unpleasant emotional state. Here is where operant conditioning enters the picture. Behaviours that are successful in reducing anxiety, such as

17. How do cognitive factors enter into anxiety disorders, particularly panic disorder? What research supports these explanations?

18. Explain anxiety disorders in terms of classical conditioning, negative reinforcement, and observational learning.

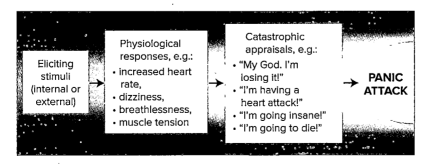

FIGURE 16.11 Current cognitive explanations of panic attacks depict a process in which normal manifestations of anxiety are appraised catastrophically, ultimately resulting in a full-blown panic attack.

compulsions or phobic avoidance responses, are strengthened through a process of negative reinforcement. Thus, the obsessive-compulsive mother's scrubbing ritual reduces anxiety about contamination, and the water phobic's avoidance of swimming prevents her from experiencing anxiety. In the case of agoraphobia, remaining at home also serves as a *safety signal*, a place where the person is unlikely to experience a panic attack (Brown & Barlow, 2009). Again, anxiety reduction reinforces the response of staying at home (Figure 16.12). Unfortunately, successful avoidance, while producing an immediate positive benefit, prolongs the problem in the long run. It prevents the learned anxiety response from being extinguished, which would occur eventually if these people exposed themselves to the feared stimuli enough times without experiencing the feared consequences.

Sociocultural Factors

Social and cultural factors also play a role in the development of anxiety disorders (Lopez & Guarnaccia, 2000). The role of culture is most dramatically shown in **culture-bound disorders** that occur only in certain places. *Koro* is a Southeast Asian anxiety disorder in which a man fears that his penis is going to retract into his abdomen and kill him. Another culture-specific disorder, found in Japan, is a social phobia called *Taijin Kyofushu* (Tanaka-Matsumi, 1979). People with this disorder are pathologically fearful of offending others by emitting offensive odours, blushing, staring inappropriately, or having a blemish or improper facial expression. Taijin Kyofushu has been attributed to the Japanese cultural

value of extreme interpersonal sensitivity and to cultural prohibitions against expressing negative emotions (Kleinknecht et al., 1997; Russell, 1989; Ono et al., 2001; Torwin et al., 2004).

Several culture-bound anxiety-based disorders occur in North America. *Windigo* is an anxiety disorder found among certain North American Aboriginals. Persons with Windigo are fearful of being possessed by monsters who will turn them into homicidal cannibals. A more familiar culturally based anxiety occurs in *anorexia nervosa*. Though formally classified as an eating disorder, anorexia nervosa has a strong phobic component, namely the fear of getting fat. This eating disorder is found almost exclusively in developed countries, in which the emphasis on being thin has become a cultural obsession (Becker et al., 1999).

Eating Disorders

Victims of **anorexia nervosa** have an intense fear of being fat and severely restrict their food intake to the point of self-starvation. Despite looking emaciated and weighing less than 85 percent of what would be expected for their age and height, anorexics continue to view themselves as fat (Figure 16.13). They often crave food but have what amounts to an eating phobia that can be life-threatening. About 90 percent of anorexics are female, mostly adolescents and young adults (Becker et al., 1999). Anorexia causes menstruation to stop, strains the heart, produces bone loss, and increases the risk of death (Neumäker, 2000). In 1982, the death of a famous singer, Karen Carpenter, was attributed to heart strain caused by her anorexia.

---

19. Describe four culture-bound disorders that involve anxiety.

20. Describe some of the symptoms and causes of anorexia and bulimia.

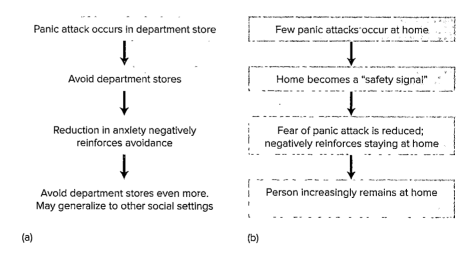

(a)

Panic attack occurs in department store
↓
Avoid department stores
↓
Reduction in anxiety negatively reinforces avoidance
↓
Avoid department stores even more. May generalize to other social settings

(b)

Few panic attacks occur at home
↓
Home becomes a "safety signal"
↓
Fear of panic attack is reduced; negatively reinforces staying at home
↓
Person increasingly remains at home

FIGURE 16.12 Panic and agoraphobia. This diagram illustrates how panic disorders contribute to the development of agoraphobia. Negative reinforcement through anxiety reduction fosters avoidance of feared situations (a), as well as an attraction to safety signals, such as one's own home (b), where panic does not occur.

(both): © Ed Quinn/Corbis

FIGURE 16.13 Anorexia nervosa is a potentially life-threatening disorder in which people virtually starve themselves to be thin. This anorexic woman returned to normal weight after therapy.

People who suffer from **bulimia nervosa** are overly concerned with becoming fat, but instead of self-starvation they binge eat and then purge the food, usually by inducing vomiting or using laxatives. Bulimics often consume 2000 to 4000 calories during binges, and in some cases may consume 20 000 calories per day (Crandall, 1989; Geracioti et al., 1995). About 90 percent of bulimics are female. A number of female celebrities (e.g. Demi Lovato, Kesha, Lady Gaga) have been very open about their struggle with bulimia.

Although most bulimics are of normal body weight, repeated purging can produce severe physical consequences, including gastric problems and badly eroded teeth. Some surveys indicate that up to 10 percent of university women exhibit symptoms of bulimia, although its general prevalence among North American women is 1 to 3 percent—compared with 0.5 percent for anorexia (Becker et al., 1999; Hudson et al., 2007).

Causes of Anorexia and Bulimia

What motivates people to develop such abnormal eating patterns? The answer—as with general eating regulation—seems to lie in a combination of environmental, psychological, and biological factors. Anorexia and bulimia are more common in industrialized cultures in which beauty is equated with "thinness." Indeed, as found by Cheryl Thomas of the University of Windsor, many women who immigrate to Western countries are at risk of developing eating disorders (Geller & Thomas, 1999). Variations in beauty norms among different ethnic groups

also may help to explain why, in North America, eating disorders are more common among Whites than Blacks (Zhang & Snowden, 1999). Consistent with objectification theory, a study of 16- to 21-year-old female university students suggests that a cultural emphasis on viewing one's body as an object contributes to eating disorders (Noll & Fredrickson, 1998).

Cultural norms alone cannot account for eating disorders, because only a small percentage of women within a particular culture are anorexic or bulimic. Some researchers believe that personality factors are another piece of the puzzle. Anorexics often are perfectionists: high achievers who often strive to live up to lofty self-standards, including distorted standards concerning an acceptably thin body (Garfinkel & Garner, 1982). In one study, Monique Smeets (1999) showed anorexic and normal women a "morphing movie" in which a woman's thin body transforms into an obese one. When asked to judge the transition points at which the body changes from "thin" to "normal," "fat," and "obese," anorexics set harsher standards (e.g., lower weight levels to meet the transition point) for their own and other women's bodies.

For anorexics, losing weight becomes a battle for success and control: "Me versus food, and I'm going to win." Their perfectionism and need for control may stem partly from their upbringing (Chan & Ma, 2002). Anorexics describe their parents as disapproving and as setting abnormally high achievement standards, and they report more stressful events related to their parents than do non-anorexics (Waller & Hartley, 1994).

A different pattern emerges for bulimics, who tend to be depressed and anxious, exhibit low impulse control, and seem to lack a stable sense of personal identity and self-sufficiency (Strober & Humphrey, 1987). Bingeing is often triggered by life stress, and guilt and self-contempt follow it. The purging may be a means of reducing depression and anxiety triggered by the bingeing (Waters et al., 2001).

On the biological side, genetic factors may create a predisposition toward eating disorders. Concordance rates for eating disorders are higher among identical twins than fraternal twins, and higher among first-degree relatives than second- or third-degree relatives (Kortegaard et al., 2001). Anorexics and bulimics exhibit abnormal activity of serotonin and other body chemicals that help to regulate eating (Bruch, 1973; Walsh & Devlin, 1998). However, because the findings are correlational, it is not clear whether these chemical abnormalities help to cause eating disorders, or are a reaction to self-starvation and binge-purge eating.

Many researchers believe that these physiological changes initially are a *response* to abnormal eating patterns; but, once started, they *perpetuate* eating and digestive irregularities (Walsh & Devlin, 1998). For example, because leptin is secreted by fat cells and anorexics have low fat mass, the amount of leptin circulating in their bloodstream is abnormally low (Mantzoros et al., 1997). But when anorexics begin to eat more, their leptin levels rebound more quickly than their weight gain. Because leptin is a signal that reduces appetite, this leptin rebound may make it more difficult for anorexics to keep gaining weight (Walsh & Devlin, 1998). Similarly, stomach acids expelled into the mouth during vomiting cause bulimics to lose taste sensitivity, making the normally unpleasant taste of vomit more tolerable (Rodin et al., 1990). This helps to perpetuate bulimics' willingness to keep purging in this manner.

Treating eating disorders is difficult and may take years, but with professional help about half of anorexics and bulimics fully recover (Becker et al., 1999; Walsh & Devlin, 1998). Others are able to eat more normally but maintain their preoccupation with weight.

MOOD (AFFECTIVE) DISORDERS

Another set of emotion-based disorders are the **mood disorders,** which involve depression and mania (excessive excitement). Together with anxiety disorders, mood disorders are the most frequently experienced psychological

Review

- Anxiety involves four components: (1) subjective-emotional feelings of tension and discomfort; (2) cognitive processes involving worry, perceptions of threat, and lack of control; (3) excessive physiological arousal; and (4) behaviours that reflect the anxious state and often are designed to escape or avoid the feared object or situation.

- Anxiety disorders include phobic disorder (an irrational fear of a specific object or situation), generalized anxiety disorder (recurrent anxiety reactions that are difficult to link to specific environmental stimuli), and panic disorder.

- OCD, which involves uncontrollable and unwelcome thoughts and repetitive behaviours, has an anxiety component, but is now a separate disorder in the DSM-5.

- Biological factors in anxiety disorders include both genetic and biochemical processes, possibly involving the action of neurotransmitters, such as GABA, within parts of the brain that control emotional arousal.

- Psychoanalytic theorists believe that neurotic anxiety results from the inability of the ego's defences to deal with internal psychological conflicts. The cognitive perspective stresses the role of cognitive distortions, including the tendencies to magnify the degree of threat and danger and, in the case of panic disorder, to misinterpret normal anxiety symptoms in ways that can evoke panic.

- The behavioural perspective views anxiety as a learned response established through classical conditioning or vicarious learning. The avoidance responses in phobias and compulsive disorders are seen as operant responses that are negatively reinforced through anxiety reduction.

- Sociocultural factors are also involved in anxiety disorders, as illustrated by certain culture-bound anxiety disorders. The greater prevalence of anxiety disorders in women has been explained in both biological and sociocultural terms.

- Anorexia and bulimia are eating disorders that have serious physical consequences, occur more often in cultures that value thinness, and are associated with different psychological profiles and childhood patterns of family interaction.

disorders (Kessler et al., 1994; Robins & Regier, 1991). Anxiety and mood disorders have a high *comorbidity* (co-occurrence). About half of all depressed people also experience an anxiety disorder (National Institute of Mental Health, 2008).

Depression

Almost everyone has experienced depression, at least in its milder and more temporary forms. Loss and pain are inevitable parts of life, and when they occur, most of us feel blue, sad, discouraged, apathetic, and passive. The future looks bleak, and some of the zest goes out of living. Such reactions are normal; at any given point in time, 25 to 30 percent of university undergraduates are experiencing mild depression (Seligman, 1991). These feelings usually fade away after the event has passed or as the person becomes accustomed to the new situation. In clinical depression, however, the frequency, intensity, and duration of depressive symptoms are out of proportion to the person's life situation (Oatley & Jenkins, 1992). Thus, some people may respond to a minor setback or loss with an intense **major depression** that leaves them unable to function effectively in their lives. This disorder occurs in 16.6 percent of Americans during their lifetimes (Kessler et al., 2005). In Canada, the rate is a little lower—about 10 percent of those over the age of 18 will suffer from major depression in their lifetimes (Canadian Mental Health Association, 2010). Other people exhibit a less intense form of depression called chronic depressive disorder (known as **dysthymia** in the DSM-IV-TR) that has less dramatic effects on personal and occupational

functioning. Dysthymia is, however, a more chronic and long-lasting form of misery, occurring for years on end with intervals of normal mood that never last more than a few weeks or months.

Although depression is primarily a disorder of mood, there are three other types of symptoms: cognitive symptoms, motivational symptoms, and somatic (physical) symptoms (Figure 16.14).

The *negative mood state* is the core feature of depression. When depressed people are asked how they feel, they most commonly report sadness, misery, and loneliness. Whereas people with anxiety disorders retain their capacity to experience pleasure, depressed people lose it (Mineka et al., 1998; Ruscio et al., 2007). Activities that used to bring satisfaction and happiness feel dull and flat. Even biological pleasures, such as eating and sex, lose their appeal.

Cognitive symptoms are also a central part of depression. Depressed people have difficulty concentrating and making decisions. They usually have low self-esteem, believing that they are inferior, inadequate, and incompetent. When setbacks occur in their lives, depressed people tend to blame themselves; when failure has not yet occurred, they expect that it will and that it will be caused by their own inadequacies. Depressed people almost always view the future with great pessimism and hopelessness (Clark et al., 1999).

Motivational symptoms in depression involve an inability to get started and perform behaviours that might produce pleasure or accomplishment. A depressed student may be unable to get out of bed in the morning, let alone go to

21. Differentiate between major depression and dysthymia.

22. Describe the four classes of symptoms that characterize (a) depression and (b) mania.

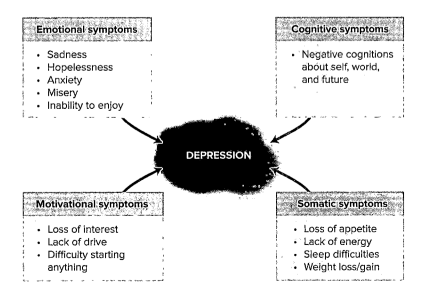

FIGURE 16.14 Depression includes emotional, cognitive, motivational, and somatic features.

class or study. Everything seems too much of an effort. In extreme depressive reactions, the person may have to be prodded out of bed, clothed, and fed. In some cases of severe depression, movements slow down and the person walks or talks slowly and with excruciating effort.

Somatic (bodily) symptoms often include loss of appetite and weight loss in moderate and severe depression. Sleep disturbances, particularly insomnia, commonly occur. Sleep disturbance and weight loss lead to fatigue and weakness, which tend to add to the depressed feelings. Depressed people also may lose sexual desire and responsiveness. In mild depression, weight gain sometimes occurs as a person eats compulsively.

Bipolar Disorder

When a person experiences only depression, the disorder is called unipolar depression. In **bipolar disorder,** depression (which is usually the dominant state) alternates with periods of **mania,** a state of highly excited mood and behaviour that is quite the opposite of depression. In a manic state, mood is euphoric and cognitions are grandiose. The person believes there are no limits to what can be accomplished and does not recognize the negative consequences that may ensue if grandiose plans are acted on. At a motivational level, manic behaviour is hyperactive. The manic person engages in frenetic activity, be it in work, in sexual relationships, or elsewhere. The 19th-century composer Robert Schumann produced 27 works during one manic year, but his productivity ground to a halt when he sank back into the depressive phase of his bipolar disorder (Jamison, 1995). Manic people can become very irritable and aggressive when their momentary goals are frustrated in any way (Miklowitz, 2007).

In a manic state, speech is often rapid or pressured, as if the person must say as many words as possible in the time allotted. With all this flurry of activity comes a greatly lessened need for sleep. Manic people may go for several days without sleeping, until exhaustion inevitably sets in and the mania slows down. The following case illustrates a manic episode:

> Robert B, a 56-year-old dentist, awoke one morning with the idea that he was the most gifted dental surgeon in his tri-state area; his mission then was to provide service for as many persons as possible so that they could benefit from his talents. Consequently, he decided to enlarge his

two-chair practice to a 20-chair one, and his plan was to reconstruct his two dental offices into 20 booths so that he could simultaneously attend to as many patients. That very day he drew up the plans for this arrangement and telephoned a number of remodellers and invited them to submit bids for the work.

> Toward the end of that day he became irritated with the "interminable delays" and, after he attended to his last patient, rolled up his sleeves and began to knock down the walls of his dental offices. When he discovered that he couldn't manage this chore with the sledgehammer he had purchased for this purpose earlier, he became frustrated and proceeded to smash his more destructible tools, washbasins, and X-ray equipment. He justified this behaviour in his own mind by saying, "This junk is not suitable for the likes of me; it'll have to be replaced anyway."

> He was in perpetual motion and his speech was "overexcited." When Robert was later admitted to a hospital, he could not sit in his chair; instead he paced the office floor like a caged animal. (Kleinmuntz, 1980, pp. 309–310)

Prevalence and Course of Mood Disorders

Epidemiological studies suggest that, at this moment, about one in 20 North Americans is severely depressed (Satcher, 1999). Statistically, your chances of having a depressive episode of clinical proportions at least once in your lifetime is about one in five (Kessler et al., 2005). No age group is exempt from depression. It appears in infants as young as six months who have been separated from their mothers for prolonged periods. The rate of depressive symptoms in children and adolescents is as high as the adult rate (Essau & Petermann, 1999).

Data from numerous studies indicate that depression is on the rise in young groups, with the onset of depression increasing dramatically in 15- to 19-year-olds (Burke et al., 1991; LeBrun, 2007). People born after 1960 are ten times more likely to experience depression than are their grandparents, even though their grandparents have lived much longer (Seligman, 1989). The reasons for this striking increase are not totally clear, but we will consider one possible explanation later (Costello et al., 2006; Lewinsohn et al., 1993).

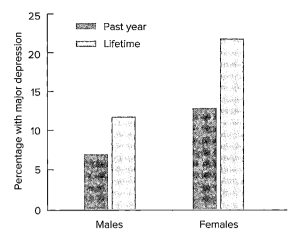

FIGURE 16.15 Prevalence rates for major depression in men and women.

Source: Data from Kessler, R.C., Berglund, P., Demler, O., Jin, R., Merikangas, K.R, & Walters, E.E. (2005). Lifetime prevalence and age-of-onset distributions of DSM-IV disorders in the National Comorbidity Survey replication. *Archives of General Psychiatry, 62*, 593–602.

The prevalence of depressive disorders is similar across socioeconomic and ethnic groups, but there is a major sex difference in our culture. Though men and women do not differ in prevalence of bipolar disorder, women appear to be about twice as likely as men to suffer unipolar depression (Figure 16.15). Women are most likely to suffer their first episode of depression in their 20s, men in their 40s (Keyes & Goodman, 2006). Biological theories suggest that genetic factors, biochemical differences in the nervous system, or the monthly premenstrual depression that many women experience could increase vulnerability to depressive disorders (Donaldson, 1998). In contrast, environmental theories focus on possible cultural causes. One suggestion is that the traditional sex role expectation for females in Western cultures is to be passive and dependent in the face of stress or loss and to focus on their feelings, whereas men are more likely to distract themselves through activities such as physical activity and drinking (Nolen-Hoeksema et al., 1994).

Most people who suffer depressive episodes never seek treatment. What is likely to happen to such people? Perhaps the one positive thing that can be said about depression is that it usually dissipates with time. After the initial episode, which typically comes on suddenly after a stressful experience, depression typically lasts an average of five to ten months when untreated (Tollefson, 1993).

Once a depressive episode has occurred, one of three patterns may follow. In perhaps half of all cases, depression will never recur. Many other cases show a second pattern: recovery with recurrence. On average, these people will remain symptom-free for perhaps three years before experiencing another depressive episode of about the same severity and duration. The time interval between subsequent episodes of depression tends to become shorter over the years (Rubin, 2000). Finally, about 10 percent of people who have a major depressive episode will not recover and will remain chronically depressed (Figure 16.16).

Manic episodes, though less common than depressive reactions, are far more likely to recur. Fewer than 1 percent of the population experience mania, but more than 90 percent of those who do have a recurrence (American Psychiatric Association, 1994; Kessler et al., 1994).

Causal Factors in Mood Disorders

Biological Factors

Both genetic and neurochemical factors have been linked to depression (Donaldson, 1998). Genetic factors surface in both twin and adoption studies (McGuffin et al., 2005). Identical twins have a concordance rate of about 67 percent for experiencing clinical depression, compared with a rate of only 15 percent for

23. How prevalent is depression in men and women? Why the difference? What is its course if left untreated, and its likelihood of recurrence?

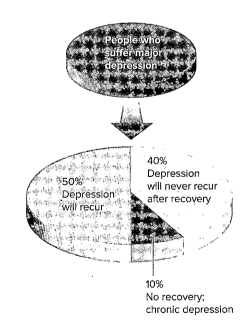

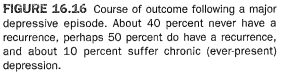

FIGURE 16.16 Course of outcome following a major depressive episode. About 40 percent never have a recurrence, perhaps 50 percent do have a recurrence, and about 10 percent suffer chronic (ever-present) depression.

fraternal twins (Gershon et al., 1989). Among adopted people who developed depression, biological relatives were found to be eight times more likely than adoptive relatives to also suffer from depression (Wender et al., 1986). What is likely inherited is a predisposition to develop a depressive disorder, given certain kinds of environmental factors such as significant losses and low social support (Brown & Barlow, 2009; Jang, 2005). .

Two genetically based temperament systems discussed in Chapter 11, the behavioural inhibition system (neuroticism) and the behavioural activation system (extraversion) are heavily involved in the development of mood disorders (Brown, 2007). You'll recall that the behavioural activation system (BAS) is reward-oriented and activated by cues that predict future pleasure, whereas the behavioural inhibition system (BIS) is pain-avoidant and generates fear and anxiety. Depression is predicted by high BIS sensitivity and low BAS activity. Mania, on the other hand, is linked to high reward-oriented BAS functioning, and scores on the personality variable of extraversion (tied heavily to the BAS) predicts the future development of bipolar mania (Lonnqvist et al., 2009). Cues connoting potential reward, achievement gratification, and goal attainment trigger BAS activation, leading to the manic person's elevated positive emotions and expectations, high activity level, and self-confidence. With clear failure, however, BAS deactivation can cause a flip-flop into feelings of depression (Alloy et al., 2009).

Increasingly, biological research has focused on the possible role of brain chemistry in depression. One influential theory holds that depression is a disorder of motivation caused by underactivity in a family of neurotransmitters that include norepinephrine, dopamine, and serotonin. These transmitters, which are involved in the BAS, play important roles in brain circuits that produce reward and pleasure. When neural transmission decreases in these brain regions, the result is the lack of pleasure and loss of motivation that characterize depression (Areán, 2007). Also in support of this theory, several highly effective antidepressant drugs operate by increasing the activity of these neurotransmitters, thereby further stimulating the neural systems that underlie positive mood and goal-directed behaviour. A study by Lescia Tremblay and colleagues (2002) tested the amount of reward experienced by depressed patients when these centres were activated by a stimulant drug that produces pleasure. Severely

depressed individuals showed a much stronger pleasure response to the drug than did nondepressed people, supporting the hypothesis of a "pleasure deficit" in the brain (Figure 16.17). Later research by Ian Gotlib and colleagues (2004a), using fMRI readings of emotion areas of the brain, showed low levels of neuron responsiveness to both happy and sad scenes, as if the emotion response systems had shut down. This may account for the lack of positive emotionality and the "emptiness" of the depressive emotional experience.

Bipolar disorder, in which depression alternates with less frequent periods of mania, has been studied primarily at the biological level because it appears to have a stronger genetic basis than does unipolar depression (Young & Joffe, 1997). Among both men and women, the lifetime risk of developing a bipolar disorder is just below 1 percent. Yet about 50 percent of patients with bipolar disorder have a parent, grandparent, or child with the disorder (Barondes, 1999; Rubin, 2000). The concordance rate for bipolar disorder is five times higher in

© Purestock/Getty Images

FIGURE 16.17 Women who suffer from postpartum depression can lose the capacity to experience pleasure while interacting with their babies. Reductions in depression can restore the brain's capacity to generate normal levels of pleasure during maternal interactions.

identical twins than in fraternal twins, suggesting a genetic link.

Manic disorders may stem from an *overproduction* of the same neurotransmitters that are underactive in depression. This might explain the symptom picture that is quite the opposite of that seen in depression. Significantly, lithium chloride, the drug most frequently used to calm manic disorders, works by decreasing the activity of these transmitters in the brain's motivational/pleasure activation system (LeMoal, 1999; Robinson, 1997).

Psychological Factors

Biological factors seem to increase vulnerability to certain types of psychological and environmental events that then can trigger the disorders. Other perspectives specify what those events might be.

Personality-based vulnerability. Psychoanalysts Karl Abraham (1911) and Sigmund Freud (1917) believed that early traumatic losses or rejections create vulnerability for later depression by triggering a grieving and rage process that becomes part of the individual's personality (Figure 16.18). Subsequent losses and rejection reactivate the original loss and cause a reaction

© Alan Oddie/Photo Edit, Inc.

FIGURE 16.18 Early catastrophic losses are thought by psychoanalysts to increase vulnerability to later depressive disorders.

not only to the current event, but also to the unresolved loss from the past.

Were he alive today, Freud would surely point to research by British sociologists George Brown and Terrill Harris (1978) to support his theory of early loss. Brown and Harris interviewed women in London and found that the rate of depression among women who had lost their mothers before age 11 and who had also experienced a severe recent loss was almost three times higher than the rate of depression among women who had experienced a similar recent loss but had not lost their mothers before age 11. Other research has shown that death of the father while a child is young is also associated with a greatly increased risk of later depression (Barnes & Prosen, 1985; Bowlby, 2000a).

The humanistic perspective also addresses causes of depression. In attempting to explain the dramatic increase in depression among people born after 1960, Martin Seligman (1989) has suggested that the "me" generation, with its overemphasis on individuality and personal control, has sown the seeds for its own depression. Because people define their self-worth in terms of individual attainment and have lesser commitment to traditional values of family, religion, and the common good, they are likely to react much more strongly to failure, to view negative events as reflecting their own inadequacies, and to experience a sense of meaninglessness in their lives.

Cognitive processes. According to Aaron Beck (1976), depressed people victimize themselves through their own beliefs that they are defective, worthless, and inadequate. They also believe that whatever happens to them is bad, and that negative things will continue happening because of their personal defects (Clark et al., 1989). This **depressive cognitive triad** of negative thoughts concerning (1) the world, (2) oneself, and (3) the future seems to pop into consciousness automatically, and many depressed people report that they cannot control or suppress the negative thoughts (Wenzlaff et al., 1988). Depressed people also tend to recall most of their failures and few of their successes, and they tend to focus much of their attention on their perceived inadequacies (Haaga et al., 1991; Clark et al., 1999). Depressed people also detect pictures of sad faces at lower exposure times and remember them better than do nondepressed people

26. What evidence is there to support the notion that early losses create a risk factor for later depression?

27. How does Seligman explain the dramatic increase in depression among people born after 1960?

28. Describe (a) the cognitive triad and (b) the depressive attributional pattern described by Beck.

(Gotlib et al., 2004b), indicating a perceptual and memory sensitivity to the negative, and they are more likely to distort their memories of negative events. Such thoughts trigger depressed affect.

As noted in the discussion of self-enhancement tendencies in Chapter 11, most people tend to take personal credit for the good outcomes in their lives and to blame their misfortunes on factors outside of themselves, thereby maintaining and enhancing their self-esteem. According to Beck, depressed people do exactly the opposite: They interpret successes or other positive events as being due to factors outside the self, while attributing negative outcomes to personal factors (Figure 16.19). Beck believes that this **depressive attributional pattern** of taking no credit for successes but blaming themselves for failures maintains depressed people's low self-esteem and their belief that they are worthless failures. Quite literally, they can't win, even when they do!

Not surprisingly, low self-esteem operates as a significant risk factor for later depression. This was established in two large-scale longitudinal studies in which over 4000 adults ranging in age from 18 to 88 years were followed for four to nine years. At all age levels, low self-esteem predicted later depressive episodes (Orth et al., 2009).

Another prominent cognitive account of depression, **learned helplessness theory,**

holds that depression occurs when people expect that bad events will occur and that there is nothing they can do to prevent or cope with them (Abramson et al., 1978; Seligman & Isaacowitz, 2000). The depressive attributional pattern just described plays a central role in the learned helplessness model; but learned helplessness theorists take it a step further by specifying what the negative attributions for failure are like. They suggest that chronic and intense depression occurs as the result of negative attributions for failure that are *personal* ("It's all *my* fault"), *stable* ("I'll *always* be this way"), and *global* ("I'm a *total* loser"). Thus, people who attribute negative events in their lives to factors such as low intelligence, physical repulsiveness, or an unlovable personality tend to believe that their personal defects will render them helpless to avoid negative events in the future, and therefore they are at significantly greater risk of depression.

Mania is dominated by quite another pattern of thinking. The person in a manic state is expansive, optimistic, and excited—all emotions linked with the behavioural activation system. In a longitudinal study, Lauren Alloy and colleagues (2009) compared 195 people with bipolar disorder with a demographically matched group of persons without bipolar disorder. They found that cognitions involving autonomy (a focus on individualistic achievement and self-sufficiency), high performance standards ("A person should do well at everything"), and a tendency toward self-criticism when goals are not obtained predicted not only bipolar group membership but also the occurrence of future hypomanic episodes.

Learning and environmental factors. Peter Lewinsohn and his colleagues (1985) believe that depression is usually triggered by a loss, some other punishing event, or by a drastic decrease in the amount of positive reinforcement that the person receives from her or his environment (Figure 16.20). As the depression begins to take hold, people stop performing behaviours that previously provided reinforcement, such as hobbies and socializing. Depressed people also tend to generate additional negative life events through their negative moods, pessimism, and reduced functioning (Harkness & Stewart, 2009). Moreover, depressed people tend to make those who come

29. According to learned helplessness theory, what kinds of attributions trigger depression?

30. How does Lewinsohn's learning theory explain the spiralling downward course that occurs in severe depression?

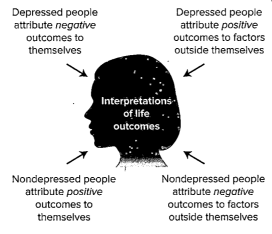

Depressive attributional pattern

Depressed people attribute *negative* outcomes to themselves

Depressed people attribute *positive* outcomes to factors outside themselves

Interpretations of life outcomes

Nondepressed people attribute *positive* outcomes to themselves

Nondepressed people attribute *negative* outcomes to factors outside themselves

Self-enhancement attributional pattern (nondepressed people)

FIGURE 16.19 Cognitive theorists believe that the attributional patterns of depressed people are the opposite of the self-enhancing patterns that characterize nondepressed people.

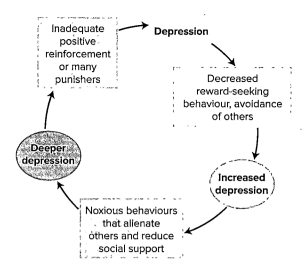

FIGURE 16.20 Lewinsohn's behavioural model of depression focuses on the environmental causes and effects of depression. Depression results from loss of positive reinforcement and produces further decline in reinforcement and social support in a vicious cycle.

in contact with them feel anxious, depressed, and hostile (Joiner & Coyne, 1999). Eventually, these other people begin to lose patience, failing to understand why the person doesn't "snap out of it." This diminishes social support still further and may eventually cause depressed people to be abandoned by those who are most important to them (Nezlek et al., 2000). Longitudinal studies show that reductions in social support are a good predictor of subsequent depression (Burton et al., 2004).

Behavioural theorists believe that to begin feeling better, depressed people must break this vicious cycle by initially forcing themselves to engage in behaviours that are likely to produce some degree of pleasure. Eventually, positive reinforcement produced by this process of *behavioural activation* will begin to counteract the depressive affect, undermine the sense of hopelessness that characterizes depression, and increase feelings of personal control over the environment (Martell et al., 2004).

Environmental factors may also help to explain why depression tends to run in families. Constance Hammen (1991) studied the family histories of depressed people and concluded that children of depressed parents often experience poor parenting and many stressful experiences as they grow up. As a result, they may fail to develop good coping skills

and a positive self-concept. They therefore are vulnerable later in life to stressful events that can trigger depressive reactions. This conclusion is supported by findings that children of depressed parents exhibit a significantly higher incidence of depression and other disorders as adolescents and young adults (Lieb et al., 2002; Halligan et al., 2007).

Sociocultural Factors

Although depression is found in virtually all cultures, its prevalence, symptom pattern, and causes reflect cultural variation (Lopez & Guarnaccia, 2000). For example, compared with Western nations, the prevalence of depressive disorders is far lower in Hong Kong and Taiwan, where strong connections to family and other groups help to reduce the negative impact of loss and disappointments and provide strong social support when they occur (Tseng et al., 1990).

Cultural factors also can affect the ways in which depression is manifested. Feelings of guilt and personal inadequacy seem to predominate in North American and western European countries, whereas somatic symptoms of fatigue, loss of appetite, and sleep difficulties are more often reported in Latin, Chinese, and African cultures (Manson, 1994).

Finally, cultural factors may influence who develops depression. As noted earlier, women are about twice as likely as men to report feeling depressed in technologically advanced countries such as Canada, the United States, and other Western nations (Keyes & Goodman, 2006). Yet this sex difference is not found in developing countries (Culbertson, 1997; Nolen-Hoeksema, 1990). In the United States, White Americans are approximately 50 percent more likely than are Black Americans to suffer from depression in their lifetimes, but Black Americans typically experience more severe and disabling symptoms than do White Americans (Williams et al., 2007). At present, we do not know why these patterns occur, but attempts are under way to learn more about how the cultural environment influences the development of depression.

At one time or another, many depressed people consider suicide as a way to escape from the unhappiness of their lives. This chapter's *Applications* feature examines suicide, its causes, and what can be done to prevent this tragic event.

31. What is the relation between depression and suicide? What are the major motives and risk factors for suicide? Describe four practical guidelines for helping a suicidal person.

32. How are cultural factors related to the prevalence, manifestation, and sex differences in depression?

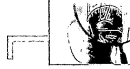

Applications

UNDERSTANDING AND PREVENTING SUICIDE

Suicide is defined as the willful taking of one's own life. The World Health Organization estimates that nearly 500000 people worldwide commit suicide annually, about 1.4 per minute. Nearly 4000 suicides a year are recorded in Canada, and there are up to 100 times as many attempts. Suicide is the second most common cause of death, surpassed only by accidents, for those in the 15- to 24-year-old age bracket (Statistics Canada, 2013). In North America, suicide rates for 15- to 24-year-olds tripled between 1960 and 1992, but have fallen off in recent years (National Center for Health Statistics, 2009; Figure 16.21). In Canada, the suicide rate for 15- to 19-year-olds (11.5 per 100000 population) is somewhat lower than the rate for adults (15.8 per 100000 population; Statistics Canada, 2013). In a survey of students in Grades 7–12, a British Columbia study found that 34 percent knew someone who had attempted suicide and 7 percent had tried themselves (Mood Disorders Society of Canada, 2009).

Women make about three times as many suicide attempts as men, but men are four times more likely to actually kill themselves (Canadian Mental Health Association, 2016; National Institute of Mental Health, 2009). These differences may be due to (1) a higher incidence of depression in women and (2) men's choice of more lethal methods, such as shooting themselves or jumping off buildings. The suicide rate for both men and women is higher among those who have been divorced or widowed. Women who commit suicide have a relatively greater tendency to be motivated by failure in love relationships, whereas men have a greater tendency to be motivated by failure in their occupations (Shneidman, 1976). A history of sexual or physical abuse significantly increases the likelihood of later

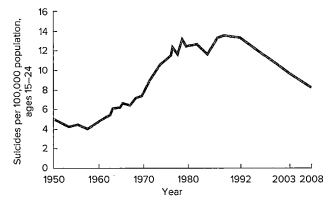

FIGURE 16.21 Suicide rate per 100 000 persons aged 15 to 24, from 1950 to 2008.

Source: Data from National Center for Health Statistics. (2009). *Health in America,* 2008. Hyattsville, MD: Author.

suicide attempts (Fergusson & Lynskey, 1997; Garnefski & Arends, 1998).

Depression, whether unipolar or bipolar, is one of the strongest predictors of suicide (Goldston et al., 2006; Ostacher & Eidelman, 2006). About 15 percent of clinically depressed individuals eventually will kill themselves, a rate that is 22 to 36 times higher than the suicide rate for the general population. An estimated 80 percent of suicidal people are significantly depressed (Yen et al., 2003). It is noteworthy, however, that suicide does not usually occur when depression is deepest. Instead, suicide often occurs unexpectedly as a depressed (or bipolar) person seems to be emerging from depression and feeling better. The lifting of depression may provide the energy needed to complete the suicidal act, without affecting the person's underlying sense of hopelessness and despair.

Motives for Suicide

There appear to be two fundamental motivations for suicide: the desire to end one's life and the desire to manipulate and coerce other people into doing what the suicidal person wants (Beck et al., 1979). Those who wish to end their lives basically have given up. They see no other way to deal with intolerable emotional distress, and in death they see an end to their problems. In one report, 56 percent of suicide attempts were classified as having been motivated by the desire to die (Beck, 1976). These attempts were accompanied by high levels of depression and hopelessness, and they tended to be more lethal than other suicide attempts.

The second primary motivation for suicide is manipulation of others. Many *parasuicides* (suicide attempts that do not end in death) are cries for help or attempts to coerce people into meeting one's needs. Trying to prevent a lover from ending a relationship or trying to dramatize one's suffering are manipulative motives. Manipulative suicide attempters tend to use less lethal means (such as drug overdoses or wrist-slashing) and to make sure help is available. In the report cited earlier (Beck, 1976), 13 percent of the suicide attempts were classified as manipulative. The remaining 31 percent combined the two types of motivation. Other contributors to suicidal ideation and behaviour are a desire to no longer be a burden to others and a sense of social alienation (Joiner et al., 2009). A small minority of suicides result from altruistic decisions to sacrifice one's life for the survival of others. Examples are the soldier who dives on a hand grenade to save comrades or a mother who elects to give birth rather than aborting her baby, knowing that she will die in the process.

Warning Signs for Suicide

The best predictor of suicide attempts in both men and women is a verbal or behavioural threat to commit suicide, and such threats should always be taken seriously. One of

continued

the most destructive myths about suicide is that people who talk openly about suicide don't actually carry out the act. Yet research shows that a high proportion of suicide attempts—perhaps 80 percent—are preceded by some kind of warning (Bagley & Ramsay, 1997; Chiles & Strossahl, 1995). Sometimes the warning is an explicit statement of intent, such as "I don't want to go on living" or "I won't be a burden much longer." Other times, the warnings are more subtle, as when a person expresses hopelessness about the future, withdraws from others or favourite activities, gives away treasured possessions, or takes unusual risks. Other important risk factors are a history of previous suicide attempts and a detailed plan that involves a lethal method (Chiles & Strosahl, 1995; Shneidman, 1998). Substance use and abuse also increase suicide risk (Yen et al., 2003).

Suicide Prevention

Much has been learned about the dynamics and prevention of suicide as a result of scientific research. These findings provide guidelines for preventing this tragic answer to life's problems. For example, another myth about suicide is that broaching the topic with a potentially suicidal person may prompt the person to carry out the act. In truth, the best first step if you suspect that someone may be suicidal is to ask the person directly whether he or she is considering suicide: "Have you thought about hurting yourself or ending your life?" If the person responds affirmatively, try to find out whether or not he or she has a plan or a timetable in mind. Do not be hesitant to approach the person. *Diffusion of responsibility* (discussed in Chapters 2 and 13) could result in your assuming that someone else is helping

a potentially suicidal person, when in fact no one is (Kalafat et al., 1993). Your ultimate goal should be to help the person to receive assistance from a qualified professional as soon as possible, not to treat the person yourself. Nonetheless, you can take some immediate steps that may be helpful.

Many suicidal people feel alone in their misery. It is important to provide social support and empathy at this critical juncture. An expression of genuine concern can pave the way for other potentially helpful interventions (Barnett & Porter, 1998). For example, a frank discussion of the problem that is foremost in the person's life can be helpful. Suicidal people often feel totally overwhelmed by life, and focusing on a specific problem may help the person realize that it is not unsolvable and need not cloud his or her total perception of life.

When people are distressed and hopeless, their time orientation tends to narrow, and they have difficulty seeing beyond their current distress. Try to help the person see his or her present situation within a wider time perspective and to consider positive possibilities that might exist in the future. In particular, discuss reasons for continuing to live, and focus on any doubts the person might have about electing suicide. For example, if the person indicates that his or her family will suffer greatly from the suicide, adopt this as one of your arguments for a different solution to the problem. Many suicidal people would like to feel that they do not have to commit suicide. Capitalize on such feelings.

If a person is suicidal, stay with him or her and seek professional assistance. Most cities have suicide prevention centres that offer 24-hour services, including telephone and direct counselling. These centres usually are listed under *suicide* or *crisis* in the phone book.

Review

- Mood disorders include several depressive disorders and bipolar disorder, in which intermittent periods of mania (intense mood and behaviour activation) occur. Depression has four sets of symptoms: emotional, cognitive, motivational, and somatic. The symptoms of negative emotions and thoughts, loss of motivation, and behavioural slowness are reversed in mania.

- Both genetic and neurochemical factors have been linked to depression. One prominent biochemical theory links depression to an underactivity of neurotransmitters (norepinephrine, dopamine, and serotonin) that activate brain areas involved in pleasure and positive motivation. Drugs that relieve depression increase the activity of these transmitters. Bipolar disorder seems to have an even stronger genetic component than unipolar depression does.

- Psychoanalytic theorists view depression as a long-term consequence of traumatic losses and rejections early in life that create a personality vulnerability pattern.

- Cognitive theorists emphasize the role of negative beliefs about the self, the world, and the future (the depressive triad) and describe a depressive attributional pattern in which negative outcomes are attributed to personal causes and successes to situational causes. Seligman's theory of learned helplessness suggests that attributing negative outcomes to personal, stable, and global causes fosters depression.

- The behavioural approach focuses on the vicious cycle in which depression-induced inactivity and aversive behaviours reduce reinforcement from the environment and thereby increase depression still further.

- Manipulation and a desire to escape distress are the two major motives for suicide. The risk for suicide increases if the person is depressed and has a lethal plan and a past history of parasuicide.

Levels of Analysis — Anxiety and Mood Disorders

Although the core emotions in the anxiety and mood disorders seem quite different, they tend to co-occur in many people. Typical results were obtained in a study of 1127 outpatients who had either anxiety or mood disorder diagnoses. Incidence results indicated that 55 percent of the patients had both anxiety and depression symptoms at the time of assessment, a figure that rose to 76 percent when lifetime prevalence was studied (Brown et al., 2001). This high level of comorbidity has led some clinical scientists to suspect that common causal factors underlie both disorders, with different combinations resulting in either anxiety or depression, or both. One such theory has been proposed by David Barlow (2002; Suarez et al., 2009). Termed the *triple vulnerability model of emotional disorders,* it draws on the biological, psychological, and environmental levels of analysis.

ENVIRONMENTAL

- Environmental life events that involve traumatic conditioning of fear and anxiety and severe losses that trigger depression prime people for later episodes of anxiety and depression.
- Another environmental vulnerability factor is growing up with depressed parents or with parents who indoctrinate in children the message that the world is a dangerous place that one is powerless to cope with.
- Negative life events that might not overwhelm a person without the triple vulnerability factors can trigger an anxiety or affective disorder in a vulnerable person.

BIOLOGICAL

- Biological vulnerability comes from genetic factors that favour ascendancy of the BIS over the BAS. There is a well-established heritability of 0.30 to 0.50 percent in BIS sensitivity, priming BIS-sensitive people to experience anxiety and depression in response to threat or loss.
- An additional (and probably related) factor is a highly reactive sympathetic nervous system that overreacts to threat and increases the ease with which conditioned anxiety responses can be established.

PSYCHOLOGICAL

- Psychological vulnerability is related to cognitive factors and coping strategies. The development of irrational ideas that generate depression or anxiety create a psychological world that primes people for emotional disorders.
- Likewise, ineffective coping strategies such as avoidance, blaming others, and wishful thinking, combined with low levels of self-efficacy that inhibits use of more adaptive problem-focused and social-support coping, help to create negative life events and interfere with acting adaptively.

The triple vulnerability model is promising because it accounts for much of what we know about the causal factors in anxiety. What implications does it have for treating anxiety disorders? We will describe treatment approaches to anxiety in Chapter 17.

FIGURE 16.22

SOMATIC SYMPTOM DISORDERS

33. Describe the varieties of somatic symptom disorder. What causal factors might be involved in these disorders?

Somatic symptom disorders (formerly known as **somatoform disorders**) involve physical complaints or disabilities that suggest a medical problem, but which have no known biological cause and are not produced voluntarily by the person (Kirmayer & Looper, 2007). People who become unduly alarmed about any physical symptom they detect and are convinced that they have or are about to have a serious illness used to diagnosed with hypochondriasis, but in the DSM-5, the likely diagnosis would be illness anxiety disorder. People with **pain disorder** experience intense pain that either is out of proportion to whatever medical condition they have or for which no physical basis can be found. Somatic symptom disorders differ from *psychophysiological disorders,* in which psychological factors cause or contribute to a real medical condition, such as an ulcer, asthma, hypertension (chronic high blood pressure), or a cardiac problem. In peptic ulcers, for example, a stress-produced outpouring of peptic acid into the stomach produces an actual lesion in the stomach wall. The resulting pain is therefore caused by the actual physical damage. In a somatic symptom disorder, no physical basis for the pain would be found.

Perhaps the most fascinating of the somatoform disorders is **functional neurological** symptom disorder (known as **conversion disorder** in the DSM-IV-TR), in which serious neurological symptoms, such as paralysis, loss of sensation, or blindness suddenly occur. In such cases, electrophysiological recordings and brain imaging indicate that sensory and motor pathways in the brain are intact (Black et al., 2004). People with conversion disorders often exhibit *la belle indifference,* a strange lack of concern about their symptom and its implications (Pajer, 2000a). In some cases, the complaint itself is physiologically impossible. An example is the so-called "glove anaesthesia" in which a person loses all sensation below the wrist. As Figure 16.23 shows, the hand is served by nerves that also provide sensory input above the hand, making glove anaesthesia anatomically impossible.

Functional neurological symptom disorders are relatively rare, occurring in about three in 1000 North Americans during peacetime (American Psychiatric Association, 1994), but such disorders occur more frequently under wartime conditions (Slavney, 1990). Thus, a soldier about to return to the trauma of combat may suddenly develop blindness or paralysis for which no physical cause can be found.

Although "psychogenic blindness" is quite rare in the general population, researchers have discovered the largest known civilian group of people in the world having trauma-induced blindness. They are Cambodian refugees who escaped from their country and settled in Long Beach, California. These survivors of the "killing fields" of Cambodia were subjected to unspeakable horror at the hands of the Khmer Rouge in the years following the Vietnam War (Cooke, 1991). More than 150 of them are functionally blind, even though their eyes appear intact and electrophysiological monitoring shows that visual stimuli "register" in their visual cortex (Figure 16.24). The doctors who studied this remarkable group are convinced that they are not faking blindness. Many of the victims reported that their blindness occurred suddenly after witnessing traumatic scenes of murder. Were the sights from the outer world so painful that their visual systems shut down involuntarily? The following intriguing question has yet to be answered: How might cultural factors have affected the development of this response to trauma?

To Freud, such symptoms were a symbolic expression of an underlying conflict that aroused so much anxiety that the ego kept the conflict in the unconscious by converting the anxiety into a physical symptom that in some way symbolized the conflict. Contemporary psychodynamic theorists continue to accept this explanation (Fisher & Greenberg, 1996). In one of Freud's cases, a young woman who was forced to take care of her hostile, verbally abusive, and unappreciative father suddenly developed paralysis in her arm. According to Freud, this occurred when her repressed hostile impulses threatened to break through and cause her to strike him by using that arm (Freud, 1935).

A predisposition to somatic symptom disorders may involve a combination of biological and psychological vulnerabilities (e.g., smaller pituitary gland volume, Atmaca et al., 2016). Somatic symptom disorders tend to run

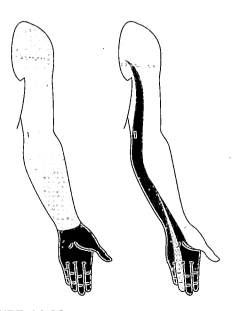

FIGURE 16.23 Glove anaesthesia is a conversion disorder in which all feeling is lost below the wrist. The skin areas served by nerves in the arm make this symptom physiologically impossible.

© Steve Smith

FIGURE 16.24 A physician examines one of the Cambodian refugees who appear to be suffering from psychologically induced blindness. There is nothing wrong with their eyes, but they cannot see.

Strasburger and Waldvogel (2015) report that a blind woman spontaneously regained her eyesight when she switched into one of her alters. Visual areas in the cortex remained inactive when she was blind and then recovered when she could see.

As dramatic as these physiological differences between DID alters might appear, they are not universally accepted by critics, who correctly point out that many of the observations are based on uncontrolled case studies. Could the average person asked to role-play separate personalities exhibit such differences as well? Indeed, there is some evidence that EEG differences can be produced by such role-playing in normal individuals (Coons et al., 1982), but so far none of the other more exotic physiological phenomena just described have been shown in role-playing controls (Gleaves, 1996). In some studies, such as the visual acuity and eye muscle study just described, role players have been unable to produce the responses shown by DID patients. In addition, a recent study by Reinders et al. (2012) demonstrates that role-playing controls could not mimic differences in fMRI patterns or in cerebral blood flow exhibited by individuals with DID. Nor are they able to "fake" the personality profiles of patients with DID (Brand & Chasson, 2015). Nonetheless, it is clear that additional controlled studies of physiological alterations are needed.

Some critics consider the notion of multiple personalities to be nothing more than science fiction, and they dispute the existence of DID as a valid clinical disorder (Beahrs, 1994; Spanos, 1994; Piper & Mersky, 2004). Troubling to many psychologists and legal experts is a tendency for some people who have committed serious crimes to disclaim personal responsibility on the grounds that they are DID victims and that one of the alternative personalities committed the crime (Beahrs, 1994). Other critics wonder if DID is, in reality, a therapist-produced phenomenon, as suggested earlier in this chapter.

In some instances, clients have filed lawsuits against therapists, charging them with creating the disorder in them. In one bizarre case, a Wisconsin woman and her insurance company successfully sued a psychiatrist who used hypnosis to allegedly unearth 120 different personalities in her, including Satan and a duck, and then billed the insurance company at the higher group therapy rate on the grounds that he was treating multiple people! The woman charged the therapist with implanting false memories of sexual abuse, rape, being pushed into an open grave, and aborting a baby. She maintained that she had never had any of the memories before beginning therapy and that the false memories caused nightmares, flashbacks, suicidal impulses, and, eventually, the need for hospitalization (*Associated Press*, December 12, 1997). Such extreme instances, which by no means typify the efforts of ethical therapists to help their clients, serve to fuel the concerns of critics.

Is DID real? Suppose it were to be convincingly demonstrated in experimental studies that role playing by average people can produce all the DID phenomena described at the beginning of this feature. Would this prove that true dissociation does not occur in *any* of the cases seen by mental-health workers? Not at all, supporters maintain, any more than a compelling depiction of a schizophrenic person by a skilled actor such as Jack Nicholson would prove that all cases of schizophrenia involve nothing more than acting. The controversy that swirls around DID may help to fuel continued investigation of the cognitive and physiological phenomena that are seen in DID. Such research may advance our understanding of factors that can produce dramatic alterations in memory, physiological responses, and behaviour.

Visual evoked potentials
Average of five separate trials

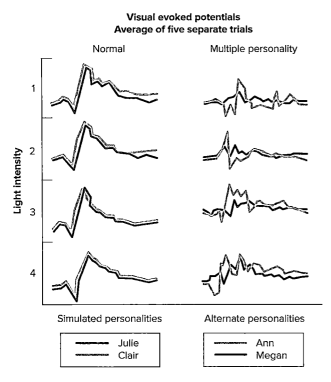

FIGURE 16.25 Comparisons of evoked potentials of a DID patient (Ann and her alternate personality, Megan) and a control participant (Julie) simulating a second personality (Clair) to four levels of visual stimulation. The DID patient's EEG records differed more from each other.

Source: Adapted from Putnam, F.W. (1984). The psychophysiologic investigation of multiple personality disorder: A review. *Psychiatric Clinics of North America, 7*, 31–39.

- Somatic symptom disorders involve physical complaints that do not have a physiological explanation. They include pain disorders, and conversion disorders in which a physical symptom or disability occurs in the absence of physical pathology.

- Familial similarities in somatic symptom disorders may have a biological basis, or they may be the result of environmental shaping through attention and sympathy. Patients with somatic symptom disorder may be highly vigilant and reactive to somatic symptoms. Such disorders tend to occur with greater frequency in cultures that discourage open expression of negative emotions.

- Dissociative disorders involve losses of memory and personal identity. The major dissociative disorders are dissociative amnesia, dissociative fugue, and dissociative identity disorder (DID).

- The trauma-dissociation theory holds that DID emerges when children dissociate to defend themselves from severe physical or sexual abuse. This model has been challenged by other theorists who believe that multiple personalities result from role immersion and therapist suggestion.

SCHIZOPHRENIA

Of all the psychological disorders, schizophrenia is the most serious and, in many ways, the most puzzling and difficult to treat (Hogarty, 2003; McKenna, 2007). Despite many theories of schizophrenia and thousands of research studies, a complete understanding of this disorder continues to elude us.

Schizophrenia is a psychotic disorder that involves severe disturbances in thinking, speech, perception, emotion, and behaviour (Herz & Marder, 2002). The term *schizophrenia* was introduced by the Swiss psychiatrist Eugen Bleuler in 1911. Literally, the term means "split mind," which often has led people to confuse schizophrenia with DID or with a Dr. Jekyll–Mr. Hyde phenomenon. But multiple personality is not what Bleuler had in mind when he coined the term. Instead, Bleuler intended to suggest that certain psychological functions, such as thought, language, and emotion, which are joined together in normal people, are somehow split apart or disconnected in schizophrenia. Schizophrenia affects approximately 1 percent of the population in Canada (Schizophrenia Society of Canada, 2013)—slightly higher than reported for some other countries (Dealberto, 2013).

Characteristics of Schizophrenia

A diagnosis of schizophrenia requires evidence that a person misinterprets reality and exhibits disordered attention, thought, or perception. In addition, withdrawal from social interaction is common, communication is strange or inappropriate, personal grooming may be neglected, and behaviour may become disorganized (American Psychiatric Association, 2000, 2013; Paris, 2013).

The schizophrenic thought disorder sometimes includes delusions (Nadelson & Reinburg, 1999). **Delusions** are false beliefs that are sustained in the face of evidence that normally would be sufficient to destroy them. A schizophrenic person may believe that his brain is being turned to glass by ray guns operated by his enemies from outer space or that Jesus Christ is a special agent of his. The first is a *delusion of persecution*, the second a *delusion of grandeur*.

Several aspects of thought disorder were described by a schizophrenic during a period of recovery:

> The most wearing aspect of schizophrenia is the fierce battle that goes on inside my head in which conflicts become unresolvable. I am so ambivalent that my mind can divide on a subject, and those two parts subdivide over and over until my mind feels like it is in pieces, and I am totally disorganized. At other times, I feel like I am trapped inside my head, banging against its walls, trying desperately to escape while my lips can utter only nonsense. (*New York Times*, March 18, 1986, p. C12)

Perceptual disorganization and disordered thought become more pronounced as people progress into a schizophrenic condition (McKenna & Oh, 2003). Unwanted thoughts constantly intrude into consciousness (Morrison, 2006). What the world might come to look like from inside the schizophrenic mind is illustrated in art by patients during periods

37. What is meant by the term *schizophrenia?* What are the major cognitive, behavioural, emotional, and perceptual features of these disorders?

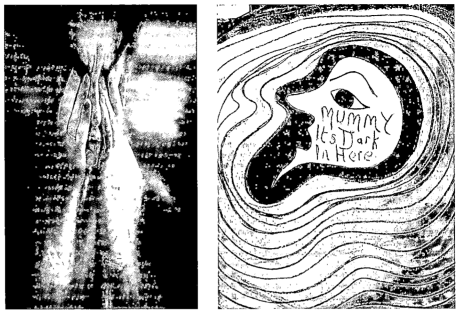

(left): © Tom and Dee Ann McCarthy/Corbis; (right): © Bettman/Corbis

FIGURE 16.26 (a) Patients diagnosed with schizophrenia are tormented by bizarre and intrusive thoughts and images. (b) This picture, drawn by a patient diagnosed with schizophrenia, may offer insights into his subjective world.

of disturbance (Figure 16.26). Some experience **hallucinations**—false perceptions that have a compelling sense of reality. Auditory hallucinations (typically voices speaking to the patient) are most common, although visual and tactile hallucinations may also occur. This patient describes his hallucinations:

> Recently, my mind has played tricks on me, creating The People inside my head who sometimes come out to haunt me and torment me. They surround me in rooms, hide behind trees and under the snow outside. They taunt me and scream at me and devise plans to break my spirit. The voices come and go, but The People are always there, always real. (*New York Times*, March 18, 1986, p. C12)

The language of schizophrenic patients is often disorganized and can contain strange words:

> I am here from a foreign university . . . and you have to have a "plausity" of all acts of amendment to go through for the children's code . . . and it is no mental disturbance or "putenance"... it is an "amorition" law ... it is like their "privatilinia." (Vetter, 1969, p. 189)

Patients' language sometimes contains word associations that are based on rhymes or other associations rather than meaning. Consider the following conversation between a psychologist and a hospitalized schizophrenic:

After two weeks, the psychologist said to him: "As you say, you are wired precisely wrong. But why won't you let me see the diagram?" Carl answered: "Never, ever will you find the lever, the eternalever that will sever me forever with my real, seal, deal, heel. It is not on my shoe, not even on the sole. It walks away." (Rosenhan & Seligman, 1989, p. 369)

Emotions can be affected in a number of ways. Many people with schizophrenia have *blunted affect*, manifesting less sadness, joy, and anger than most people. Others have *flat affect*, showing almost no emotion at all. Their voices are monotonous, their faces impassive. *Inappropriate affect* can also occur, as in the following case:

> The psychologist noted that Carl "smiles when he is uncomfortable, and smiles more when in pain. He cries during television comedies. He seems angry when justice is done, frightened when someone compliments him, and roars with laughter on reading that a young child was burned in a tragic fire. (Rosenhan & Seligman, 1989, p. 369)

Subtypes of Schizophrenia

Schizophrenia has cognitive, emotional, and behavioural facets that can vary widely from case to case. The DSM-IV-TR differentiated among four major subtypes of schizophrenia: paranoid, disorganized, catatonic, and undifferentiated. However, these subtypes have been eliminated in the DSM-5, due to lack of reliability in validity in diagnosis. A diagnosis of catatonia may still be given, but it may be in the context of schizophrenia, depression, bipolar disorder, or some other disorder. Individuals with catatonia show striking motor disturbances, ranging from muscular rigidity to random or repetitive movements. Catatonics sometimes alternate between stupor-ousstates in which they seem oblivious to reality and agitated excitement during which they can be dangerous to others. While in a stuporous state, they may exhibit a *waxy flexibility* in which their limbs can be moulded by another person into grotesque positions that they will then maintain for hours (Figure 16.27).

In addition to a formal DSM-5 classification of schizophrenia, many mental-health workers and researchers categorize schizophrenic reactions into two main categories on the basis of two classes of symptoms. **Type I schizophrenia** is characterized by a predominance of **positive symptoms,** such as delusions, hallucinations, and disordered speech and thinking. These symptoms are called *positive* because they represent added pathological extremes of normal processes. **Type II schizophrenia** features **negative symptoms**—an absence of normal reactions— such as lack of emotional expression, loss of motivation, and an absence of normal speech (Herz & Marder, 2002).

The distinction between positive and negative symptom subtypes seems to be an important one. Researchers have found differences in brain function between schizophrenics having positive symptoms and those with primarily negative symptoms (Gur et al., 1998; Zakzanis, 1998). Negative symptoms are likely to be associated with a long history of poor functioning prior to hospitalization and with a poor outcome following treatment (McGlaskan & Fenton, 1992). In contrast, positive symptoms are associated with good functioning prior to breakdown and a better prognosis for eventual recovery, particularly if the symptoms came on suddenly and were preceded by a history of relatively good adjustment (Fenton & McGlaskan, 1991a, 1991b).

Schizophrenia afflicts only 1 to 2 percent of the population worldwide, yet schizophrenic patients occupy about half of all psychiatric hospital beds (Satcher, 1999). Many others barely function as homeless "street people" in large cities (Herman et al., 1998). About 10 percent of people with schizophrenia remain permanently impaired, and 65 percent show intermittent periods of normal functioning. The other 25 percent recover from the disorder (American Psychiatric Association, 2000). Schizophrenia affects equal numbers of males and females, but it appears earlier in males, frequently between the ages of 15 and 30 (Jeste & Heaton, 1994). The estimated cost (both direct and indirect) to the Canadian economy from schizophrenia is about $6.85 billion per year (Mood Disorders Society of Canada, 2009).

38. Distinguish between Type I and Type II schizophrenia. How are positive and negative symptoms related to past history and future prognosis?

Causal Factors in Schizophrenia

Because of the seriousness of the disorder and the many years of anguish and incapacitation that its victims are likely to experience, schizophrenia is perhaps the most widely researched of the psychological disorders. There is a growing consensus that schizophrenia results from a biologically based vulnerability factor that is set into motion by psychological and environmental events (Gottesman, 1991; Herz & Marder, 2002; McGuffin et al., 2005).

Biological Factors

Biological factors are prominently involved in schizophrenia (Abi-Dargham & Guillin, 2007). Genetic, biochemical, and brain factors have been investigated.

Genetic predisposition. Strong evidence exists for a genetic predisposition to schizophrenia, though the specific genes involved and their roles in creating the disposition are still unknown (Benes, 2010; Hall et al., 2007; McGuffin et al., 2005). As Figure 16.28 shows,

39. Describe the evidence for genetic and neurological factors in schizophrenia

FIGURE 16.27 The woman pictured here exhibits catatonic rigidity. She might hold this position for several hours.

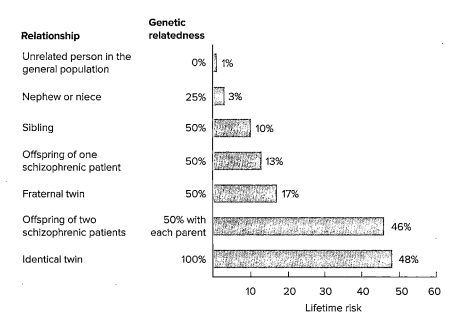

Relationship	Genetic relatedness		Lifetime risk
Unrelated person in the general population	0%		1%
Nephew or niece	25%		3%
Sibling	50%		10%
Offspring of one schizophrenic patient	50%		13%
Fraternal twin	50%		17%
Offspring of two schizophrenic patients	50% with each parent		46%
Identical twin	100%		48%

10   20   30   40   50   60
Lifetime risk

FIGURE 16.28 The degree of risk for developing schizophrenia in one's lifetime correlates highly with the degree of genetic relationship with someone who has that disorder. These data summarize the results of 40 concordance studies conducted in many countries.

Source: Based on data from Gottesman, I.I. (1991). *Schizophrenia genesis: The origins of madness.* New York, NY: W.H. Freeman.

the closer the biological relationship to a person diagnosed with schizophrenia, the greater the risk for developing the disorder during one's lifetime (Gottesman, 1991). Twin studies show that identical twins have higher concordance rates than fraternal twins, and adoption studies show much higher concordance with biological parents than with adoptive parents (Jang, 2005; Kety, 1988). But, again, genetics do not by themselves account for the development of schizophrenia. If they did, the concordance rate in identical twins would be 100 percent, not 48 percent (Ingraham & Kety, 2000).

Brain abnormalities. Brain scans have indicated a number of structural abnormalities in the brains of schizophrenic patients (Figure 16.29). According to the neurodegenerative hypothesis, destruction of neural tissue can cause schizophrenia (Weinberger & McClure, 2002). MRI studies have shown mild to moderate *brain atrophy*, a general loss or deterioration of neurons in the cerebral cortex and limbic system, together with enlarged ventricles (cavities that contain cerebrospinal fluid; Figure 16.29). The atrophy is centred in brain regions that influence cognitive processes and emotion, which may help to

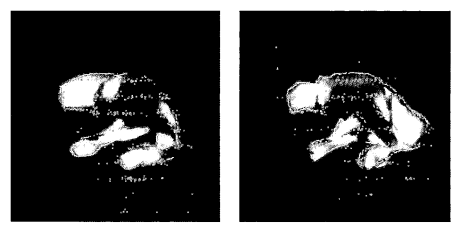

(both): © Nancy C. Andreason/The National Institute of Mental Health

FIGURE 16.29 Schizophrenia and the brain. One difference between the brains of schizophrenics and non-schizophrenics is enlarged ventricles (the butterfly-shaped spaces seen in the middle of the MRIs) in the schizophrenic brain (bottom). Findings like these support the position that brain abnormalities play a role in schizophrenia.

explain the thought disorders and inappropriate emotions that are seen in such patients. Likewise, MRI images of the thalamus, which collects and routes sensory input to various parts of the brain, reveal abnormalities (Williamson, 2006). This may help to account for the disordered attention and perception reported by schizophrenic patients whose cerebral cortex may be getting garbled or unfiltered information from the thalamus (Andreason et al., 1994). All these structural differences are more common in patients who exhibit the negative-symptom pattern (Herz & Marder, 2002). As we have seen, these patients have a poorer chance of recovery than those with the positive-symptom pattern. In addition, cannabis use by males during adolescence can increase the risk for schizophrenia through a mechanism that effectively thins cortical tissue (French et al., 2015).

Biochemical factors. Dopamine, a major excitatory transmitter substance, may play a key role in schizophrenia. The **dopamine hypothesis** states that the symptoms of schizophrenia—particularly positive symptoms—are produced by overactivity of the dopamine system in areas of the brain that regulate emotional expression, motivated behaviour, and cognitive functioning (Heinrichs, 2001; Howes & Kapur, 2009). People diagnosed with schizophrenia have more dopamine receptors on neuron membranes than do non-schizophrenics, and these receptors seem to be overreactive to dopamine stimulation (Black et al., 1988; Wong et al., 1986). Additional support comes from the finding that the effectiveness of antipsychotic drugs used to treat schizophrenia is directly related to their effectiveness in reducing dopamine-produced synaptic activity (Creese et al., 1976; Green, 1997). Other neurotransmitter systems are probably involved in this complex disorder as well. But dopamine is not the whole story, and recent research has shown that the dopamine system is part of a much larger and complex network in which a deficiency of neural input from cortical areas also plays a role (Benes, 2009).

The biological findings concerning schizophrenia are intriguing. What is not clear is whether they cause the disorder or are caused by it. Future research is almost certain to reveal other biological bases for the complex disorders of schizophrenia.

Psychological Factors

Freud and other psychoanalytic thinkers viewed schizophrenia as a retreat from unbearable stress and conflict. For Freud, schizophrenia represented an extreme example of the defence mechanism of **regression,** in which a person retreats to an earlier and more secure (even infantile) stage of psychosocial development in the face of overwhelming anxiety. Other psychodynamic thinkers, focusing on the interpersonal withdrawal that is an important feature of schizophrenia, view the disorder as a retreat from an interpersonal world that has become too stressful to deal with. Although Freud's regression explanation has not received much direct research support (Fisher & Greenberg, 1996), the belief that life stress is a causal factor is generally accepted today (Airey & Sodhi, 2007; Crook & Copolov, 2000).

Some cognitive theorists believe that schizophrenics have a defect in the attentional mechanism that filters out irrelevant stimuli, so that they are overwhelmed by both internal and external stimuli. Thus, sensory input becomes a chaotic flood, and irrelevant thoughts and images flash into consciousness. The stimulus overload produces distractibility, thought disorganization, and the sense of being overwhelmed by disconnected thoughts and ideas. As one schizophrenic noted, "Everything seems to come pouring in at once . . . I can't seem to keep anything out" (Carson et al., 1988, p. 329). The recent MRI findings of thalamic abnormalities just described may help to explain how this stimulus overload could occur through malfunction of the brain's "switchboard." Schizophrenic thought processes may be linked to deficits in the executive functions of the frontal lobe (Kerns & Berenbaum, 2002, 2003). In one study, schizophrenic patients pressed a key to signal the experimenter when they were hearing voices or experiencing a strange visual experience. PET scans performed at these times showed that the auditory or visual areas of the cortex were highly active, but there was no activity in the prefrontal cortex, whose functioning helps us distinguish reality from fantasy (Silbersweig et al., 1995).

Environmental Factors

Stressful life events seem to play an important role in the emergence of schizophrenic behaviour (McKenna, 2007). These events tend to cluster in the two or three weeks preceding the "break" when the acute signs of the disorder appear (Day et al., 1987). Stressful life events seem to interact with biological or personality vulnerability factors. A highly vulnerable person may require little in the way of life stress to reach the breaking point (Fowles, 1992; van Praag, 2004). In one study, psychotic

40. What is the dopamine hypothesis? What evidence supports it?

41. What concepts do (a) psychoanalytic and (b) cognitive theorists use to explain the symptoms of schizophrenia?

and nonpsychotic people rated their emotional responses as they encountered stressful events in their daily lives. Psychotic individuals reacted to their stressors with more intense negative emotions, suggesting that emotional overreactivity may be a vulnerability factor (Myin-Germeys et al., 2001). In a longitudinal study, Nancy Docherty and colleagues (2009) tested schizophrenic patients and matched normal controls for emotional reactivity, and then followed the two groups for nine months. They found that, as a group, the schizophrenic patients were more emotionally reactive and that the more reactive the patients were, the more likely they were to respond to stressful life events with an increase in psychotic symptoms.

Family dynamics have long been a prime suspect in the origins of schizophrenia, but the search for parent or family characteristics that might cause the disorder has been largely unsuccessful. Significantly, children of biologically normal parents who are raised by schizophrenic adoptive parents do not show an increased risk of developing schizophrenia (Kety, 1988). Although persons with schizophrenia often come from families with problems, the nature and seriousness of those problems are not different from those of families in which non-schizophrenics are raised. There is evidence that early childhood trauma increases one's risk of schizophrenia, but more research is needed before firm conclusions can be drawn (Morgan & Fisher, 2007).

This does not mean that family dynamics are not important; rather, it may mean that a biological vulnerability factor must be present if stressful familial events are to cause their damage. Indeed, there is evidence that this vulnerability factor may appear early in life. In one study, researchers analyzed home movies showing children who were later to develop schizophrenic behaviours, as well as movies of their non-schizophrenic brothers and sisters. Even at these early ages—sometimes as young as two years of age—preschizophrenic children tended to show more odd and uncoordinated movements and less emotional expressiveness, especially for positive emotions (Grimes & Walker, 1994). These behavioural oddities may not only reflect a vulnerability factor, but also help to create environmental stress by evoking negative reactions from others.

Although researchers have had difficulty pinpointing family factors that contribute to the *initial* appearance of schizophrenia, one

consistent finding is that previously hospitalized schizophrenics are more likely to relapse if they return to a home environment that is high in a factor called **expressed emotion** (Vaughn & Leff, 1976). Expressed emotion involves high levels of *criticism* ("All you do is sit in front of that TV"), *hostility* ("We're getting sick and tired of your craziness"), and *overinvolvement* ("You're not going out unless I go with you"). One review of 26 studies showed that within 9 to 12 months of their return home, an average relapse rate of 48 percent occurred in patients whose families were high in expressed emotion, compared with a relapse rate of 21 percent when families were low in this factor (Kavanagh, 1992). Before we conclude that high expressed emotion causes patients to relapse, however, we should note a finding from another study in which researchers videotaped actual interactions involving patients and their families (Rosenfarb et al., 1995). Analyses of the videotapes revealed that families high in expressed emotion did indeed make more negative comments to patients when they engaged in strange behaviours, but they also showed that the patients in these families engaged in about four times as many strange and disruptive behaviours, clouding the issue of what causes what. Thus, high expressed emotion may be either a cause of or a response to patients' disordered behaviours.

Sociocultural Factors

Sociocultural factors are undoubtedly linked to schizophrenia (Murray et al., 2003). Many studies have found that the prevalence of schizophrenia is highest in lower socioeconomic populations (Figure 16.30). Why is this? Is poverty a cause of schizophrenia, or is it an effect of the disorder? Two theories give opposite answers. The *social causation hypothesis* attributes the higher prevalence of schizophrenia to the higher levels of stress that low-income people experience, particularly within urban environments. In contrast, the *social drift hypothesis* proposes that, as people develop schizophrenia, their personal and occupational functioning deteriorates, so that they drift down the socioeconomic ladder into poverty and migrate to low-cost urban environments. Perhaps social causation and social drift are both at work, since the factors that link poverty, social and environmental stressors, and schizophrenia are undoubtedly complex.

In contrast to most of the disorders we have described so far, schizophrenia may

42. How successful have researchers been in identifying family factors that cause schizophrenia? What role does expressed emotion play as a family variable?

43. Contrast the social causation and social drift hypotheses concerning social class and the prevalence of schizophrenia

- Schizophrenia is a psychotic disorder featuring disordered thinking and language; poor contact with reality; flat, blunted, or inappropriate emotion; and disordered behaviour. The cognitive portion of the disorder can involve delusions (false beliefs) or hallucinations (false perceptions).

- Mental-health workers often categorize individuals with schizophrenia based on the nature of the symptoms: positive versus negative. Positive symptoms, such as delusions or hallucinations, predict a better outcome than negative symptoms, such as lack of emotional expression.

- There is strong evidence for a genetic predisposition to schizophrenia that makes some people particularly vulnerable to stressful life events. The dopamine hypothesis states that schizophrenia involves overactivity of the dopamine system, resulting in too much stimulation.

- Psychoanalytic theorists regard schizophrenia as a profound regression to a primitive stage of psychosocial development in response to unbearable stress, particularly within the family. Stressful life events do often precede a schizophrenic episode, but researchers have not been successful in identifying a family pattern related to the onset of schizophrenia. However, negative expressed emotion is a family variable related to relapse among formerly hospitalized schizophrenic individuals.

- Cognitive theorists focus on the thought disorder that is central to schizophrenia. One idea is that people with schizophrenia have a defect in their attentional filters, so that they are overwhelmed by internal and external stimuli and become disorganized. Deficiencies may also exist in the executive functions needed to organize behaviour.

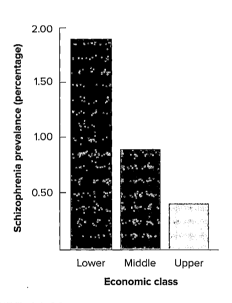

FIGURE 16.30 Relation between economic status and the prevalence of schizophrenia. Is economic status a cause or an effect of schizophrenia?

Source: Based on data from Keith, S.J., Regier, D.A., & Rae, D.S. (1991). "Schizophrenic disorders." In L.N. Robins & D.A. Regier (Eds.), *Psychiatric disorders in America: The Epidemiological Catchment Area Study.* New York, NY: Free Press.

be a "culture-free" disorder. A worldwide epidemiological study sponsored by the World Health Organization indicated that the prevalence of schizophrenia is not dramatically different throughout the world (Jablensky et al., 1992). Other researchers, however, have reported striking differences in rates (e.g., McGrath, 2006). Whatever the actual difference

in prevalence, researchers have found that the likelihood of *recovery* is greater in developing countries than in developed nations such as the United States and Canada. This may reflect a stronger community orientation and greater social support extended to disturbed people in developing countries (Tanaka-Matsumi & Draguns, 1997).

PERSONALITY DISORDERS

People diagnosed with **personality disorders** exhibit stable, ingrained, inflexible, and maladaptive ways of thinking, feeling, and behaving. When they encounter situations in which their typical behaviour patterns do not work, unresolved conflicts tend to re-emerge, they are likely to intensify their inappropriate ways of coping, and their emotional controls may break down (Lenzenweger & Clarkin, 2005; Millon et al., 2004).

Table 16.3 briefly describes the six personality disorders included in the DSM-5. As many as 10 to 15 percent of adults in the United States, Canada, and European countries may have personality disorders. A study in Norwayfound a prevalence rate of 13.4 percent, equally distributed among men and women. The most frequently encountered were avoidant and obsessive-compulsive personality disorders (Torgerson et al., 2001).

Among the personality disorders, the most destructive to society is the *antisocial*

TABLE 16.3 DSM-5 Personality Disorders and Their Major Features

Antisocial personality disorder: Severe irresponsible and antisocial behaviour beginning in childhood and continuing past age 18; impulsive need gratification and lack of empathy for others; often highly manipulative and seem to lack conscience

Narcissistic personality disorder: Grandiose fantasies or behaviour, lack of empathy, and oversensitivity to evaluation; constant need for admiration from others; proud self-display

Borderline personality disorder: Pattern of severe instability of self-image, interpersonal relationships, and emotions, often expressing alternating extremes of love and hatred toward the same person; high frequency of manipulative suicidal behaviour

Avoidant personality disorder: Extreme social discomfort and timidity; feelings of inadequacy and fearfulness of being negatively evaluated

Obsessive-compulsive personality disorder: Extreme perfectionism, orderliness, and inflexibility; preoccupied with mental and interpersonal control

Schizotypal personality disorder: Odd thoughts, appearance, and behaviour, and extreme discomfort in social situations

Source: Based on DSM-5, American Psychiatric Association, 2013.

personality disorder (Livesley, 2003). This personality disorder has received by far the greatest attention from clinicians and researchers over the years (Reich, 2006). A second personality disorder that is attracting a great deal of current attention is the *borderline personality disorder.* We will focus on these two disorders.

Antisocial Personality Disorder

In the past, individuals with antisocial personality disorder have been referred to as *psychopaths* or *sociopaths.* As Robert Hare of the University of British Columbia describes in his book *Without Conscience: The Disturbing World of the*

Psychopaths among Us (2001), people with antisocial personality disorder are among the most interpersonally destructive and emotionally harmful individuals. Males outnumber females three to one in this diagnostic group (American Psychiatric Association, 2000; Paris, 2013).

People with **antisocial personality disorder** seem to lack a conscience (Black, 2015). In the 19th century, they were sometimes referred to as "moral imbeciles." They exhibit little anxiety or guilt and tend to be impulsive and unable to delay gratification of their needs. Actual antisocial behaviour occurs in only a portion of psychopathic individuals (Figure 16.31).

44. Describe the major characteristics of antisocial personality disorder.

(left): © Paramount Pictures/Photofest, NY; (right): © Miramax Films. Photographer: Richard Foreman/Photofest, NY

FIGURE 16.31 Violent psychopaths have frequently been represented on the screen. An example is the cold-blooded hitman chillingly portrayed by Javier Bardem in the film *No Country for Old Men* (2007).

Many subclinical psychopaths flourish in settings, including politics and business, where their charisma, manipulativeness, false sincerity, and ability to deceive others can pay off. Spectacular political scandals and business schemes attest to what happens when psychopathic tendencies are not sufficiently self-regulated (Millon & Davis, 2000).

Research shows that there are two behavioural clusters of behaviours associated with psychopathy. The first cluster consists of selfishness, callousness, and interpersonal manipulation, and the second represents impulsivity, instability, and social deviance (Raine, 2008). A diagnosis of antisocial personality disorder is likely to require both behaviour clusters. Many subclinical psychopaths have only the first cluster (plus impulsivity, to varying degrees). Nonetheless, they can cause considerable harm because of their loose moral standards, ability to deceive others, and lack of empathy. They also exhibit a lack of emotional attachment to other people, as suggested in this report by a man diagnosed as having an antisocial personality:

> When I was in high school my best friend got leukemia and died and I went to his funeral. Everybody else was crying . . . (but) . . . I suddenly realized I wasn't feeling anything at all. . . . That night I thought about it some more and found I wouldn't miss my mother and father if they died and that I wasn't too nuts about my brothers and sisters for that matter. I figured there wasn't anybody I really cared for but, then, I didn't need any of them anyway so I rolled over and went to sleep. (McNeil, 1967, p. 87)

Lack of the capacity to care about others can make antisocial individuals a danger to society (Black, 1999; Hare, 2001). For example, murderers Charles Manson, Paul Bernardo (Figure 16.32), and Jeffrey Dahmer failed to show any remorse for their serial murders or sympathy for their victims. Although antisocial individuals often verbalize feelings and commitments with great sincerity, their behaviours indicate otherwise. They often appear very intelligent and charming, and they have the ability to rationalize their inappropriate behaviour so that it appears reasonable and justifiable. Consequently, they are often virtuosos at manipulating others and talking their way out of trouble. One researcher who wanted to study non-incarcerated antisocial personalities quickly attracted 25 of them from the Boston area with the following classified ad:

© Phil Snell/The Canadian Press

FIGURE 16.32 The murderer Paul Bernardo exhibited many features of the antisocial personality, including a charismatic personality and an ability to injure others without remorse or guilt.

> Wanted: Charming, aggressive, carefree people who are impulsively irresponsible but are good at handling people and at looking after Number One. Send name, address, phone, and short biography proving how interesting you are to . . . (Widom, 1983, p. 72)

People with antisocial personalities also display a perplexing failure to respond to punishment. Because of their lack of anxiety, punishment does not deter them from engaging in self-defeating or illegal acts again and again. As a result, some of them develop imposing prison records.

To be diagnosed as having an antisocial personality disorder, a person must be at least 18 years of age. However, the diagnostic criteria also require substantial evidence of antisocial behaviour before the age of 15, including such acts as habitual lying, early and aggressive sexual behaviour, excessive drinking, theft, vandalism, and chronic rule violations at home and school. Thus, antisocial personality disorder is the culmination of a behaviour pattern that typically begins in childhood (Kernberg, 2000; Paris, 2013).

Causal Factors

Biological, psychological, and environmental factors are all implicated in the development of psychopathy.

Biological factors. Biological research on antisocial personality disorder has focused on both genetic and physiological factors.

45. How are biological factors implicated in the antisocial personality disorder?

Evidence for a genetic predisposition is shown in consistently higher rates of concordance for antisocial behaviour in identical twins than in fraternal twins (Airey & Sodhi, 2007). Heritability is between 0.40 and 0.50 for antisocial behaviour in children, adolescents, and adults (Bouchard, 2004). Adoption studies suggest a similar conclusion. When researchers compared the criminal records of men who had been adopted early in life with those of their biological fathers and their adoptive fathers, they found that the criminality rate was nearly twice as high if the biological father had a criminal record and the adoptive father did not, clearly suggesting the operation of genetic factors (Cloninger & Gottesman, 1989).

46. How are classical conditioning and modelling concepts used to account for the development of antisocial personality disorder?

How might genetic factors predispose individuals to engage in antisocial behaviour? One clue might lie in the relative absence of anxiety and guilt that seems to characterize antisocial personality disorder. Many researchers have suggested that the physiological basis for the disorder might be some dysfunction in brain structures that govern emotional arousal and behavioural self-control, particularly the amygdala and the prefrontal cortex (Blair, 2005; Raine, 2008). Dysfunction in these two areas would result in behavioural impulsiveness and a chronically underaroused state that impairs avoidance learning, causes boredom, and encourages a search for excitement (Arnett, 1997; Ishikawa et al., 2001). In support of a physiological basis, both children and adults with antisocial behaviour patterns have lower heart rates, particularly when under stress (Ortiz & Raine, 2004). MRIs also reveal that antisocial individuals have subtle neurological deficits in the prefrontal lobes—the seat of executive functions such as planning, reasoning, and behavioural inhibition; these neurological deficits are associated with reduced autonomic activity (Raine et al., 2000). Recently, Checknita et al. (2015) have shown that the monoamine oxidase A (MAOA) gene is deficient in individuals with antisocial personality disorder. MAOA regulates serotonin, and deficient regulation can lead to impulsive aggression. Thus, it appears, as long suspected, that severely antisocial individuals may indeed be wired differently at a neurological level, responding with less arousal and greater impulsiveness to both pleasurable and unpleasant stimuli (Raine, 2008).

Psychological and environmental factors. Psychodynamic theorists regard antisocial people as lacking a conscience. Psychoanalytic theorists suggest that such people lack anxiety and guilt because they did not develop an adequate superego (Gabbard, 1990). In the absence of a well-developed superego, the restraints on the id are reduced, resulting in impulsive and hedonistic behaviour. The failure to develop a strong superego is thought to result from inadequate identification with appropriate adult figures because these figures were either physically or psychologically unavailable to the child (Kernberg, 2000). In support of this position, the absence of the father from the home is related to a higher incidence of antisocial symptoms in children, even when socioeconomic status is equated (Pfiffner et al., 2001).

Cognitive theorists believe that an important feature in antisocial individuals is their consistent failure to think about or anticipate the long-term negative consequences of their acts. As a result, they behave impulsively, thinking only of what they want at that moment (Bandura, 1997). From this perspective, a key to preventing psychopaths from getting into trouble is to help them develop the cognitive controls (i.e., the executive functions) needed to think before acting impulsively.

Learning through modelling may also play an important role. Antisocial individuals often come from homes in which parents exhibit a good deal of aggression and are inattentive to their children's needs (Rutter, 1997). Such parents provide role models for both aggressive behaviour and disregard for the needs of others. Another important environmental factor is exposure to deviant peers. Children who become antisocial often learn some of their deviant behaviours from peer groups that both model antisocial behaviour and reinforce it with social approval (Bandura, 1997). It is easy to see how such environmental factors, combined with a possible genetic predisposition for antisocial behaviour, would encourage the development of deviant behaviour patterns (Van Goozen et al., 2007).

Like some biological theories, learning explanations suggest that people with antisocial personality disorder lack impulse control. Learning theorists believe that poor impulse control occurs in these individuals because of an impaired ability to develop conditioned fear responses when punished, which would correspond with the lower physiological arousal and amygdala activity identified with brain recordings (Raine, 2008). This results in a deficit in avoidance learning. Hans Eysenck (1964) maintained that developing a conscience depends on the ability to learn fear and inhibitory avoidance responses, and people who fail to do so will be less able to inhibit their behaviour. In accord with this hypothesis, Adrian Raine and colleagues (1996) did a 14-year follow-up of males who had been subjected at age 15 to a classical conditioning procedure in which a soft tone was used as the CS and a loud, aversive tone as the UCS. Conditioned fear was measured by the participants' skin-conductance response when the CS occurred after a number of pairings with the loud UCS. The researchers found that men who accumulated a criminal record by age 29 had shown much poorer fear conditioning at age 15 than had those with no criminal record.

Borderline Personality Disorder

The borderline personality disorder has become the focus of intense interest among clinical researchers because of its chaotic effects on those who suffer from the disorder, their families, and their therapists. The disorder may occur in 3 to 5 percent of the general population (Clarkin et al., 1992; Selby & Joiner, 2009). About two-thirds of those diagnosed are women.

Before 1980, the term *borderline* referred to an intermediate level of disturbance between neurotic and psychotic. Now, however, **borderline personality disorder (BPD)** refers to a collection of symptoms characterized primarily by serious instability in behaviour, emotion, identity, and interpersonal relationships. A central feature of borderline is *emotional dysregulation,* an inability to control negative emotions in response to stressful life events, many of which borderline individuals themselves cause (Linehan & Dexter-Mazza, 2008; Selby et al., 2009).

Borderline individuals have intense and unstable personal relationships, and they experience chronic feelings of extreme anger, loneliness, and emptiness, as well as momentary losses of personal identity (Kuo & Linehan, 2009). They are inclined to engage in impulsive behaviour, such as running away, promiscuity, binge eating, and drug abuse, and their lives are often marked by repetitive self-destructive behaviours, such as self-mutilation and suicide attempts that seem designed to call forth a "saving" response from other people in their lives (McMurran et al., 2007).

BPD is highly associated with a number of other disorders, including mood disorders, PTSD, and substance-abuse disorders. In one study, the BPD symptoms of emotional instability and impulsivity predicted recurrent problems in academic achievement and social relationships two years later (Bagge et al., 2004). One intensive study of 57 people diagnosed with BPD revealed a total of 42 suicide threats, 40 drug overdoses, 36 instances of self-mutilation and cutting, 38 episodes of drug abuse, 36 instances of promiscuity with near-strangers, and 14 accidents, mainly caused by reckless driving (Linehan, 1993).

The chaos that marks the lives of borderline patients extends to their relationships with their psychotherapists. Borderline patients are considered to be among the most difficult clients to treat because of their clinging dependency, their irrational anger, and their tendency to engage in manipulative suicide threats and gestures as efforts to control the therapist (Linehan, 1993). Many borderline individuals, 6 to 10 percent in various large-scale studies, eventually do kill themselves, either by miscalculation or by design (Davis et al., 1999; Pompili et al., 2009).

Causal Factors

Borderline people tend to have chaotic personal histories marked by interpersonal strife, sexual and physical abuse, and inconsistent parenting (Kuo et al., 2015). This history is sometimes reflected in their earliest memories. In one study, borderline and normal participants were asked to describe their earliest memories in life. When the researchers analyzed the content of the memory reports, they found that the borderline respondents reported six times more events in which someone had treated them in a malevolent manner or had injured them emotionally or physically. Borderline individuals also viewed potential helpers as far less helpful to them (Nigg et al., 1992). Parents of many borderline individuals are described as abusive, rejecting, and non-affirming, and some theorists suggest that an early lack of acceptance by parents may cripple self-esteem and lead to clinging dependency and an inability to cope with separation (Cardasis et al., 1997). As they mature, the behaviours of borderline individuals tend to evoke negative reactions and rejection from others, affirming their sense of worthlessness and their view of the world as malevolent.

Psychoanalyst Otto Kernberg has focused on the dramatic changes that borderline people exhibit in their relationships with others (Kernberg, 1984; Kernberg & Caligor, 2005). Their sudden and vitriolic shifts from extreme love and clinging dependence to intense hatred or feelings of abandonment reflect a cognitive process that he calls **splitting,** the failure to integrate positive and negative aspects of

(left): © Sunset Boulevard/Corbis; (right): Paramount Pictures/Photofest

FIGURE 16.33 Actress Glenn Close's portrayal of Alex in the movie *Fatal Attraction* illustrates the tendency of people with BPD to show dramatic shifts in their relationships. During her affair with Dan, played by Michael Douglas, Alex goes from consuming love to a homicidal rage in which she tries to murder her lover with a butcher knife when he tries to end the relationship.

another's behaviour (e.g., a parent who is usually accepting but sometimes voices disapproval) into a coherent whole. As a result, the borderline individual may react as if the other person had two separate identities, one deserving of love and the other of hatred. Whichever of these seemingly independent images the borderline individual is reacting to at the moment totally determines how she or he relates or feels (Figure 16.33). Borderline individuals also have a bias to the interpret emotional expressions of others as more intense, thus magnifying their reaction (Daros et al., 2014). Together with severe problems in emotional control, splitting makes for chaotic and unpredictable relationships.

Biological factors also seem to be at work (Depue & Lenzenweger, 2005; Leichsenring et al., 2011). Close relatives of those with BPD are five times more likely than those in the general population to also have the disorder (Torgerson, 2000). The emotional explosiveness and impulsivity of borderlines may also reflect some biological abnormality in neurotransmitter systems or areas of the brain that contribute to emotional self-regulation (Gurvitz et al., 2000). It seems entirely possible that BPD reflects an interaction between biological factors and an early history of trauma, rejection, and psychological if not physical abandonment. Finally, sociocultural factors may also contribute to this disorder. Cases of BPD seem to increase in societies that are unstable and rapidly changing, leaving some of their members with a sense of emptiness, problems of identity, and fears of abandonment (Paris, 1993).

In Review

- Personality disorders are rigid, maladaptive patterns of behaviour that characterize an individual's behaviour over a long time.

- Antisocial personality disorder is the most studied of the personality disorders. It is characterized by an egocentric and manipulative tendency toward immediate self-gratification, a lack of empathy for others, a tendency to act out impulsively, and a failure to profit from punishment.

- Research on antisocial personality disorder suggests that genetic and physiological factors that result in underarousal may contribute to the disorder's causes. Psychoanalysts view the disorder as a failure to develop a superego, which might otherwise restrain the individual's impulsive

self-gratification. Learning explanations focus on the failure of punishment to inhibit maladaptive behaviours and exposure to aggressive, uncaring models. It seems likely that there is a genetic predisposition that increases the risk of antisocial behaviour, especially if the person is exposed to deviant models.

- Borderline personality disorder is characterized by serious instability in behaviour, emotion, interpersonal relationships, and personal identity, as well as impulsive and self-destructive behaviours. The disorder is associated with abusive parenting.

DISORDERS OF CHILDHOOD AND OLD AGE

Childhood Disorders

Psychological disorders can occur at any point in the lifespan. Mental health professionals have observed symptoms resembling clinical depression in infants, and older children exhibit a wide range of problem behaviours (Mash & Barkley, 2003). In one study of several thousand children between the ages of two and five, researchers diagnosed more than 20 percent of the children with a DSM disorder and considered half of these to be significantly impaired by their symptoms (Lavigne et al., 1996). Similar levels of incidence and impairment exist in children between the ages of 9 and 17 (Satcher, 1999). In Canada, mental disorders in youth are second only to injuries in terms of hospital expenditures (Canadian Mental Health Association, 2016).

Other studies show that only about 40 percent of children with psychological disorders receive professional attention, and only half of this group is seen by qualified mental health professionals (Satcher, 1999). In contrast, nearly three-quarters of children with physical handicaps receive professional treatment. Failure to treat childhood behaviour disorders not only results in needless distress for children and families, but such disorders tend to continue into adulthood as psychological problems. In one New Zealand study, four in five adults with diagnosed DSM disorders had histories of childhood or adolescent problems that also met DSM criteria (Newman et al., 1996).

Although many childhood disorders are the subject of current research, two are receiving particular attention. *Attention deficit/ hyperactivity disorder* is of interest because it is the most frequently diagnosed childhood disorder. *Autism* is being scrutinized because it is becoming more common and is one of the most baffling disorders.

Attention Deficit/Hyperactivity Disorder

In **attention deficit/hyperactivity disorder (ADHD)**, problems may take the form of inattention, hyperactivity/impulsivity, or a combination of the two. Ratings by teachers and parents indicate that 7 to 10 percent of American children meet DSM-5 criteria for the disorder. Similar results are reported for Canadian children and for children in most countries around the world, making ADHD the most common childhood disorder. The disorder occurs at least four

times more frequently in boys than in girls. Boys are more likely to exhibit aggressive and impulsive behaviours, whereas girls are more likely to be primarily inattentive (Poremba & Poremba, 2007). Some professionals believe that the ADHD diagnosis is applied too liberally, since normal children also exhibit the behaviours in question. They worry that some children may be labelled and medicated inappropriately (Carlson, 2000).

It may be tempting to assume that children routinely outgrow ADHD, but follow-up studies of individuals diagnosed with the disorder suggest that for 50 to 80 percent, the problems persist into adolescence and, for 30 to 50 percent, into adulthood (Biederman, 1998). Overall, adults with ADHD have more occupational, family, emotional, and interpersonal problems.

Despite many years of research, the precise causes of ADHD are unknown. Genetic factors are probably involved, as concordance rates are higher in identical than in fraternal twins. In adoption studies of ADHD children, the children's biological parents are more likely to have ADHD than the adoptive parents (Smalley et al., 2000). Experts have long suspected that the disorder has a biological basis, but EEG studies of electrical brain activity and imaging studies of brain structures and neurotransmitters have failed to reveal consistent differences between people with ADHD and control groups (Green, 1999, Lam et al., 2006). This may be due to the fact that ADHD is a multifaceted disorder with several subcategories of biological patterns. There may be some deficiency in the fibre bundles joining the frontal cortex to other brain areas (Chiang et al., 2015), but more research is needed. Environmental factors such as inconsistent parenting are also involved, perhaps in complex combinations with biological factors.

Autistic Spectrum Disorder

One of the most mysterious and perplexing of all disorders is autism. First identified by the American psychiatrist Leo Kanner in 1943, **autistic spectrum disorder** is a long-term disorder characterized by extreme unresponsiveness to others, poor communication skills, and highly repetitive and rigid behaviour patterns. In 2000, it was estimated that autism affects about one in every 2000 children, about 80 percent of them boys (American Psychiatric Association, 2000). But the rate has been steadily climbing. The current estimate from the Centers for Disease Control (2013) is that autism affects one in 50 children. Typically appearing in the first three years of life in the form of unresponsiveness and lack of interest in others, autism tends to be a lifelong disorder. Approximately 70 percent remain severely disabled into adulthood and cannot lead independent lives. More than two-thirds have intellectual disability, with IQs below 70 and frequently below 35. The rest have normal to above-average intelligence. But even the highest-functioning adults with autism have problems in communication, restricted interests and activities, and difficulty relating to others (Hillman et al., 2007).

Lack of social responsiveness to others is a central feature of autism. Autistic infants typically do not reach out to or even make eye contact with their parents. They seem not to recognize or care who is around them. Autistic children do not engage in normal play with either adults or peers and often do not even acknowledge their presence.

Language and communication difficulties are also common, with half of autistic children not developing language. The language that does develop is often strange, involving repetition of words or phrases with little recognition of meaning. Many engage in *echolalia*, the exact echoing of phrases spoken by others.

Sameness and routine are very important, and autistic children become extremely upset at even minute changes. The movement of a piece of furniture even slightly or the change of one word in a song may evoke a tantrum. Some theorists believe that sameness is an attempt to avoid overstimulation, but nobody knows for sure.

Autistic individuals have repetitive and stereotyped behaviour patterns and interests (Figure 16.34). They may spend their time

47. How does ADHD differ from autism?

48. How are biological factors implicated in autism?

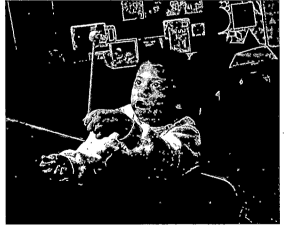

© Robin Sachs/PhotoEdit, Inc.

FIGURE 16.34 People with autism often engage in odd and repetitive stereotyped behaviours. For example, an autistic child may manipulate an object for hours at a time, showing no interest in playing with other children or relating to adults.

spinning objects, playing with objects such as jar tops, flicking their fingers, or rocking their bodies. Some engage in self-injurious behaviours, such as banging their heads against sharp objects or biting chunks of flesh out of their bodies, and these children may have to be physically restrained.

A few autistic people, such as the man portrayed by Dustin Hoffman in *Rain Man*, exhibit extraordinary *savant* (from the French word for "wise," or "learned") abilities. A common savant skill is calendar calculation. An autistic person with this ability could tell you in an instant what day of the week your birthday will fall on in 2039. Others can perfectly reproduce any song or commercial after hearing it once. Sometimes these skills give the impression of superior intelligence, even in people who have an intellectual disability.

Causal factors. Leo Kanner (1943), who first described childhood autism, offered a psychodynamic explanation. He speculated that these children had been driven into their own worlds by a cold and ungiving family environment during infancy. Parents (particularly the mother) were described as "refrigerator parents" who had thawed out just long enough to conceive a child. These were purely theoretical statements, and no evidence for such a family pattern has ever existed, but generations of parents who were exposed to this hypothesis suffered the agony of thinking they had caused their child's autistic disorder.

Today, it is widely accepted that autism has a biological basis (Mak-Fan et al., 2013; Vaccarino & Smith, 2009). What that might be remains undetermined, however. Widespread anomalies in the structures and functioning of the brain have been found in autistic children. For example, brain-imaging studies show that the brains of autistic children are 5 to 10 percent larger than average at 18 months to four years of age. There is also evidence of accelerated pruning of neural connections during early life, and prefrontal-cortex development is also abnormal. Finally, brain scans of autistic individuals reveal abnormal development in the cerebellum, which coordinates movement and is involved in shifting attention (Courchesne et al., 2003). The precise manner in which these brain differences are related to autism is the subject of extensive current research.

Genetic factors have been linked to autism. Recent molecular-genetics studies suggest that there may be four to six major genes and

20 to 30 others that contribute to a lesser degree (Piven et al., 2013). It also appears that different genes may be involved for boys than for girls (Schellenberg et al., 2006). Siblings of autistic children are 200 times more likely to have the disorder than are children in the general population, and concordance is highest in identical twins (Piven et al., 1997). One notable finding is that many relatives of autistic children, though not manifesting the disorder themselves, have unusual personality characteristics that parallel autism, including aloofness and very narrow and specialized interests (Rutter, 2000).

Another line of research is examining autism from the *theory of mind* perspective. As discussed in Chapter 12, theory of mind refers to an awareness of what others are thinking and how they may be reacting internally. Normal children become aware of some characteristics of other people's thinking by age three or four (Ritblatt, 2000). Autistic people seem to have poorly developed skills in this area, making it difficult for them to communicate with others or understand how other people might be internally reacting to them (Heerey et al., 2003). Autistic children also show poor comprehension of others' emotional responses, such as expressions of distress (Dawson et al., 2004). Theory of mind deficits could severely impair language and social development, and they are a strong focus of current research on autism.

Finally, a significant controversy has arisen concerning the possible role of children's vaccinations as a cause of autism. The controversy has stimulated a significant amount of research. A recent review of the scientific evidence led to the following conclusion:

> The parents should not be apprehensive about the fact that immunization is likely to risk the protection of the child. There is no evidence that *autism* is caused by any vaccine or any additive or preservative ever used in one. There have been large, well-controlled studies done all over the Western world that have confirmed this finding over and over again. A comparison of the risk factors, such as death or disabilities, as a result of not vaccinating a child is significantly larger than the risk of causing an autism spectrum disorder by immunizing. (Rhea, 2009, p. 962)

In fact, the original article suggesting a link between autism and vaccinations has been shown to be fraudulent. The journal, *The Lancet*, fully retracted the paper in 2010, and the author, Andrew Wakefield, was found guilty of professional misconduct.

Dementia in Old Age

> I fear I am not in my perfect mind.
> Methinks I should know you, and know this man;
> Yet I am doubtful, for I am mainly ignorant
> What place this is, and all the skill I have
> Remembers not these garments; nor I know not
> Where I did lodge last night.

> (Shakespeare, *King Lear*, Act IV, Scene 7)

In his characterization of the elderly King Lear, William Shakespeare captured the onset of **dementia**, the gradual loss of cognitive abilities that accompanies brain deterioration and interferes with normal functioning. In people with dementia, a progressive atrophy, or degeneration, of brain tissue occurs as a result of disease or injury. Depending on the cause, dementia can occur at any point in the lifespan, but elderly people are at greater risk than the general population. More than a dozen types and causes of dementia exist, the most common being Alzheimer's disease, Parkinson's disease, Huntington's disease, and Creutzfeldt-Jakob disease. Complications from high blood pressure and stroke may also be causes.

Regardless of the specific diagnosis, when dementia begins after age 65, it is labelled *senile dementia*. A large Canadian study indicated an overall rate of senile dementia of about 8 percent, and a female-to-male ratio of about two to one. The prevalence rates were 2.4 percent between ages 65 and 74, 11 percent for those between 75 and 84, and 34.5 percent for those 85 and older (Costa, 1996). More than half of those over age 65 living in institutions had dementia.

The onset of dementia is typically gradual, as is the appearance of symptoms. Memory impairment, poor judgment, confusion, language problems, and disorientation may appear gradually or sporadically. Memory for recent events is particularly affected, and the person may seem to live in the past because those memories are largely intact.

It is important to recognize that simple forgetfulness is not necessarily a symptom of dementia. Individuals who are developing dementia typically have episodes of distress because they feel confused; they may make nonsensical remarks, lose the procedural ability to perform familiar tasks, or even undergo marked personality change. Over half the cases diagnosed as senile dementia show various combinations of depression, anxiety, agitation, paranoid reactions, and disordered thinking that may resemble schizophrenia (American Psychiatric Association, 2000).

Alzheimer's disease is the leading cause of dementia in the elderly, accounting for about 60 percent of senile dementias. The Alzheimer Society of Canada (Alzheimer Society, 2010) estimates that approximately 500 000 Canadians have Alzheimer's or a related disorder. Within a generation, it is predicted that this number will be 1.1 million. The disorder is caused by deterioration in the frontal and temporal lobes of the brain, including the hippocampus, a subcortical structure involved in memory. Medical and mental-health professionals typically diagnose Alzheimer's by observing and interviewing the patient, but a postmortem microscopic examination of brain tissue is necessary to determine whether the patient had the tangled clumps of neurons and patches of disintegrating nerve cell branches called *plaques* that characterize the disease. A key to Alzheimer's disease is the destruction of cells that produce acetylcholine, a neurotransmitter that is critically involved in the neural processes underlying memory. One focus of current research is the development of drugs that might prevent the destruction of acetylcholine, enhance acetylcholine production, or directly stimulate acetylcholine receptors.

As people live longer lives, finding a cure for Alzheimer's disease and other forms of senile

49. What are the causes of Alzheimer's disease?

dementia becomes more urgent. Until then, many of us can expect our own family members to become Alzheimer's patients. Being a caregiver or watching the disease develop in a loved one is a painful and frustrating experience. In the advanced stages of the disease, the patient may not recognize even close family members. In addition, he or she may lose the ability to speak, walk, and control bladder and bowel functions. People with Alzheimer's also experience considerable stress as they feel their minds slipping away and their environment becoming more confusing.

A CLOSING THOUGHT

All of us do the best we can to adapt to the many demands we face during the course of our lives. In this chapter, we have seen the intense personal and societal suffering that occurs when biologically and experientially produced vulnerabilities combine with stressful demands to create psychological disorders. It is our hope that this discussion has increased your understanding of and compassion for those who suffer from these disorders. No one wants to be dysfunctional and miserable, and everyone deserves the opportunity to live a meaningful and fulfilling life. In the next chapter, we will focus on what can be done through psychological and biological treatments to ease the suffering that results from psychological disorders.

Review

- Psychological disorders can occur at any point in the lifespan, and epidemiological data show that both children and adolescents exhibit a variety of disorders. Moreover, many childhood disorders are precursors for psychological disorders in adulthood.

- ADHD and autistic spectrum disorder originate in childhood and often persist into adulthood. ADHD can involve inattention, hyperactivity, or a combination of the two.

- Autistic spectrum disorder is a severe disorder that involves extreme unresponsiveness to others, poor communication skills, and highly

repetitive and rigid behaviour. Both disorders appear to have biological underpinnings, but the nature of these causal factors is not fully understood.

- Cognitive deterioration, or dementia, can occur at any point in life but is especially prevalent in old age. Alzheimer's disease accounts for more than half of senile dementias. Other diseases, brain damage, and strokes also produce dementias.

Gaining Direction

What are the issues?	What does it mean to be "insane"? If you are suffering from a mental disorder, can you be held responsible for your actions? Leah was starting to fear for her life as Tony continued to threaten her. Was he really at risk for violent	action? Why did Tony believe that imposters had been planted in his family? Capgras is a very rare disorder—what might predispose you to having such an affliction?
What do we need to know?	What is Capgras syndrome? Can anyone get Capgras? What is going on in the person's mind? Why would you not recognize someone you knew for a long time?	Is this treatable? Can Capgras be drug-induced? What is the insanity defence?
Where can we find the information to answer these questions?	We need to start by looking at the various types of mental disorders. Which ones involve delusions or hallucinations? Perhaps Capgras is a subset of schizophrenia. If so, delusions could be drug-induced. The underlying problem in schizophrenia is an oversupply of dopamine.	Perhaps Capgras results from a similar neuro-transmitter imbalance. Finally, you may want to look for various legal decisions involving Capgras. Was Tony Rosato treated fairly by the legal system?

Treatment of Psychological Disorders

CHAPTER ⟩
OUTLINE

THE HELPING RELATIONSHIP

PSYCHODYNAMIC THERAPIES
Psychoanalysis
Brief Psychodynamic Therapies

HUMANISTIC PSYCHOTHERAPIES
Client-Centred Therapy
Gestalt Therapy

COGNITIVE THERAPIES
Ellis's Rational-Emotive Therapy (RET)
Beck's Cognitive Therapy

BEHAVIOUR THERAPIES
Classical Conditioning Treatments
  Focus on Neuroscience: The Neuroscience of
  Treating Unipolar Depression
  Frontiers: Virtual Reality as a Therapeutic Technique
Operant Conditioning Treatments
Modelling and Social Skills Training

"THIRD-WAVE" COGNITIVE-BEHAVIOURAL
THERAPIES

Mindfulness-Based Treatments

CULTURAL AND GENDER ISSUES IN
PSYCHOTHERAPY
Cultural Factors in Treatment Utilization
Gender Issues in Therapy

EVALUATING PSYCHOTHERAPIES
Psychotherapy Research Methods
Factors Affecting the Outcome of Therapy
  Research Foundations: Drug versus Psychological
  Treatments for Depression: A Randomized Clinical Trial

BIOLOGICAL APPROACHES TO TREATMENT
Drug Therapies
Electroconvulsive Therapy
Psychosurgery
Mind, Body, and Therapeutic Interventions

PSYCHOLOGICAL DISORDERS AND SOCIETY
Deinstitutionalization
Preventive Mental Health

A FINAL WORD
  Applications: When and Where to Seek Therapy

> It is a process, a thing-in-itself, an experience, a relationship, a dynamic.
> —Carl Rogers

 Jane Webber's life changed suddenly in 1994. She was always tired and fluorescent lights began to bother her. She loved coffee, but remembers that one day, it simply did not appeal to her any more. She felt that "all the colour had gone out of her world." Jane, from Colborne, Ontario, suffered from severe depression. Medication and various forms of psychotherapy did not work for her and the only option that doctors could recommend was electroconvulsive therapy (ECT)—delivering an electric

Centre for Addiction and Mental Health (CAMH)

What are the
issues here?

What do we need
to know?

Where can
we find the
information to
answer these
questions?

current to her brain, which results in a grand mal seizure. While ECT was effective, she had to have the treatment twice a month and the side effects—disorientation, headache, and some memory loss—were getting worse. She was not sure that she could continue doing this.

But then a new procedure became available on an experimental basis. Toronto's Centre for Addiction and Mental Health was running clinical trials on a procedure known as magnetic seizure therapy (MST). Jane dons a helmet-like headset that looks like a pair of headphones on the top of her skull. For treatment, magnetic pulses are delivered to small, targeted areas in her prefrontal cortex. A seizure is induced, but only in the target area. Jane reports that she has never felt this good in a long time. And there are no side effects.

There are only a handful of MST centres in the world. Canada has two of them.

What is the most effective way to treat an individual who is suffering from a psychological disorder? Is inducing a seizure an acceptable approach? Why? This chapter explores the many approaches used to treat psychological disorders, as well as the critical issue of their effectiveness. Although first-person reports suggest that many people derive considerable benefit from psychotherapy, psychologists demand much more in the way of evidence. Nearly 40 years of research on psychological treatments has taught us that the question of efficacy, or treatment outcome, is a tremendously complex one that has no simple answers. Yet, as we shall see, much has been learned about the effectiveness of these various therapeutic approaches and about the factors that influence treatment outcome.

THE HELPING RELATIONSHIP

The basic goal of all treatment approaches is to help people change maladaptive, self-defeating thoughts, feelings, and behaviour patterns so that they can live happier and more productive lives. The relationship between the client and the person providing help is a prime ingredient of therapeutic success (Cahill et al., 2013; Gabbard et al., 2005; Greenberg, 2014; Norcross, 2003). Within that helping relationship, therapists use a variety of treatment techniques to promote positive change in the client. These techniques vary widely, depending on the therapists' own theories of cause and change, and they may range from biomedical approaches (such as administering psychoactive drugs) to a wide range of psychological treatments. Both of these elements, relationship and techniques, are important to the success of the treatment enterprise (Figure 17.1).

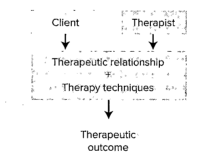

© Photodisc/Veer

FIGURE 17.1 The process of therapy involves a relationship between a client and a therapist who applies the techniques dictated by his or her approach to treatment. The quality of the therapeutic relationship, the therapy technique used, and the client's commitment to change all influence the outcome.

A majority of people with mental-health problems first seek help not from mental-health professionals, but from family members, physicians, members of the clergy, acquaintances, or self-help groups (Seligman, 1995). Often, however, these sources of psychological support are not enough, and distressed people are increasingly seeking help from professional counsellors and therapists. Surveys indicate that nearly 30 percent of North Americans have sought psychological counselling from professionals at

1. What two therapeutic elements combine in the treatment of behaviour disorders?

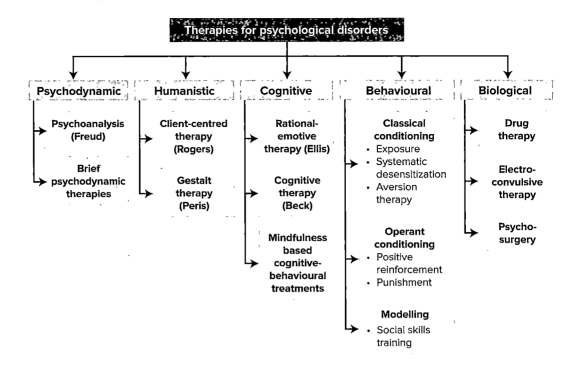

FIGURE 17.2 An overview of the major treatment approaches to the behaviour disorders, organized according to five major perspectives on behaviour.

some point in their lives, a dramatic rise from the 13 percent who had done so in the mid-1950s (Gaylin, 2000; Meredith, 1986). These people receive treatment from mental-health professionals who fall into several categories.

Counselling and clinical psychologists make up one group. These psychologists, who typically hold a Ph.D. (Doctor of Philosophy) or Psy.D. (Doctor of Psychology) degree, have received five or more years of intensive training and supervision in a variety of psychotherapeutic techniques as well as training in research and psychological assessment techniques. The Psy.D. is not currently offered at Canadian universities, but a number of American schools have this degree program. A second group, *psychiatrists*, are medical doctors who specialize in psychotherapy and biomedical treatments, such as drug therapy.

In addition to psychologists and psychiatrists, a number of other professionals provide treatment. These professionals typically receive master's degrees based on two years of highly focused and practical training. They include *psychiatric social workers*, who often work in community agencies; *marriage and family counsellors*, who specialize in problems arising from family relations; *pastoral counsellors*, who tend to focus on spiritual issues; and *abuse counsellors*, who work with substance and sexual abusers and their victims.

Having previewed the nature of therapy and those who provide it, we now consider the therapeutic approaches that have developed within the major perspectives on human behaviour. Figure 17.2 provides an overview of the therapies we will consider.

PSYCHODYNAMIC THERAPIES

The psychodynamic approach to psychotherapy focuses on internal conflict and unconscious factors that underlie maladaptive behaviour. The historical roots of psychodynamic approaches are to be found in Sigmund Freud's development of psychoanalysis. The term *psychoanalysis* refers not only to Freud's theory of personality, but also to the specific approach to treatment that he developed. Although both the theory and the techniques of therapy were later modified by his followers and those who defected to pursue rival approaches, the psychodynamic principles underlying Freud's approach continue to exert a major influence today.

Psychoanalysis

The goal of psychoanalysis is to help clients achieve **insight**, the conscious awareness of the psychodynamics that underlie their problems.

2. What is the major therapeutic goal in psychoanalysis?

Such awareness permits clients to adjust their behaviour to their current life situations, rather than continuing to repeat the old maladaptive routines learned in childhood. Analysts believe that, as the client repeatedly encounters and deals with buried emotions, motives, and conflicts both within and outside of therapy, the psychic energy that was previously devoted to keeping the unconscious conflict under control can be released and redirected to more adaptive ways of living (Gabbard, 2004).

Free Association

Freud believed that mental events are meaningfully associated with one another, so that clues to the contents of the unconscious are to be found in the constant stream of thoughts, memories, images, and feelings we experience. In his technique of **free association,** Freud asked his clients to recline on a couch and to report verbally without censorship any thoughts, feelings, or images that entered awareness. Freud sat out of sight behind the client so that the client's thought processes would be determined primarily by internal factors (Figure 17.3).

The analyst does not expect that free association necessarily will lead directly to unconscious material, but rather that it will provide clues concerning important themes or issues (Hoffer & Youngren, 2004). For example, a client's stream of thoughts may suddenly stop after she has mentioned her father, suggesting the possibility that she was approaching a "loaded" topic that activated repressive defences.

Dream Interpretation

Psychoanalysts believe that dreams express impulses, fantasies, and wishes that the client's defences keep in the unconscious during waking

© Bruce Ayres/Stone/Getty Images

FIGURE 17.3 In classical Freudian psychoanalysis the client reclines on a couch, with the analyst sitting out of the client's view.

hours (Erdelyi, 2014; Glucksman, 2001). Even in dreams, which Freud termed "the royal road to the unconscious," defensive processes usually disguise the threatening material to protect the dreamer from the anxiety that the material might evoke. In dream interpretation, the analyst tries to help the client search for the unconscious material contained in the dreams. One means of doing so is to ask the client to free associate to each element of the dream and to help the client arrive at an understanding of what the symbols in the dream really represent. Several authors (e.g., Erdelyi, 2014; Graveline & Wamsley, 2015) have argued that there is a rough correlation between content in the waking world and the dream world, suggesting that dreams do express concerns that the individual has.

Resistance

Although clients come to therapists for help, they also have a strong unconscious investment in maintaining the status quo. After all, their problems result from the fact that certain unconscious conflicts are so painful that the ego has resorted to maladaptive defensive patterns to deal with them. These avoidance patterns emerge in the course of therapy as **resistance,** defensive manoeuvres that hinder the process of therapy. Resistance can be manifested in many different ways. A client may experience difficulty in free-associating, may come late or "forget about" a therapy appointment, or may avoid talking about certain topics. Resistance is a sign that anxiety-arousing sensitive material is being approached. An important task of analysis is to explore the reasons for resistance, both to promote insight and to guard against the ultimate resistance: the client's decision to drop out of therapy prematurely.

Transference

As noted earlier, the analyst sits out of view of the client and reveals nothing to the client about himself or herself. Nonetheless, clients will eventually begin to project onto the "blank screen" of the therapist important perceptions and feelings related to their underlying conflicts. **Transference** occurs when the client responds irrationally to the analyst as if he or she were an important figure from the client's past. Transference is considered a most important process in psychoanalysis, for it brings out into the open repressed feelings and maladaptive behaviour patterns that the therapist can point out to the client.

Transference takes two basic forms. *Positive transference* occurs when a client transfers

3. How are free association and dream analysis used in psychoanalysis?

4. How do resistance and transference reflect underlying conflicts?

feelings of intense affection, dependency, or love to the analyst, whereas *negative transference* involves irrational expressions of anger, hatred, or disappointment. Analysts believe that until transference reactions are analyzed and resolved, there can be no full resolution of the client's problems. In the following excerpt from a psychoanalytic session, a client traces her transference reaction to its source and then recognizes the operation of similar reactions in other relationships:

Client: I don't want to like you. I'd rather not like you.

Therapist: I wonder why?

Client: I feel I'll be hurt. Liking you will expose me to being hurt.

Therapist: But how do you feel about me?

Client: I don't know. I have conflicting emotions about you. Sometimes I like you too much and sometimes I get mad at you for no reason. I often can't think of you, even picture you. . . . Yes, I don't want to like you. If I do, I won't be able to help myself. I'll get hurt. But why do I feel or insist that I'm in love with you?

Therapist: Are you?

Client: Yes. And I feel so guilty and upset about it. At night I think of you and get sexual feelings and it frightens me.

Therapist: Do I remind you of anyone?

Client: Yes. (Pause) There are things about you that remind me of my brother. (Laughs) I realize this is silly.

Therapist: Mmhmm.

Client: My brother Harry, the one I had the sex experiences with when I was little. He made me do things I didn't want to. I let him fool with me because he made me feel sorry for him.

Therapist: Do you have any of the same feelings toward me?

Client: It's not that I expect that anything will really happen, but I just don't want to have feelings for you. . . . I know it's the same thing. I'm afraid of you taking advantage of me. If I tell you I like you, that means you'll make me do what you want.

Therapist: Just like Harry made you do what he wanted.

Client: Yes. I didn't want to let him do what he did, but I couldn't help myself. I hated myself. That's why. I know it now because there is no reason why I should feel you

are the same way. That's why I act that way with other people too. . . . I don't like to have people get too close to me. The whole thing is the same as happens with you. It's all so silly and wrong. You aren't my brother and the other people aren't my brother. I never saw the connection until now. (Wolberg, 1967, pp. 660–661)

In this interchange, we see both positive and negative transference reactions based on an important past relationship. The client's feelings about her brother continue to be played out in her fear of getting close to others, including the analyst, and becoming vulnerable to being exploited once again.

Interpretation

How can analysts help clients detect and understand resistance, the meaning of dream symbols, and transference reactions? The analyst's chief therapeutic technique for these purposes is interpretation of the material the client presents. An **interpretation** is any statement by the therapist intended to provide the client with insight into his or her behaviour or dynamics. An interpretative statement confronts clients with something that they have not previously admitted into consciousness: "It's almost as if you're angry with me without realizing it."

A general rule in psychoanalytic treatment is to interpret what is already near the surface and just beyond the client's current awareness. Offering "deep" interpretations of strongly defended unconscious dynamics is considered poor technique because even if they are correct, such interpretations are so far removed from the client's current awareness that they cannot be informative or helpful (Levenson, 2002). This is one reason that, even after the analyst fully understands the causes of the client's problems, psychoanalysis may require several more years of treatment. It is the client who must eventually arrive at the insight.

Brief Psychodynamic Therapies

Classical psychoanalysis as practised by Freud (and a declining number of contemporary analysts) is an expensive and time-consuming process, for the goal is no less than rebuilding the client's personality. In classical psychoanalysis, it is not uncommon for a client to be seen five times a week for five years or more. Today, however, many therapists consider this level of client and therapist commitment both impractical and

5. What are interpretations, and how are they used by analysts?

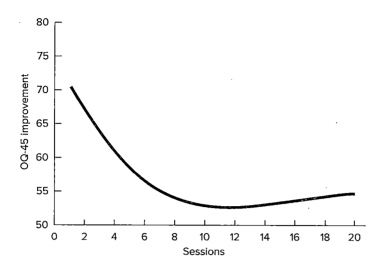

FIGURE 17.4 Decrease in psychological symptoms as a function of number of sessions seen in psychotherapy. The highest rate of improvement is seen early in treatment. Results like these have helped to stimulate the development of short-term treatments.

Source: Baldwin, S.A., Berkeljan, A., Atkins, D.C., & Nielsen, J.A., Rates of change in naturalistic psychotherapy: Contrasting dose–effect and good-enough level models of change. (2009). *Journal of Consulting and Clinical Psychology*, 2009, Vol 77 (2) Figure 1, p. 207. Copyright © 2009 American Psychological Association. Reprinted by permission.

unnecessary. Their conclusion is supported by several psychotherapy studies that measured the degree of improvement that occurred over the course of therapy. The results of a recent study involving 4676 clients and 204 therapists in a university counselling centre shows rate of improvement on the Outcome Questionnaire-45: a measure of psychological symptoms and unhappiness. As Figure 17.4 shows, by the tenth session, most of the improvements had occurred. The researchers also found that regardless of how many sessions the clients attended, the rate of improvement was highest at the beginning and decreased over time (Baldwin et al., 2009). A study of more than 4000 clients seen in therapy in the United Kingdom also found that clinically significant change did not increase in clients seen for more than ten sessions (Stiles et al., 2008).

However, other researchers have argued that psychoanalysis may be more effective than is suggested by early research, citing problems with methodology and inherent difficulties of conducting controlled, randomized studies of psychodynamic therapy (Leichsenring, 2005). Leichsenring conducted a meta-analytic review of research on psychodynamic and psychoanalytic therapies and concluded that psychoanalytic therapy is more effective in treating psychological disorders than are shorter forms of psychodynamic therapy. The authors of a three-year, randomized controlled clinical trial of 326 therapy clients in Helsinki, Finland, similarly reported that while short-term psychodynamic therapy was more effective than

long-term therapy in decreasing symptoms of depression and anxiety in the first year of the study, and there were no differences between therapy groups after two years, at the three-year follow-up the clients in the long-term psychodynamic therapy group showed significantly greater improvement than those in the short-term therapy groups (Knekt et al., 2008). It seems that, while brief psychodynamic therapies offer several advantages and have great potential to help people, for some individuals or for certain disorders, psychoanalytic or long-term psychodynamic therapies may be more effective treatments than brief psychodynamic therapies.

Like psychoanalysis, brief psychodynamic psychotherapies emphasize understanding the maladaptive influences of the past and relating them to current patterns of self-defeating behaviour. Many of these brief therapies utilize basic concepts from psychoanalysis, such as the importance of insight and the use of interpretation, but they employ them in a more focused and active fashion (Levenson, 2002). The therapist and client are likely to sit facing each other, and conversation typically replaces free association. Clients are seen once or twice a week rather than daily, and the goal is typically limited to helping the client deal with specific life problems rather than attempting a complete rebuilding of the client's personality. Therapy, therefore, is more likely to focus on the client's current life situations than on past childhood experience, and may teach the client specific interpersonal and emotion-control skills (Benjamin, 2003).

- Psychodynamic therapists view maladaptive behaviours as symptoms of an underlying conflict that needs to be resolved if behaviour is to change.

- The goal of Freudian psychoanalysis is to help clients achieve insight into the unconscious dynamics that underlie their behaviour disorders so that they can deal adaptively with their current environment.

- The chief means for promoting insight in psychoanalysis are the therapist's interpretations of free associations, dream content, resistance, and transference reactions.

- Brief psychodynamic therapies have become increasingly popular alternatives to lengthy psychoanalysis. Their goal is also to promote insight, but they tend to focus more on current life events. Interpersonal therapy is a structured therapy that focuses on addressing current interpersonal problems and enhancing interpersonal skills.

6. What two research results favour the use of brief therapies over classical psychoanalysis? How do brief psychodynamic therapies differ from classical psychoanalysis?

One brief psychodynamic therapy is called **interpersonal therapy** (Weissman & Markowitz, 1994, 2002). This therapy, which is highly structured and seldom takes longer than 15 to 20 sessions, focuses on the client's current interpersonal problems. These include dealing with role disputes such as marital conflict, adjusting to the loss of a relationship or to a changed relationship, and identifying and correcting deficits in social skills that make it difficult for the client to initiate or maintain satisfying relationships. The therapist collaborates very actively with the client in finding solutions to these problems. In controlled outcome studies, interpersonal therapy has proven to be one of the more effective current therapies for depression (Chambless & Hollon, 1998; Coren & Frosh, 2010), and for somatic system disorder (Sattel et al., 2012).

HUMANISTIC PSYCHOTHERAPIES

In contrast to psychodynamic theorists, who view behaviour as a product of unconscious processes, humanistic theorists view humans as capable of consciously controlling their actions and taking responsibility for their choices and behaviour. These theorists also believe that everyone possesses inner resources for self-healing and personal growth, and that disordered behaviour reflects a blocking of the natural growth process. This blocking is brought about by distorted perceptions, lack of awareness about feelings, or a negative self-image.

When these assumptions about human nature are applied to psychotherapy, they inspire treatments that are radically different from psychoanalysis. Humanistic psychotherapy is seen as a human encounter between equals. The

7. What is the goal of humanistic therapies, and how do the therapies try to achieve this goal?

8. Define the three important therapist attributes described by Rogers.

therapist's goal is to create an environment in which clients can engage in self-exploration and remove the barriers that block their natural tendencies toward personal growth (Hoffman et al., 2013; Greenberg & Rice, 1997). These barriers often result from childhood experiences that fostered unrealistic or maladaptive standards for self-worth. When people try to live their lives according to the expectations of others rather than in terms of their own desires and feelings, they often feel unfulfilled and empty, and unsure about who they really are as people.

In contrast to psychoanalytic therapy, humanistic approaches focus primarily on the present and future instead of the past. Therapy is directed at helping clients become aware of feelings as they occur rather than at achieving insight into the childhood origins of the feelings.

Client-Centred Therapy

The best-known and most widely used form of humanistic therapy is the client-centred (now sometimes called *person-centred*) approach developed by Carl Rogers (1959, 1980; Figure 17.5). In the 1940s, Rogers began to depart from psychoanalytic methods. He became convinced that the important "active ingredient" in therapy is the relationship that develops between client and therapist, and he began to focus his attention on the kind of therapeutic environment that seemed most effective in fostering self-exploration and personal growth (Bozarth et al., 2002). Rogers's research and experiences as a therapist identified three important and interrelated therapist attributes:

1. **Unconditional positive regard** is communicated when therapists show clients that they genuinely care about and accept them, without judgment or evaluation. The

FIGURE 17.5 "Psychotherapy is the releasing of an already existing capacity in a potentially competent individual, not the expert manipulation of a more or less passive personality."—Carl Rogers

therapist also communicates a sense of trust in clients' ability to work through their problems. In part, this sense of trust is communicated in the therapist's refusal to offer advice or guidance.

2. **Empathy,** the willingness and ability to view the world through the client's eyes, is a second vital factor. In a good therapeutic relationship, the therapist comes to sense the feelings and meanings experienced by the client and communicates this understanding to the client. The therapist does this by *reflecting* back to the client what he or she is communicating—perhaps by rephrasing something the client has just said in a way that captures the meaning and emotion involved.

3. **Genuineness** is the third important therapist attribute. There must be consistency between the way the therapist feels and the way he or she behaves. A therapist must be open enough to honestly express feelings, whether positive or negative. In the case of negative feelings, this may seem to be contradictory to the attribute of unconditional positive regard, but that is not necessarily the case. Indeed, the most striking demonstration of both attributes occurs when a therapist can express displeasure with a client's behaviour and at the same time communicate acceptance of the client as a person. For example, a therapist might say, "I feel frustrated with the way

you handled that situation because I want things to work out better than that for you."

Rogers believed that when therapists can express these three critical therapeutic attributes, they create a situation in which the client feels accepted, understood, and free to explore basic attitudes and feelings without fear of being judged or rejected. Within such a relationship, clients experience the courage and freedom to grow.

These therapeutic attitudes are exhibited in the following excerpt from one of Rogers's therapy sessions:

Client: I cannot be the kind of person I want to be. I guess maybe I haven't the guts or the strength to kill myself, and if someone else would relieve me of the responsibility or I would be in an accident, I—just don't want to live.

Rogers: At the present time things look so black that you can't see much point in living. (Note the use of empathic reflection and the absence of any criticism.)

Client: Yes, I wish I'd never started this therapy. I was happy when I was living in my dream world. There I could be the kind of person I wanted to be. But now there is such a wide, wide gap between my ideal and what I am. . . . (Notice how the client responds to reflection with more information.)

Rogers: It's really tough digging into this like you are and at times the shelter of your dream world looks more attractive and comfortable. (Reflection.)

Client: My dream world or suicide. . . . So I don't see why I should waste your time coming in twice a week—I'm not worth it—what do you think?

Rogers: It's up to you. . . . It isn't wasting my time. I'd be glad to see you whenever you come, but it's how you feel about it. (Note the genuineness in stating an honest desire to see the client and the unconditional positive regard in trusting her capacity and responsibility for choice.)

Client: You're not going to suggest that I come in oftener? You're not alarmed and think I ought to come in every day until I get out of this?

Rogers: I believe you're able to make your own decision. I'll see you whenever you want to come. (Trust and positive regard.)

Client: (Note of awe in her voice.) I don't believe you are alarmed about—I see—I may be afraid of myself but you aren't afraid for me. (She experiences the therapist's confidence in her.)

Rogers: You say you may be afraid of yourself and are wondering why I don't seem to be afraid for you. (Reflection.)

Client: You have more confidence in me than I have. I'll see you next week, maybe. (Based on Rogers, 1951, p. 49)

(The client did not attempt suicide.)

Source: Excerpt from Carl R. Rogers, *Client-Centered Therapy*, p. 49, Copyright © 1951 by Cengage Learning, Inc. Reproduced by permission. www.cengage.com/permissions.

Rogers believed that, as clients experience a constructive therapeutic relationship, they exhibit increased self-acceptance, greater self-awareness, enhanced self-reliance, increased comfort with other relationships, and improved life functioning (Rogers, 1959). Research does indicate that therapists' characteristics have a strong effect on the outcome of psychotherapy. Therapy is most likely to be successful when the therapist is perceived as genuine, warm, and empathic (Sachse & Elliott, 2002; Suminson & Law, 2006). Almost three decades after Rogers's death, the person-centred approach remains an influential force (Ahammed & Cherian, 2013; Cain, 2010; Gonçalves et al., 2012).

Gestalt Therapy

9. How is Gestalt therapy derived from Gestalt psychology principles?

Frederick S. (Fritz) Perls, a European psychoanalyst who was trained in Gestalt psychology, developed another humanistic approach to treatment. As noted in Chapter 5, the term *gestalt* ("organized whole") refers to perceptual principles through which people actively organize stimulus elements into meaningful "whole" patterns. Ordinarily, in whatever we perceive, whether external stimuli, ideas, or emotions, we concentrate on only part of our whole experience—the figure—while largely ignoring the background against which the figure appears. For people who have psychological difficulties, that background includes important feelings, wishes, and thoughts that are blocked from ordinary awareness because they would evoke anxiety. Gestalt therapy's goal is to bring them into immediate awareness so that the client can be "whole" once again.

Gestalt therapy is often carried out in groups, and Gestalt therapists have developed a variety of imaginative techniques to help clients "get in touch with their inner selves." These methods are much more active and dramatic than client-centred approaches, and are sometimes even confrontational in nature. Therapists often ask clients to role-play different aspects of themselves so that they may directly experience their inner dynamics. In the *empty-chair technique,* a client may be asked to imagine his mother sitting in the chair, and then carry on a conversation in which he alternatively role-plays his mother and himself, changing chairs for each role and honestly telling her how he feels about important issues in their relationship. These techniques can evoke powerful feelings and make clients aware of unresolved issues that affect other relationships in their lives as well.

Despite their common commitment to humanistic principles, Rogers and Perls differed sharply in their attitudes toward doing research on humanistic therapies. Rogers was committed to research that would help to identify the factors that contribute to therapeutic success. He was a pioneer in tape-recording therapy sessions and analyzing them to study what went on in therapy (Rogers & Dymond, 1954). In contrast, Perls had a strongly anti-scientific attitude that kept him and his followers from doing systematic research on the effectiveness of Gestalt therapy. As a result, the influence of the Gestalt movement began to wane following Perls's death in 1970. More recently, however, some clinical researchers have begun assessing the effects of Gestalt techniques.

Leslie Greenberg and Wanda Malcolm (2002) tested the effects of the empty-chair technique in helping clients resolve "unfinished business" with significant others in their past lives. The clients were seen for 12 to 14 hourly sessions. One client was a submissive middle-aged man who had felt humiliated and emotionally rejected by his mother's hurtful teasing and public humiliation of him as a child. Here is a sample of the client's (C) empty-chair statements to his mother (M) over several sessions:

C: You were self-centered and you didn't care too much about me and the way I was brought up as far as my emotions go.

M: (as client occupies her chair) What are you talking about? What do you mean? I gave you the best years of my life. Somebody had to look after you. I did the best I could.

C: I was hurt so much. I carry that. I lost some of that warmth inside me. It affects the way I have relationships. The way

I relate to myself. The way I feel about myself. All these years I thought I was a joke. This is what I carry (crying). I'm ashamed of myself.

M: Yes, I know I did some of those things you said. And I could have been a better mother, but I guess I was young. I was still a child myself. I couldn't give you the emotional stability you wanted. . . . I'm sorry that it had an effect on you.

C: As a little boy I couldn't tell you "Stop it. Don't do it. Keep away." But I can tell you now that I resent you for it and I won't forgive you. . . . I'm not going to dance around you any more. I'm going to stand up for myself. I think it's about time. (p. 408)

Greenberg and Malcolm then had clinicians listen to tapes of these sessions. The clinicians judged 13 of 32 clients to have completely resolved their unfinished business, as evidenced by affirmation of the self as worthwhile and either an increased understanding, empathy, or forgiveness of the other person or the ability to hold the other accountable for wrongdoing. Compared with those who did not reach complete resolution, resolved clients expressed more intense emotions during the empty-chair exercise and had significantly better treatment outcomes on measures of psychological distress, self-esteem, and improvement in interpersonal problems. Figure 17.6 shows pretreatment and post-treatment scores on a measure of interpersonal problems for the resolved and unresolved clients. Although both groups showed therapeutic gains, only those shown by the resolved group were statistically significant. Paivio and Greenberg (1995) have also demonstrated that the empty-chair

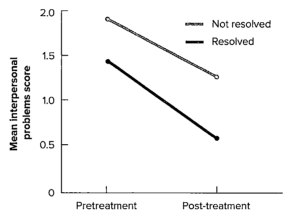

FIGURE 17.6 Use of the Gestalt therapy empty-chair technique to facilitate the resolution of unfinished business with significant others. Those clients judged to have achieved a full resolution of the past conflicts over the course of treatment showed a significant reduction in scores on a self-report measure of current interpersonal difficulties.

Source: Based on Greenberg, L.S., & Malcolm, W. (2002). Resolving unfinished business: Relating process to outcome. *Journal of Consulting and Clinical Psychology, 70,* 406–416.

exercise is more effective than simply receiving information about resolving "unfinished business." Today, the empty-chair exercise is one of several Gestalt techniques being incorporated into non-humanistic therapies as well (Cain & Seeman, 2002; Lazarus, 1995).

COGNITIVE THERAPIES

As we have seen, many behaviour disorders involve maladaptive ways of thinking about oneself and the world. Cognitive approaches to psychotherapy focus on the role of irrational and self-defeating thought patterns, and therapists who employ this approach try to help clients discover and change the cognitions that underlie their problems.

In contrast to psychoanalysts, cognitive therapists do not emphasize the importance of unconscious psychodynamic processes. They do, however, point out that, because our habitual thought patterns are so well-practised and ingrained, they tend to "run off" almost automatically, so that we may be only minimally aware of them and simply may accept them as reflecting "reality" (Clark et al., 1999). Thus, clients often need help in identifying the beliefs, ideas, and self-statements that trigger maladaptive emotions and behaviours. Once identified, these cognitions can be challenged and, with practice and effort, changed. Since there is a focus on both thoughts and behaviours, this type of therapy is often referred to as cognitive behaviour therapy (CBT). Albert Ellis and Aaron Beck are the most influential figures in the cognitive approach to therapy.

Ellis's Rational-Emotive Therapy (RET)

10. What do *ABCD* stand for in rational-emotive therapy, and how is this model used in therapy?

Albert Ellis, originally trained as a psychoanalytic therapist, became convinced that irrational thoughts, rather than unconscious dynamics, were the most immediate cause of self-defeating emotions. Ellis's theory of emotional disturbance and his rational-emotive therapy are embodied in his ABCD model (Figure 17.7):

- *A* stands for the *activating event* that seems to trigger the emotion.
- *B* stands for the *belief system* that underlies the way in which a person appraises the event.
- *C* stands for the emotional and behavioural *consequences* of that appraisal.
- *D* is the key to changing maladaptive emotions and behaviours: *disputing*, or challenging, an erroneous belief system.

Ellis (Figure 17.8) pointed out that people are accustomed to viewing their emotions (*C*'s) as being caused directly by events (*A*'s). Thus, a young man who is turned down for a date may feel rejected and depressed. However, Ellis would insist that the woman's refusal is *not* the true reason for the emotional reaction. Rather, that reaction is caused by the young man's irrational belief that "to be a worthwhile person, I must be loved and accepted by virtually everyone, especially those I consider important." If the young man does not want to feel depressed and rejected, this belief must be countered and replaced by a more rational interpretation (e.g., "It would have been nice if she had accepted my invitation, but I don't

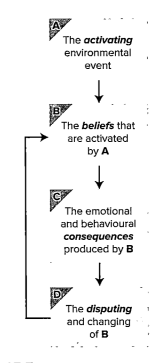

A The *activating* environmental event

B The *beliefs* that are activated by **A**

C The emotional and behavioural *consequences* produced by **B**

D The *disputing* and changing of **B**

FIGURE 17.7 Albert Ellis's ABCD model describes his theory of the cause—and cure—of maladaptive emotional responses and behaviours. In therapy, the goal is to discover, dispute, and change the client's maladaptive beliefs.

© Courtesy Dr. Albert Ellis

FIGURE 17.8 "The essence of effective therapy according to rational-emotive therapy is full tolerance of people as individuals combined with a ruthless campaign against their self-defeating ideas. . . . These can be easily elicited and demolished by any scientist worth his or her salt; and the rational-emotive therapist is exactly that: an exposing and nonsense-annihilating scientist."—Albert Ellis

TABLE 17.1 Irrational Ideas That Cause Disturbance, and Alternatives That Might Be Offered by a Rational-Emotive Therapist

Irrational Belief	Rational Alternative
It is a dire necessity that I be loved and approved of by virtually everyone for everything I do.	Although we might prefer approval to disapproval, our self-worth need not depend on the love and approval of others. Self-respect is more important than giving up one's individuality to buy the approval of others.
I must be thoroughly competent and achieving to be worthwhile. To fail is to be a failure.	As imperfect and fallible human beings, we are bound to fail from time to time. We can control only effort; we have incomplete control over outcome. We are better off focusing on the process of doing rather than on demands that we do well.
It is terrible, awful, and catastrophic when things are not the way I demand that they be.	Stop catastrophizing and turning an annoyance or irritation into a major crisis. Who are we to demand that things be different from what they are? When we turn our preferences into dire necessities, we set ourselves up for needless distress. We had best learn to change those things we can control and accept those that we can't control (and be wise enough to know the difference).
Human misery is externally caused and forced on one by other people and events.	Human misery is produced not by external factors but rather by what we tell ourselves about those events. We feel as we think, and most of our misery is needlessly self-inflicted by irrational habits of thinking.
Because something deeply affected me in the past, it must continue to do so.	We hold ourselves prisoner to the past because we continue to believe philosophies and ideas learned in the past. If they are still troubling us today, then it is because we are still propagandizing ourselves with irrational nonsense. We can control how we think in the here and now and thereby liberate ourselves from the "scars" of the past.

need to turn it into a catastrophe and believe that no one will ever care about me.").

Rational-emotive therapists introduce clients to common irrational ideas (Table 17.1) and then train them to ferret out the particular ideas that underlie their maladaptive emotional responses. Clients are given homework assignments to help them analyze and change self-statements. They also may be asked to place themselves in challenging situations and practise control over their emotions by using the new self-statements. For example, a shy person might be required to go to a party and practise rational thoughts that counteract social anxiety. By learning and practising cognitive coping responses, clients eventually can modify underlying belief systems in ways that enhance well-being (Bora et al., 2013; David et al., 2005; Dryden, 2002). RET also has been applied successfully to help elite athletes cope with beliefs and emotions related to sport performance (e.g., Turner et al., 2014a, 2014b).

Beck's Cognitive Therapy

Like Ellis, Aaron Beck's goal is to point out errors of thinking and logic that underlie emotional disturbance and to help clients identify and reprogram their overlearned "automatic" thought patterns (Figure 17.9). In treating depressed clients, a first step is to help clients realize that their thoughts, not the situation, cause their maladaptive emotional reactions.

© Courtesy Dr. Aaron T. Beck

FIGURE 17.9 "The formula for treatment may be stated in simple terms: The therapist helps the patient to identify his warped thinking and to learn more realistic ways to formulate his experience."—Aaron Beck

This realization sets the stage for identifying and changing the maladaptive thoughts.

> *Client:* I get depressed when things go wrong. Like when I fail a test.
>
> *Beck:* How can failing a test make you depressed?
>
> *Client:* Well, if I fail, I'll never get into law school.

Beck: So failing a test means a lot to you. But if failing a test could drive people into clinical depression, wouldn't you expect everyone who failed a test to have a depression? Did everyone who failed get depressed enough to require treatment?

Client: No, but it depends on how important the test was to the person.

Beck: Right, and who decides the importance?

Client: I do.

Beck: Now what did failing mean?

Client: (Tearful) That I couldn't get into law school.

Beck: And what does that mean to you?

Client: That I'm just not smart enough.

Beck: Anything else?

Client: That I can never be happy.

Beck: And how do those thoughts make you feel?

Client: Very unhappy.

Beck: So it is the *meaning* (italics added) of failing a test that makes you very unhappy. In fact, believing that you can never be happy is a powerful factor in producing unhappiness. So you get yourself into a trap—by definition, failure to get into law school equals "I can never be happy." (Based on Beck et al., 1979, pp. 145–146)

Source: Excerpt from A.T. Beck, A.J. Rush, B.F. Shaw & G. Emery, *Cognitive Therapy of Depression*, pp. 145-146, 1979. New York: Guilford. Reprinted by permission of Guilford Publications, Inc.

11. Which disorders have responded most favourably to Beck's cognitive therapy? What is the focus of the therapy in these disorders?

Beck's contributions to the understanding and treatment of depression have made his cognitive therapy a psychological treatment of choice for that disorder. Cognitive therapy with booster sessions after depression decreased resulted in improvement maintenance in 97 percent of depressed clients, with non-recurrence of depression in 75 percent (Vittengl et al., 2009). Cognitive therapy has been extended to the treatment of anger disorders, anxiety disorders, personality disorders, and eating disorders with equally encouraging results (Butler et al., 2006; Craske, 1999; Lambert et al., 2004). For example, Donald Meichenbaum's work (e.g., Meichenbaum, 1991) on **self-instructional training** has been very influential in treatments related to stress and coping. As we shall see, elements of cognitive therapy are frequently combined with other therapeutic techniques to form highly effective treatments for a variety of disorders. Cognitive therapy is considered the treatment of choice for unipolar depression and can affect underlying physiological components, as discussed in the *Focus on Neuroscience* feature for this chapter.

BEHAVIOUR THERAPIES

In the 1960s, behavioural approaches emerged as a dramatic departure from the assumptions and methods that characterized psychoanalytic and humanistic therapies. The new practitioners of behaviour therapy denied the importance of inner dynamics. Instead, they insisted that (1) behaviour disorders are learned in the same ways normal behaviours are, and (2) these maladaptive behaviours can be unlearned by application of principles derived from research on classical conditioning and operant conditioning. Behaviourists demonstrated that these learning procedures could be applied to change the behaviours of schizophrenics, to effectively treat anxiety disorders, and to modify many child and adult behaviour problems that seemed resistant to traditional therapy approaches (Hersen, 2002).

In Chapter 7, we described three important learning mechanisms: classical conditioning, operant conditioning, and modelling. We now consider therapy techniques based on each of these forms of learning.

Classical Conditioning Treatments

Classical conditioning procedures have been used in two major ways. First, they have been used to reduce, or decondition, anxiety responses. Second, they have been used in attempts to condition new anxiety responses to a particular class of stimuli, such as alcoholic beverages or inappropriate sexual objects. The most commonly used classical conditioning procedures are exposure therapies, systematic desensitization, and aversion therapy.

Exposure: An Extinction Approach

From a behavioural point of view, phobias and other fears result from classically conditioned emotional responses (e.g., Rachman, 1991). The conditioning experience is assumed to involve a pairing of the phobic object (the neutral stimulus) with an aversive unconditioned stimulus (UCS). As a result, the phobic stimulus becomes a conditioned stimulus (CS) that elicits the

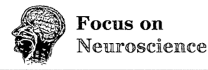

Focus on Neuroscience

THE NEUROSCIENCE OF TREATING UNIPOLAR DEPRESSION

Cognitive behaviour therapy (CBT) is viewed as the treatment of choice for unipolar depression (Kuyken, Dalglish, & Holden, 2007). The goal of this approach is to identify maladaptive thoughts and behaviours and, through therapy, help the patient to think more rationally. But what changes are going on in the brain while this is happening?

As discussed in Chapter 16, depression may stem from the underactivity of certain neurotransmitters such as norepinephrine, dopamine, and serotonin (collectively known as the *monoamines*). Drug treatments for depression target these monoamines, resulting in higher levels of the neurotransmitters in specific brain areas. Working with a group of depressed patients, Kennedy et al. (2001) report increased activity (via PET scan) in much of the prefrontal cortex, parietal cortex, and the cingulate cortex (area above the corpus callosum) following six weeks of treatment with the antidepressant drug Paxil. This increased activity reflects a return to "normal" levels and further illustrates the involvement of the cortex and limbic system in depression. Would we expect similar changes using a talking therapy?

In a study also using PET scans (Meyer et al., 2004), no global differences were found between patients with and without major depression. But for the depressed group, reduced serotonin transport was observed for those who expressed higher levels of dysfunctional beliefs. Thus, it would appear that maladaptive thoughts are related to lower levels of serotonin and, consequently, CBT should be a very effective treatment. Indeed, changes in brain function can be noted following a course of CBT treatment. Goldapple et al. (2004) have demonstrated that those patients who were successfully treated with CBT showed a change in function (as measured by PET) in both the limbic system and the cortex. Compared with a group of patients treated with paroxetine (Paxil), there were specific changes for CBT in both the frontal cortex and the hippocampus. So it would appear that talking therapy can alter brain function in much the same way that drug treatments do.

The DSM-5 calls for increased attention to the biological underpinnings of various psychological disorders (American Psychiatric Association, 2013; Phillips, 2007). To this end, various researchers are trying to develop screening tests for disorders based on neuroimaging. Siegle and colleagues (2006) presented a series of emotional words to both a group of unmedicated patients with unipolar depression and a comparison group of individuals who had never experienced depression. All participants rated the personal relevance of these words while undergoing an fMRI scan. Following this task, the depressed group received 16 sessions of CBT. Those participants who reacted with low levels of activity in the cingulate cortex and high levels in the amygdala when processing negative emotional words showed the most improvement after CBT. Siegle et al. (2006) note that the cingulate cortex is involved in the regulation of activity in the limbic system. Thus, depressed individuals showing this lack of regulation are precisely those who will benefit from CBT since CBT will help them regain emotional control. More recently, Grotegerd et al. (2012) have demonstrated unique pattern differences between unipolar and bipolar depression. Unipolar depression is associated with activity in the prefrontal and orbital frontal regions, while bipolar disorder was more specific to the dorsolateral prefrontal area.

---

conditioned response (CR) of anxiety. According to the two-factor learning theory discussed in Chapter 7, avoidance responses to the phobic situation are then reinforced by anxiety reduction (operant conditioning based on negative reinforcement). Thus, a person who is injured in an automobile accident may find herself afraid to ride in a car. Moreover, each time she avoids exposure to cars, her avoidance response is strengthened through anxiety reduction.

According to this formulation, the most direct way to reduce the fear is through a process of classical extinction of the anxiety response. This reduction requires **exposure** to the feared CS in the absence of the UCS

while using **response prevention** to keep the operant avoidance response from occurring. This is the theoretical basis for the exposure approach (Abramowitz, 2013; Marks, 1991; Zinbarg et al., 1992). The client may be exposed to real-life stimuli (a treatment known as **flooding;** Figure 17.10) or may be asked to imagine scenes involving the stimuli (referred to as **implosion therapy**). Of course, these stimuli will evoke considerable anxiety, but the anxiety will extinguish in time if the person remains in the presence of the CS and the UCS does not occur.

Exposure has proved to be a highly effective technique for extinguishing anxiety responses

12. What are the classical and operant conditioning procedures used in exposure therapy? How was this procedure used to treat agoraphobics?

13. Which specific attributes of VR make it potentially useful in therapy? What evidence is there that VR can work therapeutically?

14. How does systematic desensitization differ from exposure in terms of its (a) underlying principle and (b) specific techniques?

© Geri Engberg/The Image Works

FIGURE 17.10 A behaviour therapist guides and supports a client with a dog phobia during an in vivo exposure therapy session. As a result of exposure, the man's anxiety will extinguish, and he will be able to interact more comfortably with this animal and other dogs.

in both animals and humans (Craske & Mystkowski, 2006; Spiegler & Guevremont, 2003). It is considered the treatment of choice for post-traumatic stress disorder (PTSD; DiMauro, 2014; Zoellner et al., 2009). In one study, agoraphobics who feared leaving the safety of their homes and going into public places were treated. The researchers used an exposure therapy that required these clients to confront feared situations such as driving alone and going into crowded shopping centres. Both before and after the exposure therapy, each client was assessed on a series of real-life performance tasks. For example, an agoraphobic who feared being in public might be asked to go and stand in a long checkout line in a crowded supermarket. Before exposure treatment began, the phobics were able to pass only 27 percent of these performance tasks. At the end of treatment, they were able to perform 71 percent of the tasks. Moreover, this degree of improvement was maintained or even increased at follow-ups ranging from three months to two years (Williams et al., 1989). These are extremely encouraging results, since agoraphobics are difficult to treat with nonbehavioural methods. An additional advantage is that clients can administer exposure treatment to themselves under a therapist's direction, with high success rates (Marks, 1991). Stanley Rachman at the University of British Columbia also reports success with using behavioural methods for the treatment of obsessive-compulsive disorder (Rachman, Hodgson, & Marks, 1997). Patients who were rated as "moderately incapacitated"

were helped effectively with a treatment based on flooding.

New technologies are allowing therapists to treat anxiety disorders in a very realistic but safe manner. This chapter's *Frontiers* feature focuses on attempts to use the high-tech capabilities of virtual reality as a therapy tool.

Systematic Desensitization: A Counterconditioning Approach

In 1958, Joseph Wolpe helped to launch the behaviour therapy movement with his introduction of **systematic desensitization**, a new learning-based treatment for anxiety disorders. Wolpe also presented impressive outcome data for 100 phobics he had treated with the technique. Systematic desensitization remains a widely used treatment today. In many controlled studies, its success rate in treating a wide range of phobic disorders has been 80 percent or better (Rachman, 2000; Spiegler & Guevremont, 2003). Systematic desensitization has also been used to treat test anxiety (Maredpour et al., 2012), math anxiety (Zettle, 2012), and anxiety due to highway driving (Iglesias & Igleslas, 2013).

Wolpe viewed anxiety as a classically conditioned emotional response. His goal was to eliminate the anxiety by using a procedure called **counterconditioning,** in which a new response that is incompatible with anxiety is conditioned to the anxiety-arousing CS.

The first step in systematic desensitization is to train the client in the skill of voluntary muscle relaxation. Next, the client is helped to construct a **stimulus hierarchy** of 10 to 15 scenes relating to the fear. The hierarchy is carefully arranged in roughly equal steps from low-anxiety scenes to high-anxiety ones. Table 17.2 shows a stimulus hierarchy that was used in treating a university student with high test anxiety.

In the desensitization sessions, the therapist deeply relaxes the client and then asks the client to vividly imagine the first scene in the hierarchy (the least anxiety-arousing one) for several seconds. The client can't be both relaxed and anxious at the same time, so if the relaxation is strong enough, it replaces anxiety as the CR to that stimulus—the counterconditioning process. When the client can imagine that scene for increasingly longer periods without experiencing anxiety, the therapist proceeds to the next scene. Once low-arousal scenes have been deconditioned, some of the total anxiety has been reduced, and the person is now able to imagine more anxiety-arousing

VIRTUAL REALITY AS A THERAPEUTIC TECHNIQUE

Almost all therapeutic perspectives are based on the assumption that therapy outcomes are likely to be most favourable if clients are able to vividly experience or re-experience important environmental, emotional, and relationship elements that underlie their problems. **Virtual reality (VR)** involves the use of computer technology to create highly realistic "virtual environments" that simulate actual experience so vividly that they evoke many of the same reactions that a comparable real-world environment would create. Observers typically wear helmets containing two small video monitors (one for each eye) attached to a high-speed computer. The image to each eye is slightly different to produce binocular depth perception cues that result in a three-dimensional image. With the aid of position-tracking devices, the computer monitors the person's physical movements and adjusts the images and sounds accordingly. Thus, observers have a vivid experience of *presence* in a "different place" when navigating through the virtual world. This power to immerse the user in a simulated environment derives not so much from the realism of the displays as from the fact that perception and action are integrated as they are in real life (North et al., 2002).

Several other aspects of VR heighten its potential usefulness as a therapy tool. VR is highly flexible and programmable, allowing a therapist to present a variety of controlled situations and monitor their effects on a client. Scenes can easily be changed, depending on the actions of the client. Moreover, the therapist can don his or her own helmet and accompany the client into the virtual world, experiencing exactly what the client does and providing input to the client at appropriate moments. These shared experiences in the virtual world could enable clients to overcome old problems, experiment with new social roles, and learn new skills with the guidance of the therapist.

VR's use in psychotherapy is in its infancy, but it has already been applied to a variety of problems (Hoffman et al., 2001; Rothbaum et al., 2000). Most of these applications have been in the treatment of phobias and PTSD, where VR allows clients to interact with feared stimuli or situations while undergoing exposure or systematic desensitization therapy. For example, researchers have produced simulations of heights (e.g., a virtual elevator that could produce the sensations of being at various heights under different conditions, such as with or without walls, inside or on the outside of a building). Compared with a no-treatment control group of height phobics, those who received a seven-session VR-graded exposure treatment showed a significant reduction in anxiety and less avoidance of heights. Over a third of the VR participants spontaneously exposed themselves to heights after the treatment, including one who rode up

72 stories in a glass-walled elevator (Rothbaum et al., 1995). VR therapy has also been applied successfully to fear of flying by taking the client on trips, accompanied by the therapist, in a virtual Apache helicopter that takes off and flies over the airport and city (Klein, 1999; North et al., 1997). More recent work uses VR to treat body image disorders (Ferrer-Garcia & Gutierrez-Maldonado, 2012), social anxiety (Page et al., 2013), and gambling disorder (Giroux et al., 2013).

A case study by Albert Carlin, Hunter Hoffman, and Suzanne Weghorst (1997) provides an example of how several sensory modalities can be combined to immerse people in a virtual environment. The client was a 37-year-old woman with a debilitating spider phobia that had interfered with her life for 20 years. At the time she entered treatment, any encounter with a spider or a spider web evoked panic, weeping, and shame about her "out of control" fear. She took elaborate precautions to avoid spiders, including fumigating and vacuuming her car before entering it, sealing her bedroom door and windows with duct tape each night, placing each piece of her clothing in a separate plastic bag immediately after washing or ironing it, and avoiding the outdoors where she might encounter a spider. Even viewing photographs or drawings of spiders evoked anxiety.

Over a period of 12 weekly sessions, VR was used to create a "virtual kitchen" in which the client had encounters with either a small black spider in a web or a large brown virtual spider with a furry texture. Using a computer mouse to move about the three-dimensional virtual kitchen and a glove that operated her "virtual hand" inside the scene, the client exposed herself to spider experiences that gradually increased in intensity (Figure 17.11). When she opened a cupboard in the kitchen, she might encounter a spider that would crawl toward her. The spiders were preprogrammed to jump into the air when touched, swing toward her in their webs, and engage in other frightening behaviours. Later in treatment, when she began touching the large hairy brown spider with her virtual hand, another sensory modality was brought into the virtual world in the form of a palm-sized replica of a fur-covered Guyana bird-eating tarantula. When the client reached out with her virtual hand to touch the brown spider, her real hand encountered the furry tarantula, and any movement of the toy spider caused a similar movement of the virtual spider. These experiences, which evoked considerable anxiety at first, resulted in a dramatic reduction in spider anxiety both within the virtual world and in her real-life environment. Her ritualistic avoidance behaviours disappeared and she was able to stand over a spider that she encountered in her home for 20 minutes, to crush another one, and to go camping for the first time since adolescence. Controlled experimental studies have since confirmed the effectiveness of VR treatment for a variety

continued

Courtesy of Hunter Hoffman; photo by Mary Levin, University of Washington.

FIGURE 17.11 Virtual reality (VR) was used to treat this spider phobic. The client views a virtual "spider world" inside the helmet. Psychologist Hunter Hoffman brings a virtual spider (shown on monitor) closer by slowly moving the VR position sensor in his right hand closer to the client's face. The sensor also can be attached to a furry toy spider to increase stimulus exposure.

of phobias and anxiety disorders (Parsons & Rizzo, 2008; Powers & Emmelkamp, 2008).

The promising results achieved so far point to the need for systematic studies of VR therapy to explore several questions. Is it more effective than exposure through imagination or in real life? Is it cost effective in terms of computer and programming costs and number of therapy sessions needed? Up to now, most VR applications have depicted physical aspects of the environment. Can it be extended to social situations in which a client might be able to have realistic interaction with significant virtual others from the client's past or present life? Could it be used in aversion therapies to classically condition negative emotional responses to depictions of children, in the case of pedophiles, or to alcohol, in the case of alcoholics? With respect to anxiety disorders, Rizzo has maintained that VR is quite effective in the treatment of a variety of problems, from occupational rehabilitation to PTSD (e.g., Rizzo & Kim, 2005). Indeed, Rizzo and his colleagues (e.g., Reger et al., 2009; Rizzo et al., 2008) and others (e.g., McCann et al., 2014) have reported that VR can have a positive effect on war veterans who suffer from post-traumatic stress. However, the effectiveness may not extend to other psychological disorders. But with respect to anxiety disorders, the data are very promising. Opris et al. (2012) report that a meta-analysis of the existing studies indicates that VR is much more successful than the waitlist control procedure, and is at least as effective as either a conventional behavioural treatment or CBT. Recently, researchers have argued for a move to augmented reality (AR) platforms rather than virtual (e.g., Baus & Bouchard, 2014). AR allows for an integration of the real world with the digital and can be much more engaging (consider the success of Pokemon Go). In addition, AR may be less expensive and more readily available to clients. Giglioli et al. (2015) report remarkable success with AR in the treatment of specific phobias (particularly involving small animals or insects). AR has even been used to treat phantom pain (Ortiz-Catalan et al., 2014).

TABLE 17.2 A Stimulus Hierarchy Used in the Systematic Desensitization Treatment of a Test-Anxious University Student

Scene 1	Hearing about someone else who has a test
Scene 2	Instructor announcing that a test will be given in three weeks
Scene 3	Instructor reminding class that there will be a test in two weeks
Scene 4	Overhearing classmates talk about studying for the test, which will occur in one week
Scene 5	Instructor reminding class of what it will be tested on in two days
Scene 6	Leaving class the day before the exam
Scene 7	Studying the night before the exam
Scene 8	Getting up the morning of the exam
Scene 9	Walking toward the building where the exam will be given
Scene 10	Walking into the testing room
Scene 11	Instructor walking into room with tests
Scene 12	Tests being passed out
Scene 13	Reading the test questions
Scene 14	Watching others finish the test
Scene 15	Seeing a question I can't answer
Scene 16	Instructor waiting for me to finish the test

ones without becoming anxious. Desensitization also can be accomplished through carefully controlled exposure to a hierarchy of real-life situations (**in vivo desensitization**). For example, an individual with a height phobia might actually stand on a stepstool and, eventually, walk across a suspension bridge while voluntarily relaxed, rather than simply imagining the scenes. Both desensitization approaches are highly effective in reducing anxiety (Hersen, 2003; Zettle, 2012).

Although both exposure therapy based on extinction and systematic desensitization are very effective in reducing fear responses, systematic desensitization is sometimes preferred because the client will experience far less anxiety during the treatment. Then again, exposure often reduces anxiety more quickly than does systematic desensitization (Bruce & Sanderson, 1998).

Aversion Therapy

For some clients, the therapeutic goal is not to reduce anxiety, but to actually condition it to a particular stimulus so as to reduce deviant approach behaviours. In **aversion therapy**, the therapist pairs a stimulus that is attractive to a person and that stimulates deviant or self-defeating behaviour (the CS) with a noxious UCS in an attempt to condition an aversion to the CS. For example, aversion treatment for alcoholics may involve injecting clients with a nausea-producing drug, and then having them drink alcohol (the CS) as nausea (the UCS) develops. Similarly, pedophiles (child molesters) have undergone treatment in which strong electric shock is paired with slides showing children similar to those the offenders sexually abused (Figure 17.12). To measure the effects of the treatment on males, readings from a physiological recording device that measures penile blood volume responses to the slides can be compared before and after treatment (Drucker, 2014; Sandler, 1986).

Aversion therapies have been applied to a range of disorders with variable results. In one study of 278 alcoholics who underwent aversion therapy, 190 (63 percent) were still abstinent a year after treatment ended. Three years later, a third of the patients were still abstinent, an impressive result given the traditionally high relapse rate of chronic alcoholics (Moos & Moos, 2006). Unfortunately, however, treatment effects from aversion therapies often fail to generalize from the treatment setting to the real world. Some experts believe

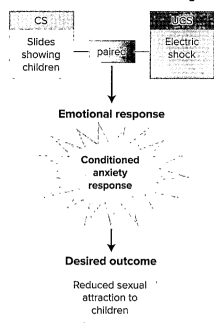

Classical aversion conditioning

Slides showing children — paired — Electric shock

Emotional response

Conditioned anxiety response

Desired outcome

Reduced sexual attraction to children

FIGURE 17.12 The classical conditioning that occurs in aversion therapy is illustrated in the treatment of a pedophile who receives electric shocks when pictures of children are presented. The goal of the treatment is the development of a conditioned anxiety response that reduces the sexual attractiveness of children.

15. How does classical conditioning underlie aversion therapy? What additional training can enhance its effectiveness?

that aversion therapy is most likely to succeed if it is part of a more comprehensive treatment program in which the client also learns specific coping skills for avoiding relapses (Marlatt & Gordon, 1985).

Operant Conditioning Treatments

The term **behaviour modification** refers to treatment techniques that involve the application of operant conditioning procedures in an attempt to increase or decrease a specific behaviour. These techniques may use any of the operant procedures for manipulating the environment that were discussed in Chapter 7: positive reinforcement, extinction, negative reinforcement, or punishment. The focus in behaviour modification is on externally observable behaviours, and measurement of the behaviours targeted for change occurs throughout the treatment program. This measurement allows the therapist to track the progress of the treatment program and to make modifications if behaviour change begins to lag.

Behaviour modification techniques have been applied successfully to many different behaviour disorders. They have yielded particularly impressive results when applied to populations that are difficult to treat with more traditional therapies, such as chronic hospitalized schizophrenics, profoundly disturbed children, and mentally disabled individuals (Eikeseth et al., 2002; Martin & Pear, 2010). We now consider the use of positive reinforcement and punishment in two of these populations.

Positive Reinforcement

One of the dangers of long-term psychiatric hospitalization is the gradual loss of social, personal-care, and occupational skills needed to survive outside the hospital. Such deterioration is common among chronic schizophrenic patients who have been hospitalized for an extended period. Verbal psychotherapies have had very limited success in rebuilding such skills.

16. How do token economies work, and what evidence exists for their effectiveness?

In the 1960s, Teodoro Ayllon and Nathan Azrin (1968) introduced a revolutionary approach to the behavioural treatment of hospitalized schizophrenics. The **token economy** is a system for strengthening desired behaviours—such as personal grooming, appropriate social responses, housekeeping behaviours, working on assigned jobs, and participation in vocational training programs—through the systematic application of positive reinforcement. Rather than giving tangible reinforcers, such as food or grounds privileges,

a kind of "menu" is derived in which a specified number of plastic tokens is given for performance of each desired behaviour. The tokens can be redeemed by the patients for a wide range of tangible reinforcers, such as a private room, exclusive rental of a radio or TV set, selection of personal furniture, freedom to leave the ward and walk around the grounds, recreational activities, and items from the hospital commissary. The long-term goal of token economy programs is to get the desired behaviours started with tangible reinforcers until they eventually come under the control of social reinforcers and self-reinforcement processes (such as self-pride), which will be needed to maintain them in the world outside the hospital. When this begins to occur, the tokens can be phased out and the desired behaviours continue to occur (Kazdin, 2003).

Token economy programs have proven highly effective with some of the most challenging populations. Figure 17.13 shows how quickly the introduction of a token economy increased the work behaviour of chronic schizophrenic patients who were supposedly too disturbed to engage in a work-retraining program (Ayllon & Azrin, 1965). In another study, a token economy program was carried out over a four-year period with severely disturbed schizophrenic patients who had been hospitalized an average of more than 17 years. During the course of the

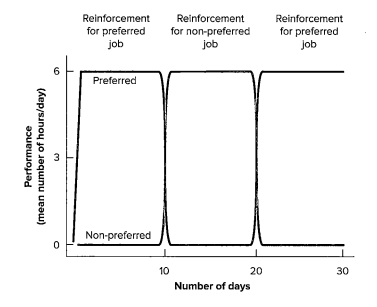

FIGURE 17.13 Average number of hours hospitalized schizophrenic patients worked per day on a job they preferred and a job they did not prefer when tokens were used as reinforcement. Notice how quickly and how strongly their behaviour was influenced by the reinforcement contingency.

Source: Data from Ayllon, T., & Azrin, N.H. (1965). The measurement and reinforcement of behavior of psychotics. *Journal of the Experimental Analysis of Behavior*, 8(6), Nov 1965, 357-383.

program, 98 percent of the patients from the behavioural treatment program were able to be released from the hospital (most to shelter-care facilities in the community), compared with only 45 percent of a control group that received the normal hospital treatments (Paul & Lentz, 1977). Token economies have also been applied successfully within business, school, prison, and home environments to increase desirable behaviours (Hulac, 2010; Martin & Pear, 2010, Slocum & Vollmer, 2015).

Therapeutic Use of Punishment

In the view of most psychologists, punishment is the least preferred way to control behaviour because of its aversive qualities and the potential negative side effects described in Chapter 7. Therefore, before deciding to use punishment as a therapeutic technique, therapists ask themselves two important questions: (1) Are there alternative, less painful approaches that might be effective? (2) Is the behaviour to be eliminated sufficiently injurious to the individual or to society to justify the severity of the punishment?

Sometimes, the answers to these questions lead to a decision to use punishment. For example, some of the most startling self-destructive behaviours imaginable occur in certain severely disturbed autistic children. Such children may strike themselves repeatedly, bang their heads on sharp objects, bite or tear pieces of flesh from their bodies, or engage in other self-mutilating behaviours. O. Ivar Lovaas (1977), a UCLA psychologist who pioneered the use of operant conditioning techniques in the treatment of such children, successfully eliminated such behaviours with a limited number of contingent electric shocks. One seven-year-old boy had been self-injurious for five years and had to be kept in physical restraints. During one 90-minute period when his restraints were removed, he struck himself more than 3000 times. With the consent of his parents, shock electrodes were attached to the boy, and he was given a painful electric shock each time he struck himself. Only 12 shocks were needed to virtually eliminate the self-destructive behaviour. In another case, 15 shocks eliminated self-destructive behaviour in a severely disturbed girl with a history of banging her head against objects. In a large-scale review of treatment techniques for autism spectrum disorder, DiGennaro-Reed et al. (2012) report that therapeutic punishment has been used in about 18 percent of cases involving the treatment of stereotypic behaviours (such as rocking, spinning, mouthing, etc.). Punishment is never employed without the consent of the client or the client's legal guardian in the event that the client is mentally incompetent to give consent.

Modelling and Social Skills Training

Modelling is one of the most important and effective learning processes in humans, and modelling procedures have been used to treat a variety of behavioural problems. One of the most widely used applications is designed to teach clients social skills that they lack.

In **social skills training,** clients learn new skills by observing and then imitating a model who performs a socially skilful behaviour. In the following example, a therapist served as a model for his client, a socially anxious university student who had great difficulty asking women for dates. The client began by pretending to ask for a date over the telephone:

> *Client:* By the way (pause), I don't suppose you want to go out Saturday night?
>
> *Therapist:* Up to actually asking for the date you were very good. However, if I were the girl, I might have been offended when you said, "By the way." It's like asking her out is pretty casual. Also, the way you posed the question, you are kind of suggesting to her that she doesn't want to go out with you. Pretend for the moment I'm you. Now, how does this sound: *"There's a movie at the Varsity Theatre that I want to see. If you don't have other plans, I'd very much like to take you."*
>
> *Client:* That sounded good. Like you were sure of yourself and like the girl, too.
>
> *Therapist:* Why don't you try it? (Masters et al., 1988, p. 100)

Social skills training has been used with many populations, including individuals who have minor deficits in social skills, delinquents who need to learn how to resist negative peer pressures, and even hospitalized schizophrenic patients who need to learn social skills to function adaptively outside the hospital (Kurtz & Mueser, 2008; Rao et al., 2008). It is often used in conjunction with other psychological or biological treatments to "jump start" new

17. Under what conditions is punishment used as a behaviour modification technique? What evidence is there for its effectiveness?

18. How is modelling used in social skills training? How is self-efficacy involved in its effectiveness?

adaptive behaviours that then can be strengthened by natural reinforcers in the client's everyday environment.

Research demonstrates that a key factor underlying the effectiveness of social skills training is increased self-efficacy. When clients come to believe that they are capable of performing the desired behaviours, they succeed in doing so (Bandura, 1997; Maddux, 1999). Observing successful models also increases self-efficacy by encouraging the view, "If she can do that, so can I."

"THIRD-WAVE" COGNITIVE-BEHAVIOURAL THERAPIES

Since the 1950s, behaviour therapies have developed through three phases. The first phase treatments were based on animal models of classical and operant conditioning and explicitly excluded cognitive principles. The second wave, beginning in the 1960s and 1970s, was the emergence of cognitive-behavioural approaches such as rational-emotive behaviour therapy (Ellis), cognitive therapy (Beck), and modelling and role-playing approaches (Bandura). Collectively, these were called *cognitive-behavioural therapies*.

The past two decades have seen the emergence of so-called "third wave" cognitive-behavioural approaches (Hayes et al., 2006; Ost, 2008). These therapies incorporate the concepts of mindfulness as a central objective to behaviour change, and they represent the addition of humanistic concepts and Eastern methods of behaviour therapy. They include a variety of mindfulness-based approaches to various problems, such as acceptance and commitment therapy, and dialectical behaviour therapy.

Mindfulness-Based Treatments

Mindfulness is a mental state of awareness, focus, openness, and acceptance of immediate experience. It also involves a nonjudgmental appraisal, so that in a state of mindfulness, difficult thoughts and feelings have much less impact. In some ways, mindfulness is like the *association cognitive techniques* (focusing nonjudgmentally on the sensations rather than trying to distract oneself) that increase the ability to tolerate painful stimuli (Chapter 5).

An important tool for learning mindfulness is a meditation technique in which people develop a tranquil state and focus closely on their sensations, thoughts, and feelings, allowing them to come and go without a struggle. The meditation technique is being incorporated into a variety of cognitive behavioural treatments, including mindfulness-based stress reduction (MBSR; McCown & Riebel, 2010; Kabat-Zinn et al., 1992) and mindfulness-based relapse prevention (MBRP; Bowen et al., 2009). As a stress management approach, mindfulness meditation reduces physiological arousal, and the detached cognitive outlook helps to free people from emotion-escalating emotional processes. It is being successfully applied to treat a variety of stress-related medical conditions and psychological disorders, including anxiety and depression (Hofmann et al., 2010; Marino et al., 2015; McCown & Riebel, 2010) and problem gambling (Toneatto et al., 2014). Mindfulness meditation has also been added to the relapse prevention techniques discussed in Chapter 15. Here, it is used to prevent relapse by increasing awareness of thoughts and emotions that trigger lapses, thereby interrupting the previous cycle of automatic substance abuse behaviour. It also helps abusers deal with a lapse by helping to neutralize self-blame and thoughts of hopelessness, which often turn lapses into complete relapses by producing the abstinence violation effect. In a study by Sarah Bowen and colleagues (2009), MBRP was applied to substance abusers who had completed intensive in-patient or outpatient treatment. As shown in Figure 17.14, compared with the control group that received traditional community aftercare, the MBRP group had less than half the number of days of alcohol or drug use in the two months following treatment. However, the group difference was no longer evident at four months after treatment, suggesting the need for booster sessions. MBRP, though promising, needs to be compared with relapse prevention treatment without the mindfulness procedure to see if it adds to the traditional procedures.

Acceptance and Commitment Therapy

Developed by Steven Hayes (Hayes et al., 2006), **acceptance and commitment therapy (ACT)** also focuses on the process of mindfulness as a vehicle for change. An important difference in emphasis from traditional cognitive therapy is that instead of teaching people to exert control over their thoughts and feelings, the ACT therapist teaches clients to "just notice," accept, and embrace them, even previously unwanted ones. This matter-of-fact acceptance of a thought

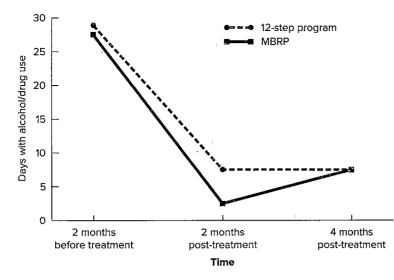

FIGURE 17.14 Number of days of alcohol or drug use reported during the two months previous to mindfulness-based relapse prevention or 12-step treatment and two and four months post-treatment.

Source: Data from Bowen, S., Chawla, N., Collins, S.E., Witkiewits, K., Hsu, S., Grow, J., . . . Marlatt, A. (2009). Mindfulness-based relapse prevention for substance use disorders: A pilot efficacy trial. *Substance Abuse, 30*, 295–305.

(e.g., "I am thinking that he doesn't like me" by a social phobic) helps to reduce the emotional impact of the thought and to defuse the anxiety it would ordinarily evoke. Even if anxiety were to be aroused, it would simply be examined and accepted as a temporary experience.

The "commitment" part of the treatment lies in examining one's life, deciding what is most important to one's true self, and setting life goals in accordance with those values. The therapist then helps the client develop strategies to work toward those goals and to remain committed to them. Although solid randomized clinical trials of ACT are rare, more than 30 efficacy studies have been reported, with moderate therapeutic effect sizes. The American Psychological Association has listed it as an empirically supported treatment "with modest research report."

Dialectical Behaviour Therapy

Dialectical behaviour therapy (DBT) is a treatment developed specifically for the treatment of borderline personality disorder. As described in Chapter 16, this complex disorder is characterized by chaotic interpersonal relationships, poor emotional control, self-destructive behaviours, and low self-esteem. As many as 70 to 80 percent make suicide attempts, and about 10 percent eventually kill themselves (Chapman, 2010). Other self-destructive behaviours, such as cutting themselves, also occur when under stress. Borderline clients are among the most challenging to treat because of the severity and diversity of symptoms, suicide potential, and tendency to have stormy relationships with therapists and drop out of therapy.

Treating clients with such a diversity of problems requires a variety of techniques. Therefore, DBT, developed by Marsha Linehan (1993), includes a "package" of elements from cognitive, behavioural, humanistic, and psychodynamic therapies. Behavioural techniques are used to help clients learn interpersonal, problem-solving, and emotion-control skills. Cognitive approaches are employed to help clients learn more adaptive thinking about the world, relationships, and themselves. A psychodynamic element traces the history of early deprivation and rejection that created many of the problems. Finally, a humanistic emphasis on acceptance of thoughts and feelings has been added to help clients better tolerate unhappiness and negative emotions as they occur. Mindfulness procedures are a foundation for the other skills taught in DBT because they help clients accept and tolerate the powerful emotions they experience in their lives. The goal is to become capable of calmly recognizing situations, thoughts, and their impact, rather than being overwhelmed or avoiding them. DBT is intensive in nature, with clients seen in both individual and group sessions by multiple therapists for up to 150 hours. Because of the diversity of skill-building techniques that it contains, DBT is increasingly being applied to many other types of disorders as well (Galietta et al., 2010).

A major goal in treatment is to bring self-destructive behaviours, such as suicide attempts and self-mutilation, under control. DBT seems to be uniquely effective in this regard. In a comprehensive clinical trial (Linehan et al., 2006), 101 borderline clients were randomly assigned to either DBT or community treatment by nonbehavioural therapists identified as experts in treating difficult clients. Clients were treated for a year and then were followed up on for an additional year so researchers could assess outcomes.

As shown in Figure 17.15, DBT was successful in reducing self-destructive behaviour over the two-year period. Although treatment gains were achieved in both treatment conditions, the rate of suicide attempts and psychiatric hospitalizations for suicidal idealization were about twice as high in the nonbehavioural condition compared with DBT. Borderline clients were also less likely to drop out of DBT (19 percent compared with 41 percent in the community therapy condition).

The third-wave therapies have yielded promising results in initial studies, but they do not yet have the research base of older cognitive-behavioural treatments. However, a recent meta-analysis of the available data suggests that ACT is quite effective, even in comparison with cognitive-behavioural therapy (Ruiz, 2012).

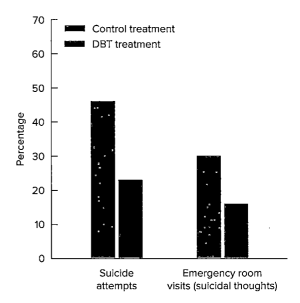

FIGURE 17.15 Percentages of borderline personality disorder clients treated with dialectical behaviour therapy or nonbehavioural therapy who made suicide attempts or visits to hospital emergency rooms because of suicidal thoughts.

Source: Data from Linehan, M.M., Comtois, K.A., Murray, A.M., Brown, M.Z., Gallop, R.J., Heard, H.L., . . . Lidenboim, N. (2006). Two-year randomized controlled trial and follow-up of dialectical behavior therapy vs. therapy by experts for suicidal behaviors and borderline personality disorder. *Archives of General Psychiatry, 63,* 757–766.

Additional well-designed clinical trials are needed to determine their overall effectiveness, the range of disorders that can be treated with them, and the specific contribution of mindfulness procedures (Ost, 2008; Pull, 2009).

·ꞮꞮꞮ Review

- Cognitive and behaviour therapies are among the most popular and effective approaches to psychological treatment.

- Ellis's rational-emotive therapy and Beck's cognitive therapy focus on discovering and changing maladaptive beliefs and logical errors of thinking that underlie maladaptive emotional responses and behaviours.

- Behavioural treatments based on classical conditioning are directed at modifying emotional responses. Exposure to a CS and prevention of avoidance responses promote extinction. Exposure may be provided in vivo (real life), through imagination, or through virtual reality (VR) technology.

- Systematic desensitization is designed to countercondition a response to anxiety-arousing stimuli that is incompatible with anxiety, such as relaxation. Aversion therapy is used to establish a conditioned aversion response to an inappropriate stimulus that attracts the client.

- Operant procedures have been applied successfully in many behaviour modification programs. The token economy is a positive reinforcement program designed to strengthen adaptive behaviours. Punishment has been used to reduce self-destructive behaviours in disturbed children.

- Modelling is an important component of social skills training programs, which help clients learn and rehearse more effective social behaviours.

- More recent cognitive-behavioural therapies feature a component of mindfulness. These newer procedures include acceptance and commitment therapy and dialectical behaviour therapy.

CULTURAL AND GENDER ISSUES IN PSYCHOTHERAPY

Psychological treatments reflect the cultural context in which they develop. Within the dominant cultures of western Europe and North America, personal problems are seen as originating within people in the form of dysfunctional thinking, conflict, and stress responses. People are assumed capable of expressing their feelings and taking personal responsibility for improving themselves. We can easily see these values and assumptions reflected in the therapies we have discussed. Psychodynamic, humanistic, and cognitive treatments all focus on changing these internal factors.

These values are not shared by all cultures and ethnic groups, however. For example, people from some Asian cultures might view the "therapeutic" expression of hostility toward one's parents as unthinkable (Hall & Okazaki, 2003). Likewise, the suggestion that assertiveness training would be helpful in competing more successfully with others and standing up for one's rights might be appalling to a person from a highly collectivistic culture (Cooper & Denner, 1998). Given diverse cultural norms and values, we should not be surprised that some individuals from non-Western cultures view psychotherapy as a totally inappropriate, and even shameful, option for the solution of their problems in living (Foulks et al., 1995).

Cultural Factors in Treatment Utilization

Although overall rates of psychopathology do not differ greatly between ethnic groups, utilization of mental-health services is far lower for minority groups than it is for the majority White population (Wang et al., 2002; Lai, 1995). Even when minorities do seek out mental-health services, they often fail to stay in treatment. As a result, many problems that could benefit from psychological treatment go untreated (Sue, 1998; Wang et al., 2002). The growing cultural diversity in North America (Toronto was recently named the most culturally diverse city in the world) has important implications for the practice of psychotherapy, and researchers are trying to identify the barriers to psychological treatment and what can be done to lower them.

Psychologists Derald Sue and David Sue (1999) have identified several of these barriers. One of them is a cultural norm against turning to professionals outside one's own culture for help. Instead, the family, clergy, acupuncturists, herbalists, and folk healers are looked to for assistance. Moreover, many minority members have a history of frustrating experiences with White bureaucracies that make them unwilling to approach a hospital or mental-health centre. There may also be language barriers.

Sometimes, access to treatment is a major problem. Because many minority groups suffer high rates of unemployment and poverty, they may not be able to afford therapy. In addition, many community mental-health agencies and professional therapists may be located outside the areas in which the underserved populations live.

But, according to Stanley Sue and Nolan Zane (1987; also Griner & Smith, 2006), the biggest problem of all is that there are too few skilled counsellors who can provide culturally responsive forms of treatment. Therapists often have little familiarity with the cultural backgrounds and personal characteristics of ethnic groups other than their own. Sometimes they operate on the basis of inaccurate stereotypes, which can result in unrealistic and possibly inappropriate goals and expectations on the part of the therapist, as well as great difficulty in establishing the positive relationship that has been shown to be a powerful factor in therapeutic success.

What can be done to increase the access of culturally diverse groups to psychological treatment? One answer is to take therapy to the people. Studies have shown that establishing mental-health service agencies in minority population areas increases utilization of mental-health services, particularly if agencies are staffed by culturally skilled counsellors (Sue, 1998). Giuseppe Costantino and colleagues (2009) found that *cultural congruence*—treatment that is consistent with cultural beliefs and expectations—predicted good therapy outcomes for elderly Hispanic clients. Similarities in language and context are both important for successful outcomes (Chowdhard et al., 2014), especially in First Nations populations (Gone, 2013). Another solution might be to train more therapists from these ethnic groups. Stanley Sue and his colleagues (1991) found that dropout rates were reduced and the number of therapy sessions increased when clients saw ethnically similar therapists. However, for clients who elect to remain in therapy, it has *not* been demonstrated that treatment outcomes are better for clients who are seen by therapists from their own ethnic group. What seems more important than ethnic match is that the therapist and client form a good relationship and share similar viewpoints regarding goals for treatment and preferred means for resolving problems (Figure 17.16).

19. What factors serve as barriers to therapy for ethnic minorities?

© Ed Lallo/Index Stock

FIGURE 17.16 Research suggests that the outcome of therapy with minority populations is affected more by the cultural sensitivity and competency of the therapist than it is by the ethnic similarity of therapist and client.

20. What skills are found in culturally competent therapists?

Stanley Sue (1998) suggests that therapists with **cultural competence** are able to use knowledge about the client's culture to achieve a broad understanding of the client. At the same time, they are attentive to how the client may differ from the cultural stereotype, thereby balancing cultural understanding with the individual characteristics and needs of the client. They also are able to introduce *culture-specific elements* into the therapy. Thus, a therapist might draw on some of the techniques used by folk healers within that culture to effect changes in the client. For example, Wendt and Gone (2012) have argued that psychotherapy in a First Nations community should incorporate elements of the healing culture within that community, such as a healing lodge or survival camp. Obviously, this would require a good working knowledge of the culture from which the client comes, plus a willingness to take advantage of what "works" in that culture (Mishne, 2002).

Can therapists be trained to be more culturally sensitive? Indeed they can. In one study, experienced African-American and White therapists were assigned to either a four-hour cultural sensitivity training program or a control condition that received no training. The therapists then treated African-American clients from the community, and the outcome of therapy was carefully assessed. The results showed that exposure to the ethnic training was more important to therapeutic outcome than whether the therapist was African-American or White. Clients rated the therapists who had received training (whether African-American or White) as having greater empathy and expertise, and these clients also attended more therapy sessions (Wade & Bernstein, 1991). Thus, it appears that cultural sensitivity can be acquired and used to enhance the process of therapy for members of minority cultures.

Gender Issues in Therapy

Even within the same culture, the lives of men and women can differ in many ways, as can the life demands they are called on to cope with. As we saw in Chapter 16, psychological disorders, particularly those involving anxiety and depression, occur more frequently among women in Western cultures. This may reflect the impact of specific stressors that women face, such as poverty (women are overrepresented below the poverty level); lack of opportunity fostered by sexism; strains created by the demanding multiple roles of mother, worker, and spouse among married women; and the violence and histories of abuse that many have been subjected to. In many instances, psychological problems arise not so much from internal problems and conflicts, as from oppressive elements in the familial, social, and political

In Review

- Research has shown that members of minority groups underutilize mental-health services. Barriers include lack of access to therapists who can provide culturally responsive forms of treatment. More important to outcome than a cultural match is a therapist who can understand the client's cultural background and share viewpoints on therapy goals and the means used to achieve them. Culturally competent therapists take into account both cultural and individual factors to understand and treat the client.

- For female clients, the most helpful therapist is one who is aware of oppressive environmental conditions and is willing to support life goals that do not necessarily conform to gender expectations. Whether the therapist is a man or a woman seems less important to outcome than gender sensitivity.

worlds. As women strive for more egalitarian relationships with men and for equal opportunity to develop their potential, they often meet external barriers that are deeply embedded in their culture's traditional sex roles (Worell & Remer, 2003).

In the eyes of many therapists, it may be more important to focus on what can be done to change women's life circumstances than to help them adapt to sex-role expectations that constrain them (Brown, 1994). It is important for both men and women therapists to support people in making choices that meet their needs, whether it be a man who wishes to stay at home and care for children or a woman who wants a career in the military. Consistent with the research on cultural similarity between therapist and client, research on therapy with women clients indicates that it is not necessary that women be treated by female therapists. Rather, what seems important is the therapist's sensitivity to gender issues (Worell & Remer, 2003).

EVALUATING PSYCHOTHERAPIES

Given the human suffering created by psychological disorders, the effects of psychotherapy have both personal and societal implications. Practising clinicians and clinical researchers want to know which approaches are most effective, what kinds of problems are best treated with each approach, and what "active ingredients" of each treatment produce its effects. Following a long-standing tradition in medicine, the impetus today is toward *evidence-based practice* (Freeman & Power, 2007).

Today the basic question "Does psychotherapy work?" is viewed as a gross oversimplification of a much more involved question known as the **specificity question:** "Which types of therapy, administered by which kinds of therapists to which kinds of clients having which kinds of problems, produce which kinds of effects?" After half a century of psychotherapy research involving many hundreds of studies, this complex question still is not fully answered (Snyder & Ingram, 2000; Kazdin, 2008). Nonetheless, for many reasons, this question demands answers. Selecting and administering the most appropriate kind of intervention is vital in human terms. It is also important for economic reasons. Billions of dollars are spent each year on psychological treatments, and an increasing share of these costs is being paid by so-called "third parties,"

such as insurance companies, health maintenance organizations, and government agencies. As the costs rise, those who bear the financial burden increase their demands for accountability and demonstration that the treatments are useful (Baker et al., 2009).

Designing good psychotherapy research is one of the most challenging tasks in all of psychology because many variables cannot be completely controlled. In contrast to laboratory studies, in which the experimental conditions can be highly standardized, therapist-client interactions are by their nature infinitely varied. Another difficulty involves measuring the effects of psychotherapy. Figure 17.17 shows some of the typical ways of measuring change. These measures differ in the outcome variable assessed (emotions, thoughts, or behaviours) and in the source of the data (client, therapist, or other informants). Which measures of change are most important or valid? A behaviourist will insist that direct observations of behaviour are the best measures, whereas a psychodynamic therapist may be most interested in how clients feel and how much insight they have achieved into the childhood roots of their problems. A humanistic therapist may place the greatest stock in self-concept changes. What if one set of measures indicates improvement, another indicates no change, and a third suggests that the client is worse off than before treatment? How should we evaluate the effects of the therapy? These are just a few of the vexing issues that can arise in psychotherapy research.

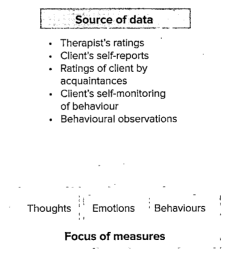

FIGURE 17.17 The measures used to assess the outcome of psychotherapy may come from a variety of data sources, and they may measure different aspects of the client's functioning.

21. What is the "specificity question" in psychotherapy research?

22. What types of measures are used to assess the outcome of therapy?

Psychotherapy Research Methods

In the 1930s and 1940s, individual case studies provided most of the psychotherapy outcome data. Indeed, Freud and other psychoanalysts opposed the use of experimental methods to evaluate psychoanalysis, insisting that case studies left no doubt as to its effectiveness (Fisher & Greenberg, 1996; Rosenzweig, 1992). They assumed that without therapy, patients would not improve, and they saw plenty of people who did improve in analysis.

In 1952, British psychologist Hans Eysenck mounted a frontal assault on this assumption. Using recovery data from insurance companies on people who applied for disability because of psychological problems, Eysenck (1952) concluded that the rate of **spontaneous remission**—symptom reduction in the absence of any treatment—was as high as the success rates reported by psychotherapists. He therefore concluded that troubled people who receive psychotherapy are no more likely to improve than are those who go untreated. He also pointed out, quite correctly, that virtually all the existing outcome data were based on therapists' evaluations of their clients' improvement, and he suggested that these evaluations could be biased by therapists' needs to see themselves as competent and successful.

Eysenck's conclusions sparked intense debate—even outrage—among clinicians, and it now appears that his conclusions were overly pessimistic. More importantly, Eysenck's challenge stimulated a vigorous increase in research on psychotherapy and the development of more sophisticated methods for evaluating treatment outcomes. Fifty years and many hundreds of studies later, we have reached the point where the American Psychological Association's Division of Clinical Psychology has taken the lead in reviewing all this research to identify *empirically validated therapies* that research shows to be effective for specific disorders (APA Task Force on Psychological Intervention Guidelines, 1995; DeRubeis & Crits-Christoph, 1998; Kazdin & Weisz, 2003).

What Is a Good Psychotherapy Research Design?

For many of the reasons discussed in Chapter 2, in which we discussed experimental methods and their value in drawing conclusions about causality, most psychotherapy researchers favour **randomized clinical trials (RCTs),** involving participants who have well-defined psychological disorders and who are similar on other variables that might affect response to treatment

(e.g., age and ethnic status). These individuals are randomly assigned either to an experimental condition that gets the treatment or a control condition (Kazdin, 2003). The control group may be either a no-treatment condition or (even better) a **placebo control group** that gets an intervention that is not expected to work but that controls for client expectations of improvement because clients are being seen by a therapist and think they're getting an effective treatment. (Clients in the control group, whether it be a no-treatment or placebo condition, are often given the real treatment later for ethical reasons.)

Another control condition, which avoids the ethical dilemma of withholding or delaying treatment for some people, involves randomly assigning participants to either the treatment being studied or another kind of treatment that has proven effective for that disorder. If the treatment being tested in the experimental condition is equally or more effective than the established treatment, the new therapy is deemed effective. Sometimes, the design of a study involves a group in which the treatment is combined with another intervention, such as a drug treatment. It is then possible to see if the group that received the drug *plus* therapy does better than the groups that got only the drug or only the therapy (Hollon, 1996).

To *standardize* the treatment, much as one would do in a laboratory experiment, the APA treatment evaluation group recommends that there be a manual containing procedures that the therapists have to follow exactly, and that therapists' compliance with these procedures be evaluated by observing them or taping their sessions. Some therapists, particularly those who do psychodynamic or humanistic therapies, object to this requirement on the grounds that every therapy case they see is different in its course, client characteristics, and procedures used. As a result, most of the current empirically validated therapies are cognitive-behavioural in nature, because these therapies are more often "manualized" into a step-by-step procedure that therapists can apply in a uniform manner. However, there is a movement toward standardizing even psychodynamically oriented therapies so that they can be evaluated more effectively (Crits-Christoph, 1992; Weissman & Markowitz, 1994).

In evaluating the treatment, at least some of the measures of improvement should be behavioural in nature. Interviewers or observers should not know what condition the clients were in so as to minimize experimenter bias in evaluating change during

---

23. Describe Eysenck's challenge to therapy effectiveness and the data on which it was based.

24. Summarize desirable standards for designing psychotherapy research studies with regard to design, treatment standardization, and follow-up.

interviews or behavioural observations following treatment.

Finally, researchers should collect follow-up data. This step is extremely important, for we want to know not only how the treatment conditions differ at the end of the clinical trial, but also how lasting the effects are. For example, in some studies comparing psychotherapy for depression with the effects of antidepressant drugs, the drug treatment effects occurred more quickly and were stronger at the end of the treatment period, suggesting

drug therapy's superiority. But follow-up data showed psychotherapy ultimately to be more effective, with fewer relapses into depression because clients had learned specific psychological skills that they could apply after therapy ended (Hollon & Beck, 1994; Weissman & Markowitz, 1994). Figure 17.18 summarizes in schematic form the procedures used in conducting an RCT to evaluate a treatment. It also shows how many factors must be taken into account to ensure meaningful scientific results.

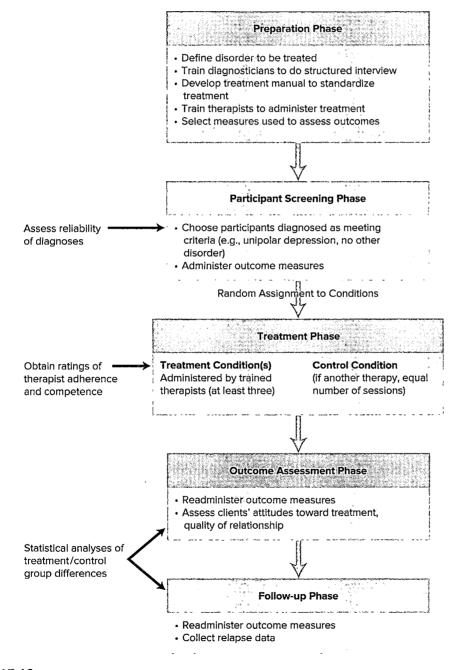

FIGURE 17.18 Phases and procedures in a well-designed randomized clinical trial.

Meta-Analysis: A Look at the Big Picture

As discussed in Chapter 2, the technique of **meta-analysis** allows researchers to combine the results of many studies to arrive at an overall conclusion. In the psychotherapy research literature, they can compute an **effect size statistic** that represents a common measure of treatment effectiveness. The effect size tells researchers what percentage of clients who have received therapy had a more favourable outcome than that of the average control client who did not receive the treatment.

In 1977, Mary Ann Smith and Gene Glass used meta-analysis to combine the effects of 375 studies of psychotherapy, involving 25 000 clients and 25 000 control participants. These studies differed in many ways, but they all compared a treatment condition with a control condition. The results indicated that the average therapy client had a more favourable outcome than 75 percent of the untreated cases. Smith and Glass therefore disputed Eysenck's earlier conclusion, maintaining that therapy does indeed have positive effects beyond spontaneous remission. More recent meta-analyses support this conclusion. Robert Grissom (1996) found that, across a large number of studies, clients who received therapy were likely to have a more favourable outcome than 70 percent of those in no-treatment control conditions and 66 percent of those in placebo conditions.

What about differences among therapies? Smith and Glass broke down their meta-analysis in terms of many of the therapies described in this chapter. As shown in Figure 17.19, psychodynamic, client-centred, and behavioural approaches were quite similar in their effectiveness, and all of them seemed to yield somewhat more positive effects than Gestalt therapy. A more recent meta-analysis of brief psychodynamic therapy outcome studies supports a similar conclusion: That form of therapy yielded significantly better outcomes than did no-treatment or placebo control conditions but did not differ in effectiveness from other forms of therapy with which it was compared (Anderson & Lambert, 1997). This finding of similar efficacy for widely differing therapies has been termed the **dodo bird verdict,** after the dodo bird's statement in *Alice in Wonderland* that "Everybody has won and all must have prizes" (Luborsky et al., 2002). Other researchers challenge this conclusion, maintaining that lumping together studies involving different kinds of clinical problems may mask *differential effectiveness*—that is, the fact that specific therapies might be highly effective for treating some

Therapies:

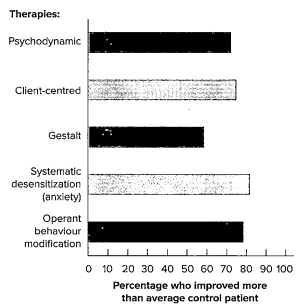

FIGURE 17.19 This meta-analysis of 375 studies of psychotherapy outcome yielded effectiveness data on various types of psychotherapy. The bars indicate the percentage of treated clients who improved more than the average control client.

Source: Data from Smith, M.L., & Glass, G.V. (1977). Meta-analyses of psychotherapy outcome studies. *American Psychologist*, 32(9), Sep 1977, 752-760. Copyright © 1977 by the American Psychological Association. Reproduced with permission. The use of APA information does not imply endorsement by APA.

25. How is meta-analysis used to assess therapy effects? What have meta-analyses shown about overall effectiveness and the effects of different forms of therapy?

clinical disorders but not others (Beutler, 2002; Westen & Morrison, 2001).

The very definition of therapy "success" is a topic of debate. How much do clients have to improve to have a successful outcome? Is therapy successful if deeply depressed clients show a statistically significant decrease in self-report scores of depression following therapy but their scores still fall within the clinically depressed range? According to Neil Jacobson and colleagues (1996), **clinical significance** would require that at the end of therapy, clients' depression scores fall within the range for nondepressed people. This is, of course, a more stringent definition of therapeutic success than the one used in most meta-analyses (i.e., greater positive change in a treatment group than in a control group of similarly depressed clients) and would undoubtedly indicate lower levels of therapeutic success for most treatments.

In evaluating the results of meta-analyses, we should remember that the studies lumped together in a meta-analysis may differ in many ways, including the nature and severity of the problems that were treated, the outcome measures that were used, and the quality of the methodology. Psychotherapy researchers point out that combining good studies with less adequate ones can produce misleading results (Kazdin, 2003; Matt & Navarro, 1997). When studies that meet rigorous research standards are compared in meta-analyses with less rigorous studies, the rigorous studies tend to yield more favourable outcomes for therapy conditions (Matt & Navarro, 1997). Apparently, the rigorous methods used in such studies allow effective therapies to show their true effects.

Survey Research

Another approach to evaluating the effectiveness of psychotherapy is to survey large numbers of people who have been in therapy and measure their reactions to the experience. A good example of the survey approach is a study carried out by the periodical *Consumer Reports (CR;* Seligman, 1995). One form of *CR*'s 1994 annual study, mailed to 184 000 randomly selected subscribers, contained a section on stress and mental health. Readers were asked to complete the mental health section if they had sought help for emotional problems in the past three years. A total of 22 000 readers responded to the questionnaire—a 13 percent response rate that is typical of *CR* surveys. Of these, 35 percent reported that they had a mental-health problem, and 40 percent (approximately 2900 respondents) of this group reported that they had sought professional help from a psychologist, psychiatrist, social worker, or marriage counsellor. The respondents were asked to indicate how much they improved as a result of treatment and how satisfied they were with the treatment the received.

Forty-two percent of the respondents said that they had been helped "A lot" and 44 percent said they had been helped "Somewhat." Eighty-nine percent were somewhat or very satisfied with the treatment they received. *CR* consultant Martin Seligman concluded that "*CR* has provided empirical validation of the effectiveness of therapy" (1995, p. 974). Further, he concluded that the survey method used in this study might actually have provided data that are more representative of real-life outcomes than data yielded by highly controlled clinical trials.

Factors Affecting the Outcome of Therapy

Clearly, not everyone who enters therapy profits from it. There is even evidence that some clients—perhaps 10 percent—may get worse

| **Thinking critically** |

DO SURVEY RESULTS PROVIDE AN ACCURATE PICTURE OF TREATMENT EFFECTIVENESS?

Based on what you've already learned about research methods, do you agree with Seligman's conclusion that the *CR* data may be a more valid reflection of therapy success than data from randomized clinical trials? Can you think of any aspects of the *CR* methods that might limit your ability to conclude how effective psychotherapy is?

Think about it, and then see the Answers section at the end of the book.

as a result of treatment (Binder & Strupp, 1997; Lambert et al., 1986). What then are the factors that influence treatment outcome? Three sets of factors have been the focus of research designed to answer this question: client variables, therapist variables, and technique variables (Figure 17.20).

As far as client variables are concerned, three important factors are an openness to therapy, self-relatedness, and the nature of the problem. **Openness** involves clients' general willingness to invest themselves in therapy and take the risks required to change themselves. **Self-relatedness** refers to their ability to experience and understand internal states such as thoughts and emotions, to be attuned to the processes that go on in their relationship with their therapist, and to be able to apply what they learn in therapy to their lives

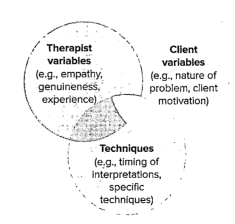

FIGURE 17.20 Research on factors that influence therapy outcome has focused on three sets of interacting variables: client factors, therapist factors, and technique factors.

26. What were the major findings of the *CR* survey? On what bases could its conclusions be criticized?

27. What client variables are important to treatment outcome?

outside of treatment (Howard et al., 1993). The third important client factor is the nature of the problem and its degree of "fit" with the therapy being used. For example, specific problems, such as phobias, may respond best to a behavioural anxiety-reduction treatment, such as systematic desensitization or exposure, whereas a more global problem, such as a search for self-discovery and greater meaning in life, may respond better to a psychodynamic, cognitive, or humanistic approach.

A second important determinant of therapy outcome is the quality of the relationship that the therapist is able to establish with the client (Teyber & McClure, 2000). Carl Rogers's emphasis on the importance of therapist qualities such as empathy, unconditional acceptance of the client as a person, and genuineness has been borne out in a great many studies (Beutler et al., 1994; Norcross, 2003). The establishment of an empathic, trusting, and caring relationship forms the foundation on which the specific techniques employed by the therapist can have their most beneficial effects (Blackstone, 2007). Indeed, Kazdin (2008) reports that quality of the therapeutic relationship accounts for about 30 percent of the variance in treatment outcome. When therapists do not manifest these behaviours, the effects of therapy are not simply null; clients can actually get worse. For example, hostile interchanges between therapist and client can contribute to a *deterioration effect* in therapy (Binder & Strupp, 1997).

We do not mean to imply that as long as a therapist has a good relationship with a client, it does not matter what therapy techniques are used or how they are used. It does matter. Therapists must be skilled in what they do. For example, a large-scale study at the University of Pennsylvania revealed that the correctness of the interpretations made by psychoanalytic therapists, as measured by expert ratings, was related to more positive treatment outcome (Crits-Christoph et al., 1988). Likewise, in a detailed analysis of the audiotaped therapy sessions of 21 psychotherapists, Enrico Jones and colleagues (1988) found that the most effective therapists adjusted their techniques to the specific needs of their clients. They concluded that "general relationship factors, such as therapeutic alliance, are closely bound with the skillful selection and application of psychotherapeutic techniques" (Jones et al., 1988, p. 55). If therapy is to be effective, clients must remain

in treatment long enough for the therapeutic relationship and techniques to have their effects. For this reason, new research is focusing on the **dose-response effect,** the relation between the amount of treatment received and the quality of the outcome. One review of 29 randomized controlled clinical trials primarily involving cognitive and behavioural treatments found that between 58 and 67 percent of clients showed clinically significant improvement within an average of 13 sessions (Hansen et al., 2002). These rates are quite consistent with those typically found in research settings. The reviewers then turned to what occurs in the "real world" of clinical practice, examining the treatment records of 6072 clients seen in a variety of naturalistic settings, including employee assistance programs, community and university counselling centres, and health maintenance organizations. Here they found that the average number of treatment sessions given was fewer than five, and the rate of improvement in this sample was only about 20 percent. These results suggest that many clients seen in these naturalistic settings do not remain in therapy long enough to realize its potential benefits. One possible reason is that many insurance plans limit their coverage to a number of treatment sessions that is too low to expect meaningful improvement.

Despite dramatic differences in the techniques they employ, various therapies tend to enjoy similar success rates, probably because people who differ on the client variables are lumped together. This finding has led many experts to search for **common factors** shared by these diverse forms of therapy that might contribute to their success. These common factors include the following:

- faith in the therapist and a belief on the part of clients that they are receiving help;

- a plausible explanation for their problems, and an alternative way of looking at themselves and their problems;

- a protective setting in which clients can experience and express their deepest feelings within a supportive relationship;

- an opportunity to practise new behaviours; and

- increased optimism and self-efficacy.

The complexities of psychotherapy pose a formidable challenge for clinical researchers. This chapter's *Research Foundations* feature describes one notable attempt to assess client perceptions of treatment outcome.

28. Which therapist factors affect treatment outcome?

29. Define and give examples of common factors in psychotherapy.

Research Foundations

DRUG VERSUS PSYCHOLOGICAL TREATMENTS FOR DEPRESSION: A RANDOMIZED CLINICAL TRIAL

Introduction

Depression is one of the most prevalent psychological disorders, and its successful treatment is a major mental-health priority. As noted in this chapter, the most widely used treatments during the past decade have been cognitive therapy, interpersonal psychotherapy, and drug treatments, all of which have proven effective in 30 to 50 percent of treated cases. Although antidepressant drug treatment has outperformed cognitive therapy in some studies, at the end of the clinical trial, many clients do not want to continue to take drugs, experience severe side effects if they do take them, or discontinue their use, resulting in poor maintenance of positive effects. Moreover, drug treatments do not teach clients effective coping skills that may help them counter depression in the future.

The new treatment tested in this study was behavioural activation therapy. The treatment is derived from a behavioural theory of depression that focuses on the spiralling loss of positive reinforcement that occurs in depression as clients stop engaging in positive behaviours and alienate others with their inertia and depressed moods (Lewinsohn et al., 1985). The goal is to increase behaviours that will increase positive reinforcement that counters depression and helps clients regain enjoyment in their lives. This study is the first to compare the effects of behavioural activation therapy with the effects produced by cognitive therapy and antidepressant drug treatment.

Method

A total of 241 people between the ages of 18 and 60 years who met DSM criteria for major depressive disorder were randomly assigned to one of four conditions: behavioural activation therapy, cognitive therapy, drug treatment, or a drug placebo condition. The clients underwent treatment for 16 weeks. Those in the antidepressant medication condition received the SSRI drug paroxetine (Paxil). A set of outcome measures was administered before treatment, after eight weeks, and after 16 weeks. These included the Beck Depression Inventory, a self-report measure of depression, and the Hamilton Rating Scale for Depression, which was based on a clinical interview by a psychologist or a psychiatrist who was unaware of which condition the client was in.

Behavioural activation treatment seeks to identify and engage clients in activities that are reinforcing and consistent with life goals. Clients monitor their moods and behaviours and work with their therapist to design and

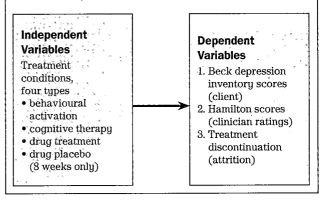

Design

Question: What are the comparative effects of behavioural activation, cognitive therapy, and antidepressant drugs in the treatment of depression?

Type of Study: *Experimental* (randomized clinical trial)

Independent Variables
Treatment conditions, four types
- behavioural activation
- cognitive therapy
- drug treatment
- drug placebo (8 weeks only)

→

Dependent Variables
1. Beck depression inventory scores (client)
2. Hamilton scores (clinician ratings)
3. Treatment discontinuation (attrition)

schedule daily routines designed to get them engaged with their social and physical environment in productive ways. This may include forcing themselves to participate in social or physical exercise activities that they formerly enjoyed. They also learn and practice ways to avoid negative thinking by redirecting their attention toward their immediate experiences in the real world. In the cognitive therapy condition, clients focused on identifying and changing automatic thought patterns that create depression.

In accordance with empirically supported treatment principles, therapists closely followed manuals prepared for each therapy to standardize treatment. To make sure that the therapists in the treatment conditions were conducting the treatments as designed, outside experts in each treatment rated videotaped sessions for "treatment adherence." These ratings indicated that all the treatments were appropriately delivered.

For ethical reasons, the placebo condition was maintained for only eight weeks, after which members of that condition were given the option of receiving any of the other treatments. (Their data were not included in the assessment of the three treatment conditions described below.)

Results

As in previous research, the highest treatment drop-out (attrition) rate was in the drug therapy condition, where 44 percent of the clients either refused the treatment or dropped out during the study. By comparison, the attrition

continued

TABLE 17.3 **Percentage of Severely Depressed Clients Who Showed Response (Improvement) and Remission (Normalization) after Behavioural Activation, Cognitive Therapy, and Antidepressant Drug Treatments**

| | Outcome Measure | | | |
| | Beck Depression Inventory (Client Self-Report) | | Hamilton Depression Rating Scale (Clinician Rating) | |
Condition	Percent Response*	Percent Remission**	Percent Response*	Percent Remission**
Behavioural Activation	76	52	60	54
Cognitive Therapy	48	40	56	35
Drug Treatment	49	42	40	23

*At least 50 percent decrease in depression scores

**Depression decrease into normal range

Source: Data from Dimidjian, S., Hollon, S.D., Dobson, K.S., Schmaling, K.B., Kohlenberg, R.J., Addis, M.E., . . . Jacobson, N.S.D. (2006). Randomized trial of behavioral activation, cognitive therapy, and antidepressant medication in the acute treatment of adults with major depression. *Journal of Consulting and Clinical Psychology, 74,* 658–670.

rates were only 16 percent in the behavioural activation condition and 13 percent in the cognitive therapy condition. Two levels of improvement were assessed on the Beck self-report and Hamilton clinical ratings of depression. Response to treatment was defined as a clinically significant decrease of at least 50 percent in depression scores. Remission was declared when a client's scores dropped below the clinical depression cut-off point into the normal range for nondepressed people.

On the basis of the pretreatment scores that were used to match the treatment groups for severity of depression, the clinical researchers divided the clients into low- and high-severity groups and compared the treatments within the two severity groups. In the low-severity group, all the treatments resulted in improvement (including the placebo condition at eight weeks). There was no statistical difference between the groups, although cognitive therapy had the highest overall response and remission rates (65 percent and 55 percent, respectively).

Table 17.3 shows the response and remission results for the severely depressed clients. Here, behavioural activation proved to be superior to the other treatments, with the drug group doing generally more poorly than the cognitive therapy group. Clients who had been treated with behavioural activation indicated that they felt less depressed than the other treatment groups, and clinical interviewer ratings also indicated a better outcome.

Discussion

This randomized clinical trial is highly significant and exceptionally well-controlled. The investigators made certain that the treatments were being delivered as intended. Clinicians who conducted the clinical interviews and provided Hamilton ratings of depression were blind to the experimental conditions. The groups were equivalent in depression at the beginning of treatment so that it was possible to plot improvement in a meaningful fashion.

This study reflects the scientific strategy of comparing new treatments with already established ones. Based on the results of this study and an earlier one (Jacobson et al., 2001), behavioural activation therapy appears to be a highly promising treatment, particularly for severely depressed people. In particular, its superiority over drug treatment provides an alternative to antidepressants, which many people refuse to take or discontinue as unpleasant side effects arise. For severely depressed clients, behavioural activation was also superior to cognitive therapy, which has been the favoured psychological treatment for depression. It appears that cognitive therapy may still be the treatment of choice for less depressed individuals, however. The different effects of the two psychological treatments as a function of severity of depression is an important finding, for it helps to answer the practical question of which treatment is most effective for which clinical population.

The results of this study were measured at the end of the 16-week treatment period. A follow-up study is needed to examine how long-lasting the positive treatment effects are. Typically, psychological treatments have done better at follow-up because many people in drug conditions discontinue their drugs or become dissatisfied and seek alternate treatments. Behavioural activation may be especially effective in the longer run because it helps clients make lifestyle changes that should provide them with continuing positive reinforcement. It remains to be seen whether future research will support this expectation.

Source: S. Dimidjian, S.D. Hollon, K.S. Dobson, K.B. Schmaling, R.J. Kohlenberg, M.E. Addis, R. Gallop, J.B. McGlinchey, D.K. Markley, J.K. Gollan, D.C. Atkins, D.L. Dunner, and N.S. Jacobson (2006). Randomized trial of behavioral activation, cognitive therapy, and antidepressant medication in the acute treatment of adults with major depression. *Journal of Consulting and Clinical Psychology, 74,* 658–670.

Review

- Eysenck challenged the effectiveness of psychotherapy and stimulated the use of increasingly more sophisticated research methods to evaluate the outcomes of various therapies. The randomized clinical trial is the most powerful approach to researching the effects of therapy, and a number of standards have been established for conducting psychotherapy research.

- Meta-analysis is a method for combining the results of many studies into an effect size statistic. Meta-analyses of treatment outcome studies found more improvement in therapy clients than in 70 to 75 percent of control clients and little difference in effectiveness among various therapies (the so-called "dodo bird verdict"). The *Consumer Reports* study of client self-report suggested high levels of client satisfaction.

- Three sets of interacting factors affect the outcome of treatment: client characteristics (including the nature of the problem), therapist characteristics, and therapy techniques.

- Client variables that contribute to therapy success include openness, self-relatedness, and a good match between the nature of the problem and the kind of therapy being received.

- A crucial factor in the success of various therapies is the quality of the relationship that the therapist establishes with the client. The three therapist characteristics suggested by Rogers—empathy, unconditional positive regard, and genuineness—are particularly important.

- Factors common to many therapies, such as faith in the therapist, a protected environment for self-exploration, and the ability to try out new behaviours, contribute to therapeutic outcome.

BIOLOGICAL APPROACHES TO TREATMENT

In the previous chapter, we found that biological factors play an important role in many psychological disorders. Thus, a direct biological approach designed to alter the brain's functioning is an alternative (or an addition) to psychological treatment.

Drug Therapies

Drug therapies are the most commonly used biological interventions. Discoveries in the field of *psychopharmacology* (the study of how drugs affect cognitions, emotions, and behaviour) have revolutionized the treatment of the entire range of behaviour disorders. Each year, more than 200 million prescriptions are filled for drugs that affect mood, thought, and behaviour (Lieberman & Tasman, 2006). Indeed, Canada is the second largest consumer of prescription psychoactive drugs, per capita, in the world (Canadian Centre on Substance Abuse, 2016). The most commonly prescribed drugs fall into three major categories: anti-anxiety drugs, antidepressant drugs, and anti-psychotic drugs.

Anti-Anxiety Drugs

Surveys have shown that more than 15 percent of Americans between the ages of 18 and 74 use anti-anxiety or tranquilizing drugs such as

Valium, Xanax, and BuSpar (Schatzberg et al., 2010). Xanax is the most prescribed drug in North America, with over 50 million prescriptions issued in 2015—more than one prescription per second. Health Canada (2014) notes that about 10 percent of Canadians report using an anti-anxiety drug at least once a year. These drugs are designed to reduce anxiety as much as possible without affecting alertness or concentration. Sometimes anti-anxiety drugs are used in combination with other therapies to help clients cope successfully with problematic situations (Stahl, 2000). A temporary reduction in anxiety resulting from the use of a drug may allow a client to enter anxiety-arousing situations and learn to cope more effectively with them.

One drawback of anti-anxiety drugs is psychological and physical dependence that can result from their long-term use. As with any other addictive drug, people who have developed physiological dependence on tranquilizers may experience characteristic withdrawal symptoms, such as intense anxiety, nausea, and restlessness when they stop taking them (Lieberman, 1998). Another problem is that anxiety symptoms often return when people stop taking the drugs.

A newer anti-anxiety drug, *buspirone* (BuSpar), is slow acting, has fewer fatiguing side effects, and seems to have less potential for abuse. It has proven effective in the treatment

30. How do anti-anxiety drugs achieve their effects? Do they have any drawbacks?

of generalized anxiety and PTSD (Lieberman, 1998; Stahl, 2000). Additionally, it has been shown to reduce the likelihood of risky sexual behaviours (such as refusing to use a condom) in cocaine abusers (Bolin et al., 2016). Like the other anti-anxiety drugs, BuSpar works by slowing down excitatory synaptic activity in the nervous system. One mechanism for doing so is by enhancing the postsynaptic activity of GABA, an inhibitory transmitter that reduces neural activity in areas of the brain associated with emotional arousal (Gorman, 2002; Rosenbaum et al., 2009).

Antidepressant Drugs

31. How do the three classes of antidepressant drugs achieve their effects biologically? How effective are they compared to/combined with psychotherapy?

Antidepressant drugs fall into three major categories: tricyclics (e.g., Elavil, Tofranil); *monoamine oxidase (MAO) inhibitors* (e.g., Nardil, Parnate); and *selective serotonin reuptake inhibitors* (SSRIs; e.g., Prozac, Zoloft, Paxil, Lexapro, Celexa). The first two classes increase the activity of the excitatory neurotransmitters norepinephrine and serotonin, whose lowered level of activity in brain regions involved in positive emotion and motivation is related to depression. The tricyclics work by preventing reuptake of the excitatory transmitters into the presynaptic neurons, allowing them to continue stimulating postsynaptic neurons. The MAO inhibitors reduce the activity of monoamine oxidase, an enzyme that breaks down the neurotransmitters in the synapse.

MAO inhibitors have more severe side effects than the tricyclics. They can cause dangerous elevations in blood pressure when taken with certain foods, such as cheeses and some types of wine. Many patients have abandoned their antidepressant medications because of severe side effects (Pompili et al., 2009). The SSRIs were designed to decrease side effects by increasing the activity of just one transmitter, serotonin (Marangell, 2002). Like the other antidepressants, however, SSRIs do have side effects. For example, about 30 percent of patients on Prozac report nervousness, insomnia, sweating, joint pain, or sexual dysfunction (Hellerstein et al., 1993). Nonetheless, the SSRIs are gradually replacing the tricyclics because, in addition to milder side effects, they reduce depressive symptoms more rapidly and also reduce anxiety symptoms, including panic disorder, obsessive-compulsive behaviours, and social phobia (Lickey & Gordon, 1991; Lieberman, 1998; Schatzberg et al., 2010). Figure 17.21 shows how the SSRIs produce their effects. A great deal of attention has been

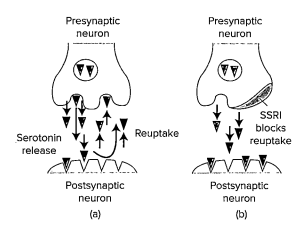

FIGURE 17.21 Serotonin activity is low in many depressed clients. When a presynaptic neuron releases serotonin into the synaptic space, a pumplike reuptake mechanism begins to pull neurotransmitter molecules back into the "sending" neuron, limiting the stimulation of the postsynaptic neuron (a). By blocking the reuptake of serotonin into the presynaptic neuron (b), the selective serotonin reuptake inhibitors (SSRIs) allow serotonin to continue its stimulation of postsynaptic neurons.

drawn to the possible relationship between SSRI usage and suicide. Indeed, warnings have been placed on the packaging of these antidepressants, cautioning patients about the risk of suicidal thoughts, particularly in children. Jureidini et al. (2004) report that the data from various clinical trials is conflicting. In a large meta-analysis of clinical trial data, the authors point out that the effectiveness of SSRIs is considerably lower than we would like. In addition, adverse effects (such as suicidal thoughts) may be vastly underestimated. Many authors do report that suicidal thoughts decreased with the administration of SSRIs (e.g., Ghaziuddin, et al., 2014; Grunebaum et al., 2013). In contrast, Khan et al. (2003) argue that we should look at actual suicides and not just increased risk. They examined the U.S. Food and Drug Administration (FDA) summary reports for controlled clinical trials of nine antidepressants. Of the 48 277 patients who participated in the trials, 77 committed suicide. The rates were comparable for SSRIs (e.g., Prozac) and standard antidepressants (e.g., Welbutrin XL). Goldberg (2006) reports that suicide rates for children are actually lower for those on high levels of SSRIs. Recently, several large-scale studies have shown that suicide rates have actually increased since the addition of warnings on packaging. Increases were highest in groups not on antidepressants (Isacsson & Ahlner, 2013; Katz et al., 2008). More research is needed to assess this question.

Increasingly, depression researchers are studying the effects of combining drugs and psychotherapy. A meta-analysis of such studies revealed that recovery rates for psychotherapy and the combined treatments did not differ, but that both were superior to drug therapy alone (Furukawa et al., 2006). Moreover, relapse rates are lower for psychotherapy than for drugs, particularly if patients stop taking their medication (Kazdin, 2008). Following successful drug therapy, about half of all patients later relapse (Rush et al., 2009).

Antipsychotic Drugs

Perhaps the most dramatic effects of drug therapy have occurred in the treatment of severely disordered people, permitting many of them to function outside of the hospital setting (Shorter, 1998). As shown in Figure 17.22, a sharp decline in the number of in-patients in public mental hospitals has occurred since 1955, when antipsychotic drugs were first introduced on a wide scale.

The revolution in drug therapy for severe psychological disorders began when it was accidentally discovered that reserpine, a drug derived from the root of the snakeroot plant, calmed psychotic patients. This discovery resulted in the development of synthetic antipsychotic drugs (also called *major tranquilizers*) used today to treat schizophrenic disorders. The primary effect of the major

tranquilizers is to decrease the action of dopamine, the neurotransmitter whose overactivity is thought to be involved in schizophrenia (Schatzberg et al., 2005). These drugs have dramatic effects in reducing positive symptoms, such as hallucinations and delusions. However, they have little effect on negative symptoms, such as apathy and withdrawal, and 20 to 40 percent of people with schizophrenia get little or no relief from them (Rosenbaum et al., 2009). Antipsychotic drugs are now so widely used that nearly all schizophrenic patients living in the United States, Canada, and western Europe have received them at one time or another. Because patients often relapse very quickly if they stop taking the drugs, it is common practice to recommend that the medication be continued indefinitely once the individual has returned to the community (Carpenter & Heinrichs, 1983).

Although antipsychotic drugs have allowed many patients to be released from hospitals and reduced the need for padded cells, straitjackets, and other restraints that were used to control the behaviour of hospitalized patients, these drugs can produce a severe movement disorder known as **tardive dyskinesia** (Cho & Lee, 2013; Kane, 2006). Uncontrollable and grotesque movements of the face and tongue are especially prominent in this disorder, and sometimes the patient's arms and legs flail uncontrollably. Tardive dyskinesia can be more debilitating than the psychotic symptoms that prompted the drug treatment, and it appears to be irreversible once it develops (Barnes, 1994). Within four years of beginning antipsychotic medications, about 20 percent of young adults and 30 percent of those over 55 develop tardive dyskinesia symptoms (Schatzberg et al., 2010).

Researchers are working to develop new drugs that can control schizophrenic symptoms without producing side effects, such as the devastating symptoms of tardive dyskinesia. A new drug called *clozapine* (Clozaril) reduces not only positive symptoms, but also negative ones, and it appears not to produce tardive dyskinesia (Lieberman, 1998). Unfortunately, it produces a fatal blood disease in 1 to 2 percent of people who take it, requiring expensive weekly blood tests for patients who use the medication. Haas et al. (2007) examined the data for all patients taking clozapine between 1993 and 2003. In this group, 116 developed the infection and 12 died. Typically, onset of the disease is early in treatment and young people are most

32. What is tardive dyskinesia, and how is it caused?

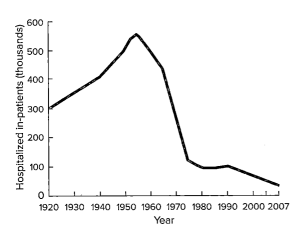

FIGURE 17.22 Antipsychotic drugs have revolutionized the treatment of severely disturbed individuals, allowing many of them to leave mental hospitals. Note the decline in hospitalized in-patients that occurred following the introduction of antipsychotic drugs in the mid-1950s.

Source: National Institute of Mental Health. (2008). "The numbers count: Mental disorders in America." November 19, 2008.

likely to be adversely affected. These newer, "second-generation" antipsychotics have not yet been studied extensively, but the existing research findings on the effectiveness and side effects of these new drugs are promising (Leucht et al., 2009).

Antipsychotic drugs often can be used effectively in conjunction with psychotherapy. For example, drugs may be used to bring psychotic symptoms under control so that other approaches such as social skills training, family therapy, and group therapy can be applied to maintain the initial improvement.

Electroconvulsive Therapy

Another biologically based treatment, **electroconvulsive therapy (ECT)**, was based on the observation by a Hungarian physician that schizophrenia and epilepsy rarely occur in the same person. (Apparently, he didn't stop to consider the fact that the probability of epilepsy and any other disorder occurring together is very low.) The physician therefore suggested that seizure induction might be useful in the treatment of schizophrenia. Two Italian physicians, Ugo Cerletti and Lucio Bini, began to treat schizophrenic patients by attaching electrodes to their skulls and inducing a seizure by means of an electric current administered to the brain.

33. Which disorders do and do not respond favourably to ECT?

When ECT was first introduced in the 1930s, it was applied to a wide range of disorders, but later research revealed that it cannot relieve anxiety disorders and it is of questionable value for schizophrenic patients (Herrington & Lader, 1996; Weiner & Coffey, 1988). However, ECT can be useful in treating severe depression, particularly if there is a high risk of suicide (Fink et al., 2014). In such cases, the use of antidepressant drugs may be impractical because they likely will take several weeks to begin reducing the depression. In contrast, the effects of ECT can be immediate, and controlled studies indicate that 60 to 70 percent of severely depressed people given ECT improve (Rey & Walter, 1997).

Dramatizations of ECT in the mass media sometimes portray a procedure that appears barbaric. In early applications of ECT, a wide-awake patient was strapped to a table, electrodes were attached to the patient's scalp, and roughly 100 volts of electricity was applied to the brain, producing violent convulsions and momentary unconsciousness. Sometimes, the seizures were so violent that patients fractured their arms or legs.

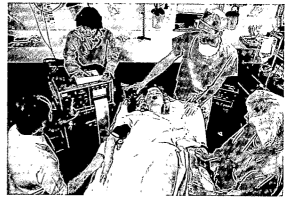

© Stephen Frisch/McGraw-Hill

FIGURE 17.23 A severely depressed and possibly suicidal patient is prepared for an ECT session. The patient has been sedated and given a muscle relaxant to minimize limb movements during the brief electrical stimulation of the brain. The rubber object in her mouth prevents her from biting her tongue or damaging her teeth during the convulsion.

Today, however, the procedure is quite different (Figure 17.23). A patient is first given a sedative and a muscle relaxant to prevent injuries from convulsions. The patient is then placed on a well-padded mattress, and electrodes are attached to his or her scalp. A modified procedure in which electrodes are placed on only one side of the head is often used (Martin, 1986). The duration of the shock is less than a second, causing a seizure of the central nervous system. There is little observable movement in the patient, other than a twitching of the toes and a slight facial grimace. The patient wakes up 10 to 20 minutes after ECT, possibly with a headache, sore muscles, and some confusion. Recently, scientists have been able to calibrate the amount of electric current a patient needs so that treatments can be individualized, and research is being carried out to determine whether certain drugs can further reduce seizure-induced confusion and amnesia.

ECT has many critics, despite its effectiveness in alleviating major depression. Critics note that even when the effects are dramatically positive, the possibility of a depressive relapse is high, perhaps 85 percent (Swartz, 1995). Although current methods prevent the physical injuries that occurred in earlier times, other concerns have been raised about the safety of ECT. In some instances, permanent memory loss has been reported, and there is also concern about possible permanent brain damage when ECT is used repeatedly. Today, the number of ECT treatments is limited to fewer than ten, but in the past, many patients received numerous treatments.

Steps have been taken to increase the safety of ECT, and available scientific evidence suggests that today's ECT is a safer treatment than were previous forms (Weiner et al., 2013). MRI studies of the brains of patients who received brief pulse treatment to both sides of the brain revealed no evidence of brain damage (Coffey et al., 1991). After reviewing both sides of the issue, the American Psychiatric Association (1990) concluded that this therapy should be regarded as a useful procedure for major depression in patients who cannot take or do not respond to medication, and has published guidelines for its use.

Psychosurgery

Psychosurgery refers to surgical procedures that remove or destroy brain tissue to change disordered behaviour. It is the least used of the biomedical procedures, but this was not always the case. In the 1930s, before the advent of antipsychotic drugs, Portuguese surgeon Egas Moniz reported that cutting the nerve tracts that connect the frontal lobes with subcortical areas of the brain involved in emotion resulted in a calming of psychotic and uncontrollably violent patients. The operation eliminated emotional input from the limbic system into the areas of the brain connected with executive functions of planning and reasoning. Walter Freeman developed a ten-minute *lobotomy* operation performed by inserting an ice pick–like instrument with sharp edges through the eye socket into the brain, then wiggling it back and forth to sever the targeted nerve tracts. During the 1930s and 1940s, tens of thousands of patients—50 000 in the United States alone—underwent the operation. Moniz received a Nobel Prize for his contribution (Shorter, 1998).

Initial enthusiasm for lobotomy was soon replaced by a sober recognition that the massive neural damage it caused had severe side effects on mental and emotional functioning, including seizures, stupor, memory and reasoning impairment, and listlessness. With the development of antipsychotic drugs in the 1950s, lobotomies decreased and are hardly ever used today. However, more precise and limited psychosurgery procedures still are used at times in the most extreme cases and when every other avenue has been tried (Pressman,

1998). One procedure called *cingulotomy* involves cutting a small fibre bundle near the corpus callosum that connects the frontal lobes with the limbic system. Cingulotomy has been used successfully in treating severe depressive and obsessive-compulsive disorders that have failed to improve with drug treatment or psychotherapy. However, this more limited procedure also can produce side effects, including seizures (Herrington & Lader, 1996; Pressman, 1998). Appropriately, cingulotomy and other forms of psychosurgery are considered to be last-resort procedures. New advances in technology and functional imaging techniques, coupled with an ever-increasing understanding of neurological and physiological underpinnings of behaviour, may soon give rise to a new generation of highly sophisticated psychosurgical techniques with greater effectiveness and fewer side effects than currently available techniques (Feldman & Goodrich, 2001; Mashour et al., 2005).

34. What were the rationale and effects of prefrontal lobotomy?

Mind, Body, and Therapeutic Interventions

The impact of drug and electroconvulsive therapies on psychological disorders illustrates once again the important interactions between biological and psychological phenomena. In the final analysis, both psychological and biological treatments affect brain functioning in ways that can change disordered thoughts, emotions, and behaviour. Moreover, they may constitute different routes to the same changes, as illustrated in a study by Tomas Furmark and colleagues (2002) at Uppsala University in Sweden. The researchers randomly assigned patients with social phobia to nine-week treatments that involved either drug therapy with an SSRI or a course of cognitive and behavioural psychotherapy involving exposure to feared social situations and cognitive modification of anxiety-arousing thoughts. Before and after treatment, the participants received PET scans while they gave a hastily prepared speech to a group of six to eight persons standing around the scanner bed. They also provided subjective ratings of their anxiety during the procedure. Uniformly high anxiety scores were reported by all participants prior to treatment.

In general, both treatments were effective, although overall the psychological treatment produced a stronger reduction in fear and social phobia symptoms than did the drug treatment. Nonetheless, when the researchers compared the pretreatment and post-treatment PET scans of those participants who responded to the two treatments with reduced social anxiety, the psychotherapy and drug groups showed basically the same changes in cerebral blood flow from the first speech situation to the second. These changes involved reduced neural activity in an "anxiety circuit" made up of the amygdala, the hippocampus, and areas of the temporal cerebral cortex (Figure 17.24). Treatment nonresponders did not show these brain changes. Thus, different forms of therapy, whether "psychological" or "biological" in nature, may result in similar changes at a neurological level and, ultimately, at a behavioural level. One suggestion is that medication can help to prime the neural network changes needed for recovery, thus allowing psychotherapies to work more effectively (Castrén, 2009).

An important factor to keep in mind is that drug treatments, however effective they may be in modifying some disordered behaviours in the short term, do not "cure" the disorder. They suppress symptoms but do not teach the client coping and problem-solving skills that might be used to deal with stressful life situations (DeLongis, 2000; Nezu et al., 2000). Many therapists believe that one of the major benefits of psychological treatments is their potential not only for helping clients deal with current problems but also for increasing their personal resources so that they might enjoy a higher level of adjustment and life satisfaction in the future (Hollon, 1996).

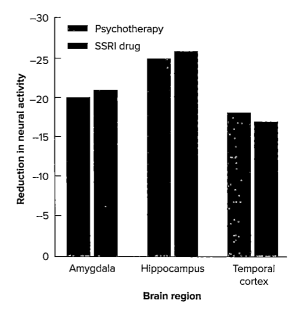

FIGURE 17.24 Effects of psychotherapy and drug therapy on brain activity in clients treated for social phobia. Clients who responded to the treatments with reduced anxiety showed nearly identical changes in PET-scan recordings of neural activity in three areas of the brain whose activation is thought to underlie anxiety.

Source: Based on Furmark, T., Tillfors, M., Marteinsdottir, I., Fischer, H., Pissiota, A., Langstroem, B., & Fredrikson, M. (2002). Common changes in cerebral blood flow in patients with social phobia treated with citalopram or cognitive-behavioral therapy. *Archives of General Psychiatry, 59*, 425–433.

We have now considered a wide spectrum of approaches to treating abnormal behaviour. Figure 17.25 summarizes the mechanisms for therapeutic change that are emphasized by the various psychological and biological approaches.

In Review

- Drugs have revolutionized the treatment of many behaviour disorders and have permitted many hospitalized patients to function outside of institutions. Drugs and psychotherapy may be combined to hasten the relief of symptoms while establishing more effective coping responses to deal with the sources of the disorder. Effective drug treatments exist for anxiety, depression, and schizophrenia. Some of these drugs have undesirable side effects and can be addictive. All of them affect neurotransmission within the brain, and they work on specific classes of neurotransmitters.

- Electroconvulsive therapy is used less frequently than in the past, and its safety has been increased. It is used primarily to treat severe depression, particularly when a strong threat of suicide exists.

- Psychosurgery techniques have become more precise, but they are still generally used only after all other treatment options have failed.

- Studies have shown similar alterations of brain functioning in successful treatment, whether the treatment involves drug treatment or psychotherapy.

Levels of Analysis | Therapeutic Change

Interacting biological, psychological, and environmental factors are involved in the positive changes produced by the psychological and biological therapies we have described. Here are some of the factors identified in scientific research.

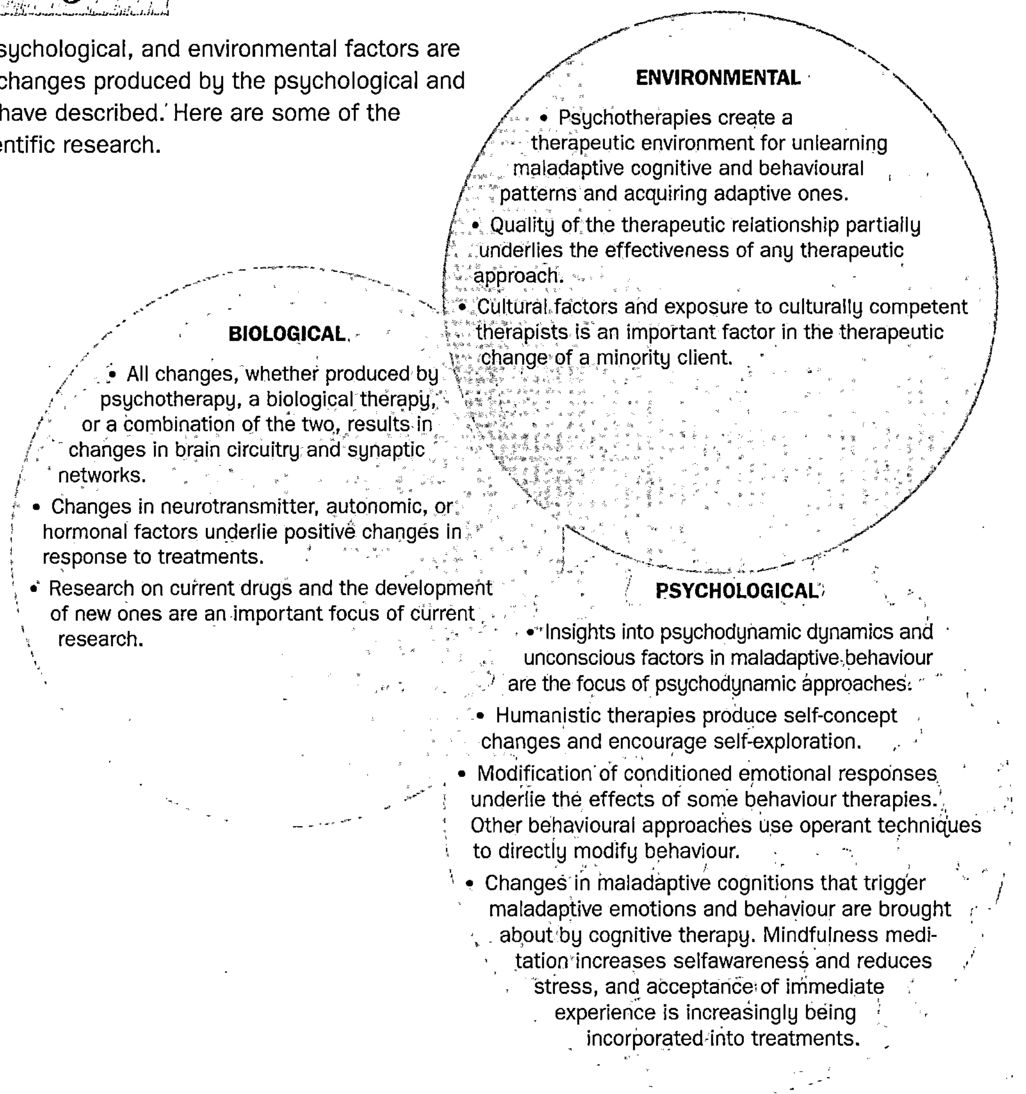

ENVIRONMENTAL

- Psychotherapies create a therapeutic environment for unlearning maladaptive cognitive and behavioural patterns and acquiring adaptive ones.
- Quality of the therapeutic relationship partially underlies the effectiveness of any therapeutic approach.
- Cultural factors and exposure to culturally competent therapists is an important factor in the therapeutic change of a minority client.

BIOLOGICAL

- All changes, whether produced by psychotherapy, a biological therapy, or a combination of the two, results in changes in brain circuitry and synaptic networks.
- Changes in neurotransmitter, autonomic, or hormonal factors underlie positive changes in response to treatments.
- Research on current drugs and the development of new ones are an important focus of current research.

PSYCHOLOGICAL

- Insights into psychodynamic dynamics and unconscious factors in maladaptive behaviour are the focus of psychodynamic approaches.
- Humanistic therapies produce self-concept changes and encourage self-exploration.
- Modification of conditioned emotional responses underlie the effects of some behaviour therapies. Other behavioural approaches use operant techniques to directly modify behaviour.
- Changes in maladaptive cognitions that trigger maladaptive emotions and behaviour are brought about by cognitive therapy. Mindfulness meditation increases selfawareness and reduces stress, and acceptance of immediate experience is increasingly being incorporated into treatments.

FIGURE 17.25

PSYCHOLOGICAL DISORDERS AND SOCIETY

Since the days of insane asylums, first established in the 16th century to segregate the insane from society, severe behaviour disorders have been treated in institutional settings. This move toward institutionalization was pioneered by Dorothy Dix, who travelled throughout Canada and the United States promoting the humane treatment of people with mental disorders. Her pleas did not fall on deaf ears. For example, in 1852, the Nova Scotia legislature enacted a statute founding a provincial asylum

for the "proper keeping of lunatics and idiots." The Provincial Hospital for the Insane was constructed and the first patient was admitted in 1858. The name was changed to the Nova Scotia Hospital for the Insane in 1900, and parts of the facility still stand today. By the early 1900s most provinces had similar institutions. However, it was readily apparent to mental-health experts that, although there were some high-quality institutions, many public mental hospitals were not fulfilling their intended role as treatment facilities. They were overcrowded, understaffed, and underfinanced. Many of them could provide little more than minimal custodial care and a haven from the stresses and demands of the outer world. Moreover, people who were admitted to such hospitals often sank into a chronic "sick" role in which passive dependence and "crazy" behaviour not only were tolerated, but also expected (Goffman, 1961; Scheff, 1966). They lost the self-confidence, motivation, and skills needed to re-enter and adapt to the outside world, and had little chance of surviving outside the hospital.

Deinstitutionalization

35. What is the rationale for deinstitutionalization? What prevents it from achieving its goals?

By the 1960s, the stage was set for a new approach to the treatment of behaviour disorders. Concern about the inadequacies of mental hospitals, together with the ability of antipsychotic drugs to "normalize" patients' behaviour, resulted in a **deinstitutionalization** movement to transfer the primary focus of treatment from the mental institution to the community.

In 1957, the Canadian government passed legislation to partially fund provincial hospital insurance plans, providing for universal health care (Saskatchewan had actually established public health insurance ten years earlier). However, the plan did not extend to mental institutions. Thus, the provinces were forced to find alternative methods to care for those with psychological disorders. Psychiatric units were added to many of the regular hospitals and community services were established—both partially covered by federal transfer payments. Community mental-health centres are designed to provide comprehensive services to their local communities. Their major function is to provide outpatient psychotherapy and counselling so that clients can remain in their normal social and work environments. For example, the Centre for Addiction and Mental Health in Toronto provides care for people with mental health issues and addiction problems. Many have crisis centres and telephone "hot lines" to respond to emergency situations encountered by people in the community. Finally, community mental-health centres provide education and training, and some operate as research facilities.

Combined with the development of effective drug treatments, the impact of deinstitutionalization on the treatment of behaviour disorders has been dramatic. According to the U.S. National Institute of Mental Health, 77.4 percent of all patients were being treated as in-patients in public and private hospitals in 1955. By 1990, the in-patient figure had shrunk to 27.1 percent. As Figure 17.26 indicates, the average length of hospitalization for patients having severe

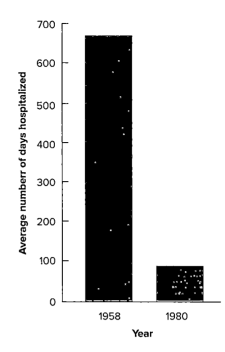

FIGURE 17.26 Average length of psychiatric hospitalization at Veterans Administration Hospitals in 1958 and 1980.

Source: Data from National Institute of Mental Health. (1992). *Psychiatric hospitalization in the United States*. Rockville, MB: Author.

(typically schizophrenic) disorders also has decreased markedly. In Canada, the deinstitutionalization movement resulted in an 80 percent decrease in the number of institutionalized patients.

The concept of community treatment is a good one, since it allows people to remain in their social and work environments and to be treated with minimal disruption of their lives. However, it requires the availability of high-quality mental health care in community clinics, halfway houses, sheltered workshops, and other community facilities. When these facilities are available, deinstitutionalization can work. Unfortunately, however, many communities never were able to fund the needed facilities, and the 1980s saw sharp cutbacks in federal funding of community mental-health centres. As a result, many patients are being released into communities that are ill-prepared to care for their needs. The result is a *revolving door phenomenon*, involving repeated rehospitalizations. Nearly three-quarters of all hospital admissions involve formerly hospitalized patients. While in the hospital, they respond well to antipsychotic medication and are soon released back into a community that cannot offer them the care they require. Soon they stop taking their

© David Litschel/Alamy Stock Photo

FIGURE 17.27 The revolving door phenomenon created by inadequate funding of community-based treatment facilities has produced a large population of severely disturbed homeless people who live on our nation's streets.

medication. In the absence of treatment, their condition deteriorates to the point where they must be hospitalized, and so the cycle begins again. One result is a growing population of disturbed and homeless people who have nowhere to go for help (Figure 17.27). In some provinces with large urban populations, the largest mental wards exist not in hospitals but on city streets. The United States has as many as one million homeless people, and approximately a third have a severe mental disorder, typically schizophrenia (Torrey, 1997). Estimates in Canada are proportionately similar—approximately 25 to 50 percent of the homeless have been hospitalized for a mental disorder in the past three years (Mental Health Commission of Canada, 2013; Wasylenki et al., 1993).

Deinstitutionalization can work only if society has the will to make it work. Time will tell if funding will be provided for the community programs needed to slow the revolving door and provide the help so desperately needed by the many people who are being left without treatment and without hope.

Preventive Mental Health

Up to now, we have focused entirely on what can be done to help people once they have developed a behaviour disorder. Successful treatment is one way to reduce the toll of human suffering produced by failures to adapt. Another way is to try to *prevent* the development of disorders through psychological intervention. In terms of economic, personal, and societal costs, it may indeed be the case that

"an ounce of prevention is worth a pound of cure." If current efforts to enhance personal well-being and slow the rise of health care costs are to be successful, then the prevention of behaviour disorders must be a focal point in social policy (Munoz et al., 1996).

People may become vulnerable to psychological disorders as the result of situational factors, personal factors, or both. Thus, prevention can be approached from two perspectives (Figure 17.28). **Situation-focused prevention** is directed at reducing or eliminating the environmental causes of behaviour disorders or at enhancing situational factors that help to prevent the development of disorders. Psychologist George Albee (1996), who champions this approach, insists that prevention must focus on efforts to reduce the stresses of unemployment, economic exploitation, discrimination, and poverty. Programs designed to enhance the functioning of families, reduce stress within organizations, provide better educational opportunities for children, and develop a sense of "connection" to other people and the community at large all have the potential to help to prevent the development

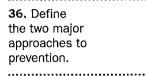

36. Define the two major approaches to prevention.

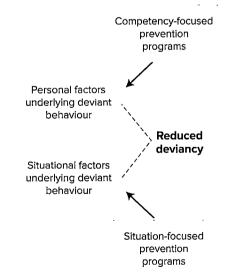

FIGURE 17.28 Two approaches to prevention of psychological disorders, based on the principle that deviant behaviour represents the interaction of personal and situational factors. Situation-focused approaches increase situational protective factors or reduce vulnerability factors in the environment. Competency-focused approaches reduce personal vulnerability factors or strengthen personal competencies and coping skills.

At various points throughout the text, we have briefly described statistical procedures to help you understand the information being presented. This appendix discusses statistics in greater detail and focuses on the concepts underlying these procedures. Our goal is to help you understand how psychologists use statistics in their research.

For some students, the prospect of studying statistics evokes visions of complex higher mathematics. You will find, however, that if you can add, subtract, multiply, and divide, you can easily perform basic statistical operations.

DESCRIPTIVE STATISTICS

Psychological research often involves a large number of measurements. Typically, it is difficult to make sense of the data merely by examining the individual scores of each participant. **Descriptive statistics** summarize and describe the characteristics of a set (also called a *distribution*) of scores.

To summarize a set of scores, we might first construct a **frequency distribution,** which shows how many participants received each score. For example, suppose that 50 university students took a 32-item psychological test that measured their level of self-esteem. The frequency distribution in Table A.1 tells us that two participants had scores of 30, 31, or 32; one had a score of 27, 28, or 29;

eleven had scores of 15, 16, or 17; and so on. Note that the researcher chose to use *intervals* of three points (e.g., 30–32) rather than to show the number (frequency) of participants who obtained each of the 33 possible (0–32) scores. She could have done the latter if she had wished to break down the scores even further. The number of intervals chosen is somewhat arbitrary, but frequency distributions often contain 10 to 12 categories.

This frequency distribution tells us at a glance about certain characteristics of the data, such as whether scores tend to cluster in one region of the distribution or are scattered throughout. We can easily convert these data into a **histogram,** which is a graph of a frequency distribution. Typically, the scores (or in this case, score intervals) are plotted along the horizontal axis (i.e., *x-axis,* or *abscissa)*, and the frequencies are plotted on the vertical axis (i.e., *y-axis,* or *ordinate)*. This method produces a column or bar above each score or score interval that shows how frequently the score occurred. Figure A.1 represents a histogram of the self-esteem scores for our sample of 50 university students.

MEASURES OF CENTRAL TENDENCY

Frequency distributions and histograms give us a general picture of how scores are distributed. **Measures of central tendency** describe a distribution in terms of a

TABLE A.1 Frequency Distribution of Self-Esteem Scores

Self-Esteem Scores	Frequency
30–32	2
27–29	1
24–26	4
21–23	6
18–20	9
15–17	11
12–14	8
9–11	3
6–8	4
3–5	1
0–2	1

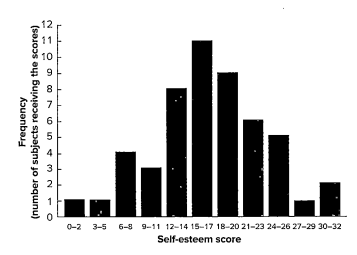

FIGURE A.1 A histogram of the self-esteem distribution shown in Table A.1.

TABLE A.2   Annual Salaries of 10 Employees

Employee		Annual Salary (X)
1.	Honest Al	$205 000
2.	Honest Al's mother	205 000
3.	Johnson	20 000
4.	Hussein	19 500
5.	Jones	19 000
6.	Chen	18 000
7.	Brown	17 500
8.	Chu	17 000
9.	Mullins	16 500
10.	Watson	16 000
$N = 10$		$\Sigma X = \$553\ 500$

Mode = The score that occurs most often—in this case, $205 000.

Mean = The arithmetic average, computed by the following formula:

$$M = \frac{\Sigma X}{N} = \frac{553\ 500}{10} = 55\ 350$$

Median = The point above and below which there is an equal number of scores. In this case, because there is an even number of scores, the median is midway between the fifth- and sixth-ranked salaries—that is, $18 500.

single statistic that is in some way "typical" of the sample as a whole. There are three commonly used measures of central tendency: the *mode*, the *mean*, and the *median*. For example, Table A.2 shows the salaries of the ten employees who work at Honest Al's Savings and Loan Corporation. Our task is to arrive at a single number that somehow typifies the salaries of the group as a whole.

The **mode** is the most frequently occurring score in a distribution. At Honest Al's, the modal salary is $205 000, because it is the only salary received by more than one person. Although the mode is easy to identify in a distribution, it is not always the most representative score, particularly if it falls far from the centre of the distribution. Clearly, $205 000 is not the "typical" salary of the ten employees, because eight of them receive $20 000 or less.

The most commonly used measure of central tendency, the **mean**, represents the arithmetic average of a set of scores. The mean is calculated by adding up all the scores and dividing by the number of scores. The statistical formula for computing the mean is

$$M = \frac{\Sigma X}{N}$$

X is the symbol for an individual score, N denotes the number of scores, and M is the symbol for the mean of the individual scores. The Greek letter Σ (sigma) means

"the sum." Thus, to compute the mean of the salaries at Honest Al's, we simply add up the individual salaries and divide the total by 10, the number of salaries. As Table A.2 shows, the mean salary at Honest Al's is $55 350.

Would you be tempted to go to work at Honest Al's if, during a job interview, Al told you that "our average salary is $55 350 per year"? Your negative answer to this question illustrates a shortcoming of the mean as a measure of central tendency. The mean can be strongly affected by one or more extremely high or low scores that are not representative of the group as a whole. In this case, the high salaries of Honest Al and his mother increased the mean to a figure more than twice as great as the salary of the next highest paid employee (i.e., Johnson). Thus, we cannot consider the mean to be representative of the salaries of Honest Al's employees.

Our third measure of central tendency, the **median**, is the point that divides the distribution in half when the individual scores are arranged in order from lowest to highest. In other words, half of the remaining scores lie above the median and half below it. If there is an odd number of scores, there will be one score that is exactly in the middle. If there were 11 salaries in Table A.2, the sixth-ranked score would be the median, because five scores would fall above and five below. In a distribution having an even number of scores, the median is halfway between the two middle scores. In our salary distribution, the median is the point halfway between employee 5 ($19 000) and employee 6 ($18 000), or $18 500.

The median has an important property that the mean does not have: It is unaffected by extreme scores. Whether Honest Al makes $205 000 or $500 000, the median remains the same. Therefore, the median is more representative of the group as a whole in instances when there are very extreme scores. In Honest Al's case, the median figure of $18 500 is more representative of the "typical" employee's salary than is the mean figure of $55 350 or the modal figure of $205 000. The median, however, can fail to capture important information. For example, suppose that employee 3 (Johnson) and employee 4 (Hussein) each received an $80 000 raise. In this case, the median would not change, because the "middle score" would still be the midpoint between employees 5 (Jones) and 6 (Chen). The mean, however, would increase to $71 350 ($713 500/10) and reflect the fact that Honest Al is being more generous in paying some of his employees.

Measures of Variability

Measures of central tendency provide us with a single score that typifies the distribution. But to describe a distribution adequately, we need to know more. One key question concerns the amount of variability, or spread, that exists among scores. Do they tend to cluster closely about the mean, or do they vary widely? **Measures of variability** provide information about the spread of scores in a distribution.

The **range**, which is the difference between the highest and the lowest score in a distribution, is the simplest but least informative measure of variability. At Honest Al's, the range is $205 000 − $16 000 = $189 000. As another example, if we have a distribution of 20 IQ scores and the highest IQ is 150 and the lowest is 70, then the range is 150 − 70 = 80. But suppose the other 18 people all have IQs of 110. If we knew only the range of scores, we might be led to believe that the scores in this distribution vary far more than they actually do. Thus, it would be more useful to know how much, on average, each IQ score varies or deviates from the mean of the distribution.

To do this we first create a *deviation score* (represented by a lowercase x) that measures the distance between each score (X) and the mean (M). To provide a simple example, suppose we have two distributions, A and B, each composed of ten scores. Looking at the "X (score)" column in Table A.3 for each distribution, you can see that although each distribution has a mean of 10, the scores in distribution B are more spread out than in distribution A. Now for each score we compute how much it differs from the mean (i.e., $x = X − M$). At this stage, you might think that to measure the variability of each distribution we need only add up its deviation scores and then compute the average deviation. But we have

a problem. Even though distribution B is more spread out than distribution A, adding up the deviation scores for each distribution yields a sum of zero ($\Sigma x = 0$). In fact, the sum of deviation scores for any distribution will always add up to zero.

To avoid this problem we must get rid of the plus and minus signs that end up cancelling each other out. As the rightmost column under each distribution in Table A.3 shows, we achieve this goal by taking each deviation score, squaring it, and then adding up these squared deviation scores. This produces a sum of 20 for distribution A and 356 for distribution B. Now we divide by 10 (i.e., the number of scores in each distribution) to find the average squared deviation. This statistic, called the **variance**, is the average of the squared deviation scores about the mean. You can see that the variance for distribution B (35.6) is considerably greater than the variance for distribution A (2.00), reflecting the greater spread of the scores in B.

The most popular measure of variability, the **standard deviation (SD)**, is the square root of the variance. Because we had to square the deviation scores to compute the variance, we now return to the original scale of measurement by taking the square root of the variance. Thus, the standard deviation describes variability

TABLE A.3 Computation of the Variance and Standard Deviation for Two Distributions of Scores with Identical Means ($M = 10$)

Distribution A			Distribution B		
X (score)	X − M = x	x²	X (score)	X − M = x	x²
12	+2	4	18	+8	64
12	+2	4	18	+8	64
11	+1	1	15	+5	25
11	+1	1	15	+5	25
10	0	0	10	0	0
10	0	0	10	0	0
9	−1	1	5	−5	25
9	−1	1	5	−5	25
8	−2	4	2	−8	64
8	−2	4	2	−8	64
$\Sigma X = 100$	$\Sigma x = 0$	$\Sigma x^2 = 20$	$\Sigma X = 100$	$\Sigma x = 0$	$\Sigma x^2 = 356$
$N = 10$			$N = 10$		
$M = 10.00$			$M = 10.00$		

x (deviation) $= X − M$

variance $= \frac{\Sigma x^2}{N} = \frac{20}{10} = 2.00$ variance $= \frac{\Sigma x^2}{N} = \frac{356}{10} = 35.6$

SD (standard deviation $= \sqrt{2.00} = 1.414$ $SD = \sqrt{35.6} = 5.967$

in the same units of measurement as the original data. You can see in Table A.3 that the standard deviation from the mean of distribution B (5.967) is more than four times greater than the standard deviation from the mean of distribution A (1.414).

THE NORMAL CURVE

The **normal curve** is a symmetrical bell-shaped curve that represents a theoretical distribution of scores in the population. In the normal curve, 50 percent of the cases fall on each side of the mean, and the median and mode have the same value as the mean. Figure A.2 shows that in a normal curve, as we move away from the mean, the frequency of each score steadily decreases. The normal curve is important because many variables in the population—weight, height, IQ, and anxiety, to name a few—are distributed in a way that approximates the normal curve. Thus, a few people are extremely tall or short, a greater number of people are moderately tall or short, and most are close to average in height.

The normal curve has several key properties. The most important of these is that the standard deviation can be used to divide the normal curve into areas containing known percentages of the population. In a normal curve, about two-thirds of the scores fall within plus or minus 1 standard deviation of the mean; about 95 percent of cases fall within plus or minus 2 standard deviations; and nearly all the cases fall between 3 standard deviations above and 3 standard deviations below the mean. Therefore, if we know that a psychological characteristic or any other variable is normally distributed, then we can deduce more information about it. For example, IQ scores as measured by the Wechsler intelligence tests (see Chapter 10) are normally distributed with a mean of 100 and a standard deviation of 15.

Knowing this, we can use our knowledge of the normal curve to answer questions like these:

1. What percentage of people have IQs between 70 and 130? (Approximately 95 percent. These scores are −2 SD and +2 SD from the mean, respectively. As Figure A.2 shows, this area below the curve includes 13.59 + 34.13 + 34.13 + 13.59 percent of the cases, or 95.44 percent.)

2. My IQ is 115, so where does that place me? (115 is +1 SD above the mean, so as Figure A.2 shows, about 16 percent of the population will have a higher IQ, and 84 percent will have a lower IQ. That is, the area to the right of +1 SD represents 13.59 + 2.14 + 0.13 percent of the cases, or 15.86 percent.)

3. What is the probability that a person selected at random from the population will have an IQ of 145 or more? (About one-eighth of 1 percent. This probability corresponds to the area under the curve beyond + 3 SD, or 0.13 percent.)

These examples point to a major use of the normal curve: It allows us to estimate the probability that a given event will occur. Indeed, the statistical tests we describe next are methods for arriving at probability statements based on the assumption that the variables being investigated are normally distributed.

STATISTICAL METHODS FOR DATA ANALYSIS

Given a set of data for any single variable, such as the scores of a sample of people on a self-esteem test, we use descriptive statistics to summarize the characteristics of those data. But psychologists do more than describe variables individually. They seek to explain and predict behaviour by examining how variables are *related* to one another. The following statistical methods are used to analyze relations among variables and draw inferences about the meaning of those relations.

Accounting for Variance in Behaviour

Behaviour varies. It varies between individuals (e.g., some people are more aggressive or helpful than others), and it varies for the same individual across time and situations (a person may perform a task well under some conditions but more poorly under other circumstances). Explaining why variations in behaviour occur (i.e., accounting for variance) is a central goal of psychological science.

As an example, suppose we want to examine how the number of bystanders present during an emergency influences the speed with which they assist a person in distress. In this instance, the number of bystanders is the independent variable, and the speed of helping is the dependent variable. We conduct an experiment, randomly

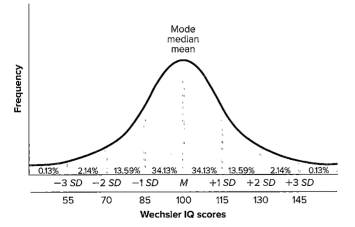

FIGURE A.2 The normal curve, showing the percentage of cases falling within each area of the normal distribution and also showing Wechsler IQ scores that correspond to standard deviation (SD) units.

assign participants to different conditions (one, two, or four bystanders present), and find that, overall, bystanders who were alone responded most quickly and groups of four responded most slowly. We also find that the speed of response varied even within each condition; for example, among those bystanders who were alone, some simply responded more quickly than others. Maybe they were in a better mood, had more altruistic personalities, and so on.

In any experiment, the total amount of variation in people's behaviour (e.g., speed of helping) may be divided into two components: the amount of *variance accounted for* by the differences in the independent variable(s) being manipulated (e.g., being placed alone or with other bystanders) and the amount of variance that is left over and therefore must be due to other factors (e.g., participants' mood, personality). Thus,

Total = Variance accounted + Variance not
variance   for (due to   accounted for
            independent   (due to random,
            variables)   unmeasured, or
                           uncontrolled
                           factors)

In our experiment, suppose a statistical analysis reveals that 20 percent of the total variance in the speed with which participants helped a person in distress can be accounted for by our independent variable: the number of other bystanders present. Figure A.3 shows this schematically. The other 80 percent of the variance in speed of helping is due to other factors that were not controlled in the experiment. Some of these other factors, which are random and beyond the control of the experimenter, produce what is called *error variance*. For example, some participants may have been momentarily bored or preoccupied with personal problems and thus responded more slowly than they otherwise would have. The rest of the unexplained variance results from factors that systematically affect the speed of helping but which the researcher either does not know about or were not controlled for in the experiment. Such variables may include the participants' personality characteristics or mood, the victim's gender, the nature of the emergency, and so forth. In future research, we might introduce additional independent variables, such as manipulating (i.e., creating) an environment that puts bystanders in a good or bad mood just prior to the emergency. By studying other independent variables, we attempt to increase the amount of variance accounted for, thereby increasing the size of the "accounted for" area in Figure A.3. Perhaps we will find that by knowing both the number of bystanders present and the participants' mood, we can now account for 35 percent of the variance in people's speed of helping.

From this perspective, understanding and/or predicting behaviour involves isolating factors that account for

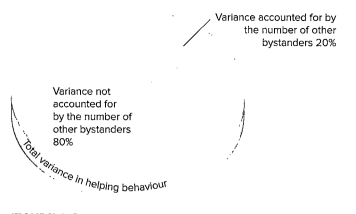

FIGURE A.3 The total amount of variation in the dependent variable (speed of responding to another person in distress) is represented within the circle. The total variance may be divided into one portion accounted for by the independent variable (number of bystanders) and another portion not accounted for by the independent variable.

behavioural variance. The more important a particular variable is, the more variance it helps us account for. To be sure, we can never completely eliminate the random factors that produce error variance. But as scientific research proceeds, the goal is to discover new variables that account for additional portions of the total variance in people's behaviour.

Correlational Methods

The concept of *variance accounted for* applies not only to experiments but also to correlational studies. As discussed in Chapter 2, correlational research does not involve manipulating independent variables. Rather, it involves measuring two or more variables and determining whether changes in one variable are associated with changes in the other. Suppose that we administer two psychological tests—one measuring self-esteem and the other measuring depression—to 200 adults. On each test we will find that the scores vary: Some people will have higher self-esteem than others, and some will be more depressed than others. The question is this: Is there a relation between the variance in self-esteem scores and the variance in depression scores? Stated differently, as self-esteem scores (variable X) become higher or lower (i.e., as they move further away from the mean of X), do depression scores (variable Y) tend to become either higher or lower (i.e., move away from the mean of Y) in a systematic manner?

The Correlation Coefficient

Relations between variables can differ in *direction* (positive or negative) and in *strength*. To illustrate, imagine that we have a sample of six people, with scores on two variables (X and Y) for each person. Table A.4 shows five hypothetical sets of X and Y scores for these six people.

TABLE A.4   Five Data Sets Illustrating Various Relations That May Exist between Two Variables

Participant	Set A		Set B		Set C		Set D		Set E	
	X	*Y*	*X*	*Y*	*X*	*Y*	*X*	*Y*	*X*	*Y*
1	1	2	1	4	1	5	1	6	1	12
2	2	4	2	5	2	8	2	8	2	10
3	3	6	3	2	3	6	3	10	3	8
4	4	8	4	10	4	2	4	4	4	6
5	5	10	5	6	5	6	5	2	5	4
6	6	12	6	8	6	7	6	1	6	2
$N = 6$	$r = +1.00$		$r = +0.58$		$r = 0.00$		$r = +0.75$		$r = -1.00$	

Each set consists of the scores of six people on two variables, X and Y. The product–moment correlation coefficient (r) has been computed for each set. The computational formula for r is as follows:

$$r = \frac{N(\Sigma X_i Y_i) - (\Sigma X_i)(\Sigma Y_i)}{\sqrt{[N(\Sigma X_i^2) - (\Sigma X_i)^2][N(\Sigma Y_i^2) - (\Sigma Y_i)^2]}}$$

Where X_i = Each person's score on variable X; ΣX_i = sum of Xs

Y_i = Each person's score on variable Y; ΣY_i = sum of Ys

N = Total number of people

In set A the relation between variables X and Y is positive in direction. That is, higher scores on variable X are associated with higher scores on Y, and lower scores on X are associated with lower scores on Y. In contrast, set E reveals a negative relation. Here, higher scores on X are associated with lower Y scores, and vice versa. In set C the pairs of X and Y scores bear no clear relation to each other: They are not correlated. As scores on X change, scores on Y do not change in any consistent manner. Thus, in sets A, C, and E, we see three different types of relations—positive, none, and negative.

To illustrate how relations between variables differ in strength, let us compare set A with set B. In set A, there is a perfect positive relation between X and Y: As each X score increases by a constant amount (in this case, by 1), each Y score also increases by a constant amount (in this case, by 2). In set B, individuals having higher X scores also tend to have higher Y scores, but this positive relation is not as consistent as in Set A. For example, in set B participant 3 has a higher X score than participant 2 yet a lower Y score. Likewise, compare set E with set D. Set E displays a perfect negative relation: As each X score increases by a constant amount, each Y score decreases by a constant amount. In set D, the negative relation between X and Y is not as consistent and thus is not as strong.

The **Pearson product-moment correlation coefficient** is a statistic that reflects the direction and strength of the relation between two variables. The correlation coefficient (designated r) can range in magnitude from −1.00 to +1.00. If $r = +1.00$, this reflects a perfect positive relation between X and Y scores, as in set A of Table A.4. A correlation coefficient of −1.00 signifies a perfect negative

relation, as in set E. Correlations close to 0.00 indicate no systematic relation between the variables, as in set C.

In actual research, a correlation of −1.00 or +1.00 is rare; psychological variables tend to be imperfectly correlated with each other. More typically, correlation coefficients might resemble those in sets B ($r = +0.58$) and D ($r = -0.75$). Remember that it is the magnitude of the correlation coefficient and not its sign (direction) that indicates the degree to which two variables are related to each other. Thus, X and Y are more strongly related in set D ($r = -0.75$) than in set B ($r = +0.58$), even though the correlation in set D is negative.

How shall we interpret a correlation coefficient? A correlation of +0.50, for example, *does not* mean that X and Y are 50 percent related. Rather, squaring the correlation coefficient (r^2) indicates the amount of variance that the two variables share or have in common. Stated another way, r^2 tells us how much of the variance in one measure can be accounted for by differences in the other measure. For example, suppose we obtain a correlation of +0.50 between scores on a mechanical aptitude test and grades in a university engineering course. As illustrated in Figure A.4, squaring the correlation coefficient ($+0.50^2 = 0.25$) tells us that 25 percent of the total variance in course grades can be accounted for by differences in mechanical aptitude scores. Obviously, the more highly two variables are correlated, the more common variance they share. If the two variables in Figure A.4 correlated +0.70, the area of overlap would include about half of each circle, because $(+0.70)^2 = 0.49$. Finally, if two variables are perfectly correlated, the two circles in Figure A.4 would overlap completely.

means for the two samples would vary in each experiment. For example, the next three times we performed the study the means might be 2.94 (experimental) versus 2.77 (control), 3.34 versus 2.31, and 2.89 versus 2.83, yielding differences between the groups of 0.17, 1.03, and 0.06, respectively. By repeating the experiment a great many times, we could create a distribution of experimental versus control difference scores, and mathematical theory tells us that this distribution would be a *normal* distribution. This gives us the key. Because we have a normal distribution, just as we previously assessed the exact likelihood of randomly selecting a person with an IQ of 145, we can now determine the likelihood of randomly obtaining a difference of any particular size between our sample means. But to do this, we must first know what the mean and standard deviation of our distribution of differences are. As we've seen, one way to determine these values would be to perform our experiment a large number of times. But, fortunately, we can estimate these values on the basis of a single experiment and thereby avoid the need for many replications.

To do this, we use an approach to statistical analysis that involves testing the **null hypothesis**, which states that any observed differences between the samples are due to chance. We begin by assuming that the null hypothesis is true—that there is no real difference, for example, in grade point average between the populations of trained and untrained test-anxious students. If the null hypothesis is true, then if we repeated our experiment a great many times, we would expect the mean of our distribution of difference scores to be zero. Therefore, the normal distribution of difference scores would cluster around this mean of zero. The standard deviation of this normal distribution can be estimated from the standard deviations of the two samples, although the mathematics need not concern us here.

In our hypothetical experiment, we obtained grade point means of 3.17 for the experimental group and 2.61 for the control group, a difference of +0.56. Let us now suppose that the standard deviation of our distribution of differences between means was estimated on the basis of our samples to be 0.25. Thus, our obtained difference of +0.56 is slightly more than 2 SD above the mean (0) of the null hypothesis distribution. From the properties of the normal curve, we know that more than 95 percent of the cases fall in the area of the curve between −2 SD and +2 SD. Thus, *if the null hypothesis were true*, we would expect a difference in means as large as 0.56 (either above or below zero) less than 5 percent of the time on the basis of chance factors. This probability level meets the criterion for statistical significance described earlier. In view of this fact, we would reject the null hypothesis and conclude that there is a real difference in grade point average in the two populations. Thus, our experimental hypothesis that the stress-management program resulted in a higher level of academic performance would be supported.

Note that we used the term *supported*, not *proven*, because we are making an inference based on a probability statement. There is, after all, some possibility (though less than 5 percent) that the null hypothesis is true and this really was a chance finding. Note also that this statistical analysis does not tell us why the stress-management group performed better (e.g., Did they perform better because of the program's content or the mere attention they received?). This is one reason why repeating or replicating research studies is so valuable. If another study—particularly one with more control groups—also yields statistically significant results, we can have more confidence that the difference we obtained reflects a real relation between the independent and dependent variables. But no matter how many times we repeat the experiment, we shall never move from the world of probability into the world of absolute truth.

CHAPTER 1

Are the Students Lazy?

It may be tempting to blame the students' unresponsiveness on laziness, but a radical behaviourist would not focus on internal mental states to explain their inaction. First, to say that students are unresponsive *because* they're lazy doesn't explain anything. Consider this reasoning: How do we know that the students are lazy? Answer: because they are unresponsive. Therefore, if we say that students are lazy because they're unresponsive and then turn around and conclude that students are unresponsive because they are lazy, all we are really saying is that "students are unresponsive because they are unresponsive." This is not an explanation at all but rather an example of circular reasoning.

From a behavioural perspective, people's actions are shaped by the environment and learning experiences. Put yourself in the hypothetical role of the high school teacher: You may not realize it, but when students sit quietly, you smile and seem more relaxed. When students participate in class discussions, you are quick to criticize their ideas. In these ways you may have taught your students to behave passively.

To change their behaviour, you can modify their educational environment so that they will learn new responses. Reward behaviours that you want to see (raising hands, correctly answering questions, and so on). For example, praise students not only for giving correct answers but also for participating. If an answer is incorrect, point this out in a nonpunitive way while still reinforcing the student's participation.

Modifying the environment to change behaviour is often not as easy as it sounds, but this example illustrates one way a behaviourist might try to rearrange the environmental consequences rather than jump to the conclusion that the situation is hopeless.

CHAPTER 2

Should You Trust Internet and Pop Media Surveys?

Typical Internet, magazine, and phone-in surveys share two major problems. First, people who choose to respond are entirely *self-selected* (rather than selected by the researcher), and the resulting samples likely do not even represent the entire population of people who use the Internet, subscribe to that magazine, or watch that TV show, respectively. Perhaps those who respond are more motivated, have a more helpful personality, or differ in some other important way from those who don't respond.

Second, it is unlikely that samples of Internet users, magazine subscribers, and TV news viewers represent the population at large (e.g., North American adults). Do you think that the readers of *Cosmopolitan, Wired, Guns & Ammo,* or any magazine typify the general population? Because Internet and pop media surveys do not use random sampling, they are likely to generate samples that are not representative of the broader population.

Surely, many news organizations sponsor high-quality surveys conducted by professional pollsters. The key is that these surveys, such as political polls, use appropriate random-sampling procedures to obtain representative samples.

Finally, be aware that some psychologists, especially those who study people's personality and social behaviours, are increasingly using the Internet to collect research data. As users surf the Web, they may find a site that invites them to participate in an experiment or take a psychological test. These studies are not surveys that critically depend on having representative samples of the broader population. Rather, they typically examine relations among variables and underlying psychological principles. Some researchers question the validity of such Internet-based studies, but proponents have shown that most of these concerns are unfounded. More research is needed, but thus far it seems that Internet-based studies of this type yield findings that are consistent with those obtained from more traditional types of methods (Best et al., 2001; Gosling et al., 2004).

Does Eating Ice Cream Cause People to Drown?

Just because two variables are correlated, we cannot conclude that they are causally related. First, consider the bidirectionality problem. We don't see any likely way that drownings could cause the rest of the public to eat more ice cream, so let's rule that out. Can we conclude, then, that more ice cream consumption causes more drownings? We suppose that, in a few cases, gorging on ice cream shortly before swimming might enhance the risk of drowning. But nationally, how often is this likely to happen?

Now consider the third-variable problem. What other factors might cause people to eat more ice cream and also lead to an increase in drownings? The most obvious third variable is "daily temperature" (or "month of the year"). Summer months bring hotter days, and people eat more ice cream in hot weather. Likewise, on hotter days drownings increase simply because so many more people go swimming. In short, the most reasonable conclusion is that the ice cream–drowning correlation is due to a third variable.

CHAPTER 3

Do the Sexes Differ?

First, you may have recognized that although the right hemisphere of women was more active during a language task, what we have is a correlation between task performance and biological activity. Does this activity play a causal role in task performance? Is it necessary for task performance? We do not know at this point. Another question we might ask is whether women are more likely than men to experience language deficits if they suffer right-hemisphere damage. If so, this would indicate that right-hemisphere activation is more important for women. In fact, we do know that women are *not* more likely than men to become aphasic if they suffer right-hemisphere damage (Brogdal, 2010). Clearly, we have more to learn about possible sex differences in lateralization, but we are learning which questions to ask.

CHAPTER 4

Natural Selection and Genetic Diseases

Genetics research shows that in most cases, there is not a one-to-one relation between a particular gene and a particular trait. Most traits involve the influence of many genes, and a given gene can contribute to many traits. Traits, therefore, come in packages, with some of the traits in the package being adaptive while others may be neutral or even maladaptive. In fact, cystic fibrosis (CF) is one such example. CF is the most commonly inherited disorder among people of European descent. Why would such a damaging genetic trait survive in the gene pool?

Geneticists have found that people with CF also have a trait that slows the release of salts into the intestine (Allen, 2010). Some scientists believe that this related trait might have helped save carriers from severe dehydration and death from the diarrheal diseases that killed seven out of every ten newborns in medieval Europe. Perhaps CF was preserved in the population because another part of the trait package made carriers more likely to survive and pass on their genes.

Let us now consider sickle-cell anemia. Many people of African descent suffer from this genetically caused blood disorder that lowers one's life expectancy. Why would a disorder that decreases survival be preserved in a population? The answer may be that despite its negatives, the sickle-cell gene has an important redeeming quality:

it makes people more resistant to malaria, the most lethal disease in the African environment. Because it enhanced survival from malaria, the sickle-cell trait became more common among Africans and can therefore be seen as a product of natural selection.

These examples show us that we should be careful not to oversimplify the concept of adaptation and assume that any trait that survives, whether physical or psychological, is always of benefit to the species.

CHAPTER 5

Why Does That Rising Moon Look So Big?

To begin with, let's emphasize the obvious: the moon is not actually larger when it's on the horizon. Photographs show that the size of the image cast on the retina is exactly the same in both cases. So what psychologists call the *moon illusion* must be created by our perceptual system. Though not completely understood, the illusion seems to be a false perception caused by cues that ordinarily contribute to maintaining size constancy. The chief suspect is apparent distance, which figures importantly in our size judgments. One theory holds that the moon looks bigger as it's rising over the horizon because we use objects in our field of vision, such as trees, buildings, and landscape features, to estimate its distance. Experiments have shown that objects look farther away when viewed through filled spaces than they do when viewed through empty spaces (such as the sky overhead). Filled space can make objects look as much as 2.5 to 4 times farther away. According to the theory, the perceptual system basically says, "If the size of the retinal image is the same but it's farther away, then it must be bigger." This explanation can't be the whole story, however, because some people perceive the moon on the horizon as being closer, rather than farther away. If something the same size seems closer, it will look larger even though it isn't. It may be that there are individual differences in the size-judgment processes that cause the illusion, so that no single explanation applies to everybody.

Explain This Striking Illusion

To analyze your experience, it is important to understand that both the "tent" and the "corner" cast identical images on your retina. After perceiving the tent for a while, your brain shifted to the second perceptual hypothesis. When the object looked like a tent, all the depth information was consistent with that perception. But when you began to see it as a corner and then moved your head slowly back and forth, the object seemed to twist and turn as if it were made of rubber. This occurred because, when you moved, the image of the near point of the fold moved across your retina faster than the image of the far point. This is the normal pattern of stimulation for points at different depths and is known as motion parallax. Thus, when you were seeing a tent, the monocular cue of motion parallax was consistent with the shape of the object. But when the object was later seen as standing upright, all the points along the fold appeared to be the same distance away, yet they were moving at different rates of speed! The only way your brain could maintain its "corner" perception in the face of the motion parallax cues was to see the object as twisting and turning. Again, as in other illusions, forcing all of the sensory data to fit the perceptual hypothesis produced an unusual experience.

CHAPTER 6

Early Birds, Climate, and Culture

As a critical thinker, keep in mind that correlation does not establish causation. This is a correlational study. The major variables (climate, students, morningness) were not manipulated; they were only measured. The association between climate and morningness might be causal, but we must consider other possible explanations.

First, why might climate affect morningness? The researchers hypothesized that to avoid performing daily activities during the hottest part of the day, people who live in warmer climates adapt to a pattern of rising early in the morning, a finding consistent with a prior study that revealed strong tendencies toward morningness among Brazilians (Benedito-Silva et al., 1989).

Second, as the authors note, these results could be due to factors other than climate. The Netherlands, England, and the United States share a northern-European heritage, and perhaps some aspect of this common background predisposes people toward less morningness. Yet, say the authors, India's cultural traditions are distinct from those of Spain and Colombia, so it is difficult to apply the "common cultural heritage" argument to explain the greater morningness found among students from these countries. If not cultural heritage, perhaps the greater industrialization and summertime use of air-conditioned home and work environments in the Netherlands, England, and the United States reduce the necessity for residents to adapt circadian cycles to local climate conditions. Aware of their study's limitations, the authors suggest that climate may be just one of several factors that contribute to cross-cultural differences in morningness.

Hypnosis and Amazing Feats

For any causal claim, it is important for critical thinkers to think about the concept of control groups. You should keep this question in mind: What would have happened anyway, even without this special treatment or intervention? Applied to hypnosis, the key question is whether people can exhibit these same amazing feats when they are not hypnotized. When a stage hypnotist gets someone to perform the human plank, the audience attributes this feat to the hypnotic trance. What the audience doesn't know is that an average man suspended in this manner

can support about 140 kilograms on his chest with little discomfort and no need of a hypnotic trance.

As for the allergy experiment, we must ask whether allergic people might show the same reactions if they were not hypnotized. Indeed, the experiment included eight nonhypnotized control participants (Ikemi & Nakagawa, 1962). When blindfolded and exposed to a toxic leaf but misled to believe that it was harmless, they did not show an allergic response. Conversely, when their arm was rubbed with a harmless leaf but they were falsely told it was toxic, they had an allergic reaction. In short, the nonhypnotized people responded the same way as the hypnotized subjects.

Other research shows that under hypnosis, vision can improve and stomach acidity can increase. However, well-controlled studies show that nonhypnotized subjects can exhibit these same responses (Spanos & Chaves, 1988). As with placebo effects and other mind–body interactions, people's beliefs and expectations can produce real physiological effects.

CHAPTER 7

Was the Little Albert Study Ethical?

Imagine that we are reviewing this research proposal in 1918.

If you initially thought that you would not approve this study, consider the following:

- Suppose the experimenters obtain Albert's parents' informed consent.
- Although Albert will experience short-term stress, consider the enormous potential benefits of this study. It may revolutionize thinking about phobias and lead to effective treatments that benefit countless people with phobias.
- Suppose the experimenters promise to use learning principles to extinguish Albert's phobia immediately after the study.

Would you now approve the study?

If your initial (or new) judgment is to approve this study, consider the following:

- Based on learning theory, is there not a long-term risk that the phobia will generalize to other stimuli?
- If a phobia is successfully conditioned, is it guaranteed that Albert will receive treatment to eliminate it? Has the treatment been tested with humans? What is the failure rate? If there already is good evidence that it is effective, why conduct this study?

Applying today's ethical standards, we believe this research proposal would have be rejected. There was insufficient evidence at the time to support the effectiveness of phobia extinction treatment with humans. An ethical alternative approach would have been to study whether learning-based treatments could effectively treat patients who already had phobias.

Can You Explain the Supermarket Tantrum?

The father's initial refusal to buy candy is followed by an aversive stimulus (the tantrum). This punishes the father's response, and after two tantrums he no longer refuses the request. When the father eventually gives in, this removes an aversive stimulus (the tantrum), which negatively reinforces (strengthens) the response of giving in. Thus, the father's response of refusing to buy candy is weakened by punishment, and the response of giving in is strengthened by negative reinforcement. Just as important, the child has learned that throwing a tantrum pays off. The tantrum was positively reinforced by the consequence of getting candy.

CHAPTER 8

Would Perfect Memory Be a Gift or a Curse?

No doubt, perfect memory would have advantages, but were you able to think of any liabilities? Russian newspaper reporter S.V. Shereshevskió—arguably the most famous mnemonist in history—had a remarkable capacity to remember numbers, poems in foreign languages, complex mathematical formulas, nonsense syllables, and sounds. Psychologist Aleksandr Luria (1968), who studied "S." for decades, describes how S. was tyrannized by his seeming inability to forget meaningless information. Almost any stimulus might unleash a flood of trivial memories that dominated his consciousness and made it difficult for him to concentrate or think abstractly.

S.'s experience may have been atypical, but perfect memory could indeed clutter up our thinking with trivial information. Moreover, perfect memory would deprive us of one of life's blessings: the ability to forget unpleasant experiences from our past. As illustrated in this chapter, imperfect memory allows us to view our past through slightly rosy glasses (Bahrick et al., 2008).

Would a perfect memory help you perform better on exams? On test questions calling only for definitions, formulas, or facts—probably so. But on questions asking you to apply concepts, synthesize ideas, analyze issues, and so forth, perfect memory might be of little benefit unless you also understood the material. In his graduate school classes,

> Rajan had a tendency to try to commit the reading assignments to memory and reproduce them on tests. The strategy . . . is counterproductive in graduate courses where students are asked to apply their knowledge and understanding to new situations. . . . When taking tests, Rajan would write furiously . . . in hopes that the correct answer was somewhere in his response. . . . As he progressed in our graduate program, he tended to rely less on the

strategy of memorizing everything and more on trying to understand and organize the information. (Thompson et al., 1993, p. 15)

Rajan's extraordinary memory for numbers did not extend to reading or visual tasks, but even if yours did, it still might tempt you to focus too heavily on sheer memorization and cause you to neglect paying attention to the meaning of the material. In sum, although imperfect memory can be frustrating and have serious consequences (as when eyewitnesses identify the wrong suspect), we should also appreciate how our memory system is balanced between the adaptiveness of remembering and the benefits of forgetting.

(By the way, in case you're curious, the current confirmed record for recalling pi is 67 890 digits, held by Chao Lu of China. To put this feat in perspective, imagine the next 19 pages of this textbook filled up with nothing but numbers!)

CHAPTER 9

Discerning the Deep Structure of Language

The final words on the grave marker ("No Les No More") consist of a single surface structure with two possible deep structures. First, given the preceding words on the tombstone, the phrase "No Les No More" could be a play on words, which in this case is meant to represent the expression "No Less, No More." In other words, Lester Moore was killed by exactly four bullets, no less, no more. Or, the deep structure of "No Les No More" can be interpreted as meaning that Lester is no longer among the living. Thus, like the sentence "The police must stop drinking after midnight," the inscription on this tombstone has an ambiguous deep structure.

Sometimes, interpreting ambiguous sentences yields humorous results. For example, a newspaper headline that reads "Squad Helps Dog Bite Victim" is intended to mean that the squad helps the victim of a dog bite. But another deep structure is that the squad helped the dog to bite the victim!

The Sleeping Policeman

This actual event illustrates how top-down processing and pragmatics affect our ability to understand language. First, I (your author, M.W.P.) didn't take the storekeeper's words literally; I did not expect to see a police officer sleeping on the side of the road!

Second, in England (and Ireland and Scotland), the taverns often have wonderfully colourful names: The Drunken Duck, The Black Swan, and so on. Given this knowledge, would it change your interpretation of *the sleeping policeman?* Indeed, I assumed that the storekeeper was referring to a pub or perhaps a restaurant— and I interpreted his spoken words as *The Sleeping Policeman.* Unfortunately, driving along the road, I saw nothing but farmland and homes. I returned to town and asked the storekeeper, "When you say *Sleeping Police-man*, are you referring to a pub?" He chuckled and said, "Oh no, no. You know . . . it's that long thing in the road . . . the thing that slows you down." "Ah," I replied, "at home we call them speed bumps!"

My prior top-down knowledge about the names of English pubs shaped my assumption that *the sleeping policeman* referred to a pub. When I later asked English friends if they had heard of the term *sleeping policeman*, about half said no. Thus, the storekeeper made an erroneous assumption as well—namely, that visitors would have the background to understand the meaning of the local idiom *sleeping policeman*. This reflects a breakdown in pragmatics: it violates the rule of clarity. Can you think of idioms (e.g., "give me a hand," "that's cool") that have obvious meaning to you but which may have a literal interpretation that could confuse a foreign visitor?

CHAPTER 10

Are Gifted Children Maladjusted?

Like the intellectually disabled, the gifted are often the victims of stereotypes. Some characterize them as "geeks" and "nerds" who are eccentric and socially maladjusted. As is the case with many stereotypes, there is a grain of truth here. A review of the scientific literature on giftedness by Ellen Winner (2000) revealed that nearly a fourth of children with truly exceptional IQs at the high end of the gifted range (around 180) have social and psychological problems, about twice the rate found in nongifted children. Such children often have different interest patterns and encounter difficulty finding like-minded peers to relate to, resulting in solitude and loneliness. The research also revealed, however, that the vast majority of these highly intelligent children show adequate adjustment, providing evidence against any stereotype that would be applied to gifted children in general.

Consider also a project begun in the 1920s by Lewis Terman, the psychologist who developed the Stanford-Binet test. Terman identified 1528 California children who had a mean IQ of 150 and began an extensive study of them that continued for over 70 years. Terman and the researchers who inherited the project found the "Termites," as they were called, to be above average not only in intelligence but also in height, weight, strength, physical health, emotional adjustment, and social maturity. They continued to exhibit high levels of adjustment throughout their adolescent and adult years. By midlife, the 1528 Termites had authored 92 books, 2200 scientific articles, and 235 patents. Their marriages tended to be happy and successful, and they seemed well adjusted psychologically (Sears, 1977). Nonetheless, some of the Termites underachieved and experienced social and psychological problems. These individuals tended to come from lower-socioeconomic backgrounds and to have parents who did not emphasize success or convey success

expectations. The results were lowered motivation to achieve and a lack of confidence that they could accomplish their goals. Findings such as these show that capitalizing on one's high IQ requires an interest in some domain and the motivation to develop one's gifts.

CHAPTER 11

Is Maslow's Need Hierarchy Valid?

More than most psychological theories of motivation, Maslow's model appropriately emphasizes that diverse motives influence human behaviour. The concepts of need progression and need regression seem to make intuitive sense. Motives do become stronger and weaker as circumstances change, and it seems logical that when people are starving, finding food becomes more important than contemplating beauty and truth.

Critics, however, have long questioned the validity of the need hierarchy and have argued that the concept of "self-actualization" is vague and hard to measure (Heylighen, 1992). The ordering of needs seems arbitrary, and the concepts of need progression and regression cannot account for important aspects of motivated behaviour. How does the hierarchy explain why a person in a war zone would create works of art, or why political protestors go on hunger strikes or risk their physical safety to defend abstract principles they believe in? Does a need for knowledge and understanding really become prominent only after needs for social belonging and self-esteem are met? Throughout evolution, was seeking esteem and recognition more important and adaptive to our ancestors than acquiring knowledge to help them survive?

Finally, rather than viewing the journey toward self-actualization as a relatively independent striving to maximize one's potential, some modern humanists view the entire process as more relationship-oriented (Hanley & Abell, 2002). In their view, healthy social relationships not only satisfy deficiency needs for belonging and esteem but also are important for achieving and expressing self-actualization.

Despite these drawbacks, by calling attention to the human desire for growth and incorporating diverse motives, the intuitive appeal of Maslow's model has influenced thinking in fields such as philosophy, education, and business (Zinovieva, 2001).

Can You Fool a Lie Detector?

Considering what you have learned about the physiology of emotion, do you think emotional arousal can tell us whether someone is telling the truth or lying? Emotional responses are accompanied by physiological responses that we have less control over than we do with numerous other behaviours. The polygraph measures respiration, heart rate, and skin conductance (a measure of sweat gland activity)—behaviours seemingly outside of our control. Polygraph examiners compare physiological responses to critical questions ("Were you present at the riot after the Stanley Cup game?") with responses to control questions that make no reference to the crime or crime scene ("Do you watch hockey?"). If there is a response to the critical question but not to the control question, the interpretation is that the examinee lied when responding to the critical question, that made him or her anxious, and the physiological changes accompanying anxiety were detected by the polygraph.

The issue, however, is whether the response to a critical question means that the person was lying. Herein lies one major problem with polygraph tests. Innocent people may appear guilty when doubt, fear, or lack of confidence increases their autonomic activity (Iacono, 2008; Lilienfeld et al., 2010). Even thoughts like "What if my answer makes me look guilty, even though I'm not?" or "I'm nervous and my voice sound shaky, does that make me seem guilty?" in response to a critical question could send the polygraph pens moving in a way that suggests a lie. Similarly, the content of a question that refers to a grisly crime may generate an emotional response regardless of a person's guilt or innocence. Research on polygraph tests has found an especially high rate of false positives; that is, identification of an innocent person as guilty (Honts & Perry, 1992).

Not only can innocent people appear guilty, but guilty people can learn to "beat" the polygraph and appear innocent. Someone may appear innocent by generating a response to both critical and control questions or by generating no response to any question. By biting their tongue, curling their toes, or contracting their anal sphincter when control questions are asked, people can produce an arousal response to those questions that is similar to the response that occurs when they actually lie on critical questions. Conversely, if someone was guilty of a crime but had no remorse or emotional reaction to the crime, or if they were sufficiently practised in relaxation techniques, critical questions may not generate any change despite the person's guilt.

Tellingly, William Casey, Director of the U.S. Central Intelligence Agency (CIA) in the 1980s, used to delight in his ability to fool the lie detector (Carlson & Hatfield, 1992). Fred Fay, a prison convict who had been falsely convicted of murder partly on the basis of a polygraph test, also became an expert at defeating polygraph tests (too late, unfortunately, for his acquittal). On one occasion, Fay coached 27 fellow inmates who were scheduled for polygraph tests. All of the inmates told Fay they were guilty of the relevant crimes. Yet after only 20 minutes of instruction, 23 of the 27 inmates managed to beat the polygraph (Lykken, 1981). Such results sharply contradict the notion of an infallible lie detector.

Misgivings about the validity of polygraph tests are supported by studies in which experienced polygraph examiners were given the polygraph records of suspects known to be either innocent or guilty on the basis of other evidence. The experts were asked to judge the guilt or innocence of the suspects. They usually did quite well in identifying the guilty, attaining accuracy rates of 80 to 98 percent (Honts & Perry, 1992). However, they were less accurate in identifying the innocent, judging as many as 55 percent of the truly innocent suspects to be guilty in some studies (Kleinmuntz & Szucko, 1984; Lykken, 1984). These error rates call into question the adage that an innocent person has nothing to fear from a polygraph test. On the other hand, guilty people who fail polygraph tests sometimes confess to the crime as a result (Ruscio, 2005).

Largely because of an unacceptably high likelihood that an innocent person might be judged guilty, the American Psychological Association has supported legal challenges to polygraph testing. Congressional testimony by psychologists strongly influenced passage of the U.S. Employee Polygraph Protection Act of 1988, which prohibits most nongovernmental polygraph testing. Moreover, polygraph results alone cannot be used to convict people of crimes in most jurisdictions (Daniels, 2002). Nonetheless, local and federal governments continue to use polygraph tests in internal criminal investigations and in police officer and national security screening, despite the weight of research evidence against their validity for these purposes (Cochrane et al., 2003; Kleiner, 2002).

CHAPTER 12

Shy Child, Shy Adult?

Researchers have conducted longitudinal studies to find out whether temperament characteristics identified in children predict their adult temperaments. For example, in the United States and Sweden, inhibited 8- to 12-year-old boys are more likely than their non-inhibited peers to delay marriage and fatherhood, while shy American girls are more likely to quit work and become homemakers after marriage (Caspi et al., 1988; Kerr et al., 1996). What about temperament in early childhood? Denise Newman and colleagues (1997) measured the temperament of 961 New Zealanders at age three, based on a 90-minute observation of each child. At age 21, participants were studied again. Compared with three-year-olds with a "well-adjusted temperament," those who were "undercontrolled" (i.e., irritable, impulsive, inattentive) reported more antisocial behaviour in adulthood and greater conflict in family and romantic relationships, and they were more likely to have been fired from a job. In contrast, children with an "inhibited temperament" (i.e., socially shy and fearful) reported having less overall companionship in adulthood. Attempts to relate certain temperament characteristics to adult psychopathology—such as the characteristic of childhood behavioural inhibition (similar to extreme shyness)—with later anxiety disorders have had some degree of success (Tincas, Benga, & Fox, 2006).

While there is evidence that temperament can be relatively stable as the individual ages, predicting how any individual infant or child will turn out as an adult is very difficult. Many factors influence development, and even during childhood strong temperaments often mellow (Pfeifer et al., 2002). Furthermore, temperament classifications vary depending on context and observers (parents versus trained observers; e.g., Hane, Fox, Polak-Toste, Ghera, & Gunner, 2006). Given these considerations, it is remarkable that Newman and colleagues were able to use a mere 90 minutes of observing three-year-olds to predict (albeit modestly) different patterns of adult adjustment 18 years later.

Cohabitation as a "Trial Marriage"

Large national surveys in several countries, including Canada, Germany, Sweden, and the United States, have found that premarital cohabitation is associated with a *higher* risk of subsequent divorce (Heaton, 2002). For example, according to Statistics Canada, in 2002 Canadian couples who cohabited before marriage were twice as likely to separate than those who did not cohabit. Many researchers, however, believe that the cohabitation-divorce relation does not reflect cause and effect. Rather, couples who choose to cohabit before marriage appear to differ psychologically from couples who do not cohabit first. They tend to be less religious and less committed to their partners and to marriage as an institution (Stanley et al., 2006). Taken together, these pre-existing factors would increase the risk of divorce even if these couples had not cohabited before tying the knot. In some studies, when researchers focus on cohabiting couples who start out with a strong orientation toward marriage, they find that the risk of divorce is no higher and the quality of marital relations is no poorer than among couples who did not cohabit prior to marriage (Bruederl et al., 1997). Still, research does *not* support the view that, overall, cohabitation reduces the risk of subsequent divorce.

CHAPTER 13

Does Pure Altruism Really Exist?

Do you believe that people ever help others for purely altruistic reasons? Perhaps your response is "Sure. Some Good Samaritans care only about the victim's welfare and even help people at a cost to themselves." Certainly, people make anonymous donations to charities and help strangers when no one (including the recipient) is taking note of their good deeds. In such cases, we can seemingly rule out motives for helping based on gaining recognition or others' approval. But still, doesn't helping someone make us feel good about ourselves?

Moreover, by helping someone, don't we feel better knowing that the person's plight has been reduced? According to the *negative state relief model*, high

empathy causes us to feel distress when we learn of others' suffering, so by helping them we reduce our own personal distress—a self-focused, egoistic goal, not an altruistic one (Cialdini et al., 1987).

Batson and many psychologists believe that while egoistic motives account for some prosocial behaviour, at times people do help others for purely altruistic reasons (Batson, 2006). Yet other psychologists remain unconvinced, arguing that some negative state relief is always involved (Cialdini et al., 1997).

Recent brain-imaging findings add some provocative fuel to this debate. Empathizing with someone else's pain does not produce the same sensations (i.e., somatosensory cortex activation) that we experience when we are in pain, but it does activate many of the brain areas (e.g., other parts of the cortex, brain stem, thalamus, and cerebellum) that process emotional aspects of our own pain (Singer et al., 2004). Moreover, people who feel greater empathy for another's pain experience greater activation in these brain areas. So what do you think? Does this suggest that when helping behaviour stems from empathy, it does indeed involve negative state relief and therefore is not purely altruistic?

CHAPTER 14

Is Self-Actualization a Useful Scientific Construct?

Self-actualization is a centrepiece of some humanistic theories, but it is troublesome from a scientific perspective. Some critics believe that it is impossible to define an individual's actualizing tendency except in terms of the behaviour that it supposedly produces. This would be an example of circular reasoning: Why did the person achieve such success? Because of self-actualization. How do we know self-actualization was at work? Because the person achieved great success.

Unless a construct can be operationally defined in a manner independent of the phenomenon it is supposed to cause, it is not scientifically useful. A construct must also be measurable. While it is true that concepts related to the self-actualization motive (such as people's beliefs that they are fulfilling their potential) could potentially be measured, most psychologists suggest that rather than being a scientific construct, self-actualization is better considered a philosophical concept.

Criminal Profiling: Analyzing the Criminal Mind

Television shows such as *Criminal Minds* and *CSI: Crime Scene Investigation* have popularized the idea that profilers can analyze the criminal mind based on crime-scene data and their expert knowledge of personality and behaviour. The use of criminal profiling has been documented in a number of countries, including Canada (Clark, 2002; Snook, 2009), and many police officials and mental-health professionals believe that profilers provide unique insights that assist in solving crimes (Snook et al., 2008).

The evidence, however, suggests a more modest conclusion about the usefulness of profiles. Brent Snook, of Memorial University, Newfoundland, and colleagues reviewed the results of controlled studies of profiling and found that expert profilers did only slightly better than university students and psychologists without forensic experience in overall accuracy of their predictions (Snook et al., 2007). Even more surprising was the finding that profilers were actually *less* accurate than the nonexperts when describing offenders' physical characteristics (e.g., sex, race, and age), personality-related characteristics (e.g., motives, thought processes, guilt), and personal characteristics (e.g., education, social class, marital status).

Why does profiling enjoy such a high profile and high level of credibility? One reason is that sometimes profilers are correct and these "hits" are widely reported because they are newsworthy. This provides exposure to successful but not unsuccessful outcomes. A second reason is that profilers often provide information on the *number* of correct predictions they have made but not on the *percentage* of correct predictions (Snook et al., 2008). It might impress you that in 21 criminal cases expert profilers provided a total of 158 correct descriptions of criminals' personal characteristics. However, you might be less impressed when you learn that in these 21 cases the profilers made a total of 880 descriptive statements; that is, 82 percent of their statements were incorrect (Alison et al., 2003).

Another issue is that we tend to find vague, general statements believable. If we told you that we had developed a new personality test and according to our test "you sometimes have doubts about some of your abilities," "you have a short attention span when dealing with boring people," "you have a desire to be liked and admired by others," and "you are strongly committed to a successful future," you might think we had a pretty good test. But if we gave those statements to 50 of your classmates, they would probably think the same thing even though they differ from you in important ways. Snook and colleagues (2007) found that many of the statements made by profilers were vague, widely applicable statements such as "the person has sexual concerns, has had conflicts with his family, and has trouble controlling his impulses when stress becomes overwhelming or things get very boring," or (in the case of a serial axe murderer) "the perpetrator has mental-health issues." The problem is that such statements are likely to apply to a very large proportion of the criminal (and even non-criminal) population. Vague, broadly applicable statements can also be found in areas such as astrology.

What is the *thinking critically* verdict on criminal profiling? Particularly when traditional intuitive methods are used, there is little evidence that profiling provides

consistent, useful descriptions. Accuracy may improve with new approaches that use scientifically based statistical methods (Goodwill et al., 2009). However, such methods will also bear the burden of demonstrating "beyond a reasonable doubt" that profiling improves on what police already do to identify and apprehend criminals.

CHAPTER 15

Do Stressful Events Cause Psychological Distress?

As we noted, the relation between stress and distress is correlational. Time to think critically and challenge the causal interpretation. Certainly, it is possible that life stress causes psychological distress—and there are various kinds of evidence to suggest that it does. But it is also possible that distress may be the causal factor instead of the effect. That is, distressed people may be more likely than nondistressed people to remember and report negative things that have happened to them. Or they may tend to view events as negative, whereas those not experiencing distress may view the same events as neutral or even positive. Moreover, psychological distress could actually cause people to behave in ways that produce more negative events. For example, research has shown that anxious and depressed people often evoke negative reactions from others because of their gloomy outlook and their tendency to frustrate others' attempts to help them feel better (remember our discussion of reciprocal determinism from Chapter 14).

And that is not all: Another possibility is that some other variable causes both negative life events *and* psychological distress to go up or down, thus creating an apparent relation between them. The Big Five personality trait of Neuroticism, discussed in Chapter 14, might be such a third variable. We know that people who are high in neuroticism have a tendency to experience a lot of negative emotions *and* to get themselves into stressful situations through their self-defeating behaviours (Lahey, 2009). Differences in neuroticism could thus cause the relation between stress and distress.

These different causal possibilities remind us that stressful life events are part of a network of causal relations and that stressful life events can function as either a cause or an effect.

CHAPTER 16

"Do I Have That Disorder?"

Wondering if you have a psychological disorder when reading a description of it is quite understandable. We all experience problems in living at various times, and we may react in ways that bear similarities to the disorders described in this chapter. Logically, seeing such a similarity does not necessarily mean that you have the disorder at a clinically significant level. On the other hand, if you find that maladaptive behaviours such as those described in this chapter are interfering with your happiness or personal effectiveness, then you should not hesitate to seek professional assistance in changing these behaviours. In addition to the three D's discussed earlier (distress, dysfunction, and deviance), you will want to consider the frequency with which the particular behaviours or experiences occur, as well as their intensity and their duration. When problem behaviours occur frequently, are intense, and/or last for a long time, they are more likely to be clinically significant. In such a case, it is important not to let any stigma you might attach to having a psychological problem keep you from acting in your best interest and discussing your problem with a mental-health professional.

CHAPTER 17

Do Survey Results Provide an Accurate Picture of Treatment Effectiveness?

Seligman's conclusion that the *CR* survey provides a realistic appraisal of treatment effects is thought-provoking, but before you accept this conclusion, you should consider some of the survey's shortcomings. First, consider the nature of the *CR* sample. Only 1.6 percent of the original 184 000 people contacted described their therapy experience. Is it possible that among the other 98.4 percent are a significant number of people who had been in therapy with unfavourable results and chose not to share their experiences? If so, the effectiveness of therapy could be exaggerated in this self-selected sample.

Second, what about the nature and quality of the data? We have only global, after-the-fact reports from clients. There is no way to corroborate respondents' reports with other sources of data. How do we know that they are not biased by memory distortions or by rationalizing their investment ("If I spent that much time and money, I must

have gotten better")? Rationalization could also account for the apparent superiority of long-term therapy, where more time and money were expended, as well as the tendency to return the questionnaire and share the success story.

Third, what has the *CR* study told us about the more important specificity question? We don't know if some matches of clinical problems with specific forms of therapy yielded better outcomes than others. In fact, we can't even be sure about what kinds of therapy were administered, because respondents didn't describe their treatments in detail.

Fourth, how about the absence of a control group? Can we rule out spontaneous remission of symptoms? As we saw in Chapter 15, many mental-health problems (e.g., depression and anxiety) fluctuate or improve with time. People who are assessed at their low points, when they are most likely to seek therapy, are almost certain to improve, with or without therapy (Mintz et al., 1996). Could this factor alone explain the respondents' perceptions that they had improved? As Seligman himself conceded, "Because there are no control groups, the *CR* . . . study cannot tell us directly whether talking to sympathetic friends or merely letting time pass would have produced just as much improvement as treatment by a mental-health professional" (1995, p. 972). Despite the interpretive challenges that attend community studies like this, psychotherapy researchers agree that it is critically important to see how well the treatment principles and techniques identified in controlled studies work in the real world (Westen et al., 2004). One way to accomplish this is by systematically measuring the variables of interest within individual cases being seen by practising therapists in the community. A large number of single-client case studies containing such measurement can provide important data on the effectiveness of specific therapies and the factors that influence those outcomes (Goldfried & Eubanks-Carter, 2004).

GLOSSARY

A

abnormal behaviour behaviour that is personally distressful, personally dysfunctional, and/or so culturally deviant that other people judge it to be inappropriate or maladaptive

absolute refractory period a time of recovery during which a cell membrane is not excitable and cannot generate another action potential

absolute threshold the lowest intensity at which a stimulus can be detected correctly 50 percent of the time

abstinence violation effect a reaction that can occur when substance misusers fail to remain abstinent and view the lapse as proof that they will never be strong enough to resist temptation; may result in a total relapse

acceptance and commitment therapy (ACT) a therapy that focuses on the process of mindfulness as a vehicle for change; teaches clients to "just notice," accept, and embrace their thoughts and feelings to reduce the anxiety they would ordinarily evoke

accommodation the process by which new experiences cause existing schemas to change

acetylcholine (ACh) an excitatory neurotransmitter that operates at synapses with muscles and is also the transmitter in some neural networks involved in memory

achievement goal theory a theory of achievement motivation that stresses the goals (ego versus mastery) and motivational climates that influence achievement strivings

achievement test a measure of an individual's degree of accomplishment in a particular subject or task based on a relatively standardized set of experiences

action potential a nerve impulse resulting from the depolarization of an axon's cell membrane

action potential threshold the intensity of stimulation (excitatory minus inhibitory) needed to produce an action potential

activation-synthesis theory the theory that dreams represent the brain's attempt to interpret random patterns of neural activation triggered by the brain stem during REM sleep

adaptations changes that allow organisms to meet recurring environmental challenges to their survival, thereby increasing their reproductive ability

adolescence the period of development and gradual transition between childhood and adulthood

adolescent egocentrism highly self-focused thinking, particularly in the earlier teenage years

adoption study a research method in behaviour genetics in which adopted people are compared on some characteristic with both their biological and adoptive parents in an attempt to determine how strong a genetic component the characteristic might have

aerobic exercise sustained activity that elevates the heart rate and body's need for oxygen

agoraphobia a phobia centred around open spaces and public places

alcohol myopia when intoxicated, a "short-sightedness" in thinking (a failure to consider consequences) caused by an inability to pay attention to as much information as when sober

algorithms procedures, such as mathematical formulas, that automatically generate correct solutions to problems

all-or-none law the fact that an action potential is not proportional to the intensity of stimulation; a neuron either fires with maximum intensity or it does not fire (compare with *graded potential*)

alleles the two genes, one on each chromosome, that control the same trait

alpha waves a brain-wave pattern of 8 to 12 cycles per second that is characteristic of humans in a relaxed waking state

altruism behaviour that occurs when one individual helps another, but in so doing accrues some cost

Alzheimer's disease a brain disorder that is the leading cause of dementia in the elderly, accounting for about 60 percent of senile dementias

amphetamine psychosis schizophrenia-like hallucinations and delusions that occur when the brain's dopamine activity is artificially increased far beyond normal levels by continuous, heavy amphetamine use

amplitude the vertical size of the sound wave, which gives rise to the perception of loudness and is measured in terms of decibels

amygdala a limbic system structure that helps to organize emotional response patterns

analytic psychology Jung's expansion of Freud's notion of the unconscious; Jung believed that humans possess not only a personal unconscious based on their life experiences, but also a collective unconscious that consists of memories accumulated throughout the entire history of the human race

anorexia nervosa an eating disorder involving a severe and sometimes fatal restriction of food intake

anterograde amnesia memory loss for events that occur after the initial onset of amnesia

antisocial personality disorder a disorder involving behaviour that is interpersonally destructive and emotionally harmful and exhibits a lack of conscience

anxiety disorders a group of behaviour disorders in which anxiety and associated maladaptive behaviours are the core of the disturbance

aphasia the loss of ability to understand speech (receptive aphasia) or produce it (productive aphasia)

applied behaviour analysis a process (also called *behaviour modification*) in which operant conditioning is combined with scientific data collection to solve individual and societal problems

applied research research involving the application of scientific knowledge to solve practical problems

approach-approach conflict a conflict in which an individual is simultaneously attracted to two incompatible positive goals

approach-avoidance conflict a conflict in which an individual is simultaneously attracted to and repelled by the same goal

aptitude test a measure of a person's ability to profit from further training or experience in an occupation or a skill; usually based on a measure of skills gained over a person's lifetime rather than during a specific course of study

archetypes in Jung's theory, innate concepts and memories (e.g., God, the hero, the good mother); memories that reside in the collective unconscious

archival measures records or documents that already exist

assimilation in cognitive development, the process by which new experiences are incorporated into existing schemas

association cortex the areas of the cerebral cortex that do not have sensory or motor functions but are involved in the integration of neural activity that underlies perception, language, and other higher-order mental processes

associative network the view that long-term memory is organized as a massive network of associated ideas and concepts

attachment the strong emotional bond that develops between children and their primary caregivers

attention-deficit/hyperactivity disorder (ADHD) disorder in which problems may take the form of attentional difficulties, hyperactivity-impulsivity, or a combination of the two that results in impaired functioning

attitude a positive or negative evaluative reaction toward a stimulus (e.g., toward a person, action, object, or concept)

attributions judgments about the causes of our own and other people's behaviour and outcomes

authoritarian parents caregivers who exert control over their children but do so within a cold, unresponsive, or rejecting relationship

authoritative parents caregivers who are controlling, but warm; they establish and enforce clear rules within a caring, supportive atmosphere

autistic spectrum disorder long-term disorder characterized by extreme unresponsiveness to others, poor communication skills, and highly repetitive and rigid behaviour patterns

automatic processing mental activities that occur automatically and require minimal or no conscious control or awareness

autonomic nervous system the branch of the peripheral nervous system that stimulates the body's involuntary muscles (e.g., heart) and internal organs

availability heuristic a guideline used to make likelihood judgments based on how easily examples of that category of events come to mind, or are "available" in memory

aversion therapy the pairing of a CS that currently evokes a positive but maladaptive response with a noxious UCS in an attempt to condition repulsion toward the CS

avoidance conditioning the conditioning of an organism to perform a response to avoid an undesirable consequence

avoidance-avoidance conflict a conflict in which an individual must choose between two alternatives, both of which she or he wishes to avoid

axon an extension from one side of the neuron cell body that conducts nerve impulses to other neurons, muscles, or glands

B

basal ganglia a part of the brain made up of five distinct structures that is critical for voluntary motor control

basic research research designed to obtain knowledge for its own sake

basilar membrane a membrane that runs the length of the cochlea and contains the organ of Corti and its sound receptor hair cells

behaviour genetics the scientific study of the role of genetic inheritance in behaviour

behaviour modification therapeutic procedures based on operant conditioning principles, such as positive reinforcement, operant extinction, and punishment

behavioural assessment explicit coding system devised by psychologists that contains the behavioural categories of interest

behavioural neuroscience the study of brain processes and other physiological functions that underlie our behaviour, sensory experiences, emotions, and thoughts

behavioural perspective a view that emphasizes the manner in which the environment and the learning experiences it provides shape and control behaviour

behaviourism school of psychology that emphasizes the role of learning and environmental control over behaviour, and maintains that the proper subject matter of psychology is observable behaviour; John Watson and B.F. Skinner were major figures in behaviourism

belief bias the tendency to abandon logical rules and form a conclusion based on one's existing beliefs

beta waves a brain-wave pattern of 15 to 30 cycles per second that is characteristic of humans who are in an alert waking state

between groups (or between subjects) design a common experimental design in which each experimental group is composed of a different set of participants

binocular cues depth cues that require the use of both eyes

binocular disparity the binocular depth cues produced by the projection of slightly different images of an object on the retinas of the two eyes

biological perspective perspective that focuses on the role of biological factors

in behaviour, including biochemical and brain processes as well as genetic and evolutionary factors

biologically based mechanisms mechanisms that receive input from the environment, process the information, and respond to it

biopsychology (neuroscience) a subfield of psychology that focuses on the biological underpinnings of behaviour

bipolar cells the second layer of retinal cells with which the rods and cones synapse

bipolar disorder mood disorder in which intermittent mania appears against a background of depression

blindsight a disorder in which people are blind in part of their visual field yet, in special tests, respond to stimuli in that field despite reporting that they cannot see those stimuli

blood-brain barrierr specialized lining of cells in the brain's blood vessels that screen out foreign substances while letting nutrients pass through to neurons

borderline personality disorder (BPD) a collection of symptoms characterized primarily by serious instability in behaviour, emotion, identity, and interpersonal relationships

bottom-up processing perceptual processing that begins with the analysis of individual elements of the stimulus and works up to the brain's integration of them into a unified perception

brain stem the portion of the brain formed by the swelling of the spinal cord as it enters the skull; its structures regulate basic survival functions of the body, such as heart rate and respiration

British empiricism 17th-century school of philosophy championed by John Locke, according to which all the contents of the mind are gained experientially through the senses; this notion was later a cornerstone for the behaviourists' position that we are shaped through our experiences

Broca's area a region of the left frontal lobe involved in speech production

bulimia nervosa a disorder involving the bingeing and purging of food, usually by vomiting or laxative use, because of a concern with becoming fat

bystander effect the finding that the presence of multiple bystanders inhibits each person's tendency to help, largely because of social comparison or diffusion of responsibility

C

case study an in-depth analysis of an individual group or an event

catharsis the discharge of aggressive energy and temporary reduction of the impulse to aggress argued to occur through performing an act of aggression

CCK (cholecystokinin) a peptide that appears to decrease eating and thereby helps to regulate food intake

central nervous system portion of the nervous system that includes the brain and spinal cord

central route to persuasion occurs when people think carefully about a message and are influenced because they find the arguments compelling

cephalocaudal principle the tendency for physical development to proceed in a head-to-foot direction

cerebellum a convoluted hindbrain structure involved in motor coordination and some aspects of learning and memory

cerebral cortex the grey, convoluted outer covering of the brain that is the seat of higher-order sensory, motor, perceptual, and mental processes

chaining an operant conditioning procedure used to develop a sequence (chain) of responses by reinforcing each response with the opportunity to perform the next response

chromosomes tightly coiled strands of deoxyribonucleic acid (DNA) and protein that contain the genes

chunking combining individual items into larger units of meaning

circadian rhythms biological cycles within the body that occur on an approximately 24-hour cycle

classical conditioning a procedure in which a formerly neutral stimulus (the conditioned stimulus) comes to elicit a conditioned response by virtue of being paired with an unconditioned stimulus that naturally elicits a similar response (the unconditioned response)

clinical psychology the study and treatment of mental disorders

clinical significance a definition of therapeutic success in which, at the end of therapy, an individual getting treatment for a particular disorder falls within the range of people not experiencing that particular disorder rather than simply experiencing the disorder less often

cochlea a small coil-shaped structure of the inner ear that contains the receptors for sound

cognitive appraisal the process of making judgments about situations, personal capabilities, likely consequences, and the personal meaning of consequences

cognitive-arousal model of love the view that passionate love has interacting cognitive and physiological components

cognitive behaviourism behavioural approach that incorporates cognitive concepts, suggesting that the environment influences our behaviour by

affecting our thoughts and giving us information; these cognitive processes allow us to control our behaviour and the environment

cognitive map a mental representation of the spatial layout of an area

cognitive neuroscience the study of the brain activity of people engaging in cognitive tasks

cognitive perspective psychological perspective that views humans as rational information processors and problem solvers, and focuses on the mental processes that influence behaviour

cognitive-process dream theories theories that focus on how (rather than why) we dream, and propose that dreaming and waking thought are produced by the same mental systems in the brain

cognitive process theories approaches to intelligence that analyze the mental processes that underlie intelligent thinking

cognitive psychology the study of mental processes, especially from a model that views the mind as an information processor

common factors therapeutic elements that are possessed by virtually any type of therapy and which may contribute to the similar positive effects shown by many different treatment approaches

communicator credibility how believable a communicator is

companionate love an affectionate relationship characterized by commitment and caring about the partner's well-being; sometimes contrasted with passionate love, which is more intensely emotional

compensatory response bodily response that opposes a drug's effects and occurs in an attempt to restore homeostasis

competency a legal decision that a defendant is mentally capable of understanding the nature of criminal charges, participating meaningfully in a trial, and consulting with a lawyer

competency-focused prevention prevention programs that are designed to enhance the personal resources needed to cope with situations that might otherwise cause psychological disorders

compulsion a repetitive act that the person feels compelled to carry out, often in response to an obsessive thought or image

computerized axial tomography (CT) scan a method of scanning the brain with narrow beams of X-rays that are then analyzed and combined by a computer to provide pictures of brain structures from many different angles

concept a mental category containing similar objects, people, and events

concordance the likelihood that two people share a particular characteristic

concrete operational stage in Piaget's theory, the stage of cognitive development during which children can perform basic mental operations concerning problems that involve tangible (i.e., "concrete") objects and situations

conditioned response (CR) in classical conditioning, a response to a conditioned stimulus; the CR is established by pairing a conditioned stimulus with an unconditioned stimulus that evokes a similar response

conditioned stimulus (CS) a neutral stimulus that comes to evoke a conditioned response after being paired with an unconditioned stimulus

conditioned taste aversion a learned repulsion to a food that formerly was neutral or desired, by virtue of pairing the food with an aversive UCS (e.g., nausea, stomach illness)

conditions of worth internalized standards of self-worth fostered by conditional positive regard from others

conduction deafness hearing loss caused by damage to the mechanical system that conducts sound waves to the cochlea

cones photoreceptors in the retina that function best in bright light and are differentially sensitive to red, green, or blue wavelengths; the retina's colour receptors

confirmation bias the tendency to seek and favour information that reinforces our beliefs rather than to be open to disconfirming information

confounding of variables in an experiment, the intertwining of the independent variable with another, uncontrolled variable, preventing people from being able to tell which variable is responsible for changes in the behaviour of interest (i.e., the dependent variable)

congruence consistency between self-perceptions and experience

consciousness our moment-to-moment awareness of ourselves and our environment; consciousness involves selective attention to ongoing thoughts, perceptions, and feelings

conservation the principle that basic properties of objects, such as their mass or quantity, stay the same (are "conserved") even though their outward appearance may change

construct validity the extent to which a test measures the psychological construct (e.g., intelligence, anxiety) that it is purported to measure

content validity the extent to which test items adequately sample the domain that the test is supposed to measure (e.g., intelligence, mathematical reasoning)

context-dependent memory the phenomenon that it is typically easier to remember something in the same environment in which it was originally learned or experienced

continuous reinforcement schedule a reinforcement schedule in which each correct response is followed by reinforcement

control group in an experiment, the group that is not exposed to the treatment, or which receives a zero level of the independent variable

controlled (effortful) processing mental processing that requires some degree of volitional control and attentiveness

conventional moral reasoning moral judgments that are based on conformity to social expectations, laws, and duties

convergence a binocular depth cue produced by the muscles that rotate the eyes as they focus on nearby objects

conversion disorder disorder in which serious neurological symptoms, such as paralysis, loss of sensation, or blindness, suddenly occur

cooperation situations in which one individual helps another and in so doing gains some advantage

coping self-efficacy beliefs relating to our ability to deal effectively with a stressful stimulus or situation, including pain

corpus callosum a broad band of white, myelinated fibres that connect the left and right cerebral hemispheres and allow the two hemispheres to communicate with each other

correlation coefficient a statistic that indicates the direction and strength of a relation between two variables

correlational research research that measures two or more naturally occurring variables, and examines whether they are statistically related

cortisol a hormone produced during a period of stress that triggers an increase in blood sugars, which is then provided to the skeletal muscles along with additional oxygen; also suppresses the immune system

counterbalancing a procedure in which participants in an experiment are exposed to all the conditions; the order of conditions is varied so that no condition has an advantage relative to the others

counterconditioning the process of conditioning an incompatible response to a particular stimulus to eliminate a maladaptive response (e.g., anxiety), as occurs in systematic desensitization

creativity the ability to produce something that is both new and valuable

criterion-related validity the ability of test scores to correlate with meaningful criterion measures

critical period a time period in which exposure to particular kinds of

stimulation (e.g., perceptual) is required for normal development to occur

cross-cultural replication the process of repeating a study to determine whether the original findings generalize across different cultures

cross-sectional design a research design that simultaneously compares people of different ages at a particular point in time

crystallized intelligence (g_c) intellectual abilities that depend on a store of information and the acquisition of particular skills (contrast to fluid intelligence)

cultural competence a set of therapeutic skills (including scientific mindedness), the ability to consider both cultural and individual factors, and the capacity to introduce culture-specific elements into therapy with people from minority cultures

cultural psychology the study of how culture is transmitted to a society's members

culture the enduring values, beliefs, behaviours, and traditions that are shared by a large group of people and passed from one generation to the next

culture-bound disorders behaviour disorders whose specific forms are restricted to one particular cultural context

D

dark adaptation the progressive increase in brightness sensitivity that occurs over time as photopigments regenerate themselves during exposure to low levels of illumination

debriefed the action of telling deceived experiment participants the true purpose of the study at the end of the experiment

decay theory the theory that with time and disuse the physical memory trace in the nervous system fades away

decibel (db) a logarithmic measure of sound intensity

decision criterion in signal detection theory, the potentially changing standard of how certain a person must be that a stimulus is present in order to report its presence

declarative memory our memory for factual knowledge, which is composed of two subcategories: knowledge pertaining to personal experience (episodic memory) and knowledge of general facts and language (semantic memory)

deductive reasoning reasoning from a general principle to a specific case

deep structure a linguistic term that refers to the underlying meaning of a spoken or written sentence; the meanings that make up deep structure are stored as concepts and rules in long-term memory

defence mechanisms unconscious processes by which the ego prevents the expression of anxiety-arousing impulses or allows them to appear in disguised forms

deindividuation a state of increased anonymity in which a person, often as part of a group or crowd, engages in disinhibited behaviour

deinstitutionalization the attempt to move the primary locus of treatment from mental hospitals to the community

delay discounting the decrease in value of a future incentive as a function of its distance in time

delay of gratification the ability to forgo immediate rewards for delayed but more satisfying outcomes

delta waves low-frequency, high-amplitude brain waves that occur in stage 3 sleep and predominate in stage 4 sleep

delusions false beliefs, often involving themes of persecution or grandeur, that are sustained in the face of evidence that normally would be sufficient to destroy them

dementia the gradual loss of cognitive abilities that accompanies brain deterioration and interferes with normal functioning

dendrites small branching fibres that extend from the soma of a neuron and receive messages from adjacent neurons

dependent variable in an experiment, the factor that is measured by the researcher and which presumably is influenced by the independent variable

depolarization the reversal of the resting potential of a neuron's cell membrane that produces the action potential

depressants drugs—including alcohol, barbiturates, and tranquilizers—that reduce neural activity and may decrease feelings of tension and anxiety

depressive attributional pattern the tendency of depressed people to attribute negative outcomes to their own inadequacies and positive ones to factors outside themselves

depressive cognitive triad negative thoughts concerning (1) the world, (2) oneself, and (3) the future that people with depression cannot control or suppress

deprivation experiment method of determining the critical periods during which certain experiences must occur for the related brain mechanisms to develop normally

descriptive research research in which the main goal is to carefully describe how organisms behave, particularly in natural settings

descriptive statistics data that summarize and describe the characteristics of a set of scores

developmental psychology a subfield of psychology that examines changes in our biological, physical, psychological, and behavioural processes as we age

dialectical behaviour therapy (DBT) a cognitive-behavioural treatment developed specifically for borderline personality disorder

difference threshold the smallest difference between two stimuli that people can perceive 50 percent of the time

discourse the sixth level of the hierarchical structure of language in which sentences are combined into paragraphs, articles, books, conversations, and so forth

discrimination treating people unfairly based on the group to which they belong

discrimination (classical conditioning) the occurrence of a CR to one stimulus but not to another stimulus

discriminative stimulus an antecedent stimulus that signals the likelihood of certain consequences if a response is made

displacement the capacity of language to represent objects and conditions that are not physically present

display rules culturally influenced standards for the circumstances and manner in which specific emotions are expressed

dissociation theories (of hypnosis) the view that hypnosis is an altered state involving a division ("dissociation") of consciousness; one theory proposes that the hypnotized person simultaneously experiences two streams of consciousness that are cut off from each other

dissociative amnesia disorder in which a person responds to a stressful event with extensive but selective memory loss

dissociative disorders disorders that involve a major dissociation of personal identity or memory

dissociative fugue a dissociative phenomenon in which a person loses all sense of personal identity and wanders to another place and establishes a new identity

dissociative identity disorder (DID) a dissociative disorder in which two or more separate identities or personalities coexist within an individual

divergent thinking a creative form of thinking that involves the generating of novel ideas that diverge from the normal ways of thinking about something

divided attention the ability to perform more than one activity at the same time

dodo bird verdict the finding of similar efficacy for widely differing therapies

domain-specific adaptations adaptations designed to solve a particular problem

dominant gene a gene that, when present, will produce a particular characteristic

door-in-the-face technique a manipulation technique in which a persuader makes a large request, expecting you to reject it, and then presents a smaller request

dopamine an excitatory neurotransmitter whose overactivity may underlie some of the disordered behaviours seen in schizophrenia

dopamine hypothesis view that the symptoms of schizophrenia are produced by overactivity of the dopamine system in areas of the brain that regulate emotional expression, motivated behaviour, and cognitive functioning

dose-response effect the relation between the amount of treatment received and the quality of the outcome

double-blind procedure a procedure in which both the participant and the experimenter are kept unaware of the research condition to which the participant has been assigned

drive theory the theory that physiological disruptions to homeostasis produce states of internal tension (called *drives*) that motivate an organism to behave in ways that reduce this tension

dual coding theory the theory that, if we encode information by using both verbal and imagery codes, the chances improve that at least one of the two codes will be available later to support recall

dual-process theory the modern colour vision theory that posits cones that are sensitive to red, blue, and green, and opponent processes at the level of ganglion cells and beyond

dynamic testing after standard testing the examiner gives the respondent guided feedback on how to improve performance and observes how the person uses the information

dysthymia a depressive mood disorder of moderate intensity that occurs over a long period of time but does not disrupt functioning as a major depression does

E

ecstasy MDMA (3, 4-m ethylened ioxym etha mphetamine); a derivative of amphetamine that acts on several neurotransmitters, including dopamine, but primarily alters serotonin functioning by causing the release of serotonin and blocking its reuptake

effect size statistic common measure of treatment effectiveness

ego the "executive" of the personality that is partly conscious and that mediates among the impulses of the id, the prohibitions of the superego, and the dictates of reality

egocentrism difficulty in viewing the world from someone else's perspective

elaborative rehearsal focusing on the meaning of information or relating it to other things we already know

electroconvulsive therapy (ECT) a biomedical technique involving the application of electrical current to the brain that is used primarily to reduce severe depression

electroencephalogram (EEG) a device used to record the simultaneous activity of many thousands of neurons through electrodes attached to the scalp

embryo scientific term for the prenatal organism during the second week through the eighth week after conception

emotion a pattern of cognitive, physiological, and behavioural responses to situations and events that have relevance to important goals or motives

emotion regulation the processes by which we evaluate and modify our emotional reactions

emotion-focused coping coping strategies directed at minimizing or reducing emotional responses to a stressor

emotional intelligence ability to respond adaptively in the emotional realm by reading and responding appropriately to others' emotions, to be aware of one's own emotions and have the ability to control them, and to delay gratification

empathy the capacity for experiencing the same emotional response being exhibited by another person; in therapy, the ability of a therapist to view the world through the client's eyes and to understand the client's emotions

empathy-altruism hypothesis the theory that pure altruism does exist, and that it is produced by empathy

empirical approach an approach to test construction in which items (regardless of their content) are chosen that differentiate between two groups that are known to differ on a particular personality variable

encoding getting information into the memory system by translating it into a neural code that the brain processes and stores

encoding specificity principle observation that memory is enhanced when conditions present during retrieval match those that were present during encoding

endorphins natural opiate-like substances that are involved in pain reduction

episodic memory our store of factual knowledge concerning personal experience—when, where, and what happened in the episodes of our lives

equal status contact a prejudice reduction principle based on the idea that prejudice among people is most likely to be reduced when they (1) engage in sustained close contact, (2) have equal status, (3) work to achieve a common goal that requires cooperation, and (4) are supported by broader social norms

escape conditioning a form of learning in which the organism learns to perform a behaviour to escape from an aversive stimulus

evolution a change over time in the frequency with which particular genes—and the characteristics they produce—occur within an interbreeding population

evolutionary/circadian sleep models the view that in the course of evolution each species developed an adaptive circadian sleep-wake pattern that increased its chances of survival in relation to its environmental demands

evolutionary personality theory a recently developed attempt to account for personality traits in terms of the evolutionary history of the human species; these traits are thought to develop from processes of natural selection

evolutionary psychology a field of study that focuses on the role of evolutionary processes (especially natural selection) in the development of adaptive psychological mechanisms and social behaviour in humans

expectancy a cognitive theory that goal-directed behaviour is jointly influenced by (1) the person's expectancy that a particular behaviour will contribute to reaching the goal and (2) how positively or negatively the person values the goal

expectancy × value theory a cognitive theory that goal-directed behaviour is jointly influenced by (1) the person's expectancy that a particular behaviour will contribute to reaching the goal and (2) how positively or negatively the person values the goal

experiment a research method in which the researcher manipulates an independent variable under controlled conditions and measures whether this produces changes in a dependent variable

experimental group in an experiment, the group that receives a treatment or is exposed to an active level of the independent variable

experimental psychology a subfield of psychology that focuses on learning, sensory systems, perception, and motivational states

experimenter expectancy effects subtle and unintentional ways in which an experimenter influences participants to behave in a way that will confirm the experimenter's hypothesis

explicit memory conscious or intentional memory retrieval

exposure a behaviour therapy treatment in which clients are presented, either in vivo or in their imagination, with fear-inducing stimuli, thus allowing extinction to occur

exposure therapies Therapeutic techniques designed to extinguish anxiety responses by exposing clients to anxiety-arousing stimuli or situations while preventing escape or avoidance

expressed emotion a family interaction pattern involving criticism, hostility, and overinvolvement that is associated with relapse when formerly hospitalized schizophrenic patients return home

expressive behaviours observable behavioural indications of subjectively experienced emotions

external validity the degree to which the results of a study can be generalized to other people, settings, and conditions

extinction (classical conditioning) weakening and eventual cessation of a CR caused by the presentation of the CS without the UCS

extinction (operant conditioning) occurs when the absence of reinforcement for a previously reinforced response causes that response to weaken and eventually to stop

extrinsic motivation motivation to perform a behaviour to obtain external rewards and reinforcers, such as money, status, attention, and praise

F

facial feedback hypothesis the notion that somatic feedback from facial muscles provides feedback to the brain and influences emotional experience

factor analysis a statistical technique that permits a researcher to reduce a large number of measures to a small number of clusters or factors; it identifies the clusters of behaviour or test scores that are highly correlated with one another

feature detectors sensory neurons that respond to particular features of a stimulus, such as its shape, angle, or colour

fetal alcohol spectrum disorders (FASD) a range of mild to severe developmental abnormalities produced by prenatal exposure to alcohol

fetal alcohol syndrome (FAS) a severe group of abnormalities that result from prenatal exposure to alcohol

fetus the scientific term for the prenatal organism from the ninth week after conception until birth

figure-ground relations perceptual organization in which a focal stimulus is perceived as a figure against a background of other stimuli

fixed-interval (FI) schedule a reinforcement schedule in which the first correct response occurring after a constant time interval is reinforced

fixed-ratio (FR) schedule a reinforcement schedule in which reinforcement is given after a constant number of correct responses

flashbulb memories recollections that seem so vivid and clear that we can picture them as if they were a "snapshot" of a moment in time

flooding a treatment in exposure therapy when a client is exposed to real-life stimuli

fluid intelligence (g_f) the ability to deal with novel problem-solving situations for which personal experience does not supply a solution (contrast to *crystallized intelligence*)

foot-in-the-door technique a manipulation technique in which the persuader gets someone to comply with a small request first and later presents a larger request

forebrain brain structures above the midbrain, including the thalamus, hypothalamus, limbic system, and the cerebral hemispheres; involved in higher-order sensory, motor, and cognitive functions

formal operational stage in Piaget's theory, a period in which individuals are able to think logically and systematically about both concrete and abstract problems, form hypotheses, and test them in a thoughtful way

fovea a small area in the centre of the retina that contains only cones and in which visual acuity is greatest

framing the idea that the same information, problem, or options can be structured and presented in different ways

free association in psychoanalysis, the procedure of verbalizing all thoughts that enter consciousness without censorship

frequency in audition, the number of cycles per second in a sound wave, responsible for the pitch of the sound; the measure of frequency is the hertz (Hz), which equals one cycle per second

frequency distribution a method of summarizing a set of scores by showing how many participants received each score

frequency theory the theory of pitch perception that holds that the number of nerve impulses sent to the brain by the hair cells of the cochlea corresponds to the frequency of the sound wave; this theory is accurate at low frequencies

frontal lobe the anterior (front) portion of the cerebral hemispheres that includes Broca's speech production area, the motor cortex, and associative cortex involved in planning and problem solving

frustration-aggression hypothesis the view that (1) frustration inevitably leads to aggression, and (2) all aggression is the result of frustration

fully functioning persons Rogers's term for self-actualized people who are free from unrealistic conditions of worth and who exhibit congruence, spontaneity, creativity, and a desire to develop still further

functional fixedness a phenomenon often found in problem-solving tasks in which the customary use of an object interferes with its use in a novel situation

functional neurological symptom disorder a somatic symptom disorder (formerly known as *conversion disorder*) in which the patient experiences physical symptoms (e.g., lack of feeling in hands), but these symptoms are neurologically impossible; there is no damage to any part of the sensory system

functionalism an early school of American psychology that focused on the functions of consciousness and behaviour in helping organisms adapt to their environment and satisfy their needs

fundamental attribution error a tendency to underestimate the impact of the situation and overestimate the role of personal factors when explaining other people's behaviour

fundamental emotional patterns basic emotional response patterns that are believed to be innate

G

g **factor** general intelligence, a component of intellectual performance according to Spearman

ganglion cells the third layer of retinal cells with which the bipolar cells synapse and whose axons form the optic nerve

gate control theory theory that proposes that the experience of pain results from the opening and closing of "gating mechanisms" in the nervous system

gender constancy the understanding that being male or female is a permanent part of a person

gender identity the sense of "femaleness" or "maleness" that is an integral part of our identity

gender schemas organized mental structures that contain our understanding of the attributes and behaviours that are appropriate and expected for males and females

general adaptation syndrome (GAS) Selye's description of the body's responses to a stressor, which includes successive phases of alarm reaction, resistance, and exhaustion

generalized anxiety disorder a chronic state of diffuse, or "free-floating," anxiety that is not attached to specific situations or objects

generativity a characteristic of symbols of language that can be combined to generate an infinite number of messages that have novel meaning

genes the biological units of heredity, located on the chromosomes

genetic determinism the view (sometimes erroneous) that genes have invariant and unavoidable effects

genotype the specific genetic makeup of an individual, which may or may not be expressed in the observable phenotype

genuineness the ability of a therapist to honestly express his or her feelings to a client

Gestalt laws the laws of perceptual organization advanced by the Gestalt psychologists—namely, similarity, proximity, closure, and continuity

Gestalt psychology a German school of psychology that emphasized the natural organization of perceptual elements into wholes, or patterns, as well as the role of insight in problem solving

ghrelin a hormone secreted by the stomach and small intestine that increases food intake and thoughts of food

glucose a simple sugar that is the body's (and especially the brain's) major source of immediately usable fuel

graded potential a change in the electrical potential of a neuron that is proportional to the intensity of the incoming stimulation, but not sufficient to produce an action potential

grammar the set of rules that dictate how symbols can be combined to create meaningful units of communication

group polarization the tendency for the "average" opinion of group members to become more extreme when like-minded people discuss an issue

groupthink the tendency of group members to suspend critical thinking because they are motivated to seek agreement

gustation the sense of taste

H

habituation a decrease in the strength of response to a repeated stimulus

hallucinations false perceptions that have a compelling sense of reality

hallucinogens drugs—such as LSD and PCP—that distort or intensify sensory experience and evoke hallucinations and disordered thought processes

hardiness a stress-resistant personality pattern that involves the factors of commitment, control, and challenge

harm reduction a prevention strategy that is designed not to eliminate a problem behaviour but to reduce its harmful consequences

health-compromising behaviours behaviours, such as poor dietary habits and unprotected sexual activity, that impair health and reduce longevity

health-enhancing behaviours behaviours, such as exercise and good dietary habits, that support and increase health and longevity

health psychology the study of psychological and behavioural factors in the prevention and treatment of illness and in the maintenance of health

heritability coefficient the extent to which the degree of variation in a particular characteristic among a group of people can be attributed to genetic factors

hertz (Hz) the measure of sound wave frequency as cycles per second

heuristics a method of problem solving characterized by quick and easy search procedures

higher-order conditioning in classical conditioning, when a neutral stimulus becomes a CS after it is paired with another CS (rather than with the original UCS)

hippocampus a structure of the limbic system that plays a key role in the formation and storage of memories

histogram a graph of a frequency distribution

homeostasis the maintenance of biological equilibrium, or balance, within the body

humanistic perspective a psychological perspective that emphasizes personal freedom, choice, and self-actualization

hyperopia a visual deficit sometimes called *farsightedness* in which the lens focuses the image behind the retina, reducing acuity for nearby objects

hypnosis a condition of enhanced suggestibility in which some people are able to experience imagined test suggestions as if they were real

hypnotic susceptibility scale a set of induction procedures and test questions that enable researchers to measure a person's responsiveness to hypnotic suggestion

hypothalamus a forebrain structure located below the thalamus and above the pituitary gland that controls autonomic and hormonal processes and plays a major role in many aspects of motivation and emotional behaviour

hypothesis a tentative explanation or prediction about some phenomenon

I

icon   a trace memory

id   the primitive and unconscious part of the personality that contains the instincts

if . . . then . . . behaviour consistency   consistency in behaviour, but only within similar situations

illusions   incorrect perceptions based on false perceptual hypotheses that often result from constancies that do not apply to the stimuli in question

imaginal thought   a form of thinking that uses images that can be from any sense modality

implicit memory   the ability of memory to influence our behaviour without conscious awareness

implosion therapy   a treatment in exposure therapy when a client is asked to imagine scenes involving the stimuli

imprinting   in some species, a sudden, biologically primed form of attachment

in vivo desensitization   carefully controlled exposure to a hierarchy of real-life situations

inattentional blindness   the failure of unattended stimuli to register in consciousness

incentive   an environmental stimulus or condition that motivates behaviour

incomplete disclosure (or deception)   occurs when participants are misled about the nature of a study

incubation   a phenomenon in which the solution to a problem suddenly appears in consciousness after a problem solver has stopped thinking about it for a while

independent variable   in an experiment, the factor that is manipulated by the researcher

inductive reasoning   reasoning that proceeds from a set of specific facts to a general conclusion or principle

indulgent parents   caregivers who have warm and caring relationships with their children but do not provide much guidance and discipline

industrial-organizational (I/O) psychology   a subfield of psychology that examines people's behaviour in the workplace

infantile amnesia   an inability to remember personal experiences from the first few years of our lives

inferential statistics   tell us how confident we can be in drawing conclusions or inferences about a population based on findings obtained from a sample

informational social influence   following the opinions or behaviour of other people because we believe they have accurate knowledge and what they are doing is "right"

informed consent   the principle that, prior to agreeing to participate in research, a person should be fully informed about the procedures, risks involved, and the right to withdraw at any time without penalty

insanity   a legal decision that a defendant was so severely impaired at the time a crime was committed that he or she was incapable of appreciating the wrongfulness of the act or of controlling his or her behaviour

insight   in Gestalt psychology, the sudden perception of a useful relationship or a solution to a problem; in psychoanalysis, the conscious awareness of unconscious dynamics that underlie psychological problems

insomnia   a sleep disorder involving chronic difficulty in falling asleep, staying asleep, or experiencing restful sleep

instinct   an inherited characteristic, common to all members of a species, that automatically produces a particular response when the organism is exposed to a particular stimulus

instinctive drift   the tendency for innate behaviours to override a conditioning procedure, thus making it difficult to create or maintain a conditioned response

instrumental behaviours   emotional coping behaviours that are directed at achieving the goal or performing the task that is relevant to the emotion

intelligence   a concept that refers to individual differences in the ability to acquire knowledge, to think and reason effectively, and to deal adaptively with the environment

intelligence quotient (IQ)   originally defined as mental age (MA) divided by chronological age (CA) multiplied by 100 (IQ = (MA/CA) × 100); an IQ of 100 indicates an individual is average for his or her age group; IQ scores are today based on norms derived from people of various ages

interaction   in analyzing causal factors, the influence that the presence or strength of one factor can have on other causal factors

interjudge reliability   the extent to which different observers or scorers agree in their scoring of a particular test or observed behaviour

internal consistency   the extent to which items within a psychological test correlate with one another, indicating that they are measuring a common characteristic

internal-external locus of control   Rotter's generalized expectancy that one's outcomes are under personal versus external control

internal validity   the degree to which an experiment produces clear causal conclusions; internal validity is high when there is no confounding of variables

interneurons   neurons that are neither sensory nor motor neurons, but perform associative or integrative functions within the nervous system

interpersonal therapy   a form of brief therapy that focuses on the client's interpersonal problems and seeks to develop new interpersonal skills

interpretation   in psychoanalysis, a statement made by the analyst that is intended to promote insight in the client

intrinsic motivation   the motivation to perform a behaviour simply because one finds it interesting or enjoyable for its own sake

J

just world hypothesis   holds that because people want to view the world as fair, they perceive that people get what they deserve and deserve what they get

K

kin selection   the view that organisms are most likely to help others with whom they share the most genes—namely, their offspring and genetic relatives

kinesthesis   the body sense that provides feedback on the position and movements of our body parts

knockout procedure   a technique in which a gene is made inoperative; the function of the targeted gene is inferred by the differences between an organism with a normally functioning gene and one in which the gene does not function (the knockout)

knowledge-acquisition components   allow us to learn from our experience, store information in memory, and combine new insight with previously acquired information

L

language   a system of symbols and rules for combining them that can produce an almost infinite number of possible messages and meanings

language acquisition device (LAD)   according to Noam Chomsky, an innate biological mechanism that contains the general grammatical rules common to all languages

language acquisition support system (LASS)   according to Jerome Bruner, the factors in the social environment that facilitate the learning of a language

lapse a one-time return to an undesirable behaviour pattern, usually in a high-risk situation

latent learning learning that occurs in the absence of reinforcement, but which is not displayed until reinforcement is later introduced into the situation

lateralization the localization of a function in either the right or left cerebral hemisphere

law of effect Thorndike's concept that a response followed by satisfying consequences will become more likely to occur, whereas a response followed by unsatisfying consequences will become less likely to occur

learned helplessness theory a theory of depression that states that if people are unable to control life events, they develop a state of helplessness that leads to depressive symptoms

learning a relatively enduring change in an organism's behaviour or performance capabilities that occurs as a result of experience

lens the transparent structure behind the pupil that changes its shape to focus images on the retina

leptin a hormone secreted by fat cells that decreases general appetite

levels of analysis an approach to analyzing behavioural phenomena and their causal factors in terms of biological, psychological, and environmental factors

levels of processing the concept that the more deeply we process information, the better it will be remembered

life event scales questionnaires that measure the number (and, sometimes, the intensity) of positive and negative life events that have occurred over a specific period of time

limbic system a group of subcortical structures, including the hippocampus and amygdala, which are involved in organizing many goal-directed and emotional behaviours

linguistic relativity hypothesis the idea, suggested by Benjamin Whorf, that people's language determines the ways in which they perceive and think about their world

long-term memory our vast library of durable stored memories

long-term potentiation an enduring increase in synaptic strength that occurs after a neural circuit is rapidly stimulated

longitudinal design research that repeatedly tests the same cohort as it grows older

lowballing a manipulation technique in which a persuader gets someone to commit to some behaviour and then increases the "cost" of that same behaviour

M

magnetic resonance imaging (MRI) a procedure that produces a highly detailed image of living tissue based on the tissue's response to a magnetic field; can be used to study both structure and, in the case of functional MRI (fMRI), brain functions as they occur

maintenance rehearsal the simple mental repetition of information

major depression a mood disorder characterized by intense depression that interferes markedly with functioning

mania a state of intense emotional and behavioural excitement in which a person feels very optimistic and energized

mastery orientation an achievement goal orientation in which success is defined in terms of personal improvement and enjoyment

mastery-approach goals goals related to the desire to master a task and learn new knowledge and skills

mastery-avoidance goals goals that reflect a fear of not performing up to one's own standards

matching effect in romantic relationships, the tendency for partners to have a similar level of physical attractiveness

maturation a genetically programmed, biological process that governs our growth

mean a measure of central tendency; the arithmetic average of a set of scores

means-end analysis a heuristic problem-solving device in which people first define a subgoal they hope to achieve (an "end"), compare that subgoal to their present state of knowledge and, if there is discrepancy, try to find the means to reduce the difference

measures of central tendency a distribution in terms of a single statistic that is in some way "typical" of the sample as a whole

measures of variability information about the spread of scores in a distribution

median a measure of central tendency; the point that divides the distribution in half when the individual scores are arranged in order from lowest to highest

meditation a wide range of different practices that self-regulate attention, the mind, and, in some cases, physiological response

medulla a brain stem structure that controls vital functions, including heartbeat and respiration

melatonin a hormone, secreted by the pineal gland, that has a relaxing effect on the body and promotes readiness for sleep

memory the processes that allow us to record and later retrieve experiences and information

memory codes visual, phonological, semantic, or motor encoding that stores information so it can be retained in short-term and long-term memory

memory consolidation the creation and binding together of neural codes that allow information to be transferred from short-term memory into long-term memory

menstrual synchrony the tendency for some women who live together over time to become more similar to one another in the timing of their menstrual cycles

mental age the mental level at which a child is performing as determined by a "standardized interview" in which the child responds to a series of questions

mental image a representation of a stimulus that originates inside your brain rather than from external sensory input

mental representations cognitive representations of the world, including images, ideas, concepts, and principles, that are the foundations of thinking and problem solving

mental set the tendency to stick to problem-solving strategies or solutions that have worked in the past

mere exposure effect the tendency to evaluate a stimulus more favourably after repeated exposure to it

meta-analysis a statistical procedure for combining the results of different studies that examine the same topic

metabolism the rate of energy expenditure by the body

metacognition a person's awareness and understanding of his or her own cognitive abilities

metacomponents higher-order processes used to plan and regulate task performance (triarchic theory)

midbrain brain structures above the hindbrain that are involved in sensory and motor functions and in attention and states of consciousness

mind–body dualism the philosophical position that the mind is a nonphysical entity that is not subject to physical laws and cannot be reduced to physical processes; body and mind are separate entities

mindfulness a mental state of awareness, focus, openness, and acceptance of immediate experience

Minnesota Multiphasic Personality Inventory (MMPI) a widely used personality test whose items were developed by using the empirical approach and comparing various kinds of psychiatric patients with normal patients

misinformation effect the distortion of a memory by misleading post-event information

mode a measure of central tendency; the most frequently occurring score in a distribution

monism the philosophical position that mental events are reducible to physical events in the brain, so that "mind" and body are one and the same

monocular cues depth cues that require only one eye; include linear perspective, decreasing size, height in the horizontal plane, texture, clarity, light and shadow, motion parallax, and interposition

monogamous mating system a mating system in which parents stay together, at least until their young are self-sufficient

mood-congruent recall tendency to recall information or events that are congruent with our current mood

mood disorders psychological disorders whose core conditions involve maladaptive mood states, such as depression or mania

morpheme the smallest unit of meaning in a given language; English morphemes include whole words, prefixes, and suffixes; there are over 100 000 English morphemes

motivation a process that influences the direction, persistence, and vigour of goal-directed behaviour

motivational interviewing a treatment approach that avoids confrontation and leads clients to their own realization of a problem and to increased motivation to change

motor cortex cortical area in the back of the frontal lobes that controls voluntary movements on the opposite sides of the body

motor neurons specialized neurons that carry neural messages from the brain and the spinal cord to the muscles and the glands

motoric thought mental representations of motor movements, such as throwing an object

multimodal treatments substance abuse interventions that combine a number of treatments, such as aversion therapy and coping skills training

myelin sheath a fatty insulating substance on the axon of some neurons that increases the speed of neural transmission

myopia a visual defect, sometimes called *nearsightedness*, in which the lens focuses distant images in front of the retina rather than on it

N

narcolepsy a sleep disorder that involves extreme daytime sleepiness and sudden, uncontrollable sleep attacks during waking hours

natural selection the evolutionary process through which characteristics that increase the likelihood of survival are preserved in the gene pool and thereby become more common in a species over time

naturalistic observation a method in which the researcher observes behaviour in a natural setting and tries to avoid influencing the participants being observed

need for achievement the desire to accomplish tasks and attain standards of excellence

need for positive regard an innate need to be positively regarded by others and by oneself

need for positive self-regard in Rogers's personality theory, the psychological need to feel positively about oneself that underlies self-enhancement behaviours

need hierarchy Maslow's view that human needs are arranged in a progression, beginning with deficiency needs and then reaching growth needs

negative correlation as scores on one variable change, scores on a second variable change in the opposite direction

negative punishment the removal of a (positive) stimulus following an undesired response to weaken it (e.g., TV privileges are taken away from a misbehaving child who wants attention)

negative reinforcement a response is strengthened by the subsequent removal of a (noxious) stimulus

negative state relief model the view that empathy does not lead to pure altruism, but instead, that high empathy causes us to feel distress when we learn of others' suffering, so that by helping them we reduce our own personal distress

negative symptoms schizophrenic symptoms that reflect a lack of normal reactions, such as emotions or social behaviours

neglectful parents caregivers who provide neither warmth, nor rules, nor guidance

nerve deafness hearing loss caused by damage to the cochlear receptor cells or the auditory nerve

neural network a model in which each concept stored in memory is represented by a unique pattern of distributed and simultaneously activated nodes that process information in parallel; also known as a *parallel distributed processing model*

neural plasticity the ability of neurons to modify their structure and function in response to experiential factors or injury

neuromodulators neurotransmitter substances that are released by neurons and circulate within the nervous system to affect the sensitivity of many neurons to their natural transmitter substances

neurons nerve cells that constitute the basic building blocks of the nervous system

neurotic anxiety in psychoanalytic theory, a state of anxiety that arises when impulses from the id threaten to break through into behaviour

neuroticism a personality trait that involves the tendency to experience high levels of negative affect and to behave in self-defeating ways

neurotransmitters chemical substances that are released from the axons of one neuron, travel across the synaptic space, and bind to specially keyed receptors in another neuron, where they produce a chemical reaction that is either excitatory or inhibitory

night terrors a disorder in which a sleeper—often feeling a strong sense of dread or danger—becomes aroused to a near panic state; the sleeper may suddenly sit up, let out a blood-curdling scream, and thrash about or flee to another room, as if trying to escape

norm of reciprocity the norm that when other people treat us well, we should respond in kind

normal curve a symmetrical bell-shaped curve that represents a theoretical distribution of scores in the population

normal distribution a frequency distribution in the shape of a symmetrical or bell-shaped curve that satisfies certain mathematical conditions deduced from the theory of probability

normative social influence conformity motivated by gaining social acceptance and avoiding social rejection

norms test scores derived from a relevant sample used to evaluate individuals' scores; behavioural "rules"

nucleus accumbens one of the structures of the limbic system; is involved in reward and motivation

null hypothesis an approach to statistical analysis that states that any observed differences between the samples are due to chance

O

object permanence the recognition that an object continues to exist even when it can no longer be seen

object relations the images or mental representations that people form of themselves and other people as a result of early experience with caregivers

observational learning learning through observing the behaviour of a model

obsession an unwanted and disturbing thought or image that invades consciousness and is very difficult to control

obsessive-compulsive disorder (OCD) an anxiety disorder characterized by persistent and unwanted thoughts and compulsive behaviours

occipital lobe the rearmost portion of the cerebral cortex that contains the primary visual sensory area

olfaction the sense of smell

olfactory bulb a forebrain structure immediately above the nasal cavity

openness a willingness to invest oneself in the process of therapy that predicts favourable therapeutic outcomes

operant conditioning a type of learning in which behaviour is modified by its consequences, such as by reinforcement, punishment, and extinction

operant discrimination an operant response that occurs when a particular antecedent stimulus is present, but not when another antecedent stimulus is present

operant extinction the weakening and eventual disappearance of a response because it is no longer reinforced

operant generalization an operant response occurs to a new antecedent stimulus that is similar to the original antecedent stimulus

operational definition defining a concept or variable in terms of the specific procedures used to produce or measure it

opiates opium and drugs derived from it, such as morphine, codeine, and heroin; opiates provide pain relief and cause mood changes, which may include euphoria

opponent-process theory the theory proposed by Hering that the retina contains three sets of colour receptors that respond differentially to red-green, blue-yellow, and black-white; the opponent processes that result can produce a perception of any hue

optic nerve a bundle of ganglion cell axons in the retina that transmits visual information to the brain

organ of Corti structure embedded in the basilar membrane that contains the hair cell receptors for sound

outcome bias the extent that a test underestimates a person's true intellectual ability

overconfidence the tendency to overestimate one's correctness in factual knowledge, beliefs, and decisions

overlearning continued rehearsal past the point of initial learning that significantly improves performance on memory tasks

P

pain disorder a somatoform disorder in which the person's complaints of pain cannot be accounted for in terms of physical damage

panic disorder an anxiety disorder characterized by unpredictable panic attacks and a pervasive fear that another will occur; may also include a resulting agoraphobia

parallel processing our ability to use our senses to take in a variety of information about an object and construct a unified image of its properties

parasympathetic nervous system the branch portion of the autonomic nervous system that slows down bodily processes to conserve energy and reduce arousal

paraventricular nucleus (PVN) a cluster of neurons in the hippocampus packed with receptor sites for transmitters that stimulate or reduce appetite

parental investment theory the view, based on evolutionary theory, that the gender with a greater investment (higher costs) in producing offspring will be more selective in choosing a mate

parietal lobe the cerebral region behind the frontal lobe that contains the somatic sensory cortex and Wernicke's speech comprehension area

partial reinforcement schedule a schedule in which reinforcement follows some correct responses but not others

partial report method used to measure iconic memory and demonstrate that memory span for a visual stimulus is longer than suggested by full reporting

passionate love a form of love that involves intense emotional arousal and yearning for one's partner

Pearson product-moment correlation coefficient a statistic that reflects the direction and strength of the relation between two variables

perception the process of organizing stimulus input and giving it meaning

perceptual constancies the ability to recognize stimulus characteristics—size, colour, and so on—under varying conditions

perceptual schemas internal representations that contain the essential features of an object of perception

perceptual set a readiness to perceive stimuli in a particular way

performance components the actual mental processes used to perform a task (triarchic theory)

performance orientation from achievement goal theory, a person defines success relative to how his or her behaviour, or performance, compares to that of others; also referred to as "ego goals"

because the individual is preoccupied with him- or herself and how he or she appears to others

performance-approach goals behaviour is motivated by the desire to outperform others; it reflects a competitive orientation that focuses on being better than other people

performance-avoidance goals behaviour is motivated by the desire to avoid being outperformed by others; that is, the goal is to avoid failure

peripheral nervous system all the neurons that connect the central nervous system with the sensory receptors, the muscles, and the glands

peripheral route to persuasion occurs when people do not scrutinize a message and are influenced mostly by other factors, such as a speaker's attractiveness or a message's emotional appeal

personal constructs in George Kelly's personality theory, the cognitive categories used to sort events and make comparisons among people and events

personality the biologically and environmentally determined characteristics within a person that account for distinctive and relatively enduring patterns of thinking, feeling, and acting

personality disorder stable, inflexible, and maladaptive personality styles

personality psychology a subfield of psychology that focuses on the study of human personality

perspective a theoretical vantage point from which to analyze behaviour and its causes

phenotype the observable characteristics produced by one's genetic endowment

pheromones chemical signals found in natural body scents

phobias strong and irrational fears of particular objects or circumstances

phoneme the smallest unit of sound in a language; these are the vowel and consonant sounds that are recognized in any given language; English has 45 phonemes

photopigments protein molecules within the rods and cones whose chemical reactions when absorbing light result in nerve impulses being generated

place theory the theory of pitch perception that holds that sound frequencies are coded in terms of the portion of the basilar membrane where the fluid wave in the cochlea peaks; this theory accounts for perception of frequencies above 4000 Hz

placebo an inactive or inert substance that has no medicinal value but is believed by a patient to be helpful

placebo control group a control group that receives an intervention that is assumed to have no therapeutic value

placebo effect a change in behaviour that occurs because of the expectation or belief that one is receiving a treatment

pleasure principle the drive for instant need gratification that is characteristic of the id

polyandry a mating system in which one female mates with many males

polygenic transmission a number of genes working together to create a particular phenotypic characteristic

polygraph a research and clinical instrument that measures a wide array of physiological responses

polygynandry a mating system in which all members of a group mate with all other members of that group

polygyny a mating system in which one male may mate with many females

pons a brain stem structure having sensory and motor tracts whose functions are involved in sleep and dreaming

population in a survey, the entire set of individuals about whom we wish to draw a conclusion

positive correlation as scores on one variable change, scores on a second variable change in the same direction

positive psychology movement the study of human strengths, fulfillment, and optimal living

positive punishment occurs when a response is weakened by the subsequent presentation of a (noxious) stimulus

positive reinforcement a response is strengthened by the subsequent presentation of a (positive) stimulus

positive symptoms schizophrenic symptoms such as delusions, hallucinations, and disordered speech and thinking

positron emission tomography (PET) scan a procedure that provides a visual display of the absorption of a radioactive substance by neurons, indicating how actively they are involved as the brain performs a task

post-formal thought the ability to reason logically about opposing points of view and to accept contradictions and irreconcilable differences

post-traumatic stress disorder (PTSD) a pattern of distressing symptoms, such as flashbacks, nightmares, avoidance, and anxiety responses that recur after a traumatic experience

postconventional moral reasoning moral judgments that are based on a system of internalized, well-thought-out moral principles

pragmatics in language learning, a knowledge of the practical aspects of using language

preconventional moral reasoning in Kohlberg's stage model, moral reasoning based on anticipated punishments or rewards

predictive bias a test bias that occurs if the test successfully predicts criterion measures for some groups but not for others

preferential looking procedure a study type used by Fantz to research infants' visual preferences

prefrontal cortex the area of the frontal lobe just behind the eyes and forehead that is involved in the executive functions of planning, self-awareness, and responsibility

prejudice a negative attitude toward people based on their membership in a group

preoperational stage in Piaget's model, a stage of cognitive development in which children represent the world symbolically through words and mental images, but do not yet understand basic mental operations or rules

preparedness the notion that evolutionary factors have produced an innate readiness to learn certain associations that have had survival implications in the past

primacy effect (impression formation) our tendency to attach more importance to the initial information that we learn about a person

primary appraisal the initial appraisal of a situation as benign, irrelevant, or threatening; a perception of the severity of demands

primary mental abilities spatial ability, perceptual speed, numerical ability, verbal meaning, memory, verbal fluency, and inductive reasoning; defined by L. L. Thurstone on the basis of his factor analysis of intelligence test items

primary reinforcers positive reinforcers that satisfy biological needs, such as food and water

primary visual cortex the area of the occipital lobe which receives impulses generated from the retina via the thalamus and analyzes visual input by using its feature detectors

priming the activation of one concept (or one unit of information) by another

proactive interference occurs when material learned in the past interferes with recall of newer material

problem-focused coping coping strategies that involve direct attempts to confront and master a stressful situation

problem-solving dream models the view that dreams can help us find creative solutions to our problems and conflicts because they are not constrained by reality

problem-solving schemas step-by-step scripts for selecting information and solving specialized classes of problems

procedural memory memory that is reflected in learned skills and actions; also known as *non-declarative memory*

projective tests tests, such as the Rorschach and the TAT, that present ambiguous stimuli to the subject; the responses are assumed to be based on a projection of internal characteristics of the person onto the stimuli

proposition a statement that expresses an idea in subject-predicate form

propositional thought thinking that takes the form of verbal sentences that we say or hear in our minds

prospective memory remembering to perform an activity in the future

protective factors environmental or personal resources that help people fare better in the face of stress

prototype the most typical and familiar members of a class that defines a concept

proximodistal principle the principle that physical development begins along the innermost parts of the body and continues toward the outermost parts

psychic energy generated by instinctual drives, this energy powers the mind and constantly presses for either direct or indirect release

psychoanalysis the analysis of internal and primarily unconscious psychological forces

psychodynamic perspective a psychological perspective that focuses on inner personality dynamics, including the role of unconscious impulses and defences, in understanding behaviour

psycholinguistics the scientific study of the psychological aspects of language, such as how people understand, produce, and acquire language

psychological test a method for measuring individual differences related to some psychological construct, based on a sample of relevant behaviour obtained under standardized conditions

psychology the scientific study of behaviour and its causes

psychometrics the study of the statistical properties of psychological tests; the psychometric approach to intelligence focuses on the number and nature of abilities that define intelligence

psychophysics the study of relations between the physical characteristics of stimuli and the sensory experiences they evoke

psychosocial stages a sequence of eight developmental stages proposed by Erikson, each of which involves a different "crisis" (i.e., conflict) over how we view ourselves

psychosurgery surgical procedures, such as lobotomy or cingulotomy, in which brain tissue involved in a behaviour disorder is removed or destroyed

puberty a period of rapid maturation in which one becomes capable of sexual reproduction

punishment a response is weakened by an outcome that follows it

R

random assignment a procedure in which each participant has an equal likelihood of being assigned to any one group within an experiment

random sampling a method of choosing a sample in which each member of the population has an equal opportunity to be included in the sample

randomized clinical trial (RCT) a research design that involves the random assignment of clients having specific problems to an experimental (therapy) group or to a control condition so as to draw sound causal conclusions about the therapy's efficacy

range in statistics, the difference between the highest and the lowest score in a distribution; the simplest but least informative measure of variability

rape trauma syndrome a pattern of cognitive, emotional, and behavioural responses that occurs in response to the trauma of being raped

rational approach an approach to test construction in which test items are made up on the basis of a theorist's conception of a construct

reaction range the genetically influenced limits within which environmental factors can exert their effects on an organism

reaction time how rapidly a person responds to a stimulus

realistic conflict theory the theory that competition for limited resources fosters prejudice

reality principle the ego's tendency to take reality into account and to act in a rational fashion in satisfying its needs

receptor sites protein molecules on neurons' dendrites or soma that are specially shaped to accommodate a specific neurotransmitter molecule

recessive gene a gene whose characteristic will be masked by a corresponding dominant gene; its characteristic will be expressed if the correspondent gene is also recessive

reciprocal determinism Bandura's model of two-way causal relations between people, behaviour, and the environment

recombinant DNA procedures genesplicing procedures that can be used to produce new life forms, such as bacteria, that can produce scarce chemical materials, such as human growth hormone

regression a psychoanalytic defence mechanism in which a person retreats back to an earlier stage of development in response to stress

reinforcement the strengthening of a response by an outcome that follows it

relapse a complete return to a previous undesirable behaviour and an abandonment of attempts to change

reliability in psychological testing, the consistency with which a measure assesses a given characteristic, or different observers agree on a given score; the degree to which clinicians show high levels of agreement in their diagnostic decisions

REM sleep a recurring sleep stage characterized by rapid eye movements, increased physiological arousal, paralysis of the voluntary muscles, and a high rate of dreaming

REM-sleep behaviour disorder a sleep disorder in which the loss of muscle tone that causes normal REM-sleep paralysis is absent, thereby enabling sleepers to move about—sometimes violently—and seemingly "act out" their dreams

remote behaviour sampling researchers and clinicians collect samples of behaviour from respondents as they live their daily lives

repeated measures (or within subjects) design each participant in an experiment is exposed to all the conditions of an independent variable

replication the process of repeating a study to determine whether the original findings can be duplicated

representative sample a sample that accurately reflects the important characteristics of the population

representativeness heuristic a guide in estimating the probability that an object or event belongs to a certain category based on the extent to which it represents a prototype of that category

repression the basic defence mechanism that actively keeps anxiety-arousing material in the unconscious

residential school syndrome a set of long-lasting symptoms, similar to PTSD, suffered by some individuals who attended residential schools away from their communities

resilience the ability to withstand psychological stress

resistance largely unconscious manoeuvres that protect clients from dealing with anxiety-arousing material in therapy

response prevention the prevention of escape or avoidance responses during exposure to an anxiety-arousing CS so that extinction can occur

resting potential in the electrical activity of neurons, the internal difference of

the sodium ions outside of a cell and the negatively charged protein ions inside the cell

restoration model the theory that sleep recharges our run-down bodies and allows us to recover from physical and mental fatigue

reticular formation a structure extending from the hindbrain into the midbrain that plays a central role in consciousness and attention, in part by alerting and activating higher brain centres (ascending portion), and by selectively blocking some inputs from admission to higher regions in the brain (descending portion)

retina the light-sensitive back surface of the eye that contains the visual receptors

retrieval the process of accessing information in long-term memory

retrieval cue any stimulus, whether internal or external, that stimulates the activation of information stored in longterm memory

retroactive interference newly acquired information interferes with the ability to recall information learned at an earlier time

retrograde amnesia memory loss for events that occurred prior to the onset of amnesia

reuptake process whereby transmitter substances are taken back into the pre-synaptic neuron so that they do not continue to stimulate postsynaptic neurons

rods visual receptors that function under low levels of illumination and do not give rise to colour sensations

rotating shiftwork a forward-rotating work schedule that changes work shifts by extending a worker's "waking day" rather than compressing it

S

sample in a survey, a subset of individuals drawn from the population

scatterplots a graph commonly used to examine correlational data; each pair of scores on variable X and variable Y is plotted as a single point

schema a "mental framework"—an organized pattern of thought about some aspect of the world, such as a class of people, events, situations, or objects

schizophrenia a psychotic disorder involving serious impairment of attention, thought, language, emotion, and behaviour

script a mental framework concerning a sequence of events that usually unfolds in a regular, almost standardized order

seasonal affective disorder (SAD) a disorder in which depressive symptoms appear or worsen during certain seasons of the year (typically, fall and winter) and then improve during the other seasons

secondary appraisal one's judgment of the adequacy of personal resources needed to cope with a stressor

secondary, or conditioned, reinforcer a stimulus that acquires reinforcing qualities by being associated with primary reinforcers

seeking social support a class of coping strategies that involves turning to others for assistance and emotional support in times of stress

self in Rogers's theory, an organized, consistent set of perceptions and beliefs about oneself

self-actualization in humanistic theories, an inborn tendency to strive toward the realization of one's full potential

self-concept one's beliefs and perceptions about oneself

self-consistency an absence of conflict among self-perceptions

self-determination theory a theory about motivation that focuses on three fundamental psychological needs: competence, autonomy, and relatedness

self-efficacy the conviction that we can perform the behaviours necessary to produce a desired outcome

self-enhancement processes whereby one enhances positive self-regard

self-esteem how positively or negatively we feel about ourselves

self-fulfilling prophecy when people's erroneous expectations lead them to act in a way that brings about the expected behaviours, thereby confirming the original impression

self-instructional training a cognitive coping approach of giving adaptive self-instructions to oneself at crucial phases of the coping process

self-monitoring a personality trait that reflects people's tendencies to regulate their social behaviour in accord with situational cues as opposed to internal values, attitudes, and needs

self-perception theory the theory that we make inferences about our own attitudes by observing how we behave

self-relatedness the ability to be flexible to change, to listen carefully to the therapist, and to use constructively what is learned in therapy

self-serving bias the tendency to make relatively more personal attributions for success and situational attributions for failure

self-verification the tendency to try to verify or validate one's existing self-concept—that is, to satisfy congruence needs

semantic memory general factual knowledge about the world and language, including memory for words and concepts

semantics rules for connecting symbols to what they represent

sensation the process by which stimuli are detected, transduced into nerve impulses, and sent to the brain

sensitization an increase in the strength of response to a repeated stimulus

sensorimotor stage in Piaget's theory, the stage of cognitive development in which children understand their world primarily through sensory experience and physical (motor) interaction with objects

sensory adaptation diminishing sensitivity to an unchanging stimulus with the passage of time as sensory neurons habituate to the stimulation

sensory memory memory processes that retain incoming sensory information just long enough for it to be recognized

sensory neurons specialized neurons that carry messages from the sense organs to the spinal cord and brain

sensory prosthetic devices devices that provide sensory input that can, to some extent, substitute for what blind and deaf people are not supplied by their sensory receptors

separation anxiety distress experienced by infants when they are separated from a primary caregiver, peaking around age 12 to 16 months

sequential design repeatedly testing several age cohorts as they grow older

serial position effect the finding that recall is influenced by a word's position in a series of items

serotonin a neurotransmitter that seems to underlie positive mood states; underactivity may be a factor in depression

sex-role stereotypes beliefs about the types of characteristics and behaviours that are appropriate for boys versus for girls

sex-typing treating others differently based on whether they are female or male

sexual orientation a person's emotional and erotic preference for partners of a particular sex

sexual response cycle a physiological response to sexual stimulation that involves stages of excitement, plateau, orgasm, and resolution

shadowing an experimental procedure used in attention research in which a person simultaneously receives two or more messages, is asked to focus on one of them, and then is asked to report on the other messages as well

shaping an operant conditioning procedure in which reinforcement begins

with a behaviour that the organism can already perform, and then is made contingent on behaviours that increasingly approximate the final desired behaviour

short-term memory type of memory that holds the information that we are conscious of at any given time; also called *working memory*

signal detection theory a theory that assumes that stimulus detection is not based on a fixed absolute threshold but rather is affected by rewards, punishments, expectations, and motivational factors

situation-focused intervention prevention efforts that focus on altering environmental conditions that are known to promote the development of psychological disorders

Skinner box an experimental chamber in which animals learn to perform operant responses, such as bar presses or pecking responses, so that the learning process can be studied

slow-wave sleep stages 3 and 4 of sleep, in which the EEG pattern shows large, slow brain waves called *delta waves*

social anxiety disorder an excessive and inappropriate fear of social situations in which a person might be evaluated and possibly embarrassed; formerly known as *social phobia*

social cognitive theory a cognitive-behavioural approach to personality, developed by Albert Bandura and Walter Mischel, that emphasizes the role of social learning, cognitive processes, and self-regulation

social-cognitive theory (of hypnosis) the view that hypnotic experiences occur because people are highly motivated to assume the role of being "hypnotized"

social comparison the act of comparing one's personal attributes, abilities, and opinions to those of other people

social Darwinism a distortion of Darwinism that argues if the more fit are more successful, then those at the top of the social and economic ladder must be most fit of all

social desirability bias tendency of people to exaggerate their positive and minimize their negative qualities

social exchange theory a theory proposing that a social relationship can best be described in terms of exchanges of rewards and costs between the two partners

social facilitation an increased tendency to perform one's dominant response in the mere presence of others

social identity theory the theory that prejudice stems from a need to enhance our self-esteem

social learning theory Bandura's former name for *social-cognitive theory*

social loafing the tendency for people to expend less individual effort when working in a group than when working alone

social norms shared expectations about how people should think, feel, and behave

social phobia excessive and inappropriate fear of social situations in which a person might be evaluated and possibly embarrassed; also known as *social anxiety disorder*

social psychology a subfield of psychology that examines people's thoughts, feelings, and behaviour pertaining to the social world

social role a set of norms that characterizes how people in a given social position ought to behave

social skills training a technique in which a client learns more effective social behaviours by observing and imitating a skillful model

socialization the process by which we acquire the beliefs, values, and behaviours of a group

sociobiology an evolutionary theory of social behaviour that emphasizes the role of adaptive behaviour in maintaining one's genes in the species' gene pool

sociocultural perspective a perspective that emphasizes the role of culture and the social environment in understanding commonalties and differences in human behaviour

somatic nervous system the branch of the peripheral nervous system that provides input from the sensory receptors and output to the voluntary muscles of the body

somatic sensory cortex cortical strips in the front portions of the parietal lobes that receive sensory input from various regions of the body

somatic symptom disorders disorders in which people complain of bodily symptoms that cannot be accounted for in terms of actual physical damage or dysfunction; formerly known as *somatoform disorders.*

somatic theory of emotion a modern emotion theory inspired by the James-Lange theory that emphasizes the causal role of bodily responses in the experiencing of emotion

somatoform disorders disorders in which people complain of bodily symptoms that cannot be accounted for in terms of actual physical damage or dysfunction; also known as *somatic symptom disorders*

source confusion tendency to recall something or recognize it as familiar, but to forget where it was encountered

specific phobia irrational and excessive fear of specific objects or situations that pose little or no actual threat

specificity question the ultimate question of psychotherapy research: Which types of therapy, administered by which kinds of therapists to which kinds of clients having which kinds of problems produce which kinds of effects?

speech segmentation perceiving where each word within a spoken sentence begins and ends

splitting the failure to integrate positive and negative aspects of another's behaviour into a coherent whole

spontaneous recovery in classical conditioning, the reappearance of a previously extinguished conditioned response after a period of time has passed following extinction

spontaneous remission improvements in symptoms in the absence of any therapy

standard deviation (SD) the square root of the variance

standardization in psychological testing, (1) creating a standard set of procedures for administering a test or making observations, and (2) deriving norms to which an individual's performance can be compared

state-dependent memory theory that our ability to retrieve information is greater when our internal state at the time of retrieval matches our original state during learning

static testing a traditional approach to testing whereby very detailed instructions must be closely adhered to in order to make sure that all testees are responding to as similar a stimulus situation as possible so that their scores will be solely a reflection of their ability

statistical significance a term that suggests that it is unlikely that a particular finding occurred by chance alone

stereotype a generalized belief about a group or category of people

stereotype threat according to Claude Steele, the idea that stereotypes create a fear and self-consciousness among stereotyped group members that they will "live up" to other people's stereotypes

stimulants drugs that stimulate neural activity, resulting in a state of excitement or aroused euphoria

stimulus generalization a CR occurs to stimuli other than the original CS, based on the similarity of these stimuli to the CS

stimulus hierarchy in systematic desensitization, the creation of a series of anxiety-arousing stimuli that are ranked in terms of the amount of anxiety they evoke

storage the retention of information over time

Strange Situation Test (SST) a standardized procedure for examining infant

attachment whereby an infant first plays with toys in his or her mother's presence and then is observed in the presence of a stranger

stranger anxiety distress over contact with strangers that typically develops in the first year of infancy and dissipates in the second year

stress a pattern of cognitive appraisals, physiological responses, and behavioural tendencies that occurs in response to a perceived imbalance between situational demands and the resources available to cope with them

stressors situations that place demands on organisms that tax or exceed their resources

stroboscopic movement illusory movement produced when a light is briefly flashed in darkness and then, a few milliseconds later, another light is flashed nearby

structuralism an early German school of psychology established by Wilhelm Wundt that attempted to study the structure of the mind by breaking it down into its basic components, thought to be sensations

subgoal analysis a problem-solving heuristic in which people attack a large problem by formulating subgoals, or intermediate steps toward a solution

sublimation the channelling of unacceptable impulses into socially accepted behaviours, as when aggressive drives are expressed in violent sports

subliminal stimulus a stimulus that is received by the senses but not perceived consciously

substance dependence a maladaptive pattern of substance use that causes significant distress or substantially impairs a person life; diagnosed as occurring "with physiological dependence" if drug tolerance or withdrawal symptoms have developed

suicide the willful taking of one's own life

superego the moral arm of the personality that internalizes the standards and values of society and serves as the person's conscience

suprachiasmatic nuclei (SCN) the brain's master "biological clock," located in the hypothalamus, that regulates most circadian rhythms

surface structure a linguistic term for the words and organization of a spoken or written sentence; two sentences with different surface structure may still mean the same thing

survey research a method in which questionnaires or interviews are used to obtain information about many people

sympathetic nervous system the branch of the autonomic nervous system that has an arousal function on the body's internal organs, speeding up bodily processes and mobilizing the body

synaesthesia a condition in which stimuli are experienced not only in the normal sensory modality, but in others as well

synapse the microscopic space between neurons over which the nerve impulse is biochemically transmitted

synaptic cleft a tiny gap between the axon terminal of one neuron and the dendrite of the next neuron

synaptic vesicles chambers within the axon that contain the neurotransmitter substance

syntax the rules for the combination of symbols within a given language

systematic desensitization an attempt to eliminate anxiety by using counterconditioning, in which a new response that is incompatible with anxiety is conditioned to the anxiety-arousing conditioned stimulus

T

tardive dyskinesia an irreversible motor disorder that can occur as a side effect of certain antipsychotic drugs

taste buds the receptors for taste in the tongue and in the roof and back of the mouth that are sensitive to the qualities of sweet, sour, salty, and bitter

TDF (testis determining factor) gene a gene on the Y chromosome that triggers male sexual development

temperament a biologically based general style of reacting emotionally and behaviourally to the environment

temporal lobe the portion of the cortex that lies below the parietal lobes and is the major site of auditory input to the brain

teratogens environmental (non-genetic) agents that cause abnormal prenatal development

test-retest reliability the extent to which scores on a presumably stable characteristic are consistent over time

thalamus a major sensory integration and relay centre in the forebrain, sometimes referred to as the brain's *sensory switchboard*

THC (tetrahydrocannabinol) the major active ingredient in marijuana

theory a set of formal statements that explain how and why certain events or phenomena are related to one another

theory of cognitive dissonance the theory that people strive to maintain consistency in their beliefs and actions, and that inconsistency creates dissonance—unpleasant arousal that motivates people to restore balance by changing their cognitions

theory of mind beliefs about the "mind" and the ability to understand other people's mental states

theory of planned behaviour view that our intention to engage in a behaviour is strongest when we have a positive attitude toward that behaviour, when subjective norms (our perceptions of what other people think we should do) support our attitudes, and when we believe that the behaviour is under our control

theory of reciprocal altruism view that altruism is long-term cooperation; one individual may help another but that assistance will be reciprocated at some time in the future

three-stratum theory of cognitive abilities a theory that supports three levels of mental skills—general, broad, and narrow—arranged in a hierarchical model

token economy a procedure in which desirable behaviours are reinforced with tokens or points that can later be redeemed for other reinforcers

tolerance a condition in which increasingly larger doses of a drug are required to produce the same level of bodily response; caused by the body's compensatory responses

top-down processing perceptual processing in which existing knowledge, concepts, ideas, or expectations are applied to make sense of incoming stimulation

transduction the conversion of one form of energy into another; in sensation, the process whereby physical stimuli are translated into nerve impulses

transfer of excitation a misinterpretation of one's state of arousal that occurs when arousal actually is caused by one source, but the person attributes it to another source

transference the psychoanalytic phenomenon in which a client responds irrationally to the analyst as if the latter were an important person from the client's past who plays an important role in the client's dynamics

transtheoretical model identifies six major stages in the process of how people change: precontemplation, contemplation, preparation, action, maintenance, and termination

trauma-dissociation theory a theory that accounts for the development of dissociative identity disorder in terms of dissociation as a defence against severe childhood abuse or trauma

triangular theory of love the view that various types of love result from different combinations of three core factors: intimacy, commitment, and passion

triarchic theory of intelligence Sternberg's theory of intelligence that distinguishes between analytical, practical, and creative forms of mental ability

trichromatic theory the colour vision theory originally advanced by Young and Helmholtz that there are three types of colour receptors in the retina and that combinations of activation of these receptors can produce perception of any hue in the visible spectrum

twin studies a behaviour genetics method in which identical (monozygotic) and fraternal (dizygotic) twins are compared on some characteristic; this method is particularly informative if the twins have been raised in different environments

two-factor theory of avoidance learning theory that avoidance learning first involves the classical conditioning of fear, followed by learning operant responses that avoid an anticipated aversive stimulus and thus are reinforced by anxiety reduction

two-factor theory of emotion Schachter's theory that the intensity of physiological arousal determines perceived intensity of emotion, whereas the appraisal of environmental cues tells us which emotion we are experiencing

Type I schizophrenia subtype of schizophrenia characterized by a predominance of positive symptoms

Type II schizophrenia subtype of schizophrenia characterized by negative symptoms

Type A personality a behavioural pattern involving a sense of time urgency, pressured behaviour, and hostility that appears to be a risk factor in coronary heart disease

Type B personality a relaxed and agreeable personality type, with little sense of time urgency

U

unconditional positive regard a communicated attitude of total and unconditional acceptance of another person that conveys the person's intrinsic worth

unconditioned response (UCR) a response (usually reflexive or innate) that is elicited by a specific stimulus (the UCS) without prior learning

unconditioned stimulus (UCS) a stimulus that elicits a particular reflexive or innate response (the UCR) without prior learning

unobtrusive measurement recording behaviour in a way that keeps participants unaware that they are being observed

V

validity the extent to which a test measures what it is supposed to; the degree to which a diagnostic system's categories contain the core features of the behaviour disorders and permit differentiation among the disorders

variable any characteristic of an organism or situation that can differ

variable-interval (VI) schedule a schedule in which reinforcement follows the first correct response that occurs after an average (but variable) time interval following the last reinforced response

variable-ratio (VR) schedule a schedule in which reinforcement is based on an average but variable number of responses

variance the average of the squared deviation scores about the mean

vestibular sense the sense of body orientation or equilibrium

virtual reality (VR) the use of computer technology to create highly realistic "virtual environments" that simulate actual experience so vividly that they evoke many of the same reactions that a comparable real-world environment would create

visual acuity the ability to see fine detail

visual agnosia a disorder in which an individual is unable to visually recognize objects

visual association cortex cortical areas in the occipital, parietal, and temporal lobes that analyze visual stimuli sent to the primary visual cortex in relation to stored knowledge and that establish the "meaning" of the stimuli

vulnerability factors predispositions that can have a biological basis, such as our genotype, a brain malfunction, or a hormonal factor

vulnerability-stress model a model that explains behaviour disorders as resulting from predisposing biological or psychological vulnerability factors that are triggered by a stressor

W

Weber's law the principle that to perceive a difference between two stimuli, the stimuli must differ by a constant percentage or ratio

Wernicke's area an area of the left temporal lobe that is involved in speech comprehension

wisdom a system of knowledge about the meaning and conduct of life

wish fulfillment in Freudian theory, the partial or complete satisfaction of a psychological need through dreaming or waking fantasy

withdrawal the occurrence of compensatory responses after drug use is discontinued, causing a person to experience physiological reactions opposite to those that had been produced by the drug

working memory a more current name for short-term memory, reflecting the fact that it consciously processes, codes, and "works on" information

Y

yo-yo dieting a form of weight monitoring that results in big up-and-down weight fluctuations; increases the risk of dying from cardiovascular disease

Z

zone of proximal development the difference between what a child can do independently, and what the child can do with assistance from adults or more advanced peers

zygote the fertilized egg

Aaron, S. (1986). *Stage fright.* Chicago, IL: University of Chicago Press.

Abbate, C.S., Ruggieri, S., & Boca, S. (2013). The effect of prosocial priming in the presence of bystanders. *The Journal of Social Psychology, 153*(5), 619–622.

Abe, N., Okuda, J., Suzuki, M., Sasaki, H., Matsuda, T., Mori, E., Takada, M., & Fuji, T. (2008). Neural correlates of true memory, false memory, and deception. *Cerebral Cortex, 18,* 2811–2819.

Abel, T., & Kandel, E. (1998). Positive and negative regulatory mechanisms that mediate long-term memory storage. *Brain Research Reviews, 26,* 360–378.

Abi-Dargham, A., & Guillin, A. (Eds.). (2007). *Integrating the neurobiology of schizophrenia.* New York, NY: Elsevier Science.

Abraham, K. (1911/1968). Notes on the psychoanalytic investigation and treatment of manic-depressive insanity and allied conditions. In K. Abraham, *Selected Papers of Karl Abraham.* New York, NY: Basic Books.

Abramowitz, A.J., & Caron, M.L. (2010). Psychological and neuropsychological testing. In M.K. Dulcan (Ed.), *Dulcan's textbook of child and adolescent psychiatry* (pp. 135–148). Arlington, VA: American Psychiatric Publishing.

Abramowitz, J.S. (2013). *The impact of dementia on Canadian society.* Retrieved The practice of exposure therapy: Relevance of cognitive-behavioral theory and extinction theory. *Behavior Therapy, 44*(4), 548–558.

Abrams, D.A., Ryali, S., Chen, T., Chordia, P., Khouzam, A., Levitin, D.L., & Menon, V. (2013). Inter-subject synchronization of brain responses during natural music listening. *European Journal of Neuroscience, 37,* 1458–1469.

Abramson, L.Y., Seligman, M.E., & Teasdale, J.D. (1978). Learned helplessness in humans: Critique and reformulation. *Journal of Abnormal Psychology, 87*(1), 49–74.

Achter, J., Lubinski, D., & Benbow, C.P. (1996). Multipotentiality among the intellectually gifted: "It was never there and already it's vanishing." *Journal of Counseling Psychology, 43*(1), 65–76.

Adachi, P.J.C., & Willoughby, T. (2013). Demolishing the competition: The longitudinal link between competitive video games, competitive gambling, and aggression. *Journal of Youth and Adolescence, 42*(7), 1090–1104.

Adair, R.K. (1990). *The physics of baseball.* New York, NY: Harper & Row.

Adams, D.B. (2006). Brain mechanisms of aggressive behavior: An updated review. *Neuroscience and Biobehavioral Reviews, 30,* 304–318.

Adamuti-Trache, M. (2013). Language acquisition among adult immigrants in Canada: The effect of premigration language capital. *Adult Education Quarterly, 63*(2), 103–126.

Adelmann, P.K., & Zajonc, R.B. (1989). Facial efference and the experience of emotion. *Annual Review of Psychology, 40,* 249–280.

Adler, A. (1927). *The practice and theory of individual psychology.* New York, NY: Harcourt.

Adler, A.B., Bliese, P.D., McGurk, D., Hoge, C.W., & Castro, C.A. (2009). Battlemind debriefing and battlemind training as early interventions with soldiers returning from Iraq: Randomization by platoon. *Journal of Consulting and Clinical Psychology, 77,* 928–940.

Adolphs, R., Tranel, D., Damasio, H., & Damasio, A. (1994). Impaired recognition of emotion in facial expressions following bilateral damage to the human amygdala. *Nature, 372,* 669–672.

Aggleton, J.P. (1993). The contribution of the amygdala to normal and abnormal emotional states. *Trends in Neurosciences, 16,* 328–333.

Agnew, H.W., Jr., Webb, W.B., & Williams, R.L. (1967). Comparison of stage four and 1-REM sleep deprivation. *Perceptual and Motor Skills, 24,* 851–858.

Ahadi, S., & Diener, E. (1989). Multiple determinants and effect size. *Journal of Personality and Social Psychology, 56,* 398–406.

Ahammed, S., & Cherian, I. (2013). The future of humanistic psychology: Towards a self with expanded horizons. *The Humanistic Psychologist, 41*(4), 364–370.

Ahn, H.J. (2005). Child care teachers' strategies in children's socialization of emotion. *Early Child Development & Care, 175,* 49–61.

Ai, A.L., Peterson, C., & Ubelhor, D. (2002). War-related trauma and symptoms of posttraumatic stress disorder among adult Kosovar refugees. *Journal of Traumatic Stress, 15,* 157–160.

Aiello, R., & Sloboda, J.A. (1994). *Musical perceptions.* Oxford, UK: Oxford University Press.

Ainslie, G. (2001). *Breakdown of will.* New York, NY: Cambridge University Press.

Ainsworth, M.D. (1979). Attachment as related to mother-infant interaction. *Advances in the Study of Behavior, 9,* 1–51.

Ainsworth, M.D.S. (1967). *Infancy in Uganda: Infant care and the growth of love.* Baltimore, MD: Johns Hopkins University Press.

Ainsworth, M.D.S. (1989). Attachments beyond infancy. *American Psychologist, 44,* 709–716.

Ainsworth, M.D.S., Blehar, M.C., Waters, E., & Wall, S. (1978). *Patterns of attachment: A psychological study of the strange situation.* Hillsdale, NJ: Erlbaum.

Airey, D., & Sodhi, M. (2007). *Schizophrenia.* New York, NY: Chelsea House.

Aitken, S., & Bower, T.G. (1982). Intersensory substitution in the blind. *Journal of Experimental Child Psychology, 33,* 309–323.

Ajzen, I. (1991). The theory of planned behavior. *Organizational Behavior and Human Decision Processes, 50,* 179–211.

Ajzen, I. (2015). The theory of planned behaviour is alive and well, and not ready to retire: A commentary on sniehotta, presseau, and araújo-soares. *Health Psychology Review, 9*(2), 131–137.

Akerstedt, T. (1988). Sleepiness as a consequence of shift work. *Sleep, 11,* 17–34.

Akerstedt, T., Kecklund, G., & Hoerte, L.G. (2001). Night driving, season and the risk of highway accidents. *Sleep, 24,* 401–406.

Akimova, S., Lanzenberger, R., & Kasper, S. (2009). The serotonin-1A receptor in anxiety disorders. *Biological Psychology, 66,* 627–635.

Alam, N., Kumar, S., Rai, S., Methippara, M., Szymusiak, R., & McGinty, D. (2009). Role of adenosine Al receptor in the perifornical-lateral hypothalamic area in sleep-wake regulation in rats. *Brain Research, 1304,* 96–104.

Albee, G.W. (1996). Revolutions and counterrevolutions in prevention. *American Psychologist, 51,* 1130–1133.

Alcock, J. (2005). *Animal behavior: An evolutionary approach* (8th ed.). Sunderland, MA: Sinauer Associates.

Alcock, J.E. (2003). Give the null hypothesis a chance: Reasons to remain doubtful about the existence of psi. In J.E. Alcock, J.E. Burns, & A. Freeman (Eds.), *Psi wars: Getting to grips with the paranormal* (pp. 29–50). Charlottesville, VA: Imprint Academic.

Alcock, J.E. (2010). The parapsychologist's lament. In S. Krippner & H.L. Harris (Eds.), *The neurobiology of psychics, mediums, and other extraordinary people.* Santa Barbara, CA: Praeger/ABC-CLIO.

Aldwin, C.M. (2007). *Stress, coping, and development: An integrative perspective* (2nd ed.). New York, NY: Guilford Press.

Alexander, G.M., & Sherwin, B.B. (1993). Sex steroids, sexual behavior, and selection attention for erotic stimuli in women using oral contraceptives. *Psychoneuroendocrinology, 18,* 91–102.

Alexander, N. (1996). Barriers to sexually transmitted diseases. *Science and Medicine, 3*(2), 32–41.

Alfieri, T., Ruble, D.N., & Higgins, E.T. (1996). Gender stereotypes during adolescence: Developmental changes and the transition to junior high school. *Developmental Psychology, 32,* 1129–1137.

Alison, L.J., Smith, M.D., Eastman, O., & Rainbow, L. (2003). Toulmin's philosophy of argument and its relevance to offender profiling. *Psychology, Crime, and Law, 9,* 173–183.

Alitto, H.J., & Usrey, W.M. (2015). Surround suppression and temporal processing of visual signals. *Journal of Neurophysiology, 113,* 2605–2617.

Allen, J. (2010). *Cystic fibrosis.* New York: Taylor and Francis.

Allen, M. (1991). Meta-analysis comparing the persuasiveness of one-sided and two-sided messages. *Western Journal of Speech Communication, 55,* 390–404.

Allen, M. (2004). Reading achievement of students in French immersion programs. *Educational Quarterly Review, 9*(4), 25–30.

Allen, M., D'Alessio, D., & Brezgel, K. (1995). A meta-analysis summarizing the effects of pornography: II. Aggression after exposure. *Human Communication Research, 22,* 258–283.

Allmer, H. (2005). Physical activity and cognitive functioning in aging. *Journal of Public Health, 13*(4), 185–188.

Alloy, L.B., Abramson, L.Y., Walshaw, P.D., Gerstein, P.D., Keyser, J.D., Whitehouse, W.G., ... Harmon-Jones, E. (2009). Behavioral approach system (BAS)–relevant cognitive styles and bipolar spectrum disorders: Concurrent and prospective associations. *Journal of Abnormal Psychology, 118*, 459–471.

Allport, G.W. (1935). Attitudes. In C. Murchison (Ed.), *Handbook of social psychology*. Worcester, MA: Clark University Press.

Allport, G.W. (1937). *Personality: A psychological interpretation*. New York, NY: Holt, Rinehart & Winston.

Allport, G.W. (1954). *The nature of prejudice*. Cambridge, MA: Addison-Wesley.

Allport, G.W., & Odbert, H.S. (1936). Trait names: A psycho-lexical study. *Psychological Monographs, 47* (Whole No. 211).

Allport, G.W., & Postman, L.J. (1947). *The psychology of rumor*. New York, NY: Holt.

Alterovitz, S.S.R., & Mendelsohn, G.A. (2009). Partner preferences across the life span: Online dating by older adults. *Psychology and Aging, 24*, 513–517.

Altman, I., & Taylor, D.A. (1973). *Social penetration: The development of interpersonal relationships*. New York, NY: Holt, Rinehart & Winston.

Altman, J., & Bayer, S.A. (1996). *Development of the cerebellar system: In relation to its evolution, structure and functions*. Boca Raton, FL: CRC Press.

Alzheimer Society. (2010). *Rising Tide: The impact of dementia on Canadian society*. Retrieved November 21, 2013, from http://www.alzheimer.ca/~/media/Files/national/Advocacy/ASC_Rising_Tide_Full_Report_e.ashx.

Amato, P.R., & Afifi, T.D. (2006). Feeling caught between parents: Adult children's relations with parents and subjective well-being. *Journal of Marriage and Family, 68*, 222–235.

Ambady, N., & Skowronski, J.J. (Eds.). (2008). *First impressions*. New York, NY: Guilford Press.

American Cancer Society. (1997). *Smoking facts and figures*. New York, NY: Author.

American Psychiatric Association. (1990). *The practice of ECT: Recommendations for treatment, training, and privileging*. Washington, DC: American Psychiatric Press.

American Psychiatric Association. (1994). *Diagnostic and statistical manual of mental disorders* (4th ed.). Washington, DC: Author.

American Psychiatric Association. (2000). *The diagnostic and statistical manual of mental disorders, fourth edition, text revision (DSM-IV)*. Washington, DC: Author.

American Psychiatric Association. (2010). *Work group proposals for DSM-V disorders*. Retrieved February 18, 2010, http://www.DSM5.org.

American Psychiatric Association. (2013). *Diagnostic and statistical manual of mental disorders* (5th ed.). Arlington, VA: American Psychiatric Publishing.

American Psychological Association Committee on Animal Research and Ethics. (2005). 2005 annual report. Retrieved November 17, 2010, from http://www.apa.org/pubs/info/reports/index.aspx.

American Psychological Association Task Force on Psychological Intervention Guidelines. (1995). *Template for developing guidelines: Interventions for mental disorders and psychological aspects of physical disorders*. Washington, DC: American Psychological Association.

American Psychological Association. (2005). *New definition: Hypnosis*. Retrieved December 14, 2009, from http://www.apa.org/divisions/div30/define_hypnosis.html.

American Psychological Association. (2016). http://www.apa.org/topics/hypnosis/.

American Psychological Society. (2003). *History of APS*. Retrieved from http://www.psychologicalscience.org/about/history.html.

American Psychology Society. (2009). About APS. Retrieved November 22, 2010, from http://www.psychologicalscience.org/index.php/about.

Anand, B.K., & Brobeck, J.R. (1951). Hypothalamic control of food intake in rats and cats. *Yale Journal of Biology and Medicine, 24*, 123–140.

Anderson, C.A. (1999). Attributional style, depression, and loneliness: A cross-cultural comparison of American and Chinese students. *Personality and Social Psychology Bulletin, 25*, 482–499.

Anderson, C.A. (2001). Heat and violence. *Current Directions in Psychological Science, 10*, 33–38.

Anderson, C.A. (2012). Climate change and violence. In D.J. Christie (Ed.), *The Encyclopedia of Peace Psychology*. Hoboken, NJ: Wiley.

Anderson, C.A., & Bushman, B.J. (2001). Effects of violent video games on aggressive behavior, aggressive cognition, aggressive affect, physiological arousal, and pro-social behavior: A meta-analytic review of the scientific literature. *Psychological Science, 12*, 353–359.

Anderson, C.A., & Bushman, B.J. (2002). Human aggression. *Annual Review of Psychology, 15*, 503–514.

Anderson, C.A., Shibuya, A., Ihori, N., Swing, E.L., Bushman, B.J., Sakamoto, A., ... Saleem, M. (2010). Violent video game effects on aggression, empathy, and pro-social behavior in Eastern and Western countries: A meta-analytic review. *Psychological Bulletin, 136*, 151–173.

Anderson, E.M., & Lambert, M.J. (1995). Short-term dynamically oriented psychotherapy: A review and meta-analysis. *Clinical Psychology Review, 15*, 503–514.

Anderson, M.C., & Neely, J.H. (1996). Interference and inhibition in memory retrieval. In E.L. Bjork & R.A. Bjork (Eds.), *Memory. Handbook of perception and cognition* (2nd ed.). San Diego, CA: Academic Press.

Anderson, N.D., & Craik, F.I.M. (2000). Memory in the aging brain. In E. Tulving & F.I.M. Craik (Eds.), *The Oxford handbook of memory* (pp. 411–426). New York, NY: Oxford University Press.

Anderson, P.L., Price, M., Edwards, S.M., Obasaju, M.A., Schmertz, S.K., Zimand, E., & Calamaras, M.R. (2013). Virtual reality exposure therapy for social anxiety disorder: A randomized controlled trial. *Journal of Consulting and Clinical Psychology, 81*(5), 751–760.

Andreasen, N.C. (1988). Brain imaging: Applications in psychiatry. *Science, 239*, 1381–1388.

Andreason, N.C., Arndt, S., Swayze, V., Cizadlo, T., Flaum, M., O'Leary, D., ... Yuh, W.T. (1994). Thalamic abnormalities in schizophrenia visualized through magnetic resonance image averaging. *Science, 266*, 294–298.

Andrés, P. (2003). Frontal cortex as the central executive of working memory: Time to revise our view. *Cortex, 39*, 871–895.

Ankney, C.D. (1992). Sex differences in relative brain size: The mismeasure of women, too? *Intelligence, 16*, 329–336.

Antfolk, C., Bjorkman, A., Frank, S., Sebelius, F., Lundborg, G., & Rosen, B. (July 2012). Sensory feedback from a prosthetic hand based on air-mediated pressure from the hand to the forearm skin. *Journal of Rehabilitation Medicine, 44*(8), 702–707.

Anthony, J.C. (2006). The epidemiology of cannabis dependence. In R.A. Roffman & R.S. Stephens (Eds.), *Cannabis dependence: Its nature, consequences and treatment* (pp. 58–104). Cambridge, UK: Cambridge University Press.

Antony, M.M., & Swinson, R.P. (2000). Specific phobia. In M.M. Antony & R.P. Swinson (Eds.), *Phobic disorders and panic in adults: A guide to assessment and treatment* (pp. 79–104). Washington, DC: American Psychological Association.

Antrobus, J. (1991). Dreaming: Cognitive processes during cortical activation and high afferent thresholds. *Psychological Review, 98*, 96–121.

APA Monitor. (1997, December). *Author, 28*(12).

Arbuckle, T.Y., Gold, D.P., Andres, D., Schwartzman, A., & Chaikelson, J. (1992). The role of psychosocial context, age, and intelligence in memory performance of older men. *Psychology and Aging, 7*, 25–36.

Archer, J. (2006). Testosterone and human aggression: An evaluation of the challenge hypothesis. *Neuroscience and Biobehavioral Reviews, 30*, 319–345.

Arendt, J. (2005). Melatonin: Characteristics, concerns, and prospects. *Journal of Biological Rhythms, 20*, 291–303.

Arendt, J. (2009). Managing jet lag: Some of the problems and possible new solutions. *Sleep Medicine Reviews, 13*, 249–256.

Arendt, J., Skene, D.J., Middleton, B., Lockley, S.W., & Deacon, S. (1997). Efficacy of melatonin treatment in jet lag, shift work, and blindness. *Journal of Biological Rhythms, 12*, 604–617.

Armitage, C.J. (2005). Can the theory of planned behavior predict the maintenance of physical activity? *Health Psychology, 24*(3), 235–245.

Arnett, J.J. (1999). Adolescent storm and stress, reconsidered. *American Psychologist, 54*, 317–326.

Arnett, J.J. (2001). Conceptions of the transition to adulthood: Perspectives from adolescence through midlife. *Journal of Adult Development, 8*, 133–143.

Arnett, P.A. (1997). Autonomic responsivity in psychopaths: A critical review and theoretical proposal. *Clinical Psychology Review, 17*, 903–936.

Aron, A., & Westbay, L. (1996). Dimensions of the prototype of love. *Journal of Personality and Social Psychology, 70*, 535–551.

Aronson, E., & Patnoe, S. (1997). *The jigsaw classroom: Building cooperation in the classroom* (2nd ed.). New York, NY: Longman.

Aronson, E., Turner, J.A., & Carlsmith, J.M. (1963). Communicator credibility and communication discrepancy as determinants of opinion change. *Journal of Abnormal and Social Psychology, 67*, 31–36.

Aronson, J., Lustina, M.J., Good, C., Keough, K., Steele, C.M., & Brown, J. (1999). When white men can't do math: Necessary and sufficient factors in stereotype threat. *Journal of Experimental Social Psychology, 35*, 29–46.

Arrigo, J.M., & Pezdek, K. (1997). Lessons from the study of psychogenic amnesia. *Current Directions in Psychological Science, 6*, 148–152.

Arundale, R.B. (2005). Pragmatics, conversational implicature, and conversation. In K.L. Fitch & R.E. Sanders (Eds.), *Handbook of language and social interaction* (pp. 41–63). Mahwah, NJ: Erlbaum.

Asch, S.E. (1946). Forming impressions of personality. *Journal of Abnormal and Social Psychology, 41*, 258–290.

Asch, S.E. (1951). Effects of group pressure upon the modification and distortion of judgment. In H. Guetzkow (Ed.), *Groups, leadership, and men.* Pittsburgh, PA: Carnegie Press.

Asch, S.E. (1956). Studies of independence and conformity: A minority of one against a unanimous majority. *Psychological Monographs, 70* (Whole No. 416).

Aschemann-Witzel, J., & Niebuhr Aagaard, E.M. (2014). Elaborating on the attitude–behaviour gap regarding organic products: Young danish consumers and in-store food choice. *International Journal of Consumer Studies, 38*(5), 550–558.

Aserinsky, E., & Kleitman, N. (1953). Regularly occurring periods of ocular motility and concomitant phenomena during sleep. *Science, 118,* 361–375.

Asimov, I. (1997). *Isaac Asimov's book of facts.* New York, NY: Random House/Wings Books.

Askew, C., Hagel, A., & Morgan, J. (2015). Vicarious learning of children's social-anxiety-related fear beliefs and emotional Stroop bias. *Emotion, 15*(4), 501–510.

Assanand, S.P., Pinel, J.P., & Lehman, D.R. (1998). Teaching theories of hunger and eating: Overcoming students' misconceptions. *Teaching of Psychology, 25,* 44–46.

Associated Press. (1997, December 12).

Astington, J.W., & Gopnik, A. (1991). Theoretical explanations of children's understanding of the mind. *British Journal of Developmental Psychology, 9,* 7–31.

Atchison, M., & McFarlane, A.C. (1994). A review of dissociation and dissociative disorders. *The Australian and New Zealand Journal of Psychiatry, 28*(4), 591–599.

Athens, E.S., Vollmer, T.R., & Pipkin, C.C.S.P. (2007). Shaping academic task engagement with percentile schedules. *Journal of Applied Behavior Analysis, 40,* 475–488.

Atkinson, J.W. (Ed.). (1958). *Motives in fantasy, action, and society.* Princeton, NJ: Van Nostrand.

Atkinson, J.W. (1964). *An introduction to motivation.* Princeton, NJ: Van Nostrand.

Atkinson, R.C., & Shiffrin, R.M. (1968). Human memory: A proposed system and its control processes. In K.W. Spence & J.T. Spence (Eds.), *Advances in the psychology of learning and motivation: Research and theory* (Vol. 2). New York, NY: Academic Press.

Atmaca, M., Baykara, S., Mermi, O., Yildirim, H., & Akaslan, U. (2016). Pituitary volumes are changed in patients with conversion disorder. *Brain Imaging and Behavior, 10*(1), 92–95.

Audero, E., Mlinar, B., Baccini, G., Skachokova, Z.K., Corradetti, R., & Gross, C. (2013). Suppression of serotonin neuron firing increases aggression in mice. *The Journal of Neuroscience, 33*(20), 8678–8688.

Auerbach, S.M. (1989). Stress management and coping research in the health care setting: An overview and methodological commentary. *Journal of Consulting and Clinical Psychology, 57,* 388–395.

Averill, J.A. (1980). A constructivist view of emotion. In R. Plutchik & H. Kellerman (Eds.), *Emotion: Theory, research and experience* (Vol. 1, pp. 305–339). New York, NY: Academic Press.

Avila-White, D., Schneider, A., & Domhoff, G.W. (1999). The most recent dreams of 12–13-year-old boys and girls: A methodological contribution to the study of dream content in teenagers. *Dreaming: Journal of the Association for the Study of Dreams, 9,* 163–171.

Ayllon, T., & Azrin, N.H. (1965). The measurement and reinforcement of behavior of psychotics. *Journal of the Experimental Analysis of Behavior, 8,* 357–383.

Ayllon, T., & Azrin, N.H. (1968). *The token economy: A motivational system for therapy and rehabilitation.* New York, NY: Appleton-Century-Crofts.

Azeredo, C.M., Rinaldi, A.E.M., de Moraes, C.L., Levy, R.B., & Menezes, P.R. (2015). School bullying: A systematic review of contextual-level risk factors in observational studies. *Aggression and Violent Behavior, 22,* 65–76.

Baars, B.J. (2007). The global workspace theory of consciousness. In M. Velmans & S. Schneider (Eds.), *The Blackwell companion to consciousness.* Malden, MA: Blackwell.

Babichev, A., Cheng, S., & Dabaghian, Y.A. (2016). Topological schemas of cognitive maps and spatial learning. *Frontiers in Computational Neuroscience, 10,* 18–35.

Bach-y-Rita, P. (2004). Tactile sensory substitution studies. In M.C. Roco & C.D. Montemagno (Eds.), *The co-evolution of human potential and converging technologies* (pp. 83–91). New York, NY: New York Academy of Sciences.

Back, M.D., Schmukle, S.C., & Egloff, B. (2008). Becoming friends by chance. *Psychological Science, 19,* 439–440.

Backhaus, W.G., Kliegl, R., & Werner, J.S. (Eds.). (1998). *Color vision: Perspectives from different disciplines.* New York, NY: Walter De Gruyter.

Baddeley, A. (1998). Recent developments in working memory. *Current Opinion in Neurobiology, 8,* 234–238.

Baddeley, A. (2003). Working memory: Looking back and looking forward. *Nature Reviews Neuroscience, 4*(10), 829–839.

Baddeley, A. (2007). *Working memory, thought, and action.* London, UK: Oxford University Press.

Baddeley, A. (2010). Long-term and working memory: How do they interact? In L. Bäckman & L. Nyberg (Eds.), *Memory, aging and the brain: A Festschrift in honour of Lars-Göran Nilsson* (pp. 18–30). New York, NY: Psychology Press.

Baddeley, A.D. (1966). Short-term memory for word sequences as a function of acoustic, semantic, and formal similarity. *Quarterly Journal of Experimental Psychology, 18,* 362–365.

Baddeley, A.D. (1990). *Human memory: Theory and practice.* Boston, MA: Allyn & Bacon.

Baert, A., Hartvig, N.V., Stokilde-Jorgensen, H., & Mammen, J. (1999). Methodological advances. *Magnetic Resonance Materials in Physics, Biology and Medicine, 8* (Suppl.), 98–99.

Baeyens, F., Wrzesniewski, A., De Houwer, J., & Eelen, P. (1996). Toilet rooms, body massages, and smells: Two field studies on human evaluative odor conditioning. *Current Psychology: Developmental, Learning, Personality, & Social, 15,* 77–96.

Bagge, C., Nickell, A., Stepp, S., Durrett, C., Jackson, K., & Trull, T.J. (2004). Borderline personality disorder features predict negative outcomes 2 years later. *Journal of Abnormal Psychology, 113,* 279–288.

Bagley, C., & Ramsay, R. (1997). *Suicidal behaviour in adolescents and adults: Research, taxonomy and prevention.* Ashgate, UK: Ashgate.

Bagot, R.C., van Hasselt, F.N., Champagne, D.L., Meaney, M.J., Krugers, H.J., & Joels, M. (2009). Maternal care determines rapid effects of stress mediators on synaptic plasticity in adult rat hippocampal dentate gyrus. *Neurobiology of Learning and Memory, 92,* 292–300.

Bahrick, H.P. (1984). Semantic memory content in permastore: Fifty years of memory for Spanish learned in school. *Journal of Experimental Psychology: General, 113,* 1–29.

Bahrick, H.P., Bahrick, P.O., & Wittlinger, R.P. (1975). Fifty years of memory for names and faces: A cross-sectional approach. *Journal of Experimental Psychology: General, 104,* 54–75.

Bahrick, H.P., Hall, L.K., & Berger, S.A. (1996). Accuracy and distortion in memory for high school grades. *Psychological Science, 7,* 265–271.

Bailey, J.M., & Pillard, R.C. (1991). A genetic study of male sexual orientation. *Archives of General Psychiatry, 48,* 1089–1096.

Bailey, J.M., Pillard, R.C., Neale, M.C., & Agyei, Y. (1993). Heritable factors influence sexual orientation in women. *Archives of General Psychiatry, 50,* 217–223.

Baillargeon, R. (1987). Object permanence in 3 1/2- and 4 1/2-month-old infants. *Developmental Psychology, 23,* 655–664.

Baker, E., Baibazarova, E., Ktistaki, G., Shelton, K.H., & Van Goozen, S.H.M. (2012). Development of fear and guilt in young children: Stability over time and relations with psychopathology. *Development and Psychopathology, 24,* 833–845.

Baker, L.H., Cooney, N.L., & Pomerleau, O.F. (1987). Craving for alcohol: Theoretical processes and treatment procedures. In W.M. Cox (Ed.), *Treatment and prevention of alcohol problems: A resource manual* (pp. 184–204). New York, NY: Academic Press.

Baker, T.B., McFall, R.M., & Shoham, V. (2009). Current status and future prospects of clinical psychology: Toward a scientifically principled approach to mental and behavioral health care. *Psychological Science in the Public Interest, 9,* 67–103.

Baldwin, E. (1993). The case for animal research in psychology. *Journal of Social Issues, 49,* 121–131.

Baldwin, S.A., Berkeljon, A., Atkins, D.C., Olsen, J.A., & Nielsen, S.L. (2009). Rates of change in naturalistic psychotherapy: Contrasting dose-effect and good-enough level models of change. *Journal of Consulting and Clinical Psychology, 77,* 203–211.

Ballard, C. (2010). *Understanding the senses.* New York, NY: Rosen Central.

Ballenger, J.C. (2000). Panic disorder and agoraphobia. In G. Fink (Ed.), *Encyclopedia of stress* (Vol. 3). San Diego, CA: Academic Press.

Baltes, P., & Staudinger, U.M. (2000). Wisdom: A meta-heuristic (pragmatic) to orchestrate mind and virtue toward excellence. *American Psychologist, 55,* 122–136.

Baltes, P.B., & Kunzmann, U. (2004). The two faces of wisdom: Wisdom as a general theory of knowledge and judgment about excellence in mind and virtue vs. wisdom as everyday realization in people and products. *Human Development, 47,* 290–299.

Bandura, A. (1965). Influence of models' reinforcement contingencies on the acquisition of imitative responses. *Journal of Personality and Social Psychology, 1,* 589–595.

Bandura, A. (1969). *Principles of behavior modification.* New York, NY: Holt, Rinehart & Winston.

Bandura, A. (1973). *Aggression: A social learning analysis.* Englewood Cliffs, NJ: Prentice Hall.

Bandura, A. (1977). *Social learning theory.* Englewood Cliffs, NJ: Prentice Hall.

Bandura, A. (1978). The self system in reciprocal determinism. *American Psychologist, 33,* 344–358.

Bandura, A. (1986). *Social foundations of thought and action: A social-cognitive theory.* Englewood Cliffs, NJ: Prentice Hall.

Bandura, A. (1988). Mechanisms of moral disengagement in terrorism. In W. Reich (Ed.), *The psychology of terrorism: Behaviors, worldviews, states of mind.* New York, NY: Cambridge University Press.

Bandura, A. (1989). Social cognitive theory. *Annals of Child Development, 6,* 3–58.

Bandura, A. (1991). Human agency: The rhetoric and the reality. *American Psychologist, 46,* 157–162.

Bandura, A. (1997). *Self-efficacy: The exercise of control.* New York, NY: W.H. Freeman.

Bandura, A. (1999a). Cognitive social learning theory of personality. In D. Cervone & Y. Shoda (Eds.), *The coherence of personality* (pp. 185–241). New York, NY: Guilford Press.

Bandura, A. (1999b). Social cognitive theory: An agentic perspective. *Asian Journal of Social Psychology, 2,* 21–41.

Bandura, A. (2000a). Health promotion from the perspective of social cognitive theory. In P. Norman, C. Abraham, & M. Conner (Eds.), *Understanding and changing health and behaviour.* Reading, UK: Harwood.

Bandura, A. (2000b). Self-efficacy: The foundation of agency. In W.J. Perrig & A. Grob (Eds.), *Control of human behavior, mental processes, and consciousness: Essays in honor of the 60th birthday of August Flammer.* Mahwah, NJ: Lawrence Erlbaum Associates.

Bandura, A. (2001). Social cognitive theory: An agentic perspective. *Annual Review of Psychology, 52,* 1–26.

Bandura, A. (2002). Environmental sustainability by sociocognitive deceleration of population growth. In P. Schmuck & W.P. Schultz (Eds.), *Psychology of sustainable development* (pp. 208–238). Dordrecht, Netherlands: Kluwer.

Bandura, A. (2006). *Applied psychology: New frontiers and rewarding careers* (pp. 53–79). Mahwah, NJ: Lawrence Erlbaum Associates Publishers.

Bandura, A., & Cervone, D. (1983). Self-evaluative and self-efficacy mechanisms governing the motivational effects of goal systems. *Journal of Personality and Social Psychology, 45,* 1017–1028.

Bandura, A., & Kupers, C.J. (1964). Transmission of patterns of self-reinforcement through modeling. *Journal of Abnormal and Social Psychology, 69,* 1–9.

Bandura, A., & Mischel, W. (1965). Modification of self-imposed delay of reward through exposure to live and symbolic models. *Journal of Personality and Social Psychology, 2,* 698–705.

Bannerman, R.L., Milders, M., de Gelder, B.D., & Sahraie, A. (2009). Orienting to threat: Faster localization of fearful facial expressions and body postures revealed by saccadic eye movements. *Proceedings in Biological Science, 276,* 1635–1641.

Barac, R., & Blalystock, E. (2012). Bilingual effects on cognitive and linguistic development: Role of language, cultural background, and education. *Child Development, 83*(2), 413–422.

Barber, J. (1977). Rapid induction analgesia: A clinical report. *American Journal of Clinical Hypnosis, 19,* 138–143.

Barber, J.P., & Sharpless, B.A. (2015). On the future of psychodynamic therapy research. *Psychotherapy Research, 25*(3), 309–320.

Barefoot, J.C., Dodge, K.A., Peterson, B.L., Dahlstrom, W.G., & Williams, R.B. (1989). The Cook-Medley Hostility Scale: Item content and ability to predict survival. *Psychosomatic Medicine, 51,* 46–57.

Bargh, J.A., & Chartrand, T.L. (1999). The unbearable automaticity of being. *American Psychologist, 54,* 462–479.

Bargh, J.A., & Morsella, E. (2010). Unconscious behavioral guidance systems. In C.R. Agnew, D.E. Carlston, W.G. Graziano, & J.R. Kelly (Eds.), *Then a miracle occurs: Focusing on behavior in social psychological theory and research* (pp. 89–118). New York, NY: Oxford University Press.

Bar-Haim, Y., Lamy, D., Pergamin, L., Bakermans-Kranenburg, M., & van Ijzendoorn, M.H. (2007). Threat-related attentional bias in anxious and non-anxious individuals: A meta-analytic study. *Psychological Bulletin, 133,* 1–24.

Barkow, J.H. (1992). Beneath new culture is old psychology: Gossip and social stratification. In J.H. Barkow, L. Cosmides, & J. Tooby (Eds.), *The adapted mind: Evolutionary psychology and the generation of culture.* London, UK: Oxford University Press.

Barlow, D.H. (1997). Cognitive-behavioral therapy for panic disorder: Current status. *Journal of Clinical Psychiatry, 58* (Suppl. 2), 32–36.

Barlow, D.H. (2002). *Anxiety and its disorders.* New York, NY: Guilford Press.

Barnes, G.E., & Prosen, H. (1985). Parental death and depression. *Journal of Abnormal Psychology, 94,* 64–69.

Barnes, T.R. (Ed.). (1994). *Antipsychotic drugs and their side effects.* San Diego, CA: Academic Press.

Barnett, J.E., & Porter, J.E. (1998). The suicidal patient: Clinical and risk management strategies. In L. VandeCreek & S. Knapp (Eds.), *Innovations in clinical practice: A source book* (Vol. 16). Sarasota, FL: Professional Resource Press.

Barnett, W.S., & Camilli, G. (2002). Compensatory preschool education, cognitive development, and "race." In J. Fish (Ed.), *Race and intelligence: Separating science from myth* (pp. 369–406). Mahwah, NJ: Erlbaum.

Baron, P., & Hanna, J. (1990). Egocentrism and depressive symptomatology in young adults. *Social Behavior and Personality, 18,* 279–285.

Baron, R.S., Cutrona, C.E., Hicklin, D., Russell, D.W., & Lubaroff, D.M. (1990). Social support and immune responses among spouses of cancer patients. *Journal of Personality and Social Psychology, 59,* 344–352.

Baron, R.S., Vandello, J.A., & Brunsman, B. (1996). The forgotten variable in conformity research: Impact of task importance on social influence. *Journal of Personality and Social Psychology, 71,* 915–927.

Barondes, S.H. (1999). *Mood genes: Hunting for origins of mania and depression.* New York, NY: Oxford University Press.

Barrera, D., & Simpson, B. (2012). Much ado about deception: Consequences of deceiving research participants in the social sciences. *Sociological Methods & Research, 41,* 383–413.

Barrett, G.V., & Depinet, R.L. (1991). A reconsideration of testing for competence rather than intelligence. *American Psychologist, 46,* 1012–1024.

Barrett, P.T., & Eysenck, H.J. (1992). Brain evoked potentials and intelligence: The Hendrickson paradigm. *Intelligence, 16,* 361–381.

Barrow, C.J. (2003). *Environmental change and human development: The place of environmental change in human evolution.* New York, NY: Oxford University Press.

Barsalou, L.W. (1992). *Cognitive psychology: An overview for cognitive scientists.* Hillsdale, NJ: Erlbaum.

Barsky, A.J. (1992). Amplification, somatization, and the somatoform disorders. *Psychosomatics, 33,* 28–34.

Bartholomew, D.J. (2004). *Measuring intelligence: Facts and fallacies.* New York, NY: Cambridge University Press.

Bartlett, D.J., Marshall, N.S., Williams, A., & Grunstein, R.R. (2008). Predictors of primary medical care consultation for sleep disorders. *Sleep Medicine, 9,* 857–864.

Bartlett, F.C. (1932). *Remembering: A study in experimental and social psychology.* New York, NY: Cambridge University Press.

Barton, J.J., Press, D.Z., Keenan, J.P., & O'Connor, M. (2002). Lesions of the fusiform face area impair perception of facial configuration in prosopagnosia. *Neurology, 58*(1), 71–78.

Bartoshuk, L.M., & Beauchamp, G.K. (1994). Chemical senses. *Annual Review of Psychology, 45,* 419–449.

Bassett, A.M., & Baker, C. (2015). Normal or abnormal? 'Normative uncertainty' in psychiatric practice. *Journal of Medical Humanities, 36*(2), 89–111.

Batson, C.D. (2006). "Not all self-interest after all": Economics of empathy-induced altruism. In D. De Cremer, D.M. Zeelenberg, & J.K. Murnighan (Eds.), *Social psychology and economics* (pp. 281–299). Mahwah, NJ: Erlbaum.

Batson, C.D., Ahmad, N., Lishner, D.A., & Tsang, J.A. (2002). Empathy and altruism. In C.R. Snyder & S.J. Lopez (Eds.), *Handbook of positive psychology* (pp. 485–498). London, UK: Oxford University Press.

Batson, C.D., Duncan, B.D., Ackerman, P., Buckley, T., & Birch, K. (1981). Is empathic emotion a source of altruistic motivation? *Journal of Personality and Social Psychology, 40,* 290–302.

Batson, C.D., Sager, K., Garst, E., & Kang, M. (1997). Is empathy-induced helping due to self-other merging? *Journal of Personality and Social Psychology, 73,* 495–509.

Battista, S.R., Stewart, S.H., Fulton, H.G., Steeves, D., Darredeau, C., & Gavric, D. (2008). A further investigation of the relations of anxiety sensitivity to smoking motives. *Addictive Behaviors, 33,* 1402–1408.

Bauer, K.E., & McCanne, T.R. (1980). Autonomic and central nervous system responding during hypnosis and simulation of hypnosis. *International Journal of Clinical and Experimental Hypnosis, 28,* 148–163.

Baum, A., & Posluszny, D.M. (1999). Health psychology: Mapping bio-behavioral contributions to health and illness. *Annual Review of Psychology, 50,* 137–164.

Baum, A., Krantz, D.S., & Gatchel, R.J. (1997). *An introduction to health psychology* (3rd ed.). Boston, MA: McGraw-Hill.

Baumeister, R.F. (1999). Self-concept, self-esteem and identity. In V.J. Derlega, B.A. Winstead, & W.H. Jones (Eds.), *Personality: Contemporary theory and research* (2nd ed.). Chicago, IL: Nelson-Hall Publishers.

Baumeister, R.F., & Leary, M.R. (1995). The need to belong: Desire for interpersonal attachments as a fundamental human motivation. *Psychological Bulletin, 117,* 497–529.

Baumeister, R.F., & Tice, D.M. (1990). Anxiety and social exclusion. *Journal of Social and Clinical Psychology, 9,* 165–195.

Baumeister, R.F., Smart, L., & Boden, J.M. (1996). Relation of threatened egotism to violence and aggression: The dark side of high self-esteem. *Psychological Review, 103*, 5–33.

Baumrind, D. (1964). Some thoughts on ethics of research: After reading Milgram's behavioral study of obedience. *American Psychologist, 19*, 421–423.

Baumrind, D. (1967). Child care practices anteceding three patterns of preschool behavior. *Genetic Psychology Monographs, 75*, 43–88.

Baumrind, D. (1991). Parenting styles and adolescent development. In J. Brooks-Gunn, R. Lerner, & A.C. Petersen (Eds.), *The encyclopedia of adolescence* (pp. 746–758). New York, NY: Garland.

Bauserman, R. (1996). Sexual aggression and pornography: A review of correlational research. *Basic and Applied Social Psychology, 18*, 405–427.

Baxter, L.R., Schwartz, J.M., Mazziota, J.C., Phelps, M.E., Pahlm J.J., & Guze, B.H.(1988). Cerebral glucose metabolic rates in non-depressed patients with obsessive-compulsive disorder. *American Journal of Psychiatry, 145*(12), 1560–1563.

Bazzett, T.J. (2008). *An introduction to behavior genetics.* Sunderland, MA: Sinauer Associates.

Beahrs, J.O. (1994). Dissociative identity disorder: Adaptive deception of self and others. *Bulletin of the American Academy of Psychiatric Law, 22*, 223–237.

Beaman, A.L., Barnes, P.J., Klentz, B., & McQuirk, B. (1978). Increasing helping rates through information dissemination: Teaching pays. *Personality and Social Psychology Bulletin, 4*, 406–411.

Beatty, M.J., Heisel, A.D., Hall, A.E., Levine, T.R., & La France, B.H. (2002). What can we learn from the study of twins about genetic and environmental influences on interpersonal affiliation, aggressiveness, and social anxiety? A meta-analytic study. *Communication Monographs, 69*, 1–18.

Beauchamp, G.K., & Bartoshuk, L. (Eds.). (1997). *Tasting and smelling* (2nd ed.). Philadelphia, PA: Academic Press.

Bechara, A., Damasio, A.R., Damasio, H., & Anderson, S.W. (1994). Insensitivity to future consequences following damage to human prefrontal cortex. *Cognition, 50*, 7–15.

Beck, A.T. (1976). *Cognitive therapy and the emotional disorders.* New York, NY: International Universities Press.

Beck, A.T. (1991). Cognitive therapy: A 30-year retrospective. *American Psychologist, 46*, 368–375.

Beck, A.T. (2002). *Cognitive therapy and the emotional disorders.* New York, NY: International Universities Press.

Beck, A.T., Rush, A.J., Shaw, B.F., & Emery, G. (1979). *Cognitive therapy of depression.* New York, NY: Guilford Press.

Becker, A.E., Grinspoon, S.K., Klibanski, A., & Herzog, D.B. (1999). Current concepts: Eating disorders. *New England Journal of Medicine, 340*, 1092–1098.

Becker, J. (2004). Reconsidering the role of overcoming perturbations in cognitive development: Constructivism and consciousness. *Human Development, 47*, 77–93.

Bedny, M., Richardson, H., & Saxe, R. (2015). "Visual" cortex responds to spoken language in blind children. *The Journal of Neuroscience, 35*(33), 11674–11681.

Bedont, J.L., & Blackshaw, S. (2015). Constructing the suprachiasmatic nucleus: A watchmaker's

perspective on the central clockworks. *Frontiers in Systems Neuroscience, 9.* Retrieved from http://search.proquest.com/docview/1710262577?accountid=15115.

Beeney, J.E., Wright, A.G.C., Stepp, S.D., Hallquist, M.N., Lazarus, S.A., Beeney, J.R.S., ... Pilkonis, P.A. (2016). Disorganized attachment and personality functioning in adults: A latent class analysis. *Personality Disorders: Theory, Research, and Treatment,* doi: http://dx.doi.org/10.1037/per0000184.

Beidel, D.C., & Stipelman, B. (2007). Anxiety disorders. In M. Hersen, S.M. Turner, & D.C. Beidel (Eds.), *Adult psychopathology and diagnosis* (pp. 349–409). Hoboken, NJ: Wiley.

Beidel, D.C., & Turner, S.M. (2007). *Shy children, phobic adults: Nature and treatment of social anxiety disorders.* Washington, DC: American Psychological Association.

Beilcock, S.L., & Carr, T.H. (2001). On the fragility of skilled performance: What governs choking under pressure? *Journal of Experimental Psychology: General, 130*, 701–725.

Bekesy, G. (1957). The ear. *Scientific American, 230*, 66–78.

Belbin, O., Beaumont, H., Warden, D., Smith, A.D., Kalsheker, N., & Morgan, K. (2009). PSEN polymorphisms alter the rate of cognitive decline in sporadic Alzheimer's disease patients. *Neurobiology of Aging, 30*, 1992–1999.

Belchior, P., Marsiske, M., Sisco, S.M., Yam, A., Bavelier, D., Ball, K., & Mann, W.C. (2013). Video game training to improve selective visual attention in older adults. *Computers in Human Behavior, 29*(4), 1318–1324.

Belke, T.W., & Pierce, W.D. (2009). Body weight manipulation, reinforcement value and choice between sucrose and wheel running: A behavioral economic analysis. *Behavioural Processes, 80*, 147–156.

Bell, A.P., Weinberg, M.S., & Hammersmith, S.K. (1981). *Sexual preference: Its development in men and women.* Bloomington, IN: Indiana University Press.

Bell, E., Schermer, J.A., & Vernon, P.A. (2009). The origins of political attitudes and behaviours: An analysis using twins. *Canadian Journal of Political Science, 42*, 855–879.

Bell, J.H., & Bromnick, R.D. (2003). The social reality of the imaginary audience: A ground theory approach. *Adolescence, 38*, 205–219.

Belloc, N.B. (1973). Relationship of health practices and mortality. *Preventive Medicine, 2*, 67–81.

Bem, D.J. (1972). Self-perception theory. In L. Berkowitz (Ed.), *Advances in experimental social psychology* (Vol. 6, pp. 1–62). New York, NY: Academic Press.

Bem, D.J. (1996). Exotic becomes erotic: A developmental theory of sexual orientation. *Psychological Review, 103*, 320–335.

Bem, D.J. (2011). Feeling the future: Experimental evidence for anomalous retroactive influences on cognition and affect. *Journal of Personality and Social Psychology, 100*(3), 407–425.

Bem, D.J., & Honorton, C. (1994). Does psi exist? Replicable evidence for an anomalous process of information transfer. *Psychological Bulletin, 115*, 4–18.

Bem, S.L. (1981). Gender schema theory: A cognitive account of sex typing. *Psychological Review, 88*, 354–364.

Benedito-Silva, A.A., Menna-Barreto, I.S., Cipolla-Neto, J., Marques, N., & Tenreiro, S. (1989). A self-evaluation questionnaire for the

determination of morningness-eveningness types in Brazil. *Chronobiologia, 16*, 311.

Benes, F.M. (2009). Neural circuitry models of schizophrenia: Is it dopamine, GABA, glutamate, or something else? *Biological Psychiatry, 65*, 1003–1005.

Benes, F.M. (2010). Relationship of GAD regulation to cell cycle and DNA repair in GABA neurons in the adult hippocampus. *Cell Cycle, 9*(4), 625–627.

Bengtson, V.L. (2001). Beyond the nuclear family: The increasing importance of multigenerational bonds. *Journal of Marriage and the Family, 63*, 1–16.

Benjamin, A.S., & Craik, F. (2001). Parallel effects of aging and time pressure on memory for source: Evidence from the spacing effect. *Memory & Cognition, 29*, 691–697.

Benjamin, L.S. (2003). *Interpersonal reconstructive therapy: Promoting change in nonresponders.* New York, NY: Guilford Press.

Benjamin, L.T., Cavell, T.A., & Shallenberger, W.R. (1984). Staying with initial answers on objective tests: Is it a myth? *Teaching of Psychology, 11*, 133–141.

Bennett, D.S., Marini, V.A., Berzenski, S.R., Carmody, D.P., & Lewis, M. (2013). Externalizing problems in late childhood as a function of prenatal cocaine exposure and environmental risk. *Journal of Pediatric Psychology, 38*, 296–308.

Bennett, H.L. (1983). Remembering drink orders: The memory skills of cocktail waitresses. *Human Learning, 2*, 157–169.

Bennett, J.E., & Sekaquaptewa, D. (2014). Setting an egalitarian social norm in the classroom: Improving attitudes towards diversity among male engineering students. *Social Psychology of Education, 17*(2), 343–355.

Bennett, N.G., Blanc, A.K., & Bloom, D.E. (1988). Commitment and the modern union: Assessing the link between premarital cohabitation and subsequent marital stability. *American Sociological Review, 53*, 127–138.

Benoit, D., & Parker, K.C.H. (1994). Stability and transmission of attachment across three generations. *Child Development, 65*, 1444–1456.

Benski, C., & Scientists from CRSSA. (1998). Testing new claims of dermo-optical perception. *Skeptical Inquirer, 22*(1), 21–26.

Benson, N., Hulac, D.M., & Bernstein, J.D. (2013). An independent confirmatory factor analysis of the wechsler intelligence scale for Children—Fourth edition (WISC-IV) integrated: What do the process approach subtests measure? *Psychological Assessment, 25*(3), 692–705.

Ben-Zur, H. (2009). Coping styles and affect. *International Journal of Stress Management, 16*, 87–101.

Berg, C.A. (2000). Intellectual development in adulthood. In R.J. Sternberg (Ed.), *Handbook of intelligence* (pp. 117–140). New York, NY: Cambridge University Press.

Berg, K.M., & Boswell, A.E. (1998). Infants' detection of increments in low- and high-frequency noise. *Perception and Psychophysics, 60*, 1044–1051.

Berger, C.C., & Henrik Ehrsson, H. (2014). The fusion of mental imagery and sensation in the temporal association cortex. *The Journal of Neuroscience, 34*(41), 13684–13692.

Berger, M., Vollmann, J., Hohagen, F., Koenig, A., Lohner, H., Voderholzer, U., & Riemann, D. (1997). Sleep deprivation combined with consecutive sleep phase advance as a fast-acting therapy in depression: An open pilot trial in medicated and unmedicated patients. *American Journal of Psychiatry, 154*, 870–872.

Berger, R.J., & Phillips, N.H. (1995). Energy conservation and sleep. *Behavioural Brain Research, 69*, 65–73.

Berkowitz, L. (1990). On the formation and regulation of anger and aggression. *American Psychologist, 45*, 494–503.

Berkowitz, L., & LePage, A. (1967). Weapons as aggression-eliciting stimuli. *Journal of Personality and Social Psychology, 7*, 202–207.

Berman, S., Ozkaragoz, T., Young, R.M., & Noble, E.P. (2002). D2 dopamine receptor gene polymorphism discriminates two kinds of novelty seeking. *Personality and Individual Differences, 33*, 867–882.

Bernstein, S.E., & Carr, T.H. (1996). Dual-route theories of pronouncing printed words: What can be learned from concurrent task performance? *Journal of Experimental Psychology: Learning, Memory, and Cognition, 22*(1), 86–111.

Berry, J.W., Poortinga, Y.H., Segall, M.H., & Dasen, P. (2002). *Cross-cultural psychology: Research and applications* (2nd ed.). New York, NY: Cambridge University Press.

Berscheid, E. (1984). *The problem of emotion in close relationships.* New York, NY: Plenum Press.

Berthoud, H.R. (2002). Multiple neural systems controlling food intake and body weight. *Neuroscience and Biobehavioral Reviews, 26*, 393–428.

Betancourt, H., & Blair, I. (1992). A cognition (attribution)-emotion model of violence in conflict situations. *Personality and Social Psychology Bulletin, 18*, 343–350.

Beucke, J.C., Sepulcre, J., Talukdar, T., Linnman, C., Zschenderlein, K., Endrass, T., ... Kathmann, N. (2013). Abnormally high degree connectivity of the orbitofrontal cortex in obsessive-compulsive disorder. *JAMA Psychiatry, 70*(6), 619–629.

Beutler, L.E. (2002). The dodo bird is extinct. *Clinical Psychology: Science and Practice, 9*, 30–34.

Beutler, L.E., Machado, P.P., & Neufeldt, S.A. (1994). Therapist variables. In A.E. Bergin & S.L. Garfield (Eds.), *Handbook of psychotherapy and behavior change* (4th ed.). New York, NY: Wiley.

Beyer, S. (1990). Gender differences in the accuracy of self-evaluations of performance. *Journal of Personality and Social Psychology, 59*, 960–970.

Bialystok, E. (1997). Effects of bilingualism and biliteracy on children's emerging concepts of print. *Developmental Psychology, 33*, 429–440.

Bialystok, E. (2001). *Bilingualism in development: Language, literacy, & cognition.* New York, NY: Cambridge University Press.

Bialystok, E., Barac, R., Blaye, A., & Poulin-Dubois, D. (2010). Word mapping and executive functioning in young monolingual and bilingual children. *Journal of Cognition and Development, 11*, 485–508.

Bialystok, E., & Martin, M.M. (2004). Attention and inhibition in bilingual children: Evidence from the dimensional change card sort task. *Developmental Science, 7*, 325–339.

Biederman, J. (1998). Attention-deficit/hyperactive disorder: A life-span perspective. *Journal of Clinical Psychology, 59*, 1–13.

Biemiller, A., & Slonim, N. (2001). Estimating root word vocabulary growth in normative and advantaged populations: Evidence for a common sequence of vocabulary acquisition. *Journal of Educational Psychology, 93*, 498–520.

Biener, L., & Boudreau, L. (1991). Social power and influence. In R.M. Baron, W.G. Graziano, & C. Stangor (Eds.), *Social psychology.* Fort Worth, TX: Holt, Rinehart & Winston.

Bierhoff, H.W. (2005). The psychology of compassion and prosocial behaviour. *Compassion: Conceptualisations, Research and Use in Psychotherapy*, 148–167.

Biller, J., Brazis, P., & Masdeu, J.C. (2006). *Localization in clinical neurology.* Philadelphia, PA: Lippincott, Williams, & Wilkins.

Billings, A.G., & Moos, R.H. (1984). Coping, stress, and social resources among adults with unipolar depression. *Journal of Personality and Social Psychology, 46*, 877–891.

Binder, J.L., & Strupp, H.H. (1997). "Negative process": A recurrently discovered and underestimated facet of therapeutic process and outcome in the individual psychotherapy of adults. *Clinical Psychology, Science & Practice, 4*, 121–139.

Birdsong, D., & Molis, M. (2001). On the evidence for maturational constraints in second-language acquisition. *Journal of Memory and Language, 44*, 235–249.

Bireta, T.J., & Simels, B.A. (2009). The isolation effect and advertising: Are unusual advertisements remembered better? In M.R. Kelley (Ed.), *Applied Memory* (pp. 57–72). Hauppauge, NY: Nova Science.

Birney, D.P., & Sternberg, R.J. (2006). Intelligence and cognitive abilities as competencies in development. In E. Bialystok & F.I.M Craik (Eds.), *Lifespan cognition: Mechanisms of change* (pp. 315–330). New York, NY: Oxford University Press.

Biswas-Diener, R., Kashdan, T.B., & King, L.A. (2009). Two traditions of happiness research, not two distinct types of happiness. *The Journal of Positive Psychology: Dedicated to furthering research and promoting good practice, 4*, 208–211.

Björkqvist, K. (1997). The inevitability of conflict, but not of violence: Theoretical considerations on conflict and aggression. In D.P. Fry & K. Björkqvist (Eds.), *Cultural variation in conflict resolution: Alternatives to violence* (pp. 25–35). Mahwah, NJ: Erlbaum.

Bjørnebekk, A., Fjell, A.M., Walhovd, K.B., Grydeland, H., Torgersen, S., & Westlye, L.T. (2013). Neuronal correlates of the five factor model (FFM) of human personality: Multimodal imaging in a large healthy sample. *Neuroimage, 65*, 194–208.

Black, D.N., Seritan, A.L., Taber, K.H., & Hurley, R.A. (2004). Conversion hysteria: Lessons from functional imaging. *Journal of Neuropsychiatry & Clinical Neurosciences, 16*, 245–251.

Black, D.W. (1999). *Bad boys, bad men: Confronting antisocial personality disorder.* New York, NY: Oxford University Press.

Black, D.W. (2015). The natural history of antisocial personality disorder. *The Canadian Journal of Psychiatry / La Revue Canadienne de Psychiatrie, 60*(7), 309–314.

Black, D.W., Yates, W.R., & Andreasen, N.C. (1988). Schizophrenia, schizophreniform disorder, and delusional paranoid disorders. In J.A. Talbott, R.E. Hales, & S.C. Yudofsky (Eds.), *Textbook of psychiatry.* Washington, DC: American Psychiatric Press.

Blackstone, J. (2007). *The empathic ground: Intersubjectivity and nonduality in the psychotherapeutic process.* Albany, NY: State University of New York Press.

Blackwood, D. (2000). Genetic predispositions to stressful conditions. In G. Fink (Ed.), *Encyclopedia of stress* (Vol. 2). San Diego, CA: Academic Press.

Blader, S.L., & Tyler, T.R. (2002). Justice and empathy: What motivates people to help others? In M. Ross & D.T. Miller (Eds.), *The justice motive in everyday life* (pp. 226–250). New York, NY: Cambridge University Press.

Blair, J. (2005). *Development of the psychopath: Emotion and the brain.* St. Louis, MO: Blackwell.

Blair, S.N., Kohl, H.W., III, Paffenbarger, R.S., Jr., Clark, D.G., Cooper, K.H., & Gibbons, L.W. (1989). Physical fitness and all-cause mortality: A prospective study of healthy men and women. *Journal of the American Medical Association, 262*, 2395–2401.

Blakemore, C., & Cooper, G.F. (1970). Development of the brain depends on visual environment. *Nature, 228*, 477–478.

Blakeslee, B., & McCourt, M.E. (2015). What visual illusions tell us about underlying neural mechanisms and observer strategies for tackling the inverse problem of achromatic perception. *Frontiers in Human Neuroscience, 9.* Retrieved from http://search.proquest.com/docview/1705048747?accountid=15115.

Blanchard, C.M., Courneya, K.S., Rodgers, W.M., Daub, B., & Knapik, G. (2002). Determinants of exercise intention and behavior during and after phase 2 cardiac rehabilitation: An application of the theory of planned behavior. *Rehabilitation Psychology, 47*, 308–323.

Blanton, H., Pelham, B.W., DeHart, T., & Carvallo, M. (2001). Overconfidence as dissonance reduction. *Journal of Experimental Social Psychology, 37*, 373–385.

Blascovich, J., Mendes, W.B., Hunter, S.B., & Salomon, K. (1999). Social "facilitation" as challenge and threat. *Journal of Personality and Social Psychology, 77*, 68–77.

Blascovich, J., Wyer, N.A., Swart, L.A., & Kibler, J.L. (1997). Racism and racial categorization. *Journal of Personality and Social Psychology, 72*, 1364–1372.

Blass, E.M., Ganchrow, J.R., & Steiner, J.E. (1984). Classical conditioning in newborn humans 2–48 hours of age. *Infant Behavior and Development, 7*, 223–235.

Blass, T. (2008). What can Milgram's obedience experiments contribute to our understanding of followership? In R.E. Riggio, I. Chaleff, & J. Lipman-Blumen (Eds.), *The art of followership: How great followers create great leaders and organizations* (pp. 195–208). San Francisco, CA: Jossey-Bass.

Blass, T. (Ed.). (2000). *Obedience to authority: Current perspectives on the Milgram paradigm.* Mahwah, NJ: Erlbaum.

Blass, T., & Schmitt, C. (2001). The nature of perceived authority in the Milgram paradigm: Two replications. *Current Psychology: Developmental, Learning, Personality, & Social, 20*, 115–121.

Blessing, W.W. (1997). *The lower brainstem and bodily homeostasis.* New York, NY: Oxford University Press.

Block, J.J. (2007). Lessons from Columbine: Virtual and real rage. *American Journal of Forensic Psychiatry, 28*(2), 1–27.

Block, N. (2002). How heritability misleads about race. In J.M. Fish (Ed.), *Race and intelligence: Separating science from myth* (pp. 281–296). Mahwah, NJ: Erlbaum.

Blodgett, H.C. (1929). The effect of the introduction of reward on the maze performance of rats. *University of California Publications in Psychology, 4*(8), 114–126.

Blodgett, R. (1986, May). Lost in the stars: Psychics strike out (again). *People Expression, 32–35.*

Bloom, F.E. (2000). *Brain, mind and behavior.* San Francisco, CA: W.H. Freeman.

Bloomfield, K., Greenfield, T.K., Kraus, L., & Augustin, R. (2002). A comparison of drinking patterns and alcohol-related problems in the United States and Germany, 1995. *Substance Use and Misuse, 37,* 399–428.

Blosser, J.L. (2000). *Pediatric traumatic brain injury: Proactive intervention.* Belmont, CA: Thompson Wadsworth.

Blum, K., Chen, A.L.C., Giordano, J., Borsten, J., Chen, T.J.H., et al. (2012). The addictive brain: All roads lead to dopamine. *Journal of Psychoactive Drugs, 44*(2), 134–143.

Bobo, L. (1988). Attitudes toward the black political movement: Trends, meaning, and effects of racial policy preferences. *Social Psychology Quarterly, 51,* 287–302.

Bochner, S., & Insko, C.A. (1966). Communicator discrepancy, source credibility, and opinion change. *Journal of Personality and Social Psychology, 4,* 614–621.

Boes, A.D., Bechara, A., Tranel, D., Anderson, S.W., Richman, L., & Nopoulos, R. (2009). Right ventromedial prefrontal cortex: A neuroanatomical correlate of impulse control in boys. *Social Cognitive and Affective Neuroscience, 4,* 1–9.

Bogale, B.A., Kamata, N., Mioko, K., & Sugita, S. (2011). Quantity discrimination in jungle crows. *Corvus macrohynchos. Animal Behaviour, 82,* 635–641.

Bolin, B.L., Lile, J.A., Marks, K.R., Beckmann, J.S., Rush, C.R., & Stoops, W.W. (2016). Buspirone reduces sexual risk-taking intent but not cocaine self-administration. *Experimental and Clinical Psychopharmacology, 24*(3), 162–173.

Bolles, R.C. (1979). *Learning theory* (2nd ed.). New York, NY: Holt, Rinehart & Winston.

Bolles, R.C. (1980). Some functionalistic thought about regulation. In F.M. Toates & T.R. Halliday (Eds.), *Analysis of motivational processes.* London, UK: Academic Press.

Bolles, R.C., & Beecher, M.D. (Eds.). (1988). *Evolution and learning.* Hillsdale, NJ: Erlbaum.

Bonanno, G.A. (2009). *The other side of sadness: What the new science of bereavement tells us about life after loss.* New York, NY: Basic Books.

Bonanno, G.A., Galea, S., Bucciarelli, A., & Vlahov, D. (2007). What predicts psychological resilience after disaster? The role of demographics, resources, and life stress. *Journal of Consulting and Clinical Psychology, 75,* 671–282.

Bonci, D.M.O., Neitz, M., Neitz, J., de Lima Silveira, L.C., & Ventura, D.F. (2013). The genetics of new world monkey visual pigments. *Psychology & Neuroscience, 6*(2), 133–144.

Bond, C.F., Jr., & Titus, L.J. (1983). Social facilitation: A meta-analysis of 241 studies. *Psychological Bulletin, 94,* 265–292.

Bond, R., & Smith, P.B. (1996). Culture and conformity: A meta-analysis of studies using Asch's (1952b, 1956) line judgment task. *Psychological Bulletin, 119,* 111–137.

Boneva, B., Frieze, I.H., Ferligoj, A., Pauknerova, D., & Orgocka, A. (1998). Achievement, power, and affiliation motives as clues to (e)migration desires: A four country comparison. *European Psychologist, 3,* 247–254.

Bonnel, A.M., & Hafter, E.R. (1998). Divided attention between simultaneous auditory and visual signals. *Perception and Psychophysics, 60,* 179–190.

Bonvillian, J.D., & Patterson, F.G.P. (1997). Sign language acquisition and the development of meaning in a lowland gorilla. In C. Mandell & A. McCabe (Eds.), *The problem of meaning: Behavioral and cognitive perspectives* (pp. 181–220). Amsterdam, Netherlands: North-Holland/Elsevier Science.

Booth, A., & Amato, P.R. (2001). Parental predivorce relations and offspring post-divorce well-being. *Journal of Marriage and the Family, 63,* 197–212.

Booth-Kewley, S., & Friedman, H.S. (1987). Psychological predictors of heart disease: A quantitative review. *Psychological Bulletin, 101,* 343–362.

Bootzin, R.R. (1979). Effects of self-control procedures for insomnia. *American Journal of Clinical Biofeedback, 2,* 70–77.

Bora, C.H., Vernon, A., & Trip, S. (2013). Effectiveness of a rational emotive behavior education program in reducing teachers' emotional distress. *Journal of Cognitive and Behavioral Psychotherapies, 13*(2), 585–604.

Boring, E.G. (1950). *A history of experimental psychology.* New York, NY: Appleton-Century-Crofts.

Born, S., Levit, A., Niv, M.Y., Meyerhof, W., & Behrens, M. (2013). The human bitter taste receptor TAS2R10 is tailored to accommodate numerous diverse ligands. *The Journal of Neuroscience, 33*(1), 201–213.

Borod, J.C. (2000). *The neuropsychology of emotion.* New York, NY: Oxford University Press.

Botman, H.I., & Crovitz, H.F. (1989). Dream reports and autobiographical memory. *Imagination, Cognition and Personality, 9,* 213–224.

Botvinick, M.M., & Plaut, D.C. (2006). Short-term memory for serial order: A recurrent neural network model. *Psychological Review, 113*(2), 201–233.

Bouchard, C., Tremblay, A., Despres, J.P., Nadeau, A., Lupien, P.J., & Theriault, G. (1990). The response to long-term overfeeding in identical twins. *The New England Journal of Medicine, 322,* 1477–1482.

Bouchard, T.J. (2004). Genetic influence on human psychological traits. *Current Directions in Psychological Science, 13,* 148–151.

Bouchard, T.J., Jr. (2014). Genes, evolution and intelligence. *Behavior Genetics, 44*(6), 549–577.

Bouchard, T.J., Lykken, D.T., McGue, M., Segal, N.L., & Tellegen, A. (1990). Sources of human psychological differences: The Minnesota study of twins reared apart. *Science, 250,* 223–228.

Bouchard, T.J., & McGue, M. (1981). Familial studies of intelligence: A review. *Science, 212,* 1055–1059.

Bould, H., Joinson, C., Sterne, J., & Araya, R. (2013). The Emotionality Activity Sociability Temperament Survey: Factor analysis and temporal stability in a longitudinal cohort. *Personality and Individual Differences, 54,* 628–633.

Bovbjerg, D.H. (2006). The continuing problem of post-chemotherapy nausea and vomiting: Contributions of classical conditioning. *Autonomic Neuroscience: Basic & Clinical, 129,* 92–98.

Bowen, S., Chawla, N., Collins, S.E., Witkiewitz, K., Hsu, S., Grow, J., ... Marlatt, A. (2009). Mindfulness-based relapse prevention for substance use disorders: A pilot efficacy trial. *Substance Abuse, 30,* 295–305.

Bower, G.H. (2000). A brief history of memory research. In E. Tulving & F.I.M. Craik (Eds.), *The Oxford handbook of memory* (pp. 3–32). New York, NY: Oxford University Press.

Bower, G.H. (2008). The evolution of a cognitive psychologist: A journey from simple behaviors to complex mental acts. *Annual Review of Psychology, 59,* 1–27.

Bower, G.H., Clark, M.C., Lesgold, M.A., & Winzenz, D. (1969). Hierarchical retrieval schemes in recall of categorized word lists. *Journal of Verbal Learning and Verbal Behavior, 8,* 323–343.

Bowlby, J. (1958). The nature of the child's tie to his mother. *International Journal of Psychoanalysis, 39,* 350–373.

Bowlby, J. (1969). *Attachment and loss: Vol. 1 Attachment.* New York, NY: Basic Books.

Bowlby, J. (1973). *Attachment and loss: Vol. 2 Separation: Anxiety and anger.* London, UK: Hogarth.

Bowlby, J. (2000a). *Loss: Sadness and depression.* New York, NY: Basic Books.

Bowlby, J. (2000b). *Separation: Anxiety and anger.* New York, NY: Basic Books.

Boyanowsky, E.O., & Griffiths, C.T. (1982). Weapons and eye contact as instigators or inhibitors of aggressive arousal in police-citizen interaction. *Journal of Applied Social Psychology, 12,* 398–407.

Bozarth, J.D., Zimring, F.M., & Tausch, R. (2002). Client-centered therapy: The evolution of a revolution. In D.J. Cain (Ed.), *Humanistic psychotherapies: Handbook of research and practice.* Washington, DC: American Psychological Association.

Braadbaart, L., de Grauw, H., Perrett, D.I., Waiter, G.D., & Williams, J.H.G. (2014). The shared neural basis of empathy and facial imitation accuracy. *NeuroImage, 84,* 367–375.

Bradizza, C.M., & Stasiewkz, P.R. (2009). Alcohol and drug use disorders. In K. Salzinger & M.R. Serper (Eds.), *Behavioral mechanisms and psychopathology: Advancing the explanation of its nature, cause, and treatment.* Washington, DC: American Psychological Association.

Bram, A.D. (2014). Object relations, interpersonal functioning, and health in a nonclinical sample: Construct validation and norms for the TAT SCORS-G. *Psychoanalytic Psychology, 31*(3), 314–342.

Brand, B.L., & Chasson, G.S. Distinguishing simulated from genuine dissociative identity disorder on the MMPI-2. *Psychological Trauma: Theory, Research, Practice and Policy, 7*(1), 93–101.

Brand, M. (2007). Cognitive profile of patients with alcoholic Korsakoff's syndrome. *International Journal on Disability and Human Development, 6,* 161–170.

Brand, M., Eggers, C., Reinhold, N., Fujiwara, E., Kessler, J., Dieter Heiss, W., & Markowitsch, H.J. (2009). Functional brain imaging in 14 patients with dissociative amnesia reveals right inferolateral prefrontal hypometabolism. *Psychiatry Research: Neuroimaging, 174*(1), 32–39.

Bransford, J.D., & Johnson, M.K. (1972). Contextual prerequisites for understanding: Some investigations of comprehension and recall. *Journal of Verbal Learning and Verbal Behavior, 11,* 717–726.

Brantley, P., & Garrett, V.D. (1993). Psychobiological approaches to health and disease. In P.B. Sutker & H.E. Adams (Eds.), *Comprehensive handbook of psychopathology* (2nd ed.). New York, NY: Plenum Press.

Brasfield, C. (2001). Residential school syndrome. *BC Medical Journal, 43*(2), 78–81.

Brauer, M. (2001). Intergroup perception in the social context: The effects of social status and group membership on perceived out group homogeneity and ethnocentrism. *Journal of Experimental Social Psychology, 37,* 15–31.

Bray, J.H., & Berger, S.H. (1993). Developmental Issues in Step Families Research Project: Family relationships and parent-child interactions. *Journal of Family Psychology, 7,* 76–90.

Bredy, T., Weaver, I., Champagne, F., & Meaney, M. (2001). Stress, maternal care, and neural development in the rat. In C.A. Shaw & J.C. McEachern (Eds.), *Toward a theory of neuroplasticity* (pp. 288–300). Philadelphia, PA: Psychology Press.

Breedlove, S.M. (1992). Sexual differentiation of brain and behavior. In J.B. Becker, S.M. Breedlove, & D. Crews (Eds.), *Behavioral endocrinology.* Cambridge, MA: MIT Press.

Brehm, J.W., & Self, E.A. (1989). The intensity of motivation. *Annual Review of Psychology, 40,* 109–131.

Breland, K., & Breland, M. (1961). The misbehavior of organisms. *American Psychologist, 16,* 681–684.

Breland, K., & Breland, M. (1966). *Animal behavior.* New York, NY: Macmillan.

Bremner, J.D. (2000). Neurobiology of post-traumatic stress disorder. In G. Fink (Ed.), *Encyclopedia of stress* (Vol. 3, pp. 186–191). San Diego, CA: Academic Press.

Bremner, J.D. (2005). *Brain imaging handbook.* New York, NY: Norton.

Brennan, S., & Taylor-Butts, A. (2008). *Sexual assaults in Canada 2004 and 2007.* Canadian Centre for Justice Statistics Profile Series. Statistics Canada. http://www.statcan.gc.ca /pub/85f0033m/85f0033m2008019-eng.pdf.

Breslau, N.S., Davis, G.C., Andreski, P., Peterson, E.L., & Schultz, L.R. (1997). Sex differences in posttraumatic stress disorder. *Archives of General Psychiatry, 54,* 1044–1048.

Bresnahan, M.J., Levine, T.R., Shearman, S.M., Lee, S.Y., Park, C.Y., & Kiyomiya, T. (2005). A multimethod multi-trait validity assessment of self-construal in Japan, Korea, and the United States. *Human Communication Research, 31,* 33–59.

Brewer, K.R., & Wann, D.L. (1998). Observational learning effectiveness as a function of model characteristics: Investigating the importance of social power. *Social Behavior and Personality, 26,* 1–10.

Brewin, C.R. (2012). A theoretical framework for understanding recovered memory experiences. In R.F. Belle (Ed.), *True and false recovered memories: Toward a reconciliation of the debate.* Nebraska Symposium on Motivation. Online publication. doi: 10.1007/978-1-4614-1195-6_5.

Bridgeman, B. (2003). *Psychology and evolution: The origins of mind.* Thousand Oaks, CA: Sage.

Briere, J., & Lanktree, C. (1983). Sex role-related effects of sex bias in language. *Sex Roles, 9,* 625–632.

Briggs, J.L. (1970). *Never in anger.* Cambridge, MA: Harvard University Press.

Bright, C.N., & Penrod, B. (2009). An evaluation of the overjustification effects across multiple contingency arrangements. *Behavioral Interventions, 24,* 185–194.

Bringmann, W.G., & Abresch, J. (1997). Clever Hans: Fact or fiction? In W.G. Bringmann, H.E. Luck, R. Miller, & C.E. Early (Eds.), *A pictorial history of psychology* (pp. 77–82). Chicago, IL: Quintessence Publishing Co Inc.

Brisson, J., de Chantal, P., Forgues, H.L., & Markovits, H. (2014). Belief bias is stronger when reasoning is more difficult. *Thinking & Reasoning, 20*(3), 385–403.

Broadbent, D.E. (1958). *Perception and communication.* London, UK: Pergamon Press.

Broberg, D.J., & Bernstein, I.L. (1987). Candy as a scapegoat in the prevention of food aversions in children receiving chemotherapy. *Cancer, 60,* 2344–2347.

Brochu, P.M., Gawronski, B., & Esses, V.M. (2008). Cognitive consistency and the relation between implicit and explicit prejudice: Reconceptualizing old-fashioned, modern, and aversive prejudice. In M.A. Morrison, & T.G. Morrison (Eds.), *The psychology of modern prejudice* (pp. 27–50). Hauppauge, NY: Nova Science Publishers.

Brogdal, P. (2010). *The central nervous system: Structure and function.* New York: Oxford University Press.

Brosch, T., Schiller, D., Mojdehbakhsh, R., Uleman, J.S., & Phelps, E.A. (2013). Neural mechanisms underlying the integration of situational information into attribution outcomes. *Social Cognitive and Affective Neuroscience, 8*(6), 640–646.

Brown, A.D. (2013). Temporal weighting of binaural cues for sound localization (Order No. AAI3542099). Available From PsycINFO. (1411062000; 2013–99180–326). Retrieved from http://search.proquest.com/docview/1411062000? accountid=15115.

Brown, A.S. (1991). A review of the tip-of-the-tongue experience. *Psychological Bulletin, 109,* 204–223.

Brown, G.D.A., Neath, I., & Chater, N. (2007). A temporal ratio model of memory. *Psychological Review, 114,* 539–576.

Brown, G.W., & Harris, T.O. (1978). *Social origins of depression.* London, UK: Tavistock Press.

Brown, I., & Percy, M. (Eds.). (2007). *A comprehensive guide to intellectual and developmental disabilities.* Baltimore, MD: Paul H. Brookes Publishing Company.

Brown, J.D. (1998). *The self.* Boston, MA: McGraw-Hill.

Brown, J.D., & McGill, K.L. (1989). The cost of good fortune: When positive life events produce negative health consequences. *Journal of Personality and Social Psychology, 57,* 1103–1110.

Brown, L.S. (1994). *Subversive dialogues: Theory in feminist therapy.* New York, NY: Basic Books.

Brown, L.S. (2000). The controversy concerning recovered memory of traumatic events. In A.Y. Shalev, R. Yehuda, & A.C. McFarlane (Eds.), *International handbook of human response to trauma.* New York, NY: Kluwer Academic/ Plenum Press.

Brown, R. (1958). How shall a thing be called? *Psychological Review, 65*(1), 14–21.

Brown, R. (1973). *A first language: The early stages.* Cambridge, MA: Harvard University Press.

Brown, S.L., Nesse, R.M., Vinokur, A.D., & Smith, D.M. (2003). Providing social support may be more beneficial than receiving it: Results from a prospective study of mortality. *Psychological Science, 14,* 320–327.

Brown, T.A. (2007). Temporal course and structural relations among dimensions of temperament and DSM-IV anxiety and mood disorder constructs. *Journal of Abnormal Psychology, 116,* 313–328.

Brown, T.A., & Barlow, D.H. (2009). A proposal for a dimensional classification system based on the shared features of the DSM-IV anxiety and mood disorders: Implications for assessment and treatment. *Psychological Assessment, 21,* 256–271.

Brown, T.A., Di-Nardo, P.A., Lehman, C.L., & Campbell, L.A. (2001). Reliability of DSM-IV anxiety and mood disorders: Implications for the classification of emotional disorders. *Journal of Abnormal Psychology, 110,* 49–58.

Brown, T.S., & Wallace, P. (1980). *Physiological psychology.* New York, NY: Academic Press.

Brownell, K.D. (1994). *The LEARN program for weight control.* Dallas, TX: American Health.

Brownell, K.D., & Rodin, J. (1994). The dieting maelstrom: Is it possible and advisable to lose weight? *American Psychologist, 49,* 781–791.

Bruce, T.J., & Sanderson, W.C. (1998). *Specific phobias: Clinical applications of evidence-based psychotherapy.* Northvale, NJ: Jason Aronson.

Bruch, H. (1973). *Eating disorders: Obesity, anorexia nervosa, and the person within.* New York, NY: Basic Books.

Bruck, M., Ceci, S.J., & Hembrooke, H. (1998). Reliability and credibility of young children's reports: From research to policy and practice. *American Psychologist, 53,* 136–151.

Bruederl, J., Diekmann, A., & Engelhardt, H. (1997). Does a trial marriage increase divorce risk? Empirical study of the Families Survey. *Koelner Zeitschrift fuer Soziologie und Sozialpsychologie, 49,* 205–222.

Bruner, J. (1983). *Child's talk: Learning to use language.* New York, NY: Norton.

Bruss, P.J., & Mitchell, D.B. (2009). Memory systems, processes, and tasks: Taxonomic clarification via factor analysis. *American Journal of Psychology, 122,* 175–189.

Bryan, J., III. (1986). *Hodgepodge: A commonplace book.* New York, NY: Ballantine.

Buck, L., & Axel, R. (1991). A novel multigene family may encode odorant receptors: A molecular basis for odor recognition. *Cell, 65,* 175–187.

Bulayeva, K., Lesch, K., Bulayev, O., Walsh, C., Glatt, S., Gurgenova, F., ... Thompson, P.M. (2015). Genomic structural variants are linked with intellectual disability. *Journal of Neural Transmission, 122*(9), 1289–1301.

Bulkeley, K., & Kahan, T.L. (2008). The impact of September 11 on dreaming. *Consciousness and Cognition: An International Journal, 17,* 1248–1256.

Bullier, J. (2002). Neural basis of vision. In H. Pashler & S. Yantis (Eds.), *Steven's handbook of experimental psychology: Vol. 1 Sensation and perception* (3rd ed., pp. 1–40). New York, NY: Wiley.

Bumpass, L.L., & Sweet, J.A. (1989). National estimates of cohabitation. *Demography, 26,* 615–625.

Burgaleta, M., Head, K., Alverez-Linera, J., Martinez, K., Escorial, S., Haier, R., & Colom, R. (2012). Sex differences in brain volume are related to specific skills, not to general intelligence. *Intelligence, 40*(1), 60–68.

Burger, J.M. (1991). Changes in attributions over time: The ephemeral fundamental attribution error. *Social Cognition, 9,* 182–193.

Burger, J.M. (2000). *Personality* (5th ed.). Belmont, CA: Wadsworth.

Burger, J.M. (2009). Replicating Milgram: Would people still obey today? *American Psychologist, 64,* 1–11.

Burgess, A.W., & Holmstrom, L.L. (1974). Rape trauma syndrome. *The American Journal of Psychiatry, 131,* 981–986.

Burke, K.C., Burke, J.D., Rae, D.S., & Regier, D.A. (1991). Comparing age at onset of major depression and other psychiatric disorders by birth cohorts in five U.S. community populations. *Archives of General Psychiatry, 48,* 789–795.

Burkholder, G.J., Evers, K.A., Burbank, P.M., & Riebe, D. (2002). Application of the transtheoretical model to several problem behaviors. In P.M. Burbank & D. Riebe (Eds.), *Promoting exercise and behavior change in older adults: Interventions with the transtheoretical model* (pp. 85–145). New York, NY: Springer Publishing Co.

Burns, M.E., & Arshavsky, V.Y. (2005). Beyond counting photons: Trials and trends in vertebrate visual transduction. *Neuron, 48,* 387–401.

Burns, M.O., & Seligman, M.E.P. (1989). Explanatory style across the life span: Evidence for stability over 52 years. *Journal of Personality and Social Psychology, 56,* 471–477.

Burroughs, S.M., & Eby, L.T. (1998). Psychological sense of community at work: A measurement system and explanatory framework. *Journal of Community Psychology, 26,* 509–532.

Burton, E., Stice, E., & Seeley, J.R. (2004). A prospective test of the stress-buffering model of depression in adolescent girls: No support once again. *Journal of Consulting and Clinical Psychology, 72,* 689–697.

Busey, T.A., Tunnicliff, J.J., Loftus, G.R., & Loftus, E.F. (2000). Accounts of the confidence-accuracy relation in recognition memory. *Psychonomic Bulletin and Review, 7,* 26–48.

Bushman, B.J., & Bonacci, A.M. (2002). Violence and sex impair memory for television ads. *Journal of Applied Psychology, 87,* 557–564.

Bushman, B.J., Wang, M., & Anderson, C.A. (2005). Is the curve relating temperature to aggression linear or curvilinear: Assaults and temperature in Minneapolis reexamined. *Journal of Personality and Social Psychology, 89*(1), 62–65.

Buss, D.M. (1985). Human mate selection. *American Scientist, 73,* 47–51.

Buss, D.M. (1989). Sex differences in human mate preferences: Evolutionary hypotheses tested in 37 cultures. *Behavioral and Brain Sciences, 12,* 1–49.

Buss, D.M. (1995). Evolutionary psychology: A new paradigm for psychological science. *Psychological Inquiry, 6,* 1–30.

Buss, D.M. (1999). Human nature and individual differences: The evolution of human personality. In L.A. Pervin & O.P. John (Eds.), *Handbook of personality: Theory and research* (2nd ed.). New York, NY: Guilford Press.

Buss, D.M. (2007). *Evolutionary psychology. The new science of the mind.* Boston, MA: Allyn & Bacon.

Buss, D.M., Abbott, M., Angleitner, A., Asherian, A., Biaggio, A., Blanco-Villasenor, A., ... Kuo-Shu, Y. (1990). International preferences in selecting mates: A study of 37 cultures. *Journal of Cross-Cultural Psychology, 21,* 5–47.

Buss, D.M., & Dedden, L.A. (1990). Derogation of competitors. *Journal of Social and Personal Relationships, 7,* 395–422.

Buster, J.E., Kingsberg, S.A., Aguirre, O., Brown, C., Breaux, J.G., Buch, A., & Casson, P. (2005). Testosterone patch for low sexual desire in surgically menopausal women: A randomized trial. *Obstetrics & Gynecology, 105,* 944–952.

Butera, F., & Levine, J. (2009). *Coping with minority status: Responses to exclusion and inclusion.* New York, NY: Cambridge University Press.

Butler, A.C., Chapman, J.E., Forman, E.M., & Beck, A.T. (2006). The empirical status of cognitive-behavioral therapy: A review of meta-analyses. *Clinical Psychology Review, 26*(1), 17–31.

Buunk, B.P., & Dijkstra, P. (2001). Rationalizations and defensive attributions for high-risk sex among heterosexuals. *Patient Education and Counseling, 45,* 127–132.

Buysse, D.J., Frank, E., Lowe, K.K., & Cherry, C.R. (1997). Electroencephalographic sleep correlates of episode and vulnerability to recurrence in depression. *Biological Psychiatry, 41,* 406–418.

Buzsáki, G. (1989). Two-stage model of memory trace formation: a role for "noisy" brain states. *Neuroscience, 31*(3), 551–570.

Byer, C.O., Shainberg, L.W., & Galliano, G. (1999). *Dimensions of human sexuality* (5th ed.). Boston, MA: McGraw-Hill.

Byer, C.O., Shainberg, L.W., & Galliano, G. (2002). *Dimensions of human sexuality* (6th ed.). Boston, MA: McGraw-Hill.

Byne, W. (1997). Why we cannot conclude that sexual orientation is primarily a biological phenomenon. *Journal of Homosexuality, 34,* 73–80.

Byrd, M.R., Richards, D.F., Hove, G., & Frima, P.C. (2002). Treatment of early onset hair pulling as a simple habit. *Behavior Modification, 26,* 400–411.

Byrne, D. (1997). An overview (and underview) of research and theory within the attraction paradigm. *Journal of Social and Personal Relationships, 14,* 417–431.

Byrne, D., Ervin, C.R., & Lamberth, J. (1970). Continuity between the experimental study of attraction and real-life computer dating. *Journal of Personality and Social Psychology, 16,* 157–165.

Byrne, D., & Greendlinger, V. (1989). *Need for affiliation as a predictor of classroom friendships.* Unpublished manuscript, State University of New York at Albany.

Byrne, D., & Nelson, D. (1965). Attraction as a linear function of proportion of positive reinforcements. *Journal of Personality and Social Psychology, 1,* 659–663.

Byrne, D., & Osland, J.A. (2000). Sexual fantasy and erotica/pornography: Internal and external imagery. In L.T. Szuchman & F. Muscarella (Eds.), *Psychological perspectives on human sexuality.* New York, NY: Wiley.

Cabeza, R., Nyberg, L., & Park, D.C. (2005). *Cognitive neuroscience of aging: Linking cognitive and cerebral aging.* New York, NY: Oxford University Press.

Cacioppo, J.T., Petty, R.E., Feinstein, J.A., & Jarvis, W.B.G. (1996). Dispositional differences in cognitive motivation: The life and times of individuals varying in need for cognition. *Psychological Bulletin, 119,* 197–253.

Cacioppo, J.T., Petty, R.E., & Morris, K.J. (1983). Effects of need for cognition on message evaluation, recall, and persuasion. *Journal of Personality and Social Psychology, 45,* 805–818.

Cadet, J.L. (2016). Epigenetics of stress, addiction, and resilience: Therapeutic implications. *Molecular Neurobiology, 53*(1), 545–560.

Cahill, J., Paley, G., & Hardy, G. (2013). What do patients find helpful in psychotherapy? implications for the therapeutic relationship in mental health nursing. *Journal of Psychiatric and Mental Health Nursing, 20*(9), 782–791.

Cahn, B.R., & Polich, J. (2006). Meditation states and traits: EEG, ERP, and neuroimaging studies. *Psychological Bulletin, 132,* 180–211.

Cai, D., Pearce, K., Chen, S., & Glanzman, D.L. (2011). Protein kinase M maintains long-term sensitization and long-term facilitation in *Aplysia. Journal of Neuroscience, 31,* 6421–6431.

Cai, L., Chan, J.S.Y., Yan, J.H., & Peng, K. (2014). Brain plasticity and motor practice in cognitive aging. *Frontiers in Aging Neuroscience, 6,* 31.

Cain, D.J. (2010). *Person-centered psychotherapies.* Washington, DC: American Psychological Association.

Cain, D.J., & Seeman, J. (Eds.). (2002). *Humanistic psychotherapies: Handbook of research and practice.* Washington, DC: American Psychological Association.

Cairns, H. (1952). Disturbances of consciousness in lesions of the mid-brain and diencephalon. *Brain, 75,* 107–114.

Caldji, C., Diorio, J., & Meaney, M.J. (2000). Variations in maternal care in infancy regulate the development of stress reactivity. *Biological Psychiatry, 48,* 1164–1174.

Caldwell, A.B. (1994). *The profile of Jeffrey Dahmer* (videotape). Los Angeles, CA: Caldwell Report, Inc.

Calkins, S.D., & Johnson, M.C. (1998). Toddler regulation of distress to frustrating events: Temperamental and maternal correlates. *Infant Behavior and Development, 21,* 379–395.

Callahan, C.M., Moon, T.R., Oh, S., Azano, A.P., & Hailey, E.P. (2015). What works in gifted education: Documenting the effects of an integrated curricular/instructional model for gifted students. *American Educational Research Journal, 52*(1), 137–167.

Calvete, E., Orue, I., & Hankin, B.L. (2015). A longitudinal test of the vulnerability-stress model with early maladaptive schemas for depressive and social anxiety symptoms in adolescents. *Journal of Psychopathology and Behavioral Assessment, 37*(1), 85–99.

Cameron, J.J., Stinson, A.A., & Wood, J.V. (2013). The bold and the bashful: Self-esteem, gender, and relationship initiation, *Social Psychological and Personality Science,* published online 13 February 2013, http://spp.sagepub.com/content/early/2013/02/13/1948550613476309.full.pdf+html.

Camilleri, C., & Malewska-Peyre, H. (1997). Socialization and identity strategies. In J.W. Berry, P.R. Dasen, & T.S. Saraswathi (Eds.), *Handbook of cross-cultural psychology: Basic processes and human development* (2nd ed., Vol. 2). Boston, MA: Allyn & Bacon.

Campbell, A., Shirley, L., & Candy, J. (2004). A longitudinal study of gender-related cognition and behaviour. *Developmental Science, 7,* 1–9.

Campbell, S.S. (1993). Seasonal effects on sleep. In M.A. Carskadon (Ed.), *Encyclopedia of sleep and dreaming.* New York, NY: Macmillan.

Campbell, T.S., Labelle, L.E., Bacon, S.L., Fairs, P., & Carlson, L.E. (2012). Impact of Mindfulness-Based Stress Reduction (MBSR) on attention, rumination and resting blood pressure in women with cancer: A waitlist-controlled study. *Journal of Behavioral Medicine, 35,* 262–271.

Campfield, L.A. (1997). Metabolic and hormonal controls of food intake: Highlights of the last 25 years: 1972–1997. *Appetite, 29,* 135–152.

Canadian Cancer Society. (2016). http://www.cancer.ca/en/cancer-information/cancer-101/what-is-a-risk-factor/tobacco/#ixzz4ARAwRQwj.

Canadian Centre on Substance Abuse. (2016). Ottawa, Ontario, 2016.

Canadian Community Epidemiology Network on Drug Use. (2001). Lifetime use of alcohol and illicit drugs. CCSA-CCLAT reports.

Canadian Community Health Survey. (2004). Canadian Community Health Survey. Retrieved from http://www.hc-sc.gc.ca/fn-an/surveill/nutrition/commun/index-eng.php.

Canadian Institutes for Health Information. (2009). Health care spending. Retrieved from http://www.cihi.ca/cihi-ext-portal/internet/en/document/spending+and+health+workforce/spending/.

Canadian Institutes for Health Information. (2010). Major findings from the Canadian alcohol and drug use monitoring survey. Canadian Institutes for Health Information and Statistics Canada.

Canadian Mental Health Association. (2009). Mental Health/Mental Illness Fast Facts. Retrieved from http://www.cmha.ca/.

Canadian Mental Health Association. (2010). Mental Illness Statistics. Retrieved from http://www.cmha.ca/bins/site_page .asp?cid=284-285-1258-1404&lang=1.

Canadian Psychological Association. (2000). *Canadian code of ethics for psychologists* (3rd ed.). Retrieved November 17, 2010, from http://www .cpa.ca/.../Canadian%20Code%20of%20Ethics%20 for%20Psycho.pdf.

Canivez, G.L., & Watkins, M.W. (1998). Long-term stability of the Wechsler Intelligence Scale for Children (3rd ed.). *Psychological Assessment, 10,* 285–291.

Cannon, W. (1927). The James-Lange theory of emotions: A critical examination and an alternate theory. *American Journal of Psychology, 39,* 106–124.

Cannon, W.B. (1929). *Bodily changes in pain, hunger, fear, and rage.* New York, NY: Appleton-Century.

Cannon, W.B. (1932). *The wisdom of the body.* New York, NY: W.W. Norton.

Cannon, W.B., & Washburn, A.L. (1912). An explanation of hunger. *American Journal of Physiology, 29,* 441–454.

Canton, J. (2012). Math, monkeys, and the developing brain. *Proceedings of the National Academy of Science, Supplement 1,* 109, 10725–10732.

Caporael, L.R. (1997). The evolution of truly social cognition: The core configurations model. *Personality and Social Psychology Review, 1,* 276–298.

Carbon, C. (2014). Understanding human perception by human-made illusions. *Frontiers in Human Neuroscience, 8.* Retrieved from http:// search.proquest.com/docview/1648594706?acco untid=15115.

Cardasis, W., Hochman, J.A., & Silk, K.R. (1997). Transitional objects and borderline personality disorder. *American Journal of Psychiatry, 154,* 250–255.

Cardeña, E., Lynn, S.J., & Krippner, S. (2000). Introduction: Anomalous experiences in perspective. In E. Cardeña, S.J. Lynn, & S. Krippner (Eds.), *Varieties of anomalous experience: Examining the scientific evidence.* Washington, DC: American Psychological Association.

Carey, G., & Gottesman, I.I. (1981). Twin and family studies of anxiety, phobic, and obsession disorders. In D.F. Klein & J. Rabkin (Eds.), *Anxiety: New research and changing concepts.* New York, NY: Raven Press.

Carlin, A.S., Hoffman, H.G., & Weghorst, S. (1997). Virtual reality and tactile augmentation in the treatment of spider phobia: A case report. *Behaviour Research and Therapy, 35,* 153–158.

Carlson, C. (2000). ADHD is overdiagnosed. In R.L. Atkinson, R.C. Atkinson, E.E. Smith, D.J. Bem, & S. Nolen-Hoeksema (Eds.), *Hilgard's introduction to psychology* (13th ed.). Fort Worth, TX: Harcourt Brace.

Carlson, E.A., & McAndrew, F.T. (2004). Body shape ideals and perceptions of body shape in Spanish and American college students. *Perceptual and Motor Skills, 99,* 1071–1074.

Carlson, J.G., & Hatfield, E. (1992). *Psychology of emotion.* Fort Worth, TX: Harcourt Brace Jovanovich.

Carmody, J., & Baer, R.A. (2008). Relationships between mindfulness practice and levels of mindfulness, medical and psychological symptoms and well-being in a mindfulness-based stress reduction program. *Journal of Behavioral Medicine, 31,* 23–33.

Carnagey, N.L., & Anderson, C.A. (2005). The effects of reward and punishment in violent video games on aggressive affect, cognition, and behavior. *Psychological Science, 16,* 882–889.

Carnagey, N.L., Anderson, C.A., & Bushman, B.J. (2007). The effect of video game violence on physiological desensitization to real-life violence. *Journal of Experimental Social Psychology, 43,* 489–496.

Carney, D.N., Bunn, P.A., Gazdar, A.F., Pagan, J.A., & Minna, J.D. (1981). *Academy of Science U.S.A., 78,* 3185–3189.

Carney, L.H. (2002). Neural basis of audition. In H. Pashler & S.Yantis (Eds.), *Steven's handbook of experimental psychology: Vol. 1 Sensation and perception* (3rd ed., pp. 341–396). New York, NY: Wiley.

Carney, R.N., Levin, J.R., & Levin, M.E. (1994). Enhancing the psychology of memory by enhancing memory of psychology. *Teaching of Psychology, 21,* 171–174.

Carnicero, J.A.C., Perez-Lopez, J., Salinas, M.D.C.G., & Martinez-Fuentes, M.T. (2000). A longitudinal study of temperament in infancy: Stability and convergence of measures. *European Journal of Personality, 14,* 21–37.

Carpenter, P.A., Just, M.A., & Shell, P. (1990). What one intelligence test measures: A theoretical account of the processing in the Raven Progressive Matrices Test. *Psychological Review, 97,* 404–431.

Carpenter, R., & Robson, J. (Eds.). (1999). *Vision research: A practical guide to laboratory methods.* New York, NY: Oxford University Press.

Carpenter, W.T., Jr., & Heinrichs, D.W. (1983). Early intervention, time-limited, targeted pharmacotherapy of schizophrenia. *Schizophrenia Bulletin, 9,* 533–542.

Carr, D., & Friedman, M.A. (2005). Is obesity stigmatizing? Body weight, perceived discrimination, and psychological well-being in the United States. *Journal of Health and Social Behavior, 46*(3), 244–259.

Carr, F. (2016). Emotion: Waves of fear. *Nature Reviews Neuroscience.* doi:10.1038/nrn.2016.32

Carrere, S., Buehlman, K.T., Gottman, J.M., Coan, J.A., & Ruckstuhl, L. (2000). Predicting marital stability and divorce in newly-wed couples. *Journal of Family Psychology, 14,* 42–58.

Carroll, C.R. (1993). *Drugs in modern society.* Madison, WI: Brown & Benchmark.

Carroll, J.B. (1993). *Human cognitive abilities: A survey of factor-analytic studies.* New York, NY: Cambridge University Press.

Carruthers, M. (1981). Field studies: Emotion and betablockade. In M.J. Christie & P.G. Mellett (Eds.), *Foundations of psychosomatics* (pp. 223–241). Chichester, UK: Wiley.

Carson, R.C., Butcher, J.N., & Coleman, J.C. (1988). *Abnormal psychology and modern life* (8th ed.). Glenview, IL: Scott, Foresman.

Carter, S.J., & Cassaday, H.J. (1998). State dependent retrieval and chlorpheniramine. *Human Psychopharmacology: Clinical and Experimental, 13,* 513–523.

Cartwright, R.D. (1977). *Night life: Explorations in dreaming.* Englewood Cliffs, NJ: Prentice-Hall.

Cartwright, R.D. (1991). Dreams that work: The relation of dream incorporation to adaptation to stressful events. *Dreaming: Journal of the Association for the Study of Dreams, 1,* 3–9.

Carvacho, H., Zick, A., Haye, A., González, R., Manzi, J., Kocik, C., & Bertl, M. (2013). On the relation between social class and prejudice: The roles of education, income, and ideological attitudes. *European Journal of Social Psychology, 43*(4), 272–285.

Carver, C.S., & Scheier, M.F. (2000). *Perspectives on personality* (4th ed.). Boston, MA: Allyn & Bacon.

Carver, C.S., & Scheier, M.F. (2003). *Perspectives on personality* (5th ed.). Boston, MA: Allyn & Bacon.

Carver, C.S., Scheier, M.F., & Weintraub, J.K. (1989). Assessing coping strategies: A theoretically based approach. *Journal of Personality and Social Psychology, 56,* 267–283.

Carver, C.S., & White, T.L. (1994). Behavioral inhibition, behavioral activation and affective responses to impending reward and punishment: The BIS/BAS scales. *Journal of Personality and Social Psychology, 67,* 319–333.

Caryl, P.G. (1994). Early event-related potentials correlate with inspection time and intelligence. *Intelligence, 18,* 15–46.

Caspi, A., Elder, G.H., & Bem, D.J. (1988). Moving away from the world: Life course patterns of shy children. *Developmental Psychology, 24,* 824–831.

Caspi, A., & Herbener, E.S. (1990). Continuity and change: Assortative marriage and the consistency of personality in adulthood. *Journal of Personality and Social Psychology, 58,* 250–258.

Caspi, A., & Roberts, B.W. (1999). Personality continuity and change across the life course. In L.A. Pervin & O.P. John (Eds.), *Handbook of personality: Theory and research.* New York, NY: Guilford Press.

Castrén, E. (2009). Neural plasticity and recovery from depression. *Duodecim, 125,* 1781–1786.

Castro-Alamancos, M.A. (2004). Absence of rapid sensory adaptation in neocortex during information processing states. *Neuron, 41*(3), 455–464.

Catalano, R., Novaco, R.W., & McConnell, W. (2002). Layoffs and violence revisited. *Aggressive Behavior, 28*(3), 233–247.

Cataldo, A.M., & Cohen, A.L. (2015). The effect of emotional state on visual detection: A signal detection analysis. *Emotion, 15*(6), 846–853.

Catchpole, C.K., & Rowell, A. (1993). Song sharing and local dialects in a population of the European wren (Troglodytes troglodytes). *Behaviour, 125,* 67–78.

Cattell, R.B. (1965). *The scientific analysis of personality.* Chicago, IL: Aldine.

Cattell, R.B. (1971). *Abilities: Their growth, structure, and action.* Boston, MA: Houghton Mifflin.

Cattell, R.B. (1990). Advances in Cattellian personality theory. In L.A. Pervin (Ed.), *Handbook of personality: Theory and research* (pp. 101–110). New York, NY: Guilford Press.

Caughlin, J.P., & Malis, R.S. (2004). Demand/ withdraw communication between parents and adolescents: Connections with self-esteem and substance use. *Journal of Social and Personal Relationships, 21,* 125–148.

CBC. (2011). Alcohol causes 2.5 million deaths a year: WHO. *CBC News,* Friday, February 11, 2011, http://www.cbc.ca/news/health /story/2011/02/11/health-alcohol-deaths.html.

CBC. (2016). Retrieved from http://www.cbc.ca /news/canada/ottawa/new-study-finds. -fentanyl-deaths-on-the-rise-in-canada-1.3187722.

CCSA. (2015). CCENDU Bulletin, August 2015. Retrieved from http://www.ccsa.ca/Resource%20 Library/CCSA-CCENDU-Fentanyl-Deaths -Canada-Bulletin-2015-en.pdf.

Ceci, S.J. (1996). *On intelligence: A bio-ecological treatise on intellectual development.* Cambridge, MA: Harvard University Press.

Ceci, S.J., Bruck, M., & Battin, D.B. (2000). The suggestibility of children's testimony. In D.F. Björklund (Ed.), *False-memory creation in children and adults: Theory, research, and implications* (pp. 166–197). Mahwah, NJ: Erlbaum.

Ceci, S.J., Loftus, E.F., Leichtman, M.D., & Bruck, M. (1994). The possible role of source misattributions in the creation of false beliefs among preschoolers. *International Journal of Clinical and Experimental Hypnosis, 42,* 304–320.

Ceci, S.J., & Williams, W.M. (1997). Schooling, intelligence, and income. *American Psychologist, 52,* 1051–1058.

Centers for Disease Control and Prevention. (1988). *Posttraumatic stress disorders.* Atlanta, GA: Author.

Centers for Disease Control and Prevention. (1994). *Addressing emerging infectious disease threats: A prevention strategy for the United States.* Washington, DC: Author.

Centers for Disease Control and Prevention. (2002). *Statistics on addictive behaviors.* Atlanta, GA: Author.

Centers for Disease Control and Prevention. (2003). *HIV/AIDS statistics.* Atlanta, GA: Author.

Centre for Addiction and Mental Health. (2001). Info on cannabis (marijuana). Retrieved from http://www.camh.net/About_Addiction_Mental_Health/AMH101/top_searched_cannabis.html.

Cervone, D. (1992). The role of self-referent cognitions in goal-setting, motivation, and performance. In M. Rabinowitz (Ed.), *Applied Cognition.* New York, NY: Ablex.

Cha, M. (2016). The mediation effect of mattering and self-esteem in the relationship between socially prescribed perfectionism and depression: Based on the social disconnection model. *Personality and Individual Differences, 88,* 148–159.

Chaiken, S., & Maheswaran, D. (1994). Heuristic processing can bias systematic processing: Effects of source credibility, argument ambiguity, and task importance on attitude judgment. *Journal of Personality and Social Psychology, 66,* 460–473.

Chakeres, D.W., Nornstein, R., & Kangarlu, A. (2003). Randomized comparison of cognitive function in humans at 0 and 8 Tesla. *Journal of Magnetic Resonance Imaging, 18,* 342–345.

Chalmers, D.J. (1995). The puzzle of conscious experience. *Scientific American, 273*(6), 80–86.

Chambless, D.L., & Hollon, S.D. (1998). Defining empirically supported therapies. *Journal of Consulting and Clinical Psychology, 66,* 7–18.

Champagne, F.A., Weaver, I.C., Diorio, J., Dymov, S., Szyf, M., & Meaney, M.J. (2006). Maternal care associated with methylation of the estrogen receptor-alpha1b promoter and estrogen receptor-alpha expression in the medial preoptic area of female offspring. *Endocrinology, 147,* 2909–2915.

Chan, Z.C.Y., & Ma, J.L.C. (2002). Family themes of food refusal: Disciplining the body and punishing the family. *Health Care for Women International, 23,* 49–58.

Chandler, M.J., Lacritz, L.H., Cicerello, A.R., Chapman, S.B., Honig, L.S., Weiner, M.F., & Cullum, C.M. (2004). Three-word recall in normal aging. *Journal of Clinical and Experimental Neuropsychology, 26,* 1128–1133.

Chang, E.C. (1998). Dispositional optimism and primary and secondary appraisal of a stressor: Controlling for confounding influences and relations to coping and psychological and physical adjustment. *Journal of Personality and Social Psychology, 74,* 1109–1120.

Chapell, M.S., Blanding, Z.B., Silverstein, M.E., Takahashi, M., Newman, B., Gubi, A., & McCann, N. (2005). Test anxiety and academic performance in undergraduate and graduate students. *Journal of Educational Psychology, 97,* 268–274.

Chaplin, T.M., Cole, P.M., & Zahn-Waxler, C. (2005). Parental socialization of emotion expression: Gender differences and relations to child adjustment. *Emotion, 5,* 80–88.

Chapman, A.L. (2010). Borderline personality disorder. In D. McKay, J.S. Abramowitz, & S. Taylor (Eds.), *Cognitive-behavioral therapy for refractory cases: Turning failure into success.* Washington, DC: American Psychological Association.

Chappell, M., & Humphreys, M.S. (1994). An autoassociative neural network for sparse representations: Analysis and application to models of recognition and cued recall. *Psychological Review, 101,* 103–128.

Chartrand, T.L., & Bargh, J.A. (2002). Nonconscious motivations: Their activation, operation, and consequences. In A. Tesser, D.A. Stapel, & J.V. Wood (Eds.), *Self and motivation: Emerging psychological perspectives.* Washington, DC: American Psychological Association.

Chase, W.G., & Simon, H.A. (1973). Perception in chess. *Cognitive Psychology, 4,* 55–81.

Chaudhuri, A. (2013). Biological properties of transduction mechanisms in sensory systems. *Expanding horizons of the mind sciences.* (pp. 69–91) Novinka/Nova Science Publishers, New York, NY. Retrieved from http://search.proquest.com/docview/1536026358?accountid=15115.

Checknita, D., Maussion, G., Labonte, B., Comai, S., Tremblay, R.E., Vitaro, F., ... Turecki, G. (2015). Monoamine oxidase A gene promoter methylation and transcriptional downregulation in an offender population with antisocial personality disorder. *The British Journal of Psychiatry, 206*(3), 216–222.

Chekroud, A.M., Everett, J.A.C., Bridge, H., & Hewstone, M. (2014). A review of neuroimaging studies of race-related prejudice: Does amygdala response reflect threat? *Frontiers in Human Neuroscience, 8.* Retrieved from https://www.lib.uwo.ca/cgi-bin/ezpauthn.cgi?url=http://search.proquest.com/docview/1555966744?accountid=15115.

Chen, C., Greenberger, E., Leter, J., Dong, Q., & Guo, M.S. (1998). A cross-cultural study of family and peer correlates of adolescent misconduct. *Developmental Psychology, 34,* 770–781.

Chen, H., Charlat, O., Tartaglia, L.A., Woolf, E.A., Weng, X., & Ellis, S.J. (1996). Evidence that the diabetes gene encodes the leptin receptor: Identification of a mutation in the leptin receptor gene in db/db mice. *Cell, 84,* 491–495.

Chen, H., & Lan, W. (2006). Adolescents' perceptions of their parents' academic expectations: Comparison of American, Chinese-American, and Chinese high school students. *Family Therapy, 33,* 113–118.

Chen, S., English, T., & Peng, K. (2006). Self-verification and contextualized self-views. *Personality and Social Psychology Bulletin, 32*(7), 930–942.

Chen, S.C. (1937). Social modification of the activity of ants in nest-building. *Physiological Zoology, 10,* 420–436.

Cheng, D.T., Knight, D.C., Smith, C.N., & Helmstetter, F.J. (2006). Human amygdala activity during the expression of fear responses. *Behavioral Neuroscience, 120,* 1187–1195.

Chenoweth, D. (2002). *Evaluating worksite health promotion.* Champaign, IL: Human Kinetics.

Chiang, H., Chen, Y., Lo, Y., Tseng, W.I., & Gau, S.S. (2015). Altered white matter tract property related to impaired focused attention, sustained attention, cognitive impulsivity and vigilance in attention-deficit/hyperactivity disorder. *Journal of Psychiatry & Neuroscience, 40*(5), 325–335.

Chiappelli, F. (2000). Immune suppression. In G. Fink (Ed.), *Encyclopedia of stress* (Vol. 2). San Diego, CA: Academic Press.

Chiauzzi, E., Brevard, J., Thum, C., Decemberle, S., & Lord, S. (2008). MyStudentBody-Stress: An online stress management intervention for college students. *Journal of Health Communication, 13,* 555–572.

Chiles, J.A., & Strosahl, K.D. (1995). *The suicidal patient: Principles of assessment, treatment, and case management.* Washington, DC: American Psychiatric Press.

Chiriboga, D.A. (1989). Mental health at the midpoint: Crisis, challenge, or relief? In S. Hunter & M. Sundel (Eds.), *Midlife myths: Issues, findings, and practice implications* (pp. 116–144). Newbury Park, CA: Sage.

Chisholm, K. (1998). A three-year follow-up of attachment and indiscriminate friendliness in children adopted from Romanian orphanages. *Child Development, 69,* 1092–1106.

Chiu, I.M., Heesters, B.A., Ghasemlou, N., Von Hehn, C.A., Zhao, F., Tran, J., ... Woolf, C.J. (2013). Bacteria activate sensory neurons that modulate pain and inflammation. *Nature, 501*(7465), 52–57.

Cho, C., & Lee, H. (2013). Oxidative stress and tardive dyskinesia: Pharmacogenetic evidence. *Progress in Neuro-Psychopharmacology & Biological Psychiatry, 46,* 207–213.

Choca, J.P., Shanley, L.A., & Van Denburg, E. (1992). *Interpretive guide to the Millon Clinical Multiaxial Inventory.* Washington, DC: American Psychological Association.

Choi, I., Dalal, R., Kim Prieto, C., & Park, H. (2003). Culture and judgement of causal relevance. *Journal of Personality and Social Psychology, 84,* 46–59.

Choleris, E., Clipperton-Allen, A.E., Gray, D.G., Diaz-Gonzalez, S., & Welsman, R.G. (2011). Differential effects of dopamine receptor D1-type and D2-type antagonists and phase of the estrous cycle on social learning of food preferences, feeding, and social interactions in mice, *Neuropsychopharmacology, 36,* 1689–1702.

Chomsky, N. (1965). *Aspects of a theory of syntax.* Cambridge, MA: MIT Press.

Chomsky, N. (1972). *Language and mind.* New York, NY: Harcourt.

Chomsky, N. (1987). Language in a psychological setting. *Sophia Linguistica: Working Papers in Linguistics, 22.* Tokyo, Japan: Sophia University.

Chowdhary, N., Jotheeswaran, A.T., Nadkarni, A., Hollon, S.D., King, M., Jordans, M.J.D., ... Patel, V. (2014). The methods and outcomes of cultural adaptations of psychological treatments for depressive disorders: A systematic review. *Psychological Medicine, 44*(6), 1131–1146.

Christianson, S.A., & Nilsson, L.G. (1989). Hysterical amnesia: A case of aversively motivated isolation of memory. In T. Archer & L.G. Nilsson (Eds.), *Aversion, avoidance, and anxiety: Perspectives on aversively motivated behavior* (pp. 289–310). Hillsdale, NJ: Erlbaum.

Creese, I., Burd, D.R., & Snyder, S.H. (1976). Dopamine receptor binding predicts clinical and pharmacological potencies of antischizophrenic drugs. *Science, 192*, 481–483.

Crits-Christoph, P. (1992). The efficacy of brief dynamic psychotherapy: A meta-analysis. *American Journal of Psychiatry, 149*, 151–158.

Crits-Christoph, P., Cooper, A., & Luborsky, L. (1988). The accuracy of therapists' interpretations and the outcome of dynamic psychotherapy. *Journal of Consulting and Clinical Psychology, 56*, 490–495.

Crocker, J. (2002). Contingencies of self-worth: Implications for self-regulation and psychological vulnerability. *Self and Identity, 1*, 143–149.

Crocker, J., & Park, L.E. (2004). The costly pursuit of self-esteem. *Psychological Bulletin, 130*, 392–414.

Crook, J.M., & Copolov, D.L. (2000). Schizophrenia. In G. Fink (Ed.), *Encyclopedia of stress* (Vol. 3). San Diego, CA: Academic Press.

Cross, S.E., & Markus, H.R. (1999). The cultural constitution of personality. In L.A. Pervin & O.P. John (Eds.), *Handbook of personality: Theory and research* (2nd ed.). New York, NY: Guilford Press.

Crowley, K. (2008, June 27). "Game Boy" havoc on LI—teens busted in "grand theft auto" spree. *New York Post*. Retrieved February 12, 2010, from http://proquest.umi.com/pqdweb?index=2&did=15 01482521&SrchMode=1&sid=1&Fmt=3&VInst=PR OD&VType=PDQ&RQT=309VName=PQD& TS=1267587664&clientId=8991.

Crowley, K., Callanan, M.A., Tenenbaum, H.R., & Allen, E. (2001). Parents explain more often to boys than to girls during shared scientific thinking. *Psychological Science, 12*, 258–261.

Croyle, R.T., & Cooper, J. (1983). Dissonance arousal: Physiological evidence. *Journal of Personality and Social Psychology, 45*, 782–791.

Cruse, D., Chennu, S., Chatelle, C., Bekinschtein, T.A., Fernandez-espejo, D., Pickard, J.D., Laureys, S., & Owen, A.M. (2012). Bedside detection of awareness in the vegetative state: A cohort study. *Lancet, 378*, 2088–2094.

Cserr, H.F., & Bundgaard, M. (1986). The neuronal micro-environment: A comparative view. *Annals of the New York Academy of Science, 481*, 1–6.

Csikszentmihalyi, M. (1990). *Flow: The psychology of optimal experience*. New York, NY: Harper & Row.

Cue, D.K., Hendershot, C.S., George, W.H., Norris, J., & Heiman, J.R. (2007). Alcohol's effects on sexual decision making: An integration of alcohol myopia and individual differences. *Journal of Studies on Alcohol and Drugs. 68*, 843–851.

Culbertson, F.M. (1997). Depression and gender: An international review. *American Psychologist, 52*, 25–31.

Culham, J. (2004). Neuroimaging investigations of visually guided grasping. In N. Kanwisher & J. Duncan (Eds.), *Functional brain imaging of human cognition: Attention and performance XX* (pp. 415–436). Oxford, UK: Oxford University Press.

Cummings, L. (2005). *Pragmatics: A multidisciplinary perspective*. Mahwah, NJ: Erlbaum.

Cunillera, T., Toro, J.M., Sebastian-Galles, N., & Rodriguez-Fornells, A. (2006). The effects of stress and statistical cues on continuous speech segmentation: An event-related brain potential study. *Brain Research, 1123*, 168–178.

Cunningham, W.A., Johnson, M.K., Raye, C.L., Gatenby, J.C., Gore, J.C., & Banaji, M.R. (2004).

Separate neural components in the processing of black and white faces. *Psychological Science, 15*, 12806–12813.

Curci, A., & Luminet, O. (2009). Flashbulb memories for expected events: A test of the emotional-integrative model. *Applied Cognitive Psychology, 23*, 98–114.

Curry, F., Elliot, A.J., Fonseca, D.D., & Moller, A.C. (2006). The social-cognitive model of achievement motivation and the 2 × 2 achievement goal framework. *Journal of Personality and Social Psychology, 90*, 666–679.

Curry, O., Roberts, S.G.B., & Dunbar, R.I.M. (2013). Altruism in social networks: Evidence for a "kinship premium." *British Journal of Psychology, 104*(2), 283–295.

Curtis, C.E., & D'Esposito, M. (2003). Persistent activity in the prefrontal cortex during working memory. *Trends in Cognitive Sciences, 7*(9), 415–423.

Curtis, G.C., Magee, W.J., Eaton, W.W., Wittchen, H-U., & Kessler, R.C. (1998). Specific fears and phobias: Epidemiology and classification. *British Journal of Psychiatry, 173*, 112–117.

Curtiss, S. (1977). *Genie: A psychological study of a modern day "wild child."* New York, NY: Academic Press.

Cyranoski, D. (2012). Neuroscience: The mind reader. *Nature, 485*, 178–180.

Cytowic, R.E. (2002). *Synesthesia: A union of the senses* (2nd ed.). Boston, MA: MIT Press.

Cytowic, R.E., & Eagleman, D.M. (2009). *Wednesday is indigo blue: Discovering the brain of synesthesia*. Cambridge, MA: MIT Press.

Dabaghian, Y., Brandt, V.L., & Frank, L.M. (2014). Reconceiving the hippocampal map as a topological template. *Elife, 3*, e03476, doi: 10.7554/eLife.03476.

Daily Mail. (2009). Girls trapped in storm drain use Facebook to call for help ... instead of phoning emergency services. *Daily Mail*, 8 September 2009. http://www.dailymail.co.uk /news/article-1211909/Girls-trapped-storm-drain-use-Facebook-help–instead-phoning-emergency-services.html.

Dalenberg, C.F., Brand, B.L., Gleaves, D.H., Dorahy, M.J., Loewenstein, R.J., et al. (2012). Evaluation of the evidence for the Trauma and Fantasy Models of Dissociation. *Psychological Bulletin, 138*, 550–588.

Dalgarno, P. (2007). Subjective effects of Salvia divinorum? *Journal of Psychoactive Drugs, 39*, 143–149.

Dallow, A. (Director). (2007, April 11). Voice flame extinguisher [Television series episode]. In J. Hunt (Producer), *MythBusters*. San Francisco, CA: Beyond Television Productions.

Dalton, A.L., & Daneman, M. (2006). Social suggestibility to central peripheral misinformation. *Memory, 14*(4), 468–501.

Dalton, P. (2002). Olfaction. In H. Pashler & S. Yantis (Eds.), *Steven's handbook of experimental psychology: Vol. 1 Sensation and perception* (3rd ed., pp. 641–746). New York, NY: Wiley.

Daly, M., & Wilson, M. (1988). *Homicide*. New York, NY: Aldine de Gruyter.

Daly, M., Wilson M., & Vasdev, S. (2001). Income inequality and homicide rates in Canada and the United States. *Canadian Journal of Criminology, 43*, 219–236.

Daly, M., Wilson, M., & Weghorst, S.J. (1982). Male sexual jealousy. *Ethology and Sociobiology, 3*, 11–27.

Damasio, A.R. (2005). Emotions and feelings: A neurobiological perspective. In A.S.R. Manstead,

N.H. Frijda, A.H. Fischer, & K. Oatley (Eds.), *Feelings and Emotions: The Amsterdam Symposium* (pp. 49–57). New York, NY: Cambridge University Press.

Damasio, H. (1989). Neuroimaging contributions to the understanding of aphasia. In F. Boller & J. Grafman (Eds.), *Handbook of Neuropsychology* (Vol. 2). Amsterdam, Netherlands: Elsevier.

Dandeneau, S.D., Baldwin, M.W., Baccus, J.R., Sakellaropoulop, M., & Pruessner, J.C. (2007). Cutting stress off at the pass: Reducing vigilance and responsiveness to social threat by manipulating attention. *Journal of Personality and Social Psychology, 93*, 651–666.

Daniels, K., Toth, J., & Jacoby, J. (2006). The aging of executive functions. In E. Bialystok & F.I.M Craik (Eds.), *Lifespan cognition: Mechanisms of change* (pp. 96–111). New York, NY: Oxford University Press.

Dark, K., Peeke, H.V., Ellman, G., & Salfi, M. (1987). Behaviorally conditioned histamine release: Prior stress and conditionability and extinction of the response. *Annals of the New York Academy of Sciences, 496*, 578–582.

Darley, J.M., & Gross, P.H. (1983). A hypothesis-confirming bias in labeling effects. *Journal of Personality and Social Psychology, 44*, 20–33.

Darley, J.M., & Latané, B. (1968). Bystander intervention in emergencies: Diffusion of responsibility. *Journal of Personality and Social Psychology, 8*, 377–383.

Daros, A.R., Uliaszek, A.A., & Ruocco, A.C. (2014). Perceptual biases in facial emotion recognition in borderline personality disorder. *Personality Disorders: Theory, Research, and Treatment, 5*(1), 79–87.

Darragh, M., Chang, J.W., Booth, R.J., & Consedine, N.S. (2015). The placebo effect in inflammatory skin reactions: The influence of verbal suggestion on itch and weal size. *Journal of Psychosomatic Research, 78*(5), 489–494.

Darwin, C. (1859). *On the origin of species by means of natural selection*. London, UK: Murray.

Darwin, C. (1871). *The descent of man, and selection in relation to sex*. New York: Appleton & Co.

Darwin, C.R. (1872/1965). *The expression of emotions in man and animals*. Chicago, IL: University of Chicago Press.

Dasen, P.R., Barthélémy, D., Kan, E., Kouamé, K., Daouda, K., Adjéi, K.K., & Assandé, N. (1985). N'glouele, l'intelligence chez les Baoulé [N'glouele, intelligence according to the Baoulé]. *Archives de Psychologie, 53*, 293–324.

Datta Gupta, N., Etcoff, N.L., & Jaeger, M.M. (2015). Beauty in mind: The effects of physical attractiveness on psychological well-being and distress. *Journal of Happiness Studies*, doi:http:// dx.doi.org/10.1007/s10902-015-9644-6.

Dauvilliers, Y., Jennum, P., & Plazzi, G. (2013). Rapid eye movement sleep behavior disorder and rapid eye movement sleep without atonia in narcolepsy. *Sleep Medicine, 14*(8), 775–781.

Davey, G.C.L. (1995). Preparedness and phobias: Specific evolved associations or a generalized expectancy bias? *Behavioral and Brain Sciences, 18*, 289–325.

David, D., Szentagotai, A., Eva, K., & Macavei, B. (2005). A synopsis of rational-emotive behavior therapy (REBT): Fundamental and applied research. *Journal of Rational-Emotive and Cognitive-Behavior Therapy, 23*(3), 175–221.

Davidoff, J. (2004). Coloured thinking. *Psychologist, 17*, 570–572.

Davidowicz, L.S. (1975). *The war against the Jews, 1933-1945*. New York, NY: Holt, Rinehart & Winston.

Davidson, M.C., Amso, D., Anderson, L.C., & Diamond, A. (2006). Development of cognitive control and executive functions from 4 to 13 years: Evidence from manipulations of memory, inhibition, and task switching. *Neuropsychologia, 44*(11), 2037-2078.

Davidson, R.J. (1998). Affective style and affective disorders: Perspectives from affective neuroscience. *Cognition and Emotion, 12,* 307-320.

Davidson, R.J. (2000). Affective style, psychopathology, and resilience: Brain mechanisms and plasticity. *American Psychologist, 55,* 1196-1214.

Davidson, R.J. (2003). Affective neuroscience and psychophysiology: Toward a synthesis. *Psychophysiology, 40,* 655-665.

Davidson, R.J., Coe, C.C., Dolski, I., & Donzella, B. (1999). Individual differences in prefrontal activation asymmetry predict natural killer cell activity at rest and in response to challenge. *Brain, Behavior, and Immunity, 13,* 93-108.

Davidson, R.J., & Fox, N.A. (1988). Cerebral asymmetry and emotion: Developmental and individual differences. In D.L. Molfese & S.J. Segalowitz (Eds.), *Brain lateralization in children: Developmental implications* (pp. 191-206). New York, NY: Guilford Press.

Davidson, R.J., & Fox, N.A. (1989). Frontal brain asymmetry predicts infants' response to maternal separation. *Journal of Abnormal Psychology, 98,* 127-131.

Davidson, W.B., & Cotter, P.R. (1997). Psychological sense of community and newspaper readership. *Psychological Reports, 80,* 659-665.

Davis, C., Patte, K., Levitan, R., Reid, C., Tweed, S., & Curtis, C. (2007). From motivation to behaviour: A model of reward sensitivity, overeating, and food preferences in the risk profile for obesity. *Appetite, 48,* 12-19.

Davis, C.G., Nolen, H.S., & Larson, J. (1998). Making sense of loss and benefiting from the experience: Two construals of meaning. *Journal of Personality and Social Psychology, 75,* 561-574.

Davis, C.J., Knopik, V.S., Olson, R.K., Wadsworth, S.J., & DeFries, J.C. (2001). Genetics and environmental influences on rapid naming and reading ability. *Annals of Dyslexia, 51,* 231-247.

Davis, C.M., & Bauserman, R. (1993). Exposure to sexually explicit materials: An attitude change perspective. *Annual Review of Sex Research, 4,* 121-209.

Davis, E.P., Sandman, C.A., Buss, C., Wing, D.A., & Head, K. (2013). Fetal glucocorticoid exposure is associated with preadolescent brain development. *Biological Psychiatry, 74*(9), 647-655.

Davis, K., Christodoulou, J., Seider, S., & Gardner, H. (2011). The theory of multiple intelligences. In R.J. Sternberg & S.B. Kaufman (Eds.), *The Cambridge Handbook of Intelligence.* Cambridge: Cambridge University Press.

Davis, M. (1992). The role of the amygdala in fear and anxiety. *Annual Review of Neuroscience, 15,* 311-327.

Davis, M. (2003). MRC Cognition and Brain Sciences Unit. Cambridge University. Retrieved December 18, 2009, from http://www.mrccbu.cam.ac.uk/people/matt.davis.

Davis, M.H., & Johnsrude, I.S. (2007). Hearing speech sounds: top-down influences on the interface between audition and speech perception. *Hearing Research, 229*(1-2), 132-147.

Davis, T., Gunderson, J.G., & Myers, M. (1999). Borderline personality disorder. In D.G. Jacobs (Ed.), *The Harvard Medical School Guide to s uicide assessment and intervention.* San Francisco, CA: Jossey-Bass.

Daw, J., Guo, G., & Harris, K.M. (2015). Nurture net of nature: Re-evaluating the role of shared environments in academic achievement and verbal intelligence. *Social Science Research, 52,* 422-439.

Dawes, R.M. (1994). *House of cards: Psychology and psychotherapy built on myth.* New York, NY: Free Press.

Dawkins, R. (2006). *The selfish gene* (revised ed.). New York, NY: Oxford University Press.

Dawson, W.A. (1993). Aboriginal dreaming. In M.A. Carskadon (Ed.), *Encyclopedia of sleep and dreaming.* New York, NY: Macmillan.

Dawson-McClure, S.R., Sandler, I.N., Wolchik, S.A., & Millsap, R.E. (2004). Risk as a moderator of the effects of prevention programs for children from divorced families: A six-year longitudinal study. *Journal of Abnormal Child Psychology, 32,* 175-190.

Day, R., Nielsen, J.A., Korten, A., Ernberg, G., Dube, K.C., Gebhart, J., ... Olatawura, M. (1987). Stressful life events preceding the acute onset of schizophrenia. *Culture, Medicine, and Psychiatry, 11,* 123-205.

Dealberto, M. (2013). Are the rates of schizophrenia unusually high in canada? A comparison of canadian and international data. *Psychiatry Research, 209*(3), 259-265.

Deary, I.J., Spinath, F.M., & Bates, T.C. (2006). Genetics of intelligence. *European Journal of Human Genetics, 14*(6), 690-700.

Deary, I.J., Whiteman, M.C., Starr, J.M., Whalley, L.J., & Fox, H. (2004). The impact of childhood intelligence on later life: Following up the Scottish Medical Surveys of 1932 and 1947. *Journal of Personality and Social Psychology, 86,* 130-147.

De Castro, J. (2002). The influence of heredity on self-reported sleep patterns in free-living humans. *Physiology & Behavior, 76,* 479-486.

De Cremer, D., & van Lange, P.A.M. (2001). Why prosocials exhibit greater cooperation than proselfs: The roles of social responsibility and reciprocity. *European Journal of Personality, 15,* 5-18.

DeCasper, A.J., & Fifer, W.P. (1980). Of human bonding: Newborns prefer their mothers' voices. *Science, 208,* 1174-1176.

DeCasper, A.J., & Spence, M.J. (1986). Prenatal maternal speech influences newborns' perceptions of speech sounds. *Infant Behavior and Development, 9,* 133-150.

DeCharms, R., & Moeller, G.H. (1962). Values expressed in American children's readers: 1800 to 1950. *Journal of Abnormal and Social Psychology, 64,* 135-142.

Deci, E.L., & Ryan, R.M. (1985). *Intrinsic motivation and self-determination in human behavior.* New York, NY: Plenum Press.

Deci, E.L., & Ryan, R.M. (2000). The "what" and "why" of goal pursuits: Human needs and the self-determination of behavior. *Psychological Inquiry, 11,* 227-268.

Deci, E.L., & Ryan, R.M. (2002). *Handbook of self-determination theory research.* Rochester, NY: University of Rochester Press.

Deci, E.L., & Ryan, R.M. (2009). Self-determination theory: A consideration of human motivational universals. In P.J. Corr & G. Matthews (Eds.), *The Cambridge handbook of personality psychology* (pp. 441-456). Cambridge, UK: Cambridge University Press.

Deckersbach, T., Miller, K.K., Klibanski, A., Fischman, A., Dougherty, D.D., Blais, M.A., ... Rauch, S.L. (2006). Regional cerebral brain metabolism correlates of neuroticism and extraversion. *Depression and Anxiety, 23,* 133-138.

Deffenbacher, K.A., Bernstein, B.H., & Penrod, S.D. (2006). Mugshot exposure effects: Retroactive interference, mugshot commitment, source confusion, and unconscious transference. *Law and Human Behavior, 30,* 287-307.

DeFries, J.C., Singer, S.M., Foch, T.T., & Lewitter, F.I. (1978). Familial nature of reading disability. *British Journal of Psychiatry, 132,* 361-367.

de Geus, E.J.C. (2000). Aerobics in stress reduction. In G. Fink (Ed.), *Encyclopedia of stress* (Vol. 1). San Diego, CA: Academic Press.

Dehaene, S., Izard, V., Pica, P., & Spelke, E. (2006). Core knowledge of geometry in an Amazonian indigene group. *Science, 311,* 381-384.

Dekker, E., & Groen, J. (1956). Reproducible psychogenic attacks of asthma. *Journal of Psychosomatic Research, 1,* 56-67.

Delahunt, P.B., Ball, K.K., Roenker, D.L., Hardy, J.L., Mahncke, H.W., & Merzenich, M.M. (2009). Computer-based cognitive training to facilitate neural plasticity. *Gerontechnology, 8,* 52-53.

Dell, P.F., & O'Neil, J.A. (Eds.). (2009). *Dissociation and the dissociative disorders: DSM-V and beyond.* New York, NY: Routledge/Taylor & Francis Group.

DeLongis, A. (2000). Coping skills. In G. Fink (Ed.), *Encyclopedia of stress* (Vol. 1). San Diego, CA: Academic Press.

Demarest, J., & Allen, R. (2000). Body image: Gender, ethnic, and age differences. *Journal of Social Psychology, 140,* 465-472.

De Martino, B., Camerer, C.F., & Adolphs, R. (2010). Amygdala damage eliminates monetary loss aversion. *Proceedings of the National Academy of Sciences, 107*(8), 3788-3792.

Dement, W.C. (1978). *Some must watch while some must sleep.* New York, NY: Norton.

Dement, W.C. (2005). History of sleep medicine. *Neurologic Clinics, 23,* 945-965.

Démonet, J.F., Thierry, G., & Cardebat, D. (2005). Renewal of the neurophysiology of language: Functional neuroimaging. *Physiological Reviews, 85,* 49-95.

Denzin, N.K. (2010). *Childhood socialization* (Rev. 2nd ed.). New Brunswick, NJ: Transaction.

Department of Health and Human Services. (1998). *National Household Survey On Drug Abuse: Population Estimates 1997.* Rockville, MD: Author.

Depue, R.A., & Lenzenweger, M.F. (2005). A neurobehavioral dimensional model of personality disorders. In M.F. Lenzenweger & J.F. Clarkin (Eds.), *Major theories of personality disorder* (pp. 391-454). New York, NY: Guilford Press.

Der, G., Batty, G.D., & Deary, I.J. (2009). The association between IQ in adolescence and a range of health outcomes at 40 in the 1979 US National Longitudinal Study of Youth. *Intelligence, 37,* 573-580.

DeRubeis, R.J., & Crits-Christoph, P. (1998). Empirically supported individual and group psychological treatments for adult mental disorders. *Journal of Consulting and Clinical Psychology, 66,* 37-52.

De Silva, P., & Rachman, J. (1998). *Obsessive-compulsive disorders.* New York, NY: Oxford University Press.

De Souza, C.M., & Hidalgo, M.P.L. (2014). Midpoint sleep on school days is associated with depression among adolescents. *Chronobiology International, 31*, 199–205.

D'Espositio, M.D. (2003). *Neurological Foundations of Cognitive Neuroscience.* Boston, MA: MIT Press.

Dessens, A.B., Cohen, K.P.T., Mellenbergh, G.J., van der Poll, N., Koppe, J.G., & Boer, K. (1999). Prenatal exposure to anticonvulsants and psychosexual development. *Archives of Sexual Behavior, 28*, 31–44.

Deuker, L., Olligs, J., Fell, J., Kranz, T.A., Mormann, F., Montag, C., ... Axmacher, N. (2013). Memory consolidation by replay of stimulus-specific neural activity. *The Journal of Neuroscience, 33*(49), 19373–19383.

Deutsch, M., & Gerard, H.B. (1955). A study of normative and informational social influence upon individual judgment. *Journal of Abnormal and Social Psychology, 51*, 629–636.

Deutschenbaur, L., Beck, J., Kiyhankhadiv, A., Mühlhauser, M., Borgwardt, S., Walter, M., ... Lang, U.E. (2016). Role of calcium, glutamate and NMDA in major depression and therapeutic application. *Progress in Neuro-Psychopharmacology & Biological Psychiatry, 64*, 325–333.

DeValois, R.L., & DeValois, K.K. (1988). *Spatial vision.* New York, NY: Oxford University Press.

Devane, W.A., Hanus, L., Breuer, A., Pertwee, R.G., Stevenson, L.A., & Griffin, G. (1992). Isolation and structure of a brain constituent that binds to the cannabinoid receptor. *Science, 18*, 1946–1949.

DeVries, H., Mudde, A.N., Dijkstra, A., & Willemsen, M.C. (1998). Differential beliefs, perceived social influences, and self-efficacy expectations among smokers in various motivational phases. *Preventive Medicine, 27*, 681–689.

DeVries, R., Hildebrandt, C., & Zan, B. (2000). Constructivist early education for moral development. *Early Education and Development, 11*, 9–35.

Dewsbury, D.A. (1988). The comparative psychology of monogamy. In D.W. Leger (Ed.), *Comparative perspectives in modern psychology* (pp. 1–50). Nebraska Symposium on Motivation. Lincoln, NE: University of Nebraska Press.

Dewsbury, D.A. (1997). In celebration of the centennial of Ivan P. Pavlov's (1897/1902) *The Work of the Digestive Glands. American Psychologist, 52*, 933–935.

DeYoung, C.G. (2013). The neuromodulator of exploration: A unifying theory of the role of dopamine in personality. *Frontiers in Human Neuroscience,* doi: 10.3389/fnhum.2013.00762.

DeYoung, C.G., Peterson, J.B., & Higgins, D.M. (2005). Sources of openness/intellect: Cognitive and neuropsychological correlates of the fifth factor of personality. *Journal of Personality, 73*, 825–858.

De Zeeuw, C.I., & Cicirata, F. (2005). *Creating coordination in the cerebellum.* St. Louis, MO: Elsevier Science/Mosby.

Diacon, S., & Hasseldine, J. (2007). Framing effects and risk perception: The effect of prior performance presentation format on investment fund choice. *Journal of Economic Psychology, 28*, 31–52.

Diaz, J. (1997). *How drugs influence behavior: A neurobehavioral approach.* Upper Saddle River, NJ: Prentice Hall.

Dickinson, A. (1997). Bolles's psychological syllogism. In M.E. Bouton, M.S. Fanselow, &

S. Michael (Eds.), *Learning, motivation, and cognition: The functional behaviorism of Robert C. Bolles.* Washington, DC: American Psychological Association.

Dickinson, C.A., & Intraub, H. (2009). Spatial asymmetries in viewing and remembering scenes: Consequences of an attentional bias? *Attention, Perception, & Psychophysics, 71*, 1251–1262.

DiClemente, C.C. (2003). *Addiction and change: How addictions develop and addicted people recover.* New York, NY: Guilford Press.

Diener, E. (2000). Subjective well-being: The science of happiness and a proposal for a national index. *American Psychologist, 55*, 34–43.

Diener, E., & Biswas-Diener, R. (2008). *Happiness: Unlocking the mysteries of psychological wealth.* Malden, MA: Blackwell.

Diener, E., & Seligman, M.E.P. (2002). Very happy people. *Psychological Science, 13*, 81–84.

Diener, E., Suh, E., Lucas, R.E., & Smith, H.L. (1999). Subjective well-being: Three decades of progress. *Psychological Bulletin, 125*, 276–302.

Dienes, Z., Brown, E., Hutton, S., Kirsch, I., Mazzoni, G., & Wright, D.B. (2009). Hypnotic suggestibility, cognitive inhibition, and dissociation. *Consciousness and Cognition: An International Journal, 18*, 837–884.

DiFonzo, N., Bourgeois, M.J., Suls, J., Homan, C., Stupak, N., Brooks, B.P., Ross, D.S., & Bordia, P. (2013). Rumor clustering, consensus, and polarization: Dynamic social impact and self-organization of hearsay. *Journal of Experimental Social Psychology, 49*(3), 378–399.

DiGennaro, F.D., Hirst, J.M., & Hyman, S.R. (2012). Assessment and treatment of stereotypic behavior in children with autism and other developmental disabilities: A thirty year review. *Research in Autism Spectrum Disorders, 6*(1), 422–430.

Di Lorenzo, P.M., & Youngentob, S.L. (2013). Taste and olfaction. Handbook of psychology, vol. 3: Behavioral neuroscience (2nd ed., pp. 272–305). New York: John Wiley & Sons Ltd.

DiMauro, J. (2014). Exposure therapy for posttraumatic stress disorder: A meta-analysis. *Military Psychology, 26*(2), 120–130.

Dimberg, U., & Thunberg, M. (1998). Rapid facial reactions to emotional facial expressions. *Scandinavian Journal of Psychology, 39*, 39–46.

Dimberg, U., Thunberg, M., & Elmehed, K. (2000). Unconscious facial reactions to emotional facial expressions. *Psychological Science, 11*, 86–89.

Dimidjian, S., Hollon, S.D., Dobson, K.S., Schmaling, K.B., Kohlenberg, R.J., Addis, M.E., ... Jacobson, N.S.D. (2006). Randomized trial of behavioral activation, cognitive therapy, and antidepressant medication in the acute treatment of adults with major depression. *Journal of Consulting and Clinical Psychology, 74*, 658–670.

Dindia, K. (2002). Self-disclosure research: Knowledge through meta-analysis. In M. Allen, R.W. Preiss, B.M. Gayle, & N.A. Burrell (Eds.), *Interpersonal communication research: Advances through meta-analysis* (pp. 169–186). Mahwah, NJ: Erlbaum.

Dion, K.K., Berscheid, E., & Walster, E. (1972). What is beautiful is good. *Journal of Personality and Social Psychology, 24*, 285–290.

Dishman, R.K. (1982). Compliance/adherence in health-related exercise. *Health Psychology, 1*, 237–267.

Dishman, R.K. (1988). Behavioral barriers to health-related physical fitness. In L.K. Hall & G.C. Meyer (Eds.), *Epidemiology, behavior change,*

and interventions in chronic disease. La Crosse exercise and health series. Champaign, IL: Life Enhancement Publications.

Dixon, M., & Laurence, J.R. (1992). Two hundred years of hypnosis research: Questions resolved. Questions unanswered. In E. Fromm & M.R. Nash (Eds.), *Contemporary hypnosis research* (pp. 34–63). New York, NY: Guilford Press.

Dixon, N.F. (1981). *Preconscious processing.* New York, NY: Wiley.

Docherty, N.M., St-Hillaire, A., Aakre, J.M., & Seghers, J.P. (2009). Life events and high trait reactivity predict psychotic symptom increase in schizophrenia. *Schizophrenia Bulletin, 35*, 638–645.

Doell, R.G. (1995). Sexuality in the brain. *Journal of Homosexuality, 28*, 345–354.

Doherty, T.S., Forster, A., & Roth, T.L. (2016). Global and gene-specific DNA methylation alterations in the adolescent amygdala and hippocampus in an animal model of caregiver maltreatment. *Behavioural Brain Research, 298*, 55–61.

Doi, H., & Shinohara, K. (2015). Unconscious presentation of fearful face modulates electrophysiological responses to emotional prosody. *Cerebral Cortex, 25*, 817–832.

Doka, K.J. (1995). Coping with life-threatening illness: A task model. *Omega: Journal of Death and Dying, 32*, 111–122.

Dolezal, H. (1982). *Living in a world transformed: Perceptual and performatory adaptation to a visual distortion.* New York, NY: Academic Press.

Dollard, J., Doob, L., Miller, N., Mowrer, O.H., & Sears, R.R. (1939). *Frustration and aggression.* New Haven, CT: Yale University Press.

Domhoff, G.W. (1999). Drawing theoretical implications from descriptive empirical findings on dream content. *Dreaming: Journal of the Association for the Study of Dreams, 9*, 201–210.

Domhoff, G.W. (2005). Refocusing the neurocognitive approach to dreams: A critique of the Hobson versus Solms debate. *Dreaming: Journal of the Association for the Study of Dreams, 15*, 3–20.

Domhoff, G.W. (2011). The neural substrate for dreaming: Is it a subsystem of the default network *Consciousness and Cognition, 20*, 1163–1174.

Domhoff, G.W., & Schneider, A. (2008). Similarities and differences in dream content at the cross-cultural, gender, and individual levels. *Consciousness and Cognition: An International Journal, 17*, 1257–1265.

Domino, G., & Domino, M.L. (2006). *Psychological testing: An introduction,* New York, NY: Cambridge University Press.

Domjan, M., Greene, P., & North, N.C. (1989). Contextual conditioning and the control of copulatory behavior by species-specific sign stimuli in male Japanese quail. *Journal of Experimental Psychology: Animal Behavior Processes, 15*, 147–153.

Donahoe, J.W., & Palmer, D.C. (1994). *Learning and complex behaviour.* Needham Heights, MA: Allyn & Bacon.

Donaldson, D. (1998). *Psychiatric disorders with a biochemical basis.* New York, NY: Parthenon.

Donnerstein, E., & Berkowitz, L. (1981). Victim reactions in aggressive erotic films as a factor in violence against women. *Journal of Personality and Social Psychology, 41*, 710–724.

Donnerstein, E., & Malamuth, N. (1997). Pornography: Its consequences on the observer.

In L.B. Schlesinger & E. Revitch (Eds.), *Sexual dynamics of antisocial behavior* (2nd ed.). Springfield, IL: Charles C Thomas.

Doppelt, J.E., & Wallace, W.L. (1955). Standardization of the Wechsler Adult Intelligence Scale for older persons. *Journal of Abnormal and Social Psychology, 51*, 312–330.

Dor, D. (2014). *The social origins of language.* New York: Oxford University Press.

Dorahy, M.J., Brand, B.L., Şar, V., Krüger, C., Stavropoulos, P., Martínez-Taboas, A., ... Middleton, W. (2014). Dissociative identity disorder: An empirical overview. *Australian and New Zealand Journal of Psychiatry, 48*(5), 402–417.

Dornbusch, S.M., Ritter, P.L., Liederman, P.H., Roberts, D.F., & Fraleigh, M.J. (1987). The relation of parenting style to adolescent school performance. *Child Development, 58*, 1244–1257.

Dossenbach, M., & Dossenbach, H.D. (1998). *All about animal vision.* Chicago, IL: Blackbirch Press.

Dovidio, J., Glick, P., & Rudman, L.A. (Eds.). (2005). *On the nature of prejudice: Fifty years after Allport.* Malden, MA: Blackwell Publishing.

Dovidio, J.F. (1984). Helping behavior and altruism: An empirical and conceptual overview. In L. Berkowitz (Ed.), *Advances in experimental social psychology* (Vol. 17). New York, NY: Academic Press.

Dovidio, J.F., Kawakami, K., & Gaertner, S.L. (2000). Reducing contemporary prejudice: Combating bias at the individual and intergroup levels. In S. Oskamp (Ed.), *Reducing prejudice and discrimination.* Mahwah, NJ: Erlbaum.

Dovidio, J.F., Kawakami, K., Johnson, C., Johnson, B., & Howard, A. (1997). On the nature of prejudice: Automatic and controlled processes. *Journal of Experimental Social Psychology, 33*, 510–540.

Dovidio, J.F., Piliavin, J.A., Gaertner, S.L., Schroeder, D.A., & Clark, R.D., III. (1991). The arousal cost-reward model and the process of intervention: A review of the evidence. In M.S. Clark (Ed.), *Prosocial behavior. Review of personality and social psychology* (Vol. 12). Newbury Park, CA: Sage.

Dozza, M., Flannagan, C.A.C., & Sayer, J.R. (2015). Real-world effects of using a phone while driving on lateral and longitudinal control of vehicles. *Journal of Safety Research, 55*, 81–87.

Drake, M.E., Pakalnis, A., & Denio, L.C. (1988). Differential diagnosis of epilepsy and multiple personality: Clinical and EEG findings in 15 cases. *Neuropsychiatry, Neuropsychology, and Behavioral Neurology, 1*, 131–140.

Drew, T., Võ, M.L., & Wolfe, J.M. (2013). The invisible gorilla strikes again: Sustained inattentional blindness in expert observers. *Psychological Science, 24*(9), 1848–1853.

Driskell, J.E., Willis, R.P., & Copper, C. (1992). Effect of overlearning on retention. *Journal of Applied Psychology, 77*, 615–622.

Drucker, D.J. (2014). The penile strain gauge and aversion therapy: Measuring and fixing the sexual body. *The Machines of Sex Research* (pp. 19–43). New York, NY: Springer.

Drukin, K. (1998). Implicit content and implicit processes in mass media use. In K. Kirsner, C. Speelman, M. Mayberry, A. O'Brien-Malone, M. Anderson, & C. MacLeod (Eds.), *Implicit and explicit mental processes* (pp. 273–290). Mahwah, NJ: Erlbaum.

Dryden, W. (Ed.). (2002). *Handbook of individual therapy.* Thousand Oaks, CA: Sage.

Du, X., Liu, Y., & Li, Y. (2003). The effect of familiarity on out-group homogenicity. *Psychological Science (China), 26*(4), 625–627.

Ducci, F., & Goldman, D. (2008). Genetic approaches to addiction: Genes and alcohol. *Addiction, 103*, 1414–1428.

Dumanis, S.B., DiBattista, A.M., Miessau, M., Moussa, C.E.H., & Rebeck, G.W. (2013). APOE genotype affects the pre-synaptic compartment of glutamatergic nerve terminals. *Journal of Neurochemistry, 124*(1), 4–14.

Duncan, B.L. (1976). Differential social perception and attribution of intergroup violence: Testing the lower limits of stereotyping of blacks. *Journal of Personality and Social Psychology, 34*, 590–598.

Duncan, I.J.H., Widowski, T.M., Malleau, A.E., Lindberg, A.C., & Petherick, J.C. (1998). External factors and causation of dustbathing in domestic hens. *Behavioural Processes, 43*, 219–228.

Dunlosky, J., & Lipko, A.R. (2007). Metacomprehension: A brief history and how to improve its accuracy. *Current Directions in Psychological Science, 16*, 228–232.

Dunn, J., & Plomin, R. (1990). *Separate lives: Why siblings are so different.* New York, NY: Basic Books.

Dunne, M.P., Bailey, J.M., Kirk, K.M., & Martin, N.G. (2000). The subtlety of sex-atypicality. *Archives of Sexual Behavior, 29*, 549–565.

Dutton, D.G. (2006). *The abusive personality: Violence and control in intimate relationships.* New York: Guilford Press.

Dutton, D.G., & Aron, A.P. (1974). Some evidence for heightened sexual attraction under conditions of high anxiety. *Journal of Personality and Social Psychology, 30*, 510–517.

Duvander, A.Z.E. (1999). The transition from cohabitation to marriage: A longitudinal study of the propensity to marry in Sweden in the early 1990s. *Journal of Family Issues, 20*, 698–717.

Dweck, C. (1999). *Self theories: Their role in motivation, personality, and development.* Philadelphia: Psychology Press/Taylor and Francis.

Dwyer, D. (2007). *The pharmacology of neurogenesis and neuroenhancement.* New York, NY: Academic Press.

Dyken, M.E., Lin-Dyken, D.C., Seaba, P., & Yamada, T. (1995). Violent sleep-related behavior leading to subdural hemorrhage. *Archives of Neurology, 52*, 318–321.

Eacott, M.J., & Crawley, R.A. (1998). The offset of childhood amnesia: Memory for events that occurred before age 3. *Journal of Experimental Psychology: General, 127*, 22–33.

Eagly, A.H., & Crowley, M. (1986). Gender and helping behavior: A meta-analytic review of the social psychological literature. *Psychological Bulletin, 100*, 283–308.

Eagly, A.H., & Wood, W. (1999). The origins of sex differences in human behavior: Evolved dispositions versus social roles. *American Psychologist, 54*, 408–423.

Eagly, A.H., & Wood, W. (2006). Three ways that data can misinform: Inappropriate partialling, small samples, and, anyway, they're not playing our song. *Psychological Inquiry, 17*, 131–137.

Eagly, A.H., & Wood, W. (2013). The nature-nurture debates: 25 years of challenges in understanding the psychology of gender. *Perspectives on Psychological Science, 8*(3), 340–357.

Easterbrooks, M.A., Kotake, C., Raskin, M., & Bumgarner, E. (2016). Patterns of depression among adolescent mothers: Resilience related to father support and home visiting program. *American Journal of Orthopsychiatry, 86*(1), 61–68.

Eastwick, P.W., & Gardner, W.L. (2009). Is it a game? Evidence for social influence in the virtual world. *Social Influence, 4*, 18–32.

Eaton, J. (2001). Management communication: The threat of groupthink. *Corporate Communications, 6*, 183–192.

Ebbinghaus, H. (1885/1964). *Über das Gedächtnis: Untersuchungen Zur Experimentellen Psychologie (Memory: A contribution to experimental psychology).* (H.A. Ruger & C.E. Bussenius, Trans.). New York, NY: Dover. (Original work published 1885).

Eberhardt, J.L. (2005). Imaging race. *American Psychologist, 60*, 2181–2190.

Echt, K.V., Morrell, R.W., & Park, D.C. (1998). Effects of age and training formats on basic computer skill acquisition in older adults. *Educational Gerontology, 24*, 3–25.

Eckensberger, L.H., & Zimba, R.F. (1997). The development of moral judgment. In J.W. Berry, P.R. Dasen, & T.S. Saraswathi (Eds.), *Handbook of cross-cultural psychology* (2nd ed., Vol. 2). Boston, MA: Allyn & Bacon.

Eckhardt, C.I., & Kassinove, H. (1998). Articulated cognitive distortions and cognitive deficiencies in maritally violent men. *Journal of Cognitive Psychotherapy, 12*, 231–250.

Edvardsen, J., Torgersen, S., Røysamb, E., Lygren, S., Skre, I., Onstad, S., & Øien, P.A. (2009). Unipolar depressive disorders have a common genotype. *Journal of Affective Disorders, 117*, 30–41.

Edwards, D.C. (1998). *Motivation and emotion: Evolutionary, physiological, cognitive and social influences.* Thousand Oaks, CA: Sage.

Eelen, P., & Vervliet, B. (2006). Fear conditioning and clinical implications: What can we learn from the past? In M.G. Craske, D. Hermans, & D. Vansteenwegen (Eds.), *Fear and learning: From basic processes to clinical implications.* Washington, DC: American Psychological Association.

Ehlers, C.L., Gizer, I.R., Vieten, C., Gilder, D.A., Stouffer, G.M., Lau, P., & Morrow, A.L. (2010). Cannabis dependence in the San Francisco family study: Age of onset of use, DSM-IV symptoms, withdrawal, and heritability. *Addictive Behaviors, 35*, 102–110.

Ehrman, J. (2003). *Clinical exercise psychology.* Champaign, IL: Human Kinetics.

Eibl-Eibesfeldt, I. (1973). The expressive behavior of the deaf-and-blind children. In M. von Cranach & I. Vine (Eds.), *Social communication and movement.* New York, NY: Academic Press.

Eibl-Eibesfeldt, I. (1998). Us and the others: The familial roots of ethnonationalism. In I. Eibl-Eibesfeldt & F. Salter (Eds.), *Indoctrinability, ideology and warfare* (pp. 21–54). New York, NY: Berghahn Books.

Eikeseth, S., Smith, T., Jahr, E., & Eldevik, S. (2002). Intensive behavioral treatment at school for 4- to 7-year-old children with autism: A 1-year comparison controlled study. *Behavior Modification, 26*(1), 49–68.

Einstein, G.O., McDaniel, M.A., Manzi, M., Cochran, B., & Baker, M. (2000). Prospective memory and aging: Forgetting intentions over short delays. *Psychology and Aging, 15*(4), 671–683.

Eisenberg, N. (2000). Emotion, regulation, and moral development. *Annual Review of Psychology, 51*, 665–697.

Eisenberg, N. (2002). Emotion related regulation and its relation to quality of social functioning. In W. Hartup & R.A. Weinberg (Eds.), *Child psychology in retrospect and prospect: In celebration of the 75th anniversary of the Institute of Child Development. The Minnesota symposia on child psychology* (Vol. 32). Mahwah, NJ: Erlbaum.

Eisenberg, N., & Mussen, P.H. (1989). *The roots of prosocial behavior in children.* Cambridge, UK: Cambridge University Press.

Eisenberg, N., & Valiente, C. (2002). Parenting and children's prosocial and moral development. In M.H. Bornstein (Ed.), *Handbook of parenting: Vol. 5 Practical issues in parenting* (2nd ed.). Mahwah, NJ: Erlbaum.

Eisenberger, N.I., Taylor, S.E., Gable, S.L., Hilmert, C.J., & Lieberman, M.D. (2007). Neural pathways link social support to attenuated neuroendocrine stress responses. *NeuroImage, 35,* 1601–1612.

Ekman, P. (1973). *Darwin and facial expression: A century of research in review.* New York, NY: Academic Press.

Ekman, P. (1982). Felt, false and miserable smiles. *Journal of Nonverbal Behavior, 6,* 238–252.

Ekman, P. (1994). Strong evidence for universals in facial expressions: A reply to Russell's mistaken critique. *Psychological Bulletin, 115,* 268–287.

Ekman, P., & Friesen, W.V. (1987). *Facial action coding system.* Palo Alto, CA: Consulting Psychologists Press.

Ekman, P., Friesen, W.V., & O'Sullivan, M. (1988). Smiles when lying. *Journal of Personality and Social Psychology, 54,* 414–420.

Ekman, P., Levenson, R.W., & Friesen, W.V. (1983). Autonomic nervous system activity distinguishes among emotions. *Science, 221,* 1208–1210.

Elbert, T., Pantev, C., Wienbruch, C., Rockstroh, B., & Taub, E. (1995). Increased cortical representation of the fingers of the left hand in string players. *Science, 270,* 305–307.

Eldevik, S., Jahr, E., Eikeseth, S., Hastings, R.P., & Huges, C.J. (2010). Cognitive and adaptive behavior outcomes of behavioral intervention for young children with intellectual disability. *Behavior Modification, 34,* 16–34.

Elek, J.K., Ware, L.J., & Ratcliff, J.J. (2012). Knowing when the camera lies: Judicial instructions mitigate the camera perspective bias. *Legal and Criminological Psychology, 17,* 123–135.

Elhalal, A., Davelaar, E.J., & Usher, M. (2014). The role of the frontal cortex in memory: An investigation of the von restorff effect. *Frontiers in Human Neuroscience, 8.*

Elias, B., Mignone, J., Hall, M., Hong, S.P., Hart, L., & Sareen, J. (2012). Trauma and suicide behaviour histories among a Canadian indigenous population: An empirical exploration of the potential role of Canada's residential school system. *Social Science & Medicine, 74*(10), 1560–1569.

Elkind, D. (1967). Egocentrism in adolescence. *Child Development, 38,* 1025–1034.

Elliot, A.J., & Church, M.A. (1997). A hierarchical model of approach and avoidance achievement motivation. *Journal of Personality and Social Psychology, 72,* 218–232.

Elliot, A.J., & McGregor, H.A. (1999). Test anxiety and the hierarchical model of approach and avoidance achievement motivation. *Journal of Personality and Social Psychology, 76,* 628–644.

Elliot, A.J., & McGregor, H.A. (2001). A 2 × 2 achievement goal framework. *Journal of Personality and Social Psychology, 80,* 501–519.

Elliot, A.J., Chirkov, V.I., Kim, Y., & Sheldon, K.M. (2001). A cross-cultural analysis of avoidance (relative to approach) personal goals. *Psychological Science, 12,* 505–510.

Elliot, A.J., McGregor, H.A., & Gable, S. (1999). Achievement goals, study strategies, and exam performance: A mediational analysis. *Journal of Educational Psychology, 91,* 549–563.

Elliott, M.A., Armitage, C.J., & Baughan, C.J. (2007). Using the theory of planned behaviour to predict observed driving behaviour. *British Journal of Social Psychology, 46*(1), 69–70.

Ellis, A. (1962). *Reason and emotion in psychotherapy.* New York, NY: Lyle Stuart.

Elovainio, M., & Kivimaki, M. (2009). Models of personality and health. In P.J. Corr & G. Matthews (Eds.), *The Cambridge handbook of personality psychology.* Cambridge, UK: Cambridge University Press.

Emens, J.S., Yuhas, K., Rough, J., Kochar, N., Peters, D., & Lewy, A.J. (2009). Phase angle of entrainment in morning- and evening-types under naturalistic conditions. *Chronobiology International, 26,* 474–493.

Emerson, R.M. (1966). Mount Everest: A case study of communication feedback and sustained group goalstriving. *Sociometry, 29,* 213–227.

Emery, C.E., Jr. (2001). Cracked crystal balls? Psychics' predictions for past year a litany of prognostive failures. *The Skeptical Inquirer, 25*(1), 7–8.

Endler, N.S. (1982). *Holiday of darkness: A psychologist's personal journey out of his depression.* New York, NY: Wiley.

Endress, A.D., & Potter, M.C. (2014). Large capacity temporary visual memory. *Journal of Experimental Psychology: General, 143*(2), 548–565.

Enoch M.A. (2011). The role of early life stress as a predictor for alcohol and drug dependence. *Psychopharmacology (Berlin), 214*(1), 17–31.

Enquist, M., & Leimar, O. (1990). The evolution of fatal fighting. *Animal Behaviour, 39,* 1–9.

Epling, W.F., & Pierce, W.D. (1992). *Solving the anorexia puzzle: A scientific approach.* Toronto, ON: Hogrefe & Huber.

Epps, J., & Kendall, P.C. (1995). Hostile attributional bias in adults. *Cognitive Therapy and Research, 19,* 159–178.

Epps, J., Monk, C., Savage, S., & Marlatt, G.A. (1998). Improving credibility of instructions in the balanced placebo design: A misattribution manipulation. *Addictive Behaviors, 23,* 427–435.

Epstein, J.A., & Harackiewicz, J.M. (1992). Winning is not enough: The effects of competition and achievement orientation on intrinsic interest. *Personality and Social Psychology Bulletin, 18,* 128–138.

Epstein, M.A., & Bottoms, B.L. (2002). Explaining the forgetting and recovery of abuse and trauma memories: Possible mechanisms. *Child Maltreatment: Journal of the American Professional Society on the Abuse of Children, 7,* 210–225.

Epstein, R., Kirshnit, C.E., Lanza, R.P., & Rubin, L.C. (1984). "Insight" in the pigeon: Antecedents and determinants of an intelligent performance. *Nature, 308,* 61–62.

Epstein, S. (1983). Aggregation and beyond: Some basic issues on the production of behavior. *Journal of Personality, 51,* 360–392.

Erdberg, P. (2000). Rorschach assessment. In G. Goldstein & M. Hersen (Eds.), *Handbook of psychological assessment* (3rd ed., pp. 437–450). New York, NY: Elsevier.

Erdelyi, M.H. (1995). *Psychoanalysis: Freud's cognitive psychology.* New York, NY: W.H. Freeman.

Erdelyi, M.H. (2014). The interpretation of dreams, and of jokes. *Review of General Psychology, 18*(2), 115–126.

Erez, A., & Isen, A.M. (2002). The influence of positive affect on the components of expectancy motivation. *Journal of Applied Psychology, 87*(6), 1055–1067.

Ericsson, K.A., & Polson, P.G. (1988). An experimental analysis of the mechanisms of a memory skill. *Journal of Experimental Psychology: Learning, Memory, and Cognition, 14,* 305–316.

Erikson, E.H. (1959/1980). *Identity and the life cycle.* New York, NY: W.W. Norton.

Erikson, E.H. (1968). *Identity, youth and crisis.* New York, NY: W.W. Norton.

Erikson, E.H., Erikson, J.M., & Kivnick, H.Q. (1986). *Vital involvement in old age.* New York, NY: W.W. Norton.

Eriksson, P.S., Perfilieva, E., Bjork-Erikkson, T., Alborn, A.M., Nordborg, C., Peterson, D.A., & Gage, F.H. (1998). Neurogenesis in the adult human hippocampus. *Nature Medicine, 4*(11), 1313–1317.

Eron, L.D. (1987). The development of aggressive behavior from the perspective of a developing behaviorism. *American Psychologist, 42,* 435–442.

Eron, L.D. (2000). A psychological perspective. In V.B. Van Hasselt & M. Hersen (Eds.), *Aggression and violence: An introductory text.* Boston, MA: Allyn & Bacon.

Errázuriz, P., Constantino, M.J., & Calvo, E. (2015). The relationship between patient object relations and the therapeutic alliance in a naturalistic psychotherapy sample. *Psychology and Psychotherapy: Theory, Research and Practice, 88*(3), 254–269.

Esparza, J., Fox, C., Harper, I.T., Bennett, P.H., Schulz, L.O., Valencia, M.E., & Ravussin, E. (2000). Daily energy expenditure in Mexican and USA Pima Indians: Low physical activity as a possible cause of obesity. *International Journal of Obesity and Related Metabolic Disorders, 24,* 55–59.

Essau, C.A., & Petermann, F. (1999). *Depressive disorders in children and adolescents: Epidemiology, risk factors, and treatment.* Northvale, NJ: Jason Aronson.

Essau, C.A., & Trommsdorff, G. (1996). Coping with university-related problems: A cross-cultural comparison. *Journal of Cross-Cultural Psychology, 27,* 315–328.

Esser, J.K., & Lindoerfer, J.S. (1989). Groupthink and the space shuttle Challenger accident: Toward a quantitative case analysis. *Journal of Behavioral Decision Making, 2,* 167–177.

Esses, V.M., & Hodson, G. (2006). The role of lay perceptions of ethnic prejudice in the maintenance and perpetuation of ethnic bias. *Journal of Social Issues, 62,* 453–456.

Esses, V.M., & Zanna, M.P. (1995). Mood and the expression of ethnic stereotypes. *Journal of Personality and Social Psychology, 69,* 1052–1068.

Essock-Vitale, S.M., & McGuire, M.T. (1985). Women's lives viewed from an evolutionary perspective: II. Patterns of helping. *Ethology and Sociobiology, 6,* 155–173.

Estes, T.H., & Vaughn, J.L. (1985). *Reading and learning in the content classroom: Diagrams and instructional strategies* (3rd ed.). Boston, MA: Allyn & Bacon.

Ethier, C., Gallego, J.A., & Miller, L.E. (2015). Brain-controlled neuromuscular stimulation to drive neural plasticity and functional recovery. *Current Opinion in Neurobiology, 33,* 95–102.

Etzold, E. (2006). Does psi exist and can we prove it? Belief and disbelief in parapsychology. *European Journal of Parapsychology, 21,* 38–57.

Everitt, B.J., Parkinson, J.A., Olmstead, M.C., Arroyo, M., Robledo, P., & Robbins, T.W. (1999). Associative processes in addiction and reward. The role of amygdala-ventral striatal subsystems. *Annals of the New York Academy of Sciences, 877*, 412–438.

Exner, J.E., Jr., & Erdberg, P. (2005). *The Rorschach: A comprehensive system, Vol. 2: Advanced interpretation* (3rd ed.). Hoboken, NJ: John Wiley & Sons.

Eysenck, H.J. (1952). The effects of psychotherapy: An evaluation. *Journal of Consulting Psychology, 16*, 319–324.

Eysenck, H.J. (1964). *Crime and personality.* Boston, MA: Houghton Mifflin.

Eysenck, H.J. (1967). *The biological basis of personality.* Springfield, IL: Charles C. Thomas.

Eysenck, H.J. (1990). Biological dimensions of personality. In L.A. Pervin (Ed.), *Handbook of personality: Theory and research.* New York, NY: Guilford Press.

Eysenck, H.J. (1991). Dimensions of personality: 16, 5, or 3? Criteria for a taxonomic paradigm. *Personality and Individual Differences, 12*, 773–790.

Eysenck, H.J. (1993). Creativity and personality: Word association, origence, and psychoticism. *Creativity Research Journal, 7*, 209–216.

Eysenck, M.W. (1989). Personality, stress arousal, and cognitive processes in stress transactions. In R.W.J. Neufeld (Ed.), *Advances in the investigation of psychological stress.* New York, NY: Wiley.

Fabbro, F. (2001). The bilingual brain: Bilingual aphasia. *Brain & Language, 79*, 201–210.

Facon, B., Sahiri, S., & Rivière, V. (2008). A controlled single-case treatment of severe long-term selective mutism in a child with mental retardation. *Behavior Therapy, 39*, 313–321.

Fagley, N.S. (1987). Positional response bias in multiple-choice tests of learning: Its relation to testwiseness and guessing strategy. *Journal of Educational Psychology, 79*, 95–97.

Fain, G.L. (1999). *Molecular and cellular physiology of neurons.* Cambridge, MA: Harvard University Press.

Faith, M.S., Matz, P.E., & Jorge, M.A. (2002). Obesity depression associations in the population. *Journal of Psychosomatic Research, 53*, 935–942.

Falkner, A.L., Dollar, P., Perona, P., Anderson, D.J., & Lin, D. (2014). Decoding ventromedial hypothalamic neural activity during male mouse aggression. *The Journal of Neuroscience, 34*(17), 5971–5984.

Fallon, A.E., & Rozin, P. (1985). Sex differences in perceptions of desirable body shape. *Journal of Abnormal Psychology, 94*, 102–105.

Fantz, R.L. (1961, May). The origin of form perception. *Scientific American,* 66–72.

Fardo, F., Allen, M., Jegindò, E.E., Angrilli, A., & Roepstorff, A. (2015). Neurocognitive evidence for mental imagery-driven hypoalgesic and hyperalgesic pain regulation. *NeuroImage, 120*, 350–361.

Farina, B., Della Marca, A., & Grochocinski, V.J. (2003). Microstructure of sleep in depressed patients according to the cyclic alternating pattern. *Journal of Affective Discord, 77*, 227–235.

Fayad, J.N., Otto, S.R., Shannon, R.V., & Brackmann, D.E. (2008). Cochlear and brainstem auditory prostheses for hearing restoration: Cochlear and brain stem implants. *Proceedings of the IEEE, 96*, 1085–1095.

Fazio, R.H. (2001). On the automatic activation of associated evaluations: An overview. *Cognition and Emotion, 15*, 115–141.

Fazio, R.H., Jackson, J.R., Dunton, B.C., & Williams, C.J. (1995). Variability in automatic activation as an unobtrusive measure of racial attitudes: A bona fide pipeline? *Journal of Personality and Social Psychology, 69*, 1013–1027.

Fazio, R.H., Zanna, M.P., & Cooper, J. (1977). Dissonance and self-perception: An integrative view of each theory's proper domain of application. *Journal of Experimental Social Psychology, 13*, 464–479.

Feeny, N.C., & Foa, E.B. (2000). Sexual assault. In G. Fink (Ed.), *Encyclopedia of stress* (Vol. 3). San Diego, CA: Academic Press.

Fein, S., & Spencer, S.J. (1997). Prejudice as self-image maintenance: Affirming the self through derogating others. *Journal of Personality and Social Psychology, 73*, 31–44.

Feingold, A. (1988). Matching for attractiveness in romantic partners and same-sex friends: A meta-analysis and theoretical critique. *Psychological Bulletin, 104*, 226–235.

Feingold, A. (1992). Good-looking people are not what we think. *Psychological Bulletin, 11*, 304–341.

Feingold, A., & Mazzella, R. (1998). Gender differences in body image are increasing. *Psychological Science, 9*, 190–195.

Feldman, M.A., Garrick, M., & Case, L. (1997). The effects of parent training on weight gain of nonorganic-failure-to-thrive children of parents with intellectual disabilities. *Journal on Developmental Disabilities, 5*, 47–61.

Feldman, R.P., & Goodrich, J.T. (2001). Psychosurgery: A historical overview. *Neurosurgery, 48*(3), 647–659.

Feldman-Barrett, L., Niedenthal, P.M., & Winkielman, P. (Eds.). (2007). *Emotion and consciousness.* New York, NY: Guilford Press.

Feliciano, L., & Areán, P.A. (2007). Mood disorders: Depressive disorders. In M. Hersen, S.M. Turner, & D.C. Beidel (Eds.), *Adult psychopathology and diagnosis* (pp. 286–316). Hoboken, NJ: Wiley.

Felmlee, D.H. (1998). "Be careful what you wish for ...": A quantitative and qualitative investigation of "fatal attractions." *Personal Relationships, 5*, 235–253.

Felsen, G., & Dan, Y. (2005). A natural approach to studying vision. *Nature Neuroscience, 8*(12), 1643–1646.

Fenichel, G. (2006). *Neonatal neurology.* St. Louis: Mosby.

Fenigstein, A. (2015). Milgram's shock experiments and the nazi perpetrators: A contrarian perspective on the role of obedience pressures during the holocaust. *Theory & Psychology, 25*(5), 581–598.

Fenn, K.M., & Hambrick, D.Z. (2015). General intelligence predicts memory change across sleep. *Psychonomic Bulletin & Review, 22*(3), 791–799.

Fenn, K.M., & Hambrick, D.Z. (2015). General intelligence predicts memory change across sleep. *Psychonomic Bulletin & Review, 22*(3), 791–799.

Fenton, W.S., & McGlaskan, T.H. (1991a). Natural history of schizophrenia subtypes: I. Longitudinal study of paranoid, hebephonic, and undifferentiated schizophrenia. *Archives of General Psychiatry, 48*, 969–977.

Fenton, W.S., & McGlaskan, T.H. (1991b). Natural history of schizophrenia subtypes: II. Positive and negative symptoms and long-term course. *Archives of General Psychiatry, 48*, 978–986.

Ferguson, C.J. (2008). The school shooting/violent video game link: Casual relationship or moral panic? *Journal of Investigative Psychology and Offender Profiling, 5*, 25–37.

Ferguson, C.J., & Kilburn, J. (2009). The public health risks of media violence: A meta-analytic review. *Journal of Pediatrics, 154*, 759–763.

Ferguson, C.J., & Kilburn, J. (2010). Much ado about nothing: The misestimation and overinterpretation of violent video game effects in Eastern and Western nations: Comment on Anderson et al. (2010). *Psychological Bulletin, 136*, 174–178.

Ferguson, E.D. (2000). *Motivation: A biosocial and cognitive integration of motivation and emotion.* New York, NY: Oxford University Press.

Fergusson, D.M., & Lynskey, M.T. (1997). Physical punishment/maltreatment during childhood and adjustment in young adulthood. *Child Abuse and Neglect, 21*, 617–630.

Fernald, A., Taeschner, T., Dunn, J., Papousek, M., De Boysson-Bardies, B., & Fukui, I. (1989). A crosscultural study of prosodic modification in mothers' and fathers' speech to preverbal infants. *Journal of Child Language, 16*, 477–501.

Fernichel, G. (2006). *Neonatal neurology.* St. Louis, MO: Mosby.

Ferrer-García, M., & Gutiérrez-Maldonado, J. (2012). The use of virtual reality in the study, assessment, and treatment of body image in eating disorders and nonclinical samples: A review of the literature. *Body Image, 9*(1) 1–11.

Ferster, C.B., & Skinner, B.F. (1957). *Schedules of reinforcement.* Englewood Cliffs, NJ: Prentice-Hall.

Festinger, L. (1954). A theory of social comparison processes. *Human Relations, 2*, 117–140.

Festinger, L. (1957). *A theory of cognitive dissonance.* Stanford, CA: Stanford University Press.

Festinger, L., & Carlsmith, J.M. (1959). Cognitive consequences of forced compliance. *Journal of Abnormal and Social Psychology, 58*, 203–210.

Festinger, L., Pepitone, A., & Newcomb, T. (1952). Some consequences of deindividuation in a group. *Journal of Abnormal and Social Psychology, 47*, 382–389.

Festinger, L., Schachter, S., & Back, K. (1950). *Social pressures in informal groups: A study of a housing community.* New York, NY: Harper.

Fichera, L.V., & Andreassi, J.L. (1998). Stress and personality as factors in women's cardiovascular reactivity. *International Journal of Psychophysiology, 28*, 143–155.

Fiedler, K. (2000). Toward an integrative account of affect and cognition phenomena using the BIAS computer algorithm. In J.P. Forgas (Ed.), *Feeling and thinking: The role of affect in social cognition* (pp. 223–252). New York, NY: Cambridge University Press.

Field, T. (2002). Preterm infant massage therapy studies: An American approach. *Seminars in Neonatology, 7*, 487–494.

Field, T., Diego, M.A., Hernandez-Reif, M., Deeds, O., & Figuereido, B. (2006). Moderate versus light pressure massage therapy leads to greater weight gain in preterm infants. *Infant Behavior & Development, 29*, 574–578.

Field, T.M., Schanberg, S.M., Scafidi, F., Bauer, C.R., Vega-Lahr, N., Garcia, R., ... Kuhn, C.M. (1986). Tactile/kinesthetic stimulation effects on preterm neonates. *Pediatrics, 77*, 654–658.

Fields, H.L. (2005). *Pain: Mechanisms and management.* New York, NY: McGraw-Hill.

Fink, M., Kellner, C.H., & McCall, W.V. (2014). The role of ECT in suicide prevention. *The Journal of ECT, 30*(1), 5–9.

Finley, J.R., Benjamin, A.S., & McCarley, J.S. (2014). Metacognition of multitasking: How well do we predict the costs of divided attention?

Journal of Experimental Psychology: Applied, 20(2), 158–165.

Fish, J.M. (2002). The myth of race. In J.M. Fish (Ed.), *Race and intelligence: Separating science from myth* (pp. 113–141). Mahwah, NJ: Erlbaum.

Fishbein, M. (1980). A theory of reasoned action: Some applications and implications. In H.E. Howe & M.M. Page (Eds.), *Nebraska Symposium on Motivation* (Vol. 27, pp. 65–116). Lincoln, NE: University of Nebraska Press.

Fishbein, M., & Ajzen, I. (1974). Attitudes toward objects as predictors of single and multiple behavioral criteria. *Psychological Review, 81,* 59–74.

Fisher, R.J., & Ma, Y. (2014). The price of being beautiful: Negative effects of attractiveness on empathy for children in need. *Journal of Consumer Research, 41*(2), 436–450.

Fisher, S., & Greenberg, R.P. (1996). *Freud scientifically reappraised: Testing the theories and therapy.* New York, NY: Wiley.

Fisher, W.A., Kohut, T., Salisbury, C.M.A., & Salvadori, M.I. (2013). Understanding human papillomavirus vaccination intentions: Comparative utility of the theory of reasoned action and the theory of planned behavior in vaccine target age women and men. *Journal of Sexual Medicine, 10*(10), 2455–2464.

Fiske, S.T. (2002). What we know about bias and intergroup conflict, the problem of the century. *Current Directions in Psychological Science, 11,* 123–128.

Fitch, G.M., Soccolich, S.A., Guo, F., McClafferty, J., Fang, Y., Olson, R.L., Perez, M.A., Hanowski, R.J., Hankey, J.M., & Dingus, T.A. (2013). *The Impact of Hand-Held and Hands-Free Cell Phone Use on Driving Performance and Safety-Critical Event Risk.* Transportation Research Board, National Academies of Science.

Flavell, J.H. (1970). Developmental studies of mediated behavior. In H.W. Reese & L.P. Lipsett (Eds.), *Advances in child development and behavior* (Vol. 5, pp. 181–211). New York, NY: Academic Press.

Flavell, J.H., Miller, P.H., & Miller, S.A. (1993). *Cognitive development* (3rd ed.). Upper Saddle River, NJ: Prentice-Hall.

Fleeson, W. (2004). Moving personality beyond the person-situation debate. *Current Directions in Psychological Science, 13,* 83–87.

Flege, J., Yeni-Komshian, G., & Liu, S. (1999). Age constraints on second language learning. *Journal of Memory and Language, 41,* 78–104.

Fleming, I., Baum, A., & Weiss, L. (1987). Social density and perceived control as mediators of crowding stress in high-density residential neighborhoods. *Journal of Personality and Social Psychology, 52,* 899–906.

Flinn, M.V. (1997). Culture and the evolution of social learning. *Evolution and Human Behavior, 18,* 23–67.

Flores, J.A., Galan-Rodriguez, B., Ramiro-Fuentes, S., & Fernandez-Espejo, E. (2006). Role for dopamine neurons of the rostral linear nucleus and periaqueductal gray in the rewarding and sensitizing properties of heroin. *Neuropsychopharmacology, 31,* 1475–1488.

Floyd, R.L., O'Connor, M.J., Sokol, R.J., Bertrand, J., & Cordero, J.F. (2005). Recognition and prevention of fetal alcohol syndrome. *Obstetrics & Gynecology, 106,* 1059–1064.

Flynn, J.R. (1987). Massive IQ gains in 14 nations. What IQ tests really measure. *Psychological Bulletin, 101*(2), 171–191.

Flynn, J.R. (1998). IQ gains over time: Toward finding the causes. In U. Neisser (Ed.), *The rising curve: Long-term gains in IQ and related measures.* Washington, DC: American Psychological Association.

Foa, E.B., Hearst-Ikeda, D., & Perry, K.J. (1995). Evaluation of a brief cognitive-behavioral program for the prevention of chronic PTSD in recent assault victims. *Journal of Consulting and Clinical Psychology, 63,* 948–955.

Folkard, S. (2008). Shift work, safety, and aging. *Chronobiology International, 25,* 183–198.

Folkman, S., & Lazarus, R.S. (1988). Coping as a mediator of emotion. *Journal of Personality and Social Psychology, 54,* 466–475.

Follette, W.C., & Davis, D. (2009). Clinical practice and the issue of repressed memories: Avoiding an ice patch on the slippery slope. In W. O'Donohue & S.R. Graybar (Eds.), *Handbook of contemporary psychotherapy: Toward an improved understanding of effective psychotherapy* (pp. 47–74). Thousand Oaks, CA: Sage.

Ford, T.M., Liwag, M., Michelle, G., & Foley, L.A. (1998). Perceptions of rape based on sex and sexual orientation of victim. *Journal of Social Behavior and Personality, 13,* 253–262.

Fordyce, W.E. (1988). Pain and suffering: A reappraisal. *American Psychologist, 43,* 276–283.

Forgas, J.P. (Ed.). (2000). *Feeling and thinking: The role of affect in social cognition.* New York, NY: Cambridge University Press.

Fossion, R., & Zapata-Fonseca, L. (2015). The scientific method. Aging research—methodological issues (pp. 9–25). Cham, Switzerland: Springer International Publishing.

Foster, C.A., Witcher, B.S., Campbell, W.K., & Green, J.D. (1998). Arousal and attraction: Evidence for automatic and controlled processes. *Journal of Personality and Social Psychology, 74,* 86–101.

Foulkes, D. (1962). Dream reports from different states of sleep. *Journal of Abnormal and Social Psychology, 65,* 14–25.

Foulkes, D. (1982). REM-dream perspectives on the development of affect and cognition. *Psychiatric Journal of the University of Ottawa, 7,* 48–55.

Foulkes, D. (1985). *Dreaming: A cognitive-psychological analysis.* Hillsdale, NJ: Erlbaum.

Foulkes, D. (1999). *Children's dreaming and the development of consciousness.* Cambridge, MA: Harvard University Press.

Foulks, F.F., Bland, I.J., & Shervington, D. (1995). Psychotherapy across cultures. *Review of Psychiatry, 14,* 511.

Foushee, H.C. (1984). Dyads and triads at 35,000 feet: Factors affecting group process and aircrew performance. *American Psychologist, 39,* 885–893.

Fouts, R.S., Fouts, D.H., & Van Cantfort, T.E. (1989). The infant Loulis learns signs from other cross-fostered chimpanzees. In R.A. Gardner, B.T. Gardner, & T.E. Van Cantfort (Eds.), *Teaching sign language to chimpanzees* (pp. 280–292). Albany, NY: State University of New York Press.

Fowles, D.C. (1992). Schizophrenia: Diathesis-stress revisited. *Annual Review of Psychology, 43,* 303–336.

Fox, N.A., & Davidson, R.J. (1991). Hemispheric specialization and attachment behaviors: Developmental processes and individual differences in separation process. In J.L. Gewirtz & W.M. Kurtines (Eds.), *Interactions with attachment.* Hillsdale, NJ: Erlbaum.

Fox, N.A., Henderson, H.A., Marshall, P.J., Nichols, K.E., & Ghera, M.M. (2005). Behavioral inhibition: Linking biology and behavior within a developmental framework. *Annual Review of Psychology, 56,* 235–262.

Fox, P.T. (1997). The growth of human brain mapping. *Human Brain Mapping, 5,* 1–2.

Fox, R., Aslin, R.N., Shea, S.L., & Dumais, S.T. (1980). Stereopsis in human infants. *Science, 207,* 323–324.

Fraley, R.C., & Shaver, P.R. (2008). Attachment theory and its place in contemporary personality theory. In O.P. John, R.W. Robins, & L.A. Pervin (Eds.), *Handbook of personality theory and research* (3rd ed., pp. 518–541). New York, NY: Guilford Press.

Francis, G. (February 2012). Too good to be true: Publication bias in two prominent studies from experimental psychology. *Psychonomic Bulletin & Review, 19*(2), 151–156.

Franco, A.H.R., Butler, H.A., & Halpern, D.F. (2015). Teaching critical thinking to promote learning. *The Oxford handbook of undergraduate psychology education* (pp. 65–74). New York, NY: Oxford University Press.

Franić, S., Dolan, C.V., Broxholme, J., Hu, H., Zemojtel, T., Davies, G.E., … Boomsma, D.I. (2015). Mendelian and polygenic inheritance of intelligence: A common set of causal genes? using next-generation sequencing to examine the effects of 168 intellectual disability genes on normal-range intelligence. *Intelligence, 49,* 10–22.

Frank, N.C., Spirito, A., Stark, L., & Owens-Stively, J. (1997). The use of scheduled awakenings to eliminate childhood sleepwalking. *Journal of Pediatric Psychology, 22,* 345–353.

Fredrickson, B.L. (1998). What good are positive emotions? *Review of General Psychology, 2,* 300–319.

Fredrickson, B.L., & Roberts, T.A. (1997). Objectification theory: Toward understanding women's lived experiences and mental health risks. *Psychology of Women Quarterly, 21,* 173–206.

Fredrickson, B.L., Roberts, T.A., Noll, S.M., Quinn, D.M., & Twenge, J.M. (1998). That swimsuit becomes you: Sex differences in self-objectification, restrained eating, and math performance. *Journal of Personality and Social Psychology, 75,* 269–284.

Freeman, C., & Power, M. (2007). *Handbook of evidence-based psychotherapy.* Hoboken, NJ: Wiley.

French, L., Gray, C., Leonard, G., Perron, M., Pike, B., Richer, L., … Paus, T. (2015). Early cannabis use, polygenic risk score for schizophrenia and brain maturation in adolescence. *JAMA Psychiatry, 72*(10), 1002–1011.

Freud, S. (1900/1953). The interpretation of dreams. In J. Strachey (Ed.), *The standard edition of the complete psychological works of Sigmund Freud* (Vols. 4 & 5). London, UK: Hogarth. (Original work published 1900).

Freud, S. (1917/1957). Mourning and melancholia. In J. Strachey (Ed.), *The standard edition of the complete psychological works of Sigmund Freud* (Vol. 14). London, UK: Hogarth. (Original work published 1917).

Freud, S. (1923). *The ego and the id.* New York, NY: W.W. Norton.

Freud, S. (1935). *A general introduction to psychoanalysis.* New York, NY: Washington Square Press.

Friedlander, L., & Desrocher, M. (2006). Neuroimaging studies of obsessive-compulsive disorder in adults and children. *Clinical Psychology Review, 26*(1), 32–49.

Friedman, H. (Ed.). (1991). *Hostility, coping, and health.* Washington, DC: American Psychological Association.

Friedman, H., & DiMatteo, M.R. (1989). *Health psychology.* New York, NY: Prentice Hall.

Friedman, H.S., Tucker, J.S., Schwartz, J.E., Tomlinson-Keasy, C., Wingard, L., & Criqui, M.H. (1995). Psychosocial and behavioral predictors of longevity: The aging and death of the Termites. *American Psychologist, 50,* 69–78.

Friendly, M., & Beach, J. (2005). Early childhood education and care in Canada (6th ed., 232 pp.) CRRU publications. May. Retrieved from http://www.ccsd.ca/factsheets/family/index.htm.

Frijda, N.H., Manstead, A.S.R., & Bem, S. (Eds.). (2005). *Emotions and beliefs: How feelings influence thoughts.* New York, NY: Cambridge University Press.

Frisby, J.P. (1980). *Seeing: Illusion, brain, and mind.* Oxford, UK: Oxford University Press.

Frisco, M.L., & Williams, K. (2003). Perceived housework equity, marital happiness, and divorce in dual earner households. *Journal of Family Issues, 24,* 51–73.

Fristoe, N.M., Salthouse, T.A., & Woodard, J.L. (1997). Examination of age-related deficits on the Wisconsin Card Sorting Test. *Neuropsychology, 11,* 428–436.

Fritsch, J. (1999, May 25). 95% regain lost weight. Or do they? *The New York Times,* F7.

Frodi, A.M., Lamb, M.E., Leavitt, L.A., Donovan, W.L., Neff, C., & Sherry, D. (1978). Fathers' and mothers' responses to the faces and cries of normal and premature infants. *Developmental Psychology, 14,* 490–498.

Froger, C., Taconnat, L., Landré, L., Beigneux, K., & Isingrini, M. (2008). Effects of level of processing at encoding and types of retrieval task in mild cognitive impairment and normal aging. *Journal of Clinical and Experimental Neuropsychology, 31,* 312–321.

Fromm, E. (1956). *The art of loving.* New York, NY: Harper.

Fuligni, A.J. (1998). Authority, autonomy, and parent-adolescent conflict and cohesion: A study of adolescents from Mexican, Chinese, Filipino, and European backgrounds. *Developmental Psychology, 34,* 782–792.

Funk, S.C. (1992). Hardiness: A review of theory and research. *Health Psychology, 11,* 335–345.

Furmark, T., Tillfors, M., Marteinsdottir, I., Fischer, H., Pissiota, A., Langstroem, B., & Fredrikson, M. (2002). Common changes in cerebral blood flow in patients with social phobia treated with citalopram or cognitive-behavioral therapy. *Archives of General Psychiatry, 59,* 425–433.

Furukawa, T.A., Watanabe, N., & Churchill, R. (2006). Psychotherapy plus antidepressant for panic disorder with or without agoraphobia: Systematic review. *British Journal of Psychiatry, 188,* 305–312.

Gabbard, C., & Ammar, D. (2008). The effect of response-delay on estimating reachability. *International Journal of Neuroscience, 118,* 1502–1514.

Gabbard, G.O. (1990). *Psychodynamic psychiatry in clinical practice.* Washington, DC: American Psychiatric Press.

Gabbard, G.O. (2004). *Long-term psychodynamic psychotherapy.* Washington, DC: American Psychiatric Publishing.

Gabbard, G.O., Beck, J., & Holmes, J. (2005). *Oxford textbook of psychotherapy.* New York, NY: Oxford University Press.

Gabrieli, J.D.E. (1998). Cognitive neuroscience of human memory. *Annual Review of Psychology, 49,* 87–115.

Gabrieli, J.D.E., Desmond, J.E., Demb, J.B., & Wagner, A.D. (1996). Functional magnetic resonance imaging of semantic memory processes in the frontal lobes. *Psychological Science, 7,* 278–283.

Gainotti, G. (1972). Emotional behavior and hemispheric side of lesion. *Cortex, 8,* 41–55.

Galanaki, E.P. (2012). The imaginary audience and the personal fable: A test of Elkind's theory of adolescent egocentrism. *Psychology, 3,* 457–466.

Galanter, E. (1962). Contemporary psychophysics. In R. Brown (Ed.), *New directions in psychology.* New York, NY: Holt, Rinehart & Winston.

Galati, D., & Lavelli, M. (1997). Neonate and infant emotion expression perceived by adults. *Journal of Nonverbal Behavior, 21,* 57–83.

Galea, S., Ahern, J., Resnick, H., Kilpatrick, D., Bucuvalas, M., Gold, J., & Vlahov, D. (2002). Psychological sequelae of the September 11 terrorist attacks in New York City. *New England Journal of Medicine, 346,* 982–987.

Galef, B.G., Jr., & Giraldeau, L-A. (2001). Social influences on foraging in vertebrates: Causal mechanisms and adaptive functions. *Animal Behaviour, 61,* 3–15.

Galef, B.G., Jr., & Whiskin, E.E. (2000). Demonstration of a socially transmitted flavor aversion in rats? Kuan and Colwill (1997) revisited. *Psychonomic Bulletin and Review, 7,* 631–635.

Galef, B.G., Jr., & Whiskin, E.E. (2001). Interaction of social and individual learning in food preferences of Norway rats. *Animal Behaviour, 62,* 41–46.

Galek, J., LeBeouf, R.A., Nelson, L.D., & Simmons, J.P. (2012). Correcting the past: Failure to replicate psi. *Journal of Personality and Social Psychology, 103*(6).

Galietta, M., Fineran, V., Fava, J., & Rosenfeld, B. (2010). Antisocial and psychopathic individuals. In D. McKay, J.S. Abramowitz, & S. Taylor (Eds.), *Cognitive-behavioral therapy for refractory cases: Turning failure into success.* Washington, DC: American Psychological Association.

Gallagher, A.M., De Lisi, R., Holst, P.C., McGillicuddy-De Lisi, A.V., Morely, M., & Cahalan, C. (2000). Gender differences in advanced mathematical problem solving. *Journal of Experimental Child Psychology, 75*(3), 165–190.

Gallese, V. (2013). Mirror neurons, embodied simulation and a second-person approach to mind-reading. *Cortex, 49,* 2954–2956.

Gallistel, C.R., & Gelman, R. (2000). Non-verbal numerical cognition: From reals to integers. *Trends in Cognitive Sciences, 4,* 59–65.

Gallivan, J.P., Cavina-Pratesi, C., & Culham, J.C. (2009). Is that within reach? fMRI reveals that the human superior parieto-occipital cortex encodes objects reachable by the hand. *The Journal of Neuroscience, 29,* 4381–4391.

Gallup, G.G., Jr. (1970). Chimpanzees: Self-recognition. *Science, 167,* 86–87.

Galton, F. (1869). *Hereditary genius: An inquiry into its laws and consequences.* New York, NY: Appleton.

Galton, F. (1883). *Inquiries into human faculty and its development.* London, UK: Dent.

Gangestad, S.W., Haselton, M.G., & Buss, D.M. (2006). Evolutionary foundations of cultural variation: Evoked culture and mate preferences. *Psychological Inquiry, 17,* 75–95.

Ganis, G., Thompson, W.L., & Kosslyn, S.M. (2004). Brain areas underlying visual mental imagery and visual perception: An fMRI study. *Cognitive Brain Research, 20,* 226–241.

Gannon, P.J., Holloway, R.L., Broadfield, D.C., & Braun, A.R. (1998). Asymmetry of chimpanzee planum temporale: Human-like pattern of Wernicke's brain language area homolog. *Science, 279,* 220–222.

Garbarino, J. (1995). The American war zone: What children can tell us about living with violence. *Journal of Developmental and Behavioral Pediatrics, 16,* 431–435.

Garbutt, J.C. (2009). The state of pharmacotherapy for the treatment of alcohol dependence. *Journal of Substance Abuse Treatment, 36,* S15–S23.

Garcia, J., & Koelling, R.A. (1966). The relation of cue to consequence in avoidance learning. *Psychonomic Science, 4,* 123–124.

Garcia, J., Lasiter, P.S., Bermudez, R.F., & Deems, D.A. (1985). A general theory of aversion learning. *Annals of the New York Academy of Sciences, 443,* 8–21.

Garcia-Palacios, A., Hoffman, H., Carlin, A.C., Furness T.A., III, & Botella, C. (2002). Virtual reality in the treatment of spider phobia: A controlled study. *Behaviour Research and Therapy, 40,* 983–993.

Gardiner, J.M., Gawlick, B., & Richardson, K.A. (1994). Maintenance rehearsal affects knowing, not remembering; elaborative rehearsal affects remembering, not knowing. *Psychonomic Bulletin and Review, 1,* 107–110.

Gardner, H. (2000). *Multiple intelligences: The theory in practice.* New York, NY: Basic Books.

Gardner, H. (2003). Three distinct meanings of intelligence. In R.J. Sternberg, J. Lautrey, & T.I. Lubart (Eds.), *Models of intelligence: International perspectives.* Washington, DC: American Psychological Association.

Gardner, R.A., & Gardner, B.T. (1969). Teaching language to a chimpanzee. *Science, 165,* 664–672.

Garfinkel, P.E., & Garner, D.M. (1982). *Anorexia nervosa: A multidimensional perspective.* New York, NY: Brunner-Mazel.

Garland, D.J., & Barry, J.R. (1991). Cognitive advantage in sport: The nature of perceptual structures. *American Journal of Psychology, 104,* 211–228.

Garlick, D. (2002). Understanding the nature of the general factor of intelligence: The role of individual differences in neural plasticity as an explanatory mechanism. *Psychological Review, 109,* 116–136.

Garmezy, N. (1983). *Stress, coping and development in children.* New York, NY: McGraw-Hill.

Garnefski, N., & Arends, E. (1998). Sexual abuse and adolescent maladjustment: Differences between male and female victims. *Journal of Adolescence, 21,* 99–107.

Garoff-Eaton, R.J., Slotnick, S.D., & Schacter, D.L. (2006). Not all false memories are created equal: The neural basis of false recognition. *Cerebral Cortex, 16*(11), 1645–1652.

Gathercole, S.E., Pickering, S.J., Knight, C., & Stegmann, Z. (2004). Working memory skills and educational attainment: Evidence from national curriculum assessments at 7 and 14 years of age. *Applied Cognitive Psychology, 18,* 1–16.

Gaucher, D., Wood, J.V., Stinson, D.A., Forest, A.L., Holmes, J.G., & Logel, C. (2012). Perceived regard explains self-esteem differences in expressivity. *Personality and Social Psychology Bulletin, 38,* 1144–1156.

Gawronski, B. (2007). Attitudes can be measured! But what is an attitude? *Social Cognition, 25,* 573–581.

Gawronski, B., Deutsch, R., Mbirkou, S., Seibt, B., & Strack, F. (2008). When "just say no" is not enough: Affirmation versus negation training and the reduction of automatic stereotype activation. *Journal of Experimental Social Psychology, 44,* 370–377.

Gaylin, G. (2000). *Talk is not enough: How psychotherapy really works.* Boston, MA: Little, Brown.

Gazit, I., & Terkel, J. (2003). Explosives detection by sniffer dogs following strenuous physical activity. *Applied Animal Behaviour Science, 81,* 149–161.

Gazzaniga, M.S., Steen, D., & Volpe, B.T. (1979). *Functional neuroscience.* New York, NY: Harper & Row.

Geary, D.C. (2005). *The origin of mind: Evolution of brain, cognition, and general intelligence.* Washington, DC: American Psychological Association.

Gegenfurtner, K.R., & Kiper, D.C. (2003). Color vision. *Neuroscience, 26*(1), 181–206.

Gelade, G.A. (2008). IQ, cultural values and the technological achievement of nations. *Intelligence, 36,* 711–718.

Geldard, F.A. (1962). *Fundamentals of psychology.* New York, NY: Wiley.

Gelernter, J., & Stein, M.B. (2009). Heritability and genetics of anxiety disorders. In M.M. Antony & M.B. Stein (Eds.), *Oxford handbook of anxiety and related disorders* (pp. 87–96). New York, NY: Oxford University Press.

Geller, G., & Thomas, C.D. (1999). A review of eating disorders in immigrant women: Possible evidence for a culture-change model. *Eating Disorders: The Journal of Treatment and Prevention, 7,* 279–297.

Gelman, S.A., Taylor, M.G., & Nguyen, S.P. (2004). Mother-child conversations about gender. *Monographs of the Society for Research in Child Development, 69,* vii–127.

Genesee, F., & Gandara, P. (1999). Bilingual education programs: A cross-national perspective. *Journal of Social Issues, 55,* 665–685.

Gentile, D.A., Lynch, P.J., Linder, J.R., & Walsh, D.A. (2004). The effects of violent video game habits on adolescent hostility, aggressive behaviors, and school performance. *Journal of Adolescence, 27,* 5–22.

Gentilucci, M., & Volta, R.D. (2008). Spoken language and arm gestures are controlled by the same motor control system. *The Quarterly Journal of Experimental Psychology, 61*(6), 944–957.

George, W.H., Stoner, S.A., Norris, J., Lopez, P.A., & Lehman, G.L. (2000). Alcohol expectancies and sexuality: A self-fulfilling prophecy analysis of dyadic perceptions and behavior. *Journal of Studies on Alcohol, 61,* 168–176.

Geracioti, T.D., Loosen, P.T., Ebert, M.H., & Schmidt, D. (1995). Fasting and postprandial cerebrospinal fluid glucose concentrations in healthy women and in an obese binge eater. *International Journal of Eating Disorders, 18,* 365–369.

Geraerts, E., Lindsay, D.S., Merckelbach, H., Jelicic, M., Raymaekers, L., Arnold, M.M., & Schooler, J.W. (2009). Cognitive mechanisms underlying recovered-memory experiences of childhood sexual abuse. *Psychological Science, 20*(1), 92–98.

Geraerts, E., Schooler, J.W., Merckelbach, C., Jelicic, M., Beatrijs, H.B., & Ambadar, Z. (2007). The reality of recovered memories: Corroborating continuous and discontinuous memories of childhood sexual abuse. *Psychological Science, 18,* 564–568.

Gershoff, E.T. (2008). *Report on physical punishment in the United States: What research tells us about its effects on children.* Columbus, OH: Center for Effective Discipline.

Gershon, E.S., Berrettini, W.H., & Golden, L.E. (1989). Mood disorders: Genetic aspects. In H.I. Kaplan & B.J. Sadock (Eds.), *Comprehensive textbook of psychiatry.* Baltimore, MD: Williams & Wilkins.

Ghaziuddin, N., Merchant, C., Dopp, R., & King, C. (2014). A naturalistic study of suicidal adolescents treated with an SSRI: Suicidal ideation and behavior during 3-month post-hospitalization period. *Asian Journal of Psychiatry, 11,* 13–19.

Ghetti, S., Qin, J., & Goodman, G.S. (2002). False memories in children and adults: Age, distinctiveness, and subjective experience. *Developmental Psychology, 38,* 705–718.

Ghodse, H. (2007). 'Uppers' keep going up. *British Journal of Psychiatry, 191,* 279–281.

Gibbs, J., Young, R.C., & Smith, G.P. (1973). Cholecystokinin decreases food intake in rats. *Journal of Comparative and Physiological Psychology, 84,* 488–495.

Gibson, E.J., & Walk, R.D. (1960). The "visual cliff." *Scientific American, 202,* 64–71.

Gibson, J.J. (1979). *The ecological approach to visual perception.* Boston, MA: Houghton Mifflin.

Gibson, P.A., Baker, E.H., & Milner, A.N. (2016). The role of sex, gender, and education on depressive symptoms among young adults in the united states. *Journal of Affective Disorders, 189,* 306–313.

Giedd, J.N. (2004). Structural magnetic resonance imaging of the adolescent brain. *Annals of the New York Academy of Sciences, 2021,* 77–85.

Giedd, N., Lein, E.S.,Sestan, N., Weinberger, D.R., & Casey, B. (2014), Adolescent mental health— opportunity and obligation. *Science, 346,* 547–549.

Giglioli, I., Pallavicini, F., Pedroli, E., Serino, S., & Riva, G. (2015). Augmented reality: A brand new challenge for the assessment and treatment of psychological disorders. *Computational and Mathematical Methods in Medicine, 2015,* 862942.

Gilbert, D.T., & Malone, P.S. (1995). The correspondence bias. *Psychological Bulletin, 117,* 21–38.

Gillespie, M. (1999, April 30). *Americans have very mixed opinions about blame for Littleton shootings.* Gallup News Service. Princeton, NJ: Gallup Organization.

Gillette, M.U. (1986). The suprachiasmatic nuclei: Circadian phase-shifts induced at the time of hypothalamic slice preparation are preserved in vitro. *Brain Research, 379,* 176–181.

Gilligan, C. (1982). *In a different voice: Psychological theory and women's development.* Cambridge, MA: Harvard University Press.

Giroux, I., Faucher-Gravel, A., St-Hilaire, A., Boudreault, C., Jacques, C., & Bouchard, S. (2013). Gambling exposure in virtual reality and modification of urge to gamble. *Journal of CyberPsychology and Social Networking, 16*(3), 224–231.

Glanzer, M. (1972). Storage mechanisms in recall. In G.H. Bower (Ed.), *The psychology of learning and motivation: Advances in research and theory* (Vol. 5). New York, NY: Academic Press.

Glanzer, M., & Cunitz, A.R. (1966). Two storage mechanisms in free recall. *Journal of Verbal Learning and Verbal Behavior, 5,* 351–360.

Glanzman, D.L. (2009). Habituation in aplysia: The Cheshire cat of neurobiology. *Neurobiology of Learning and Memory, 92,* 147–154.

Glaser, R., & Bassok, M. (1989). Learning theory and the study of instruction. *Annual Review of Psychology, 40,* 631–666.

Gleason, J-B., & Ely, R. (2002). Gender differences in language development. In A. McGillicuddy-De Lisi & R. De Lisi (Eds.), *Biology, society, and behavior: The development of sex differences in cognition. Advances in applied developmental psychology* (Vol. 21). Westport, CT: Ablex.

Gleaves, D.H. (1996). The sociocognitive model of dissociative identity disorder: A re-examination of the evidence. *Psychological Bulletin, 120,* 42–59.

Glenberg, A.M., Sanocki, T., Epstein, W., & Morris, C. (1987). Enhancing calibration of comprehension. *Journal of Experimental Psychology: General, 116,* 119–136.

Glick, P., & Fiske, S.T. (1999). Gender, power dynamics, and social interaction. In M.M. Ferree, J. Lorber, & B.B. Hess (Eds.), *Revisioning gender. The gender lens.* (Vol. 5, pp. 365–398). Thousand Oaks, CA: Sage.

Glock, S., & Kneer, J. (2009). Game over? The impact of knowledge about violent digital games on the activation of aggression-related concepts. *Journal of Media Psychology: Theories, Methods, and Applications, 21,* 151–160.

Glucksman, M.L. (2001). The dream: A psychodynamically informative instrument. *Journal of Psychotherapy Practice and Research, 10,* 223–230.

Gobet, F., & Simon, H.A. (1998). Expert chess memory: Revisiting the chunking hypothesis. *Memory, 6*(3), 225–255.

Gobet, F., Lane, P.C.R., Croker, S., Cheng, D.C.H., Jones, G., Oliver, L., & Pine, J.M. (2001). Chunking mechanisms in human learning. *Trends in Cognitive Sciences, 5*(6), 236–243.

Goddard, A.W., Mason, G.F., Almai, A., Rothman, D.L., Behar, K.L., Ognen, A.C.P., ... Krystal, J.H. (2001). Reductions in occipital cortex GABA levels in panic disorder detected with 1H-magnetic resonance spectroscopy. *Archives of General Psychiatry, 58,* 556–561.

Goddard, H.H. (1917). Mental tests and the immigrant. *Journal of Delinquency, 2,* 243–277.

Godden, D.R., & Baddeley, A.D. (1975). Contextdependent memory in two natural environments: On land and under water. *British Journal of Psychology, 66,* 325–332.

Goddings, A.L., Mills, K.L., Clasen, L.S., Giedd, J.N., Viner, R.M., & Blakemore, S.J. (2014). The influence of puberty on subcortical brain development. *NeuroImage, 88,* 242–251.

Goel, V., & Dolan, R.J. (2003). Explaining modulation of reasoning by belief. *Cognition, 87*(1), B11–B22.

Goffman, E. (1961). *Asylums: Essays on the social situation of mental patients and other inmates.* New York, NY: Doubleday.

Goldapple, K., Segal, Z., Garson, C., Lau, M., Bieling, P., Kennedy, S., & Mayberg, H. (2004). Modulation of cortical-limbic pathways in major depression: Treatment-specific effects of cognitive behavior therapy. *Archives of General Psychiatry, 61*(1), 34–41.

Goldberg, I. (2006). SSRIs and suicide. *American Journal of Psychiatry, 163,* 898–904.

Goldberg, L.R. (1981). Unconfounding situational attributions from uncertain, neutral, and ambiguous ones: A psychometric analysis of descriptions of oneself and various types of others. *Journal of Personality and Social Psychology, 41,* 517–552.

Goldberg, S. (1991). Recent developments in attachment theory and research. *Canadian Journal of Psychiatry, 36,* 393–400.

Golden, C., Golden, C.J., & Schneider, B. (2003). Cell phone use and visual attention. *Perceptual and Motor Skills, 97*, 385–389.

Goldstein, B. (2002). *Sensation and perception* (6th ed.). Belmont, CA: Wadsworth.

Goldstein, G. (2000). Comprehensive neuropsychological assessment batteries. In G. Goldstein & M. Hersen (Eds.), *Handbook of psychological assessment* (3rd ed., pp. 231–262). New York, NY: Elsevier.

Goldston, D.B., Reboussin, B., & Daniel, S.S. (2006). Predictors of suicide attempts: State and trait components. *Journal of Abnormal Psychology, 115*, 842–849.

Gonçalves, M.M., Mendes, I., Cruz, G., Ribeiro, A.P., Sousa, I., Angus, L., & Greenberg, L.S. (2012). Innovative moments and change in client-centered therapy. *Psychotherapy Research, 22*(4), 389–401.

Gone, J.P. (2013). Redressing first nations historical trauma: Theorizing mechanisms for indigenous culture as mental health treatment. *Transcultural Psychiatry, 50*(5), 683–706.

Gong, T., & Shuai, L. (2015). Modeling coevolution between language and memory capacity during language origin. *PLoS ONE, 10*(11). Retrieved from http://search.proquest.com/docview/1767920721?accountid=15115.

Goodale, M.A. (2000). Perception and action in the human visual system. In M.S. Gazzaniga (Ed.), *The new cognitive neurosciences* (2nd ed.). Cambridge, MA: MIT Press.

Goodale, M.A., & Milner, A.D. (1992). Separate visual pathways for perception and action. *Trends Neuroscience, 15*, 20–25.

Goodall, J. (1971). *In the shadow of man.* London, UK: William Collins.

Goodall, J. (1986). *The chimpanzees of Gombe: Patterns of behavior.* Cambridge, MA: Harvard University Press.

Goode, W.J. (1959). The theoretical importance of love. *American Sociological Review, 24*, 38–47.

Goodman, G.S., Quas, J.A., & Ogle, C.M. (2010). Child maltreatment and memory. *Annual Review of Psychology, 61*, 325–351.

Goodman, G.S., Quas, J.A., Batterman-Faunce, J.M., Riddlesberger, M.M., & Kuhn, J. (1994). Predictors of accurate and inaccurate memories of traumatic events experienced in childhood. *Consciousness and Cognition: An International Journal, 3*, 269–294.

Goodman, W. (1982, August 9). Of mice, monkeys and men. *Newsweek*, 61.

Goodrick, S. (2014). Defining narcolepsy. *The Lancet Neurology, 13*(6), 542.

Goodwill, A.M., Alison, L.J., & Beech, A.R. (2009). What works in offender profiling? A comparison of typological, thematic, and multivariate models. *Behavioral Sciences and the Law, 27*, 507–529.

Gorman, J.M. (2002). Treatment of generalized anxiety disorder. *Journal of Clinical Psychiatry, 63* (Suppl. 8), 17–23.

Gosling, P., Denizeau, M., & Oberlé, D. (2006). Denial of responsibility: A new mode of dissonance reduction. *Journal of Personality and Social Psychology, 90*(5), 722–733.

Gosling, S.D., Vazire, S., Srivastava, S., & John, O.P. (2004). Should we trust web-based studies? A comparative analysis of six preconceptions about Internet questionnaires. *American Psychologist, 59*, 93–104.

Gothard, S.I., & Ivker, N.A.C. (2000). The evolving law of alleged delayed memories of childhood sexual abuse. *Child Maltreatment Journal of the American Professional Society on the Abuse of Children, 5*, 176–189.

Gotlib, I.H., & Hammen, C.L. (2010). *Handbook of depression* (2nd ed.). New York, NY: The Guilford Press.

Gotlib, I.H., Kasch, K.L, Traill, S., Joormann, J., Arnow, B.A., & Johnson, S.L. (2004a). Coherence and specificity of information-processing biases in depression and social phobia. *Journal of Abnormal Psychology, 113*, 386–398.

Gotlib, I.H., Krasnoperova, E., Yue, D.N., & Joormann, J. (2004b). Attentional biases for negative interpersonal stimuli in clinical depression. *Journal of Abnormal Psychology, 113*, 127–135.

Gottesman, I.I. (1991). *Schizophrenia genesis: The origins of madness.* New York, NY: W.H. Freeman.

Gottfredson, N.C., & Hussong, A.M. (2013). Drinking to dampen affect variability: Findings from a college student sample. *Journal of Studies on Alcohol and Drugs, 74*, 576–583.

Gottfried, A.E., Fleming, J.S., & Gottfried, A.W. (1998). Role of cognitively stimulating home environment in children's academic intrinsic motivation: A longitudinal study. *Child Development, 69*, 1448–1460.

Gottfried, T. (2000). *Should drugs be legalized?* Brookfield, CT: Twenty-First Century.

Gottman, J., & Silver, N. (2012). *What makes love last? How to build trust and avoid betrayal.* New York, NY: Simon & Schuster.

Gottman, J., Swanson, C., & Murray, J. (1999). The mathematics of marital conflict: Dynamic mathematical nonlinear modeling of newlywed marital interaction. *Journal of Family Psychology, 13*, 3–19.

Gottman, J.M. (1994). *What predicts divorce? The relationship between marital processes and marital outcomes.* Hillsdale, NJ: Erlbaum.

Gottman, J.M., Coan, J., Carrere, S., & Swanson, C. (1998). Predicting marital happiness and stability from newlywed interactions. *Journal of Marriage and the Family, 60*, 5–22.

Gottman, J.M., & DeClaire, J. (2002). *The relationship cure: A five-step guide to strengthening your marriage, family, and friendships.* New York, NY: Three Rivers Press.

Gould, E., Reeves, A.J., Graziano, M.S.A., & Gross, C.G. (1999). Neurogenesis in the neocortex of adult primates. *Science*, 548–552.

Govorun, O., Fuegen, K., & Payne, B.K. (2006). Stereotype focus and defensive projection. *Personality and Social Psychology Bulletin, 32*, 781–793.

Graber, J.A., Seeley, J.R., Brooks-Gunn, J., & Lewinsohn, P.M. (2004). Is pubertal timing associated with psychopathology in young adulthood? *Journal of the American Academy of Child & Adolescent Psychiatry, 43*, 718–726.

Graber, M.A., & Graber, A. (2013). Internet-based crowdsourcing and research ethics: The case for IRB review. *Journal of Medical Ethics: Journal of the Institute of Medical Ethics, 39*(2), 115–118.

Gracely, R.H., Farrell, M.J., & Grant, M.A.B. (2002). Temperature and pain perception. In H. Pashler & S. Yantis (Eds.), *Steven's handbook of experimental psychology: Vol. 1 Sensation and perception* (3rd ed.). New York, NY: Wiley.

Graf, P., & Schacter, D.L. (1985). Implicit and explicit memory for new associations in normal and amnesic subjects. *Journal of Experimental Psychology: Learning, Memory, and Cognition, 11*, 501–518.

Graham, J.D., Sonne, M.W.L., & Bray, S.R. (2014). It wears me out just imagining it! mental imagery leads to muscle fatigue and diminished performance of isometric exercise. *Biological Psychology, 103*, 1–6.

Graham, S., Hudley, C., & Williams, E. (1992). Attributional and emotional determinants of aggression among African-American and Latino young adolescents. *Developmental Psychology, 28*, 731–740.

Grant, H.M., Bredahl, L.C., Clay, J., Ferrie, J., Groves, J.E., McDorman, T.A., & Dark, V.J. (1998). Context-dependent memory for meaningful material: Information for students. *Applied Cognitive Psychology, 12*, 617–623.

Grasshoff, C., Netzhammer, N., Schweizer, J., Antkowiak, B., & Hentschke, H. (2008). Depression of spinal network activity by thiopental: Shift from phasic to tonic GABA [sub]A[/sub] receptor-mediated inhibition. *Neuropharmacology, 55*, 793–802.

Gratton, A., & Wise, R.A. (1994). Drug- and behaviour-associated changes in dopamine-related electrochemical signals during intravenous cocaine self-administration in rats. *Journal of Neuroscience, 14*, 4130–4146.

Graveline, Y.M., & Wamsley, E.J. (2015). Dreaming and waking cognition. *Translational Issues in Psychological Science, 1*(1), 97–105.

Green, D.P., Glaser, J., & Rich, A. (1998). From lynching to gay bashing: The elusive connection between economic conditions and hate crime. *Journal of Personality and Social Psychology, 75*(1), 82–92.

Green, J.T., & Woodruff-Pak, D.S. (2000). Eyeblink classical conditioning: Hippocampal formation is for neutral stimulus associations as cerebellum is for association-response. *Psychological Bulletin, 126*, 138–158.

Green, M. (1999). Diagnosis of attention-deficit/hyperactivity disorder. *Technical Review Number 3, Publication No. 99–0050.* Rockville, MD: Agency for Health Care Policy and Research.

Green, M.F. (1997). *Schizophrenia from a neurocognitive perspective: Probing the impenetrable darkness.* Boston, MA: Allyn & Bacon.

Greenberg, L. (2014). The therapeutic relationship in emotion-focused therapy. *Psychotherapy, 51*(3), 350–357.

Greenberg, L.S., & Malcolm, W. (2002). Resolving unfinished business: Relating process to outcome. *Journal of Consulting and Clinical Psychology, 70*, 406–416.

Greenberg, L.S., & Rice, L.N. (1997). Humanistic approaches to psychotherapy. In P.L. Wachtel & S.B. Messer (Eds.), *Theories of psychotherapy: Origins and evolution.* Washington, DC: American Psychological Association.

Greene, K., Krcmar, M., Walters, L.H, Rubin, D.L., & Hale, J.L. (2000). Targeting adolescent risk-taking behaviors: The contribution of egocentrism and sensation seeking. *Journal of Adolescence, 23*, 439–461.

Greene, R.L. (1992). *Human memory: Paradigms and paradoxes.* Hillsdale, NJ: Erlbaum.

Greene, R.W., & Ollendick, T.H. (2000). Behavioral assessment of children. In G. Goldstein & M. Hersen (Eds.), *Handbook of psychological assessment* (3rd ed., pp. 453–470). New York, NY: Elsevier.

Greenfield, P.M. (1998). The cultural evolution of IQ. In U. Neisser (Ed.), *The rising curve: Long-term gains in IQ and related measures.* Washington, DC: American Psychological Association.

Greenleaf, E. (1973). "Senoi" dream groups. *Psychotherapy: Theory, Research and Practice, 10,* 218–222.

Greeno, C.G., & Wing, R.R. (1994). Stress-induced eating. *Psychological Bulletin, 115,* 444–464.

Greenwald, A.G. (1992). New look 3: Unconscious cognition reclaimed. *American Psychologist, 47,* 766–779.

Greenwald, A.G., & Banaji, M.R. (1995). Implicit social cognition: Attitudes, self-esteem, and stereotypes. *Psychological Review, 102,* 4–27.

Greenwald, A.G., McGhee, D.E., & Schwartz, J. (1998). Measuring individual differences in implicit cognition: The implicit association test. *Journal of Personality and Social Psychology, 74,* 1464–1480.

Gregory, M.D., Kippenhan, J.S., Dickinson, D., Carrasco, J., Mattay, V.S., Weinberger, D.R., & Berman, K.F. (2016). Regional variations in brain gyrification are associated with general cognitive ability in humans. *Current Biology,* April.

Gregory, R.J. (1998). *Foundations of intellectual assessment: The WAIS-III and other tests in clinical practice.* Boston, MA: Allyn & Bacon.

Gregory, R.L. (1966). *Eye and brain.* New York, NY: McGraw-Hill.

Gregory, R.L. (2005). *Illusion: The phenomenal brain.* New York, NY: Oxford University Press.

Gregory, R.L., & Gombrich, E.H. (Eds.). (1973). *Illusion in Nature and Art.* London, UK: Duckworth.

Grice, H.P. (1975). Logic and conversation. In P. Cole & J.L. Morgan (Eds.), *Syntax and semantics: Vol. 3 Speech acts.* New York, NY: Seminar.

Grierson, B. (2010). The incredible flying nonagenarian. *NY Times Magazine,* November 25, 2010. http://www.nytimes.com/2010/11/28 /magazine/28athletes-t.html?pagewanted =1&_r=0.

Grigorenko, E.L. (2003). Selected links between nutrition and the mind. In R.J. Sternberg, J. Lautrey, & T.I. Lubart (Eds.), *Models of intelligence: International perspectives.* Washington, DC: American Psychological Association.

Grigorenko, E.L., Jarvin, L., & Sternberg, R.J. (2002). School-based tests of the triarchic theory of intelligence: Three settings, three samples, three syllabi. *Contemporary Educational Psychology, 27*(2), 167–208.

Grimes, K., & Walker, E.F. (1994). Childhood emotional expressions, educational attainment, and age at onset of illness in schizophrenia. *Journal of Abnormal Psychology, 103,* 784–790.

Griner, D., & Smith, T. (2006). Culturally adapted mental health intervention: A meta-analytic review. *Psychotherapy: Theory, Research, Practice, Training. Special issue: Culture, race, and ethnicity in psychotherapy, 43*(4), 531–548.

Grissom, R.J. (1996). The magical number 7 plus or minus 2: Meta-meta-analysis of the probability of superior outcome in comparisons involving therapy, placebo, and control. *Journal of Consulting and Clinical Psychology, 64,* 973–982.

Groepper, D., Veach, P.M., LeRoy, B.S., & Bower, M. (2015). Ethical and professional challenges encountered by laboratory genetic counselors. *Journal of Genetic Counseling, 24*(4), 580–596.

Gronnerod, C. (2003). Temporal stability in the Rorschach method: A meta-analytic review. *Journal of Personality Assessment, 80,* 272–293.

Groppa, S., Oliviero, A., Eisen, A., Quartarone, A., Cohen, L.G., Mall, V., Kaelin-Lang, A., Mima, T., Rossi, S., Thickbroom, G.W., Rossini, P.M., Ziemann, U., Valls-Solé, J., & Siebner, H.R. (2012).

A practical guide to diagnostic transcranial magnetic stimulation: Report of an IFCN committee. *Clinical Neurophysiology, 123*(5), 858–882.

Gross, J.J. (1998). The emerging field of emotion regulation: An integrative review. *Review of General Psychology. Special issue: New directions in research on emotion, 2,* 271–299.

Gross, J.J. (1999). Emotion and emotion regulation. In L.A. Pervin & O.P. John (Eds.), *Handbook of personality: Theory and research* (2nd ed.). New York, NY: Guilford Press.

Grossberg, S., Finkel, L., & Field, D. (Eds.). (2005). *Vision and brain: How the brain sees: New approaches to computer vision.* St. Louis, MO: Elsevier.

Grotegerd, D., Suslow, T., Bauer, J., Ohrmann, P., Arolt, V., Stuhrmann, A., Heindel, W., Kugel, H., & Dannlowsk, U. (2012). Discriminating unipolar and bipolar depression by means of fMRI and pattern classification: a pilot study. *European Archives of Psychiatry and Clinical Neuroscience, 263*(2), 119–131.

Groth-Marnat, G. (1999). *Handbook of psychological assessment.* New York, NY: Wiley.

Groth-Marnat, G. (2003). *Handbook of psychological assessment* (4th ed.). Hoboken, NJ: Wiley.

Grunebaum, M.F., Keilp, J.G., Ellis, S.P., Sudol, K., Bauer, N., Burke, A.K., ... Mann, J.J. (2013). SSRI versus bupropion effects on symptom clusters in suicidal depression: Post hoc analysis of a randomized clinical trial. *Journal of Clinical Psychiatry, 74*(9), 872–879.

Guan, Y., Chen, S.X., Levin, N., Bond, M.H., Luo, N., Xu, J., ... Han, X. (2015). Differences in career decision-making profiles between American and Chinese university students: The relative strength of mediating mechanisms across cultures. *Journal of Cross-Cultural Psychology, 46*(6), 856–872.

Guéguen, N. (2002). Foot in the door technique and computer mediated communication. *Computers in Human Behavior, 18,* 11–15.

Guilford, J.P. (1959). Three faces of intellect. *American Psychologist, 14,* 469–479.

Guilford, J.P. (1967). *The nature of human intelligence.* New York, NY: McGraw-Hill.

Guinness book of records. (2000). Stamford, CT: Guinness Media.

Gulevich, G., Dement, W., & Johnson, L. (1966). Psychiatric and EEG observations on a case of prolonged (264 hours) wakefulness. *Archives of General Psychiatry, 15,* 29–35.

Gump, L.S., Baker, R.C., & Roll, S. (2000). Cultural and gender differences in moral judgment: A study of Mexican Americans and Anglo-Americans. *Hispanic Journal of Behavioral Sciences, 22,* 78–93.

Guo, G. (2006). Genetic similarity shared by best friends among adolescents. *Twin Research and Human Genetics, 9,* 113–121.

Guo, T., Ji, L.J., Spina, R., & Zhang, Z. (2012). Culture, temporal focus, and the values of the past and the future. *Personality and Social Psychology Bulletin, 38*(8), 1030–1040.

Gur, R.E., Cowell, P., Turetsky, B.I., Gallacher, F., Cannon, T., Bilker, W., & Gur, R.B. (1998). A follow-up magnetic resonance imaging study of schizophrenia: Relationship of neuroanatomical changes to clinical and neurobehavioral measures. *Archives of General Psychiatry, 55,* 145–152.

Gurvitz, I.G., Koenigsberg, H.W., & Siever, L.J. (2000). Neurotransmitter dysfunction in patients with borderline personality disorder. *Psychiatric Clinics of North America, 23,* 27–40.

Gustavson, C.R., Garcia, J., Hankins, W.G., & Rusiniak, K.W. (1974). Coyote predation control by aversive conditioning. *Science, 184,* 581–583.

Gustavson, C.R., & Gustavson, J.C. (1985). Predation control using conditioned food aversion methodology: Theory, practice, and implications. *Annals of the New York Academy of Sciences, 443,* 348–356.

Guthrie, J.P., Ash, R.A., & Bendapudi, V. (1995). Additional validity evidence for a measure of morningness. *Journal of Applied Psychology, 80,* 186–190.

Haaga, D.A.F., Dyck, M.J., & Ernst, D. (1991). Empirical status of cognitive theory of depression. *Psychological Bulletin, 110,* 215–236.

Haas, S.J., Hill, R., Krum, H., Liew, D., Tonkin, A., Demos, L., ... McNeil, L. (2007). Clozapine-associated myocarditis: A review of 116 cases of suspected myocarditis associated with the use of clozapine in Australia during 1993–2003. *Drug Safety, 30*(1), 47–57.

Haász, J., Westlye, E.T., Fjær, S., Espeseth, T., Lundervold, A., & Lundervold, A.J. (2013). General fluid-type intelligence is related to indices of white matter structure in middle-aged and old adults. *NeuroImage, 83,* 372–383.

Hafen, B.Q., & Hoeger, W.W.K. (1998). *Wellness: Guidelines for a healthy lifestyle.* Englewood, CO: Morton.

Hagen, C., & Wilson, J. (2013). New implant helps boy hear for first time. *CNN Health,* 11:41 a.m., June 21.

Haier, R.J., Colom, R., Schroeder, D.H., & Condon, C.A. (2009). Gray matter and intelligence factors: Is there a neuro-g? *Intelligence, 37,* 136–144.

Haier, R.J., Jung, R.E., Yeo, R.A., Head, K., & Alkire, M.J. (2005). The neuroanatomy of general intelligence: Sex matters. *NeuroImage, 25,* 320–327.

Haier, R.J., Siegel, B.V., Crinella, F.M., & Buchsbaum, M.S. (1993). Biological and psychometric intelligence: Testing an animal model in humans with positron emission tomography. In D.K. Detterman (Ed.), *Individual differences and cognition: Current topics in human intelligence* (Vol. 3). Norwood, NJ: Ablex.

Haines, R.F. (1991). A breakdown in simultaneous information processing. In G. Obrecht & L.W. Stark (Eds.), *Presbyopia research* (pp. 171–175). New York, NY: Plenum Press.

Halaas, J.L., Gajiwala, K.S., Maffei, M., Cohen, S.L., Chait, B.T., & Rabinowitz, D. (1995). Weight-reducing effects of the plasma protein encoded by the obese gene. *Science, 269,* 543–546.

Halari, R., Hines, M., Kumari, V., Mehrotra, R., Wheeler, M., Ng, V., & Sharma, T. (2005). Sex differences and individual differences in cognitive performance and their relationship to endogenous gonadal hormones and gonadotropins. *Behavioral Neuroscience, 119,* 104–117.

Hale, C.R., Casey, J.E., & Ricciardi, P.W.R. (2014). A cluster analytic study of the wechsler intelligence test for children-IV in children referred for psychoeducational assesment due to persistent academic difficulties. *Archives of Clinical Neuropsychology, 29*(1), 132–142.

Hall, C.S. (1984). "A ubiquitous sex difference in dreams" revisited. *Journal of Personality and Social Psychology, 46,* 1109–1117.

Hall, C.S., & Van de Castle, R. (1966). *The content analysis of dreams.* New York, NY: Appleton-Century-Crofts.

Hall, D.R., & Zhao, J.Z. (1995). Cohabitation and divorce in Canada: Testing the selectivity hypothesis. *Journal of Marriage and the Family,* 57, 421–427.

Hall, G.C.N., & Okazaki, S. (2003). *Asian American psychology: The science of lives in context.* Washington, DC: American Psychological Association.

Hall, G.S. (1904). *Adolescence* (Vols. 1 & 2). New York, NY: Appleton-Century-Crofts.

Hall, H., Lawyer, G., Sillen, A., Jonsson, E.G., Agartz, I., Terenius, L., & Arnborg, S. (2007). Potential genetic variants in schizophrenia: A Bayesian analysis. *World Journal of Biological Psychiatry, 8,* 12–22.

Hall, J.A.Y., & Kimura, D. (1995). Sexual orientation and performance on sexually dimorphic tasks. *Archives of Sexual Behavior, 24,* 395–407.

Hall, W., & Degenhardt, L. (2009). Adverse health effects of non-medical cannabis use. *Lancet, 37,* 1383–1391.

Halligan, P.W., Fink, G.R., Marshall, J.C., & Vallar, G. (2003). Spatial cognition: Evidence from visual neglect. *Trends in Cognitive Sciences, 7,* 125–133.

Halligan, S., Murray, C., Martins, C., & Cooper, P.J. (2007). Maternal depression and psychiatric outcomes in adolescent offspring: A 13-year longitudinal study. *Journal of Affective Disorders, 97*(1–3), 145–154.

Halpern, B.P. (2002). Taste. In H. Pashler & S. Yantis (Eds.), *Steven's handbook of experimental psychology: Vol. 1 Sensation and perception* (3rd ed., pp. 653–690). New York, NY: Wiley.

Halpern, C.T., Udry, J.R., Campbell, B., & Suchindran, C. (1999). Effects of body fat on weight concerns, dating, and sexual activity: A longitudinal analysis of Black and White adolescent girls. *Developmental Psychology, 35,* 721–736.

Halpern, D.F. (2004). *Sex differences in cognitive abilities* (3rd ed.). Mahwah, NJ: Erlbaum.

Halpern, D.F., & Tan, U. (2001). Stereotypes and steroids: Using a psychobiosocial model to understand cognitive sex differences. *Brain and Cognition, 45,* 392–414.

Haluk, D.M., & Wickman, K. (2010). Evaluation of study design variables and their impact on food-maintained operant responding in mice. *Behavioural Brain Research, 207,* 394–401.

Hamilton, A.F. (2013). Reflecting on the mirror neuron system in autism: A systematic review of current theories. *Developmental Cognitive Neuroscience, 3,* 91–105.

Hamilton, R.J. (1985). A framework for the evaluation of the effectiveness of adjunct questions and objectives. *Review of Educational Research, 55,* 47–85.

Hamilton, W.D. (1964). The genetical theory of social behaviour, I, II. *Journal of Theoretical Biology, 12,* 12–45.

Hamm, A.O. (2009). Specific phobias. *Psychiatric Clinics of North America, 16,* 577–591.

Hammen, C. (1991). *Depression runs in families: The social context of risk and resilience in children of depressed mothers.* New York, NY: Springer-Verlag.

Hampson, E., & Kimura, D. (1988). Reciprocal effects of hormonal fluctuations on human motor and perceptual-spatial skills. *Behavioral Neuroscience, 102*(3), 456–459.

Hampson, E., & Kimura, D. (1992). Sex differences and hormonal influences on cognitive function in humans. In J.B. Becker, S.M. Breedlove, & D. Crews (Eds.), *Behavioral endocrinology.* Cambridge, MA: MIT Press.

Hampson, S.E. (2012). Personality processes: Mechanisms by which personality traits "get

outside the skin." *Annual Review of Psychology, 63,* 315–339.

Hampson, S.E., & Friedman, H.S. (2008). Personality and health: A lifespan perspective. In O.P. John, R.W. Robins, & L.A. Pervin (Eds.), *Handbook of personality: Theory and research* (3rd ed., pp. 770–794). New York, NY: Guilford Press.

Hampstead, B.M., & Koffler, S.P. (2009). Thalamic contributions to anterograde, retrograde, and implicit memory: A case study. *The Clinical Neuropsychologist, 23,* 1232–1249.

Han, S.H., Northoff, G., Vogeley, K., Wexler, B.E., Kitayama, S., & Varnum, M.E.W. (2013). A cultural neuroscience approach to the biosocial nature of the human brain. *Annual Review of Psychology, 64,* 335–359.

Han, Z., Bi, Y., Chen, J., Chen, Q., Yong, H., & Caramazza, A. (2013). Distinct regions of right temporal cortex are associated with biological and human-agent motion: Functional magnetic resonance imaging and neuropsychological evidence. *Journal of Neuroscience, 33*(39), 15442–15443.

Hancock, P.A., & Desmond, P.A. (2000). *Stress, workload and fatigue.* Mahwah, NJ: Lawrence Erlbaum Associates.

Hane, A.A., Fox, N.A., Polak-Toste, C., Ghera, M., & Gunner, B. (2006). Contextual basis of maternal perceptions of infant temperament. *Developmental Psychology, 42,* 1077–1088.

Hankin, B.L., Kassel, J.D., & Abela, R.Z. (2005). Adult attachment dimensions and specificity of emotional distress symptoms: Prospective investigations of cognitive risk and inter-personal stress generation as mediating mechanisms. *Personality and Social Psychology Bulletin, 31,* 136–151.

Hanley, S.J., & Abell, S.C. (2002). Maslow and relatedness: Creating an interpersonal model of self-actualization. *Journal of Humanistic Psychology, 42,* 37–56.

Hannon, E.E., & Trainor, L.J. (2007). Music acquisition: Effects of enculturation and formal training on development. *Trends in Cognitive Sciences, 11*(11), 466–472.

Hansen, C.H., & Hansen, R.D. (1988). Finding the face in the crowd: An anger superiority effect. *Journal of Personality and Social Psychology, 54,* 917–924.

Hansen, J., & Wänke, M. (2009). Liking what's familiar: The importance of unconscious familiarity in the mere-exposure effect. *Social Cognition, 27,* 161–182.

Hansen, N.B., Lambert, M.J., & Forman, E.M. (2002). The psychotherapy dose-response effect and its implications for treatment delivery services. *Clinical Psychology: Science and Practice, 9,* 329–343.

Hardt, O., Migues, P.V., Hastings, M., Wong, J., & Nader, K. (2010). PKM maintains 1-day- and 6-day-old long-term object location but not object identity memory in dorsal hippocampus. *Hippocampus, 20*(6), 691 695.

Hardy, C., & Latané, B. (1986). Social loafing on a cheering task. *Social Science, 71,* 165–172.

Hare, R.D. (2001). *Without conscience: The disturbing world of the psychopaths among us.* New York, NY: Guilford Press.

Harkness, K.L., & Stewart, J.O. (2009). Symptom specificity and the prospective generation of life events in adolescence. *Journal of Abnormal Psychology, 118,* 278–287.

Harley, K., & Reese, E. (1999). Origins of autobiographical memory. *Developmental Psychology, 35,* 1338–1348.

Harlow, H.F. (1958). The nature of love. *The American Psychologist, 13,* 673–685.

Harlow, H.F., & Suomi, S.J. (1970). The nature of love simplified. *American Psychologist, 25,* 161–168.

Harlow, J., & Roll, S. (1992). Frequency of day residue in dreams of young adults. *Perceptual and Motor Skills, 74,* 832–834.

Harlow, J.M. (1868). Recovery from the passage of an iron bar through the head. *Massachusetts Medical Society, 2,* 327.

Harmon-Jones, E., Brehm, J.W., Greenberg, J., Simon, L., & Nelson, D.E. (1996). Evidence that the production of aversive consequences is not necessary to create cognitive dissonance. *Journal of Personality and Social Psychology, 70,* 5–16.

Harrington, D.M., Block, J.H., & Black, J. (1987). Testing aspects of Carl Rogers's theory of creative environments: Child-rearing antecedents of creative potential in young adolescents. *Journal of Personality and Social Psychology, 52,* 851–856.

Harris, S.L. (1981). A letter from the editor on loss and trust. *The Clinical Psychologist, 34*(3), 3.

Harrison, A.G., Holmes, A., Silvestri, R., & Armstrong, I.T. (2015). Implications for educational classification and psychological diagnoses using the Weschsler Adult Intelligence Scale-Fourth Edition with Canadian versus American norms. *Journal of Psychoeducational Assessment,* Feb., 0734282915573723.

Harrison, J.E., & Baron-Cohen, S.C. (1997). Synaesthesia: A review of psychological theories. In J.E. Harrison & S.C. Baron-Cohen (Eds.), *Synaesthesia: Classic and contemporary readings.* Oxford, UK: Blackwell.

Hart, J.W., Bridgett, D.J., & Karau, S.J. (2001). Coworker ability and effort as determinants of individual effort on a collective task. *Group Dynamics, 5,* 181–190.

Hart, W., Albarracín, D., Eagly, A.H., Lindberg, M.J., Merrill, L., & Brechan, I. (2009). Feeling validated versus being correct: A meta-analysis of selective exposure to information. *Psychological Bulletin, 135,* 555–588.

Hartmann, E. (1977). L-tryptophane as an hypnotic agent: A review. *Waking & Sleeping, 1,* 155–161.

Hartshorne, H., & May, A. (1928). *Studies in the nature of character, Vol. 1: Studies in deceit.* New York, NY: Macmillan.

Hasan, Y., Begue, L., Scharkow, M., & Bushman, B.J. (2013). The more you play, the more aggressive you become: A long-term experimental study of cumulative violent video game effects on hostile expectations and aggressive behavior. *Journal of Experimental Social Psychology, 49*(2), 224–227.

Hassabis, D., Kumaran, D., Vann, S.D., & Maguire, E.A. (2007). Patients with hippocampal amnesia cannot imagine new experiences. *Proceedings of the National Academy of Sciences, 104*(5), 1726–1731.

Hassin, R.R., Uleman, J.S., & Bargh, J.A. (2005). *The new unconscious.* New York, NY: Oxford University Press.

Hastings, P., & Grusec, J.E. (1997). Conflict outcome as a function of parental accuracy in perceiving child cognitions and affect. *Social Development, 6,* 76–90.

Hatfield, E. (1988). Passionate and companionate love. In R.J. Sternberg & M.L. Barnes (Eds.), *The psychology of love.* New Haven, CT: Yale University Press.

Hatfield, E., & Rapson, R.L. (1987). Passionate love/ sexual desire: Can the same paradigm explain both? *Archives of Sexual Behavior, 16,* 259–278.

Hathaway, S.R., & McKinley, J.C. (1983). *The Minnesota Multiphasic Personality Inventory manual.* New York, NY: Psychological Corporation.

Haugtvedt, C.P., Petty, R.E., & Cacioppo, J.T. (1992). Need for cognition and advertising: Understanding the role of personality variables in consumer behavior. *Journal of Consumer Psychology, 1,* 239–260.

Hauri, P. (1982). *The sleep disorders* (2nd ed.). Kalamazoo, MI: Upjohn Corp.

Hawkins, D.L., Pepler, D.J., & Craig, W.M. (2001). Naturalistic observations of peer interventions in bullying. *Social Development, 10,* 512–527.

Hawkins, K.A., & Trobst, K.K. (2000). Frontal lobe dysfunction and aggression: Conceptual issues and research findings. *Aggression and Violent Behavior, 5,* 147–157.

Hayes, S.C., Luoma, J., Bond, F., Masuda, A., & Lillis, J. (2006). Acceptance and commitment therapy: Model, processes, and outcomes. *Behaviour Research and Therapy, 44,* 1–25.

Haynes, S.G., Feinleib, M., & Kannel, W.B. (1980). The relationship of psycho-social factors in coronary heart disease in the Framingham study: Study III: Eight-year incidence of coronary heart disease. *American Journal of Epidemiology, 111,* 37–58.

Haynes, S.N. (2000). Behavioral assessment of adults. In G. Goldstein & M. Hersen (Eds.), *Handbook of psychological assessment* (3rd ed., pp. 471–502). New York, NY: Elsevier.

Haynes, S.N., Price, M.G., & Simons, J.P. (1975). Stimulus control treatment of insomnia. *Journal of Behavior Therapy and Experimental Psychiatry, 6,* 279–282.

Hayslip, B., & Panek, P.E. (2002). *Adult development and aging.* New York, NY: Harper & Row.

Hazan, C., & Diamond, L.M. (2000). The place of attachment in human mating. *Review of General Psychology, 4,* 186–204.

Hazen, N.L., & Durrett, M.E. (1982). Relationship of security of attachment to exploration and cognitive mapping abilities in 2-year-olds. *Developmental Psychology, 18,* 751–759.

He, M., Walle, E.A., & Campos, J.J. (2015). A cross-national investigation of the relationship between infant walking and language development. *Infancy, 20*(3), 283–305.

He, X.X., Nebert, D.W., Vasiliou, V., Zhu, H., & Shertzer, H.G. (1997). Genetic differences in alcohol drinking preference between inbred strains of mice. *Pharmacogenetics, 7,* 223–233.

Health Canada. (2002). A report on mental illnesses in Canada. Retrieved November 22, 2010, from http://www.phac-aspc.gc.ca/publicat/miic-mmac/index-eng.php.

Health Canada. (2008). Canadian Addiction Survey (CAS): A national survey of Canadians' use of alcohol and other drugs: Substance use by Canadian youth. Retrieved November 17, 2010, from http://www.hc-sc.gc.ca/hc-ps/pubs/adp-apd/cas_youth-etc_jeunes/chap3_page3-eng.php.

Health Canada. (2011). Canadian Alcohol and Drug Use Monitoring Survey. http://www.hc-sc.gc.ca/hc-ps/drugs-drogues/stat/_2011/summary-sommaire-eng.php#a3.

Health Canada. (2012). Canadian Alcohol and Drug Use Monitoring Survey (CADUMS). http://www.hc-sc.gc.ca/hc-ps/drugs-drogues/stat/_2011/summary-sommaire-eng.php.

Hearold, S. (1986). A synthesis of 1043 effects of television on social behavior. In G. Comstock (Ed.), *Public communications and behavior* (Vol. 1, pp. 66–135). New York, NY: Academic Press.

Heath, A.C., Todorov, A.A., Nelson, E.C., Madden, P.A.F., Bucholz, K.K., & Martin, N.G. (2002). Gene–environment interaction effects on behavioral variation and risk of complex disorders: The example of alcoholism and other psychiatric disorders. *Twins Research, 5,* 30–37.

Heath, R.G. (1972). Pleasure and brain activity in man. *Journal of Nervous and Mental Disease, 154,* 3–18.

Heaton, T.B. (2002). Factors contributing to increasing marital stability in the U.S. *Journal of Family Issues, 23,* 392–409.

Heavey, E. (2015). Review of phantom limb: Amputation, embodiment, and prosthetic technology. *Sociology of Health & Illness, 37*(5), 800–801.

Hebb, D.O. (1949). *The organization of behavior.* New York, NY: Wiley.

Heckers, S., & Konradi, C. (2000). Anatomic and molecular principles of psychopharmacology: A primer for psychiatrists. *Child and Adolescent Psychiatric Clinics of North America, 9,* 1–22.

Heckhausen, H. (1991). *Motivation and action* (2nd ed.). New York, NY: Springer-Verlag.

Heerey, E.A., Keltner, D., & Capps, L.M. (2003). Making sense of self-conscious emotion: Linking theory of mind and emotion in children with autism. *Emotion, 3,* 394–400.

Hefferon, K., & Boniwell, I. (2011). *Positive psychology: Theory, research and applications.* Maidenhead, UK: Open University Press/McGraw Hill.

Heider, F. (1958). *The psychology of interpersonal relations.* New York, NY: Wiley.

Heim, C., & Nemeroff, C.B. (2001). The role of childhood trauma in the neurobiology of mood and anxiety disorders: Preclinical and clinical studies. *Biological Psychiatry, 49*(12), 1023–1039.

Heiman, J. (1975). Women's sexual arousal: The physiology of erotica. *Psychology Today, 8,* 90–94.

Heiman, J.R. (1977). A psychophysiological exploration of sexual arousal patterns in females and males. *Psychophysiology, 14,* 266–274.

Heimpel, S.A., Wood, J.V., Marshall, M.A., & Brown, J.D. (2002). Do people with low self-esteem really want to feel better? Self-esteem differences in motivation to repair negative moods. *Journal of Personality and Social Psychology, 82,* 128–147.

Heinrichs, R.W. (2001). *In search of madness: Schizophrenia and neuroscience.* New York, NY: Oxford University Press.

Heller, M.A., & Schiff, W. (Eds.). (1991). *The psychology of touch.* Hillsdale, NJ: Erlbaum.

Hellerstein, D., Yanowitch, P., Rosenthal, J., Samstag, L.W., Maurer, M., Kasch, K., ... Winston, A. (1993). A randomized double-blind study of fluoxetine versus placebo in the treatment of dysthymia. *American Journal of Psychiatry, 150,* 1169–1175.

Helmreich, R.L. (1997, May). Managing human error in aviation. *Scientific American,* 62–67.

Henry, J.D., MacLeod, M.S., Phillips, L.H., & Crawford, J.P. (2004). A meta-analytical review of prospective memory and aging. *Psychology and Aging, 19*(1), 27–39.

Herculano-Houzel, S. (2014). The glia/neuron ratio: How it varies uniformly across brain structures and species and what that means for brain physiology and evolution. *Glia, 62*(9), 1377–1391.

Herdt, G., & Lindenbaum, S. (Eds.). (1992). *Social analysis in the time of AIDS.* Newbury Park, CA: Sage.

Herek, G.M. (2000). The psychology of sexual prejudice. *Current Directions in Psychological Science, 9,* 19–22.

Herek, G.M. (2002). Gender gaps in public opinion about lesbians and gay men. *Public Opinion Quarterly, 66,* 40–66.

HeretoHelp. (2016). http://www.heretohelp.bc.ca/wellness-module/wellness-module-6-getting-a-good-nights-sleep.

Herman, D.B., Susser, E.S., Jandorf, L., Lavelle, J., & Bromet, E.J. (1998). Homelessness among individuals with psychotic disorders hospitalized for the first time: Findings from the Suffolk County Mental Health Project. *American Journal of Psychiatry, 155,* 109–113.

Hernandez, L., & Hoebel, B.G. (1988). Food reward and cocaine increase extracellular dopamine in the nucleus accumbens as measured by microdialysis. *Life Sciences, 42,* 1705–1712.

Herndon, P., Myers, B., Mitchell, K., Kehn, A., & Henry, S. (2014). False memories for highly aversive early childhood events: Effects of guided imagery and group influence. *Psychology of Consciousness: Theory, Research, and Practice, 1*(1), 20–31.

Herrington, R., & Lader, M.H. (1996). *Biological treatments in psychiatry* (2nd ed.). New York, NY: Oxford University Press.

Herrnstein, R.J., & Murray, C. (1994). *The bell curve: Intelligence and class struggle in American life.* New York, NY: Free Press.

Hersen, M. (2002). *Clinical behavior therapy: Adults and children.* New York, NY: Wiley.

Hersen, M. (2003). *Effective brief therapies.* New York, NY: Academic Press.

Herskovits, M.J. (1948). *Man and his works.* New York, NY: Knopf.

Hertwig, R., & Ortmann, A. (2008). Deception in experiments: Revisiting the arguments in its defense. *Ethics & Behavior, 18,* 59–92.

Herz, M., & Marder, S. (2002). *Schizophrenia: A comprehensive text.* New York, NY: Williams & Wilkins.

Hess, E.H. (1959). Imprinting. *Science, 130,* 133–141.

Hess, W.R. (1965). Sleep as phenomenon of the integral organism. In K. Akert, C. Bally, & J.P. Schade (Eds.), *Sleep mechanisms.* New York, NY: Elsevier.

Hetherington, A.W., & Ranson, S.W. (1942). The spontaneous activity and food intake of rats with hypothalamic lesions. *American Journal of Physiology, 136,* 609–617.

Hetherington, E.M. (1998). Relevant issues in developmental science: Introduction to the special issue. *American Psychologist, 53,* 93–94.

Hetherington, E.M., & Stanley-Hagan, M. (2002). Parenting in divorced and remarried families. In M.H. Bornstein (Ed.), *Handbook of parenting: Being and becoming a parent* (2nd ed., Vol. 3). Mahwah, NJ: Erlbaum.

Hetherington, E.M., Bridges, M., & Insabella, G.M. (1998). What matters? What does not? Five perspectives on the association between marital transitions and children's adjustment. *American Psychologist, 53,* 167–184.

Hetherington, E.M., Parke, R.D., & Locke, V.O. (1999). *Child psychology: A contemporary viewpoint* (5th ed.). Boston, MA: McGraw-Hill.

Hewstone, M., Rubin, M., & Willis, H. (2002). Intergroup bias. *Annual Review of Psychology, 53,* 575–604.

Heylighen, F. (1992). A cognitive-systemic reconstruction of Maslow's theory of self-actualization. *Behavioral Science, 37,* 39–58.

Hibbard, S. (2003). A critique of Lilienfeld et al.'s (2000) "The scientific status of projective techniques." *Journal of Personality Assessment, 80,* 260–271.

Hickok, J.T., Roscoe, J.A., & Morrow, G.R. (2001). The role of patients' expectations in the development of anticipatory nausea related to chemotherapy for cancer. *Journal of Pain and Symptom Management, 22,* 843–850.

Higgins, A. (1991). The Just Community approach to moral education: Evolution of the idea and recent findings. In W.M. Kurtines & J.L. Gerwirtz (Eds.), *Handbook of moral behavior and development,* (Vol. 3). Hillsdale, NJ: Erlbaum.

Higham, T., Basell, L., Jacobi, R., Wood, R., Ramsey, C.B., & Conard, N.J. (2012). Testing models for the beginnings of the Aurignacian and the advent of figurative art and music: The radiocarbon chronology of Geißenklösterle. *Journal of Human Evolution, 62*(6), 664–676.

Hilgard, E.R. (1977). *Divided consciousness: Multiple controls in human thought and action.* New York, NY: Wiley.

Hilgard, E.R. (1994). Neodissociation. In S.J. Lynn, & J.W. Rhue (Eds.), *Dissociation: Clinical and theoretical perspectives* (pp. 32–51). New York, NY: Guilford Press.

Hill, C.A. (1987). Affiliation motivation: People who need people but in different ways. *Journal of Personality and Social Psychology, 52,* 1008–1018.

Hill, J.L., Brooks-Gunn, J., & Waldfogel, J. (2003). Sustained effects of high participation in an early intervention for low-birth-weight premature infants. *Developmental Psychology, 39,* 730–744.

Hill, J.O., & Peters, J.C. (1998). Environmental contributions to the obesity epidemic. *Science, 280,* 1371–1374.

Hill, M.M., Dodson, B.B., Hill, E.W., & Fox, J. (1995). An infant sonicguide intervention program for a child with a visual disability. *Journal of Visual Impairment and Blindness, 89,* 329–336.

Hillman, D.C., Siffre, M., Milano, G., & Halberg, F. (1994). Free-running psycho-physiologic circadians and three-month pattern in a woman isolated in a cave. *New Trends in Experimental and Clinical Psychiatry, 10,* 127–133.

Hillman, J.L., Neubrander, J., & Snyder, S.J. (2007). *Childhood autism.* New York, NY: Routledge.

Hines, M. (2005). *Brain gender.* New York, NY: Oxford University Press.

Hines, M., & Gorski, R.A. (1985). Hormonal influences on the development of neural asymmetries. In D.F. Benson & E. Saidel (Eds.), *The Dual Brain* (pp. 75–96). New York, NY: Guilford Press.

Hobson, A. (1988). Psychoanalytic dream theory: A critique based upon modern neurophysiology. In P. Clark & C. Wright (Eds.), *Mind, psychoanalysis and science.* Oxford, UK: Basil Blackwell.

Hobson, J.A. (2007). Current understanding of cellular models of REM expression. In D. Barrett & P. McNamara (Eds.), *The new science of dreaming: Vol. 1 Biological aspects.* Westport, CT: Praeger/Greenwood.

Hobson, J.A., & McCarley, R.W. (1977). The brain as a dream state generator: An activation-synthesis hypothesis of the dream process. *American Journal of Psychiatry, 134,* 1335–1348.

Hobson, J.A., Pace-Schott, E.F., & Stickgold, R. (2000). Dreaming and the brain: Toward a cognitive neuroscience of conscious states. *Behavioral and Brain Sciences, 23,* 793–842.

Hobson, J.A., Stickgold, R., Pace, S., & Edward, F. (1998). The neuropsychology of REM sleep dreaming. *Neuroreport: An International Journal for the Rapid Communication of Research in Neuroscience, 9,* R1–R14.

Hobson-West, P. (2012). Ethical boundary-work in the animal research laboratory. *Sociology, 46,* 649–663.

Hodges, J., & Tizard, B. (1989). Social and family relationships of ex-institutional adolescents. *Journal of Child Psychology and Psychiatry, 30,* 77–97.

Hodson, H. (2014). Dolphin whistle instantly translated by computer. *New Scientist, 2962,* March.

Hoebel, B.G. (1997). Neuroscience and appetitive behavior research: 25 years. *Appetite, 29,* 119–133.

Hoeksema, V.O., Claudia, Y.D., Gaillard, A.W.K., & Buunk, B.P. (1998). Social loafing under fatigue. *Journal of Personality and Social Psychology, 75,* 1179–1190.

Hoffart, A., & Martinson, E.W. (1991). Mental health locus of control in agoraphobia and depression: A longitudinal study of inpatients. *Psychological Reports, 68,* 1011–1018.

Hoffer, A., & Youngren, V.R. (2004). Is free association still at the core of psychoanalysis? *International Journal of Psychoanalysis, 85,* 1489–1492.

Hoffman, H.G., Patterson, D.R., Canougher, G.J., & Sharar, S.R. (2001). Effectiveness of virtual reality-based pain control with multiple treatments. *Clinical Journal of Pain, 17,* 229–235.

Hoffman, L., Lopez, A.J., & Moats, M. (2013). Humanistic psychology and self-acceptance: The strength of self-acceptance The strength of selfacceptance. In M. Bernard (Ed.), *The strength of self-acceptance* (pp. 3–17). New York, NY: Springer.

Hofman, M.A. (2015). Evolution of the human brain: From matter to mind. *Handbook of intelligence: Evolutionary theory, historical perspective, and current concepts* (pp. 65–82). New York, NY: Springer Science + Business Media.

Hofmann, S.G., Sawyer, A.T., Witt, A.A., & Oh, D. (2010). The effect of mindfulness-based therapy on anxiety and depression: A meta-analytic review. *Journal of Consulting and Clinical Psychology, 78*(2), 169–183.

Hogan, M. (2014). Reflections on positive psychology. *PsycCRITIQUES, 59*(12).

Hogan, R. (1983). A socioanalytic theory of personality. In M. Page & R. Dienstbier (Eds.), *Nebraska Symposium on Motivation, 1982.* Lincoln, NE: University of Nebraska Press.

Hogarty, G.E. (2003). *Personal therapy for schizophrenia and related disorders.* New York, NY: Guilford Press.

Holahan, C.J., & Moos, R.H. (1990). Life stressors, resistance factors, and improved psychological functioning: An extension of the stress resistance paradigm. *Journal of Personality and Social Psychology, 58,* 909–917.

Hollis, K.L. (1997). Contemporary research on Pavlovian conditioning: A "new" functional analysis. *American Psychologist, 52,* 956–965.

Hollon, S.D. (1996). The efficacy and effectiveness of psychotherapy relative to medications. *American Psychologist, 51,* 1025–1030.

Hollon, S.D., & Beck, A.T. (1994). Cognitive and cognitive-behavioral therapies. In A.E. Bergin & S.L. Garfield (Eds.), *Handbook of psychotherapy and behavior change.* New York, NY: Wiley.

Holmes, M.R., & St.-Lawrence, J.S. (1983). Treatment of rape-induced trauma: Proposed behavioral conceptualization and review of the literature. *Clinical Psychology Review, 3,* 417–433.

Holmes, T.H., & Rahe, R.H. (1967). The social readjustment rating scale. *Journal of Psychosomatic Research, 11,* 213–218.

Holsboer, F., & Ising, M. (2010). Stress hormone regulation: Biological role and translation into therapy. *Annual Review of Psychology, 61,* 81–109.

Homan, K., McHugh, E., Wells, D., Watson, C., & King, C. (2012). The effect of viewing ultra-fit images on college women's body dissatisfaction. *Body Image, 9,* 50–56.

Honey, P.L., & Galef, B.G., Jr. (2004). Long-lasting effects of rearing by an ethanol-consuming dam on voluntary ethanol consumption by rats. *Appetite, 43,* 261–268.

Honolulu Star-Bulletin. (1980, January 6).

Honts, C.R., & Perry, M.V. (1992). Polygraph admissibility: Changes and challenges. *Law and Human Behavior, 16,* 357–379.

Hooper, J., & Teresi, M. (1986). *The three-pound universe.* New York, NY: Macmillan.

Hopf, W.H., Günter, L., & Weiss, R.H. (2008). Media violence and youth violence: A 2-year longitudinal study. *Journal of Media Psychology: Theories, Methods, and Applications, 20,* 79–96.

Hopko, D.R., & Mullane, C.M. (2008). Exploring the relation of depression and overt behavior with daily diaries. *Behaviour Research and Therapy, 46,* 1085–1089.

Horn, J.L. (1985). Remodeling old models of intelligence. In B.B. Wolman (Ed.), *Handbook of intelligence* (pp. 257–300). New York, NY: John Wiley & Sons.

Horn, J.L., & Cattell, R.C. (1966). Refinement and test of the theory of fluid and crystallized general intelligences. *Journal of Educational Psychology, 57,* 253–270.

Horn, J.L., & Masunaga, H. (2000). On the emergence of wisdom: Expertise development. In W.S. Brown (Ed.), *Understanding wisdom: Sources, science, and society* (pp. 245–276). Philadelphia, PA: Templeton Foundation Press.

Horn, J.L., & Noll, J. (1997). Human cognitive capabilities: Gf-Gc theory. In D.P. Flanagan, J.L. Genshaft, & P.L. Harrison (Eds.), *Contemporary intellectual assessment: Theories, tests, and issues.* New York, NY: Guilford Press.

Hornak, J.P. (2000). The basics of MRI. Retrieved from http://www.cis.rit.edu/htbooks/mri/.

Horton, C.L., & Malinowski, J.E. (2015). Autobiographical memory and hyperassociativity in the dreaming brain: Implications for memory consolidation in sleep. *Frontiers in Psychology, 6.*

House, J.S., Landis, K.R., & Umberson, D. (1988). Social relationships and health. *Science, 241,* 540–545.

Hovland, C.I., Janis, I., & Kelley, H.H. (1953). *Communication and persuasion.* New Haven, CT: Yale University Press.

Hovland, C.I., & Sears, R. (1940). Minor studies of aggression: Correlation of lynchings with economic indices. *Journal of Psychology, 9,* 301–310.

Howard, I.P. (2002). Depth perception. In H. Pashler & S.Yantis (Eds.), *Steven's handbook of experimental psychology: Vol. 1 Sensation and perception* (3rd ed., pp. 77–120). New York, NY: Wiley.

Howard, K.I., Lueger, R.J., Maling, M.S., & Martinovich, Z. (1993). A phase model of psychotherapy outcome: Causal mediation of change. *Journal of Consulting and Clinical Psychology, 61,* 678–685.

Howes, O., McCutcheon, R., & Stone, J. (2015). Glutamate and dopamine in schizophrenia: An update for the 21st century. *Journal of Psychopharmacology, 29*(2), 97–115.

Howes, O.D., & Kapur, S. (2009). The dopamine hypothesis of schizophrenia: version III—the final common pathway. *Schizophrenia Bulletin, 35*(3), 549–562.

Hsieh, A.Y., Tripp, D., & Ji, L.J. (2011). The influence of ethnic concordance and discordance on verbal reports and nonverbal behaviors of pain. *Pain, 152*(9), 2016–2022.

Hubbard, E.M., & Ramachandran, V.S. (2005). Neurocognitive mechanisms of synesthesia. *Neuron, 48*, 509–520.

Hubel, D.H., & Wiesel, T.N. (1979). Brain mechanisms of vision. *Scientific American, 241*, 150–162.

Hubel, D.H., & Wiesel, T.N. (2005). *Brain and visual perception: The story of a 25-year collaboration.* New York, NY: Oxford University Press.

Hubert, V., Beaunieux, H., Chételat, G., Platel, H., Landeau, B., Viader, F., ... Eustache, F. (2009). Age-related changes in the cerebral substrates of cognitive procedural learning. *Human Brain Mapping, 30*, 1374–1386.

Hublin, C., Kaprio, J., Partinen, M., Heikkila, K., & Koskenvuo, M. (1997). Prevalence and genetics of sleepwalking: A population-based twin study. *Neurology, 48*, 177–181.

Hublin, C., Kaprio, J., Partinen, M., & Koskenvuo, M. (2001). Parasomnias: Co-occurrence and genetics. *Psychiatric Genetics, 11*, 65–70.

Huddy, L., & Birtanen, S. (1995). Subgroup differentiation and subgroup bias among Latinos as a function of familiarity and positive distinctiveness. *Journal of Personality and Social Psychology, 68*, 97–108.

Hudson, J.I., Hiripi, E., Pope, H.G., & Kessler, R.C. (2007). The prevalence and correlates of eating disorders in the National Comorbidity Survey replication. *Biological Psychiatry, 61*(3) 348–358.

Hudson, W. (1960). Pictorial depth perception in subcultural groups in Africa. *Journal of Social Psychology, 52*, 183–208.

Huesmann, L.R. (1997). Observational learning of violent behavior: Social and biosocial processes. In A. Raine, P.A. Brennan, D.P. Farrington, & S.A. Mednick (Eds.), *Biosocial bases of violence.* New York, NY: Plenum Press.

Huesmann, L.R. (2007). The impact of electronic media violence: Scientific theory and research. *Journal of Adolescent Health, 41*, S6–S13.

Huesmann, L.R. (2010). Nailing the coffin shut on doubts that violent video games stimulate aggression: Comment on Anderson et al. (2010). *Psychological Bulletin, 136*, 179–181.

Huesmann, L.R., Moise-Titus, J., Podolski, C.L., & Eron, L.D. (2003). Longitudinal relations between children's exposure to TV violence and their aggressive and violent behavior in young adulthood: 1977–1992. *Developmental Psychology, 39*, 201–221.

Huff, R.M., & Kline, M.V. (Eds.). (1999). *Promoting health in multicultural populations: A handbook for practitioners.* Thousand Oaks, CA: Sage.

Hughes, C., Lorden, S.W., Scott, S.V., Hwang, B., Derer, K.R., & Rodi, M.S. (1998). *Journal of Applied Behavior Analysis, 31*, 431–446.

Hulac, D. (2010). *Behavioral interventions in schools.* London, UK: Routledge.

Hull, C.L. (1943). *Principles of behavior: An introduction to behavior theory.* New York, NY: Appleton-Century.

Hull, C.L. (1951). *Essentials of behavior.* New Haven, CT: Yale University Press.

Hulstijn, J.H. (2005). Theoretical and empirical issues in the study of implicit and explicit second-language learning. *Studies in Second Language Acquisition, 27*, 129–140.

Human Genome Project. (2007). Retrieved May 16, 2007, from http://www.genome.gov/.

Human Genome Project. (2010). Retrieved from http://www.genome.gov/.

Humphrey-Murto, S., Leddy, J.J., Wood, T.J., Puddester, D., & Moineau, G. (2014). Does emotional intelligence at medical school admission predict future academic performance? *Academic Medicine, 89*(4), 638–643.

Humphriss, N. (1989, November 20). Letters. *Time*, 12.

Hunecke, M., Haustein, S., Böhler, S., & Grischkat, S. (2010). Attitude-based target groups to reduce the ecological impact of daily mobility behavior. *Environment and Behavior, 42*, 3–43.

Hunt, E. (1995). The role of intelligence in modern society. *American Scientist, 83*, 356–368.

Hunt, E. (1997). The status of the concept of intelligence. *Japanese Psychological Research, 39*, 1–11.

Hunt, E. (2007). P-FIT: A major contribution to theories of intelligence. *Behavioral and Brain Sciences, 30*, 158–159.

Hunter, J.E., & Hunter, R.F. (1984). Validity and utility of alternative predictors of job performance. *Psychological Bulletin, 96*, 72–98.

Huon, G.F., Mingyi, Q., Oliver, K., & Xiao, G. (2002). A large-scale survey of eating disorder symptomatology among female adolescents in the People's Republic of China. *International Journal of Eating Disorders, 32*, 192–205.

Hupbach, A., Hardt, O., Gomez, R., & Nadel, L. (2008). The dynamics of memory: Context-dependent updating. *Learning & Memory, 15*(8), 574–579.

Hussaini, S.A., Komischke, B., Menzel, R., & Lachnit, H. (2007). Forward and backward second-order Pavlovian conditioning in honeybees. *Learning & Memory, 14*, 678–683.

Huston, T.L. (1973). Ambiguity of acceptance, social desirability, and dating choice. *Journal of Experimental Social Psychology, 9*, 32–42.

Huttenlocher, P.R. (2002). *Neural plasticity.* Cambridge, MA: Harvard University Press.

Huurre, T., Junkkari, H., & Aro, H. (2006). Long-term psychosocial effects of parental divorce: A follow-up study from adolescence to adulthood. *European Archives of Psychiatry and Clinical Neuroscience, 256*, 256–263.

Hyde, J.S., & DeLamater, J. (2000). *Understanding human sexuality* (7th ed.). Boston, MA: McGraw-Hill.

Hyde, J.S., & DeLamater, J. (2003). *Understanding human sexuality* (8th ed.). Boston, MA: McGraw-Hill.

Hyde, K.L., Lerch, J., Norton, A., Forgeard, M., Winner, E., Evans, A.C., & Schlaug, G. (2009). Musical training shapes structural brain development. *The Journal of Neuroscience, 29*, 3019–3025.

Hyde, M., Ferrie, J., Higgs, P., Mein, G., & Nazroo, J. (2004). The effects of pre-retirement factors and retirement route on circumstances in retirement: Findings from the Whitehall II study. *Ageing & Society, 24*, 279–296.

Hyman, R. (1994). Anomaly or artifact? Comments on Bem and Honorton. *Psychological Bulletin, 115*, 19–24.

Hysek, C., Schmid, Y., Simmler, L.D., Domes, G., Heinrichs, M., Eisenegger, C., ... Liechti, M.E. (2014). MDMA enhances emotional empathy and prosocial behavior. *Social Cognitive and Affective Neuroscience, 9*(11), 1645–1652.

Iacono, W.G. (2008). Effective policing: Understanding how polygraph tests work and are used. *Criminal Justice and Behavior, 35*, 1295–1308.

Iglesias, A., & Iglesias, A. (2013). Phobia treated with hypnotic systematic desensitization: A case report. *American Journal of Clinical Hypnosis, 56*, 143–151.

Ikeda, H., Ikeda, E., Shiozaki, K., & Hirayasu, Y. (2014). Association of the five factor personality model with prefrontal activation during frontal lobe task performance using two channel near infrared spectroscopy. *Psychiatry and Clinical Neurosciences, 68*(10), 752–758.

Ikemi, Y., & Nakagawa, A. (1962). A psychosomatic study of contagious dermatitis. *Kyushu Journal of Medical Science, 13*, 335–350.

Inagaki, T.K., & Eisenberger, N.I. (2016). Giving support to others reduces sympathetic nervous system-related responses to stress. *Psychophysiology, 53*(4), 427–435.

Ingelhart, R., & Rabier, J.R. (1986). Aspirations adapt to situations—but why are the Belgians so much happier than the French? A cross-cultural study of the quality of life. In F.M. Andrews (Ed.), *Research on the quality of life.* Ann Arbor, MI: Institute for Social Research, University of Michigan.

Ingham, A.G., Levinger, G., Graves, J., & Peckham, V. (1974). The Ringelmann effect: Studies of group size and group performance. *Journal of Experimental Social Psychology, 10*, 371–384.

Ingold, C.H. (1989). Locus of control and use of public information. *Psychological Reports, 64*, 603–607.

Ingraham, L.J., & Kety, S.S. (2000). Adoption studies of schizophrenia. *American Journal of Medical Genetics, 97*(1), 18–22.

Inhelder, B., & Piaget, J. (1958). *The growth of logical thinking from childhood to adolescence.* New York, NY: Basic Books.

Institute of Medicine. (1990). *Broadening the base of treatment for alcohol problems.* Washington, DC: National Academy Press.

International Human Genome Sequencing Consortium. (2001). Initial sequencing and analysis of the human genome. *Nature, 409*, 860–921.

Intraub, H., Gottesman, C.V., & Bills, A.J. (1998). Effects of perceiving and imagining scenes on memory for pictures. *Journal of Experimental Psychology: Learning, Memory, and Cognition, 24*, 186–201.

Intraub, H., Gottesman, C.V., Willey, E.V., & Zuk, I.J. (1996). Boundary extension for briefly glimpsed photographs: Do common perceptual processes result in unexpected memory distortions? *Journal of Memory and Language, 35*, 118–134.

Iranzo, A., & Aparicio, J. (2009). A lesson from anatomy: Focal brain lesions causing REM sleep behavior disorder. *Sleep Medicine, 10*, 9–12.

Irie, M., Maeda, M., & Nagata, S. (2001). Can conditioned histamine release occur under urethane anesthesia in guinea pigs? *Physiology and Behavior, 72*, 567–573.

Irwin, A.R., & Gross, A.M. (1995). Cognitive tempo, violent video games, and aggressive behavior in young boys. *Journal of Family Violence, 10*, 337–350.

Irwin, J.R., & McCarthy, D. (1998). Psychophysics: Methods and analyses of signal detection. In K.A.

Lattal & M. Perone (Eds.), *Handbook of research methods in human operant behavior: Applied clinical psychology.* New York, NY: Plenum Press.

Isaacs, K.S. (1998). *Uses of emotion: Nature's vital gift.* New York, NY: Praeger.

Isaacson, R.L. (2002). Unsolved mysteries: The hippocampus. *Behavioral and Cognitive Neuroscience Reviews, 1,* 87–107.

Isacsson, G., & Ahlner, J. (2013). Antidepressants and the risk of suicide in young persons—prescription trends and toxicological analyses. *British Journal of Psychiatry* (July 24), 1–19.

Ishigami, Y., & Klein, R.M. (2009). Is a hands-free phone safer than a handheld phone? *Journal of Safety Research, 40,* 157–164.

Ishihara, K., Miyake, S., Miyasita, A., & Miyata, Y. (1992). Morningness-eveningness preference and sleep habits in Japanese office workers of different ages. *Chronobiologia, 19,* 9–16.

Ishikawa, S.L., Raine, A., Lencz, T., Bihrle, S., & Lacasse, L. (2001). Autonomic stress reactivity and executive functions in successful and unsuccessful criminal psychopaths from the community. *Journal of Abnormal Psychology, 110,* 423–432.

Ispas, D., Iliescu, D., Ilie, A., & Johnson, R.E. (2014). Exploring the cross-cultural generalizability of the five-factor model of personality: The Romanian neo PI-R. *Journal of Cross-Cultural Psychology, 45*(7), 1074–1088.

Itard, J.M.G. (1894/1962). *The wild boy of Aveyron* (G. Humphrey & M. Humphrey, Trans.). New York, NY: Appleton-Century-Crofts. (Original work published 1894).

Ito, H. (1984). Possibility of "invasion" in the sensory area. *Behavioral and Brain Sciences, 7,* 341–342.

Ito, T.A., & Bartholow, B.D. (2009). The neural correlates of race. *Trends in Cognitive Sciences, 13*(12), 524–531.

Ito, T.A., & Cacioppo, J.T. (2000). Electrophysiological evidence of implicit and explicit categorization processes. *Journal of Experimental Social Psychology, 36,* 660–676.

Itti, L., & Rees, G. (2005). *Neurobiology of attention.* St. Louis, MO: Elsevier.

Iwasa, N. (2001). Moral reasoning among adults: Japan-U.S. comparison. In H. Shimizu & R.A. LeVine (Eds.), *Japanese frames of mind: Cultural perspectives on human development* (pp. 51–83). New York, NY: Cambridge University Press.

Izard, C. (Ed.). (1982). *Measuring emotions in infants and children.* Cambridge, UK: Cambridge University Press.

Izard, C.E. (1989). The structure and functions of emotions: Implications for cognition, motivation, and personality. In I.S. Cohen (Ed.), *The G. Stanley Hall lecture series* (Vol. 9). Washington, DC: American Psychological Association.

Izard, E.E. (1984). Emotion-cognition relationships and human development. In C.E. Izard, J. Kaga, & R.B. Zajonc (Eds.), *Emotions, cognition and behavior.* Cambridge, UK: Cambridge University Press.

Jablensky, A., Sartorius, N., Ernberg, C., Anker, M., Korten, A., Cooper, J.E., ... Bertelsen, A. (1992). Schizophrenia: Manifestation, incidence, and course in different cultures: A World Health Organization ten country study. *Psychological Medicine Monograph Supplement, 20.* Cambridge, UK: Cambridge University Press.

Jackendoff, R. (1996). The architecture of the linguistic-spatial interface. In P. Bloom, M.A. Peterson,

L. Nadel, & M.F. Garrett, (Eds.), *Language and space. Language, speech, and communication* (pp. 1–30). Cambridge, MA: MIT Press.

Jackson, A., Morrow, J., Hill, D., & Dishman, R. (1999). *Physical activity for health and fitness.* Champaign, IL: Human Kinetics.

Jackson, N., & Butterfield, E. (1986). A conception of giftedness designed to promote research. In R.J. Sternberg & J.E. Davidson (Eds.), *Conceptions of giftedness.* New York, NY: Cambridge University Press.

Jacobson, N.S., Gottman, J.M., Gortner, E., Berns, S., & Shortt, J.W. (1996). Psychological factors in the longitudinal course of battering: When do the couples split up? When does the abuse decrease? *Violence & Victims, 11,* 371–392.

Jacobson, N.S., Martell, C.R., & Dimidjian, S. (2001). Behavioral activation therapy for depression: Returning to contextual roots. *Clinical Psychology: Science and Practice, 8,* 255–270.

Jaeggi, S.M., Buschkuehl, M., Jonides, J., & Perrig, W.J. (2008). Improving fluid intelligence with training on working memory. *Proceedings of the National Academy of Sciences, 105*(19), 6829–6833.

Jaffee, S.R., Price, T.S., & Reyes, T.M. (2013). Behavior genetics: Past, present, future. *Development and Psychopathology, 25*(4), 1225–1242.

James, T.W., Culham, J., Humphrey, G.K., Milner, A.D., & Goodale, M.A. (2003). Ventral occipital lesions impair object recognition but not object-directed grasping: An fMRI study. *Brain, 126,* 2463–2475.

James, W. (1879). Are we automata? *Mind, 4,* 1–22.

James, W. (1890/1950). *Principles of psychology* (Vol. 2). New York, NY: Dover Publications.

James, W. (1902). *The varieties of religious experience: A study in human nature.* New York, NY: Longmans, Green.

Jamison, K. (1995, February). Manic-depressive illness and creativity. *Scientific American,* 63–67.

Jang, K. (2005). *The behavioral genetics of psychopathology: A clinical guide.* Hillsdale, NJ: Erlbaum.

Jang, K.L., Lam, R.W., Livesley, W.J., & Vernon, P.A. (1997). Gender differences in the heritability of seasonal mood change. *Psychiatry Research, 70*(3), 145–154.

Jang, K.L., Vernon, P.A., & Livesley, W.J. (2000). Personality disorder traits, family environment, and alcohol misuse: A multivariate behavioural genetic analysis. *Addiction, 95,* 873–888.

Janis, I.L. (1983). *Groupthink: Psychological studies of policy decisions and fiascos* (2nd ed.). Boston, MA: Houghton Mifflin.

Janoski, T., Musick, M., & Wilson, J. (1998). Being volunteered? The impact of social participation and pro-social attitudes on volunteering. *Sociological Forum, 13,* 495–519.

Janssens, J.M.A.M., & Dekovic, M. (1997). Child rearing, prosocial moral reasoning, and prosocial behaviour. *International Journal of Behavioral Development, 20,* 509–527.

Janus, S.S., & Janus, C.L. (1993). *The Janus report on sexual behavior.* New York, NY: Wiley.

Jasinska, K.K., & Petitto, L.A. (2013). How age of bilingual exposure can change the neural systems for language in the developing brain: A functional near infrared spectroscopy investigation of syntactic processing in monolingual and bilingual children. *Developmental Cognitive Neuroscience, 6,* 87–101.

Jay, T., King, K., & Duncan, T. (2006). Memories of punishment for cursing. *Sex Roles, 55,* 123–133.

Jeffery, K.J. (2008). The place cells—Cognitive map or memory system? In S.J.Y. Mizumori (Ed.), *Hippocampal place fields: Relevance to learning and memory* (pp. 59–72). New York, NY: Oxford University Press.

Jeffery, R.W., & Wing, R.R. (1995). Long-term effects of interventions for weight loss using food provisions and money incentives. *Journal of Consulting and Clinical Psychology, 63,* 793–796.

Jemmott, J.B., Jemmott, L.S., & Fong, G.T. (1998). Abstinence and safer sex HIV risk-reduction interventions for African American adolescents. *Journal of the American Medical Association, 279,* 1529–1536.

Jencks, C., & Phillips, M. (Eds.). (1998). *The Black-White test score gap.* Washington, DC: Brookings Institution.

Jenike, M.A. (1998). *Obsessive-compulsive disorders.* St. Louis, MO: Mosby.

Jenkins, J., Simpson, A., Dunn, J., Rasbash, J., & O'Connor, T.G. (2005). Mutual influence of marital conflict and children's behavior problems: Shared and nonshared family risks. *Child Development, 76,* 24–39.

Jennings, B.M. (1990). Stress, locus of control, social support, and psychological symptoms among head nurses. *Research in Nursing and Health, 13,* 393–401.

Jennum, P., Frandsen, R., & Knudsen, S. (2013). Characteristics of rapid eye movement sleep behavior disorder in narcolepsy. *Sleep and Biological Rhythms, 11,* 65–74.

Jensen, A.R. (1980). *Bias in mental testing.* New York, NY: Free Press.

Jensen, A.R. (1998). The g factor and the design of education. In R.J. Sternberg & W.M. Williams (Eds.), *Intelligence, instruction, and assessment: Theory into practice* (pp. 111–132). Mahwah, NJ: Erlbaum.

Jensen, L.A., Arnett, J.J., Feldman, S.S., & Cauffman, E. (2004). The right to do wrong: Lying to parents among adolescents and emerging adults. *Journal of Youth and Adolescence, 33,* 101–112.

Jensen, R. (2006). Behaviorism, latent learning, and cognitive maps: Needed revisions in introductory psychology textbooks. *The Behavior Analyst, 29,* 187–209.

Jequier, E., & Tappy, L. (1999). Regulation of body weight in humans. *Physiological Reviews, 79,* 451–480.

Jeste, D., & Heaton, S. (1994). How does late-onset compare with early-onset schizophrenia? *Harvard Mental Health Letter, 49,* 132–139.

Ji, L.J., Schwarz, N., & Nisbett, R.E. (2000). Culture, autobiographical memory in cross-cultural studies. *Personality and Social Psychology Bulletin, 26*(5), 586–594.

Ji, L.J., Zhang, Z., & Nisbett, R.E. (2004). Is it culture, or is it language? Examination of language effects in cross-cultural research on categorization. *Journal of Personality and Social Psychology, 87*(1), 57–65.

Jiang, T., & Gore, J.S. (2015). The relationship between autonomous motivation and goal pursuit: A cross-cultural perspective. *Asian Journal of Social Psychology,* doi:http://dx.doi.org/10.1111/ajsp.12115.

Joanisse, M.F. (2009). Model-based approaches to child language disorders. In R.G. Schwartz (Ed.), *Handbook of child language disorders.* New York, NY: Psychology Press.

Johnson, A.M., Wadsworth, J., Wellings, K., & Bradshaw, S. (1992). Sexual lifestyles and HIV risk. *Nature, 360,* 410–412.

Johnson, B.T. (1991). Insights about attitudes: Meta-analytic perspectives. *Personality and Social Psychology Bulletin, 17,* 289–299.

Johnson, D.W., & Johnson, R.T. (2000).The three Cs of reducing prejudice and discrimination in children and adolescents. In S. Oskamp (Ed.), *Reducing prejudice and discrimination* (pp. 239–268). Mahwah, NJ: Erlbaum.

Johnson, J.G., Cohen, P., Smailes, E.M., Kasen, S., & Brook, J.S. (2002). Television viewing and aggressive behavior during adolescence and adulthood. *Science, 295,* 2468–2471.

Johnson, J.S., & Newport, E.L. (1989). Critical period effects on universal properties of language: The influence of maturational state on the acquisition of English as a second language. *Cognitive Psychology, 21*(1), 60.

Johnson, J.S., & Newport, E.L. (1991). Critical period effects on universal properties of language: The status of subjacency in the acquisition of a second language. *Cognition, 39,* 215–258.

Johnson, K.R., & Johnson, S.L. (2014). Cross-national prevalence and cultural correlates of bipolar I disorder. *Social Psychiatry and Psychiatric Epidemiology, 49*(7), 1111–1117.

Johnson, M.W., Richards, W.A., & Griffiths, R.R. (2008). Human hallucinogen research: Guidelines for safety. *Journal of Psychopharmacology, 22,* 603–620.

Johnson, S., Cooper, C., Cartwright, S., Donald, I., Taylor, P., & Millet, C. (2005). The experience of work-related stress across occupations. *Journal of Managerial Psychology, 20,* 178–187.

Johnson-Laird, P.N. (2001). Mental models and deduction. *Trends in Cognitive Sciences, 5*(10), 434–442.

Johnson-Laird, P.N. (2010). Mental models and human reasoning. *Proceedings of the National Academy of Sciences, 107*(43), 18243–18250.

Johnson-Laird, P.N., Byrne, R.M., & Schaeken, W. (1992). Propositional reasoning by model. *Psychological Review, 99*(3), 418–439.

Johnston, M.S., Kelley, C.S., Harris, F.F., & Wolf, M.M. (1966). An application of reinforcement principles to development of motor skills of a young child. *Child Development, 37,* 379–387.

Johnston, V.S., Hagel, R., Franklin, M., Fink, B., & Grammer, K. (2001). Male facial attractiveness: Evidence for hormone-mediated adaptive design. *Evolution and Human Behavior, 22,* 251–267.

Joiner, T.E., & Coyne, J.C. (Eds.). (1999). *The interactional nature of depression: Advances in interpersonal approaches.* Washington, DC: American Psychological Association.

Joiner, T.E., Alfano, M.S., & Metalsky, G.I. (1992). When depression breeds contempt: Reassurance seeking, self-esteem, and rejection of depressed college students by their roommates. *Journal of Abnormal Psychology, 101,* 165–173.

Jones, B.C., Little, A.C., Feinberg, D.R., Penton-Voak, I.S., Tiddeman, B.P., & Perrett, D.I. (2004). The relationship between shape symmetry and perceived skin condition in male facial attractiveness. *Evolution and Human Behavior, 25,* 24–30.

Jones, D. (1996). *Physical attractiveness and the theory of sexual selection.* Ann Arbor, MI: University of Michigan Press.

Jones, E., Cumming, J.D., & Horowitz, M.J. (1988). Another look at the nonspecific hypothesis of therapeutic effectiveness. *Journal of Consulting and Clinical Psychology, 56,* 48–55.

Jones, E.E., & Harris, V.A. (1967). The attribution of attitudes. *Journal of Experimental Social Psychology, 3,* 2–24.

Jones, E.G. (2006). *The thalamus.* New York, NY: Cambridge University Press.

Jones, G.V. (1990). Misremembering a common object: When left is not right. *Memory and Cognition, 18,* 174–182.

Jones, M.C. (1924). A laboratory study of fear: The case of Peter. *Pedagogical Seminary, 31,* 308–315.

Jonsson, T., Stefansson, H., Steinberg, S., Jonsdottir, I., Jonsson, P.V., Snaedal, J., Bjornsson, S., Huttenlocher, J., Levey, A.I., Lah, J.J., Rujescu, D., Hampel, H., Giegling, I., Andreassen, O.A., Engedal, K., Ulstein, I., Djurovic, S., Ibrahim-Verbaas, C., Hofman, A., Ikram, M.A., van Duijn, C.M., Thorsteinsdottir, U., Kong, A., Stefansson, K. (2013). Variant of *TREM2* associated with the risk of Alzheimer's Disease. *New England Journal of Medicine, 368,* 107–116.

Jordan, P.H. (2016). Individual therapy with a child of divorced parents. *Journal of Clinical Psychology, 72*(5), 430–443.

Joseph, B. (2014). What is residential school syndrome? http://www.ictinc.ca/blog/what-is-residential-school-syndrome.

Joseph, R. (2000). The evolution of sex differences in language, sexuality, and visual-spatial skills. *Archives of Sexual Behavior, 29,* 35–66.

Josephson, W.L. (1987). Television violence and children's aggression: Testing the priming, social script, and disinhibition predictions. *Journal of Personality and Social Psychology, 53,* 882–890.

Joslyn, S., & Hunt, E. (1998). Evaluating individual differences in response to time-pressure situations. *Journal of Experimental Psychology: Applied, 4,* 16–43.

Joslyn, S.L., Nadav-Greenberg, L., Taing, M.U., & Nichols, R.M. (2009). The effects of wording on the understanding and use of uncertainty information in a threshold forecasting decision. *Applied Cognitive Psychology, 23,* 55–72.

Julien, R. (2008). *A primer of drug action* (11th ed.). New York, NY: Worth.

Jung, D-I., Ha, J., Kang, B.T., et al. (2009). A comparison of autologous and allogenic marrow-derived myeschemal stem cell transplantation in canine spinal cord injury. *Journal of the Neurological Sciences, 285,* 67–77.

Jureidini, J.N., Doecke, C.J., Mansfield, P.R., Haby, M.H., Menkes, D.B., & Tomkin, A.L. (2004). Efficacy and safety of antidepressants for children and adolescents. *British Medical Journal, 328,* 879–883.

Jurkowitz, M. (2002, October 2). Appeals court holds key in battle over regulation of violent video games. *Boston Globe,* D1.

Kabat-Zinn, J. (1994). *Wherever you go, there you are: Mindfulness meditation in everyday life.* New York, NY: Hyperion.

Kabat-Zinn, J. (2003). Mindfulness-based interventions in context: Past, present, and future. *Clinical Psychology: Science and Practice, 10,* 144–158.

Kabat-Zinn, J., Massion, A.O, Kristeller, J., Peterson, L.G., Fletcher, K.E., Pbert, L., ... Santorelli, S.F. (1992). Effectiveness of a meditation-based stress reduction intervention in the treatment of anxiety disorders. *American Journal of Psychiatry, 149,* 936–943.

Kagan, J. (1989). Temperamental contributions to social behavior. *American Psychologist, 44,* 668–674.

Kagan, J., Kearsley, R.B., & Zelazo, P. (1978). *Infancy: Its place in human development.* Cambridge, MA: Harvard University Press.

Kagan, J., Reznick, S., & Snidman, N. (1988). Biological bases of childhood shyness. *Science, 240,* 167–171.

Kagitáibasi, C. (1997). Individualism and collectivism. In J.W. Berry, M.H. Segall, & C. Kagitáibasi (Eds.), *Handbook of cross-cultural psychology* (2nd ed., Vol. 3). Boston, MA: Allyn & Bacon.

Kaheman, D. (2011). *Thinking fast and slow.* New York: Farrar, Straus & Giroux.

Kaheman, D., & Klein, G. (2009). Conditions for intuitive expertise: A failure to disagree. *American Psychologist, 64*(6), 515–526.

Kahleova, H., Belinova, L., Hill, T., & Pelikanova, T. (2012). Two meals a day are better than six for patients with Type 2 diabetes. Presentation at the annual meeting of American Diabetes Association, Philadelphia, June, 2012.

Kahn, A., Kahn, S., Kolts, R., & Brown, W.A. (2003). Suicide rates in clinical trials of SSTRs, other antidepressants, and placebo: Analysis of FDA report. *American Journal of Psychiatry, 160,* 790–792.

Kahn, S., Zimmerman, G., Csikszentmihalyi, M., & Getzels, J.W. (1985). Relations between identity in young adulthood and intimacy at midlife. *Journal of Personality and Social Psychology, 49,* 1316–1322.

Kahneman, D., & Tversky, A. (1979). Prospect theory: An analysis of decisions under risk. *Econometrica, 47,* 263–291.

Kahneman, D., & Tversky, A. (1982). On the study of statistical intuitions. *Cognition, 11,* 123–141.

Kaia, L., Pullmann, H., & Allik, J. (2007). Personality and intelligence as predictors of academic achievement: A cross-sectional study from elementary to secondary school. *Personality and Individual Differences, 42,* 444–451.

Kail, R. (1991). Developmental change in speed of processing during childhood and adolescence. *Psychological Bulletin, 109,* 490–501.

Kaiser, A., Haller, S., & Nitsch, C. (2009). On sex/gender related similarities and differences in fMRI language research. *Brain Research Reviews, 61,* 49–59.

Kaku, M. (2004). *Einstein's cosmos: How Albert Einstein's vision transformed our understanding of space and time.* New York, NY: Norton.

Kalafat, J., Elias, M., & Gara, M.A. (1993). The relationship of bystander intervention variables to adolescents' responses to suicidal peers. *Journal of Primary Prevention, 13,* 231–244.

Kalaitzaki, A.E., Birtchnell, J., Hammond, S., & De Jong, C. (2015). The shortened Person's relating to others questionnaire (PROQ3): Comparison of the internet-administered format with the standard-written one across four national samples. *Psychological Assessment, 27*(2), 513–523.

Kalick, S.M., & Hamilton, T.E., III. (1988). Closer look at a matching simulation: Reply to Aron. *Journal of Personality and Social Psychology, 54,* 447–451.

Kalish, R.A., & Reynolds, D.K. (1977). The role of age in death attitudes. *Death Education, 1,* 205–230.

Kaltiala-Heino, R., Marttunen, M., Rantanen, P., & Rimpela, M. (2003). Early puberty is associated with mental health problems in middle adolescence. *Social Science & Medicine, 57,* 1055–1064.

Kampmann, K.M., Volpicelli, J.R., Mulvaney, F., Rukstalis, M., Alterman, A.I., Pettinati, H., ... O'Brien, C.P. (2002). Cocaine withdrawal severity and urine toxicology results from treatment entry predict outcome in medication trials for cocaine dependence. *Addictive Behaviors, 27,* 251–260.

Kandel, E.R. (2001). The molecular biology of memory storage: A dialogue between genes and synapses. *Science, 294*, 1030–1038.

Kandel, E.R., & Hawkins, R.D. (1992). The biological basis of learning and individuality. *Scientific American, 267*, 78–87.

Kandler, C. (2012). Knowing your personality is knowing its nature: The role of information accuracy of peer assessments for heritability estimates of temperamental and personality traits. *Personality and Individual Differences, 53*, 387–392.

Kane, H.D., & Brand, C.R. (2006). The variable importance of general intelligence (*g*) in the cognitive abilities of children and adolescents. *Educational Psychology, 26*, 751–767.

Kane, J.M. (2006). Tardive dyskinesia circa 2006. *American Journal of Psychiatry, 16*, 1316–1318.

Kaner, A. (1995). Physical attractiveness and women's lives: Findings from a longitudinal study. *Dissertation Abstracts International: Section B: The Sciences and Engineering, 56*, 2942.

Kanetsuna, T., Smith, P.K., & Morita, Y. (2006). Coping with bullying at school: Children's recommended strategies and attitudes to school-based interventions in England and Japan. *Aggressive Behavior, 32*, 570–580.

Kanner, L. (1943). Autistic disturbance of affective contact. *Nervous Child, 12*, 17–50.

Kaplan, H., & Dove, H. (1987). Infant development among the Ache of eastern Paraguay. *Development Psychology, 23*, 190–198.

Kaplan, R.M., & Saccuzzo, D.P. (2009). *Psychological Testing: Principles, Applications, and Issues.* Belmont, CA: Wadsworth.

Kaprio, J., Koskenvu, M., & Rita, H. (1987). Mortality after bereavement: A prospective study of 95,647 widowed persons. *American Journal of Public Health, 77*, 283–287.

Karau, S.J., & Hart, J.W. (1998). Group cohesiveness and social loafing: Effects of a social interaction manipulation on individual motivation within groups. *Group Dynamics, 2*, 185–191.

Karau, S.J., & Williams, K.D. (1993). Social loafing: A meta-analytic review and theoretical integration. *Journal of Personality and Social Psychology, 65*, 681–706.

Karau, S.J., & Williams, K.D. (2001). Understanding individual motivation in groups: The collective effort model. In M.E. Turner (Ed.), *Groups at work: Theory and research. Applied social research.* Mahwah, NJ: Erlbaum.

Karimizadeh, A., Mahnam, A., Yazdchi, M.R., & Besharat, M.A. (2015). Individual differences in personality traits: Perfectionism and the brain structure. *Journal of Psychophysiology, 29*(3), 107–111.

Karon, B.P. (2002). Psychoanalysis: Legitimate and illegitimate concerns. *Psychoanalytic Psychology, 19*, 564–571.

Kassel, J.D., Wardle, M.C., Heinz, A.J., & Greenstein, J.E. (2010). Cognitive theories of drug effects on emotion. In J.D. Kassel (Ed.), *Substance abuse and emotion.* Washington, DC: American Psychological Association.

Katapodi, M.C., Facione, N.C., Humphreys, J.C., & Dodd, M.J. (2005). Perceived breast cancer risk: Heuristic reasoning and search for a dominance structure. *Social Science & Medicine, 60*, 421–432.

Katz, J., & Melzack, R. (1990). Pain "memories" in phantom limbs: Review and clinical observations. *Pain, 43*, 319–336.

Kaufman, A.S., & Kaufman, N. (1997). The Kaufman Adolescent and Adult Intelligence Test. In D.P.

Flanagan, J.L. Genshaft, & P.L. Harrison (Eds.), *Contemporary intellectual assessment: Theories, tests, and issues.* New York, NY: Guilford Press.

Kavanagh, D. (1992). Schizophrenia. In P.H. Wilson (Ed.), *Principles and practice of relapse prevention* (pp. 157–191). New York, NY: Guilford Press.

Kawakami, K., Dovidio, J.F., Moll, J., Hermsen, S., & Russin, A. (2000). Just say no (to stereotyping): Effects of training in the negation of stereotypic associations on stereotype activation. *Journal of Personality and Social Psychology, 78*, 871–888.

Kaysen, D., Atkins, D.C., Simpson, T.L., Stappenbeck, C.A., Blayney, J.A., Lee, C.M., & Larimer, M.E. (2013). Proximal relationships between PTSD symptoms and drinking among female college students: Results from a daily monitoring study. *Psychology of Addictive Behaviors,* online first publication, August 5, 2013. doi: 10.1037/a0033588.

Kazdin, A.E. (1975). The impact of applied behavior analysis on diverse areas of research. *Journal of Applied Behavior Analysis, 8*, 213–229.

Kazdin, A.E. (2008). Evidence-based treatment and practice: New opportunities to bridge clinical research and practice, enhance the knowledge base, and improve patient care. *American Psychologist, 63*, 146–159.

Kazdin, A.E. (Ed.). (2003). *Methodological issues and strategies in clinical research* (3rd ed.). Washington, DC: American Psychological Association.

Kazdin, A.E., & Weisz, J.R. (2003). *Evidence-based psychotherapies for children and adolescents.* New York, NY: Guilford Press.

Keith, S.J., Regier, D.A., & Rae, D.S. (1991). Schizophrenic disorders. In L.N. Robins & D.A. Regier (Eds.), *Psychiatric disorders in America: The Epidemiological Catchment Area Study.* New York, NY: Free Press.

Kelley, H.H. (1950). The warm-cold variable in first impressions of persons. *Journal of Personality, 18*, 431–439.

Kelley, H.H. (1973). The process of causal attribution. *American Psychologist, 28*, 107–128.

Kelley, P., Lockley, S.W., Foster, R.G., & Kelley, J. (2015). Synchronizing education to adolescent biology: "let teens sleep, start school later." *Learning: Media and Technology, 40*, 210–226.

Kelly, G. (1955). *The psychology of personal constructs.* New York, NY: Norton.

Kelly, G.F. (2001). *Sexuality today: The human perspective* (7th ed.). Boston, MA: McGraw-Hill.

Kelly, J.A., St. Lawrence, J.S., Hood, H.V., & Brasfield, T.L. (1989). Behavioral intervention to reduce AIDS risk activities. *Journal of Consulting and Clinical Psychology, 57*, 60–67.

Kelly, J.B. (2012). Risk and protective factors associated with child adolescent adjustment following separation and divorce. In K. Kuehnle, & L. Drozd (Eds.), *Parenting plan evaluations: Applied research for the family court* (pp. 49–84). New York: Oxford University Press.

Kelly, T.A., & Strupp, H.H. (1992). Patient and therapist values in psychotherapy: Perceived changes, assimilation, similarity, and outcome. *Journal of Consulting and Clinical Psychology, 60*, 34–40.

Keltner, D., & Ekman, P. (2000). Facial expression of emotion. In M. Lewis & J.M. Haviland-Jones (Eds.), *Handbook of emotions* (2nd ed.). New York, NY: Guilford Press.

Kemeny, M.E. (2004). The psychobiology of stress. *Current Directions in Psychological Science, 12*, 124–129.

Kempermann, G. (2005). *Adult neurogenesis: Stem cells and neural development in the adult brain.* New York, NY: Oxford University Press.

Kenardy, J., Brown, W.J., & Vogt, E. (2001). Dieting and health in young Australian women. *European Eating Disorders Review, 9*, 242–254.

Kennedy, S.H., Evans, K.R., Krüger, S., Mayberg, H.S., Meyer, J.H., McCann, S., ... Vaccarino, F.J. (2001). Changes in regional brain glucose metabolism measured with positron emission tomography after paroxetine treatment of major depression. *American Journal of Psychiatry, 158*, 899–905.

Kenrick, D.T., & Funder, D.C. (1988). Profiting from controversy: Lessons from the person-situation debate. *American Psychologist, 43*, 23–34.

Kenrick, D.T., & Funder, D.C. (1991). The person-situation debate: Do personality traits really exist? In N.J. Derlega, B.A. Winstead, & W.H. Jones, (Eds.), *Personality: Contemporary theory and research.* Chicago, IL: Nelson-Hall.

Kensinger, E., & Schacter, D. (2005a). Emotional content and reality monitoring ability: fMRI evidence for the influences of encoding processes. *Neuropsychologia, 43*, 1429–1443.

Kensinger, E., & Schacter, D. (2005b). Memory accuracy versus memory assignment: An fMRI study of reality-monitoring ability. *Journal of Cognitive Neuroscience, 96*.

Kensinger, E.A., & Schacter, D.L. (2006). Reality monitoring and memory distortion: Effects of negative, arousing content. *Memory & Cognition, 34*(2), 251–260.

Kentridge, R.W., Heywood, C.A., & Weiskrantz, L. (2004). Spatial attention speeds discrimination without awareness in blindsight. *Neuropsychologia, 42*, 831–835.

Kernberg, O. (1976). *Object relations theory and clinical psychoanalysis.* New York, NY: Jason Aronson.

Kernberg, O.F. (1984). *Severe personality disorders.* New Haven, CT: Yale University Press.

Kernberg, O.F. (2000). *Personality disorders in children and adolescents.* Poulsbo, WA: H-R Press.

Kernberg, O.F., & Caligor, E. (2005). A psychoanalytic theory of personality disorders. In M.F. Lenzenweger & J.F. Clarkin (Eds.), *Major theories of personality disorder* (pp. 114–156). New York, NY: Guilford Press.

Kerns, J.G., & Berenbaum, H. (2002, 2003). Cognitive impairments associated with formal thought disorder in people with schizophrenia. *Journal of Abnormal Psychology, 111*, 211–224.

Kerr, M., Lambert, W.W., & Bem, D.J. (1996). Life course sequelae of childhood shyness in Sweden: Comparison with the United States. *Developmental Psychology, 32*, 1100–1105.

Kerstholt, J.H., & Eikelboom, A.R. (2007). Effects of prior interpretation on situation assessment in crime analysis. *Journal of Behavioral Decision Making. Special issue: Decision making and the law, 20*, 455–465.

Kessels, R.P.C., & Postma, A. (2006). Object-location memory in ageing and dementia. In T. Vecchi & G. Bottini (Eds.), *Imagery and spatial cognition: Methods, models and cognitive assessment* (pp. 227–243). Amsterdam, Netherlands: Benjamins.

Kessler, R.C., & Wittchen, H.U. (2002). Patterns and correlates of generalized anxiety disorder in community samples. *Journal of Clinical Psychiatry, 63* (Suppl. 8), 4–10.

Kessler, R.C., Berglund, P., Demler, O., Jin, R., Merikangas, K.R., & Walters, E.E. (2005). Lifetime prevalence and age-of-onset distributions of *DSM-IV* disorders in the National Comorbidity Survey replication. *Archives of General Psychiatry, 62*, 593–602.

Kessler, R.C., McGonagle, K.A., Zhao, S., & Nelson, C. (1994). Lifetime and 12-month prevalence of DSM-III-R psychiatric disorder in the United States: Results from the National Comorbidity Survey. *Archives of General Psychiatry, 51*, 8–19.

Kety, S., Rosenthal, D., Wender, P.H., Schulsinger, F., & Jacobson, B. (1978). The biological and adoptive families of adopted individuals who become schizophrenic: Prevalence of mental illness and other characteristics. In L.C. Wynne, R.L. Cromwell, & S. Matthysse (Eds.), *The nature of schizophrenia: New approaches to research and treatment.* New York, NY: Wiley.

Kety, S.S. (1988). Schizophrenic illness in the families of schizophrenic adoptees: Findings from the Danish national sample. *Schizophrenia Bulletin, 1988*(14), 217–222.

Keyes, C.L.M., & Waterman, M.B. (2003). Dimensions of well-being and mental health in adulthood. In M.H. Bornstein, L. Davidson, C.L.M. Keyes, & K.A. Moore (Eds.), *Well-being: Positive development across the life course: Crosscurrents in contemporary psychology.* Mahwah, NJ: Erlbaum.

Keyes, L.M., & Goodman, S.H. (2006). *Women and depression: A handbook for social, behavioral, and biomedical sciences.* New York, NY: Cambridge University Press.

Khan, A.U., & Olson, D.L. (1977). Deconditioning of exercise-induced asthma. *Psychosomatic Medicine, 39*, 382–392.

Khoury, B., Lecomte, T., Fortin, G., Masse, M., Therien, P., et al. (2013). Mindfulness-based therapy: A comprehensive meta-analysis. *Clinical Psychology Review 33*, 763–771.

Khoury, R.M. (1985). Norm formation, social conformity, and the confederating function of humor. *Social Behavior and Personality, 13*, 159–165.

Kiecolt-Glaser, J., McGuire, L., Robles, T.F., & Glaser, R. (2002). Emotions, morbidity, and mortality: New perspectives from psychoneuroimmunology. *Annual Review of Psychology, 53*, 83–107.

Kiecolt-Glaser, J.K., Glaser, R., Cacioppo, J.T., & Malarkey, W.B. (1998). Marital stress: Immunologic, neuroendocrine, and autonomic correlates. *Annals of the New York Academy of Sciences, 840*, 656–663.

Kiecolt-Glaser, J.K., Graham, J.E., Malarkey, W.B., Porter, K., Lemeshow, S., & Glaser, R. (2008). Olfactory influences on mood and autonomic, endocrine, and immune function. *Psychoneuroendocrinology, 33*, 328–339.

Kihlstrom, J. (2008). The psychological unconscious. In O.P. John, R.W. Robins, & L.A. Pervin (Eds.), *Handbook of personality theory and research* (3rd ed.). New York, NY: Guilford Press.

Kihlstrom, J.F. (1999). The psychological unconscious. In L.A. Pervin & O.P. John (Eds.), *Handbook of personality: Theory and research.* New York, NY: Guilford Press.

Killen, M., Ardila-Rey, R., Barakkatz, M., & Wang, P.L. (2000). Preschool teacher's perceptions about conflict resolution, autonomy, and the group in four countries: United States, Colombia, El Salvador, and Taiwan. *Early Education and Development, 11*, 73–92.

Kim, K., & Johnson, M.K. (2014). Extended self: spontaneous activation of medial prefrontal cortex by objects that are "mine." *Social Cognitive and Affective Neuroscience, 9*, 1006–1012.

Kimble, D.P. (1992). *Biological psychology* (2nd ed.). Fort Worth, TX: Harcourt Brace Jovanovich.

Kimura, D. (1973). The asymmetry of the human brain. *Scientific American, 228*, 70–78.

Kimura, D. (1992). Sex differences in the brain. *Scientific American, 267*, 119–195.

Kimura, K., Tachibana, N., Aso, T., Kimura, J., & Shibasaki, H. (1997). Subclinical REM sleep behavior disorder in a patient with corticobasal degeneration. *Sleep, 20*, 891–894.

Kinsey, A.C., Pomeroy, W.B., & Martin, C.E. (1948). *Sexual behavior in the human male.* Philadelphia, PA: Saunders.

Kinsey, A.C., Pomeroy, W.B., Martin, C.E., & Gebhard, P.H. (1953). *Sexual behavior in the human female.* Philadelphia, PA: Saunders.

Kirchengast, S., & Hartmann, B. (2003). Nicotine consumption before and during pregnancy affects not only newborn size but also birth modus. *Journal of Biosocial Science, 35*, 175–188.

Kirk, K.M., Bailey, J.M., & Martin, N.G. (2000). Etiology of male sexual orientation in an Australian twin sample. *Psychology, Evolution, and Gender, 2*, 301–311.

Kirmayer, L.J., & Looper, K. (2007). Somatoform disorders. In M. Hersen, S.M. Turner, & D.C. Beidel (Eds.), *Adult psychopathology and diagnosis* (pp. 410–472). Hoboken, NJ: Wiley.

Kirsch, I. (2001). The response set theory of hypnosis: Expectancy and physiology. *American Journal of Clinical Hypnosis, 44*, 69–73.

Kirsch, I., & Lynn, S.J. (1998a). Dissociation theories of hypnosis. *Psychological Bulletin, 123*, 100–115.

Kirsch, I., & Lynn, S.J. (1998b). Social cognitive alternatives to dissociation theories of hypnotic involuntariness. *Review of General Psychology, 2*, 66–80.

Kirsch, I., & Lynn, S.J. (1999). Automaticity in clinical psychology. *American Psychologist, 54*, 504–515.

Kirsch, I., Lynn, S.J., Vigorito, M., & Miller, R.R. (2004). The role of cognition in classical and operant conditioning. *Journal of Clinical Psychology, 60*, 369–392.

Kiyatkin, E.A., & Gratton, A. (1994). Electrochemical monitoring of extracellular dopamine in nucleus accumbens of rats lever-pressing for food. *Brain Research, 652*, 225–234.

Klahr, D., & Simon, H.A. (1999). Studies of scientific discovery: Complementary approaches and convergent findings. *Psychological Bulletin, 125*, 524–543.

Klapwijk, E.T., Goddings, A., Burnett Heyes, S., Bird, G., Viner, R.M., & Blakemore, S. (2013). Increased functional connectivity with puberty in the mentalising network involved in social emotion processing. *Hormones and Behavior, 64*(2), 314–322.

Klauer, K.C., & Musch, J. (2003). Affective priming: Findings and theories. In J. Musch & K.C. Klauer (Eds.), *The psychology of evaluation: Affective processes in cognition and emotion* (pp. 7–49). Mahwah, NJ: Erlbaum.

Klauer, K.C., Musch, J., & Naumer, B. (2000). On belief bias in syllogistic reasoning. *Psychological Review, 107*(4), 852–884.

Kleider, H.M., Knuycky, L.R., & Cavrak, S.E. (2012). Deciding the fate of others: The cognitive underpinnings of racially biased juror decision making. *Journal of General Psychology, 139*, 175–196.

Klein, M. (1991). The emotional life and ego-development of the infant with special reference to the depressive position. In P. King & R. Steiner (Eds.), *The Freud-Klein controversies, 1941–45.* New Library of Psychoanalysis. New York, NY: Tavistock/Routledge.

Klein, R.M. (1999). The Hebb legacy. *Canadian Journal of Experimental Psychology, 53*, 1–3.

Klein, S.B., & Mowrer, R.R. (1989). *Contemporary learning theories. Vol I: Pavlovian conditioning and the status of tradition.* Hillsdale, NJ: Erlbaum.

Kleinknecht, R.A., Dinnel, D.L., Kleinknecht, E.E., Hiruma, N., & Harada, N. (1997). Cultural factors in social anxiety: A comparison of social phobia symptoms and Taijin Kyofusho. *Journal of Anxiety Disorders, 2*, 157–177.

Kleinmuntz, B. (1980). *Essentials of abnormal psychology* (2nd ed.). New York, NY: Harper & Row.

Kleitman, N. (1963). *Sleep and wakefulness* (2nd ed.). Chicago, IL: University of Chicago Press.

Klemmensen, R., Hatemi, P.K., Hobolt, S.B., Skytthe, A., & Nørgaard, A. (2012). Heritability in political interest and efficacy across cultures: Denmark and the United States. *Twin Research and Human Genetics, 15*, 15–20.

Kline, D.W. (1994). Optimizing the visibility of displays for older observers. *Experimental Aging Research. Special issue: Human factors and the aging driver, 20*, 11–23.

Kline, G.H., Stanley, S.M., Markman, H.J., Olmos-Gallo, P.A., St. Peters, M., Whitton, S.W., & Prado, L.M. (2004). Timing is everything: Pre-engagement cohabitation and increased risk for poor marital outcomes. *Journal of Family Psychology, 18*, 311–318.

Kluckhohn, C., & Murray, H.A. (1953). Personality formation: The determinants. In C. Kluckhohn, H.A. Murray, & D.M. Schneider (Eds.), *Personality in nature, society, and culture* (pp. 53–71). New York, NY: Alfred A. Knopf.

Kluft, R.P. (1999). True lies, false truths, and naturalistic raw data: Applying clinical research findings to the false memory debate. In L.M. Williams & V.L. Banyard (Eds.), *Trauma and memory* (pp. 319–330). Thousand Oaks, CA: Sage.

Knafo, D. (2009). Freud's memory erased. *Psychoanalytic Psychology, 26*, 171–190.

Knekt, P., Lindfors, O., Harkanen, T., Valikoski, M., Virtala, E., Laaksonen, M.A., ... & Renlund, C. (2008). Randomized trial on the effectiveness of long-and short-term psychodynamic psychotherapy and solution-focused therapy on psychiatric symptoms during a 3-year follow-up. *Psychological Medicine, 38*(5), 689–704.

Knoblauch, K. (2002). Color vision. In H. Pashler & S. Yantis (Eds.), *Steven's handbook of experimental psychology: Vol. 1 Sensation and perception* (3rd ed., pp. 41–76). New York, NY: Wiley.

Knowles, J.H. (1977). The responsibility of the individual. In J.H. Knowles (Ed.), *Doing better and feeling worse: Health in the United States* (pp. 57–80). New York, NY: Norton.

Kobasa, S.C., Maddi, S.R., Puccetti, M.C., & Zola, M.A. (1985). Effectiveness of hardiness, exercise and social support as resources against illness. *Journal of Psychosomatic Research, 29*, 525–533.

Koch, C. (2004). *The quest for consciousness: A neurobiological approach.* Denver, CO: Roberts.

Kochanska, G., Aksan, N., Knaack, A., & Rhines, H.M. (2004). Maternal parenting and children's conscience: Early security as moderator. *Child Development, 75*, 1229–1242.

Kochanska, G., Casey, R.J., & Fukumoto, A. (1995). Toddlers' sensitivity to standard violations. *Child Development, 66,* 643–656.

Kochanska, G., Forman, D.R., Aksan, N., & Dunbar, S.B. (2005). Pathways to conscience: Early mother-child mutually responsive orientation and children's moral emotion, conduct, and cognition. *Journal of Child Psychology and Psychiatry, 46,* 19–34.

Koenig, H.G., Pargament, K.L., & Nielsen, J. (1998). Religious coping and health status in medically ill hospitalized older adults. *Journal of Nervous and Mental Disease, 186,* 513–521.

Koerner, N., Tallon, K., & Kusec, A. (2015). Maladaptive core beliefs and their relation to generalized anxiety disorder. *Cognitive Behaviour Therapy, 44*(6), 441–455.

Koestner, R., & McClelland, D.C. (1990). Perspectives on competence motivation. In L.A. Pervin (Ed.), *Handbook of personality theory and research.* New York, NY: Guilford Press.

Kohlberg, L. (1963). The development of children's orientations toward a moral order: I. Sequence in the development of moral thought. *Human Development, 6,* 11–33.

Kohlberg, L. (1984). *The psychology of moral development: Essays on moral development* (Vol. 2). New York, NY: Harper & Row.

Köhler, W. (1925). *The mentality of apes* (2nd revised ed.) (Ella Winter, Trans.). New York, NY: Harcourt.

Kohut, H. (1975). The psychoanalyst in the community of scholars. *The Annals of Psychoanalysis, 3,* 341–370.

Kohut, H. (1977). *The restoration of self.* New York, NY: International Universities Press.

Kolata, G. (2009, November 16). Panel urges mammograms at 50, not 40. *New York Times.* Retrieved February 2, 2010, from http://www.nytimes.com/2009/11/17/health/17cancer.html.

Kolb, B. (1989). Brain development, plasticity, and behavior. *American Psychologist, 44,* 1203–1212.

Kolb, B., & Whishaw, I.Q. (1989). Plasticity in the neocortex: Mechanisms underlying recovery from early brain damage. *Progress in Neurobiology, 32,* 235–276.

Kolb, B., & Whishaw, I.Q. (1998). Brain plasticity and behavior. *Annual Review of Psychology, 49,* 43–64.

Kolb, B., & Whishaw, I.Q. (2003). *Fundamentals of human neuropsychology* (5th ed.). New York, NY: Worth.

Kolb, B., & Whishaw, I.Q. (2005). *An introduction to brain and behavior* (2nd ed.). New York, NY: Worth.

Kollar, E.J., & Fisher, C. (1980). Tooth induction in chick epithelium: Expression of quiescent genes for enamel synthesis. *Science, 207,* 993–995.

Koluchova, J. (1972). Severe deprivation in twins: A case study. *Journal of Child Psychology and Psychiatry, 13,* 107–114.

Koluchova, J. (1991). Severely deprived twins after 22 years of observation. *Studiea Psychologica, 33,* 23–28.

Konkle, A.T.M., Kubela, S.L., & Bielajew, C. (2000). The effects of cholecystokinin on stimulation-induced feeding and self-stimulation. *Behavioural Brain Research, 107,* 145–152.

Koriat, A., & Björk, R.A. (2005). Illusions of competence in monitoring one's knowledge during study. *Journal of Experimental Psychology: Learning, Memory, and Cognition, 31,* 187–194.

Koriat, A., Goldsmith, M., & Pansky, A. (2000). Toward a psychology of memory accuracy. *Annual Review of Psychology, 51,* 481–537.

Korpi, E.R. (1994). Role of GABA-sub(A) receptors in the actions of alcohol and in alcoholism: Recent advances. *Alcohol and Alcoholism, 29,* 115–129.

Kortegaard, L., Hoerder, K., Joergensen, J., Gillberg, C., & Kyvik, K.O. (2001). A preliminary population-based twin study of self-reported eating disorder. *Psychological Medicine, 31,* 361–365.

Koss, M.P., Gidycz, C.A., & Wisniewski, N. (1987). The scope of rape: Incidence and prevalence of sexual aggression and victimization in a national sample of higher education students. *Journal of Consulting and Clinical Psychology, 55,* 162–170.

Kosslyn, S.M., Ball, T.M., & Reiser, B.J. (1978). Visual images preserve metric spatial information: Evidence from studies of image scanning. *Journal of Experimental Psychology: Human Perception and Performance, 4,* 47–60.

Kosslyn, S.M., Thompson, W.L., & Ganis, G. (2006). *The case for mental imagery.* New York, NY: Oxford University Press.

Kottak, C.P. (2000). *Cultural anthropology* (8th ed.). Boston, MA: McGraw-Hill.

Kraft, C.L. (1978). A psychophysical contribution to air safety: Simulator studies of visual illusions in night visual approaches. In H.L. Pick, Jr., H.W. Leibowitz, J.E. Singer, A. Steinschneider, & H.W. Stevenson (Eds.), *Psychology: From research to practice* (pp. 363–385). New York, NY: Plenum Press.

Krahé, B., & Altwasser, C. (2006). Changing negative attitudes towards persons with physical disabilities: An experimental intervention. *Journal of Community & Applied Social Psychology, 16,* 59–69.

Krain, A.L., Gotimer, K., Hefton, S., Ernst, M., Castellanos, F.X., Pine, D.S., & Milham, M.P. (2008). A functional magnetic resonance imaging investigation of uncertainty in adolescents with anxiety disorders. *Biological Psychiatry, 63,* 563–568.

Kramer, D.A. (1983). Post-formal operations? A need for further conceptualization. *Human Development, 26,* 91–105.

Kramer, M.S., Aboud, F., Mironova, E., Vanilovich, I., Platt, R.W., Matush, L., & Shapiro, S. (2008). Breastfeeding and child cognitive development: New evidence from a large randomized trial. *Archives of General Psychiatry, 65,* 578–584.

Krasnegor, N.A., Lyon, G.R., & Goldman, R.P.S. (1997). *Development of the prefrontal cortex: Evolution, neurobiology, and behavior.* Baltimore, MD: Paul H. Brookes.

Kraus, N., & Chandrasekaran, B. (2010). Music training for the development of auditory skills. *Nature Reviews Neuroscience, 11*(8), 599–605.

Kraut, R., Olson, J., Banaji, M., Bruckman, A., Cohen, J., & Cooper, M. (2004). Psychological research online: Report of board of scientific affairs' advisory group on the conduct of research on the internet. *American Psychologist, 59,* 105–117.

Krebs, D.L., & Denton, K. (1997). Social illusions and self-deception: The evolution of biases in person perception. In J.A. Simpson & D.T. Kenrick (Eds.), *Evolutionary social psychology* (pp. 21–48). Mahwah, NJ: Lawrence Erlbaum.

Krech, D. (1978). Quoted in M.C. Diamond, The aging brain: Some enlightening and optimistic results. *American Scientist, 66,* 66–71.

Krevans, J., & Gibbs, J.C. (1996). Parents' use of inductive discipline: Relations to children's empathy and prosocial behavior. *Child Development, 67,* 3263–3277.

Krishna, A. (2009). *Sensory marketing: Research on the sensuality of products.* Chicago, IL: Taylor & Francis.

Krizan, Z., & Baron, R.S. (2007). Group polarization and choice-dilemmas: How important is self-categorization? *European Journal of Social Psychology, 37,* 191–201.

Krohn, M.D. (1976). Inequality, unemployment and crime: Cross-national data and criminology theories. *Criminology, 24,* 269–295.

Krosnick, J.A., Betz, A.L., Jussim, L.J., & Lynn, A.R. (1992). Subliminal conditioning of attitudes. *Personality and Social Psychology Bulletin, 18,* 152–162.

Krueger, R.F., & Caspi, A. (1993). Personality, arousal, and pleasure: A test of competing models of interpersonal attraction. *Personality and Individual Differences, 14,* 105–111.

Kruger, J., Wirtz, D., & Miller, D.T. (2005). Counterfactual thinking and the first instinct fallacy. *Journal of Personality and Social Psychology, 88,* 725–735.

Kruglanski, A.W. (2004). *The psychology of closed mindedness.* New York, NY: Psychology Press.

Ksir, C.J., Hart, C.I., & Ray, O.S. (2008). *Drugs, society, and human behavior.* New York, NY: McGraw-Hill.

Kübler-Ross, E. (1969). *On death and dying.* New York, NY: Macmillan.

Kubota, J.T., & Ito, T.A. (2007). Multiple cues in social perception: The time course of processing race and facial expression. *Journal of Experimental Social Psychology, 43,* 738–752.

Kuhl, P.K. (2004). Early language acquisition: cracking the speech code. *Nature Reviews Neuroscience, 5*(11), 831–843.

Kulik, J.A., & Mahler, H.I.M. (1989). Stress and affiliation in a hospital setting: Pre-operative roommate preferences. *Personality and Social Psychology Bulletin, 15,* 183–193.

Kulik, J.A., Mahler, H.I.M., & Moore, P.J. (1996). Social comparison and affiliation under threat: Effects of recovery from major surgery. *Journal of Personality and Social Psychology, 66,* 301–309.

Kumar, S., Porcu, P., Werner, D.F., Matthews, D.B., Diaz-Granados, J.L., Helfand, R.S., & Morrow, A.L. (2009). The role of GABAA receptors in the acute and chronic effects of ethanol: A decade of progress. *Psychopharmacology, 205,* 529–564.

Kuncel, N.P., Hezlett, S.A., & Ones, D.S. (2004). Academic performance, career potential, and job performance: Can one construct predict them all? *Journal of Personality and Social Psychology, 86,* 148–161.

Kunzendorf, R.G., Papoutsakis, E., Watson, G., McArdle, E., Monroe, L., Gauthier, A., & Tassone, S. (2007). The archaic belief in dream visitations as it relates to "seeing ghosts," "meeting the lord," as well as "encountering extraterrestrials." *Imagination, Cognition and Personality, 27,* 71–85.

Kunzman, U., & Baltes, P.B. (2003). Beyond the traditional scope of intelligence: Wisdom in action. In R.J. Sternberg, J. Lautrey, & T.I. Lubart (Eds.), *Models of intelligence: International perspectives.* Washington, DC: American Psychological Association.

Kuo, P., Kalsi, G., Prescott, C.A., Hodgkinson, C.A., Goldman, D., Alexander, J., ... Riley, B.P. (2009). Associations of glutamate decarboxylase genes with initial sensitivity and age-at-onset of alcohol dependence in the Irish Affected Sib Pair Study of Alcohol Dependence. *Drug and Alcohol Dependence, 101,* 80–87.

Kuo, J.R., Khoury, J.E., Metcalfe, R., Fitzpatrick, S., & Goodwill, A. (2015). An examination of the relationship between childhood emotional abuse and borderline personality disorder features: The role of difficulties with emotion regulation. *Child Abuse & Neglect, 39*, 147–155.

Kuo, J.R., & Linehan, M.M. (2009). Disentangling emotion processes in borderline personality disorder: Physiological and self-reported assessment of biological vulnerability, baseline intensity, and reactivity to emotionally evocative stimuli. *Journal of Abnormal Psychology, 118*, 531–544.

Kurtz, M.M., & Mueser, K.T. (2008). A meta-analysis of controlled research on social skills training for schizophrenia. *Journal of Consulting and Clinical Psychology, 76*(3), 491–504.

Kurzban, R., Burton-Chellew, M., & West, S.A. (2015). The evolution of altruism in humans. *Annual Review of Psychology, 66*, 575–599.

Kurzweil, E. (1989). *The Freudians: A comparative perspective.* New Haven, CT: Yale University Press.

Kuyken, W., Dalgleish, T., & Holden, E.R. (2007). Advances in cognitive-behavioural therapy for unipolar depression. *Canadian Journal of Psychiatry, 52*, 5–13.

LaBar, K.S., & LeDoux, J.E. (2006). Fear and anxiety pathways. In S.O. Moldin & J.L. Rubenstein (Eds.), *Understanding autism: From basic neuroscience to treatment.* Boca Raton, FL: CRC Press.

LaBar, K.S., & Phelps, E.A. (1998). Arousal-mediated memory consolidation: Role of the medial temporal lobe in humans. *Psychological Science, 9*, 490–493.

Labbate, L.A., Rosenbaum, J., Arana, G.W., Fava, M. (2009). *Handbook of psychiatric drug therapy.* Chicago, IL: Lippincott.

Lachman, M.E. (2004). Development in midlife. *Annual Review of Psychology, 55*, 305–331.

Lack, D. (1968). *Ecological adaptations for breeding in birds.* London, UK: Methuen.

Lacks, P., Bertelson, A.D., Gans, L., & Kunkel, J. (1983). The effectiveness of three behavioral treatments for different degrees of sleep onset insomnia. *Behavior Therapy, 14*, 593–605.

Lagerspetz, K.Y., Tirri, R., & Lagerspetz, K.M. (1968). Neurochemical and endocrinological studies of mice selectively bred for aggressiveness. *Scandinavian Journal of Psychology, 9*, 157–160.

Lai, D.W.L. (1995). *Needs assessment on the Chinese community in Calgary: Final report.* Calgary, AB: Calgary Chinese Community Service Association.

Laible, D., & Thompson, R.A. (2000). Mother-child discourse, attachment security, shared positive affect, and early conscience development. *Child Development, 71*, 1424–1440.

Lakein, A. (1973). *How to get control of your time and your life.* New York, NY: Peter H. Wyden.

Lam, K.S., Aman, M.G., & Arnold, L.E. (2006). Neurochemical correlates of autistic disorder: A review of the literature. *Research in Developmental Disabilities, 27*(3), 254–289.

Lambert, L., Passmore, H., & Holder, M.D. (2015). Foundational frameworks of positive psychology: Mapping well-being orientations. *Canadian Psychology/Psychologie Canadienne, 56*(3), 311–321.

Lambert, M.J., Bergin, A.E., & Garfield, S.L. (2004). Introduction and Historical Overview. In M.J. Lambert, *Bergin and Garfield's Handbook of Psychotherapy and Behavior Change* (5th ed., pp. 3–15). New York: John Wiley & Sons.

Lambert, M.J., Shapiro, D.A., & Bergin, A.E. (1986). The effectiveness of psychotherapy. In S.L. Garfield & A.E. Bergin (Eds.), *Handbook of psychotherapy and behavior change* (3rd ed.). New York, NY: Wiley.

Lambert, W.E. (1992). Challenging established views on social issues: The power and limitations of research. *American Psychologist, 47*, 533–542.

Lambert, W.E., Genesee, F., Holobow, N., & Chartrand, L. (1993). Bilingual education for majority English-speaking children. *European Journal of Psychology of Education, 8*, 3–22.

Lamborn, S.D., Mounts, N.S., Steinberg, L., & Dornbusch, S.M. (1991). Patterns of competence and adjustment among adolescents from authoritative, authoritarian, indulgent, and neglectful families. *Child Development, 62*, 1049–1065.

Lampinen, J.M., & Schwartz, R.M. (2000). The impersistence of false memory persistence. *Memory, 8*(6), 393–400.

Lamport, M., & Richards, F.A. (2003). Four post-formal stages. In J. Demick & C. Andreoletti, (Eds.), *Handbook of adult development. The Plenum series in adult development and aging* (pp. 199–219). New York, NY: Kluwer Academic/Plenum Press.

Land, B.B., & Seeley, T.D. (2004). The grooming invitation dance of the honeybee. *Ethology, 110*, 1–10.

Landesman, S., & Ramey, C.T. (1989). Developmental psychology and mental retardation: Integrating scientific principles with treatment practices. *American Psychologist, 44*, 409–415.

Landfield, P., Baskin, R.K., & Pitler, T.A. (1981). Brain-aging correlates: Retardation by hormonal-pharmacological treatments. *Science, 214*, 581–583.

Landfield, P., Waymire, J., & Lynch, G. (1978). Hippocampal aging and adrenocorticoids: A quantitative correlation. *Science, 202*, 1098–1101.

Landry, M., & Raz, A. (2015). Hypnosis and imaging of the living human brain. *American Journal of Clinical Hypnosis, 57*(3), 285–313.

Landström, S., Strömwall, L.A., & Alfredsson, H. (2016). Blame attributions in sexual crimes: Effects of belief in a just world and victim behavior. *Nordic Psychology, 68*(1), 2–11.

Landy, F.J. (2005). Some historical and scientific issues related to research on emotional intelligence. *Journal of Organizational Behavior, 26*(4), 411–424.

Lane, R.D., Reiman, E.M., Ahern, G.L., & Schwartz, G.E. (1997). Neuroanatomical correlates of happiness, sadness, and disgust. *American Journal of Psychiatry, 154*, 926–933.

Laney, C., & Loftus, E.F. (2005). Traumatic memories are not necessarily accurate memories. *Canadian Journal of Psychiatry, 50*(13), 823–828.

Laney, C., & Loftus, E.F. (2010). Truth in emotional memories. In B.H. Bornstein & R.L. Wiener (Eds.), *Emotion and the law: Psychological perspectives* (pp. 157–186). New York, NY: Springer.

Langer, E. (1989). *Mindlessness.* Reading, MA: Addison-Wesley.

Langlois, J.H., & Roggman, L.A. (1990). Attractive faces are only average. *Psychological Science, 1*, 115–121.

Langlois, J.H., Kalakanis, L., Rubenstein, A.J., Larson, A., Hallam, M., & Smoot, M. (2000). Maxims or myths of beauty? A meta-analytic and theoretical review. *Psychological Bulletin, 126*, 390–423.

Lanier, C.A. (2001). Rape accepting attitudes: Precursors to or consequences of forced sex. *Violence Against Women, 7*, 876–885.

Lanius, R.A., Williamson, P.C., Densmore, M., Boksman, K., Neufeld, R.W., Gati, J.S., & Menon, R.S. (2004). The nature of traumatic memories: A 4-T fMRI functional connectivity analysis. *American Journal of Psychiatry, 161*, 36–44.

LaPiere, R.T. (1934). Attitudes and actions. *Social Forces, 13*, 230–237.

LaPointe, L.L. (2005). *Aphasia and related neurogenic language disorders* (3rd ed.). New York, NY: Thieme New York.

Larivée, S., Normandeau, S., & Parent, S. (2000). The French connection: Some contributions of French language research in the post-Piagetian era. *Child Development, 71*, 823–839.

Larsen, R.J., & Buss, D.M. (2010). *Personality psychology: Domains of knowledge about human behavior* (4th ed.). New York, NY: McGraw-Hill.

Larsen, S.R. (1965). *Strategies for reducing phobic behavior.* Stanford, CA: Stanford University Press.

Larson, C.L., Schaefer, H.S., Siegle, G.J., Jackson, C.A., Anderle, M.J., & Davidson, R.J. (2006). Fear is fast in phobic individuals: Amygdala activation in response to fear-relevant stimuli. *Biological Psychiatry, 60*(4), 410–417.

Larson, R.W., Hansen, D.M., & Moneta, G. (2006). Differing profiles of developmental experiences across types of organized youth activities. *Developmental Psychology, 42*, 849–863.

Larson, S.J., & Siegel, S. (1998). Learning and tolerance to the ataxic effect of ethanol. *Pharmacology, Biochemistry and Behavior, 61*, 131–142.

Lashley, K.S. (1930). The mechanism of vision: 1. A method for rapid analysis of pattern-vision in the rat. *Journal of Genetic Psychology, 37*, 453–460.

Lashley, K.S. (1950). In search of the engram. In *Symposium of the Society for Experimental Biology* (Vol. 4). New York, NY: Cambridge University Press.

Lassiter, G.D., Diamond, S.S., Schmidt, H.C., & Elek, J.K. (2007). Evaluating videotaped confessions: Expertise provides no defense against the camera-perspective effect. *Psychological Science, 18*, 224–226.

Latané, B., & Bourgeois, M.J. (2001). Successfully simulating dynamic social impact: Three levels of prediction. In J.P. Forgas & K.D. Williams (Eds.), *Social influence: Direct and indirect processes. The Sydney symposium of social psychology.* Philadelphia, PA: Psychology Press.

Latané, B., & Darley, J.M. (1968). Group inhibition of bystander intervention in emergencies. *Journal of Personality and Social Psychology, 10*, 215–221.

Latané, B., & Darley, J.M. (1970). *The unresponsive bystander: Why doesn't he help?* New York, NY: Appleton-Century-Crofts.

Latané, B., Liu, J.H., Nowak, A., Bonevento, M., & Zheng, L. (1995). Distance matters: Physical space and social impact. *Personality and Social Psychology Bulletin, 21*, 795–805.

Latané, B., & Nida, S. (1981). Ten years of research on group size and helping. *Psychological Bulletin, 89*, 308–324.

Latané, B., & Rodin, J. (1969). A lady in distress: Inhibiting effects of friends and strangers on bystander intervention. *Journal of Experimental Social Psychology, 5*, 189–202.

Lau, H.L., Timbers, T.A., Mahmoud, R., & Rankin, C.H. (2013). Genetic dissection of memory for associative and non-associative learning in

Caenorhabditis elegans. *Genes, Brain & Behavior, 12,* 210–223.

Lau, R.R., & Russell, D. (1980). Attribution in the sports pages. *Journal of Personality and Social Psychology, 39,* 29–38.

Laumann, E.O., Gagnon, J.H., Michael, R.T., & Michaels, S. (1994). *The social organization of sexuality: Sexual practices in the United States.* Chicago, IL: University of Chicago Press.

Lavigne, J.V., Gibbons, R.D., Christoffel, K.K., & Arend, R. (1996). Prevalence rates and correlates of psychiatric disorders among preschool children. *Journal of the American Academy of Child & Adolescent Psychiatry, 35,* 204–214.

Lawler, K.A., & Schmied, L.A. (1992). A prospective study of women's health: The effects of stress, hardiness, locus of control, Type A behavior, and physiological reactivity. *Women & Health, 19,* 27–41.

Lazarus, A.A. (1995). Multimodal therapy. In R.J. Corsini & D. Wedding (Eds.), *Current psychotherapies* (5th ed.). Itaska, IL: Peacock.

Lazarus, R.S. (1991). Progress on a cognitive-motivational-relational theory of emotion. *American Psychologist, 46,* 819–834.

Lazarus, R.S. (1998). *Fifty years of the research and theory of R.S. Lazarus: An analysis of historical and perennial issues.* Mahwah, NJ: Erlbaum.

Lazarus, R.S. (2001). Relational meaning and discrete emotions. In B.K. Scherer, A. Schorr, & T. Johnstone (Eds.), *Appraisal processes in emotion: Theory, methods, research* (pp. 37–67). New York, NY: Oxford University Press.

Lazarus, R.S. (2006). Emotions and interpersonal relationships: Toward a person-centered conceptualization of emotions and coping. *Journal of Personality, 74,* 9–46.

LeBel, E.P., & Peters, K.R. (January 2011). Fearing the future of empirical psychology: Bem's (2011) evidence of psi as a case study of deficiencies in modal research practice. *Review of General Psychology, 15*(4), 371–379.

LeBon, G. (1895). *Psychologies des foules.* Paris, France: Oleon.

Lebrun, M. (2007). *Student depression.* Lanham, MD: Rowman & Littlefield Education.

Lecat, B., Hilton, D.J., & Crano, W.D. (2009). Group status and reciprocity norms: Can the door-in-the-face effect be obtained in an out-group context? *Group Dynamics: Theory, Research, and Practice, 13,* 178–189.

Lecompte, V., Moss, E., Cyr, C., & Pascuzzo, K. (2014). Preschool attachment, self-esteem and the development of preadolescent anxiety and depressive symptoms. *Attachment & Human Development, 16*(3), 242–260.

Ledford, J.R., & Wolery, M. (2015). Observational learning of academic and social behaviors during small-group direct instruction. *Exceptional Children, 81*(3), 272–291.

LeDoux, J.E. (1986). Cognitive-emotional interactions in the brain. *Cognition and Emotion, 3,* 267–289.

LeDoux, J.E. (1992). Systems and synapses of emotional memory. In L.R. Squire, N.M. Weinberger, G. Lynch, & J.L. McGaugh (Eds.), *Memory: Organization and locus of change* (pp. 205–216). New York, NY: Oxford University Press.

LeDoux, J.E. (1996, 1998). *The emotional brain.* New York, NY: Simon & Schuster.

LeDoux, J.E. (2000). Emotion circuits in the brain. *Annual Review of Neuroscience, 23,* 155–184.

LeDoux, J.E. (2006). Fear and anxiety pathways. In S.O. Moldin & J.R.L. Rubenstein, (Eds.),

Understanding autism: From basic neuroscience to treatment. Boca Raton, FL: CRC Press.

Lee, C.H. (2009). Testing the role of phonology in reading: Focus on sentence processing. *Journal of Psycholinguistic Research, 38,* 333–344.

Lee, K., & Freire, A. (1999). Effects of face configuration change on shape perception: A new illusion. *Perception, 28,* 1217–1226.

Leech, J., Mazzone, S.B., & Farrell, M.J. (2012). The effect of placebo conditioning on capsaicin-evoked urge to cough. *Chest, 142*(4), 951–957.

Lefaucheur, J.P., André-Obadia, N., Antal, A., Ayache, S.S., et al. (2014). Evidence-based guidelines on the therapeutic use of repetitive transcranial magnetic stimulation (rTMS). *Clinical Neurophysiology, 125*(11), 2150–2206.

Lehmann, D., Pascual-Marqui, R.D., Strik, W.K., & Koenig, T. (2010). Core networks for visual-concrete and abstract thought content: A brain electric microstate analysis. *NeuroImage, 49,* 1073–1079.

Lehmann-Haupt, C. (1988, August 4). Books of the times: How an actor found success, and himself. *New York Times,* 2.

Leibenluft, E. (1999). Gender differences in mood and anxiety disorders: From bench to bedside. Washington, DC: American Psychiatric Press.

Leibowitz, S.F. (1992). Hypothalamic neurochemical systems mediate drug effects on food intake. *International Journal of Obesity and Related Metabolic Disorders, 15,* 701A–702A.

Leichsenring, F. (2005). Are psychodynamic and psychoanalytic therapies effective? A review of empirical data. *The International Journal of Psychoanalysis, 86*(3), 841–868.

Leichsenring, F., Leibing, E., Kruse, J., New, A.S., & Leweke, F. (2011). Borderline personality disorder. *The Lancet, 377*(9759), 74–84.

Leichtman, M.D., & Ceci, S.J. (1995). The effects of stereotypes and suggestions on preschoolers' reports. *Developmental Psychology, 31,* 568–578.

Leigh, B.C., & Stall, R. (1993). Substance use and risky sexual behavior for exposure to HIV: Issues in methodology, interpretation, and prevention. *American Psychologist, 48,* 1035–1045.

Leigland, S. (2000). On cognitivism and behaviorism. *American Psychologist, 55,* 273–274.

Leising, D., Rogers, K., & Ostner, J. (2009). The undisordered personality: Assumptions underlying personality disorder diagnoses. *Review of General Psychology, 13,* 230–241.

Leitenberg, H., & Henning, K. (1995). Sexual fantasy. *Psychological Bulletin, 117,* 469–496.

Lenzenweger, M.F., & Clarkin, J.F. (Eds.). (2005). *Major theories of personality disorder.* New York, NY: Guilford Press.

Leon, D.A., Lawlor, D.A., Clark, G.D., & Macintyre, S. (2009). The association of childhood intelligence with mortality risk from adolescence to middle age: Finding of the Aberdeen Children of the 1950's cohort study. *Intelligence, 37,* 517–634.

Leondes, C.T. (1997). *Medical imaging systems techniques and applications: Brain and skeletal systems.* New York, NY: Gordon and Breach.

Leor, J., Poole, W.K., & Kloner, R.A. (1996). Sudden cardiac death triggered by an earthquake. *New England Journal of Medicine, 334,* 413–419.

Lepper, M.R., Greene, D., & Nisbett, R.E. (1973). Undermining children's intrinsic interest with extrinsic reward: A test of the "overjustification" hypothesis. *Journal of Personality and Social Psychology, 28,* 129–137.

Lerner, M.J. (1980). *The belief in a just world: A fundamental delusion.* New York, NY: Plenum Press.

Lett, B.T., Grant, V.L., Byrne, M.J., & Koh, M.T. (2000). Pairings of a distinctive chamber with the after-effect of wheel running produce conditioned place preference. *Appetite, 34,* 87–94.

Lett, B.T., Grant, V.L., & Koh, M.T. (2001). Naloxone attenuates the conditioned place preference induced by wheel running in rats. *Physiology & Behavior, 72,* 355–358.

Lett, B.T., Grant, V.L, Koh, M.T., & Flynn, G. (2002). Prior experience with wheel running produces cross-tolerance to the rewarding effect of morphine. *Pharmacology, Biochemistry and Behavior, 72,* 101–105.

Lett, B.T., Grant, V.L., Koh, M.T., & Smith, J.F. (2001). Wheel running simultaneously produces conditioned taste aversion and conditioned place preference in rats. *Learning and Motivation, 32,* 129–136.

Leucht, S., Corves, C., Arbter, D., Engel, R.R., Li, C., & Davis, J.M. (2009). Second-generation versus first-generation antipsychotic drugs for schizophrenia: A meta-analysis. *The Lancet, 373*(9657), 31–41.

Levenson, H. (2002). *Concise guide to brief dynamic and interpersonal therapy.* Washington, DC: American Psychiatric Press.

Levenson, R.W. (1992). Autonomic nervous system differences among emotions. *Psychological Science, 3,* 23–27.

Levin, L.H., & Reppy, W.A. (2015). Reforming the politics of animal research. *Journal of Medical Ethics: Journal of the Institute of Medical Ethics, 41*(7), 563–566.

Levine, R., Sato, S., Hashimoto, T., & Verma, J. (1995). Love and marriage in eleven cultures. *Journal of Cross-Cultural Psychology, 26,* 554–571.

Levinson, D.J. (1986). A conception of adult development. *American Psychologist, 41,* 3–13.

Levinson, D.J. (1990). A theory of life structure development in adulthood. In C.N. Alexander & E.J. Langer (Eds.), *Higher stages of human development: Perspectives on adult growth.* New York, NY: Oxford University Press.

Levinson, D.J., Darow, C.N., Klein, E.B., Levinson, M.H., & McKee, B. (1978). *The seasons of a man's life.* New York, NY: Knopf.

Levinthal, C.E. (2005). *Drugs, behavior and modern society* (4th ed.). Aukland, New Zealand: Pearson Education.

Levinthal, C.F. (2010). *Drugs, behavior, and modern society.* New York: McGraw-Hill.

Levis, D.J. (1989). The case for a return to a two-factor theory of avoidance: The failure of non-fear interpretations. In S.B. Klein, B. Stephen, & R.R. Mowrer (Eds.), *Contemporary learning theories: Pavlovian conditioning and the status of traditional learning theory.* Hillsdale, NJ: Erlbaum.

Levitin, D.L. (2006). *This is your brain on music: The science of a human obsession.* New York: Dutton.

Levitin, D.L. (2008). *The world in six songs: How the musical brain created human nature.* Toronto: Viking Canada.

Levitin, D.L. (2012). What does it mean to be musical? *Neuron, 73*(4), 633–637.

Levitsky, D.A. (2005). The non-regulation of food intake in humans: Hope for reversing the epidemic of obesity. *Physiology & Behavior, 86,* 623–632.

Levy, D.A. (2010). *Tools of critical thinking: Metathoughts for psychology* (2nd ed.). Prospect Heights, IL: Waveland Press.

Levy, S., Marrow, L., Bagley, C., & Lippman, M. (1989). Survival hazards analysis in first recurrent breast cancer patients: Seven-year follow-up. *Psychosomatic Medicine, 50,* 520–528.

Lewin, K. (1935). *A dynamic theory of personality*. New York, NY: McGraw-Hill.

Lewin, R. (1998). *The origin of modern humans*. New York, NY: American Scientific Library.

Lewin, T. (2009, October 23). No Einstein in your crib? Get a refund. *New York Times*. Retrieved February 5, 2010, from http://www.nytimes.com/2009/10/24/education/24baby.html.

Lewinsohn, P.M., Gotlib, I.H., Lewinsohn, M., Seeley, J.R., & Allen, N.B. (1998). Gender differences in anxiety disorders and anxiety symptoms in adolescents. *Journal of Abnormal Psychology, 107*, 109–117.

Lewinsohn, P.M., Hoberman, H., Teri, L., & Hantzinger, M. (1985). An integrative theory of depression. In S. Reiss & R. Bootzin (Eds.), *Theoretical issues in behavior therapy*. New York, NY: Academic Press.

Lewinsohn, P.M., Hops, H., Roberts, R.E., Seeley, J.R., & Andrews, J.A. (1993). Adolescent psychopathology: I. Prevalence and incidence of depression and other DSMIII-R disorders in high school students. *Journal of Abnormal Psychology, 102*, 133–144.

Lewis, M. (1999). On the development of personality. In L.A. Pervin & O.P. John (Eds.), *Handbook of personality: Theory and research* (2nd ed.). New York, NY: Guilford Press.

Lewis, M. (2000). The emergence of human emotions. In M. Lewis & J.M. Haviland-Jones (Eds.), *Handbook of emotions* (2nd ed., pp. 265–280). New York, NY: Guilford Press.

Leyens, J.P., Camino, L., Parke, R.D., & Berkowitz, L. (1975). Effects of movie violence on aggression in a field setting as a function of group dominance and cohesion. *Journal of Personality and Social Psychology, 32*, 346–360.

Li, M., D'Arcy, C., & Meng, X. (2015). Maltreatment in childhood substantially increases the risk of adult depression and anxiety in prospective cohort studies: Systematic review, meta-analysis, and proportional attributable fractions. *Psychological Medicine*, doi: http://dx.doi.org/10.1017/S0033291715002743.

Li, R., Polat, U., Makous, W., & Bavelier, D. (2009). Enhancing the contrast sensitivity function through action video game training. *Nature Neuroscience, 12*(5), 549–551.

Li, S. (2001). How close is too close? A comparison of proxemic reactions of Singaporean Chinese to male intruders of four ethnicities. *Perceptual and Motor Skills, 93*, 124–126.

Li, S., & Li, Y. (2007). How far is far enough?: A measure of information privacy in terms of interpersonal distance. *Environment and Behavior, 39*(3), 317–331.

Li, W., Liu, H., Yu, M., Zhang, X., Zhang, Y., et al. (2015). Folic acid alters methylation profile of jak-stat and long-term depression signaling pathways in Alzheimer's disease models. *Molecular Neurobiology*, Dec. 1, 2015.

Libertus, K., Joh, A.S., & Needham, A.W. (2015). Motor training at 3 months affects object exploration 12 months later. *Developmental Science*, doi: http://dx.doi.org/10.1111/desc.12370.

Lickey, M.E., & Gordon, B. (1991). *Medicine and mental illness: The use of drugs in psychiatry*. New York, NY: W.H. Freeman.

Lidz, C.S. (1997). Dynamic assessment approaches. In D.P. Flanagan, J.L. Genshaft, & P.L. Harrison (Eds.), *Contemporary intellectual assessment: Theories, tests, and issues*. New York, NY: Guilford Press.

Lieb, R., Isensee, B., Hoefler, M., Pfister, H., & Wittchen, H.U. (2002). Parental major depression and the risk of depression and other mental disorders in offspring: A prospective-longitudinal community study. *Archives of General Psychiatry, 59*, 365–374.

Lieberman, J., & Tasman, A. (2006). *Handbook of psychiatric drugs*. New York, NY: John Wiley & Sons.

Lieberman, J.A. (1998). *Psychiatric drugs*. Philadelphia, PA: Saunders.

Lieberman, M.D., & Eisenberger, N.I. (2009). Pains and pleasures of social life. *Science, 323*, 890–891.

Liedtke, W.B. (2006). *TRP ion channel function in sensory transduction and cellular signaling cascades*. San Francisco, CA: Taylor & Francis.

Lijffijt, M., Hu, K., & Swann, A.C. (2014). Stress modulates illness-course of substance use disorders: a translational review. *Front Psychiatry, 5*(83.10), 3389.

Lilienfeld, S.O., Kirsch, I., Sarbin, T.R., Lynn, S.J., Chaves, J.F., Ganaway, G.K., & Powell, R.A. (1999). Dissociative identity disorder and the socio-cognitive model: Recalling the lessons of the past. *Psychological Bulletin, 125*, 507–523.

Lilienfeld, S.O., Lynn, S.J., Ruscio, J., & Beyerstein, B.L. (2010). *50 great myths of popular psychology: Shattering widespread misconceptions about human behavior*. London, UK: Wiley-Blackwell.

Lin, J.Y., Murray, S.O., & Boynton, G.M. (2009). Capture of attention to threatening stimuli without perceptual awareness. *Current Biology, 19*, 1118–1122.

Lindell, A.K., & Lamb, J.A.G. (2008). Priming vs. rhyming: Orthographic and phonological representations in the left and right hemispheres. *Brain and Cognition, 68*, 193–203.

Linehan, M.M. (1993). *Cognitive-behavioral treatment of borderline personality disorder*. New York, NY: Guilford Press.

Linehan, M.M., & Dexter-Mazza, E.T. (2008). Dialectical behavior therapy for borderline personality disorder. In D.H. Barlow (Ed.), *Clinical handbook of psychological disorders: A step-by-step treatment manual* (4th ed.). New York, NY: Guilford Press.

Linehan, M.M., Comtois, K.A., Murray, A.M., Brown, M.Z., Gallop, R.J., Heard, H.L., ... Lidenboim, N. (2006). Two-year randomized controlled trial and follow-up of dialectical behavior therapy vs. therapy by experts for suicidal behaviors and borderline personality disorder. *Archives of General Psychiatry, 63*, 757–766.

Linver, M.R., Brooks-Gunn, J., & Kohen, D.E. (2002). Family processes as pathways from income to young children's development. *Developmental Psychology, 38*, 719–734.

Linville, P.W., & Jones, E.E. (1980). Polarized appraisals of out-group members. *Journal of Personality and Social Psychology, 38*, 689–703.

Linz, D., & Donnerstein, E. (1989). The effects of countertransformation on the acceptance of rape myths. In D. Zillmann & J. Bryant (Eds.), *Pornography: Research advances and policy considerations* (pp. 259–288). Hillsdale, NJ: Erlbaum.

Lippa, R.A. (2005). *Gender, nature, and nurture*. Hillsdale, NJ: Erlbaum.

Lisman, J.E., & Grace, A.A. (2005). The hippocampal-VTA loop: controlling the entry of information into long-term memory. *Neuron, 46*(5), 703–713.

Liu, W.T., Humayun, M.S., & Liker, M.A. (2008). Implantable biomimetic microelectronics systems. *Proceedings of the IEEE, 96*, 1073–1074.

Liu, W-Y., Weber, B., Reuter, M., Markett, S., & Chu, W-C. (2013). The Big Five of personality and structural imaging revisited: A VBM-DARTEL study. *NeuroReport: For Rapid Communication of Neuroscience Research, 24*, 375–380.

Livesley, W.J. (2003). *Practical management of personality disorder*. New York, NY: Guilford Press.

Livingstone, M. (2000). Is it warm? Is it real? Or just low spatial frequency? *Science, 290*(5495), 1299.

Livingstone, M., & Hubel, D. (1994). Segregation of form, color, movement, and depth: Anatomy, physiology, and perception. In H. Gutfreund, & G. Toulouse (Eds.), *Biology and computation: A physicist's choice. Advanced series in neuroscience* (pp. 596–605). Singapore: World Scientific.

Lloyd, E.A., & Feldman, M.W. (2002). Evolutionary psychology: A view from evolutionary biology. *Psychological Inquiry, 13*, 150–156.

Locke, E.A., & Latham, G.P. (2002). Building a practically useful theory of goal setting and task motivation: A 35-year odyssey. *American Psychologist, 57*, 705–717.

Loehlin, J.C. (1992). *Genes and environment in personality development*. Newbury Park, CA: Sage.

Loewenstein, R.J. (1991). Psychogenic amnesia and psychogenic fugue: A comprehensive review. In A. Tasman & S.M. Goldfinger (Eds.), *American Psychiatric Press review of psychiatry* (Vol. 10). Washington, DC: American Psychiatric Association.

Loewi, O. (1935). Humoral transmission of nervous impulses. *Nature, 135*, 1082–1083.

Loewi, O. (1960). An autobiographical sketch. *Perspectives in Biology, 4*, 3–25.

Loftus, E.F., & Burns, T.E. (1982). Mental shock can produce retrograde amnesia. *Memory and Cognition, 10*, 318–323.

Loftus, E.F., & Loftus, G.R. (1980). On the permanence of stored information in the human brain. *American Psychologist, 35*, 409–420.

Loftus, E.F., & Palmer, J.C. (1974). Reconstruction of automobile destruction: An example of the interaction between language and memory. *Journal of Verbal Learning and Verbal Behavior, 13*, 585–589.

Loftus, E.F., & Pickrell, J.E. (1995). The formation of false memories. *Psychiatric Annals, 25*, 720–725.

Logie, R.H., & Maylor, E.A. (2009). An internet study of prospective memory across adulthood. *Psychology and Aging, 24*, 767–774.

Logothetis, N.K., Pauls, J., Augath, M., Trinath, T., & Oeltermann, A. (2001). Neurophysiological investigation of the basis of the fMRI signal. *Nature, 412*, 150–157.

Logue, A.W. (1991). *The psychology of eating and drinking* (2nd ed.). New York, NY: W.H. Freeman.

Lomber, S.J., & Eggermont, J.J. (2006). *Reprogramming the cerebral cortex: Plasticity following central and peripheral lesions*. New York, NY: Oxford University Press.

London, K., Bruck, M., Ceci, S.J., & Shuman, D.W. (2005). Disclosure of child sexual abuse: What does the research tell us about the ways that children tell? *Psychology, Public Policy and Law, 11*(1), 199–226.

London, K., Bruck, M., Wright, D.B., & Ceci, S.J. (2008). Review of the contemporary literature on how children report sexual abuse to others: Findings, methodological issues, and implications for forensic interviewers. *Memory, 16*, 29–47.

Lonnqvist, J-E., Verkasalo, M., Haukka, J., Nyman, K., Tiihonen, J., Laaksonen, I., ... Henriksson, M. (2009). Premorbid personality factors in schizophrenia and bipolar disorder: Results from a large cohort study of male conscripts. *Journal of Abnormal Psychology, 118*, 418–423.

Lonsdorf, E.V. (2006). What is the role of mothers in the acquisition of termite-fishing behaviors in wild chimpanzees (Pan troglodytes schweinfurthii)? *Animal Cognition, 9*, 36–46.

Lopez, A.C., & McDermott, R. (2012). Adaptation, heritability, and the emergence of Evolutionary Political Science. *Political Psychology, 33*, 343–362.

Lopez, S.J., Pedrotti, J.T., & Snyder, C.R. (2015). Positive psychology: The scientific and practical explorations of human strengths (3rd ed.). Thousand Oaks, CA: Sage Publications, Inc.

Lopez, S.R., & Guarnaccia, P.J. (2000). Cultural psychopathology: Uncovering the social world of mental illness. *Annual Review of Psychology, 51*, 571–598.

Lorenz, K. (1937). The companion in the bird's world. *Auk, 54*, 245–273.

Lorenz, K. (1966). *On aggression.* New York, NY: Harcourt Brace Jovanovich.

Lount, R.B., Jr., & Wilk, S.L. (2014). Working harder or hardly working? Posting performance eliminates social loafing and promotes social laboring in workgroups. *Management Science, 60*(5), 1098–1106.

Lovaas, O.I. (1977). *The autistic child.* New York, NY: Irvington.

Lovallo, W. (2005). *Stress and health: Biological and psychological interactions.* Newbury Park, CA: Sage.

Low, L-F., & Anstey, K.J. (2009). Dementia literacy: Recognition and beliefs on dementia of the Australian public. *Alzheimer's & Dementia, 5*, 43–49.

Lubinski, D. (2004). Introduction to the special section on cognitive abilities: 100 years after Spearman's (1904) "'General intelligence,' objectively determined and measured." *Journal of Personality and Social Psychology, 86*, 96–111.

Luborsky, L., Rosenthal, R., Diguer, L., Andrusyna, T.P., Berman, J.S., Jeffrey, S., Levitt, J.T., Seligman, D.A., & Krause, E.D. (2002). The dodo bird verdict is alive and well—mostly. *Clinical Psychology: Science and Practice, 9*, 2–12.

Lucassen, A. (2012). Ethical implications of new genetic technologies. *Developmental Medicine & Child Neurology, 54*, 196.

Luchins, A. (1957a). Primacy-recency in impression formation. In C. Hovland, W. Mandell, E. Campbell, T. Brock, A. Luchins, & A. Cohen (Eds.), *The order of presentation in persuasion.* New Haven, CT: Yale University Press.

Luchins, A. (1957b). Experimental attempts to minimize the impact of first impressions. In C. Hovland, W. Mandell, E. Campbell, T. Brock, A. Luchins, & A. Cohen (Eds.), *The order of presentation in persuasion.* New Haven, CT: Yale University Press.

Luchins, A.J. (1942). Mechanization in problem solving: The effect of Einstellung. *Psychological Monographs, 54*, 6 (Whole No. 248).

Luck, S.J., & Vecera, S.P. (2002). Attention. In H. Pashler & S. Yantis (Eds.), *Steven's handbook of experimental psychology: Vol. 1 Sensation and perception* (3rd ed., pp. 235–286). New York, NY: Wiley.

Luders, E., Narr, K.L., Thompson, P.M., & Toga, A.W. (2009). Neuroanatomical correlates of intelligence. *Intelligence, 37*, 156–163.

Luna, B., Paulsen, D.J., Padmanabhan, A., & Geier, C. (2013). The teenage brain cognitive control and motivation. *Current directions in psychological science, 22*(2), 94–100.

Luo, S., & Zhang, G. (2009). What leads to romantic attraction: Similarity, reciprocity, security, or beauty? Evidence from a speed-dating study. *Journal of Personality, 77*, 933–964.

Lupien, S.J., King, S., Meaney, M.J., & McEwen, B.S. (2001). Can poverty get under your skin? Basal cortisol levels and cognitive function in children from low and high socioeconomic status. *Development & Psychopathology, 13*, 653–676.

Luria, A.R. (1968). *The mind of a mnemonist: A little book about a vast memory.* New York, NY: Basic Books.

Lydic, R., & Biebuyck, J.F. (Eds.). *Clinical physiology of sleep.* New York, NY: Oxford University Press.

Lykken, D.T. (1981). *A tremor in the blood: Uses and abuses of the lie detector.* New York, NY: Plenum Press.

Lykken, D.T. (1984). Polygraph interrogation. *Nature, 307*, 681–684.

Lykken, D.T. (2006). The mechanism of emergenesis. *Genes, Brain, & Behavior, 5*, 306–310.

Lykken, D.T., Bouchard, T.J., McGue, M., & Tellegen, A. (1993). Heritability of interests: A twin study. *Journal of Applied Psychology, 78*, 649–661.

Lyn, H., & Savage-Rumbaugh, S. (2013). The use of emotion symbols in language-using apes. In S. Watanabe & S. Kuczaj (Eds.), *Emotions of animals and humans: Comparative perspectives, the science of the mind.* Japan: Springer.

Lynch, M.A. (2004). Long-term potentiation and memory. *Physiological Reviews, 84*(1), 87–136.

Lynn, E.J. (1971). Amphetamine abuse: A "speed" trap. *Psychiatric Quarterly, 45*, 92–101.

Lynn, R. (2009). What has caused the Flynn effect? Secular increases in the Development Quotients of infants. *Intelligence, 37*, 16–24.

Lynn, R., & Cheng, H. (2013). Recent data for majority and racial minority differences in intelligence of 5-year-olds in the United Kingdom. *Intelligence, 41*(5), 452–455.

Lynn, S.J., Boycheva, E., Deming, A., Lilienfeld, S.O., & Hallquist, M.N. (2009). Forensic hypnosis: The state of the science. In J.L. Skeem, K.S. Douglas, & S.O. Lilienfeld (Eds.), *Psychological science in the courtroom: Consensus and controversy* (pp. 80–99). New York, NY: Guilford Press.

Lynne, S.J., Lillenfeld, S.O., Merckelbach, H., Giesbrecht, T., & van der Kloet, D. (2012). Dissociation and dissociative disorders: Challenging conventional wisdom. *Current Directions in Psychological Science, 21*(1), 48–53.

Lyons, L. (2005, November). Paranormal beliefs come (super)naturally to some. *Gallup USA.* Retrieved January 12, 2009, from http://www.gallup.com/poll/19558/Paranormal-Beliefs-Come-SuperNaturally-Some.aspx.

Lyons, M.J., Schultz, M., Neale, M., Brady, K., Eisen, S., Toomey, R., ... Tsuang, M. (2006). Specificity of familial vulnerability for alcoholism versus major depression in men. *The Journal of Nervous and Mental Disease, 194*, 809–817.

Maass, A., & Clark, R.D., III. (1984). Hidden impact of minorities: Fifteen years of minority influence research. *Psychological Bulletin, 95*, 428–450.

MacAndrew, C., & Edgerton, R.B. (1969). *Drunken comportment: A social explanation.* Chicago, IL: Aldine.

Maccari, S., Krugers, H.J., Morley-Fletcher, S., Szyf, M., & Brunton, P.J. (2014). The consequences of early-life adversity: neurobiological, behavioural and epigenetic adaptations. *Journal of Neuroendocrinology, 26*, 707–723.

Maccoby, E.E., & Jacklin, C.N. (1974). *The psychology of sex differences.* Stanford, CA: Stanford University Press.

Maccoby, E.E., & Maccoby, N. (1954). The interview: A tool of social science. In G. Lindzey (Ed.), *Handbook of social psychology.* Cambridge, MA: Addison-Wesley.

Maccoby, E.E., & Martin, J.A. (1983). Socialization in the context of the family: Parent-child interaction. In E.M. Hetherington (Ed.), *Handbook of child psychology: Socialization, personality, and social development.* New York, NY: Wiley.

MacCoun, R.J. (1998). Toward a psychology of harm reduction. *American Psychologist, 53*, 1199–1208.

MacDonald, T.K., Fong, G.T., Zanna, M.P., & Martineau, A.M. (2000). Alcohol myopia and condom use: Can alcohol intoxication be associated with more prudent behavior? *Journal of Personality and Social Psychology, 78*, 605–619.

MacDonald, T.K., Zanna, M.P., & Fong, G.T. (1995). Decision making in altered states: Effects of alcohol on attitudes toward drinking and driving. *Journal of Personality and Social Psychology, 68*, 973–985.

Maciejewski, P.K., Zhang, B., Block, S.D., & Prigerson, H.G. (2007). An empirical examination of the stage theory of grief. *JAMA: Journal of the American Medical Association, 297*, 716–723.

Mack, A. (2003). Inattentional blindness: Looking without seeing. *Current Directions in Psychological Science, 12*, 180–184.

Maddox, K.B., & Gray, S.A. (2002). Cognitive representations of black Americans: Reexploring the role of skin tone. *Personality and Social Psychology Bulletin, 28*, 2250–2259.

Maddux, J.E. (1999). Personal efficacy. In V.J. Derlega, B.A. Winstead, & W.H. Jones (Eds.), *Personality: Contemporary theory and research.* Chicago, IL: Nelson-Hall.

Madon, S., Willard, J., Guyll, M., Trudeau, L., & Spoth, R. (2006). Self-fulfilling prophecy effects of mothers' beliefs on children's alcohol use: Accumulation, dissipation, and stability over time. *Journal of Personality and Social Psychology, 90*, 911–926.

Maes, H.H.M., Neale, M.C., & Eaves, L.J. (1997). Genetic and environmental factors in relative body weight and human adiposity. *Behavior Genetics, 27*, 325–351.

Magnuson, S. (1986). "A serious deficiency": The Rogers Commission faults NASA's "flawed" decision-making process. *Time* (Intl. Ed.), 40–42.

Mahler, M. (1968). *On human symbiosis and the vicissitudes of individuation: Infantile psychosis.* New York, NY: Basic Books.

Mahoney, M.J. (1980). *Abnormal psychology: Perspectives on human variance.* New York, NY: Harper & Row.

Maio, G.R., & Olson, J.M. (Eds.). (2000). *Why we evaluate: Functions of attitudes.* Mahwah, NJ: Erlbaum.

Major, B., Carrington, P.I., & Carnevale, P.J.D. (1984). Physical attractiveness and self-esteem: Attributions for praise from an other-sex evaluator. *Personality and Social Psychology Bulletin, 10*, 43–50.

Mäkelä, K. (1997). Drinking, the majority fallacy, cognitive dissonance and social pressure. *Addiction, 92*, 729–736.

Mak-Fan, K., Morris, D., Vidal, J., Anagnostou, E., Roberts, W., & Taylor, M.J. (2013). White matter and development in children with an autism spectrum disorder. *Autism, 17*(5), 541–557.

Malamuth, N.M. (1998). The confluence model as an organizing framework for research on sexually aggressive men: Risk moderators, imagined aggression, and pornography consumption. In R.G. Geen & E. Donnerstein (Eds.), *Human aggression: Theories, research, and implications for social policy* (pp. 230–243). San Diego, CA: Academic Press.

Maldonado, R., & Rodriguez de Fonseca, F. (2002). Cannabinoid addiction: Behavioral models and neural correlates. *Journal of Neuroscience, 22,* 3326–3331.

Malouf, J.M., Rooke, S.E., & Schutte, N.S. (2008). The heritability of human behavior: Results of aggregating meta-analyses. *Current Psychology, 27,* 153–161.

Mancini, A.D., & Bonanno, G.A. (2012). *Trauma therapy in context: The science and craft of evidence-based practice.* Washington, DC: American Psychological Association.

Mandler, G. (1984). *Mind and body: Psychology of emotion and stress.* New York, NY: W.W. Norton.

Mann, L. (1981). The baiting crowd in episodes of threatened suicide. *Journal of Personality and Social Psychology, 41,* 703–709.

Manning, W.D., & Smock, P.J. (2002). First comes cohabitation then comes marriage? A research note. *Journal of Family Issues, 23,* 1065–1087.

Manolo, E. (2002). Uses of mnemonics in educational settings: A brief review of selected research. *Psychologia, 45*(2), 69–79.

Manson, J.E., Colditz, G.A., Stampfer, M.J., Willett, W.C., Rosner, B., Monson, R.R., ... Hennekens, C.H. (1990). A prospective study of obesity and risk of coronary heart disease in women. *New England Journal of Medicine, 322,* 882–888.

Manson, S.M. (1994). Culture and depression: Discovering variations in the experience of illness. In W.J. Lonner & R.S. Malpass (Eds.), *Psychology and culture* (pp. 285–290). Boston, MA: Allyn & Bacon.

Mäntylä, T. (1986). Optimizing cue effectiveness: Recall of 500 and 600 incidentally learned words. *Journal of Experimental Psychology: Learning, Memory, and Cognition, 12,* 66–71.

Mäntylä, T., & Nilsson, L.G. (1988). Cue distinctiveness and forgetting: Effectiveness of self-generated retrieval cues in delayed recall. *Journal of Experimental Psychology: Learning, Memory, and Cognition, 14,* 502–509.

Mantzoros, C., Flier, J.S., Lesem, M.D., Brewerton, T.D., & Jimerson, D.C. (1997). Cerebrospinal fluid leptin in anorexia nervosa: Correlation with nutritional status and potential role in resistance to weight gain. *The Journal of Clinical Endocrinology and Metabolism, 82,* 1845–1851.

Maquet, P., Laureys, S., Peigneux, P., Fuchs, S., Petiau, C., Phillips, C., ... Smith, C. (2000). Experience-dependent changes in cerebral activation during human REM sleep. *Nature Neuroscience, 3,* 831–836.

Marangell, L.B. (2002). *Concise guide to psychopharmacology.* Washington, DC: American Psychiatric Publishing.

Marcia, J.E. (1966). Development and validation of ego identity status. *Journal of Personality and Social Psychology, 3,* 551–558.

Marcia, J.E. (2002). Adolescence, identity, and the Bernardone family. *Identity, 2,* 199–209.

Maredpour, A. Najafi, M., & Rafat-Mah, M. (2012). The comparison of the effectiveness of systematic desensitization, study skills and combination method in decreasing test anxiety. *Journal of Clinical Psychology, 4*(1), 55–64.

Mares, D. (2013). Climate change and levels of violence in socially disadvantaged neighborhood groups. *Journal of Urban Health, 90*(4), 768–783.

Margolin, G., & Wampold, B.E. (1981). Sequential analysis of conflict and accord in distressed and nondistressed marital partners. *Journal of Consulting and Clinical Psychology, 49,* 554–567.

Marian, V., Spivey, M., & Hirsch, J. (2003). Shared and separate systems in bilingual language processing: Converging evidence from eyetracking and brain imaging. *Brain and Language, 86,* 70–82.

Marini, Z.A., & Case, R. (1994). The development of abstract reasoning about the physical and social world. *Child Development, 65,* 147–159.

Marino, P., DePasquale, A., & Sirey, J.A. (2015). Cognitive behavior therapy with mindfulness and acceptance skills for the treatment of older adults. *Clinical Case Studies, 14*(4), 262–273.

Markey, P.M. (2000). Bystander intervention in computer mediated communication. *Computers in Human Behavior, 16,* 183–188.

Markovitz, H., & Nantel, G. (1989). The belief-bias effect in the production and evaluation of logical conclusions. *Memory and Cognition, 17,* 11–17.

Marks, I.M. (1977). Phobias and obsessions: Clinical phenomena in search of laboratory models. In J. Maser & M.E.P. Seligman (Eds.), *Psychopathology: Experimental models.* San Francisco, CA: W.H. Freeman.

Marks, I.M. (1987). *Fear, phobias, and rituals: Panic, anxiety, and their disorders.* New York, NY: Oxford University Press.

Marks, I.M. (1991). Self-administered behavioural treatment. *Behavioural Psychotherapy, 19,* 42–46.

Markus, H.R., & Kitayama, S. (1999). Culture and the self: Implications for cognition, emotion, and motivation. In R.F. Baumeister (Ed.), *The self in social psychology. Key readings in social psychology* (pp. 339–371). New York, NY: Psychology Press.

Marlatt, G.A. (1987). Alcohol, the magic elixir: Stress, expectancy, and the transformation of emotional states. In E. Gottheil, K.A. Druley, S. Pashko, & S.P. Weinstein (Eds.), *Stress and addiction.* New York, NY: Brunner/Mazel.

Marlatt, G.A. (1996). Taxonomy of high-risk situations for alcohol relapse: Evolution and development of a cognitive-behavioral model. *Addiction, 91* (Suppl.), S37–S49.

Marlatt, G.A. (Ed.). (1998). *Harm reduction: Pragmatic strategies for managing high-risk behaviors.* New York, NY: Guilford Press.

Marlatt, G.A., & Gordon, J.R. (1985). *Relapse prevention: Maintenance strategies in the treatment of addiction.* New York, NY: Guilford Press.

Marlatt, G.A., & Kaplan, B.E. (1972). Self-initiated attempts to change behavior: A study of New Year's resolutions. *Psychological Reports, 30,* 123–131.

Marlatt, G.A., & Witkiewitz, K. (2002). Harm reduction approaches to alcohol use: Health promotion, prevention, and treatment. *Addictive Behaviors, 27,* 867–886.

Marlatt, G.A., Baer, J.S., Kivlahan, D.R., Dimeff, L.A., Larimer, M.E., Quigley, L.A., ... Williams, E. (1998). Screening and brief intervention for high-risk college student drinkers: Results from a 2-year follow-up assessment. *Journal of Consulting and Clinical Psychology, 66,* 604–615.

Marsat, G., & Pollack, G.S. (2006). A behavioral role for feature detection by sensory bursts. *Journal of Neuroscience, 26,* 10542–10547.

Marschark, M., & Mayer, T.S. (1998). Interactions of language and memory in deaf children and adults. *Scandinavian Journal of Psychology, 39,* 145–148.

Marsh, H.W. (1990). A multidimensional, hierarchical model of self-concept: Theoretical and empirical justification. *Educational Psychology Review, 2,* 77–172.

Marsh, R.L., Hicks, J.L., & Landau, J.D. (1998). An investigation of everyday prospective memory. *Memory and Cognition, 26,* 633–643.

Marshall, L.H., & Magoun, H.W. (1997). *Discoveries in the human brain: Neuroscience prehistory, brain structure, and function.* New York, NY: Humana Press.

Marshall, M.A., & Brown, J.D. (2006). Trait aggressiveness and situational provocation: A test of the traits as situational sensitivities (TASS) model. *Personality and Social Psychology Bulletin, 32,* 422–458.

Marshall, N.L. (2004). The quality of early child care and children's development. *Current Directions in Psychological Science, 13,* 165–168.

Marshall, P.J., & Fox, N.A. (2000). Emotion regulation, depression, and hemispheric asymmetry. In S.L. Johnson, A.M. Hayes, T.M. Field, P.M Schneiderman, & P.M. McCabe (Eds.), *Stress, coping, and depression* (pp. 35–50). Mahwah, NJ: Erlbaum.

Marsland, A.L., Bachen, E.A., Cohen, S., Rabin, B., & Manuck, S. (2002). Stress immune reactivity and susceptibility to infectious disease. *Physiology & Behavior, 77,* 711–716.

Martell, C., Addis, M., & Dimidjian, S. (2004). Finding the action in behavioral activation: The search for empirically supported interventions and mechanisms of change. In S.C. Hayes, V.M. Follette, & M.M. Linehan (Eds.), *Mindfulness and acceptance: Expanding the cognitive-behavioral tradition* (pp. 152–167). New York, NY: Guilford Press.

Martin Surbeck, M., & Hohmann, G. (2015). Social preferences influence the short-term exchange of social grooming among male bonobos. *Animal Cognition, 18,* 573–579.

Martin, B.A. (1986). Electroconvulsive therapy: Contemporary standards of practice. *Canadian Journal of Psychiatry, 31,* 759–771.

Martin, C.L., & Ruble, D. (2004). Children's search for gender cues: Cognitive perspectives on gender development. *Current Directions in Psychological Science, 13,* 67–70.

Martin, G.L., & Pear, J. (2010). *Behavior modification.* Piscataway, NJ: Prentice Hall.

Martin, J.E., & Dubbert, P.M. (1985). Adherence in exercise. In R.I. Terjung (Ed.), *Exercise and sport sciences review* (Vol. 13). New York, NY: Macmillan.

Martin, S.J., Grimwood, P.D., & Morris, R.G.M. (2000). Synaptic plasticity and memory: An evaluation of the hypothesis. *Annual Review of Neuroscience, 23*(1), 649–711.

Martinez-Conde, S., Macknik, S.L., & Hubel, D.H. (2004). The role of fixational eye movements in visual perception. *Nature Reviews Neuroscience, 5,* 229–240.

Masataka, N. (2007). Music, evolution and language. *Developmental Science, 10,* 35–39.

Mascaro, N., & Rosen, H. (2006). The role of existential meaning as a buffer against stress. *Journal of Humanistic Psychology, 46,* 168–190.

Mascolo, M.E., & Li, J. (Eds.). (2004). *Culture and developing selves: Beyond dichotomization.* San Francisco, CA: Jossey-Bass.

Mash, E.J., & Barkley, R.A. (2003). *Child psychopathology* (2nd ed.). New York, NY: Guilford Press.

Mashour, G.A., Walker, E.E., & Martuza, R.L. (2005). Psychosurgery: Past, present, and future. *Brain Research Reviews, 48*(3), 409–419.

Maslow, A.H. (1954). *Motivation and personality.* New York, NY: Harper.

Massen, C., Vaterrodt-Plünnecke, B., Krings, L., & Hilbig, B.E. (2009). Effects of instruction on learners' ability to generate an effective pathway in the method of loci. *Memory, 17,* 724–731.

Masten, A.S., & Coatsworth, J.D. (1998). The development of competence in favorable and unfavorable environments: Lessons from research on successful children. *American Psychologist, 53,* 205–220.

Masterpasqua, F. (2009). Psychology and epigenetics. *Review of General Psychology, 13,* 194–201.

Masters, W., & Johnson, V. (1966). *Human sexual response.* London, UK: Churchill.

Masters, W.H., Johnson, V.E., & Kolodny, R.C. (1988). *Human Sexuality* (3rd ed.). Boston, MA: Little, Brown.

Matarazzo, J.D. (1980). Behavioral health and behavioral medicine: Frontiers for a new health psychology. *American Psychologist, 35,* 807–817.

Mather, G. (2006). *Foundations of perception.* Hove, UK: Psychology Press/Erlbaum.

Matson, J.L. (Ed.). (2009). *Practitioner's guide to applied behavior analysis for children with autism spectrum disorders.* New York, NY: Springer-Verlag.

Matson, J.L., & Gardner, W.I. (1991). Behavioral learning theory and current applications to severe behavior problems in persons with mental retardation. *Clinical Psychology Review, 11,* 175–183.

Matsumoto, D., & Hull, P. (1994). Cognitive development and intelligence. In D. Matsumoto (Ed.), *People: Psychology from a cultural perspective.* Pacific Grove, CA: Brooks/Cole.

Matsumoto, D., & Willingham, B. (2006). The thrill of victory and the agony of defeat: Spontaneous expressions of medal winners of the 2004 Athens Olympic Games. *Journal of Personality and Social Psychology, 91,* 568–581.

Matt, G.E., & Navarro, A.M. (1997). What meta-analyses have and have not taught us about psychotherapy effects: A review and future directions. *Clinical Psychology Review, 17,* 1–32.

Matthen, M. (2007). *Seeing, doing, and knowing: A philosophical theory of sense perception.* New York, NY: Oxford University Press.

Matthews, G., Roberts, R.D., & Zeidner, M. (2004). Seven myths about emotional intelligence. *Psychological Inquiry, 15,* 179–196.

Mattys, S.L. (2000). The perception of primary and secondary stress in English. *Perception & Psychophysics, 62,* 253–265.

Matud, M.P. (2004). Gender differences in stress and coping styles. *Personality and Individual Differences, 37,* 1401–1415.

Maurer, D., & Mondloch, C.J. (2006). *Processes of change in brain and cognitive development: Attention and performance.* New York, NY: Oxford University Press.

Maurer, D., Mondloch, C.J., & Lewis, T.L. (2007). Sleeper effects. *Developmental Science, 10,* 40–47.

Mauro, R., Sato, K., & Tucker, J. (1992). The role of appraisal in human emotions: A cross-cultural study. *Journal of Personality and Social Psychology, 62,* 301–317.

May, M. (2007). *Sensation and perception.* New York, NY: Chelsea House.

May, R. (1961). The emergence of existential psychology. In R. May (Ed.), *Existential psychology.* New York, NY: Random House.

Mayer, J.D., Roberts, R.D., & Barsade, S.G. (2008). Human abilities: Emotional intelligence. *Annual Review of Psychology, 59,* 507–536.

Mayer, J.D., Salovey, P., & Caruso, D.R. (2004). Emotional intelligence: Theory, findings, and implications. *Psychological Inquiry, 15,* 197–215.

Mayer, R.E. (2000). Intelligence and education. In R.J. Sternberg (Ed.), *Handbook of intelligence* (pp. 519–531). New York, NY: Cambridge University Press.

Mayr, U. (2009). Sticky plans: Inhibition and binding during serial-task control. *Cognitive Psychology, 59,* 123–153.

McAdams, D.P., & de St. Aubin, E. (Eds.). (1998). *Generativity and adult development: How and why we care for the next generation.* Washington, DC: American Psychological Association.

McAdams, D.T. (1992). The five-factor model in personality: A critical appraisal. *Journal of Personality and Social Psychology, 60,* 329–361.

McAdams, S., & Drake, C. (2002). Auditory perception and cognition. In H. Pashler & S. Yantis (Eds.), *Steven's handbook of experimental psychology: Vol. 1 Sensation and perception* (3rd ed., pp. 397–452). New York, NY: Wiley.

McAuley, E. (1992). The role of efficacy cognitions in the prediction of exercise behavior in middle-aged adults. *Journal of Behavioral Medicine, 15,* 65–88.

McCabe, J.A. (2015). Location, location, location! demonstrating the mnemonic benefit of the method of loci. *Teaching of Psychology, 42*(2), 169–173.

McCall, W.V., & Edinger, J.D. (1992). Subjective total insomnia: An example of sleep state misperception. *Sleep, 15,* 71–73.

McCann, R.A., Armstrong, C.M., Skopp, N.A., Edwards-Stewart, A., Smolenski, D.J., June, J.D., ... Reger, G.M. (2014). Virtual reality exposure therapy for the treatment of anxiety disorders: An evaluation of research quality. *Journal of Anxiety Disorders, 28*(6), 625–631.

McCann, U.D., Szabo, Z., Scheffel, U., Dannals, R.F., & Ricaurte, G.A. (1998). Positron emission tomographic evidence of toxic effect of MDMA ("Ecstasy") on brain serotonin neurons in human beings. *Lancet, 352,* 1433–1437.

McCarley, R.W. (1998). Dreams: Disguise of forbidden wishes or transparent reflections of a distinct brain state? In R.M. Bilder & F.F. LeFever (Eds.), *Neuroscience of the mind on the centennial of Freud's Project for a Scientific Psychology: Annals of the New York Academy of Sciences* (Vol. 843). New York, NY: New York Academy of Sciences.

McClelland, D.C. (1989). *Human motivation.* New York, NY: Cambridge University Press.

McClelland, D.C., Atkinson, J.W., Clark, R.A., & Lowell, E.L. (1953). *The achievement motive.* New York, NY: Appleton-Century-Crofts.

McClelland, J.L., & Rumelhart, D.E. (1985). Distributed memory and the representation of general and specific information. *Journal of Experimental Psychology: General, 114,* 159–188.

McClintock, M.K. (1971). Menstrual synchrony and suppression. *Nature, 229,* 244–245.

McConnell, J.V. (1962). Memory transfer through cannibalism in planarians. *Journal of Neuropsychiatry, 3* (Suppl. 1), 542–548.

McCown, D., & Reibel, D. (2010). Mindfulness and mindfulness-based stress reduction. In D.A. Monti & B.D. Beitman (Eds.), *Integrative psychiatry.* New York, NY: Oxford University Press.

McCoy, D.F., Roszman, T.L., Miller, J.S., Kelly, K.S., & Titus, M.J. (1986). Some parameters of conditioned immunosuppression. Species difference and CS-US delay. *Physiology and Behavior, 36,* 731–736.

McCrae, R.R., & Costa, P.T. (1990). *Personality in adulthood.* New York, NY: Guilford Press.

McCrae, R.R., & Costa, P.T. (2003). *Personality in adulthood: A Five-Factor Theory perspective.* New York, NY: Guilford Press.

McCrae, R.R., & Costa, P.T. (2008). The five-factor theory of personality. In O.P. John, R.W. Robins, & L.A. Pervin (Eds.), *Handbook of personality theory and research* (3rd ed.). New York, NY: Guilford Press.

McCullough, M.E., Worthington, E.L., Jr., & Rachal, K.C. (1997). Interpersonal forgiving in close relationships. *Journal of Personality and Social Psychology, 73,* 321–336.

McDaniel, M.A. (2005). Big-brained people are smarter: A meta-analysis of the relationship between in vivo brain volume and intelligence. *Intelligence, 33,* 337–346.

McDaniel, M.A., & Einstein, G.O. (1993). The importance of cue familiarity and cue distinctiveness in prospective memory. *Memory, 1,* 23–41.

McDaniel, M.A., Einstein, G.O., Stout, A.C., & Morgan, Z. (2003). Aging and maintaining intentions over delays: Do it or lose it. *Psychology and Aging, 18,* 823–835.

McDaniel, M.A., Glisky, E.L., Guynn, M.J., & Routhieaux, B.C. (1999). Prospective memory: A neuropsychological study. *Neuropsychology, 13,* 103–110.

McDermott, J.H. (2014). *Audition. The Oxford handbook of cognitive neuroscience, vol. 1: Core topics* (pp. 135–170). New York, NY: Oxford University Press.

McEvoy, S.P., Stevenson, M.R., McCartt, A.T., Woodward, M., Haworth, C., Palamara, P., & Cercarelli, R. (2005). Role of mobile phones in motor vehicle crashes resulting in hospital attendance: A case-crossover study. *BMJ: British Medical Journal, 331,* 428.

McFarlane, A. (1975). Olfaction in the development of social preferences in the human neonate. *Ciba Foundation Symposium, 33,* 103–117.

McGinnis, M. (1994). The role of behavioral research in national health policy. In S.J. Blumenthal, K. Matthews, & S.M. Weiss (Eds.), *New research frontiers in behavioral medicine: Proceedings of the national conference.* Washington, DC: NIH Publications.

McGinty, D.J., & Sterman, M.B. (1968). Sleep suppression after basal forebrain lesions in the cat. *Science, 160,* 1253–1255.

McGlaskan, T.H., & Fenton, W.S. (1992). The positive-negative distinction in schizophrenia: Review of natural history validators. *Archives of General Psychiatry, 49,* 63–72.

McGown, P.O., Sasaki, A., D'Alessio, A.C.D., Dymov, S., Labonte, B., Szyf, M., ... Meaney, M.J. (2009). Epigenetic regulation of the glucocorticoid receptor in human brain associates with childhood abuse. *Nature Neuroscience, 12,* 342–348.

McGrath, J.J. (2006). Variations in the incidence of schizophrenia: Data versus dogma. *Schizophrenia Bulletin, 32,* 195–197.

McGuffin, P., Owen, M.J., & Gottesman, I.I. (Eds.). (2005). *Psychiatric genetics and genomics.* New York, NY: Oxford University Press.

McIntosh, D.N., Silver, R.C., & Wortman, C.B. (1993). Religion's role in adjustment to a negative life event: Coping with the loss of a child. *Journal of Personality and Social Psychology, 65*, 812–821.

McIntosh, D.N., Zajonc, R.B., Vig, P.S., & Emerick, S.W. (1997). Facial movement, breathing, temperature, and affect: Implications of the vascular theory of emotional efference. *Cognition and Emotion, 11*(2), 171–195.

McKenna, P. (2007). *Schizophrenia.* Philadelphia, PA: Taylor & Francis.

McKenna, P., & Oh, T. (2003). *Formal thought disorder in schizophrenia.* New York, NY: Cambridge University Press.

McKey, R., Conndelli, L., Gansin, H., Barrett, B., McConkey, C., & Plantz, M. (1985). *The impact of Head Start on children, families and communities (Final report of the Head Start Evaluation, Synthesis and Utilization Project).* Washington, DC: CSR, Inc.

McKim, W.A. (2000). *Drugs and behavior* (4th ed.). Upper Saddle River, NJ: Prentice Hall.

McKimmie, B.M., Terry, D.J., & Hogg, M.A. (2009). Dissonance reduction in the context of group membership: The role of metaconsistency. *Group Dynamics: Theory, Research, and Practice, 13*, 103–119.

McKown, C. (2005). Applying ecological theory to advance the science and practice of school-based prejudice reduction interventions. *Educational Psychologist, 40*, 177–189.

McMurran, M., Conor, D., Christopher, G., & Huband, N. (2007). The relationship between personality disorders and social problem solving in adults. *Personality and Individual Differences, 42*, 145–155.

McNally, L. (2013). Semantics and pragmatics. *WIREs Cognitive Science, 4*(3), 285–297.

McNally, R.J., & Geraerts, E. (2009). A new solution to the recovered memory debate. *Perspectives on Psychological Science, 4*, 126–134.

McNeil, E.B. (1967). *The quiet furies: Man and disorder.* Englewood Cliffs, NJ: Prentice Hall.

McNulty, J.K., & Karney, B.R. (2004). Positive expectations in the early years of marriage: Should couples expect the best or brace for the worst? *Journal of Personality and Social Psychology, 86*, 729–743.

McVey, G.L., Tweed, S., & Blackmore, E. (2004). Dieting among preadolescent and young adolescent females. *Canadian Medical Association Journal, 170*, 1559–1561.

McVey, G.L., Tweed, S., & Blackmore, E. (2005). Correlates of dieting and muscle gaining behaviors in 10–14-year-old males and females. *Preventive Medicine, 40*, 1–9.

Meacham, J.A., & Singer, J. (1977). Incentive effects in prospective memory. *Journal of Psychology, 97*, 191–197.

Meaney, M.J. (2003). Plasticity and health: Social influences on gene expression and neural development. In F. Kessel & P.L. Rosenfield (Eds.), *Expanding the boundaries of health and social science: Case studies in interdisciplinary innovation* (pp. 147–174). London, UK: Oxford University Press.

Meaney, M.J., Aitken, D.H., Bhatnagar, S., Van Berkel, C., & Sapolsky, R.M. (1988). Postnatal handling attenuates the neuroendocrine, anatomical, and cognitive impairments related to the aged hippocampus. *Science, 238*, 766–768.

Meaney, M.J., Mitchell, J.B., Aitken, D.H., Bhatnagar, S., Bodnoff, S.R., & Sarrieau, A. (1991). The effects of neonatal handling on the development of the adrenocortical response to stress: Implications for neuropathology and cognitive deficits in later life. *Psychoneuroendocrinology, 16*, 85–103.

Mebane-Sims, I. (2009). 2009 Alzheimer's disease facts and figures. *Alzheimer's & Dementia, 5*, 234–270.

Medhus, S., Rognli, E.B., Gossop, M., Holm, B., Mørland, J., & Bramness, J. (2015). Amphetamine-induced psychosis: Transition to schizophrenia and mortality in a small prospective sample. *The American Journal on Addictions, 24*(7), 586–589.

Medieros, J.A. (2006). *Cone shape and color vision: Unification of structure and perception.* Blountsville, AL: Fifth Estate.

Meehl, P.E. (1995). "Is psychoanalysis one science, two sciences, or no science at all? A discourse among friendly antagonists": Comment. *Journal of the American Psychoanalytic Association, 43*, 1015–1023.

Meeus, W.H.J., & Raaijmakers, Q.A.W. (1986). Administrative obedience: Carrying out orders to use psychological-administrative violence. *European Journal of Social Psychology, 16*, 311–324.

Meeus, W.H.J., & Raaijmakers, Q.A.W. (1995). Obedience in modern society: The Utrecht studies. *Journal of Social Issues, 51*, 155–175.

Megargee, E.I. (1966). Undercontrolled and overcontrolled personality types in extreme antisocial aggression. *Psychological Monographs, 80* (Whole No. 611).

Meichenbaum, D. (1985). *Stress inoculation training.* New York, NY: Pergamon Press.

Meichenbaum, D. (1991). Evolution of cognitive behavior therapy: Origins, tenets and clinical examples. In J. Zeig (Ed.), *The evolution of psychotherapy, II* (pp. 114–121). New York, NY: Brunner/Mazel.

Meilman, P.W. (1979). Cross-sectional age changes in ego identity status during adolescence. *Developmental Psychology, 15*, 230–231.

Meleski, M.E., & Damato, E.G. (2003). HIV exposure: Neonatal considerations. *Journal of Obstetric, Gynecologic, and Neonatal Nursing, 32*, 109–116.

Meltzoff, A.N., & Moore, M.K. (1977). Imitation of facial and manual gestures by human neonates. *Science, 198*, 75–78.

Meltzoff, A.N., & Moore, M.K. (2000). Resolving the debate about early imitation. In D. Muir & A. Slater (Eds.), *Infant Development: The Essential Readings.* (pp. 176–181). Oxford, UK: Blackwell.

Melzack, R., & Wall, P.D. (1982). *The challenge of pain.* New York, NY: Basic Books.

Menary, K., Collins, P.F., Porter, J.N., Muetzel, R., Olson, E.A., Kumar, V., ... Luciana, M. (2013). Associations between cortical thickness and general intelligence in children, adolescents and young adults. *Intelligence, 41*(5), 597–606.

Mendel, R., Traut-Mattausch, E., Jonas, E., Leucht, S., Kane, J.M., Maino, K., Kissling, W., & Hamann, J. (2011). Confirmation bias: Why psychiatrists stick to wrong preliminary diagnoses. *Psychological Medicine, 41*, 2651–2659.

Menon, D.K., Owen, A.M., Williams, E., Minhas, P.S., Allen, C.M.C., Boniface, S., & Pickard, J.D. (1998). Cortical processing in the persistent vegetative state. *Lancet, 352*(9123), 200.

Menon, U., & Schweder, R.A. (1994). Cultural psychology and the power of shame in Orissa, India. In S. Kitayama & H. Markus (Eds.), *Emotion and culture.* Washington, DC: American Psychological Association.

Mental Health Commission of Canada. (2013). *Housing and homelessness.* Retrieved on November 22, 2013, from http://www.mentalhealthcommission.ca/.

Menzies, R.G., & Clarke, J.C. (1995). The etiology of acrophobia and its relationship to severity and individual response patterns. *Behaviour Research and Therapy, 33*, 795–803.

Meredith, N. (1986). Testing the talking cure. *Science, 232*, 31–37.

Merikle, P.M., & Daneman, M. (1998). Psychological investigations of unconscious perception. *Journal of Consciousness Studies, 5*, 5–18.

Merikle, P.M., & Skanes, H.E. (1992). Subliminal self-help audiotapes: A search for placebo effects. *Journal of Applied Psychology, 77*, 772–776.

Merikle, P.M., Smilek, D., & Eastwood, J.D. (2001). Perception without awareness: Perspectives from cognitive psychology. *Cognition, 79*, 115–134.

Merrill, E.C., & Lookadoo, R. (2004). Selective search for conjunctively defined targets by children and young adults. *Journal of Experimental Child Psychology, 89*, 72–90.

Mersch, P.P.A., Middendorp, H.M., Bouhuys, A.L., Beersma, D.G.M., & van den Hoofdakker, R.H. (1999). Seasonal affective disorder and latitude: A review of the literature. *Journal of Affective Disorders, 53*, 35–48.

Mersky, J., & Topitzes, J. (2009). Comparing early adult outcomes of maltreated and non-maltreated children: A prospective longitudinal investigation. *Children and Youth Services Review.* Advance online publication. doi: 10.1016/j.childyouth.2009.10.018.

Merz, C.J., Tabbert, K., Schweckendiek, J., Klucken, T., Vaitl, D., Stark, R., & Wolf, O.T. (2010). Investigating the impact of sex and cortisol on implicit fear conditioning with fMRI. *Psychoneuroendocrinology, 35*, 33–46.

Mesquita, B., & Markus, H.R. (2005). Culture and emotion: Models of agency as sources of cultural variation in emotion. In A.S.R. Manstead, N.H. Frijda, A.H. Fischer, & K. Oatley (Eds.), *Feelings and emotions: The Amsterdam Symposium.* New York, NY: Cambridge University Press.

Mesquita, B., Frijda, N.H., & Scherer, K.R. (1997). Culture and emotion. In J.W. Berry, P.R. Dasen, & T.S. Saraswathi (Eds.), *Handbook of cross-cultural psychology: Vol. 2 Basic processes and human development* (2nd ed., pp. 255–298). Boston, MA: Allyn & Bacon.

Messenger, J.C. (1971). Sex and repression in an Irish folk community. In D.S. Marshall & R.C. Suggs (Eds.), *Human sexual behavior.* Englewood Cliffs, NJ: Prentice Hall.

Messner, M., Reinhard, M., & Sporer, S.L. (2008). Compliance through direct persuasive appeals: The moderating role of communicator's attractiveness in interpersonal persuasion. *Social Influence, 3*, 67–83.

Messner, S.F. (1982). Societal development, social equality, and homicide: A cross-national test of a Durkheimian model. *Social Forces, 61*, 225–240.

Metcalfe, J., & Mischel, W. (1999). A hot/cool-system analysis of delay of gratification: Dynamics of willpower. *Psychological Review, 106*, 3–19.

Meyer, C.B., & Taylor, S.E. (1986). Adjustment to rape. *Journal of Personality and Social Psychology, 50*, 1226–1234.

Meyer, J.H., Houle, S., Sagrati, S., Carella, A., Hussey, D.F., Ginovart, N., ... Wilson, A.A. (2004). Brain serotonin transporter binding potential measured with carbon 11-labeled DASB positron emission tomgraphy: Effects of major depressive episodes and severity of dysfuntional attuties. *Archives of General Psychiatry, 61,* 1271–1279.

Meyer, T.A., Svirsky, M.A., Kirk, K.I., & Miyamoto, R.T. (1998). Improvements in speech perception by children with profound prelingual hearing loss: Effects of device, communication mode, and chronological age. *Journal of Speech, Language, and Hearing Research, 41,* 846–858.

Mezulis, A.H., Hyde, J.S., & Abramson, L.Y. (2006). The developmental origins of cognitive vulnerability to depression: Temperament, parenting, and negative life events in childhood as contributors to negative cognitive style. *Developmental Psychology, 42,* 1012–1025.

Michael, R.T., Gagnon, J.H., Laumman, E.O., & Kolata, G. (1994). *Sex in America: A definitive survey.* Boston, MA: Little, Brown.

Michaels, J.W., Blommel, J.M., Brocato, R.M., Linkous, R.A., & Rowe, J.S. (1982). Social facilitation and inhibition in a natural setting. *Replications in Social Psychology, 2,* 21–24.

Mignot, E. (1998). Genetic and familial aspects of narcolepsy. *Neurology, 50,* S16–S22.

Miklowitz, D.J., & Johnson, S.L. (2007). Mood disorders: Bipolar disorders. In M. Hersen, S.M. Turner, & D.C. Beidel (Eds.), *Adult psychopathology and diagnosis* (pp. 317–348). Hoboken, NJ: Wiley.

Mikulincer, M., & Shaver, P.R. (2009). Attachment theory: II. Development, psychodynamic, and optimal-functioning aspects. In P.J. Corr & G. Matthews (Eds.), *The Cambridge handbook of personality psychology.* Cambridge, UK: Cambridge University Press.

Miles, C., & Hardman, E. (1998). State dependent memory produced by aerobic exercise. *Ergonomics, 41,* 20–28.

Miles, H.L., Mitchell, R.W., & Harper, S.E. (1996). Simon says: The development of imitation in an enculturated orangutan. In A.E. Russon, K.A. Bard, & A. Kim (Eds.), *Reaching into thought: The minds of the great apes* (pp. 278–299). Cambridge, UK: Cambridge University Press.

Milgram, S. (1974). *Obedience to authority: An experimental view.* New York, NY: Harper & Row.

Millar, M.G., & Millar, K.U. (1996). The effects of direct and indirect experience on affective and cognitive responses and the attitude-behavior relation. *Journal of Experimental Social Psychology, 32,* 561–579.

Miller, A.G. (1986). *The obedience experiments: A case study of controversy in social science.* New York, NY: Praeger.

Miller, B.C., Fan, X., Christensen, M., Grotevant, H.D., & van Dulmen, M. (2000). Comparisons of adopted and nonadopted adolescents in a large, nationally representative sample. *Child Development, 71,* 1458–1473.

Miller, C.T., & Downey, K.T. (1999). A meta-analysis of heavyweight and self-esteem. *Personality and Social Psychology Review, 3,* 68–84.

Miller, G.A. (1956). The magical number seven, plus or minus two: Some limits on our capacity for processing information. *Psychological Review, 63,* 81–97.

Miller, G.E., Chen, E., & Zhou, E.E. (2007). If it goes up, must it come down? Chronic stress and the hypothalamic-pituitary-adrenocortical axis in humans. *Psychological Bulletin, 133,* 25–45.

Miller, J.D., Morin, L.P., Schwartz, W.J., & Moore, R.Y. (1996). New insights into the mammalian

circadian clock: State of the art review. *Sleep, 19,* 641–667.

Miller, J.G. (1984). Culture and the development of everyday social explanation. *Journal of Personality and Social Psychology, 46,* 961–978.

Miller, J.G., Bersoff, D.M., & Harwood, R.L. (1990). Perceptions of social responsibility in India and in the United States: Moral imperatives or personal decisions? *Journal of Personality and Social Psychology, 58,* 33–47.

Miller, J.L., Weiss, L.G., Beal, A.L., Saklofske, D.H., Zhu, J., & Holdnack, J.A. (2015). Intelligent use of intelligence tests: Empirical and clinical support for Canadian WAIS–IV norms. *Journal of Psychoeducational Assessment, 33*(4), 312–328.

Miller, K.F., & Stigler, J.F. (1987). Counting in Chinese: Cultural variation in a basic cognitive skill. *Cognitive Development, 2,* 279–305.

Miller, K.F., Kelly, M., & Zhou, X. (2005). Learning mathematics in China and the United States: Cross-cultural insights into the nature and course of preschool mathematical development. In J.I.D. Campbell (Ed.), *Handbook of mathematical cognition* (pp. 163–177). New York, NY: Psychology Press.

Miller, K.J., Gleaves, D.H., Hirsch, T.G., Green, B.A., Snow, A.C., & Corbett, C.C. (2000). Comparisons of body image dimensions by race/ethnicity and gender in a university population. *International Journal of Eating Disorders, 27,* 310–316.

Miller, L., & Budd, J. (1999). The development of occupational sex-role stereotypes, occupational preferences and academic subject preferences in children at ages 8, 12, and 16. *Educational Psychology, 19,* 17–35.

Miller, N.E. (1944). Experimental studies of conflict. In J. McV Hunt (Ed.), *Personality and the behavior disorders* (Vol. 1, pp. 431–465). New York, NY: Ronald Press.

Miller, N.S. (1997). Clinical approach to diagnosis of comorbid addictive and psychiatric disorders. *Psychiatric Rehabilitation Skills, 2,* 77–90.

Miller, S.D., Blackburn, T., Scholes, G., White, G.L., & Mamales, N. (1991). Optical differences in multiple personality disorder: A second look. *Journal of Nervous and Mental Disease, 179,* 132–135.

Miller, S.L., Zielaskowski, K., & Plant, A. (2012). The basis of shooter bias: Beyond cultural stereotypes. *Personality and Social Psychology Bulletin, 38*(10), 1358–1356.

Miller, T.Q. (2000). Type A behavior. In G. Fink (Ed.), *Encyclopedia of stress.* San Diego, CA: Academic Press.

Miller, T.W., & Leukefeld, C. (1995). Multinational efforts in substance abuse prevention. *Journal of Contemporary Psychotherapy, 25,* 243–252.

Miller, W.R., & Rollnick, S. (2002). *Motivational interviewing* (2nd ed.). New York, NY: Guilford Press.

Miller, W.R., & Rose, G.S. (2009). Toward a theory of motivational interviewing. *American Psychologist, 64,* 527–537.

Milligan, C.E., & Schwartz, L.M. (1997). Programmed cell death during animal development. *British Medical Bulletin, 53,* 570–590.

Milling, L.S. (2008). Recent developments in the study of hypnotic pain reduction: A new golden era of research? *Contemporary Hypnosis, 25,* 165–177.

Millon, T., & Davis, R. (2000). *Personality disorders in modern life.* New York, NY: Wiley.

Millon, T., Millon, C.M., Meagher, D., Meagher, S., Grossman, S., & Ramnath, R. (2004). *Personality

disorders in modern life* (2nd ed.). New York, NY: Wiley.

Milner, B. (1965). Memory disturbances after bilateral hippocampal lesions. In P. Milner & S. Glickman (Eds.), *Cognitive processes and the brain.* Princeton, NJ: D. Van Nostrand.

Milner, B., Petrides, M., & Smith, M.L. (1985). Frontal lobes and the temporal organization of memory. *Human Neurobiology, 4,* 137–142.

Milrod, B., Busch, F., Cooper, A., & Shapiro, T. (1997). *Manual of panic-focused psychodynamic psychotherapy.* Washington, DC: American Psychiatric Press.

Miltenberger, R.G. (2016). *Behavior modification: Principles and procedures* (6th ed.) Boston, MA: Cengage Learning.

Milton, J., & Wiseman, R. (1999). Does psi exist? Lack of replication of an anomalous process of information transfer. *Psychological Bulletin, 125,* 387–391.

Milton, J., & Wiseman, R. (2001). Does psi exist? Reply to Storm and Ertel. *Psychological Bulletin, 127,* 434–438.

Milyavskaya, M.G., Gingras, I., Mageau, G.A., Koestner, R., Gagnon, H., Fang, J., & Boiche, J. (2009). Balance across contexts: Importance of balanced need satisfaction across various life domains. *Personality and Social Psychology Bulletin, 35,* 1031–1045.

Mineka, S., Watson, D., & Clark, L.A. (1998). Comorbidity of anxiety and unipolar mood disorder. *Annual Review of Psychology, 49,* 377–412.

Mineka, S., & Zinbarg, R. (1998). Experimental approaches to the anxiety and mood disorders. In J.G. Adair, D. Belanger, & K.L. Dion (Eds.), *Advances in psychological science, Vol. 1: Social, personal, and cultural aspects* (pp. 429–454). Hove, UK: Psychology Press/Erlbaum.

Mineka, S., & Zinbarg, R. (2006). A contemporary learning theory perspective on the etiology of anxiety disorders: It's not what you thought it was. *American Psychologist, 61*(1), 10–26.

Mioranzza, S., Nunes, F., Marques, D.M., Fioreze, G.T., Rocha, A.S., Botton, P.H.S., & Porciúncula, L.O. (2014). Prenatal caffeine intake differently affects synaptic proteins during fetal brain development. *International Journal of Developmental Neuroscience, 36,* 45–52.

Miranda, R. Jr., Meyerson, L.A., Long, P.J., Marx, B.P., & Simpson, S.M.. (2002). Sexual assault and alcohol use: Exploring the self-medication hypothesis. *Violence and Victims, 17,* 205–217.

Mischel, W. (1973). Toward a cognitive social learning reconceptualization of personality. *Psychological Review, 80,* 252–283.

Mischel, W. (1984). Convergences and challenges in the search for consistency. *American Psychologist, 39,* 351–364.

Mischel, W. (1999). Personality coherence and dispositions in a cognitive-affective personality system (CAPS) approach. In D. Cervone & Y. Shoda, (Eds.), *The coherence of personality: Social cognitive bases of consistency, variability, and organization* (pp. 37–66). New York, NY: Guilford Press.

Mischel, W. (2004). Toward an integrated science of the person. *Annual Review of Psychology, 55,* 1–22.

Mischel, W., Ebbesen, E.B., & Raskoff, Z.A. (1972). Cognitive and attentional mechanisms in delay of gratification. *Journal of Personality and Social Psychology, 21,* 204–218.

Mischel, W., & Shoda, Y. (1998). Reconciling processing dynamics and personality dispositions. *Annual Review of Psychology, 49,* 229–258.

Mischel, W., & Shoda, Y. (1999). Integrating dispositions and personality dynamics within a unified theory of personality: The cognitive-affective personality system (CAPS). In L.A. Pervin & O.P. John (Eds.), *Handbook of personality: Theory and research* (2nd ed.). New York, NY: Guilford Press.

Mischel, W., Shoda, Y., & Rodriguez, M.L. (1989). Delay of gratification in children. *Science, 244,* 933–938.

Mischel, W., Shoda, Y., & Smith, R.E. (2004). *Introduction to personality: Toward an integration.* New York, NY: Wiley.

Mishne, J. (2002). *Multiculturalism and the therapeutic process.* New York, NY: Guilford.

Mitchell, J.B., & Gratton, A. (1991). Opioid modulation and sensitization of dopamine release elicited by sexually relevant stimuli: A high speed chronoamperometric study in freely behaving rats. *Brain Research, 551,* 20–27.

Moayedi, M., & Davis, K.D. (2013). Theories of pain: From specificity to gate control. *Journal of Neurophysiology, 109*(1), 5–12.

Moe, A., & De Benji, R. (2005). Stressing the efficacy of the loci method. Oral presentation and the subject-generation of the loci pathway with expository passages. *Applied Cognitive Psychology, 19*(1), 95–106.

Moen, P., Kim, J.E., & Hofmeister, H. (2001). Couples' work/retirement transitions, gender, and marital quality. *Social Psychology Quarterly, 64,* 55–71.

Moffitt, T., Caspi, A., & Rutter, M. (2006). Measured gene-environment interactions in psychopathology: Concepts, research strategies, and implications for research, intervention, and public understanding of genetics. *Perspectives on Psychological Science, 1,* 5–27.

Molenberghs, P., Cunnington, R., & Mattingley, J. (2009). Is the mirror neuron system involved in imitation? A short review and meta-analysis. *Neuroscience & Biobehavioral Reviews, 33*(1), 975–980.

Molfese, D.L., & Molfese, V.J. (2002). *Developmental variations in learning: Applications to social, executive function, language, and reading skills.* Mahwah, NJ: Erlbaum.

Möller, I., & Krahé, B. (2009). Exposure to violent video games and aggression in German adolescents: A longitudinal analysis. *Aggressive Behavior, 35,* 75–89.

Monahan, J.L., Murphy, S.T., & Zajonc, R.B. (2000). Subliminal mere exposure: Specific, general, and diffuse effects. *Psychological Science, 11,* 462–466.

Money, J. (1987). Sin, sickness or status. *American Psychologist, 42,* 384–399.

Monk, T.H., Folkard, S., & Wedderburn, A.I. (1996). Maintaining safety and high performance on shiftwork. *Applied Ergonomics, 27,* 17–23.

Montgomery, H., Lipshitz, R., & Brehmer, B. (Eds.). (2005). *How professionals make decisions.* Mahwah, NJ: Erlbaum.

Monti, M.M., Vanhaudenhuyse, A., Coleman, M.R., Boly, M., Pickard, J.D., Tshibanda, L., Owen, A.M., & Laureys, S. (2010). Willful modulation of brain activity in disorders of consciousness. *New England Journal of Medicine, 362,* 579–589.

Monti-Bloch, L., & Grosser, B.I. (1991). Effect of putative pheromones on the electrical activity of the human vomeronasal organ and olfactory epithelium. *Journal of Steroid Biochemistry and Molecular Biology, 39,* 573–582.

Moore, K.A., Guzman, L., Hair, E., Lippman, L., & Garrett, S. (2004). Parent-teen relationships and interactions: Far more positive than not. *Child Trends Research Brief,* publication no. 2004–25. Retrieved February 20, 2007, from http://www .childtrends.org/Files/Parent_TeenRB.pdf.

Moore, T.M., Scarpa, A., & Raine, A. (2002). A meta-analysis of serotonin metabolite 5 HIAA and antisocial behavior. *Aggressive Behavior, 28,* 299–316.

Moorhead, G., Ference, R., & Neck, C.P. (1991). Group decision fiascoes continue: Space shuttle Challenger and a revised groupthink framework. *Human Relations, 44,* 539–550.

Moos, R.H., & Moos, B.S. (2006). Rates and predictors of relapse after natural and treated remission from alcohol use disorders. *Addiction, 101,* 212–222.

Moran, J.M., Jolly, E., & Mitchell, J.P. (2014). Spontaneous mentalizing predicts the fundamental attribution error. *Journal of Cognitive Neuroscience, 26*(3), 569–576.

Moreland, J.L., Dansereau, D.F., & Chmielewski, T.L. (1997). Recall of descriptive information: The roles of presentation format, annotation strategy, and individual differences. *Contemporary Educational Psychology, 22,* 521–533.

Morewedge, C.K., & Norton, M.I. (2009). When dreaming is believing: The (motivated) interpretation of dreams. *Journal of Personality and Social Psychology, 96,* 249–264.

Morford, J.P. (2003). Grammatical development in adolescent first-language learners. *Linguistics, 41,* 681–721.

Morgan, C., & Fisher, H. (2007). Environment and schizophrenia: Environmental factors in schizophrenia: Childhood trauma—a critical review. *Schizophrenia Bulletin, 33*(1), 3–10.

Morgan, O., Vicente, J., Griffiths, P., & Hickman, M. (2008). Trends in overdose deaths from drug misuse in Europe: What do the data tell us? *Addiction, 103,* 699–700.

Morgan, W. (1997). *Physical activity and mental health.* Philadelphia, PA: Taylor & Francis.

Morgenstern, J., Labouvie, E., McCrady, B.S., Kahler, C.W., & Frey, R.M. (1997). Affiliation with Alcoholics Anonymous after treatment: A study of therapeutic effects and mechanisms of action. *Journal of Consulting and Clinical Psychology, 65,* 768–777.

Mori, D., Chaiken, S., & Pliner, P. (1987). "Eating lightly" and the self-presentation of femininity. *Journal of Personality and Social Psychology, 53,* 693–702.

Morrell, M.J., Dixen, J.M., Carter, C.S., & Davidson, J.M. (1984). The influence of age and cycling status on sexual arousability in women. *American Journal of Obstetrics and Gynecology, 148,* 66–71.

Morris, D., Collett, P., Marsh, P., & O'Shaughnessy, M. (1979). *Gestures.* New York, NY: Stein & Day.

Morris, M.K., Laney, C., Bernstein, D.M., & Loftus, E.F. (2006). Susceptibility to memory distortion: How do we decide it has occurred? *American Journal of Psychology, 119,* 255–274.

Morris, J.S., Büchel, C., & Dolan, R.J. (2001). Parallel neural responses in amygdala subregions and sensory cortex during implicit fear conditioning. *NeuroImage, 1,* 1044–1052.

Morris, J.S., Oehman, A., & Dolan, R.J. (1998). Conscious and unconscious emotional learning in the human amygdala. *Nature, 393,* 467–470.

Morris, R., & Becker, J. (2005). *Cognitive neuropsychology of Alzheimer's disease.* New York, NY: Oxford University Press.

Morris, R.G., Garrud, P., Rawlins, J.N., & O'Keefe, J. (1982). Place navigation impaired in rats with hippocampal lesions. *Nature, 297,* 681–683.

Morrison, D.C. (1988). Marine mammals join the navy. *Science, 242,* 1503–1504.

Morrison, S. (2006). *Hypothalamus: Brainstem interactions in homeostasis.* New York, NY: Springer.

Morrongiello, B.A., Fenwick, K.D., & Chance, G. (1998). Crossmodal learning in newborn infants: Inferences about properties of auditory-visual events. *Infant Behavior & Development, 21,* 543–553.

Moscovici, S. (1985). Social influence and conformity. In G. Lindzey & E. Aronson (Eds.), *Handbook of social psychology* (3rd ed.). New York, NY: Random House.

Moskowitz, A., Stein, J.A., & Lightfoot, M. (2013). The mediating roles of stress and maladaptive behaviors on self-harm and suicide attempts among runaway and homeless youth. *Journal of Youth and Adolescence, 42,* 1015–1027.

Moss, C.S. (1972). *Recovery with aphasia.* Urbana, IL: University of Illinois Press.

Mousikou, P., Coltheart, M., Saunders, S., & Yen, L. (2010). Is the orthographic/phonological onset a single unit in reading aloud? *Journal of Experimental Psychology: Human Perception and Performance, 36,* 175–194.

Mowrer, O.H. (1947). On the dual nature of learning: A reinterpretation of "conditioning" and "problem solving." *Harvard Educational Review, 17,* 102–150.

Muchinsky, P.M. (2000). *Psychology applied to work* (6th ed.). Pacific Grove, CA: Brooks/Cole.

Muehlenkamp, J.J. (2005). Self-injurious behavior as a separate clinical syndrome. *American Journal of Orthopsychiatry, 75,* 324–333.

Mueller, U., Zelazo, P.D., Leone, T., & Hood, S. (2004). Interference control in a new rule use task: Age-related changes, labeling, and attention. *Child Development, 75,* 1594–1609.

Muir, D., & Hains, S. (2004). The U-shaped developmental function for auditory localization. *Journal of Cognition and Development, 1,* 123–130.

Muir, D., Humphrey, D., & Humphrey, G.K. (1994). Patterns and space perception in young infants. *Spatial Vision, 8,* 141–165.

Muir, D., & Slater, A. (2004). The scope and methods of developmental psychology. In A. Slater & G. Bremner (Eds.), *Developmental Psychology: An introduction.* Oxford, UK: Blackwell.

Muir, D.W., & Mitchell, D.E. (1975). Behavioural deficits in cats following early selective visual exposure to contours of a single orientation. *Brain Research, 85,* 459–477.

Müller, U., & Carpendale, J.I.M. (2011). Reevaluation of Piaget's concept of egocentrism: New perspectives on a misunderstood idea. *New Ideas in Psychology, 29,* 325–326.

Mulligan, N.W., & Dew, I.T.Z. (2009). Generation and perceptual implicit memory: Different generation tasks produce different effects on perceptual priming. *Memory and Cognition, 35,* 1522–1538.

Mumme, D.L., Fernald, A., & Herrera, C. (1996). Infants' responses to facial and vocal emotional signals in a social referencing paradigm. *Child Development, 67,* 3229–3237.

Munafo, M.R. (2009). Behavioral genetics: From variance to DNA. In P.J. Corr & G. Matthews (Eds.), *The Cambridge handbook of personality psychology* (pp. 287–305). Cambridge, UK: Cambridge University Press.

Munoz, R.F., Mrazek, P.J., & Haggerty, R.J. (1996). Institute of Medicine Report on Prevention of Mental Disorders: Summary and commentary. *American Psychologist, 51,* 1116–1122.

Murphy, J.M., Gatto, G.J., Waller, M.B., McBride, W.J., Lumeng, L., & Li, T.K. (1986). Effects of scheduled access on ethanol intake by the alcohol-preferring (P) line of rats. *Alcohol, 3,* 331–336.

Murphy, S.L. (2000). Deaths: Final data for 1998. *National Vital Statistics Reports* (NCHS), *26,* 73.

Murray, C. (1998). *Income, inequality, and IQ.* Washington, DC: American Enterprise Institute.

Murray, H.A. (1971). *Thematic apperception test.* Cambridge, MA: Harvard University Press.

Murray, R., Jones, P.B., Susser, E., van Os, J., & Cannon, M. (2003). *The epidemiology of schizophrenia.* New York, NY: Cambridge University Press.

Murthy, P., Kudlur, S., George, S., & Mathew, G. (2009). A clinical overview of fetal alcohol syndrome. *Addictive Disorders & Their Treatment, 8,* 1–12.

Muscatell, K.A., Eisenberger, N.I., Dutcher, J.M., Cole, S.W., & Bower, J.E. (2016). Links between inflammation, amygdala reactivity, and social support in breast cancer survivors. *Brain, Behavior, and Immunity, 53,* 34–38.

Musella, D.P. (2005). Gallup poll shows that Americans' belief in the paranormal persists. *The Skeptical Inquirer, 29,* 5.

Musicek, F.E., & Baran, J. (2006). *The auditory system: Anatomy, physiology, and clinical correlates.* Boston, MA: Allyn & Bacon.

Myers, B., Myers, J., Herndon, P., Broszkiewicz, N., & Tar, M. (2015). Beliefs about therapist suggestiveness and memory veracity in recovered-memory therapy: An analogue study. *Professional Psychology: Research and Practice, 46*(4), 270–276.

Myin-Germeys, I., van Os, J., Schwartz, J.E., Stone, A.A., & Delespaul, P.A. (2001). Emotional reactivity to daily life stress in psychosis. *Archives of General Psychiatry, 58,* 1137–1144.

Na, E.Y., & Loftus, E.F. (1998). Attitudes toward law and prisoners, conservative authoritarianism, attribution, and internal-external locus of control: Korean and American law students and undergraduates. *Journal of Cross Cultural Psychology, 29,* 595–615.

Naci, L., Cusack, R., Jia, V.Z., & Owen, A.M. (2013). The brain's silent messenger: Using selective attention to decode human thought for brain-based communication. *Journal of Neuroscience, 33*(22), 9385–9393.

Nadelson, C.C., & Reinburg, C.E. (Eds.). (1999). *Schizophrenia: Losing touch with reality.* Broomall, UK: Chelsea House.

Nadler, A., & Ben-Slushan, D. (1989). Forty years later: Long-term consequences of massive traumatization as manifested by Holocaust survivors from the city and the Kibbutz. *Journal of Consulting and Clinical Psychology, 57,* 287–293.

Naglieri, J.A. (2015). Hundred years of intelligence testing: Moving from traditional IQ to second-generation intelligence tests. *Handbook of intelligence: Evolutionary theory, historical perspective, and current concepts* (pp. 295–316). New York, NY: Springer Science + Business Media.

Nakayama, K., & Tyler, C.W. (1981). Psychophysical isolation of movement sensitivity by removal of familiar position cues. *Vision Research, 21,* 427–433.

Narrow, W.E., Rae, D.S., Robins, L.N., & Regier, D.A. (2002). Revised prevalence based estimates of mental disorders in the United States: Using a clinical significance criterion to reconcile 2 surveys' estimates. *Archives of General Psychiatry, 59,* 115–123.

Nathan, P.E., & Langenbucher, J.W. (1999). Psychopathology: Description and classification. *Annual Review of Psychology, 50,* 79–107.

National Center for Health Statistics. (2008). *Health, United States 2008.* Hyattsville, MD: Author.

National Center for Health Statistics. (2009). *Health in America, 2008.* Hyattsville, MD: Author.

National Center on Addiction and Drug Abuse. (2005). *National survey of American attitudes on substance abuse X: Teens and parents.* Retrieved March 4, 2007, from http://www.casacolumbia.org/Absolutenm/articlefiles/Teen_Survey_Report_2005.pdf.

National Highway Traffic Safety Administration. (2000). *Traffic Safety Facts 1998: Alcohol* (DOT HS 808 950). Retrieved from http://www.nhtsa.dot.gov/people/ncsa/factsheet.html.

National Institute of Mental Health. (1992). *Psychiatric hospitalization in the United States.* Rockville, MD: Author.

National Institute of Mental Health. (2008). The numbers count: Mental disorders in America. Retrieved November 19, 2009, from http://www.nimh.nih.gov/health/publications/the-numberscount-mental-disorders-in-america/index.shtml.

National Institute of Mental Health. (2009). Suicide in the U.S.: Statistics and prevention. Retrieved February 22, 2010, from http://www.nimh.gov/health/publications/suicide-in-the-us-statistics-and-prevention/index/shtml.

National Institutes of Health. (2002). *Alzheimer's disease: Unraveling the mystery.* NIH Publication 02-3782. Bethesda, MD. Retrieved from http://www.alzheimers.org/unraveling/unraveling.pdf.

National Institutes of Health. (2010). Human Genome Project Information. Retrieved from http://www.nlm.nih.gov/medlineplus/genetictesting.html.

National Safety Council. (1992). *Blood alcohol level and risk of having an automobile accident.* Washington, DC: Author.

National Sleep Foundation. (2000). *2000 omnibus sleep in America poll.* Retrieved from http://www.sleepfoundation.org/publications/2000poll.html#9.

National Sleep Foundation. (2016). Retrieved from https://sleepfoundation.org/sleep-tools-tips/healthy-sleep-tips.

National Task Force on the Prevention and Treatment of Obesity. (1994). Weight cycling. *Journal of the American Medical Association, 272,* 1196–1202.

National television violence study (Vol. 3). (1998). Thousand Oaks, CA: Sage/Author.

National Transportation Safety Board. (1979, June). *Aircraft accident report* (NTSB-AAR-79- 7). Washington, DC: NTSB Bureau of Accident Investigations.

National Weight Control Registry. (2000). Retrieved from http://www.uchsc.edu/nutrition/nwcr.htm.

Natsoulas, T. (1999). An ecological and phenomenological perspective on consciousness and perception: Contact with the world at the very heart of the being of consciousness. *Review of General Psychology, 3,* 224–245.

Naumann, P.P., Vazire, S., Rentfrow, P.J., & Gosling, S.D. (2009). Personality judgments based on physical appearance. *Personality and Social Psychology Bulletin, 35,* 1661–1671.

Naveh, B.M., & Jonides, J. (1984). Cognitive load and maintenance rehearsal. *Journal of Verbal Learning and Verbal Behavior, 23,* 494–507.

Nederkoorn, C., Smulders, F.T.Y., & Jansen, A. (2000). Cephalic phase responses, craving and food intake in normal subjects. *Appetite, 35,* 45–55.

Needham, A., Barrett, T., & Peterman, K. (2002). A pick-me-up for infants' exploratory skills: Early simulated experiences reaching for objects using "sticky" mittens enhances young infants' object exploration skills. *Infant Behavior and Development, 25,* 279–295.

Neisser, U. (1967). *Cognitive psychology.* New York, NY: Appleton-Century-Crofts.

Neisser, U., Bouchard, T.J., Jr., Boykin, A.W., Brody, N., Ceci, S.J., Halpern, D.F., ... Urbina, S. (1998). Intelligence: Knowns and unknowns. In M.E. Hertzig & E.A. Farber (Eds.), *Annual progress in child psychiatry and child development: 1997* (pp. 95–134). Bristol, PA: Brunner/Mazel.

Neisser, U., & Harsch, N. (1993). Phantom flashbulbs: False recollections of hearing the news about Challenger. In E. Winograd & U. Neisser (Eds.), *Affect and accuracy in recall: Studies of "flashbulb" memories.* New York, NY: Cambridge University Press.

Nelson, C.A., Monk, C.S., Lin, J., Carver, L.J., Thomas, K.M., & Truwit, C.L. (2000). Functional neuroanatomy of spatial working memory in children. *Developmental Psychology, 36,* 109–116.

Nelson, T.D. (2013). The neurobiology of stereotyping and prejudice. In D.D. Franks & J.H. Turner (Eds.), *Handbook of Neurosociology.* New York, NY: Springer.

Neumäker, K.J. (2000). Mortality rates and causes of death. *European Eating Disorders Review, 8,* 181–187.

Neuschatz, J.S., Lawson, D.S., Swanner, J.K., Meissner, C.A., & Neuschatz, J.S. (2008). The effects of accomplice witnesses and jailhouse informants on jury decision making. *Law and Human Behavior, 32,* 137–149.

New York Times. (1986, March 18). C12.

New York Times. (1987, October 13). C11.

Newcomb, M.D., & Harlow, L.L. (1986). Life events and substance use among adolescents: Mediating effects of perceived loss of control and meaninglessness in life. *Journal of Personality and Social Psychology, 51,* 564–577.

Newcombe, N.S., & Uttal, D.H. (2006). Whorf versus Socrates, round 10. *Trends in Cognitive Sciences, 10,* 394–396.

Newell, A., & Simon, H.A. (1972). *Human problem solving.* Englewood Cliffs, NJ: Prentice Hall.

Newlin, D.B., & Thomson, J.B. (1997). Alcohol challenge with sons of alcoholics: A critical review and analysis. In G.A. Marlatt & G.R. VandenBos (Eds.), *Addictive behaviors: Readings on etiology, prevention and treatment.* Washington, DC: American Psychological Association.

Newman, D.L., Caspi, A., Moffitt, T.E., & Silva, P.A. (1997). Antecedents of adult interpersonal functioning: Effects of individual differences in age 3 temperament. *Developmental Psychology, 33,* 206–217.

Newmark, C.S. (2005). *Major psychological assessment instruments.* Austin, TX: PRO-ED.

Newson, R.S., & Kemps, E.B. (2006). Cardiorespiratory fitness as a predictor of successful cognitive ageing. *Journal of Clinical and Experimental Neuropsychology, 28,* 949–967.

Nezami, E., & Butcher, J.N. (2000). Objective personality assessment. In G. Goldstein & M. Hersen (Eds.), *Handbook of psychological assessment* (3rd ed., pp. 413–436). New York, NY: Elsevier.

Nezlek, J.B., Hampton, C.P., & Shean, G. (2000). Clinical depression and day-to-day social interaction in a community sample. *Journal of Abnormal Psychology, 109*, 11–19.

Nezu, A.M., Nezu, C.M., & D'Zurilla, T.J. (2000). Problem-solving skills training. In G. Fink (Ed.), *Encyclopedia of stress* (Vol. 3). San Diego, CA: Academic Press.

NICHD Early Child Care Research Network. (2001). Child care and family predictors of preschool attachment and stability from infancy. *Developmental Psychology, 37*, 847–862.

NICHD Early Child Care Research Network. (2002). Early child care and children's development prior to school entry: Results from the NICHD Study of Early Child Care. *American Educational Research Journal, 39*, 133–164.

NICHD Early Child Care Research Network. (2006). Child-care effect sizes for the NICHD Study of Early Child Care and Youth Development. *American Psychologist, 61*, 99–116.

Nichols, P.L. (1984). Familial mental retardation. *Behavior Genetics, 14*, 161–170.

Nickerson, R.S., & Adams, M.J. (1979). Long term memory for a common object. *Cognitive Psychology, 11*, 287–307.

Nickerson, R.S., & Adams, M.J. (1982). Long-term memory for a common object. In U. Neisser (Ed.), *Memory observed* (pp. 163–175). San Francisco, CA: W.H. Freeman.

Nicks, S.D., Korn, J.H., & Mainieri, T. (1997). The rise and fall of deception in social psychology and personality research, 1921 to 1994. *Ethics and Behavior, 7*, 69–77.

Nicoladis, E., & Genesee, F. (1997). Language development in preschool bilingual children. *Journal of Speech-Language Pathology & Audiology, 21*, 258–270.

Nigg, J.T., Lohr, N.E., Westen, D., & Gold, L.J. (1992). Malevolent object representation in borderline personality disorder and major depression. *Journal of Abnormal Psychology, 101*, 61–67.

Niles, S. (1998). Achievement goals and means: A cultural comparison. *Journal of Cross Cultural Psychology, 29*, 656–667.

Nirenberg, S., & Pandarinath, C. (2012). Retinal prosthetic strategy with the capacity to restore normal vision. *PNAS, 109*(37), 15012–15017.

Nisbett, R.E. (1998). Race, genetics, and IQ. In C. Jencks & M. Phillips (Eds.), *The Black-White test score gap.* Washington, DC: Brookings Institution.

Nisbett, R.E. (2003). *The geography of thought: How Asians and Westerners think differently … and why.* New York, NY: Free Press.

Nisbett, R.E., & Miyamoto, Y. (2005). The influence of culture: Holistic versus analytic perception. *Trends in Cognitive Sciences, 9*(10), 467–473.

Nisbett, R.E., Aronson, J., Blair, C., Dickens, W., Flynn, J., Halpern, D.F., & Turkheimer, E. (2012). Intelligence: New findings and theoretical developments. *American Psychologist, 67*(2), 130–159.

Nisbett, R.E., Peng, K., & Choi, I. (2008). Culture and systems of thought: Holistic versus analytic cognition. In J.E. Adler & L.J. Lance (Eds.), *Reasoning: Studies of human inference and its foundations* (pp. 956–985). New York, NY: Cambridge University Press.

Nisbett, R.E., Peng, K., Choi, I., & Norenzayan, A. (2001). Culture and systems of thought: Holistic vs. analytic cognition. *Psychological Review, 108*, 291–310.

Nixon, M.K., Cloutier, P., & Jansson, S.M. (2008). Nonsuicidal self-harm in youth: A population-based survey. *Canadian Medical Association Journal, 178*, 306–312.

Nolen-Hoeksema, S. (1990). *Sex differences in depression.* Stanford, CA: Stanford University Press.

Nolen-Hoeksema, S. (2006). *Sex differences in depression.* Stanford, CA: Stanford University Press.

Nolen-Hoeksema, S., Parker, L.E., & Larson, J. (1994). Ruminative coping with depressed mood following loss. *Journal of Personality and Social Psychology, 67*, 97–107.

Noll, S.M., & Fredrickson, B.L. (1998). A mediational model linking self-objectification, body shame, and disordered eating. *Psychology of Women Quarterly, 22*, 623–636.

Nolte, J. (1998). *The human brain: An introduction to its functional anatomy.* St. Louis, MO: Mosby.

Norcross, J.C. (2003). *Psychotherapy relationships that work: Therapist contributions and responsiveness to patients.* New York, NY: Oxford University Press.

Norcross, J.C., Pfund, R.A., & Prochaska, J.O. (2013). Psychotherapy in 2022: A Delphi poll on its future. *Professional Psychology: Research and Practice, 44*(5), 363–370.

Norcross, J.C., Ratzin, A.C., & Payne, D. (1989). Ringing in the New Year: The change processes and reported outcomes of resolutions. *Addictive Behaviors, 14*, 205–212.

Norman, G. (2013). Working memory and mental workload. *Advances in Health Sciences Education, 18*(2), 163–165.

Normann, R.A., Maynard, E.M., Guillory, K.S., & Warren, D.J. (1996). Cortical implants for the blind. *IEEE Spectrum, 33*, 54–59.

Normann, R.A., Maynard, E.M., Rousche, P.J., & Warren, D.J. (1999). A neural interface for a cortical vision prosthesis. *Vision Research, 39*, 2577–2587.

North, M., North, S.M., & Coble, J.R. (2002). Virtual reality therapy: An effective treatment for psychological disorders. In K.M. Stanney (Ed.), *Handbook of virtual environments: Design, implementation, and applications. Human factors and ergonomics* (pp. 165–178). Mahwah, NJ: Erlbaum.

North, M.M., North, S.M., & Coble, J.R. (1997). Virtual reality therapy for fear of flying. *American Journal of Psychiatry, 154*, 130.

Norton, G.R., Harrison, B., Haunch, J., & Rhodes, L. (1985). Characteristics of people with infrequent panic attacks. *Abnormal Psychiatry, 94*, 216–221.

Nosek, B.A., Banaji, M.R., & Greenwald, A.G. (2002). Harvesting implicit group attitudes and beliefs from a demonstration web site. *Group Dynamics: Theory, Research and Practice, 6*, 101–115.

Nossal, C.J.V., & Hall, E. (1995). Choices following antigen entry: Antibody formation or immunologic tolerance? *Annual Review of Immunology, 13*, 171–204.

Nunn, J.A., Gregory, L.J., Brammer, M., William, S.C.R., Parslow, D.M., Morgan, J.M., … Gray, J.A. (2002). Functional magnetic resonance imaging of synesthesia: Activation of V4/V8 by spoken words. *Nature Neuroscience, 5*, 371–375.

Nye, R.D. (1996). *Three psychologies: Perspectives from Freud, Skinner, and Rogers* (4th ed.). Pacific Grove, CA: Brooks/Cole.

Oatley, K., & Jenkins, J.M. (1992). Human emotions: Function and dysfunction. *Annual Review of Psychology, 43*, 55–85.

O'Brien, C.P. (1997). Recent developments in the pharmacotherapy of substance abuse. In G.A. Marlatt & G.R. VandenBos (Eds.), *Addictive behavior: Readings on etiology, prevention and treatment.* Washington, DC: American Psychological Association.

Ockene, J.K., Emmons, K.M., Mermelstein, R.J., Perkins, J.A., Bonollo, D., Voorhees, C.C., & Hollis, J.F. (2001). Relapse and maintenance issues for smoking cessation. *Health Psychology, 19*, 17–31.

O'Connor, D.B., Archer, J., Hair, W.M., & Wu, F.C.W. (2002). Exogenous testosterone, aggression, and mood in eugonadal and hypogonadal men. *Physiology and Behavior, 75*, 557–566.

O'Donohue, W., & Elliot, A. (1992). The current status of posttraumatic stress disorder as a diagnostic category: Problems and proposals. *Journal of Traumatic Stress, 5*, 421–439.

Oehman, A., Flykt, A., & Esteves, F. (2001). Emotion drives attention: Detecting the snake in the grass. *Journal of Experimental Psychology, 130*, 466–478.

Ohayon, M.M. (2008). From wakefulness to excessive sleepiness: What we know and still need to know. *Sleep Medicine Reviews, 12*, 129–141.

Ohayon, M.M., Guilleminault, C., & Priest, R.G. (1999). Night terrors, sleepwalking, and confusional arousals in the general population: Their frequency and relationship to other sleep and mental disorders. *Journal of Clinical Psychiatry, 60*, 268–276.

Ohbuchi, K., & Kambara, T. (1985). Attacker's intent and awareness of outcome, impression management, and retaliation. *Journal of Experimental Social Psychology, 21*, 321–330.

Ohira, K., Kobayashi, K., Toyama, K., Nakamura, H.K., Shoji, H., et al. (2013). Synaptosomal-associated protein 25 mutation induces immaturity of the dentate granule cells of adult mice. *Molecular Brain, 6.* Retrieved from http://www.molecularbrain.com/content/6/1/12.

Öhman, A. (2000). Anxiety. In G. Fink (Ed.), *Encyclopedia of stress* (Vol. 1). San Diego, CA: Academic Press.

Öhman, A. (2008). Fear and anxiety: Overlaps and dissociations. In M. Lewis, J. Haviland-Jones, & L.F. Barrett (Eds.), *Handbook of emotions* (3rd ed., pp. 709–729). New York, NY: Guilford Press.

Öhman, A., Fredrikson, M., & Hugdahl, K. (1978). Towards an experimental model for simple phobic reactions. *Behavioural Analysis and Modification, 2*, 97–114.

Öhman, A., & Soares, J.J. (1993). On the automatic nature of phobic fear: Conditioned electrodermal responses to masked fear-relevant stimuli. *Journal of Abnormal Psychology, 102*, 121–132.

Öhman, A., & Soares, J.J.F. (1998). Emotional conditioning to masked stimuli: Expectancies for aversive outcomes following nonrecognized fear-relevant stimuli. *Journal of Experimental Psychology: General, 127*, 69–82.

Öhman, A., & Wiens, S. (2005). The concept of an evolved fear. In A.S.R. Manstead, N.H. Frijda, A.H. Fischer, & K. Oatley (Eds.), *Feelings and emotions: The Amsterdam Symposium.* New York, NY: Cambridge University Press.

O'Keefe, G.S., & Clarke, K. (2011). The impact of social media on children, adolescents, and families. *Pediatrics, 127*, 800–804.

O'Keefe, J., & Dostrovsky, J. (1971). The hippocampus as a spatial map. Preliminary evidence from unit activity in the freely-moving rat. *Brain Res, 34*, 171–175.

Olafson, E., & Lederman, C.S. (2006). The state of the debate about children's disclosure patterns in child sexual abuse cases. *Juvenile and Family Court Journal, 57,* 27–40.

Olds, J. (1958). Self-stimulation of the brain. *Science, 127,* 315–324.

Olds, J., & Milner, P. (1954). Positive reinforcement produced by electrical stimulation of septal area and other regions of rat brain. *Journal of Comparative and Physiological Psychology, 47,* 419–427.

O'Leary, A., & The National Institute of Mental Health Multisite HIV Prevention Trial Group. (2001). Social-cognitive theory mediators of behavior change in the National Institute of Mental Health Multisite HIV Prevention Trial. *Health Psychology, 20,* 369–376.

Oleson, T. (2002). Auriculotherapy stimulation for neuro-rehabilitation. *NeuroRehabilitation, 17,* 49–62.

Ollendick, T.H., & Muris, P. (2015). The scientific legacy of Little Hans and Little Albert: Future directions for research on specific phobias in youth. *Journal of Clinical Child & Adolescent Psychology, 44*(4), 689–706.

Olsen, J.A., & Akirav, E.M. (2015). Remyelination in multiple sclerosis: Cellular mechanisms and novel therapeutic approaches. *Journal of Neuroscience Research, 93*(5), 687–696.

Olson, E.J., Boeve, B.F., & Silber, M.H. (2000). Rapid eye movement sleep behavior disorder: Demographic, clinical and laboratory findings in 93 cases. *Brain: A Journal of Neurology, 123,* 331–339.

Olson, J.M., Vernon, P.A,. Harris, J.A., & Jang, K.L. (2001). The heritability of attitudes: A study of twins. *Journal of Personality and Social Psychology, 80,* 845–860.

Olson, M.A., & Fazio, R.H. (2003). Relations between implicit measures of prejudice: What are we measuring? *Psychological Science, 14,* 636–639.

Oltman, P.K. (1968). A portable rod-and-frame apparatus. *Perceptual and Motor Skills, 26,* 503–506.

Ono, Y., Yoshimura, K., Yamauchi, K., Asai, M., Young, J., Fujihara, S., & Kitamura, T. (2001). Taijin Kyofusho in a Japanese community population. *Transcultural Psychiatry, 38*(4), 506–514.

Opriş, D., Pintea, S., García-Palacios, A., Botella, C., Szamosközi, Ş., & David, D. (2012). Virtual reality exposure therapy in anxiety disorders: A quantitative meta-analysis. *Depression and Anxiety, 29,* 85–93.

Orbuch, T.L., House, J.S., Mero, R.P., & Webster, P.S. (1996). Marital quality over the life course. *Social Psychology Quarterly, 59,* 162–171.

Ormel, J., & Wohlfarth, T. (1991). How neuroticism, long-term difficulties, and life situation change influence psychological distress. *Journal of Personality and Social Psychology, 60,* 744–755.

Orne, M.T. (1959). The nature of hypnosis: Artifact and essence. *Journal of Abnormal and Social Psychology, 58,* 277–299.

Orne, M.T. (1962). On the social psychology of the psychological experiment: With particular reference to demand characteristics and their implications. *American Psychologist, 17,* 776–783.

Orne, M.T., & Evans, F.J. (1965). Social control in the psychological experiment: Antisocial behavior and hypnosis. *Journal of Personality and Social Psychology, 1,* 189–200.

Orr, A.L. (1998). *Issues in aging and vision: A curriculum.* Washington, DC: American Foundation for the Blind Press.

Orth, U., Robins, R.W., Trzesniewski, K.H., Maes, J., & Schmitt, M. (2009). Low self-esteem is a risk factor for depressive symptoms from young adulthood to old age. *Journal of Abnormal Psychology, 118,* 472–478.

Ortiz, J., & Raine, A. (2004). Heart rate level and antisocial behavior in children and adolescents: A meta-analysis. *Journal of the American Academy of Child & Adolescent Psychiatry, 43,* 154–162.

Ortiz-Catalan, M., Sander, N., Kristoffersen., M.B., Håkansson, B., & Brånemark, R. (2014). Treatment of phantom limb pain (PLP) based on augmented reality and gaming controlled by myoelectric pattern recognition: a case study of a chronic PLP patient. *Frontiers in Neuroscience, 8,* 24. doi: 10.3389/fnins.2014.00024.

Ost, J., Granhag, P.A., Udell, J., & Roos af Hjelmsäter, E. (2008). Familiarity breeds distortion: The effects of media exposure on false reports concerning media coverage of the terrorist attacks in London on 7 July 2005. *Memory, 16,* 76–85.

Ost, J., Vrij, A., Costall, A., & Bull, R. (2002). Crashing memories and reality monitoring: Distinguishing between perceptions, imaginations and false memories. *Applied Cognitive Psychology, 16,* 125–134.

Öst, L.G. (2008). Efficacy of the third wave of behavioral therapies: A systematic review and meta-analysis. *Behaviour Research and Therapy, 46*(3), 296–321.

Ostacher, M.J., & Eidelman, P. (2006). Suicide in bipolar depression. In R.S. El-Mallakh & S.N. Ghaemi (Eds.), *Bipolar depression: A comprehensive guide* (pp. 117–145). Arlington, VA: American Psychiatric Publishing.

Ostrovsky, Y., Andalman, A., & Sinha, P. (2007). Vision following extended congenital blindness. *Psychological Science, 17,* 1009–1014.

Ouimette, P.C., Finney, J.W., & Moos, R.H. (1997). Twelve-step and cognitive-behavioral treatment for substance abuse: A comparison of treatment effectiveness. *Journal of Consulting and Clinical Psychology, 65,* 230–240.

Overy, K. (2003). Dyslexia and music: From timing deficits to musical intervention. *Annals of the New York Academy of Science, 999,* 497–505.

Owen, A.M., Coleman, M.R., Boly, M., Davis, M.H., Laureys, S., & Pickard, J.D. (2006). Detecting awareness in the vegetative state. *Science, 313*(5792), 1402.

Owen, P.R., & Laurel-Seller, E. (2000). Weight and shape ideals: Thin is dangerously in. *Journal of Applied Social Psychology, 30,* 979–990.

Oyserman, D., Coon, H.M., & Kemmelmeier, M. (2002). Rethinking individualism and collectivism: Evaluation of theoretical assumptions and meta-analyses. *Psychological Bulletin, 128*(1), 3–72.

Packard, E. (2007). That teenage feeling. *Monitor on Psychology, 38,* 20–24.

Paffenbarger, R.S., Jr., Hyde, R.T., Wing, A.L., & Hsieh, C.C. (1986). Physical activity, all-cause mortality, and longevity of college alumni. *New England Journal of Medicine, 314,* 605–613.

Page, S. (1999). Accommodating persons with AIDS: Acceptance and rejection in rental situations. *Journal of Applied Social Psychology, 29*(2), 261–270.

Paivio, A. (1969). Mental imagery is associative learning and memory. *Psychological Review, 76,* 241–263.

Paivio, A. (1995). Imagery and memory. In M.S. Gazzaniga (Ed.), *The cognitive neurosciences.* Cambridge, MA: MIT Press.

Paivio, A. (2006). *Mind and its evolution: A dual coding theoretical approach.* Mahwah, NJ: Erlbaum.

Paivio, S.C., & Greenberg, L.S. (1995). Resolving "unfinished business": Efficacy of experiential therapy using empty-chair dialogue. *Journal of Consulting and Clinical Psychology, 63,* 419–425.

Pajer, K. (2000a). Antisocial disorders. In G. Fink (Ed.), *Encyclopedia of stress* (Vol. 1). San Diego, CA: Academic Press.

Pajer, K. (2000b). Hysteria. In G. Fink (Ed.), *Encyclopedia of stress* (Vol. 2). San Diego, CA: Academic Press.

Pal, M., Ebrahimi, S., Oh, G., Khare, T., Zhang, A. et al. (2016). High precision DNA modification analysis of *HCG9* in major psychosis. *Schizophrenia Bulletin, 42,* 170–177.

Palfai, T., & Jankiewicz, H. (1991). *Drugs and human behavior.* Dubuque, IA: William C. Brown.

Palmer, J.A., & Palmer, L.K. (Eds.). (2002). *Evolutionary psychology: The ultimate origins of human behavior* (Vol. 15). Needham Heights, MA.: Allyn & Bacon.

Palmer, S.E. (2002). Perceptual organization in vision. In H. Pashler & S. Yantis (Eds.), *Steven's handbook of experimental psychology: Vol. 1 Sensation and perception* (3rd ed., pp. 177–234). New York, NY: Wiley.

Palmere, M., Benton, S.L., Glover, J.A., & Ronning, R. (1983). Elaboration and recall of main ideas in prose. *Journal of Education Psychology, 75,* 898–907.

Pan, Y. (2015). Development of young adolescents' self-esteem and influencing factors: A longitudinal analysis. *Acta Psychologica Sinica, 47*(6), 787–796.

Panksepp, J. (1998). *Affective neuroscience: The foundations of human and animal emotions.* Oxford, UK: Oxford University Press.

Panksepp, J. (2005). Basic affects and the instinctual emotion system of the brain: The primordial sources of sadness, joy and seeking. In A.S.R. Manstead, N.H. Frijda, A.H. Fischer, & K. Oatley (Eds.), *Feelings and emotions: The Amsterdam Symposium.* New York, NY: Cambridge University Press.

Pansu, P., Lima, L., & Fointiat, V. (2014). When saying no leads to compliance: The door-in-the-face technique for changing attitudes and behaviors towards smoking at work. *European Review of Applied Psychology / Revue Européenne de Psychologie Appliquée, 64*(1), 19–27.

Pantev, C., Dinnesen, A., Ross, B., Wollbrink, A., & Knief, A. (2006). Dynamics of auditory plasticity after cochlear implantation: A longitudinal study. *Cerebral Cortex, 16,* 31–36.

Pantev, C., Oostenveld, R., Engelien, A., Ross, B., Roberts, L.E., & Hoke, M. (1998). Increased auditory cortical representation in musicians. *Nature, 392,* 811–814.

Papanicolaou, A.C. (1989). *Emotion: A reconsideration of the somatic theory.* New York, NY: Gordon and Breach.

Paparrigopoulos, T.J. (2005). REM sleep behavior disorder: Clinical profiles and pathophysiology. *International Review of Psychiatry, 17,* 293–300.

Paquette, D. (2004). Theorizing the father-child relationship: Mechanisms and developmental outcomes. *Human Development, 47,* 193–219.

Paquette, D., & Bigras, M. (2010). The risky situation: A procedure for assessing the father-child activation relationship. *Early Child Development and Care, 180,* 33–50.

Parapsychology Association. (2008). *Frequently asked questions.* Retrieved October 3, 2009, from http://www.parapsych.org/faq_file2.html#11.

Paris, J. (1993). *Borderline personality disorder*. Washington, DC: American Psychiatric Press.

Paris, J.P. (2013). *The intelligent clinician's guide to DSM-5*. New York: Oxford University Press.

Park, C.L., Armeli, S., & Tennen, H. (2004). Appraisal-coping goodness of fit: A daily internet study. *Personality and Social Psychology Bulletin, 30*, 558–569.

Park, D.C., Smith, A.D., & Cavanaugh, J.C. (1990). Metamemories of memory researchers. *Memory and Cognition, 18*, 321–327.

Parker, A. (2000). A review of the ganzfeld work at Gothenburg University. *Journal of the Society for Psychical Research, 64*, 1–15.

Parker, C.R., Bolling, M.Y., & Kohlenberg, R.J. (1998). Operant theory of personality. In D.F. Barone, M. Hersen, & V.B. Van Hasselt (Eds.), *Advanced personality* (pp. 155–172). New York, NY: Plenum Press.

Parker, K.J., Buckmaster, C.L., Justus, K.R., Schatzberg, A.F., & Lyons, D.M. (2005). Mild early life stress enhances prefrontal-dependent response inhibition in monkeys. *Biological Psychiatry, 57*, 848–855.

Parker, L.A., Kwiatkowska, M., & Mechoulam, R. (2006). Delta-9-tetrahydrocannabinol and cannabidiol, but not ondansetron, interfere with conditioned retching reactions elicited by a lithium-paired context in *Suncus murinus:* An animal model of anticipatory nausea and vomiting. *Physiology & Behavior, 87*, 66–71.

Parkinson, A.J., Parkinson, W.S., Tyler, R.S., Lowder, M.W., & Gantz, B.J. (1998). Speech perception performance in experienced cochlear-implant patients receiving the SPEAK processing strategy in the Nucleus Spectra-22 cochlear implant. *Journal of Speech, Language, and Hearing Research, 41*, 1073–1087.

Parrott, A.C. (1999). Does cigarette smoking cause stress? *American Psychologist, 54*, 817–820.

Parrott, A.C. (2002). Human psychopharmacology of Ecstasy (MDMA): A review of 15 years of empirical research. *Human Psychopharmacology Clinical and Experimental, 16*, 557–577.

Parrott, A.C. (2006). MDMA in humans: Factors which affect the neuropsychobiological profiles of recreational ecstasy users, the integrative role of bioenergetic stress. *Journal of Psychopharmacology, 20*, 147–163.

Parsons, T.D., & Rizzo, A.A. (2008). Affective outcomes of virtual reality exposure therapy for anxiety and specific phobias: A meta-analysis. *Journal of Behavior Therapy and Experimental Psychiatry, 39*(3), 250–261.

Partain, C. (2006). Clinical potential of brain mapping using MRI. *Journal of Magnetic Resonance Imaging, 23*, 785–786.

Passie, T., Halpern, J.H., Strichenoth, D.O., Emrich, H.M., & Hintzen, A. (2008). The pharmacology of lysergic acid diethylamide: A review. *CNS Neuroscience & Therapeutics, 14*, 295–314.

Patil, P.G., & Turner, D.A. (2008). The development of brain-machine interface neuroprosthetic devices. *Neurotherapeutics, 5*, 137–146.

Patterson, D.R. (2004). Treating pain with hypnosis. *Current Directions in Psychological Science, 13*, 252–255

Patterson, G.R. (1982). *Coercive family processes*. Eugene, OR: Castalia Press.

Patterson, G.R., Littman, R.A., & Bricker, W. (1967). Assertive behavior in children: A step toward a theory of aggression. *Monographs of the Society for Research in Child Development, 32* (Whole No. 5).

Patton, D., Brown, D., Broszeit, B., & Dhaliwal, J. (2001). *Substance use among Manitoba high school students, 2001*. Winnipeg, MB: Addictions Foundation of Manitoba.

Pauk, W., & Fiore, J.P. (2000). *Succeed in college!* Boston, MA: Houghton Mifflin.

Paul, G.L., & Lentz, R.J. (1977). *Psychosocial treatment of chronic mental patients: Milieu versus social learning programs*. Cambridge, MA: Harvard University Press.

Paulhus, D.L. (1991). Measurement and control of response bias. In J. Robinson, P. Shaver, & L. Wrightsman (Eds.), *Measures of personality and social psychological attitudes* (pp. 17–59). Toronto, ON: Academic Press.

Paulhus, D.L., Harms, P.D., Bruce, M.N., & Lysy, D.C. (2003). The over-claiming technique: Measuring self-enhancement independent of ability. *Journal of Personality and Social Psychology, 84*, 890–904.

Paulson, T. (2004, December 14). Thought powers computer. *Seattle Post-Intelligencer*, A1.

Paunonen, S.V. (2003). Big Five factors of personality and replicated predictions of behavior. *Journal of Personality and Social Psychology, 84*, 411–424.

Pavlov, I.P. (1923/1928). *Lectures on conditioned reflexes: Twenty-five years of objective study of the higher nervous activity (behaviour) of animals* (W.H. Gantt, Trans.). New York, NY: International Publishers. (Original work published 1923).

Paz-Alonzo, P.M., Ogle, C.M., & Goodman, G. (2013). Children's memory in "scientific case studies" of child sexual abuse: A review. In B.S. Cooper et al. (Eds.), *Applied issues in investigative interviewing, eyewitness memory, and credibility assessment*. New York, NY: Springer.

Pea, R., Nass, C., Meheula, L., Rance, M., Kumar, A., Bamford, H., Nass, M., Simha, A., Stillerman, B., Yang, S., & Zhou, M. (2012). Media use, face-to-face communication, media multitasking, and social well-being among 8- to 12-year-old girls. *Developmental Psychology, 48*, 327–336.

Peacock, K.W. (2010). *Biotechnology and genetic engineering*. New York, NY: Facts on File, Inc.

Pearlin, L.I., & Schooler, C. (1978). The structure of coping. *Journal of Health and Social Behavior, 19*, 2–21.

Pearsall, M.J., Christian, M.S., & Ellis, A.P.J. (2010). Motivating interdependent teams: Individual rewards, shared rewards, or something in between. *Journal of Applied Psychology, 95*, 183–191.

Pederson, D.R., Gleason, K.E., Moran, G., & Bento, S. (1998). Maternal attachment representations, maternal sensitivity, and the infant-mother attachment relationship. *Developmental Psychology, 34*, 925–933.

Pederson, N.L., Plomin, R., McClearn, G.E., & Griberg, L. (1988). Neuroticism, extraversion, and related traits in adult twins reared apart and reared together. *Journal of Personality and Social Psychology, 55*, 950–957.

Pedrotti, F.L., & Pedrotti, L.S. (1997). *Optics and vision*. Englewood Cliffs, NJ: Prentice Hall.

Pelé, M., & Sueur, C. (2013). Decision-making theories: Linking the disparate research areas of individual and collective cognition. *Animal Cognition, 16*, 543–556.

Pelham, W.E., Jr., Massetti, G.M., Wilson, T., Kipp, H., Myers, D., Newman Standley, B.B., ... Waschbusch, D.A. (2005). Implementation of a comprehensive schoolwide behavioral intervention: The ABC Program. *Journal of Attention Disorders, 9*, 248–260.

Pelletier, D.L., & Frongillo, E.A. (2003). Changes in child survival are strongly associated with changes in malnutrition in developing countries. *Journal of Nutrition, 133*, 107–119.

Pendlebury, S.T. (2007). *Neurological case histories*. New York, NY: Oxford University Press.

Penfield, W. (1975). *The mystery of the mind: A critical study of consciousness and the human brain*. Princeton, NJ: Princeton University Press.

Penfield, W., & Perot, P. (1963). The brain's record of auditory and visual experience. *Brain, 86*, 595–696.

Pennycook, G., Cheyne, J.A., Koehler, D.J., & Fugelsang, J.A. (2013). Belief bias during reasoning among religious believers and skeptics. *Psychonomic Bulletin & Review, 20*(4), 806–811.

Peper, J.S., & Dahl, R.E. (2013). The teenage brain: Surging hormones—Brain-behavior interactions during puberty. *Current Directions in Psychological Science, 22*, 134–139.

Peplau, L.A., Garnets, L.D., Spalding, L.R., Conley, T.D., & Veniegas, R.C. (1998). A critique of Bem's "Exotic Becomes Erotic" theory of sexual orientation. *Psychological Review, 105*, 387–394.

Perani, D., Colombo, C., Bressi, S., Bonfanti, A., Grassi, F., Scarone, S., ... Fazio, F. (1995). PET study in obsessive–compulsive disorder: A clinical metabolic correlation study after treatment. *British Journal of Psychiatry, 166*(2), 244–250.

Perani, D., Paulesu, E., Galles, N.S., Dupoux, E., & Dehaene, S. (1998). The bilingual brain: Proficiency and age of acquisition of the second language. *Brain, 121*, 1841–1852.

Perdue, C.W., Dovidio, J.F., Gurtman, M.B., & Tyler, R.B. (1990). Us and them: Social categorization and the process of intergroup bias. *Journal of Personality and Social Psychology, 59*, 475–486.

Perlman, M., & Clark, N. (2015). Learned vocal and breathing behavior in an enculturated gorilla. *Animal Cognition, 18*(5), 1165–1179.

Pernollet, J.C., Sanz, G., & Briand, L. (2006). Olfactory receptors and odour coding. *Comptes Rendus Biologies, 329*, 679–690.

Perrett, D.I., Lee, K.J., Penton-Voak, I., Rowland, D., Yoshikawa, S., Burt, D.M., ... Akamatsu, S. (1998). Effects of sexual dimorphism on facial attractiveness. *Nature, 394*, 884–887.

Perruchet, P., Grégoire, L., Aerts, K., & Poulin-Charronnat, B. (2015). Dissociating conscious expectancies from automatic-link formation in an electrodermal conditioning paradigm. *Psychological Research*, doi: http://dx.doi.org/10.1007/s00426-015-0676-7.

Pert, C.B. (1997). *Molecules of emotion: Why you feel the way you feel*. New York, NY: Simon & Schuster.

Peterson, C., & Park, C. (1998). Learned helplessness and explanatory style. In D.F. Barone, M. Hersen, & V.B. Van Hasselt (Eds.), *Advanced personality* (pp. 287–310). New York, NY: Plenum Press.

Peterson, C., & Seligman, M.E.P. (1987). Explanatory style and illness. *Journal of Personality, 55*, 237–265.

Peterson, C., Seligman, M.E.P., & Vaillant, G.E. (1988). Pessimistic explanatory style is a risk factor for physical illness: A thirty-five-year longitudinal study. *Journal of Personality and Social Psychology, 55*, 23–27.

Peterson, C., & Whalen, N. (2001). Five years later: Children's memory for medical emergencies. *Applied Cognitive Psychology, 15*, 7–24.

Peterson, L.R., & Peterson, M.J. (1959). Short term retention of individual verbal items. *Journal of Experimental Psychology, 58*, 193–198.

Petrides, K.V., Pérez-González, J.C., & Furnham, A. (2007). On the criterion and incremental validity of trait emotional intelligence. *Cognition and Emotion, 21*(1), 26–55.

Petrill, S. (2003). The development of intelligence: Behavior genetics approaches. In R.J. Sternberg, J. Lautrey, & T.I. Lubart (Eds.), *Models of intelligence: International perspectives.* Washington, DC: American Psychological Association.

Petrosini, L., De Bartolo, P., Foti, F., Gelfo, F., Cutuli, D., Leggio, M.G., et al. (2009). On whether the environmental enrichment may provide cognitive and brain reserves. *Brain Research Reviews, 61*, 221–239.

Petrovic, P., Kalso, E., Petersson, M.K., & Ingvar, M. (2002, February). Placebo and opioid analgesia: Imaging a shared neuronal network. *Science Express Reports*, 17–22.

Petryshen, T.L., Kaplan, B.J., Liu, M.F., de French, N.S., Tobias, R., Hughes, M.L., & Field, L.L. (2001). Evidence for a susceptibility locus on chromosome 6q influencing phonological coding dyslexia. *American Journal of Medical Genetics (Neuropsychiatric Genetics), 105*, 507–517.

Pettigrew, T.F., & Meertens, R.W. (1995). Subtle and blatant prejudice in western Europe. *European Journal of Social Psychology, 25*, 57–76.

Pettigrew, T.F., & Tropp, L.R. (2000). Does intergroup contact reduce prejudice: Recent meta-analytic findings. In S. Oskamp (Ed.), *Reducing prejudice and discrimination. The Claremont Symposium on Applied Social Psychology* (pp. 93–114). Mahwah, NJ: Erlbaum.

Pettit, M., & Vigor, J. (2015). Pheromones, feminism and the many lives of menstrual synchrony. *BioSocieties, 10*(3), 271–294.

Petty, R.E., & Cacioppo, J.T. (1986). *Communication and persuasion: Central and peripheral routes to attitude change.* New York, NY: Springer-Verlag.

Petty, R.E., & Wegener, D.T. (1998). Attitude change: Multiple roles for persuasion variables. In D.T. Gilbert, S.T. Fiske, & G. Lindzey (Eds.), *The handbook of social psychology* (4th ed., Vol. 1, pp. 323–390). Boston, MA: McGraw-Hill.

Petty, R.E., Fleming, M.A., Priester, J.R., & Feinstein, A.H. (2001). Individual versus group interest violation: Surprise as a determinant of argument scrutiny and persuasion. *Social Cognition, 19*, 418–442.

Pezdek, K. (2002). Event memory and autobiographical memory for the events of September 11, 2001. Manuscript submitted for publication.

Pezdek, K. (2012). Fallible eyewitness memory and identification. In Cutler, B.L. (Ed.), *Conviction of the innocent: Lessons from psychological research* (pp. 105–124). Washington, DC: American Psychological Association.

Pezzuti, L., & Orsini, A. (2016). Are there sex differences in the Wechsler Intelligence Scale for Children—fourth edition? *Learning and Individual Differences*, doi: http://dx.doi.org/10.1016/j.lindif.2015.12.024.

Pfeffer, K., Cole, B., & Dada, M.K. (1998). Attributions for youth crime among British and Nigerian primary school children. *Journal of Social Psychology, 138*, 251–253.

Pfeifer, M., Goldsmith, H.H., Davidson, R.J., & Rickman, M. (2002). Continuity and change in inhibited and uninhibited children. *Child Development, 73*, 1474–1485.

Pfiffner, L.J., McBurnett, K., & Rathouz, P.J. (2001). Father absence and familial antisocial characteristics. *Journal of Abnormal Child Psychology, 29*, 357–367.

Phelps, E.A. (2005). The power of the subliminal: On subliminal persuasion and other potential applications. In R.R. Hassin, J.S. Uleman, & J.A. Bargh (Eds.), *The New Unconscious* (pp. 61–76). New York, NY: Oxford University Press.

Phelps, E.A., O'Connor, K.J., Cunningham, W.A., Funayama, E.S., Gatenby, J.C., Gore, J.C., & Banaji, M.R. (2000). Performance on indirect measures of race evaluation predicts amygdala activation. *Journal of Cognitive Neuroscience, 12*, 5729–5738.

Phelps, E.A., O'Connor, K.J., Gatenby, C., Gore, J.C., Grillon, C., & Davis, M. (2001). Activation of the left amygdala to a cognitive representation of fear. *Nature Neuroscience, 4*, 437–441.

Phillips, A.G., Blaha, C.D., Pfaus, J.G., & Blackburn, J.R. (1992). Neurobiological correlates of positive emotional states: Dopamine, anticipation and reward. In K.T. Strongman (Ed.), *International review of studies on emotion* (Vol. 2, pp. 31–50). New York, NY: John Wiley & Sons.

Phillips, A.G., & Silvia, P.J. (2005). Self-awareness and the emotional consequences of self-discrepancies. *Personality and Social Psychology Bulletin, 31*, 703–713.

Phillips, L.H., Kriegiel, M., & Martin, M. (2006). Age and planning tasks: The influence of ecological validity. *International Journal of Aging and Human Development, 62*(2), 175–184.

Phillips, M. (2007). The emerging role of neuroimaging in psychiatry: Characterizing treatment-relevant endophenotypes. *American Journal of Psychiatry, 164*, 697–699.

Phillips, M., Brooks, G.J., Duncan, G.J., Klebanov, P., & Crane, J. (1998). Family background, parenting practices, and the Black-White test score gap. In C. Jencks & M. Phillips (Eds.), *The Black-White test score gap* (pp. 103–145). Washington, DC: Brookings Institution.

Phillipson, S.N., & McCann, M. (2007). *Conceptions of giftedness: Socio-cultural perspectives.* Mahwah, NJ: Erlbaum.

Piaget, J. (1926). *The language and thought of the child.* New York, NY: Meridian Books.

Piaget, J. (1970). Piaget's theory. In P.H. Mussen (Ed.), *Carmichael's manual of child psychology* (Vol. 1). New York, NY: Wiley.

Piaget, J. (1977). *The development of thought: Equilibration of cognitive structure.* New York, NY: Viking.

Pickering, A.D., & Gray, J.A. (1999). The neuroscience of personality. In L.A. Pervin & O.P. John (Eds.), *Handbook of personality: Theory and research.* New York, NY: Guilford Press.

Pickrell, J.E., Bernstein, D., & Loftus, E.F. (2003). The misinformation effect. In R. Pohl (Ed.), *Cognitive illusions: Fallacies and biases in thinking, judgment, and memory* (pp. 345–362). London, UK: Psychology Press.

Pierce, G.R., Ptacek, J.T., Taylor, B., Yee, P.L., Henderson, C.A., Lauventi, H.J., & Loffredo, C.M. (1998). The role of dispositional and situational factors in cognitive interference. *Journal of Personality and Social Psychology, 75*, 1016–1031.

Piffer, L., Agrillo, C., & Hyde, D.C., (2012). Small and large number discrimination in guppies. *Animal Cognition, 15*, 215–221.

Pilbeam, D. (1984). The descent of hominoids and hominids. *Scientific American, 250*, 84–87.

Pilcher, J.J., & Huffcutt, A.J. (1996). Effects of sleep deprivation on performance: A meta-analysis. *Sleep, 19*, 318–326.

Pilla, M., Perachon, S., Sautel, F., Garrido, F., Mann, A., Wermuth, C.G., ... Sokoloff, P. (1999). Selective inhibition of cocaine seeking behaviour by a partial dopamine D3 receptor agonist. *Nature, 400*, 371–375.

Pinel, J.P., Assanand, S., & Lehman, D.R. (2000). Hunger, eating and ill health. *American Psychologist, 55*, 1105–1116.

Pinel, J.P.J. (1997). *Biopsychology.* Boston, MA: Allyn & Bacon.

Pinker, S. (2000). *Words and rules: The ingredients of language.* New York, NY: Basic Books.

Pinker, S. (2003). Language as an adaptation to the cognitive niche. *Studies in the Evolution of Language, 3*, 16–37.

Piper, A., & Merskey, H. (2004). The persistence of folly: A critical examination of dissociative identity disorder. Part I. The excesses of an improbable concept. *Canadian Journal of Psychiatry, 49*, 592–600.

Pitel, S., & Solomon, R. (2013). Estimating the number and cost of impairment-related traffic crashes in Canada: 1999 to 2010. Oakville, ON: MADD Canada.

Pitman, R.K., Shalev, A.Y., & Orr, S.P. (2000). Post-traumatic stress disorder: Emotion, conditioning, and memory. In M.S. Gazzaniga (Ed.), *The new cognitive neurosciences* (2nd ed., pp. 1133–1148). Cambridge, MA: MIT Press.

Pittenger, D.J. (2003). Internet research: An opportunity to revisit classic ethical problems in behavioral research. *Ethics & Behavior, 13*, 45–60.

Pitts, M.A., Martinez, A., & Hillyard, S.A. (2012). Visual processing of contour patterns under conditions of inattentional blindness. *Journal of Cognitive Neuroscience, 24*(2), 287–303.

Pitz, G.F., & Sachs, N.J. (1984). Judgment and decision: Theory and application. *Annual Review of Psychology, 35*, 139–163.

Piven, J., Saliba, K., Bailey, J., & Arndt, S. (1997). An MRI study of autism: The cerebellum revisited. *Neurology, 13*, 546–551.

Piven, J., Vieland, V.J., Parlier, M., Thompson, A., O'Conner, I., Woodbury-Smith, M., ... Szatmari, P. (2013). A molecular genetic study of autism and related phenotypes in extended pedigrees. *Journal of Neurodevelopmental Disorders, 5*(1), 1–15.

Plant, E.A., & Peruche, B.M. (2005). The consequences of race for police officers' responses to criminal suspects. *Psychological Science, 16*, 180–183.

Plant, E.A., Peruche, B.M., & Butz, D.A. (2005). Eliminating automatic racial bias: Making race non-diagnostic for responses to criminal suspects. *Journal of Experimental Social Psychology, 41*, 141–156.

Plantinga, J., & Trainor, L.J. (2009). Melody recognition by two-month-old infants. *Journal of Acoustical Society of America, 125* (Published online 21 JASA Express Letters. doi: 10.1121/1.3049583" January 2009).

Platt, M.L., & Pearson, J.M. (2016). Dopamine: Context and counterfactuals. *Proceedings of the National Academy of Sciences, 113*(1), 22–23.

Plaud, J.J., & Plaud, D.M. (1998). Clinical behavior therapy and the experimental analysis of behavior. *Journal of Clinical Psychology, 54*, 905–921.

Plomin, R. (1997). *Behavioral genetics.* New York, NY: St. Martin's Press.

Plomin, R., Asbury, K., & Dunn, J. (2001). Why are children in the same family so different? Non-shared environment a decade later. *Canadian Journal of Psychiatry, 46*, 225–233.

Plomin, R., & Caspi, A. (1999). Behavior genetics and personality. In L.A. Pervin & O.P. John (Eds.), *Handbook of personality: Theory and research* (2nd ed.). New York, NY: Guilford Press.

Plomin, R., DeFries, J.C., & Fulker, D.W. (2007). *Nature and nurture during infancy and early childhood.* New York, NY: Cambridge University Press.

Plomin, R., & Haworth, C.M.A. (2009). Genetics of high cognitive abilities. *Behavior Genetics, 39,* 347–349.

Plomin, R., & Spinath, F.M. (2004). Intelligence: Genetics, genes, and genomics. *Journal of Personality and Social Psychology, 86,* 112–129.

Ploner, M., Gross, J., Timmerman, L., & Schnitzler, A. (2006). Pain processing is faster than tactile processing in the human brain. *Journal of Neuroscience, 26,* 10879–10882.

Plotkin, S.A. (2006). The history of rubella and rubella vaccination leading to elimination. *Clinical Infectious Diseases, 43,* S164–S168.

Plous, S. (1996a). Attitudes toward the use of animals in psychological research and education: Results from a national survey of psychologists. *American Psychologist, 51,* 1167–1180.

Plous, S. (1996b). Attitudes toward the use of animals in psychological research and education: Results from a national survey of psychology majors. *Psychological Science, 7,* 352–358.

Plous, S., & Herzog, H.A. (2000). Poll shows researchers favor lab animal protection. *Science, 290,* 711.

Plutchik, R. (1991). *The emotions.* Lanham, MD: University Press of America.

Plutchik, R. (1994). *Psychology of emotion.* Reading, MA: Addison-Wesley.

Pollack, I., & Pickett, J.M. (1964). Intelligibility of excerpts from fluent speech: Auditory vs. structural context. *Journal of Verbal Learning and Verbal Behavior, 3,* 79–84.

Pompili, M., Serafini, G., Del Casale, A., Rigucci, S., Innamorati, M., Girardi, P., … Lester, D. (2009). Improving adherence in mood disorders: The struggle against relapse, recurrence and suicide risk. *Expert Reviews in Neurotherapy, 9,* 985–1004.

Pool, R. (1994). *The dynamic brain.* Washington, DC: National Academy Press.

Poremba, M., & Poremba, A. (2007). *Attention-deficit/hyperactivity disorder (ADHD).* New York, NY: Chelsea House.

Pornari, C.D., & Wood, J. (2010). Peer and cyber aggression in secondary school: The role of moral disengagement, hostile attribution bias, and outcome expectancies. *Aggressive Behavior, 36,* 81–94.

Porter, N.P., & Geis, F.L. (1981). Women and nonverbal leadership cues: When seeing is not believing. In C. Mayo & N.M. Henley (Eds.), *Gender and nonverbal behavior.* New York, NY: Springer-Verlag.

Porter, S., Bellhouse, S., McDougall, A., ten Brinke, L., & Wilson, K. (2010). A prospective investigation of the vulnerability of memory for positive and negative emotional scenes to the misinformation effect. *Canadian Journal of Behavioural Science/Revue Canadienne des Sciences du Comportement, 42,* 55–61.

Posada, G., Jacobs, A., Richmond, M.K., Carbonell, O.A., Alzate, G., Bustamante, M.R., & Quiceno, J. (2002). Maternal caregiving and infant security in two cultures. *Developmental Psychology, 38,* 67–78.

Posner, M.I., & Rothbart, M.K. (2007a). Learning to look. In M.I. Posner & M.K. Rothbart (Eds.), *Educating the human brain.* Washington, DC: American Psychological Association.

Posner, M.I., & Rothbart, M.K. (2007b). *Educating the human brain.* Washington, DC: American Psychological Association. .

Posthuma, D., & de Geus, E.J.C. (2006). Progress in the molecular-genetic study of intelligence. *Current Directions in Psychological Science, 15,* 151–155.

Posthuma, D., Mulder, E.J.C.M., Boomsma, D.I., & de Geus, E.J.C. (2002). Genetic analysis of IQ, processing speed and stimulus response in congruency effects. *Biological Psychology, 61*(1–2), 157–182.

Posthuma, D., Neale, M.C., Boomsma, D.I., & de Geus, E.J.C. (2001). Are smarter brains running faster? Heritability of alpha peak frequency, IQ, and their interrelation. *Behavior Genetics, 31,* 567–579.

Postman, L., & Phillips, L.W. (1965). Short-term temporal changes in free recall. *Quarterly Journal of Experimental Psychology, 17,* 132–138.

Postman, L., & Underwood, B.J. (1973). Critical issues in interference theory. *Memory and Cognition, 1,* 19–40.

Postmes, T., & Spears, R. (1998). Deindividuation and antinormative behavior: A meta-analysis. *Psychological Bulletin, 123,* 238–259.

Poulin-Dubois, D., Serbin, L.A., & Derbyshire, A. (1988). Toddlers' intermodal and verbal knowledge about gender. *Merrill-Palmer Quarterly, 44,* 338–354.

Poulin-Dubois, D., Serbin, L.A., Kenyon, B., & Derbyshire, A. (1994). Infants' intermodal knowledge about gender. *Developmental Psychology, 30,* 436–442.

Poulin-Lord, M.P., Barbeau, E.B., Soulières, I., Monchi, O., Doyon, J., Benali, H., & Mottron, L. (2014). Increased topographical variability of task-related activation in perceptive and motor associative regions in adult autistics. *Neuroimage: Clinical, 4,* 444–453.

Powell, M.C., & Fazio, R.M. (1984). Attitude accessibility as a function of repeated attitudinal expression. *Personality and Social Psychology Bulletin, 10,* 139–148.

Powell, R.W., & Curley, M. (1976). Instinctive drift in nondomesticated rodents. *Bulletin of the Psychonomic Society, 8,* 175–178.

Powers, M.B., & Emmelkamp, P.M. (2008). Virtual reality exposure therapy for anxiety disorders: A meta-analysis. *Journal of Anxiety Disorders, 22*(3), 561–569.

Powers, T.L., & Jack, E.P. (2013). The influence of cognitive dissonance on retail product returns. *Psychology & Marketing, 30*(8), 724–735.

Powley, T.L., & Kessey, R.E. (1970). Relationship of body weight to the lateral hypothalamic feeding syndrome. *Journal of Comparative and Physiological Psychology, 70,* 25–36.

Prapavessis, H., Gaston, A., & DeJesus, S. (2015). The theory of planned behavior as a model for understanding sedentary behavior. *Psychology of Sport and Exercise, 19,* 23–32.

Pressley, M., Snyder, B.L., Levin, J.R., Murray, H.G., & Ghatala, E.S. (1987). Perceived readiness for examination performance (PREP) produced by initial reading of text and text containing adjunct questions. *Reading Research Quarterly, 22,* 219–236.

Pressman, J.D. (1998). *Last resort: Psychosurgery and the limits of medicine.* New York, NY: Cambridge University Press.

Pressman, S.D., & Cohen, S. (2005). Does positive affect influence heath? *Psychological Bulletin, 131,* 925–971.

Preti, G., Cutler, W.B., Garcia, G.R., Huggins, G.R., & Lawley, J.J. (1986). Human axillary secretions influences women's menstrual cycles: The role of donor extract from females. *Hormones and Behavior, 20,* 473–480.

Price, R.A., Charles, M.A., Pettitt, D.J., & Knowler, W.C. (1993). Obesity in Pima Indians: Large increases among post–World War II birth cohorts. *American Journal of Physical Anthropology, 92,* 473–479.

Pridmore, R.W. (2013). Single cell spectrally opposed responses: Opponent colours or complementary colours? *Journal of Optics, 10.* Online publication. doi: 1007 /s12596-012-0090-0.

Prigerson, H., Maciejewski, P.K., & Rosenheck, R.A. (2002). Population attributable fractions of psychiatric disorders and behavioral outcomes associated with combat exposure among U.S. men. *American Journal of Public Health, 92*(1), 59–63.

Priluck, R., & Till, B.D. (2004). The role of contingency awareness, involvement, and need for cognition in attitude formation. *Journal of the Academy of Marketing Science, 32,* 329–344.

Pritchard, R.D., Hollenback, J., & DeLeo, P.J. (1980). The effects of continuous and partial schedules of reinforcement on effort, performance, and satisfaction. *Organizational Behavior and Human Decision Processes, 25,* 336–353.

Pritchard, R.M. (1961). Stabilized images on the retina. *Scientific American,* 72–78.

Probst, L.R., Ostrom, R., Watkins, P., Dean, T., & Mashburn, D. (1992). Comparative efficacy of religious and non-religious cognitive-behavioral therapy for the treatment of clinical depression in religious individuals. *Journal of Consulting and Clinical Psychology, 60,* 94–103.

Prochaska, J., & DiClemente, C. (1984). *The transtheoretical approach: Crossing traditional boundaries of therapy.* Homewood, IL: Dow Jones-Irwin.

Prochaska, J.O., Norcross, J.C., & DiClemente, C.C. (1994). *Changing for good.* New York, NY: Avon Books.

Project MATCH Research Group. (1997). Matching alcoholism treatments to client heterogeneity: Project MATCH post-treatment drinking outcomes. *Journal of Studies on Alcohol, 58,* 7–29.

Pruden, S.M., Hirsh-Pasek, K., & Golinkoff, R.M. (2006). The social dimension in language development: A rich history and a new frontier. In P.J. Marshall & N.A. Fox (Eds.), *The development of social engagement: Neurobiological perspectives* (pp. 118–152). New York, NY: Oxford University Press.

Public Health Agency of Canada. (2015). HIV and AIDS in Canada: Surveillance Report to December 31, 2014. Ottawa: Minister of Public Works and Government Services Canada, http://healthycanadians.gc.ca/publications /diseases-conditions-maladies-affections /hiv-aids-surveillance-2014-vih-sida/index-eng. php?page=10#t21.

Pugh, G.E. (1977). *The biological origin of human values.* New York, NY: Basic Books.

Pull, C.B. (2009). Current empirical status of acceptance and commitment therapy. *Current Opinion in Psychiatry, 22*(1), 55–60.

Putnam, F.W. (1984). The psychophysiologic investigation of multiple personality disorder: A review. *Psychiatric Clinics of North America, 7,* 31–39.

Putnam, F.W. (1989). *Diagnosis and treatment of multiple personality disorder.* New York, NY: Guilford Press.

Putnam, F.W. (1998). *Dissociation in children and adolescents: A developmental perspective.* New York, NY: Guilford Press.

Putnam, F.W. (2000). Dissociative disorders. In A.J. Sameroff & M. Lewis (Eds.), *Handbook of developmental psychopathology* (2nd ed., pp. 739–754). New York, NY: Cambridge University Press.

Putri, N.L. (2015). The usage of extinction and positive reinforcement procedures to reduce the tantrums behavior on early age children with autism. *International Journal of Scientific Research and Education, 3*(05).

Pylyshyn, Z.W. (2003). Return of the mental image: Are there really pictures in the brain? *Trends in Cognitive Sciences, 7*(3), 113–118.

Pyszczynski, T., & Greenberg, J. (1987). Toward an integration of cognitive and motivational perspectives on social inference: A biased hypothesis-testing model. In L. Berkowitz (Ed.), *Advances in experimental social psychology* (Vol. 20, pp. 297–340). Orlando, FL: Academic Press.

Pyszczynski, T., Hamilton, J.C., Greenberg, J., & Becker, S.E. (1991). Self-awareness and psychological dysfunction. In C.R. Snyder & D.O. Forsyth (Eds.), *Handbook of social and clinical psychology: The health perspective.* New York, NY: Pergamon Press.

Quera-Salva, M.A., Guilleminault, C., Claustrat, B., Defrance, A., Gajdos, P., McCann, C.C., & De Lattre, J. (1997). Rapid shift in peak melatonin secretion associated with improved performance in short shift work schedule. *Sleep, 20,* 1145–1150.

Quinn, P.C., & Bhatt, R.S. (2006). Are some gestalt principles deployed more readily than others during early development? The case of lightness versus form similarity. *Journal of Experimental Psychology: Human Perception and Performance, 32,* 1221–1230.

Quinn, P.C., Brown, C.R., & Streppa, M.L. (1997). Perceptual organization of complex visual configurations by young infants. *Infant Behavior and Development, 20,* 35–46.

Quinsey, V.L., Maguire, A., & Varney, G.W. (1983). Assertion and overcontrolled hostility among mentally disordered murderers. *Journal of Consulting and Clinical Psychology, 51,* 550–566.

Quintero, N. (1980). Coming of age the Apache way. *National Geographic, 157*(2), 262–271.

Rachlin, H. (1995). *Introduction to modern behaviorism.* New York, NY: W.H. Freeman.

Rachlin, H. (2000). Discounting in judgments of delay and probability. *Journal of Behavioral Decision Making, 13,* 145–159.

Rachman, S. (1998). *Anxiety.* Mahwah, NJ: Erlbaum.

Rachman, S. (2000). Joseph Wolpe: Obituary. *American Psychologist, 55,* 431–432.

Rachman, S., & Hodgson, R. (1968). Experimentally-induced "sexual fetishism": Replication and development. *Psychological Record, 18,* 25–27.

Rachman, S.J. (1991). Neo-conditioning and the classical theory of fear acquisition. *Clinical Psychology Review, 11,* 155–173.

Rachman, S.J., & Hodgson, R.J. (1980). *Obsessions and compulsions.* Englewood Cliffs, NJ: Prentice Hall.

Rachman, S.J., Hodgson, R., & Marks, I.M. (1997). The treatment of chronic obsessive-compulsive

disorder. In D.J. Stein & M.H. Stone (Eds.), *Essential papers on obsessive-compulsive disorder.* New York, NY: New York University Press.

Radcliffe, R.A., Erwin, V.G., Bludeau, P., Deng, X., Fay, T., Floyd, K.L., & Deitrich, R.A. (2009). A major QTL for acute ethanol sensitivity in the alcohol tolerant and non-tolerant selected rat lines. *Genes, Brain & Behavior, 8,* 611–625.

Radel, R., Sarrazin, P., Jehu, M., & Pwlletire, L. (2013). Priming motivation through unattended speech. *British Journal of Social Psychology.* Online publication. doi: 10.1111/bjsp.12030.

Radin, D.I. (2006). *Entangled minds: Extrasensory experiences in a quantum reality.* New York, NY: Simon & Schuster.

Radoeva, P.D., Prasad, P., Brainard, D.H., & Aguirre, G.K. (2008). Neural activity within area VI reflects unconscious visual performance in a case of blindsight. *Journal of Cognitive Neuroscience, 20,* 1927–1939.

Rahman, Q. (2005). Fluctuating asymmetry: Second to fourth finger length ratios and human sexual orientation. *Psychoneuroendocrinology, 30,* 382–391.

Raichle, M.E. (1994). Images of the mind: Studies with modern imaging techniques. *Annual Review of Psychology, 45,* 333–356.

Raichle, M.E., MacLeod, A.M., Snyder, A.Z., Powers, W.J., Gusnard, D.A.,& Shulman, G.L. (2001). A default mode of brain function. *Proceedings of the National Academy of Sciences, U.S.A., 98,* 676–682.

Raine, A. (2002). Annotation: The role of prefrontal deficits, low autonomic arousal and early health factors in the development of antisocial and aggressive behavior in children. *Journal of Child Psychology and Psychiatry and Allied Disciplines, 43,* 417–434.

Raine, A. (2008). From genes to brain to antisocial behavior. *Current Directions in Psychological Science, 17,* 323–328.

Raine, A., Buchsbaum, M., & LaCasse, L. (1997). Brain abnormalities in murderers indicated by positron tomography. *Biological Psychiatry, 42,* 495–508.

Raine, A., Lencz, T., Bihrle, S., LaCasse, L., & Colletti, P. (2000). Reduced prefrontal gray matter volume and reduced autonomic activity in antisocial personality disorder. *Archives of General Psychiatry, 57,* 119–127.

Raine, A., Lencz, T., Taylor, K., Hellige, J.B., Bihrle, S., Lacarre, L., Lee, M., ... Colletti, P. (2003). Corpus callosum abnormalities in psychopathic antisocial individuals. *Archives of General Psychiatry, 60,* 1134–1142.

Raine, A., Meloy, J.R., Bihrle, S., Stoddard, J., LaCasse, L., & Buchsbaum, M.S. (1998). Reduced prefrontal and increased subcortical brain functioning assessed using positron emission tomography in predatory and affective murderers. *Behavioral Sciences and the Law, 16,* 319–332.

Rakfeldt, J., Rybash, J.M., & Roodin, P.A. (1996). Affirmative coping: A marker of success in adult therapeutic intervention. In M.L. Commons, J. Demick, & C. Goldberg (Eds.), *Clinical approaches to adult development* (pp. 295–310). Norwood, NJ: Ablex.

Rako, S., & Friebely, J. (2004). Pheromonal influences on sociosexual behavior in postmenopausal women. *Journal of Sex Research, 41,* 372–380.

Ramey, C., & Ramey, S. (1998). Early intervention. *American Psychologist, 53,* 210–225.

Ramey, C.T., Ramey, S.L., & Lanzi, R.G. (1998). Differentiating developmental risk levels for families

in poverty: Creating a family typology. In M. Lewis & C. Feiring (Eds.), *Families, risks, and competence* (pp. 187–206). Mahwah, NJ: Erlbaum.

Ramus, F., Hauser, M.D., Miller, C., Morris, D., & Mehler, J. (2000). Language discrimination by human newborns and by cotton-top tamarin monkeys. *Science, 288*(5464), 349–351.

Rangmar, J., Hjern, A., Vinnerljung, B., Strömland, K., Aronson, M., & Fahlke, C. (2015). Psychosocial outcomes of fetal alcohol syndrome in adulthood. *Pediatrics, 135*(1), e52–e58.

Rao, P.A., Beidel, D.C., & Murray, M.J. (2008). Social skills interventions for children with Asperger's syndrome or high-functioning autism: A review and recommendations. *Journal of Autism and Developmental Disorders, 38*(2), 353–361.

Raphling, D.L. (1998). Aggression: Its relation to desire and self-interest. *Journal of the American Psychoanalytic Association, 46,* 797–811.

Rapoport, J.L. (1991). Recent advances in obsessive–compulsive disorder. *Neuropsychopharmacology 5,* 1–10.

Rasmussen, A.M., & Charney, D.S. (2000). Posttraumatic therapy. In G. Fink (Ed.), *Encyclopedia of stress* (Vol. 2). San Diego, CA: Academic Press.

Ratcliff, R., Thapar, A., & McKoon, G. (2006). Aging and individual differences in rapid two-choice decisions. *Psychonomic Bulletin & Review, 13,* 626–635.

Rauch, S.L., Shin, L.M., & Phelps, E.A. (2006). Neurocircuitry models of posttraumatic stress disorder and extinction: Human neuroimaging research— past, present, and future. *Biological Psychiatry, 60,* 376–382.

Rauch, S.L., van der Kolk, B.A., Fisler, R.E., Alpert, N.M., Orr, S.P., Savage, C.R., ... Pitman, R.K. (1996). A symptom provocation study of posttraumatic stress disorder using positron emission tomography and script-driven imagery. *Archives of General Psychiatry, 53,* 380–387.

Rauscher, F.H., Shaw, G.L., & Ky, K.N. (1993). Music and spatial task performance. *Nature, 365,* 611.

Raven, B.H. (1998). Groupthink, Bay of Pigs, and Watergate reconsidered. *Organizational Behavior and Human Decision Processes, 73,* 352–361.

Raven, J. (1962). *Colored progressive matrices.* New York, NY: The Psychological Corporation.

Ravussin, E., & Gautier, J.F. (1999). Metabolic predictors of weight gain. *International Journal of Obesity and Related Metabolic Disorders, 23* (Suppl. 1), 37–41.

Ravussin, E., Valencia, M.E., Esparza, J., Bennett, P.H., & Schulz, L.O. (1994). Effects of a traditional lifestyle on obesity in Pima Indians. *Diabetes Care, 17,* 1067–1074.

Rawlinson, G. (1999, May 29). Reibadailty. *New Scientist.* Retrieved February 5, 2010, from http://www.newscientist.com/issue/2188.

Ray, O.S., & Ksir, C. (1987). *Drugs, society and human behavior* (4th ed.). St. Louis, MO: Mosby.

Ray, O.S., & Ksir, C.J. (2004). *Drugs, society and human behavior* (9th ed.). Boston, MA: McGraw-Hill.

Ray, W.J. (2000). *Methods: Toward a science of behavior and experience* (6th ed.). Belmont, CA: Wadsworth.

Rayner, K., White, S.J., Johnson, R.L., & Liversedge, S.P. (2006). Raeding wrods with jubmled lettres: There is a cost. *Psychological Science, 17,* 192–193.

Rechtschaffen, A., Bergmann, B.M., Gilliland, M.A., & Bauer, K. (1999). Effects of method, duration, and sleep stage on rebounds from sleep deprivation in the rat. *Sleep, 22,* 11–31.

Regan, D.T., Williams, M., & Sparling, S. (1972). Voluntary expiation of guilt: A field experiment. *Journal of Personality and Social Psychology, 24*, 42–45.

Reger, G.M, Gahm, G.A., Rizzo, A.A., Swanson, R., & Duma, S. (2009). Soldier evaluation of the virtual reality Iraq. *Telemedicine and e-Health, 15*(1), 101–104.

Rehm, J., & Weeks, J. (2005). Abuse of controlled prescription drugs. In *Substance abuse in Canada: Current challenges and choices*. Ottawa, ON: Canadian Centre on Substance Abuse.

Rehm, J., Baliunas, D., Brochu, S., Fischer, B., Gnam, W., Patra, J., Popova, S., Sarnocinska-Hart, A., & Taylor, B. (2006). *The costs of substance abuse in Canada 2002*. Ottawa, ON: Canadian Centre on Substance Abuse.

Reich, T.W. (2006). *Personality disorders research*. London, UK: Brunner-Routledge.

Reichl, A.J. (1997). In-group favouritism and out-group favouritism in low status minimal groups: Differential responses to status-related and status-unrelated measures. *European Journal of Social Psychology, 27*, 617–633.

Reid, A.K., & Staddon, J.E.F. (1998). A dynamic route finder for the cognitive map. *Psychological Review, 105*, 585–601.

Reilly, T. (2009). The body clock and athletic performance. *Biological Rhythm Research, 40*, 37–44.

Reisberg, D. (1997). *Cognition: Exploring the science of the mind*. New York, NY: W.W. Norton.

Remland, M.S., Jones, T.S., & Brinkman, H. (1995). Interpersonal distance, body orientation, and touch: Effects of culture, gender, and age. *Journal of Social Psychology, 135*, 281–297.

Rendell, P.G., & Thomson, D.M. (1993). The effect of aging on remembering to remember: An investigation of simulated medication regimens. *Australian Journal on Ageing, 12*, 11–18.

Rendell, P.G., & Thomson, D.M. (1999). Aging and prospective memory: Differences between naturalistic and laboratory tasks. *Journals of Gerontology: Series B: Psychological Sciences and Social Sciences, 54B*(4), 256–269.

Rensink, R.A. (2002). Change detection. *Annual Review of Psychology, 53*, 247–277.

Renzulli, J.S. (2002). Emerging conceptions of giftedness: Building a bridge to the new century. *Exceptionality, 10*, 67–75.

Repous, G., & Baddeley, A. (2006). The multicomponent model of working memory: Explorations in experimental cognitive psychology. *Neuroscience, 139*, 5–21.

Reppucci, N.D., Wollard, J.L., & Fried, C.S. (1999). Social, community, and preventive interventions. *Annual Review of Psychology, 1*, 387–415.

Rescorla, R.A. (1968). Probability of shock in the presence and absence of CS in fear. *Journal of Comparative and Physiological Psychology, 66*, 1–5.

Rescorla, R.A., & Solomon, R.L. (1967). Two-process learning theory: Relationships between Pavlovian conditioning and instrumental learning. *Psychological Review, 74*, 151–182.

Rescorla, R.A., & Wagner, A.R. (1972). A theory of Pavlovian conditioning: Variations in the effectiveness of reinforcement and non-reinforcement. In A.H. Black & W.F. Prokasky (Eds.), *Classical conditioning: II. Current research and theory* (pp. 64–99). New York, NY: Appleton-Century-Crofts.

Resick, P. (2005). *Stress and trauma*. San Francisco, CA: Taylor & Francis.

Resnick, S.M., Pham, D.L., Kraut, M.A., Zonderman, A.B., & Davatzikos, C. (2003). Longitudinal magnetic resonance imaging studies of older adults: A shrinking brain. *Journal of Neuroscience, 23*, 3295–3301.

Revell, V.L., & Eastman, C.I. (2005). How to trick Mother Nature into letting you fly around or stay up all night. *Journal of Biological Rhythms, 20*, 353–365.

Rey, J.M., & Walter, G. (1997). Half a century of ECT use in young people. *American Journal of Psychiatry, 154*, 595–602.

Rezayof, A., Alijanpour, S., Zarrindast, M.R., & Rassouli, Y. (2008). Ethanol state-dependent memory: Involvement of dorsal hippocampal muscarinic and nicotinic receptors. *Neurobiology of Learning and Memory, 89*, 441–447.

Rhea, P. (2009). Parents ask: Am I risking autism if I vaccinate my children? *Journal of Autism and Developmental Disorders, 39*, 962–963.

Rhee, S.H., & Waldman, I.D. (2002). Genetic and environmental influences on antisocial behavior: A meta-analysis of twin and adoption studies. *Psychological Bulletin, 128*, 490–529.

Rhodes, G. (2006). The evolutionary psychology of facial beauty. *Annual Review of Psychology, 57*, 199–226.

Rhodes, G., Yoshikawa, S., Clark, A., Lee, K., McKay, R., & Akamatsu, S. (2001). Attractiveness of facial averageness and symmetry in non-Western cultures: In search of biologically based standards of beauty. *Perception, 30*, 611–625.

Richard, S., Davies, D.C., & Faure, J.M. (2000). The role of fear in one-trial passive avoidance learning in Japanese quail chicks genetically selected for long or short duration of the tonic immobility reaction. *Behavioural Processes, 48*, 165–170.

Richardson, D.R. (1991). Interpersonal attraction and love. In R.M. Baron, W.G. Graziano, & C. Stangor (Eds.), *Social psychology*. Fort Worth, TX: Holt, Rinehart & Winston.

Rideout, V.J., Foehr, U.G., & Roberts, D.F. (2010). *Generation M2: Media in the lives of 8–18-year-olds*. Retrieved from Kaiser Family Foundation website: http://www.kff.org/entmedia/mh012010pkg.cfm.

Ridout, B., & Campbell, A. (2014). Using facebook to deliver a social norm intervention to reduce problem drinking at university. *Drug and Alcohol Review, 33*(6), 667–673.

Riefer, D.M., Keveri, M.K., & Kramer, D.L.F. (1995). Name that tune: Eliciting the tip-of-the-tongue experience using auditory stimuli. *Psychological Reports, 77*, 1379–1390.

Riesen, A.R. (1965). Effects of early deprivation of photic stimulation. In S. Oster & R. Cooke (Eds.), *The biosocial basis of mental retardation*. Baltimore, MD: Johns Hopkins University Press.

Rilling, M. (1996). The mystery of the vanished citations: James McConnell's forgotten 1960s quest for planarian learning, a biochemical engram, and celebrity. *American Psychologist, 51*, 589–598.

Rips, L.J. (1997). Goals for a theory of deduction: Reply to Johnson-Laird. *Minds & Machines, 7*, 409–424.

Ritblatt, S.N. (2000). Children's level of participation in a false-belief task, age, and theory of mind. *Journal of Genetic Psychology, 161*, 53–64.

Ritchie, C.W., Ames, D., Clayton, T., & Lai, R. (2004). Meta-analysis of randomized trials of the efficacy and safety of donepezil, galantamine, and rivastigmine for the treatment of Alzheimer disease. *American Journal of Geriatric Psychiatry, 12*, 358–369.

Rivera-Tovar, L.A., & Jones, R.T. (1990). Effect of elaboration on the acquisition and maintenance of cardiopulmonary resuscitation. *Journal of Pediatric Psychology, 15*, 123–138.

Rizzo, A., & Kim, G.J. (2005). A SWOT analysis of the field of virtual reality rehabilitation and therapy. *Presence: Teleoperators and Virtual Environments, 14*(2), 99–146.

Rizzo, A.A., Parsons, T., Pair, J., McLay, R., Johnston, S., Perlman, K., ... Difede, J. (2008). Clinical results from the virtual Iraq exposure therapy application for PTSD. Retrieved from http://www.dtic.mil/cgi-bin/GetTRDoc?Location=U2&doc=GetTRDoc.pdf&AD=ADA505737.

Rizzolatti, G., Cattaneo, L., Fabbri-Destro, M., & Rozzi, S. (2014). Cortical mechanisms underlying the organization of goal-directed actions and mirror neuron-based action understanding. *Physiological reviews, 94*(2), 655–706.

Rizzolatti, G., Fadiga, L., Gallese, V., & Fogassi, L. (1996). Premotor cortex and the recognition of motor actions, *Cognitive Brain Research, 3*, 131–141.

Rizzolatti, G., & Sinigaglia, C. (2010). The functional role of the parieto-frontal mirror circuit: interpretations and misinterpretations. *Nature Reviews Neuroscience, 11*, 264–274.

Roberts, B.W., Wood, D., & Caspi, A. (2008). The development of personality traits in adulthood. In O.P. John, R.W. Robins, & L.A. Pervin (Eds.), *Handbook of personality theory and research* (3rd ed.). New York, NY: Guilford Press.

Roberts, W.A. (2010). "Counting" serially presented stimuli by human and nonhuman primates and pigeons. *Learning and Motivation, 41*, 241–251.

Robins, R.W., Gosling, S.D., & Craik, K.H. (1999). An empirical analysis of trends in psychology. *American Psychologist, 54*, 117–128.

Robins, R.W., Norem, J.K., & Cheek, J.M. (1999). Naturalizing the self. In L.A. Pervin & O.P. John (Eds.), *Handbook of personality: Theory and research* (2nd ed.). New York, NY: Guilford Press.

Robinson, D. (1997). *Neurobiology*. New York, NY: Springer-Verlag.

Robinson, D., Wu, H., Munne, R., Ashtari, M., Alvir, J.J., Lerner, G., ... Bogerts, B. (1995). Reduced caudate nucleus volume in obsessive-compulsive disorder. *Archives of General Psychiatry, 52*(5), 393–398.

Robinson, D.T., Clay-Warner, J., Moore, C.D., Everett, T., Watts, A., Tucker, T.N., Thai, C. (2012). Toward an unobtrusive measure of emotion during interaction: Thermal imaging techniques. In Will Kalkhoff, Shane R. Thye, Edward J. Lawler (Eds.), *Biosociology and Neurosociology* (Advances in Group Processes, Vol. 29, pp. 225–266). Wagon Lane, UK: Emerald Group Publishing Limited.

Robles, T.F., & Kiecolt-Glaser, J.K. (2003). The physiology of marriage: Pathways to health. *Physiology & Behavior, 79*, 409–416.

Rodgers, J.E. (1982). The malleable memory of eyewitnesses. *Science Digest, 3*, 32–35.

Rodin, J. (1978). Has the distinction between internal versus external control of feeding outlived its usefulness? In G.A. Bray (Ed.), *Recent advances in obesity research* (Vol. 2). London, UK: Newman.

Rodin, J. (1981). Current status of the internal-external hypothesis for obesity: What went wrong? *American Psychologist, 36*, 361–372.

Rodin, J., Bartoshuk, L., Peterson, C., & Schank, D. (1990). Bulimia and taste: Possible interactions. *Journal of Abnormal Psychology, 99*, 32–39.

Rodin, J., Wack, J., Ferrannini, E., & Defronzo, R.A. (1985). Effect of insulin and glucose on feeding behavior. *Metabolism, 34*, 826–831.

Roelofs, K., Hoogduin, K.A.L., Keijsers, G.P.J., Naering, G.W.B, Moene, F.C., & Sandijck, P. (2002). Hypnotic susceptibility in patients with conversion disorder. *Journal of Abnormal Psychology, 111*, 390–395.

Roeser, R.W., Schonert-Reichl, K.A., Jha, A., Cullen, M., Wallace, L., Wilensky, R., Oberle, E., Thomson, K., Taylor, C., & Harrison, J. (2013). Mindfulness training and reductions in teacher stress and burnout: Results from two randomized, waitlist-control field trials. *Journal of Educational Psychology, 105*, 787–804.

Roeser, R.W., Skinner, E., Beers, J., & Jennings, P.A. (2012). Mindfulness training and teachers' professional development: An emerging area of research and practice. *Child Development Perspectives, 6*, 167–173.

Rogers, C.R. (1951). *Client-centered therapy.* Boston, MA: Houghton Mifflin.

Rogers, C.R. (1959). A theory of therapy, personality and interpersonal relationships, as developed in the client-centered framework. In S. Koch (Ed.), *Psychology: A study of a science* (Vol. 3). New York, NY: McGraw-Hill.

Rogers, C.R. (1980). *A way of being.* Boston, MA: Houghton Mifflin.

Rogers, C.R., & Dymond, R.F. (1954). *Psychotherapy and personality change: Coordinated studies in the client-centered approach.* Chicago, IL: University of Chicago Press.

Rogers, E.J., Vaughan, P.W., Swalahe, R.M.A., Rao, N., & Sood, S. (1996). *Effects of an entertainment-education radio soap opera on family planning and HIV/AIDS prevention behavior in Tanzania.* Unpublished manuscript, Department of Communication and Journalism, University of New Mexico at Albuquerque.

Rohrer, J.H., Baron, S.H., Hoffman, E.L., & Swander, D.V. (1954). The stability of autokinetic judgments. *Journal of Abnormal and Social Psychology, 49*, 595–597.

Rohsenow, D.J., & Marlatt, G.A. (1981). The balanced placebo design: Methodological considerations. *Addictive Behaviors, 6*, 107–122.

Rohsenow, D.J., & Smith, R.E. (1985). Stress management training as a prevention program for heavy social drinkers: Cognitions, affect, drinking, and individual differences. *Addictive Behaviors, 10*, 45–54.

Roland, P.E. (1997). *Brain activation.* New York, NY: Wiley.

Rolls, B.J., Morris, E.L., & Roe, L.S. (2002). Portion size of food affects energy intake in normal-weight and overweight men and women. *American Journal of Clinical Nutrition, 76*, 1207–1213.

Rolls, B.J., Rolls, E.T., Rowe, E.A., & Sweeney, K. (1981). Sensory specific satiety in man. *Physiology and Behavior, 27*, 137–142.

Rolls, E.T. (2000). Memory systems in the brain. *Annual Review of Psychology, 5*, 599–630.

Rolls, E.T. (2010). The affective and cognitive processing of touch, oral texture, and temperature in the brain. *Neuroscience and Biobehavioral Reviews, 34*, 237–245.

Rolls, E.T., & Deco, G. (2002). *Computational neuroscience of vision.* London, UK: Oxford University Press.

Romeo, R.D., & McEwen, B.S. (2006). Stress and the adolescent brain. *Annals of the New York Academy of Sciences, 1094*, 202–214.

Ron, M.A., & David, A.S. (1997). *Disorders of brain and mind.* Cambridge, UK: Cambridge University Press.

Ronquillo, J., Denson, T.F., Lickel, B., Lu, Z., Nandy, A., & Maddox, K.B. (2007). The effects of skin tone on race-related amygdala activity: An fMRI investigation. *Social Cognitive and Affective Neuroscience, 2*(1), 39–44.

Roos, S. (2013). The Kübler-Ross Model: An esteemed relic. *Gestalt Review, 17*, 312–315.

Rosch, E. (1973). On the internal structure of perceptual and semantic categories. In T.E. Moore (Ed.), *Cognitive development and the acquisition of language.* New York, NY: Academic Press.

Rosch, E. (1977). Human categorization. In N. Warren (Ed.), *Advances in cross-cultural psychology* (Vol. 1). London, UK: Academic Press.

Rose, S.A., Feldman, J.F., Jankowski, J.J., & Van Rossem, R. (2012). Information processing from infancy to 11 years: Continuities and prediction of IQ. *Intelligence, 40*(5), 445–457.

Rosen, C.S. (2000). Integrating stage and continuum models to explain processing of exercise messages and exercise initiation among sedentary college students. *Health Psychology, 19*, 172–180.

Rosenbaum, A., Abend, S.S., Gearan, P.J., & Fletcher, K.E. (1997). Serotonergic functioning in partner-abusive men. In A. Raine, P.A. Brennan, D.P. Farrington, & S.A. Mednick (Eds.), *Biosocial bases of violence.* New York, NY: Plenum Press.

Rosenbaum, M.E. (1986). The repulsion hypothesis: On the on-development of relationships. *Journal of Personality and Social Psychology, 51*, 1156–1166.

Rosenbloom, T. (2006). Driving performance while using cell phones: An observational study. *Journal of Safety Research, 37*, 207–212.

Rosenfarb, I.S., Goldstein, M.J., Mintz, J., & Nuechterlein, K.H. (1995). Expressed emotion and subclinical psychopathology observable within the transactions between schizophrenic patients and their family members. *Journal of Abnormal Psychology, 104*, 259–267.

Rosenhan, D. (1973). On being sane in insane places. *Science, 179*, 250–258.

Rosenhan, D.L., & Seligman, M.E.P. (1989). *Abnormal psychology* (2nd ed.). New York, NY: W.W. Norton.

Rosenman, R.H., Brand, R.J., Jenkins, C.D., Friedman, M., Straus, R., & Wurm, M. (1975). Coronary heart disease in the Western Collaborative Group Study: 8½ year follow-up. *Journal of the American Medical Association, 233*, 872–877.

Rosenthal, N.E., & Wehr, T.A. (1987). Seasonal affective disorders. *Psychiatric Annals, 17*, 670–674.

Rosenthal, R., Archer, D., DiMatteo, M.R., Koivumaki, J.H., & Rogers, P.L. (1974). Body talk and tone of voice: The language without words. *Psychology Today, 8*, 64–71.

Rosenzweig, M.R. (1984). Experience, memory, and the brain. *American Psychologist, 39*, 365–376.

Rosenzweig, S. (1992). Freud and experimental psychology: The emergence of idiodynamics. In S. Koch & D.E. Leary (Eds.), *A century of psychology as science.* Washington, DC: American Psychological Association.

Ross, C.A. (2009). Errors of logic and scholarship concerning dissociative identity disorder. *Journal of Child Sexual Abuse, 18*, 221–231.

Ross, L. (2001). Getting down to fundamentals: Lay dispositionism and the attributes of psychologists. *Psychological Inquiry, 12*, 37–40.

Ross, L., & Nisbett, R.E. (1991). *The person and the situation: Perspectives of social psychology.* New York, NY: McGraw-Hill.

Ross, R.J., Ball, W.A., Sullivan, K.A., & Caroff, S.N. (1989). Sleep disturbance as the hallmark of posttraumatic stress disorder. *American Journal of Psychiatry, 146*, 697–707.

Rossell, S.L., Bullmore, E.T., Williams, S.C.R., & David, A.S. (2002). Sex differences in functional brain activation during a lexical visual field task. *Brain and Language, 80*, 97–105.

Rothbaum, B.O., Anderson, P., Zimand, E., Hodges, L., Lang, D., & Wilson, J. (2006). Virtual reality exposure therapy and standard (in vivo) exposure therapy in the treatment of fear of flying. *Behavior Therapy, 37*, 80–90.

Rothbaum, B.O., Hodges, L.F., Kooper, R., Opdyke, D., Williford, J.S., & North, M. (1995). Virtual reality graded exposure in the treatment of acrophobia: A case report. *Behavior Therapy, 26*, 547–554.

Rothbaum, B.O., Hodges, L., Smith, S., Lee, J.H., & Prince, L. (2000). A controlled study of virtual reality exposure therapy for the fear of flying. *Journal of Consulting and Clinical Psychology, 68*, 1020–1026.

Rotheram-Borus, M.J., Desmond, K., Comulada, W.S., Arnold, E.M., & Johnson, M. (2008). Reducing risky sexual behavior and substance abuse among currently and formerly homeless adults living with HIV. *American Journal of Public Health, 98*, 409–417.

Rotter, J.B. (1954). *Social learning and clinical psychology.* Englewood Cliffs, NJ: Prentice Hall.

Rotter, J.B. (1966). Generalized expectancies for internal versus external control of reinforcement. *Psychological Monographs, 80* (Whole No. 609).

Rotton, J., & Cohn, E.G. (2000). Violence is a curvilinear function of temperature in Dallas: A replication. *Journal of Personality and Social Psychology, 78*, 1074–1081.

Rouw, R., & Scholte, H.S. (2007). Increased structural connectivity in grapheme-color synesthesia. *Nature Neuroscience, 10*, 792–797.

Rovere, H., Rossini, S., & Reimão, R. (2008). Quality of life in patients with narcolepsy: A WHOQOL-brief study. *Arquivos de Neuro-Psiquiatria, 66*, 163–167.

Rowden, P., Watson, B., Haworth, N., Lennon, A., Shaw, L., & Blackman, R. (2016). Motorcycle riders' self-reported aggression when riding compared with car driving. *Transportation Research Part F: Traffic Psychology and Behaviour, 36*, 92–103.

Rowe, D.C. (1999). Heredity. In V.J. Derlega, B.A. Winstead, & W.H. Jones (Eds.), *Personality: Contemporary theory and research.* Chicago, IL: Nelson-Hall.

Rowley, J.T., Stickgold, R., & Hobson, J.A. (1998). Eyelid movements and mental activity at sleep onset. *Consciousness and Cognition: An International Journal, 7*, 67–84.

Rubin, D.C., & Kozin, M. (1984). Vivid memories. *Cognition, 16*, 81–95.

Rubin, R.T. (2000). Depression and manic-depressive illness. In G. Fink (Ed.), *Encyclopedia of stress* (Vol. 1). San Diego, CA: Academic Press.

Rubonis, A.V., & Bickman, L. (1991). Psychological impairment in the wake of disaster: The disaster-psychopathology relationship. *Psychological Bulletin, 109*, 384–399.

Rudatsikira, E., Muula, A.S., & Siziya, S. (2008). Variables associated with physical fighting among US high-school students. *Clinical Practice and Epidemiology in Mental Health, 4.* Online publication. doi:10.1186/1745-0179-4-16.

Ruffman, R., Perner, J., Naito, M., Parkin, L., & Clements, W.A. (1998). Older (but not younger) siblings facilitate false belief understanding. *Developmental Psychology, 34*, 161–174.

Ruger, M., St. Hilaire, M.A., Brainard, G.C., Khalsa, S.B., Kronauer, R.E., Czeisler, C.A., & Lockley, S.W. (2012). Human phase response curve to a single 6.5 h pulse of short-wavelength light. *The Journal of Physiology, 591,* 353–363.

Ruiz, F.J. (2012). Acceptance and commitment therapy versus traditional cognitive behavioral therapy a systematic review and meta-analysis of current empirical evidence. *International Journal of Psychology and Psychological Therapy, 12*(3), 333–358.

Rumbaugh, D.M. (1990). Comparative psychology and the great apes: Their competency in learning, language, and numbers. *Psychological Record, 40,* 15–39.

Rumstein, M.O., & Hunsley, J. (2001). Interpersonal and family functioning of female survivors of childhood sexual abuse. *Clinical Psychology Review, 21,* 471–490.

Runquist, W.N. (1975). Interference among memory traces. *Memory and Cognition, 3,* 143–159.

Ruscio, M.G., Sweeny, T., Hazelton, J., Suppatkul, P., & Carter, C.S. (2007). Social environment regulates corticotrophin releasing factor, corticosterone and vasopressin in juvenile prairie voles. *Hormones and Behavior, 51,* 54–61.

Rush, A.J., Crismon, M.L., Toprac, M.G., Trivedi, M.H., Rago, W.V., Shon, S., & Altshuler, K.Z. (1998). Consensus guidelines in the treatment of major depressive disorder. *Journal of Clinical Psychiatry, 59* (Suppl. 20), 73–84.

Rush, A.J., Warden, D., Wisniewski, S.R., Fava, M., Trivedi, M., Gaynes, B.N., & Nierenberg, A.A. (2009). STAR*D: Revising conventional wisdom. *CNS Drugs, 23,* 627–647.

Rushton, J.P. (1989). Genetic similarity, human altruism, and group selection. *Behavioral and Brain Sciences, 12,* 503–559.

Rushton, J.P. (1995). Asian achievement, brain size, and evolution: Comments on A.H. Yee. *Educational Psychology Review, 7*(4), 373–380.

Rushton, J.P. (2012). No narrowing in mean Black–White IQ differences—Predicted by heritable *g. American Psychologist, 67*(6), 500–501.

Rushton, J.P., & Davison, A.C. (2009). Whole brain size and general mental ability: A review. *International Journal of Neuroscience, 119,* 691–731.

Russell, J.A. (1994). Is there universal recognition of emotion from facial expressions? A review of the cross-cultural studies. *Psychological Bulletin, 115,* 102–141.

Russell, J.C. (1989). Anxiety disorders in Japan: A review of the Japanese literature on Shinkeishitsu and Taijin Kyofushu. *Culture, Medicine, and Psychiatry, 13,* 391–403.

Russell, P.A., Deregowski, J.B., & Kinnear, P.R. (1997). Perception and aesthetics. In J.W. Berry, P.R. Dasen, & T.S. Saraswathi (Eds.), *Handbook of cross-cultural psychology, Vol. 2: Basic processes and human development* (2nd ed., pp. 107–142). Boston, MA: Allyn & Bacon.

Rusting, C.L., & DeHart, T. (2000). Retrieving positive memories to regulate negative mood: Consequences for mood-congruent memory. *Journal of Personality and Social Psychology, 78*(4), 737–752.

Rutter, D.R. (2000). Attendance and reattendance for breast cancer screening: A prospective 3-year test of the Theory of Planned Behaviour. *British Journal of Health Psychology, 5,* 1–13.

Rutter, M. (2014). Nature-nurture integration. *Handbook of developmental psychopathology* (3rd ed.,

pp. 45–65). New York, NY: Springer Science + Business Media.

Rutter, M.L. (1997). Nature-nurture integration: The example of antisocial behavior. *American Psychologist, 52,* 390–398.

Ryan, L., & Eich, E. (2000). Mood dependence and implicit memory. In E. Tulving (Ed.), *Memory, consciousness, and the brain: The Tallinn Conference* (pp. 91–105). Philadelphia, PA: Psychology Press/Taylor & Francis.

Ryan, R.M., & Lynch, J. (1989). Emotional autonomy versus detachment: Revisiting the vicissitudes of adolescence and young adulthood. *Child Development, 60,* 340–356.

Ryder, N., & Leinonen, E. (2014). Pragmatic language development in language impaired and typically developing children: Incorrect answers in context. *Journal of Psycholinguistic Research, 43*(1), 45–58.

Ryle, A. (2010). Cognitive analytic therapy. In N. Kazantzis, M.A. Reinecke, & A. Freeman (Eds.), *Cognitive and behavioral theories in clinical practice* (pp. 244–277). New York, NY: Guilford Press.

Saad, L. (1999, April 23). *Public views Littleton tragedy as sign of deeper problems in country.* Gallup News Service. Princeton, NJ: Gallup Organization.

Saari, L.M., Johnson, T.R., McLaughlin, S.D., & Zimmerle, D.M. (1988). A survey of management training and education practices in U.S. companies. *Personnel Psychology, 41,* 731–743.

Sachse, R., & Elliott, R. (2002). Process-outcome research on humanistic therapy variables. In D.J. Cain (Ed.), *Humanistic psychotherapies: Handbook of research and practice.* Washington, DC: American Psychological Association.

Sack, R.L., & Lewy, A.J. (1997). Melatonin as a chronobiotic: Treatment of circadian desynchrony in night workers and the blind. *Journal of Biological Rhythms, 12,* 595–603.

Sacks, O. (1985, 1986). *The man who mistook his wife for a hat and other clinical tales.* New York, NY: Summit Books/Simon & Schuster.

Sacks, O. (1993). To see and not to see: A neurologist's notebook. *The New Yorker, 59,* 69.

Sadoski, M., Kealy, W.A., Goetz, E.T., & Paivio, A. (1997). Concreteness and imagery effects in the written composition of definitions. *Journal of Educational Psychology, 89,* 518–526.

Saffran, E.M., Schwartz, M.F., & Martin, O.S.M. (1980). Evidence from aphasia: Isolating the components of a production model. In B. Butterworth (Ed.), *Language production.* London, UK: Academic Press.

Sagi, A., & Hoffman, M.L. (1976). Empathic distress in the newborn. *Developmental Psychology, 12,* 175–176.

Saito, A., & Shinozuka, K. (2013). Vocal recognition of owners by domestic cats (Felis catus). *Animal Cognition. 16,* 685–690.

Sakellaropoulo, M., & Baldwin, M.W. (2006). The hidden sides of self-esteem: Two dimensions of implicit self-esteem and their relation to narcissistic reactions. *Journal of Experimental Social Psychology, 43,* 995–1001.

Saklofske, D.H., Austin, E.J., Galloway, J., & Davidson, K. (2007). Individual difference correlates of health-related behaviours: Preliminary evidence for links between emotional intelligence and coping. *Personality and Individual Differences, 42,* 491–502.

Saling, L.L., & Phillips, J.G. (2007). Automatic behaviour: Efficient not mindless. *Brain Research Bulletin, 73,* 1–20.

Salovey, P., Mayer, J.D., & Rosenhan, D.L. (1991). Mood and helping: Mood as a motivator of helping and helping as a regulator of mood. In M.S. Clark (Ed.), *Prosocial behavior* (Vol. 12). Newbury Park, CA: Sage.

Salovey, P., & Pizzaro, D.A. (2003). The value of emotional intelligence. In R.J. Sternberg, J. Lautrey, & T.I. Lubart (Eds.), *Models of intelligence: International perspectives.* Washington, DC: American Psychological Association.

Salthouse, T.A. (2004). What and when of cognitive aging. *Current Directions in Psychological Science, 13,* 140–144.

Saltzman, A.L. (2000). The role of the obedience experiments in Holocaust studies: The case for renewed visibility. In T. Blass (Ed.), *Obedience to authority: Current perspectives on the Milgram paradigm* (pp. 125–144). Mahwah, NJ: Erlbaum.

Salvatore, J.E., & Dick, D.M. (2015). Gene-environment interplay: Where we are, where we are going. *Journal of Marriage and Family, 77*(2), 344–350.

Sana, F., Weston, T., & Cepeda, N.J. (2013). Laptop multitasking hinders classroom learning for both users and nearby peers. *Computers & Education, 62,* 24–31.

Sandler, J. (1986). Aversion methods. In F.H. Kanfer & A.P. Goldstein (Eds.), *Helping people change: A textbook of methods* (3rd ed.). New York, NY: Pergamon Press.

Sanes, J.R., & Masland, R.H. (2015). The types of retinal ganglion cells: Current status and implications for neuronal classification. *Annual Review of Neuroscience, 38,* 221–246.

Sarason, I.G., & Sarason, B.R. (1990). Test anxiety. In H. Leitenberg (Ed.), *Handbook of social and evaluation anxiety* (pp. 475–495). New York, NY: Plenum Press.

Sarason, I.G., Sarason, B.R., Pierce, G.R., Shearin, E.N., & Sayers, M.H. (1991). A social learning approach to increasing blood donations. *Journal of Applied Social Psychology, 21,* 896–918.

Saremi, M., Grenèche, J., Bonneford, A., Rohmer, O., Eschenlauer, A., & Tassi, P. (2008). Effects of nocturnal railway noise on sleep fragmentation in young and middle-aged subjects as a function of type of train and sound level. *International Journal of Psychophysiology, 70,* 184–191.

Sasseville, A., Benhaberou-Brun, D., Fontaine, C., Charon, M.C., & Hébert, M. (2009). Wearing blue-blockers in the morning could improve sleep of workers on a permanent night schedule: A pilot study. *Chronobiology International, 26,* 913–925.

Sataloff, J., & Thayer, R. (2006). *Hearing loss.* New York, NY: Marcel Dekker.

Satcher, D. (1999). *Mental health: A report of the Surgeon General.* Washington, DC: U.S. Department of Health and Human Services.

Satcher, D. (2000). *Mental health: A report of the Surgeon General.* Washington, DC: U.S. Department of Health and Human Services.

Sattel, H., Lahmann, C., Gundel, H., Guthrie, E., Kruse, J., Noll-Hussong, M., Ohmann, C., Ronel, J., Sack, M., Sauer, N., Schneider, G, & Henningsen, P. (2012). Brief psychodynamic interpersonal psychotherapy for patients with multisomatoform disorder: Randomised controlled trial. *British Journal of Psychiatry, 203*(3), 60–67.

Saurer, T.B., James, S.G., Carrigan K.A., & Lysle, D.T. (2008). Neuroimmune mechanisms of opioid-mediated conditioned immunomodulation. *Brain, Behavior, & Immunity, 22,* 89–97.

Savage, P.J., & Bennett, P.H. (1992). Obesity and diabetes in American Indians and their inter-relationships among the Pima Indians of Arizona. In E.W. Haller & L.P. Aitken (Eds.), *Mashkiki: Old medicine nourishing the new. American Indians and Alaska Natives in biomedical research careers.* Lanham, MD: University Press of America.

Savage-Rumbaugh, E.S., McDonald, K., & Sevcik, R.A. (1986). Spontaneous symbol acquisition and communicative use by pygmy chimpanzees (pan paniscus). *Journal of Experimental Psychology: General, 115,* 211–235.

Savage-Rumbaugh, E.S., Murphy, J., Sevcik, R.A., Brakke, K.E., Williams, S.L., & Rumbaugh, D.M. (1993). Language comprehension in ape and child. *Monographs of the Society for Research in Child Development, 58*(233), 1–254.

Sawle, G.V., Hymas, N.F., Lees, A.J., & Frackowiak, R.S.J. (1991). Obsessional slowness: Functional studies with positron emission tomography. *Brain, 114,* 2191–2202.

Saxena, S., Brody, A.L., Schwartz, J.M., & Baxter, L.R. (1998). Neuroimaging and frontal-subcortical circuitry in obsessive-compulsive disorder. *British Journal of Psychiatry, 173*(35S), 26–37.

Scarr, S. (1992). Developmental theories for the 1990s: Development and individual differences. *Child Development, 63,* 1–19.

Scarr, S., & McCartney, K. (1983). How do people make their own environments: A theory of geno-type environment effects. *Child Development, 54,* 424–435.

Scarr, S., & Weinberg, R.A. (1977). Intellectual similarities within families of both adopted and biological children. *Intelligence, 32,* 170–190.

Schachter, S. (1959). *The psychology of affiliation: Experimental studies of the sources of gregariousness.* Stanford, CA: Stanford University Press.

Schachter, S. (1966). The interaction of cognitive and physiological determinants of emotional state. In C.D. Spielberger (Ed.), *Anxiety and behavior.* New York, NY: Academic Press.

Schachter, S. (1968). Obesity and eating. *Science, 16,* 751–756.

Schachter, S. (1982). Recidivism and self-cure of smoking and obesity. *American Psychologist, 37,* 436–444.

Schachter, S., & Wheeler, L. (1962). Epinephrine, chlorpromazine, and amusement. *Journal of Abnormal and Social Psychology, 65,* 121–128.

Schacter, D.L. (1992). Understanding implicit memory: A cognitive neuroscience approach. *American Psychologist, 47,* 559–569.

Schacter, D.L., & Curran, T. (2000). Memory without remembering and remembering without memory: Implicit and false memories. In M.S. Gazzaniga (Ed.), *The new cognitive neurosciences* (2nd ed., pp. 829–841). Cambridge, MA: MIT Press.

Schaie, K.W. (1994). The course of adult intellectual development. *American Psychologist, 49,* 304–313.

Schaie, K.W. (1998). The Seattle Longitudinal Studies of adult intelligence. In M. Lawton & T.A. Salthouse (Eds.), *Essential papers on the psychology of aging.* New York, NY: University Press.

Schaie, K.W. (2005). *Developmental influences on adult intelligence: The Seattle Longitudinal Study.* London, UK: Oxford University Press.

Schaller, M., & Crandall, C.S. (Eds.). (2004). *The psychological foundations of culture.* Mahwah, NJ: Erlbaum.

Schaller, M., Norenzayan, A., Heine, S.J., Yamagishi, T., & Kameda, T. (Eds.). (2010). *Evolution,*

culture, and the human mind. New York, NY: Psychology Press.

Schatzberg, A.F., Cole, J.O., & DeBattista, C. (2005). *Manual of clinical psychopharmacology.* Washington, DC: American Psychiatric Publishing.

Schatzberg, A.F., Cole, J.O., & DeBattista, C. (2010). *Manual of clinical psychopharmacology.* Washington, DC: American Psychiatric Publishing.

Scheele, D., Kendrick, K.M., Khouri, C., Kretzer, E., Schläpfer, T.E., Stoffel-Wagner, B., ... & Hurlemann, R. (2014). An oxytocin-induced facilitation of neural and emotional responses to social touch correlates inversely with autism traits. *Neuropsychopharmacology, 39*(9), 2078–2085.

Scheff, T.J. (1966). *Being mentally ill: A sociological theory.* Chicago, IL: Aldine.

Scheier, M.F., & Carver, C.S. (1985). Optimism, coping, and health: Assessment and implications of generalized outcome expectancies. *Health Psychology, 4,* 219–247.

Schellenberg, E.G., Corrigall, K.A., Dys, S.P., & Malti, T. (2015). Group music training and children's prosocial skills. *PLoS ONE, 10*(10). Retrieved from https://www.lib.uwo.ca/cgi-bin /ezpauthn.cgi?url=http://search.proquest.com /docview/1751223261?accountid=15115.

Schellenberg, G.D., Dawson, G., Sung, Y.J., Estes, A., Munson, J., Rosenthal, E., ... Wijsman, E.M. (2006). Evidence for genetic linkage of autism to chromosomes 7 and 4. *Molecular Psychiatry, 11,* 979–989.

Schenck, C.H., Hurwitz, T.D., & Mahowald, M.W. (1993). REM sleep behavior disorder: A report on a series of 96 consecutive cases and a review of the literature. *Journal of Sleep Research, 2,* 189–224.

Schenck, C.H., Milner, D.M., Hurwitz, T.D., & Bundlie, S.R. (1989). A polysomnographic and clinical report on sleep-related injury in 100 adult patients. *American Journal of Psychiatry, 146,* 1166–1173.

Scherer, K. (1984). On the nature and function of emotion: A component process approach. In K. Scherer & P. Ekman (Eds.), *Approaches to emotion.* Hillsdale, NJ: Erlbaum.

Scherer, K. (1998). The role of injustice in the elicitation of differential emotional reactions. *Personality and Social Psychology Bulletin, 24,* 769–783.

Scherer, K.R. (1988). *Facets of emotion: Recent research.* Hillsdale, NJ: Erlbaum.

Schermer, J.A., Johnson, A.M., Jang, K.L., & Vernon, P.A. (2015). Phenotypic, genetic, and environmental relationships between self-reported talents and measured intelligence. *Twin Research and Human Genetics, 18*(1), 36–42.

Schibler, U. (2006). Circadian time keeping: The daily ups and downs of genes, cells, and organisms. *Progress in Brain Research, 153,* 271–282.

Schiff, M., & Lewontin, R. (1986). *Education and class: The irrelevance of IQ genetic studies.* Oxford, UK: Clarendon Press.

Schiff, W., & Foulke, E. (Eds.). (2010). *Tactual perception: A sourcebook.* New York, NY: Cambridge University Press.

Schimanski, L.A., & Nguyen, P.V. (2005). Impaired fear memories are correlated with subregion-specific deficits in hippocampal and amygdalar LTP. *Behavioral Neuroscience, 119,* 38–54.

Schimmack, U., Oishi, S., Furr, M., & Funder, D.C. (2004). Personality and life satisfaction: A facet-level analysis. *Personality and Social Psychology Bulletin, 30,* 1062–1075.

Schlegel, A., & Barry, H. (1991). *Adolescence: An anthropological inquiry.* New York, NY: Free Press.

Schlesinger, L.B. (Ed.). (2007). *Explorations in criminal psychopathology: Clinical syndromes with forensic implications.* Springfield, IL: Charles C Thomas.

Schmajuk, N.A., & Holland, P.C. (Eds.). (1998). *Occasion setting: Associative learning and cognition in animals.* Washington, DC: American Psychological Association.

Schmid, D.A., Held, K., Ising, M., Uhr, M., Weikel, J.C., & Steiger, A. (2005). Ghrelin stimulates appetite, imagination of food, GH, ACTH, and cortisol, but does not affect leptin in normal controls. *Neuropsychopharmacology, 30,* 1187–1192.

Schmidt, F.L., & Hunter, J. (2004). General mental ability in the world of work: Occupational attainment and job performance. *Journal of Personality and Social Psychology, 86,* 162–173.

Schmithorst, V.J., & Holland, S.K. (2007). Sex differences in the development of neuroanatomical functional connectivity underlying intelligence found using Bayesian connectivity analysis. *NeuroImage, 35,* 406–419.

Schmitt, D.P., Shackelford, T.K., & Buss, D.M. (2001). Are men really more "oriented" toward short-term mating than women? A critical review of theory and research. *Psychology, Evolution and Gender, 3,* 211–239.

Schmolck, H., Buffalo, E.A., & Squire, L.R. (2000). Memory distortions develop over time: Recollections of the O.J. Simpson trial verdict after 15 and 32 months. *Psychological Science, 11,* 39–45.

Schneider Helmert, D. (1985). Overestimation of hypnotic drug effects by insomniacs: A hypothesis. *Psychopharmacology, 87,* 107–110.

Schneider, W., Kron, V., Hunnerkopf, M., & Krajewski, K. (2004). The development of young children's memory strategies: First findings from the Wurzburg Longitudinal Memory Study. *Journal of Experimental Child Psychology, 88,* 193–209.

Schoen, L.M. (1996). Monopoly: Board games and mnemonics. *Teaching of Psychology, 23,* 30–32.

Schoop, V.M., Gardziella, S., & Muller, C.M. (1997). Critical period-dependent reduction of the permissiveness of cat visual cortex tissue for neuronal adhesion and neurite growth. *European Journal of Neuroscience, 9,* 1911–1922.

Schore, A.N. (2002). Dysregulation of the right brain: A fundamental mechanism of traumatic attachment and the psychopathogenesis of post-traumatic stress disorder. *Australian and New Zealand Journal of Psychiatry, 36,* 9–30.

Schraw, G., Crippen, K.J., & Hartley, K. (2006). Promoting self-regulation in science education: Metacognition as part of a broader perspective on learning. *Research in Science Education, 36*(1–2), 111–139.

Schul, Y., Mayo, R., & Burnstein, E. (2004). Encoding under trust and distrust: The spontaneous activation of incongruent cognitions. *Journal of Personality and Social Psychology, 86,* 668–679.

Schulz, R., & Aderman, D. (1980). Clinical research and the stages of dying. In R.A. Kalish (Ed.), *Death, dying, and transcending.* Farmingdale, NY: Baywood.

Schunk, D.H., Pintrich, P.R., & Meese, J. (2007). *Motivation in education: Theory, research, and application.* Englewood Cliffs, NJ: Prentice Hall.

Schüssler, P., Kluge, M., Yassouridis, A., Dresler, M., Uhr, M., & Steiger, A. (2012). Ghrelin levels increase after pictures showing food. *Obesity, 20,* 1212–1217.

Schwartz, B.L. (1998). Illusory tip-of-the-tongue states. *Memory, 6,* 623–642.

Schwartz, R. (1984). Body weight regulation. *University of Washington Medicine, 10,* 16–20.

Schwarz, J. (2009, June 11). If the shoe fits, duck: A real-life example of humans' dual vision system. *University of Washington News and Information.* Retrieved November 17, 2009, from www.uwnews.org.

Schwarzer, R. (1998). Stress and coping from a social-cognitive perspective. *Annals of the New York Academy of Sciences, 851,* 531–537.

Schweinhart, L.J., & Weikart, D.P. (1998). High Scope/Perry Preschool Program effects at age twenty-seven. In J. Crane (Ed.), *Social programs that work* (pp. 148–162). New York, NY: Russell Sage.

ScienceDaily. (2009, November 11). Human-machine interface is essential link in ground-breaking prosthetic hand. Retrieved December 7, 2009, from http://www.sciencedaily.com/releases/2009/11/091104132708.htm.

Scoboria, A., Mazzoni, G., Kirsch, I., & Milling, L.S. (2002). Immediate and persisting effects of misleading questions and hypnosis on memory reports. *Journal of Experimental Psychology: Applied, 8,* 26–32.

Scott, T.R. (1992). Taste, feeding, and pleasure. In A.N. Epstein & A.R. Morrison. (Eds.), *Progress in psychobiology and physiological psychology.* San Diego, CA: Academic Press.

Scott, T.R., & Giza, B.K. (1993). Gustatory control of ingestion. In D.A. Booth (Ed.), *Neurophysiology of ingestion. Pergamon studies in neuroscience.* Oxford, UK: Pergamon Press.

Scoville, W.B., & Milner, B. (1957). Loss of recent memory after bilateral hippocampal lesions. *Journal of Neurology, Neurosurgery, and Psychiatry, 20,* 11–21.

Sears, D.O., & Kinder, D.R. (1985). Whites' opposition to busing: On conceptualizing and operationalizing group conflict. *Journal of Personality and Social Psychology, 48,* 1141–1147.

Segall, M.H., Campbell, D.T., & Herskovits, M.J. (1966). *The influence of culture on visual perception.* Oxford, UK: Bobbs-Merrill.

Segerdahl, P., Fields, W., & Savage-Rumbaugh, E.S. (2006). *Kanzi's primal language: The cultural initiation of primates into language.* New York, NY: Palgrave Macmillan.

Segerstrom, S.C., & Miller, G.E. (2004). Psychological stress and the human immune system: A meta-analytic study of 30 years of inquiry. *Psychological Bulletin, 130,* 601–630.

Segerstrom, S.C., Taylor, S.E., Kemeny, M.E., & Fahey, J.L. (1998). Optimism is associated with mood, coping and immune change in response to stress. *Journal of Personality and Social Psychology, 74,* 1646–1655.

Seilabipour, N.M., Fallah, S.M., Kazemi, H., & Shariat, S.V. (2013). Phantom limb correlates among amputee war veterans. *Advances in Cognitive Science, 15*(258), 32–39.

Sekuler, R., Watamaniuk, S., & Blake, R. (2002). In H. Pashler & S. Yantis (Eds.), *Steven's handbook of experimental psychology: Vol. 1 Sensation and perception* (3rd ed.). New York, NY: Wiley.

Selby, E.A., & Joiner, T.E. (2009). Cascades of emotion: The emergence of borderline personality disorder from emotional and behavioral dysregulation. *Review of General Psychology, 13,* 219–229.

Selby, E.A., Anestis, M.D., Bender, T.W., & Joiner, T.E. (2009). An exploration of the emotional cascade model in borderline personality disorder. *Journal of Abnormal Psychology, 118,* 375–387.

Seligman, M.E.P. (1970). On the generality of the laws of learning. *Psychological Review, 77,* 406–418.

Seligman, M.E.P. (1971). Phobias and preparedness. *Behavior Therapy, 2,* 307–320.

Seligman, M.E.P. (1989). Research in clinical psychology: Why is there so much depression today? In I.S. Cohen (Ed.), *The G. Stanley Hall lecture series* (Vol. 9). Washington, DC: American Psychological Association.

Seligman, M.E.P. (1991). *Learned optimism.* New York, NY: Knopf.

Seligman, M.E.P. (1995). The effectiveness of psychotherapy: The *Consumer Reports* study. *American Psychologist, 50,* 965–974.

Seligman, M.E.P. (1999). The president's address. *American Psychologist, 54,* 559–562.

Seligman, M.E.P. (2002). *Authentic happiness: Using the new positive psychology to realize your potential for lasting fulfillment.* New York: Free Press.

Seligman, M.E.P., & Csikszentmihalyi, M. (2000). Positive psychology: An introduction. *American Psychologist, 55,* 5–14.

Seligman, M.E.P., & Isaacowitz, D.M. (2000). Learned helplessness. In G. Fink (Ed.), *Encyclopedia of stress* (Vol. 2). San Diego, CA: Academic Press.

Selye, H. (1956). *The stress of life.* New York, NY: McGraw-Hill.

Selye, H. (1976). *The stress of life.* New York, NY: McGraw-Hill.

Sergios, P.A., & Cody, J. (1985, 1986). Importance of physical attractiveness and social assertiveness skills in male homosexual dating behavior and partner selection. *Journal of Homosexuality, 12,* 71–84.

Serpell, R. (2000). Intelligence and culture. In R.J. Sternberg (Ed.), *Handbook of intelligence.* New York, NY: Cambridge University Press.

Servos, P., Engel, S.A., Gati, J., & Menon, R. (1999). fMRI evidence for an inverted face representation in human somatosensory cortex. *NeuroReport, 10,* 1393–1395.

Sexton, M.M. (1979). Behavioral epidemiology. In O.F. Pomerleau & J.P. Brady (Eds.), *Behavioral Medicine: Theory and Practice.* Baltimore, MD: Williams & Wilkins.

Shaffer, D.R. (1989). *Developmental psychology: Childhood and adolescence* (2nd ed.). Pacific Grove, CA: Brooks/Cole.

Shair, H.N., Barr, G.A., & Hofer, M.A. (Eds.). (1991). *Developmental psychobiology.* New York, NY: Oxford University Press.

Shanab, M.E., & Yahya, L.A. (1977). A behavioral study of obedience in children. *Journal of Personality and Social Psychology, 35,* 530–536.

Shanahan, T.L., Kronauer, R.E., Duffy, J.F., Williams, G.H., & Czeisler, C.A. (1999). Melatonin rhythm observed throughout a three-cycle bright-light stimulus designed to reset the human circadian pacemaker. *Journal of Biological Rhythms, 14,* 237–253.

Shanks, D.R. (2010). Learning: From association to cognition. *Annual Review of Psychology, 61,* 273–301.

Shapiro, C.M., Bortz, R., Mitchell, D., Bartel, P., & Jooste, P. (1981). Slow-wave sleep: A recovery period after exercise. *Science, 214,* 1253–1254.

Shapiro, J.R., King, E.B., & Quiñones, M.A. (2007). Expectations of obese trainees: How stigmatized trainee characteristics influence training effectiveness. *Journal of Applied Psychology, 92,* 239–249.

Sharkey, K.M. (1993). Short sleepers in history and legend. In M.A. Carskadon (Ed.), *Encyclopedia of sleep and dreaming.* New York, NY: Macmillan.

Shaver, P., Hazan, C., & Bradshaw, D. (1988). Love as attachment: The integration of three behavioral systems. In R.J. Sternberg & M.L. Barnes (Eds.), *The psychology of love.* New Haven, CT: Yale University Press.

Shaver, P.R., & Clark, C.L. (1996). Forms of adult romantic attachment and their cognitive and emotional underpinnings. In G.G. Noam & K.W. Fischer (Eds.), *Development and vulnerability in close relationships. The Jean Piaget symposium series.* Mahwah, NJ: Erlbaum.

Shaver, P.R., & Mikulincer, M. (2009). Attachment theory: I. Motivational, individual differences and structural aspects. In P.J. Corr & G. Matthews (Eds.), *The Cambridge handbook of personality psychology.* Cambridge, UK: Cambridge University Press.

Shaw, J.A. (2000). Narcissism as a motivational structure: The problem of personal significance. *Psychiatry, Interpersonal and Biological Processes, 63,* 219–230.

Shaywitz, B.A., Shaywitz, S.E., Pugh, K.R., et al. (1995). Sex difference in the organization of the brain for language. *Nature, 373,* 607–609.

Shead, N.W., Walsh, K., Taylor, A., Derevensky, J.L., & Gupta, R. (2011). Youth gambling prevention: Can public service announcements featuring celebrity spokespersons be effective? *International Journal of Mental Health and Addiction, 9,* 165–179.

Sheehan, P.W., Green, V., & Truesdale, P. (1992). Influence of rapport on hypnotically-induced pseudomemory. *Journal of Abnormal Psychology, 101,* 690–700.

Sheldon, K.M., & Kasser, T. (2001). Getting older, getting better? Personal strivings and psychological maturity across the life span. *Developmental Psychology, 37,* 491–501.

Sheldon, K.M., Joiner, T.E., Pettit, J.W., & Williams, G. (2003). Reconciling humanistic ideals and scientific clinical practice. *Clinical Psychology: Science and Practice, 10,* 302–315.

Shepard, R.N., & Metzler, J. (1971). Mental rotation of three-dimensional objects. *Science, 171,* 701–703.

Shepherd, C., McCann, H., & Halliday, G.M. (2009). Variations in the neuropathology of familial Alzheimer's disease. *Neuropathologica, 118,* 37–52.

Shepherd, G. (1997). *The synaptic organizer of the brain.* New York, NY: Oxford University Press.

Sherif, M. (1935). A study of some social factors in perception. *Archives of Psychology* (No. 187).

Sherif, M., Harvey, O., White, B., Hood, W., & Sherif, C. (1961). *Intergroup conflict and cooperation: The Robbers Cave experiment.* Norman, OK: University of Oklahoma Press.

Sherman, P.W. (1977). Nepotism and the evolution of alarm calls. *Science, 197,* 1246–1253.

Sherwood, L. (1991). *Fundamentals of physiology: A human perspective.* St. Paul, MN: West.

Shneidman, E.S. (1998). *The suicidal mind.* New York, NY: Oxford University Press.

Shoda, Y., & Mischel, W. (2000). Reconciling contextualism with the core assumptions of personality psychology. *European Journal of Personality, 14,* 462–484.

Shoda, Y., Mischel, W., & Wright, J.C. (1994). Intra-individual stability and patterning of behavior: Incorporating psychological situations into the idiographic analysis of personality. *Journal of Personality and Social Psychology, 65*, 1023–1035.

Shorey, H.S., & Snyder, C.R. (2006). The role of adult attachment styles in psychopathology and psychotherapy outcomes. *Review of General Psychology, 10*, 1–20.

Shorter, E. (1998). *A history of psychiatry: From the era of the asylum to the age of Prozac.* New York, NY: Wiley.

Shostack, M. (1981). *Nisa: The life and words of a !Kung woman.* Cambridge, MA: Harvard University Press.

Shultz, K.S., Morton, K.R., & Weckerle, J.R. (1998). The influence of push and pull factors on voluntary and involuntary early retirees' retirement decision and adjustment. *Journal of Vocational Behavior, 53*, 45–57.

Sia, C.L., Tan, B.C.Y., & Wei, K.K. (2002). Group polarization and computer mediated communication: Effects of communication cues, social presence, and anonymity. *Information Systems Research, 13*, 70–90.

Siegel, A., & Victoroff, J. (2009). Understanding human aggression: New insights from neuroscience. *International Journal of Law and Psychiatry, 32*, 209–215.

Siegel, A., Roeling, T.A.P., Gregg, T.R., & Kruk, M.R. (1999). Neuropharmacology of brain-stimulation-evoked aggression. *Neuroscience and Biobehavioral Reviews, 23*, 359–389.

Siegel, R.K. (1986). MDMA: Medical use and intoxication. *Journal of Psychoactive Drugs, 18*, 349–353.

Siegel, S. (1984). Pavlovian conditioning and heroin overdose: Reports from overdose victims. *Bulletin of the Psychonomic Society, 22*, 428–430.

Siegel, S., & Allan, L.G. (1996). The widespread influence of the Rescorla-Wagner model. *Psychonomic Bulletin and Review, 3*, 314–321.

Siegle, G.J., Carter, C.S., & Thase, M.E. (2006). Use of fMRI to predict recovery from unipolar depression with cognitive behavior therapy. *American Journal of Psychiatry, 163*, 735–738.

Siegler, R.S. (1996). *Emerging minds: The process of change in children's thinking.* New York, NY: Oxford University Press.

Siever, L.J., Buchsbaum, M.S., New, A.S., Spiegel, C.J., Wei, T., & Hazlett, E.A. (1999). d,l-fenfluramine response in impulsive personality disorder assessed with [^{18}F]fluorodeoxyglucose positron emission tomography. *Neuropsychopharmacology, 20*, 413–423.

Sieverding, M., Matterne, U., & Ciccarello, L. (2010). What role do social norms play in the context of men's cancer screening intention and behavior? Application of an extended theory of planned behavior. *Health Psychology, 29*, 72–81.

Sigala, N., & Logothetis, N.K. (2002). Visual categorization shapes feature selectivity in the primate temporal cortex. *Nature, 415*, 318–320.

Signorelli, N., Gross, L., & Morgan, M. (1982). Violence in television programs: Ten years later. In D. Pearl, L. Bouthilet, & J. Lazar (Eds.), *Television and behavior: Ten years of scientific progress and implications for the eighties* (pp. 158–173). Rockville, MD: National Institute of Mental Health.

Silberswerg, D.A., Stern, E., Frith, C., Cahill, C., Holmes, A., Grootoonik, S., ... Frackowiak, R.S.J. (1995). A functional neuroanatomy of hallucinations in schizophrenia. *Nature, 378*, 176–179.

Silveri, M.M., Rohan, M.L., Pimentel, P.J., Gruber, S.A., Rosso, I.M., & Yureelun-Todd, D.A. (2006). Sex differences in the relationship between white matter microstructure and impulsivity in adolescents. *Magnetic Resonance Imaging, 24*, 833–841.

Simkin, L.R., & Gross, A.M. (1994). Assessment of coping with high risk situations for exercise relapse among healthy women. *Health Psychology, 13*, 274–277.

Simmons, J.V. (1981). *Project sea hunt: A report on prototype development and tests. Technical Report 746.* San Diego, CA: Naval Ocean Systems Center.

Simms, L.J., Prisciandaro, J.J., Krueger, R.F., & Goldberg, D.P. (2012). The structure of depression, anxiety and somatic symptoms in primary care. *Psychological Medicine, 42*(1), 15–28.

Simner, J., & Hubbard, E.M. (2014). *The Oxford handbook of synesthesia.* New York, NY: Oxford University Press.

Simon, C. (2007). *Neurology.* New York, NY: Oxford University Press.

Simon, H.A. (1990). Invariants of human behavior. *Annual Review of Psychology, 41*, 1–20.

Simons, D.J., & Chabris, C.F. (1999). Gorillas in our midst: Sustained inattentional blindness for dynamic events. *Perception, 28*, 1059–1074.

Simons, J.S., & Spiers, H.J. (2003). Prefrontal and medial temporal lobe interactions in long-term memory. *Nature Reviews Neuroscience, 4*(8), 637–648.

Simonton, D.K. (1999). Creativity and genius. In L.A. Pervin & O.P. John (Eds.), *Handbook of personality: Theory and research* (2nd ed.). New York, NY: Guilford Press.

Simonton, D.K. (2001). Talent development as a multidimensional, multiplicative, and dynamic process. *Current Directions in Psychological Science, 10*, 39–43.

Simpaio, E., Maris, S., & Bach-y-Rita, P. (2001). Brain plasticity: "Visual" acuity of blind persons via the tongue. *Brain Research, 908*, 204–207.

Singer, J.L. (1988). Sampling ongoing consciousness and emotional experience: Implications for health. In M.J. Horowitz (Ed.), *Psychodynamics and cognition.* Chicago, IL: University of Chicago Press.

Singer, J.L. (1999). Repression, dissociation and our human stream of consciousness: Memory as a constructive, creative process. In S. Taub (Ed.), *Recovered memories of child sexual abuse: Psychological, social, and legal perspectives on a contemporary mental health controversy.* Springfield, IL: Charles C Thomas.

Singer, J.L., & Salovey, P. (1988). Sampling ongoing consciousness and emotional experience: Implications for health. In M.J. Horowitz (Ed.), *Psychodynamics and cognition* (pp. 33–80). Chicago, IL: University of Chicago Press.

Singer, T., Verhaeghen, P., Ghisletta, P., Lindenberger, U., & Baltes, P.B. (2003). The fate of cognition in very old age: Six-year longitudinal findings in the Berlin Aging Study (BASE). *Psychology and Aging, 18*, 318–331.

Singh, R., Gupta, M., & Dalal, A.K. (1979). Cultural difference in attribution of performance: An integration-theoretical analysis. *Journal of Personality and Social Psychology, 37*, 1342–1351.

Singh-Manous, A., Hillsdon, M., Brunner, E., & Marmot, M. (2005). Effects of physical activity on cognitive functioning in middle age: Evidence from the Whitehall II Prospective Cohort study. *American Journal of Public Health, 95*, 2252–2258.

Single, E., Robson, L., Zie, X., & Rehm, J. (1996). *The costs of substance abuse in Canada.* Ottawa, ON: Canadian Centre on Substance Abuse.

Siu, O. (2003). Job stress and job performance among employees in Hong Kong: The role of Chinese work values and organizational commitment. *International Journal of Psychology, 38*, 337–347.

Skinner, B.F. (1938). *The behavior of organisms: An experimental analysis.* New York, NY: Appleton-Century.

Skinner, B.F. (1948). *Walden two.* New York, NY: Macmillan.

Skinner, B.F. (1953). *Science and human behavior.* New York, NY: Macmillan.

Skinner, B.F. (1957). *Verbal behavior.* New York, NY: Prentice Hall.

Skinner, B.F. (1961). Why we need teaching machines. *Harvard Educational Review, 31*, 377–398.

Skinner, B.F. (1971). *Beyond freedom and dignity.* New York, NY: Knopf.

Skinner, B.F. (1989a). Teaching machines. *Science, 243*, 1535.

Skinner, B.F. (1989b). The origins of cognitive thought. *American Psychologist, 44*, 13–18.

Skinner, B.F. (1990). Can psychology be a science of mind? *American Psychologist, 45*, 1206–1210.

Sklar, L.S., & Anisman, H. (1981). Stress and cancer. *Psychological Bulletin, 89*, 369–406.

Skodol, A.E., & Bender, D.S. (2009). The future of personality disorders in DSM-V. *American Journal of Psychiatry, 166*, 388–391.

Skoyles, J.R. (1997). Evolution's "missing link": A hypothesis upon neural plasticity, prefrontal working memory and the origins of modern cognition. *Medical Hypotheses, 48*, 499–501.

Slater, C.L. (2003). Generativity versus stagnation: An elaboration of Erikson's adult stage of human development. *Journal of Adult Development, 10*, 53–65.

Slavney, P.R. (1990). *Perspectives on hysteria.* Baltimore, MD: Johns Hopkins University Press.

Sloan, D.M., & Marx, D. (2004). A closer examination of the structured written disclosure procedure. *Journal of Consulting and Clinical Psychology, 72*, 165–175.

Sloan, D.M., Feinstein, B.A., & Marx, B.A. (2009). The durability of beneficial health effects associated with expressive writing. *Anxiety, Stress & Coping, 22*, 509–523.

Slocum, S.K., & Vollmer, T.R. (2015). A comparison of positive and negative reinforcement for compliance to treat problem behavior maintained by escape. *Journal of Applied Behavior Analysis, 48*(3), 563–574.

Slotnick, S., & Schacter, D. (2004). A sensory signature that distinguishes true from false memories. *Nature Neuroscience, 7*, 664–672.

Slotnick, S.D., Thompson, W.L., & Kosslyn, S.M. (2005). Visual mental imagery induces retinotopically organized activation of early visual areas. *Cerebral Cortex, 15*, 1570–1583.

Slotnick, S.D., Thompson, W.L., & Kosslyn, S.M. (2012). Visual memory and visual mental imagery recruit common control and sensory regions of the brain. *Cognitive Neuroscience, 3*(1), 14–20.

Slovic, P., & Peters, E. (2006). Risk perception and affect. *Current Directions in Psychological Science, 15*, 322–325.

Slovic, P., Fischhoff, B., & Lichtenstein, S. (1988). Response mode, framing, and information processing effects in risk assessment. In D.E. Bell & H. Raiffa (Eds.), *Decision making: Descriptive, normative, and prescriptive interactions* (pp. 152–166). New York, NY: Cambridge University Press.

Small, D.M., Gregory, M.D., Mak, Y.E., Gitelman, D., Mesulam, M.M., & Parrish, T. (2003). Dissociation of neural representation of intensity and affective valuation in human gustation. *Neuron, 39*(4), 701–711.

Smalley, S.L., McGough, J.J., Del'Homme, M., New-Delmann, J., Gordon, E., Kim, T., ... McCracken, J.T. (2000). Familial clustering of symptoms and disruptive behaviors in multiplex families with attention-deficit/hyperactivity disorder. *Journal of the American Academy of Child & Adolescent Psychiatry, 39*, 1135–1143.

Smeets, M.A.M. (1999). Body size categorization in anorexia nervosa using a morphing instrument. *International Journal of Eating Disorders, 25*, 451–455.

Smilek, D., & Frischen, A. (2013). The "cold" and "hot" sides of attention. The Oxford handbook of social cognition (pp. 313–328). New York, NY: Oxford University Press.

Smith, A.T., Snowden, R.J., & Milne, A.B. (1995). Is global motion really based on spatial integration of local motion signals? *Ophthalmic Literature, 48*, 228.

Smith, B.D. (1998). *Psychology: Science and understanding.* New York, NY: McGraw-Hill.

Smith, C., & Lapp, L. (1991). Increases in number of REMs and REM density in humans following an intensive learning period. *Sleep, 14*, 325–330.

Smith, C., & Rose, G.M. (1997). Post-training paradoxical sleep in rats is increased after spatial learning in the Morris water maze. *Behavioral Neuroscience, 111*, 1197–1204.

Smith, C.A., & Ellsworth, P.C. (1985). Patterns of cognitive approach in emotion. *Journal of Personality and Social Psychology, 48*, 813–838.

Smith, C.A., & Kirby, L.D. (2004). Appraisal as a pervasive determinant of anger. *Emotion, 4*, 133–138.

Smith, C.L., Johnson, J.L., & Hathaway, W. (2009). Personality contributions to belief in paranormal phenomena. *Individual Differences Research, 7*, 85–96.

Smith, C.S., Folkard, S., Schmieder, R.A., Parra, L.F., Spelten, E., Almiral, H., et al. (2002). Investigation of morning-evening orientation in six countries using the preferences scale. *Personality and Individual Differences, 32*, 949–968.

Smith, C.T., Nixon, M.R., & Nader, R.S. (2004). Posttraining increases in REM sleep intensity implicate REM sleep in memory processing and provide a biological marker of learning potential. *Learning and Memory, 11*, 714–719.

Smith, D. (2002, October). The theory heard 'round the world. *Monitor on Psychology, 33*(9), http://www.apa.org/monitor/oct02/theory.html.

Smith, E.R., & Zarate, M.A. (1992). Exemplar-based model of social judgment. *Psychological Review, 99*, 3–21.

Smith, G.E., Housen, P., Yaffe, K., Ruff, R., Kennison, R.F., Mahncke, H.W., & Zelinski, E.M. (2009). A cognitive training program based on principles of brain plasticity: Results from the Improvement in Memory with Plasticity-based Adaptive Cognitive Training (IMPACT) study. *Journal of the American Geriatric Society, 57*, 594–603.

Smith, J.W., & Frawley, P.J. (1993). Treatment outcome of 600 chemically dependent patients treated in a multimodal in-patient program including aversion therapy and pentothal interviews. *Journal of Substance Abuse Treatment, 10*, 359–369.

Smith, M.J., Thirthalli, J., Abdallah, A.B., Murray, R.M., & Cottler, L.B. (2009). Prevalence of psychotic symptoms in substance users: A comparison across substances. *Comprehensive Psychiatry, 50*, 245–250.

Smith, M.L., & Glass, G.V. (1977). Meta-analyses of psychotherapy outcome studies. *American Psychologist, 32*, 752–760.

Smith, R.E. (1989). Effects of coping skills training on generalized self-efficacy and locus of control. *Journal of Personality and Social Psychology, 56*, 228–233.

Smith, R.E. (1996). Performance anxiety, cognitive interference, and concentration enhancement strategies in sports. In I.G. Sarason, G.R. Pierce, & B.R. Sarason (Eds.), *Cognitive interference: Theories, methods, and findings* (pp. 261–284). Mahwah, NJ: Erlbaum.

Smith, R.E., Leffingwell, T.R., & Ptacek, J.T. (1999). Can people remember how they coped? Factors associated with discordance between same-day and retrospective reports. *Journal of Personality and Social Psychology, 76*, 1050–1061.

Smith, R.E., & Rohsenow, D.J. (1987). Cognitive-affective stress management training: A treatment and resource manual. *Social and Behavioral Science Documents, 17*(2), Document No. 2829.

Smith, R.E., & Shoda, Y. (2009). Personality as a cognitive-affective processing system. In P.J. Corr & G. Matthews (Eds.), *The Cambridge handbook of personality psychology.* Cambridge, UK: Cambridge University Press.

Smith, R.E., & Smoll, F.L. (1997). Coaching the coaches: Youth sports as a scientific and applied behavioral setting. *Current Directions in Psychological Science, 6*, 16–21.

Smith, R.E., Smoll, F.L., & Schutz, R.W. (1990). Measurement and correlates of sport-specific cognitive and somatic trait anxiety: The Sport Anxiety Scale. *Anxiety Research, 2*, 263–280.

Smith, S.L., & Donnerstein, E. (1998). Harmful effects of exposure to media violence: Learning of aggression, emotional desensitization, and fear. In R.G. Geen, G. Russell, & E. Donnerstein (Eds.), *Human aggression: Theories, research, and implications for social policy* (pp. 168–203). San Diego, CA: Academic Press.

Smith, S.M., & Rothkopf, E.Z. (1984). Contextual enrichment and distribution of practice in the classroom. *Cognition and Instruction, 1*, 341–358.

Smith, S.M., McIntosh, W.D., & Bazzini, D.G. (1999). Are the beautiful good in Hollywood? An investigation of the beauty-and-goodness stereotype on film. *Basic and Applied Social Psychology, 21*, 69–80.

Smithson, J., Lewis, S., Cooper, C., & Dyer, J. (2004). Flexible working and the gender pay gap in the accountancy profession. *Work, Employment and Society, 18*, 115–135.

Smoll, F.L., Smith, R.E., Barnett, N.P., & Everett, J.J. (1993). Enhancement of children's self-esteem through social support training for youth sport coaches. *Journal of Applied Psychology, 78*, 602–610.

Snook, B. (2009). Criminal profiling: International theory, research, and practice. *Canadian Journal of Criminology and Criminal Justice/Revue canadienne de criminologie et de justice penale, 51*, 123–124.

Snook, B., Cullen, R.M., Bennell, C., Taylor, P.J., & Gendreau, P. (2008). The criminal profiling illusion: What's behind the smoke and mirrors? *Criminal Justice and Behavior, 35*, 1257–1276.

Snook, B., Eastwood, J., Gendreau, P., Goggin, C., & Cullen, R.M. (2007). Taking stock of criminal profiling: A narrative review and meta-analysis. *Criminal Justice and Behavior, 34*, 437–453.

Snow, M.E., Jacklin, C.N., & Maccoby, E.E. (1983). Sex-of-child-differences in father-child interaction at one year of age. *Child Development, 54*, 227–232.

Snyder, C.R. (Ed.). (2001). *Coping with stress: Effective people and processes.* New York, NY: Oxford University Press.

Snyder, C.R., & Ingram, R.E. (2000). Psychotherapy: Questions for an evolving field. In C.R. Snyder & R.E. Ingram (Eds.), *Handbook of psychological change: Psychotherapy processes and practices for the 21st century.* New York, NY: John Wiley & Sons.

Snyder, C.R., & Lopez, S.J. (2007). *Positive psychology: The scientific and practical explorations of human strengths.* Thousand Oaks, CA: Sage Publications, Inc.

Snyder, F. (1970). The phenomenology of dreaming. In L. Madow & L. Snow (Eds.), *The psychodynamic implications of the physiological studies on dreams.* Springfield, IL: Charles C Thomas.

Snyder, M. (1974). Self-monitoring of expressive behavior. *Journal of Personality and Social Psychology, 30*, 526–537.

Snyder, M. (1987). *Public appearances/private realities: The psychology of self-monitoring.* New York, NY: W.H. Freeman.

Snyder, M., Berscheid, E., & Glick, P. (1985). Focusing on the exterior and the interior: Two investigations of the initiation of personal relationships. *Journal of Personality and Social Psychology, 48*, 1427–1439.

Snyder, S.H. (1977). Opiate receptors and internal opiates. *Scientific American, 236*, 44–56.

Sober, E., & Wilson, D.S. (1998). *Unto others: The evolution and psychology of unselfish behavior.* Cambridge, MA: Harvard University Press.

Sohn, C.H., & Lam, R.W. (2005). Update on the biology of seasonal affective disorder. *CNS Spectrums, 10*, 635–646.

Soler, M.J., & Ruiz, J.C. (1996). The spontaneous use of memory aids at different educational levels. *Applied Cognitive Psychology, 10*, 41–51.

Solms, M. (2002). Dreaming: Cholinergic and dopaminergic hypotheses. In E. Perry, H. Ashton, & A. Young (Eds.), *Neurochemistry of consciousness: Neurotransmitters in mind. Advances in consciousness research* (pp. 123–132). Amsterdam, Netherlands: Benjamins.

Sommer, I.E.C., Aleman, A., Bouma, A., & Kahn, R.S. (2004). Do women really have more bilateral language representation than men? A meta-analysis of functional imaging studies. *Brain, 127*(8), 1845–1852.

Son, L.K., & Metcalfe, J. (2000). Meta-cognitive and control strategies in study-time allocation. *Journal of Experimental Psychology: Learning, Memory, and Cognition, 26*, 204–221.

Song, H., Zou, Z., Kou, J., Liu, Y., Yang, L., Zilverstand, A., ... Zhang, X. (2015). Love-related changes in the brain: A resting-state functional magnetic resonance imaging study. *Frontiers in Human Neuroscience, 9*. Retrieved from https://www.lib.uwo.ca/cgi-bin/ezpauthn.cgi?url=http://search.proquest.com/docview/1710261472?accountid=15115.

Sorenson, S.B. (2002). Preventing traumatic stress: Public health approaches. *Journal of Traumatic Stress, 15,* 3–7.

Sorrentino, R.M., Bobocel, D.R., Gitta, M.Z., Olson, J.M., & Hewitt, E.C. (1988). Uncertainty orientation and persuasion: Individual differences in the effects of personal relevance on social judgements. *Journal of Personality and Social Psychology, 55,* 357–371.

Sorrentino, R.M., Otsubo, Y., Yasunaga, S. Nezlek, J., Kouhara, S., & Shuper, P. (2005). Uncertainty orientation and social behavior: Individual differences within and across cultures. In R.M. Sorrentino, D. Cohen, J.M. Olson, & M.P. Zanna (Eds.), *Culture and social behavior: The Ontario Symposium* (Vol. 10, pp. 181–205). New York, NY: Lawrence Earlbaum Associates.

Sotres-Bayon, F., Cain, C.K., & LeDoux, J.E. (2006). Brain mechanisms of fear extinction: Historical perspectives on the contribution of prefrontal cortex. *Biological Psychiatry, 60,* 329–336.

Soussignan, R. (2002). Duchenne smile, emotional experience, and autonomic reactivity: A test of the facial feedback hypothesis. *Emotion, 2,* 52–74.

Soussignan, R., Schaal, B., Marlier, L., & Jiang, T. (1997). Facial and autonomic responses to biological and artificial olfactory stimuli in human neonates: Re-examining early hedonic discrimination of odors. *Physiology and Behavior, 62,* 745–758.

South, S.C., Reichborn-Kjennerud, T., Eaton, N.R., & Krueger, R.F. (2015). Genetics of personality. *APA handbook of personality and social psychology, volume 4: Personality processes and individual differences* (pp. 31–60). Washington, DC: American Psychological Association.

Southwick, S.M., Vythilingam, M., & Charney, D.S. (2005). The psychology of depression and resilience to stress: Implications for prevention and treatment. *Annual Review of Clinical Psychology, 1,* 255–291.

Sowell, E.R., Thompson, P.M., Tessner, K.D., & Toga, A.W. (2001). Mapping continued brain growth and gray matter density reduction in dorsal frontal cortex: Inverse relationships during post-adolescent brain maturation. *Journal of Neuroscience, 21,* 8819–8829.

Spanos, N.P. (1991). A sociocognitive approach to hypnosis. In S.J. Lynn & J.W. Rhue (Eds.), *Theories of hypnosis: Current models and perspectives* (pp. 43–82). New York, NY: Guilford Press.

Spanos, N.P. (1994). Multiple identity enactments and multiple personality disorder: A sociocognitive perspective. *Psychological Bulletin, 116,* 143–165.

Spanos, N.P., & Chaves, J.F. (Eds.). (1988). *Hypnosis: The cognitive-behavioral perspective.* Buffalo, NY: Prometheus Books.

Sparkes, S., Grant, V.L., & Lett, B.T. (2003). Role of conditioned taste aversion in the development of activity anorexia. *Appetite, 41,* 161–165.

Sparks, G.G., & Miller, W. (2001). Investigating the relationship between exposure to television programs that depict paranormal phenomena and beliefs in the paranormal. *Communication Monographs, 68,* 98–113.

Spearman, C. (1923). *The nature of "intelligence" and the principles of cognition.* London, UK: Macmillan.

Specht, J., Luhmann, M., & Geiser, C. (2014). On the consistency of personality types across adulthood: Latent profile analyses in two large-scale panel studies. *Journal of Personality and Social Psychology, 107*(3), 540–556.

Spector, P.E. (1997). The role of frustration in anti-social behavior at work. In R.A. Giacalone & J. Greenberg (Eds.), *Antisocial behavior in organizations* (pp. 1–17). Thousand Oaks, CA: Sage.

Speisman, J., Lazarus, R.S., Mordkoff, A., & Davidson, L. (1964). Experimental reduction of stress based on ego-defense theory. *Journal of Abnormal and Social Psychology, 68,* 367–380.

Spencer, S.J., Steele, C.M., & Quinn, D.M. (1999). Stereotype threat and women's math performance. *Journal of Experimental Social Psychology, 35,* 4–28.

Sperdin, H.F., Spierer, L., Becker, R., Michel, C.M., & Landis, T. (2015). Submillisecond unmasked subliminal visual stimuli evoke electrical brain responses. *Human Brain Mapping, 36*(4), 1470–1483.

Sperling, G. (1960). The information available in brief visual presentations. *Psychological Monographs: General and Applied, 74*(11), 1–30.

Sperling, G. (1984). A unified theory of attention and signal detection. In R. Parasuraman & D.R. Davies (Eds.), *Varieties of attention.* New York, NY: Academic Press.

Sperry, R.W. (1970). *Perception in the absence of neocortical commissures.* Association for Research in Nervous and Mental Disease, Perception and Its Disorders. New York, NY: Williams & Wilkins.

Spiegel, D., Lewis-Fernández, R., Lanius, R., Vermetten, E., Simeon, D., & Friedman, M. (2013). Dissociative disorders in DSM-5. *Annual Review of Clinical Psychology, 9,* 299–326.

Spiegler, M.D., & Guevremont, D.C. (2003). *Contemporary behavior therapy.* Belmont, CA: Wadsworth.

Spina, R., Ji, L.J., Ross, M., Li, Y., & Zhang, Z. (2010). Why best can't last: Cultural differences in anticipating regression toward the mean. *Asian Journal of Social Psychology, 13,* 153–162.

Spitzer, R.L. (1975). More on pseudoscience in science and the case for psychiatric diagnosis: A critique of D.L. Rosenhan's "On Being Sane in Insane Places" and "The Contextual Nature of Psychiatric Diagnosis." *Archives of General Psychiatry, 33,* 459–470.

Spitzer, R.L., Skodol, A.E., Gibbon, M., & Williams, J.B.W. (1983). *Psychopathology: A casebook.* New York, NY: McGraw-Hill.

Sprafkin, J.N., Liebert, R.M., & Poulos, R.W. (1975). Effects of a prosocial televised example on children's helping. *Journal of Experimental Child Psychology, 20,* 119–126.

Sprecher, S. (2001). A comparison of emotional consequences of and change in equity over time using global and domain specific measures of equity. *Journal of Social and Personal Relationships, 18,* 477–501.

Sprecher, S., & Regan, P.C. (1998). Passionate and companionate love in courting and young married couples. *Sociological Inquiry, 68,* 163–185.

Sprecher, S., Barbee, A., & Schwartz, P. (1995). "Was it good for you, too?" Gender differences in first sexual intercourse experiences. *Journal of Sex Research, 32,* 13–15.

Springer, S. (1997). *Left brain, right brain.* San Francisco, CA: W.H. Freeman.

Squire, L.H., & Domhoff, G.W. (1998). The presentation of dreaming and dreams in introductory psychology textbooks: A critical examination with suggestions for textbook authors and course instructors. *Dreaming: Journal of the Association for the Study of Dreams, 8,* 149–168.

Squire, L.R. (1987). *Memory and brain.* Oxford, UK: Oxford University Press.

Squire, L.R., & Zola-Morgan, S. (1991). The medial temporal lobe memory system. *Science, 253,* 1380–1386.

Squire, L.R., Stark, C.E.L., & Clark, R.E. (2004). The medial temporal lobe. *Annual Review of Neuroscience, 27,* 279–306.

Sroufe, L. (2002). From infant attachment to promotion of adolescent autonomy: Prospective, longitudinal data on the role of parents in development. In J.G. Borkowski, S.L. Ramey, & M. Bristol-Power (Eds.), *Parenting and the child's world: Influences on academic, intellectual, and social-emotional development. Monographs in parenting.* Mahwah, NJ: Erlbaum.

Staats, H., van Leeuwen, E., & Wit, A. (2000). A longitudinal study of informational interventions to save energy in an office building. *Journal of Applied Behavior Analysis, 33,* 101–104.

Stahl, S.M. (2000). *Essential psychopharmacology: Neuroscientific basis and clinical applications* (2nd ed.). New York, NY: Cambridge University Press.

Stalder, D.R., & Baron, R.S. (1998). Attributional complexity as a moderator of dissonance-produced attitude change. *Journal of Personality and Social Psychology, 75,* 449–455.

Staniloiu, A., & Markowitsch, H.J. (2014). Dissociative amnesia. *The Lancet Psychiatry, 1*(3), 226–241.

Stanley, B.G., Kyrkouli, S.E., Lampert, S., & Leibowitz, S.F. (1986). Neuropeptide Y chronically injected into the hypothalamus: A powerful neurochemical inducer of hyperphagia and obesity. *Peptides, 7,* 1189–1192.

Stanley, S.M., Rhoades, G.K., & Markman, H. (2006). Sliding versus deciding: Inertia and the premarital cohabitation effect. *Family Relations: Interdisciplinary Journal of Applied Family Studies, 55,* 499–509.

Stanton, S.J., Beehner, J.C., Saini, E.K., Kuhn, C.M., & LaBar, K.S. (2009). Dominance, politics, and physiology. *PLoS ONE, 4*(10), 7453. Retrieved from http://www.plosone.org/article /info%3Adoi%2F10.1371%2Fjournal.pone.0007543.

Stark, E. (1989, May). Teen sex: Not for love. *Psychology Today,* 10–11.

Statistics Canada. (1997). Canada's alcohol and other drugs survey 1994.

Statistics Canada. (2001). 2001 Census of Canada. Retrieved November 17, 2010, from http://www12 .statcan.ca/english/census01/home/index.cfm.

Statistics Canada. (2002). Profile of languages in Canada: Provinces and territories. Retrieved from http://www12.statcan.ca/english/census01 /Products/Analytic/companion/lang/provs.cfm.

Statistics Canada. (2002). Suicides and suicide rates, by sex and age group. Retrieved from http:// www40.statcan.gc.ca/l01/cst01/hlth66d-eng.htm.

Statistics Canada. (2004). General Social Survey. Retrieved from http://www.statcan.gc.ca/pub/85 -002-x/85-002-x2007001-eng.pdf.

Statistics Canada. (2004). Stress, health, and the benefit of social support. Health Reports. Article abstract retrieved from http://www.statcan.gc.ca /pub/11-002-x/2004/02/03404/4155300-eng.htm.

Statistics Canada. (2005). General Social Survey, http://www.statcan.gc.ca/pub/11-008-x/2008001 /t/10553/5214754-eng.htm.

Statistics Canada. (2006). Measuring violence against women: Statistical trends. Retrieved from http://www.statcan.gc.ca/pub/85-570 -x/2006001/4054094-eng.htm.

Statistics Canada. (2007). Canadian internet use survey. Retrieved from http://www.statcan.gc.ca /cgi-bin/imdb/p2SV.pl?Function=getSurvey&SDD S=4432&lang=en&db=imdb&adm=8&dis=2.

Statistics Canada. (2007). Leading causes of death by selected age groups and sex, Canada. Retrieved from http://www.statcan.gc.ca/.

Statistics Canada. (2009). Health in Canada: Lifestyle and social conditions, CANSIM Table 105-0501. Retrieved from http://www40.statcan.ca/101/cst01/health79a-eng.htm.

Statistics Canada. (2010). *General Social Survey—2010: Overview of the Time Use of Canadians*. http://www.statcan.gc.ca/pub/89-647-x/89-647-x2011001-eng.pdf.

Statistics Canada. (2010). Population by sex and age group. Retrieved November 10, 2010, from http://www40.statcan.gc.ca/101/cst01/demo10a-eng.htm?sdi=age.

Statistics Canada. (2012). CANSIM, table 105-0501. http://www.statcan.gc.ca/tables-tableaux/sum-som/101/cst01/health79b-eng.htm.

Statistics Canada. (2012). *The Daily*, September 27. http://www.statcan.gc.ca/daily-quotidien/120927/dq120927b-eng.htm.

Statistics Canada. (2013). CANSIM, table 105-0501. http://www.statcan.gc.ca/tables-tableaux/sum-som/101/cst01/health82b-eng.htm?sdi=body%20mass%20index.

Statistics Canada. (2013). Control and sale of alcoholic beverages, for the year ending March 31, 2012 (correction). *The Daily*, http://www.statcan.gc.ca/daily-quotidien/130411/dq130411a-eng.htm.

Statistics Canada. (2013). The evolution of English–French bilingualism in Canada from 1961 to 2011. Retrieved from http://www.statcan.gc.ca/pub/75-006-x/2013001/article/11795-eng.htm.

Statistics Canada. (2014). Child Care in Canada. Catalogue no. 89-652-X—No. 005.

Statistics Canada. (2015a). *Health Fact Sheets—Perceived Life Stress, 2014*, http://www.statcan.gc.ca/pub/82-625-x/2015001/article/14188-eng.htm.

Statistics Canada. (2015b). *Health Fact Sheet* 82-625-X. http://www.statcan.gc.ca/pub/82-625-x/2015001/article/14185-eng.htm.

Statistics Canada. (2016a). CANSIM, table 105-0501 and Catalogue no. 82-221-X. http://www.statcan.gc.ca/tables-tableaux/sum-som/101/cst01/health79b-eng.htm.

Statistics Canada. (2016b). CANSIM, table 105-0501 and Catalogue no. 82-221-X. http://www.statcan.gc.ca/tables-tableaux/sum-som/101/cst01/health73b-eng.htm.

Staub, E. (1996). Cultural-society roots of violence: The examples of genocidal violence and of contemporary youth violence in the United States. *American Psychologist, 51*, 117–132.

Stearns, S., & Hoekstra, R. (2005). *Evolution*. New York, NY: Oxford University Press.

Steele, C.M. (1997). A threat in the air: How stereotypes shape intellectual identity and performance. *American Psychologist, 52*, 613–629.

Steele, C.M., & Baumeister, R.F. (1999). The psychology of self-affirmation: Sustaining the integrity of the self. *Key Readings in Social Psychology*. New York, NY: Psychology Press.

Steele, C.M., & Josephs, R.A. (1990). Alcohol myopia: Its prized and dangerous effects. *American Psychologist, 45*, 921–933.

Steele, J., James, J.B., & Barnett, R.C. (2002). Learning in a man's world: Examining the perceptions of undergraduate women in male-dominated academic areas. *Psychology of Women Quarterly, 26*, 46–50.

Steeves, J.K.E., Culham, J.C., Duchaine, B.C., Pratesi, C.C., Valyear, K.F., Schindler, I., ... Goodale, M.A. (2006). The fusiform face area is not sufficient for face recognition: Evidence from a patient with dense prosopagnosia and no occipital face area. *Neuropsychologia, 44*, 594–609.

Stein, D.J., & Hollander, E. (2002). *Textbook of anxiety disorders*. Washington, DC: American Psychiatric Press.

Stein, M., Federspiel, A., Koenig, T., Wirth, M., Strik, W., Wiest, R., & Dierks, T. (2012). Structural plasticity in the language system related to increased second language proficiency. *Cortex, 48*, 458–465.

Steinberg, L. (2008). A social neuroscience perspective on adolescent risk-taking. *Developmental Review, 28*(1), 78–106.

Steinberg, L., Lamborn, S.D., Darling, N., & Mount, N.S. (1994). Over-time changes in adjustment and competence among adolescents from authoritative, authoritarian, indulgent, and neglectful families. *Child Development, 65*, 754–770.

Stel, M., & Koningsbruggen, G.M. (2015). I need you closer to me: Effects of affiliation goals on perceptions of interpersonal distance. *European Journal of Social Psychology*, doi: http://dx.doi.org/10.1002/ejsp.2124.

Stella, N., Schweitzer, P., & Piomelli, D. (1997). A second endogenous cannabinoid that modulates long-term potentiation. *Nature, 388*, 773–778.

Stellar, E. (1954). The physiology of motivation. *Psychological Review, 61*, 5–22.

Stephan, W.G. (1990). School desegregation: Short-term and long-term effects. In H. Knopke (Ed.), *Opening doors: An appraisal of race relations in America*. Tuscaloosa, AL: University of Alabama Press.

Steptoe, A. (2000). Control and stress. In G. Fink (Ed.), *Encyclopedia of stress* (Vol. 1). San Diego, CA: Academic Press.

Steptoe, A., & Wardle, J. (2001). Locus of control and health behaviour revisited: A multivariate analysis of young adults from 18 countries. *British Journal of Psychology, 92*, 659–672.

Stern, M. (2006). *Cognitive reserve: Theory and applications*. San Francisco, CA: Taylor & Francis.

Sternberg, K.J., Lamb, M.E., Esplin, P.W., Opbach, Y., & Hershkowitz, I. (2002). Using a structure interview protocol to improve the quality of investigative interviews. In M.L. Eisen (Ed.), *Memory and suggestibility in the forensic interview: Personality and Clinical Psychology Series* (pp. 409–436). Mahwah, NJ: Erlbaum.

Sternberg, R.J. (1988). Triangulating love. In R.J. Sternberg & M.L. Barnes (Eds.), *The psychology of love*. New Haven, CT: Yale University Press.

Sternberg, R.J. (1997). Construct validation of a triangular love scale. *European Journal of Social Psychology, 27*, 313–335.

Sternberg, R.J. (2003). A broad view of intelligence: The theory of successful intelligence. *Consulting Psychology Journal: Practice and Research, 55*(3), 139–154.

Sternberg, R.J. (2004). Culture and intelligence. *American Psychologist, 59*, 325–338.

Sternberg, R.J. (2006). The nature of creativity. *Creativity Research Journal, 18*, 87–98.

Sternberg, R.J. (2007). *Wisdom, intelligence, and creativity synthesized*. New York: Cambridge University Press.

Sternberg, R.J., & Davidson, J.E. (Eds.). (2005). *Conceptions of giftedness*. New York, NY: Cambridge University Press.

Sternberg, R.J., & Grigorenko, E.L. (2006). Cultural intelligence and successful intelligence. *Group & Organization Management, 31*(1), 27–39.

Sternberg, R.J., & Kaufman, S.B. (2012). Trends in intelligence research. *Intelligence, 40*(2), 235–236.

Sternberg, R.J., Lautrey, J., & Lubart, T.I. (2003). *Models of intelligence: International perspectives*. Washington, DC: American Psychological Association.

Sternberg, R.J., Nokes, C., Geissler, P., Prince, R., Okatcha, F., Bundy, D.A., & Grigorenko, E.L. (2001). The relationship between academic and practical intelligence: A case study in Kenya. *Intelligence, 29*, 401–418.

Stetson, B.A., Rahn, J.M., Dubbert, P.M., Wilner, B.I., & Mercury, M.G. (1997). Prospective evaluation of the effects of stress on exercise adherence in community-residing women. *Health Psychology, 16*, 515–520.

Steuber, D., Lueck, M., & Roth, G. (2006). The violent brain. *Scientific American Mind, 17*, 20–27.

Stevens, S.J., & Bogart, J.C. (1999). Reducing HIV risk behavior of drug-involved women: Social, economic, medical, and legal constraints. In W.N. Elwood (Ed.), *Power in the blood: A handbook on AIDS, politics, and communication. Communication series: Applied communications*. Mahwah, NJ: Lawrence Erlbaum Associates.

Stewart, J. (2000). Pathways to relapse: The neurobiology of drug- and stress-induced relapse to drug taking. *Journal of Psychiatry and Neuroscience, 25*, 125–136.

Stewart, J. (2002). Modulation of the subjective and physiological effects of drugs by contexts and expectations—the search for mechanisms: Comment on Alessi, Roll, Reilly, and Johanson (2002). *Experimental and Clinical Psychopharmacology, 10*, 96–98.

Stewart, J., & Wise, R.A. (1992). Reinstatement of heroin self-administration habits: Morphine prompts and naltrexone discourages renewed responding after extinction. *Psychopharmacology, 108*, 79–84.

Stewart, T.L., Latu, I.M., Kawakami, K., & Myers, A.C. (2010). Consider the situation: Reducing automatic stereotyping through situational attribution training. *Journal of Experimental Social Psychology, 46*, 221–225.

Stice, E., Spoor, S., Bohon, C., Veldhuizen, M.G., & Small, D.M. (2008). Relation of reward from food intake and anticipated food intake to obesity: A functional magnetic resonance imaging study. *Journal of Abnormal Psychology, 117*(4), 924–935.

Stickgold, R., Pace, S.E., & Hobson, J.A. (1994). A new paradigm for dream research: Mentation reports following spontaneous arousal from REM and NREM sleep recorded in a home setting. *Consciousness and Cognition: An International Journal, 3*, 16–29.

Stiles, W., Barkham, M., Connell, J., & Mellor-Clark, J. (2008). Responsive regulation of treatment duration in routine practice in United Kingdom primary care settings: Replication in a larger sample. *Journal of Consulting and Clinical Psychology, 76*, 298–305.

Stine-Morrow, E.A.L., Parisi, J.M., Morrow, D.G., & Park, D.C. (2008). The effects of an engaged lifestyle on cognitive vitality: A field experiment. *Psychology and Aging, 23*, 778–786.

Stockhorst, U., Steingrueber H-J., Enck, P., & Klosterhalfen, S. (2006). Pavlovian conditioning of nausea and vomiting. *Autonomic Neuroscience: Basic & Clinical, 129,* 50–57.

Stone, A.A., Shiffman, S.S., & DeVries, M. (2000). Rethinking our self-report assessment methodologies: An argument for collecting ecologically valid, momentary measurements. In D. Kahneman, E. Diener, & N. Schwarz (Eds.), *Understanding quality of life: Scientific perspectives on enjoyment and suffering.* New York, NY: Russel Sage Foundation.

Stone, J., & Cooper, J. (2001). A self-standards model of cognitive dissonance. *Journal of Experimental Social Psychology, 37,* 228–243.

Stone, K., & Church, S.L. (1968). *Personality theories.* San Francisco, CA: Jossey-Bass.

Storm, L., & Ertel, S. (2001). Does psi exist? Comments on Milton and Wiseman's (1999) meta-analysis of Ganzfield research. *Psychological Bulletin, 12,* 424–433.

Storms, M.D. (1973). Videotape and the attribution process: Reversing actors' and observers' points of view. *Journal of Personality and Social Psychology, 27,* 165–175.

Stormshak, E.A., Bierman, K.L., McMahon, R.J., & Lengua, L.J. (Conduct Problems Prevention Research Group). (2000). Parenting practices and child disruptive behavior problems in early elementary school. *Journal of Clinical Child Psychology, 29,* 17–29.

Strack, F., Martin, L.L., & Stepper, S. (1988). Inhibiting and facilitating conditions of facial expressions: A non-obtrusive test of the facial feedback hypothesis. *Journal of Personality and Social Psychology, 54,* 768–777.

Strasburger, H., & Waldvogel, B. (2015). Sight and blindness in the same person: Gating in the visual system. *PsyCh Journal, 4,* 178–185.

Stratton, G. (1896). Some preliminary experiments on vision without inversion of the retinal image. *Psychological Review, 3,* 611–617.

Strawbridge, W.J., Shema, S.J., Cohen, R.D., Roberts, R.E., & Kaplan, G.A. (1998). Religion buffers effects of some stressors on depression but exacerbates others. *Journal of Gerontology, 53,* 118–126.

Strayer, D.A., & Drews, F.A. (2004). Profiles in driver distraction: Effects of cell phone conversations on younger and older drivers. *Human Factors, 46,* 640–649.

Strayer, D.L., Drews, F.A., & Johnston, W.A. (2003). Cell-phone induced failures of visual attention during simulated driving. *Journal of Experimental Psychology: Applied, 9,* 23–32.

Streissguth, A.P. (2001). Recent advances in fetal alcohol syndrome and alcohol use in pregnancy. In D.P. Agarwal & H.K. Seitz (Eds.), *Alcohol in health and disease* (pp. 303–324). New York, NY: Marcel Dekker.

Strentz, T., & Auerbach, S.M. (1988). Adjustment to the stress of simulated captivity: Effects of emotion-focused versus problem-focused preparation on hostages differing in locus of control. *Journal of Personality and Social Psychology, 55,* 652–660.

Stricker, E.M., & Verbalis, J.G. (1987). Biological bases of hunger and satiety. *Annals of Behavioral Medicine, 9,* 3–8.

Striedter, G.F. (2005). *Principles of brain evolution.* Springfield, IL: Sinauer.

Strober, M., & Humphrey, L.L. (1987). Familial contributions to the etiology and course of anorexia nervosa and bulimia. *Journal of Consulting and Clinical Psychology, 55,* 654–659.

Strong, R.E., Marchant, B.K., Reimherr, F.W., Williams, E., Soni, P., & Mestas, R. (2009).

Narrow-band blue-light treatment of seasonal affective disorder in adults and the influence of additional nonseasonal symptoms. *Depression and Anxiety, 26,* 273–278.

Strube, M.J. (1989). Evidence for the type in Type A behavior: A taxometric analysis. *Journal of Personality and Social Psychology, 56,* 972–987.

Strunk, D.R., & Adler, A.D. (2009). Cognitive biases in three prediction tasks: A test of the cognitive model of depression. *Behaviour Research and Therapy, 47,* 34–40.

Stryer, L. (1987). The molecules of visual excitation. *Scientific American, 257,* 42–50.

Stukas, A.A., Snyder, M., & Clary, E.G. (1999). The effects of "mandatory volunteerism" on intentions to volunteer. *Psychological Science, 10,* 59–64.

Stunkard, A.J., Harris, J.R., Pedersen, N.L., & McClearn, G.E. (1990). The body-mass index of twins who have been reared apart. *New England Journal of Medicine, 322,* 1483–1487.

Suarez, L.M., Bennett, S.M., Goldstein, C.R., & Barlow, D.H. (2009). Understanding anxiety disorders from a "triple vulnerability" framework. In M.M. Antony & M.B. Stein (Eds.), *Oxford handbook of anxiety and related disorders* (pp. 153–172). New York, NY: Oxford University Press.

Sue, D.W., & Sue, D. (1999). *Counseling the culturally different: Theory and practice* (2nd ed.). New York, NY: Wiley.

Sue, S. (1998). In search of cultural competence in psychotherapy and counseling. *American Psychologist, 53,* 440–448.

Sue, S., Fujino, D., Hu, L.N., Takeuchi, D., & Zane, N. (1991). Community mental health services for ethnic minority groups: A test of the cultural responsiveness hypothesis. *Journal of Consulting and Clinical Psychology, 59,* 533–540.

Sue, S., & Zane, N. (1987). The role of culture and cultural techniques in psychotherapy. *American Psychologist, 42,* 37–45.

Suggs, R. (1962). *The hidden worlds of Polynesia.* New York, NY: Harcourt.

Suicide Information and Education Centre. (1996). 1996 cause of death statistics.

Suinn, R.M., Osborne, D., & Winfree, P. (1962). The self-concept and accuracy of recall of inconsistent self-related information. *Journal of Clinical Psychology, 18,* 473–474.

Suls, J., Green, P., & Hillis, S. (1998). Emotional reactivity to everyday problems, affective inertia, and neuroticism. *Personality and Social Psychology Bulletin, 24,* 127–136.

Sumsion, T., & Law, M. (2006). A review of evidence on the conceptual elements informing client-centred practice. *Canadian Journal of Occupational Therapy, 73*(3), 153–162.

Sun, M-K. (2005). *Cognition and mood interactions.* New York, NY: Nova Science.

Super, C.M., & Harkness, S. (1997). The cultural structuring of child development. In J.W. Berry, P.R. Dasen, & T.S. Saraswathi (Eds.), *Handbook of cross-cultural psychology* (2nd ed., Vol. 2). Boston, MA: Allyn & Bacon.

Super, D.E. (1957). *The psychology of careers.* New York, NY: Harper & Row.

Sussman, N.M., & Rosenfeld, H.M. (1982). Influence of culture, language, and sex on conversational distance. *Journal of Personality and Social Psychology, 42,* 66–74.

Sutherland, R., & Hayne, H. (2001). Age-related changes in the misinformation effect. *Journal of Experimental Child Psychology, 79*(4), 388–404.

Sutton, S.K. (2002). Incentive and threat reactivity: Relations with anterior cortical activity. In D. Cervone & W. Mischel (Eds.), *Advances in personality science.* New York, NY: Guilford Press.

Suzuki, L.A., Naqvi, S., & Hill, J.S. (2014). Assessing intelligence in a cultural context. APA handbook of multicultural psychology, vol. 1: Theory and research (pp. 247–266). Washington, DC: American Psychological Association.

Svirsky, M.A., Teoh, S.W., & Neuburger, H. (2004). Development of language and speech perception in congenitally, profoundly deaf children as a function of age at cochlear implantation. *Audiology and Neurotology, 9*(4), 224–233.

Swain, I., Zelazo, P.R., & Clifton, R. (1993). Newborn infants' memory for speech sounds retained over 24 hours. *Developmental Psychology, 29,* 312–323.

Swann, W.B. (1966). *Self-traps: The elusive quest for higher self-esteem.* New York, NY: W.H. Freeman.

Swann, W.B., & Bosson, J.K. (2008). Identity negotiation: A theory of self and social interaction. In O.P. John, R.W. Robins, & L.A. Pervin (Eds.), *Handbook of personality theory and research* (3rd ed.). New York, NY: Guilford Press.

Swann, W.B., Jr., Stein-Seroussi, A., & Giesler, R.B. (1992). Why people self-verify. *Journal of Personality and Social Psychology, 62,* 392–401.

Swartz, C. (1995). Setting the ECT stimulus. *Psychiatric Times, 12*(6).

Syka, J., & Merzenich, M.M. (2005). *Plasticity and signal representation in the auditory system.* New York, NY: Springer.

Szelenberger, W., Niemcewicz, S., & Dabrowska, A.J. (2005). Sleepwalking and night terrors: Psychopathological and psychophysiological correlates. *International Review of Psychiatry, 17,* 263–270.

Szeszeko, P.R., MacMillan, S., McMeniman, M., Chen, S., Baribault, K., Lim, K.O., ... Rosenberg, D.R. (2004). Brain structural abnormalities in psychotropic drug-naïve pediatric patients with obsessive-compulsive disorder. *American Journal of Psychiatry, 161,* 1049–1056.

Szkrybalo, J., & Ruble, D.N. (1999). "God made me a girl": Sex-category constancy judgments and explanations revisited. *Developmental Psychology, 35,* 392–402.

Szymusiak, R. (1995). Magnocellular nuclei of the basal forebrain: Substrates of sleep and arousal regulation. *Sleep, 18*(6), 478–500.

Tajfel, H. (1970). Experiments in intergroup discrimination. *Scientific American, 223,* 96–102.

Tajfel, H., & Turner, J.C. (1986). The social identity theory of intergroup behavior. In S. Worchel & W.G. Austin (Eds.), *The psychology of intergroup relations* (2nd ed.). Chicago, IL: Nelson-Hall.

Tajfel, H., Turner, J.C., Jost, J.T., & Sidanius, J. (2004). The social identity theory of intergroup behavior. In J.T. Jost & J. Sidanius (Eds.), *Political psychology: Key readings. Key readings in social psychology* (pp. 276–293). New York, NY: Psychology Press.

Takahashi, Y. (1990). Is multiple personality disorder really rare in Japan? *Dissociation: Progress in the Dissociative Disorders, 3,* 57–59.

Talarico, J.M., & Rubin, D.C. (2003). Confidence, not consistency, characterizes flashbulb memories. *Psychological Science, 14*(5), 455–461.

Talbot, D. (2003). Advanced brain imaging. *Technological Review(Cambridge, Mass), 105,* 64.

Tallal, P., & Gaab, N. (2006). Dynamic auditory processing, musical experience and language development. *Trends in Neurosciences, 29*(7), 382–390.

Tal-Or, N., & Papirman, Y. (2007).The fundamental attribution error in attributing fictional figures' characteristics to the actors. *Media Psychology, 9,* 331–345.

Talwar, V., & Lee, K. (2008). Socio-cognitive correlates of children's lying behaviour: Conceptual understanding of lying, executive functioning, and false beliefs. *Child Development, 79,* 866–881.

Tamagawa, R., Giese-Davis, J., Speca, M., Doll, R., Stephen, et al. (2013). Trait mindfulness, repression, suppression, and self-reported mood and stress symptoms among women with breast cancer. *Journal of Clinical Psychology, 69,* 264–277.

Tamres, L.K., Janicki, D., & Helgeson, V.S. (2002). Sex differences in coping behavior: A meta-analytic review and an examination of relative coping. *Personality and Social Psychology, 6,* 2–30.

Tanaka-Matsumi, J. (1979). Taijin Kyofushu: Diagnostic and cultural issues in Japanese psychiatry. *Culture, Medicine, and Psychiatry, 3,* 231–245.

Tanaka-Matsumi, J., & Draguns, J. (1997). Culture and psychopathology. In J.W. Berry, M.H. Segall, & C. Kagitáibasi (Eds.), *Handbook of cross-cultural psychology* (Vol. 3). Boston, MA: Allyn & Bacon.

Tarr, M.J., & Vuong, Q.C. (2002). Visual object recognition. In H. Pashler & S. Yantis (Eds.), *Steven's handbook of experimental psychology: Vol. 1 Sensation and perception* (3rd ed., pp. 284–314). New York, NY: Wiley.

Tatlisumak, T., & Fisher, M. (2006). *Handbook of experimental neurology: Methods and techniques in animal research.* New York, NY: Cambridge University Press.

Taylor, C., Schloss, K., Palmer, S.E., & Franklin, A. (2013). Color preferences in infants and adults are different. *Psychonomic Bulletin & Review, 20*(5), 916–922.

Taylor, J., Deane, F., & Podd, J. (2002). Driving-related fear: A review. *Clinical Psychology Review, 22,* 631–645.

Taylor, R.D., & Wang, M.C. (Eds.). (2000). *Resilience across contexts: Family, work, culture, and community.* Mahwah, NJ: Erlbaum.

Taylor, S.E. (1991). Health psychology: The science and the field. In A. Monat & R.S. Lazarus (Eds.), *Stress and coping: An anthology* (3rd ed.). New York, NY: Columbia University Press.

Taylor, S.E. (1999). *Health psychology* (2nd ed.). Boston, MA: McGraw-Hill.

Taylor, S.E. (2009). *Health psychology* (7th ed.). New York, NY: McGraw-Hill.

Taylor, S.E., & Brown, J.D. (1988). Illusion and well-being: A social psychological perspective on mental health. *Psychological Bulletin, 103,* 193–210.

Taylor, S.E., Eisenberger, N.I., Saxbe, D., Lehman, B.J., & Lieberman, M.D. (2006). Neural responses to emotional stimuli are associated with childhood family stress. *Biological Psychiatry, 60,* 296–301.

Taylor, S.E., Kemeny, M.E., Reed, G.M., Bower, J.E., & Gruenwald, T.L. (2000). Psychological resources, positive illusions, and health. *American Psychologist, 55,* 99–109.

Teachman, B.A., Gapinski, K.D., Brownell K.D., Rawlins, M., & Jeyaram, S. (2003). Demonstrations of implicit anti-fat bias: The impact of providing causal information and evoking empathy. *Health Psychology, 22,* 68–78.

Teasdale, J.D., & Fogarty, F.J. (1979). Differential affects of induced mood on retrieval of pleasant and unpleasant events from episodic memory. *Journal of Abnormal Psychology, 88,* 248–257.

Teghtsoonian, R. (1971). On the exponents in Stevens' law and the constant in Ekman's law. *Psychological Review, 78,* 71–80.

Tellegen, A., Lykken, D.T., Bouchard, T.J., Wilcox, K.J., Segal, N.L., & Rich, S. (1988). Personality similarity in twins reared apart and together. *Journal of Personality and Social Psychology, 54,* 1031–1039.

Templeton, L.M., & Wilcox, S.A. (2000). A tale of two representations: The misinformation effect and children's developing theory of mind. *Child Development, 71,* 402–416.

Tenenbaum, H.R., & Leaper, C. (2002). Are parents' gender schemas related to their children's gender related cognitions? A meta-analysis. *Developmental Psychology, 38,* 615–630.

Tenenbaum, H.R., & Leaper, C. (2003). Parent-child conversations about science: The socialization of gender inequities? *Developmental Psychology, 39,* 34–47.

Terman, L.M., & Merrill, M.A. (1972). *Stanford-Binet intelligence scale, form L—M* (3rd ed.). Boston, MA: Houghton Mifflin.

Terracciano, A., Abdel-Khalek, A.M., Adam, N., Adamvova, L., Ahn, C-K., Alansari, B.M., ... McCrae, R.R. (2005). National character does not reflect mean personality trait levels in 49 cultures. *Science, 310,* 96–100.

Terrace, H.M., Petitto, L.A., Sanders, R.J., & Bever, T.G. (1979). Can an ape create a sentence? *Science, 206,* 891–902.

Terrace, H.S. (1979). *Nim.* New York, NY: Knopf.

Terrier, L., Marfaing, B., & Boldi, M. (2013). Door-in-the-face: Is it really necessary that both requests be made by the same requester? *Psychological Reports, 113*(2), 675–682.

Tesser, A., & Shaffer, D. (1990). Attitudes and attitude change. *Annual Review of Psychology, 41,* 479–523.

Testa, M., Fillmore, M.T., Norris, J., Abbey, A., Curtin, J.J., Leonard, K.E., ... Hayman, L.W., Jr. (2006). Understanding alcohol expectancy effects: Revisiting the placebo condition. *Alcoholism: Clinical and Experimental Research, 30,* 339–348.

Teyber, E., & McClure, F. (2000). Therapist variables. In C.R. Snyder & R.E. Ingram (Eds.), *Handbook of psychological change: Psychotherapy processes and practices for the 21st century.* New York, NY: Wiley.

Thelen, E., Fisher, D.M., & Ridley-Johnson, R. (1984). The relationship between physical growth and a newborn reflex. *Infant Behavior and Development, 7,* 479–493.

Thibaut, J.W., & Kelley, H.H. (1959). *The social psychology of groups.* New York, NY: Wiley.

Thiede, K.W., & Anderson, M.C.M. (2003). Summarizing can improve metacomprehension accuracy. *Contemporary Education Psychology, 28,* 129–160.

Thoits, P. (1983). Dimensions of life events that influence psychological distress: An evaluation and synthesis of the literature. In H.B. Kaplan (Ed.), *Psychological stress: Trends in theory and research.* New York, NY: Academic Press.

Thomas, A., & Chess, S. (1977). *Temperament and development.* New York, NY: Brunner/Mazel.

Thomas, L. (1974). *The lives of a cell.* New York, NY: Viking.

Thomas, S.L., Skitka, L.J., Christen, S., & Jurgena, M. (2002). Social facilitation and impression formation. *Basic and Applied Social Psychology, 24,* 67–70.

Thomas, W.P., & Collier, V.P. (1997). *School effectiveness for language minority students.*

Washington, DC: National Clearinghouse for Bilingual Education.

Thompson, J.G. (1988). *The psychobiology of emotions.* New York, NY: Plenum Press.

Thompson, P.M., Giedd, J.N., Woods, R.P., Macdonald, D., Evans, A.C., & Toga, A.W. (2000). Growth patterns in the developing brain detected by using continuum mechanical tensor maps. *Nature, 404,* 190–193.

Thompson, R.F. (1985). *The brain: An introduction to neuroscience.* New York, NY: W.H. Freeman.

Thompson, W.F., Schellenberg, E.G., & Husain, G. (2001). Arousal, mood, and the Mozart effect. *Psychological Science, 12,* 248–251.

Thomson, J. (1887). *Through Masai land: A journey of exploration through the snow-clad volcanic mountains and strange tribes of eastern equatorial Africa.* London, UK: Low, Marston, Searle, & Rivington.

Thorndike, E.L. (1898). *Animal intelligence: An experimental study of the associative processes in animals.* New York, NY: Macmillan.

Thorndike, E.L. (1911). *Animal intelligence: Experimental studies.* New York, NY: Macmillan.

Thornhill, R., & Gangestad, S.W. (2006). Facial sexual dimorphism, developmental stability, and susceptibility to disease in men and women. *Evolution and Human Behavior, 27,* 131–144.

Thorpe, S.J., Gegenfurtner, K.R., Fabre-Thorpe, M., & Bülthoff, H.H. (2001). Detection of animals in natural images using far peripheral vision. *European Journal of Neuroscience, 14*(5), 869–876.

Thurstone, L.L. (1938). *Primary mental abilities.* Chicago, IL: University of Chicago Press.

Tilker, H.A. (1970). Socially responsible behavior as a function of observer responsibility and victim feedback. *Journal of Personality and Social Psychology, 14,* 95–100.

Tinbergen, N. (1951). *The study of instinct.* Oxford, UK: Clarendon Press.

Tincas, I., Benga, O., & Fox, N.A. (2006). Temperamental predictors of anxiety disorders. *Cognition, Brain, Behavior, 10,* 489–515.

Tinsley-Li, S., & Jenkins, S. (2007). Impact of race and ethnicity on the expression, assessment, and diagnosis of psychopathology. In M. Hersen, S.M. Turner, & D.C. Beidel (Eds.), *Adult psychopathology and diagnosis* (pp. 101–124). Hoboken, NJ: Wiley.

Tix, A.P., & Frazier, P.A. (1998). The use of religious coping during stressful life events: Main effects, moderation, and mediation. *Journal of Consulting and Clinical Psychology, 66,* 411–422.

Tizard, B., & Hodges, J. (1978). The effect of early institutional rearing on the development of eight-year-old children. *Journal of Child Psychology and Psychiatry, 19,* 99–118.

Tjepkema, M. (2004). Use of cannabis and other illicit drugs. *Health Reports, 15*(4), 43–47.

Tobin, S.J., & Raymundo, M.M. (2009). Persuasion by causal arguments: The motivating role of perceived causal expertise. *Social Cognition, 27,* 105–127.

Todd, K.J., Serrano, A., Lacaille, J.C., & Robitaille, R. (2006). Glial cells in synaptic plasticity. *Journal of Physiology—Paris, 99,* 75–83.

Todorov, A., & Bargh, J.A. (2002). Automatic sources of aggression. *Aggression and Violent Behavior, 7,* 53–68.

Tollefson, G.D. (1993). Major depression. In D.L. Dunner (Ed.), *Current psychiatric therapy.* Philadelphia, PA: Saunders.

Tolman, E.C. (1948). Cognitive maps in rats and men. *Psychological Review, 55,* 189–208.

Tolman, E.C., & Honzik, C.H. (1930). Introduction and removal of reward and maze performance in rats. *University of California Publications in Psychology, 4*, 257–275.

Toma, C., & Butera, F. (2009). Hidden profiles and concealed information: Strategic information sharing and use in group decision making. *Personality and Social Psychology Bulletin, 35*, 793–806.

Tomarken, A.J., & Keener, A.D. (1998). Frontal brain asymmetry and depression: A self-regulatory perspective. *Cognition and Emotion. Special issue: Neuropsychological perspectives on affective and anxiety disorders, 12*(3), 387–420.

Tomkins, S.S. (1991). *Affect, imagery, consciousness, Vol. 3: Anger and fear.* New York, NY: Springer.

Toneatto, T., Pillai, S., & Courtice, E.L. (2014). Mindfulness-enhanced cognitive behavior therapy for problem gambling: A controlled pilot study. *International Journal of Mental Health and Addiction, 12*(2), 197–205.

Tonigan, J.S., Toscova, R., & Miller, W.R. (1996). Meta-analysis of the literature on Alcoholics Anonymous: Sample and study characteristics moderate findings. *Journal of Studies on Alcohol, 57*, 65–72.

Tooby, J., & Cosmides, L. (1992). The psychological foundations of culture. In J.H. Barkow, L. Cosmides, & J. Tooby (Eds.), *The adapted mind* (pp. 19–136). New York, NY: Oxford University Press.

Tooby, J., & Cosmides, L. (2005). Conceptual foundations of evolutionary psychology. In D.M. Buss (Ed.), *The handbook of evolutionary psychology* (pp. 5–67). Hoboken, NJ: Wiley.

Torgersen, S., Myers, J., Reichborn-Kjennerud, T., Røysamb, E., Kubarych, T.S., et al. (2012). The heritability of Cluster B personality disorders assessed both by personal interview and questionnaire. *Journal of Personality Disorders, 26*, 848–866.

Torgerson, S. (2000). Genetics of patients with borderline personality disorder. *Psychiatric Clinics of North America, 23*, 1–9.

Torgerson, S., Kringlen, E., & Cramer, V. (2001). The prevalence of personality disorders in a community sample. *Archives of General Psychiatry, 58*, 590–596.

Tornick, J.K., & Gibson, B.M. (2013).Tests of inferential reasoning by exclusion in Clark's nutcrackers (Nucifraga columbiana). *Animal Cognition, 16*, 583–597.

Törnros, J., & Bolling, A. (2006). Mobile phone use— effects of conversation on mental workload and driving speed in rural and urban environments. *Transportation Research Part F: Traffic Psychology and Behaviour, 9*, 298–306.

Toro-Morn, M., & Sprecher, S. (2003). A cross-cultural comparison of mate preferences among university students: The United States vs. the People's Republic of China (PRC). *Journal of Comparative Family Studies, 34*, 151–170.

Torrey, E.F. (1997). *Out of the shadows: Confronting America's mental illness crisis.* New York, NY: Wiley.

Trainor, L.J., Tsang, C.D., & Cheung, V.H.W. (2002). Preference for sensory consonance in 2- and 4-month-old infants. *Music Perception, 20*, 187–194.

Travers, K.R., & Lyvers, M. (2005). Mood and impulsivity of recreational Ecstasy users in the week following a "rave." *Addiction Research & Theory, 13*, 43–52.

Treffner, P.J., & Barrett, R. (2004). Hands-free mobile phone speech while driving degrades coordination and control. *Transportation Research Part F: Traffic Psychology and Behaviour, 7*, 229–246.

Tremblay, L.K., Naranjo, C.A., Cardenas, L., Hermann, N., & Busto, U.E. (2002). Probing brain reward system function in major depressive disorder: Altered response to extroamphetamine. *Archives of General Psychiatry, 59*, 409–417.

Tremblay, M.A., Blaanchard, C.M., Taylor, S., & Pelletier, L.G. (2009). Work Extrinsic and Intrinsic Motivation Scale: Its value for organizational psychology research. *Canadian Journal of Behavioural Science, 41*, 213–226.

Tremblay, R.E., Pagani-Kurtz, L., Mâsse, L.C., Vitaro, F., & Pihl, R.O. (1995). A bimodal preventive intervention for disruptive kindergarten boys: Its impact through mid-adolescence. *Journal of Consulting and Clinical Psychology, 63*, 560–568.

Triandis, H.C. (1989). Cross-cultural studies of individualism and collectivism. In J.J. Berman (Ed.), *Nebraska Symposium on Motivation.* Lincoln, NE: University of Nebraska Press.

Triandis, H.C. (2001). Individualism–collectivism and personality. *Journal of Personality, 69*, 907–924.

Triandis, H.C., & Suh, E.M. (2002). Cultural influences on personality. *Annual Review of Psychology, 53*, 133–160.

Trimble, M. (2003). *Somatoform disorders.* New York, NY: Cambridge University Press.

Triplett, N. (1898). The dynamogenic factors in pacemaking and competition. *American Journal of Psychology, 9*, 507–533.

Trivers, R. (1971). The evolution of reciprocal altruism. *Quarterly Review of Biology, 46*, 35–57.

Trivers, R.L. (1972). Parental investment and sexual selection. In B. Campbell (Ed.), *Sexual selection and the descent of man* (pp. 136–179). Chicago, IL: Aldine-Atherton.

Troll, L.E. (1985). *Early and middle adulthood* (2nd ed.). Monterey, CA: Brooks/Cole.

Truell, A.D., Bartlett, J.E., & Alexander, M.W. (2002). Response rate, speed and completeness: A comparison of Internet-based and mail surveys. *Behavioral Research Methods, Instruments, & Computers, 34*, 46–49.

Truscott, S.D., & Frank, A.J. (2001). Does the Flynn effect affect IQ scores of students classified as LD? *Journal of School Psychology, 39*, 319–334.

Tsai, J.L., Levenson, R.W., & McCoy, K. (2006). Cultural temperamental variations in emotional response. *Emotion, 6*, 484–497.

Tsai, J.L., Louie, J.Y., Chen, E.E., & Uchida, Y. (2007). Learning what feelings to desire: Socialization of ideal affect through children's storybooks. *Personality and Social Psychology Bulletin, 33*, 17–30.

Tse, D., Langston, R.F., Kakeyama, M., Bethus, I., Spooner, P.A., Wood, E.R., & Morris, R.G. (2007). Schemas and memory consolidation. *Science, 316*(5821), 76–82.

Tseng, W.S., Asai, M., Liu, J., Wibulswadi, P., Suryani, L.K., Wen, J-K., ... Heiby, E. (1990). Multi-cultural study of minor psychiatric disorders in Asia: Symptom manifestations. *International Journal of Social Psychiatry, 36*, 252–264.

Tsien, J.Z. (2007). The memory code. *Scientific American, 297*(1), 52–59.

Tsujimoto, S., Yahamoto, T., Kawaguchi, H., Koizumi, H., & Sawaguchi, T. (2004). Prefrontal cortical activation associated with working memory in adults and preschool children: An event-related optical topography study. *Cerebral Cortex, 14*(7), 703–712.

Tucker, P., & Aron, A. (1993). Passionate love and marital satisfaction at key transition points in the family life cycle. *Journal of Social and Clinical Psychology, 12*, 135–147.

Tucker, V.A. (2000). The deep fovea, sideways vision and spiral flight paths in raptors. *Journal of Experimental Biology, 203*, 3745–3754.

Tulving, E. (2002). Episodic memory: From mind to brain. *Annual Review of Psychology, 53*, 1–25.

Tulving, E., & Psotka, J. (1971). Retroactive inhibition in free recall: Inaccessibility of information available in the memory store. *Journal of Experimental Psychology, 87*, 1–8.

Tulving, E., & Thomson, D.M. (1973). Encoding specificity and retrieval processes in episodic memory. *Psychological Review, 80*, 359–380.

Tung, M., Huang, J.Y., Keh, H.C., & Wai, S.S. (2009). Distance learning in advanced military education: Analysis of joint operations course in the Taiwan military. *Computers & Education, 53*, 653–666.

Tuomi, I. (2013). *Educational Neurosciences—More Problems than Promise?* Bangkok: UNESCO.

Turk, D.C. (2001). Physiological and psychological bases of pain. In A. Baum, T.A. Revenson, & J.R. Singer (Eds.), *Handbook of health psychology.* Mahwah, NJ: Erlbaum.

Turk, D.C., & Melzack, R. (2001). *Handbook of pain assessment* (2nd ed.). New York, NY: Guilford Press.

Turnbull, C.M. (1961). Some observations regarding the experiences and behavior of the Ba Mbuti pygmies. *American Journal of Psychology, 74*, 304–308.

Turner, M.E., Pratkanis, A.R., & Struckman, C.K. (2007). Groupthink as social identity maintenance. In A.R. Pratkanis (Ed.), *The science of social influence: Advances and future progress.* New York, NY: Psychology Press.

Turner, M.J., Barker, J.B., & Slater, M.J. (2014a). The season-long effects of rational emotive behavior therapy on the irrational beliefs of professional academy soccer athletes. *International Journal of Sport Psychology, 45*(5), 429–451.

Turner, M.J., Slater, M.J., & Barker, J.B. (2014b). Not the end of the world: The effects of rational-emotive behavior therapy (REBT) on irrational beliefs in elite soccer academy athletes. *Journal of Applied Sport Psychology, 26*(2), 144–156.

Tusing, K.J., & Dillard, J.P. (2000). The psychological reality of the door-in-the-face: It's helping, not bargaining. *Journal of Language and Social Psychology, 19*, 5–25.

Tversky, A., & Kahneman, D. (1982). Judgements of and by representativeness. In D. Kahneman, P. Slovic, & A. Tversky (Eds.), *Judgement under uncertainty: Heuristics and biases* (pp. 23–31). Cambridge, MA: Cambridge University Press.

Tversky, B., & Tuchin, M. (1989). A reconciliation of the evidence on eyewitness testimony: Comments on McCloskey and Zaragoza. *Journal of Experimental Psychology: General, 118*, 86–91.

Tye, M. (1991). *The imagery debate.* Cambridge, MA: MIT Press.

Tyson, G.A., & Hubert, C.J. (2002). Cultural differences in adolescents' explanations of juvenile delinquency. *Journal of Cross-Cultural Psychology, 3*(5), 459–463.

Tzuriel, D. (2000). Dynamic assessment of young children: Educational and intervention perspectives. *Educational Psychology Review, 12*(4), 385–435.

Underwood, B.J. (1970). A breakdown of the total-time law in free-recall learning. *Journal of Verbal Learning and Verbal Behavior, 9*, 573–580.

United Nations. (2002). *Report on the global reach of AIDS*. New York, NY: Author.

Unsworth, G., Devilly, G.J., & Ward, T. (2007). The effect of playing violent video games on adolescents: Should parents be quaking in their boots? *Psychology, Crime & Law, 13*, 383–394.

Urry, H.L., Nitschke, J.B., Dolski, I., Jackson, D.C., Dalton, K.M., Mueller, C.J., ... Davidson, R.J. (2004). Making a life worth living: Neural correlates of well-being. *Psychological Science, 15*, 367–372.

Urry, H.L., van Reekum, C.M., Johnstone, T., Kalin, N.H., Thurow, M.E., Schaefer, H.S., ... Davidson, R.J. (2006). Amygdala and ventromedial prefrontal cortex are inversely coupled during regulation of negative affect and predict the diurnal pattern of cortisol secretion among older adults. *Journal of Neuroscience, 26*, 4415–4425.

U.S. Public Health Service. (1979). *Healthy people: The Surgeon General's report on health promotion and disease prevention*. Washington, DC: U.S. Government Printing Office.

Uttl, B., & Graf, P. (1993). Episodic spatial memory in adulthood. *Psychology and Aging, 8*, 257–273.

Vaccarino, F.M., & Smith, K.M. (2009). Increased brain size in autism—what it will take to solve a mystery. *Biological Psychiatry, 66*, 313–315.

Vakil, E. (2012). Neuropsychological assessment: Principles, rationale, and challenges. *Journal of Clinical and Experimental Neuropsychology, 34*(2), 135–150.

Valberg, A. (2006). *Light vision color*. New York, NY: Wiley.

Valent, P. (1998). Effects of the Holocaust on Jewish child survivors: Traumas and latent disturbances 50 years later. *Psyche: Zeitschriftfuer Psychoanalyse und ihre Anwendungen, 52*, 751–771.

Valent, P. (2000a). Stress effects of the Holocaust. In G. Fink (Ed.), *Encyclopedia of stress* (Vol. 3). San Diego, CA: Academic Press.

Valent, P. (2000b). Survivor guilt. In G. Fink (Ed.), *Encyclopedia of stress* (Vol. 3). San Diego, CA: Academic Press.

Vallone, R.P., Griffin, D., Lin, S., & Ross, L. (1990). Overconfident prediction of future actions and outcomes by self and others. *Journal of Personality and Social Psychology, 58*, 582–592.

Valsiner, J., & Lawrence, J.A. (1997). Human development in culture across the life span. In J.W. Berry, P.R. Dasen, & T.S. Saraswathi (Eds.), *Handbook of cross-cultural psychology* (Vol. 2). Boston, MA: Allyn & Bacon.

Valverde, C. (2010). *Genetic screening of newborns: An ethical inquiry*. New York: Nova Science Publishers.

Valyear, K.F., Culham, J.C., Sharif, N., Westwood, D., & Goodale, M.A. (2006). A double dissociation between sensitivity to changes in object identity and object orientation in the ventral and dorsal visual streams: A human fMRI study. *Neuropsychologia, 44*, 218–228.

Van Damme, I., & Seynaeve, L. (2013). The effect of mood on confidence in false memories. *Journal of Cognitive Psychology, 25*(3), 309–318.

Vandell, D.L., Burchinal, M.R., Belsky, J., Owen, M.T., Friedman, S.L., ...Weinraub, M. (2005). *Early child care and children's development in the primary grades: Follow-up results from the NICHD Study of Early Child Care*. Paper presented at the biennial meeting of the Society for Research in Child Development, Atlanta, Georgia.

van de Rijt, A., & Macy, M.W. (2006). Power and dependence in intimate exchange. *Social Forces, 84*, 1455–1470.

van De Ruit, M., Perenboom, M.J.L., & Grey, M.J. (2015). TMS brain mapping in less than two minutes. *Brain Stimulation, 8*(2), 231–239.

van der Hart, O., & Nijenhuis, E. (2009). Dissociative disorders. In P.H. Blaney & T. Millon (Eds.), *Oxford textbook of psychopathology* (2nd ed., pp. 452–481). New York, NY: Oxford University Press.

Van Goozen, S., Fairchild, G., Snoek, H., & Harold, G. (2007). The evidence for a neurobiological model of childhood antisocial behavior. *Psychological Bulletin, 133*, 149–182.

Van Houten, R., & Retting, R.A. (2001). Increasing motorist compliance and caution at stop signs. *Journal of Applied Behavior Analysis, 34*, 185–193.

van Ijzendoorn, M. (1995). Adult attachment representations, parental responsiveness, and infant attachment: A meta-analysis of the Adult Attachment Interview. *Psychological Bulletin, 117*, 387–403.

VanItallie, T.B., & Kissileff, H.R. (1990). Human obesity: A problem in body economics. In E.M. Stricker (Ed.), *Handbook of behavioral neurobiology, Vol. 10: Neurobiology of food and fluid intake* (pp. 183–206). New York, NY: Plenum Press.

van Kesteren, Marlieke T.R., Rijpkema, M., Ruiter, D.J., Morris, R.G.M., & Fernández, G. (2014). Building on prior knowledge: Schema-dependent encoding processes relate to academic performance. *Journal of Cognitive Neuroscience, 26*(10), 2250–2261.

Van Overschelde, J.P., Rawson, K.A., Dunlosky, J., & Hunt, R.R. (2005). Distinctive processing underlies skilled memory. *Psychological Science, 16*(5), 358–361.

van Praag, H.M. (2004). *Stress, vulnerability and depression*. New York, NY: Cambridge University Press.

van Strien, N.M., Cappaert, N.L.M., & Witter, M.P. (2009). The anatomy of memory: An interactive overview of the parahippocampal–hippocampal network. *Nature Reviews Neuroscience, 10*, 272–282.

Van Yperen, N. (2006). A novel approach to assessing achievement goals in the context of the 2 × 2 framework: Identifying distinct profiles of individuals with different dominant achievement goals. *Personality and Social Psychology Bulletin, 32*, 1432–1445.

Van Zomeren, A.H., & Brouwer, W.H. (1994). *Clinical neuropsychology of attention*. New York, NY: Oxford University Press.

Vargha-Khadem, F., Gadian, D.G., Watkins, K.E., Connelly, A., Van Paesschen, W., & Mishkin, M. (1997). Differential effects of early hippocampal pathology on episodic and semantic memory. *Science, 277*, 376–380.

Varney, N.R., & Roberts, R.J. (1999). *The evaluation and treatment of mild traumatic brain injury*. Mahwah, NJ: Erlbaum.

Vartanian, L.R. (2000). Revisiting the imaginary audience and personal fable constructs of adolescent egocentrism: A conceptual review. *Adolescence, 35*, 639–661.

Vasilaki, E.I., Hosier, S.G., & Cox, W.M. (2006). The efficacy of motivational interviewing as a brief intervention for excessive drinking. A meta-analytic review. *Alcohol and Alcoholism, 41*, 328–335.

Vaughan, P.W., Rogers, E.M., Singhal, A., & Swalehe, R.M. (2000). Entertainment-education and HIV/AIDS prevention: A field experiment in Tanzania. *Journal of Health Communication, 5*, 81–100.

Vaughn, C., & Leff, J. (2006). The measurement of expressed emotion in the families of psychiatric patients. *British Journal of Clinical Psychology, 15*(2), 157–165.

Vaughn, L. (2016). *The power of critical thinking: Effective reasoning about ordinary and extraordinary claims* (5th ed.). New York, NY: Oxford University Press.

Vazire, S., & Gosling, S.D. (2004). e-Perceptions: Personality impressions based on personal websites. *Journal of Personality and Social Psychology, 87*, 123–132.

Velotis, C.M. (2006). *New developments in anxiety disorders research*. Hauppauge, NY: Nova Biomedical Books.

Venter, J.C., Adams, M.D., Myers, E.W., Li, P.W., Mural, R.J., Sutton, G.G., ... Zhu, X. (2001). The sequence of the human genome. *Science, 291*, 1304–1351.

Verghese, P. (2001). Visual search and attention: A signal detection theory approach. *Neuron, 31*(4), 523–535.

Vernon, P.A., Martin, R.A., Schermer, J.A., Cherkas, L.F., & Spector, T.D. (2008). Genetic and environmental contributions to humor styles: A replication study. *Twin Research and Human Genetics, 11*, 44–47.

Verplanken, B., & Holland, R.W. (2002). Motivated decision making: Effects of activation and self centrality of values on choices and behavior. *Journal of Personality and Social Psychology, 82*, 434–447.

Vervliet, B., Vansteenwegen, D., & Eelen, P. (2006). Generalization gradients for acquisition and extinction in human contingency learning. *Experimental Psychology, 53*, 132–142.

Vésteinsdóttir, V., Reips, U., Joinson, A., & Thorsdottir, F. (2015). Psychometric properties of measurements obtained with the Marlowe–Crowne social desirability scale in an icelandic probability based internet sample. *Computers in Human Behavior, 49*, 608–614.

Vetter, H.J. (1969). *Language behavior and psychopathology*. Chicago, IL: Rand McNally.

Viemeroe, V. (1996). Factors in childhood that predict later criminal behavior. *Aggressive Behavior, 22*(2), 87–97.

Villarreal, D.M., Do, V., Haddad, E., & Derrick, B.E. (2002). NMDA receptor antagonists sustain LTP and spatial memory: Active processes mediate LTP decay. *Nature Neuroscience, 5*, 48–52.

Vincent, N., Cox, B., & Clara, I. (2009). Are personality dimensions associated with sleep length in a large nationally representative sample? *Comprehensive Psychiatry, 50*, 158–163.

Vitaliano, P.P., Young, H.M., & Zhang, J. (2004). Is caregiving a risk factor for illness? *Current Directions in Psychological Science, 13*, 13–16.

Vittengl, J.R., Clark, L.A., & Jarrett, R.B. (2009). Continuation-phase cognitive therapy's effects on remission and recovery from depression. *Journal of Consulting and Clinical Psychology, 77*, 367–371.

Vogels, T.P., Rajan, K., & Abbott, L.F. (2005). Neural network dynamics. *Annual Review of Neuroscience, 28*, 357–376.

Vogels, W.W.A., Dekker, M.R., Brouwer, W.H., & deJong, R. (2002). Age-related changes in event-related prospective memory performance: A comparison of four prospective memory tasks. *Brain and Cognition, 49*, 341–362.

von Frisch, K. (1974). Decoding the language of the bee. *Science, 185*, 663–668.

von Senden, M. (1960). *Space and sight: The perception of space and shape in the congenitally blind before and after operation.* (P. Heath, Trans.). New York, NY: Free Press.

Vormfelde, S.V., Hoell, I., Tzvetkov, M., Jamrozinski, K., Sehrt, D., Brockmöller, J., & Leibing, E. (2006). Anxiety- and novelty seeking-related personality traits and serotonin transporter gene polymorphisms. *Journal of Psychiatric Research, 40,* 568–576.

Vouimba, R.M., Yaniv, D., & Richter-Levin, G. (2007). Glucocorticoid receptors and beta-adrenoreceptors in basolateral amygdala modulate synaptic plasticity in hippocampal dentate gyrus but not in area CA1. *Neuropharmacology, 52,* 244–252.

Vral, A., Thierens, H., Baeyens, A., & De Ridder, L. (2002). The micronucleus and g(2)-phase assays for human blood lymphocytes as biomarkers of individual sensitivity to ionizing radiation: Limitations imposed by intra-individual variability. *Radiation Research, 157,* 472–477.

Vrij, A., van der Steen, J., & Koppelaar, L. (1994). Aggression of police officers as a function of temperature: An experiment with the Fire Arms Training System. *Journal of Community and Applied Social Psychology, 4,* 365–370.

Vurpillot, E. (1968). The development of scanning strategies and their relation to visual differentiations. *Journal of Experimental Child Psychology, 6,* 632–650.

Vygotsky, L.S. (1935/1978). *Mind in society: The development of higher psychological processes.* Cambridge, MA: Harvard University Press.

Vygotsky, L.S. (1962). *Thought and language.* Cambridge, MA: MIT Press.

Wacha, V.H., & Obrzut, J.E. (2007). Effects of fetal alcohol syndrome on neuropsychological function. *Journal of Developmental and Physical Disabilities, 19,* 217–226.

Wachs, T.D. (2000). *Necessary but not sufficient: The respective roles of single and multiple influences on individual development.* Washington, DC: American Psychological Association.

Wadden, T.A., Brownell, K.D., & Foster, G.D. (2002). Obesity: Responding to the global epidemic. *Journal of Consulting and Clinical Psychology, 70,* 510–525.

Wadden, T.A., Vogt, R.A., Andersen, R.E., Bartlett, S.J., Foster, G.D., Kuehnel, R.H., ... Steen, S.N. (1997). Exercise in the treatment of obesity: Effects of four interventions on body composition, resting energy expenditure, appetite, and mood. *Journal of Consulting and Clinical Psychology, 66,* 269–277.

Wade, C., & Cirese, S. (1992). *Human sexuality* (2nd ed.). Chicago, IL: Harcourt Brace Jovanovich.

Wade, N.J., & Swanston, M. (2001). *Visual perception: An introduction.* New York, NY: Psychology Press.

Wade, P., & Bernstein, B. (1991). Culture sensitivity training and counselor's race: Effects on Black female clients' perceptions and attrition. *Journal of Counseling Psychology, 38,* 9–15.

Wagenmakers, E.-J., Wetzels, R., Borsboom, D., & van der Maas, H.L.J. (2011). Why psychologists must change the way they analyze their data: The case of psi: Comment on Bem (2011). *Journal of Personality and Social Psychology, 100,* 426–432.

Wagner, A.D., Schacter, D., Rotte, M., Koutstaal, W., Meril, A., Dale, A., ... Buckner, R. (1998). Building memories: Remembering and forgetting of verbal experiences as predicted by brain activity. *Science, 281,* 1188–1191.

Wagstaff, G.F. (2009). Is there a future for investigative hypnosis? *Journal of Investigative Psychology and Offender Profiling, 6,* 43–57.

Wagstaff, G.F., Cole, J., Wheatcroft, J., Anderton, A., & Madden, H. (2008). Reducing and reversing pseudo-memories with hypnosis. *Contemporary Hypnosis, 25,* 178–191.

Wahlsten, D. (1999). Single-gene influences on brain and behavior. *Annual Review of Psychology, 50,* 599–624.

Wahlsten, V.S., & Sarman, I. (2013). Neurobehavioural development of preschool-age children born to addicted mothers given opiate maintenance treatment with buprenorphine during pregnancy. *Acta Paediatrica, 102,* 544–549.

Wainwright, P.E., Simpson, J.R., Cameron, R., Hoffman-Goetz, L., Winfield, D., McCutcheon, D., & MacDonald, M. (1990). Effects of treadmill exercise on weight cycling in female mice. *Physiology and Behavior, 49,* 639–642.

Wakefield, J.C. (2006). Normal inability versus pathological disability: Why Ossorio's definition of mental disorder is not sufficient. *Clinical Psychology: Science and Practice, 4,* 249–258.

Wakefield, J.C. (2013). The DSM-5 debate over the bereavement exclusion: Psychiatric diagnosis and the future of empirically supported treatment. *Clinical Psychology Review, 33(7),* 825–845.

Wakefield, M., Reid, Y., Roberts, L., Mullins, R., & Gillies, P. (1998). Smoking and smoking cessation among men whose partners are pregnant: A qualitative study. *Social Science and Medicine, 47,* 657–664.

Walen, S.R., & Roth, D. (1987). A cognitive approach. In J.H. Geer & W.T. O'Donohue (Eds.), *Theories of human sexuality.* New York, NY: Plenum Press.

Walker, M.P. (2005). A refined model of sleep and the time course of memory formation. *Behavioral and Brain Sciences, 28,* 51–104.

Walker, M.P. (2008). Cognitive consequences of sleep and sleep loss. *Sleep Medicine, 9* (Suppl. 1), S29–S34.

Walker, M.P., & Stickgold, R. (2006). Sleep, memory, and plasticity. *Annual Review of Psychology, 57,* 139–166.

Walker, P.L. (2001). A bioarchaeological perspective on the history of violence. *Annual Review of Anthropology, 30,* 573–596.

Wallbott, H., & Scherer, K. (1988). How universal and specific is emotional experience? Evidence from 27 countries and five continents. In K. Scherer (Ed.), *Facets of emotion: Recent research* (pp. 31–56). Hillsdale, NJ: Erlbaum.

Wallenius, M., & Punamäki, R.L. (2008). Digital game violence and direct aggression in adolescence: A longitudinal study of the roles of sex, age, and parent-child communication. *Journal of Applied Developmental Psychology, 29,* 286–294.

Wallentin, M. (2009). Putative sex differences in verbal abilities and language cortex: A critical review. *Brain and Language, 108,* 175–183.

Waller, G., & Hartley, P. (1994). Perceived parental style and eating psychopathology. *European Eating Disorders Review, 2,* 76–92.

Wallis, D.J., & Hetherington, M.M. (2004). Stress and eating: The effects of ego-threat and cognitive demand on food intake in restrained and emotional eaters. *Appetite, 43(1),* 39–46.

Wallis, T.S., & Horswill, M.S. (2007). Using fuzzy signal detection theory to determine why experienced and trained drivers respond faster than novices in a hazard perception test. *Accident Analysis & Prevention, 39(6),* 1177–1185.

Wallston, K.A. (1993). Hocus-pocus, the focus isn't strictly on locus: Rotter's social learning theory

modified for health. *Cognitive Therapy and Research, 16,* 183–199.

Walsh, B.T., & Devlin, M.J. (1998). Eating disorders: Progress and problems. *Science, 280,* 1387–1390.

Walster, E., Aronson, V., Abrahams, D., & Rottman, L. (1966). The importance of physical attractiveness in dating behavior. *Journal of Personality and Social Psychology, 4,* 508–516.

Walther, E. (2002). Guilty by mere association: Evaluative conditioning and the spreading attitude effect. *Journal of Personality and Social Psychology, 82,* 919–934.

Wand, T., Hudson, S., & Marshall, W. (1996). Attachment style in sex offenders: A preliminary study. *Journal of Sex Research, 33,* 17–26.

Wang, G., Mao, L., Ma, Y., Yang, X., Cao, J., Liu, X., ... & Han, S. (2011). Neural representations of close others in collectivistic brains. *Social Cognitive and Affective Neuroscience, 7(2),* 222–229.

Wang, P.S., Demler, O., & Kessler, R.C. (2002). Adequacy of treatment for serious mental illness in the United States. *American Journal of Public Health, 92,* 92–98.

Wang, S., Baillargeon, R., & Paterson, S. (2005). Detecting continuity violations in infancy: A new account and new evidence from covering and tube events. *Cognition, 95,* 129–173.

Wang, S.H., & Morris, R.G.M. (2010). Hippocampal-neocortical interactions in memory formation, consolidation, and reconsolidation. *Annual Review of Psychology, 61,* 49–79.

Wang, T., Brownstein, R., & Katzev, R. (1989). Promoting charitable behaviour with compliance techniques. *Applied Psychology: An International Review, 38,* 165–183.

Ward, J. (2008). *The frog who croaked blue: Synesthesia and the mixing of the senses.* London, UK: Routledge.

Ward, S.L., & Overton, W.F. (1990). Semantic familiarity, relevance, and the development of deductive reasoning. *Developmental Psychology, 26,* 488–493.

Warga, C. (1987). Pain's gatekeeper. *Psychology Today, 21,* 50–59.

Warneken, F., & Tomasello, M. (2006). Altruistic helping in human infants and young chimpanzees. *Science, 311,* 1301–1303.

Watanabe, H., Sato, C., Kuramochi, T., Nishino, H., & Mizunami, M. (2008). Salivary conditioning with antennal gustatory unconditioned stimulus in an insect. *Neurobiology of Learning and Memory, 90,* 245–254.

Waters, A., Hill, A., & Waller, G. (2001). Bulimics' response to food cravings: Is binge eating a product of hunger or emotional state. *Behaviour Research and Therapy, 39,* 877–886.

Waters, A.M., Henry, J., & Neumann, D.L. (2009). Aversive Pavlovian conditioning in childhood anxiety disorders: Impaired response inhibition and resistance to extinction. *Journal of Abnormal Psychology, 118,* 311–321.

Watkins, D., Cheng, C., Mpofu, E., Olowu, S., Singh-Sengupta, S., & Regmi, M. (2003). Gender differences in self-construal: How generalizable are Western findings? *Journal of Social Psychology, 143,* 501–519.

Watkins, L.R., & Maier, S.F. (2003). When good pain turns bad. *Current Directions in Psychological Science, 12,* 232–236.

Watson, D., Clark, L.A., & Tellegen, A. (1988). Development and validation of brief measures of positive and negative affect: The PANAS scales. *Journal of Personality and Social Psychology, 54,* 1063–1070.

Watson, D.L., & Tharp, R.G. (1997). *Self-directed behavior: Self-modification for personal adjustment* (6th ed.) Belmont, CA: Brooks/Cole.

Watson, J.B. (1924). *Behaviorism.* New York, NY: People's Institute.grefe, Inc.

Watson, J.B., & Rayner, R. (1920). Conditioned emotional reactions. *Journal of Experimental Psychology, 3,* 1–14.

Watson, J.C., & Greenberg, L.S. (1998). Humanistic and experiential theories of personality. In D.F. Barone, M. Hersen, & V.B. Van Hasselt (Eds.), *Advanced personality* (pp. 81–102). New York, NY: Plenum Press.

Watt, C.A., & Irwin, H.J. (2010). Processes underlying the phenomena of mysterious minds: Laboratory evidence for ESP. In S. Krippner, & H.L. Friedman (Eds.), *Mysterious minds: The neurobiology of psychics, mediums, and other extraordinary people.* Santa Barbara, CA: Praeger/ABC-CLIO.

Wauterickx, N., Gouwy, A., & Bracke, P. (2006). Parental divorce and depression: Long-term effects on adult children. *Journal of Divorce & Remarriage, 45,* 43–68.

Webb, W.B. (1974). Sleep as an adaptive response. *Perceptual and Motor Skills, 38,* 1023–1027.

Webb, W.B. (1994). Prediction of sleep onset. In R.D. Ogilvie & J.R. Harsh. (Eds.), *Sleep onset: Normal and abnormal processes.* Washington, DC: American Psychological Association.

Webster, D.M., Richter, L., & Kruglanski, A.W. (1996). On leaping to conclusions when feeling tired: Mental fatigue effects on impressional primacy. *Journal of Experimental Social Psychology, 32,* 181–195.

Webster, J.D. (1997). Attachment style and well-being in elderly adults: A preliminary investigation. *Canadian Journal on Aging, 16,* 101–111.

Wechsler, D. (1991). WISC III: Wechsler Intelligence Scale for Children (3rd ed.). San Antonio, TX: The Psychological Corporation.

Wechsler, D. (1997). Wechsler Adult Intelligence Scale (3rd ed.). San Antonio, TX: The Psychological Corporation.

Wechsler, H., Davenport, A., Dowdall, G., Hoeykins, B., & Castillo, S. (1994). Health and behavioral consequences of binge drinking in college: A national survey of students at 140 campuses. *Journal of the American Medical Association, 272,* 1672–1677.

Weg, R.B. (1983). Changing physiology of aging: Normal and pathological. In D.S. Woodruff & J.E. Birren (Eds.), *Aging: Scientific perspectives and social issues* (2nd ed.). Monterey, CA: Brooks/Cole.

Wegner, D.M., Wenzlaff, R.M., & Kozak, M. (2004). Dream rebound: The return of suppressed thoughts in dreams. *Psychological Science, 15,* 232–236.

Weiland, J.D., & Humayun, M.S. (2008). Visual prosthesis. *Proceedings of the IEEE, 96,* 1076–1084.

Weinberg, R.S., & Genuchi, M. (1980). Relationship between competitive trait anxiety, state anxiety, and golf performance: A field study. *Journal of Sport Psychology, 2,* 148–154.

Weinberger, D.R., & McClure, R.K. (2002). Neurotoxicity, neuroplasticity, and magnetic resonance imaging morphometry: What is happening in the schizophrenic brain? *Archives of General Psychiatry, 59,* 553–559.

Weiner, B. (1985). An attributional theory of achievement motivation and emotion. *Psychological Review, 92,* 548–573.

Weiner, B. (1992). *Human motivation: Metaphors, theories, and research.* Newbury Park, CA: Sage.

Weiner, B. (1996). Searching for order in social motivation. *Psychological Inquiry, 7,* 199–216.

Weiner, R., Lisanby, S.H., Husain, M.M., Morales, O.G., Maixner, D.F., Hall, S.E., et al. (2013). Electroconvulsive therapy device classification: Response to FDA advisory panel hearing and recommendations. *Journal of Clinical Psychiatry, 74*(1), 38–42.

Weiner, R.D., & Coffey, C.E. (1988). Indications for the use of electroconvulsive therapy. In A.J. Francis & R.E. Hales (Eds.), *Review of Psychiatry* (Vol. 7). Washington, DC: American Psychiatric Press.

Weinert, F.E., & Hany, E.A. (2003). The stability of individual differences in intellectual development. In R.J. Sternberg, J. Lautrey, & T.I. Lubart (Eds.), *Models of intelligence: International perspectives.* Washington, DC: American Psychological Association.

Weingardt, K.R., & Marlatt, G.A. (1998). Harm reduction and public policy. In G.A. Marlatt (Ed.), *Harm reduction: Pragmatic strategies for managing high-risk behaviors* (pp. 353–378). New York, NY: Guilford Press.

Weingarten, H.P. (1983). Conditioned cues elicit feeding in sated rats: A role for learning in meal initiation. *Science, 220,* 431–433.

Weinstein, L., Perez-Rodriguez, M., & Siever, L. (2014). Personality disorders, attachment and psychodynamic psychotherapy. *Psychopathology, 47*(6), 425–436.

Weissman, M.M., & Markowitz, J.C. (1994). Interpersonal psychotherapy: Current status. *Archives of General Psychiatry, 51,* 599–606.

Weissman, M.M., & Markowitz, J.C. (2002). Interpersonal psychotherapy for depression. In I.H. Gotlib & C.L. Hammen (Eds.), *Handbook of Depression* (pp. 404–421). New York, NY: Guilford Press.

Weissman, M.M., Geshon, E.S., Kidd, K.K., Prusoff, B.A., Leckman, J.F., Dibble, E., ... Guroff, J.J. (1984). Psychiatric disorders in the relatives of probands with affective disorders. *Archives of General Psychiatry, 41,* 13–21.

Weitlauf, J., Smith, R.E., & Cervone, D. (2000). Generalization effects of coping skills training: Influences of self-defense training on women's efficacy beliefs, assertiveness, and aggression. *Journal of Applied Psychology, 85,* 625–633.

Weitzenhoffer, A.M., & Hilgard, E.R. (1962). *Stanford Hypnotic Susceptibility Scale: Form C.* Palo Alto, CA: Consulting Psychologists Press.

Weller, A., & Weller, L. (1997). Menstrual synchrony under optimal conditions: Bedouin families. *Journal of Comparative Psychology, 111,* 143–151.

Weller, A., & Weller, L. (1998). Prolonged and very intensive contact may not be conducive to menstrual synchrony. *Psychoneuroendocrinology, 23,* 19–32.

Weller, L., Weller, A., Koresh, H.K., & Shoshan, B.R. (1999). Menstrual synchrony in a sample of working women. *Psychoneuroendocrinology, 24,* 449–459.

Wender, P.H., Kety, S.S., Rosenthal, D., Schulsinger, F., Ortmann, J., & Lunde, I. (1986). Psychiatric disorders in the biological and adoptive families of adopted individuals with affective disorders. *Archives of General Psychiatry, 43,* 923–929.

Wendt, D.C., & Gone, J.P. (2012). Rethinking cultural competence: Insights from indigenous community treatment settings. *Transcultural Psychiatry, 49*(2) 206–222.

Wenzlaff, R.M., & Wegner, D.M. (2000). Thought suppression. *Annual Review of Psychology, 51,* 59–91.

Wenzlaff, R.M., Wegner, D.M., & Roper, D.W. (1988). Depression and mental control: The resurgence of unwanted negative thoughts. *Journal of Personality and Social Psychology, 55,* 882–892.

Werker, J. (1989). Becoming a native listener. *American Scientist, 77,* 54–59.

Werker, J.F., & Byers-Heinlein, K. (2008). The youngest bilinguals: First steps in perception and comprehension of language. *Trends in Cognitive Sciences, 12*(4), 144–151.

Werker, J.F., & Tees, R.C. (1992). The organization and reorganization of human speech perception. *Annual Review of Neuroscience, 15,* 86–101.

Werner, E.E., & Smith, R.S. (1982). *Vulnerable but invincible: A longitudinal study of resilient children.* New York, NY: McGraw-Hill.

Werth, J.L., Jr., Blevins, D., Toussaint, K.L., & Durham, M.R. (2002). The influence of cultural diversity on end of life care and decisions. *American Behavioral Scientist, 46,* 204–219.

Wertheimer, M. (1912). Experimentelle studien über das Gesehen von Bewegung. *Zeitschrift fuer Psychologie, 61,* 161–265.

Westen, D. (1998). The scientific legacy of Sigmund Freud: Toward a psychodynamically informed psychological science. *Psychological Bulletin, 24,* 333–371.

Westen, D., & Gabbard, G. (1999). Psychoanalytic approaches to personality. In L.A. Pervin & O.P. John (Eds.), *Handbook of personality: Theory and research* (2nd ed.). New York, NY: Guilford Press.

Westen, D., & Morrison, K. (2001). A multidimensional meta-analysis of treatments for depression, panic, and generalized anxiety disorder: An empirical examination of the status of empirically supported therapies. *Journal of Consulting and Clinical Psychology, 69,* 875–889.

Westen, D., Gabbard, G.O., & Ortigo, K.M. (2008). Psychoanalytic approaches to personality. In O.P. John, R.W. Robins, & L.A. Pervin (Eds.), *Handbook of personality theory and research* (3rd ed.). New York, NY: Guilford Press.

Westen, D., Novotny, C.M., & Thompson-Brenner, H. (2004). The empirical status of empirically supported psychotherapies: Assumptions, findings, and reporting in controlled clinical trials. *Psychological Bulletin, 130,* 631–663.

Weston, S.J., Hill, P.L., & Jackson, J.J. (2015). Personality traits predict the onset of disease. *Social Psychological and Personality Science, 6*(3), 309–317.

Wethington, E. (2000). Expecting stress: Americans and the "midlife crisis." *Motivation and Emotion, 24,* 85–103.

Wetter, D.W., Fiore, M.C., Gritz, E.R., Lando, H.A., Stitzer, M.L., ... Baker, T.B. (1998). The Agency for Health Care Policy and Research smoking cessation clinical practice guideline: Findings and implications for psychologists. *American Psychologist, 53,* 657–669.

Whalley, L.J., & Deary, I.J. (2001). Longitudinal cohort study of childhood IQ and survival up to age 76. *British Medical Journal, 322,* 819–822.

Wheeler, R.E., Davidson, R.J., & Tomarken, A.J. (1993). Frontal brain asymmetry and emotional reactivity: A biological substrate of affective style. *Psychophysiology, 30,* 82–89.

Whitam, F.L., & Mathy, R.M. (1991). Childhood cross-gender behavior of homosexual females in Brazil, Peru, the Philippines, and the United States. *Archives of Sexual Behavior, 20,* 151–170.

White, E.J., Hutka, S.A., Williams, L.J., & Moreno, S. (2013). Learning, neural plasticity and sensitive periods: Implications for language acquisition, music training and transfer across the lifespan. *Frontiers in Systems Neuroscience, 7.* doi: http://dx.doi.org/10.3389/fnsys.2013.00090.

White, G.L. (1980). Physical attractiveness and courtship progress. *Journal of Personality and Social Psychology, 39,* 660–668.

White, K.M., Hogg, M.A., & Terry, D.J. (2002). Improving attitude behavior correspondence through exposure to normative support from a salient ingroup. *Basic and Applied Social Psychology, 24,* 91–103.

White, N.M., & Milner, P.M. (1992). The psychobiology of reinforcers. *Annual Review of Psychology, 43,* 443–472.

White, P.A. (2009). Property transmission: An explanatory account of the role of similarity information in casual inference. *Psychological Bulletin, 135,* 774–793.

White, T., & Nelson, C.A. (2004). Neurobiological development during childhood and adolescence. In R.L. Findling & S.C. Schulz (Eds.), *Schizophrenia in adolescents and children: Assessment, neurobiology, and treatment.* Baltimore, MD: Johns Hopkins University Press.

Whitehouse, W.G., Orne, E.C., & Dinges, D.F. (2008). Eyewitness memory: Can suggestion be minimized in the investigative interview? *The Forensic Examiner, 17,* 66–75.

Whorf, B.L. (1956a). *Language, thought, and reality: Selected writings of Benjamin Lee Whorf,* J.B. Carroll, ed. Cambridge, MA: MIT Press.

Whorf, B.L. (1956b). Science and linguistics. In J.B. Carroll (Ed.), *Language, thought and reality: Selected writings of Benjamin Lee Whorf.* Cambridge, MA: MIT Press.

Widiger, T.A., & Smith, G.T. (2008). Personality and psychopathology. In O.P. John, R.W. Robins, & L.A. Pervin (Eds.), *Handbook of personality: Theory and research* (3rd ed.). New York, NY: Guilford Press.

Widiger, T.A., Livesley, T.A., & Clark, L.A. (2009). An integrative dimensional classification of personality disorder. *Psychological Assessment, 21,* 243–255.

Widom, C.S. (1983). A methodology for studying non-institutionalized psychopaths. In R.D. Hare & D.A. Schaling (Eds.), *Psychopathic behavior: Approaches to research.* Chichester, UK: Wiley.

Wiedeman, A.M., Black, J.A., Dolle, A.L., Finney, E.J., & Coker, K.L. (2015). Factors influencing the impact of aggressive and violent media on children and adolescents. *Aggression and Violent Behavior, 25,* 191–198.

Wiedenfeld, S.A., O'Leary, A., Bandura, A., Brown, S., Levine, S., & Raska, K. (1990). Impact of perceived self-efficacy in coping with stressors on components of the immune system. *Journal of Personality and Social Psychology, 59,* 1082–1094.

Wilbrecht, L., & Nottebohm, F. (2003). Vocal learning in birds and humans. *Mental Retardation and Developmental Disabilities Research Reviews, 9,* 135–148.

Wilcox, S., & Storandt, M. (1996). Relations among age, exercise, and psychological variables in a community sample of women. *Health Psychology, 15,* 110–113.

Wilder, D.A., Austin, J., & Casella, S. (2009). Applying behavior analysis in organizations: Organizational behavior management. *Psychological Services, 6,* 202–211.

Wilkin, B. (2011). Ethical issues in genetics. *Journal of Paediatrics and Child Health, 47,* 668–671.

Wilkins, A.J., & Baddeley, A.D. (1978). Remembering to recall in everyday life: An approach to absent-mindedness. In M.M. Grueneberg, P.E. Morris, & R.N. Sykes (Eds.), *Practical aspects of memory.* London, UK: Academic Press.

Willenberg, H.S., Bornstein, S.R., & Crousos, G.P. (2000). Stress-induced disease: Overview. In G. Fink (Ed.), *Encyclopedia of stress* (Vol. 3). San Diego, CA: Academic Press.

Williams, C. (2001). *You snooze, you lose?—Sleep patterns in Canada.* Canadian Social Trends, Statistics Canada—Catalogue No. 11-008, 10–14.

Williams, D., & Skoric, M. (2005). Internet fantasy violence: A test of aggression in an online game. *Communication Monographs, 72,* 217–233.

Williams, D.R., Gonzalez, H.M., Neighbors, H., Nesse, R., Abelson, J.M., Sweetman, J., & Jackson, J.S. (2007). Prevalence and distribution of major depressive disorder in African Americans, Caribbean blacks, and non-Hispanic whites: Results from the National Survey of American Life. *Archives of General Psychiatry, 64*(3), 305–315.

Williams, S.L., Kinney, P.J., & Falbo, J. (1989). Generalization of therapeutic changes in agoraphobia: The role of perceived self-efficacy. *Journal of Consulting and Clinical Psychology, 57,* 436–442.

Williams, T.J., Pepitone, M.E., Christensen, S.E., Cooke, B.M., Huberman, A.D., & Breedlove, N.J. (2000). Finger length patterns and human sexual orientation. *Nature, 404,* 455–456.

Williams, W.L., & Burkholder, E. (2008). Response chaining. In W.T. O'Donohue & J.E. Fisher, (Eds.), *Cognitive behavior therapy: Applying empirically supported techniques in your practice* (2nd ed.). Hoboken, NJ: Wiley.

Williamson, P. (2006). *Mind, brain, and schizophrenia.* New York, NY: Oxford University Press.

Willingham, W.W., Rock, D.A., & Pollack, J. (1990). Predictability of college grades: Three tests and three national samples. In W.W. Willingham & C. Lewis (Eds.), *Predicting college grades: An analysis of institutional trends over two decades.* Princeton, NJ: Educational Testing Service.

Wills, T.A., & Shinar, O. (2000). Measuring perceived and received social support. In S. Cohen, L. Underwood, & B.H. Gottlieb (Eds.), *Social support measurement and intervention.* New York, NY: Oxford University Press.

Wilson, D.A., Best, A.R., & Sullivan, R.M. (2004). Plasticity in the olfactory system: Lessons for the neurobiology of memory. *Neuroscientist, 10,* 513–524.

Wilson, E.O. (1980). *Sociobiology.* Cambridge, MA: Harvard University Press.

Wilson, M., & Daly, M. (1985). Competitiveness, risk-taking and violence: The young male syndrome. *Ethology and Sociobiology, 6,* 59–73.

Wilson, M., & Daly, M. (1992). The man who mistook his wife for a chattel. In J. Barkow, L. Cosmides, & J. Tooby (Eds.), *The adapted mind: Evolutionary psychology and the generation of culture* (pp. 289–326). London, UK: Oxford University Press.

Windholz, G. (1997). Ivan P. Pavlov: An overview of his life and psychological work. *American Psychologist, 52,* 941–946.

Winkler, I., Korzyukov, O., Gumenyuk, V., Cowan, N., Linkenkaer, H.K., Ilmoniemi, R.J., ... Naeaetaenen, R. (2002). Temporary and longer term retention of acoustic information. *Psychophysiology, 39,* 530–534.

Winne, P.H., & Hadwin, A.F. (1998). Studying as self-regulated learning. In D.J. Hacker, J. Dunlosky, & A.C. Graesser (Eds.), *Metacognition in educational theory and practice* (pp. 277–304). Mahwah, NJ: Erlbaum.

Winnepenninckx, B., Rooms, L., & Kooy, R.F. (2003). Mental retardation: A review of the genetic causes. *British Journal of Developmental Disabilities, 49,* 29–44.

Winner, E. (2000). The origins and ends of giftedness. *American Psychologist, 55,* 159–169.

Winograd, E., Goldstein, F.C., Monarch, E.S., Peluso, J.P., & Goldman, W.P. (1999). The mere exposure effect in patients with Alzheimer's disease. *Neuropsychology, 13,* 41–46.

Wise, R.A. (1996). Addictive drugs and brain stimulation reward. *Annual Review of Neuroscience, 19,* 319–340.

Wise, R.A. (2004). Dopamine, learning and motivation. *Nature Reviews Neuroscience, 5,* 483–494.

Wise, R.A., & Rompre, P.P. (1989). Brain dopamine and reward. *Annual Review of Psychology, 40,* 191–226.

Witelson, S.F., Kigar, D.L., & Harvey, T. (1999). The exceptional brain of Albert Einstein. *Lancet, 353,* 2149–2153.

Witkin, H.A., Dyk, R.B., Faterson, H.F., Goodenough, D.R., & Karp, S.A. (1962). *Psychological differentiation.* New York, NY: Wiley.

Wittchen, H.U., Zhao, S., Kessler, R.C., & Eaton, W.W. (1994). DSM-III-R generalized anxiety disorder in the National Comorbidity Survey. *Archives of General Psychiatry, 51,* 355–364.

Witte, K., & Allen, M. (2000). A meta-analysis of fear appeals: Implications for effective public health campaigns. *Health Education and Behavior, 27,* 591–615.

Wixted, J.T. (1991). Conditions and consequences of maintenance rehearsal. *Journal of Experimental Psychology: Learning, Memory, and Cognition, 17,* 963–973.

Wixted, J.T. (2004). The psychology and neuroscience of forgetting. *Annual Review of Psychology, 55,* 235–269.

Wolberg, L.R. (1967). *The technique of psychotherapy* (2nd ed.). New York, NY: Grune & Stratton.

Wolken, J.J. (1995). *Light detectors, photoreceptors, and imaging systems in nature.* New York, NY: Oxford University Press.

Wolpe, J. (1958). *Psychotherapy by reciprocal inhibition.* Stanford, CA: Stanford University Press.

Wong, D.F., Wagner, H.N., Jr., Tune, L.E., Donnals, R.F., Pearlson, G.D., Links, J.M., ... Wilson, A.A. (1986). Positron emission tomography reveals elevated D2 dopamine receptors in drug-naive schizophrenics. *Science, 234,* 1558–1563.

Wong, M.M., & Csikszentmihalyi, M. (1991). Affiliation motivation and daily experience: Some issues on gender differences. *Journal of Personality and Social Psychology, 60,* 154–164.

Wong, P.C., Perrachione, T.K., & Parrish, T.B. (2007). Neural characteristics of successful and less successful speech and word learning in adults. *Human Brain Mapping, 28,* 995–1006.

Wood, E. Nosko, A., Desmarais, S., Ross, C., & Irvine, C. (2006). Online and traditional paper-and-pencil survey administration: Examining experimenter presence, sensitive material and long surveys. *The Canadian Journal of Human Sexuality, 15,* 147–155.

Wood, J.M., Nezworski, M.T., Lilienfeld, S.O., & Garb, H.N. (2003). *What's wrong with the Rorschach? Science confronts the controversial inkblot test.* San Francisco, CA: Jossey-Bass.

Wood, J.V., Heimpel, S.A., & Michela, J.L. (2003). Savoring versus dampening: Self-esteem differences in regulating positive affect. *Journal of Personality and Social Psychology, 85,* 566–580.

Wood, J.V., Heimpel, S.A., Newby-Clark, I.R., & Ross, M. (2005). Snatching defeat from the jaws of victory: Self-esteem differences in the experience and anticipation of success. *Journal of Personality and Social Psychology, 89,* 764–780.

Wood, S.L., & Swait, J. (2002). Psychological indicators of innovation adoption: Cross classification based need for cognition and need for change. *Journal of Consumer Psychology, 12,* 1–13.

Wood, W. (2000). Attitude change: Persuasion and social influence. *Annual Review of Psychology, 51,* 539–570.

Wood, W., & Eagly, A.H. (2000). A call to recognize the breadth of evolutionary perspectives: Sociocultural theories and evolutionary psychology. *Psychological Inquiry, 11,* 52–55.

Wood, W., Lundgren, S., Ouellete, J.A., Busceme, S., & Blackstone, T. (1994). Minority influence: A meta-analytic review of social influence processes. *Psychological Bulletin, 115,* 323–345.

Woodcock, R.W. (1997). The Woodcock-Johnson Tests of Cognitive Ability—Revised. In D.P. Flanagan, J.L. Genshaft, & P L. Harrison (Eds.), *Contemporary intellectual assessment: Theories, tests, and issues.* New York, NY: Guilford Press.

Woodley, M.A., & Meisenberg, G. (2012). Ability differentials between nations are unlikely to disappear. *American Psychologist, 67(6),* 501–502.

Woodruff-Pak, D.S. (1993). Eyeblink classical conditioning in H.M.: Delay and trace paradigms. *Behavioral Neuroscience, 107,* 911–925.

Woods, S.C., & Seeley, R.J. (2002). Hunger and energy homeostasis. In H. Pashler & R. Gallistel (Eds.), *Steven's handbook of experimental psychology: Vol. 3 Learning, motivation, and emotion* (3rd ed.). New York, NY: Wiley.

Woods, S.C., Seeley, R.J., Porte, D., & Schwartz, M.W. (1998). Signals that regulate food intake and energy homeostasis. *Science, 280,* 1378–1387.

Woody, E., & Sadler, P. (1998). On reintegrating dissociated theories: Comment on Kirsch and Lynn. *Psychological Bulletin, 123,* 192–197.

Woody, E.Z., & Szechtman, H. (2011). Adaptation to potential threat: The evolution, neurobiology, and psychopathology of the security motivation system. *Neuroscience & Biobehavioral Reviews, 35(4),* 1019–1033.

Word, C.O., Zanna, M.P., & Cooper, J. (1974). The nonverbal mediation of self-fulfilling prophecies in interracial interaction. *Journal of Experimental Social Psychology, 10,* 109–120.

Worell, J., & Remer, P.P. (2003). *Feminist perspectives in therapy: Empowering diverse women.* New York, NY: Wiley.

World Health Organization. (2004). *Global summary of the AIDS epidemic, December, 2004.* Geneva, Switzerland: Author.

World Health Organization. (2015). http://www.who .int/mediacentre/factsheets/fs110/en/. Accessed July 25, 2016.

Wouters-Adriaens, M., & Westerterp, K. (2006). Basal metabolic rate as a proxy for overnight energy expenditure: The effect of age. *British Journal of Nutrition, 95,* 1166–1170.

Wrangham, R.W. (1993). The evolution of sexuality in chimpanzees and bonobos. *Human Nature, 4,* 47–79.

Wrangham, R.W., & Peterson, D. (1996). *Demonic males.* Boston, MA: Houghton Mifflin.

Wright, M.J., & Myers, C.R. (1982). *History of Academic Psychology in Canada.* Toronto, ON: C.J. Ho.

Wu, M., Kujawa, A., Lu, L.H., Fitzgerald, D.A., Klumpp, H., Fitzgerald, K.D., Monk, C.S., Phan, K.L. (2016). Age-related changes in amygdala-frontal connectivity during emotional face processing from childhood into young adulthood. *Human Brain Mapping, 37,* 1684–1695.

Wu, X., & Foster, D.J. (2014). Hippocampal replay captures the unique topological structure of a novel environment. *The Journal of Neuroscience, 34(19),* 6459–6469.

Wyer, R.S., Bodenhausen, G.V., & Gorman, T.F. (1985). Cognitive mediators of reactions to rape. *Journal of Personality and Social Psychology, 48,* 324–338.

Wylie, R.C. (1989). *Measures of self-concept.* Lincoln, NE: University of Nebraska Press.

Wyman, A.J., & Vyse, S. (2008). Science versus the stars: A double-blind test of the validity of the NEO five-factor inventory and computer-generated astrological natal charts. *Journal of General Psychology, 135,* 287–300.

Wynn, K. (1992). Addition and subtraction by human infants. *Nature, 358,* 749–750.

Wynn, K. (1998). An evolved capacity for number. In D.D. Cummins & C. Allen (Eds.), *The evolution of mind* (pp. 107–126). New York, NY: Oxford University Press.

Xue, G., Lu, Z., Levin, I.P., Weller, J.A., Li, X., & Bechara, A. (2009). Functional dissociations of risk and reward processing in the medial prefrontal cortex. *Cerebral Cortex, 19(5),* 1019–1027.

Yalom, I.D. (1980). *Existential psychotherapy.* New York, NY: Basic Books.

Yamagata, S., Suzuki, A., Ando, J., Ono, Y., Kijima, N., Yoshimura, K., ... Jang, K.L. (2006). Is the genetic structure of human personality universal? A cross-cultural twin study from North America, Europe, and Asia. *Journal of Personality and Social Psychology, 90,* 987–998.

Yang, J., & Hofman, J. (2015). Action observation and imitation in autism spectrum disorders: an ALE meta-analysis of fMRI studies. *Brain Imaging and Behavior, 24,* 1–19.

Yardley, L., & Donovan-Hall, M. (2007). Predicting adherence to exercise-based therapy in rehabilitation. *Rehabilitation Psychology, 52(1),* 56–64.

Yarmey, D. (1993). Stereotypes and recognition memory for faces and voices of good guys and bad guys. *Applied Cognitive Psychology, 7(5),* 419–431.

Yarmey, D. (2001). Expert testimony: Does eyewitness memory research have probative value for the courts? *Canadian Psychology, 42(2),* 92–100.

Yarmey, D., & Yarmey, M. (1997). Eyewitness recall and duration estimates in field settings. *Journal of Applied Social Psychology, 27(4),* 330–344.

Yen, S., Shea, T., Pagano, M., Sanislow, C.A., Grilo, C.M., McGlashan, T., ... Morey, L.C. (2003). Axis I and Axis II disorders as predictors of prospective suicide attempts: Findings from the Collaborative Longitudinal Personality Disorders Study. *Journal of Abnormal Psychology, 112,* 375–381.

Yerkes, R.M., & Dodson, J.D. (1908). The relation of strength of stimulus to rapidity of habit-formation. *Journal of Comparative and Physiological Psychology, 18,* 459–482.

Yin, T.C.T., & Kuwada, S. (1984). Neuronal mechanisms of binaural interaction. In G.M. Edelman, W.M. Cowan, & W.E. Gall (Eds.), *Dynamic aspects of neocortical function.* New York, NY: Wiley.

Yiu, W-Y., Weber, B., Reuter, M., Markett, S., Chu, W-C., & Montag, C. (2013). The Big Five of Personality and structural imaging revisited: A VBM-DARTEL study. *Neuroreport, 24,* 375–380.

Young, A.W. (2003). Face recognition with and without awareness. In A. Cleeremans (Ed.), *The unity of consciousness: Binding, integration, and dissociation.* New York: Oxford University Press.

Young, L.R., & Joffe, R.T. (1997). *Bipolar disorder: Biological models and their clinical application.* New York, NY: Marcel Dekker.

Youngstedt, S.D., O'Connor, P.J., & Dishman, R.K. (1997). The effects of acute exercise on sleep: A quantitative synthesis. *Sleep, 20,* 203–214.

Yuan, Y., Zhang, Z., Bai, F., You, J., Yu, H., Shi, Y., & Liu, W. (2009). Genetic variation in apolipoprotein E alters regional gray matter volumes in remitted late-onset depression. *Journal of Affective Disorders, 121,* 273–277.

Yuille, J.C., & Tollestrup, P. (1990). Some effects of alcohol on eyewitness memory. *Journal of Applied Psychology, 75(3),* 268–273.

Yuille, J.C., Tollestrup, P., Marxsen, D., Porter, S., & Herve, H. (1998). An exploration on the effects of marijuana on eyewitness memory. *International Journal of Law and Psychiatry, 21(1),* 117–128.

Zadra, A., Pilon, M., & Montplaisir, J. (2008). Polysomnographic diagnosis of sleepwalking: Effects of sleep deprivation. *Annals of Neurology, 63,* 513–519.

Zahava, S., & Ginzburg, K. (1998). War trauma and the aged: An Israeli perspective. In J. Lomranz (Ed.), *Handbook of aging and mental health: An integrative approach. The Plenum series in adult developing and aging.* New York, NY: Plenum Press.

Zahava, S., Shklar, R., Singer, Y., & Mikulincer, M. (2006). Reactions to combat stress in Israeli war veterans twenty years after the 1982 Lebanon war. *Journal of Mental and Nervous Disease, 194,* 935–939.

Zahn-Waxler, C., Radke-Yarrow, M., & King, R.A. (1979). Child rearing and children's prosocial initiations towards victims of distress. *Child Development, 50,* 319–330.

Zahn-Waxler, C., Radke-Yarrow, M., Wagner, E., & Chapman, M. (1992). Development of concern for others. *Developmental Psychology, 28,* 126–136.

Zajonc, R.B. (1965). Social facilitation. *Science, 149,* 269–274.

Zajonc, R.B., Murphy, S.T., & Inglehart, M. (1989). Feeling and facial efference: Implications of a vascular theory of emotion. *Psychological Review, 96,* 395–416.

Zakzanis, K.K. (1998). Neuropsychological correlates of positive vs. negative schizophrenic symptomatology. *Schizophrenia Research, 29,* 227–233.

Zambelis, T., Paparrigopoulos, T., & Soldatos, C.R. (2002). REM sleep behaviour disorder associated with a neurinoma of the left pontocerebellar angle. *Journal of Neurology, Neurosurgery, & Psychiatry, 72,* 821–822.

Zanker, J. (2010). *Sensation, perception, and action: A functional perspective.* New York, NY: Macmillan.

Zanna, M.P., & Cooper, J. (1974). Dissonance and the pill: An attribution approach to studying the arousal properties of dissonance. *Journal of Personality and Social Psychology, 29,* 703–709.

Zanna, M.P., Olson, J.M., & Fazio, R.H. (1980). Attitude-behavior consistency: An individual difference perspective. *Journal of Personality and Social Psychology, 38,* 432–440.

Zaragoza, M.S., & Mitchell, K.J. (1996). Repeated exposure to suggestion and the creation of false memories. *Psychological Science, 7,* 294–300.

Zautra, A.J. (2003). *Emotions, stress, and health.* New York, NY: Oxford University Press.

Zayas, V., & Shoda, Y. (2007). Predicting preferences for dating partners from past experiences of psychological abuse: Identifying the psychological ingredients of situations. *Personality and Social Psychology Bulletin, 33,* 123–138.

Zebrowitz, L.A., Voinescu, L., & Collins, M.A. (1996). "Wide-eyed" and "crooked-faced": Determinants of perceived and real honesty across the life span. *Personality and Social Psychology Bulletin, 22,* 1258–1269.

Zechner, U., Wilda, M., Kehrer-Sawatzki, H., Vogel, W., Fundele, R., & Hameister, H. (2001). A high density of X-linked genes for general cognitive ability: A runaway process shaping human evolution? *Trends in Genetics, 17,* 697–701.

Zeki, S. (2007). The neurobiology of love. *FEBS letters, 581,* 2575–2579.

Zelazo, P.D., Mueller, U., Frye, D., & Marcovitch, S. (2003). The development of executive function in early childhood. *Monographs of the Society for Research in Child Development, 68*(274), 138–151.

Zettle, R.D. (2012). Acceptance and commitment therapy (ACT) vs. systematic desensitization in treatment of mathematics anxiety. *The Psychological Record, 53*(2), 197–215.

Zhang, A.Y., & Snowden, L.R. (1999). Ethnic characteristics of mental disorders in five U.S. communities. *Cultural Diversity and Ethnic Minority Psychology, 5,* 134–146.

Zhang, Q., & Haydon, P.G. (2005). Role for gliotransmission in the nervous system. *Journal of Neural Transmission, 112,* 121–125.

Zhang, T-Y., & Meaney, M.J. (2010). Epigenetics and the Environmental Regulation of the Genome and Its Function. *Annual Review of Psychology, 61,* 439–466.

Zhang, Y., Proenca, R., Maffei, M., & Barone, M., Leopold, L., & Friedman, J.M. (1994). Positional cloning of the mouse obese gene and its human homologue. *Nature, 372,* 425–432.

Zhao, W., Yao, S., Li, Q., Geng, Y., Ma, X., Luo, L., ... Kendrick, K.M. (2016). Oxytocin blurs the self-other distinction during trait judgments and reduces medial prefrontal cortex responses. *Human Brain Mapping,* doi: http://dx.doi.org/10.1002/hbm.23190.

Zhuikov, A.Y., Couvillon, P.A., & Bitterman, M.E. (1994). Quantitative two-process analysis of avoidance conditioning in goldfish. *Journal of Experimental Psychology: Animal Behavior Processes, 20,* 32–43.

Zillmann, D. (1979). *Hostility and aggression.* New York, NY: Halsted Press.

Zillmann, D. (1984). *Connections between sex and aggression.* Hillsdale, NJ: Erlbaum.

Zillmann, D. (1994). Erotica and family values. In D. Zillmann, J. Bryant, & A.C. Huston (Eds.), *Media, children, and the family: Social scientific, psychodynamic, and clinical perspectives* (pp. 199–214). Hillsdale, NJ: Erlbaum.

Zimbardo, P.G., Haney, C., Banks, W.C., & Jaffe, D. (1973, April 8). The mind is a formidable jailer: A Pirandellian prison. *New York Times Magazine,* 38–60.

Zimmerman, F.J., Christakis, D.A., & Meltzoff, A.N. (2007). Associations between media viewing and language development in children under age 2 years. *The Journal of Pediatrics, 151,* 364–368.

Zinbarg, R.E., Barlow, D.H., Brown, T.A., & Hertz, R.M. (1992). Cognitive-behavioral approaches to the nature and treatment of anxiety disorders. *Annual Review of Psychology, 43,* 235–268.

Zoellner, L.A., Feeny, N.C., & Bittinger, J.N. (2009). What you believe is what you want: Modeling PTSD-related treatment preferences for sertraline or prolonged exposure. *Journal of Behaviour Therapy and Experimental Psychiatry, 40,* 455–467.

Zubieta, J-K., Smith, Y.R., Bueller, J.A., Xu, Y., Kilbourn, M.R., Jewett, D.M., ... Stohler, C.S. (2001). Regional *mu* opioid receptor regulation of sensory and affective dimensions of pain. *Science, 293,* 311–315.

Zuckerman, M. (2005). *Psychobiology of personality* (2nd ed.). New York, NY: Cambridge University Press.

Zuckerman, M., Hall, J.A., DeFrank, R.S., & Rosenthal, R. (1976). Encoding and decoding of spontaneous and posed facial expressions. *Journal of Personality and Social Psychology, 34,* 966–977.

Zuk, J., Benjamin, C., Kenyon, A., & Gaab, N. (2014). Behavioral and neural correlates of executive functioning in musicians and non-musicians. *PLoS ONE, 10*(9), e0137930. doi: 10.1371/journal.pone.0137930.

A

AA: Project MATCH Research Group, 623
Aaron, S., 608, 609
Abbate, C.S.. 537
Abbott, L.F., 290
Abe, N., 308
Abel, T., 311
Abi-Dargham, A., 667
Abraham, K., 655
Abrams, D.A., 103
Abramson, L.Y., 656
Abramowitz, A.J., 44
Abramowitz, J.S., 695
Abresch, J., 268
Achter, J., 389
Adachi, P., 546
Adair, R.K., 179
Adams, A, 2
Adams, D.B., 540
Adams, M.J., 285, 298, 299
Adamuti-Trache, M., 328
Addis, M.E., 714
Adelmann, P.K., 440
Aderman, D., 496
Adler, A., 398, 554, 724
Adler, A.D., 27
Adolphs, R., 90, 532
Afifi, T.D., 473, 474
Aggleton, J.P., 540
Ahadi, S., 572, 573
Ahammed, S., 690
Ahlner, J., 716
Ahn, H.J., 466
Ai, A.L., 598
Aiello, R., 148
Ainslie, G., 424
Ainsworth, M.D.S., 468, 469, 470, 472
Airey, D., 669, 674
Aitken Schermer, J., 122
Ajzen, I., 505
Akerstedt, T., 200
Akimova, S., 646
Akirav, E.M., 73
Al-Maliki, N., 172
Alam, N., 207
Albee, G.W., 723, 724
Alcock, J., 62, 163, 331
Aldwin, C.M., 593, 609, 611

Alexander, M.W., 49
Alfieri, T., 475
Alitto, H.J., 89
Allan, L.G., 269
Allen, M., 326, 406, 508
Allison, D.B., 409
Allmer, H., 487
Alloy, L.B., 654, 656
Allport, G.W., 504, 533, 535, 549, 567
Alterovitz, S.S.R., 527
Altman, I., 526
Altman, J., 88
Altwasser, C., 535
Alzheimer, A., 301
Alzheimer Society, 301, 680
Amato, D., 1–2
Amato, P.R., 473, 474
Ambady, N., 503
American Anti-Vivisection Society, 65
American Psychiatric Association, 97, 246, 391, 392, 599, 633, 636, 637, 653, 661, 665, 667, 672, 677, 680, 695, 719
American Psychology Society, 31
American Psychological Association, 12, 31, 230, 502, 517, 546, 566, 572, 575, 576, 579, 605, 627, 687, 703, 708, 710, 724
Ames, A., 182
Ames, E., 470
Anand, B.K., 403
Anderson, 345
Anderson, C.A., 502, 542, 543, 545, 546
Anderson, E.M., 710
Anderson, J.L., 261
Anderson, M.C., 300
Anderson, M.C.M., 33, 351, 352
Anderson, N.D., 302
Andreason, N.C., 85, 669
Andreassi, J.L., 607
Andrés, P., 309
Anisman, H., 600

Ankney, C.D., 379
Anmar, D., 196
Anstey, K.J., 487
Antfolk, C., 169
Anthony, J.C., 227
Antony, M.M., 246
Antrobus, J., 211, 214, 215, 216
APA Monitor, 307
APA Task Force on Psychological Intervention Guidelines, 708
Aparicio, J., 210
Aquino, K., 436
Arbeau, K., 450
Arbib, M.A., 333
Arbuckle, T., 485
Archer, J., 129
Areán, 654
Arends, E., 658
Arendt, J., 145
Armitage, C.J., 505
Arnett, J.J., 479, 487, 489, 490, 491, 495
Arnett, P.A., 674
Aron, A., 529
Aron, A.P., 441, 528
Aronson, E., 508, 535
Aronson, J., 535
Arshavsky, V.Y., 151
Arterberry, M.A., 453
Arundale, R.B., 321
Asbury, K., 122
Asch, S.E., 503, 512, 513
Aschemann-Witzel, J., 505
Aserinsky, E., 202, 203
Asimov, I., 644
Askew, C., 271
Assanand, S.P., 400
Associated Press, 664
Astington, J.W., 464
Atchison, M., 663
Athens, E.S., 259
Atkins, D.C., 687, 714
Atkinson, J.W., 396, 420, 422
Atkinson, R.C., 278, 280
Atmaca, M., 661
Audero, E., 541
Auerbach, S.M., 613
Averill, J.A., 426

Avila-White, D., 212
Axel, R., 163
Ayearst, L.E., 48
Ayllon, T., 700
Azeredo, C.M., 47
Azrin, N.H., 700

B

Baars, B.J., 193, 197
Babichev, A., 266, 267
Bainbridge, K., 194
Bach-y-Rita, P., 167
Back, M.D., 524
Backhaus, W.G., 154
Baddeley, A.D., 280, 281, 282, 284, 294, 302
Baer, J.L., 417
Baer, R.A., 612
Baert, A., 87
Baeyens, F., 245
Bagge, C., 675
Bagley, C., 659
Bagot, R.C., 601
Bahrick, H.P., 282, 297, 298, 304, 485
Bailey, J.M., 419
Baillargeon, R., 461
Baker, C., 632
Baker, E., 467
Baker, E.H., 28
Baker, L.H., 624
Baker, T.B., 707
Baldwin, E., 65
Baldwin, J., 11
Baldwin, M.W., 567, 567
Baldwin, S.A., 687
Ball, K., 150
Ballard, C., 162
Ballenger, J.C., 643
Baltes, P., 347
Baltes, P.B., 347, 364
Bamford, H., 466
Banaji, M.R., 49, 145
Bandura, A., 15, 33, 271, 272, 274, 474, 542, 573, 574, 575, 576, 577, 578, 579, 581, 605, 674, 702
Bannerman, R.L., 172
Bannister, R., 580
Bar-Haim, Y., 647
Barac, R., 326

Baran, J., 159, 161
Barber, J.P., 13
Bard, L.L., 438, 441
Barefoot, J.C., 607
Barendse, M.E.A., 405
Bargh, J.A., 13, 146, 195, 196, 558
Barkley, R.A., 677
Barkow, J.H., 136
Barlow, D.H., 637, 641, 645, 646, 647, 648, 654, 660
Barnes, G.E., 655
Barnes, T.R., 717
Barnett, J.E., 659
Barnett, W.S., 385
Barnfield, A.M.C., 474
Baron, R.S., 507, 513, 520, 602
Barondes, S.H., 654
Barrera, D., 64
Barrett, G.V., 385
Barrett, P.T., 378
Barrett, R., 195
Barrow, C.J., 124
Barry, H., 478
Barry, J.R., 288
Barsalou, L.W., 278
Barsky, A.J., 662
Bartholow, B.D., 532
Bartholomew, D.J., 361, 371
Bartlett, F., 304, 305
Bartlett, F.C., 209, 287
Bartlett, J.E., 49
Barton, J.J., 145
Bartoshuk, L., 162, 163, 164
Bassett, A.M., 632
Bassok, M., 32
Batson, C.D., 537
Battista, S.R., 254
Baum, A., 618, 620, 624
Baumeister, R.F., 127, 523, 561, 564, 565
Baumrind, D., 472, 515
Baus, O., 698
Bauserman, R., 415, 416
Bavelier, D., 150
Baxter, L.R., 645
Bayer, S.A., 88
Bazzett, T.J., 117
BC Partners for Mental Health, 206

Beahrs, J.O., 664
Beaman, A.L., 540
Beatty, M.J., 540
Beauchamp, G.K., 162, 163, 164
Bechara, A., 98
Beck, A.T., 27, 655, 658, 692, 693, 694, 702, 709
Beck, J., 27
Becker, A.E., 648, 649, 650
Becker, C.B., 462
Becker, J., 78
Becker, R., 146
Bedny, M., 322
Bedont, J.L., 198, 199
Beecher, M.D., 237
Beeney, J.E., 557
Behrens, M., 163
Beidel, D.C., 642, 644
Beilcock, S.L., 195
Belbin, O., 301
Belchior, P., 150
Bell, A.P., 418
Bell, E., 122, 129
Bell, J.H., 483
Bell, R., 289
Belloc, N.B., 618
Bellugi, U., 430
Bem, D.J., 8, 62, 63, 419, 507
Bem, S.L., 566
Ben-Slushan, D., 597
Ben-Zur, H., 609
Bender, D.S., 638
Benes, F.M., 667, 669
Bengtson, V.L., 492, 493
Benjamin, A.S., 485
Benjamin, L.S., 687
Benjamin, L.T., 34
Bennett, D.S., 451
Bennett, H.L., 297
Bennett, J.E., 511
Bennett, P.H., 409
Benoit, D., 493
Bento, S., 470
Berenbaum, H., 669
Berg, K.M., 255
Berg, C.A., 364
Berger, C.C., 350
Berger, M., 27
Berger, R.J., 208
Berger, S.H., 473
Berkowitz, L., 416, 417, 541, 543, 544
Berlitz, M.D., 325
Bernstein, B., 706
Bernstein, I.L., 262
Bernstein, S.E., 319
Berra, Y., 195
Berridge, K.C., 405
Berry, J.W., 461
Berscheid, E., 529

Berthoud, H.R., 403, 404
Betancourt, H., 542
Beucke, J.C., 645
Beutler, L.E., 710, 712
Beyer, S., 566
Bhatt, R.S., 454
Bialystok, E., 325, 326, 328
Bickman, L., 597
Biebuyck, J.F., 209
Biederman, J., 677
Biemiller, A., 324
Biener, L., 512
Bierhoff, H.W., 272
Bigras, M., 474
Biller, J., 99
Billings, A.G., 614
Binder, J.L., 711, 712
Binet, A., 358–359, 360, 457
Bini, L., 718
Birch, 422
Birdsong, D., 327, 328
Bireta, T.J., 293
Birney, D.P., 365
Birtanen, S., 533
Birtchnell, J., 49
Biswas-Diener, R., 628, 630
Bjork, R.A., 350
Björkqvist, K., 541, 542
Black, D.N., 661
Black, D.W., 669, 672, 673
Blackshaw, S., 198, 199
Blackstone, J., 712
Blackwood, D., 644
Blader, S.L., 539
Blair, I., 542
Blair, J., 674
Blair, S.N., 619
Blakemore, C., 185, 186
Blakeslee, B., 181
Blanchard, C.M., 505
Blanton, H., 344
Blascovich, J., 509, 534
Blass, E.M., 453
Blass, T., 515, 516
Blessing, W.W., 88
Bleuler, E., 665
Block, J.J., 545
Block, N., 385, 386
Blodgett, H.C., 270
Bloom, F.E., 70
Bloomfield, K., 228
Blosser, J.L., 104
Blum, K., 77, 78, 91
Bobo, L., 534
Bochner, S., 508
Boden, J.M., 564
Boersma, M., 397
Boes, A.D., 430
Bogale, B.A., 268

Bogart, J.C., 621
Bolin, B., 716
Bolles, R.C., 237, 267, 400
Bolling, A., 61
Bonacci, A.M., 298, 543
Bonanno, G.A., 496, 605
Bonaparte, N., 205
Bonci, D.M.O., 151
Bond, C., 510
Bond, M.H., 19
Bond, R., 513
Boneva, B., 423
Bonnel, A.M., 171
Boniwell, I., 629
Bonvillian, J.D., 331
Booth, R.J., 59
Booth-Kewley, S., 607
Bora, C., 693
Boren, E., 276
Borgwardt, S., 27
Boring, E.G., 22
Born, S., 163
Borod, J.C., 9, 90
Borsboom, D., 63
Bosboom, D., 63
Bosson, J.K., 560
Boswell, A.E., 255
Botman, H.I., 212
Botvinick, M.M., 290
Bouchard, C., 115, 409, 540
Bouchard, S., 698
Bouchard, T.J., 117, 118, 119, 120, 380, 674
Boudreau, L., 512
Bould, H., 467
Bourgeois, M.J., 40
Bovbjerg, D.H., 262
Bowen, S., 702, 703
Bower, G.H., 277, 285, 289, 296
Bowers, K., 232
Bowlby, J., 27, 468, 469, 555, 655
Bowring, J., 325
Boyanowsky, E.O., 544
Boyce, J.A., 410
Boyce, W., 103
Bozarth, J.D., 688
Braadbaart, L., 97
Bradizza, C.M., 219
Braid, J., 230, 232
Brand, B.L., 664
Brand, C.R., 371
Brand, M., 301, 663
Bransford, J.D., 287
Brantley, P., 601
Brasfield, C., 599
Brauer, M., 533
Bray, J.H., 473
Bredy, T., 601
Breedlove, S.M., 413
Brehm, J.W., 397

Breland, K., 263
Breland, M., 263
Bremner, J.D., 85, 646
Brennan, S., 416
Breslau, N.S., 599
Bresnahan, M.J., 566
Brewer, K.R., 272
Brewin, C.R., 308
Briand, L., 163
Bridgeman, B., 128
Bright, C.N., 398
Briere, J., 329
Briggs, J.L., 434
Bringmann, W.G., 268
Brislin, R., 28
Brisson, J., 337
Broadbent, D.E., 17
Brobeck, J.R., 403
Broberg, D.J., 262
Broca, P., 83, 95
Brochu, P.M., 531
Bromnick, R.D., 483
Brosch, T., 500
Broszeit, B., 226
Brouwer, W.H., 89
Brown, A.D., 161
Brown, A.S., 299, 300
Brown, C.R., 454
Brown, D., 226
Brown, G.D.A., 299
Brown, G.W., 27, 655
Brown, I., 391
Brown, J.D., 252, 254, 563, 565, 566
Brown, L.S., 707
Brown, M., 563
Brown, R., 324, 325
Brown, S.L., 628
Brown, T.A., 623, 637, 646, 647, 648, 654, 660
Brown, T.S., 401
Brownell, H., 620
Brownell, K.D., 409
Browning, E.B., 528
Bruce, M.N., 43
Bruce, T.J., 647, 699
Bruch, H., 650
Bruck, M., 295, 308
Bruner, J., 324
Brunner, E., 487
Bruss, P.J., 292
Bryan, J., III., 297, 325
Buck, L., 163
Buckmaster, C.L., 601
Budd, J., 475
Bulayeva, K., 391
Bulkeley, K., 212
Bullier, J., 150, 156
Bülthoff, H.H., 172
Bumgarner, 27
Bundgaard, M., 71
Bunn, T., 237

Burbank, P.M., 616
Burgaleta, M., 387
Burger, J.M., 501, 517, 575
Burgess, C.A., 232, 597
Burke, K.C., 652
Burkholder, E., 254
Burkholder, G.J., 616
Burns, M.O., 151, 571, 572
Burroughs, S.M., 523
Burton, E., 657
Burton-Chellew, M., 23
Busey, T.A., 294
Bush, G., 172
Bushman, B.J., 298, 542, 543, 545
Buss, D.M., 20, 23, 24, 125, 128, 132, 133, 134, 135, 137, 396, 433, 524, 527, 528, 560, 571
Buster, J.E., 414
Butcher, J.N., 585, 589
Butera, F., 4, 513
Butler, A.C., 694
Butler, H.A., 6
Butterfield, E., 390
Buunk, B.P., 507
Buysse, D.J., 27
Buzsaki, G., 311
Byer, C.O., 411, 413, 417
Byers-Heinlein, K., 455
Byne, W., 419, 420
Byrd, M.R., 260
Byrne, D., 414, 417, 523, 524

C
Cabeza, R., 73
Cacioppo, J.T., 507, 508, 532
Cadet, J.L., 110, 623
Cahill, K., 683
Cahn, B.R., 230
Cai, D., 102, 239
Cain, C.K., 429
Cain, D.J., 690, 691
Cairns, H., 92
Caldji, C., 601
Caldwell, A.B., 586
Caligor, E., 675
Calkins, S.D., 541
Calkins, M.W., 12
Callahan, H.L., 390
Calment, J., 495
Calvete, E., 636
Calvo, E., 557
Cambridge University, 6
Cameron, C.F., 90
Cameron, J.J., 563
Camilleri, C., 488

Camilli, G., 385
Campbell, A., 475, 511
Campbell, S.S., 204
Campbell, T.S., 612
Campos, J.J., 456
Canadian Association
    of Genetic
    Counsellors, 114
Canadian Cancer
    Society, 622
Canadian Centre
    on Substance
    Abuse, 715
Canadian Community
    Epidemiology
    Network on Drug
    Use, 226
Canadian Council on
    Animal Care, 65
Canadian Department
    of Justice, 640
Canadian Hearing
    Society, 162
Canadian Institutes
    for Health
    Information, 616
Canadian Institutes
    of Health
    Research, 63
Canadian Mental Health
    Association, 592,
    632, 651, 658,
    677, 726
Canadian Psychological
    Association, 31,
    64, 726
Canadian Sleep
    Society, 206
Canadian Tobacco
    Use Monitoring
    Survey, 76
Canfield, 164
Canivez, G.L., 373
Cannon, W.B., 396, 401,
    438, 439, 441
Canton, J., 268
Caporael, L.R., 24
Carbon, C.C., 175
Cardasis, W., 675
Cardeña, E., 62
Carey, G., 645
Carlin, A.S., 697
Carlsmith, J.M., 36,
    37, 506
Carlson, C., 677
Carlson, E.A., 406
Carlson, J.G., 425
Carlson, L.E., 612
Carmody, J., 612
Carnagey, N.L., 545
Carney, L.H., 160, 161
Carney, R.N., 287
Carnicero, J.A.C., 467
Caron, M.L., 44

Carpendale, J.I.M., 464
Carpenter, K., 648
Carpenter, P.A., 378
Carpenter, W.T., Jr., 717
Carpenter, R., 152
Carr, D., 529
Carr, F., 263
Carr, M.F., 311
Carr, T.H., 195, 319
Carrere, S., 530
Carroll, C.R., 623
Carroll, J.B., 364, 365
Carroll, J.S., 416
Carruthers, M., 597
Carson, R.C., 643, 669
Carter, H., 447
Carter, S.J., 295
Cartwright, R.D., 212
Carvacho, H., 529
Carver, C.S., 554, 572,
    582, 606, 609,
    614
Caryl, P.G., 378
Case, L., 46
Case, R., 461
Caspi, A., 121, 524, 528,
    550, 571
Cassaday, H.J., 295
Castrén, E., 720
Castro, D.C., 405
Castro-Alamancos,
    M.A., 148
Catalano, R., 534
Cataldo, A.M., 146
Catchpole, C.K., 331
Cattell, R.B., 345, 363,
    364, 568
Cattell, R.C., 485
Caughlin, J.P., 488
CBC, 225, 622
CCSA, 225
Ceausescu, N., 470
Ceci, S.J., 381, 386
Celera Genomics, 110
Centerbar, D., 428, 440
Centers for Disease
    Control (CDC),
    412, 598, 616, 621,
    677
Centre for Addiction
    and Mental Health,
    226, 682, 683, 722
Cerletti, U., 718
Cervone, D., 579
Cha, M., 27
Chabris, C.F., 171
Chaffin, R., 387
Chaiken, S., 508
Chakeres, D.W., 86
Chalmers, D., 192
Chambless, D.L., 688
Champagne, F., 111, 601
Chan, Z.C.Y., 649
Chance, G., 453

Chandler, M.J., 301
Chandrasekaran, B.,
    390
Chang, E.C., 606
Chang, J.W., 59
Chapell, M.S., 33
Chaplin, T.M., 615
Chapman, A.L., 703
Chapman, S.B., 102
Chappell, M., 289
Charbonnier, L., 405
Charcot, J., 551
Charney, D.S., 724
Chartrand, T.L., 195,
    196, 558
Chase, W.G., 288, 346
Chasson, G.S., 664
Chaudhuri, A.R., 144
Checknita, D., 674
Chekroud, A.M., 532
Chen, C., 488, 489
Chen, H. 402, 423
Chen, S., 343
Chen, S.C., 509
Chen, S.X., 19
Cheng, H., 384
Cheng, S., 266
Chenoweth, D., 619
Cherian, I., 690
Chess, S., 467
Chiang, H.-L., 677
Chiappelli, F., 596
Chiauzzi, E., 611
Chiles, J.A., 659
Chiriboga, D.A., 492
Chirkov, V.I., 615 ·
Chisholm, K., 470
Chiu, I.M., 144
Cho, C.H., 717
Choca, J.P., 573
Choi, I., 19, 502
Choleris, E., 271
Chomsky, N., 17, 315,
    323, 331
Chowdhard, 705
Christianson, S.A., 294
Christoff, K., 309
Christy, C.A., 539
Chung, V.H.W., 455
Church, S.L., 550
Church, M.A., 420
Churchill, W., 205, 634
Chwalisz, K., 439
Chwilla, D.J., 289
Cialdini, R.B., 517,
    518, 537
Cianelli, S.N., 331
Ciarello, C., 101
Cicchetti, D., 101
Cicirata, F., 88
Cicirelli, V.G., 496
Cigales, M., 164
Cinnirella, M., 513
Cirelli, S.N., 207

Cirese, S., 412
Clamp, G., 169
Clark, C.L., 555
Clark, D.A., 644, 651,
    655, 692
Clark, D.M., 647
Clark, E.V., 321
Clark, K.B., 18
Clark, M.P., 18
Clark, M.S., 540
Clark, N., 333
Clark, R.D., III, 513
Clark, S.S., 539
Clark, W.R., 139
Clark v. Arizona, 640
Clarke, A.D.B., 325
Clarke, A.M., 325
Clarke, J.C., 647
Clarke, K., 466
Clarkin, J.F., 671, 675
Clarkson-Smith, L., 486
Clement, K., 403
Clements, A.M., 101
Clifasefi, S.L., 171
Clifton, R., 453
Clinton, B., 158
Cloninger, C.R., 117,
    228, 674
Clore, G.L., 428, 440
Clowey, 323
Coalson, D.L., 373
Coan, J.A., 611
Coates, D., 450
Coatsworth, J.D.,
    383, 604
Coccaro, E.F., 540
Cody, J., 535
Coffey, C.E., 718, 719
Cohen, A.L., 146
Cohen, D.A., 290
Cohen, K.M., 419
Cohen, N.J., 310
Cohen, S., 593, 598, 602,
    603, 605, 628
Cohn, E.G., 541
Colby, A., 477
Cole, P.M., 615
Cole, S.L., 405
Coleman, D.L., 402
Collaer, M.L., 419
Collier, G., 401
Collier, V.P., 326
Collings, P., 347
Collins, A.M., 289
Collins, D.W., 386
Colom, R., 364, 379
Colonius, H., 147
Columbia Accident
    Investigation
    Board, 522
Committee on Animal
    Research and
    Ethics (CARE), 65
Commons, M.L., 253

Comuzzie, A.G., 409
Conrad, R., 280
Consedine, N.S., 59
Constantine, M.G., 207
Constantino, M., 557
Consumer Reports, 711
Contrada, R.J., 607
Cook, E.W., 404
Cooke, P., 661
Coomans, C.P., 198, 199
Coon, H.M., 19
Cooney, R., 485
Coons, P.M., 664
Cooper, C.R., 705
Cooper, G., 185, 186
Cooper, J., 506, 507, 508
Coopersmith, S., 564
Coplan, R.J., 450
Copolov, D.L., 669
Cordova, J.V., 492
Coren, A., 688
Coren, S., 201, 205
Corina, D.P., 101
Cormack, A., 85
Corrigan, P.W., 639
Cosmides, L., 23, 124,
    125, 136
Costa, P.T., 120, 494,
    569, 570, 585, 679
Costantino, G., 705
Costello, E.J., 652
Cotter, P.R., 523
Couchman, J.J., 352
Courchesne, E., 678
Courneya, K.S., 505, 619
Cousins, S.D., 566
Cowan, C.P., 492
Cowan, N., 280
Cowan, P.A., 492
Cox, J.E., 404
Coyne, J.C., 598, 657
Craig, W.M., 47
Craik, F.I.M., 284, 285,
    302, 485
Cramer, P., 554
Crandall, C.S., 510, 529,
    649
Crano, W.D., 504
Craske, M., 646, 647,
    694, 696
Crawford, C.B., 261
Crawford, M., 387
Crawley, R.A., 302
Creese, I., 669
Crippen, K.J., 350
Crits-Christoph, P., 708,
    712
Crocker, J., 564
Crook, J.M., 669
Cross, S.E., 565
Crovitz, H.F., 212
Crowley, K., 474, 539
Crowley, M., 545
Croyle, R.T., 507

Cruse, D., 194
Cserr, H.F., 71
Csikszentmihalyi, M., 523, 584, 629, 630
Cue, D.K., 221
Culbertson, F.M., 28, 657
Culham, J., 45, 145
Cullen, M., 612
Cummings, L., 321
Cunillera, T., 320
Cunitz, A.R., 283
Cunningham, M.R., 135
Cunningham, W.A., 532
Cunnington, R., 97
Curci, A., 293
Curran, T., 304
Curry, F., 421, 422
Curry, O., 127, 136
Curtis, C.E., 309
Curtis, G.C., 642
Curtiss, S., 325
Cyr, C., 557
Cyranoski, D., 194
Cytowic, R.E., 142, 143

D
da Vinci, L., 141, 176, 205
Dabaghian, Y., 267
Dahl, R.E., 479
Dahmer, J., 586
Daily Mail, 466
Dalai Lama, 498
Dalenberg, C.F., 663
Dalgarno, P., 228
Dalgleish, T., 695
Dalton, A.L., 307
Dalton, P., 163
Daly, M., 23, 137
Damasio, A.R., 96, 428, 430
Damasio, H., 95, 96
Damato, E.G., 450
Dan, Y., 172
Dandeneau, S.D., 567
Daneman, M., 145, 307
Dangerfield, R., 414
Daniels, K., 364
D'Arcy, C., 27
Darley, J.M., 37, 38, 39, 40, 41, 43, 58, 61, 64, 504, 533, 538, 439
Daros, A.R., 676
Darragh, M., 59
Darwin, C., 11, 12, 22, 23, 107, 124, 128, 139, 269, 358, 389, 432
Dasen, P., 461
Datta Gupta, A., 525
Dauvilliers, Y., 209, 210

Davey, G.C.L., 263
David, A.S., 85
David, D., 693
Davidoff, J., 328
Davidowicz, L.S., 516
Davidson, J.E., 389
Davidson, L., 443
Davidson, M.C., 463
Davidson, R.J., 163, 430, 616
Davidson, W.B., 523
Davis, C.G., 607
Davis, C.M., 415
Davis, D., 300, 308
Davis, K., 367
Davis, K.D., 165
Davis, M., 6, 7, 90
Davis, M.H., 173
Davis, R., 637, 673
Davis, T., 675
Davis, T.E., 450
Davison, A.C., 378, 379
Dawes, R.M., 587
Dawkins, R., 125
Dawson, 679
Dawson, W.A., 210
Dawson-McClure, S.R., 473
Day, R., 669
De Benji, R., 296
De Bono, E., 356
De Castro, J., 205, 408
De Cremer, D., 536
de Fonseca, F.R., 226
de Geus, E.J.C., 381, 618
De Jesus, S., 505
De Jong, C., 49
De Martino, B., 90
de Moraes, C.L., 47
De Silva, P., 644
de Souza, A., 482
de St. Aubin, 491
De Young, C.G., 573
De Zeeuw, C.I., 88
Dealberto, M-J., 665
Deary, I.J., 373, 374, 381
DeCasper, A.J., 453
DeCharms, R., 423
Deci, E.L., 399, 564
DeClaire, J., 530
Deco, G., 151
Dedden, L.A., 137
Deffenbacher, K.A., 307
DeFries, J.C., 118
Degenhardt, L., 227
Dehaene, S., 328
DeHart, T., 295
Dekovic, M., 537
Delahunt, P.B., 487
DeLamater, J., 411, 414, 450
Dell, P.F., 662
DeLongis, A., 720
Demarest, 406

Dement, W.C., 201, 205, 211
Démonet, J.F., 322, 329
Denzin, N.K., 466
Denner, J., 705
Denton, K., 503
Department of Health and Human Services, 228
Depinet, R.L., 385
Depue, R.A., 676
Der, G., 374
Deregowski, 187, 188
DeRubeis, R.J., 708
Descartes, R., 11
Desmarais, S., 49
Desmond, P.A., 596
D'Espositio, M., 309
D'Espositio, M.D., 554
Despres, J.P., 115
Desrocher, M., 645
Dessens, A.B., 419
Deuker, L., 311
Deutsch, M., 512
Deutschenbaur, L., 27
DeValois, K.K., 154
DeValois, R.L., 154
Devane, W.A., 226
Devlin, M.J., 650
DeVries, H., 617
DeVries, R., 457
Dew, I.T.Z., 292
Dewsbury, D.A., 131, 240
Dexter-Mazza, E.T., 675
DeYoung, C.G., 571
Dhaliwal, J., 226
Diacon, S., 338
Diamond, L.M., 528
Diaz, C., 634
Diaz, J., 217, 219
Dick, D.M., 9
Dickens, C., 192
Dickinson, A., 238
Dickinson, C.A., 305
DiClemente, C., 616
DiClemente, C.C., 625
Diener, E., 15, 50, 51, 439, 494, 560, 572, 573, 628
Dienes, Z., 232, 233, 234
DiFonzo, N., 40
DiGennaro, F.D., 701
Dijkstra, P., 507
Dillard, J.P., 518
DiLorenzo, P.M., 162
DiMatteo, M.R., 600, 618
DiMauro, J., 696
Dimberg, U., 195, 432
Dimidjian, S., 714
Dindia, K., 526
Dion, K.K., 525, 529
Diorio, J., 601
Dishman, R.K., 619

Dix, D., 721
Dixon, N.F., 146
Dobson, K.S., 714
Docherty, N.M., 670
Dodson, J.D., 435
Doell, R.G., 419
Doherty, T.S., 111
Doka, K.J., 496
Dolan, R.J., 337
Dolezal, H., 187
Dollard, J., 541
Domhoff, G.W., 212, 213, 214, 215
Domino, G., 583
Domino, M.L., 583
Donahoe, J.W., 239
Donaldson, D., 653
Donnerstein, E., 416, 417, 543
Donovan-Hall, M., 505
Doppelt, J.E., 485
Dor, D., 315
Dorahy, M., 663
Dornbusch, S.M., 472
Dossenbach, H.D., 150
Dossenbach, M., 150
Dostrovsky, J., 266
Douglas, K., 432
Dovidio, J.F., 531, 532, 535, 539
Dozza, M., 53, 61
Draguns, J., 228, 662, 671
Drake, C., 175
Drake, M.E., 662
Drew, T., 171
Drews, F.A., 61
Driskell, J.E., 296
Drucker, D.J., 699
Drukin, K., 146
Dryden, W., 693
Du, X., 533
Dubbert, P.M., 619
Ducci, F., 623
Dumanis, S.B., 113
Duncan, B.L., 533
Duncan, I.J.H., 510
Dunlosky, J., 33
Dunn, J., 119, 122
Dunne, M.P., 418
Dunner, D.I., 714
Durrett, M.E., 468
Dutton, D.G., 441, 529, 556
Duvander, A.Z.E., 493
Dweck, C., 420
Dwyer, D., 104
Dyken, M.E., 210
Dymond, R.F., 690
Dzhafarov, E.N., 147

E
Eacott, M.J., 302
Eagleman, D.M., 143

Eagly, A.H., 9, 134, 528, 539
Eastman, C.I., 200
Eastwick, P.W., 518
Eaton, J., 522
Ebbinghaus, H., 16, 277, 297, 298
Eberhardt, J.L., 532
Eby, L.T., 523
Echt, K.V., 486
Eckensberger, L.H., 477, 537
Eckhardt, C.I., 543
Edgerton, R.B., 228
Edinger, J.D., 209
Edvardsen, J., 27
Edwards, D.C., 425
Edwards, J.R., 598
Eggermont, J.J., 104
Ehlers, C.L., 220
Ehrman, J., 618, 619
Eibl-Eibesfeldt, I., 137, 433
Eich, E., 295
Eidelman, P., 658
Eikelboom, A.R., 522
Eikeseth, S., 700
Einstein, A., 36, 348, 379
Einstein, G.O., 302
Eisenberg, N., 465, 536, 537, 540
Eisenberger, N.I., 18, 603, 604
Ekman, P., 127, 431, 433, 434, 436
Elbert, T., 102
Eldevik, S., 15
Elek, J.K., 5
Elhalal, A., 303, 309
Elkind, D., 483
Elliot, A., 599
Elliot, A.J., 420, 615
Elliot, M.S., 505
Elliott, R., 421, 690
Ellis, A., 692, 693, 702
Ellithorpe, M.E., 436, 437
Ellsworth, P.C., 428
Elovainio, M., 616
Ely, R., 322
Emens, J.S., 199
Emerson, R.M., 422
Emery, C.E., Jr., 62
Emmelkamp, P.M., 698
Enck, P., 262
Endler, N.S., 27
Endress, A.D., 280
Engel, S.A., 94
Enquist, M., 541
Epps, J., 542
Epstein, J.A., 422
Epstein, S., 573
Erdberg, P., 587
Erdelyi, M.H., 558, 685

Erez, A., 397
Ericsson, K.A., 285
Erikson, E.H., 466, 467, 468, 470, 482, 487, 488, 491, 494, 554
Eriksson, P.S., 104
Eron, L.D., 272, 541, 543, 544
Errázuriz, P., 557
Escher, M.C., 179
Esdaile, J., 231
Esparza, J., 409
Essau, C.A., 615, 652
Esser, J.K., 522
Esses, V.M., 531, 532
Essock-Vitale, S.M., 136
Esterbrooks, 27
Estes, T.H., 33
Ethier, C., 101
Evans, F.J., 230
Evanshen, T., 310
Everitt, B.J., 220
Evers, C., 404
Evers, K.A., 616
Ewoldsen, D.R., 436
Exner, J.E., Jr., 587
Eysenck, H.J., 120, 378, 568, 569, 571, 598, 674, 708

F
Fabbro, F., 329
Fabre-Thorpe, M., 172
Facon, B., 254
Fagley, N.S., 33
Fain, G.L., 75
Faith, M.S., 408
Falkner, A.L., 540
Fallah, S., 165
Fallon, A.E., 406, 407
Fantz, R.L., 126, 452, 453
Fardo, F., 231
Farina, B., 27
Farwell, L., 395, 396
Fayad, J.N., 169
Fazio, R.H., 63, 505, 507, 531
Feeny, N.C., 597
Fein, S., 534
Feingold, A., 406, 525
Feinstein, B.A., 614
Feldman-Barrett, L., 427
Feldman, M.A., 46
Feldman, M.W., 139
Feldman, R.P., 719
Felmlee, D.H., 524
Felsen, G., 172
Fenichel, G., 101
Fenigstein, A., 516
Fenn, K.M., 363
Fenton, W.S., 667
Fenwick, K.D., 453
Ferguson, C.J., 545, 546

Ferguson, E.D., 589
Ferguson, R., 399
Fergusson, D.M., 658
Fernald, A., 324
Fernichel, G., 71
Ferrer-García, M., 697
Ferster, C.B., 255
Fessler, D.M.T., 436
Festinger, L., 36, 37, 506, 518, 523, 524
Fichera, L.V., 607
Fiedler, K., 295
Field, T., 164, 264, 456
Fields, H.L., 165
Fifer, W.P., 453
Fink, M., 718
Finley, J.R., 196
Fiore, J.P., 32
Fish, J.M., 384
Fishbein, M., 505
Fisher, C., 108
Fisher, D.M., 456
Fisher, H., 669
Fisher, J., 505
Fisher, M., 82
Fisher, R.J., 525
Fisher, S., 13, 212, 557, 646, 661, 670, 708
Fishman, I., 430
Fiske, S.T., 529, 532
Fitch, G.M., 53
Flannagan, C., 53
Flavell, J.H., 464
Fleeson, W., 574
Flege, J., 328
Fleming, I., 541
Flinn, M.V., 315, 523
Flores, J.A., 225
Flynn, J.R., 375, 376
Foa, E.B., 597, 647, 724
Fogarty, F.J., 295
Folkard, S., 200
Folkman, S., 609
Follette, W.C., 300, 308
Fong, G.T., 222
Foo Fighters, 162
Food and Drug Administration (FDA), 716
Ford, H., 581
Ford, T.M., 539
Fordyce, W.E., 165
Forgas, J.P., 427
Forster, A., 111
Fossion, R., 37
Foster, D.J., 266, 311
Foulke, E., 164
Foulkes, D., 203, 211, 214
Foulks, F.F., 705
Foushee, H.C., 517
Fouts, D.H., 331
Fouts, R.S., 331
Fowles, D.C., 669

Fox, K.C.R., 213, 214
Fox, N.A., 99, 163, 430, 467
Fox, P.T., 22
Fox, R., 454
Fraley, R.C., 555
Francis, G., 8
Franco, A.H.R., 6
Franic, 119
Frank, A.J., 376
Frank, N.C., 210
Frank, R., 96
Franz, S., 22
Frawley, P.J., 624
Frazier, P.A., 602
Fredrickson, B.L., 406, 425, 649
Freeman, C., 707
Freeman, D., 436
Freeman, W., 719
Freire, A., 16, 553
French, L., 669
Freud, S., 12–13, 193, 195, 212, 213, 244, 300, 389, 398, 491, 543, 550, 551, 552, 553, 554, 555, 558, 559, 586, 636, 646, 655, 661, 669, 685, 708
Friebely, J., 164
Friedlander, L., 645
Friedman, H., 600, 618
Friedman, H.S., 602, 607
Friedman, M.A., 529
Friesen, W.V., 433, 434, 436
Frijda, N.H., 427, 435
Frisby, J.P., 181
Frischen, A., 171
Frisco, M.L., 492
Fristoe, N.M., 486
Fritsch, G., 83
Fritsch, J., 409
Frodi, A.M., 426
Froger, C., 284
Fromm, E., 528
Frongillo, E.A., 456
Frosh, S., 688
Fuegen, K., 554
Fuligni, A.J., 488
Fulker, D.W., 118
Funder, D.C., 572, 573
Funk, S.C., 605
Furmark, T., 719, 720
Furukawa, T.A., 717

G
Gaab, N., 390
Gabbard, C., 196
Gabbard, G.O., 554, 674, 683, 685
Gabrieli, J.D.E., 284, 290, 296, 309, 310

Gage, P., 45, 96, 98
Gainotti, G., 430
Galaburda, A.M., 96
Galanaki, E.P., 483
Galati, D., 427
Galea, S., 212, 599
Galef, B.G., Jr., 228, 270, 271
Galek, J., 63
Galietta, M., 704
Gall, F.J., 22
Gallagher, A.M., 386
Gallagher, D., 439
Gallego, J.A., 101
Gallese, V., 97
Gallistel, C.R., 268
Gallivan, J.P., 284
Gallop, R., 704
Gallup, G., 193
Gallup Polls, 501
Galton, F., 277, 358, 377, 379
Ganchrow, J.R., 453
Gandara, P., 326
Gangestad, S.W., 132, 135, 527
Ganis, G., 309, 350
Gannon, P.J., 101
Garb, H.N., 587
Garbarino, J., 604
Garbutt, J.C., 245
Garcia, J., 261
Garcia-Palacios, A., 246
Gardiner, J.M., 281, 285
Gardner, B.T., 331
Gardner, H., 367
Gardner, R., 205
Gardner, R.A., 331
Gardner, W.I., 252
Gardziella, S., 104
Garfinkel, P.E., 649
Garland, D.J., 288
Garlick, D., 378
Garmezy, N., 604
Garnefski, N., 658
Garner, D.M., 649
Garoff-Eaton, R.J., 304
Garrett, V.D., 601
Garrick, M., 46
Gathercole, S.E., 463
Gati, J., 94
Gaucher, D., 563
Gautier, J.F., 403
Gaylin, G., 683
Gawronski, B., 504, 535
Gazit, I., 259
Gazzaniga, M.S., 88, 104, 403
Geary, D.C., 125, 126
Gegenfurtner, K.R., 154, 172
Geis, F.L., 533
Geiser, C., 550
Gelade, G.A., 374

Gelernter, J., 645
Geller, G., 649
Gelman, R., 268
Gelman, S.A., 474
Genesee, F., 325, 326
Genovese, K., 37, 38, 39, 41, 538
Gentile, D.A., 543, 545
Gentilucci, M., 322
Genuchi, M., 438
George, 229
Geracioti, T.D., 649
Geraerts, E., 300, 307, 308
Gerard, H.B., 512
Gershoff, E.T., 252
Gershon, E.S., 654
Ghasemlou, N., 144
Ghaziuddin, M., 716
Gherardini, L., 176
Ghetti, S., 293
Ghodse, H., 223
Giacomantonio, S., 539
Gibbs, J., 401
Gibbs, J.C., 537
Gibson, B.M., 269
Gibson, E.J., 184
Gibson, J.J., 181
Gibson, P.A., 28
Giedd, J.N., 112, 479
Giftakis, J.E., 269
Giglioli, I.A.C., 698
Gilbert, D.T., 501
Gill, K., 498, 499
Gillespie, M., 501
Gillette, M.U., 199
Gilligan, C., 477
Ginzburg, K., 597
Giraldeau, L-A., 271
Giroux, I., 697
Giza, B.K., 163
Glanzer, M., 282, 283
Glanzman, D.L., 238
Glaser, R., 32
Glass, G.V., 710
Gleaves, D.H., 234, 664
Gleason, J-B., 322
Gleason, K.E., 470
Glenberg, A.M., 33
Glick, P., 532
Glock, S., 545
Glucksman, M.L., 685
Gobet, F., 286, 288
Goddard, A.W., 646
Goddard, H.H., 386
Godden, D.R., 294
Goddings, A-L., 479, 481
Goel, V., 337
Goffman, E., 722
Goldapple, K., 695
Goldberg, I., 716
Goldberg, L.R., 128
Goldberg, S., 493
Golden, C., 171

Gollan, J.K., 714
Goldman, D., 623
Goldstein, B., 180
Goldstein, G., 370
Goldstein, J.H., 264
Goldston, D.B., 658
Gombrich, E.H., 187
Gonçalves, M.M., 690
Gone, J.P., 705, 706
Gong, T., 316
Goodale, M.A., 44, 45, 196
Goodall, J., 47, 69, 131, 136, 137, 138
Goode, W.J., 20
Goodman, S.H., 653, 657
Goodman, W., 65
Goodrich, J.T., 719
Goodrick, S., 209
Gopnik, A., 464
Gordon, B., 716
Gordon, J.R., 624, 699
Gore, J.S., 19
Gorman, J.M., 716
Gorski, R.A., 388
Gosling, P., 507
Gosling, S.D., 49, 583
Gothard, S.I., 308
Gotlib, I.H., 27, 654, 656
Gottesman, I.I., 117, 645, 667, 668, 674
Gottfredson, N.C., 613
Gottfried, A.E., 422
Gottfried, T., 226
Gottman, J., 530, 531
Gould, E., 104
Govorun, O., 554
Graber, A., 65
Graber, J.A., 479
Graber, M.A., 65
Grabowski, T., 96
Grace, A.A., 310
Gracely, R.H., 164, 165
Graf, P., 290, 485
Graham, J.D., 350
Graham, S., 542
Grant, H.M., 295
Grasshoff, C., 221
Gratton, A., 91
Graveline, Y.M., 685
Gray, J.A., 571
Gray, S.A., 532
Green, B., 513
Green, D.P., 534
Green, J.T., 313
Green, M., 677
Green, M.F., 669
Greenberg, J., 565
Greenberg, L.S., 607, 683, 688, 690, 691
Greenberg, R.P., 13, 212, 557, 646, 661, 669, 708
Greendlinger, V., 523

Greene, K., 483
Greene, R.L., 299
Greene, R.W., 584
Greenfield, P.M., 381
Greenleaf, E., 211
Greeno, C.G., 408
Greenwald, A.G., 49, 145, 531, 532, 558
Gregory, R.J., 373, 379
Gregory, R.L., 175, 181, 187
Grey, M.J., 84
Grice, H.P., 321
Grierson, B., 480
Griffiths, C.T., 544
Grigorenko, E.L., 366, 377, 385
Grimes, K., 670
Griner, D., 705
Grissom, R.J., 710
Groepper, D., 113
Gronnerod, C., 587
Groppa, S., 84
Gross, A.M., 545, 619
Gross, J.J., 429
Gross, P.H., 504, 533
Grossberg, S., 157
Grosser, B.I., 164
Grotegerd, D., 695
Groth-Marnat, G., 371, 589
Gruber, M.J., 303
Grunebaum, M.F., 716
Grunstein, M., 139
Grusec, J.E., 489
Guan, Y., 19
Guarnaccia, P.J., 28, 648, 657
Guéguen, N., 518
Guevremont, D.C., 696
Guilford, J.P., 345, 363
Guillin, A., 667
Guinness Book, 408
Gulevich, G., 205
Gump, L.S., 477
Guo, G., 489
Guo, T., 26
Gur, R.E., 667
Gurvitz, I.G., 676
Gustavson, C.R., 65, 262
Gustavson, J.C., 65, 262
Gutiérrez-Maldonado, J., 697

H
Haaga, D.A.F., 655
Haas, S.J., 717
Haasz, J., 364
Hadwin, L., 191, 192
Hadwin, A.F., 352
Hafen, B.Q., 620
Hafter, E.R., 171
Hagel, A., 271

Hagen, C., 169
Haidt, J., 436
Haier, R.J., 378, 379
Hains, S., 454
Halaas, J.L., 402
Halari, R., 389
Hale, J.B., 373
Hall, C.S., 211, 212
Hall, E., 144
Hall, G.C.N., 705
Hall, G.S., 487
Hall, H., 667
Hall, J.A.Y., 389
Hall, W., 227
Halligan, P.W., 350
Halligan, S., 657
Halpern, B.P., 162, 163
Halpern, C.T., 407
Halpern, D.F., 6, 386, 387
Haluk, D.M., 255
Hambrick, D.Z., 363
Hamilton, D.R., 97
Hamilton, R.J., 32
Hamilton, T.E., III, 525
Hamilton, W.D., 136
Hamm, A.O., 245
Hammen, C., 27, 657
Hammond, S., 49
Hampson, E., 386, 388
Hampson, S.E., 571, 602
Hampstead, B.M., 310
Han, X., 19
Hancock, P.A., 596
Hanes, 171
Hankin, B.L., 555
Hannon, E.E., 390
Hans, 18
Hansen, C.H., 172
Hansen, J., 524
Hansen, N.B., 712
Hansen, R.D., 172
Hany, E.A., 364
Harackiewicz, J.M., 422
Hardman, E., 295
Hardt, O., 310
Hardy, C., 520
Hare, R.D., 672, 673
Harkness, K.L., 656
Harkness, S., 238
Harley, K., 302
Harlow, H.F., 164, 468, 470
Harlow, J., 212
Harlow, J.M., 96
Harlow, L.L., 229
Harmon-Jones, E., 507
Harms, P.D., 43
Harrington, D.M., 564
Harrington, T., 396
Harris, E., 499, 501
Harris, J.A., 122
Harris, S.L., 726
Harris, T.O., 27, 655

Harris, V.A., 500, 501
Harrison, A., 375
Harsch, N., 293
Hart, J.W., 520
Hart, W., 5
Hartley, A.A., 486
Hartley, K., 350
Hartley, P., 649
Hartmann, B., 450
Hasan, Y., 546
Haselton, M.G., 132
Hashimoto, T., 20
Hassabis, D., 300
Hasseldine, J., 338
Hassin, R.R., 195
Hastings, P., 489
Hatfield, E., 425, 528, 429
Hathaway, S.R., 585
Haugtvedt, C.P., 508
Hauri, P., 202
Hawkins, D.L., 47, 50
Hawkins, K.A., 541
Hawkins, R.D., 239
Haworth, C.M.A., 21
Haydon, P.G., 71
Hayes, S.C., 702
Hayman, A., 276
Hayne, H., 306
Haynes, 32
Haynes, S.G., 606
Haynes, S.N., 584
Hayslip, B., 480
Hazan, C., 528
Hazen, N.L., 468
He, M., 456
He, X.X., 227
Health Canada, 28, 76, 217, 220, 412, 622, 715
Hearold, S., 536
Heath, A.C., 228
Heath, R.G., 91
Heaton, S., 667
Heavey, E.E.L., 164
Hebb, D.O., 21, 95
Heckers, S., 217
Heckhausen, H., 422
Heerey, E.A., 679
Heesters, B.A., 144
Hefferon, K., 629
Heider, F., 499
Hein, C., 646
Heiman, J., 415
Heimpel, S.A., 561, 563
Heinrichs, D.W., 717
Heinrichs, R.W., 669
Helgeson, V.S., 614
Heller, M.A., 164
Hellerstein, D., 716
Helmreich, R.L., 517
Henner, M., 277
Henning, K., 414
Henrik Ehrsson, H., 350

Henry, J.D., 302
Herbener, E.S., 528
Herculano-Houzel, S., 71
Herdt, G., 622
Herek, G.M., 531, 633
HeretoHelp, 206
Hering, E., 154
Herman, D.B., 667
Hernandez, L., 91
Herndon, P., 308
Herrington, R., 718, 719
Herrnstein, R.J., 384
Hersen, M., 694, 699
Herskovits, M.J., 238
Hertwig, R., 64
Herz, M., 665, 667, 669
Herzing, D., 333
Hess, E.H., 468
Hess, W.R., 207
Hetherington, A.W., 403
Hetherington, E.M., 383, 449, 472
Hetherington, M.M., 408
Hewstone, M., 533, 535
Heylighen, F., 398
Hibbard, S., 587, 588
Hickok, J.T., 262
Hidalgo, M.P., 482
Higgins, A., 476
Higham, T., 103
Hilgard, E.R., 230, 232
Hill, C.A., 523
Hill, J.L., 383
Hill, J.O., 409
Hill, P.L., 571
Hillman, D.C., 199, 678
Hillsdon, M., 487
Hines, M., 386, 387, 388, 419
Hippocrates, 108, 635
Hitzig, E., 83
Hobbes, T., 11
Hobson, A., 212
Hobson, J.A., 204, 212, 216
Hobson-West, P., 65
Hodges, J., 471
Hodgkin, A., 71
Hodgson, R., 245, 644, 696
Hodson, G., 532
Hoebel, B.G., 91, 163
Hoeger, W.W.K., 620
Hoeksema, V.O., 520
Hoekstra, R., 124
Hoffart, A., 575
Hoffer, A., 685
Hoffman, H.G., 697, 698
Hoffman, L., 688
Hoffman, M.L., 426
Hofman, P., 97, 98, 127
Hofmann, S.G., 702
Hogan, C., 16

Hogarty, G.E., 665
Hohmann, G., 136
Holahan, C.J., 597, 609
Holden, E.R., 695
Holder, M.D., 16
Holland, P.C., 250, 269
Holland, R.W., 16
Holland, S.K., 379
Hollander, E., 642
Hollis, K.L., 267
Hollon, S.D., 688, 708, 709, 720
Holmes, M.R., 593
Holmes, T.H., 597
Holmstrom, 597
Holsboer, F., 596, 597, 601
Homan, C., 406
Honey, P.L., 228
Honolulu Star-Bulletin, 435
Honts, C.R., 432
Honzik, C.H., 270
Hooper, J., 70
Hopf, W.H., 546
Hopko, D.R., 28
Horn, J.L., 346, 363, 364, 485
Hornak, J.P., 85
Horney, K., 554
Horswill, M.S., 147
Horton, C.L., 206
Hounsfield, G., 85
House, J.S., 602
Hovland, C.I., 508, 534
Howard, I.P., 180
Howard, K.I., 712
Howes, O., 78
Howes, O.D., 669
Hsieh, A.Y., 26
Hu, K., 624
Hubbard, E.M., 142, 143
Hubel, D., 180
Hubel, D.H., 94, 148, 156, 157
Hubert, C.J., 502
Hubert, V., 312
Hublin, C., 210
Huddy, L., 533
Hudson, 649
Hudson, S., 493
Hudson, W., 187
Hudson, W.D., 333
Huesmann, L.R., 272, 542, 543, 544
Huff, R.M., 622
Huffcutt, A., 205
Hughes, C., 260
Hulac, D., 701
Hull, C.L., 397, 398
Hull, P., 461
Hulstijn, J.H., 329
Human Genome Project, 109, 110

Humayun, M.S., 168
Humphrey, D., 452
Humphrey, G.K., 11, 45, 452
Humphrey, L.L., 650
Humphrey-Murto, S., 369
Humphreys, M.S., 289
Humphriss, N., 523
Hunecke, M., 505
Hunsley, J., 414
Hunt, E., 364, 378, 384, 385, 438
Hunter, J., 362, 374
Hunter, J.E., 374
Hunter, R.F., 374
Huon, G.F., 407
Hupbach, A., 295
Hurwitz, T.D., 210
Husain, G., 58
Hussaini, S.A., 243
Hussong, A.M., 613
Huston, T.L., 525
Huttenlocher, P.R., 104
Hutzler, F., 176
Huurre, T., 473
Huxley, A., 71
Hyde, J.S., 411, 414, 450
Hyde, K.L., 390
Hyde, M., 494
Hysek, C.M., 539

I

Iglesias, A., 696
Ikeda, H., 571
Ikemi, Y., 231
Ilie, A., 569
Iliescu, D., 569
Inagaki, T.K., 604
Ingelhart, R., 494
Ingham, A.G., 519
Ingold, C.H., 575
Ingraham, L.J., 668
Ingram, R.E., 707
Inhelder, B., 484
Insko, C.A., 508
Institute of Medicine, 623
International Human Genome Sequencing Consortium, 110
Intraub, H., 305
Iranzo, A., 210
Irie, M., 245
Irvine, C., 49
Irwin, A.R., 545
Irwin, J.R., 147
Isaacowitz, D.M., 656
Isaacs, K.S., 425
Isacsson, G., 716
Isaacson, R.L., 90
Isen, A.M., 397

Ishigami, Y., 53, 61
Ishihara, K., 199
Ishikawa, S.L., 674
Ising, M., 596, 598, 601
Isles, A.R., 110
Ispas, D., 569
Itard, J.M.G., 470
Ito, H., 88
Ito, T.A., 532
Itti, L., 171
Ivker, N.A.C., 308
Iwasa, N., 477
Izard, C., 432, 433, 434, 465
Izard, C.E., 426

J

Jablensky, A., 671
Jack, E.P., 506
Jackendoff, R., 280
Jackson, A., 620
Jackson, J.H., 83
Jackson, J.J., 571
Jackson, N., 390
Jacobson, N.S., 710, 714
Jadhav, S.P., 311
Jaeggi, S.M., 364
Jaffee, S.R., 21
James, T.W., 45, 145
James, W., 12, 128, 191, 193, 234, 278, 396, 397, 438, 439, 440, 452
Jamison, K., 652
Jang, K., 644, 654, 668
Jang, K.L., 122
Janicki, D., 614
Janis, I.L., 520
Jankiewicz, H., 228
Janoski, T., 536, 540
Janssens, J.M.A.M., 537
Janus, C.L., 414
Janus, S.S., 414
Jasinska, K., 329
Jay, T., 252
Jeffery, K.J., 266
Jeffery, R.W., 620
Jemmott, J.B., 621
Jencks, C., 384
Jenike, M.A., 44
Jenkins, J., 473
Jenkins, J.M., 651
Jenkins, S., 636
Jennings, B.M., 575
Jensen, A.R., 377, 384, 385
Jensen, L.A., 488, 489
Jensen, R., 266
Jequier, E., 403
Jeste, D., 667
Jha, A., 612
Ji, L.J., 26
Jiang, T., 19, 452

Joanisse, M.F., 290
Joffe, R.T., 654
Joh, A.S., 456
John, O.P., 49, 569
Johnson, A.M., 418
Johnson, B.T., 508
Johnson, D.F., 401
Johnson, D.W., 535, 636
Johnson, J.G., 543
Johnson, J.S., 325, 327
Johnson, L., 205
Johnson, M.C., 541
Johnson, M.K., 562
Johnson, M.W., 226
Johnson, M.K., 287
Johnson, R.E., 569
Johnson, R.L., 7
Johnson, R.T., 535, 636
Johnson, S., 612
Johnson, V., 412, 413
Johnson-Laird, P., 335, 337
Johnsrude, I.S., 173
Johnston, V.S., 526
Johnston, W.A., 56
Joiner, T.E., 598, 657, 658, 675
Joinson, A., 49
Jones, B.C., 526
Jones, E., 712
Jones, E.E., 500, 533
Jones, E.G., 89
Jones, G.V., 285, 298
Jones, M.C., 244
Jones, R.T., 285
Jonides, J., 285
Jonsson, T., 301
Jordan, P.H., 473
Joseph, R., 387, 599
Josephs, R.A., 221
Josephson, W.L., 544
Joslyn, S., 438
Joslyn, S.L., 4
Julien, R., 217, 218
Jung, C., 554, 555
Jung, D.-I., 105
Jureidini, J.N., 716
Jurkowitz, M., 544
Justus, K.R., 601

K

Kabat-Zinn, J., 612, 702
Kagan, J., 22, 467, 469
Kagitáibasi, C., 488
Kahan, T.L., 212
Kaheman, D., 341
Kahleova, H., 5
Kahn, S., 468
Kahneman, D., 337, 341, 342
Kaia, L., 373
Kail, R., 463
Kail, R.V., 474

Kaiser, A., 322
Kaku, M., 348
Kalafat, J., 659
Kalaitzaki, A.E., 49
Kali, R., 463
Kalick, S.M., 525
Kalish, R.A., 496
Kaltiala-Heino, R., 479
Kambara, T., 541
Kampmann, K.M., 220
Kandel, E.R., 239, 311
Kandler, C., 120
Kane, H.D., 371
Kane, J.M., 717
Kaner, A., 525
Kanetsuna, T., 47
Kangarlu, A., 86
Kanner, L., 677, 678
Kaplan, B.E., 624
Kaplan, R.M., 370
Kaprio, J., 600
Kapur, S., 669
Karau, S.J., 520
Karimizadeh, M., 573
Karney, B.R., 492
Karon, B.P., 300
Kashimoto, R.K., 110
Kasparov, G., 346
Kassel, J.D., 217
Kasser, T., 491
Kassinove, H., 543
Katapodi, M.C., 341
Katz, J., 164, 716
Kaufman, A.S., 371
Kaufman, N., 371
Kaufman, S.B., 363
Kavanagh, D., 670
Kawakami, K., 535
Kaysen, D., 260, 599, 613
Kazdin, A., 700, 707, 708, 711, 712, 717
Kazemi, H., 165
Keenan, J.P., 145
Keener, A.D., 430
Keith, S.J., 671
Keller, H., 395
Kelley, H., 500
Kelley, H.H., 177, 526
Kelley, J.B., 473, 474, 482
Kellman, P.J., 453
Kelly, G.F., 411, 414, 418, 559
Kelly, J.A., 621, 622
Kelly, T.A., 726
Keltner, D., 433
Kemeny, M.E., 595
Kemmelmeier, 19
Kempermann, G., 104
Kemps, E.B., 487
Kenardy, J., 407, 410
Kendall, P.C., 542

Kennedy, J.F., 205, 520
Kennedy, S.H., 695
Kenrick, D.T., 572, 573
Kentridge, R.W., 197
Ker, 405
Kernberg, O.F., 13, 555, 673, 674, 675
Kerns, J.G., 669
Kersholt, J.H., 522
Kessels, R.P.C., 485
Kessey, R.E., 400
Kessler, R.C., 494, 642, 643, 644, 646, 651, 652, 653
Ketellar, T., 127
Kety, S., 115
Kety, S.S., 668, 670
Keyes, C.L.M., 493
Keyes, L.M., 653, 657
Khan, 716
Khoury, B., 612
Khoury, R.M., 511
Kiecolt-Glaser, J.K., 44, 530, 600, 610
Kierkegaard, S., 40
Kihlstrom, J.F., 145, 232, 233, 558
Kilburn, J., 546
Kim, G.J., 698
Kim, K., 562
Kim, Y., 615
Kimble, D.P., 600
Kimura, D., 99, 386, 387, 388, 389
Kimura, K., 210
Kinnear, P.R., 187, 188
Kinsey, A.C., 411, 418
Kiper, D.C., 154
Kirby, L.D., 428
Kirchengast, S., 450
Kirk, K.M., 419
Kirmayer, L.J., 660
Kirsch, I., 230, 232, 233, 234, 264
Kirschmann, A., 11
KISS, 162
Kissileff, H.R., 410
Kitayama, S., 423
Kitzinger, C., 65
Kitzinger, J., 65
Kivimaki, M., 616
Kiyatkin, E.A., 91
Kiyhankhadiv, A., 27
Klahr, D., 41
Klauer, K.C., 63, 337
Klebold, D., 499, 501
Klein, G., 341
Klein, M., 555, 697
Klein, R.M., 53, 61
Klein, S.B., 242
Kleinknecht, R.A., 648
Kleinmuntz, B., 652
Kleitman, N., 201, 202, 203

Klem, B., 252
Klemmensem, R., 129
Klieder, H.M., 5
Kline, M.V., 622
Klosterhalfen, S., 262
Kluckhohn, C., 550
Kluft, R.P., 307
Knafo, D., 300
Knekt, P., 687
Kneer, J., 545
Knoblauch, K., 154
Knowles, J.H., 615
Kobasa, S.C., 604, 605
Koch, C., 148, 197, 334
Kochanska, G., 465, 477, 478
Koelling, R.A., 261
Koenig, H.G., 607
Koerner, N., 643
Koestner, R., 422
Koffler, S.P., 310
Kohlberg, L., 475, 476
Kohlenberg, R.J., 714
Köhler, W., 264, 265, 268
Kohut, H., 398, 555
Kohut, T., 417
Kolata, G., 5
Kolb, B., 455
Kolb, Z.B., 70, 72, 75, 89, 92, 101, 109, 379
Kolk, H.H.J., 289
Kollar, E.J., 108
Koluchova, J., 470
Konkle, A.T.M., 401
Konradi, C., 217
Koriat, A., 287, 350
Korn, J.H., 64
Kortegaard, L., 650
Kosslyn, S.M., 349
Kotake, 27
Kotelko, O., 480
Kottak, C.P., 305, 523
Kozin, M., 293
Krahé, B., 535, 546
Krain, A.L., 4
Kramer, D.A., 485
Kramer, M.S., 456
Krasnegor, N.A., 96
Kraus, N., 390
Krauss, K., 314
Kraut, R., 49
Krebs, D.L., 503
Krech, D., 105
Krevans, J., 537
Krijn, M., 246
Krippner, S., 62
Krishna, A., 171
Krizan, Z., 520
Kroese, F.M., 404
Krosnick, J., 145
Krueger, R.F., 524
Kruger, J., 34

Kruglanski, A.W., 503
Ksir, C.J., 73, 76, 223, 226, 227, 229
Kubler-Ross, E., 495, 496
Kubota, J.T., 532
Kuhl, P.K., 323
Kuijer, R.G., 410
Kulik, J.A., 523
Kumar, A., 466
Kumar, S., 220
Kuncel, N.P., 362, 373, 374, 385
Kunzendorf, R.G., 62
Kunzmann, U., 347, 364
Kuo, J.R., 675
Kuo, P., 228
Kupers, C.J., 576, 577
Kurzweil, E., 554
Kurtz, M.M., 701
Kurzban, R., 23
Kuwada, S., 161
Kuyken, W., 695
Ky, K.N., 58

L
La Cerra, P., 132
LaBar, K.S., 13, 312
Lacaille, J.C., 71
Lachman, M.E., 494
Lack, D., 131
Lader, M.H., 718, 719
Lagenbucher, J.W., 637
Lagerspetz, K.Y., 540
Lai, D.W.L., 705
Laible, D., 477
Lakein, A., 32
Lam, K.S., 677
Lam, R.W., 122, 200
Lamb, J.A.G., 101
Lambert, L., 16
Lambert, M.J., 694, 710, 711
Lambert, W.E., 326
Lamborn, S.D., 472
Lampinen, J.M., 300
Lamport, M., 485
Lan, W., 423
Land, B.B., 331
Landesman, S., 383
Landfield, P., 601
Landis, T., 146
Landon, A., 49
Landry, M., 233
Landstrom, S., 539
Landy, F.J., 369
Lane, R.D., 98
Laney, C., 278, 308
Lang, U.E., 27
Lange, C., 438
Langer, E., 195
Langlois, J.H., 525, 526
Lanier, C.A., 542

Lanktree, C., 329
LaPiere, R., 505
LaPointe, L.L., 322
Lapp, L., 208
Larivée, S., 462
Larsen, R.J., 560
Larson, C.L., 645
Larson, R.W., 489
Larson, S.J., 219
Lashley, K.S., 21, 22, 255, 309
Lassiter, G.D., 5
Latané, B., 37, 38, 39, 40, 41, 43, 58, 61, 64, 520, 524, 538, 539
Latham, G.P., 579, 580
Lau, H.L., 238
Lau, R.R., 502
Laumann, E.O., 411, 414, 415, 418
Laurel-Seller, E., 406
Lavelli, M., 427
Lavigne, J.V., 677
Law, M., 690
Lawler, K.A., 605
Lawrence, J.A., 478
Lazarus, R.S., 425, 427, 440, 441, 442, 443, 444, 592, 593, 594, 609, 691
Leaper, C., 462, 474
Leary, M.R., 523, 564
LeBel, E.P., 8, 36, 37, 63
Leblanc, K.H., 397
LeBeouf, R.A., 63
LeBon, G., 518
Lebrun, M., 652
Lecat, B., 518
Lecompte, V., 557, 562
Ledford, J., 272
LeDoux, J.E., 13, 90, 91, 196, 263, 312, 429, 603
Leduc, A., 315
Lee, C.H., 280
Lee, H.J., 717
Lee, K., 16, 464
Leech, J., 59
Lefaucher, J.P., 84
Leff, J., 670
Lehman, D.R., 400
Lehmann-Haupt, C., 432
Lehmann, D., 309
Leibenluft, E., 646
Leibowitz, S.F., 403
Leichsenring, F., 676, 687
Leigh, B.C., 221
Leigland, S., 264
Leimar, O., 541
Leinonen, E., 321
Leising, D., 632
Leitenberg, H., 414

LeMoal, H., 655
Lentz, R.J., 701
Lenzenweger, M.F., 671, 676
Leon, D.A., 374
Leondes, C.T., 87, 101
Leor, J., 600
LePage, A., 544
Lerner, M.J., 539
Leucht, S., 717
Leukefeld, C., 623
Leutgeb, J.K., 311
Levenson, H., 686, 687
Levenson, R.W., 431, 615
Levin, L.H., 65
Levin, N., 19
Levine, J., 513
Levine, R., 20
Levinson, D.J., 491, 494
Levinthal, C.E., 622
Levinthal, C.F., 76, 77, 220, 221, 225, 226
Levis, D.J., 258
Levit, A., 163
Levitin, D.L., 103, 104
Levitsky, D.A., 407
Levy, S., 606
Levy, D.A., 6
Levy, R.B., 47
Lewin, K., 423
Lewin, R., 125
Lewin, T., 7
Lewinsohn, P.M., 28, 646, 652, 656, 713
Lewis, J., 107–108
Lewis, M., 465, 550
Lewis, T.L., 186, 452, 454
Lewontin, R., 120, 381
Lewy, A., 199
Leyens, J.P., 544
Li, J., 488
Li, M., 27
Li, R., 150
Li, S., 511
Li, Y., 511
Libertus, K., 456
Lickey, M.E., 716
Lidz, C.S., 376, 377
Lieb, R., 657
Lieberman, J., 715, 716, 717
Lieberman, M.D., 18
Liedtke, W.B., 144
Lijffijt, M., 624
Lilienfeld, S.O., 234, 560, 587, 640
Lin, J.Y., 172
Lincoln, A., 634
Lindell, A.K., 101
Lindenbaum, S., 622
Lindoerfer, J.S., 522
Linehan, M.M., 675, 703, 704

Linver, M.R., 472
Linville, P.W., 533
Linz, D., 417
Lipko, A.R., 33
Lippa, R.A., 386, 387
Liu, L., 311
Liu, W.T., 168
Lisman, J.E., 310
Liversedge, S.P., 7
Livesley, W.J., 122, 672
Livingstone, M., 156, 176, 180
Lloyd, E.A., 139
Locke, E.A., 579, 580
Locke, J., 11, 13
Locke, V.O., 449
Lockhart, R.S., 284, 285
Loehlin, J.C., 117
Loewenstein, R.J., 662
Loewi, O., 73
Loftus, E.F., 17, 278, 289, 306, 308, 309, 502
Loftus, G.R., 309
Logie, R.H., 302
Logothetis, N.K., 45, 347
Logue, A.W., 403, 409
Lomber, S.J., 104
Lonnqvist, J-E., 654
Lonsdorf, E.V., 47
Lookadoo, R., 463
Looper, K., 660
Lopez, A.C., 129
Lopez, S.J., 16, 628
Lopez, S.R., 28, 648, 657
Lorenz, K., 468, 543
Louca, M., 205, 206
Lount, R.B., Jr., 520
Lovaas, O.I., 252, 701
Lovallo, W., 599
Low, L-F., 487
Lowenstein, 545
Lubinski, D., 362, 372, 374, 381, 393
Lubitz, A., 1
Luborsky, L., 710
Lucassen, A., 112, 113
Luchins, A., 503
Luchins, A.J., 339
Luck, S.J., 161, 171
Luders, E., 378, 379
Ludlow, C., 663
Luhmann, M., 550
Luminet, O., 293
Luna, B., 463, 480, 481, 484
Lundemo, T., 334
Luo, N., 19
Luo, S., 524
Lupien, P.J., 115
Lupien, S.J., 601
Luria, A.R., 142
Lydic, R., 209

Lykken, D.T., 22, 117, 121, 380, 432
Lyn, S.J., 332
Lynch, J., 399
Lynch, M.A., 311
Lynn, R., 376, 384
Lynn, S.J., 62, 232, 233, 663
Lynskey, M.T., 658
Lyons, D.M., 601
Lyons, L., 62
Lyons, M.J., 227
Lysy, D.C., 43
Lyvers, M., 224

M
Ma, J.L.C., 649
Ma, Y., 525
Maass, A., 513
MacAndrew, C., 228
Maccari, S., 111
Maccoby, E.E., 472, 584
Maccoby, N., 584
MacCoun, R.J., 626
MacDonald, T.K., 221, 222, 234
Maciejewski, P.K., 496
Mack, A., 171
Macknik, S.L., 148
Macy, M.W., 526
Maddox, K.B., 532
Maddux, J.E., 578, 579, 702
Madon, S., 504
Maes, H.H.M., 409
Magnuson, S., 522
Magoun, H.W., 89
Maheswaran, D., 508
Mahler, H.I.M., 523, 555
Mahowald, M.W., 210
Maidment, N.T., 397
Maier, S.F., 165
Mainieri, T., 64
Maio, G.R., 504, 507
Major, B., 525
Mak-Fan, S., 678
Mäkelä, K., 507
Malamuth, N.M., 416, 417
Malcolm, W., 690, 691
Maldonado, R., 226
Malewska-Peyre, H., 488
Malinowski, J.E., 206
Malis, R.S., 488
Malone, P.S., 501
Malouf, J.M., 115
Malzahn, A.M., 397
Mancini, A.D., 496, 605
Mandel, H., 634, 635
Mandler, G., 425
Mann, L., 518, 519
Mann, W., 150

Manning, W.D., 493
Manolo, E., 286
Manson, J.E., 620
Manson, S.M., 657
Mäntylä, T., 281, 285, 292, 293
Mantzoros, C., 650
Maquet, P., 208
Marangell, L.B., 716
Marcia, J.E., 487
Marder, S., 665, 667, 669
Maredpour, A., 696
Mares, D., 542
Margolin, G., 530
Marian, V., 329
Marini, Z.A., 461
Marino, P., 702
Markey, P.M., 539
Markley, D.K., 714
Markovitz, H., 337
Markowitsch, H.J., 663
Markowitz, J.C., 687, 708, 709
Marks, I.M., 262, 695, 696
Markus, H.R., 423, 428, 565
Marlatt, G.A., 220, 229, 623, 624, 625, 626, 699
Marlier, L., 452
Marmot, M., 487
Marsat, G., 157
Marschark, M., 325
Marsh, H.W., 566
Marsh, R.L., 302
Marshall, L.H., 89
Marshall, M.A., 563
Marshall, N.L., 471
Marshall, P.J., 99, 430
Marshall, W., 493
Marsiske, M., 150
Marsland, A.L., 599
Martell, C., 657
Martin, B.A., 718
Martin, C.L., 474
Martin, G.L., 700, 701
Martin, J.E., 619
Martin, M.M., 326
Martin, O.S.M., 95
Martin, S.J., 311
Martinez, R., 529
Martinez-Conde, S., 148
Martinson, E.W., 575
Marx, B., 613, 614
Masataka, N., 455
Mascaro, N., 607
Mascolo, M.E., 488
Mash, E.J., 677
Mashour, G.A., 719
Masland, R.H., 156
Maslow, A.H., 15, 16, 398, 399, 523, 558, 627

Massen, C., 287
Masten, A.S., 383, 604
Masterpasqua, F., 9, 108
Masters, W., 412, 413
Masters, W.H., 81, 701
Masunaga, H., 346, 364
Matarazzo, J.D., 615
Mather, G., 143
Mathy, R.M., 418
Matson, J.L., 252, 260
Matsumoto, D., 434, 461
Matt, G.E., 711
Matthen, M., 145, 173
Matthews, G., 369
Mattingley, J.B., 97
Mattys, S.L., 320
Matud, M.P., 614
Maurer, D., 142, 186, 452, 454
Mauro, R., 428
May, M., 143, 152, 156
May, R., 607
Mayer, J.D., 367, 368, 369
Mayer, R.E., 363, 381
Mayer, T.S., 325
Maylor, E.A., 302
Mayr, U., 299
Mazzella, R., 406
McAdams, D.P., 491
McAdams, D.T., 573
McAdams, S., 175
McAndrew, F.T., 406
McAuley, E., 619
McCabe, J., 287
McCall, W.V., 209
McCann, M., 224, 390
McCann, R.A., 698
McCarley, R.W., 212
McCarthy, D., 147
McCartney, K., 379
McClelland, D.C., 420, 422, 589
McClelland, J.L., 289
McClintock, M.K., 164
McClure, F., 712
McClure, R.K., 668
McConnell, J.V., 309
McCourt, M.E., 181
McCown, D., 624, 702
McCoy, K., 615
McCrae, R.R., 120, 494, 569, 570, 585
McCullough, M.E., 542
McCutcheon, R., 78
McDaniel, M.A., 302, 379, 485
McDermott, J.H., 159
McDermott, R., 129
McDowd, J.M., 485
McEvoy, S.P., 53
McEwen, B.S., 603
McFarlane, A., 126
McFarlane, A.C., 663

McFerran, B., 436
McGinty, D.J., 204
McGlaskan, T.H., 667
McGlinchey, J.B., 714
McGown, P.O., 601
McGrath, J.J., 671
McGregor, H.A., 421
McGue, M., 117
McGuffin, P., 113, 653, 667
McGuire, M.T., 136
McIntosh, D.N., 440
McKenna, P., 665, 665, 669
McKey, R., 382
McKimmie, B.M., 506, 507
McKinley, J.C., 585
McKown, C., 535
McMurran, M., 675
McNally, L., 321
McNally, R.J., 300, 307
McNeil, E.B., 673
McNulty, J.K., 492
McVey, G.L., 407, 409, 410
Meacham, J.A., 302
Meaney, M.J., 110, 111, 601
Medhus, S., 223
Medieros, J.A., 153
Meehl, P.E., 557
Meertens, R.W., 534
Meeus, W.H.J., 515
Megargee, E.I., 543
Meheula, I., 466
Meichenbaum, D., 694
Meilman, P.W., 488
Meisenberg, G., 384
Meleski, M.E., 450
Meltzoff, A.N., 453
Melzack, R., 164, 165
Mendel, G., 108
Mendel, R., 5
Mendelsohn, G.A., 527
Menezes, P.R., 47
Meng, X., 27
Menon, D.K., 194
Menon, R., 94
Menon, U., 434
Mental Health Commission of Canada, 632, 723
Menzies, R.G., 647
Meredith, N., 683
Merikle, P.M., 145, 146
Merrill, M.A., 359
Merrill, E.C., 463
Merskey, H., 663
Mersky, J., 471, 664
Merzenich, M.M., 159
Mesquita, B., 428, 434, 435
Messenger, J.C., 415

Messner, M., 508
Metcalfe, J., 253, 350
Metzler, J., 348, 349
Meunier, C.L., 397
Meyer, C.B., 597, 599
Meyer, J.H., 695
Meyer, T.A., 169
Meyerhof, W., 163
Michael, R.T., 412, 418, 524
Michaels, J., 510
Michel, C.M., 146
Michela, J.L., 563
Mignot, E., 209
Miklowitz, D.J., 652
Mikulincer, M., 470, 555, 611
Miles, C., 295
Miles, H.L., 331
Milgram, S., 513, 514, 515, 516
Millar, K.U., 505
Millar, M.G., 505
Miller, A.G., 515
Miller, B.C., 409
Miller, D.T., 34
Miller, G.A., 280, 286
Miller, G.E., 595, 599, 600
Miller, J.D., 198
Miller, J.G., 502, 536, 537
Miller, J.L., 375
Miller, K.F., 330
Miller, L., 475
Miller, L.E., 101
Miller, N.S., 424, 622
Miller, R., 198
Miller, S.D., 662, 663
Miller, T.Q., 607
Miller, T.W., 623
Miller, W., 62
Miller, W.R., 623
Milligan, C.E., 104
Milling, L.S., 231, 233
Millon, T., 637, 671, 673
Milne, A.B., 156
Milner, A.D., 44, 45
Milner, A.N., 28
Milner, B., 21, 90, 98, 277, 290, 310
Milner, P.M., 21, 91, 277
Milrod, B., 643
Miltenberger, R.G., 15
Milyavskaya, M.G., 399
Mineka, S., 646, 647, 651
Mioranzza, S., 451
Miranda, R. Jr., 613
Mischel, W., 253, 424, 554, 572, 573, 574, 577, 581, 582
Mishne, J., 706
Mitchell, D.B., 292
Mitchell, D.E., 186

Mitchell, K.J., 307
Mitchell, J.B., 91
Miyamoto, Y., 187
Moayedi, M., 165
Moe, A., 296
Moeller, G.H., 423
Moen, P., 494
Moffitt, T., 9
Molaison, H., 277
Molenberghs, P., 97
Molfese, D.L., 391
Molfese, V.J., 391
Molis, M., 327, 328
Möller, I., 546
Monahan, J.L., 524
Mondloch, C.J., 142
Monell Chemical Senses Center, 164
Money, J., 419
Moniz, E., 98, 719
Montgomery, H., 346
Monti-Bloch, L., 164
Mood Disorders Society of Canada, 658, 667
Moore, K.A., 488
Moore, M.K., 453
Moore, T.M., 541
Moorhead, G., 522
Moos, B.S., 699
Moos, R.H., 597, 609, 614, 699
Moran, G., 470
Moran, J.M., 500
Mordkoff, A., 443
Moreland, J.L., 32
Morewedge, C.K., 211
Morford, J.P., 325
Morgan, C., 670
Morgan, J., 271
Morgan, K., 303
Morgan, O., 225
Morgan, W., 628
Morgenstern, J., 624
Mori, D., 406
Morina, N., 247
Morita, Y., 47
Morrell, M.J., 414
Morris, D., 434
Morris, E.K., 278
Morris, E.L., 408
Morris, J.S., 266, 434, 510
Morris, R., 78
Morris, R.G.M., 311
Morrison, K., 710
Morrison, S., 90, 665
Morrongiello, B.A., 453
Morrow, G.R., 262
Morsella, E., 13
Moscovici, S., 513
Moskowitz, A., 613
Moss, C.S., 99
Moss, E., 557
Mousikou, P., 2

Mowrer, O.H., 258
Mowrer, R.R., 242
Muchinsky, P.M., 398
Muehlenkamp, J.J., 613
Mueller, P.A., 303
Mueser, K.T., 701
Muhlhauser, M., 27
Muir, D., 452, 454
Muir, D.W., 186
Mullane, C.M., 28
Muller, C.M. 104
Müller, U., 464
Mulligan, N.W., 292
Mumme, D.L., 426
Munafo, M.R., 571
Munoz, R.F., 723
Murdaugh, D.L., 404
Muris, P., 244, 245, 246
Murphy, J.M., 227
Murphy, S.L., 615
Murray, C., 374, 384
Murray, H.A., 550
Murray, R., 670
Murthy, P., 450
Muscatell, K.A., 603
Musch, J., 63
Musella, D.P., 62
Musicek, F.E., 159, 161
Mussen, P.H., 536
Myers, B., 308
Myers, C.R., 11, 29, 30
Mystkowski, J.L., 696
Myin-Germeys, I., 670

N
Na, E.Y., 502
Naci, L., 194
Nadeau, A., 115
Nadelson, C.C., 665
Nadler, A., 597
Naglieri, J.A., 361
Nairne, J.S., 289
Nakagawa, A., 231
Nakayama, K., 181
Nantel, G., 337
Napi, R.E., 414
Narrow, W.E., 642
Nass, C., 466
Nass, M., 466
Nathan, P.E., 637
National Association of Broadcasters, 145
National Center for Health Statistics, 618, 658
National Center on Addiction and Drug Abuse, 488
National Highway Traffic Safety Administration, 221

National Institute of Child Health and Human Development (NICHD), 471, 472
National Institute of Mental Health, 632, 651, 658, 663, 722
National Institutes of Health, 113, 301
National Safety Council, 221
National Sleep Foundation, 205, 206, 208
National Task Force, 409
National Television Violence Study, 543, 544
National Transportation Safety Board, 517
National Weight Control Registry, 409
Natsoulas, T., 192
Natural Sciences and Engineering Research Council (NSERC), 63
Naumann, P.P., 583
Navarro, A.M., 711
Naveh, B.M., 285
Nederkoorn, C., 410
Needham, A., 456
Neely, J.H., 300
Neisser, U., 279, 293, 376
Neitz, J., 151
Neitz, M., 151
Nelson, C.A., 282, 480
Nelson, D., 524
Nelson, L.D., 63
Nelson, T.D., 532
Nemeroff, C.B., 646
Neuberger, H., 324
Neuhaus, I.M., 508
Neumäker, K.J., 648
Neuschatz, J.S., 500
New York Times, 604, 665, 666
Newcomb, M.D., 229
Newcombe, N.S., 328
Newell, A., 340, 347
Newlin, D.B., 227
Newman, D.L., 22, 677
Newmark, C.S., 360
Newport, E.L., 325, 327
Newson, R.S., 487
Newton, I., 348
Nezami, E., 585, 589
Nezlek, J.B., 28, 657
Nezu, A.M., 720
Nezworski, M.T., 587
Ng, R., 430

Nguyen, P.V., 311
Nichols, P.L., 392
Nickerson, R.S., 285, 298, 299
Nicks, S.D., 64
Nicoladis, E., 326
Nida, S., 40, 61
Nigg, J.T., 555, 675
Nijenhuis, E., 662
Niles, S., 423
Nilsson, L.G., 292, 294
Nirenberg, S., 168
Nisbett, R.E., 19, 26, 187, 377, 384, 385, 500, 501, 502
Niv, M.Y., 163
Nixon, M.K., 613
Nixon, R., 520
Nolen-Hoeksema, S., 28, 653, 657
Noll, J., 364
Noll, S.M., 649
Nolte, J., 70
Norcross, J.C., 247, 624, 683, 712
Norenzayan, A., 19
Norman, K.A., 282
Normann, R.A., 168
Nornstein, R., 86
North, M., 697
Norton, G.R., 644
Norton, M.I., 211
Nosek, B.A., 49
Nosko, A., 49
Nossal, C.J.V., 144
Nottebohm, F., 331
Nouchi, R., 289
Nunn, J.A., 143
Nye, R.D., 566

O
Oatley, K., 651
Obama, B., 129
O'Brien, C.P., 219
Ockene, J.K., 624
O'Connor, D.B., 541
O'Connor, K., 644
O'Connor, M., 145
Odbert, H.S., 567
O'Donohue, W., 599
Oehman, A., 172
Ogawa, T., 196
Oh, T., 665
Ohayon, M.M., 210
Ohbuchi, K., 541
Ohira, K., 113
Öhman, A., 262, 427, 646, 647
Okazaki, S., 705
O'Keefe, G.S., 466
O'Keefe, J., 266, 267
Okubo, C., 196
Olds, J., 21, 91
O'Leary, A., 621

Oleson, T., 166
Oliver, M.B., 436
Olivier, L., 608
Ollendick, T.H., 244, 245, 246, 584
Olsen, J.A., 73
Olson, E.J., 210
Olson, J.M., 122, 504, 505, 507
Olson, M.A., 531
Oltman, P.K., 388
O'Neil, J.A., 662
O'Neil, K., 450
Ono, Y., 648
Onyper, S., 303
Oppenheimer, D.M., 303
Opriş, D., 698
Orbuch, T.L., 492
Ormel, J., 598
Orne, M.T., 230, 233
Orr, A.L., 150
Orsini, A., 386
Orth, U., 656
Ortiz, J., 674
Ortiz-Catalan, M., 698
Ortmann, A., 64
Osland, J.A., 414, 417
Ost, J., 294, 704
Öst, L.G., 702
Ostacher, M.J., 658
Ostlund, S.B., 397
Ostrovsky, Y., 188
Otero, M., 176
Otis, A., 360
Ouimette, P.C., 625
Overton, W.F., 461
Overy, K., 390
Owen, A.M., 194
Owen, P.R., 406
Oyserman, D., 19

P
Pablos, A., 176
Packard, E., 482
Paffenbarger, R.S., Jr., 619
Pagano, B., 306
Page, S., 505
Paiva, T., 205, 206
Paivio, A., 287, 297
Paivio, S.C., 691
Pajer, K., 661
Pal, S., 110
Palfai, T., 228
Palmer, D.C., 239
Palmer, J.A., 396
Palmer, J.C., 306
Palmer, L.K., 396
Palmer, S.E., 156
Palmere, M., 285, 296
Pan, C-Y., 560, 562
Pandarinath, C., 168
Panek, P.E., 480

Panksepp, J., 427, 431
Pansu, P., 518
Pantev, C., 169, 390
Papanicolaou, A.C., 438
Paparrigopoulos, T.J., 210
Papirman, Y., 501
Paquette, D., 474
Parapsychology Association, 62
Paris, J.P., 638, 665, 672, 673, 676
Park, C., 606
Park, D.C., 296, 297
Park, L.E., 564
Parke, R.D., 449
Parker, I., 574
Parker, K.C.H., 493
Parker, K.J., 601
Parkinson, A.J., 169
Parrott, A.C., 224
Parsons, T.D., 698
Partain, C., 45
Pascuzzo, K., 557
Passmore, H.A., 16
Pasteur, L., 644
Patil, P.G., 167
Patnoe, S., 535
Patterson, D.R., 231
Patterson, F.G.P., 331
Patterson, G.R., 472, 542
Patton, D., 226
Pauk, W., 32
Paul, G.L., 701
Paulhus, D.L., 43, 48
Paulson, T., 334
Paunonen, S.V., 570
Pavlov, I.P., 14, 83, 240, 241, 242, 243, 268, 336
Payne, B.K., 554
Pea, R., 466
Peacock, K.W., 112, 113
Pear, J., 700, 701
Pearlin, L.I., 614
Pearsall, M.J., 520
Pearson, J.M., 263
Pederson, N.L., 121
Pederson, D.R., 470
Pedrotti, F.L., 150
Pedrotti, J.T., 16
Pedrotti, L.S., 150
Peek, K., 356–357
Pelé, M., 269
Pelham, W.E., Jr., 44
Pelletier, D.L., 456
Pemberton, J., 224
Pendlebury, S.T., 89
Penfield, W., 82, 83, 84, 309
Peng, K., 19
Pennycook, G., 337
Penrod, B., 398
Peper, J.S., 479

Peplau, L.A., 420
Pepler, D.J., 47
Perani, D., 329, 645
Percy, M., 391
Perdue, C.W., 534
Perenboom, M.J., 84
Perlman, M., 333
Perls, F.S., 690
Pernollet, J.C., 163
Perrachione, T.K., 390
Perrett, D.I., 526
Perruchet, P., 267
Perry, M.V., 432
Pert, C.B., 430
Petermann, F., 652
Peters, E., 337, 338
Peters, J.C., 409
Peterson, C., 302, 606
Peterson, D., 138
Peters, K.R., 63
Peterson, L.R., 281
Peterson, M.J., 281
Petitto, L.A., 329
Petrides, K.V., 369
Petrides, M., 98
Petrill, S., 119
Petrosini, L., 487
Pettigrew, T.F., 534, 535
Pettit, M., 164
Petty, R.E., 506, 507, 508
Pezdek, K., 293, 306
Pezzuti, L., 386
Pfeffer, K., 502
Pfiffner, L.J., 674
Pfungst, O., 268
Phelps, E.A., 312, 428, 532
Phillips, A.G., 91, 565
Phillips, J.G., 195
Phillips, L.H., 302
Phillips, L.W., 283
Phillips, M., 384, 385, 695
Phillips, N.H., 208
Phillipson, S.N., 390
Piaget, J., 17, 457, 458, 459, 460, 461, 462, 464, 475, 482, 484
Pickering, A.D., 571
Pickett, J.M., 320
Pickrell, J.E., 278, 308
Pierce, G.R., 438
Piffer, L., 268
Pila, E., 406
Pilbeam, D., 23, 315
Pilcher, J.J., 205
Pillard, R.C., 419
Pinel, J.P., 400
Pinel, J.P.J., 400, 403, 541
Pinker, S., 315, 323
Piper, A., 663, 664

Pitel, S., 622
Pitman, R.K., 598, 647
Pitt, B., 69
Pittenger, D.J., 64
Pitts, M.A., 171
Piven, J., 679
Pizzaro, D.A., 369
Plant, E.A., 536
Plantinga, J., 455
Platt, M.L., 263
Plaud, D.M., 258
Plaud, J.J., 258
Plaut, D.C., 290
Ploner, M., 165
Plomin, R., 21, 115, 117, 119, 121, 122, 373, 379, 380, 391, 571
Plotkin, S.A., 450
Plourde, M-A., 237
Plous, S., 65
Plutchik, R., 432, 433
Polat, U., 150
Polich, J., 230
Pollack, G.S., 157
Pollack, I., 320
Polson, P.G., 285
Pompili, M., 675, 716
Pool, R., 94, 184
Poremba, A., 677
Poremba, M., 677
Pornari, C.D., 542
Porter, J.E., 659
Porter, N.P., 533
Porter, S., 306
Posada, G., 470
Posluszny, D.M., 618, 620
Posner, M.I., 18, 101, 187
Posthuma, D., 377, 381
Postma, A., 485
Postman, L.J., 283, 299, 533
Postmes, T., 519
Potter, M.C., 280
Poulin-Dubois, D., 474
Poulin-Lord, M.P., 97
Powell, M.C., 505
Power, M., 707
Powers, M.B., 698
Powers, T.K., 506
Powley, T.L., 400
Prapavessis, H., 505
Press, D.Z., 145
Pressley, M., 33
Pressman, J.D., 719
Pressman, S.D., 605
Preti, G., 164
Price, R.A., 409, 415
Price, T.S., 21
Pridmore, R.W., 154
Prigerson, H., 598
Priluck, R., 245
Prinz, J., 195

Prislin, R., 504
Pritchard, R.D., 256
Pritchard, R.M., 148
Probst, L.R., 726
Prochaska, J., 616, 617
Prosen, H., 655
Pruden, S.M., 323
Psotka, J., 299, 300
Public Health Agency of Canada, 621
Pugh, G.E., 87
Pull, C.B., 704
Punamäki, R.L., 546
Putnam, F.W., 234, 662, 663
Putri, M., 251
Pylyshyn, Z.W., 349
Pyszczynski, T., 295, 565

Q
Quera-Salva, M.A., 201
Quinn, P.C., 454
Quinsey, V.L., 543

R
Raaijmakers, Q.A.W., 515
Rabier, J.R., 494
Rachlin, H., 424
Rachman, S., 245, 696
Rachman, S.J., 644, 694, 696
Radcliffe, R.A., 227
Radel, R., 146
Radin, D.I., 62
Radoeva, P.D., 197
Rahe, R.H., 593
Rahman, Q., 419
Raichle, M.E., 86, 101, 213
Raiford, S.E., 373
Raine, A., 98, 541, 542, 673, 674, 675
Rajan, K., 290
Rakfeldt, J., 485
Rako, S., 164
Ramachandran, V.S., 143
Ramey, C., 383
Ramey, C.T., 382, 383
Ramey, S., 383
Ramon y Cajal, S., 73
Ramsay, R., 659
Ramus, F., 333
Rance, M., 466
Randi, J., 62
Rangmar, J., 101
Rankin, C., 238
Ranson, S.W., 403
Rao, P.A., 701
Raphling, D.L., 543
Rapoport, J.L., 645
Rapson, R.L., 529

Raskin, 27
Rasmussen, A.M., 724
Ratcliff, R., 485
Rauscher, F.H., 58
Raven, B.H., 522
Raven, J., 377
Ravussin, E., 403, 409
Rawlinson, G., 6
Ray, O.S., 73, 229
Ray, W.J., 59
Raymundo, M.M., 508
Rayner, K., 7
Rayner, R., 244
Raz, A., 233
Rechtschaffen, A., 208
Rees, G., 171
Reese, E., 302
Regan, D.T., 539
Regan, P.C., 528
Reger, G.M., 698
Regier, D.A., 651
Rehm, J., 622
Reibel, D., 624
Reich, T.W., 672
Reichl, A.J., 533
Reid, A.K., 264
Reilly, T., 200
Reinburg, C.E., 665
Reinders, 664
Reips, U-D., 49
Reisberg, D., 195, 281, 289
Remer, P.P., 707
Remland, M.S., 511
Rendell, P.G., 302
Rensink, R.A., 148
Renzulli, J.S., 389
Repous, G., 282
Reppucci, N.D., 383
Reppy, W., 65
Rescorla, R.A., 258, 267
Resick, P., 597
Resnick, S.M., 480
Retting, R.A., 260
Revell, V.L., 200
Rey, J.M., 718
Reyes, T.M., 21
Reynolds, D.K., 496
Rezayof, A., 295
Rhea, P., 679
Rhee, S.H., 121
Rhodes, G., 526
Rhodes, L., 23
Rice, K., 142
Rice, L.N., 688
Richard, S., 242
Richards, F.A., 485
Richardson, D.R., 525
Rideout, V.J., 466
Ridley-Johnson, R., 456
Ridout, B., 511
Riebe, D., 616
Reibel, D., 702
Ridder, D.T.D., 404

Riefer, D.M., 300
Riesen, A.R., 186
Rilling, M., 309
Rinaldi, A.E.M., 47
Ringelmann, M., 519
Rips, L.J., 335, 340
Ritblatt, S.N., 679
Ritchie, C.W., 301
Rivera-Tovar, L.A., 285
Rizzo, A.A., 698
Rizzo, S., 247
Rizzolatti, G., 97, 271, 333
Roberts, B.W., 550, 571
Roberts, R.J., 104
Roberts, T.A., 406
Roberts, W.A., 268
Robins, L.N., 651
Robins, R.W., 15, 565
Robinson, D., 92, 645, 655
Robinson, D.T., 44
Robitaille, R., 71
Robles, T.F., 610
Robson, J., 152
Rodgers, J.E., 306
Rodin, J., 409, 410, 539, 620, 650
Roelofs, K., 662
Roeser, R.W., 612, 613
Rogers, C.R., 16, 559, 564, 565, 566, 682, 688, 689, 690, 712
Roggman, L.A., 526
Rohrer, J.H., 511
Rohsenow, D.J., 229
Roland, P.E., 27
Roll, S., 212
Rollnick, S., 623
Rolls, B.J., 407, 408
Rolls, E.T., 21, 45, 151, 310
Romeo, R.D., 603
Rompre, P.P., 91
Ron, M.A., 85
Ronquillo, J., 532
Roos, S., 496
Roosevelt, F., 49
Roper, J., 436
Rosato, T., 631, 632
Rosch, E., 26, 328, 335
Roscoe, J.A., 262
Rose, G.M., 208
Rose, G.S., 623
Rose, S.A., 463
Rosen, C.S., 619
Rosen, H., 607
Rosenbaum, A., 541
Rosenbaum, M.E., 524, 716, 717
Rosenbloom, T., 195
Rosenfarb, I.S., 670
Rosenfeld, H.M., 511
Rosenhan, D., 639

Rosenhan, D.L., 666
Rosenman, R.H., 606
Rosenthal, N.E., 200
Rosenthal, R., 433
Rosenzweig, M.R., 9, 102, 263
Rosenzweig, S., 554, 708
Ross, C., 49
Ross, C.A., 663
Ross, L., 500, 501
Ross, M., 26
Ross, R.J., 307
Rossell, S.L., 322, 323
Roth, D., 414
Roth, T.L., 111
Rothbart, M.K., 18, 101, 187
Rothbaum, B.O., 697
Rotheram-Borus, M.J., 621
Rothkopf, E.Z., 296
Rotter, J.B., 573, 574, 575
Rotton, J., 541
Rousseau, J-J., 382
Rouw, R., 143
Rowden, L.J., 541
Rowe, D.C., 120
Rowell, A., 331
Rowley, J.T., 211
Rozin, P., 406, 407
Rubin, D.C., 293, 294
Rubin, R.T., 27, 653, 654
Ruble, D.N., 474
Rubonis, A.V., 597
Rudatsikira, E., 545
Ruffman, R., 462, 464
Ruger, A.T., 482
Ruiz, F.J., 704
Ruiz, J.C., 286, 296
Rumbaugh, D.M., 331
Rumelhart, D.E., 289
Rumstein, M.O., 414
Runquist, W.N., 300
Ruscio, M.G., 651
Rush, A.J., 717
Rushton, J.P., 378, 379, 384, 540
Russell, D., 502
Russell, J.A., 434
Russell, J.C., 648
Russell, P.A., 187, 188
Rusting, C.L., 295
Rutter, D.R., 505
Rutter, M.L., 9, 674, 679
Ryan, L., 295
Ryan, R.M., 399, 564
Ryder, N., 321
Ryle, A., 13

S
Saad, L., 501
Sabido, M., 272
Saccuzzo, D.P., 370

Sachse, R., 690
Sacks, O., 69, 95, 96, 99, 173, 188
Sack, R.L., 199, 201
Sadler, P., 233
Sadoski, M., 287
Saffran, E.M., 95
Sagan, Carl, 1
Sagi, A., 426
Saito, A., 269
Sakellaropoulo, M., 567
Saklofske, D.H., 369
Saladin, M.E., 269
Saling, L.L., 195
Salovey, P., 367, 368, 369, 539
Salthouse, T.A., 485
Saltzman, A.L., 516
Salvatore, J.E., 9
Sana, F., 196
Sanderson, W.C., 647, 699
Sandler, J., 699
Sanes, J.R., 156
Sanz, G., 163
Sanzio, R., 180
Sarason, B.R., 33, 420
Sarason, I.G., 33, 272, 420, 539, 540
Saremi, M., 204
Sarman, I., 451
Sasseville, A., 200
Sataloff, J., 161
Satcher, D., 27, 652, 667, 677
Sato, S., 20
Sattel, H., 688
Sauer, N., 245
Saunders, B., 65
Savage, P.J., 409
Savage-Rumbaugh, E.S., 332
Sawle, G.V., 645
Sayer, J., 53
Saxena, S., 645
Scarr, S., 118, 379, 381
Schemer, J.A., 122
Schaal, B., 452
Schacter, D.L., 290, 291, 292, 304
Schacter, S., 409, 440, 441, 443, 444, 523, 617
Schaefer, H.S., 611
Schaie, K.W., 264, 364, 486
Schaller, M., 18, 510
Schatzberg, A.F., 76, 601, 715, 716, 717
Scheele, D., 562
Scheff, T.J., 722
Scheier, M.F., 554, 572, 582, 606

Schellenberg, E.G., 58, 540
Schellenberg, G.D., 679
Schenck, C.H., 210
Scherer, K.R., 425, 428, 435
Schermer, J.A., 381
Schibler, U., 199
Schiff, M., 120, 381
Schiff, W., 164
Schimanski, L.A., 311
Schimmack, U., 570
Schizophrenia Society of Canada, 665
Schlegel, A., 478
Schlesinger, L.B., 640
Schmajuk, N.A., 250, 269
Schmaling, K.B., 714
Schmid, D.A., 402
Schmidt, F.L., 362, 374
Schmied, L.A., 605
Schmithorst, V.J., 379
Schmitt, C., 515
Schmitt, D.P., 527
Schnall, S., 436
Schneider, A., 212
Schneider, W., 464
Schneider Helmert, D., 209
Schneidman, 658, 659
Schoen, L.M., 287
Scholte, H.S., 143
Schonert-Reichl, K.A., 612
Schooler, C., 614
Schoop, V.M., 104
Schraw, G., 350
Schul, Y., 508
Schulz, R., 496
Schuman, R., 652
Schulze, B., 325
Schunk, D.H., 421
Schüssler, P., 402, 410
Schwartz, B.L., 300
Schwartz, L.M., 104
Schwartz, M.F., 95
Schwartz, N., 26
Schwartz, R., 403
Schwartz, R.M., 300
Schwarz, J., 172
Schwarzer, R., 614
Schweder, R.A., 434
Schweinhart, L.J., 383
ScienceDaily, 169
Scoboria, A., 232
Scott, T.R., 163
Scoville, W.B., 21, 90, 310
Sears, D.O., 504
Sears, R., 534
Seehagen, S., 303
Seeley, R.J., 400, 402, 403

Seeley, T.D., 331
Seeman, J., 691
Segerdahl, P., 332
Segerstrom, S.C., 599, 600, 606
Seilabipour, N., 165
Sekaquaptewa, D., 511
Sekuler, R., 181
Selby, E.A., 675
Self, E.A., 397
Seligman, M.E.P., 50, 51, 261, 262, 572, 606, 627, 628, 629, 630, 651, 652, 655, 656, 666, 683, 711
Selye, H., 591, 593, 595
Sergios, P.A., 535
Serpell, R., 120, 381, 385
Serrano, A., 71
Servos, P., 94
Sexton, M.M., 615
Seynaeva, L., 306
Shaffer, D., 507
Shaffer, D.R., 460, 461
Shair, H.N., 94
Shakespeare, W., 679
Shanab, M.E., 516
Shanahan, T.L., 199
Shanks, D.R., 238
Shapiro, C.M., 207
Shapiro, J.R., 504
Shariat, S.V., 165
Sharif, N., 45
Sharkey, K.M., 205
Sharpless, B.A., 13
Shaughnessy, 4
Shaver, P.R., 470, 555, 611
Shaw, G.L., 58
Shaw, J.A., 606
Shaywitz, B.A., 101
Shead, N.W., 272
Sheehan, P.W., 232
Sheldon, K.M., 399, 491, 615
Shepard, R.N., 348, 349
Shepherd, C., 301
Shepherd, G., 104
Sherif, M., 511, 534
Sherman, P.W., 135, 136
Sherrington, C., 73
Sherwood, L., 78
Shiffrin, R.M., 278, 280
Shinar, O., 602
Shinozuka, K., 269
Shneidman, E.S., 658, 659
Shoda, Y., 556, 557, 572, 573, 574, 581, 584
Shorey, H.S., 557
Short, M.A., 205, 206
Shorter, E., 98, 717, 719
Shostak, M., 130
Shuai, L., 316

Shultz, K.S., 494
Sia, C.L., 520
Siegel, A., 540, 541
Siegel, S., 219, 224, 269
Siegle, G.J., 695
Siegler, R.S., 463
Siever, L.J., 541
Sieverding, M., 505
Sigala, N., 347
Silbersweig, D.A., 669
Silver, N., 531
Silveri, M.M., 480
Silvers, J.A., 436
Silvia, P.J., 565
Simha, A., 466
Simels, B.A., 293
Simkin, L.R., 619
Simmons, J.P., 63
Simmons, J.V., 259
Simms, 641
Simner, J., 142
Simon, C., 70, 82, 89, 92
Simon, H.A., 41, 288, 315, 340, 346, 347
Simons, D.J., 171
Simons, J.S., 310
Simonton, D.K., 345, 389
Simpaio, E., 167
Simpson, B., 64
Singer, J., 302
Singer, J.L., 300, 584
Singer, T., 486
Singh, R., 502
Singh-Manous, A., 487
Sinigaglia, C., 97
Sisco, S.M., 150
Siu, O., 493
Skanes, H.E., 146
Skinner, B.F., 14–15, 17, 83, 248, 249, 255, 259, 263, 264, 324
Sklar, L.S., 600
Skodol, A.E., 638
Skoric, M., 546
Skowronski, J.J., 503
Skoyles, J.R., 95
Slater, C.L., 491
Slavney, P.R., 661
Sloan, D.M., 613, 614
Sloboda, J.A., 148
Slocum, S.K., 701
Slonim, N., 324
Slotnick, S.D., 350
Slovic, P., 337, 338, 342
Small, D.M., 163
Smalley, S.L., 677
Smart, L., 564
Smeets, M.A.M., 649
Smeets, P.A., 404, 405
Smilek, D., 171
Smith, A.T., 156
Smith, B.D., 552
Smith, C., 208
Smith, C.A., 428

Smith, C.L., 62, 487
Smith, C.S., 199
Smith, D., 272
Smith, E.R., 335
Smith, G.T., 637
Smith, J.W., 624
Smith, K.M., 678
Smith, M.A., 710
Smith, M.J., 224
Smith, M.L., 98, 705,
Smith, P.B., 513
Smith, P.K., 47
Smith, R.E., 420, 573, 574, 581, 593, 609
Smith, R.S., 604
Smith, S.M., 296, 525
Smith, T., 705
Smithson, J., 493
Smock, P.J., 493
Smoll, F.L., 564
Snow, M.E., 474
Snowden, L.R., 649
Snowden, R.J., 156
Snyder, C.R., 16, 557, 573, 628, 707
Snyder, F., 211
Snyder, M., 165, 525
Soares, J.J., 646
Soares, J.J.F., 262
Sober, E., 24
Social Sciences and Humanities Research Council (SSHRC), 63, 64
Sodhi, M., 669, 674
Sohn, C.H., 200
Soler, M.J., 286, 296
Solms, M., 212
Solomon, R., 622
Solomon, R.L., 258
Sommer, I.E.C., 322
Son, L.K., 350
Song, H., 529
Sorenson, S.B., 599
Sorrentino, R.M., 508
Soto, K., 591
Sotres-Bayon, F., 429
Soussignan, R., 440, 452
South, S.C., 120
Southwick, S.M., 605
Sowell, E.R., 455, 479
Spanos, N.P., 232, 234, 663, 664
Sparks, G.G., 62
Spear, L.P., 479
Spearman, C., 362
Spears, R., 519
Specht, J., 550
Spector, P.E., 541
Speisman, J., 443
Spence, M.J., 453
Spencer, H., 139
Spencer, S.J., 534, 535
Sperdin, H.F., 146

Sperling, G., 171, 278, 279
Sperry, R.W, 99
Spiegel, D., 662, 663
Spiegler, M.D., 696
Spielberg, S., 343
Spierer, L., 146
Spiers, H.J., 310
Spina, R., 26
Spinath, F.M., 117, 373, 379, 380, 391
Spitzer, R.L., 639, 643
Sprafkin, J.N., 272, 536
Sprecher, S., 411, 527, 528
Springer, J., 107–108
Springer, S., 101
Spurzheim, J.C., 22
Squire, L.H., 214
Squire, L.R., 290, 310
Srivastava, S., 49, 569
Sroufe, L., 468
St.-Lawrence, J.S., 597
Staats, H., 260
Staddon, J.E.F., 264
Stahl, S.M., 715, 716
Stalder, D.R., 507
Stall, R., 221
Stanford Sleep Disorders Center, 209
Staniloiu, A., 663
Stanley, B.G., 403
Stanton,. S.J., 129
Stark, E., 411
Stasiewkz, P.R., 219
Statistics Canada, 205, 220, 325, 408, 416, 471, 473, 493, 494, 583, 592, 600, 615, 619, 622, 658
Staub, E., 518
Staudinger, U.M., 347
Stearns, S., 124
Steele, C.M., 221, 534, 535, 565
Steeves, J.K., 145
Stein, D.J., 642
Stein, M., 329
Stein, M.B., 645
Steinberg, L., 472, 481
Steiner, J.E., 453
Steingrueber H-J., 262
Stel, M., 524
Stella, N., 226
Stellar, E., 403
Stephan, W.G., 535
Steptoe, A., 575, 605
Sterman, M.B., 204
Stern, M., 374
Stern, W., 359–360
Sternberg, R.J., 337, 345, 357, 361, 363, 365, 366, 371, 377, 389, 528

Stetson, B.A., 601
Steuber, D., 98
Stevens, S.J., 621
Stewart, J., 227, 397
Stewart, J.O., 656
Stewart, T.L., 499, 534
Stice, 408
Stickgold, R., 203, 208
Stigler, J.F., 330
Stiles, W., 687
Stillerman, B., 466
Stine-Morrow, E.A.L., 487
Stockhorst, U., 262
Stone, A.A., 584
Stone, J., 78, 506
Stone, K., 550
Storandt, M., 619
Storms, M.D., 501
Stormshak, E.A., 252, 542
Strack, F., 440
Strasburger, H., 664
Stratton, G., 186
Strauss, E., 370
Strawbridge, W.J., 608
Strayer, D.A., 61
Strayer, D.L., 56, 57
Streppa, M.L., 454
Stricker, E.M., 401
Striedter, G.F., 87, 125
Strober, M., 650
Strong, R.E., 200
Strosahl, K.D., 659
Strube, M.J., 606
Strunk, D.R., 27
Strunkard, A., 409
Strupp, H.H., 711, 712, 726
Stryer, L., 152
Studte, S., 303
Stukas, A.A., 540
Stunkard, A.J., 409
Suarez, L.M., 660
Sue, D., 705
Sue, D.W., 705
Sue, S., 705, 706
Sueur, C., 269
Suggs, R., 415
Suh, E.M., 19
Sumsion, T., 690
Suinn, R.M., 565
Suls, J., 598
Suls, J.M., 602, 614, 616, 619
Sun, M.-K., 595
Surbeck, M., 136
Suomi, S.J., 470
Super, C.M., 238
Super, D.E., 493
Sussman, N.M., 511
Sutherland, R., 306
Sutton, S.K., 430
Suzuki, L., 377

Svirsky, M.A., 324
Swalehe, R.M., 274
Swain, I., 453
Swait, J., 508
Swann, A.C., 624
Swann, W.B., 560
Swann, W.B., Jr., 565
Swanston, M., 175
Swartz, C., 718
Swinson, R.P., 246
Syka, J., 159
Szelenberger, W., 210
Szeszeko, P.R., 645
Szkrybalo, J., 474
Szymusiak, R., 204

T
Tait, R.W., 269
Tajfel, H., 533, 534
Takahashi, Y., 663
Tal-Or, N., 501
Talarico, J.M., 294
Talbot, D., 45
Tallal, P., 390
Talwar, V., 464
Tamagawa, R., 614
Tamres, L.K., 614
Tan, U., 387
Tanaka-Matsumi, J.,
    228, 648, 662, 671
Tappy, L., 403
Tarr, M.J., 157
Tasman, A., 715
Tatlisumak, T., 82
Taylor, 242
Taylor, C., 453
Taylor, D.A., 526
Taylor, R.D., 724
Taylor, S.E., 433, 565,
    593, 595, 597, 599,
    600, 601, 605, 607,
    613, 614, 616, 618,
    620, 623, 625, 628
Taylor-Butts, A., 416
Teachman, B.A., 408
Teasdale, J.D., 295
Tees, R.C., 95
Teghtsoonian, R., 147
Theide, K.W., 351, 352
Tellegen, A., 117, 121
Tenenbaum, H.R.,
    462, 474
Teoh, S.W., 324
Teresi, M., 70
Terkel, J., 259
Terman, L.M., 359, 360
Terracciano, A., 48
Terrace, H.S., 331
Terrier, L., 518
Tesser, A., 507
Teyber, E., 712
Tharp, R.G., 32, 33
Thatcher, M., 205
Thayer, R., 161

Theriault, G., 115
Thibaut, J.W., 526
Thiede, K.W., 33, 351,
    352
Thoits, P., 593
Thomas, A., 467
Thomas, C., 569
Thomas, C.D., 649
Thomas, L., 163
Thomas, S.L., 510
Thomas, W.P., 326
Thompson, J.G., 429
Thompson, P.M., 45
Thompson, R.A., 477
Thompson, R.F., 312
Thompson, W.F., 58
Thomson, D.M., 294
Thomson, D.M., 302
Thomson, J., 434
Thomson, J.B., 227
Thorndike, E.L., 14, 83,
    248, 264
Thornhill, R., 132, 135
Thorpe, S.J., 172
Thorsdottir, F., 49
Thunberg, M., 432
Thurstone, L.L., 363
Tice, D.M., 127
Tilker, H.A., 516
Till, B.D., 245
Tinbergen, N., 540
Tinsley-Li, S., 636
Titchener, E., 11
Titus, L., 510
Tix, A.P., 602
Tizard, B., 471
Tobin, S.J., 508
Todd, K.J., 71
Todorov, A., 146
Tollefson, G.D., 653
Tollestrup, P., 307
Tolman, E.C., 265, 266,
    268, 269, 270
Toma, C., 4
Tomarken, A.J., 430
Tomasello, M., 537
Tomkins, S.S., 432,
    433, 434
Tomlin, L., 631
Toneatto, T., 702
Tonigan, J.S., 624
Tooby, J., 23, 124,
    125, 136
Topitzes, J., 471
Torgerson, S., 122,
    671, 676
Tornick, J.K., 269
Törnros, J., 61
Torrey, E.F., 723
Torwin, 648
Trainor, L.J., 390, 455
Tran, J., 144
Trapnell, P.D., 48
Travers, K.R., 224

Treffner, P.J., 195
Tremblay, A., 115
Tremblay, L.K., 654
Tremblay, M.A., 399
Triandis, H.C., 19,
    502, 565
Trimble, M., 662
Triplett, N., 18, 509
Tripp, D., 26
Trivers, R.L., 130,
    131, 136
Trobst, K.K., 541
Troll, L.E., 480
Trommsdorff, G., 615
Tropp, L.R., 535
Truell, A.D., 49
Truscott, S.D., 376
Trzesniewski, K.H., 561
Tsai, J.L., 615
Tsang, C.D., 455
Tse, D., 287
Tseng, W.S., 657
Tsien, J.Z., 280
Tsujimoto, S., 282
Tuchin, M., 306
Tucker, P., 528
Tucker, V.A., 151
Tulving, E., 284, 290,
    294, 299, 300
Tung, M., 259
Tuomi, 22
Turk, D.C., 165
Turnbull, C.M., 184
Turner, D.A., 167
Turner, J.C., 534
Turner, M.E., 521
Turner, M.J., 693
Turner, S.M., 642
Tusing, K.J., 518
Tversky, A., 337, 341,
    342
Tversky, B., 306
Twain, M., 236
Tye, M., 287
Tyler, C.W., 181
Tyler, T.R., 539
Tyson, G.A., 502
Tzuriel, D., 377

U
U.S. Public Health
    Service, 615
Underwood, B.J., 296,
    299
Unsworth, G., 546
Urry, H.L., 603
Usrey, W.M., 89
Uttal, D.H., 328
Uttl, B., 485

V
Vaccarino, F.M., 678
Vakil, E., 82
Valberg, A., 152, 154

Valent, P., 597, 598
Valiente, C., 537
Vallone, R.P., 344
Valsiner, J., 478
Valyear, K.F., 45
Valverde, C., 113
Van Damme, I., 306
Van de Castle, R., 211,
    212
van de Rijt, A., 526
van de Ruit, M., 84
van der Hart, O., 662
van der Laan, L.N., 405
Van der Maas, H.L.J., 63
Van Goozen, S., 674
Van Houten, R., 260
van Ijzendoorn, M., 555
van Kesteren, M.T.R.,
    288
Van Koningsbruggen,
    G.M., 524
van Lange, P.A.M., 536
Van Overschelde,
    J.P., 283
van Praag, H.M., 669
van Strien, N.M., 310
Van Yperen, N., 421, 422
Van Zomeren, A.H., 89
Vandell, D.L., 472
VanItallie, T.B., 410
Vargha-Khadem, F., 290
Varney, N.R., 104
Vasilaki, E.I., 623
Vaughan, P.W., 274
Vaughn, J.L., 33
Vaughn, 6, 670
Vazire, S., 49, 583
Vecera, S.P., 161, 171
Velotis, C.M., 644
Venter, J.C., 110
Ventura, D.F., 151
Verbalis, J.G., 401
Verbeek, G., 175
Verghese, P., 147
Verma, J., 20
Vernon, P.A., 122, 129
Verplanken, B., 16
Vésteinsdóttir, V., 49
Vetter, H.J., 666
Vicary, J., 145
Viemeroe, V., 543
Viergever, M.A., 405
Vigor, J., 164
Villarreal, D.M., 299
Vincent, N., 205
Vitaliano, P.P., 600
Vittengl, J.R., 694
Vo, M.L.H., 171
Vogels, T.P., 290
Vogels, W.W.A., 302
Voigt, H., 539
Vollmer, T.R., 701
Volta, R.D., 322
Voltaire, 297

von Bekesy, G., 161
von Frisch, K., 331
Von Hehn, C.A., 144
von Osten, W., 268
von Senden, M., 188
von Helmholtz, H., 153,
    154
Vormfelde, S.V., 122
Vouimba, R.M., 601
Vral, A., 125
Vrij, A., 542
Vuong, Q.C., 157
Vurpillot, E., 463
Vygotsky, L.S., 26, 462
Vyse, S., 7

W
Wachs, T.D., 263
Wadden, T.A., 407, 620
Wade, C., 412
Wade, N.J., 175
Wade, P., 706
Wagenmakers, E-J., 63
Wagner, A.R., 267
Wagstaff, G.F., 230, 232
Wahlsten, D., 109, 112
Wahlsten, V.S., 451
Wainwright, P.E., 410
Wakefield, A., 679
Wakefield, J.C., 632, 633
Wakefield, M., 451
Waldman, I.D., 121
Waldvogel, B., 664
Walen, S.R., 414
Walk, R.D., 184
Walker, E.F., 670
Walker, M.P., 207, 208
Walker, P.L., 633
Wall, P.D., 165
Wallace, P., 401
Wallace, W.L., 485
Wallbott, H., 428
Walle, E.A., 456
Wallenius, M., 546
Wallentin, M., 101
Waller, G., 649
Wallis, D.J., 408
Wallis, T.S., 147
Wallston, K.A., 575, 602,
    614, 616, 619
Walsh, B.T., 650
Walster, E., 524
Walter, G., 718
Walter, M., 27
Walther, E., 245
Wampold, B.E., 530
Wamsley, E.J., 685
Wand, T., 493
Wang, C., 560
Wang, M.C., 724
Wang, P.S., 705
Wang, S., 461
Wang, S.H., 311
Wang, T., 518

Wänke, M., 524
Wann, D.L., 272
Ward, S.L., 461
Ward, J., 143
Wardle, J., 575
Warga, C., 164
Warneken, F., 537
Washburn, A.L., 401
Wasyleski, D.A., 723
Watanabe, H., 239
Waterman, M.B., 493
Waters, A., 650
Waters, A.M., 647
Watkins, D., 566
Watkins, L.R., 165
Watkins, M.W., 373
Watson, D.L., 32, 33
Watson, J., 69
Watson, J.B., 14, 15, 83, 244, 245
Watson, J.C., 607
Watts, B., 417
Wauterickx, N., 473
Weaver, I., 601
Webb, W.B., 207, 208
Webber, J., 682, 683
Weber, E., 147
Webster, D.M., 503
Webster, J.D., 493
Wechsler, D., 360, 370
Wechsler, H., 626
Weg, R.B., 480
Wegener, D.T., 506
Weghorst, S., 697
Weghorst, S.J., 137
Wehr, T.A., 200
Weikart, D.P., 383
Weiland, J.D., 168
Weinberg, R.A., 381
Weinberg, R.S., 438
Weinberger, D.R., 668
Weiner, B., 422, 499, 539
Weiner, R., 719
Weiner, R.D., 718
Weinert, F.E., 364
Weingardt, K.R., 626
Weingarten, H.P., 408
Weinstein, A., 557
Weissman, M.M., 27, 688, 708, 709
Weisz, J.R., 708
Weitlauf, J., 578
Weller, A., 164

Weller, L., 164
Weller, R.E., 404
Wen, B., 110
Wender, P.H., 654
Wendt, D.C., 706
Wenzlaff, R.M., 655
Werker, J.F., 95, 454, 455
Werner, E.E., 604
Wernicke, C., 83, 94
Werth, J.L., Jr., 496
Wertheimer, M., 181
West, S.A., 23
Westbay, L., 528
Westen, D., 195, 398, 554, 637, 710
Westerterp, K., 208
Weston, S., 571
Westwood, D., 45
Wethington, E., 494
Wetter, D.W., 627
Wetzels, R., 63
Wever, R.A., 199
Whalen, N., 302
Whalley, L.J., 374
Wheeler, L., 444
Whishaw, I.Q., 70, 72, 75, 89, 92, 101, 109, 379
Whiskin, E.E., 271
Whitam, F.L., 419
White, E.J., 325
White, G.L., 525
White, K.M., 505
White, N.M., 91
White, P.A., 5
White, T., 480
White, S.J., 7
Whitehouse, W.G., 232
Who, The, 162
Whorf, B.L., 26, 328
Wickman, K., 255
Widiger, T.A., 637, 638
Widom, C.S., 673
Wiedenfeld, S.A., 605
Wiens, S., 427
Wiesel, T.N., 94, 156, 157
Wilbrecht, L., 331
Wilcox, S., 619
Wilder, D.A., 260
Wilk, S.L., 520
Wilkins, A.J., 302
Willenberg, H.S., 600
Williams, C., 205

Williams, D., 546
Williams, D.R., 657
Williams, K., 492
Williams, K.D., 520, 615
Williams, R.L., 208
Williams, S.L., 696
Williams, T.J., 419
Williams, W.L., 254
Williams, W.M., 381
Williamson, P., 669
Willingham, B., 434
Willingham, W.W., 374
Willoughby, T., 546
Wills, T.A., 602, 604
Wilson, D.A., 163
Wilson, D.S., 23, 24
Wilson, E.O., 128, 137
Wilson, J., 169
Wilson, M., 23, 137, 138
Wilson, M.A., 311
Windholz, G., 240
Wing, R.R., 408, 620
Winkler, I., 278
Winne, P.H., 352
Winnepenninckx, B., 391
Winner, E., 390
Winograd, E., 524
Wirtz, D., 34
Wise, R.A., 91
Witelson, S.F., 379
Witkiewitz, K., 623
Witkin, H.A., 388
Wittchen, H.U., 643
Witte, K., 508
Wixted, J.T., 285, 300
Wohlforth, T., 598
Wolberg, L R., 686
Wolery, M., 272
Wolfe, J.M., 171
Wolken, J.J., 151
Wolpe, J., 696
Wong, D.F., 669
Wong, M.M., 523
Wong, P.C., 390
Wood, E., 49
Wood, J., 542
Wood, J.M., 587
Wood, J.V., 563
Wood, S.L., 508
Wood, W., 9, 134, 508, 513, 528
Woodcock, R.W., 371

Woodley, M.A., 384
Woodruff-Pak, D.S., 290, 313
Woods, S.C., 400, 402, 403
Woody, E., 233
Woolf, C.J., 144
Word, C.O., 534
Worell, J., 707
World Association of Sleep Medicine, 205, 206
World Health Organization (WHO), 412, 621, 622, 658, 671
Wouters-Adriaens, M., 208
Wrangham, R.W., 131, 138
Wright, H., 411
Wright, M.J., 11, 29, 30
Wright, T., 205
Wu, X., 266
Wu, Y.I., 479, 481
Wundt, W., 11, 12
Wyer, R.S., 539
Wylie, R.C., 589
Wyman, A.J., 7
Wynn, K., 461, 462

X
Xu, J., 19
Xue, G., 98

Y
Yahya, L.A., 516
Yalom, I.D., 607
Yam, A., 150
Yamagata, S., 121
Yang, L.G., 561, 562, 563
Yang, S., 466
Yang, Y.S., 97, 98
Yardley, L., 505
Yarmey, D., 306, 307
Yarmey, M., 307
Yassa, M.A., 303
Yen, S., 658, 659
Yerkes, R.M., 435
Yin, T.C.T., 161
Young, A.W., 196
Young, L.R., 654
Young, T., 153, 154

Youngentob, S.L., 162
Youngren, V.R., 685
Youngstedt, S.D., 207
Yuan, J., 196
Yuan, Y., 301
Yuille, J.C., 307
Yurgelun-Todd, D.A., 482

Z
Zadra, A., 210
Zahava, S., 597
Zahn-Waxler, C., 426, 615
Zajonc, R.B., 440, 509
Zakzanis, K.K., 667
Zane, N., 705
Zanker, J., 156, 165
Zanna, M.P., 222, 505, 507, 531
Zapata-Fonseca, L., 37
Zaragoza, M.S., 307
Zarate, M.A., 335
Zautra, A.J., 592, 593
Zayas, V., 556, 557
Zebrowitz, L.A., 529
Zechner, U., 391
Zeki, S., 529
Zelazo, P.R., 453, 469
Zettle, R.D., 696, 699
Zhang, A.Y., 649
Zhang, G., 524
Zhang, Q., 71
Zhang, T-Y., 110, 111, 601
Zhang, Y., 402
Zhang, Z., 26
Zhao, F., 144
Zhao, X-H., 562, 563
Zhou, M., 466
Zhuikov, A.Y., 258
Zillmann, D., 417, 529, 542
Zimba, R.F., 477, 537
Zimbardo, P.G., 510, 519
Zimmerman, F.J., 7
Zinbarg, R., 647
Zinbarg, R.E., 695
Zoellner, L.A., 696
Zola-Morgan, S., 290
Zubieta, J-K., 166
Zuckerman, M., 433, 571
Zuk, J., 390

A

Abecedarian Program, 382–383
abnormal, 632–634
abnormal behaviour, 633
absentmindedness, 297
absolute refractory period, 72
absolute threshold, 144
abstinence violation effect, 625
abstract reasoning, 483–484
abuse counselors, 684
abusive emotional
 relationships, 556–557
academic performance
 enhancement strategies,
 32–34, 283–289, 296–297
acceptance, 495
acceptance and commitment
 therapy (ACT), 702–703
accommodation, 458
acetylcholine (ACh), 76, 77–78
achievement goal theory,
 420–421
achievement motivation,
 420–423
achievement test, 371
acid, 230
acquired immune deficiency
 syndrome (AIDS), 621
 social-cognitive theory, 274
acquisition, 240–242
acquisition of language. See
 language acquisition
action potential, 71–73
action potential threshold, 73
activation-synthesis theory,
 212
activational effects, 413
acupuncture, 166
adaptation theories of
 learning, 237–239
 behaviourism, 237–238
 biological factors, 238
 biology and environment,
  237–238
 habituation, 238–239
 sensitization, 239
adaptations, 125, 148
adaptive mechanisms, 124–126
 adaptations, 125–126
 evolution, 124
 natural selection, 124–125
addiction to drugs, 219–220
additive colour mixture, 153
adenosine, 76, 207

ADHD (attention deficit/
 hyperactivity disorder),
 677
adolescence, 478–497
 adult, 479
 analysis, 495
 brain, 479–480
 brain development, 481–482
 cognitive development,
  483–484
 early experience and,
  111–112
 emotional changes, 487
 epigenetics and, 111–112
 foreclosure, 487
 identity achievement, 487
 identity diffusion, 487
 moratorium, 487
 personality development,
  487–491
 physical development,
  479–483
 reasoning and information
  processing, 483–484
 relationships with parents,
  488–489
 relationships with peers,
  488–489
 search for identity, 487–488
 social-emotional
  development, 487–491
 transition to adulthood,
  489–491
adolescent egocentrism, 483
adoption study, 115–116
adulthood, 478–497
 adolescent, 478–479
 analysis, 495
 attachment, 493
 brain, 480, 483
 career, 493–494
 cognitive development,
  483–487
 cohabitation, 493
 critical events, 491
 death, 495–496
 dying, 495–496
 family, 492–493
 golden years, 494
 information processing and
  memory, 485
 intellectual changes,
  485–486
 marriage, 492–493

 mid-life crisis, 494
 personality development,
  489–496
 physical development, 480
 post-formal thought,
  484–485
 retirement, 494
 social development, 489–496
 stages, 491
 transition to, 489–491
aerobic exercise, 618
affective disorders. See mood
 disorders
affective neuroscience,
 428–430
affective style, 428–430
affiliation, 523
affiliative people, 396
afterimage, 154
age of viability, 449
aggression, 137–138, 272,
 540–547
 amygdala, 540
 analysis, 547
 biological factors, 540–541
 environmental factors,
  541–542
 evolutionary psychology,
  137–138
 frontal lobes, 541
 hypothalamus, 540
 media violence, 543–544
 modelling, 542
 psychological factors,
  542–543
 reinforcement, 542
 serotonin, 541
 social, 541
 testosterone, 541
 video game violence,
  545–546
agnosia, 95
agonist, 76, 217
agoraphobia, 642, 643
agreeableness, 120, 570
AIDS (acquired immune
 deficiency syndrome), 621
 social-cognitive theory, 274
airline safety, 517
alarm reaction, 595
alcohol, effects of, 76, 220–221,
 227, 228, 622
alcohol myopia, 221, 222–223
algorithm, 340

all-or-none law, 73
alleles, 109
allergens, 245
alpha waves, 201
altered consciousness, 217–234
 drugs. See drugs and altered
  consciousness
 hypnosis, 230–234
 meditation, 230
altered state of
 consciousness, 192
alters, 662
altruism, 135–136, 537
Alzheimer's disease (AD), 113,
 301, 680
 genetic determinism, 139
 long-term memory, 301
 neurotransmitters, 77
 working memory, 301
Ames room, 182
amnesia, 277, 300–302
amotivational syndrome, 226
amphetamine psychosis, 223
amphetamines, 76, 77, 217–218,
 223–224, 227
amplitude, 158
amygdala, 90–91, 166
 aggression, 540
 anxiety disorder, 645
 biological treatments for
  disorders, 720
 emotion, 428–429
 fear-conditioning, 263
 memory, 312
 obsessive compulsive
  disorder, 646
 social support, 603–604
 unipolar depression, 695
analytic psychology, 555
analytical intelligence, 366
androgens, 413, 414, 449
androgynous gender
 identity, 475
angel dust, 226
anger, 495
animal cognition, 268–269
animal magnetism, 230
animal research ethical
 standards, 65
animal training, 259, 263
anorexia nervosa, 648, 649–650
antagonist, 76, 218
antecedents, 249
anterograde amnesia, 300

anti-anxiety drugs, 715–716
antidepressant drugs, 78, 716–717
antipsychotic drugs, 78, 218, 717–718
antisocial personality disorder, 671–675
  biological factors, 673–674
  psychological and environmental factors, 674–675
anvil (incus), 159
anxiety disorders, 641–650
  analysis, 660
  anxiety responses, 641
  biological factors, 644–646
  defined, 641
  eating disorder, 648–650
  generalized anxiety disorder, 643
  obsessive-compulsive disorder (OCD), 644–648
  panic disorder, 643–644
  phobic disorder, 642
  psychological factors, 646–658
  sociocultural factors, 648
anxious-avoidant infants, 470
anxious-resistant infants, 470
aphasia, 98, 322
ApoE gene, 301
applications of classical conditioning, 694–699
  aversion therapy, 699
  exposure therapy, 245, 694–696
applied behaviour analysis, 259–260
applied research, 8
approach-approach conflict, 424
approach-avoidance conflict, 424
aptitude test, 371
archetypes, 555
archival measures, 44
Argus II, 168
Army Alpha, 360
Army Beta, 360
arousal, 414
Art of Loving, The (Fromm), 528
Asperger syndrome, 97
assimilation, 458
association cognitive techniques, 702
association cortex, 93, 95–96
associative network, 289
attachment, 468–470
  abusive romantic relationships, 556–557
  adulthood, 493
  deprivation, 470–471

process, 468–469
  types, 469–470
attention, 171–172, 271
attention deficit hyperactivity disorder (ADHD), 677
attitude, 504–508
  defined, 504
  influence on behaviour, 505
  influenced by behaviour, 505–507
  persuasion, 507–508
  self-perception, 507
attraction, 523–528
  affiliation, 523
  close relationships, 526–527, 530–531
  initial, 523–526
  sociocultural and evolutionary views, 527–528
attribution, 499–502
  bias, 500–502
  culture, 502
  personal, 499–500
  situational, 499–500
attribution of intentionality, 542
audition, 144, 158–162
  hearing loss, 161–162
  locating sound, 161
  pitch and loudness, 159–161
  sensory prosthetics, 167, 168–169
  transduction, 159
auditory habituation procedure, 453
auditory working memory, 282
authoritarian parent, 472
authoritative parent, 472
autism, 97, 357, 677
autistic spectrum disorder, 97–98, 677–678
autokinetic effect, 511
automatic processing, 195, 283–284
autonomic feedback, 438–439
autonomic nervous system, 80–81, 428–432
autonomy, 399
availability heuristic, 342–343
aversion therapy, 245, 698, 699
aversive punishment, 251
avoidance-avoidance conflict, 424
avoidance conditioning, 258
avoidant personality disorder, 672
awareness, 194, 269
axon, 70
axon terminals, 70

B
backward pairing, 242, 269
barbiturate, effect, 76, 221, 227
bargaining, 495

basal forebrain, 204
basal ganglia, 89–90
basal metabolic rate, 480
basal metabolism, 400
basic research, 8
basilar membrane, 159
Battlemind, 724
Beck Depression Inventory, 713–714
Beck's cognitive therapy, 693–694
behaviour, 10–24
  analysis, 24–29
  attitude, affect on, 505–507
  attitude's influence on, 505
  behavioural genetics, 112–117
  behavioural perspective, 13–15, 24
  biological perspective, 20–24
  cognitive perspective, 16–18, 24
  common beliefs, 4–5
  comparison, 24
  critical thinking, 6–8
  culture, 26
  defined, 2
  evolutionary psychology, 128–138
  genetic influences on, 118–123
  historical context, 18–19
  humanistic perspective, 15–16, 24
  influence of genetics, 118–123
  language, 26
  psychodynamic perspective, 12–13, 24
  sociocultural perspective, 18–19, 24
  summary of themes, 29
behaviour genetics, 21–22, 112–117
  adoption study, 115–116
  genetic counselling, 113–114
  heredity, 114–115
  personality, 120–122
  twin studies, 116–117, 118, 120, 121
behaviour modification, 15, 259–260, 699–700, 699–701
behaviour tendencies, 426
behaviour therapies, 694–702
  classical conditioning, 694–699
  modelling, 701–702
  operant conditioning, 699–701
  social skills training, 701–702
behavioural activation, 657
behavioural activation system (BAS), 654

behavioural assessment, 584
behavioural component of emotions, 432–438
  affective style, 428–430
  culture, 434–435
  elevation, 436–437
  evolution, 432–433
  expressive behaviours, 432
  facial expression, 433–434
  instrumental behaviours, 435, 438
behavioural inhibition, 467
behavioural inhibition system (EIS), 654
behavioural measures, consciousness, 193
behavioural neuroscience, 20–21
behavioural perspective, 13–15, 24
behaviourism, 14–15, 237–238
belief bias, 337
beliefs, 238
Bell Curve, The (Herrnstein and Murray), 384
belongingness, 16
beta waves, 201
between groups design, 55
between subjects design, 55
bidirectionality problem, 51
Big Five, 120, 569–570
  See also Five Factor Model
bilingualism, 325–328, 329
binaural ability, 161
binding problem, 143
binge drinking, 626–627
binocular cues, 179
binocular disparity, 180
biological approaches to psychological disorder, 715–721
  drug therapies, 715–718
  electroconvulsive therapy, 718–719
  mind-body, and therapeutic interventions, 719–720
  psychosurgery, 719
biological clock, 200
  synchronizing, 198–199
biological factors in
  aggression, 540–541
  antisocial personality disorder, 673–674
  anxiety disorder, 644–646
  autism, 678–679
  borderline personality disorder, 676
  childhood development, 456–457
  drug use and effects, 227–229
  eating disorders, 650
  emotion, 428–432
  evolution, 124–126

language acquisition, 323
learning, 238
mood disorders, 653–655
obesity, 408–409
obsessive-compulsive
disorder, 644–646
personality disorder,
673–674
personality trait, 571
prenatal development,
449–450
schizophrenia, 667–669
sexual response cycle,
412–413
sleep, 204
biological level of analysis, 8,
9, 24
aggression, 547
anxiety and mood
disorders, 660
behaviour genetics, 123
brain, behaviour and
environment, 105
conceptions of
personality, 588
depression, 28
drug-induced states, 229
emotion, 445
intellectual functioning, 393
language, 330
learning, 273
lifespan development, 495
measuring exam stress, 42
memory, 312
perception, 189
sleep and dreaming, 215
stress and coping, 608
therapeutic change, 721
thinking processes, 353
biological perspective, 10,
20–24
behaviour genetics, 21–22
behavioural neuroscience,
20–21
evolutionary psychology,
22–24
history, 10–12
biologically based
mechanisms, 124
biology and learning, 261–264
brain, the, 263–264
classical conditioning, vs.,
261–262
fear preparedness, 262–263
operant conditioning, vs.,
263
biology of memory, 309–313
declarative memory, 310,
312
formation, 311
long-term memory,
310–313
procedural memory,
312–313

sensory memory, 309
working memory, 309
bionic hand, 169
biopsychology, 3
bipedal locomotion, 125
bipolar cells, 151
bipolar disorder, 652, 654
blind spot, 151
blindsight, 197
blood alcohol level (BAL),
221, 227
blood-brain barrier, 71,
217–218
blunted affect, 666
bodily-kinesthetic
intelligence, 367
body image, 406
body senses, 164, 166, 170
borderline personality
disorder, 672, 675–676
biological factors, 676
causal factors, 675–676
sociocultural factors, 676
bottom-up processing,
170–171, 319
botulism, 78
boundary extension, 305
brain, 82
adolescent, 479–480
adult, 480, 483
intelligence, 379
mental image, 350
neuroscience, 45
plasticity, 101–105, 378
brain atrophy, 668
brain development
adolescents, 479–480,
481–482
children, 455–457
brain evolution, 125–126
brain fingerprinting, 395–396
brain function
affective style, 428–430
aggression, 540–541
anxiety disorder, 646
behaviour. See neural basis
of behaviour
biological approaches to
treatment, 715–720
circadian rhythms,
198–199
communication systems,
73–79
depression, 654
dreaming, 208
drugs, 217–218
emotion, 428–432
fear conditioning, 269
hunger and eating
regulation, 400–411,
403, 404–405
hypnosis and, 233–234
intelligence, 379

language acquisition,
321–322, 329
learning, 263–264
memory, 311
obsessive-compulsive
disorder (OCD), 645
personality traits, 571
schizophrenia, 668–669
sleep, 213
stereotyping, 532
stress, 603–604
thought, 334–335
unipolar depression, 695
brain recovery. See neural
plasticity
brain research, 82–87
cortical map, 83–84
destruction and stimulation
techniques, 82, 84
electrical recording, 84
imaging, 22, 45, 84–87
neuropsychological tests, 82
brain stem, 88
brain structure, 87–105
adolescence, 479–480
amygdala, 90
basal ganglia, 89–90
cerebellum, 88
cerebral cortex, 92–98
children, 455
forebrain, 89–91
hemispheric lateralization,
98–101
hindbrain, 88
hypothalamus, 90
limbic system, 90–91
midbrain, 89
neural plasticity, 101–105
stem, 88
thalamus, 89
BrainPort V100, 167
breast cancer, 139
brief psychodynamic
therapies, 686–688
brightness constancy, 177–178
British empiricism, 11
Broca's area, 94–95, 98,
321–322
bulimia nervosa, 649–650
bullying, 47
BuSpar, 715
buspirone, 715
bystander apathy, 37
bystander effect, 38, 539, 540.
See also altruism
bystander intervention, 38

C
caffeine, 76, 303
"Canadian Code of Ethics for
Psychologists," 64
cannabinoids, 226
capabilities, 237

capillaries, 217
careers, adulthood and,
493–494
case study
advantages of, 46–47, 57
defined, 46, 57
limitations, 47, 57
cataplexy, 209
catastrophic events, 593, 597
catatonic schizophrenia,
666–667
catharsis, 543
catharsis principle, 416
Cattell personality factors,
567–568
caudate nucleus, 66
cause-effect relations, 47
CCK (cholecystokinin), 401
cell body, 70
cells, 109
central control mechanism,
165
central executive, 282
central fissure, 92
central nervous system, 79,
81–87
brain, 82
brain research, 82–87
spinal cord, 81–82
central route to persuasion,
508
centration, 459
cephalocaudal principle, 455
cerebellum, 88, 312, 356
cerebral cortex, 92–98
association cortex, 93, 95–96
Broca's area, 94–95
frontal lobes, 92, 96, 98
memory, 309
motor cortex, 93
role and structure, 92–93
sensory cortex, 93–94
Wernicke's area, 94
chaining, 254
child-directed speech, 323
childhood amnesia. See
infantile amnesia
childhood development,
451–478
brain growth, 455–457
cognitive development,
457–464
environment and culture,
456–457
language, 324–325
moral development,
75–478
motor development, 455–457
newborn, 452–454
personality development,
465–475
physical growth, 455–457
sensory-perceptual
development, 454–455

childhood development,—*Cont.*
    social-emotional
        development, 465–475
    theory of mind, 464
childhood disorders, 677–679
    attention deficit/
        hyperactivity disorder
        (ADHD), 677
    autistic spectrum disorder,
        677–678
    causal factors , 678–679
childhood memories, 307–308
childhood psychological
    disorder, 677–679
cholecystokinin (CCK), 401,
    402
cholesterol, 618
chromosome, 108–109
chronic depressive disorder,
    651
chronic stress, 595–597
chunking, 281, 286
cingulotomy, 719
circadian rhythms, 197–201
    brain, 198–200
    disruptions, 200–201
    environment, 198–200
clairvoyance, 62
clarity, 180
classical conditioning, 219,
    237, 249
classical conditioning theory
    of learning, 239–245
    applications, 243–245
    defined, 239
    Pavlov's research, 240
    principles, 240–243
classical conditioning
    treatments, 694–699
classically conditioned
    responses, 290
client-centred therapy, 688–690
clinical psychology, 2
clinical significance, 710
clozapine, 717
cocaine, 77, 224–225, 227
cochlea, 159
cochlear implant, 169
coding systems, 44
cognition in conditioning, 237,
    266–270
cognition-arousal relations,
    442–444
cognitive appraisal, 426
cognitive behaviour therapy
    (CBT), 695
cognitive behaviourism, 15
cognitive development in
    children, 457–464
    assessment of Piaget's
        stages, 461–462
    information processing,
        462–464

Piaget's stages, 457–461
social context, 462
theory of mind, 464
cognitive dissonance, 506, 507
cognitive functioning,
    maintaining, 486–487
cognitive map, 266–267
cognitive model of learning,
    264–270
    classical conditioning, and,
        266–269
    cognitive maps, 266–267
    insights, 264–265
    operant conditioning, and,
        269–270
cognitive neuroscience, 17–18
cognitive perspective, 16–18,
    24
    functionalism, 11–12, 16
    Gestalt psychology, 16, 17
    learning, 238
    modern, 17–18
    origins, 16
    prejudice, 532–534
    renewed interest, 16–17
    structuralism, 11–12, 16
cognitive process theories,
    365–366
cognitive protective factors
    and stress, 601–608
cognitive psychology, 2–3, 17,
    195–196
cognitive revolution, 17
cognitive psychology, 2–3,
    12, 17
cognitive revolution, 17
cognitive therapies, 691–694
    Beck's cognitive therapy,
        693–694
    Ellis's rational-emotive
        therapy, 692–693
cognitive-affective personality
    system (CAPS), 581
cognitive-arousal model of
    love, 529
cognitive-behaviour therapy
    (CBT), 692, 695, 698
cognitive-process dream
    theory, 214
cohabitation, 493
collective effort model, 520
collective unconscious, 555
collectivism, 19
combating substance abuse,
    622–627
    harm reduction strategies,
        625–627
    motivational interviewing,
        623
    multimodal treatments,
        623–624
    relapse prevention, 624–625
commitment, 528

Committee for Skeptical
    Inquiry, 62
common chemical sense, 162
common factors, 712
communication systems,
    425–426. *See also*
    language
communicator credibility,
    507–508
comorbidity, 651
companionate love, 528
compensatory responses, 219
competence motivation, 399
competency (legal), 640
competency-focused
    prevention, 724
competition, 137–138
compulsions, 644
computer-assisted
    instruction, 259
computerized axial
    tomography (CT) scan,
    84, 85
concept, 335
concordance, 115
concrete operational stage,
    459, 460
conditional positive regard,
    564
conditioned attraction, 245
conditioned reinforcers,
    252–253
conditioned response (CR), 241
conditioned stimulus (CS), 241
conditioned taste aversion, 261
conditions of worth, 564
conduction deafness, 161
cones, 150
confederates, 512
confidence, 539
confirmation bias, 5, 343
conflict as motivation, 423–424
conformity, 511–518
    destructive obedience,
        514–515, 516
    factors, 512–513
    minority influence, 513
    obedience, 513
    resisting compliance,
        517–518
confounding of variables,
    58–59
congruence, 560
conscience, 477–478
conscientiousness, 120, 570
conscious, 551
conscious mind, 193
consciousness, 192–197
    characteristics, 192–193
    cognitive unconscious, 193,
        195–196
    emotional unconscious,
        193, 196

measuring, 193
modular mind, 197
neural basis, 196–197
consequences, 249, 250–254
conservation, 459
consistency paradox, 581
consistent observations, 44
constraint and stress,
    613–614
construct, 372
construct validity, 372, 373
construction of memory,
    304–308
    biology, 309–313
    childhood memories,
        307–308
    distortion, 304–306
    forgetting, 312
    misinformation effect,
        306–307
    recovered memory,
        307–308
    source confusion, 306–307
consummate love, 528
contact comfort, 468
content validity, 372, 373
context, 143, 182
context-dependent memory,
    294–295
contingencies, 249
continuous reinforcement, 255
continuous reinforcement
    schedule, 255
control, 41
control group, 55
controlled (effortful)
    processing, 195
conventional moral
    reasoning, 476
conventional wisdom, 4–5
convergence, 180
conversion disorder, 661
conversion hysteria, 551
cooperation, 135
cooperative learning
    programs, 535
coping self-efficacy, 605
coping strategies and stress,
    599, 608–615
    constraint, 613–614
    culture, 614–615
    effectiveness, 609, 611, 613
    gender, 614–615
    mindfulness, 612–613
    physical contact, 610–611
cornea, 149
corpus callosum, 98, 99, 101,
    356
correlation coefficient, 51–52
correlational research, 50–53,
    57
    causation, 50–51
    components, 50

correlational coefficient, 51–52
prediction, 52–53
correlational studies, 52
cortex, 695
cortical implants, 168
cortical map, 83–84
cortisol, 595–596, 601
couches, 2
counselling and clinical psychologists, 684
counterattitudinal behaviour, 506
counterbalancing, 55
counterconditioning, 696
CR (conditioned response), 241
crack, 224
cramming, 33
creative intelligence, 366
creative problem solving, 345–346
creativity, 345
Creutzfeld-Jakob disease, 679
criminal behaviour, 98
criterion measure, 373
criterion-related validity, 372, 373
critical period, 185–186, 468
critical thinking, 6–8
behaviour, 6–8
potential costs of failure of, 7–8
critical thinking skills, 66
criticism, 670
cross-cultural psychology, 18, 238
cross-cultural replication, 61
cross-sectional design, 448
crosstalk, 75
crowd behaviour, 518–519
crowding, 541
crystal meth, 223–224
crystallized intelligence, 363–364, 485
CS (conditioned stimulus), 241
CT (computerized axial tomography), 85
cued recall, 292
cues, 221
cultural competence, 706
cultural congruence, 705
cultural influence in
abnormality, 633–634
achievement, 422–423
anxiety disorders, 648
attribution, 502
behaviour therapies, 18–19, 21
coping strategies, 614–615
childhood development, 456–457
disorders, 636

drug use and effects, 227–229
eating disorders, 649–650
emotional expression, 434–435
identity formation, 488
intelligence, 382–386
mate seeking, 527–528
mood disorders, 657
moral reasoning, 477
norm formation, 511
perception, 187–188
prejudice, 536–537
psychotherapy, 705–706
schizophrenia, 670–671
self-concept, 565–566
sexuality, 414–417
social learning, 536–537
social thinking and perception, 502
stress, 614–615
cultural psychology, 18
culturally competent therapist, 706
culture, 18
behaviour, 26
hunger and weight regulation, 407–408
language, 26
love and marriage, 20
culture-bound disorders, 648. See also cultural influence
cumulative recorder, 248
curiosity, 37, 303
Cyberball, 603–604
cyberporn, 416
cytokines, 165

D
D.F. case, 145–146, 196
dark adaptation, 152
data, 40
date rape drugs, 77
daycare controversy, 471–472
daydreams, 213–214
day-night cycle, 197–198
db (decibels), 158, 159
deactivated transmitter, 75
death, 495–496
stages of, 495
debriefing, 64
decay theory, 299
deception, 64
decibels (db), 158, 159
decision criterion, 146
declarative memory, 290, 310, 312
deductive reasoning. 336, 337, 338
Deep Maple, 110
deep structure, 317–318
default mode network,, 562
defence mechanisms, 552

deficiency needs, 398
deindividuation, 518
deinstitutionalization, 722–723
delay discounting, 424
delay of gratification, 253
delta waves, 202
delusion of grandeur, 665
delusion of persecution, 665
delusions, 665
dementia, 301, 679–680
denial, 495, 553
dendrites, 70
deoxyribonucleic acid (DNA), 108
dependent variable, 54
depolarization, 71
depressants, 220–221, 227
alcohol, 220–221, 227
alcohol myopia study, 221, 222–223
barbiturates, 221, 227
depression, 27–28, 495, 651–652, 694
biological level of analysis, 27, 28
causal factors in, 28, 653–657
clinical trials, 713–714
environmental level of analysis, 27–28
neurotransmitters and, 27
psychological level of analysis, 28
sociocultural environment, 28
depressive attributional pattern, 656
depressive cognitive triad, 655
deprivation experiment, 185
depth of processing, 284
descriptive research, 46–50
case studies, 46–47
defined, 46
naturalistic observation, 47–48, 57
survey research, 48–50, 57
desire, 414
destruction and stimulation techniques, 82, 84
destructive obedience, 516
deterioration effect, 712
developmental psychology, 3, 447–497
adolescence, 478–496
adulthood, 478–496
childhood, 451–478
developmental functions, 449
environmental influences, 450–451
genetics, 449–450
issues, 447

lifespan development, 495
prenatal development, 449–451
research design, 448
sex determination, 449–450
deviance, 633
devil's tuning fork, 182
diagnosing psychological disorders, 636–641
Diagnostic and Statistical Manual of Mental Disorders, Fifth Edition (DSM-5), 97, 634, 637–638
diagnostic labelling issues, 638–641
dialectical behaviour therapy (DBT), 703–704
diathesis-stress model. *See* vulnerability-stress model
dichromat, 155
DID (dissociative identity disorder), 234, 662
difference threshold, 147
differential effectiveness, 710
diffusion of responsibility, 39, 538, 659
digit-span task, 280
digit-span test, 280
Directed Questions Method, 32–33
discourse, 318
discriminate attachment, 469
discrimination, 243, 254–255, 529–536. *See also* prejudice
discriminative stimulus, 250, 255
disequilibrium, 458
disorders of childhood, 677–679
disorders of old age, 679–680
disorganized schizophrenia, 666
displacement, 317, 553
display rules, 434
dissociation theory (of hypnosis), 232
dissociative amnesia, 662
dissociative disorders, 662–664
dissociative fugue, 662
dissociative identity disorder (DID), 234, 662
distraction, 337
distributed practice, 296
divergent thinking, 345
divided attention, 195
division of awareness, 232
divorce and childhood development, 473–474
dizygotic twins, 116
DNA (deoxyribonucleic acid), 108
DNA-methylation, 110, 111–112

dodo bird verdict, 710
domain-specific adaptations, 126
dominance hierarchies, 137
dominance position, 137
dominant gene, 109
dominant response, 509
door-in-the-face technique, 517
dopamine, 76, 77, 78, 217, 654, 669, 695
dopamine hypothesis, 669
dose-response effect, 712
double-blind procedure, 60
Down syndrome, 391
dream interpretation, 685
dreaming, 210–216. *See also* REM sleep
    content, 211–212
    daydreams, 213–214
    latent content, 212
    manifest content, 212
    nightmares, 210
    reasons, 212–216
    sleep cycle, 211
drive theory, 397
drives, 397
drug abuse, 397
drug therapy for psychological disorder, 715–718
drug-induced states of consciousness, 229
drugs and altered consciousness, 217–229, 715–718
    anti-anxiety drugs, 715–716
    antidepressant drugs, 716–717
    antipsychotic drugs, 717–718
    brain functioning and, 76–77, 217–218
    decision making and, 222–223
    depressants, 220–221, 227
    determinants, 227–229
    hallucinogens, 226, 227
    marijuana, 226–227
    opiates, 225, 227
    psychoactive, 76
    sedatives, 76
    stimulants, 223–225, 227
    tolerance, 218–220
    withdrawal, 218–220
drunken invincibility, 223
DSM-5. *See Diagnostic and Statistical Manual of Mental Disorders, Fifth Edition*
dual coding theory, 287, 297
dual instinct model, 398
dual-process theory, 154
dualism, 11
dying, 495–496
dynamic testing, 376

dysfunctional, 633
dysthymia, 651

E

ear, 159, 160
easy lay, 77
eating disorders, 406–407, 648–650
echoic store, 278
echolalia, 678
echolocation, 167
ecstasy (MDMA), 224
ECT (electroconvulsive therapy), 718–719
EEG (electroencephalogram), 84
effect size statistic, 710
effortful processing, 283
ego, 552
egocentrism, 459–460
elaborative rehearsal, 281, 285, 296
electrical recording, 84
electroconvulsive therapy (ECT), 718–719
electroencephalogram (EEG), 84
elevation, 436–437
elicited responses, 247
embedded human, 18–19
embryo, 449
embryonic stage, 449
emitted responses, 247
emotion, 424–445
    adaptive function, 425–426
    adaptive value, 425–426
    analysis, 445
    affective style, 428–430
    autonomic feedback, 438–439
    behavioural component, 426, 432–438
    Cannon-Bard theory, 438–440
    childhood, 465
    cognition-arousal relations, 442–444
    cognitive component, 427–428
    cognitive-affective theories, 440–441
    dual system processing, 429
    facial feedback, 440
    framing, 337–338
    function of, 424–438
    James-Lange somatic theory, 438
    nature of, 426–438
    physiological component, 428–432
    stimuli, 425, 426, 427
emotion-focused coping, 609

emotion regulation, 465–466, 542
emotional arousal, 581
emotional competence, 370
emotional dysregulation, 675
emotional intelligence, 367–370
emotional unconscious, 196
emotions, 425
empathy, 97, 432, 537, 542, 689
empathy-altruism hypothesis, 537
empirical approach, 585
empirical evidence, 4
empirically validated therapies, 708
empty-chair technique, 690
encoding, 277
encoding failure, 298–299
encoding information into memory, 283–289
    chunking, 285–286
    levels of processing, 284
    mnemonic devices, 286–287
    organization, 285–287
    prior knowledge, 287–289
    processing effort, 283–284
    rehearsal, 284–285
    schemas, 287–289
    visual imagery, 287
encoding specificity principle, 294
endocrine system, 595
endorphins, 77, 78, 165–166
engram, 309, 309
environment, intelligence, 379–382
environmental factors in aggression, 541–542
    antisocial personality disorder, 674–675
    attention, 171–172
    autism, 679
    childhood development, 456–457
    drugs, 227–229
    genes, 109–110
    hunger, 407–408
    learning, 263–264
    mood disorders, 656–657
    obesity, 408–409
    personality disorder, 674–675
    prenatal development, 450–451
    schizophrenia, 669–670
    sexuality, 414–417
environmental level of analysis, 8, 9, 25
    aggression, 547
    anxiety and mood disorders, 660
    behaviour genetics, 123

brain, behaviour and environment, 105
conceptions of personality, 588
depression, 28
drug-induced states, 229
emotion, 445
intellectual functioning, 393
language, 330
learning, 273
lifespan development, 495
measuring exam stress, 42
memory, 312
perception, 189
sleep and dreaming, 215
stress and coping, 608
therapeutic change, 721
thinking processes, 353
epigenetics, 109–110, 111–112
episodic buffer, 282
episodic memory, 290
equal status contact, 535
equilibrium, 458
Erikson's psychosocial stages, 467–468
erogenous zones, 553
escape conditioning, 258
establishment phase of career, 493
estrogen, 413
ethical standards in research, 63–65
ethics review boards, 64
ethnicity, intelligence, 384–386
event-related potentials (ERPs), 84
evidence gathering, 39–40
evidence-based practice, 707
evolution, 124
    human nature and, 125–126
    theory of, 11
evolution and behaviour. *See* evolutionary psychology
evolutionary noise, 125
evolutionary personality theory, 128
evolutionary psychology, 12, 22–24, 128–139
    adaptive mechanisms, 124–126
    aggression, 137–138
    altruism, 135–136
    competition, 137–138
    errors and misunderstandings, 138–139
    instinct theory, 396
    mate preference, 131–135
    mating systems, 130–131
    natural selection, 22
    parenting, 130–131
    personality, 128, 130

evolutionary view of attraction, 527–528
evolutionary/circadian sleep models, 207–208
exam stress, measuring, 42
examples, linking new information to, 296
excitatory transmitter, 74, 220
excitement phase, 412
executive dysfunction model, 645
executive functions, 98, 282
exercise, 618–619
exhaustion, 596
existential intelligence, 367
expectancy, 267, 269, 574
expectancy × value theory, 397
experiment, 53–57
  between-groups design, 55
  between-subjects design, 55
  characteristics, 53–54
  control group, 55
  counterbalancing, 55
  defined, 53
  dependent variable, 54
  design, 55–56
  experimental group, 55
  independent variable, 54
  interaction, 56
  logic of, 54
  one independent variable example, 55
  placebo effect, 59–60
  random assignment, 55
  repeated measures design, 55
  two independent variables example, 56–57
  within-subjects design, 55
experimental group, 55
experimental methods, 46
experimental psychology, 3
experimenter expectancy effects, 60
expert knowledge, 288, 305
expertise, 346–347
  credibility, 508
  memory, 346–347
  nature of, 346
  schemas, 288–289, 344, 346
explicit memory, 291–292
exploration stage of career, 493
exposure, 695
exposure therapies, 245, 694–696
expressed emotion, 670
Expression of Emotions in Man and Animals, The (Darwin), 432
expressive behaviours, 426, 432

external aids, 296
external validity, 61
extinction, 242
  operant conditioning, 250–251
  partial reinforcement, 257–258
extinction trial, 242
extrasensory perception (ESP), 62–63
extraversion, 117, 128, 567, 570
extraversion-introversion, 120, 128
extrinsic motivation, 398
eye, 149–150
eyewitness testimony, 307
Eysenck's Extraversion-Stability model, 568–569

F
Facial Action Coding System (FACS), 433
facial attractiveness, 525–526
facial expressions, 433–434
facial feedback, 440
facial feedback hypothesis, 440
FACS (Facial Action Coding System), 433
factor analysis, 361–362, 567
false belief tasks, 464
false memories, 232
family, adulthood, 492–493
family environment, intelligence, 385
farsightedness, 150
FAS (fetal alcohol syndrome), 450
FASD (fetal alcohol spectrum disorders), 450
fear, acquiring and overcoming, 244–245
fear conditioning, 261–262
fear of failure, 420
feature detectors, 142, 156
fetal alcohol spectrum disorders (FASD), 450
fetal alcohol syndrome (FAS), 450
fetal stage, 449
Fentanyl, 225
fetus, 449
FI (fixed-interval) schedule, 257
fight-or-flight response, 431, 596
figure-ground relations, 173–174
finding meaning in stressful life events, 607–608
first instinct fallacy, 34
fissure, 92, 103

Five Factor Model, 120, 128, 569–570, 589, 638
fixation, 554
fixed schedule, 256
fixed-interval (FI) schedule, 256, 257
fixed-ratio (FR) schedule, 256
fixed-role therapy, 559
flashbulb memories, 293
flat affect, 666
flooding, 695
fluid intelligence, 364, 485
flunitrazepam, 77
Flynn effect, 375–376
  intelligence and, 375
fMRI (functional MRI), 85, 87, 322
folk wisdom, 4
foot-in-the-door technique, 518
forebrain, 89–91
foreclosure, 487
forgetting, 297–302, 312
  amnesia, 300–302
  analysis, 312
  process, 297–298
  prospective memory, 302
  reasons, 298–300
formal operational stage, 459, 461
forward pairing, 269
forward short-delay pairing, 242
forward trace pairing, 242
fovea, 151
FR (fixed-ratio) schedule, 256
framing, 337–338
Fraser's spiral, 174
fraternal twins, 116–117, 118
free association, 13, 685
free nerve endings, 164
free will, 15
free-running circadian rhythm, 199, 200
French immersion programs, 326
frequency, 158
frequency theory, 160
Freud's psychoanalytic theory. *See* psychodynamic perspective of personality
frontal cortex, 83
  criminal behaviour, 96
  human aggression, 96
frontal lobe, 92, 96, 98
  aggression, 541
frustration-aggression hypothesis, 541
fully functioning persons, 564–565
functional fixedness, 345
functional MRI (fMRI), 85, 87, 322

functional neurological symptom disorder, 660–661
functionalism, 11–12, 16
fundamental attribution error, 500–501
fundamental emotional patterns, 433
fusiform face area (FFA), 194
fusiform facial area (FFA), 145

G
g factor, 362–363, 366
  genes, 380
GABA, 75, 76, 77, 220, 221, 646, 716
GAD (generalized anxiety and worry disorder), 643
gamma hydroxybutyrate (GHB), 77
gamma-aminobutyric acid. *See* GABA
ganglion cells, 151
GAS (general adaptation syndrome), 595
gate control theory, 165
g_c-g_f model, 364
gender
  anxiety disorders, 646
  attraction differences in, 523–528
  brain size and, 379, 379
  career paths and, 493–494
  coping strategies and, 614–615
  helping, 539
  intelligence and, 386–387
  language acquisition, 321–322
  mate seeking, 133–134
  mood disorders and, 657
  moral reasoning and, 477
  prejudice, 529–534
  psychotherapy, 706–707
  schemas, 566
  self-concept, 565–566
  sexual response cycle, 412–413
  stress and, 614–615
  suicide and, 658
gender constancy, 474
gender identity, 474
gender schema, 566
gene knockout, 112, 113
gene therapy, 113–114
general adaptation syndrome (GAS), 595
general intelligence, 362
general mental capacity, 362
general paresis, 635
generalizability of underlying principle, 61
generalization, 47, 243

generalized anxiety and worry disorder (GAD), 643
generalized expectancy, 575
Generation X, 492
generativity, 317
generativity versus stagnation, 491
genes, 108–109
  environmental effects on, 109–110
  g factor, 379
  intelligence, 379–381
genetic determinism, 139
genetic engineering, 112
genetic influences on behaviour, 118–123
  drug use and effects, 227–229
  intelligence, 118–119
  personality, 120–123
  reaction range, 119–123
genetics, 108–117
  behaviour genetics, 112–117
  chromosomes, 108–109
  counselling, 113–114
  engineering, 112
  epigenetics, 109–110
  genes, 108–109
  genetic code mapping, 110
  obesity, 408–409
  influence on behaviour, 118–123
genotype, 108
genuineness, 689
germinal stage, 449
Gestalt, 173, 690
Gestalt laws, 174–175
Gestalt psychology, 16, 17
Gestalt therapy, 690–691
GHB, 77
ghrelin, 402
glial cells, 70, 165
global workspaces, 197
glove anaesthesia, 661
glucose, 401, 402
glutamate, 75, 77
glutamic acid, 75, 77
goal-corrected partnership, 469
goal setting and self-efficacy, 579–580
golden years, 494
gonadotropins, 413
gonads, 413
graded potential, 73
grammar, 316
group influence on performance, 519–522
group polarization, 520
groupthink, 520–522
growth needs, 398
growth stage of career, 493
gum chewing and memory, 303
gustation (taste), 144, 162–163

H
habituation, 48, 148, 237, 238–239
hallucinations, 666
hallucinogens, 226, 227
Hamilton Rating Scale for Depression, 713–714
hammer (malleus), 159
happiness, 628
hardiness, 604–605
harm reduction, 625–627
Head Start programs, 382
health promotion, 615–622
  health psychology, 616
  health-compromising behaviours, 616, 621–622
  health-enhancing behaviours, 616, 618–620
  transtheoretical model, 616–618
health psychology, 616, 618–620
health-compromising behaviours, 616, 621–622
health-enhancing behaviours, 616, 618–620
hearing, 144. See also audition
heat, 542
Hebb synapse, 95
height in the horizontal plane, 180
helpful role model, 539
hemispheric lateralization, 98–101, 430
Hereditary Genius (Galton, 1869), 358
heredity, 114
  intelligence, 118–119, 379–382
heritability, 114, 129
heritability coefficient, 114–115
heritability estimates, 115
heroin, 225
heroin junkie, 220
hertz (Hz), 158
heuristics, 340–343
  availability, 342–343
  defined, 340
  means-ends analysis, 340
  representational, 341–342
  subgoal analysis, 340
  Tower-of-Hanoi problem, 340–341
  uncertainty, 341–343
hidden observer, 232
hierarchy, 285–286
high internal validity, 58
High/Scope Perry Preschool Program, 383
higher-order conditioning, 243
hindbrain, 88

hindsight understanding, 40–41
hippocampus, 90
  biological treatments for disorders, 720
  memory, 301, 310
  stress, 601
historical perspective on psychological disorders, 634–636
HIV (human immunodeficiency virus), 621
Holocaust, 516
homeostasis, 81, 218–219, 396
hormones, 431–432
  intelligence, 388–389
  sexual motivation, 413–414
host personality, 662
hostility, 670
human agency, 576–577
Human Genome Project, 110
human growth hormone, 112
human immunodeficiency virus (HIV), 621
human nature, 126–127
human plank, 231
human research ethical standards, 63–65
humanism, 15
humanistic perspective, 15–16, 24
humanistic perspective of personality, 558–567
  culture and gender, 565–566
  evaluation, 566–567
  fully functioning persons, 564–565
  need for positive regard, 564
  personal constructs, 559
  the self, 560
  self-enhancement, 565
  self-esteem, 560–564
  self theory, 559–566
  self-verification, 565
  success and self-esteem, 562–563
humanistic psychotherapies, 688–691
  client-centred therapy, 688–690
  Gestalt therapy, 690–691
hunger and weight regulation, 400–411
  culture, 407–408
  environmental factors, 407–408
  obesity, 408–409
  physiology of hunger, 400–403
  psychology of hunger, 405–407, 408–409
hunger pangs, 401
hunter and gatherer, 115, 132
hunter and protector, 125
Huntington's disease, 679

hyperopia, 150
hyperpolarize, 75
hypnagogic state, 211
hypocretin, 210
hypnosis, 230–234
  behaviour, 230–232
  memory, 231–232, 237
  pain tolerance, 231
  science, 230
  theories, 232–234
hypnotic amnesia, 231
hypnotic induction, 230
hypnotic susceptibility scale, 230
hypnotic susceptibility scales, 230
hypothalamus, 90
  aggression, 540
hypothesis, 39
Hz (hertz), 158

I
icon, 279
iconic memory, 279, 281
iconic store, 278
id, 551–552
ideal selves, 566
identical twins, 116–117, 118–119, 120
identity achievement, 487
identity diffusion, 487
identity versus role confusion, 487
if ... then ... behaviour consistencies, 581
if-then hypothesis, 336
illness prevention. See health promotion
illusion of unanimity, 521
illusions, 181–183
imagery, memory, 297
imagery neurons, 350
imaginal thought, 335
imaginary audience, 483
immediate performance feedback, 259
immune system, training, 245
implicit association test, 531
implicit memory, 292
implosion therapy, 695
impression forming, 503–504
imprinting, 468
in vivo desensitization, 699
in-group favouritism, 533
inappropriate affect, 666
inattentional blindness, 171
incentive, 397
incentive value, 397
incidence, 641
inclusion programs, 392
incomplete disclosure, 64
incongruent recall, 295
incubation, 345

incus (anvil), 159
independent intelligence, 367
independent variable, 54
indiscriminate attachment, 469
individualism, 19, 490
inductive reasoning, 336, 338
indulgent parent, 472
industrial-organizational (I/O)
　　psychology, 3
industry, 467
infantile amnesia, 302
inferiority, 467
inferiority complex, 554
information processing,
　　memory, 277–283,
　　483–484, 485
information search, 463
informational social influence,
　　512, 520
informed consent, 64
inhibitory transmitter, 75, 220
inner ear, 159
insanity (legal), 640
insight, 264–265, 684
insomnia, 209
instinct, 396
instinctive drift, 263
instrumental behaviours, 426,
　　435, 438
instrumental learning, 248
integrated network of
　　predictions, 41
integrity versus despair, 491
intellectualization, 553
intelligence, 357–393
　　academic performance,
　　　373–374
　　achievement tests, 371
　　analysis, 393
　　aptitude tests, 371
　　auditory processing, 390
　　brain, 378, 379
　　brain size, 379
　　broader conceptions,
　　　367–370
　　cognitive process theories,
　　　365–366
　　cognitively disabled,
　　　390–393
　　crystallized intelligence,
　　　363–364
　　cultural influence, 377–378
　　defined, 357
　　early childhood
　　　interventions, 382–383
　　emotional intelligence,
　　　367–370
　　environment, 118–119,
　　　379–382
　　ethnicity, 384–386
　　extremes, 389–393
　　family environment, 385–386
　　fluid intelligence, 364
　　Flynn effect, 375–376

Gardner's multiple
　　intelligences, 367
gender, 386–387
gender differences, 386–387
genes, 118–119, 379–381
genetic differences, 384, 386
genotype, 381
giftedness, 389–390
group differences, 382–387
heredity, 118–119, 379–382
historical perspective,
　　358–361
hormones, 388–389
income, 374–375
intelligence quotient (IQ),
　　119, 359
job performance, 374–375
longevity, 374
measurement of, 370–378
musical training, 390
nature of, 361–370
nature-nurture debate,
　　385–386
neural efficiency, 377–378
non-Western cultures,
　　377–378
psychological test
　　standards, 372–377
psychometrics theories,
　　361–365
social environment, 385–386
Stanford-Binet scales, 360
testing, 358–361
twins, 380–381
Wechsler scales, 360, 370
intelligence quotient (IQ),
　　119, 359
intelligence tests, 44, 371
interaction, 28, 56, 290
interference, 296–297
　　memory and, 296–297
interference theory, 299
interhemispheric
　　communication, 101
interjudge reliability, 372, 373
intermittent reinforcement, 255
internal consistency, 372, 373
internal validity, 58
　　high, 58
　　low, 58
internal-external locus of
　　control, 574–575
*International Statistical
　　Classification of
　　Diseases*, 637
Internet questionnaires, 49, 50
interneurons, 79
interpersonal intelligence, 367
interpersonal therapy, 688
interposition, 180
interpretation, 686
Interpretation of Dreams, The
　　(Freud) 551
interval schedules, 256

interviews, 583–584
intimacy, 528
intimacy versus isolation, 491
intrapersonal intelligence, 367
intrinsic motivation, 398
introspection, 11
introversion-extraversion, 120,
　　128, 567, 569
ion channels, 71
ions, 71
IQ (intelligence quotient), 359
iris, 149
isolation, 470
isolation studies, 199

J
jet lag, 200, 204
jumbled word challenge, 2, 6–7
just noticeable difference
　　(jnd), 147
just world hypothesis, 539

K
Kaufman Adolescent and Adult
　　Intelligence Test, 371
kin selection theory, 136
kinesthesis, 93, 166
Kitty Genovese case, 37–39,
　　41, 538
knockout procedure, 112
knowledge, 266, 344, 346
　　acquisition, 344, 346
knowledge-acquisition
　　components, 366
Kohlberg's stages of moral
　　reasoning, 475–476
Korsakoff's syndrome, 300–301

L
L-Dopa, 78
la belle indifference, 661
labelling, diagnostic, 638–641
LAD (language acquisition
　　device), 323
language, 315–333
　　acquisition, 323–325
　　adaptive functions, 315–316
　　analysis, 330
　　animals and, 331–333
　　behaviour and, 26
　　bilingualism, 325–328, 329
　　bottom-up processing, 319
　　brain functions, 321–322, 323
　　brain-imaging, 322, 329
　　critical period hypothesis,
　　　327
　　culture and, 26
　　defined, 315
　　functional MRIs, 322
　　functions, 321–322
　　grammar, 316
　　hemispheres, 321–322
　　hemispheric lateralization,
　　　101

hierarchical structure of,
　　318, 319
influence on thinking,
　　328–330
learning mechanisms, 316
mental image, 349–350
observational learning, 316
pragmatics, 320–321
producing, 318–323
properties of, 316–317
rules of, 316–317
semantics, 317
sensitive period, 327
sex differences, 321–322
social context, 320–321
social rules, 321
social units, 315
structure, 317–318
symbols, 316
syntax, 316
top-down processing,
　　319–320
trial and error learning, 316
understanding, 318–323
language acquisition, 323–325
　　animals and, 331–333
　　biology of, 323
　　children and, 324–325
　　gender difference, 321–322
　　second language, 325–328,
　　　329
　　social process of, 323–324
language acquisition device
　　(LAD), 323
language acquisition support
　　system (LASS), 324
language structure, 317–318
lapse, 624
late adulthood, 479
latent content, 212
latent learning, 269–270
lateral hypothalamus (LH), 403
lateral occipital area (LOA),
　　145
lateralization, 98
law of closure, 174
law of continuity, 174
law of effect, 14, 248
law of parsimony, 41
law of proximity, 174
law of similarity, 174
learned helplessness, 656
learned helplessness theory,
　　656
learned response. *See*
　　conditioned response
learning, 237–274
　　adaptation theories, 237–239
　　analysis, 273
　　biological factors, 238
　　biology, 261–264
　　classical conditioning,
　　　239–245
　　cognitive model, 264–270

learning, —Cont.
  cross-cultural psychology, 238
  defined, 237
  drug tolerance and, 219
  newborn, 453–454
  operant conditioning, 247–260
  partial reinforcement, 255–256, 257–258
  therapy, 245, 246–247
  through observation, 270–272
  virtual learning, 245, 246–247
learning to learn approach, 382
learning trial, 241
left-hemisphere lateralization, 99
lens, 150
leptin, 402–403, 650
lesions, 82
levels of analysis, 8–9, 24–29
levels of processing, 284
life event scales, 593
lifespan development, analysis, 495
light, 179
limbic system, 90–91, 429–429, 695
linear perspective, 180
linguistic intelligence, 367
linguistic relativity hypothesis, 328
Little Albert study, 244
lobotomy, 719
locus of control, 574–575
long-term memory, 282–295
  Alzheimer's disease and, 301
  children, 463–464
  defined, 282–283
  encoding, 283–289
  retrieval, 292–295
  storage, 289–292
  types, 290–292
long-term potentiation (LTP), 311
longhand writing, 303
longitudinal design, 448
Lorge-Thorndike Intelligence Test, 360
loss aversion, 90
loudness, 159–161
love, 20, 528–529
low internal validity, 58
lowballing, 518
LSD, 226

M
magnetic resonance imaging (MRI), 84, 86–87
magnetic seizure therapy (MST), 683

mainstreaming, 392
maintenance rehearsal, 281, 285
maintenance stage of career, 493
major depression, 651
major tranquilizers, 717
major negative events, 593
malleus (hammer), 159
mania, 652
manic disorders, 655
manifest content, 212
marijuana, 226–227
marriage, 20, 492–493, 530–531
marriage and family counselors, 684
massed learning, 33
massed practice, 296
mastery-approach goals, 421
mastery-avoidance goals, 421
mastery orientation, 420, 421
matching effect, 525
mate preference, 131–135
mate seeking, 525–525
maturation, 455
Mayer-Salovey-Caruso Emotional Intelligence Test (MSCEIT), 367–369
MDMA, 224
meaning, 16
meaningful positions, 288
means-ends analysis, 340
measurement bias, 47
measuring variables, 41–45
  behavioural measures, 43–45
  physiological measures, 44–45
  report by others, 43
  self-reporting, 43
media violence and aggression, 543–544
meditation, 230
medulla, 88
melatonin, 198
memory, 277–313
  biology, 309–313
  construction, 304–308, 309
  declarative, 290, 310, 312
  defined, 277
  encoding, 283–289
  enhancement strategies, 283–287, 303
  expert schemas, 346–347
  forgetting, 297–302, 309
  hypnosis, 231–232
  imagery, 297
  improving, 296–297
  information processing, as, 277–283, 483–484, 485
  interference, 296–297
  long-term, 290, 310
  network, 289–290

neural networks, 289
  procedural, 312–313
  recovered memory, 307–308
  recovery, 307–308
  retrieval, 292–295
  storage, 289–292
  three-component model, 278–283
memory code, 280
memory consolidation, 310
memory trace, 279
memory transfer, 308
menarche, 479
menopause, 480
menstrual synchrony, 164
mental age, 359
mental coaches, 382
mental competence, 367
mental event, 551
mental health professionals, 683–684
mental image, 347–350
  brain, 350
  defined, 347
  language, 349–350
  mental rotation, 348–349
  perception, 349
mental representations, 315
mental rotation, 348–349
mental set, 339, 503–504
mental shortcuts, 5
mental telepathy, 62
mere exposure effect, 524
mere presence, 509
mescaline, 226
mesmerism, 230
messenger molecules, 165
meta-analysis, 61, 710
metacognition, 350–352
metacomponents, 365
metacomprehension, 350, 351–352
metamemory, 350
meth mouth, 224
method of loci, 287
method of successive approximations, 254
microstressors, 593
mid-life crisis, 494
midbrain, 89
middle adulthood, 479
middle ear, 159
mind, 2
mind, body, and therapeutic interventions, 719–720
mind-body dualism, 11
mind-body interaction, 9
mind guards, 521
mindfulness, 612–613, 702
mindfulness-based relapse prevention (MBRP), 702

mindfulness-based stress reduction (MBSR), 702
mindfulness-based treatments, 702–704
mindfulness meditation, 624
Minnesota Multiphasic Personality Inventory (MMPI), 585, 586
Minnesota Twin Study, 121
minority influence, 513
mirror neurons, 97–98
misinformation effect, 306
MMPI (Minnesota Multiphasic Personality Inventory), 585, 586
mnemonics, 286–287, 296
modelling, 271–272, 542
modelling therapy, 701–702
moderate degree of discrepancy, 508
moderate fear, 508
modulatory control model, 645
Mona Lisa, 176
mongolism, 391
monism, 11
monoamine, 695
monoamine oxidase (MAO) inhibitors, 716
monoamine oxidase A (MAOA) gene, 674
monochromat, 155
monocular cues, 179–180
monogamous mating system, 131
monozygotic twins, 116
mood-congruent recall, 295
mood-dependent memory, 295
mood disorders, 650–660
  analysis, 660
  biological factors, 653–655
  bipolar disorder, 652
  depression, 651–652
  patterns, 653
  personality factors, 655
  prevalence and course, 652–653
  psychological factors, 655–657
  sociocultural factors, 657
  suicide, 658–659
mood-incongruent recall, 295
moral development, 475–478
  culture and gender, 477
  Kohlberg's stages of moral reasoning, 475–476
  moral behaviour and conscience, 477–478
moral imbeciles, 672
moratorium, 487
morning person, 199
morpheme, 318
morphine, 788
motion parallax, 180

motivated forgetting, 300
motivation, 271, 396–424
  achievement, 420–423
  achievement needs, 422
  adaptive significance, 396
  conflict as motivation,
    423–424
  cultural influences, 422–423
  defined, 396
  expectancy theories of,
    397–398
  family influences, 422–423
  hunger and weight
    regulation, 400–411
  sexual, 411–420
  situational factors, 422
  theories, 396–400
motivation theories, 396–400
  drive, 396–397
  expectancy, 397–398
  humanistic, 398–400
  incentive, 397–398
  instinct, 396
  psychodynamic, 398–400
motivational interviewing, 623
motive for success, 420
motor cortex, 93
motor development in
    children, 456
motor nerves, 80
motor neurons, 79, 80
motoric thought, 335
Mozart effect, 58–59
MRI (magnetic resonance
    imaging), 84, 86–87
Müller-Lyer illusion, 183,
    187–188
multiculturalism, 326
multimodal treatments,
    623–624
multiple intelligences, 367, 389
multiple personality disorder.
    See dissociative identity
    disorder (DID)
multiple sclerosis, 73
multiple-act behaviour
    criterion, 505
music, 103–104
musical intelligence, 367
mutations, 124
My Lai massacre, 513
myelin sheath, 73
myopia, 150

N
napping, and memory, 303
nanometres, 149
narcissistic personality
    disorder, 672
narcolepsy, 209–210
natural reflex. *See*
    unconditioned response
natural selection, 22, 124–125

naturalistic intelligence, 367
naturalistic observation,
    47–48, 57
nature of therapy, 684
nature-nurture debate, 9, 571
  intelligence and, 385
Necker cube, 175
need achievement, 422
need for achievement, 422–423
need for affiliation, 523
need for cognition, 508
need for positive regard, 564
need for positive self-regard,
    564
need hierarchy, 398
negative correlation, 51–52
negative mood state, 651
negative punishment, 251, 252
negative reinforcement, 250,
    251
negative reinforce, 250
negative state relief model, 537
negative symptoms, 667
negative transference, 686
neglectful parents, 472
NEO Personality Inventory
    (NEO-PI), 570
neoanalysts, 554
neoanalytic theory, 554–555
neo-Piagetians, 462
nerve deafness, 162
nerve function, 71–73
  action potential, 71–73
  electrical properties, 71–73
  impulse, 71–73
  myelin sheath, 73
nerve impulse, 71–73
nervous system, 79–105
  brain structures and
    functions, 87–105
  central system, 79, 81–87
  neural plasticity, 101–105
  peripheral system, 79–81
  research and imaging, 84–87
nervous system healing,
    102–105. *See also* neural
    plasticity
neural basis of behaviour,
    70–79
  nerve function, 71–73
  neuron communication,
    73–79
  neurons, 70–73
neural efficiency, intelligence,
    377–378
neural network, 289–290
neural plasticity, 101–105
  recovery of function,
    102–105
  role of early experience,
    101–102
neurogenesis, 104, 105
neuromodulators, 79

neuron, suicide apparatus, 104
neuron communication, 73–79
  deactivation, 74–75
  drugs, 217–218
  excitation, 74–75
  inhibition, 74–75
  neurotransmitter, 73–74, 77
  specialized transmitter
    systems, 75–79
  synapse, 73
neurons, 70–71
  electrical activity, 71–73
  motor, 79, 80
  sensory, 79
  specialized, 142
neuropeptide Y, 402, 403
neuropsychological tests, 44,
    82
neuroscience
  human brain, 45
  imaging studies, 22
neurotic anxiety, 646
neuroticism, 117, 120, 570,
    571, 598
neurotransmitters, 21, 27,
    73–74, 76, 77, 217, 646
  depression and, 27
neutral stimulus, 240
newborn development,
    452–454
nicotine, 76, 91
night person, 199
night shiftwork, 200
night terrors, 210
nightmares, 210
nightwork, 201
node, 290
nodes of Ranvier, 73
nondeclarative memory, 290
nonsense syllables, 297
norepinephrine, 76, 77, 654, 695
norm of reciprocity, 517,
    536–537
norm of social responsibility,
    537
normal distribution, 375
normative social influence,
    512, 520
norms, 18, 238, 375, 414–415,
    633
nucleus, 109
nucleus accumbens, 91
Nuremberg trials, 513
nurturer of children, 125

O
obedience, 513. *See also*
    conformity
  dilemma of, 514–515
obesity, 408–409
object permanence, 459
object relations theories, 555
objectification theory, 406

observational learning, 237,
    270–272, 580
  applications, 272
  Bandura's social-cognitive
    theory, 271–272
  defined, 270
  imitations of aggression and
    prosocial behaviour,
    272
  modelling process,
    271–272
  self-efficacy, 271–272
  sex-role stereotyping, 474
observer bias, 47
obsessions, 644
obsessive-compulsive disorder
    (OCD), 644–648
occipital lobe, 92, 94
OCD (obsessive-compulsive
    disorder), 644–648
old-age disorders, 679–680
olfaction (smell), 144, 162,
    163–164
olfactory bulb, 163
Ontario Human Rights
    Commission, 384
open-mindedness, 37
openness, 120, 128, 570, 711
operant conditioning, 237,
    247–260
  ABCs of, 249
  antecedents, 250
  applications, 259–260
  avoidance learning, 258
  chaining, 254
  classical conditioning
    versus, 249
  consequences, 250–254
  contingencies, 249
  defined, 248
  discrimination, 255
  escape conditioning, 258
  fear conditioning, 258
  generalization, 254–255
  language acquisition, 324
  negative punishment, 252
  negative reinforcement, 250
  operant extinction,
    250–251
  positive punishment,
    251–252
  positive reinforcement, 250
  primary reinforcers, 252
  schedules of reinforcement,
    255–257
  secondary reinforcers,
    252–253
  sex-role stereotyping, 474
  shaping, 254
  Skinner's analysis, 248–250
  Thorndike's law of effect,
    248

operant conditioning —*Cont.*
   timing of consequences,
      253–254
   two-factor theory of
      avoidance learning, 258
operant conditioning
   therapies, 699–701
operant discrimination, 255
operant discrimination
   training, 255
operant extinction, 250–251
operant generalization,
   254–255
operational definition, 42, 372
opiates, 165, 217, 225, 227
opium, 78
opponent-process theory,
   153, 154
optic chiasm, 99
optic nerve, 151
optimism, 605–606
organ of Corti, 159, 160, 167
organizational effects, 413
organized cooperative
   groups, 138
organizing information, 296
orgasm phase, 413
orphanages, 470–471
Otis-Lennon School Ability
   Test, 360
out-group derogation, 533
out-group homogeneity bias,
   533
outcome, 526–527
outcome bias, 385
Outcome Questionnaire-45, 687
outside-the-box thinking, 338
oval window, 159
Over-Claiming Questionnaire
   (OCQ), 43
overconfidence, 343–344
overcontrolled hostility, 543
overinvolvement, 670
overjustification hypothesis,
   398
overlearning, 296
overt behaviour measures,
   43–45
oxycodone, 225

P
pain, 165
pain disorder, 660
pain tolerance, hypnosis, 231
painful stimuli, 541
panic disorder, 643–644
paradoxical sleep, 203
parallel distributed processing
   (PDP) models, 290
parallel processing, 157
parallel reality, 210
paranoid schizophrenia, 666
paranormal phenomena, 62–63

parasuicide, 658
parasympathetic nervous
   system, 81, 596
paraventricular nucleus
   (PVN), 403
parental investment, 130–131,
   132
parenting styles, 472
parietal lobe, 92, 93
Parkinson's disease, 78, 90, 679
partial reinforcement, 255–256
   extinction, 257–258
   learning, 257–258
partial report, 279
passion, 528
passionate love, 528
pastoral counselors, 684
Pavlovian conditioning. *See*
   classical conditioning
pay for performance, 256
peptides, 401
perceived intent, 542
perceived responsibility, 539
perceived selves, 566
perception, 143, 170–189
   attention factor, 171–172
   bottom-up processing,
      170–171
   constancies, 177–178
   culture, 187–188
   depth and distance, 179–180
   development, 184–189
   early experience, 185–186
   expectation, 176–177
   Fraser's spiral, 174
   Gestalt laws, 174–175
   hypothesis testing, 175
   illusion, 181–183
   mental image, 349
   movement, 180–181
   organization and structure,
      173–175
   restored sensory capacity,
      188–189
   top-down processing, 171
perception and social thinking,
   499–508
   attitude, 504–508
   attribution, 499–502
   impression forming, 503–504
perceptual constancies,
   177–178
perceptual schema, 175
perceptual set, 176–177
perceptual speed, 485
performance anxiety, 414
performance attainment, 578
performance components,
   365–366
performance orientation,
   420, 421
performance-approach goals,
   421

performance-avoidance
   goals, 421
peripheral nervous system,
   79–81
   autonomic nervous system,
      80–81
   somatic nervous system,
      79–80
peripheral route to
   persuasion, 508
person-centred therapy. *See*
   client-centred therapy
person-situation interaction,
   592
personal adaptation, 237, 238
personal change process,
   616–618
personal construct theory, 559
personal constructs, 559
personal fable, 483
personal growth, 15
personal (internal)
   attributions, 499–500
personal space, 511
personal unconscious, 555
personality, 465, 550–589
   analysis, 588
   behaviour genetics,
      120–122
   biological perspectives,
      567–573
   defined, 550
   drug use and effects, 229
   evolutionary personality
      theory, 128, 130
   humanistic perspective,
      558–567
   personality assessment,
      582–589
   psychodynamic perspective,
      550–558
   social cognitive theories,
      573–582
   trait perspective, 567–573
personality assessment,
   582–589
   behavioural assessment, 584
   interviews, 583–584
   measurement approaches,
      582–583
   personality scales, 585–586
   projective tests, 586–589
   remote behaviour sampling,
      584
   theory and assessment, 589
personality development in
   adolescents and adults,
      487–496
   career, 493–494
   death and dying, 495–496
   marriage and family,
      492–493
   mid-life crisis, 494

relationship with parents
   and peers, 488–489
retirement, 494
search for identity, 487–488
stages versus critical events
   in adulthood, 491
transition to adulthood,
   489–491
personality development in
   children, 465–475
   attachment, 468–470
   attachment deprivation,
      470–471
   daycare, 471–472
   divorce and remarriage
      effect, 473–474
   early emotions, 465–466
   emotion regulation, 465–466
   Erikson's psychosocial
      stages, 467–468
   gender identity, 474–475
   parenting styles, 472
   social media, 466
   socialization, 474–475
   temperament as predictor,
      466–467
personality disorders, 671–676
   antisocial personality
      disorder, 671–675
   borderline personality
      disorder, 672, 675–676
   types, 672
personality factors, 606–607
personality psychology, 3
personality scales, 585–586
personality tests, 44
perspectives, 10
perspectives on behaviour. *See*
   behaviour
persuasion, 507–508
PET (positron emission
   tomography), 21, 84,
      85–86
phantom limb sensation,
   164–165
phencyclidine, 226
phenotype, 108
pheromones, 164
phi phenomenon, 181
Phineas Gage case, 96, 98
phobias, 642
phobic disorder, 642
phonemes, 318, 454
phonemic encoding, 284
phonological encoding, 284
phonological loop, 282
phosphenes, 168
photopigments, 151
photoreceptors, 150–151
phrenology, 22
physical attractiveness,
   524–525
physical effects of stress,
   599–601

physiological component of emotions, 428–432
physiological measures, 44–45
consciousness, 193
physiological psychology, 21
physiological reaction to stress, 609–613
physiological vs. psychological dependence, 219
physiology, 11
physiology of hunger, 400–405
brain mechanisms, 403–405
meal signals, 400–402
signal regulating appetite, 402–403
physiology of sex, 412–414
Piaget's stages of cognitive development, 457–462
assessment, 461–462
concrete operational stage, 459, 460
formal operational stage, 459, 461
preoperational stage, 459–460
sensorimotor stage, 458–459
pineal gland, 198
pitch, 103, 159–161
pituitary gland, 90
place cells, 266–267
place theory, 161
placebo, 59
placebo control group, 59, 708
placebo effect, 59–60, 195
placenta, 449
plaques, 301, 680
plateau phase, 413
pleasure principle, 552
political interest, 129
politics, 129
polyandry, 131
polygenic transmission, 109
polygraph, 431
polygynandry, 131
polygyny, 130
pons, 88
Ponzo illusion, 181
population, 48
pornography, 416–417
positive correlation, 51
positive psychology, 16, 627–630
positive psychology movement, 16
positive punishment, 251–252
positive reinforcement, 250, 251, 700–701
positive reinforce, 250
positive symptoms, 667
positive transference, 685–686
positron emission tomography (PET), 21, 84, 85–86
post-formal thought, 484–485

post-traumatic stress disorder (PTSD), 247, 598–599
postconventional moral reasoning, 476
posthypnotic amnesia, 231–232
practical intelligence, 366
pragmatics, 320–321
precognition, 62
preconscious, 551
preconscious mental events, 193
preconventional moral reasoning, 476
prediction, 41, 52–53
predictive bias, 385
pre-existing guilt, 539
predictive validity, 373
preferential looking procedure, 452, 453
prefrontal asymmetry, 430
prefrontal cortex, 98, 429, 603–604, 645
prefrontal lobotomies, 98
prejudice, 523, 529–536
cognitive causes, 532–533
motivation, 534
overt and covert, 529, 531
reducing, 535–536
self-fulfillment, 534–535
stereotyping, 532
premises, 336
prenatal critical period, 450
prenatal development, 449–451
preoperational stage, 459–460
preparedness, 261
presence, 18
prevalence, 641–642
preventive mental health, 723–725
primacy effect, 282, 503
primary appraisal, 594
primary mental abilities, 363
primary reinforcer, 252
primary sex characteristics, 479
primary visual cortex, 156
priming, 289, 292
priming tasks, 292
prioritizing, 32
prosocial behaviour, 536–540
increasing, 539–540
when people help, 538–539
who people help, 539
why people help, 536–537
proactive interference, 299
problem solving. 338–344
algorithms, 340
confirmation bias, 343
creativity guidelines, 345–346
evaluating results, 340
formulating solutions, 339
heuristics, 341–343

overconfidence, 343–344
problem-solving schemas, 340–341
testing solutions, 339–340
uncertainty, 341–343
understanding the problem, 338
problem-focused coping, 609
problem-solving dream model, 212, 214
problem-solving schemas, 340–341
procedural memory, 290, 312–313
projection, 553
projective tests, 586–589
proposition, 335
propositional thought, 335
prosocial behaviour, 272
prosopagnosia, 145–146
prospective memory, 302, 485
protective factors, 601–608
coping self-efficacy, 605
finding meaning in stressful life events, 607–608
hardiness, 604–605
optimism, 605–606
personality factors, 606–607
social support, 602–604
prototype, 335
provocation, 541
proximity, 523–524
proximodistal principle, 455
pseudoinsomniacs, 209
pseudomemories, 232
pseudoscience, 7
pseudoscientific misinformation, 66
psilocybin, 226
psychiatric revolution, 78, 218
psychiatric social workers, 684
psychiatrists, 684
psychic energy, 551
psychic phenomena, 62–63
psychoanalysis, 12–13, 684–686
psychodynamic, 13
psychodynamic perspective, 12–13, 24
psychodynamic perspective of personality, 550–558
dynamics of personality, 552–553
evaluation, 557–558
Freud's psychoanalytic theory, 212, 551
neoanalytic approach, 554–555, 557
object relations approach, 554–555, 557
psychic energy, 551
psychoanalysis, 12–13
psychoanalytic theory research, 554

psychosexual development, 553–554
structure of personality, 551–552
psychodynamic therapies, 684–688
brief psychodynamic therapy, 686–688
psychoanalysis methods, 684–686
psychogenic blindness, 661
psycholinguistics, 3, 315
psychological disorders, 632–680
abnormality, 632–634
analysis, 660
anxiety disorders, 641–650
childhood disorders, 677–679
diagnosing, 636–641
diagnostic labelling, 638–641
dissociative disorders, 662–664
historical perspective, 634–636
insanity, 639–640
mood disorder, 650–659
old age disorders, 679–680
personality disorders, 671–676
schizophrenia, 665–671
scope and nature, 632–634
somatic symptom disorders, 660–662
treatment, 682–727
psychological disorders and society, 721–725
deinstitutionalization, 722–723
preventive mental health, 723–725
psychological effects of stress, 597–598
psychological factors in
antisocial personality disorder, 674–675
anxiety disorder, 646–648
autism, 678
borderline personality disorder, 675–676
mood disorders, 655–657
personality disorders, 674–675
schizophrenia, 669
psychological level of analysis, 8, 9, 24–25
aggression, 547
anxiety and mood disorders, 660
behaviour genetics, 123
brain, behaviour and environment, 105
conceptions of personality, 588

psychological level,—*Cont.*
depression, 28
drug-induced states, 229
emotion, 445
intellectual functioning, 393
language, 330
learning, 273
lifespan development, 495
measuring exam stress, 42
memory, 312
perception, 189
sleep and dreaming, 215
stress and coping, 608
therapeutic change, 721
thinking processes, 353
psychological sense of
community, 523
psychological test, 44,
372–377
norms, 375
reliability, 372–373
standardization, 375–377
validity, 373–375
psychological well-being,
597–598
psychological vs. physiological
dependence, 219
psychologists, 2, 30
psychology, 2
basic and applied science, 8
Canadian history, 29–30
empirical evidence and, 4
fields of, 30–31
goals of, 8
modern-day, 29–30
nature of, 2–9
perspectives on behaviour,
10–24
research ethics, 63–65
research methods, 46–57
research validity, 58–61
science, as, 4–5
scientific approach, 4–5
scientific hub, 4
scientific principles in, 37–45
specialty areas, 30
work setting, 31
psychology of aggression,
542–543
psychology of hunger,
405–407
psychology of sex, 414
psychometric approach to
intelligence, 361–365
psychometrics, 361
psychopaths. *See* antisocial
personality disorder
psychopharmacology, 715
psychophysics, 11, 144
psychophysiological
disorders, 660

psychosexual development,
553–554
psychosocial stages, 467–468
psychosomatic diseases, 597
psychosurgery, 719
psychotherapies, evaluating,
707–712
common factors between
therapies, 712
factors affecting outcome,
711–712
research methods and
design, 708–711
specificity question, 707
psychoticism-self-control, 569
PTSD. *See* post-traumatic
stress disorder (PTSD)
puberty, 479
punishers, 249
punishment, 249, 701
pupil, 149
puzzle box, 248
PVN (paraventribular
nucleus), 403

R
radical behaviourism, 15
Rain Man, 356, 678
random assignment, 55
random positions, 288
random sampling, 49
randomized clinical trial,
713–714
rape trauma syndrome, 597
rapid eye movements (REMs),
203. *See also* REM sleep
ratio schedule, 256
rational approach, 585
rational-emotive therapy
(Ellis), 692–693
rationalization, 553
Raven Progressive Matrices,
377
RBD (REM-sleep behaviour
disorder), 210
reaction formation, 553, 557
reaction range, 119–123
reaction time, 43
realistic conflict theory, 534
reality principle, 552
reasoning, 335–338
adolescence, 483–484
belief bias, 337
deductive, 336
distraction, 337
emotions, 337–338
framing, 337–338
inductive, 336
irrelevant information, 337
stumbling blocks in, 337–338
recall, 291, 485
recency effect, 282, 503

receptor sites, 74
recessive gene, 109
reciprocal determinism, 574
recognition, 291
recombinant DNA procedures,
112
recovered memory, 307–308
refractory period, 72, 413
refrigerator parents, 678
regression, 669
reinforcement, 248, 542
reinforcement value, 574
reinforcers, 249
relapse, 624
relapse prevention, 624–625
relatedness, 399
relative size, 180
relearning, 297
reliability, 44, 372–373, 583, 636
reliable, 44
REM density, 224
REM rebound effect, 208
REM sleep, 202–203
disorder, 210
dreaming, 203, 209,
213–214
learning and memory, 206,
208
patterns, 203
restoration, and, 207
REM sleep paralysis, 203
REM-sleep behaviour disorder
(RBD), 210
remarriage and childhood
development, 473–474
remote behaviour sampling,
584
repeated measures design, 55
replication, 61
representative sample, 48
representativeness heuristic,
341–342
repression, 13, 300, 552, 553
reproduction, 271
research ethical standards,
63–65
research methods, 46–57
comparison of methods, 57
correlational research,
50–53
descriptive, 46–50
experiments, 53–57
research validity issues, 58–61
confounding of variables,
58–59
example, 62–63
expectancy effect, 60
generalizing findings, 61
placebo effect, 59–60
replicating findings, 61
residential school syndrome,
599

receptor sites, 74
resilience, 605
resistance, 596, 685
resistance to extinction, 251
resolution phase, 413
response cost, 252
response prevention, 695
resting potential, 71
restoration model, 207
retention, 271
reticular formation, 89
reticulum, 89
retina, 150
retinal implant, 167–168
retirement, 494
retrieval, 278
retrieval cue, 292
retrieval failure, 299–300
retrieval of memory,
292–295
context effects, 294–295
cues, 292–293
distinctiveness, 293–294
enhancement strategies,
296–297
mood effects, 295
state effects, 295
retroactive interference, 299
retrograde amnesia, 300
retrospective memory, 302
reuptake, 75
revolving door phenomenon,
722
rising-curve phenomenon, 376
rites of passage, 478
road rage, 541
Rod-and-Frame test, 388
rods, 150
Rogers's self theory, 559–567
fully functioning persons,
564–565
need for positive regard, 564
research, 565–566
the self, 560
self-esteem, 560–564
rohypnol, 77
role conflict, 510
roller coaster gene, 122
roofies, 77
rope, 77
Rorschach inkblots, 587
Rosenberg Self-esteem Scale,
562
rotating shiftwork, 201
rouge test, 193

S
SAD (seasonal affective
disorder), 200
sample, 48
sample bias, 49
satiety signals, 400–401
savants, 678

scatterplot, 52
Schacter-Singer theory of
emotion. *See* two-factor
theory of emotion
schedules of reinforcement,
255
schema, 287, 344, 346
expertise, 288–289, 346–347
gender, 566
impression forming, 503–504
memory distortion, 304–306
mental framework, 287–288
Piaget's stages, 458
problem solving, 345–346
schizophrenia, 665–671
antipsychotic drugs, 717–718
biological factors, 667–669
characteristics, 665–666
electroconvulsive therapy,
718–719
environmental factors,
669–670
psychological factors, 669
sociocultural factors, 670
subtypes, 666–667
token economy, 700
schizotypal personality
disorder, 672
science, 4
scientific principles in
psychology, 37–45
attitudes, 37, 39
defining variables, 41–45
development theory, 41
hindsight understanding,
40–41
measuring variables, 41–45
process steps, 39–40
scientific process, 39–40
scientific progress, 5
SCN (suprachiasmatic nuclei),
198–199
script, 344, 346
seasonal affective disorder
(SAD), 200
secondary (conditioned)
reinforcers, 252–253
secondary appraisal, 594
secondary sex characteristics,
479
seeing tongue, 167
seeking social support, 609
selective attention, 193
selective mutism, 254
selective serotonin reuptake
inhibitors (SSRIs), 78, 716
self, 560
self-actualization, 15, 398,
558, 565
self-censorship, 521
self-concept, 560
self-consistency, 560

self-correcting process, 5
self-determination theory, 399
self-disclosure, 526
self-efficacy, 271, 539, 578
bystander effect, 539, 540
coping, 605
goal setting, 579–580
research, 578–581
self-enhancement, 565
self-esteem, 560–564
self-esteem and success
research, 562–563
self-fulfilling prophecy, 504
self-instructional training, 694
self-justification, 506, 542
self-monitoring, 572
self-paced learning, 259
self-perception theory, 507
self-reactiveness, 578
self-reinforcers, 537
self-relatedness, 711
self-report, 193
self-report measures, 43
self-serving bias, 501–502
self-verification, 565
semantic encoding, 284
semantic memory, 290
semantics, 317
semicircular canals, 166
senile dementia, 679
sensation, 143. *See also*
sensory systems, sensory
processes
sensitive period, 468
sensitization, 237, 239
sensorimotor state, 458–459
sensory adaptation, 148
learning, 239
sensory cortex, 93–94
sensory memory, 278, 309
sensory nerves, 80
sensory neurons, 79
sensory processes, 143–148.
See also sensory systems
difference threshold,
147–148
sensory adaptation, 148
signal detection theory, 144,
146–147
stimulus detection, 144
sensory prosthetics, 167–169
sensory registers, 278
sensory systems, 149–170. *See
also* sensory processes
audition, 158–162
body senses, 166, 170
endorphins, 165–166
gustation (taste), 162–163
olfaction (smell), 162,
163–164
pain, 165

spinal and brain
mechanisms, 165
tactile senses, 164–165
vision, 149–158
sensory-perception
development in children,
454–455
separation anxiety, 469
sequential design, 448
serial position effect, 282, 293
serotonin, 77, 78, 224, 654, 695
aggression, 541
set point, 396, 400
sex-role stereotypes,
474–475
sex-typing, 474
sexual dysfunction, 414
sexual fantasy, 414
sexual motivation, 411–420
cultural and environmental
influences, 414–417
orientation, 417–420
patterns, 411–412
physiology of sex, 412–414
psychology of sex, 414
sexual orientation, 417–420
biological influences,
418–419
defined, 417
determinants of, 418–420
environmental influences,
419–420
prevalence of different, 418
sexual response cycle, 412–413
sexual strategies theory, 527
sexual violence, 416–417
sfumato, 176
shadow, 179
shadowing, 171
shape constancy, 177
shaping, 254
shooter bias, 536
short-term memory, 280–282
capacity, 280–281
defined, 280
digit-span task, 280
duration, 280–281
memory codes, 280
putting to work, 281–282
units, 281
shrinks, 2
signal detection theory,
146–147
similarity, 524, 539
simultaneous pairing, 242, 269
situation-focused prevention,
723
situational (external)
attributions, 499–500
16 Personality Factor
Questionnaire (16PF),
567–568

size constancy, 178
skepticism, 37
Skinner box, 248
skin senses, 164–166
sleep, 201–216
biological regulation, 204
brain and environment, 204
deprivation, 205
disorder, 208–210
dreaming, 210–216
healthy, 206–207
learning and memory, 206,
208
pattern, 204, 208
reason for, 207–208
regulation, 204
stages, 201–203
sleep spindles, 202
sleep terrors, 210
sleep thoughts, 203
sleepwalking, 210
slow-wave sleep, 202
SmartHand, 169
smell, sense of, 144, 163–164
social aggression, 541
social anxiety disorder, 642
social causation hypothesis,
670
social cognitive theorists, 573
social cognitive theory,
271–272, 274
social cognitive theory (of
hypnosis), 232–233
social cognitive theory of
personality, 573–582
Albert Bandura and, 575–
581
consistency paradox, 581
evaluation, 581–582
expectancy, 574
if… then… behaviour
consistencies, 581
locus of control, 574–575
reciprocal determinism, 574
reinforcement value, 574
self-efficacy, 578–581
social comparison, 523, 538
social compensation, 520
social customs, 238
social Darwinism, 139
social desirability bias, 43
social drift hypothesis, 670
social-emotional development
in adolescents and adults,
487–496
career, 493–494
death and dying, 495–496
marriage and family,
492–493
mid-life crisis, 494
relationship with parents
and peers, 488–489

social-emotional development
in adolescents and
adults—*Cont.*
retirement, 494
search for identity, 487–488
stages versus critical events
in adulthood, 491
transition to adulthood,
489–491
social-emotional development
in children, 465–475
attachment, 468–470
attachment deprivation,
470–471
daycare, 471–472
divorce and remarriage
effect, 473–474
early emotions, 465–466
emotion regulation, 465–466
Erikson's psychosocial
stages, 467–468
gender identity, 474–475
parenting styles, 472
social media, 466
socialization, 474–475
temperament as predictor,
466–467
social engineering, 15
social exchange theory, 526
social facilitation, 509–510
social identity theory, 534
social influence, 509–522
conformity, 511–518
crowd behaviour, 518–519
group influence on
performance, 519–522
mere presence of others,
509–510
norms, 510–511
social facilitation, 509–510
social interest, 554
social isolation, 610–611
social learning theory, 271,
416, 536–537
social loafing, 519–520
social media, 466
social norm, 510
social organization, 125
social phobia, 642
social psychologists, 18
social psychology, 4
social relations, 523–546
affiliation, 523
aggression, 540–546
attraction, 523–528
discrimination, 529–536
love, 528–529
prejudice, 529–536
prosocial behaviour,
536–540
social responsibility, 537
social role, 510

social skills training, 701–702
social structure theory, 528
social support and stress,
602–604, 609
social thinking and perception.
See perception and social
thinking
socialization, 18, 474
society and psychological
disorder, 721–725
sociobiology, 23, 24
sociocultural environment,
depression, 28
sociocultural factors
anxiety disorder, 648
mood disorders, 657
schizophrenia, 670–671
sociocultural perspective,
18–19, 24
sociocultural view of
attraction, 527–528
sociopaths. *See* antisocial
personality disorder
soma, 70
somatic nervous system, 79–80
somatic sensory cortex, 93–94
somatic symptom disorders,
660–662
somatic theory of emotions, 438
somatoform disorders, 660–662
Sonicguide, 167
S-O-R model of learning, 264
sound, 158
sound localization, 161
sound waves, 158
source confusion, 306–307
source monitoring error, 306–307
spatial memory, 485
specific phobias, 642
specificity question, 707
speech comprehension, 94–95
speech production, 94–95
speech segmentation, 320
spinal cord, 81–82
spinal reflexes, 81
split brain, 99–101, 195
splitting, 675–676
spontaneous recovery, 242–243
spontaneous remission, 708
spreading activation, 289
SST (Strange Situation Test),
469
stage-matched interventions,
617
standardization, 375–377
Stanford Prison Study, 510–511
Stanford-Binet, 359, 360, 362,
371, 375, 376, 377
stapes (stirrup), 159
state of consciousness, 192
state-dependent memory, 295
static testing, 376

stereotype, 5, 503, 533
stereotype threat, 534
stereotyping, 532
Sternberg Triarchic Ability
Test (STAT), 371
stimulants, 223–225, 227
stimuli, 425
arousing, 415
emotion, 427
painful, 541
stimulus control, 255
stimulus generalization, 243
stimulus hierarchy, 696
stimulus-response (SR)
psychology, 264
stirrup (stapes), 159
stomach and intestinal
distention, 401
storage, 278
storage of memory, 289–292
Strange Situation Test (SST),
469
stranger anxiety, 469
stratified random sampling, 49
stress, 591–615
analysis, 608
chronic stress, 595–597
coping self-efficacy, 605
coping strategies, 608–615
finding meaning, 607–608
general adaptation
syndrome (GAS),
595–597
hardiness, 604–605
health, 597–601
illness, 599–601
immune system
functioning, 600
memory impairment, 601
mindfulness, 612–613
nature, 592–597
optimism, 605–606
personality factors, 606–607
physical contact, 610–611
physical effects, 599–601
post-traumatic stress
disorder, 598–599
psychological effects,
597–598
response, 594–595
social support protective
factors, 602–604
stressors, 592–593
success, 594–595
vulnerability and protective
factors, 601–608
stress management, 608–613
stress-resilience in children,
605
stressor, 592–593, 636
striving for superiority, 554
stroboscopic movement, 181

structural encoding, 284
structuralism, 11–12, 16
structure of language, 317–318
structured interview, 583–584
study strategies, 32–33
subgoal analysis, 340
subjective norms, 505
sublimation, 553
subliminal perception, 145–
146, 195, 196
subliminal stimulus, 145–146
substance dependence, 219–
220. *See also* combatting
substance abuse
subtractive colour mixture, 153
suffering, 165
suicide, 658–659
sulcus, 103
superego, 552
suprachiasmatic nuclei (SCN),
198–199
surface structure, 317
survey research, 48–50,
57, 711
syllogism, 336
sympathetic nervous system,
80–81, 595–596
synaesthesia, 142–143
synapse, 73
synaptic cleft, 73
synaptic transmission. *See*
neuron communication
synaptic vesicles, 74
syntax, 316
systematic desensitization,
696, 698–699
systematic observations, 4

T
tabula rasa, 14, 238
tactile senses, 164–165
Taijin Kyofushu, 648
tangles, 301
tardive dyskinesia, 717
taste, 144, 162–163
taste buds, 163
taste sense, 162–163
TAT (Thematic Apperception
Test), 587–589
TDF (testis determining factor)
gene, 449
telegraphic speech, 324
temperament, 466–467
temporal lobe, 92, 94
teratogens, 450
test preparation, 33
test-retest reliability, 372, 373
test-taking strategies, 33–34
test-wiseness, 33
testis determining factor (TDF)
gene, 449
testosterone, 541

tetrahydrocannabinol (THC), 226
texture, 180
thalamus, 89, 166, 310
THC (tetrahydrocannabinol), 226
Thematic Apperception Test (TAT), 587–589
theory, 40
theory building, 40
theory development, 40
theory of cognitive dissonance, 506
theory of evolution, 11
theory of mind, 464, 679
theory of planned behaviour, 505
theory of reciprocal altruism, 136
theory of social impact, 40
theory of successful intelligence, 377
therapeutic behaviour change analysis, 721
therapists, 683
therapy, 2, 245, 246–247, 725–726
thinking, 334–354
  analysis, 353
  brain and mind, 334–335
  concepts, 335
  expertise, 346–347
  knowledge, 344–346
  mental imagery, 347–350
  metacognition, 350, 352–353
  metacomprehension, 351–352
  problem solving, 338–344
  propositions, 335
  reasoning, 335–338
  wisdom, 347
third-variable problem, 51
"third-wave cognitive-behavioural therapies, 702–704
threat, 560
three-component model of memory, 278–283
  iconic memory, 279, 281
  long-term memory, 282–283
  sensory memory, 278
  short-term memory, 280–282
three-stratum theory of cognitive abilities, 364–365
timbre, 103
time management strategies, 32
tip-of-the-tongue (TOT) phenomenon, 300
tobacco, 76, 622
token economy, 259, 700

tolerance, 218–220
tonotopic map, 103
tool use, 125
top-down processing, 171, 319–320
touch, 144, 164–165
Tower-of-Hanoi problem, 340–341
tracts, 80
Trail Making Test, 82
trait perspective of personality, 567–573
  behaviour, 570–571
  biological factors, 571
  brain, 571
  Cattell personality factors, 567–568
  evaluation, 573
  Eysenck's Extraversion-Stability model, 568–569
  factor analysis, 567
  Five Factor Model, 569–570, 589
  stability of traits, 571–573
tranquilizer, effect, 76, 221, 227
transaction, 592
transcranial magnetic stimulation (TMS), 84
transduction, 142, 144, 151, 159
transfer of excitation, 529
transference, 685–686
transtheoretical model, 616–618
trauma-dissociation theory, 662
treatment group, 59
treatment of psychological disorders, 682–727
  analysis, 721
  behaviour therapies, 694–702
  biological approaches, 715–720
  cognitive therapies, 691–694
  cultural issues, 705–706
  drug versus psychological treatments, 713–714
  evaluating therapies, 707–712
  gender issues, 706–707
  helping relationship, 683–684
  humanistic psychotherapies, 688–691
  mental health professionals, 683–684
  nature of therapy, 684
  psychodynamic therapies, 684–688
  psychological disorders and society, 721–725

"third-wave" cognitive-behavioural therapies, 702–704
  virtual reality (VR) therapy, 697–698
trephination, 635
tri-council policy for ethical conduct, 64
triangular theory of love, 528
triarchic theory of intelligence, 365
trichromat, 155
trichromatic theory, 153–154
tricyclics, 716
Trier Social Stress Test (TSST), 604
triple vulnerability model of emotional disorders, 660
trustworthiness, 508
truth value, 324
twin studies, 116–117, 118, 120, 121
twins, intelligence, 380–381
two-factor theory of avoidance learning, 258
two-factor theory of emotion, 441
two-sided refutational approach, 508
two-way causality problem, 51
Type A personality, 606
Type B personality, 606
type I schizophrenia, 667
type II schizophrenia, 667

U
UCR (unconditioned response), 241
UCS (unconditioned stimulus), 241
umami, 163
umbilical cord, 449
unconditional positive regard, 564, 688–689
unconditioned response (UCR), 241
unconditioned stimulus (UCS), 241
unconscious, 551
unconscious events, 195
undifferentiated schizophrenia, 666
unipolar depression, 695
universal grammar, 323
universality principle, 476
unlearned reflex. See unconditioned response
unobtrusive measures, 44
us-them thinking, 532–533
USS Vincennes, 176–177

V
validity, 58, 372, 373–375, 583, 636
validity scales, 585
Valium, 715
variable, 41–42, 50, 51
  manipulation, 53
variable-interval (VI) schedule, 256, 257
variable-ratio (VR) schedule, 256–257
variable schedules, 256
vasocongestion, 413
vegetative state, 194
ventromedial hypothalamus (VMH), 403
verbal persuasion, 581
vestibular apparatus, 166
vestibular sacs, 166
vestibular sense, 166
VI (variable-interval) schedule, 256, 257
Victor case study, 470
video game violence and aggression, 545–546
virtual reality (VR), 245, 246–247, 697–698
virtual reality (VR) therapy, 245, 246–247, 697–698
virtual reality exposure therapy (VRET), 246–247
vision, 144, 149–158
  acuity, 151
  analysis and reconstruction of visual scenes, 155–158
  brightness, 151–152
  colour blindness, 155
  colour vision theory, 152–155
  dark adaptation, 152
  eye, 149–150
  feature detectors, 156
  photoreceptors, 150–151
  sensory prosthetics, 167–168
  transduction, 151
  visual association cortex, 157
  visual perception analysis, 189
visual acuity, 151
visual agnosia, 196
visual association cortex, 157
visual cliff, 184
visual cortex, 168, 322
visual habituation procedure, 454
visual perception, analysis, 189
visual-spatial working memory, 282
visuospatial intelligence, 367
visuospatial sketchpad, 282

voluntary responses, 247
VR (variable-ratio) schedule, 256–257
VR (virtual reality), 245, 246–247, 697–698
VRET (virtual reality exposure therapy), 246–247
vulnerability, 636
vulnerability factors, 601–602
vulnerability-stress model, 636

W
WAIS (Wechsler Adult Intelligence Scale), 360, 370, 373

Weber fraction, 147
Weber's law, 147–148
Wechsler Adult Intelligence Scale (WAIS), 360, 370, 373
Wechsler Intelligence Scale for Children (WISC), 360, 370, 371, 373
Wechsler Preschool and Primary Scale of Intelligence (WPPSI), 360
Wechsler tests (WAIS-IV, WAIS-V), 360
weight control, 619–620
Wernicke's area, 92, 94, 322
Windigo, 648

WISC (Wechsler Intelligence Scale for Children), 360, 370, 371, 373
wisdom, 347
wish fulfillment, 212
withdrawal, 218–220
within subjects design, 55
Without Conscience: The Disturbing World of the Psychopaths among Us (Hare), 672
Woodcock-Johnson Psycho-Educational Battery, 371
working memory, 278, 280, 281, 309

Alzheimer's disease (AD), 301
children, 463–464

X
Xanax, 715

Y
yo-yo dieting, 620
young adulthood, 479
Young-Helmholtz theory, 153–154

Z
zone of proximal development, 462
zygote, 108, 449